A GREEK-ENGLISH LEXICON
of the
SEPTUAGINT

T. MURAOKA

A GREEK-ENGLISH LEXICON of the SEPTUAGINT

PEETERS
LOUVAIN - PARIS - WALPOLE, MA
2009

A CIP record for this book is available from the Library of Congress.

ISBN 978-90-429-2248-8
D. 2009/0602/87

PRINTED IN BELGIUM

Peeters, Warotstraat 50, B-3020 Herent

To Keiko my wife,

who has suffered me so long

and

who has suffered with me and for me so much.

INTRODUCTION[*]

There is now hardly any need to justify the compiling of a Septuagint lexicon. The need of a modern scientific Septuagint lexicon was justly recognised by many leading scholars and by the International Organization for Septuagint and Cognate Studies.[1] Since one could hardly disagree with Schürer, who says: "Die Grundlage aller jüdisch-hellenistischen Bildung ist die alte anonyme griechische Übersetzung der heiligen Schriften, die unter dem Namen der Septuaginta .. bekannt und durch die Überlieferung der christlichen Kirche uns vollständig erhalten ist. Ohne sie ist das hellenistische Judentum ebenso wenig denkbar, wie die evangelische Kirche Deutschlands ohne Luthers deutsche Bibelübersetzung,"[2] one wonders how much longer the serious scientific study of this document could be contemplated without the proper tools of the trade such as a dictionary and a grammar. Whatever merits one may still accord to Schleusner's justly famous *Lexicon*,[3] there is not a shadow of doubt that it needs to be superseded. Apart from the fundamental fact that his dictionary is not a dictionary in the usual sense of the term, but rather a collection of philological notes made from the perspective of the Hebrew[4] word or words which a given Greek word translates in the Septuagint, the lexicon was published decades before the discovery of Greek papyri and inscriptions, which revolutionised our perception of the nature of the language of the Greek Bible. The importance of the Septuagint does not lie merely in its value for historians of Early Judaism, but also in the fact that it embodies quite a sizeable amount of texts witnessing to Hellenistic, Koiné Greek. Some of the current lexica such as Liddell, Scott and Jones, and Bauer do make fairly frequent references to the Septuagint, but their treatment, by universal agreement, leaves much to be desired.[5] Furthermore, the last several decades have witnessed remarkable revived interests in the Septuagint, not only on the part of scholars interested in the history of the text of the Hebrew Bible, but also those who study the Septuagint as a Greek text with its own interests and perspectives, not necessarily as a translated text. All these considerations make it imperative that we should have an up-to-date and scientific dictionary of the Septuagint. It was against this backgroud that in the mid eighties I set out, together with Dr J.A.L. Lee, of Sydney University, in the compiling of a lexicon of the Septuagint of the Twelve Prophets.

Scope

The present dictionary covers the entire Septuagint, including the so-called deuterocanonical books or apocrypha. Furthermore, the following data have also been systematically covered for this lexicon:

a) the Antiochene or proto-Lucianic version in the books of 4 Kingdoms, namely Samuel and Kings of the Hebrew Bible, and the book of Chronicles,[6] and for these books the so-called Kaige recension and/or the text-

[*] A revised version of the Introduction to our 2002 lexicon, *A Greek-English Lexicon of the Septuagint: Chiefly of the Pentateuch and the Twelve Prophets* (Leuven: Peeters, 2002).

[1] For a brief history of a never completed project launched by this organization with a view to filling this gap, see Muraoka 1986b, esp. 255f., and Muraoka 1990: vii-viii. See further E. Tov, "Some thoughts on a lexicon of the LXX," *BIOSCS* 9 (1976) 14-46.

[2] E. Schürer, *Geschichte des jüdischen Volkes im Zeitalter Jesu Christi*, Bd. 3 (Leipzig, 1909), p. 424. Incidentally, in the English translation as revised and edited by G. Vermes et al. (Edinburgh, 1986), the closing sentence of the above quote reads: "Without it the religion of the Greek-speaking Jews was as unthinkable as the Church of England without the Authorised Version" (vol. III.1, 474).

[3] J.F. Schleusner, *Novus thesaurus philologico-criticus sive lexicon in LXX et reliquos interpretes graecos ac scriptores apocryphos veteris testamenti*, 5 vols. (Leipzig, 1820). For an evaluation of this dictionary, see J. Lust, "J.F. Schleusner and the lexicon of the Septuagint," *ZAW* 102 (1990) 252-62.

[4] In this Introduction "Hebrew" is mostly a shorthand including also Aramaic.

[5] On some methodological flaws in the former work in this regard, see Caird 1968, Caird 1969, and Lee 1969.

[6] For this the Spanish edition by N. Fernández Marcos & J.R. Busto Saiz, *El Texto Antioqueno de la Biblia griega*, has been used: 1-2 Samuel (Madrid, 1989), 1-2 Kings (Madrid, 1992), and 1-2 Chronicles (Madrid, 1996). Cf. also N. Fernández Marcos, V. Spottorno Díaz-Caro and J.M. Cañas Reíllo, *Índice griego-hebreo del Texto Antioqueno en los libros históricos*, 2 vols. (Madrid, 2005).

form presented in the edition by Rahlfs have also been fully investigated, and most of the variations between the two have been noted when instances are cited from these books with the form in the Antiochene version marked with *L*,

b) the Antiochene text of Judges[7] in addition to two versions of Judges, represented mainly by the codices A and B respectively,

c) Esther: both versions, the Old Greek, marked with o', and the so-called Alpha text, marked with *L*; six additional chapters enumerated from A to F, following the Göttingen edition by Hanhart,

d) Daniel: both the Old Greek and the so-called Theodotionic version, marked with LXX and TH respectively,

e) Job: the astericised passages or portions, marked with ¶,

f) what is printed in smaller typeface in Ziegler's edition of Ben Sira, representing a later Greek recension, marked here with ¶,

g) both versions of Tobit marked with $\mathfrak{G}^{I}$ and $\mathfrak{G}^{II}$ respectively and as printed in Hanhart's edition,

h) Ode 12, also known as Prayer of Manasseh.

Basic approach to the Septuagint lexicography

The Septuagint can be approached from a variety of angles, and this is true even when one's interests are basically those of a lexicographer. Focusing for the moment on those parts of the Septuagint which are a translation from a Semitic original – and they form the bulk of the Septuagint – a Septuagint lexicographer must ask himself a series of questions: what does he understand by the meaning or usage of a given Septuagint Greek word or form?, what significance is to be attached to the Semitic text behind the translation?, what is he going to do when the Greek text reads rather oddly or makes no good sense at all?, and so on. These are some of the complexities arising from the fact that here we are dealing with a translated text, which adds a third dimension, that of translator in addition to the author of the original text and the reader of the resultant translation.[8] If one is, in contrast, to define the meaning of a word in an original composition, one would attempt to determine what its author presumably meant and had in mind. However, the translator's intention is something rather elusive and not easy to comprehend with confidence. Reference to the original text, even if one is reasonably certain as to what the translator's text (*Vorlage*) read, does not necessarily remove all ambiguity. This is not to speak of the possibility, and even the likelihood, that the translator may have found the meaning of the Hebrew text obscure, totally unintelligible or susceptible of more than one interpretation, just as we do today. Following a series of exploratory studies and debates,[9] we have come to the conclusion that we had best read the Septuagint as a Greek document and try to find out what sense a reader in a period roughly 250 B.C. - 100 A.D. who was ignorant of Hebrew or Aramaic might have made of the translation, although we did compare the two texts all along. Thus we agree, for instance, with M. Harl,[10] who at Ho 13.8 ἄρκος ἀπορουμένη assigns the latter word the meaning 'famished,' thus 'a hungry bear,' despite the underlying Hebrew word שַׁכּוּל 'bereaved, robbed of cubs.'[11]

It is in line with this approach that we consider it justifiable and useful to refer, where appropriate, to daughter versions based on the Septuagint on the one hand, and Greek patristic commentaries on the Septuagint on the other,[12] although we are not particularly concerned with specifically Christian interpretation necessarily embedded in those daughter versions and commentaries, for our basic starting point is the Septuagint as a document of Hellenistic Judaism.

[7] In the absence of an edition of this recension for the book of Judges, it has been tentatively reconstructed from two uncials, K and Z, and several minuscules, *glnwptv* in particular, on the basis of the data to be found in the Larger Cambridge Septuagint.

[8] For a discussion of some theoretical aspects of the question, see E.A. Nida, *Toward a Science of Translating* (Leiden, 1964), esp. pp. 145-55.

[9] Some details arising from this exploration may be found in Muraoka 1990 as well as E. Tov, "Some thoughts" (n. 1 above) 23f. and idem, "Three dimensions of LXX words," *RB* 83 (1976) 529-44.

[10] Harl, *Langue*, p. 38, and *pace* Bons 2001, which is followed by Joosten in *BA* ad loc.

[11] Note the Ethiopic version, which has *reḥub* 'hungry.' The use of ἀτεκνόω or ἀποτεκνόω elsewhere in the LXX (including Ho 9.12) is obviously closer to the Hebrew meaning, and for some reason or other neither was used in our passage.

[12] We have occasionally consulted commentators such as Jerome, though writing in Latin, had themselves consulted the LXX.

An alternative approach is represented by J. Lust, E. Eynikel and K. Hauspie in their *Lexicon* (2003). For the translated parts of the LXX they attempt to understand the LXX Greek in relation to its Semitic original. The interlinear model advocated by Pietersma and partly applied to the LXX lexicography also belongs here.[13]

Jewish Greek?

The nature of the Septuagint Greek has been debated for quite some time. Since we do not believe that this is the appropriate place for engaging with that debate, we would simply like to state our position that we regard the language of the Septuagint to be a genuine representative of the contemporary Greek, that is to say, the Greek of the Hellenistic and Early Roman periods, though necessarily influenced by the grammar and usage of Aramaic and Hebrew from which the bulk of the Septuagint was translated, the nature and degree of that influence varying from translator to translator and from question to question.[14]

Whilst every effort has been made to consult and assimilate the standard works such as Preisigke's *Wörterbuch*, Moulton and Miligan's *Vocabulary*, the series *New Documents*, and many other studies, it has not proved practicable to comb through more recent publications of Greek papyri and inscriptions the results of which have not yet been fully incorporated into the standard reference works and other studies which have been consulted by us. See also our remark below (under **Layout**) on the symbol (*).

Textual basis

As we believe in the basic tenet of the Lagardian Ur-Septuaginta hypothesis, we submit that the fruits of study and work undertaken along that line should be fully utilised. We have thus adopted as our textual basis the excellent critical edition prepared by R. Hanhart, W. Kappler, O. Munnich, U. Quast, A. Rahlfs, J.W. Wevers and J. Ziegler.[15] For books for which the critical Göttingen edition is not available yet, we have based our investigation on Rahlfs's Handausgabe (1935) with occasional use of the Cambridge Larger Septuagint.[16]

Textual criticism and variants

We do not believe that we are obliged to redo all of the detailed textcritical work already competently undertaken by Ziegler and others for the Göttingen edition. Thus our lexicon is essentially based on the critical text as established by them. Only in a handful of places was it deemed justified to depart from their text, which is clearly indicated in the lexicon.[17] However, where variant readings (abbreviated as "v.l.") recorded by Ziegler and others or even readings attested by no Greek manuscript but established on their own authority with "scripsi" as at Ho 12.6 ἔλπιζε, for which the entire body of Greek manuscripts reads ἔγγιζε and rightly so in our view, were judged to be of some relevance for determining the sense of a given Greek lexeme or its usage, they are duly mentioned: for examples of the former category, see our entries for παρά **III 2**, and ὡς **I 9**. Finally, it goes without saying that textual criticism and lexicography sometimes inform each other, and future students of the Septuagint may find in this lexicon something useful for their textcritical work.[18]

[13] For our critique of this position, see Muraoka 2008b.

[14] Here is a considered opinion of one of the leading *savants* of the Septuagint and its language, M. Harl in Dogniez and Harl 2001.9: "le grec de la LXX est un vrai grec, non pas un grec bâtard." The reader interested in details and the recent discussion of the question is referred to Lee 1983.11-30; Harl, Dorival & Munnich 1988.233-35; G.H.R. Horsley, "The fiction of Jewish Greek," in G.H.R. Horsley, *New Documents Illustrating Early Christianity*, vol. 5 (Macquarie University, 1989), pp. 5-40.

[15] In the case of Ezekiel, however, we have deviated somewhat more frequently in favour of the papyrus 967 parts of which were not available to Ziegler, the editor of the critical Göttingen edition of the book.

[16] On the Antiochene recension, however, see above under **Scope**, pp. vii-viii.

[17] An example is our preference of ἐπ' ἐμὲ to Wevers's ἐπ' ἐμοὶ at Nu 11.13; see s.v. ἐπί **III 7**.

[18] To illustrate, at Am 8.1 some witnesses (V A') read ὁρᾷς instead of βλέπεις, which is Ziegler's preferred reading. Whilst we do not know the editor's reason for his decision at this point, a lexicographer may point out that in the Twelve Prophets the verb used in a question, which is the case in our passage, is consistently βλέπω, and ὁράω is used in a reply to it.

Nor does our lexicon deal with data gathered in the second apparatus of the Göttingen edition, the so-called "Three" or Hexaplaric materials. In addition to the reason advanced above, these data are mostly fragmentary and remain at word level, which does not provide a sufficient basis for lexicographical analysis.[19]

Fully fledged lexicon

Our lexicon is meant to be a fully fledged lexicon. As can be seen from the full explanation provided below under **Layout**, it provides as much information as considered necessary and desirable regarding the morphology, syntagmatics, paradigmatics, and semantics. Thus it differs in nature and conception from two recent related publications,[20] though both cover the entire Septuagint.

Following the model example of S.R. Driver, who was put in charge of the bane of any lexicographer, the so-called particles such as prepositions and conjunctions for 'BDB,'[21] we have given full attention to those short but highly versatile words, some of which, e.g. the prepositions ἐν, ἐπί, the definite article, the verb εἰμί, occur with frustrating frequency, but play extremely important roles from the point of view of communication and language functioning. In some such cases the line between lexicography and grammar tends to become blurred.

Working method

Whilst not every scholar publicises details of how he works, we would like to share this information with the reader so that our lexicon may be better understood and more effectively used, and also in the interest of the furtherance of our discipline.[22]

Whereas we, like many other colleagues in the field, have made extensive and grateful use of the essential tool of every scholar interested in the Septuagint, namely Hatch and Redpath's concordance (hencefoward: HR), and indeed we would rather doubt that we would have ever proceeded with the project but for this tool, we did not think it sound method to work from it, the main reason being that it does not provide enough context for serious lexicographical work. In order to determine the meaning of a word, one needs to read it at least in the whole sentence of which it forms a part. It is further axiomatic to see it in paradigmatic relationships, namely by taking into account synonymic, antonymic, or some other semantically associated word or words with which it occurs. This sort of essential information cannot, in most cases, be retrieved from the concordance. To illustrate, working from the concordance alone one would not notice two interesting points about the use of βλέπω in the Twelve Prophets: firstly, it occurs parallel to ὁράω, and secondly, when it does so, the former is used in a question, and the latter in a reply to it. Thus we started from the actual text, the whole text. Actually we began with the book of Obadiah. Each word occurring in the book was studied in its full context. Excepting a relatively small number of lexemes occurring even in our limited corpus with considerable frequency, the entries for all the lexemes occurring in Obadiah were completed by studying at the same time all other passages in the remaining books of the corpus where those lexemes occur. Important to point out in this connection is that we tried to study a given lexeme in relation to another lexeme or lexemes which are semantically associated with it in one way or another.[23] Without having a full inventory of all

[19] One would presumably have to modify this position somewhat when it comes to certain Septuagint books.

[20] *A Greek-English Lexicon of the Septuagint* as compiled by J. Lust, E. Eynikel and K. Hauspie (Stuttgart, 2003) and F. Rehkopf, *Septuaginta-Vokabular* (Göttingen, 1989). On the former, cf. the present writer's review in *Bib.* 75 (1994) 434-9.

[21] F. Brown, S.R. Driver and Ch.A. Briggs, *A Hebrew and English Lexicon of the Old Testament* (Oxford, 1907).

[22] This section describes our method adopted while working on the first edition of our lexicon for the Twelve Prophets, though basically the same method has also been applied in the subsequent phases of our work.

[23] Whilst fully cognizant of Wartburg's criticism of the traditional alphabetical arrangement as unscientific, we agree with Silva in thinking that it still has much to commend itself: M. Silva in *BIOSCS* 11 (1978) 23. Although a work such as J.P. Louw and E.A. Nida, *Greek-English Lexicon of the New Testament Based on Semantic Domains*, 2 vols. (New York, 1988), has very much of interest and value to offer, comparison with a standard dictionary such as Bauer's makes it plain that the former has its limitations (as they themselves are aware; see E.A. Nida and J.P. Louw, *Lexical Semantics of the Greek New Testament* [Atlanta, GA 1992], pp. 109, 114; see a reivew article by J.A.L. Lee in *FN* 5 [1992] 167-90), and we perhaps need both.

lexemes occurring in the Twelve Prophets it was not possible to start with fully mapped-out semantic fields of the whole vocabulary of our corpus.[24] Such networks of relationship continued to be built up by taking note of semantically related lexemes used in conjunction with the lexeme under study. Thus when the book of Obadiah was finished, we had completed rather more entries than the number of lexemes actually occurring in the book. Those related words occurring outside of Obadiah and our corpus were sought out with the help of HR. Proceeding in this manner book after book, we reached the last book of the corpus, Joel, when there were a rather small number of lexemes still remaining to be studied. A handful of lexemes and passages which had not been registered by Hatch and Redpath as occurring in our corpus were also picked up on the way. Information on those relatively few, high-frequency lexemes kept being collected, and their entries were completed towards the end of the whole work.

Words in context

A word is hardly ever used in isolation and on its own, but normally occurs in conjunction with another word or words. Such collocations help to establish the semantic 'profile' of the word concerned. Two words which are closely related may not wholly share their 'partners,' each thus gaining its individuality. Such information about collocations a given word enters provides important clues for defining its senses and determining its semantic 'contours.' It concerns questions such as what sorts of adjective a given noun is qualified by or what sorts of nouns or nominal entities a given verb takes as its grammatical subject or object.[25] In addition to these semantic collocations, the question of syntactic collocations is equally important: which case (genitive, dative or accusative) and which preposition a given verb governs.

Illustrative examples and references

Every dictionary user knows from experience that it is always useful to have definitions and uses of a word amply illustrated by actual examples. Here we have decided to err on the generous side. We trust, however, that this will serve good purpose in the long run. For every single sense and use, at least one applicable passage is mentioned, and rather often the actual Greek text is quoted, an English translation of which is enclosed within single quotes. Sometimes it was thought better to give the general idea of the context in which the word concerned occurs, and then an English translation of the sentence was given enclosed within double quotes with the occasional insertion of a relevant Greek word or words: e.g., ἀλλά, **2 b**, **d**.

Biblical references follow the numeration of chapter and verse as in the Septuagint, and the information on discrepancies in this regard between the Greek and Hebrew Bibles is not given, information which is readily available in the Göttingen critical edition or Rahlfs's Handausgabe.

Here we would like to draw the user's attention to not infrequent discrepancies in the system and mode of citation between the various, commonly used editions of the Septuagint themselves on the one hand, and between them and HR on the other. Our system is that of the critical Göttingen edition except for Ne (= Nehemiah), for which we follow HR, so that Ne 1.3 corresponds to 2E 11.3 in Hanhart's critical edition. When one has no easy access to the critical Göttingen edition, one ought to bear in mind that many of these discrepancies often boil down to a difference of one verse: e.g., Ps 84.2 (Göttingen and Rahlfs) = 84.1 (HR), which is also the case in books other than Psalter, for instance, Exodus. Another significant discrepancy concerns six additional passages in the book of Esther, which have been designated by Hanhart with the uppercase letters A to F with running verse numbers within each passage: e.g. Es A 2 in our and Hanhart's system corresponds to Es 1.1[b] in Rahlfs's Handausgabe and Es 1.1 in HR.

[24] Though highly useful in its way, X. Jacques's *List of Septuagint Words Sharing Common Elements* (Rome, 1972) does not always provide the sort of information we are after, for its principle is that of derivation and etymology. From a synchronic point of view, words sharing a common stem do not necessarily form a semantically related group: e.g. γινώσκω and ἀναγινώσκω have very little in common for our purpose, whereas βλέπω and ὁράω must be looked at together. Or again, ἔχω, κατάσχεσις 'possession,' and κάτοχος 'holding back,' all three are grouped together under ἔχω.

[25] See M. Silvas, *Biblical Words & their Meaning. An Introduction to Lexical Semantics* (Grand Rapids, 1983), pp. 142f., 160.

Definition, not translation equivalents[26]

Most bilingual or multilingual dictionaries give a translation equivalent or equivalents in the (target) language or languages other than the source language, words of which are being described in the dictionary in question. Such translation equivalents may or may not be accompanied by phrases or short sentences designed to illustrate the usage of the source language word concerned. The philosophy behind such a lexicographical approach is largely pragmatic and traditional: the average potential user of such a dictionary, reading a text in the foreign language concerned, wants to know how to "translate" an unfamiliar word occurring in the text. However, it is every average student's common knowledge that the use of such a pragmatically conceived and designed bi-/multilingual dictionary does often prove rather demanding. Finding in one's Spanish-English dictionary Sp. *otoño* glossed as "autumn, fall (US)," one would be able to cope without much trouble. But how about Sp. *orden* glossed as "order"? The Engl. *order* without further qualification is so vague: 'order' as in "a strict order," "the Franciscan order," "everything is in order," "maintain law and order," "talents of the first order," "alphabetical order," "to place an order for some commodity," and quite a few other possibilities. Even for a reasonably experienced student, choosing between such a wide array of diverse equivalents can be difficult.[27]

There is another potential difficulty to be borne in mind: that is the likelihood that the user of such a dictionary does not have the target language as his or her native language. This would certainly be the case with our own dictionary. Then the very pragmatic consideration dictates that something must be done to minimise the margin of misunderstanding and ensure the optimal communication between the author of a dictionary and its user. This is one major reason that we have chosen to go for definition, to describe senses of a given word in sentence form or as fragments of a sentence. This method is used not just in monolingual dictionaries. An outstanding example of the method applied to a bilingual dictionary is P.G.W. Glare (ed.), *Oxford Latin Dictionary* (Oxford, 1968-82).

Another consideration is more theoretical. In Bauer's New Testament Greek dictionary (BAGD) the definition of ἄγω begins with "**1**. *lead* - **a**. *lead, bring* ..." Whatever the dash after the first *lead* might be supposed to mean, 'to lead' and 'to bring' are, semantically speaking, two quite distinct things; they simply do not suffice as the definition of a sense of the verb in question.[28] Thus the method being adopted here makes one consider precisely what a given lexeme means. Given the fact that a given word in one language hardly ever fully overlaps with some word in another language, the translation equivalent method is bound to be imprecise, approximate or potentially misleading. We have tried to adhere to the principle of definition, though it has not always proven easy. The so-called function words such as prepositions, the article, conjunctions, for example, do not easily lend themselves to this method, constituting virtually *sui generis*.

The definition is italicised. Occasionally, when we saw fit, we *added* a translation equivalent or equivalents enclosed within single quotes: for example, ἀρήν is defined as *the young of sheep*, immediately followed by 'lamb.'

Where there is no or little likelihood of misunderstanding, we have given what might look like translation equivalents: e.g., τροφός *wet-nurse* instead of *woman employed to suckle another's child*. These are, in fact, single-word definitions.[29]

Layout

The typical entry consists of three main sections: for example,

A **ἀγνοέω**: aor. ἠγνόησα, inf. ἀγνοῆσαι; pf. ἠγνόηκα, ptc. ἠγνοηκώς, pass. ἠγνοημένος.

B **1**. *to act in ignorance*: περὶ τῆς ἀγνοίας αὐτοῦ, ἧς ἠγνόησεν καὶ αὐτὸς οὐκ ᾔδει Le 5.18, cf. Nu 12.11; ἔθνος ἀγνοοῦν καὶ δίκαιον Ge 20.4. **b**. *to do in ignorance*: pass., 2M 11.31.

[26] For a general discussion on definition to be preferred to gloss, see Lee 2003a. esp. 15-30, and for a nuanced exposition of pros and cons of the former, Thompson 2003. 114-19.

[27] For a discussion of methodological as well as practical reasons for preferring translation equivalents, see also E. Eynikel, "La lexicographie de la Septante: aspects méthodologiques," in *RSR* 73 (1999) 135-50, esp. 142-44. See also Roberts 2004.

[28] In the thoroughly revised edition by Danker (2000: BDAG) these translation equivalents are preceded by: "to direct the movement of an object from one position to another."

[29] An insight owed to Dr J.A.L. Lee in his review of the 2002 edition of our lexicon: *BIOSCS* 37 (2004) 134.

2. *to sin by wilfully ignoring and disregarding divine injunctions*: μὴ ἀγνόει Ho 4.15, Si 5.15; + cogn. acc., ἄγνοιαν μεγάλην 1K 14.24; + ματαιόομαι 26.21.

3. *to fail to discern*: ***o*** τι Wi 5.12. **b**. *to be unaware of*: a fact, + inf., Wi 7.12; + ὅτι 12.10. **c**. *to be unknown to one*: ὁ ἀγνοῶν 'the stranger' Wi 19.14 (‖ ἀλλότριος 'alien' vs. 15).

4. *to fail* or *to refuse to acknowledge the existence or reality of*: + acc., God Wi 15.11.

C Cf. ἄγνοια, ἀγνόημα, ἄγνωστος, γινώσκω: Bultmann, *TDNT* 1.115f.; Muraoka 1983.51f.

Section A, following the bold-faced headword, gives the following information:

Morphology. If the headword is a verb as in the example above, it lists forms of the tenses/moods other than the present and imperfect attested in our corpus. Where two or more forms belong to one tense, the name of the tense is not repeated, but the forms are marked off by a comma, not a semicolon.

If the headword is a noun, its genitive singular form is given, followed by its gender classification as in: "διαφθορά, ᾶς. f." In the case of an adjective, its singular feminine and neuter form follow the entry word as in: "διπλοῦς, ῆ, οῦν."

Occasionally the morphological inventory lists non-standard forms, e.g. ἐκρίνοσαν under κρίνω as an indicative, aorist, active 3pl. This, however, does not mean that this is the only form attested in our corpus for this inflectional category, for the standard form ἔκριναν *is* attested indeed.

The symbol ʃ means that all the passages in which the headword occurs in the corpus are mentioned in the entry. Out of a total of 9,548 head-words entered in this lexicon, 5,548 are so marked.

The asterisk, *, signifies that the word is not attested earlier than the Septuagint. The decision in this regard, mostly dependent on Liddell, Scott, and Jones's dictionary, can be debatable. Many papyri and other epigraphical material are undated or cannot be dated with confidence. Words so marked do not have to be neologisms created by Septuagint translators. When a word or usage marked with an asterisk is attested in Polybius, for instance, it is likely that its absence prior to the Septuagint is due to incomplete attestation, for Polybius is hardly under direct influence of the Septuagint. In this connection it may be interesting to know whether an etymologically and semantically related word or words are attested earlier than the entry word. The information on this matter is given as in: "βδέλυγμα, τος. n. * (βδελύσσω: Aristoph. +; so βδελυγμός)."[30] These neologims amount to about 1,900, roughly one fifth of the total LXX vocabulary. The asterisk is also used in the main body of the entry (e.g. under ἐνώπιος **II 2**), the following section, where the uncertainty equally prevails, and perhaps to a greater degree.

Section B is the main body of any entry, defining senses of the headword and describing its usage in accordance with our approach outlined above. A sense definition with occasional listing of a translation equvalent(s) enclosed with single quotes is marked off by a colon from the following description of the uses of the headword in the sense so defined. Here we would draw the user's particular attention to the use of semicolon. For example, Section **B** of the entry ὀργή reads as follows:

indignation, *wrath*: mostly of God's wrath, which is implied also in Zp 1.15 and Hb 3.2. Thus ὀ. κυρίου Mi 7.9, Zp 1.18, 2.2; ἐγένετο ὀ. μεγάλη παρὰ τοῦ κυρίου Zc 7.12; ‖ θυμός Ex 15.7 (see vs. 8), De 9.19, 29.23, Ho 13.11, Mi 5.15, Na 1.6, Zp 2.2; often combined w. θυμός for the effect of intensification as in ὁ θ. τῆς ~ῆς μου Nu 14.34, De 29.24, ὀ. θυμοῦ κυρίου Nu 25.4, κατὰ τὴν ~ὴν τοῦ θυμοῦ μου Ho 11.9, sim. Jn 3.9, Na 1.6*b*, Zp 3.8; ‖ ζῆλος Zp 1.18, 3.8, Zc 1.15; ‖ θυμός and παροξυσμός De 29.28; opp. to an attitude of love and care, Ho 14.5; opp. ἔλεος, Hb 3.2, Si 5.6; results in perdition, destruction, Ho 11.9, Am 4.10, Jn 3.9; in punishment, Mi 5.15; provoked by sins and disobedience, ~ὴν κυρίου ὑποίσω, ὅτι ἥμαρτον αὐτῷ Mi 7.9; Zc 7.12; w. obj. gen. in ἐν τῇ ~ῇ ὑμῶν Am 4.10; + εἴς τινα 1E 8.21 (‖ ἐπί τινα 2E 7.23); as cogn. obj. Ὠργίσθη κύριος .. ~ὴν μεγάλην Zc 1.2,

[30] See also M. Harl, "Problèmes de traduction du Pentateuque de la Septante dans une langue moderne," *Annali di Scienze Religiose* 1 (1996) 33-56. A convenient list of LXX neologisms, though confined to those occurring more than three times in the LXX, is Schröder 2001.

so 15; ἡμέρα ~ῆς Zp 1.15 (ǁ ἡ. θλίψεως καὶ ἀνάγκης, ἡ. ἀωρίας καὶ ἀφανισμοῦ), 18, 2.3; as adverbial adjunct, θυμωθεὶς ~ῇ κύριος ἐπὶ Μωυσῆν Ex 4.14; 32.10. **b**. hum. anger: ἐθυμώθη ~ῇ Ge 39.19; royal, ~ῃ καὶ χόλῳ 3M 5.1. **c**. w. no moral connotation: pl. and of raging wild animals, 2M 4.25.

The use of the semicolon on line 2 after "2.2" means that the combination ὀργὴ κυρίου occurs in our corpus at Mi 7.9, Zp 1.18 and 2.2, whereas the word occurs in conjunction with or parallel to θυμός at Ex 15.7, De 9.19 ... and so on. Thus, in order to gain an overall picture of the use of a given lexeme, the reader would be best advised to go through this section or a major sense division indicated by a bold-faced Arabic numeral or an upper case, bold-faced Roman numeral from the beginning to the end.

In the interest of economical use of space and resources, headwords are often abbreviated: when a headword occurs in a given citation in the form as given at the start of the entry printed bold, then its first letter only, or the first two letters in case of a diphthong, is given, followed by a full stop as in "ὀ. κυρίου" above for "ὀργὴ κυρίου." Otherwise the symbol "~" is used as in "~ὴν μεγάλην" (line 11 above) for "ὀργὴν μεγάλην."

The text is cited as it appears in the passage concerned. However, where the information provided concerns a particular phrase, idiom or the use of an associated word, synonym, antonym and the like, this does not necessarily apply. For example, on line 11 above the phrase ἡμέρα ὀργῆς appears in the form ἡμέρᾳ ὀργῆς at Zp 1.18, preceded by the preposition ἐν. Furthermore, a semantically associated word is generally given in the headword form. Thus under διαφεύγω one reads "Am 9.1 (ǁ διασῴζομαι)," whereas the actual form used in the passage mentioned is διασωθῇ. Likewise, we may omit mentioning a variant reading when such does not affect the point concerned: e.g., under φυλάσσω, **2**, 4K 6.9 is quoted with παρελθεῖν, for which the Lucianic recension[31] has διελθεῖν, which, however, is not mentioned, since we are interested in the syntagm <φυλάσσω + μή + inf.>. Moreover, particles such as δέ, γάρ or the definite article may be omitted when not affecting the description in a given entry; in the case of the definite article, its presence may apply only to the immediately following reference, but not necessarily to (all of) the subsequent reference(s).[32] Likewise, a pronoun has sometimes been replaced by a substantive to which it refers: e.g., under ἀντιλαμβάνομαι **1**, + ἐπιστήμης Ba 3.21 is mentioned, whilst the actual text reads αὐτῆς. Such a replacement is usually marked with a single ^ (e.g. ^ἐπιστήμης) or with ^..^ (e.g. ^ταῖς ὁδοῖς τοῦ κυρίου^, s.v. πορεύομαι **II 3**).

Under **Words in context** above we have referred to the notion of syntactic relationships a given lexeme may enter. To give part of this sort of information the symbols ***s*** and ***o*** (bold-faced as well as italic) are used, meaning "subject" and "object." These concepts are broadly understood here in terms of "deep structure," not "surface structure." For instance, under γεννάω one reads: "*to bring forth, bring into existence*: ***o*** hum. child - υἱοὺς καὶ υἱοὺς τῶν υἱῶν 'sons and grandsons' De 4.25; τέκνα ἀλλότρια ἐγεννήθησαν αὐτοῖς 'bastards were born to them' Ho 5.7." Here the grammatical subject of the passive form of the verb τέκνα ἀλλότρια, in the underlying active transform, however, is its grammatical object.

s is further extended to adjectives and substantives. Thus, under ἐπέτειος, "***s*** μίσθιος" signifies that μίσθιος may appear as the subject in a clause such as ἐπέτειος ὁ μίσθιος 'the labourer is hired for one year,' though in its only occurrence in the LXX the adj. is used attributively: μετὰ μισθίου ἐπετείου Si 37.11. Likewise βδέλυγμα 'abomination' we find "***s*** shepherd .. law-breaker .. sexual immoralities .. etc.," a catalogue of entities and actions which can constitute the predicate of a clause "τὸ βδέλυγμά ἐστιν .."

When a headword is thought to have more than one distinct sense, its multiple senses are divided by Roman numerals printed in bold typeface like **1**, **2**, **3** etc. Often under one such sense further division may be made as **a**, **b**, **c** etc. Such a subdivision is considered useful to identify distinct sets of references, diverse syntagmatic features, but sometimes a sense which can somehow be subsumed under a major subdivision, e.g.

31 When we cite from 1-4Kg, Ch, and Jd, the Lucianic recension is always consulted.

32 Thus under **λόγιον 3**, one reads, ".. λ. τῶν κρίσεων Ex 28.15; τῆς κρίσεως 28.23, Si 45.10." At Si 45.10, however, the text actually reads: λογίῳ κρίσεως.

under the headword ἄρχω we have first "**3**. mid. *to begin, make beginning, commence*," subsequently "**b**. *to be the first* to do sth."

Section C lists, where appropriate, a word or group of words semantically associated with the headword. Where the list is long, one headword is chosen to which reference is made in the same section of every other word on the list. This is the case with words constituting the semantic field of physical destruction, the complete list of which consists of 79[33] items and may be found under ἀφανίζω. In other words, the same list under ἀφανίζω is not repeated another 78 times.

Another type of information provided in this section is secondary literature. In addition to monographs, journal articles and the like dealing with individual lexemes, reference is often made to such major works as Preisigke's dictionary, Moulton and Milligan's *Vocabulary*, Shipp's monograph on Modern Greek illuminating Ancient Greek (full details under **Abbreviations** below). It has been part of our policy to mention these works only when they make some substantive contribution to our understanding of the semantics of the headword in question. Thus reference would be found lacking to many headwords in this dictionary, though they are mentioned and discussed in, for instance, Spicq's valuable *Theological Lexicon*[34] and Kittel's *Theological Dictionary*. The same applies to journal articles, encyclopaedia entries, and monographs.

The list of paradigmatically relevant lexemes is introduced with "Cf." with the letter C in upper case. The list may be followed, separated with a colon, by a reference or references to secondary literature. E.g., under τύχη: "Cf. δαίμων, μόρος: Schmidt 4.375f.; Bauernfeind, *TDNT* 8.240f." Where such information applies specifically to part of the entry, it may be inserted at the appropriate place within the body of the entry. Thus, again under τύχη, Section **B** of the entry ends with: "Is 65.11 (‖ δαίμων), cf. Seeligmann 1948.99f.," which signifies that the reference to Seeligmann's work applies to Is 65.11 only. In the case of entries which have multiple divisions marked off by the use of Roman numerals (I, II etc.), Arabic numerals, letters of the Latin alphabet whether in upper-case or lower-case, all these bold-faced, Section **C** is indented as under τροφή:

τροφή, ῆς. f.

1. *food*: διαδώσει ~ήν 'will distribute food' Ge 49.27; ἀγγέλων ~ήν .. ἄρτον ἀπ' οὐρανοῦ Wi 16.20.

2. *upbringing*: Si 22.7¶.

Cf. ἔδεσμα, τρέφω: Moussy 85-8.

Finally, in some entries we mention a reference or references preceded by "Del." as under τύχη where we read: "Del. 2M 7.37 v.l." This does not necessarily mean that the entire verse is to be deleted, but only the noun τύχη attested in some manuscripts instead of ψυχή, which has been adopted by R. Hanhart, the editor of the critical edition of the book. This type of data, however, is only partially presented. The full data will be published in the future publication mentioned below in f.n. 35.

In the first two editions of this dictionary (1993; 2002) most entries concluded with **Section D**, which is about the relationship between the Septuagint and its Hebrew original. Seeing, however, this section is not integral to the LXX lexicography as such, it has been deleted from this edition.[35] The only exceptions are a small number of particles, e.g. ἅμα, for which HR provide no information.

In the main section of the entry which includes references where the Hebrew or Aramaic lexeme or phrase has been identified as rendering the Greek word of the entry, this link is marked by using the italicised lower-case letters of the alphabet appearing in the list at the end of the entry.

[33] Even this list is not absolutely complete, for not every derivative such as nouns is included, but looking up any word appearing on the list would lead the reader to such derivatives. The author is contemplating presenting data in this section in a more illuminating format.

[34] Though this is an extremely useful and informative work, the user ought to be aware that references given by Spicq, especially those from the LXX, do not always contain a given lexeme under discussion, though the general idea which the author is discussing is there.

[35] We hope to publish these data in a single volume incorporating our *Hebrew/Aramaic Index to the Septuagint: Keyed to the Hatch-Redpath Concordance* (Grand Rapids, MI, 1998), replacing the original HR's reverse index in the 1998 reprint of HR brought out by the same publisher.

Of other symbols used. (†) indicates the doubt as to whether or not the Greek word concerned was meant by the translator to be a straightforward equivalent of the putative Hebrew or Amamaic word in the MT. (-) indicates that the translator's Greek text most probably had no Hebrew or Aramaic word corresponding to the Greek headword. (?) is a symbol of despair, indicating our inability to establish any relationship of equivalence between the Greek word concerned and the supposed Hebrew original of the translator. All this is the same as in HR. With (fr) we mean to say that our translator, who seems, in the passage concerned, to have had basically the same Hebrew text as the Massoretic text, without vowels and other Massoretic signs, of course, but decided to exercise, for some reason or other, a measure of freedom, deliberately not translating his Hebrew text as he had it.

Because of the considerable length of time that has elapsed since we started working on this project sometime in mid 1984, we fear, there may be spotted signs of inconsistency in the matter of organisation and presentation of data. We only hope that they will not result in serious breakdown in communication between the compiler of the dictionary and its user.

It is our most pleasant duty to record here in writing our very sincere thanks to various individuals and organisations which have contributed to the production of this present volume. First, Dr J.A.L. Lee of Sydney, Australia, the author of a pioneering work in the field of Septuagintal lexicography (*A Lexical Study of the Septuagint Version of the Pentateuch* [1983]), who as full partner in the project up to mid 1989, read, with his characteristic care and attention to both details and general, methodological aspects, my initial draft of about 250 entries for our 1993 lexicon for the Twelve Prophets, thereby contributing very substantially to their more or less definitive writing. I learned a great deal from, and thoroughly enjoyed, exchanges of correspondence with him and several precious sessions we spent in each other's company. The Faculty of Arts of the University of Melbourne, where I worked from 1980 to 1991, provided a considerable amount of resources for this project. Dr R.G. Jenkins, a former colleague of mine at the same institution, assisted me generously on countless occasions with his expert knowledge of computer technology. I also made grateful use of a neatly handwritten Hebrew index[36] to HR prepared by my wife, Keiko, with all page references converted to actual Greek words.

The task of expanding the 1993 small-scale lexicon for the Twelve Prophets to incorporate data chiefly from the Pentateuch was assisted by a number of organisations and individuals, to all of which/whom I am profoundly indebted. The Netherlands Organisation for Scientific Research (NWO) granted me a substantial fund which released me for one full year from my teaching duties at Leiden University. My previous employer, Leiden University, is also to be thanked for exempting me from all my teaching duties for a year. Prof. Dr. A. Aejmelaeus of the University of Göttingen showed great interest in the project and proposed me to the Alexander von Humboldt Foundation, which conferred on me a most generous research award, enabling me to work on the project intensively for a year in Göttingen. Prof. Aejmelaeus also saw to it that during my stay in Göttingen I was provided with a paid assistant, the luxury enjoyed for the first (and alas last) time in my working life, in the person of Mr Oleg Lazarenco, who dutifully and efficiently discharged quite a few onerous tasks on my behalf, including a systematic check of names of LXX books and literally thousands of references mentioned in the lexicon. He also proffered his considered view on various substantive issues. Any typographical or material errors that might still remain are, however, entirely mine. I am also grateful to the Faculty of Divinity at Göttingen for accommodating me as a visiting professor, and the Septuaginta-Unternehmen, the facilities of which were made available to me. The Rev. Dr. Max Rogland offered his services yet again, by going through a near-definitive version of the lexicon, improving the quality of its English at countless places. Thanks are also due to Messers. Peeters Sr and Jr for agreeing to publish this work and their enthusiasm and encouragement shown to me over so many years, and likewise to their printer of this volume, Drukkerij Orientaliste, for the excellent technical execution and converting the entire file of my 1993 lexicon to the proper Macintosh format.

[36] Which formed the basis of the *Index* mentioned in the preceding footnote.

ἄνθρωπος γεννᾶται κόπῳ.
Man is born to toil. (Job 5.7)

χάριτι δὲ θεοῦ εἰμι ὅ εἰμι,
καὶ ἡ χάρις αὐτοῦ ἡ εἰς ἐμὲ οὐ κενὴ ἐγενήθη,
ἀλλὰ περισσότερον αὐτῶν πάντων ἐκοπίασα,
οὐκ ἐγὼ δὲ ἀλλὰ ἡ χάρις τοῦ θεοῦ ἡ σὺν ἐμοί.

It is by God's grace that I am what I am today,
and His grace for me has not been wasted,
but rather I toiled more than all of them put together,
yet not I, but God's grace which is ever with me. (1Cor 15.10)

οὐκ εἰς κενὸν ἔδραμον οὐδὲ εἰς κενὸν ἐκοπίασα.
I have not run in vain nor have I toiled in vain. (Phil 2.16)

Oegstgeest, The Netherlands
6th October, 2008.

Prof. emer. Dr. Takamitsu Muraoka.
Leiden University

ABBREVIATIONS

1. **General**

abl.: ablative
abs.: absolute, i.e. used without an object or any similar essential modifier; gen. abs., genitive absolute
acc.: accusative case
Ach: Achmimic (Coptic) version
act.: active voice
adj.: adjective (-val, -vally)
adv.: adverb (-ial, -ially)
AE: *L'Année épigraphique*
Aeg: *Aegyptus*
ag.n.: agent noun, nomen agentis
AJBI: *Annual of the Japanese Biblical Institute*
AJP: *American Journal of Philology*
AJSL: *American Journal of Semitic Languages and Literatures*
alm.: almost
alr.: already
alw.: always
AN: *Abr-Nahrain*
anarth.: anarthrous, i.e. lacking the definite article
AnCl: *L'Antiquité Classique*
AO: *Archiv Orientální*
aor.: aorist tense
Apol: Apollinarius of Laodicaea, quoted from PG 33
app.: apposition; appositional
Aq: Aquila
Arb: Arabic (version)
Ar: Aramaic
Arm: Armenian (version)
art.: (definite) article
Ath: St Athanasius, quoted from PG 27.
attr.: attributive(ly)
BA: *La Bible d'Alexandrie*, ed. M. Harl, G. Dorival, O. Munnich (Paris, 1986-)
Bas. Magn.: Basilius Magnus of Caesarea, quoted from PG 29
BH: Biblical Hebrew
Bib.: *Biblica*
BIOSCS: *Bulletin of the International Organization for Septuagint and Cognate Studies*
bis: 'occurring twice'
BNAW: Beihefte *Zeitschrift für Neutestamentliche Wissenschaft*
Bo: Bohairic (Coptic) version
BZ: *Biblische Zeitschrift*
BZAW: Beihefte *Zeitschrift für Alttestamentliche Wissenschaft*
c.: cum 'together with, in conjunction with'; common gender, i.e. used irrespectively whether masculine or feminine; century
caus.: causative
CÉg: *Chronique d'Égypte*
Chr: Chrysostom, cited from PG 69; for Job from Hagedorn 1990
Cl. Gk: Classical Greek
cl.: clause
ClPh: *Classical Philology*
ClQu: *The Classical Quarterly*
Co: Coptic (version)
cogn.obj.: cognate object, i.e. a grammatical object derived from the same root or stem as that of the verb of which it is the object
coll.: collective (singular)
com.: commodi, in "dat. com." (= dative of advantage)
comp.: comparative degree (of adjectives, adverbs)
conj.: conjunction
cp.: compare
CPR: Corpus papyrorum Raineri
Cyr.: Cyril of Alexandria, quoted for the XII Prophets from Ph.E. Pusey (ed.), *Sancti patris nostri Cyrilli Alexandrini in XII prophetas*, 2 vols. (Oxford, 1868); other books from PG
dat.: dative case
def.: definite
dep.: deponent (i.e., passive in form only)
dim.: diminutive
dir.: direct
ditt.: dittography
div.: division in "word div."
DJD: *Discoveries in the Judaean Desert* (Oxford)
DN: divine name
du.: dual
Engl.: English
Epiph: Epiphanius
esp.: especially
ÉC: *Les études classiques*
Eth: Ethiopic (version)
ETL: *Ephemerides Theologicae Lovanienses*
euph.: euphemism, euphemistic
Eus.: Eusebius of Caesarea, commentary on Isaiah, quoted from J. Ziegler, *Der Jesajakommentar* [Eusebius Werke 9] (Berlin, 1975)
Euth.: Euthymius Zigabenus, quoted from PG
Evagrius: P. Géhin, *Évagre le Pontique, Scholies aux Proverbes* [SC 340] (Paris, 1987)
ex.: example
exc.: except; exception(s)
excl.: exclamatory
f.: feminine gender
fig.: figure, figurative(ly)
FN: *Filología Neotestamentaria*

f.n.: footnote
foll.: following *or* followed
fr.: 'free rendering' (see above, Introduction, p. xvi)
freq.: frequent(ly)
Fschr: Festschrift
fut.: future tense
GCS: Die griechischen christlichen Schriftsteller der ersten drei Jahrhunderte.
gen.: genitive case; general(ly)
Gk: Greek
GN: geographical name
GRBS: *Greek, Roman, and Byzantine Studies*
hapl.: haplography
Heb.: Hebrew
hi.: Hifil
hishtaf.: Hishtafel
hith.: Hithpael
ho.: Hofal
hum.: human
ib.: ibidem, 'in the work or passage or chapter just mentioned'
idiom.: idiomatic(ally)
i.e.: id est (= that is to say)
impers.: impersonal
impf.: imperfect tense
impv.: imperative mood
incom.: incommodi, in "dat. incom." (= dative case of disadvantage)
ind.: indicative mood
indecl.: indeclinable
inf.: infinitive
infl.: influence(d)
inst.: instrumental
interj.: interjection
intr.: intransitive
interr.: interrogative
JBL: *Journal of Biblical Literature*
Jer.: Jerome
JJS: *Journal of Jewish Studies*
JNWSL: *Journal of Northwest Semitic Languages*
JSJ: *Journal for the Study of Judaism*
JSS: *Journal of Semitic Studies*
JThSt: *Journal of Theological Studies*
Jul.: Job commentary by Julian the Arian, ed. Hagedorn (1973)
K: Ketiv
κτλ: καὶ τὰ λοιπά 'et cetera'
L: Lucianic version or recension; *L* Mad, Madrid ed., N. Fernández Marcos and J.R. Busto Saiz, *El Texto antioqueno de la biblia griega* (Madrid, 1989-96)
La: Old Latin version
leg.: legendum (= to be emended to)
lit.: literal(ly)
loc.: in "ad loc." (= 'at *or* the place in question'); = loci 'of place'
LXX: Septuagint
m.: masculine gender
met.: by metonymy
metaph.: metaphorical(ly)
metath.: metathesis
meton.: metonymy, metonymical
MH: Mishanic Hebrew
mid.: middle voice
MM: J.H. Moulton and G. Milligan, *The Vocabulary of the Greek Testament* (London, 1930)
MT: Massoretic text of the Hebrew Bible
n.: neuter gender *or* noun
NAWG: *Nachrichten von der Akademie der Wissenschaften zu Göttingen*
neg.: negative *or* negator
ni.: Nifal
nom.: nominative case; nominal
NT: *Novum Testamentum*
NTS: *New Testament Studies*
num.: numeral
O: Origenic recension
o: object of a verb (see above, Introduction, p. xiv)
obj.: object of a verb; objective in "obj.gen." (= objective genitive)
obl.: oblique (case), viz. case other than nom. and voc.
Ol.: Olympiodorus, commentary on Job (Hagedorn 1984)
om.: omit(s)
opp.: opposed to, opposite = used alongside the antonym mentioned
opt.: optative mood
Or.: Origen; commentary on Job quoted from Hagedorn (1994-2000); on Ezekiel from Baehrens
פ': = פְּלוֹנִי "somebody"
pass.: passive (voice)
perh.: perhaps
pers.: person (as against "rei": see below; divine beings included)
pf.: perfect tense
PG: J.P. Migne (ed.), *Patrologia Graeca* (Paris, 1844ff.)
pi.: Piel
PL: J.P. Migne (ed.), *Patrologia Latina* (Paris, 1844ff.)
pl.: plural
plpf.: pluperfect tense
PN: personal name
poet.: poetic
poss.: possibly *or* possessive
postp.: postposition
pu.: Pual
pr.: praemittit, 'prefixes, adds before'; 'preface'
prec.: preceding, immediately preceding entry *or* preceded
pred.: predicative *or* predicatively
prep.: preposition
pres.: present tense
prob.: probably
Proc.: Procopius of Gaza, quoted from Migne's edition
prol.II: Prologue of Ben Sira in MS 248
pron.: pronoun

ptc.:	participle
Q:	Qere
QH:	Qumran Hebrew
q.v.:	quod vide, 'see under the item just mentioned'
Ra:	A. Rahlfs, *Septuaginta* (Stuttgart, 1935)
RB:	*Revue biblique*
RdP:	*Revue de philologie de littérature et d'histoire anciennes*
RÉA:	*Revue des études anciennes*
ref.:	reference; referring
refl.:	reflexive
RÉG:	*Revue des études grecques*
rei:	'of a thing' as against "pers." 'of a person'
rel.:	relative; = reliqui, 'remaining (manuscripts)'
Rev:	Revelation, i.e. the Apocalypse of St John
RH:	Rabbinic Hebrew
RHPR:	*Revue d'histoire et de philosophie religieuses*
Riv.Fil.:	*Rivista di Filologia*
RMPh:	*Rheinisches Museum für Philologie*
RSPT:	*Revue des sciences philosophiques et théologiques*
RSR:	*Revue des sciences religieuses*
RTP:	*Revue de théologie et de philosophie*
s.:	sub, 'under'; singular
s:	subject (see Introduction, p. xiv)
sbd:	somebody
SBFLA:	*Studium biblicum franciscanum, Liber annuus*
SC:	Sources Chrétiennnes
sc.:	scilicet, 'that is to say, the following is to be understood as implied, though not explicitly stated'
SCS:	Septuagint and Cognate Studies
SEG:	*Supplementum Epigraphicum Graecum*
sg.:	singular
sim.:	similar(ly) *or* simile
simp.:	simplex (verb: as against compound)
SP:	*Studia papyrologica*
spec.:	specifically
sth:	something
subj.:	subjunctive mood *or* subject of a clause or sentence *or* subj.gen. = subjective genitive
subs.:	immediately following entry
subst.:	substantive, substantivally used = adjective used as a noun
suf.:	suffix
super.:	superlative degree (of adjectives and adverbs)
Supp.:	Supplement
s.v.:	sub voce, 'under the word in question'
Syh:	Syrohexapla
Sym:	Symmachus
syn.:	synonym, synonymous(ly)
Syp:	Syropalestinian version
Syr:	Syriac
ter.:	tertio, 'occurring three times'
Th:	Theodore, quoted from the edition by H.N. Sprenger, *Theodori Mopsuesteni commentarius in XII prophetas* (Wiesbaden, 1977); Theodotion.
TH:	Theodotionic version or recension
Thdt:	Theodotion
ThLZ:	*Theologische Literaturzeitung*
Tht:	Theodoret, quoted from Migne's edition
Thph:	Theophrastus, quoted from Migne's edition
tit.:	title
tr.:	transitive
Trg:	Targum
TrgJon:	Targum Jonathan (ed. A. Sperber)
Trg N:	Targum Neofiti.
TrgOnk:	Targum Onkelos (ed. A. Sperber)
t.t.:	technical term
txt?:	uncertain whether the received Hebrew text is in order or not
v.:	vide, 'See'
vb. fin.:	verbum finitum, i.e. a verb inflected for person and number in addition to tense, mood, and voice
viz.:	videlicet, 'namely'
v.l.:	varia lectio, 'variant reading'
v.n.:	verbal noun
voc.:	vocative case *or* vocalisation
Vorl.:	Vorlage, i.e. a Hebrew or Aramaic text which lay before a translator
vs.:	verse *or* versus
VT:	*Vetus Testamentum*
VTS:	Supplements to *Vetus Testamentum*
w.:	with
XII:	the Twelve (Minor) Prophets
Z:	*Zeitschrift*
ZAW:	*Zeitschrift für die alttestamentliche Wissenschaft*
ZNW:	*Zeitschrift für die neutestamentliche Wissenschaft*
ZPE:	*Zeitschrift für Papyrologie und Epigraphik*
Zgl:	Joseph Ziegler

2. **Books of the Bible** (mostly in accordance with Hatch and Redpath's concordance)

Ge	Genesis
Ex	Exodus
Le	Leviticus
Nu	Numbers
De	Deuteronomy
Jo	Joshua
Jd	Judges
Ru	Ruth
1-4K	1-4 Kingdoms
1-2C	1-2 Chronicles
1-2E	1-2Ezra
Ne	Nehemiah[37]
To	Tobit
Ju	Judith

[37] Nehemiah MT chapters 1-13 = chapters 11-23 in the Göttingen edition, R. Hanhart, *Esdrae Liber II*.

Es	Esther	Na	Nahum
Jb	Job	Hb	Habakkuk
Ps	Psalms	Zp	Zephaniah
Pr	Proverbs	Hg	Haggai
Ec	Ecclesiastes	Zc	Zechariah
Wi	Wisdom of Solomon	Ma	Malachi
Od	Odes	Is	Isaiah
PSol	Psalms of Solomon	Je	Jeremiah
Ct	Canticles	Ba	Baruch
Si	Ben Sira	La	Lamentations
Ho	Hosea	Ep Je	Epistle of Jeremiah
Am	Amos	Ez	Ezekiel
Mi	Micah	Da	Daniel
Jl	Joel	Su	Susannah
Ob	Obadiah	Bel	Bel and the Dragon
Jn	Jonah	1-4M	1-4Mccabees

New Testament and the Dead Sea Scrolls

Mt	Matthew	1-2 Tim	1-2 Timothy
Mk	Mark	1-2Pet	1-2 Peter
Lk	Luke	Heb	Hebrews
Joh	John	Jas	Epistle of James
Acts	The Acts of the Apostles	Rev	Revelation
Rom	Romans	Ep. Arist.	Epistle of Aristeas
1-2Cor	1-2 Corinthians	1QapGen	Genesis Apocryphon
Eph	Ephesians	1QS	The Community Rule
Phil	Philippians	8QMez	8Q Mezuzah
1-2 Thes	1-2 Thessalonians	CD	Damascus Document

Classical authors

Aes.	Aeschylus	Joseph.	Josephus
Aristot.	Aristoteles	Luc.	Lucianus
Aristoph.	Aristophanes	Lys.	Lysias
Demosth.	Demosthenes	Pl.	Plato
Eur.	Euripides	Plut.	Plutarch
Hdt.	Herodotus	Polyb.	Polybius
Hip.	Hippocrates	Soph.	Sophocles
Hom.	Homer	Thuc.	Thucydides
Isoc.	Isocrates	Xen.	Xenophon

3. **Other symbols**

::	opposite, differently than.
*	a Greek headword, a sense or a usage so marked is not attested prior to the LXX (see above p. xiii)
∫	All passages where the headword occurs in the LXX or the usage concerned occurs are mentioned in the body of the article (see above, p. xiii).
x∫	The listing is incomplete, esp. in lists of Semitic equivalents at the end of some entries, e.g. ἐάν.
(†)	The LXX translator did not have in mind the Hebrew word standing in the Massoretic text when he used the Greek headword concerned (see above, p. xvi).
‖	'parallel to'
+	a) used when a lexeme is found with a synonym joined by καί or ἤ, e.g. under ταλαιπωρία: "+ σύντριμμα Is 59.7." b) indicates that more references can be mentioned, though used only selectively. c) indicates in lists of Semitic equivalents that the references mentioned are to be added.
-	indicates in lists of Semitic equivalents that the references mentioned are to be deleted.
~	used to give a compound word in an abbreviated form. More than a prefix may be abbreviated: e.g., ~μήσας for an aor. ptc. of κατατολμάω. used to abbreviate a cited form (see above, p. xiv).
(-)	In the apparent Vorlage there is no Hebrew or Aramaic word which would correspond to the Greek entry word.

(?)	We cannot establish the Aramaic or Hebrew word which a given Greek headword is supposed to have translated (see above, p. xvi).
¶	Added at the end of references found in the asstericised Origenic recension in the book of Job, and what is printed in a smaller font in Ziegler's ed. of Sira.
^ ^	enclose a word or words marked by a pronoun in the actual text (see above, p. xiv).
⸢ ⸣	enclose a variant reading.

BIBLIOGRAPHY

AB: *The Anchor Bible*. Eds: W.F. Albright and D.N. Freedman (Garden City, N.Y.)

Abel: F.-M. Abel, *Grammaire du grec biblique suivie d'un choix de papyrus* (Paris, 1927).

—. 1948. "Éclaircissement de quelques passages des Maccabées," *RB* 55.184-94.

—. ^{2}1949. *Les livres des Maccabées* (Paris).

Aejmelaeus, A. 1982. *Parataxis in the Septuagint: A Study of the Renderings of the Hebrew Coordinate Clauses in the Greek Pentateuch* (Helsinki).

—. 1985. "OTI *causale* in Septuagintal Greek," in N. Fernández Marcos (ed.), *La Septuaginta en la investigacion contemporanea* (V Congreso de la IOSCS, Madrid), 115-32.

—. 1987. "The significance of clause connectors in the syntactical and translation-technical study of the Septuagint," in Cox, *VI Congress*, 361-80.

—. 1990. "OTI *recitativum* in Septuagintal Greek," in D. Fraenkel, U. Quast and J.W. Wevers (eds), *Studien zur Septuaginta: Robert Hanhart zu Ehren* (Göttingen), 74-82.

—. 2003. "'Rejoice in the Lord!'. A lexical and syntactical study of the semantic field of joy in the Greek Psalter," on Baasten and van Peursen 2003.501-21.

Aerts, W.J. 1965. *Periphrastica. An Investigation into the Use of* εἶναι *and* ἔχειν *as Auxiliaries or Pseudo-auxiliaries in Greek from Homer up to the Present Day* (Amsterdam).

Aitken, J.K. 2000. "ΣΧΟΙΝΟΣ in the Septuagint," *VT* 50.433-44.

—. 2007. *The Semantics of Blessing and Cursing in Ancient Hebrew* [*ANES* Supplement 23] (Leuven).

Albrektson, B. 1963. *Studies in the Text and Theology of the Book of Lamentations with a Critical Edition of the Peshitta Text* (Lund).

Albright, W.F. 1955. "Some Canaanite-Phoenician sources of Hebrew wisdom," in H.H. Rowley (ed.), *Wisdom in Israel and in the Ancient Near East* [VTS 3], 1-15 (Leiden).

Alexandre, M. 1988. *Le Commencement du livre Genèse I-V. La version grecque de la Septante et sa réception* [Christianisme Antique 3] (Paris).

Allen, W.C. 1894. "On the meaning of προσήλυτος in the Septuagint," *The Expositor* 4.264-75.

Amigues, S. 1980. "Remarques sur la syntaxe de ΠΡΙΝ," *ÉC* 48.193-210.

—. 2005. "Les animaux nommés σκώληξ dans les *Indica* de Ctésias, *FGrH* 45(46)," *RdP* 79.7-15.

Amouretti, M.C. 1988. "La viticulture antique: contraintes et choix techniques," *RÉA* 90.5-17.

Amstutz, J. 1968. ΑΠΛΟΤΗΣ. *Eine begriffsgeschichtliche Studie zum jüdisch-christlichen Griechisch* (Bonn).

Amusin, I.D. 1986. "I termini designanti la schiavitù nell'Egitto ellenistico in base ai dati dei Settanta," in I. Biezunska Malowist (ed.), *Schiavitù e produzione nella Roma repubblicana* (Roma), 107-46.

Anz: H.A. Anz, *Subsidia ad cognoscendum Graecorum sermonem vulgarem e Pentateuchi versione alexandrina repetita* (Halle, 1894).

Arieti, J.A. 1974. "The vocabulary of Septuagint Amos," *JBL* 93.338-47.

Armoni, Ch. 2003. "Zur Bedeutung von μετάβολος in den Papyri und Ostraka," *ZPE* 145.213-8.

Aubin, P. 1963. *Le Problème de la <<Conversion>>: Étude sur un terme commun à l'hellénisme et au christianisme des trois premiers siècles* (Paris).

Auvray, P. 1957. "Notes sur le prologue de l'Ecclésiastique," in R. Tournay (ed.), *Mélanges bibliques rédigés en l'honneur de André Robert* (Paris), 281-7.

Auwers, J.-M. 2005. "L'apport du texte long du Siracide au lexique du grec biblique," in F. García Martínez and M. Vervenne (eds), *Interpreting Translation: Studies on the LXX and Ezekiel* [Fschr J. Lust] (Leuven), 33-44.

Avalos, H. 1989. "δεῦρο / δεῦτε and the imperatives of הלך: New criteria for the 'Kaige' recensions of Reigns," *EB* 47.165-76.

Azar, M. 1995. *The Syntax of Mishnaic Hebrew* [in Heb.] (Jerusalem).

Baasten, M.F.J., and W.Th. van Peursen. 2003. *Hamlet on a Hill: Semitic and Greek Studies Presented to Professor T. Muraoka on the Occasion of his Sixty-Fifth Birthday* [Orientalia Lovaniensia Analecta 118] (Leuven - Paris - Dudley, MA).

Baehrens, W.A. 1925. *Origenes Werke*, Bd. 8 [GCS] (Leipzig).

BAGD: W. Bauer (W.F. Arndt and F.W. Gingrich), *A Greek-English Lexicon of the New Testament and Other Early Christian Literature*, rev. and ed. by F.W. Danker (Chicago/London, ^{2}1979).

Bagnall, R.S. 1999. "The date of *P. Kell.* I G. 62 and the meaning of χωρίον," *CÉg* 74.329-33.

Bain, D. 1999. "Some addenda and corrigenda to the revised Supplement to Liddell and Scott," *Glotta* 75.121-33.

Bakker, W.F. 1974. *Pronomen abundans and pronomen coniunctum* (Amsterdam).

Balode, S. & J. Blomqvist, 2002. "ὀπίσω with genitive in extra-biblical Greek," *Eranos* 100.101-8.

Barr, J. 1961. *The Semantics of Biblical Language* (London).

—. 1962. *Biblical Words for Time* (London).

—. 1967. “Seeing the wood for the trees? An enigmatic ancient translation,” *JSS* 12.11-20.

—. 1974. “ΕΡΙΖΩ and ΕΡΕΙΔΩ in the Septuagint: a note principally on Gen. xlix. 6,” *JSS* 19.198-215.

—. 1975. “בארץ ~ΜΟΛΙΣ: Prov. xi.31, I Pet. iv.18,” *JSS* 20.149-64.

—. 1980. “The meaning of ἐπακούω and its cognates in the LXX,” *JThSt* 31.67-72.

—. 1987. “Words for love in Biblical Greek,” in L.D. Hurst & N.T. Wright (eds), *The Glory of Christ in the New Testament* [Fschr G.B. Caird] (Oxford), 3-18.

Barth, G. 1982. “Pistis in hellenistischer Religiosität,” *ZNW* 73.110-26.

Barthélemy, D. 1963. *Les Devanciers d’Aquila* [SVT 10] (Leiden).

—. 1972. “Le papyrus Bodmer 24 jugé par Origène,” J. Schreiner (ed.), *Wort, Lied und Gottesspruch* [Fschr J. Ziegler] (Würzburg), 11-19.

—. 1980. “La qualité du Texte Massorétique de Samuel,” in E. Tov (ed.), *The Hebrew and Greek Texts of Samuel* (Jerusalem), 1-44.

Bartina, S. 1965. “ὀθόνια ex papyrorum testimoniis linteamina,” *SP* 4.27-38.

Battaglia, E. 1989. *‘Artos’: Il lessico della panificazione nei papiri greci* (Milano).

Bauer: W. Bauer, *Griechisch-deutsches Wörterbuch zu den Schriften des Neuen Testaments und der frühchristlichen Literatur,* 6., völlig neu bearbeitete Auflage von K. und B. Aland (Berlin / Hawthorne, 1988).

Bauer, J. 1957. “Πῶς in der griechischen Bibel,” *NT* 2.81-91.

Baumgarten, J.M. 1984. “On the non-literal use of *ma‘ăśēr/dekatē*,” *JBL* 103.245-51.

BD: F. Blass and A. Debrunner, *Grammatik des neutestamentlichen Griechisch* (Göttingen, ^{9}1954).

BDAG: *A Greek-English Lexicon of the New Testament and Other Early Christian Literature*, rev. and ed. by F.W. Danker, based on Walter Bauer’s *Griechisch-deutsches Wörterbuch zu den Schriften des Neuen Testaments und der frühchristlichen Literatur,* sixth edition, ed. Kurt Aland and Barbara Aland, with Viktor Reichmann and on previous English editions by W.F. Arndt. F.W. Gingrich and F.W. Danker (Chicago/London, 2000).

BDB: F. Brown, S.R. Driver & Ch.A. Briggs, *A Hebrew and English Lexicon of the Old Testament* (Oxford, 1907).

BDF: F. Blass and A. Debrunner (tr. and rev. by R.W. Funk), *A Greek Grammar of the New Testament and Other Early Christian Literature* (Chicago/London, 1961).

BDR: F. Blass and A. Debrunner, *Grammatik des neutestamentlichen Griechisch.* Bearbeitet von F. Rehkopf (Göttingen, ^{14}1975).

Beekes, R.S.P. 2002. “Hom. γέφυρα, and Arm. *kamurǰ* ‘bridge,’” *Glotta* 78.12-21.

Beentjes, P.C. 1992. “‘You have given a road in the sea.’ What is Wisdom 14,3 talking about?” *ETL* 68.136-41.

Ben-Ḥayyim, Z. 1965. “Traditions in the Hebrew language, with special reference to the Dead Sea Scrolls,” *Scripta Hierosolymitana* 4 (Jerusalem), 200-14.

—. 1974. “Word studies” [in Heb.], in E.Y. Kutscher, S. Lieberman and M.Z. Kaddari (eds), *Henoch Yalon Memorial Volume* (Jerusalem, 1974), 46-58.

Ben-Yehuda, E. 1908-59. *Thesaurus totius hebraitatis et veteris et recentioris* (Jerusalem).

Bengston, H. 1944. *Die Strategie in der hellenistischen Zeit. Ein Beitrag zum antiken Staatsrecht.* Teil 2 (München).

Bergson, L. 1995. “στάς, ἑστώς κτλ. Entbehrliches und ergänzendes Partizip,” *Eranos* 93.65-8.

Berenguer Sánchez, J.A. 1989. “ἀρνόν en *PGurob* 22 y el empleo del término ἀρνίον en los papiros documentales,” *Emerita* 57.277-88.

Bergren, Th.A. and R.A. Kraft, 1992. “ἁλίσκω (ἁλίσκομαι) in Greek Jewish Scriptures: Profile of a difficult Greek verb,” *Bulletin of the John Rylands University Library of Manchester* 74, 3.53-66.

Bernand, A. 1977. *Pan du désert* (Leiden).

Berthiaume, G. 1982. *Les Rôles du Μάγειρος* [*Mnemosyne* Suppl. 70] (Leiden).

Bertram, G. 1932. “Der Begriff der Erziehung in der griechischen Bibel: Imago Dei,” in H. Bornkamm, *Imago dei: Beiträge zur theologischen Anthropologie* [Fschr G. Krüger] (Giessen), 33-51.

—. 1958. “ἹΚΑΝΟΣ in den griechischen Übersetzungen des ATs als Wiedergabe von *schaddaj*,” *ZAW* 70.20-31.

—. 1964-66. “‘Hochmut’ und verwandte Begriffe im griechischen und hebräischen Alten Testament,” *Die Welt des Orients* 3.32-43.

Bewer, J.A. 1938. Rev. of A.Ch. Johnson et al., *The John H. Scheide Biblical Papyri: Ezekiel*, *JBL* 57.421-5.

Beyer, K. 1962. *Semitische Syntax im Neuen Testament* (Göttingen).

Bickerman, E.J. 1944. “Héliodore au temple de Jérusalem,” *Annuaire de l’Institut de philologie et d’histoire orientales et slaves* 7 (1939-44) 5-40.

—. 1962. “Bénédiction et prière,” *RB* 69.524-32.

—. 1976. *Studies in Jewish and Christian History*, vol. 1 (Leiden).

Bieżuńska-Małowist, I. 1974-7. *L’esclavage dans l’Égypte gréco-romaine*, 2 vols. (Wrocław).

Biscardi, A. 1985. “Osservazioni critiche sulla terminologia ΔΙΑΘΗΚΗ - ΔΙΑΤΙΘΕΣΘΑΙ,” in P. Dimakis et al. (eds), *Symposion 1979: Vorträge zur griechischen und hellenistischen Rechtsgeschichte*, 23-35.

Blank, Sh.H. 1930. “The LXX renderings of Old Testament terms for law,” *HUCA* 7.259-83.

Blomqvist, J. 1969. *Greek Particles in Hellenistic Prose* (Lund).

—. 1974. “Juxtaposed τε καί in post-classical prose,” *Hermes* 102.170-8.

——. 1985. "Textual and interpretational problems in Sirach," *Eranos* 83. 33-43.

Bogaert, P.-M. 1981. "L'orientation du parvis du sanctuaire dans la version grecque de l'Exode (*Ex.*, 27, 9-13 LXX)," *AnCl* 50.79-85.

Bogner, H. 1941. "Was heisst μοιχεύειν?," *Hermes* 76.318-20.

Bolkestein, J.C. 1936. "Ὅσιος *en* Εὐσεβής. *Bijdrage tot de godsdienstige en zedelijke terminologie van de Grieken. Avec un résumé en français* (Amsterdam).

Bonneau, D. 1982. "Le drymos (δρυμός), marais du Fayoum, d'après la documentation papyrologique," in *L'Étyptologie en 1979. Axes prioritaires de recherches*, 2 vols., I.181-90 (Paris).

Bons, E. 1994. "Ἐλπίς comme l'espérance de la vie dans l'au-delà dans la littérature juive hellénistique," in R. Kuntzmann (ed.), *Le Dieu qui vient* [Fschr B. Renaud] (Paris), 345-70.

——. 2001. "La signification de ἄρκος ἀπορουμένη en LXX Osée xiii 8," *VT* 51.1-8.

——. 2007. "Le verbe ΚΤΙΖΩ comme terme technique de la création dans la Septante et dans le Nouveau Testament," in Joosten and Tomson, 1-15.

Borger, R. 2000. "Der Bogenköcher im Alten Orient, in der Antike und im Alten Testament," *NAWG*, Ph.-His. Kl. 2000-2.39-84.

Borthwick, E.K. 2001. "A rare meaning of the verb τέμνω," *Eranos* 99.72-4.

Boucher, P.-M. 2008. "ΓΕΝΝΗΘΗΝΑΙ ΑΝΩΘΕΝ: La valeur de l'adverbe ΑΝΩΘΕΝ en Jn 3,3 et 7," *RB* 115.191-215, 568-95.

Boyd-Taylor, C. 2001. "The evidential value of Septuagintal usage for Greek lexicography: Alice's reply to Humpty Dumpty," *BIOSCS* 34.47-80.

——. 2004. "Lexicography and interlanguage—Gaining our bearings," *BIOSCS* 37.55-72.

——. 2005. "Calque-culations—Loan words and the lexicon," *BIOSCS* 38.79-100.

Bratsiotis, N.P. 1966. "נֶפֶשׁ - ψυχή. Ein Beitrag zur Erforschung der Sprache und der Theologie der Septuaginta," VTS 15.58-89.

Braunert, H. 1971. "αγοραστής," *ZPE* 8.118-22.

Brent Sandy, D. 1984. "Oil specifications in the papyri: what is ΕΛΑΙΟΝ?," *Atti del XVII Congresso Internazionale di Papirologia*, vol. 3 (Napoli), 1317-23.

Brock, S.P. 1973. "An unrecognised occurrence of the month name Ziw (2 Sam. xxi 9)" *VT* 23.100-3.

——. 1996. *The Recensions of the Septuagint Version of I Samuel* (Torino).

Brockington, L.H. 1951. "The Greek translator of Isaiah and his interest in δόξα," *VT* 1.23-32.

Brongers, 1965. "Bemerkungen zum Gebrauch des adverbialen *w^e'attāh* im Alten Testament," *VT* 15.289-99.

Brooke & Lindars: G.J. Brooke & B. Lindars. 1992. *Septuagint, Scrolls and Cognate Writings* [SCS 33] (Atlanta).

Brown, J.P. 1980. "The sacrificial cult and its critique in Greek and Hebrew (II)," *JSS* 25.1-7.

Bruce, F.F. 1952. *The Acts of the Apostles. The Greek Text with Introduction and Commentary* (London).

Bruneau, Ph. 1967. "Deux noms antiques de pavement: ΚΑΤΑΚΛΥΣΤΟΝ et ΛΙΘΟΣΤΡΩΤΟΝ," *Bulletin de correspondance hellénique* 91.423-46.

Brunschwig, J. 1973. "Sur quelques emplois d'ὄψις," *Zetesis* [Fschr E. de Strycker] (Antwerpen / Utrecht), 24-39.

De Bruyne, D.D. 1921. "Notes de philologie biblique," *RB* 30.400-9.

Buscemi, M. 1979. "Ἐξαιρέομαι, verbo di liberazione," *SBFLA* 29.293-314.

Busch, S. 2002. "Lautes und leises Lesen in der Antike," *RMPh* NF 145.1-45.

Busto Saiz, J.R. 1991. "The meaning of Wisdom 2.9a," in Cox (1991), 355-9.

Byl, S. 2001. "Les infirmités physiques de la vieillesse dans les épigrammes de l'*Anthologie Palatine*," *RÉG* 114.439-55.

Cacciari, A. 2006. "Una nota su ὀλιγοστός (Mi 5,1 LXX)," in R. Pierri (ed.), *Grammatica intellectio Scripturae. Saggi filologici di greco biblico* (Jerusalem), 157-62.

Cadell, H. 1973. "Papyrologica: à propos de πυρός et de σῖτος," *CÉg*48.329-38.

——. 1994. "Vocabulaire de l'irrigation: la Septante et les papyrus," in B. Menn (ed.), *Les problèmes institutionnels de l'eau en Égypte ancienne et dans l'Antiquité méditerranéenne* (Le Caire), 103-17.

——. 1995. "Vocabulaire de la législation ptolémaïque: Problème du sens de *dikaiôma* dans la Pentateuque," in Dorival and Munnich (eds), 206-21.

Caird, G.B. 1968. "Towards a lexicon of the Septuagint. I," *JThSt* 19.453-75.

——. 1969. "Towards a lexicon of the Septuagint. II," *JThSt* 20.21-40.

Caragounis, C.C. 1974. "ΟΨΩΝΙΟΝ: a reconsideration of its meaning," *NT* 16.35-57.

Carden, R. 1974. *The Papyrus Fragments of Sophocles* [Texte und Kommentare 7] (Berlin / New York).

Casabona, J. 1966. *Recherches sur le vocabulaire des sacrifices en grec, des origines à la fin de l'époque classique* (Aix-en-Provence).

Casanova, G. 1982. "Le parole dell'amore nei papiri: osservazioni su ἐράω e corradicali," *Anagennesia* 2.213-26.

Casarico, L. 1984. "ΕΟΡΤΗ e ΠΑΝΗΓΥΡΙΣ," *Aeg* 64.135-62.

Casevitz, M. 1985. *Le Vocabulaire de la colonisation en grec ancien. Étude lexicologique: les familles de* κτίζω *et de* οἰκέω – οἰκίζω (Paris).

——. 1995. "Les mots de la lapidation dans la Bible," in Dorival and Munnich (eds), 223-52.

——. 1996. "Note sur ἐρυσίβη (à propos des exemples du mot chez les Septante," *Revue de philologie* 70.211-5.

Ceresa-Gastaldo, A. 1953. "ἀγάπη nei documenti estranei all' influsso biblico," *Rivista di filologia e di istruzione classica* NS 31.347-55.
Cerfaux, L. 1933a. "Le nom divin «Kyrios» dans la Bible grecque," *RSPT* 20.27-51.
—. 1933b. "«Adonai» et «Kyrios»," *RSPT* 20.417-52.
Cerunda, A.V. 1975. "'Considerar', acepción axiológica de καλέω y su presencia en la Biblia," *Augustinianum* 15.445-55.
Ceulemans, R. and D. de Crom. 2007. "Greek renderings of the Hebrew lexeme צמה in LXX Canticles and Isaiah," *VT* 57.511-23.
Chadwick: Chadwick, J., *Lexicographia Graeca: Contributions to the Lexicography of Ancient Greek* (Oxford, 1996).
Chamberlain, G.A. 1994. "Cultic vocabulary in the Septuagint,' *BIOSCS* 27.21-8.
Chantraine, P. 1955. "Les noms de l'agneau en grec: ἀρήν et ἀρνός," in H. Krahe (ed.), *Corolla Linguistica* [Fschr F. Sommer] (Wiesbaden), 12-19.
—. 1964. "Grec αἴθριον," *Recherches de papyrologie* 3.7-15.
Chepey, S.D. 2002. "Samson the 'Holy One': A suggestion regarding the reviser's use of ἅγιος in Judg 13,7; 16,17 LXX Vaticanus," *Bib.* 83.97-9.
Cifoletti, G. 1974. "ΑΠΟΔΕΧΟΜΑΙ nella diplomazia imperiale (a proposito di *P. Med.* 70/01)," *Incontri linguistici* 1 (Trieste), 55-60.
Cimosa, M. 1985. *Il vocabolario di preghiera nel Pentateuco greco dei LXX* (Rome).
Clark, K.W. 1972. "The meaning of ΑΡΑ," in E.H. Barth and R.E. Cocroft (eds) [Fschr F.W. Gingrich] (Leiden), 70-84.
Coin-Longeray, S. 2001. "Πενία et πένης: Travailler pour ivvre?," *RdP* 75.249-56.
Coleman, N.D. 1927. "Some noteworthy uses of εἰ or εἶ in Hellenistic Greek with a note on St Mark viii 12," *JThSt* 28.159-67.
Connolly, R.H. 1924. "'The meaning of ἐπίκλησις': a reply," *JThSt* 25.337-64.
Cook, J. 1997. *The Septuagint of Proverbs. Jewish and/or Hellenistic Proverbs? Concerning the Hellenistic Colouring of LXX Proverbs* [VTS 69] (Leiden).
Cornill, C.H. 1886. *Das Buch des Propheten Ezechiel* (Leipzig).
Corssen, P. 1918. "Über Bildung und Bedeutung der Komposita ψευδοπροφήτης, ψευδόμαντις, ψευδόμαρτυς," *Sokrates: Zeitschrift für das Gymnasialwesen* NF 6.106-14.
Cox (ed.), *VI Congress*: C.E. Cox (ed.), *VI Congress of the International Organization for Septuagint and Cognate Studies. Jerusalem 1986* [SCS 23] (Atlanta, 1987).
—. 1981. "Εἰσακούω and ἐπακούω in the Greek Psalter," *Bib.* 62.251-8.
—. 1990. "Vocabulary for wrongdoing and forgiveness in the Greek translations of Job," *Textus* 15.119-30.
Cox (ed.), *VII Congress*: C.E. Cox (ed.), *VII Congress of the International Organization for Septuagint and Cognate Studies. Leuven 1989* [SCS 31] (Atlanta, 1991).
CPR: *Corpus Papyrorum Raineri Archiducis Austriae* (Vienna, 1895-).
Croughs, M. 2002. "Vertaler, dichter en exegeet: De Septuaginta-vertaling van Jesaja 57 vergeleken met de Masoretische tekst en de teksten uit Qumran," M.A. (Theol.) thesis, Leiden.
Cunen, F. 1959. "Les pratiques divinatoires attribuées à Joseph d'Égypte," *RSR* 33.396-404.
Dafni, E.G. 2001a. "איש הרוח - ἄνθρωπος πνευματοφόρος (Hos 9:7): Zur Theologie der Sprache des Hoseabuches," in Sollamo and Sipilä 2001, 247-67.
—. 2001b. "σάρξ μου ἐξ αὐτῶν (LXX-Hosea ix 12): Zur Theologie der Sprache der Septuaginta," *VT* 51.336-53.
—. 2002. "נחש - ΟΦΙΣ. Genesis 3 und Jesaja 27,1 auch im Lichte von I Kön. 22,19-23, Hiob 1,6-12; 2,1-7 und Sach. 3,1-2," *BIOSCS* 35.47-54.
Dalman, G. [2]1930. *Die Worte Jesu* (Leipzig).
Dancy, J.C. 1954. *A Commentary on I Maccabees* (Oxford).
Daniel, S. 1966. *Recherches sur le vocabulaire du culte dans la Septante* (Paris).
Daris, S. 1983. "Ricerce di papirologia documentaria. II," *Aeg* 63.117-69.
Debrunner, A. 1925. "Zur Übersetzungstechnik der Septuaginta: Der Gebrauch des Artikels bei κύριος," BZAW 41.69-78.
Deissmann, A. 1895. *Bibelstudien* (Marburg).
—. 1903. "ἱλαστήριος und ἱλαστήριον. Eine lexikalische Studie," *ZNW* 4.193-212.
—. 1921. "Das sog. vierte Buch der Makkabäer," in E. Kautzsch (ed.), *Die Apokryphen und Pseudepigraphen des Alten Testaments*, II (Tübingen), 149-77.
—. [4]1923. *Licht vom Osten*. Tübingen.
Delling, G. 1952. "ΜΟΝΟΣ ΘΕΟΣ," *ThLZ* 77.469-76.
Demont, P. 1978. "Remarques sur le sens de τρέφω," *RÉG* 91.358-84.
Denooz, L. 2002. "Emplois de μίγνυμι et de ses composés. Sémantique grecque et statistique," *L'Antiquité classique* 71.65-84.
Des Places, É. 1975. "Un terme biblique et platonicien: ἀκοινώνητος," in *Forma futuri* [Fschr M. Pellegrino] (Torino), 154-8.
DGE: Adrados, F.R. (ed.), *Diccionario griego-español* (Madrid, 1986-).

Dimant, D. 1981. "A cultic term in the Psalms of Solomon in the light of the Septuagint," *Textus* 9. נא-כח+

Dines, J. 2007. "Light from the Septuagint on the New Testament - or vice versa?," in Joosten and Tomson, 17-34.

Dodd, C.H. 1930-31. "ΙΛΑΣΚΕΣΘΑΙ, its cognates, derivatives, and synonyms in the Septuagint," *JThSt* 32.352-60.

—. 1935. *The Bible and the Greeks* (London).

Dörrie, H. 1955. "Ὑπόστασις: Wort- und Bedeutungsgeschichte," *NAWG*, I. Phil.-histr. Klasse, Jahrgang 1955, Nr. 3, 35-92.

Dogniez, C. 1997. "Le Dieu des armées dans le Dodekapropheton: quelques remarques sur une initiative de traduction," Taylor 1997.19-36.

—. 2001. "Fautes de traduction, ou bonnes traductions? Quelques exemples pris dans la LXX des Douze Petits Prophètes," Taylor 2001.241-61.

—. 2002. "The Greek renderings of Hebrew idiomatic expressions and their treatment in the Septuagint lexica," *JNWSL* 28.1-17.

Dogniez, C. and M. Harl (eds), 2001. *La Bible des Septante: Le Pentateuque d'Alexandrie, Texte grec et traduction* (Paris).

Dorival, G. 1995. "Les phénomènes d'intertextualité dans le livre grec des *Nombres*," in Dorival and Munnich (eds), 253-85.

—. 1996. "Dire en grec les choses juives," *RÉG* 109.527-47.

Dorival, G. and O. Munnich (eds). 1995. *ΚΑΤΑ ΤΟΥΣ Ο' Selon les Septante. Trente études sur la Bible grecque des Septante en hommage à Marguerite Harl* (Paris).

Drescher, J. 1970. "Graeco-Coptica II," *Le Muséon* 83.139-55.

—. 1976. "Graeco-Coptica: Postscript," *Le Muséon* 89.307-21.

Drexhage, H.-J. 1991. "Einige Bemerkungen zu den ἔμποροι und κάπηλοι im römischen Ägypten (1.-3.Jh.n.)," *Münstersche Beiträge zur antiken Handelsgeschichte,* 10.28-46.

Drew-Bear, T. 1972. "Some Greek words: Part I," *Glotta* 50.61-96.

Drew Griffiths, R. 1997. "Criteria for evaluating hypothetical Egyptian loan-words in Greek: the case of Αἴγυπτος," *Illinois Classical Studies* 22.1-6.

Driver, S.R. [2]1913. *Notes on the Hebrew Text and the Topography of the Books of Samuel* etc. (Oxford).

Du Plessis, P.J. 1959. "ΤΕΛΕΙΟΣ: The idea of perfection in the New Testament," Diss. Kampen.

Dupont, J. 1961. "Τὰ ὅσια Δαυιδ τὰ πιστά (Ac xiii 34 = Is lv 3)," *RB* 68.91-114.

—. 1967. "Les «simples» (*petâyim*) dans la Bible et à Qumrân. À propos des νήπιοι de Mt. 11,25; Lc. 10,21," in *Studi sull' Oriente e la Bibbia* [Fschr G. Rinaldi] (Genova), 329-36.

Evans, T.V. 1999. "The comparative optative: a Homeric reminiscence in the Greek Pentateuch?," *VT* 49.487-504.

—. 2001. *Verbal Syntax in the Greek Pentateuch. Natural Greek Usage and Hebrew Interference* (Oxford).

—. 2003. "The last of the optatives," *ClPh* 98.70-80.

—. 2005. "Periphrastic tense forms in the Greek Tobit," in F. García Martínez and M. Vervenne (eds), *Interpreting Translation: Studies on the LXX and Ezekiel* [Fschr J. Lust] (Leuven), 109-17.

Eynikel, E. and K. Hauspie, 1997. "The use of *καιρός* and *χρόνος* in the Septuagint," *ETL* 73.369-85.

—. 2004. "The use of δράκων in the Septuagint," in B. Taylor et al. (eds), *Biblical Greek Language and Lexicography* [Fsch F.W. Danker] (Grand Rapids), 126-35.

Eynikel, E. and J. Lust. 1991. "The use of δεῦρο and δεῦτε in the LXX," *ETL* 67.57-68.

Fascher, E. 1927. ΠΡΟΦΗΤΗΣ. *Eine sprach- und religionsgeschichtliche Untersuchung* (Gießen).

—. 1954. "Theologische Beobachtungen zu δεῖ im Alten Testament," *ZNW* 45.244-52.

—. 1971. "Zum Begriff des Fremden," *ThLZ* 96.161-8.

Fehling, D. 1969. "Noch einmal der passer solitarius und der passer Catullus," *Philologus* 113.217-24.

Fernández Marcos, N. 1980. "Nueva acepción de ΤΕΡΑΣ en las «Vidas de los profetas»," *Sefarad* 40.27-39.

—. 1995. "La reanimación del hijo de la Sunamita en el texto antioqueno," in Dorival and Munnich 1995.119-28.

Festugière, A.-J. 1949. *La Sainteté* (Paris).

Fiedler, M.J. 1972. "Δικαιοσύνη in der diaspora-jüdischen und intertestamentarischen Literatur," *JSJ* 1.120-43.

Finkelberg, A. 1995. "On the history of the Greek ΚΟΣΜΟΣ," *Harvard Studies in Classical Philology* 98 (1998) 103-36.

Fisher, N.R.E. 1992. HYBRIS. *A Study in the Values of Honour and Shame in Ancient Greece* (Warminster).

Fitzmyer, J.A. [2]1995. *The Aramaic Inscriptions of Sefire* (Rome).

—. 2003. *Tobit* (Berlin / New York).

Flashar, M. 1912. "Exegetische Studien zum Septuagintapsalter," *ZAW* 32.81-116.

Fohrer, G. 1969. "σῴζω, σωτηρία, und σωτήριος im Alten Testament," *BZAW* 115.275-93.

Frankel, *Einfl.*: Z. Frankel, *Über den Einfluss der palästinischen Exegese auf die alexandrinische Hermeneutik* (Leipzig, 1831).

Frankel, *Vorstudien*: Z. Frankel, *Vorstudien zu der Septuaginta* (Leipzig, 1841).

Freund, R.A. 1990. "From kings to archons," *Scandinavian Journal of the Old Testament* 2.58-72.

Frey, J.-B., 1930. "La signification du terme πρωτότοκος d'après une inscription juive," *Bib* 11.373-90.

Fridrichsen, A. 1938. "Ἰσόψυχος = ebenbürtig, solidarisch," *Symbolae Osloenses* 18.42-9.

Fuchs, E. 1977. "Gloire de dieu, gloire de l'homme: Essai sur les terms *kauchasthai, kauchèma, kauchèsis* dans la Septante," *RTP* 27.321-32.

Gagliano, C.L. 2000. "A proposito di ἐν μάνδρᾳ in P. Oxy. 984,"*Aeg.* 80.99-115.

G.D.K.: G.D. Kilpatrick, *The Principles and Practice of New Testament Textual Criticism. Collected Essays.* [ed. J.K. Elliott] (Leuven, 1990).

Georgacas, D.J. 1958. "A contribution to Greek word history, derivation and etymology," *Glotta* 36.100-22.

Gerhardt, M.I. 1965. "The ant-lion. Nature study and the interpretation of a biblical text, from the Physiologus to Albert the Great," *Vivarium* 3.1-23.

Ghiron-Bistagne, P. 1983. "L'emploi du terme grec πρόσωπον dans l'Ancien et le Nouveau Testament," in C. Froidefond (ed.), *Mélanges E. Delebecque* (Aix-en-Provence), 157-74.

GI: F. Montanari, *Vocabolario della Lingua Greca.* Torino 2004².

Gignac: F.T. Gignac, *A Grammar of the Greek Papyri of the Roman and Byzantine Periods*, 2 vols. (Milan, 1976-81).

Gilbert, M. 1976. "La conjecture μετριότητι en Sg 12,22a," *Bib.* 57.550-3.

—. 1985. "'On est puni par où l'on pèche'," in A. Caquot et al. (eds), *Mélanges bibliques et orientaux en l'honneur de M. Mathias Delcor* [AOAT 215] (Neukirchen-Vluyn), 183-91.

Görg, M. 2001. "Die Septuaginta im Kontext spätägyptischer Kultur: Beispiele lokaler Inspiration bei der Übersetzungsarbeit am Pentateuch," in H.-J. Fabry and U. Offerhaus (eds), *Im Brennpunkt: Die Septuaginta. Studien zur Entstehung und Bedeutung der griechischen Bibel* (Stuttgart / Berlin / Köln), 115-30.

Goldstein, J.A. 1983. *II Maccabees* [*AB* 41A] (Garden City, NY).

Gooding, D.W. 1965. ",The Septuagint version of Solomon's misconduct," *VT* 15.325-35.

—. 1976. *Relics of Ancient Exegesis: A Study of the Miscellanies in 3 Reigns 2* (Cambridge).

—. 1981. Review of Olley 1979, *JThSt* 32.204-12.

Gorman, R. 2001. "οἱ περί τινα in Strabo," *ZPE* 136.201-13.

Grayston, K. 1981. "Ἱλάσκεσθαι and related words in LXX," *NTS* 27.640-56.

Grobel, K. 1954. "Σῶμα as 'self, person' in the Septuagint," in W. Eltester (ed.), *Neustestamentliche Studien für Rudolf Bultmann zu seinem siebzigsten Geburtstag* etc. [BZNW 21] (Berlin W), 52-9.

Guinot, J.-N. 1989. "Sur le vêtement du grand prêtre: le δῆλος était-il une pierre divinatoire?" *Vetera Christianorum* 26.23-48.

Gundry, R.H. 1976. *Sōma in Biblical Theology with Emphasis on Pauline Anthropology* (Cambridge).

Gurtner, D.M. 2005. "LXX syntax and the identity of the NT veil," *NT* 47.344-53.

Guyot, P. 1980. *Eunuchen als Sklaven und Freigelassene in der griechisch-römischen Antike* [Stuttgarter Beiträge zur Geschichte und Politik 14] (Stuttgart).

Habermann, W. 1988. "Lexikalische und semantische Untersuchung am griechischen Begriff βύρσα," *Glotta* 66.93-9.

Habicht, Ch. 1976. *2. Makkabäerbuch*, in *Jüdische Schriften aus hellenistisch-römischer Zeit*, Bd. I, *Historische und legendarische Erzählungen* (Gütersloh).

Hagedorn, D. 1973. *Der Hiobkommentar des Arianers Julian* (Berlin / New York).

—. 1984. *Olympiodor, Diakon von Alexandria*: *Kommentar zu Hiob* (Berlin / New York).

—. 1990. *Johannes Chrysostomos Kommentar zu Hiob* (Berlin / New York).

Hagedorn, U. and D. 1990. *Johannes Chrysostomos Kommentar zu Hiob.* Berlin / New York.

—. 1994-2000. *Die älteren griechischen Katenen zum Buch Hiob* (Berlin / New York).

—. & Worp, K.A. 1980. "Von κύριος zu δεσπότης. Eine Bemerkung zur Kaisertitulatur im 3./4. Jhdt.," *ZPE* 39.165-77.

Halleux, R. 1973. "Le sens d'ἄσημος dans le papyrus chimique de Leyde et dans l'alchimie gréco-étyptienne," *CÉg* 48.370-80.

Hamm, W. 1969. *Der Septuaginta-Text des Buches Daniel (Kap. 1-2) nach dem Kölner Teil des Papyrus 967* (Bonn).

Hanhart, R. 1974. *Text und Textgeschichte des 1. Esrabuches* (Göttingen).

—. 1992. "The translation of the Septuagint in light of earlier tradition and subsequent influences," in Brooke & Lindars, 339-79.

—. 2003. *Text und Textgeschichte des 2. Esrabuches* (Göttingen).

Harl, M. 1992. *La Langue de Japhet. Quinze études sur la Septante et le grec des chrétiens* (Paris).

—. 1999. "Le sens et l'histoire du mot λῆμμα comme intitulé d'une prophétie," in *BA* 23.4-9, 302-310.

—. 2001. "Glossaire," in Dogniez, C. and M. Harl 2001:861-906.

Harl, M., G. Dorival and O. Munnich. 1988. *La Bible grecque des Septante: Du judaïsme hellénistique au christianisme ancien* (Paris).

Hatch, E. 1889. *Essays in Biblical Greek* (Oxford).

Hauspie, K. 2001. "πίπτω ἐπὶ πρόσωπόν μου: A set phrase in Ezekiel?," in Taylor 2001.513-30.

—. 2003. "La version de la Septante d'Ézéchiel: Traduction annotée d'Ez 1-24 et étude du grec d'Ézéchiel par une sélection de particularités lexicales et grammaticales," in 2 parts. Diss. Leuven.

—. 2003a. "ζῶ ἐγώ, λέγει κύριος, εἰ μήν ... dans la Septante d'Ézéchiel," *BIOSCS* 36.3-25.

—. 2004. "The LXX quotations in the LSJ Supplements of 1968 and 1996," in B. Taylor et al. (eds), *Biblical Greek Language and Lexicography* [Fsch F.W. Danker] (Grand Rapids), 108-25.

——. 2005. "'Ακούω dans le livre d'Ézéchiel. Étude sémantique en vue d'une traduction française et anglaise," in F. García Martínez and M. Vervenne (eds), *Interpreting Translation: Studies on the LXX and Ezekiel* [Fschr J. Lust] (Leuven), 177-92.

——. 2006. "Proposition complétive avec τοῦ et l'infinitif dans la Septante d'Ézéchiel," in R. Pierri (ed.), *Grammatica intellectio Scripturae. Saggi filologici di greco biblico* (Jerusalem), 163-82.

Heidland, H.-W. 1936. *Die Anrechnung des Glaubens zur Gerechtigkeit. Untersuchungen zur Begriffsbestimmung von* חשׁב *und* λογίζεσθαι [Beiträge zur Wissenschaft vom Alten und Neuen Testament 71] (Stuttgart).

Heinen, H. 1984. "Zur Terminologie der Sklaverei im ptolemäischen Ägypten: ΠΑΙΣ und ΠΑΙΔΙΣΚΗ in den Papyri und der Septuaginta," *Atti del XVII Congresso Internazionale dei Papirologia*, vol. 3 (Napoli), 1287-95.

Helbing, *Gram.*: R. Helbing, *Grammatik der Septuaginta. Laut- und Wortlehre* (Göttingen, 1907).

Helbing, *Kasus.*: R. Helbing, *Die Kasussyntax der Verba bei den Septuaginta. Ein Beitrag zur Hebraismenfrage und zur Syntax der* Κοινή (Göttingen, 1928).

Heltzer, M. 1988. "ΜΙΣΘΩΤΟΣ im Buche 'Judith'," in M. Wissemann (ed.), *Roma renascens: Beiträge zur Spätantike und Rezeptionsgeschichte* [Fschr I. Opelt] (Frankfurt am Main / Bern / New York / Paris),118-24.

Hesseling, D.C. 1911. "Zur Syntax von ἄρχομαι und Verw.," *Byzantinische Zeitschrift* 20.147-64.

Hilhorst, A. 1982. "Darius' pillow (1 Esdras iii 8)," *JThSt* NS 33.161-3.

——. 1989. "'Servir Dieu,' dans la terminologie du judaïsme hellénistique et des premières générations chrétiennes de langue grecque," in A.A.R. Bastiaensen et al. (eds), *Fructus centesimus* [Fschr G.J.M. Bartelink, *Instrumenta Patristica* 19], 177-92.

Hill, D. 1967. *Greek Words and Hebrew Meanings* (Cambridge).

Hollexaux, M. 1942. "«Ceux qui sont dans le bagage»," in id., *Études d'épigraphie et d'histoire grecques*, III (Paris), 15-26.

Horsley, G.H.R. 1994. Review of Muraoka 1993 in *AN* 32.110-4.

HTM: *The Psalter according to the Seventy of St. David, the Prophet and King* etc. (Holy Transfiguration Monastery, Boston, 1974).

Humbert: J. Humbert, *Syntaxe grecque* (Paris, 1960).

Husson: G. Husson, *OIKIA. Le Vocabulaire de la maison privée en Égypte d'après les papyrus grecs* (Paris, 1983).

——. 1967. "Recherches sur les sens du mot ΠΡΟΑΣΤΙΟΝ dans le grec d'Égypte," *Recherches du papyrologie*, IV.187-200.

——. 1983. "Un sens méconnu de θυρίς et de *fenestra*," *Journal of Juristic Papyrology* 19.155-62.

——. 1988. "Le paradis de délices (Genèse 3,23-24)," *RÉG* 101.64-73.

Huys, M. 1989. "ΕΚΘΕΣΙΣ and ΑΠΟΘΕΣΙΣ: the terminology of infant exposure in Greek antiquity," *AnCl* 58.190-7.

Index 1E: T. Muraoka, *A Greek-Hebrew/Aramaic Index to 1Esdras* (Chico, CA, 1984).

Irmscher, J. 1950. *Götterzorn bei Homer* (Leipzig).

Jacobson, H. 2000. "LXX Genesis 43:23: ἵλεως ὑμῖν," *Textus* 20.39-41.

Japheth: Japheth, S. 1993. *I & II Chronicles* [The Old Testament Library] (London).

Jarick, J. 1990. *Gregory Thaumatourgos' Paraphrase of* Ecclesiastes [SCS 29] (Atlanta, GA).

Jeremias, J. 1939. "Beobachtungen zu neutestamentlichen Stellen an Hand des neugefundenen griechischen Henoch-Textes," *ZNW* 38.115-24.

JM: P. Joüon and T. Muraoka, *A Grammar of Biblical Hebrew* [Subsidia biblica 27] (Roma, [2]2006).

Jobes, K. 1991. "Distinguishing the meaning of Greek verbs in the semantic domain of worship," *FN* 7.183-91.

Jobes, K.H. and M. Silva. 2000. *Invitation to the Septuagint* (Grand Rapids, MI).

Johannessohn, *Kasus*: M. Johannessohn, *Der Gebrauch der Kasus und Präpositionen in der Septuaginta* (Berlin, 1910).

Johannessohn, *Präp.*: M. Johannessohn, *Der Gebrauch der Präpositionen in der Septuaginta* (Berlin, 1926).

Johannessohn, M. 1926. "Das biblische καὶ ἐγένετο und seine Geschichte," *Z. für vergleichende Sprachforschung* 53.161-212.

——. 1939-40. "Das biblische καὶ ἰδού in der Erzählung samt seiner hebräischen Vorlage," *Z. für vergleichende Sprachforschung* 66.145-95; 67.30-84.

Joly, R. 1968. *Le Vocabulaire chrétien de l'amour est-il original?* Φιλεῖν *et* 'Αγαπᾶν *dans le grec antique* (Bruxelles).

Jones, C.P. 1987. "Στίγμα: Tatooing and branding in Graeco-Roman antiquity," *J. of Roman Studies* 77.139-55.

——. 1996. "ἔθνος and γένος in Herodotus," *ClQu* 46.315-20.

Jones, D. 1955. "ἀνάμνησις in the LXX and the interpretation of 1Cor. xi. 25," *JThSt* 6.183-91.

Joosten, J. 2003. "«Père, j'ai péché envers le ciel et devant toi» Remarques exégétiques et textuelles sur Luc 15, 18.21," *RHPR* 83.145-56.

——. 2004. "חסד 'bienveillance' et ἔλεος 'pitié': Réflexions sur une équivalence lexicale dans la Septante," in E. Bons (ed.), *«Car c'est l'amour qui me plait, non le sacrifice...»: Recherches sur Osée 6:6 et son interprétation juive et chrétienne* (Leiden), 25-42.

——. 2005. "Source-language oriented remarks on the lexicography of the Greek versions of the Bible," *ETL* 81.152-64.

——. 2006. "L'agir humain *devant* Dieu. Remarques sur une tournure remarquable de la Septante," *RB* 113.5-17.

——. 2007. "«À Dieu ne plaise» (Matthieu 16,22). La provenance et l'arrière-plan de l'expression ΙΛΕΩΣ ΣΟΙ," in Joosten and Tomson, 155-67.

Joosten and Tomson: Joosten, J. and P.J. Tomson (eds), *Voces biblicae. Septuagint Greek and its Significance for the New Testament* (Peeters: Leuven, 2007).

Julia, M.-A. 2001. "Les particules αὐτάρ et ἀτάρ: passerelles entre la structuration syntaxique et la structuration informative de l'énonce," *Revue de philologie* 75.83-98.

Kallitsunakis, J.E. 1926. "'ΟΨΟΝ und 'ΟΨΑ'ΡΙΟΝ. Ein Beitrag zur griechischen Semasiologie," in *Beiträge zur griechischen und lateinischen Sprachforschung* [Fschr P. Kretschmer] (Wien / Leipzig / New York), 96-106.

Kamphausen, A. In E. Kautzsch (ed.), *Die Apokryphen und Pseudepigraphen des Alten Testaments*, Bd. 1 (Tübingen, 1900).

Karrer, M. 2007. "Ῥίζα - Wurzel und Geschlecht. Ein Motiv zwischen griechischer Antike, Septuaginta und Neuem Testament," in Joosten and Tomson, 63-98.

—. 2008. "Umfang und Text der Septuaginta: Erwägungen nach dem Abschluss der deutschen Übersetzung II, Probleme der wiederzugebenden Textgestalt," in M. Karrer and W. Kraus (eds), *Die Septuaginta — Texte, Kontexte, Lebenswelten* (Tübingen), 8-63.

Katz, P. 1946. "ΚΑΤΑΠΑΥΣΑΙ as a corruption of ΚΑΤΑΛΥΣΑΙ in the LXX," *JBL* 65.319-24.

—. 1946a. "Notes on the Septuagint: IV. Ἔα δέ *Let alone* in Job," *JThSt* 47.168f.

—. 1956. Rev. of J. Wackernagel, *Kleine Schriften* I & II (Göttingen, 1953), in *TLZ* 81.603-7.

—. 1960. "πρεσβυτέριον in I Tim. 4.14 and Susanna 50," *ZNW* 51.27-30.

Kaupel, H. 1935-36. "'Sirenen' in der Septuaginta," *BZ* 23.158-65.

Keil: C.F. Keil in C.F. Keil and F. Delitzsch, *Commentary on the Old Testament* [reprint] (Grand Rapids, 1988).

Kerr, A.J. 1988. "ΑΡΡΑΒΩΝ," *JThSt* 39.92-7.

KG: R. Kühner and B. Gerth, *Ausführliche Grammatik der griechischen Sprache: Satzlehre* (Hannover / Leipzig, [3]1904).

Kießling, E. 1927. "Die Aposkeuai und die prozessrechtliche Stellung der Ehefrau im ptolemäischen Ägypten," *Archiv für Papyrusforschung und verwandte Gebiete*, 8.240-9.

—. 1956. "Über den Rechtsbegriff der Paratheke," in *Akten des VIII. internationalen Kongresses für Papyrologie. Wien 1955* (Wien), 69-78.

Kilpatrick, G.D. 1942. "A theme of the Lucan passion story and Luke xxiii. 47," *JThSt* 43.34-6.

—. 1961. "The meaning of θύειν in the New Testament," *BiTr* 12.130-2. [= G.D.K. 1990.201-4].

—. 1963. "Atticism and the text of the Greek New Testament," in J. Blinzler (ed), *Neustestamentliche Aufsätze* [Fschr J. Schmid, Regensburg] [= G.D.K. 1990.15-32].

—. 1967. "The aorist of γαμεῖν in the New Testament," *JThSt* 18.139f. [= G.D.K. 1990.187f.].

—. 1973. "Κύριος again," in P. Hoffmann (ed.), *Orientierung an Jesus. Zur Theologie der Synoptiker* [Fschr J. Schmid, Freiburg / Basel / Wien], 214-9 [= G.D.K. 1990.216-22].

—. 1977. "Ecclecticism and Atticism," *ETL* 53.107-12 [= G.D.K. 1990.73-9].

—. 1983a. "Atticism and the future of Ζῆν," *NT* 25.146-51 [= G.D.K. 1990.195-200].

—. 1983b. "ἐπιθύειν and ἐπικρίνειν in the Greek Bible,' *ZNW* 74.151-3.

Kindstrand, J.F. 1983. "ΘΥΡΟΚΟΠΟΣ. A study of the Greek compounds with -κόπος, -κοπία and -κοπέω in the Classical and Hellenistic periods," *AnCl* 52.86-109.

Kittel, R. 1921. "Die Psalmen Salomos," in E. Kautzsch (ed.), *Die Apokryphen und Pseudepigraphen des Alten Testaments*, II (Tübingen), 127-48.

Klauck, H.-J. 1980. "θυσιαστήριον. Eine Berichtigung," *ZNW* 71.274-7.

Klíma, O. 1955. "Pāqīd - διδάσκαλος," *AO* 23.481.

Koch, K. 1987. *Deuterokanonische Zusätze zum Danielbuch. Entstehung und Textgeschichte* [Alter Orient und Altes Testament 38/1-2] (Neukirchen-Vluyn).

Koonce, K. 1988. "ΑΓΑΛΜΑ and ΕΙΚΩΝ," *AJP* 109.108-10.

Korn, J.H. 1937. ΠΕΙΡΑΣΜΟΣ. *Die Versuchung des Gläubigen in der griechischen Bibel* [Beiträge zur Wissenschaft vom Alten und Neuen Testament 20] (Stuttgart).

Kraabel, A.T. 1969. "Ὕψιστος and the synagogue at Sardis," *Greek, Roman, and Byzantine Studies* 10.81-93.

Kraft, *Sept. Lexicography*: R.A. Kraft (ed.), *Septuagintal Lexicography* [SCS 1] (Missoula, 1972).

—. 1972a. "EIS NIKOS = Permanently/Successfully: 1 Cor 15.54, Matt 12.20," in Kraft, *Sept. Lexicography*, 153-6.

—. 1972b. "Preparatory remarks to the lexical "Probes"," *Sept. Lexicography*, 157-78.

Kraus, Th.J. 1999. "'Uneducated', 'Ignorant', even 'Illiterate'? Aspects and background for an understanding of ἀγράμματοι and ἰδιῶται in Acts 4.13," *NTS* 45.434-49.

Krischer, T. 1981. "Σιγᾶν und σιωπᾶν," *Glotta* 59.93-107.

—. 1984. "Νόος, νοεῖν, νόημα," *Glotta* 62.141-9.

Kuhlmann, P. 1997-98. "Εἷς als Indefinitpronomen im Griechischen in diachroner Sicht," *Glotta* 74.76-93.

Lampe: G.W.H. Lampe (ed.), *A Patristic Greek Lexicon* (Oxford, 1961-8).

Larcher, C. 1983-4. *Le Livre de la sagesse ou la sagesse de Salomon*, 2 vols. (Paris).

Lauer, S. 1955. "Eusebes logismos in IV Macc.," *JJS* 6.170f.

Laurentin, A. 1964. "עַתָּה καὶ νῦν Formule caractéristique des textes juridiques et liturgiques (à propos de Jean 17,5)," *Bib.* 45.168-95.

Lazarenco, O. 2002. "Does ἀδολεσχέω mean 'To meditate' in the LXX?," *BIOSCS* 35.110-20.

Le Déaut, R. 1964. "Φιλανθρωπία dans la littérature grecque jusqu'au Nouveau Testament," in *Mélanges Eugène Tisserant. Vol. I. Écriture sainte — Ancient Orient* (Rome), 253-94.

Ledogar, R.J. 1967. "Verbs of praise in the LXX translation of the Hebrew canon," *Bib.* 48.29-56.

Lee: Lee, J.A.L. *A Lexical Study of the Septuagint Version of the Pentateuch* [SCS 14] (Chico, 1983).

—. 1969. "A note on Septuagint material in the Supplement to Liddell and Scott," *Glotta* 47.234-42.

—. 1972. "Αποσκευή in the Septuagint," *JThSt* 23.430-7.

—. 1980a. "Equivocal and stereotyped renderings in the LXX," *RB* 87.104-17.

—. 1980b. "The future of Ζῆν in Late Greek," *NT* 22.289-98.

—. 1985. "Some features of the speech of Jesus in Mark's Gospel," *NT* 27.1-26.

—. 1990. "συνίστημι: a sample lexical entry," in Muraoka 1990.49-82.

—. 1997. "Hebrews 5:14 and ἕξις: A history of misunderstanding," *NT* 39.151-76.

—. 2003. "*A Lexical Study* thirty years on, with observations on 'order' words in the LXX Pentateuch," in Paul, Sh. et al. (eds), *Emanuel: Studies in Hebrew Bible, Septuagint and Dead Sea Scrolls in Honor of Emanuel Tov* (Leiden, 2003), 513-24.

—. 2003a. *A History of New Testament Lexicography* (Frankfurt am Main).

—. 2004. Rev. of Muraoka 2002 in *BIOSCS* 37.127-39.

—. 2007. "Ἐξαποστέλλω," in Joosten and Tomson, 99-114.

Lefebvre, Ph. 1995. "Les mots de la Septante ont-ils trois dimensions? Φωστῆρες εἰς ἀρχάς Gn 1.16," in Dorival and Munnich (eds), 299-320.

LEH: J. Lust, E. Eynikel and K. Hauspie, *A Greek-English Lexicon of the Septuagint*, rev. ed. (Stuttgart, 2003).

Leivestad, R. 1966. "ΤΑΠΕΙΝΟΣ - ΤΑΠΕΙΝΟΦΡΩΝ," *NT* 8.36-47.

Lewis, N. 1960. "*Leitourgia* and related terms," *GRBS* 3.175-84.

Lieberman, S. 1934. "Ben Sira à la lumière du Yerouchalmi," *RÉJ* 97.50-7.

—. 1962. *Hellenism in Jewish Palestine* (New York).

—. 1965. *Greek in Jewish Palestine* etc (New York).

Lightfoot, J.B. 1895 [1957]. *Notes on the Epistles of St Paul* (Grand Rapids).

Lindblom, J. 1921. *Skandalon: eine lexikalisch-exegetische Untersuchung* (Uppsala).

Lindhagen, C. 1950. "ΕΡΓΑΖΕΣΘΑΙ Apc 18:17, Hes 48:18.19, Die Wurzel ΣΑΒ Π im NT und AT: Zwei Beiträge zur Lexikographie der griechischen Bibel," *Uppsala Universiteits Årsskrift* 5.5-26, 27-69.

LN: J.P. Louw and E.A. Nida (eds), *Greek-English Lexicon of the New Testament Based on Semantic Domains*, 2 vols. (New York, 1988).

Loader, J.A. 1973. "An explanation of the term prosēlutos," *NT* 15.270-7.

Lowe, A.D. 1967. "The origin of οὐαί," *Hermathena* 105.34-9.

LSJ: H.G. Liddell, R. Scott & H.S. Jones, *A Greek-English Lexicon* (Oxford, [9]1940).

LSG: *Revised Supplement* to LSJ by P.G.W. Clare (Oxford, 1996).

Lührmann, D. 1971. "Epiphaneia: Zur Bedeutungsgeschichte eines griechischen Wortes," in G. Jeremias et al. (eds), *Tradition und Glaube: das frühe Christentum in seiner Umwelt* [Fschr K.G. Kuhn] (Göttingen), 185-99.

—. 1973. "Pistis im Judentum," *ZNW* 64.19-38.

Lust, J. 1992."Ἕδρα and the Philistine plague," in Brooke & Lindars, 569-97.

Lyonnet, S. 1958. "Le sens de πειράζειν en Sap 2,24 et la doctrine du péché originel," *Bib* 39.27-36.

Lys, D. 1966. "The Israelite soul according to the LXX," *VT* 16.181-228.

—. 1986. "L'arrière-plan et let connotations vétérotestamentaires de σάρξ et de σῶμα (Étude préliminaire)," *VT* 36.163-204.

Malingrey, A.-M. 1961. "'Philosophia.' Étude d'un groupe de mots dans la littérature grecque, des Présocratiques au IVe siècle après J.-C.," *Études et commentaires* 40.

Mandilaras: B.G. Mandilaras, *The Verb in the Greek non-literary Papyri* (Athens, 1973).

Manson, T.W. 1945. "Ἱλαστήριον," *JThSt* 46.1-10.

Margolis, M.L. 1909. "The particle ἤ in Old Testament Greek," *AJSL* 25.257-75.

—. 1912-13. "The mode of expressing the Hebrew *'ā'id* in the Greek Hexateuch," *AJSL* 29.237-60.

Masson, M. 1986. "Σφαῖρα, σφαιρωτήρ: Problème d'étymologie grecque," *Bulletin de la Société de Linguistique de Paris*, 81.231-52.

Mateos, J. 1990. "σάββατα, σάββατον, προσάββατον, παρασκευή," *FN* 3.19-38.

Mayerson, Ph. 2000. "The meaning and function of ληνός and related features in the production of wine," *ZPE* 131.161-7.

—. 2002. "Qualitative distinctions for ἔλαιον (oil) and ψωμίον (bread)," *Bulletin of the American Society of Papyrologists* 39.101-9.

—. 2003. "ἀμπελουργός: More than a "vine dresser"," *Bulletin of the American Society of Papyrologists* 40.187-90.

Mayser: E. Mayser, *Grammatik der griechischen Papyri aus der Ptolemäerzeit* (Berlin, 1906-70)[I.1 and 2 - 2nd ed.].

Mazzucco, C. 2006. "Εἰς τί; «Perché?» (Mc 15,34)," in R. Pierri (ed.), *Grammatica intellectio Scripturae. Saggi filologici di greco biblico* (Jerusalem), 205-13.

Meadowcroft, T.J. 1996. "καταστροφή: a puzzling LXX translation choice in Hosea viii 7a," *VT* 46.539-43.

Mealand, D.L. 1990. "The close of *Acts* and its Hellenistic Greek vocabulary," *NTS* 36.583-97.

Merkelbach, R. 1970. "Σημεῖον im Liebesepigramm," *ZPE* 6.245f.

——. 1971. "σωτήρ 'Arzt'," *ZPE* 8.14.

Metzler, K. 1991. *Der griechische Begriff des Verzeihens* [Wissenschaftliche Untersuchungen zum Neuen Testament. 2. Reihe 44] (Tübingen).

Meyer, B. 1984. ΧΑΛΚΙΟΝ, ΧΑΛΚΙΟΝ ΜΟΛΥΒΔΟΥΝ et ΧΑΛΚΙΟΝ ΧΑΛΚΟΥΝ, *Atti del XVII Congresso Internazionale di Papirologia*, vol. 3 (Napoli), 1303-8.

Michaelis, W. 1954. "Der Beitrag der Septuaginta zur Bedeutungsgeschichte von πρωτότοκος," in *Sprachgeschichte und Wortbedeutung* [Fschr. A. Debrunner] (Bern), 313-20.

Milgrom, J. 2001. *Leviticus 23-27* [AB 3B] (Garden City, NY).

Mitchell, L.G. 1997. "Φιλία, εὔνοια, and Greek interstate relations," *Antichton* 31.28-44.

MM: J.H. Moulton and G. Milligan, *The Vocabulary of the Greek Testament* (London, 1930).

Moatti-Fine, J. 1995. "La «tâche du traducteur» de *Josué / Jésus*," in Dorival and Munnich (eds), 321-30.

Mohrmann, Ch. 1954. "Note sur *doxa*," in *Sprachgeschichte und Wortbedeutung* [Fschr. A. Debrunner] (Bern), 321-8.

Monro, D.B. 1891. *A Grammar of the Homeric Dialect* (Oxford).

Monsengwo Pasinya, L. 1973. *La notion de* Nomos *dans le Pentateuque grec* (Rome).

Montevecchi, O. 1957. "Pantokrator," in *Studi in onore di Aristide Calderini e Roberto Paribeni* (Milano), 401-32.

Morenz, S. 1964. "Ägyptische Spuren in den Septuaginta," A. Stuiker and A. Hermann (eds), *Mullus* [Fschr. Theodor Klauser] (München), 250-8.

Mortari: *La Bibbia dei LXX. 1. Il Pentateuco* a cura di Luciana Mortari (Roma, 1999).

Moulton: J.H. Moulton. *A Grammar of New Testament Greek*. Vol. I. Prolegomena (Edinburgh, ^{3}1908).

Moussy, C. 1969. *Recherches sur* τρέφω *et les verbes grecs signifiants* «nourir» (Paris).

Mühlenberg, E. 1975-78. *Psalmenkommentare aus der Katenenüberlieferung*. 3 vols. (Berlin / New York).

Munnich, O. 1979. "L'opacité sémantique de la *Septante*," *Silento* 5-6.333-51.

——. 1986. "Note sur la Bible de Philon: κλοποφορεῖν / *κλοποφρονεῖν en *Gen*. 31,26 et en *Leg. All*. III, 20," in A. Caquot et al. (eds), *Hellenica et Judaica. Hommages à Valentin Nikiprowetzky* ז"ל (Leuven / Paris), 43-51.

Munz, R. 1921. "Über γλῶττα und διάλεκτος und über ein posidonianisches Fragment bei Strabo. Ein sprachwissenschaftlich-philologischer Exkurs zu Posidonius bei Strabo C 176 über dialektische Verschiedenheiten bei den Griechen," *Glotta* 11.85-94.

Muraoka, T. 1964. "The use of ὡς in the Greek Bible," *NT* 8.51-72.

——. 1970. "Is the Septuagint Amos viii 12—ix 10 a separate unit?," *VT* 20.496-500.

——. 1973a. "Literary device in the Septuagint," *Textus* 8.20-30.

——. 1973b. "Purpose or result? ὥστε in Biblical Greek," *NT* 15.205-19.

——. 1978. "On the so-called *dativus ethicus* in Biblical Hebrew," *JThSt* NS 29. 495-8.

——. 1983. "Hosea IV in the Septuagint version," *AJBI* 9.24-64.

——. 1984. "On Septuagint lexicography and patristics," *JThSt* 35.441-8.

——. 1986a. "Hosea V in the Septuagint version," *AN* 24.120-38.

——. 1986b. "Towards a Septuagint lexicography," in Cox 1986.255-76.

——. (ed.). 1990. *Melbourne Symposium on Septuagint Lexicography* [SCS 28] (Atlanta, GA).

——. 1990a. "Septuagintal lexicography: Some general issues," in Muraoka 1990.17-47.

——. 1991. "Hebrew hapax legomena and Septuagint lexicography," in Cox 1989.205-22.

——. 1993. *A Greek-English Lexicon of the Septuagint (Twelve Prophets)* (Leuven).

——. 2000. "How to analyse and translate the idiomatic phrase מִי יִתֵּן," *BIOSCS* 33.47-52.

——. 2001a. "Translation technique and beyond," in Sollamo and Sipilä 2001.13-22.

——. 2001b."Pairs of synonyms in the Septuagint Psalms," in R.J.V. Hiebert et al. (eds), *The Old Greek Psalter* [Fschr A. Pietersma] (Sheffield), 36-43.

——. 2001c. "'Three of them' and 'the three of them' in Hebrew," *Ancient Near Eastern Studies* 38.215f.

——. 2002. *A Greek-English Lexicon of the Septuagint. Chiefly of the Pentateuch and the Twelve Prophets* (Leuven).

——. 2005. "Apports de la LXX dans notre compréhension de l'hébreu et du grec et de leur vocabulaire," J. Joosten and Ph. le Moigne (eds), *L'apport de la Septante aux études sur l'Antiquité* (Paris), 57-68.

——. 2005a. "Why not a Morgenthaler for the Septuagint?," in F. García Martínez and M. Vervenne (eds), *Interpreting Translation: Studies on the LXX and Ezekiel* [Fschr J. Lust] (Leuven), 301-09.

——. 2005b. "Gleanings of a Septuagint lexicographer," *BIOSCS* 38.101-8.

——. 2006. "On the syntax of verba iubendi in the Septuagint," in R. Pierri (ed.), *Grammatica intellectio Scripturae: Saggi filologici di Greco biblico in onore di Lino Cignelli OFM* (Jerusalem), 69-80.

——. 2008a. "Septuagint lexicography and Hebrew etymology," in A. Voitila & J. Jokiranta (eds.), *Scripture in Transition, Essays on Septuagint, Hebrew Bible, and Dead Sea Scrolls* (Fschr. R. Sollamo) (Leiden). 463-69.

——. 2008b. "Recent discussions on the Septuagint lexicography with special reference to the so-called interlinear model," in M. Karrer and W. Kraus (eds), *Die Septuaginta - Texte, Kontexte, Lebenswelten* (Tübingen), 221-35.

Muraoka - Malessa: T. Muraoka and M. Malessa. 2002. "A deuteronomistic formula <שׁמר + עשׂה>," *VT* 52.548-50.

Muraoka - Porten: T. Muraoka and B. Porten. ^{2}2003. *A Grammar of Egyptian Aramaic* (Leiden).

Naumann, W. 1913. *Untersuchungen über den apokryphen Jeremiasbrief* [BZAW 25] (Gießen).

ND: G.H.R. Horsley and S.L. Llewelyn, *New Documents Illustrating Early Christianity*, vols. 1-8 (Macquarie University/Grand Rapids, 1981-97).
Neirynck, F. 1977. "Παρακύψας βλέπει: Lc 24,12 et Jn 20,5," *ETL* 53.113-52.
—. 1979. "Εἰς τὰ ἴδια: Jn 19,27 (et 16,32)," *ETL* 55.357-65.
Nestle, E. 1895. "חבר = ἔθνος," *ZAW* 15.288-90.
—. 1903. "Sykophantia im biblischen Griechisch," *ZNW* 4.271f.
—. 1904. "Zur aramäischen Bezeichnung der Proselyten," *ZNW* 5.263f.
Nielsen, K. 1986. *Incense in Ancient Israel* (Leiden).
North, H. 1966. Sophrosyne. *Self-knowledge and Self-restraint in Greek Literature* (Ithaca).
North, J.L. 1973. "'Ακηδία and ἀκηδιᾶν in the Greek and Latin Bible tradition," in E.A. Livingstone (ed.), *Studia Evangelica* VI [TU 112] (Berlin), 387-92.
O'Callaghan, J. 1971. "El vocativo singular de ἀδελφός en el griego bíblico," *Bib.* 52.217-25.
O'Connor, M. and J.A.L. Lee. 2007. "A problem in biblical lexicography: The case of Hebrew *ṭap* and Greek *aposkeuē*," *ZAW* 119.403-9.
Olley, J.W. 1979. *'Righteousness' in the Septuagint of Isaiah: A Contextual Study* (Missoula).
—. 1980. "The translator of the Septuagint of Isaiah and 'righteousness'," *BIOSCS* 13.58-74.
Orlinsky, H.M. 1937. "'Αποβαίνω and ἐπιβαίνω in the Septuagint of Job," *JBL* 56.361-7.
—. 1962. "Studies in the Septuagint of the Book of Job," *HUCA* 33.119-51.
Ottley: R.R. Ottley, *The Book of Isaiah according to the Septuagint (Codex Alexandrinus). Translated and Edited.* 2 vols. (London / Cambridge, 1904-6).
Owen, E.C.E. 1929. "ἀποτυμπανίζω, ἀποτυμπανισμός (τυμπανισμός), τυμπανίζω, τύμπανον (τύπανον)," *JThSt* 30.259-66.
—. 1931. "Δαίμων and cognate words," *JThSt* 32.133-266.
—. 1932. "Δόξα and cognate words," *JThSt* 33.132-50, 265-79.
Paeslack, M. 1953/54. "Zur Bedeutungsgeschichte der Wörter φιλεῖν 'lieben,' φιλία 'Liebe,' 'Freundschaft,' φίλος 'Freund' in der Septuaginta und im Neuen Testament (unter Berücksichtigung ihrer Beziehungen zu ἀγαπᾶν, ἀγάπη, ἀγαπητός," *Theologia Viatorum* 5.51-142.
Paradise, B. 1986. "Food for thought: The Septuagint translation of Genesis 1.11-12," J.D. Martin and Ph.R. Davies (eds), *A Word in Season* [Fschr W. McKane] (Sheffield), 177-204.
Passoni Dell'Acqua, A. 1974. "Σκυλμός," *Aeg.* 54.197-202.
—. 1976. "Euergetes," *Aeg.* 56.177-91.
—. 1981. "Richerche sulla versione dei LXX e i papiri, I Pastophorion," *Aeg.* 62.171-211.
—. 1982. "Richerche sulla versione dei LXX e i papiri, II Nomós; III Andrizomai," *Aeg.* 62.173-94.
—. 1983. "Indagine lessicale su ἐρευνάω e composti: dall'età classica a quella moderna," *Anagennesis* 3.201-326.
—. 1984. "Καταπάτησις: Storia del termine, con un papiro inedito (*PMed. Inv.* 63, Ispezione di un terreno)," in *Atti del XVII congresso internazionale di papirologia*, III (Napoli), 1309-15.
—. 1986. "L'imagine del «calpestare» dall'A.T. ai padri della chiesa," *Anagennesis* 4.63-129.
—. 1988. "La terminologia dei reati nei προστάγματα dei Tolemei e nella versione dei LXX," *Proceedings of the XVIII International Congress of Papyrology* (Athens), II.335-50.
—. 1998. "Notazione cromatiche dall'Egitto greco-romano. La versione dei LXX e i papiri," *Aeg.* 78.77-115.
—. 2000. "La figura dei θεόμαχος nella letteratura giudaico-ellenistica: Un ritratto per antitesi del monarca ellenistico ideale," S. Graziani (ed.), *Studi sul vicino oriente antico dedicati alla memoria di Luigi Cagni* (Napoli), 1963-81.
—. 2002. "Gli editti di liberazione nella letteratura giudaico-ellenistica: Intento storico ed apologetico," *Materia giudaica* 7.55-65.
Pax, E. 1955. *ΕΠΙΦΑΝΕΙΑ: Ein religionsgeschichtlicher Beitrag zur biblischen Theologie* (München).
Pelletier, A. 1960. Article "Pain de proposition," in *Dictionnaire de la Bible*: Supplément, VI (Paris), cols. 965-76.
—. 1962. *Flavius Josèphe, Adapteur de la Lettre d'Aristée. Une Réaction atticisante contre la Koinè.* Diss. Paris.
—. 1967a. "Une particularité du rituel des 'Pains d'oblation' conservée par la Septante," *VT* 17.364-7.
—. 1967b. "Note sur les mots διατριβή, ἱερόν, διάθεσις dans *P. Gen.* inv. 108," *Recherches de papyrologie* 4.175-86.
—. 1972. "*Sabbata*, transcription grecque de l'araméen," *VT* 22.436-47.
—. 1982. "L'autorité divine d'après le Pentateuque grec," *VT* 32.236-42.
Pendrick, G. 1995. "ΜΟΝΟΓΕΝΗΣ," *NTS* 41.587-600.
Penna, A. 1965. "Διαθήκη e συνθήκη nei libri dei Maccabei," *Bib.* 46.149-80.
Pennington, J.T. 2003. "'Heaven' and 'Heavens' in the LXX: Exploring the relationship between שָׁמַיִם and οὐρανός," *BIOSCS* 36.39-59.
Perlitt, L. 1990. "Dtn 1,12 LXX," in D. Fraenkel / U. Quast / J.W. Wevers (eds), *Studien zur Septuaginta - Robert Hanhart zu Ehren* (Göttingen), 299-311.
Perpillou-Thomas, F. 1989. "*P.Sorb. inv.* 2381: γρύλλος, καλαμαύλης, χορός," *ZPE* 78.153-5.
Petersen, H. 1986. "Wörter zusammengesetzt mit ΑΜΦΙ," *Glotta* 64.198.
Pierri, R. 2006. "La congiunzione ὅτι nel greco biblico," in R. Pierri (ed.), *Grammatica intellectio Scripturae. Saggi filologici di greco biblico* (Jerusalem), 81-108.

Pietersma, A. 2002. "᾿Επίχειρον in Greek literature," *JNWSL* 28.101-8.

—. 2003. "When Dauid fled Abessalom: a commentary on the third psalm in Greek," in Fshcr. E. Tov [see above under Lee], 645-59.

Poland, F. 1931. "Συμβίωσις," in *Paulys Real-enczyclopädie der classischen Altertumswissenschaft*, IV 1 (Stuttgart), cols.1075-82.

Popper, J. 1862. *Der biblische Bericht über die Stiftshütte* (Leipzig).

P.Oxy: *Oxyrhynchus Papyri* (London, 1898-).

P.Paris: Letronne, J.A., W. Brunet de Presle and E. Egger (eds), *Notices et textes des papyrus du Musée du Louvre et de la Bibliothèque Impériale* (Paris, 1865).

Préaux, C. 1931. "῞Οτι suivi d'un discours direct après un verbe *dicendi*," *CÉg* 11.414f.

Preisigke: F. Preisigke, E. Kießling, H.-A. Rupprecht & A. Jördens, *Wörterbuch der griechischen Papyrusurkunden mit Einschluss der griechischen Inschriften, Aufschriften, Ostraka, Mumienschilder usw. aus Ägypten*, 4 vols. with Supplements (Berlin/Amsterdam/Wiesbaden, 1925-91).

PSI: *Papiri greci e latini.*

Psichari: J. Psichari, "Essai sur le grec de la Septante," *RÉJ* 55 (1908) 161-208.

Radt, S. 1980. "Noch einmal Aischylos, *Niobe* Fr. 162 N[2] (278 M.)," *ZPE* 38.47-58.

Rahlfs, A. 1930. Rev. of A. Sperber, *Septuaginta-Probleme I*, *ThLZ* 55.104-6.

Raurell, F. 1986. "The polemical role of the ἄρχοντες and ἀφηγούμενοι in Ez LXX," in J. Lust (ed.), *Ezekiel and his Book* (Leuven), 85-9.

—. 1990. "The religious meaning of «δόξα» in the Book of Wisdom," M. Gilbert (ed.), *La Sagesse de l'Ancien Testament* [Bibliotheca Ephemeridum Thaologicarum Lovaniensium 51] (Leuven), 370-83.

Read-Heimerdinger, J. 2006. "Luke's use of ὡς and ὡσεί: Comparison and correspondance as a means to convey his message," in R. Pierri (ed.), *Grammatica intellectio Scripturae. Saggi filologici di greco biblico* (Jerusalem), 251-74.

Redditt, P.L. 1983. "The concept of *Nomos* in Fourth Maccabees," *CBQ* 45.249-70.

Reekmans, T. 1985. "᾿Αργός and its derivatives in the papyri," *CÉg* 60.275-91.

Rehrl, S. 1961. *Das Problem der Demut in der profangriechischen Literatur im Vergleich zu Septuaginta und Neuem Testament* (Münster).

Reiling, J. 1971. "The use of ΨΕΥΔΟΠΡΟΦΗΤΗΣ in the Septuagint, Philo and Josephus," *NT* 13.147-56.

Renehan: R. Renehan, *Greek Lexicographical Notes. A Critical Supplement to the Greek-English Lexicon of Liddell-Scott-Jones*, 2 vols. (Göttingen, 1975-82).

Repo, E. 1951-4. *Der Begriff "Rhēma" im Biblisch-Griechischen. Eine traditionsgeschichtliche und semologische Untersuchung*, 2 vols. (Helsinki).

Reumann, J. 1958. "'Stewards of God' – Pre-Christian religious application of οἰκονόμος in Greek," *JBL* 77.339-49.

Riesenfeld, H. 1963. "Zu μακροθυμεῖν (Lk 18,7)," in J. Blinzler, O. Kuss, and F. Mußner, *Neutestamentliche Aufsätze* [Fschr J. Schmid] (Regensburg), 214-7.

Rigsby, K.J. 1976. "Teiresias as magus in *Oedipus Rex*," *Greek, Roman and Byzantine Studies* 17.109-14.

Robert, L. 1937. *Études anatoliennes. Recherches sur les inscriptions grecques de l'Asie Mineure* (Paris).

—. 1938. *Études épigraphiques et philologiques* (Paris).

—. 1960. "Recherches épigraphiques," *RÉAnc* 62.276-361.

—. 1989. "Le serpent Glycon d'Abônouteichos à Athèbes et Artémis d'Éphèse à Rome," in id., *Opera Minora Selecta*, V (Amsterdam), 747-69.

Roberts, T. 2004. "A review of *BDAG*," in B.A. Taylor et al. (eds), *Biblical Greek Language and Lexicography* [Fschr F.W. Danker (Grand Rapids, MI), 53-65.

Rödiger, R. 1917. "Βούλομαι und ἐθέλω, eine semasiologische Untersuchung," *Glotta* 8.1-24.

Rösel, M. 1994. *Übersetzung als Vollendung der Auslegung. Studien zur Genesis-Septuaginta* [BZAW 223] (Berlin / New York).

—. 2001. "Die Psalmüberschriften des Septuagintapsalters," in E. Zenger (ed.), *Die Septuaginta-Psalter: Sprachliche und theologische Aspekte* (Freiburg), 125-48.

Rogland, M. 2008. "μακροθυμεῖν in Ben Sira 35:19 and Luke 18:7: A lexicographical note," *NT* [forthcoming].

Romeo, A. 1949. "Il termine ΛΕΙΤΟΥΡΓΙΑ nella grecità biblica," *Miscellanea Liturgica in honorem L. Cuniberti Mohlberg* [Bibliotheca Ephemerides Liturgicae 23] (Roma), 467-519.

Romilly, J. de. 1979. *La douceur dans la pensée grecque* (Paris).

Roux, G. 1961a. "Le sens de τύπος," *RÉA* 63.5-14.

—. 1961b. *L'architecture de l'argolide aux IVe et IIIe siècles avant J.-C.* (Paris).

Rowley, H.H. 1951. "A note on the LXX text of 1Sam. xv:22a," *VT* 1.67f.

Ruffing, K. 1999. *Weinbau im römischen Ägypte* [Pharos. Studien zur griechisch-römischen Antike 12] (St. Katharinen).

Rundgren, F. 1957. "Zur Bedeutung von *ΟΙΚΟΓΕΝΗΣ* in 3. Esra 3,1," *Eranos* 55.145-52.

Rupprecht, H.-A. 1994. *Kleine Einführung in die Papyruskunde* (Darmstad).

Russo, S. 1999. "I gioielli nei papiri di età greco-romana," Ph.D. diss. Florence.

Rydén, L. 1961. "LXX Sirach 37,2," *Eranos* 59.40-4.

Ryssel, V. 1900. Commentary on Ben Sirach and the prayer of Manasseh in E. Kautzsch (ed.), *Die Apokryphen und Pseudepigraphen des Alten Testaments* (Tübingen).

Samuel, A.E. 1965. "The role of paramone clauses in ancient documents," *Journal of Juristic Papyrology* 15.221-311.

—. 1966. "The judicial competence of oikonomos in the third century B.C.," *Atti dell'XI Congresso Internazionale di Papirologia* (Milano), 444-50.

SB: *Sammelbuch griechischer Urkunden aus Ägypten*. 1915-83.

Scarpat, G. 1989-99. *Libro della Sapienza. Testo, traduzione, introduzione e commento*. 3 vols. (Brescia).

Scharbert, J. 1972. "Fleisch, Geist und Seele in der Pentateuch-Septuaginta," in J. Schreiner (ed.), *Wort, Lied und Gottesspruch: Beiträge zur Septuaginta* [Fschr J. Ziegler] (Würzburg), I.121-43.

Schenker, A. 1999. "ΔΙΑΘΗΚΗ pour ברית. L'option de traduction de la LXX à la double lumière du droit successoral de l'Égypte ptolémaïque et du livre de la Genèse," in J.-M. Auwers and A. Wénin, *Lectures et relectures de la Bible* [Fshcr P.-M. Bogaert] (Leuven), 125-31.

—. 2000. "Le contrat successoral en droit gréco-égyptien et la διαθήκη dans la Septante," *Z. für Altorientalische und Biblische Rechtsgeschichte* 6.175-85. [= "The inheritance contract in Greco-Egyptian law and διαθήκη in the Septuagint," *Journal of Biblical Text Research* 7 (2000) 36-49.]

Scherer, J. 1975. "Note de frais concernant l'élevage de cinq veaux (*P. Sorbonne Inv.* 2393)," in J. Bingen et al. (eds), *Le Monde grec* [Fschr. C. Préaux] (Bruxelles), 578-84.

Schermann, Th. 1910. "Εὐχαριστία und εὐχαριστεῖν in ihrem Bedeutungswandel bis 200 n. Chr.," *Philologus* 69.375-410.

Schleusner: J.F. Schleusner, *Novus thesaurus philologico-criticus sive lexicon in LXX et reliquos interpretes graecos ac scriptores apocryphos veteris testamenti*, 5 vols. (Lepzig, 1820-21).

Schmidt: J.H. Heinrich Schmidt. *Synonymik der griechischen Sprache*, 4 vols. (Leipzig, 1876-86).

Schmitt, A. 1974. "Interpretation der Genesis aus hellenistischem Geist," *ZAW* 86.137-63.

Schnebel, M. 1925. *Die Landwirtschaft im hellenistischen Ägypte* [Münchener Beiträge zur Papyrusforschung und antiken Rechtsgeschichte 7] (München).

Scholl, R. 1983. *Sklaverei in den Zenonpapyri. Eine Untersuchung zu den Sklaventermini, zum Sklavenerwerb und Sklavenflucht* [Trier Historische Forschungen 4] (Trier).

—. 1984. "Zur Bezeichnung ἱερόδουλος im griechisch-römischen Ägypten," in *Atti del XVII Congresso Internazionale di Papirologia*, III (Napoli), 977-83.

Schoonheim, P.L. 1966. "Der alttestamentliche Boden der Vokabel ὑπερήφανος Lukas I 51," *NT* 8.235-46.

Schreiner, J. 1972. "Anti in der Septuaginta," in J. Schreiner (ed.), *Wort, Lied und Gottesspruch* [Fschr J. Ziegler] (Würzburg), 171- 6.

Schröder, Ch. 2001. "Alphabetische Zusammenstellung afffälliger Neologismen," in H.-J. Fabry and U. Offerhaus (eds), *Im Brennpunkt: Die Septuaginta. Studien zur Entstehung und Bedeutung der griechischen Bibel* (Stuttgart / Berlin / Köln), 61-70.

Schwyzer: E. Schwyzer (and A. Debrunner), *Griechische Grammatik*, 2 vols. (München, ^{2}1953-9).

—. 1935. "Altes und Neues zu (hebr.-)griech. σάββατα, (griech.-)lat. *sabbata* usw.," *Z. für vergleichende Sprachforschung auf dem Gebiete der indogermanischen Sprachen* 62.1-16.

Seeligmann, I.L. 1990 (1940). "Problems and perspectives in modern Septuagint research," *Textus* 15.169-232 [originally publ. in Dutch].

—. 1948. *The Septuagint Version of Isaiah. A Discussion of its Problems* (Leiden).

Segal: M.H. Segal, ספר בן סירא השלם (Jerusalem, ^{2}1958).

Segalla, G. 1965. "La volontà di Dio nei LXX in rapporto al TM: θέλημα, *rāṣôn, ḥēfeṣ*," *Rivista Biblica* 13.121-43.

Selb, W. 1974. "Διαθήκη im Neuen Testament," *JJS* 25.183-96.

Shaw, F. 2004-05. "χορηγία at 2 Maccabees 4.14," *Bulletin of Judaeo-Greek Studies* 35.34-6.

Shipp: G.P. Shipp, *Modern Greek Evidence for the Ancient Greek Vocabulary* (Sydney, 1979).

Smend, R. 1906. *Die Weisheit des Jesus Sirach erklärt* (Berlin).

Soisalon-Soininen, *Infinitive*: I. Soisalon-Soininen, *Die Infinitive in der Septuaginta* (Helsinki, 1965).

—. 1979. "Renderings of Hebrew comparative expressions with *min* in the Greek Pentateuch," *BIOSCS* 12.27-42.

—. 1987. *Studien zur Septuaginta-Syntax*, (eds) A. Aejmelaeus and R. Sollamo (Helsinki).

F. de P. Solà, 1966. "El uso de artículos delante de las palabras θεός y κύριος en las cartas cristianas del siglo V," *Atti dell'XI Congresso Internazionale di Papirologia* (Milano), 126-34.

Sollamo, *Semiprep.*: R. Sollamo, *Renderings of Hebrew Semiprepositions in the Septuagint* (Helsinki, 1979).

—. 1991. "The pleonastic use of the pronoun in connection with the relative pronoun in the Greek Pentateuch," in Cox (ed.), *VII Congress*, 75-85.

—. 2005. "An example of consistency: Interpretation by the translator of the Greek Genesis in rendering the Hebrew semipreposition לפני," in A. Mustakallio (ed.), *Lux Humana, Lux Aeterna* [Fschr L. Aejmelaeus] (Helsinki / Göttingen), 3-12.

Sollamo, R. and S. Sipilä (eds), 2001. *Helsinki Perspectives on the Translation Technique of the Septuagint: Proceedings of the IOSCS Congress in Helsinki 1999* (Helsinki / Göttingen).

Souter: Souter, A., *A Pocket Lexicon of the Greek New Testament* (Oxford, 1916).

Spicq: C. Spicq, *Theological Lexicon of the New Testament*, 3 vols., ET J.D. Ernest (Peabody, Mass., 1994), tr. of *Lexique théologique du Nouveau Testament* (Paris, 1991).

—. 1947. "Bénigté, mansuétude, douceur, clémence," *RB* 54.321-39.

—. 1957. "Ἐπιποθεῖν, désirer ou chérir?," *RB* 64.184-95.

—. 1973. "Note sur μορφή dans les papyrus et quelques inscriptions," *RB* 80.37-45.

—. 1978. "Le vocabulaire de l'esclavage dans le Nouveau Testament," *RB* 85.201-26.

—. 1985. Article "Religion (vertu de)," in *Supplémant au Dictionare de la Bible*, x (Paris), cols. 210-40.

Stählin, G. 1930. *Skandalon: Untersuchungen zur Geschichte eines biblischen Begriffs* (Gütersloh).

Stanton, G.R. 1988. "Τέκνον, παῖς and related words in Koine Greek," *Proceedings of the XVIII International Congress of Papyrology* (Athens) I.463-80.

Steinmueller, J.E. 1951. "Ἐρᾶν, φιλεῖν, ἀγαπᾶν in extra-biblical and biblical sources," in A. Metzinger (ed.), *Miscellanea biblica et orientalia* [Fschr R.P.A. Miller, Rome], 404-23.

Stoop - van Paridon, P.W.T. 2005. *The Song of Songs. A Philological Analysis of the Hebrew Book* שִׁיר הַשִּׁירִים [*Ancient Near Eastern Studies* Supplement 17] (Leuven).

Streane, A.W. 1896. *The Double Text of Jeremiah (Massoretic and Alexandrian Compared* etc.) (Cambridge).

Swinn, S.P. 1990. "ἀγαπᾶν in the Septuagint," in Muraoka (ed.) 1990.49-82.

TAD: Porten, B. and A. Yardeni, *Textbook of Aramaic Documents from Ancient Egypt*: *Newly Copied, Edited and Translated into Hebrew and English* (Jerusalem / Winona Lake, 1986-93).

Taillardat, J. 1978. "Le thème ψαλ- ψελ- en grec (ψάλιον, ψέλιον, ψαλίς, σπαλίων)," *RÉG* 91.1-11.

—. 1999. "Ἀγκών «baie»," *Revue de philologie* 73.253-5.

Talshir, Z. 2001. *I Esdras. A Text-critical Commentary* [SCS 50] (Atlanta).

Tarelli, C.C. 1950. "Ἀγάπη," *JThSt* NS 1.64-8.

Taylor, B.A. (ed.) 1997. *IX Congress of the IOSCS* (Atlanta).

—. (ed.) 2001. *X Congress of the IOSCS* (Atlanta).

—. 2003. "The NETS translation of 1 Reigns: Lexical issues," *BIOSCS* 36.75-85.

—. 2004. "Hebrew to Greek: A semantic study of σπεύδω for the New English Translation of the Septuagint," in B. Taylor et al. (eds), *Biblical Greek Language and Lexicography* [Fsch F.W. Danker] (Grand Rapids), 136-48.

TDNT: G. Kittel, *Theological Dictionary of the New Testament*, 10 vols., tr. by G.W. Bromiley (Grand Rapids, 1964-76) from *Theologisches Wörterbuch zum Neuen Testament* (Stuttgart, 1933-78).

Thack.: H. St J. Thackeray, *A Grammar of the Old Testament in Greek according to the Septuagint*. Vol. I. Introduction, Orthography and Accidence (Cambridge, 1909).

Thibaut, A. 1988. *L'infidélité du peuple élu: Ἀπειθῶ entre la bible hébraïque et la bible latine* [Collectanea biblica latina 17] (Rome/Turnhout).

Thomas, D.W. 1960. "The Septuagint's rendering of שנות לב טוב in Ecclus xxxiii: 13" *VT* 10.456.

Thompson, A. 2003. Review of Lee 2003a, *BIOSCS* 36.113-26.

Thrall, M.E. 1962. *Greek Particles in the New Testament* (Leiden).

Tigner, St. S. 1974. "Some LSJ addenda and corrigenda," *Glotta* 52.192-206.

Tomsin, A. 1952. "Étude sur les πρεσβύτεροι des villages de la χώρα égyptienne," *Bulletin: Académie royale de Belgique*, 38.95-130.

Tomson, P.J. 2007. "Blessing in disguise: ΕΥΛΟΓΕΩ and ΕΥΧΑΡΙΣΤΕΩ between 'biblical' and everyday Greek usage," in Joosten and Tomson, 35-61.

Torallas Tovar, S. and A. Maravela-Solbakk. 2001. "Between necromancers and ventriloquists: the ἐγγαστρίμυθοι in the *Septuaginta*," *Sefarad* 61.419-37.

Torm, F. 1934. "Der Pluralis οὐρανοί," *ZNW* 33.48-50.

Tosato, A. "Sulle origini del termine *akrobustía* (prepuzio, incirconcisione)," *Bibbia e Oriente* 24 (1982) 43-9.

Tov, E. 1990. "Greek words and Hebrew meanings," in Muraoka 1990.83-126.

Townshend, R.B. 1913. "Fourth Maccabees," in R.H. Charles (ed.), *The Apocrypha and Pseudepigrapha of the Old Testament in English*, vol. 2, Pseudepigrapha (Cambridge).

Trédé, M. 1984. "Καιρός: problème d'étymologie," *RÉG* 97.xi-xvi.

Tréheux, J. 1987. "Κοινόν," *RÉG* 89.39-46.

Trench: R.C. Trench, *Synonyms of the New Testament* (Grand Rapids, 1953 [= repr. of (London, 1880)]).

Troxel, R.L. 1992. "ἘΣΧΑΤΟΣ and eschatology in LXX-Isaiah," *BIOSCS* 25.18-27.

Turner, C.H. 1926. "Ο ΥΙΟΣ ΜΟΥ Ο ΑΓΑΠΗΤΟΣ," *JThSt* 27.113-29.

Turner, *Syntax*: J.H. Moulton, *A Grammar of New Testament Greek*. Vol. III, Syntax by N. Turner (Edinburgh, 1963).

Tyrer, J.W. 1924. "The meaning of ἐπίκλησις," *JThSt* 25.139-50.

Utzschneider, H. 2001. "Das griechische Michabuch—Zur Probe übersetzt und erläutert im Rahmen des Projekts „Septuaginta-Deutsch—Das Griechische Alte Testament in Übersetzung," in H.-J. Fabry and U. Offerhaus (eds), *Im Brennpunkt: Die Septuaginta, Studien zur Entstehung und Bedeutung der griechischen Bibel* (Stuttgart / Berlin / Köln), 213-50.

van Daalen, D.H. 1982. "The *'ēmunah* / πίστις of Habakkuk 2.4 and Romans 1.17," in E.A. Livingstone (ed.), *Studia Evangelica,* vol. VII [Texte und Untersuchungen 126] (Berlin), 523-8.

van den Eynde, S. 2005. "Blessed by God - Blessed be God. Εὐλογέω and the concept of blessing in the LXX with special attention to the book of Ruth," in F. García Martínez and M. Vervenne (eds), *Interpreting Translation: Studies on the LXX and Ezekiel* [Fschr J. Lust] (Leuven), 415-36.

Vandersleyen, C. 1973. "Le mot λαός dans la langue des papyrus grecs," *CÉg* 48. 339-49.

van der Kooij, A. 1987. "The Old Greek of Isaiah 19:16-25: Translation and interpretation," Cox (ed.) 1987.127-66.

—. 1998. *The Oracle of Tyre. The Septuagint of Isaiah XXIII as Version and Vision* [SVT 71] (Leiden).

—. 2003. "On the use of βωμός in the Septuagint," in Baasten and van Peursen 2003.601-7.

van der Meer, M.N. 2006. "Provenance, profile, and purpose of the Greek Joshua," in M.K.H. Peters, *XII Congress of the IOSCS* [SCS 54] (Atlanta), 55-80.

—. 2008. "Trendy translations in the Septuagint of Isaiah. A study of the vocabulary of the Greek Isaiah 3,18-23 in the light of contemporary sources," in M. Karrer and W. Kraus (eds), *Die Septuaginta — Texte, Kontexte, Lebenswelten* (Tübingen), 581-96.

van Herten, J. 1934. Θρησκεία Εὐλάβεια Ἱκέτης. *Bijdrage tot de kennis der religieuze terminologie in her grieksch* (Amsterdam).

van Leeuwen, W.S. 1940. *Eirene in het Nieuwe Testament* (Wageningen).

van Menxel, F. 1983. Ἐλπίς. *Espoir. Espérance. Études sémantiques et théologiques du vocabulaire de l'ésperance dans l'Héllenisme et le Judaïsme avant le Nouveau Testament* (Frankfurt a. M. / Bern / New York).

Waanders, F.M.J. 1983. *The History of ΤΕΛΟΣ and ΤΕΛΕΩ in Ancient Greek* (Amsterdam).

Wackernagel, J. 1969 (1905). *Kleine Schriften* I. (Göttingen).

Wagner, Ch. 1999. *Die Septuaginta-Hapaxlegomena im Buch Jesu Sirach. Untersuchungen zu Wortwahl und Wortbildung unter besonderer Berücksichtigung des textkritischen und übersetzungstechnischen Aspekts* [BZAW 282] (Berlin / New York).

Wallace, D.H. 1966. "A note on μορφή," *Theologische Zeitschrift* 22.19-25.

Walters: P. Walters (formerly Katz), ed. by D.W. Gooding, *The Text of the Septuagint: its Corruptions and their Emendation* (Cambridge, 1973).

Watson, N.M. 1960. "Some observations on the use of δικαιόω in the Septuagint," *JBL* 79.255-66.

Weierholt, K. 1932. "Zum Ausdruck οἱ περί τινα in den Maccabäerbüchern," *Symbolae Osloenses* 11.69-71.

Wellhausen: J. Wellhausen, *Die kleinen Propheten: Skizzen und Vorarbeiten* (Göttingen, ^{4}1963).

—. 1871. *Der Text der Bücher Samuelis untersucht* (Göttingen).

Wells, L. 1998. *The Greek Language of Healing from Homer to the New Testament Times* (Berlin / New York).

Wevers, J.W. 1978. *Text History of the Greek Deuteronomy* (Göttingen).

—. 1982. *Text History of the Greek Numbers* (Göttingen).

—. 1986. *Text History of the Greek Levicitus* (Göttingen).

—. 1990. *Notes on the Greek Text of Exodus* [SCS 30] (Atlanta, GA).

—. 1992. *Text History of the Greek Exodus* (Göttingen).

—. 1993. *Notes on the Greek Text of Genesis* [SCS 35] (Atlanta, GA).

—. 1995. *Notes on the Greek Text of Deuteronomy* [SCS 39] (Atlanta, GA).

—. 1997. *Notes on the Greek Text of Leviticus* [SCS 44] (Atlanta, GA).

—. 1998. *Notes on the Greek Text of Numbers* [SCS 46] (Atlanta, GA).

Wickenhauser, A. 1910. "Ἐνώπιος - ἐνώπιον - κατενώπιον," *BZ* 8.267-70.

Wiedemann, A. 1890. *Herodots zweites Buch mit sachlichen Erläuterungen* (Leipzig).

Wifstrand, A. 1965. "Lukas xviii. 7," *NTS* 10.72-4.

Wilcken: L. Mitteis & U. Wilcken, *Grundzüge und Chrestomathie der Papyruskunde* (Leipzig / Berlin, 1921).

Wilhelm, A. 1937. "Zu einigen Stellen der Bücher der Makkabäer," *Anzeiger der Akademie der Wissenschaften in Wien, Philosophisch-historische Klasse* 74.15-30.

Will, Éd. 1975. "Notes sur ΜΙΣΘΟΣ," in J. Bingen et al. (eds), *Le Monde grec: Pensée, littérature, histoire, documents* [Fschr C. Préaux] (Brussels), 426-38.

Will, E. 1987. "Qu'est-ce qu'une βᾶρις?," *Syria* 64.253-9.

Williger, E. 1922. Ἅγιος: *Untersuchungen zur Terminologie des heiligen in den hellenisch-hellenistischen Religionen* (Giessen).

Wilson, J.R. 1980. "KAIROS as 'due measure'," *Glotta* 58.177-204.

Winston, D. 1979. *The Wisdom of Solomon* [AB 43] (Garden City, NY).

Wissemann, M. 1988. "ΚΕΦΑΛΗ = 'Schwadron, Schar'? Spätantike Übersetzungen als Hilfsmittel moderner Lexikologie," in M. Wissemann (ed.), *Roma renascens: Beiträge zur Spätantike und Rezeptionsgeschichte* [Fschr I. Opelt] (Frankfurt a.M. / Bern / New York / Paris), 377-84.

Witherington III, B. 1993. "Not so idle thoughts about εἰδωλόθυτον," *Tyndale Bulletin* 44.237-54.

Witt, R.E. 1933. Ὑπόστασις, in H.G. Wood (ed.), *Amicitiae corolla* [Fschr J.R. Harris] (London), 319-43.

Wodke, W. 1977. "Oikos in der Septuaginta: Erste Grundlagen," in O. Rössler (ed.), *Hebraica* (Marburger Studien zur Afrika- und Asienkunde B/4) (Berlin), 57-140.

Wolfson, H.A. 1947. "On the Septuagint use of *to hagion* for the temple," *JQR* 38.109f.

Wollentin, U. 1961. "Ὁ Κίνδυνος in den Papyri," Diss. Köln.

Wolters, A. 1999. "Semantic borrowing and inner-Greek corruption in LXX Zechariah 11:8," *JBL* 118.685-707.

Woo, S.-H. 2006. "Études sur le système verbal dans la Septante de Job," diss. Strasbourg.

Wooden, R.G. 2008. "The φορολόγος of 2 Esdras," in M. Karrer and W. Kraus (eds), *Die Septuaginta - Texte, Kontexte, Lebenswelten* (Tübingen), 248-57.

Wright, B.G. 1997. "Δοῦλος and Παῖς as translations of עבד: Lexical equivalences and conceptual transformations," Taylor 1997.263-77.

Youtie, H.C. 1970. "σημεῖον in the papyri and its significance for Plato, Epistle 13 (360a - b)," *ZPE* 6.105-16.

——. 1978. "Wörterbuch I, s.v. ΒΡΕΧΩ (1)," *ZPE* 30.191f.

Ysebaert, J. 1973. "Propitiation, expiation and redemption in Greek biblical terminology," in *Mélanges Christine Mohrmann* (Utrecht / Antwerpen), 1-12.

Ziegler, J. 1934. *Untersuchungen zur Septuaginta des Buches Isaias* (Münster i. W.).

——. 1958. *Beiträge zur Jeremias-Septuaginta* (Göttingen).

——. 1985. *Beiträge zum griechischen Iob*, Mitteilungen des Septuaginta-Unternehmens XVIII] (Göttingen).

Ziesler, J.A. 1983. "ΣΩΜΑ in the Septuagint," *NT* 25.133-45.

Zijderveld, C. 1934. Τελετή. *Bijdrage tot de kennis der religieuze terminologie in het Grieks* (Purmerend).

A

ἆ.ʃ

exclamation expressing consternation on realising one's own terrifying predicament: Jd 6.22, 11.35 A (B: οἴμμοι). Cf. οἴμμοι.

Ααρωνίδης, ου. m.ʃ *

descendant of Aaron: 4M 7.12.

ἀβασίλευτος, ον.ʃ

having no ruler: ***s*** locusts, Pr 30.27. Cf. βασιλεύς.

ἄβατος, ον.

impassable: ***s*** γῆ ἄ. [= ἔρημος] Le 16.22, ἐν γῇ ἐρήμῳ καὶ ~ῳ καὶ ἀνύδρῳ '.. and waterless' Ps 62.2, γῆ ἄνυδρος καὶ ἄ. Je 28.43, ἐν γῇ ἀπείρῳ καὶ ἀβάτῳ 'in a vast land with no end in sight and forbidding for journeymen' 2.6; 'not fordable,' swelling wadi (χειμάρρους) Am 5.24; ἔρημος Je 12.10; not easily accessible to pedestrians - ~ον γῆν ἥτις οὐ κατοικηθήσεται 6.8, ἐν γῇ ~ῳ καὶ οὐχ ὁδῷ Ps 106.40; τὸν ~ον ἡμῖν ναόν 'the temple, which is off-limits to us' 3M 5.43. **b**. subst.n. *tract of land not amenable to easy and regular passage*: ~ον καὶ ἀοίκητον Jb 38.27¶ (‖ ἔρημος vs. 26), sim. Wi 11.2; ἀπὸ ἀνθρώπου καὶ κτήνους Je 39.43 (‖ ἔρημος 40.10). **c**. *deserted and waste*: subst. n., ἔσονται εἰς ~ον καὶ ἀπώλειαν Je 30.2.

Cf. ἀβατάω, ἔρημος: Muraoka 1973a:22; LSG, s.v.

ἀβατόω: aor.subj.pass. ἀβατωθῶ.ʃ

to make ἄβατος **c**: pass., ***o*** dwelling-place, Je 29.21. Cf. ἄβατος, ἔρημος.

ἀβλαβής, ές.ʃ

causing no harm: ***s*** the sun, Wi 18.3. **b**. *suffering no harm*: ***s*** hum., Wi 19.6. Cf. βλάπτω.

ἀβοηθησία, ας. f.ʃ

want of help: Si 51.10. Cf. ἀβοήθητος.

ἀβοήθητος, ον.ʃ

cut off from help, 'helpless': ***s*** ἄνθρωπος Ps 87.5, ἑαυτῷ 'unable to help himself' 2M 3.28, ψυχή Wi 12.6. Cf. βοηθός, ἀβοηθησία.

ἀβουλεύτως. adv.ʃ

indiscreetly, against the best counsel: 1M 5.67.

ἀβουλία, ας. f.ʃ

thoughtlessness: Ba 3.28 (‖ τὸ μὴ ἔχειν φρόνησιν), Pr 14.17 (:: φρόνιμος).

ἅβρα, ας. f.

female personal servant, 'maid': on a journey, Ge 24.61; in the service of Pharaoh's daughter, Ex 2.5; lady-in-waiting, τὴν ~αν αὐτῆς (i.e. Judith's) τὴν ἐφεστῶσαν πᾶσιν τοῖς ὑπάρχουσιν αὐτῆς '.. who was in charge of all her possessions' Ju 8.10; ἀφῆκεν (sc. Judith) τὴν ~αν αὐτῆς ἐλευθέραν 16.23; in Esther's service, Es 2.9; αἱ ~αι καὶ οἱ εὐνοῦχοι τῆς βασιλίσσης 4.4 LXX (= κοράσιον 4.11*L*). Cf. δούλη, λάτρις, παιδίσκη, κοράσιον: Renehan 2.9.

Ἀβραμιαῖος, α, ον.

Abramic: ***s*** hum., 4M 9.21.

Ἀβραάμιτις, ιδος. f.ʃ

Abrahamic faith: 4M 18.20.

ἀβροχία, ας. f.ʃ

prolonged want of rain, 'drought': Je 14.1, 17.8, Si 32.26. Cf. βρέχω.

ἄβρωτος, ον.ʃ

inedible: ***s*** hum. bones, Pr 24.22e. Cf. βιβρώσκω.

ἄβυσσος, ον.

*subst. f. ἡ ~ος, *source of water located exceedingly deep below* – σκότος ἐπάνω τῆς ~ου Ge 1.2; τὴν ~ον τὴν πολλήν Am 7.4; Hb 3.10; αἱ πηγαὶ τῆς ~ου 'the fountains of the deep' Ge 7.11, 8.2, De 8.7, cf. πηγαὶ ~οι 'the sources (of the Nile being) deep down in the ground' Hdt. 2.28; ἀπὸ ~ων πηγῶν κάτωθεν De 33.13; καταβαίνουσιν ἕως τῶν ~ων Ps 106.26 (:: οὐρανοί); source of rivers, Ez 31.4; ‖ θάλασσα Jb 28.14¶, Ps 32.7, 134.6; more than one envisaged, 41.8; opp. οὐρανοί 106.26. Cf. Jeremias, *TDNT* 1.9f.

ἀγαθοποιέω: aor.subj. ~ποιήσω, opt.3s. ~ποιήσαι, inf. ~ποιῆσαι.ʃ *

1. *to act* or *do things for the benefit of*: abs. and ***s*** God, 2M 1.2, Zp 1.12 (:: κακόω); ***s*** hum., To 12.13 𝔊[I]; + dat. com., 1M 11.33; + acc. pers., Jd 17.13 A (B: ἀγαθύνω τινι).

2. *to do* sth *for the benefit of*: + double acc., τὰ ἀγαθὰ ἐκεῖνα, ὅσα ἂν ἀγαθοποιήσῃ κύριος ἡμᾶς 'those good things which the Lord might do for us' Nu 10.32. On the double acc., see ποιέω **I 2**.

Cf. ἀγαθός, ἀγαθοποιός, ἀγαθύνω, κακόω.

ἀγαθοποιός, όν.ʃ

disposed to acts of ἀγαθοποιέω (q.v.), 'beneficent': ***s*** γυνή (:: πονηρία) Si 42.14. Cf. ἀγαθοποιέω and κακοποιός.

ἀγαθός, ή, όν; comp. ἀγαθώτερος.

1. *flowing from kind and generous character*: subst., ἐπὶ πᾶσιν τοῖς ~οῖς, οἷς ἐποίησεν αὐτοῖς κύριος Ex 18.9; τὰ ~ὰ αὐτοῦ 'his (viz. God's) kindnesses' Ho 3.5; Si 18.15 (‖ δόσις); + εἰρήνη 2E 9.12; λαλέω ~ά 'speak kindly' 4K 25.28.

2. *good and acceptable*: morally, subst., οὐκ οἴδασιν ~ὸν οὐδὲ κακόν Nu 14.23, sim. De 1.39; ἀπεστρέψατο ~ά 'rejected the good' Ho 8.3; μνήμης ~ῆς ἀξία 'deserving respectful memory' 2M 7.20; ἄξονας ~ούς 'right courses' Pr 2.9. **b**. *acceptable in general*: εἰ ἐπὶ τὸν βασιλέα ~όν 'if the King pleases' Ne 2.5; Es 5.18 *L*; ἐφ' ὑμῖν ~όν 1C 13.2; ~ῇ συνέσει .. 'intelligent' 1K 25.3.

3. *useful, desirable*, often subst.: anarthrous, ὅπως .. λάβητε ~ά Ho 14.3; εἰς ~ά 'to sbd's advantage' Ge 50.20 (:: εἰς πονηρά), Am 9.4 (:: εἰς κακά), Mi 1.12, De 28.11; μνήσθητί μου εἰς ~όν .. 'Remember for my good ..' Ne 5.19; τὴν ζωὴν καὶ τὸν θάνατον, τὸ ἀγαθὸν καὶ τὸ κακόν 30.15; εἴ τι ~όν Zc 9.17 (|| καλόν); διαχυθήσονται πόλεις ἐν ~οῖς 'cities will be flooded with good things' 1.17, ζήσεται ἐν ~οῖς Is 55.3, κατάλυμα ~ῶν 'five-star residence' Si 14.25; articular, ἐν τοῖς ἀγαθοῖς σου 'when you are prosperous' 6.11 (:: ταπεινοῦμαι), sim. 12.9 (:: ἐν τοῖς κακοῖς, cf. Lk 16.25), τὰ ~ὰ Ιερουσαλημ 'well-being, prosperity of J.' Ps 127.5 but τὰ ~ά σου 'your kindnesses' Si 12.1, cf. "no kindness (~ά) will be shown to one who habitually causes mischiefs" 12.3; τὰ πάντα ~ὰ Αἰγύπτου Ge 45.20; τὰ ἀγαθὰ τῆς γῆς Is 58.13, cf. ἀνεβίβασεν αὐτοὺς ἐπὶ τὴν ἰσχὺν τῆς γῆς '.. the most fertile part of the land (?)' De 32.13, ~ὰ κυρίου, .. γῆν σίτου καὶ οἴνου .. Je 38.12.

***4**. *joyful*: *s* heart, ἐν εὐφροσύνῃ καὶ ἐν ~ῇ καρδίᾳ De 28.47, sim. Ec 9.7; λαμπρὰ καρδία καὶ ~ή Si 33.13[b]. **b**. *conducive to joy*: *s* holiday, ἑορτή '(happy) holiday' Zc 8.19; ἀπὸ ὀδύνης εἰς ~ὴν ἡμέραν, ἄγειν ὅλον ~ὰς ἡμέρας γάμων καὶ εὐφροσύνης 'from sorrow to a joyous day, to celebrate the whole (month) as joyous days of weddings and cheer' Es 9.22 o'; εὐαγγελία ~ή 'cheerful news' 2K 18.27; ἐν φιλίᾳ αὐτῆς τέρψις ~ή 'in friendship with her [= wisdom] is joyous pleasure' Wi 8.18, ἐπιθυμία ~ή 'hearty delight' Si 14.14; with sensual connotation, Ct 1.2; subst.n., ποιέω ~όν Ec 3.12 (|| εὐφραίνομαι).

5. *performing* or *functioning well*, 'capable': *s* δρομεύς 'good (i.e. fast) runner' Pr 6.11.

6. articular and n.pl.: *goods, possessions*, ἀπὸ τῶν καμήλων τοῦ κυρίου αὐτοῦ καὶ ἀπὸ πάντων τῶν ~ῶν τοῦ κυρίου αὐτοῦ Ge 24.10; ἐξελοῦμαι τὰ ~ὰ αὐτῶν 'I will take away their goods' Mi 7.3; spec. *crops and products of nature* (cf. BDAG, s.v., 1**b**β), κατὰ τὸ πλῆθος τῶν καρπῶν αὐτῆς .. κατὰ τὰ ~ὰ τῆς γῆς Ho 10.1, τὰ ~ὰ τῆς γῆς φάγεσθε Is 1.19, sim. Je 2.7.

On the partial synonymity of ἀγαθός and καλός, see esp. Zc 9.17.

Cf. ἀγαθοποιέω, ἀγαθύνω, ἀγαθότης, ἀγαθωσύνη, φιλάγαθος, βελτίων, βέλτιστος, καλός, χρηστός, ἐλεήμων, συμφέρω, ὠφελέω, κακός, πονηρός: Grundmann, *TDNT* 1.10f., 13-5.

ἀγαθότης, ητος. f.

moral integrity: Si 45.23, Wi 1.1. Cf. ἀγαθός.

ἀγαθόω: fut. ἀγαθώσω; aor. inf. ἀγαθῶσαι.*

to act benevolently towards: + acc., *s* div., *o* hum., Je 51.27 (:: κακόω), 39.41; + dat. pers., 1K 25.31B*bis* (*L*: ἀγαθύνω, καλῶς ποιέω). Cf. κακόω, ἀγαθύνω, εὐεργετέω.

ἀγαθύνω: fut.pass. ~θυνθήσομαι; aor. ἠγάθυνα, inf. ~θῦναι, impv. ἀγάθυνον, subj. ~θύνω, opt.3s ~θύναι, pass. ἠγαθύνθην, subj. ~θυνθῶ.*

1. *to conduct oneself in accordance with good ethical standards*: Ps 35.4; τοῦ ποιῆσαι τὸ εὐθές 4K 10.30.

2. *to act kindly and confer benefits on*: + dat. pers., Ps 48.19, 124.4 (*s* God); + acc. pers., 50.20.

3. *to adorn*: *s* woman, τὴν κεφαλὴν αὐτῆς 4K 9.30 (*L* κοσμέω); *s* God, ***o*** τὸ ὄνομά τινος 3K 1.47.

4. *to cause to excede in quality*: + acc., τὸ ἔλεός σου τὸ ἔσχατον ὑπὲρ τὸ πρῶτον Ru 3.10.

5. *to cause to become cheerful*: ἀγαθυνάτω σε ἡ καρδία σου Ec 11.9.

6. pass. *to be found* or *considered acceptable, desirable*: 2E 7.18; ἐν ὀφθαλμοῖς τινος 1M 1.12, ἐνώπιόν σου Ne 2.5; impers., 2.6, ἐπί τινι (pers.) Da 6.23 TH. **b**. *to become attracted* to a proposal: *s* καρδία Jd 18.20.

***7**. mid. *to become cheerful*: *s* καρδία 2K 13.28B, Jd 16.25; hum., τῇ καρδίᾳ 19.22 A, cf. ἀγαθός **4**.

ἀγαθῶς. adv.ʃ

1. *in fitting manner*: 1K 20.7, To 13.10 𝔊[I].

2. *thoroughly*: 4K 11.18.

ἀγαθωσύνη, ης. f.*

1. *good, kindly disposition*: ἠγάπησας κακίαν ὑπὲρ ~ην 'you loved wickedness more than ..' Ps 51.5; divine, Ne 9.25. **b**. *deeds and behaviour indicative of kindly disposition*: ~ην, ἣν ἐποίησεν μετὰ Ισραηλ Jd 8.35 A (B: τὰ ἀγαθά), *s* hum.

***2**. *materially agreeable state of affairs*, 'prosperity, well-being': ἐν βασιλείᾳ σου καὶ ἐν ~ῃ σου τῇ πολλῇ 'in ruling positions ..' Ne 9.35; opp. κακία Ec 7.14.

***3**. *advantage*: μνήσθητί μου, ὁ θεὸς ἡμῶν, εἰς ~ην 'Remember me .. in my favour' Ne 13.31, cf. εἰς ἀγαθόν 5.19.

Cf. ἀγαθός, κακία.

ἀγαλλίαμα, ατος. n.*

joy: + εὐφροσύνη Is 16.10 (of harvesters), 22.13, 51.3; αἰώνιον 60.15; + αἴνεσις 35.10. Cf. ἀγαλλιάομαι, εὐφροσύνη, χαρά.

ἀγαλλιάομαι: fut. ἀγαλλιάσομαι; aor. ἠγαλλιασάμην, impv. ἀγαλλίασαι, 3s ἀγαλλιάσθω, subj. ἀγαλλιάσωμαι, opt.3pl. ἀγαλλιάσαιντο. On the ending ~ιάω as indicative of strong emotions, see Schwyzer 1.732. *

to rejoice: abs. ἀγαλλιᾶσθε καὶ εὐφραίνεσθε Is 12.6, ἐν εὐφροσύνῃ 65.14; + acc., τὴν δικαιοσύνην σου 50.16, τὸ ἔλεός σου Ps 58.17; + dat. pers., αὐτῷ [= κυρίῳ] ἐν τρόμῳ '.. in trepidation' 2.11, τῷ θεῷ τῷ βοηθῷ ἡμῶν '.. our helper' 80.2, + dat. rei, τῇ δικαιοσύνῃ σου 144.7; + ἐν – εὐφρανθήσομαι καὶ ἀγαλλιάσομαι ἐν σοί 9.3, ἐν τῷ κυρίῳ Hb 3.18 (|| χαίρω), ἐν τοῖς ἔργοις τῶν χειρῶν σου Ps 91.5; + ἐπί τινι– ἐπὶ τῷ σωτηρίῳ σου 9.15, ἀγαλλιάσαιντο καὶ εὐφρανθείησαν ἐπὶ σοί 39.17; + ἐπί τι– ἐπὶ τὰ λόγιά σου 118.162; + πρός τινα To 13.13 𝔊[II] (𝔊[I] ἐπί τινι); + inf., Ps 18.6. **b**. verbally manifested: *s* γλῶσσα Ps 15.9, 50.16, χείλη 'lips' 70.23; ᾄσατε καὶ ἀγαλλιᾶσθε καὶ ψάλατε 97.4; || ἀλαλάζω 80.2, || ἐξερεύγομαι 'utter' 144.7, κράζω Is 65.14. **c**. tinged with pride: Je 30.4; || καυχάομαι 3M 2.17, Ps 31.11, 149.5. **d**. non-hum. *s*: ἔρημος Is 35.1, γῆ Ps 95.11 (|| εὐφραίνομα, χαίρω), ὄρη 97.8, ξύλα 95.12.

Used mostly of religious ecstasy and very common in Ps and Is (ca. 85%): with no religious connotation – *s* Si 30.3 (out of pride), Ct 1.4, Ps 12.5, 18.6, 125.6, θυγατέρες ἀπεριτμήτων 'daughters of the uncircumcised' 2K 1.20 (|| εὐφραίνομαι).

Cf. ἀγαλλίαμα, εὐφραίνω, τέρπομαι, χαίρω: Shipp 24; Bultmann, *TDNT* 1.19f.; Aejmelaeus 2003. 503-7.

ἀγαλλίασις, εως. f. *

v.n. of ἀγαλλιάομαι: + αἴνεσις Is 51.11; αἰνέσω ἐν ~σει PSol 5.1.

ἄγαλμα, ατος. n.ʃ

object of pagan worship: ἐπερωτήσουσιν τοὺς θεοὺς αὐτῶν καὶ τὰ ~ατα αὐτῶν καὶ τοὺς ἐκ τῆς γῆς φωνοῦντας .. 'they will enquire .. those who utter sounds out of the ground ..' Is 19.3, Πέπτωκε Βαβυλῶν, καὶ πάντα τὰ ~ατα αὐτῆς καὶ τὰ χειροποίητα αὐτῆς '.. and her handmade idols' 21.9, ~ατα χρυσᾶ καὶ ἀργυρᾶ 'silver and golden ..' 2M 2.2. Alw. in pl. Cf. εἴδωλον, χειροποίητος: Koonce 1988. Del. Ba 4.34 v.l.

ἄγαμος, ον.ʃ

unmarried: *s* hum. male, 4M 16.9.

ἄγαν. adv.ʃ

to considerable degree, 'very much': 3M 4.11. Cf. λίαν, σφόδρα.

ἀγανακτέω: fut. ~τήσω; aor. ἠγανάκτησα, ptc. ἀγανακτήσας.ʃ

1. *to stir oneself violently*: *s* sea-water signalling God's wrath, κατά τινος Wi 5.22.

2. *to be violently displeased*: *s* hum., Bel 28 TH, ἐφ' οἷς 'at which (= the idols)' Wi 11.27; divine justice, ἐφ' οἷς 'at which situation' 4M 4.21.

Cf. θυμόω: Schmidt 3.560-2; Spicq 1.5-7.

ἀγαπάω: fut. ἀγαπήσω, pass. ~πηθήσομαι; aor. ἠγάπησα, inf. ἀγαπῆσαι, ptc. ἀγαπήσας, impv. ἀγάπησον, subj. ἀγαπήσω, opt.3s ἀγαπήσαι, pass. ἠγαπήθην; pf. ἠγάπηκα, ptc.pass. ἠγαπημένος; plpf. ἠγαπήκειν.

1. *to treat with affection*: + τινα **a**. of man in relation to woman, παρὰ τὸ ἀγαπᾶν αὐτὸν αὐτήν 'because he was in love with her' Ge 29.20; 24.67; τὴν παρθένον 34.3; ἀγάπησον γυναῖκα ἀγαπῶσαν πονηρά Ho 3.1; father to son, Ge 37.3 (|| φιλέω vs. 4), 22.2, mother to son, 25.28; τὸν κύριόν μου (hum. master) καὶ τὴν γυναῖκα καὶ τὰ παιδία Ex 21.5; hum. to hum., ἀγαπήσεις τὸν πλησίον σου Le 19.18; husband to wife, De 21.15; harlot to her clients, Ez 16.37 (:: μισέω). **b**. of God in relation to hum.: διὰ τὸ ἀγαπᾶν αὐτὸν τοὺς πατέρας σου De 4.37; ἀγαπᾷ ὁ θεὸς τοὺς υἱοὺς Ισραηλ Ho 3.1; οὐ μὴ προσθήσω τοῦ ἀγαπῆσαι αὐτούς 9.15; ἀγάπησιν αἰώνιον ἠγάπησά σε Je 38.3; Zc 10.6, Ma 1.2*ter*; Αβρααμ, ὃν ἠγάπησα Is 41.8, Αβρααμ τῷ ἠγαπημένῳ σου 2C 20.7 (*L* τοῦ φίλου σου); πόλις ἠγαπημένη [= Jerusalem] Si 24.11. **c**. *s* impers.: αἱ παρακλήσεις σου ἠγάπησαν τὴν ψυχήν μου Ps 93.19.

2. *to display respect for and accept authority of*: of hum. in relation to God, τοῖς ἀγαπῶσίν με καὶ τοῖς φυλάσσουσιν τὰ προστάγματά μου Ex 20.6, De 5.10 (opp. μισέω); foll. by φυλάσσω τὰς ἐντολὰς αὐτοῦ 7.9, sim. 11.τὸν νόμον Ps 118.163; ἀγαπᾶτε κύριον .. ἐξ ὅλης τῆς καρδίας ὑμῶν καὶ ἐξ ὅλης τῆς ψυχῆς ὑμῶν De 13.3, πάσῃ ζωῇ σου Si 13.14¶; τὸ ὄνομα τοῦ κυρίου Is 56.6; *o* hum., Si 47.16.

3. *to take delight in*: + acc. rei, ματαιότητα Ps 4.3 (|| ζητέω), ἀδικίαν 10.4, πονηρά Ho 3.1; ἀτιμίαν 4.18; δῶρα 8.9, δόματα 9.1; θυσιαστήρια ἠγαπημένα 'altars dear (to them)' 8.11; νεῖκος 10.11; κίνδυνον 'danger' Si 3.26; μεμισήκαμεν τὰ πονηρὰ καὶ ἠγαπήκαμεν τὰ καλά Am 5.15; ἔλεος Mi 6.8; ὅρκον ψευδῆ 'false oath' Zc 8.17; ἀλήθειαν .. εἰρήνην 8.19, δικαιοσύνην 1C 29.17 (*s* God), Is 61.8 (:: μισέω), σοφίαν .. ζωήν Si 4.12; μαστούς σου 'your breasts' Ct 1.5, ἀργύριον 'money' Ec 5.9; + acc. pers., ὑπὲρ τὴν ἀγάπην, ἣν ἠγάπησεν αὐτήν 'more than the love with which he had loved her' 2K 13.15 (:: μισέω and w. ref. to carnal lust); "he took a liking to him" 1K 16.21 (|| εὗρεν χάριν ἐν ὀφθαλμοῖς μου vs. 22); ἐγένοντο οἱ ἐβδελυγμένοι ὡς οἱ ἠγαπημένοι 'the detested have turned into the beloved' Ho 9.10. **b**. + ἐν: Ma 2.11. **c**. + inf.: καταδυναστεύειν Ho 12.7, ἀκούειν Si 6.33; Pr 20.13, see s.v. φιλέω **1 a**.

Cf. ἀγάπη, ἀγάπησις, ἀγαπητός, ἔραμαι, στέργω, φιλέω, βδελύσσω, μισέω: Trench 41-4; Schmidt

3.474-91; Tarelli; Stauffer, *TDNT* 1.38-41; Steinmueller 406-13; Ceresa-Gastaldo; Paeslack; Georgacas 105f.; Spicq 1.8-22; *ND* 3.15; Swinn; Joly; Barr 1987; LSG s.v.; Muraoka 2001a:16f.

ἀγάπη, ης. f.

intense affection and attachment: between man and woman, ὑπὲρ τὴν ἀγάπην, ἣν ἠγάπησεν αὐτήν 'more than the love with which he had loved her' 2K 13.15 (:: μῖσος and w. ref. to carnal lust); τετρωμένη ~ης 'love-sick' Ct 2.5, cf. ἐπεί μ' ἔρως ἔτρωσεν Eurip. *Hipp.* 392; ἐξεγείρητε τὴν ~ην 2.7, κραταιὰ ὡς θάνατος ἀ. '.. as powerful as death' 8.6, σβέσαι τὴν ~ην .. ἐὰν δῷ ἀνὴρ τὸν πάντα βίον αὐτοῦ ἐν τῇ ~ῃ 'to extinguish .. if a man gives all his possessions for love' 8.7; opp. μῖσος Ec 9.1; passion, 9.6 (ǁ ζῆλος 'zeal'); for God, τελειώσεως 'in mature age' Je 2.2; ἐν ~ῃ προσμενοῦσιν αὐτῷ 'will remain loyal to Him in love' Wi 3.9; for wisdom, 6.18. Cf. ἀγαπάω, ἀγάπησις, φιλία: Paeslack 74-81; Ceresa-Castaldo; LSG s.v.

ἀγάπησις, εως. f.ʃ

1. *intense affection and attachment*, 'love, affection': of God (= *s*), ἐν δεσμοῖς ~εώς μου 'with the bonds of my love' Ho 11.4; ~ιν κραταιάν Hb 3.4; Zp 3.17, ~ιν αἰώνιον Je 38.3 (cogn. obj.); ἐν ~ει κεκοιμημένοι 'died, loved (by God?) Si 48.11; of illicit heterosexual relationship in a fig. of Israel's breach of faith – τοῦ ζητῆσαι ~ιν 2.33; between men, between man and woman, ἐθαυμαστώθη ἡ ἀ. σου ἐμοὶ ὑπὲρ ~ιν γυναικῶν 'your love was to me more marvellous than that of women' 2K 1.26*L*, cf. Paeslack 75; between people, μῖσος ἀντὶ τῆς ~εώς μου Ps 108.5; cogn. dat., Pr 30.15; υἱὸς ~εως 'beloved son' PSol 13.9 (ǁ πρωτότοκος 'firstborn son').

2. v.n. of ἀγαπάω **2**: ***o*** God: Si 1.10¶ (a manifestation of wisdom); wisdom, 40.20. φιλοσοφ~ lexemes occur only in 4M and Da LXX 1.20 (at which latter w. ref. to Babylonian scholars and ǁ TH μάγοι); as cogn. obj., 2K 13.15*L* (B: ἀγάπη).

Cf. ἀγαπάω, ἀγαπητός, μῖσος.

ἀγαπητός, ή, όν.

beloved, dearly loved: *s* hum., τὸν υἱόν σου τὸν ~όν, ὃν ἠγάπησας Ge 22.2; Μία σοι ὑπῆρχεν θυγάτηρ ~ή 'you had only one, beloved daughter' To 3.10 𝔊II, μονογενὴς αὐτῷ ~ή Jd 11.34A (B: om. ἀ., cf. *BA* ad loc.); subst. m., + obj. gen. pers., πένθος ~οῦ 'lamenting of a beloved one' Am 8.10, Je 6.26; κοπετὸν ὡς ἐπ' ~όν 'mourning ..' Zc 12.10; Ἄισω τῷ ἠγαπημένῳ ᾆσμα τοῦ ἀγαπητοῦ Is 5.1; τοὺς ~οὺς τῆς χήρας '.. of the widow' Ba 4.16; οἱ ~τοί σου Ps 59.7. On the "only" child being specially dear, see Homer, *Od.* 2.365 μοῦνος ἐὼν ~ός. **b**. *s inan.*, τὰ σκηνώματά σου 'your dwellings' Ps 83.2.

Cf. ἀγαπάω, προσφιλής: Turner 1926; Chadwick 32-4; Lee 2003a: 193-211.

ἀγαπητῶς. adv.ʃ

gladly: Si prol. II.

ἀγαυρίαμα, ατος.ʃ *

pride (in sensu bono): Is 62.7; τὸ ἀ. αὐτῆς ἔσται εἰς πένθος '.. will turn into grief' Ba 4.34.

ἀγαυριάομαι.ʃ*

to boast: ἐπὶ ξίφεσιν 'of swords' Jb 3.14. Cf. γαυριάω, καυχάομαι.

ἀγγεῖον, ου. n.

container for holding liquids or dry substances: for corn, Ge 42.25; out of which to drink, πίνεται ἐν παντὶ ~ῳ Le 11.34; ἀ. ὀστράκινον ἐφ' ὕδατι ζῶντι 'an earthen vessel with fresh water' 14.5; ἐλαίου 'for oil' Nu 4.9. Cf. ἄγγος.

ἀγγελία, ας. f.

what is reported about, 'news': ἤκουσε τὴν ~ίαν ὅτι .. 1K 4.19; ἀγαθὴ Pr 12.25; ἀ. σου '.. concerning you' Na 3.19. Cf. ἄγγελος and λόγος: Schniewind, *TDNT* 1.59f

ἄγγελος, ου. m.

1. human *messenger*: ἀπέστειλεν Ιακωβ ~ους ἔμπροσθεν αὐτοῦ πρὸς Ησαυ Ge 32.3; ἄ. κυρίου, sent by God Hg 1.13; in order to carry out a divine mission, Ge 19.1 (= οἱ ἄνδρες 18.22); in order to convey a divine message, Ma 1.1, w. ref. to Levi, 2.7; an eschatological figure, 3.1*a*; ἄ. τῆς διαθήκης 3.1*b*; ǁ πρέσβυς Is 63.9. **b**. *that which gives warning of sth to come*: θανάτου Pr 16.14.

*__2__. *supernatural being mediating between God and human(s)*, 'angel': ἄ. κυρίου τοῦ θεοῦ Ge 16.7, ~οι θεοῦ De 32.43 (ǁ υἱοὶ θεοῦ); is introduced as ἀνήρ (Zc 1.8) as well as ὁ ἄ. κυρίου 1.11; interprets a vision to a prophet, 1.9; more than one are introduced, 2.3; inhabiting heaven, Ge 21.17, 22.11; guiding the Israelites, Ex 14.19; ἡγούμενος 23.23; προπορεύσεται πρὸ προσώπου σου 32.34; protecting guardian, φυλάξῃ σε ἐν τῇ ὁδῷ 23.20, ἀγαθὸς ἄ. 2M 11.6, 15.3; harmful, ~οι πονηροί Ps 77.49; ǁ λειτουργός 103.4, ǁ παῖς Jb 4.18. For a later attestation of ἄγγελος in sense **2** in an apparently non-Judaeo-Christian setting, see *ND* 5.73.

Cf. ἀνα~, ἀπαγγέλλω, εὐαγγελίζω, ἀγγελία, πρέσβυς, κηρύσσω: Grundmann, *TDNT* 1.74-6; *ND* 3.28.

ἄγγος, ους. n.ʃ

container: for grapes picked, De 23.25; ἄ. ἰξευτοῦ 'fowler's basket' Am 8.1*bis*; ὀστράκινον 'earthen' Je 19.11; for water, 3K 17.10. **b**. cooking utensil: Ez 4.9.

Cf. ἀγγεῖον, κάλαθος, κανοῦν, κάρταλλος, κόφινος. See Renehan, 1.10.

ἀγελαῖος, α, ον.ʃ
consisting of common, ordinary folk: *s* ὄχλος 'crowd' 2M 14.23.

ἀγέλη, ης. f.
congregation: of animals, καμήλων Is 60.6, ποιμνίων 1K 24.4, αἰγῶν 'of goats' Ct 4.1; of people, 4M 5.4; ‖ ποίμνιον Pr 27.23, 1K 17.34. Cf. ἀγεληδόν, βουκόλιον, ποίμνη, ποίμνιον, συναγωγή: Shipp 25f.; Schmidt 4.576-8.

ἀγεληδόν. adv.ʃ
en masse: of hums., 2M 3.18, 14.14. Cf. ἀγέλη.

ἀγερωχία, ας. f.ʃ
1. *arrogance*: ‖ ὑπερηφανία 2M 9.7; + ὕβρις 3M 2.3.
2. *revelry*: ‖ εὐφροσύνη Wi 2.9.
Cf. ἀγέρωχος, ὕβρις, ὑπερηφανία.

ἀγέρωχος, ον.ʃ
arrogant: *s* νοῦς 3M 1.25. Cf. ἀγερωχία, ὑπερήφανος.

ἁγιάζω: fut. ἁγιάσω, pass. ἁγιασθήσομαι; aor. ἡγίασα, impv. ἁγίασον, mid. ἁγίασαι, subj. ἁγιάσω, inf. ἁγιάσαι, ptc. ἁγιάσας, pass. ἡγιάσθην, impv. 3pl. ἁγιασθήτωσαν, subj. ἁγιασθῶ, inf. ἁγιασθῆναι, ptc. ἁγιασθείς; pf. ἡγίακα, ptc.pass. ἡγιασμένος.*
1. *to designate as* ἅγιος (q.v.) *and treat accordingly*, 'to consecrate': *o* a specific day, Ge 2.3 (of the institution of the sabbath); a newly born life, Ex 13.2, ‖ ἀφαιρέω 13.12; for a cultic or sacral office, ἡγιασμένος Am 2.12 (‖ προφήτης), poss. also De 33.3; τοὺς κλητοὺς αὐτοῦ 'those who have been called by Him' Zp 1.7. **b**. *to treat as* ἅγιος: + acc., Μνήσθητι τὴν ἡμέραν τῶν σαββάτων ἁγιάζειν αὐτήν Ex 20.8; με [= God] ἐναντίον υἱῶν Ισραηλ Nu 20.12; De 32.51; κύριον αὐτὸν ἁγιάσατε Is 8.13, τὸ ὄνομά μου .. καὶ τὸν ἅγιον Ιακωβ 29.23; mid., + ἀφορίζω, acc., Mt Sinai, Ex 19.23. **c**. *to declare* or *institute as holy* (ἅγιος): + acc. priests, 28.37; νηστείαν 'fasting' Jl 1.14, 2.15; ἐκκλησίαν 'assembly' 2.16; πόλεμον 'to declare a holy war' 3.9; food and drink, and opp. μιαίνω Hg 2.12; robe for cultic use, Le 16.4; a people with *s* God, ἐγὼ κύριος ὁ ἁγιάζων ὑμᾶς Ex 31.13; an object offered with a vow, and + ἅγιος as pred., ἁγιάσῃ τὴν οἰκίαν αὐτοῦ ἁγίαν τῷ κυρίῳ Le 27.14, cf. Pr 20.25.
2. *to render fit to participate in cultic rituals*: + acc. pers., Ex 19.14 (‖ ἁγνίζω vs. 10); by undergoing some ritual(s)(?), ἑαυτούς τῷ κυρίῳ 1E 1.3; pass. Ex 19.22.
3. *to enlist and deploy* troops: + acc. pers., ἐπ' αὐτὴν ἔθνη Je 28.27.
Cf. ἁγίασμα, ἁγιασμός, ἅγιος, ἁγνίζω, ἀφιερόω, ἀφορίζω, βεβηλόω, μιαίνω: Procksch, *TDNT* 1.111.

ἁγίασμα, ατος. n.*
1. *sanctuary*: Ex 15.17 (‖ κατοικητήριον); βασιλέως 'built by a king' Am 7.13; ‖ τὸ ὄρος τὸ ἅγιον Is 63.18; πόλις ~ατος Si 36.18, PSol 8.4.
***2**. *sacred offering*, Zc 7.3 (θυσίαι, Tht, PG 81.1908); σταφυλὴ τοῦ ~ατός σου 'grapes dedicated by you' Le 25.5.
3. *an object possessing sanctity*: ἁ. κυρίου, ref. to a golden plate, Ex 28.32; Ez 20.40.
Cf. ἁγιάζω, ἁγιασμός, ἁγιαστήριον, ἅγιος, ἱερόν.

ἁγιασμός, οῦ. m. *
***1**. *consecration* for a cultic or sacral office: Am 2.11 (‖ προφήτης), cf. s.v. ἁγιάζω, **1**; as a sacrifice, θυσία ~οῦ Si 7.31; + ἱεράτευμα 'priesthood' 2M 2.17.
2. *sanctity*: ὄνομα ~οῦ Si 17.10; τὸν οἶκον τοῦ ~οῦ 3M 2.18; ἅγιε παντὸς ~οῦ κύριε 2M 14.36.
Cf. ἁγιάζω, ἁγίασμα and ἅγιος: Procksch, *TDNT* 1.113.

ἁγιαστήριον, ου.* n.
sanctuary: Le 12.4; τοῦ θεοῦ Ps 72.17, 82.13. Cf. ἁγίασμα, ἱερός.

ἁγιαστία, ας. f.ʃ *
sacred ritual: 4M 7.9. Cf. ἅγιος.

ἅγιος, α, ον.
holy, sacred **a**. *s* the God of Israel: ὁ θεὸς ὁ ἅ. μου Hb 1.12; ὁ ἅ. (‖ ὁ θεός) 3.3; ‖ θεός Ho 11.9; ὁ ἅγιος τοῦ Ισραηλ Is 1.4, τοῦ ~ου Ισραηλ 5.19. **b**. *s* people, *dedicated to the divine*: ἄνδρες ἅγιοι ἔσεσθέ μοι [= τῷ θεῷ] Ex 22.31, ἔθνος ~ον 19.6; Ἅγιοι ἔσεσθε, ὅτι ἐγὼ ἅ., κύριος ὁ θεὸς ὑμῶν Le 19.2; λαὸς ἅ. De 7.6, λ. ἅ. κυρίῳ τῷ θεῷ σου 14.2, λ. ἅ. θεοῦ Ho 11.12; οἱ ἅγιοι αὐτοῦ 'His saints' Am 4.2, Zc 14.5; Nazirite, Nu 6.5 and Samson, Jd 13.7B, 16.17B (see *BA* ad loc. and Chepey); angels, To 11.14. **c**. *s* things: ἁγία στολή Ex 28.2 (priestly robe); τὰς στολὰς τὰς ~ας Ααρων 35.18 (‖ λειτουργικάς 31.10); ἔλαιον 30.25 (used in cult); κρέας 'meat' offered to God, Hg 2.12, πρόβατα Ez 36.38, ἄρτοι 1K 21.5 (:: βέβηλος); the holy temple (οἶκος), Mi 1.2; ναός Jn 2.5, 8, Hb 2.20; Zion the holy mountain (ὄρος) Zc 8.3, Zp 3.11, Jl 2.1, 3.17, Ob 16, cf. 17; οὐρανός Ps 19.7, οὐρανοί Wi 9.10; γῆ of the Land of Israel, Ex 3.5, Zc 2.12, Wi 12.3; πόλις Is 52.1, 66.20, To 13.9𝔊[I] (Jerusalem); νεφέλαι'clouds' Zc 2.13 (because of their proximity to God's abode? – cf. Th. 339); λίθοι 9.16; τῷ κυρίῳ παντοκράτορι 'to the almighty Lord' 14.20, 21; λέβης 'pot' 14.21; God's name, Ps 110.9 (+ φοβερός), Is 60.9, Si 47.10; God's spirit (πνεῦμα), Ps 50.13; ὑπὲρ τῶν σεμνῶν καὶ ~ων νόμων 'for the sake of the revered and holy laws' 2M 6.28 – for this rare use of ἅ. with νόμος, albeit in pl., see τὴν

κειβωτὸν ἀνέθηκεν νόμῳ ἁγίῳ 'dedicated the ark for the holy law' in a synagogue dedicatory inscription (*ND* 4.112) and ὁ νόμος ἅ. καὶ ἡ ἐντολὴ ~α Rom 7.12. **d**. subst. n.: τὸ ἅγιον τῶν ἁγίων 'the holy of holies' Ex 26.33, 30.10, Ez 41.4; ἅγιον ἁγίων 'sth absolutely sacred' Le 27.28; τὸ ἅγιον 'the sanctuary' Ex 28.3, also pl.– Le 19.30, 20.3, 21.12, Ez 37.36; ἐν ~οις Is 57.15 (ǁ ἐν ὑψίστοις); τὰ ἅγια 'the holy things (offered to God)' Ex 28.34 (cogn. obj. of ἁγιάζω); sacrifices, Le 22.10, De 12.26, τὰ ~α τῶν ~ων Ez 42.13; opp. τὰ βέβηλα and ǁ τὰ καθαρά Le 10.10; to defile (βεβηλόω) τὰ ἅγια, w. ref. to holy rituals (Cyr, II.217), the temple (ναός, Th, 296) Zp 3.4, ǁ οἶκος κυρίου Je 28.51, or divine service (θεραπεία τοῦ θεοῦ, Th, 413) Ma 2.11; f. with ἡμέρα understood, ἁγία ἑβδομάδων 'the holiday of weeks' To 2.1 𝔊^II^.

Cf. ἁγιάζω, ἁγίασμα, ἁγιασμός, ἁγιαστήριον, ἁγιαστία, ἁγιότης, ἁγιωσύνη, ἁγνός, καθαρός, βέβηλος, βεβηλόω, ἱερός, ναός, σεμνός, τέμενος: Schmidt 4.338-40; Trench 327-30; Williger 1922.84-7; Wolfson 1947; Festugière; Procksch, *TDNT* 1.96f.; Barr 1961.282-7; Dimant 1981; *ND* 4.111f.; *BA* 3:29f.; LSG s.v.; Harl 2001.872-6.

ἁγιότης, ητος. f.ʃ*

sanctity: of a particular day, 2M 15.2. Cf. ἅγιος.

ἁγιωσύνη, ης. f.*

holiness: God's, Ps 29.5; of the Jerusalem Temple, 2M 3.12 (ǁ σεμνότης). Cf. ἅγιος, σεμνότης.

ἀγκάλη, ης. f.ʃ

bent arm: to pick up a falling person with, Es D 8; lover's, Pr 5.20; holding a sleeping baby, 3K 3.20. Cf. ἀγκών, βραχίων.

ἀγκαλίς, ίδος. f.ʃ

sheaf: Jb 24.19.

ἄγκιστρον, ου. n.

fishing-hook: Hb 1.15; ***o*** of βάλλω Is 19.8 (***s*** fisher); ἀνάξω σε ἐν τῷ ~ῳ μου 'I shall haul you up with my ..' Ez 32.3, sim. Jb 40.25. Cf. ἀγκωνίσκος.

ἀγκύλη, ης. f.

1. *loop*: at the edge of a curtain, Ex 26.4.

2. *curtain-ring, hook*: Ex 37.15.

ἀγκών, ῶνος. m.ʃ

elbow: χειρός Ez 13.18; part of the arm, Jb 31.22, 4M 10.6; πῆξις ~ος (ref. to leaning on it during meals) Si 41.19; ἐπὶ τοῦ θρόνου 2C 9.18. Cf. βραχίων: Taillardat; LSG s.v.

ἀγκωνίσκος, ου. m. Dim. of ἀγκών.ʃ *

small hook: Ex 26.17. Cf. ἄγκιστρον.

ἁγνεία, ας. f.ʃ

1. *consecration*: ὁ νόμος τῆς ~ας Nu 6.21; cogn. acc., ἀφαγνίσασθαι ~αν κυρίῳ 6.2.

2. *purity*: religious, 2C 30.19, 1M 14.36.

Cf. ἁγνίζω: Hauck, *TDNT* 1.123. Del. 2M 14.13 v.l.

ἁγνίζω: fut.mid. ἁγνισθήσομαι; aor. ἥγνισα, inf. ἁγνίσαι, mid. ἡγνισάμην, pass. ἡγνίσθην, ptc. ἁγνισθείς, impv.act. ἅγνισον, mid. ἅγνισαι, pass. ἁγνίσθητι; pf.ἥγνικα, ptc.pass. ἡγνισμένος.

to render fit to participate in cultic rituals: + acc. pers., Ex 19.10 (ǁ ἁγιάζω vs. 14); ǁ ἀφαγνίζω Nu 19.12; by means of water, 31.23, 2M 1.33; εἰς ἡμέραν σφαγῆς 'for a day of slaughter' Je 12.3. **b**. mid.: Is 66.17 (+ καθαρίζομαι); ἀπὸ οἴνου '(by abstaining) from wine' Nu 6.3; 8.21; so as to take part in a holy war, 1K 21.6 (ǁ ἁγιάζω), Jo 3.5; + ἁγιάζω 2C 29.5.

Cf. ἁγιάζω, ἅγνισμα, ἁγνισμός, ἁγνεία, ἀφαγνίζω: LSG s.v.

ἅγνισμα, ατος. n.ʃ

v.n. of ἁγνίζω (q.v.): Nu 19.9. Cf. ἁγνίζω, ἁγνισμός.

ἁγνισμός, οῦ. m.

1. v.n. of ἁγνίζω, q.v.: of Levites, Nu 8.7; by means of ὕδωρ ~οῦ ib.; σποδιὰ ~οῦ 'ashes of ..' 19.17.

2. *religious, moral purity*: εὑρήσετε ~ὸν ταῖς ψυχαῖς ὑμῶν Je 6.16.

Cf. ἁγνίζω: Hauck, *TDNT* 1.124.

ἀγνοέω: aor. ἠγνόησα, inf. ἀγνοῆσαι; pf. ἠγνόηκα, ptc. ἠγνοηκώς, pass. ἠγνοημένος.

1. *to act in ignorance*: περὶ τῆς ἀγνοίας αὐτοῦ, ἧς ἠγνόησεν καὶ αὐτὸς οὐκ ᾔδει Le 5.18, cf. Nu 12.11; ἔθνος ἀγνοοῦν καὶ δίκαιον Ge 20.4. **b**. *to do in ignorance*: pass., 2M 11.31.

2. *to sin by wilfully ignoring and disregarding divine injunctions*: μὴ ἀγνόει Ho 4.15, Si 5.15; + cogn. acc., ἄγνοιαν μεγάλην 1K 14.24; + ματαιόομαι 26.21.

3. *to fail to discern*: ***o*** τι Wi 5.12. **b**. *to be unaware of*: a fact, + inf., Wi 7.12; + ὅτι 12.10. **c**. *to be unknown to one*: ὁ ἀγνοῶν 'the stranger' Wi 19.14 (ǁ ἀλλότριος 'alien' vs. 15).

4. *to fail* or *to refuse to acknowledge the existence or reality of*: + acc., God Wi 15.11.

Cf. ἄγνοια, ἀγνόημα, ἄγνωστος, γινώσκω: Bultmann, *TDNT* 1.115f.; Muraoka 1983.51f.

ἀγνόημα, ατος. n.ʃ

1. *error made through ignorance*: μήποτε ἀ. ἐστιν 'perhaps it is a mistake' Ge 43.12. **b**. with moral nuance: ταῖς ἁμαρτίαις μου καὶ τοῖς ~ασίν μου To 3.3, cf. Ju 5.20, ǁ ἁμάρτημα Si 23.2, 1M 13.39.

2. *that which one is ignorant of*: ~ατα ^σοφίας^ Si 51.19.

Cf. ἀγνοέω, ἄγνοια, ἁμαρτία, ἁμάρτημα: Trench 247f.; Bultmann, *TDNT* 1.115.

ἄγνοια, ας. f.
error made through ignorance: with moral nuance, περὶ τῆς ~ας αὐτοῦ, ἧς ἠγνόησεν καὶ αὐτὸς οὐκ ᾔδει Le 5.18; ὃς ἂν φάγῃ ἅγια κατὰ ~αν 22.14; ἐπήγαγες ἐφ' ἡμᾶς ~αν Ge 26.10; ǁ ἁμαρτία 2C 28.13, 1E 8.72. **b**. *ignorance*: PSol 13.7; + λήθη 'forgetfulness' 4M 1.5.
Cf. ἀγνοέω, ἀγνόημα, γνῶσις: Bultmann, *TDNT* 1.116-8.

ἄγνος, ου. f.ʃ
chaste-tree: Le 23.40, Jb 40.22.

ἁγνός, ή, όν.
pure and free from stain: morally, *s* παρθένος 4M 18.7; God's words Ps 11.7, ὁ φόβος κυρίου 18.10, καρδία Pr 20.9; the fire of an altar, 2M 13.8; subst.m.pers., Pr 15.26, n.pl. παρθενίας 4M 18.8. Cf. ἀναγνεία, καθαρός: Schmidt 4.343f.; Trench 332-4; Bultmann, *TDNT* 1.118, Hauck 1.122.

ἀγνωσία, ας. f.
ignorance: Jb 35.16¶; θεοῦ (obj. gen.) Wi 13.1. Cf. γνῶσις, ἀγνοέω.

ἄγνωστος, ον.ʃ
unknown: *s* place, 2M 2.7, + dat. pers. 1.19; animal, Wi 11.18; journey, 18.3. Cf. ἀγνοέω, ἄδηλος, γνωστός: Bultmann, *TDNT* 1.119-21.

ἄγονος, ον.ʃ
childless: *s* a woman who lost child through a stillbirth, Ex 23.26 (ǁ στεῖρα); gender-neutral, Jb 30.3¶; also including animals, De 7.14 (ǁ στεῖρα). Alw. indicative of misery. Cf. στεῖρα and ἄτεκνος.

ἀγορά, ᾶς. f.
1. *commercial activities*: ἔδωκαν τὴν ~άν σου 'generated your business' Ez 27.12 (*s* metals as commodities), 27.16.
2. *market-place*: 1E 2.17.

ἀγοράζω: fut. ἀγοράσω; aor.inf. ἀγοράσαι, impv. ἀγόρασον; pf.ptc.pass. ἠγορασμένος.
to purchase: abs., Ge 41.57, 42.5 (:: πωλέω vs. 6), ὁ ἀγοράζων ὡς ὁ πωλῶν '.. as seller' Is 24.2; + acc. rei, βρώματα 'foods' Ge 42.7; + dat. pers., ἀγοράσομέν σοι βρώματα 43.4; 44.25; παρά τινος De 2.6 (ǁ λαμβάνω ἀργυρίου); + gen. pretii, τοῦ ἀργυρίου Ba 1.10, ὀλίγου Si 20.12 (:: ἀποτιννύω); ἐν ἀργυρίῳ 1C 21.24 (ǁ 2K 24.24 κτάομαι). Cf. ἀγορασμός, ἀγοραστής, κτάομαι, πωλέω, πριάομαι.

ἀγορανομία, ας. f.ʃ
office of the clerk of a market: 2M 3.4.

ἀγορασμός, οῦ. m.
1. *act of purchasing*: + πρᾶσις 'sale' Si 27.2; κρεῶν 'of meat' Pr 23.21.
2. *that which has been purchased*: τὸν ~ὸν τῆς σιτοδοσίας ὑμῶν 'what you have purchased of the grain allocated to you' Ge 42.19. **b**. *that which is to be sold*, 'merchandise': Ne 10.31 (+ πρᾶσις).
Cf. ἀγοράζω, πρᾶσις.

ἀγοραστής, οῦ. m.ʃ
procurement officer: king's, To 1.13 𝔊[I]. Cf. ἀγοράζω: Braunert 1971.

ἀγρεύω: aor.subj.pass. ἀγρευθῶ.ʃ
to take by hunting: + acc., τὴν θήραν 'the game' Ho 5.2; *o* lion, Jb 10.16. **b**. metaph. 'to capture, trap': παρανομίαι ἄνδρα ἀγρεύουσιν 'deeds of lawlessness ..' Pr 5.22; pass. and *o* hum., σοῖς ὀφθαλμοῖς 'with your own eyes' 6.25; hum. soul, 6.26.
Cf. θηρεύω, κυνηγέω: Shipp 28f.; Muraoka 1986a.122f.

ἀγριαίνω: fut.pass. ~ανθήσομαι.ʃ
to make angry: pass., *s* hum., Da 11.11 TH (LXX παροργίζω). Cf. θυμόω, ὀργίζομαι.

ἀγριομυρίκη, ης.ʃ*
tamarisk: ἐν τῇ ἐρήμῳ Je 17.6.

ἄγριος, α, ον.
1. *living in the wild*: θηρία ἄγρια 'wild animals' Ex 23.11, De 7.22; Is 56.9 (ǁ θ. τοῦ δρυμοῦ); θ. ἄ. τῆς γῆς Le 26.22, ὄνοι ~οι '.. asses' Je 14.6; vegetation, 4K 4.39.
2. *malignant*: ψώρα 'itch' Le 21.20, De 28.27.
3. *harsh and fierce* in force: *s* κύματα 'waves' Wi 14.1; ὠμότης 'cruelty' 3M 7.5. **b**. in character, 'savage': *s* lion, 4M 16.3.
Cf. ἀγρός, ἄγροικος, ἀγρίως, ἀγριότης, ἀπηνής, βάρβαρος, ὠμός: Schmidt 3.72f.

ἀγριότης, τος. f.ʃ
fierceness: of elephants on battlefield, 2M 15.21. Cf. ἄγριος.

ἀγριόω: aor.ptc.pass. ἀγριωθείς.ʃ
to make wild and savage: pass., *o* elephants, 3M 5.2. Cf. ἐξαγριαίνω.

ἀγρίως. adv.ʃ
harshly and fiercely: treatment, + βαρβάρως 2M 15.2. Cf. ἄγριος.

ἄγροικος, ον.ʃ
1. *dwelling in the fields*, 'rustic, wild': ἄνθρωπος Ge 16.12 (Ishmael); Ησαυ ἄνθρωπος εἰδὼς κυνηγεῖν ἄ., Ιακωβ δὲ ἄνθρωπος ἄπλαστος οἰκῶν οἰκίαν '.. knowing how to hunt .. not fully shapen, living indoors' 25.27.
2. *uncivilised, rough*: *s* manners, 2 Ma 14.30 (ǁ αὐστηρός 'harsh').
Cf. ἀγρός, ἄγριος.

ἀγρός, οῦ. m.
1. *field for agricultural cultivation*: φάγῃ τὸν χόρτον τοῦ ~οῦ 'you shall eat the grass of the field' Ge 3.18; containing a plot for burial, 25.9, 49.29; χέρσον ~οῦ 'dry clot of a field' Ho 10.4; ὡς ἀ. ἀροτριασθήσεται 'will be ploughed as a field' Mi 3.12; ἀπόλωλε τρυγητὸς ἐξ ~οῦ 'there is no crop to be had in the field' Jl 1.11; τὰ ξύλα τοῦ ~οῦ 'the

(fruit-)trees of the field' 1.12; ἡ ἄμπελος ἐν τῷ ~ῷ 'the grapevine ..' Ma 3.11; γενήματα ~ῶν 'agricultural products' De 32.13; object of plundering, Mi 2.2, 4; ‖ ἀμπελών 'vineyard' Nu 20.17, 21.22; pl., De 11.15, 32.13. **b**. as against house: Ge 39.5, Ex 20.17.

2. *area of land outside of settled area*: χλωρὸν ~οῦ 'wild vegetation' Ge 2.5; θηρία ~οῦ 'wild beasts' 2.19; ἀ. τῆς γῆς 'open country' Le 25.31; ἐν πόλει .. καὶ ἐν ~ῷ De 28.3.

Cf. ἄρουρα, πεδίον, πόλις: Schmidt 3.69f.

ἀγρυπνέω: aor. ἠγρύπνησα, ptc. ἀγρυπνήσας.

1. *to lie awake without sleeping*: Ps 101.8; *s* night watchman, 126.1, + φυλάσσω 1E 8.58, + τηρέω 2E 8.29, ἐπὶ σορῷ 'by a coffin' Jb 21.32¶, ἐπ' ἐμαῖς θύραις 'at my doors' Pr 8.34.

2. *to remain watchful and attentive*: Wi 6.15; ἐπὶ τὰ κακά Da 9.14 LXX (TH γρηγορέω).

Cf. ἀγρυπνία, γρηγορέω.

ἀγρυπνία, ας. f.

1. *insomnia*: Si 34.2, 42.9.

2. *alertness*: Si prol. 31, πλούτου 'over wealth' 34.1 (‖ μέριμνα 'worry'). **b**. *concentration of mind*: εἴς τι 'directed towards ..' 38.26; + inf., 38.27, 28.

Cf. ἀγρυπνέω.

ἄγρωστις, ιδος, acc. ~ιν. f.ʃ

dog's-tooth grass (LSJ): De 32.2; ξηρά 'dry' Is 9.18, ‖ χόρτος ξηρός 'dry grass' 37.27; a symbol of uncontrollable noisome growth, Ho 10.4; Mi 5.7. Cf. Ziegler 1934.181f.

ἄγυια, ᾶς (also pl. acc.). f.ʃ On the accentuation, see Schwyzer I 541.

street: pl., of a city, 3M 1.20 (:: indoors), 4.3. Cf. ὁδός: Shipp 30f.

ἀγχιστεία, ας. f.

1. v.n. of ἀγχιστεύω, **2 b**: Ru 4.6.

***2**. *dismissal* from official position: τῆς ἱερατείας 'from priesthood' Ne 13.29.

Cf. ἀγχιστεύω.

ἀγχιστεύς, έως. m.

the nearest of kin: Ru 3.9. **b**. entitled to avenge a kinsman's death: τοῦ αἵματος 2K 14.11.

ἀγχιστευτής, τοῦ. m.ʃ

= ἀγχιστεύς (q.v.): Ru 4.1.

ἀγχιστεύω: fut. ἀγχιστεύσω; aor.pass. ἠγχιστεύθην, impv. ἀγχίστευσον, inf.act. ἀγχιστεῦσαι, subj. ἀγχιστεύσω.

1. *to be near in blood-relationship*: ὁ ἀγχιστεύων ὁ ἔγγιστα αὐτοῦ 'his nearest kin' Le 25.25.

2. *to act as the nearest of kin*: abs., Ru 4.6[1, 3]; + ἀγχιστείαν as cogn. acc., 4.6[2]. Cf. Moatti-Fine 323f. **b**. *to lay claim to* or *in respect of as the nearest of kin*: + acc. pers., by marrying a widow, Ru 3.13; + acc. rei, κληρονομίαν Nu 36.8; ὁ ἀγχιστεύων τὸ αἷμα 'the blood-relation who is entitled to avenge his kinsman's death' 35.19 +; = τοῦ αἵματος De 19.6, 12.

***3**. *to dismiss* from official position: pass., ἀπὸ τῆς ἱερατείας 'from priesthood' 2E 2.62 (v.l. ἐξώσθησαν), Ne 7.64 (v.l. ἀπώσθησαν), cf. ἐξεβλήθησαν .. ἐκ τῆς τιμῆς 'were expelled from the office' Joseph. *Ant*. xi 71.

Cf. ἀγχιστεία, ἐγγίζω: Walters 149f.; Muraoka 2005b.101-4.

ἄγχω: aor.inf. ἄγξαι.ʃ

to constrict: + acc., τὰς σιαγόνας 'the jaws (of horses and mules with bridles and muzzles)' Ps 31.9, σῶμα 4M 11.11; + acc. pers., 10.7 (to break his spirit by torturing), cf. μου τὸν λογισμόν 9.17. Cf. ἀπάγχομαι, ἀποπνίγω.

ἄγω: fut. ἄξω, inf. ἄξειν, pass. ἀχθήσομαι, ptc. ἀχθησόμενος; aor. ἤγαγον, inf.act. ἀγαγεῖν, mid. ἀγαγέσθαι, ptc. ἀγαγών, impv. ἄγαγε, 2pl. ἀγάγετε, subj. ἀγάγω, pass. ἤχθην, inf. ἀχθῆναι, ptc. ἀχθείς, opt.3s ἀχθείη; pf.act.3pl. ἀγειόχασιν (the spelling ἀγειοχ- is not attested prior to the second cent. BCE: Mayser I 2.105), inf. ἀγηοχέναι, ptc. ἀγηοχώς, pass. ἦγμαι.

1. *to cause to move with one*: of going, pass. αἰχμάλωτος ἀχθήσεται ἀπὸ τῆς γῆς αὐτοῦ 'will be forced to leave their own land as captives' Am 7.11, 17; αἱ δοῦλαι αὐτῆς ἤγοντο ὡς περιστεραί 'her maid-servants were led away like doves' Na 2.8; 'to drive (cattle)' – τὰ κτήνη καὶ τοὺς βόας Ge 46.32; πρόβατα ὑπὸ τὴν ἔρημον Ex 3.1; beast of burden as ***o*** understood, 4K 4.24; wagon, 1C 13.7; ἐπί τινα (so as to attack) Ez 38.17; πρός τινα, Le 13.2; of legal proceeding, τὴν γυναῖκα αὐτοῦ πρὸς τὸν ἱερέα Nu 5.15; ***o*** captives, Is 20.4, the blind 42.16, ***o*** troops understood, 2M 12.38. **b**. ἄγω ἐπὶ πέρας 'to achieve a goal, accomplish': + acc., Es B 3, Si prol. 33, cf. ἐπὶ τέλος 1C 29.19. **c**. of coming: τὸν ἀδελφὸν ὑμῶν .. ἀγάγετε πρός με Ge 42.20; τοὺς κληρονόμους ἀγάγω σοι 'bring the heirs to you' Mi 1.15; ἐγὼ ἄγω δοῦλόν μου Zc 3.8. **d**. metaph.: εἰς λαογραφίαν '(to be forced) to register oneself' 3M 2.28, εἰς κατάστεμα μανιῶδες 'into a state of madness' 5.45.

2. *to organise and hold* a formal, public event: + acc., τὸ πάσχα 1E 1.1, τὸν καθαρισμὸν τοῦ ἱεροῦ 'the purification of the temple' 2M 1.18, ἀγών 'athletic games' 4.18, γάμος 'wedding' To 11.19. Cf. s.v. ποιέω **I 10**.

3. *to treat*: + acc. pers., ὡς ἀδελφόν Si 30.39.

4. *to bring up as parent*: + acc. pers. (son), εἰς τὴν ἡλικίαν ταύτην 'to this point in your life' 2M 7.27; + ἐκτρέφειν 'to nurture' 1M 6.15.

5. *to maintain* a certain attitude: + acc., πρὸς αὐτὸν τὴν εὐμένειαν 'goodwill towards him' 2M 6.29, εἰρήνην 12.12, ἡσυχίαν 'quiet' Pr 11.12.

6. Ἄγε urging sbd to take an initiative, foll. asyndetically by an impv.: Ἄγε δὴ αὐλίσθητι '.., spend a night!' Jd 19.6B (A: ἀρξάμενος).

7. mid. *to take to oneself* as wife: + acc., νύμφην ἐμαυτῷ 'bride ..' Wi 8.2. Cf. Renehan 2.10.

Cf. ἀν~, δι~, εἰσ~, ἐξ~, ἐπ~, ἐπαν~, ἐπισυν~, κατ~, παρ~, περι~, προ~, προσ~, συνάγω, ἀγωγή, συναγωγή, ὀχλαγωγέω, φωταγωγέω, αἴρω, φέρω: Schmidt 3.168-71, 173-80; Shipp 32-8.

ἀγωγή, ῆς. f.

way in which one performs as leader: military, 4K 9.20*L*. **b**. metaph. *way in which one leads one's life or manages affairs*: Es 2.20 o', 10.3 o', 2M 4.16; ***o*** of ἄγω, 6.8. Cf. ἄγω: Schmidt, *TDNT* 1.128f.; Pelletier 1962.301-3; Spicq 1.29-31.

ἀγών, ῶνος. m.

struggle to be gone through and overcome: Is 7.13; ἐν ἀγῶνι θανάτου '.. in a life-or-death struggle' Es C 12; τὸν .. ~να νικήσασα '.. overcoming' Wi 4.2. **b**. contest in sports: 2M 4.18; military, 10.28; ἐν τοῖς περὶ τῆς πατρίδος ~ῶσιν 'in the struggles for their fatherland' 14.18, διὰ τὴν τοῦ ~ῶνος σπουδήν 'in the heat of the struggle' 14.43.

Cf. ἀγωνίζομαι.

ἀγωνία, ας. f.

frightening agony: τὴν κατὰ ψυχὴν ~αν 2M 3.16. Cf. ἀγωνιάω, φόβος: Stauffer, *TDNT* 1.140.

ἀγωνιάω: aor.ptc. ἀγωνιάσας.ʃ

to be in frightening agony: Da 1.10 LXX (TH φοβέομαι), Es D 8, 2M 3.21; ὑπέρ τινος 1K 4.13 *L* (B: ἐξίστημι). Cf. ἀγωνία, φοβέομαι.

ἀγωνίζομαι: aor. ἠγωνισάμην, impv. ἀγώνισαι, inf. ~νίσασθαι.

to engage in a combat, 'struggle': military, γενναίως 'nobly' 2M 8.16, μέχρι θανάτου περὶ νόμων 13.14; metaph., ἕως θανάτου .. περὶ ἀληθείας Si 4.28 (ǁ πολεμέω), περὶ τοῦ Δανιηλ .. τοῦ ἐξελέσθαι αὐτόν '.. to rescue him' Da TH 6.14. Cf. ἄγων, ἀγωνιστής, ἀντ~, ἐν~, προαγωνίζομαι: Stauffer, *TDNT* 1.135f.

ἀγωνιστής, οῦ. m.ʃ

protagonist: ἀρετῆς 'for virtue' 4M 12.14. Cf. ἀγωνίζομαι.

ἀδαμάντινος, η, ον.ʃ

adamantine: ***s*** τεῖχος 'wall' Am 7.7; metaph., 'resolute,' ***s*** mind, 4M 16.13. Cf. ἀδάμας.

ἀδάμας, αντος. m.

adamant (very hard metal): ἐγὼ ἐντάσσω ~τα ἐν μέσῳ λαοῦ μου Am 7.8. Cf. ἀδαμάντιος.

ἀδάμαστος, ον.ʃ

not broken yet, 'untamed': ***s*** horse in a fig. of insubordination, Si 30.8 (ǁ ἀνειμένος). **b**. *insurmountable*: ***s*** πάθη 'sufferings' 4M 16.13.

ἄδεια, ας.ʃ

state of having no cause to fear: Wi 12.11, 2M 11.30; + gen. obj., 3M 7.12. Cf. δέος, ἀδεῶς: Schmidt 3.530.

ἄδειπνος, ον.ʃ

without the evening meal: Da 6.18 TH (LXX νήστης). Cf. δεῖπνον.

ἀδελφή, ῆς. f.

closely related female: female sibling, 'sister', ἀδελφή μου Ge 20.2 (Abraham of Sarah), sim. To 5.21, 7.11 𝔊[II]; sharing common descent, religion, etc., 'sister'; so referred to by her brother *and* other family members, 24.59, 60; εἴπατε .. τῇ ~ῇ ὑμῶν Ἠλεημένη 'Say to your sister, "Beloved"' Ho 2.1; as an endearing term, ἀ. μου νύμφη 'my dearie bride' Ct 4.9; metaph., w. ref. to wisdom, Pr 7.4. Cf. ἀδελφός.

ἀδελφιδός, οῦ. m. *

son of brother or sister, 'nephew': Ct 1.13+, but cf. *DGE* s.v.

ἀδελφικῶς. adv.ʃ

in a manner befitting brotherhood: to die, 4M 13.9. Cf. ἀδελφός, ἀδελφοπρεπῶς.

ἀδελφοκτόνος, ον.ʃ

murdering a brother or *sister*: ***s*** θυμός 'passion' Wi 10.3.

ἀδελφοπρεπῶς. adv.ʃ *

in a manner befitting a brother: to die, 4M 10.12. Cf. ἀδελφικῶς.

ἀδελφός, οῦ, voc. ἄδελφε. m.

1. *closely related male, male sibling*, 'brother': ἐν τῇ κοιλίᾳ ἐπτέρνισε τὸν ~ὸν αὐτοῦ 'in the womb he kicked his brother with his heel' Ho 12.3; Ps 49.20, 68.9 (ǁ ὁ υἱὸς τοῦ μητρός σου); οὐκ ἀ. ἦν Ησαυ τῷ Ιακωβ; Ma 1.2. **b**. *blood relation, kinsman*: ref. to uncle and nephew, ἄνθρωποι ~οί Ge 13.8, 29.12; To 1.21; ref. to husband, 7.11 𝔊[II]. **c**. 'ally', οὐκ ἐμνήσθησαν διαθήκης ~ῶν 'they did not remember an agreement as allies' Am 1.9, cf. 1.11; φίλοι καὶ σύμμαχοι καὶ ~οί 1M 14.40; from king to his regent, 2M 11.23. **d**. sg. in generic sense and of members of same religious community – De 22.1; τὸν ~όν σου Ιακωβ (as against the Edomites) Ob 10; 12; εἴπατε τῷ ~ῷ ὑμῶν· Λαός Ho 2.1; pl. Mi 5.3; ǁ γείτων Je 29.11; + φίλος 3M 3.10; ǁ ὁμοεθνής 2M 12.6. **e**. *fellow member of faith community*: Ἐβραῖον τῶν ἑαυτοῦ ~ῶν τῶν υἱῶν Ισραηλ Ex 2.11; οἱ ~οὶ ὑμῶν πᾶς ὁ οἶκος Ισραηλ Le 10.6; opp. ἄνθρωπος ἀλλότριος De 17.15, sim. 23.20; pl., in addressing members of one's own community: 'Friends!, Folks!' Ge 19.7.

***2**. in Hebraistic expressions of reciprocity: with ἕκαστος (q.v.): εἶπαν δὲ ἕκαστος πρὸς τὸν ~ὸν αὐτοῦ 'they said to one another' Ge 37.19; ἐγκατελίπετε ἕκαστος τὸν ~ὸν αὐτοῦ 'you abandoned one another' Ma 2.10; Hg 2.23, Jl 2.8, Zc 7.9, 10; ἕκαστος τῷ πλησίον καὶ τῷ ~ῷ Is 41.6; with ἄνθρωπος– ἄνθρωπος τὸν ~ὸν αὐτοῦ οὐκ ἐλεήσει 9.19; ἄνθρωπος τὸν ~ὸν αὐτοῦ καὶ ἄνθρωπος τὸν πλησίον αὐτοῦ 19.2; with οὐδείς– οὐκ εἶδεν οὐδεὶς τὸν ~ὸν αὐτοῦ Ex 10.23. **b.** ‖ ὁ πλησίον αὐτοῦ, ὁ ἔγγιστα αὐτοῦ: Ex 32.27; Je 23.35.

***3.** in a formal address in direct speech to a stranger(s): ἀδελφοί, πόθεν ἐστὲ ὑμεῖς; 'Gentlemen, where are you from?' Ge 29.4, ἄνδρες ~οί 4M 8.19.

4. *colleague* at work: ἱερεὺς ἀ. 'fellow-priest' 1E 1.12.

Cf. ἀδελφή, ἀδελφικῶς, πλησίον, ἔγγιστα. On the accentuation of the vocative, see Katz 1956.604; O'Callaghan.

ἀδελφότης, ητος. f. *

brotherhood: + φιλία 1M 12.10 (between nations); between individuals of a religious community, 4M 9.23.

ἀδέσποτος, ον.ʃ

without master: *s* carriage-driver, Si 20.32¶. Cf. δεσπότης.

ἀδεῶς. adv.ʃ

fearlessly: 3M 2.32. Cf. ἄδεια.

ἄδηλος, ον.

unknown, uncertain: subst.n., 3M 1.17, and *o* of δηλόω Ps 50.8 (+ κρύφιος); ἐλπίς 2M 3.34. Cf. ἄγνωστος: Schmidt 3.435.

ᾅδης, ου; voc. ᾅδη. m.

Hades, the underworld as the abode of the dead: κατάξετέ μου τὸ γῆρας μετὰ λύπης εἰς ~ου Ge 42.38, 44.29; ἕως ᾅδου κάτω De 32.22; εἰς ~ου Am 9.2; ἐκ κοιλίας ~ου Jn 2.3; ‖ θάνατος Ps 17.6, Jb 33.22; + ἀπώλεια 'perdition' Pr 15.11; insatiable, 27.20 (+ ἀπώλεια), PSol 4.13. **b.** personified: ἐκ χειρὸς ~ου ῥύσομαι .. ποῦ τὸ κέντρον σου, ᾅδη; Ho 13.14 (‖ θάνατος); Hb 2.5 (ditto); ὁ ᾅ. κάτωθεν ἐπικράνθη '.. was embittered' Is 14.9. On the gen. as in εἰς ᾅδου, see BDF, § 162 (8).

Cf. θάνατος: Jeremias, *TDNT* 1.146-9.

ἀδιάκριτος, ον.ʃ

undistinguished from one another: παιδεῖαι ~οι 'an assortment of teachings' Pr 25.1.

ἀδιαλείπτως. adv.

without a let-up, non-stop: pray, 1M 12.11, 2M 13.12, 3M 6.33; punish, 2M 3.26. Cf. ἀκατάλυτος: Spicq 1.32-4.

ἀδιάλυτος, ον.ʃ

incapable of dissolution: *s* περιστόμιον 'the opening of a garment' Ex 36.31. Cf. διαλύω.

ἀδιάπτωτος, ον.ʃ

not liable to mislead, 'infallible': *s* prudence, Wi 3.15.

ἀδιάστροφος, ον.ʃ

unflinching: *s* πίστις 'loyalty' 3M 3.3.

ἀδιάτρεπτος, ον.ʃ*

unwilling to have one's course of action altered, 'headstrong': *s* daughter, Si 26.10, 26.25¶, 42.11.

ἀδιάφορος, ον.ʃ

unimportant: Si 20.17¶.

ἀδιεξέταστος, ον.ʃ*

that would not stand up to examination: *s* λόγοι Si 21.18.

ἀδικέω: fut. ἀδικήσω, inf. ἀδικήσειν; aor. ἠδίκησα, subj. ἀδικήσω, ptc. ἀδικήσας, inf. ἀδικῆσαι, pass. ἀδικηθῆναι; pf.pass. ἠδίκημαι, ptc.act. ἠδικηκώς, pass. ἠδικημένος.

morally to wrong (τινα), *act wrongly against*: abs. 2K 24.17B (‖ κακοποιέω); use of false weights, Ps 61.10; ἀδικήσειν με Ge 21.23; τὸν πλησίον Le 19.13; opp. εὖ ποιέω τινα Ju 11.4; pass., ἀδικοῦμαι ἐκ σοῦ 'I am being wronged by you' Ge 16.5; ἀδικούμενος καὶ διαρπαζόμενος '.. and plundered' De 28.29; Hb 1.2. **b.** + acc. of wrong deed: τὸ ἀδίκημα, ὃ ἠδίκησεν Le 6.4, sim. Ez 39.26; + ἐπί τινι: ἐπὶ τοῖς δικαιώμασί σου Ba 2.12; *+ ἐν – ἐν διαθήκῃ σου Ps 43.18, ἐν τῇ ἀληθείᾳ μου 88.34, ἐν κυρίῳ 2C 26.16; + inf., τὸ μὴ ἀκοῦσαι Is 21.3. **c.** + double acc.: ἠδίκησέν τι τὸν πλησίον 'has wronged the neighbour in one way or another' Le 6.2, τί ἠδίκησά σε; Je 44.18, Pr 24.29. **d.** syn.: ἡμάρτομεν .. ἠνομήσαμεν, ἠδικήσαμεν Ps 105.6, ἡμάρτομεν, ἠσεβήσαμεν, ἠδικήσαμεν Ba 2.12, ἡμάρτομεν, ἠσεβήσαμεν, ἠδικήσαμεν καὶ ἀπέστημεν καὶ παρήλθομεν τὰς ἐντολάς σου Da LXX 9.5 (TH ἡμ., ἠδ., ἠνομήσαμεν καὶ ἀπ. καὶ ἐξεκλίναμεν ἀπὸ τῶν ἐντολῶν σου), sim. 3K 8.47. The wronged party is generally human (exc. Ez 17.21 v.l. ἐν ἐμοί), but see Ba 2.12 and 2E 10.13.

Cf. ἀδικία, ἀδίκημα, ἁμαρτάνω, ἀνομέω, ἀσεβέω, κατακονδυλίζω: Schrenk, *TDNT* 1.157-60.

ἀδίκημα, ατος. n.

wrong done, misdeed: τὸ ἀ. μου Ge 31.36 (‖ ἁμάρτημα); περιεῖλε κύριος τὰ ~ατά σου 'the Lord has removed your misdeeds' Zp 3.15; ‖ ἀκαθαρσία Lv 16.16. Cf. ἀδικία: Schrenk, *TDNT* 1.161-3.

ἀδικία, ας. f.

act contravening law, wrongdoing, iniquity: οὐκ ἀπέχεσθε ἀπὸ τῶν ~ῶν τῶν πατέρων ὑμῶν, ἐξεκλίνατε νόμιμά μου καὶ οὐκ ἐφυλάξασθε Ma 3.7; τέκνα ~ας Ho 10.9; ζυγὸς ~ας 'false scales' 12.7; ‖ αἵματα 'murderous acts' Mi 3.10, Hb 2.12, cf. Jl 3.19, Na 3.1; ‖ ἁμαρτία Ge 50.17, Ho 8.13, 9.9, Mi 7.19; ‖ ἀσέβεια Ho 10.13, Mi 7.18; ‖ μάταια Zp 3.13; ‖ ἁμαρτία and ἀνομία Le 16.21; ‖ ἁμάρτημα, ἁμαρτία De 19.15; ‖ ὁδὸς πονηρά Jn 3.8; ‖ κακία and associated with deception, Ho 7.1; opp. ἀγαθά

14.3, ἀλήθεια Ma 2.6, κρίμα Zp 3.5, δικαιοσύνη Pr 15.29a, τὸ δίκαιον 2M 10.12; ἀφαιρῶν ἀνομίας καὶ ~ας καὶ ἁμαρτίας Ex 34.7, Nu 14.18; not attributable to God, De 32.4. **b**. *penalty for wrongdoing*: Ez 18.19; 4K 7.9*L* (B: ἀνομία).

Cf. ἀδικέω, ἀδίκημα, ἄδικος, ἀνομία, ἁμαρτία, ἀσέβεια, δίκη, δικαιοσύνη: Schrenk, *TDNT* 1.155-7.

ἄδικος, ον.

unjust: *s* μάρτυς 'witness' Ex 23.1, De 19.16; ζυγὸν ἄ. 'false scales' Am 8.5; λόγοι ~οι Is 59.13, χείλη 'lips' Pr 4.24; ἔργα 11.18; ὁδός Ps 118.128 (|| ἀδικία 104); θυμός 'anger' Si 1.22; οἶνος 1E 4.37; δεσμά 'fetters' 3M 6.27; subst. m., || sinners, Wi 14.31, || ἀσεβής Jb 16.11; opp. δίκαιοι Pr 13.23, 17.25; n. *injustice*, ἐπ' ἀδίκῳ 'falsely' Le 19.12; οὐ ποιήσετε ~ον ἐν κρίσει 19.15; Zp 3.5; λαλεῖ ~α Is 9.17, 59.13, προφητεύω ~α Je 5.31, || ψευδῆ 34.11f.; opp. ἀλήθεια 1E 4.36; + ἄνομος Ez 21.3, 4. Cf. ἀδικία, ἄνομος, παράνομος, δίκαιος: Schrenk, *TDNT* 1.149-52.

ἀδίκως. adv.

in unjust manner: ὀμόσῃ ἀ. 'swear ..' Le 6.3, 4; ἀπολλύμενον 'perishing' 3M 6.3. Cf. ἄδικος.

ἀδόκητος, ον.ʃ

unexpected: *s* φόβος 'fear' Wi 18.17. Cf. ἀπροσδόκητος.

ἀδόκιμος, ον.ʃ

having failed a test, counterfeit: *s* ἀργύριον Is 1.22, Pr 25.4. Cf. δόκιμος: Lee 1969.239.

ἀδολεσχέω: fut. ἀδολεσχήσω; aor. ἠδολέσχησα, inf. ἀδολεσχῆσαι.

1. *to chatter*: μὴ ἀδολέσχει ἐν πλήθει πρεσβυτέρων 'Do not chatter among a gathering of elderly people' Si 7.14; μὴ πολλὰ ἀδολέσχει 35.9; κατ' ἐμοῦ 'against me' Ps 68.13 (|| ψάλλω).

*2. *to meditate, ponder* (< 'to talk to oneself'?): abs. Ge 24.63; νυκτὸς μετὰ τῆς καρδίας μου ἠδολέσχουν Ps 76.7 (|| ἔσκαλλεν τὸ πνεῦμά μου 'my spirit probed,' and διελογισάμην vs. 6); + ἐν – ἐν τοῖς ἐπιτηδεύμασίν σου 'on your deeds' 76.13 (|| μελετάω), ἐν ταῖς ἐντολαῖς σου 118.15 (|| κατανοέω, μελετάω); ἐν τοῖς δικαιώμασίν σου 118.23 (|| καταλαλέω), 118.48 (|| μελετάω vs. 47), || συνετίζω 'to inculcate' 118.27.

Cf. ἀδολεσχία, διαλογίζομαι, διανοέομαι, καταδολεσχέω, ~λαλέω, ~νοέω, μελετάω: Schmidt 1.169f.; Munnich 1979.346-50; Lazarenco.

ἀδολεσχία, ας. f.

inner, mental struggle: 1K 1.16, Ps 54.3. **b**. *thought resulting from such*: διηγήσαντό μοι ~ας Ps 118.85. Cf. ἀδολεσχέω.

ἀδόλως. adv.ʃ

without guile: Wi 7.13. Cf. δόλος, ἁπλῶς.

ἀδοξέω: fut. ἀδοξήσω.ʃ

to be held in low esteem: *s* τὸ εἶδός σου .. ἡ δόξα σου 'your appearance ..' Is 52.14. Cf. ἀδοξία, ἐξουδενόω.

ἀδοξία, ας. f.ʃ

low esteem, ill repute: Si 3.11 (|| ἀτιμία vs. 10). Cf. ἀτιμία, δόξα, ἀδοξέω, ἄδοξος.

ἄδοξος, ον.ʃ

held in low esteem: *s* hum., Si 10.31, 1M 2.8. Cf. ἀδοξία.

ἀδρανής, ές.ʃ

not possessed of requisite strength: *s* idols, ταῖς χερσίν Wi 13.19. Cf. ἀδύνατος.

ἁδρός, ά, όν.

subst. m. *person in leadership position*, 'chief': τῆς πόλεως 4K 10.6; Is 34.7, Je 5.5, Jb 29.9; τιμὴν θέσθαι ~οῖς 'to pay respect to ..' 34.19 (|| ἔντιμος). Cf. ἄρχων, ἡγεμών.

ἁδρύνω: aor.pass. ἡδρύνθην, ptc. ἁδρυνθείς, inf. ἁδρυνθῆναι, subj. ἁδρυνθῶ; pf.ptc.pass. ἡδρυμμένος.

1. pass. = act. intr., *to mature, grow*: *s* child, Jd 13.24B (A αὐξάνομαι), 11.2, Ex 2.10; lamb, 2K 12.3B (*L* συντρέφομαι); plants, Ps 143.12.

2. pass. = act. intr., *to show off, swagger*: 1M 8.14.

ἀδυναμέω.ʃ*

to be incapable of achieving an aim: *s* hum. and + dat., "our ability is not up to some of the .. words" Si prol. 20. Cf. ἀδυναμία, δυναμέω, ἀδυνατέω: Wagner 117-9.

ἀδυναμία, ας. f.ʃ

inability, helplessness: ἀποθανεῖται ἐν ~ίᾳ 'will die in helplessness' Am 2.2; pl. 3M 2.13. Cf. ἀδύνατος and ἀδυνατέω.

ἀδυνατέω: fut. ἀδυνατήσω; aor.subj. ἀδυνατήσω.ʃ

1. *to be impossible*: *s* *thing, ἐνώπιόν τινος Zc 8.6; μὴ ἀδυνατεῖ παρὰ τοῦ θεοῦ ῥῆμα; 'Is anything impossible with God?' Ge 18.14; Ἐὰν ἀδυνατήσῃ ἀπὸ σοῦ ῥῆμα 'Should anything turn out to be too difficult for you' De 17.8; + inf., 2K 13.2*L*, οὐκ ἀδυνατεῖ παρὰ σοὶ σῴζειν 2C 14.10; + acc. pers., πᾶν μυστήριον οὐκ ἀδυνατεῖ σε 'no mystery is beyond you' Da 4.6 TH; + dat. pers., ἀδυνατεῖ σοι οὐθέν Jb 10.13, 42.2.

2. *to be unable to cope*: *s* hum., ἀδυνατήσῃ ταῖς χερσίν 'is struggling (financially)' Le 25.35; ἐν αὐτοῖς 'with them (= opponents)' or '(many) among them' Is 8.15 (militarily); γόνασιν ἀδυνατοῦσιν θάρσος περιέθηκας 'you have given support to struggling knees' Jb 4.4. **b**. = οὐ δύναμαι 'to be unable to do': + inf., Wi 12.9, 13.16.

Cf. ἀδύνατος, ἀδυναμέω, ἀδυναμία.

ἀδύνατος, ον.

1. *lacking ability, weak*: ὁ ἀ. λεγέτω ὅτι Ἰσχύω ἐγώ 'Let the weak say "I have strength"' Jl 3.10; ἀ.

τοῖς ὀφθαλμοῖς 'unable to see' To 2.10, 5.9 𝔊II; + ἀσθενής Jb 36.15. **b.** *financially disadvantaged*: ‖ πτωχός Ep Je 27; δεήσεως ἐν ἀνάγκῃ ὄντων ἀδυνάτων 'supplication of the destitute in dire straits' Jb 36.19. **c.** *s* inanimate: night, Hades Wi 17.14; βία 'force' 4M 11.26.

2. *impossible*: Pr 30.18; n.sg. impers. and + inf. as subj., τὴν σὴν χεῖρα φυγεῖν ~όν ἐστιν 'it is impossible to get away from your hand' Wi 16.15; 2M 4.6.

Cf. δυνατός, ἀδυνατέω, ἀδρανής: Spicq 1.35-8.

ᾄδω: fut. ᾄσω, mid. ᾄσομαι; aor. ᾖσα, subj. ᾄσω, impv. ᾆσον.

to sing, chant: abs. ᾄσατε καὶ ἀγαλλιᾶσθε καὶ ψάλατε Ps 97.4; *s* hum. and + acc. (song) and dat. pers., τὴν ᾠδὴν ταύτην τῷ θεῷ Ex 15.1; τῷ ἠγαπημένῳ ᾆσμα Is 5.1; τὸ ᾆσμα τοῦτο Nu 21.17; *o* ψαλμός Ps 7.1, αἴνεσις 105.12; ‖ ψάλλω 67.5, ‖ αἰνέω Je 20.13; ‖ παίζω 37.19; ‖ ἐξάρχω Ju 16.1; ‖ ὑμνέω 1C 16.9. **b.** *to sing of*: + acc. of subject-matter, ἔλεος καὶ κρίσιν Ps 100.1.

Cf. ᾆσμα, αἰνέω, μελῳδέω, παίζω, προαναμέλπω, ὑμνέω, ψάλλω, ᾠδή.

ἀεί. adv.

always, ever: Si 22.22¶; Is 42.14; ἀ. πάσας τὰς ἡμέρας 51.13. **b.** used attrib.: εἰς τὸν ἀ. χρόνον 'for perpetuity' 3M 3.29, εἰς τοὺς ἀ. χρόνους 7.23.

Cf. πάντοτε, αἰώνιος.

ἀειγενής, ές.ʃ

everlasting: subst.m., Si 24.18¶. Cf. αἰώνιος, subs.: Auwers 35f.

ἀέναος, ον.ʃ

everlasting: *s* hill (θίς) Ge 49.26, Ba 5.7; βουνός De 33.15 (‖ ἀρχή); arm (βραχίων) 33.27; God, Jb 19.25; ever-flowing river (ποταμός) Wi 11.6; life (ζωή) 2M 7.36. Cf. αἰώνιος, μόνιμος, prec.

ἀεργός, ον.ʃ

slothful: subst.m., Pr 13.4, 15.19 (:: ἀνδρεῖος), 19.15. Cf. ὀκνηρός, ἀνδρεῖος.

ἀετός, οῦ. m.

eagle, mostly in simile: forbidden as food, Le 11.13, De 14.12; ὡσεὶ ἐπὶ πτερύγων ~ῶν 'like on the wings of ..' Ex 19.4; ὡσεὶ ὅρμημα ~οῦ 'like a swoop of ..' De 28.49; ὡς ἀ. σκεπάσαι νοσσιὰν αὐτοῦ 'just as an eagle protects her nestlings' 32.11; of boldness, Mi 1.16, cf. Cyr. I 624; of a bird soaring to the sky, ἐὰν μετεωρισθῇς ὡς ἀ. Ob 4; eager to consume its prey, ὡς ἀ. πρόθυμος εἰς τὸ φαγεῖν Hb 1.8. Cf. LSG s.v.

ἄζυμος, ον.

unleavened: ἄρτους ~ους πεφυραμένους ἐν ἐλαίῳ 'unleavened bread kneaded in oil' Ex 29.2, Le 2.4; subst. (ἄρτος understood), ~ους ἔπεψεν 'baked unleavened loaves of bread' Ge 19.3; ἐγκρυφία 'cake' Ex 12.39; n.pl. 'unleavened loaves (eaten at the feast of the passover), ἑορτὴ ~ων 'the feast of the unleavened loaves,' i.e. the Passover 23.15, 34.18, 1E 1.17; ~α ἐπὶ πικρίδων ἔδονται 'they shall eat .. with chicories' Ex 12.8. Cf. ἄρτος, ζύμη.

Ἀζωτιστί. adv.ʃ

in the language of Azotus: Ne 13.24.

ἀηδία, ας. f.ʃ

odious, disagreeable situation: Pr 23.29. Cf. ἡδονή.

ἀήρ, ἀέρος.

gassy substance in the atmosphere, 'air': τὸ πνεῦμα διαχυθήσεται ὡς χαῦνος ἀ. 'the spirit will be diffused like thin air' Wi 2.3; pl. διὰ τῶν ἀέρων τρέχοντας ἱππεῖς 'horses leaping through the air' 2M 5.2, σκοτεινὸν ὕδωρ ἐν νεφέλαις ἀέρων 'dark water in misty clouds' Ps 17.12. Cf. πνεῦμα, πνοή: Schmidt 1.611-5.

ἀθανασία, ας. f.

immortality: ~ας δένδρον Si 19.19¶; Wi 3.4. Cf. ἀθάνατος, ἀφθαρσία, θάνατος: Bultmann, *TDNT* 3.22-5.

ἀθάνατος, ον.

immortal: *s* hum. Si 17.30; δικαιοσύνη Wi 1.15, νίκη 'triumph' 4M 7.3, ψυχή 18.23. Cf. ἀθανασία, ἄφθαρτος, θνητός.

ἀθέμιτος, ον.ʃ

unlawful: *s* pork, 2M 7.1, words uttered, 10.34; hum., 3M 5.20; subst.n., cultic offerings, 2M 6.5. Cf. ἄθεσμος, ἄνομος, παράνομος, θέμις: Oepke, *TDNT* 1.166.

ἀθεσία, ας. f.ʃ

1. v.n. of ἀθετέω: sense **2**, Je 20.8; sense **1**, Da 9.7 TH.

2. *breach of faith*, 'treachery': 1M 16.17; 2M 15.10 (‖ τῶν ὅρκων παράβασις).

Cf. ἀθετέω.

ἄθεσμος, ον.ʃ*

unlawful: *s* πρόθεσις 'purpose' 3M 5.12. Cf. ἀθέμιτος, ἀθέσμως: Oepke, *TDNT* 1.167; Renehan 2.13. Del. 3M 6.26 v.l. (> ἀθέσμως).

ἀθέσμως. adv.ʃ

in unlawful manner: 3M 6.26.

ἀθετέω: fut. ἀθετήσω, pass. ἀθετηθήσομαι; aor. ἠθέτησα, inf. ἀθετῆσαι, subj. ἀθετήσω, pass. ἀθετηθῶ; pf. ἠθέτηκα, ptc. ἠθετηκώς.

1. *to refuse to recognise the claim and obligation due to*: *s* child disowning *o* (acc.) his parents, Is 1.2 (:: γινώσκω vs. 3); De 21.14. **b.** to act accordingly against sbd (εἴς τινα), 'to betray the faith and trust of sbd else': + εἴς τινα – ὡς ἀθετεῖ γυνὴ εἰς τὸν συνόντα αὐτῇ, οὕτως ἠθέτησεν εἰς ἐμὲ οἶκος Ισραηλ Je 3.20; + dat. (God), 3K 8.50; *+ ἔν τινι (pers.) 2C 10.19 (‖ 3K 12,19 εἰς), 4K 1.1, 18.20 (Hebraism?, but cf. Lampe, s.v.); ὑποκάτωθεν χειρὸς Ιουδα 'in an attempt to set oneself free from the yoke of ..' 4K 8.20; + εἴς τι 1C 2.7. **c.** in dealing w. sbd (ἔν τινι), Ex 21.8, 4K 1.1, La 1.2, Da TH 9.7. **d.** abs. σύνοδος ἀθετούντων 'a bunch of disowners, rejecters' Je 9.2; ὀμνύων τῷ πλησίον αὐτοῦ καὶ οὐ ἀθετῶν Ps 14.4; Ju 14.18; w. a cogn. obj., ἀθετήματα Je 12.1, 2C 36.14.

2. *to reject and treat as invalid and meaningless*: + acc. rei, τὸν νόμον Is 24.16; Ez 22.26; τοὺς λόγους σου Je 15.16, λογισμοὺς λαῶν .. καὶ βουλὰς ἀρχόντων Ps 32.10 (‖ διασκεδάζω); 88.35 (‖ βεβηλόω); ἀλήθειαν 131.11; τὴν προσταγὴν τοῦ βασιλέως Da LXX 3.95, ὁρκισμόν 'oath' 1M 6.62, cf. 2C 36.13; others' toils (πόνους) Wi 5.1; pass. Is 31.2. **b.** *to abrogate, annul*, 1M 11.36; 14.44 (‖ ἀντειπεῖν), 45 (‖ παρά τι ποιεῖν 'to act against'), διαστάλσεις 'terms of an agreement' 2M 13.25. **c.** abs. and ‖ ἀνομέω: Is 21.2.

3. *to disprove the claim* of supremacy *made by*, alm. = 'vanquish': + acc. pers., Ju 16.5.

Cf. ἀκυρόω, ἀθεσία, ἀθέτημα: Spicq 1.39f.; Lee 1969.239.

ἀθέτημα, ατος. n.ʃ

an instance of refusing to recognise (God's) *claim and obligation due to Him*: as cogn. obj. of ἀθετέω (q.v.), Je 12.1, 3K 8.50, ~ματα βδελυγμάτων ἐθνῶν 2C 36.14. Cf. ἀθετέω.

ἀθέτησις, εως. f.ʃ

refusal to recognise authority of sbd: + ἀσέβεια 1K 24.12. Del. Je 12.1, Da TH 9.7, 2M 14.28 v.l.

ἀθεώρητος, ον.ʃ

invisible: *s* dashing animals, Wi 17.19. Cf. θεωρέω, ἀόρατος.

ἀθλητής, οῦ. m.

athlete: metaph. of martyrs, γενναῖος 'noble' 4M 6.10. Cf. ἐναθλέω: Stauffer, *TDNT* 1.167f.

ἄθλιος, α, ον.ʃ

wretched: *s* hum., 3M 5.37, προσδοκία 'expectation' 49. Cf. τρισάθλιος, μέλεος, τάλας, μακάριος: Schmidt 4.436-8; Shipp 45.

ἀθλοθετέω.ʃ *

to award the prize of a contest: 4M 17.12. Cf. ἆθλον.

ἆθλον, ου. n.ʃ

prize of contest: of athletic contest, Wi 4.2; of moral struggle, ἀρετῆς 4M 9.8. Cf. ἀθλοθετέω.

ἀθλοφόρος, ον.ʃ

bearing away the prize: *s* μήτηρ, 4M 18.23; subst. m., 'prize-winner,' 15.29.

ἀθροίζω: fut. ἀθροίσω; aor. ἤθροισα, impv. ἄθροισον, pass. ἠθροίσθην, impv.2pl. ἀθροίσθητε.

to bring together: + acc., αὐτοὺς εἰς χεῖρας μαχαίρας Je 18.20; *o* troops, 1M 3.13. **b.** pass. w. intr. sense, *to come together, gather*: in order to hear sbd speak, Ge 49.2 (‖ συνάγομαι vs. 1); ἐπὶ Μωυσῆν Nu 20.2 (to protest). Cf. ἄθροισμα, ἀθρόος, συναθροίζω, συνάγω.

ἄθροισμα, ατος. n.ʃ

large group: of troops, + ἐκκλησία 1M 3.13. Cf. ἀθροίζω, ἐκκλησία, ὄχλος, πλῆθος, συναγωγή.

ἀθρόος, α, ον.ʃ

assembled: *s* guests, 3M 5.14. Cf. ἀθροίζω.

ἀθυμέω: aor. ἠθύμησα, ptc. ἀθυμήσας.

to feel despondent: *s* καρδία De 28.65; πόλις – δι' ἔνδειαν 'because of scarce supplies' Is 25.4; hum., συνεχύθη καὶ ἠθύμει 'was upset and despondent' 1M 4.27; Ju 7.22; ὑπέρ τινος 2K 6.8. Cf. ἀθυμία, θαρσέω, ἀποκακέω.

ἀθυμία, ας. f.ʃ

despondency: Ps 118.53, 1K 1.6. Cf. ἀθυμέω. Del. 2M 10.13 v.l.

ἄθυτος, ον.ʃ

not fit to be offered as sacrifice: Le 19.7. Cf. θύω.

ἀθῷος, ον.

1. *immune*: legally, ἀθῷος ἀπὸ τῆς ἀρᾶς μου .. ἀ. ἀπὸ τοῦ ὁρκισμοῦ μου Ge 24.41 (‖ καθαρός vs. 8); Ex 21.19, Nu 5.19; ἔναντι κυρίου καὶ ἀπὸ Ισραηλ, free from obligations imposed on members of a divinely constituted Israelite confederation 32.22 (sense **2.** also implied, see ‖ ἁμαρτήσεσθε ἔναντι κυρίου vs. 23); + dat. rei, ὅρκῳ Jo 2.17, 19, 20; free from military service, De 24.5. **b.** *exempt from accountability for that which one might do to* sbd: ἀπό τινος Jd 15.3 A.

2. *not deserving punishment*, 'innocent': *s* hum., ἀθῷον καὶ δίκαιον οὐκ ἀποκτενεῖς Ex 23.7, χερσίν Ps 23.4 (‖ καθαρός); πατάξαι ψυχὴν αἵματος ~ου 'to strike the life of a man innocent of murder' De 27.25 (‖ αἷμα ἀναίτιον 19.10); ἀπὸ Κυρίου '(safe) from (the punishment by) the Lord' 2K 3.28; ἀπὸ ἀνομίας Jb 10.14; αἷμα ~ον 'blood of an innocent person' Je 7.6; God, Ps 17.26.

Cf. ἀθῳόω, καθαρός, ἀναίτιος, ἀκατάγνωστος.

ἀθῳόω: fut. ἀθῳώσω, pass. ἀθῳωθήσομαι; aor.subj. ἀθῳώσω, pass. ἀθῳωθῶ, impv. ἀθῴωσον; pf.pass. ἠθῴωμαι.

to leave unpunished: abs., ἀθῳῶν οὐκ ἀθῳώσει κύριος 'the Lord will certainly not leave (the guilty) unpunished' Na 1.3; Jl 3.21 (neg. ‖ ἐκδικέω); + acc. rei (offence), τὰς ἀδικίας αὐτῶν Je 18.23; + acc. pers., 26.28; βλάσφημον ἀπὸ χειλέων αὐτοῦ 'a blasphemer from his utterances' Wi 1.6. **b.** *to protect* from assailants (in court?): + acc. pers., ἀπὸ τῶν καταδιωκόντων με Je 15.15; pass., ἀπό τινος (enemies) Jd 15.3 B.

Cf. ἀθῷος.

αἴγειος, α, ον.
of a goat: *s* hair (θρίξ) Ex 25.4 (sth valuable); without θρίξ, Nu 31.20. Cf. αἴξ.

αἰγιαλός, οῦ. m.ʃ
stretch of land at the edge of an expanse of water: sea-shore, Jd 5.17 A (B: παραλία). Cf. χεῖλος: Schmidt 3.103-6.

αἰγίδιον, ου. n.ʃ
Dim. of αἴξ, *kid*: 1K 10.3 (*L* ἔριφος). Cf. αἴξ.

Αἰγύπτιος, α, ον.
Egyptian: παιδίσκη ~ία 'an Egyptian handmaid' Ge 16.1; ἀνὴρ ~ος 39.1; subst. οἱ ~οι 12.12. Cf. Drew Griffiths.

Αἴγυπτος, ου. f.
Egypt: κατέβη εἰς ~ον Ge 12.10; ἐν (ὅλῃ) γῇ ~ῳ for .. Αἰγύπτου Ge 41.19, Ex 6.28, Le 19.34, Nu 8.17, De 1.30, Je 39.20 +.

αἰδέομαι: aor. ᾐδεσάμην, pass. ᾐδέσθην, ptc. αἰδεσθείς.
1. *to feel ashamed of*: + acc., ἀπάτην 'deceit' Ju 9.3; + inf., 4M 12.11.
2. *to pay regard to*: + acc., οὐκ αἰδεσθεὶς τὸ δίκαιον 'with no regard for justice' 2M 4.34, πρόσωπον Pr 24.23, σου τὴν ἡλικίαν 'your (venerable) age' 4M 5.7.
Cf. αἰδώς, αἰσχύνομαι, καταιδέομα, ἀναιδής: Schmidt 3.536-8; Shipp 45-7.

αἰδήμων, ον, gen. ονος.ʃ
modest in attitude: *s* hum. 2M 15.12, 4M 8.3. Cf. αἰδώς.

ἀΐδιος, η, ον.ʃ
everlasting: *s* light, Wi 7.26; life, 4M 10.15 (‖ αἰώνιος). Cf. αἰώνιος: Sasse, *TDNT* 1.168.

αἰδοῖον, ου. n.ʃ
pudenda: male, Ez 23.20 (‖ σάρξ). Cf. αἰσχύνη, ἀσχημοσύνη.

αἰδώς, οῦς, acc. ~ῶ. f.ʃ
1. *sense of modesty*: befitting young women, 3M 1.19.
2. *sense of respect* for others: for the elderly, 3M 4.6.
Cf. αἰδήμων, ἀναίδεια, αἰσχύνη, ἐντροπή: Trench 66-9; Bultmann, *TDNT* 1.169-71; Spicq 1.41-4.

αἰθάλη, ης. f.ʃ
soot: καμιναίας 'of furnace' Ex 9.8 (turning into κονιορτός on falling on the ground, vs. 9), 10. Cf. σποδός.

Αἰθιοπία, ας. f.
Ethiopia: Ge 2.13.

Αἰθιόπισσα, ης. f.ʃ
Ethiopian woman: γυνὴ Αἰ. Nu 12.1.

Αἰθίοψ, οπος. m.
Ethiopian: Ez 29.10.

αἴθριον, ου. n.
the main hall: τοῦ οἴκου 'of the temple' Ez 9.3. Cf. Chantraine 1964, esp. 9f.; Husson 29-36.

αἴθριος, ον.ʃ
kept in the open air: "(sleeping at night) outdoors" Jb 2.9c; στῆναι ~οι 'stand ..' 1E 9.11.

αἰκία, ας. f.
act of torture: 2M 7.42; pl. 3M 4.14. Cf. αἰκισμός, βάσανος, στρέβλη.

αἰκίζομαι: aor.ptc. αἰκισάμενος, pass. αἰκισθείς; pf.ptc.pass. ᾐκισμένος.
to torture: pass., 2M 7.1; w. act. sense, 7.13, 4M 1.11. Cf. αἰκία, βασανίζω, καταικίζω.

αἰκισμός, οῦ. m.
v.n. of αἰκίζω: 2M 8.17; torture suffered, 4M 6.9. Cf. αἰκία, αἰκίζω.

αιλαμ. n.
= אֵילָם 'porch': 1K 6.36, Ez 40.9+.

Αἰλαμίτης, ου. m.
subst.m.pl., *Elam*: Is 11.11+. Del. Je 36.24,31 v.l.

αἴλουρος, ου. m./f.ʃ
domestic cat: Ep Je 21.

αἷμα, ατος. n.
1. *blood*: αἷ. περιτομῆς 'of circumcision' Ex 4.25; τῆς διαθήκης 24.8; ῥύσις ~ατος 'menstruation' Le 15.25; in description of a supernatural, eschatological phenomenon, αἷ. καὶ πῦρ καὶ ἀτμίδα καπνοῦ 'blood and fire and vapour of smoke' Jl 2.30; in which life consists, ψυχῆς Ge 9.4; ref. to its red colour, μεταστραφήσεται .. ἡ σελήνη εἰς αἷ. 'the moon will change into blood' Jl 2.31; of sacrificial animals, Ex 29.12, Zc 9.7; with ritually purifying power, καθαρισμοῦ τῶν ἁμαρτιῶν Ex 30.10; associated with murder, Ge 4.10, αἷ. καὶ θάνατος Ez 28.23; ἐξεχεεῖ τὸ αἷ. αὐτῶν ὡς χοῦν Zp 1.17; τὸ αἷ. αὐτοῦ ἐπ' αὐτὸν ἐκχυθήσεται Ho 12.14; αἷ. δίκαιον 'innocent blood,' i.e. murder of innocent person, Jl 3.19, Jn 1.14, cf. αἷ. δικαίου Pr 6.17; αἷ. ἀναίτιον De 19.10; πατάξαι ψυχὴν ~ατος ἀθῴου 27.25; ‖ μοιχαλίς 'adulteress' Ez 23.45; often in pl. αἵματα ἐφ' αἵμασι μίσγουσι 'they mix blood with blood' Ho 4.2; *acts of murder*, ‖ ἀδικίαι Mi 3.10, Hb 2.12; ‖ ἀσέβειαι 2.8, 17; πόλις ~άτων ὅλη ψευδὴς ἀδικίας πλήρης Na 3.1, ἀνὴρ ~άτων 2K 16.8, Ps 5.7, 25.9; ἐπὶ τοῖς ~ασί σου τοῖς γεγενημένοις ἐν μέσῳ σου 'over your acts of murder which have taken place in your midst' Ez 22.13; of death sentence obtained unjustly, εἰς ~ατα δικάζονται 'they go to law, demanding a death sentence' Mi 7.2 (cf. Thph PG 126.1169); τὸ αἷ. αὐτοῦ ἐκζητεῖται 'his murder is being revenged' Ge 42.22; De 17.8; ref. to a husband avenging his wife's adultery (?), Si 9.9.
b. In a rendering of a post-Biblical idiom בָּשָׂר וָדָם to denote transient human existence: σὰρξ καὶ αἷμα Si

17.31 (|| γῆ καὶ σποδός 'dust and ashes' vs. 32), sim. 14.18, cf. Behm, *TDNT* 1.172.

2. *dark-red liquid*: αἷ. σταφυλῆς, fig. 'wine' and || οἶνος Ge 49.11, De 32.14; Si 39.26; αἷ. σταφυλῆς καὶ μόρων 'juice of grapes and mulberries' 1M 6.34.

Cf. αἱμάσσω, αἱμοβόρος, αἱμορρέω: Behm, *TDNT* 1.172-7.

αἱμάσσω: aor.inf. αἱμάξαι∫.

to cause hemorrage to: + acc. (part of the body), πλευράν Si 42.5 (through a punitive blow).

αἱμοβόρος, ον.∫

bloodthirsty: *s* hum., + φονώδης 'murderous' 4M 10.17.

αἱμορροέω.∫

to have discharge of blood: *s* menstruating woman, Le 15.33. Cf. ῥέω.

αἱμωδιάω: fut. ~διάσω; aor. ᾑμωδίασα.∫

to trill with slight pain: **s* teeth on eating unripe, sour grapes, Je 38.29; 38.30 (|| γομφιάζω Ez 18.2). Cf. γομφιάζω.

αἴνεσις, εως. f.*

act of praising in religious sense and vocally: θυσία ~εως σωτηρίου Le 7.3; μετὰ φωνῆς ~εως καὶ ἐξομολογήσεως Jn 2.10; ~εως αὐτοῦ (obj. gen.) πλήρης ἡ γῆ Hb 3.3; αἴ. καὶ ἀγαλλίαμα Is 35.10, ἀγαλλίασις καὶ αἴ. 51.11; + εὐφροσύνη, μεγαλειότης Je 40.9. **b**. *object of praising*: ἡ δόξα μου καὶ ἡ αἴ. μου κύριος Is 12.2.

Cf. αἰνέω and ἐξομολόγησις.

αἰνετός, ή, όν.

praiseworthy: *s* fruits (not necessarily cultic offerings), ὁ καρπὸς αὐτοῦ ἅγιος καὶ αἰ. τῷ κυρίῳ Le 19.24; πόλις Je 30.14; God and + μέγας Ps 47.2, 144.3; hum. 2K 14.25, god PSol 3.1. Cf. αἰνέω and ὑπεραινετός.

αἰνέω: fut. αἰνέσω; aor. ᾔνεσα, subj. αἰνέσω, inf. αἰνέσαι, impv.2pl αἰνέσατε, opt. 3pl αἰνέσαισαν.

to praise, extol: abs. Je 38.5, 7, ***so*** pers., σὲ αἰνέσαισαν οἱ ἀδελφοί σου Ge 49.8, ***o*** (acc.) God, Is 38.18 (|| εὐλογέω), φωνῇ μεγάλῃ Jb 38.7 (*s* angels), || δοξάζω Ps 21.24, || ἐξομολογέω Si 51.12; *s* nature, Ps 68.35; in religious sense and + acc. rei, αἰνέσετε τὸ ὄνομα τοῦ κυρίου Jl 2.26, || εὐλογέω Ps 144.2, || ὑμνέω Si 51.11, ἐν χορῷ 'with a dance' Ps 149.3 (|| ψάλλω); ἐπὶ τῷ θεῷ .. ῥῆμα .. λόγον 55.11; + dat. dei, Je 20.13 (|| ᾄδω), τῷ θεῷ 4.2 (|| εὐλογέω); and + ἐπί τι Ps 118.164; + dat. rei, τῷ ὀνόματί σου PSol 5.1. Cf. αἴνεσις, ἐπαινέω, αἶνος, ἐγκωμιάζω, εὐφημέω, εὐλογέω, ἐξομολογέω, κατευφημέω, προαναμέλπω: Ledogan 34-6.

αἴνιγμα, ατος. n.

1. *dark saying*: a form of divine revelation, ἐν εἴδει καὶ οὐ δι' ~άτων '.. and not through riddles' Nu 12.8; general, λύσεις ~άτων 'answers to riddles' Wi 8.8, ἐν αἰνίγμασιν παραβολῶν Si 39.3, ἐν παραβολαῖς ~άτων 47.15, διανοούμενος ~ατα 'pondering over riddles' Da LXX 8.23 (|| προβλήματα ib. TH).

***2**. *taunt*: ἔσῃ .. ἐν ~ατι καὶ ἐν παραβολῇ .. De 28.37.

Cf. παραβολή: Kittel, *TDNT* 1.178.

αἰνιγματιστής, οῦ. m.∫ *

one who speaks riddles: Nu 21.27. Cf. αἴνιγμα.

αἶνος, ου. m.

verbal expression of praise: Ps 8.3; ᾠδῆς τῷ Δαυιδ 'in the form of dirge ..' 90 tit.; ῥηθήσεται αἰ. Si 15.10; in worship, ἐν ~ῳ καὶ ἀνθομολογήσει τῷ κυρίῳ 2E 3.11, + ψαλμός Ju 16.1. **b**. musical: ἐν ~οις καὶ παμμελέσιν ὕμνοις 'in .. and all sorts of hymns' 3M 7.16, ὑμνοῦντες ~ον 2C 23.13.

Cf. αἰνέω, ἔπαινος.

αἴξ, γός. c.

goat: sacrificial animal, τριετίζουσαν 'three-year-old' Ge 15.9 (|| δάμαλις, κριός, τρυγών, περιστερά); subsumed, together with ἀρήν, under πρόβατα, 30.32; || μόσχος, πρόβατον Le 17.3. Cf. αἰγίδιον, αἰπόλιον, αἰπόλος, ἔριφος, πρόβατον, τράγος, χίμαρον.

αἰπόλιον, ου. n.∫

herd of goats: Pr 30.31. Cf. αἰπόλος, αἴξ.

αἰπόλος, ου. m.∫

= prec.: Am 7.14. Cf. ποίμνη, αἰπόλιον.

αἵρεσις, εως. f.∫

choice: of course of action, συνετέλεσαν ἀδικίαν ἐξ ~εως αὐτῶν Ge 49.5; κατὰ πᾶσαν ~ιν αὐτῶν 'in keeping with whatever choice they have made' Le 22.18 (|| κατὰ πᾶσαν ὁμολογίαν αὐτῶν); κατὰ ~ιν 'according to their free will' 22.21; ἐξ ~εως αὐτῶν 'at their own discretion' 1M 8.30.

Cf. αἱρετίζω, ἐκλογή.

αἱρετίζω: fut. αἱρετιῶ; aor. ᾑρέτισα, mid. ᾑρετισάμην; pf. ᾑρέτικα.

to choose as desirable, prefer: + acc. pers., αἱρετιεῖ με ὁ ἀνήρ μου Ge 30.20; Nu 14.8; Χαναναίους Ho 4.18; of divine election, Hg 2.24, Ez 20.5; τὴν Ιερουσαλημ Zc 1.17 (|| ἐλεέω), 2.12; αἱρετιῶ αὐτοὺς ὃν τρόπον αἱρετίζει ἄνθρωπος τὸν υἱὸν αὐτοῦ τὸν δουλεύοντα αὐτῷ 'I shall choose them as a man chooses his son to serve him' Ma 3.17 (cf. Tht PG 81.1984: προτιμῶντος); παρὰ πάντα τὰ ἔθνη 'in preference to all the (other) nations' PSol 9.9; ***o*** τὸ πρόσωπόν σου '(I have decided to pay respect) due to you' 1K 25.35 (*L* ἐντρέπομαι); + inf., Ju 11.1, mid. and || ἐκλέγομαι Ps 131.13; + acc. rei, τὰς ἐντολάς σου 118.173; *ἔν τινι (pers.) [Heb. calque] 2C 29.11. Cf. αἱρέω, αἵρεσις, αἱρετός, αἱρετίς, ἐκλέγω.

αἱρετίς, ίδος. f.∫*

female chooser: *s* Wisdom, + gen., Wi 8.4. Cf. αἱρετίζω.

αἱρετισμός, οῦ. m.ʃ

adherence to unorthodox practices, 'heresy': 4K 12.17*L*. Cf. LSG s.v.

αἱρετός, ή, όν.

chosen as the better or *the best, preferable*: + gen., Pr 16.16a, + ὑπέρ and acc., 16.16b, + ἤ Si 20.25; *s* inf., Su 23 TH (LXX: κάλλιον), 2M 7.14; subst.m., God's elect (?), Si 11.31. Cf. αἱρετίζω, αἱρέω.

αἱρέω: aor.mid. εἱλάμην, impv.2pl. ἕλεσθε, subj. ἑλῶμαι.

mid. *to choose as one's own*: + acc., τὸν θεὸν εἵλου σήμερον εἶναί σου θεόν De 26.17; κύριος εἵλατό σε σήμερον γενέσθαι αὐτῷ λαὸν περιούσιον 26.18; τὸν θάνατον ἢ τὴν ζωήν 'death rather life' Je 8.3; κρίσιν ἑλώμεθα ἑαυτοῖς Jb 34.4¶; *o* καιρόν 'moment for an action' PSol 17.21. **b**. as desirable and preferable: + acc. pers., 1K 19.1 (impf.; *L* ἀγαπάω); + inf., 2M 11.25 (pres.; ‖ αἱρετίζω vs. 24), cf. Renehan 2.15.

Cf. αἱρετίζω, ἐκλέγω, ἀνθ~, προαιρέω.

αἴρω: fut. ἀρῶ, pass. ἀρθήσομαι; aor. ἦρα, impv. ἆρον, inf. ἆραι, ptc. ἄρας, subj. ἄρω, opt.3s. ἄραι, pass. ἤρθην, subj. ἀρθῶ, impv. ἄρθητι, 3s ἀρθήτω, inf. ἀρθῆναι, ptc. ἀρθείς; pf. ἦρκα, pass. ἦρμαι.

1. *to move sth upwards vertically*, 'pick up, lift': + acc. pers. ἄρατέ με καὶ ἐμβάλετέ με εἰς τὴν θάλασσαν 'pick me up and cast me into the sea' Jn 1.12; hands in prayer, Mi 2.1, Ps 27.2, cf. πρὸς σὲ .. τὴν ψυχήν μου 24.1, 85.4; in taking a vow, εἰς τὸν οὐρανὸν τὴν χεῖρά μου De 32.40 (*s* God!), Ez 36.7, ἄνω τὰς χεῖρας 1E 9.47, ἐναντίον τοῦ κυρίου, gesture of hostility Jb 15.25; one's eyes to see, ἦρα τοὺς ὀφθαλμούς μου καὶ εἶδον Zc 1.18, ἄρατε εἰς τὸν οὐρανὸν τοὺς ὀφθαλμοὺς ὑμῶν καὶ ἐμβλέψατε .. Is 51.6, εἰς ὕψος 4K 19.22, εἰς εὐθεῖαν 'straight' Je 3.2; ἄρης τοὺς ὀφθαλμούς σου ἐπ' αὐτούς 'set your eyes on them' Ez 23.27; τὸ πρόσωπον εἰς τὸν οὐρανόν 1E 4.58; with no guilt-feeling, πρός τινα 2K 2.22, in entreaty PSol 5.10; τὸν πόδα σου ἐπ' ἔργῳ Is 58.13 (to set out: ‖ ἐξαίρω τοὺς πόδας Ge 29.1); με, from low-lying Egypt to Canaan, 47.30; κεφαλήν 'to rise in eminence' Si 20.11, with self-confidence Is 8.8, a sign of defiance and challenge Jd 8.28, Zc 2.4; σημεῖον '(hoist) a flag' Is 13.2, 33.23, Je 6.1; ὅπλα 'weapons' 50.10. **b**. *to raise to a higher level*, but not physically: τὴν φωνήν: 1K 24.17, 30.4 (*L* ἐπαίρω).

2. *to remove by lifting*: *o* τοὺς θεοὺς τοὺς ἀλλοτρίους 'the alien gods' Ge 35.2; neck, Mi 2.3; yoke, 1M 13.41. **b**. upward movement not implied: τινα Ps 151.4.

3. *to take up and carry*: *o* μερίδας παρ' αὐτοῦ πρὸς αὐτούς 'portions (of a meal)' Ge 43.34; ζυγόν 'yoke' La 3.27, ἐφ' ἑαυτῷ 3.28; cadaver, Le 11.40; θυσίας Ps 95.8; σημεῖον 'flag' Is 11.12.

4. *to bear with, endure*: + acc. pers., Jb 21.3, cf. v.l. βαστάσατε and Jul. and Ol. ad loc.

5. *to carry, transport*: ἐπ' ὤμων 'on shoulders' Nu 7.9, Is 46.7, 60.4, ἐπὶ χειρῶν Ps 90.12; *s* donkey, Ge 45.23; *o* load, 44.1; 46.5; τὴν σκηνὴν (sc. τοῦ μαρτυρίου) καὶ πάντα τὰ σκεύη αὐτῆς Nu 1.50; τὴν κιβωτὸν τῆς διαθήκης κυρίου De 31.9; πῦρ in an earthen lamp, Is 30.14. **b**. weapons of one's superior: πρὸς τὸ παιδάριον τὸν αἴροντα τὰ σκεύη αὐτοῦ Jd 9.54A, ὁ αἴρων τὰ ὅπλα αὐτοῦ 1K 17.7; prob. one's own weapons, αἴροντες θυρεὸν καὶ δόρυ 1C 12.24*L* (AB+: θυρεοφόροι καὶ δορατοφόροι, ὁπλοφόρων αἰρόντων θυρεοὺς καὶ δόρατα 2C 14.7), cf. s.v. φέρω **2a**.

6. *to bear and uphold*: *o* part of a structure, altar, Ex 27.7.

7. *to take away*: + acc., ὄνειδος 'reproach' Ps 151.7; τὸ ἀνόμημα τῆς δούλης σου 'the iniquity of your handmaid' 1K 25.28 (= 'overlook'?), ἁμάρτημα 15.25, cf. Jeremias, *TDNT* 1.185f. **b**. unjustly or by force: τὸ δίκαιον τοῦ δικαίου 'the justice of the just' Is 5.23; καταλελειμμένα ᾠά 'eggs left (after mother birds having been killed)' 10.14 (‖ καταλαμβάνω), μνήμην τινος 'that which reminds of sbd's existence' Pr 1.12; pass., *o* συμμαχία 'allies' Is 16.4 (‖ ἀπόλλυμι), ὁ ἀσεβής 26.10 (‖ παύω), ὁ δίκαιος 57.1 (‖ ἀπόλλυμι), εὐφροσύνη καὶ ἀγαλλίαμα ἐκ τῶν ἀμπελώνων σου 16.10.

8. *to be dressed in as office-bearer*: + acc., ἐφουδ 1K 2.28.

9. *to cause to emerge*: + acc. rei, ἔχθραν 'hostility' 1M 13.17.

Cf. ἀντ~, ἐξ~, ἐπαίρω, ἄρσις, ἀρτός, ἄγω, φέρω.

αἰσθάνομαι: fut. ~θηθήσομαι, ~θανθήσομαι; aor. mid. ᾐσθόμην, inf. αἰσθέσθαι, subj. αἰσθηθῶ, opt. αἰσθοίμην.

1. *to grasp mentally*: ‖ ὁράω Is 33.11; + a ὅτι-clause, 49.26, 2K 12.19 *L* (B: νοέω); + an interr. cl., ‖ γινώσκω Jb 23.5. **b**. *to become aware of*: + gen., τοῦ κυρίου Wi 11.13.

2. *to notice by senses* what is happening: Ep Je 19, 23.

Cf. γινώσκω, νοέω, συνίημι, αἴσθησις, αἰσθητήριον, αἰσθητικός, ἀναισθητέω.

αἴσθησις, εως. f.

act of perceiving and discerning: πνεῦμα ~εως as divine gift, Ex 28.3. **b**. *ability to perceive and discern*: Ep Je 41; ἐν ~ει 'with full consciousness (of pain)' Ju 16.17; + ἔννοια Pr 1.4, ‖ σοφία 1.7. **c**. *that which one has perceived and discerned*: Si 22.19.

Cf. γνῶσις, αἰσθάνομαι: Naumann 35, Delling, *TDNT* 1.187f.; Hauspie 2004.119.

αἰσθητήριον, ου. n.ʃ

sense organ: τῆς καρδίας μου Je 4.19; 4M 2.22. Cf. αἰσθάνομαι.

αἰσθητικός, ή, όν.ʃ

perceptive: *s* καρδία Pr 14.10, 30. Cf. αἰσθάνομαι.

αἴσχιστος. ⇒ subs.

αἰσχρός, ά, όν; superl. αἴσχιστος.

1. *ugly in look and appearance*: *s* cattle, βόες .. ~αὶ τῷ εἴδει Ge 41.3, 19 (:: καλαὶ τῷ εἴδει vs. 2, 19 and || πονηραὶ καὶ ~αί vs. 19); ὄψις 'outward look' 41.21.

2. *revolting*: *s* βάσανος 'torture' 3M 3.27.

3. *shameful*: *s* conduct, 4M 16.17.

Cf. αἰσχρῶς, κακός, πονηρός, εὐδιδής, καλός: LSG s.v.

αἰσχρῶς. adv.ʃ

in shameful manner: φεύγων 'fleeing' 2M 11.12; τελευτῶσιν 'they die' Pr 15.10. Cf. αἰσχύνη.

αἰσχύνη, ης. f.

1. *sense of shame*: περιβαλεῖται ~ην 'she will enwrap herself with shame' Mi 7.10; καλύψει σε ἀ. Ob 10; ἐβουλεύσω ~ην τῷ οἴκῳ σου 'you counselled shame to your house' Hb 2.10; + ἐντροπή Ps 34.26. **b**. *loss of face* arising from guilt: αἰ. τῶν προσώπων Ba 1.15, sim. Da 9.7; Is 3.9; arising from failure, 30.3 (|| ὄνειδος), from ill repute, Si 6.1. **c**. *that of which one feels* or *ought to feel ashamed*: ἀπηλλοτριώθησαν εἰς ~ην 'they shamelessly estranged themselves' Ho 9.10; euphemistically with ref. to pudenda, δείξω ἔθνεσι τὴν ~ην σου 'I will show nations your pudenda' Na 3.5 (|| ἀτιμία), Ez 16.36, πατρός 'father-in-law's' 22.10; Is 20.4 (with a comma before τὴν αἰσχύνην *pace* Zgl); προφήτης ~ης 3K 18.19 (Baal's prophet).

Cf. (κατ)αισχύνω, αἰσχυντηρός, αἰσχρῶς, ἀναίδεια, αἰδοῖον, αἰδώς, ἀσχημοσύνη, ἐντροπή, ὄνειδος, ἀτιμία: Trench 66-9.

αἰσχυντηρός, ά, όν.ʃ

bashful, modest: *s* hum., Si 35.10, 42.1, γυνή 26.15. Cf. αἰσχύνη.

αἰσχύνω: fut.pass. ~χυνθήσομαι; impf. ᾐσχυνόμην; aor. ᾔσχυνα, pass. ᾐσχύνθην, impv. αἰσχύνθητι, ptc. αἰσχυνθείς, subj. αἰσχυνθῶ, opt.2pl. αἰσχυνθείητε, 3pl. αἰσχυνθείησαν; pf.pass. ᾔσχυμμαι.

I. act. *to transform into sth shameful*: + acc., χαράν 'a joyous occasion' Jl 1.12.

II. pass. *to be made to feel ashamed* (for some wrongdoing, error): ἐν τῇ βουλῇ αὐτοῦ 'of its decision' Ho 10.6; ἐπὶ τῷ παραπτώματι αὐτῆς 'of its transgression' Zc 9.5; ἐπὶ τοῖς Αἰθίοψιν 'over the Ethiopians' Is 20.5, + ἀτιμόω Je 22.22; opp. εὐφραίνομαι Is 65.13; ἀπὸ καυχήσεως 'because of boasting' Je 12.13; || καταισχύνω Ps 6.11.

III. mid. *to feel ashamed*: Ge 2.25; + cogn. acc., αἰσχύνην Is 42.17; + ἐντρέπομαι 41.11, Ez 36.32; ἀπό τινος 'by virtue of respect due to' περί τινος 'over some deed' - ἀπὸ πατρὸς καὶ μητρὸς περὶ πορνείας Si 41.17; || ἀπό τινος 'over some deed' - ἀπὸ ὁράσεως γυναικὸς ἑταίρας 'over staring at a woman of the streets' 41.20; + acc. pers., "before our forefathers" 4M 9.2; + ptc., Wi 13.17. **b**. embarrassment: Jd 3.25.

2. *to show respect to*: + acc., πρεσβύτην 'an elderly person' Ba 4.15; πρόσωπον Pr 22.26, πρόσωπα δικαίων 28.21.

3. *to feel overawed by*: + acc. pers., Jb 32.21 (|| ἐντρέπομαι); w. negative connotation, + φοβέομαι Pr 29.25.

4. *to feel diffident about and hesitate* to do: + inf., ὁμολογῆσαι ἐφ' ἁμαρτίαις σου 'to admit your sins' Si 4.26; 2E 8.22 (|| ἐντρέπομαι 1E 8.51).

Cf. αἰσχύνη, ἐπ~, καταισχύνω, ἐντρέπω: Schmidt 3.538-41; Bultmann, *TDNT* 1.189.

αἰτέω: fut. αἰτήσω, mid. αἰτήσομαι; aor. ᾔτησα, impv. αἴτησον, subj. αἰτήσω, inf. αἰτῆσαι, mid. ᾐτησάμην, impv. αἴτησαι, inf. αἰτήσασθαι, ptc. αἰτησάμενος; pass.ptc. αἰτηθείς.

1. *to ask for*: abs. ὁ ἄρχων αἰτεῖ Mi 7.3; παρά τινος + acc., αἰτήσει γυνὴ παρὰ γείτονος .. σκεύη '.. from a neighbour some vessels' .. Ex 3.22; || θέλω Ps 39.7; λόγον ᾔτησεν 'asked to have a word' 4M 5.14; τινά τι Jb 6.22 (|| ἐπιδέομαι), αἰτοῦσί με .. κρίσιν Is 58.2. **b**. mid., + of the acc. of the thing asked for, τί κύριος .. αἰτεῖται παρὰ σοῦ De 10.12, Αἰτεῖσθε παρὰ κυρίου ὑετόν 'Ask the Lord for rain' Zc 10.1, αἴτησαι σεαυτῷ σημεῖον παρὰ κυρίου Is 7.11, πόλιν Jo 19.50; || ἀξιόω 1E 4.46; + inf. cl., τὴν ψυχὴν ʳL: τῇ ψυχῇ˥ αὐτοῦ ἀποθανεῖν 3K 19.4; τινα εἰς ἀπώλειαν 'to be destroyed' Es E 13; + cogn. acc., αἴτημα 1K 1.17, αἴτησιν μίαν αἰτοῦμαι παρὰ σοῦ 3K 2.16; τινά τι, Jo 15.18 (|| τι παρά τινος Jd 1.14), Jo 14.12, ζωὴν ᾐτήσατό σε Ps 20.5. **c**. mid. *to ask for permission to leave the presence of*: ᾐτησάμην παρὰ τοῦ βασιλέως 'I took leave of the king' Ne 13.6. ***d**. mid. *to ask for a favour of being allowed* to do sth: + ptc., δεόμενός σου Od 12.13.

2. *to borrow*: + acc. and παρά τινος, Ex 22.14.

Cf. αἴτημα, αἴτησις, δέομαι, ἐρωτάω: Schmidt 1.193f.; Stählin, *TDNT* 1.190-2

αἴτημα, ατος. n.

that which one asks for: Ps 105.15, τῆς καρδίας σου 36.4, ψυχῆς PSol 6.6; + ἀξίωμα Es 5.7, 7.2; cogn. obj. of αἰτέω 1K 1.17. Cf. αἰτέω.

αἴτησις, εως. f.

act of asking for: as cogn. obj., Jd 8.24 A (B: αἴτημα), 3K 2.16. **b**. *that which one asks for*: Jb 6.8.

Cf. αἰτέω, αἴτημα, δέησις.

αἰτία, ας. f.

1. *punishable guilt*: μείζων ἡ αἰτία μου Ge 4.13.

2. *accusation*: βασιλική 'by a king' Jb 18.14; ἐν ~ᾳ φόνου 'charged with murder' Pr 28.17. **b**. *reason for accusation*: 1M 9.10.

3. *that which causes sth*: 1E 2.19, 4M 1.16.

Cf. αἰτιάομαι, αἴτιος.

αἰτιάομαι: fut. αἰτιάσομαι.ʃ

to lay the blame at the door of: + acc., τὸν θεόν Pr 19.3, τὸν καιρόν 'the current (economic situation)' Si 29.5; 4M 2.19. Cf. αἰτία, ἐγκαλέω, κατηγορέω: Schmidt 1.150-4.

αἴτιος, α, ον.

responsible for a wrongdoing or sth that ought not to have happened: + τοῦ inf., "the downfall of a tyranny" 4M 1.11; for a punishable deed, Su 53 TH (LXX ἔνοχος); + gen. of crime, ἀπωλείας '(attempted) destruction' Bel 42, τῆς ὅλης κακίας 2M 4.47, ἀθῴων αἱμάτων 'innocent death' Es 7.23 *L* (ο' μέτοχος 'partaker'). **b**. *bearing the responsibility for*: + gen., τῶν ψυχῶν 'for (the security of) the lives' 1K 22.22.

Cf. αἰτία, ἔνοχος.

αἰφνίδιος, ον.ʃ

unexpected, unforeseen: *s* sth undesirable, ἀφασία 'onslaught of aphasia' 2M 14.17, ταραχή 'disruption' 3M 3.24; φόβος and + ἀπροσδόκητος Wi 17.15. Cf. αἰφνιδίως, ἐξαίφνης, ἀπροσδόκητος: Spicq 1.49-52.

αἰφνιδίως. adv.ʃ

unexpectedly: 2M 5.5, 14.22. Cf. αἰφνίδιος, ἄφνω.

αἰχμαλωσία, ας. f.

1. *state of being a captive*, 'captivity': πορεύσονται οἱ βασιλεῖς αὐτῆς ἐν ~ᾳ 'her kings will go as captives' Am 1.15; πορευθῶσιν ἐν ~ᾳ πρὸ προσώπου τῶν ἐχθρῶν αὐτῶν '.. ahead of their enemies' 9.4; ἐξελεύσεται τὸ ἥμισυ τῆς πόλεως ἐν ~ᾳ 'half of the city will leave in captivity' Zc 14.2; ἀποδώσονται αὐτοὺς εἰς ~αν 'they will sell them into captivity' Jl 3.8; τὰ ἐκ τῆς ~ας 'the things of the captivity' Zc 6.10.

2. collectively, *captives, people residing in a foreign land as a consequence of lost war*: ἐν τῷ ἐπιστρέφειν με τὴν ~αν τοῦ λαοῦ μου 'when I bring back the captives of my people' Ho 6.11; also + ἐπιστρέφω Am 9.14, Jl 3.1, Zp 3.20; + ἀποστρέφω 2.7 – in all these places the noun is possibly abstract, i.e. sense **1**. in the sense of 'to turn the captivity'; as a cogn. obj., αἰχμαλωτεῦσαι αὐτοὺς ~αν Am 1.6; συνέκλεισαν ~αν τοῦ Σαλωμων εἰς τὴν Ἰδουμαίαν 'they confined Solomon's captives in Idumea' Am 1.9; numerous as sand, συνάξει ὡς ἄμμον ~αν Hb 1.9; applied to cavalry horses, ἵππων σου Am 4.10; ‖ ἀποικία Je 37.18; αἰ. παροικίας 1E 5.7. For single captives, αἰχμάλωτος is used. **b**. *place of captivity*: εἴσελθε εἰς τὴν ~αν Ez 3.11; 3.15, 11.24.

3. coll., *prisoners of war*: κατεπρονόμευσαν ἐξ αὐτῶν ~αν Nu 21.1; ‖ σκῦλα, προνομή 31.12; poss. including non-combatants, Is 20.4.

Cf. αἰχμαλωτεύω, αἰχμαλωτίς, and αἰχμάλωτος.

αἰχμαλωτεύω: fut. αἰχμαλωτεύσω, pass. ~θήσομαι; aor. ᾐχμαλώτευσα, inf. αἰχμαλωτεῦσαι, subj. ~τεύσω, ptc. ~τεύσας, pass. ᾐχμαλωτεύθην; pf.pass.3sg ᾐχμαλώτευται, ptc.pass. ᾐχμαλωτευμένος.

to take as prisoner (of war), *to take captive*: + acc. pers. Ge 14.14; πάντα τὰ σώματα αὐτῶν καὶ πᾶσαν τὴν ἀποσκευὴν αὐτῶν καὶ τὰς γυναῖκας αὐτῶν 'all their slaves and all their little ones and ..' 34.29; δύναμιν αὐτοῦ Ob 11; + acc. rei, ἀποσκευήν 'baggage' 1C 5.21; + a cogn. obj., αἰχμαλωσίαν τοῦ Σαλωμων Am 1.6; + an emphasising ptc., αἰχμαλωτευομένη ~τευθήσεται 5.5; ᾐχμαλωτεύθησαν ἀπὸ σοῦ 'they have been taken away from you as captives' Mi 1.16.

Cf. αἰχμαλωτίζω and αἰχμαλωσία.

αἰχμαλωτίζω: fut.pass. αἰχμαλωτισθήσομαι; aor. ᾐχμαλώτισα, ptc. ~τίσας, pass. ~τισθείς, inf. ~τισθῆναι; pf. ᾐχμαλώτικα.

Syn. w. αἰχμαλωτεύω (q.v.): λαὸς Συρίας Am 1.5 (v.l. ~τευθήσεται). **b**. metaph.: "her beauty captivated his soul" Ju 16.9 (‖ ἁρπάζω), cf. συναρπάζω.

Cf. αἰχμαλωτεύω.

αἰχμαλωτίς, ίδος. f.ʃ

person kept in confinement and unable to escape, 'captive': ἀπήγαγες τὰς θυγατέρας μου ὡς ~ίδας 'led my daughters away like captives' Ge 31.26; ἐν τῷ λάκκῳ 'in the dungeon' Ex 12.29 (unlikely a female prisoner). Cf. αἰχμαλωσία, αἰχμάλωτος.

αἰχμάλωτος, ον.

1. *captured*: *s* animal, ~ον γένηται Ex 22.10.

2. subst., *person to be moved to a foreign land as a consequence of lost war*: αἰ. ἀχθήσεται ἀπὸ τῆς γῆς αὐτοῦ Am 7.11, 17; εἰς μετοικεσίαν πορεύσεται αἰ. Na 3.10.

Cf. αἰχμαλωσία.

αἰών, ῶνος. m.

1. *very long stretch of time ahead*: adv. acc., τὸν ~να ζήσονται Zc 1.5; πάντα τὸν ~να 'for ever' To 6.18 𝔊II; βασιλεύων τὸν ~να καὶ ἐπ' ~να καὶ ἔτι Ex 15.18; εἰς τὸν ~να 'for ever' Ge 3.22, De 13.16; Jl 3.20 (‖ εἰς γενεὰς γενεῶν), Is 57.16 (‖ διὰ παντός), Ps 48.10 (‖ εἰς τέλος); εἰς τὸν ~να τοῦ ~ος 9.6, εἰς τοὺς ~νας 47.15, εἰς τοὺς ~νας τῶν ~νων 83.5, To 14.15 𝔊II, 4M 18.24; εἰς πάντας τοὺς ~νας To 13.4; εἰς τὸν ~να εἰς τὰς γενεὰς αὐτῶν Ex 40.13; εἰς τὸν ~να καὶ ἐπέκεινα 'for ever and even beyond' Mi 4.5, .. καὶ ἔτι To 13.18 𝔊II, PSol 9.11; εἰς τὸν ~να χρόνον 'for a long time to come' Ex 14.13, Is 13.20 (‖ διὰ πολλῶν γενεῶν), 34.10; ἐν τῷ ~νι 'all the time, always' Wi 4.2; ἕως τοῦ ~νος

Ge 13.15; ἕως ~ος καὶ ἕως τοῦ ~νος τῶν ~ων Da 7.19; ἕως ~νος Ma 1.4; δι' αἰώνων Si 17.8¶. **b**. w. neg., εἰς τὸν ~να 'never ever' Si 12.10. **c**. attrib. gen.: θεμέλιον ~νος 'everlasting foundation' Si 1.15, εὐφροσύνην ~νος 2.9; ὄνομα ~νος 'enduring reputation' 15.6, διαθήκη ~ος 17.12, γενεαὶ ~ων 24.33; ἀνάπαυσις ~νος 30.17 (ref. to death), κοίμησις ~νος 'eternal sleep' 46.19, νεκροὶ ~νος La 3.6, Ps 142.3; οἶκος ~νος 'grave' Ec 12.5.

2. *remote past*: καθὼς αἱ ἡμέραι τοῦ ~νος Am 9.11, Mi 7.14, cf. De 32.7 (ǁ γενεαὶ γενεῶν); Ma 3.4 (ǁ καὶ καθὼς τὰ ἔτη τὰ ἔμπροσθεν); κατὰ τὰς ἡμέρας τοῦ ~νος Si 50.23; ἐξ ἡμερῶν ~νος Mi 5.2, ἐξ ~νος 1E 2.19; πρὸ (τοῦ) ~νος 'long ago' Ps 73.12, Si 24.9, To 6.18; πρὸ τῶν ~ων Ps 54.20; ἀπ' ~νος 'long ago (from now)' Je 2.20; οἱ γίγαντες οἱ ἀπ' ~νος 'the giants of the olden days' Ge 6.4, λαὸς ~νος Ez 26.20; ὅμοιος αὐτῷ οὐ γέγονεν ἀπὸ τοῦ ~νος 'the like of it has not happened for a long time' Jl 2.2, for a similar expression, cp. Joh 9.32 and a 3rd (CE) cent. papyrus, *P.Oxy*.42 (1974) 3065 discussed at *ND* 4.58. **b**. *the whole of one's past*: Ps 89.8.

3. combining **1** and **2**: πρὸ τοῦ ~νου καὶ εἰς τὸν ~να Si 42.21; ἀπὸ τοῦ νῦν καὶ ἕως εἰς τὸν ~να Mi 4.7, ἐξ ~νος καὶ ἕως ~νος Je 7.7, ἀπ' ~νος καὶ ἕως ~νος 25.5. Perh. belongs here σὺ εἶ ὁ κύριος ὁ θεὸς τῶν ~νων Si 36.22.

Cf. αἰώνιος, γενεά: Shipp 49f.; Sasse, *TDNT* 1.199-201.

αἰώνιος, ον.

1. *lasting for very long, everlasting*: εἰς γενεὰς ~ους 'for eternal generations' Ge 9.12; *s* διαθήκη 9.16, Nu 25.13, Is 24.5, 2K 23.5; πρόσταγμα 'prescription' Je 5.22; θεὸς αἰ. Ge 21.33 and Is 40.28 (a title of κύριος), without θεός Ba 4.10, 24; *s* κάτοχος 'eternal check' Jn 2.7, πορεία Hb 3.6*b*, εὐφροσύνη Is 35.10, ἀγαλλίαμα 51.11; τόπος To 3.6 (for the dead); ὄλεθρος 'perdition' 4M 10.15 (ǁ ἀΐδιος), πῦρ 'fire (of punishment)' 12.12 (ǁ πυκνός 'frequent'), πύλη 'gate' Ps 23.7.

2. *having existed very long, long past*, 'ancient': *s* ὄρος Mi 2.9, βουνός Hb 3.6*a*; ἐμνήσθη ἡμερῶν ~ων 'he remembered the olden days' Is 63.11, ἔτη Ps 76.6 (ǁ ἀρχαῖος).

Cf. αἰών, ἀεί, ἀειγενής, ἀέναος, ἀΐδιος, βεβαίως, ἀρχαῖος, παλαιός, νέος, ἀκαριαῖος, βραχύς.

ἀκαθαρσία, ας. f.

1. *religiously* or *morally impure object*: w. ref. to female pudenda, τὴν ~αν αὐτῆς Ho 2.10.

2. *ceremonially unclean state*: Le 7.10; arising from menstruation, 18.19, Ez 22.10; of fruit-trees, Le 19.23; of animals, 20.25.

3. *immorality, moral* or *religious depravity*: Mi 2.10; ψυχῆς Pr 6.16; deed characterised by such, and in pl. Na 3.6 (ǁ βδελυγμός), Ez 39.24 (ǁ ἀνομήματα).

Cf. ἀκάθαρτος, μάκρυμμα.

ἀκάθαρτος, ον.

Opp. καθαρός (q.v.), *impure*: in ritual, ceremonial sense, ἅψηται παντὸς πράγματος ~ου 'touches any unclean thing whatsoever' Le 5.2; ἐπὶ ψυχῇ ἀνθρώπου 'on account of a human corpse' Nu 9.6; subst. and ǁ βέβηλος, Le 10.10, + ἀπερίτμητος Is 52.1; *s* food, Ho 8.13; γῆ, i.e. outside of Israel. **b**. in religious, moral sense: *s* τὸ πνεῦμα τὸ ἀ. Zc 13.2; ~α χείλη 'impure lips' Is 6.5; hum., 35.8.

Cf. ἀκαθαρσία, βέβηλος, καθαρός.

ἄκαιρος, ον.ʃ

ill-timed: *s* μῦθος 'story' Si 20.19, διήγησις 22.6. Cf. καιρός, ἀκαίρως, ἄωρος, εὔκαιρος, καίριος.

ἀκαίρως. adv.ʃ

in ill-timed manner: Si 35.4. Cf. ἄκαιρος, εὐκαίρως.

ἀκακία, ας. f.

moral *innocence*: Ps 7.9 (ǁ δικαιοσύνη), τῆς καρδίας 77.72. Cf. ἄκακος.

ἄκακος, ον.

1. *impeccable*: *s* hum., morally Ps 24.21 (+ εὐθής), Jb 2.3 (+ ἀληθινός, ἄμεμπτος, θεοσεβής), 8.20 (:: ἀσεβής), ǁ χρηστός Pr 2.21; subst. m. hum., ǁ the god-fearing, opp. the lawless PSol 12.4.

2. *simple-minded, naive*: *s* blissfully ignorant, sacrificial lamb, Je 11.19, νοῦς 'mind' Wi 4.12 (ǁ καλός); subst.m. hum., Pr 1.4 (wanting in πανουργία 'astuteness'); ǁ ἀπαίδευτος 8.5; opp. πανοῦργος 'clever, astute' 14.15 (gullible), 21.11. Cf. *BA* ad Pr 1.4 and Lampe, s.v. ἀκακία, ἄκακος.

Cf. ἀκακία: Trench 206-8; Spicq 1.53-5.

ἀκάλυπτος, ον.ʃ

uncovered: *s* face, To 2.9 𝔊[I]; head, Ep Je 30 (mourners). Cf. ἀκατακάλυπτος, καλύπτω, ἀκαλύπτως.

ἀκαλύπτως. adv.ʃ

unveiled: 3M 4.6.

ἀκάν, νος. m.ʃ Also spelled ἀκχάν.*

thistle: 4K 14.9.

ἄκανθα, ας. f.

thorny or *prickly plant*: growing on barren, desolate land, ~αι ἐν τοῖς σκηνώμασιν αὐτῶν Ho 9.6, sim. ~αι καὶ τρίβολοι Ge 3.18 (farmers' curse) and σταφυλὴν .. ~ας Is 5.2; χέρσος καὶ ἄ. 'barren land and ..' 7.24, sim. 7.23, 25; fig. of painful experience, Ps 31.4. Cf. ἀκάνθινος, τρίβολος: Shipp 108f.

ἀκάνθινος, η, ον.ʃ

having thorns: *s* ξύλον Is 34.13. Cf. ἄκανθα.

ἀκάρδιος, ον.ʃ

wanting in sound judgement and discretion: + μωρός Je 5.21; Pr 10.13, 17.16; Si 6.20 (ǁ ἀπαί-

ἀκούω: fut. ἀκούσω (Is 6.9), ἀκούσομαι, ptc. ἀκουσόμενος, pass. ἀκουσθήσομαι; aor. ἤκουσα, subj. ἀκούσω, impv. ἄκουσον, ptc. ἀκούσας, inf. ἀκοῦσαι, opt.3s ἀκούσαι, pass. ἠκούσθην, impv.3s ἀκουσθήτω, subj.3s ἀκουσθῇ, inf. ἀκουσθῆναι; pf. ἀκήκοα, ptc. ἀκηκοώς, pass.3s ἤκουσται; plpf. ἀκηκόειν.

1. of sense perception: *to hear*, + acc. τὸ ὄνομα Ιακωβ 'the name of J. (mentioned)' Ge 29.13; τὴν ἀγγελίαν σου 'the news about you' Na 3.19; φωνήν Ge 3.8, pass. Is 15.4; ῥήματα 27.34, 31.1; + gen. rei ῥημάτων 24.52; τῆς κραυγῆς αὐτῶν Ex 3.7; φωνῆς μου Jn 2.3; τῆς φωνῆς κυρίου Hg 1.12; + gen. pers., ἤκουσα αὐτῶν λεγόντων .. Ge 37.17; περί σου λεγόντων .. 41.15; ἵνα ἀκούσῃ ὁ λαὸς λαλοῦντός μου Ex 19.9; + ὅτι– ἐν τῷ ἀκοῦσαι αὐτὸν ὅτι ὕψωσα τὴν φωνήν μου 'on hearing me raising my voice' Ge 39.15. **b**. *to hear the sound of*: pass., ***o*** builder's instruments, 3K 6.7. **c**. *to learn of*: οὐ μὴ ἀκουσθῇ τὰ ἔργα σου 'your deeds will not be heard of' Na 2.14; ἠκούσθη ταῦτα εἰς τὰ ὦτα κυρίου Is 5.9; ὀνειδισμοὺς Μωαβ 'learn (by hearing) of calumnies of Moab' Zp 2.8, τὴν ὕβριν Μωαβ Is 16.6, τὰ κακά 'the calamities' Jb 2.11; + ὅτι (news): Ge 14.14, Zc 8.23; + acc. and inf., 2M 11.24; + acc. and ptc., 3M 4.12. **d**. pass. *to be made heard*: μὴ ἀκούσθῃ ἐκ τοῦ στόματος ὑμῶν 'should not be mentioned by you' Ex 23.13; ***o*** voice, Jd 18.25. **e**. ‖ βλέπω: Is 6.9.

2. attentively, with intention, *to listen*: abs., Ge 27.5 (foll. by a gen.abs.), Nu 23.18 (‖ ἐνωτίζω), 'Αναγγείλατε .. καὶ ἀκουσθήτω 'Announce .. and be heard' Je 4.5; + acc., ***o*** λόγον 'to heed sbd's advice' Ju 7.9, λόγον κυρίου Ho 4.1; τὸν λόγον τοῦτον Am 3.1, 4.1; ψαλμὸν ὀργάνων σου οὐκ ἀκούσομαι 5.23; τὰς ἐντολὰς κυρίου De 11.27, 28; ταῦτα Ho 5.1; λόγους Mi 1.2; φωνήν σου Mi 6.1; τὴν κρίσιν τοῦ κυρίου 6.2; τοὺς λόγους τούτους ἐκ στόματος τῶν προφητῶν Zc 8.9; ἐὰν ἀκούσητε .. θῆσθε εἰς τὴν καρδίαν ὑμῶν Ma 2.2; + εἰς - εἰς τὰ ἐνύπνια Je 36.8; τί τινος (pers.) Jo 1.17; + ἐπί τινι - ἐπὶ τῷ κρίματι αὐτῶν 4K 17.40B. **b**. approvingly and sympathetically: + gen. rei, φωνῆς αὐτῆς Ge 21.12; τοῦ ἐνυπνίου τούτου 37.6; τῆς φωνῆς κυρίου Hg 1.12; τῆς φωνῆς τῆς γυναικός Ge 3.17; ‖ ἐνωτίζομαι 4.23; ἤκουσεν Μωυσῆς τῆς φωνῆς τοῦ γαμβροῦ, καὶ ἐποίησεν ὅσα αὐτῷ εἶπεν Ex 18.24; ἀκοῇ ἀκούσητε τῆς ἐμῆς φωνῆς καὶ φυλάξητε τὴν διαθήκην μου 19.5; τῶν λόγων τοῦ προφήτου De 13.3; τοῦ νόμου αὐτοῦ Is 42.24, ‖ ὑπακούω 2M 7.30; + gen. pers., ἄκουσον ἡμῶν Ge 23.6; 27.8, 28.7; + cogn. dat., ἀκοῇ ἀκούσῃς τῆς φωνῆς τοῦ κυρίου Ex 15.26; 23.22. **c**. + λόγον and ‖ φωνῆς: ἀκούετε τῆς φωνῆς μου .. ἀκούετε τοὺς λόγους μου Is 18.23, sim. 32.9. **d**. opp. ἀπειθέω Ez 3.27. **e**. pass., ἀκουσθήσῃ 'you will get a hearing' Si 36.5.

3. *to consent*: ἤκουσαν οἱ ἀδελφοὶ αὐτοῦ Ge 37.27.

4. *to hear and comprehend*: ἵνα μὴ ἀκούσωσιν ἕκαστος τὴν φωνὴν τοῦ πλησίον 'so that they will not understand one another' Ge 11.7; ἀκούει Ιωσηφ· ὁ γὰρ ἑρμηνευτὴς ἀνὰ μέσον αὐτῶν ἦν 'Joseph understood, for there was an interpreter between them' 42.23, see also 11.7, 4K 18.26 ‖ Is 36.11; + gen. rei, φωνῆς De 28.49; Je 5.15. See Aes., *Prom.* 448.

5. *to hear oneself called*: προδότης 'traitor' 2M 10.13. **b**. *to hear oneself spoken of in public*: καλῶς 'well spoken-of' 2M 14.37.

On the syntax (gen. or acc.), see Helbing, *Kasus*. 150ff.; BDF, § 173, 416.1; Hauspie 2005.

Cf. ἀκοή, ἀκουστός, ἀκουστής, ἀντ~, εἰσ~, ἐν~, ἐπ~, ὑπακούω, φιληκοΐα, ἐνωτίζομαι, ἀκροάομαι, ἀνήκοος: Schmidt 1.273-7.

ἄκρα, ας. f.

citadel built on a steep rock overhanging a town (LSJ): De 3.11; Δαυιδ 'of D.' Is 22.9; metaph., ***s*** mind, 4M 7.5. Cf. ἀκρόπολις, φρούριον.

ἀκρασία, ας. f.ʃ

lack of self-control: pl., manifestations of such, ‖ ἁμαρτία PSol 4.3. Cf. ἀκρατής, ἐγκράτεια. Del. 1M 6.26 v.l.

ἀκρατής, ές.ʃ

not having command over: *+ dat., γλώσσῃ Pr 27.20a.

ἄκρατος, ον.ʃ

unmixed, neat: ***s*** οἶνος Ps 7.49, Je 32.1, 3M 5.2, PSol 8.14. Cf. κεράννυμι.

ἀκριβάζω: aor.pass. ἠκριβάσθην, impv.mid. ἀκρίβασαι.ʃ *

1. *to prove accurate*: pass. and ***o*** hum., προφήτης 'as a prophet' Si 46.15.

2. *to describe accurately*: περί τινος 'about ..' 2K 1.19.

Cf. ἀκριβής, ἐξακριβάζω: Caird 1968.456.

ἀκρίβασμα, ατος. n.ʃ

accurate instruction: divine, + πρόσταγμα, κρίμα, ἐντολή 3K 2.3. Cf. ἀκριβάζω.

ἀκριβασμός, οῦ. m.ʃ *

accurate investigation: καρδίας Jd 5.15A (B: ἐξετασμός). Cf. Caird 1968.456f.; Walters 205f.; LSG s.v.

ἀκρίβεια, ας. f.

precision: ἐν ~ᾳ Si 16.25 (‖ ἐν σταθμῷ), ζυγοῦ καὶ σταθμίων 'of scales and weights' 42.4. **b**. *precise information*: Da 7.16. Cf. ἀκριβής.

ἀκριβής, ές.
precise: *s* παροιμία Si 18.29, πανουργία 19.24, ἐπιστήμη 35.3, μαρτυρία 34.24 (|| πιστός vs. 23), ὅραμα Da 2.45 LXX, λόγος 6.12 LXX. Cf. ἀκριβάζω, ἀκρίβασμα, ἀκριβασμός, ἀκριβεία, ἀκριβῶς.

ἀκριβῶς. adv.ʃ
accurately, with precision: ἐξετάσωσιν 'examine' De 19.18; εἰκάσαι 'to infer' Wi 19.18; ἐζήτουν ἀ. περὶ τοῦ θηρίου 'investigated .. about the animal' Da TH 7.19. Cf. ἀκριβής.

ἀκρίς, ίδος. f.
grasshopper: sg. used collectively, destructive of crops, De 28.38; τὰ κατάλοιπα τῆς κάμπης κατέφαγεν ἡ ἀ. 'locusts ate up what had been left over by caterpillars' Jl 1.4; ἡ ἀ. καὶ ὁ βροῦχος καὶ ἡ ἐρυσίβη καὶ ἡ κάμπη 2.25; ἀ. ἐπιβεβηκυῖα ἐπὶ φραγμόν 'locusts which landed on a hedge' Na 3.17; ἀτμὶς ἀπὸ ~ίδων Ho 13.3 (v. s.v. ἀτμίς); plague as divine punishment, ἐπάγω ~ίδα πολλὴν ἐπὶ πάντα τὰ ὅριά σου Ex 10.4; symbol of smallness, Nu 13.34; pl. in a figure of swarming assailants, Je 28.14, ὡς ~ίδων πλῆθος 28.27; sg. collectively, πολὺς .. ὡς ἀ. Ju 2.20, ἀ. εἰς πλῆθος Jd 6.5. Cf. ἀττέλεβος, ἀττάκης, βροῦχος, ὀφιομάχης, κάμπη.

ἀκρίτως. adv.ʃ
unjustly: "you are destroying us .." 1M 2.37; 15.33.

ἀκρόαμα, ατος. n.ʃ
entertainment with music and stories: Si 35.4. Cf. ἀκροάομαι.

ἀκροάομαι: fut. ἀκροάσομαι; aor.impv. ἀκρόασαι.
to listen attentively: + acc. rei, τὰ πάντα Wi 1.10 (*s* οὖς), διήγησιν 'discourse' Si 6.35; + cogn. obj., ἀκρόασιν πολλήν Is 21.7. Cf. ἀκροατής, ἀκρόαμα, ἀκρόασις, ἀκούω, εἰσακούω, προσέχω: Schmidt 1.277-79.

ἀκρόασις, εως. f.
attentive listening: Γίνου ταχὺς ἐν ~ει σου 'Be quick in ..' Si 5.11, cf. ταχὺς εἰς τὸ ἀκοῦσαι Jas 1.19; as cogn. obj., ἀκρόασαι ~ιν πολλήν Is 21.7. **b**. *sign of response to vocal signal*: 3K 18.26, 4K 4.31.
Cf. ἀκοή, ἀκροάομαι, ἐπακρόασις.

ἀκροατής, οῦ. m.ʃ
attentive listener: ref to diviner (?), συνετός Is 3.3; οὖς ~οῦ 'the ear of ..' Si 3.29; prol. II. Cf. ἀκροάομαι, ἀκουστής.

ἀκροβυστία, ας.*
foreskin: to be circumcised, περιτμηθήσεσθε τὴν σάρκα τῆς ~ας 'you shall have the flesh of your foreskin excised around' Ge 17.11; τὴν ~αν τοῦ υἱοῦ αὐτῆς Ex 4.25. **b**. metaph.: περιέλεσθε τὴν ~αν τῆς καρδίας ὑμῶν 'Remove ..' Je 4.4.
Cf. περιτομή: Schmidt, *TDNT* 1.225f.; Tosato 1982; BDF § 120.4.

ἀκρογωνιαῖος, ον.ʃ*
situated at the extreme angle: λίθον .. ~ον 'corner (foundation)-stone' Is 28.16.

ἀκρόδρυα, ων. n.pl.
"*fruits grown on upper branches of trees*, esp. *hard-shelled fruits*" (LSJ): To 1.7 𝔊II; Ct 4.13. Cf. καρπός.

ἀκρόπολις, εως. f.
citadel: of Jerusalem, 2M 4.12. Cf. ἄκρα.

ἄκρος, α, ον.
situated at the farthest end: *s* θεμέλιος οὐρανοῦ 'the base of the sky' Is 13.5. **b**. subst. n., *farthest end, extremity*: of a stone pillar (στήλη), Ge 28.18; of a staff (ῥάβδος) 47.31; τὸ ἄ. τοῦ ἱματίου αὐτοῦ 'the skirt of his garment' Hg 2.12*bis*; ἄκρον χειρός .. ἄ. ποδός 'thumb .. big toe' Ex 29.20, Jd 1.6 (pl.); τοῦ οὐρανοῦ De 4.32; ἀπ' ~ου τοῦ οὐρανοῦ ἕως ~ου τοῦ οὐρανοῦ 30.4; ἀπ' ~ου τῆς γῆς ἕως ~ου τῆς γῆς De 13.7, 28.64, Je 12.12; ἐπ' ~ου μετεώρου 'on the top end (of olive trees)' Is 17.6; pl. ἀπ' ~ων ὁρίων Αἰγύπτου ἕως ~ων 'from one end of the territory of Egypt to the other' Ge 47.21; ἕως ~ων τῆς γῆς 'to the ends of the earth' Mi 5.5, ἐκ τῶν τεσσάρων ~ων τοῦ οὐρανοῦ 'from the four ends ..' Je 25.16. **c**. vertically: of a mountain, Ex 34.2; ἐπ' ἄκρων τῶν ὀρέων Is 2.2, τῶν τειχέων 'of the walls' Pr 1.21; ἀπ' ~ου τοῦ ὄρους τοῦ ὑψηλοῦ Is 28.4. **d**. used pred.: ἐν ~ῳ τῷ σκήπτρῳ 'with the tip of the staff' 1K 14.43 (*L* τοῦ σκήπτρου).
Cf. ἀκρωτήριον, ἀκμή: Schmidt 3.86f.

ἀκρότομος, ον.ʃ
having vertical, steep face: *s* πέτρα 'rock' De 8.15, Wi 11.4, Ps 135.16, Si 40.15; ὄρος Jb 40.20, λίθος '(stone-) slab' 3K 6.7; subst., Ps 113.8 (f. and || πέτρα and || Wi 11.4), Si 48.17, Jb 28.9¶. **b**. *sharp at edges*: *s* stone, Jo 5.2; stone-knife, 5.3.

ἀκροφύλαξ, ακος. m.ʃ
citadel guard: 4M 3.13. Cf. φύλαξ.

ἀκρωτηριάζω.ʃ
to cut off hands and feet of: mode of torture, + acc. pers., 2M 7.4, 4M 10.20.

ἀκρωτήριον, ου. n.ʃ
extremities, farthest end: of body, hands and feet, fingers and toes, and subst.n.pl., of sacrificial animal, Le 4.11; ἀπὸ τῶν πόλεων ~ων αὐτοῦ 'from its outlying cities' Ez 25.9; w. ref. to the far north, Jb 37.9; subst.n.sg., ἀ. πέτρας 1K 14.4. Cf. ἄκρος: Schmidt 3.88.

ἀκτίς, ῖνος. f.ʃ
ray: of the sun, Si 43.4, Wi 2.4, 16.27.

ἀκύματος, ον.ʃ
unaffected by troubles, 'calm': *s* βίος 'life' Es B 2 o' (*L* ἀτάραχος). Cf. ἀτάραχος.

ἄκυρος, ον.ʃ

of no consequence: *s* βουλή Pr 1.25, λόγος 5.7.

ἀκυρόω: aor. ἠκύρωσα, inf. ἀκυρῶσαι, subj. ἀκυρώσω.

1. *to repel, beat off* an assailant: metaph., + acc., οἶστρον '(carnal) impulse' 4M 2.3, ^παθήματα^ 'passions' 2.18; pass., *o* ἐπιθυμίαι 'desires' 2.1.

2. *to deny the validity of, belittle*: *o* directives (|| παραβαίνω) 1E 6.31; + acc., βουλήν Es 1.12 *L*, πρόσταγμα 1.16 *L*; ἐπινοίας 'designs' 4M 17.2 (|| καταλύω). **b.** *to treat as valueless and meaningless*: + acc., δόξαν '(one's) reputation' 4M 5.18.

Cf. ἀθετέω, ἐξουδενόω, κυρόω.

ἀκχάν. ⇒ ἀκάν.

ἀκώλυτος, ον.ʃ

having complete freedom of action: *s* spirit of Wisdom, Wi 7.22. Cf. κωλύω.

ἄκων. adv.ʃ

against one's own will: to transgress, Jb 14.17; to do a favour, 4M 11.12. Cf. ἀκουσιάζομαι, ἑκών.

ἀλάβαστρος, ου. m.ʃ

vase: 4K 21.13B (*L* πυξίον).

ἀλαζονεία, ας. f.

arrogant, pretentious overestimation of self: Wi 5.8 (|| ὑπερηφανία), 2M 9.8; + κενοδοξία, μεγαλαυχία 4M 2.15, + κενοδοξία 8.19. Cf. ἀλαζονεύομαι, γαυρίαμα, κόμπος: Schmidt 4.209f.

ἀλαζονεύομαι.ʃ

to speak with ἀλαζονεία (q.v.): ἐνώπιον βασιλέως 'in front of a king' Pr 25.6. **b.** *to claim with* ἀλαζονεία sbd or sth to be: + double acc., πατέρα θεόν Wi 2.16.

Cf. ἀλαζονεία, ἀλαζών, μεγαλύνω.

ἀλαζών, όνος. m./f.ʃ

person inclined to the attitude of ἀλαζονεία (q.v.): ἀνὴρ ἀ. Hb 2.5; υἱοὶ ~όνων 'young lions(?)' Jb 28.8 (|| λέων), + αὐθάδης 'self-willed,' θρασύς 'bold' Pr 21.24. Cf. ἀλαζονεία, μεγαλύνω, ὑπερήφανος: Trench 98-105; Delling, *TDNT* 1.226f.; Spicq 1.63-5.

ἀλάλαγμα, ατος. n.ʃ

= ἀλαλαγμός, q.v.: raised by ecstatic troops, || κραυγή 1K 4.6 *L*; fig. of arrogance, PSol 17.6, emended from ἀλλάγματος. Cf. κραυγή.

ἀλαλαγμός, οῦ. m.

loud noise: heard at a site of disaster, Je 20.16 (|| κραυγή); made by cattle being slaughtered, 32.22; cry of joy, Ps 26.6; of praise, 32.3; of public celebration, + χαρά 'joy' 3M 4.1; battle-cry, Jo 6.20. Cf. ἀλαλάζω, κραυγή, φωνή.

ἀλαλάζω: fut. ἀλαλάξω; aor. ἠλάλαξα, impv. ἀλάλαξον, subj. ἀλαλάξω.

to shout: out of grief, Je 4.8 (+ κόπτομαι), || κράζω 29.2, 30.3; out of joy and + dat. pers., τῷ θεῷ Ps 80.2 (|| ἀγαλλιάομαι), 97.4 (also || ᾄδω, ψάλλω), ἐν φωνῇ ἀγαλλιάσεως 'with a sound of joy' 46.2, ἐν ψαλμοῖς 94.2, ἐπί τινα Ez 27.30 (|| κράζω); φωνῇ μεγάλῃ Ju 14.9, ἀλαλαγμῷ μεγάλῳ Jo 6.20. Cf. ἀλαλαγμός, ἀλάλαγμα, κράζω, ὀλολύζω.

ἄλαλος, ον.ʃ

incapable of speech: *s* χείλη 'lips' Ps 30.19; 37.14, cf. ἄ. ἀνθρώποις σκιά 'a shadow, mute to men' (*s* a deceased person) *ND* 4.149. Cf. λαλέω, κωφός, ἀφασία.

ἅλας. ⇒ ἅλς.

ἀλάστωρ, ορος. m.

1. *avenging spirit* or *deity*: 4M 11.23.

2. *he whose deeds deserve vengeance*: 2M 7.9; ἀ. τύραννος 4M 9.24.

ἀλγέω: fut. ἀλγήσω; aor. ἤλγησα.ʃ

to suffer acute pain: *s* hum. and + acc. (suffering part), τὴν κοιλίαν μου 'my belly' Je 4.19, τὴν κεφαλήν μου 4K 4.19*L*, τραῦμα 'wound' Jb 16.6; πτωχὸς καὶ ἀλγῶν Ps 68.30; hum. body, Jb 14.22 (|| πενθέω); mental and *s* hum., ἐπὶ σοί 'over you' 2K 1.26; birds, τῇ στοργῇ 'from affection' 4M 14.17. Cf. ἀλγηδών, πενθέω, συναλγέω, ὠδίνω: Schmidt 2.605.

ἀλγηδών, όνος. f.

acute pain: σκληρά 'severe' 2M 6.30; Ps 37.18; + ὀδύνη 2M 9.9; bodily, σωμάτων 4M 3.18. Cf. ἀλγέω, ἄλγημα, ὀδύνη, πόνος: Schmidt 2.603f.

ἄλγημα, ατος. n.

= ἀλγηδών, q.v.: Ps 38.3; mental, Ec 2.23 (+ θυμός). Cf. ἀλγηδών.

ἀλγηρός, ά, όν.ʃ*

causing pain, 'painful, smarting': *s* πληγή 'a blow (sustained)' Je 10.19, 37.12; εἰς ~όν 'ending up in pains' 37.13.

ἄλγος, ους. n.ʃ

grief: La 1.12; τῶν τραυματιῶν 'of wounds' Ps 68.27; ἀ. καρδίας καὶ πένθος Si 26.6, κατὰ καρδίαν ἐνεστός 'lodged in his heart' 2M 3.17. Cf. λύπη, ὀδύνη, πένθος: Schmidt 2.597, 601f.

ἀλεεύς, έως. m. Also ἁλιεύς (an older form).

fisherman: operating in the Nile, Is 19.8; ἐν πλοίοις ἁλιέων 'in fishermen's boats' Jb 40.31. **b.** emissary sent out to gather scattered coreligionists, Je 16.16 (|| θηρευτής), cf. ποιήσω ὑμᾶς ~εῖς ἀνθρώπων Mt 4.19.

Cf. ἁλιεύω.

ἄλειμμα, ατος. n.ʃ

that which is used for anointing, 'unguent': ἔλαιον ἄ. χρίσεως ἅγιον Ex 30.31; cogn. obj., ἄ. οὐκ ἠλειψάμην 'I have not applied unguent' Da TH 10.3 (LXX ἔλαιον); fig., ἄ. εὐφροσύνης Is 61.3. Cf. ἀλείφω.

ἀλείφω: fut. ἀλείψω, mid. ἀλείψομαι; aor. ἤλειψα, subj. ἀλείψω, mid. ἠλειψάμην, inf. ἀλείψασθαι; pf.ptc.pass. ἠλειμμένος.

to spread sticky, fluid-like substance *over the surface of*, 'to anoint': ***o*** στήλη 'stela, pillar' Ge 31.13, τοῖχος 'wall' Ez 13.10; person, Ex 40.13; sbd inducted as priest, Nu 3.3; metaph., *to oil sbd's palm* in order to ingratiate oneself with him, Ez 22.28. **b**. mid., abs., 2K 12.20 (*L* χρίω); one's own body with ἔλαιον (acc.) 'olive oil' Mi 6.15, Da 10.3 LXX (TH ἄλειμμα) (with no ceremonial significance); ἐν ἐλαίῳ Es 2.12 o'.

Cf. λιπαίνω, χρίω, ἄλειμμα, ἀλοιφή, ἐξαλείφω.

ἄλεκτος, ον.ʃ

impossible to express verbally: ***s*** sorrow, 3M 4.2. Cf. λέγω.

ἀλεκτρυών, όνος. m.ʃ

cock: crowing (κράζω) at the dawn, 3M 5.23. Cf. ἀλέκτωρ: Shipp 55f.

ἀλέκτωρ, ορος. m.ʃ

synonym of prec.: Pr 30.31. Cf. ἀλεκτρυών: Bain 122.

ἄλευρον, ου. n.

wheat-meal: Ho 8.7, Is 47.2; ἀ. κρίθινον 'barley meal' Nu 5.15 (cultic offering). Cf. σῖτος, ἀλέω.

ἀλέω: aor.impv. ἄλεσον.ʃ

to grind: + acc., hard stuff for food, ἄλευρον 'wheat-meal' Is 47.2. Cf. ἄλευρον, ἀλήθω, καταλέω.

ἀλήθεια, ας. f.

1. *truthfulness, sincerity* (of character, thought or conduct): ***s*** man, ǁ ἔλεος Ho 4.1; ǁ εἰρήνη Zc 8.19; ὀμόσῃ μετὰ ~ας 'swear ..' Je 4.2, πορεύεσθαι ἐν ~είᾳ 3K 2.4, + ἐν πίστει 4K 20.3*L*, + δικαιοσύνη To 14.7 𝔊[I]; opp. πορνεία 'carnal lust' To 8.7; a gift of God, Mi 7.20 (ǁ ἔλεος); an attribute of God, Ge 24.27, 32.10, Zc 8.8 (+ δικαιοσύνη), 1E 4.40; νόμος ~ας Ma 2.6.

2. *faithfulness*: ποιήσεις ἐπ' ἐμὲ ἐλεημοσύνην καὶ ~αν Ge 47.29, ~αν ἐποίησας Ne 9.33, ἐργάζομαι ἐν ~ᾳ 'work dutifully' Si 7.20; + κρίσις.

3. *truth* (opp. lie): λαλεῖτε ~αν Zc 8.16, cf. Ps 14.2 (:: δολόω vs. 3), μὴ ἀντίλεγε τῇ ~ᾳ Si 4.25; ἐπ' ~ας 'based on truth' De 22.20; οὐκ ἔστιν ἐν τῷ στόματι αὐτῶν ἀ. Ps 5.10, λόγον ~ας 118.43, ῥήματα ~ας Ju 10.13; Pr 8.7.

4. *accordance with reality*: ἐπ' ~ας οἶδα ὅιτ οὕτως ἐστίν Jb 9.2, ἐπ' ~ας ἠρήμωσαν 'it is a known fact that they demolished' Is 37.17 ǁ 4K 19.17*L* (B+ ǁ ~ᾳ); κατὰ ~αν .. θεῖος 'truly divine' 4M 5.18; πεποιθότες ἐπὶ τὸν θεὸν .. τῇ ~ᾳ 'trusting .. actually' Is 10.20; ταῖς ~αις 'as a matter of fact' Es E 10, 2M 3.9, 'in truth' 7.6; μισθὸς ~ας 'true reward' Pr 11.18.

5. *a means of revealing* or *arriving at correct decision* (?): carried by the high priest in his oracular pouch – combined with δήλωσις – ἀρχιερεὺς ἐνδεδυμένος τὴν δήλωσιν καὶ τὴν ~αν 'the high priest wearing ..' 1E 5.40; Ex 28.26, Le 8.8; δῆλοι καὶ ἀ. De 33.8.

Cf. ἀληθής, ἀληθινός, ψεῦδος: Schmidt 4.290-2; Bultmann, *TDNT* 1.238-44; Spicq 1.66-86.

ἀληθεύω: fut. ἀληθεύσω; aor.impv. ἀλήθευσον.ʃ

1. *to tell the truth*: abs. Pr 21.3, εἰ ἀληθεύετε ἢ οὔ Ge 42.16; πάντα ἀλήθευσον 'Tell the whole truth' 20.16. Cf. *ND* 4.145.

2. *to declare to be true*: + acc., βουλήν Is 44.26 (ǁ ἵστημι).

3. *to prove true*: ἀπὸ ψευδοῦς τί ἀληθεύσει; Si 31.4.

Cf. ἀληθής, ψεύδομαι.

ἀληθής, ές.

1. *being in accordance with the true state of affairs*: ~ές ἔσται τὸ ῥῆμα τὸ παρὰ τοῦ θεοῦ Ge 41.32; ~ὴς σαφῶς ὁ λόγος De 13.14; ἴδωμεν εἰ οἱ λόγοι αὐτοῦ ~εῖς 'let's see if his words are true' Wi 2.17; (τὸ) ~ές 'the truth' 4M 5.10, Jb 42.7f.

2. *rightly so called, not spurious*: ***s*** god, Wi 12.27.

3. *in the habit of speaking truth*, 'honest': ἀνὴρ ἀ. Ne 7.2. **b**. *sincere*: ***s*** desire, Wi 6.17.

4. *indicative of integrity of character*: ***s*** deed, Jb 5.12; 17.10; god, + χρηστός 'kindly' Wi 15.1 (or: **3a**).

Cf. ἀλήθεια, ἀληθινός, ἀληθῶς, ἀληθεύω, ψευδής, ἀψευδής: LSG s.v.

ἀληθινός, ή, όν.

1. *truthful*: ***s*** God, μακρόθυμος καὶ πολυέλεος καὶ ἀ. Ex 34.6, Nu 14.18 (His truthfulness manifesting itself in His concern about maintenance of justice and righteousness), sim. Ps 85.15; hum., ἀ., ἄμεμπτος, δίκαιος, θεοσεβής '.., impeccable, .. God-fearing' Jb 1.1; μετὰ ἀληθείας ἐν καρδίᾳ ~ῇ Is 38.3; ǁ δίκαιος Jb 17.8, 27.17; ǁ καθαρός 4.7; + πιστός 3M 2.11.

2. *authentic, as it should be*: ***s*** God's works or deeds, De 32.4; Jerusalem, Zc 8.3; ὁδός 'way of life' Is 65.2, grape-vine Je 2.21 (:: ἀλλότριος).

3. *not fraudulent*: ***s*** στάθμιον ~ὸν καὶ δίκαιον .. μέτρον ~ὸν καὶ δίκαιον 'accurate and honest weight .. measure' De 25.15. **b**. *according with the principle of justice*: divine judgement, Ps 18.10, Da 3.27 LXX (TH ἀληθείας); + δίκαιος To 3.2 𝔊[I].

4. = ἀληθής **1**: ***s*** message (λόγος) 3K 10.6, Da 10.1 TH (LXX ἀληθής), ῥῆμα κυρίου ἐν (τῷ) στόματί σου 3K 17.24; χείλη 'lips' Pr 12.19.

5. = ἀληθής **2**: ***s*** god, Is 65.16, 2C 15.3.

Cf. ἀλήθεια, ἀληθινῶς, δίκαιος: Trench 26-30; Bultmann, *TDNT* 1.249f.; Spicq 1.84f.

ἀληθινῶς. adv.ʃ
1. *correctly and without erring*: ὁρῶν Nu 24.3, 15.
2. *in accordance with truth*: οὐκ ἐπορεύθημεν ἀ. ἐνώπιόν σου To 3.5 𝔊II (𝔊I ἐν ἀληθείᾳ); 14.6; πεπαιδευμένος ἀ. 'having obtained sound education' Si 42.8.
3. *sincerely, genuinely*: αἰσχυντηρός 'shamefaced' Si 42.1.
Cf. ἀληθής, ἀληθῶς, ὄντως.

ἀλήθω.ʃ
to grind: ***o*** hard stuff for food, ἐν τῷ μύλῳ 'with the mill' Nu 11.8; ***s*** women, Ec 12.3,4. Cf. ἀλέω.

ἀληθῶς. adv.
in accordance with what has been stated, affirming its veracity: ˀΑρά γε ἀ. τέξομαι; 'Am I really going to have a baby, I wonder?' Ge 18.13, Εἰ ἀ. ἄρα δικαιοσύνην λαλεῖτε; Ps 57.2; ἀ. ἀδελφή μού ἐστιν 'she is indeed a sister of mine' Ge 20.12; πῶς γνωστὸν ἔσται ἀ. ὅτι ..; 'how could one indeed find out that ..?' Ex 33.16; ἀ. γέγονεν τὸ ῥῆμα 'it has indeed happened' De 17.4. **b**. in response, 'Yes, indeed': Je 35.6, Da 3.91 TH.
Cf. ἀληθής, ἀληθινῶς, ὄντως.

ἀλιάετος, ου. m.ʃ On the spelling, see Walters 80f.
sea-eagle: forbidden as food, Le 11.13, De 14.12.

ἁλιεύς: ⇒ ἁλεεύς.

ἁλιεύω: fut. ἁλιεύσω.ʃ
to catch: ***s*** fisherman (fig.) and + acc. pers., Je 16.16 (|| θηρεύω). Cf. ἁλεεύς.

ἁλίζω: fut.pass. ἁλισθήσομαι; aor.pass. ἡλίσθην; pf.ptc.pass. ἡλισμένος.ʃ
to apply salt: + acc., food, ἁλὶ ἁλισθήσεται '.. with salt' Le 2.13 (cultic offering); a new-born baby, Ez 16.4; fish, To 6.6 𝔊II. Cf. ἅλς, ταριχεύω.

ἅλιμος, ον.ʃ
pertaining to the sea: subst.n.pl., *seaside* Je 17.6; seaside vegetation as food for the hungry, Jb 30.4a¶, b.

ἀλισγέω: fut. ἀλισγήσω; aor.act. ἠλίσγησα, pass. subj. ἀλισγηθῶ; pf.ptc.pass. ἠλισγημένος.ʃ
to destroy the purity or *sanctity of*: **a**. ἀλισγήσει ψυχὴν αὐτοῦ ἐν ἐδέσμασιν ἀλλοτρίοις 'he will defile his soul with a stranger's foods' Si 40.29. **b**. ritually: pass., ***o*** rei, ἄρτους ἠλισγημένους Ma 1.7; τράπεζα κυρίου ἠλισγημένη ἐστι 'the table (on which offerings are set) ..' 1.12; ***o*** hum., ἀλισγηθῇ ἐν τῷ δείπνῳ τοῦ βασιλέως .. 'through the meal ..' Da LXX 1.8 (|| συμμολύνω).
Cf. βεβηλόω and μολύνω.

ἁλίσκομαι: fut. ἁλώσομαι; aor. ἑάλων, inf. ἁλῶναι, ptc. ἁλούς, subj. ἁλῶ; pf. ἑάλωκα, ptc. ἑαλωκώς. Defective passive.
1. *to be captured*: red-handed, κλέπτων 'in an act of theft' De 24.7; ὑπὸ τῆς παγίδος 'by the trap' Is 24.18, ἐν ^παγίδι^ Si 27.26, παγίδι 27.29. Cf. φωράω. **b**. *to be conquered* as a result of military defeat and ***s*** city, Zc 14.2, Is 30.13; Babylon, Je 27.2, 9; + θηρεύομαι 28.41.
2. *to be convicted* in a law-court: ὁ ἁλοὺς διὰ τοῦ θεοῦ 'the one who has been convicted through God' Ex 22.9.
Cf. αἵρω, ἅλωσις, εὐάλωτος, κατα~, προκαταλαμβάνω: Ziegler 1934.197f.; Bergren & Kraft.

ἀλιτήριος, ον.
sinning: subst.m., non-Jew, 2M 12.23, 13.4. Cf. ἁμαρτωλός.

ἀλκή, ῆς. f.ʃ
might: military, 3M 3.18; + δυναστεία 6.12; || κυριεία Da 11.4 LXX. Cf. δύναμις, ἰσχύς: Schmidt 3.676-8. Del. Si 29.13, 2M 12.28 v.l.

ἀλλά. On the elision of the final vowel, see BDF, § 17.
1. 'but, however' (indicating transition to a new subject-matter): Ge 40.14, Ma 2.16.
2. 'but, rather' (indicating contrast and preceded by a negative statement): Οὐ κληρονομήσει οὗτος, ἀλλ' ὃς ἐξελεύσεται ἐκ σοῦ, οὗτος κληρονομήσει σε Ge 15.4. **b**. combined w. ἤ (q.v.) and foll. by a clause, Am 7.14 "I was not a prophet nor a prophet's son, ἀλλ' ἢ αἰπόλος ἤμην"; Ho 1.6, 7.14; foll. by a phrase, οὐχ ὑμεῖς με ἀπεστάλκατε, ἀλλ' ἢ ὁ θεός Ge 45.8. Οὐκ ἐν δυνάμει μεγάλῃ οὐδὲ ἐν ἰσχύι, ἀλλ' ἢ ἐν πνεύματί μου 'not with great strength nor with force, but with my spirit' Zc 4.6. **c**. introduces a protest or dissent: Ἀλλ' ὡσεὶ πόρνῃ χρήσονται τῇ ἀδελφῇ ἡμῶν; 'But should they treat our sister like a whore?' Ge 34.31. Cf. Renehan 1.22. **d**. preceded by a rhetorical question anticipating a negative answer: "Who on earth could be free from filth? Why, nobody (ἀλλ' οὐθείς)" Jb 14.4, cf. Fr. *mais personne*. **e**. ἀλλ' ὅτι = ἀλλά: Es 6.13 *L*.
3. *in spite of that, notwithstanding*: ὧδε οὐκ ἐποίησα οὐδέν, ἀλλ' ἐνέβαλόν με εἰς τὸν λάκκον τοῦτον 'here I have done nothing (wrong), and yet they have thrown me into this pit' Ge 40.15; Pr 29.19.
4. ἀλλ' ἤ 'other than, except': οὐδὲ ἐγὼ ἤκουσα ἀλλ' ἢ σήμερον 'nor have I heard (about it) but today' Ge 21.26; τί κύριος .. αἰτεῖται παρὰ σοῦ ἀλλ' ἢ φοβεῖσθαι κύριον ..; De 10.12; τί κύριος ἐκζητεῖ παρὰ σοῦ ἀλλ' ἢ τοῦ ποιεῖν .. 'what does the Lord require of you other than practising ..?' Mi 6.8; Ma 2.16; foll. by a gen. abs., ἀλλ' ἢ συμπορευομένου σου μεθ' ἡμῶν 'unless you go with us' Ex 33.16. **b**. preceded by a negator, 'no .. but': οὐκ ἔστιν τοῦτο ἀλλ' ἢ οἶκος θεοῦ 'this is nothing but God's dwelling' Ge 28.17; χήραν .. οὐ λήμψεται, ἀλλ' ἢ παρθένον ἐκ τοῦ γένους αὐτοῦ λήμψεται γυναῖκα 'he shall not take a widow .. but (only) a virgin from his class shall he take for wife' Le 21.14;

negation implied by an oath formula with εἰ, Is 62.9; 1K 2.30. **c**. without ἤ: οὐκ ἐξιλασθήσεται .. ἀλλ' ἐπὶ τοῦ αἵματος .. 'will not be purged .. except with the blood of ..' Nu 35.33. **d**. introduces a qualifying statement or condition: Je 33.15, Da 10.21 TH; without ἤ - "I will let you go, but don't go too far away (ἀλλ' οὐ μακρὰν ..)" Ex 8.28; Nu 18.15. ***e**. ὅτι ἀλλ' ἤ, ὅτι being a calque of כִּי: 1K 21.4 (*L* εἰ μή), 21.7 (*L* om. ὅτι), 30.17 (*L* om. ὅτι), 2K 19.29 (*L* om. ὅτι), 4K 5.15, Ec 5.10; + a clause, 1K 30.22 (*L* ἀλλά), Jd 15.13 B, cf. *BA* 9.1, p. 43f.

5. strongly disjunctive: "Even if a woman forgot them, *I* would not forget you (ἀλλ' ἐγὼ ..)" Is 49.15.

6. introduces an answer in reply to a question which implies an element of uncertainty or doubt on the part of the interrogator, 'Let me assure you, you must believe me': 1K 21.6.

Cf. ἀτάρ, χωρίς.

ἀλλαγή, ῆς. f.ʃ

alternation: τροπῶν 'of the solstices' Wi 7.18. Cf. ἀλλάσσω, μεταβολή.

ἄλλαγμα, ατος. n.

1. *that which replaces* sth or sbd else: Le 27.10, 33.

2. *payment made for service rendered* or *in return for sth purchased*: ἐν ~ατι 'for a price' La 5.4; κυνός 'of a dog [= male prostitute]' De 23.18 (‖ μίσθωμα πόρνης 'harlot's fee'); virtually = 'bribe', λαμβάνοντες ~ατα Am 5.12 (cf. Tht PG 81.1689 δωροδοκία); 'value', ἄ. σου 'a price-tag on you' Is 43.3, τὸ ἄ. αὐτῆς σκεύη χρυσᾶ '.. golden vessels' Jb 28.17¶; "their prices were rather depressed" Ps 43.13.

3. *changing* into sth else: ἐν ~ασιν ταπεινώσεως 'when things have begun to take a downward turn' or 'at the cost of your humbling experiences' Si 2.4.

Cf. ἀλλάσσω: Caird 1968.457.

ἀλλάσσω: fut. ἀλλάξω, mid. ἀλλάξομαι, pass. ἀλλαγήσομαι; aor. ἤλλαξα, impv.2pl. ἀλλάξατε, subj. ἀλλάξω, inf. ἀλλάξαι, mid. ἠλλαξάμην, pass.subj. ἀλλαγῶ.

1. tr. *to make other than it is now*, 'change, alter': + acc., ἤλλαξεν τὸν μισθόν μου τῶν δέκα ἀμνῶν 'he changed my wages to the tune of ten lambs' Ge 31.7 (‖ παρελογίσω τὸν μισθόν μου δέκα ἀμνάσιν 31.41); τὰς στολὰς ὑμῶν 'your clothes' 35.2; ἀλλάξουσιν ἰσχύν 'will have the energy recharged' Is 40.31, 41.1. **b**. *to act in contravention of*: + acc. rei, 2E 6.11 (‖ παραβαίνω 1E 6.31).

2. *to take in exchange for* another, 'substitute, replace': abs. Ne 9.26; for sth else (dat.), Ex 13.13 (‖ λυτρόομαι 34.20); καλὸν πονηρῷ οὐδὲ πονηρὸν καλῷ Le 27.10; *τι ἕν τινι Si 30.29. **b**. mid. and no 2nd term mentioned – θεοὺς αὐτῶν Je 2.11, τὴν δόξαν αὐτοῦ ib.; τι ἀντί τινος 1M 1.29; act. in the same sense, ἤλλαξε τὴν στολὴν τῆς φυλακῆς αὐτοῦ 'he changed his prison clothes' Je 52.33.

3. *to give in exchange for* sth else: + acc., τὰ προστάγματα Is 24.5 (for the worse); *τι ἕν τινι - τὴν δόξαν αὐτῶν ἐν ὁμοιώματι μόσχου Ps 105.20; ἕνεκεν διαφόρου 'for the sake of money' Si 7.18.

4. mid. *to alternate and be replaced by sth else*: *s* καιροί Da 4.13, 22 TH (‖ ἀλλοιόομαι 4.20 TH); ἀλλασσόμεναι στολαὶ ἱματίων 'changes of robes' Jd 14.13 B, 4K 5.5. **b**. pass. *to change in character*: Wi 12.10.

Cf. ἄλλαγμα, ἀλλαγή, ἀντ~, μεταλλάσσω, ἀλλοιόω.

ἀλλαχῇ. adv.ʃ

in another place: ἄλλος ἀ. 'one here and another there' 2M 12.22, Wi 18.18. Cf. ἄλλος, πανταχῇ.

ἀλλαχόθεν. adv.ʃ

from other quarters: by adducing other sources in an argument, + πολλαχόθεν 4M 1.7. Cf. πανταχόθεν, πολλαχόθεν.

ἀλλήλω. Alw. pl. and in obl. cases.

each other, one another: ἔθηκεν αὐτὰ ἀντιπρόσωπα ἀλλήλοις 'placed them facing one another' Ge 15.10; κατεφίλησαν ~ήλους 'they kissed each other' Ex 4.27; κατέναντι ~ων 'in front of one another' Am 4.3.

ἀλλογενής, ές.

1. *born from parents of another race, alien*, i.e. other than Israelite, and with an accompanying connotation of hostility, incongruity, etc.: ἐξ ~ῶν ἐθνῶν Ge 17.27; υἱοὶ ἀλλογενεῖς ἀπερίτμητοι Ez 44.7; subst. Ex 12.43, Le 22.25 (barred from Israelite religious activities); Ob 11, Jl 4.17, ‖ οἱ ποιοῦντες ἄνομα 'those who act against the law' Ma 4.1; ‖ ἀλλότριος Ob 11, ἀλλόφυλος Is 61.5, Zc 9.6; + πάροικος PSol 17.27.

2. *born into another* (non-priestly) *family*: Ex 29.33, 30.33.

On a possible Jewish origin of the word, see Deissmann 1923.62f.; MM, s.v. and Büchsel, *TDNT* 1.266f.

Cf. ἀλλότριος, ἀλλοεθνής, ἀλλόφυλος, ἀλλόχθων, ξένος, συγγενής.

ἀλλόγλωσσος, ον.ʃ

speaking a foreign language: *s* ἔθνος Ba 4.15, λαός Ez 3.6 (‖ ἀλλόφωνος). Cf. ἀλλόφωνος, γλῶσσα.

ἀλλοεθνής, ές.ʃ

pertaining to an ethnic group other than one's own: 3M 4.6. Cf. ἀλλογενής.

ἄλλοθεν. adv.ʃ

from elsewhere: Es 4.14 o'.

ἀλλοιόω: fut. ἀλλοιώσω, pass. ἀλλοιωθήσομαι, ptc. ~ωθησόμενος; aor. ἠλλοίωσα, inf. ἀλλοιῶσαι, impv. ἀλλοίωσον, subj. ἀλλοιώσω, pass. ἠλλοιώθην, subj. ἀλλοιωθῶ, ptc. ἀλλοιωθείς; pf.pass. ἠλλοίωμαι, ptc. ἠλλοιωμένος.

1. *to make different*: + acc., τὸ πρόσωπον αὐτοῦ Ps 33.1, Si 12.18; ‖ διαχωρίζω 36.8, 11; pass. *to become different*: οὐκ ἠλλοίωμαι 'I have not changed' Ma 3.6; Da 7.28 TH (LXX διαφέρω); by disguising oneself, 1K 28.8*L*; *s* ὁ καιρός Da 2.9 LXX; moon, Si 27.11.

2. *to discard and replace*: + acc., τὰ ἱμάτια τῆς φυλακῆς 'prison uniform' 4K 25.29; = wilfully ignore, + acc. (royal edict) Da 3.95 TH (LXX ἀθετέω), 6.8.

3. pass. intr. *to become estranged*: + gen. pers., 1M 11.12.

Cf. ἀλλάσσω, ἄλλος, ἀλλοίωσις, ἀλλοτριόω, ἐξαλλοιόω, διαφέρω, μεταβάλλω, ~πίπτω, ~στρέφω, ~σχηεματίζω: Schmidt 4.567-9.

ἀλλοίωσις, εως. f.

act of becoming different: Ps 76.11; ref. to changing phases of the moon, Si 43.8. Cf. ἀλλοιόω.

ἅλλομαι: fut. ἁλοῦμαι; aor. ἡλάμην.

to leap: "the lame will leap like a deer" Is 35.6, "four-footed animals which leap on the ground' Jb 41.17; *s* shafts of lightning, ἐπὶ σκοπόν 'on to a target' Wi 5.21; a divine spirit, ἐπ' αὐτόν Jd 14.6 B (A: κατευθύνω 'to descend straight'). Cf. ἀφ~, δι~, ἐν~, ἐξ~, ἐφάλλομαι, ἅλμα, ἀναβράσσω, πηδάω, σκιρτάω: Schmidt 1.536-46.

ἄλλος, η, ον.

other than what has been mentioned or is in view: ἄλλαι ἑπτὰ βόες 'another seven cows' Ge 41.3 (‖ vs. 19 ἑπτὰ βόες ἕτεραι); οὐκ ἄ. ἐποίησε 'it is not another person who has done (so)' Ma 2.15; Τί ἄλλο ἀλλ' ἢ σπέρμα .. 'what other than offspring ..?' ib. **b.** *additional*: ἄλλα τάλαντα δέκα 'further 10 talents' 1E 4.52.

The distinction between ἄλλος and ἕτερος does not appear to be maintained: see esp. the alternation between the two at Ge 41.3 and 19 on the one hand, and between Jb 1.16, 17 and 18 on the other. Cf. καρδίαν ἄλλην 1K 10.9 (*L* ἑτέραν).

Cf. ἄλλως, ἕτερος, ἔτι, λοιπός: Schmidt 4.559f., 562-7; Trench 357-61; Shipp 58-61.

ἄλλοτε.ʃ

at another time: 2M 13.10. Cf. ποτέ.

ἀλλότριος, α, ον.

1. *coming from another society* or *ethnic group*: ἀπὸ παντὸς υἱοῦ ~ου, ὃς οὐκ ἔστιν ἐκ τοῦ σπέρματός σου Ge 17.12; πάροικός εἰμι ἐν γῇ ~ᾳ Ex 2.22; *s* ἔθνος 21.8; ‖ πάροικος De 14.20; opp. ἀδελφός 17.15, 23.20; subst., 29.22.

2. *foreign, alien*: contrary to what is proper and natural, thus with ref. to paganism, θεοί Ge 35.2, Ho 3.1, and perh. on the basis of this frequent collocation (first Ge 35.2), 'associated with a pagan religion and its practices'; τέκνα w. ref. to children born from ethnically foreign mothers and thus exposed to foreign religious influences Ho 5.7 (see Muraoka 1986a:126f); ὡς ~α ἐλογίσθησαν θυσιαστήρια '(their) altars were considered alien,' ib. 8.12; πῦρ ~ον, ὃ οὐ προσέταξεν κύριος αὐτοῖς Le 10.1, sim. Nu 26.61; ἐνδύματα 'incongruous, alien (cultic) vestments' Zp 1.8; γῆ 'land (of exile)' PSol 9.1; + gen., τῆς σῆς δυνάμεως 'to your authority' Wi 12.15, τῆς δικαίας γνώμης Pr 2.16, cf. ἀπὸ τοῦ θεοῦ ἡμῶν PSol 17.13; subst., μακαρίζομεν ~ους 'we congratulate foreigners' who are not burdened with our religious obligations, Ma 3.15; ‖ βδελύγματα De 32.16. Cf. θεοὶ ἕτεροι, see under ἕτερος. **b.** subst., *a person of the other sex other than one's spouse*: Si 23.22 (‖ ἀλλότριος ἀνήρ vs. 23); married woman, Pr 5.20 (‖ μὴ ἰδία), 6.24 (‖ γυνὴ ~α 7.5), 23.33.

3. *other than oneself, stranger* with the implication that he is sbd hostile or harmful to oneself, subst.: ὡς αἱ ~αι λελογίσμεθα αὐτῷ Ge 31.15; κατέφαγον ~οι τὴν ἰσχὺν αὐτοῦ, αὐτὸς δὲ οὐκ ἔγνω 'strangers devoured his resources without his knowledge' Ho 7.9, sim. 8.7; ~οι εἰσῆλθον εἰς πύλας αὐτοῦ 'foreigners,' who are enemy troops, Ob 11 (‖ ἀλλογενής); ἐν ἡμέρᾳ ~ων 'on the day of foreigners,' i.e. when they triumph, ib. 12; ‖ ξένος La 5.2. Cf. Preisigke, s.v. **5** "unpassend, ungehörig" and **6** "illegitim" (of children). **b.** with no negative connotation: subst., 'sbd else' Pr 27.2. **c.** *belonging to someone other than oneself*: τράπεζα ~α 'sbd else's table' Si 40.29.

4. *unfavourably disposed*, 'hostile': + gen., τῶν αὐτοῦ πραγμάτων 'towards his government' 2M 4.21, sim. 14.26.

5. *unfamiliar, unusual*: Is 28.21.

Cf. ἀλλογενής, ἀλλοτριότης, ἀλλοτρίως, ἀλλοτριόω, ἀλλοτρίωσις, ἀλλόφυλος, ξένος, ἐγχώριος.

ἀλλοτριότης, ητος. f.ʃ

state of being alien to one's own outlook and stance: PSol 17.13.

ἀλλοτριόω: fut.pass. ἀλλοτριωθήσομαι; aor.mid. ἠλλοτριώθην.ʃ

1. mid. *to feign to be a stranger and to keep a distance*: + ἀπό τινος, Ge 42.7; 1M 6.24; + dat. pers., 11.53, 15.27.

2. *to ostracise, treat as alien*: pass., ἀπὸ τοῦ πλήθους τῆς αἰχμαλωσίας 'from the group of returnees from the exile' 1E 9.4.

Cf. ἀλλότριος.

ἀλλοτρίως. adv.ʃ

in strange manner: Is 28.21. Cf. ἀλλότριος.

ἀλλοτρίωσις, εως. f.ʃ
1. *that which is alien*: Ne 13.30.
2. *indifferent stranger who keeps aloof*: Je 17.17.
Cf. ἀλλότριος.

ἀλλοφυλέω: aor.inf. ~φυλῆσαι.ʃ
to adopt foreign culture: 4M 18.5 (‖ ἐκδιαιτάω). Cf. ἀλλόφυλος.

ἀλλοφυλισμός, οῦ. m.ʃ
alien, foreign culture: 2M 4.13 (‖ Ἑλληνισμός), 6.24.

ἀλλόφυλος, ον.
of another race: τέκνα πολλὰ ~α Is 2.6. **b**. subst. pl.: Γαλιλαία ~ων Jl 3.4, cf. Cyr. I 350 for their identification with Philistines); used esp. w. ref. to Philistines, οἱ κατάλοιποι τῶν ~ων (resident in Ekron) Am 1.8; Γεθ (Gath) ~ων 6.2; of Cappadocian provenance, 9.7; to be expelled by residents of Shephelah, Ob 19; inhabitants of Canaan, Zp 2.5; ὕβρις ~ων Zc 9.6; ‖ ἀλλογενής Is 61.5; distinct from Greek colonists in Alexandria, 3M 3.6.
Cf. ἀλλογενής, ἀλλότριος, ἀλλοφυλέω, ἀλλόχθων.

ἀλλόφωνος, ον.ʃ
speaking a foreign language: *s* λαός Ez 3.6 (‖ ἀλλόγλωσσος). Cf. ἀλλόγλωσσος.

ἄλλως. adv.
1. *in some other way*: ἄ. ἢ .. '.. than' Jb 40.8; Es 1.19 LXX (‖ *L* ἄλλῃ), ἄ… ἐὰν μὴ .. 'unless ..' Wi 8.21.
2. *in some other respects*: 4M 4.13.
3. *in vain*: Jb 11.12. **b**. *for no good reason*, 'wrongly': 4M 5.18 (:: κατὰ ἀλήθειαν 'in accordance with truth').
4. καὶ ἄ. 'and besides' 4M 1.2.
5. ἄ. καὶ ἄ. 'here and there': 3M 1.20.
Cf. ἄλλος.

ἅλμα, ατος. n.ʃ
act of leaping, v.n. of ἅλλομαι: of horse, Jb 39.25.

ἅλμη, ης.ʃ
1. unproductive *soil saturated with salt*: Ps 106.34 (‖ γῆ καρποφόρος).
2. *brine*: Si 39.23 (:: ὕδωρ).
Cf. ἁλμυρίς, ἅλς.

ἁλμυρίς, ίδος.ʃ
unproductive *soil saturated with salt*: Jb 39.6¶ (‖ ἔρημος). Cf. ἅλμη, ἁλμυρός, ἅλς.

ἁλμυρός, ά, όν.ʃ
saturated with salt: *s* γῆ Je 17.6. Cf. ἅλμη.

ἀλοάω: pres.impv. ἀλόα; fut. ἀλοήσω, fut. ἀλοηθήσομαι; aor. ἠλόησα.ʃ
1. *to thresh* unprocessed grain: *s* ox, De 25.4, hum. 1C 21.20.
2. *to crush and destroy*: + acc. pers. Mi 4.13, Jd 8.16 B (A: καταξαίνω); πόλεις ὀχυράς 'fortified cities' Je 5.17; + acc. rei, σάρκας '(their) flesh' Jd 8.7 B (A: καταξαίνω).
3. *to move over and crush* that which is underneath: *s* wheels of a wagon, Is 41.15; *o* mountains ib. (‖ λεπτύνω), houses Je 28.33.
Cf. ἀλόητος, ἅλων, ἀφανίζω, καταλοάω: Caird 1968.114f.; LSG s.v.

ἀλογέω: aor.inf.pass. ἀλογηθῆναι.ʃ
to pay no regard to: *o* hum., 2M 12.24

ἀλογιστία, ας. f.ʃ
senselessness: characteristic of certain deeds and behaviours, 2M 14.8, 3M 5.42. Cf. ἀλόγιστος.

ἀλόγιστος, ον.ʃ
1. *not lending itself to logical explanation*: *s* hum. death, Si 18.9¶; ὕβρις 3M 6.12; hum. desire, 4M 3.11; course of action, 6.18, 16.23.
2. *incapable of logical reasoning*: *s* child, Wi 12.25.
Cf. ἀλογίστως, παράδοξος: Schmidt 3.654f.

ἀλογίστως. adv.ʃ
in a manner contrary to logical explanations: 4M 6.14. Cf. ἀλόγιστος.

ἄλογος, ον.
1. *lacking in eloquence*: *s* hum., Ex 6.12 (‖ ἰσχνόφωνος vs. 30).
2. *not to be counted, null and void*: αἱ ἡμέραι αἱ πρότεραι ~οι ἔσονται Nu 6.12.
3. *lacking in intelligence*: *s* hum., 3M 5.40; ζῷα 'animals' 4M 14.14.
4. *not consonant with reason*, 'irrational' *s* hum. anger, PSol 16.10. Or: *not based on reality*, 'groundless, unfounded.'
Cf. ἀλόγως, ἄνους, βραδύγλωσσος, ἰσχνόφωνος, μάταιος, κενός.

ἀλόγως. adv.ʃ
against the best counsel: 3M 6.25. Cf. ἄλογος.

ἀλόητος, ου. m.ʃ
act of threshing: καταλήμψεται ὁ ἀ. τὸν τρύγητον 'the threshing will last up to the time of harvesting' Am 9.13, sim. Le 26.5 (v.l. ἄμητος for ἀλ.).
Cf. ἀλοάω, ἄμητος and τρύγητος.

ἀλοιφή, ῆς. f.ʃ
1. *act of painting over* in order to erase a writing on a surface: as dat. cog. ~ῇ ἐξαλείψω τὸ μνημόσυνον Αμαληκ 'I shall completely erase the memory of A.' Ex 17.14.
2. *that which has been painted*: ἐπὶ τοίχου 'on a wall' Jb 33.24; cogn. obj. of ἀλείφω, Ez 13.12.
3. *act of forming sticky material* (viz. clay) into brick: πλίνθου 'of brick' Mi 7.11.
Cf. ἀλείφω, ἐξάλειψις.

ἅλς, ός. m. Also spelled ἅλας.
salt: ἁλὶ ἁλισθήσεται 'shall be rubbed with salt' Le 2.13, sim. Ez 16.4; θημωνιὰ ἁλός 'a heap of

salt' Zp 2.9; διαθήκη ἁλός Nu 18.19, 2C 13.5; θεῖον καὶ ἅλς κατακεκαυμένος 'brimstone and burnt salt' De 29.23; ἡ κοιλὰς τῶν ἁλῶν 'the Valley of the Salt' 1C 18.12. Cf. ἁλυκός, ἁλίζω, ἅλμη: Shipp 53f.

ἄλσος, ους. n.

grove: site of pagan cult, Ex 34.13, De 7.5 (|| βωμός, στήλη, γλυπτά), sim. 12.3; + Βααλιμ Jd 3.7; Mi 5.14; ἄ. δρυμοῦ '.. of thicket' 3.12, Je 33.18; a hiding-place, Je 4.29. Cf. τέμενος.

ἀλσώδης, ες; gen. ~ους.

belonging to a (heathen sacred) *grove*: *s* ξύλον Je 3.6, 4K 16.4 (a site for heathen cult); with no negative connotation, στελέχη ~δη 'branches (typical of a well-appointed sacred) grove' Je 17.8; οἶκοι ~εις 'buildings on sacred precincts' Ez 19.6.

ἁλυκός, ή, όν.

pertaining to salt (ἅλς): ἡ φάραγξ ἡ ~ή Ge 14.3 || ἡ κοιλὰς ἡ ~ή 14.8, 10, both ref. to the basin of the Dead Sea; ἡ θάλασσα ἡ ~ή Nu 34.3, 12, De 3.17 (= יָם הַמֶּלַח) || ἡ θάλασσα τῶν ἁλῶν Ge 14.3. Cf. ἅλς.

ἁλυσιδωτός, ή, όν.*

wrought in chain fashion: *s* ἔργον Ex 28.22, θώραξ 'coat of mail' 1K 17.5; = subst.n., 1M 6.35. Cf. ἅλυσις.

ἅλυσις, εως. f.∫

chain as instrument for binding: metaph., Wi 17.18. Cf. ἁλυσιδωτός.

ἄλφιτον, ου. n.

groats: food for hum. consumption, Ju 10.5, Ru 2.14. Cf. ἄλευρον: Renehan 1.23f.; LSG s.v.

ἀλφός, οῦ. m.∫

dull-white leprosy (LSJ): Le 13.39.

ἅλων, gen. ἅλω or ἅλωνος, dat. ἅλῳ or ἅλωνι, acc. ἅλωνα; pl.acc. ἅλω. c.

threshing-floor: Ex 22.6; ἅ. σίτου Ho 9.1, πλησθήσονται αἱ ~ες Jl 2.24; ἅ. καὶ ληνός '.. and wine-press' Ex 22.29, De 16.13, Ho 9.2; χοῦς ἀποφυσώμενος ἀφ' ~ος 'chaff blown away from a threshing-floor' 13.3; δράγματα ('sheaves') ~ος Mi 4.12. **b.** *crops to be processed on a threshing-floor*: Jb 39.12, Ru 3.2.

Cf. ἀλοάω: Ziegler 1934.185f.; Shipp 62.

ἀλώπηξ, εκος. m./f.

fox: La 5.18; contemptible animal, Ne 4.3.

ἅλως. ⇒ ἅλων.

ἅλωσις, εως. f.∫

v.n. of ἁλίσκομαι, **1**: Je 27.46.

ἅμα.

I. adv. *jointly*: κατοικεῖν ἅμα 'to live together' Ge 13.6(*b*bis); ἅπας ὁ λαὸς ἅμα 19.4(†); ἅ. πάντες Is 31.3(*b*); οἱ δύο ἅμα Ge 22.6(*b*). **b.** *as everybody else*: Ps 13.3(*b*). **c.** *both* in a formula <A καὶ B ἅμα> 'A and B alike': οἱ ἄνομοι καὶ οἱ ἁμαρτωλοὶ ἅ Is 1.28(*b*), 31(-), πατέρες καὶ υἱοὶ ἅ. Je 6.21(*b*); 1E 7.10(*i*); with three terms, μοσχάριον καὶ ταῦρος καὶ λέων ἅ. 'a calf and a bull and a lion altogether' Is 11.6(*b*); ἅ. with the first term, 11.14(*b*); <ἅμα .. καὶ .. ἅμα .. >, Is 3.16(-); <ἅμα A καὶ B>, Is 18.6(*b*), Si 16.19(*g*). **d.** *likewise*: καὶ ἅμα διὰ γραπτῶν 'and likewise in writing' (i.e., not only orally) 1E 2.2(*h*); 'or alternatively' 3K 18.27(-).

II. prep. w. dat., *together with*: ἅμα αὐτῷ De 32.43(*f*), ἅμα φυλαῖς Ισραηλ '.. the tribes of Is.' 33.5(*e*).

2. *immediately following in time*: ἅμα τῇ ἡμέρᾳ 'the moment it was day' Mi 2.1(*a*), ἅ. ἡμέρᾳ 1M 4.6, ἕως ἅ. τῷ ἡλίῳ 'until daybreak' Ne 7.3(-); + τῷ and inf aor., ἅ. τῷ ἀνατεῖλαι τὸν ἥλιον 'immediately with sunrise' Jn 4.8(*a*); Ez 17.10(*a*), Ps 36.20(*a*), 3M 3.25, 4M 4.29; pres. inf., 23.40(-); + τοῦ and inf. aor., Jd 3.21A (B: dat.)(-).

Cf. ἐπί **III 12**, ὁμοθυμαδόν, and ὁμοῦ.

a) -כּ [Mi 2.1, MT -בּ]; *b*) יַחְדָּו; *c*) אֵת; *d*) עַל; *e*) יַחַד; *f*) עִם; *g*) אַף; *h*) גַּם; *i*) כְּאֶחָד. Del. Ge 46.8, De 22.22 v.l.

ἀμαθία, ας. f.∫

refusal to learn: PSol 18.4. Cf. μανθάνω.

ἅμαξα, ης. f.

wagon used for transporting persons and / or goods: Ge 45.19; γέμουσα καλάμης 'laden with straw' Am 2.13; for threshing, Is 25.10.

ἀμάραντος, ον.∫

unfading: *s* σοφία, + λαμπρός 'resplendent' Wi 6.12. Cf. μαραίνω.

ἁμαρτάνω: fut. ἁμαρτήσω, mid. ἁμαρτήσομαι; aor. ἥμαρτον, 3pl. ἡμάρτοσαν, inf. ἁμαρτεῖν, impv.3s ἁμαρτησάτω, ptc. ἁμαρτών, subj. ἁμάρτω; pf. ἡμάρτηκα, ptc. ἡμαρτηκώς.

1. *to act sinfully*: abs. 2K 14.27*L* (|| κακοποιέω), of idol worship, Ho 13.2; against sbd τινι– God, 1Kg 1.25 (|| εἰς ἄνθρωπον), Ho 4.7, Mi 7.9; ἐναντίον τοῦ θεοῦ Ge 39.9 (|| ποιέω ῥῆμα πονηρόν); ἔναντι κυρίου ἀκουσίως ἀπὸ τῶν προσταγμάτων κυρίου 'against the Lord unwillingly in contravention of the Lord's injunctions' Le 4.2; εἰς ἐμέ Ge 20.6, εἰς τὸν θεὸν αὐτῶν Ju 5.20; πρός με Ex 23.33; ἐνώπιόν μου 32.33. **b**. against a hum.: + dat. pers., τῷ κυρίῳ αὐτῶν τῷ βασιλεῖ Αἰγύπτου Ge 40.1; εἰς σέ 43.9, εἰς πλῆθος πόλεως Si 7.7; εἰς αἷμα ἀθῷον 'innocent blood' 1K 19.5; πρὸς τὸν πατέρα Ge 44.32; treason against ruler, 3K 1.21*L*. **c**. ἐναντίον κυρίου τοῦ θεοῦ ὑμῶν καὶ εἰς ὑμᾶς Ex 10.16. **d**. opp. ἀθῷος εἰμί: Nu 32.23 (:: εἰμι ἀθῷος vs. 22). **e**. on various combinations of synonyms, see under ἀδικέω, and on the rection, cf. Joosten 2003.

2. *to commit* a sinful act (acc.): ἁμαρτίαν μεγάλην Ex 32.30; ἀδικίαν Ho 12.8; cf. ἡ ἁμαρτία, ἣν ἥμαρτον ἐν αὐτῇ Le 4.14; ἕν τι τούτων 5.4; ἁμαρτιῶν, ὧν ἡμάρτοσάν μοι Je 40.8.

3. *to fail to be available*: *s* food (δίαιτα) Jb 5.24.

Cf. ἁμαρτία, ἁμάρτημα, ἁμαρτωλός, ἐφ~, ἐξαμαρτάνω, ἀδικέω, ἀσεβέω, πλημμελέω: Quell, *TDNT* 1.267-9; Betram, ib. 286-9; Stählin, ib. 293-6; Rengstrof, ib. 320-4.

ἁμάρτημα, ατος. n.

1. *sinful act*: τὸ ἁ. μου Ge 31.36 (ǁ ἀδίκημα); manifested by βωμοί 'altars' Ho 10.8; ǁ σκληρότης, ἀσέβημα De 9.27; ǁ ἀδικία, ἁμαρτία 19.15; ǁ ἀνομία Is 58.1; θανάτου 'punishable by death' De 22.26; νόμου 'against the law' Wi 2.12.

2. *failure to achieve an aim*: παιδείας ἡμῶν 'of our education' Wi 2.12.

*3. *penalty incurred for committing a sin*: ἐδέξατο .. διπλᾶ τὰ ~τα αὐτῆς Is 40.2, cf. ἁμαρτία **4**.

*4. *slaughtered animal offered to atone* ἁμάρτημα: Le 4.29.

Cf. ἁμαρτία, ἁμαρτάνω, ἀσέβημα: Trench 241f.

ἁμαρτία, ας. f.

1. *sinful act*: ǁ ἀδικία Ge 50.17, Ho 8.13, Mi 7.19; ǁ ἀνομία Is 5.18; ǁ ἀδικία and ἀνομία Le 16.21, ἀφαιρῶν ἀνομίας καὶ ἀδικίας καὶ ~ας Ex 34.7, Nu 14.18; ǁ ἀδικία, ἁμάρτημα De 19.15; ǁ ἀσέβεια Mi 1.5, 3.8, 6.7; punishable, ἐκδικήσει ~ας Ho 9.9 (ǁ ἀδικία), sim. Am 3.2; ἀφανιῶ σε ἐπὶ ταῖς ~αις σου 'shall obliterate you on account of your sins' Mi 6.13; ἰσχυρά 'grave' Am 5.12 (consisting in social injustices and ǁ ἀσέβεια); μεγάλη Ge 18.20, 20.9. **b**. cogn. obj. of ἁμαρτάνω Le 19.22. **c**. obj. of ποιέω Nu 5.7, De 9.21. **d**. τὸ περὶ ~ας 'an offering for sin' Le 14.13, Ba 1.10, see s.v. περί **I 3b**. **e**. *transgression, violation*: διαθήκης '(against the terms) of covenant' Da 11.32 LXX.

2. *state of being sinful*: ἐν ~ᾳ ἐσμεν περὶ τοῦ ἀδελφοῦ ἡμῶν 'we are guilty over our brother' Ge 42.21.

*3. *slaughtered animal offered to atone* ἁμαρτία: μοσχάριον ~ας Ex 29.36; Le 4.29; ~ας λαοῦ μου φάγονται 'they shall eat the sin-offerings of my people' Ho 4.8 (Muraoka 1983.36) or '.. feast on the sins .. (i.e. by encouraging people to sin and offer more sin-offerings),' cf. Daniel 299-328.

*4. *penalty incurred for committing a sin*: λήμψεται τὴν ~αν Le 5.1; 19.8, Nu 14.34; pl. 1E 8.83, Is 13.11. Cf. ἁμάρτημα **3**.

Cf. ἁμαρτάνω, ἁμάρτημα, φιλαμαρτήμων, ἀδικία, ἀμβλοκία, ἀσέβεια, πλημμέλεια: Trench 240f.

ἁμαρτωλός, όν.

given to ἁμαρτία (q.v.): ἔθνος ~όν Is 1.4 (ǁ πλήρης ἁμαρτιῶν), 1M 1.34 (ǁ ἄνδρας παρανόμους), cf. ἔθνος ~ῶν To 13.6 𝔊[I]; ῥίζα ~ός 1.10; ἀνὴρ ~ός Si 27.30, cf. s.v. ἀνήρ **3**; ἀνθρώπων ~ῶν Nu 32.14, cf. s.v. ἄνθρωπος **3f**; Si 5.9, 6.1. **b**. mostly subst., 'sinner': in relation to God, πονηροὶ καὶ ~οὶ ἐναντίον τοῦ θεοῦ Ge 13.13; βασιλεία ~ῶν Am 9.8; object of divine punishment, τελευτήσουσι πάντες ~οὶ λαοῦ μου 9.10; opp. εὐσεβής Si 36.14; ǁ ἀσεβής, λοιμός Ps 1.1, + πονηρός 9.35; opp. δίκαιος 1.5.

Cf. ἁμαρτία, ἀλιτήριος: Deissmann 1923.91f.

ἀμάσητος, ον.ʃ*

unchewed: *s* food, Jb 20.18. Cf. μάσσομαι.

ἀμαυρός, ά, όν.

not clearly visible, 'dim, faint': *s* infection of leprous skin, Le 13.4 (:: τηλαυγής). Cf. ἀμαυρόω, τηλαυγής, φανερός: LSG s.v.

ἀμαυρόω: fut.pass. ἀμαυρωθήσομαι; aor.pass. ἠμαυρώθην.ʃ

1. *to render blind*: *o* eyes, pass., De 34.7, Si 43.4

2. *to make dim, obscure*: fig., "Bewitching power of wickedness obscures τὰ καλά" Wi 4.12.

3. *to cause to lose lustre*: *o* gold, Πῶς ἀμαυρωθήσεται χρυσίον; La 4.1.

Cf. ἀμαυρός, ἀπαμαυρόω.

ἀμάχως. adv.ʃ

without strife: βιώσεται 'he will live' Si 19.6¶. Cf. μάχη.

ἀμάω: fut. ἀμήσω; aor.subj. ἀμήσω, impv. ἄμησον.ʃ

to reap, harvest: abs., σπείραντες ἀμήσατε Is 37.30; σὺ σπερεῖς καὶ οὐ μὴ ἀμήσῃς 'you will sow but never harvest' Mi 6.15; + acc. rei, τὰ αὐτόματα τὰ ἀναβαίνοντα 'what grows of itself' Le 25.11 (ǁ τρυγάω); ἀμητὸν ἐν τῷ ἀγρῷ De 24.19; σπέρμα σταχύων Is 17.5. Cf. ἄμητος, εἰσφέρω, θερίζω, τρυγάω: Shipp 63.

ἀμβλακία, ας. f.ʃ

error: moral, ǁ ἁμαρτία 3M 2.19.

ἀμβλύνω: aor.pass. ἠμβλύνθην.ʃ

pass. *to lose power and effectiveness*: ἠμβλύνθησαν οἱ ὀφθαλμοὶ αὐτοῦ τοῦ ὁρᾶν 'his eyes became too dim to see' Ge 27.1 (in old age). Cf. ἀμβλυωπέω, ἐκλείπω.

ἀμβλυωπέω.ʃ

to suffer from dysfunction as an organ of visual perception: *s* hum. eye, 3K 12.24[i] (in old age). Cf. ἀμβλύνω.

ἀμβρόσιος, α, ον.ʃ

divinely excellent: *s* τροφή 'food' Wi 19.21.

ἀμέθυστος, ου. m.

amethyst: Ex 28.19, Ez 28.13.

ἀμείδητος, ον.ʃ *

not smiling: *s* πρόσωπον Wi 17.4. Cf. μειδιάω.

ἀμέλγω: aor. ἤμελξα.ʃ

to squeeze out milk: + acc., γάλα 'milk' Pr 30.33; metaph., + acc. pers., ὥσπερ γάλα με ἤμελξας Jb

10.10 (‖ τυρόω 'to curdle'). Cf. γάλα, τυρόω, ἄμελξις.

ἀμελέω: aor. ἠμέλησα, ptc. ἀμελήσας.ʃ

to be unconcerned and indifferent to: + gen. pers., Je 4.12, 38.32; + gen. rei, τῶν θυσιῶν 2M 4.14 (‖ καταφρονέω and see Spicq 1.91, n. 18), τοῦ δικαίου Wi 3.10. Cf. ἀμελῶς, ἐπιμελέομαι, μέλω, ὀλιγωρέω, παρ~, ὑπεροραω: Schmidt 2.634f.

ἄμελξις, εως. f.ʃ

v.n. of ἀμέλγω: Jb 20.17. Cf. ἀμέλγω.

ἀμελῶς. adv.ʃ.

in indifferent manner: ποιῶν τὰ ἔργα κυρίου ἀ. Je 31.10. Cf. ἐπιμελῶς, ἀμελέω.

ἄμεμπτος, ον.

irreproachable (morally): *s* hum., γίνου ἀ. Ge 17.1; Jb 1.1; θεῷ 'in relation to God' Wi 10.5; ‖ ὅσιος 10.15, ‖ καθαρός Jb 4.17, ‖ δίκαιος 9.20, 12.4. Cf. ἄμωμος, ἀνέγκλητος, μέμφομαι: Trench 380; MM s.v.; *ND* 4.141.

ἀμέμπτως. adv. ʃ

impeccably: Es B 4 o'. Cf. ἄμεμπτος: *ND* 4.141.

ἀμερής, ές.ʃ

incapable of further division, minuscule: *s* χρόνος '(very brief) moment' 3M 5.25, 6.29. Cf. μερίζω.

ἀμέριμνος, ον.ʃ

not affected by worries and anxiety: *s* hum., Wi 6.15; wisdom, 7.23. Cf. μέριμνα.

ἀμεσσαῖος, ον.ʃ *

positioned in the middle between two sides: *s* hum., 1K 17.23*L*. Cf. μέσος.

ἀμετάθετος, ον.ʃ

not amenable to a change of attitude or stance: *s* hum., 3M 5.1; plan, 5.12. Cf. μετατίθημι.

ἀμέτρητος, ον.ʃ

immeasurably great in quantity or size: εἰς χώραν μεγάλην καὶ ~ον Is 22.18; ὕδωρ 3M 2.4 (of the Noachic flood), τὴν ἀπέραντον καὶ ~ον γῆν 'the limitless ..' 2.9, τὴν ~ον αὐτῶν πληθύν 'their immeasurably large number' 4.17; *s* γῆ 3M 2.9, κτίσις 'the created world' Si 16.17, ὄλβος'happiness' 30.15, divine mercy, Od 12.6 (+ ἀνεξιχνίαστος 'inscrutable'); ὁ οἶκος τοῦ θεοῦ Ba 3.25 (+ ὑψηλός). Cf. μετρέω.

ἄμητος, ου. m.

act of harvesting, reaping: Ge 45.6 (‖ ἀροτρίασις 'ploughing'); τῷ σπόρῳ καὶ τῷ ~ῳ κατάπαυσις 'you shall not engage in seeding and harvesting' Ex 34.21, + σπορά 'sowing' 4K 19.29; συνάγων καλάμην ἐν ~ῳ 'gathering straw in harvest' Mi 7.1 (‖ τρύγητος). Cf. ἀμάω, ἀλόητος, ἀροτρίασις, τρύγητος.

ἀμητός, οῦ. m.

crop ripe for harvesting: δρέπανον ἐπ' ~όν 'sickle ..' De 16.9, δρέπανον οὐ μὴ ἐπιβάλης ἐπὶ τὸν ~ὸν τοῦ πλησίον σου 23.24; εἰσέλθῃς εἰς ~ὸν τοῦ πλησίον σου ib.; ἀμήσῃς ~ὸν ἐν τῷ ἀγρῷ σου 'harvest crop in your field' 24.19; συναγάγῃ ~ὸν ἑστηκότα Is 17.5; ~οῦ εἰσφερομένου '.. ingathered' 23.3. Cf. ἄμητος, ἀμάω. On the distinction between ἀμητός and ἄμητος, see Walters 226f.

ἀμήχανος, ον.ʃ

inconceivable, unthinkable: *s* action, 2M 3.12.

ἀμίαντος, ον.ʃ

morally *undefiled*: *s* hum., Wi 3.13; prizes in sports, 4.2; body, 8.20; temple, 2M 14.36, 15.34. Cf. μιαίνω.

ἀμιξία, ας. f.ʃ

dissociation from the ruler or ruling authority, 'sedition, revolt': 2M 14.3 (v.l. ἐπιμιξία 'commingling'), 38, see *DGE* s.v. Cf. μίγνυμι.

ἀμισθί. adv.ʃ

without being paid for labour: Jb 24.6. Cf. μισθός.

Αμμανίτης, ου.

an Ammonite: Ge 19.38 +.

ἄμμος, ου. f.

fine particle of earth, 'sand': ἔκρυψεν αὐτὸν ἐν τῇ ~ῳ 'hid him in the sand' Ex 2.12; in a simile of large quantity, εἰ δύναταί τις ἐξαριθμῆσαι τὴν ~ον τῆς γῆς 'if someone can count up the sand of the earth' Ge 13.16, cf. 28.14, 32.12; ἦν ὁ ἀριθμὸς τῶν υἱῶν Ισραηλ ὡς ἡ ἄ. τῆς θαλάσσης Ho 1.10; πληθυνῶ τὸ σπέρμα σου ὡς τοὺς ἀστέρας τοῦ οὐρανοῦ καὶ ὡς τὴν ~ον τὴν παρὰ τὸ χεῖλος τῆς θαλάσσης '.. the stars .. the beach' Ge 22.17; σῖτον ὡς τὴν ~ον τῆς θαλάσσης πολὺν σφόδρα 41.49; ὑπὲρ ~ον τῆς θαλάσσης 'more than ..' Je 15.8.

Cf. γῆ, ἀμμώδης, ψάμμος.

ἀμμώδης, ες.ʃ

sandy: ἀνάβασις 'climbing a sandy ground' Si 25.20. Cf. ἄμμος.

ἀμνάς, άδος. f.*

fem. of ἀμνός 'lamb': ἑπτὰ ~άδας προβάτων Ge 21.28; cultic offering, ~άδα ἢ χίμαιραν '.. or a female kid' Le 5.6; μικρά 'small' 2K 12.3. Cf. ἀμνός, πρόβατον.

ἀμνημονέω: aor.subj. ἀμνημονήσω.ʃ

to fail to retain in memory: + gen., Si 37.6 (‖ ἐπιλανθάνομαι). Cf. ἐπιλανθάνω, μιμνήσκομαι, ἀμνησία.

ἀμνησία, ας. f.ʃ

act of mentally not retrieving the past, 'amnesia, forgetfulness': κακῶν 'of hardships' Si 11.25. Cf. μιμνήσκομαι, ἀμνημονέω, ἀμνηστία, λήθη, ἐπιλησμονή.

ἀμνησικακία, ας.ʃ*

act of bestowing amnesty: 3M 3.21.

ἀμνήστευτος, ον.ʃ

unbetrothed: *s* παρθένος Ex 22.16. Cf. μνηστεύω.

ἀμνηστία, ας. f.ʃ
= ἀμνησία, q.v.: + gen. rei, Wi 14.26, 19.4.

ἀμνός, οῦ. m.
lamb: for cultic use, Ex 12.5 (+ ἔριφος), Le 14.10 (+ πρόβατον); νεμήσει αὐτοὺς κύριος ὡς ~όν 'the Lord will feed them as a lamb' Ho 4.16; ἀ. ἐκ προβάτων De 14.4 (‖ μόσχος, χίμαρον). Cf. ἀμνάς, ἀρήν, πρόβατον: Chantraine 1955; LSG s.v.

ἀμοιρέω.ʃ
to have no share in: + gen., γνώσεως Si 3.25¶ (‖ ἀπορέω). Cf. ἄμοιρος.

ἄμοιρος, ον.ʃ
having a share of sth *withheld*: + gen., Wi 2.9. Cf. ἀμοιρέω.

ἀμόλυντος, ον.ʃ
undefiled: *s* spirit of Wisdom, Wi 7.22. Cf. μολύνω.

ἀμόρα, ας. f.ʃ
sweet cake: Ct 2.5. Cf. ἀμορίτης.

ἀμορίτης, ου. m.ʃ*
= ἀμόρα: 1C 16.3.

Αμορραῖος.
Amorite: Ge 10.16 +.

ἄμορφος, ον.ʃ
amorphous: *s* ὕλη 'material' Wi 11.17. Cf. μορφή.

ἄμπελος, ου. f.
grape-vine: ἄ. εὐκληματοῦσα 'a well-growing ..' Ho 10.1 (ref. to Israel); ἐξανθήσει ὡς ἄ. τὸ μνημόσυνον αὐτοῦ 'his memory will blossom like ..' 14.8; ἡ ἄ. ἐξηράνθη Jl 1.12; οὐ μὴ ἀσθενήσῃ ὑμῖν ἡ ἄ. ἐν τῷ ἀγρῷ Ma 3.11; ἡ ἄ. δώσει τὸν καρπὸν αὐτῆς Zc 8.12; ἀναπαύσεται ἕκαστος ὑποκάτω ~ου αὐτοῦ Mi 4.4, sim. Zc 3.10; κληματίς, σταφυλή De 32.32; ‖ συκῆ Nu 20.5, Ho 2.12; ‖ συκῆ, ῥόα De 8.8; also φοῖνιξ, μῆλον and other fruit-trees, Jl 1.12; fig. of wisdom, Si 24.17, of wife Ps 127.3. Cf. ἀμπελών, σταφυλή.

ἀμπελουργός, οῦ. m.
vineyard specialist: ‖ ἀροτήρ 'plougher' Is 61.5, ‖ γεωργός 'peasant' Je 52.16, 4K 25.12*L*. Cf. Mayerson 2003.

ἀμπελών, ῶνος. m.
vineyard: ‖ ἐλαιών Ex 23.11, De 6.11; ‖ ἀγρός Nu 20.17, 21.22; ‖ συκών, ἐλαιών, and κῆπος Am 4.9; ~ῶνας .. ἐφυτεύσατε 'you planted ..' 5.11. **b**. *fruits of vineyard*: ‖ ἐλαιών Jo 24.13.
Cf. ἄμπελος, ἐλαιών, κῆπος, συκών: Shipp 65; Lee 107.

ἀμπλακία: ⇒ ἀμβλακία.

ἀμύγδαλον, ου. n.ʃ
almond-tree: Ec 12.5. Cf. Shipp 66f.

ἀμύθητος, ον.
unquantifiably many or *much*: opp. ὀλίγος Jb 8.7; *s* hum., 36.28. Cf. πολύς.

ἄμυνα, ας. f.ʃ
v.n. of ἀμύνω **2**: ἐχθρῶν 'by enemies' Wi 5.17.

ἀμύνω: aor.mid. ἠμυνάμην, inf. ἀμύνασθαι, subj. ἀμύνωμαι.
1. *to help and defend*: + acc., τῷ βραχίονι αὐτοῦ 'with his arm' Is 59.16.
2. *to ward off* an assailant: + acc., Es 6.13, E 20, Ps 117.10; ἐχθρούς Jo 10.13, Wi 11.3. **b**. *to reject* sth undesirable or unlawful: 2M 6.20.
Cf. ἄμυνα, ἀπ~, ἐπαμύνω: LSG s.v.

ἀμφήκης, ες.ʃ
two-edged: *s* sword, 2K 20.8*L*.

ἀμφιά/έζω: aor. ἠμφίασα, mid. ἠμφια/εσάμην, impv. mid. ἀμφίασαι.ʃ
to clothe: Jb 31.19; mid., 'to wear, put on' and metaph., + acc., κρῖμα 29.14 (‖ ἐνδύω), δόξαν καὶ τιμήν 40.10, λόγους ἀδίκους 4K 17.9. Cf. ἐνδύω.

ἀμφίασις, εως. *
clothes: Jb 22.6; 24.7 (‖ ἱμάτιον). Cf. ἱμάτιον, ἀμφιάζω.

ἀμφιβάλλω: fut. ~βαλῶ.ʃ
to move by throwing over a large area, 'cast': *o* ἀμφίβληστρον 'net' Hb 1.17. Cf. ἀμφίβληστρον, ἀμφιβολεύς, βάλλω.

ἀμφίβληστρον, ου. n.
casting-net: for fishing, εἵλκυσεν αὐτὸν ἐν ~ῳ 'drew it with a net' Hb 1.15 (‖ σαγήνη); ἀμφιβάλλειν ἀ. 'to cast a net' 1.17; 1.16; for hunting(?), πεσοῦνται ἐν ~ῳ Ps 140.10 (‖ παγίς 'trap' vs. 9). Cf. ἀμφιβάλλω, δίκτυον, σαγήνη: Trench 236; Petersen 198.

ἀμφιβολεύς, έως. m.ʃ*
he who fishes with ἀμφίβληστρον (q.v.): Is 19.8 (‖ οἱ βάλλοντες σαγήνας). Cf. LSG s.v.

ἀμφιλαφής, ές.ʃ
thickly grown: *s* branch, Wi 17.18.

ἀμφίταπος, ου.ʃ
rug or *carpet with pile on both sides* (LS): + κοίτη 'bed' 2K 17.28; Egyptian import, Pr 7.16. Cf. ψιλή.

ἄμφοδον, ου. n.ʃ
quarter of a town: Je 17.27, 30.16.

ἀμφοτεροδέξιος, ον.ʃ *
able to use left and right hands equally well: *s* hum., Jd 3.15.

ἀμφότερος, α, ον. Alw. pl.
the two mentioned earlier or *implied*: διέθεντο ~οι διαθήκην 'the two made a covenant' Ge 21.27, ἔκλαυσαν ~οι 'they both wept' 33.4; ἀνὰ μέσον ~ων 'between the two of them' Zc 6.13. **b**. used predicatively: ~α τὰ μέρη αὐτοῦ 'both sides of it' Ex 26.19, ἐπ' ~ων τῶν σταθμῶν 'on both of the door-posts' 12.22, ~ους τοὺς νεφρούς Le 3.10 (‖ τοὺς δύο νεφρούς 4.9); 1K 5.4. ***c**.ʃ καὶ ἀμφότερ~ may conclude a sentence to reinforce the fact that the pre-

ceding statement equally applies to both subjects mentioned therein: .. βδέλυγμα κυρίῳ .. ἐστιν καὶ ~α 'they are an abomination to the Lord, both of them' De 23.18; οὖς ἀκούει καὶ ὀφθαλμὸς ὁρᾷ· κυρίου ἔργα καὶ ~α 'the ear hears and the eye sees; they are both the Lord's work' Pr 20.12, see also 20.10: in all three cases the Heb. reads גַּם שְׁנֵיהֶם and the form of ἀμφ. is n.pl. irrespective of the gender and number of the two nouns concerned while the suffix attached to the Hebrew numeral is invariably masculine. Cf. ἀπέθανον καί γε ἀμφότεροι, Μααλων καὶ Χελαιων Ru 1.5.

Cf. δύο, ἑκάτερος: Shipp 67; Muraoka 2001c.

ἄμωμος, ον.

unblemished, impeccable: *s* sacrificial animals, δάμαλιν ~ον, ἥτις οὐκ ἔχει ἐν αὐτῇ μῶμον 'a heifer ..' Nu 19.2; Ex 29.1, 38, Le 1.3, 22.19; ἀμνοὺς ἐνιαυσίους ~ους Nu 28.3; human moral character, γινώσκει κύριος τὰς ὁδοὺς τῶν ~ων Ps 36.18, γυνὴ ~ος Si 40.19, poss. physical features included, νεανίσκους ~ους καὶ εὐειδεῖς καὶ ἐπιστήμονας .. '.. handsome and knowledgeable ..' Da LXX 1.4; human conduct, πορευόμενος ἐν ὁδῷ ~ῳ Ps 100.6 (cf. πορευόμενος ~ος καὶ ἐργαζόμενος δικαιοσύνην 14.2), γενηθήτω ἡ καρδία μου ~ος ἐν τοῖς δικαιώμασίν σου 118.80; in general, ἱερεῖς ~ους θελητὰς νόμου '.. devoted to the law' 1M 4.42; ὁ νόμος κυρίου ~ος Ps 18.8, God's way 17.31 ‖ hum.'s way 17.33. Cf. μῶμος, ἄμεμπτος, ἀνέγκλητος.

ἄν. Never clause-initial.

1. Used in the apodosis of a hypothetical condition, with an aor., and immediately before or after it: Εἰ εὗρον χάριν ἐναντίον σου, οἰωνισάμην ἄν 'If I were favourably regarded by you, I would have guessed' Ge 30.27; εἰ ἀνήγγειλάς μοι, ἐξαπέστειλα ἄν σε .. 'if you had let me know, I would have sent you off ..' 31.27; ποῦ ἂν ἀπερρίφης .. οὐκ ἂν ἔκλεψαν .. οὐκ ἂν ὑπελίποντο .. 'where would you have been cast away? .. would they not have stolen ..? would they not have left ..? Ob 5; Nu 16.14. **b**. + an aor. opt.: πῶς ἂν κλέψαιμεν .. 'how could we have stolen ..?' Ge 44.8.

2. With another conjunction and subj.: ἡνίκα ἄν Ge 24.41, 27.40; ὅπως ἄν Ho 2.3, Am 9.12 v.l; καθὼς ἄν Ho 7.12; καθὰ ἄν Ge 19.8; ἐν παντὶ τόπῳ, οὗ ἂν .. Ex 20.24. **b**. In a generalising relative clause: ὃς ἄν + subj., Ge 2.17, 15.14, 44.9; + indic. 2.19; ὅσος ἄν + subj., Ge 11.6, Jl 2.32. On ὡς ἄν, see under ὡς, and on the variation between ἐάν and ἄν, see Wevers, *Notes* ad Ge 2.19.

3. In an independent clause with ἄν and an opt.aor., indicating a possibility: πῶς ἂν γένοιτο ἑσπέρα 'How on earth could an evening come round?' De 28.67; εἰσέλθοις ἄν 'you could enter' 33.7; reinforced by ἴσως 'perhaps' 4M 1.5. **b**. Also w. an indic. aor.: ἀπήλλαξεν γὰρ ἂν πόνον 'for he could have removed pain' Jb 3.10; 3.13.

4. Introduces a conditional clause (= ἐάν): οὐδ' ἂν ἔρχησθε 'not even if you came' Is 1.12, sim. 58.5; + subj. aor., 4M 16.11; + opt. aor., 5.30. Cf. BDF § 107.

5. With an impf. or aor. indic. in a subordinate clause indicates iterativity: + impf., Ez 1.12, 20; + aor., 10.11.

Cf. ἐάν.

ἀνά prep. Mostly compounded with μέσον and gen.

I. ἀνὰ μέσον + gen. *in the midst of, amongst*: w. a pl. noun, ἀδελφῶν Ho 13.15; τῶν ἀστρῶν Ob 4; τῶν ὀρέων Zc 1.8; ἀνὰ μέσον αὐτῶν 'between them' Ge 42.23.

2. *between* two or more distinct parties: to judge, arbitrate, ἀ. μ. λαῶν πολλῶν Mi 4.3; ἀμφοτέρων Zc 6.13; τῶν χειρῶν σου 13.6; two parties specified, ἀ. μέσον ἐμοῦ καὶ σοῦ Ge 13.7; ἀ. μ. τῆς κρηπῖδος καὶ τοῦ θυσιαστηρίου 'between the platform and the altar' Jl 2.17; ἀ. μ. τοῦ δουλεύοντος θεῷ καὶ τοῦ μὴ δουλεύοντος Ma 3.18; τοῦ συνίειν ἀ. μ. ἀγαθοῦ καὶ κακοῦ 'to be intelligent enough to tell the good from the evil' 3K 3.9; same noun repeated, ἀνὰ μέσον ὕδατος καὶ ὕδατος 'between one mass of water and the other' Ge 1.6, ἀ. μ. ποίμνης καὶ ποίμνης 32.16; *ἀνὰ μέσον repeated, ἀ. μ. τοῦ φωτὸς καὶ ἀ. μ. τοῦ σκότους 1.4; ἀ. μ. τῆς ἡμέρας καὶ ἀ. μ. τῆς νυκτός 1.14; ἀ. μ. τῆς γῆς καὶ ἀ. μ. τοῦ οὐρανοῦ Zc 5.9; Juda and Israel, 11.14; ἀ. μ. δικαίου καὶ ἀ. μ. ἀνόμου 3.18; ‖ ἀνὰ μέσον not repeated, Le 20.25; a third party added, i.e. between A and B on the one hand, and between A and C on the other – ἀ. μ. ἐμοῦ καὶ ὑμῶν καὶ ἀ. μ. πάσης ψυχῆς Ge 9.12; ἀ. μ. ἐμοῦ καὶ ἀ. μ. σοῦ καὶ ἀ. μ. τοῦ σπέρματός σου 17.7; ἀ. μ. τι καί τινος– ἀ. μ. αἷμα καὶ αἵματος 'a case involving two possible decisions relating to homicide' De 17.8.

II. + acc., distributively, 'each': ἐνώτια χρυσᾶ ἀνὰ δραχμὴν ὁλκῆς 'golden ear-rings each a drachm in weight' Ge 24.22, ἑκατὸν ἄνδρας ἀ. πεντήκοντα ἐν σπηλαίῳ '100 men, 50 each in a cave' 3K 18.13. **b**. w. pleonastic μέσον: ἀ. μέσον τῶν δέκα ἡμερῶν 'every ten days' Ne 5.18. ***c**. calqued on עַל־יַד: ἀ. χεῖρα ὁδοῦ .. 2K 15.2 (*L* ἐπὶ τῆς ὁδοῦ 'by the roadside ..'). Cf. κατά **II 8**. See Johannessohn, *Präp.* 169.

Cf. μεταξύ: Johannessohn, *Präp.* 169-73; Sollamo, *Semiprep.* 347f.

ἀναβαθμίς, μίδος. f.ʃ *

step, stair with which to ascend: οὐκ ἀναβήσῃ ἐν ~ίσιν 'thou shalt not ascend by steps' Ex 20.26; 4K 9.13*L* (B: ἀναβαθμός). Cf. ἀναβαίνω, ἀναβαθμός.

ἀναβαθμός, οῦ. m.

1. *stage in ascending or descending scale*: 'degree' on a sun-dial, ἀνέβη ὁ ἥλιος τοὺς δέκα ~ούς, οὓς κατέβη ἡ σκιά 'the sun went up by the ten degrees, by which the shadow (on the dial) had gone down' Is 38.8, sim. ‖ 4K 20.9*L* (B: βαθμός).

2. = ἀναβαθμίς (q.v.): Ez 40.6 (‖ κλιμακτήρ vs. 22), Ps 119.1+; up to a throne, 3K 10.19.

Cf. ἀναβαθμίς, βαθμός.

ἀναβαίνω: fut. ~βήσομαι; aor. ἀνέβην, subj. ~βῶ, inf. ~βῆναι, impv.2sg. ~βηθι, 3s ~βήτω, ptc. ~βάς; pf.ptc. ~βεβηκώς.

1. *to ascend*, 'go/come up.' **a**. Physically, to a higher place: abs., Ge 46.29 (mounting a carriage [ἅρμα]); ἐπὶ τὴν κορυφὴν τοῦ βουνοῦ 'to the top of the hill' Ex 17.10; ἀπὸ Αραβωθ .. ἐπὶ τὸ ὄρος .. ἐπὶ κορυφὴν Φασγα De 34.1; ἐπὶ (v.l. εἰς) τὸ ὄρος Hg 1.8, cf. Ex 34.4 (‖ εἰς vs. 2); ἐπ' αὐτήν [= ὁδόν] Is 35.9 (not necessarily an elevated highway); ἐπί τινα Ge 38.12; ἐν ἀναβαθμίσιν ἐπὶ τὸ θυσιαστήριον 'to the altar by steps' Ex 20.26, ἐπὶ βωμόν Je 31.35, cf. 3K 18.29 (*s* cultic offering); ἐξ Αἰγύπτου .. εἰς τὴν ἔρημον Ge 13.1; εἰς τὸ ὄρος Ex 19.12; εἰς τὸν οὐρανόν De 30.12, Am 9.2 (last: opp. κατάγω), ἕως τῶν οὐρανῶν Ps 106.26 (:: καταβαίνω and *s* waves of the sea); from a river, Ex 8.3 (*s* frogs); from a fountain, Ge 24.16 (:: καταβαίνω); from Egypt to Canaan, πρὸς τὸν παῖδά σου 44.24 (:: καταβαίνω vs. 23); ἐντεῦθεν .. εἰς τὴν γῆν .. Ex 33.1; οἱ ἄγγελοι τοῦ θεοῦ ἀνέβαινον καὶ κατέβαινον ἐπ' αὐτῆς Ge 28.12; ἀνέβη ὁ θεὸς ἀπ' αὐτοῦ 35.13; ὡς ἄνδρες πολεμισταὶ ἀ. ἐπὶ τὰ τείχη 'like soldiers they will climb on to the walls' Jl 2.7, sim. 9; + acc. loci (so already in Hom., οὐρανόν *Il*. 1.497), Φάραγγα βότρυος Nu 32.9, τὴν πόλιν 1K 9.14 (*L* εἰς ..), ὄρη Ps 103.8 (*s* flood waters); returnees from exile, Ju 4.3, εἰς τὴν Ιερουσαλημ 1E 2.5. See Na 2.8, which is obscure. **b**. Heading for a more desirable or important destination: ἐκ τῆς γῆς, poss. alluding to the Exodus, Ho 1.11; εἰς 'Ασσυρίους 'to Assyria' (in order to seek help) 8.9; εἰς λαὸν παροικίας μου Hb 3.16; said to a man of authority, Οὐκ ἀναβαίνομεν 'We are not coming' Nu 16.12, 14; ἐπὶ τὴν πύλην ἐπὶ τὴν γερουσίαν De 25.7; 'Ανάβαινε πρός με 'Come to me' (or poss. lit. to a high-ranking person seated at a higher level) Pr 25.7. **c**. Up into a temple often situated on elevated ground: εἰς τὸν οἶκον Ων Ho 4.15; εἰς τὸ ὄρος κυρίου καὶ εἰς τὸν οἶκον τοῦ θεοῦ Ιακωβ Mi 4.2, cf. ἀναβήσομαι πρὸς τὸν θεὸν Ex 32.30; of an annual pilgrimage to Jerusalem, κατ' ἐνιαυτὸν τοῦ προσκυνῆσαι .. καὶ τοῦ ἑορτάζειν Zc 14.16; εἰς Ιερουσαλημ, 17; 18*bis*, 19. **d**. *s* vegetation, 'to come up, shoot up': στάχυες 'ears of corn' Ge 41.5 (‖ vs. 6 ἀναφύω); χλωρόν De 29.23 (‖ ἀνατέλλω); ἄκανθα καὶ τρίβολοι ἐπὶ τὰ θυσιαστήρια Ho 10.8; ἄνθος 'flower' Is 5.24, 11.1 (‖ ἐξέρχομαι); Le 25.5. **e**. a stream of water gushing up out of the ground: πηγή Ge 2.6; ὡς ποταμὸς συντέλεια Am 8.8, 9.5 (‖ καταβαίνειν), Je 26.7, 8 - on the use in papyri of this verb on the flooding of the Nile, see Preisigke, s.v.; ὡς ἀναβαίνει ἡ θάλασσα τοῖς κύμασιν αὐτῆς 'as the sea mounts with its waves' Ez 26.3. **f**. foul odour rising: σαπρία, βρόμος Jl 2.20, ὀσμή (of corpses) Is 34.3. **g**. a cry, clamour: βοὴ πρός τινα Ex 2.23; κραυγή Jn 1.2, Je 14.2. **h**. Embarking a ship: εἰς ^τὸ πλοῖον^ Jn 1.3 v.l. (for ἐμβαίνω). **i**. of mounting a horse: ἐφ' ἵππον Ho 14.4; ἱππέως ἀναβαίνοντος Na 3.3; *s* copulating animals, ἐπὶ τὰ πρόβατα καὶ τὰς αἶγας Ge 31.10, 12. **j**. *s* flame: φλὸξ τῆς γῆς ὡσεὶ ἀτμὶς καμίνου 'a flame of the (burning) land like a steam of furnace' Ge 19.28, sim. καπνός 'smoke' Is 34.10; ἀτμίς 'smoke (of incense)' Ez 8.11. **k**. overshadowing cloud lifting, ἀπὸ τῆς σκηνῆς Ex 40.30; Nu 9.21.

*2. *to emerge, make appearance* with no upward movement necessarily implied: *s* a threatening object or person with hostile intent: abs. Jl 3.9; ἀκρὶς ἐπὶ τὴν γῆν καὶ κατέδεται πᾶσαν βοτάνην .. 'locusts .. upon the earth and devour every plant ..' Ex 10.12; a lion out of its lair, Je 4.7. **b**. *s* anger: ἀναβῆναι θυμὸν εἰς ἐκδίκησιν Ez 24.8, ἀναβήσεται ὁ θυμός μου καὶ ὁ ζῆλός μου 38.18f.; 2K 11.20; + ἐπί τινα Ps 77.21; ἔν τινι 2C 36.16. Cf. ἀναφέρω **5**. **c**. welcome object: food in the wilderness, Ex 16.13. **d**. daybreak: ἀνέβη ὁ ὄρθρος 'the day broke' Ge 32.26, 1K 9.26, *s* τὸ πρωί Jd 19.25 B (A: ὁ ὄρθρος). **e**. *s* thought: οὐκ ἀναβήσεται αὐτῶν ἐπὶ τὴν καρδίαν Is 65.16 (‖ ἐπέρχομαι), ῥήματα Ez 38.10, ἐπὶ τὸ πνεῦμα ὑμῶν 20.31, cf. Je 28.50, λάλημα γλώσσῃ 'as the talk of the town' Ez 36.3, ἐν τοῖς ὠσίν μου '(reached) me as a report' 4K 19.28; inf., 12.5; δόξα θεοῦ Ισραηλ Ez 9.3, sim. 11.23. **f**. process: ἴασις 'healing' Je 8.22, cf. s.v. ἀνάγω **5**. **g**. medical symptom: λεύκωμα 'white film' To 6.9 $\mathfrak{G}^{II}$.

3. *to advance and reach a higher position*: on socio-economic ladder, ἐπὶ σὲ ἄνω ἄνω De 28.43 (:: καταβαίνω), cf. ἀναβῇ Βαβυλὼν ὡς ὁ οὐρανός Je 28.53; in military and/or political terms, Da 11.23 TH; ἀνέβη μῆκος τῶν ἔργων 'the (building) works made quite a progress' 2C 24.13.

*4. *to go away* (?): ἀναβήτω φθορὰ ζωῆς μου 'may the decay of my life be removed!' Jn 2.7 (MT: /taʿal miššaḥat ḥayyay/). On this semantic development, cf. עלה ni. and MH/Jewish Aramaic סלק 'to ascend' > הסתלק 'to disappear, go away.' Cf. ἀνέβη ἡ νεφέλη ἀπὸ τῆς σκηνῆς 'the cloud lifted from the tent' Nu 10.11, sim. 9.17, 21, Ex 40.31 and 'Εκχωρήσατε 'Depart!' for הֵרֹמּוּ Nu 16.45; ἀνέβη ἡ δύναμις τῶν Χαλδαίων ἀπὸ Ιερουσαλημ 'the Chaldaean army lifted its siege from J.' Je 44.11 (|| ἀποτρέχοντες ἀπελεύσονται vs. 9; Trg. *'istallaq* 'disappeared'), ἀναβήσεται ἀπ' ἐμοῦ 3K 15.19 (|| 2C 16.3 ἀπελθέτω ἀπ' ἐμοῦ 'let him get off my back'), 4K 12.19, cf. ἀπελεύσεται (MT: *ya'ăle*) ἀφ' ἡμῶν Je 21.2. See also Renehan 2.22 on an intr. ἀνάγω (sc. ἑαυτόν) 'to withdraw, retreat.' See also s.v. ἀνάγω **4** and ὑψόω **3**.

*__5__. *to set out on a military campaign*: εἰς πόλεμον 3K 22.15; *s* an army, ἐπὶ τὴν γῆν μου 'advance against my land' Jl 1.6, ἐπὶ Ιερουσαλημ πολεμῆσαι αὐτήν Is 7.1, sim. 36.10; Jl 3.12, cf. Ob 21, Na 2.2; ἐπὶ τὸν λαόν μου Ez 38.16; πρὸς τὸ ἔθνος Nu 13.31; εἰς τὴν 'Ιουδαίαν Is 7.6, εἰς σέ Je 31.18. See also s.v. ἀνάγω **3**.

Cf. ἀναβαθμίς, ἀνάβασις, ἀναβάτης, ἐμ~, ἐπι~, κατα~, συναναβαίνω, ἀναβιβάζω, ἀνάγω, ἀνατέλλω: Schmidt 1.477-504.

ἀναβάλλω: aor. ἀνέβαλον, mid. ἀνεβαλόμην; pf. ptc.mid. ~βεβλημένος.ʃ

I. act., *to toss*: + acc., ἐπὶ τὴν γῆν To 6.4 𝔊[I]; 4M 9.12.

2. *to wear*: + acc., στολήν 'garment' Si 50.11 (|| ἐνδιδύσκομαι).

II. mid. *to get into action*: abs., Ps 77.21, or poss. *to put off an action*.

2. *to dismiss the case of as of no consequence and urgency*: + acc. pers., τὸν χριστόν σου Ps 88.39, cf. Acts 24.22.

3. *to throw over own shoulder and wear*: + acc., φῶς ὡς ἱμάτιον Ps 103.2; διπλοΐδα ἀναβεβλημένος 'clothed with a double cloak' 1K 28.14.

Cf. ἀναβράσσω, ἐνδιδύσκω, ἐνδύω: LSG s.v.; Joosten 2005.155-63.

ἀνάβασις, εως. f.

1. *ascent*: w. ref. to the Exodus, ἐκ γῆς Αἰγύπτου Ho 2.15; θυσιαστηρίου ἁγίου Si 50.11; of sunrise at dawn, τοῦ ὄρθρου Ne 4.21. **b**. metaph., *upward struggle*: Ps 83.6.

2. *ascending road*: Is 15.5; ὁ οἰκοδομῶν εἰς τὸν οὐρανὸν ~ιν 'one who builds a passage up into the sky' Am 9.6, cf. ἀναβαίνω, **1a**.

*__3__. *that which has emerged*: fruits, crop, || καρπός Ez 47.12; thought, plan Ps 83.6, cf. ἀναβαίνω **2** and Ath. ad loc., or poss. **1b**.

Cf. ἀναβαίνω: LSG s.v.

ἀναβαστάζω: aor. ἀνεβάστασα.ʃ *

to grasp and move upwards: τι Jd 16.3.

ἀναβάτης, ου. m.

person mounted: of charioteer, ἅρματα καὶ ~αι Ex 14.23, Hg 2.22; of cavalry, ἵπποι καὶ ~αι αὐτῶν ib., sim. De 20.1; ~αι ἵππων Zc 10.5; ἀναβάτας ἱππεῖς .. ~ην ὄνου καὶ ~ην καμήλου Is 21.7. Cf. ἀναβαίνω, ἔφιππος. Del. 1M 4.36, 5.25 v.l.

ἀναβιβάζω: fut. ~βιβῶ, ~βιβάσω, pass. ~βιβασθήσομαι; aor. ἀνεβίβασα, impv. ~βίβασον, inf. ~βιβάσαι, ptc. ~βιβάσας, pass. ἀνεβιβάσθην.

1. *to cause to move higher*, causative of ἀναβαίνω: + acc., ἀνεβίβασαν τὸν Ιωσηφ ἐκ τοῦ λάκκου Ge 37.28; εἰς γῆν ῥέουσαν γάλα καὶ μέλι 'into a land flowing with milk and honey' Ex 3.17; ἐπὶ τὸ ἅρμα 'on to the carriage' Ge 41.43; ἐπὶ τὰ ὑποζύγια 'on to the beasts of burden' Ex 4.20; ἀναβιβῶ ἐπὶ πᾶσαν ὀσφῦν σάκκον 'I will bring sackcloth on everybody's loins' Am 8.10; ἀναβήσονται οἱ βάτραχοι .. ἀνεβιβάσθη ὁ βάτραχος Ex 8.4-6; ἐπὶ τὴν ἰσχὺν τῆς γῆς De 32.13, cf. ἐπὶ τὰ ἀγαθὰ τῆς γῆς Is 58.14; of the Exodus, ἀνεβίβασάν σε ἐκ γῆς Αἰγύπτου Ex 32.4; χοῦν ('dust') ἐπὶ τὴν κεφαλὴν αὐτῶν La 2.10 (mourners). **b**. *o* cultic offerings: ὁλοκαυτώματα Ex 32.6; μόσχον καὶ κριὸν ἐπὶ τὸν βωμόν Nu 23.4 (|| ἀναφέρω vs. 2), θυσίας Is 57.7 (|| ἀναφέρω vs. 6).

2. *to cause to launch a military attack*, caus. of ἀναβαίνω **5**: + acc. pers. (attacker), ἐπί τινα (the attacked) 1E 1.49, ἵππον ἐπὶ ^τὴν γῆν^ Je 28.27.

Cf. βιβάζω, ἐπιβιβάζω, ἀναβαίνω, ἀνάγω, ἀναφέρω.

ἀναβίωσις, εως. f.ʃ*

act of reactivating: ζωῆς 2M 7.9.

ἀναβλαστάνω: fut. ~βλαστήσω.ʃ

to emerge: *s* plant, Jb 8.19; metaph., πόνος 5.6. Cf. βλαστάνω.

ἀναβλέπω: fut.mid. ~βλέψομαι; aor. ἀνέβλεψα, ptc. ~βλέψας, inf. ~βλέψαι, impv. ἀνάβλεψον.

1. *to look upwards*: εἰς τὸν οὐρανόν Ge 15.5; εἰς τὸν οὐρανὸν ἄνω Is 8.21, 2M 7.28; to notice sth as a result, ἀναβλέψας τοῖς ὀφθαλμοῖς αὐτοῦ εἶδεν, καὶ ἰδοὺ .. Ge 18.2, 22.13; 24.63; 24.64, 37.25, 43.29 (without poss. pron.); ἀναβλέψας .. εἶδεν 33.1; ἀναβλέψας .. καὶ ἰδὼν .. De 4.19; ἀνάβλεψον τοῖς ὀφθαλμοῖς σου καὶ ἴδε τί .. Zc 5.5, cf. ἀναβλέψατε εἰς ὕψος τοὺς ὀφθαλμοὺς [acc.!] ὑμῶν καὶ ἴδετε· τίς ..; Is 40.26 (see Renehan, 1.26), sim. To 3.12 𝔊[II]; ἀναβλέψατε ἰδεῖν Is 42.18; τὰ κτήνη τοῦ πεδίου ἀ. πρὸς σέ 'the beasts of the field looked up to you (for help)' Jl 1.20; πρὸς βορρᾶν καὶ λίβα καὶ ἀνατολὰς καὶ θάλασσαν 'towards the north, south, east and west' Ge 13.14; κατὰ θάλασσαν .. De 3.27.

2. *to recover eyesight*: *s* hum., To 14.2. **b**. *to gain in sharpness*: *s* eyes,1K 14.27.

Cf. ἀνάβλεψις, βλέπω, εἶδον, ὁράω.

ἀνάβλεψις, εως. f.ʃ

v.n. of ἀναβλέπω, *recovering of sight*: τυφλοῖς ~ιν Is 61.1.

ἀναβοάω: fut. ~βοήσω; aor. ἀνεβόησα, inf. ~βοῆσαι, ptc. ~βοήσας.

1. *to shout, cry aloud*: + κλαίω Ge 21.16; + λαλέω Zc 6.8; for help and + πρός τινα - ἕκαστος πρὸς τὸν θεὸν αὐτῶν 'each to his god' Jn 1.5, πρὸς κύριον De 26.7, Jn 1.14, sim. 3.8; + acc. (God) 3M 5.51.

*2. *to give out* sound, noise: φωνήν Ge 27.38; φωνὴν μεγάλην καὶ πικράν σφόδρα 27.34, cf. βοήσας τῇ φωνῇ αὐτοῦ 29.11 and φωνῇ βοήσονται Is 24.14.

Cf. βοάω and κράζω.

ἀναβολή, ῆς. f.∫ .

1. *that which is thrown back over the shoulder*, 'mantle' (LSJ): Ez 5.3; *o* of ἐκτινάσσω 'shake out' Ne 5.13.

2. *that which swells higher than the surrounding surface*: ref. to hip-joint (?) 2S 10.4 *L* ‖ 2C 19.4.

Cf. ἀναβάλλω: LSG s.v.

ἀναβράσσω: aor. ἀνέβρασα, inf. ~βράσαι.∫

1. *to jump*: *s* chariot on uneven ground, φωνὴ .. ἅρματος ἀναβράσσοντος Na 3.2.

2. tr. *to cause to move swiftly upwards*: + acc., ἐκ βάθους ἀβύσσου 'from the depths of the sea' Wi 10.19; ῥάβδον 'stick' (for divination) Ez 21.21.

Cf. ἀναβάλλω, ἅλλομαι.

ἀναγγέλλω: fut. ἀναγγελῶ, mid. ~λήσομαι; aor. act. ἀνήγγειλα, subj. ἀναγγείλω, impv. ἀνάγγειλον, ptc. ἀναγγείλας, inf. ἀναγγεῖλαι, pass. ἀνηγγέλην, subj. ἀναγγελῶ; pf. ἀνήγγελκα.

1. *to inform*: + dat. pers., Ge 9.22, 24.23, σοι εἰς τὰ ὦτα Ez 24.26; and + acc. rei, ἀνάγγειλόν μοι τὸ ὄνομά σου Ge 32.29; ὑμῖν τὰ ῥήματα κυρίου De 5.5, τὸν νόμον .. ὑμῖν 24.8, ἡμῖν τὴν ὁδὸν αὐτοῦ Is 2.3; αὐτῇ τὴν πᾶσαν καρδίαν αὐτοῦ '.. everything with utmost honesty' Jd 16.17 B; + cogn. acc. ἀγγελίαν Is 28.9; *Hebraistically with a third complement, ἀναγγειλάτωσαν ἡμῖν ἀπόκρισιν τὴν ὁδόν 'let them report to us, indicating the route' De 1.22; and + πρός τινα Ex 19.9; εἰς τὸν οἶκον Δαυιδ Is 7.2; and + ὅτι – τίς ἀνήγγειλέν σοι ὅτι γυμνὸς εἶ; Ge 3.11; 21.7, 29.12; + λέγων ὅτι 45.26; + λέγων and a direct speech, Ex 13.8, Le 14.35; without λέγων, Ex 20.22; + indir. question, ἀνάγγειλόν μοι ποῦ βόσκουσιν Ge 37.16; and + εἰ, 43.6; ἀνηγγέλη σοι .. τί καλόν; Mi 6.8. **b**. impers. pass., ἀνηγγέλη τῷ Αβρααμ λέγοντες .. Ge 22.20; Ex 18.6; + ὅτι Ge 31.22, 48.1, Ex 14.5; περὶ αὐτῆς ἀνηγγέλη σοι Is 38.16; 2K 10.5*L* (B: ἀπ~). **c**. not necessarily orally: De 8.3. **d**. ἐπερώτησον .. ἀναγγελεῖ 'Ask .. he will tell ..' De 32.7 (‖ λέγω). **e**. not orally, *to reveal, help recognise*: τὰ περὶ αὐτοῦ 'a thing or two about him' Si 19.30.

2. *to make publicly known*, 'announce': ‖ εὐαγγελίζομαι 2K 1.20; + acc., διαθήκην De 4.13, ἐν τοῖς ἔθνεσι τὰ ἔνδοξα αὐτοῦ Is 12.4, τὴν δικαιοσύνην σου 38.19; ‖ ἀκουστὸν ποιέω Je 27.2; + dat. pers., κρίσιν De 17.9; 17.10; νόμον 24.8; ἁμαρτίαν Is 3.9 (‖ ἐμφανίζω), γνῶσιν Ps 18.3. **b**. *+ acc. pers. (to whom a message is conveyed): Jb 36.33¶.

3. *to make public announcement*: Ἀναγγείλατε .. καὶ ἀκουσθήτω 'Announce .. and be heard' Je 4.5; ‖ παραγγέλλω 26.14; + περί τινος, De 13.9; + ὅτι, 30.18 (‖ διαμαρτύρομαι vs. 19).

Cf. ἀπ~, δι~, ἐξ~, κατα~, παρα~, προσαγγέλλω, ἀγγελία, διαμαρτύρομαι, κηρύσσω: on the synonymity with ἀπαγγέλλω and a diachronic development (ἀπα~ > ἀνα~), see Anz 27f.; Schniewind, *TDNT* 1.61-3; Kilpatrick 1990.28.

ἀναγινώσκω: fut. ~γνώσομαι; aor. ἀνέγνων, impv. ~γνωθι, inf. ~γνῶναι, subj. ~γνῶ, pass. ἀνεγνώσθην, ptc. ~γνωσθείς; pf.ptc.pass. ἀνεγνωσμένος.

to read aloud in public: + acc. rei (what is written), τὸν νόμον τοῦτον ἐναντίον παντὸς Ισραηλ εἰς τὰ ὦτα αὐτῶν '.. in their earshot' De 31.11; ἔξω νόμον 'read the law outside' Am 4.5; τοὺς λόγους τούτους Je 3.12. **b**. acc. (document): ἐπιστολήν 1E 2.22, βιβλίον .. εἰς τὰ ὦτα τοῦ λαοῦ Ex 24.7, ἐν τῷ βιβλίῳ τῷ ἀνεγνωσμένῳ ἐναντίον τοῦ βασιλέως 2C 34.24; ἐν ὠσί τινος Je 43.14, Ne 13.1; + *ἔν τινι – ἐν τῷ βιβλίῳ νόμου τοῦ θεοῦ Ne 8.8, ἐν τῷ χαρτίῳ 'the roll' Je 43.6, cf. 43.8, 10, Mt 12.5: Spicq 1.101f. **c**. *to recite a story about*: + dat. pers. and acc., 4M 18.11. **d**. ὁ ἀναγινώσκων *one who reads the Scriptures regularly* or *recites them publicly*, 'Bible scholar' Si prol. 4, cf. πρὸς Ἔσδραν τὸν ἱερέα καὶ ἀναγνώστην τοῦ νόμου 1E 8.8, and Auvray 1957. 284.

Cf. ἀνάγνωσις, ἀναγνώστης, παραναγινώσκω: Busch.

ἀναγκάζω: fut. ἀναγκάσω; aor. ἠνάγκασα, inf. ἀναγκάσαι, ptc.pass. ἀναγκασθείς; pf.ptc.pass. ἠναγκασμένος.

to compel to do: + inf., οὕτως ἀναγκάζει ποιεῖν 1E 3.23; + acc. pers., ἕτερος τὸν ἕτερον ἀναγκάζοντες ἀναφέρουσιν τοὺς φόρους τῷ βασιλεῖ 4.6; + acc. and inf., τοὺς πάντας ἠνάγκασαν φυγεῖν 'they compelled everyone to flee' 2M 11.11; pass., ἀναγκασθεὶς παρέδωκεν αὐτοῖς τὸν Δανιηλ Da TH Bel 30, ἠναγκάζετο φαγεῖν ὕειον κρέας '.. to eat pork' 6.18. Cf. ἀνάγκη, καταναγκάζω.

ἀναγκαῖος, α, ον.∫

in need of urgent attention: *s* matter (inf. cl.), Si prol. 30, 2M 9.21; πράγματα 'business, affairs' 4.23. **b**. *indispensable*, 'a bare minimum': *s* ὄρεξις 'appetite' Wi 16.3; λόγος 'rational consideration,' εἰς ἐπιστήμην παντί 'to everybody in pursuit of knowledge' 4M 1.2.

Cf. II δέω, χρή.

ἀνάγκη, ης. f.
plight with little scope for manoeuvring: ἡμέρα θλίψεως καὶ ~ης Zp 1.15 (ǁ ἀωρία), θησαυρίζεις .. εἰς ἡμέραν ~ης To 4.9; παραδώσω αὐτοὺς εἰς ~ας πάσαις ταῖς βασιλείαις Je 15.4; ἐν ἀνάγκῃ ἄνθρωπον ὄντα Ep Je 36 (ǁ τυφλός, χήρα), δεήσεως ἐν ~ῃ ὄντων ἀδυνάτων 'supplication of the destitute in dire straits' Jb 36.19; alw. (7x) pl. in Ps, ἐκ τῶν ~ῶν μου ἐξάγαγέ με 24.17, θλίψεις καὶ ~αι (Ra ~η) εὕροσάν με 118.143; ἄνδρα ἐν ~αις Jb 30.25 (ǁ ἀδύνατος); δι' ~ης 'perforce' Si 20.14¶, κατ' ~ην 2M 15.2, δι' ~ην 'under coertion' 4M 8.14, 'under duress with no other option' PSol 5.6; μετὰ πικρᾶς ~ης 'under bitter constraint' 2M 6.7; τῶν παθῶν ~αι 'the shackles of passions' 4M 3.17; pl., ref. to mental and physical tortures, μέχρι θανάτου 5.37. Cf. ἀναγκάζω, ἀναγκαῖος, ἀωρία, θλῖψις: Schmidt 3.682f.

ἀναγνεία, ας. f.ʃ*
abominable wickedness: 2M 4.13. Cf. ἁγνός.

ἀναγνωρίζω.ʃ
mid., *to reveal one's identity*: + dat. pers., Ge 45.1. Cf. γνωρίζω.

ἀνάγνωσις, εως. f.ʃ
1. *act of reading* (not necessarily in public): τοῦ νόμου καὶ τῶν προφητῶν .. Si prol. 9f.; ib. 17.
2. *that which is publicly read*: ἐμφυσιοῦντες ἅμα τὴν ~ιν 'interpreting the text as it was read' 1E 9.48; συνῆκεν .. ἐν τῇ ~ει Ne 8.8.
Cf. ἀναγινώσκω, ἀναγνώστης.

ἀναγνώστης, ου. m.
public reader, also competent to teach and interpret: Ἔσδρας ὁ ἱερεὺς καὶ ἀ. τοῦ νόμου τοῦ θεοῦ 1E 8.19 +. Cf. ἀναγινώσκω: LSG s.v.

ἀναγορεύω: aor.inf.pass. ~γορευθῆναι ʃ
to designate: + double acc., πατέρα Es E 11. Cf. ἐπι~, καλέω, ὀνομάζω.

ἀναγραφή, ῆς. f.ʃ
written record: + ὑπομνήματα 'memoranda' 2M 2.13. Cf. ἀναγράφω, ἀπογραφή.

ἀναγράφω: aor. ἀνέγραψα, inf. ~γράψαι; pf.pass.3s ἀναγέγραπται.
1. *to record in writing*: + acc., words said, 1M 14.22; epitaph, 4M 17.8; ***o*** personal deeds, 1E 1.22; ἐν τῇ βιβλίῳ 1.31.
2. *to enrol* in a register: + acc. pers., 2M 4.9.
Cf. γράφω.

ἀνάγω: fut. ἀνάξω; aor. ἀνήγαγον, impv. ἀνάγαγε, ptc. ~γαγών, pass. ἀνήχθην, ptc. ~χθείς, subj.act. ἀναγάγω.
1. *to cause to move from a lower to a higher position*: + acc., ***s*** God leading Israel from Egypt up to Canaan thought of as lying on a higher ground, Ge 50.24; κατάγει εἰς ᾅδου καὶ ἀνάγει 1K 2.6, sim. To 13.2, Wi 16.13; ***s*** Moses, Ex 33.12; εἰς τὴν ἔρημον ταύτην Nu 20.4; as causative of ἀναβαίνω, cp. ἀνάγαγε τοὺς βατράχους 'Bring the frogs up' Ex 8.5 with ἀναβήσονται οἱ βάτραχοι 8.4; in fire, ἀνήγαγον ἐν πυρὶ τὰς παρεμβολὰς ὑμῶν 'I sent your encampments up in fire' Am 4.10; ***o*** the water of a river to cause flooding, ἐφ' ὑμᾶς τὸ ὕδωρ τοῦ ποταμοῦ τὸ ἰσχυρόν Is 8.7, ἐπὶ σὲ τὴν ἄβυσσον Ez 26.19, cf. τὸν Νεῖλον ἀναγέτω Luc. *DDeor*. 3; νεφέλας Je 28.16; the dead out of the grave, 1K 28.8. **b**. ἀνάγω μηρυκισμόν 'to chew the cud': Le 11.3 +, and ǁ μα/ηρυκάομαι μηρυκισμόν. **c**. of movement from the south to the north, ἀνήγαγεν αὐτὴν ἐπὶ πᾶσαν γῆν Αἰγύπτου 'it [= the south wind] brought it [= locusts] up on to the whole land of Eg.' Ex 10.14. **d**. of movement to a more central position: νεφέλας ἐξ ἐσχάτου τῆς γῆς 'clouds from the end of the earth' Je 10.13; from exile, 16.15. **e**. = ἄγω: τινα ἐπὶ χειρός τινος 'to deliver to be executed by ..' 4K 10.24 (*L* εἰσάγω); 'to lead, guide τινα' Ps 77.52 (ǁ vs. 53 ὁδηγέω).
2. *to cause to move back* to the point of origin: ἀνάξω αὐτὸν πρὸς σέ Ge 42.37; Je 38.9.
3. caus. of ἀναβαίνω **5**, *to deploy*: + acc., ἐπ' αὐτὰς ὄχλον Ez 23.46, ἐπὶ σὲ ἔθνη πολλά 26.3.
4. *to remove, do away with*: + acc. pers., ἐν ἡμίσει ἡμερῶν μου 'halfway my life' Ps 101.25, cf. Trg תסלקני מן עלמא and ἀναβαίνω **4**.
5. *to cause to emerge*, 'to effect': + acc., ἴαμα 'cure' Je 37.17 (ǁ ἰατρεύω), συνούλωσιν ('complete cure') καὶ ἴαμα 40.6 (ditt.), cf. ἀνέβη ἴασις 8.22 and τὰ ἰάματα .. ἀνατελεῖ Is 58.8.
6. mid./pass. *to put out to sea, sail*: 2M 5.9.
Cf. (κατ)άγω, ἀναβαίνω, ~βιβάζω, ~τέλλω, συναναφέρω, ἄναξις.

ἀναγώγως. adv.ʃ
in rude manner: 2M 12.14.

ἀναδείκνυμι: fut. ~δείξω, pass. ἀναδειχθήσομαι; aor. ἀνέδειξα, impv. ~δειξον, inf. ~δεῖξαι, ptc. ~δείξας, pass. ἀνεδείχθην; pf. ~δέδειχα, ptc.pass. ~δεδειγμένος.
1. *to lift up and show*: + double acc., 3M 6.8.
2. *to declare in public* to the effect that ..: + double acc., τὴν πόλιν .. ἐλευθέραν 'the city to be free' 2M 9.14. **b**. *to declare in public* as elected or appointed to the office of: + double acc., τὸν Ἰεχονίαν .. βασιλέα 1E 1.32 (ǁ κατέστησαν .. εἰς βασιλέα 2C 36.1); pass. 1.41; as designated for a certain function, τῷ ὀνόματι .. σου 'for your .. name' 3M 2.14.
3. *to make an appointment* of office-holder: + acc., κριτάς 'judges' 1E 8.23; 2M 9.23; στρατηγόν 'governor' 14.12.

4. *to disclose*: + acc. rei, *s* God, ταῦτα 2M 2.8; pass. and *o* God, Hb 3.2 (|| γνωρίζω and ἐπιγινώσκω).

Cf. δείκνυμι, γνωρίζω, καθίστημι: Schlier, *TDNT* 2.30.

ἀνάδειξις, εως. f.ʃ

indication: ἡ σελήνη .. ~ιν χρόνων Si 43.6 (|| σημεῖον).

ἀναδενδράς, άδος. f.ʃ

vine that grows up trees (LSJ): Ez 17.6. Cf. Schnebel 255; Ruffing 72.

ἀναδέχομαι: aor.ptc. ~δεξάμενος.ʃ

to accept: willingly, + acc. (difficult fate), 2M 6.19; *o* task, mission, + inf. 8.36. Cf. Spicq 1.105f.

ἀναδίδωμι: fut. ~δώσω; aor.ptc. ~δούς.ʃ

1. *to communicate orally* a signal: + σύνθημα 'watchword' 2M 13.15.

2. intr. *to burst out*: *s* εὐφροσύνη 'joy' Si 1.23.

ἀνάδυσις, εως.ʃ

act of emerging from beneath: of dry land in the midst of the sea, Wi 19.7.

ἀναζευγνύω: fut. ~ζεύξω; aor. ἀνεζεύγνυσα, ἀνέζευξα, impv.3pl. ~ζευξάτωσαν, ptc. ~ζεύξας.

to break up one's quarters and march forth: Ex 14.15; σὺν τῇ ἀπαρτίᾳ αὐτῶν 'with their baggage' 40.30; ἐπὶ Βαιτυλουα 'to attack B.' Ju 7.1; εἰς τὸν λαὸν αὐτοῦ 'back to his army' 7.7; ἀπὸ τοῦ ποταμοῦ 1E 8.60 (|| ἐξαίρω 2E 8.31); ἐκεῖθεν 'from there' 2M 12.29. Cf. ἀναζυγή, ἀπαίρω, ἐξαίρω.

ἀναζέω.ʃ

I. tr. *to make bubble up*: τὴν ἄβυσσον ὡς χαλκίον 'the deep like a copper cauldron' Jb 41.23.

II. intr. *to bubble up, boil up*: *s* boils on the skin, Ex 9.9, 10; worms, ἐκ τῶν ὀφθαλμῶν 2M 9.9.

Cf. ζέω.

ἀναζητέω: aor. ἀνεζήτησα, opt.3s ~ζητήσαι, ptc. ~ζητήσας, pass. ἀνεζητήθην.ʃ

1. *to investigate*: + acc., τὴν ἀνομίαν μου Jb 10.6 (|| ἐξιχνιάζω), 3.4.

2. *to seek for*: pass., *o* pers., 2M 13.21.

Cf. ζητέω, ἐξιχνιάζω.

ἀναζυγή, ῆς. f.ʃ*

v. n. of ἀναζευγνύω: Ex 40.32; ~ὴν ποιήσασθαι 'to make a retreat' 2M 9.2; opp. ἔφοδος 'attack' 13.26. Cf. ἀναζευγνύω.

ἀναζώννυμι: aor.ptc.mid.~ζωσάμενος; pf.ptc.mid. ἀνεζωσμένος.ʃ *

to gird up: + acc., ἰσχυρῶς τὴν ὀσφὺν αὐτῆς 'strongly her (own) loins' Pr 31.17. **b**. *to fasten securely to own body*: + acc. rei, τὰ σκεύη τῆς παρατάξεως 'the battle-gear' Jd 18.16B (A: περι~).

Cf. ζώννυμι.

ἀναζωπυρέω: aor. ἀνεζωπύρησα.ʃ

to regain strength: *s* τὸ πνεῦμα Ιακωβ Ge 45.27; 1M 13.7.

ἀναθάλλω: aor. ἀνέθαλα, subj. ~θάλω, opt.3s ~θάλοι. *

to sprout afresh: *s* a plant, Wi 4.4; fig., the bones of the dead, Si 46.12, 49.10; ἀνέθαλε Εφραιμ, καθ' ἑαυτόν 'E. has sprouted again against itself' Ho 8.9; on the interpretation of ἀνέθαλε as aor., and not impf., hence not causative 'make to flourish' (impf.), see Walters, 307; *s* ἡ σάρξ μου Ps 27.7; εὐοδία Si 11.22. **b**. causative: *o* ξύλον ξηρόν 'dry tree' (:: ξηραίνω) Ez 17.24, καρπούς Si 50.10; metaph., εἰρήνην καὶ ὑγιείαν 1.18.

Cf. θάλλω, ἀνατέλλω.

ἀνάθεμα, ατος. n. Also spelled ἀνάθημα.

*__1__. *that which* or *he who has been consigned by cursing to destruction*: κυρίῳ σαβαωθ Jo 6.17; cogn. obj. of ἀνατίθημι Le 27.28; w. ref. to a hum., De 7.26. ***b**. *act of consigning by cursing to destruction*: Zc 14.11; as symbolic place-name, Nu 21.3; as cogn. obj., ~ατι ἀναθεματιεῖτε De 13.15, 20.17.

2. *that which has been dedicated*: as offering to God, 2M 2.13, εἰς ἀ. θεῷ Ju 16.19.

Cf. ἀνατίθημι, ἀναθεματίζω: Behm, *TDNT* 1.354f.; Harl 2001.866-8.

ἀναθεματίζω: fut. ~θεματιῶ, pass. ~θεματισθήσομαι; aor. ἀνεθεμάτισα, inf. ~θεματίσαι; pf.ptc.pass. ~τεθεματισμένος.*

to consign by cursing to destruction*: Nu 18.14; + acc., ^τὸν λαόν^ καὶ τὰς πόλεις αὐτοῦ 21.2, 3; *o* property, 2E 10.8. **b. actually and accordingly destroy: ἐν φόνῳ μαχαίρας, ἀναθέματι .. ^τὴν πόλιν^ καὶ πάντα ἐν αὐτῇ De 13.15; ἐν στόματι ῥομφαίας Jo 6.21, ἀνεθεμάτισαν αὐτὴν καὶ ἐξωλέθρευσαν αὐτούς Jd 1.17A; *o* hum., Da 11.44 TH (LXX ἀφανίζω), Jd 21.11. Cf. Moatti-Fine 325-9.

Cf. ἀνάθεμα, ἀνιερόω, ἀφανίζω: Deissmann 1923.74.

ἀνάθημα. ⇒ ἀνάθεμα.

ἀναίδεια, ας.ʃ

shamelessness, chutspah: + αἰσχύνη Si 22.52. Cf. ἀναιδής, αἰδώς.

ἀναιδής, ές.ʃ

1. *wanting in regard and respect for others' needs and feelings*, 'ruthless, pitiless': *s* pers., ἔθνος ~ὲς προσώπῳ De 28.50, ἔθνος ~ὲς καὶ ἀλλόγλωσσον '.. speaking a foreign tongue' Ba 4.15; βασιλεύς Da 8.23; *s* γνώμη 'decision' Da TH 2.15 (|| LXX πικρῶς).

2. *wanting in self-respect and restraint*, 'unashamed, shameless': *s* dogs, οἱ κύνες ~εῖς τῇ ψυχῇ, οὐκ εἰδότες πλησμονήν '.. not knowing what it is to be filled' Is 56.11; ψυχή Si 23.6 (|| 'gluttony and lust'); ὀφθαλμός of an undisciplined, coquettish woman, 26.11, indicative of unrestrained, shameless appetite, 1K 2.29; πρόσωπον Pr 7.13, leading to a quarrel 25.23; προσώπῳ Ec 8.1; στόμα of a shameless beggar, Si 40.30; behaviour, ἀποστροφὴ τῇ ψυχῇ 'foresaking' Je 8.5.

Cf. ἀναίδεια, ἀναιδῶς, αἰδέομαι, ἄνοικτος: Spicq 1.41-4; LSG s.v.

ἀναιδῶς. adv.∫

shamelessly: Pr 21.29. Cf. ἀναιδής.

ἀναίρεσις, εως. f.

v.n. of ἀναιρέω **1**: ἀπόκτεινόν με ~ει Nu 11.15; || ἀφανισμός, σφαγή 2M 5.13; Jd 15.17, cf. Syh. *qeṭlā'* and *BA* ad loc. Cf. ἀναιρέω.

ἀναιρέω: fut. ἀνελῶ, pass. ἀναιρεθήσομαι; aor.act. ἀνεῖλον, mid. 1aor.3s ἀνείλατο, 2aor. ἀνειλόμην, inf.act. ἀνελεῖν, impv. ἄνελε, mid. ἀνελοῦ, 2pl. ἀνέλεσθε, subj.act. ἀνέλω, ptc. ἀνελών, mid. ἀνελόμενος, opt.3s ἀνέλοι, pass. ἀνῃρέθην, inf. ἀναιρεθῆναι, ptc. ~ρεθείς; pf.inf.pass. ἀνῃρῆσθαι, ptc. pass. ἀνῃρημένος.

1. *to do away with by killing*: abs., Nu 31.19; + acc. pers., Ge 4.15, Ex 2.14, Nu 35.31 (|| θανατόω); + ἀποκτείνω Jo 11.17; *o* snake (δράκων, ὄφις), with a sword (μάχαιρα) Is 27.1; μαχαίρᾳ 'with a sword' Ex 15.9; ἐν φόνῳ μαχαίρας De 13.15, θανάτῳ Je 18.21; λιμῷ 'through famine' Is 14.30; *s* animal, Ex 21.29, anger Jb 5.2.

2. *to overwhelm mentally and cause to be carried away* to act in a certain way: pass., *o* hum., 4M 4.13.

3. mid. *to pick up*: + acc., Ex 2.5, Nu 16.37, 2K 22.17*L* (B: ἕλκω), 4K 2.13*L* (B: ὑψόω).

4. mid. *to take up and carry off*: + acc. rei, Da 1.16; + acc. pers., To 2.4.

Cf. ἀναίρεσις, ἀναλαμβάνω, ἀφανίζω.

ἀναισθητέω.∫

to be mentally obtuse: *s* the silly, Si 22.13¶. Cf. αἰσθάνομαι.

ἀναίτιος, ον.

guiltless: *s* αἷμα ~ον 'blood of an innocent person' De 19.10 (|| αἷμα ἀθῷον 27.25); 'guiltless person' Da LXX Su 62. Cf. ἀθῷος.

ἀναιτίως. adv.∫

in spite of the absence of guilt: to kill, 4M 12.14.

ἀνακαινίζω: fut. ~καινιῶ, pass. ~καινισθήσομαι; aor.impv. ~καίνισον, pass. ἀνεκαινίσθην.∫

to cause to revert to former condition: + acc., ἡμέρας ἡμῶν La 5.21, the surface of the earth, Ps 103.30; pass., *s* pain 38.3, 1M 6.9, youthful vigour Ps 102.5. Cf. ἐγκαινίζω.

ἀνακαίω: fut. ~καύσω; aor. ἀνέκαυσα, ptc. ~καύσας, pass. ἀνεκαύθην.

1. *to set fire to*: + acc., ἐν πυρί Ez 5.2; πυράς 'burning missiles' Ju 7.5.

2. *to set on fire*, 'kindle': pass. *to become hot*: *s* oven, Ho 7.6 (|| θερμαίνομαι vs. 7); ὡς πυρὸς φέγγος 'like the light of a fire' 6.

3. *to ignite*: + acc., πῦρ Ez 24.10; metaph., pass., φιλία ὡς πῦρ ἀνακαίεται Si 9.8.

Cf. καίω, ἐκ~, κατακαίω, ἀνάπτω.

ἀνακαλέω: aor. ἀνεκάλησα, ptc. ~καλέσας, pass. ~κληθείς; pf.act. ~κέκληκα, mid. ~κέκλημαι.

***1**. *to summon for a task*: + acc. pers., Le 1.1; pass. and + ἐξ ὀνόματος 'by name' Nu 1.17 (|| ἐπίκλητος); mid. Ex 31.2 (|| act. 35.30).

2. *to call to*: + acc., συναγωγήν Nu 10.2; 4M 14.17.

Cf. ἐπίκλητος.

ἀνακαλύπτω: fut. ~καλύψω, pass. ~καλυφθήσομαι; aor. ἀνεκάλυψα, opt.3s ~καλύψαι, pass. ἀνεκαλύφθην, inf. ~καλυφθῆναι, impv.mid. ~κάλυψαι; pf.ptc.pass. ~κεκαλυμμένος.∫

1. *to remove* that which covers: + acc., συγκάλυμμα τοῦ πατρὸς αὐτοῦ De 22.30 (|| ἀπο~ 27.20).

2. *to remove a covering from*: + acc. and pass., τὸ πρόσωπόν μου ἀνακεκαλυμμένον διὰ τὸ καῦμα 'with my face uncovered because of the heat' To 2.9 𝔊[II] (|| ἀκάλυπτος 𝔊[I]); fig., νοῦν ἀνθρώπων '(enlightens) the mind of men' Jb 33.16.

3. *to disclose and render visible*: + acc., βαθέα ἐκ σκότους 'the depth out of darkness' Jb 12.22 (|| ἐξαγάγω εἰς φῶς), βάθη ποταμῶν ἀνεκάλυψεν 28.11 (|| δείκνυμι εἰς φῶς); τὰ κρυπτὰ 'the hidden treasures' Is 22.9, 'hide-outs' Je 29.11, 'the buttocks' 13.22; mid. τὰς πολιάς 'own pubic hairs' Is 47.2 (|| ἀποκαλύπτω); metaph. of God, ὁ ἀνακαλύπτων μυστήρια Da LXX 2.29 (|| TH ἀποκαλύπτων), τὰ βαθέα καὶ σκοτεινά 'the profound and obscure' 2.22, τὰ ἔργα τοῦ θεοῦ To 12.7 (:: κρύπτω), φωστῆρα 'a ray (of hope)' 1E 8.76; *o* a state of affairs, pass. ἐν τοῖς ὠσὶ κυρίου 'in the ears (!) ..' Is 22.14; τὸ αἷμα 26.21 (evidence of murder and:: κατακαλύπτω), τὰς ἀνομίας Jb 20.27, τὰς ἁμαρτίας PSol 2.17. **b**. mid., *to reveal oneself* or *itself* from a state of invisibility, *become visible*: abs. and addressed to those who are in the dark, Is 49.9; ἀνεκαλύφθη τὰ θεμέλια τῆς οἰκουμένης 'the foundations of the world emerged' Ps 17.16 (|| ὤφθησαν); w. ref. to female pudenda, Is 47.3 (|| φανήσονται).

***4**. *to expose and render defenceless*, having a protective cover removed (?): τὰς πύλας 'the gates (as the first line of defence)' Is 22.8, τὴν οἰκουμένην 24.1; 20.4 (add a comma, *pace* Zgl and with Ottley).

Cf. ἀπο~, κατακαλύπτω.

ἀνακάμπτω: fut. ~κάμψω; aor. ἀνέκαμψα, impv. ἀνάκαμψον, ptc. ~κάμψας.

intr. *to return, move back*: ἀπὸ πύλης ἐπὶ πύλην 'from one gate to another' Ex 32.27; Zc 9.8 (|| διαπορεύομαι); + dat. pers., Je 15.5, Jb 39.4¶; *s* a divorcee to her former husband (πρὸς αὐτόν) Je 3.1; river water, εἰς θάλασσαν Si 40.11 (|| ἀναστρέφω); ||

ἀποστρέφω 2K 1.22B (*L* ἀναστρέφω), 1C 19.5 || 2K 10.5*L* (B: ἐπιστρέφομαι). **b.** + inf., *to repeat*: 1E 8.84.

Cf. ἀνα~, ἀπο~, ἐπιστρέφω.

ἀνάκειμαι.ʃ

to lie at dining-table: 1E 4.10, To 9.6𝔊II. Cf. συνανάκειμαι, ἀνα~, κατακλίνω, ἀναπίπτω.

ἀνακηρύσσω: aor. ἀνεκήρυξα.ʃ

to make public proclamation about: τινί (pers.) τι, 4M 17.23. Cf. κηρύσσω.

ἀνακλάω.ʃ

to bend back: pass., ***o*** hum. body, 4M 11.10.

ἀνάκλησις, εως. f.ʃ

invitation to return home: from the Babylonian exile, Si prol. II.

ἀνακλίνω: aor.inf. ~κλῖναι, subj.pass. ~κλιθῶ, impv. pass.2pl. ~κλίθητε.ʃ

to lie down for a meal: 3M 5.16, εἰς τὴν θυσίαν 1K 16.5*L* (B: κατα~) Cf. ἀνάκλισις, κατακλίνω, ἀνάκειμαι, ἀναπίπτω.

ἀνάκλισις, εως. f.ʃ

v.n. of ἀνακλίνω (q.v.): Ct 1.12. Cf. ἀνακλίνω.

ἀνάκλιτος, ον.ʃ

for reclining: subst.n.(?), *reclining chair* Ct 3.10 (|| στῦλος).

ἀνακοινόω: aor.mid.ptc. ~κοινωσάμενος.ʃ

mid. *to communicate and share a message* with sbd: τινι 2M 14.20.

ἀνακομίζω: aor.mid.inf. ~κομίσασθαι, ptc. ~κομισθείς.

1. mid. *to bring back with one*: + acc., bodies left lying on battlefield, 2M 12.39.

2. mid. intr. *to return to a point of origin*: ***s*** hum., 3M 1.1. Cf. ἐπιστρέφω.

3. mid. *to regain*: + acc., ἱερόν 'temple' 2M 2.22.

ἀνακόπτω: aor. ἀνέκοψα.ʃ

to repulse: + acc., ὁρμήν 'impulse' Wi 18.23; ***o*** threatening billows, 4M 13.6; pass., ***o*** passions, 1.35 (|| ἀνέχω, φιμόω).

ἀνακράζω: fut. ἀνακεκράξομαι (on morphology, s.v. κράζω); 1aor. ἀνέκραξα, 2aor. ἀνέκραγα, impv. ~κραγε, ptc. ~κραγών.

to speak loudly, cry out: ***s*** pers., Zc 1.14, 17 (foll. by λέγω and dir. speech); to God, εἰς οὐρανόν 3M 6.17; ***s*** God Jl 3.16; εἰς τὰ ὦτά μου φωνῇ μεγάλῃ Ez 9.1. Cf. κράζω.

ἀνακρεμάννυμι, ~μάζω: aor.pass. ἀνεκρεμάσθην.ʃ

pass. *to become suspended high up*: above the ground, 2K 18.9*L*. Cf. κρεμάζω.

ἀνακρίνω: fut. ~κρινῶ; aor.ptc. ~κρίνας.

to subject to examination: abs. Su 48; + acc. pers., 51 TH (LXX ἐτάζω); orally, 13 LXX. Cf. ἀνάκρισις, ἐτάζω, ζητέω.

ἀνάκρισις, εως. f.ʃ

v.n. of ἀνακρίνω: + ἐξέτασις 3M 7.5.

ἀνακρούω.ʃ

1. *to begin* a tune *first*, 'strike up': + acc., φωνὴν ἁρμονίας 'sound of music' Ez 23.42; Jd 5.11B, ἐν ὀργάνοις 2K 6.14; + ὀρχέομαι 'to dance' 6.16.

2. *to express musically*: abs., ἐν λόγοις θεοῦ 1C 25.5; + acc. rei, ἐν κινύρᾳ .. ἐξομολόγησιν καὶ αἴνεσιν τῷ κυρίῳ 1C 25.3.

ἀνακύπτω: aor.inf. ~κύψαι, ptc.f. ~κύψασα.ʃ

to look upwards: Da Su 35 LXX (TH ἀναβλέπω), Jb 10.15.

ἀναλαμβάνω: fut. ~λήμψομαι, pass. ~λημφθήσομαι; aor. ἀνέλαβον, sub. ~λάβω, inf. ~λαβεῖν, ptc. ~λαβών, impv. ~λαβε, opt. ~λάβοιμι, pass. ἀνελήμφθην, inf. ~λημφθῆναι, ptc. ~λημφθείς.

1. *to take up, pick up, lift*: + acc., ἐπὶ τὰς ἁμάξας 'on to the wagons' Ge 46.5; ἐπ' ὤμων 'on shoulders' Ez 12.6; τὰ σκεύη τὰ πολεμικά 'the weapons' De 1.41, ὅπλα καὶ ἀσπίδας 'small and large shields' Je 26.3; αὐτὸν (= Ephraim) ἐπὶ τὸν βραχίονά μου Ho 11.3 (out of paternal care and affection), ***o*** hum. about to collapse, ἐπὶ τὰς ἀγκάλας αὐτοῦ 'into his arms' Es D 8; in order to *carry* and ***s*** wind, ***o*** locusts, Ex 10.13, 19; τὴν σκηνὴν τοῦ Μολοχ Am 5.26 (cf. the use of the impf. ἀνελάμβανον in the exposition part of the commentary by Cyr. [I.474.6]); τὸ μέτρον Zc 5.9; + acc. and gen. (part of the first entity), με τῆς κορυφῆς μου 'me (by) the crown of my head' Ez 8.3; musical instrument, Jb 21.12.

2. *to transport to a higher location*: αὐτὸν .. εἰς γῆν Χαναάν Ge 50.13; ***s*** sirocco, Jb 27.21¶; ***o*** Enoch, ἀπὸ τῆς γῆς Si 49.14, cf. 48.9, Acts 1.2, 11; Elisha up into heaven, ἀπὸ σοῦ 4K 2.9f.; τὸ πνεῦμά μου To 3.6. **b.** *to transport* generally: Ez 8.3*b*; metaph., εἰρήνην τῷ λαῷ Ps 71.3.

3. *to direct and turn upwards*: + acc., ἀνάλαβε ὀφθαλμούς σου .. καὶ ἴδε .. Je 13.20, εἰς τὸν οὐρανόν Da 4.31 TH; καρδίας ἡμῶν ἐπὶ χειρῶν πρὸς ὑψηλὸν ἐν οὐρανῷ La 3.41 (***s*** prayer).

4. *to pick out, select*: + acc. ἀ. με κύριος ἐκ τῶν προβάτων Am 7.15, sim. and || simp. 2.11, || ἐκλέγομαι 'to choose' Ps 77.70; + acc. pers., 1E 1.32; ***o*** troops, 2M 12.38.

5. *to receive in one's care and charge*: ἀναλαβὼν ὁ παῖς (= Abraham's servant) τὴν Ρεβέκκαν ἀπῆλθεν Ge 24.61 (or: *to take along* on a journey); τὸν πατέρα ὑμῶν 45.19; τὴν γυναῖκαι καὶ τὰ παιδία Ex 4.20; τὰ πρόβατα καὶ τοὺς βόας ὑμῶν 12.32; ἐπὶ τῶν μεταφρένων αὐτῶν 'on their back' De 32.11 (***s*** eagles); διὰ μνήμης '(to commit) to memory' 2M 2.25.

6. *to react verbally to what has been said* or *to a situation*, 'to respond': ἀναλαβοῦσα .. ἔδωκεν φωνήν Nu 14.1, Da 3.51 LXX, cf. LSJ s.v. **II 4**.

*7. *to start off uttering* in response: ἀναλαβὼν τὴν παραβολὴν αὐτοῦ εἶπεν Nu 23.7 +; ἀνάλαβε ἐπὶ χειλέων θρῆνον Je 7.29; 1M 1.27; ᾠδήν 3M 6.32; τὴν διαθήκην μου διὰ στόματός σου Ps 49.16 (ǁ διηγέομαι). See also λαμβάνω **I 10**; ὑπολαμβάνω **3**.

*8. *to get into action*: ἀναλαβόντες φεύγετε 'Off and flee' Je 4.6, cf. Syh /'ašqel(w)/ 'depart.'

9. *to decide to make use of resources of*: ἀναλάβοι θάρσος 'let him pluck up courage' Jb 17.9, ἐπιστήμην 'knowledge' 36.3, λογισμὸν ἀστεῖον 'noble mind' 2M 6.23.

10. *to accept and submit oneself to*: + acc. rei, ὄλεθρον 'ruin' 3M 6.30.

11. *to confiscate*: ὑμῶν τὰ ὑπάρχοντα εἰς τὸ βασιλικόν 'your properties into the royal treasury' Da 2.5 LXX, sim. To 1.20 𝔊[II]. Cf. LSG s.v.

Cf. ἀναλημπτέος, ἀνάλημψις, λαμβάνω, ἀνάγω, ἀναβιβάζω, ἀναιρέω, ἐκλέγομαι.

ἀναλάμπω: fut. ~λάμψω; aor. ἀνέλαμψα, subj. ἀναλάμψω.

to shine brightly: ὅπως μὴ ἀναλάμψῃ ὡς πῦρ ὁ οἶκος Ιωσηφ Am 5.6; *s* the sun, 2M 1.22; hum. face, Jb 11.15; God, ἐν σκότει 'in darkness' 2K 22.29*L* (ǁ φωτίζω). Cf. λάμπω, στίλβω, φαίνω.

ἀνάλγητος, ον.ʃ

indisposed towards toil and hardship: *s* hum., Pr 14.23. Cf. κόπος, μόχθος.

ἀναλέγω: aor. ἀνέλεξα, mid.ptc. ~λεξάμενος.ʃ

1. *to bring to one place* multiple objects *that are found in various locations*: + acc., σχίζας 'darts' 1K 20.38.

2. *to pick out as especially noteworthy*: τὸν λόγον ἐκ τοῦ στόματος αὐτοῦ 3K 21.33.

3. mid., + ἑαυτόν, *to recover from mental shock*, 'pick up pieces': 3M 2.24.

ἀνάλημμα, ατος. n.ʃ

retaining wall: περιβόλου 'of an enclosure' Si 50.2; πόλεως 2C 32.5.

ἀναλημπτέος, ον.ʃ

liable to confiscation: 2M 3.13. Cf. ἀναλαμβάνω.

ἀναλημπτήρ, ῆρος.ʃ *

vessel into which sth is collected, 'bowl; ladle': temple fixture, 2C 4.16. Cf. κρατήρ.

ἀνάλημψις, εως. f.ʃ

v.n. of ἀναλαμβάνω, *act of being taken up into heaven upon death*: simply death, PSol 4.18.

ἀναλίσκω: fut. ἀναλώσω, pass. ~λωθήσομαι; aor. ἀνήλωσα, subj. ἀναλώσω, ptc. ~λώσας, pass. ἀνηλώθην, subj. ἀναλωθῶ; pf.pass.3s ἀνήλωται.

1. *to spend and use*: pass., for cultic purposes, 1E 6.29; generic, + acc. rei, εἰς ἐργασίαν τροφῆς 'for preparation of a meal' Wi 13.12.

2. *to destroy* (+ acc.): *s* fire, πῦρ ἀνήλωσε τὰ ὡραῖα τῆς ἐρήμου 'a fire destroyed the beautiful things of the wilderness' Jl 1.19, cf. 1.20; τὰ ἔμπροσθεν αὐτοῦ ἀναλίσκον πῦρ 2.3; famine, ἀναλώσει ὁ λιμὸς τὴν γῆν Ge 41.30; ἐν θανάτῳ Ez 5.12 (ǁ συντελέω); *o* limbs, Nu 14.33; hum., Is 66.17.

3. *to consume* (foods and drinks): *o* τὰ τῆς θυσίας 2M 1.31.

Cf. ἐξ~, καταναλίσκω, ἀνάλωμα, ~λωσις, ἀφανίζω, κατεσθίω.

ἀναλογίζομαι: aor. ἀνελογισάμην, ptc. ~λογισάμενος.ʃ

to consider carefully: Is 44.19 (ǁ λογίζομαι); + acc. rei, 3M 7.7, PSol 8.7. Cf. λογίζομαι.

ἀναλόγως. adv.ʃ

in analogous manner: Wi 13.5. Cf. ὁμοίως.

ἀναλύω: fut.pass. ~λυθήσομαι; aor. ἀνέλυσα, ptc. ~λύσας, pass. ἀνελύθην; pf.~λέλυκα, ptc. ~λελυκώς.

1. *to undo*:'to revoke (a previous decision)' 3M 5.40; pass. 'to melt' Si 3.15 (*s* frost and sins).

2. *to depart*: at the end of a gathering, εἰς τὸν κοιτῶνα '(retired) to his bed-chamber' 1E 3.3; suspending what one is doing, To 2.9 𝔊[I]; so as to return to an army base, 2M 8.25.

3. *to return to the point of origin*: ἐξ ᾅδου Wi 2.1; ἀνελύθη εἰς ἑαυτόν '(the parted air) closed up again' 5.12.

4. *to acquit*: + gen. rei, πάσης αἰτίας 'of every charge' 3M 7.7.

ἀνάλωμα, ατος. n.ʃ

expense: 4K 12.13*L* (B: ἐξωδιάζομαι). Cf. ἀναλίσκω.

ἀνάλωσις, εως. f.ʃ

1. *depletion, bankruptcy*: divine punishment and ǁ ἔνδεια, ἐκλιμία 'deprivation, exceeding hunger' De 28.20.

2. *act of consuming*: by fire, Ez 15.4, 6; child sacrifice, 16.20.

Cf. ἀναλίσκω.

ἀναμάρτητος, ον.ʃ

committing or *having committed no sin*: *s* hum. and opp. ἁμαρτωλός De 29.19; τῆς τῶν ~ων νηπίων παρανόμου ἀπωλείας 'the lawless destruction of the innocent infants' 2M 8.4; 12.42. Cf. ἁμαρτωλός.

ἀνάμειξις, εως. f.ʃ

v.n. of ἀναμίγνυμι: w. ref. to intermarriage, PSol 2.13.

ἀναμένω: fut. ~μενῶ; aor. ἀνέμεινα, impv. ~μεινον.ʃ

1. *to anticipate eagerly the coming of*: + acc., κρίσιν Is 59.11, σωτηρίαν Ju 8.17, μισθόν 'wages' Jb 7.2, τὸ ἔλεος αὐτοῦ Si 2.7, good harvest 6.19; + εἰς – εἰς φῶς Je 13.16.

2. *to remain* without making a move and anticipating a favourable development: Ju 7.12; ἀναμένω χρόνον ἔτι μικρὸν προσδέχομενος .. Jb 2.9a. **b**. *to delay, put off*: + inf., ἐπιστρέψαι πρὸς κύριον 'to return ..' Si. 5.7 (‖ ὑπερβάλλω); μακροθυμῶν .. κολάσαι 'patiently .. to punish' 2M 6.14.

Cf. μένω.

ἀναμίγνυμι: aor.inf. ~μεῖξαι; pf.ptc.pass. ~μεμειγμένος, inf. ~μεμῖχθαι.ʃ

to mix: + acc., σεμίδαλιν 'fine flour' Ez 46.14; Da 2.41 TH (LXX συμ.), 2.43 TH (LXX παρα.). **b**. pass., + dat., χαλκῷ καὶ σιδήρῳ .. ἐν μέσῳ ἀργυρίου 'with copper and iron .. amongst silver' Ez 22.18; ἐν .. φυλαῖς 'mingled .. among tribes' Es B 4.

Cf. μίγνυμι, ἀνάμειξις.

ἀναμιμνήσκω: fut.pass. ~μνησθήσομαι; aor. ἀνέμνησα, impv. ~μνησον, inf. ~μνῆσαι, pass. ἀνεμνήσθην, subj. ~μνησθῶ, opt.3s ~μνησθείη, impv. ~μνήσθητι.

1. *to recall to mind*: + acc., τὴν ἁμαρτίαν μου ἀναμιμνήσκω σήμερον Ge 41.9; θυσία μνημοσύνου ἀναμιμνήσκουσα ἁμαρτίαν Nu 5.15; pass. ἀναμνησθήσεσθε ἔναντι κυρίου 'you shall be remembered before the Lord' 10.9; + gen., Si 3.15; + ὅτι 4M 16.18.

2. pass. and ***o*** ἀνομία Ps 108.14, ἁμαρτία Jb 24.20. **b**. with active force, *to make mention of*: + acc., ὄνομα θεῶν ἑτέρων οὐκ ἀναμνησθήσεσθε Ex 23.13.

Cf. ἀνάμνησις, μιμνήσκομαι: Schmidt 1.316f.

ἀνάμνησις, εως. f.ʃ

v.n. of ἀναμιμνήσκω **1**.: εἰς ~ιν Le 24.7, Ps 37 tit, 69 tit, Wi 16.6; Nu 10.10. Cf. ἀναμιμνήσκω: Behm, *TDNT* 1.348; Jones 1955; Caird 1968.458; Daniel 235f.

ἀναμοχλεύω.ʃ

to sever by a lever: limbs, 4M 10.5.

ἀναμφισβητήτως. adv.ʃ

without dispute: 1E 6.29.

ἄνανδρος, ον.

cowardly: ***s*** hum., 4M 5.31. Cf. ἀνδρεῖος, δειλόψυχος.

ἀνανεάζω: aor. ἀνενέασα.ʃ

to regain youthful spirit: 4M 7.13. Cf. νέος, νεάζω.

ἀνανεόω: fut. ~νεώσω; aor.mid.inf. ~νεώσασθαι, ptc. ~νεωσάμενος.

1. *to rejuvenate*: + acc., τὸ σῶμα αὐτοῦ Jb 33.24.

2. mid. *to restore*: + acc., εἰρήνην Es B 2, τὴν φιλίαν .. κατὰ τὸ πρότερον 'the friendship .. up to the former level' 1M 12.1, τὴν ἐξ ἀρχῆς φιλίαν καὶ συμμάχιαν '.. and alliance' 15.17; τὴν εὐνομίαν 'the adherence to the law' 4M 18.4.

Cf. νέος, ἀνανέωσις, ἀνακαινίζω: *ND* 3.61f; LSG s.v.

ἀνάνευσις, εως. f.ʃ

negative decision: Ps 72.4. Cf. ἀνανεύω: Caird 1968.458f.

ἀνανεύω: aor. ἀνένευσα, inf. ~νεῦσαι, subj. ~νεύσω.ʃ

to indicate that one does not consent or *approve*: abs., Ex 22.17, Nu 30.6 and 12 (:: παρασιωπάω vs. 5); ἀπό τινος (pers.) 30.9; + τοῦ inf., Ne 9.17. Cf. βούλομαι + neg., ἀνάνευσις.

ἀνανέωσις, εως. f.ʃ

v.n. of ἀνανεόω **2**: 1M 12.17.

ἀναντλέω: fut.~λήσω.ʃ

to endure patiently: + acc. rei, Jb 19.26; κακά Pr 9.12. Cf. ὑποφέρω.

ἀναξηραίνω: fut. ~ξηρανῶ; aor.impv.2pl ~ξηράνατε.ʃ

to dry up: + acc. rei, φλέβας 'blood-vessels' Ho 13.15 (‖ ἐρημόω, καταξηραίνω), καρπούς 'fruits' Je 27.27, χῶραν 'field' Si 43.3; metaph., ψυχήν 14.9. Cf. ξηραίνω.

ἀνάξιος, ον.ʃ

1. *worthless*: subst.n., Je 15.19 (:: τίμιος).

2. *not becoming and worthy of honourable position or treatment*: ***s*** hum., Od 12.14; adv. subst.n.pl., ~α δυναστεύω 'to exercise authority unworthily' Es E 7 o'; subst. m., Si 25.8.

Cf. ἀναξίως, τίμιος.

ἄναξις, εως. f.ʃ *

act of bringing back, 'restoration': χριστοῦ αὐτοῦ PSol 18.5. Cf. ἀνάγω.

ἀναξίως. adv.ʃ

in a manner unworthy of: + gen., 2M 14.42. Cf. ἀνάξιος.

ἀνάπαλιν. adv.ʃ

on the contrary: Wi 19.21.

ἀνάπαυμα, ατος. n.ʃ

= ἀνάπαυσις, q.v.: τῷ πεινῶντι 'to the hungry' Is 28.12; θάνατος ἀνδρὶ ἀ. Jb 3.23. Cf. ἀναπαύω.

ἀνάπαυσις, εως. f.

1. *rest*: freedom from tiring activity, τοῖς ποσὶν αὐτῆς (of a dove looking for a spot for putting its feet down) Ge 8.9; οἶκος ~εως 'a permanent, stable place of its own' 1C 28.2; ἐπὶ κοίτης 'in bed' Si 40.5; σάββατα ἀ. ἁγία τῷ κυρίῳ αὔριον Ex 16.23; free from anxiety, Mi 2.10, Is 23.12, cf. Si 28.16 (‖ ἡσυχία); free from labour, ref. to sabbath, Le 16.31 ref. to death, ἀ. αἰῶνος Si 30.17, νεκροῦ 38.23, cf. Jb 7.18 and LSG s.v.; a state after death, Wi 4.7.

2. *being freed from danger or threat*, 'liberation': ἡμέρα ~εως Es 9.17 o'.

Cf. ἀναπαύω.

ἀναπαύω: fut. ~παύσω, mid. ~παύσομαι; aor. ἀνέπαυσα, mid. ἀνεπαυσάμην, inf. ~παύσασθαι, impv.

~παυσαι, subj. ~παύσωμαι, pass. ἀνεπαύθην; pf. mid. ~πέπαυμαι.

1. *to put an end to*: + acc. rei, τὸν θυμόν μου 'my rage' Zc 6.8.

2. *to give rest*: *s* God, *o* hum., De 28.65, ἐκ τῆς ὀδύνης .. δουλείας σκληρᾶς 'from stress .. hard slavery' Is 14.3, σε ἀπὸ πάντων τῶν ἐχθρῶν σου 2K 7.11; *s* and *o* hum., Si 3.6; mentally, 1K 16.16.

3. mid. *to take rest, leave off working*: τῇ ἡμέρᾳ τῇ ἑβδόμῃ ἀναπαύσῃ Ex 23.12; ἀναπαύσεται ἕκαστος ὑποκάτω ἀμπέλου αὐτοῦ 'each will take rest under his vine' Mi 2.4; ἐν ἡμέρᾳ θλίψεως 'on a distressful day' Hb 3.16; *s* flock of sheep, Ge 29.2; agricultural land, Le 25.2, cf. Shipp 69; lion, Nu 24.9 (:: ἀνίστημι), De 33.20; opp. κοπιάω La 5.5. **b**. *to let up, decrease pressure*: *s* creditor, harsh taskmaster Is 14.4. **c**. *to call the day*: ἐπὶ τοῖς κακοῖς, οἷς ἐποίησα ὑμῖν Je 49.10.

4. mid. *to stop moving and come to rest*: ἀναπαύσεται ἐπ' αὐτὸν πνεῦμα τοῦ θεοῦ Is 11.2, κρίμα 32.16 (|| κατοικέω); *s* swarms of insects, 7.19 (|| καταπαύω Ex 10.14), birds, Ez 31.13; God dwelling restfully, Is 57.15 (|| κατοικέω), the deceased Si 22.11; anger, Ec 7.9.

5. mid. *to be* or *become free from agitation and worries*: οὔτε εἰρήνευσα οὔτε ἡσύχασα οὔτε ἀνεπαυσάμην Jb 3.26; ὑπνώσας ἀνεπαυσάμην 'upon sleeping (an eternal sleep) ..' 3.13 (|| ἡσυχιάζω), μετὰ τῶν πατέρων Si 47.23. **b**. *to be relieved of, freed from*: + gen., μόχθων 'toils' Jb 2.9d, θυμοῦ 13.13; ἀπὸ τῶν πολεμίων '(got rid) of the enemies' Es 9.16 o', ἀπὸ τῶν ἐχθρῶν 9.22 o'.

Cf. ἀνάπαυσις, ἐπανα~, προσανα~, συναναπαύω, παύω, εἰρηνεύω, ἡσυχάζω, καθίζω: Shipp 69, s.v. ἀνάπαυμα.

ἀναπείθω: aor. ἀνέπεισα.ʃ

to persuade and convince: + acc. pers. and by deception, Je 36.8, 1M 1.11. Cf. πείθω.

ἀναπείρω.ʃ

to pierce through: 2M 12.22.

ἀναπέμπω: aor.inf. ~πέμψαι.ʃ

to send: + dat. and acc. pers., Es 7.36*L*. Cf. πέμπω.

ἀναπετάννυμι: aor.ptc. ~πετάσας.ʃ

to spread out: + acc., πτέρυγας 'wings' Jb 39.26.

ἀναπηδάω: aor. ἀνεπήδησα.

to leap up: *s* fish out of a river, To 6.3 𝔊[I]; astonished or in panic, *s* hum., ἀπὸ τῆς τραπέζης 1K 20.34, ἀπὸ τοῦ θρόνου αὐτοῦ Es D 8 o' (*L* κατα~), enraged 7.9*L*. Cf. πηδάω, ἀν~, ἐξανίστημι.

ἀνάπηρος, ον.ʃ

maimed: *s* hum., τοῖς ὀφθαλμοῖς To 14.2 𝔊[II], τοῖς μέλεσιν 'in the limbs' 2M 8.24.

ἀναπιδύω. On the spelling, see Katz 66.ʃ

to gush forth: ποταμὸς .. καὶ πηγή 'a river .. and a fountain' Pr 18.4.

ἀναπίπτω: fut. ἀναπεσοῦμαι; aor. ἀνέπεσα, ptc. ἀναπεσών, impv. ἀνάπεσε.ʃ

to lie down, recline: to sleep, Ju 12.16; and *s* wild animal, ὡς λέων καὶ ὡς σκύμνος Ge 49.9; for a meal, To 2.1, Si 35.2; to rest, Si 25.18, 35.2; to have sexual intercourse, μετ' αὐτῆς Su 37 TH. Cf. ἀνακλίνω.

ἀναπλάσσω: aor.mid. ἀνεπλασάμην.ʃ

to mould: mid., *s* potter, + acc. rei, σκεύη 'vessels' Wi 15.7. Cf. πλάσσω.

ἀναπληρόω: fut. ~ρώσω, pass. ~ρωθήσομαι; aor. ἀνεπλήρωσα, pass. ἀνεπληρώθην, subj. ~ρωθῶ; pf.pass. ~πεπλήρωμαι.ʃ

1. *to fill a void by supplying* what is lacking: + acc., ἀνεπλήρωσεν σάρκα ἀντ' αὐτῆς 'he applied a piece of flesh in its place' Ge 2.21; fig., οὔπω ἀναπεπλήρωνται αἱ ἁμαρτίαι τῶν Ἀμορραίων 15.16, σύνεσιν Si 24.26 (|| πίμπλημι).

2. *to complete*: + acc., τὰ ἕβδομα ταύτης 'the seven-day marriage feast of this (girl)' Ge 29.28. Cf. LSG s.v.

3. *to go through* a certain period of time, engaged in a certain activity: + acc., μῆνας δεκαδύο '12 months' Es 2.12 o'.

4. *to increase abundantly*: + acc., τὸν ἀριθμὸν τῶν ἡμερῶν 'the length of life' Ex 23.26.

5. pass. *to elapse*: *s* a period of time, ἀνεπληρώθησαν ἑπτὰ ἡμέραι Ex 7.25; Le 12.6 (|| πληροῦμαι); αἱ ἡμέραι τοῦ πένθους 'the days of sorrow' Is 60.20. Cf. συμπλήρωσις **1**.

Cf. πληρόω.

ἀναπλήρωσις, εως. f.

1. *act of reaching the full extent of* and subsequent suspension of: ὀνειδισμοῦ Ιηρουσαλημ 'the disgrace of J.' Da 9.2 LXX (TH: συμπλήρωσις).

2. *coming true* of what has been promised or foretold: 1E 1.54 (|| πληρόομαι 2C 36.21).

Cf. συμπλήρωσις, συντέλεια.

ἀναπνεύω: aor.inf. ~πνεῦσαι.ʃ

to enjoy a respite: Jb 9.18. Cf. ἀναψύχω.

ἀναποδίζω: aor. ἀνεπόδισα, ptc.~δίσας.ʃ

intr. *to move backwards*: *s* sun, Si 48.23; hum., 2M 14.44. Cf. ἀναποδισμός, ἀνα~, ἐπιστρέφω.

ἀναποδισμός, οῦ. m.ʃ *

v.n. of ἀναποδίζω, 'reversal': τελευτῆς 'of (hum.) death' Wi 2.5. Cf. ἀναποδίζω.

ἀναποιέω: pf.ptc.pass. ~πεποιημένος.

to prepare by mixing various ingredients: + acc. and pass., θυσία ἀναπεποιημένη ἐν ἐλαίῳ Le 6.40; ἄρτους ἀναπεποιημένους Nu 6.15; ἄχυρα ἀναπεποιημένα ἐν κριθῇ 'straw mixed with barley' Is 30.24. Cf. ποιέω: Ziegler 1934.187f.

ἀναπτερόω: aor. ἀνεπτέρωσα; pf.ptc.pass. ἀνεπτερωμένος.ʃ
to excite with expectation: + acc. pers., Si 31.1, Ct 6.5; pass., Pr 7.11.

ἀναπτέρωσις, εως. f.ʃ *
v.n. of ἀναπτερόω: PSol 4.12.

ἀναπτύσσω: fut. ~πτύξω; aor. ἀνέπτυξα.ʃ
1. *to unfold*: + acc., τὸ ἱμάτιον 'the garment' De 22.17, Jd 8.25; ^βιβλίον^ 'letter' 4K 19.14.
2. *to make an aperture in*: pass., *o* windows, Ez 41.16, ναός τετράγωνα '.. at four corners' 41.21.

ἀνάπτω: fut. ἀνάψω, pass. ἀναφθήσομαι; aor. ἀνῆψα, inf. ~άψαι, pass. ἀνήφθην, subj. ἀναφθῶ.
1. *to set on fire, kindle* (+ τι): *o* θυσιαστήριον Ma 1.10, γῆν Je 9.12; hum. and fig. ἀνάψει αὐτοὺς ἡ ἡμέρα ἡ ἐρχομένη Ma 4.1; coals, Ps 17.9; *s* flame, φλὸξ ἀνῆψε πάντα τὰ ξύλα τοῦ ἀγροῦ 'a flame set all the trees of the field on fire' Jl 1.19; mid. 2.3.
2. *to cause to flare up*: *s* πῦρ, *o* φλόξ 'flame' La 2.3; *o* πῦρ 4.11, Ez 20.47, πῦρ ἐν ταῖς πύλαις 'in the gates' Je 17.27, πῦρ ἐπὶ τὰ τείχη .. 'on the walls' Am 1.14; πυράς 2M 10.36. **b.** pass., intr. *to flare up*: πῦρ ἀνήφθη Ps 77.21, πυρά 2M 1.22, φλόξ 1.32.
Cf. (ὑφ)άπτω, ἐμπίμπρημι, καίω.

ἀναρίθμητος, ον.
countless: *s* people, ἔθνος .. ἰσχυρὸν καὶ ~ον Jl 1.6; possessions (?) Jb 31.25; life-span, Si 37.25; deeds, 3M 2.26. Cf. ἀριθμός, μυριοπλάσιος.

ἀναρπάζω.ʃ
to carry out highway robbery on: + acc. pers., Jd 9.25 A (B: δια~). Cf. ἁρπάζω.

ἀναρρήγνυμι: fut. ~ρρήξω; aor. ἀνέρρηξα.ʃ
to rip up: + acc., child 4K 2.24; pregnant woman, 8.12 (*L* δια~), 15.16 (id.). Cf. (δια)ρρήγνυμι, ἀνασχίζω.

ἀνασκάπτω: aor. ἀνέσκαψα; pf. ptc. pass. ἀνεσκαμμένος.ʃ
1. *to make by excavating*: *o* λάκκον 'pit' Ps 7.16 (+ ὀρύσσω).
2. *to uproot*: *o* grape-vine, Ps 79.17.

ἀνασκολοπίζω: aor.inf. ~πίσαι.ʃ
to impale: + acc. pers., Es 6.14*L*. Cf. σταυρόω.

ἀνασπάω: fut. ἀνασπάσω; aor. ἀνέσπασα, subj. ~σπάσω.ʃ
to pull up from a lower position: + acc., ἐκεῖθεν (viz. from Hades) ἡ χείρ μου ἀνασπάσει αὐτούς Am 9.2 (opp. κατάγω), ἐκ τοῦ λάκκου 'out of the pit' Da 6.17 LXX (|| αἴρω); συντέλειαν ἐν ἀγκίστρῳ ἀνέσπασε 'he pulled up destruction (!) with a hook' Hb 1.15. Cf. ἀπο~, ἐκ~, ἐπι~, κατασπάω.

ἀνάστασις, εως. f.
1. *arising*: from seat, La 3.63; from grave, 'resurrection,' 2M 12.43, sim. 7.14; as part of the title of a psalm, Ps 65, cf. Karrer 2006. § 4.1.
2. *act of presenting oneself* at a meeting etc.: εἰς ἡμέραν ~εώς μου εἰς μαρτύριον 'for the day when I turn up to testify (in a court)' Zp 3.8.
Cf. ἀνίστημι.

ἀναστατόω: fut. ~στατώσω.ʃ *
to unsettle: + acc., ^πᾶσαν τὴν γῆν^ Da 7.23 LXX. Cf. Shipp 70.

ἀναστέλλω: aor.pass. ἀνεστάλην.ʃ
1. *to remove, make away with*: pass. ἀνεστάλη ἡ γῆ ἀπὸ προσώπου αὐτοῦ 'the earth was removed from His presence' Na 1.5.
2. *to push back and block the way forward*: *o* enemies and pass., 1M 7.24.
Cf. ἀφανίζω.

ἀναστενάζω: aor. ἀνεστέναξα, ptc. ἀναστενάξας.
to groan: out of grief, La 1.4, πικρά 'bitterly' Si 25.18; in dire straits, Su 22 TH. Cf. στενάζω.

ἀνάστημα, ατος. n.ʃ
1. *height*: κέδρος τὸ ἀ. αὐτῆς 'its height is that of a cedar' Zp 2.14.
2. *some structure that goes up under a building*, 'foundation, prop'(?): ὑποστήσομαι τῷ οἴκῳ μου ἀ. τοῦ μὴ διαπορεύεσθαι μηδὲ ἀνακάμπτειν Zc 9.8. **b.** ref. to garrison: τῶν ἀλλοφύλων 1K 10.5; Ju 9.10.
3. *that which has come into being* (of animate beings): πᾶν τὸ ἀ., ὃ ἦν ἐπὶ προσώπου πάσης τῆς γῆς, ἀπὸ ἀνθρώπου ἕως κτήνους καὶ ἑρπετῶν καὶ τῶν πετεινῶν τοῦ οὐρανοῦ Ge 7.23 (|| ἐξανάστασις vs. 4).
4. *regaining of former strength*, 'restoration': Ju 12.8.
Cf. ἀνίστημι, ἐξανάστασις, ὕψος: LSG s.v.; Hauspie 2004.113.

ἀναστρατοπεδεύω: aor. ἀνεστρατοπέδευσα.ʃ
to move military camp: πρός τινα 2M 3.35.

ἀναστρέφω: fut. ~στρέψω, mid.~στραφήσομαι; aor. ἀνέστρεψα, impv. ~στρεψον, subj. ~στρέψω, ptc. ~στρέψας; pf.mid. ἀνέστραμμαι, 3s ἀνέστραπται.
1. intr. *to turn back, return* to point of origin: πρὸς αὐτὸν Ge 8.11; ἀπὸ τῆς κοπῆς .. εἰς τὴν κοιλάδα 14.17; ἐπὶ τὸν λάκκον 37.29; Da 11.9 TH (LXX ἐπι~); || διοδεύειν Zc 7.14, cf. Lee 82; Jd 3.19A (B: ὑπο~). **b.** metaph., in repentance: Πρός με ἀνάστρεψον Je 3.7. **c.** *to go back* as against 'to come back' (ἐπι~): 3K 13.10 (:: vs. 9 ἐπι~), 19.15, 20. **d.** tr. and caus., *o* τὴν αἰχμαλωσίαν Ιακωβ Ez 39.25; τοὺς ἀγγέλους αὐτοῦ κενούς 'his envoys empty-handed' Ju 1.11.
2. *to change the course of action and leave off*: + neg. and inf., μὴ καταδιώκειν 1K 23.28, cf. ἀπο~, ἐπιστρέφω.
3. *to turn upside down*: + acc. (tent), ἄνω Jd 7.13 B.

4. *to remove* from a public office: + acc. pers., ἀπὸ στάσεως αὐτῶν Si 36.12.

5. mid. *to busy oneself* with sth, *engage oneself* in sth: ἀναστρεφομένους '(temple) functionaries, officials' Zc 3.7 (cf.Th, 343 ἐκτελοῦντες λειτουργίαν; Cyr. II 319 συνιερατεύοντας καὶ συλλειτουργοῦντας ἀγγέλους); ἐν ἔργοις αὐτῶν Si 38.25, ἐν αἰνίγμασιν 39.3; ἐν ἀδικίαις Ez 22.7; ἐν μέσῳ αὐτῶν 'in their midst' 3.15, sim. 19.6, Pr 8.20 (ǁ περιπατέω), 3M 2.30; ὀρθῶς '(conduct oneself) uprightly' Ez 22.30, ἄμωμος ἐν δικαιοσύνῃ 'impeccably with righteousness' Pr 20.7; + ptc. pres., 3M 1.24. ***b**. + πρός τινα, turning one's attention to sbd: πρὸς προσήλυτον .. μετὰ κρίματος Ez 22.29.

6. mid. *to dwell* in a certain place *and lead one's life* there: Jo 5.6.

Cf. ἀνακάμπτω, ἀναποδίζω, ἐπανα~, ἐπι~, συνανα~, ὑποστρέφω, στρέφω, κατέρχομαι: LSG s.v.

ἀναστροφή, ῆς. f.ʃ

1. *way in which one conducts oneself*: To 4.14 𝔊[I], 2M 6.23.

2. *reversal of fortune*: 2M 5.8.

ἀνασύρω: aor.impv.mid. ~συραι.ʃ

to pull up that which covers part of one's body to expose it: + acc., τὰς κνήμας 'the legs' Is 47.2 (prior to wading a stream).

ἀνασχίζω: aor.ptc. ~σχίσας, impv. ~σχισον.ʃ

to rip up: *o* foetus, Am 1.13; ἰθχύν 'fish' To 6.4 𝔊[II] (𝔊[I] ἀνατέμνω), 6 𝔊[II]. Cf. σχίζω, ἀναρρήγνυμι, ἀνατέμνω.

ἀνασῴζω: aor.pass.ptc. ~σωθείς; pf.ptc.pass. ~σεσῳσμένος.

1. act. *to rescue*: + acc. τὸν λαόν μου Zc 8.7, ψυχήν Je 28.6 (ǁ φεύγω). Pass.: παραγενόμενος δὲ τῶν ἀνασωθέντων τις 'one of the survivors appeared' Ge 14.13; Ez 33.21. See *ND* 4.142. **b**. *to protect from mortal attack*: pass., *o* hum., 3M 7.20.

2. mid. *to escape in an attempt to rescue oneself*: ἐξολεθρεῦσαι τοὺς ἀνασῳζομένους 'to destroy those who were trying to escape' Ob 14; εἰς Σιων ἀνασῴζεσθε 'flee into Zion' Zc 2.7; Am 9.1, Jl 2.3, 32; φεύγω καὶ ἀ. Je 27.28, sim. 26.6; ἐκ ῥομφαίας Ez 6.8.

Cf. σῴζω.

ἀνατείνω: aor. ἀνέτεινα, ptc. ~τείνας.ʃ

to extend upwards: τὰς χεῖρας εἰς τὸν οὐρανόν 'the hands to heaven' 2M 15.21, ὑψηλοὺς .. τοὺς ὀφθαλμούς 'high .. his eyes' 4M 6.6, τὰ ὄμματα πρὸς τὸν θεόν 26. Cf. τείνω, ἐκτείνω.

ἀνατέλλω: fut. ~τελῶ; aor. ἀνέτειλα, inf. ~τεῖλαι, subj. ~τείλω, impv.3s ~τειλάτω, opt.3s ~τείλαι; pf. ~τέταλκα.

1. *to spring up, sprout*: *s* plants, Ge 2.5, 19.25 (ἐκ τῆς γῆς), Ho 10.4, Zc 6.12, Is 44.4; hair on a shaven head, Jd 16.22 A (B: βλαστάνω), beard 2K 10.5; hum., alm. = 'to thrive' Pr 11.28. **b**. caus.: + acc., *to make spring up, sprout*: abs., De 29.23 (ǁ ἀναβαίνω); ἀκάνθας καὶ τριβόλους ἀνατελεῖ σοι 'it (= ἡ γῆ) will make thorns and thistles grow for you' Ge 3.18, cf. Anz 10.

2. of heavenly bodies, *to rise above the horizon, come up*: *s* the sun, ἀνέτειλεν αὐτῷ ὁ ἥλιος Ge 32.31; Jn 4.8; ἄστρον 'star' Nu 24.17 (ǁ ἀνίστημι); ἀνατελεῖ ὑμῖν .. τὸ ὄνομά μου ἥλιος δικαιοσύνης Ma 4.2; opp. δύνω Ec 1.5; metaph. ἡ δόξα κυρίου ἐπὶ σὲ ανατέταλκεν Is 60.1 (after ἥκει σου τὸ φῶς), 58.10.

3. in general, *to appear, become visible*: *s* hair, Le 13.37; θρίξ 'pubic hair' Ez 16.7; κέρας 'horn' 29.21; ἁφή 'leprous infection' Le 14.43, λέπρα 2C 26.20; ἔτι ὅρασις εἰς καιρὸν καὶ ἀνατελεῖ εἰς πέρας Hb 2.3, cf. 8Ḥev ἐμφανήσεται; δικαιοσύνη .. πλῆθος εἰρήνης Ps 71.7; *s* hum., ὡς χόρτον 'like grass' 91.8, ζωή Jb 11.17.

4. tr. *to cause to come into being*: ἀνατειλάτω ἡ γῆ ἔλεος Is 45.8, ἀνατελεῖ κύριος δικαιοσύνην 61.11.

Cf. ἀναβαίνω, ἀνάγω, ἀναθάλλω, ἀναφαίνω, ἐξ~, προανατέλλω, ἀνατολή, βλαστάνω, δύω.

ἀνατέμνω: aor.inf. ~τέμε.ʃ

to cut open: + acc. rei, fish To 6.5 𝔊[I] (𝔊[II] ~σχίζω).

ἀνατίθημι: fut.act. ἀναθήσω; aor. ἀνέθηκα, subj. ~θῶ, mid. ἀνεθέμην, inf. ~θέσθαι, ptc.pass. ~τεθείς, subj.pass. ~τεθῶ.

I. act. *to dedicate* (to a divine being): + acc. and dat., πᾶν ἀνάθεμα, ὃ ἂν ἀναθῇ ἄνθρωπος τῷ κυρίῳ Le 27.28; τί τινι – ἀναθήσεις τῷ κυρίῳ τὸ πλῆθος αὐτῶν 'you will dedicate to the Lord a great number of them' Mi 4.13; 2M 5.16 (Kappler: ἀνίστημι); pregnantly, εἰς τὸ 'Αστρατεῖον '(depositing them) in the Astarte temple' 1K 31.10 (or: = τίθημι).

II. mid. *to communicate* (intimate knowledge): τί τινι – ἀναθέσθαι τι αὐτῇ 'to communicate anything to her' Mi 7.5; + περί τινος 2M 4.9.

Cf. ἀνάθεμα.

ἀνατίκτω.ʃ

to give birth anew: τινα 4M 16.13. Cf. τίκτω, γεννάω.

ἀνατιναγμός, οῦ. m.ʃ*

shaking up and down: of violent action, ἐκτιναγμὸς καὶ ἀ. καὶ ἐκβρασμὸς .. Na 2.11. Cf. ἐκτιναγμός.

ἀνατολή, ῆς. f.

1. v.n. of ἀνατέλλω: **1** χλόης 'of grass' PSol 5.9; **3** σελήνης 'of the moon' Is 60.19, ἡλίου 'of the sun' Da 4.28 LXX. **b**. *the sunlight at dawnbreak*: 2M 10.28, cf. φωτός Wi 16.28.

2. in pl. *the quarter of sunrise,* 'east': ἀπὸ ~ῶν ἡλίου Ma 1.11 (ǁ δυσμαί), De 4.41; ἀπὸ ~ῶν ἡλίου μέχρι δυσμῶν Ps 49.1, 3M 4.15; ἀφ' ἡλίου ~ῶν Is 9.12 (opp. ἀφ' ἡλίου δυσμῶν), Jb 1.3; ἀπὸ γῆς ~ῶν Zc 8.7 (ǁ δυσμαί); ἐξ ~ῶν 'to the east' 14.4*a*, sim. ἐπὶ θάλασσαν .. ἐπ' ~άς 'westwards .. eastwards' Ge 28.14; κατὰ ~άς 2.8, κατ' ἀνατολὰς ἡλίου Nu 21.11; ὄρος ~ῶν 'a mountain in the east' Ge 10.30, πρὸς ~άς Zc 14.4*b* (ǁ πρὸς θάλασσαν); πρὸς ~ὰς εἰς γῆν ~ῶν Ge 25.6; κατὰ θάλασσαν καὶ βορρᾶν καὶ λίβα καὶ ~άς De 3.27. Also δυσμή, when in the sense of 'west,' appears alw. in the pl.

3. *shoot of plants*: as a name, Zc 3.8, 6.12; a messianic figure, δικαία Je 23.5; ἀγροῦ 'of a field' Ez 16.7.

Cf. ἀνατέλλω, ἀπηλιώτης, βορρᾶς, δυσμή, νότος.

ἀνατρέπω: fut. ~τρέψω; aor.pass. ἀνετράπην, subj. ~τραπῶ.

1. *to overthrow*: τοῦ πεσεῖν 'to fall' Ps 117.13; + acc., city towers, To 13.12 𝔊[II]; pregnantly, εἰς βόθρον '(and hurl you) into a pit' Si 12.16, ἀγαθὰ ἐγγύου 'favours given by a guarantor' 29.16; ζωὴν ἀσεβῶν 'the life of the godless' Pr 10.3 (ǁ λιμοκτονέω 'starve to death').

2. *to dishearten*: pass., ***o*** hum., Ju 16.11 (ǁ πτοέω).

3. *to turn back, put to flight*: ***o*** hum. (defeated commander), ἀπὸ προσώπου τινός 1M 6.6. **b**. *to force to abandon* a course of action: pass. and + gen., τοῦ θράσους 'the audacity' 2M 5.18.

4. *to render ineffective and harmless*: ***o*** ὀργάς 'anger' Pr 21.14.

ἀνατραπῇ Ec 12.6 is perh. to be emended to ἀναρραγῇ 'to snap': LEH, s.v.

ἀνατρέφω: aor.pass. ἀνετράφην, ptc. ~τραφείς.

to help and take care for sth *to grow and mature*, 'rear, bring up': ***o*** hum. infant, Wi 7.4. **b**. of intellectual, religious education: 4M 10.2, cf. Spicq 1.115f.

Cf. ἀνατροφή.

ἀνατρέχω: aor. ἀνέδραμον, ptc. ~δραμών.ʃ

to move with speed towards sbd or sth: abs., To 11.9 𝔊[II] (𝔊[I] προσ~), εἰς τὰς ἐπάνω σατραπείας 'into the upper provinces' 2M 9.25, ἐπὶ τὸ τεῖχος 'on to the wall' 14.43. Cf. τρέχω, σπεύδω.

ἀνατροπή, ῆς. f.ʃ

1. *upsetting, overturning*: ἀ. θολερᾷ 'unclear drink which causes the loss of mental equilibrium (?)' Hb 2.15.

2. *ruin*: βιαία 'violent ruin' 3M 4.5.

ἀνατροφή, ῆς. f.ʃ

v.n. of ἀνατρέφω, 'rearing of child': 4M 16.8. Cf. ἀνατρέφω, παιδεία.

ἀνατυπόω: aor.ptc.mid. ~τυπωσάμενος.ʃ

mid. *to form a mental image of*: + acc., τὴν ὄψιν 'his appearance' Wi 14.17.

ἀναφαίνομαι: fut. ~φανοῦμαι; aor. ἀνεφάνην, subj. ~φανῶ, opt.3s ~φανείη.

1. *to make appearance*: ***s*** goats, Ct 6.5; εἰρήνη Jb 11.18.

2. pass. *to give the impression of* or *to be seen as* being so and so: + inf., 4M 1.4 (ǁ φαίνομαι vs. 3); + adj., δίκαιος ἀναφανοῦμαι Jb 13.18.

Cf. φαίνω, ἀνατέλλω, ὁράω: LSG s.v.

ἀναφάλαντος, ον.ʃ *

having a receding hairline (LSG): Le 13.41. Cf. ἀναφαλάντωμα.

ἀναφαλάντωμα, ατος. n.ʃ *

part affected by the condition of ἀναφάλαντος (q.v.): Le 13.42, 43. Cf. ἀναφάλαντος, φαλάκρωμα.

ἀναφέρω: fut. ἀνοίσω, pass. ἀνενεχθήσομαι; aor. ἀνήνεγκα, impv. ἀνένεγκε, inf. ἀνενέγκαι, ptc. ἀνενέγκας, subj. ἀνενέγκω, pass. ἀνηνέχθην; pf. ἀνενήνοχα, ptc.f. ἀνενηνοχυῖα, pass. ἀνηνεγμένος.

1. *to take to a higher position*: + acc., cultic offerings to an altar, ὁλοκαρπώσεις ἐπὶ τὸ θυσιαστήριον Ge 8.20; εἰς ὁλοκάρπωσιν ἐφ' ἓν τῶν ὀρέων 22.2; ἐπὶ τὸν βωμόν Nu 23.2 (ǁ ἀναβιβάζω vs. 4); ἐκ τοῦ λάκκου 'out of the pit' Da 6.23 TH; torch, Jd 20. 38 A. **b**. *to mount* on sth else: κόσμον χρυσοῦν ἐπὶ τὰ ἐνδύματα ὑμῶν 'golden decorative pieces on your garments' 2K 1.24.

2. *to present*: as a cultic offering, + acc., οὐκ ἀνοίσεις ἐπ' αὐτοῦ θυμίαμα ἕτερον 'you shall not offer on it [= altar] a foreign incense' Ex 30.9; ὁλοκαυτώματα κυρίῳ 30.20, δῶρα κυρίῳ Is 18.7; τὸ δράγμα ἔναντι κυρίου 'the sheaf ..' Le 23.11; θυσίας Is 57.6 (ǁ ἀναβιβάζω); υἱοὺς καὶ θυγατέρας .. τῷ βασιλεῖ Je 39.35; ἐπὶ τὸν βωμόν Nu 23.30. **b**. ***o*** ὕμνους τῷ εὐοδώσαντι 'hymns to one who had given success' 2M 10.7. **c**. not cultic: ***o*** agricultural produce, τῷ βασιλεῖ 1E 4.6; φόρους 'tributes' ib. **d**. personal gift: τινί (pers.) τι 1K 18.27.

3. *to communicate, transmit* to a higher authority: τοὺς λόγους αὐτῶν πρὸς τὸν θεόν Ex 18.19, cf. Jb 7.13; τὸ ῥῆμα τὸ ὑπέρογχον ἀνοίσουσιν ἐπὶ σέ 'the difficult matter they will refer to you' Ex 18.22; De 1.17. Cf. Spicq 1.117, n. 4. **b**. *to utter*: + acc. rei, ἀπὸ χειλέων 'from my lips' Pr 8.6.

4. *to bring back* to the point of origin: θηριάλωτον οὐκ ἀνενήνοχά σοι 'I have not brought back to you any cattle caught and torn by wild beasts' Ge 31.39. **b**. *to repay*: ἀναφερέτω σοι χάριν 'expecting a return of favour from him' Si 8.19.

5. *to make appear*: ***s*** vine, βλαστούς 'flowers' Ge 40.10. **b**. fig., θυμὸν κατὰ τὸ κρίμα '(gave vent) to his righteous indignation' 1M 2.24, cf. ἀναβαίνω **2 b**.

6. *to carry* that which one is not obligated to: τὴν πορνείαν ὑμῶν '(the consequences of) your whoredom' Nu 14.33; τὰς ἁμαρτίας αὐτῶν αὐτὸς ἀνοίσει .. αὐτὸς ἁμαρτίας πολλῶν ἀνήνεγκε Is 53.11f.

7. *to fetch*: + acc. rei, Da 5.2 LXX (TH φέρω).

Cf. ἀναφορά, ἀναφορεύς, ἀναβιβάζω, προσ~, συναναφέρω, φέρω, δωρέω: Weiss, *TDNT* 9.60.

ἀναφορά, ᾶς. f.ʃ

**cultic offering*: Nu 4.19; θυσίαν .. ~ὰν καὶ ὁλοκαυτώματα Ps 50.21. Cf. ἀναφέρω, ἀναφορεύς.

ἀναφορεύς, έως. m.*

carrying-pole: for carrying the ark of testimony, Ex 25.12, 13, Nu 4.10; used to carry clusters of grapes, 13.24. Cf. ἀναφέρω.

ἀναφράσσω.ʃ*

to block up: ***o*** breaches in a ruined wall, Ne 4.7. Cf. φράσσω.

ἀναφύω: fut. ~φύσω; aor.pass. ἀνεφύην.ʃ

1. *to let grow*: ***s*** land, ***o*** vegetation, Is 34.13.

2. mid. *to grow in size* or *quantity*: vertically, ***s*** στάχυες 'ears of corn' Ge 41.6 (|| vs. 5 ἀναβαίνω), κέρας 'horn' Da 7.8 LXX (TH: ἀναβαίνω), 8.9 LXX (TH: ἐξέρχομαι); mice, 1K 5.6.

Cf. φύω, ἀναβαίνω.

ἀναφωνέω.

to make a loud sound: + dat. (musical instrument), 1C 15.28; ἐν κυμβάλοις 'with cymbals' 16.5. Cf. φωνέω.

ἀναχαίνω: aor.ptc. ~χανών.ʃ

to open the mouth: abs., to eat, 2M 6.18. Cf. χαίνω.

ἀναχωρέω: aor. ἀνεχώρησα, impv. ~χώρησον, ptc. ~χωρήσας, inf. ~χωρῆσαι.

to withdraw in order to flee a danger: abs. To 1.19 $\mathfrak{G}^{I}$ ($\mathfrak{G}^{II}$: ἀποδιδράσκω 'to run away,' sim. 1K 20.1*L*, cf. 25.10), "he dodged (scil. the spear hurled at him)" 19.10 (+ διασῴζομαι); ἀπὸ προσώπου Φαραω Ex 2.15; Nu 16.24 (|| ἀφίστημι vs. 27); ἀπὸ φωνῆς ἱππέως .. Je 4.29; εἰς τὰ ὀπίσω 'backwards' Ps 113.5 (|| φεύγω), modestly Pr 25.9; to seek seclusion, Ιακωβ εἰς πεδίον Συρίας Ho 12.12; πρός τινα 2M 10.13; ***s*** troops, 1K 13.6 *L*. Cf. the application of ἀ. to run-away slaves as in *PSI* VI 667.85.4f.

Cf. ἐκχωρέω, ἀφίστημι, ἀποδιδράσκω, φεύγω.

ἀνάψυξις, εως. f.ʃ

respite, being released from distressful condition: γέγονεν ἀ. Ex 8.15. Cf. ἀναψύχω, ἀναψυχή: *ND* 4.261f.

ἀναψυχή, ῆς. f.

relief from worries and distress: πεπλούτηκα, εὕρηκα ~ὴν ἐμαυτῷ 'I have become wealthy and found myself relief' Ho 12.8; ἐξήγαγες ἡμᾶς εἰς ~ήν Ps 65.12. Cf. ἀναψύχω, ἀνάψυξις.

ἀναψύχω: fut.ptc. ~ψύξων; aor. ἀνέψυξα, subj. ~ψύξω; pf.ptc. ἀνεψυχώς.ʃ

1. *to seek cool shelter in hot weather*: 2M 4.46.

2. *to have temporary relief and respite*: ***s*** lowly members of a household resting on sabbaths, Ex 23.12 (|| ἀναπαύομαι); ἄνες μοι, ἵνα ἀναψύξω 'Just give me a break, please' Ps 38.14; ἔπιεν (sc. ὕδωρ) καὶ ἐπέστρεψεν τὸ πνεῦμα αὐτοῦ ἐν αὐτῷ καὶ ἀνέψυξεν (B: ἔζησεν) Jd 15.19, τὸν ἄρτι βραχέως ἀνεψυχότα λαόν 'the people who had just sighed a brief sigh of relief' 2M 13.11; 1K 16.23, 2K 16.14 (at latter || ἀναπαύομαι *L*).

Cf. ἀναψυχή, ἀνάψυξις, καταψύχω, ἀναπαύομαι, ἀναπνεύω: Spicq 1.120f.

ἀνδραγαθέω: aor. ἠνδραγάθησα, inf. ~γαθῆσαι, ptc. ~γαθήσας.

to act bravely on the battlefield: 1M 5.61; + cogn. acc., 16.23. Cf. subs.

ἀνδραγαθία, ας. f.

manly virtue, bravery: Es 10.2 o', 1M 5.56, 4M 1.8. Cf. prec.: Renehan 2.26.

ἀνδράποδον, ου. n.ʃ

one taken in war and sold as a slave (LSJ): 3M 7.5. Cf. δοῦλος: Schmidt 4.126f.; Spicq 1978. 201-4.

ἀνδρεία, ας. f.

1. *brave attitude*: divine attribute, Ps 67.7; king's, Ep Jer 58; soldiers', ἀποθνῄσκω ἐν ~ᾳ 1M 9.10; martyrs', 4M 1.4; in a list of Stoic moral ideals, + ὑπομονή 'endurance' 1.11, + δικαιοσύνη, σωφροσύνη 1.6, also + φρόνησις 1.18.

2. *industry, hard-working life-style*: || μόχθος Ec 4.4, cf. ἀνδρεῖος **2**.

Cf. ἀνδρεῖος.

ἀνδρεῖος, α, ον.

1. *staunch*: ***s*** γυνή 'wife' Si 26.2, 28.15, Pr 12.4, 31.10, To 6.12 $\mathfrak{G}^{II}$ (the last two poss. **2**), cf. Arist. *Pol.* 1277ᵇ22 (***s*** women).

2. *industrious*: opp. ἀεργός 'lazy' Pr 13.4, 15.19; opp. ὀκνηρός 'slothful' 11.16, cf. 10.4; ἐν ἀσεβείαις 28.3.

3. *courageous*: ***s*** βασιλεία 4M 2.23.

Cf. ἄνανδρος, ἀνδρεία, ἀνδρειόω, ἐπανδρόω, θρασύς: Schmidt 3.544f.

ἀνδρειόω: aor.ptc. ἀνδρειώσας.ʃ *

to give courage to: + acc., 4M 15.23, or poss. read ἀνδρείως (so Deissmann 1921 ad loc.). Cf. ἀνδρεῖος.

ἀνδρείως. adv.ʃ

bravely: 2M 6.27. Cf. ἀνδρωδῶς. Del. 1M 9.10, 2M 14.43 v.l.

ἀνδρίζομαι: fut. ἀνδριοῦμαι; aor. ἠνδρισάμην, impv. ἄνδρισαι.

1. *to conduct oneself in a resolute manner*: ἀνδρίζου Mi 4.10 (to a woman in labour); ἀνδρίζου καὶ ἴσχυε 'Be a man ..' De 31.6 (foll. by μὴ φοβοῦ μηδὲ δειλία), 7, 23, ἴσχυε καὶ ἀνδρίζου Jo 1.6; ἐν τῷ νόμῳ 1M 2.64; τῇ ἰσχῦι Na 2.2; ἀνδρίζου, καὶ κραταιούσθω ἡ καρδία σου Ps 26.14; ἀνδριοῦμαι Je 2.25 (a defiant response).

2. *to act in a manner typical of men*: ἐν οἴνῳ Si 34.25. **b**. *to perform the man's part in sexual intercourse* (LSG): ἐπὶ τὸ παιδάριον 4K 4.35*L*.

Cf. ἀνήρ, ἰσχύω, κραταιόω: Passoni Dell'Acqua 1982.178-94; Fernández Marcos 1995.

ἀνδρόγυνος, ου. m.ʃ
effeminate person: Pr 18.8, 19.15. Cf. Walters 122.

ἀνδροφονέω: aor.ptc. ~φονήσας.ʃ
to murder sbd: abs., 4M 9.15. Cf. ἀνδροφόνος.

ἀνδροφόνος, ον.ʃ
subst.m. *murderer of humans*: 2M 9.28. Cf. φονεύς.

ἀνδρόω: aor.pass.subj. ἀνδρωθῶ, ptc. ~ρωθείς.ʃ
pass. *to reach manhood*: Jb 27.14, 33.25. Cf. Renehan 2.26.

ἀνδρωδῶς. adv.ʃ
courageously: on battlefield 1M 6.31, 2M 14.43. Cf. ἀνδρείως.

ἀνεγείρω: aor.ptc. ἀνεγείρας.ʃ
to help rise again, 'rebuild': + acc. οἰκόπεδα 'ruins' Si 49.13. Cf. ἐγείρω: Renehan 2.26f., s.v. ἀνέγερσις.

ἀνέγκλητος, ον.ʃ
occasioning no reproach, 'blameless': *s* hum., 3M 5.31. Cf. ἄμεμπτος: Grundmann, *TDNT* 1.356f.

ἀνείκαστος, ον.ʃ*
considerable in extent and effect: *s* βοή 'outcry' 3M 1.28.

ἀνειλέω: aor. ἀνείλησα.ʃ
to unroll: + acc., Ez 2.10.

ἄνειμι: pres.ptc.m.sg. ἀνιών.ʃ
to ascend: *s* hum., 4M 4.10. Cf. ἀναβαίνω.

ἀνεκλιπής, ές.ʃ*
never ceasing to exist and be available: *s* wisdom compared to treasure, Wi 7.14, sim. 8.18. Cf. ἐκλείπω.

ἀνελεημόνως. adv.ʃ
mercilessly: Jb 6.21, 30.21. Cf. ἀνελεήμων, ἐλεήμων.

ἀνελεήμων, όνος.
merciless: *s* hum., Jb 19.13, Pr 5.9; ἄγγελον 'angel' 17.11; τὰ σπλάγχνα τῶν ἀσεβῶν 'the bowels of the impious' 12.10; infanticide, Wi 12.5; wrath, 19.1. Cf. ἀνηλεής, ἐλεήμων, ἀνελεημόνως.

ἀνέλπιστος, ον.ʃ
having lost hope: ἔθνος ~ον καὶ καταπεπατημένον 'a nation hopeless and trampled' Is 18.2 (:: ἔθνος ἐλπίζον .. vs. 7). Cf. ἀνελπίστως, ἐλπίζω, ἀπροσδόκητος: Schmidt 3.589f.

ἀνελπίστως. adv.ʃ
unexpectedly: Wi 11.7. Cf. ἀνέλπιστος, ἀπροσδοκήτως.

ἄνεμος, ου. m.

1. *air in more or less rapid motion*, 'wind': ἄ. νότος 'south wind' Ex 10.13; καύσωνα ~ον 'a burning-hot wind' Ho 13.15; ‖ καταιγίς Is 17.13, 57.13; fig. of elusiveness, Si 31.2, of evanescence or ephemeralness Pr 9.12a, 11.29, Ec 5.15.

*__2__. *one of the four cardinal points*: ἐκ τῶν τεσσάρων ~ων τοῦ οὐρανοῦ Zc 2.6, sim. Da 8.8, 11.4; εἰς πάντα ἄνεμον 'in every direction' Ez 5.10.

Cf. καταιγίς, λαῖλαψ, πνεῦμα.

ἀνεμοφθορία, ας. f. *
damaging by wind: divine punishment and ‖ ὤχρα 'mildew' De 28.22; ‖ ἀφορία Hg 2.17. Cf. ἀνεμόφθορος and φθορά.

ἀνεμόφθορος, ον. *
damaged by wind: στάχυες λεπτοὶ καὶ ~οι 'lean and wind-blasted ears of corn' Ge 41.6; ~α ἔσπειραν 'they sowed wind-damaged (seeds)' Ho 8.7. Cf. prec.

ἀνεμπόδιστος, ον.ʃ
not being disadvantaged by any impediment: *s* ἔργον 'work' Wi 17.20, ὁδός 'road' 19.7. Cf. ἐμποδίζω, ἀπαραπόδιστος.

ἀνεξέλεγκτος, ον.ʃ
not amenable to critical examination: *s* παιδεία Pr 10.17; καρδία βασιλέως '(inscrutable) mind ..' 25.3. Cf. ἐξελέγκω.

ἀνεξικακία, ας. f.ʃ
forbearance shown when wronged: Wi 2.19. Cf. ὑπομονή.

ἀνεξιχνίαστος, ον.
unfathomable: *s* God's deeds, Jb 5.9 (+ μέγας, ἔνδοξος, ἐξαίσιος); God's mercy, + ἀμέτρητος Od 12.6. Cf. ἐξιχνιάζω.

ἀνεπιεικής, ές.ʃ
unfair: *s* γνώμη 'decision' Pr 12.26. Cf. ἐπιεικής.

ἀνεπιστρέπτως. adv.ʃ
with utter indifference: 3M 1.20.

ἀνερευνάω.ʃ
to search thoroughly: mid., κατὰ τὸ .. στρατόπεδον 'throughout the encampment' 4M 3.13. Cf. ἐρευνάω.

ἀνέρχομαι: aor. ἀνῆλθον.ʃ
to go back to the point of origin: *s* hum., 3K 13.12. Cf. ἔρχομαι.

ἄνεσις, εως. f.

1. *licence* to act in a certain way: + inf., Si 15.20; ἄ. καὶ ἄφεσις 'permission to go away' 1E 4.62. **b**. *freedom of action resulting from restriction lifted*: Si 26.10. **c**. *freedom from routine employment*, 'spare time': ‖ ἀργία Wi 13.13.

2. *insufficient attention and neglect* to keep to the instruction: ~ιν ποιῆσαι περὶ τούτου 2E 4.22.

Cf. ἀνίημι.

ἀνετάζω.ʃ

to subject to examination: abs. and + ἐκζητέω Jd 6.29; oral and + double acc., ἀλλήλους τὴν αἰτίαν Su 14 TH. Cf. ἐτάζω.

ἄνευ. prep. w. gen.

with absence of, 'without': ἄ. θεοῦ Ge 41.16(*c*); ἄ. σου 'without your permission' 41.44(*c*), ἄ. κυρίου Is 36.10(*d*); ἄ. ἀργυρίου 'free without paying silver' Ex 21.11(*a*), ἄ. ἀργυρίου καὶ τιμῆς οἴνου Is 55.1(*g*); εἰ πεσεῖται ὄρνεον ἐπὶ τὴν γῆν ἄ. ἰξευτοῦ; 'would a bird fall on to the ground without a fowler?' Am 3.5(*a*); εἰ βρωθήσεται ἄρτος ἄ. ἁλός; 'would bread be eaten without salt?' Jb 6.6(*f*); + inf. ἄ. τοῦ συλλαβεῖν τι 'without having caught anything' Am 3.5(*b*). **b**. postp.: πάσης αἰδοῦς ἄ. 'absolutely shamelessly' 3M 4.5.

Cf. ἄτερ, χωρίς: Renehan 2.28; Muraoka 2005a. 302f.

a) אַיִן; *b*) לֹא; *c*) בִּלְעָד; *d*) מִבִּלְעָד; *e*) בְּלִי; *f*) מִבְּלִי; *g*) בְּלֹא; *h*) Ar. לָא בְּ.

ἀνευρίσκω: aor.ptc.mid. ἀνευράμενος.ʃ

to find out after a search: τι 4M 3.14. Cf. εὑρίσκω.

ἀνέφικτος, ον.ʃ

beyond reach: *s* heaven as God's abode, ἀνθρώποις 3M 2.15. Cf. ἀφικνέομαι.

ἀνέχω: fut. ἀνέξω, mid. ἀνέξομαι; aor.act. ἀνέσχον.

I. act., *to hold back, withhold, refuse to grant*: ἀνέσχον ἐξ ὑμῶν τὸν ὑετόν 'I withheld rain from you' Am 4.7; ἀνέξει ὁ οὐρανὸς ἀπὸ δρόσου 'the heavens will hold back dew' Hg 1.10, cf. ἀνέσχεν οὐρανόν Si 48.3 (*s* Elijah). Both constructions illustrated here, i.e. the use of ἐκ and ἀπό, are prob. Hebraistic, though on the latter, cf. Plutarch 2.514a ἑαυτὸν ἀπό τινος in the sense of "to keep oneself away from." See also Renehan, 1.30f. **b**. *to deny complete freedom of action and restrain*: pass., ***o*** passions, 4M 1.35 (|| ἀνακόπτω, φιμόω). **c**. *to refrain from* doing: + inf., 3K 12.24[z], PSol 17.18, cf. **II b**.

II. mid., *to put up with, bear with*: abs., ἀνέχεταί μου ἡ ψυχή Jb 6.11 (|| ὑπομένω); + gen. pers., οὐκ ἠδύνατο Ιωσηφ ἀνέχεσθαι πάντων τῶν παρεστηκότων αὐτῷ Ge 45.1; Is 46.4; + gen. rei, ὀσμῆς 'stench' 2M 9.12; + gen. abs., 3M 1.22; + acc., τὰς νουμηνίας ὑμῶν .. 'your new-moon festivals .. I cannot stand' Is 1.13 (|| μισέω). **b**. *to restrain oneself so as not to react*: Is 42.14, 64.12 (|| σιωπάω).

Cf. ἀντέχω, κωλύω, μακροθυμέω, ὑποστέλλω, ὑποφέρω, φέρω: Schmidt 1.424-41.

ἀνεψιός, οῦ. m.ʃ

male cousin: as husband, Nu 36.11; To 7.2 𝔊[I] (|| 𝔊[II] ἀδελφός), 9.6 𝔊[II]. Cf. Shipp 72f.

ἀνήκεστος, ον.ʃ

incapable of its severe impact being alleviated: *s* συμφορά 'calamity' Es E 5, ἀλγηδών 'pain' 2M 9.5, φόνος '(inescapable) death' 3M 3.25. Cf. ἀνίατος.

ἀνήκοος, ον.

unwilling to listen, disobedient: subst. and *s* human, Nu 17.10; καρδία ἀ. καὶ ἀπειθής Je 5.23; opp. ὑπήκοος 'obedient' Pr 13.1. Cf. ἀκούω, ὑπακούω, ὑπήκοος, ἀπειθής.

ἀνήκω.ʃ

1. *to have come up to* a place: *s* hum., 1K 27.8.

2. *to be concerned* with (εἰς): Si prol. 13.

3. *to be appropriate*: *s* τόπος 1M 10.40.

4. *to belong as right* to sbd (τινι): *s* amount of money, 1M 10.42, 11.35.

5. *to be of interest* or *relevance* to sbd (τινι): Jo 23.14, 2M 14.8.

ἀνήλατος, ον.ʃ

not struck with a hammer: *s* ἄκμων 'anvil' Jb 41.16.

ἀνηλεής, ές.ʃ

merciless: *s* elephants, 3M 5.10. Cf. ἀνελεήμων, ἐλεήμων.

ἀνήνυτος, ον.ʃ

impossible to complete: *s* task, 3M 4.15. Cf. τελείωσις.

ἀνήρ, ἀνδρός. m.

1. *male person*, 'man': κοίτη ~ός 'intercourse with a male' Nu 31.35 (|| κ. ἄρσενος vs. 17, 18); γένῃ ~ρί 'have (sexual) relationships with a male' Ho 3.3; οὐ μάχαιρα ~ρὸς οὐδὲ μ. ἀνθρώπου Is 31.8; male adult ready to marry, To 1.9; he who has reached manhood, 1M 13.53. **b**. specifically *husband*: πρὸς τὸν ~ρα σου ἡ ἀποστροφή σου Ge 3.16; με ἀγαπήσει ὁ ἀ. μου 29.32; ἐγὼ οὐκ ἀ. αὐτῆς Ho 2.2; τὸν ~ρα μου τὸν πρότερον 'my former husband' 2.7, 16; τὸν ~ρα αὐτῆς τὸν παρθενικόν 'the husband of her youth' Jl 1.8; sexual partner, θυγατέρες, αἳ οὐκ ἔγνωσαν ~ρα 'daughters who have not yet had sex with a man' Ge 19.8. **c**. harlot's male client: Ez 16.32, if παρὰ τοῦ ἀνδρὸς αὐτῆς is to be construed with λαμβάνουσα.

2. *person*, maleness not being prominent: people belonging to a certain geographical location ~ρῶν (בֵּית) Χαρραν Am 1.5; οἱ ~ρες Νινευη 'the citizens of Nineveh, Ninevites' Jn 3.5; οἱ ~ρες τῆς πόλεως Ge 20.2; οἱ ~ρες τοῦ τόπου 'the local folks' 26.7, 29.22 (and also at 20.2 possibly 'males'). **b**. *personnel*: ὁ βασιλεὺς καὶ οἱ ~ρες αὐτοῦ 'the king and his men' Zc 7.2; οἱ ἡγεμόνες .. καὶ οἱ ~ρες αὐτῶν Je 47.7; Ju 10.13. **c**. a near-synonym of τις, 'any given person (or: 'people' in pl.), often in a generalising statement, ἀνὴρ ὃς ἂν δῷ τῷ ἱερεῖ, αὐτῷ ἔσται 'whosoever gives to the priest, it shall be his' Nu 5.10; ἐχθροὶ ~ρὸς οἱ ~ρες οἱ ἐν τῷ οἴκῳ αὐτοῦ 'the very people who live under his own roof will be his enemies' Mi 7.6; δέκα ~ρες 'ten people' Am 6.9, Zc 8.23; ~ρες τῶν πρεσβυτέρων 'some of the elders' Je 33.17, Ez 14.1; οἱ ~ρες τῆς διαθήκης σου 'your allies' Ob 7; ~ρες εἰρηνικοί 'confederates' ib.; ~ρες σεσωσμένοι 'survivors' 21 (cf. Jn 1.10*bis*, 13, 16); ~ρας δυνατούς Na 2.4 (cf. Zp 1.12, Zc 1.8, 10, 2.5, 6.12); 4K 4.29 (*L* τις). ***d**. Hebraistically + negator = *nobody*: τῶν ἐθνῶν οὐκ ἔστιν ἀ. μετ' ἐμοῦ Is 63.3. **e**. ‖ ἄνθρωπος: Is 2.9, 5.15, 31.8, 56.2, cf. the use of ~ρες as against ἄνθρωπος, the main character of a story (Abraham's servant), "his men" Ge 24.32. ***f**. the generalising function is reinforced by Hebraistically repeating ἀνήρ: 'Ανδρὸς ~ρὸς ἐὰν παραβῇ ἡ γυνὴ αὐτοῦ 'Should the wife of any man go astray ..' Nu 5.12; 'Ανδρὶ ἀνδρί .. 'To any person ..' Le 15.2. **g**. in a public address: ῎Ανδρες 'Gentlemen!' 1E 3.17. ***h**. Hebraistically and collectively, ἀνὴρ Ισραηλ 'Israelites': 1K 4.10, 17.

3. Pleonastically, (usually) preceding another noun denoting a class of men of some profession or disposition [not necessarily Hebraism – already in Homer, e.g. *Iliad* 2.1 ἀνέρες ἱπποκορυσταί 'arrangers of chariots'; see LSJ + LSG, s.v. VI, 1 and BDAG, s.v. **1 d** α]: ~ρες κτηνοτρόφοι 'cattlemen' Ge 46.32, ἀ. γεωργός 49.15, ἀ. τέκτων Is 41.7, ~ρὸς πειρατοῦ 'brigand' Ho 6.8, ~ρες πολεμισταί Jl 2.7, 3.9, ~ρες λῃσταί Ez 22.9, ~ρες φίλοι Je 20.10, καταφρονητὴς ἀ. ἀλαζών Hb 2.5, Zp 3.4; ~ρες τερατοσκόποι Zc 3.8 (cf. ~ρὸς Ἰουδαίου 'a Jew' Zc 8.23); ~ρα πολίτην 13.7, ἀ. σφενδονήτης 'slinger' Ju 6.12, ἀ. ἁμαρτωλός Si 10.23. **b**. voc.: ~ρες ἱερεῖς Bel 15-17 LXX. **c**. preceding a PN: ὁ ἀ. Ἰούδας 1M 5.63. Cf. ἄνθρωπος **3 f**, γυνή **1 c**.

***4**. *each*, Hebraistically together with ἑαυτοῦ etc.: w. a pl. verb, παρεμβαλοῦσιν οἱ υἱοὶ Ισραηλ, ἀ. ἐν τῇ ἑαυτοῦ τάξει 'the children of Is. shall encamp, each in his own quarters' Nu 1.52.

Cf. ἄνθρωπος, ἀνδρίζομαι, ἄρσην, γυνή: Schmidt 2.385-8.

ἀνθαιρέω.∫∫

to choose instead of sth else (gen.): mid., τι Pr 8.10. Cf. αἱρέω.

ἀνθέμιον, ου. n.∫

small flower: Ec 12.6. Cf. ἄνθος: Caird 1968.459f.

ἀνθέω: fut. ἀνθήσω; impv. ἄνθησον, ptc.n.sg. ἀνθῆσαν, subj. ἀνθήσω, opt.3s ἀνθήσαι; pf. ἤνθηκα.

to blossom: ἀνθήσει ὡς κρίνον 'it will blossom as a lily' Ho 14.6, sim. Is 35.1; εἰς ἀμητόν 17.11; + cogn. acc., ἄνθος 18.5, Si 39.14; *s* ῥάβδος 'staff' Ez 7.10 (‖ ἐξανίστημι), ἄνθος Jb 14.2, τὰ ἀγαθὰ αὐτοῦ 'his goods' 20.21; metaph., δίκαιος ὡς φοῖνιξ ἀνθήσει 'a righteous man shall flourish like a palm-tree' Ps 91.13. Cf. ἐξανθέω, κυπρίω, and ἄνθος.

ἄνθινος, η, ον.∫

like flowers: subst., decorative knob on a garment, Ex 28.30. Cf. ἄνθος.

ἀνθίστημι: ἀντιστήσομαι; 1aor. ἀντέστησα, subj. ἀντιστήσω; 2aor. ἀντέστην, inf. ἀντιστῆναι, impv.3s. ἀντιστήτω, ptc. ἀντιστάς; pf. ἀνθέστηκα, ptc. ἀνθεστηκώς; plpf. ἀνθειστήκειν.

I. tr. (1aor.) *to set against*: μήποτε ἀντιστήσῃ σου τὴν ὁλκήν 'in case he outweighs you' Si 8.2. **b**. *to instigate, incite*: ***o*** (population understood?) 2K 5.6B (*L* ἀφίστημι), poss. intr.

II. intr. (fut.mid., 2aor., pf., plpf.) *to stand against*: esp. in battle, + dat. pers., ἐχθροῖς Le 26.37, τοὺς ὑπεναντίους τοὺς ἀνθεστηκότας ὑμῖν Nu 10.9; ἐξ ἐναντίας 'opposed to (the enemy),' Ob 11, Hb 1.9; ἔναντι ἐκκλησίας Si 46.7; ἐναντίον μου Da 10.13 LXX; κατὰ πρόσωπόν τινος De 7.24, 9.2, 11.25; κατενώπιόν τινος Jo 1.5; in a court, κατὰ τοῦ ἀδελφοῦ αὐτοῦ De 19.18, μοι Is 50.8; + dat. rei, κρίματι αὐτοῦ Jb 9.19, sim. Wi 12.12, τοῖς λόγοις σου Ju 8.28. **b**. fig.: ἡ αἰσχύνη τοῦ προσώπου αὐτῶν ἀντέστη αὐτοῖς 'the loss of face came to confront them' Is 3.9, cf. 59.12; αἱ ἁμαρτίαι ἡμῶν ἀντέστησαν ἡμῖν 'our sins were to our disadvantage' Je 14.7.

2. *to rise* in rebellion or opposition: + πρός τινα Ho 14.1 (against one's own god); + dat. pers. 'to challenge,' θεῷ Ma 3.15, sim. Je 27.44 (‖ ἵστημι κατὰ πρόσωπόν τινος), 27.24 (‖ πρός τινα vs. 29), τῇ δεξιᾷ σου Ps 16.7; βασιλεῦσιν 1E 2.18; τῇ φωνῇ ^τοῦ θεοῦ^ Ju 16.14; εἰς ἔχθραν 'as an enemy' Mi 2.8; ἀπὸ ὄπισθεν τοῦ θεοῦ 'having ceased following God' Is 59.13. Cf. στασιάζω, συναφίστημι.

3. *to withstand* sbd else's anger: ἐν ὀργῇ θυμοῦ αὐτοῦ Na 1.6 (‖ ὑφίστημι ἀπὸ προσώπου ὀργῆς αὐτοῦ).

4. *to emerge to replace*: + ἀντί τινος Ba 3.19.

Cf. ἵστημι, καθίστημι.

ἀνθομολογέομαι: fut. ~γήσομαι; aor. ἀνθωμολογησάμην.

1. *to admit openly*: abs., one's fault as ***o*** understood, 1E 8.88, Si 20.3; + dat., τῷ ὑψίστῳ Da LXX 4.34 (+ αἰνέω and ‖ ἐξομολογέομαι), σοι Ps 78.13; εἰς οὐρανὸν .. ἐπὶ τῇ .. σωτηρίᾳ '.. over the rescue' 3M 6.33.

2. *to give formal consent* to a request: + dat. pers. and inf., Es 7.21 *L*.

Cf. ἀνθομολόγησις, ἐξομολογέομαι.

ἀνθομολόγησις, εως. f.∫

v.n. of ἀνθομολογέω: Si 17.27 (‖ αἰνέω, ἐξομολόγησις), ἐν αἴνῳ καὶ ~ει 2E 3.11.

ἄνθος, ους. n.

flower: ἄ. παραπορευόμενον 'an evanescent flower' Zp 2.2. **b**. decorative element in the fabric of an ephod, καταμεμιγμένα ἐν ~εσιν 'intermingled with flowers' Ex 28.14; ἄ. σμύρνης ἐκλεκτῆς '.. of choice myrrh' 30.23 (for cultic use). Cf. ἀνθέω, ἄνθινος, διανθίζω, ἐξανθέω: Schmidt 2.487-9.

ἀνθρακιά, ᾶς. f.∫

burning charcoal: Si 11.32, 4M 9.20. Cf. ἄνθραξ.

ἀνθράκινος, ον. n.∫

made of a carbuncle: *s* κυλίκιον 'small cup' Es 1.7 o'. Cf. ἄνθραξ.

ἄνθραξ, ακος. m.

1. precious stone of dark-red colour, including the *carbuncle, ruby* and *garnet* (LSJ, s.v.): Ge 2.12, Ex 28.18; + βήρυλλος 'beryl' To 13.17 𝔊I; as a cosmetic ingredient, Is 54.11; λίθος ~ος Ez 10.9.

2. *coal*: πυρεῖον πλῆρες ~άκων 'censer full of coals' Le 16.12; πυρός 'burning' Is 5.24, used at an altar, 6.6; for baking, 44.19. **b**. *coal-fire*: fig. of sth remaining alive and giving hope for the future, 2K 14.7B (*L* σπινθήρ 'spark').

Cf. ἀνθρακιά.

ἀνθρωπάρεσκος, ου.∫

man-pleaser: Ps 52.6, PSol 4 tit.

ἀνθρώπινος, η, ον.

1. *human*: *s* ἁμαρτία Nu 5.6; ὀστοῦν 'bone' 19.16, 18; βίος 'life' Jb 10.5; flesh and blood, Wi 12.5; πρᾶγμα 'matter', opp. θεῖος 4M 1.16, 4.13.

***2**. *humane*: *s* παρηγορία 'exhortation' 4M 5.12.

Cf. ἄνθρωπος, θεῖος: Schmidt 2.388-91; Shipp 74f.

ἄνθρωπος, ου. m.

1. *man* (with no particular reference to maleness), *human being*: **a**. in general, πνεῦμα ~ου 'man's spirit' Zc 12.1; often in pl. ἀτεκνωθήσονται ἐξ ~ων 'they will be made childless by (?) men' Ho 9.12; ἐν διαφθορᾷ ~ων 11.4; κατορθῶν ἐν ~οις οὐχ ὑπάρχει Mi 7.2, sim. Am 4.13; with the generic def. art. καὶ ἐκθρίψω τοὺς ~ους Zp 1.17; Hg 1.11, πάντας τοὺς ~ους Zc 8.10; 11.6; sg. with generic force, ὅπως ἐξαρθῇ ἄ. ἐξ ὄρους Ησαυ 'so that people may be exterminated from the mountain of Esau' Ob 9, ἄ. τοῦ Ιουδα Is 5.3; coll., εἶπον ~ῳ Ιουδα καὶ τοῖς κατοικοῦσιν Ιερουσαλημ 'Say to the people of J...' Je 42.12. Esp. υἱοὶ ~ων 'sons of men' Mi 5.7, Jl 1.12; ‖ ἀνήρ Is 56.2. **b**. opp. a divine being, θεὸς ἐγώ εἰμι καὶ οὐκ ἄ. Ho 11.9; ~ον καὶ οὐ θεόν Is 31.3; εἰ πτερνιεῖ ἄ. θεόν 'would a man cheat God?' (or: 'would anybody ..: cf. Epiph III.218 with τις) Ma 3.8; Ge 4.1 (MT: *yhwh* - cf. Rösel 102); τοῦ θεοῦ [= Moses] Ps 89.1, applied to a prophet 3K 12.22, David 2C 8.14; God addressing - ἄ~πε Mi 6.8. **c**. opp. animals, πᾶν τὸ ἀνάστημα .. ἀπὸ ~ου ἕως κτήνους καὶ ἑρπετῶν καὶ τῶν πετεινῶν τοῦ οὐρανοῦ Ge 7.23; ἐάν τε κτῆνος ἐάν τε ἄ., οὐ ζήσεται 'whether it be an animal or a human, it shall not live' Ex 19.13; θύσατε ~ους, μόσχοι γὰρ ἐκλελοίπασι 'sacrifice humans, for calves have perished' Ho 13.2; οἱ ~οι καὶ τὰ κτήνη καὶ οἱ βόες καὶ τὰ πρόβατα Jn 3.7; more valued than κολόκυνθα 'a gourd' Jn 4.10f.; ‖ τετράπους 'quadruped' Ex 8.16. **d**. opp. fishes, ποιήσεις τοὺς ~ους ὡς τοὺς ἰχθύας τῆς θαλάσσης Hb 1.14. **e**. of particular individuals, τοῦ ~ου τούτου Jn 1.14. **f**. pl. 'mankind, humanity': ἡ βίβλος γενέσεως ~ων Ge 5.1. **g**. ~οι πόλεως 'townsfolk' Ge 24.43. **h**. legal body w. ref. to husband: Nu 5.15.

2. *man* w. special reference to males in generic statements: καταλείψει ἄ. τὸν πατέρα αὐτοῦ καὶ τὴν μητέρα αὐτοῦ καὶ προσκολληθήσεται πρὸς τὴν γυναῖκα αὐτοῦ Ge 2.24, οὐ δύνανται οἱ ~οι εἶναι χωρὶς τῶν γυναῖκων 'menfolk can't do without womenfolk' 1E 4.17; 9.40 (‖ ἀνήρ vs. 41).

3. With weakened force: like Engl. *one* and qualified by an adj. or ptc. ἄ. ὁ πνευματοφόρος Ho 9.7, ὡς ἄ. παραβαίνων διαθήκην 6.7, ὡς ῥαπίζων ἄ. ἐπὶ τὰς σιαγόνας αὐτοῦ 11.4, ἄ. ἐργαζόμενος τὴν γῆν Zc 13.5, τὸν ~ον τὸν ποιοῦντα ταῦτα Ma 2.12; ‖ ἀνήρ Is 2.9. **b**. almost = τις, esp. in a conditional or associated clause: Ἄ. ἐξ ὑμῶν ἐὰν προσαγάγῃ Le 1.2 (‖ ψυχή 2.1); ὃν τρόπον ἐὰν φύγῃ ἄ. ἐκ προσώπου τοῦ λέοντος Am 5.19, ἐὰν λάβῃ ἄ. κρέας ἅγιον Hg 2.12, ὅταν ἐξεγερθῇ ἄ. ἐξ ὕπνου αὐτοῦ Zc 4.1, ἐὰν προφητεύσῃ ἄ. ἔτι 13.3, ὃν τρόπον αἱρετίζει ἄ. τὸν υἱὸν αὐτοῦ τὸν δουλεύοντα αὐτῷ 'in the way someone chooses his son to serve him' Ma 3.17 (or a contrast with God intended?). ***c**. ἄ. ἄ. 'every person' Ez 14.4, 7; 'anybody' Le 17.3, cf. ἀνήρ **1 i**. **d**. w. negative = *none*: οὐκ ἦν ἄ. τῶν ἐπεσκεμμένων .. 'there was none of those who had been counted ..' Nu 26.64; Je 4.29, 41.9, 48.4. ***e**. in a Hebraic expression of reciprocity, εἶπεν ἄ. τῷ πλησίον αὐτοῦ 'they said to one another' Ge 11.3, ἄ. πρὸς ~ον καὶ ἄ. πρὸς τὸν πλησίον αὐτοῦ Is 3.5; w. a pl. verb, ὤμοσαν ἄ. τῷ πλησίον αὐτοῦ 'they swore to each other' Ge 26.31; ὃς ἀποκαταστήσει .. καρδίαν ~ου πρὸς τὸν πλησίον αὐτοῦ 'who will return the heart of a person to his fellow-man' Ma 4.5 (cf. Cyr. II 624 τῆς ἀλλήλων ἀγάπης 'the mutual love'); ἄ. τὸν ἀδελφὸν αὐτοῦ καὶ ἄ. τὸν πλησίον αὐτοῦ Is 19.2; ἄ... τῇ ὁδῷ αὐτοῦ 'each .. by his own way' 53.6. **f**. pleonastically with another noun following: ἐκ χειρὸς ~ου ἀδελφοῦ 'from a brother' Ge 9.5; ἄ. γεωργὸς γῆς 'farmer' ib. 9.20; ~οι ἀδελφοί 13.8; οἱ ~οι οἱ Μαδιηναῖοι 37.28; θυγάτηρ ~ου ἱερέως Le 21.9; ~ων κυρίων σκληρῶν Is 19.4, ~ον δότην 'giver' Si 3.17; ἄ. following, ἀναβάται ~οι 'horsemen' Is 22.6. Cf. ἀνήρ **3**, γυνή **1 c**.

Cf. ἀνήρ, ἀνθρώπινος, βροτός: Schmidt 2.385-8; Jeremias, *TDNT* 1.364f.

ἀνθυφαιρέω: fut.pass. ~ρεθήσομαι.ʃ
to deduct: ***s*** an amount of money, ἀπὸ τῆς συντιμήσεως αὐτοῦ 'from its total assessment' Le 27.18. Cf. ἀφαιρέω.

ἀνίατος, ον.ʃ
incurable: ***s*** hum., De 32.24; *unbeatable*, ***s*** θυμὸς ἀσπίδων 'the wrath of vipers (the harmful effect of which is incurable)' 32.33, cf. ἡμέρα κυρίου ~ος .. θυμοῦ καὶ ὀργῆς Is 13.9; πατάξας θυμῷ πληγῇ ~ῳ 14.6, ἐπάταξεν .. ~ῳ καὶ ἀοράτῳ πληγῇ 'with an incurable and invisible blow' 2M 9.5; συντριβή Pr 6.15; *to be written off*, ***s*** ξύλον 'timber' Jb 24.20; subst.n.sg. εἰς ~ον '(are doomed) to hopeless (situation)' La 4.3; pl. used adverbially, 'incurably' Je 8.18. Cf. ἰάομαι, ἀνήκεστος, στερεός **3**.

ἀνιερόω: fut.pass. ἀνιερωθήσομαι; aor.ptc. ἀνιερώσας.ʃ
to treat as sacred: + acc., days of celebration, 3M 7.20. **b**. *to confiscate for cultic purposes*: ***o*** cattle, 1E 9.4 (|| ἀναθεματίζω 2E 10.8).
Cf. ἀναθεματίζω.

ἀνίημι: pres.inf. ἀνιέναι; fut. ἀνήσω; 1aor. ἀνῆκα, pass. ἀνέθην, 2aor.subj. ἀνῶ, inf. ἀνεῖναι, impv. ἄνες, ptc. ἀνείς; pf.pass. ἀνεῖμαι, ptc.pass. ἀνειμένος.

1. *to let loose, free*: pass. στέλεχος ἀνειμένον 'a trunk let loose,' thus growing luxuriantly Ge 49.21; μοσχάρια ἐκ δεσμῶν ἀνειμένα 'young calves let loose from tethers' Ma 4.2, δέσμιοι ἀνειμένοι 'prisoners ..' Jb 3.18 (see Walters 316); ὑπὸ φλόγος ἀνειμένης 'by a flame let loose (among stubble)' Is 5.24 (or: 'running wild, coursing beyond control'); χεῖρας 25.11 (at a target); child left to himself to act as he pleases, Si 30.8 (|| unbroken horse); ἀπὸ ζυγοῦ 'from a yoke' 2C 10.9 (|| vs. 4 ἀφίημι). **b**. *to utter a sound*: *φωνήν understood, Is 42.2 (|| κράζω).

2. *to let go unpunished*: + acc. pers., πάντα τὸν τόπον ἕνεκεν τῶν πεντήκοντα δικαίων Ge 18.24 (|| vs. 26 ἀφίημι 'forgive'), Is 2.9; + acc. (sin), ἁμαρτήματα καὶ ἀνομήματα Jo 24.19, τὰς ἁμαρτίας Is 1.14; + dat. pers., ***s*** God, Od 12.13.

3. *to leave unused*: ***o*** agricultural land, Ex 23.11; ἄνες τὴν χεῖρά σου 'Hands off!' 2K 24.16. **b**. *to choose not to derive benefit from*: + acc., "the 7th year and exaction of debts" Ne 10.31.

4. *to leave uncared for*, 'desert, forsake': abs. and || σιωπάω Is 62.1; + acc. pers. and ***s*** God, De 31.6, 8 (|| ἐγκαταλείπω), Is 2.6; ***o*** ἀμπελῶνα 'vineyard' 5.6, φροντίδας 'concerns' 1K 9.5 *L* (om. B); pass., Is 3.8, flock (or: sheep-fold) 27.10 (|| καταλελειμμένος).

5. *to release tension on*, 'slacken': ἄνες χεῖρας αὐτῷ 'allow him to idle away' Si 30.34; pass., χεῖρες ἀνειμέναι Is 35.3 (|| feeble knees), 37.27. **b**. *to let one's hands off*: ἀφ' ἡμῶν 2C 10.10 (|| 3K 12.10 κουφίζω 'to lighten'). **c**. mid. *to deal gently*: abs., Wi 16.24. **d**. intr. (also pass.) *to lose intensity*: ἀνῆκε (B: ἀνέθη) τὸ πνεῦμα αὐτῶν ἀπ' αὐτοῦ 'their mood against him quietened' Jd 8.3.

6. *to allow* to do: + dat. pers. and ἵνα, Ps 38.14; + inf., Jd 11.17*L*. **b**. *to concede and allow* sbd to do sth by granting a period of time: + dat. pers. and acc., ἡμῖν (*L* ἡμᾶς) ἑπτὰ ἡμέρας '(Give) us a grace period of seven days' 1K 11.3. **c**. *to leave alone without interfering* or *harassing*: + acc. pers., Ἄνες (B: Ἄφες) αὐτήν 'Leave her alone' 4K 4.27*L*.

7. *to neglect* to do: + τοῦ inf., 1K 12.23 (*L* διαλείπω). **b**. *to call off a plan*: + inf., 1K 23.13; ἀνῇ ⸢ἀπ' ἐμοῦ⸣ (B om.) Σαουλ τοῦ ζητεῖν με 'Saul gets off my back, hunting me' 27.1.

8. *to cease* doing: λαλῶν understood, Ἄνες 'Hold on!' 1K 15.16.

Cf. ἄνεσις, ἐγκατα~, καταλείπω, παραλύω, ἀφίημι, ἐλευθερόω, ἐνδίδωμι, χαλάω: Schmidt 3.263-5; Ziegler 1934.179f.

ἀνίκητος, ον.
invincible: ***s*** hum., 2M 11.13; ἐπιστήμη 'knowledge' 4M 11.21, λογισμός 'rational will' 11.27, προνοία '(divine) providence' 3M 4.21, δύναμις '(divine) power' 6.13. Cf. νίκη, ἀκαταμάχητος, ἀνυπέρβλητος.

ἀνίπταμαι.ʃ
to fly upwards: ***s*** birds, Is 16.2. Cf. πέτομαι.

ἀνίστημι: pres.ptc. ἀνιστάμενος, ἀνιστῶν; fut. ἀναστήσω, ~στήσομαι, inf. ~στήσεσθαι, ptc. ~στήσων; 1aor. ἀνέστησα, impv. ἀνάστησον, inf. ~στῆσαι, opt.3s ~στήσαι, pass.subj. ~σταθῶ, ptc. ~σταθείς; 2aor. ἀνέστην, subj. ἀναστῶ, impv. ἀνάστηθι, ἀνάστα (sg.) (the latter not exclusively poetical, *pace* Thack. 254: see Jn 1.2 ἀνάστηθι || ib. 6 ἀνάστα, ib. 3.2 ἀνάστηθι; see also 2E 10.3f.), 2pl. ~στητε, 3s. ~στήτω, pl. ~στήτωσαν, inf. ~στῆναι, ptc. ~στάς; pf. ἀνέστακα. For details of morphology, see Thack. 247f., 252-5.

I. tr. (pres.act., fut.act., 1aor.) **1**. *to cause or help to stand up again, raise again*: ***o*** an object which has fallen, De 22.4, Am 5.2, Je 27.32 (:: πίπτω); ἀναστήσω τὴν σκηνὴν Δαυιδ τὴν πεπτωκυῖαν καὶ ἀνοικοδομήσω τὰ πεπτωκότα αὐτῆς καὶ τὰ κατεσκαμμένα αὐτῆς 'I will restore the fallen tent of David and rebuild its debris and its ruins' Am 9.11; τὸν ναὸν τοῦτον Hg 2.9; a lion lying in rest, Nu 24.9; of 'restoring' a numerically diminished nation to its former size, τίς ἀναστήσει τὸν Ιακωβ; ὅτι ὀλιγοστός ἐστι Am 7.2, 5; ἀπὸ γῆς πένητα 1K 2.8 (|| ἐγείρω). **b**. *to hold upright*: + acc., 3K 7.11. ***c**. *to enhance the repuation and estimation of* (?): τινα Pr 31.28.

2. *to establish anew*: ***o*** covenant, ***s*** God, ἀνίστημι τὴν διαθήκην μου ὑμῖν Ge 9.9 (ǁ ἵστημι πρός τινα 9.11), μετὰ σοῦ Ez 16.62; λόγον 13.6.

3. *to cause to come into existence*: + acc. pers., ἀνάστησον σπέρμα τῷ ἀδελφῷ σου 'Raise offspring for your brother' Ge 38.8 (through levirate marriage); προφήτην De 18.15; βασιλέα χώρας Ep Je 52, αὐτοῖς τὸν βασιλέα αὐτῶν PSol 17.21; ἀναστήσαι σε κύριος ἑαυτῷ λαὸν ἅγιον 'May the Lord raise you as his holy people' De 28.9; τὸ ὄνομα τοῦ ἀδελφοῦ αὐτοῦ ἐν Ισραηλ 25.7 (:: ἐξαλείφω vs. 6). **b**. *to help become reality*: + acc., τὸ ῥῆμα αὐτοῦ 3K 8.20, τὸν λόγον αὐτοῦ 2C 6.10, προφητείαν Da 11.14 LXX (TH στῆσαι ὅρασιν); τὸ ὄνομα τοῦ τεθνηκότος ἐπὶ τῆς κληρονομίας αὐτοῦ '(to ensure) the future of the inheritance under the name of the deceased' Ru 4.5.

4. *to cause to become alive again after death*: abs., ἰατροὶ οὐ μὴ ἀναστήσωσι Is 26.14, sim. Ps 87.11; + acc. pers., ὁ τοῦ κόσμου βασιλεὺς ἀποθανόντας ἡμᾶς .. εἰς αἰώνιον ἀναβίωσιν ζωῆς ἡμᾶς ἀναστήσει 'the king of the universe will raise us into an eternal second life, us who died ..' 2M 7.9; ***s*** God, Jb 42.17αα².

5. *to erect*: + acc., ***o*** a structure, σκηνήν Ex 26.30, ἱερόν 'temple' 2M 14.33, θρόνον 3K 9.5; opp. καθαιρέω Nu 1.51 (ǁ ἵστημι 10.21); στήλην as object of (pagan) worship, Le 26.1. Cf. συνίστημι **I 8**, στηλόω.

6. *to assign* to office or task: + acc. and dat. (com.) pers. ποιμένας 'shepherds' Je 23.4, ἀνατολὴν δικαίαν 'a righteous scion' 23.5; ἐπ' αὐτοὺς ποιμένα Ez 34.23, χριστόν 2K 23.1*L*; 'to reassign' divisions of priests which had lapsed, 2C 23.18; εἰς δόξαν 'to an honourable office' PSol 2.31.

II. intr. (pres.mid., fut.mid., 2aor.) **1**. *to stand up, rise*: from lying position, Ge 19.33; from sitting position, ἀπὸ τοῦ νεκροῦ 'from the corpse' 23.3 (*pace* Wevers ad loc.); ἀπὸ τοῦ φρέατος 46.5, ἀπὸ (B: ἐκ) τῆς γῆς 2K 12.20 *L* (B: ἐκ); from sleep, (τὸ) πρωΐ 'early' Ge 21.14, 22.3, 24.54 +; from a dream, Es A 9 *L*; of one lying in sick bed, so 'recover,' ἀναστησόμεθα καὶ ζησόμεθα Ho 6.2l, ἐκ τῆς μαλακίας αὐτοῦ 'from his ailment' Is 38.9; ἀπὸ ταπεινώσεως 'from a fast' 2E 9.5. Opp. to falling (πίπτω): Am 5.2, 8.14, Mi 7.8, Je 8.4, PSol 3.10. **b**. w. hostile intent, e.g. 'to attack': ἐπί τινα– ἀνέστη Καιν ἐπὶ Αβελ .. καὶ ἀπέκτεινεν αὐτόν Ge 4.8; Am 7.9; εἰς πόλεμον Je 29.15, εἰς βοήθειαν Ps 34.2; κατά τινα Da 11.7 LXX. ***c**. w. weakened basic meaning, in urging one to act or signalling an action taken with clear intent - Hebraistic (note esp. ἐπεσπούδαζον .. λέγοντες Ἀναστὰς λάβε .. Ge 19.15, ἀναστὰς κάθισον '.. sit up!' 27.19, ἀνάστηθι κάθισον Is 52.2, and ἀνάστηθι εἰς τὴν ἀνάπαυσίν σου Ps 131.8): ἀνάστητε καὶ ἐξέλθατε Ge 19.14, Ex 12.31; ἀνάστηθι καὶ πορεύου Mi 2.10; w. first verb as ptc., ἀναστὰς λάβε .. Ge 19.15 (ǁ ἀνάστηθι, λάβε τὸ παιδίον 21.18 addressed to sbd seated), ἀναστάντες ἐπορεύθησαν 22.19; ἀναστὰς Μωυσῆς ἐρρύσατο αὐτάς 'M. got into action and rescued them' Ex 2.17; also in two imperatives joined by καί, Mi 4.13, Jn 1.2, 3; without καί, Ge 13.17, 21.18, Mi 6.1, Jn 1.6, 3.2, 3; with a second verb as hortatory subj., ἀνάστητε καὶ ἐξαναστῶμεν ἐπ' αὐτὴν εἰς πόλεμον Ob 1, cf. ἐγείρω **6 b**, ἐξανίστημι **II b**.

2. *to make appearance*: ἀνέστη βασιλεὺς ἕτερος ἐπ' Αἴγυπτον 'there appeared a different king in Egypt' Ex 1.8; ἐν σοὶ προφήτης De 13.1, ἀντ' αὐτοῦ 'to succeed him' 1M 3.1; οἱ υἱοὶ ὑμῶν, οἳ ἀναστήσονται μεθ' ὑμᾶς De 29.22; ἐξαίφνης ἀναστήσονται δάκνοντες αὐτόν Hb 2.7; ***s*** rei, διάνοιαι ἐπὶ τὸν βασιλέα 'designs against the king' Da 11.14 LXX.

3. *to present oneself*: for a meeting, debate etc. and challenging, ἔναντι Μωυσῆ Nu 16.2, foll. by συνέστησαν ἐπὶ Μωυσῆν καὶ Ααρων ..; as rebels 32.14; ***s*** φωνὴ ἐπὶ σὲ εἰς κρίσιν Is 54.17; in court, ἐν κρίσει .. ἐν βουλῇ Ps 1.5 (to defend oneself or as judge), μάρτυρες 34.11.

4. *to become alive again after death*: "the dead will arise (ἀναστήσονται) and those in graves will rise (ἐγερθήσονται)" Is 26.19, cf. Da LXX 12.2 (TH ἐγερθήσονται), Jb 14.12, 41.17αα¹; προσδοκᾶν ἐλπίδας ἀναστήσεσθαι 'to look to the prospects of resurrection' 2M 7.14 (ǁ ἀνάστασις); 12.44 (ǁ ἀνάστασις vs. 43); εἰς ζωὴν αἰώνιον PSol 12.

5. *to come true*: οἱ λόγοι τοῦ κυρίου .. ἐπὶ Ισραηλ 1E 1.22.

Cf. ἀντ~, διανί~, ἐξανίστημι, ἵστημι, ἀνάστασις, ἐγείρω: Shipp 75-80; Oepke, *TDNT* 1.368-70.

ἄνισχυς, υ.*ʃ**

without strength: Is 40.30. Cf. ἰσχύς, ἰσχυρός.

ἀνόητος, ον.

wanting in understanding: ***s*** animals, Ps 48.13, 21 (ǁ οὐ συνίημι); subst.m., hum., De 32.31, παιδεία ~ου καὶ μωροῦ 'education of the unintelligent and stupid' Si 42.8; Pr 15.21 (:: φρόνιμος), seeks wisdom, 17.28. **b**. *indicative of want of understanding*: ***s***, deed, 4M 5.9, 10.

Cf. ἄνους, ἀσύνετος, μωρός, σοφός, φρόνιμος.

ἄνοια, ας. f.

lack of understanding, 'folly': Ps 21.3; ἀ. ἀφρόνων Pr 14.8 (opp. σοφία); typical of youth, 22.15, + νεότης 'youth' Ec 11.10; typical of animals, Wi 15.18. Cf. ἀνόητος, σοφία.

ἀνοίγω: fut.act. ἀνοίξω, pass. ἀνοιχθήσομαι, ἀνεῳχθήσομαι, ἀνοιγήσομαι; aor.act. ἤνεῳξα, ἀνέῳξα, ἤνοιξα, ptc. ἀνοίξας, subj. ἀνοίξω, impv. ἄνοιξον, inf. ἀνοῖξαι, opt.3s ἀνοίξαι; pass. ἠνεῴχθην, ἠνοίχθην, ptc. ἀνοιχθείς, inf. ἀνοιγῆσαι; pf.ptc.pass. ἀνεῳγμένος, ἠνοιγμένος; plpf.pass.3s ἀνέῳκτο.

1. tr. *to open*: ***o*** θυρίδα 'window' Ge 8.6; ὀφθαλμούς 'to reveal' 21.19, ὀφθαλμοὶ τυφλῶν Is 35.5 (pass.), τὰ ὦτα 'the ears' 42.20, 1C 17.25 (ǁ 7.27 ἀποκαλύπτω); χείλη 'lips' Ps 50.17, Jb 11.5; μήτραν 'womb (of a barren woman)' Ge 29.31, 30.22; σιτοβολῶνας 'granaries' 41.56; μαρσίππους 'bags' 43.21; σκεῦος 'vessel' Nu 19.15; τὸν θησαυρὸν αὐτοῦ τὸν ἀγαθόν, τὸν οὐρανόν De 28.12; θησαυρούς 'store-houses' Am 8.5; στόμα 'mouth' Ex 4.12 (to give facility of speech), Ez 33.22 (:: συνέχω), 16.63 (so as to speak); ***s*** generous giver, χεῖρας '(grudgingly clenched) hands' De 15.8, χεῖρα Ps 103.28, 144.16 (***s*** God), ἐν ἐλέει PSol 5.12; πύλας 'gates' or suchlike understood, σοι De 20.11, cf. Pl., *Prot.* 310b; ἀνοίξας ἡ γῆ τὸ στόμα καταπίεται αὐτούς Nu 16.30 (in order to devour), sim. De 11.6; λάκκον 'cistern' Ex 21.33; τοὺς καταρράκτας τοῦ οὐρανοῦ 'the sluices of the sky' Ma 3.10; pass., ***o*** ἡ γῆ Nu 16.32; πύλαι 'gates' Na 3.13, θύρα Jb 31.32, πόλις Jo 8.17 (left undefended); Is 60.11 (:: κλείω), οὐρανοί Ez 1.1, τάφος 'grave' Ps 5.10. **b.** *to lift siege*: Je 13.19 (:: συγκλείσω 'to lay siege'). **c.** pass. with intr. force: οἱ καταρράκται τοῦ οὐρανοῦ ἠνεῴχθησαν 'the sluices of the sky opened' Ge 7.11, cf. Si 43.14. θυρίδες ἐκ τοῦ οὐρανοῦ Is 24.18, ἠνοίχθη ἡ γῆ Ps 105.17, cf. τὴν πύλην τὴν σιδηρᾶν .. ἥτις αὐτομάτη ἠνοίγη αὐτοῖς 'the iron gate .., which opened to them of itself' Acts 12.10, and more examples at Spicq 1.231, n. 1.

2. *to make an aperture in a surface and cause to emerge* that which is underneath: ἀνοίξω ἐπὶ τῶν ὀρέων ποταμοὺς καὶ ἐν μέσῳ πεδίῳ πηγάς Is 41.18. **b.** metaph., *to bring into the open, disclose*: + acc., πικρίαν ψυχῆς μου 'bitterness of my soul' Jb 7.11

Cf. διανοίγω, ἀποκαλύπτω, καμμύω, συγκλείω.

ἀνοικοδομέω: fut. ~ήσω, pass. ~ηθήσομαι; aor. ἀνῳκοδόμησα, subj. ἀνοικοδομήσω, pass. ~μηθῶ.

1. *to rebuild* (a destroyed building or city): De 13.16; ἀνοικοδομήσω τὰ πεπτωκότα αὐτῆς 'I will rebuild its ruins' Am 9.11*a* (ǁ ἀνίστημι), sim. Da 11.14 LXX; τὰς ἐρήμους Ma 1.4; pass. and ***o*** the temple in Jerusalem, Zc 1.16; a kingdom, Je 18.9 (:: ἐξαίρω, ἀπόλλυμι vs. 7), a nation, 24.6.

2. *to wall up*: + acc., ὁδούς Ho 2.6 (ǁ φράσσω), La 3.9 (ǁ ἐμφράσσω), 3.5.

*3. pass. *to prosper, achieve distinction*: ἀνοικοδομοῦνται ποιοῦντες ἄνομα 'those who act unlawfully prosper' Ma 3.15.

Cf. οἰκοδομέω and εὐθηνέω.

ἄνοικτος, ον.ʃ

ruthless: ***s*** ψυχή 3M 4.4. Cf. ἀναιδής, ἀπότομος.

ἀνομβρέω: fut. ἀνομβρήσω; aor. ἀνώμβρησα.ʃ

to pour forth: metaph., + acc., παροιμίας 'parables' Si 18.29, ῥήματα σοφίας 39.6, σοφίαν 50.27. Cf. ἐξομβρέω.

ἀνομέω: fut. ἀνομήσω; aor. ἠνόμησα, subj. ἀνομήσω, inf.pass. ἀνομηθῆναι.

1. *to act in breach of law* (νόμος): of idolatry, Ex 32.7, De 4.16, 25; ἀνομίᾳ ἀνομήσετε 31.29; Am 4.4 (v.l. ἀσεβέω); ǁ ἀθετέω Is 21.2; εἴς τινα 'against sbd' Nu 32.15, Je 2.29; τινα Ez 22.11 (of raping a woman and ǁ ταπεινόω); + acc. rei, διαθήκην Da 11.32 TH. **b.** on various combinations of synonyms, see under ἀδικέω.

2. *to declare to be* ἄνομος *and treat as such*: pass., ***o*** hum., 3K 8.32.

Cf. ἀνομία, ἄνομος, νόμος, παρανομέω, and ἀσεβέω.

ἀνόμημα, ατος. n.

1. *act of transgression of the law*: Le 20.14, De 15.9; ǁ ἀκαθαρσίαι Ez 39.24.

2. *punishment for transgression of the law*: λήμψεται ἀ. αὐτοῦ Le 17.16; La 5.7.

Cf. ἀνομία.

ἀνομία, ας. f.

1. *act which is in breach of law* (νόμος): ~αν ποιεῖν Ho 6.9; ἀφαιρῶν ~ας καὶ ἀδικίας καὶ ἁμαρτίας Ex 34.7, Nu 14.18; ἀφῄρηκα τὰς ~ας σου Zc 3.4; 5.8 (ǁ ἀδικία, vs. 6); ὅρια ~ας 'domain of lawlessness' Ma 1.4; ταῖς ~αις τῆς πόλεως Ge 19.15; + ἀδικία, ἁμαρτία Le 16.21; ǁ ἁμαρτία Is 5.18, ǁ ἁμάρτημα 58.1; ~ᾳ ἀνομήσετε De 31.29; verbally manifested, Is 3.8.

2. *consequences of an act* as defined under **1.**, 'penalty': προσδέξονται τὰς αὐτῶν ~ας Le 26.43; 2E 9.13.

Cf. ἀδικία, ἁμαρτία, ἀνόμημα, ἀσέβεια: Trench 243f.

ἀνόμοιος, ον.ʃ

dissimilar to: + dat., Wi 2.15. Cf. ὅμοιος, διαφέρω.

ἄνομος, ον.

unlawful, in breach of law (νόμος): θησαυροὺς ~ους 'ill-gotten treasures' Mi 6.10[2]; ***s*** pers., and + πονηρός Is 9.17; ἔθνος 10.6. **b.** subst. pers. οἶκος ~ου Mi 6.10[1]; εἰ δικαιωθήσεται ἐν ζυγῷ ἀ. ..; 6.11; ἔβαλες εἰς κεφαλὰς ~ων θάνατον Hb 3.13; opp. δίκαιος and ǁ ὁ μὴ δουλεύων θεῷ Ma 3.18, ǁ ἀσεβής Is 55.7, + ἄδικος Ez 21.3, 4; subst. n. pl. ποιοῦντες ~α καὶ ἀντέστησαν θεῷ Ma 3.15, sim. 4.1.; διδάσκοντα ~α Is 9.15.

Cf. ἀνομία, ἀνόμημα, ἀνόμως, ἄδικος, ἀθέμιτος, ἀθέμιστος, ἔκθεσμος, δίκαιος, νόμος, παράνομος.

ἀνόμως. adv.ʃ

in a manner contravening laws: 2M 8.17. Cf. ἄνομος, παρανόμως.

ἀνόνητος, ον.ʃ

unprofitable: *s* κόποι 'toils' Wi 3.11 (|| ἄχρηστος 'useless'), gestation (of foetus) 4M 16.7 (|| μάταιος 'vain,' ἄκαρπος 'fruitless'), marriage 16.9. Cf. ἄχρηστος, ἀνωφελής.

ἀνορθόω: fut. ~θώσω; aor. ἀνώρθωσα, ptc. ~θώσας, inf. ~θῶσαι, pass. ἀνωρθώθην; pf.ptc.pass. ἀνωρθωμένος.

*__1__. *to establish firmly*: + acc., τὴν οἰκουμένην ἐν τῇ σοφίᾳ αὐτοῦ Je 10.12 (|| ποιέω), τὴν γῆν 40.2 (*s* God), τὸν θρόνον αὐτοῦ εἰς τὸν αἰῶνα 2K 7.13; + acc. pers., ἐκ ταπεινώσεως Si 11.12; pass. ὁ οἶκος Δαυιδ 1C 17.24.

*__2__. *to make stand erect*: + acc., τοὺς κατερραγμένους 'those who were cast down' Ps 144.14 (|| ὑποστηρίζω); τρίχας 'hair' Si 27.14. **b**. pass. *to stand erect*: ἀνέστημεν καὶ ἀνωρθώθημεν Ps 19.9; horizontally, οἱ μαστοί σου ἀνωρθώθησαν 'your breasts were formed' Ez 16.7.

3. *to set right*, 'correct': ἡ παιδεία σου ἀνώρθωσέν με Ps 17.36.

ἀνορύσσω.ʃ

to dig up that which has been buried: ***o*** θησαυρούς 'treasures' Jb 3.21, ἐν πεδίῳ 39.21. Cf. ὀρύσσω.

ἀνόσιος, α, ον.ʃ

opposed to piety: *s* hum., 2M 7.34, + ἀσεβής 4M 12.11, + βέβηλος 3M 2.2; βουλή 'plot' 5.8, τελετή '(pagan) mystic rite' Wi 12.4; subst.n.pl. ~α ἐποίουν Ez 22.9. Cf. ὅσιος, ἀνοσίως.

ἀνοσίως. adv.ʃ

in impious manner: + συντελέω 'perpetrate' Es E 7 o', + κατεγχειρέω 'plot' 3M 1.21.

ἄνους, ουν.

characterised by lack of understanding and intelligence, 'silly': ἦν Εφραιμ ὡς περιστερὰ ἄ. '.. a silly dove' Ho 7.11; *s* hum., ἄφρων καὶ ἄ. Ps 48.11. Cf. ἀνόητος, ἄφρων, μωρός, συνίημι, συνετός: Schmidt 3.651f.

ἀνοχή, ῆς. f.ʃ

opportunity for an action: + inf., 1M 12.25. Cf. καιρός.

ἀνταγωνίζομαι.ʃ

to contend as opponent: 4M 17.14. Cf. ἀγωνίζομαι, ἀνταγωνιστής, μάχομαι.

ἀνταγωνιστής, οῦ. m.ʃ

combatant: παθῶν 'against passions' 4M 3.5. Cf. ἀνταγωνίζομαι.

ἀνταίρω: aor. ἀντῆρα, subj. ἀντάρω.ʃ

to raise sth with hostile intent: οὐκέτι μὴ ἀντάρῃ ἔθνος ἐπ' ἔθνος ῥομφαίαν 'nations will no longer raise a sword against one another' Mi 4.3 (|| λαμβάνω Is 2.4); τὴν χεῖρα αὐτοῦ ἐπὶ τὸν βασιλέα 2K 20.21*L* (B: ἐπαίρω). Cf. αἴρω.

ἀντακούω: fut.mid. ~κούσομαι.ʃ

to listen in turn: opp. λέγω Jb 11.2. Cf. ἀκούω.

ἀντάλλαγμα: : ατος. n.

that which is given or taken as having equal value: to sth (gen.), Jb 28.15¶, δώσω σοι ἀργύριον ἀ. (*L*: ἄλλαγμα) ἀμπελῶνός σου 'I shall pay you silver to the value of your vineyard' 3K 20.2, φίλου πιστοῦ οὐκ ἔστιν ἀ. 'one cannot put a price on a loyal friend' Si 6.15 (|| σταθμός); "they do not recognise any alternative course" Ps 54.20; of Noah replacing the existing human race and making a new start, Si 44.17. Cf. ἄλλαγμα, ἀνταλλάσσω.

ἀνταλλάσσω: fut. ~λλάξω, mid. ~λλάξομαι.ʃ

to give in exchange for: + acc., Jb 37.4; + acc. and gen., οὐδενὸς λύτρου τὴν ἔχθραν '(will not give up his) enmity for any compensation' Pr 6.35. Cf. ἀντάλλαγμα, ἀλλάσσω.

ἀντάμειψις, εως. f.ʃ*

requital: Ps 118.112.

ἀνταναιρέω. fut. ~νελῶ, pass. ~ρεθήσομαι; aor.subj. ~νέλω, pass. ἀντανηρέθην, subj. ~ρεθῶ.

to render non-existent, 'obliterate': + acc., τὰ κρίματά σου ἀπὸ προσώπου αὐτοῦ Ps 9.26, πολέμους 45.10, τὸ πνεῦμα τὸ ἅγιόν σου ἀπ' ἐμοῦ 50.13; τὸ πνεῦμα αὐτῶν 'their breath (as a sign of life)' 103.29, τὴν ψυχήν μου 140.8; moon, 71.7 (w. ref. to eclipse?); shadow (at the evening), 108.23; εὐχαριστίαν 'sense of gratitude' Es E 4 o' (*L* ἀναι~). Cf. ἀφανίζω: Flashar 1912.96-8.

ἀντανακλάω.ʃ

to reflect: pass., ***o*** echo, Wi 17.19.

ἀντανίστημι: 2aor. ἀντανέστην.ʃ

to emerge to replace that which existed earlier: *s* hum., ἀντ' αὐτῶν 'in their place' Ba 3.19. Cf. ἀνίστημι.

ἀνταποδίδωμι: fut.act. ~δώσω, ptc. ~δώσων, pass. ~δοθήσομαι; aor. ἀνταπέδωκα, subj. ἀνταποδῶ, impv. ~δος, inf. ~δοῦναι.

1. *to requite, repay*: abs. and *s* God, De 32.35, ὑπὲρ ἐμοῦ 'for my sake' Ps 137.8; for evil done, τινί (pers.) τι – ἀδικίαν αὐτοῖς Le 18.25; διπλᾶς τὰς ἀδικίας αὐτῶν '(repay) their iniquities double' Je 16.18; διαβούλια '(evil) schemes, deliberations' Ho 4.9, ὀνειδισμόν 'reproach (brought upon God)' 12.14; τινί (pers.) περί τινος (deed) and cogn. obj. (ἀνταπόδοσις) Jd 16.28 B; + πρός τινα Jb 21.19. **b**. + κατά τι (deed): κατὰ τὰ ἐπιτηδεύματα αὐτοῦ 'in accordance with his practices' Ho 12.2, κατὰ τὰ ἔργα αὐτῆς Je 27.29. **c**. with ἀνταπόδομα as cogn. obj., τὸ ἀνταπόδομα ὑμῶν εἰς κεφαλὰς ὑμῶν Jl 3.4*b*, 7, sim. Ob 15; μὴ ἀνταπόδομα ὑμεῖς ἀνταποδίδοτέ μοι; Jl 3.4*a*; and + acc. rei (= the wrong done), ἀνταπόδομα ἀνταποδῷ ἡμῖν πάντα τὰ κακά Ge 50.15; Je 28.24. **d.** with ἀνταπόδοσις as cogn. obj., φωνὴ κυρίου ἀνταποδιδόντος ἀνταπόδοσιν τοῖς ἀντικειμένοις '.. to the adversaries' Is 66.6; 59.18. **e.** for good done: + τι only, πονηρὰ ἀντὶ καλῶν Ge 44.4, ἀντὶ ἀγαθῶν κακά Je 18.20; ταῦτα κυρίῳ De 32.6; καρπὸν χειλέων 'fruit of lips, i.e. thanksgiving, praises etc. (see Cyr. I 278 and Th 75)' Ho 14.3; χάριν 'favour done' Si 3.31, 30.6, 32.3. **f.** τι (reward): σοι ἀγαθά Pr 25.22.

2. *to recompense, make amends* for damage and discomfort sustained, + ἀντί τινος (thing): ἀντὶ τῶν ἐτῶν 'for the years (of a natural calamity)' Jl 2.25, ἀντὶ μιᾶς ἡμέρας παροικεσίας σου διπλᾶ ἀ. σοι 'for one day of your stay in a foreign land I will recompense you double' Zc 9.12.

3. *to mete out* as recompense: + dat. pers., τοῖς μισοῦσιν De 32.43² and acc., δίκην τοῖς ἐχθροῖς 32.41, τοῖς ἔθνεσιν .. ἐκδίκησιν Si 32.23; || ἐκδικέω De 32.43¹; κρίσιν Is 35.4; + a cogn. obj., ἀνταπόδοσιν ὄνειδος τοῖς ὑπεναντίοις 'open humiliation to the antagonists' 59.18.

Cf. ἀνταπόδοσις, ἀνταπόδομα, ἀνταπο~, ἀποτίνω.

ἀνταπόδομα, ατος. n.

what is rendered as recompense, retribution: for evil deeds in conjunction with the related verb ἀνταποδίδωμι– ἀνταποδώσω τὸ ἀ. ὑμῶν εἰς κεφαλὰς ὑμῶν 'I will return your recompense on your heads' Jl 3.4*b*, 7, sim. Ob 15; Jl 3.4*a*, Ps 27.4; Jd 14.4 A (B: ἐκδίκησις 'retribution'); reward for good deeds, Si 2.9; return on invested efforts, 20.10. **b.** 'kick-back': Is 1.23 (|| δῶρον).

Cf. ἀνταποδίδωμι, ἀνταπόδοσις, ἐκδίκησις.

ἀνταπόδοσις, εως. f.

act of retribution, rendering recompense for evil done: αἱ ἡμέραι τῆς ~εως, || ἐκδίκησις Ho 9.7, ἐνιαυτὸς ~εως κρίσεως Σιων Is 34.8, ἡμέρα ~εως 61.2; as acc. cogn. φωνὴ κυρίου ἀνταποδιδόντος ~ιν τοῖς ἀντικειμένοις '.. to the adversaries' 66.6; ἁμαρτωλῶν Ps 90.8 (obj. gen.). Cf. ἀνταποδίδωμι, ἀνταπόδομα: Caird 1968.460.

ἀνταποθνῄσκω: fut. ~θανοῦμαι.ʃ

to die as a punishment: Ex 22.3. Cf. ἀποθνῄσκω.

ἀνταποκρίνομαι: aor. ἀνταπεκρίθην, inf. ~κριθῆναι.ʃ *

to reply to: κατὰ πρόσωπόν μου Jb 16.8¶, πρὸς αὐτήν Jd 5.29A (B: ἀποκρίνομαι); + acc. rei, ῥήματα αὐτοῦ Jb 32.12¶; τῷ Αβεννηρ ῥῆμα 2K 3.11*L* (B: ἀπο~). Cf. ἀνταπόκρισις, ἀποκρίνομαι.

ἀνταπόκρισις, εως. f.ʃ *

answer, response: σοι δώσω ~ιν Jb 13.22; 34.36. Cf. ἀνταποκρίνομαι.

ἀνταποστέλλω: aor. ἀνταπέστειλα.ʃ

to send a message in response: + λέγων foll. by a message, 3K 21.10. Cf. ἀποστέλλω.

ἀνταποτίνω: fut. ~τείσω.ʃ

to requite: αὐτῷ *s* God, ἀγαθά 1K 24.20 (*L* ἀνταποδίδωμι). Cf. ἀνταποδίδωμι.

ἀντεῖπον (aor.): fut. 1pl. ἀντεροῦμεν, ptc. ἀντερῶν, inf. ἀντερεῖν; aor. inf. ἀντειπεῖν, ptc. ~ειπών, subj. ἀντείπω.

to say by way of contradiction and gainsay: + acc. rei, Jb 20.2; + acc. and dat., κακὸν καλῷ 'evil for good' Ge 24.50; τί ἀντεροῦμεν τῷ κυρίῳ; 'what could we say and contradict our Lordship?' 44.16. **b.** *to register orally dissent* or *disapproval*: + dat. pers. (sbd in authority), Is 10.15, τῷ κυρίῳ μου Ju 12.14, τῷ βασιλεῖ Es 1.17, Ιωβ (winner of a debate) Jb 32.1; + dat. rei (authoritative), τοῖς ὑπ' αὐτοῦ ῥηθησομένοις 'what is going to be said by him' 1M 14.44; Es 8.8; πρὸς ἕνα λόγον αὐτοῦ Jb 9.3.

Cf. ἀντιλέγω, ἀντίρρησις, εἶπον.

ἀντέχω: pres.subj.mid. ~έχωμαι; fut.mid. ἀνθέξομαι; aor. ἀντέσχον.

I. *to hold out without giving in*: *s* city under siege, 4M 7.4.

II. mid. *to be adherent of, devoted to*: + gen., κρίματος De 32.41; τοῦ κυρίου Zp 1.6 (|| ζητέω); τῆς διαθήκης μου Is 56.4, 6, τοῦ νόμου Je 2.8, τῶν προσταγμάτων μου 51.10, ^σοφίας^ Pr 3.18 (|| ἐπερείδομαι 'to lean on'); objects of pagan worship, Je 8.2. **b.** + *dat., νεκρῷ 'a lifeless (god)' Si 18.29¶. **c.** ἐν τούτῳ Ec 7.18.

2. *to resist*: abs. Ne 4.16; + dat., τῷ ὀνόματι τῆς πόλεως τῆς ἁγίας Is 48.2 (|| ἀντιστηρίζω).

3. *to hold out a helping hand to*: abs., Jb 33.24; + gen.pers., Pr 4.6.

4. *to hold out and endure without reacting*: Si 1.23 (*s* μακρόθυμος).

5. *to hold on to*: + gen. (land), 1M 15.34.

Cf. ἀνέχω, μακροθυμέω.

ἀντηχέω.ʃ

to echo back: *s* βοή Wi 18.10. Cf. ἠχέω.

ἀντί, prep. w. gen.

1. Precedes a noun of commodity or service to be obtained in return for payment or giving of equivalent amount: μεμίσθωμαι γάρ σε ἀ. τῶν μανδραγορῶν 'for I have hired you for the mandrakes' Ge 30.16(*c*); κτᾶσθαι ἐν ἀργυρίῳ πτωχοὺς καὶ ταπεινὸν ἀ. ὑποδημάτων 'to acquire the poor with silver and the lowly for footwear' Am 8.6(*d*); τὰ κοράσια ἐπώλουν ἀ. οἴνου Jl 3.3(*c*); + ἀνταποδιδόναι, Jl 2.25(*b*), Zc 9.12(†).

2. Precedes a noun of commodity to be given in return for service rendered: δώσω σοι καὶ ταύτην ἀ. τῆς ἐργασίας, ἧς ἐργᾷ παρ' ἐμοὶ .. 'I shall give you this also for the labour you are going to perform with me ..' Ge 29.27(*c*); δώσω ὑμῖν ἄρτους ἀ. τῶν κτηνῶν ὑμῶν 47.16(*c*).

3. Precedes a noun of deed(s) which is requited, whether positively (reward) or, mostly, negatively (punishment): **a**. ἀ. τοῦ αἵματος αὐτοῦ ἐκχυθήσεται 'in return for his blood (his own blood) shall be shed' Ge 9.6(*c*); δώσει ψυχὴν ἀ. ψυχῆς, ὀφθαλμὸν ἀ. ὀφθαλμοῦ, ὀδόντα ἀ. ὀδόντος, χεῖρα ἀ. χειρός, πόδα ἀ. ποδός .. Ex 21.23f.(*j*), sim. De 19.21(*c*); ἀ. ὕβρεως αὐτῶν Zp 2.10(*j*); ἀγαθὰ ἀνθ' ὧν ποιεῖτε μεθ' ἡμῶν 'good deeds in return for what you do to us' 1M 10.27. **b**. Often in the form ἀνθ' ὧν introducing a clause the verb of which is in the past and specifies a commendable or (mostly) punishable deed, and such a clause usually follows the main clause: ἐνευλογηθήσονται .. ἀνθ' ὧν ὑπήκουσας τῆς ἐμῆς φωνῆς Ge 22.18(*k*), 26.5(*k*); ἀποστρέψει τὸ πρόσωπον αὐτοῦ ἀπ' αὐτῶν .. ἀνθ' ὧν ἐπονηρεύσαντο Mi 3.4(*e*); De 22.29(*o*) (|| ὅτι 22.24); Ho 8.1(*g*), Am 1.3(*i* and || ἕνεκεν + inf. vs. 6), 9(*i* || + ἕνεκα + inf. vs. 11), 13(*i*), 2.1(*i*), 6(*i*), Mi 5.15(*a*), Jl 3.5(*a*), 19(*a*), Zc 1.15(*a*), 12.10(*a*?), 13.4(*h*), Ma 2.9(*f*); followed by the main clause, Am 5.11(*i*), Hg 1.9(*g*), Is 3.16(*q*), Pr 1.32(*s*), cf. Spicq 1.122-5. **c**. ἀνθ' ὧν = ἀντὶ τούτων with anaphoric force: Ju 9.3. **d**. ἀνθ' ὧν ὅσα = causal ὅτι: preceding the main cl., Jd 2.20(*u*), 4K 21.11(*u*). **e**. + inf., only in Ez: ἀ. τοῦ λέγειν σε Ez 29.9(*g*); ἀ. τοῦ γενέσθαι τὰ πρόβατά μου .. ἀ. τούτου .. 34.8f(*g, r*), cf. **4 b**. Cf. **8 b** below.

4. Precedes a noun of ground or reason: ἀ. κόπων Hb 3.7(*j*), ἀ. τούτου Ez 28.7(*r*); PSol 17.6. **b**. + inf.: ἀ. τοῦ ἀτιμασθῆναι ὑμᾶς .. διὰ τοῦτο .. 36.3f.(*m, r*), 36.6(*g*), cf. **3 d** above.

5. *as a substitute for*: ἀ. Αβελ, ~ον ἀπέκτεινεν Καιν Ge 4.25(*j*); ἀ. Ισαακ 22.13(*j*); μὴ ἀ. θεοῦ ἐγώ εἰμι ..; 'surely I cannot act in God's place ..?' 30.2(*j*); ἀνθ' ὧν = ἀντὶ τούτων with anaphoric force, 'instead of which' Wi 16.20. Cf. ἀνεπλήρωσεν σάρκα ἀντ' αὐτῆς 'replaced it with flesh' Ge 2.21(*j*).

6. *in succession to*: ἐβασίλευσεν ἀντ' αὐτοῦ 'succeeded him as king' Ge 36.34(*j*); ὁ ἱερεὺς ὁ ἀντ' αὐτοῦ τῶν υἱῶν αὐτοῦ 'the priest to succeed him among his sons' Ex 29.30(*j*).

7. *analogously to, just like*: ἀ. τῶν πατέρων ὑμῶν 'just like your forefathers' Nu 32.14(*j*). Cf. δουλεύειν ἀ. ἀργυρωνήτων 'to serve just like purchased slaves' Demosth. 17.3.

8. ἀνθ' ὧν ὅτι *in place of, instead of*: ἀνθ' ὧν ὅτι ἦτε ὡσεὶ τὰ ἄστρα τοῦ οὐρανοῦ De 28.62(*o*). **b**. *as retribution for*, ἀνθ' ὧν ὅτι (*L* om. ὅτι) ἐποίησεν τὸ ῥῆμα τοῦτο 2K 12.6(*k*), .. ἐξουδένωσας 12.10(*t*) (*L* ἕνεκεν τούτου ὅτι); Ez 36.34(*o*); without ὅτι, Je 7.13(*g*), 1E 4.42, cf. **3 b** above.

Cf. διά, ὑπέρ: Trench 311-3; Johannessohn, *Präp.* 198-201; Schreiner 1972.

a) אֲשֶׁר; *b*) אֵת; *c*) בְּ; *d*) בַּעֲבוּר; *e*) כַּאֲשֶׁר; *f*) אֲשֶׁר כְּפִי; *g*) יַעַן; *h*) לְמַעַן; *i*) עַל; *j*) תַּחַת; *k*) עֵקֶב אֲשֶׁר; *l*) אֶל־תַּחַת; *m*) יַעַן וּבְיַעַן; *n*) חֵלֶף; *o*) תַּחַת אֲשֶׁר; *p*) עֵקֶב; *q*) יַעַן כִּי; *r*) ἀντὶ τούτοὺ לָכֵן; *s*) כִּי; *t*) עֵקֶב כִּי; *u*) יַעַן אֲשֶׁר.

ἀντιβάλλω.ʃ

to present for consideration: τι πρός τινα 2M 11.13. Cf. Spicq 1.126f.

ἀντίγραφον, ου. n.

copy of a document: ἐπιστολῆς Ep Je inscr., 1E 6.7. Cf. ἀφόμοιος.

ἀντιγράφω: aor. ἀντέγραψα.

to write back to reply: + dat. pers., 1E 2.21. **b**. *to write in reply*: + acc. rei, ἐπιστολήν 1M 8.22.

Cf. γράφω.

ἀντιδίδωμι: impf. ἀντεδιδόμην.ʃ

1. *to give in return* for a service rendered or a commodity purchased: + dat. pers. and acc. rei, μισθούς Ex 27.15.

2. *to give* sth *instead*: ἀπὸ τῶν ὀσπρίων 'some pulse' Da 1.16 LXX (TH: δίδωμι).

Cf. δίδωμι.

ἀντιδικέω: aor. ἀντεδίκησα.

1. *to play the defendant against*: in court, + acc. pers., Jd 6.31 A.

2. *to act rebelliously*: + πρός τινα Es 3.16 *L*.

ἀντίδικος, ου. m.

1. *plaintiff*: κατεδυνάστευσεν .. τὸν ~ον αὐτοῦ 'oppressed its plaintiff' Ho 5.11.

2. *opponent, adversary*: Is 41.11, Es 8.11 o' (|| ἀντικείμενος), Si 33.9 (|| ἐχθρός); God's, 1K 2.10; hum., in a law-court, Pr 18.17.

Cf. Schrenk, *TDNT* 1.373f.

ἀντιδοξέω.ʃ

to take a view opposed to that of: + dat. pers., Es C 2 o'.

ἀντίζηλος, ου. f.ʃ *

rival: of rival wife in polygamy, γυναῖκα ἐπὶ ἀδελφῇ αὐτῆς οὐ λήμψῃ ~ον 'you shall not take a wife as rival in addition to her sister' Le 18.18; 1K 1.6*L*; γυνὴ ἀ. ἐπὶ γυναικί Si 26.6; 37.11.

ἀντίθετος, ον.ʃ

opposed: πρός τινα Es B 4 o'; subst.m. 'opponent' 2K 23.5*L*; n.pl., *counter-arguments*, ἀποκριθῆναι ~α Ιωβ 'to refute J.'s argument' Jb 32.3. Cf. ἐχθρός.

ἀντικαθίζω: aor. ἀντεκάθισα.ʃ

to cause to live, replacing present dweller: *o* colonist, 4K 17.26. Cf. καθίζω.

ἀντικαθίστημι: fut.mid. ~καταστήσομαι; 1aor.act. ~κατέστησα, 2aor. ~κατέστην.ʃ

1. tr. (1aor.act.): *to present instead*: + acc. pers., Jo 5.7.

2. intr. (2aor.act., fut.mid.): *to stand up with hostile intent, confront*: ἀ. ἡ ᾠδὴ αὕτη κατὰ πρόσωπον De 31.21; εἰς ἔχθραν Mi 2.8 v.l. (Zgl: ἀντέστη), see Spicq 1.128f.

Cf. ἀνθίστημι and ἵστημι.

ἀντικαταλλάσσω.ʃ

1. mid. *to exchange*: + acc, τὰ χρήματα περὶ τοῦ ζῆν 'money for life' 3M 2.32.

2. mid. *to be comparable in value*: Si 46.12.

ἀντίκειμαι: fut. ἀντικείσομαι.

1. *to act as opponent of* sbd (τινι): *s* διάβολος Zc 3.1; God and + dat. pers., Ex 23.22; hum., φωνὴ κυρίου ἀνταποδιδόντος ἀνταπόδοσιν τοῖς ἀντικειμένοις '.. meting out retribution to the adversaries' Is 66.6; ‖ ἀντίδικος 41.11.

2. *to assume a certain stance towards*: + dat. pers., Jb 18.25.

Cf. ἐχθρεύω: Lee 82; Spicq 1.129f.

ἀντικρίνω: fut.mid. ~κρινοῦμαι.ʃ

to contend against: mid., in court, + dat. pers., Jb 9.32; 11.3.

ἄντικρυς. Used adverbially.ʃ

right opposite: situated, 3M 5.16. Del. Ne 12.8 v.l.

ἀντιλαμβάνομαι: fut. ~λήμψομαι, ptc. ~λημψόμενος; aor. ἀντελαβόμην, inf. ~λαβέσθαι, impv. ~λαβοῦ, opt.3s ~λάβοιτο.

1. *to lay hold of, grasp*: + gen., τῆς χειρὸς τοῦ πατρὸς αὐτοῦ Ge 48.17, to help Is 51.18, to encourage Je 23.14 (cf. Chr PG 64.945 συνηγόρουν); ἐν δικαιοσύνῃ καὶ κρίματι Is 9.7 (of management of a kingdom with a firm hand of justice, cf. Syp: *yšwy* 'he shall direct'); ^ἐπιστήμης Ba 3.21.

2. *to secure*: + gen., ἀντιλήμψομαι θεοῦ μου ὑψίστου Mi 6.6; Is 64.7. See MM, 47b.

3. *to hold fast, adhere to*: + gen., ἀληθείας Is 26.3, θεῶν ἀλλοτρίων 'alien gods' 3K 9.9.

4. *to come to the assistance of*: abs., Is 63.5; + gen. pers., Le 25.35; χειρῶν πονηρῶν 'evil people' Je 23.14; τῇ χειρί μου 'with my hand' Ez 20.5; + dat. pers., 1C 22.17, cf. Helbing, *Kasus*. 127; *s* God, Ps 3.6, God's ἔλεος and ἀλήθεια 39.12. ***b**. + χεῖρά τινος (pers.): χεῖρα πτωχοῦ Ez 16.49, cf. Helbing, *Kasus*. 127.

Cf., ἀντιλήμπτωρ, βοηθέω, συναντι~, ὑπολαμβάνω.

ἀντιλάμπω: aor. ptc. ~λάμψας.ʃ

to shine in opposition to another source of light: *s* φῶς 2M 1.32. Cf. λάμπω.

ἀντιλέγω. See also under ἀντεῖπον.

1. *to challenge the authority of, object to*: abs., Is 22.22; 50.5, 65.2 (+ ἀπειθέω); + dat., τῇ ἀληθείᾳ Si 4.25; πρὸς τὸν λόγον σχετλιάζοντος ἀντιλέγοντός τε 'protesting his speech indignantly' 4M 4.7.

2. *to impeach*: pass. ἀντιλεγόμενος ἱερεύς 'an impeached priest' Ho 4.4.

Cf. ἀντεῖπον: Renehan 1.34.

ἀντιλήμπτωρ, ορος. m. Freq. in Ps. *

helper: *s* God, Ps 3.4, 17.3; τῆς ψυχῆς μου 53.6; ‖ καταφυγή, βοηθός 58.17, ‖ σωτήρ 61.3, τῆς σωτηρίας μου 88.27, ‖ ῥύστης, ὑπερασπίστης 143.2; hum. Si 13.22. Cf. ἀντιλαμβάνω, βοηθός.

ἀντίλημψις, εως. f.

1. *help*: from God, Ps 21.20 (‖ βοήθεια), military 82.9; ἀνθρώπων 'by men' Si 51.7; pl. 2M 8.19 (‖ βοήθεια vs. 20).

2. *act of attaining*: τῶν ἰδίων 'of one's own aims' 2M 11.26.

Cf. βοήθεια.

ἀντιλογία, ας. f.

dispute: Ex 18.16; ὕδωρ ~ας Nu 20.13, 27.14, Ps 80.8; De 17.8; ἀνὰ μέσον ἀνθρώπων 25.1; + κρίσις 2K 15.4B (‖ *L* om. ἀ.). Cf. *ND* 2.78. **b**. *verbal attack*: Pr 17.11, Ps 17.44, 79.7; γλωσσῶν 30.21.

Cf. ἀντιλέγω.

ἀντιμαρτυρέω.ʃ

to make a case in front of a hostile audience: κατὰ πρόσωπον 'in direct confrontation' 2M 7.6. Cf. μαρτυρέω.

ἀντίον, ου. n.

the upper cross-beam of a loom: as standard for comparison of a spear-shaft, 2K 21.19. Cf. Shipp 83; Caird 1968.460.

ἀντίπαλος, ον.ʃ

subst.m. *antagonist*: military, 2M 14.17, 3M 1.5. Cf. ἐχθρός, πολέμιος.

ἀντιπαραβάλλω: pf.ptc.pass. ~βεβλημένος.ʃ

to contrast: + dat., Si 23.12.

ἀντιπαράγω.ʃ

to march parallel with: + dat. pers., 1M 13.20.

ἀντιπαραγωγή, ῆς. f.ʃ

hostility, opposition: + dat., Es B 5 o' (*L* ἐναντία παραγωγή).

ἀντιπαρατάσσομαι.ʃ

to take hostile attitude: + dat., βασιλεῦσιν 1E 2.22 (‖ 2E ἐπαίρομαι 4.19).

ἀντιπαρέρχομαι: aor. ἀντιπαρῆλθον.ʃ

to come along and help against an enemy: *s* God, Wi 16.10.

ἀντιπίπτω.ʃ

1. *to position itself* or *oneself opposite* sth else: ἀλλήλαις εἰς ἑκάστην Ex 26.5; ἕτερον τῷ ἑτέρῳ 26.17.

2. *to set oneself against*: + inf., Nu 27.14.

Cf. πίπτω, ἀπειθέω: Lee 1969.239.

ἀντιποιέω: fut. ~ποιήσομαι, pass. ~ποιηθήσομαι; aor.mid.inf. ~ποιήσασθαι.ʃ

1. *to do the same* as done by the other party *in re-*

taliation: impers.pass., ὡσαύτως ἀντιποιηθήσεται αὐτῷ Le 24.19.

2. *to resist*: + dat., τῇ χειρὶ αὐτοῦ Da TH 4.32.

3. *to lay claim to*: + gen., τῆς βασιλείας 1M 15.3.

ἀντιπολεμέω.ʃ

to wage war against: + acc. pers., Is 41.12 (ǁ παροινέω). Cf. πολεμέω.

ἀντιπολιτεύομαι.ʃ

mid. *to be* or *act as political opponent*: πρός τινα 'against sbd' 4M 4.1.

ἀντιπράττωʃ

to act in defiance of: + dat., τῷ βασιλεῖ 2M 14.29.

ἀντιπρόσωπος, ον.

facing: + dat., ἔθηκεν αὐτὰ ~α ἀλλήλοις 'placed them facing one another' Ge 15.10; ~οι ἀντιπίπτουσαι ἀλλήλαις εἰς ἑκάστην 'facing each other, falling one upon the other' Ex 26.5. **b**. subst.n., *frontline*: τοῦ πολέμου 2K 10.9, cf. ǁ ~οι τοῦ πολεμεῖν 1C 19.10.

Cf. ἐναντίον.

ἀντίπτωμα, ατος. n.ʃ*

1. *act of stumbling against sth and falling*: metaph., Si 35.20.

2. *falling out with each other*: + ἐρεθισμός 'strife' Si 34.29.

Cf. σκάνδαλον.

ἀντίρρησις, εως. f.ʃ

verbal protest, 'objection': Ec 8.11. Cf. ἀντεῖπον, ἀντιρρητορεύω.

ἀντιρρητορεύω: aor.ptc. ~ρρητορεύσας.ʃ

to deliver a counter-speech against (dat.): ταῖς .. παρηγορίαις 'against the exhortations ..' 4M 6.1. Cf. ἀντίρρησις, ἀντεῖπον.

ἀντιστήριγμα, ατος. n.ʃ

one which or *that which provides support*: τὰ ~ατα Αἰγύπτου 'the supporters of E.' Ez 30.6; κύριος ἀ. μου Ps 17.19. Cf. στήριγμα, ἐπιστήριγμα.

ἀντιστηρίζω: aor.impv.mid.2pl. ~στηρίσασθε.ʃ

I. act. *to render support to*: κύριος ἀντιστηρίζει χεῖρα αὐτοῦ [= one who has fallen] Ps 36.24.

II. mid. *to put up resistance*: ἐπὶ τῷ θεῷ Is 48.2 (ǁ ἀντέχομαι).

2. *to seek support, rely*: ἐπὶ τῷ θεῷ (ǁ πέποιθα) Is 50.10.

Cf. ἀντιτάσσω.

ἀντιτάσσω: fut.mid. ~τάξομαι.

mid. *to align oneself against* (sbd τινι): ἀντιτασσόμενος ἀντιτάξομαι αὐτοῖς 'I shall become their sworn enemy' Ho 1.6, cf. 3K 11.34; ὑπερηφάνοις 'the arrogant' Pr 3.34; against God, Es C 4 o'; "no evil will be a match for her [= wisdom]" Pr 3.15, cf. Caird 1968.460. **b**. + dat. rei: *to behave against* (royal directive) Es 3.4 o'.

Cf. ἀντιστηρίζω.

ἀντιτίθημι: fut. ~θήσω; 2aor.ptc. ~θείς.ʃ

to place in place of sth else: ἀντί τινος Le 14.42. **b**. *to set* sth *against* sth else: τί τινι - τῇ ἐπιθυμίᾳ τὸν λογισμόν 'the rational will against the desire' 4M 3.16. Cf. τίθημι.

ἀντιφιλοσοφέω: aor. ἀντεφιλοσόφησα.ʃ*

to argue back with own philosophy: + dat. pers., 4M 8.15. Cf. φιλοσοφέω.

ἀντιφωνέω: aor.ptc. ~φωνήσας.ʃ

to answer by letter to: + dat. pers., 1M 12.18.

ἀντίψυχος, ον.ʃ

given for the sake of: + gen. pers. (beneficiary), 4M 6.29; people's sin, 17.21.

ἀντλέω: fut. ἀντλήσω; aor. ἤντλησα, impv. ἄντλησον, inf. ἀντλῆσαι ʃ

to draw (drinking water for humans or livestock): abs. Ge 24.20 (from a well [φρέαρ]), Ex 2.16; 2.17, 19 (*s* a man); + acc., ὕδωρ (*s* young girls and from a well [πηγή]) Ge 24.13; fig. ἀντλήσετε ὕδωρ μετ' εὐφροσύνης ἐκ τῶν πηγῶν τοῦ σωτηρίου Is 12.3. Cf. ὑδρεύομαι.

ἀντοφθαλμέω; aor.inf. ~μῆσαι.ʃ

to confront and defy: + dat., ἡδοναῖς Si 19.5¶, σοι Wi 12.14.

ἄντρον, ου. n.ʃ

inner chamber of a palace, poss. *cellar*: 3K 16.18, cf. Caird 1968.460f.

ἀντρώδης, ες.ʃ

similar to cave: *s* οἶκος 2M 2.5.

ἄνυδρος, ον.

lacking water, waterless: *s* γῆ Ho 2.3 (resulting from drought), γῆ ἄ. ǁ ἔρημος Ez 19.12, + ἄκαρπος Je 2.6; εἰς ἀφανισμὸν ~ον ὡς ἔρημον 'into a parched wasteland like a wilderness' Zp 2.13; subst.n., ἐν δίψει καύματος ἐν ~ῳ 'in thirst from heat in waterless land' De 32.10; f., γῆ or ἔρημος understood, Is 35.7, 43.19 (at latter ǁ ἔρημος), cf. γῆ ἄ. καὶ ἄβατος Je 28.43. Cf. ὕδωρ, ξηρός, ὑγρός.

ἀνυπέρβλητος, ον.ʃ

incapable of being overthrown, 'invincible': *s* God, Ju 16.13. Cf. ἀνίκητος.

ἀνυπερθέτως.ʃ

without delay: 3M 5.20, 42.

ἀνυπόδετος, ον.ʃ On the form (for Cl. ~ητος), see Thack. 80.

without wearing anything on one's feet, 'barefooted': of mourner - ἀ. καὶ γυμνή '.. and naked' Mi 1.8 (the same collocation occurs at Is 20.2, 3), 2K 15.30. Cf. ὑπόδημα.

ἀνυπόκριτος, ον.ʃ

sincere and not put on: *s* κρίσις 'justice' Wi 5.18, ἐπιταγή 'authentic (command)' 18.16. Cf. γνήσιος, ὑποκρίνομαι: Spicq 1.134-6.

ἀνυπομόνητος, ον.ʃ
unbearable: subst.n., a demanding, 'killing' task, καταφθαρήσῃ ~τῳ Ex 18.18. Cf. ὑπομένω.

ἀνυπονόητος, ον.ʃ
unsuspected: subst.m., Si 11.5. Cf. ἀδόκητος.

ἀνυπόστατος, ον.ʃ
irresistible: *s* flood-water, Ps 123.5, δύναμις 'armed forces' 2M 1.13, army commander, 8.5; God's anger, Od 12.5 (|| ἄστεκτος). Cf. ὑφίστημι: Renehan 2.30.

ἀνυψόω: fut. ἀνυψώσω; aor. ἀνύψωσα, inf. ἀνυψῶσαι, pass. ἀνυψώθην, inf. ~υψωθῆναι. *
to lift up, raise: + acc., φωνήν Si 21.20, ἐκ γῆς 46.20, fallen temple, 49.12, its foundations 2E 4.12; tree, Da 4.19 LXX; metaph., ἀπὸ κοπρίας πένητα 'the poor from a rubbish-tip' Ps 112.7; δόξαν Si 1.19, κέρας λαοῦ 47.5, κεφαλήν 11.1, 12, 38.3 (of gaining public recognition), ψυχήν 31.20, καρδίαν 40.26 (sense of self-importance); ἱκετείαν '(the voice of) supplication' 51.9; opp. ταπεινόω 7.11, 1K 2.7; τὸν λόγον αὐτοῦ ἕως τῶν νεφελῶν 'praised his speech to the skies' Si 13.23, ὡς ἄστρα 44.21; pass., ἀπὸ τοῦ οἴνου 'elated, "high" with wine' Da 5 pr. LXX. **b**. *to add to the extent and intensity of*: + acc., ὀργήν 'anger' Si 28.10. **c**. pass. *to gain height*: *s* Wisdom, ὡς κέδρος 'like a cedar' Si 24.13, ὡς φοῖνιξ 'like a palm-tree' 24.14.
Cf. ὑψόω.

ἀνύω.ʃ
to accomplish, effect: + acc., μηδέν 'nothing' 4M 9.12. Cf. ποιέω.

ἄνω. adv.; comp. ἀνώτερος, α, ον; sup. ~τατος, η, ον.
1. *high above*: ἐν τῷ οὐρανῷ ἄ. καὶ .. ἐν τῇ γῇ κάτω Ex 20.4, sim. De 4.39; ἔχει σκέλη ἀνώτερον τῶν ποδῶν 'has legs above the feet' Le 11.21; attr., τῆς ἄ. ὁδοῦ Is 7.3.
2. *upwards*: ἀναβήσεται ἄ. ἄ. 'shall rise very high' De 28.43 (:: κάτω κάτω); Is 34.10; αἴροντες ἄ. τὰς χεῖρας 1E 9.47. **b**. *towards higher ground*: of the Nile, To 8.3 𝔊[II]. *c. ἕως ἄνω, calqued on Heb. לְמַעְלָה 'exceedingly': 2K 26.8.
3. adj., *upper*: ἡ ἀνωτέρα τῶν πλευρῶν 'the side-chamber above' Ez 41.7. **b**. *higher*: ἡ ἄ. Γαλιλαία 'Northern Galilee' To 1.2 𝔊[II], ἡ ἄνω Κιλικία Ju 2.21; τὰ ἀνώτατα Αἰγύπτου 'Upper Egypt' 8.3 𝔊[I]; εἰς τοὺς ἄ. τόπους 'into the inland region' lying higher than the coastal area, 2M 9.23.
Cf. ἄνωθεν, ἐπάνω, ὑπεράνω, κάτω. Del. De 30.12 v.l.

ἄνωθεν.
A. adv. **1**. *at the top*: Ge 6.16.
2. *high above*: ἀπὸ τῆς δρόσου τοῦ οὐρανοῦ ἄ. 'from the dew of heaven above' Ge 27.39.
3. *fresh from the start*, 'anew': πάλιν ἄ. Wi 19.6, cf. Boucher on Joh 3.3.
B. prep. + gen. **1**. *from above*: ἄ. τοῦ ἱλαστηρίου Ex 25.21.
2. *positioned above*: Ex 38.5.
Cf. ἄνω, ἀπάνωθεν, κάτωθεν.

ἀνώνυμος, ον.ʃ
having no name: *s* idols, Wi 14.27. Cf. ὄνομα.

ἀνωφελής, ές.ʃ
being of no use and profit: *s* pagan idols and subst. n., Is 44.10, Je 2.8; γογγυσμός 'grumbling' Wi 1.11, ἁμαρτία PSol 16.8, ὑετὸς λαβρὸς καὶ ἀ. 'impetuous, .. rain' Pr 28.3. Cf. ὠφελέω, ἀσύμφορος, ἀχρεῖος, ἄχρηστος.

ἀξία, ας. f.ʃ
value and estimation appropriate to sbd or sth (gen.): κατὰ τὴν ἀξίαν αὐτοῦ Si 38.17 (|| κατὰ τὴν κρίσιν αὐτοῦ vs. 16); 10.28. Cf. τιμή.

ἀξίνη, ης. f.
axe for hewing wood: De 19.5; w. (ἐκ)κόπτω 'to fell, chop,' Is 10.15, Je 26.22, Ps 73.6. Cf. Shipp 84f.

ἀξιόπιστος, ον.ʃ
worthy of belief, 'credible': *s* dream, 2M 15.11; hum. Pr 28.20. **b**. *worthy of trust*: *s* wounds inflicted, Pr 27.6. Cf. πιστός.

ἄξιος, α, ον.
1. *accurately corresponding, comparable*: ἀργυρίου τοῦ ~ου 'for the right amount of silver' (as price) Ge 23.9; + gen., ^σοφίας^ '(comparable in value) to wisdom' Pr 3.15.
2. *proper, appropriate*: + inf. ~ον ἐπιβλέψαι ..; 'is it proper (for me) to look forward to ..?' Ma 2.13.
3. *deserving, worthy of*: + gen., πληγῶν 'beatings' De 25.2; Jb 11.6, Es 7.4 o', θανάτου 2K 12.5*L*; + inf., Wi 18.4, ἀποθανεῖν 4M 4.12; subst. m., 2M 15.21. **b**. subst. n.sg. used adv., *in a manner befitting*: + gen., τῆς ἡλικίας 'the age' 4M 5.11.
Cf. ἀξιόω, ἀξίως, ἁρμόνιος.

ἀξιόω: fut. ἀξιώσω; aor. ἠξίωσα, subj. ἀξιώσω, inf. ἀξιῶσαι, ptc. ἀξιώσας; pass. ἠξιώθην; pf.pass. ἠξίωμαι.
1. *to deem deserving of*: + inf., οὐκ ἠξιώθην καταφιλῆσαι τὰ παιδία μου 'I was not given a chance to kiss my children' Ge 31.28. Cf. Lee 69f. **b**. + acc. pers. and gen. rei, ὁ θεὸς εὐεργεσιῶν ἠξίωσε τὸν λαὸν αὐτοῦ Si prol. II, ταφῆς 'of burial' 2M 9.15.
2. *to put a request to*: + acc. pers., ἀξιῶ σε, μὴ ὀκνήσῃς ἐλθεῖν πρός με 'Do not delay your coming to me, please' Nu 22.16; + inf., 2M 9.26 (+ παρακαλέω), 12.11, Ep Je 41; περὶ ἐμοῦ 'on my behalf' To 1.21; περὶ ἁμαρτιῶν Da 4.30a LXX (|| δέομαι), περὶ ζωῆς (|| ἐπικαλέομαι, ἱκετεύω); ὑπέρ τινος 2K 12.16*L* (B: ζητέω); + ὡς + subj., Da

1.8 TH (LXX ἵνα); + ἵνα + subj. 2.16 LXX (TH ὅπως), 2M 2.8, + ὅπως + subj. To 10.7 𝔊II; + acc. rei, Es 5.6; + double acc., ὅ σε ἀξιῶ 1E 4.46 (ll αἰτέομαι); + cogn. acc., ἀξίωμα Da 6.5 LXX (ll εὔχομαι); + *παρά τινος (pers.) 6.7 LXX.

3. *to think highly of*: + acc., εἰρήνην Is 33.7.

4. *to think fit and consent*: + inf., τοῦ δεηθῆναι 'to supplicate' Je 7.16; 2M 4.19.

5. *to think wishfully*: + inf., 2M 5.4.

Cf. αἰτέω, δέομαι, ἐπικαλέω, ἱκετεύω, ἄξιος, προσ~, καταξιόω: LSG s.v.

ἀξίωμα, ατος. n.

1. *juridical decision, assessment* of damage: δώσει μετὰ ~ατος 'he shall pay in accordance with the assessment' Ex 21.22.

2. *request*: Τί θέλεις .. καὶ τί σού ἐστιν τὸ ἀ.; Es 5.3; ll αἴτημα 5.7, 7.2, 3; εἰσέλθοι τὸ ἀ. μου ἐνώπιόν σου 'May my request come before you' Ps 118.170; ll εὐχή and cogn. obj. of ἀξιόω Da LXX 6.5, 7, 12.

3. *honour and respect accorded*: κείμενος ἐν ~ατι 'a dignitary' 2M 4.31.

Cf. ἀξιόω, αἴτημα, εὐχή.

ἀξίως. adv.ʃ

in a respectable and fitting manner: Si 14.11; *in a manner deserving of* (τινος), Wi 7.15, ἐκολάσθησαν ἀ. 'deservedly punished' 16.1.

ἄξων, ονος. m.

1. *axle*: τῶν ἁρμάτων 'of the chariots' Ex 14.25; στρεφόμενος 'turning' Si 36.5.

2. metaph., *path of action*: Pr 2.9, 18, ll ὁδός 9.12b.

ἀοίδιμος, ον.ʃ

famous in song: *s* martyr's death, 4M 10.1. Cf. LSG s.v.

ἀοίκητος, ον.

uninhabited or *uninhabitable*: ἀ... οὐκ ἀνοικοδομηθήσεται ἔτι De 13.16; ἐν γῇ ~ῳ Ho 13.5 (as explanatory gloss for ἐν τῇ ἐρήμῳ); *s* οἶκος Jb 15.28 (ll ἔρημος), 8.14, ἔρημος Wi 11.2, χώρα (?) 'area' Pr 8.26; subst. n., ἄβατον καὶ ~ον Jb 38.27¶ (ll ἔρημος vs.26), f. Jo 13.3. Cf. οἰκέω.

ἄοκνος, ον.ʃ

not idle: *s* hum., Pr 6.11a. Cf. ὀκνηρός.

ἀορασία, ας. f.

blindness: meted out as punishment, ἐπάταξαν ~ᾳ Ge 19.11; πατάξαι σε κύριος παραπληξίᾳ καὶ ~ᾳ καὶ ἐκστάσει διανοίας 'May the Lord strike you with madness and blindness and mental derangement' De 28.28. Cf. ἀόρατος, τυφλός.

ἀόρατος, ον.ʃ

incapable of being seen with the eye, 'invisible': of the earth (γῆ) in the primaeval period, ἀ. καὶ ἀκατασκεύαστος '.. and incomplete' Gn 1.2; ἀποκρύφους ~ους '(otherwise) invisible hidden objects' Is 45.3; ἀνιάτῳ καὶ ~ῳ πληγῇ 'with an incurable and invisible plague' 2M 9.5.

Cf. ὁρατός, ἀορασία, ἀθεώρητος, ἀφανής, ἀπόκρυφος, ὁράω: Michaelis, *TDNT* 5.368-70.

ἀπαγγελία, ας. f.ʃ

act of passing news on: cogn. dat., Ru 2.11. Cf. ἀπαγγέλλω.

ἀπαγγέλλω: fut. ἀπαγγελῶ, pass. ἀπαγγελήσομαι; aor. ἀπήγγειλα, subj. ἀπαγγείλω, impv. ἀπάγγειλον, inf. ἀπαγγεῖλαι, ptc. ἀπαγγείλας, pass. ἀπηγγέλην, inf. ~γγελθῆναι; pf. ἀπήγγελκα, ptc. ἀπηγγελκώς.

1. *to tell in the way of explaining* or *interpreting* a mystery, riddle, etc.: of mantic revelation, ἐν ῥάβδοις 'by means of sticks' Ho 4.12; "Tell us on whose account this disaster is on us" Jn 1.8; 1.10; ἐπιστήμην Si 16.25; + dat. pers., περί τινος 1E 3.16 (ll δηλόω 15), ὑπέρ τινος 2K 10.5*L* (B: ἀν~); μοι τὸ πρόβλημα '.. the riddle' Jd 14.12; abs., ll διηγέομαι 'recount' Ps 54.18. **b**. + acc. rei, 'to explain the meaning of' – ὁ ἀπαγγέλλων αὐτό [= ἐνύπνιον 'dream, vision'] τῷ Φαραω sought among ἐξηγηταί and σοφοί of the land, Ge 41.8, cf. 41.24 (+ μοι); opp. ἀποκρύπτω 'conceal' Wi 6.22.

2. *to announce, make public proclamation*: + ὅτι, Am 4.5; + dat. pers. foll. by direct speech, 3.9.

3. *to inform*: + dat. pers., Ge 14.13, 21.26; κατὰ τὴν ἐπερώτησιν ταύτην 'in response to this questioning' 43.7; and also + acc. rei, αὐτῷ πάντα τὰ συμβάντα αὐτοῖς λέγοντες .. 'all that had happened to them ..' 42.29; πᾶσαν τὴν δόξαν μου .. καὶ ὅσα εἴδετε 45.13; and ὅτι, 12.18; and εἰ 'whether' 24.49; τίς ὁ μισθός σού ἐστιν 'what your hire is' 29.15; + καί λέγω and direct speech, 46.31 (ll λέγων 47.1); δραμοῦσα ἡ παῖς ἀπήγγειλεν εἰς τὸν οἶκον τῆς μητρὸς αὐτῆς κατὰ τὰ ῥήματα ταῦτα 24.28 where εἰς is pregnant: the girl ran into the house, not the household (*pace* Wevers ad loc.) to break the news; περί τινος 26.32.

4. *to pass on* a piece of verbal communication: + dat. pers. and acc. rei, αὐτῷ τὰ ῥήματα τοῦ κυρίου Ge 44.24; *o* news and pass., ἀπηγγέλη Ῥεβεκκᾳ τὰ ῥήματα Ησαυ τοῦ υἱοῦ αὐτῆς .. 27.42; impers. and foll. by ὅτι recitativum, 48.1; by λέγοντες and direct speech, 38.13, 24; + dat. pers., 48.2. **b**. a step to be taken: + dat. pers. and inf. clause, Ju 2.7.

5. *to proclaim in public as significant* or *noteworthy*: + acc. rei εἰρήνην Na 1.15 (ll εὐαγγελίζομαι); τινί τι – τῷ Ιακωβ ἀσεβείας αὐτοῦ Mi 3.8; εἰς ἀνθρώπους τὸν χριστόν 'the anointed one amongst people' Am 4.13.

Cf. ἀπαγγελία, ἄγγελος, ἀναγγέλλω, εὐαγγελίζω, κηρύσσω, μεταδίδωμι: Schniewind, *TDNT* 1.65f.

ἀπαγορεύω: pf.ptc.pass. ἀπηγορευομένος.ʃ
to regard and treat as non-permissible for use by sbd (dat.): pass., *o* (non-kosher) foods, 4M 1.34 (|| ἀπεῖπον vs. 33). Cf. ἀπεῖπον.

ἀπάγχομαι: aor. ἀπηγξάμην, inf. ἀπάγξασθαι.ʃ
to hang oneself: To 3.10, 2K 17.23. Cf. ἄγχω.

ἀπάγω: fut. ἀπάξω, pass. ἀπαχθήσομαι; aor. ἀπήγαγον, impv. ἀπάγαγε, subj. ἀπαγάγω, opt.3s ἀπαγάγοι, pass. ἀπήχθην, impv.2pl ἀπάχθητε, inf. ἀπαχθῆναι, subj. ἀπαχθῶ; pf.ptc.pass. ἀπηγμένος; plpf.pass.3s ἀπῆκτο.
to lead or *carry away*: + acc., Ge 31.18; *o* purchased goods, τὸν ἀγορασμὸν τῆς σιτοδοσίας ὑμῶν 'what you purchased of your allocated grain' 42.19; ὁδοὺς οὐκ ἀγαθάς 'towards wrong paths' Pr 16.29; *o* enemy troops, πρός σε Jd 4.7 Ra (B: ἐπ~). **b**. often under unfavourable conditions or to an unenviable destination, *o* hum., ὡς αἰχμαλωτίδας μαχαίρᾳ 'like captives under (the threat of) a sword' Ge 31.26; εἰς ἔθνος De 28.36 (exile), εἰς γῆν ἀλλοτρίαν 'to a foreign land' PSol 9.1, || ὁδηγέω Ps 59.11; pass., *o* one sentenced guilty and led away, Ge 39.22, 40.3, cf. 42.16, ἐπὶ θανάτῳ Ep Je 17, εἰς ἡμέραν ὀργῆς Jb 21.30¶.
Cf. (συναπ)άγω ἀπαγωγή: LSG, s.v.

ἀπαγωγή, ῆς. f.ʃ
**carrying off to prison*: 1E 8.24 (|| δεσμά 2E 7.26); τοὺς ἐν ~ῇ οὐκ ἔλυσε 'he did not release those in his train' Is 14.17; ἐμπεσεῖν εἰς ~ήν 10.4; De 32.36. Cf. ἀπάγω: Ottley ad Is 10.4, 14.17; Walters 129f.; *BA* ad De 32.36.

ἀπαδικέω: fut. ~κήσωʃ *
to withhold wrongfully: + acc., μισθὸν πένητος καὶ ἐνδεοῦς 'wages of a poor and needy person' De 24.14. Cf. ἀδικία.

ἀπαιδευσία, ας. f.
1. *ignorance*: περὶ τῆς ~ας σου ἐντράπηθι 'Feel ashamed of your ignorance' Si 4.25.
2. *lack of discipline*: ἀ. γλώσσης 'undisciplined speech, unrestrained tongue' Ho 7.16.
Cf. ἀπαίδευτος.

ἀπαίδευτος, ον.
uneducated: *s* hum., Si 6.20, ἔθνος Zp 2.1 (cf. TrgJon ad loc. "not desirous of sitting to study the Law"), λαός Is 26.11, βασιλεύς Si 10.3, ψυχαί Wi 17.1; subst.m. || ἄκακος 'simple-minded' Pr 8.5. Cf. παιδεύω and ἀπαιεδυσία.

ἀπαίρω: fut. ἀπαρῶ; aor. ἀπῆρα, subj. ἀπάρω, impv. ἄπαρον, 2pl. ἀπάρατε, ptc. ἀπάρας; pf. ἀπῆρκα.
1. *to remove*: + acc., Ps 77.26.
2. *to lead away* from danger: τινα Ps 77.52 (|| ἀνάγω).
3. *to depart, move off*: abs. Ge 12.9, 46.1; ἀπὸ ἀνατολῶν 13.11; ἐκεῖθεν 26.21; ἐντεῦθεν 37.17; εἰς Σκηνάς 33.17; ἐπὶ τὰ ὄρη Na 3.18; ἐκ Ραμεσση εἰς Σοκχωθα Ex 12.37. **b**. caus.: + acc., troops, Jd 4.7 *L*, 1M 6.33.
Cf. ἄπαρσις, ἐξαίρω, ἔρχομαι, οἴχομαι, πορεύομαι.

ἀπαιτέω: fut. ἀπαιτήσω; aor.ptc.pass. ἀπαιτηθείς.
to demand to have returned or *repaid*: abs. Si 20.15 (:: δανίζω 'lend'); + acc. pers. (debtor), τὸν ἀδελφόν σου De 15.2, sim. Ne 5.7; + acc. rei (debt), τὸν ἀλλότριον ἀπαιτήσεις ὅσα ἂν ᾖ σοι παρ' αὐτῷ 'you shall demand the foreigner to repay what is owed by him to you' De 15.3; οἱ ἀπαιτοῦντες κυριεύουσιν ὑμῶν 'the creditors are lording it over you' Is 3.12; τὴν ῥάβδον τῶν ἀπαιτούντων.'the stick of ..' 9.4; || ἐπισπουδαστής 14.4; pass., *o* τὸ τῆς ψυχῆς .. χρέος 'the soul which was on loan' Wi 15.8. Cf. ἀπαίτησις.

ἀπαίτησις, εως. f.ʃ
v.n. of ἀπαιτέω: as dat. cogn., Ne 5.7; χειρός (leg. χρέος ?) 10.31; μὴ αὐτὸν θλίψῃς ἐν ~ει 'do not harass him ..' Si 34.31; ποιουμένου τὴν ~ιν 2M 4.28. Cf. ἀπαιτέω, ἐπαίτησις.

ἀπαλείφω: fut. ~λείψω; aor. ἀπήλειψα, impv. ἀπάλειψον, inf. ἀπαλεῖψαι; pf.ptc.pass. ἀπηλειμμένος.ʃ
to make traces of existence disappear, 'wipe off': *s* God and *o* pers. and other creatures, ἀπαλείψω τὸν ἄνθρωπον .. ἀπὸ προσώπου τῆς γῆς Ge 6.7 (|| ἐξαλείφω 7.4); pass. ἀπηλειμμένων Is 5.17 (Zgl ἀπειλημμένων < ἀπολαμβάνω), see Schleusner s.v. ἀπολαμβάνω; *o* vase, 4K 21.13; moral defects, ἀνομίας .. ἁμαρτίας Is 44.22; Da LXX 9.24, 3M 2.19. Cf. ἀλείφω, ἐξαλείφω, ἀφανίζω.

ἀπαλλάσσω: fut. ~λλάξω; aor. ἀπήλλαξα, pass. ἀπηλλάγην, inf. ~λλάξαι, impv.3s ~λλαξάτω, ptc.pass. ἀπαλλαγείς, subj.act. ἀπαλλάξω, pass. ἀπαλλαγῶ, opt.act.3s ἀπαλλάξαι; pf. ἀπήλλαχα.
1. *to do away with*: ἀπ' αὐτῶν 'some of them' Ex 19.22 (with partitive ἀπό and || ἀπόλλυμι vs. 24); + acc. pers., Is 10.7 (|| ἐξολεθρεύω), ^πόλιν^ Je 39.31; τὴν ψυχήν μου Jb 7.15. **b**. *to pronounce and treat as invalid*: μου τὴν ἀκακίαν 'my innocence' Jb 27.5, μου τὸ κρίμα 34.5.
2. *to keep away* from: + acc., ἀπὸ θανάτου τὰ ὀστᾶ μου 'my bones ..' Jb 7.15.
3. *to remove*: abs., Jb 9.12; + acc., ἀπ' ἐμοῦ τὴν ῥάβδον '.. the rod' 9.34.
4. intr. *to move away* from where one is at the moment: pass. in form, εἰς τὴν πόλιν 3M 6.30, εἰς μνῆμα 'into the grave' Jb 10.19; + gen., τῆς κακίας 'from the wickedness' Wi 12.2, 20; *to be released and spared*: τῶν βασάνων 'from the tortures' 4M 9.16, cf. ἀπαλλαχθῆνα[ι τῶν] κακῶν ἀνθρώπων

τὰς ἐπιβουλάς 'to get rid of the wicked people with their intrigues' *ND* 4.155 (l. 8).

Cf. ἀφανίζω.

ἀπαλλοτριόω: fut. ~τριώσω; aor. ἀπηλλοτρίωσα, pass. ἀπηλλοτριώθην, impv. ἀπαλλοτριώθητι, subj. ~τριωθῶ; pf.ptc.pass. ἀπηλλοτριωμένος.ʃ

1. tr. *to turn into an outsider*: + acc. and gen., σε τῶν ἰδίων σου '.. to your own folk' Si 11.34. **b**. *to excommunicate, ostracise*: τινα Jo 22.25. **c**. mid. *to become an outsider*: + dat., ἀπηλλοτριωμένοις .. τοῖς ἀδελφοῖς μου καὶ ξένος τοῖς υἱοῖς τῆς μητρός μου Ps 68.9 (ǁ ξένος).

2. *to render alien*: fig., ἀπηλλοτρίωσαν τὸν τόπον τοῦτον .. ἐθυμίασαν .. θεοῖς ἀλλοτρίοις '.. burned incense to alien gods' Je 19.4. **b**. mid. *to conduct oneself as alien* (ἀλλότριος), departing from the proper religious, moral standards: ἀπηλλοτριώθησαν εἰς αἰσχύνην '.. shamefully' Ho 9.10; *s* ἁμαρτωλοί Ps 57.4 (ǁ πλανάομαι); heart, τὰς καρδίας αὐτῶν τὰς ἀπηλλοτριωμένας ἀπ' ἐμοῦ Ez 14.5; + gen., τῶν πατριῶν δογμάτων 'from the ancestral teachings' 3M 1.3.

3. tr. *to alter*: *o* σημεῖα 'signs, tokens' Jb 21.29¶.

*__4__. mid./pass. *to break with the past and leave elsewhere*: ἐκ μέσου Βαβυλῶνος Je 27.8, cf. κινήθητε Aq and Sym ad loc.

Cf. ἀλλότριος.

ἀπαλλοτρίωσις, εως.ʃ

v.n. of ἀπαλλοτριόω: see s.v. **2 b**, ἡ ἀ. τῆς πορνείας σου Je 13.27. **b**. *treating as not belonging to one's own circle and rejecting*: Jb 31.3¶ (ǁ ἀπώλεια).

ἁπαλός, ή, όν.ʃ

1. *soft to the touch, tender*: *s* calf (μοσχάριον) to be slaughtered for meat, Ge 18.7 (καὶ καλόν); δύο ἐρίφους ~οὺς καὶ καλούς 'two tender and good goats' 27.9; γῆ Wi 15.7.

2. *easily injured*, 'delicate': *s* παιδία Ge 33.13; person and + τρυφερός, De 28.54, 56, Is 47.1. **b**. *of tender age*: *s* παιδάριον 'lad' 1C 22.5; + νέος 29.1.

Cf. ἁπαλότης, ἁπαλύνω, τρυφερός.

ἁπαλότης, τος. f.ʃ

1. *being soft to the touch*: τὰ ἄκρα τῆς ~τος 'the tender ends (of a cedar tree)' Ez 17.4; αἱ ῥίζαι τῆς ~τος 'the tender roots (of a vine)' 17.9.

2. *being liable easily to be injured*: + τρυφερότης, De 28.56.

Cf. ἁπαλός and τρυφερότης.

ἁπαλύνω: fut. ~νῶ; aor.pass. ἡπαλύνθην.ʃ

to soften: *o* flesh of baby's body, Jb 33.25; metaph., *o* God's words, Ps 54.22; human heart, 4K 22.19. Cf. ἁπαλός.

ἀπαμαυρόω: aor.pass. ἀπημαυρώθην.ʃ

to deprive of the ability to see: pass., τοῦ βλέπειν τοῖς ὀφθαλμοῖς Is 44.18. Cf. ἀμαυρόω, τυφλόω.

ἀπαμύνω.ʃ

to ward off: abs., 4M 14.19. Cf. ἀμύνω, ἐπαμύνω.

ἀπαναίνομαι: aor.mid. ἀπηνηνάμην.ʃ

to refuse: to do, + inf., Ps 76.3; to take notice of (acc. pers.), ἱκέτην θλιβόμενον 'a suppliant in distress' Si 4.4, τὴν συμβουλίαν μου 'my counsel' 6.23, νουθέτημα 'warning' Jb 5.17; ἔν τινι Si 41.4.

ἀπαναισχυντέω: aor. ἀπηναισχύντησα.ʃ

to behave shamelessly: *s* harlot, πρός τινα Je 3.3. Cf. αἰσχύνομαι.

ἀπανίστημι: fut.mid. ~ναστήσομαι.ʃ

to move away and shun: ἀπὸ λογισμῶν ἀσυνέτων 'unwise thoughts' Wi 1.5 (ǁ φεύγω).

ἀπαντάω: fut. ἀπαντήσω, mid. ἀπαντήσομαι; aor. ἀπήντησα, impv. ἀπάντησον, inf. ἀπαντῆσαι, ptc. ἀπαντήσας, subj. ἀπαντήσω; pf. ἀπήντηκα.

1. *to come face to face with*: + dat. pers., αὐτοῖς ὡς ἄρκος '.. like a bear' Ho 13.8; τί ἀπαντήσει ὑμῖν ἐπ' ἐσχάτων τῶν ἡμερῶν; 'what is going to confront you on the last of the days?' Ge 49.1; τῷ λόγῳ πρῶτος '(had a go at) it [= the medical treatment] as the first (patient)' Pr 26.18.

2. *to chance upon*: + dat. ἀπήντησεν τόπῳ 'came to a certain spot' Ge 28.11; Τί ταῦτά σοί ἐστιν, πᾶσαι αἱ παρεμβολαὶ αὗται, αἷς ἀπήντηκα; 'What are these to you, all these encampments I have come upon?' 33.8.

3. *to befall*: *s* disaster, + dat. pers., Jb 4.12, κακόν Si 36.1, ἀδικία 1K 28.10, ταῦτα 'these things' Je 13.22; illness, Si 34.22; ἐπὶ Αθουρ καὶ Νινευη To 14.4 𝔊[II].

4. *to present oneself*: "friends turn up at the right moment (εἰς καιρόν)" Si 40.23; 43.22; for a public meeting, 1E 9.4.

5. *to treat, deal with*: + dat. pers., χειρίστως 'worse' 2M 7.39; ὡς ἔστιν ἀγαθὸν ἐν ὀφθαλμοῖς σου 'as you see fit' Ju 3.4; τῷ προσώπῳ σου ἐν εἰρήνῃ 'receive you peaceably' 7.15, εἰρηνικῶς 1M 5.25; with harmful intent, ἐν ἐμοί Jd 15.12 A (B: συν~), εἴς τινα 1K 22.17, 18; + dat. pers., Jd 18.25 A (B: συν~). **b**. mid., forcibly: + dat. pers. and inf., Ru 1.16.

Cf. ἀπάντησις, συναντάω: LSG s.v.

ἀπαντή, ῆς. f. *

= ἀπάντησις **1**: εἰς ~ὴν αὐτοῦ Jd 4.22A (B: εἰς συνάντησιν αὐτῷ), 2K 10.5 (*L* εἰς ἀπάντησιν αὐτῶν); ἐξῆλθεν ἡ κραυγὴ εἰς ~ιν 'the wailing rang out to greet (her)' 3K 12.24[n].

ἀπάντημα, ατος. n.ʃ

that which befalls sbd and harms: 3K 5.18, Ec 9.11; healthwise, To 6.7. Cf. συνάντημα.

ἀπάντησις, εως. f.

1. *act of moving* towards sbd *in order to meet* him: + gen., διώκων εἰς ~ιν διώκοντος Je 28.31 (w. ref. to a relay of messengers), τινος 1K 25.32 (*L* τινι; ǁ

vs. 34 τινι, *L* τινος), To 11.16 $\mathfrak{G}^{II}$ ($\mathfrak{G}^{I}$ εἰς συνάντησίν τινι), Jd 11.31 A (B: εἰς συνάντησίν τινος), 11.34 A (B: εἰς ὑπάντησιν); + dat., Jer 48.6; to confront in a battle, 1E 1.23 (‖ συνάντησις 2C 35.20), 1M 12.41. **b**. *act of coming together as marriage partners at a wedding*: 3M 1.19.

2. *attitude shown* to other people: ἥμερος 'civil' 2M 12.30.

3. *act of perceiving and processing* incoming data: Es E 9 o'.

Cf. ἀπαντάω, ἀπαντή, συν~, ὑπάντησις.

ἀπάνωθεν.

I. adv. *from above*: from heaven, Jb 31.1¶ (‖ ἐξ ὑψίστων).

II. prep. + gen. *from .. high up*: ἀ. (*L* ἀπὸ; ‖ B vs. 21 ἐπάνωθεν) τοῦ τείχους '(shoot arrows) from the wall above' 2K 11.20; almost = ἀπό: ἀπέστη .. ἀ. αὐτοῦ 'had left him' Jd 16.20B (A: ἀπ' αὐτοῦ; *s* the Lord whose power had lain on him), 2K 20.21 (*L*: ἀπό), ἀ. τοῦ θυσιαστηρίου 3K 1.53 (*s* sbd who had been embracing the altar for protection).

Cf. ἄνωθεν, ἐπάνωθεν, ἀπό. Del. 4K 2.3,5, 10.31, Am 2.9 v.l.

ἅπαξ. adv.

once: ἔτι ἅ. 'yet once' Ge 18.32, Hg 2.6; πλὴν ἔτι τὸ ἅ. τοῦτο 'only once more now' Jd 16.28 A; ἅ. τοῦ ἐνιαυτοῦ 'once per year' Ex 30.10, Le 16.34; εἰς ἅ. 'once and for all' Nu 16.21, 45, Jo 10.42; ἅ. καὶ δίς 'once or twice' De 9.13, Ne 13.20, 1M 3.30; τὸ ἅ. 'for once' Jd 15.3; τὸ ἅ. τοῦτο 'this time round' 2K 17.7B; ὡς ἅ. καὶ ἅ. 'as in the past' Jd 16.20 B (A: καθὼς ἀεί), 20.30 B (A: καθὼς ..), 1K 3.10 B (*L* ὡς ἅ. καὶ δίς). Cf. δίς, πολλάκις, ποσάκις: Spicq 1.139f.

ἀπαραίτητος, ον.ʃ

1. *not to be affected by circumstances*: *s* ὑπομονή '(unshakable) patience' Si 20.32¶; ὄμβρος '(unmerciful) storm' Wi 16.16.

2. *unavoidable*: *s* ἔνδεια 'want' Wi 16.4.

ἀπαράλλακτος, ον.ʃ

unchangeable: *s* εὔνοια 'goodwill' Es 3.16 *L*.

ἀπαραλλάκτως. adv.ʃ

unchangeably: Es B 3 o'.

ἀπαραπόδιστος, ον.ʃ

unimpeded: *s* εὐστάθεια '(political) stability' 3M 6.28. Cf. ἀνεμπόδιστος.

ἀπαρασήμαντος, ον.ʃ*

unnoticed: *s* special day, 2M 15.36 (:: ἐπίσημος). Cf. ἄσημος, ἐπίσημος.

ἀπαρέσκω: aor. ἀπήρεσα.ʃ

to reject as unacceptable, disapprove of: + dat., Si 21.15. Cf. ἀρέσκω.

ἀπαρνέομαι: fut. ~νήσομαι.ʃ

to disown: + acc., τὰ χειροποίητα αὐτῶν 'their handmade (idols)' Is 31.7. Cf. ἀρνέομαι: LSG s.v.

ἄπαρσις, εως. f.ʃ

v.n. of ἀπαίρω, 'departure, setting out on a journey': τὰς ~εις αὐτῶν καὶ τοὺς σταθμοὺς αὐτῶν 'their departures and stages' Nu 33.2. Cf. ἀπαίρω.

ἀπαρτία, ας. f.ʃ

1. *baggage* carried by travellers, often troops: Ex 40.30, Ez 25.4, Ju 2.17; τῆς δυνάμεως 'of the army' 3.10; pl. Nu 10.12, Ju 7.18.

2. collectively, *people dependent on main characters on a move*: w. ref. to children of defeated troops, πᾶν ἀρσενικὸν ἐν πάσῃ τῇ ~ᾳ Nu 31.17; πᾶσαν τὴν ~αν τῶν γυναικῶν 31.18; ‖ livestock and other property, De 20.14.

Cf. ἀποσκευή.

ἀπαρχή, ῆς. f.

first-fruits, firstling: designated as cultic offerings, ἅλωνος καὶ ληνοῦ 'of a threshing floor and winepress' Ex 22.28 (‖ πρωτότοκος); τὰς ~ὰς τῶν πρωτογενημάτων τῆς γῆς 23.19; τῶν καρπῶν τῆς γῆς σου De 26.2; δράγμα ~ὴν τοῦ θερισμοῦ 'a sheaf, the first-fruits of your harvest' Le 23.10; σίτου καὶ οἴνου .. 'of grain and wine ..' 2C 31.5, τὰ ἐπιδέκατα καὶ αἱ ~αὶ ὑμῶν 'the tithes ..' Ma 3.8; to be offered to God, λάβετέ μοι ~άς Ex 25.2 (with the added nuance of "choice, excellent" – *BA* ad loc.); ὁλοκαυτώματα .. θυσιάσματα .. ~ὰς .. εὐχὰς .. ἑκούσια .. πρωτότοκα De 12.6; not necessarily agricultural or dairy products, Ex 25.3, 39.1 (metals); κυρίου Nu 31.29; τῶν χειρῶν De 12.11, Si 32.10; δομάτων Ez 20.31; χειλέων ref. to religious songs, PSol 15.3 (‖ καρπὸς χειλέων). Cf. ἄρχω, ἀπάρχομαι, πρωτότοκος.

ἀπάρχομαι: aor. ἀπηρξάμην.

to dedicate: + dat. pers. and acc. rei, 2C 35.7 (‖ δωρέομαι 1E 1.7); ***o*** offerings to God, τινι Pr 3.9. Cf. ἀπαρχή: Robert 1938.38-45.

ἅπας, ἅπασα, ἅπαν. Declined like πᾶς. Often with πᾶς as variant.

entire, whole: **a**. pseudo-attributive, ἅπας ὁ λαὸς ἅμα Ge 19.4, ἅπασαν τὴν βουλὴν αὐτῶν 'all of their design' Je 18.23; οὐ .. τὸν ἅπαντα χρόνον 'not .. at any point in time, never' De 22.19, 29, τῆς ἁπάσης κτίσεως 3M 2.7. **b**. *every, all*: + pl. noun, ἅπασι τοῖς Ἰουδαίοις .. ἅπαντας τοὺς λόγους Je 33.2; + dem. pron., ἅπαντες οὗτοι 4M 1.9. **c**. substantivally: n. ἅπαν Le 6.22, 8.27; art., pl. and + negating morpheme, τῶν ἁπάντων ἀπροσδεής 'in need of nothing' 3M 2.9.

Cf. πᾶς, ὅλος, σύμπας: Schmidt 4.543-6.

ἀπασπάζομαι: aor.ptc. ~σπασάμενος.ʃ *

to say farewell: To 10.12 $\mathfrak{G}^{II}$. Cf. ἀσπάζομαι.

ἀπατάω: fut. ἀπατήσω, pass. ἀπατηθήσομαι; aor. ἠπάτησα, inf. ἀπατῆσαι, impv. ἀπάτησον, pass. ἠπατήθην, ptc. ἀπατηθείς, subj. ἀπατήσω, pass. ἀπατηθῶ.

1. *to lead astray*: into committing a wrong deed and + acc. pers., ἡ ὄφις ἠπάτησέν με Ge 3.13; παρθένον ἀμνήστευτον 'an unbetrothed girl' Ex 22.16, καιρὸν ἀπατῆσαι αὐτήν 'a chance to seduce her' Ju 12.16; + inf., 2C 18.2. **b**. resulting in misjudgement or wrong decision: with misleading words or argument, ὑμᾶς Εζεκίας λόγοις Is 36.14; ἐν τῷ στόματι and ‖ ψεύδομαι Ps 77.36; *s* God, Μή σε ἀπατάτω ὁ θεός σου .. λέγων Is 37.10; Je 4.10; κάλλος 'good looks' Da Su 56 LXX (‖ TH ἐξαπατάω), τὸ πρόσωπόν μου εἰς ἀπώλειαν Ju 13.16; Je 29.9.

2. *to allow to have fun*: δὸς καὶ λάβε καὶ ἀπάτησον τὴν ψυχήν σου 'Give and take, and enjoy yourself' Si 14.16 (‖ ζητέω τρυφήν 'to seek pleasure'), sim. 30.23, cf. ἡ ἀπάτη τοῦ πλούτου Mk 4.19 (‖ ἐπιθυμίαι): Spicq 1.153-5.

Cf. ἀπάτησις, ἐξαπατάω, κεπφόω, πλανάω: Oepke, *TDNT* 1.384f.

ἀπάτη, ης. f.

deceit: Ju 9.3; ~ης ὄφις 'snake of ..' 4M 18.8.

ἀπάτησις, εως. f.ʃ.

v.n. of ἀπατάω, **2**: εἰς ~ιν ὀφθαλμῶν ἀνδρῶν 'to gratify the men's eyes' Ju 10.4.

ἀπαύγασμα, ατος. n.ʃ *

reflected light: *s* Wisdom, Wi 7.26. Cf. φῶς.

ἀπαυτομολέω: fut. ~μολήσω.ʃ

to flee in fear: abs. Pr 6.11a; + gen. rei, 4M 12.16. Cf. αὐτομολέω, φεύγω.

ἀπεῖδον: aor.subj. ~ίδω, ptc. ἀπ/φιδών; the aor. of ἀφοράω.ʃ.

to observe visually with exclusive attention: + acc. and ptc., 3M 6.8; + πρός τι 4M 17.23. **b**. *to find out by observation*: + interr. clause, ἕως οὗ ἀπίδῃ τί ἔσται τῇ πόλει'until he found out what would become of the city' Jn 4.5.

Cf. εἶδον, ἀποβλέπω, ἀφοράω.

ἀπείθεια, ας. f.

disobedience: 4M 8.9. Cf. ἀπειθέω.

ἀπειθέω: fut. ἀπειθήσω; aor. ἠπείθησα, subj. ἀπειθήσω, ptc. ~θήσας.

1. *to be recalcitrant, disobedient*: abs. ὁ υἱὸς ἡμῶν ἀπειθεῖ καὶ ἐρεθίζει De 21.20; opp. ἀκούω Ez 3.27; οἱ ἄρχοντες αὐτῶν ἀπειθοῦντες Ho 9.15; + dat. pers., πρόσεχε σεαυτῷ καὶ εἰσάκουε αὐτοῦ καὶ μὴ ἀπείθει αὐτῷ 'make sure that you hearken unto him, and do not disobey him' Ex 23.21; κυρίῳ Nu 11.20, 14.43; + acc., τὰ πρὸς κύριον 'in matters pertaining to the Lord' De 9.7, 24, Is 3.8 (on the syntax, see *BA* ad De 1.36 and Thibaut 85); + ἀντιλέγω Is 65.2; ‖ ἁμαρτάνω Ba 1.18; opp. εὐπειθέω 4M 8.5; + gen. rei, τῶν ἐντολῶν Jo 5.6, ῥημάτων αὐτοῦ Si 2.15, sim. 16.28; *ἔν τινι - ἐν νόμῳ 23.23; *πρός τινα Ba 1.19, cf. Helbing, *Kasus*. 204f.; *s* νῶτος '(hum.) back' Ne 9.29. **b**. *to put up resistance against*: + dat. rei, ^τοῖς προστάγμασιν^ Le 26.15 (:: ὑπακούω), τῷ ῥήματι κυρίου De 1.26, 9.23, φόβῳ κυρίου Si 1.28; πονηρίᾳ Is 7.16, τῇ πορείᾳ τῆς ὁδοῦ τοῦ λαοῦ τούτου 8.11.

2. *to refuse* to act in a certain way: 4K 5.16 (*L* οὐ θέλω); + inf. τοῦ προσέχειν 'to take notice' Zc 7.11, τοῦ κατασκηνῶσαι Ps 67.19; τοῦ εἰσακοῦσαι Ne 9.17*L*.

Cf. ἀπείθεια, ἀπειθής, εὐπειθέω, οὐ θέλω, πείθω, παρακούω.

ἀπειθής, ές.ʃ

recalcitrant, inclined to refuse compliance: *s* hum., υἱὸς ἀ. καὶ ἐρεθιστής 'disobedient and quarrelsome son' De 21.18 (cf. 21.20 ὁ υἱὸς ἡμῶν ~εῖ καὶ ἐρεθίζει); ἔθνος ἀ. Si 16.6 (‖ ἁμαρτωλός); βασιλεία 47.21; λαός Is 30.9; καρδία ἀνήκοος καὶ ἀ. Je 5.23; τὴν καρδίαν αὐτῶν ἔταξαν ~ῆ τοῦ μὴ εἰσακούειν τοῦ νόμου μου 'their mind was set defiantly not to listen to my law' Zc 7.12; subst., Nu 20.10. Cf. ἀπειθέω, ἀνήκοος.

ἀπεικάζω: aor. ἀπείκασα.ʃ

to make sth *in such a way that it resembles* sth else: + acc. and dat., ‖ ὁμοιόω Wi 13.13. Cf. ἀπείκασμα, ὁμοιόω.

ἀπείκασμα, ατος. n.ʃ

that which is made to resemble sth: *s* idols, ζῴων Wi 13.10. Cf. ἀπεικάζω, μίμημα.

ἀπειλέω: fut. ἀπειλήσω; aor.inf. ~λῆσαι, ptc. ~λήσας, pass. ~ληθῆναι.

to speak in threatening manner: abs. Si 19.17; + dat. pers., ἀπειλεῖ σοι τοῦ ἀποκτεῖναί σε Ge 27.42; θαλάσσῃ Na 1.4 (*s* God); pass. Nu 23.19, ***o*** God Ju 8.16. **b**. *to speak threateningly to* sbd (dat.) *by mentioning* sth (acc.) as a means of intimidation: θάνατον ἡμῖν 4M 9.5.

Cf. ἀπειλή, διαπειλέω.

ἀπειλή, ῆς. f.

threatening action, utterance or *attitude*: Hb 3.12 (‖ θυμός); τοῦ κυρίου 2K 22.16*L* (B: ἐπιτίμησις 'reprimand'); σάλος (q.v.) ~ῆς Zc 9.14; ἐπὶ ἁμαρτωλούς Od 12.5. Cf. ἀπειλέω: Drescher 1976.308-10.

I. **ἄπειμι**: fut. ἀπέσομαι.

1. *to be alien* to, *have nothing to do* with: + ἀπό τινος - Ισραηλ οὐκ ἄπεστιν ἀπ' ἐμοῦ Ho 5.3; Jb 6.13.

2. *to be away*, not affecting or harming: *s* μάχη καὶ ἔχθρα 'strife and hostility' Pr 25.10. **b**. *to be absent*: τῆς ἀπὸ σοῦ σοφίας ἀπούσης 'in the absence of your wisdom' Wi 9.6; ἀπόντες καὶ παρόντες 'whether absent or present' 11.11.

Cf. πάρειμι.

II. **ἄπειμι**: pres.ptc.sg.gen. ἀπιόντος; impf.3s. ἀπῄει.ʃ *to move away*: abs. Ex 33.8; πρός τινα 2M 12.1; in retreat, 13.22; εἰς τὸ ἱερόν 4M 4.8. Cf. ἀπέρχομαι, οἴχομαι.

ἀπεῖπον: aor.act. ἀπεῖπον, mid.2s ἀπείπω, 3s ἀπείπατο, impv.pl. ἀπείπασθε; pf.ptc.pass. ἀπειρημένος.ʃ

1. *to rescind* an agreement: abs. Zc 11.12.

2. *to forbid access to*: pass., + acc.rei, πρὸς τὰς ἀπειρημένας τροφάς 'to the forbidden foods' 4M 1.33 (|| ἀπαγορεύω vs. 34); + dat. pers., ἐκ τῶν ἐθνῶν, ὧν ἀπεῖπεν κύριος τοῖς υἱοῖς Ισραηλ 3K 11.2.

3. *to disown*: + acc., ἔργα χειρῶν σου Jb 10.3; + acc. pers., Wi 11.14, "(God's) grace was withdrawn from me" Jb 6.14 (|| ὑπερεῖδον).

Cf. ἀπαγορεύω.

ἀπειράγαθος, ον.ʃ*

unacquainted with goodness: ***s*** hum., Es E 4.

ἀπείργω.ʃ

to disallow having to do with (ἀπό τινος): τινα and ***s*** νόμος 2M 12.40.

I. ἄπειρος, ον.ʃ

boundless: ἐν γῇ ~ῳ καὶ ἀβάτῳ 'in a vast land with no end in sight and forbidding to journeymen' Je 2.6.

Cf. ἀπέραντος, πέρας.

II. ἄπειρος, ον.ʃ

inexperienced: νεώτερος ~ος 'inexperienced younger one' Nu 14.23; ***s*** shepherd Zc 11.15, warrior 1K 17.39*L*; idol, Wi 13.18. Cf. πεῖρα, πολύπειρος.

ἀπεκδίδωμι: pf.pass.2s ἀπεκδέδοσαι.ʃ

to give in marriage: || ἐκδίδωμι, + dat. pers. (masc.), To 3.8 𝔊II.

ἀπέκτασις, εως. f.ʃ *

act of spreading and expanding: νεφέλης 'of clouds' Jb 36.29¶. Cf. ἔκτασις.

ἀπελαύνω: fut. ἀπελάσω; aor ἀπήλασα, impv. ἀπέλασον.ʃ

to drive away: + acc., stranded sheep, ἀπὸ παντὸς τόπου Ez 34.12; 1Kg 6.8; fear, Wi 17.8. Cf. ἐλαύνω.

ἀπελέγχω.ʃ

to rebuke in public: abs., 2M 4.33; + acc. pers., 4M 2.11. Cf. ἐλέγχω.

ἀπελέκητος, ον.

unwrought: ***s*** building material, 3K 6.1[a] (stone), 10.11 (timber). Cf. πελεκάω, πελεκητός.

ἀπελευθερόω: aor.pass. ἀπηλευθερώθην.ʃ

to set free: ***o*** slave and pass., Le 19.20. Cf. ἐλευθερόω.

ἀπελπίζω: aor. ἀφήλπισα, subj. ~ελπίσω, ptc. ~ελπίσας; pf.ptc.pass. ~ηλπισμένος. On φ for π, see Thack. § 8.2-3.ʃ

1. *to lose* or *have lost hope*, 'despair': Si 22.21, 27.21; voluntarily, 'to give up hope,' 2M 9.18.

2. *to rob of hope*, 'drive to despair': + acc.pers. and pass., ἀπηλπισμένων σωτὴρ 'saviour of those in despair' Ju 9.11 (|| ἀπεγνωσμένος), φωνὴ ἀπηλπισμένων Es C 30; || πτωχός Is 29.19.

Cf. ἐλπίζω, ἀπογινώσκω: Spicq 1.156-8.

ἀπέναντι.

I. prep. *opposite, facing*: Ge 49.30; + gen. ἔναντι κυρίου ἀ. τοῦ θυσιαστηρίου Le 6.14; ἀ. τοῦ προσώπου τῆς σκηνῆς Nu 19.4; ἀ. τοῦ προσώπου μου ἐγένοντο 'they emerged before my face' Ho 7.2; ἐκάθισεν ἀ. τῆς πόλεως 'he sat facing the city' Jn 4.5; ἀ. τῶν ὀφθαλμῶν μου 'whilst I am watching' Is 1.16, ἀ. τοῦ ἡλίου 'in broad daylight' Nu 25.4, PSol 2.12 (κατέναντι .. vs. 11); metaph., "his outlook leaves no room for the fear of God" Ps 35.2. **b**. postposition and + gen.: τῆς κιβωτοῦ ἀ. Jo 9.2d (or poss. adv. and the gen. to be construed with the preceding ἔνθεν καὶ ἔνθεν 'on either side of the ark opposite').

II. adv. *in a space facing*: ἀ. ὄψῃ τὴν γῆν 'you shall see the land opposite you' De 32.52; Ez 40.2; ἔσται ἀ. 'will stand aloof (unconcerned)' or 'will assume a hostile attitude' Si 37.4.

Cf. ἐναντίος, κατέναντι: Shipp 87; Sollamo, *Semiprep*. 154f., 317-9.

ἀπενεόομαι: aor. ἀπηνεώθην.ʃ*

to become dumbfounded: Da 4.16 TH. Cf. κωφός.

ἀπένθητος, ον.ʃ

unmourned on death: ***s*** hum., 2M 5.10. Cf. πενθέω.

ἀπέραντος, ον.ʃ

infinite: ***s*** number, Jb 36.26¶; κτίσας τὴν ~ον καὶ ἀμέτρητον γῆν 'having created the boundless and immeasurable earth' 3M 2.9. Cf. I ἄπειρος, πέρας: Schmidt 4.513f.; Spicq 1.159.

ἀπερείδομαι: aor. ἀπηρεισάμην, subj. ἀπερείσωμαι.

1. *to position firmly*: 1E 1.39 (|| τίθημι 2C 36.7); + acc. rei, τὰς χεῖρας ἐπὶ τὸν τοῖχον 'the hands on to the wall' Am 5.19; Jd 6.37*AL* (B: τίθημι). **b**. *to position oneself firmly*, ref. to military operation, ἐπὶ Ιερουσαλημ Ez 24.2.

2. *to deposit*, ***o*** ^ἱερὰ σκεύη^ Da 1.2 LXX (TH εἰσφέρω), 1E 1.39.

Cf. τίθημι.

ἀπερικάθαρτος, ον.ʃ

unpurged, unpurified: ***s*** fruits, Le 19.23 (:: ἅγιος vs. 24). Cf. περικαθαρίζω, ἀκάθαρτος.

ἀπερίσπαστος, ον.ʃ

free from distractions and annoyances: ***s*** hum., Si 41.1. **b**. *having one's attention not distracted from*: + gen., Wi 16.11, cf. Scarpat 3.199 and Clemens Alex. *Stromata*, 7.64.2 ~ον τῆς πρὸς τὸν κύριον ἀγάπης.

Cf. περισπάω: Spicq 1.160f.

ἀπερίτμητος, ον.*
uncircumcised: *s* hum. male, ἀ. ἄρσην Ge 17.14; fig. καρδία Le 26.41, ἀλλογενὴς ἀ. καρδίᾳ .. καὶ ἀ. σαρκί Ez 44.9, σαρκὶ .. καρδίας Je 9.26; *s* τὰ ὦτα αὐτῶν 'their ears' 6.10; subst., Ex 12.48, ἀ. καὶ ἀκάθαρτος Is 52.1. Cf. *PCair. Zen.* 76 (3 c. BCE: non-Jewish instance). Cf. περιτέμνω.

ἀπέρχομαι: fut. ἀπελεύσομαι; aor. ἀπῆλθον, ptc. ἀπελθών, impv. ἄπελθε, 2pl. ἀπέλθατε, subj. ἀπέλθω, inf. ἀπελθεῖν; plpf. ἀπεληλύθειν.

1. *to depart* from one place to another: abs., Ge 14.11 (ǁ ἀποίχομαι); ǁ ἀποτρέχω Ex 3.21, 21.5 (see vs. 2), 7; εἰς γῆν Ge 3.19, Jb 7.21; εἰς τὴν ὁδόν Ge 19.2, cf. ὁδόν 2K 4.7; εἰς τὴν ἑαυτοῦ ὁδόν Ge 32.1; εἰς τὸν τόπον μου 30.25; Ἄπελθε ἀφ' ἡμῶν 'Leave us' 26.16, cf. Je 21.2; ἐκεῖθεν Ge 26.17; ὀπίσω αὐτοῦ 'following him' Jb 21.33¶; of death, πρὸς τοὺς πατέρας σου μετ' εἰρήνης Je 15.15, cf. πρὸ τοῦ με ἀπελθεῖν καὶ οὐκέτι μὴ ὑπάρξω 'before I depart and be no more around (in life)' Ps 38.14, see also Si 14.19; in order to perform a task, Ex 12.21; family reunion, εἰς τὴν πατριὰν αὐτοῦ Le 25.10 (ǁ ἐπανέρχομαι vs. 13); departure from the right path, De 17.3. **b**. no new destination indicated: Ex 19.13; *s* servant, ἐλεύθερος δωρεάν 'as a free man for no payment' 21.2; ἐν αἰχμαλωσίᾳ 'as captives' De 28.41; God, Nu 12.9; fig. of apostasy, Je 5.23.

2. *to depart and arrive* at another place: *s* possession once sold, εἰς τὴν κατέσχεσιν αὐτοῦ Le 25.27.

Cf. (ἀπ)οίχομαι, ὑπάγω, ἀποπηδάω, ἀποτρέχω.

ἀπευθανατίζω.ʃ*
to die a good death: 2M 6.28. Cf. ἀποθνήσκω.

ἀπεχθάνομαι: aor.ptc. ἀπεχθόμενος.ʃ
to incur hatred of: + dat. pers., 3M 2.30. Cf. ἀπέχθεια, μισέω.

ἀπέχθεια, ας.ʃ
hatred: 3M 4.1. Cf. ἀπεχθής, ἀπεχθάνομαι, μῖσος.

ἀπεχθής, ές.ʃ
1. *inclined towards intense hate*: *s* διάθεσις 'attitude' 2M 5.23.

2. *liable to arouse hatred*: *s* hum., 3M 3.4.

Cf. ἀπέχθεια, ἀπεχθῶς, μισητός, στυγνός: Schmidt 3.498f.

ἀπεχθῶς. adv.ʃ
adv. of ἀπεχθής: ἀ. ἔχω 'to be in hating mood' 3M 5.3; Wi 19.15.

ἀπέχω: fut.mid. ἀφέξομαι; aor. ἀπέσχον, impv.mid. ἀπόσχου; pf.act. ἀπέσχηκα, mid. ἀπέσχημαι.

1. *to be unavailable, be in short supply*: *s* needs for cultic services, ἀπέσχηκεν ἐξ οἴκου θεοῦ θυσία καὶ σπονδή 'sacrifices and libations have run out in the house of your God' Jl 1.13 (cf. ἐξῆρται θυσία καὶ σπονδὴ .. 1.9).

2. *to be at some distance*: οὐκ ἀπέσχον μακράν 'had not (yet) gone far' Ge 44.4; ἔθνος μακρὰν ἀπέχον 'a people far away' Jl 3.8; + gen., ἐὰν μακρότερον ἀπέχῃ σου ὁ τόπος De 12.21, Βαιθσούροις .. Ἱεροσολύμων ἀπέχοντι ὡσεὶ σταδίους πέντε 'Bethzur was .. about five leagues from J.' 2M 11.5, ὁδὸν ἡμερῶν δύο To 5.6 𝔊II; + ἀπό τινος – ἡ καρδία αὐτῶν πόρρω ἀπέχει ἀπ' ἐμοῦ 'their heart is miles apart from me' Is 29.13 (:: ἐγγίζω), ὁ τόπος ἦν μακρὰν ἀπέχων ἀπ' αὐτῶν 1M 8.4.

3. *to have received as one's due*: ***o*** silver, τὸ ἀργύριον ὑμῶν .. ἀπέχω Ge 43.23; τοὺς κλήρους ἡμῶν Nu 32.19. See Deissmann 1923.88-90; MM s.v. and Spicq 1.164-7.

4. mid. *to keep a distance*: οὐκ ἀπέχεσθε ἀπὸ τῶν ἀδικιῶν τῶν πατέρων ὑμῶν 'you do not keep away from the wrong-doings of your forefathers' Ma 3.7, ἀπόσχου ἀπὸ μάχης 'Move away from a quarrel' Si 28.8, ἀπὸ παντὸς πονηροῦ πράγματος Jb 1.1 (cf. ἔκκλινε ἀπὸ παντὸς κακοῦ Pr 3.7), ἀπὸ τῶν ἁγίων μου Ez 8.6, ἀπὸ γυναικός 1K 21.6 (abstinence; ǁ φυλάσσομαι vs. 5), cf. 4M 1.34; + gen., τοῦ τόπου 1E 6.26, τῶν ὁδῶν ἡμῶν ὡς ἀπὸ ἀκαθαρσιῶν Wi 2.16, σου [= God] PSol 8.32; + negated inf., Ἀπεσχήμεθα τοῦ μὴ ποιεῖν .. 'We have refrained from doing ..' Je 7.10; with no negator, εὖ ποιεῖν Pr 3.27; not coming to aid, ἕκαστος ἀπὸ τοῦ ἀδελφοῦ αὐτοῦ οὐκ ἀφέξεται 'nobody will stand aloof from his mate' Jl 2.8; out of fear and + ἀπό τινος (pers.) De 18.22; + acc., τὴν χεῖρα ἀπ' ἐμοῦ Jb 13.21. **b**. *to neglect doing* what one ought to do: + inf., Pr 23.13.

Cf. ἐκκλίνω.

ἀπηλιώτης, ου. m.
east: τῷ κλίτει τῷ πρὸς ~ην 'to the east side' Ex 27.11; πρὸς νότον καὶ ~ην 'to the south and east' Ju 7.18; ἀπὸ ~ου ἕως βορρᾶ 'from east to north' Ez 20.47. Cf. ἀνατολή: Popper 174-6; Deissmann 1895.139.

ἀπήμαντος, ον.
1. *unharmed*: *s* hum., 2M 12.25 (ǁ σῷος vs. 24).

2. *doing no harm*: *s* wisdom, ǁ φιλάγαθος Wi 7.22.

Cf. ἀσινής, σῷος.

ἀπηνής, ές.ʃ
not gentle but rough to senses: *s* din of falling stones, Wi 17.19; wild animals, ib. Cf. ἄγριος, σκληρός.

ἄπιος, ου. m.ʃ
pear-tree: 1C 14.14, 15.

ʾἈπις, ιδος. f.ʃ
Apis, a bull worshipped in Egypt: ǁ μόσχος Je 26.15.

ἀπιστέω.
to refuse to put trust in: + acc. rei, τὴν τοῦ θεοῦ δίκην 2M 8.13; + dat. pers., ^τῷ κυρίῳ^ Wi 1.2 (|| πειράζω); pass., ἐπί τινι (rei) 'over sth' 12.17. Cf. πιστεύω, ἀπιστία.

ἀπιστία, ας. f.ʃ
faithlessness: Wi 14.25. Cf. ἄπιστος.

ἄπιστος, ον.ʃ
1. *distrustful*: subst.m., hum., : : πιστός Pr 17.6a.
2. **not inspiring trust*: φύτευμα ~ον καὶ σπέρμα ~ον 'unpromising plant ..' Is 17.10.
Cf. πιστός, ἀπιστία.

ἄπλαστος, ον.ʃ
not fully formed and set: *s* human character, ἄνθρωπος ἄ. Ge 25.27. Cf. Shipp 87.

ἀπλάστως. adv.ʃ
**unsuspectingly* (?): 2K 15.11*L*.

ἄπλατος, ον.ʃ
immense in area: 3M 4.11.

ἀπληστεύομαι.ʃ
to be insatiable: Si 34.17, 37.29. Cf. ἄπληστος.

ἀπληστία, ας. f.ʃ
insatiability, greed: Si 37.30, 31. Cf. ἄπληστος.

ἄπληστος, ον.
insatiate, greedy: *s* ἀνήρ Si 34.20, ὀφθαλμός Pr 27.20 (|| οὐκ ἐμπίμπλαται), Ps 100.5. Cf. ἀπληστεύομαι.

ἁπλοσύνη, ης. f.ʃ
sincerity: Jb 21.23¶. Cf. ἁπλοῦς.

ἁπλότης, ητος. f.
1. *moral integrity*: Su 62[a] LXX; 1M 2.37.
2. *sincerity without duplicity*: καρδίας 'single-mindedness' Wi 1.1, 1C 29.17. **b.** τῇ ~τι αὐτῶν 'in their blissful ignorance' 2K 15.11.
Cf. ἁπλοῦς: Amstutz, esp. 21-41; Bauernfeind, *TDNT* 1.386f.

ἁπλοῦς, ῆ, οῦν.ʃ
entertaining no ulterior motive: acting out of pure compassion, *s* ψυχή of alms-giver, Pr 11.25. Cf. ἁπλότης, γνήσιος, νόθως, πολύπλοκος: BDAG s.v. and *ND* 5.77.

ἁπλόω: fut. ἁπλώσω.ʃ
to characterise by sincerity: + acc., τὴν ὁδόν σου Jb 22.3¶. Cf. ἁπλοῦς.

ἁπλῶς. adv.ʃ
in simple, not elaborate or devious manner: Pr 10.9 (|| πεποιθώς 'trusting'; opp. διαστρέφων 'perverse'), 2M 6.6, Wi 16.27. Cf. ἁπλοῦς, ἀδόλως, γνησίως.

ἄπνοος, ον.ʃ
incapable of breathing: *s* idols, Wi 15.5. Cf. πνοέω.

ἀπό. prep. w. gen.; ἀφ' foll. by a rough breathing.
1. *away from* ("removal or dissociation"): ἀτεκνωθῶ ἀ. τῶν δύο ὑμῶν 'I lost two of you, my children' Ge 27.45; ἐξηλείφθησαν ἀ. τῆς γῆς 'they were obliterated from the earth' 7.23; λάβε τὴν ψυχήν μου ἀπ' ἐμοῦ 'Take my life from me' Jn 4.3; Ἀποστρέψατε ἀ. τῶν ὁδῶν ὑμῶν τῶν πονηρῶν 'Turn away from your wicked ways' Zc 1.4; ἀπόσχου ἀπὸ μάχης 'Move away from a quarrel' Si 28.8; ἐπέστρεψεν ἀ. ἀδικίας 'he turned away from unlawfulness' Ma 2.6; ἀπόλωλεν ἀ. τῆς γῆς 'perished from the earth' Mi 7.2; συντρίψω τὴν ῥάβδον αὐτοῦ ἀπό σου 'I shall break his staff off you' Na 1.13; ἐξανέστη ἀ. τοῦ θρόνου αὐτοῦ καὶ περιείλατο τὴν στολὴν αὐτοῦ ἀφ' ἑαυτοῦ 'he got up from his throne and took off his garment' Jn 3.6; + μετοικίζομαι Ho 10.5; pregnantly, θάψω τὸν νεκρόν μου ἀπ' ἐμοῦ 'I shall bury my dead (to dispose of the corpse)' Ge 23.4 (|| ἀ. προσώπου μου vs. 8), οὐ τελευτήσει ἀ. πάντων τῶν τοῦ Ισραηλ υἱῶν ῥητόν 'none of the specified things shall die on the children of Israel' Ex 9.4, Σίγα ἀπ' ἐμοῦ 'Shut up, and leave me alone' To 10.7 𝔊[II]; ἁμάρτῃ ἔναντι κυρίου ἀκουσίως ἀ. τῶν προσταγμάτων κυρίου Le 4.2; ἐξεπόρνευσαν ἀ. τοῦ θεοῦ 'they fornicated, thus straying away from their God' Ho 4.12, sim. Ez 23.5, σκιάζειν αὐτῷ ἀ. τῶν κακῶν 'to provide him with a shade against his hardships' Jn 4.6; κοπάσει ἡ θάλασσα ἀφ' ἡμῶν 'the sea will become calm (and keep) away from us' 1.11; ἵνα μὴ ὑψωθῇ ἡ καρδία αὐτοῦ ἀ. τῶν ἀδελφῶν αὐτοῦ 'lest his heart should get puffed up, neglecting his brethren' De 17.20; ἄβατος ἀ. ἀνθρώπου καὶ κτήνους 'deserted by ..' Je 39.43, sim. 40.10, Ba 2.23. Cf. γενόμενοι ἀ. τῆς δεήσεως 'having come away from the prayer' 2M 10.27, γενόμενοι ἀ. τῆς χρείας 'having finished the business' 15.28 (see ἀπὸ δείπνου γένωνται 'having finished the dinner' Hdt 2.78), and see ἀπ' ἀγορᾶς Mk 7.5 and MM s.v ἀπό. **b.** + verbs of fleeing: φεύγω Ex 4.3, Ho 1.2; ἀ. τῆς φωνῆς αὐτῶν Nu 16.34; ἀ. πάσης ἁμαρτίας To 4.21 𝔊[II] (𝔊[I] ἀφίστημι). **c.** of waking up from sleep or intoxication: ἐξηγέρθη Ιακωβ ἀ. τοῦ ὕπνου Gn 28.16; ἐξένηψεν Νωε ἀ. τοῦ οἴνου 'N. awoke ..' 9.24; ἀ. τοῦ οἴνου γενηθῶσιν 1E 3.22. **d.** + verbs of withholding, preventing etc.: ἀνέξει ἀ. δρόσου 'will withhold dew' Hg 1.10; τὸ μνημεῖον αὐτοῦ κωλύσει ἀ. σοῦ 'will withhold his tomb from you' Ge 23.6, sim. 2K 13.13, 3K 21.7; οὐκ οἰκτιρήσω ἀπὸ διαφθορᾶς αὐτῶν 'I shall not pity (them so much as to be deterred) from destroying them' Je 13.14. **e.** + verbs of stopping an activity: κατέπαυσεν .. ἀ. πάντων τῶν ἔργων αὐτοῦ 'he rested from all his tasks' Ge 2.2, cf. 5.29, μὴ καταπαύσωμεν αὐτοὺς ἀ. τῶν ἔργων 'let's not ease pressure off their toil' Ex 5.5, and πρεσβῦται ἀ. πύλης κατέπαυσαν 'the elders stayed away

from (their duties) at the city gate' La 5.14; παῦσον τὴν γλῶσσάν σου ἀ. κακοῦ 'Stop your tongue from evil' Ps 33.14, παῦσαι ἀ. ὀργῆς 'leave your anger off' 36.8 (|| ἐγκαταλείπω). **f.** + verbs of fearing (mental distancing, shrinking or recoiling from): εὐλαβέομαι Zp 3.12; πτοέομαι Hb 3.16; φοβέομαι Mi 7.17, ἀ. τῶν λόγων Is 37.6. **g.** + verbs of concealing: οἱ κεκρυμμένοι ἀ. σοῦ De 7.20, παράκλησις κέκρυπται ἀπὸ ὀφθαλμῶν μου 'consolation is hidden from my eyes' Ho 13.14, ὁ στεναγμός μου ἀ. σοῦ οὐκ ἐκρύβη 'my groan did not go unnoticed by you' Ps 37.10, μὴ κρύψης ἀπ' ἐμοῦ ῥῆμα Je 45.14; 'Απεκρύβη ἡ ὁδός μου ἀ. τοῦ θεοῦ Is 40.27. **h.** + verbs of rescuing: ῥύομαι – ἀπὸ τῶν ποιμένων 'from the shepherds' Ex 2.19; διασῴζω – ἀπὸ τῶν ἐχθρῶν ὑμῶν Nu 10.9, cf. ὑπελείφθη ἀ. τῆς χαλάζης 'survived the hail' Ex 10.15. **i.** + adj.: ἀθῷος ἔσῃ ἀ. τῆς ἀρᾶς μου 'you will be exempt from my curse' Ge 24.41, ἀ. ἀνομίας οὐκ ἀθῷόν με πεποίηκας Jb 10.14; καθαρὸς ἔσῃ ἀ. τοῦ ὅρκου τούτου 'you shall not be bound by this oath' Ge 24.8, cf. MM s.v. ἀπό.

2. *starting from* ("origin or starting point"): of place, φωνὴ κραυγῆς ἀ. πύλης 'a noisy sound originating in a gate' Zp 1.10; ἀπὸ τούτων διεσπάρησαν ἐπὶ πᾶσαν τὴν γῆν 'from these they spread over the whole earth' Ge 9.19; "it is the Lord who has sent me to do all this work, ὅτι οὐκ ἀπ' ἐμαυτοῦ" Nu 16.28; ἀπ' ἐμαυτοῦ 'of my own accord' 4M 11.3, cf. "on my own, i.e. unaided" P.Oxy 3314, 9. **b.** of time, ἀ. τῆς ἡμέρας ταύτης καὶ ὑπεράνω 'from this day onwards' Hg 2.15, sim. 2.18; ἀ. τῆς σήμερον καὶ ἐπέκεινα 'from today onwards' 1M 10.30; ἀπὸ τοῦ νῦν καὶ εἰς τὸν ἅπαντα χρόνον 'from now on for ever' 11.36, ἀπὸ τοῦ νῦν καὶ εἰς τὸν αἰῶνα Is 59.21, .. ἕως τοῦ αἰῶνος Ps 112.2; ἀποθανοῦμαι ἀ. τοῦ νῦν 'I could die at any time henceforward' Ge 46.30; ἀ. μήτρας .. ἀ. γαστρός 'from the moment of their leaving their mother's womb (or: from the time when they were still inside ..) ..' Ps 57.4; ἀφ' ὅτε 2E 5.12. On ἀφ' οὗ and ἀφ' ἧς, see under ὅς **e**. **c.** ἀπὸ .. ἕως .. marking the two extreme ends of a scale: πᾶν τὸ ἀνάστημα .. ἀ. ἀνθρώπου ἕως κτήνους .. Ge 7.23, Le 27.28; εἰ ἀ. σπαρτίου ἕως σφαιρωτῆρος ὑποδήματος λήμψομαι 'I shall not take from a cord to a shoe thong' Ge 14.23; ἀ. νεανίσκου ἕως πρεσβυτέρου 'from young to old' 19.4; τὸ κλέμμα ἀπό τε ὄνου ἕως προβάτου 'the stolen object ranging from donkey to sheep' Ex 22.4; ἀ. μεγάλου αὐτῶν ἕως μικροῦ αὐτῶν Jn 3.5; ἀ. ἀνατολῶν ἡλίου ἕως δυσμῶν 'from where the sun rises to where it sets' Ma 1.11, cf. .. μέχρι δυσμῶν Ps 112.3; ἀπό τινος .. ἐπί τι Ez 43.14. **d.** indicates a point of time in the past: τὸν ἀπ' ἀρχῆς ποιήσαντα 'the one who made at the beginning' Is 22.11, καθὼς ἦσαν ἀπ' ἀρχῆς 'as they were previously' Ez 16.55; καθὼς ἀπ' ἀρχῆς 'as at the beginning' Zc 12.7, cf. Ne 12.46; ἀ. τοῦ αἰῶνος 'from the ancient times,' i.e. 'ever' (+ neg.) Jl 2.2, cf. Ge 6.4. Cf. ἐκ.

3. "source or collection" out of which selection is made: ἔλαβον ἑαυτοῖς γυναῖκας ἀ. πασῶν, ὧν ἐξελέξαντο Ge 6.2; λήμψεται Ιακωβ γυναῖκα ἀ. τῶν θυγατέρων τῆς γῆς ταύτης 27.46 (|| ἐκ 28.1); πάσῃ ψυχῇ τῇ ζώσῃ μεθ' ὑμῶν ἀ. ὀρνέων καὶ ἀ. κτηνῶν .. 'every living being .. (consisting) of birds ..' 9.10; ἀ. παντὸς γενήματος ἐμπορευσόμεθα 'we shall trade in every kind of produce' Am 8.6; 'Απὸ τῶν παιδίων τῶν 'Εβραίων τοῦτο 'This is one of the Hebrew children' Ex 2.6; ὀπίσω θεῶν ἑτέρων ἀ. τῶν θεῶν τῶν ἐθνῶν 'behind alien gods out of the gods of the nations' De 6.14; pregnant and partitive, ἅψηται .. ἀ. παντὸς τούτων 'touches any of these' Hg 2.13. Perh. belongs here ἔσεσθέ μοι λαὸς περιούσιος ἀπὸ πάντων τῶν ἐθνῶν '.. (distinct) from all the nations' Ex 19.5 in view of ἐξελέξατο κύριος .. γενέσθαι σε αὐτῷ λαὸν περιούσιον ἀπὸ πάντων τῶν ἐθνῶν τῶν ἐπὶ προσώπου τῆς γῆς 'the Lord chose ..' De 14.2, though possible Hebraism (מִן of comparison) is not to be precluded, cf. σὲ προείλατο κύριος .. εἶναι αὐτῷ λαὸν ~ον παρὰ πάντα τὰ ἔθνη '.. dearer than ..' 7.6. **b.** The so-called partitive genitive is replaced by ἀπό: φάγομαι ἀ. τῆς θήρας σου Ge 27.25 || φάγε τῆς θήρας μου vs. 19; λήμψῃ ἀ. τοῦ ὕδατος τοῦ ποταμοῦ Ex 4.9; λήμψῃ ἀ. τοῦ αἵματος τοῦ μόσχου 29.12 || λήμψῃ τοῦ αἵματος αὐτοῦ vs. 20; Ἄνθρωπος ἄνθρωπος τῶν υἱῶν Ισραηλ καὶ ἀ. τῶν υἱῶν τῶν προσηλύτων Le 17.8; ἀ. τοῦ σπέρματός σου οὐ δώσεις .. 18.21 || δῷ τοῦ σπέρματος αὐτοῦ 20.2; δώῃ σοι .. ἀ. τῆς δρόσου τοῦ οὐρανοῦ Ge 27.28; ἔλαβεν ἀ. τῶν λίθων τοῦ τόπου 28.11; τί εὗρες ἀ. πάντων τῶν σκευῶν τοῦ οἴκου σου; 31.37; ὄνους αἴροντας ἀ. πάντων ἀγαθῶν Αἰγύπτου 45.23; ἕν τι ἀπ' αὐτῶν 'one of them' Le 4.2; || ἐκ La 3.19. Cf. Εὐλογημένος ἀ. τέκνων, Ασηρ 'Blessed (being) among children, A.' De 33.24. Hardly partitive in ἔφαγον ἀ. πάντων 'I ate all of it' Ge 27.33. See ἐκ **3**.

4. *on account of, caused by*: οὐκ ἀποθανεῖται πᾶσα σὰρξ ἔτι ἀ. τοῦ ὕδατος τοῦ κατακλυσμοῦ '.. from the flood water' Ge 9.11; οὐκ ἀριθμηθήσεται ἀ. τοῦ πλήθους 'will not be able to be counted because of (their) multitude' 16.10, 32.12; ἀ. τοῦ γήρους 'due to his advanced age' 48.10; τῆς κραυγῆς αὐτῶν ἀκήκοα ἀ. τῶν ἐργοδιωκτῶν 'I have heard their call of distress caused by the taskmasters' Ex 3.7; διψῶντες .. ἀ. ἀνθρώπων ἀσεβῶν 'being made to thirst at the hands of infidels' Is 25.5; τὰ ὄρη ἐσαλεύθησαν ἀπ' αὐτοῦ 'the mountains shook at him' Na 1.5 (|| ἀ. προσώπου αὐτοῦ); ἀ. πλήθους ἡμερῶν 'on account of his old age' Zc 8.4; 8.10; ἐνέπεσεν εἰς ἀρρωστίαν ἀ. τῆς λύπης 'fell ill from sorrow' 1M 6.8; Jo 22.20. **b.** ἀφ' οὗ *because*: ἀφ' οὗ ἔντιμος ἐγένου 'since you became precious' Is 43.4. **c.** + inf., Is 50.2, 4M 6.7. **d.** source of knowledge: ἀπὸ τούτων 'on these grounds' Ep Je 28 (|| ὅθεν vss. 14, 22).

5. *through the agency of*: with a passive verb, αἱ πέτραι διεθρύβησαν ἀπ' αὐτοῦ 'the rocks were broken in pieces by him' Na 1.6 (v.l. ὑπ'); κατοικηθήσεται .. ἀ. πλήθους ἀνθρώπων 'will be populated by a multitude of people' Zc 2.4; συνετρίβη τὸ δεξιὸν μέρος ἀπ' αὐτῶν 'the right wing was crushed by them' 1M 9.15, sim. 8.6, 10.82; ἀνενεχθήσεται .. ἀπὸ λαοῦ Is 18.7 (|| ἐκ); 23.13; Ez 36.12 (|| ὑπό vs. 13). **b.** a pass. verb understood: ἀδικία ἀπ' αὐτῶν Ge 6.13. Cf. ἀποπέσοιν ἀ. τῶν ἐχθρῶν μου 'May I fall away at the hands of my enemies' Ps 7.5. **c.** virtually passive: ἀδοξήσεται ἀπὸ ἀνθρώπων τὸ εἶδός σου 'your appearance will be held in low esteem by men' Is 52.14; Ge 4.11, 2M 7.14.

6. *by means of*: ἀ. τοῦ αἵματος .. αὐτὸ καθαριεῖ 'with blood .. he shall cleanse it' Ex 30.10.

7. phrases: ἀπὸ προσώπου (q.v.) and ἀπὸ χειρός (q.v.).

8. indicates a position relative to a given point of reference: ἀ. ἀνατολῶν 'to the east' Ge 11.2, 13.11; ἀ. ἀνατολῶν ἡλίου De 4.41 (|| κατ' ἀνατολὰς ἡλίου 4.47, 49, Nu 21.11); ἀ. λιβός Nu 34.4; ἀ. ἀνατολῶν καὶ δυσμῶν καὶ βορρᾶ καὶ θαλάσσης Ps 106.3; ἀ. γωνίας τοῦ οἴκου 'at the corner of the house' 2C 4.10. Cf. ἐκ **10**.

*__9__. Hebraistically, *in excess of capacity* or *ability of*: τὸ ῥῆμα, ὃ ἂν σκληρὸν ᾖ ἀφ' ὑμῶν 'a matter which you are not able to cope with' De 1.17; ἀδυνατήσῃ ἀ. σοῦ ῥῆμα 'a matter is beyond your competence' 17.8; πολλὴ ἀπὸ σοῦ ἡ ὁδός 'the journey might turn out to be too much for you' 3K 19.7; στενὸς ἀφ' ἡμῶν 'too narrow for us' 4K 6.1. Cf. Soisalon-Soininen 1979.39f. **b.** = ἤ of comparison: ἀ. θαλάσσης ἐπληθύνθη 'became vaster than the sea' Si 24.29.

10. *worth*: ἤνεγκαν ἀσπίδα χρυσῆν ἀ. μνῶν χιλίων 'they brought a gold shield valued at 1.000 minas' 1M 15.18, cf. Johannessohn, *Kasus*, 35, n. 2.

*__11__. The noun governed by ἀπό may refer to an entity between which and the entity marking the subject of the clause or indicated by a direct object in it the relationship of equation is no longer applicable: ἐκλείψει ἡ βασιλεία .. ἀ. λαοῦ Is 7.8, ἐκόψαμεν αὐτὴν ἀ. ἔθνους 'we cut her down so that she was no longer a nation' Je 31.2, ἀπολεῖται Μωαβ ἀ. ὄχλου 31.42, cf. τὴν Ανα .. μετέστησεν τοῦ μὴ εἶναι ἡγουμένην 3K 15.13.

Cf. ἐκ, παρά, ὑπό: Johannessohn, *Präp.*, 271-83; LSG s.v.

ἀποβαίνω: fut. ~βήσομαι, ptc. ~βησόμενος; aor. ἀπέβην, subj. ~βῶ.

1. *to happen to, befall*: + dat. pers., τί τὸ ἀποβησόμενον αὐτῷ 'what was going to happen to him' Ex 2.4.

2. *to acquire the character of*, 'become': ἀποβήσεται ὑμῖν σοφία 'it will become unto you wisdom' Jb 13.5; 13.12; σοφὸς γένῃς .. κακὸς ἀποβῇς Pr 9.12, ἀπέβης μοι ἀνελεήμων [*pace* Zgl: ἐπέβης .. ἀνελεημόνως] 'you became to me merciless' Jb 30.21; + εἴς τι – εἰς σωτηρίαν 13.16, εἰς πάθος 30.31; ἀπέβησαν ὥσπερ ὄνοι 'became like asses' 24.5. Cf. s.v. γίνομαι **3**.

3. *to achieve its aim* (?): *s* φλόξ 'flame' Jb 18.5.

Cf. συμβαίνω, γίνομαι: Orlinsky 1937.

ἀποβάλλω: fut. ~βαλῶ; aor. ἀπέβαλον; pf.ptc. ~βεβληκώς.

1. *to reject* as unacceptable, undesirable: + acc., Συρίαν De 26.5; πατέρα ἢ μητέρα Pr 28.24; To 11.8 𝔊I.

2. *to remove from oneself*: 'to shed', τερέβινθος ἀποβεβληκυῖα τὰ φύλλα 'a terebinth which has shed its leaves' Is 1.30.

ἀποβάπτω: aor.ptc. ~βάψας.ʃ

to drain: abs., 2M 1.21.

ἀποβιάζομαι.ʃ

to treat with violence: + acc. pers., πένητα 'a poor man' Pr 22.22.

ἀποβλέπω: aor. ἀπέβλεψα.

1. *to turn exclusive attention* to: ἐπί + acc., ἐπὶ θεοὺς ἀλλοτρίους 'to alien gods' Ho 3.1; + εἰς– εἰς τὸν πένητα (|| ἐξετάζω 'examine') Ps 10.4, ditto w. hostile intent 9.29, cf. εἰς τὸ ὀψώνιον ἀποβλέπω 'I eagerly look forward to my pay' *PSI* 414, 9, ἀπέβλεπεν .. εἰς τὴν μισθαποδοσίαν Heb 11.26, and ἀφορῶντες .. εἰς Ἰησοῦν 12.2; + interr. clause, τί ποιήσει .. '(eager to find out) what He is going to do ..' PSol 3.5 (|| ἀποσκοπεύω).

2. *to turn attention away from, disregard*: abs. ἀποβλέποντες ἀποβλέπετε Ma 3.9. The v.l. at Ma 3.9 with εἰς αὐτά, the pron. apparently referring back to "the tithes", is prob. an attempt to interpret the verb in sense **1**, and Th 424 with ἐπί τινα μεγίστην ὠφέλειαν ἀφορῶντες is in the same spirit, whereas the Eth's use of the verb *ta'awwara* "he neglected, despised" attests to sense **2**. See Muraoka 1990a: 45.

3. *to divert attention elsewhere and move away*: ποῦ ἀπέβλεψεν; Ct 6.1 (|| ποῦ ἀπῆλθεν ..;).

Cf. βλέπω, ἀπεῖδον, ἀποσκοπεύω, ἀφοράω: Spicq 1.174f.

ἀπόβλημα, ατος. n.ʃ
that which is cast off as not needed: Wi 13.12,13.
ἀπογαλακτίζω: aor. ἀπεγαλάκτισα, subj. ~τίσω, pass. ~τίσθην; pf.ptc.pass. ~γεγαλακτισμένος.
to wean: ***s*** woman and + acc. pers. 1K 1.22, Ho 1.8; pass., ηὐξήθη τὸ παιδίον καὶ ἀπεγαλακτίσθη 'the child grew and became weaned' Ge 21.8; ἀπὸ γάλακτος 'off milk' Is 28.9 (ἀπεσπασμένος ἀπὸ μαστοῦ 'drawn away from the breast'). Cf. γάλα.
ἀπογεύομαι: aor.ptc. ~γευσάμενος.
to partake of: abs., 4M 10.1; + gen. rei, foods 4.26. Cf. γεύω, ἐσθίω.
ἀπογινώσκω: aor. ἀπέγνων; pf.ptc.pass. ἀπεγνωσμένος.ʃ
1. *to renounce*: + acc. pers., τοὺς ἀδελφοὺς αὐτοῦ De 33.9.
2. *to give up as hopeless*: Ju 9.11 (|| ἀσθενῶν, ἀπηλπισμένος); + acc., τὰ κατ' ἐμαυτόν 'my situation' 2M 9.22.
3. *to reject as of slight value*: pass., + ἀτιμόω, and ***o*** rei, 1K 15.9*L* (B: ἐξουδενόω).
ἀπόγονος, ον.
descended from: + gen., Ju 5.6, Wi 7.1; subst.m., τῶν γιγάντων 'of the giants' 2K 21.10*L* (= B 11). Cf. ἔκγονος, σπέρμα, φυτόν **2**.
ἀπογραφή, ῆς. f.
1. *act of registering oneself*: as inhabitant in a state, 3M 2.32.
2. *document which records data systematically and in an orderly fashion*: Ιερεμίας 2M 2.1, ἀληθείας Da 10.21 LXX.
Cf. ἀναγραφή, ἀπογράφω, γραφή.
ἀπογράφω: aor.inf.pass. ἀπογραφῆναι, ptc.mid. ~γραψάμενος, impv.mid. ~γραψαι.
1. mid. *to note down in writing*: for one's own use, + acc. rei, σεαυτῷ Pr 22.20 (|| ἐπι~ 7.3); on request and + τινα (his name), πρὸς αὐτούς Jd 8.14 A (B: ἔγραψε πρὸς αὐτὸν τὰ ὀνόματα ..).
2. mid. *to register oneself*: as inhabitant in a state, 3M 2.29. **b**. *to register* sbd else: abs. 3M 6.34; τινα 6.38.
Cf. γράφω, ἀπογραφή.
ἀποδείκνυμι: aor. ἀπέδειξα, subj. ~δείξω, inf. ~δεῖξαι, opt. ~δείξαιμι pass. ἀπεδείχθην, ptc.pass. ἀποδειχθείς; pf.ptc.pass. ~δεδειγμένος.
1. *to show forth* sbd or sth as so and so: + double acc., τὰ ὀστᾶ αὐτοῦ κενά Jb 33.21. **b**. mid. *to demonstrate through deed*: ἐν τῇ εὐνοίᾳ .. ἀποδεδειγμένος 'having proved himself through his goodwill' Es B 3; + dat. pers. and acc. rei, ἐμοὶ .. βεβαίαν πίστιν 'firm loyalty' 3M 5.31. **c**. by way of argument: dat. pers., ὑμῖν ὅτι .. Da 4.34c LXX, + acc. rei, ἀπό τινος 'on the basis of ..' 4M 1.8.
2. *to decide and arrange formally*: + dat. pers., To 3.8𝔊[II].
3. *to appoint and assign*: + double acc., αὐτὸν ἄρχοντα Da 2.48 LXX (TH: καθίστημι); pass., κριταί 'as judges' Su TH 5; κοράσια ἀποδεδειγμένα αὐτῇ 'servant-girls assigned to her' Es 2.10 o'; ἡμέραι ἀποδεδειγμέναι 'days appointed as festivals' 1M 10.34; ἐν τοῖς ἀποδεδειγμένοις τῷ δήμῳ βιβλίοις 'among the documents designated for the public' 14.23.
Cf. ἀπόδειξις, δείκνυμι, ἀποφαίνω: Schmidt 3.405f.
ἀπόδειξις, εως. f.ʃ
1. v.n. of ἀποδείκνυμι **1 a**: 3M 4.20.
2. *act of presenting orally and in public*: ἱστορίας 'of history' 4M 3.19.
ἀποδειροτομέω.ʃ
to cut off in order to slaughter: pass., + acc., κεφαλήν 4M 15.20. Cf. ἀφανίζω.
ἀποδεκατίζω: aor. ἀπεδεκάτισα.ʃ
= ἀποδεκατόω: To 1.7 𝔊[II].
ἀποδεκατόω: fut. ἀποδεκατώσω; aor.inf. ~δεκατῶσαι.* (ἀποδεκατεύω 'to dedicate a tithe [τῷ θεῷ] *SEG* 9.72.56, LSG)
to set apart a tenth of: δεκάτην or ἐπιδέκατον as cogn. obj., + gen. πάντων .. δεκάτην ἀποδεκατώσω αὐτά σοι Ge 28.22; δεκάτην ἀποδεκατώσεις παντὸς γεμήματος .. '.. of every produce ..' De 14.21; πᾶν τὸ ἐπιδέκατον τῶν γενημάτων 26.12; + acc. of a tenth of which is to be taken, σπέρματα .. ἀμπελῶνας 'seeds .. vineyards' 1K 8.15. Cf. δεκατόω, δέκατος, ἐπιδέκατον.
ἀποδεσμεύω.ʃ *
to bind fast: + acc., λίθον ἐν σφενδόνῃ 'a stone in a sling' Pr 26.8. Cf. δεσμεύω.
ἀπόδεσμος, ου. m.ʃ
sachet: στακτῆς 'of myrrh' Ct 1.13.
ἀποδέχομαι: aor. ἀπεδεξάμην, ptc.mid. ~δεξάμενος, pass. ~δεχθείς.
1. *to show understanding for*: + acc., the tears of a daughter about to marry, To 7.16 𝔊[I].
2. *to receive* guest *kindly*: τινα 2M 13.24; pass., 3.9.
3. *to approve of*: + acc., τὴν ἡμετέραν παρουσίαν 'our presence' 3M 3.17.
4. *to receive an oral report*: abs., 3M 5.27.
***5**. *to thank*: + τινα 2M 3.35, see Bickerman 1944. 31, n. 155.
Cf. δέχομαι: Cifoletti; Spicq 1.176f.
ἀποδέω: fut. ~δήσω; pf.ptc.pass. ~δεδεμένος.ʃ
to bind: + acc., πῦρ ἐν τῷ κόλπῳ 'fire in his bosom' Pr 6.27; wine-bottle, Jo 9.4. Cf. δέω.
ἀποδιαστέλλω: fut. ~στελῶ; pf.ptc.pass. ~διεσταλμένος.ʃ

1. *to divide and apportion*: + dat. pers. and acc. rei, τῷ λαῷ τούτῳ τὴν γῆν Jo 1.6.

2. *to distinguish*: as forbidden (ἀθέμιτος), *o* cultic offerings, 2M 6.5.

Cf. διαιρέω, μερίζω.

ἀποδιδράσκω: fut. ~δραμοῦμαι; 1aor. ἀπέδρασα, 2aor. ἀπέδραν / ἀπέδρων, impv. ἀπόδραθι, subj. ~δρῶ.

to run away: from danger or discomfort and *s* maltreated maidservant, ἀπὸ προσώπου αὐτῆς Ge 16.6; 27.43; ἀπ' αὐτῶν Ju 11.3; εἰς τὴν Μεσοποταμίαν εἰς τὸν οἶκον τοῦ πατρὸς τῆς μητρός σου Ge 28.2; πρός τινα 3K 2.39; κρυφῇ 'by stealth' Ge 31.26 (cf. λάθρᾳ 'secretly' *P.Oxy.Turner* 41.18), ἐν σπουδῇ 'fast' Da 10.7 LXX (TH φεύγω); with the superior's or master's consent, Le 25.41. **b**. *to depart and be no more present*: ἀπέδρα ὀδύνη καὶ λύπη καὶ στεναγμός 'pain, sorrow and sigh are gone' Is 35.10, 51.11, ὥσπερ σκιά 'as a shadow' Jb 14.2.

Cf. ἀναχωρέω, ἀποτρέχω, διαδιδράσκω, ἐκτοπίζω, φεύγω: Schmidt 1.524-34.

ἀποδίδωμι: pres.ptc.act. ~διδούς, opt.3s ~διδοῖ; fut.act. ~δώσω, inf. ~δώσειν, mid. ~δώσομαι, pass. ~δοθήσομαι; aor.act. ἀπέδωκα, impv. ἀπόδος, subj. ἀποδῶ, inf. ~δοῦναι, mid.indic. ἀπεδόμην, impv. ἀπόδου, inf. ~δόσθαι, subj. ἀποδῶμαι, 2sg ~δῷ, ptc. ~δόμενος, indic.pass. ἀπεδόθην, opt.3s ~δοθείη; pf.ptc. ~δεδωκώς, pass. ~δεδομένος.

I. act. *to pay* a vow: + acc., De 23.21; and dat. ὅσα εὐξάμην ἀποδώσω σοι 'all that I vowed I will pay you' Jn 2.10; ἀπόδος τὰς εὐχάς σου Na 1.15.

2. *to give* what is due to proper owner: + acc. and dat., ἀπόδος τὴν γυναῖκα τῷ ἀνθρώπῳ Ge 20.7; opp. δίδωμι, 20.14; ἀπόδος τὰς γυναῖκας μου καὶ τὰ παιδία, περὶ ὧν δεδούλευκά σοι '.. my wives and the kids for whom I have laboured for you' 30.26; αὐτὸν τῷ πατρὶ αὐτοῦ 37.22; τὴν σύνταξιν τῆς πλινθείας ἀποδώσετε 'you are going to deliver the quota of brick production' Ex 5.18, cf. Da 2.9 LXX; τὴν γῆν τῆς κληρονομίας Nu 36.2; pass. ἀπεδόθη μοι τὸ ἀργύριον Ge 42.28; *o* cultic offerings, Ex 22.30; vengeance, ἐκδίκησιν παρὰ κυρίου τῇ Μαδιαν Nu 31.3; ἀνταπόδομα La 3.64, εἰς κεφαλὴν αὐτῶν Si 17.23; κακὰ ἀντὶ ἀγαθῶν 1M 16.17, καταξίαν .. κρίσιν 'a fitting penalty' Es E 18 o' (*L* δίκη); + gen. pretii, but no acc., 1K 6.3 (*L* ὑπὲρ τῆς βασάνου δῶρα). **b**. *to give back* to owner: *o* what has been (wrongly) taken away, De 28.31, Da 4.30c LXX. **c**. ἀ. τινι λόγον 'to report to, be responsible to sbd' 2C 34.28, Da 6.2 TH.

3. *to make amends for* (a wrongdoing): + dat. (wronged party), Nu 5.7; + acc. (wrongdoing) and acc. (amount of compensation), πλημμέλειαν τὸ κεφάλαιον '.. the capital' Nu 5.7; ἀποδοῦναι αὐτῷ τὸ πλημμέλημα πρὸς αὐτόν 5.8 (αὐτόν = one who is paid on behalf of the wronged party?).

4. *to yield*: *o* agricultural produce, τὰ ξύλα τῶν πεδίων ἀποδώσει τὸν καρπὸν αὐτῶν Le 26.4 (‖ δίδωμι), σοι τὸ σπόρον '.. the crop' Jb 39.12.

5. *to make return for*, 'to requite': + acc. (deed) and ἐπί τινα– θεὸς ζηλωτὴς ἀποδιδοὺς ἁμαρτίας πατέρων ἐπὶ τέκνα Ex 20.5, De 5.9 (.. τοῖς μισοῦσίν με), sim. Nu 14.18; εἰς τὸν κόλπον αὐτῶν τὰς ἁμαρτίας αὐτῶν .. τὰ ἔργα αὐτῶν .. '.. into their lap' Is 65.6, sim. Je 39.18, Ps 78.12, κατὰ πρόσωπον αὐτοῦ 'to his face' To 14.10 𝔊[II]; + dat. pers. and *s* God, De 7.10, cf. Is 26.12, καθὰ ποιεῖ ἕκαστος αὐτῶν Jb 34.11, κατὰ τὰς ὁδοὺς αὐτοῦ Si 11.26; εἰς κεφαλάς PSol 2.24; pass. Jb 24.20. **b**. *to give* in return for: + acc. rei, κακὰ ἀντὶ ἀγαθῶν Pr 17.13.

6. *to deliver over* to an undesirable fate, 'to consign, relegate': κόνει τὰς κόμας 'the hair to dust' 3M 1.18. Cf. ἀπέδωκεν 'took his life in his own hands' 4M 12.19.

II. mid. *to sell*: + acc., εἰς Αἴγυπτον Ge 45.4; τὴν ἑαυτοῦ θυγατέρα οἰκέτιν 'one's own daughter as slave' Ex 21.7 (‖ πωλέω vs. 8); + acc. and dat. pers., ἀπόδου μοι .. τὰ πρωτοτόκιά σου 'Sell me your right of primogeniture' Ge 25.31; τὴν γῆν αὐτῶν τῷ Φαραω 47.20; τοὺς υἱοὺς Ισραηλ τοῖς υἱοῖς τῶν Ἑλλήνων Jl 3.6; + acc. and εἰς χεῖράς τινος– ἀποδώσομαι τοὺς υἱοὺς ὑμῶν .. εἰς χεῖρας υἱῶν Ιουδα .. εἰς αἰχμαλωσίαν εἰς ἔθνος μακρὰν ἀπέχον Jl 3.8; + cogn. obj., πρᾶσιν Le 25.14 (:: κτάομαι); + gen. of price, De 14.24, Pr 28.21; ἀπέδοντο ἀργυρίου δίκαιον 'they sold a righteous man for silver' Am 2.6; Jl 3.7, cf. ἄνευ τιμῆς 'without price' Ps 43.13.

2. *to withdraw care and favour from and to deliver over* in favour of one of the warring parties: + acc. pers., De 32.30 (‖ παραδίδωμι); ἐν χειρί τινος 'through the (hostile) agency of' Jd 2.14, 4.2, 10.7; εἰς χεῖράς τινος 3.8A (B: ἐν χειρί), 1K 12.9.

Cf. ἀνταποδίδωμι, ἀπόδομα, δίδωμι, πωλέω.

ἀποδιώκω: aor. ἀπεδίωξα.ʃ

to hunt down with hostile intent: τινα La 3.43. Cf. διώκω.

ἀποδοκιμάζω: fut. ~μῶ, pass. ~μασθήσομαι; aor. ἀπεδοκίμασα, subj. ~μάσω; pf.ptc.pass. ἀποδεδοκιμασμένος.

to reject as "Failed" after testing: *o* metal, Je 6.30, stone as building material Ps 117.22; + ἀπωθέω Je 7.29; hum., 14.19, 38.35. Cf. δοκιμάζω.

ἀπόδομα, ατος. n.*

that which is returned to owner: of Levites, Nu 8.11; cogn. obj. of ἀποδίδωμι 8.13, 16 (‖ δόμα 3.9). Cf. ἀποδίδωμι, δόμα, δίδωμι.

ἀπόδοσις, εως. f.ʃ
act of returning to owner (ἀποδίδωμι): as cogn. dat., De 24.13; pecuniary debt, Si 29.5. Cf. ἀποδίδωμι.

ἀποδοχεῖον, ου. n.ʃ
storage place: Si 1.17; ὑδάτων 'cistern' 39.17 (|| θημωνιά), 50.3.

ἀποδύρομαι.ʃ
to lament bitterly: τι 3M 4.12.
Cf. θρηνέω.

ἀποδύω: aor.mid. ἀπεδυσάμην.ʃ
mid. *to take off*: + acc. rei (one's own clothes), Es 6.16 *L* (:: ἐνδύομαι; || περιαιρέομαι vs. 15). Cf. ἐκ~, ἐνδύω, περιαιρέω.

ἀποθαυμάζω: aor. ἀπεθαύμασα, ptc.~μάσας.ʃ
to be astonished: abs., Da 4.16 LXX; + εἰς Si 40.7; marvelling, ἐπί τινι Si 11.13; τινα ἔν τινι 47.17. Cf. θαυμάζω.

ἀποθερίζω: aor. ἀπεθέρισα.ʃ
to make an end of, destroy: + acc. pers., τοὺς προφήτας Ho 6.5 (|| ἀποκτείνω). Cf. ἀποκτείνω and ἀφανίζω.

ἀποθήκη, ης. f.
1. *keeping temporarily unused*: καταλίπετε αὐτὸ εἰς ~ην ἕως πρωΐ 'Keep it stored away till the morning' Ex 16.23.
2. *that which is stored and kept unused*: αἱ ~αί σου καὶ τὰ ἐγκαταλείμματά σου '.. and your left-overs' De 28.5, 17.
3. *storeroom*: Je 27.26, Ez 28.13.
Cf. ἀποτίθημι.

ἀποθησαυρίζω.ʃ
to store away: abs., Si 3.4. Cf. θησαυρίζω.

ἀποθλίβω: aor. ἀπέθλιψα.ʃ
to press hard against sth: + acc., τὸν πόδα Βαλααμ 'B.'s leg (against the wall)' Nu 22.25. Cf. θλίβω.

ἀποθνῄσκω: fut. ~θανοῦμαι; aor. ἀπέθανον, inf. ~θανεῖν, ptc. ~θανών, impv.3s ~θανέτω, subj. ~θάνω, opt.3s ~θάνοι. For the pf. and plpf., θνῄσκω is used.
to come to the end of one's physical existence: *s* hum., οὐκ ἀποθανεῖται πᾶσα σὰρξ .. Ge 9.11; ἐν ἀδυναμίᾳ .. μετὰ κραυγῆς 'powerless, screaming' Am 2.2; opp. ζάω– ἵνα ζῶμεν καὶ μὴ ἀποθάνωμεν Ge 42.2; καλὸν ἀποθανεῖν με ἢ ζῆν Jn 4.8; Zc 11.9 (|| ἐκλείπω); θανάτῳ Ge 2.17, Nu 26.65; ἐν θανάτῳ Je 14.15 (|| συντελέομαι); ἀπὸ τοῦ ὕδατος 'of water' (as cause) Ge 9.11; and animals, 7.21, Le 11.39; as a result of divine punishment, Ge 38.11, Le 8.35, τῇ ἀσεβείᾳ αὐτοῦ 'on account of his ungodliness' Ez 33.9, ἐν τῇ ἀδικίᾳ 33.13. Cf. προσαπο~, συναπο~, θνῄσκω, θάνατος, ἀπευθανατίζω, ἐκλείπω, κάμνω, τελευτάω, ζάω: Schmidt 4.55-8.

ἀποικεσία, ας. f.
(enforced) *emigration*: υἱοὶ ~ας 2E 6.16 (ref. to returnees from the Babylonian exile); with υἱοί understood, 9.4. **b**. *community far away from home*: 4K 19.25, 24.15B.
Cf. ἀποικία, ἀποικίζω, ἀποικισμός.

ἀποικία, ας. f.
1. *act of being forced to move to a new dwelling-place*: Je 13.19, 30.3, Jd 18.30 B (A: μετοικεσία); κατὰ τὴν ~αν 'during the exile' 3M 6.10.
2. *group of individuals forcefully moved to a new dwelling-place*: ἁ. Ιουδα 'Judaean exiles' Je 35.4; 37.18 (|| αἰχμαλωσία); αἰχμαλωσία ~ας 2E 2.1.
Cf. ἀποικίζω, ἀποικεσία, ἀποικισμός.

ἀποικίζω: aor. ἀπῴκισα, inf. ἀποικίσαι, pass. ἀπῳκίσθην, ptc. ἀποικίσας, pass. ἀποικισθείς, inf. ~κισθῆναι; pf.pass. ἀπῴκισμαι.
to force to move to a new dwelling-place: + acc. pers., Je 24.1; ἐξ Ιερουσαλημ 34.17, εἰς Βαβυλῶνα 2E 5.12; pass., Je 13.19. **b**. mid. *to move away abandoning* one who or that which is to be cared for: δόξα Ισραηλ 1K 4.22.
Cf. ἀποικία, ἀποικισία, ἀποκισμός, ἐκβράζω, μεταγίνομαι, μεταίρω, μετοικίζω.

ἀποκισμός, οῦ. m.
v.n. of ἀποικίζω: Je 26.19; || θάνατος, ῥομφαία 50.11; γῆ ~οῦ Ba 2.30, 32. Cf. ἀποικίζω.

ἀποίχομαι: impf. ἀπῳχόμην. Impf. also seems to double as aor.ʃ#
to go away, quit: abs. Ge 14.12 (|| vs. 11 ἀπέρχομαι); ἀπ' αὐτοῦ '(took leave) of him' 26.31; ἐκ προσώπου μου 'from my presence' Ho 11.2; εἰς τὴν Μεσοποταμίαν Ge 28.6; εἰς τὰς κοίτας αὐτῶν 'into their bedrooms' Ju 13.1; πρὸς τὸν κύριον αὐτῶν 6.13. Cf. οἴχομαι, ἀπέρχομαι, ἀποχωρέω, πορεύομαι.

ἀποκαθαίρω: aor.subj.mid. ~καθάρωμαι,.ptc.pass. ~θαρθείς.
1. mid. *to cleanse oneself*: Jb 9.30 (|| ἀπολούομαι).
2. *to remove*: ἁμαρτίαν To 12.9𝔊II (𝔊I ~καθαρίζω); intr. pass., "cloud cleared away from the sky" Jb 7.9.
Cf. καθαίρω, ἀποκαθαρίζω, ἀπολούω.

ἀποκαθαρίζω: fut. ~ριῶ; aor.opt.3s ~ρίσαι.ʃ
1. *to remove* moral blemish: + acc., ἁμαρτίαν To 12.9𝔊I (𝔊II ~καθαίρω).
2. *to cleanse*: morally, ἑαυτόν Jb 25.4.
Cf. καθαρίζω, ἀποκαθαίρω.

ἀποκάθημαι.
to sit apart: *s* menstruating woman, Le 15.33; ἀκαθαρσίαν τῆς ἀποκαθημένης Ez 36.17, ἐν ἀκαθαρσίαις ἀποκαθημένη 22.10, ὕδωρ ἀποκαθημένης 'fluid [= urine?] of a menstruating woman' Is 30.22. Cf. κάθημαι.

ἀποκαθίστημι: fut. ~καταστήσω, pass. ~κατασταθήσομαι; impf.3pl ἀπεκαθίστων; 1aor. ἀπεκατέστησα, impv. ~κατάστησον, inf. ~καταστῆσαι, subj. ~καταστήσω, opt.3s ~καταστήσαι, pass. ἀπεκατεστάθην, inf. ~κατασταθῆναι, ptc. ~κατασταθείς; 2aor. ἀπεκατέστην, impv. ~κατάστηθι, 3s ~καταστήτω, subj. ~στῶ.

I. tr. (fut., 1aor.) **1.** *to restore* as in former condition: + acc. τὸν λίθον .. εἰς τὸν τόπον αὐτοῦ Ge 29.3; ἀποκαταστήσει σε ἐπὶ τὴν ἀρχιοινοχοΐαν σου 'he will restore you to your office of chief cupbearer' 40.13; ἐπὶ τὴν ἀρχὴν αὐτοῦ 'to his office' 40.21; καθὼς ἡμέρα γενέσεως αὐτῆς 'as on the day of her birth' Ho 2.3, καθὼς ἦσαν ἀπ' ἀρχῆς Ez 16.55, ὡς ἦν τὸ πρότερον 'as it was before' 1M 15.3; εἰς τοὺς οἴκους αὐτῶν 11.11; ἐν πύλαις κρίμα Am 5.15; "will redirect the heart of a father towards his son" Ma 4.5; τὴν ψυχήν μου Ps 34.17; + dat. com., τὴν κληρονομίαν μου ἐμοί Ps 15.5, σοι δίαιταν '.. dwelling' Jb 8.6, Da 4.33 LXX (pass.); pass., *o* Tyre, πάλιν .. εἰς τὸ ἀρχαῖον 'back to her former status' Is 23.16; fallen soldiers separated from their forefathers, 2M 12.39. **b.** into a fomer dwelling-place: Je 16.15, 23.8, 24.6. **c.** w. ref. to medical cure: abs., Jb 5.18 (reinforced by πάλιν). **d.** *to cause to return*: + acc. pers., εἰς Ιερουσαλημ 1E 5.2, ὑγιαίνοντας 'safe and sound' To 5.17 𝔊II, 'unharmed' 2M 11.25; pass., intr. *to return*: εἰς Ιερουσαλημ 1E 1.29.

*__2__. *to pay* what is due: ἀπεκατέστησεν Αβρααμ τῷ Εφρων τὸ ἀργύριον Ge 23.16.

*__3__. *to depose*: + acc. pers., τοῦ μὴ βασιλεύειν 1E 1.33.

*__4__. *to deploy*: pass., *o* elephants, ἐπὶ μέρος εὔκαιρον 'at a strategic position' 2M 15.20.

II. intr. (2aor.) *to return* to former condition: πάλιν ἀπεκατέστη εἰς τὴν χρόαν τῆς σαρκὸς αὐτοῦ 'it [= the hand] regained the colour of his flesh' Ex 4.7, cf. Le 13.16; ἀποκαταστήτω τὸ ὕδωρ .. ἀπεκατέστη τὸ ὕδωρ Ex. 14.26f.; a sword back into its sheath, Je 29.6.

Cf. ἵστημι: Oepke, *TDNT* 1.387f.; LSG s.v.

ἀποκαίω.ʃ

to consume by fire: pass., *o* hum. flesh of martyrs, 4M 15.20. Cf. καίω: LSG s.v.

ἀποκακέω: aor. ἀπεκάκησα.ʃ

to feel depressed: *s* ἡ ψυχὴ αὐτῆς Je 15.9. Cf. ἀθυμέω.

ἀποκάλυμμα, ατος. n.ʃ

that which has been disclosed: Jd 5.2B. Cf. ἀποκαλύπτω.

ἀποκαλύπτω: fut.act. ~καλύψω, pass. ~καλυφθήσομαι; aor. ἀπεκάλυψα, subj. ἀποκαλύψω, inf. ~καλύψαι, impv. ~κάλυψον, pass. ἀπεκαλύφθην, inf. ~λυφθῆναι, ptc. ~λυφθείς; pf.ptc.pass. ~κεκαλυμμένος.

1. *to uncover and bring into view* what is invisible (and ought to so remain): + acc. τὴν ἀσχημοσύνην σου 'your pudenda' to have sexual intercourse Ex 20.26, sim. Le 18.6, αἰσχύνην πατρός Ez 22.10; συγκάλυμμα τοῦ πατρὸς αὐτοῦ De 27.20 (by sleeping with one's stepmother and ‖ ἀνα~ 22.30); κεφαλήν 'unveil' Nu 5.18; τὰ θεμέλια αὐτῆς ἀποκαλύψω 'I shall reveal its foundations (, causing the building to collapse)' Mi 1.6, sim. Ez 13.14, and cf. Na 2.8; ἀποκαλύψω τὰ ὀπίσω σου ἐπὶ τὸ πρόσωπόν σου καὶ δείξω ἔθνεσιν τὴν αἰσχύνην σου Na 3.5, sim. Je 13.26; metaph., τὸν βραχίονα .. ἐνώπιον πάντων τῶν ἐθνῶν Is 52.10 (God's might), pass. and + dat. pers., 53.1.

2. *to remove a cover* or *a veil from*: + acc., τοὺς ὀφθαλμοὺς Βαλααμ Nu 22.31, sim. and pass. 24.4 (while in sleep); + acc. (veiled woman) Su 32 (:: κατακαλύπτω TH); *o* hum. ears (alw. ὠτίον, not οὖς exc. Ru 4.4), so as to enable communication, 2K 7.27 (‖ ἀνοίγω 1C 17.25), 1K 9.15, sim. 20.2 (*L* + acc. rei [that which is to be revealed]). **b.** *to remove* a cover: + acc., κατακάλυμμα Is 47.2.

3. *to bring into the open, make public knowledge of*: ἀποκαλύψω τὴν ἀκαθαρσίαν αὐτῆς ἐνώπιον τῶν ἐραστῶν αὐτῆς Ho 2.10, *o* βαθέα καὶ σκοτεινά 'profound and obstruse matters' Da 2.22 LXX, μάχην ὀνειδισμοῦ σου '(make) the quarrel (public), causing you disgrace' Si 6.9, μυστήρια 'secrets' Si 27.16, Da 2.28 TH (LXX φωτίζω); pass., *o* μυστήριον - τῷ Δανιηλ ἐν ὁράματι τῆς νυκτός Da 2.19 TH (LXX δηλόω), ἡ ἀδικία .. καὶ ἡ κακία Ho 7.1; + ἐπί and acc. (Hebraism?), 'to point to, draw attention to' La 2.14, 4.22; opp. κρύπτω Pr 11.13, *o* ἔλεγχος 'reproach' 27.5.

4. *to make known* what is unknown: παιδείαν ('instruction'?) πρὸς τοὺς δούλους αὐτοῦ Am 3.7, πρὸς κύριον τὴν ὁδόν σου Ps 36.5; τὴν δικαιοσύνην αὐτοῦ 97.2 (‖ γνωρίζω); + dat. pers. 1K 3.7B (*L* πρός τινα). **b.** mid.: *s* God, πρός τινα 1K 2.27.

Cf. ἀποκάλυμμα, ἀποκάλυψις, ἀνα~, ἐκκαλύπτω, δείκνυμι, δηλόω, μηνύω, φανερόω, φωτίζω, (ἀπο)κρύπτω: Spicq 2.248-50.

ἀποκάλυψις, εως.ʃ

act of uncovering, exposing: μητρός 'mother's (pudenda),' i.e. incest 1K 20.30; ἔργων Si 11.27 (upon death), μυστηρίου '(divulging) of secrets' 22.22, λόγων κρυφίων 'secret matters' 42.1. Cf. ἀποκαλύπτω.

ἀπόκειμαι.

to be kept reserved: + dat. pers., τὰ ἀποκείμενα αὐτῷ Ge 49.10; *s* reward, 2M 12.45, death 4M 8.11.

ἀποκενόω: fut. ~κενώσω; aor.subj.~κενώσω.ʃ
1. *to strip* sbd *bare of his possessions*: τινα Si 13.5.
2. idiom., τοὺς πόδας 'to empty the bowel, relieve oneself': Jd 3.24B.

ἀποκεντέω: aor. ἀπεκέντησα, impv. ~κέντησον.ʃ
to pierce through with a view to killing: + acc. pers., διὰ τῆς μήτρας αὐτῆς 'through her womb' Nu 25.8; Zp 1.10; with a sword, 1K 31.4 (*L* ἐκ~), Ez 21.11. Cf. ἀποκέντησις, (ἐκ)κεντέω, ἀποκτείνω.

ἀποκέντησις, εως. f.ʃ* (ἀποκεντέω: Hippocrates +)
v.n. of ἀποκεντέω: ἐξαγαγεῖν εἰς ~ιν τὰ τέκνα αὐτοῦ 'leading their children out to pierce through (with a sword)' Ho 9.13. Cf. ἀποκεντέω.

ἀποκεφαλίζω: aor. ἀπεκεφάλισα.ʃ
to behead: + acc. pers., 1K 31.9*L*, Ps 151.7.

ἀποκιδαρόω: fut. ~κιδαρώσω.*ʃ
to take the κίδαρις (q.v.) *off*: τὴν κεφαλήν Le 10.6, 21.10 (as a sign of mourning and ‖ rending one's garment).

ἀποκλαίω: fut. ~κλαύσομαι.ʃ
to weep aloud: + dat. pers., Je 31.32. **b.** mid. = act., Pr 26.24; ἐπί τινι Je 38.15.
Cf. κλαίω.

ἀποκλάω: aor. ἀπέκλασα.ʃ
to chop a small part of: + acc., ξύλον 4K 6.6*L* (B: ~κνίζω 'to nip off'). Cf. κλάω.

ἀπόκλεισμα, ατος. n.ʃ
guard-house: Je 36.26.

ἀποκλείω: fut. ~κλείσω, pass. ~κλεισθήσομαι; aor. ἀπέκλεισα, impv. ~κλεισον, inf.pass. ~κλεισθῆναι; pf.pass.3s ~κέκλεισται, ptc.pass. ~κεκλεισμένος.
1. *to shut*: abs., ἐφ' ἑαυτούς '(shut) themselves in' Jd 9.51A; + acc. rei, τὴν θύραν τοῦ οἴκου 'the door of the house' Ge 19.10, ἐπί τινα 4K 4.4*L* (B: κατά τινος); lions' mouths, Da 6.18 LXX (‖ ἐμφράσσω 22 TH).
2. *to shut in, confine*: + acc., εἰς ὀχύρωμα καὶ εἰς δεσμωτήριον 'into a fortress and prison' Is 24.22, εἰς τὴν χεῖρά μου 1K 17.46, sim. 24.19, 26.8; 2K 18.28.
3. *to shut out*: pass., Ps 67.31; to deny entry, + acc. pers., 1M 5.47, 10.75, Jd 20.48 A.
4. *to close off*: τὰ περὶ τὴν μήτραν αὐτῆς 'the area around her womb' 1K 1.5 (‖ vs. 6 συγκλείω); pass., *o* city (if not ὁ δοῦλός σου) 23.12.
Cf. κλείω, συγκλείω.

ἀποκλίνω: aor. ἀπέκλινα.ʃ
1. *to make change the direction of movement*: + acc. rei, εἰς οἶκον .. 2K 6.10B (*L* ἐκ~).
2. intr. *to change the direction of movement*: εἰς Μααφα 1M 5.35.
Cf. ἐκκλίνω.

ἀποκλύζω.ʃ
to wash clean by pouring a quantity of water over: *o* cultic vessels understood, 2C 4.6.

ἀποκνίζω: fut. ~κνίσω, ~κνιῶ; aor. ἀπέκνισα.
to sever and remove a part from the whole of, 'to nip off': *o* the head of a sacrificial animal, κεφαλήν Le 1.15; ἀπὸ τοῦ σφονδύλου 'off the neck' 5.8 (mistranslation in view of the foll. καὶ οὐ διελεῖ 'shall not sever [it]'); ξύλον 4K 6.6 (*L* ~κλάω 'to chop off'); καρδίας Ez 17.22; of pruning, 4M 1.29. Cf. ἀποκόπτω **1**.

ἀποκομίζω: fut.ptc. ~κομιῶν.ʃ
to carry back sth to where it belongs or its destination: abs., 2M 2.15; + acc., ἀγγελίαν 'message' Pr 26.16.

ἀποκόπτω: fut. ~κόψω; aor. ἀπέκοψα, pass. ~κόπην; pf.pass.ptc. ἀποκεκομμένος.
1. *to remove by severing and cutting off*, 'amputate': + acc. (of persons' limbs), χεῖρα De 25.12. **b.** pass. and + acc. pers. whose limbs are amputated: Jd 1.7; τὰ γεννητικά 'the genitalia' understood, θλαδίας καὶ ἀποκεκομμένος De 23.1.
2. *to stop conferring*: *o* ἔλεος Ps 76.9.
Cf. ἀφαιρέω, κόπτω, ἀποκνίζω.

ἀποκοσμέω: aor. ἀπεκόσμησα.ʃ
to remove from the world: + acc. pers., 2M 4.38. Cf. ἀφανίζω.

ἀπόκρημνος, ον.ʃ
precipitous: *s* rim, 2M 13.5. Cf. ἀπορρώξ.

ἀποκρίνομαι: fut. ~κριθήσομαι; aor. ἀπεκρίθην, impv. ~κρίθητι, ptc. ~κριθείς, subj. ~κριθῶ, inf. ~κριθῆναι, mid. ἀπεκρινάμην ("solemn" - Thack. 239), impv. ~κριναι; pf.3s ~κέκριται.
Often followed by καὶ εἶπον etc.
1. *to respond verbally* to a question: ἀπεκρίθησαν .. καὶ εἶπαν Οὔ 'they answered .. saying, "No"' Hg 2.12; ὁ δὲ ἀποκριθεὶς εἶπεν .. Ge 18.9; + dat. pers. τί ἀπεκρίθη αὐτῷ; Mi 6.5; and ἐπί τινι (subject-matter) Da 3.16 LXX (TH περί τινος). **b.** *to say in response, as a reaction* (in a dialogue): εἰρηνικὰ ἀποκριθῶσίν σοι De 20.11, sim. Si 4.8, κακά Pr 15.28; οὐδεὶς ἀπεκρίθη αὐτῷ λόγον Is 36.21; κρίσιν Jb 40.2¶; even introducing a question, Zc 4.11, 6.4. Cf. Ge 41.16, see **3**. **c.** *to act verbally in response to a circumstance*: ὠργίσθη .. ἀποκριθεὶς .. εἶπεν Ge 31.36; ἀπεκρίθη κύριος καὶ εἶπε τῷ λαῷ αὐτοῦ Jl 2.19; πρός με Hb 2.2 (.. καὶ εἶπε); even introducing a question, Da 3.14 TH (LXX συνιδών 'having realised'); 1K 14.28. Cf. Mk 9.6, 10.13f. **d.** ἀποκρίνομαι ῥῆμα, *to report*: + dat. pers., Nu 13.27, cf. 22.8. **e.** act. *to confront with questions*: τινα 1K 20.12. **f.** as a witness in a court, prob. Hebraism (< עָנָה): κατά τινος 'against sbd,' ἐνώπιον κυρίου 1K 12.3; 14.39, 2K 1.16.

2. *to respond to a request*: οἱ ἱερεῖς αὐτῆς μετὰ μισθοῦ ἀπεκρίνοντο 'her priests would respond in return for payment' Mi 3.11.

*3. *to meet the demand of* (?): ἀποκρίνεσθε αὐτά Zp 2.3 (cf. Th 289 and Tht PG 81.1845); ἄνευ θεοῦ οὐ ἀποκριθήσεται τὸ σωτήριον Φαραω 'without God the security of Ph. could not be vouchsafed (?)' Ge 41.16; + dat. rei, Pr 15.33 (?).

Cf. ἀπόκρισις, ἀνταποκρίνομαι, ὑπολαμβάνω: Shipp 88f.

ἀπόκρισις, εως. f.

reply to a question or query: ἀναγγειλάτωσαν ἡμῖν ~ιν 'let them announce a reply to us' De 1.22; πρὸς ταῦτα 'as regards these matters' Jb 40.4; ***o*** of δίδωμι Si 8.9. Cf. ἀποκρίνομαι.

ἀποκρυβή, ῆς. f.ʃ *

that which does not allow sth to be seen, 'cover': ἀ. προσώπου Jb 24.15¶. Cf. ἀποκρύπτω.

ἀποκρύπτω: fut.~κρύψω, pass. ~κρυβήσομαι; aor. ἀπέκρυψα, subj. ~κρύψω, ptc. ~κρύψας, pass. ἀπεκρύβην, subj. ~κρυβῶ, impv. ~κρύβηθι; pf.ptc.pass. ~κεκρυμμένος.

to remove and make invisible: + acc., μωρίαν ('stupidity') .. σοφίαν Si 41.15; ὀφθαλμούς '(to turn) a blind eye' 1K 12.3 *L*; pass., *to be* or *become invisible, unnoticeable*, Ἀπεκρύβη ἡ ὁδός μου ἀπὸ τοῦ θεοῦ Is 40.27; οὐ μὴ ἀποκρυβῇ ἀπὸ σοῦ οὐθέν 'nothing will remain unnoticed by you' Je 39.17; + acc., ἀποκρυβήσεται τὴν θέρμην αὐτοῦ 'will remain unaffected by its [sun's] heat' Ps 18.7; ***o*** hum., 2M 10.37; and + dat. pers., μυστήρια Wi 6.22; mid., + acc. rei, 7.13. Cf. (συναπο)κρύπτω, ἀποκρυβή, ~κρυφή, κρυφός, λανθάνω, ἀποκαλύπτω.

ἀποκρυφή, ῆς. f.*

hiding-place: νέφη ἀ. αὐτοῦ, καὶ οὐχ ὁρασθήσεται 'Clouds are his hiding-place, and it will remain invisible' Jb 22.14¶; dark place, Ps 17.12. Cf. ἀποκρύπτω.

ἀπόκρυφος, ον.

a. *kept out of sight* deliberately: ἔλαβε τοὺς θησαυροὺς τοὺς ~ους οὓς εὗρε 1M 1.23; θησαυροὺς ~ους ἀοράτους 'invisible, hidden treasures' Is 45.3. Hence safe from hostile agents or forces: ἐσκέπασέν με ἐν ~ῳ τῆς σκηνῆς αὐτοῦ Ps 26.5; κατακρύψεις .. ἐν ~ῳ τοῦ προσώπου σου ἀπὸ ταραχῆς ἀνθρώπων 30.21.

b. Not necessarily intentionally, *invisible, not easily observable*: ~α μέρη 'hidden parts' Si 23.19; ~ος ἀγρυπνία 'sleeplessness suffered unknown to others' 42.9; often subst. in n.pl. of esoteric, abstruse matters – ἀποκαλύπτων ἴχνη ~ων 'revealing the traces of hidden matters' 42.19; ‖ βαθέα 'profound matters' Da TH 2.22 (‖ ἐν τῷ σκότει and LXX σκοτεινός); ‖ αἴνιγμα Si 39.3; of future events, ὑπέδειξεν τὰ ἐσόμενα καὶ τὰ ~α πρὶν ἢ παραγενέσθαι αὐτά 'he showed things to come and what is (still) unobservable before it arrives' 48.25; ἐν ~ῳ 'in a secret place, hiding place' De 27.15, cf. Is 4.6 (‖ ἐν σκέπῃ); ἐνεδρεύει ἐν ~ῳ ὡς λέων 'lie in ambush ... like a lion' Ps 9.30; ἐν ~οις 'in secret, unnoticed', ἐν ~οις ἀποκτεῖναι ἀθῷον 'to murder an innocent person in secret' 9.29.

Cf. ἀποκρύπτω, ~κρυβή, ~κρυφή, κρυπτός, αἴνιγμα, βαθύς, λάθρᾳ, σκοτεινός.

ἀποκτείνω or ἀποκτέννω (the latter in Jo 8.24, 4Ki 17.25, 1E 4.7, Hb 1.17, Is 66.3, To 𝔊II 3.8*bis*, 6.14, 15, 14.11, Ps 77.34, 100.8, Da 2.13 TH; Wi 16.14): fut. ~κτενῶ; aor. ἀπέκτεινα, subj. ἀποκτείνω, ptc. ~κτείνας, impv. ἀπόκτεινον, inf. ~κτεῖναι, pass. ἀπεκτάνθην, inf. ~κτανθῆναι; pf. ἀπέκταγκα, inf.pass. ἀπεκτονῆσθαι.

to terminate physical life of, 'kill': abs., De 32.39 (:: ζῆν ποιέω); + acc. pers. and wrongfully, 'to murder,' Αβελ, ὃν ἀπέκτεινεν Καιν Ge 4.25; δίκαιον μετὰ ἀσεβοῦς 18.25; αὐτὴν ἐν δίψει Ho 2.3; ‖ ἀπόλλυμι Is 14.20, ‖ φονεύω Ps 93.6; ***o*** babes, Ho 9.16; Am 2.3 (‖ ἐξολεθρεύω), 4.10 (‖ ἐξαποστέλλω θάνατον); ἐν λιμῷ 'with lack of food' Ex 16.3; ἐν ῥομφαίᾳ 'with a sword' Am 4.10; fishes, Ps 104.29; ***s*** God as punishment, Ge 38.7 (‖ θανατόω vs. 10); Ex 4.23; human and not wrongfully, Ge 42.37; punishment, θανάτῳ ἀποκτενεῖτε αὐτούς Ex 22.19; μαχαίρᾳ 22.24; Le 20.4 (‖ ἀπόλλυμι vs. 3); opp. περιποιέω 'to keep alive' Ge 12.12, Nu 22.33, ζωγρέω 31.18. **b**. metaph. *to ruin*: τινα Pr 21.25.

Cf. ἀποθνήσκω, θανατόω, κατακτείνω, λιμοκτονέω, φονεύω, ἀφανίζω, ζωγρέω, περιποιέω.

ἀποκυέω: aor.ptc. ~κυήσας.ʃ

to give birth to: ***s*** mother, + acc., εὐσέβειαν 4M 15.17. Cf. κύω, γεννάω, (ἀπο)τίκτω: Spicq 1.178-80.

ἀποκυλίω: aor. ἀπεκύλισα, subj. ~κυλίσω.ʃ

to roll away to enable free access: + acc., λίθον ἀπὸ τοῦ στόματος τοῦ φρέατος 'a stone from the top of the well' Ge 29.3, 8, 10, cf. λίθους *AE* 1923.39 (4 c. BCE); τὸ σῶμα ἀπὸ τῆς στρωμνῆς 'the corpse from the bed' Ju 13.9.

ἀποκωλύω: aor. ἀπεκώλυσα, subj. ἀποωλύσω, inf. ~κωλῦσαι, ptc. ~κωλύσας.

1. *to withhold*: + acc., καὶ ἐπὶ νεκρῷ μὴ ἀποκωλύσῃς χάριν 'do not withhold kindness even from the dead' Si 7.33; ἀπό τινος (pers.) 3K 21.7; ‖ ὑφαιρέω Ec 2.10.

2. *to prevent* sbd from doing: + acc. pers. 1K 25.7; and μὴ inf., 25.33 (‖ simp. vs. 26) ‖ τοῦ inf., vs. 34; 1E 2.24 (‖ καταργέω 2E 4.21).

3. *to deprive* sbd *of freedom of movement by confining* him to a space: + acc. pers., εἰς οἶκον 'indoors' 1K 6.10 (*L* ἀποκλείω 'to shut up').

Cf. κωλύω, εἴργω, καταργέω.

ἀποκωφόω: fut.pass. ~κωφωθήσομαι; aor.subj.pass. ~κωφωθῶ. *

1. *to make incapable of hearing*, 'deafen': pass. τὰ ὦτα αὐτῶν ἀποκωφωθήσονται 'their ears will be deafened' Mi 7.16.

2. *to make incapable of speaking*: pass. τὴν γλῶσσάν σου συνδήσω, καὶ ἀποκωφωθήσῃ 'I shall tie your tongue, and you shall become dumb' Ez 3.26.

Cf. κωφός.

ἀπολακτίζω: aor. ἀπελάκτισα.ʃ

to kick: abs., De 32.15, symbolic of rebellion?

ἀπολαμβάνω: aor. ἀπέλαβον, ptc. ~λαβών; pf.ptc. ἀπειληφώς, pass. ἀπειλημμένος.ʃ

1. *to cause to move away* from where one presently is, 'lead aside': + acc. pers., 2M 4.46, κατ' ἰδίαν 'in private' 6.21.

2. *to receive, be given*: τοὺς κλήρους αὐτῶν 'their shares' Nu 34.14 (‖ λαμβάνω vs. 15), "pure and immortal souls from (παρὰ τοῦ) God" 4M 14.23.

3. *to capture from enemies in military operation*: + acc., places, 2M 8.6.

Cf. λαμβάνω.

ἀπόλαυσις, εως. f.ʃ

enjoyment: non-material, σωτηρίας 3M 7.16. Cf. ἀπολαύω, μετουσία, ὄνησις.

ἀπολαύω: aor. ἀπέλαυσα, subj. ~λαύσω.

to take delight in, enjoy: + gen., φιλίας 'love-making' Pr 7.18 (‖ ἔρως), 4M 8.5, ἡδέων 'pleasures (of meals)' 5.9, τοῦ βίου 16.18. Cf. ἀπόλαυσις: Spicq 1.181f.

ἀπολέγω: impf.mid. ἀπελεγόμην.ʃ

mid. *to give up on* (sth τι): τὴν ψυχήν Jn 4.8.

ἀπολείπω: fut. ~λείψω; 1aor.ptc. ~λείψας, 2aor. ἀπέλιπον, impv.3s. ~λιπέτω, ptc. ~λιπών, pass. ἀπελείφθην, subj. ~λειφθῶ, ptc. ~λειφθείς; pf.ptc.pass. ~λελειμμένος.ʃ

1. *to be wanting in*: + gen., τῆς πλινθείας τὸ καθῆκον τῇ ἡμέρᾳ 'in brick production in respect of the day's quota' Ex 5.19.

2. *to leave behind*: unfinished or unconsumed and + ἀπό τινος – οὐκ ἀπολείψετε ἀπὸ τῶν κρεῶν εἰς τὸ πρωΐ 'you shall not leave over any of the meat till the following morning' Le 22.30; Ex 12.10; unharmed, *o* hum., pass. Jd 9.5A (B: κατα~). **b**. as undesirable and break ties with: ἀπολιπέτω ὁ ἀσεβὴς τὰς ὁδοὺς αὐτοῦ Is 55.7, ἁμαρτίας Si 17.25; διδασκαλίαν Pr 2.17 (‖ ἐπιλανθάνω), ἀφροσύνην 'folly' 9.6. **c**. *to leave helpless*, 'abandon': σωτηρία αὐτοὺς ἀπολείψει Jb 11.20. **d**. not taking along with one and to take care of matters during one's temporary absence: Σίμωνα .. ἐν τῇ πόλει 1M 9.65, κρυπτῶς κατόπισθεν αὐτῶν 'secretly behind them' 10.79; pass. ἀπολελειμμένον ἐπὶ τῶν πραγμάτων 'left behind in charge of the matters' 2M 13.23; ἀπολειπόμενοι κατὰ τὴν πόλιν 'left behind throughout the city' 3M 1.17. **e**. as legacy: μνήμειον αἰώνιον τοῖς μετ' ἐμέ 'an eternal memory with my descendants' Wi 8.13; 10.8, 14.6. **f**. *to lose possession of*: καὶ ἐὰν ἀπολείπῃ σύνεσιν 'even if his mental faculty should fail him' Si 3.13.

3. *to cease* to do: + ptc., προφερόμενος 'persist in saying' 3M 1.12; + inf., Pr 19.27; + a negatived inf., τοῦ μηκέτι οἰκοδομεῖν 2C 16.5 (‖ καταπαύω and 3K 15.21 δια~).

4. mid. *to absent oneself*: 4K 10.21; τοῦ πορευθῆναι '(neglected) to go' 1K 30.21*L* (on the syntax, cf. τοῦ δείπνου .. ἀπολέλειπται 'was absent .. from the meal' Joseph. *Antiq*. 6.236).

Cf. ἀπο~, καταλείπω, καταπαύω, συντελέω: Spicq 1.183-5.

ἀπολεπίζω: fut. ~λεπίσω; aor. ἀπελέπισα.ʃ

tr. *to peel off*: abs. To 11.13 𝔊II; + acc., λευκώματα 'white films' 11.8 𝔊II. Cf. λεπίζω.

ἀπολήγω.ʃ

to cease to exist: *s* kingdom, Da 2.26 LXX. Cf. ἀπόλλυμι.

ἀπολιθόω: aor.impv.pass.3pl. ~λιθωθήτωσαν.ʃ

to turn into stone, 'petrify': pass., *o* hum., Ex 15.16. Cf. λίθος.

ἀπόλλυμι, ἀπολλύω: fut.act. (cf. Thack. 230) ἀπολῶ, ~λέσω, mid. ἀπολοῦμαι; 1aor. ἀπώλεσα, subj. ἀπολέσω, inf. ~λέσαι, ptc. ~λέσας, impv. ~λεσον; 2aor.mid. ἀπωλόμην, subj. ἀπόλωμαι, inf. ~λέσθαι, ptc. ~λόμενος, impv.3pl ~λέσθωσαν, opt.2s ~λοιο, 3s ~λοιτο, 3pl. ~λοιντο; 1pf.ptc. ἀπολωλεκώς; 2pf. ἀπόλωλα, ptc. ἀπολωλώς.

I. intr. (fut.mid., 2aor.mid, 2pf.). **1**. *to perish* as a result of violence or calamity: *s* individual human or group, ἀπόλωλεν Αἴγυπτος Ex 10.7; ἀπολοῦνται οἱ κατάλοιποι τῶν ἀλλοφύλων Am 1.8 (‖ ἐξολεθρεύω and ἐξαίρομαι), οἱ ἐχθροὶ Ιουδα Is 11.13; ὅπως διασώσῃ ὁ θεὸς ἡμᾶς καὶ μὴ ἀπολώμεθα Jn 1.6, sim. 1.14, 3.9; ἐκ τοῦ λαοῦ αὐτοῦ Ex 30.38; ἐκ μέσου τῆς συναγωγῆς Nu 16.33; + dat. cogn., ἀπωλείᾳ De 4.26, 30.18; a thing, οἶκοι ἐλεφάντινοι 'houses of ivory' Am 3.15, fortress Is 23.14; as a result of divine punishment, *s* sinners Ps 67.3 (‖ ἐκλείπω), 72.27 (‖ ἐξολεθρεύω), virtually Is 41.11 (+ ἔσονται ὡς οὐκ ὄντες).

2. *to be unavailable, be taken away* from (ἀπό / ἐκ): ἀπολεῖται φυγὴ ἐκ δρομέως 'a runner will be deprived of a chance to run away' Am 2.14, sim. Je 32.21; ἀπολεῖται βασιλεὺς ἐκ Γαζης Zc 9.5; ἀπόλωλε τρυγητὸς ἐξ ἀγροῦ Jl 1.11; ἡ βουλή σου ἀπώλετο Mi 4.9, ἐκ συνετῶν (‖ οἴχομαι) Je 30.1; οὐκ ἀπολεῖται νόμος ἀπὸ ἱερέως καὶ βουλὴ ἀπὸ συνετοῦ καὶ λόγος ἀπὸ προφήτου 18.18, sim. Ez

7.26. **b**. *not to be found, have vanished, have gone missing* (from [ἀπό / παρά] the sphere of): *s* piece of property gone missing, ἀπόληται παρ' αὐτοῦ καὶ εὕρῃς De 22.3; ἀπόλωλεν εὐλαβὴς ('the pious') ἀπὸ τῆς γῆς Mi 7.2; ὑπὸ νύκτα ἐγενήθη καὶ ὑπὸ νύκτα ἀπώλετο 'came into being overnight and vanished overnight' Jn 4.10; τοὺς ἀπολομένους Ισραηλ 'those of Is. who had gone missing' Is 11.12 (|| διεσπαρμένους 'scattered'), ἀπὸ προσώπου σου Ps 9.4; *s* καρδία 'courage, will to keep on going' Je 4.9; ὅρασις 'vision' Ez 12.22, ὕβρις 33.28, ἐλπίς 37.11; τὸ ὄνομα αὐτοῦ Ps 40.6; sheep, Je 27.6, Ps 118.176, τὸ ἀπολωλὸς ζητήσω Ez 34.16 (|| πλανάομαι); τὸ μνημόσυνον αὐτῶν 'their traces' Ps 9.7, sim. Jb 18.17 (|| οὐχ ὑπάρχω); ἡμέρα Jb 3.3. **c**. *to go astray*: ἐξ ὁδοῦ δικαίας '(to lose the sight of) the path of righteousness' Ps 2.12.

II. tr. (act.pres., fut., 1aor., 1pf.) *to destroy*: + acc. pers., ἀπόλλυμεν .. τὸν τόπον τοῦτον Ge 19.13; σῳζόμενον Nu 24.19; τοὺς κατοικοῦντας ἐπὶ τῆς γῆς ἀπὸ προσώπου ὑμῶν 33.55 (:: καταλείπω); σοφοὺς ἐκ τῆς Ἰδουμαίας Ob 8; ἀπολῶ ὑμᾶς ἐκ κατοικίας 'I shall wipe you out of existence' Zp 2.5; τὸν Ἀσσύριον 2.13; ἁμαρτωλούς Is 13.9; + acc. rei ὕβριν ἀνόμων Is 13.11, ἰσχύν 23.11 (economic); ^τὴν ψυχήν^ ἐκ τοῦ λαοῦ αὐτῆς Le 17.10 (|| ἐξολεθρεύω vs. 9); θηρία πονηρά 'harmful animals' Le 26.6; ἅρματα 'chariots' Mi 5.10; || ἐκτρίβω De 2.12, 28.24, 52; || ἀποκτείνω Is 14.20, || ἐξαίρω Je 18.7; + dat. cogn., ἀπωλείᾳ μεγάλῃ De 7.23 (|| ἐξολεθρεύω), 12.2; τὸ ὄνομα αὐτῶν 7.24, 12.3, Is 14.22; ***o*** mental vigour, Ec 7.7; divine punishment, Le 20.3; ἐν τάχει διὰ τὰ πονηρὰ ἐπιτηδεύματά σου 'with speed on account of your evil deeds' De 28.20 (|| ἐξολεθρεύω); πατάξω αὐτοὺς θανάτῳ καὶ ἀπολῶ αὐτούς Nu 14.12; *s* anger, Pr 15.1; by torture, 4M 8.9.

2. *to conceal and make inaccessible*, thus effectively destroying: + acc. rei, κατέκρυψεν αὐτὰ .. καὶ ἀπώλεσεν Ge 35.4; τὴν σοφίαν τῶν σοφῶν Is 29.14 ("from the wise": || κρύπτω).

3. *to take away*: + acc., ἀπ' αὐτῶν φωνὴν χαρᾶς Je 25.10, cf. 28.55 (|| δίδωμι εἰς ὄλεθρον).

4. *to lose*: + acc., ἀπολωλεκὸς βουλήν 'at their wits' end' De 32.28, καρδίαν Is 46.12, cf. μωρὸς καὶ ἀκάρδιος Je 5.21; ὑπομονήν 'patience' Si 2.14, αἰσχύνην 'a sense of shame' 29.14, φιλίαν 27.18; ***o*** money lent, 8.12, cf. 29.10; ὀφθαλμούς 'to become blind' To 7.7 𝔊[I] (𝔊[II] τυφλόομαι).

Cf. ἀπώλεια, ἐξ~, προσ~, συναπόλλυμι, ὄλλυμι, διό~, ἐξόλλυμι, ἀπολήγω, ἀφανίζω, ἐκλείπω, ἐξαναλίσκω, ἐξολεθρεύω, ὄλεθρος: Oepke, *TDNT* 1.394-6.

ἀπολογέομαι: fut. ~λογήσομαι; aor. ἀπελογησάμην.ʃ

to speak in defence of oneself: abs. Je 38.6, 2M 13.26; πρός τινα 'before sbd (= a judge or prosecutor) Je 12.1. Cf. ἀπολόγημα, ἀπολογία.

ἀπολόγημα, ατος.ʃ

that which is said in defence of sbd accused: Je 20.12. Cf. ἀπολογέομαι, ἀπολογία.

ἀπολογία, ας.ʃ

that which can be adduced in defence of sbd accused: Wi 6.10. Cf. ἀπολογέομαι, ἀπολόγημα.

ἀπόλοιπος, ον.

remaining over: subst.n., space, Ez 41.9 (976: λοιπά). Cf. κατάλοιπος, λοιπός.

ἀπολούω: aor.subj.mid. ~λούσωμαι.ʃ

mid. *to wash oneself clean*: χιόνι 'with snow' Jb 9.30 (|| ἀποκαθαίρω). Cf. λούω, ἀπονίπτω.

ἀπόλυσις, εως. f.ʃ

v.n. of ἀπολύω 'to allow to leave a meeting or work-place': 3M 6.37, 40.

ἀπολυτρόω: fut. ~ρώσω; pf.pass.ptc. ~λελυτρωμένος.ʃ

1. *to release from bondage on payment of ransom*: + acc. pers. (a maid), Ex 21.8.

2. mid. *to ransom*: Ὦ ἐπιφανὴς καὶ ἀπολελυτρωμένη 'O the distinguished and ransomed (city)!' Zp 3.2.

Cf. λυτρόομαι, ἀπολύτρωσις.

ἀπολύτρωσις, εως. f.ʃ

emancipation, liberation: fig., from paganism, ὁ χρόνος μου τῆς ~εως ἦλθεν Da LXX 4.30c. Cf. ἀπολυτρόω, λυτρόομαι, ἐκλύτρωσις: Büchsel, *TDNT* 4.351-6.

ἀπολύω: aor. ἀπέλυσα, inf. ~λῦσαι, ptc. ~λύσας, pass. ἀπελύθην, inf. ~λυθῆναι, subj. ~λυθῶ; pf. impv.pass.3pl. ~λελύσθωσαν.

I. act. *to make depart*, 'dismiss': + acc. pers., Ps 33.1, handmaid, Su 36 TH; troops, 1M 11.38; a bird out of your hand, Si 27.19; of divorce, 1E 9.36; ἐκ τοῦ παρόντος ἡμᾶς ζῆν 'from our present life' 2M 7.9 (by killing us).

2. *to allow to walk out from a court as innocent*: + acc. pers., τοὺς αἰτίους 'the guilty' Su 53 TH (:: κατακρίνω; LXX ἀφίημι); ἀπὸ τῶν κατηγορημένων '(acquitted) of the charges' 2M 4.47; ἀκατάγνωστοι 'innocent' ib.

3. *to release, set free*: from a bond, + gen.(abl.), τῆς ἀνάγκης To 3.6 𝔊[I] (𝔊[II] + ἀπό); from financial debt, 1M 10.43; τοῦ θανάτου 2M 6.21, τῆς ἁμαρτίας 12.45; so as to allow freedom of action, 10.21.

II. mid. *to depart*: εἰς τὴν παρεμβολήν 'into the encampment' Ex 33.11; Es 2.14 *L* (o'); of death, abs. Nu 20.29, To 3.6; ἄτεκνος 'childless' Ge 15.2, cf. ἀπὸ τῆς γῆς To 3.13; Soph. *Ant*. 1268 ἔθανες, ἀπελύθης; Anz 29.

Cf. ἀπέρχομαι.

ἀπομαίνομαι: aor.subj. ~μανῶ.ʃ
to become insane: Da 12.4 LXX. Cf. μαίνομαι.

ἀπομαρτυρέω: aor.ptc. ~ρήσας.ʃ
to bear witness to: τι 2M 12.30. Cf. μαρτυρέω.

ἀπομάσσω: aor.mid. ἀπεμαξάμην.ʃ
to wipe off: mid., + acc. (one's own) tears, To 7.17 𝔊II. Cf. ἐκμάσσω.

ἀπομάχομαι.ʃ
to fight enemies off: abs., 2M 12.27. Cf. μάχομαι.

ἀπομέμφομαι: fut. ~μέμψομαι.ʃ
to rebuke: + acc. pers., ἑαυτόν Jb 33.27. Cf. μέμφομαι.

ἀπομερίζω: fut. ~μεριῶ; aor.impv. ~μέρισον.ʃ
1. *to divide* into multiple parts: + acc., χώραν Da 11.39 LXX (TH διαιρέω).
2. *to accord as due to*: + acc. and dat., δόξαν τῇ .. ἡμέρᾳ (the sabbath) 2M 15.2.
Cf. μερίζω.

ἀπόμοιρα, ας. f.ʃ
portion dedicated to God: Ez 45.20 (967 ἀφαίρεμα).

ἀπόμυγμα, ατος. n.ʃ *
snuffed out wick (?): fig. of sth trivial, λύχνου 'of a lamp' 2K 23.6*L* (‖ ἄκανθα 'thorn').

ἀπονέμω: aor. ἀπένειμα, ptc. ~νείμας.ʃ
to allow to have a share of, apportion: + acc. and dat., ἀπένειμεν κύριος .. αὐτὰ [= heavenly bodies] πᾶσιν τοῖς ἔθνεσιν De 4.19; τοῖς τεμένεσι δωρεὰς ἀπονείμας 'having granted gifts to the shrines' 3M 1.7; 3.16. Cf. διανέμω, μερίζω: Schmidt 4.611f.

ἀπονίπτω: aor. ἀπένιψα, ptc.mid. ~νιψάμενος.ʃ
to wash clean: + acc., ἅρμα 'chariot' 3K 22.38; metaph., ἔξοδον 'way-out' Pr 30.12. **b**. mid. Pr 30.20. Cf. νίπτω, ἀπολούω.

ἀπονοέω: aor.pass. ἀπενοήθην; pf.inf.pass. ~νενοῆσθαι.ʃ
1. pass. *to lose all sense*: 1E 4.26.
2. pass. *to rebel*: 2M 13.23, cf. στασιάζω, συναφίστημι.

ἀπόνοια, ας. f.ʃ
madness: Si 22.13, 4M 12.3; *s* λόγοι 2M 6.29. Cf. μανία.

ἄπονος, ον.ʃ
causing no pain: *s* catapult as an instrument of torture, 4M 11.26. Cf. πόνος.

ἀποξαίνω.ʃ*
to cut off pieces of sbd's skin: pass., *o* hum., + acc., ταῖς μάστιξιν τὰς σάρκας 'pieces of his flesh with whips' 4M 6.6.

ἀποξενόω: aor.ptc. ~ξενώσας, subj.pass. ~ξενωθῶ.ʃ
to expel to a foreign land: + acc. pers., τῆς πατρίδος 'from homeland' 2M 5.9, ἐκ τῶν ἰδίων τόπων 'out of one's (familiar) places' Pr 27.8.

ἀποξηραίνω: fut.pass. ~ξηρανθήσομαι; aor. ἀπεξήρανα, ptc. ~ξηράνας, pass. ἀπεξηράνθην.
to make dry: + acc., ὕδωρ Jo 4.23, θάλασσαν ib., τὸν Ιορδάνην 5.1; pass. *to dry up, wither*: *s* a plant, Jn 4.7. Cf. ξηραίνω.

ἀποξύω: fut. ~ξύσω; aor.inf.pass. ~ξυσθῆναι; pf.ptc. pass. ἀπεξυσμένος.
to clean by scraping undesirable things *off*: + acc. rei, τὴν οἰκίαν ἔσωθεν κύκλῳ 'the inside of the house all round' Le 14.41; stones of house, 14.42.

ἀποπαρθενόω: aor.inf. ~θενῶσαι.ʃ
to deflower: + acc., νεάνιδα 'maiden' Si 20.4. Cf. παρθένος, διαπαρθενεύω.

ἀποπειράω.ʃ
mid. *to put to a test*: + gen. pers., Pr 16.29. Cf. πειράζω.

ἀποπεμπτόω: aor.impv.3pl. ~πεμπτωσάτωσαν.ʃ *
1. *to take a fifth part of*: + acc. πάντα τὰ γενήματα τῆς γῆς Αἰγύπτου Ge 41.34.
2. *to set apart a fifth part to give*: + dat. pers., Ge 47.26.
Cf. πέμπτος.

ἀποπηδάω: aor. ἀπεπήδησα, impv. ~πήδησον.
to walk away: + ἀπό τινος– ἀπ' ἐμοῦ Ho 7.13; Na 3.7 v.l.; *s* young lion, Ez 19.3. Cf. ἀπέρχομαι.

ἀποπιάζω: aor. ἀπεπίασα.ʃ
to squeeze so as to get the contents out: acc., πόκον 'fleece' Jd 6.38 A [B: ἐκ~] (to press dew out). Cf. πιάζω, ἐκπιάζω.

ἀποπίπτω: fut. ~πεσοῦμαι; aor.ptc. ~πεσών, impv. 3pl ~πεσάτωσαν, opt.1s ~πέσοιν (on which last, see Walters 23f.).ʃ
1. *to fall off*: *s* vegetation, τὰ ἀποπίπτοντα τοῦ θερισμοῦ 'gleanings' Le 19.9, 23.22; στάχυς ἀπὸ καλάμης αὐτόματος ἀποπεσών 'an ear of corn falling off of its own from the stalk' Jb 24.24; Ps 36.2, 89.6; φῶς τοῦ προσώπου μου Jb 29.24¶.
2. *to fail to achieve*: abs., κενός 'empty-handed' Ps 7.5; + gen., ἐπιτηδευμάτων 'aims' Ju 11.6; + ἀπό τινος – ἀπὸ τῶν διαβουλίων αὐτῶν 'their designs' Ps 5.11; PSol 4.16.
Cf. πίπτω.

ἀποπλανάω: fut. ~νήσω; aor. ἀπεπλάνησα, subj. pass. ~νηθῶ.
to lead astray: + acc., hum. in a figure of sheep, Je 27.6; morally, Pr 7.21(‖ ἐξοκέλλω); 'to deceive' Si 13.6, pass. 13.8, ταῖς διανοίαις 'in mind' 2M 2.2. Cf. ἀποπλάνησις, πλανάω, ἐξοκέλλω.

ἀποπλάνησις, εως. f.ʃ
wandering away from the truth: *s* τῆς καρδίας De 29.19; Si 31.12. Cf. ἀποπλανάω, πλανάω.

ἀποπλύνω: aor.impv.mid. ~πλυναι; pf. ἀπέπλυνα.ʃ
to wash in order to remove dirt: mid. ἐν νίτρῳ 'with washing powder' Je 2.22. **b**. *to wash* sth *off*:

mid. + acc., ἀπόπλυναι ἀπὸ κακίας τὴν καρδίαν σου Je 4.14. **c**. act.: *o* sbd else's dirt, ἀπέπλυνα τὸ αἷμά σου ἀπὸ σοῦ Ez 16.9 (|| λούω). Cf. πλύνω.

ἀποπνέω.ʃ
to breathe one's last: || ἀποψύχω 4M 15.18. Cf. ἀποψύχω, ψυχουλκέομαι.

ἀποπνίγω: aor.act. ἀπέπνιξα.ʃ
to kill by external compression of throat: λέων .. ἀπέπνιξε (*o* prey) Na 2.13; σου τοὺς ἄνδρας To 3.8 𝔊[I]. Cf. πνιγμός, περιπνίγω, ἄγχω, στραγγαλάω.

ἀποποιέομαι: fut. ~ποιήσομαι; aor. ἀπεποιησάμην, subj. ~ποιήσωμαι.
1. *to disown*: + acc. pers., τὸν ἄκακον 'the innocent' Jb 8.20, τὰ ἔργα τῶν χειρῶν σου 14.15; + acc. rei, μου τὸ κρίμα 40.8.
2. *to do away with*: + acc., φόβον Jb 15.4. Cf. ἀφανίζω.

ἀποπομπαῖος, α, ον.ʃ *
carrying away evil: subst., Le 16.8 (|| κύριος), 10. Cf. ἀποπομπή: *BA* ad Le 16.8.

ἀποπομπή, ῆς. f.ʃ *
act of getting rid of evil: Le 16.10. Cf. ἀποπομπαῖος.

ἀποπρατίζομαι.ʃ *
to sell: + acc. rei, To 1.7 𝔊[I]. Cf. πιπράσκω.

ἀποπτύω: aor.inf. ~πτύσαι.ʃ
to reject with contempt: τι 4M 3.18.

ἀπόπτωμα, ατος. n.ʃ
deviation from or *failure to meet the right* moral *norm*, 'lapse': Jd 20.6, 10 B (A: ἀφροσύνη).

ἀποργίζομαι: pf.3s ἀπώργισται.ʃ
to distance oneself in anger: *s* God, 2M 5.17. Cf. ὀργίζομαι.

ἀπορέω: fut. ~ρήσω, pass. ~ρηθήσομαι; aor.pass. ptc., ~ρηθείς.
1. mid. *to worry, not knowing what to do*: ἐφοβήθη .. σφόδρα καὶ ἠπορεῖτο Ge 32.7; τῇ ψυχῇ αὐτοῦ 1M 3.31.
2. pass. *to be in dire, severe difficulty*: *s* ἡ γῆ Is 24.19; hum. and financially, Le 25.47; militarily, 2M 8.20. **b**. act. w. same meaning: + inf., Wi 11.17. **c**. *to be left wanting*: food, *famished* (τροφῆς understood) — ἄρκος ἀπορουμένη 'a famished bear' Ho 13.8 (cf. Eth /reḫub/); also act. and + gen., φωτός Si 3.25¶ (|| ἀμοιρέω), ἄρτων 10.27; Pr 31.11.
Cf. ἀπορία, ἐξαπορέομαι, ἐνδέω **II**, ὑστερέω: Bons 2001.

ἀπορία, ας.ʃ
1. *physical discomfort*: divine punishment and || ψώρα 'itch' and ἴκτερος 'jaundice' Le 26.16; || πυρετός 'fever,' ῥῖγος 'chill' etc. De 28.22.
2. *helplessness with no way-out*: ἀ. στενὴ καὶ σκότος Is 8.22; ἀ. κατίσχυσέ με '.. overpowered me' Je 8.21; cogn. dat., ~ᾳ ἀπορηθήσεται ἡ γῆ Is 24.19; ἄνδρα ἐν ~ᾳ αὐτοῦ 'in his financial trouble' Si 4.2, sim. Pr 28.27; + ὀδύνη, πενία, and || λύπη PSol 4.15.
Cf. ἀπορέω, εὐπορία.

ἀπορρέω: fut. ~ρυήσομαι; aor. ἀπερρύην.ʃ
1. *to flow off*: *s* blood, 4M 10.8, *s* dew, ἐκ τοῦ πόκου 'from the fleece' Jd 6.38A.
2. *to leave one's position*: *s* troops, 1M 9.7; heart, ἐκ τοῦ τόπου αὐτῆς Jb 37.1¶; leaves of tree falling off, Ps 1.3.
Cf. ἀπόρροια, ῥέω.

ἀπορρήσσω: fut. ἀπορρήξω, pass. ~ραγήσομαι; aor. ἀπέρρηξα.
1. *to tear away*: + acc. and ἀπό τινος, Le 13.56; τὴν ψυχήν 'breathed his last' 4M 9.25 cf. ἀποψύχω.
2. intr. *to move with some speed and suddenly away from one's usual location*, 'break away': of young animals from their mothers, Jb 39.4¶.

ἀπόρρητος, ον.ʃ
unfit to be said in public: Si 13.22.

ἀπορρίπτω: fut. ἀπορρίψω, pass. ~ρριφήσομαι; aor.act. ἀπέρριψα, impv. ἀπόρριψον, subj. ~ρρίψω, inf. ~ρρίψαι, pass. ἀπερρίφην, subj. ~ρριφῶ; pf.pass. ἀπέρριμμαι, ptc.pass. ἀπερριμμένος.
to throw away: + acc., lit. εἰς βάθη καρδίας θαλάσσης 'into the depth of the midst of the sea' Jn 2.4; as useless, εἰς τὸ ὄρος Am 4.3, εἰς γῆν Je 22.26; μακρὰν ἀπ' ἐμοῦ 'far from me' PSol 2.4; *o* (acc.) sbd or sth contemptible, objectionable, burdensome etc., βδελύγματα Ez 20.8 (|| ἐγκαταλείπω), ἀφ' ἡμῶν ζυγόν '.. yoke' Ps 2.3; and + dat., τῷ κυνί 'to a dog' Ex 22.31; a staff, Zc 11.10, 14; thrown out of a house by thieves or robbers, Ob 5; of rejection of a leader, βασιλέα ὡς φρύγανον 'throw out a king like firewood' Ho 10.7, ἡγούμενοι λαοῦ μου ἀπορριφήσονται ἐκ τῶν οἰκίων τρυφῆς αὐτῶν Mi 2.9; of God, με ὀπίσω τοῦ σώματός σου Ez 23.35; *s* God, ὑμᾶς ἀπὸ προσώπου μου Je 7.15; ἀπὸ ἑαυτῶν πάσας τὰς ἀσεβείας ὑμῶν Ez 18.31; of forgiven sins, εἰς τὰ βάθη τῆς θαλάσσης πάσας τὰς ἁμαρτίας ὑμῶν Mi 7.19, cf. Is 38.17; τὰ ἐπιτηδεύματα 'the customary practices' Jd 2.19; *o* God, Ez 23.35; ἀπό τινος 'to be robbed of it' - ἀπὸ κληρονομίας 'of their inheritance' PSol 9.1. **b**. *to remove by force*, 'banish, expel': + acc. pers., "from this land to the land unfamiliar to you" Je 16.13, sim. 22.26, cf. 28.6, 29.5.
Cf. ῥίπτω, βάλλω.

ἀπόρροια, ας. f.ʃ
act of flowing out or *that which flows out*, 'emanation': τῆς δόξης Wi 7.25. Cf. ἀπορρέω.

ἀπορρώξ, ῶγος. m./f.ʃ
precipitous: *s* πέτρα 'rock' 2M 14.45. **b**. subst. *precipice, cliff*: 4M 14.16. Cf. ἀπόκρημνος.

ἀποσάσσω: aor. ἀπέσαξα.ʃ
to take a load off: τὰς καμήλους Ge 24.32.

ἀποσβέννυμι: fut.act. ~σβέσω, pass. ~σβεσθήσομαιʃ
1. *to put out* fire: "water will put out a blazing fire' Si 3.30; pass. "her lamp does not go out the whole night" Pr 31.18.
2. *to cause to cease to exist*: "it [= wind] destroys young green grass like fire" Si 43.21; pass. *to cease to exist*: ***s*** τὰ ὄρη καὶ οἱ βουνοὶ καὶ οἱ δρυμοί 'the mountains, valleys and thickets' Is 10.18 (as a result of bush-fire).
Cf. σβέννυμι, ἀφανίζω.

ἀποσείω.ʃ
mid. *to shake* one's own limb(s) away from sth: τὰς χεῖρας ἀποσειόμενος ἀπὸ δώρων 'refusing to accept bribes' Is 33.15. Cf. σείω, κινέω.

ἀποσημαίνω: aor.inf.pass. ~σημανθῆναι.ʃ
to notify: pass., + dat. pers., περί τινος 1E 6.6. Cf. γνωρίζω.

ἀποσιωπάω: aor. ἀπεσιώπησα.ʃ
to keep quiet: ***s*** hum., Je 45.27. Cf. σιωπάω.

ἀποσκαρίζω: aor. ἀπεσκάρισα.ʃ * (but ἀπα~ in Aristoph. and Menander).
to convulse, gasping for air, and give up the ghost: Jd 4.21.

ἀποσκεδάννυμι: fut. ~σκεδάσω.ʃ
to cast off as useless, wrong etc.: + acc. rei, 4M 5.10. Cf. ἀπορρίπτω.

ἀποσκευάζω: inf. ~σκευάσαι.ʃ
to strip of furniture: + acc., οἰκίαν Le 14.36. Cf. ἀποσκευή.

ἀποσκευή, ῆς. f.
1. *possessions carried by a person on a move*, 'baggage': Ge 14.12; μετὰ ~ῆς πολλῆς 15.14; ἀπήγαγεν πάντα τὰ ὑπάρχοντα αὐτοῦ καὶ τὴν ~ὴν αὐτοῦ 31.18; "sent the wives, children and also (!) the baggage (τὴν ἄλλην ~ήν) in advance" 2M 12.21.
2. collectively *infants*: πάντα τὰ σώματα αὐτῶν καὶ πᾶσαν τὴν ~ὴν αὐτῶν καὶ τὰς γυναῖκας αὐτῶν 'all their slaves and all their little ones ..' Ge 34.29; αἱ γυναῖκες αὐτῶν καὶ τὰ τέκνα αὐτῶν καὶ ἡ ἀ. αὐτῶν Nu 16.27; πᾶν ἀρσενικὸν .. [14]πλὴν τῶν γυναικῶν καὶ τῆς ~ῆς 'every male .. except the women and ..' De 20.13f.
3. collectively *family members other than male adults* such as wives and children: ἵνα ζῶμεν καὶ μὴ ἀποθάνωμεν καὶ ἡμεῖς καὶ σὺ καὶ ἡ ἀ. ἡμῶν Ge 43.8; οἱ ἄνδρες πλὴν τῆς ~ῆς 'the men exclusive of the dependants' Ex 12.37; Jd 18.21 *L* (A: πανοικία, B: τέκνα); ‖ κτήνη 'livestock' Nu 32.24; ἀ... γυναῖκες .. καὶ κτήνη 32.26; the only pl. in the LXX, 32.16 (‖ sg. at vs. 24).
Cf. ἀποσκευάζω, ἀπαρτία, ὑπάρχοντα (ptc.n.pl. of ὑπάρχω): Kießling 1927, esp. 243 w. ref. to wives and children of soldiers on military duties away from home; Holleaux; Lee 101-7; id. 1972; *BA* 2.39; O'Connor and Lee; LSG s.v.

ἀποσκηνόω: aor.ptc. ~σκηνώσας, subj. ~σκηνώσω.ʃ
to fold and shift a tent to live elsewhere*: Ge 13.18; metaph., ***s* God, ἀφ' ἡμῶν PSol 7.1. Cf. σκηνή.

ἀποσκληρύνω: impf. or aor. 3s ἀπεσκλήρυνεν.ʃ
to deal harshly with: + acc., τὰ τέκνα αὐτῆς Jb 39.16¶. Cf. σκληρύνω.

ἀποσκοπεύω: fut. ~σκοπεύσω; aor. ἀπεσκόπευσα.ʃ * (~σκοπέω: Soph. +)
to watch, look intently at: ἀποσκοπεύσω τοῦ ἰδεῖν τί λαλήσει ἐν ἐμοί Hb 2.1; + acc. pers., Ju 10.10, + εἴς τινα La 4.17f.; + interr. cl., ὅθεν ἥξει σωτηρία αὐτοῦ '(eager to find out) where his salvation is going to come from' PSol 3.5 (‖ ἀποβλέπω). Cf. σκοπεύω, ἀποσκοπέω, ἀποβλέπω.

ἀποσκοπέω.ʃ
to keep watch over: + acc., 1C 12.30. Cf. ἀποσκοπεύω.

ἀποσκορακίζω: fut. ~κιῶ; aor. ἀπεσκοράκισα, subj. ~κίσω.ʃ
1. *to send away* as not needed, 'discharge': + acc. (troops), 1M 11.55.
2. *to send to the devil*, 'curse': + acc. pers., Is 17.13 (‖ διώξω), Ps 26.9.

ἀποσκορκισμός, οῦ. m.ʃ
v.n. of ἀποσκορακίζω, sense **2**, 'execration': + ἐκδίκησις Is 66.15 (executed by God). Cf. Caird 1968.461; LSG s.v.

ἀποσκυθίζω.ʃ
to scalp in a Sythian fashion: 4M 10.7.

ἀποσοβέω.ʃ
to scare away: + acc. (predator), birds and beasts coming at human corpses, De 28.26, Je 7.33, sim. Si 22.20.

ἀπόσπασμα, ατος. n.ʃ
1. v.n. of ἀποσπάω, or an agent of such an action: Je 26.20.
2. *that which is removed by force*: w. ref. to a shock of hair cut off from a Nazirite's head (?), La 4.7.

ἀποσπάω: fut. ~σπάσω; aor.ptc. ~σπάσας, subj.pass. ~σπασθῶ, opt.3s ἀποσπάσοι; pf.ptc.pass. ἀπεσπασμένος.
1. tr. *to remove by force*: ***o*** testicles (understood), Le 22.24 (castrated animal, unfit for offering); hum., ἀπὸ τῆς γῆς αὐτῶν Je 12.14 (‖ ἐκβάλλω), babies from mother's breast, Is 28.9 (‖ ἀπογαλακτίζω).
2. *to cause to move away from where sbd is stationed*, 'lure away': + acc. pers. (enemy troops), ἀπὸ τῆς πόλεως Jo 8.6, cf. Jd 20.32A (ἐκ~).
3. intr. *to leave* a place *and move farther*: ἐκεῖθεν 2M 12.10.

Cf. ἀπόσπασμα, ἐκθλίβω, ἐκτομίας, θλαδίας.

ἀποστάζω.ʃ

to cause to fall drop by drop: + acc. rei, "your lips .. honey" Ct 4.11; "the mouth of the righteous .. wisdom" Pr 10.31; χάριτας 'charms' 10.32. **b**. intr.: "honey .. from the lips of .." Pr 5.3.

Cf. ἀποσταλάζω.

ἀποσταλάζω: fut. ~λάξω.ʃ *

to let drip: fig. and + acc. rei, ἀποσταλάξει τὰ ὄρη γλυκασμόν 'the mountains will drip sweet wine' Am 9.13, Jl 3.18. Cf. σταλάσσω, ἀποστάζω.

ἀποστασία, ας. f.ʃ

v.n. of ἀφίστημι, sense **II 5**: religious apostasy, Jo 22.22; Je 2.19 (ǁ κακία), 2C 29.19, 1M 2.15. Cf. ἀποστάσιον, ἀπόστασις, ἀποστατεῖν, ἀποστάτης, ἀποστάτις, ἀφίστημι: Schlier, *TDNT* 1.513.

ἀποστάσιον, ου. n.ʃ

act of parting with, severing of relationship with: βιβλίον ~ου 'a bill of divorce' to be written by a husband and handed to his wife, De 24.1, Is 50.1, Je 3.8. Cf. ἀφίστημι, ἀποστασία.

ἀπόστασις, εως. f.

acting in contravention of terms agreed, usually with a superior individual or group, 'rebellion, revolt': ~εις καὶ πολέμους .. συντελοῦντες 1E 2.23; ~εις καὶ φυγαδεῖαι '.. and defections' 2E 4.19. **b**. v.n. of ἀφίστημι **II 5**, 'apostasy': cogn. dat., ἀπέστη ~ει ἀπὸ κυρίου 2C 28.19; + ἁμαρτία 33.19. Cf. ἀφίστημι, ἀποστασία.

ἀποστατέω: aor.inf. ~τῆσαι, subj. ~τήσω.ʃ

to rebel: abs., 1M 11.1, Ne 6.6; + ἐπί τινα - ἐπὶ τὸν βασιλέα 2.19; acting against and dissociating oneself from (ἀπό) - ἀπὸ τῶν δικαιωμάτων σου Ps 118.118, ἀφ' ἡμῶν 1M 13.16, 2M 5.11. Cf. ἀφίστημι, ἀποστασία.

ἀποστάτης, ου. m.

one who renounces one's allegiance to sbd else: ἀπὸ τοῦ κυρίου Nu 14.9; political rebel, 1E 2.19; religious apostate, τῶν νόμων 2M 5.8, and adj. used, τέκνα ~άται Is 30.1; δράκων 'snake' Jb 26.13. Cf. ἀφίστημι, ἀποστασία.

ἀποστάτις, ιδος. f. of ~στάτης used adj.*

rebellious: *s* city, Ιερουσαλημ, τὴν πόλιν τὴν ~τιν καὶ πονηράν 1E 2.17; 2.19. Cf. ἀφίστημι, ἀποστασία.

ἀποστέλλω: fut. ἀποστελῶ, pass. ~σταλήσομαι; aor.act. ἀπέστειλα, impv. ἀπόστειλον, ptc. ~στείλας, inf. ~στεῖλαι, subj. ~στείλω, opt.3s. ~στείλαι, pass. ἀπεστάλην, subj. ἀποσταλῶ, impv. ~στάληθι, ptc. ~σταλείς; pf. ἀπέσταλκα, pass. ἀπέσταλμαι, ptc.pass. ἀπεσταλμένος; plpf. ἀπεστάλκειν.

1. *to send, dispatch* (+ acc.) on a mission: *o* pers., πρός τινα– ἀπέστειλε πρέσβεις πρὸς Βαλααμ 'he sent emissaries to B.' Nu 22.5; ἄγγελον αὐτοῦ ἔμπροσθέν σου Ge 24.7; ἐπί τινα Zc 2.8 (enemy), Da 10.11 LXX (TH πρός τινα); ἐπὶ ὕδωρ 'to fetch water' Je 14.3; + dat. (com.) pers. Ma 4.4; bird, Ge 8.7; με ἀπεστάλκατε ὧδε 45.8;. The mission is indicated by an inf.– ἀπέστειλεν τὸν κόρακα τοῦ ἰδεῖν εἰ κεκόπακεν τὸ ὕδωρ 'sent a raven to see whether the water had abated' Ge 8.7. Acc. obj. of emissary elided: Ge 20.2, 27.45, 31.4, Ex 9.27, Je 9.17; foll. by πρός τινα λέγων and dir. speech with a message, Ge 38.25. Often used of God sending a human agent; cf. "pour désigner l'envoi d'un subordonné par son supérieur," Bernand 1977.256, and Joh 13.16. **b**. *o* rei, τὸν χιτῶνα Ge 37.32; ἐν χειρὶ τοῦ ποιμένος 'by the shepherd' 38.20; ἀποστείλαι κύριος ἐπὶ σὲ τὴν εὐλογίαν De 28.8 (ǁ ἐξαποστείλαι .. τὴν ἔνδειαν '.. poverty' vs. 20); ὀργήν 'fury' Ex 15.7, εἰς κεφαλὰς αὐτῶν Ju 9.9; φόβον 'fear' Ex 23.27; πνεῦμα 'wind' 15.10; ἐφ' ὑμᾶς τὰ θηρία τὰ ἄγρια τῆς γῆς '.. wild beasts' Le 26.22 (divine punishment); πληγὰς .. νόσους De 29.22, πῦρ Ez 39.6, λύτρωσιν Ps 110.9, θάνατον Is 9.8, PSol 7.4; χεῖρα '(harmful) hand' Ex 9.15, Jb 1.11, but merely 'to put out' Ct 5.4; ἐπιστολήν 2E 4.11, ὑετόν 'rain' Ju 8.31, ἄρτον Ec 11.1. **c**. message: τοὺς λόγους κυρίου, οὓς ἀπέστειλεν 'the message of the Lord, which He had entrusted (him with)' Ex 4.28. **d**. w. double acc. (pers. and message): τὸν λόγον, ὃν ἂν ἀποστείλῃ σε κύριος πρὸς ἡμᾶς 'a message with which the Lord would send you to us' Je 49.5; 49.21, 50.1. **e**. with no obj., *to send a message over*: De 19.12, 1E 1.43; ἐπί τινα 'to send for, summon' Su 29[2] TH (LXX: καλέω). **f**. *to designate* or *mention through a messenger*: περὶ πάντων, ὧν ἀπέσταλκας πρός με 'about all that you have indicated..' 3K 5.22, ἕως τοῦ τόπου, οὗ ἐὰν ἀποστείλῃς πρός με 'up to the point which you might indicate..' 5.23. **g**. ǁ ἐξαποστέλλω: cp. Nu 13.3, 4 and 17, De 28.8 and 20.

2. *to take leave of and send away* (+ acc.): ἀπέστειλεν αὐτήν Ge 21.14; pass. 44.3.

3. *to send away as unwanted*: + acc. pers., με ἀφ' ὑμῶν Ge 26.27.

4. *to allow to leave*: ἀπόστειλόν με, ἵνα ἀπέλθω .. 'Let me leave, so that I may depart ..' Ge 30.25; 32.26, 43.14, De 22.7; τὸν παῖδα .. καὶ τὴν παιδίσκην Je 41.10 (ǁ ἐξαποστέλλω vs. 9).

Cf. ἀντ~, ἐξ~, ἐπ~, προ~, προσ~, συναποστέλλω, πέμπω: Rengstorf, *TDNT* 1.400-3; Spicq 1.186-94, esp. 186f.

ἀποστενόω: pf.ptc.pass. ἀπεστενωμένος.ʃ

to straiten: metaph., *o* heart, Es D 5 (from angst).

ἀποστέργω: fut. ~στέρξω.ʃ
to empty of love: + acc., καρδίαν De 15.7 (‖ κατισχύω 2.30).

ἀποστερέω: fut. ~στερήσω; aor.subj. ~στερήσω, inf.pass. ~στερηθῆναι.
1. *to withhold unjustly*: + acc. rei, τὰ δέοντα καὶ τὸν ἱματισμὸν καὶ τὴν ὁμιλίαν 'the necessities and the clothes and sexual intercourse' Ex 21.10; sbd (τινος) of sth (τι)– μισθὸν μισθωτοῦ 'a labourer (his) pay' Ma 3.5, μισθὸν μισθίου Si 31.27; ‖ ἀφαιρέομαι 31.25.
2. *to deprive* sbd (τινα) of sth (τινος): Si 29.6, ἑαυτοὺς τοῦ γλυκέος κόσμου 'ourselves of this sweet world' 4M 8.23 (‖ ἐξάγω).
Cf. στερέω

ἀποστολή, ῆς. f.
1. v.n. of ἀποστέλλω **4**: as cogn. dat., De 22.7.
***2.** *expulsion* to a foreign land: divine punishment and + μάχαιρα, λιμός Je 39.36, sim. Ba 2.25. See LSG and *GI*.
3. *parting gift*: pl., 1E 9.51; for a daughter to be married off, 3K 5.14[b]. **b.** *gift*: Ct 4.13, 1M 2.18, 2M 3.2.
***4.** *mission discharged*: δι' ἀγγέλων πονηρῶν 'through evil angels (acting on God's behalf)' Ps 77.49. See HTM.
5. *exempting from duties*: discharge from armed service, Ec 8.8, cf. Jarick 208f.
***6.** *shoot* of a plant: metaph. for female breasts, Ct 4.13.
Cf. ἀποστέλλω: LSG s.v.

ἀποστρεβλόω.ʃ *
to place under severe physical pain: pass., *o* limbs, 2M 9.7.

ἀποστρέφω: fut. ~στρέψω, pass. ~στραφήσομαι; aor.act. ἀπέστρεψα, inf. ~στρέψαι, impv. ~στρεψον, ptc. ~στρέψας, subj. ~στρέψω, mid. ἀπεστρεψάμην, opt. 3s ~στρέψαιτο, pass. ἀπεστράφην, impv. ~στράφητι, ptc. ~στραφείς, inf. ~στραφῆναι, subj. ~στραφῶ, opt.3pl ~στραφείησαν; pf. ἀπέστροφα, pass.3s ἀπέστραπται, ptc.pass. ἀπεστραμμένος.
I. tr. **1.** *to turn away, divert*: + acc., τὸ πρόσωπον αὐτοῦ ἀπ' αὐτῶν, out of displeasure De 31.17 (‖ καταλείπω), 18, 32.20, Mi 3.4, lack of compassion Si 4.4 (‖ ὀφθαλμόν vs. 5, and cf. PSol 2.8 ἀπὸ ἐλέους αὐτῶν [gen. obj.]), Si 14.8 (‖ ὑπερoράω), but πρὸς τὸν τοῖχον 'towards the wall (so as to keep his mind away from other concerns?)' 4K 20.2; + acc. pers., αὐτὸν κενόν '.. empty-handed' Si 29.9; μὴ ἀποστρέψῃς τὸ πρόσωπόν σου (*L*: μου) .. οὐκ ἀποστρέψω σε 3K 2.20 (refusal to grant a request), sim. Ex 3.6 (out of a sense of awe); in order (not) to see, εἰς τὴν ἔρημον Nu 24.1, τοῦ μὴ βλέπειν Ps 9.32 (to look away), ἀπὸ τῶν ἁμαρτιῶν μου 50.11; τὸν ὀφθαλμόν 'turn a blind eye (to the needy)' Pr 28.27, τοὺς ὀφθαλμούς μου ἀφ' ὑμῶν Is 1.15; ἡμᾶς ἀπὸ τῆς ὁδοῦ ταύτης 30.11, ἐκ τῆς ὁδοῦ τῆς πονηρᾶς Ez 18.23; σε ἐκ πορνείας 16.41, ἐκ τῆς δικαιοσύνης αὐτοῦ 18.24; *o* course of water, τὸ ὕδωρ τῆς ἀρχαίας κολυμβήθρας εἰς τὴν πόλιν 'the water of the ancient pool into the city' Is 22.9; τὸν πόδα σου ἀπὸ τῶν σαββάτων 'refrain from going about secular businesses on sabbaths' 58.13, σὸν πόδα ἀπὸ ὁδοῦ κακῆς Pr 4.27, ἐξ ἀδικίας τὴν χεῖρα αὐτοῦ Ez 18.8 (‖ ἀπό vs. 17), τὴν χεῖρά σου 'your (helping) hand' Ps 73.11, τὴν βοήθειαν 88.44; φρονίμους εἰς τὰ ὀπίσω '(send) the sages packing' Is 44.25, cf. La 2.3. **b.** *to dissuade*: + acc. pers.: 1M 9.9, cf. ἀποτρέπω **b**. **c.** *to reject*: τὴν ὕβριν Na 2.3, τὰς ἑορτὰς καὶ τὰς νουμηνίας αὐτῆς Ez 23.34; τὴν δέησιν ἡμῶν 'our supplicaiton' PSol 5.5; ὀπίσω τοῦ νώτου αὐτοῦ 'behind his back' Si 21.15 (‖ ἀπαρέσκω); pass., *o* "the mouths of the infidels" Pr 10.32. **d.** *to remove, do away with*: μαλακίαν ἀφ' ὑμῶν 'ailment from you' Ex 23.25; αὐτοὺς [= enemies] πρὸ προσώπου σου De 9.3 (‖ ἀπόλλυμι); τὴν αἰχμαλωσίαν αὐτῶν Zp 2.7; joyous holidays, Ho 2.11; βασιλείαν 1.4; ἀσεβείας Is 59.20, ἀσέβειαν ἐκ τῆς γῆς Ez 23.48, ὀργήν (‖ ἀπωθέω) Si 1.21; διαθήκην .. ὄπισθεν αὐτῶν Je 39.40. **e.** *to deny access* (?): + acc. pers. Mi 2.4 (αὐτόν = a hostile surveyor, so Cyr. I 628 and Thph PG 126.1081), cf. ἀποστρέψω αὐτοὺς τοῦ μὴ ποιμαίνειν τὰ πρόβατά μου 'I shall deny them the right to herd my sheep' Ez 34.10. **f.** *to avert*: *o* divine anger, Pr 29.8 (see Ibn Ezra ad loc.), ἀπὸ Ισραηλ Nu 25.4, sim. Je 18.20 and cf. τὴν χεῖρα τὴν ὑψηλήν Is 14.27 (God's punitive hand), cf. La 2.8[1] (Zgl: ἐπι~); hum. anger, Pr 15.1. **g.** mid. *to turn away, reject*: ἀγαθά Ho 8.3 (opp. καταδιώκω); + acc. pers. 3K 8.57 (‖ ἐγκαταλείπομαι), Zc 10.6; *o* sth desirable, 3M 3.22; *to deny oneself*, + acc. rei, ἡδονάς 'pleasures' 4M 1.33, φύσεως χάριτας 'nature's gifts' 5.9, ὄρεξιν 'appetite' Wi 16.3.
2. *to cause to move back* to a point of departure: + acc., ἀποστρέψω τὸν υἱόν σου εἰς τὴν γῆν, ὅθεν ἐξῆλθες ἐκεῖθεν; 'Shall I return your son to the land where you came from?' Ge 24.5; 28.15; μετὰ σωτηρίας εἰς τὸν οἶκον τοῦ πατρός μου 'safely to my father's house' 28.21; τὸ ἀργύριον τὸ ἀποστραφὲν ἐν τοῖς μαρσίπποις ὑμῶν ἀποστρέψατε μεθ' ὑμῶν 'take back the silver returned in your bags with you' 43.12; Je 35.3 (‖ ἐπιστρέφω vs. 6); ἐκ τῆς γῆς ταύτης εἰς τὴν γῆν τῶν πατέρων ὑμῶν Ge 48.21; εἰς Αἴγυπτον De 28.68; ἑαυτὸν ἐπὶ τὸ ἅρμα αὐτοῦ '.. to his chariot' 1E 1.26; πρός τινα Ex 10.8; *o* stray cattle and + dat. pers. (owner), Ex 23.4, De 22.1; ἀποικίαν Je 37.3; τὰ κακὰ τοῖς ἐχθροῖς μου

Ps 53.7, τὴν κακίαν Jd 9.56 A (B: ἐπι~; A vs. 57 ἐπι~ εἰς τὴν κεφαλήν τινος), 1K 25.39 (*L* ἐπι~). **b.** *to make undone*: + acc., Is 43.13.

3. *to restore, recover* what has been lost: possessions and people, πᾶσαν τὴν ἵππον .. τὸν ἀδελφὸν αὐτοῦ .. τὰ ὑπάρχοντα αὐτοῦ καὶ τὰς γυναῖκας καὶ τὸν λαόν 'the entire cavalry .. his possessions ..' Ge 14.16; pass., ἀπεστράφη ὅριον Ισραηλ αὐτοῖς 4K 13.5.

4. pass. *to let go of, let go unpunished*: + acc. pers. Am 1.3, 6, 9, 11, 13, 2.1, 4, 6.

II. intr. **1.** *to turn back, revert*: εἰς τὴν γῆν Ge 3.19; εἰς Αἴγυπτον Ex 13.17, Nu 14.3, Ho 8.13; εἰς τὸν τόπον αὐτοῦ Ge 18.33; εἰς τὸν ᾅδην Ps 9.18; ἐκεῖθεν Ge 18.22; πρός τινα, Ex 4.18; ‖ ἐπιστρέφω 4.21 (vs. 20), Nu 23.6 (vs. 5). **b.** pass. in form: ὧδε Ge 15.16; πρὸς τὴν κυρίαν σου Ge 16.9 (said to a runaway maidservant); εἰς τὴν γῆν τοῦ πατρός σου 31.3, εἰς τὴν παρεμβολήν Nu 14.45, εἰς τοὺς οἴκους ὑμῶν De 5.30; ὀπίσω La 1.8, εἰς τὰ ὀπίσω Ps 34.4, 39.15; opp. ἐξέρχομαι Is 45.23. **c.** *to turn away, dissociate oneself*: ἀπ' αὐτῶν Ge 42.24; ἀπὸ τῆς ὁδοῦ αὐτοῦ τῆς πονηρᾶς καὶ ἀπὸ τῆς ἀδικίας Jn 3.8, sim. 3.10, Zc 1.4, Je 18.11; ἀποστρέψει ἐξ ὀργῆς θυμοῦ αὐτοῦ Jn 3.9; ὁ ἀποστρέφων οὐκ ἐπιστρέψει Je 8.4; ἐν τῷ ἀποστρέψαι δίκαιον ἀπὸ τῆς δικαιοσύνης αὐτοῦ .. τὸν ἁμαρτωλὸν ἀπὸ τῆς ἀνομίας αὐτοῦ Ez 33.18f.; + cogn. acc., ἀποστροφήν Je 8.5; pass. ἀποστραφῇ .. ἀπὸ θυμοῦ τῆς ὀργῆς αὐτοῦ De 13.17; + acc. pers. (!), Je 15.6, cf. τὸ θεῖον 'the divine will' Eur., *Supp.* 159. **d.** *to abandon*, withdrawing aid and protection: **s** God, ἀπό σου De 23.14; hum., Si 29.7. **e.** pass. in form, *to leave* the current (right) path or course of action: abs., Jd 2.19 (*pace BA* ad loc.), ἀπεστράφητε ἀπειθοῦντες κυρίῳ Nu 14.43 (*pace* Wevers: "again" = ἐπι~), ἀπὸ ^κυρίου^ 32.15, sim. Jo 22.18, 29 (‖ ἀφίστημι), Je 3.19, εἰς τὰ ὀπίσω 'backwards (defeated)' Is 42.17, Ps 9.4; giving up a chase, 17.38, + a negatived inf., 2C 11.4 τοῦ μὴ πορευθῆναι, τοῦ μὴ διώκειν 2K 18.16 (*L* κατα~), cf. ἀπὸ τοῦ διώκειν 1M 4.16 (Kappler: ἐπι~); + gen., λοιδορίας 'railing' Pr 20.3. **f.** *to be turned away, depart*, so as to be no longer affecting: ἕως τοῦ ἀποστρέψαι τὸν θυμὸν .. τοῦ ἀδελφοῦ σου ἀπὸ σοῦ, καὶ ἐπιλάθηται .. Ge 27.45; ἡ ὀργή μου ἀπ' αὐτῶν Ho 14.5; οὐκ ἀπεστράφη ὁ θυμός Is 5.25, sim. Je 2.35.

2. *to turn round and start moving in the opposite direction*: ἀποστρέψας .. κατέβη ἀπὸ τοῦ ὄρους Ex 32.15; εἰς φυγήν Je 33.13, ἀπὸ σιδήρου '(recoil) from a sword' Jb 39.22.

*__3.__ pass. *to be transformed and become*: εἰς οὐθέν Ho 7.16 (‖ γίνομαι; cf. Th PG 66.169 ἔδειξα ὄντας τὸ μηθέν).

Cf. ἀποστροφή, ἐπιστρέφω, ἀφανίζω.

ἀποστροφή, ῆς. f.

1. *return, coming* or *going back*: ἐπὶ τὸ αὐτὸ θήσομαι τὴν ~ὴν αὐτῶν 'I shall effect their return together' Mi 2.12; εἰς ^τὴν γὴν^ Si 16.30 (on death); 1K 7.18.

2. *turning* to sbd *for companionship and intimacy*: between a male and a female, πρὸς τὸν ἄνδρα σου ἡ ἀ. σου Ge 3.16; πρὸς σὲ ἡ ἀ. αὐτοῦ 4.7, cf. Ct 7.11 (ἐπιστροφή) and Alexandre 318f.

3. *group of returnees*: Ez 16.53.

4. v.n. of ἀποστρέφω: De 22.1 (q.v. **I 2**), 31.18 and Si 41.21 (q.v. **I 1a**), Je 5.6 + 8.5 + 18.12 + 3M 2.10 (q.v. **II 1e**).

Cf. ἀποστρέφω, ἐπιστροφή, ἐπάνοιδος.

ἀποστύφω: fut. ~στύψω.ʃ

to draw together: **s** medicine, To 11.8 𝔊[II].

ἀποσυνάγω: fut. ~άξω; aor.inf. ~άξαι.ʃ

to help sbd *be freed from*: ἀυτὸν ἀπὸ τῆς λέπρας αὐτοῦ 'from his leprosy' 4K 5.3B, 6, 7. **b.** *to remove* sth troublesome: + acc., ἀπ' αὐτοῦ τὴν λέπραν αὐτοῦ 4K 5.3*L*; ^τὸ λεπρὸν^ ἀπὸ τῆς σαρκός μου 5.11*L*.

ἀποσύρω: fut. ~συρῶ; aor. ἀπέσυρα.ʃ

to remove from a surface: to skim off, + acc., ὕδωρ μικρόν Is 30.14 (with an earthen vessel); scalp, 4M 9.28. Cf. LSG s.v.

ἀποσφάζω: aor.ptc. ἀποσφάξας.ʃ

to slaughter en mass: τινα 4M 2.19. Cf. σφάζω.

ἀποσφενδονάω: aor.pass. ἀπεσφενδονήθην.ʃ

to hurl from or *as from a sling* (LSJ): pass., ***o*** hum., εἰς κάμινον 'into a furnace' 4M 16.21. Cf. σφενδόνη.

ἀποσφράγισμα, ατος. n.ʃ

signet-ring as symbol of authority: worn on the right hand, Je 22.24; ὁμοιώσεως (q.v.) Ez 28.12 (‖ στέφανος κάλλους). Cf. σφραγίς.

ἀποσχίζω: aor.mid. ἀπεσχίσθην, impv.mid. ~σχίσθητι.ʃ

mid. *to separate oneself, detach oneself*: ἐκ μέσης τῆς συναγωγῆς ταύτης Nu 16.21; 16.26; ἀπεσχίσθη λίθος ἐξ ὄρους Da 2.34 TH; ἀπὸ οἴκου κυρίου 2C 26.21. Cf. σχίζω, ἀφορίζω.

ἀποτάσσω: aor. ἀπέταξα, inf.mid. ~τάξασθαι; pf.ptc. pass. ~τεταγμένος.

1. *to set apart*: pass., οἶκος ἀποτεταγμένος 'designated, special cell' Je 20.2. **b.** *to station* a military unit: + acc., δύναμιν 1M 4.61, φρουράν 'garrison' 6.50, ἀποτεταγμένοι ἐν Συρίᾳ 'troops stationed in Syria' 1E 6.26.

2. mid. *to bid adieu*: + dat., τῇ καρδίᾳ μου ἐπὶ παντὶ τῷ μόχθῳ 'to leave off troubling my mind over all that toil' Ec 2.20.

ἀποτείνω: fut. ~τενῶ.ʃ

to continue doing: + inf.,* οὐ μακρὰν ἀποτενεῖτε πορευθῆναι 'you are not going to go on too far' Ex

8.28, cf. + ptc. at Plutarch 2.60a μαχόμενοι. Cf. παύω.

ἀποτελέω: aor.pass. ἀπετελέσθην.ʃ

1. *to cause to come true*: ***o*** dream, Es 7.53 *L*.

2. *to cause to acquire the (desirable) quality of*: ἐπιτερπῆ τὴν χάριν 'the attraction more enjoyable' 2M 15.39.

ἀποτέμνω: aor. ἀπέτεμον, impv. ~τεμε, ptc. ~τεμών.ʃ

to cut off and sever: + acc., σελίδας ξυρῷ γραμματέως 'columns of a papyrus roll with a scribe's knife' Je 43.23, τὴν κεφαλὴν .. καὶ τὴν χεῖρα 2M 15.20; 4M 15.20 (ǁ ἀποδειροτομέω 'to decapitate'); + acc. pers., *to decapitate* Jd 5.26A (*L*: σφυροκοπέω 'to beat with a hammer'), *to sever* a relationship Si 25.26 (***o*** wife). Cf. τέμνω, ἀποτομή.

ἀποτηγανίζω: aor. ἀπετηγάνισα.ʃ

to eat broiled: + acc. pers., ἐν πυρί Je 36.22. Cf. LSG s.v.

ἀποτίθημι: fut.act. ~θήσω; 1aor.act. ἀπέθηκα, impv. ἀπόθες, inf. ~θεῖναι, mid. ἀπεθέμην, impv. ~θου, ptc. ~θέμενος.

to put away: for storage and + acc., εἰς διατήρησιν Ex 16.33; detention, εἰς φυλακήν Le 24.12, Nu 15.34; official garment, στολήν Le 16.23, στέφανον Ez 21.26 (ǁ ἀφαιρέω); σποδόν 'ashes (of a burnt sacrificial animal)' Nu 19.9; ***o*** valuable objects, 1E 6.18. **b**. mid. ***o*** that which one has on oneself, τὰ σκεύη ἀφ' ἑαυτοῦ 'weapons' 1K 17.22 *L*, ἐσθῆτα 'robe' 2M 8.35.

Cf. τίθημι, ἀποθήκη.

ἀποτίκτω: aor.ptc.pass. ~τεχθείς.

to give birth to: pass., ***o*** hum. baby, 4M 13.21. Cf. τίκτω, ἀποκυέω.

ἀποτίναγμα, ατος. n.ʃ *

coarse and broken part of flax prepared for spinning: Jd 16.9 A.

ἀποτινάσσω: aor. ἀπετίναξα; pf.mid.3s ~τετίνακται.ʃ

to shake a burden or constraint *off*: + acc., ἁγίασμα 'sanctuary' La 2.7; mid., Jd 16.20A (B: ἐκ~). **b**. *to stop concerning oneself about*: + acc., τὸ ῥῆμα τῶν ὄνων 'the matter of the donkeys' 1K 10.2.

Cf. ἀφανίζω, ἐκτινάσσω.

ἀποτιννύω.ʃ

1. *to pay* for commodities purchased: + double acc., ἀποτιννύων αὐτὰ ἑπταπλάσιον 'paying for them sevenfold' Si 20.12 (:: ἀγοράζω).

2. *to pay compensation for*: + acc., ἀπετίννυον παρ' ἐμαυτοῦ κλέμματα ἡμέρας 'I would pay damages out of my own pocket for those stolen by day' Ge 31.39; ἃ οὐχ ἥρπασα, τότε ἀπετίννυον 'I would recompense for what I did not rob' Ps 68.5.

Cf. ἀποτίνω.

ἀποτίνω: fut. ~τείσω, ~τίσω, ptc. ~τείσων; aor.subj. ~τείσω, impv. ~τισον, opt.3s ~τείσαι.

1. *to give as compensation for damage* either in cash or kind: + acc., πλὴν τῆς ἀργίας αὐτοῦ ἀποτείσει καὶ τὰ ἰατρεῖα 'in addition to (the lost income due to) his unemployment he shall also pay the doctor's fee' Ex 21.19; ταῦρον ἀντὶ ταύρου 'a bull for a bull' 21.36; πέντε μόσχους .. ἀντὶ τοῦ μόσχου 22.1; ψυχὴν ἀντὶ ψυχῆς Le 24.18; 1K 2.20 (*L* ἀνταποδίδωμι).

2. *to make compensation for*: + acc., ἅρπαγμα Ez 33.15; 2K 12.6; Is 9.5. **b**. *to give reward for*: + acc., τὴν ἐργασίαν σου 'your endeavour' Ru 2.12.

3. *to give that which is due*: + acc., εὐχάς 'vows' 2K 15.7. **b**. *to repay*: abs. Si 8.13; + acc., τὸ κεφάλαιον 'the principal' Le 6.5, τὸ δάνειον 'the debt' 4K 4.7*L* (B: τόκους 'interests'); opp. δανείζομαι 'borrow' Ps 36.21.

4. *to make pay for, punish for*: + acc. rei, παρὰ σοῦ ἀποτείσει [for ἀποτείσεται] ^ἀδικίαν^ Jb 34.33¶.

Cf. ἀνταποδίδωμι, τίνω.

ἀποτομή, ῆς. f.ʃ

piece chopped off (?): Jd 5.26A. Cf. ἀποτέμνω.

ἀπότομος, ον.ʃ

relentless: ***s*** βασιλεύς Wi 11.10, πολεμιστής 'warrior' 18.15; ὀργή '(divine) wrath' 5.20, κρίσις '(divine) judgement' 6.5 (ǁ ἰσχυρός 'strict' vs. 8), λόγος '(divine) word' 12.9. Cf. ἀποτόμως. ἀναιδής, ἄνοικτος.

ἀποτόμως. adv.ʃ

relentlessly: Wi 5.22. Cf. ἀπότομος.

ἀποτρέπω: aor.ptc.pass. ~τραπείς.ʃ

to turn away: + acc., ἐλεγμούς 'criticism' Si 20.29. **b**. orally, *to dissuade*: 3M 1.23; + acc. pers., ἵνα μὴ ἀποθάνωσιν 'from dying' 4M 16.12, cf. ἀποστρέφω **I 1 b**.

ἀποτρέχω: fut. ~δραμοῦμαι; aor. ἀπέδραμον.

to depart, leave sbd's presence quickly: λαβὼν ἀπότρεχε 'Take (her and) be off!' Ge 12.19, 24.51; εἰς τὴν γῆν τῆς γενέσεώς σου 32.9 (ǁ ἀποστρέφομαι 31.3); εἰς οἶκον Si 35.11; εἰς τὸν τόπον μου Nu 24.14; πρός τινα 22.13; ǁ ἀπέρχομαι Ex 3.21; ***s*** king's female companion for the night, Es 2.14 o' (*L* ἀπολύομαι); slave, ἐλεύθερος (ǁ ἀπέρχομαι) Ex 21.5; 21.7; emissaries, Nu 22.13; people on the run, Je 41.21; To 8.3 $\mathfrak{G}^{II}$ ($\mathfrak{G}^{I}$ φεύγω); of death, ἐκ τοῦ ζῆν 14.3 $\mathfrak{G}^{I}$, τὴν ὁδὸν καθὰ καὶ πάντες οἱ ἐπὶ τῆς γῆς Jo 23.14. Cf. τρέχω, ἀπέρχομαι, ἀποδιδράσκω: Schmidt 1.524-34; *ND* 4.97.

ἀποτρίβω: fut.mid. ~τρίψομαι; aor.mid.impv. ἀπότριψαι.ʃ

mid. *to get rid of*: + acc., τὸν μόσχον σου 'your calf' Ho 8.5 (object of worship); νόμιμα 'regulations' Mi 7.11; ref. to beheading, Jd 5.26 A.

ἀποτροπιάζομαι.ʃ*
to offer as sacrifice so as to avert evil: + acc. and dat. pers., Ez 16.21, cf. Hauspie 2002.103.

ἀποτρυγάω: aor. ἀπετρύγησα.ʃ
to pluck (fruit): fig. of destructive action, + acc. pers., ἀρχὰς ἐθνῶν Am 6.1 (Th 137 περικόψας .. ἀφελών; Tht PG 81.1693 ἀναλώσας). Cf. τρυγάω and ἀφανίζω.

ἀποτυγχάνω: aor. ἀπέτυχον.ʃ
to fail to obtain: *+ acc. rei, Jb 31.16.

ἀποτυμπανίζω: fut.pass. ~τυμπανισθήσομαι; aor. pass. ἀπετυμπανίσθην.ʃ
to terminate the life of, 'destroy, kill': pass., ***o*** animal, Da 7.11 LXX (TH ἀναιρέω); hum., by torturing, 3M 3.27. Cf. ἀφανίζω: LSG s.v.

ἀποτυφλόω: aor. ἀπετύφλωσα, inf.pass. ~λωθῆναι.ʃ
to cause the loss of ability to see, 'blind': pass., as a result of disease, To 2.10 𝔊[II]; fig., ξένια καὶ δῶρα ἀποτυφλοῖ ὀφθαλμοὺς σοφῶν 'favours and gifts ..' Si 20.29 (‖ ἐκτυφλόω De 16.19); + acc. pers., ἀπετύφλωσεν αὐτοὺς ἡ κακία αὐτῶν Wi 2.21. Cf. ἀποτύφλωσις, ἐκτυφλόω, τυφλός, τυφλόω.

ἀποτύφλωσις, εως. f.ʃ
v.n. of ἀποτυφλόω: Zc 12.4. Cf. ἀποτυφλόω.

ἀποφαίνω: aor. ἀπέφηνα, mid. ἀπεφηνάμην, ptc. mid., ~φηνάμενος, inf.act. ~φῆναι.

1. *to show by reasoning*: + double acc., δικαίους ὑμᾶς Jb 27.5.

2. mid. *to declare an opinion*: + inf., 2M 6.23; + dir. speech, 15.4.

Cf. ἀποδείκνυμι, ἐκφαίνω: Schmidt 3.406f.

ἀποφέρω: fut.act. ἀποίσω, mid. ἀποίσομαι, pass. ἀπενεχθήσομαι; aor.act. ἀπήνεγκα, impv. ἀπένεγκε, ptc. ἀπενέγκας, mid. ἀπενεγκάμενος, inf. mid. ἀπενέγκασθαι, opt.3s ἀπενέγκαιτο, pass. ἀπηνέχθην; pf.ptc.pass. ἀπενηνεγμένος.

1. *to cause to move away with one* from where the object presently or normally is: + acc., αὐτὸν εἰς 'Ασσυρίους δήσαντες ἀπήνεγκαν ξένια τῷ βασιλεῖ Ιαριμ 'they carried him away, bound, to Assyria as gifts to King J.' Ho 10.6; Ποῦ αὗται ἀποφέρουσι τὸ μέτρον; 'Where do they take this measure-line to?' Zc 5.10; ***o*** τὸ ὄνειδός μου 'my shame' 2K 13.13B; unlawfully or by force, Ez 38.13 (‖ προνομεύω, σκυλεύω); mid., + acc., Jb 15.28.

2. *to sustain*: + acc., ἁμαρτίαν 'the penalty of sin' Le 20.19 (‖ κομίζομαι vs. 17), βάσανον 'severe punishment' Ez 32.30 (‖ λαμβάνω vs. 24); πρόστιμον 'penalty' 2M 7.36.

3. mid. *to gain*: γέρας 'office of distinction' Es B 3.

Cf. φέρω, κομίζω.

ἀποφεύγω: fut.~φεύξομαι.ʃ
to run away out of fear: Si 22.22. Cf. φεύγω: Schmidt 3.244-7.

ἀποφθέγγομαι: fut. ~φθέγξομαι; aor. ἀπεφθεγξάμην. *(ἀπόφθεγμα: Xen. +)
to make pronouncement: ***s*** God's wicked enemies, ἐν τῷ στόματι αὐτῶν Ps 58.8; oracle-giver, diviner, ἀποφθεγγόμενοι οὐκ ἔσονται ἐν σοί 'there will be no diviners amongst you' Mi 5.12; 1K 28.9*L* (B: γνώστης); + acc., μάταια Ez 13.9; w. a cogn. obj., μάταια ἀποφθέγματα 13.19; also playing musical instruments in temple service, 1C 25.1, cf. 25.5 and Japheth ad 25.1. Cf. ἀπόφθεγμα, φθέγγομαι and μάντις.

ἀπόφθεγμα, ατος. n.ʃ
that which is pronounced, uttered: divine and ‖ ῥήματα De 32.2; μάταια ~ατα 'worthless ..' Ez 13.19; συνετῶν ἀνδρῶν 'of sages' Si prol. II. Cf. ἀποφθέγγομαι, ῥῆμα.

ἀποφράσσω: aor. ἀπέφραξα, pass. ἀπεφράγην.ʃ
not to allow to function by way of obstruction: + acc., προσευχήν μου 'my prayer' La 3.8; pass., ***o*** στόμα 1M 9.55.

ἀποφυσάω.ʃ
tr. *to blow away*: χνοῦς ἀποφυσώμενος ἀφ' ἅλωνος 'chaff blown away from a threshing-floor' Ho 13.3. Cf. ἐκ~ and ἐμφυσάω.

ἀποχέω: fut. ~χεῶ; aor. ἀπέχεα. Also ~χύννω.ʃ
to cause to flow out: abs., 2K 13.9*L* (B: κατακενόω 'to empty'), + μεθύσκομαι La 4.21 ('to throw up after excessive drinking' [?], cf, Syh /tsapqin/; εἰς τὰ σκεύη 4K 4.4B (*L* ἐκχέω); + acc., αἷμα 3K 22.35B. Cf. ἐκχέω, χέω, κατακενόω.

ἀποχύννω.⇒ ἀποχέω.

ἀποχωρέω: pf.ptc. ~κεχωρηκώς.ʃ
to move away: out of fear, ὀπίσω 'backwards, i.e. retreat' Je 26.5, εἰς ἄσυλον τόπον 'into a safe place' 2M 4.33, τοὺς ἀποχωροῦντας ἐξ αὐτῶν 'the deserters from among their ranks' 3M 2.33. Cf. ἀποχώρησις, ἀπέρχομαι, ἀποίχομαι: LSG s.v.

ἀποχώρησις, εως. f.ʃ
act of temporarily leaving the area of one's current activity: ref. to relieving oneself, Jd 3.24A. Cf. ἀποχωρέω.

ἀποχωρίζω: pf.ptc.pass. ~κεχωρισμένος.ʃ
to set apart: τὸ ἀποκεχωρισμένος τοῦ οἴκου 'the area of the temple set apart (for the purpose)' Ez 43.21. Cf. χωρίζω.

ἀποψύχω.ʃ
to breathe one's last: ‖ ἀποπνέω 4M 15.18. Cf. ἀποπνέω, ψυχουλκέομαι: Schmidt 2.291-4.

ἄπρακτος, ον.ʃ
having failed to achieve an aim, 'unsuccessful': ***s*** hum., + ἔκβολος 'frustrated' Ju 11.11; 2M 12.18.

b. *unable to achieve anything*, 'powerless': *s* hum., 3M 2.22.

ἀπρεπής, ές.ʃ

not befitting: + dat., ἀπρεπὲς ἡμῖν δρᾶμα 'a role not befitting us' 4M 6.17.

ἀπρονοήτως. adv.ʃ

not having thought through beforehand, 'just off-hand': 3M 1.14. Cf. ἀπρόπτωτος.

ἀπρόπτωτος, ον.ʃ

well thought over and not rash: *s* συμμαχία 'alliance' 3M 3.14. Cf. ἀπρονοήτως.

ἀπροσδεής, ές.ʃ

not being in need of: + gen., 1M 12.9, τῶν ὅλων 'anything' 2M 14.35; τῶν ἁπάντων 3M 2.9. Cf. ἐνδεής.

ἀπροσδόκητος, ον.

experienced as a surprise, unexpected: *s* undesirable development, 3M 4.2 (ǁ ἐξαίφνης), + αἰφνίδιος 'sudden' Wi 17.15. Cf. ἀπροσδοκήτως, προσδοκάω, ἀπρόσκοπος, ἀδόκητος, αἰφνίδιος, ἀνυπονόητος: Schmidt 3.589f.

ἀπροσδοκήτως. adv.ʃ

unexpectedly: 2M 8.6, 12.37. Cf. ἀπροσδόκητος.

I **ἀπρόσκοπος**, ον.ʃ

free from stumbling-blocks: *s* even road free from pot-holes, Si 35.21, poss. II in the sense of *unexplored, uncharted*. Cf. προσκόπτω.

II **ἀπρόσκοπος**, ον.ʃ

unsuspected, unexpected: *s* gathering of a crowd, 3M 3.8. Cf. ἀπροσδόκητος.

ἄπταιστος, ον.ʃ

not fallen as victim of hostilities: *s* hum., 3M 6.39.

ἀπτόητος, ον.ʃ

fearless: *s* Babylon, Je 27.2. Cf. πτοέω, θρασύς.

ἅπτομαι: fut. ἅψομαι; aor. ἡψάμην, subj. ἅψωμαι, inf. ἅψασθαι, impv. ἅψαι, ptc. ἁψάμενος; pf.3s ἧπται, ptc. ἡμμένος.

1. *to touch*: + gen., Ge 3.3, Hg 2.12; τῷ ἅψασθαι αὐτῆς [grape-vine] ἄνεμον Ez 17.10; euphemism for sexual intercourse, οὐχ ἥψατο αὐτῆς Ge 20.4; + gen. and with harmful, malicious intent, τοῦ ἀνθρώπου τούτου ἢ τῆς γυναικὸς αὐτοῦ 26.11, τῆς κληρονομίας μου [= Israel] Je 12.14; with a weapon, 2K 5.8; *s* μάχαιρα Je 4.10; fire, Da 3.94 LXX (TH κυριεύω). **b**. *to befall and to cause harm to*: + gen. pers., *s* βάσανος 'torture' Wi 3.1, πεῖρα θανάτου 'the experience of death' 18.20. **c**. with partitive ἀπό: ἀπὸ ἀκαθαρσίας Le 5.3, ἀπὸ πάντων 15.10, Nu 16.26, Ἐὰν ἅψηται μεμιαμμένος ἐπὶ ψυχῇ ἀπὸ παντὸς τούτων 'if one who is defiled by a corpse touched any of these things' Hg 2.13: see Helbing, *Kasus*. 124.

2. *to reach, get as far as*: + ἕως– ἕως πύλης λαοῦ μου Mi 1.9; + acc., πόλεις Ιαζηρ Je 31.32; + gen., νεφῶν 'clouds' Jb 20.6, ἄστρων 'stars' 2M 9.10; *s* calamity, Jd 20.41 A (:: ἀφάπτομαι vs. 34). **b**. metaph.: ἥψατο ἕως τῆς καρδίας (ǁ ψυχῆς 4.10) σου 'affected even your heart' Je 4.18.

Cf. ἐφάπτω, θιγγάνω: Schmidt 1.232-7; Trench 58-60.

ἅπτω: aor. ἧψα, ptc. ἅψας.ʃ

to cause to glow, 'kindle': + acc., τὸν λύχνον 'the lamp' To 8.13 𝔊II; πῦρ εἰς φαῦσιν '.. in order to give light' Ju 13.13. Cf. ἀν~, ἐξάπτω, καίω.

ἄπυρος, ον.ʃ

not yet treated with fire: *s* gold, Is 13.12. Cf. πυρόω.

ἀπωθέω: fut. ἀπώσομαι, pass. ἀπωσθήσομαι; aor. mid. ἀπωσάμην, inf. ἀπώσασθαι, ptc. ἀπωσάμενος, impv. ἄπωσαι, subj.2s ἀπώσῃ, pass. ἀπώσθην, inf. ἀπωσθῆναι, subj. ἀπωσθῶ, opt.3pl ἀπώσειεν; pf. mid. and pass. ἀπῶσμαι, pass.ptc. ἀπωσμένος.

1. *to reject*: + acc., σὺ ἐπίγνωσιν ἀπώσω, κἀγὼ ἀπώσομαι σὲ τοῦ ἱερατεύειν μοι 'you rejected knowledge, and I will also reject you (and not allow you) to serve me as priest' Ho 4.6; 9.17, Mi 4.7; τὸν λόγον κυρίου Je 23.17, τὸν νόμον κυρίου Am 2.4; ἑορτάς 5.21 (ǁ μισέω), θυσιαστήριον La 2.7; τὸν ἄνδρα αὐτῆς καὶ τὰ τέκνα αὐτῆς Ez 16.45, τὴν πόλιν .. τὴν Ιερουσαλημ 4K 23.27; ἀπῶσμαι ἐξ ὀφθαλμῶν σου 'I have been rejected from your presence' Jn 2.5; ǁ ἐξωθέω and opp. εἰσδέχομαι 'to welcome, accept' Mi 4.6, cf. Zp 3.19 (ǁ ἐκπιέζω); ἐκ φωτὸς εἰς σκότος Jb 18.18, + ἀποδοκιμάζω Je 7.29; ἀπώσατο ἐξ εἰρήνης ψυχήν μου 'he denied my soul peace' La 3.17; mid. and ǁ ἐξουδενέω Ez 21.10, Ps 88.39, ǁ ἐξουδενόω 1K 16.1*L* (see 15.26), ǁ ἀτιμάζω Pr 19.26.

2. *to remove*: + acc. pers., 4K 4.27; + acc. rei, οὐ ἀπώσεται ὀνείδη 'he will not remove reproaches' Mi 2.6, ἁμαρτήματα Si 1.21¶ (*s* wisdom and ǁ ἀποστρέφω); μακρὰν ἀπὸ σοῦ 'far from you' Pr 4.24.

3. *to leave off*: ***o*** τι, lamentation 3M 6.32.

Cf. ἀπωσμός, ἐξωθέω, προσαπωθέω, ἐκπιέζω, ἐξουδενέ/όω, εἰσδέχομαι, and μισέω.

ἀπώλεια, ας. f.

1. *loss* of property: Ex 22.9. **b**. *lost piece of property*: εὗρεν ~αν Le 6.3; De 22.3.

2. *ruin, destruction*: collective, national, ἐν ~ᾳ τῶν ἀδελφῶν ἡμῶν Nu 20.3; ἀ. ἐν τῷ λαῷ σου Ho 10.14, λαὸς ~ας 'destined for perdition' Is 34.5; ἐν ἡμέρᾳ ~ας αὐτῶν Ob 12, 13 (ǁ ὄλεθρος, πόνος); ~ᾳ ἀπολεῖσθε De 4.26, 30.18, sim. 7.23; ἀφανισμὸς ~ας Je 12.11; + ἔξαρσις 12.17, + συντέλεια 1M 3.42; opp. σωτηρία Wi 18.7. **b**. *termination of life*, 'perdition': personified, ἡ ἀ. καὶ ὁ θάνατος εἶπαν Jb 28.22; ǁ τάφος 'grave' Ps 87.12; + ᾅδης Pr 15.11, 27.20, ǁ ᾅδης Jb 26.6¶; active, παράνομος 'unlawful' 2M 8.4. **c**. metaph.: Pr 10.11 (:: ζωή).

Cf. ἀπόλλυμι, ἀφανισμός, ὄλεθρος.

ἀπῶρυξ, υγος.f.ʃ

layer of a vine (LSJ): Ez 17.6.

ἀπωσμός, οῦ. m.ʃ*

v.n. of ἀπωθέω, *rejection*: La 1.7.

ἀπωτέρω. Comp. of ἄπωθεν.ʃ

farther away: opp. ἔγγιστα Da 9.7 LXX (TH μακρός).

ἄρα.

1. Inferential particle, 'then, so': against classical usage, at the beginning, Εἶπα γάρ Ἄρα οὐκ ἔστιν .. 'for I thought, Well then there is no ..' Ge 20.11(*c*), sim. Ps 72.13(*f*); ἄρα γε γυνή σού ἐστιν 'she is your wife then' Ge 26.9(*d*); ἄρα γε ἀπατῶν ἠπάτησας 'then you have indeed deceived' Je 4.10(*e*); Wi 5.6; at the beginning of an apodosis, ἄρα ψεύδεις ἦσαν .. Ho 12.11(?). **b**. not clause-initial: Ps 7.5(-), 6(-); following a conditional cl., Jb 31.8(-).

2. Adds a sense of diffidence on the part of the speaker: in a politely phrased conditional clause, εἰ ἄρα εὗρον χάριν ἐναντίον σου Ge 18.3(*b*); εἰ ἄρα δυνήσομαι .. 'if I could at all ..' Nu 22.11(*a*); Ἐὰν ἄρα Ez 2.5(-).

Cf. διότι, τοίνυν: Clark 1972; Shipp 90.

a) εἰ ἄρα אוּלַי; *b*) נָא; *c*) רַק; *d*) ἄρα γε אַךְ הִנֵּה; *e*) אָכֵן; *f*) אַךְ;?) [Ho 12.11 MT *ʾk*, see s.v. ἆρα].

ἆρα.ʃ

Interrogative particle expressing "impatience or anxiety" (LSJ, s.v.): ἆρα προσθήσω τοῦ ἐπιβλέψαι πρὸς τὸν ναὸν τὸν ἅγιόν σου; Jn 2.5; reinforced by γέ – ἆρά γε ἀληθῶς τέξομαι; 'Am I really going to have a baby, I wonder?' Ge 18.13; 37.10.

ἀρά, ᾶς. f.

1. *act of cursing*: in a catalogue of vices, ἀ. καὶ ψεῦδος καὶ φόνος καὶ κλοπὴ καὶ μοιχεία Ho 4.2; ὅρκος ἀρᾶς Nu 5.21; ἀ. καὶ ὅρκος Ne 10.29. **b**. *words of curse consigning a person* or *object to divine punishment*: Zc 5.3. **c**. *target of curse*: + ὀνειδισμός Je 49.18. **d**. *accursed condition*: τὰ κακὰ καὶ ἡ ἀ. Ba 1.20; ‖ στεναγμός 'groan' PSol 4.14.

2. *a pact with a curse attached in case of breach*: Γενέσθω ἀ. ἀνὰ μέσον ἡμῶν καὶ ἀνὰ μέσον σοῦ, καὶ διαθησόμεθα μετὰ σοῦ διαθήκην Ge 26.28; ἀθῷος ἔσῃ ἀπὸ τῆς ἀρᾶς μου 'my curse will have no effect upon you' 24.41 (‖ ὁρκισμός); ‖ διαθήκη Ez 17.16, ἐν τῇ διαθήκῃ κυρίου .. καὶ ἐν ταῖς ἀραῖς αὐτοῦ De 29.12.

Cf. κατάρα, ὅρκος, ὁρκισμός, εὐλογία.

Ἀράβισσα, ας. f.ʃ

Arabian woman: Jb 42.17ca.

Ἀραβία, ας. f.

Arabia: Hb 1.8.

ἀράομαι: pres.subj.3s. ἀρᾶται; fut. ἀράσομαι; aor. mid.inf. ἀράσασθαι, impv.mid. ἄρασαι, subj. ἀράσωμαι.

to pronounce curse upon, utter words consigning a person or *object to an odious state*: *s* hum. and + acc. rei and dat. com., ἄρασαί μοι τὸν λαὸν τοῦτον Nu 22.6 (‖ καταράομαι and:: εὐλογέω; ‖ ἐπικαταράομαι vs. 17), 11, 23.7; *s* God, 23.8; hum. and + acc. pers., Jd 17.2 B (A: ἐξορκίζω), + dat. pers. Jo 24.9, 1K 14.24. Cf. ἀρά, (ἐπι)καταράομαι, εὐλογέω.

ἀραρότως. adv.ʃ

in full and strict conformity with an instruction given: 3M 5.3.

ἀράχνη, ης. f.

spider: ἱστὸς ἀράχνης 'a spider's web' Is 59.5; ‖ σής 'moth' Jb 27.18. **b**. *spider's web*: Jb 8.14.

Ἄραψ, βος.m.

Arab: Is 13.20 +.

ἀργέω: aor. ἤργησα.ʃ

to neglect work, 'be idle': *s* servant, Si 30.36. **b**. *to be at a standstill*: *s* work, 1E 2.25, 2E 4.24. **c**. *to rest from work*: *s* hum., Ec 12.3; Jews on a sabbath day, 2M 5.25.

Cf. ἀργία, ἀργός, καταργέω: Delling, *TDNT* 1.452.

ἀργία, ας. f.ʃ

want of employment: as a result of an injury, Ex 21.19; νηστείαν καὶ ~αν Is 1.13 (rest on sabbath); Si 30.37; χειρῶν Ec 10.18 (‖ ὀκνηρία 'idleness'); ἥξει ἐπὶ τὴν ~αν αὐτοῦ 'will attack him with his pants down' Da LXX 11.7. **b**. *freedom from routine employment*, 'spare time': ‖ ἄνεσις Wi 13.13.

Cf. ἔργον, ἀργέω, ὀκνηρία, σχολή: Daris 158-61; Reekmans, esp. 281f.

ἀργός, ή, όν.ʃ

1. *not working when one* or *it ought to be*: *s* hum., ‖ ὀκνηρός'lazy' Si 37.11; τὰ τῆς σοφίας σου ἔργα 'the works of your wisdom' Wi 14.5.

2. *incapable of working*: *s* feet, πρὸς ἐπίβασιν 'for a walk' Wi 15.15.

3. *unwrought, unprocessed*: *s* rough stones, 3K 6.7.

Cf. ἀεργός, ὀκνηρός: Spicq 1.195-8.

ἀργυρικός, ή, όν.ʃ

pertaining to money: *s* ζημία 'a fine' 1E 8.24.

ἀργύριον, ου. n.

1. *silver* as material (= ἄργυρος): "I shall test them by fire as silver is tested by fire" Zc 13.9 (‖ χρυσίον), sim. Ma 3.3*bis*; material for making images, Ho 8.4 (‖ χρυσίον), 13.2, Hb 2.19 (ditto); "you will take silver and gold, and make crowns" Zc 6.11; as valuable possession, "she hoarded silver as dust and gold as mud of roads" 9.3; Zp 1.18, Ho 9.6, cf. Am 2.6, Jl 3.5 (‖ χρυσίον), Zp 1.11 (see under ἐπαίρω); more valuable than iron, Is 60.17; || κτήνη 'livestock' and χρυσίον Ge 13.2; as payment, ~ου τοῦ ἀξίου 'for the right amount of silver' 23.9; λήμψεσθε .. ~ου De 2.6 (|| ἀγοράζω).

2. *silver coin* as monetary unit: πεντεκαίδεκα ~ου '15 pieces of silver' Ho 3.2. Cf. Lee 64f. and Preisigke, s.v.

3. *money* in general: ψυχὴν ἔγκτητον ~ου 'slaves purchased with ..' Le 22.11, κτᾶσθαι ἐν ~ῳ πτωχούς Am 8.6; Mi 3.11 (|| δῶρον, μισθός).

4. *property* or *possession acquired by payment*: Ex 21.21.

Cf. ἀργυροῦς, ἄργυρος, χρυσίον, χαλκός.

ἀργυροκοπέω.ʃ*

to work as ἀργυροκόπος (q.v.): Je 6.29.

ἀργυροκόπος, ου. m.ʃ

silversmith: Jd 17.4B (*L*+: χωνευτής); Je 6.29 (poss. *one who coins money*). Cf. ἀργυροχόος: *ND* 4.7f.

ἀργυρολόγητος, ον.ʃ*

subject to a levy in money: ***s*** city, 2M 11.3.

ἄργυρος, ου. m.

silver: αἱ βάσεις περιηργυρωμέναι ~ῳ 'the bases being plated with silver' Ex 27.11. Cf. ἀργύριον.

ἀργυροῦς, ᾶ, οῦν.

made of silver: σκεύη ~ᾶ καὶ χρυσᾶ 'silver and golden implements' Ge 24.53, θεοὺς ~οῦς καὶ θεοὺς χρυσοῦς Ex 20.23; subst., ~ᾶ καὶ χρυσᾶ ἐποίησε τῇ Βααλ 'she fashioned silver and golden (images) to Baal' Ho 2.8. **b**. *piece of silver* used to settle commercial transaction, "they weighed as my wage 30 pieces of silver (τριάκοντα ~οῦς)" Zc 11.12.

Cf. ἀργύριον and χρυσοῦς.

ἀργυροχόος, ου. m.ʃ *

silversmith: || χρυσουργός .. χαλκοπλάστης 'goldsmith .. coppersmith' Wi 15.9. Cf. ἀργυροκόπος, χρυσοχόος.

ἀργύρωμα, ατος. n.

silver plate: pl., Ju 12.1; + χρύσωμα 1M 15.32.

ἀργυρώνητος, ον.ʃ

bought with silver: ***s*** slave Ge 17.12, 13, Ex 12.44 (all:: οἰκέτης 'homegrown'); πάροικος καὶ μισθωτὸς καὶ ἀ. Ju 4.10. Cf. ἀργύριον.

ἀρδαλόω: pf.ptc.pass. ἠρδαλωμένος.ʃ

to smear and make dirty: ***o*** stone, Si 22.1.

ἄρδην. adv.ʃ

utterly, wholly: χαλκᾶ ἄ. 'entirely of bronze' 3K 7.31 B (*L* ἦν); πατάξω τὴν γῆν ἄ. 'I shall deal the earth a deadly blow' Ma 4.5. See Renehan 2.36f.

ἀρέσκεια, ας. f.ʃ

that which pleases others: external charm or attraction, Pr 31.30 (|| κάλλος).

ἀρέσκω: fut. ἀρέσω; aor. ἤρεσα, subj. ἀρέσω, inf. ἀρέσαι, impv.3s ἀρεσάτω, opt.3s ἀρέσαι.

to be found acceptable, often impersonally used in the third person singular: abs., 4M 8.26; to sbd τινι– καθὰ ἂν ἀρέσκῃ ὑμῖν 'as it pleases you' Ge 19.8; οὗ ἄν σοι ἀρέσκῃ 'wherever you fancy' 20.15; ἤρεσεν αὐτῷ 'he approved of it' Le 10.20; εἰ μή σοι ἀρέσκει 'if you don't approve of it' Nu 22.34; εἰ ἀρέσει τῷ θεῷ 23.27; + δοκεῖ τινι Jo 9.25; + ἐναντίον τινός– Οὗ ἀρέσκει ἐναντίον αὐτῶν 'where they please' Nu 36.6; + ἐνώπιόν τινος Ju 7.16. **b**. w. explicit ***s***: ἤρεσαν οἱ λόγοι ἐναντίον Εμμωρ Ge 34.18; Ἤρεσεν τὰ ῥήματα ἐναντίον Φαραω 41.37; ἀρέσει τῷ κυρίῳ θυσία Ιουδα 'Judah's sacrifice will be pleasing to the Lord' Ma 3.4; + ἐνώπιον - ἤρεσεν ἐνώπιόν (v.l. ἐναντίον) μου τὸ ῥῆμα De 1.23; Jd 14.1 A (:: ἐν ὀφθαλμοῖς τινος vs. 3; εὐθής εἰμι B ib.), Je 18.4. **c**. w. a ὅτι-clause as ***s***: 3K 3.10. **d**. *to make oneself attractive* to sbd, *to ingratiate*: ἀρέσαι .. ἡ γυνή μου ἑτέρῳ Jb 31.10.

Cf. ἀρεστός, εὐαρεστέω.

ἀρεστός, ή, όν.

pleasing to senses: visually and ***s*** tree, ἀ. τοῖς ὀφθαλμοῖς ἰδεῖν Ge 3.6; ὡς ἄν σοι ~ὸν ᾖ 'as you please' 16.6. **b**. morally *pleasing*: ποιῆσαι .. ὡς ~ὸν ἐνώπιον αὐτῶν Ne 9.24, τῷ θεῷ 2E 7.18 (|| τὸ θέλημα τοῦ θεοῦ 1E 8.16). **c**. subst., alw. n. w. moral application, τὰ ~ὰ ἐναντίον αὐτοῦ ποιήσῃς Ex 15.26, ^κυρίῳ^ Si 19.19¶; τὸ ~ὸν καὶ τὸ καλὸν ἔναντι κυρίου De 6.18, 12.25, 28 (|| τὸ κ. καὶ τὸ ἀ… 13.18); ἕκαστος τὸ ~ὸν ἐναντίον αὐτοῦ 12.8; τὰ ~ὰ ἐνώπιόν σου Is 38.3; τὰ ~ὰ τῆς καρδίας αὐτῶν τῆς κακῆς Je 9.14, .. πονηρᾶς 16.12, sim. 18.12.

Cf. ἀρέσκω, δεκτός, καλός.

ἀρεταλογία, ας. f.ʃ*

sounds praising God's wonders: Si 36.19.

ἀρετή, ῆς. f.

1. *laudatory praise*: God's, ἐκάλυψεν οὐρανοὺς ἡ ἀ. αὐτοῦ 'the praise of Him filled heavens' Hb 3.3 (|| αἴνεσις); αὐτὸς λήμψεται ~ήν Zc 6.13; pl., ματαίων 'of vain things' Es C 21. Cf. ἀ. || ἔπαινος Phil. 4.8.

2. *excellent feature and property*: pl., God's, Is 42.8, 12 (|| δόξα, so 2Pet 1.3), Is 43.21, 63.7; ***s*** φρόνησις 'prudence' 4M 1.2. **b**. of soldiers, 'valour': 2M 10.28. **c**. *moral excellence*, 'virtue': Wi 4.1.

Cf. αἴνεσις: Bauernfeind, *TDNT* 1.457-61.

ἀρήγω.ʃ

to come to aid of sbd: abs., 3M 4.16.

Cf. ἐπαρήγω, βοηθέω: Schmidt 4.157f., 161.

ἀρήν, ἀρνός. m.

the young of sheep, 'lamb': προβάτων Si 47.3; ὡς ~νες ἐπὶ ἄγρωστιν 'as lambs (or: sheep) on the grass' Mi 5.7, γαλαθηνός 'sucking' Si 46.16; food, στέαρ ἀρνῶν καὶ κριῶν, υἱῶν ταύρων καὶ τράγων 'fat of lambs and rams, of calves and kids' De 32.14. Cf. ἀμνός, ἀρνίον, πρόβατον: Chantraine 1955.

ἀρθρέμβολον, ου. n.ʃ

instrument of torture applied to limbs: 4M 8.13. **b.** adj., *used in order to torture*: *s* ὄργανον 4M 10.5. Cf. βασανιστήριον.

ἄρθρον, ου. n.ʃ

joint (anatomical t.t.): τῆς καρδίας Jb 17.11; 4M 9.17. Cf. Schmidt 4.625f.

ἀριθμέω: fut. ἀριθμήσω, pass. ~μηθήσομαι; aor. ἠρίθμησα, impv. ἀρίθμησον, inf. ἀριθμῆσαι, pass.opt.3s ἀριθμηθείη; pf.pass.3s ἠρίθμηται.

1. *to count*: + acc., τοὺς ἀστέρας 'the stars' Ge 15.5, ὑετόν 'rain' Jb 28.26; pass., ἡ ἄμμος τῆς θαλάσσης 'the sand of the sea' Ge 32.12.

2. *to consider as part of* (+ εἴς τι): pass., Jb 3.6 (ǁ εἶναι εἴς τι).

3. *to muster*: + acc. pers., Ge 14.14 (as a fighting force). **b.** *to enumerate and evaluate*: + acc. rei, Pr 8.21a.

4. *to go through* a specified length of time (acc.): ἀριθμήσετε πεντήκοντα ἡμέρας 'you shall count fifty days' Le 23.16.

Cf. ἀριθμός, ἀριθμητός, ἐξ~, κατα~, παρ~, συναριθμέω.

ἀριθμητός, ή, όν.

counted: *s* a period of time, Jb 14.5; and allotted, ἔτη ~ά 'predetermined life-span' 16.22.

Cf. ἀριθμέω.

ἀριθμός, οῦ. m.

1. *sum total, aggregate* of countable objects: οὐ γὰρ ἦν ἀ. 'for it was innumerable' Ge 41.49, ὑπὲρ ~όν 'beyond reckoning' Ps 39.6; τῶν ἡμερῶν σου Ex 23.26; ὁ ἀ. τῶν υἱῶν Ισραηλ Ho 1.10; ǁ μέτρον 'measure', σταθμός 'weight' Wi 11.20; ~ῷ παρῆλθον 'they paraded, while being counted (?)' Is 34.16. **b.** ἡμέρας ~ῷ 'only for a few days' Nu 9.20 (:: ἡμέρας πλείους 9.19), ἄνδρας ~ῷ 'a few men' Ez 12.16; ὀλίγοι ~ῷ 'few in number' De 4.27; ἐν ~ῷ 'in small numbers' (?) Ez 20.37, 1M 9.65, cf. ἐν ~ῷ ἡμερῶν Si 37.25, "a good life is short-lived (ἀ. ἡμερῶν)" 41.13; ~ῷ τεσσαράκοντα '40 in number' Ez 25.3, τὸν ~ὸν πεντακόσιοι '50 in number' Su 30 LXX, ὄντας ~ὸν ἑξακισχιλίους 'being 60,000 in number' 2M 8.16; ἐπὶ τὸν ~ὸν αὐτῶν 'on their number, i.e. on all of them' or 'their troops' (**3**) Is 34.2. **c.** ref. to an unquantifiable entity: τῆς συνέσεως αὐτοῦ 'his ability to comprehend' Ps 146.5.

2. *a small, negligible number*: "the survivors will be few and far between" Is 10.19; ἡμέραι ~οῦ 'a short period' Si 17.2.

3. *unit of troops*: Is 34.2.

4. *act of counting*, 'census-taking': cogn. obj. of ἀριθμέω, 2C 2.16.

Cf. (ἐξ)αριθμέω, ἀναρίθμητος, μέτρον, σταθμός.

ἀριστάω: aor.inf. ἀριστῆσαι, impv. ἀρίστησον.

to eat the midday meal: Ge 43.25; To 2.1 𝔊II (𝔊I ἐσθίω). The time of the meal concerned cannot always be established with certainty.

ἀριστεία. ας. f.ʃ

excellence: moral and religious, 4M 12.16. Cf. ἄριστος.

ἀριστερός, ά, όν.

of the left hand side (opp. right): *s* χείρ Le 14.15; χείρ understood, ἐν τῇ ~ᾷ 'in his left hand' Ge 48.13 (:: δεξιά); οὐκ ἔγνωσαν .. ~ὰν αὐτῶν Jn 4.11 (:: δεξιά). **b.** subst.: n.pl., εἰ σὺ εἰς ἀριστερά, ἐγὼ εἰς δεξιά 'if you go left, I'll go right' Ge 13.9, ἐκ δεξιῶν .. ἐκ ~ῶν Ez 1.10; adv. 'to the left' Jb 23.9¶, cf. LSG s.v.; rarely n.sg., εἰς ~ὸν αὐτοῦ Ec 10.2. **c.** elliptically: ἵνα ἐπιστρέψω εἰς δεξιὰν ἢ εἰς ~άν 'in order that I may turn to the right or to the left' Ge 24.49; δεξιὰν οὐδὲ ~άν Nu 22.26; δεξιὰ ἢ ~ά 'whether to the right or to the left' De 17.20; εἴτε δεξιὰ εἴτε ~ά Is 30.21 δεξιὰ οὐδὲ ~ά 2.27, 17.11. **d.** in combination with δεξιά, the latter precedes: see examples above. **e.** subst. 'the north' ἐν ~ᾷ Δαμασκοῦ 'to the north of D.' Ge 14.15; ἐξ ~ῶν .. 'to the north of ..' To 1.2 𝔊II.

Cf. εὐώνυμος and δεξιός.

ἀριστεύω.ʃ

to prove stronger: κατά τινος 'than ..' 4M 1.18.

ἄριστον, ου. n.

meal: luncheon, 2K 24.15; quite substantial, 'dinner' 3K 2.46[e], To 2.1. Cf. δείπνιον.

ἄριστος, η, ον.ʃ

best: *s* soldiers, 2M 13.15; pilot of ship, 4M 7.1. Cf. ἀριστεία, βέλτιστος, καλός, κάλλιστος, κρείσσων, χείριστος: Schmidt 4.305f. Del. 3M 3.14 v.l.

ἀρκεύθινος, η, ον.ʃ

pertaining to ἄρκευθος (q.v.): *s* ξύλον, + κέδρινος, πεύκινος 2C 2.7; 3K 6.31. Cf. ἄρκευθος.

ἄρκευθος, ου. f.ʃ

juniper tree: ἄ. πυκάζουσα 'leafy juniper tree' Ho 14.9. Cf. ἀρκεύθινος.

ἀρκέω: fut. ἀρκέσω; aor.pass. ἠρκέσθην, ptc.pass. ἀρκεσθείς.

to suffice: + dat. pers., ἕκαστος τὸ ἀρκοῦν αὐτῷ συναριθμήσετε εἰς πρόβατον 'you shall each recruit people sufficient in number for one sheep' Ex 12.4; ἀρκέσει αὐτοῖς 'it will be enough to meet their needs' Nu 11.22*bis*, ἀρκέσει μοι τὸ δοθέν 'what I have been given will suffice for me' PSol 16.12. **b.** pass. *to be satisfied, content*: + dat., 2M

5.15. **c**. impers. ἀρκεῖ 'Good enough, no more needed!' Pr 30.16 (‖ ἱκανόν vs. 15).

Cf. δι~, ἐξαρκέω, ἱκανός: Kittel, *TDNT* 1.464-7.

ἄρκος, ου. c.

bear: likely to attack humans, 1K 17.34; ἐμπέσῃ αὐτῷ ἡ ἄ. 'a bear attacks him' Am 5.19 (‖ λέων); Ho 13.8.

᾿Αρκτοῦρος, ου. m.ʃ

the star *Arcturus*: Jb 9.9.

ἅρμα, ατος. n.

1. *war-chariot*: ἔζευξεν Φαραω τὰ ~ατα αὐτοῦ 'Ph. harnessed his chariots' Ex 14.6; οὐδὲ ἐν πολέμῳ οὐδὲ ἐν ~ασιν Ho 1.7; 10.13; καταστρέψω ~ατα καὶ ἀναβάτας 'I shall overthrow chariots with (their) riders' Hg 2.22; drawn by horses, ψόφος ~άτων καὶ ἱππευόντων 'sound of chariots and horsemen' Mi 1.13, cf. Na 2.4, 3.2, Zc 6.2, 3; ‖ ἵππος, Mi 5.10, Zc 9.10, Is 2.7. **b**. *warrior mounted on a chariot*: Jd 4.13 *L*. **c**. ἅ. χερουβιν Si 49.8.

2. *vehicle for transport of persons*, 'carriage': ἀνεβίβασεν αὐτὸν ἐπὶ τὸ ἅ. τὸ δεύτερον τῶν αὐτοῦ 'he put him on the second of his carriages' Ge 41.43; ~ατα καὶ ἱππεῖς 50.9, .. καὶ ἵπποι Je 17.25.

Cf. ἵππος.

ἁρματηλάτης, ου. m.ʃ

chariot-driver: 1K 8.11*L*, 2M 9.4.

ἁρμόζω: fut. ἁρμόσω; aor. ἥρμοσα, mid.impv. ἅρμοσαι; pf.ptc.pass. ἡρμοσμένος.

1. *to fit together, join*: + acc. rei, χορδήν 'a string' Na 3.8.

2. *to set in order*: 'to tune' + acc. rei, harp Ps 151.2, ὄργανον '(tongue as) musical instrument' PSol 15.3; κοινολογίαν 'coordinating consultation' 2M 14.22.

3. *to befit*: αἰδώς '(befitting) sense of modesty' 3M 1.19; + dat., Pr 17.7. **b**. *to give* that which is *befitting*: pass., + dat., ***o*** wife, Pr 19.14.

Cf. ἁρμόνιος.

ἁρμονία, ας. f.ʃ

1. *counterpart which fits sth else and holds it fast*: Ez 37.7.

2. *music*: φωνὴ ~ας Ez 23.42.

ἁρμόνιος, ον.ʃ

suited, fitting: πρός + acc., Wi 16.20. Cf. ἁρμόζω, ἄξιος.

ἁρμός, οῦ. m.ʃ

joint: in masonry, λίθων Si 27.2; in the body, 4M 10.5. Cf. LSG s.v.

ἀρνέομαι: fut. ἀρνήσομαι; aor. ἠρνησάμην, ptc. ἀρνησάμενος.ʃ

1. *to say that a statement heard or presented is untrue*: ἠρνήσατο .. λέγουσα Ge 18.15.

2. *to deny the value or validity of*: + acc. rei, θεσμόν 'law' 4M 8.7, ἀδελφότητα 'brotherhood' 10.15.

3. *to refuse* to do: + inf., Wi 12.27, 16.16, 17.10.

Cf. ἀπ~, ἐξαρνέομαι, ὁμολογέω: Schlier, *TDNT* 1.469-71; Spicq 1.199-205.

ἀρνίον, ου. n.

(little) *lamb*: ἀ. προβάτων Ps 113.4, 6 (‖ κριοί 'rams'), Je 27.45; to be slaughtered, 11.19. Cf. ἀρήν, πρόβατον: Berenguer Sánchez 1989.

ἀροτήρ, ῆρος. m.ʃ

ploughman: Is 61.5.

ἀροτρίασις, εως. f.ʃ *

v.n. of ἀροτριάω **1**: Ge 45.6 (‖ ἄμητος 'harvesting'), 1K 8.12 *L* (om. B) (‖ θερισμός, τρύγητος). Cf. ἀροτριάω and ἄμητος.

ἀροτριάω: fut. ἀροτριάσω, pass. ~τριαθήσομαι; aor. ἠροτρίασα.

1. *to plough* (a field): ἐν μόσχῳ καὶ ὄνῳ 'with an ox and an ass' De 22.10, ἐν βουσίν 'with cows' 3K 19.19; ὡς ἀγρὸς ἀροτριαθήσεται Mi 3.12, πᾶν ὄρος ἀροτριώμενον ἀροτριαθήσεται 'every mountain shall be deeply ploughed' (Ottley) Is 7.25; ὁ ἀροτριῶν καὶ ὁ σπείρων 'the plougher and the sower' Si 6.19; ***s*** cattle, Jb 1.14; ***o*** τὴν γῆν Is 45.9, ἀγρός 'field' and pass., Je 33.18; cogn. obj., ἀροτρίασιν 1K 8.12 *L* (om. B; + θερίζω, τρυγᾶν); ἐν δαμάλει 'with a heifer' Jd 14.18 B.

*__2__. *to sow*, unless a calque on Heb. חָרַשׁ 'to devise, design': metaph. and + acc., ψεῦδος ἐπ' ἀδελφῷ σου Si 7.12, ἄτοπα 'wrong things' Jb 4.8.

Cf. ἀροτρίασις, ἄροτρον, ἄρουρα: Lee 113.

ἄροτρον, ου. n.

plough: ‖ δρέπανον 'sickle' Mi 4.3, Jl 3.10, Is 2.4; ‖ δόρα Si 38.25. Cf. ἀροτριάω.

ἀροτρόπους, οδος. m.ʃ*

ploughshare: Jd 3.31B.

ἄρουρα, ας. f.

tilled land: Ge 21.33. Cf. ἀγρός: Schmidt 3.70f.; Barr 1967.

ἁρπαγή, ῆς. f.

1. *act of unlawfully seizing* sbd else's possession: Le 6.2; widows as victims, Is 10.2 (‖ προνομή); To 3.4 $\mathfrak{G}^{II}$ (‖ αἰχμαλωσία, θάνατος); εἰς φόνον καὶ ~ήν Ju 2.11; pl. 1M 13.34.

2. *unlawfully seized article*: sg. collectively, of prey caught by a lion Na 2.13 (‖ θήρα); property of the poor, Is 3.14.

Cf. ἅρπαγμα, ἁρπάζω, λάφυρον.

ἅρπαγμα, ατος. n.

unlawfully or violently seized article: ἀποδῷ τὸ ἅ., ὃ ἥρπασεν 'he should return ..' Le 6.4; offered to God, Ma 1.13; ***s*** lions' prey, Ez 19.3. Cf. ἁρπαγή and ἁρπάζω.

ἁρπάζω: fut. ἁρπάσω, mid. ἁρπῶμαι; aor. ἥρπασα, subj. ἁρπάσω, inf. ἁρπάσαι, ptc. ἁρπάσας, pass. ἡρπάγην; pf. ἥρπακα, ptc.pass. ἡρπασμένος.

1. *to seize unlawfully* (sth [acc.] that does not belong to oneself): *s* lion, Am 3.4, Na 2.13, cf. Ho 5.14, Mi 5.8; hum., ἅρπαγμα, ὃ ἥρπασεν Le 6.4; *o* donkey, ἀπὸ σοῦ De 28.31 (:: ἀποδίδωμι), κρίμα πενήτων 'the just share of the poor' Is 10.2, ἅρπαγμα Ez 18.7, δίαιταν 'residence' Jb 20.19.

2. *to rob*: + acc. pers., πτωχόν Ps 9.30.

3. *to tear away, forcibly remove*: + acc. rei, 2K 23.21B (*L* and || 1C 11.23 ἀφαιρέω); *o* hum., Ge 37.33 (possibly **1**), Wi 4.11 (from this world); skin and flesh, Mi 3.2, cf. Ho 6.1; ὀρφανὸν ἀπὸ μαστοῦ 'an orphan from the breast' Jb 24.9.

4. *to seize*: φρίκην αὐτοῦ 'awe of him' Am 1.11.

5. *to captivate, allure*: + acc., ὀφθαλμόν τινος Ju 16.9 (|| αἰχμαλωτίζω).

Cf. ἀνα~, δι~, συναρπάζω, ἁρπαγή, ἁρπαγμός, ἅρπαξ, ἀφαιρέω, λαφυρέω, λεηλατέω, λωποδέω, προνομεύω.

ἅρπαξ, αγος. m./f.ʃ

rapacious animal: λύκος ἅ. 'rapacious wolf' Ge 49.27. Cf. ἁρπάζω.

ἀρραβών, ῶνος. m.ʃ An Aramaic loanword (עֵרָבוֹן).

sth of value which is handed over as security that a promise will be fully kept, 'pledge': Ge 38.17; Τίνα τὸν ~ῶνά σοι δώσω 'what shall I give you as the pledge?' 38.18; κομίσασθαι τὸν ~ῶνα παρὰ τῆς γυναικός 'to retrieve the pledge from the woman' 38.20. See MM s.v.; Kerr 1988; LSG s.v.

ἀρρενωδῶς. adv.ʃ*

bravely: *s* soldiers, 2M 10.35.

ἄρρηκτος, ον.ʃ

unbreakable: *s* πέδαι 'fetters' 3M 4.9. Cf. ῥήγνυμι.

ἄρριζος, ον.ʃ

without roots: metaph. and *s* hum., Jb 31.8. Cf. ῥίζα.

ἀρρωστέω: aor. ἠρρώστησα, inf. ~στῆσαι.

to fall ill or *to suffer illness*: *s* hum., 2K 12.15; Si 18.21; εἰς θάνατον (*L* and || 2C 32.24 ἕως .. ~ου) 'critically' 4K 20.1; + cogn. acc., ἀρρωστίαν 13.14. Cf. ἀρρώστημα, ἀρρωστία, ἐνοχλέω.

ἀρρώστημα, ατος. n.

sickness: μακρόν 'chronic' Si 10.10, ἔμμονον 'ditt.' 30.17, βαρύ 'severe' 34.2. Cf. ἀρρωστία, ἀσθένεια, μαλακία, ὑγίεια.

ἀρρωστία, ας. f.

1, *sickness*: Ps 40.4; love-sickness, 2K 13.2 *L*; cogn. obj., ἠρρώστησε .. ~αν κραταιάν 3K 12.24[h].

2. *sickening, disheartening state of affairs*, 'general malaise': Ec 5.12, + ματαιότης 'futility' 6.2.

Cf. ἄρρωστος, ἀρρώστημα, μαλακία.

ἄρρωστος, ον.ʃ

sickly: subst., and of ceremonially unacceptable sacrificial animal, Ma 1.8 (|| τυφλός 'blind' and χωλός 'lame'); *s* hum., Si 7.35. Cf. ἀρρωστία, ἐνοχλέω, ἀσθενής, ῥώμη: Schmidt 3.701f.; *ND* 3.63.

ἀρσενικός, όν.

belonging to the male sex: *s* εἰκών 'idol' Ez 16.17; subst. πᾶν ~όν 'every male' Ge 17.10 (w. ref. to human male: παιδίον understood[?] and || πᾶν ἄρσεν 17.23), Ex 34.23, De 16.16 (irrespective of age); πᾶν ~ὸν τῶν ἱερέων Le 6.18; || θηλυκός 'female' Nu 5.3; pl.n. τὰ ~ά Ex 13.12, 34.19. Cf. ἄρσην, θηλυκός: Shipp 99f.

ἄρσην (ἄρρην), εν; gen. ~ενος.

male: of animal, Ge 1.27 (opp. θῆλυς), Le 1.3; subst. and hum., ἀπερίτμητος ἄ. 'uncircumcised male' Ge 17.14; 34.24 (|| ἀρσενικός vs. 25); κοίτη ἄρσενος 'intercourse with a male' Nu 31.17 (|| κ. ἀνδρός vs. 35), cf. LSG, s.v. Cf. ἀνήρ, ἀρσενικός, θῆλυς.

ἄρσις, εως. f.

1. v.n. of αἴρω **1**: πυρός 'of (torch-)fire' Jd 20.41*L*.

2. *that which is lifted and carried*, 'load, burden': Ps 80.7; ἦρεν ~ιν ἡμῖν 2K 19.43, καμήλων 4K 8.9; 7.8. Cf. αἴρω.

ἀρτάβη, ης. f.ʃ

Egyptian dry measure of capacity: of seeds, Is 5.10; of flour, Bel 3. Cf. LSG s.v.

ἀρτήρ, ῆρος. m.ʃ

**that with which one carries things*: Ne 4.17.

ἄρτι. adv.

just now: Da 9.22 LXX (TH νῦν). **b**. ref. to the past, *just at that moment*: Ju 9.1, ἄ. αὐτοῦ καταλήξαντος *just as he finished*' 2M 9.5; *just a short while before*, 3.28.

Cf. ἀρτίως, νῦν, πάλαι: Shipp 101f.

ἀρτίως. adv.ʃ

= ἄρτι: τότε καὶ ἀ. 2K 15.34. Cf. προσαρτίως.

ἀρτοκοπικός, ή, όν.ʃs

belonging to a baker or *baking*: subst.n., some baked food, 1C 16.3.

ἄρτος, ου. m.

1. *bread*: as essential to man's physical existence, alm. = "food," φάγῃ τὸν ἄ. σου Ge 3.19; δῷ μοι ~ον φαγεῖν καὶ ἱμάτιον περιβαλέσθαι 'gives me bread to eat and clothes to put on' 28.20 (basic needs for human subsistence), sim. De 10.18 (provided by God), cf. ἀπ' οὐρανοῦ Wi 16.20, ἄ. ἐξ οὐρανοῦ Ne 9.15, ἄ. οὐρανοῦ Ps 77.24, ἀγγέλων Ps 77.25; || οἶνος and ὕδωρ Ex 23.25; λιμὸς ~ου 'famine of food' Am 8.11; ἄ. πένθους 'mourners' bread' Ho 9.4*a*, ἤσθιον τὸν ~ον μετὰ πένθους To 2.5 𝔊[II], cf. ἄ. θλίψεως 'bread on reduced rations' Is 30.20 (|| ὕδωρ στενόν), ἄ. θ. καὶ ὕδωρ θ. 3K 22.27; as cultic offering, Hg 2.12 (sg. and along w. other kinds

of offerings), ἄ. ἐν πρώτοις 'shewbread' Si 45.20 = ~οι τοῦ προσώπου Ne 10.33; pl. w. ref. to varieties of offerings, προσάγοντες πρὸς τὸ θυσιαστήριόν μου ~ους ἠλισγημένους 'bringing to my altar polluted foods' Ma 1.7; Ho 9.4*b*. **b**. *meal*, more idiomatically in the pl. (**2**): ὅπως ~ον φάγῃ 'so that he may dine (with us)' Ex 2.20.

2. pl. *food*: μετ' ἐμοῦ φάγονται ~ους 'they are going to dine with me' Ge 43.16; ~ους καὶ ἀσκὸν ὕδατος '.. and a skinful of water' 21.14; Παράθετε ~ους 43.31; ἔνδεια ~ων 'shortage of food' Am 4.6; τοὺς ~ους μου καὶ τὸ ὕδωρ μου καὶ τὰ ἱμάτιά μου .. καὶ πάντα ὅσα μοι καθήκει Ho 2.5; τῶν ἐθνῶν To 1.10; manna Ex 16.4, but sg. 2.20, Ne 9.15, Wi 16.20, Ps 77.24, 104.40. **b**. sg and metaph., συνέσεως Si 15.3 (‖ ὕδωρ σοφίας); pl., Pr 20.13.

Cf. ὕδωρ, τροφή: Behm, *TDNT* 1.476f.; Daniel 131-43; Shipp 102f.; Battaglia 74-8.

ἀρτός, ή, όν.ʃ *

to be carried: Nu 4.27. Cf. αἴρω.

ἀρχαῖος, α, ον.

having come into existence long ago, 'ancient': *s* κολυμβήθρα 'pool' Is 22.9, ἐξ ~ων ἡμερῶν Is 37.26. ἐν ἡμέραις ~αις Ps 43.2, ‖ αἰώνιος 76.6, ~αι γενεαί '.. generations' Si 2.10, φίλος 9.10, φιλία 2M 6.21; χείρ '(old) hand' Wi 13.10, βουλή 'decision, design' Is 25.1; subst. n., ἀποκατασταθήσεται εἰς τὸ ~ον 'will be restored to its former status' 23.16; τὰ ~α 43.18 (‖ τὰ πρῶτα), Ps 138.5 (:: τὰ ἔσχατα), Wi 8.8 (:: τὰ μέλλοντα 'the future'); m. ~οι 'predecessors' Si 39.1. Cf. αἰώνιος, παλαιός, νέος: Schmidt 2.79-87; Trench 249-53; Delling, *TDNT* 1.486f.

ἀρχή, ῆς. f.

1. *beginning, commencement*: ἀ. λόγου κυρίου ἐν Ωσηε 'here begins the Lord's pronouncement through Hosea' Ho 1.2. **b**. *beginning, starting point*: temporally, and specifically 'the primaeval era' – ἐν ~ῇ ἐποίησεν ὁ θεὸς τὸν οὐρανὸν καὶ τὴν γῆν Gn 1.1, cf. ὄρη ~ῆς 'very ancient mountains' De 33.15 (‖ βουνοὶ ἀέναοι 'eternal hills') and θεοῦ ~ῆς .. βραχιόνων ἀενάων '.. of eternal arms' 33.27, and Rösel 28f.; υἱοὶ βασιλέων τῶν ἐξ ~ῆς 'descendants of ancient kings' Is 19.11, ἀπὸ γενεῶν ~ῆς 41.4, ἐξ ἡμερῶν ~ῆς 'in the primaeval era' 4K 19.25*L*, οἱ γίγαντες .. οἱ ἀπ' ~ῆς 'the giants of olden days' Ba 3.26; ποιήσει κεφαλὴν καὶ οὐράν, ἀρχὴν καὶ τέλος 'he will make head and tail, beginning and end' Is 19.15, cf. 9.14f.; ἀπ' ~ῆς 'from the very beginning' Hb 1.12, 'a long time ago' Is 22.11, 'previously, formerly' Ez 16.55; foll. by ἐξ ἡμερῶν αἰῶνος Mi 5.2 (cf. Ge 1.1), by ἡμερῶν εἰς ἡμέρας 'at the beginning of every year' 2K 14.26; ἐξ ~ῆς Is 40.21, Si 15.14; ἀπ' ~ῆς τοῦ ἐνιαυτοῦ καὶ ἕως συντελείας τοῦ ἐνιαυτοῦ 'from the beg. of the year to the end ..' De 11.12; 'former times'– καθὼς ἀπ' ~ῆς 'as before' Zc 12.7, ὡς τὸ ἀπ' ~ῆς Is 1.26 (‖ ὡς τὸ πρότερον), 2.5; ‖ ἔμπροσθεν Ez 36.11; spatially, ἐπ' ~ὰς πασῶν τῶν ὁδῶν αὐτῆς 'at the top of all her roads' Na 3.10, ἐξόδων La 2.19, 4.1; of branches at the source of a river, ἀφορίζεται εἰς τέσσαρας ~άς 'splits into four new rivers' Ge 2.10, cf. τρισὶν ~αῖς 'in three detachments' 1K 13.17. **c**. *the first to have arrived* among a group of entities: ἀ. τέκνων 'the first-born child': Ge 49.3, De 21.17 [= πρωτότοκος υἱός]; ἀ. μηνῶν 'the first month (of a year)' Ex 12.2 (glossed as πρῶτός ἐστιν ὑμῖν ἐν τοῖς μησὶν τοῦ ἐνιαυτοῦ); *the first to be reached, the nearest end*, Jd 7.11 B (A: μέρος), 7.17 B. **d**. τὴν ~ήν: adv., 'at the beginning; initially; previously'– θυσιαστηρίου, οὗ ἐποίησεν ἐκεῖ τὴν ~ήν 'the altar that he had previously constructed there' (*pace BA* – 'l'autel qu'il avait fondé là') Ge 13.4; καθὰ καὶ τὴν ~ήν 'as before' 41.21; 43.18, 20; ~ήν 'to begin with, at first' 2E 8.18. **e**. ἀρχῆς adv., 'at the beginning': Wi 14.6. **f**. spatially: ἐν ~ῇ τοῦ λαοῦ 'in the front seat ..' 3K 20.9. **g**. λαμβάνω ~ήν, an obscure, mechanical (?) rendering of /nāśā' rōʾš/ 'to take a headcount' Nu 1.2, 26.2, cf. 4.22 λάβε τὴν ~ήν 'Take the sum total' for the same Heb. idiom. Cf. κεφάλαιον **2**.

2. *rule, dominion*: over sth τινος – δυναστῶν Am 6.7; ἡ ἀ. ἡ πρώτη Mi 4.8; pl.(!), εἰς ~ὰς τῆς ἡμέρας .. εἰς ~ὰς τῆς νυκτός Ge 1.16, cf. vs. 18 ἄρχειν τῆς ἡμέρας, and τῷ ποιήσαντι .. τὸν ἥλιον εἰς ἐξουσίαν τῆς ἡμέρας Ps 135.7f. (cf. Lefebvre 1995; Dines 2007.26-30) and ἐκραταιώθησαν αἱ ~αὶ αὐτῶν '.. has been strengthened' 138.17; ἡ γῆ ~ῆς αὐτοῦ 'his empire' Je 41.1. **b**. *domain, realm over which one's sovereignty extends*: Ob 20; ἧς ἡ ἀ. θάλασσα 'whose dominion is the sea' Na 3.8; Da TH 11.41 (or: 'the elite, the upper echelon'); + τιμή, βασιλεία 7.14 TH. **c**. *one who rules*: ἐθνῶν Nu 24.20, Am 6.1; οἴκου Ιακωβ Mi 3.1; Na 1.6; of military leader, θήσονται ἑαυτοῖς ~ὴν μίαν Ho 1.11; head of a household, αἱ ~αὶ πατριᾶς Λευιτῶν Ex 6.25 (‖ ἀρχηγός vs. 14); ταπεινή 'lowly' Ez 29.14; Ne 9.17; + βασιλεύς PSol 2.30. **d**. *leadership position*: of military commander, Jd 20.18 B; of temple staff, 1C 26.10; high priest, 4M 4.17. Cf. συναρχία.

3. *high office*: τὴν ~ήν σου τὴν προτέραν 'your former office' Ge 40.13.

4. *the far end*: Ex 36.24; ὁδοῦ Ez 16.25, 21.20, cf. LSG, s.v. **b**. vertically: *the top* or *summit* of a mountain range, τοῦ Λιβάνου Je 22.6; of a tree, Ez 31.3, 10.

5. *that which is fundamental and of prime importance*: ἀ. ζωῆς ὕδωρ καὶ ἄρτος καὶ ἱμάτιον καὶ οἶκος Si 29.21, ἀ. σοφίας φόβος θεοῦ Ps 110.10, Pr 1.7, sim. Si 1.14; ἀ. ^σοφίας^ ἡ ἀληθεστάτη παιδείας ἐπιθυμία '.. the most sincere desire for instruction' Wi 6.17; ἀ. γενημάτων 'the best product' Je 2.3, ἀ. γλυκασμάτων 'the best among sweet foods' Si 11.3, ἀ. πλάσματος κυρίου Jb 40.19; ἀ. τῆς δυναστείας αὐτῶν 'the mainstay of their strength' Je 25.15; elite troops or aristocracy, Da 11.41 TH.

*6. *division of an army*, 'company' (calque on Heb. ראשׁ): Jd 7.16, 1K 11.11, 1M 5.33.

Cf. ἀρχῆθεν, ἄρχω, φιλαρχία, μεσότης, συντέλεια, τέλος, τυραννίς: Delling, *TDNT* 1.481; Dines 2007.24f.

ἀρχηγέτης, ου. m.ʃ

leader: ἱστορίας '(leading) historian' 2M 2.30. Cf. ἄρχω, ἡγέομαι.

ἀρχηγός, όν.

subst. **1**. *prime mover, leader*: ~οὶ οἴκων πατριῶν Ex 6.14 (ǁ ἀρχαί vs. 25); Ισραηλ 'of Is.' Nu 10.4 (ǁ ἄρχων), Μωαβ 'of Moab' 24.17; λαῶν De 33.21 (ǁ ἄρχων); military, Jd 11.11 B (A: ἡγούμενος), Ju 14.2; of a maiden, + πατήρ Je 3.4; ~οὺς παρθένους 'leading virgins' La 2.10; ἀ. ἁμαρτίας αὐτή ἐστι τῇ θυγατρὶ Σιων 'she leads the daughter of Zion into sin' Mi 1.13, τῆς κακίας 1M 9.61.

2. *initiator*: λόγων εἰρηνικῶν 'of peaceful dialogue' 1M 10.47.

Cf. ἀρχή, ἄρχων, ἡγέομαι, καθηγημών: Delling, *TDNT* 1.487; Casevitz 1985.246-8.

ἀρχῆθεν. adv.ʃ

from the beginning: 3M 3.21. Cf. ἀρχή: Shipp 103.

ἀρχιδεσμοφύλαξ, κος. m.* ʃ

chief jailer: Ge 39.21f.; δεσμωτηρίου 39.23. Cf. ἀρχιδεσμώτης.

ἀρχιδεσμώτης, ου.ʃ

governor of prison: Ge 40.4. Cf. prec.

ἀρχιεράομαι.ʃ *

to serve as high priest: 4M 4.18. Cf. ἀρχιερεύς, ἀρχιερατεύω.

ἀρχιερεύς, έως. m.

high priest: ὁ ἀ. ὁ κεχρισμένος 'the anointed ..' Le 4.3; τοῦ ἔθνους σου 1M 10.20 (royal appointment). Cf. ὁ ἱερεὺς ὁ μέγας Nu 35.25, ἱ. ὁ μέγας Si 50.1; ἱ. μ. 1M 14.20. Cf. ἱερεύς, ἀρχιεράομαι: Schrenk, *TDNT* 3.265-70.

ἀρχιερατεύω.ʃ

to serve as high priest: 1M 14.47. Cf. ἀρχιεράομαι.

ἀρχιερωσύνη, ης. f.

office of high priest: 1M 7.21; up for sale, 2M 11.3; ancestral glory, 14.7; life appointment, 4M 4.1.

ἀρχιευνοῦχος, ου. m. *

chief eunuch: Da 1.3. Cf. εὐνοῦχος.

ἀρχιμάγειρος, ου.*

chief cook: of a royal court and wielding considerable authority, τῷ σπάδοντι Φαραω, ~ῳ 'to the eunuch of Ph., chief cook' Ge 37.36.

ἀρχιοινοχοΐα, ας. f.ʃ *

office of ἀρχιοινοχόος (q.v.): Ge 40.13. Cf. ἀρχιοινοχόος.

ἀρχιοινοχόος, ου. m.*

chief cupbearer: in the court of Pharaoh, and eunuch, Ge 40.1; in the court of Sennacherib and with additional functions, καὶ ἐπὶ τοῦ δακτυλίου καὶ διοικητὴς καὶ ἐκλογιστὴς ἐπὶ Σενναχηρειμ βασιλέως Ἀσσυρίων 'also in charge of the signet-ring, steward, accountant to S. ..' To 1.22 𝔊[II]. Cf. ἀρχιοινοχοΐα.

ἀρχιπατριώτης, ου.ʃ*

head of a family: Jo 21.1, Da 3.94 LXX.

ἀρχισιτοποιός, οῦ. m. *

chief baker: in the court of Pharaoh, and eunuch, Ge 40.1.

ἀρχιστράτηγος, ου. m.

commander-in-chief: τῆς δυνάμεως αὐτοῦ Ge 21.22; 1K 12.9. Cf. στρατηγός.

ἀρχισωματοφύλαξ, κος. m.ʃ *

head of security service: 1K 28.2; king's eunuchs, Es 2.21.

ἀρχιτεκτονέω: aor. ἠρχιτεκτόνησα, inf. ~νῆσαι.ʃ

1. *to work as commissioner of building works*: Ex 31.4, 35.32.

2. *to design and construct*: + acc. rei, τὰ ὑφαντὰ καὶ τὰ ῥαφιδευτὰ .. 'things woven and embroidered ..' Ex 37.21.

Cf. ἀρχιτέκτων.

ἀρχιτεκτονία, ας. f.ʃ *

architecture: ἔργα ~ας Ex 35.32. Cf. ἀρχιτέκτων.

ἀρχιτέκτων, ονος.ʃ m.

master builder: a member of working-class, and no intellectual, τέκτων καὶ ἀ. Si 38.27; σοφός Is 3.3; οἰκίας and with overall responsibility, 2M 2.29. Cf. ἀρχιτεκτονέω, ἀρχιτεκτονία, τέκτων: Spicq 1.209-11.

ἀρχίφυλος, ου. m. *

chief of tribe: ǁ γερουσία, κριταί, γραμματοεισαγωγεῖς De 29.10; Jo 21.1. Cf. φύλαρχος.

ἄρχω: fut. ἄρξω, mid. ἄρξομαι; aor.act. ἦρξα, ptc. ἄρξας, impv. ἄρξον, inf. ἄρξαι, mid. ἠρξάμην, inf. ἄρξασθαι, ptc. ἀρξάμενος, impv. ἄρξαι, subj. ἄρξωμαι; pf.mid, ἦργμαι.

1. *to rule*: abs. Ho 8.4 (ǁ βασιλεύω), ἄρχουσαι 'the upper rank among royal consorts' 3K 11.1; μετὰ κρίσεως Is 32.1; + gen. rei, τῆς ἡμέρας καὶ τῆς νυκτός Ge 1.18; τῶν ἰχθύων τῆς θαλάσσης καὶ τῶν πετεινῶν τοῦ οὐρανοῦ καὶ τῶν κτηνῶν .. ib. 26; τῆς γῆς Is 14.9; + gen. pers., Ge 4.7; πάσης γῆς

Αἰγύπτου 45.26; ἐθνῶν πολλῶν De 28.12; + ἐν - ἐν χώραις La 1.1, ἐν ἡμῖν Jd 8.22A*L* (B: ἡμῶν).

2. *to manage, administer*:+ gen., τῷ παιδὶ αὐτοῦ τῷ πρεσβυτέρῳ τῆς οἰκίας αὐτοῦ τῷ ἄρχοντι πάντων τῶν αὐτοῦ 'to his elderly servant of his household in charge of all his affairs' Ge 24.2; ἐν ἀργυρίῳ 2E 8.17.

3. mid. *to begin, make beginning, commence*: ἀπὸ τοῦ πρεσβυτέρου ἀρξάμενος .. ἕως ἦλθεν ἐπὶ τὸν νεώτερον 'beginning from the eldest .. till he got to the youngest' Ge 44.12; ἤρξατο εἰς ἀγαθά 'began (to act) for her good' Mi 1.12, ἀρχομένη (corrupted to ἐρ~; propos. Muraoka, see MT) .. ἑωθινή 'starting early in the morning' Am 7.1; + inf. (either pres. or aor.) Ge 2.3, 18.27, Nu 16.46 (‖ ἐνάρχω vs. 47), Ho 5.11, 6.11, 7.5; + τοῦ inf., Mi 6.13, Jn 3.4, Ez 13.6; + a second vb fin., 'to start by doing ..', ἤρξατο .. καὶ ἐφύτευσεν ἀμπελῶνα '(after the flood) he started by planting a vineyard' Ge 9.20; 2E 3.8; *s* battle, 1M 5.31; + gen., τῆς ὑποθέσεως 'the fundamental' 4M 1.12; v. n., 2C 20.22, 2M 2.32. **b**. *to be the first* to do sth: οὗτος ἤρξατο εἶναι γίγας 'he was the first to become a giant' Ge 10.8.

***4**. *to act forthwith*: ἀρξάμενος αὐλίσθητι 'Stay overnight. No argument!' Jd 19.6 A (B: Ἄγε δὴ ..).

Cf. ἀρχή, ἄρχων, ἐν~, ἐπ~, κατάρχω, ἀπαρχή, ἡγέομαι, τελέω: Hesseling.

ἄρχων, οντος. m.

1. *one who rules*, with less power and authority than βασιλεύς: local chieftain, τῆς γῆς Ge 34.2, "world leaders (in commerce)" Is 23.8; Ge 42.6 (of Joseph as governor of Egypt and ‖ ὁ κύριος τῆς γῆς vs. 30, so also 45.8f.); Ho 12.11; w. gen. of subjects or domain, τῶν ἐμῶν κτηνῶν 'my cattle' Ge 47.5; Ho 7.16, Am 2.3, Zp 3.3; τῆς συναγωγῆς Ex 16.22, τῆς στρατιᾶς De 20.9, βασιλείας Da 10.13, 20 TH (LXX στρατηγός), τῆς πόλεως Jd 9.30, Ju 6.14, τῶν ἱερέων Ne 12.7; domain indicated by ἔν τινι, Mi 5.2; appointed with anointment, Ho 8.10; named, ὡς ἄ. Σαλαμαν 10.14; ‖ βασιλεύς 3.4, Is 32.1, Je 39.32 (and following it, but preceding it at Nu 21.18), Ho 7.3 (cf. 7.5), 13.10; "kings, priests and ἄρχοντες" Je 4.9 + Am 1.15, κριτὴν .. καὶ ~τας 2.3, ἄ... καὶ κριτής Mi 7.3; subordinate to Pharaoh, 'courtier' Ge 12.15; τοῦ βασιλέως Da 2.15 TH; ‖ ἡγούμενος Ge 49.10, ‖ προηγούμενος De 20.9, ‖ ἀφηγούμενος Ez 12.10; ‖ ἡγεμών Ex 15.15; τοῦ λαοῦ and ‖ θεοί 22.28; a disguised reference to a pagan deity (MT: Moloch), Le 18.21, 20.2; ‖ ἀρχηγός De 33.21; + ἡγούμενος 1M 9.30. **b**. f., ἀρχούσας θυγατέρας Σιων 'the leading ladies of Z.' Is 3.17; 2C 35.25.

2. *he who is charged with important functions*: δώρων Je 28.59.

Cf. ἄρχω, ἀρχηγός, ἐθνάρχης, ἀρχή, μόναρχος, ἡγέομαι, πρύτανις, τύραννις: Delling, *TDNT* 1.488f.; Raurell 1986; Freund.

ἀρωδιός. ⇒ ἐρωδιός.

ἄρωμα, ατος. n.

aromatic substance: 2C 9.1 (‖ 3K 10.2 ἥδυσμα), Si 24.15.

ἀσάλευτος, ον.ʃ

immovable: subst., either n.sg. or pl., σημεῖον ἐπὶ τῆς χειρὸς καὶ ~ον/α πρὸ ὀφθαλμῶν Ex 13.16, De 6.8, 11.18. Cf. σαλεύω: Frankel *Einfl*. 89-91; *BA* 2.52-5, 5.45f.

ἀσβόλη, ης. f.ʃ

soot: symb. of blackness, La 4.8.

ἀσέβεια, ας. f.

impiety, ungodliness: ‖ ἀδικία, Ho 10.13; τὸν πλοῦτον αὐτῶν ~ας Mi 6.12; ταλαιπωρίαν καὶ ~αν Hb 1.3; opp. δικαιοσύνη De 9.4; ἀ. ἁμαρτίας (gen.) Ps 31.6; ref. to illicit sexual intercourse, Ez 22.11, taking of bribes Jb 36.18. **b**. *act of impiety, ungodliness*: πληροῦντας .. ~ας καὶ δόλου Zp 1.9; pl. Ho 11.12 (‖ ψεῦδος); ἐπὶ ταῖς τρισὶν ~αις Δαμασκοῦ Am 1.3; 5.12 (‖ ἁμαρτία); committed against humans, διὰ τὴν σφαγὴν καὶ τὴν ~αν τὴν εἰς τὸν ἀδελφόν σου Ob 10, cf. διὰ αἵματα ἀνθρώπων καὶ ~ας γῆς Hb 2.8.

Cf. ἀσεβέω, ἀσέβημα, ἀσεβής, ἄνομος, ἀδικία, ἁμαρτία: Trench 242; Foerster, *TDNT* 7.187f.

ἀσεβέω: fut. ἀσεβήσω; aor. ἠσέβησα, subj. ἀσεβήσω, inf. ἀσεβῆσαι, ptc. ~βήσας; pf. ἠσέβηκα, ptc. ἠσεβηκώς.

to act impiously: abs., through incest, Le 20.12; εἴς τινα, God, Ho 7.13, Zp 3.11, 2M 4.17 (on εἰς, cf. ἀ. ἐς τὸν νηόν Hdt. 8.129), ἀπὸ τοῦ θεοῦ Ps 17.22; κατὰ τοῦ νόμου μου Ho 8.1; ‖ ἀνομέω Am 4.4, Je 2.29; + ψεύδομαι Is 59.13, + ἁμαρτάνω, ἀδικέω Ba 2.12. **b**. *to act impiously in respect of*: + acc. rei, God's law, Zp 3.4; (right) path, Ez 16.26; πολλά 1E 1.47; + an inf. specifying the impiety, De 18.20; ἀσεβείαν Ez 18.31. **c**. on various combinations of synonyms, see under ἀδικέω.

Cf. ἀσέβεια, ἀσέβημα, ἀνομέω.

ἀσέβημα, ατος. n.ʃ

impious deed: pl. τὰ ~ατα καὶ ἐπὶ τὰ ἁμαρτήματα De 9.27; La 1.14, 4.22; of sexual impropriety, Le 18.17. Cf. ἀσεβής, ἀσέβεια.

ἀσεβής, ές.

ungodly, impious: liable to founder in God's straight ways, and opp. δίκαιος, Ge 18.23, Ho 14.10, cf. ἀ. καταδυναστεύει τὸν δίκαιον 'an ungodly person prevails over the just person' Hb 1.4, sim. ἐν τῷ καταπίνειν ~ῆ τὸν δίκαιον 1.13. **b**. subst.: ἀποκτεῖναι δίκαιον μετὰ ~οῦς Ge 18.25; συντέλεια εἰς ~εῖς ἥξει ἀνθεστηκότας .. Hb 1.9; 1.13; ‖ ἄνομος

Is 55.7; ‖ ἁμαρτωλός, λοιμός Ps 1.1; + ἁμαρτωλός Pr 11.31.

Cf. ἀσέβεια, ἀσεβέω, ἀσέβημα, ἄνομος, δίκαιος.

ἀσέλγεια, ας. f.ʃ

licentious life-style: 3M 2.26, + μοιχεία 'adultery' Wi 14.26. Cf. Trench 53-8.

ἄσημος, ον.ʃ

having no distinguishing marks: *s* livestock (πρόβατα), Ge 30.42; τετράδραχμον χρυσοῦν ~ον 'uncoined, plate of gold worth four drachms' Jb 42.11; not easily identifiable person, 3M 1.3. Cf. ἐπίσημος, σημεῖον: Shipp 105; Halleux.

ἄσηπτος, ον.

not liable to decay or *corruption*: *s* ξύλα, "of *Acacia tortilis*" (LSJ) Ex 25.5; building material, 25.9; for ark of testimony (κιβωτὸν μαρτυρίου) ib.; poles (ἀναφοραί) 25.12; pillar (στῦλος) 26.15; bar (μοχλός) 25.27; altar (θυσιαστήριον) 27.1; pole (σκυτάλη) 30.5; ξύλον ~ον ἐκλέγεται τέκτων 'a carpenter chooses durable timber' Is 40.20.

Cf. σήπω.

ἀσθένεια, ας. f.

weakness: physical, material Je 6.21; φωνῆς Ec 12.4. **b**. moral malaise or failure: Je 18.23.

Cf. ἀσθενέω, ἀρρώστημα.

ἀσθενέω: fut. ἀσθενήσω; aor. ἠσθένησα, subj. ἀσθενήσω, inf. ~νῆσαι, ptc. ~νήσας; pf.ptc. ἠσθενηκώς.

1. *to be weak, not able to function properly*, 'fail': lit., *s* ῥομφαία Ho 11.6; οὐ μὴ ἀσθενήσῃ ὑμῖν ἡ ἄμπελος ἐν τῷ ἀγρῷ 'the vine in the field will not fail you' Ma 3.11; militarily Je 26.6 (+ πίπτω), Na 3.3, Da 11.41 TH; morally and spiritually Ho 5.5, ταῖς διανοίαις αὐτῶν 'mentally' 1M 11.49, cf. Is 32.4; οἱ ἀσεβεῖς ἀσθενήσουσι ἐν αὐταῖς 'the ungodly will grow weak on them (= the paths of the Lord) Ho 14.10; ἐν τῇ πορείᾳ αὐτῶν 'in the course of their journey' Na 2.6; *s* soul, μηδὲ ἡ ψυχή σου ἀσθενείτω ἀπὸ τῶν δύο ξύλων Is 7.4 (‖ φοβέομαι); sheep Ez 34.4 (‖ ἐκλείπω vs. 16); ἡ ἰσχύς μου La 1.14, Ps 30.11; ὕβρις 'insolence' Je 27.32.

*__2__. *to cease to be what used to be and be transformed*: *s* the time of twilight, εἰς τὴν ἑσπέραν Jd 19.9 B (A: κλίνω).

*__3__. tr. *to cause* (τινα) *to fail*: πολλοὺς ἐν νόμῳ Ma 2.8.

Cf. ἀσθενής, ἀσθένεια, ἐξασθενέω, μαλακίζομαι, νόσος, ὀδύνη, σθένω, ὑγιαίνω.

ἀσθενής, ές.

1. *sick, unhealthy* in body: *s* ὀφθαλμός Ge 29.17.

2. *weak and easily defeated*: physically, *s* potential enemy, Nu 13.19 (:: ἰσχυρός), βασιλεία Ez 17.14; sheep, 34.20 (:: ἰσχυρός); idols, Wi 13.17. **b**. mentally: *s* λογισμός 'rational will' 4M 7.20.

Cf. ἀσθενέω, ἰσχυρός, ἄρρωστος, ὑγιής.

ἀσθενόψυχος, ον.ʃ *

weak-minded: *s* woman, 4M 15.5.

ἄσθμα, ατος. n.ʃ

breath: Wi 11.18. Cf. πνοή.

ἀσθμαίνω.ʃ

to breathe hard: from indigestion, Si 34.19.

ἀσίδηρος, ον.ʃ

not made of iron: *s* εἱρκτή 'prison' Wi 17.16.

ἀσινής, ές.ʃ

unharmed: *s* hum., 3M 6.7, 7.20. Cf. ἀπήμαντος: Shipp 105.

ἀσιτέω: fut. ἀσιτήσω.ʃ

to abstain from meals, 'to fast': ‖ νηστεύω Es 4.16 o'; 1M 3.17. Cf. νηστεύω.

ἀσιτί. adv.ʃ

with no food provided: for labourer, Jb 24.6. Cf. σῖτος.

ἀσκέω.ʃ

to observe duly: + acc., sabbath, 2M 15.4. Cf. ἄσκησις, τιμάω.

ἄσκησις, εως. f.ʃ

practice and training: ἐν νόμῳ 4M 13.22. Cf. ἀσκητής: Windisch, *TDNT* 1.494-6.

ἀσκητής, οῦ. m.ʃ

one who practises sth *regularly*: εὐσεβείας 'of piety' 4M 12.11. Cf. ἄσκησις: LSG s.v.

ἀσκοπυτίνη, ης. f.ʃ

leathern canteen: for wine, Ju 10.5.

ἀσκός, οῦ. m.

bag made of skin to hold liquid: ἔπλησεν τὸν ~ὸν ὕδατος 'filled the skin bag with water' Ge 21.19; 21.15; for wine, Jo 9.4, Je 13.12, for milk Jd 4.19. **b**. a quantity of water held in such a bag: ἄρτους καὶ ~ὸν ὕδατος Ge 21.14.

Cf. κάδος, κάλπη, ὑδρία.

ᾆσμα, ατος. n.

song: ᾖσεν ᾆ. 'sang a song' Nu 21.17; Ἄισω τῷ ἠγαπημένῳ ᾆσμα τοῦ ἀγαπητοῦ Is 5.1; θυγατὴρ ~ατος 'songstress' Ec 12.4; ‖ ὕμνος Ps 39.3. Cf. ᾄδω.

ἀσμενίζω: aor. ἠσμένισα.ʃ

to be glad and satisfied: *s* hum., 1K 6.19. Cf. ἄσμενος, χαίρω.

ἄσμενος, η, ον.ʃ

glad: 2M 10.33. As in Cl. Gk, with a verb, hence = ἀσμένως. Cf. ἀσμένως, ἀσμενίζω: Schmidt 2.560f.

ἀσμένως.

gladly, readily: 2M 4.12. Cf. ἄσμενος.

ἀσπάζομαι: fut.ptc. ἀσπασμένος; aor. ἠσπασάμην, inf. ἀσπάσασθαι.

to say words of greeting to: abs., Si 41.20; + acc. pers., ἀλλήλους Ex 18.7, εἰρηνικῶς 1M 7.29. Cf. ἀπασπάζομαι: Windisch, *TDNT* 1.496-8.

ἀσπάλαθος, ου. m.ʃ
camel's thorn: fragrant, Si 24.15 (+ κιννάμωμον). Cf. Shipp 108f.

ἀσπάλαξ, ακος. m.ʃ
blind-rat, Spalax typhlus (LSJ): ceremonially unclean, Le 11.30.

ἀσπιδίσκη, ης. f. Alw. pl.
ornamental small shield: on an ephod, ἐκ χρυσίου καθαροῦ 'made of pure gold' Ex 28.13; 28.25; of a temple, 1M 4.57 (‖ στέφανοι χρυσοῖ 'golden crowns'). Cf. ἀσπίς I and LSG, s.v.

I **ἀσπίς**, ίδος. f.
shield: ὅπλα καὶ ~ίδας 'large and small shields' Je 26.3; ‖ δόρυ 'spear' Si 29.13; + γαῖσος 'spear,' τόξον 'bow' Ju 9.7, λόγχη 'lance' 2M 15.11; made of copper, 1K 17.6. Cf. δόρα, θυρεός, ὅπλον, ὑπασπιστής.

II **ἀσπίς**, ίδος. f.
asp, Egyptian cobra (LSJ): θυμὸς ~ίδων ἀνίατος 'incurable venom (?) of ..' De 32.33, ἰὸς ~ίδων 'venom of ..' Ps 13.3; dangerous, Is 11.8, flying, 30.6; ‖ ὄφις Ps 57.5, ‖ βασίλισκος 90.13. Cf. δράκων and ὄφις.

Ἀσσύριος, α, ον.
Assyrian: subst. m.pl., 'Assyria' as a geographical area, Ge 25.18; Is 7.18 (‖ Αἴγυπτος); as a political entity, Nu 24.22, τὸν βασιλέα τῶν ~ων Is 7.17; f.sg., *the land of Assyria*, 4M 13.9.

ἀσταθής, ές.ʃ
unstable: *s* mind, 3M 5.39.

Ἀσταρτεῖον, ου. n.
temple containing a statute of Astarte: 1K 31.10.

Ἀστάρτη, ης. f.
Astrarte: object of pagan worship of Phoenician origin, Jd 2.13, 3K 11.6.

ἄστεγος, ον.ʃ
1. *having no roof over one's head*: πτωχοὺς ~ους 'the homeless poor' Is 58.7, cf. στέγη.
2. *not being able to keep silence*: *s* στόμα Pr 26.28, ἄ. χείλεσιν 'a man of loose tongue' 10.8.

ἀστεῖος, α, ον.ʃ
1. *charming*: *s* baby, Ex 2.2; man, Jd 3.17; woman, ἐν τῷ εἴδει σου 'in your appearance' Ju 11.23, τῷ εἴδει Da LXX Su 7.
2. *proper, appropriate*: *s* ἡ ὁδός σου Nu 22.32.
3. *showing signs of good upbringing and education*: *s* λογισμός 'reasoning' 2M 6.23.
Cf. ἀστείως, καλός, ὡραῖος: Schmidt 2.505; Trench 387f.

ἀστείως. adv.ʃ
in a proper and appropriate manner: πάνυ καλῶς καὶ ἀ. πράττων 'acting well and most properly' 2M 12.43. Cf. ἀστεῖος.

ἄστεκτος, ον.ʃ
incapable of being borne up against, 'unendurable': *s* the magnificence of God's glory, Od 12.5 (‖ ἀνυπόστατος).

ἀστήρ, έρος. m.; mostly in pl. (sg.: Si 50.6).
star as heavenly luminary: ὥσπερ ὁ ἥλιος καὶ ἡ σελήνη καὶ ἕνδεκα ἀστέρες Ge 37.9, sim. De 4.19; οἱ ~ες δύσουσι φέγγος αὐτῶν 'the stars will lose their brightness' Jl 3.15 (‖ ἥλιος and σελήνη), οἱ ~ες τοῦ οὐρανοῦ .. τὸ φῶς οὐ δώσουσι Is 13.10; created by God along with the sun and the moon, Ge 1.16, Je 38.36; pl. as a figure of exceedingly great number, ἀρίθμησον τοὺς ~ας, εἰ δυνήσῃ ἐξαριθμῆσαι αὐτούς Ge 15.5; πληθυνῶ τὸ σπέρμα σου ὡς τοὺς ~ας τοῦ οὐρανοῦ καὶ ὡς τὴν ἄμμον τὴν παρὰ τὸ χεῖλος τῆς θαλάσσης 22.17, sim. 26.4, De 1.10 (the latter with ἄστρα). Cf. ἄστρον, ἀστραπή, ἰσάστερος, ἥλιος, σελήνη.

ἀστοχέω.ʃ
to fail to take advantage of: + gen., γυναικὸς σοφῆς Si 7.19, διηγήματος γερόντων 'a talk by elderly folks' 8.9. Cf. LSG s.v.

ἀστράγαλος, ου. m.ʃ
1. *one of the vertebrae* of the neck: of sheep, Zc 11.16.
2. *knuckle* (LSG): pl. χειρός Da TH 5.5, 24.
Cf. ἀστραγαλωτός: Caird 1968.461f.

ἀστραγαλωτός, ή, όν.ʃ
**long enough to reach the ankles*: *s* χιτών 2K 13.18*L*, 19*L*. Cf. ἀστράγαλος.

ἀστραπή, ῆς. f.
lightning: accompanying a theophany, Ex 19.16; ~αὶ διατρέχουσαι 'flashing (across the sky)' Na 2.5; φέγγος ~ῆς ὅπλων 'the brightness of lightning of arms' Hb 3.11; ἐξελεύσεται ὡς ἀ. βολίς 'an arrow will dash out ..' Zc 9.14; associated with rain-storm, Je 10.13, 28.16. Cf. ἀστήρ, δι~, ἐξ~, περιαστράπτω.

ἀστράπτω: aor. ἤστραψα, impv. ἄστραψον.ʃ
to hurl a flashing object: + cogn. acc., ἀστραπήν 'lightning' Ps 143.6, 2K 22.15*L*; σπινθῆρας 'sparks' Wi 11.18. Cf. ἀστραπή.

ἀστρολόγος, ου. m.ʃ
astrologer: τοῦ οὐρανοῦ Is 47.13.

ἄστρον, ου. n; mostly in pl. (sg. 2/38).
star: Ob 4; object of worship, τὸ ἄ. τοῦ θεοῦ ὑμῶν Am 5.26; ‖ sun and moon, Jl 2.10; in sim. of great numbers, ἐπλήθυνεν ὑμᾶς .. ὡσεὶ τὰ ~α τοῦ οὐρανοῦ τῷ πλήθει De 1.10, sim. Ge 22.17, 26.4 (with ἀστήρ); ὑπὲρ τὰ ~α τοῦ οὐρανοῦ 'more than the stars of the sky' Na 3.16. Cf. ἀστήρ, ἥλιος, σελήνη.

ἀστυγείτων, ον.ʃ
situated nearby: πόλις 'city' 2M 6.8.

ἀσυλία, ας. f.ʃ
inviolability: of the Jerusalem temple, + σεμνότης 2M 3.12.
Cf. ἄσυλος, συλάω: *ND* 4.168f.

ἄσυλος, ον.ʃ
protected from violence: *s* soul, Pr 22.23; place, 2M 4.33; subst.n., 'sanctuary' 4.34. Cf. ἀσυλία.

ἀσύμφορος, ον.ʃ
not beneficial: τινι Pr 25.20. Cf. ἀνωφελής, σύμφορος.

ἀσύμφωνος, ον.ʃ
1. *wanting in harmony, discordant*: *s* βοή Wi 18.10.
2. *not agreeable and acceptable to*: + dat. pers., Bel 15-7 LXX.

ἀσύνετος, ον.
wanting in understanding: *s* ἔθνος De 32.21; τῇ καρδίᾳ Ps 75.6; subst.m., 91.7, Si 22.13 (|| ἄφρων). Cf. συνίημι, ἀνόητος, ἄνους, ἄφρων, μωρός.

ἀσυνθεσία, ας. f.ʃ*
v.n. of ἀσυνθετέω: 2E 9.2, 4, 10.6; Je 3.7. Cf. subs.

ἀσυνθετέω: aor. ἠσυνθέτησα, subj. ~τήσω, inf. ~τῆσαι; pf. ἠσυνθέτηκα.*
to act against agreement and be unfaithful to: abs., ἀπέστρεψαν καὶ ἠσυνθέτησαν Ps 77.57; + dat. pers., τῇ γενεᾷ τῶν υἱῶν σου 72.15, τῷ θεῷ 2E 10.2; ἔν τινι– ἐν τῷ θεῷ Ne 13.27. Cf. ἀσυνθεσία, ἀσύνθετος, συνθήκη.

ἀσύνθετος, ον. Only in Je.*
given to ἀσυνθετέω (q.v.): *s* pers., Ιουδα Je 3.7 +. Cf. ἀσυνθετέω.

ἀσυρής, ες.ʃ
lewd, morally filthy: *s* ἀπαιδευσία Si 23.13. Cf. LSG s.v.

ἀσφάλεια, ας. f.
absence of danger, 'security, safety': mostly with military connotation, κατοικήσετε μετὰ ~ας ἐπὶ τῆς γῆς ὑμῶν Le 26.5 (|| πεποιθώς 25.18, 19); De 12.10; ὠχύρωσεν αὐτὴν πρὸς ~αν τῆς χώρας 'fortified it with a view to the security of the country' 1M 14.37; ἕνεκεν ~ας τῆς πρὸς τοὺς ἐναντιουμένους ἡμῖν 'in the interest of security in view of our enemies' 1E 8.51; σῷα διαφυλάσσειν μετὰ πάσης ~ας 'to keep absolutely safe and secure' 2M 3.22; μετὰ πάσης ~ας αὐτοῖς ἐπιβαλεῖν 'to attack them with no risk whatsoever' 15.1; τὴν ἀσπιδῶν καὶ λογχῶν ~αν 'the security provided by shields and spears' 15.11; w. ref. to potential security risk of captives, 3M 5.5. **b**. with no military connotation: ἐθεμελίωσεν τὴν γῆν ἐπὶ τὴν ~αν αὐτῆς 'he laid the foundation of the earth on a secure basis' Ps 103.5, cf. ἀσφαλῆ βάσιν Wi 4.3.
Cf. ἀσφαλής, ἀσφαλίζω, ἀσφαλῶς, ἐλπίς: Spicq 1.212-9.

ἀσφαλής, ές.
1. *free from danger*: ἡ ὁδὸς ἀ. To 5.16 𝔊[II], ἐν κύμασιν τρίβον ~ῆ 'a safe course amidst the waves' Wi 14.3; ἀ. βάσις 'secure foundation' 4.3; *s* καρδία Pr 15.7. **b**. *capable of providing security and safety*: *s* wisdom, Pr 3.18.
2. *self-assured, self-confident*: πνεῦμα .. βέβαιον, ~ές, ἀμέριμνον .. 'steadfast, secure, carefree ..' Wi 7.23.
Cf. ἀσφάλεια.

ἀσφαλίζω: aor.mid. ἠσφαλισάμην, ptc. ἀσφαλισάμενος.ʃ
to make secure against attack or *danger*, 'fortify': + acc., τὴν πύλην 'the gate' Ne 3.15; + acc. pers., Wi 4.17; διεφύλαξεν αὐτὸν .. καὶ ἀπὸ ἐνεδρευόντων ἠσφαλίσατο 'he kept him .. and secured him against those who lay in wait' 10.12; σιδήρῳ 'with iron' 13.15; ἠσφαλισάμην σε τῇ δεξιᾷ τῇ δικαίᾳ μου 'I secured you with my righteous right hand' Is 41.10 (+ ὁ ἐνισχύσας σε καὶ ἐβοήθησά σοι). Cf. ἀσφάλεια, παρασφαλίζω, προασπίζω: Shipp 110; LSG s.v.

ἀσφαλτόπισσα, ας. f.ʃ *
compound of asphalt and pitch: used to coat a floating basket, Ex 2.3. Cf. ἄσφαλτος.

ἄσφαλτος, ου. f.ʃ
bitumen, pitch: as coating material against moisture, Ge 6.14; building material substituted by clay (πηλός) 11.3; φρέατα ~ου 'asphalt pits' 14.10. Cf. ἀσφαλτόω and ἀσφαλτόπισσα.

ἀσφαλτόω: fut. ~τώσω.ʃ *
to smear with pitch: ***o*** ship (κιβωτός) and + dat. instr. (τῇ ἀσφάλτῳ) Ge 6.14. Cf. ἄσφαλτος.

ἀσφαλῶς. adv.ʃ
1. *encountering no danger*: εἰσῆλθον εἰς τὴν πόλιν ἀ. Ge 34.25, ἵνα βαδίσῃ Ισραηλ ἀ. Ba 5.7, ἤρχοντο ἀ. καὶ τεταγμένως 'kept moving, .. in orderly fashion' 1M 6.40.
2. *in safe keeping*: θὲς ἀ. To 6.5 𝔊[I].
3. *with conviction and confidence*: ἀ. εἰδότες 'with sure knowledge' Wi 18.6; ἐγνωκότες ἀ. 3M 7.6.
Cf. ἀσφαλής.

ἀσχημονέω: fut. ~νήσω.
1. *to incur disgrace*: ἐναντίον σου De 25.3.
2. *to behave in an indecent, disgraceful manner*: *s* young woman, ἦσθα γυμνὴ καὶ ἀσχημονοῦσα Ez 16.7, 22.
Cf. ἀσχημοσύνη, ἀσχήμων.

ἀσχημοσύνη, ης. f.

1. *something unseemly not in keeping with codes of decorum* or *meant for public exposure*: οἶκος καλύπτων ~ην 'a house providing privacy' Si 29.21; euphemistically w. ref. to **a**. *private parts, pudenda*: ἀποκαλύψης τὴν ~ην σου Ex 20.26; καλύψαι ~ην 28.38; ἱμάτιον ~ης 'a garment to cover private parts' 22.27; ἴδῃ τὴν ~ην αὐτῆς καὶ αὕτη ἴδῃ τὴν ~ην αὐτοῦ Le 20.17; τοῦ πατρός σου 'of your mother-in-law's' 20.11; of woman, καλύπτειν τὴν ~ην Ho 2.9; ~ην αὐτῆς οὐ συγκαλύψει Si 26.8 (of a drunken woman exposing herself in public?); **b**. *ordure*, human *feces*, De 23.13; ἀ. πράγματος 23.14.

2. *disgrace, discredit*: ~ην βασιλέως .. ἰδεῖν 2E 4.14 (gen. obj.); La 1.8.

Cf. ἀσχημονέω, ἀσχήμων, αἰδοῖον, αἰσχύνη.

ἀσχήμων, ον.ʃ

unseemly, shameful: *s* deed, ἄσχημον πρᾶγμα De 24.1 (ground for divorce), Su 63 TH, cf. ἄσχημον ἐποίησεν κοιμηθείς μετὰ τῆς θυγατρὸς Ιακωβ Ge 34.7; death Wi 2.20; retreat 2M 9.2; woman, Si 26.24¶ (:: εὐσχήμων). Cf. ἀσχημονέω, εὐσχήμων: Schmidt 4.358f.

ἀσχολέω: fut.mid. ~ληθήσομαι.ʃ

mid. *to occupy oneself* with (ἐν): intellectually, Si 39.1. Cf. ἀσχολία.

ἀσχολία, ας. f.ʃ

v.n. of ἀσχολέομαι: hum. existence itself, Si 40.1. **b**. *that which occupies one*: 3M 5.34. Cf. ἀσχολέω.

ἀσωτία, ας f.ʃ

extravagant, spendthrift life-style: 2M 6.4 (+ κῶμος), Pr 28.7. Cf. ἄσωτος: Trench 53-8; Foerster, *TDNT* 1.506f.; Spicq 1.220-2.

ἄσωτος, ον.ʃ

indulging in ἀσωτία: *s* hum., Pr 7.11. Cf. ἀσωτία.

ἄτακτος, ον.ʃ

disorderly: *s* δρόμος 'running' 3M 1.19. Cf. ἀταξία, τεταγμένως: Spicq 1.223-6.

ἀταξία, ας. f.ʃ

disorderliness: γάμων 'of marriages' Wi 14.26. Cf. ἄτακτος, εὐταξία.

ἀτάρ.ʃ

Marks a rapid transition to another thought: Jb 6.21, 7.11. Cf. ἀλλά: Ziegler 1985.111; Julia.

ἀταραξία, ας. f.ʃ

lack of undesirable *disturbance*: μετὰ ~ας ζῆν 'to live ..' 4M 8.26. Cf. ταράσσω.

ἀτάραχος, ον.ʃ

unaffected by disturbances, 'trouble-free, calm': *s* βίος Es 3.15 *L* (o' ἀκύματος), πράγματα 'government' Es B 7 o' (+ εὐσταθής), βασιλεία E 8, 2M 11.23. Cf. τάραχος, ἀκύματος.

ἄταφος, ον.ʃ

not properly buried: *s* dead hum., 2M 5.10. Cf. θάπτω.

ἅτε. adv.ʃ

seeing that: + gen. abs., 1M 1.29.

ἀτείχιστος, ον.ʃ

unwalled: *s* city, Nu 13.20 (:: τειχήρης), Pr 25.28. Cf. τεῖχος, τειχήρης.

ἀτεκνία, ας. f.

state of being childless: χηρεία καὶ ἀ. 'widowhood ..' Is 47.9. **b**. *loss of children*: 4M 18.9. Cf. ἄτεκνος, εὐτεκνία.

ἄτεκνος, ον.ʃ

childless: ἀποθανεῖν ~ον Si 16.3; as punishment for a crime, ~οι ἀποθανοῦνται Le 20.20, 21; *s* aged married male, ἀπολύομαι ἄ. 'I am departing childless' Ge 15.2; woman, ἄ. καὶ χήρα '.. and widowed' Is 49.21, see also Je 18.21 (punishment). Cf. ἄγονος and ἀτεκνόω.

ἀτεκνόω: fut. ἀτεκνώσω, pass. ~νωθήσομαι; aor. ἠτέκνωσα, pass. ἠτεκνώθην, subj. ἀτεκνωθῶ, inf. ἀτεκνωθῆναι; pf.pass. ἠτέκνωμαι, ptc. ἠτεκνωμένος.

to cause loss of child: *s* μάχαιρα 'sword' De 32.25, La 1.20; *o* father, Ge 42.36; women, 1K 15.33 (*s* sword); pass. *to lose child* or *young*, ἀτεκνωθῶ ἀπὸ τῶν δύο ὑμῶν Ge 27.45, cf. ἀτεκνωθήσονται ἐξ ἀνθρώπων 'they shall lose (all) people' Ho 9.12; *o* livestock, Ge 31.38, bear 2K 18.8B. **b**. *to be incapable of producing children*: *s* womb, μήτραν ἀτεκνοῦσαν καὶ μαστοὺς ξηρούς 'a sterile womb and dry breasts' Ho 9.14; sheep, Ct 4.2.

Cf. ἄτεκνος, ἄγονος, τέκνον.

ἀτέλεια, ας. f.ʃ

exemption from public duties or *payment of taxes* or *dues*: + ἄφεσις 1M 10.34. Cf. τέλος.

ἀτέλεστος, ον.ʃ

incapable of achieving maturity: *s* child Wi 3.16; tree's branch, 4.5. Cf. LSG s.v.

ἀτελής, ές.ʃ

1. *not having reached the end* or *destination*: ~έσιν ὥραις 'out of season, prematurely' Wi 10.7.

2. *ineffectual*: *s* oath, 3M 5.42.

Cf. τέλος.

ἀτενίζω: aor.inf. ἀτενίσαι.ʃ

1. *to observe closely*: εἰς τὴν τοῦ βασιλέως πρόθεσιν 'the king's purpose' 3M 2.26; + εἶδον Od 12.9. On the rection, see BDAG s.v.

2. *to take great care*: + ὅπως 1E 6.27.

Cf. ἐνατενίζω, κατανοέω: Spicq 1.227f.

ἄτερ. prep. c. gen.ʃ

not having at one's disposal: 2M 12.15. Cf. ἄνευ.

ἀτιμάζω: fut.pass. ἀτιμασθήσομαι; aor. ἠτίμασα, inf. ἀτιμάσαι, ptc. ἀτιμάσας, subj. ἀτιμάσω, pass.

ἠτιμάσθην, inf. ἀτιμασθῆναι.

1. *to dishonour, rob* sbd *of honour*: + acc. pers., υἱὸς ἀτιμάζει πατέρα Mi 7.6; πατέρα αὐτοῦ ἢ μητέρα αὐτοῦ De 27.16; pass., ἠτιμάσθη ἡ κυρία ἐναντίον αὐτῆς 'the mistress lost face on account of her' Ge 16.4; ***o*** husband, ἐν ὑπερηφανίᾳ Si 26.26¶ (:: τιμάω); former elite, Is 5.15 (|| ταπεινοῦμαι), δόξα 16.14, πᾶν ἔνδοξον 23.9; + acc. rei, γῆρας 'old age' Pr 30.17 (|| καταγελάω).

2. *to form* or *hold a low view of*: τινα 1K 17.42 (*L* ἐξουδενόω).

Cf. ἀτιμάω, ἀτιμόω, ἀτιμία, τιμή, τίμιος, ἐξουδενόω, ταπεινόω, δόξα.

ἀτιμασμός, οῦ.ʃ

dishonour, disgrace: 1M 1.40 (:: δόξα). Cf. ἀτιμία.

ἀτιμάω: pf. ἠτίμακα.ʃ

to treat with disdain: τινα 2K 19.44*L* (B: ὑβρίζω). Cf. ἀτιμάζω.

ἀτίμητος, ον.ʃ

priceless: ***s*** citizenship, 3M 3.23; stone, Wi 7.9. Cf. τιμή.

ἀτιμία, ας. f.

1. *infamy, ignominy*: πλησμονὴν ~ας ἐκ δόξης πίε 'Drink a full measure of ignominy from glory (?)' Hb 2.16[2], opp. δόξα also 2.16[1], Ho 4.7, Si 5.13, 29.6, Pr 3.35; that which brings about disrepute and discredit, Na 3.5 (|| αἰσχύνη); opp. τιμή Is 10.16; + ὀνειδισμός Je 23.40, || ὁ. Ez 36.15, + ὄνειδος Pr 18.3; pl., 6.33; arising from one's humble station in society, 12.9; ***o*** of λαμβάνω 'to be subjected to' 39.26; || ἀδοξία Si 3.10. **b**. *sense* or *fear of disgrace*: Si 21.24. **c**. w. ref. to private parts: Je 13.26.

*__2__. *worthlessness*: Ep Je 25.

Cf. ἀτιμάζω, ἄτιμος, ταπείνωσις, τιμή, and δόξα.

ἄτιμος, ον.

not warranting any special honour or respect: ***s*** hum. and subst., ὁ ἄ. πρὸς τὸν ἔντιμον 'the man in the street up against the notable' Is 3.5; τὸ εἶδος αὐτοῦ 'his outward appearance' 53.3, γῆρας 'old age' Wi 3.17, πτῶμα 'corpse' 4.19; πηλοῦ τε ἀτιμότερος ὁ βίος αὐτοῦ 'his life is less worthy even than clay' 15.10; σπέρμα 'offspring' Si 10.19 (:: ἔντιμος). Cf. ἀτιμία, ἔντιμος.

ἀτιμόω: fut.pass. ~μωθήσομαι; aor. ἠτίμωσα, pass. ἠτιμώθην, subj. ἀτιμωθῶ; pf.pass.ptc. ἠτιμωμένος.

1. *to dishonour, humiliate*: + acc. pers., 1C 18.5; ***o*** God, 1K 2.30; nation, Ob 2; + ἔκ τινος Ez 16.54; + αἰσχύνω Je 22.22; + acc. rei, ἀράν Ez 17.16, ὁρκωμοσίαν 17.18.

*__2__. *to consider of slight value*: + acc., + ἐξουδενόω 1K 15.9.

Cf. ἀτιμάζω, ἀτιμάω, ἐξατιμόω.

ἀτιμώρητος, ον.ʃ

unpunished, let go with impunity: οὐκ ἀ. ἔσται Pr 11.21, 19.5, 28.20. Cf. τιμωρέω.

ἀτμίς, ίδος. f.ʃ

gaslike substance which shoots up unbroken and continuously: oven flame, φλὸξ τῆς γῆς ὡσεὶ ἀ. καμίνου Ge 19.28; τηγάνου 'of frying-pan' 2M 7.5; πυρός 'of fire' Si 38.28; πυρώδης 'fiery' 43.4, cf. 22.24; θυμιάματος 'of incense' Le 16.13, Ez 8.11; λιβάνου 'of frankincense' Si 24.15; ***s*** Wisdom, ἀ. .. τῆς τοῦ θεοῦ δυνάμεως Wi 7.25; ἀ. ἀπὸ ἀκρίδων 'haze-like swarm of locusts (which fly off in a short while)' Ho 13.3.

ἀτοπία, ας. f.ʃ

morally wrong deed: Ju 11.11.

ἄτοπος, ον.

morally wrong, improper: alw. subst.n., ***s*** deeds, ~α πράξας Jb 27.6, also w. πράσσω, 36.21, Pr 30.20, 2M 14.23, w. ποιέω Jb 34.12. Cf. ἀτοπία.

ἄτρακτος, ου. m.ʃ

spindle: Pr 31.19.

ἀτραπός, οῦ. f.

1. *path*: Jb 6.19, 24.13 (|| ὁδός), Si 5.9. **b**. *short cut* not meant for normal, public traffic, and contrasted with ὁδός Jd 5.6B (|| ὁδοὺς διεστραμμένας).

2. *track left* by a moving object: by a ship's keel, Wi 5.10 (|| ἴχνος).

Cf. ἴχνος, ὁδός: Schmidt 4.637f.

ἄτρυγος, ον.ʃ

without lees, 'pure': ***s*** ἔλαιον .. ἄτρυγον καθαρόν 'oil .. clarified, pure' Ex 27.20.

ἄτρωτος, ον.

invulnerable: ***s*** hum., on battlefield 2M 8.36; καρδία resistant to humane sentiments, 3M 5.47. Cf. τιτρώσκω.

ἀττάκης, ου. m.ʃ *

kind of *locust*: edible and || βροῦχος, ἀκρίς Le 11.22. Cf. ἀκρίς.

ἀττέλεβος, ου. m.ʃ

locust: ἐξῆλατο ὡς ἀ. 'hopped off like locust' Na 3.17. Cf. ἀκρίς: Shipp 112f.

ἀτυχέω.ʃ

to find oneself in ἀτυχία (q.v.): Pr 27.10.

ἀτυχία, ας.ʃ

untoward circumstances, 'misfortune': 2M 12.30, pl. 14.14 (+ συμφορά and:: εὐημερία). Cf. ἀτυχέω, ταλαιπωρία, συμφορά, εὐημερία: Schmidt 4.409-13.

αὐγάζω.

to appear bright* or *white*: ***s* cancerous part of the body, Le 13.24; αὐγάσματα αὐγάζοντα λευκαθίζοντα 13.38. Cf. αὔγασμα, αὐγέω, αὐγή, λάμπω, λευκαθίζω, καταυγάζω.

αὔγασμα, ατος. m.ʃ
1. *that which appears bright* or *white*: cancerous, ~ατα αὐγάζοντα λευκαθίζοντα Le 13.38, 39.
2. *shining brightness*: of bow, Si 43.11.
Cf. αὐγάζω, λευκαθίζω: Kittel, *TDNT* 1.507f.

αὐγέω.ʃ *
to shine, glitter: *s* λύχνος 'lamp' Jb 29.3. Cf. αὐγάζω, στίλβω.

αὐγή, ῆς. f.ʃ
1. *daybreak, dawn*: opp. ἀωρία 'midnight' Is 59.9.
2. *gleam, sheen*: of a burning object, τὰς ~ὰς τοῦ φέγγους 2M 12.9.
Cf. αὐγάζω: Schmidt 1.563-98; Shipp 115.

αὐθάδεια, ας. f.ʃ
arrogance: αὐ. καὶ πλοῦτος ἀσεβῶν '.. and wealth of the ungodly' Is 24.8. Cf. αὐθάδης, ὑπερηφανία and LSG, s.v.

αὐθάδης, ες.ʃ
self-willed and arrogant: *s* hum., σκληρὸς αὐ. Ge 49.3; accursed, 49.7 (‖ σκληρύνεται); + θρασύς 'bold,' ἀλαζών 'boastful' Pr 21.24. Cf. αὐθάδεια, ὑπερήφανος: Trench 349-51; Bauernfeind, *TDNT* 1.508f.; Spicq 1.229f.

αὐθαιρέτως. adv.
of one's own accord: 2M 6.19, 3M 7.10. Cf. ἑκών, ἑκουσίως: Schmidt 3.612f.; *ND* 4.127f.

αὐθέντης, ου. m.ʃ
murderer: used adj., γονεῖς 'parents' Wi 12.6. Cf. φονεύς: Shipp 115.

αὐθεντία, ας. f.ʃ
autonomous district: 3M 2.29.

αὐθημερινός, ή, όν.ʃ
having to do with a single day: *s* μίσθιος '(day) labourer' Jb 7.1. **b**. adv. subst.n.sg., *the same day*: without waiting a day, Pr 12.16.
Cf. αὐθημερόν.

αὐθημερόν. adv.ʃ
on the very day, on the same day: De 24.15, Pr 12.16. Cf. αὐθημερινός.

αὐθωρί. adv.ʃ *
instantly: Da 3.15 LXX (TH αὐτῇ τῇ ὥρᾳ), 3M 3.25. Cf. εὐθύς, εὐθέως.

αὐλαία, ας. f.
curtain: of a tabernacle, Ex 26.1.

αὐλαῖος, α, ον.ʃ
belonging to the court (αὐλή): *s* θύρα 'door' 2M 14.41. Cf. αὐλή.

αὖλαξ, ακος. f.
furrow: in vineyard, Nu 22.24; ἐν πεδίῳ Jb 39.10; τῆς γῆς Ps 64.11, Jb 31.38. Cf. Shipp 116.

αὐλάρχης, ου. m.ʃ *
chief of the royal court (?): 2K 8.18. Cf. αὐλαρχία.

αὐλαρχία, ας. f.ʃ *
office of αὐλάρχης (q.v.): 3K 2.46[h].

αὐλέω.ʃ
to play on the flute: 3K 1.40*L*. Cf. αὐλός.

αὐλή, ῆς. f.
1. *a fairly large enclosure within a building*: of tabernacle, Ex 27.9; temple court, Zc 3.7, Is 1.11; ἁγία Ps 28.2; royal, Je 30.6. On αὐλή attached to private houses, see Husson, 45-54 and LSG, s.v.
2. *dwelling-place*: στρουθῶν 'of sparrows' Is 34.13 (‖ ἔπαυλις); king's quarters in an encampment, 2M 13.15.
Cf. αὐλαῖος, τέμενος: LSG s.v.

αὐλίζω: fut. αὐλισθήσομαι; aor. ηὐλίσθην, impv. αὐλίσθητι, 3s αὐλισθήτω, inf. αὐλισθῆναι, subj. αὐλισθῶ, opt.3s αὐλισθείη.
I. mid. *to take up one's temporary abode*: metaph. and *s* ψυχή Ps 24.13, πλάνος 'error' Jb 19.4; hum., ἐν σκέπῃ τοῦ θεοῦ Ps 90.1; *+ acc. loci, πόλεις Jb 15.28; δρόσος 'dew' 29.19¶. **b**. not necessarily temporary, 'to reside': ὑπὸ τοὺς κλάδους ^τῆς σοφίας^ 'under the branches of ..' Si 14.26, ἐν οἴκῳ παιδείας 51.23; *s* δύναμις Jb 41.14, ἁμαρτία PSol 3.6, ἀδικία ἐν μέσῳ αὐτῶν 'injustice in their midst' 17.27 (‖ κατοικέω), wages unpaid παρὰ σοί To 4.14 𝔊[I]. **c**. *to sleep*: Da 6.18 LXX (TH κοιμάομαι).
2. *to come to rest and stop*: *s* activity, κλαυθμός 'weeping' Ps 29.6.
II. act. *to cause to take up one's temporary abode*: ἐπὶ διώρυγας ὑδάτων 'beside canals' Je 38.9.

αὐλός, οῦ. m.
flute: an instrument which makes a booming noise, αὐ. βομβήσει Je 31.36; used on festive occasions, αὐ. καὶ ψαλτήριον ἡδύνουσιν μέλη '.. and harps accompany sweet melodies' Si 40.22, μετὰ κιθάρας καὶ ψαλτηρίου καὶ τυμπάνων καὶ ~ῶν Is 5.12, μετὰ μουσικῶν, τυμπάνων καὶ ~ῶν 'with music, timbrels and flutes' (or: 'musical instruments, [such as] ..') 1E 5.2, ἐξέλιπεν αὐ. καὶ κινύρα 'there was no flute or harp around' 1M 3.45; on religious holidays, ὡσεὶ εὐφραινομένους εἰσελθεῖν μετὰ ~οῦ εἰς τὸ ὄρος τοῦ κυρίου Is 30.29; in a military band, μετὰ ~ῶν καὶ κιθάρας πολεμήσουσιν 30.32. See *BA* 9.1, p. 84f. Cf. αὐλέω: LSG s.v.

αὐλών, ῶνος. m.
glen: ‖ πεδινή Je 31.8; 1C 10.7 (‖ κοιλάς 1K 30.7), 3M 6.17. Cf. κοιλάς, φάραγξ.

αὐξάνω, also αὔξω: fut. αὐξανῶ, pass. αὐξηθήσομαι; aor. ηὔξησα, impv. αὔξησον, pass. ηὐξήθην, ptc. αὐξηθείς, subj. αὐξηθῶ, opt.act.3s αὐξήσαι; pf.pass.ptc. ηὐξημένος.
I. act. tr., *to cause to grow in quantity*: *s* God blessing ***o*** hum., Ge17.6;17.20, 28.3, Le 26.9 (‖ πληθύνω); Ge 26.22 (‖ πλατύνω); 41.52 (:: ταπεί-

νωσις); in size, *s* soil and orchard, ὡς γῆν αὔξουσαν τὸ ἄνθος καὶ ὡς κῆπον τὰ σπέρματα αὐτοῦ Is 61.11. **b**. *to cause to grow rich in possessions*: ὁ κύριος ηὔξησεν τὸν Ιωβ Jb 42.10. **c**. *to enhance the stature of*: + acc. pers., ἐναντίον τινός Jo 4.14 (|| ὑψόω 3.7).

II. pass. intr. *to grow in quantity* or *size*: *s* living creatures exclusive of humans, Ge 1.22 (+ πληθύνομαι), including humans 8.17, humans 9.1, 35.11, 47.27, Ex 1.7, Je 23.3 (latter two || πληθύνω), Nu 24.7 (|| ὑψόω); infant Ge 21.8, 20, youths 25.27; υἱός 49.22; εἰς πλῆθος 30.30 (:: μικροί); kingdom, εἰς ὕψος 1C 14.2; the moon, Si 43.8. **b**. *to come into being*: ἐκ σπέρματος αὐτοῦ 'out of his offspring' Je 22.30.

Cf. αὔξησις, ἐπ~, συναύξω, πληθύνω, πλεονάζω.

αὔξησις, εως. f.ʃ

increase in prestige: of temple, 2M 5.16. Cf. αὐξάνω.

αὔρα, ας. f.ʃ

gentle breeze: opp. καταιγίς 'tempest' Ps 106.29; λεπτή 'fine, faint' 3K19.12; + φωνή Jb 4.16. Cf. πνεῦμα.

αὔριον.

the following day: counting from the point of speech, 'tomorrow', used adjectivally, ἐν τῇ ἡμέρᾳ τῇ αὔ. Ge 30.33. **b**. used as an indeclinable fem. subst. in a variety of syntagms, all meaning 'tomorrow' adverbially: αὔ. Ex 8.29, cf. ἑορτὴ κυρίου αὔ. 'tomorrow it is going to be a festival for the Lord' 32.5; ταύτην τὴν ὥραν αὔ. 'this time tomorrow' 9.18; σήμερον καὶ αὔ. 'today and ..' 19.10; εἰς αὔ. 8.10; ἐν τῇ αὔ. 8.23; τῇ αὔ. Le 7.6; τὴν αὔ. Es 9.13 o'. **c**. counting from the point of reference in the past, 'the next day, the day after': καὶ ἐγένετο μετὰ τὴν αὔ. Ex 32.30.

Cf. ἐπαύριον, σήμερον.

αὐστηρία, ας. f.ʃ

attitude of being αὐστηρός (q.v.): 2M 14.30. Cf. αὐστηρός.

αὐστηρός, ά, όν.ʃ

not gentle nor affectionate, 'rough': *s* behaviour, 2M 14.30. Cf. αὐστηρία, σκληρός: Trench 46-9.

αὐτάρκεια, ας. f.ʃ

state of having necessities provided: for hum. subsistence, PSol 5.16.

αὐταρκέω: aor. αὐτάρκησα.ʃ

**to supply with necessities*: + acc. pers. and *s* God, αὐτάρκησεν αὐτὸν ἐν γῇ ἐρήμῳ De 32.10.

αὐτάρκης, ες.

sufficient in oneself: ~η μοί ἐστιν 'I have enough' Si 5.1, 11.23; *s* hum. 40.18 ('self-employed'?,:: ἐργάτης), wine 34.28, torment 4M 9.9; + δέοντα 'necessities' Pr 30.8. Cf. αὐταρκέω.

αὐτίκα. adv.ʃ

without long interval from the point of reference: 'shortly,' 4M 1.12; 2.8. Cf. εὐθύς.

αὐτοδέσποτος, ον.ʃ

able to claim sovereignty over: *s* λογισμός 'reason,' + gen., παθῶν 'passions' 4M 1.1, 7, 13.1; || αὐτοκράτωρ 1.30. Cf. δεσπότης, κύριος.

αὐτόθεν. adv.ʃ

from this place: To 8.21 𝔊[II].

αὐτόθι. adv.

at the place named: 1E 8.41 (|| ἐκεῖ 2E 8.15). **b**. *at this point* in the course of a narrative, 2M 15.37.

Cf. ἐκεῖ.

αὐτοκράτωρ, ορος. m./f.

complete master: + gen., *s* λογισμός 'rational will,' παθῶν 'of passions' 4M 1.7, ἀλγηδόνων 'of sufferings' 4.28, || ἡγεμών, αὐτοδέσποτος 1.30. Cf. ἡγεμών, αὐτοδέσποτος.

αὐτόματος, η, ον.ʃ

self-acting: *s* plant, τὰ ~α τὰ ἀναβαίνοντα τοῦ ἀγροῦ 'that which grows of itself (without having been sown, but from seeds fallen in the course of harvesting)' Le 25.5, τὰ ~α τὰ ἀναβαίνοντα αὐτῆς 25.11 (second crop), cf. τὰ ~α 'that which grows of itself' 4K 19.29*L* (B+: τὰ ἀνατέλλοντα 'that which grows'), cf. ~η ἡ γῆ καρποφορεῖ Mk 4.28 (without a farmer tending after sowing the seed); στάχυς ἀπὸ καλάμης ~ος ἀποπεσών 'an ear of corn fallen off of itself from the stalk' Jb 24.24; ~η πυρά 'self-kindled fire' Wi 17.6; πεσεῖται ~α τὰ τείχη τῆς πόλεως 'the walls .. will fall of themselves' Jo 6.5: Spicq 1.231-4. Cf. ἑκών: Schmidt 3.614f.

αὐτομολέω: aor. ηὐτομόλησα, ptc. αὐτομολήσας.

to desert: *s* soldier, Ju 16.12; + μετά τινος (to join the side of) 2K 10.19B, 1M 7.19, πρός τινα Jo 10.1; young girl running away from parental authority, 1K 20.30. Cf. ἀπαυτομολέω, ἀποδιδράσκω, ἀναχωρέω.

αὐτός, ή, ό. pron.

Reference to a definite person or thing spoken or written about.

1. anaphoric, i.e. referring back to what has been mentioned before, and used in all oblique cases, genders, and numbers: ἐν αὐτῇ = ἐν Νινευη τῇ πόλει Jn 1.2; the gen. follows the head noun immediately, δύναμιν αὐτοῦ Ob 11; predicative, τὰ οὐκ ὄντα αὐτοῦ 'what does not belong to him' Hb 2.6. **b**. The nom. may be used for the sake of contrast: αὐτοὶ .. ἐγὼ .. Ma 1.4; also when a new subject is added, εἶδον .., αὐτοὶ καὶ ὁ πατὴρ αὐτῶν 'they saw .., they and their father' Ge 42.35; with the same force in an oblique case alongside a pronoun in the 1st or 2nd person - ὑμῖν αὐτοῖς 'yourselves' Ge 47.24, Nu 35.11. **c**. Reinforces an emphatic nom. pers. pron.: αὐτοὶ ὑμεῖς πορευόμενοι .. 'you yourselves go..' Ex 5.11; αὐτὸς σύ 33.15; αὐτός following – σὺ εἶ αὐτὸς ὁ βασιλεύς μου Ps 43.5, "Are you none other than Asael?" 2K 2.20; without the nom.pers.pron., αὐτοὶ ἑωράκατε 'you yourselves have seen' Ex 19.4; αὐτοὶ δὲ βαδίσατε 'you, however, go' Ge 42.19; Jb 18.2. **d**. An oblique case form may substitute for a reflexive pronoun: φερνῇ φερνιεῖ αὐτὴν αὐτῷ γυναῖκα 'he shall take her for himself as a wife by paying her price' Ex 22.16, ὑμῖν αὐτοῖς De 4.16 (|| ὑμῖν ἑαυτοῖς vs. 23); ἐπισυνάξει πρὸς αὐτὸν πάντα τὰ ἔθνη 'he will gather to himself all the nations' Hb 2.5. **e**. refers to a preceding substantive in extraposition: ἀπὸ τοῦ ξύλου .. οὐ φάγεσθε ἀπ' αὐτοῦ Ge 2.17; Je 28.19.

2. with the definite article, ὁ αὐτός, ἡ αὐτή, τὸ αὐτό, *the same, the selfsame*: μέτρον τὸ αὐτὸ ἔσται πάσαις ταῖς αὐλαίαις 'all the curtains shall have the same measurement' Ex 26.2; πρὸς τὴν αὐτὴν παιδίσκην 'to the same handmaid' Am 2.7; τοῦ αὐτοῦ ἔτος 'of that year' Es 8.9; + dat., τὴν αὐτὴν τῷ .. γέροντι μανίαν 'the madness identical with that of the old man' 4M 8.5; 10.2; νόμῳ τῷ αὐτῷ 'by a law, the one common to them all' 13.24. **b**. without a substantive, εἰς τὸ αὐτό 'to the same place' Ma 2.3, 2M 14.21; ἐπὶ τὸ αὐτό 'at the same time' Na 1.9, see further s.v. ἐπί **III 12**; ἐν τῷ αὐτῷ 'in the same place (?)' Ho 11.8, Zc 10.4; 'in the same (garment)' De 22.11; 'all together' Je 13.14; κατὰ τὸ αὐτό 'likewise' Ex 26.24, ἕκαστος κατὰ τὸ αὐτό Is 56.11, κατὰ τὰ αὐτά Ge 45.23, Ez 45.25 (v.l. at latter - κατὰ ταῦτα); τὸ δ' αὐτὸ καὶ πνεῦμα 'Likewise wind' Ep Je 60. **c**. = **5** below: ἐν τῇ αὐτῇ νυκτί 'on that very night' Da 5 pr. LXX. **d**. ὁ αὐτός etc., *the said, the above-named*: Pr 6.13 (|| ὁ τοιοῦτος 14). **e**. w. crasis, αὑτός = ὁ αὐτός: 4M 10.2.

3. *the former*, parallel to οὗτος 'the latter': Hb 2.19.

4. fossilised adv. αὐτοῦ *at this place* 'here': καθίσατε αὐτοῦ 'Sit here!' Ge 22.5; Ex 24.14, Nu 9.8, 22.8, 32.6; in indirect discourse, = 'there,' 3M 5.17. Cf. ὧδε.

5. precedes an articular noun phrase and emphasises the identity, 'the very': αὐτὴν τὴν ἡμέραν ταύτην 'this very day' Le 23.14; ἐν αὐτῇ τῇ ἡμέρᾳ ταύτῃ 'on this very day' 23.28, 29; αὐτῇ τῇ ἡμέρᾳ 'on the very day' To 14.10 𝔊II; 1E 6.3 (|| 2E 5.3), αὐτῇ τῇ ὥρᾳ 'at that moment' Da 3.6 TH, ἐν αὐτῇ τῇ ὥρᾳ ἐκείνῃ 5.5 LXX; ὑπ' αὐτὴν τὴν ἀκρόπολιν 'under the citadel of all places' 2M 4.12.

Cf. MM s.v.

αὐτοσχεδίως. adv.ʃ*

without previous planning, 'by mere chance': Wi 2.2.

αὑτοῦ, ῆς etc.

= ἑαυτοῦ, ῆς etc. (q.v.): εὗρον αὑτοῖς ἀνάπαυσιν 'they found their own resting-place' Is 34.14; 2M 8.30.

αὐτόχθων, ον; gen. ονος.

of native stock, indigenous: ἔν τε τοῖς γιώραις καὶ ~οσιν τῆς γῆς 'among the resident aliens and the natives of the land' Ex 12.19; opp. προσήλυτος 12.48 (|| ἐγχώριος vs. 49), Le 16.29, 17.15; 20.4 (|| τὸ ἔθνος τὸ ἐπὶ τῆς γῆς 20.2), Nu 15.13, 14, opp. πάροικος Je 14.8; ὑμῖν [= Israelites] καὶ τῷ προσηλύτῳ καὶ τῷ ~ονι Nu 9.14. Cf. ἐγχώριος, προσήλυτος, ἀλλογενής, ἀλλόφυλος: Harl 2001. 889.

αὐχήν, ένος. m.

neck: vulnerable part of body, Ps 128.4; μεταβάλλω ~ένα 'take to one's heels' Jo 7.8, sim. ἐπιστρέφω ~ένα 7.12, δίδωμι ~ένα 2C 29.6; καταπατέω ~ένα 'to walk over ..' 2K 22.41*L*.

αὐχμός, οῦ. m.ʃ

drought: Je 31.31. Cf. αὐχμώδης, ἀβροχία.

αὐχμώδης, ες.ʃ

dusty as a result of the lack of moisture: πύργος ποιμνίου αὐ. 'a dusty tower of the flock' Mi 4.8; *s* γῆ 'region' 1K 23.14 (*L* ὄρος), ὄρος 23.15 (*L* ἔρημος), ἔρημος 26.2; subst.f., γῆ (?) understood, 23.19, 26.1.

Cf. αὐχμός, ξηρός: Schmidt 2.326f.

ἀφαγνίζω: fut. ἀφαγνιῶ, pass. ~νισθήσομαι; aor. inf.act. ~νίσαι, mid. ~νίσασθαι, pass.subj. ~νισθῶ.

to purify: + acc. rei, οἰκίαν 'a house (contaminated with leprous infection)' Le 14.49 ('decontaminate,' Wevers ad loc.); objects, Nu 31.20; ἐν τῷ αἵματι τοῦ ὀρνιθίου 'with the blood of the bird' Le 14.52; + acc. pers., Nu 8.6, 21; + acc. cogn., ἁγνείαν κυρίῳ ἀπὸ οἴνου '.. (by abstaining) from wine ..' 6.2; || ἁγνίζω 19.12; ἂν μιανθῇ καὶ μὴ ἀφαγνισθῇ 19.20. Cf. ἁγνίζω, καθαρίζω.

ἀφαίρεμα, ατος. n.*

that which has been deducted in advance and set apart: a sacrificial animal and a cogn. obj., τὸν βραχίονα τοῦ ~ατος .. ὃς ἀφήρηται Ex 29.27; Le 14.21; τὸ τέλος κυρίῳ τὸ ἀ. τοῦ θεοῦ Nu 31.40; || πρωτότοκος Ex 22.29; also || ἀπαρχή Ez 44.30 (967 ἀφόρισμα). Cf. ἀφαιρέω.

ἀφαίρεσις, εως. f.ʃ

v.n. of ἀφαιρέω **1**: μερίδος καὶ δόσεως Si 41.21; 3M 1.1.

ἀφαιρέω: fut.act. ἀφελῶ, mid. ἀφελοῦμαι, pass. ἀφαιρεθήσομαι; aor.act. ἀφεῖλον, impv. ἄφελε, 3s ἀφελέτω, inf. ἀφελεῖν, ptc. ἀφελών, subj. ἀφέλω, mid. ἀφειλάμην, impv. ἀφελοῦ, 2pl ἀφέλεσθε, inf. ἀφελέσθαι, ptc. ἀφελόμενος, subj. ἀφέλωμαι, pass.ind. ἀφηρέθην, ptc. ἀφαιρεθείς, opt.3s ἀφαιρεθείη; pf.act. ἀφῄρηκα, pass. ἀφῄρημαι, ptc. ἀφῃρημένος; plpf.pass.3s ἀφῄρητο.

1. *to remove and cause to disappear*: + acc., ἀνομίας καὶ ἀδικίας καὶ ἁμαρτίας Ex 34.7, Nu 14.18, πονηρίας Is 1.16, κακίας Je 11.15, ἀδικίαν καὶ ταλαιπωρίαν (‖ ἐξαίρω); στολάς 'garments' Ex 33.5; concealing hand, 33.23; τὰ ἱμάτια τὰ ῥυπαρὰ ἀπ' αὐτοῦ 'the filthy clothes from him' Zc 3.4*a*; τὸν σάκκον Is 20.2; φραγμόν 5.5 (‖ καθαιρέω), κίδαριν 'turban' Ez 21.26 (‖ ἀποτίθημι); ***o*** office-holder and pass., ἐκ τῆς οἰκονομίας σου καὶ ἐκ τῆς στάσεώς σου 'from your stewardship and your position' Is 22.19; ***o*** δόξα 22.25; leadership, 3.1-3; δάκρυον ἀπὸ παντὸς προσώπου· τὸ ὄνειδος τοῦ λαοῦ 25.8; ὅρια ἐθνῶν '(dismantle) the boundaries between nations' 10.13; that which is perceived to be a burden, τὸν ὀνειδισμὸν ἡμῶν 'our disgrace' 4.1, ἀφέλετε ἀφ' ἡμῶν τὸν τρίβον τοῦτον καὶ .. τὸν ἅγιον τοῦ Ισραηλ 30.11; ἀπὸ δικαίου ὀφθαλμοὺς αὐτοῦ 'disregard the cause of the righteous' Jb 36.7¶; pass. ὕβρις Zc 10.11 (‖ περιαιρεῖσθαι); οὐ γὰρ ἀφαιρεῖται ἀπὸ τῆς συντάξεως ὑμῶν οὐθέν 'for your quota is not to be reduced at all' Ex 5.11; φόβος .. ζυγός Is 10.27; beheading, κεφαλήν Ge 40.19, 1M 7.47. **b.** 'to excise, delete': οὐκ ἀφελεῖτε ἀπ' αὐτοῦ De 4.2 (:: προστίθημι 'to add'), sim. 12.32, Ec 3.14, 1M 8.30. **c.** 'to take away' that which has been given: ***o*** allocated land, ἐκ τῆς κατασχέσεως .. ἐκ τοῦ κλήρου τῆς κληρονομίας Nu 36.3 (‖ ἀπό vs. 4); + τινός τι Is 28.18, Da 4.28 LXX, Pr 26.7, Es 8.2 o', Jb 24.7 (Zgl's ψυχῆς > ἐν ψύχει).

2. *to shift positions of*: + acc. rei, ἀπὸ τῆς κεφαλῆς Εφραιμ ἐπὶ τὴν κεφαλὴν Μανασση Ge 48.17.

3. *to deduct in advance and set apart* from the rest: + acc. and ‖ ἁγιάζω, Ex 13.12, see *BA* 2.44f.; + ἀφαίρεμα as cogn. obj., Ex 35.24; ἀφαίρεμα ἀφόρισμα κυρίῳ Nu 15.19; τέλος κυρίῳ παρὰ τῶν ἀνθρώπων 31.28. Cf. ἀφαίρεμα.

4. mid. *to cause the loss of*, 'deprive, seize': abs. and opp. δίδωμι Jb 1.21; + acc. περὶ τῶν φρεάτων τοῦ ὕδατος, ὧν ἀφείλαντο οἱ παῖδες τοῦ Αβιμελεχ 'over the water wells, which A.'s servants had seized' Ge 21.25; πάντα τὰ κτήνη 31.9; τὰ ἱμάτιά μου Ho 2.9 (‖ κομίζομαι); ἐλπίδα 'hope' Mi 2.8; τὴν ζωήν σου Si 9.13; ***o*** sth burdensome, τὴν ὀδύνην τῆς ψυχῆς Is 38.14f.; ἐμβίωσιν 'livelihood' Si 31.26 (‖ ἀποστερέω); own clothes, Es C 13 o' (*L* + ἀφ' ἑαυτῆς); own high office, 2M 14.7. **b.** + gen. of sbd to be deprived or robbed, πάντα τὸν πλοῦτον καὶ τὴν δόξαν, ἣν ἀφείλατο ὁ θεὸς τοῦ πατρὸς ἡμῶν Ge 31.16., poss. also 31.9; τοῦ πλησίον ἀφέλωνταί τι Is 5.8; ἀμφίασιν ψυχῆς αὐτῶν 'garments ..' Jb 24.10; τὴν ψυχὴν ἀφαιρεῖται τῶν κεκτημένων 'robs the soul of those who have got (gifts)' Pr 22.9a. **c.** + ἀπό τινος– Μήποτε ἀφέλῃ (v.l. ἀφέλῃς) τὰς θυγατέρας σου ἀπ' ἐμοῦ Ge 31.31.

Cf. ἀφαίρεμα, ἀφαίρεσις, ἐξ~, καθ~, παρ~, περι~, ὑφαιρέω, ἁγιάζω, περικαθαρίζω, ἀφορίζω, ἀποκόπτω.

ἀφάλλομαι: aor. ἀφηλάμην.ʃ

to move away quickly: ***s*** the sun, Na 3.17; of apostasy, ἀπ' ἐμοῦ Ez 44.10; thief, ἐκ πόλεως εἰς πόλιν Si 36.31. Cf. ἐξ~, ἐφάλλομαι.

ἀφανής, ές.

invisible: ***s*** hum., Jb 24.20; treasures, Si 20.30 (‖ κεκρυμμένος). Cf. ἀόρατος.

ἀφανίζω: fut.act. ἀφανιῶ, pass. ἀφανισθήσομαι; aor. ἠφάνισα, inf. ἀφανίσαι, impv. ἀφάνισον, subj. ἀφανίσω, opt.3s ἀφανίσαι, pass. ἠφανίσθην, subj. ἀφανισθῶ, impv.2pl ἀφανίσθητε; pf.pass. ἠφάνισμαι, ptc. ἠφανισμένος.

1. *to cause to disappear*: + acc., βατράχους ἀπὸ σοῦ .. ἐκ τῶν οἰκιῶν ὑμῶν 'frogs ..' Ex 8.9 (‖ περιαιρέω vs. 8, 11); ζύμην 'leaven, yeast' 12.15; ἀφανιῶ τὸ πρόσωπον αὐτοῦ εἰς τὴν θάλασσαν τὴν πρώτην Jl 2.20; pass. ἀφανίσθητε 'Vanish!' Hb 1.5. Cf. ἀφανής.

2. *to destroy*, + acc.: ***o*** agricultural produce, ἄμπελον .. συκᾶς Ho 2.12, ποίμνια Jl 1.18; ἀμπελών 'vineyard' Ct 2.15; βωμοί 'altars' Am 7.9, οἶκος Si 21.18, πόλεις Ez 36.36 (‖ καθαιρέω,:: καταφυτεύω), Am 9.14, Mi 5.14, γωνίαι 'corners' Zp 3.6; νόμιμα 'legislations' Mi 6.15; τὸ ὄνομά μου 1K 24.22 (‖ ἐξολεθρεύω); θησαυροί 'treasures' Jl 1.17 (‖ κατασκάπτω); γῆν Ez 19.7 (‖ ἐξερημόω); ***o*** hum., De 7.2, 19.1, Ho 5.15, 10.2, 14.1, Mi 6.13, Zp 2.9, + ἀποκτείνω Da 11.44 LXX (TH ἀναθεματίζω); *to put down*, dangerous domestic animal, Ex 21.29, 36 (or: *to keep away from the public*, cf. *BA* ad loc.).

3. pass. *to suffer lack* (*of* ἔκ τινος): ἡ γῆ ἀφανισθήσεται .. ἐκ διοδεύοντος καὶ ἀναστρέφοντος 'the land will have absolutely nobody travelling through and returning' Zc 7.14.

Cf. ἀφανισμός, ἀλοάω, ἀναθεματίζω, (ἀντ)αναιρέω, ἀναλίσκω, ἀναστέλλω, ἀποδειτρομέω, ἀποθερίζω, ~κοσμέω, ~λλυμι, ~ποιέομαι, ~σβέννυμι, ~στρέφω, ~τρυγάω, ~τυμπανίζω, ἀφαιρέω, ἀχρειόω, βιβρώσκω, διαπαύω, ~τήκω, ~φθείρω, διόλλυμι, ἐκκόπτω, ~λείπω, ~πίνω, ~πορθέω, ~ριζόω, ~τρίβω, ἐξαίρω, ~αλείφω, ~αναλίσκω, ~ερημόω, ~ολεθρεύω, ~όλλυμι, ἐξωθέω, ἐπαναιρέω, ἐσθίω, θλάω, θραύω, καθαιρέω, καταβάλλω, ~βιβρώσκω, ~άγω, ~κόπτω, ~ναλίσκω, ~ποντίζω, ~σκάπτω, ~σπάω, ~στρέφω, ~σφάζω, ~τήκω,

~τρώγω, κατεσθίω, ἀπο~, κατα~, κτείνω, λικμάω, λύω, ὀλεθρεύω, ὄλλυμι, παίω, παραναλίσκω, πατάσσω, παύω, περιαιρέω, πορθέω, πυρπολέω, σβέννυμι, συγκλάω, ~χέω, συμπεραίνω, συντελέω, ~τρίβω, ~εκτρίβω, (ἀπο)σφάζω, τύπτω, φθείρω, φονεύω, χειρόομαι: Shipp 117.

ἀφανισμός, οῦ. m.

ruin, destruction, annihilation: πεδίον ~οῦ 'plain of perdition' Jl 2.3, 3.19; ἡμέρα ἀωρίας καὶ ~οῦ 'a day of calamity and ruin' Zp 1.15; ‖ διαρπαγή 1.13, cf. 2.4; εἶναι εἰς ~όν 'to be destined to ruin' Mi 7.13, Jl 3.19, Zp 2.4; γίνεσθαι εἰς ~όν 'to meet perdition, be destroyed' Ho 5.9, Zp 3.1; τιθέναι or τάσσειν εἰς ~όν 'to condemn to perdition' Mi 1.7, Jl 1.7, Zp 2.13, εἰς ~ὸν καὶ εἰς ὄλεθρον Ez 6.14, εἰς ~ὸν καὶ εἰς συριγμόν '.. being whistled at' Je 19.8, cf. ὅπως παραδῶ σε εἰς ~όν Mi 6.16; ἀ. ἀπωλείας 'utter destruction' Je 12.11; ‖ ἀναίρεσις, σφαγή 2M 5.12. **b**. as dat. cogn., ~ῷ ἀφανιεῖς αὐτούς De 7.2; Je 12.11. Cf. ἀφανίζω, ἀπώλεια, διαρπαγή, ὄλεθρος.

ἀφάπτω: fut. ἀφάψω; aor.mid.impv. ἄφαψαι; pf. mid.3s ἀφῆπται.

to tie and fasten: + acc., αὐτὰ εἰς σημεῖον ἐπὶ τῆς χειρός σου De 6.8, sim. 11.18; metaph., ἐπὶ σῇ ψυχῇ Pr 6.21. **2**. mid., metaph. *to gain total control over*: + gen. pers., *s* κακία 'calamity' Jd 20.34 A (:: ἅπτομαι vs. 41). Cf. ἐφάπτομαι.

ἀφασία, ας. f.ʃ

inability to speak: out of astonishment, Es 6.17 *L*, 2M 14.17. Cf. ἄλαλος.

ἀφεγγής, ές.ʃ

without light: *s* παρακάλυμμα 'veil' Wi 17.3. Cf. σκοτεινός.

ἄφεδρος, ου. f.*

menstruation: χωρισμὸς ~ου 'separation due to ..' Le 12.2; ἀκαθαρσίαν ~ου 15.26; 2K 11.4*L* (B: ἀκαθαρσία); πρὸς γυναῖκα ἐν ~ῳ οὖσαν Ez 18.6, cf. ἀποκάθημαι; αἵματος PSol 8.12.

ἀφειδῶς. adv.

1. *relentlessly, mercilessly*: 2M 5.6.

2. *ungrudgingly, lavishly*: οἰκτίρω 'to show mercy' Pr 21.26.

Cf. φείδομαι.

ἀφελπίζω:⇒ ἀπελπίζω.

ἀφελῶς. adv.ʃ

without taking recourse to intricate or ingenous skills or devices: 3K 22.34*L*.

ἄφεμα, ατος. n.ʃ

amount of taxation or *tribute that has been exempted*: cogn. acc. of ἀφίημι 1M 10.28, 13.37. Cf. ἀφίημι.

ἄφεσις, εως. f.

1. *making go away*, 'dismissal': + obj.gen. pers., Ex 18.2 (divorce?); scapegoat, Le 16.26, on which latter cf. Dogniez - Harl 2001 n. ad loc.; ἄνεσις καὶ ἄ. 'permission to go away' 1E 4.62.

2. *channel* for accumulated water to flow through: of wadi, ἐξηράνθησαν ~εις ὑδάτων 'river-beds dried up' Jl 1.20, θαλάσσης 2K 22.16, fig. of streams of tears, La 3.48; αἱ ~εις Ιουδα ῥυήσονται ὕδατα 3.18 (‖ πηγή). Cf. the use of the word in the sense of 'sluice gates' in papyri, see Preisigke I 245, s.v. **12**.

3. *releasing* from use, bondage, debt: to be announced every fifty years – διαβοήσετε ~ιν Le 25.10; τὸ ἔτος τῆς ~εως 25.13 (‖ ἐνιαυτὸς ~εως 25.10), Ez 46.17; of agricultural land, Ex 23.11; of slaves, καλέσαι ~ιν Je 41.8; of captives, κηρύξαι αἰχμαλώτοις ~ιν Is 61.1; of debts, τοῦ ἀδελφοῦ σου ~ιν ποιήσεις τοῦ χρέους σου 'you shall write off the debt owed by your brother to you' De 15.3, ἀπόστελλε τεθραυσμένους ἐν ~ει 'free those crushed under heavy debts' Is 58.6; τὸ ἔτος τὸ ἕβδομον, ἔτος τῆς ~εως 15.9, ἐνιαυτὸς ~εως 31.10; royal amnesty, Es 2.18, ἡμέραι ἀτελείας καὶ ~εως 'days of immunity and ..' 1M 10.34.

4. *permission*: Ju 11.14 cf. ἐπιχώρησις.

Cf. ἀφίημι: Spicq 1.239f.; Harl 2001.898f.

ἀφεύκτως.ʃ

inescapably: 3M 7.9.

ἀφή, ῆς. f.

1. **infection*, esp. of leprosy: λέπρας Le 13.2, De 24.8.

2. *part of body infected by leprosy*: Le 13.49.

3. *injury*: De 17.8, 21.5 (‖ ἀντιλογία 'dispute'). **b**. mental: καρδίας 'being conscience-stricken' 3K 8.38, ‖ 2C 6.29 καρδίας understood.

4. v.n. of ἅπτομαι: as cogn. dat., Je 31.9.

ἀφηγέομαι: fut. ἀφηγήσομαι.

to serve as leader of: + gen. pers., ὁ λαός σου, οὗ σὺ ἀφηγῇ Ex 11.8; military, τοῦ πολεμῆσαι Jd 1.1; + gen. rei, political or administrative, τῶν ἐπὶ τῆς βασιλείας .. πραγμάτων 'the running of the kingdom' 4M 12.5; subst. ptc., ἀφηγούμενος 'leader' Ez 11.1, ‖ ἄρχων 12.10. Cf. ἡγέομαι, ἀφήγημα, ἄρχω: Raurell 1986.

ἀφήγημα, ατος. n.ʃ

directive issued by a leader: τῆς ψυχῆς 4M 14.6. Cf. ἀφηγέομαι.

ἀφθαρσία, ας. f.

immortality: of hum., Wi 2.23; originally divine property, 6.19; prize won by martyrs, 4M 17.12. Cf. ἄφθαρτος, φθείρω, ἀθανασία.

ἄφθαρτος, ον.ʃ

immortal: *s* divine spirit, Wi 12.1, νόμου φῶς 18.4. Cf. ἀφθαρσία, ἄφθορος, ἀθάνατος, εὔφθαρτος, φθαρτός.

ἄφθονος, ον.ʃ
liberal and generous in provision: ***s*** χορηγία 'provision' 3M 5.2; πηγή 'spring' 4M 3.10. Cf. φθόνος.

ἀφθόνως. adv.ʃ
liberally and generously, 'ungrudgingly': Wi 7.13. Cf. ἄφθονος.

ἀφθορία: ⇒ ἀφορία.

ἄφθορος, ον.ʃ
uncorrupted: w. ref. to virgn, Es 2.2 o'.
Cf. ἄφθαρτος, φθορά.

ἀφιερόω: aor.subj. ἀφιερώσω.ʃ
to consecrate: ἑαουτοὺς τῷ θεῷ 4M 13.13. Cf. ἁγιάζω.

ἀφίημι, ἀφίω: pres.ind.2s ἀφεῖς, inf. ἀφιέναι; fut: ἀφήσω, pass. ἀφεθήσομαι; aor.act. ἀφῆκα, impv. 2s ἄφες, pl. ἄφετε, 3s ἀφέτω, ptc. ἀφείς, inf. ἀφεῖναι, subj. ἀφῶ, pass. ἀφέθην, inf. ἀφεθῆναι, ptc. ἀφεθείς; pf.ptc.pass. ἀφειμένος.

1. *to forgive*: ***o*** pers, μείζων ἡ αἰτία μου τοῦ ἀφεθῆναί με 'my guilt is too grave for me to be forgiven' Ge 4.13; + acc. of sin and dat. pers., Ἄφες αὐτοῖς τὴν ἀδικίαν καὶ τὴν ἁμαρτίαν 50.17, sim. Nu 14.19, ***s*** God Ex 32.32, ἀφῆκας τὰς ἀνομίας τῷ λαῷ σου Ps 84.3 (ǁ ἐκάλυψας); pass. ἀφεθήσεται αὐτοῖς ἡ ἁμαρτία Le 4.20 ǁ impers., ἀφεθήσεται αὐτῷ 4.31, 35, sim. Nu 15.25; ***s*** God and + acc. pers., πάντα τὸν τόπον δι' αὐτούς Ge 18.26 (ǁ ἀνίημι vs. 24).

2. *to refrain from exacting*: + acc., χρέος 'debt' De 15.2, φόρους .. κτηνῶν 'taxes on cattle' 1M 10.33. **b**. *to exempt*: abs., ἀπὸ δουλείας .. ἀπὸ ζυγοῦ 'from slavery .. from yoke' 2C 10.4 (ǁ vs. 9 ἀνίημι); + acc. pers., ἀπὸ τῶν φόρων 'from payment of tributes' 1M 10.29; ἀφ' ἡμῶν 2C 10.10 (***o*** ζυγόν implied). Cf. χρεοκοπέομαι.

3. *to allow, give a free hand*: + acc., Ex 22.5; and + inf., οὐκ ἀφῆκά σε ἅψασθαι αὐτῆς 'I did not let you touch her' Ge 20.6; Ex 12.23, Nu 22.13; + indic. fut., Ἄφετέ με πικρῶς κλαύσομαι 'Allow me to wail bitterly' Is 22.4; Ru 2.16. Cf. δίδωμι **16**, ἐπιτρέπω, συγχωρέω. **b**. w. the collateral notion of abandoning sbd to his fate (see below **9**): + inf., με πεσεῖν Si 23.1.

4. *to entrust*: + acc. pers., ἐν χειρὶ διαβουλίου αὐτοῦ 'to the domain of his (own) decision' Si 15.14.

5. *to let go of*: abs. and:: ἐπιλαμβάνομαι 'hold fast to' Pr 4.13; + acc., ἐν τῷ ἀφιέναι αὐτὴν τὴν ψυχήν 'as she was about to breathe her last' Ge 35.18; ***o*** scapegoat, Le 16.10; πᾶσαν ψυχὴν .. ἐλευθέραν δωρεάν 'set everybody .. free for no payment' 1M 10.33; ἐξουσίαν 'authority (over)' 10.32.

6. *to pronounce innocent*: + acc. pers., τοὺς ἐνόχους 'the guilty' Su 53 LXX (TH ἀπολύω).

7. *to leave behind* without taking along: + acc., ἀδελφὸν ἕνα ἄφετε ὧδε μετ' ἐμοῦ Ge 42.33; τὰ κτήνη ἐν τῷ πεδίῳ 'the cattle in the field' Ex 9.21; σε γυμνήν 'unclothed' Ez 16.39, σεαυτόν Si 6.3; ἐν γραφῇ 39.32; ***o*** cultic offerings, ἀπέναντι κυρίου De 26.10; food unconsumed, To 2.4 𝔊[II].

8. *to emit*: + φωνήν – φωνὴν μετὰ κλαυθμοῦ Ge 45.2.

9. *to stop taking interest in and caring for*: + acc., τὴν κληρονομίαν μου (= Israel and ***s*** God) Je 12.7 (ǁ ἐγκαταλείπω).

10. *to leave* in a certain state: + double acc., τοὺς υἱοὺς αὐτῶν ἀπεριτμήτους 'to leave .. uncircumcised' 1M 1.48. **b**. *to leave unharmed*, 'spare': τινα Jd 2.21 (ǁ καταλείπω), 23, 3.1.

11. *to depart from* when one ought to stay put: + acc., τόπον σου 'your post' Ec 10.4. **b**. intr.: μὴ ἀφέτω ἡ χείρ σου 'Let your hand not leave off (working)' Ec 11.6.

Cf. ἄφεσις, ἄφεμα, ἐξαφίημι, καταλείπω, ἱλάσκομαι, ἀν~, παρ~, προΐημι.

ἀφικνέομαι: fut. ἀφίξομαι; aor.mid. ἀφικόμην, subj. ἀφίκωμαι, opt.3s ἀφίκοιτο; pf. ἀφῖγμαι.
to reach: ἧς ἡ κεφαλὴ ἀφικνεῖτο εἰς τὸν οὐρανόν 'its [= the ladder's] top reached the sky' Ge 28.12; ἕως πρὸς ἄνθρωπόν τινα .. 38.1; ἀφίκοιτό μου ἡ δέησις πρὸς κύριον 'May my entreaty reach ..' Jb 16.20; οὐκ ἀφίκοντο εἰς τὰς ἡμέρας τῶν ἐτῶν τῆς ζωῆς τῶν πατέρων μου 'have not got as far as the length of my fathers' lives' Ge 47.9; εἰς γενεὰς γενεῶν Ju 8.32; εἰς τὰ ἔσχατα Jb 11.7; πρὸς τέλος 'the ultimate' 2M 6.15; + dat. pers., ***s*** sth undesirable Pr 1.27. **b**. *to reach the end, having done enough*: Si 43.27, 30.

Cf. ἄφιξις, ἀνέφικτος, ἐξικνέομαι, καταντάω, φθάνω: Schmidt 1.513.

ἄφιξις, εως. f.ʃ
arrival: 3M 7.18. Cf. ἀφικνέομαι, ἄφοδος.

ἀφίστημι: pres.impv.mid. ἀφίστω; impf.mid. ἀφιστάμην; fut. act. ἀποστήσω, mid. ~στήσομαι, pass. ~σταθήσομαι; 1aor.act. ἀπέστησα, inf. ἀποστῆσαι, ptc.~στήσας, impv. ~στησον, pass.subj. ἀποσταθῶ; 2aor.act. ἀπέστην, 3pl ἀπέστησαν, impv.act. ἀπόστηθι, ἀπόστα (poet.), 2pl ~στητε, 3pl ~στήτωσαν, subj. ἀποστῶ, inf. ~στῆναι, ptc. ~στάς, opt.3s ~σταίη; pf. ἀφέστηκα (intr.), ἀφέστακα (tr.), ptc. ἀφεστηκώς(intr.).

I. tr. (pres./fut.act., 1aor., pf. ἀφέστακα), *to keep at a distance*: ἀπέστησεν ὁδὸν τριῶν ἡμερῶν ἀνὰ μέσον αὐτῶν καὶ ἀνὰ μέσον Ιακωβ 'he put a distance of three days' journey between them and J.' Ge 30.36; ἀπόστησον ἀπ' ἐμοῦ τὰς μάστιγάς σου '.. your whips' Ps 38.11; τὴν προσευχήν μου καὶ τὸ ἔλεος αὐτοῦ ἀπ' ἐμοῦ 65.20; τὸν Ιουδαν ἀπὸ τοῦ προσώπου μου 4K 23.27; *o* divine blessings, αἱ ἁμαρτίαι ὑμῶν ἀπέστησαν τὰ ἀγαθὰ ἀφ' ὑμῶν Je 5.25 (‖ ἐκκλίνω), divine commandments, Ps 17.23; λύπην μακρὰν ἀπὸ σοῦ 'pain ..' Si 30.23, ὕπνον 'sleep' 34.1, 42.9, πλημμέλειαν 'error' 38.10, θυμόν 'anger' Ec 11.10 (‖ παράγω); + gen., τῆς οἰκίας 'from their home' 3M 6.25. **b**. *to alienate*: + acc. pers., Si 47.23.

2. *to remove*: from office, 'depose,' *o* one anointed to an office, Da 9.26 LXX (TH ἐξολεθρεύω), cf. ἀπέστησε τῆς ἐξουσίας αὐτῶν 'relieved .. of their office' 7.12 LXX. **b**. *to annul wrongfully*: *o* institution, θυσίαν Da 11.31 LXX (TH μεθίστημι).

3. *to divert*: + acc., τὴν καρδίαν τῶν υἱῶν Ισραηλ, ὅπως μὴ εἰσέλθωσιν .. Nu 32.9 (‖ διαστρέφετε τὰς διανοίας .. μὴ διαβῆναι .. vs. 7); De 1.28; ἀπεστήσαμεν ὀπίσω τὴν κρίσιν 'we shunted justice to the backseat' Is 59.14; με ἀπὸ τῆς μάχης 1E 1.28. **b**. from the right course: of apostasy, τὸν υἱόν σου ἀπ' ἐμοῦ De 7.4; ἀπὸ κυρίου 13.10; συνετούς Si 19.2. **c**. *to cause to revolt*: abs., 2K 5.6*L* (B: ἀνθίστημι), poss. intr.

II. intr. (mid. fut. and 2aor., pf. ἀφέστηκα), **1**. *to move* from place A to place B permanently: change of dwelling-place - ἀπέστη ἐκεῖθεν εἰς τὸ ὄρος Ge 12.8; ἀπόστα ἐκεῖ 'Move on there!' 19.9.

2. *to desert, move away*: abs. 'to disappear' Si 39.9; + ἀπό τινος– ἀφίστατο ὁ ὕπνος ἀπὸ τῶν ὀφθαλμῶν μου 'sleep kept eluding me' Ge 31.40; ἡ νεφέλη ἀπέστη ἀπὸ τῆς σκηνῆς 'the cloud lifted from the tent' Nu 12.10; ἀφέστηκεν ὁ καιρὸς ἀπ' αὐτῶν 'they have had their day' 14.9; ἀπὸ τῆς καρδίας σου De 4.9; κρίσις 'justice' Is 59.9; ἀφέστη ἡ ψυχὴ αὐτῆς ἀπ' αὐτῶν 'she lost interest in them' Ez 23.17; ὁ λόγος ἀπ' ἐμοῦ ἀπέστη 'the issue has been finalised, as far as I am concerned' Da 2.5 TH, sim. 2.8 TH; *s* God's indifference, μακρόθεν Ps 9.22, ἀπ' ἐμοῦ 37.22 (‖ ἐγκαταλείπω), 34.22; *s* hum., + gen., τοῦ κυρίου Wi 3.10, ὁδῶν αὐτῶν PSol 18.12. **b**. involuntarily, *to become disjointed*: *s* collar-bone from shoulder-blade, Jb 31.22.

3. *to be at some distance*: ἀποστησόμεθα ἕτερος ἀπὸ τοῦ ἑτέρου 'we shall keep a distance from each other' Ge 31.49; μακρὰν ἀφέστηκεν ἀφ' ἡμῶν Is 59.11.

4. *to take leave of, resign*: abs., οὐκ ἀπέστη, ἕως .. 'he did not stop (his action) until ..' PSol 4.10; ἀπὸ τῆς λειτουργίας 'from the (cultic) service' Nu 8.25.

5. *to distance oneself*: abs., 1E 1.25 (military withdrawal); ἀποστῆσαι καὶ ὑπεριδεῖν τὸ ῥῆμα κυρίου 'to revolt and disregard the word of the Lord' Nu 31.16; of religious apostasy, ἀπὸ θεοῦ De 32.15 (‖ ἐγκαταλείπω), ἀπὸ λατρείας πατέρων 'the ancestral religion' 2.19; Jo 22.18, 29 (‖ ἀποστρέφω), Da 9.5 (‖ LXX παρέρχομαι, TH ἐκκλίνω), ὁ ἀφεστηκώς 'apostate' Ez 20.38 (‖ ἀσεβής), ἀπὸ διαθήκης ἁγίας 1M 1.15; of political rebellion, Ge 14.4, ἀπό τινος 2C 36.5[a] (‖ ἀθετέω 2K 24.1); Nu 14.31; 16.27 (‖ ἀναχωρέω vs. 24); ἀπὸ παντὸς ῥήματος ἀδίκου 'from any kind of unjust statement' Ex 23.7, ἀπὸ πονηρίας .. ἀπὸ ἀδικίας Si 32.5; ἀπὸ (B: om.) ὄπισθεν ^Κυρίου^ 4K 18.6*L*; ἐπάνωθεν (*L* ἀπὸ) ἁμαρτιῶν 4K 10.31; μὴ ἀποστῇ ἡ ψυχή μου ἀπὸ σοῦ Je 6.8, sim. 14.19, Ez 23.28 (latter ‖ μισέω); w. ref. to breach of treaty, 17.15; + gen., ἀκαθάρτων La 4.15 (:: ἅπτομαι).

6. *to be* or *become unservicable*: *s* unsafe roads, To 1.15 𝔊[II].

7. *to cease to be available*, 'run out': *s* olive-oil, 4K 4.4 *L* (‖ simp., vs. 6).

Cf. ἀποστασία, ἀποστάσιον, ἀποστατέω, ἀποστάτης, ἀποστάτις, διαστρέφω, ἐκκλίνω.

ἄφνω. adv.

at an unexpected moment and with speed: ἄ. ἔπεσε Βαβυλων '.. B. fell' Je 28.8; 4.20; πατάξαι αὐτοὺς ἄ. 'attack them ..' 1M 4.2; ‖ ὁμοίως καταιγίδι 'like a hurricane' Pr 1.27. Cf. αἰφνιδίως: Schmidt 2.164-7.

ἀφοβία, ας.ʃ

want of a sense of respect and awe towards God: opp. φόβος κυρίου Pr 15.16. Cf. φόβος.

ἄφοβος, ον.

without fear: *s* hum., Si 5.5. Cf. ἀφόβως, φόβος.

ἀφόβως. adv.ʃ

fearing nothing: Pr 1.33. Cf. ἄφοβος.

ἀφόδευμα, ατος. n.ʃ

excrement: birds', To 2.10 𝔊[II]. Cf. βόλβιτον, κόπρος, προχώρημα.

ἀφοδεύω: aor. ἀφώδευσα.ʃ

to discharge as excrement: *s* birds, + acc. rei, θερμόν 'warm dropping' To 2.10 𝔊[I].

ἄφοδος, ου. f.ʃ

departure: 3M 7.10. Cf. ἄφιξις.

ἀφόμοιος, ον.ʃ

subst., *copy* of a document: Si prol. 29 (v.l. ἀφορμή 'occasion'). Poss. "an example of considerable intellectual pursuit," cf. Auvray 1957.285-7. Cf. ἀντίγραφον: Wagner 119f.

ἀφομοιόω: aor.pass.subj. ~μοιωθῶμαι, ptc. ~μοιωθείς; pf. ἀφωμοίωμαι, ptc.pass. ἀφωμοιωμένος.

pass. *to become like*: + dat., τοῖς ἀλλοφύλοις Ep Je 4. Cf. ὁμοιόω, ἀφόμοιος: Naumann 36. Del. Wi 13.14 v.l.

ἀφοράω.ʃ

to turn exclusive attention to: εἰς θεόν 4M 17.10, cf. ἀφορῶντες .. εἰς Ἰησοῦν Heb 12.2. Cf. ἀποβλέπω, ἀπεῖδον: Spicq 1.247-9.

ἀφόρητος, ον.ʃ
such that one cannot put up with, 'unbearable, intolerable': τὸ τῆς ὀσμῆς ~ον βάρος 'the unbearably thick stench' 2M 9.10. Cf. φέρω.

ἀφορία, ας. f.ʃ
failure of agricultural crops: as punitive, natural disaster along with ἀνεμοφθορία and χάλαζα Hg 2.17. Cf. φέρω.

ἀφορίζω: fut. ἀφοριῶ; aor.act. ἀφώρισα, subj. ἀφορίσω, inf. ἀφορίσαι, ptc. ἀφορίσας, mid.impv. ἀφόρισαι, pass. ἀφωρίσθην, impv. ἀφορίσθητι, ptc. ἀφορισθείς; pf.pass. ἀφώρισμαι, ptc. ἀφωρισμένος.

I. *to sever*: ἀ. ὑμῖν τὸν ὦμον 'I sever the shoulder for you (?)' Ma 2.3, cf. Tht PG 81.1969 and Th 410; με .. ἀπὸ τοῦ λαοῦ αὐτοῦ Is 56.3.

2. *to set apart, separate*: + acc. pers., Ex 19.12; ὑμᾶς ἀπὸ πάντων τῶν ἐθνῶν εἶναι ἐμοί Le 20.26; παρὰ τῶν υἱῶν Ισραηλ Nu 8.11; τὸν οἶκον Ιακωβ, ὃν ἀφώρισεν ἐξ Αβρααμ Is 20.22; sacrificial animals, ἀνὰ μέσον τῶν κτηνῶν τῶν καθαρῶν καὶ ἀνὰ μέσον τῶν κτηνῶν τῶν ἀκαθάρτων Le 20.25; + cogn. obj. ἀφόρισμα ἔναντι κυρίου Ex 29.24, Le 14.12, cf. ἀφαίρεμα ἀφοριεῖτε Nu 15.20; ***o*** leper, 'quarantine' (Wevers) Le 13.4; πόλεις for fugitives, De 4.41; mid. ἀφόρισαι τὸ ὄρος καὶ ἁγίασαι αὐτό Ex 19.23.

3. *to mark out an area for*: + acc., θρόνον 'throne' Pr 8.27.

4. *to give as a special gift*: + dat. com. and acc. rei, Ps 67.10; ***o*** funds earmarked for a special purpose, 4M 3.20; as a tribute (?), 2K 8.1.

II. mid. *to split* into more than one part: ἀφορίζεται εἰς τέσσαρας ἀρχάς 'it splits into four tributaries' Ge 2.10; ἐκ τούτων ἀφωρίσθησαν 'from these they split off' 10.5.

2. *to distance oneself*: Is 52.11.

Cf. ἀφόρισμα, ἀποσχίζω, ἀφαιρέω, διορίζω, ἁγιάζω, διαστέλλω.

ἀφόρισμα, ατος. n.

1. *act of setting apart* for sacerdotal office: as cogn. obj. of ἀφορίζω, Ex 29.24, Le 10.15, 14.12.

2. *object set apart*: τοῦ ἁγίου 'for use in the sanctuary' Ex 36.38; ‖ ἀφαίρεμα Le 10.14; ἀφαίρεμα ἀ. κυρίῳ Nu 15.19; Ez 44.29; plot of land, Nu 35.3.

Cf. ἀφορίζω, ἀφορισμός.

ἀφορισμός, οῦ. m.ʃ
*= ἀφόρισμσ **2**: Ez 20.31 (‖ ἀπαρχὴ δομάτων); ἀπαρχὴ ~οῦ 20.40, 48.8. Cf. ἀφορισμός.

ἀφορμή, ῆς. f.ʃ
occasion for an act, source of inspiration: Ez 5.7, Pr 9.9, 3M 3.2. Cf. Bertram, *TDNT* 5.472-4.

ἀφορολόγητος, ον.ʃ
exempt from payment of tribute: ***s*** land, 1E 4.50, 1M 11.28.

ἀφρονεύομαι: ἠφρονευσάμην.ʃ *
to act foolishly: οἱ ποιμένες ἠφρονεύσαντο Je 10.21. Cf. ἀφρόνως.

ἀφρόνως. adv.ʃ *
in a foolish manner, without exercising discretion: ἀ. ἔπραξας 'you have acted foolishly' Ge 31.28. Cf. ἀφροσύνη, ἀφρονεύομαι, φρόνιμος.

ἀφροσύνη, ης. f.
act of folly: committed by a woman who married in an unchaste state, De 22.21; + μάταια La 2.14. **b**. *foolishness*: Ps 68.6; opp. φρόνησις Pr 9.6.

Cf. ἄφρων: Bertram, *TDNT* 9.225.

ἄφρων, ον; gen. ονος.
silly: ***s*** hum., Is 59.7, Je 17.11, ‖ ἀσύνετος Ps 91.7, ‖ μωρός 93.8; subst. hum., 38.9, + ἄνους 48.11, + παράνομος Pr 6.12; opp. φρόνιμος 11.29. Cf. ἀφροσύνη, ἀκάρδιος, ἄνους, ἀσύνετος, μωρός, νήπιος, σώφρων, φρόνιμος.

ἀφυλάκτως. adv.ʃ
not watched, by stealth: Ez 7.22.

ἀφυστερέω: aor. ἀφυστέρησα, subj. ~ρήσω.ʃ
to withhold from oneself, deprive oneself of: ἀπὸ ἀγαθῆς ἡμέρας 'occasional pleasure' Si 14.14; + acc., τὸ μάννα .. ἀπὸ στόματος αὐτῶν Ne 9.20.

ἄφωνος, ον.
giving out no sound, 'speechless, silent': Is 53.7; stunned, 2M 3.29.

ἀχανής, ές.ʃ
wide-open: threatening to engulf, ***s*** σκότος 'darkness' Wi 19.17. Cf. χαίνω.

ἄχαρις, ρι.ʃ
unpleasant: ***s*** hum., Si 20.19. Cf. χάρις: LSG s.v.

ἀχάριστος, ον.
ungrateful: ***s*** hum., Si 29.17. **b**. *indicative of ungratefulness*: ***s*** n.pl., acts typical of such an attitude, Si 29.25. Cf. ἀχαρίστως.

ἀχαρίστως. adv.ʃ
ungratefully or *ungraciously*: Si 18.18. Cf. ἀχάριστος.

ἀχάτης, ου. m.
agate: Ex 28.19, Ez 28.13.

ἄχι. n. *ʃ Egypt. loan-word.
reed-grass: grazing-ground for cattle by the Nile, Ge 41.2, 18; growing by a river, ἄ. ἐπὶ παντὸς ὕδατος καὶ χείλους ποταμοῦ Si 40.16; τὸ ἄ. τὸ χλωρὸν τὸ κύκλῳ τοῦ ποταμοῦ 'the green reed-grass around the river' Is 19.7.

ἀχρεῖος, ον.ʃ

1. *useless*: ***s*** σκεῦος .. συντριβέν 'a broken instrument' Ep Je 15.

2. *out of keeping with one's character* or *situation* (cf. LSG), 'unseemly': ***s*** hum., ἐν ὀφθαλμοῖς σου 2K 6.22.

Cf. ἄχρηστος, ἀχρειότης, ἀχρειόω, ἀνωφέλης: Shipp 120-2.

ἀχρειότης, ητος. f.ʃ *
refusal to make oneself useful, 'idleness': ἡ ἀ. μήτηρ ἐστὶν τοῦ λιμοῦ '.. leads to hunger' To 4.13 𝔊[I]. Cf. ἀχρεῖος.

ἀχρε(ι)όω: fut. ἀχρειώσω; aor.inf. ἀχρεῶσαι, pass. ἠχρεώθην; pf. ἠχρείωκα.ʃ
1. *to render useless*: + acc., τὰ ἔνδοξα αὐτῆς 1E 1.53; ***o*** and pass., κλάδοι 'branches' Je 11.16, δένδρον Da LXX 4.11; agricultural land, μερίδα ἀγαθήν 'a good plot' 4K 3.19.
*__2__. *to destroy physically*: ***s*** lions, ***o*** human, Da LXX 6.21.
3. *to render morally corrupt*: ***o*** hum. and pass., Ps 13.3 ‖ 52.4 (‖ ἐκκλίνω).
Cf. ἀχρεῖος, ἀφανίζω.

ἄχρηστος, ον.
useless: ***s*** σκεῦος 'vessel, instrument' Ho 8.8, ἔργα 'works' Wi 3.11, καρπός '(unripe, inedible) fruit' 4.5, λίθος 13.10, ὕδωρ '(waste) water' 16.29, τέκνον Si 16.1, with limbs mutilated 2M 7.5; τόπος 3M 3.29. Cf. ἀχρεῖος, εὔχρηστος, χρήσιμος, ἀνόνητος, ἀνωφελής.

ἄχρι.ʃ
up to, as far as: **I a**. prep. + gen. and local, ἄ. περάτων 'up to the borders' Es *L* B 15 (LXX μέχρι); Jd 11.33 B (-). **b**. temporal, ἄ. οὗ + subj. aor. 'until' Jb 32.11¶(*a*); + gen., ἄ. αἰῶνος 'for ever' 2M 14.15.
II conj., **as long as*: ἄ. Ἰούδας περίεστιν 'as long as J. is around' 2M 14.10.
Cf. ἕως, μέχρι.
**a*) עַד.

ἄχυρον, ου. n.
1. *straw* left after threshing: fodder for livestock, ἄχυρα καὶ χορτάσματα ταῖς καμήλοις 'straw and fodder for the camels' Ge 24.32, λέων καὶ βοῦς ἅμα φάγονται ~α 'a lion and an ox alike shall eat straw' Is 11.7, sim. 65.25; for horses, 3K 5.1; material for manufacturing of bricks, Ex 5.7; stubble as substitute, καλάμη εἰς ~α 5.12; building material, συμπατήθητι ἐν ~οις 'Be trampled in straw' Na 3.14; fig. of sth worthless and:: σῖτος Je 23.28. Cf. καλάμη.
2. *chaff and grain* separated from the straw and grain: ἐν ἅλωνι 'on a threshing-floor' Da 2.35 LXX.
Cf. χόρτασμα: Chadwick 56-9.

ἀψευδής, ές.ʃ
containing no falsehood: ***s*** γνῶσις 'knowledge' Wi 7.17.

ἄψυχος, ον.ʃ
having no soul: ***s*** εἴδωλα idols, Wi 14.29; 13.17. Cf. ψυχή.

ἀωρία, ας. f.ʃ
1. *hard time, distressful plight*: ἡμέρα ~ας Zp 1.15 (‖ θλῖψις and ἀνάγκη; 8Ḥev, ἀπορία).
2. *midnight, the dead of night*: Is 59.9 (:: αὐγή 'dawn' and ‖ σκότος); Ps 118.147; 1E 1.13.
Cf. ἀνάγκη and θλῖψις.

ἄωρος, ον.
too early and happening before the desired or normal time: ***s*** pers. dying an untimely death, Jb 22.16 ¶, Pr 11.30, + πρεσβύτης 'elderly' Is 65.20, πένθος 'mourning' Wi 14.15; fruits, εἰς βρῶσιν 'for consumption' 4.5. Cf. ἀωρία.

B

Βαβυλών, ῶνος. f.
Babylon: Ge 10.10 +.

Βαβυλώνιος, α, ον. f.
subst.f.sg. *Babylon*: Is 11.11 +.

βαδίζω: fut. βαδιοῦμαι; aor.subj. βαδίσω, impv. βάδισον, inf. βαδίσαι, ptc. βαδίσας.

1. *to walk*: *s* moth, ἐπὶ κανόνος, '(crawls) on a rod' Mi 7.4; Is 40.31 (ǁ τρέχω).

2. *to go, proceed*: *s* ship, πλοῖον βαδίζον εἰς Θαρσις 'a boat sailing to Tarshish' Jn 1.3.

3. In the impv.: in the pres. asyndetically with another verb in the aor., urging sbd (lower in standing) to an action: βάδιζε ἄπελθε Ex 4.19; βάδιζε κατάβηθι 32.7; βάδιζε ἄπαρον De 10.11; βάδιζε λάβε σεαυτῷ γυναῖκα Ho 1.2, sim. Am 7.12, 15; syndetically, βάδιζε καὶ ὁδήγησον Ex 32.34; βάδιζε .. καὶ ἄγαγε .. To 2.2 𝔊II. **b.** both verbs in the pres.: βάδιζε καὶ ποίει 2K 7.3. **c.** both verbs in the aor.: βαδίσατε καὶ ἀπαγάγετε Ge 42.19; Βαδίσατε πάλιν, ἀγοράσατε 44.25, cf. βαδίσαντες ἀγοράσατε Is 55.1; βάδισον εἰπὸν De 5.30, βαδίσας στῆσον Is 21.6. **d.** β. alone, βάδισον πρὸς Φαραω Ex 7.15; βάδιζε ὑγιαίνων 'in peace' 4.18. **e.** βαδίσατε καὶ μὴ ὀλέσητε τὸν Ισραηλ '.. destroy I. not' Je 38.2.

Cf. ἔρχομαι, πορεύομαι: Schmidt 1.477-504; Shipp 122-4.

βάδος > **βάτος**.

βαθέως. adv.ʃ
in a profound manner: βαθέως βουλὴν ποιοῦντες 'do deep thinking' Is 29.15. Cf. βαθύς.

βαθμός, οῦ. m.
step: οἴκου Δαγων 'of Dagon's house' 1K 5.5, θυρῶν 'doorstep, threshold' Si 6.36; degree on a sundial, 4K 20.9 (*L* ἀναβαθμός). Cf. ἀναβαθμός: Shipp 124f.; LSG s.v.

βάθος, ους. n.
deep place, often a figure of a distressful, desperate personal situation: 'deep water', mostly pl. – τὰ ~η τῆς θαλάσσης Am 9.3, Mi 7.19, Is 51.10; ~η καρδίας θαλάσσης 'the depth of the heart of the sea' Jn 2.4, cf. ἐκ ~ους κοιλίας ᾅδου Si 51.5 and β. θαλάσσης 3M 2.7, β. ὕδατος Ez 27.34; τὰ ~η τῶν ποταμῶν Zc 10.11; abs., ἐκ ~έων ἐκέκραξά σε Ps 129.1; sg., εἰς β. ἢ εἰς ὕψος Is 7.11; "May I be rescued from my enemies and ἐκ τοῦ ~ους τῶν ὑδάτων" Ps 68.15; δώσει ῥίζαν εἰς β. 'puts down a deep root' Wi 4.3; the lowest part of a structure, Ez 43.14. **b.** under the ground, βάθη τῆς γῆς Ez 26.20 (ǁ βόθρος), 31.14 γῆς β. (ǁ βόθρος), τὸ β. τῆς γῆς 32.18 (ǁ βόθρος); ἐν βάθει βόθρου 32.21, 22, ἐν βάθει ἀβύσσων Si 24.5; ἐκ ~ους ἀβύσσου Wi 10.19. **c.** metaph.: β. κακῶν 'the depth of the disaster' Pr 18.3, cf. Aes. *Pers*. 465; β. καρδίας ἀνθρώπου Ju 8.14.

Cf. βαθύς, ἄβυσσος, βόθρος, ὕψος: Schlier, *TDNT* 1.517f.

βάθρον ⇒ βάραθρον.

βαθύγλωσσος ⇒ βαθύχειλος.

βαθύνω: aor.impv.2pl. βαθύνατε, pass. ἐβαθύνθην.ʃ
to dig deep: a trench or cave for hiding (?), εἰς κάθισιν Je 29.9, 30.8. **b.** fig., ἐβαθύνθησαν οἱ διαλογισμοί σου 'your thoughts were profound' Ps 91.6.

Cf. βαθύς: LSG s.v.

βαθύς, εῖα, ύ.

1. when looking from above, *extending far downwards*, 'deep': *s* φάραγξ 'valley' Is 30.33, βόθρος 'pit' Pr 22.14, ὕδωρ 18.4, ποτήριον 'cup' Ez 23.32.

2. *not easily comprehensible*, 'profound; inscrutable': *s* βουλή 'design' Is 31.6, ἀνακαλύπτων τὰ ~έα καὶ σκοτεινά 'disclosing things profound and obscure' Da 2.22 LXX, sim. Jb 12.22; καρδία '(human) mind' Je 17.9.

3. *reaching great extent*: *s* λήθη 'oblivion' Wi 16.11, ὕπνος 'sleep' Si 22.9, 3M 5.12; εἰρήνη 'peace' 4M 3.20.

Cf. βαθύνω, βάθος.

βαθύφωνος, ον.ʃ*
of deep, i.e. *hollow voice*: *s* pers. (diviner), Is 33.19. Cf. LSG s.v.

βαθύχειλος, ον.ʃ*
speaking an unintelligible language: *s* hum., + βαρύγλωσσος Ez 3.5. Cf. ἰσχνόφωνος, ψελλίζω: Caird 1968.462.

βαΐνη, βάϊον > **βάϊς**.

βαίνω: pf.ptc. βεβηκώς; plpf. βεβήκειν.ʃ

1. *to tread*: *s* οὐχὶ πεῖραν ἔλαβεν ὁ ποὺς αὐτῆς βαίνειν ἐπὶ τῆς γῆς 'her foot did make no attempt to tread on the land' De 28.56.

2. (pl)pf., *to stand*: ἐπισφαλῶς βεβηκότα 'precariously poised' Wi 4.4; βεβήκει ἐπὶ γῆς 'stood on earth' 18.16; 3M 6.31.

Cf. βῆμα, ἀνα~, δια~, ἐμ~, ἐπι~, κατα~, προ~, προσαναβαίνω, πορεύομαι, ἵστημι: Shipp 125f.

βάϊς, acc. βάϊν.ʃ On the spelling, see Katz 102f.
palm-leaf: 1M 13.37, 51.

βακτηρία, ας. f.
staff: ἐν ταῖς χερσὶν ὑμῶν Ex 12.11; καρυΐνη 'made of nut-wood' Je 1.11, εὐκλεής 'splendid'

31.17; ‖ ῥάβδος ib., Ps 22.4; for disciplinary punishment, Pr 13.24. Cf. ῥάβδος.

βακχούρια, ων. n.pl.ʃ
= Heb. /bikkurim/ 'first-fruits' Ne 13.31.

βάλανος, ου. f.
oak-tree: burial place, β. πένθους '.. of grief' Ge 35.8; known for its height, δένδρον ~ου Is 2.13. **b.** *gates of oak*; *bars of oak on doors* (?): ‖ θύραι Je 30.9. **c.** *acorn*: ‖ τερέβινθος Is 6.13.
Cf. δρῦς.

βαλλάντιον, ου. n.
bag: Jb 14.17; money-bag, To 1.14𝔊II; ‖ μαρσίππιον Pr 1.14. Cf. μαρσίππιον, δεσμός **2**: Rengstorf, *TDNT* 1.525f.

βάλλω: fut. βαλῶ; aor. ἔβαλον, subj. βάλω, impv. βάλε, ptc. βαλών, pass. ἐβλήθην, ptc. βληθείς; pf.ptc.pass. βεβλημένος.

1. *to throw*: + acc., χῶμα 'heap of earth' "thrown up against the walls of cities to take them" (LSJ, s.v. χῶμα) Hb 1.10; βέλος 'arrow' Is 37.33 (cf. ἐπὶ σκοπόν 'at a target' Wi 5.12), cf. τόξοις 'with bows' Ps 77.9 and βέλεσιν 'with arrows' 2C 26.15 (calqued on בַּחִצִּים); ἄγκιστρον εἰς τὸν ποταμόν .. σαγήνας 'fishing-hook into the river .. and nets' Is 19.8; κλήρους 'to cast lots' Jl 3.3, Ob 11, Na 3.10, Jn 1.7*bis*, cf. σχοίνιον ἐν κλήρῳ 'cast a line for the lot' Mi 2.5 (see under κλῆρος) and βαλεῖτε αὐτὴν [= τὴν γῆν] ἐν κλήρῳ ὑμῖν Ez 47.22 (‖ διαμερίζω 'divide' vs. 21); κλήρους understood, 1K 14.42 (*L* + κλῆρον); pass. εἰς μέσον τῆς καμίνου 'into the furnace' Da TH 3.21 (‖ LXX ἐμβάλλω). **b.** + ἔν τινι: ἐν λίθοις ἐπ' αὐτούς Ju 6.12.

2. more generally, *to set*, *place*: + acc., τὸ ῥῆμα, ὃ ἂν βάλῃ ὁ θεὸς εἰς τὸ στόμα μου Nu 22.38 (‖ ἐμβάλλω 23.5); ἔβαλες εἰς κεφαλὰς ἀνόμων θάνατον 'you have brought down death on to the heads of the wicked' Hb 3.13 (‖ ἐξεγείρω); ῥίζας 'to put down roots' Ho 14.6, ἐπὶ ἰκμάδα 'towards moisture' Je 17.8; λίθον γωνιαῖον 'corner-stone' Jb 38.6.

3. mid. *to throw oneself down to lie and rest*: *s* hum., Jd 7.12B.

Cf. ἀμφι~, ἐκ~, ἐμ~, ἐπι~, κατα~, περιβάλλω, κρημνίζω, ῥάσσω, ῥίπτω, τίθημι: Schmidt 3.151-3; Shipp 129-31; LSG s.v. ad fin.

βάμμα, ατος. n.ʃ
dyed stuff: Jd 5.30. Cf. βάπτω.

βαπτίζω: aor.mid. ἐβαπτισάμην.ʃ

1. mid. *to immerse oneself*: so as to wash oneself, ἐπὶ τῆς πηγῆς τοῦ ὕδατος 'by the spring ..' Ju 12.7; therapeutic, ἐν τῷ Ἰορδάνῃ 4K 5.14, ritual, ἀπὸ νεκροῦ Si 31.30.

2. act. and fig. *to affect thoroughly*: ἡ ἀνομία με βαπτίζει 'I am thoroughly soaked with lawlessness' Is 21.4.

Cf. βάπτω: Oepke, *TDNT* 1.529-36; LSG s.v.

βαπτός, ή, όν.ʃ
placed in liquid, 'dipped': τιάραι ~αί 'dyed tiaras' Ez 23.15. Cf. βάπτω.

βάπτω: fut. βάψω, pass. βαφήσομαι; aor.act. ἔβαψα, ptc. βάψας, mid. ἐβαπτισάμην, pass. ἐβάφην, subj. βαφῶ.

1. *to place* into liquid, 'dip, immerse': εἰς τὸ ὕδωρ Nu19.18; + acc., τὸν δάκτυλον εἰς τὸ αἷμα 'the finger into the blood' Le 4.6; ἐν ἐλαίῳ τὸν πόδα αὐτοῦ 'his foot in oil' De 33.24; ἐν αἵματι Ps 67.24, ἐν ῥύπῳ 'in dirt' Jb 9.31; ὕδατι 4K 8.15*L* (B: ἐν τῷ ὕδατι); into sth that contains liquidlike substance, εἰς τὸ κηρίον 'into the honeycomb' 1K 14.27 (*L* ἐμ~). **b.** mid. 'to bathe': ἐν τῷ Ἰορδάνῃ 4K 5.14 (‖ λούομαι vs. 13)

2. *to moisten by forming contact with liquid*: ἀπὸ τοῦ αἵματος Ex 12.22; τὸν δάκτυλον ἀπὸ τοῦ αἵματος τοῦ μόσχου Le 4.17; ἀπὸ τοῦ ἐλαίου 14.16; ἀπὸ τῆς δρόσου τοῦ οὐρανοῦ τὸ σῶμα αὐτοῦ ἐβάφη 'his body was wetted with the dew ..' Da TH 4.30, 5.21; *o* feet, εἰς μέρος τοῦ ὕδατος τοῦ Ιορδάνου Jo 3.15; ὕδατι 4K 8.15 *L* (v.l. ἐν τῷ ὕδατι = MT).

Cf. βαπτός, βαπτίζω, βαφή, ἐμβάπτω, βάμμα: Chadwick 59-62; LSG s.v.

βάραθρον, ου. n.ʃ
pit: πηλοῦ β. '.. of (thrown-away, used) clay' Is 14.23 (fig. of ruin). Cf. βάθρος, λάκκος.

βάρβαρος, ον.

1. *uncultured*, *barbarous*: *s* hum., Ez 21.31, λαός Ps 113.1 (ref. to Egyptians as seen by Israel and speaking a language other than Hebrew!), ~α πλήθη '.. hordes' (ref. to Syrians under Antiochus) 2M 2.21, ἔθνη 10.4.

2. *savage*: *s* θήρ 'beast' 2M 4.25.

Cf. βαρβαρόω, βαρβάρως, ἄγριος: Windisch, *TDNT* 1.546-51.

βαρβαρόω: pf.ptc.pass. βεβαρβαρωμένος.ʃ
pass. *to become barbarous*: *s* hum., 2M 13.9. Cf. βάρβαρος.

βαρβάρως. adv.ʃ
savagely: treatment, + ἀγρίως 2M 15.2. Cf. βάρβαρος, ἀγρίως.

βαρέως. adv.ʃ

1. *very slowly and reluctantly* in action or reaction: τοῖς ὠσὶν αὐτῶν β. ἤκουσαν Is 6.10, cf. βαρύνω **3**.

2. β. φέρω 'to be annoyed, vexed': Μὴ β. φέρε, κύριε 'No offence, sir' Ge 31.35; ἐπὶ τοῖς γεγόνοις 'over what happened' 2M 11.1; ὑπὲρ τῶν συνθηκῶν 'over the agreements' 14.27.

3. *guided by a firm and resolute attitude*: to oppose sbd., 3M 3.1; to endure a suffering, 4M 9.28.

Cf. κούφως: Chadwick 71-3.

βᾶρις, εως. f.

1. *tower* as part of a city-wall: La 2.5 (|| ὀχύρωμα), τεῖχος ~εων 2.7; || τεῖχος 2C 36.19.

2. *citadel, fortified city*: Da 8.2 TH (LXX πόλις); + πόλις ὀχυρά 2C 17.12 *L* (v.l. οἴκησις); + πύργος 27.4 *L* (dit.).

Cf. Shipp 132; Walters 304f.; LSG s.v.

βάρος, ους. n.ʃ

1. quantifiable *weight*: οὐτὲ οἱ βουνοὶ ὑποστήσουσιν τὸ β. αὐτῶν 'nor would the hills be able to stand their (= the enemies') weight' Ju 7.4, παντὶ τῷ βάρει .. ἐξώρμησε 'dashed out .. with his full weight' 3M 5.47.

2. *load to be carried*: β. ὑπὲρ σὲ μὴ ἄρῃς 'Don't lift a load too heavy for you' Si 13.2; Jd 18.21 B. **b**. fig., τὸ τῆς ὀσμῆς ἀφόρητον β. 2M 9.10 (of the oppressive, unbearable stench of a decaying corpse).

Cf. βαρύς: Schrenk, *TDNT* 1.553f.; LSG s.v.

βαρύγλωσσος, ον.ʃ*

speaking an unbearable (foreign) *language*: λαὸς βαθύχειλος καὶ ~ος Ez 3.5. Cf. LSG s.v.; Hauspie 2003.I 24.

βαρυηχής, ές.ʃ

emitting loud noise: *s* θόρυβος 'commotion' 3M 5.48.

βαρυθυμέω: aor. ἐβαρυθύμησα.ʃ *

to become sullen: *s* hum., Nu 16.15; ἐν Ισραηλ 'against ..' 3K 11.25; heaven, PSol 2.9 (|| βδελύσσω). Cf. βαρύθυμος, θυμός.

βαρύθυμος, ον.ʃ

sullen: *s* θράσος 'rashness' 3M 6.20. Cf. βαρυθυμέω.

βαρυκάρδιος, ον.ʃ*

not readily responding: *s* hum., Ps 4.3. Cf. βαρύνω: Caird 1968.462.

βαρύνω: fut.pass. βαρυνθήσομαι; aor. ἐβάρυνα, subj. βαρύνω, impv. βάρυνον, pass. ἐβαρύνθην, ptc. βαρυνθείς, subj. βαρυνθῶ; pf.pass. βεβάρυμμαι.

1. *to make heavy*: + acc., ships fully laden, Ez 27.25; τὸν κλοιὸν ἡμῶν 'our collar' 3K 12.4 (:: κουφίζω 'to lighten'), ἐφ' ἡμᾶς 12.24p, sim. Hb 2.6 (κλοιός, fig. of burden of taxes and tributes, cf. Tht PG 81.1820; Thph PG 126.857); τὸν ζυγόν Is 47.6, χαλκόν μου 'my fetter' La 3.7; τὰ βρώματα τῆς τραπέζης αὐτοῦ 'the levies for paying the costs of his dining and wining' 3K 12.24p; w. ref. to locust (? βροῦχος), βαρυνθήσῃ ὡς βροῦχος Na 3.15 (cf. Cyr. II 63); πᾶν τὸ στρατόπεδον βαρύνεσθαι τὴν σαπρίαν 'the stink of the decomposing corpses hung thick over the entire camp' 2M 8.9. **b**. pass. *to be heavy*: ὑπὲρ μόλιβον '(heavier) than lead' Si 22.14.

2. *to make unbearable*: + acc. and fig., Ἐβαρύνατε ἐπ' ἐμὲ τοὺς λόγους ὑμῶν 'your remarks were intolerable to me' Ma 3.13, sim. Jb 35.16¶; pass., βαρυνέσθω τὰ ἔργα τῶν ἀνθρώπων τούτων Ex 5.9; ἐβαρύνθη ὁ πόλεμος 'the battle became intolerably fierce' 1M 9.17, sim. Jd 20.34, ἐπὶ Σαουλ 1C 10.3. ***b**. idiom., βαρύνεται χείρ τινος ἐπί τινα: w. ref. to military pressure, Jo 19.48a, Jd 1.35, 1K 5.6 (:: 6.5 κουφίζω 'to lighten'), PSol 2.22; mental pressure, Ps 31.4; general, PSol 5.6.

3. *to make unreceptive, unresponsive*: ἐβάρυνεν Φαραω τὴν καρδίαν αὐτοῦ Ex 8.32, cf. βαρύς **4**; *s* God, ἐβάρυνα αὐτοῦ τὴν καρδίαν 10.1; τὰ ὦτα αὐτῶν ἐβάρυναν τοῦ μὴ εἰσακούειν Zc 7.11, sim. Is 33.15 and 59.1; mid., *s* sleepy eyes, 1K 3.2, cf. Mt 26.43. Cf. βαρέως **1** and στερεόω **2**.

4. *to weigh down*: metaph., + acc., ψυχήν Wi 9.15 (|| βρίθω).

5. *to become unfavourably disposed*: βεβάρυνται ἡ καρδία Φαραω τοῦ μὴ ἐξαποστεῖλαι τὸν λαόν Ex 7.14 (|| σκληρύνω vs. 3 and κατισχύω vs. 13); βαρυνθήσεται ἡ ψυχή μου ἐπ' αὐτούς 'my attitude towards them will become unfriendly' Zc 11.8.

7. *to become a burden*: ἐπὶ σέ 2K 13.25*L* (B: κατα~).

6. *to mount a heavy attack*: βεβάρυνται ὑπὲρ πάντα τὰ σκεύη τὰ ἐπιθυμητὰ αὐτῆς '.. at all its attractive utensils'(?) Na 2.10 (cf. Th 249).

Cf. βαρύς, βρίθω, κατισχύω, σκληρύνω, κουφίζω: Wolters 685-8.

βαρύς, εῖα, ύ.

1. *relatively heavy in weight*: *s* hands, Ex 17.12 (so felt because of fatigue), oppressive Jb 23.2; old man (clumsy and heavy-footed?) 1K 4.18.

2. *comprising many individuals*: *s* an army, ἐν ὄχλῳ ~εῖ καὶ ἐν χειρὶ ἰσχυρᾷ 'with a huge army ..' Nu 20.20; 1M 1.17; ἵππον καὶ ἅρμα καὶ δύναμιν ~εῖαν 4K 6.14; ἐν δυνάμει ~είᾳ 'with a large entourage (and perh. also an army of bodyguards?) 2C 9.1, 4K 18.17 (|| πολλή Is 36.2); a body of people, λαός 3K 3.9; of worshippers, ἐν λαῷ βαρεῖ αἰνέσω σε Ps 34.18 (|| ἐν ἐκκλησίᾳ πολλῇ); συμπόσιον βαρύ 'grand banquet' 3M 6.33.

3. *unbearable* (mentally): βαρὺ αὐτῷ κατεφάνη 'it appeared to him unbearable' Ge 48.17; *s* task, βαρύ σοι τὸ ῥῆμα τοῦτο, οὐ δυνήσῃ ποιεῖν σὺ μόνος 'this matter is too onerous for you, you won't be able to execute it on your own' Ex 18.18, ~εῖα ἡ δουλεία ἐπὶ τὸν λαόν Ne 5.18, sim. κλοιός 'collar (of bondage)' 3K 12.4; φορτίον 'burden' Ps 37.5 (of sins weighing heavily on one's conscience), ζυγός 'yoke (of human existence)' Si 40.1 (|| ἀσχολία 'occupation'), κλοιός 'a collar (around the neck)' in a fig. of oppressive servitude (δουλεία) 3K 12.4, νύξ '(oppressive) night' Wi 17.21; ὀργή 'anger' Pr 27.3.

4. *unreceptive, unresponsive*: *s* hum. heart, 4K 14.10*L*.

5. *serious in effect*: πτῶσις 'fall' Na 3.3, ἀρρώστημα 'illness' Si 34.2, ὀργή '(intense) fury' 3M 5.1, 47.

6. *weighty*, 'important': βαρύτερος τοῦ πατρός σου ἡμέραις 'weightier than your father in terms of age' Jb 15.10¶, cf. **1** above; + ἐπίδοξος Da 2.11 LXX.

Cf. βαρύνω, βαρέως, βαρυωπέω, βάρος, ἐλαφρός, κοῦφος: Schrenk, *TDNT* 1.556f.; Spicq 1.252-5; Chadwick 64-73.

βαρυτέρως. Adv. derived from the comp. of βαρύς.ʃ

more violently: of hostility, 3M 3.1 (see s.v. βαρύς **5**).

βαρυωπέω: aor. ἐβαρυώπησα.ʃ *

to be dim-sighted: οἱ ὀφθαλμοὶ αὐτοῦ ἐβαρυώπησαν ἀπὸ τοῦ γήρους 'because of his old age' Ge 48.10.

βασανίζω: fut. βασανίσω, ~ιῶ; aor. ἐβασάνισα, impv. βασάνισον, ptc. ~ίσας, pass. ἐβασανίσθην, pass. βασανισθείς.

to torment: + acc. pers., ἐν παιδείᾳ 'by chastising' Si 4.17 (*s* wisdom); ∥ κολάζω 'to punish' Wi 16.1; martydom, 4M 8.2; on battlefield, *s* God's hand, 1K 5.3. Cf. βάσανος, προβασανίζω, αἰκίζω, στρεβλόω, τροχίζω.

βασανιστήριον, ου. n.

instrument of torture: pl., 4M 6.1. Cf. βασανίζω, ἀρθρέμβολον, δακτυλήθρα, ζώπυρον, καταπέλτης, καυτήριον, λέβης, νευρά, ὀβελίσκος, πρίων, σκέπαρνον, σκορπίος, στρέβλη, στρεβλωτήριον, σφήν, τήγανον, τρίβολος **2**, τροχαντήριον, τροχός.

βάσανος, ου. f.

torture, torment: Ez 3.20, Wi 2.19, τὸν διὰ τῶν ~ων θάνατον 4M 9.5, + ὕβρις 'insulting' Wi 2.19; severe punishment, β. ἀδικιῶν '.. for unlawfulnesses' Ez 7.19, + στρέβλαι Si 30.35; *o* of κομίζομαι Ez 16.52, of λαμβάνω 32.16, of ἀποφέρω 32.30; very often pl. in 4M. **b**. *exceeding hardship*: β. καὶ θλῖψις Ez 12.18 (∥ ὀδύνη).

Cf. βασανίζω, βασανιστήριον, αἰκία, στρέβλη: Caird 1968.462; Lee 1969.238f.; Schneider, *TDNT* 1.561-3

βασιλεία, ας. f.

1. *dominion, reigning, supreme authority*: ἀποστρέψω ~αν οἴκου Ισραηλ Ho 1.4; οἶκος ~ας 'royal palace' Am 7.13 (∥ ἁγίασμα βασιλέως); ἔσται τῷ κυρίῳ ἡ β. 'the dominion will be the Lord's' Ob 21; Mi 4.8 (∥ ἀρχή); Nu 21.18 (∥ κυριεύω); τοῦ θεοῦ Wi 10.10, σκῆπτρα ~ας 'sceptres of ..' 10.14; Si 10.8. **b**. *act* or *manner of ruling and controling*: σώφρονά τε καὶ δικαίαν καὶ ἀγαθὴν καὶ ἀνδρείαν 4M 2.23. **c**. *period of reign*: Ἐγένετο δὲ ἐν τῇ ~ᾳ .. 'Now it was during the reign of .. ' Ge 14.1. **d**. *position of supreme rulership*: 'queenship' (LSG, s.v.), ἡ β. δοθήτω ἄλλῃ '.. be given to another woman' Es 1.18*L*.

2. *territory ruled by* βασιλεύς, 'kingdom, empire': τὰς κρατίστας ἐκ πασῶν τῶν ~ῶν τούτων 'the most powerful of all these kingdoms' Am 6.2; τῶν ἁμαρτωλῶν, which is to be obliterated from upon the face of the earth, 9.8; ∥ ἔθνη, Na 3.5; Wi 6.4, Si 44.3.

Cf. βασιλεύς and βασιλεύω: Schmidt, *TDNT* 1.574-6; Spicq 1.256-71.

βασίλειον, ου. n.

royal residence, 'palace': pl. τὰ ~α διέπεσε 'the royal palace collapsed' Na 2.7; 2K 11.2*L*, Da 5.1 pr. LXX. Cf. βασιλεύς.

βασίλειος, ον.

1. *possessing characteristics of* βασιλεύς, 'royal': β. ἱεράτευμα 'royal body of priests' Ex 19.6. **b**. subst.n.sg. 'rule, kingship': + ἰσχύς, ἐξουσία 1E 4.40; 4.43, Wi 1.14.

2. *belonging to king* or *to royal house*: *s* πόλις De 3.10, σκηνή 'tent in a battlefield' 4K 3.8. **b**. *tiara*: ἐπὶ τὴν κεφαλὴν αὐτοῦ 2K 1.10 (∥ διάδημα), 2C 23.11; ∥ διάδημα Wi 5.16.

Cf. βασιλεύς, βασιλικός, διάδημα.

βασιλεύς, έως, voc. βασιλεῦ. m.

supreme ruler, 'king': ruling over a ciy, τῆς Νινευη 'over N.' or 'resident in N.'(?) Jn 3.6, cf. ὁ β. τοῦ οὐρανοῦ To 1.18 𝔊II; over nations, ἐθνῶν Ge 17.16, Nu 21.18; over deities, κύριε βασιλεῦ τῶν θεῶν De 9.26; β. ~έων Ez 26.7 (Nebuchadnezzar); over a state, Σαμαρεια Ho 10.7; β. Ισραηλ 11.1; θρόνος ~έων 'royal throne' Hg 2.22; δύναμις ~έων ib.; in apposition and following a king's name, Δαυιδ τὸν ~έα Ho 3.5, Δαρείου τοῦ ~έως 1E 7.4 (∥ τοῦ ~έως Δαρείου vs. 1); of God, β. μέγας ἐγώ εἰμι Ma 1.14, cf. LSG, s.v.; β. Ισραηλ κύριος ἐν μέσῳ σου Zp 3.15, τὸν ~έα κύριον σαβαωθ Is 6.5; ∥ ἄρχων Nu 21.18 (following it), Is 32.1, Ho 3.4 (preceding it), 7.3, 13.10; β. δίκαιος Is 32.1; β. τοῦ οὐρανοῦ 1E 4.58, τῶν οὐρανῶν 3M 2.2; β. βασιλέων 2E 7.12, Nebuchadnezzar, Da 2.37. Cf. ἄρχων, βασιλεία, βασίλειος, βασίλειον, βασιλεύω, βασιλικός, βασίλισσα, παμβασιλεύς, ἡγέομαι, and τύραννος: Kleinknecht, *TDNT* 1.565f. On the divine title βασιλεὺς τῶν θεῶν, see Morenz 252f. and Görg 116-8. See also Pelletier 1962.288-95.

βασιλεύω: fut. βασιλεύσω; aor. ἐβασίλευσα, impv. βασίλευσον, inf. βασιλεῦσαι, ptc. βασιλεύσας; pf. βεβασίλευκα.

1. *to rule as king*: *s* hum., οἱ βασιλεῖς οἱ βασιλεύσαντες ἐν Εδωμ Ge 36.31; ἐπί τινος (hum.), Jd

9.8 (*L*: ἐπί τινα); *s* God and ἐπί τινα – βασιλεύσει κύριος ἐπ' αὐτοὺς ἐν ὄρει Σιων ἀπὸ τοῦ νῦν εἰς τὸν αἰῶνα Mi 4.7; ‖ κυριεύω Ge 37.8; + cogn. acc., βασιλείαν Da 7.27 LXX. **b.** + gen.: τῆς Ἰουδαίας Is 1.1. **c.** *to become king*: 2K 15.10; + gen., τῆς Ἰουδαίας 1E 1.37.

*__2__. *to make king*: ἑαυτοῖς ἐβασίλευσαν καὶ οὐ δι' ἐμοῦ 'they made sbd king by themselves, and not through me' Ho 8.4; + acc. pers., αὐτῆς τὸν υἱὸν Ταβεηλ 'the son of T. over her' Is 7.6; Je 44.1, Ez 17.16, Jb 34.30¶; ἐπὶ Ιουδαν 2C 36.10. **b.** *to appoint as ruler*: αὐτοῖς βασιλέα 1K 8.22; ἐφ' ἑαυτοὺς βασιλέα 2C 21.8.

Cf. βασιλεία, βασιλεύς, ἄρχω, κυριεύω, παραβασιλεύω.

βασιλικός, ή, όν.

pertaining to βασιλεύς: ὁδῷ ~ῇ 'by the royal road' Nu 20.17, 21.22; *s* δεῖπνον 'meal' Da 1.13 LXX, οἶνος Es 1.7 *L*; λογισμός 'rational will' 4M 14.2. **b.** subst.n. 'royal decree' Es 1.19 o'; 'royal treasury' 2M 3.13; pl., τὰ ~ά 'the king's account': 1E 1.7, 'royal taxes; payment due to the royal treasury' 1M 10.43, 11.34, 15.8.

Cf. βασιλεύς, βασίλειος.

βασιλίσκος, ου.ʃ m.

kind of dangerous serpent, perh. *Egyptian cobra* (LSJ): Is 59.5; + ἀσπίς 'asp' Ps 90.13.

βασίλισσα, ης. f.

1. = βασίλεια 'queen': 3K 10.1, Je 30.6; τοῦ οὐρανοῦ 51.17.

2. *king's spouse*: ‖ παλλακίς 'concubine' Ct 6.8.

Cf. βασιλεύς.

βάσις, εως. f.

1. v.n. of βαίνω, *act of walking*: Wi 13.18.

2. *base* of a structure: of tabernacle post, Ex 26.19; 26.32 (:: κεφαλίς); of altar, 29.12, De 12.27; of washing-tub, Ex 30.28, Le 8.11; of a plant, Wi 4.3.

3. *that on which one stands*: for a harlot to attract potential clients, Ez 16.31, 39.

Cf. κεφαλίς.

βασκαίνω: fut. βασκανῶ.ʃ

to be unable to bear sbd (acc.) *being happy or enjoying*, 'begrudge': ἑαυτόν Si 14.6; *Hebraistically with ὀφθαλμῷ – πονηρὸς ὁ βασκαίνων ὀφθαλμῷ 14.8; "the brother, the wife in his (own) bosom .." De 28.54; τῷ ὀφθαλμῷ αὐτῆς τὸν ἄνδρα αὐτῆς ἐν τῷ κόλπῳ αὐτῆς καὶ τὸν υἱὸν .. 28.56. Cf. βασκανία, βάσκανος: Delling, *TDNT* 1.594f.; Caird 1968. 463; Spicq 1.272-6.

βασκανία, ας. f.

1. *bewitching power*: φαυλότητος Wi 4.12.

2. *backbiting*: + φιλονεικία 'contentiousness' 4M 1.26.

Cf. βασκαίνω.

βάσκανος, η, ον.

of begrudging disposition, 'mean, niggardly': *s* hum., Si 14.3; subst., δόσις ~ου 'gift from ..' 18.18; 37.11. Cf. βασκαίνω; LSG s.v.

βάσταγμα, ατος. n.

load to be carried: on sabbaths – μὴ αἴρετε ~ατα .. μὴ ἐκφέρετε .. Je 17.21f., *o* of εἰσφέρω 17.24; fig., mental burden, 2K 15.33 (*L*: φορτίον). Cf. βαστάζω, γόμος, φορτίον.

βαστάζω: fut. βαστάσω; aor. ἐβάσταξα, impv. βάσταξον, ptc. βαστάσας.ʃ

to carry a load: abs. Ru 2.16; a burden of tributes understood, 4K 18.14; + acc., Si 6.25; + gen., τῆς κόμης τῆς κεφαλῆς αὐτοῦ 'by the hair of ..' Da Bel 36 TH. Cf. δυσβάστακτος, φέρω: Schmidt 3.185-7; Shipp 132-7.

I **βάτος**, ου. m./f.

bramble, Rubus ulmifolius (LSJ): Ex 3.2; τῷ ὀφθέντι ἐν τῇ ~ῳ 'to the one who appeared in the bramble' De 33.16; noisome plant, Jb 31.40 (‖ κνίδη 'nettle').

II **βάτος**, ου. m.

liquid measure: 2E 7.22. Cf. LSG s.v.

βάτραχος, ου. m.

frog: its appearance en masse as a divine punishment, ἐγὼ τύπτω πάντα τὰ ὅριά σου τοῖς ~οις Ex 8.2; Ps 77.45, 104.30, Wi 19.10; rivers as their habitat, Ex 8.3; also canals and marshlands, 8.5. Cf. Shipp 138-41.

βαφή, ῆς. f.ʃ

act of dipping in water: during the smeltering of iron, Si 34.26. **b.** *dyed stuff*: Jd 5.30A (B: βάμμα). Cf. βάπτω.

βδέλλα, ας. f.ʃ

leech: Pr 30.15.

βδέλυγμα, τος. n. * (βδελύσσω: Aristoph. +; so βδελυγμός).

what is abominable, loathsome: β. ἐστί τοῖς Αἰγυπτίοις Ge 43.32; synonymously by means of a gen., β. τῶν Αἰγυπτίων Ex 8.26; ~ατα κυρίου, ἃ ἐμίσησεν De 12.31; *s* shepherd, Ge 46.34; lawbreaker, De 25.16; ritually unclean animal, Le 5.2; unclean food (?) Je 4.1; β. ἐγένετο (by disobeying the Law) Ma 2.11; ἐκ μέσων ὀδόντων, ref. to sacrificial meat offered to idols, Zc 9.7 (‖ αἷμα), cf. Pr 15.8 (:: δεκτός 'acceptable'); ways of the impious, 15.9, sexual immoralities, Le 18.26, 20.13; valuable possessions of pagans, β. κυρίῳ De 7.25; objects of pagan worship, τὰ ~ατα αὐτῶν καὶ τὰ εἴδωλα αὐτῶν 29.17; ‖ ἀλλότριοι 'heathen (gods)' 32.16, cf. β. ἐρημώσεως '.. which leads to desolation' Da 11.31 LXX, 1M 1.54; for Ashtart, 3K 11.6 ‖ προσόχθισμα 2C15.16; τὰ ~ατα .. τὰ ἀργυρᾶ καὶ τὰ χρυσᾶ Is 2.20; ὀφθαλμῶν 'eyed (with affection)'

Ez 20.7; ‖ ἀνομία 36.31. Cf. βδελυγμός, βδελύσσω, ἀλλότριος, προσόχθισμα: Foerster, *TDNT* 1.598-600.

βδελυγμός, οῦ. m. * (⇒ βδέλυγμα)
loathsomeness: ‖ ἀκαθαρσία Na 3.6. Cf. βδέλυγμα and βδελύσσω.

βδελυκτός, ή, όν. *
loathed: *s* hum., 2M 1.27. Cf. βδελύσσω.

βδελυρός, ά, όν.ʃ
disgusting: *s* hum., Si 41.5. Cf. σχέτλιος.

βδελύσσω: fut. βδελύξομαι, βδελυχθήσομαι; aor. act. ἐβδέλυξα, subj. βδελύξω, inf. βδελύξαι, mid. ἐβδελυξάμην, pass. ἐβδελύχθην; pf.pass. ἐβδέλυγμαι, ptc. ἐβδελυγμένος.

I. act. **1**. *to make hateful*: + acc., ἐβδελύξατε τὴν ὀσμὴν ἡμῶν ἐναντίον Φαραω 'you made personae non gratae of us with Ph.' Ex 5.21; pass. νόμιμα ἐβδελυγμένα 'hateful customs' Le 18.30.

2. *to render abominable*: + acc., τὰς ψυχὰς ὑμῶν Le 11.43 (‖ μιαίνομαι), 20.25, ἐν παντὶ ἀκαθάρτῳ 1M 1.48; pass. and *o* hum., Ps 52.2.

II. mid. **1**. *to loathe, dislike intensely*: *o* acc. pers., Le 20.23, De 23.7; + acc. rei, λόγον ὅσιον, and ‖ μισέω Am 5.10; τὴν ὕβριν Ιακωβ, and ‖ μισέω 6.8, ἀδικίαν Ps 118.163; κρίμα Mi 3.9; βρῶμα Ps 106.18; *ἀπό τινος, Ex 1.12 (Heb. מִפְּנֵי); *s* God, οὐ βδελύξεται ἡ ψυχή μου ὑμᾶς Le 26.11; the earth, PSol 2.9; pass. οἱ ἐβδελυγμένοι, ref. to idols, and opp. ἀγαπάω Ho 9.10; νεκρός Is 14.19.

2. *to treat as abominable*: + acc., θνησιμαῖα 'dead bodies' Le 11.11; + dat. cogn. βδελύγματι De 7.26 (+ προσοχθίζω).

3. *to act abominably*: towards sbd (acc.), Ge 26.29 (:: χράομαί τινι καλῶς); + epexegetic inf., 3K 20.26; + καί and a vb. fin., 4K 21.9*L*.

Cf. βδέλυγμα, βδελυγμός, βδελυκτός, βδελυρός, μισέω, προσοχθίζω, στυγέω: Caird 1968.463; Harl 2001.862-4.

βέβαιος, α, ον.
solid, firm: *s* πίστις '(unswerving) loyalty' Es B 3, 3M 5.31; εὐνοία 'good-will' 7.7; πνεῦμα .. ~ον, ἀσφαλές Wi 7.23. Cf. βεβαιόω, βεβαίως, βεβαίωσις: Schlier, *TDNT* 1.600-3.

βεβαιόω: aor. ἐβεβαίωσα, impv. βεβαίωσον.ʃ
to confer firm and solid status on: + acc. pers., ἐβεβαίωσάς με ἐνώπιόν σου εἰς τὸν αἰῶνα Ps 40.13, βεβαίωσόν με ἐν τοῖς λόγοις σου 118.28. Cf. βέβαιος.

βεβαίως. adv.ʃ
1. *for perpetuity*: Le 25.30.

2. *firmly*: β. ὅρκον ὁρισάμενος 'firmly swearing an oath' 3M 5.42.

Cf. βέβαιος, αἰώνιος.

βεβαίωσις, εως. f.ʃ
act of making last for perpetuity: ἡ γῆ οὐ πραθήσεται εἰς ~ιν 'the land shall not be sold in perpetuity' Le 25.23; προσοχὴ νόμων β. ἀφθαρσίας 'attention to laws ensures immortality' Wi 6.18. Cf. βέβαιος.

βέβηλος, η, ον.
profane: opp. ἅγιος and ‖ ἀκάθαρτος – διαστεῖλαι ἀνὰ μέσον τῶν ἁγίων καὶ τῶν ~ων 'to draw a line between the sacred and the secular' Le 10.10, sim. Ez 22.26 (ἀκάθαρτος); opp. ἅγιος 'designated for cultic use,' *s* ἄρτος 1K 21.5, ὁδός 21.6. **b**. w. pejorative connotation: "taking the sacred (ἱερά) vessels with polluted (μιεραῖς) hands, and sweeping away with profane (βεβήλοις) hands the votive offerings .." 2M 5.16; *s* hum., PSol 2.13, ‖ ἀνόσιος 3M 2.2; κρέα '(sacrificial) meat' PSol 8.12; hum. mouth, 3M 4.16; subst.m., 7.15; + ἄνομος Ez 21.25; opp. ὅσιος PSol 4.1.

Cf. βεβηλόω, ἅγιος, ἀκάθαρτος, κοινός: Trench 374-7; Hauck, *TDNT* 1.604f.

βεβηλόω: fut. βεβηλώσω; aor. ἐβεβήλωσα, sub. βεβηλώσω, inf. ~λῶσαι, pass. ἐβεβηλώθην, subj. βεβηλωθῶ, ptc. βεβηλωθείς; pf.pass. βεβήλωμαι, ptc. βεβηλωμένος. * (βέβηλος: Soph. +)
to profane, desecrate what is holy and sacred, or honourable: *o* sabbath, Ex 31.14 (:: ἅγιος), Is 56.6 (:: φυλάσσομαι); τὸ ὄνομα τὸ ἅγιον Le 18.21; τὸ ὄνομα τοῦ θεοῦ 19.12, Am 2.7, sim. Le 20.3, Ma 1.12; τὰ ἅγια (q.v.) Nu 18.32, Zp 3.4, τὰ ἅγια κυρίου Le 19.8, Ma 2.11, sim. Ez 22.26; εἰς τὴν γῆν τὸ ἁγίασμα αὐτοῦ Ps 88.40 (razing it to the ground); τὸ θυσιαστήριον 1M 4.38; τὴν γῆν μου Je 16.18, τὴν διαθήκην τῶν πατέρων 'the ancestral covenant' (by disobeying it) Ma 2.10, διαθήκην ἁγίαν 1M 1.63, τὰ δικαιώματά μου Ps 88.32; one's daughter by forcing her into prostitution, Le 19.29, cf. γυναῖκα πόρνην καὶ βεβηλωμένην 21.7 and ἐβεβηλώθη ὁ λαὸς ἐκπορνεῦσαι Nu 25.1; ‖ μιαίνω Le 20.31; the family name, τὸ ὄνομα τοῦ πατρὸς αὐτῆς 21.9; τὸ σπέρμα αὐτοῦ 21.15; τὸ ῥῆμα αὐτοῦ 'his pledge' Nu 30.3; βασιλέα .. καὶ ἄρχοντας La 2.2 (leadership in whom the divine sanctity is invested); *o* God, Ez 13.19. Cf. βέβηλος, βεβήλωσις, ἀλισγέω, μιαίνω, μολύνω, ἁγιάζω: Spicq 1.284-6.

βεβήλωσις, εως. *f.
v.n. of βεβηλόω: w. obj.gen., Le 21.4 (through contact with corpses); ἐκ τῆς ~εως ἡγιασμένα Ju 4.3 (of cultic installations); ‖ ἀκάθαρτος 1M 1.48, ‖ ἀκαθαρσία 3M 2.17. Cf. βεβηλόω.

βέλος, ους. n.
arrow: weapon, De 32.23, 42; ἐν τοῖς ~εσιν αὐτῶν πεσοῦνται 'will fall with their arrows' Jl 2.8 (‖ ὅπλον); μετὰ ~ους καὶ τοξεύματος 'with ar-

rows and missiles' Is 7.24; instrument of divine punishment, La 3.12. **b**. euphemism for phallus: Si 26.12.

Cf. βολίς, III ἰός, ὅπλον, σκορπίδιον, σχίζα, τόξον, τόξευμα: Hauck, *TDNT* 1.608f.

βελόστασις, εως. f. *

battery of engines for waging a war: Je 28.27, Ez 4.2, 17.17, + μηχαναί 1M 6.20.

βελτίων, βέλτιον. adj., comp. of ἀγαθός; super. βέλτιστος, η, ον.

1. *more* or *the most desirable* or *preferable*: βέλτιον δοῦναί με αὐτὴν σοὶ ἢ δοῦναί με αὐτὴν ἀνδρὶ ἑτέρῳ 'it is better for me to give her to you than for me to give her to another man' Ge 29.19; βέλτιον ἡμῖν ἐστιν ἀποστραφῆναι εἰς Αἴγυπτον 'it is better for us to return to Egypt' Nu 14.3; ἐν τῇ βελτίστῃ γῇ κατοίκισον 'live in the best area' Ge 47.6; τὰ βέλτιστα τοῦ ἀγροῦ αὐτοῦ 'the best (part) of his field' Ex 22.5; ‖ κρείσσων Pr 8.19.

2. *morally acceptable*: *s* ὁδοὶ καὶ ἔργα Je 33.13.

Cf. ἀγαθός, καλός, κρείσσων, ἄρτιστος, χείρων: Schmidt 4.306f.

Βηλεῖον, ου. n.ʃ

temple for Bel: Bel 22 LXX.

βῆμα, ατος. n.

1. *step* made while one walks: β. ἀνθρώπου 'the way one walks, one's gait' Si 19.30; met. of tiny area covered by a single step, β. ποδός De 2.5.

2. *raised place*: προσῆλθεν ἐπὶ τὸ β. 'went up to the platform' 2M 13.26; wooden, 1E 9.42, Ne 8.4.

Cf. βαίνω, διάβημα; LSG s.v.

***βηρύλλιον**, ου. n. Dim. of βήρυλλος.

beryl: Ex 28.20, Ez 28.13. Cf. βήρυλλος.

βήρυλλος, ου. f.ʃ

beryl: To 13.17 𝔊ᴵ. Cf. βηρύλλιον.

βία, ας. f.

force: adverbial dat., κατεδυνάστευον .. τοὺς υἱοὺς Ισραηλ βίᾳ 'lorded it over the Israelites with force' Ex 1.13 (‖ μετὰ βίας vs. 14); διεθρύβη τὰ ὄρη βίᾳ 'the mountains broke up to pieces violently' Hb 3.6; βίᾳ μετὰ ἰσχύος Is 63.1; κατεδουλοῦντο αὐτοὺς μετὰ βίας 'they made forced slaves of them' Ex 1.14; through strenuous efforts, Da 11.17 LXX. **b**. *that which is obtained by force*: Ne 5.14, cf. ἄρτοι ~ας 5.18.

Cf. βιάζομαι, βίαιος, δύναμις, ἰσχύς, κράτος, στιβαρός: Schmidt 3.678-82; Shipp 147f.; *ND* 7.130-62.

βιάζομαι: aor. ἐβιασάμην, inf. βιάσασθαι, ptc. βιασάμενος, subj. βιάσωμαι, pass. ἐβιάσθην.

1. *to exert force and pressure* on sbd (τινα) or sth (τι): verbally, 'to urge, insist' – ἐβιάσατο καὶ ἔλαβεν Ge 33.11, Jd 19.7; physically, + inf., μὴ βιαζέσθωσαν ἀναβῆναι 'Don't let them force their way' Ex 19.24; of rape, βιασάμενος κοιμηθῇ μετ' αὐτῆς De 22.25, 28; + acc. pers., τὴν γυναῖκα Es 7.8 o' (*L* ἐκ~); + acc. rei, θύραν '(forcing the) door' 2M 14.41, ῥοῦν ποταμοῦ '(to swim) against the current' Si 4.26; τὸν αὐτοῦ τρόπον 'his natural life-style' 4M 2.8; πρὸς τὴν μιαροφαγίαν 'so as to make eat defiled food' 11.25. **b**. *to detain* a visitor *to stay on*: Jd 13.16A (*L*: παρα~., B: κατέχω)

2. *to make special efforts and put up resistance against*: + acc., ἀνάγκην 4M 8.24.

Cf. βία, δια~, ἐκ~, παραβιάζομαι: Spicq 1.287-91.

βίαιος, α, ον.

possessed of great power, 'strong, powerful': *s* wind (ἄνεμος), Ex 14.21, πνεῦμα Is 11.15, ποταμός 59.19, κλύδων 'wave' Wi 19.7, χείμαρρος 'torrent' 2K 22.5*L*, βέλος 'arrow' Jb 34.6¶; πάθη 'passions' 4M 2.15. Cf. βία, δυνατός, ἰσχυρός, κραταιός.

βιαίως. adv.ʃ

with force, forcefully: ὕδωρ β. ἀνέμῳ φερόμενον 'water mightily borne by wind' Je 18.14, ἐν ἡμέρᾳ μιᾷ β. εἰς τὸν ᾅδην κατελθόντες 'violently descending into Hades in a single day' Es B 7; Is 30.30 (‖ βίᾳ). Cf. βία, ἰσχυρῶς, κραταιῶς, στιβαρῶς.

βιβάζω: aor.inf.pass. βιβασθῆναι.ʃ

to mount to have sexual intercourse: *s* animal and *o* woman, γυνή, ἥτις προσελεύσεται πρὸς πᾶν κτῆνος βιβασθῆναι αὐτὴν ὑπ' αὐτοῦ Le 20.16; 18.23. Cf. ἀναβιβάζω: Bain 124f.

βιβλιαφόρος, ου. m.ʃ

letter-carrier: of the Persian Empire, Es 3.13, 8.10 o'. Cf. LSG s.v.

βιβλιοθήκη, ης. f.

library: 2E 6.1 (‖ βιβλιοφυλάκιον 1E 6.22), βασιλική 'royal' Es 2.23.

βίβλινος. ⇒ βύβλινος.

βιβλίον, ου. n.

1. *writing material*: To 7.13.

2. *book*: κατάγραψον .. ἐν ~ῳ 'Put down .. in a book' Ex 17.14; γράψει εἰς β. De 17.18; διαθήκης 1M 1.57 (‖ τοῦ νόμου), Ex 24.7, τοῦ νόμου De 28.61, ὁράσεως 'of a vision' Na 1.1, μνημοσύνου 'of memoranda' Ma 3.16; τὰ ~ία τὰ ἅγια 1M 12.9; ἡμερῶν ἀρχιερωσύνης αὐτοῦ 'of records of his high priesthood' 16.24.

3. *sealed letter*: Is 37.14, 3K 20.8.

4. *official document*: β. κτήσεως 'bill of purchase' Je 39.11, συνοικήσεως '(marriage) certificate' To 7.13 𝔊ᴵᴵ, ἀποστασίου '(bill) of divorce' De 24.1, συνοδίας '(list) of fellow-travellers' Ne 7.5.

Cf. γράφω: Schrenk, *TDNT* 1.615-8.

βιβλιοφυλάκιον, ου. n.ʃ

archive: βασιλικόν 'royal' 1E 6.20, 22.

βίβλος, ου. f.

1. *written piece*: ἐξάλειψόν με ἐκ τῆς ~ου, ἧς ἔγραψας 'Expunge me from the book which you have written' Ex 32.32; β. ζώντων Ps 68.29; β. νόμου κυρίου 2C 17.9, β. διαθήκης θεοῦ Si 24.23; ἱερά 2M 8.23.

2. *division of a written composition*: Αὕτη ἡ β. γενέσεως οὐρανοῦ καὶ γῆς 'this is the chapter concerning the emergence of heaven and earth' Ge 2.4. Cf. βιβλίον.

βιβρώσκω: fut.pass. βρωθήσομαι; aor.pass. ἐβρώθην, subj. βρωθῶ, opt.3pl βρωθείησαν; pf. βέβρωκα, inf. βεβρωκέναι, pass. βεβρῶσθαι, ptc.pass. βεβρωμένος; plpf. βεβρώκειν. Used in the LXX virtually exclusively in fut.pass., aor.pass., and pf. in complementary distribution with ἐσθίω (q.v.), cp. Ez 18.15 w. vs. 11.

to eat up, consume: pass. ***o*** paschal lamb, Ex 12.46; sacrificial meal, Le 19.6, De 12.23 (|| ἐσθίω); leaven, i.e. leavened bread, Ex 13.3; καρπός Le 19.23; 6.16 (|| act. ἔδομαι), ἄρτος Jb 6.6; + dat cogn., βρώσει βρωθῇ Le 19.7; ὑπὸ σητός 'by a moth' Is 51.8. **b**. generally of consuming food with no nuance of eating *up*: ἄρτον, and + πίνω ὕδωρ 1K 30.12; ***o*** βρῶμα 2K 19.43*L*. **c**. metaph. of destruction, Na 1.10; ***o*** ἀνομία Is 9.18; reproach by people, ὑπὸ χρόνου 51.8, δίαιτα 'abode' Jb 5.3.

Cf. βρῶμα, βρῶσις, βρώσιμος, οἰωνόβρωτος, σητόβρωτος, ἄβρωτος, ἐσθίω, κατεσθίω, ἀφανίζω.

βῖκος, ου. m.ʃ

jar: Je 19.1, 10. Cf. Shipp 148.

βίος, ου. m.

1. *life lived*: ἀνθρώπου ἐπὶ τῆς γῆς Jb 7.1; ἀνθρώπινος 10.5; ἡμέραι τοῦ ~ου αὐτοῦ 14.14. **b**. *life-style*: Wi 2.15 (|| τρίβος), cf. διαγωγή, δρόμος.

2. *livelihood, means of living*: ἐλάττωσις ~ου 'diminution of ..' Si 34.4; || ζωή Pr 5.9.

3. *the world we live in*: Wi 10.8, 14.21.

Cf. βιοτεύω, βιότης, ἐμβίωσις, ζωή: Schmidt 4.41-51; Trench 91-5; Bertram, *TDNT* 2.851-4.

βιοτεύω.ʃ

to conduct a life in a certain manner: ἐννόμως 'in accordance with the law' Si prol. 35. Cf. βιόω, ζάω: Wagner 120f.

βιότης, τητος. f.ʃ

life lived: Pr 5.23. Cf. βίος **1**

βιόω: fut. βιώσω; aor.subj. βιώσω, ptc. βιώσας.

1. *to remain in life*: πολὺν χρόνον Jb 29.18 (*s* plant and hum.); Si 19.6¶.

2. *to lead a life*: + acc., ζωὴν ἐπαιτήσεως 'a beggar's life' Si 40.28, μετὰ εὐλογιστίας 'based on sound thinking' 4M 5.22.

Cf. βιοτεύω, ἐπι~, κατα~, συμβιόω, βίωσις, ζάω.

βίωσις, εως. f.ʃ*

act of leading a life: ἔννομος 'in conformity with the law' Si prol. 14. Cf. βιόω: Wagner 120f.

βλαβερός, ά, όν.ʃ

liable to cause damage: vinegar to the teeth or smoke to the eyes, τινι Pr 10.26. Cf. βλάπτω, ἀβλαβής: Spicq 1.292.

βλάβη, ης. f.ʃ

physical *damage*, 'wound, injury': Wi 11.19. Cf. βλάπτω.

βλάπτω: aor.pass. ἐβλάβην.

to cause damage: financial, To 12.2, physical 2M 12.22; + acc. rei, mental, καρδίαν Pr 25.20a. **b**. pass. *to suffer the damage of*: τοῦ μὴ γνῶναι 'not to get to know' Wi 10.8.

Cf. βλαβερός, βλάβη, ἀβλαβής, καταβλάπτω.

βλαστάνω, -τάω, -τέω: fut. ~τήσω; aor. ἐβλάστησα, impv. βλάστησον, subj. βλαστήσω; pf. βεβλάστηκα: the earlier form with Nu only at Jd 16.22B.

1. *to cause* sth (acc.) *to sprout*: ***s*** earth (γῆ), ***o*** grass, seeds, and trees Ge 1.11; ***s*** rod, ***o*** almonds Nu 17.8; ***s*** coppice, ***o*** trees, Ec 2.6; χάριν Si 24.17; obj. understood, πεδία τῆς ἐρήμου '(the plants of) the plains of the wilderness' Jl 2.22.

2. *to sprout*: ***s*** rod, εἰς οἶκον Λευι Nu 17.8 (|| ἐκβλαστάνω vs. 5); metaph., ***s*** hum. and + ἐξανθέω 'to blossom' Is 27.6; παράνομος 2K 23.5B; Si 39.13; hair on a shaven head, Jd 16.22 B (A: ἀνατέλλω).

Cf. βλάστημα, βλαστός, ἀνα~, ἐκβλαστάνω, ἀνατέλλω, θάλλω.

βλάστημα, ατος. n.ʃ

that which has grown (of plant): β. κέδρων ἐν τῷ Λιβάνῳ 'a young cedar in Lebanon' Si 50.12. Cf. βλαστάνω, βλαστός.

βλαστός, οῦ.

bud or *shoot*: of vine, Ge 40.10; ἐκ ~οῦ .. ἀνέβης 49.9 (Wevers: *shoot* = *cub*); ἐξήνεγκεν ~όν Nu 17.8; metaph., Jb 30.12. Cf. βλαστάνω: Schmidt 2.477f.

βλασφημέω: aor. ἐβλασφήμησα, subj. ~μήσω.

to speak ill of: esp. of a divine being, abs. ἐβλασφήμουν καὶ λόγους ἀθεμίτους προΐεντο '.. kept uttering outrageous words' 2M 10.34; εἰς τὸν κύριον Da 3.96 LXX, εἰς τὸν Βηλ Bel 9 TH; ^λόγους^ ⌜εἰς ἐμέ⌝ (B: om.) 4K 19.6; + ὀνειδίζω 19.22; + acc. and pass., τὸ ὄνομά μου Is 52.5, + cogn. acc. To 1.18 𝔊[II]. Cf. βλασφημία, βλάσφημος, διαβάλλω, δυσφημέω, κακολογέω, λοιδορέω, εὐλογέω εὐφημέω: Wackernagel I 741-4; Beyer, *TDNT* 1.621f.

βλασφημία, ας. f.

v.n. of βλασφημέω: περὶ τῶν γενομένων εἰς τὸ ὄνομα αὐτοῦ ~ῶν 'about the blasphemies committed against his name' 2M 8.4; ἡ φωνὴ τῶν ~ῶν σου Ez 35.12, εἴπῃ ~αν κατὰ τοῦ θεοῦ Da 3.96 TH. Cf. βλασφημέω.

βλάσφημος, ον.

given to committing βλασφημία: ~οις καὶ βαρβάροις ἔθνεσι 2M 10.4; subst. m. ὡς β. ὁ ἐγκαταλιπὼν πατέρα 'he who abandons his own father is no different from a blasphemer' Si 3.16, + ἀνδρόφονος 'murderer' 2M 9.28; burned alive, 10.36. Cf. βλασφημέω.

βλέπω: fut.act. βλέψω, mid. βλέψομαι; aor.impv. βλέψον, subj. βλέψω. Only rarely used in tenses other than the pres., fut., and impf.

1. *to perceive with the eyes*, 'see' (= ὁράω): in XII, all in a question, τί σὺ βλέπεις (v.l. ὁρᾷς); Am 8.1; Zc 4.2, 5.2 (|| ὁρᾶν and in reply); πῶς ὑμεῖς βλέπετε αὐτόν; Hg 2.3; *s* eyes and foll. by an object ὅτι-clause, οἱ ὀφθαλμοὶ ὑμῶν βλέπουσιν .. ὅτι .. Ge 45.12; || ἀκούω Is 6.9; *o* πτωχείαν 'conditions of poverty' La 3.1. **b**. *to be gifted with special insight*: προφήτης formerly known as βλέπων 1K 9.9; 1C 9.22, 29.29, cf. ὁ ὁρῶν, s.v. ὁράω **I 2 c**. **c**. pass. *to be visible, showing*: || ὑπερέχω 3K 8.8 || 2C 5.9.

2. *to regard with the eyes*: *s* eyes, σφακελίζοντες εἰς αὐτά 'strained, with a yearning after them' De 28.32; *+ ἔν marking sustained interest and concern: ἐν νεφέλαις Ec 11.4; + εἰς - εἰς τράπεζαν ἀλλοτρίαν 'sbd else's dinner-table' Si 40.29, εἰς ὑπερηφανίαν αὐτῶν Ju 9.9; + ἐπί - ἐπὶ πτώσει ἐχθρῶν 'to feast one's eyes on enemies' downfall' Si 25.7.

3. *to have sound eye-sight*, 'keen-sighted': βλέποντα καὶ τυφλόν 'seeing and blind' Ex 4.11.

4. *to face, be turned* in a certain direction: *s* a geographical feature, κατὰ πρόσωπον τῆς ἐρήμου 'towards the wilderness' Nu 21.20 (of the plain of Moab), κατὰ ἀνατολάς 'the east' Ez 46.1 (967: rel. πρός), πρὸς βορρᾶν 'the north' 8.3, ἀπέναντί τινος 42.7, εἴς τι 42.8, Pr 16.25.

5. *to take into consideration*: + ὅτι Su 51[a] LXX.

6. *to cause the look of one's face to assume the character of*: + acc. rei, λεῖα '(to look) gentle and peaceable' Pr 12.13a.

7. *to see to it* that sth happens: + impv., 2K 15.27.

Cf. ἀνα~, ἀπο~, ἐπι~, προβλέπω, ὑποβλέπομαι, εἶδον, θεάομαι, θεωρέω, ὁράω, καθοράω, τυφλός: Schmidt 1.253-60; Shipp 151-7; Lee 131-41; LSG s.v.

βλέφαρον, ου. n. Alw. pl.

eyelid: Je 9.18, Ps 10.4,130.4 (|| ὀφθαλμός); of an adulterous woman, Pr 6.25.

βοάω: fut. βοήσομαι; aor. ἐβόησα, subj. βοήσω, ptc. βοήσας, impv. βόησον.

1. *to shout, cry out*: βοήσας τῇ φωνῇ αὐτοῦ ἔκλαυσεν 'crying aloud, he wept' Ge 29.11; appealing to God, πρός + acc., 4.10 (*s* hum. φωνή), Ho 7.14, Jl 1.19, Jn 2.3, Hb 1.2; and + περί τινος Ex 8.12, 1K 7.9 (*L* ὑπὲρ Ισραηλ); κατὰ σοῦ πρὸς κύριον De 15.9; ἐπί τινα Je 31.31; accusing (?) and metaph., λίθος ἐκ τοίχου βοήσεται 'a stone will cry out from a wall' Hb 2.11 (|| φθέγγομαι); μετ' εὐφροσύνης Is 14.6; for help, φωνῇ μεγάλῃ Ge 39.14; + ὑψόω φωνήν 39.15; *s* roaring, predatory animal, Is 5.29, 31.4 (at latter || κράζω); in sorrow, 15.4; ἡ καρδία .. ἐν ἑαυτῇ 15.5; σύντριμμα καὶ σεισμός 'destruction and quake' ib. **b**. *to utter loudly*: + acc. rei, Τί βοᾷς πρός με; 'What are you clamouring to me for?' or 'Why ..?' Ex 14.15, τί βοήσω; Is 43.6; τὸ ὄνομα αὐτοῦ 12.4 (|| ὑμνέω), εὐφροσύνην 44.23.

2. *to address and call on* for an action: τινα Jd 4.10B (A: παραγγέλλω τινι).

Cf. ἀνα~, δια~, ἐκ~, ἐπι~, καταβοάω, βοή, κράζω, φθέγγομαι, λέγω: Schmidt 1.126-8; Shipp 157f.; Stauffer, *TDNT* 1.625-8.

βοή, ῆς. f.

shouting voice, 'cry': ἀνέβη ἡ β. αὐτῶν πρὸς τὸν θεὸν ἀπὸ τῶν ἔργων Ex 2.23; of mourning, + κλαυθμός 'weeping,' στεναγμός 'groaning' Ju 14.16; + εὐφροσύνη 'joy' 3M 7.16. Cf. βοάω, κραυγή, φωνή.

βοήθεια, ας. f.

1. *help provided*: Ps 21.20 (|| ἀντίλημψις); military, Je 44.7.

2. *he who or that which provides help*: νόμον εἰς ~αν ἔδωκεν Is 8.20, φυγεῖν .. εἰς ~αν 20.6; || ὠφέλεια 30.5; God, Je 16.19 (|| ἰσχύς, καταφυγή 'might, refuge').

Cf. βοηθέω, βοήθημα, βοηθός, ἐπικουρία, τιμωρία.

βοηθέω: fut. βοηθήσω, ptc. βοηθήσων, pass. βοηθηθήσομαι; aor. ἐβοήθησα, impv. βοήθησον, inf. βοηθῆσαι, ptc. βοηθήσας, subj. βοηθήσω, opt.3s. βοηθήσαι, pass. ἐβοηθήθην, inf. βοηθηθῆναι; pf.pass. βεβοήθημαι.

to provide help: + dat. pers., Ge 49.25, cf. τῇ διαφθορᾷ σου τίς βοηθήσει; 'who is going to help (you) as you are being ruined?' Ho 13.9; πένητι ἐκ πτωχείας 'the poor out of his poverty' Ps 106.41; + λυτρόω 43.27; pass. ὑπό τινος Is 30.2 (|| σκεπάζω 'protect'); + cogn. acc., βοήθειαν μικράν Da 11.34 TH. Cf. βοηθός, βοήθεια, βοήθημα, ἀντιλαμβάνω, ἀρήγω, ἐπαρήγω, σκεπάζω, ἀβοηθησία, ἀβοήθητος: Schmidt 4.153-8, 161.

βοήθημα, ατος. n.ʃ

help provided: on battlefield, 2M 15.8; Wi 17.12. Cf. βοήθεια.

βοηθός, οῦ. m.

helper: of a woman as as her husband's aid, β. κατ' αὐτόν 'cut out for him' Ge 2.18 (|| β. ὅμοιος αὐτῷ vs. 20, cf. To 8.6), β… στήριγμα '.. support' ib., cf. β. κατ' αὐτὸν καὶ στῦλον ἀναπαύσεως

'.. column for rest' Si 36.24; β. καὶ σκεπαστὴς ἐγένετό μοι εἰς σωτηρίαν Ex 15.2; Na 3.9; God, ὁ θεὸς τοῦ πατρός μου β. μου, καὶ ἐξείλατό με ἐκ χειρὸς Φαραω '.. and rescued me out of the hand of Ph.' Ex 18.4; ἐκ τῶν ἐχθρῶν De 33.7, ἀπὸ ἐχθρῶν Jb 22.25; || σκέπη Is 25.4; || ἀντιλαμβάνομαι 63.5, || σωτήρ 17.10, || ἀντιλήμπτωρ Ps 17.3, + ὑπερασπιστής 32.20, 39.18. Cf. βοηθέω.

βόθρος, ου. m.

pit dug in the ground: ὀρύσσω ~ον 'I shall dig a pit' Zc 3.9; Am 9.7; ἐμπεσεῖται εἰς ~ον 'he will fall into ..' Ps 7.16; || παγίς 56.7. Cf. βάθος, βάραθρον, βόθυνος, λάκκος, τρώγλη: Shipp 158f.

βόθυνος, ου. m.

= βόθρος, q.v.: || φόβος, παγίς 'trap' Is 24.17, Je 31.43; ἐμπεσεῖται εἰς τὸν ~ον Is 24.18; β. λάκκου 51.1; in the cliffs as a bird's nest, Je 31.28. See Renehan 1.55.

βοΐδιον, ου. n.ʃ

dim. of βοῦς: Je 27.11. Cf. βοῦς: Shipp 159.

βόλβιτον, ου. n.ʃ

excrement: cow-dung, fig. of valueless object, Zp 1.17 (|| χοῦς), βοῶν Ez 4.15; β. κόπρου ἀνθρωπίνης 4.12. Alw. pl. exc. Si 22.2. Cf. LSG, s.v. Cf. κόπρος.

βολή, ῆς. f.ʃ

1. *act of hurling*: βελῶν 'of arrows' 2M 5.3. Cf. πυροβόλος, λιθοβόλος.

2. *a distance covered by a piece of hurled weapon*: τόξου 'a bow-shot' Ge 21.16.

3. *ray*: ἡλίου ~αί 'sunbeams' 3M 5.26.

Cf. βάλλω: Schmidt 3.161.

βολίς, ίδος. f. *

thrown weapon: ~ίδι κατατοξευθήσεται 'will be shot down with a missile' Ex 19.13; || ὅπλα Hb 3.11; hurled at an enemy's sides, Nu 33.55; thrust in one's eyes and affecting one's vision, Jo 23.13; fast-moving like lightning (ἀστραπή) Zc 9.14, cf. ~ες ἀστραπῶν 'shafts of lightning' Wi 5.21. **b**. weapon in general: λιμοῦ 'of famine' Ez 5.16; verbal, γλώσσης ἀδίκου Si 51.6.

Cf. βέλος and ὅπλον: Borger 2000; Caird 1968.463.

βομβέω: fut. βομβήσω; aor. ἐβόμβησα.ʃ

to emit a loud noise: ***s*** God's heart like a flute, Je 31.36; roaring billows (κύματα) 38.36; the sea, 1C 16.32. Cf. ἠχέω, φωνέω: Schmidt 3.341f.

βόμβησις, εως. f.ʃ*

buzzing, huge crowd: of people, Ba 2.29.

βοοζύγιον, ου. n.ʃ*

ox-yoke: Si 26.7. Cf. ζυγός.

βορά, ᾶς. f.

food of carnivorous animals: Jb 4.11. Cf. βρῶμα, ἔδεσμα.

βόρβορος, ου. m.ʃ

mire, filth: in a dungeon, Je 45.6. Cf. Shipp 161.

βορρᾶς, gen. ᾶ, acc. ᾶν; βορέας, gen. ου, acc. αν. m. On the form, see Thack. 123f. and Shipp 161-3. Used alw. anarthrously.

1. *north wind*: Jb 26.7¶. **b**. ἄνεμος βορρέας Pr 25.23.

2. *north*: πρὸς ~ᾶν καὶ λίβα καὶ ἀνατολὰς καὶ θάλασσαν 'towards the north, south, east and west' Ge 13.14; κατὰ θάλασσαν καὶ ~ᾶν καὶ λίβα καὶ ἀνατολάς De 3.27; ἀπὸ γῆς ~ᾶ Zc 2.6; καταιγὶς ~έου 'north wind' (|| νότος) Si 43.17.

Cf. ἀνατολή, δυσμή, θάλασσα, λίψ, νότος: Shipp 161-3.

βόσκημα, ατος. n.

1. *fatted beast*: 2M 12.11; cultic offerings, 2C 7.5 (|| *L* πρόβατα).

*__2__. *feeding ground*: for sheep, θήσω πᾶσαν τρίβον εἰς β. Is 49.11, β. προβάτου 7.25 (|| καταπάτημα βοός), ποιμένων 'of shepherds' 32.14.

Cf. βόσκω.

βόσκω: fut. βοσκήσω, pass. βοσκηθήσομαι; aor. ἐβόσκησα, subj.pass. βοσκηθῶ.

1. *to help eat standing grass in the open*: abs. Ge 29.7; + acc., πρόβατα 29.9; 37.12 (|| vs. 13 ποιμαίνω), ποίμνιον Je 38.10; ἐν νομῇ Ez 34.14; fig., ***o*** hum., τὸν οἶκόν σου 3K 12.16, and pass. ὡς ταῦροι 'like bulls' Is 5.17, πτωχοί 14.30.

2. mid. *to eat standing grass in the open*, 'to graze': ***s*** cattle, ἐν τῷ ἄχει 'on the reed-grass' Ge 41.2 (***s*** βόες 'cows' and || vs. 3,18 νέμω), λύκοι καὶ ἄρνες 'wolves and lambs' Is 65.25; ***o*** (place), τόπον πίονα καὶ εὐρύχωρον 'a fertile and spacious plot' 30.23.

Cf. κατα~, συμβόσκω, βόσκημα, ποιμαίνω, νέμω, κατανέμομαι, ἐσθίω, τρέφω: Schmidt 4.588f.; Trench 84-6; Moussy 11-9.

βόστρυχος, ου. m.

lock of hair: Ct 5.2; κεφαλῆς Jd 16.14A (B: σειρά). Cf. θρίξ, σειρά.

βοτάνη, ης. f.

growth on land, 'plant, herbage': χόρτου 'of grass' Ge 1.11 (|| ξύλον); ἐπὶ τῆς γῆς Ex 9.22; τῆς γῆς 10.12; ἐν τῷ πεδίῳ 9.25; τοῦ πεδίου Ex 10.15; ἐν ἀγρῷ Zc 10.1; || χόρτος Je 14.6; medicinal, Wi 16.12. Cf. δάσος, δένδρον, ξύλον, παμβότανον, πόα, φυτόν, χλόη, χόρτος: Shipp 163.

βοτρύδιον, ου. n.ʃ

Dim. of βότρυς, q.v.: β. μικρά Is 18.5.

βότρυς, υος. m.

bunch or *cluster* of grapes: πέπειροι οἱ ~υες σταφυλῆς 'the bunches of grapes (were) ripe' Ge 40.10; ἀμπέλου Ct 7.9 (compared to female breasts); κύπρου 'of camphor' Ct 1.14; ῥὼξ ἐν βότρυι 'berry amid a cluster' Is 65.8; πικρίας 'of bitterness' De 32.32; *o* of κόπτω 'to cut' Nu 13.24, 25. Cf. σταφυλή: Shipp 163f.

βούβαλος, ου. m.ʃ

African *antelope*: ritually clean food, De 14.5.

βούκεντρον, ου.ʃ *

ox-goad: 1K 13.21*L*; fig. of pungent words of sages, Ec 12.11. Cf. κέντρον.

βουκόλιον, ου. n.

herd of cattle: ‖ κτῆνος Ex 13.12 (sacrificial animals); μοσχάρια ἐκ μέσου ~ων 'calves out of herds of cattle' Am 6.4 (‖ ποίμνιον); ~α βοῶν 'herds of cattle' De 28.4, 28.18, 51, Jl 1.18 (‖ ποίμνια προβάτων); ἐκ τῶν ~ων καὶ ἐκ τῶν προβάτων καὶ ἐκ τῶν αἰγῶν Le 22.19; τὸν καρπὸν τῆς γῆς .. τὰ ~α τῶν βοῶν .. καὶ τὰ ποίμνια τῶν προβάτων De 7.13. Cf. βοῦς, ἀγέλη, ποίμνιον.

βουλευτήριον, ου. n.

senate chamber: 1M 8.15. Cf. βουλεύω.

βουλευτής, οῦ. m.ʃ

counsellor: βασιλεὺς β. γῆς Jb 3.14; ‖ κριτής 12.17. Cf. βουλεύω, συμβουλευτής.

βουλευτικός, ή, όν.ʃ

capable of deliberating: *s* καρδία Pr 24.6. Cf. βουλεύω.

βουλεύω: fut. βουλεύσομαι; aor.act. ἐβούλευσα, mid. ἐβουλευσάμην, inf. βουλεύσασθαι, ptc. βουλευσάμενος, subj. βουλεύσωμαι, impv. βούλευσαι; pf. βεβούλευμαι. Mostly mid.

1. *to deliberate, ponder* (+ τι): πονηρὰ βουλευόμενος (v.l. λογιζόμενος) ἐναντία 'planning evil things in opposition' Na 1.11; ἡ βουλὴ τῶν πονηρῶν ἄνομα βουλεύσεται Is 32.7, *o* συνετά 32.8; πλείονα βουλεύου 'think further' 16.3; πρὸς ἑαυτοὺς .. ποῦ συναποκρυβῶσι .. 'among themselves where to hide ..' Ep Je 48; βουλευόμενος 'senator' 1M 8.15.

2. *to resolve* to do sth: abs. κατ' ἐμοῦ εἰς πονηρά .. περὶ ἐμοῦ εἰς ἀγαθά 'to my disadvantage .. to my benefit' Ge 50.20; + acc., τί ἐβουλεύσατο κατὰ σοῦ ..'what he has decided against you' Mi 6.5, περὶ αὐτοῦ 'about him' Wi 4.17; αἰσχύνην τῷ οἴκῳ σου Hb 2.10; + cogn. acc., βουλὴν πονηρὰν καθ' ἑαυτῶν Is 3.9, περὶ σοῦ 7.5, ἐπί τινα 14.26, 19.12, 23.8, Je 29.21 (last ‖ λογίζομαι); + inf., 2C 30.2, 3M 1.10.

3. mid. *to offer advice*: + dat. pers., Si 37.8; ἐβουλεύσατο καρδία μου ἐπ' ἐμέ 'it appeared to me advisable' Ne 5.7. **b**. *to seek advice, consult*: μετά τινος Si 37.10; πρός τινα 4K 6.8B (*L* dat.).

Cf. βουλή, βουλευτήριον, βουλευτικός, ἐπίβουλος, διαβουλεύω, διανοέομαι, λογίζομαι, μελετάω.

βουλή, ῆς. f.

1. *decision*: Ge 49.6 (‖ σύστασις); ἡ β. σου ἀπώλετο 'your decision has come to naught' Mi 4.9, αἱ ~αὶ ὑμῶν '.. concerning you' Is 41.21 (‖ κρίσις); ‖ λογισμός Mi 4.12; β. εἰρηνική 'peaceful counsel' Zc 6.13; πονηρά Is 3.9; ἐπ' ἐμὲ εἰς θάνατον Je 18.23; ‖ ὁδοί Is 55.7; δότε (B: φέρετε) ἑαυτοῖς ~ήν 'Decide among yourselves' Jd 20.7, 2K 16.20*L* (B: φέρετε); θήσομαι ~ὰς ἐν ψυχῇ μου 'I shall think plans over' Ps 12.3; pl., ‖ ὁδοί Is 55.7; β. ἀγαθή 1M 4.45; as cogn. acc., βουλή, ἣν βεβούλευται Is 14.26, Je 27.45. **b**. *decision-making faculty*: ἀπολωλεκὸς ~ήν 'at their wits' end' De 32.28 (‖ ἐπιστήμη); ‖ σοφία Je 29.8; residing with elders and ‖ ὅρασις, νόμος Ez 7.26; ἀνὴρ ~ῆς 'a man capable of wise decision' 1M 2.65. **c**. *decision-making body or process*: σύγκλητοι ~ῆς 'council members' Nu 16.2 (‖ ἀρχηγοὶ συναγωγῆς), ἁγίων 'of the saints' Ps 88.8, δικαίων 1.5, εὐθείων 'of the upright' 110.1 (‖ συναγωγή); civic, λαοῦ Si 38.32. Cf. συμβοῦλιον.

2. *deliberation, act of pondering*: βαθέως ~ὴν ποιοῦντες 'do deep thinking' Is 29.15 (human as against divinely inspired), βαθὴν ~ὴν βουλευόμενοι 31.6; πρὸ πάσης πράξεως β. 'Before acting, always think first' Si 37.16; Jd 19.30.

Cf. βουλεύω, συμβοῦλιον, γνώμη, κρίσις: Schrenk, *TDNT* 1.633f.

βούλημα, ατος. n.ʃ

that which one intends: 2M 15.5, 4M 8.18.

βούλομαι: impf. ἠβουλόμην (on ἠ-, see Thack. § 16.3), ἐβουλόμην; fut. βουλήσομαι; aor. ἐβουλήθην, subj. βουληθῶ.

1. *to wish, desire*: abs. ὃν τρόπον ἐβούλου πεποίηκας 'you have done as you wished' Jn 1.14; + inf., εἰδέναι βούλει ὅτι .. 'do you wish to have the knowledge that ..,' ironically for 'you ought to know already ..' Ex 10.7; + ἵνα with a subj. of the same person as that of the lead verb, Is 42.21 (v.l. βουλεύομαι). **b**. *to desire to have, long for*: + acc., στέαρ ἀρνῶν 'the fat of lambs (as a cultic offering)' Is 1.11; εἴδωλα 1.29 (‖ ἐπιθυμέω); divine message, Je 6.10; θάνατον Ez 33.11 (‖ θέλω 18.23, 32); μοὶ κακά Ps 69.3 (‖ θέλω 39.15); ἔν τινι 1K 18.25B (*L* acc.), 2K 24.3B (*L* θέλω).

2. *to consent*: mostly c. neg., 'to refuse,' + inf. οὐ βούλεται .. πορευθῆναι Ge 24.5 (‖ θέλω vs. 8); Ex 4.23, 8.2, 21; 10.3 (‖ θέλω vs. 4), 22.17 (‖ ἀνανεύω).

Cf. ἐπιθυμέω, ἐπιποθέω, εὐδοκέω, θέλω, ὁμείρομαι, προσδέχομαι: Schmidt 3.602-10, 617f.; Shipp 166f.; Rödiger; Schrenk, *TDNT* 1.629-32.

βουνίζω: aor. ἐβούνισα; pf.ptc.pass. βεβουνισμένος.ʃ *

to make a heap of: + dat. com. pers.), ἄλφιτον 'groats' Ru 2.14; pass., *o* sheaves of harvested crop (?), 2.16.

βουνός, οῦ. m.

1. *small mountain, high ground*: οἱ ~οὶ ῥυήσονται γάλα 'the hills will flow with milk' Jl 3.18 (|| ὄρος); less prominent than ὄρος - μετεωρισθήσεται ὑπεράνω τῶν ~ῶν '(the mountain [ὄρος] of the Lord) will tower over the hills' Mi 4.1, sim. Is 2.2; place for cultic activities, Ho 4.13 (|| ὄρος), 10.9*a*; κατὰ τὰς ἡμέρας τοῦ ~οῦ 9.9 (where the MT means 'Gibeah' w. ref. to the infamous incident there [Jd 19f.]; so identified in Cyr. I 195 and Thph PG 126.726); || ὑψηλά and as suited for making public announcements, 5.8; its large quantity of soil being capable of burying one, 10.8 (|| ὄρος); β. ὑψηλός and || ὄρος Is 2.14, τὰ ὄρη καὶ οἱ βουνοὶ καὶ οἱ δρυμοί '.. and thickets' 10.18; ὄρη, φάραγγες, νάπαι Ez 6.3.

2. *cairn*: made of stones, Ge 31.46. **b.** *pile*: of heads of hum. corpses, 4K 10.8.

Cf. θίς, ὄρος: Schmidt 3.94; Shipp 167-70; Lee 167-70.

βοῦς, οός, dat. βοΐ, acc.pl. βόας. m./f.

ox or *cow*: βουκόλια βοῶν 'herds of cattle' Jl 1.18; οἱ ἄνθρωποι καὶ τὰ κτήνη καὶ οἱ βόες καὶ τὰ πρόβατα 'men and animals, cattle and sheep' Jn 3.7, ὄνοι added Nu 31.28, also || κτῆνος, ἵππος, ὑποζύγιον, κάμηλος, πρόβατον Ex 9.3; || πρόβατα in Hb 3.17; πρόβατα καὶ βόες καὶ σκηναί Ge 13.5 (= vs. 6 τὰ ὑπάρχοντα); κτήνη προβάτων καὶ κτήνη βοῶν και γεώργια πολλά '.. and many fields' 26.14. Cf. κτῆνος, μόσχος, μοσχάριον, πρόβατον, and βουκόλιον.

βούτομον, ου. m.ʃ

sedge: Jb 8.11 (|| πάπυρος), 40.21 (+ πάπυρος, κάλαμος).

βούτυρον, ου. n.

butter: β. καὶ γάλα '.. and milk' Ge 18.8, β. βοῶν καὶ γάλα προβάτων De 32.14, β. καὶ μέλι φάγεται '.. and honey' Is 7.15; ἐχέοντό μου αἱ ὁδοὶ ~ῳ 'my ways were poured with ..' Jb 29.6.

βραβεύω: aor. ἐβράβευσα.ʃ

to act as umpire in: + acc. rei and dat. pers. (com.), ἄγωνα 'race' Wi 10.12. Cf. συμβραβεύω: Stauffer, *TDNT* 1.637f.

βραγχιάω: aor. ἐβραγχίασα.ʃ

to suffer hoarseness: *s* λάρυγξ Ps 68.4. Cf. Shipp 172.

βραδέως. adv.ʃ

slowly: 2M 14.17 (v.l. βραχέως 'for a short while'). Cf. βραδύνω, ταχέως.

βραδύγλωσσος, ον.ʃ *

slow of tongue: ἰσχνόφωνος καὶ β. 'having impediment in speech and ..' Ex 4.10. Cf. ἄλογος, ἰσχνόφωνος, ψελλίζω.

βραδύνω: fut. βραδυνῶ; aor. ἐβράδυνα, subj. βραδύνω.ʃ

1. *to be slow in acting*, 'loiter, sit idle': εἰ μὴ ἐβραδύναμεν, ἤδη ἂν ὑπεστρέψαμεν δίς 'if we had not dillydallied, by this time we would have returned there twice' Ge 43.10; ὁ κύριος οὐ μὴ βραδύνῃ Si 32.22; τοῖς μισοῦσιν 'to the enemies' De 7.10.

2. tr. *to cause to come late*: τὴν σωτηρίαν τὴν παρ' ἐμοῦ οὐ βραδυνῶ 'I shall not delay my salvation' Is 46.13 (:: ἐγγίζω).

Cf. ἐγγίζω, μακροθυμέω, νωθρός, ταχύνω, ὑστερέω, χρονίζω.

βραχέως. adv.

for a short while, temporarily: 2M 5.17. **b.** ἄρτι β. indicates that a given state had prevailed just a short while: 2M 13.11.

Cf. βραχύς.

βραχίων, ονος. m.

1. *arm* extending from the hand up to the shoulder: τὰ νεῦρα ~όνων χειρῶν αὐτοῦ 'the sinews of the arms of his hands' Ge 49.24; ἀνέλαβον αὐτὸν ἐπὶ τὸν ~ονά μου 'I took him up on my arm' Ho 11.3 (of a caring parent), cf. Is 40.11; seat of strength [cf. LSG s.v.], ἰσχὺς ~όνων ἀενάων 'might of eternal arms' De 33.27; of divine might, ἐν χειρὶ κραταιᾷ .. καὶ ἐν ~ονι ὑψηλῷ 'with a mighty hand .. and an uplifted arm' Ex 6.1, sim. De 3.24, 7.19; ἐν ἰσχύι μεγάλῃ καὶ ἐν ~ονι ὑψηλῷ Ex 32.11; ἐν τῷ ~ονι τῆς δυνάμεώς σου Ps 88.11, κατὰ τῆς ἰσχύος τοῦ ~ονος αὐτοῦ Is 62.8, κράτει ~ονός σου Wi 12.22; hum., σάρκα βραχίονος 'physical (or: military) strength' Je 17.5; β. κραταιός 'powerful ..' Jb 26.2 (|| ἰσχύς), κράτος ~ονος 'power of ..' Wi 11.21; δεξιος Si 33.7.

2. *shoulder of an animal*: of a sacrificial animal, Ex 29.22, De 18.3.

Cf. ἀγκάλη, ἀγκών, πῆχυς, χείρ, ἐπίχειρον, πῆχυς: Shipp 174f.; Schlier, *TDNT* 1.639f.

βραχύς, εῖα, ύ.

slight: in significance: τὰ βραχέα τῶν κριμάτων 'the easier of the cases' Ex 18.22 (:: ὑπέρογχος). **b.** in number: ἐν ἀριθμῷ βραχεῖ De 26.5; 28.62 (:: πλῆθος), ἀριθμῷ Ps 104.12 (|| 1C 16.19 ὀλιγοστός). **c.** in quantity: ~υ τοῦ μέλιτος 'a bit of the honey' 1K 14.29. **d.** in length of time: subst. n., βραχύ τι 'for a short while' Is 57.17; πρὸ ~έως 'just a while ago' 4M 9.5; poss. 'a short distance' 2K 16.1B (*L* μικρόν); χρόνον understood, 2M 7.36 (|| βραχέως vs. 33). **e.** in degree: Ps 8.6; παρὰ ~ύ 'almost' 93.17; κατὰ ~ύ 'little by little' Wi 12.8. **f.** subst. n., βραχεῖ *expressed in few words*, 'in brief' 3M 4.14.

Cf. ἀκαριαῖος, βραχέως, βραχυτελής, μέγας, μακρός, πλῆθος, πολύς, ὑπέρογχος.

βραχυτελής, ές.ʃ
ending shortly: *s* βίος 'life' Wi 15.9.

βρέφος, ους. n.
baby: about to be born, Si 19.11; infant, 1M 1.61, 4M 4.25. Cf. νήπιος, παιδάριον, ὑποτίθιος: Shipp 175; *ND* 4.40f.

βρέχω: fut.act. βρέξω, pass. βραχήσομαι; aor. ἔβρεξα, inf. βρέξαι.ʃ
1. *to cause to descend* from the sky: *s* God and *o* "rain" understood, οὐ ἔβρεξεν ὁ θεὸς ἐπὶ τὴν γῆν 'God had not yet sent rain on the earth' Ge 2.5; ἐπί + acc. of place on which it rains, ἐπὶ πόλιν Am 4.7[1, 2, 4]; + ὑετόν – β. ὑμῖν ὑετὸν πρόϊμον καὶ ὄψιμον 'early and late rain' Jl 2.23, εἰς αὐτὸν (= τὸν ἀμπελῶνα 'vineyard') ὑετόν Is 5.6; κύριος ἔβρεξεν ἐπὶ Σόδομα καὶ Γόμορρα θεῖον καὶ πῦρ 'brimstone and fire' Ge 19.24, sim. Ez 38.22; 'hail' (χάλαζα) Ex 9.23 (ǁ ὕω vs. 18), ἔβρεξεν αὐτοῖς μαννα φαγεῖν Ps 77.24 ǁ ἐπ' αὐτοὺς .. σάρκας vs. 27. **b**. *to cause sth to descend on*: pass., *o* rain understood, μερὶς μία βραχήσεται 'one part (of the land) will have rainfall' Am 4.7[3], γῆ ἡ οὐ βρεχομένη Ez 22.24.
2. *to cause to be moistened* through some liquid descending on it: ἐν δάκρυσίν μου τὴν στρωμνήν μου βρέξω 'I shall soak my couch with my tears' Ps 6.7; pass., βραχήσεται τὰ ὄρη ἀπὸ τοῦ αἵματος αὐτῶν 'the mountains will be showered upon by their [= fallen soldiers'] blood' Is 34.3.
Cf. ἀβροχία, ἐπιβρέχω, βροχή, ὑετός, ὑετίζω, ὕω: Shipp 176; Lee 122-4; Youtie 1978.

βρίθω.ʃ
to weigh down: + acc., νοῦν 'mind' Wi 9.15 (ǁ βαρύνω). Cf. βαρύνω: Shipp 176f.

I **βρόμος**, ου. m.ʃ
foul odour: ἀναβήσεται ὁ β. αὐτοῦ 'its stink will rise' (ǁ σαπρία) Jl 2.20; opp. ὀσμή 'fragrance' Jb 6.7; foul smells of animal, Wi 11.18. Fig., αἱ ἡμέραι μου παρῆλθον ἐν ~ῳ 'my days have been spent in a "stinking" condition' (?) Jb 17.11.
On the variant spelling βρῶμος and the semantic development from 'noise' to 'stink,' see Walters 72f., Muraoka 1991.207, and Shipp 177. Cf. ὀσμή, προσόζω, σαπρία.

II **βρόμος**, ου. m.ʃ
oats: Jb 6.7, or I βρόμος.

βροντάω: fut. βροντήσω; aor. ἐβρόντησα.
to give out loud noise, 'thunder': *s* God, Ps 28.3, ἐξ οὐρανοῦ 17.14, ἀπ' οὐρανοῦ Si 46.17, ἐν φωνῇ μεγάλῃ 1K 7.10; + acc., θαυμάσια 'wondrously' Jb 37.5¶. Cf. βροντή.

βροντή, ῆς. f.
thunder: Am 4.13; + σεισμός 'earthquake' Is 29.6, Es A 4.

βροτός, οῦ. m. Only in Jb (17x), cf. Ziegler 1985.111.
human being: Jb 4.17 (ǁ ἀνήρ), 10.4 (ǁ ἄνθρωπος); mortal, ὀλιγόβιος 'short-lived' 14.1; 14.10. Cf. ἀνήρ, ἄνθρωπος: Schmidt 2.392f.

βροῦχος, ου. m.
locust: destructive of agricultural crops, and ǁ ἀκρίς Am 7.1, Jl 1.4, Ps 104.34 (innumerable); κατέφαγεν ἡ ἀκρὶς καὶ ὁ β. καὶ ἡ ἐρυσίβη καὶ ἡ κάμπη Jl 2.25; edible and ǁ ἀκρίς, ἀττάκης Le 11.22. Cf. ἀκρίς, ἀττάκης, κάμπη: Shipp 178.

βροχή, ῆς. f.ʃ
rain: Ps 67.10, 104.32. Cf. βρέχω, ὑετός.

βρόχος, ου. m.
noose: around the neck of a captive, 3M 4.8; ǁ παγίς Si 51.3, Pr 6.5; fig. of seductive speech, 7.21. Cf. παγίς.

βρυγμός, οῦ. m.ʃ
v.n. of βρύχω, q.v.: Si 51.3; lion's Pr 19.12. Cf. βρύχω.

βρύχω: fut. βρύξω; aor. ἔβρυξα.
to gnash the teeth to show hostility: ὀδόντας La 2.16, out of chagrin Ps 111.10; ἐπί τινα 34.16. Cf. βρυγμός.

βρῶμα, ατος. n. Used mostly in the pl.
1. *foodstuff*: ἀπὸ πάντων ~άτων, ἃ ἔδεσθε Ge 6.21; agricultural produce, 41.35, Is 62.8 (ǁ σῖτος; also γενήματα Ge 41.34), Jl 2.23; Pr 23.6 (ǁ ἐδέσματα vs. 3); cultic offering, τὰ ἐπιτιθέμενα ~ατα Ma 1.7; Hb 1.16, Hg 2.12; essential for subsistence and ǁ ὕδωρ De 2.6; for predatory birds, Ps 78.2. **b**. *game* to be caught in a snare or trap: Si 50.3. **c**. cooked: 2K13.10, τὰ ~ματα τῶν τραπεζῶν 'the foods on the tables' 2C 9.4.
***2**. *moth-eating* or *corrosion*: Ep Je 11 (ǁ ἰός 'rust').
Cf. βρῶσις, κατάβρωμα, βιβρώσκω, ἔδεσμα, σκεύασμα: Naumann 36; Behm, *TDNT* 1.642-5.

βρώσιμος, ον.ʃ
capable of bearing edible fruit: ξύλον ~ον 'fruit-tree' Le 19.23, Ne 9.25, Ez 47.12. Cf. βιβρώσκω.

βρῶσις, εως. f.
food: agricultural produce, Hb 3.17*a*, Ma 3.11; game, Ge 25.28; for cattle, Hb 3.17*b*; corpses, τὰ θνησιμαῖα αὐτῶν β. τοῖς πετεινοῖς τοῦ οὐρανοῦ καὶ τοῖς θηρίοις τῆς γῆς 'their corpses (shall be) food for the birds of the sky and the beasts of the earth' Je 41.20; + πόσις Da 1.10. So also most likely καλὸν τὸ ξύλον εἰς ~ιν Ge 3.6 rather than "suited for the purpose of eating". **b**. cooked: Ps 77.30, Jb 34.3¶.
2. v.n. of βιβρώσκω, *act of eating*: as a dat. cogn., βρώσει φάγῃ 'you may indeed eat' Ge 2.16, βρώσει βρωθῇ Le 19.7, ἄρτου Ps 13.4; πρόβατα ~εως 'sheep as food' 43.12; ὀρνέων 'by birds' De 32.24, also by predatory animals Je 15.3 (ǁ διαφθορά).
Cf. βιβρώσκω, βρῶμα, κατάβρωμα.

βρωτός, ή, όν.ʃ
to be eaten: subst.n., 'food' Jd 14.14 B (A: βρῶσις), ποτὰ καὶ ~ά 'drinks and foods' 1E 5.53, σίτου 'of grain' Jb 33.20 (: : βρῶσις). Cf. βιβρώσκω, βρῶσις, βρῶμα.

βύβλινος, ον.ʃ
made of βύβλος 'papyrus': *s* ἐπιστολή Is 18.2.

βύβλος. ⇒ βίβλος.

βυθίζω: aor. ἐβύθισα.ʃ
tr. *to drown*: acc. pers., 2M 12.4. Cf. Shipp 180.

βυθός, οῦ. m.
the depth of the sea, 'bottom': κατέδυσαν εἰς ~όν ὡσεὶ λίθος 'went down into the bottom of the sea like a stone' Ex 15.5; ἔρριψας εἰς ~ὸν ὡς λίθον Ne 9.11; ἐν ~οῖς θαλάσσης Ps 67.23; ἰλὺς ~οῦ 'mire of ..' 68.3; μηδὲ καταπιέτω με β. 'nor may the depth drown me' 68.16. Cf. βαθύς, ἔδαφος, πυθμήν, ῥίζωμα.

βυθοτρεφής, ές.ʃ*
being nourished in the deep: *s* Jonah, 3M 6.8.

βύρσα, ας. f.
skin stripped off, *hide*: of calf, Le 8.17; of human, Jb 16.15; of river-monster, 40.31. Cf. δέρμα: Habermann.

βύσσινος, η, ον.
made of βύσσος (q.v.): *s* στολή 'garment' Ge 41.42, κίδαρις 'tiara' Ex 28.35, χιτὼν 'tunic' 36.35, περιβόλαια 'garments' Ez 16.13; subst. ~α (sc. ἱμάτια) Is 3.23 (+ ὑακίνθια, κόκκινα), Es 1.6[1] (+ καρπάσινος), 1.6[2] (+ πορφυροῦς). Cf. βύσσος, λινοῦς, ὀθόνιον: Passoni dell'Acqua 1998.95-7.

βύσσος, ου. f.
fine linen made from flax: κεκλωσμένη 'spun' Ex 25.4, 26.1 (|| ὑάκινθος, πορφύρα, κόκκινος). **b**. linen garment, Ez 16.10. **c**. poss. fishing-net made of *Indian cotton*: Is 19.9 (|| λίνον).
Cf. βύσσινος.

βύω.ʃ
to stuff full: c. acc., τὰ ὦτα 'the ears' (hence deaf) Ps 57.5. Cf. κωφός.

βῶλαξ, ακος. f.ʃ
lump of earth: γῆς Jb 7.5.

βῶλος, ου. m./f.ʃ
1. *mass* of sth *stuck together*: "drops of dew (δρόσου)" Jb 38.28, σιδήρου 'of iron' Si 22.15.
2. *soil*: in which a grape-vine grows, Ez 17.7, 10.

βωμός, οῦ. m.
altar with a base: pertaining to pagan or illegitimate cult, τοὺς ~οὺς αὐτῶν καθελεῖτε Ex 34.13, De 7.5, 12.3 (|| στήλη, ἄλσος, τὰ γλυπτά); ἐξαρθήσονται ~οὶ Ων, ἁμαρτήματα τοῦ Ισραηλ 'the altars of On, the sins of Is., shall be removed' Ho 10.8 (|| θυσιαστήριον); ~οὶ τοῦ γέλωτος Am 7.9, τοῦ Ταφεθ Je 7.31. **b**. applied to cultic sites of the Israelite religion, Nu 3.10; in the Jerusalem Temple, 2M 2.19, 13.8, Si 50.12, 14 (|| θυσιαστήριον 11, 14), but ref. to a pagan altar at 2M 10.2: : θυσιαστήριον vs. 3 (in the Jerusalem Temple).
Cf. ἄλσος, ἐσχάρα, θυσιαστήριον, στήλη: Trench 364-6; Brown; Hanhart 1992.346f.; Daniel 15-53; van der Kooij 2003.

Γ

γάζα, ης. f. Pers. word.

valuable objects, 'treasure': Is 39.2 (|| θησαυροί); ἐν τῷ οἴκῳ τῆς ~ης τοῦ βασιλέως 2E 5.17; important official documents included, 6.1. **b.** = οἶκος ~ης 'treasury': 2E 7.21.

γαζαρηνός, οῦ. m.

Ar. loanword < גָּזַר 'astrologer': Da 2.27.

γαζοφυλάκιον, ου. n.

treasury: ἱερόν 1E 5.44; 4M 4.3, 6.

γαζοφύλαξ, κος. m.

treasurer: 1E 2.10. Cf. γαζοφυλάκιον.

γαῖα, ας. f.

poet. syn. of γῆ: Ps 48.12; οἱ λαοὶ τῶν ~ῶν 2E 3.3; οἱ θεοὶ τῶν ~ῶν 4K 18.35. Cf. γῆ: Caird 1968.463f.

γαῖσος, ου. m.ʃ*

a sort of *javelin*: Jo 8.18,19; + ἀσπίς, τόξον, σφενδόνη Ju 9.7, see *BA* ad Jo 8.18.

γάλα, ακτος. n.

milk: βούτυρον καὶ γ. 'butter and milk' Ge 18.8, sim. De 32.14; γῆν ῥέουσαν γ. καὶ μέλι 'a land flowing with milk and honey' Ex 3.8, De 6.3 +; οἱ βουνοὶ ῥυήσονται γ. 'the hills will flow with milk' Jl 3.18; προβάτων De 32.14; symb. of whiteness, La 4.7. Cf. ἀπογαλακτίζω and γαλαθηνός.

γαλαθηνός, ή, όν.ʃ

milk-sucking: *s* μοσχάριον 'calf' Am 6.4, 1K 28.24 *L*, ἀρήν 'lamb' Si 46.16,1K 7.9. Cf. γάλα.

γαλακτοποτέω.ʃ

to drink milk: *s* baby, 4M 13.21. Cf. γάλα.

γαλακτοτροφία, ας. f.ʃ

act of suckling: 4M 16.7. Cf. γάλα.

γαλεάγρα, ας. f.ʃ

cage for beasts: + κημός Ez 19.9.

γαλῆ, ῆς. f.ʃ

weasel: ritually unclean, Le 11.29. See Shipp 185.

γαληνός, όν.ʃ

free from agitation: *s* course taken by sailing ships, 4M 13.6. Cf. λαῖλαψ: Schmidt 4.263f.

γαμβρεύω: aor.subj. γαμβρεύσω, inf. γαμβρεῦσαι, mid.impv. γάμβρευσαι.ʃ

to form kinship relationship by marriage: πρὸς αὐτούς De 7.3; mid. + acc. pers., αὐτήν Ge 38.8 (the widow of a brother, levirate marriage). Cf. γαμβρός, ἐπιγαμβρεύω, ἐπιγαμία, συγκαταμίγνυμι.

γαμβρός, οῦ. m.

person connected by marriage, 'in-law': ~οὶ ἢ υἱοὶ ἢ θυγατέρες Ge 19.12; τοὺς ~οὺς αὐτοῦ τοὺς εἰληφότας τὰς θυγατέρας αὐτοῦ 'his in-laws who had taken his daughters (in marriage)' 19.14; wife's father, Ex 3.1, 18.1, Jd 1.16B (A: πενθερός); son-in-law, 1K 18.18*L*. Cf. γαμβρεύω: Shipp 185f.

γαμετή, ῆς. f.ʃ

duly married female spouse: 4M 2.11. Cf. γυνή: Schmidt 2.397f.; Shipp 186f.

γαμέω: aor. ἐγάμησα, inf. γῆμαι, ptc. γήμας.ʃ

to enter marital relationship: *s* man, abs. 2M 14.25, + acc. pers. (fem.), Es F 3 o'. Cf. γαμικός, γάμος, γαμβρεύω, συνοικέω, ~οικίζω: Shipp 187; Kilpatrick 1990.187f.

γαμικός, ή, όν.ʃ

pertaining to marriage: *s* παστός 'bridal chamber' 3M 4.6.

γάμος, ου. m.

wedding-feast: ἐποίησεν ~ον 'held a wedding reception' Ge 29.22; pl., celebrations associated with wedding, Es 2.18 o', To 9.2 𝔊II (𝔊I sg.), sg. 11.19 𝔊I. Cf. γαμέω, νύμφευσις: Shipp 187f.

γάρ.

Never clause-initial, usually second position in clause.

1. Indicates a reason or provides an explanation of the preceding statement: Noah and his family are told to enter the ark with animals ἔτι γὰρ ἡμερῶν ἑπτὰ ἐγὼ ἐπάγω ὑετόν 'for in seven more days I shall bring rain down' Ge 7.4; "my soul will grieve for them, καὶ γὰρ αἱ ψυχαὶ αὐτῶν ἐπωρύοντο ἐπ' ἐμέ 'for their souls also howled over me'" Zc 11.8; Θύσατε ἀνθρώπους, μόσχοι γὰρ ἐκλελοίπασι 'Sacrifice humans, for bulls have died out' Ho 13.2; "Jethro .. heard all that the Lord had done to Israel .." ἐξήγαγεν γὰρ κύριος τὸν Ισραηλ ἐξ Αἰγύπτου 'namely, the Lord ..' Ex 18.1. **b.** in a reply to a question introduced by τί ὅτι 'why?' Ge 26.9.

2. See under εἰ.

3. Indicates what would ensue when that which is indicated in a preceding statement becomes a reality: Is 13.10, 15.

4. καὶ γάρ introduces an additional statement, which also explains the preceding: "Become farmers now. καὶ γὰρ πλοῖα οὐκέτι ἔρχεται ἐκ Καρχηδόνος 'besides, ships are not going to arrive from Carthage any more'" Is 23.10; Ps 40.10, 83.4. ***b.** asseverative, *indeed*, *surely*: κεκράξονται, καὶ γὰρ ὑμνήσουσιν Ps 64.14; γῆ ἐσείσθη, καὶ γὰρ οἱ οὐρανοὶ ἔσταξαν 'the earth shook, indeed the sky dripped' 67.9 (|| Jd 5.4 v.l. καὶ γὲ ἔσταξεν .. καὶ γὲ ..), καὶ γ. καὶ Ασσουρ 'indeed even A.' Ps 82.9; 15.6, 18.12, 57.3, 61.3, 70.22, 76.18, 95.10, 118.23, 24, 138.10.

Cf. ὅτι.

γαστήρ, τρός. f.

belly: of a woman, ἐν ~ρὶ ἔχω 'to be pregnant' Ge 16.4, Ex 21.22, Ho 14.1, Is 7.14, so Hdt. 3.32, ἐκ πορνείας Ge 38.24, || συλλαμβάνω Jd 13.3 A || B; λαμβάνω ἐν ~ρί 'to become pregnant' Ge 25.21, Ex 2.2, Is 8.3, *s* hum. male, Nu 11.12 (|| τίκτω), ἐξ αὐτοῦ 'by him' Ge 38.18; || κοιλία 25.23, Jd 13.5B, || μήτρα Ps 57.4; ἐκ ~ὸς μητρός μου 'from the time when I was still in my mother's womb' 138.13. **b**. the destination of consumed food: πληρῶσαι ~ρα αὐτοῦ 'fills his belly' Jb 20.23, τοὺς ~ὸς ἕνεκεν τὰ θεῖα παραβεβηκότας 'those who have transgressed the divine injunctions for the love of their belly' 3M 7.11.

Cf. κοιλία, μήτρα, συλλαμβάνω: Spicq 1.294.

γαστριμαργία, ας. f.ʃ

gluttony: 4M 1.3. Cf. γαστρίμαργος.

γαστρίμαργος, ον.ʃ

gluttonous: 4M 2.7. Cf. γαστριμαργία.

γαυρίαμα, ατος. n.ʃ *

1. *boasting*: Jb 4.10; of Goliath, Si 47.4.

2. *that which awakens a sense of pride*: Si 43.1; Ju 10.8, σὺ γ. μέγα τοῦ Ισραηλ 15.9.

Cf. γαυριάω, ἀλαζονεία: Schmidt 4.214-6.

γαυριάω: aor. ἐγαυρίασα, subj. γαυριάσω.ʃ

to act with a sense of pride: Jb 39.21; γαυριᾷ τόξον καὶ μάχαιρα 'a bow and a sword are proudly displayed' 39.23; ἐν βραχίονι πεζῶν '.. the force of infantry' Ju 9.7; ἐπὶ κακίᾳ Si 11.16¶; mid., Si 22.8¶; as victors, 2K 1.20*L* (B: ἀγαλλιάομαι 'to exult'). Cf. γαυριόω, ἀγαυριάομαι, καυχάομαι.

γαυριόω: fut.mid. γαυριωθήσομαι.ʃ *

to bear oneself proudly, prance: *s* lion, Nu 23.24. Cf. γαυρίαμα, γαυριάω, γαυρόω.

γαυρόω: aor.ptc.mid. γαυρωθείς; pf.ptc.mid. γεγαυρωμένος.ʃ

= γαυριόω: *s* king, + dat., τῇ εὐημερίᾳ 'over the success' 3M 3.11; over innumerable troops, 6.5; ἐπὶ ὄχλοις ἐθνῶν 'over many nations' Wi 6.2.

Cf. γαυριάω.

γέ

Never clause-initial and gives prominence to the preceding constituent: ἆρά γε: Ge 18.13, 37.10; ἄρα 26.9, Je 4.10; καὶ προβιβάσαι γε ἔδωκεν αὐτῷ 'also gave him the ability to instruct' Ex 35.34; καί γε / καίγε Jd 1.3A, Ru 2.15, 1K 18.5, La 1.8, 2.9, 3.8, Jb 30.2¶; εἰ δὲ μή γε Da 3.15, Bel 8 LXX. **b**. καί γε preceded by a negator: κ. γ. ἕνα '(not) even one' 2K 17.12B. **c**. foll. by a redundant καί: καί γε καὶ Ιουδας 4K 17.19. **d**. καί γε .. καὶ .. 'both .. and ..': Ru 1.5, Ec 2.8. **e**. ἔγωγε 'even I': contrary to what might be expected, 4M 8.10.

Cf. Barthélemy1963.31-47.

γεῖσος, ους. n. *

projecting part: 'cornice' Je 52.22; of slaughtering-table, Ez 40.43.

γειτνιάω.ʃ

to be adjacent: + dat., Su TH 4, 2M 9.25. Cf. γείτων.

γείτων, ονος. m.

neighbour: || σύσκηνος Ex 3.22; γ. πλησίον 'next door neighbour' 12.4; + πλησίον Je 6.21; || ἀδελφός 29.11. Cf. γειτνιάω, πλησίον, σύσκηνος.

γειώρας. ⇒ γιώρας.

γελάω: fut. γελάσω, mid. γελάσομαι; aor. ἐγέλασα, subj. γελάσω.

to laugh: in disbelief, ἐγέλασεν καὶ εἶπεν ἐν τῇ διανοίᾳ Ge 17.17; ἐγέλασεν ἐν ἑαυτῇ 18.12, cf. ἐγέλασσε δέ οἱ φίλον ἦτορ 'he laughed within himself' Hom., *Il*. 21.389. **b**. in derision: πικρῷ λόγῳ 'with a sharp tongue' Je 20.8; + ἐπί τινι (rei) La 1.7; + ἐπί τινα Ps 51.8; + dat. rei, Jb 19.7; 22.19 (|| μυκτηρίζω); κατ' ἐμοῦ τοῦτον τὸν γέλωτα 4M 5.28. **c**. friendly gesture, 'to smile': + πρός τινα Jb 29.24.

Cf. γέλως, γελοιάζω, ἐκ~, ἐπι~, κατα~, προσ~, συγγελάω, μειδιάω, μυκτηρίζω: Schmidt 4.188f.; Rengstorf, *TDNT* 1.658-62.

γελοιάζω.ʃ

to jest, joke: ἔδοξεν γελοιάζειν 'he appeared to be joking' Ge 19.14. Cf. γελάω, γελοιασμός, γελοιαστής, μωκάομαι. On the word-formation, see BDF § 108, 3.

γελοιασμός, οῦ. m.ʃ

butt of jesting: εἰς ~ὸν ἦν Je 31.27 (|| γέλως). Cf. γελοιάζω.

γελοιαστής, οῦ. m.ʃ

jester: Jb 31.5. Cf. γελοιάζω.

γελοῖος, α, ον.

deserving of being laughed at, 'ludicrous': *s* deed, 4M 1.5; argument, 3.1. Cf. Schmidt 4.189f.

γέλως, ωτος. m.

1. *laughter*: βωμοὶ τοῦ ~τος 'joyous altars' Am 7.9; derisive, as cogn. obj. of γελάω 4M 5.28.

2. happy *occasion of laughter*: ~τά μοι ἐποίησεν κύριος 'the Lord gave me food for laughter' Ge 21.6; Ec 10.19.

3. *laughing-stock*: Je 20.7; || γελοιασμός 31.26, ψαλμός La 3.14, || θρύλημα Jb 17.6; || παραβολὴ ὀνειδισμοῦ 'the butt of insult' Wi 5.3.

Cf. γελάω, εὐφροσύνη, τέρψις, χαρά, καταγέλως.

γεμίζω: aor.impv. γέμισον, ptc. γεμίσας.ʃ

caus. of γέμω, *to fill*: + acc. rei, πορεῖα 'pack animals' Ge 45.17; and + dat. rei, 3M 5.47. Cf. γέμω, πίμπλημι: Shipp 192f.

γέμω.

to be fully loaded: *s* beast of burden or wagon and + gen. of load, αἱ κάμηλοι αὐτῶν ἔγεμον θυμιαμάτων .. 'their camels were fully laden with spices ..' Ge 37.25; ἡ ἅμαξα ἡ γέμουσα καλάμης 'the wagon laden with straw' Am 2.13; ἀρᾶς τὸ στόμα αὐτοῦ γέμει '.. is full of curses' Ps 9.28, δέους καὶ ταραχῆς 'of fear and disturbance' 2M 3.30.

Cf. γεμίζω, πίμπλημι, πλήρης, πληρόω.

γενεά, ᾶς. f.

1. *period of time in which a whole body of people born about same time live*, 'generation': τὰ τέκνα αὐτῶν εἰς ~ὰν ἑτέραν Jl 1.3; ἕως ἐτῶν εἰς ~ὰς ~ῶν 'for generations of years' 2.2; εἰς ~ὰς ~ῶν 3.20, cf. De 32.7 (ǁ ἡμέραι αἰῶνος); εἰς γενεὰς αἰωνίους 'for eternal generations' Ge 9.12, εἰς ~άς 'for generations to come' Is 34.10; εἰς τὰς ~ὰς ὑμῶν Ex 12.14; μνημόσυνον ~ῶν ~αῖς 'a memory for many generations to come' 3.15; Is 58.12; τίς διηγήσεται τὴν ~ὰν αὐτου; 'who is going to tell his life-story?' 53.8; εἰς ~ὰν καὶ ~άν 'for many generations' La 5.19, ἀπὸ ~ᾶς εἰς ~άν Ps 9.27.

2. *whole body of people born about same time*, 'contemporaries,' always used collectively: Ge 6.9, 7.1.

3. *whole body of blood-relations*: Ge 43.7; εἰς τὴν γῆν μου καὶ εἰς τὴν ~άν μου Nu 10.30; γενεαὶ Ενακ 13.23.

4. *birthplace*: Ge 31.3 (ǁ ἡ γῆ τοῦ πατρός σου and 31.13, 32.9 ἡ γῆ γενέσεώς σου); Le 25.41.

5. *single step in descent*: ἕως τρίτης ~ᾶς Ge 50.23.

6. *that which is produced*, 'product': Pr 22.4.

Cf. αἰών, γένεσις, γενεαλογέω.

γενεαλογέω: aor.pass. ἐγενεαλογήθην.ʃ

to trace a pedigree of: pass., εἰς πρωτοτόκια 'back to the rank of first-born' 1C 5.1. Cf. γενεά.

γενέθλιος, ον.ʃ

pertaining to birth: γ. ἡμέρα 'birthday' 2M 6.7. Cf. γένεσις.

γένειον, ου. n.ʃ

chin: 4M 9.28, 15.15. Cf. LSG s.v.

γενεσιάρχης, ου. m.ʃ*

creator: *s* God, τοῦ κάλλους 'of the beauty' Wi 13.3. Cf. κτίστης, γενεσιουργός.

γενεσιουργός, οῦ. m.ʃ

concerned with the act of generating: subst.m., *creator*, *s* God, Wi 13.5 (ǁ γενεσιάρχης). Cf. γενεσιάρχης.

γένεσις, εως. f.

1. *coming into being*: ἡ βίβλος ~εως οὐρανοῦ καὶ γῆς 'the chapter concerning the emergence of heaven and earth' Ge 2.4; εἰς τὴν γῆν τῆς ~εώς σου 'to the land of your birth' 31.13 (ǁ γενεά vs. 3), 32.9; ἡμέρα ~εως αὐτῆς 'the day when she was born' Ho 2.3, sim. Ge 40.20; κατὰ τὰς ~εις αὐτῶν 'according to their date of birth,' i.e. from the oldest to the youngest Ex 28.10; ǁ ῥίζα 'origin' Ez 16.3. **b**. *reproductive system*: ~εως ἐναλλαγή 'interchange of sex roles' Wi 14.26. **c**. *family tie*: 4M 15.25.

2. *physical existence and living*: πᾶσαι αἱ ἡμέραι τῆς ~εώς μου 'all my life so far' Ju 12.18. **b**. *that which came into being and exists*: pl., the universe and nature, Wi 1.14; coll. sg., 'offspring' 18.12.

3. pl., *a listing of descendants in chronological order*, 'genealogy': αὗται δὲ αἱ ~εις τῶν υἱῶν Νωε 'the following is the genealogy of Noah's descendants' Ge 10.1; Ex 6.24.

Cf. γενεά, γενέθλιος, γενετή, γενέτις, γέννησις, γίνομαι.

γενετή, ῆς. f.ʃ

time of birth: ἐκ ~ῆς προσήλυτος 'προσήλυτος by birth' Le 25.47; ἐκ ~ῆς μου Es C 16 o'. Cf. γενεά: Shipp 193.

γενέτις, ιδος. f.ʃ

one who brings into existence: + obj. gen., Wi 7.12. Cf. γένεσις.

γένημα, ατος. n. Also γέννημα; on the orthographical differentiation and its possible semantic implications, see Thack. § 7.38.

that which is produced, 'product, produce': agricultural produce, ἀγροῦ De 14.21; πάντα τὰ ~ατα τῆς γῆς Αἰγύπτου Ge 41.34 (ǁ βρώματα vs. 35); τὰ ~ατα τῆς γῆς σου De 28.4 (ǁ καρπός 7.13); ἀγρῶν 32.13; ἡ γῆ δώσει τὰ ~ατα αὐτῆς 'the earth will yield its produce' Zc 8.12 (ǁ καρπός); σπέρματος De 14.21; τὸ γ. καὶ τὸ σπέρμα .. ἀμπελῶνος 22.9; ~ατα ἐν ἀμπέλοις Hb 3.17; ἀπὸ παντὸς ~ατος ἐμπορευσόμεθα 'we shall trade in every kind of produce' Am 8.6; ǁ καρπός Le 19.25, De 26.2 (see vs. 10); fig., ~ατα δικαιοσύνης Ho 10.12, τῶν ἔργων αὐτῶν Is 3.10; *s* hum., Si 10.18 (ǁ ἄνθρωποι), 1M 1.38 (ǁ τέκνον). Cf. καρπός, ἐκφόριον: Preisigke, s.v.; Lee 99; Shipp 193; Georgacas 118.

γενικός, ή, όν.ʃ

pertaining to birth: ~ὴ γραφή 'genealogy, birth certificate' 1E 5.49.

γενναῖος, α, ον.

noble of mind or *character*: *s* ὑπόδειγμα 'example' 2M 6.28; φρόνημα 'thought' 7.21; ἀθλητής 'athlete' 4M 6.10; martyr's blood, 7.8; ἀγών 'struggle' 16.16. Cf. γενναιότης, γενναίως.

γενναιότης, ητος. f.ʃ

nobility of mind or character: 2M 6.31; τῆς πίστεως 4M 17.2. Cf. γενναῖος.

γενναίως. adv.

1. *nobly*: τεθνηκέναι 'to have died' 1M 4.35, + προθύμως καὶ γ. 'eagerly and ..' 2M 6.28.

2. *in a manner conducive to maximum effects*: 2M 14.31.

γεννάω: fut. γεννήσω, pass. γεννηθήσομαι; aor. ἐγέννησα, 3pl. ἐγεννῶσαν, ptc. γεννήσας, subj. γεννήσω, inf. γεννῆσαι, pass. ἐγεννήθην, subj. γεννηθῶ, ptc. γεννηθείς; pf. γεγέννηκα, pass. γεγέννημαι, ptc. γεγεννηκώς, pass. γεγεννημένος.

to bring forth, bring into existence: ***o*** hum. child, υἱοὺς καὶ υἱοὺς τῶν υἱῶν 'sons and grandsons' De 4.25; τέκνα ἀλλότρια ἐγεννήθησαν αὐτοῖς 'bastards were born to them' Ho 5.7; 9.16; nations, δώδεκα ἔθνη Ge 17.20; *s* parents, ὁ πατὴρ αὐτοῦ καὶ ἡ μήτηρ αὐτοῦ οἱ γεννήσαντες αὐτόν Zc 13.3; father, μετὰ τὸ γεννῆσαι αὐτὸν τὸν Ενως 'after he begot Enosh' Ge 5.7, Je 16.3 (latter || τίκτω *s* mother), 2C 24.3, ὁ γεννήσας 'the begetter' Si 22.4, ἐξ αὐτῆς To 1.9; τὰ ἔκγονα, ἃ ἐὰν γεννήσῃς Ge 48.6; God, Ps 2.7, θεὸν τὸν γεννήσαντά σε De 32.18 (|| τὸν ποιήσαντα αὐτόν vs. 15); *s* animals Ez 31.6, wisdom Pr 8.25 (|| κτίζω vs. 22). Cf. γένημα, γέννησις, γεννητός, γεννήτωρ, ἔκγονος, γίνομαι, ἀποκυέω, κτίζω, λοχεύομαι, τίκτω: Schmidt 4.62f., 76-9; Büchsel, *TDNT* 1.668f.

γέννημα. ⇒ γένημα.

γέννησις, εως. f.ʃ

1. v.n. of γεννάω: Si 22.3.

2. *offspring*: 1C 4.8.

Cf. γένεσις.

γεννητός, ή, όν.

born, begotten: subst.m., γ. γυναικός 'hum. being' Jb 11.2+, and only in Jb. Cf. γεννάω.

γεννήτωρ, ορος. m.ʃ

begetter, 'parent': || συγγένεια Si 22.7¶.

γένος, ους. n.

1. *division into which entities are classified*, 'kind, sort, species': κατὰ γένος 'in accordance with species' Ge 1.11; κατὰ γένη αὐτῶν ib. 21; κατὰ γ. αὐτῶν ib. 25, 8.19; πάντα τὰ θηρία κατὰ γ. 'all the animals per species' 7.14; γ. ἓν καὶ χεῖλος ἕν 11.6.

2. *society of individuals with common beliefs and ancestry*: ἐξολεθρευθήσεται ἡ ψυχὴ ἐκείνη ἐκ τοῦ ~ους αὐτῆς Ge 17.14; 25.17 (|| λαός vs. 8 w. ref. to Israelites, see Rösel 236f.), τὸ γ. μου τὸ ἐκλεκτόν Is 43.20 (|| λαός); "I shall be God of γ. Ισραηλ and they shall be λαός for me" Je 38.1; τις τοῦ ~ους μου 'someone of my household' Ge 26.10; τὸ γ. τῶν υἱῶν Ισραηλ Ex 1.9 (|| ἔθνος), 5.14; γ. Ἰουδαίων Es 5.23 *L*; a priestly class, Le 21.13; ἀπὸ ~ους τοῦ βασιλέως 'of royal lineage' Je 48.1, ἐκ τοῦ βασιλικοῦ ~ους Da 1.3 LXX (TH σπέρμα); τὸ γ. Ἰουδαῖος 'Jew by descent' 3M 1.3, τὸ γ. ἱερεύς 'priest by birth' 4M 5.4; || ὁ ὅμοιός τινος Si 13.16.

3. *offspring*: pl., hum., || γονεῖς 'parents' 4M 15.13.

Cf. ἔθνος, λαός: Jones 1996.

γεραιός, ά, όν.

aged: *s* hum., subst., + πρεσβύτερος 3M 1.23; opp. νήπιος 'infant' 3.27. Cf. γέρων.

γεραίρω.ʃ

mid. *to celebrate*: εἰς εὐφροσύνην 'for fun's sake' 3M 5.17.

γέρας, ως. n.ʃ

1. *honour*: δεύτερον γ. 'the second highest position' Es B 3.

2. *reward*: ψυχῶν ἀμώμων 'due to blameless souls' Wi 2.22 (|| μισθός).

3. *perquisite* received by priests at sacrifices (LSJ): Nu 18.8.

Cf. δόμα.

γερουσία, ας. f.

assembly of elders: a decision-making body in ancient Israel, συνάγαγε τὴν ~αν τῶν υἱῶν Ισραηλ Ex 3.16; 24.9 (|| πρεσβύτεροι vs. 1); Le 9.1 (|| priests), De 5.23 (|| ἡγούμενοι); 21.2 (|| κριταί); 29.10 (|| ἀρχίφυλοι, κριταί, γραμματοεισαγωγεῖς) at the city gate, 22.15; πόλεως 25.8; παντὸς δήμου Ισραηλ Ju 4.8, τῶν Ἰουδαίων 2M 11.27. Cf. πρεσβύτερος: LSG s.v. and Dorival 1996.535.

γέρων, οντος. m.

old man: Jb 32.9 (|| πολυχρόνιος), Si 25.5 (|| πρεσβύτερος vs. 4). **b**. *member of* γερουσία, 'senator': 2M 6.1, but cf. Wilhelm 20-2.

Cf. γεραιός, πρεσβύτερος, νέος.

γεῦμα, ατος. n.

taste: Ex 16.31; εἰ δὲ καὶ γ. ἐν ῥήμασιν κενοῖς; 'is there taste in empty words at all?' Jb 6.6; εἰληφὼς γ. τῆς τῶν Ἰουδαίων εὐτολμίας 'having had a taste of the daring of the Jews' 2M 13.18; || ὀσμή 'smell' Je 31.11. Cf. γεύω, γεῦσις.

γεῦσις, εως. f.

1. *that which is to be tasted*: food, ξένη 'unfamiliar' Wi 16.2, 3.

2. *act of tasting*: οἴνου Da TH 5.2 (|| πίνω LXX ib.).

Cf. γεύω, γεῦμα.

γεύω: fut. γεύσομαι; aor.act.impv. γεῦσον, mid. ἐγευσάμην, impv.3pl. γευσάσθωσαν, subj. γεύσωμαι, inf. γεύσασθαι, ptc. γευσάμενος.

to give a taste of: + acc. pers., γεῦσόν με ἀπὸ τοῦ ἑψέματος τοῦ πυρροῦ τούτου 'Give me a taste of that red boiled stuff' Ge 25.30. **b**. mid. *to taste* foodstuff, *take* food *and feed oneself with*: abs. 'to dine' To 2.4 𝔊I; + acc. rei, μὴ γευσάσθωσαν μηδὲν μηδὲ νεμέσθωσαν μηδὲ ὕδωρ πιέτωσαν Jn 3.7, λάρυγξ σῖτα γεύεται 'a palate tastes foods' Jb 12.11, φάρυγξ γεύεται βρώματα θήρας '.. various kinds of meat of game' Si 36.24; To 7.11 𝔊I (|| ἐσθίω 𝔊II); +

neg. for fasting, + gen. rei, ἄρτου οὐκ ἐγεύσατο οὐδὲ ὕδωρ ἔπιεν 1E 9.2 (*s* mourner), + ἀπό τινος – ἄρτου ἢ ἀπὸ παντός τινος 2K 3.35 (*L* om. ἀπό). **b**. fig., 'to experience': + acc. rei, καρδία συνετὴ (sc. γεύεται) λόγους ψευδεῖς Si 36.24; + ἔκ τινος – πλοῦτον, ἐξ οὗ οὐ γεύσεται 'wealth which he will not enjoy' Jb 20.18; *+ a ὅτι-clause, ἐγεύσατο ὅτι καλόν ἐστι τὸ ἐργάζεσθαι 'he found out by experience that it is good to work' Pr 31.18, cf. γεύσασθε καὶ ἴδετε ὅτι χρηστὸς ὁ κύριος '.. that the Lord is kind' Ps 33.9 (quoted without καὶ ἴδετε at 1Pet 2.3, cf. BDAG, s.v.).

Cf. ἀπογεύομαι, γεῦμα, ἐσθίω: Behm, *TDNT* 1.675-7.

γέφυρα, ας. f.∫

dyke: Is 37.25. Cf. Beekes.

γεώδης, ες.∫

pertaining to the earth: *s* σκῆνος 'tent' (= hum. body) Wi 9.15, ὕλη '(soil as) material' 15.13. Cf. γῆ.

γεωμετρία, ας. f.∫

land-survey: Is 34.11.

γεωμετρικός, ή, όν.∫

**pertaining to land-surveying*: σχοινίον ~όν 'land-surveyor's measuring-line' Zc 2.1. Cf. μέτρον and γῆ.

γεωργέω.

to work at as farmer: + acc., γῆν 1E 4.6.

γεωργία, ας. f.∫

agricultural work, farming: Si 7.15, 2M 12.1.

γεώργιον, ου. n.

1. *agricultural field*: nomad's property, κτήνη προβάτων καὶ κτήνη βοῶν καὶ ~ια πολλά '.. and many fields' Ge 26.14; γεωργὸν καὶ τὸ γ. αὐτοῦ Je 28.23.

2. *husbandry*: ξύλου 'of (fruit-)trees' Si 27.6.

Cf. ἀγρός, γῆ.

γεωργός, όν.

subst. *one who cultivates land*, 'farmer': ἄνθρωπος ~ὸς γῆς Ge 9.20; ἀνὴρ γ. 49.15; κληθήσεται γ. εἰς πένθος 'a farmer will be called upon to act as (professional) mourner' Am 5.16; ‖ ποιμήν 'shepherd' Wi 17.17, Je 28.23; ‖ ἀμπελουργός 'vine-dresser' 52.16. Cf. γεωργός, γεωργία, γῆ, ἀμπελουργός, παγγέωργος, ποιμήν.

γῆ, ῆς, pl. γεῶν, f.

1. *land and sea*, opp. sky: ἀνὰ μέσον τῆς γῆς καὶ ἀνὰ μέσον τοῦ οὐρανοῦ Zc 5.9; συσκοτάσει ἐπὶ τῆς γῆς ἐν ἡμέρᾳ τὸ φῶς 'the light (shining) upon the earth will lose its brightness' Am 8.9; cf. τὸν οὐρανὸν καὶ τὴν γῆν καὶ τὴν θάλασσαν καὶ τὴν ξηράν Hg 2.6, 21 (comprising the whole physical universe).

2. *subterranean space*: κατέβη εἰς γῆν Jn 2.7.

3. *lower level and surface*: ταπεινῶν ἕως τῆς γῆς 'lowering to the ground' Ps 146.6.

4. *land, ground*, opp. sea: name given to the dry land at the creation of the universe, Ge 1.10; θηρία τῆς γῆς Zp 2.14; Jn 1.13; also opp. sky, ἐποίησεν κύριος τὸν οὐρανὸν καὶ τὴν γῆν καὶ τὴν θάλασσαν καὶ πάντα τὰ ἐν αὐτοῖς Ex 20.11. **b**. sphere of human habitation: τοὺς κατοικοῦντας τὴν γῆν Zp 1.18. **c**. the entire inhabited sphere, 'the world': πάντα τὰ ἔθνη τῆς γῆς Ge 22.18; πάντας τοὺς θεοὺς τῶν ἐθνῶν τῆς γῆς Zp 2.11; ἐν πᾶσι τοῖς λαοῖς τῆς γῆς 3.20; ‖ ἄνθρωποι Hb 2.17; ‖ ἔθνη 3.12. **d**. belonging to or inhabited by a particular ethnic group or nation, often w. a qualifying adjective or gen.: γ. Σεναααρ Ge 11.2; ἐκ τῆς γῆς σου 12.1; Αἰγύπτου 21.21; Ex 11.6 (‖ γῆ Αἴγυπτος vs. 5); Αἰγύπτων Ho 12.9; Βαβυλῶνος Zc 5.11; γ. Χανααν Ge 16.3 ‖ τῶν Χαναναίων Ob 20; ἀλλοφύλων 'of foreign ethnic groups' Zp 2.5; θελητή 'desirable' Ma 3.12; γῆς βορρᾶ 'northern region' Zc 6.8. **e**. agricultural land: τὸν καρπὸν τῆς γῆς Ma 3.11; ἐργαζόμενος τὴν γῆν 'working the land' Ge 4.2, Zc 13.5; ἄνθρωπος γεωργὸς γῆς Ge 9.20. **f**. in contrast to floored surface: προσεκύνησεν ἐπὶ τὴν γῆν 'prostrated on the ground, threw himself on to the ground' Ge 18.2.

5. *area, region*: οὐδείς ἐστιν ἐπὶ τῆς γῆς .. 'there is nobody in this area ..' Ge 19.31; εἰς γῆν πρὸς λίβα 'into the southern region' 20.1; εἰς τὴν γῆν τὴν ὑψηλήν 22.2; ἀπέλθω εἰς τὸν τόπον μου καὶ εἰς τὴν γῆν μου 30.25.

6. *population inhabiting the earth*: κρίνων πᾶσαν τὴν γῆν Ge 18.25; εὐλαβείσθω ἀπὸ προσώπου αὐτοῦ πᾶσα ἡ γῆ 'let all the earth fear him' Hb 2.20; πᾶσα ἡ γῆ ‖ πᾶσα σάρξ 'all mankind' Is 66.16; Je 34.5.

7. *fine particles lying on ground*, 'dust': food for snakes, fig. of land-crawling creatures, Ge 3.14, cf. ὄφις (sc. φάγεται) γῆν ὡς ἄρτον Is 65.25; substance from which man is made, and thus his origin (cf. LSG, s.v.), γῆ εἶ καὶ εἰς γῆν ἀπελεύσῃ Ge 3.19, cf. Si 17.1, 36.10, To 3.6, and τῆς γῆς τυγχάνω of burial upon death at 2M 13.7; θυσιαστήριον ἐκ γῆς ποιήσετέ μοι Ex 20.24; γῆν καταπάσασθε καταγέλωτα ὑμῶν 'Sprinkle your laughable object with dust' Mi 1.10; in self-depreciation, ἐγώ εἰμι γῆ καὶ σποδός 'I am soil and dust' Ge 18.27; fig. of large quantity, Jb 27.16.

Cf. γαῖα, γεώδης, γεωμετρικός, γεωργός, θάλασσα, ξηρός, οὐρανός, τόπος (for **4**), ἔδαφος: Schmidt 3.57-60.

γηγενής, ές.

earthborn: subst., υἱὸς ~οῦς 'a son of an earthborn being' Je 30.11 (‖ ἄνθρωπος), 39.20, ~οῦς ἀπόγονος 'descendant of ..' Wi 7.1; ~εῖς Ps 48.3 (‖ οἱ υἱοὶ τῶν ἀνθρώπων).

γῆρας, gen. ους/ως, dat. ~ει, ~ᾳ. n.; Thack 149f.
a phase of life when one is old, 'old age': dying ἐν γήρει καλῷ 'in good old age' Ge 15.15, 25.8; ἐν τῷ γήρει μου 21.7; ἕως ~ους καὶ πρεσβείου Ps 70.18; υἱὸς ~ους 'a son (born) in (father's) old age' Ge 37.3; παιδίον γήρως 44.20; metonymically (Wevers), κατάξετέ μου τὸ γ. μετὰ λύπης εἰς ᾅδου 'you are going to send this old man in sorrow ..' 42.38, 44.29; eye-sight failing, 48.10; opp. νεότης Si 25.3. Cf. γέρων: Byl.

γηράσκω, γηράω: fut. γηράσω; aor. ἐγήρασα, inf. γηρᾶσαι, subj. γηράσω; pf. γεγήρακα.
to become old: in age and *s* hum., Ge 18.13, τοῦ μὴ εἶναι ἀνδρί 'too old to marry a man' Ru 1.12; ἡλικία 'age of a hum.' Jb 29.18; root of a plant, 14.8. Cf. γέρων, γῆρας, κατα~, συγ~, συγκαταγηράω.

γηροβοσκέω: aor. ἐγηροβόσκησα.ʃ
to look after in old age: + acc. pers., To 14.13 $\mathfrak{G}^{II}$.

γῆρος. n. = γῆρας, q.v.

γίγαρτον, ου. n.ʃ
grape-stone: Nu 6.4.

γίγας, αντος. m.
giant: of the primaeval era, Ge 6.4 (called <u>ἄνθρωποι</u> ὀνομαστοί); 10.8; of the post-primaeval era and terrifying, 14.5; Nu 13.34 (opp. ἀκρίδες 'grasshoppers'). **b**. *person wielding enormous power*: ~τα καὶ ἰσχύοντα Is 3.2; ‖ ἄρχων Ez 39.18, ‖ βασιλεύς Ps 32.16, συναγωγὴ ~ων Pr 21.16; warriors, Is 13.3, μαχαῖραι ~ων Ez 32.12; ὑψηλὸς γ. Ju 16.6 (‖ τίταν).
Cf. Schmitt 152f.

γίνομαι: pres.impv.sg. γίνου; fut. γενήσομαι, γενηθήσομαι, ptc. γενησόμενος; aor. ἐγενόμην, ἐγενήθην, inf. γενέσθαι, γενηθῆναι, ptc. γενόμενος, γενηθείς, impv. γενοῦ, 3s γενηθήτω, 3pl γενέσθωσαν, subj. γένωμαι, γενηθῶ, opt. γενοίμην, 3s γένοιτο; pf. γέγονα, 3pl γεγόνασιν, ptc. γεγονώς, mid. γεγένημαι, inf. γεγενῆσθαι, ptc. γεγενημένος; plpf.3s ἐγεγόνει.

1. *to happen, take place*: καὶ ἔγενετο οὕτως 'it so happened' Ge 1.6; ἐγενήθη αὐτοῖς οὕτως 42.25; ἐπ' ἐμὲ ἐγένετο πάντα ταῦτα 42.36; *s* μάχη 'strife' 13.7; κρίσις 'a court case' Hb 1.3; ἀνομίαι Ez 9.4; μὴ γένηται τὸ ῥῆμα καὶ μὴ συμβῇ 'what has been said does not materialise and happen' De 18.22; *s* inf., Ne 6.16; + dat. pers. and inf., μὴ γένοιτο τοῖς παισίν σου ποιῆσαι κατὰ τὸ ῥῆμα τοῦτο 'God forbid that thy servants should act in such a way' Ge 44.7; 44.17, 3K 20.3, 1M 13.5; + acc. pers. and inf., μὴ γένοιτο ἡμᾶς ἀποστραφῆναι .. Jo 22.29 (‖ ἡμῖν 24.16); + inf. alone, 1M 9.10; Γένοιτο, γένοιτο 'So be it, so be it; Hear!, hear!' (an expression of concurrence) Nu 5.22, Ps 71.19, Si 50.29¶, Ju 13.20, sim. De 27.15-26.

2. *to come into existence, emerge*: Γενηθήτω φῶς, καὶ ἐγένετο φῶς 'Let there be light! ..' Ge 1.3, cf. Alexandre 89f.; καὶ ἐγένετο ἑσπέρα καὶ ἐγένετο πρωΐ 'and there came an evening and a morning' 1.8; ἐγένετο ὁ ὑετὸς ('rain') ἐπὶ τῆς γῆς 7.12; κατακλυσμός 'flood' 7.17, λιμός 'famine' 12.10, ἀκρίς 'locusts' Ex 10.14, σκότος 'darkness' 10.21, κλύδων μέγας 'a billow' Jn 1.4; "when you cast into a barley container 20 measures, there come out (only) ten measures of barley (ἐγένετο κριθῆς δέκα σάτα)" Hg 2.16; ποῦ ἐστιν ἡ πόρνη ἡ γενομένη ἐν Αιναν ..; 'where is the harlot who made her appearance in Ainan ..?' Ge 38.21; οἱ προφῆται οἱ γεγονότες πρότεροί μου 'the prophets who preceded me' Je 35.8; ‖ κτίζομαι Ex 9.24 (see ἔκτισται vs. 18), Ps 32.9, 148.5, ‖ πλάσσομαι 89.2; κολυμβήθρα γεγονυία 'artificial pool' Ne 3.16. **b**. 'to be born', ἐν τῇ γῇ, ᾗ ἐγενήθη 'in the land in which he was born' Ge 11.28; εἰς τὴν γῆν μου, οὗ ἐγενόμην 'my homeland' 24.4 (‖ ἐγενήθην vs. 7); + dat. pers., ἐγενήθη τῷ Ενωχ Γαιδαδ 'G. was born to E.' 4.18; τοῦ υἱοῦ αὐτοῦ τοῦ γενομένου αὐτῷ, ὃν ἔτεκεν αὐτῷ Σάρρα 21.3. **c**. + dat. pers., 'to acquire', ἐγένετο αὐτῷ κτήνη προβάτων .. Ge 26.14; ἐγένετο ἡ γῆ τῷ Φαραω 47.20. **d**. *to come up as a case for a debate*: Ἐὰν γένηται παῖς παρθένος .. καὶ εὑρὼν αὐτὴν ἄνθρωπος ἐν πόλει .. 'should it be a case of a young woman .. whom a man comes across in a city ..' De 22.23. **e**. ingressive of εἰμί 'to be present, situated (at a certain location)': 'to betake oneself,' ὅταν μέλλῃς γίνεσθαι μετ' αὐτῆς 'when you are about to join her in bed' To 6.18 $\mathfrak{G}^{II}$, ἐγενήθη ἐπὶ τὴν καρδίαν σου 3K 8.18 B (‖ ἦλθεν ἐπὶ τὴν καρδίαν σου), cf. συγγίνομαι; εἰς τὴν Περσίδα γενόμενος .. 'having entered Persia ..' 2M 1.13, γενομένου δέους ἐπὶ τοὺς πολεμίους 'fear having descerded upon the warriors' 12.22, σὺν τοῖς πρεσβυτέροις γενόμενος 'having got together with the elders' 13.13; Ez 31.13; ἐγενήθη ἐπ' ἐμὲ χεὶρ κυρίου 33.22, ἐγένοντό σοι ἐπὶ δυσμὰς δυσμῶν 'they went for you to the farthest west' 27.9, cf. ἐγίνετο ἐπὶ Γύνδῃ ποταμῷ Herod. 1.189; ὁ ὕπνος αὐτοῦ ἐγένετο ἀπ' αὐτοῦ 'he lost sleep' Da 2.1 TH; γενόμενοι ἀπὸ τῆς δεήσεως 'having come away from the prayer' 2M 10.27; περὶ τὴν γεωργίαν ἐγίνοντο 'went about their farming' 12.1. **f**. esp. in the standing expression ἐγένετο λόγος κύριου πρός PN, introducing a divine pronouncement to a human intermediary, Jn 1.1, 3.1; Zc 1.1; Hg 1.1, 3, 2.20; λόγος κυρίου, ὃς ἐγενήθη πρὸς Σοφονίαν Zp 1.1; of a prophetic message, Λόγοι Αμως, οἳ ἐγένοντο ἐν νακκαριμ Am 1.1; sim. with ῥῆμα, Ge 15.1, ἐπὶ Ιερεμίαν Je 1.1 (‖ vs. 2 λόγος .. πρὸς αὐτόν); with φωνὴ θεοῦ Ge 15.4; γενηθῆναι φωνὰς θεοῦ καὶ χάλαζαν καὶ πῦρ Ex 9.28; ἐγενήθη πνεῦμα θεοῦ ἐπ' αὐτῷ Nu 23.6 (|| ἐγένετο 24.2).

3. *to become, acquire the character of, be transformed into*: ποιμήν 'shepherd' Ge 4.2, στήλη ἁλός 'salt pillar' 19.26; τοξότης 'archer' 21.20; ἐγένετο γυνὴ αὐτοῦ 24.67; βδέλυγμα ἐγένετο 'he became abomination' Ma 2.11; ἐγένετο ἡ ζωὴ Σάρρας ἔτη ἑκατὸν εἴκοσι ἑπτά 'S.'s life-span came to 127 years' Ge 23.1; ὡς ἄνθος 'like a flower' Zp 2.2; καθὼς οἱ πατέρες ὑμῶν Zc 1.4; ἐγένετο οὕτως 'it became so' Ge 1.9; τὸ πρωῒ ἐγενήθη 'it dawned' Ex 10.13; + adj., ἵνα τί περίλυπος ἐγένου; 'why have you become sorrowful?' Ge 4.6; + ptc. w. adj. force, πεποιθὼς γίνου Si 2.5, πεποιθὼς ἐγένου Is 30.12, cf. γενέσθωσαν .. ἄτεκνοι .. ἀνῃρημένοι .. πεπτωκότες Je 18.21 (pf. ptc.). **b**. + εἰς (alr. in Cl.Gk, see LSJ s.v. **II 3 c** and LSG s.v.), εἰς ψυχὴν ζῶσαν Ge 2.7, ἐγένετο ἡ πλίνθος εἰς λίθον 'a brick served as stone' 11.3, εἰς ἔθνος μέγα καὶ πολύ 18.18, εἰς δύο παρεμβολάς 32.10, εἰς ἀφανισμόν Zp 3.1, εἰς πλησμονήν Is 1.14, cf. εἰμί **3**; + dat. pers., ἐγενήθη μοι εἰς γυναῖκα Ge 20.12 (|| ἐγένετο αὐτοῦ γυνή 24.67), ἐγενήθη αὐτῇ εἰς υἱόν Ex 2.10, ἐγενόμην τῷ Ισραηλ εἰς πατέρα Je 38.9. **c**. + πρός: Si 46.4. Cf. Renehan, 2.48. Opp. εἶναι–Ἐγένετο δὲ Αβραμ ἐτῶν ἐνενήκοντα ἐννέα Ge 17.1 || Αβραμ ἦν ὀγδοήκοντα ἓξ ἐτῶν 16.16; w. respect to the Aktionsart, ἔσομαι and γένωμαι have the same value, ἔσονται .. γυναῖκες .. οἷς ἂν γένωνται γυναῖκες Nu 36.3. Cf. παρ' ἐμοὶ γενοῦ 'Come near me!' Ge 23.11.

4. *to become allied* (w. sbd τινι): of marriage relationship, θυγάτηρ .. ἐὰν γένηται ἀνδρὶ ἀλλογενεῖ Le 22.12; ἀνδρὶ ἑτέρῳ De 24.2, Je 3.1; οὐδὲ μὴ γένῃ ἀνδρί Ho 3.3; Nu 36.11, cf. συγγίνομαι and BDAG, s.v. **9**, b.

5. *to set out* doing sth (ptc., mostly pres.), marking the onset of a new action or situation: ἐγινόμην .. συγκαιόμενος 'started .. getting burned' Ge 31.40, ἡ νεφέλη ἐγένετο σκιάζουσα 'the cloud started casting a shadow' Nu 10.36, γένηται .. μισῶν τὸν πλησίον αὐτοῦ De 19.11, ἐγένοντο λογιζόμενοι κόπους 'they set out devising troubles' Mi 2.1, but cf. Zgl with the apparatus criticus ad loc.; ἐγενήθημεν εὐφραινόμενοι Ps 125.3; ἐὰν γένηται ἔτι λεγομένη ἡ παραβολὴ αὕτη ἐν τῷ Ισραηλ 'this by-word shall not get going in Israel again' Ez 18.3; Si 30.31. **b**. with an aorist form of γ. combined with a pf. mid./pass. ptc. it is a substitute for a mid./pass. pf.: ἐγένοντο αἱ χεῖρες .. ἐστηριγμέναι Ex 17.12, ἐγενόμην μεμαστιγωμένος ὅλην τὴν ἡμέραν 'I started getting tormented all day long' Ps 72.14, ἀπηλλοτριωμένος ἐγενήθην 'I became estranged' 68.9, ἐγενήθην τεταραγμένος 29.8; Ez 36.1, 34. **c**. with a pf. form of γ. combined with a pf. mid./pass. ptc. it is equivalent to a mid./pass. pf.: γεγόνασι .. ἀναμεμειγμένοι .. Ez 22.18. See LSJ s.v., **II 1**, BDF § 354, Evans 2001.224-7, and *ND* 4.66 with an illuminating example: ἐγενάμην [sic!] σου λοιπὸν ἀνεχόμενος, οὐ μέλλω σε λοιπὸν ἀνέχεσθαι 'so I did start putting up with you, but from now on I shall not put up with you.'

*__6__. καὶ ἐγένετο introduces a time-frame within which a past event took place, and with the second or subsequent verb, often prefixed with a pleonastic καί, begins the main sequence of events: καὶ ἐγένετο μετὰ τὰς ἑπτὰ ἡμέρας καὶ τὸ ὕδωρ τοῦ κατακλυσμοῦ ἐγένετο ἐπὶ τῆς γῆς 'and now after the seven days the flood-water emerged on the earth' Ge 7.10; ἐν τῷ + inf., καὶ ἐγένετο ἐν τῷ εἶναι αὐτοὺς ἐν τῷ πεδίῳ καὶ ἀνέστη Καιν .. 'when they were in the field, Cain stood up ..' 4.8, || with no second καί, 11.2; ἅμα τῷ + aor. inf., καὶ ἐγένετο ἅμα τῷ ἀνατεῖλαι τὸν ἥλιον καὶ προσέταξεν .. 'now with the sunrise he commanded ..' Jn 4.8; ἡνίκα + aor., and with no second καί - Καὶ ἐγένετο ἡνίκα ἤρξαντο οἱ ἄνθρωποι πολλοὶ γίνεσθαι ἐπὶ τῆς γῆς, καὶ θυγατέρες ἐγενήθησαν αὐτοῖς. [2]ἰδόντες δὲ οἱ υἱοὶ τοῦ θεοῦ τὰς θυγατέρας τῶν ἀνθρώπων ὅτι καλαί εἰσιν, ἔλαβον ἑαυτοῖς γυναῖκας ἀπὸ πασῶν, ὧν ἐξελέξαντο Ge 6.1f. where the onset of main actions is signalled by δέ; by καί instead, 19.17, 24.30; + ὥστε and inf., καὶ ἐγένετο ὥστε πειράσαι Jd 3.4, sim. 1K 10.9; + gen. abs., καὶ ἐγένετο Ιερεμίου παυσαμένου λαλοῦντος 'when J. stopped talking' Je 33.8; 2K 15.32*L*, 4K 19.37. At Ex 4.24 there is no explicit time reference, which is only implied: Ἐγένετο ἐν τῇ ὁδῷ .. συνήντησεν αὐτῷ ἄγγελος κυρίου 'when he was on the way ..' **b**. followed asyndetically by a clause: καὶ ἐγένετο μεθ' ἡμέρας ἤνεγκεν Καιν .. Ge 4.3 +: Johannessohn 1926.161-212; Beyer 29-62. **c**. Without the initial καί, but followed by δέ and continued without a pleonastic καί: Ἐγένετο δὲ ἐν τῇ βασιλείᾳ .. 'Now it was during the reign of .. ' Ge 14.1; Ἐγένετο δὲ ὡς ἔτεκεν .. εἶπεν Ιακωβ .. 'Now when she gave birth .., J. said ..' 30.25; 41.1; Ex 16.22. **d**. καὶ ἐγένετο not followed by a temporal adjunct: καὶ ἐγένετο πᾶς ὁ ζητῶν κύριον ἐξεπορεύετο εἰς τὴν σκηνὴν .. 'and whenever anyone was seeking the Lord, he went out into the tent ..' Ex 33.7. See Johannessohn 1926.

N.B. Many of the senses of γίνομαι may be perceived as an aoristic or ingressive variant of εἰμί: e.g., παρ' ἐμοὶ γενοῦ 'Come near me' Ge 23.11 is essentially 'Enter the state of being (εἶ) near me,' and γίνομαι on its own does not indicate physical movement; cf. γενόμενοι ἀπὸ τῆς δεήσεως 'having come away from the prayer' 2M 10.27, γενόμενοι ἀπὸ τῆς χρείας 'having finished the business' 15.28; γίνεσθαι μετ' αὐτῆς To 6.18 𝔊[II] (𝔊[I] προσπορεύῃ αὐτῇ). See **2 e** above.

Cf. εἰμί, προγίνομαι, συμβαίνω: Schmidt 2.530-3, 4.76-80.

γι(γ)νώσκω: fut. γνώσομαι, pass. γνωσθήσομαι; aor. ἔγνων, 3pl ἔγνωσαν, inf. γνῶναι, subj. γνῶ, impv. γνῶθι, 2pl γνῶτε, 3s γνώτω, ptc. γνούς, opt.1s γνῴην, 3s γνοίη, pass. ἐγνώσθην, subj. γνωσθῶ, impv. γνώσθητι, 3s γνωσθήτω, inf. γνωσθῆναι; pf. ἔγνωκα, ptc. ἐγνωκώς, pass. ἔγνωσμαι.

1. *to come to know, find out by observation* or *inquiry*: abs., οὔτε ἔγνως οὔτε ἠπίστω Is 48.8; + acc., ὅσα ἐποίησεν αὐτῷ 'what he had done to him' Ge 9.24; τὸν λογισμὸν κυρίου Mi 4.12 (ǁ συνίημι); "what she was going to face" Am 3.10; οὐκ ἔγνωσαν δεξιὰν αὐτῶν ἢ ἀριστερὰν αὐτῶν 'did not know their right hand nor their left hand' Jn 4.11; + ὅτι– κατὰ τί γνώσομαι, ὅτι .. 'How could I know that ..?' Ge 15.8; νῦν ἔγνων ὅτι .. 22.12, Ex 18.11; Ge 3.7, 8.11, 42.33, Jn 1.10, 12 (ἔγνωκα = οἶδα); + διότι Zc 2.9 (ǁ ἐπιγινώσκω 2.11); + inf. clause, Da 4.14 LXX; pass. γνωσθῇ αὐτοῖς ἡ ἁμαρτία Le 4.14, and + ptc., γινώσκεται κύριος κρίματα ποιῶν Ps 9.17. **b**. *to arrive at a solution of*: + acc. rei, πρόβλημα 'riddle' Jd 14.18 B (A: εὑρίσκω).

2. *to have in the mind, to have learnt* (= οἶδα): οὐ γ. τί ἐστι ταῦτα; Zc 4.5; + ὅτι Jn 4.2.

3. *to be* or *become acquainted w., to gain close knowledge of*: + acc. pers. Γινώσκετε Λαβαν ..; Ge 29.5; Ho 5.3; τὸν κύριον 6.3*b*, cf. 6.3*a* (abs.); ὁ θεός, ἐγνώκαμέν σε 8.2; τὰ ἔθνη Zc 7.14; + acc. rei, καλὸν καὶ πονηρόν Ge 2.17, 3.5, κοίτην ἄρσενος 'sleeping with a male' Nu 31.17 (ǁ vs. οἶδα 18), Jd 21.11 A (B: οἶδα); pass., γνωσθῇ ἡ δικαιοσύνη τοῦ κυρίου Mi 6.5; + acc. rei, τὴν δουλείαν, ἣν δεδούλευκά σοι Ge 30.26; τὸν θυμὸν τῆς ὀργῆς μου Nu 14.34; τὴν ἁμαρτίαν ὑμῶν 32.23; ἀσεβείας Am 5.12, τὴν δόξαν κυρίου Hb 2.14; ǁ ἐπίσταμαι To 5.10 𝔊[II]. **b**. pass.: ἐγνώσθη αὐτοῖς 'he [= God] became known to them' Ex 2.25; γνωσθήσομαί σοι 25.21, 29.42; ἐν ὁράματι αὐτῷ Nu 12.6; πρὸς αὐτούς Ez 20.9 (ǁ + dat. pers., vs. 5); + ἐκ 'on the basis of' Si 11.28. **c**. + inf., *to have the capability* of doing: πρὶν ἢ γνῶναι τὸ παιδίον καλεῖν πατέρα ἢ μητέρα Is 8.4, πρὶν ἢ γνῶναι αὐτὸν [= υἱός] προελέσθαι πονηρά 'before he has learned to choose evil things' 7.15 v.l. (Zgl: αὐτὸν ἢ προε.). **d**. + ptc.: γνωσθήτω ἠθετηκυῖα .. Ουαστιν Es 1.18 *L*. **e**. abs.: Is 7.15, 9.9, 50.4.

4. *to recognise, admit to acquaintance with*: ἅλων καὶ ληνὸς οὐκ ἔγνω αὐτούς 'the threshing-floor and wine-press refused to recognise them' Ho 9.2; Is 1.3 (ǁ συνίημι).

5. *to experience*: κακά 'misfortune' Mi 4.9; πάσας νόσους Αἰγύπτου τὰς πονηράς, ἃς ἑώρακας καὶ ὅσα ἔγνως De 7.15.

6. *to be* or *become aware*: "strangers devoured his resources without him becoming aware thereof" Ho 7.9*a*, sim. 7.9*b*.

7. *to recognise as one's own*: ἐπέσκεπται καὶ ἔγνω ὁ θεός 'God has considered and found out' Nu 16.5; ἔγνω αὐτοὺς ὁ θεός Ho 11.12 (cf. Th 62: οἰκειώσομαι), sim. Am 3.2; PSol 17.42.

8. *to identify*: οὐκ ἔγνω τὸν τόπον αὐτῆς Na 3.17; pass., ἔγνωσται Δαυιδ 'D. had been sighted' 1K 22.6, "his identity will be exposed" Pr 10.9.

9. *to acknowledge as true, important*, etc.: θεὸν πλὴν ἐμοῦ οὐ γνώσῃ 'you shall not recognise any other god than me' Ho 13.4; τὸ κρίμα 'to recognise the importance of justice' Mi 3.1; Ps 1.6.

10. *to take note of, not neglect* sbd who is in some special need: ἐν ἡμέρᾳ θλίψεως .. τοὺς εὐλαβουμένους αὐτόν Na 1.7.

11. *to take an interest in, concern oneself with*: οὐ γινώσκει .. οὐδὲν ἐν τῷ οἴκῳ αὐτοῦ Ge 39.8 (ǁ ᾔδει vs. 6).

12. *to admit to the veracity of* a proposition: + ὅτι, Ge 12.11, Ho 2.8, 11.3; + διότι, Zc 11.11; + ὡς Je 15.15; τῇ καρδίᾳ σου De 8.5.

13. *to have sexual intercourse*: ***s*** a hum. male, Αδαμ δὲ ἔγνω Ευαν τὴν γυναῖκα αὐτοῦ Ge 4.1, παρθένος ἦν, ἀνὴρ οὐκ ἔγνω αὐτήν 24.16; a hum. fem., θυγατέρες, αἳ οὐκ ἔγνωσαν ἄνδρα 'daughters who have not yet had sex with a man' 19.8, cf. οὐκ ἔγνω κοίτην '.. conjugal bed' Wi 3.13; both ***s*** and ***o*** hum. male, Jd 19.22. This sense is already known to Menander (4/3 c. BC).

Cf. ἐπι~, προγινώσκω, γνωρίζω, γνῶσις, αἰσθάνομαι, ἐπίσταμαι, κατανοέω, μιμνήσκω, οἶδα, συνίημι: Schmidt 1.285-8; Bultmann, *TDNT* 1.689-92, 696-701.

γιώρας, ου. m. Also γειώρας.ʃ

resident alien: γιώραις καὶ αὐτόχθοσιν τῆς γῆς 'resident aliens and natives of the land' Ex 12.19; ὁ γ. προστεθήσεται Is 14.1. Cf. πάροικος, παρεπίδημος: Nestle 1904.

γλαύξ, κός. f.ʃ

little owl: forbidden as food, Le 11.15, De 14.15.

γλεῦκος, ους. n.ʃ

unfermented grape-juice, 'must': Jb 32.19. Cf. LSG s.v.

γλυκάζω.ʃ

to have sweet taste: ***s*** μέλι 'honey' Ez 3.3. Cf. γλυκάζω.

γλυκαίνω: fut. γλυκανῶ, pass. γλυκανθήσομαι; aor. ἐγλύκανα, pass. ἐγλυκάνθην, subj. γλυκανθῶ.

to make sweet: abs., ἐν τοῖς χείλεσιν αὐτοῦ 'with his lips' Si 12.16; *o* water, Ex 15.25, food, Ps 54.15; στόμα 'flatter' Si 27.23; melodies, 47.9. **b**. pass. *to become sweet*: *s* ὕδωρ Si 38.5; φάρυγξ 'throat' Pr 24.13; κακία Jb 20.12¶; ζωή Si 40.18, μέλος 50.18. Cf. γλυκύς, γλυκασμός, γλυκάζω, πικρός: Shipp 196.

γλύκασμα, ατος. n.

sweet stuff: honey, Si 11.3; sweet drink, 1E 9.51; metaph. and ‖ honeycomb, Pr 16.24. Cf. γλυκασμός.

γλυκασμός, οῦ. m. *

sweet drink: of sweet wine (?), Am 9.13, Jl 3.18. Cf. γλυκύς, γλυκαίνω, γλύκασμα.

γλυκερός, ά, όν.ʃ

sweet to taste: *s* stolen water Pr 9.17. Cf. γλυκύς.

γλυκύς, εῖα, ύ.

sweet to taste: opp. πικρός Is 5.20; τὰ κρίματα αὐτοῦ .. γλυκύτερα ὑπὲρ μέλι .. 'sweeter than honey ..' Ps 18.10f. (cf. Si 24.20). **b**. metaph.: οὐθὲν ~ύτερον προσέχειν ἐντολαῖς κυρίου 'nothing is sweeter than heeding ..' Si 23.26, ὡς ~έα τῷ λάρυγγί μου τὰ λόγιά σου 'how sweet to my throat ..' Ps 118.103, ἐν λόγῳ Pr 16.21; λάρυγξ γ. 'sweet speech' Si 6.5; *s* κόσμος 'this world' 4M 8.23.

Cf. γλυκαίνω, γλυκασμός, γλυκερός, πικρός: LSG s.v.

γλυκύτης, ητος.ʃ

sweetness: of fruits, Jd 9.11; of God's character, Wi 16.21. Cf. γλυκύς.

γλύμμα, ατος. n.

engraved figure: σφραγῖδος 'of a seal' Ex 28.11; γλύφοντες ~ατα σφραγίδων Si 38.27; λίθοις πολυτελέσιν ~ατος σφραγῖδος 'with precious stones of an engraved seal' 45.11; object of heathen worship, ξύλον 'wooden' Is 45.20. Cf. γλύφω.

γλυπτός, ή, όν.

carved: εἰς ~ὸν θεόν Is 44.17; subst. n. of carved images for pagan worship, τὰ ~ὰ τῶν θεῶν αὐτῶν κατακαύσετε 'you shall burn ..' Ex 34.13, De 7.5 (‖ βωμοί, στήλη, ἄλσος and καθαιρέω, συντρίβω, ἐκκόπτω), sim. 12.3; τοῖς ~οῖς ἐθυμίων 'they burned incense to carved idols' Ho 11.2 (‖ Βααλιμ); Τί ὠφελεῖ ~όν, ὅτι ἔγλυψεν αὐτό; 'What use is there of a carved image, for it was carved by man?' Hb 2.18; χειροποίητα οὐδὲ ~ά, οὐδὲ στήλην .. Le 26.1; Mi 5.13; ~ὰ καὶ χωνευτά 'carved and molten images' Na 1.14; ‖ εἴδωλον Is 10.11. Cf. γλύφω, χωνευτός: Caird 1968.464; LSG s.v.

γλυφή, ῆς. f.

1. *act of engraving*: Ex 25.6, 35.9.

2. *that which has been engraved*, 'engraving': σφραγίδων 'of seals' Ex 28.21.

Cf. γλύφω.

γλύφω: fut. γλύψω; aor.act. ἔγλυψα, inf. γλύψαι, pass. ἐγλύφην; pf.ptc.pass. γεγλυμμένος.

1. *to carve*: + acc., idol, Τί ὠφελεῖ γλυπτόν, ὅτι ἔγλυψεν αὐτό; 'What is the use of a carved idol, for it was carved by man?' Hb 2.18; hum., Wi 7.1.

2. *to engrave*: ἐν αὐτοῖς τὰ ὀνόματα .. ἐπὶ τὸν λίθον 'the names into them [= stones]' Ex 28.9f., χερουβιν ἐπὶ τῶν τοίχων 'cherubs on the walls' 2C 3.7; + acc. (decorative stone), Ex 36.13; + cogn. obj. γλύμμα Si 38.27, γλυφή 2C 2.6; + double acc., τοὺς τοίχους .. ἐγκολάπτοις ἔγλυψεν ἐν γραφίδι χερουβιμ 'engraved .. with engravings with an engraving tool, cherubs' 3K 6.28 *L* (B: ἔγραψεν).

Cf. γλύμμα, γλυπτός, γλυφή, δια~, ἐγ-, ἐπιγλύφω, γράφω, κολάπτω, χαράσσω, χωνεύω.

γλῶσσα, ης. f.

1. *tongue*: inside the mouth, Zc 14.12, cleaving to the palate in thirst, La 4.4, used in lapping water, Jd 7.5, digestive organ, Jb 20.12; organ of speech, ἐλάλησα ἐν ~ῃ μου Ps 38.4, ‖ στόμα 125.2, ‖ χείλη 'lips' 119.2, Is 59.3, ‖ λάρυγξ Si 6.5; of an animal, οὐ γρύξει κύων τῇ ~ῃ αὐτοῦ 'no dog will growl with its tongue' Ex 11.7, Ju 11.19; cleaving to the palate (λάρυγξ) so as to produce dumbness, Jb 29.10 ¶; with erotic connotations (?), Is 57.4.

2. *language* as a system of verbal —mainly oral— communication: λαλοῦσαι τῇ γλώσσῃ τῇ Χανανίτιδι Is 19.18; συγχέωμεν .. αὐτῶν τὴν ~αν, ἵνα μὴ ἀκούσωσιν ἕκαστος τὴν φωνὴν τοῦ πλησίον 'Let's confuse their language so that they will not understand one another' Ge 11.7; Χαλδαίων Da 1.4 TH (LXX διάλεκτος); ἐκ πασῶν τῶν ~ῶν τῶν ἐθνῶν Zc 8.23; Zp 3.9.

3. *what is said and uttered*, 'speech': ἀπαιδευσίαν ~ης 'uncouth language' Ho 7.16; γ. δολία 'dishonest speech' Zp 3.13.

4. *people who speak a particular language*: πάντα τὰ ἔθνη καὶ τὰς ~ας Is 66.18, πάντα τὰ ἔθνη καὶ φυλὰς καὶ γλώσσας Da 3.2 LXX, sim. Ju 3.8.

5. *tongue-shaped, oblong and relatively thin object*: metal plate, χρυσῆ 'of gold' Jo 7.21.

Cf. γλωσσότμητος, ἀλλόγλωσσος, διάλεκτος, φωνή: Munz; Behm, *TDNT* 1.719-22; LSG s.v.

γλωσσόκομον, ου. n.

chest: for collected monies, 2C 24.8. Cf. κιβωτός.

γλωσσότμητος, ον.ʃ *

with the tongue cut out: *s* sacrificial animal not acceptable, Le 22.22. Cf. γλωσσοτομέω.

γλωσσοτομέω, ~ωττο~: fut. ~τομήσω; aor.inf. ~τομῆσαι.ʃ

to cut out the tongue of: + acc. pers., 2M 7.4, 4M 12.13. **b**. *to incapacitate*: metaph., + acc., τὸν λογισμόν 'the reason' 4M 10.19.

Cf. γλωσσότμητος.

γλωσσοχαριτόω.ʃ*
to flatter: Pr 28.23.
γλωσσώδης, ες.*
talkative: *s* hum., Ps 139.12, γυνή Si 25.20 (:: ἥσυχος), + μάχιμος 'quarrelsome' Pr 21.19. Cf. πολυλογία.
γλωττοτομέω = γλωσσοτομέω, q.v.
γνάθος, ου. m.
jaw: Jd 4.21. Cf. σιαγών.
γναφεύς, έως. m.
fuller: Is 7.3, 36.2.
γνήσιος, α, ον.ʃ
genuine and not guided by ulterior motives: *s* ἀδελφός 'true brother' Si 7.18 (not biological, ‖ φίλος; cf. εὔνουν ἀδελφὸν ὄντα μοι καὶ γνήσιον, οὐ τῆι φύσει μεν (ἧπερ ἦν ἀνεψιός) στρογῆι δὲ νικήσαντα καὶ τάξιν πατρός *SEG* viii 621.19-21); deed, 3M 3.19. Cf. γνησίως, ἀνυπόκριτος, ἁπλοῦς, νόθος: Spicq 1.136-8, 296-9.
γνησίως. adv.ʃ
in sincerity: 2M 14.8, 3M 3.23. Cf. γνήσιος, ἀδόλως, ἁπλῶς.
γνοφερός, ά, όν.ʃ *
dark: *s* Hades and + σκοτεινός Jb 10.21. Cf. γνόφος, γνοφώδης, σκοτεινός.
γνόφος, ου. m.
darkness: γ. οὐκ ἔχων φέγγος 'darkness lacking light' Am 5.20 (‖ σκότος); σκότος καὶ γ. Ex 14.20, Is 60.2; εἰς τὸν ~ον, οὗ ἦν ὁ θεός Ex 20.21; ἡμέρα σκότους καὶ ~ου, ἡμέρα νεφέλης καὶ ὁμίχλης Jl 2.2, Zp 1.15; juxtaposition of three nouns, σκότος γ. θύελλα 'pitch-dark stormy cloud(?)' Ex 10.22, De 4.11, 5.22, Ps 17.10; γ. καὶ νεφέλη Ez 34.12 (ref. to thick fog?), ν. καὶ γ. Ps 96.2, with 3 other nouns - ἀστραπῶν καὶ βροντῶν καὶ ~ου καὶ ἀνέμων 'of lightning and thunder and .. and winds' *ND* 4.143; fig. of sth fleeting, Is 44.22 (‖ νεφέλη). Cf. γνοφώδης, γνοφερός, γνοφόω, σκότος, φῶς: Trench 372f.; Schmidt 1.599-608.
γνοφόω: aor. ἐγνόφωσα.ʃ*
to make dark for sbd: + acc. pers. and metaph., La 2.1. Cf. γνόφος.
γνοφώδης, ες.
pitch-dark: νεφέλη γ. Ex 19.16. Cf. γνόφος, γνοφερός.
γνώμη, ης. f.
1. *plan* for action: Ps 82.4.
2. *opinion*: Si 6.23; + βουλή Da 2.14 TH (LXX γνῶσις); ὁποίας ἐστε ~ης 'what your opinion is' 2M 11.37. **b**. *sound opinion*: κατὰ ~ην Wi 7.15. **c**. *what one judges to be the best or most desirable*: κατὰ ~ην 2M 9.19.
3. *decision*: 4M 9.27. **b**. *authoritative decision and directive*: Δαρεῖος ἔθηκεν ~ην 2E 6.1 (‖ προστάσσω 1E 6.22), περὶ τίνος ἐξῆλθεν ἡ γ... ἐκ προσώπου τοῦ βασιλέως; Da 2.15 TH; ἀπὸ ~ης θεοῦ .. καὶ ἀπὸ ~ης Κύρου 2E 6.14; + inf., τίς ἔθηκεν ὑμῖν ~ην τοῦ οἰκοδομῆσαι .. 5.3; + ὅτι and fut., 6.11, + ὅτι and inf.(!) 7.13; + ὅτι and impv.(!) 7.21.
4. *consent, approval*: μετὰ ~ης τινός 2M 4.39, 1E 6.21. Cf. Renehan 2.49.
Cf. βουλή, δόξα: LSG s.v.
γνωρίζω: fut. γνωριῶ, γνωρίσω; aor. ἐγνώρισα, subj. γνωρίσω, impv. γνώρισον, inf. γνωρίσαι, pass. ἐγνωρίσθην, subj. γνωρισθῶ; pf.pass.3s ἐγνώρισται.
1. *to make known*: + dat. pers. Ho 8.4; and + acc. rei, Je 16.21 (‖ δηλόω); pass., ἐὰν γνωρίζηται ὁ ταῦρος ὅτι κερατιστής ἐστιν 'if the bull was known to be given to goring' Ex 21.36; + ptc., πονηροὶ ὄντες '(known) to be wicked' Es 3.8 *L*; ‖ διδάσκω Ps 24.4, ‖ οὐ καλύπτω 31.5.
2. *to become acquainted w.*: + acc. pers. ἑαυτούς Am 3.3 (on this sense in papyri, see Preisigke, s.v. **3**, and other evidence in BDAG, s.v. **2**); + acc. rei, Jb 34.25 (‖ καταλαμβάνω vs. 24), ^σοφίαν^ Pr 3.6.
Cf. ἀναγνωρίζω, γινώσκω, γνώριμος, ἀναγγέλλω, ἀποσημαίνω, μηνύω: Schmidt 1.285-8.
γνώριμος, ον.ʃ
known to oneself: subst., 'acquaintance' Ru 2.1, 3.2, Si 30.2, 2K 3.8; w. ref. to φρόνησις 'prudence' and ‖ ἀδελφή Pr 7.4; τινι 4M 5.4. **b**. *known* as: the content of knowledge given in a ptc. phrase, ὅθεν ~μοί εἰσιν οὐκ ὄντες θεοί 'whence you may conclude that they are no gods' Ep Je 14 (‖ γνώσεσθε ὅτι .. vs. 22, γνωστέον ἐστὶν ὅτι .. vs. 51).
Cf. Naumann 36f.; Caird 1968.464.
γνωριστής, οῦ. m.ʃ
= γνώστης, q.v.: 4K 23.24. Cf. LSG s.v.
γνῶσις, εως. f.
that which one has found out and knows: pl., θεὸς ~εων 1K 2.3, πάντων ~ιν ἔχεις 'you know everything' Es C 25; prudent deed based on such knowledge, ποιήσεις ~ιν 1C 4.10; *knowledge, understanding*: in matters of religion - οὐκ ἔχων ~ιν Ho 4.6 (‖ ἐπίγνωσις 'understanding'), φῶς ~εως 10.12; πνεῦμα ~εως καὶ εὐσεβείας Is 11.2; preserved through priestly instruction, Ma 2.7 (‖ νόμος); γ. συνέσεως Si 1.19 (+ ἐπιστήμη), cf. γ. καὶ σύνεσις Pr 2.6; + obj. gen., νόμου Si 11.15¶, ἐντολῶν κυρίου 19.19¶. **b**. general: Si 40.5. **c**. *awareness of the existence of sbd or sth*: "anybody acting wickedly will not go unnoticed by you (ἀπὸ τῆς ~εως σου)" PSol 9.3.
Cf. γινώσκω, εἴδησις, ἄγνοια.
γνωστέος, ον.ʃ
must know: τίνι οὐ ~ον ἐστὶν ὅτι .. 'Who does not have to realise that ..?' Ep Je 51. Cf. γνωστός.

γνώστης, ου. m.
one who is possessed of esoteric knowledge: 1K 28.3, 2C 35.19[a] (+ ἐγγαστρίμυθος 'ventriloquist'; || γνωριστής 4K 23.24), 21.6 (+ θελητής); God, τῶν κρυπτῶν γ. 'knowledgeable about hidden things' Su TH 42. Cf. γνωριστής, ἐγγαστρίμυθος, ἐπαοιδός: Caird 1968.464f.; LSG s.v.

γνωστός, ή, όν.ʃ
1. *known*, + dat. pers.: *s* day, Zc 14.7; + μετά τινος (Hebraism?), γνωστὰ πάντα μετὰ σοῦ To 2.14 𝔊ᴵ, cf. Pesh. /ʻammāḵ/; person, γνωστὸς μακρόθεν ὁ δυνατὸς .. 'the competent .. is widely known' Si 21.7, κύριος τοῖς Αἰγυπτίοις Is 19.21; things, τὰ ἀρεστὰ τῷ θεῷ 'that which pleases God' Ba 4.4; + ὅτι, Wi 16.28. **b**. in an officialese formula γνωστὸν ἔστω τινι 'Herewith I/we beg to inform ..': καὶ νῦν ~ὸν ἔστω τῷ κυρίῳ βασιλεῖ διότι .. 1E 2.17, sim. 6.8, 2E 4.12, 13, 5.8, Da 3.18 TH (|| LXX φανερόν).
2. *knowable*: γ. καλοῦ καὶ πονηροῦ 'knowable of good and evil' Ge 2.9.
3. subst., *acquaintance, close friend*: οἱ ἀδελφοί μου καὶ οἱ ~οί μου 'my colleagues and ..' Ne 5.10; Ps 30.12 (|| γείτων 'neighbour'), 87.19 (|| φίλος, πλησίον), alw. with a pers. poss. pron. See *ND* 4.143.
Cf. γινώσκω, γνωστῶς, γνωστέος, ἐπίγνωστος, εὔγνωστος, ὀνομαστός, ἄγνωστος, γνώριμος, περιβόητος.

γνωστῶς. adv.ʃ
with full knowledge: γ. εἴδω σε 'Let me know you fully' Ex 33.13; Pr 27.23. Cf. γινώσκω.

γογγύζω: fut. γογγύσω; aor. ἐγόγγυσα.
to grumble: *s* alw. hum., ἐπί τινα Ex 17.3, Nu 16.41 ('to take it out on sbd [= hum.]'); + acc. rei, πονηρὰ ἔναντι κυρίου 11.1, τί .. περὶ τῆς ἁμαρτίας; La 3.39; ἐναντίον μου [= κυρίου] Nu 14.27; περὶ ὑμῶν ib.; ἐπ' ἐμοί [= κυρίῳ] 14.29, ἐφ' ὑμῖν [= Moses and Aaron] 17.5; opp. ὑπακούω 'obey' Is 29.24. Cf. γόγγυσις, γογγυσμός, δια~, καταγογγύζω, σχετλιάζω: Shipp 197; Rengstorf, *TDNT* 1.728-33, 735f.

γόγγυσις, εως. f.ʃ
v.n. of γογγύζω: cogn. obj. of γογγύζω – τῶν υἱῶν Ισραηλ, ἣν ἐγόγγυσαν περὶ ὑμῶν Nu 14.27. Cf. γογγύζω, γογγυσμός.

γογγυσμός, οῦ. m.
grumble: ἐπὶ τῷ θεῷ '(directed) at God' Ex 16.7 (|| κατὰ τοῦ θεοῦ vs. 8); cogn. obj. of διαγογγύζω 16.8, of γογγύζω Nu 17.5; θροῦς ~ῶν 'noise of ..' Wi 1.10, ἀνωφελής 'unprofitable' 1.11 (|| καταλαλιά); πονηρίας Si 46.7; ῥῆμα ~οῦ Is 58.9; of grudging benefactor, PSol 5.13 (|| φειδώ). Cf. γογγύζω, διαγογγυσμός, and *ND* 4.143f.

γοερός, ά, όν.ʃ
mournful: *s* μέλος 'melody' 3M 5.25.

γοητεία, ας. f.ʃ
charming tactfulness and finesse in negotiations: 2M 12.24.

γομορ *
a definite dry measure: Ex 16.16; of barley, γ. κριθῶν Ho 3.2.

γόμος, ου. m.ʃ
load carried by beast of burden: πεπτωκὸς ὑπὸ τὸν ~ον αὐτοῦ 'fallen under (the weight of) its load' Ex 23.5; ζεύγους ἡμιόνων 'of a pair of mules' 4K 5.17. Cf. βάσταγμα, διγομία, φορτίον: Lee 62; Shipp 192f.

γομφιάζω: fut. γομφιάσω; aor. ἐγομφίασα.ʃ*
1. *to suffer pain*: *s* teeth, οἱ ὀδόντες τέκνων ἐγομφίασαν Ez 18.2 (|| αἱμωδιάω Je 38.29, 30).
2. tr. *to grind* or *gnash* teeth (acc.) out of chagrin: γομφιάσεις τοὺς ὀδόντας σου Si 30.10.
Cf. γομφιασμός, αἱμωδιάω: Caird 1968.465; LSG s.v.

γομφιασμός, οῦ. m.ʃ *
toothache: γ. ὀδόντων Am 4.6. Cf. γομφιάζω.

γονεῖς. m.pl.
parents: οἱ γονεῖς αὐτῆς καὶ τὰ τέκνα αὐτῆς Da Su 30 TH; Es 2.7 o'; in-laws, To 10.12 𝔊ᴵ; || γένη 'offspring' 4M 15.13. Cf. γεννήτωρ, μήτηρ, πατήρ, τέκνον.

γονορρυής, ές.
having a discharge of semen: Le 15.4; || λεπρός, ἀκάθαρτος Nu 5.2.

γόνος, ου. m.ʃ
1. *that which is begotten*: γονεῖς .. ἢ παίδων ~οι 'parents .. or infants' 3M 5.31.
2. *semen*: ῥέων ~ον 'having a discharge of semen' Le 15.3.
Cf. γονορρυής: Schmidt 2.430f.

γόνυ, γόνατος. n. Mostly in the pl.
knee: τέξεται ἐπὶ τῶν γονάτων μου 'she will give birth as a surrogate mother for me' Ge 30.3 (knees on which a child is placed and claimed as his or her own), cf. 48.12; ἐπὶ ~άτων παρακληθήσονται Is 66.12 (*s* infants). **b**. bent as one prays: κάμπτων ἐπὶ τὰ ~ατα αὐτοῦ καὶ προσευχόμενος 'kneeling .. and praying' Da TH 6.10, κάμψας τὰ ~ατα 1E 8.70, κλίνω ἐπὶ τὰ ~ατά μου 2E 9.5; ἔπεσεν (*L* ἔκαμψεν) ἐπὶ τὰ ~ατα 2C 6.13; sg., καρδίας Od 12.11. **c**. firm knees as a symbol of physical strength: ὑπόλυσις ~άτων 'knees becoming disjointed' Na 2.11; ἰσχύσατε, χεῖρες ἀνειμέναι καὶ ~ατα παραλελυμένα 'Be strong, o slackened hands and paralysed knees!' Is 35.3, χεῖρες παρειμέναι καὶ ~ατα παραλελυμένα Si 25.23; τὰ ~ατά μου ἠσθένησαν ἀπὸ νηστείας 'my knees weakened from fasting' Ps 108.24.
Cf. Schlier, *TDNT* 1.738-40.

γόος, ου.ʃ
act of wailing: + στεναγμός 'sigh' 3M 1.18, + κοπετός 'mourning' 4.3, + οἶκτος 'lamentation' 5.49; opp. τέρψις 'pleasure' 4.6. Cf. θρῆνος, κλαυθμός, κωκυτός, στεναγμός: Schmidt 3.385-7.

γοῦν.ʃ
1. introduces a new phase in a chain of connected events: 2M 5.21.
2. introduces an illustrative case: 4M 3.6, cf. 2.5, 8.
3. asseverative particle, *undoubtedly*: 4M 2.2.
Never word-initial.

γράμμα, ατος. n. Mostly pl.
that which is written or *engraved*: 1E 3.9; ~ατα ἐκτετυπωμένα σφραγῖδος 'letters of a seal engraved in relief' Ex 36.39; ~ατα στικτά 'tattoo marks' Le 19.28; τὰ ~ατα τὰ γραφέντα περὶ .. 'what is written about ..' Es 6.2; διδάξαι αὐτοὺς ~ατα καὶ διάλεκτον Χαλδαικήν 'to teach them to read and write Chaldaean' Da 1.4 LXX; pl., a biblical book (viz. Chronicles), Es 6.1. **b**. *missive*: Es E 17; 1M 5.10 (|| ἐπιστολή vs. 13). **c**. *written decree*: Es 4.3, 8.10.
Cf. γράφω, ἐπιστολή.

γραμματεία, ας. f.ʃ
subject of learning: Ps 70.15; σύνεσις ~ας Si 44.4.

γραμματεύς, έως.
1. *one who records*: mentioned after ἐργοδιώκτης 'taskmaster' Ex 5.6, 10; appointed by a foreign ruler's functionaries out of one's own group, 5.14; τῶν υἱῶν Ισραηλ 5.15, 19; senior functionary in a royal court, 2K 8.17 +.
2. a person in leadership position of one sort or another: civic, πρεσβύτεροι τοῦ λαοῦ καὶ ~εῖς αὐτῶν Nu 11.16, || οἰκονόμος, ὑπομνηματογράφος Is 36.3; addresses the people after the priest, De 20.5; Jd 5.14 (|| A: ἐνισυχύων); Si 10.5. **b**. low-ranking military leader: 1M 5.42.
3. *scholar*: σοφία ~έως Si 38.24.
Cf. ἀνα~, ὑπομιμνήσκω: *BA* ad Ex 5.14; *ND* 1.116.

γραμματεύω.ʃ
to serve as γραμματεύς, q.v.: Je 52.25; + διακρίνω 1C 26.29.

γραμματικός, ή, όν.ʃ
1. *pertaining to written texts*: *s* τέχνη 'discipline' Da 1.17 LXX.
2. subst. f.sg., *expertise in textual matters*: ἐν πάσῃ ~ῇ καὶ σοφίᾳ Da 1.17 TH. **b**. m., *expert in textual matters*: + σοφός Da 1.4 LXX; *good scholar* Is 33.18.

γραμματοεισαγωγεύς, έως. m.ʃ*
instructor in the law (?) with some judicial function: De 1.15; κριτὰς καὶ ~εῖς 16.18, 31.28 (the latter with πρεσβύτεροι), sim. 29.10, alw. mentioned last. Cf. γραμματεύς: Caird 1968.465; LSG s.v.

γραπτόν, οῦ. n.ʃ
written document: subst.n.pl., διὰ ~ῶν 'through written communication' 1E 2.2 (|| ἐν ~ῷ 1C 36.22, 2E 1.1), 2M 11.15. Cf. γραφή.

γραφεῖον, ου. n.ʃ
writing instrument: σιδηρόν 'iron (pen)' Jb 19.24¶. Cf. γραφίς.

γραφή, ῆς. f.
that which is written or *inscribed*: ἡ γ. γ. θεοῦ ἐστιν κεκολαμμένη .. '.. engraved' Ex 32.16; De 10.4; ἐν ~ῇ 'by letter' 2C 2.10; official document, ἀντίγραφον τῆς ~ῆς 'copy of ..' 1M 14.27, γενικὴ γ. 'genealogical record' 1E 5.39, συνοδίας '(list of) fellow-travellers' Ne 7.64; burgher-roll, Ez 13.9; containing a royal edict, Da 6.8 TH; written instruction, ἅλας οὗ οὐκ ἔστιν γ. 'salt of unspecified quantity' 2E 7.22, κατὰ τὴν ~ὴν Δαυιδ βασιλέως 2C 35.4; literary composition, Si 44.5, κατὰ τὴν ~ὴν βιβλίου Μωυσῆ 2E 6.18, Ησαιου 'of Isaiah' 4M 18.14; inscription on a tower, 3M 2.27.
Cf. γράφω, γράμμα, ἀπογραφή: Schrenk, *TDNT* 1.749-55.

γραφικός, ή, όν.ʃ
pertaining to writing: *s* κάλαμος 'pen' 3M 4.20. Cf. γράφω.

γραφίς, ίδος. f.
engraving tool: ἔπλασεν ἐν ~ίδι 'he moulded (them) .. (into ..)' Ex 32.4; γράψον εἰς αὐτὸν ~ίδι ἀνθρώπου 'Write in it [= a scroll] with a human pen' Is 8.1, ἐζωγραφημένους ἐν ~ίδι 'painted ..' Ez 23.14. Cf. γράφω, γραφεῖον, ἐγκολάπτω.

γράφω: fut. γράψω, pass. γραφήσομαι; aor. ἔγραψα, impv. γράψον, pass.3pl γραφήτωσαν, ptc. γράψας, pass. ἐγράφην, ptc. γραφείς, inf. γραφῆναι, impv.3s γραφήτω; pf. γέγραφα, pass.3s γέγραπται, ptc.pass. γεγραμμένος; plpf.pass.3s ἐγέγραπτο.
1. *to hew out*: + acc., ἐν πέτρᾳ σκηνὴν 'a habitation in a rock' Is 22.16 (|| λατομέω).
2. *to inscribe*: on a hard surface, + acc. of message, τὸν νόμον τοῦτον De 27.8; αὐτὰ ἐπὶ δύο πλάκας λιθίνας 5.22, ἐπὶ τὰς πλάκας τὰ ῥήματα 10.2, ἐπὶ τὰς φλιάς 'on the doorposts' 6.9; ἐπὶ τῶν λίθων πάντας τοὺς λόγους 27.3, cf. metaph., ἐπὶ καρδίας αὐτῶν Je 38.33.
3. *to cover with writing*: + acc. of hard surface, πλάκας λιθίνας γεγραμμένας τῷ δακτύλῳ τοῦ θεοῦ 'stone tablets inscribed by God's finger' Ex 31.18, De 9.10; stick, Ez 37.16; + double acc., τοὺς τοίχους .. γραφίδι χερουβιν 'the walls with an engraving tool cherubim' 3K 6.29 (*L* ἔγλυψεν).
4. *to produce by writing, compose*: + acc. rei, βίβλον Ex 32.32; αὐτῇ βιβλίον ἀποστασίου 'a bill

of divorce' De 24.1, 3; βιβλίον μνημοσύνου 'a book of memoranda' Ma 3.16; γραφήν 2E 4.7 pass., *o* ἐπιστολήν 2M 11.16.

5. *to record in writing*: + acc., τὰ ῥήματα κυρίου Ex 24.4; τὰς ἀράς 'the curses' Nu 5.23; τὰς ἀπάρσεις αὐτῶν 'their departures' 33.2; ᾠδήν De 31.22; πληγήν 'plague' 28.61; τὰς ἀρὰς τὰς γεγραμμένας ἐν τῷ βιβλίῳ 29.21 (ǁ τὰς κατάρας vs. 27); ὅρασιν 'a vision' Hb 2.2; πονηρίαν '(laws and sentences motivated by) wickedness' Is 10.1; and + dat. pers., 1E 6.11, τὰς ἐντολάς .. ὑμῖν 4K 17.37; + περί τινος Ps 39.8; εἰς βιβλίον De 17.18, 31.9, Je 39.10, ἐν κεφαλίδι "in a scroll' Ps 39.8; εἰς ^τόμον^ (a papyrus roll) Is 8.1; ἐπὶ βιβλίου De 37.2, ἐπὶ βιβλίῳ 2C 35.27, 1M 16.24; ἐπὶ πυξίου καὶ εἰς βιβλίον 'on a tablet ..' Is 30.8; ἐπὶ βιβλίου 4K 23.21 (*L* ἐν ..); ἐπὶ ^ῥάβδον^ Ez 37.16 (ǁ ἐπ' αὐταῖς vs. 20); ἀπὸ στόματός τινος 'as dictated by ..' Je 43.4. **b.** *to record sbd* (τινα) *by name* and assign him to a certain category: οἱ γραφεντὲς εἰς ζωήν Is 4.3, cf. ἐν τῇ βιβλίῳ τῆς ζωῆς γεγραμμένος Rev 20.15; Is 10.19, Je 17.13; εἰς τοὺς περὶ ἡμᾶς 'as our bodyguard' 1M 13.40 (ǁ ἐγ~), συμμάχους καὶ φίλους ὑμῶν 'as your allies and friends' 8.20. **c.** + acc., *to record* about sth or sbd: τὸν ἄνδρα τοῦτον ἐκκήρυκτον ἄνθρωπον 'this man as a person banished by proclamation' Je 22.30; 2C 35.26; εἰς βιβλίον To 12.20 𝔊[I]; pass. ἐν τῷ βιβλίῳ Es A 15 *L*. **d.** *to correspond by letter*: πρός τινα 2E 4.7, δέλτοις χαλκαῖς 'with bronze tablets' 1M 14.18.

6. *to impose in writing*, 'prescribe': abs., ἐπὶ τὴν βασιλείαν Es 10.1 o' (L + τὰ τέλη 'taxes'); + acc., χορηγίαν 'provision for sustenance' 1E 4.54. **b.** *to instruct in writing*: *s* sbd in authority, + dat. pers. and inf., 1M 13.37, 1E 4.55, 56; + inf. only, 6.16.

Cf. γράμμα, γραφή, γραφικός, γραφίς, γραπτόν, ἔγγραπτος, ἀντι~, ἐγ~, κατα~, προ~, ὑπογράφω, βιβλίον, ἱστορέω, κολάπτω: Schrenk, *TDNT* 1.742-6; Chadwick 79-87.

γρηγορέω: aor. ἐγρηγόρησα, impv. γρηγόρησον, pass. ἐγρηγορήθην.

1. *to be fully awake and watchful*: *s* night-watch, Ne 7.3, 1M 12.27; ἐπὶ τὴν γρηγόρησιν αὐτοῦ 'by having regard to the fact that He is also watchful' (?) PSol 3.2 (:: ὑπνόω).

2. *to pay maximum attention with a view to deal with in future*: abs. Da 9.14 TH (LXX: ἀγρυπνέω); + ἐπί and acc., ἐπὶ τοὺς λόγους μου τοῦ ποιῆσαι αὐτούς Je 1.12, "a leopard kept a watch over their cities" 5.6; 38.28; + ἐπί τινι – ἐπὶ τοῖς κακοῖς 'the calamities (to bring upon the evil-doers)' Ba 2.9.

Cf. ἀγρυπνέω, γρηγόρησις, ἐγρηγορέω.

γρηγόρησις, εως. f.ʃ *

1. *state of being fully awake and watchful*: God's, PSol 3.2, 16.4.

2. *intellectual sharpness and keenness*: + σύνεσις Da 5.11, 14 TH.

Cf. γρηγορέω.

γρύζω: fut. γρύξω; aor. ἔγρυξα.ʃ

to growl: *s* aggressive dog, οὐ γρύξει κύων τῇ γλώσσῃ αὐτοῦ 'no dog will growl with its tongue' Ex 11.7, Ju 11.19 (latter: + ἀπέναντί σου, cf. οὐκ ἔγρυξεν οὐδεὶς τῶν υἱῶν Ισραηλ τῇ γλώσσῃ αὐτοῦ Jo 10.21). Cf. ἠχέω: Schmidt 3.368.

γρύψ, πός. m.ʃ

type of vulture: forbidden as food, Le 11.13, De 14.12.

γυμνάζω.ʃ

to harass: + acc. pers., 2M 10.15. Cf. γυμνασία, γυμνάσιον.

γυμνασία, ας.ʃ

bodily training: metaph., πόνων 'in sufferings' 4M 11.20. Cf. γυμνάζω.

γυμνάσιον, ου. n.

gymnasium: κατὰ τὰ νόμιμα τῶν ἐθνῶν 'in accordance with the gentile customs' 1M 1.14; + ἐφηβίαν 'youth club' 2M 4.9.

γυμνός, ή, όν.

undressed, naked: τὰ ~ὰ τοῦ τραχήλου 'the exposed parts of the neck' Ge 27.16; of humiliated woman, ἐκδύσω αὐτὴν ~ήν 'strip her naked' Ho 2.3; Am 4.3; cf. πορεύσεται ἀνυπόδετος καὶ ~ή 'she will walk along with no shoes or clothes on' Mi 1.8. Γυμνός does not necessarily mean 'stark-naked' but 'scantly clad': one wearing only χιτών 'tunic, undergarment' may still be described as γ.: see LSJ, s.v. **5** and LSG s.v., and cf. γ. καὶ ἀνυπόδετος Is 20.2 (with no sackcloth round one's waist), ~ὴ καὶ ἀσχημονοῦσα Ez 16.7, and descriptive of a defeated nation being taken into captivity Is 20.4; ἀμφίασιν ~ῶν 'clothes of ..' Jb 22.6. Cf. γυμνότης, γύμνωσις, γυμνόω, ἀνυπόδετος.

γυμνότης, ητος. f.ʃ

lack of clothing as a form of destitution: ἐν λιμῷ καὶ ἐν δίψει καὶ ἐν ~τι καὶ ἐν ἐκλείψει πάντων 'in hunger, thirst, nakedness and lack of everything' De 28.48. Cf. γυμνός.

γυμνόω aor. ἐγύμνωσα, pass. ἐγυμνώθην.ʃ

1. *to expose oneself by taking clothes off*: mid., as a result of getting drunk, Ge 9.21.

2. *to expose* part of a human body by removing its covering: μηρὸν εἰς αἰσχύνην '(her) thigh to put her to shame' Ju 9.2, cf. LSG s.v. **1**.

3. *to remove* one's upper garment: ἐγύμνωσεν ὃν ἐνδεδύκει σάκκον '.. a sackcloth she had put on' Ju 9.1.

Cf. γυμνός.

γύμνωσις, εως. f.ʃ

state of being unclothed and naked: εἶδεν .. τὴν

~ιν τοῦ πατρὸς αὐτοῦ Ge 9.22. **b**. *part* or *whole of a naked body*: συνεκάλυψαν τὴν ~ιν τοῦ πατρὸς αὐτῶν 'they covered ..' Ge 9.23. All these passages implicitly refer to unseemingly exposed genitals.

Cf. γυμνός.

γυναικεῖος, ον.∫

pertaining to women: στολή 'garment' De 22.5; ἐκοσμήθη τῷ ἱματισμῷ καὶ παντὶ τῷ κόσμῳ τῷ ~ῳ 'was decorated with her apparel and all sorts of ladies' accessories' Ju 12.15; *s* αὐλή '(women's) court' Es 2.11; διάδημα 'diadem' 2.17. **b**. subst. n.pl.: ἐξέλειπεν Σάρρᾳ γίνεσθαι τὰ ~εῖα 'S. was missing her periods' Ge 18.11; ἠριθεύετο ἐν τοῖς ~είοις 'she worked, doing women's works' To 2.11 𝔊[I] (cf. ἐν τοῖς ἔργοις τοῖς ~οις 𝔊[II]).

Cf. γυνή.

γυναικοτραφής, ές.∫

brought up by a woman: 1K 20.30*L*.

γυναικών, ῶνος. m.

harem: Es 2.3 o'.

γύναιον. n.∫

weak woman: Jb 24.21 (ǁ στεῖρα 'barren woman').

γυνή, αικός. f.

1. *female person*, 'woman': counterpart of, and derived from ἀνήρ Ge 2.23; fig. as symbol of weakness, ὁ λαός σου ὡς ~κες 'your people are like women' Na 3.13; ἀποσκευὴ .. ~κες .. καὶ κτήνη Nu 32.26. ***b**. in Hebraistic distributive expressions: αἰτησάτω ἕκαστος παρὰ τοῦ πλησίον καὶ γ. παρὰ τῆς πλησίον 'Let each ask his neighbour and each woman her neighbour' Ex 11.2 (see under ἕκαστος); Je 9.20. ***c**. pleonastically with another noun following: ~κα παρθένον Le 21.13, τῆς ~κὸς τῆς Αἰθιοπίσσης .. ~κα Αἰθιόπισσαν Nu 12.1, γ. προφῆτις 'prophetess' Jd 4.4, ~κα παλλακήν 'concubine' 19.1, ἔργα ~κὸς πόρνης Ez 16.30, ~κὸς μοιχαλίδος 'of adulteress' Pr 30.20, cp. ~αῖκα πόρνην καὶ βεβηλωμένην Le 21.7, γ. χήρα 4M 16.10. Cf. ἀνήρ **3** and ἄνθρωπος **3f**. **d**. liable to dread: Is 19.16.

2. *wife*: γ. μου Ge 20.2 (Abraham of Sarah); γ. νεότητός σου 'the wife of your youth' Ma 2.14; γ. διαθήκης 'wife married by agreement' ib.; λάβε σεαυτῷ ~κα πορνείας 'Take for yourself a wife of fornication' Ho 1.2 (ǁ τέκνον); opp. ἀνήρ 'husband' 2.2; woman to be taken as wife, ἐδούλευσεν Ισραηλ ἐν ~κί 'Israel slaved for a future wife of his' 12.12; ἀνδρὸς γ. 'sbd else's wife' Jb 31.11.

Cf. γυναικεῖος, γύναιον φιλογύναιος, ἀνήρ, γαμετή, παλλακίς, παράκοιτος: Schmidt 2.404f.

γῦρος, ου.∫

ring, circle: τῆς γῆς Is 40.22; οὐρανοῦ Jb 22.14¶, Si 24.5. Cf. γυρόω: Shipp 205f.

γυρόω: aor. ἐγύρωσα.∫

to go round: abs., Jb 26.10¶; + acc., οὐρανόν Si 43.12. Cf. γῦρος, κυκλόω: Schmidt 4.454-6, 58f.

γύψ, πός, pl.dat. γυψίν. m.

vulture: forbidden as food, Le 11.14, De 14.13; inhabits high places, Jb 5.7; known for its sharp eyes, 28.7; ǁ ἀετός 39.27.

γωνία, ας. f.

1. *corner*: of tabernacle, Ex 26.23; of altar, 27.2; ἱλαστηρίου Ez 43.20; of defence wall, ἐπὶ τὰς ~ας τὰς ὑψηλάς Zp 1.16; of street, Pr 7.8; ἡ πύλη τῶν ~ῶν, the name of a gate of Jerusalem, Zc 14.10; κεφαλὴ ~ας 'corner-stone' Ps 117.22.

2. *person of cardinal importance, key figure*, 'ruler, chief': 1K 14.38.

Cf. γωνιαῖος.

γωνιαῖος, α, ον.∫*

positioned in a corner: *s* λίθος Jb 38.6. Cf. γωνία.

Δ

δᾳδουχία, ας.ʃ*

bearing of torch: welcoming gesture for guests, 2M 4.22.

δαιμόνιος, α, ον.

subst.n. *pseudo-divine being*: ἔθυσαν ~οις καὶ οὐ θεῷ De 32.17, sim. Ba 4.7; πάντες οἱ θεοὶ τῶν ἐθνῶν ~α Ps 95.5 (‖ 1C 16.26 εἴδωλον); recipient of child sacrifice, Ps 105.37; Ἀσμοδαῖος τὸ ~ον τὸ πονηρόν To 𝔊II 3.8; ‖ πνεῦμα πονηρόν 6.8; ‖ σειρήν Is 13.21; ‖ ὀνοκένταυρος 34.14; having no real existence, 65.3; scary, δ. μεσημβρινόν 'midday' Ps 90.6; inhabitant of ruins, Ba 4.35. Cf. θεός, πνεῦμα: Schmidt 4.1-5; Owen 1931.150-2; Foerster, *TDNT* 2.1-16.

δάκνω: fut. δήξομαι; aor. ἔδακον, subj. δάκω, pass. ptc. δηχθείς; pf.ptc.pass. δεδηγμένος.

1. *to bite*: + acc. pers. and *s* snake, πτέρναν ἵππου 'a horse's heel' Ge 49.17 (ὄφις); Nu 21.6, 8, Am 5.19 (ὄφις), 9.3 (δράκων); fig. of false prophet active outdoors, Mi 3.5; Hb 2.7.

2. pass. *to feel a sudden, sharp pain*: To 11.8 𝔊I. Cf. δῆγμα, ὀφιόδηκτος.

δάκρυον, ου; pl.dat. δάκρυσι, n. Alm. alw. in pl.

tear shed: μὴ κλαίετε ~σι 'Don't cry, shedding tears' Mi 2.6, ἐκαλύπτετε ~σι τὸ θυσιαστήριον 'you covered the altar with tears' Ma 2.13, ἀφεῖλεν ὁ θεὸς πᾶν δάκρυον ἀπὸ παντὸς προσώπου Is 25.8; "your eyes will shed (κατάξουσιν) tears" Je 13.17; ‖ κλαυθμός 38.16. Cf. δακρύω, πολύδακρυς: Shipp 207.

δακρύω: fut. δακρύσω; aor. ἐδάκρυσα, ptc. δακρύσας.

to shed tears: μηδὲ δακρυέτωσαν ἐπὶ τούτοις 'Nor let them shed tears over these matters' Mi 2.6 (‖ κλαυθμός and στεναγμός); ἐν ὀφθαλμοῖς αὐτοῦ Si 12.16; *s* hum. face, Ez 27.35. Cf. δάκρυον, κλαίω: Schmidt 1.471-6.

δακτυλήθρα, ας. f.ʃ

thumb-screw: instrument of torture, 4M 8.13. Cf. βασανιστήριον.

δακτύλιος, ου. m.

1. *signet-ring*: Ge 38.18; περιελόμενος Φαραω τὸν ~ον ἀπὸ τῆς χειρὸς αὐτοῦ 'Pharaoh, having removed the ring from his hand' 41.42; carried by a king and high-ranking priests, Bel 14 LXX.

2. *finger-ring*: woman's accessory, σφραγῖδας καὶ ἐνώτια καὶ ~ους καὶ ἐμπλόκια καὶ περιδέξια Ex 35.22, sim. Ju 10.4, Is 3.20; worn as a token of high office, Es 3.10. Cf. κόσμος **3**.

3. *ring* as part of an architectural structure: of the ark of testimony, Ex 25.11; of hearth, 27.4; beneath a golden twisted border round an altar, 30.4.

Cf. δάκτυλος, σφραγίς: Russo 163-87.

δάκτυλος, ου. m.

finger: θεοῦ as the author of an extraordinary event Ex 8.19, De 9.10, cf. Lk 11.20, ἔργα τῶν δακτύλων σου Ps 8.4 (ref. to the sky, moon and stars); of a hum., Ex 29.12, ‖ χείρ Is 2.9, 59.3; also of 'toe,' 2K 21.20; a measure of length, Je 52.21. Cf. χείρ

δαλός, οῦ. m.

piece of burning wood: δ. ἐξεσπασμένος ἐκ πυρός 'a firebrand plucked out of the fire' Am 4.11, Zc 3.2; δ. πυρός 12.6. Cf. Schmidt 2.381; Shipp 206f.

δαμάζω: fut. δαμάσω.ʃ

to bring under control: + acc., Da 2.40 TH. Cf. καταδαμάζω, ὑποτάσσω.

δάμαλις, εως. f.

young cow, 'heifer': ~ιν τριετίζουσαν 'three-year old heifer' Ge 15.9, τριετής Is 15.5 (still full of vitality); cultic offering, Nu 7.17; πυρρὰ ἄμωμος 'red, unblemished' 19.2; used in farming, δ. ἐκ βοῶν De 21.3; δ. βοῶν 1K 16.2, Is 7.21; ὡς δ. παροιστρῶσα 'as a heifer hopping mad' Ho 4.16; pugnatious, 10.11; ἐσκίρτησαν ~εις ἐπὶ ταῖς φάτναις '... leapt about the mangers' Jl 1.17; 1K 28.24*L* (B: μοσχάριον). Cf. βοῦς.

Δαμασκός, οῦ.

Damascus: Ge 14.15 +.

δανείζω: fut. δανιῶ, mid. δανιοῦμαι; aor. impv. δάνεισον, subj. δανείσω, mid. ἐδανεισάμην; pf.ptc. mid. δεδανεσμένος. On the spelling, see Walters, 29-30.

I. act. *to put out* money, 'lend': abs. Si 20.15 (:: ἀπαιτέω 'demand repayment'); + dat. pers., De 15.6; + acc. cogn., δάνειον δανιεῖς αὐτῷ 15.8; χωρὶς τόκων 'without interest' 4M 2.8.

II. mid., *to have* sth *lent to oneself*, 'borrow': ***o*** money, De 15.6; grain, Pr 20.4; τὸ πνεῦμα Wi 15.16; opp. ἀποτίνω 'repay' Ps 36.21; ὁ δανείζων ὡς ὁ δανειζόμενος 'the lender as the borrower' Is 24.2.

Cf. δάνειον, δανεισμός, δανειστής, δάνος, κιχράω.

δάνειον, ου. n.ʃ

money lent, 'loan': as cogn. obj., δ. δανιεῖς αὐτῷ De 15.8; 15.10; 24.11 (‖ ὀφείλημα vs. 10), 4M 2.8. Cf. δανείζω, ὀφείλημα.

δανεισμός, οῦ. m.ʃ
act of borrowing money: Si 18.33.

δαν(ε)ιστής, οῦ. m.
he who lent money, 'creditor': Ps 108.11; opp. χρεοφειλέτης 'debtor' Pr 29.13. Cf. δανείζω.

δάνος, ου. m.ʃ
that which has been lent: Si 29.4. Cf. δανείζω.

δαπανάω: aor.inf. δαπανῆσαι, aor. ἐδαπανήθην; pf. ptc.pass. δεδαπανημένος.
1. *to expend*: ***o*** cultic offerings, εἰς ^Βηλ^ Bel 3 TH (LXX ἀναλίσκω).
2. *to consume*: ***o*** cultic offerings, Bel 18 LXX.
3. pass. *to lose strength* or *efficacy*: ***s*** fire, 2M 1.32.
Cf. καταδαπανάω, ἀναλίσκω, ἐκλείπω.

δαπάνη, ης. f.
1. *expense*: sg., 2E 6.4, 1M 10.39, 44; pl., 3.30.
*2. *that which is supplied and consumed*: foods, Bel 8 TH, 22 LXX.
Cf. δαπάνημα, δαπανάω.

δαπάνημα, ατος. n.ʃ
1. *expense*: sg., 1E 6.24 (‖ δαπάνη 2E 6.4); χορηγεῖν .. ~ατα 'to defray ..' 2M 3.3.
*2. *that which is supplied and consumed*: foods, pl., 2M 11.31.
Cf. δαπάνη.

δάσος, ους. n.ʃ
thick growth of vegetation, 'thicket, copse': ἐν τοῖς ~εσιν τοῦ δρυμοῦ Is 9.18; ὑπὸ τὸ δ. τῆς δρυός '.. of an oak' 2K 18.9 (*L* ὑ. φυτὸν δένδρου). Cf. βοτάνη.

δασύπους, όδος.ʃ
"*Lepus timidus*" (LSJ), 'hare': forbidden food, Le 11.5, De 14.7.

δασύς, εῖα, ύ.
thickly, densely covered with distinct objects: with hair, δορὰ ~ύς 'shaggy hide' Ge 25.25 (of a new-born baby); ***s*** ἀνὴρ δ. 27.11 (:: λεῖος); χεῖρ 27.23. **b.** with leaves, κλάδους ξύλου ~εῖς 'leafy twigs of a tree' Le 23.40; ***s*** δένδρον De 12.2, Is 57.5 (site for pagan cults). **c.** with trees, ἐξ ὄρους κατασκίου ~έος 'from a shady, densely-wooded mountain' Hb 3.3.
Cf. λεῖος.

δαψιλεύομαι: aor. ἐδαψιλευσάμην.ʃ
to expend very much: ***o*** μέριμναν 'concern' understood (?), δι' ὑμᾶς 'on your account' 1K 10.2.

δαψιλής, ές.ʃ
1. *abundant in quantity*: ***s*** ὕδωρ Wi 11.7; δράκες λιβανωτοῦ 'handfuls of frankincense' 3M 5.2; θοῖνα '(sumptuous) meal' 5.31.
2. *munificent, generous*: ***s*** χεῖρ 1M 3.30.

δέ
Never occupies the initial position in a clause.
1. a transitional particle, no specific, clear contrast intended, 'now, then' (BDAG, s.v. **2**): Λάβε μοι .. ἔλαβεν δὲ αὐτῷ Ge 15.9f.; Ob 17, Jn 2.10, Hb 2.4, Zc 6.14. Marks a new stage in a series of events following one after another: [7]καὶ εἶπεν ἡ ἀδελφὴ αὐτοῦ .. [8]ἡ δὲ εἶπεν αὐτῇ ..Πορεύου. ἐλθοῦσα δὲ ἡ νεᾶνις .. [9]εἶπεν δὲ πρὸς αὐτὴν .. ἔλαβεν δὲ ἡ γυνὴ .. [10]ἁδρυνθέντος δὲ τοῦ παιδίου Ex 2.7-10. Even introduces a totally new story: Ὁ δὲ ὄφις ἦν φρονιμώτατος .. Ge 3.1; Ἐγένετο δὲ λιμὸς .. 26.1.
2. in lists of similar items or matters, bringing about clearer separation between them (BDAG, s.v. **1**), 'whereas': "you Noah and your entire immediate family go into the ark (by yourselves)," ἀπὸ δὲ τῶν κτηνῶν καθαρῶν εἰσάγαγε πρὸς σὲ .. [you need to herd them ..] Ge 7.1f. where this latter is further separated from a third entity, ἀπὸ δὲ τῶν κτηνῶν τῶν μὴ καθαρῶν ib.; ἔσται ὁ οἶκος Ιακωβ πῦρ, ὁ δὲ οἶκος Ιωσηφ φλόξ, ὁ δὲ οἶκος Ησαυ εἰς καλάμην Ob 18; Jb 19.19, 20, 23.
3. introduces a separate, but associated incident: "whilst his fellow passengers were frantically struggling with their battered ship, Ιωνας δὲ κατέβη εἰς τὴν κοίλην τοῦ πλοίου καὶ ἐκάθευδε 'Jonah went down into the hold of the ship, and was having a sleep'" Jn 1.5; Is 62.1.
4. introduces a parenthetical comment: ἡ δὲ γῆ ἦν ἀόρατος .. Gn 1.2; "This is the river which encircles the whole land of .. where gold is. τὸ δὲ χρυσίον τῆς γῆς ἐκείνης καλόν" 2.11f.; εὐλόγησεν δὲ αὐτὸν κύριος '(this is an illustration of the fact that) the Lord blessed him' 26.12; Ἔστιν κύριος ἐν τῷ τόπῳ τούτῳ, ἐγὼ δὲ οὐκ ᾔδειν 28.16; ἡ δὲ Νινευη ἦν πόλις μεγάλη 'Now N. was a large city' Jn 3.3; a parenthetical correction, ἐξῆλθεν ὁ βασιλεὺς αὐτῶν πρὸ προσώπου αὐτῶν, ὁ δὲ κύριος ἡγήσεται αὐτῶν '... but as a matter of fact the Lord will lead them' Mi 2.13.
5. contrastive and co-functioning with μέν (q.v.): ἐὰν μὲν ἄρσεν ᾖ, ἀποκτείνατε αὐτό, ἐὰν δὲ θῆλυ, περιποιεῖσθε αὐτό 'if it be male, kill him, but if it be female, let it live' Ex 1.16; εἰ μὲν .. εἰ δὲ μή, .. 32.32. **b**. also without μέν: ἐγένετο Αβελ ποιμὴν προβάτων, Καιν δὲ ἦν ἐργαζόμενος τὴν γῆν Ge 4.2; τόν τε Εφραιμ ἐν τῇ δεξιᾷ ἐξ ἀριστερῶν δὲ Ισραηλ 'E. in his right hand, but to I.'s left' 48.13; ἠγάπησα τὸν Ιακωβ, τὸν δὲ Ησαυ ἐμίσησα Ma 1.2f; Σὺ ἐφείσω .. ἐγὼ δὲ οὐ φείσομαι ..; Jn 4.10f; Hb 2.5, 19; Zc 12.4; contrast between two whole thoughts, 'and yet' Hb 3.18.
Cf. ἀλλά and μέν.

δέησις, εως. f.
v.n. of δέομαι: Is 1.15; addressed to God, Si 32.20 (‖ προσευχή vs. 21); ‖ κλαυθμός 'weeping' Je 3.21, ‖ κραυγή Ps 5.3, ‖ ἱκετεία Si 32.17, ‖ προσευχή Ps 6.10; οἶκος προσευχῆς καὶ ~εως 1M 7.37. Cf.

δέομαι, εὐχή, ἱκετηρία, προσευχή: Trench 188f.

δείδω: pf.(in pres. sense) δέδοικα, ptc. δεδοικώς; plpf.(in impf. sense) ἐδεδοίκειν.

to fear, feel scared: abs., Is 60.14; + acc., θεράπων ⌜οὐ⌝ (Zgl. om.) δεδοικὼς τὸν κύριον αὐτοῦ 'a servant not scared of his master' Jb 3.19, χεῖρα κυρίου 31.35; + a ὅτι clause, 41.2. Cf. δειλιάω, δειλόω, δεῖμα, δεινός, δέος, φοβέομαι: Schmidt 3.523-7.

δείκνυμι, δεικνύω: fut. δείξω; aor.act. ἔδειξα, inf. δεῖξαι, ptc. δείξας, impv. δεῖξον, subj. δείξω, pass. ἐδείχθην, inf. δειχθῆναι, impv.3s δειχθήτω; pf. δέδειχα, ptc.pass. δεδειγμένος.

1. *to cause to be seen*: + acc., Nu 13.27; + acc. and dat. pers., ἔδειξεν ὁ θεός σοι πάντα ταῦτα Ge 41.39, ἔθνεσι τὴν αἰσχύνην σου Na 3.5 (|| ἀποκαλύπτω); κόπους καὶ πόνους Hb 1.3; οὕτως ἔδειξέ μοι Am 7.1; + interr. cl., Ἐγὼ δείξω σοι τί ἐστι ταῦτα Zc 1.9; + ptc., ἔδειξέ μοι τὸν ἱερέα .. ἑστῶτα .. 'showed me the priest .. standing' 3.1; 4K 8.13; + ὅτι 3M 6.15. Cf. ἔδειξα τοῖς ὀφθαλμοῖς σου De 34.4. **b**. mental perception: δεῖξαι τῷ θεράποντί σου τὴν ἰσχύν σου .. καὶ τὴν χεῖρα τὴν κραταιὰν .. De 3.24, αὐτοῦ χειρὸς κράτος 'the power of his hand' 3M 5.13; σκληρά 'harsh things' Ps 59.5; 70.20; ἡμέραν ἀπωλείας Je 18.17; *o* ῥῆμα 'matter' Nu 23.3; pass., *o* πρόσταγμα Da 10.1 LXX (TH ἀποκαλύπτω).

2. *to point to*: + acc. and dat. pers., τῆν γῆν, ἣν ἄν σοι δείξω Ge 12.1; ἐν στύλῳ νεφέλης δεῖξαι αὐτοῖς τὴν ὁδόν 'with a pillar of cloud to show them the way' Ex 13.21, ἡμῖν τὴν ὁδὸν αὐτοῦ Mi 4.2.

3. *to act in such a way as to show evidence of*: πιστά 'loyalty' Ho 5.9.

4. *to show by way of instruction*: ποιήσεις μοι, κατὰ πάντα ὅσα ἐγώ σοι δεικνύω 'you shall do to me exactly as I show you' Ex 25.8; κατὰ τὸν τύπον τὸν δεδειγμένον σοι 'according to the pattern shown to you' 25.40; φόβον τοῖς ἔθνεσιν Ep Je 3; + interr. cl., De 32.20; + dat. pers. and acc., δέδειχα ὑμῖν δικαιώματα καὶ κρίσεις .. ποιῆσαι οὕτως .. 4.5; δέδειχά σοι τοῦ εὑρεῖν σε τὴν ὁδόν Is 48.17.

Cf. ἀνα~, ἀπο~, παρα~, (ὑπο)δείκνυμι, ἀποκαλύπτω, γνωρίζω, σημαίω: Schlier, *TDNT* 2.25-30.

δειλαίνω: aor.subj.pass. δειλανθῶ.ʃ

pass. *to be overcome with fright*: 1M 5.41. Cf. δειλιάω: LSG s.v.

δείλαιος, α, ον.

wretched: *s* pers., ~αία Νινευη Na 3.7 (*DJD* 8: τεταλαιπώρηκεν); || οὐαί Ho 7.13. Cf. ταλαιπωρία, δηλαϊστός.

δειλανδρέω: aor.inf. ~δρῆσαι, subj. ~δρήσω. *

to behave as coward: 2M 8.13.

δείλη, ης. f.

evening: when the day's work finishes, τὸ πρὸς ~ης 'towards the evening' Ge 24.63; τὸ πρωῒ καὶ τὸ ~ης 3K 17.6; adv. gen., ~ης καταλύσουσιν Zp 2.7; opp. πρὸς ἡμέραν 'at daybreak' Es 2.14; πρωῒ καὶ ~ης 'morning and evening' 2C 13.11; ἕως ~ης 1K 20.5, ἀπὸ πρωῒ ἕως ~ης Ex 18.14, ἐκ πρωΐθεν ἕως ~ης 1M 10.80; 2K 11.2 *L* (B: ἑσπέρα). Cf. ἑσπέρα: Johannessohn, *Präp.* 259-61.

δειλία, ας. f.

fearfulness: ἐπάξω ~αν εἰς τὴν καρδίαν αὐτῶν Le 26.36, cf. φόβον καὶ ~αν ἐπάξει ἐπ' αὐτόν Si 4.17; δ. θανάτου Ps 54.5; resulting from the removal of fortifications (?), 88.41; || ἔκλυσις 2M 3.24, || ταραχή 3M 6.19; opp. θράσος 'boldness' 1M 4.32. Cf. δειλιάω, δειλός, φόβος: Trench 34f.

δειλιαίνω: aor.subj. δειλιάνω.ʃ *

to make afraid: + acc., τὴν καρδίαν De 20.8. Cf. δειλός.

δειλιάω: fut. δειλιάσω; aor. ἐδειλίασα, subj. δειλιάσω. * (see Renehan 2.51)

to be afraid, fearful: abs. μὴ φοβεῖσθε μηδὲ δειλιάσητε De 1.21, sim. 31.6 (|| πτοέω pass.), 8, cf. 1M 3.56; *s* καρδία Ps 118.161, Si 22.16, hum. 31.16 (|| εὐλαβέομαι), ψυχή Is 13.7; hum. and + acc. rei, τὴν τῶν ἐθνῶν ἔφοδον 'the attack by the Gentiles' 2M 15.8; + ἀπό τινος, Ps 26.1, ἀπὸ φωνῆς βροντῆς 'the sound of thunder' 103.7, ἀπὸ τῶν λόγων σου 118.161; + ἐπί τινι Je 15.5; φόβῳ Ps 13.5; subst. and disqualified as soldier, 1M 3.56. Cf. δειλία, δειλός, δειλαίνω, δειλόομαι, εὐλαβέομαι, πτήσσω, πτοέω, φοβέομαι.

δειλινός, ή, όν.

pertaining to δείλη (q.v.): *s* θυσία 1E 8.69, ὁλοκαύτωσις 'burnt offering' 2C 31.3 (|| πρωϊνός). **b**. τὸ ~όν 'evening': 3K 18.29; adv. 'in the evening' Ge 3.8; Ex 29.39, 41, Le 6.20 (:: τὸ πρωΐ); τὸ πρωϊνὸν καὶ τὸ ~όν 1E 5.49.

Cf. δείλη, ἑσπέρα, πρωΐ.

δειλόομαι: aor. ἐδειλώθην, subj. δειλωθῶ.ʃ

to fear, be or *become scared of*: abs., 1M 4.21; + acc. rei, ὅρμημα 'advance (of enemies)' 4.8; + inf., 16.6. Cf. δειλιάω, δείδω, φοβέομαι. Del. 1M 5.41 v.l.

δειλός, ή, όν.

1. *fearful, fainthearted*: *s* hum., τῇ καρδίᾳ De 20.8; καρδία Si 2.12, 22.18; subst. 37.11; of punishment awaiting, Wi 4.20.

2. *deserving pity* or *contempt*, 'pitiable, contemptible': *s* λογισμοὶ θνητῶν 'thoughts of mortals' Wi 9.14.

Cf. δειλιάω, δειλόομαι, δειλία, δειλόψυχος, δείδω, φοβερός, θρασύς: Schmidt 3.528f.

δειλόψυχος, ον.∫ *
= δειλός, **1**: *s* hum. and ‖ ἄνανδρος 'cowardly' 4M 8.16; 16.5. Cf. δειλός, ἄνανδρος.

δεῖμα, ατος. n.∫
sense of dread: + ταραχή 'trepidation' Wi 17.8. Cf. φόβος.

δεινάζω: ∫*
to become angry: *s* hum., + δυσφορέω 2M 4.35, 13.25. Cf. θυμόω.

δεινός, ή, όν.
horrible: *s* πληγή 'blow' Jb 2.13, φόβος 33.15, Wi 5.2, ὄνειρος 'dream' 18.17, πόνος 'hardship' 19.16, κόλασις 'punishment' 4M 8.9, σκότος 'darkness' 2K 1.9; subst.n.pl. ~ὰ πάσχω 'suffer terribly' Si 38.16; 'terrifying instruments (of torture)' 4M 8.15. Cf. δεινῶς, πάνδεινος, δείδω, ὑπέρφοβος: Schmidt 3. 528f.

δεινῶς. adv.∫
1. *to frightening degree*: + ὀλέκω 'to cause distress' Jb 10.16; + ὀργῇ χράομαι 'to vent anger' 19.11; + θαμβοῦμαι 'to be alarmed' Wi 17.3.

2. *in vehement, forcible manner* (of style of speech): + κακίζω 'to reproach' 4M 12.2.

Cf. δεινός.

δειπνέω: fut. δειπνήσω; aor.inf. δειπνῆσαι.∫
to have a dinner, meal, to dine: ἀνέπεσαν δειπνῆσαι 'they lay down to dine' To 7.9 𝔊II; 8.1 𝔊I (‖ φαγεῖν καὶ πιεῖν 𝔊II); *s* kings, Da 11.27 LXX; ἐπὶ τραπέζης 'at a table' Pr 23.1. Cf. δεῖπνον and συνδειπνέω.

δεῖπνον, ου. n.
meal, dinner, usually sumptuous or formal: τοῦ βασιλέως Da 1.8 LXX (‖ τράπεζα TH); τῶν ἐσθιόντων τὸ βασιλικόν δ. 1.15; separate from drinks, τὸ δ. αὐτῶν καὶ τὸ οἶνον αὐτῶν 1.16 (also TH); ὁ βασιλεὺς ἐποίησεν δ. μέγα 'held a grand banquet' Da 5.1 TH (‖ LXX ἑστιατορία); taken in the evening and on a battlefield, 4M 3.9. Cf. δειπνέω, συνδειπνέω, ἄδειπνος, ἄριστον, τράπεζα.

δέκα. num.
ten: τοὺς δ. λόγους 'the decalogue' Ex 34.28. Also used as a component of numerals for teens as in πεντεκαίδεκα Ho 3.2; juxtaposed, δ. πέντε πήχεις '15 cubits' Ge 7.20; joined by καί – τριακόσιοι δ. καὶ ὀκτώ 'three hundred and eighteen' 14.14, τέσσαρας καὶ δ. ἀμνούς Nu 29.15.

δεκάδαρχος, ου. m.
leader over ten men: Ex 18.21. Cf. δέκα and LSG s.v.

δεκαδύο. num.
twelve: Ge 5.8.

δεκαέξ. num.∫
sixteen: Jo 15.41.

δεκαμηνιαῖος, α, ον.∫ *
of ten-month duration: *s* χρόνος Wi 7.2 (ref. to hum. foetus). Cf. δεκάμηνος.

δεκάμηνος, ον.∫
lasting ten months: subst.m. (χρόνος understood), 'hum. pregnancy' 4M 16.7. Cf. δεκαμηναῖος.

δεκάπηχυς, υ.∫
ten cubits long: *s* stone, 3K 7.47.

δεκαπλασιάζω: aor.impv.2pl. ~σιάσατε.∫
to repeat ten times: the action to be repeated indicated by a ptc., Ba 4.28.

δεκαπλασίων, ον.∫
tenfold: an adj. or adv. understood, Da 1.20 TH.

δεκαπλασίως. adv.∫
ten times: + comp., Da 1.20 LXX.

δέκατος, η, ον.
1. *tenth* in order: τῇ ~ῃ τοῦ μηνὸς τούτου 'on the tenth (day) of this month' Ex 12.3; νηστεία ἡ ~η Zc 8.19.

2. *one tenth*: τὸ ~ον τῶν τριῶν μέτρων 'one tenth of three measures' Ex 16.36.

3. subst. f., *one tenth of produce of land*: given to another person, ἔδωκεν αὐτῷ ~ην ἀπὸ πάντων Ge 14.20; to God as tithe, 28.22, De 14.21 (cogn. obj. of ἀποδεκατόω), Si 32.11, τῆς γῆς 'of the land' Le 27.30, τῶν γενημάτων 'of the products' To 1.6 𝔊I. See Baumgarten 246-8, Renehan 2.51, *ND* 3.65, and LSG s.v. **II 1**.

4. n. adv. δέκατον 'ten times': τοῦτο ~ον 'these ten times' Nu 14.22.

Cf. ἀποδεκατόω.

δεκατόω.∫
to tithe: abs., Ne 10.37. Cf. ἀποδεκατόω.

δεκάχορδος, ον.
having ten strings: *s* harp, Ps 32.2.

δεκτός, ή, όν. Cf. εἰσδεκτός.
acceptable: *s* cultic offering, ἔναντι κυρίου Le 1.3, Je 6.20; + dat. pers., De 33.16; παρά τινι (pers.) Pr 15.28a, 16.7; καιρός Is 49.8; prayer, Jb 33.26, χείλη δίκαια 'righteous lips' Pr 16.13; ἐπιθυμία 10.24; hum., 22.11 (to God), "decent fellows" Si 2.5; subst. λαβεῖν ~ὸν ἐκ τῶν χειρῶν ὑμῶν 'to receive an acceptable (offering) at your hands' Ma 2.13. **b**. as beneficial: + dat. pers., αὐτοῖς ἔναντι κυρίου Ex 28.34; Le 1.4, 22.19 (‖ οὐ δεχθήσεται ὑμῖν vs. 25); + gen pers., ὑμῶν 'acceptable in your favour' 19.5.

Cf. δέχομαι, (εὐ)αρεστός: Grundmann, *TDNT* 2.58f.

δέλτος, ου. f.
writing-tablet: bronze, 1M 8.22 +.

δένδρον, ου. n. Also δένδρος with dat. δένδρει De 22.6.

tree: καταψύξατε ὑπὸ τὸ δ. 'Cool off under the tree' Ge 18.4; ὑποκάτω ~ου δασέος 'under a leafy tree' De 12.2 (site of a cult), sim. Is 57.5, cf. φύλλον θάλλον ἐπὶ ~ου δασέος 'leaves thriving on ..' Si 14.18 with no cultic connotation; ὑποκάτω .. ~ου συσκιάζοντος 'under a thick-shading tree' Ho 4.13, .. συσκίου Ez 6.13; οὐκ ἐξολεθρεύσεις τὰ ~α αὐτῆς De 20.19; ζωῆς Pr 11.30 (|| ξύλον ζωῆς 3.18, Ge 2.9, Is 65.22); w. a gen. of species, δ. βαλάνου 2.13; object of pagan worship, 17.8 (|| βδέλυγμα). Cf. ξύλον.

δενδροτομέω.ʃ

to fell: + acc., φυτά 'plants' 4M 2.14.

δεξαμενή, ῆς.ʃ

trough, tank for storing water: ἔπλησαν τὰς ~ὰς ποτίσαι τὰ πρόβατα 'filled up the troughs to give water to the sheep' Ex 2.16.

δεξιάζω: aor.ptc.pass. δεξιασθείς.ʃ

to greet with the right hand: 2M 4.34 (glossed as δίδωμι δεξιάν).

δεξιός, ά, όν.

I. adj., *of the right-hand side* (opp. left): *s* χείρ Ge 48.14; ὁ ὀφθαλμὸς ὁ ~ὸς αὐτοῦ 'his right eye' Zc 11.17.

II. Subst.: **a**. f., *right hand*, χείρ understood, ἐν τῇ ~ᾷ 'in his right hand' Ge 48.13 (:: ἐν τῇ ἀριστερᾷ); ἡ ~ά σου .. ἡ ~ά σου χείρ Ex 15.6; οὐκ ἔγνωσαν ~ὰν αὐτῶν Jn 4.11 (:: ἀριστερά); the right hand as a symbol of power and might – ἡ ~ά σου .. δεδόξασται ἐν ἰσχύι· ἡ ~ά σου χείρ .. ἔθραυσεν ἐχθρούς '.. has been glorified with might .. crushed enemies' Ex 15.6; || βραχίων 'arm' Is 65.8, cf. ἀνὴρ ~ᾶς 'right-hand man' Ps 79.18; involved in the creation of the universe, Is 48.13; idiom., δίδωμι ~άν / ~άς τινι 'to make terms with sbd' 1M 6.58, 11.50 (+ ποιέω εἰρήνην w. ἡμῖν as dat. com.) || λαμβάνω ~άς 'to have terms of peace granted' 11.66, 2M 12.12, δοῦναι καὶ λαβεῖν ~άς 'to negotiate a peace treaty' 14.19; ~ὰ ὑπάρξει 'they will have (my) consent' 11.30. **b**. *right-hand side*, **i**. n.pl., εἰ σὺ εἰς ἀριστερά, ἐγὼ εἰς ~ά 'if you go left, I'll go right' Ge 13.9; ἐκ ~ῶν 'on the right' - καταφάγονται ἐκ ~ῶν 'they will eat on the right' Zc 12.6 (:: ἐξ εὐωνύμων); ἐκ ~ῶν τινος 'to the right of sbd or sth', "to Israel's right" Ge 48.13 (place of greater honour or importance,:: ἐξ ἀριστερῶν I.), sim. 3K 2.19, and cf. Pr 3.16 with Rashi ad loc.; ἐκ ~ῶν τοῦ λαμπαδίου 'to the right of the bowl' Zc 4.3 (:: ἐξ εὐωνύμων), *'to the south' Ez 16.46, To 1.2. **ii**. rarely n.sg., εἰς ~ὸν αὐτοῦ 'to his right' Ec 10.2 (:: εἰς ἀριστερὸν αὐτοῦ). **iii**. f.sg., ἵνα ἐπιστρέψω εἰς ~ὰν ἢ εἰς ἀριστεράν 'in order that I may turn to the right or to the left' Ge 24.49. **iv**. adv. n.pl., ~ὰ οὐδὲ εὐώνυμα Nu 20.17, ~ὰ καὶ εὐώνυμα 'right and left' 1M 6.45; ~ὰ ἢ ἀριστερά 'whether to the right or to the left' De 17.20; εἴτε ~ὰ εἴτε ἀριστερά Is 30.21; ~ὰ οὐδὲ ἀριστερά De 2.27, 17.11. **v**. adv. f. sg., ~ὰν οὐδὲ ἀριστεράν Nu 22.26, sim. 1M 2.22. **c**. in combination with ἀριστερά, the latter always follows: see examples above.

Cf. ἀριστερός, εὐώνυμος: Grundmann, *TDNT* 2.37-40.

δέομαι: fut. δεηθήσομαι; aor. ἐδεήθην, inf. δεηθῆναι, impv. δεήθητι, δεήθητε, ptc. δεηθείς, subj. δεηθῶ, opt.3s δεηθείη; pf. δεδέημαι.

1. *to ask humbly for help*: abs., Wi 16.25; + gen. pers., Ὁ θεός, δέομαί σου Nu 12.13; || ἐπικαλέομαι Jb 5.8; + κράζω 34.20, + εὔχομαι Da 6.8, 13 LXX; ἔκλαυσαν καὶ ἐδεήθησάν μου 'they wept and begged me' Ho 12.4, cf. δεηθῆναι τοῦ προσώπου τοῦ κυρίου καὶ ἐκζητῆσαι τὸ πρόσωπον τοῦ κυρίου Zc 8.21, sim. PSol 2.22; Ma 1.9 (|| ἐξιλάσκομαι); ἔναντι κυρίου De 9.18, 25; + κατέναντί τινος– κατέναντι κυρίου Ex 32.11, ἐνώπιόν σου Da 9.18 LXX, cf. ἔναντι κυρίου Si 39.5; δεήθητι κατὰ πρόσωπον 'Confront (Him) with a request' 17.25; + πρός τινα– πρὸς κύριον περὶ τῆν καταλελειμμένων τούτων '.. about these survivors' Is 37.4; + περί τινος (pers.) Ge 25.21, Je 7.16; περὶ πασῶν τῶν ἁμαρτιῶν De 9.18; ὑπὲρ θανάτου ῥύσεως 'for rescue from death' Si 51.9; ὑπὲρ τοῦ ὄρους τοῦ ἁγίου τοῦ θεοῦ ἡμῶν 'for the sake of ..' Da 9.20 LXX; + ἵνα 1E 4.46. In most cases God is addressed, but 4K 1.13, Pr 26.25, Jb 11.19. **b**. + cogn. acc., 3K 9.3. **c**. *to beg and ask for*, περί τινος Si 30.28; + gen. rei, Od 12.11, Jb 9.15¶, 17.1, 30.24. **d**. *to utter in supplication*: + acc., ^λόγους^ 3K 8.59. **e**. δέομαι as a humble and polite form of introductory address, Δέομαι, κύριε Ge 19.18, Ex 4.10, 32.31, Nu 12.11; Ge 44.18 (foll. by an impv.); δεόμεθα, κύριε 43.20; || ἐπικαλέομαι Jb 5.8, || ἱκετεύω 19.16; ἐν προσευχῇ Si 50.19; foll by an impv., δέομαί σου, ἴασαι αὐτήν, 'Please, cure her' Nu 12.13.

2. *to stand in need of*: ptc., οἱ δεόμενοι 'the needy people' 4M 2.8, Wi 16.25.

Cf. κατα~, προσδέομαι, δέησις, αἰτέω, ἀξιόω, ἐγτυγχάνω, ἐξιλάσκομαι, εὔχομαι, ἱκετεύω, προσεύχομαι: Trench 188f.; Cimosa 43-8; *ND* 6.145f.

δέος, ους. n.

fear: + φρικασμός 'shuddering' 2M 3.17, + φόβος 12.22, + τρόμος 'trembling' 15.23. Cf. ἄδεια, δείδω, δεῖμα, φόβος: Shipp 211f.

δέρμα, ατος. n.

1. *skin on living body*: of hum., δ. χρωτός Le 13.2, δ. ὑπὲρ ~ατος 'skin for skin' Jb 2.4; and || σάρξ and ὀστοῦν 'bone' Mi 3.2, 3, La 3.4; of animal, τῶν ἐρίφων 'of the goats' Ge 27.16; κριῶν ἠρυθροδανωμένα 'of rams dyed red' Ex 25.5.

2. *leather object*: Le 11.32.

3. *leather as material to be worked*, 'hide': ἐργάσιμον δ. Le 13.48.

Cf. δορά, δερμάτινος, βύρσα, χρώς, δέρω, ἐκδέρω.

δερμάτινος, η, ον.

made of leather: *s* χιτών 'tunic' Ge 3.21; σκεῦος Le 13.52, Nu 31.20; κάλυμμα 'covering' 4.8, ζώνη 'belt' 4K 1.8. Cf. δέρμα.

δέρρις, εως. f.

1. *curtain*: τριχίνη 'hairy' Ex 26.7; τῆς σκηνῆς 'of the tabernacle' 26.12, Nu 4.25; metaph., ἐκτείνων τὸν οὐρανὸν ὡς ~ιν 'spreading the sky ..' Ps 103.2 (ǁ ἱμάτιον).

2. *leather garment*: τριχίνη 'hairy' Zc 13.4.

Cf. ἱστίον: LSG s.v.

δέρω: aor.inf. δεῖραι.ʃ

to skin: sacrificed animal, 2C 29.34. Cf. ἐκδέρω, δέρμα: Shipp 212f.

δέσις, εως. f.ʃ

chain: golden, Si 45.11 (accessory).

δεσμεύω.

1. *to bind, tie up*: + acc. rei, δράγματα 'sheaves' Ge 37.7; πρὸς ἄμπελον τὸν πῶλον αὐτοῦ 'his colt to a vine' 49.11; τὰ ἱμάτια αὐτῶν δεσμεύοντες σχοινίοις 'tying their clothes with cords' Am 2.8; χεῖρας 'hands' 3M 5.5; + acc. pers., Jd 16.11 B (A: δέω); metaph. δεσμεύεις τὴν ψυχήν μου λαβεῖν αὐτήν 1K 24.12 (*L* συν~), cf. 25.29 (ἐνδεδεμένη).

2. *to dress* a wound with bandage or the like: + acc., σύντριμμα 'wound' Ps 146.3. Cf. καταδεσμεύω.

Cf. δέω, ἀποδεσμεύω, δεσμή, δεσμός, δέσμιος: Caird 1968.466.

δέσμη, ης. f.ʃ

bundle: ὑσσώπου 'of hyssop' Ex 12.22. Cf. δέω, δεσμεύω.

δέσμιος, ον.

subst., *one who is deprived of freedom of movement*: "you have rescued your prisoners from a pit which had no water" Zc 9.11; subst. ~οι τῆς συναγωγῆς 9.12, οἶκος ~ων Ec 4.14, ~οι ἀνειμένοι '.. set free' Jb 3.18 (see Katz 316); metaph. ~οι σκότους καὶ μακρᾶς πεδῆται νυκτός 'captives of darkness and prisoners of long night' Wi 17.2. Cf. δεσμός, δεσμώτης, δέω.

δεσμός, οῦ. m. On the pl. form, see Thack. 154 and BDF, § 49.3.

1. *that which binds and holds together*: Nu 19.15; in pl. and of chains, fetters, and the like, τοὺς ~ούς σου διαρρήξω 'I shall tear apart ..' Na 1.13; around one's neck, Hb 3.13; + κλοιοί 'collars' Je 34.1; ὡς μοσχάρια ἐκ ~ῶν ἀνειμένα 'as young calves let loose from tethers' Ma 4.2; fig., ἐν ~οῖς ἀγαπήσεως Ho 11.4; religious allegiance, Je 2.20 (ǁ ζυγός); discipline, Si 6.25; dog collar or leash, Pr 7.22.

2. *receptacle for keeping money in*, in sg.: ἀργυρίου Ge 42.27; τετρυπημένον 'full of holes' Hg 1.6. Cf. βαλλάντιον.

3. *binding agreement*: ὅρκος ~οῦ 'binding oath' Nu 30.14.

Cf. δέω, δεσμεύω, δεσμώτης, δέσμιος.

δεσμωτήριον, ου. n.

prison: ἀρχιδεσμοφύλαξ ~ου 'chief-jailer of prison' Ge 39.23; pleonastically, οἶκος ~ου Jd 16.21 B (A: οἶ. φυλακῆς). Cf. δεσμώτης, εἱρκτή, φυλακή **4**.

δεσμώτης, ου. m.ʃ

incarcerated person: οἱ ~ται τοῦ βασιλέως κατέχονται ('are detained') ἐκεῖ Ge 39.20; exiles to Babylon, Je 24.1; 36.2 (:: ἐλεύθρος), Ba 1.9. Cf. δέσμιος.

δεσπόζω. Mostly pres., once fut.(4M 5.38).

to have absolute authority and control over: abs. and *s* God, ἐν δυναστείᾳ αὐτοῦ τοῦ αἰῶνος Ps 65.7; + gen. rei, ἡ βασιλεία ^τοῦ θεοῦ^ πάντων δεσπόζει 102.19; τῶν .. κτισμάτων Wi 9.2, πάντων 12.16, τοῦ κράτους τῆς θαλάσσης Ps 88.10 (ǁ καταπραΰνω 'to humble'), ἰσχύος Wi 12.18, τῆς ζωῆς καὶ τοῦ πνεύματος 2M 14.46, πάσης .. δυνάμεως 3M 7.9, λήθης καὶ ἀγνοίας 'oblivion and ignorance' 4M 1.5 (ǁ κρατέω); + gen. pers., ὁ βασιλεὺς ὑπερισχύει καὶ κυριεύει καὶ δεσπόζει πάντων 1E 4.3; *s* women, 4.14 (ǁ κυριεύω); God, τῶν ἐθνῶν Ps 21.29, τοῦ Ιακωβ, τῶν περάτων τῆς γῆς '.. the ends of the earth' 58.14. Cf. δεσπότης, δεσποτεύω, κρατέω, κυριεύω.

δεσποτεία, ας. f.ʃ

absolute authority and control: God's, ἐν παντὶ τόπῳ τῆς ~ας αὐτοῦ Ps 102.22; and eternal, 144.13 (ǁ βασιλεία). Cf. δεσπότης, ἀρχή, βασιλεία.

δεσποτεύω.ʃ

= δεσπόζω: + acc. and *s* God, ἡ ἐνεργεία τοῦ πάντα δεσποτεύοντος 'the act of the one who ..' 3M 5.28. Cf. δεσπότης, δεσπόζω, κυριεύω.

δεσπότης, ου. m.: voc. δέσποτα.

one who wields absolute authority and control over sbd, 'lord, master': often as voc. in an address to God, δέσποτα Ge 15.2; δέσποτα κύριε 15.8, Jn 4.3, Da 9.17 LXX, cf. LSG s.v. **I 3**; δέσποτα τῶν πατέρων 1E 4.50, τῶν οὐρανῶν καὶ τῆς γῆς Ju 9.12, κύριε, πάτερ καὶ δέσποτα ζωῆς μου Si 23.1, ὁ ὢν δέσποτα κύριε Je 1.6, δέσποτα πάσης κτίσεως 3M 2.2; w. ref. to God, Su 5, ὁ πάντων δ. Wi 6.7, ὁ δ. κύριος σαβαωθ Is 1.24, 10.32. **b**. applied to hum., δέσποτα Ὀλοφέρνη Ju 5.24, ~α κύριε 5.20. **c**. general: ὑπὸ ~την ὢν Pr 6.7, δοῦλος ἅμα ~τῃ 'a slave together with his master' Wi 18.11, ὡς ~ταις δουλεύσει 'he shall serve as to his masters' 3.7; opp. οἰκέτης Pr 17.2; δ. τῶν παθῶν ἐστιν ὁ εὐσεβὴς λογισμός 'pious reason is in control of passions' 4M 6.31 (ǁ κρατέω).

Cf. δεσπόζω, δεσποτεία, δεσποτεύω, αὐτοδέσποτος, ἀδέσποτος, ἡγεμών, κύριος, δοῦλος, οἰκέτης: Schmidt 4.119f.; Trench 96-8; Rengstorf, *TDNT* 2.44-8; Schmitt 161f.; Hagedorn & Worp.

δεῦρο Indecl.

I. Introduces a proposal or request–

a. + καί and a subj. in the first person: δεῦρο καὶ ποτίσωμεν .. 'Come on, let's give drink ..' Ge 19.32; ‖ ἐλθέ Pr 7.18. **b**. without καί – νῦν οὖν δ. διαθώμεθα διαθήκην '.. let's make a covenant' Ge 31.44; δ. ἀποστείλω σε 37.13, Ex 3.10; Δ. παραλάβω σε Nu 23.27; δ. συμβουλεύσω σοι Nu 24.14; 1M 11.9; δ. ⸢L: δεῦτε καὶ⸣ πορευθῶμεν 1K 9.9 (‖ δ. καὶ π. 9.10). **c**. + impv.: Δ. εἴσελθε Ge 24.31; καὶ νῦν δ. ἄρασαι 'and now, curse' Nu 22.6, 11; 22.17, 23.7*bis*, Su 50 TH; δ. καὶ ἀναπαύου 12.13 TH; interrupted by a word other than καί - δ. σὺ βασίλευσον Jd 9.14.

II. Impv. '*Come*' addressed to one person: δ. μεθ' ἡμῶν Nu 10.29; Δ. ἔτι μετ' ἐμοῦ εἰς τόπον ἄλλον 23.13; Jd 18.19 B (A: ἐλθέ); πρός με 1K 17.44. **b**. '*Go*' said to one person: δ. πρὸς τοὺς προφήτας 4K 3.13; 1M 12.45; with no local adverbial, Da 12.9 TH (‖ LXX 'Απότρεχε).

III. adv., *to this place*: δ. νῦν ἐλήλυθα 'I have now come here' 2M14.7.

Cf. δεῦτε: Caird 1968.466.

δεῦτε.

I. **a**. Followed asyndetically and immediately by a 1st pl. hortatory subj.(aor.) proposing a joint action: δ. πλινθεύσωμεν πλίνθους 'now let us bake bricks' Ge 11.3; δ. ἀναβῶμεν 'come on, let us go up' Mi 4.2, Is 2.2; δ. βάλωμεν κλήρους 'now let us cast lots' Jn 1.7. Also Ge 11.4, 37.20, 27, Ex 1.10. **b**. δεῦτε καὶ + 1st pl. hortatory subj. aor.: δεῦτε καὶ καταβάντες συγχέωμεν .. 'come on, let's go down and confuse ..' Ge 11.7; Is 1.18, Je 28.10, Wi 2.6. **c**. followed asyndetically by a 2pl. impv.: δ. φάγετε Is 56.9; syndetically — δεῦτε καὶ ἴδετε Ps 65.5; PSol 8.16; preceded by καί and a 2pl. impv., ἐξέλθετε καὶ δ. Da 3.93 TH.

II. used as a genuine 2pl. impv., 'Come!': Is 27.11.

Cf. δεῦρο: Lust 1972; Avalos 1989.

δευτερεύω.

to serve as deputy, be second in rank: *s* priest, Je 52.24 (:: πρῶτος); τῷ βασιλεῖ Es 4.8; *s* chariot, 2C 35.24 (*L*: δεύτερος; δευτέριος 1E 1.29). Cf. LSG s.v.

δευτέριος, α, ον.ʃ

of inferior quality: *s* war-chariot, 1E 1.29 (or poss. 'spare, standby chariot').

δευτερολογέω: aor. ἐδευτερολόγησα.ʃ*

to speak a second time: renegotiation, + dat. pers. 2M 13.22.

δευτερονόμιον, ου. n. *ʃ

second Law: De 17.18, Jo 9.2c. Cf. νόμος.

δεύτερος, α, ον.

second in order: ~ου ἔτους μετὰ τὸν κατακλυσμόν 'in the second year after the innundation' Ge 11.10: ἐν τῷ ~ῳ ἔτει ἐπὶ Δαρείου 'in the second year of the reign of Darius' Hg 1.1; τοῦ προτέρου '(second) to the first' 4M 9.26; a subst. understood, δευτέρᾳ (sc. ἡμέρᾳ) σαββάτου 'on the second of the week' Ps 47.1, ἀπὸ τῆς ~ας (sc. πύλης) Zp 1.10; ἐκ ~ου 'for a second time' 1K 3.6*L* (B: τὸ δεύτερον; vs. 8 ἐν τρίτῳ), Jn 3.1, Hg 2.20, Zc 4.12, Da 2.7 LXX (TH ~ον), ἐκ ~ας Is 61.7; ἐκ ~ας 'as deputy' To 1.22, cf. Fitzmyer ad loc.; subst.m., *right-hand man*, 1K 23.17. **b**. *the other* of a pair: ὄνομα τῇ μιᾷ Αδα, καὶ ὄνομα τῇ ~ᾳ Σελλα Ge 4.19; Ex 25.11. **c**. adv. δεύτερον, 'for a second time, again': Ge 22.15, 27.36, De 9.18, Je 40.1; δεύτερον τοῦτο Jd 20.28*L*; τὸ δεύτερον 'for a second time' Ge 41.5, Le 13.5.

Cf. δευτερόω, δύο, πρῶτος: Shipp 213f.

δευτερόω: fut. δευτερώσω; aor. ἐδευτέρωσα, inf. ~ρῶσαι, subj. ~ρώσω.*

1. *to occur twice*: *s* ἐνύπνιον 'dream' Ge 41.32 (reinforced by δίς 'twice').

2. *to do again*, 'repeat': abs., Ne 13.21, 3K 18.34, Si 19.14; ἐν προσκυνήσει 'bowing down' 50.21; + acc. rei, λόγον ἐν προσευχῇ σου 'repeat yourself in prayer' 7.14, τὰς ὁδούς σου 'your practices' Je 2.36; + acc. pers., ἐδευτέρωσεν ἕκαστος τὸν παρ' αὐτοῦ 'each repeated it to the one next to him' 3K 21.20, cf. οὐ δευτερώσω αὐτῷ 1K 26.8 (*L* αὐτόν).

Cf. δεύτερος: LSG s.v.

δευτέρωσις, εως. f.ʃ *

*__1__. v.n. of δευτερόω **2**: λόγου ἀκοῆς '(repeating) what one has heard as a rumour' Si 42.1.

2. *second rank*: ἱερεὺς ~εως 'assistant priest' 4K 23.4 (*L*: δευτερεύων); 25.18.

δέχομαι: fut. δέξομαι, pass. δεχθήσομαι; aor.mid. ἐδεξάμην, impv. δέξαι, subj. δέξωμαι, inf. δέξασθαι, ptc. δεξάμενος.

to receive approvingly or *willingly*: + acc., τὸ αἷμα τοῦ ἀδελφοῦ σου Ge 4.11; μέθυσμα καὶ οἶνον ἐδέξατο καρδία λαοῦ μου 'my people's heart received drinks and wine' Ho 4.11; ἐν δόματι Ho 10.6; δῶρα Ge 33.10, 'bribes' Jb 36.18; δῶρα ἐκλεκτά 'choice gifts' Am 5.11; τὰ ἔργα τῶν χειρῶν αὐτοῦ De 33.11; ἐκ τῆς χειρός σου Ge 4.11; ἐκ τῶν χειρῶν αὐτῶν Ex 32.4; διὰ τῶν ἐμῶν χειρῶν Ge 33.10; ***o*** cultic offering, Le 19.7 (pass.), Jb 8.20; visitors, Wi 19.14; sth incorporeal, δόξαν .. καὶ ὄνομα 'glory .. and fame' 1M 2.51, παιδείαν Zp 3.2, 7, Je 5.3, 17.23, τοὺς λόγους μου καὶ τὰ νόμιμά μου Zc 1.6; εἰς τὴν καρδίαν σου 'ponder, take to heart' De 30.1, καρδίᾳ .. ἐντολάς Pr 10.8. **b**. 'to come to terms with, reconcile oneself with': δέξαι τὴν ἀδικίαν τῶν θεραπόντων τοῦ θεοῦ τοῦ πατρός σου Ge 50.17 (|| Ἄφες 'Forgive'); Si 2.4. **c**. against one's will: ἐκ χειρὸς κυρίου διπλᾶ τὰ ἁμαρτήματα αὐτῆς 'the double portion of the penalty for her sins at the hands of the Lord' Is 40.2. **d**. + dat. of beneficiary, οὐ δεχθήσεται ταῦτα ὑμῖν Le 22.25 (|| δεκτὰ ὑμῖν vs. 19). **e**. *s* receptive human ears: ***o*** divine message, Je 9.20.

Cf. ἀπο~, εἰσ~, ἐκ~, προσ~, ὑποδέχομαι, δεκτός, ἀρέσκω, ἐκ~, λαμβάνω: Schmidt 3.210-26, 230-3; Büchsel, *TDNT* 2.50-3.

I **δέω**: fut. δήσω, pass. δεθήσομαι; aor. ἔδησα, ptc. δήσας, inf. δῆσαι, subj. δήσω, mid. ἐδησάμην, pass. ἐδέθην; pf.pass. δέδεμαι, ptc. δεδεμένος.

1. *to tie*: ἐπὶ τὴν χεῖρα αὐτοῦ κόκκινον 'a scarlet string on his hand' Ge 38.28; μαστούς 'breasts' (on birth) Ez 16.4; σχοινίοις 'with cords' 27.24, ἁλύσει 'with a chain' Wi 17.18; ***o*** hands, 2K 3.34; skin of wine, Jb 32.19; horse and donkey, 4K 7.10; mid., hair of one's own head, Ju 16.8.

2. *to incarcerate, tie up*: + acc. pers., Ge 42.24, Ho 10.6, Is 3.10, ἐν πέδαις 'in fetters' Je 52.11, ἐν δεσμοῖς Ez 3.25; pass. δεθήσονται χειροπέδαις 'will be handcuffed' Na 3.10.

**3*. δέω σύνδεσμον 'to stage a conspiracy': 4K 12.21B.

Cf. ἀπο~, δια~, ἐπι~, κατα~, περι~, προσ~, συνδέω, δεσμός, δέσμιος.

II **δέω**: fut. δεήσω.

1. *to be needed*: practically, τὰ δέοντα διπλᾶ 'the necessary double portion (of food)' Ex 16.22; τὰ δέοντα καὶ τὸν ἱματισμόν 'the necessities and the clothes' 21.10; τὰ δέοντά σοι 'your expenses' To 5.15; τὰ δέοντα τῷ Σαλωμων ἐν ἡμέρᾳ μιᾷ 'Solomon's daily needs' 3K 5.2; *s* inf. clause, Ποσάκις δεῖ σοι .. προστάττειν; 'How often does one have to order you ..?' 3M 5.37; 4M 14.18. **b**. *required by a rule or law or a code of ethics*: impers. and + inf., οὐ δεῖ ποιεῖν 'not required to do' Le 4.2, 5.17; Pr 22.14[a]. **c**. *destined and inevitable*: on account of God's will or decision, ἃ δεῖ γενέσθαι μετὰ ταῦτα 'that which is to happen after this' Da 2.29 TH, τὰς ψυχάς, ἃς οὐκ ἔδει ἀποθανεῖν .. ἃς οὐκ ἔδει ζῆσαι 'the souls which should not have died .. which should not have lived' Ez 13.19. **d**. *required by virtue of logic*: ἐντεῦθεν δεῖ ὑμᾶς γνῶναι, ὅτι .. 'hence you must but conclude that ..' 1E 4.22. **e**. δέον ἐστιν 'it is proper' + inf.: Si prol. 3, 4, δέον ἐστὶν καὶ πρέπον μνημονεύειν .. 'it is proper and appropriate to remember ..' 1M 12.11; cf. δέον ἡγησάμεθα διασαφῆναι ὑμῖν 'we considered it appropriate to notify you' 2M 1.18.

2. + neg. and impers., *not permitted*: + inf., Da 6.15 TH.

Cf. ἀναγκαῖος, καθήκω, πρέπω, χρή: Schmidt 3.702-5; Grundmann, *TDNT* 2.21-5; Fascher 1954.

δή

Never clause-initial.

1. adds a sense of urgency to commands, exhortations, requests, expressions of speaker's wish, determination or emotion: + impv. λημφθήτω δὴ ὕδωρ 'Do take water' Ge 18.4(*a*); Εὐλόγησον δὴ κἀμέ, πάτερ Ge 27.34(*a*: MT נִי), 38(-); κόπασον δή 'Do cease, please' Am 7.5(*a*); ἀκούσατε δὴ ταῦτα Mi 3.1(*b*); ἄκουε δή Zc 3.8(*a*); + fut., παύσω De 32.26(-); + hortatory subj., Je 5.24(*a*); following ἰδού Is 3.1(-), Ps 132.1(-); οὐαὶ δὴ ἡμῖν La 5.16(*a*); in a plea, Παρέλθωμεν δὴ .. 'Do allow us to pass through ..' Jd 11.19 B(*a*) (:: παρελεύσομαι δὴ .. vs. 17); μὴ δή + subj., 1K 3.17(*a*).

2. asseverative particle, 'indeed; surely': Jb 6.3(*b*); μὴ δή 'O never' Ne 1.5(-), 11(-); λέγω δὴ τὴν ἀρχιερωσύνην 'I mean the highpriesthood, of course' 2M 14.7; Ὦ δή, κύριε 'Goodness me, I'm telling you, sir' 4K 6.5(*b*). **b**. confirmatory: To 12.11 𝔊[I] (𝔊[II] ἤδη). **c**. strengthens an indefinite notion: ὅθεν δή 'never mind where (it comes) from' Wi 15.12, ὅς δή ποτ' οὖν ἦν ἐκεῖ 'whoever was there' 17.16.

a) נָא; *b*) אֲהָהּ.

δῆγμα, ατος. n.ʃ

bite, sting: of snake, Wi 16.5; of locust and fly, 16.9; ~ατα ἀνθρώπων Mi 5.5. Cf. δάκνω.

δηλαϊστός, ή, όν.ʃ*

wretched, miserable: *s* pers., Ez 5.15 (+ στενακτός). Cf. δείλαιος, στενακτός, ταλαιπωρός.

δῆλος, η, ον.

1. *obvious*: ~ον ὅτι .. 4M 2.7. Cf. ἔκδηλος.

2. subst.m.pl. *some device used for discovering God's will*: κρίσις τῶν ~ων 'decision reached by means of ..' Nu 27.21; in possession of the high priest, δῆλοι καὶ ἀλήθεια De 33.8 (|| δήλωσις καὶ ἀ. Ex 28.26, Le 8.8), ~οι ἀληθείας Si 45.10; || θυσία, θυσιαστήριον, and ἱερατεία Ho 3.4; ἐρώτημα ~ων 'answer obtained by ..' Si 36.4. Cf. δήλωσις: Guinot 1989.

δηλόω: fut. δηλώσω, ptc. δηλώσων; aor. ἐδήλωσα, inf. δηλῶσαι, impv. δήλωσον, subj. δηλώσω, pass. ἐδηλώθην, inf. δηλωθῆναι; pf.ptc.pass. δεδηλωμένος, impv.3s δεδηλώσθω.

1. *to make known, disclose*: *s* God and + dat. pers. and acc. rei, τὸ ὄνομά μου οὐκ ἐδήλωσα αὐτοῖς Ex 6.3; σὺ δὲ οὐκ ἐδήλωσάς μοι ὃν συναποστελεῖς μετ' ἐμοῦ 'you have not disclosed to me whom you are going to send with me' 33.12; δηλώσουσιν τὰ δικαιώματά σου τῷ Ιακωβ De 33.10; || γνωρίζω Je 16.21, Da 7.16 LXX (TH γνωρίζω); 2.25 LXX (TH ἀναγγέλλω); ***o*** μυστήριον 2.19, 47 LXX (TH ἀποκαλύπτω), ὅραμα .. καὶ τὴν τούτου σύγκρισιν 2.26 LXX; 1K 12.23 *L* (B δείκνυμι). **b.** mid. *to reveal oneself*: + dat. pers. 1K 3.21.

2. *to explain*: + acc., λόγους 1E 3.15 (|| ἀπαγγέλλω 16). **b.** *to expound in writing*: ***o*** matters, 2M 2.23.

Cf. δήλωσις, ἀνα~, ἀπαγγέλλω, ἀποκαλύπτω, γνωρίζω, δείκνυμι: Bultmann, *TDNT* 2.61f.; Drescher 1970.139-42.

δήλωσις, εως. f.ʃ

1. *act of making clear, explaining*: ἡ δ. τῶν λόγων σου φωτιεῖ 'the explication through your words is illuminating' Ps 118.130; of a mysterious dream, Da LXX 2.27.

2. *a means of discovering God's will* (?), carried by the high priest in his oracular pouch (τὸ λόγιον τῆς κρίσεως): τὴν ~ιν καὶ τὴν ἀλήθειαν Ex 28.26, Le 8.8 (|| δῆλοι καὶ ἀ. De 33.8); ἀρχιερεὺς ἐνδεδυμένος τὴν ~ιν καὶ τὴν ἀλήθειαν 'the high priest wearing ..' 1E 5.40.

Cf. δῆλος, δηλόω, διασάφησις, σύγκρισις.

δημαγωγία, ας. n.ʃ

act of persuading and leading a public in a certain direction: w. negative connotation, + ἐπιβουλή 'plotting,' ἐπισύστασις 'rebellious action' 1E 5.70. Cf. ὀχλαγωγέω.

δημεύω: fut.pass. δημευθήσομαι.ʃ

to seize as public property: pass., ***o*** property, Da 3.96 LXX.

δημηγορέω.ʃ

to speak in public: ***s*** king, Pr 30.31; high priest, 4M 5.15.

δήμιος, ου. m.ʃ

public executioner: 2M 5.8, 7.29.

δημιουργέω: pf.ptc.pass. δεδημιουργημένος.ʃ

1. *to construct*: pass., ***o*** altar, 2M 10.2; objects of idolatry, Wi 15.13.

2. *to administer*: + acc. rei, τὸν νόμον 4M 7.8.

Cf. πλάσσω, ποιέω.

δημιουργός, οῦ. m.ʃ

perpetrator: κακῶν 2M 4.1.

δῆμος, ου. m.

1. *assembled crowd*: 1E 9.53, Ju 6.1.

2. *organised body of humans*: a component unit of the ancient Israelite society, smaller than φυλή and consisting of οἶκοι: Nu 1.20 +; Jd 13.2B, Jo 7.14. See *BA* 4:159-61; Dorival 1996.532-4. **b.** general: ἁγίων Da 8.24 LXX (TH λαὸς ..); δ. Ισραηλ Ju 4.8, τῶν Ἰουδαίων 1M 8.29 (|| ἔθνος vs. 23).

Cf. ἔθνος, λαός, ὄχλος, φυλή: Schmidt 4.572f.

δημόσιος, α, ον.ʃ

f.s. dat. adv., δημοσίᾳ *in public view*: 2M 6.10, 3M 2.27, 4.7.

δημοτελής, ές.ʃ

done or made at the public cost: ***s*** εὐωχία 'festivity' 3M 4.1.

δημότης, ου. m.ʃ

commoner: opp. βασιλεύς Wi 18.11.

διά prep.

I. + gen. **1.** *from end to end of* a circumscribed, passable space, 'through' ("extension"): ἐπορεύετο δ. τῆς ἐρήμου 'walked through the wilderness' Ge 24.62; δ. τῆς παρεμβολῆς 'through the encampment' Ex 32.27; διαπορευόμενος δι' αὐτῆς 'go through it' Zp 3.1; διῆλθε δ. μέσης τῆς πόλεως Je 44.4; entry made at an aperture, δ. θυρίδων εἰσελεύσονται 'will enter through the windows' Jl 2.9; τὰ ἐκπορευόμενα δ. τῶν χειλέων μου 'that which comes out through my lips' Ps 88.35; παρακύψας δ. τῆς θυρίδος 'peeping through the window' Ge 26.8. **b.** of time, δι' ὅλης τῆς νυκτός 1M 12.27, δι' ὅλης ἡμέρας 4M 3.7, δι' ἡμέρας καὶ νυκτός 'day and night' 2M 13.10; δι' αἰῶνος 'for ever' De 5.29, Is 60.21, δι' αἰώνων Si 17.8¶; διὰ πολλῶν γενεῶν 'throughout many generations' Is 13.20 (|| εἰς τὸν αἰῶνα χρόνον). **c.** διὰ παντός 'continuously': Ex 25.29, Le 6.13, 24.2 (|| ἐνδελεχῶς vs. 3), Ho 12.6; Ps 33.2 (|| ἐν παντὶ καιρῷ), Pr 15.15 (|| πάντα τὸν χρόνον); as attributive adj., ἄρτοι δ. παντός 'perpetual loaves' Nu 4.7, τῆς ὁλοκαυτώσεως τῆς δ. παντός 'the continuous whole-burnt-offering' 28.10, cf. ὁλοκαύτωμα ἐνδελεχισμοῦ 28.6, 23; θυσία δ. παντός Le 6.20, cf. ἡ θ. ἡ καθ' ἡμέραν Nu 4.16 and θυμίαμα ἐνδελεχισμοῦ δ. παντός Ex 30.8; ἄνδρας δ. παντός 'permanent staff' Ez 39.14, cf. ἀρχιερωσύνη .. διὰ βίου 'life highpriesthood' 4M 4.1; *δι' ὅλου – ἔρημος δι' ὅλου 'permanent wilderness' Ez 38.8, adv. 'all the time, throughout the period' 3K 10.8, 1M 6.18; *διὰ τέλους 'endlessly, perpetually' Is 62.6, Es B 7.

2. *with mediation of*: pers., δ. τοῦ θεοῦ Ge 4.1, 40.8, 1K 22.13; δ. πνεύματος τοῦ θυμοῦ σου Ex 15.8; συνέταξεν κύριος .. δ. Μωυσῆ 35.29; δ. χειρὸς Μωυσῆ Le 10.11, δέξαι τὰ δῶρα δ. τῶν ἐμῶν χειρῶν 'Accept the gifts at my hands' Ge 33.10; || ὑπό τινος Nu 4.27 and τὸ ῥηθὲν ὑπὸ κυρίου δ. τοῦ προφήτου Mt 1.22, cf. ὁ ἁλοὺς δ. τοῦ θεοῦ 'convicted through God' Ex 22.9, but possibly '*by* God' as in διά τινος .. φόνους συντελεῖσθαι 'murders .. perpetrated by one ..' 2M 4.3 and κρέα .. δι' αὐτοῦ παρασκευασθέντα 'meat .. prepared by him' 6.21; || ἐν Nu 5.8; δι' ἑαυτοῦ 'unaided' Ep Je 26.

3. indicates an indirect cause: δ. φωνῆς κυρίου 'prompted by what the Lord had said' Nu 3.16; ἐτελεύτησεν .. δ. ῥήματος κυρίου 'died .. as decreed by the Lord' De 34.5; Ex 17.1.

4. indicates a means for achieving an end: τὴν ὁδόν, δι᾽ ἧς ἀναβησόμεθα ἐν αὐτῇ De 1.22 (ǁ ἐν); ἐπηγγείλατο δ. τοῦ νόμου 'he promised ..' 2M 2.18.

5. *after the elapse of* a period of time: δι᾽ ἑπτὰ ἐτῶν De 15.1; 9.11; δ. πολλῶν γενεῶν Is 24.22, δ. χρόνου .. πολλοῦ 30.27, δ. ἡμερῶν πολλῶν Pr 7.20; μία (ǁ 2C 9.21 ἅπαξ) δ. τριῶν ἐτῶν 'one (ship) every three years' 3K 10.22.

6. in various adv. expressions: δι᾽ ἑκατέρου 'in either case' 4M 5.21; δι᾽ εὐθείας 'in a straight line' Is 59.14; δ. κενῆς 'in vain, to no purpose' Le 26.16, 'for no good, justifiable reason' Jb 2.3, Ps 24.3, Si 23.11; δ. τάχους 'instantly' Ps 6.11, Si 11.21, Est E 18 o'.

II. + acc. **1**. *for the reason, ground* or *cause of*: καταράσασθαι τὴν γῆν δ. τὰ ἔργα τῶν ἀνθρώπων 'to curse the earth on account of man's works' Ge 8.21; δ. ἁμαρτίαν αὐτοῦ ἀπέθανεν Nu 27.3; δ. τὴν σφαγὴν καὶ τὴν ἀσέβειαν (argument for a punitive action) Ob 10; δι᾽ αἵματα ἀνθρώπων 'in order to avenge murders' Hb 2.8; δι᾽ ἐμέ 'on my account' Jn 1.12; δ. τοῦτο 'for this reason' Ge 11.9; 20.2 (ǁ περί τινος 26.7 but διά τινα 26.9); διὰ τί 'why?' Le 10.17, ǁ ἵνα τί Nu 11.11, Ps 41.10; δ. τὸν μετεωρισμὸν τῆς καρδίας 'because of the elation of his mind' 2M 5.21 (ǁ ἀπὸ τῆς ὑπερηφανίας 'out of arrogance'); οἱ δ. τὸν θεὸν ἀποθνήσκοντες ζῶσιν τῷ θεῷ 'those who die for God live to Him' 4M 16.25. **b**. + articular inf., δ. τὸ εἶναι αὐτοὺς σάρκας Ge 6.3; δ. τὸ σὲ γυναῖκα αὐτοῦ εἶναι 'on the ground that you are his wife' 39.9; Ex 16.8, 17.7, 19.18, 33.3.

2. *thanks to*: ὅπως ἂν εὖ μοι γένηται δ. σέ 'so that it would turn out to my advantage thanks to you' Ge 12.13 (ǁ ἕνεκεν σοῦ); 18.26 (ǁ vs. 24 ἕνεκεν + gen.); δ. τὴν παρὰ τοῦ θεοῦ βοήθειαν 2M 12.11; σωτηρίας τῆς δ. θεὸν γενομένης αὐτοῖς 'the rescue brought about by God for them' 3M 6.36; δ. τὸν θεὸν τοῦ κόσμου μετελάβετε 'you owe to God the share you have had of the world' 4M 16.18.

3. *in the course of* a period of time: δ. τὴν ἡμέραν 1K 9.12, 13.

Cf. ἕνεκεν / ~κα, παρά **III 2**: Johannessohn, *Präp*., 235-45.

διαβάθρα, ας. f.ʃ

ladder: 2K 23.21.

διαβαίνω: fut. ~βήσομαι; aor. διέβην, subj. διαβῶ, impv. διάβηθι, inf. ~βῆναι, ptc. ~βάς.

to traverse in order to reach another place or side: abs. Am 6.2, To 11.16 𝔊[II]; + acc., ποταμόν 'a river' Ge 31.21; τὸν Ἰορδάνην Nu 32.29 (ǁ παρέρχομαι vs. 21), De 3.27, 4.21, 30.18; διάβασιν 'a ford' Ge 32.22; χειμάρρουν 'a wadi' 32.23; w. prep., δι᾽ ὕδατος Is 43.2 (ǁ διέρχομαι); εἰς τὴν γῆν Nu 32.7; ἐν μέσῳ παγίδων 'in the midst of snares' Si 9.13 (ǁ περιπατέω); ἐπὶ τὸ φρέαρ τοῦ ὅρκου 'over to the well of the oath' Am 5.5 (v.l. ἀνα~); πρὸς σέ Ge 31.52, ἐπί σε Is 45.14, πέραν τῆς θαλάσσης Ba 3.30; ǁ ὑπερβαίνω 'to cross over' Pr 9.18b, ǁ πορεύομαι 30.29; ***s*** ship, Wi 5.10.

Cf. διάβασις, διαβιβάζω, ~περάω, ~πορεύομαι, διέρχομαι.

διαβάλλω: aor. διέβαλον, ptc. ~βαλών.

to speak slanderously against: abs., 2M 3.11; + acc. pers., Da 3.8; + dat. pers. (the addressed) ib. TH; false accusation, 2M 3.11. Cf. διαβολή, διάβολος, βλασφημέω, δυσφημέω, ἐνδιαβάλλω, κακολογέω, καταλαλέω: Schmidt 1.157f.

διάβασις, εως. f.

1. *place where a river* or *a wadi is crossed over*, 'ford': διέβη τὴν ~ιν τοῦ Ιαβοκ Ge 32.22, τοῦ Ἰορδάνου Jd 12.5.

2. v.n. of διαβαίνω: ὁδὸς ~εως Is 51.10; ποταμῶν 'of rivers' PSol 6.3.

Cf. διαβαίνω.

διάβημα, ατος. n.* Alw. pl.

step taken along a path: ἐν ταῖς τρίβοις μου Ps 16.5. Cf. βῆμα. **b**. *area to be covered by a step*: ***o*** of πλατύνω 'to broaden' Ps 17.37. **c**. metaph., *course of action taken*: Pr 20.24, Jb 31.4 (ǁ ὁδός), PSol 16.9.

διαβιάζομαι: aor.ptc. ~βιασάμενος.ʃ

to act deliberately against an instruction or *request*: διαβιασάμενοι ἀνέβησαν Nu 14.44. Cf. βιάζομαι: LSG s.v.

διαβιβάζω: aor. διεβίβασα, subj. ~βιβάσω, inf. ~βιβάσαι, impv.2pl ~βιβάσατε.

to cause to cross from one side to the other: of a river crossing and + acc., πάντα τὰ αὐτοῦ 'all his possessions' Ge 32.24; τὴν ἀποσκευὴν αὐτῶν καὶ τὰς γυναῖκας αὐτῶν καὶ τὰ κτήνη αὐτῶν Nu 32.30 (ǁ διαβαίνω); + a second acc. of river, ἡμᾶς τὸν Ἰορδάνην 32.5; αὐτοὺς θάλασσαν ἐρυθράν Wi 10.18 (ǁ διάγω: of the crossing of the Red Sea); of a land, 2K 2.8*L* (B: ἀνα~). Cf. διαβαίνω.

διαβιόω: aor.subj. ~βιώσω.ʃ

to survive without dying immediately: ἡμέραν μίαν ἢ δύο Ex 21.21. Cf. ζάω.

διαβοάω: fut. ~βοήσω; aor.pass. διεβοήθην.ʃ

to announce abroad: + acc. rei and dat. pers., ἄφεσιν ἐπὶ τῆς γῆς πᾶσιν τοῖς κατοικοῦσιν αὐτήν Le 25.10; pass., διεβοήθη εἰς τὰ σκηνώματα ἡ παρουσία αὐτῆς 'her arrival was announced in the tents' Ju 10.18; ***o*** news, διεβοήθη ἡ φωνὴ εἰς τὸν οἶκον Φαραω Ge 45.16. Cf. βοάω.

διαβολή, ῆς. f.

1. *false, malicious accusation*: Si 19.15; γλώσσης 51.2. φθόνου 'arising from envy' 3M 6.7. **b**. *criticism*: Si 38.17. **c**. *prejudice*: Es 7.24 *L*.

2. *dissuasion*: εἰς ~ήν σου 'to dissuade you' Nu 22.32.

Cf. (ἐν)διαβάλλω, δυσφημία.

διάβολος, ου. m.

he who is intent on harming sbd else's wellbeing and interests: 1C 21.1, Es 8.1 (Haman), πονηρός 1M 1.36; adversary (ἀντικείμενος) of a high priest, Zc 3.1. **b.** verbally through slanderous remarks: Ps 108.6 (‖ ἁμαρτωλός), Jb 1.9. **c.** capable of harming physically: Jb 2.7 (w. the def. article from the first occurrence in the account). **d.** w. ref. to the tempter in the Garden of Eden: φθόνῳ ~ου θάνατος εἰσῆλθεν εἰς τὸν κόσμον Wi 2.24

Cf. διαβάλλω, ἐχθρός, σατανᾶς: Foerster, *TDNT* 2.72f.

διαβουλεύω.ʃ

mid. *to deliberate*: with evil intention, διαβουλευόμενοι ἐλοιδόρουν 'they reviled ..' Ge 49.23. Cf. διαβούλιον, βουλεύω.

διαβούλιον, ου. n.*

that which one deliberates to do, 'design, plan': τὰς ὁδοὺς αὐτοῦ καὶ τὰ ~α αὐτοῦ 'his practices and his designs' Ho 4.9; τὰ ~α τοῦ πνεύματος ὑμῶν 'what you have in your minds' Ez 11.5; οὐκ ἔδωκαν τὰ ~α αὐτῶν τοῦ ἐπιστρέψαι πρὸς τὸν θεὸν αὐτῶν 'they did not consider returning to their God' Ho 5.4. Cf. βουλή.

διαγγέλλω: fut. διαγγελῶ, pass. ~γγελήσομαι; aor. subj. ~γείλω, pass. διηγγέλην, subj. διαγγελῶ.ʃ

1. *to spread knowledge of, make widely known*: abs., ***s*** ἥλιος Si 43.2; ***o*** God's name, ἐν πάσῃ τῇ γῇ Ex 9.16; ***o*** God's instruction, Ps 2.7, annihilation by God, 58.13; + dat. pers. and acc. rei, πᾶσι τὸ μεγαλεῖον τοῦ θεοῦ 2M 3.34; + ὅτι 1.33; σάλπιγγος φωνῇ 'with the sound of a trumpet' Le 25.9, σάλπιγγι ib.

2. *to announce an order* to do: 3K 4.21*L*; + inf., Jo 6.10.

Cf. ἀναγγέλλω: Schniewind, *TDNT* 1.67f.

διάγγελμα, ατος. n.ʃ *

orally transmitted directive: foods and drinks so ordered and delivered, 3K 5.1. Cf. Caird 1968.467.

διαγίνομαι.ʃ

to go about one's life: πρός τι, aiming at, 2M 11.26.

διαγινώσκω: aor. διέγνωσα, impv. διάγνωθι, subj. pass. ~γνωσθῶ; pf.ptc.pass. διεγνωσμένος; plpf. διεγνώκειν.

1. *to determine* a step to be taken: + inf., Nu 33.56, Ju 11.12, 2M 9.15.

2. *to form a view on*: + indir. question, πῶς .. De 2.7; τὰ ἐν τῇ καρδίᾳ σου 8.2.

3. *to notice the presence of*, 'spy': pass., ***o*** wisdom, Pr 14.33.

Cf. διάγνωσις.

διαγλύφω: fut. ~γλύψω; pf.ptc.pass. ~γεγλυμμένος.ʃ

to engrave on: + acc., λίθους Ex 28.11; temple, Ez 41.19; part of a building, 41.20. **b.** *to engrave on with*: + double acc. and pass., βλαστοὺς κρίνου 'with flowers of lilies' 2C 4.5.

Cf. γλύφω, γράφω.

διάγνωσις, εως. f.ʃ

v.n. of διαγινώσκω, q.v.: ἡμέρα ~εως Wi 3.18 (final judgement day).

διαγογγύζω: fut. ~γογγύσω; aor. διεγόγγυσα. *

to grumble: ***s*** alw. human, abs. De 1.27; + κατά τινος (hum.), Ex 16.7, 8, Nu 16.11; + ἐπί τινα (hum.) Ex 15.24, 16.2, Nu 14.2; κατά τινος 'about sth' 14.36; + τινι ἐπί τινι 'against sbd over sth' Si 34.24. Cf. γογγύζω.

διαγορεύω: pf.ptc.pass. διηγορευμένος.ʃ

to prescribe explicitly: in writing, 1E 5.48; ***s*** law, Da Su 61 LXX.

διαγραφή, ῆς. f.ʃ

that which has been delineated, 'diagram, sketch': τοῦ οἴκου Ez 43.12. Cf. διαγράφω.

διαγράφω: fut. ~γράψω; aor.impv.3pl ~γραψάτωσαν; pf.ptc.pass. ~γεγραμμένος.

1. *to delineate*: + acc., πόλιν and on a brick, Ez 4.1; τὴν γῆν Jo 18.4.

2. *to write an order of payment for*: + acc., εἰς τὸ γαζοφυλάκιον .. τάλαντα μύρια '10,000 talents in favour of the treasury' Es 3.9. **b.** *to pay*: + acc., 2M 4.9.

Cf. διαγραφή.

διάγω: fut.act. διάξω, pass. ~χθήσομαι; aor. διήγαγον, ptc. διαγαγών.

1. *to cause to move* through: + acc., διὰ πυρός Zc 13.9; ἐν πυρὶ 4K 16.3 (hum. sacrifice) ‖ 2C 28.3 διὰ πυρός; αὐτοὺς δι' ὕδατος πολλοῦ Wi 10.18 (‖ διαβιβάζω: of the crossing of the Red Sea), sim. Ps 77.13; τὸν Ισραηλ διὰ μέσου ^τῆς ἐρυθρᾶς θαλάσσης^ 135.14; ἐν τῇ ἐρήμῳ 135.16; ὑπὸ τὴν ῥάβδον 'under the rod' Ez 20.37; τὰ σκέλη σου παντὶ παρόδῳ 'your legs to every passer-by' (of a whore's posture in copulation) 16.25. **b.** *to cause to move* away: from a danger, τινα Jb 12.17, 3M 1.3.

2. *to pass life, live*: βίον understood, Si 38.27, cf. διαγωγή. **b.** *to spend* a period of time: abs., 3M 6.35; + acc., ἡμέρας 3M 4.8, τὸ σάββατον 2M 12.38.

Cf. ἄγω, διαβιβάζω.

διαγωγή, ῆς.ʃ

life-style: Es B 5 o' (*L* παραγωγή). Cf. διάγω, παραγωγή, βίος **1 b**, δρόμος.

διαδέχομαι: aor.ptc. ~δεξάμενος.

1. *to act on behalf of*: abs. 2C 31.12, 2M 4.31; + acc. pers., τὸν βασιλέα Es 10.3.

2. *to take the place of and come after*, 'succeed': + acc., Wi 7.30, 4M 4.15. **b**. *to supplant and remove forcibly*: τινα Wi 17.21.

Cf. διάδοχος.

διαδέω: aor. διέδησα.ʃ

to bind and tie: + acc., hands and arms, ἱμᾶσιν 'with ropes' 4M 9.11. Cf. δέω.

διάδηλος, ον.ʃ

easily noticeable: οὐ ~οι ἐγένοντο ὅτι εἰσῆλθον 'it did not become apparent that they entered' Ge 41.21; Σοδομίτας ~ους ταῖς κακίαις γενομένους 'the Sodomites who stood out for their evil practices' 3M 2.5. Cf. ἐπίσημος: LSG s.v.

διάδημα, ατος. n.

diadem: δ. βασιλείας Is 62.3 (|| στέφανος), δόξης Si 47.6, γυναικεῖον Es 2.17 o'; κάλλους 'of beauty' Wi 5.16 (|| βασιλεῖον). Cf. στέφανος: Trench 78-81.

διαδιδράσκω: aor.ptc. ~δράς.ʃ

to run away: Si 11.10, 2M 8.13. Cf. ἀποδιαδιδράσκω, φεύγω: LSG s.v.

διαδίδωμι: fut. ~δώσω; aor. διέδωκα, impv. ~δος, inf. ~δοῦναι, pass. διεδόθην, ptc. ~δοθείς.

1. *to distribute*: + acc., τροφήν 'food' Ge 49.27; κληρονομίαν Si 30.32; ^τὴν ὀρεινὴν^ ἐν κλήρῳ 'the mountain region by casting lots (or: as an inheritance, s.v. ἐν **12**)' Jo 13.6 (|| μερίζω vs. 7).

2. tr. *to spread about*: + acc., εὐωδίαν 'fragrance' Si 24.15, φωνήν 39.14; δημοσίᾳ .. ψόγον 'publicly .. censure' 3M 2.26; pass., *o* φήμη 'report' 2M 4.39, 4M 4.22; πλοῦτος 'wealth' PSol 1.4.

3. intr. *to spread about*: *s* children, εἰς ῥίζαν '(to grow) into a large family' Si 23.25, smoke 2M 7.5.

Cf. δίδωμι, μερίζω.

διάδοχος, ον.

succeeding: *s* προφήτης ~ος μετ' αὐτόν Si 48.8. **b**. subst.m., *successor*: Μωυσῆ 'of M.' Si 46.1, τοῦ βασιλέως 'the king's (deputy)' 1C 18.17.

Cf. διαδέχομαι: LSG s.v.

διαδύνω: aor. διέδυν.ʃ

to move through tightly packed space, 'penetrate': *s* a stone missle, διὰ τῆς περικεφαλαίας 'through the helmet' 1K 17.49. Cf. διέρχομαι.

διαζάω: impf.3s διέζη.ʃ

to manage to live in a certain style: θηρίων τρόπον 'as wild animals' 2M 5.27. Cf. ζάω.

διάζομαι: aor. διεσάμην, subj. 2s διάσῃ.ʃ

to mount on a loom: acc., torn fishing-net, Is 19.10; locks of hair, Jd 16.13*L* (AB:ὑφαίνω), 16.14A*L*. Cf. δίασμα: LSG s.v.

διαθερμαίνω: aor.ptc. ~θερμάνας, pass. διεθερμάνθην.ʃ

to become rather warm: *s* the sun, Ex 16.21, ἡ ἡμέρα 1K 11.11; mid., hum. body, 4K 4.34.

διάθεσις, εως. f.

1. *inclination, disposition* of mind: διῆλθοσαν εἰς ~ιν καρδίας 'they set about (realising) their heart's inclination' Ps 72.7.

2. *state, condition*: τυραννικὴ ἦν ἡ δ. 'the regime was tyrannical' 3M 3.8; οἰκετικὴ δ. 'status of slave' 2.28; ἐν τῇ καλλίστῃ ~ει 'in the most splendid order' Es E 16.

3. *act of verbally representing* a situation in a certain way: ὡς ἂν ἀπὸ τῶν νομίμων αὐτοὺς κωλυόντων 'as if they were keeping them away from the laws' 3M 3.2.

Cf. διάνοια, ἕξις: LSG s.v.

διαθήκη, ης. f.

1. *compact, treaty, mutual agreement*: God initiating and mediating in establishment of such between Israel and the animal kingdom, διαθήσομαι αὐτοῖς (dat. com.) ~ην .. μετὰ τῶν θηρίων .. καὶ μετὰ τῶν πετεινῶν .. καὶ μετὰ τῶν ἑρπετῶν Ho 2.18; with humans, ~ην μετὰ Ασσυρίων διέθετο 12.1; + διατίθημι 'to establish' 2.18 (c. μετά τινος), Zc 11.10 (c. πρός τινα, cf. τῆς ~ης αὐτοῦ τῆς πρὸς Αβρααμ .. Ex 2.24, cf. Le 26.44; c. πρός τινος 2M 1.2); + ποιέω Je 41.18; of a king proposing such with his subjects, Ho 10.4; + παραβαίνω 'to contravene' 6.7, Ez 17.15; between two persons, Ge 21.27; ἀδελφῶν 'fraternal agreement' Am 1.9; οἱ ἄνδρες τῆς δ. σου 'your allies' Ob 7; of lawfully wedded wife, γυνὴ ~ης Ma 2.14; the terms of agreement expressed with an inf., διαθησόμεθα μετὰ σοῦ ~ην μὴ ποιήσειν μεθ' ἡμῶν κακόν Ge 26.28. **b**. human undertaking: Ἐποιήσαμεν ~ην μετὰ τοῦ ᾅδου Is 28.15 (|| συνθῆκαι) || δ. τοῦ θανάτου 'a pact indemnifying against death' 28.18; μετὰ τὸ συντελέσαι τὸν βασιλέα .. διαθήκην πρὸς τὸν λαόν 'after the king concluded an agreement with the people' Je 41.8; political, Ez 17.13; δ. κρίματος 'juridical agreement' Si 38.33; + dat., ὀφθαλμοῖς 'with (my) eyes' Jb 31.1¶; task agreed to, assignment Si 11.20 (|| ἔργον).

2. "*covenant*" between God and Israel: but spoken of as God's, στήσω τὴν ~ν μου πρὸς σέ 'I shall establish my covenant with you' Ge 6.18; ἡ δ. μου μετὰ σοῦ 17.4; + dat. ἀνίστημι τὴν ~ην μου ὑμῖν 9.9 (also with animals, καὶ πάσῃ ψυχῇ .. ἀπὸ ὀρνέων καὶ ἀπὸ κτηνῶν, καὶ πᾶσιν τοῖς θηρίοις τῆς γῆς); ἐγὼ τίθημί σοι ~ην Ex 34.10; τοῖς υἱοῖς Ισραηλ De 29.1; θήσομαι τὴν ~ην μου ἀνὰ μέσον ἐμοῦ καὶ ἀνὰ μέσον σοῦ Ge 17.2; παρέβησαν τὴν ~ην μου καὶ κατὰ τοῦ νόμου μου ἠσέβησαν 'they contravened ..' Ho 8.1; sealed with blood, ἐν αἵματι ~ης Zc 9.11; equated with ἡ ἐντολή 'the Torah,' ἐξαπέσταλκα πρὸς ὑμᾶς τὴν ἐντολὴν ταύτην τοῦ εἶναι τὴν ~ην μου πρὸς τοὺς Λευίτας Ma 2.4, cf. δ. τοῦ Λευι 2.8; for life and peace, ἡ δ. μου ἦν μετὰ αὐτοῦ τῆς ζωῆς καὶ τῆς εἰρήνης 2.5; εἰρήνης Nu 25.12, Ez 34.25; δ. ᾅδου 'the time appointed for death' Si 14.12; ἱερατείας αἰωνία Nu 25.13; δ. τῶν πατέρων ἡμῶν 'ancestral' Ma 2.10; αἰώνιος 'eternal' Ge 9.16, Ex 31.16, Is 55.3, δ. αἰωνία Ez 37.26; καινή 'new' Je 38.31; ὁ ἄγγελος τῆς ~ης sent by the Lord and desired by his people (?), Ma 3.1; pl. Es 7.58 *L*. **b**. also with a hum. referent in the gen., ἐμνήσθην τῆς ~ης ὑμῶν Ex 6.5 (MT "my c."); δ. Ιακωβ .. δ. Ισαακ .. δ. Αβρααμ Le 26.42; τῶν πατέρων σου De 4.31: see Wevers ad Ex 6.5. **c**. δ. ἁλός '.. of salt' Nu 18.19. **d**. obj. of: διατίθημι Ge 9.17, De 4.23, 29.1*a*; δίδωμι Nu 25.12; ἵστημι Ge 17.7, Ex 6.4, De 29.1*b*; τίθημι Ge 17.2; διατηρέω 'to keep' Ge 17.9; ὄμνυμι De 4.31; διασκεδάζω 'to annul, repeal' Zc 11.10, Je 14.21; διαφθείρω 'to set at naught' Ma 2.8; βεβηλόω 'desecrate' 2.10; παραβαίνω 'to contravene' Ho 8.1.

Pl. only once (Si 44.18); cf. συνθήκη.

Cf. διατίθημι, συνθήκη: Behm, *TDNT* 2.124-34; Penna; Selb; *ND* 6.36-9, 41-7; Biscardi; Schenker 1999 and 2000; Jobes and Silvas 200f.

διαθρύπτω: fut. ~θρύψω; aor.pass. διεθρύβην.ʃ

to break in pieces, crumble: pass., ***o*** rock, Na 1.6 (‖ τήκω), Hb 3.6 (‖ διατήκω, τήκω); hailstone, Si 43.15; fried cakes, Le 2.6, bread, πεινῶντι τὸν ἄρτον σου 'to the one who hungers ..' Is 58.7, cf. La 4.4. Cf. διακλάω.

διαίρεσις, εως. f.

1. *act of dividing*: κλήρου 'by casting lots' Si 14.15.

2. *act of dividing and apportioning*: υἱῶν 'among sons' Ju 9.4.

3. *part divided*: Ps 135.13, 2C 35.5; clan, Jd 5.15A (B: μερίς), or **b**. **b**. *that which is divided and apportioned*: Jo 19.51. **c**. *team*: 2E 6.17; of temple functionaries, 1C 24.1.

Cf. διαιρέω.

διαιρέω: fut. act. διελῶ, mid. διελοῦμαι, pass. διαιρεθήσομαι; aor. διεῖλον, subj. διέλω, inf. διελεῖν, impv.2pl διέλετε, mid. διειλάμην, inf. διελέσθαι, pass. διῃρέθην, subj. διαιρεθῶ; pf.pass. διῄρημαι, ptc.pass. διῃρημένος.

1. *to divide*: abs. Ge 4.7 (of sacrifical animal to be cut up?, see Rösel 106); ***o*** animals, μέσα 'in half' 15.10; sacrificial animals, κατὰ μέλη 'into multiple pieces' Le 1.12; τραύματα '(to split the skin and open up) wounds' (?) Si 27.25; possessions, εἰς δύο παρεμβολάς Ge 32.7; kingdom, 1K 15.29 (*L* σχίζω), Da 11.4 TH (LXX μερίζω); proceeds of a sale, Ex 21.35 (mid.); τὰ σκῦλα ἀνὰ μέσον τῶν πολεμιστῶν .. καὶ ἀνὰ μέσον .. 'the spoils between the warriors .. and ..' Nu 31.27, διαιρούμενοι σκῦλα 'divide the spoils among themselves' Is 9.3; ἐφημερίας 'divisions of temple duties by rotation' 1C 23.6; + double acc.,τρεῖς ἀρχάς 'as three detachments' Jd 7.16 A (B: εἰς ..). **b**. mid. *to divide and share* with sbd: + acc., τὴν προνομὴν μετὰ τῶν ἀδελφῶν αὐτῶν 'the spoils ..' Jo 22.8.

2. *to dispense, apportion*: + acc. rei, συντριμμὸν ἐπ' ἰσχύν Am 5.9.

3. *to sever*: ***o*** (acc.) the head of a sacrificial bird, Le 5.8.

4. *to separate*: + acc. Nu 31.42.

5. *to make a breach in a continuum and diminish*: "the number of months (of his life-span) was shortened" Jb 21.21¶.

Cf. ἀποδιαστέλλω, διχοτομέω, καταδιαιρέω, μελίζω, μερίζω, σχίζω: Schmidt 4.608-10.

δίαιτα, ας. f.

1. *way of life lived*: καθημερίνη 'daily life' Ju 12.15. Cf. ἐκδιαιτάω.

2. *dwelling, abode*: Jb 5.3; ‖ οἶκος 20.19.

Cf. διαιτάω, οἶκος.

διαιτάω: fut.mid. ~τηθήσομαι; aor. διῄτησα.ʃ

1. act. *to keep under control*: + acc., anger, 4M 2.17.

2. mid. *to subject*: + acc. and dat., πολέμου ἀκαταστασίαις τὴν ψυχήν 'one's life to the disruptions caused by wars' Si 26.27¶.

3. mid. *to have a dwelling*: Jb 30.7.

διαιτέω: aor.inf.pass. διαιτηθῆναι.ʃ *

to coax into doing sth: ***o*** God, ‖ ἀπειλέω 'to threaten' Ju 8.16.

διακαθιζάνω: pres.subj. ~άνω.ʃ *

to sit down apart to empty the bowel: ***s*** hum., ἔξω 'outdoors' De 23.13. Cf. καθίζω, κάθημαι.

διακαθίζω: aor. διεκάθισα.ʃ

to take up position*: ***s* troops, ἐπὶ Ραββαθ 'against R.' 2K 11.1 (*L* περι~). Cf. καθίζω.

διακαίω.ʃ

to burn from one end to the other of: + acc., the entrails, 4M 11.19. Cf. καίω.

διακάμπτω: aor. διέκαμψα.ʃ *

to bend over: ἐπὶ ^τὸ παιδάριον^ 4K 4.34 (*L* συγ~). Cf. κάμπτω.

διακαρτερέω: aor.subj. ~καρτερήσω.ʃ

to hold out against in difficulty: ***s*** hum., abs., Ju 7.30; + acc., τοὺς αἰκισμούς 'the pains' 4M 6.9.

διακατέχω: aor.inf. ~κατασχεῖν.ʃ

to seize: + acc., τὰς ἀναβάσεις τῆς ὀρεινῆς 'mountain passes' Ju 4.7.

διάκειμαι.ʃ

to be in a certain state or *mental disposition*: + adv., ἀσθενῶς 'ill' 2M 9.21, γνησίως 'sincerely' 3M 3.23; locational adverb, καθύπερθεν 'above (their heads)' 4.10.

διάκενος, ον.ʃ

porous: ***s*** ἄρτος Nu 21.5.

διακινδυνεύω.ʃ
to run every manner of risk: 2M 11.7. Cf. κινδυνεύω.

διακινέω: aor.pass. διεκινήθην.ʃ
to cause to move along: + acc. understood (elephants to a battlefield) 3M 5.23. **b**. pass. intr. *to move, stir*: *s* resuscitated hum., 4K 4.35*L*. Cf. κινέω.

διακλάω.ʃ
to break into small parts: abs., *o* bread to be served understood, La 4.4, cf. Is 58.7 and Je 16.7. Cf. κλάω.

διακλείω: aor.pass. διεκλείσθην.ʃ
to hem in and deny exit: pass., *o* hum., εἰς τοὺς πύργους 'into the towers' 1M 5.5.

διακλέπτω.ʃ
mid. *to act by stealth in* doing: + inf., 2K 19.4.

διακολυμβάω: aor. διεκολύμβησα.ʃ
to dive and swim across: εἰς τὸ πέραν 'to the other side' 1M 9.48.

διακομίζω: aor. διεκόμισα, ptc. ~κομίσας, pass. διεκομίσθην, ptc. ~κομισθείς.
1. *to transfer* from one place to another: *o* rei, 1E 2.13, + acc. pers., σώους 'safely' 3M 2.7.
2. mid./pass. *to betake oneself*: ὡς τὸν βασιλέα 'to the king' 2M 4.5; out of fear, 9.29; νύκτωρ ἐπὶ τὴν .. σκηνήν 'at night to the tent of ..' 3M 1.2.

διακονία, ας. f.ʃ
utensils of service: 1M 11.58. Del. Es 6.3, 5 v.l.

διάκονος, ου. m.
one who renders personal service: εὐνούχοις τοῖς ~οις τοῦ βασιλέως Es 1.10 o'; 2.2 τοῦ βασιλέως (|| *L* λειτουργός), 6.3 (|| *L* νεανίσκος); metaph., 4M 9.17. Cf. δοῦλος, θεράπων, λειτουργικός, νεανίσκος, παῖς, ὑπηρέτης, ὑπουργός: Schmidt 4.141-4; Trench 32f.; Beyer, *TDNT* 2.81, 88f.

διακοπή, ῆς. f.
1. *breach*: made in barrier, διὰ τῆς ~ῆς πρὸ προσώπου αὐτῶν διέκοψαν 'through the breach made before them they broke through' Mi 2.13; resulting from the extinction of a section of the population, Jd 21.15. Cf. ἔκρηγμα. **b**. metaph., *serious damage* liable to lead to a collapse: + συντριβή Pr 6.15.
2. *steep, narrow course* in the ground, 'gorge': χειμάρρου ἀπὸ κονίας 'of a river made from chalk' Jb 28.4¶, ὕδατος 1C 14.11, cf. Jd 5.17A (B: διέξοδος).
Cf. διακόπτω.

διακόπτω: aor. διέκοψα, inf. ~κόψαι, impv. διάκοψον, subj. ~κόψω, pass. διεκόπην.
1. *to gash*: + acc., κεφαλὰς δυναστῶν Hb 3.14, cf. διάκοψον εἰς κεφαλὰς πάντων 'Cut through the heads of all' Am 9.1.
2. *to force one's way into* an area *by destroying a barrier*: abs., Ju 2.23, διὰ τῆς διακοπῆς πρὸ προσώπου αὐτῶν διέκοψαν 'through the breach made before them they broke through' Mi 2.13, πρός τινα (commander) 4K 3.26; + acc., τὴν παρεμβολήν 'the encampment' 2K 23.16*L*; pass., *o* city, 3K 2.35[f], Je 52.7.
3. *to destroy and overcome* a barrier in order to force one's way in: + acc., πύλας 'gates' 2M 10.36; + acc. pers., lines of enemy troops, 2K 5.20; + cogn. acc., διακοπήν 2K 6.8; pass., ὡς διακόπτεται ὕδατα 'just as a sheet of water is done away with' 2K 5.20 (a poss. reminiscence of the crossing of the sea and that of the river?), cf. ὡς διακοπὴν ὕδατος 1C 14.11 and διέρρηξας πηγὰς καὶ χειμάρρους Ps 73.15. **b**. seeking a way out: pass, *o* womb, τί διεκόπη .. φραγμός; 'why has (the womb as) a barrier been cut through?' Ge 38.29.
Cf. διακοπή, κόπτω: del. 2M 10.30 v.l.

διακόσιοι, αι, α: num.
two hundred: αἶγας ~ίας '.. goats' Ge 32.14.

διακοσμέω: pf.ptc.pass. ~κεκοσμημένος.ʃ
1. *to deck out*: *o* horse with a saddle-pack, 2M 3.25.
2. *to set in order*: τὴν διασκευήν 'the battle-order' 2K 23.8*L*.
Cf. διακόσμησις, κοσμέω.

διακόσμησις, εως. f.ʃ
v.n. of διακοσμέω **1**: 2M 2.29.

διακούω.ʃ
to try a case: ἀνὰ μέσον τῶν ἀδελφῶν ὑμῶν 'between ..' De 1.16; μεσίτης .. ἀνὰ μέσον ἀμφοτέρων 'arbiter ..' Jb 9.33. Cf. ἀκούω, κρίνω.

διακρατέω: aor. διεκράτησα.ʃ
1. *to hold in possession*: acc. (land), 1E 4.50.
2. *to hold at bay*: + acc. (enemies' assault), Ju 6.12.

διακριβάζομαι: aor. διηκριβασάμην.ʃ *
to act meticulously: ἐν ποιήσει νόμου Si 51.19.

διακριβόω.ʃ
to be accurate: in description, περί τινος 2M 2.28. Del. Si 51.19 v.l.

διακρίνω: fut. ~κρινῶ, mid. ~κριθήσομαι; aor.act. διέκρινα, inf. ~κρῖναι.
1. *to pass judgement on*: + acc. pers. (multiple individuals), Ex 18.16, φόνους 'murderers' Jb 21.22, πάντα τὰ ἔθνη κυκλόθεν Jl 3.12, θεούς Ps 81.1, τὸν οἶκόν μου Zc 3.7; + dat. pers.com., De 33.7; + acc. rei, ῥήματα Jb 12.11 (*s* οὖς 'ear,' Zgl: νοῦς, but see Orlinsky 1962.148, and Jb 34.3), κρίσιν .. αὐτῶν 'a case presented to them' Ep Je 53; ἐν δικαιοσύνῃ 3K 3.9; + an indir. question, 4M 1.14.
2. *to subject to thorough examination*: *s* God, + acc., με ὡς τὸ χρυσίον Jb 23.10; hum., ῥήματα δυναστῶν 15.5.

3. mid. *to hold disputation, argue* (with sbd πρός τινα): Jl 3.2, Ez 20.35; + dat. pers., πάσῃ τῇ γῇ Je 15.10 (+ δικάζομαι).

Cf. κρίνω.

διάκρισις, εως. f.∫

separation: 'dispersal (of clouds)' Jb 37.16.

διακυβερνάω.∫

to steer through, pilot: ***s*** God, τινα 3M 6.2; divine providence, Wi 14.3. Cf. κυβερνάω.

διακύπτω: aor. διέκυψα, subj. ~κύψω.

to peep in or through: Ez 41.16; ***s*** God, La 3.50 (+ εἶδον), ἐκ τοῦ οὐρανοῦ ἐπὶ τοὺς υἱοὺς τῶν ἀνθρώπων Ps 13.2, 52.3; διὰ τῶν θυρίδων 'through the windows' 2M 3.19, sim. 2K 6.16, Jd 5.28A (B: παρα~). Cf. ἐκ~, παρακύπτω.

διακωλύω: aor.inf. ~κωλῦσαι.∫

to prevent sbd from doing sth: + acc. pers., Ju 12.7, and ptc., 4.7.

διαλαμβάνω: fut. ~λήμψομαι; aor. διέλαβον; pf. διείληφα, ptc. διειληφώς.

to perceive and realise: + acc. and ptc., Es B 5 + inf. cl. 7.23*L*, 2M 5.11; ***o*** thought, Ju 8.14 (|| ἐπιγινώσκω, κατανοέω).

διαλανθάνω: διέλαθον.∫

to act by successfully escaping sbd else's notice: abs., 2K 4.6. Cf. λανθάνω.

διαλέγομαι: fut. διαλεχθήσομαι; aor. διελεξάμην, inf.pass. ~λεγῆναι.∫

to hold a discussion or *conversation*: abs., Es D 15, ἐν συνέσει 'intelligently' Si 14.20; πρός τινα, Ex 6.27, πρὸς αὐτὸν ἰσχυρῶς Jd 8.1B (A: κρίνομαι); + dat. pers., 2M 11.20; + acc. (subject matter), Is 63.1. **b**. + dat. pers. and inf.: διαλεγῆναι τῷ Ἀδδαίῳ .. ἀποστεῖλαι ἡμῖν .. 'to talk to A. to have .. sent to us ..' 1E 8.45.

Cf. διαλογή, λαλέω: Schrenk, *TDNT* 2.93-5.

διαλείπω: fut. ~λείψω; aor διέλιπον, subj. ~λίπω, inf. ~λιπεῖν, impv. ~λιπε.

1. *to stop temporarily in the middle* of an action: abs., τοῦ μὴ διαλιπεῖν 'unceasingly' Is 5.14; foll. an impv., Καταγάγετε .. καὶ μὴ διαλιπέτωσαν Je 14.17; 9.5; *+ ἀπό - ἀπὸ τοῦ δρόμου 'running' 8.6, ἀπὸ κλαυθμοῦ .. ἀπὸ δακρύων 'from crying .. from tears' 38.16; + ptc. pres. and a negator, ποιῶν καρπόν 17.8, θυμιῶντες 51.18, καίων 'stoking (fire)' Da 3.46 TH; *+ τοῦ inf., τοῦ οἰκοδομεῖν 3K 15.21 (|| 2C 16.5 ἀπο~), but not Je 9.5 where τοῦ ἐπιστρέψαι is final-resultative; with no τοῦ, 1K 12.23 *L*.

2. *to allow* a period of time *to elapse* before taking an action: ἑπτὰ ἡμέρας 1K 10.8, διέλιπεν ἑπτὰ ἡμέρας τῷ μαρτυρίῳ '.. the instructed (date)' 13.8.

Cf. διαλιμπάνω, παύω, ἀδιαλείπτως.

διάλεκτος, ου. f.∫

language as a system for communication: Χαλδαϊκή Da 1.4 LXX (TH γλῶσσα), Es 9.26. Cf. γλῶσσα, φωνή: Schmidt 1.102-4; Munz.

διάλευκος, ον.

having white spots or *speckles*: ***s*** goat (αἶξ), Ge 30.32; he-goat (τράγος) 30.35; πρόβατον 30.39; ram (κριός) 30.40.

διάλημψις, εως. f.∫

opinion: + inf., 2M 3.32.

διαλιμπάνω.∫

= διαλείπω **1**: + ptc., οὐ διελίμπανεν θρηνοῦσα 'wouldn't stop lamenting' To 10.7 𝔊[I]. Cf. διαλείπω.

διαλλαγή, ῆς. f.∫

reconciliation, v.n. of διαλλάσσω **1 b**: Si 22.22; λοιδορίας 'of abuse' 27.21. Cf. διαλλάσσω, καταλλαγή.

διαλλάσσω: fut.mid. ~λλαγήσομαι; aor.inf. ~λλάξαι, ptc. ~λλάξας, mid.subj. ~λλαγῶ; pf.ptc.pass. διηλλαγμένος.∫

1. *to alter, transform*: + acc., βουλάς 'plans' Jb 5.12 (virtually 'to foil,' cf. ἀκύρους ἀποφαίνει 'renders invalid' Polychronios apud Hagedorn 1994 I 359, μὴ συγχωρῶν ἐπιτελεσθῆναι 'not allowing .. to be effected' Jul. ad loc., and μεταβάλλοντα, μεταλλάττοντα Chr. ad loc.), 12.20, 24, Wi 19.18. **b**. pass. *to differ*: pf.ptc., χρώμασιν διηλλαγμένοις 'with various colours' Wi 15.4; *to be at variance, in conflict* with - ἡ καρδία ἀπὸ σώματος Jb 36.28.

2. *to change the personal disposition and attitude of* after estrangement: + acc. pers., αὐτὴν ἑαυτῷ Jd 19.3A. **b**. mid. *to change one's personal disposition and attitude* after estrangement: + dat. pers., 1K 29.4, 1E 4.31.

***3**. *to give up in exchange*: + acc., τὸν βίον (in exchange for death) 2M 6.27, cf. ἀπὸ σώματος Jb 36.29.

Cf. διαλλαγή, καταλλάσσω, μεταβάλλω.

διάλλομαι.∫

to move jumping from place to place: ἐπὶ τοὺς βουνούς 'over the hills' Ct 2.8 (|| πηδάω). Cf. ἅλλομαι.

διαλογή, ῆς. f.∫

conversation: Ps 103.34, PSol 4 tit. Cf. διαλέγομαι.

διαλογίζομαι: fut. ~γιοῦμαι; aor. διελογισάμην, impv.3s ~γισάσθω.

1. *to form in the mind*, 'design, plan': abs., κατ' ἐμοῦ 'against me' Ps 139.9; + acc. rei, διαβούλιον 9.23, βουλήν 'plan' 20.12, λογισμοὺς πονηρούς 1M 11.8, κακά Pr 17.12.

2. *to reflect on, muse over*: + acc., ἡμέρας ἀρχαίας 'olden days' Ps 76.6, ταῦτα 4M 8.11; + ὑπὲρ ἀναστάσεως 'about resurrection' 2M 12.43.

Cf. λογίζομαι, διαλογισμός, ἀδολεσχέω, διανοέομαι, μελετάω: Schrenk, *TDNT* 2.95.

διαλογισμός, οῦ. m.

*1. *content of reflection* or *reasoning*: τοὺς ~οὺς τῆς καρδίας σου γνῷς Da 2.30 TH (LXX: ἃ ὑπέλαβες τῇ καρδίᾳ σου), οἱ ~οί μου .. συνετάρασσόν με 'my thoughts kept troubling me' 7.28 TH; 5.6 TH (LXX: ὑπόνοια); εἰς κακόν Ps 55.6, μάταιοι 'senseless' 93.11; God's 91.5. **b**. *plan, design*: 1M 2.63; τοὺς ~οὺς αὐτῶν ἐν ἐμοί La 2.60, κατ' ἐμοῦ 2.61.

2. *debate, discussion*: μετά τινος Si 9.15.

Cf. διαλογίζομαι, διανόημα: Schrenk, *TDNT* 2.96f.

διαλοιδόρησις, εως. f.ʃ*

railing at one another: Si 27.15. Cf. λοιδόρησις.

διάλυσις, εως. f.ʃ

v.n. of διαλύω **2**: ~ει διελύσαμεν πρός σε 'we have made a definitive end to our relationship with you' Ne 1.7. Cf. διαλύω.

διαλύω: fut. ~λύσω, pass. ~λυθήσομαι; aor. διέλυσα, inf. ~λῦσαι, pass. διελύθην, subj. ~λυθῶ; pf.pass. ~λέλυμαι.

1. *to destroy a firm bond between parts*: pass. τὰ νεῦρά μου διαλέλυται 'my sinews are taken apart' Jb 30.17; οἱ σύνδεσμοι τῆς ὀσφύος 'the joints of the loins' Da 5.6 TH; ὄρη 'mountains' 3K 19.11; Si 22.16, Is 58.6 (|| λύω); σώματα 'bodies (burnt in fire)' 4M 14.10. **b**. mid. *to become freed from a bond*: "the cords became unstuck from his arms" Jd 15.14 A (B: τήκομαι).

2. *to put an end to a firm, personal relationship*: πρός τινα – διαλύσει διελύσαμεν πρός σε 'we have made a definitive end to our relationship with you' Ne 1.7.

3. *to put an end to*: + acc., πόλεμον 3M 1.2; φιλίαν 'friendship' Si 22.20; σοφίαν PSol 4.9.

4. pass. *to be reconciled, settle a quarrel*: Pr 6.35. Cf. διαλλάσσω.

Cf. λύω, διάλυσις.

διαμαρτάνω: aor.subj. ~αμάρτω.ʃ

1. *to miss the aim*: *s* slinger, Jd 20.16 A (B: ἐξ~).

2. *to fail utterly*: Nu 15.22.

Cf. ἐξ~, ἁμαρτάνω.

διαμαρτυρέω: pf.mid. ~μεμαρτύρημαι, ptc. ~μεμαρτυρημένος.ʃ

to warn: + dat. pers., διαμαρτυρίᾳ διαμεμαρτύρηται ἡμῖν .. λέγων .. 'has sternly warned us ..' Ge 43.3; Ex 19.23, 21.36, 1K 21.3; *ἔν τινι (pers.) + inf., Ne 9.26. Cf. μαρτυρία, μαρτυρέω.

διαμαρτυρία, ας. f.ʃ

1. *a warning*: ~ᾳ διαμεμαρτύρηται ἡμῖν .. λέγων .. 'has sternly warned us ..' Ge 43.3.

2. *act of testifying*: 4M 16.16.

Cf. διαμαρτυρέω.

διαμαρτύρομαι: fut. ~μαρτυροῦμαι; aor. διεμαρτυράμην, impv. ~μάρτυραι.

1. *to testify*: *s* God, ἀνὰ μέσον σοῦ καὶ ἀνὰ μέσον γυναικὸς νεότητός σου 'between you and the wife of your youth' Ma 2.14; an angel, πρός τινα Zc 3.6.

2. *to bear witness to*: + acc. rei and dat. pers., αὐτοῖς τὰ προστάγματα τοῦ θεοῦ καὶ τὸν νόμον αὐτοῦ Ex 18.20; De 32.46.

3. *to call as witness and affirm*: + acc. pers., μάρτυρας Je 39.10 (|| ἐπιμαρτύρομαι vs. 25); and dat. pers. and ὅτι-clause, ὑμῖν .. τόν τε οὐρανὸν καὶ τὴν γῆν ὅτι ἀπωλείᾳ ἀπολεῖσθε De 4.26; + direct speech, 30.19 (|| ἀναγγέλλω vs. 18), 31.28

4. *to asseverate, state firmly*: + dat. pers., Ex 21.29; and ὅτι-clause, ὑμῖν ὅτι ἀπωλείᾳ ἀπολεῖσθε De 8.19; the message understood, Ex 19.10.

5. *to denounce solemnly*: + dat. pers. and acc. rei, τῇ Ιερουσαλημ τὰς ἀνομίας αὐτῆς Ez 16.2; 20.4.

6. *to give firm guideline to*: + dat. pers., Ex 19.21; + *ἔν τινι (pers.), Ne 9.26, 13.21.

Cf. ἐπιμαρτύρομαι, μαρτύριον, μάρτυς, μαρτύρομαι, ἀναγγέλλω: *BA* ad De 4.26.

διαμασάομαι.ʃ

to chew up: abs., Si 34.16. Cf. μασάομαι.

διαμαχίζομαι: pf. διαμεμάχισμαι.ʃ *

to strive earnestly, 'grapple (with)': *b* soul, ἐν ^σοφίᾳ^ Si 51.19.

διαμάχομαι: fut. ~μαχήσομαι.

to contend with sbd: militarily, μετὰ τοῦ στρατηγοῦ 'with the commander' Da 10.20 LXX (TH: πολεμέω). **b**. not militarily: μετὰ ἀνθρώπου δυνάστου 'with a powerful person' Si 8.1 (|| ἐρίζω vs. 2); ἐν θέρμῃ καμίνου 'in the heat of an oven' 38.28; reciprocal, 2K 14.6*L* (B simp.).

Cf. μάχομαι, διαμαχίζομαι, ἐρίζω.

διαμελίζω: fut.pass. ~μελισθήσομαι.ʃ.

to dismember: Da 3.96 LXX. Cf. (ἐκ)μελίζω.

διαμένω: fut. ~μενῶ, inf. ~μενεῖν; aor.subj. ~μείνω.

1. *to continue to exist*: εἰς τὸν αἰῶνα Je 3.5, ἡμέρας πλείους 39.14; opp. ἀπόλλυμι 'to perish' Ps 101.27; *s* ὁ λόγος σου 118.89, ἡ γῆ 90, ἡ ἡμέρα 91. **b**. in sbd's company: μετὰ σοῦ Si 12.15.

2. *to remain unaltered*: ἐν τῇ αὐτῇ .. βουλῇ '(to maintain) the same course of action' 3M 3.11; personal loyalty and friendship, αὐτῷ Si 22.23.

διαμερίζω: fut. ~μεριῶ, pass. ~μερισθήσομαι; aor. διεμέρισα, impv. ~μέρισον, ptc. ~μερίσας, mid. ~εμερισάμην, pass. διεμερίσθην.

1. *to deal out*: abs., Is 34.17; pass., *o* conquered land, Jo 21.42[a]; fields, Mi 2.4; spoils, ἐν σοί 'among you' Zc 14.1; + dat. pers., 2K 6.19; mid., + acc. rei, ἑαυτοῖς Ps 21.19; 2M 8.28 (|| μερίζω).

2. *to separate from one another*: + acc., people, Ge 49.7, De 32.8 (|| διασπείρω); pass., Ge 10.25, Ps 54.22.

Cf. διαμερισμός, μέρος, μερίζω: Schmidt 4.611.

διαμερισμός, οῦ. m.

being divided up as spoil: of cities, Mi 7.12 (|| ὁμαλισμός 'being levelled'); Ez 48.29.

διαμετρέω: fut. ~μετρήσω; aor. διεμέτρησα, inf. ~μετρῆσαι.

to measure the whole area of (+ τι): τὴν Ιερουσαλημ Zc 2.2; ἐν σχοινίοις 'with strings' 2K 8.2. Cf. ἐκ~, καταμετρέω, διαμέτρησις, μέτρον.

διαμέτρησις, εως. f.

1. v.n. of διαμετρέω, q.v.: of the city, Je 38.39; οἴκου Ez 42.15.

2. *diametre*: πήχεων δέκα τὴν ~ιν 'ten cubits in ..' 2C 4.2.

Cf. διαμετρέω.

διαναπαύω: fut. ~παύσω.ʃ

to allow to rest a while: + *s* pers. and acc. pers., οὗτος διαναπαύσει ἡμᾶς ἀπὸ τῶν ἔργων ἡμῶν καὶ ἀπὸ τῶν λυπῶν τῶν χειρῶν ἡμῶν καὶ ἀπὸ τῆς γῆς Ge 5.29. Cf. ἀναπαύω.

διανέμω: aor. διένειμα.ʃ

to designate and assign as appropriate to: + acc. and dat., θεοῖς ἑτέροις .. οὓς .. οὐδὲ διένειμεν αὐτοῖς 'other gods .. whom He did not assign to them, either' De 29.26. Cf. ἀπονέμω, μερίζω.

διανεύω.ʃ *

to signal consent by winking the eye: ὀφθαλμῷ / ~οῖς Ps 34.19, Si 27.22. Cf. ἐννεύω.

διανήθω: pf.ptc.pass. ~νενησμένος. *

to spin to manufacture fabric: + acc. and pass., κόκκινον διανενησμένον 'spun scarlet fabric' Ex 28.8. Cf. νήθω.

διανθίζω: pf.ptc.pass. διηνθισμένος.ʃ *

to adorn with flowers: *o* bed-spread, Es 1.6 o'. Cf. ἄνθος.

διανίστημι: 2aor.ptc.f.sg. διαναστᾶσα.ʃ

to terminate sleep and leave bed: opp. κοιτάζομαι De 6.7, 11.19; Ju 12.15. Cf. ἀνίστημι.

διανοέομαι: fut.pass.~νοηθήσομαι; aor. διενοήθην, ptc. ~νοηθείς, inf. ~νοηθῆναι, impv. ~νοήθητι; pf. διανενόημαι.

1. *to devise* (action): + acc. rei, Ju 9.5 (|| ἐν~), + ἐπί τι - ἐν τῇ καρδίᾳ αὐτοῦ ἐπιμελῶς ἐπὶ τὰ πονηρά Ge 6.5; + inf., τοῦ κακῶσαι ὑμᾶς Zc 8.14; 3M 1.22; || παρατάσσω 8.15. Abs. and *s* God, Ge 6.6, 8.21, Je 7.31, 19.5.

2. *to think out, design*: as architect, and abs., Ex 31.4; + cogn. obj. and acc. rei, διανόησιν, ὅσα ἂν δῷς αὐτῷ 'anything that you might suggest to him' 2C 2.13.

*__3__. *to ponder*: ἐν τοῖς προστάγμασιν κυρίου 'about the Lord's injunctions' Si 6.37 (|| μελετάω), ἐν νόμῳ ὑψίστου 38.34; ἐπί τινι 34.15 (|| νοέω), 16.20; *+ dat. rei, Da LXX 10.11 (|| TH συνίημι), poss. **4** c. dat. instr.; + acc. rei, Si 3.22, 29, ἐν καρδίᾳ 14.21 (|| ἐννοέομαι), 21.17.

*__4__. *to comprehend*: abs. Da LXX 12.10 (|| TH συνίημι); παρά τι 'regarding' 12.8 (ditto).

Cf. διανόημα, βουλεύω, διάνοια, ἀδολεσχέω, διαλογίζομαι, μελετάω, ἐννοέομαι, νοέω.

διανόημα, ατος. n.

intention, design: Is 55.9 (|| διανοία); Si 24.29 (|| βουλή); ἐπί τινα (hostile) Da 8.25 LXX. Cf. διανοέομαι, ἐννόημα.

διανόησις, εως. f.ʃ

v.n. of διανοέομαι **2**: cogn. acc., 2C 2.13.

διάνοια, ας. f.

1. *faculty of thinking and planning*, 'mind': ἔγκειται ἡ δ. τοῦ ἀνθρώπου ἐπιμελῶς ἐπὶ τὰ πονηρὰ 'man's mind is intensely occupied with evil things' Ge 8.21; ἐξέστη ἡ δ. Ιακωβ 'his mind got totally confused' 45.26; σοφὸς τῇ ~ᾳ 'intelligent' filled with divine πνεῦμα αἰσθήσεως Ex 28.3; προβιβάσαι γε ἔδωκεν ἐν τῇ ~ᾳ 'awakened in him a will to teach' 35.34; σύνεσις ~ας 35.35; οὐ μισήσεις τὸν ἀδελφόν σου τῇ ~ᾳ σου Le 19.17; ἐν τῇ ~ᾳ μου 'at my discretion' Nu 22.18 (|| παρ' ἐμαυτοῦ). **b**. || καρδία Ex 25.2, Je 38.33; Ex 35.22 (|| ψυχή vs. 21); ἐξ ὅλης τῆς ~ας σου καὶ ἐξ ὅλης τῆς ψυχῆς σου καὶ ἐξ ὅλης τῆς δυνάμεώς σου De 6.5; || φρόνησις Jo 5.1.

2. *inner being*: εἶπεν ἐν τῇ ~ᾳ 'inwardly' Ge 17.17, cf. ἐγέλασεν .. ἐν ἑαυτῇ 18.12; 27.41 (= 'determined, thought aloud'?, for Rebecca had got wind of her son's plan, vs. 42); λαλοῦντα ἐν τῇ ~ᾳ 'to think' 24.15; De 7.17; οὐδὲ ἔλαβές με εἰς τὴν ~αν οὐδὲ εἰς τὴν καρδίαν σου 'nor did you think of me ..' Is 57.11.

3. *that which one has in mind*, 'thought; intention': ἐλάλησεν κατὰ τὴν ~αν τῆς παρθένου 'talked to the girl, by taking note of her intention' Ge 34.3; διαστρέφετε τὰς ~ας τῶν υἱῶν Ισραηλ μὴ διαβῆναι .. Nu 32.7, sim. 15.39 (in contrast to visual perceptions); ἐν ~ᾳ καρδίας αὐτοῦ τῆς πονηρᾶς Ba 1.22; God's Is 55.9 (|| διανόημα). **b**. *that which a word or event signifies*: Da 9.22 LXX (TH σύνεσις).

Cf. διανοέομαι, διανόημα, διάθησις, ἔννοια: Behm, *TDNT* 4.963-5.

διανοίγω: fut. διανοίξω, pass. ~νοιχθήσομαι; aor. διήνοιξα, impv. διάνοιξον, inf. ~νοῖξαι, opt. 3s ~νοίξαι, pass. διηνοίχθην; pf.pass.3s διήνοικται.

to lay open: + acc. rei, μήτραν 'womb' Ex 13.2, 34.19, Nu 8.16 (*s* πρωτότοκος 'first-born baby'), Ez 20.26, || ἀνοίγω μήτραν (of God curing female barrenness, s.v. ἀνοίγω); στόμα Is 5.14 (so as to eat),

La 2.16 (so as to speak); χεῖρας .. πένητι 'her hands to the poor' Pr 31.20 (so as to hand alms); χαλίνους 'bridles' Hb 3.14; θύρας 'doors' Zc 11.1; ἐπὶ τὸν οἶκον Ιουδα διανοίξω τοὺς ὀφθαλμούς μου 'I shall keep my (protective) eyes open on the household of Judah' 12.4; pass. πύλαι τῶν ποταμῶν διηνοίχθησαν 'the gates (i.e. sluices?) of the rivers were laid open' Na 2.7; ἔσται πᾶς τόπος διανοιγόμενος Zc 13.1; of discerning eyes Ge 3.5; eyes of a resuscitated hum., 4K 4.35; τὴν καρδίαν ὑμῶν ἐν τῷ νόμῳ αὐτοῦ 2M 1.4. Difficult is διανοῖξαι σύνεσιν αὐτῆς Ho 2.15, a possible Christian gloss with ref. to Lk 24.45? Cf. *BA* ad loc. **b.** *to open up, gain access to*: + acc., δυναστεύματα 'military fortifications' or 'natural resources'3K 2.46[c].

Cf. ἀνοίγω: Morenz 1964.256.

διανυκτερεύω.ʃ

to pass the night: Jb 2.9c.

διανύω: aor. διήνυσα.ʃ

to complete a journey and arrive: εἰς τὸν Χάρακα 2M 12.17. Cf. παραγίνομαι: Lee 2003a: 265-78.

διαπαρατηρέομαι.ʃ *

to keep looking for a chance to assail: τινα 2K 3.30.

διαπαρθενεύω: aor. διεπαρθένευσα, pass. διεπαρθενεύθην.ʃ

to deflower: ***o*** maiden, Ez 23.3, 8. Cf. ἀποπαρθενεύω.

διαπαύω: fut. ~παύσω; aor.subj. ~παύσω.ʃ

1. *to cause to cease to exist*: οὐ διαπαύσετε ἅλα διαθήκης κυρίου ἀπὸ θυσιασμάτων ὑμῶν 'you shall not omit the salt of the covenant of the Lord from your sacrifices' Le 2.13.

2. *to cease to exist*: οὐ μὴ διαπαύσῃ ἐξ ὑμῶν ὀδύνη 'you will never be free from suffering' Ho 5.13.

Cf. ἀφανίζω.

διαπειλέω: aor.mid.ptc. ~πειλησάμενος, subj. ~πειλήσωμαι.ʃ

to threaten forcefully: + dat. pers., Ez 3.17, μετ' ὀργῆς 3M 6.23, ἐπὶ τούτοις σκληρότερον 'rather harshly for these acts' 7.6. Cf. ἀπειλέω.

διαπειράζω.ʃ *

to put to a test: τινα 3M 5.40.

διαπείρω: aor.ptc. ~πείρας.ʃ

to pierce: + acc., τὰ πλευρά 'the sides (of his body)' 4M 11.19.

διαπέμπω: aor. διέπεμψα, mid. διεπεμψάμην, ptc. ~πεμψάμενος, inf.pass. ~πεμφθῆναι.ʃ

1. *to send* with a mission: τινα πρός τινα 3M 1.8; pass. 2M 3.37.

2. *to send message*: ἐπί τινα Ju 14.12; mid. πρός τινα 1E 1.24, 2M 11.26.

3. *to spread in all directions*: mid., + acc., κακά Pr 16.28.

Cf. ἀποστέλλω, πέμπω.

διαπεράω: fut. ~περάσω; aor. διεπέρασα, inf. ~περᾶσαι.

to move across a space, 'traverse': abs., εἰς τὸ πέραν τῆς θαλάσσης 'to the land beyond the sea' De 30.13, ἐπὶ τοὺς υἱοὺς Αμμων 'attacking ..' 1M 5.6, πρὸς αὐτόν 5.41 (|| διαβαίνω vs. 40); + acc. and ***s*** Phoenician mariners, τὴν θάλασσαν Is 23.2; τὸν Εὐφράτην ποταμόν 1M 3.37, τὸν χειμάρρουν 16.6. Cf. διαβαίνω, ~βιβάζω, ~πορεύομαι, διέρχομαι.

διαπετάννυμι: aor. διεπέτασα, ptc. ~πετάσας, subj. ~πετάσω; pf.ptc. ~πεπετακώς, pass. ~πεπετασμένος.

to open and spread out: + acc. rei, δίκτυον τοῖς ποσί μου 'a net (to catch) my feet' La 1.13; ***o*** hands seeking help, 1.17, in prayer Ps 43.21, To 3.11𝕲[II]; wings, Ez 16.8; νεφέλην Ps 104.39.

διαπίπτω: fut. ~πεσοῦμαι; aor. διέπεσον, inf. ~πεσεῖν, subj. ~πέσω; pf.ptc.act. ~πεπτωκώς.

1. *to collapse, crumble*: ***s*** edifice, βασίλεια 'royal palace' Na 2.7, μηρός 'thigh' Nu 5.21, σάρκες 'pieces of human body' 2M 9.9, ἀγγεῖον 'vessel' Je 18.4, πόλις 19.12; hum., Ne 8.10.

2. *to perish*: ***s*** hum., πᾶσα γενεὰ ἀνδρῶν πολεμιστῶν 'a whole generation of warriors' De 2.14.

3. *to fail to materialise*, 'fall through': ***s*** εἷς λόγος Jo 23.14 (|| διαφωνέω), ῥῆμα To 14.4 𝕲[II], sim. Ju 6.9. Cf. διαφωνέω **2**.

4. *to go missing*: ***s*** books, 2M 2.14.

Cf. διάπτωσις, πίπτω, ἀπόλλυμι.

διαπλανάω: impf.3s διεπλάνα.ʃ

to mislead completely: τινα Jd 19.8*L*. Cf. πλανάω, ἀπατάω.

διαπλατύνω.ʃ

to make wide: Ez 41.7. Cf. πλατύνω.

διαπληκτίζομαι.ʃ *

to fight with the hands with each other: Ex 2.13.

διαπνέω: aor.subj. ~πνεύσω.ʃ

to breathe through space: ***s*** ἡ ἡμέρα 'the (new) day' Ct 2.17, 4.6. **b.** tr.: + acc., κῆπόν μου 'my orchard' Ct 4.16.

Cf. πνέω.

διαπονέω: fut.pass. ~πονηθήσομαι.ʃ

1. *to endeavour assiduously*: + inf., 2M 2.28.

2. pass. *to get tired*: physically, Ec 10.9.

Cf. MM, s.v.

διαπορεύομαι: fut. ~πορεύσομαι.

1. *to move through* a space: no space mentioned, Nu 11.8; ***s*** person, δι' αὐτῆς (= city) Zp 3.1; enemy who has breached defences, Zc 9.8; enemy's sword, PSol 13.2; ships, Ps 103.26; water, Is 30.25; || διέρχομαι– πάντα, ὅσα ἂν μὴ διαπορεύηται διὰ πυρός, διελεύσεται δι' ὕδατος Nu 31.23 (|| διέρχομαι ἐν πυρί); + acc. loci, τὴν γῆν Ez 39.14, τὴν ὑπ' οὐρανόν Jb 2.2, ἔρημον Si 8.16 (cf. δι' ἐρήμου

Pr 9.12c), τρίβους θαλασσῶν Ps 8.9 (*s* animals); fig., ἐν σκότει 81.5 (|| lit. 90.6).

2. *to conduct oneself* or *one's life* in a certain manner: ἐν προστάγμασι ζωῆς Ez 33.15; ἐν εἰκόνι 'in a phantom' Ps 38.7, ἐν πλημμελείαις 'in errors' 67.22, ἐν ἀκακίᾳ 100.2.

Cf. πορεύομαιι, διαβαίνω, διαπειράω, διέρχομα.

διάπρασις, εως. f.ʃ

act of selling to various purchasers: Le 25.33 (|| πρᾶσις vs. 28). Cf. πρᾶσις.

διαπράσσω: aor.ptc.mid. ~πραξάμενος.ʃ

to finish doing: + acc. rei, ταῦτα 2M 8.29, 10.38. Cf. ποιέω, πράσσω, συντελέω.

διαπρεπής, ές.ʃ

magnificent: *s* hum., τὴν περιβολήν 'in their robes' 2M 3.26; 10.29. Cf. ἐκπρεπής.

διαπρίω: aor. διέπρισα.ʃ

to put under the saw: with an instrument specified, ἐν πρίοσι 'with saws' 2K 12.31*L*; || 1C 20.3. Cf. πρί(ζ)ω, πρίων.

διάπτωσις, εως. f.ʃ

v.n. of διαπίπτω: Je 19.6, 14. Cf. διαπίπτω, πτῶσις.

διάπυρος, ον.ʃ

extremely hot: *s* furnace, Da 3.46 LXX, 3M 6.6.

διαπυρόω.ʃ

to subject sbd *to intense effect* of sth: pass., *o* hum., δίψῃ 'thirst' 4M 3.15.

διαριθμέω: aor.mid. διηριθμησάμην.ʃ

to take into account: τι 3M 3.6.

διαρκέω: aor.pass. διηρκέσθην.ʃ

pass. *to be content* with: + dat. rei, 3M 2.26. Cf. ἀρκέω.

διαρπαγή, ῆς. f.

act or *object of plundering, pillaging*: αἱ γυναῖκες ἡμῶν καὶ τὰ παιδία ἔσονται εἰς ~ήν '.. will become objects of plundering' Nu 14.3 (|| ἐν ~ῇ 14.31), sim. Is 5.5, ἔδωκεν εἰς ~ὴν Ιακωβ 42.24; Hb 2.7; || ἀφανισμός Zp 1.13; + προνομή 4K 21.14. Cf. διαρπάζω.

διαρπάζω: fut.mid. διαρπῶμαι, pass. διαρπαγήσομαι; aor. διήρπασα, inf. ~πάσαι, impv.3pl. ~πασάτωσαν, subj. ~πάσω, inf.pass. ~πασθῆναι, 2aor.pass. διηρπάγην, subj. ~παγῶ; pf.ptc.pass. διηρπασμένος.

to plunder: *o* area, πόλιν Ge 34.27; διαρπαγήσονται αἱ χῶραί σου Am 3.11; Zp 2.4; οἰκίαι Zc 14.2; person, ἀδικούμενος καὶ διαρπαζόμενος 'wronged and plundered' De 28.29; ὀρφανούς .. ἄνδρα Mi 2.2 (|| καταδυναστεύω), Is 42.22 (|| προνομεύω); valuable property, ἀργύριον .. χρυσίον Na 2.10; κτῆμα 'property' Si 36.30, ὑπάρχοντα 'properties' Es 3.13 o', νήπια 'infants' 3.7 *L*; || ἀφανίζω Zp 2.9; ἁρπάγματα Ez 22.29; pass. ἡ ἰσχύς σου 'your strength (is sapped)' Si 6.2. Cf. διαρπαγή, ἁρπάζω, ἐκδιδύσκω, κλοποφορέω, προνομεύω.

διαρραίνω: pf. διέρραγκα.ʃ

to scatter sth over the whole surface of sth else *in small drops or particles*, 'besprinkle': + acc., τὴν κοίτην μου κρόκῳ 'my bed with saffron' Pr 7.17. Cf. ῥαίνω.

διαρρέω: aor.pass.inf. ~ρρυῆναι.ʃ

to slip through and escape: *s* troops, 2M 10.20.

διαρρήγνυμι, ~ρρήσσω: fut.act. ~ρρήξω, pass. ~ρραγήσομαι; aor. διέρρηξα, impv. ~ρρηξον, subj. ~ρρήξω, inf. ~ρρῆξαι, ptc. ~ρρήξας, pass. διερράγην, subj. ~ρραγῶ; pf.ptc. διερρηχώς, διερρωγώς, pass. διερρηγμένος.

1. *to tear apart*: *o* the heart of a prey, Ho 13.8; *o* own clothes, as a sign of repentance, ἱμάτια Ge 37.29, 34, 44.13; as a sign of grief, Le 10.6, 21.10, Nu 14.6, 1M 2.14, χιτῶνα 2K 15.32, τὰ ἱμάτια αὐτοῦ διηρρηγότα (act.!: *L* διηρρηγμένα), Je 48.5 (+ κόπτομαι); διερρηγμένα καὶ ῥακώδη 'rags and tattered clothes' Pr 23.21; pregnant woman, Ho 14.1, 4K 15.16*L* (B: ἀνα~); δεσμούς 'fetters' Je 5.5 (|| συντρίβω), Na 1.13, Ps 2.3; σχοινία 'cords' Is 33.20; σάκκον 'sack-cloth' Ps 29.12, ὑποδήματα 'shoes' Ne 9.21; τὴν βασιλείαν σου ἐκ χειρός σου 1K 28.17, 3K 11.11; metaph., διαρρήξατε τὰς καρδίας ὑμῶν καὶ μὴ τὰ ἱμάτια ὑμῶν καὶ ἐπιστράφητε πρὸς τὸν κύριον 'Rend your hearts, and not your garments, and return to the Lord' Jl 2.13; also + cogn. acc., ^τὸ ἱμάτιον^ δώδεκα ῥήγματα 'into twelve pieces' 3K 11.30. **b.** pass. *to become broken into pieces and hang loose*: *o* garment, 2K 1.2.

2. *to divide in the middle*, 'split': + acc., διέρρηξεν θάλασσαν καὶ διήγαγεν αὐτούς Ps 77.13, πέτραν 77.15; pass., φαγὼν διερράγη ὁ δράκων 'having eaten, the snake split open' Bel TH 27.

3. *to break through* an enemy line: ἐν τῇ παρεμβολῇ 'the camp' 2K 23.16B (*L*: διακόπτω) || 1C 11.18 τὴν ~ήν.

4. *to make totally ineffective*: + acc., ἰσχὺν βασιλέων Is 45.1.

5. *to cleave* hard soil or rock and reveal: + acc., πηγὰς καὶ χειμάρρους 'fountains and torrents' Ps 73.15, πάχος γῆς 'thick soil' 140.7.

Cf. ῥήγνυμι, ῥῆγμα, διασπάω, διΐστημι.

διαρρίπτω, ~τέω: aor.impv. ~ριψον.ʃ

to throw about: *o* τοὺς λίθους τοὺς ἐκ τῆς ὁδοῦ 'the stones cleared from the road' Is 62.10; hearths of fire, Jb 41.11.

διαρρυθμίζω: aor. διερρύθμισα.ʃ

to arrange in good order: + acc., 2M 7.22.

διαρτάω: aor.inf.pass. διαρτηθῆναι, ptc. ~ρτησάμενος∫

to stay sbd's *hand*: οὐχ ὡς ἄνθρωπος ὁ θεὸς διαρτηθῆναι 'God is not like a man so as to be deterred' Nu 23.19 (|| ἀπειλέω); mid., with the collateral notion of *to have* sbd (acc.) *removed from influencial office*: τινα Es E 26*L*.

διαρτίζω: pf.pass. διήρτιμαι.∫*

to mould: ***o*** hum., ἐκ πηλοῦ 'from clay' Jb 32.6. Cf. ποιέω.

διασαλεύω: aor.pass.impv. διασαλεύθητι.∫

to shake violently: pass.= intr. διασαλεύθητι καὶ σείσθητι Hb 2.16. Cf. σαλεύω and σείω.

διασαφέω: fut.pass. ~σαφηθήσομαι; aor. διεσάφησα, subj. ~σαφήσω, inf. ~σαφῆσαι.

1. *to explain the meaning of*: τὸν νόμον De 1.5; + dat. pers., τὸ ἐνύπνιον διασαφήσητέ μοι καὶ τὴν τούτου σύγκρισιν ἀναγγείλητε Da 2.6 LXX; ἐπίκρισις ^τοῦ ἐνυπνίου^ 'the interpretation of the dream' Es A 11 *L*.

2. *to state plainly*: περὶ συμμαχίας καὶ φιλίας 'about alliance and friendship' 1M 12.8; + inf., ἡμῖν μὴ εὑρηκέναι πῦρ 'that they had not found fire' 2M 1.21; + an interrogative, τίνος ἕνεκεν 'why' 3.9; + λέγων and direct speech, 7.6; ὅσα 11.18; ***s*** law, καθὼς ὁ νόμος διασαφεῖ 10.26.

3. *to instruct plainly*: + dat. pers. and ἵνα, 2M 1.18.

Cf. διασάφησις, ἀναγγέλλω, συγκρίνω: LSG s.v.

διασάφησις, εως.* f.∫

1. *act of explaining*: + gen. obj., ^ἐνυπνίων^ 'dreams' Ge 40.8.

2. *text publicly made known*: δ. ἐπιστολῆς 2E 5.6; διατάγματος 'of decree' 7.11.

Cf. διασαφέω, σύγκρισις.

διασείω: aor. διέσεισα, ptc.pass. ~σεισθείς.∫

1. *to shake violently*: στύλους 'columns' understood as ***o***, ἐν ἰσχύι αὐτοῦ 'with his might' Jd 16.30 *L*.

2. *to extort and rob* sbd: pass., + gen., τῶν ὑπαρχόντων 'of the possessions' 3M 7.21.

διασκεδάζω, ~σκεδαννύω: fut.act. ~δάσω, pass. ~δασθήσομαι; aor.act. διεσκέδασα, inf. ~δάσαι, impv. ~δασον, subj. ~δάσω, pass. ~δασθῶ; pf.pass. διεσκέδασμαι, inf. ~σκεδάσθαι.

1. *to cause to disintegrate*: + acc. (a group of people), Ex 32.25; army troops, Is 9.11; mind, 3M 5.30.

2. *to disperse, scatter abroad*: pass., ***o*** mist, Wi 2.4.

*__3__. *to reject, throw away* as unimportant, unacceptable and the like: τὴν διαθήκην μου Ge 17.14, Le 26.15, 44, De 31.16, Zc 11.10, τὰς ἐντολὰς αὐτοῦ Nu 15.31, pass. Zc 11.11; διεσκέδασται νόμος Hb 1.4; τὴν κατάσχεσιν 'the relation (between ..)' Zc 11.14; τὴν εὐλογίαν ὑμῶν Ma 2.2, τὸ ἔλεός μου ἀπ' αὐτοῦ Ps 88.34; ἃ ὁ θεὸς .. βεβούλευται 'what God .. has decided' Is 14.27, λόγους ταπεινῶν ἐν κρίσει '.. in a court' 32.7, βουλήν 'advice' 3K 12.24ʳ (|| vs. 8 ἐγκαταλείπω). **b**. as undesirable: ***o*** ἀμβλακία 'error' 3M 2.19.

*__4__. *to prevent successful conclusion of*, 'thwart, jeopardise': + acc., βουλήν 'design, decision' Is 8.10, 19.3, Ps 32.10, Ne 4.15.

Cf. διασκορπίζω, διασπείρω.

διασκευάζω: aor.pass. διεσκευάσθην; pf.ptc.pass. διεσκευασμένος.∫

to equip for military action: pass., ***o*** hum., Jo 4.12; διεσκευάσθησαν αἱ δυνάμεις εἰς τὸν πόλεμον 'the forces were made ready for battle' 1M 6.33. Cf. διασκευή.

διασκευή, ῆς. f.∫

1. *furniture*, coll.: τῆς σκηνῆς Ex 31.7.

2. *battle order*: ἐν ~ῃ 2M 11.10; 2K 23.8*L*.

Cf. διασκευάζω.

διασκιρτάω: aor. διεσκίρτησα.∫ *

to skip around: ***s*** hum., like lambs, Wi 19.9. Cf. σκιρτάω, ἅλλομαι.

διασκορπίζω: fut. ~πιῶ, pass. ~πισθήσομαι; aor. διεσκόρπισα, subj. ~πίσω, impv. ~πισον, inf. ~πίσαι, ptc. ~πίσας, pass. διεσκορπίσθην, impv. 3pl. ~πισθήτωσαν, subj.~πισθῶ; pf.pass.ptc. διεσκορπισμένος.

to scatter abroad, disperse: + acc. pers., Nu 10.34 (enemies); Zc 1.19, 21*ter*; ἐν τοῖς ἔθνεσιν 'among the peoples' Ez 20.23 (|| διασπείρω), To 3.4 𝔊ᴵᴵ (𝔊ᴵ σκορπίζω), Je 9.16, ἐν πάσῃ τῇ γῇ Si 48.15, εἰς πάντα ἄνεμον 'in every direction' Ez 5.10; ***o*** flock, Zc 11.16, Je 23.1; treasures, 27.37; weapons (to be made ineffective), 28.20, chariots 28.22, clouds Jb 37.11¶; + dat. pers., Da 11.24 TH.

Cf. διασκορπισμός, σκορπίζω, διασκεδάζω, ἐκριπτέω, σπείρω.

διασκορπισμός, οῦ. m.

state of being dispersed: divine punishment of people, Ez 6.8, εἰς πάσας τὰς βασιλείας τῆς γῆς Je 24.9. Cf. διασκορπίζω.

δίασμα, ατος. n.

warp: Jd 16.13. Cf. διάζομαι.

διασπασμός, οῦ. m.∫

v.n. of διασπάω, q.v.: Je 15.3 (done by dogs).

διασπάω:pres.impv. ~σπα; fut. ~σπάσω; aor. διέσπασα, pass. ~σπάσθην, opt.3s ~σπάσαι.

to tear asunder: ***o*** prey, θηρία ἀγροῦ διασπάσει αὐτούς 'wild animals will tear them asunder' Ho 13.8, sim. Jd 14.6 A (B: συντρίβω); document, Is 58.6; fetters, Je 2.20, curtain 4.20, tent and grapevine La 2.6, thread Jd 16.9 A, cord ib. B; + acc. pers., διέσπασέν με κύκλῳ 'he took me apart thoroughly' Jb 19.10. Cf. διασπασμός, διαρρήγνυμι.

διασπείρω: fut. ~σπερῶ, pass. ~σπαρήσομαι; aor. διέσπειρα, inf. ~σπεῖραι, pass. διεσπάρην, inf. ~σπαρῆναι, impv. ~σπάρηθι, subj. ~σπαρῶ; pf.ptc. pass. διεσπαρμένος.

to disperse, scatter: + acc. pers., ἐν Ισραηλ Ge 49.7 (|| διαμερίζω, so De 32.8), ***o*** sheep, Ez 34.5. **b.** outside of one's own national boundaries as divine punishment: + acc. pers., εἰς τὰ ἔθνη Le 26.33, εἰς πάντα τὰ ἔθνη De 28.64, ἐν πᾶσιν τοῖς ἔθνεσιν 4.27, διασπερῶ αὐτοὺς ἐν διασπορᾷ Je 15.7, ἐν ταῖς χώραις Ez 20.23 (|| διασκορπίζω); pass., ἀπὸ τούτων διεσπάρησαν ἐπὶ πᾶσαν τὴν γῆν 'from these they spread over the entire earth' Ge 9.19; διεσπάρη ὁ λαὸς ἐν ὅλῃ Αἰγύπτῳ Ex 5.12, διεσπάρησαν ἐν τοῖς ἔθνεσι Jl 3.2; ἐκ τῆς διασπορᾶς, οὗ διεσπάρησαν ἐκεῖ Ju 5.19; τοὺς διεσπαρμένους Ιουδα Is 11.12 (|| ἀπολομένους); outside of metropolis, Es 9.19 ο'. **c.** *to send away* without offering to help, opp. συνάγω **2**: ***o*** ψυχὰς πεινώσας 'souls of the hungry' Is 32.6; pass. and ***o*** children, ἀπό τινος (the parent) Je 52.8. **d.** mid. *to spread farther away*: ***s*** battle, εἰς ὅλην τὴν πόλιν 1K 14.23, ἐπὶ προσώπου ὅλου τοῦ δρυμοῦ 'over the entire area of the coppice' 2K 18.8*L*. **e.** mid. *to dissociate oneself from a bond* to sbd *and go one's own way*: ἀπό τινος (pers.) 1K 11.11, 13.8, 11; ἐν τῷ λαῷ '(Disperse yourselves) among the people' 14.34.

Cf. διασπορά, σπείρω, διασκεδάζω, διασκορπίζω.

διασπορά, ᾶς. f.ʃ *

state of being dispersed outside of national boundaries: ἔσῃ ἐν ~ᾷ ἐν πάσαις ταῖς βασιλείαις τῆς γῆς De 28.25; δώσω ὑμᾶς εἰς ~ὰν πάσαις ταῖς βασιλείαις τῆς γῆς Je 41.17 (|| 24.9 εἰς διασκορπισμόν); ἐὰν ᾖ ἡ δ. σου ἀπ' ἄκρου τοῦ οὐρανοῦ ἕως ἄκρου τοῦ οὐρανοῦ De 30.4, sim. Ne 1.9; διασπερῶ αὐτοὺς ἐν ~ᾷ Je 15.7; Da 12.2 LXX. **b.** *land where one has been dispersed to outside of one's national boundaries*: ἀνέβησαν ἐκ τῆς ~ᾶς, οὗ διεσπάρησαν ἐκεῖ Ju 5.19. **c.** *group of people dispersed to outside of their national boundaries*: coll. τὴν ~ὰν τοῦ Ισραηλ ἐπιστρέψαι Is 49.6; ἐπισυνάγαγε τὴν ~ὰν ἡμῶν 2M 1.27, τὰς ~ὰς τοῦ Ισραηλ ἐπισυνάξει Ps 146.2; συνάγαγε τὴν ~ὰν Ισραηλ PSol 8.28.

Cf. διασπείρω, διασκεδάζω, σκορπισμός: Schmidt, *TDNT* 2.98-101.

διάσταλσις, εως. f.ʃ

exact provisions made in a treaty: 2M 13.24. Cf. διαστέλλω **4**.

διάστασις, εως. f.ʃ

difference: about religious and cultic matters, 3M 3.7.

διαστέλλω: fut.act. διαστελῶ, mid. ~στελοῦμαι, pass. ~σταλήσομαι; aor. διέστειλα, impv. διάστειλον, inf. ~στεῖλαι, ptc.act. ~στείλας, subj. ~στείλω, mid. διεστειλάμην, inf. ~στείλασθαι, subj. ~στείλωμαι, pass. διεστάλην, impv. ~στάληθι; pf.ptc.pass. διεσταλμένος.

1. *to make a distinction, separate one from another*: ἀνὰ μέσον τῶν ἁγίων καὶ τῶν βεβήλων 'between the holy and profane' Le 10.10, cf. ἅγια ἀπὸ βεβήλων Si 18.3¶; ἀνὰ μέσον ἀδελφῶν Ho 13.15; of a tactic used by a wild animal attacking a flock of sheep, Mi 5.8; τοὺς Λευίτας ἐκ μέσου τῶν υἱῶν Ισραηλ Nu 8.14, ὑμᾶς ἐκ συναγωγῆς Ισραηλ 16.9; τὸν ὄχλον Su 48 LXX (by walking in the middle of the crowd); pass., δύο λαοὶ ἐκ τῆς κοιλίας σου διασταλήσονται 'two nations will separate out of your belly' Ge 25.23; 30.40 (|| διαχωρίζω); ὑπερῷα ῥιπιστὰ διεσταλμένα θυρίσιν 'well-ventilated penthouses with windows of their own' Je 22.14; οὐ διαστελῶ 'I shall make no distinction, i.e. nobody shall escape punishment' Ez 24.14; ***o*** understood, "having drawn the curtains" Ju 14.15.

2. *to set apart*: + acc., εἰς ἄφεσιν 'for release' Le 16.26, εἰς κακά De 29.21; ὑμῖν αὐτοῖς πόλεις Nu 35.11; De 10.8, 19.2; 3K 8.53. **b.** *to assign* (to a specific task): + acc. pers., Ez 39.14; ἐπὶ τὸν οἶκον κυρίου 2C 23.18. **c.** *to allocate as a portion*: pass. (***o*** wisdom), παρὰ κυρίου Si 15.9. **d.** *to excommunicate*: 2E 10.8 (|| ἀλλοτριόω 1E 9.4). **e.** mid. *to dissociate oneself* from, *part* with: ἀπό τινος 2E 10.11 (|| χωρίζομαι 1E 9.9), cf. διΐστημι **I 4**.

3. *to dispel, disperse*: pass. οὕτως διασταλήσονται Na 1.12 (of water?).

4. *to state precisely*, 'spell out': + acc., διάστειλον τὸν μισθόν σου πρός με 'State your wage to me' Ge 30.28; τοῖς χείλεσιν 'with the lips, i.e. orally' Le 5.4, sim. Ps 105.33, μεθ' ὅρκου 'by oath' Le 5.4; as a mutual agreement, 2M 14.28; ***s*** τὰ χείλη Ps 65.14 (|| λαλέω); visually, divine epiphany 1K 3.1 (***s*** ὅρασις); didactic, + διδάσκω Ne 8.8.

5. mid. *to give express orders*: + dat. pers., Ez 3.18; + inf., 3.21. **b.** act., + dat. pers., 2E 8.24, Jd 1.19B.

6. *to discharge* an obligation: + acc., εὐχήν 'a vow' Le 22.21; abs., διαστελῶ ὑμῖν εἰς βρῶσιν 'I will pay for your food' Ma 3.11 (cf. Arb /'arsulu lakum ṭa'āman/).

Cf. δια~, ἐκ~, χωρίζω, ἀφορίζω, διαστολή, διάσταλσις, ὁρίζω: LSG s.v.

διάστημα, ατος. n.

a space between two objects or areas: δ. ποιεῖτε ἀνὰ μέσον ποίμνης καὶ ποίμνης 'keep flocks separated from one another' Ge 32.16. **b.** *a period of time*: τοῦ χρόνου Si prol. 32, 3M 4.17.

Cf. διαστέλλω.

διαστολή, ῆς. f.∫

1. *discrimination*: δώσω ~ὴν ἀνὰ μέσον τοῦ ἐμοῦ λαοῦ καὶ ἀνὰ μέσον τοῦ σοῦ λαοῦ Ex 8.23; ἄνευ ~ῆς 'indiscriminately' PSol 4.4.

2. *express, precise verbal statement*: τοῦ νόμου Nu 19.2; κατὰ τὴν ~ὴν τῶν χειλέων αὐτῆς 'in accordance with her own express, oral statement' 30.7.

3. *a tract of land agreed to be ceded* (?): διδόναι .. ~ὴν καὶ χώραν .. 1M 8.7.

Cf. διαστέλλω, ὁρισμός: Caird 1968.467f.; *BA* ad Nu 19.2 and 30.7.

διαστράπτω.∫ *

to flash like lightning: *s* fire, Wi 16.22. Cf. ἀστραπή.

διαστρεννύναι.⇒ διαστρώννυμι.

διαστρέφω: fut. ~στρέψω, pass. ~στραφήσομαι; aor. διέστρεψα, subj. ~στρέψω, pass. διεστράφην, subj. ~στραφῶ; pf.ptc.pass. διεστραμμένος.

1. *to twist about*: metaph., *o* τὸ στόμα αὐτοῦ '(change) his tune' Si 27.23.

2. *to pervert, distort*: + acc., κρίμα πένητος 'a court-case of a poor person' Ex 23.6; τὰ ὀρθά Mi 3.9; ἐξελεύσεται τὸ κρίμα διεστραμμένον 'the justice will, in the end, get perverted' Hb 1.4; ψυχάς Ez 13.18, καρδίαν δικαίου 13.22, + acc. pers., ib.; pass., διεστραμμένον 'the opposite of what is normal' 16.34, διεστραμμένα 'perversities' ib. (sexual), Pr 16.30; pass., αἱ τρίβοι αὐτῶν διεστραμμέναι 'their paths ..' Is 59.8, ὁδοί Pr 4.27a, 8.13, "detours" Jd 5.6 (*L* οὐκ εὐθείας 'not straight'); pass., *o* hum., τοὺς πόδας 'the legs (twisted; hence bent) understood (?) Ec 12.3. **b**. intr., *to conduct oneself perversely*: Ps 17.27 ‖ 2K 22.27*L* (B: στρεβλόομαι).

3. *to distract, divert*: τὸν λαόν μου ἀπὸ τῶν ἔργων Ex 5.4 (‖ καταπαύω vs. 5); διανοίας 'mind, intention' Nu 32.7 (‖ ἀφίστημι τὴν καρδίαν vs. 9), τὸν νοῦν Su 9, τὴν καρδίαν 56 TH; pass. ὀπίσω τῶν διανοιῶν ὑμῶν καὶ ὀπίσω τῶν ὀφθαλμῶν ὑμῶν '(so as to follow the direction of) your minds ..' Nu 15.39; γενεὰ σκολιὰ καὶ διεστραμμένη 'an obstinate and perverse generation' De 32.5 (‖ ἐξεστραμμένη vs. 20). Cf. σκολιός.

4. *to carry around*: + acc., Jb 37.12¶.

5. *to cause disruptions for, mess things up for*: τινα Si 11.34.

Cf. διαστροφή.

διαστροφή, ῆς. f.∫

moral perversity: ‖ κακά Pr 2.14. Cf. διαστρέφω.

διαστρώννυμι: aor. διέστρωσα.∫

to spread a couch or bed: abs., ἐπὶ τῷ δώματι 'on the roof' 1K 9.25 (*L* simp.). Cf. στρώννυμι.

διασυρίζω.∫ *

to move through a space *while making whistling noise*: *s* wind, Da 3.50. Cf. συρίζω. Del. Wi 17.18 v.l.

διασφαγή, ῆς. f.∫

**gap* in a wall in ruins: Ne 4.7.

διασφάλλω: pf.ptc.pass. διεσφαλμένος.∫

not to suceed in attaining: + gen., προθέσεως 'purpose' 3M 5.12. Cf. ἐξαμαρτάνω, ἐπιτυγχάνω.

διασχίζω: aor. διέσχισα, pass. διεσχίσθην.∫

1. *to sever* sth oblong so that it does not reach its other end: + acc., τὴν ὁδόν Wi 18.23.

2. *to disband*: *o* crowd, Ps 34.15.

Cf. σχίζω.

διασῴζω: fut. διασώσω, pass. ~σωθήσομαι; aor. διέσωσα, impv.3s διασωσάτω, inf.act. ~σῶσαι, ptc. ~σώσας, opt.3s ~σώσαι, pass. διεσώθην, inf. ~σωθῆναι, ptc. ~σωθείς, subj. ~σωθῶ; pf.pass. ~σέσῳσμαι.

to save out of difficulty and trouble: + acc. pers., *s* king, 2K 10.19*L* (B: simp.), Ho 13.10; God, ἐν τῇ ὁδῷ Ge 35.3; De 20.4, Jn 1.6, Zc 8.13; pass., *to save one's skin by fleeing*, διασωθῆναι εἰς τὸ ὄρος '.. into the mountain(s)' Ge 19.19 (‖ καταφεύγω vs. 20); ἀπὸ τῶν ἐχθρῶν ὑμῶν Nu 10.9; οὐ μὴ διασωθῇ ἐξ αὐτῶν ἀνασῳζόμενος 'any one of them attempting to escape will not succeed' Am 9.1 (‖ διαφεύγω); 2.15, Mi 6.14; pass., ἀπὸ ἰοῦ καὶ βρωμάτων 'from rust and moth-eating' Ep Je 11, ἀπὸ καύματος 'from heat' Pr 10.5; + διαφεύγω Jo 10.28+. **b**. pass. *to be spared some unpleasant experience*: διασωθήσομαι δή 'May I please be excused for my absence?' 1K 20.29 (*L* ἀπελεύσομαι δή); *to be spared disturbance*, hum. bones in a tomb, 4K 23.18*L* (B: ῥύομαι).

Cf. σῴζω.

διαταγή, ῆς. f.∫*

command: τῆς ἐπιστολῆς 'contained in the epistle' 2E 4.11. Cf. ἐντολή, διατάσσω **4**: Deissmann 1923.70f.

διάταγμα, ατος. n.

= διαταγή: 2E 7.11 (‖ πρόσταγμα 1E 8.8).

διάταξις, εως. f.

1. *manner of arranging multiple components*: ἐν ~ει 'as they were arranged' Ez 42.15, τοῦ οἴκου 42.20; 3K 6.1[d], Ps 118.91; *o* daily portion of food, 'ration' Da 1.5 TH.

2. *that which is arranged, consisting of multiple components*: of troops, Ju 1.4, 8.36; priests' timetable, work-schedule, 2C 31.16.

Cf. διατάσσω.

διατάσσω: aor. διέταξα, ptc. ~τάξας, impv. ~ταξον, mid. διεταξάμην, ptc. ~ταξάμενος; pf.ptc.pass. ~τεταγμένος.

1. *to arrange* multiple components in a certain order: + acc. rei, ὁδούς Ez 21.19; hair, Ju 10.3; troops, 2.16; chamber, 3M 1.19; roster of priestly service, 1C 9.33, cf. Ez 44.8; heavenly bodies, PSol 18.10.

2. *to assign*: "500 horsemen assigned to every animal (ἑκάστῳ θηρίῳ)" 1M 6.35; ἄρτους .. αὐτῷ 3K 11.18; οἱ διατεταγμένοι 'staff assigned various duties' Jd 3.23B.

3. *to bequeath*: pass., + acc. rei, Pr 9.12c.

4. *to prescribe as a command*: + dat. pers., pass., Jd 5.9. **b**. mid. 1K 13.11 (*L* act.); + acc. rei, ταῦτα 4M 8.3.

Cf. διάταξις.

διατείνω: fut. ~τενῶ; aor. διέτεινα, ptc. ~τείνας; pf.ptc.pass. ~τεταμένος.∫

to stretch, extend: spatially, Is 40.22, + acc., σχοινία 'cords (of trap)' Ps 139.6, temporally, ὀργήν 84.6; pass. τοξευμάτων διατεταμένων 'stretched arrows' Is 21.15. **b**. intr.: ἀπὸ πέρατος εἰς πέρας 'from one end to the other' Wi 8.1. Cf. τείνω.

διατελέω: aor. διετέλεσα.∫

to continue: 'to do' + ptc. pres., ἀπειθοῦντες διετελεῖτε De 9.7; Es E 11, 2M 5.27; Je 20.7; 'to remain' in a certain condition without a change, διετέλεσαν ἐν αἰσχύνῃ αἱ ἡμέραι μου 20.18.

διατήκω: aor.pass. διετάκην.∫

to cause to melt away and disappear: pass., διετάκη ἔθνη 'nations were brought to naught' Hb 3.6 (|| διαθρύπτω). Cf. τήκω and ἀφανίζω.

διατηρέω: fut. ~ρήσω; aor. διετήρησα, impv. ~τήρησον, ptc. ~τηρήσας, pass. διετηρήθην; pf.ptc. pass. ~τετηρημένος.

1. *to maintain without abandoning* or *annulling*: + διαθήκην Ge 17.9 (opp. διασκεδάζω, vs. 14), De 33.9 (|| φυλάσσω), τὴν ἱερατείαν ὑμῶν 'your priestly duties' Nu 18.7; ***s*** God, δικαιοσύνην Ex 34.7, ὅρκον De 7.8.

2. *to retain in memory*: + acc. rei, τὸ ῥῆμα 'the matter' Ge 37.11; ἐν τῇ καρδίᾳ αὐτοῦ Da 7.28 TH (LXX στηρίζω), cf. Lk 2.51.

3. *to have in one's care temporarily*: ***s*** wet-nurse and ***o*** infant, Ex 2.9 (+ dat. com.); the captured in war, Ju 2.10.

4. *to allow to survive*: pass. ***o*** hum., Ex 9.16; sacrificial animal, 12.6. **b**. *to sustain*: + acc. pers., || τρέφω Wi 16.26.

5. *to adhere* to an injunction: + inf. indicating the injunction, Nu 28.2; + acc., ἐντολάς Si 1.26.

6. *to cleave to and not let go of*: + acc. μῆνιν Si 28.5 || ἀνθρώπῳ συντηρεῖ ὀργήν 28.3.

7. *to guard* against some danger: + acc., τὰς χεῖρας αὐτοῦ μὴ ποιεῖν ἀδίκημα Is 55.2; ἡμᾶς ἀπὸ τῆς γενεᾶς ταύτης Ps 11.8; ἐκ θλίψεως τὴν ψυχὴν αὐτοῦ Pr 21.23, ἐξ ἀνδρῶν ἀσεβῶν 'from impious men' 2K 22.49*L* (B: ῥύομαι).

8. *to cause to remain as*: + double acc., ἀμίαντον τὸν οἶκον 'the house undefiled' 2M 14.36, sim. 15.34.

Cf. διατήρησις, τηρέω, φυλάσσω.

διατήρησις, εως. f.*

1. *conservation*: ἀποθήσεις αὐτὸ .. εἰς ~ιν εἰς τὰς γενεὰς ὑμῶν 'you shall store it .. for conservation for your generations' Ex 16.33.

2. *that which is conserved and kept*: ἀπαρχῶν Nu 18.8.

Cf. διατηρέω.

διατίθημι: fut.mid. ~θήσομαι; 1aor. διέθηκα, 2aor. mid. διεθέμην, inf. ~θέσθαι, impv. ~θου, subj.aor. act. ~θῶ, mid. ~θῶμαι.

I. act. *to deal with, handle*: + acc. pers., τί σε διαθῶ; ὡς Αδαμα θήσομαί σε ..; 'how shall I deal with you? Shall I treat you like Adama…?' Ho 11.8; Ez 16.30, 2M 9.28. Cf. LSG s.v. **A II 1**.

II. mid. *to conclude* an agreement: διέθεντο ἀμφότεροι διαθήκην 'the two made a covenant' Ge 21.27; διαθησόμεθα μετὰ σοῦ διαθήκην 26.28; πρός τινα Ex 24.8, De 4.23, 29.12; 5.2 (|| dat. pers. 5.3); διαθήκην understood, πρὸς Αβρααμ Es 4.16 *L*; esp. between God and Israel, + ἀνὰ μέσον - τὸ σημεῖον τῆς διαθήκης, ἧς διεθέμην ἀνὰ μέσον ἐμοῦ καὶ καὶ ἀνὰ μέσον πάσης σαρκός Ge 9.17; + μετὰ - διαθήσομαι αὐτοῖς διαθήκην μετὰ τῶν θηρίων τοῦ ἀγροῦ Ho 2.18; + dat. pers., Ge 15.18, Is 55.3, Je 38.31, De 29.1 (last || ἵστημι), Ps 88.4, so Aristoph. *Av*. 439; μετὰ Δαυιδ ⸢εἰρήνην⸣ (om. B) 1C 19.19*L*; ***s*** hum., Ps 49.5; ***o*** πίστιν 2E 19.38 [= Ne 10.1].

2. *to accept and submit oneself to as binding*: + acc., τὸν τῆς θειότητος νόμον 'the divine law' Wi 18.9.

3. *to put together into a coherent whole*: + acc. rei, ἀναβάσεις .. διέθετο 'he formed ideas' Ps 83.6.

4. *to impose authoritatively*: + dat. pers., ἀπὸ τῆς ὁδοῦ, ἧς διέθετο αὐτοῖς Ju 5.18.

5. *to bring* sbd *into a certain state of mind*: + τινα and adv., ὀργίλως με 'into anger' 4M 8.9.

Cf. διαθήκη: Behm, *TDNT* 2.104f.

διατίλλω: aor. διέτιλα.∫

to pull out: abs. (*hair* understood), Jb 16.12. Cf. τίλλω.

διατόνιον, ου. n.∫ *

curtain-hook or *-ring* (LSJ): Ex 35.10.

διατρέπω: aor.pass. διετράπην; pf.ptc.pass. ~τετραμμένος.∫

1. *to disturb mental serenity of*: abs., + καταισχύνω Jd 18.7 B. **b**. pass. *to be overawed by*: + acc., huge crowd, Jb 31.34; τῷ προσώπῳ Es 7.8. Cf. συγχέω **2**.

2. pass. (intr.) *to change*: of facial look, Da 1.10 LXX.

Cf. συγχέω, ταράσσω.

διατρέφω: fut. ~θρέψω, pass. ~τραφήσομαι; aor. διέθρεψα, inf. ~θρέψαι, pass. διετράφην, subj. ~τραφῶ.

to provide food regularly for sustenance: τινα 2K 19.33 (*L* χορηγέω); ***o*** hum., διατραφῇ λαὸς πολύς Ge 50.20; ὑμᾶς καὶ τὰς οἰκίας ὑμῶν ib. 21; animals (σπέρμα 'their descendants') 7.3; ἐν λιμῷ 'in famine' Ps 32.19; τὸ γῆρας σου 'your old age' 2K 19.34, τὴν πολιάν σου Ru 4.15. Cf. τρέφω, διατροφή: Moussy 1969.78.

διατρέχω: fut. ~δραμοῦμαι.ʃ

to move fast across a space from one end to the other: ***s*** fire, Ex 9.23; ὡς ἀστραπαὶ διατρέχουσαι 'as lightnings traversing (the sky)' Na 2.5; sparks, Wi 3.7; hum., 3K 18.26. Cf. τρέχω.

διατριβή, ῆς. f.

1. *pastime*: negatively perceived, Pr 14.24.

2. *place where one resides and spends days*: quarantine for lepers, Le 13.46; στρουθῶν 'of sparrows' Je 30.11; ἡδὺς ἐν οἴνων ~αῖς 'over the moon in pubs' Pr 12.11a. Cf. Pelletier 1967b.175-80.

Cf. διατρίβω.

διατρίβω: fut. ~τρίψω; aor. διέτριψα.

1. *to reside and spend days*: ἔξω τοῦ οἴκου αὐτοῦ Le 14.8; Ju 10.2.

2. *to rub hard*: + acc., ὀφθαλμούς To 11.12 𝔊[I].

Cf. διατριβή.

διατροφή, ῆς. f.ʃ

provisions for sustenance: 1M 6.49. Cf. διατρέφω.

διατυπόω.ʃ

to shape and mould: pass., ***o*** the universe, Wi 19.6.

διαυγάζω.ʃ

to become light at dawn: impers., 4K 7.5*L* (ll διαφώσκω vs.7). Cf. διαφαύσκω, ~φώσκω.

διαφαίνομαι.ʃ

to shine through: + dat. pers., Wi 17.6. Cf. φαίνω. Del. Wi 18.10 v.l.

διαφανής, ές.ʃ

translucent: indicative of high quality and ***s*** frankincense, Ex 30.34; bedspread, Es 1.6 o'; ~ῆ Λακωνικά 'Laconian see-through dresses' Is 3.22, cf. Ottley ad loc.; morbidly pale face, Da 1.13

διαφαύσκω: aor. διέφαυσα, subj. ~φαύσω.

to grow light in the early morning: ***s*** the morning, τὸ πρωΐ Ge 44.3, ὁ ὄρθρος Ju 14.2, ἡ ἡμέρα 1K 14.36 (*L* διαφωτίζω). Cf. διαφωτίζω, ~φώσκω.

διαφέρω: fut. διοίσω; aor. διήνεγκα, ptc. διενέγκας, pass. διηνέχθην, inf. διενεχθῆναι; pf.ptc. διενηνοχώς, pass. διενηνεγμένος.

1. *to transport*: ***o*** acc. (goods), 1E 5.53; a hum. corpse on the sea, PSol 2.27; wrongfully, 2M 4.39. **b**. mid. intr. *to move throughout a space*: ***s*** φωνή Wi 18.10, hum. soul PSol 16.3.

2. intr. *to be different*: ptc., παρά + acc., 'from' Da 7.3 LXX (TH παρὰ ἀλλήλων 'from one another'); + gen., 3M 6.26, οὐδέν 'in no respect' Pr 27.14; in opinion, + dat. pers. and περί τινος (matter), 2M 3.4. Cf. διΐστημι **I 3**. **b**. *to be at variance, quarrel*: Wi 18.2.

3. *to excel*: πολιᾷ 'by grey hair' 2M 15.13; in pejorative sense, κακοῖς ὑπὲρ τοὺς πρώτους 'the first ones in wickedness' Da 7.24 LXX (TH ὑπερφέρω), παρὰ πάσην τὴν γῆν 7.23 LXX (TH ὑπερέχω); σωφροσύνῃ 'in sound judgement' Es B 3.

Cf. διαφορά, φέρω, ἴσος, ὅμοιος, ἀόμοιος: Weiss, *TDNT* 9.63.

διαφεύγω: fut. ~φεύξομαι; aor. διέφυγον, subj. διαφύγω, inf. ~φυγεῖν, ptc. ~φυγών; pf. ~πέφευγα, ptc. ~πεφευγώς.

to manage to escape an assailant, danger: abs., οὐ μὴ διαφύγῃ ἐξ αὐτῶν φεύγων 'none of them will manage to escape' Am 9.1 (ll διασῴζομαι), Je 11.15, πρὸς ὑμᾶς 1M 15.21, εἰς Μαρισα 2M 12.35; with impunity, Pr 19.5; + acc. pers., πόλις, ἥτις διέφυγεν ἡμᾶς De 2.36; Is 10.14; + acc. rei, τὰς χεῖρας τοῦ θεοῦ 2M 7.31, τὴν προσημανθεῖσαν ὥραν 'the appointed hour' 3M 5.13; + διασῴζω Jo 10.28+. Cf. φεύγω: Schmidt 3.244-8.

διαφθείρω: fut. ~φθερῶ, pass. ~φθαρήσομαι; aor. act. διέφθειρα, inf. ~φθεῖραι, impv. ~φθειρον, subj. ~φθείρω, pass. διεφθάρην, inf. ~φθαρθῆναι; pf. pass. διέφθαρμαι, ptc. διεφθαρμένος; plpf.pass.3s διέφθαρτο.

1. physically *to ruin, destroy*: ***o*** hum., Je 5.26 (by means of traps), on battlefield 2K 11.1, 2M 12.23, means unspecified 1K 2.25; τὴν πόλιν 23.10, ^τὸν τόπον .. τὴν γῆν^ 4K 18.25, weapons, Na 2.3; crop, Zp 3.7, Ma 3.11; foundations of a city wall, Je 6.5, fortresses, La 2.5 (ll καταποντίζω), βασιλεία Da 2.44 TH, idols 4K 19.12; ll ἔρημος, πίπτω Is 49.19; + cogn. dat. διεθφάρητε φθορᾷ Mi 2.10; ***s*** mice ravaging the field, 1K 6.5. **b**. ***o*** quality of an obj., Je 13.7 (girdle), Jd 16.7 B (cord), festivals La 2.6, κληρονομίαν 'inheritance' Ru 4.6.

2. morally and religiously, *to corrupt*: ***o*** the Levitical covenant, Ma 2.8; hum., Je 6.28; ἐπιτηδεύματα 'practices' Ez 20.44, ἐπίθεσιν 'preoccupation' 23.11; pass., ***o*** ἐπιστήμη 28.17, hum. Ps 52.2 (+ βδελύσσομαι and ll act. 13.1), cultic offerings Ma 1.14; ῥῆμα, + ψευδής Da 2.9 TH. **b**. *to degenerate morally*: πορευθῆναι ὀπίσω θεῶν ἑτέρων Jd 2.19; Ps 13.1.

3. *to renege* on: ἀπὸ τῶν λόγων αὐτοῦ 'any of what he said' Si 47.22.

Cf. διαφθορά, φθείρω, μολύνω, ἀφανίζω: Harder, *TDNT* 9.98-100.

διαφθονέω.ʃ*

to envy: + dat. pers., Es 6.5 *L*. Cf. φθόνος.

διαφθορά, ᾶς. f.

1. v.n. of διαφθείρω, 'ruining, destruction': physically and w. obj.gen. pers. Ho 11.4, 13.9; ἐν ~ᾷ κατέσπασα ὑπερηφάνους 'I cut down the haughty with ruin' Zp 3.6; done by predatory animals and birds, Je 15.3.

2. *instrument of ruin*: Ps 9.16.

3. *abode of the dead*: καταβῆναι εἰς ~άν Ps 29.10.

Cf. διαφθείρω, φθορά: LSG s.v.

διαφλέγω: fut. ~φλέξω.ʃ*

to burn up: + acc., δρυμόν 'forest' Ps 82.15. Cf. φλέγω.

διαφορά, ᾶς. f.ʃ

difference, variety: φυτῶν 'of plants' Wi 7.20; Si prol. 26; 1M 3.18. Cf. διαφέρω, διάφορος.

διαφορέω.ʃ

to scatter all around: + acc. pers., Je 37.16 (ǁ προνομεύω). Cf. LSG s.v.

διαφόρημα, ατος. n.ʃ

that which has been scattered all around: Je 37.16 (ǁ προνομή).

διάφορος, ον.ʃ

1. *diverse, different in kind*: Le 19.19, De 22.9.

2. *distinguishing onself, excellent*: 2E 8.27 (ǁ ἐπιθυμητός 'desirable'); subst. πολλὰ ~α 'many excellent gifts' 2M 1.35.

3. subst., n., *deeds of partiality*: 1E 4.39 (ǁ λαμβάνειν πρόσωπα).

4. *ready money, cash*: Si 34.5 (ǁ χρυσίον), 7.18, 27.1; πράσεως ἐμπόρων 'arising from dealing with merchants' 42.5; τὸ πλῆθος τῶν ~ων ἀναρίθμητον 'the multitude of monies .. untold' 2M 3.6; ἡ τῶν ~ων πρᾶξις 'the collection of ..' 4.28.

Cf. διαφέρω, διαφορά, διαφόρως, χρῆμα: Weiss, *TDNT* 9.63.

διαφόρως. adv.ʃ

differently: + παρά and acc., 'from' Da 7.7 LXX. Cf. διάφορος.

διαφυλάσσω, ~ττω: fut. ~φυλάξω, pass. ~φυλαχθήσομαι; aor. διεφύλαξα, pass. διεφυλάχθην, subj. act. ~φυλάξω, impv. ~φύλαξον, inf. and opt.3s. ~φυλάξαι, ptc. ~φυλάξας; pf.ptc.pass. ~πεφυλαγμένος.

1. *to watch closely, guard carefully* against danger, corruption, negligence, etc.: + acc., τὴν αὐλήν μου 'my court' Zc 3.7; ἀπὸ γυναικὸς ὑπάνδρου 'against a married woman' Pr 6.24; pass. ἐν προφήτῃ διεφυλάχθη Ho 12.13; ***o*** betrothed woman, οἰκέτις διαπεφυλαγμένη ἀνθρώπῳ Le 19.20; ***s*** God, ***o*** pers. διαφυλάσσων σε ἐν τῇ ὁδῷ πάσῃ, οὗ ἂν πορευθῇς Ge 28.15, sim. 20, ὡς κόρην ὀφθαλμοῦ 'like the apple of an eye' De 32.10, ἄτρωτον 'so as not to get wounded' 2M 10.30; ***o*** τὰ διαβήματά μου 'my steps' PSol 16.9; ἀπὸ ἐχθρῶν 'from enemies' Wi 10.12 (***s*** wisdom, ǁ ἀσφαλίζω 'to keep safe'); + dat. com., διαφυλάξει κύριος .. σοι τὴν διαθήκην καὶ τὸ ἔλεος De 7.12.

2. *to preserve from loss* or *disappearance*: Je 3.5 (ǁ διαμένω); + acc. rei, σῷα 2M 3.15.

3. *to value highly and engage oneself eagerly in*: + acc., ματαιότητας 'vain things' Ps 30.7, ἑορτάς 'festivals' 2M 6.6, εὔνοιαν καὶ πίστιν 'goodwill and loyalty' 3M 3.3.

Cf. φυλάσσω, διαμένω.

διαφωνέω: fut. ~φωνήσω; aor. διεφώνησα; pf. διαπεφώνηκα.ʃ

1. *to be wanting, lacking*, alw. with a negator: ***s*** pers. and + gen.pl., euphemism for 'to be dead'(?), τῶν ἐπιλέκτων τοῦ Ισραηλ οὐ διεφώνησεν οὐδὲ εἷς 'none of the chosen of Is. was missing' Ex 24.11, οὐ διαφωνήσει τῶν ἀνδρῶν αὐτοῦ σὰρξ μία 'he would lose not even one of his men' Ju 10.13 (ǁ διαπίπτω); + ἀπὸ τινῶν, Nu 31.49. Cf. *ND* 2.9. **b**. both pers. and things, and + dat. pers.: οὐ διεφώνησεν αὐτοῖς ἀπὸ μικροῦ ἕως μεγάλου 1K 30.19.

2. *to fail to materialise*: ***s*** promise, prophecy, λόγος Jo 23.14 (ǁ διαπίπτω), 3K 8.56. Cf. διαπίπτω **3**.

3. *to find oneself in a hopeless situation, lost*: ἀπόλωλεν ἡ ἐλπὶς ἡμῶν, διαπεφωνήκαμεν Ez 37.11.

Cf. πίπτω: Caird 1968.468; Lee 82; LSG s.v.; *BA* 4 ad Nu 31.49.

διαφώσκω: aor. διέφωσα, inf. ~φῶσαι, subj. ~φώσω, pass. διεφώσθην. Ionic for διαφαύσκω, q.v.ʃ

to become light early in the morning: impers., Jd 19.26 B (A: ~φαύσκω), 2K 2.32*L* (B: ~φαύσκω); τὸ πρωΐ 17.22*L*; 4K 7.7*L* (ǁ διαυγάζω vs. 5). Cf. διαυγάζω, διαφαύσκω, ὑποφαίνω.

διαφωτίζω: aor.inf. ~φωτίσαι, subj. ~φωτίσω.ʃ

to grow light in the early morning: ***s*** the sun, Ne 8.3; τὸ πρωΐ 1K 14.36*L* (B: διαφαύσκω). Cf. διαφαύσκω.

διαχειρίζω: pf.inf.pass. ~κεχειρίσθαι.ʃ

to confiscate: ***o*** property, Es 7.37*L*.

διαχέω: pres.mid.subj.3s διαχέηται; fut.pass. ~χυθήσομαι; aor. διέχεα, pass. διεχύθην, subj. διαχυθῶ; pf.pass. ~κέχυμαι, ptc.pass. ~κεχυμένος.

1. act. tr. *to spread widely*, 'diffuse': τὰς ὁδούς σου εἰς ἀλλοτρίους 'your practices among alien (gods)' Je 3.13; pass., ***o*** smoke, ὑπὸ ἀνέμου 'by a wind' Wi 5.14 (ǁ διώκω). **b**. mid. intr., ***s*** symptom of disease, διαχύσει διαχέηται Le 13.22; 13.23 (:: μένω 'to remain contained'); ὕδατα Ez 30.16 (resulting from a breached dam); ἀνατολή '(the sunlight) at dawnbreak' 2M 10.28; snake's venom, Pr 23.32.

2. mid. intr. *to relax and enjoy thoroughly*: ἐν τῇ πορνείᾳ μου Je 2.20.

3. mid. intr. *to spread broadly through a space*: ***s*** air, Wi 2.3; λαλιὰ .. πανταχῇ 'a rumour .. all over the place' 2M 8.7.

4. *to permeate*: pass. διαχυθήσονται πόλεις ἐν ἀγαθοῖς 'cities will be flooded with good things' Zc 1.17.

Cf. χέω, διάχυσις.

διαχρίω: pf.ptc.pass. ~κεχρισμένος.ʃ

to apply some liquid to the entire surface of: pass., *o* bread, ἐν ἐλαίῳ 'with oil' Le 2.7, 7.2.

διάχρυσος, ον.ʃ

interwoven with gold: *s* ἱματισμός Ps 44.10, hum. Es 5.4 *L*, ἱππεύς 'horseman' 2M 5.2.

διάχυσις, εως. f.

v.n. of διαχέω, **1**: ~ει διαχέηται Le 13.22.

διαχωρέω: aor. διεχώρησα.ʃ

to split: ἀνὰ μέσον ἀμφοτέρων 'between the two of them' 4K 2.11*L* (B: διαστέλλω). Cf. διαχωρίζω.

διαχωρίζω: fut.pass.~χωρισθήσομαι; aor.act. διεχώρισα, impv. διαχώρισον, inf. ~χωρίσαι, mid./pass. διεχωρίσθην, impv. ~χωρίσθητι, inf. ~χωρισθῆναι, pf.ptc.pass. διακεχωρισμένος.

1. *to regard and declare as different and separate*: ἀνὰ μέσον τοῦ φωτὸς καὶ ἀνὰ μέσον τοῦ σκότους 'the light and the darkness' Ge 1.4; ἀνὰ μέσον ὕδατος καὶ ὕδατος 1.6; || ἀλλοιόω Si 36.8, 11.

2. *to separate out*: + acc., πᾶν πρόβατον φαιὸν ἐν τοῖς ἀρνάσιν 'every grey sheep among the rams' Ge 30.32, + dat. 2C 25.10 (*L* acc.); + dat. com., ἑαυτῷ ποίμνια καθ' ἑαυτόν Ge 30.40; for a special task, Χαλεβ .. ὁ διακεχωρισμένος Nu 32.12.

3. *to separate from one another*: *o* sheep Ez 34.12 (due to a thick fog); hum., αὐτοὺς ἀπ' ἀλλήλων Su 51, φίλους 'friends' Pr 16.28; + gen., αὐτὴν τῆς πόλεως 'it [= the citadel] from the city' 1M 12.36.

4. mid. *to part company* (with sbd ἀπό τινος): Ge 13.9, Si 6.13.

Cf. χωρίζω, διαστέλλω, ~χωρέω.

διάψαλμα, ατος. n. *

musical interlude: found between two contiguous passages of a poem, Hb 3.3, 9, 13; Ps 2.2 +; PSol 17.29. Cf. Pietersma 2003.649f.

διαψεύδομαι: aor. διεψευσάμην, subj. ~ψεύσωμαι; pf.ptc. διεψευσμένος.ʃ

1. *to deceive*: + acc. pers., 4K 4.16; abs., 1M 13.19.

2. *to fail to attain* what one had counted on (τινος): 3M 5.12.

Cf. ψεύδομαι, ἐξαμαρτάω.

διαψιθυρίζω: fut. ~ψιθυρίσω.ʃ

to whisper slanders: + acc., πολλά Si 12.18. Cf. ψιθυρίζω: Caird 1968.468.

δίγλωσσος, ον.

**double-tongued*: *s* hum., ἁμαρτωλός Si 5.9; subst.m., || ψίθυρος 'slanderer' 5.14, + ψίθυρος 28.13. Cf. LSG s.v.

διγομία, ας. f.ʃ *

double burden: Jd 5.16B. Cf. γόμος, φορτίον.

διδακτός, ή, όν.ʃ

well educated: *s* hum., θεοῦ 'by God' Is 54.13, ὑπὸ θεοῦ PSol 17.32; πολέμου '(knowledgeable about) warfare' 1M 4.7. Cf. διδάσκω, πολυμαθής.

διδασκαλία, ας. f.ʃ

what is taught, 'teaching, doctrine': of human origin, + ἔνταλμα Is 29.13; of divine origin and || προφητεία Si 24.33; learning acquired, 39.8, νεότητος 'of youth' Pr 2.17. Cf. διδάσκω, διδαχή: Rengstorf, *TDNT* 2.160f.

διδάσκαλος, ου. m.ʃ

tutor: royal, Es 6.1 o', 2M 1.10. Cf. διδάσκω: Rengstorf, *TDNT* 2.148-51; Klíma 1955.

διδάσκω: fut. διδάξω; aor. ἐδίδαξα, subj. διδάξω, impv. δίδαξον, inf. διδάξαι, pass. ἐδιδάχθην, subj. διδαχθῶ, ptc. διδαχθείς; pf. δέδειχα, δεδίδαχα, ptc.pass. δεδιδαγμένος.

to teach: + acc. pers., acc. rei, διδάξετε ^τὴν ᾠδήν^ τοὺς υἱοὺς Ισραηλ De 31.19, αὐτοὺς πόλεμον Jd 3.2, γράμματα Da 1.4, ὀπίσω τῶν εἰδώλων, ἃ ἐδίδαξαν αὐτοὺς οἱ πατέρες αὐτῶν Je 9.14; and inf. (duty), τῶν κριμάτων, ὅσα ἐγὼ διδάσκω ὑμᾶς .. ποιεῖν De 4.1; διδάξετε τὰ τέκνα ὑμῶν λαλεῖν αὐτὰ .. 11.19; || συμβιβάζω 4.10; διδάξαι ὑμᾶς δικαιώματα καὶ κρίσεις, ποιεῖν ὑμᾶς αὐτὰ .. 4.14, τοῦ ποιεῖν τὸ θέλημά σου Ps 142.10, + ἐλέγχω, παιδεύω Si 18.13, cf. Ps 93.10 (γνῶσιν); pass. + inf. δάμαλις δεδιδαγμένη ἀγαπᾶν νεῖκος 'a heifer taught to love strife' Ho 10.11; δεδιδαγμένος πόλεμον Ct 3.8, cf. εἰς παράταξιν .. εἰς πόλεμον Ps 143.1; *s* God, *o* hum., 70.17; *o* subject matter, γνῶσιν 93.10, σύνεσιν καὶ ἐπιστήμην Jb 22.2, τὸν νόμον κυρίου 1E 9.48; *s* father, *o* son, Si 30.3 (|| παιδεύω); + acc. rei (pupil), χεῖρας εἰς πόλεμον 2K 22.35. **b**. *to teach a lesson to be learned from*: ὑμᾶς τοὺς ἐν πυρὶ Ανανιαν .. 4M 18.12; with no acc. of pupils, 18.13. **c**. *to signal*: so as to make one's intention known, Pr 6.13 (|| ἐννεύω).

Cf. ἐκ~, ὑποδιδάσκω, διδαχή, διδασκαλία, διδάσκαλος, μανθάνω, παιδεύω, προβιβάζω, σοφίζω **2**, συμβιβάζω, συνετίζω: Rengstorf, *TDNT* 2.135-8.

διδαχή, ῆς. f.ʃ

v.n. of διδάσκω: Ps 59.1. Cf. διδασκαλία.

δίδραχμον, ου. n.

two drachms: Ge 20.14; τὸ ἥμισυ τοῦ ~ου .. κατὰ τὸ δ. τὸ ἅγιον εἴκοσι ὀβολοὶ τὸ δ. Ex 30.13 (as poll-tax); κατὰ τὸ δ..., εἴκοσι ὀβολοὺς τοῦ σίκλου Nu 3.47; δ. ἀργυρίου Le 27.6, De 22.29.

διδυμεύω.ʃ*

to bear twins: *s* sheep, Ct 4.2, 6.6. Cf. δίδυμος.

δίδυμος, η, ον.

double, twofold: "they hanged the king on a forked

wooden pole (ἐπὶ ξύλου ~ου)" Jo 8.29; δύο νεβροὶ ~οι 'two fawns' Ct 4.5; subst. 'twin babies' ~α ἐν τῇ κοιλίᾳ αὐτῆς 'twins in her belly' Ge 25.24; 38.27; m. (see *Greek Anthology* 5.126) pl. 'testicles' De 25.11. Cf. διδυμεύω.

δίδωμι: pres.3s δίδωσιν, διδοῖ, inf. διδόναι, ptc. διδούς; impf.pass. ἐδιδόμην; fut. δώσω, inf. δώσειν, pass. δοθήσομαι; aor. ἔδωκα, pass. ἐδόθην, inf.act. δοῦναι, pass. δοθῆναι, impv.act. δός, pl. δότε, 3s δότω, pass. 3s δοθήτω, ptc.act. δούς, pass. δοθείς, subj.act. δῶ, opt. 3s δῴη, pass.3s δοθείη; pf. δέδωκα, pass. δέδομαι, inf. δεδόσθαι, ptc. act. δεδωκώς, pass. δεδομένος.

1. *to deliver and provide* (τί τινι): δέδωκα ὑμῖν πᾶν χόρτον 'I have given you every (kind of) grass' Ge 1.29; ὁ θεός μου δῴη ὑμῖν χάριν ἐναντίον τοῦ ἀνθρώπου 43.14; τὸ ἄχυρον ἐδίδοτο ὑμῖν 'the straw used to be provided for you [and you did not have to go and get it yourselves]' Ex 5.13; ὑετὸν χειμερινὸν δώσει αὐτοῖς 'he will give them wintry rain' Zc 10.1; διδόντων μοι τοὺς ἄρτους μου Ho 2.5; + δόμα as cogn. acc., Nu 27.7.

2. *to give and place*: ὑπὸ χεῖρας ὑμῖν δέδωκα 'I have handed (them) over to your control' Ge 9.2; ἔδωκεν τὰ ἐδέσματα .. εἰς τὰς χεῖρας Ιακωβ 'handed the foods to Jacob' 27.17, cf. the occasional ἐν χειρί τινος– ἔδωκας αὐτοὺς ἐν χειρὶ θλιβόντων αὐτούς Ne 9.27 (:: ἔσωσας αὐτοὺς ἐκ χειρὸς θλιβόντων αὐτούς), 9.30, 1M 2.7, 8.25, 11.11, Da 1.1 TH, and pl., ἐν χερσὶ βασιλέως Βαβυλῶνος Je 39.3 (MT: sg., cf. JM, § 6*d*, f.n. 4); δώσεις τὸ ποτήριον Φαραω εἰς τὴν χεῖρα (sg.) αὐτοῦ Ge 40.13 (|| pl. vs. 11); πάντα .. ἔδωκεν εἰς τὰς χεῖράς μου 39.8; διὰ χειρός τινος 'to entrust to sbd, put sbd in charge'– τὸ δεσμωτήριον διὰ χειρὸς Ιωσηφ 39.22, cf. 39.4; ἐπὶ χεῖρά(ς) τινος 'as necessary expenses to be spent by' 4K 22.5 (|| dat.), 9*L* (B: sg.), 2C 34.17; τὸ σημεῖον τῆς διαθήκης, ὃ ἐγὼ δίδωμι ἀνὰ μέσον ἐμοῦ καὶ ὑμῶν Ge 9.12 (|| τίθημι vs. 13); τὸ ῥῆμά μου ἐν τῷ στόματι αὐτοῦ De 18.18, τὰ ῥήματα, ἃ ἔδωκα εἰς τὸ στόμα σου Is 59.21, οὐκ ἐδόθη εἰς τὸ στόμα αὐτῶν Mi 3.5, cf. Ez 3.3; τὸν νόμον μου .. ἔδωκα πρὸ προσώπου αὐτῶν Je 9.13. **b**. Opp. λαμβάνω - Δός μοι τοὺς ἄνδρας, τὴν δὲ ἵππον λάβε σεαυτῷ Ge 14.21; τὰς θυγατέρας ὑμῶν δότε ἡμῖν καὶ τὰς θυγατέρας ἡμῶν λάβετε τοῖς υἱοῖς ὑμῶν 34.9. **c**. In marrying away a daughter or woman: βέλτιον δοῦναί με αὐτὴν σοὶ ἢ δοῦναί με αὐτὴν ἀνδρὶ ἑτέρῳ 'it is better for me to give her to you than for me to give her to another man' Ge 29.19; δοῦναι τὴν νεωτέραν πρὶν ἢ τὴν πρεσβυτέραν 29.26; ἔδωκεν αὐτῷ τὴν Ασεννεθ θυγατέρα Πετεφρη .. αὐτῷ γυναῖκα 41.45, cf. δέδωκα τὴν παιδίσκην μου εἰς τὸν κόλπον σου 'I've given my maidservant into your bosom' 16.5 and Ἡ γυνή, ἣν ἔδωκας μετ' ἐμοῦ 3.12; a widowed daughter-in-law, οὐκ ἔδωκεν αὐτὴν αὐτῷ γυναῖκα 38.14. **d**. *to entrust* for safe-keeping: .. φυλάξαι Ex 22.7, 10; + πρός τινα Je 39.16. **e**. + εἰς 'under the sphere of authority or influence': εἰς μάχαιραν Je 15.9, 32.17, εἰς οἰκτιρμούς Ps 105.46, 3K 8.50, Ne 1.11, εἰς σωτηρίαν 2C 12.7, σεαυτὸν εἰς ἐγγύην '.. for surety' Pr 22.26, ἑαυτὸν δοὺς εἰς τὴν ἀνάγνωσιν 'having devoted himself to the study' Si prol. 7, εἰς εὐωχίαν 'to revelry' 3M 5.17; εἰς λύπην τὴν ψυχήν σου '(to allow) your mind to be occupied with pain' Si 30.21 (|| σεαυτόν), .. καρδίαν 38.20, εἰς ^ἐνύπνια^ ('dreams') τὴν καρδίαν σου 31.6, cf. ἐν καρδίᾳ αὐτοῦ ζητῆσαι νόμον 2E 7.10, εἰς τὴν καρδίαν 1E 8.25; δὸς εἰς τὰ ὦτα Ἰησοῦ ὅτι .. 'Communicate to Joshua that ..' Ex 17.14; ἐδόθησαν εἰς πτῶμα 'were condemned to a downfall' Si 34.6; + inf., "he sets his heart on ploughing" 38.26 (|| ἐπιδίδωμι), εἰς + inf. 38.27, εἰς + v.n. 38.28. Cf. **12 c** below. **f**. *to hand over* to be treated as sbd pleases: ἔδωκεν τῇ ἐρυσίβῃ τὸν καρπὸν αὐτῶν '.. their crops to rust' Ps 77.46 || παρέδωκεν εἰς χάλαζαν τὰ κτήνη αὐτῶν '.. their cattle to hail' 77.48. **g**. *to give up* sth of great value willingly for an important cause: ἑαυτὸν τοῦ σῶσαι τὸν λαὸν αὐτοῦ 1M 6.44, δότε τὰς ψυχὰς ὑμῶν ὑπὲρ διαθήκης 2.50. ***h**. δεδομένος calqued on נָתִין 'low-ranking temple staff': 1C 9.2 +.

3. *to hand over as present*: + dat. pers. and acc., δέδωκα χίλια δίδραχμα τῷ ἀδελφῷ σου Ge 20.16 (:: ἀποδίδωμι 'to give back' vs. 14); partitive gen. instead of acc., δώσω ὑμῖν πάντων τῶν ἀγαθῶν Αἰγύπτου 'I shall give you some of all the good things of Egypt' 45.18.

4. *to produce, provide*: ἡ ἄμπελος δώσει τὸν καρπὸν αὐτῆς, καὶ ἡ γῆ δώσει τὰ γενήματα αὐτῆς, καὶ ὁ οὐρανὸς δώσει τὴν δρόσον ('dew') αὐτοῦ Zc 8.12; || ἀποδίδωμι Le 26.4; 26.20, De 11.17; *s* rock, δώσει τὰ ὕδατα αὐτῆς Nu 20.8.

5. *to cause to come into existence*: ***o*** εἰρήνην Le 26.6 (:: πόλεμος), Hg 2.9; "instilling her fear (φόβον) into the minds of all her inhabitants" Ez 26.17, sim. 32.23, 32 (last: A causing B to fear C); λύπην Si 36.25.

6. *to emit, utter*: ***o*** φωνήν Nu 14.1, Am 1.2, Hb 3.10, Je 12.8, 22.20 (last || κράζω, βοάω), Pr 2.3 (|| ἐπικαλέομαι); pl. φωνάς Ex 9.23; φῶς Is 13.10; ἀνθομολόγησιν Si 17.27; ὀσμήν 'odour' Ct 1.12. **b**. *to mention and make known*: + acc., λυχνίων τὴν ὁλκήν 'the weight of lampstands' 1C 28.15.

7. *to issue a command*: + τινι and inf., ἔδωκα αὐτῷ ἐν φόβῳ φοβεῖσθαί με 'I charged him to fear me' Ma 2.5.

8. *to hand down* (sentence): κρίμα Zp 3.5.

9. *to pay*: ***o*** a fare Jn 1.3; μισθόν 'wage' Ge 30.28, Zc 11.12; a whore's fee, Ge 38.16.

10. *to cause sth* (acc.) *to attach to*, 'impute': μὴ δῷς μῶμον ἐν δόξῃ σου 'bring no stain upon your honour' Si 30.31; ἐν τοῖς λόγοις σου δώσει σκάνδαλον'he will cast your words in a bad light' 27.23. **b**. *to lay the blame for* sth (acc.) *at the door of* sbd (ἐπί τινα or κατά τινος): μὴ δῷς ἐφ' ἡμᾶς αἷμα δίκαιον 'Don't make us murderers of an innocent man' Jn 1.14, ἐπὶ σὲ πάντα τὰ βδελύγματά σου Ez 7.5, τὰς ὁδούς σου ἐπὶ σέ 7.6, cf. τὰς ὁδοὺς αὐτῶν εἰς κεφαλὰς αὐτῶν δέδωκα 9.10, 11.21, sim. 17.19, 3K 8.32 (‖ ^δικαίῳ^ κατὰ τὴν δικαιοσύνην αὐτοῦ; ‖ 2C 6.23 ἀποδίδωμι); μὴ δότω ὁ βασιλεὺς κατὰ τοῦ δούλου αὐτοῦ λόγον 'May the king not blame his servant for anything' 2K 22.15 ..

11. *to accord* (τί τινι): δόξαν (= δοξάζω) τῷ ὀνόματί μου Ma 2.2, δόξαν καὶ δικαίωμα τῷ κυρίῳ Ba 2.17, sim. 2.18, μεγαλωσύνην ^τῷ θεῷ^ To 12.6 𝔊[I]; δικαιοσύνην κυρίῳ '(ascribe) the act of justice ..' Jd 5.11; ὁσιότητα ταῖς ὁδοῖς μου 2K 22.33*L*.

12. *to cause to fall* into a certain state: + acc. and ptc., ὑμᾶς ἐξουδενωμένους 'I have allowed you to be despised' Ma 2.9; τὸν μηρόν σου διαπεπτωκότα 'your thigh to collapse' Nu 5.21; ἐν ἀρᾷ 'in an accursed state' ib.; εἰς ὀνειδισμόν 'into ignominy' Jl 2.19, εἰς ὄνειδος Ps 56.4, εἰς διαρπαγήν Is 42.24, Ez 25.7, εἰς ἀπώλειαν 32.15, εἰς φόνον Ju 2.11, εἰς ἀφανισμόν 4.1, εἰς ὄλεθρον Je 28.55, εἰς λιμόν 18.20, εἰς σάλον Ps 65.9, cf. παραδίδωμι **1**. **b**. *to consign and abandon* to undesirable treatment or destiny: οὐδὲ δώσεις τὸν ὅσιόν σου ἰδεῖν διαφθοράν 'nor will you allow your saint to see perdition' Ps 15.10 (‖ ἐγκαταλείπω); ἔδωκεν ἑαυτὸν τῷ κινδύνῳ 'he exposed himself to danger' 1M 11.23, sim. 14.29. **c**. *to entrust to deal with* in a certain way: δότε τοὺς ἄνδρας .., καὶ θανατώσομεν αὐτούς Jd 20.13 (‖ παραδίδωμι 1K 11.12), sim. 2K 14.7 (*L* παραδίδωμι). **d**. a Hebrew calque: Ez 45.6.

13. *to cause to become*: with double obj., δέδωκά σε θεὸν Φαραω 'I have made you god for Ph.' Ex 7.1; δώσω πάντας τοὺς ὑπεναντίους σου φυγάδας 'I shall put all your opponents to flight' 23.27; τίς δῴη πάντα τὸν λαὸν κυρίου προφήτας ..; Nu 11.29; δῴη σε κύριος ἐπικοπὴν ἐναντίον τῶν ἐχθρῶν σου 'may the Lord make you fall before your enemies' De 28.25; δέδωκά σε ὀλιγοστόν Ob 2; ὑμᾶς ὀνομαστούς 'famous' Zp 3.20, δοκιμαστὴν .. σε Je 6.27; + εἰς– δώσω αὐτὸν εἰς ἔθνος μέγα Ge 17.20; Je 9.11, 36.26, Ez 25.5, 26.4, εἰς καύχημα 'something to be proud of' Zp 3.20 (‖ τίθημι 3.19); also + dat. pers., ὄνειδος ἄφρονι ἔδωκάς με 'you allowed the fool to humiliate me' Ps 38.9. **b**. mentally *to represent, imagine*: + acc., τὴν καρδίαν σου ὡς καρδίαν θεοῦ Ez 28.2, cf. 1K 1.16 "Don't make a pestilent wench out of your handmaid" (εἰς θυγατέρα λοιμήν).

14. *to expend* (effort, thought etc.): οὐκ ἔδωκαν τὰ διαβούλια αὐτῶν τοῦ ἐπιστρέψαι πρὸς τὸν θεὸν αὐτῶν 'they did not give thought to returning to their God' Ho 5.4, τὴν διάνοιάν σου διανοηθῆναι Da 10.12 LXX (TH καρδίαν); καρδίας ὑμῶν καὶ ψυχὰς ὑμῶν τοῦ ζητῆσαι τῷ κυρίῳ .. 1C 22.19; δότε ἑαυτοῖς λόγον καὶ βουλήν 'Give thought and deliberate' Jd 20.7; εἰς οὐθὲν ἔδωκα τὴν ἰσχύν μου 'I expended my energy for nothing' Is 49.4; Ec 1.17.

15. *to transfer* (τί τινι): for payment, 'to sell' ἀργυρίου τοῦ ἀξίου δότω μοι αὐτό 'let him give it to me for silver as its price' Ge 23.9; Ez 27.13; as loan, τὸ ἀργύριόν σου οὐ δώσεις αὐτῷ ἐπὶ τόκῳ '.. with interest' Le 25.37; for professional processing, Jd 17.4.

16. *to allow*: + dat. pers. and inf., οὐκ ἔδωκεν αὐτῷ ὁ θεὸς κακοποιῆσαί με 'God did not allow him to wrong me' Ge 31.7, δοῦναι τῷ Ισραηλ παρελθεῖν Nu 20.21; + a verbal noun, δότε οὖν μοι κτῆσιν τάφου 'Allow me to acquire a burial-place' Ge 23.4; Si 23.4; Jd 15.1 B (A: ἀφίημι), 1K 18.2 (*L* ἀφίημι). Cf. ἀφίημι, ἐπιτρέπω, συγχωρέω.

17**. *to position, place*: ἡ γυνή, ἣν ἔδωκας μετ' ἐμοῦ Ge 3.12; ποίμνιον κατὰ μονάς 'flocks in separate groups' 32.16; δώσεις τὸ ποτήριον Φαραω εἰς τὴν χεῖρα αὐτοῦ 'you shall place Pharaoh's cup into his hand' 40.13; δοῦναι ἀναβάτας ἐπ' αὐτούς '.. riders on them [= horses]' Is 36.8; τὸ πρόσωπόν μου ἐπὶ τὴν γῆν Da 10.15; seeking, τὸ πρόσωπόν μου ἐπὶ τὸν κύριον Da 9.3 LXX, ἐκζητῆσαι τὸν κύριον 2C 20.3. **b**. idiom., + ***o πρόσωπον 'to fix one's stance': τὸ πρόσωπον ὑμῶν εἰς Αἴγυπτον Je 49.15 (to look to Egypt as allies and ‖ τίθημι vs. 17), ἐπί τινα 'against sbd' Ez 15.7, Da 11.18 LXX; + inf. of intention, 11.17 LXX (TH: τάσσω), 4K 12.18 *L* (B: τάσσω); + χεῖρα, as a gesture of consent or submission, La 5.6, Ez 17.18.

18. *to present*: sth intangible, δίδωμι ἐνώπιον ὑμῶν .. εὐλογίαν καὶ κατάραν De 11.26, πρὸ προσώπου σου 30.1, πρὸ προσώπου σου τὴν ζωὴν καὶ τὸν θάνατον, τὸ ἀγαθὸν καὶ τὸ κακόν 30.15, ἐπὶ τοὺς ἐχθρούς σου 30.7; πάντα τὰ προστάγματα ταῦτα καὶ τὰς κρίσεις ταύτας, ὅσας ἐγὼ δίδωμι ἐνώπιον ὑμῶν σήμερον 11.32; σοι ἔλεος 13.17 (‖ ἐλεέω), sim. Je 16.13, pass. Jo 11.20.

19. *to obtain for oneself*: Δῶμεν ἀρχηγόν 'Let's appoint someone our leader' Nu 14.4; δότε ἑαυτοῖς ἄνδρας σοφοὺς .. De 1.13.

20. *to grant* that a desirable or wished-for situation becomes reality: + inf. τίς δώσει εἶναι οὕτως τὴν καρδίαν αὐτῶν ..; De 5.29; Jb 19.23; Si 50.23 (|| acc.). See Muraoka 2000.

21. *to allow to perform the function proper to*: τὰ ὦτα δώσουσιν ἀκούειν Is 32.3.

22. *to give as recompense*, 'requite': + dat. pers. but no acc., ἑκάστῳ κατὰ τὴν ὁδὸν αὐτοῦ Je 39.19, κατὰ τὰ ἔργα αὐτῶν Ps 27.4 (|| ἀποδίδωμί τινι ἀνταπόδομα), cf. δώσω ἐκδίκησίν μου ἐπὶ τὴν Ἰδουμαίαν Ez 25.14.

***23**. idiom. calqued on Heb. /nātan yād/, *to pledge*: + inf., χεῖρα 2E 10.19 (|| ἐπιβάλλω 1E 9.20).

Cf. ἀπο~, ἐπι~, μετα~, παραδίδωμι, δόμα, δόσις, δῶρον, δωρέω, δότης, δοτός, βουνίζω, τίθημι, τάσσω, λαμβάνω: Schmidt 3.194-6.

διεγγυάω.ʃ

to mortgage one's property: abs., Ne 5.3. Cf. ἐγγυάω.

διεγείρω: aor.ptc. διεγείρας, pass. διεγερθείς.ʃ

1. *to make active*, 'arouse': + acc., λογισμόν 2M 7.21; emotionally, τινα 15.10. **b**. mentally: ***o*** sleeping hum., 3M 5.15.

2. mid. *to become awake* after a dream: Es A 11 o' (*L* ἀνίστημι).

3. mid. *to extend vertically*: ***s*** gate, εἰς ὕψος πηχῶν ἑβδομήκοντα 'to the height of 70 cubits' Ju 1.4.

διεκβάλλω: fut. ~βαλῶ.

mid. *to move through an area till reaching* an end-point: ἕως τινός (loci) Jo 15.4, ἐπί τι (loci) 15.7, εἴς τι (loci) 15.9. Cf. διεκβολή.

διεκβολή, ῆς. f. *

1. *way out*: τῆς πόλεως 'out of the city' Ez 48.30; for escape, Ob 14; Je 12.12.

2. *point reached by going through*, i.e. *end-point*, ~ὰς γῆς 'the ends of the earth' (cf. Cyr. πέρατα, II.418) Zc 9.10.

3. *outlet* of river: Ez 47.11.

Cf. διεκβάλλω.

διελαύνω: aor. διήλασα.ʃ

to pass through a space, 'penetrate': ***s*** tent-peg understood, ἐν τῇ γῇ Jd 4.21; + acc. loci, τὴν γναθὸν αὐτοῦ 'his jaw' 5.26A (B: διηλόω 'nail through'). Cf. διέρχομαι.

διελέγχω: fut.mid. ~λεγχθήσομαι; aor.subj.mid. ~λεγχθῶ.ʃ

mid. *to engage in critical debate* over moral issues: ***s*** God, Mi 6.2 (with sbd μετά τινος); ***s*** God and his people, δεῦτε διελεγχθῶμεν Is 1.18. Cf. ἐλέγχω.

διεμβάλλω: fut. διεμβαλῶ; aor. διενέβαλον. *

to put in through, + acc.: ***o*** μοχλούς 'bars' Ex 40.16; ἀναφορεῖς 'staves' Nu 4.6; δι' αὐτῆς 4.8.

διεμπίμπλημι.ʃ *

to fill thoroughly: pass., ***o*** hum., ὀργαῖς 'sentiments of fury' 2M 4.40. Cf. πίμπλημι.

διεξάγω: aor.ptc. ~ξαγάγων.ʃ

1. *to give effect to*: pass. οὐ διεξάγεται .. κρίμα Hb 1.4.

2. *to conduct and handle* an affair in a certain manner: ἐν πραΰτητι τὰ ἔργα σου 'in humility ..' Si 3.17; τὰ πρὸς αὐτοὺς εἰρηνικῶς 'the relationships towards them peacefully' 2M 10.12, αὐστηρότερον 'more harshly' 14.30, μετὰ ἠπιότητος 'gently' Es B 2.

διέξειμι: impf.3pl διεξῄεσαν.ʃ

to traverse the whole area: 4M 3.13.

διεξέρχομαι: fut. διεξελεύσομαι; aor. διεξῆλθον, opt.3s διεξέλθοι.

to go out through: διὰ σώματος αὐτοῦ βέλος 'an arrow .. through his body' Jb 20.25; Ez 12.5; a spear, 2K 2.23.

διεξίπταμαι: impf.mid.3pl διεξίπταντο.ʃ*

to dash out in different directions: ***s*** soldiers trying to flee, 2M 10.30 (v.l. διεκόπτοντο).

διεξοδεύω: aor. ~εξώδευσα.ʃ

to have a way out of a confined area: ***s*** flame, Da 3.48 LXX (TH διοδεύω).

διέξοδος, ου. f.

1. *place for exit*: δ. ὑδάτων 'spring of water' Ps 106.33 (|| ποταμός), 1.3, 4K 2.21; ~οι ὑδάτων 'streams of tears flowing out' Ps 118.136; τοῦ θανάτου 'from death' 67.21; breach in a fence or hedge, 143.14.

2. *the far end* of a strip of land, 'the outer limit': Nu 34.4.

Cf. ἔξοδος, εἴσοδος: Michaelis, *TDNT* 5.108f.

διέπω.ʃ

to take charge of and conduct: + acc., τὸν κόσμον Wi 9.3, δικαίως τὰ πάντα 12.15.

διερεθίζω.ʃ

to add intensity to: ***o*** fire (by fanning it) 4M 9.19.

διερευνάω.ʃ

to scrutinize: abs. Wi 13.7; ***s*** God + ***o*** τὰς βουλάς 6.3 (|| ἐξετάζω). Cf. ἐρευνάω, ἐξετάζω.

διερμηνεύω.ʃ

pass. *to be translatable as*: νεφθαρ, ὃ διερμηνεύεται καθαρισμός 2M 1.36. Cf. ἑρμηνεύω.

διέρχομαι: fut. διελεύσομαι; aor. διῆλθον, impv. δίελθε, 2pl ~έλθατε, subj. ~έλθω, inf. ~ελθεῖν, ptc. ~ελθών, opt.3s ~έλθοι; pf. ~ελήλυθα.

1. *to go through, pass through*: ἀνὰ μέσον τῶν διχοτομημάτων τούτων 'passed through those dissected pieces' Ge 15.17; victoriously or unchallenged (cf. διαπορεύομαι), Mi 5.8; + διά τινος Nu 20.17, Jl 3.17, διὰ μέσου σου Am 5.17, διὰ πυρός Is 43.2; ἐν πυρί Nu 31.23 (|| διαπορεύομαι διὰ πυρός); ἐν θαλάσσῃ στενῇ 'through a narrow sea' Zc 10.11, ἐν ποταμῷ .. ποδί 'through the river .. on foot' Ps 65.6; + acc., πᾶσαν γῆν Αἰγύπτου Ge 41.46 || ἐν γῇ

Αἰγύπτῳ Ex 12.12, ἐν αὐτῇ .. αὐτήν Ez 29.11; τὴν ἔρημον De 2.7; πύλην 'gate' Mi 2.13, θάλασσαν Je 31.32, κυμαινόμενον ὕδωρ 'billowy water' Wi 5.10 (*s* ship, ‖ διαβαίνω), μέσην τὴν Ιερουσαλημ Ez 9.4; νεφέλας Si 32.21 (*s* prayer); ^ὁδόν^ 3K 18.6; τὸν τράχηλον αὐτοῦ 'his neck' Ju 16.9 (*s* sword), τοὺς ὄχλους 'the crowd' 2M 14.45; metaph. of experiences, χείμαρρον Ps 123.4, σίδηρον 'iron (of chains)' 104.18, ἀγαθά Pr 28.10, ἐν τῷ θυμῷ αὐτῆς Si 28.19; *s* πούς Ez 29.11; πόλεμος - πόλεμος οὐ διελεύσεται διὰ τῆς γῆς ὑμῶν Le 26.5, κήρυγμα 'message' 2C 30.5. **b**. *to spread out* throughout a space: *s* clouds, Ps 17.13, Flashar 1912. 111.

2. *to go over and arrive* by traversing an intervening space: ἐκεῖθεν εἰς Εμαθ Ραββα Am 6.2 (prec. by διαβαίνω καί).

3. *to pass and move on*, Hb 1.11; *s* hum., 2K 15.34; waves, ἐπ' ἐμέ Jn 2.4, Ps 41.8, ἐπ' ἐμὲ αἱ ὀργαί σου 87.17, θάνατος καὶ αἷμα ἐπὶ σέ Ez 5.17; to sth else, of transition, εἰς παλαίωσιν 'into decay' Na 1.15.

4. *to elapse*, of time: ἡ νύξ 'the night' Ex 14.20, ὁ μήν 'the month' Am 8.5; θέρος 'summer' Je 8.20 (‖ παρέρχομαι); ἡμέρα .. φυλακὴ ἐν νυκτί '.. night-watch' Ps 89.4; πένθος 'time of mourning' 2K 11.26.

5. *to move further on*: "You stay here; I and my child shall journey on (διελευσόμεθα)" Ge 22.5.

6. *to take a step to enter* a relationship: ἐν διαθήκῃ 2C 15.12, cf. ἐνώπιον κυρίου 1K 6.20.

Cf. ἔρχομαι, διαβαίνω, ~δύνω, ~περάω, ~πορεύομαι, διελαύνω, διϊκνέομαι.

δίεσις, εως. f.ʃ

careful investigation (LSG s.v.) or *lenience*: Wi 12.20.

διεστραμμένως. adv.ʃ

in a haphazard fashion: + πορεύομαι Si 4.17. Cf. διαστρέφω.

διετηρίς, ίδος. f.ʃ *

period of two years: ἡμερῶν 2K 13.23B (*L* δύο ἔτη).

διετής, ές.ʃ

lasting two years: *s* χρόνος 2M 10.3. Cf. διετηρίς.

διευλαβέομαι: aor.ptc. ~βηθείς.ʃ

1. *to dread*: ἀπὸ προσώπου τινός, De 28.60; + acc. pers., 2M 9.29.

2. *to reverence*: + acc. pers., Jb 6.16.

Cf. εὐλαβέομαι, φοβέομαι.

διηγέομαι: fut. ~γήσομαι; aor. διηγησάμην, impv. διήγησαι, inf. ~γήσασθαι, subj. διηγήσωμαι.

to give detailed account, narrate: abs. Ps 47.13; εἰς γενεὰν ἑτέραν 'to next generation' 47.14; + acc. rei and dat. pers., τῷ Ισαακ πάντα τὰ ῥήματα Ge 24.66; τῷ Λαβαν πάντας τοὺς λόγους τούτους 29.13; τὸ ἐνύπνιον αὐτοῦ τῷ Ιωσηφ 40.9, cf. εἰς τὰ ὦτα τῶν τέκνων ὑμῶν καὶ τοῖς τέκνοις τῶν τέκνων ὑμῶν ὅσα ἐμπέπαιχα .. καὶ τὰ σημεῖά μου '.. that which I shall have mockingly done and my signs' Ex 10.2; "expounded to the whole nation how they ought to lead their lives" Es 10.3 o'; + cogn. acc., Ez 17.2; + ὑπέρ τινος - ὑπὲρ αὐτῶν τοῖς τέκνοις ὑμῶν διηγήσασθε Jl 1.3; + ἐν - ἐν τοῖς πύργοις αὐτῆς 'about her towers' Ps 47.13; Si 19.8; + ὅτι, Ex 18.8 (‖ + acc.); + λέγω and direct discourse, Nu 13.28; *s* heaven, Ps 18.2 (‖ ἀναγγέλλω), teacher Si 22.10 (‖ διδάσκω vs. 9). Cf. διήγησις, διήγημα, δυσδιήγητος, ἐκδιηγέομαι, ἐξηγέομαι, προσαναλέγομαι.

διήγημα, ατος. n.

tale told: about sbd else's misfortune, De 28.37 (‖ αἴνιγμα, παραβολή); as cogn. obj., Ez 17.2; written account, ἱστορίας 2M 2.24. Cf. διηγέομαι, διήγησις.

διήγησις, εως. f.

1. v.n. of διηγέομαι: 2M 2.32; Jd 7.15 A (B: ἐξήγησις).

2. *narrative*: δ. αὐτοῦ 'a story about him' Hb 2.6. **b**. *conversation*: ἔν τινι 'over sth' Si 38.25.

3. *educative, instructive discourse*: θεία 'conducive to piety' Si.6.35; ἐν νόμῳ 'about the law' 9.15.

Cf. διηγέομαι, διήγημα, ἐξήγησις ..

διηθέω.ʃ

to extract by filtering: pass. and *o* metal, Jb 28.1.

διήκω.ʃ

to pervade: *s* spirit of Wisdom, Wi 7.24.

διηλόω: aor. διήλωσα.ʃ *

to drive a nail through: + acc., κεφαλήν .. κρόταφον 'head .. temple' Jd 5.26B.

διηνεκῶς. adv.

persistently: to ignore, Es B 4; to persevere, 3M 3.11; to be inclined, 3.22.

δίθυμος, ον.ʃ *

at variance in respect of disposition and temperament: subst.m., hum., Pr 26.20.

διΐημι: aor.ptc.act. διείς.ʃ

to let go of: τὰς πτέρυγας '(spreading) the wings' De 32.11.

διϊκνέομαι.ʃ

to traverse a space between two objects: *s* bar, ἀπὸ τοῦ ἑνὸς κλίτους εἰς τὸ ἕτερον κλίτος 'from one side to the other' Ex 26.28. Cf. διέρχομαι.

διΐπταμαι.ʃ

to traverse by flying: *s* bird, + acc., ἀέρα 'the air' Wi 5.11. Cf. πέτομαι.

διΐστημι: pres.indic.3pl ~ιστῶσι; fut. ~στήσω; 1aor. διέστησα, subj. ~στήσω, mid. διεστησάμην; 2aor.act. διέστην; pf.ptc. διεστώς/~εστηκώς.

I. intr. (pres., 2aor., pf.) **1**. *to get divided*: *s* sea-water, Ex 15.8 (|| σχίζομαι 14.21), 4K 2.14B (|| pass. διαρρήγνυμι, *L* διαιρέομαι).

2. *to form a barrier*: τὰ ἁμαρτήματα ὑμῶν διιστῶσιν ἀνὰ μέσον ὑμῶν καὶ τοῦ θεοῦ 'Your sins come between you and God' Is 59.2.

3. *to differ* from: + gen., Es E 10. Cf. διαφέρω **2**.

4. *to part with*: + gen., religion, 3M 2.32. Cf. διαστέλλω **2e**.

II. tr. (fut., 1aor.) *to separate into multiple parts*: + acc., Ez 5.1; ἀπὸ ἔθνους εἰς ἔθνος 'among various nations' Si 28.14. **b**. *to cause discord among*: + acc. pers., φίλους καὶ οἰκείους 'friends and family members' Pr 17.9.

2. *to settle and agree upon*: + acc., τὰ πρὸς ἐμέ 'the affairs pertaining to me' To 7.11 𝔊II. **b**. mid., + inf. fut., 2M 8.10.

Cf. διαρρήγνυμι.

δικάζω: pres.mid.subj. δικάζωμαι; fut. δικάσω; aor. ἐδίκασα, impv. δίκασον, opt.3s δικάσαι, mid.subj. δικάσωμαι, impv.3s δικασάσθω.

I. act.. *to make a decision, upholding* the just cause of sbd: *s* God, ἀνὰ μέσον ἐμοῦ καὶ σοῦ 1K 24.13 (*L* κρίνω); + acc., τὰς δίκας τῆς ψυχῆς μου 'my life and death cases' La 3.58; τὴν δίκην μου ἐξ ἔθνους οὐχ ὁσίου Ps 42.1 (|| κρίνω τινα); μοι (dat. com.) ἐκ χειρός σου 1K 24.16.

2. *to sit in judgement and consider a case of*: + acc. pers., ἐνώπιον κυρίου 1K 12.7.

3. *to mete out justice to*: + acc. pers., τοὺς ἀδικοῦντάς με Ps 34.1.

II. mid. *to plead one's cause*: || ἐλέγχω Ho 4.4; πάντες εἰς αἵματα δικάζονται 'everybody demands capital punishment' Mi 7.2; + διακρίνομαι Je 15.10. **b**. *to contend in a court*: μετὰ κριτοῦ 'with a judge' Si 8.14; περί (B: ὑπέρ) τινος 'on behalf of sbd' Jd 6.31*a* A; + dat. pers., ib. *b* B; ἐν αὐτῷ 'against him' 6.32B.

Cf. δίκαιος, δικαστήριον, δικαστής.

δικαιοκρίτης, ου. m.ʃ*

righteous judge: *s* God, Es 7.24 *L*, 2M 12.41. Cf. κριτής.

δικαιολόγια, ας. f.ʃ

speech in law court: 2M 4.44.

δίκαιος, α, ον.

1. *righteous, just*: **a**. *s* person, ὁ δ. ἐκ πίστεως μου ζήσεται Hb 2.4; opp. ἄδικος Pr 17.15, ἁμαρτωλός Ps 124.3, ἄνομος Ma 3.18, ἀσεβής Ge 18.23, Ex 9.27, De 25.1, Ho 14.10, ἀ. καταδυναστεύει τὸν ~ον Hb 1.4, καταπίνειν ἀσεβῆ τὸν ~ον 1.13, παράνομος Jb 17.8; || τέλειος Ge 6.9, || θεοσεβής Ex 18.21, || ἀθῷος 23.7; ἐλεήμων καὶ οἰκτίρμων καὶ δ. Ps 111.4, sim. 114.5; = υἱὸς θεοῦ Wi 2.18; || πένης Am 2.6, 5.12 (καταπατοῦντες ~ον); of a messianic figure, δ. καὶ σῴζων Zc 9.9, ἀνατολὴ ~α Je 23.5; ~ον ὄρος τὸ ἅγιον αὐτοῦ 38.23; subst., πεντήκοντα ~οι Ge 18.24; κύριος ἀγαπᾷ ~ους Ps 145.8; *s* God, Ex 9.27, De 32.4, Ps 144.17 (latter two || ὅσιος); οὐκ ἔστιν δ. ὡς ὁ θεὸς ἡμῶν 1K 2.2, ὁ κύριος δ. ἐν μέσῳ αὐτῆς καὶ οὐ μὴ ποιήσῃ ἄδικον Zp 3.5; κριτὴς δ. Ps 8.12; ἐλεήμων ὁ κύριος καὶ δ. 114.5; δ. καὶ σωτήρ Is 45.21; μάρτυς δ. καὶ πιστός Je 49.5, cf. χείλη 'lips' Pr 16.13; *s* ὁδὸς ~α 'way of justice' Ps 2.12. **b**. w. ref. to legal justice and fairness: αἷμα ~ον 'blood of an innocent person' Jn 1.14, Jl 3.19; κρίσις ~α De 16.18, κρίμα ~ον 'just, fair judgement' Zc 7.9; ῥήματα ~α 'pronouncements of justice' Ex 23.8; subst. n., τὸ ~ον τοῦ ~ου 'the justice of the just' Is 5.23; τὸ ~ον ἐκ σου λήμψομαι 'I shall exact fair vengeance from you' 47.3; ἡ βοήθειά μου παρὰ τοῦ θεοῦ Ps 7.11, παρὰ κυρίου Pr 29.26; τὰ ~α 'the rightful claims or entitlements' 2M 13.23, Wi 19.16. **c**. πάντα τὰ ἔργα σου [= κυρίου] ~α To 3.2 𝔊II.

2. *conforming with set and agreed standards*: *s* στάθμιον ἀληθινὸν καὶ ~ον '.. weight of balance' De 25.15, sim. Pr 11.1 (:: δόλιος 'false'), ζυγὸς ~ος καὶ μέτρον ~ον Ez 45.10. Cf. LSG s.v. **B I 1**.

Cf. δικαιοσύνη, τέλειος, ὅσιος, ἀσεβής, ἄδικος, ἄνομος: Schrenk, *TDNT* 2.182-6; Kilpatrick 1942.35; Spicq 1.320-6; Muraoka 1984.443-7.

δικαιοσύνη, ης. f. Mostly in the sg.

1. *conformity to the dictates of the religion of Israel* as should characterise man's conduct: ἐλογίσθη αὐτῷ εἰς ~ην Ge 15.6, Ps 105.31; ποιεῖν ~ην καὶ κρίσιν Ge 18.19; σπείρατε εἰς ~ην Ho 10.12*a* (to be rewarded with ζωή); ~ην ζητήσατε Zp 2.3 (|| κρίμα); γενήματα ~ης 'products of ...' Ho 10.12*b*; καρπὸν ~ης Am 6.12; in contradistinction to observances of cult, Am 5.24, but cf. τῷ κυρίῳ προσάγοντες θυσίαν ἐν ~ῃ Ma 3.3; θυσία ~ης 'proper sacrifice' De 33.19; opp. ἀσέβεια 9.4; ἀνομίαν καὶ οὐ ~ην Is 5.7; || ὁσιότης De 9.5; + κρίσις Is 33.5, || κρίμα Je 22.13. **b**. practical act manifesting such a conformity: pl., Ez 33.13, Si 44.10 (practised by ἄνδρες ἐλέους), ποιοῦντες ἐλεημοσύνας καὶ ~ας To 12.9 𝔊I, sim. 2.14; pl., 1K 26.23.

2. *uprightness and righteousness* as an attribute of God's: ὁ θεὸς τῆς ~ης Ma 2.17 (who hates πονηρόν); δ. τοῦ κυρίου Mi 6.5; Τῷ κυρίῳ θεῷ ἡμῶν ἡ δ. Ba 1.15; + ἀλήθεια Ge 24.27, 32.10, Zc 8.8.

3. *divine justice*: as manifested in God's salvific acts, ~ην διατηρῶν καὶ ποιῶν ἔλεος Ex 34.7, cf. 15.13; || ἔλεος and οἰκτιρμοί as well as κρίμα Ho 2.19, Je 9.23; ἔδωκεν ὑμῖν τὰ βρώματα εἰς ~ην 'I provided you with food to demonstrate my δ. (as your saviour)' Jl 2.23; τὴν ~ην μου καὶ τὴν σωτηρίαν τὴν παρ' ἐμοῦ Is 46.13; ἐν τῇ ~ῃ σου ῥῦσαί με Ps

70.2; ἥλιος ~ης καὶ ἴασις .. Ma 4.2. **b**. God as just judge: ὁ κρίνων ~ην Ps 9.5, κρινεῖ .. ἐν ~ῃ 95.13; ὁ κύριος τῆς ~ης To 13.6.

4. *proper conduct*: Ταύτην τὴν ~ην ποιήσεις ἐπ' ἐμέ Ge 20.13.

5. *fairness and conformity to moral and ethical codes*: ἐν ~ῃ κρινεῖς Le 19.15, ‖ εὐθύτης Ps 9.9; νομὴ ~ης 'rightful pasture' Je 27.7; in a list of Stoic moral ideals, + ἀνδρεία, σωφροσύνη 4M 1.6, also + φρόνησις 1.18. **b**. concrete manifestation of such as laws and regulations: Pr 8.15.

6. *rightful entitlement*: + μερίς Ne 2.20.

Cf. δίκη, δίκαιος, δικαιόω, δικαίωμα, κρίμα: Schmidt 1.348-60; Dodd 1935.42-59; Schrenk, *TDNT* 2.195f.; Hill 104-9; Caird 1968.468; Fiedler; Olley 1979, on which see also Gooding 1981 and Muraoka 1984; Olley 1980; Renehan 1.67f, 2.56; Spicq 1.326f.; Rösel 230-7.

δικαιόω: fut. δικαιώσω, pass. δικαιωθήσομαι; aor. ἐδικαίωσα, subj. δικαιώσω, impv. δικαίωσον, inf. ~ῶσαι, ptc. ~ώσας, pass. ἐδικαιώθην, inf. δικαιωθῆναι, impv. δικαιώθητι, subj. δικαιωθῶ, opt.act. 3pl δικαιώσαισαν; pf.pass. δεδικαίωμαι, ptc. δεδικαιωμένος.

*__1__. *to declare just and righteous*, 'to vindicate': + acc. pers., τὸν ἀσεβῆ Ex 23.7, Is 5.23, Si 42.2, τὸν δίκαιον De 25.1 (:: καταγινώσκω), τὴν κληρονομίαν ἑαυτοῦ [= Israel] Es F 9 LXX; with comparative ἀπό 'more than' Je 3.11; pass. δεδικαίωται Θαμαρ ἢ ἐγώ 'T. has turned out to be right rather than I' Ge 38.26, δικαιωθήσεται .. ἄνομος Mi 6.11; ἀπὸ κυρίου Is 45.25; ἀπὸ ἁμαρτίας 'innocent of any crime' Si 26.29; ***o*** God, PSol 2.15, ἐν τοῖς λόγοις σου 'as you pronounce a verdict' Ps 50.6. **b**. *to pronounce as having acted correctly*: by carrying out a vow, Si 18.22; 13.22. **c**. *to consider just and correct*: + acc., τὸ κρίμα τοῦ θεοῦ PSol 4.8, cf. τὸν θεὸν ἐν τοῖς κρίμασιν αὐτοῦ 8.7; impers. pass., .. δικαιοῦταί σοι κληρονομῆσαι 'you can be said to be in your right to inherit ..' To 6.12 𝔊^{II} (𝔊^{I} ἐπιβάλλει), 6.13 𝔊^{II}; 12.4. **d**. *to keep in irreproachable state*: τὴν καρδίαν μου Ps 72.13.

2. *to take up the cause of* sbd *as judge*: + acc. pers., ταπεινὸν καὶ πένητα 'the underprivileged and poor' Ps 81.3 (‖ κρίνω); 2K 15.4, χήραν 'widow' Is 1.17 (‖ κρίνω).

3. *to consider in court and pronounce judgement*: pass., impers., "a verdict is out" Ez 21.13. **b**. + acc., τὰ δικαιώματά μου 'my ordinances' Ez 44.24 (967 ἐν τοῖς προστάμασίν μου), τὴν δίκην μου 'my case' Mi 7.9.

Cf. δίκη, δικαιοσύνη, καταγινώσκω, κατακρίνω: Schrenk, *TDNT* 2.212-4; Watson 1960; Hill 106-8; Spicq 1.337-43.

δικαίωμα, ατος. n.

1. *ordinance* embodying principles of the Israelite religion and handed down by God: ~ατα ἔλαβε ἐν τῷ Ισραηλ καὶ ἔθετο αὐτὰ τῇ Βααλ 'he received ordinances in Israel and established them for Baal' Ho 13.1; ἐφύλαξεν .. τὰ προστάγματά μου καὶ τὰς ἐντολάς μου καὶ τὰ ~ατά μου καὶ τὰ νόμινά μου Ge 26.5; φυλάξῃ τὰ φυλάγματα αὐτοῦ καὶ τὰ ~ατα .. καὶ τὰς ἐντολὰς .. καὶ τὰς κρίσεις .. De 11.1; ~ατα καὶ κρίσεις Ex 15.25, De 4.5; αἱ ἐντολαὶ καὶ τὰ ~ατα καὶ τὰ κρίματα, ἃ ἐνετείλατο κύριος ἐν χειρὶ Μωυσῆ Nu 36.13; προστάγματα καὶ ~ατα Ma 4.6; τὰ μαρτύρια καὶ τὰ δ. καὶ τὰ κρίματα De 4.45, 6.20, sim. 6.17; + νόμος 1M 2.21; ~ατα, ἃ παραθήσεις ἐνώπιον αὐτῶν Ex 21.1; κατὰ τὸ δ. τῶν θυγατέρων 'in accordance with the ordinance applicable to daughters' 21.9; δ. κρίσεως '.. reached by juridical process' Nu 27.11 (‖ δ. κρίματος 35.29); τοῦ νόμου 31.21. **b**. *rule of human origin prevailing in society and to be adhered to*: 1K 27.11, cf. δίκη 'custom' in Cl. Gk. and Vulg. *decretum*; Ru 4.7.

2. *state of not being guilty*, 'innocence': πρὸς σὲ ἀπεκάλυψα τὸ δ. μου Je 11.20, τῆς φωνῆς τοῦ ~ατός μου 18.19. **b**. *vocal expression over sbd's justice*: δώσουσιν δόξαν καὶ δ. τῷ κυρίῳ Ba 2.17.

*__3__. *that which one can rightfully claim as one's share and entitlement*: 1K 2.13, 8.9, 2K 19.29 (*L* δικαιοσύνη).

4. *act which is just and fair*: ***o*** of ποιέω 3K 3.28, 8.45, 59.

Cf. δίκαιος, ἐντολή, κρίμα, κρίσις, νόμιμον, πρόσταγμα: Schrenk, *TDNT* 2.219-21; Spicq 1.343f.; Tov 1990.83-96; Cadell 1995; Harl 2001.893.

δικαίως. adv.

1. *justly, in accordance with the principle of justice*: κρίνετε δ. De 1.16; δ. τὸ δίκαιον διώξῃ 'you shall justly pursue justice' 16.20.

2. *for good reason, rightly*: Δ. ἐκλήθη τὸ ὄνομα αὐτοῦ Ιακωβ Ge 27.36; δ. ἔπασχον Wi 19.13.

Cf. δίκαιος.

δικαίωσις, εως. f.ʃ

1. *administering of justice*: δ. μία ἔσται τῷ προσηλύτῳ καὶ τῷ ἐγχωρίῳ 'there shall be one justice for the resident alien and the native' Le 24.22.

2. v.n. of δικαιόω **1c**: PSol 3.3.

Cf. δίκαιος.

δικαστήριον, ου. n.ʃ

court-house, tribunal: Jd 6.32 A.

δικαστής, οῦ. m.

judge: ἄρχοντα καὶ ~ήν Ex 2.14, κριτὰς καὶ ~άς, ὅπως δικάζωσιν 1E 8.23; part of the establishment and elite of a nation, Is 3.2, Ba 2.1, ‖ βασιλεύς Wi 6.1, 9.7; ‖ πρεσβύτερος, γραμματεύς Jo 9.2d; δίφρος ~οῦ 'a judge's seat' Si 38.33; *s* God, + κριτής 1K 24.16. Cf. κριτής, δικάζω.

δίκη, ης. f.

1. *sentence* pronounced at the conclusion of a law-suit, 'verdict': ~η ἐκδικηθήτω 'let the verdict be executed on him' Ex 21.20; ποῦ ἡ δ. σου, θάνατε; 'where is your verdict, O death?' Ho 13.14; ἁμαρτανόντων Wi 14.31.

2. *law-suit*: ἐκάλεσε τὴν ~ην 'called for the lawsuit to be opened' Am 7.4; Mi 7.9; ἐποίησας τὴν κρίσιν μου καὶ τὴν ~ην μου Ps 9.5; δίκασον τὴν ~ην μου 42.1.

3. *punishment*: divine, 2M 8.11, μισοπόνηρον 'evil-hating' Es E 4, μάχαιραν ἐκδικοῦσαν ~ην διαθήκης Le 26.25, ἀνταποδώσω ~ην (|| κρίμα) De 32.41; civil, ~η ἐκδικηθήτω Ex 21.20.

4. δίκην + gen., *after the manner of* sth: νηπίων ~ην 'like infants' Wi 12.24.

Cf. δικαιόω, κρίσις: Schmidt 1.348-60; Schrenk, *TDNT* 2.178-81; Spicq 1.318-20; *BA* ad Jl 3.14.

δίκτυον, ου. n.

1. *hunting-net*: δ. ἐκτεταμένον 'a spread net' Ho 5.1; ἐπιβαλῶ ἐπ' αὐτοὺς τὸ δ. μου 'I shall cast my net upon them' 7.12; || παγίς 'snare, trap' Jb 18.8. **b**. net covering the capital of a column, 3K 7.5.

2. *lattice-work*: Je 52.22, Ct 2.9.

Cf. ἀμφίβληστρον, παγίς, σαγήνη.

δικτυόω: pf.ptc.pass. δεδικτυωμένος.ʃ

to form with network: pass., ***o*** row of bronze pomegranates, 3K 7.6.

δικτυωτός, ή, όν.ʃ

latticed: *s* part of hearth, Ex 27.4; appendage of an altar, 38.24; window, Ez 41.16; θυρίς 'window' understood, Jd 5.28 A, cf. subst. n., 4K 1.2.

διμερής, ές.ʃ

bipartite: *s* βασιλεία Da 2.41 LXX (TH διῃρημένος).

δίμετρον, ου. n.

**double measure*: 4K 7.2 (*L* δύο μέτρα). Cf. μέτρον.

δίνη, ης. f.ʃ

1. *whirlpool*: ποταμῶν Jb 28.10.

2. *whirlwind*: Jb 37.9.

διό. conj.

therefore: Ep Je 68 (|| οὖν vss. 14, 22), Jb 9.22. Del. Zp 3.8, Is 51.19 v.l.

διοδεύω: aor. διώδευσα, impv. διόδευσον, pass. διωδεύθην.

to travel through: abs. Zp 3.6; Zc 7.14 (|| ἀναστρέφω); + acc., τὴν γῆν εἰς τὸ μῆκος αὐτῆς Ge 12.6, 13.17 (+ καὶ εἰς τὸ πλάτος), paths (τρίβοι) Is 59.8, ὁδόν Ps 88.42; κύματα 'billows' Wi 14.1; wilderness and pass. (= act.) Je 9.12; *s* troops, ἐν πάσῃ τῇ χώρᾳ 1M 12.32; bird, Wi 5.11.

Cf. διαπορεύομαι, δίοδος, περιοδεύω: *ND* 4.146.

δίοδος, ου. f.

1. *way through, passage*: of a city, De 13.16, Je 7.34.

2. v.n. of διοδεύω: Wi 5.12 (|| ἐπίβασις vs. 11). Cf. ὁδός, τρίβος.

διοικέω: fut. διοικήσω.ʃ

to administer: ***o*** an area and its inhabitants, Da 3.1 LXX; + acc., λαούς Wi 8.14, ἡμᾶς 12.18, τὰ πάντα 8.1, 15.1. Cf. διοίκησις and δικοικητής.

διοίκησις, εως. f.ʃ

financial administration: To 1.21.

διοικητής, οῦ. m.ʃ

finance minister: To 1.22, Da 3.2 LXX.

διοικοδομέω: aor.subj. ~μήσω.ʃ

to build for partition: + acc., τεῖχος 'wall' Ne 2.17. Cf. οἰκοδομέω.

διόλλυμι: aor.inf. διολέσαι.ʃ

to destroy: abs., Wi 11.19; pass. *to perish*, 17.10. Cf. ἀπόλλυμι.

διόλου. adv.ʃ

regularly, all the time: Bel TH 13.

διόπερ. adv.

Introduces a logical concluson, 'therefore,' and clause-initial: Ju 8.17, 2M 5.20+.

διοράω.ʃ

to see through, see clearly: Jb 6.19. Cf. ὁράω.

διοργίζομαι: aor.ptc. ~οργισθείς.ʃ

to become very angry: + dat. pers., 3M 3.1; abs., 4.13. Cf. θυμόω, ὀργίζομαι.

διορθόω: fut.pass. ~θωθήσομαι; aor.subj. ~θώσω, impv. ~θωσον, pass. διωρθώθην, subj. ~θωθῶ.ʃ

to make straight: ***o*** way (acc.), τὰς ὁδοὺς ὑμῶν καὶ τὰ ἐπιτηδεύματα ὑμῶν '.. your conduct' Je 7.3, 5; pass., τρίβοι τῶν ἐπὶ γῆς Wi 9.18, διαβήματα 'steps' Pr 15.29b. **b**. *to erect straight*: abs. Is 62.7; pass., θρόνος 16.5.

Cf. διορθωτής.

διορθωτής, οῦ.ʃ *

ag.n. of διορθόω: *s* God, σοφῶν 'of sages' Wi 7.15 (|| ὁδηγός 'guide'). Cf. ὁδηγός.

διορίζω: fut. διοριῶ; aor. διώρισα.

1. *to serve as a partition*: *s* veil of the ark of the covenant, ἀνὰ μέσον τοῦ ἁγίου καὶ ἀνὰ μέσον τοῦ ἁγίου τῶν ἁγίων Ex 26.33; τὸ διορίζον 'partition' Ez 41.12; *s* a river flowing in the centre of a city, 2C 32.4.

2. *to mark out as distinct*: + acc., ὑμᾶς ἀπὸ πάντων τῶν ἐθνῶν Le 20.24; Jb 35.11.

3. *to make a determination*: + inf., Jo 5.6.

Cf. ἀφορίζω.

διόρυγμα, ατος. n.ʃ

a hole dug in the ground: Je 2.34; by a burglar, Ex 22.2; *burrow* of animals, Zp 2.14. Cf. διορύσσω, διῶρυξ.

διορύσσω: fut. διορύξω; aor. διώρυξα, impv. διόρυξον.

to dig through: *s* burglar and + acc., διώρυξεν ἐν σκότει οἰκίας 'he dug houses through in darkness' Jb 24.16¶; τὸν τοῖχον 'the wall' Ez 12.7; εἰς τὸν τοῖχον 12.5.

Cf. διόρυγμα, διῶρυξ.

διότι. conj.

1. causal, 'because, since, for': διότι ἔλεος θέλω 'for I desire mercy' Ho 6.6(*a*); the causal clause preceding the main clause, διότι σὺ ἐσκύλευσας ἔθνη πολλὰ, σκυλεύσουσί σε πάντες .. Hb 2.8(*a*); De 31.17(*h*), 1K 30.22*L*(*j*); ‖ ὅτι – δ. πάρεστι ἡμέρα κυρίου, ὅτι ἐγγύς Jl 2.1(*a*), sim. 2.11(*a*), 3.13(*a*), Zp 1.7(*a*). **b**. with no main clause: Ge 29.32(*a*).

2. 'that' introducing a noun clause: w. ὄμνυμι Am 4.2(*a*), 6.8(-), Je 28.14(*i*); w. ἐπιγινώσκω Jl 3.17(*a*), Zc 4.9(*a*), 6.15(*a*), Ma 2.4(*a*); w. γινώσκω Zc 2.9(*a*); τί πλέον ὅτι ἐφυλάξαμεν τὰ φυλάγματα αὐτοῦ καὶ διότι ἐπορεύθημεν ἱκέται .. 'what have we gained in that we have kept his ordinances and we have walked as suppliants ...?' Ma 3.14(*a*); w. ἐπιγινώσκω Ez 6.10(*a*) (‖ ὅτι vs. 7). **b**. introduces direct speech: Da 2.5 LXX (-).

3. Borderline cases between **1**. and **2**.: ἐνωτίζεσθε διότι πρὸς ὑμᾶς ἐστι τὸ κρίμα Ho 5.1(*a*), cf. ib. 4.1(*a*), Zc 3.8(*a*), 8.6(*a*).

4. inferential, *therefore*: Is 3.8(-).

5. redundant under Heb. infl. (כִּי): 2K 2.27B (*L* ὅτι) (*a*).

The variant ὅτι abounds: e.g., Ho 2.4, 6, 9, Am 4.2, 6.8, Mi 1.3 (*DJD* 8 +), 4.4(ib.).

Cf. ἄρα, τοίνυν.

a) כִּי; *b*) אָז; *c*) אֲשֶׁר *d*) עַל אֲשֶׁר; *e*) כַּאֲשֶׁר; *f*) רַק; *g*) תַּחַת אֲשֶׁר; *h*) הֲלֹא עַל כִּי; *i*) כִּי אִם; *j*) יַעַן אֲשֶׁר. x∫

δίπηχυς, υ.∫

having two cubits in measure: depth, Nu 11.31.

διπλασιάζω: aor.impv. ~σίασον.∫

to duplicate: + acc., Ez 21.14; φωνὴ διπλασιαζόντων πολλῶν 'an echo of a large crowd' 43.2. Cf. διπλασιασμός.

διπλασιασμός, οῦ. m.∫

act of doubling: Jb 42.1. Cf. διπλασιάζω.

διπλάσιος, α, ον.

twice as many or *much*: Si 12.5. Cf. διπλοῦς.

διπλοΐς, ΐδος. f.

**double cloak*: Ps 108.29; metaph., δικαιοσύνης Ba 5.2.

διπλοῦς, ῆ, οῦν.

twofold: *s* σπήλαιον 'cavern' Ge 23.9, λύπη 'sorrow' Wi 11.12; subst., τὰ δέοντα ~ᾶ 'the requisite double portion' Ex 16.22; ~ᾶ αὐτὰ ἀποτείσει 'he shall compensate for them double' 22.4; ~ᾶ ἀνταποδώσω σοι 'I shall recompense you double' Zc 9.12, sim. Je 16.18. Cf. δισσός, διπλασιάζω, τριπλοῦς.

δίς. adv.

twice: περὶ τοῦ δευτερῶσαι τὸ ἐνύπνιον Φαραω δίς 'as regards Pharaoh's dream having occurred twice' Ge 41.32; ἅπαξ καὶ δίς 'once and twice' De 9.13; Na 1.9; δ. ἢ τρίς 'twice or thrice' Si 13.7. **b**. *twice as many* or *much*: δ. ἑπτά 'fourteen' Le 12.5.

Cf. δύο and ἅπαξ.

δίσκος, ου. m.∫

disc thrown by athletes: 2M 4.14.

δισμύριοι, αι, α. num.

twenty thousand: 2M 5.24 +.

δισσός, ή, όν.∫

1. *twofold, twice as much as* a given quantity: τὸ ἀργύριον ~ὸν λάβετε 'take the silver doubled' Ge 43.12 (‖ διπλοῦς vs. 15); πᾶσιν ἔδωκεν ~ὰς στολάς 'gave everyone two sets of robes' 45.22; *s* σύντριμμα 'blow' Je 17.18; μέτρα ~ά 'double standards' Pr 20.10, ~ὸν στάθμιον '.. weight' 20.23 (‖ δόλιος 'fraudulent'). **b**. w. pl. noun, = δύο: Pr 31.22.

2. *forming a pair*: Si 42.24.

3. metaph. *divided*: ἐν καρδίᾳ ~ῇ 'half-heartedly' Si 1.28.

Cf. δισσῶς, διπλοῦς, δύο and δίς.

δισσῶς. adv.∫

doubly, twice as much: ἥμαρτεν δ. 'sinned doubly' Si 23.11; 4K 2.9*L* (B: διπλᾶ). Cf. δισσός.

δίστομος, ον.∫

double-edged: *s* μάχαιρα Jd 3.16, fig. of added effectiveness, Pr 5.4, ῥομφαία Ps 149.6, Si 21.3.

δισχίλιοι, αι, α: num.

two thousand: Nu 7.85. **b**. sg. with a coll. noun: ~αν ἵππον '2,000 horses' Is 36.8, so Herod. 7.158.

Cf. χίλιοι.

διτάλαντον.∫

two talents: of silver, 4K 5.23.

διυλίζω: pf.ptc.pass. διυλισμένος.∫ *(?)

to strain, filter thoroughly: pass., ***o*** good-quality wine (οἶνος), Am 6.6.

διυφαίνω: pf.ptc.pass. διυφασμένος.∫ *

to interweave: pass. and + acc., περιστόμιον 'collar' Ex 36.31. Cf. ὑφαίνω.

διφθέρα, ας. f.∫

prepared hide: ~ας δέρματα κριῶν '.. rams' skins' Ex 39.21. Cf. δορά.

δίφραξ, ακος. f.∫ A poetic equivalent of δίφρος.

chariot: 2M 14.21.

διφρεύω.∫

**to sit apart*: *s* priests, Ep Je 30. Cf. κάθημαι: Naumann 37.

δίφρος, ου. m.
seat of a person in authority: καθίσῃ ἐπὶ τοῦ ~ου τῆς ἀρχῆς αὐτοῦ De 17.18; δικαστοῦ 'of a judge' Si 38.33; for a priest, 1K 1.9; for a king, 28.23; for an important lodger, 4K 4.10; set in a city square, Jb 29.7; pl., toilet-seat, chamber-pot, Jd 3.24A. Cf. θρόνος: Renehan 1.69f.

δίχα. adv.ʃ
asunder, split: *s* kingdom, Si 47.21.

διχηλέω.
to divide the hoof: κτῆνος διχηλοῦν ὁπλήν 'an animal with a cloven hoof' Le 11.3; De 14.6.

διχομηνία, ας. f.ʃ
full moon: Si 39.12.

διχοστασία, ας. f.ʃ
dissension: 1M 3.29.

διχοτομέω: fut. διχοτομήσω.ʃ
to cut into two pieces, resulting by repetition in multiple pieces: *o* sacrificial animal, κατὰ μέλη 'each organ apart' Ex 29.17. Cf. διχοτόμημα, διαιρέω, μελίζω, μερίζω.

διχοτόμημα, ατος.ʃ
part of a thing cut in two or more: pieces of sacrificial animal, τὰ σώματα, τὰ ~ατα αὐτῶν Ge 15.11; 15.17; head not included, τὰ ~ατα καὶ τὴν κεφαλήν Le 1.8, cf. Ex 29.17; cut pieces of meat to be cooked, πᾶν δ. καλόν, σκέλος καὶ ὦμον '.. leg and shoulder' Ez 24.4*b*. Cf. διχοτομέω, διαιρέω.

δίψα, ης. f.
lack of drinking water, 'thirst': δ., οὗ οὐκ ἦν ὕδωρ De 8.15, διὰ λιμὸν καὶ ~αν ὕδατος 'due to the lack of food ..' Is 5.13, δ. ὕδατος Am 8.11 (‖ λιμός ἄρτου); ἡ γλῶσσα αὐτῶν ἀπὸ τῆς ~ης ἐξηράνθη Is 41.17; ἴαμα ~ης 'quenching ..' Wi 11.4, εἰς ~αν αὐτῶν 'so as to quench their thirst' Ne 9.15, sim. Ps 68.22, 103.11, 106.33. **b**. deadly: ἀνελεῖ αὐτοὺς ἡ δ. 'the water shortage could be their end' Ju 7.13, ἐξέλιπον ἀπὸ τῆς ~ης 7.22; Is 5.13.
Cf. δίψος, διψάω, διψώδης, λιμός.

διψάω: fut. διψήσω; aor. ἐδίψησα, subj. διψήσω, ptc. διψήσας; pf. δεδίψηκα.
to suffer from lack of water: drinking water and + dat., ὕδατι Ex 17.3; + acc. rei, ὅ τι Ru 2.9 (ref. to water); ‖ πεινάω 'to hunger' Si 24.21, Is 65.13, Je 31.25; for cultivation and *s* γῆ 32.2, 53.2, ἔρημος 35.1; metaph., Si 24.21, ἐδίψησέν σοι ἡ ψυχή μου Ps 62.2, cf. πρὸς τὸν θεόν 41.3, sim. 142.6 Aq. Cf. δίψα, δίψος: Shipp 219; Bertram, *TDNT* 2.227-9.

δίψος, ους. n.
lack of drinking water, 'thirst': ἀποκτεῖναι .. τῷ δίψει Ex 17.3, ἀποκτενῶ αὐτὴν ἐν ~ει 'I shall kill her with thirst' Ho 2.3; Am 8.13; ἐν λιμῷ καὶ ἐν ~ει καὶ ἐν γυμνότητι καὶ ἐν ἐκλείψει πάντων 'in hunger, thirst, nakedness and lack of everything' De 28.48; ἐν ~ει καύματος ἐν ἀνύδρῳ 'in thirst from heat in waterless land' 32.10. Cf. δίψα, διψάω, λιμός.

διψώδης, ες.ʃ
thirsty: subst.m.hum., Pr 9.12c. Cf. δίψα.

διωγμός, οῦ. m.ʃ
act of pursuing: Pr 11.19; chasing w. hostile intent - La 3.19, 2M 12.23. Cf. διώκω.

διωθέω.ʃ
mid. *to force one's way through*: *s* sheep, with sides and shoulders, Ez 34.21 (‖ κερατίζω). Cf. ὠθέω.

διώκω: fut. διώξω, διώξομαι; aor. ἐδίωξα, inf. διῶξαι, ptc. διώξας, impv. δίωξον, pass. ἐδιώχθην, ptc. διωχθείς.
I tr. **1**. *to chase, pursue eagerly*: w. hostile, harmful intent and abs., οὐθενὸς διώκοντος Le 26.36 (‖ κατατρέχω vs. 37); + acc. pers., Ge 14.15; ἐχθρούς 2K 22.38 (*L* κατατρέχω; ‖ ἀφανίζω 'exterminate'); ὄρνεα πετόμενα 'flying birds' Pr 9.12a; ἐν ῥομφαίᾳ τὸν ἀδελφὸν αὐτοῦ Am 1.11; non-animate *s*, τοὺς ἐχθροὺς αὐτοῦ διώξεται σκότος Na 1.8, αἷμά σε διώξεται Ez 35.6, δίκη 'justice' Wi 11.20, πόλεμος PSol 15.7, πλάνησις 'error' Is 30.28; *o* = sbd on the run, ὡς φυγάδας 'as fugitives' Wi 19.3; often w. ἕως + GN, Ge 14.15, 1M 4.15, PSol 15.10. **b**. w. intense longing: + acc., ἀνταπόδομα 'a kick-back' Is 1.23, σικερα 5.11, διάφορα 'cash' Si 34.5; ἄνεμον 31.2, καύσωνα Ho 12.1; τὸ δίκαιον De 16.20, Is 51.1 (‖ ζητέω), δικαιοσύνην Pr 15.9; λόγον θεοῦ 2E 9.4, εἰρήνην Ps 33.15 (‖ ζητέω), μάταια 'meaningless things' Pr 21.6, σχολήν 'leisurely life' 28.19, ἐργολαβίας 'profiteering' Si 29.19; + τοῦ inf., Ho 6.3.
2. *to force to move away*: + acc. pers., πόρρω 'afar' Is 17.13 (‖ ἀποσκοράκιζω); pass., mist chased by the rays of the sun, Wi 2.4, πάχνη ὑπὸ λαίλαπος διωχθεῖσα 'a frost driven away by a storm' 5.14.
3. *to harass persistently*, 'persecute': abs., Je 20.11; + acc. pers., De 30.7 (‖ μισέω), Jb 19.22, Je 17.18; pass. + instr. dat., punitive rains, hail and storms Wi 16.16.
II intr. **1**. *to move with speed* towards some place: Je 28.31, ὑμεῖς ἕκαστος εἰς τὸν οἶκον αὐτοῦ Hg 1.9, sim. Is 13.14; *s* horse, Am 6.12, Na 3.2. **b**. *to move away with speed*: ὁ γυμνὸς διώξεται Am 2.16; Is 13.14.
2. *to chase*: w. hostile intent, + ὀπίσω τινός (= sbd on the run), De 19.6, Jo 2.7 (‖ κατα~), 4K 9.27 (‖ κατα~), φεύγων διωκόμενος ὑπὸ πάντων 'fleeing, chased by everybody' 2M 5.8; + ὄπισθέν τινος 1M 4.16; often w. ἕως + GN, 1M 9.15; w. no hostile intent, 4K 5.21 (*L* κατα~); often as an abs. pres. ptc., ὁ διώκων 'pursuer, persecutor,' 1M 12.51.

Cf. διωγμός, ἀπο~, ἐκ~, κατα~, μετα~, συνδιώκω, ζητέω, τρέχω: Oepke, *TDNT* 2.228f.

διώροφος, ον.ʃ *(τριώροφος already in Hdt.)
situated at second level (of living quarters): subst., n.pl. 'second level cabins' (of ship) Ge 6.16 (|| κατάγαιος and τριώροφος). Cf. κατάγαιος, τριώροφος: LSG s.v.

διῶρυξ, γος. f.
canal: of the tributaries of the Nile, Ex 7.19, 8.5 (|| ποταμοί and ἕλη); τοῦ ποταμοῦ [= the Nile] Is 19.6; ποταμοὶ καὶ ~γες πλατεῖς καὶ εὐρύχωροι 'rivers and wide and spacious canals' 33.21; ὑδάτων Je 38.9; ἀπὸ ποταμοῦ Si 24.30 (|| ὑδραγωγός); smaller than river, ἐγένετό μοι ἡ δ. εἰς ποταμόν 24.31. Cf. ἕλος, ποταμός, τάφρος, ὑδραγωγός: Schmidt 4.639f.; Schnebel 31-3.

διωστήρ, ῆρος. m.
pole running through rings: for carrying the ark, Ex 38.4 +; of a table, 38.11.

δόγμα, ατος. n.
1. *public decree*: τὸ δ. ἐξῆλθε Da 2.13 TH; ἔθηκας δ. 'you laid down ..' 3.10 TH.
2. *that which one learns as authoritative*, 'teaching': πατρία ~ατα 'ancestral ..' 3M 1.3; 4M 10.2. Cf. δόγμα Μοιρῶν w. ref. to premature death, *ND* 4.146.

δογματίζω: aor. ἐδογμάτισα, impv.3s δογματισάτω, pass. ἐδογματίσθην; pf. δεδογμάτικα, ptc.pass. δεδογματισμένος.
to issue a decree by ordinance: + inf., 1E 6.33, Es 3.9; also + dat. pers., 2M 10.8; pass., παρὰ τοῦ βασιλέως Da 2.15 LXX, τῷ βασιλεῖ 3M 4.11.

δοκέω: fut. δόξω; aor. ἔδοξα, ptc. δόξας, subj. δόξω; pf.pass.3s δέδοκται, ptc.pass. δεδογμένος.
1. *to have the appearance of being* or *doing*, 'seem': + inf., ἔδοξεν γελοιάζειν ἐναντίον τῶν γαμβρῶν αὐτοῦ 'he appeared to be joking in the eyes of his in-laws' Ge 19.14; Jb 15.21, 20.7, 22; ἔδοξαν ἐν ὀφθαλμοῖς ἀφρόνων τεθνάναι 'they seemed, in fools' eyes, to have died' Wi 3.2 (|| λογίζομαι pass.); dat. pers. (observer), 3M 5.6, 4M 5.7, Pr 16.25.
2. *to be of opinion*: οὕτως 2M 2.29; + inf., ἔδοξεν αὐτὴν πόρνην εἶναι 'he thought her to be a prostitute' Ge 38.15; 2M 5.6, 7.16; the opinion proven wrong, 9.10.
3. impers. *to be thought good and right* by sbd or in his or her judgement (τινι) to act in a certain way: ὡς ἀρέσκει ὑμῖν καὶ ὡς δοκεῖ ὑμῖν 'as you please and as you think fit' Jo 9.25, εἰ δοκεῖ σοι, καὶ εὗρον χάριν 'if it seems right to you, and I have found favour' Es 8.5 LXX, ὅτε ἔδοξε τῷ θεῷ 2M 1.20; πᾶσαι αἱ γυναῖκες, αἷς ἔδοξεν τῇ διανοίᾳ αὐτῶν 'all the women to whom it seemed good in their minds' Ex 35.26; τῇ καρδίᾳ 25.2, τῇ ψυχῇ αὐτῶν 35.21, τῇ διανοίᾳ 35.22; + inf., 4M 11.16. **b**. *to be thought appropriate* or *suitable*: ᾧ ἐὰν δόξῃ ἐν ὀφθαλμοῖς μου 'to whomever I would consider suitable' Je 34.4.
Cf. ἔοικα, ἡγέομαι, καταφαίνω, λογίζομαι, νομίζω, οἴομαι, ὑπολαμβάνω, φαίνω: Schmidt 1.321-4, 333-47; Trench 304-8; Bertram, *TDNT* 2.233.

δοκιμάζω: fut. δοκιμῶ; aor. ἐδοκίμασα, subj. δοκιμάσω, inf. ~μάσαι, ptc. ~μάσας, impv. δοκίμασον, pass. ἐδοκιμάσθην; pf. δεδοκίμακα, ptc.pass. δεδοκιμασμένος.
1. *to subject to scrutiny*: + acc. rei, δοκιμῶ αὐτούς, ὡς δοκιμάζεται τὸ χρυσίον Zc 13.9, cf. Ps 65.10, ἐν πυρί Si 2.5, νεφροὺς καὶ καρδίας 'the livers and hearts' Je 11.20 (sim. 17.10), λόγους Jb 34.3 (|| γεύω 'to taste'; διακρίνω 'to discriminate' 12.11), τὸ πρᾶγμα 'the matter' 2M 1.34; || πυρόω Ps 16.3, 65.10, Je 9.7; + acc. pers., Ps 25.2 (|| πειράζω). **b**. 'to put to a test', abs.(?), Ps 94.9 (|| πειράζω); ἐν αὐτῷ 'with gold' (with tempting power) Si 34.10; τὴν ἀνεξικακίαν αὐτοῦ 'his forbearance' Wi 2.19 (|| ἐτάζω); τιμωρίαις 'with punishments' 3M 2.6.
2. *to approve, after scrutiny, as acceptable and authentic*: ***o*** hum., 2M 4.3; metal used as coin, χρυσίον δεδοκιμασμένον 'authenticated gold' Pr 8.10; in a simile of metal-testing, ἐδοκιμάσθην 'I was declared to be of approved quality' Zc 11.13.
Cf. δόκιμος, δοκιμασία, δοκιμαστός, ἀποδοκιμάζω, ἐτάζω, πειράζω: Trench 278f.; Grundmann, *TDNT* 2.256f.; Spicq 1.353-61, esp. 353-7.

δοκιμασία, ας. f.ʃ
testing of quality: λίθος ~ας ἰσχυρός 'a hard testing stone' (for weight-lifting contest) Si 6.21; by God, PSol 16.14. Cf. δοκιμάζω: Spicq 1.353-61, esp. 357f.

δοκιμαστός, ή, όν.ʃ
tried out, tested: ***s*** hum., Je 6.27.

δοκιμεῖον, ου. n.ʃ On the spelling, see Katz 49f., 57 and BDF § 23.
means of testing: τῇ γῇ Ps 11.7, on the dat., cf. δ. ἀργύρῳ καὶ χρυσῷ πύρωσις 'putting through fire is ..' Pr 27.21. Cf. δοκιμάζω.

δόκιμος, ον.
tested and found acceptable, genuine: ἀργυρίου ~ου ἐμπόροις 'silver current among traders' Ge 23.16; ***s*** metal, Zc 11.13. Cf. δοκιμάζω, ἀδόκιμος: Renehan 1.70; Spicq 1.358-60; LSG s.v.

δοκός, οῦ. f.
bearing-beam: ὑπὸ τὴν στέγην τῶν ~ῶν 'under the roof of beams' Ge 19.8, ὑπὸ σκέπην ~ῶν 'under the cover of ..' Si 29.22. Cf. δόκωσις: cf. *ND* 2.73f.

δόκωσις, εως. f.ʃ *
act of furnishing with rafters, roofing (LSJ): Ec 10.18. Cf. δοκός.

δόλιος, α, ον.
given to deception and falsehood: γλῶσσα ~ία 'deceitful tongue' Zp 3.13 (ǁ ἀδικία and μάταια), χείλη ~α '.. lips' Ps 11.4 (ǁ μεγαλορρήμων); *s* hum. 42.1 (+ ἄδικος), 5.7; utterances, Je 9.8; πληγή 'blow' Si 22.22; ζυγοί '(false) balances' Pr 11.1 (:: δίκαιος); subst.pl.n., + ψεῦδος PSol 12.1. Cf. δόλος, δολιότης, δολίως, ψευδής.

δολιότης, ητος. f. *
deceitfulness: Nu 25.18; pl., Ps 37.13 (ǁ ματαιότης), 72.18; verbal, 49.19 (ǁ κακία); ἄνδρες αἱμάτων καὶ ~ητος 54.24. Cf. δόλιος.

δολιόω: impf.3pl. ἐδολιοῦσαν (Thack., § 17.5).ʃ
1. *to deceive*: + acc. pers., Nu 25.18; verbal, ταῖς γλώσσαις Ps 5.10, 13.3.
2. mid. *to deal treacherously with*: ἔν τινι (pers.), Ps 104.25.
Cf. δολόω, δόλος, παρακρούομαι, παραλογίζομαι, ψεύδομαι.

δολίως. adv.ʃ
in a manner characterised by deception and falsehood: πορεύομαι Je 9.4.

δόλος, ου. m.
deception: μετὰ ~ου Ge 27.35, 34.13, ἐν ~ῳ 1M 1.30; ἀποκτεῖναι .. δόλῳ Ex 21.14, sim. De 27.24; οὐ πορεύσῃ ~ῳ ἐν τῷ ἔθνει σου Le 19.16, cf. δολίως πορεύσεται Je 9.4; στάθμια ~ου 'false weights' Mi 6.11; ǁ ἀσέβεια Zp 1.9; verbally manifested, Ps 31.2. Cf. δόλιος, δολιότης, δολιόω, ἀδόλως, ψεῦδος.

δολόω: aor. ἐδόλωσα.ʃ
to deceive, beguile: Ps 35.3; verbally, ἐν γλώσσῃ 14.3. Cf. δολιόω, δόλος.

δόμα, τος. n.
gift, present: ἔδωκεν .. δόματα Ge 25.6; ἐν δόσει ἔδωκεν δ. τοῖς ἱερεῦσιν 47.22; Ho 9.1; 10.6 (ǁ ξένια); offered to God, Ex 28.34; cultic, ἔναντι κυρίου Le 7.20, τὰ δῶρά μου ~ατά μου καρπώματά μου Nu 28.2; δ. δεδομένοι οὗτοί μοί εἰσιν ἀπὸ τῶν υἱῶν Ισραηλ 3.9 (of Levites), sim. 18.6; + δωρεά Da 2.6 TH.
Cf. δίδωμι, δῶρον, δωρεά, ἀπόδομα, ξένιος: Lee 100.

δόμος, ου. m.
course of stone or bricks in a building (LSJ): λίθινος ξυστός .. ξυλίνος 'of polished stone .. of wood' 1E 6.24.

δόξα, ης. f.
1. *status of honour and distinction*: τὴν ~αν αὐτῶν εἰς ἀτιμίαν θήσομαι 'I shall turn their glory into ignominy' Ho 4.7, opp. ἀτιμία also Si 5.13, Hb 2.16*bis*; ǁ τιμή Wi 8.10; Ho 10.5; that which a son brings to his father, Ma 1.6; in pl., Ho 9.11; δοῦναι ~αν τῷ ὀνόματί μου Ma 2.2, δὸς ~αν .. τῷ κυρίῳ Jo 7.19 (in a formula demanding honest confession of guilt; + δὸς τὴν ἐξομολόγησιν, and cf. Joh 9.24); γνῶναι τὴν ~αν κυρίου Hb 2.14; δ. τοῦ ὀνόματος κυρίου Mi 5.4; symbolised by material wealth, πάντα τὸν πλοῦτον καὶ τὴν ~αν Ge 31.16; 31.1; στέφανος ~ης Je 13.18 (royal crown), θρόνος ~ης Je 14.21; + καύχημα Si 1.11 (*s* wisdom); + πλοῦτος 'riches' Pr 3.16, 8.18. **b**. 'status symbol': pl., Ἑλληνικὰς ~ας 2M 4.15 (ǁ πατρῴους τιμάς 'ancestral values'), cf. LSG s.v. **c**. w. ref. to God, and virtually his title: τῆς δόξης σου = σοῦ Es 4.16 *L*; ἐνώπιον τῆς ~ης κυρίου To 12.12 𝔊[II] (𝔊[I] ἐν. τοῦ ἁγίου), sim. 3.16, 12.15, cf. τὴν ~αν αὐτῶν, alm. = 'their God' Ps 105.20.
2. *external splendour, magnificent appearance*: God's– τοῦ θεοῦ Ex 24.16, ἡ δ. κυρίου ὤφθη ἐν νεφέλῃ '.. appeared in the clouds' 16.10, τὴν ~αν κυρίου εἶδεν Nu 12.8, ὄψεσθε ~αν κυρίου Ex 16.7, τὴν ~αν κυρίου καὶ τὸ ὕψος τοῦ θεοῦ Is 35.2; εἰς τιμὴν καὶ ~αν Ex 28.2 (of priest's garments), cf. Is 35.2 and Jb 37.22 (also + τιμή); Τίς ἐξ ὑμῶν ὃς εἶδε τὸν οἶκον τοῦτον ἐν τῇ ~ῃ αὐτοῦ τῇ ἔμπροσθεν; 'Who is amongst you who saw this temple in its former splendour?' Hg 2.3, sim. 2.9; κάλλος οὐρανῶν δ. ἄστρων 'the beauty of the sky is .. of its stars' Si 43.9; ǁ εἶδος Is 52.14, 53.2; + χάρις Si 24.16, + πλοῦτος 24.17, 2C 18.1; that which adds to such splendour, πλήσω τὸν οἶκον τοῦτον ~ης Is 2.7; δ. τοῦ ἱματισμοῦ αὐτῶν καὶ τοὺς κόσμους αὐτῶν 3.18; pl. στολαὶ ~ῶν 'stately robes' Ex 33.5 (ǁ κόσμον), sg. σ. ~ης Si 6.29, ποδήρη ~ης 27.8. **b**. *magnificent-looking object*: of garments, περιεβάλετο τὴν δόξαν [*L* τὰ ἱμάτια τῆς δόξης] αὐτῆς καὶ γενηθεῖσα ἐπιφανὴς .. Es D 2 o' (*s* Esther); pl., + στολὰς πολέμου 1M 14.9; of army, Is 8.7. **c**. not visible: δ. φωνῆς Si 17.13.
3. *an opinion which appears to be or commonly held to be right*: κατὰ τὴν ~αν κρινεῖ (ǁ κατὰ τὴν λαλιάν 'according to the popular opinion') Is 11.3, cf. οὐ κατὰ δόξαν ἀλλὰ κατ' οὐσίαν προθυμούμενος ἐλέγχειν Plato, *Rep*. 543C, but poss. sense **1**, Cyr. ad loc, PG 70:317; κατὰ τὴν ~αν αὐτοῦ κρινοῦσιν αὐτῷ 'the court will pass a judgement in line with what he thinks right' Si 8.14 (or sense **1**: 'by having regard to his high social status'). **b**. *reputation*: favourable, ἐπὶ τῇ εὐσεβείᾳ 'of (our) piety' 4M 5.18.
*__4__. δόξα προσώπου 'partiality; favouritism': Si 32.15.

Cf. δοξάζω, δοξαστός, δόξασμα, ἔνδοξος, ἐπίδοξος, φιλοδοξία, εὐπρέπεια, τιμή, ἀδοξία, ἀτιμία: Kittel, *TDNT* 2.233-7, 242-5; Spicq 3.364-76, esp. 364-7; Owen 1932.132-50; Brockington; Mohrmann.

δοξάζω: fut. δοξάσω, pass. δοξασθήσομαι; aor. ἐδόξασα, inf. δοξάσαι, impv. δόξασον, pass. ἐδοξάσθην, ptc. δοξασθείς, subj. δοξασθῶ, inf. δοξασθῆναι; pf.pass. δεδόξασμαι, ptc. δεδοξασμένος.

1. *to bring* or *accord honour to* (+ acc.): ***o*** God, ἐνδόξως δεδόξασται Ex 15.1 (|| ἐνδοξάζομαι 14.4, 17, 18); hum., Δαυιδ 2K 10.3, υἱὸς δοξάζει πατέρα Ma 1.6, μητέρα Si 3.4, cf. 3.2 (|| τιμάω vs. 3), ἱερέα 7.31 (|| φοβέομαι), ὑψῶσαι καὶ δοξάσαι τὸ καταλειφθὲν τοῦ Ισραηλ Is 4.2; τὸ ὄνομά μου δεδόξασται ἐν τοῖς ἔθνεσι 'my name has been accorded honour amongst the nations' Ma 1.11; by means of offerings, ἐν ἀγαθῷ ὀφθαλμῷ 'generously' Si 32.10; opp. ἐξουδενόω – τοὺς φοβουμένους κύριον δοξάζει Ps 14.4; || ὑψόω Is 10.15, Ps 36.20, || ὑμνέω Is 25.1; opp. ταπεινόω La 1.8; inanimate, τὸ ἱερόν 1E 8.78; also w. cogn. acc., τὴν δόξαν κυρίου, ἣν ἐδόξασεν αὐτήν PSol 17.31. **b**. mid. 'to pursue one's own honour or good reputation' Si 3.10. **c**. mid. 'to concern oneself unduly with one's reputation': Si 10.26, 27.

2. *to accord splendour to* (+ acc.): pass., δεδόξασται ἡ ὄψις τοῦ χρωτὸς τοῦ προσώπου αὐτοῦ 'the skin of his face had taken on a resplendent look' Ex 34.29; 34.30; ***o*** hum. face, 34.35; high priest, Si 50.5.

3. *to express oneself with reverence over*: + acc., τὸ ὄνομα αὐτοῦ Is 42.10 (|| ὑμνέω), Ps 21.24 (|| αἰνέω).

Cf. δόξα, δοξαστός, δοξικός, ἐνδοξάζω: Owen 1932.265-70; Kittel, *TDNT* 2.253; Ledogar 44-9; Spicq 1.376f.; LSG s.v.

δόξασμα, ατος. n.ʃ

*= δόξα 'glory': Is 46.13; δ. Ισραηλ La 2.1. Cf. δόξα: Owen 1932.270.

δοξασμός, οῦ. m.ʃ

**glorification*: 2K 22.25*L*.

δοξαστός, ή, όν.ʃ

full of splendour and glory*: ***s* hum., ὀνομαστὸν καὶ καύχημα καὶ ~ον De 26.19. Cf. δόξα, δοξικός: Owen 1932.271.

δοξικός, ή, όν.ʃ *

matching one's high social standing, 'glorious': ***s*** robe, 2M 8.35. Cf. δόξα, δοξαστός.

δορά, ᾶς. f.ʃ

skin of body when taken off, 'hide': of animal, δ. δασύς 'shaggy hide' Ge 25.25 (of a new-born baby); of human, τὴν ~ὰν αὐτοῦ ἐξέδειραν 'they stripped his skin off' Mi 2.8; scalp, κεφαλῆς 4M 9.28. Cf. δέρμα, διφθέρα, and ἐκδέρω.

δορατοφόρος, ον.ʃ

= δορυφόρος (q.v.): + θυρεοφόρος 'armed with a long shield' 1C 12.25. Cf. δόρυ.

δοριάλωτος, ον.ʃ

taken in war: ***s*** city, w. λαμβάνω 2M 5.11, 10.24; hum., w. συλλαμβάνω 3M 1.5.

δορκάδιον, ου. n.ʃ*

Dim. of δορκάς: Is 13.14.

δορκάς, άδος. f.

gazelle: as food, De 12.15 +, often || ἔλαφος.

δόρκων, ωνος.ʃ

= δορκάς, q.v.: Ct 2.17.

δόρυ, ατος. n.

1. *spear*: || ῥομφαία Mi 4.3; || ἀσπίς 'shield' 1K 17.7, Si 29.13.

2. *shaft*: κέντρου 'of a goad' Si 38.25.

Cf. δορύφορος, ζιβύνη.

δορυφορία, ας. f.ʃ

company of spearmen: serving as bodyguard, 2M 3.28. Cf. δορύφορος.

δορύφορος, ον.

spear-bearing: subst.m., *spearman* 2M 3.24, 4M 5.2. Cf. δόρυ, δορυφορία, δορατοφόρος.

δόσις, εως. f.

1. *act of giving*: Si 1.10; + λῆμψις 41.19, 42.7.

2. *gift*: ἐν δόσει ἔδωκεν δόμα 'gave as a gift' Ge 47.22 (cf. LSG s.v.), cf. δόσει δέδοταί μοι To 2.14 𝔊[II]; ἤσθιον τὴν ~ιν 'lived on the allowance' ib.; || δῶρον Pr 21.14.

Cf. δίδωμι, δόμα, δῶρον, λῆμψις: Schmidt 3.196.

δότης, ου. m.ʃ*

giver: of alms (?), Pr 22.8a. Cf. δίδωμι.

δοτός, ή, όν.ʃ *

granted as a gift: ***s*** child of a formerly barren woman, 1K 1.11, or poss. *offered* for life-long cultic service with δώσω meaning 'I shall place.' Cf. δίδωμι.

δουλεία, ας. f.

1. *slavery, bondage*: ἐξήλθετε ἐξ Αἰγύπτου, ἐξ οἴκου ~ας Ex 13.3, sim. Le 26.45; ἐξ οἴκου ~ας ἐλυτρωσάμην σε Mi 6.4; δ. σκληρά 'harsh ..' Is 14.3; || ταπείνωσις La 1.3; Es 7.4 o' (*L* δούλωσις).

2. *service* rendered: as cogn. obj., γινώσκεις τὴν ~αν, ἣν δεδούλευκά σοι Ge 30.26, οὐ δουλεύσει σοι ~αν οἰκέτου 'he shall not serve you as a domestic slave' Le 25.39; ἀνθρώπων (obj. gen.) Ps 103.14; cultic, θεοῦ 2E 6.18 (|| ἔργα 1E 7.9).

Cf. δοῦλος, ἐλευθερία.

δουλεύω: fut. δουλεύσω; aor. ἐδούλευσα, impv. δούλευσον, inf. ~λεῦσαι, ptc. ~λεύσας, subj. ~λεύσω; pf. δεδούλευκα.

to perform the duties incumbent upon oneself *dutifully and obediently*: + dat. pers., Ge 15.14, Ex 14.5, Zc 2.9; ὁ μείζων δουλεύσει τῷ ἐλάσσονι 'the major shall serve the minor' Ge 25.23; to an uncle, 31.6; a son to his father, Ma 3.17; to God, αὐτῷ ὑπὸ ζυγὸν ἕνα '.. under a single yoke' Zp 3.9, Ma 3.14, 18*bis* (|| δίκαιος and [+ neg.] ἄνομος); w. emphasis on an attitude - ἐν καρδίᾳ τελείᾳ καὶ ψυχῇ θελούσῃ 'wholeheartedly and with a willing soul' 1C 28.9; to heathen gods, θεοῖς ἑτέροις, ξύλοις καὶ λίθοις De 28.64 (ǁ λατρεύω vs. 36), + προσκυνέω Je 13.10; ἐν γυναικί 'in return for a wife' Ho 12.12, but ἔν τινι = τινι at Si 3.7; to a hum. master, Ex 21.2 (*s* παῖς); ǁ προσκυνέω Ge 27.29; + cogn. obj. δουλεία, 30.26, so Xen. *Mem.* 3.12.2; + acc. of limitation(?), σὺ γινώσκεις ἃ δεδούλευκά σοι 'you know in what ways I have slaved for you' Ge 30.29 (ǁ ἐργάζομαι 29.27 with Laban speaking, cf. Daniel 56f.); + cogn. acc., οὐ δουλεύσει σοι δουλείαν οἰκέτου 'he shall not serve you as a domestic slave' Le 25.39, τῆς δουλείας τῆς σκληρᾶς, ἧς ἐδούλευσας αὐτοῖς Is 14.3; ἐπ' αὐτήν [= Tyre as object of military operation) Ez 29.18; ἐλευθέρωσον τοὺς δουλεύοντας 'Liberate ..' 2M 1.27. **b.** w. ref. to political subordination: to foreign rulers, Ge 14.4; δ. οἱ Αἰγύπτιοι τοῖς Ἀσσυρίοις Is 19.23.

Cf. δοῦλος, δουλεία, ἐργάζομαι, (ἀπ)ελευθερόω, λατρεύω. What is prominent is not, despite the etymology, so much (often odious) slavery and bondage as service; see also Daniel 56-61, 62f., 72f. and Harl 2001.901.

δούλη, ης. f.

1. *female slave, bondwoman*: Na 2.8; + δοῦλος Le 25.44, Jl 2.29, Is 14.2; opp. ἐλευθέρα 1M 2.11.

2. *submissive and respectful woman*: in honorific, self-effacing discourse vis-à-vis a king, as a substitute for the first person personal pronoun, ἡ δ. σου 1K 25.27.

Cf. δοῦλος, λάτρις, οἰκέτις, παιδίσκη.

δοῦλος, ου. m.

1. *male slave, bondsman*: **a.** opp. κύριος '(human) master', υἱὸς δοξάζει πατέρα καὶ δ. τὸν κύριον αὐτοῦ Ma 1.6; + δούλη Jl 2.29, Is 14.2; and lowlier than παῖς and to be recruited from amongst non-Israelites, Le 25.44. **b.** of Israelites in Egypt: Le 26.13, cf. De 32.36.

2. *submissive and respectful person*, vis à vis the God of Israel, δ. κυρίου Jn 1.9, τοῦ θεοῦ Is 42.19; applied to Moses, Ma 4.6; to Jacob and David, Ez 37.25; to a prophet, Am 3.7, Zc 1.6, Je 7.25, cf. Hg 2.23, Zc 3.8 (ǁ παῖς, q.v. **2**), to priests, Da 3.84 LXX. **b.** adj., καθαρῶν ἔργων ~α σκεύη 'vessels serving clean uses' Wi 15.7; subst., τὰ σύμπαντα δοῦλά σά 'everything is subordinate to you' Ps 118.91.

Cf. ἀνδράποδον, δούλη, δουλεύω, σύνδουλος, δεσπότης, ἐλεύθερος, κύριος, θεράπων, οἰκέτης, οἰκετικός, παῖς, ὑπουργός: Schmidt 4.124-6; Thack. 7-9; Trench 32f.; Rengstorf, *TDNT* 2.261-9; Bieżuńska-Małowist; Spicq 1978.204-14; Amusin; Spicq 1.380-3; Wright 1997; Harl 2001.902; LSG s.v.

δουλόω: fut. δουλώσω; aor.inf.pass. δουλωθῆναι, ptc.pass. δουλωθείς.ʃ

to make work as slave: harshly and + acc. pers., *s* foreign masters, Ge 15.13 (ǁ κακόω and ταπεινόω), Pr 27.8; 1M 8.11; mid. τινα Wi 19.14. **b.** metaph. *to enslave*: pass., *o* hum., + dat., τῇ ἐπιθυμίᾳ 'to the desire' 4M 3.2, τοῖς πάθεσι 'to the passions' 13.2.

Cf. δούλωσις, δοῦλος, δουλεύω.

δούλωσις, εως. f.ʃ

v.n. of δουλόω: Es 7.4 *L* (o' δουλεία). Cf. δουλόω.

δοχή, ῆς. f.ʃ

reception where guests are entertained: ἐποίησεν αὐτοῖς ~ήν Ge 26.30; 21.8 (on the weaning of an infant); βασιλεὺς Δαρεῖος ἐποίησεν ~ὴν μεγάλην πᾶσιν τοῖς ὑπ' αὐτὸν καὶ πᾶσιν τοῖς οἰκογενέσιν αὐτοῦ καὶ τοῖς μεγιστᾶσιν τῆς Μεδίας καὶ τῆς Περσίδος .. 1E 3.1; τοῖς φίλοις .. Es 1.3, 5.4 o' (ǁ πότος *L*); glossed as δεῖπνον πολυτελές 'lavish dinner' 5.16 *L*; given for a king, Es 5.8; οὐ κέκληκεν ἡ βασίλισσα .. οὐδένα εἰς τὴν ~ήν 'the queen has not invited anybody to the dinner' 5.12; εἴσελθε εἰς τὴν ~ήν 5.14; Da 5 pref. LXX ǁ ἑστιατορία LXX 5.1 and TH δεῖπνον.

Cf. δέχομαι, δεῖπνον, ἑστιατορία, πότος.

δράγμα, ατος. n.

sheaf of cut corn-stalks: δεσμεύειν ~ατα 'to bind sheaves' Ge 37.7; offering to God, Le 23.10; δ. οὐκ ἔχον ἰσχὺν τοῦ ποιῆσαι ἄλευρον 'a sheaf not enough to produce wheat-meal' Ho 8.7; ~ατα ἅλωνος 'sheaves of threshing-floor' Mi 4.12. Cf. δράξ, δράσσομαι.

δράκος, ους. n.ʃ

*= δράγμα: 3M 5.2.

δράκων, οντος. m.

snake: κατοικητήριον ~των 'a lair of ...' Je 9.10 (ǁ ἀφανισμός); poisonous and ǁ ἀσπίς De 32.33; ǁ ὄφις Jb 20.16; ~οντα ὄφιν φεύγοντα .. ὄφιν σκολιόν ('wriggling'?) Is 27.1; makes loud noise, γαυρίαμα ~των 'the exulting cry of ...' Jb 4.10; Mi 1.8 (ǁ σειρήν); harmful wild animal, ἰοβόλων ~των 'of venomous ...' Wi 16.10; ǁ λέων Jb 38.39; Ps 90.13 (also ǁ ἀσπίς). **b.** Inhabits the sea, 'sea-snake'(?): συνέτριψας τὰς κεφαλὰς τῶν ~των ἐπὶ τοῦ ὕδατος Ps 73.13; ~τες καὶ πᾶσαι ἄβυσσοι 148.7; it bites, Am 9.3; ǁ κῆτος Jb 26.13, cf. ἄξεις ~τα ἐν ἀγκίστρῳ; 'Will you catch .. with a hook?' 40.25. **c.** Worshipped by the Babylonians: Bel 23. **d.** Fig. applied to a hostile foreign power: Nebuchadnezzar, Je 28.34; Pharaoh, Ez 29.3 (inhabiting rivers), 32.2; the Roman Empire, PSol 2.25.

Cf. ἀσπίς and ὄφις. On the mythological significance of the term, see BDAG, s.v., and Foerster - Bertram, *TDNT* 2.281-3; Eynikel & Hauspie 2004. See also Renehan 1.71.

δρᾶμα, ατος. n.ʃ

role played in public: 4M 6.17.

δράξ, κός. f.*
1. *handful amount*: of fine flour (σεμίδαλις) Le 2.2, 5.12, 6.15; κριθῶν 'of barley' Ez 13.19; ἀναπαύσεως .. μόχθου 'of rest .. of toil' Ec 4.6.
2. *hand* for holding sth in: πλῆσον τὰς ~ας σου ἀνθράκων 'fill your hands with coal' Ez 10.2; for measuring, Is 40.12.
Cf. δράσσομαι, χείρ.

δραπέτης, ου. m.ʃ
runaway: 2M 8.35.

δράσσομαι: fut. δράξομαι; aor. ἐδραξάμην, impv. 2pl. δράξασθε, ptc. δραξάμενος.ʃ
1. *to grasp and take a handful of*: + acc., πλήρη τὴν δράκα ἀπὸ τῆς σεμιδάλεως 'a handful of the fine flour' Le 2.2, sim. 5.12; Nu 5.26; + partitive ἐκ, 2M 4.41.
2. *to take hold of*: + gen., τῆς κόμης τῆς κεφαλῆς αὐτοῦ 'the hair of his head' Ju 13.7, σκορπίου 'scorpion' Si 26.7 (‖ κρατέω), σκιᾶς 'shadow' 31.2; fig. and cherishingly, παιδείας Ps 2.12.
Cf. δράγμα, δράξ, κρατέω.

δραχμή, ῆς. f.
drachm: a weight of metal, Ex 39.2 [= half shekel]. **b**. *drachma*, monetary unit worth the weight of the metal concerned, ἀργυρίου 2M 4.19; To 5.15.

δράω: aor.ptc. δράσας.ʃ
1. *to act and do*: ‖ πράσσω Wi 14.10; 4M 11.4.
*__2__. *to fabricate and produce*: abs., *o* idols understood, Wi 15.6.
Cf. ἐργάζομαι, ποιέω, πράσσω: Schmidt 1.397-9.

δρεπανηφόρος, ον.ʃ
fitted with a scythe: *s* chariot, 2M 13.2. Cf. δρέπανον.

δρέπανον, ου. n.
1. *sickle*: agricultural tool, De 16.9; Mi 4.3 (‖ Is 2.4), Jl 3.10 (‖ ἄροτρον); δ. οὐ μὴ ἐπιβάλῃς τὸν ἀμητόν De 23.24.
2. *pruning-knife*: Is 18.5.
Cf. δρεπανοφόρος: Shipp 221f.

δρομεύς, έως. m.
he who runs, 'runner': ἀπολεῖται φυγὴ ἐκ ~έως 'a runner will not manage to escape' Am 2.14, ἐλαφρότερος ~έως 'faster than ..' Jb 9.25. Cf. τρέχω.

δρόμος, ου. m.
v.n. of τρέχω 'to run': 1E 4.34 (*s* the sun), Je 8.6; fig., life-style 23.10, cf. βίος **1b**, διαγωγή. Cf. τρέχω, δρομεύς.

δροσίζω: aor.ptc. δροσίσας.ʃ
to moisten with dew (δρόσος): + acc. (burning furnace), 3M 6.6. Cf. δρόσος.

δρόσος, ου. f.
dew: τοῦ οὐρανοῦ Ge 27.28 (needed for agriculture); δ. ὀρθρινή 'early morning dew' symbolic of ephemeral existence, Ho 6.4, 13.3 (‖ νεφέλη πρωϊνή); moisture needed for growth of vegetation, 14.6, Hg 1.10; originating in the sky, Zc 8.12; descending, καταβήτω De 32.2 (‖ ὑετός, ὄμβρος, νιφετός); ὄμβρος καὶ δ. Da 3.64. Cf. ὑετός, δροσίζω.

δρυμός, οῦ. m.
coppice, thicket: where wood is collected, De 19.5; habitat of lions, σκύμνοι ~οῦ Ho 13.8, λέων ἐκ ~οῦ Je 5.6, ἐν ~ῷ 12.8; Am 3.4, Mi 5.8; grazing ground for sheep, 7.14, Is 65.10; ὁ δ. ὁ σύμφυτος 'thickly wooded' Zc 11.2; ἄλσος ~οῦ 'overgrown, sacred grove' Je 33.18; τὰ ὄρη καὶ οἱ βουνοὶ καὶ οἱ δρυμοί 'the mountains, valleys and ..' Is 10.18; opp. ἡ πεδινή 32.19. Cf. ὕλη: Bonneau 1982.

δρῦς, gen. δρυός, dat. δρυί, acc. δρῦν. f.
oak-tree: of Bashan, Zc 11.2; tall (ὑψηλός) Ge 12.6, De 11.30; hard and strong, ἰσχυρὸς ἦν ὡς δ. Am 2.9; standing at a site of cult, ἔθυον ὑποκάτω δρυὸς καὶ λεύκης Ho 4.13; and named Mambre, Ge 13.18 +. Cf. βάλανος: Shipp 223; LSG s.v.

δύναμαι: pres.subj. δύνωμαι; fut. δυνήσομαι; impf. ἠδυνάμην, ἐδύνατο (Ge 13.6); aor. ἠδυνάσθην, ἠδυνήθην, inf. δυνηθῆναι, ptc. δυνηθείς, subj. δυνηθῶ, opt. δυναίμην. The η~ augment is better attested (cf. BDF, § 66, Thack. § 16, 3; Mayser, I 2.93f.); so is the "shorter" form (of Ionic origin) like ἠδυνάσθην as against ἠδυνήθην (e.g. Ho 12.4 v.l., and cf. Mayser, I 1.17, I 2.156, 158).
1. With inf., *can, to be able* (to): οὐκ ἐδύναντο κατοικεῖν ἅμα 'were not able to live together' Ge 13.6; οὐκ ἠδυνάσθη ἰάσασθαι ὑμᾶς 'he was not able to cure you' Ho 5.13; ἕως τίνος οὐ μὴ δύνωνται καθαρισθῆναι 8.5. **b**. abs. δυνάμενος θεός 'potent god' 2M 11.13. **c**. idiom. w. *s* χείρ: καθὰ ἑκάστου ἠδύνατο ἡ χείρ 'to the best of each one's ability' Ba 1.6.
2. *be permitted, allowed*: **s** pers. and + inf., De 7.22, 17.15, 22.3; Es 4.2 o' (*L* εἶναι ἐξόν).
3. *to be capable of*: + acc. rei, πάντα δύνασαι 'you are almighty' Jb 10.13, sim. Wi 7.27.
*__4__. abs., *to prevail against, defeat*: **a**. abs. "you had your way" Je 3.5. ἐνίσχυσε μετὰ ἀγγέλου καὶ ἠδυνάσθη 'he matched his strength with an angel and won' Ho 12.4; Ge 30.8. **b**. c. πρός τινα: οὐ δύναται πρὸς αὐτόν Ge 32.25; δυνατοὶ δυνησόμεθα πρὸς αὐτούς Nu 13.31; ἠδυνάσθησαν πρός σε ἄνδρες εἰρηνικοί σου 'your allies prevailed against you' Ob 7; Je 1.19, 15.20. **c**. c. dat. pers., *to prevail with*: δυνήσομαι αὐτῷ (MT: אוּכַל לֹא) Ho 11.4, Je 45.22, Ps 128.2. This use (**4**), unknown outside of the LXX, is probably a Septuagintalism modelled on Heb. /yāḵōl l-/, but cf. Helbing *Kasus*. 116 top.
Cf. ἀδυναμία, ἀδυνατέω, ἀδύνατος, δύναμις, δυναστεία, δυνάστης, δυνατός, καταδυναστεία, καταδυναστεύω, ἰσχύω, ἐνισχύω, κατισχύω.

δύναμις, εως, f.

1. *power, capability* in gen.: Zc 4.6, ‖ ἰσχύς, and opp. the power of a divine spirit; δ. μου, which the Lord God is, Hb 3.19; ἀγαπήσεις κύριον .. ἐξ ὅλης τῆς καρδίας σου καὶ ἐξ ὅλης τῆς ψυχῆς σου καὶ ἐξ ὅλης τῆς ~εώς σου De 6.5; κατὰ ~ιν τῶν χειρῶν ὑμῶν 16.17 (‖ καθότι ἰσχύει ἡ χείρ σου vs. 10); financial, Si 8.13. **b**. *powerful performance*: on battlefield, ἐποίησεν ~ιν 1K 14.48, 4K 19.23*L*. **c**. *enabling force*: ἐποπτική 'overseeing' 4M 5.13.

2. *armed military force,* as a concrete embodiment of power, alw. in sg.: **a**. of a hum. army, ἀρχιστρατηγὸς τῆς ~εως αὐτοῦ 'the commander-in-chief of his army' Ge 21.22, 26.26; ἤλπισας ἐν τοῖς ἅρμασί σου, ἐν πλήθει ~εώς σου 'you trusted your carriages, the abundance of your troops' Ho 10.13 (‖ ἅρματα 'chariots'); to be captured by enemies, Ob 11; to be attacked, ib. 13; king's army to be destroyed, Hg 2.22 (‖ ἅρματα, ἀναβάται); naval(?) power of Tyre to be hit, Zc 9.4; κυρίου Ex 12.41, τῶν Αἰγυπτίων De 11.4; δ. καὶ ἱππεῖς 2E 8.22. **b**. high-ranking army officer (?): Es 2.18 o'; dignitaries, Da 6.23 LXX **c**. of divine troops: Jl 2.11 (‖ παρεμβολή), ἡ δ. μου ἡ μεγάλη, ἣν ἐξαπέστειλα εἰς ὑμᾶς 'my large army, which I have sent against you' 2.25; ὁ θεὸς τῶν ~εων Is 42.13, κύριος τῶν ~εων Ps 47.9.

3. *constellation of powerful* celestial *bodies*: ἡ δ. τοῦ οὐρανοῦ Da 8.10 TH, 2K 17.16 (*L*: στρατιά), Ps 32.6, pl. and ‖ ἥλιος καὶ σελήνη .. τὰ ἄστρα καὶ τὸ φῶς 148.2. See also under κόσμος **1** and στρατιά.

4. *wealth* as indicative of one's power: ‖ κτήνη 'cattle,' ἔγκτητα 'possessions' Nu 31.9; μεγάλη De 8.17; to be plundered, Zp 1.13 (‖ οἱ οἶκοι); ‖ σκῦλα 'spoils' Is 8.4; ***o*** of προνομεύω 'to plunder' Ez 26.12. Cf. ἰσχύς **3**. On the nuance of "pecuniary ability, available material resources," see MM, s.v. and Preisigke, s.v. 1.

Cf. ἀλκή, δύναμαι, δυναμόω, ἰσχύς, κράτος, στρατόπεδον: Schmidt 3.663-6; Dines 2007.20f.

δυναμόω: fut. δυναμώσω; aor.impv. ~νάμωσον, pass. ἐδυναμώθην.ʃ*

to strengthen: + acc. rei Ps 67.29, διαθήκην Da 9.27 TH (LXX δυναστεύω), δυνάμεις '(he would have to) make Herculean efforts' Ec 10.10. **b**. mid. *to rely for strength*: ἐπὶ τῇ ματαιότητι αὐτοῦ 'on his vanity' Ps 51.9 (‖ ἐπελπίζω).

Cf. δύναμις.

δυναστεία, ας. f.

1. *power, strength*: ὅπλα ~ας 'powerful weapon' Na 2.4; moral?, Mi 3.8 (‖ πνεῦμα κυρίου καὶ κρίμα); bodily vitality, Ps 89.10; divine, 3M 2.6 (‖ κράτος). **b**. *powerful deed*: pl. and wrought by God, Ps 19.7, 105.2. **c**. *one who is possessed of power*: w. ref. to God, Da 11.31 TH (LXX φόβος).

2. *powerful army*: pl. Am 2.16.

3. *domination*: ἐξάγω ὑμᾶς ἀπὸ τῆς ~ας τῶν Αἰγυπτίων Ex 6.6 (‖ δουλεία; καταδυναστεία vs. 7); Ba 4.21, Ez 22.25.

Cf. δυνάστης, δύναμαι, δουλεία, καταδυναστεία.

δυνάστευμα, ατος. n.ʃ*

military fortification, 'fortress' or *natural resources*: 3K 2.46[c] (*L* 2.28: τὰ δυναστεύοντα). Cf. ὀχύρωμα.

δυναστεύω: fut. ~τεύσω; aor. ἐδυνάστευσα, inf. ~τεῦσαι, subj.~τεύσω; pf. δεδυνάστευκα.

to have and wield power: ***s*** hum., Je 13.18 (‖ βασιλεύς); king, 2K 17.10*L*; queen, 4K 10.13; ἡ διαθήκη εἰς πολλούς Da 9.27 LXX (TH δυναμόω); + acc. rei, δυναστείαν μεγάλην 11.4 LXX (TH κυριεύω), πάντα Es E 21 o'; + acc. pers., με 'over me' Si 5.3, with negative connotation 1C 16.21 (‖ Ps 104.14 ἀδικέω); + gen., ***s*** God, τῆς ἁπάσης κτίσεως 'the entire creation' 3M 2.7, πάσης δυνάμεως 5.7.

δυνάστης, ου. m.; voc. ~α.

one who is in a position of power: διὰ χεῖρα ~ου Ιακωβ Ge 49.24; Φαραω 'of Ph.' 50.4; ἀπ' ἀρχῆς ~ῶν 'from the rule of masters' Am 6.7; διέκοψας .. κεφαλὰς δυναστῶν 'you beheaded powerful men' Hb 3.14; ‖ βασιλεύς Si 10.3, Pr 8.15; opp. πτωχός Le 19.15; ‖ οἱ ἰσχύοντες Is 5.22; + ἄρχων, ἱερεύς, λαός Je 41.19; w. ref. to God of Israel, τῶν πνευμάτων καὶ πάσης ἐξουσίας 2M 3.24, τὸν μέγαν τοῦ κόσμου ~ην 12.15, τῶν οὐρανῶν 15.23. **b**. with negative connotation: ‖ ἀσεβής, Jb 15.20, 27.13.

Cf. δυναστεία, δύναμαι: Cox 1990.

δυνατός, ή, όν.

1. *physically strong and capable*: ***s*** pers., Ge 32.28, Na 2.3; subst., De 3.18; God, δ. σώσει σε Zp 3.17, κραταιὸς καὶ δ… δ. ἐν πολέμῳ Ps 23.8; Es 4.29 *L* (o' ἰσχύων); the day of the Lord, Zp 1.14; ὁ δ. = ὁ θεός Es A 9 *L*; subst. m., 'warrior,' δύναμις ~ῶν 'an army of troops' Ju 1.4; τῇ ἰσχύι Jd 6.12 A. **b**. w. ref. to moral authority or intellectual ability: ***s*** hum., + inf., λαλῆσαι Nu 22.38.

2. *in possession of abundant means*: ***s*** pers., Ma 1.14.

3. *talented, able* to perform various demanding tasks: ἄνδρες ~οί Ge 47.5 (fit to be appointed ἄρχοντες); leaders, Ex 18.25; ἐν πολέμῳ Je 48.16.

4. *can be done* or *happen*: Οὐ ~ὸν γενέσθαι οὕτως 'that is impossible' Ex 8.26. **b**. logically possible or permissible: + inf., 2M 3.6.

Cf. δύναμαι, ἀδύνατος, βίαιος, ἰσχυρός, κραταιός, παντοδύναμος.

δυνατῶς. adv.ʃ

with vigour: to examine, Wi 6.6; to work, 1C 26.8.

δύνω: ⇒ δύω.

δύο. num. nom./gen./dat,/acc. δύο; dat. δυσίν; du. δυεῖν.

two: δύο δύο ἀπὸ πάντων εἰσάξεις εἰς τὴν κιβωτόν 'you shall lead all of them by pairs into the ark' Ge 6.19; τοὺς δ. νεφρούς Le 4.9 (ǁ ἀμφοτέρους τοὺς νεφρούς 3.10); δυεῖν μοι χρήσῃ 'you will indulge me in two ways' Jb 13.20. **b**. indeclinable: δύο καλωδίοις 'with two cords' Jd 15.13 A.

Cf. δεύτερος, δίς, δώδεκα, ζεῦγος.

δυσάθλιος, ον.ʃ

most miserable: *s* expulsion, 3M 4.4. Cf. ταλαίπωρος.

δυσαίακτος, ον.ʃ *

most mournful: + πικρός, *s* μόρος 'death' 3M 6.31.

δυσάλυκτος, ον.ʃ

hard to escape: *s* ἀνάγκη Wi 17.17.

δυσβάστακτος, ον.ʃ *

difficult to carry: *s* sand, ǁ βαρύς Pr 27.3. Cf. βαστάζω.

δυσγένεια, ας. f.ʃ

low birth, 'humble origin': Si 22.7¶ (:: εὐγένεια vs. 8). Cf. ταπεινός.

δυσδιήγητος, ον.ʃ *

hard to recount: *s* God's judgements, ǁ μέγας Wi 17.1. Cf. διηγέομαι.

δυσημερία, ας. f.ʃ

misfortune: opp. εὐημερία 2M 5.6. Cf. εὐημερία, ἀτυχία, συμφορά.

δύσις, εως. f.ʃ

v.n. of δύω: of the sun, Ps 103.19. Cf. δύω.

δυσκατάπαυστος, ον.ʃ

hardly stoppable: *s* βοή 'cry (of prayer)' 3M 5.7. Cf. καταπαύω.

δυσκλεής, ές.ʃ

1. *infamous*: *s* life-style, 3M 3.23. Cf. εὐκλεής, κλέος.

2. *liable to cause a sense of shame*: *s* death, 3M 3.25.

δυσκολία, ας. f.ʃ *

being unbearable, intolerable: Jb 34.30¶ (*s* hum.). Cf. δύσκολος.

δύσκολος, ον.ʃ

hard to bear: ~α ἐποίησεν Je 29.9. Cf. σκληρός: Shipp 223f.

δύσκωφος, ον.ʃ

hard of hearing, 'deaf': δ. καὶ κωφόν 'deaf and dumb' Ex 4.11. Cf. κωφός, βραδύγλωσσος, ἰσχνόφωνος.

δυσμένεια, ας. f.

ill will, animosity: opp. εὐμένεια 2M 6.29; πρός τινα 12.3, εἴς τινα 3M 3.19. Cf. δυσμενής, εὐμένεια, ἔχθρα.

δυσμενής, ές.

hostile: *s* hum., Es B 4; φήμη 'rumour' 3M 3.2; subst.m., 3.25. Cf. δυσμενῶς, δυσμένεια, εὐμενής, ἐνάντιος, κακόφρων: Schmidt 3.496-8.

δυσμενῶς. adv.ʃ

with hostile intentions: ἔχω δ. *to be hostile* 2M 14.11. Cf. δυσμενής, εὐμενῶς.

δυσμή, ῆς. f. Alw. in pl., so also ἀνατολή when meaning 'east.'

1. *going down*, esp. of the sun, 'sunset': περὶ ἡλίου ~άς 'about the time of sunset' Ge 15.12, περὶ ~ὰς ἡλίου De 24.13; ἐπεὶ ἐγίνετο ὁ ἥλιος πρὸς ~αῖς 'when the sun was just setting' Ge 15.17; ἕως δυσμῶν ἡλίου Ex 17.12; πρὸ ~ῶν ἡλίου 22.26, πρὸς ~ὰς ἡλίου De 16.6.

2. *west*: ἀπὸ ἀνατολῶν ἡλίου ἕως ~ῶν Ma 1.11, sim. Zc 8.7; Am 6.14; ἐπὶ ~ῶν De 11.30; ἐπὶ ~ῶν Μωαβ 'on the west of M.' Nu 22.1; τῆς θαλάσσης τῆς ἐπὶ ~ῶν De 11.24; πρὸς ~αῖς 'towards the west' 1.1. **b**. ~αὶ ἡλίου 'west': De 11.30, ἀφ' ἡλίου ~ῶν Is 9.12 (ǁ ἀφ' ἡλίου ἀνατολῶν).

Cf. δύω, ἀνατολή, βορρᾶς, νότος.

δυσνοέω.ʃ

to be ill-disposed: + dat. rei, Es B 5; + dat. pers., 3M 3.24. Cf. εὐνοέω.

δυσπέτημα, ατος. n.ʃ

unfortunate event: pl., 2M 5.20 (:: εὐεργέτημα) Cf. εὐεργέτημα.

δυσπολιόρκητος, ον.ʃ

hard to besiege: *s* place, 2M 12.21. Cf. πολιορκέω.

δυσπρόσιτος, ον.ʃ

difficult to attack: *s* place, 2M 12.21.

δυσσέβεια, ας. f.ʃ

impiety: 1E 1.40, 2M 8.33. Cf. δυσσεβέω, δυσσέβημα, δυσσεβής, εὐσέβεια.

δυσσεβέω.ʃ

to act in impiety: 2M 6.13. Cf. δυσσέβεια.

δυσσέβημα, ατος. n.ʃ

act of impiety: 1E 1.49, 2M 12.3. Cf. δυσσέβεια.

δυσσεβής, ές.

infidel, impious: *s* hum., 2M 3.11; φρήν 'mind' 3M 5.47. Cf. δυσσέβεια, εὐσεβής.

δυστοκέω: aor. ἐδυστόκησα.ʃ

to have painful delivery: ἐδυστόκησεν ἐν τῷ τοκετῷ 'she had difficulties in giving birth' Ge 35.16 (ǁ σκληρῶς τίκτειν vs. 17). Cf. τίκτω.

Δύστρος, ου. m.

name of a month in the Macedonian calendar: Es A 1 *L*.

δυσφημέω: aor. ἐδυσφήμησα.ʃ

to slander: abs., 1M 7.41. Cf. δυσφημία, δύσφημος, βλασφημέω, διαβάλλω, κακολογέω, εὐφημέω.

δυσφημία, ας. f.ʃ
slanderous utterance: 1M 7.38, 3M 2.26. Cf. διαβολή.

δύσφημος, ον.ʃ
given to making slanderous remarks: *s* hum., ἔθνη 2M 13.11; subst.m., 15.32. Cf. δυσφημέω.

δυσφορέω.ʃ
to find it hard to come to terms with: ἐπί τινι 2M 4.35, περί τινος 13.25. Cf. δυσφόρως.

δυσφόρως. adv.ʃ
finding it hard to come to terms: δ. ἔφερεν 'was finding it hard ..' 2M 13.28; δ. ἔχω 3M 3.8. Cf. δυσφορέω.

δυσχέρεια, ας. f.ʃ
situation or *event difficult to handle and bear*: attendant upon a study of history, 2M 2.24; upon illness, 9.21. Cf. δυσχερής.

δυσχερής, ές.
difficult to handle and bear: *s* attack, 2M 6.3 (+ χαλεπός), fall from a moving chariot, 9.7; physical wound, 14.45. Cf. δυσχέρεια, εὐχερής.

δύσχρηστος, ον.ʃ
hard to deal with: *s* righteous and incorruptible person, δ. ἡμῖν ἐστιν Is 3.10, Wi 2.12.

δυσώδης, ες.ʃ
emitting disagreeable smell, 'stinking': *s* liquid, 4M 6.25. Cf. εὐώδης, ὀσμή.

δύω: fut. δύσομαι, causative δύσω; 1aor. ἔδυσα, 2aor. ἔδυν, subj. δύω, inf. δῦναι; pf.ptc. δεδυκώς.

1. *to move to a lower place, plunge*: of a heavenly body setting, ἔδυ ὁ ἥλιος Ge 28.11; δεδυκότος ἡλίου 'after sunset' De 23.11; δύσεται ὁ ἥλιος μεσημβρίας 'the sun will go down at noon' Am 8.9, sim. Mi 3.6; Ec 1.5 (:: ἀνατέλλω), Jd 14.18 A (B: ditto); ὡσεὶ μόλιβος ἐν ὕδατι σφοδρῷ 'like lead in mighty waters' Ex 15.10; ἔδυ ἡ κεφαλή μου Jn 2.6. **b**. fig. εἰς τὴν γῆν οἱ λόγοι σου δύσονται 'your (boasting) words will sink to the bottom of the earth' Is 29.4 (|| ταπεινόομαι).

2. *to cause to vanish*: τὰ ἄστρα δύσουσι τὸ φέγγος αὐτῶν 'the stars will lose their brightness' Jl 2.10, sim. 3.15.

Cf. δυσμή, δύνω, ἐπι~, καταδύω, δύσις.

δώδεκα. indecl. num.
twelve: δ. ἔτη 'twelve years' Ge 14.4; δ. μυριάδες 'twelve myriads' Jn 4.11. Cf. δύο and δέκα.

δωδεκαετής, ές.ʃ
aged twelve: *s* hum., 1E 5.41.

δωδεκάμηνος, ον.ʃ
of twelve months: subst. n., *a period of twelve months*, Da 4.26 TH.

δωδέκατος, η, ον.
twelfth: Nu 7.78.

δῶμα, ατος. n.

1. *housetop, roof of a building*: De 22.8; where idol-worship takes place, Zp 1.5, Je 19.13; where good view can be had, Is 22.1. Cf. στέγη.

2. *dwelling-place*: ~ατα ἐρήμου 'desert dwellings' Ma 1.3 (Zgl: δόματα, and MT תנות, but see Syh *dyr'*, Tht PG 81.1964, Schleusner, s.v., and Arb. *tana'a* 'to dwell').

Cf. οἶκος, οἰκεία: Schmidt 2.508-13; Shipp 225, and on sense **1**, see Husson 63f., esp. 64.

δωρεά, ᾶς. f.

A. *gift, present*: δώσει αὐτῷ .. ~ὰς μεγάλας; δόματα καὶ ~ὰς καὶ τιμὴν πολλὴν λήμψεσθε Da 2.6 TH; εἰς ~ὰν 'as a gift' 11.39 LXX; ἐν ~ᾷ 2M 4.30.

B. Adv. acc. ~άν, **1**. *to no purpose, not resulting in desired effect*: Ma 1.10.

2. *for receiving or giving no remuneration*: οὐ δουλεύσεις μοι δ. 'you shall not work for me for nothing' Ge 29.15; μὴ ~ὰν Ιωβ σέβεται τὸν κύριον; Jb 1.9; 2K 24.24.

3. *not required to make any payment*: ἀπελεύσεται ἐλεύθερος ~άν 'shall leave as a free man for no payment' Ex 21.2; δ. ἄνευ ἀργυρίου '.. without paying silver' 21.11; ἠσθίομεν .. δ. Nu 11.5.

4. *for no justifiable reason, undeservedly*: ἐπολέμησάν με ~άν 'waged a war against me for no good reason' Ps 118.3; La 3.52; || μάτην Ps 34.7, || ἀδίκως 34.19.

Cf. δόμα, δόσις, δῶρον: Schmidt 3.197-9.

δωρέω: aor.mid. ἐδωρησάμην, impv. δώρησαι; pf. mid. δεδώρημαι.
to present: *o* cultic offering, ἐν ᾗ δωρεῖται βρωθήσεται 'on the day when it is offered, it shall be consumed' Le 7.5; mid. and + dat. pers. and acc. (baby boy), δεδώρηταί μοι ὁ θεὸς δῶρον καλόν Ge 30.20, sim. Pr 4.2; 'to give in marriage' Si 7.25 (|| ἐκδίδωμι). Cf. δῶρον, δίδωμι, ἀνα~, προσφέρω: Schmidt 3.194-6.

δώρημα, ατος. n.ʃ
that which is presented: cultic offering, Si 31.22 (|| προσφορά vs. 21). Cf. δῶρον.

δωροδέκτης, ου. m.ʃ *
he who accepts gifts: w. ref. to bribes, Jb 15.34.

δωροκοπέω: pf.ptc.pass. δεδωροκοπημένος.ʃ*
to offer bribes: Si 32.14. **b**. *to get sbd to accept a bribe*: 3M 4.19.

δωρολήμπτης, ου. m.ʃ *
one who accepts bribes: Pr 15.27. Cf. δῶρον.

δῶρον, ου. n.
gift: Ge 24.53; δεδώρηταί μοι ὁ θεὸς δ. καλόν 30.20; cultic offerings, 4.4, τὰ ~ά μου δόματά μου καρπώματά μου Nu 28.2; ἐὰν προσαγάγῃ ~α τῷ κυρίῳ Le 1.2; || θυσία Ge 4.5, Ep Je 26; gained

through extortion, ~α ἐκλεκτά 'choice gifts' Am 5.11, cf. πᾶν ἐκλεκτὸν τῶν ~ων ὑμῶν De 12.11; bribe or payment made to influence a judge, Ex 23.7, 8, De 16.19, Is 5.23; μὴ λάβῃ δ. De 10.17; μετὰ ~ων ἔκρινον Mi 3.11; a ruler, Is 1.23; donations made by a ruler, 1E 8.13. Cf. δίδωμι, δωρεά, δώρημα, δόμα, δόσις, δωρολήμπτης, θαλλός: Schmidt 3.196f.

E

ἔα. ⇒ ἐάω **3**.

ἐάν

I. Used as an ordinary, i.e. non-Hebraising, particle of condition *if*, its basic meaning is: should A happen or be the case, B will, would, should, could, might follow or follows.

1. **a**. A (aor.subj.) + B (fut.), *even if, suppose* Ge 18.24(*h*), Ob 4*bis*(*a*), Is 1.18(*a*), Ho 8.7(ἐὰν καί: *b*), 13(-), 9.12(καὶ ἐάν: *a*), 16(καὶ ἐάν: *c*), Am 5.22(*a*), Es 4.16 o' (ἐὰν καί; *j*); **b**. *if*, Na 3.12(*a*), Hg 2.12(*f*), 2.16(*e*); *unless* Am 3.3(ἐὰν μή: *a*), Ma 2.2*bis*(*a*). Pleonastic καί prefixed to the apodosis: Zc 14.18(*a*), Ma 2.16(*e*). **c**. ἐάνπερ: 2M 3.38.

2. A (aor.subj.) + B (οὐ μή subj.): **a**. *even if* with the apodosis preceding, Hb 1.5(*e*); **b**. *unless* Am 3.7 (ἐὰν μή: *d*).

3. A (aor.subj.) + B (pres.ind.): Hb 2.4(*f*: MT /hinnē/); ἐὰν φάγητε καὶ ἐὰν πίητε, οὐχ ὑμεῖς ἔσθετε καὶ ὑμεῖς πίνετε; 'if you eat and drink, are you not eating and drinking for yourselves?' Zc 7.6*bis*(*e*).

4. A (aor.subj.) + B (pf.ind.): ἐὰν νηστεύσητε .. μὴ νενηστεύκατέ μοι; 'should you fast .., have you fasted for me at all?' Zc 7.5(*e*).

5. A (aor.subj.) + B (impv.): Hb 2.3 (v.l.: ind.)(*a*).

6. A (aor.subj.) + B (non-verbal predicate): ἐὰν προσαγάγητε τυφλὸν εἰς θυσίαν, οὐ κακόν; Ma 1.8*bis*(*e*).

7. A (aor.subj.), B (apodosis) missing: Ge 38.17(*a*); and ἐάν not in the first position: ἐν ταῖς ἡμέραις ἐκείναις ἐὰν ἐπιλαβῶνται .. Zc. 8.23(*g*).

8. A (fut.) + B (fut.): Ez 22.13(*f*: MT הִנֵּה)

9. A (nominal clause), B (fut.): Le 1.3(*a*).

10. Ἐάν may be preceded by another clause constituent: Ἄνθρωπος ἐξ ὑμῶν ἐὰν προσαγάγῃ .. Le 1.2(*e*); 4.2(*e*), Zc 8.23(*g*).

II. With a rel. pron. in a generalising statement, equivalent to ἄν: καὶ ἔσται ὅσοι ἐὰν καταλειφθῶσιν .. καὶ ἀναβήσονται 'whosoever shall be left .. shall come up' Zc 14.16(-); ὃν τρόπον ἐάν + aor. subj., *in the same way as .. might* Am 5.19(-); πᾶς ὃς ἄν (v.l. ἐάν) *whosoever*, Jl 2.32 (-); ὅσος ἐάν + subj. *whosoever*, Mi 6.14(-); ὃς ἐάν Hg 2.14(-); εἰς πάντα τόπον, οὗ ἐὰν εἰσέλθωμεν ἐκεῖ Ge 20.13(-). **b**. w. an adverbial: πᾶς τόπος, οὗ ἐὰν ὦσι 'in whichever place they are' Is 7.23(-); Je 8.3(-), Si 15.16(-); καθὼς ἐὰν .. 14.11, Da 11.3 LXX.

***III**. **a**. Partially reflecting the typical Hebrew syntax of /*whāyā* ..*w* + pf.: καὶ ἔσται A (with aor. subj.) .. καί B (fut.), Am 6.9f.(*a*), Zc 13.3(*e*); mechanically beginning with καὶ ἔσται, but rightly continuing with καὶ εἶπα (aor.), Am 7.2(*a*). **b**. Hebraistically in oaths, ἐὰν μή (w. aor.subj.) signifying, like Heb. /ʾim lōʾ/, emphatic affirmation: ἐὰν μὴ ἐμπλήσω ἰσχὺν .., Mi 3.8(*a*: MT /ʾulām/). Perh. also Ma 3.10(*a*). **c**. Hebraism in strong negation after verbs of swearing: Ne 13.25(*a*). Cf. Je 22.6(*a*), Ez 17.16(v.l. εἰ μήν)(*a*), 20.33(*a*) εἰ μήν (v.l. ἐὰν μή). **d**. The pleonastic καί (see above, **I.1b**) is also Hebraising.

IV. ἐάν τε .. ἐάν τε .. in a disjunctive statement, *whether .. or ..*: ἐάν τε κτῆνος ἐάν τε ἄνθρωπος, οὐ ζήσεται 'whether it be an animal or a human, it shall not live' Ex 19.13(*i*); ἐάν τε ἄρσεν ἐάν τε θῆλυ 'whether male or female' Le 3.1 (ǁ ἄρσεν ἢ θῆλυ vs. 6)(*i*).

Cf. εἰ.

a) אִם; *b*) אוּלַי; *c*) גַּם כִּי; *d*) כִּי אִם; *e*) כִּי; *f*) הֵן; *g*) אֲשֶׁר; *h*) -הֲ; *i*) ἐάν τε אִם; *j*) ἐὰν καί כַּאֲשֶׁר.x∫

ἔαρ, ρος. n.∫

spring: a season of the year, Ge 8.22, Zc 14.8, Ps 73.17 (ǁ θέρος 'summer'); season of flowers, ἄνθος ἔαρος 'a spring flower' Wi 2.7; ἡμέραι ἔαρος Nu 13.21. Cf. θέρος.

ἑαυτοῦ, ~ῆς, ~οῦ; pl. ~ῶν; dat. ~ῷ, ~ῇ, ~ῷ; pl. ~οῖς, ~αῖς, ~οῖς; acc. ~όν, ~ήν, ~ό; pl. ~ούς, ~άς, ~ά.

Pronouns of reflexive reference.

1. In the obl. cases, referring to the person or thing spoken of or written about: περιείλατο τὴν στολὴν αὐτοῦ ἀφ' ~οῦ 'he took his robe off himself' Jn 3.6; ἐποίησεν ~ῷ ἐκεῖ σκηνήν 'he made himself a tent there' 4.5; ἐν ~ῷ 'inwardly' contrary to outside appearance, Je 9.8; ἐν ~οῖς Ἑβραϊστὶ λεγόμενα 'said in Heb. in its own idiomatic fashion' Si prol. 22. **b**. With the use of the genitive ἑαυτοῦ etc. when qualifying a subst., the identity of the referent becomes unequivocal and emphasises the exclusive relationship: εἶπεν Λαμεχ ταῖς ~οῦ γυναιξίν Ge 4.23; τὴν ~ῆς παιδίσκην 'her own maidservant' 16.3: cf. Moulton 87-90. In our corpus the pronoun with possessive function always (18x) occurs between the def. article and the substantive except at τὸ πρόσωπον ~οῦ Ex 34.35 (v.l. αυτου).

2. In the pl., they may also refer to the speakers or the persons spoken to: ἀργύριον ἕτερον ἠνέγκαμεν μεθ' ~ῶν 'we have brought extra money with us' Ge 43.22; Εὑρήσομεν ~οῖς τοὺς κατοικοῦντας .. 'we shall find for ourselves the inhabitants ..' Zc 12.5; τοὺς τύπους αὐτῶν, οὓς ἐποιήσατε ~οῖς 'their images, which you have made for yourselves' Am 5.26. **b**. beside a preceding person. pron., ὑμῖν ἑαυτοῖς Ex 12.21; 20.23 (|| ἑαυτοῖς), Nu 16.6, De 9.16.

Cf. αὑτοῦ.

ἐάω: fut. ἐάσω; aor. εἴασα; impv. ἔασον, inf. ἐᾶσαι, subj. ἐάσω, pass. εἰάθην.

1. *to allow, permit*: + acc. and inf., Ἔασόν με εἰσελθεῖν πρὸς σέ Ge 38.16; De 9.14, Es E 19; inf. understood, 1M 12.40; no acc., To 4.10. **b**. with the nuance of lack of concern: εἴασα ἀδύνατον ἐξελθεῖν θύραν μου κόλπῳ κενῷ 'I let a man of no means go out my door with an empty bosom' Jb 31.34; 2M 13.11. **c**. *not to interfere with* sbd (τινα): + καί and a subj., ἔασόν με καὶ .. ἐκτρίψω αὐτούς 'let me obliterate them' Ex 32.10.

2. *to let alone in peace and undisturbed*: + acc. pers., Es 3.8 o'; Jb 7.19 (|| προΐημι'let go'); + acc. rei, τὴν φυὴν τῶν ῥιζῶν ἐν τῇ γῇ 'the growth of the roots in the ground' Da 4.12 TH (|| LXX ἀφίημι); tomb, 4K 23.18*L* (B: ἀφίημι); pass. 2M 6.13. **b**. + pred. adj., οὐκ ἀθῷόν με ἐάσεις 'you are not going to let me go with impunity' Jb 9.28; 2M 15.36. **c**. + ptc. and pass., εἰάθησαν .. περιβεβιωκότες 'had been allowed .. to survive' 3M 5.18.

3. ἔα δέ introduces a proposition which would be all the more true, should the preceding one be true (*a maiore ad minus*), 'let alone': Jb 15.16, 19.5, 25.6, and poss. 4.19 τοὺς δὲ κατοικοῦντας (> ἔα δέ, οἱ ~ες), Katz 1946a.

ἑβδομάς, άδος. f.

1. *group consisting of seven*: heptad of brothers, 4M 14.7. **b**. week, ἑορτὴ ~άδων Ex 34.22, De 16.10; ἑορτή understood, Nu 28.26, ἁγία ~άδων To 2.1 𝔊[II]. **c**. seven years, ἑπτὰ ~άδες ἐτῶν Le 25.8.

*__2__. *the seventh day of a week*, 'sabbath': 2M 6.11, || σάββατον 12.38.

ἑβδομήκοντα. indecl. num.

seventy: Ge 5.12; ἑ. πέντε 12.4.

ἑβδομηκοντάκις. adv.ʃ *

seventyfold, seventy times: ἑ. ἑπτά 'seventy and sevenfold' Ge 4.24 (as a considerable increase on ἑπτάκις 'sevenfold'). Cf. ἑβδομήκοντα.

ἑβδομηκοστός, ή, όν.

seventieth: Zc 1.12.

ἕβδομος, η, ον.

1. *seventh*: ἑβδόμῃ καὶ εἰκάδι τοῦ μηνός 'on the 17th (day) of the month' Ge 7.11; τῷ ~ῳ μηνί 'in the seventh month' Hg 2.1. **b**. subst.n. adv. ~ον 'seven times': 4K 5.10*L* (B: ἑπτάκις).

2. n.pl.subst. ἕβδομα 'seven-day marriage feast': συντέλεσον τὰ ἕ. ταύτης 'Sit through the seven-day marraige feast of this (girl)' Ge 29.27; || ἀνεπλήρωσεν τὰ ἕ. ταύτης 29.28. Cf. LSG s.v.

Cf. ἑπτά and ἑβδομήκοντα.

Ἑβραῖος, α, ον.

Hebrew: *s* παῖς 'domestic servant' Ex 21.2; De 15.12; Si prol. II; said by a Jew to a non-Jew, 2M 7.31. Cf. Ἑβραΐς, Ἑβραϊστί.

Ἑβραΐς, ίδος. f.ʃ

used adj., *Hebrew*: *s* φωνή 'language' 4M 12.7, 16.15. Cf. Ἑβραῖος.

Ἑβραϊστί. adv.ʃ

in Hebrew: λέγω Si prol. 22.

ἐγγαστρίμυθος, ου. m.

ventriloquist: Le 19.31, 20.6, 27 (|| ἐπαοιδός); De 18.11, Is 8.19, 19.3 (|| other kinds of pagan practitioners); woman, 1K 28.7. Cf. ἐπαοιδός, γνώστης: Torallas-Tovar and Maravela-Solbakk.

ἐγγίζω: fut. ἐγγιῶ; aor. ἤγγισα, impv. ἔγγισον, inf. ἐγγίσαι, ptc. ἐγγίσας, subj. ἐγγίσω; pf. ἤγγικα.

1. *to draw near*: abs. Ge 18.23, Am 6.3; πρός τινα– πρὸ τοῦ ἐγγίσαι αὐτὸν πρὸς αὐτούς Ge 37.18; ἔγγιζε (*pace* Zgl's ἔλπιζε) πρὸς τὸν θεόν σου Ho 12.6, sim. Zp 3.2; so as to harm, Ps 90.7; εἰς Μηδίαν To 6.6 𝔊[II] (ἐν Ἐκβατάνοις 𝔊[I]); + dat. pers., μοι Ge 27.21 (|| + πρός τινα vs. 22), w. hostile intent, Ps 54.19, εἰς παράταξιν 'for a battle' Jd 20.23 B; *s* priests in cultic service, τῷ θεῷ Ex 19.22 (|| πρὸς τὸν θεόν vs. 21), indicative of false piety Is 29.13 (:: πόρρω ἀπέχω 'far removed'), πρός με Ez 43.19; πρὸς τὸ θυσιαστήριον understood – τοῦ προσενεγκεῖν τὰς θυσίας τῷ θεῷ σου Le 21.23 (|| προσέρχομαι vs. 17); + dat. rei τῷ πολέμῳ De 20.2, cf. ἐγγιοῦσιν καὶ ἁλώσονται '.. and will be captured' Is 8.15 (poss. πολέμῳ or ἐχθροῖς understood); ὄρεσιν αἰωνίοις Mi 2.9; + dat. loc., τῇ παρεμβολῇ Ex 32.19; + τινος– τοῦ ἀδελφοῦ αὐτοῦ Ge 33.3, αὐτῆς To 6.15 𝔊[II] (for sexual intercourse); ἐκεῖ Hg 2.14; + ἐπί and acc., Ez 9.6, ἐπ' ἐμέ Ps 26.2, ἐπὶ τὸν χειμάρρουν 1M 5.40; πρὸς θύραις 'the doors' Pr 5.8; + ἕως τινός 1M 3.16, Jd 9.52, ἕως θανάτου Si 37.2, cf. Rydén; 37.30; *to verge on*, 'to be on the brink of' ἕως θανάτου 51.6; *s* ἡ ἡμέρα Ge 27.41; αἱ ἡμέραι 47.29, De 31.14; ὁ καιρός La 4.19 (|| πληρόομαι, πάρειμι); ἐν τῷ ἐγγίζειν τὰ ἔτη 'as the years approach' Hb 3.2 (|| πάρειμι), οὐ μὴ ἐγγίσῃ .. τὰ κακά Am 9.10, δικαιοσύνη Is 51.5; εἰς τὸν οὐρανὸν τὸ κρίμα αὐτῆς Je 28.9.

2. *to get to, reach* (πρός τινα): ἤγγισεν ὁ λόγος πρὸς τὸν βασιλέα 'the news reached the king' Jn 3.6, ἡ δέησίς μου ἐνώπιόν σου Ps 118.169; ἕως τοῦ βασιλέως τὸ ὄνομα αὐτοῦ 1M 3.26.

3. *to be* or *come close to the point of* doing sth: + inf., ἤγγισεν Αβραμ εἰσελθεῖν εἰς Αἴγυπτον Ge 12.11; συντρῖψαι τὴν θύραν 'breaking down the door' 19.9, τεκεῖν Is 26.17, τοῦ ἐλθεῖν Ez 36.8, παραγίνεσθαι Is 56.1. **b**. tr. *to accelerate the com-*

ing of: + acc., ἤγγισα τὴν δικαιοσύνην μου Is 46.13 (:: βραδύνω).

4. *to bring near*: αὐτοὺς πρὸς αὐτόν Ge 48.10 || αὐτοὺς αὐτῷ 48.13; ἀγρὸν πρὸς ἀγρόν Is 5.8 (appropriating another man's adjoining field, and || συνάπτω); τὰς ἡμέρας σου Ez 22.4 (|| ἄγω). **b**. *to fetch*: τινί (pers.) τι 4K 4.6*L*.

5. *to be closely related to* within a family: + dat. pers., Le 21.3 (|| ἔγγιστα vs. 2), De 25.5; ἐκ τοῦ Λευι 'descended from L.' Ez 40.46.

6. *to be near, close by*: + dat., τῶν ἐθνῶν .. τῶν ἐγγιζόντων σοι ἢ τῶν μακρὰν ἀπὸ σοῦ De 13.7; πρὸς σέ 22.2; opp. πόρρωθεν Is 33.13.

Cf. ἐγγύς, προσ~, συνεγγίζω, ἀγχιστεύω: Johannessohn, *Präp*. 264, f.n. 3; Preisker, *TDNT* 2.330; Drescher 1976. 310f.

ἔγγιστα. ⇒ ἐγγύς.

ἐγγλύφω: aor.inf.pass. ἐγγλυφῆναι; pf.ptc.pass. ἐγγεγλυμμένος.ʃ

to mark carvings on, 'engrave': pass., ***o*** ring, ἐγγεγλυμμέναι σφραγῖδες Ex 36.21; ἔν τινι– ἐν πέτραις ἐγγλυφῆναι Jb 19.24. Cf. γλύφω.

ἔγγραπτος, ον.ʃ

written: ***s*** κρίμα Ps 149.9. Cf. γράφω.

ἐγγραφή, ῆς. f.ʃ

written message, 'missive': 2C 21.12. Cf. γραφή.

ἐγγράφω: aor.impv.pass.3pl ~γραφέσθωσαν; pf.ptc. pass. ~γεγραμμένος.ʃ

1. *to record in writing*: ὁ ὅρκος ὁ ἐγγεγραμμένος ἐν τῷ νόμῳ Μωυσέως Da 9.11 LXX (TH γράφω).

2. *to enrol* for a function or assignment: pass., ***o*** hum., 1M 13.40 (|| γράφω).

3. *to name in writing*: pass., ***o*** hum., Da 12.1 LXX.

Cf. γράφω.

ἐγγυάω: fut. ἐγγυήσομαι; aor.mid. ἐνεγυησάμην, subj. ~ήσωμαι.

1. mid. *give surety*: ὑπὲρ δύναμίν σου 'beyond your means' Si 8.13; + acc. pers. ('on behalf of'), 29.14, σὸν φίλον Pr 6.1.

2. mid. *to promise to give in marriage*: + acc. pers. (woman) and dat. pers., To 6.13𝔊[II].

Cf. ἐγγύη, ἔγγυος, διεγγυάω: Spicq 1.390-5.

ἐγγύη, ης. f.

acting as guarantor: hazardous, Pr 22.26, Si 29.18. Cf. ἐγγυάω.

ἐγγύθεν. adv.ʃ

from close by: Ez 7.5, Jo 6.13. **b**. prep. c. gen., *close by*: Jo 9.16.

Cf. ἐγγύς, μακρόθεν.

ἔγγυος, ου. m.

guarantor: gracious, Si 29.15. **b**. *that which guarantees*: εὐημερίας καὶ νίκης 'of success and triumph' 2M 10.28.

Cf. ἐγγυάω.

ἐγγύς, comp. ἐγγίων, superl. ἐγγύτατος, η, ον. adv. superl. ἔγγιστα.

near, at hand: ἡ πόλις αὕτη ἐ. Ge 19.20; + gen., ἔσῃ ἐγγύς μου 45.10; ***s*** time, esp. the (eschatological) day of the Lord, ἐγγὺς ἡμέρα ἀπωλείας αὐτῶν, καὶ πάρεστιν ἕτοιμα ὑμῖν De 32.35; ἐ. ἡ ἡμέρα κυρίου Jl 1.15, 3.14, Zp 1.7, 14*a*, Is 13.6, sim. Jl 2.1; ἐπὶ πάντα τὰ ἔθνη 'to all the nations' Ob 15; ἐ. καὶ ταχεῖα 'near and speedy' Zp 1.14*b*; ἐ. ἡμέρα Μωαβ ἐλθεῖν Je 31.16; opp. πόρρω - ἐ. εἶ σὺ τοῦ στόματος αὐτῶν 'you are often on their lips' Je 12.2; readily available to help, ἐ. κύριος τοῖς ἐπικαλουμένοις αὐτόν Ps 144.18, sim. 33.19. **b**. in kinship: To 3.15. **c**. used as an attributive adj.: ἐν τῷ οἰκείῳ τῷ ἔγγιστα αὐτοῦ 'his nearest family-member' Le 21.2 (glossed as 'father, mother, sons, daughters, brothers and sisters'); τὰς πόλεις Μωαβ τὰς πόρρω καὶ τὰς ἐγγύς 'the Moabite cities far and near' Je 31.24. **d**. subst., οἱ ἔγγιστά μου 'my kinsmen' Ps 37.12; οἱ ἐγγύτατοί μου Jb 6.15. **e**. || ὁ ἀδελφὸς αὐτοῦ, ὁ πλησίον αὐτοῦ: Ex 32.27, see under ἕκαστος; ὁ ἔγγιστα || ὁ πλησίον Ps 14.3. **f**. used as a prep. with gen., only in De in our corpus: προσάξετε ἐγγὺς υἱῶν Αμμαν 'Draw near to the Ammonites' De 2.19; ἐν φάραγγι ἐγγὺς οἴκου Φογωρ 'in a wadi near the house of P.' 4.46; ἐγγὺς σοῦ τὸ ῥῆμα 'the word is near you' 30.14; 34.6.

Cf. ἐγγίζω, ἐγγύθεν, σύννεγγυς, ἔχομαι, ὑπόγυος, πέλας, μακρός, πόρρω: Preisker, *TDNT* 2.330f.

ἐγείρω: fut. ἐγερῶ, mid. ἐγερθήσομαι; aor. ἤγειρα, ptc. ἐγείρας, impv. ἔγειρον, inf. ἐγεῖραι, pass. ἠγέρθην, subj. ἐγερθῶ, impv. ἐγέρθητι.

1. *to help to rise*: ***o*** a fallen person Ec 4.10, a prostrate person Da 8.18 LXX (TH ἵστημι), ἀπὸ τῆς γῆς 2K 12.17, the poor 1K 2.8, fallen idol 5.3, fallen walls Si 49.13; temple 1E 5.43. **b**. *to force to rise*: + acc., ἐκ τῶν θρόνων αὐτῶν πάντας βασιλεῖς Is 14.9. **c**. of resurrection from death: + acc., νεκρὸν ἐκ θανάτου καὶ ἐξ ᾅδου Si 48.5, cf. πολλοὺς .. νοσέοντας ἔγειρας 'you raised many who were sick' *ND* 4.20.

2. *to wake up from sleep*: + acc., Ge 49.9; pass. with intr. force, 41.4 (having had a dream), ἐξ ὕπνου 'from sleep' Pr 6.9. νυκτός 2C 21.9 (*L* ἀνέστη).

3. *to stir, set in motion*: + acc., ἐπ' αὐτὸν πόλεμον 'started war against them' Mi 3.5; ***o*** emotion, ἀγάπην Ct 2.7, 8.4 (+ ἐξεγείρω), νεῖκος 'strife' Pr 10.12, κρίσεις 'litigations' 15.18a (|| κατασβέννυμι), ὀργάς 'sentiments of anger' 15.1, θυμόν Si 33.8, Pr 21.14; τὸ πνεῦμα βασιλέως Μήδων Je 28.11, sim. 1E 2.2 (|| ἐξεγείρω 2E 1.1), νοῦς 1E 2.8; πόλεμον '(to wage) a war' 1.23.

4. *to bring into existence*: ἐγείρει ἀνδρὶ δόξαν 'raises her husband's standing' Pr 11.16; ***o*** hum. invested with a certain function, κριτάς 'judges' Jd 2.16, σωτῆρα τῷ Ισραηλ 'saviour ..' 3.9.

*5. *to give effect to*, calque on Heb. הֵקִים: + acc., προφητείας Si 36.20.

6. mid. *to rise*: opp. κάθημαι Ps 126.2; from bed, τὸ πρωί 'in the morning' Is 5.11; opp. καθεύδω Pr 6.22; fig., "the dead will arise (ἀναστήσονται) and those in graves will rise (ἐγερθήσονται)" Is 26.19, cf. Da 12.2 TH (LXX ἀναστήσονται). *b. w. weakened basic meaning, in urging one to act or signalling an action taken with clear intent - Hebraistic, ἐγέρθητε (*L* ἀνάστητε) καὶ οἰκοδομήσατε .. 1C 22.19; 2C 22.10 (*L* ἀνέστη), cf. ἀνίστημι **II 1 c**.

Cf. ἀν~, ἐξ~, ἐπ~, συνεγείρω, ἀνίστημι: Oepke, *TDNT* 2.334f.

ἔγερσις, εως. f.ʃ

1. *act of arising*: opp. καθέδρα Ps 138.2.

2. v.n. of ἐγείρω **2**: as cogn. dat., Jd 7.19A*L*.

3. *completion of building*: τοῦ οἴκου 1E 5.59.

Cf. ἐγείρω.

ἐγκάθετος, ον.ʃ

lying in ambush: ἐπὶ θύραις αὐτῆς Jb 31.9; subst. m., ταῖς ὁδοῖς μου 19.12. Cf. ἐγκάθημαι.

ἐγκάθημαι: fut. ἐγκαθήσομαι.

1. *to sit* in ambush: ὄφις .. ἐγκαθήμενος ἐπὶ τρίβου 'a snake .. on a path' Ge 49.17; Is 8.14; || ἐνεδρεύω Ps 9.29. **b**. *to remain engaged against* a military target: 3K 11.16.

*2. *to reside*: τοὺς ἐγκαθημένους ἐν τῇ γῇ 'the local inhabitants' Ex 23.31 (εἰς τὴν γῆν Jd 2.2); ἐπὶ τῆς γῆς Ex 34.12; Le 18.25, Nu 13.19; ἡ γῆ, εἰς ἣν οὗτοι ἐγκάθηνται ἐπ' αὐτῆς 13.20; ἐχόμενός μου 'close by me' 22.5; *s* snake, ἐν μέσῳ ποταμῶν Ez 29.3.

Cf. κάθημαι, ἐγκαθίζω, ἐγκάθετος.

ἐγκαθίζω: aor. ἐνεκάθισα, subj. ~καθίσω, impv. ~κάθισον.ʃ

I. tr. *to cause to seat oneself*: ***o*** witnesses, 3K 20.10.

II. intr. *to lie in ambush*: Jo 8.9 (|| ἔνεδρα), ὡς ἔνεδρον τῷ στόματί σου Si 8.11, τῷ οἴκῳ Ισραηλ δόλῳ Ez 35.5.

Cf. ἐγκάθημαι.

ἐγκαίνια. ⇒ ἐγκαίνιος.

ἐγκαινίζω: fut. ἐγκαινιῶ; aor. ἐνεκαίνισα, impv. ἐγκαίνισον, inf. ~νίσαι, subj. ~νίσω, pass. ἐνεκαινίσθην. *

1. *to bring into existence as new*: + acc., πνεῦμα εὐθές 'upright spirit' Ps 50.12 (|| κτίζω), σημεῖα Si 36.6 (|| ἀλλοιόω), τεῖχος 'wall' Is 16.11; 'to restore' τὰς πύλας 'the (temple) gates' 1M 4.57; βασιλείαν 'kingship' 1K 11.14; ὡς τὸ πρότερον 'as the former one' 1M 5.1. **b**. mid. *to reform oneself*: Is 41.1

2. *to inaugurate* the use of: + acc. rei, a new house, De 20.5; τὸν οἶκον κυρίου 3K 8.63, τὰ ἅγια 'the sanctuary' 1M 4.36; pass. 4.54.

Cf. ἐγκαίνισις, ἐγκαινισμός, καινίζω, καινός.

ἐγκαίνιος, ον.ʃ

subst.n.pl., *feast of inauguration*: τοῦ οἴκου τοῦ θεοῦ 2E 6.16f.; τείχους 'of the wall' Ne 12.27, τῆς εἰκόνος 'of the statue' Da 3.2 TH (LXX: ἐγκαινισμός). Cf. ἐγκαινισμός.

ἐγκαίνισις, εως.ʃ *

inauguration: θυσιαστηρίου Nu 7.88. Cf. ἐγκαινίζω, ἐγκαινισμός.

ἐγκαινισμός, οῦ. m. *

inauguration: θυσιαστηρίου Nu 7.10, 1M 4.56, τοῦ οἴκου Ps 29.1, τοῦ ἱεροῦ 2M 2.9, τῆς εἰκόνος τῆς χρυσῆς 'of the golden image' Da 3.2 LXX (TH: ἐγκαίνια). Cf. ἐγκαινίζω, ἐγκαίνισις, ἐγκαίνια.

ἐγκαίω.ʃ

to paint with colours mixed with wax (LSJ): + ζωγραφέω 2M 2.29.

ἐγκαλέω: fut. ~καλέσω; aor. ἐνεκάλεσα.

1. *to take legal proceedings*: pass., περὶ .. πάσης ἀπωλείας τῆς ἐγκαλουμένης 'concerning any loss about which a case is proceeding' Ex 22.9.

2. *to castigate, bring a charge* (against sbd τινι): Zc 1.4; κατά τινος (rei) 'in respect of ..' Wi 12.12.

Cf. ἀνέγκλητος, αἰτιάομαι: Schmidt 1.155f.

ἔγκαρπος, ον.ʃ

producing fruit: *s* ξύλον Je 38.12. Cf. κατάκαρπος.

ἐγκαρτερέω.ʃ

to hold out under difficult circumstances: 4M 14.9. Cf. ὑπομένω.

ἐγκατάλειμμα, ατος. n.

that which remains behind: of crops unconsumed, αἱ ἀποθῆκαί σου καὶ τὰ ~ατά σου De 28.5, 17. **b**. survivors, ἐ. καὶ διασῳζόμενον 2E 9.14; Je 11.23. **c**. descendants: Ps 36.37, 38.

Cf. ἐγκαταλείπω, κατάλειμμα: Caird 1968.469; LSG s.v.

ἐγκαταλείπω: fut. ~λείψω, pass. ~λειφθήσομαι; aor. act. ἐγκατέλιπον, subj. ~λίπω, impv. ~λιπε, inf. ~λιπεῖν, opt. 3s ~λίποι, mid. ~λίποιτο, pass. ἐγκατελείφθην, subj. ~λειφθῶ; pf. ~λέλοιπα, ptc. ~λελοιπώς, pass. ~λέλειμμαι, ~λελειμμένος.

1. *to desert*: as an act of betrayal of trust, De 28.20; ***o*** God, 31.16, 32.15, τὸν κύριον Ho 4.10, 5.7; one's wife, Ma 2.14, 15, 16; ἕκαστος τὸν ἀδελφὸν αὐτοῦ Ma 2.10, cf. 11; οὐ μὴ ἐγκαταλίπω τοῦ ἐξαλειφθῆναι τὸν Εφραιμ 'I will not desert Ephraim to be wiped out' Ho 11.9. **b**. neglected and uncared for, ***s*** God ***o*** pers., οὐ μή σε ἐγκαταλίπω Ge 28.15; De 4.31, 31.6, 8 (both latter || ἀνίημι); Je 12.7 (|| ἀφίημι), τὴν ψυχήν μου εἰς ᾅδην Ps 15.10, εἰς τὰς χεῖρας αὐτοῦ [= of an enemy] 36.33; *s* and *o* pers., De 12.19; ‖ ἐπιλανθάνομαι 'forget' 32.18; *o* houses Is 24.12, cities, 17.9, Ez 36.4; *s* ἐ. με ἡ ἰσχύς μου Ps 37.11.

2. *to disregard* as unimportant and irrelevant: + acc. rei, τὴν δικαιοσύνην καὶ ἀλήθειαν ἀπὸ τοῦ κυρίου μου Ge 24.27 (pregnantly: 'and [withholding them] from my master'), κρίσιν θεοῦ αὐτοῦ Is 58.2, βουλήν 'advice' 3K 12.8 (‖ vs. 24ʳ διασκεδάζω; 2C 10.8 καταλείπω); land, Le 26.43; ὡς σκηνὴ ἐν ἀμπελῶνι 'like a tent in vineyard' Is 1.8; ἔλεος Jn 2.9, Si 47.22; *o* sth objectionable, τὰ ἐπιτηδεύματα 'practices' Αἰγύπτου Ez 20.8 (‖ ἀπορρίπτω). **b.** *to give up, quit:* + acc., θυμόν Ps 36.8 (‖ παύομαι ἀπό); *o* undesirable practice, Ne 5.10.

3. *to leave in the care of sbd*: pass., + dat., σοι ἐγκαταλέλειπται ὁ πτωχός Ps 9.35.

4. *to leave for future benefit*: + acc. and dat., ἐγκατέλιπεν ἡμῖν σπέρμα Is 1.9.

Cf. ἐγκατάλειμμα, ἐκ~, καταλείπω, ἀπορρίπτω, ἀφίημι.

ἐγκαταλιμπάνω.ʃ

= ἐγκαταλείπω: + acc., τὸν νόμον σου Ps 118.53.

ἐγκαταπαίζω.ʃ *

to use as plaything: pass., Jb 40.19, 41.25. Cf. παίζω.

ἔγκατον, ου. n. Alw. pl.

intestines: of fish, To 6.5𝔖ᴵᴵ, Jb 21.24; of hum. body, Ps 108.18. **b.** *the whole inside* of hum. body: Ps 50.12; brain as the centre of hum. intellect, Si 21.14.

Cf. ἔντερα, ἐγκοίλιος.

ἐγκαυχάομαι: aor. ἐνεκαυχησάμην.ʃ*

to exult: abs. Ps 73.4; + acc. rei, ἀνομίαν 51.3; + ἐν 'over' - ἐν κακίᾳ 51.3, ἐν εἰδώλοις 96.7; ἐν τῇ αἰνέσει σου 105.47. Cf. καυχάομαι: Caird 1968. 469.

ἔγκειμαι.ʃ

1. *to be involved and concerned*: + ἐπί τι - ἔγκειται ἡ διάνοια τοῦ ἀνθρώπου ἐπιμελῶς ἐπὶ τὰ πονηρὰ 'man's mind is intensely occupied with evil things' Ge 8.21; + dat., τῇ θυγατρὶ Ιακωβ 34.19.

2. *to weigh heavily upon*: + dat. pers., ὁ φόβος Μαρδοχαίου ἐνέκειτο αὐτοῖς Es 9.3 o' (*L* ἐπέπεσεν ἐπ' αὐτοῖς), ἐν τοῖς σπλάγχνοις αὐτῶν 6.5 *L*.

See Renehan 1.75 and LSG s.v.

ἐγκεντρίζω.ʃ

to sting, bite: pass., *o* hum., Wi 16.11. Cf. Caird 1968.469; LSG s.v.

ἐγκηδεύω: pf.pass.3pl ἐγκεκήδευνται.ʃ *

to bury in a place: pass., *o* hum., 4M 17.9. Cf. θάπτω.

ἐγκισσάω: impf. ἐνεκίσσων; aor. ἐνεκίσσησα, inf. ἐγκισσῆσαι, subj. ἐγκισσήσω.ʃ *

to come into heat: *s* animal, abs. Ge 31.10; εἰς τὰς ῥάβδους 30.38, κατὰ τὰς ῥάβδους 30.41; ἐν γαστρὶ λαμβάνοντα 'having become pregnant' ib.

ἐγκλείω: aor.pass.impv. ~κλείσθητι, ptc. ~κλεισθείς.ʃ

to shut in, confine: pass. and of imprisonment, 2M 5.8; mid., *to confine oneself*, Ez 3.24. Cf. κλείω.

ἔγκληρος, ον.ʃ

having a share in inheritance: *s* λαός De 4.20. Cf. κλῆρος.

ἐγκλοιόω: aor.impv.mid. ~κλοίωσαι.ʃ *

to enclose in a collar: mid., *o* understood, ἐπὶ σῷ τραχήλῳ 'on your neck' Pr 6.21 (‖ ἀφάπτω 'to fasten'). Cf. κλοιός.

ἐγκοίλιος, ον.ʃ

subst. n.pl., *intestines, internal organs*: cultic offering, Le 1.9, 13. Cf. ἔγκοιλος, κοιλία, ἔγκατον.

ἔγκοιλος, ον.ʃ

situated inside and beneath the surface of: τοῦ δέρματος 'underneath the skin' Le 13.30, 31 (‖ ταπεινὸς ἀπὸ τοῦ δέρματος vs. 3, 4, 25). Cf. ἐγκοίλιος.

ἐγκολαπτός, ή, όν.ʃ

engraved: subst.n.pl., 3K 6.29, 32. Cf. ἐγκολάπτω.

ἐγκολάπτω: pf.ptc.pass. ἐγκεκολαμμένος.ʃ

to engrave: + double acc., ἐγκολαπτὰ .. χερουβιν 3K 6.32; 6.35. Cf. κολάπτω, γλύφω.

ἐγκολλάω: fut. ~κολληθήσομαι.ʃ *(?)

to adjoin: + ἕως– ἐγκολληθήσεται φάραγξ ὀρέων ἕως Ιασολ 'the valley at the base of the mountains will join up with Jasol' Zc 14.5. Cf. προσκυρέω: Lee 1969.239.

ἔγκοπος, ον.ʃ

1. *wearied*: *s* hum., Is 43.23; ψυχή Jb 19.2.

2. *wearisome*: *s* λόγος 'matter' or 'discourse, discussion' Ec 1.8.

Cf. κόπος.

ἐγκοσμέω.ʃ

to adorn: metaph., pass., *o* hum., τῇ εὐσχημοσύνῃ 'with comliness' 4M 6.2.

ἐγκοτέω.ʃ

to bear a grudge: + dat. pers., ἐνεκότει Ησαυ τῷ Ιακωβ περὶ τῆς εὐλογίας Ge 27.41 (‖ θυμὸς καὶ ὀργή vs. 45); ἐν ὀργῇ ἐνεκότουν μοι Ps 54.4. Cf. ἐγκότημα, ἐνέχω, θυμόω, ὀργίζω.

ἐγκότημα, ατος.ʃ *

target of indignation: ἐγένετο Μωαβ εἰς γέλωτα καὶ ἐ. πᾶσι τοῖς κύκλῳ αὐτῆς 'M. became a laughing-stock and a butt of anger to all around her' Je 31.39. Cf. ἐγκοτέω.

ἐγκράτεια, ας. f.ʃ
self-control: ψυχῆς Si 18.30; 4M 5.34. Cf. ἐγκρατέω, ἀκρασία: Grundmann, *TDNT* 2.339-42.

ἐγκρατεύομαι: aor. ἐνεκρατευσάμην, inf. ~κρατεύσασθαι.ʃ
to pull oneself together to overcome emotions and passions: Ge 43.31, 1K 13.12 (on which last, see Rashi ad loc.); *to keep under control, restrain,* + dat., γλώσσῃ Si 19.6¶. Cf. Spicq 1.60-2. Cf. ἐγκράτεια.

ἐγκρατέω.ʃ
to hold on to without letting go of: + gen., Ex 9.2.

ἐγκρατής, ές.
1. *having possession of*: Si 6.27; + gen., τοῦ νόμου 15.1; of sth undesirable, 27.30.
2. *having control over*: + gen., ἐ. γίνομαι 'to overpower' Su 39 TH, To 6.4 𝔊II (+ ἐπιλαμβάνομαι), ὀχυρωμάτων 'citadels' 2M 10.15, τῆς πόλεως 13.13; ψυχῆς 'self-controlled' Si 26.15.

ἐγκρίς, ίδος. f.ʃ
kind of cake: ἐν μέλιτι 'with honey' Ex 16.31; ἐξ ἐλαίου Nu 11.8. Cf. πέμμα: LSG s.v.

ἐγκρούω: aor. ἐνέκρουσα, subj. ~κρούσω.ʃ
to hammer in: abs., (ἐν) τῷ πασσάλῳ 'with the (tent-)peg' Jd 16.13; + acc. rei, πάσσαλον 4.21 Ra (A: τίθημι, B: πήγνυμι). Cf. κρούω, κατακρούω.

ἐγκρύπτω: fut. ἐγκρύψω; aor. ἐνέκρυψα, subj.pass. ἐγκρυβῶ; pf.pass.3s ἐγκέκρυπται, ptc.pass. ἐγκεκρυμμένος.
to conceal, put out of view: + acc. pers., 1M 16.15; pass. ἐγκεκρυμμένη ἡ ἁμαρτία αὐτοῦ 'his sin is concealed' Ho 13.12; ***o*** gold plate, ἐν τῇ γῇ ἐν τῇ σκηνῇ μου Jo 7.21. Cf. κρύπτω.

ἐγκρυφίας, ου. m.
cake baked in ashes of coal fire (Schleusner): ἀζύμους 'unleavened' Ex 12.39; οὐ μεταστρεφόμενος 'not turned' Ho 7.8; ποιέω ἐ. Ge 18.6, Nu 11.8; κρίθινον 'made of barley' Ez 4.12. Cf. ἐγκρίς, πέμμα.

ἐγκτάομαι.ʃ
to acquire landed property in a foreign land *and settle* there: ἐγκτᾶσθε ἐν ^τῇ γῇ^ Ge 34.10. Cf. ἔγκτητος, κτάομαι: Renehan 1.75.

ἔγκτησις, εως. f.ʃ
cost for tenure of land: πληθύνῃ τὴν ~ιν αὐτοῦ .. ἐλαττονώσῃ τὴν ~ιν αὐτοῦ 'raises the cost of its tenure .. lowers ..' Le 25.16.

ἔγκτητος, ον.* n.ʃ
acquired: ***s*** unspecified, τὰ κτήνη .. ἔγκτητα .. δύναμιν Nu 31.9; person, ψυχή Le 22.11; γῆ in a foreign country, ἐν ταῖς οἰκίαις τῆς γῆς τῆς ~ου ὑμῖν Le 14.34. Cf. ἐγκτάομαι.

ἐγκύκλιος, ον.ʃ
to be sent round: ***s*** letter, Da 4.34b LXX.

ἐγκυλίω: fut.pass. ~κυλισθήσομαι; aor.pass. ἐνεκυλίσθην, subj. ~κυλισθῶ.ʃ
to make entry so as to engage oneself in some activity: metaph., ***s*** sinful intention, Si 37.3; *to get involved* in, ἐν ἁμαρτίαις 23.12; + dat. rei, ἔρωτι 'sensuous love' Pr 7.18.

ἔγκυος, ον.ʃ
pregnant: Si 42.10. Cf. συλλαμβάνω.

ἐγκύπτω: aor.ptc. ~κύψας.ʃ
to stoop down and peep in: εἰς τὸν λάκκον 'into the den' Bel LXX (TH ἐμβλέπω). Cf. βλέπω.

ἐγκωμιάζω.
to eulogise: τινα Pr 12.8 (:: μυκτηρίζω 'sneer'), ‖ καυχάομαι 'to brag' 27.2. Cf. ἐγκώμιον, αἰνέω.

ἐγκώμιον, ου. n.ʃ
eulogy: about hum. deeds, Es 2.23 o', Pr 10.7. Cf. ἐγκωμιάζω.

ἐγρήγορος, ον.ʃ
vigilant without sleeping: ἐπὶ τῆς κοίτης μου 'on my bed' Da 4.10 TH v.l.; subst., La 4.14. Cf. γρηγορέω.

ἐγχάσκω: pf. ἐγκέχηνα.ʃ
to long intensely (*for* εἰς): ***o*** beautiful woman, 1E 4.19. On the prep. εἰς, see its collocation with χάσκω in Philostratus, *VA* 2.7. Cf. χαίνω.

ἐγχειρέω: aor. ἐνεχείρησα.ʃ
1. *to attempt* to undertake: abs. Je 28.12; + acc. rei, λόγον 'deliberate' 18.22; temple services, 2C 23.18.
2. *to lay hands on, attack*: + dat. pers., Je 29.17.
Cf. ἐγχείρημα, ἐγχειρίζω, ἐπιχειρέω, πειράζω.

ἐγχείρημα, ατος. n.ʃ
that which is attempted: ἐ. καρδίας Je 23.20 ‖ 37.24. Cf. ἐγχειρέω.

ἐγχειρίδιον, ου. n.
1. *hand-weapon*: τόξον καὶ ἐ. Je 27.42 (‖ ζιβύνη 6.23); ‖ πέλεκυς 'battle-axe' Ep Je 14 (held in the right hand); ἐκσπάσω τὸ ἐ. μου ἐκ τοῦ κολεοῦ αὐτοῦ 'I shall draw .. out of its sheath' Ez 21.3.
2. *stone-cutting implement*: ἐ. ἐπιβέβληκας ἐπ' αὐτό [= θυσιαστήριον] Ex 20.25.
Cf. μάχαιρα, ξίφος, ῥομφαία: Caird 1968.465; LSG s.v.

ἐγχειρίζω: aor. ἐνεχείρισα.ʃ
to entrust: + dat.pers. and acc., τὰ κατὰ τὴν βασιλείαν 'the affairs of the state' Es 7.17 *L*, + inf. 7.33 *L*. Cf. ἐγχειρέω.

ἐγχέω: aor. ἐνέχεα, impv. ἔγχεον.
to pour in: abs. ἐξ ἀγγείου εἰς ἀγγεῖον 'from a vessel ..' Je 31.11; + acc. rei, τὸ ἥμισυ τοῦ αἵματος ἐνέχεεν εἰς κρατῆρας 'he poured half of the blood into bowls' Ex 24.6, ὕδωρ εἰς ^τὸν λέβητα 'the claudron'^ Ez 24.3, ζωμὸν εἰς χύτραν 'sauce into a pot' Jd 6.19A (B: βάλλω;:: ἐκχέω vs. 20); ***o*** liquid food, ἕψεμα 'pottage' 4K 4.40, 41; olive-oil, 4.5 *L* (B: ἐπι~). Cf. ἐκ~, χέω.

ἐγχρίω: impf.3pl ἐνεχρίοσαν; aor.inf.act. ~χρῖσαι, impv. ~χρισον, subj.mid. ~χρίσωμαι.ʃ

to anoint, smear: + acc. (part of sbd else's body), ἀνθρώπου ὀφθαλμούς To 6.9 𝔊II; + acc.pers. (other than *s*), ἄνθρωπον To 6.9 𝔊I; + acc. (substance), τὴν χολὴν εἰς τοὺς ὀφθαλμοὺς αὐτοῦ 'the gall (of a fish) ..' 11.8 𝔊I (𝔊II ἐμπάσσω 'sprinkle in'); + double acc., με τὰ φάρμακα 'applied the medicaments to me' To 2.10 𝔊II; mid., + acc. (part of one's own body), στίβει τοὺς ὀφθαλμούς σου 'your eyes with kohl' Je 4.30. Cf. χρίω.

ἐγχρονίζω: aor.subj. ~χρονίσω.ʃ

to remain a long time: ἐν τῷ τόπῳ Pr 9.18, ἐν οἴνοις 23.30; *s* εὐφροσύνη 'delight' 10.28 (:: ὄλλυμαι 'to perish').

ἐγχώριος, ον.

indigenous: δόμος ξύλινος ~ος 'a course of native timber' 1E 6.24. **b.** subst. *local inhabitant*: τὰς θυγατέρας τῶν ~ίων Ge 34.1; opp. προσήλυτος Ex 12.49, Le 18.26, 24.22, Nu 15.29.

Cf. αὐτόχθων, ἀλλότριος, προσήλυτος: Harl 2001.889.

ἐγώ; ἐμοῦ, μου; ἐμοί, μοι; ἐμέ, με.

Speaker's reference to himself or herself: 'I,' 'my,' 'me.'

I. 1. The nominative ἐγώ may be added to a finite verb for the sake of contrast: ἐγὼ δὲ .. θύσω σοι Jn 2.10; ἐγὼ ἐλάλησα πρὸς σέ 3.2; καὶ ἐγώ 'I in turn' Ma 2.9.

***2.** Often it is a mechanical rendition of the underlying Hebrew structure in which the use of /'ăni/ or / 'ānōḇi/ is grammatically conditioned, thus adding no emphasis: with εἶναι - ἐγώ εἰμι μεθ' ὑμῶν Hg 1.13, cp., in the reverse order (same word-order in the Heb.), μεθ' ὑμῶν ἐγώ εἰμι 2.4; with other verbs (corresponding to the Heb. participle), ἔγνωκα ἐγὼ .. (MT: /yōdēaʿ 'ānōḇi/; often following ἰδού and followed by pres. (= Heb. ptc.), ἰδοὺ ἐγὼ ἐξεγείρω .. Hb 1.6. Cf. Deissmann 1923.108-15; Mayser, II 1.63, and BDF, § 277. **b.** ἐγώ εἰμι as a rendering of / 'ānōḇi/ typical of the Kaige-Theodotionic recension: ἐγώ εἰμι ἔχρισά σε [= /'ānōḇi mšaḥtiḇā/] 2K 12.7B, ἐγώ εἰμι λαλήσω [= /'ānōḇi 'ădabbēr/] Jb 33.31¶; Jd 6.18.

II. In the oblique cases, **1.** the free-standing (i.e. not following a prep.) accusative ἐμέ is emphatic: ἐμὲ ὑμεῖς πτερνίζετε Ma 3.9 (in an emotionally charged accusation with finger-pointing). Likewise ἐμοί: Ἐπειδὴ ἐμοὶ οὐκ ἔδωκας σπέρμα .. Ge 15.3 (with an accusing tone); repeated after μοι earlier in the clause, 25.31.

2. However, with prepositions (excepting πρός as in πρός με Ge 4.10)), the ἐ-forms are the norm: ἀνὰ μέσον ἐμοῦ καὶ ὑμῶν 'between me and you' Ge 9.12; ἀπ' ἐμοῦ Jn 2.8; ἐνώπιον ἐμοῦ Hg 2.14 (v.l. μου); κατ' ἐμοῦ Ho 7.13; πλὴν ἐμοῦ 13.4; πάρεξ ἐμοῦ 13.4. On the distribution of the ἐ- forms and the shorter, enclitic forms, see, Mayser I-2.62f. and Katz, 101.

ἐδαφίζω: fut.act. ἐδαφιῶ, pass. ~φισθήσομαι; aor. ἠδάφισα.ʃ

to dash to the ground: + acc. pers., Ez 31.12; τὰ νήπια αὐτῆς ἐδαφιοῦσιν ἐπ' ἀρχὰς πασῶν τῶν ὁδῶν αὐτῆς 'they will dash its infants at the top of all its streets' Na 3.10; εἰς τὴν γῆν Is 3.26; πρὸς τὴν πέτραν Ps 136.9; μητέρα ἐπὶ τέκνοις 'mother along with her children' Ho 10.14; ὑποτίτθια 'sucklings' 14.1.

ἔδαφος, ους. n.

1. *ground*: καταβήσεται ἕως τοῦ ἐδάφους '(the wall) will be razed to the ground' Is 25.12, ὁ ναὸς .. ἐγενήθη εἰς ἔ. Ju 5.18; for pedestrians, 'pavement, walking path' Si 20.18; opp. θαλάσση Jb 9.8; the origin of human beings, Si 36.10 (‖ γῆ).

2. *the lowest part*: τῆς γῆς 'of the earth' Je 38.35, τοῦ λάκκου Da 6.24 TH. **b.** *floor* of the interior of a building: 3K 6.15, Ez 41.16, cf. σκηνῆς Nu 5.17.

Cf. γῆ: Schmidt 3.67.

ἔδεσμα, ατος. n. Alw. pl.

cooked food, 'meal': ποίησόν μοι ~ατα Ge 27.4; ἔδωκε τὰ ~ατα καὶ τοὺς ἄρτους 27.17; Pr 23.3 (‖ βρώματα vs. 6). Cf. ἐσθίω, βρῶμα, χόρτασμα.

ἕδρα, ας. f.

pl. **buttock*: affected by hemorroids, De 28.27; 1K 5.3, cf. *BA* 9.1, 96f. **b.** as object of pagan worship: 1K 5.9; golden, 5.10*L*.

Cf. Lust 1992.

ἑδράζω: fut. ἑδράσω; aor.inf.pass. ἑδρασθῆναι; pf. ptc.pass. ἡδρασμένος.ʃ

to position firmly: ***o*** mountains, Pr 8.25 (at the creation), ἀσφαλῆ βάσιν 'secure foundation' Wi 4.3. **b.** metaph., καρδία ἡδρασμένη ἐπὶ διανοίας 'a mind rooted in thought' Si 22.17. Cf. ἐμπήγνυμι.

ἐθελοκωφέω.ʃ *

to pretend to be deaf: Si 19.27. Cf. κωφός.

ἐθίζω: aor.subj. ἐθίσω; pf.ptc.pass. εἰθισμένος.ʃ

to accustom: + dat. and acc., ὅρκῳ .. τὸ στόμα μου Si 23.9; εἰθισμένη ἀπάντησις 'customary meeting' 2M 14.30. Cf. ἐθισμός, συνεθίζω. Del. Si 23.13 v.l.

ἐθισμός, οῦ. m.

that which is customary: τὰ καθ' ~ὸν τῶν γυναικῶν 'the women's usual thing, i.e. menstruation' Ge 31.35; customary habit, Si 23.14; παράνομος 'unlawful' 2M 4.11. Cf. ἔθω, ἐθίζω, ἔθος, ἦθος, νόμιμος **2**, and τρόπος **1**.

ἐθνάρχης, ου. m.ʃ

ethnarch: 1M 14.47, 15.1, 2. Cf. ἄρχων.

ἐθνηδόν. adv.ʃ *

dealing with the nation as a whole: ἀποσφάζω 'by way of genocide' 4M 2.19. Cf. ἔθνος.

ἐθνοπάτωρ, τορος.ʃ *

father of the nation: 4M 16.20.

ἐθνόπληθος, ους. n.ʃ *

large crowd: 4M 7.11. Cf. πλῆθος.

ἔθνος, ους. n.

body of people associated together sharing cultural, religious, linguistic features: **a**. sg., w. ref. to Israel, ἔσται εἰς ἔ. μέγα καὶ πολύ Ge 18.18; ἔ. ἅγιον Ex 19.6; λαὸς σοφὸς καὶ ἐπιστήμων τὸ ἔ. τὸ μέγα τοῦτο 'this populous crowd is a wise and intelligent people' De 4.6; οἱ κατάλοιποι τοῦ ~ους μου 'the remainder of my people' Zp 2.9; Ma 3.9, Zp 2.1; ǁ λαός Ge 25.23, Is 1.4, Ez 36.15; w. ref. to a specific (non-Israelite) ethnic group, Ex 1.9 (ǁ λαός vs. 22); τοὺς Χαλδαίους .. τὸ ἔ. τὸ πικρόν Hb 1.6; τὸ ἔ. τῶν Ἰουδαίων 1M 8.23 (said by non-Israelites; ǁ δῆμος vs. 29). **b**. sg. w. generic reference: παντὶ ἔθνει ἐπὶ τῆς γῆς Da 9.6 LXX (TH πρὸς πάντα τὸν λαὸν τῆς γῆς). **c**. pl. and usually large in number – note the frequent addition of πολλά as in ἔθνη μεγάλα καὶ πολλά De 7.1, ἔθνη πολλὰ καὶ ἰσχυρότερα ὑμῶν ib., ἔθνη πολλά Hb 2.8; grouped by language, ἐκ πασῶν γλωσσῶν τῶν ~ῶν Zc 8.23; not excluding Israel, πάντα τὰ ~η τῆς γῆς Ge 18.18, De 28.10, συσσείσω πάντα τὰ ~η 'I shall shake all the nations' Hg 2.7; opp. to Israel, 'gentiles', Ex 15.14; τὸ ὑπόλειμμα τοῦ Ιακωβ ἐν τοῖς ~εσιν ἐν μέσῳ λαῶν πολλῶν Mi 5.7; μακαριοῦσιν ὑμᾶς πάντα τὰ ~η 'all the nations will declare you to be happy' Ma 3.12; τὰ νόμιμα τῶν ~ῶν μάταια Je 10.3; 1M 1.14. Often ǁ or synonymous with λαός – οἱ κατάλοιποι λαοῦ μου .. οἱ κατάλοιποι ~ους μου Zp 2.9; Οὕτως ὁ λαὸς οὗτος καὶ οὕτως τὸ ~ος τοῦτο Hg 2.14; ἥξουσι λαοὶ πολλοὶ καὶ ~η πολλά Zc 8.22; 12.3*d*; πάντα τὰ ~η .. πάντας τοὺς λαούς Hb 2.5; 2.8; but prob. distinct from λαός at λαός σου τὸ ~ος τοῦτο Ex 33.13, see also De 7.6 (God does not refer to Israel as "my ἔθνος"); ǁ φυλή– πᾶσαι φυλαὶ τῆς γῆς Ge 12.3, 18.18, 22.18, 26.4, Ez 20.32, cf. λαοὶ ~ῶν 'large groups of gentiles' PSol 17.30.

Cf. γένος, δῆμος, λαός, φυλή, ἐθνηδόν, πανεθνεί: Schmidt 4.570-2; Trench 367f.; Nestle 1895; Bertram, *TDNT* 2.364-9; Jones 1996; Harl, *Langue*, 132.

ἔθος, ους. n.

= ἐθισμός: ἀσεβὲς ἔ. ὡς νόμος 'ungodly custom ..' Wi 14.16 (ǁ νόμος); κατὰ τὸ ἔ. αὐτῶν Bel 15 TH, ὡς ἔ. ἐστι 'as is customary' 1M 10.89, πατριὰ ~η 'ancestral customs' 4M 18.5. Cf. ἐθισμός: Spicq 1.405-11.

ἔθω: pf. (used as pres.) εἴωθα, ptc. εἰωθώς; plpf.3s εἰώθει.

to be accustomed to do (inf.): κατὰ τὸ εἰωθός 'as he was wont (to do)' Nu 24.1; καθὼς εἰώθει 1K 20.25*L*; Su 13 LXX; Si 37.14. Cf. ἐθισμός, ἔθος.

εἰ

1. Conditional particle, 'if': **a**. εἰ + ind., apod. with ἄν + aor.ind. marking a contrary-to-fact supposition, Ge 43.10(*c*), Nu 16.14(*d*), 22.29(*g*), Ob 5*bis*(*b*); without ἄν, 2M 4.47, 5.18; apod. with ἄν + impf., Ba 3.13. **b**. εἰ + ind. — ind., Zc 8.6(-), 11.12(*b*), Ma 1.6*bis*(*b*), 2M 5.18; εἰ + ind. — impv., Ge 15.5(*b*). The εἰ in Mi 6.8(-) is rather suspect; as it stands, the text makes no good sense, and the only Father that does have it in his lemma, Cyr, does not presuppose it in his exposition; on the contrary, he contradicts, οἶσθα ποῦ τὸ ἀγαθὸν θέλημα τοῦ θεοῦ (ed. Pusey, 1.700). Its equivalent is wanting in MT, but present in Eth. **c**. εἰ + opt.: ὡς εἴ τις λαλήσαι πρὸς τὸν ἑαυτοῦ φίλον 'as one might speak to one's own friend' Ex 33.11(*e*); De 1.31(*e*), 44(*e*), 8.5(*e*), 4M 5.19. **d**. apodosis understood: Jo 7.7(*d*), Da 3.15 LXX(*h*). **e**. elliptically: εἰ δὲ μή 'otherwise' Ge 42.16(*a*), Nu 20.18(*f*).

2. presents one's inference as an argument for an action to be undertaken, *seeing*: εἰ μή σοι ἀρέσκει 'since it does not appear to please you' Nu 22.34(*b*).

3. introduces: ***a**. direct question, Ge 3.11(*a*), 17.17a(*a*), b(*a*+*b*), 24.23 (or indir. question) (*a*), 44.19(*a*), Ex 2.14(*a*), Am 3.3(*a*), 4(*a*)*bis*, 5(*a*)*bis*, 6(*b*)*bis*, 6.10(*a*), 12(*a*)*bis*, Mi 2.7(*b*), 6.6(*a*), 7(*a*)*bis*, 11(*a*), Zc 7.3(*a*), Ma 1.9(*a*), 13(*a*), 3.8(*a*), Jn 3.9(-), 4.4(*a*), 9(*a*), Hg 1.4(*a*), 2.12(*a*), 13(*a*), Je 16.20(*a*), Da 3.14 TH(*a*), 10.20 TH(*a*); **b**. indirect question, 'whether': ὄψομαι εἰ .. εἰ δὲ μή 'I shall see whether .. or not' Ge 18.21(*a*, *b*); τοῦ γνῶναι εἰ .. ἢ οὔ 'in order to find out whether .. or not' 24.21(*a*), cf. 42.16(*a*); θέσθε ἐν ταῖς καρδίαις ὑμῶν, εἰ .. 'consider whether ..' Hg 2.19(*a*)*bis*; Am 6.2(*b*); σκέψομαι Zc 11.13(*a*); Ma 1.8(*a*)*bis*. Cf. *ND* 5.57f., 6.183.

***4**. Hebraism in strong negation after verbs of swearing: ὀμνύει .. εἰ ἐπιλησθήσεται Am 8.7(*b*); swearing implied, Ge 14.23(*b*); Ζῶ ἐγώ .. εἰ .. Nu 14.28-30(*b*); De 1.35(*b*), Ez 16.48(*b*). See under ἐάν, **III b**.

5. εἰ γάρ marking an intense wish. **a**. + opt.: εἰ γὰρ δῴη καὶ ἔλθοι μου ἡ αἴτησις 'O that he would grant that my desire be realised' Jb 6.8(-). **b**. reinforced by ὄφελον (q.v.) foll. by an aor.: εἰ γὰρ ὄφελον ἐν ᾅδῃ με ἐφύλαξας 'O that you would preserve me in Hades' Jb 14.13(-); foll. by an opt.: εἰ γὰρ ὄφελον δυναίμην .. 30.24(-).

6. εἰ .. ἢ marks a range of choices: εἰ μὲν ἀπὸ τῶν βοῶν ἢ ἀπὸ τῶν προβάτων 'whether one of the oxen or one of the sheep' Nu 15.3(-).

7. εἰ μή 'unless': Εἰ μὴ αὐτὸς σὺ πορεύῃ 'unless you yourself go' Ex 33.15(*b*); εἰ μὴ δι' ὀργὴν ἐχθρῶν 'were it not for the enemies' wrath' De 32.27(*c*); εἰ μὴ ὁ θεὸς ἀπέδοτο αὐτούς 'unless God had delivered them' 32.30(*b*). ***b**. εἰ μὴ ὅτι, introducing an unreal condition, *except that*∫: εἰ μὴ ὅτι ὁ νόμος σου μελέτη μού ἐστιν, τότε ἂν ἀπωλόμην .. 'unless your law were my concern, I would then have perished ..' Ps 118.92 (*i*), εἰ μὴ ὅτι κύριος ἦν ἐν ἡμῖν, .. ἄρα ζῶντας ἂν κατέπιον ἡμᾶς 'unless the Lord had been amongst us, .. they would surely have swallowed us alive' 123.1-3 (*i*); with no ἄν in the apodosis, but παρὰ βραχύ 'nearly' 93.17 (*i*). ***c**. ὅτι εἴ μη 'except for': ὅτι εἰ μὴ τοῦ φαγεῖν 'except eating' Ec 8.15 (*j*); 3K 17.1 (*L* ὅτι ἐάν μη) (*j*), cf. ἀλλ' ἤ, πλήν.

Cf. ἐάν.

a) -הֲ; *b*) אִם; *c*) εἰ μή לוּלֵא, לוּלֵי [+ Nu 22.33 MT *'wly*]; *d*) לוּ; *e*) ὡς εἰ כַּאֲשֶׁר; *f*) εἰ δὲ μή פֶּן; *g*) כִּי; *h*) Arm. הֵן; *i*) εἰ μὴ ὅτι לוּלֵי; *j*) ὅτι εἰ μή כִּי אם.x∫

εἶ: ⇒ ἤ.

εἶβις. ⇒ ἶβις.

εἰδέα. ⇒ ἰδέα.

εἰδέναι. ⇒ οἶδα.

εἰδέχθεια, ας. f.∫ *

odious, ugly look: Wi 16.3.

εἴδησις, εως. f.∫

knowledge: ***o*** of γινώσκω, Si 42.18. Cf. γνῶσις.

εἶδον (aor.): 3pl. εἶδον, εἴδοσαν, subj. ἴδω, inf. ἰδεῖν, ptc. ἰδών, impv. ἴδε; opt. ἴδοιμι, ἴδοις, ἴδοι. For the present, ὁράω is used.

1. *to perceive visually, notice*: abs. Ho 9.13; + acc., τὴν γύμνωσιν τοῦ πατρὸς αὐτοῦ 'the nakedness of his father' Ge 9.22, 23; τὴν νόσον .. τὴν ὀδύνην Ho 5.13; 6.10, Jn 3.10, Hg 2.3 (‖ βλέπω); ἐνύπνιον Ge 37.9 (‖ ἐνυπνιάζω), 41.1; of a prophetic message seen in a vision (?), λόγοι Αμως .. οὓς εἶδεν ὑπὲρ Ιερουσαλημ Am 1.1, sim. Mi 1.1, Hb 1.1 (λῆμμα); + acc. and ptc., τὸν Ισαακ παίζοντα Ge 26.8, ἐν τῷ ἰδεῖν αὐτὸν μὴ ὂν τὸ παιδάριον μεθ' ἡμῶν 'on his seeing that the child is not with us' 44.31, ἰδοῦσα .. τὸν ἄγγελον θεοῦ ἀνθεστηκότα ἐν τῇ ὁδῷ καὶ τὴν ῥομφαίαν ἐσπασμένην .. 'seeing God's angel having taken a hostile position and the sword drawn ..' Nu 22.23, εἶδον τὸν κύριον καθήμενον ἐπὶ θρόνου .. '.. seated on a throne' Is 6.1, κύριον .. τοῖς ὀφθαλμοῖς μου 6.5, συνηγμένα τὰ τέκνα σου 60.4, τὸν κύριον ἐφεστῶτα ἐπὶ τοῦ θυσιαστηρίου Am 9.1; Ex 23.5; + adj., ἰδόντες αὐτὸ ἀστεῖον 'seeing that he was charming' Ex 2.2; + ptc., ἴδε συνηγμένα τὰ τέκνα σου Is 60.4; + abs. gen., εἶδον .. ἐμοῦ ὄντος ἐν Σούσοις 'I saw .. myself being in Susa' Da 8.2 LXX; + adj., τὰς τραπέζας κενάς Bel 18 LXX. **b**. obj. understood: ἰδὼν δὲ Λωτ ἐξανέστη 'Lot, having spotted them, stood up' Ge 19.1, sim. 18.2.

2. *to observe, watch, behold attentively*: abs., impv. Ge 39.14, Am 6.2, Hb 1.5; ἀρεστὸν τοῖς ὀφθαλμοῖς ἰδεῖν Ge 3.6; οὐ μὴ ἴδω τὸν θάνατον τοῦ παιδίου μου 21.16; τὸ πρόσωπον Λαβαν 31.2; ***o*** τὸ πρόσωπόν τινος 'to meet him' Ge 43.3 (‖ εἶδον 44.23); ἴδετε θαυμαστά Am 3.9; "I lifted my eyes, and looked around, and behold! .." Zc 1.18, sim. 2.1, 5.1, 9; + acc. pers., Ge 12.12; + acc. rei, Hb 3.7, Zc 2.2; + interr. cl., Ge 2.19; + ptc., ἰδοῦσα δὲ Σάρρα τὸν υἱὸν Αγαρ .. παίζοντα μετὰ Ισαακ 'S., having watched Hagar's son .. playing with Isaac' Ge 21.9 (possibly sense **1**.); Jb 3.9. **b**. + ἔν marking sustained interest and concern: ἐν τῇ ταπεινώσει μου 2K 16.12 (*L* acc.), ἐν τῇ χρηστότητι τῶν ἐκλεκτῶν σου Ps 105.5, ἐν τῷ ζηλῶσαί με 4K10.16, ἐν τῷ βασιλεῖ Ct 3.11. **c**. What has been observed is given by a syndetic καί-clause: καὶ εἶδεν κύριος .. τὴν γῆν, καὶ ἦν κατεφθαρμένη .. Ge 6.12.

3. *to recognise* sth as having a certain quality, engaged in a certain activity or being in a certain state: + ὅτι– εἶδεν ὁ θεὸς ὅτι καλόν 'God saw that it was good' Ge 1.8; εἶδεν ὅτι ἐν γαστρὶ ἔχει '.. that she was with child' 16.4; ὡς σκοπὸν ἐν συκῇ πρόϊμον .. πατέρας αὐτῶν 'saw their fathers as comparable to an early watchman (?; see under σκοπός) in a figtree' Ho 9.10 (‖ εὑρίσκω); + an adjectival complement, σὲ εἶδον δίκαιον ἐναντίον μου Ge 7.1, sim. 4K 14.26; + a participial complement, Ἴδετε δή μοι ἄνδρα ὀρθῶς (*L* ἀγαθῶς) ψάλλοντα 'Do spot someone who performs music well' 1K 16.17. **b**. With an obj. of observation in the acc. foll. by a ὅτι-clause indicating the contents of the observation: ἰδόντες οἱ υἱοὶ τοῦ θεοῦ τὰς θυγατέρας τῶν ἀνθρώπων ὅτι καλαί εἰσιν Ge 6.2; ἰδόντες .. τὴν γυναῖκα ὅτι καλὴ ἦν σφόδρα 12.14; ἰδὼν Μωυσῆς τὸν λαὸν ὅτι διεσκέδασται '.. were scattered' Ex 32.25; 34.35.

4. *to find out by observation*: ἴδε εἰ ὑγιαίνουσιν οἱ ἀδελφοί σου 'Find out whether your brothers are all right' Ge 37.14; also foll. by an indirect question, τοῦ ἰδεῖν τί λαλήσει Hb 2.1; Zc 5.5.

5. *to note mentally by observation and reflection*: abs., 2K 12.19*L* (B: συνίημι), Ge 18.2b (cf. Rashi ad loc.); + acc. rei, μου .. τὴν ταπείνωσιν 'my degradation' 29.32, τὴν κάκωσιν τοῦ λαοῦ μου Ex 3.7; αὐτῶν τὴν θλῖψιν 4.31 (*s* God), οὐκ ἐνεβλέψατε εἰς τὸν ἀπ' ἀρχῆς ποιήσαντα αὐτὴν καὶ τὸν κτίσαντα αὐτὴν οὐκ εἴδετε Is 22.11; φωνήν Ez 3.13, cf. Ex 20.18; + ὅτι – Εἶδεν Ησαυ ὅτι εὐλόγησεν Ισαακ τὸν Ιακωβ καὶ ἀπῴχετο .. καὶ ἐνετείλατο .. Ge 28.6; εἶδεν Ησαυ ὅτι πονηραί εἰσιν αἱ θυγατέρες Χαναaν 28.8; 29.31, 30.1; 37.4; ἰδὼν τὴν ἀνάπαυσιν ὅτι καλή, καὶ τὴν γῆν ὅτι πίων 49.15; De 5.24; following visual perception, Is 6.9; *s* God's face, Ps 10.7.

6. *to experience*: + acc. rei, κάκωσιν 'maltreatment' Nu 11.15; οἱ νεκροὶ ζωὴν οὐ μὴ ἴδωσιν Is 26.14, τὰ ἀγαθὰ κυρίου Ps 26.13, διαφθοράν 15.10.

7. indeclinable ἴδε, drawing attention to an important statement or situation: To 2.2𝔊II, Si 28.24

Cf. ἀπ~, εἰσ~, ἐπ~, προ~, ὑπερεῖδον, βλέπω, εἰσ~, ἐμβλέπω, ὁράω, ἰδού: Michaelis, *TDNT* 5.329f.

εἶδος, ους. n.

1. *form, shape*: καλὴ τῷ ~ει καὶ ὡραία τῇ ὄψει 'comely and good-looking' Ge 29.17 (*s* woman); καλὸς τῷ ~ει καὶ ὡραῖος τῇ ὄψει 39.6 (*s* man); καλαὶ τῷ εἴδει 41.2 (*s* cattle and:: αἰσχραὶ τῷ ~ει vs. 3); θεοῦ 32.30; ὥσπερ εἶ. στερεώματος τοῦ οὐρανοῦ 'like the firmament of the sky' Ex 24.10. **b**. *attractive look*: ‖ δόξα Is 52.14, 53.2; ‖ κάλλος 53.2.

2. *that which looks like*: εἶ. πυρός 'something like fire' Nu 9.16 (‖ ὡς εἶδος πυρός vs. 15).

3. *visible form*: ἐν ~ει καὶ οὐ δι' αἰνιγμάτων '(speak) looking each other in the eye and not through riddles' Nu 12.8, φόβου 'frightening' Jb 33.16.

4. *external appearance*: La 4.8.

5. *sort, kind*: Je 15.3, Si 23.16.

Cf. ἰδέα, μορφή, ὄψις: Schmidt 4.346-8.

εἰδωλεῖον / εἰδώλιον, ου. n.*

idol's or *idols' temple*: 1E 2.9 (‖ οἶκος θεοῦ 2E 1.7); + βωμοί, τεμένη 1M 1.47.

εἰδωλόθυτος, ον.ʃ *

offered to pagan idols: s.n., κρέα 'meat' understood, 4M 5.2. Cf. Witherington.

εἴδωλον, ου. n. Often in the pl.

manually crafted object of worship: kept in a private home, Ge 31.19 (called θεοί vs. 30); made from precious metal, τὸ ἀργύριον αὐτῶν καὶ τὸ χρυσίον αὐτῶν ἐποίησαν ἑαυτοῖς ~α Ho 8.4; molten (χώνευμα), 13.2 (condemned as sinful); χωνευτά Nu 33.52 (‖ σκοπιαί 'high-places,' στῆλαι 'stelae'); ‖ γλυπτά Mi 1.7 (to be destroyed by God), Is 10.11; ἐξολεθρεύσω τὰ ὀνόματα τῶν ~ων ἀπὸ τῆς γῆς Zc 13.2; dumb (κωφός) Hb 2.18; προσεκύνησαν τοῖς ~οις Nu 25.2; τὰ ~α αὐτῶν, ξύλον καὶ λίθον, ἀργύριον καὶ χρυσίον De 29.17; 1C 16.26 (‖ Ps 95.5 δαιμόνιον). Cf. ἄγαλμα, γλυπτός, εἰκών, θεός, χώνευμα.

εἴθε.ʃ

optative particle, 'would that .., I wish that ..': + impf., Jb 9.33.

εἰκάζω: aor.inf. εἰκάσαι, subj.pass. εἰκασθῶ.

to make an inference about: pass., οὐ μὴ εἰκασθῇ 'it is unfathomable' Je 26.23; + acc., τὰ μέλλοντα εἰκάζει 'infers things to come' Wi 8.8 (:: οἶδα), ἀκριβῶς 'accurately' 19.18.

εἰκάς. num. gen. ~δος.

the twentieth day of a month: ἑβδόμῃ καὶ εἰκάδι τοῦ μηνός 'on the 27th of the month' Ge 8.4, Hg 2.1. Cf. εἴκοσι.

εἰκῇ. adv.ʃ

with no purpose in view, capriciously: to judge, Pr 28.25 (:: ἐν ἐπιμελείᾳ 'considerate').

εἰκοσαετής, ές.

of twenty years: subst. and of age, ἀπὸ ~τοῦς καὶ ἐπάνω 'from twelve years old and above' Ex 30.14, 2E 3.8.

εἴκοσι. indeclinable num.

twenty: εἴ. ἔτη 'twenty years' Ge 31.38; ἐννέα καὶ εἴκοσι 'twenty-nine' Ex 39.1. Cf. εἰκάς.

εἰκοστός, ή, όν.

twentieth in order: Ex 29.17.

εἰκότως. adv.ʃ

in a manner conforming to what appears to be right and sensible: αἰσχυνόμεθα .. εἰ. 'it is right that we should be ashamed ..' 4M 9.2. Cf. LSG s.v.

εἴκω: aor. εἶξα, inf. εἶξαι. See also under ἔοικα.ʃ

to give way to, 'yield, cede': out of fear, τινι Wi 18.25, 4M 1.6. Cf. συν~, ὑπείκω.

εἰκών, όνος. f.

1. *likeness*, 'image': Ποιήσωμεν ἄνθρωπον κατ' ~όνα ἡμετέραν 'Let us make man according to our own image' Ge 1.26, sim. Si 17.3; κατὰ τὴν ἰδέαν αὐτοῦ καὶ κατὰ τὴν ~όνα αὐτοῦ Ge 5.3; ἐν ~όνι θεοῦ ἐποίησα τὸν ἄνθρωπον 9.6; κατ' ~όνα εἰδώλων 'so that it will resemble idols' Ho 13.2; ἐν ~όνι 'as a phantom' Ps 38.7.

2. *sth made in resemblance of sth else*: ὁ θεὸς ἔκτισεν τὸν ἄνθρωπον .. καὶ ~όνα τῆς ἰδιότητος ἐποίησεν αὐτόν Wi 2.23. **b**. as object of worship, and ‖ γλυπτὸν ὁμοίωμα De 4.16; βδελυγμάτων Ez 7.20, ἐποίησεν ~όνα χρυσῆν Da 3.1. **c**. *statue*: ~νας ἀρσενικάς Ez 16.17; Da 2.31. **d**. *painting, drawing*: ἄνδρας .. ἐπὶ τοῦ τοίχου, ~ας Χαλδαίων, ἐζωγραφημένους ἐν γραφίδι 'men .. on the wall, drawings of Chaldaeans, painted with a stylus' Ez 23.14.

Cf. εἴδωλον, μορφή, ὁμοίωμα, ὁμοίωσις: Trench 49-53; Spicq 1.412-9; Koonge.

εἰλέω: aor. εἴλησα; pf.mid./pass.ptc. εἰλημένος.ʃ

1. *to place securely*: pass., ***o*** sword, ἐν ἱματίῳ 1K 21.10*L* (B: ἐνειλέω).

2. *to bind fast*: + acc., ^μηλωτήν^ 'goat-skin mantle' 4K 2.8; fig. and + dat. and acc. (part of one's own body), ἀληθείᾳ εἰλημένος τὰς πλευράς 'having fastened his sides with truth' Is 11.5 (‖ ζώννυμι).

εἰλικρινής, ές.ʃ

not containing any foreign element, 'pure': *s* emanation of divine glory, Wi 7.25. Cf. καθαρός: Spicq 1.420-3.

εἰμί: pres.ptc. ὤν, inf. εἶναι, impv.2s ἴσθι, 3s ἔστω / ἤτω, pl. ἔστωσαν; fut. ἔσομαι, ptc. ἐσόμενος, inf. ἔσεσθαι; impf. ἤμην, ἦτε; subj. ὦ; opt.3s εἴη.

1. *to exist, be present*, with or without indication of location: Οὐκ ἔστιν θεός .. οὐκ ἔστιν ποιῶν ἀγαθόν Ps 52.2; ἐκεῖ οὗ ἐστιν τὸ χρυσίον 'there where gold is' Ge 2.11; μὴ ἔστω μάχη 'Let there be no quarrel' 13.8; εἰ ἔστιν παρὰ τῷ πατρί σου τόπος ..; 'is there space at your father's ..?' 24.23; Ἔστιν κύριος ἐν τῷ τόπῳ τούτῳ 28.16; Ἐγώ εἰμι, καὶ οὐκ ἔστι μετ' ἐμὲ ἔτι 'I exist, and there is none beside me' Zp 3.1, τοῖς δαιμονίοις, ἃ οὐκ ἔστι 'to the demons who have no existence' Is 65.3; οὐκ ἔστι σύνεσις ἐν αὐτῷ 'he has no understanding' Ob 7; ἦν Ιωνας ἐν τῇ κοιλίᾳ τοῦ κήτους 'J. was in the belly of the big fish' Jn 2.1; ἔτι ὄντος μου ἐν τῇ γῇ μου 'whilst I was still in my country' 4.1; ἐγώ εἰμι μεθ' ὑμῶν 'I am with you' Hg 1.13; ‖ ὑπάρχω Zc 8.10; οὐκ ἔστι τοῦ εἶναι 'there is no way to survive' Is 14.31; ἐσόμεθα τοῦ σῶσαί σε 'we shall be there to rescue you' 2K 10.11 (*L* πορεύσομαι), hardly an error for an Epic., εἰσόμεθα (< εἶμι). **b**. Fut., *to emerge, make appearance*: ἔσται τὸ τόξον ἐν τῇ νεφέλῃ 'the (rain)bow shall appear in the cloud' Ge 9.16; ἀπὸ τοῦ λιμοῦ τοῦ ἐσομένου μετὰ ταῦτα 'because of the famine to come after that' 41.31; *to happen*, + dat. pers. and inf., μή μοι εἴη ἀποφῆναι 'Far be it from me to declare' Jb 27.5, sim. 34.10, cf. μὴ γένοιτο under γίνομαι **1**. **c**. ὁ ὤν: divine name, Ἐγώ εἰμι ὁ ὤν· .. ὁ ὢν ἀπέσταλκέν με πρὸς ὑμᾶς Ex 3.14; ὁ ὢν δέσποτα κύριε Je 1.6, 4.10, ὁ Ὢν κύριε 14.13. **d**. Impersonal with an inf., 'there is a possibility of ..ing, it is possible to ..': ἐν τόπῳ στενῷ, εἰς ὃν οὐκ ἦν ἐκκλῖναι δεξιὰν οὐδὲ ἀριστεράν 'a narrow spot in which it was not possible to turn right or left' Nu 22.26; Je 29.11, Ep Je 49, Ez 16.63, Si 14.16, 27.21; + dat. (see below **4**), οὐκ ἔστιν χαίρειν τοῖς ἀσεβέσιν 'the impious shall not be able to rejoice' Is 57.21 (‖ δύναμαι vs. 20); marks a necessity, οὐκ ἔστιν ἐπιζητῆσαι Si 40.26; 1E 1.4; marks an intention, οὐκ ἔστιν ἡμῖν θανατῶσαι ἄνδρα 2K 21.4*L*, cf. pers., ἐσόμεθα (*L* πορεύσομαι) τοῦ σῶσαί σε 'we shall be there to rescue you' 2K 10.11.

2. *to possess a certain characteristic, to be identical with* (so-called copula): its use is usually obligatory in all non-present tenses, σὺ ἦς ὡς εἷς ἐξ αὐτῶν Ob 11; τίς σου ἡ ἐργασία ἐστί; .. ἐκ ποίου λαοῦ εἶ σύ; 'what is your occupation? .. which people are you from?' Jn 1.8; ὁ οἶκός μού ἐστιν ἔρημος Hg 1.9; the copula may be left out, Τί τὸ ἔργον ὑμῶν; 'What is your occupation?' Ge 47.3 (‖ .. ἐστιν; 46.33); often in genealogies, καὶ ταῦτα τὰ ὀνόματα τῶν υἱῶν Λευι 'and the following are the names of L.'s children' Ex 6.16; Ἐγὼ κύριος 6.29; ἐγὼ κύριος ὁ θεὸς ὑμῶν Le 19.3, 4 (‖ ἐγώ εἰμι .. vs. 10, 12, 14 +); σὺ ἐλεήμων καὶ οἰκτίρμων .. 'you are merciful and compassionate ..' Jn 4.2 (v.l. + εἶ); μέγα τὸ ὄνομά μου ἐν τοῖς ἔθνεσι 'great is my name among the nations' Ma 1.11: BDF, § 127f. With ὡς: 'to be like, act like *or* as'– ἔσομαι αὐτοῖς ὡς ῥαπίζων ἄνθρωπος ἐπὶ τὰς σιαγόνας αὐτοῦ 'I shall become to them as a person slapping them on the cheek' Ho 11.4. Cf. προϋπάρχω.

*__3__. *to become* (εἰς, q.v.), *serve as*, confined to the indicative past and future tenses and the subjunctive: ὑμῖν ἔσται εἰς βρῶσιν 'they shall be your food' Ge 1.29; ἔσονται οἱ δύο εἰς σάρκα μίαν 2.24; ἔσται εἰς σημεῖον διαθήκης 'shall serve as a sign of covenant' 9.13; οὐκ ἔσται ἔτι τὸ ὕδωρ εἰς κατακλυσμὸν .. 'there shall be no repetition of that water resulting in a flooding' 9.15; ἵνα ὦσίν μοι εἰς μαρτύριον 'so that they may serve me as evidence' 21.30; ἔσται .. ὁ οἶκος Ησαυ εἰς καλάμην 'the house of Esau will become stubble' Ob 18; εἰς διαρπαγὴν .. εἰς ἀφανισμόν Zp 1.13; ἔσται εἰς οὐδέν Is 14.23; ἔσονται αὐτῷ εἰς λαόν 'they will become a people of his' Zc 2.11. On this Semitism, see BDF, § 145, 157, and the literature cited there. Cf. γίνομαι **3b**, ποιέω **I 9b**, τίθημι **3b**. **b**. without εἰς: ἔσται αἷμα Ex 7.19 (‖ μεταβαλεῖ εἰς αἷμα vs. 17). **c**. On εἰμί ἐν for εἰμί εἰς, see s.v. ἐν, **17**.

4. *to belong to, be had by* (τινι): ἡμῖν ἔσται καὶ τοῖς τέκνοις ἡμῶν 'will be ours and our children's' Ge 31.16; ἐσόμεθά σοι [= τῷ θεῷ] Ex 34.9; ἔσται τῷ κυρίῳ ἡ βασιλεία 'the kingship shall be the Lord's' Ob 21; ἔσονταί μοι 'they will be mine' Ma 3.17; cf. Ἔστιν ἡμῖν πατὴρ .. Ge 44.20, and see ἔχω, **I 2**.

*__5__. Hebraistically, and always in the form of ἔσται, introduces an utterance indicating that which may or ought to happen, with a temporal clause or phrase or a conditional clause intervening, often preceded by καί, and foll. by a finite verb, which latter in turn may or may not be preceded by καί: καὶ ἔσται ἐν τῷ συννεφεῖν με νεφέλας .. ὀφθήσεται τὸ τόξον 'when I gather clouds .. the (rain)bow shall appear' Ge 9.14; καὶ ἔσται ἐὰν μὴ πιστεύσωσίν σοι .. λήμψῃ .. Ex 4.9 (‖ ἐὰν δὲ μὴ πιστεύσωσίν σοι vs. 8); καὶ ἔσται ἐν τῇ ἡμέρᾳ ἐκείνῃ ἐξερευνήσω τὴν Ιερουσαλημ 'and when that day arrives, then I shall search J.' Zp 1.12; καὶ ἔσται καθότι διεγνώκειν ποιῆσαι αὐτούς, ποίησω ὑμᾶς 'and just as I have decided to deal with them, I shall deal with you' Nu 33.56; καὶ ἔσται ὅταν παύσῃ .. καὶ ἐπιδήσεις 'when you cease .., you shall bind' Je 28.63. Cf. καὶ ἔσται ἡ παρθένος, ᾗ ἂν ἐγὼ εἴπω .., ταύτην ἡτοίμασας .. Ge 24.14. **b**. Without the initial καί but foll. by another particle: ἔσται οὖν ὡς ἂν ἴδωσιν .. Ge 12.12; ἔσται δὲ ἡνίκα ἂν καθέλῃς, καὶ ἐκλύσεις .. 'now, when you overpower (him), then you will loosen ..' 27.40. **c**. ἔσται may be followed by a non-adverbial structure: καὶ ἔσται πᾶς ὁ εὑρίσκων με ἀποκτενεῖ με Ge 4.14; καὶ ἔσται ὁ ἄνθρωπος, ὃν ἂν ἐκλέξωμαι αὐτόν, ἡ ῥάβδος αὐτοῦ ἐκβλαστήσει 'the person whom I might choose, his staff is going to blossom' Nu 17.5. This usage and *3 **a** above attest to a complementary distribution of γίνομαι and εἶναι. **d**. Here does not belong a case such as καὶ ἔσονται .. γυναῖκες, καὶ ἀφαιρεθήσεται ὁ κλῆρος αὐτῶν 'and should they become wives .. their inheritance shall be taken away' Nu 36.3. For further details, see s.v. καί **12**.

6. Periphrastically with a ptc.: **a**. with the impf. ἦν and a pres. ptc. to indicate iteration or continuation, ἦν φεύγων 'he was running away' Jn 1.10; ‖ γίνομαι, Ge 4.2; ἦν κατοικῶν 'was resident' 14.12 (‖ vs. 13 κατῴκει); a ptc. preceding παροξύνοντες ἦτε De 9.22, sim. 9.24. **b**. with a pf. pass. ptc. and the pres. εἰμί, impf. ἦν or subj. ὦ to indicate a state arising from a past action and still existing at the moment of speech: ἠτιμωμένος σὺ εἶ 'you have been slighted' Ob 2; ἦν κατεφθαρμένη Ge 6.12. **c**. with a pf. act. ptc., ἦν ἔτι ἑστηκώς· Ge 18.22, and the subj. ὦ: ὅπως ἂν ὦ εὑρηκὼς .. Ex 33.13, ἐὰν ἐπ' αὐτῷ πεποιθὼς ᾖς 'should you be reliant on him' Is 8.14 – functionally, these belong under **b**, see under ἵστημι and πείθω. **d**. with the fut. ἔσομαι and a pres. ptc., στένων καὶ τρέμων ἔσῃ Ge 4.12; 1.6, 18.18, Ex 22.25, 25.19; De 16.15, Is 34.9, Ec 1.7; cf. πεποιθὼς ἔσομαι Is 8.17. **e**. w. the fut. ἔσομαι and a pf.ptc. to indicate a future state arising from a previous action – ἔσται τὰ βρώματα πεφυλαγμένα Ge 41.36; ἡμαρτηκὼς ἔσομαι εἰς σὲ πάσας τὰς ἡμέρας 43.9; Γαζα διηρπασμένη ἔσται 'Gaza will have been plundered' Zp 2.4; ἔσῃ ὑπερεωραμένη 'you will have been overlooked' Na 3.11. Only apparently belongs here: ἔσονται τῷ κυρίῳ προσάγοντες θυσίαν Ma 3.3. **f**. with the impv. of εἶναι: ἔστω διαχωρίζον 'Be separating …!' Ge 1.6; ἴσθι ἐστηριγμένος ἐν συνέσει σου 'hold firmly on to your understanding' Si 5.10.

Cf. BDF, § 352-4, Aerts 1965, esp. pp. 52-96, and Evans 2001.230-48.

*7. + inf., *be obliged* to do: εἶπον τίνα σοι ἔσομαι μισθὸν διδόναι 'Tell me what I'm supposed to pay you for wages' To 5.15 𝔊ᴵ, ἐσόμεθα τοῦ σῶσαί σε 'it would be up to us to rescue you' 2K 10.11B, οἱ Λευῖται ἦσασν τοῦ θύειν τὸ φασεκ 'the Levites were charged with slaughtering paschal lambs' 2C 30.17. Cf. Evans 2005.

8. foll. by a rel. pron. or adv., *there are some people who .., there are cases in which ..* etc.: ἔστι καὶ ὅτε .. 'it sometimes happens also that .. ' Ep Je 9, cf. LSJ s.v. **A IV** ad fin.

Cf. γίνομαι, ἔνειμι, περίειμι, ὑπάρχω: Schmidt 2.544-8.

εἶμι: pres.inf. ἰέναι, impv. ἴθι, 3s. ἴτω.∫

intr. *to move forward*: ἴτω πρός με Ex 32.26; Pr 6.6 (‖ πορεύομαι 8*a*), 6.3; 1K 25.15 (ἦμεν R to be read ᾖμεν). Cf. βαδίζω, ἔρχομαι, πορεύομαι, ἄν~, ἄπ~, διέξ~, ἔξ~, ἔπ~, πάρ~, περί~, πρόσειμι: Schmidt 1.477-504.

εἶν. ⇒ ἴν.

εἵνεκεν. ⇒ ἕνεκα.

εἴπερ. conj.∫

if indeed:+ ind. pres., Ju 6.9; + ind. aor., Su 54 TH. Del. 4M 11.7 v.l.

εἶπον (aor.act.ind.): fut. ἐρῶ, pass. ῥηθήσομαι, ptc. ῥηθησόμενος; aor.3pl εἴποσαν, subj. εἴπω, impv. εἰπόν or εἶπον (on the accentuation, see Walters, 99f.), ptc. εἴπας, opt.1s εἴποιμι, 3pl εἴπαισαν, εἴποιεν, pass. ἐρρέθην, inf. ῥηθῆναι, ptc. ῥηθείς; pf. εἴρηκα, pass.3pl εἴρηνται, impv.3s εἰρήσθω, ptc. εἰρημένος. For the pres. and impf., λέγω is used.

1. *to say*: καὶ ἐρεῖ Δειλαία Νινευη 'and he will say, "Wretched is Nineveh"' Na 3.7; in conjunction with ἀποκρίνομαι– ὁ δὲ ἀποκριθεὶς εἶπεν .. Ge 18.9; ἀπεκρίθησαν οἱ ἱερεῖς καὶ εἶπαν .. 'the priests answered and said ..' Hg 2.13; + dat. pers., ἐρεῖ τοῖς προεστηκόσι τῆς οἰκίας '.. to the heads of the household' Am 6.10; παντὶ ὀρνέῳ .. καὶ πρὸς πάντα τὰ θηρία 'to every bird .. and to all the animals' Ez 39.17; εἴς τινα Jb 2.9e; ἐπί τινα, Je 39.36; πρός τινα, Ge 7.1 +, cf. πρὸς τοὺς ἄρχοντας καὶ παντὶ τῷ λαῷ Je 33.11, 12; + ὅτι, Ge 12.12; + inf., ὃν εἴπατε πρός με ἀγαγεῖν 'whom you said to me you would bring' 43.29; Ex 32.13, Nu 14.10, De 9.25, Ps 105.23; εἶπεν .. ὁ θεὸς οὐ καλὸν εἶναι τὸν ἄνθρωπον μόνον 'God said that it was not good for the man to be alone' Ge 2.18. **b**. + acc. pers., concerning whom a statement was / is made: εἰπὸν ἐμὲ ὅτι Ἀδελφός μού ἐστιν 'Say about me: "He is my brother"' Ge 20.13; ἄρχοντας τοῦ λαοῦ οὐ κακῶς ἐρεῖς Ex 22.28; κρινάτω σε ὃν εἶπας Δός μοι βασιλέα 'Let him judge you concerning whom you said, "Give me a king"' Ho 13.10; Pr 24.24, Jd 7.4. **c**. impersonally: ἐρρέθη πρὸς Αβραμ Ge 15.13. **d**. not necessarily audibly, thus mentally, 'thought, reflected; thought aloud' with the foll. direct speech indicating a conclusion or decision reached: Ge

18.17, 26.28, 31.31, Nu 24.11; sim. εἶπεν ἐν ἑαυτῷ To 4.2 𝔊^{I} (𝔊^{II} ἐν τῇ καρδίᾳ αὐτοῦ), Es 6.6, εἶπεν ἐν καρδίᾳ αὐτοῦ Ps 9.27, 34.25*a* (without ἐν κ., 25*b*), εἶπας τῇ καρδίᾳ σου Is 47.10, εἴπατε τῇ διανοίᾳ Ep Je 5, μὴ εἴπῃς σεαυτῇ Es 4.13 o', cf. φησὶν ἐν ἑαυτῷ Ps 35.2 and λέγω **4**, φημί **e**, and Mk 2.8. **e**. in writing: ἐν γραφῇ 2C 2.10. **f**.. εἴπας, aor.ptc., introduces direct discourse: Ge 22.7, 46.2 (ǁ λέγων).

2. *to mention, name*: ἓν τῶν ὀρέων, ὧν ἄν σοι εἴπω 'one of the mountains that I would mention' Ge 22.2; τὸν τόπον, ὃν εἶπεν αὐτῷ ὁ θεός 22.3; 43.27, Ex 32.34, Nu 10.29, De 9.28, Ru 4.1, Ps 105.34.

3. *to command, bid*: + inf., the *s* of which often only implied, εἶπεν κύριος ποιῆσαι αὐτούς 'the Lord has commanded (us) to do them' Ex 35.1; εἶπον ἀπολῦσαί (ἀπολυθῆναί 𝔊^{II}) με ἀπὸ τῆς γῆς To 3.13 𝔊^{I}; Jb 2.3, Wi 9.8; + ὥστε and inf., Ne 13.19; + dat. pers., τῷ μωρῷ ἄρχειν Is 32.5. **b**. abs.: αὐτὸς εἶπεν, καὶ ἐγενήθησαν Ps 32.9 (ǁ ἐντέλλομαι), εἶπεν, καὶ ἔστη πνεῦμα 'He spoke, and there arose a wind' 106.25; 104.31; εἶπα καὶ ἐκαθάρισαν Ne 13.9; 13.19.

4. *to decide* to act: + inf., τοῦ ἐκχέαι Ez 20.8, 13, 21; τοῦ ἐξολεθρεῦσαι Ps 105.23; φυλάξασθαι 118.57.

5. *to propose* or *demand verbally* a course of action: + inf., Ju 5.22, 6.2.

6. *to bring to oral expression*, 'utter': ***o*** αἶνος 'praise (of God)' Si 15.10.

Cf. λέγω, ἀντ~, προσεῖπον.

εἴργω: aor. εἶρξα, pass. εἴρχθην.ʃ

to prevent to do: τοῦ οἰκοδομεῖν 1E 5.69; + gen. (action) and pass., εἴρχθησαν τῆς οἰκοδομῆς 5.70; + acc. pers., ἡμᾶς τῆς εἰσόδου 'denied us entry' 3M 3.18. Cf. καταργέω, κωλύω.

εἰρηνεύω: fut. εἰρηνεύσω; aor. εἰρήνευσα, inf. εἰρηνεῦσαι.

1. *to have peace of mind*: Jb 2.26 (ǁ ἡσυχάζω). **b**. *to live in peace*: ***s*** the country, 2C 14.5 (opp. πόλεμος), Jb 5.24.

2. *to relate in a peaceable, friendly manner*: abs. 1M 6.60; *+ dat. pers., Jb 5.23, Si 6.6; μετά τινος 3K 22.45; εἰρηνεύοντες ǁ φίλοι 28.9.

3. tr. *to keep in a peaceable state*: + acc., τὰ πρὸς αὐτούς '(to maintain a peaceful) relationship with them' 1E 8.82.

Cf. εἰρήνη.

εἰρήνη, ης. f.

1. *lack of physical strife, peaceful and harmonious state*: opp. πόλεμος, Le 26.6, Ec 3.8, Mi 2.8, 3.5, cf. 5.5; ποιέω ~ην τινι 'make peace with sbd' Is 27.5, sim. 1M 13.37; μετά τινος 6.49, 58, πρός τινα Jo 9.15, cf. Si 13.18; + συμμαχία 'alliance' 1M 8.20; μετ' ~ης 'peacefully, i.e. natural death' Ge 15.15, '(to arrive) in one piece' 3M 7.19, ἐν ~η ἀποθανῇ Je 41.5, cf. Si 44.14, 3K 2.6; ἀπαγγέλλοντος ~ην Na 1.15; τὴν ἀλήθειαν καὶ τὴν ~ην ἀγαπήσατε Zc 8.19; + ζωή Ma 2.5; opp. πόλεμος Le 26.6, Je 35.9; κατοικέω ἐπ' ~ης 'live in peace' Ez 38.11 (ǁ ἐν ἡσυχίᾳ), 14; + ἡσυχία 1C 22.9; *security, safety*, Ps 118.165.

2. *lack of mental, inner turmoil, peace of mind*: εἰ. ψυχῆς Hg 2.9; οὐκ ἔσται εἰ. ἀπὸ τῆς θλίψεως Zc 8.10 (on the use of ἀπό, see Epictetus, 3.13.10 ἀπὸ πυρετοῦ .. εἰ.); ἐν ~η κατευθύνων ἐπορεύθη μετ' ἐμοῦ Ma 2.6; a share of the righteous after death, Wi 3.3; Εἰ. εἰ. 'No worries!' Je 6.14, sim. 4K 4.23; opp. φόβος 37.5.

3. *general, material* or *physical well-being*: as divine gift, Hg 2.9, Zc 8.12, Is 26.12, 45.7, Je 36.11 (last two:: κακά), 45.4 (:: πονηρά), 16.5, 2M 1.4, 3M 2.20; effected by a hum. ruler, 1M 14.11; + πλῆθος Zc 9.10; + ὑγίεια 'health' Is 9.6, cf. Si 38.8; ἐρωτήσατε τὰ εἰς ~ην τὴν Ιερουσαλημ Ps 121.6, ἐρωτῆσαι αὐτὸν τὰ εἰς ~ην 'to ask after him' 2K 8.10, ἐπηρώτησεν .. εἰς ~ην Ιωαβ .. καὶ εἰς ~ν τοῦ πολέμου 'asked how things were with J... and with the war' 11.7 (*L* εἰ ὑγιαίνει); ἁμαρτωλῶν 'of sinners' Ps 72.3; Εἰ. ὑμῖν πληθυνθείη 'May your welfare increase!' Da 3.98 TH, 4.34c LXX, cf. **4a** and 1Pet 1.2, Jude 2.

4. *friendly words of greeting* by letter: 2E 4.17; in a greeting formula, Δαρείῳ τῷ βασιλεῖ εἰ. πᾶσα 5.7. **b**. *friendly, peaceable attitude*: 2E 9.12.

Cf. εἰρηνικός, εἰρηνεύω, εἰρηνοποιέω, ἡσυχάζω, πόλεμος: Foerster, *TDNT* 2.406-8; van Leeuwen 13-117; Spicq 1.424-38, esp. 218-20.

εἰρηνικός, ή, όν.

conducive to friendly relationship, characterised by friendly sentiments, 'friendly; peaceful': ***s*** hum., μεθ' ἡμῶν Ge 34.21, ἄνδρες ~οί 'allies', i.e. people bound by non-belligerency agreement, Ob 7 (ǁ ἄνδρες διαθήκης), sim. Je 45.22 ǁ ἀνὴρ φίλος 20.10 and ἄνθρωπος εἰρήνης Ps 40.10; opp. κατάσκοποι 'spies (with hostile intent)' Ge 42.11; οὐκ ἐδύναντο λαλεῖν αὐτῷ οὐδὲν ~όν 37.4; ὁ κριτὴς ~οὺς λόγους ἐλάλησεν 'the judge said friendly things' Mi 7.3; βουλὴ ~ή 'friendly, peaceful counsel' Zc 6.13; κρίμα ~όν 'a judgement conducive to peaceful relation' Zc 8.16; θυσία ~ή 'cultic offering made to mark a relationship restored with God' 1K 11.15 *L* (B: θ. καὶ ~ή, cf. ὁλοκαυτώματα καὶ ~άς 2K 6.17 and ὁλοκαυτώσεις .. 6.18), Pr 7.14. **b**. subst.n.: ~ὰ ἀποκριθῶσίν σοι De 20.11; 23.6; λαλεῖ ~ά Je 9.8.

Cf. εἰρήνη, εἰρηνικῶς: Foerster, *TDNT* 2.418; Daniel 288-97.

εἰρηνικῶς. adv.ʃ
in peaceful, friendly manner: w. ref. to encounter between people, 1M 5.25; greeting, 7.29,33; conduct of relationship, 2M 10.12. Cf. εἰρηνικός.

εἰρηνοποιέω.ʃ
to help foster mutual concord and peaceful relationship: Pr 10.10. Cf. εἰρήνη.

εἱρκτή, ῆς. f.ʃ
prison: Wi 17.16. Cf. δεσμωτήριον.

εἰρωνεία, ας. f.ʃ
attitude of disguising one's true intention, 'hypocrisy': 2M 13.3. Cf. ὑπόκρισις.

εἰς. Prep. foll. by acc.

1. *towards* a goal which is inside an area or in the direction of it: with verbs of movement, ἀναβαίνω Hb 3.16, cf. Am 9.6; ἀπέρχομαι Ge 3.19, ἀπορρίπτω Jn 2.4, ἀποστρέφομαι Ge 3.19, ἐπιστρέφω 2E 2.1, διώκω Hg 1.9, εἰσέρχομαι Ge 7.1, εἰσφέρω Hg 1.9, ἐκβάλλω Jn 1.15, cf. ἐκβολὴν ποιέομαι 1.5; ἐμβάλλω 1.12, ἐξαποστέλλω Ob 1*a*, ἐξεγείρω Jn 1.4, ἔρχομαι 2.8, ἥκω Ma 3.1, καταβαίνω Jn 1.3, 5, πίπτω Na 3.12, πορεύομαι Ge 27.9, Jn 3.2, 3, τρέχω Ge 18.7; φεύγω Jn 4.2; with verbs of giving or handing over, ἀνταποδίδωμι Ob 15; δίδωμι Ma 2.9; with verbs of positioning, τάσσω Hb 2.9, fig. Hg 1.5; τίθημι fig. 1.6, 2.15, μίγνυμι Ge 30.40, cf. ἀναβλέπω 15.5; with verbs of verbal communication, ἐλάλησεν αὐτῶν εἰς τὴν καρδίαν 50.21, ἀπήγγειλεν εἰς τὸν οἶκον 24.28; on λαλέω etc. εἰς τὰ ὦτά τινος, see under οὖς; λάβω αὐτὴν εἰς ἐμαυτόν 'take her [= Wisdom] in for intimate company' Wi 8.18, cf. Neirynck 1979.361. On δίδωμι εἰς χεῖράς τινος, see under χείρ **1 g**.

2. *destined for* (some use or role): ξύλον ὡραῖον εἰς ὅρασιν καὶ καλὸν εἰς βρῶσιν 'plant beautiful to gaze at and good for eating' Ge 2.9; εἰς φαῦσιν 'for illumination' 1.14; οὐχ ἱκανὸς εἰς καῦσιν 'does not suffice for burning' Is 40.16, μὴ εἶναι ἱκανοὺς εἰς πρόβατον 'there are not enough people for a sheep' Ex 12.4; ἔστωσαν εἰς σημεῖα 'Let them there be as signs!' Ge 1.14; ἔσται ὑμῖν εἰς βρῶσιν 1.29; πεφυλαγμένα .. εἰς τὰ ἑπτὰ ἔτη τοῦ λιμοῦ 'stored .. for the seven years of famine' 41.36; ὁ οἶκος Ησαυ εἰς καλάμην 'the house of Esau is to be used as stubble' Ob 18; οὐκ ἀπολείψετε ἀπὸ τῶν κρεῶν εἰς τὸ πρωΐ 'you shall not leave any of the meat for the following day' Le 22.30; ὅρασις εἰς καιρόν 'a vision is meant for some future time' Hb 2.3; εἰς θήραν παρέστησαν τὰ τέκνα αὐτῶν 'they offered their children for a prey' Ho 9.13; pregnantly – εἰς πλημμέλειαν 'in order to deal with (the) error' Le 5.18.

3. Indicates a target, aim or focus of action: εἰς ζωὴν ἀπέστειλέν με ὁ θεὸς '.. to rescue (you)' Ge 45.5, ἤχθη εἰς θάνατον 'was led away to be killed' Is 53.8 (‖ ἐπὶ σφαγήν vs. 7); ἐξῆλθες εἰς σωτηρίαν τοῦ λαοῦ σου 'you went out to rescue your people' Hb 3.13; πρόθυμος εἰς τὸ φαγεῖν 'eager to eat' Hb 1.8. Esp. of hostile action, attack: εἰς τοὺς ἄνδρας τούτους μὴ ποιήσητε μηδὲν ἄδικον 'Only to these men do not do anything unjust' Ge 19.8; Οὐ πατάξομεν αὐτὸν εἰς ψυχήν 37.21; ἁμαρτεῖν σε εἰς ἐμέ 20.6, Ἡμάρτηκα ἐναντίον κυρίου .. καὶ εἰς ὑμᾶς Ex 10.16; θυμοῖ ὀργῇ εἰς τὸν λαόν σου 'you lash out in anger at your people' 32.11; εἰς Μωαβ ποιήσω ἐκδίκησιν Ez 25.11 (see under ἐν **10**); ἐμφυσῶν εἰς πρόσωπόν σου 'blowing at your face' Na 2.2; ἀνομήσετε εἰς ὅλην τὴν συναγωγήν Nu 32.15; ἠσέβησας εἰς ἐμέ Zp 3.11; τὴν ἀσέβειαν τὴν εἰς τὸν ἀδελφόν σου Ob 10*a*; συντέλεια εἰς ἀσεβεῖς ἥξει 'an annihilation will come to the ungodly' Hb 1.9; εἰς πᾶν ὀχύρωμα ἐμπαίξεται 'he will laugh at every castle' 1.10; ἐμεγαλορρημόνησεν .. εἰς τὸν οἶκον Ισραηλ 'boasted ..' Ju 6.17; εἰς ἐμὲ ἐλογίσαντο πονηρά 'thought up wicked things against me' Ho 7.15, cf. ὑμεῖς ἐβουλεύσασθε κατ' ἐμοῦ εἰς πονηρά, ὁ δὲ θεὸς ἐβουλεύσατο περὶ ἐμοῦ εἰς ἀγαθά Ge 50.20; ἐκλεκτὴν εἰς ἀφανισμόν 'singled out for devastation' Zc 7.14; εἰς τὸν πένητα ἀποβλέπουσιν Ps 10.4, ἀτενίζοντας εἰς τὴν τοῦ βασιλέως πρόθεσιν 'closely observing the king's purpose' 3M 2.26. Cf. ἐκπορνεύειν αὐτοὺς εἰς τοὺς ἄρχοντας Le 20.5 and εἰς τὰς θυγατέρας Μωαβ Nu 25.1 (with the notion of illicit sexual desire directed at sbd). **b**. εἰς τὸ + inf. indicates a purpose: εἰς τὸ πιεῖν Ge 30.38 (‖ πιεῖν); εἰς τὸ ἱερατεύειν μοι Ex 28.4. **c**. εἰς τί 'for what purpose?': Jd 5.17 B (A: ἵνα τί), cf. Mazzucco. **d**. *paying attention to*: 1K 12.1B (*L* κατὰ πάντα). **e**. On εἰς συνάντησίν τινι, see s.v. συνάντησις.

4. Indicates an extent of time: εἰς τὸν αἰῶνα 'for ever' Ob 10*b*, cf. ἕως εἰς τὸν αἰῶνα Mi 4.7; εἰς τὸν αἰῶνα χρόνον Is 13.20, εἰς τὸν ἅπαντα χρόνον 1M 15.8; τοῦ σπέρματός σου μετὰ σὲ εἰς γενεὰς αὐτῶν Ge 17.7; εἰς χιλίας γενεάς De 7.9; εἰς χιλιάδας 'up to a thousand generations' Je 39.18, Ex 34.7; εἰς γενεὰν ἑτέραν 'into another generation' Jl 1.3; εἰς γενεὰς γενεῶν 2.2; ποιήσετε τὴν ἡμέραν εἰς τὰς ἑπτὰ ἡμέρας 'do every day for the seven days' Nu 28.24; οὐχ ὑπελίποντο εἰς τὸ πρωΐ 'they did not stay on till the morning' Zp 3.3; "my questioning lasts into the early hours of the morning (εἰς τὰς πρωΐας)" Ps 72.14. On εἰς ὥρας 'on time,' see under ὥρα.

5. Marks a point in future towards which sth takes place: "they will return towards the evening (εἰς ἑσπέραν)" Ps 58.7; εἰς τὰς τρεῖς ἡμέρας 'within the (prescribed) three-day period' 2E 10.9.

6. Indicates transformation, added to the predicate of a nominal clause: ἔσται μοι κύριος εἰς θεόν 'the Lord will become my god' Ge 28.21, see under εἰμί, **3**; ἀφορίζεται εἰς τέσσαρας ἀρχάς 'it splits into four tributaries' 2.10; ἐγένετο ἡ πλίνθος εἰς λίθον 'a brick served them as stone' 11.3; ἔστωσαν ὑμῖν εἰς κατάσχεσιν 'Let them become your possession' Le 25.45. **b**. the transitive transform of the preceding: ἔταξα τὰ ὄρη αὐτοῦ εἰς ἀφανισμόν 'I turned his mountains into desolation' Ma 1.3; ποιῶ εἰς περιποίησιν 3.17; ποιήσω σε εἰς ἔθνος μέγα Ge 12.2, 46.3; ἵνα στήσῃ σε ἑαυτῷ εἰς λαόν De 29.13; θήσομαί σε εἰς παράδειγμα Na 3.6; μεταστρέψω τὰς ἑορτὰς ὑμῶν εἰς πένθος Am 8.10; ᾠκοδόμησεν .. τὴν πλευράν .. εἰς γυναῖκα 'built .. the rib into a woman' Ge 2.22; ἔλαβον αὐτὴν ἐμαυτῷ εἰς γυναῖκα 12.19; δώσω αὐτὸν εἰς ἔθνος μέγα 17.20; τὴν ῥάβδον τὴν στραφεῖσαν εἰς ὄφιν 'the staff changed to a snake' Ex 7.15, μετέβαλεν πᾶν τὸ ὕδωρ .. εἰς αἷμα 'he changed all the water .. into blood' 7.20; "call upon him as a god (εἰς θεόν)" Ju 3.8.

7. Indicates a state to which an action leads: δώσω .. τὴν γῆν .. εἰς κατάσχεσιν αἰώνιον 'as eternal possession' Ge 17.8, 48.4; ἐφάγετε καὶ οὐκ εἰς πλησμονήν, ἐπίετε καὶ οὐκ εἰς μέθην Hg 1.6; εἰς κενόν 'to no purpose' Hb 2.3. Also ἄνδρα ἀπέκτεινα εἰς τραῦμα ἐμοί καὶ νεανίσκον εἰς μώλωψ ἐμοί Ge 4.23? But perhaps 'in the face of' (BDAG, s.v. **10** a): cf. Harl *BA*, Wevers and Rösel ad loc. Cf. also δὸς λόγον μου .. εἰς τραῦμα καὶ μώλωψ αὐτῶν Ju 9.13 and εἰς πῆχυν συντελέσεις αὐτὴν ἄνωθεν 'Finish it (as) one cubit (in width) at the top' Ge 6.16.

8. Synonymous with ἐν: 'at the time of'– εἰς τὸν καιρὸν τοῦτον ἐν τῷ ἐνιαυτῷ τῷ ἑτέρῳ 'at this time next year' Ge 17.21; εἰς τὸ γῆρας 'in old age' 21.2 (|| ἐν τῷ γήρει μου vs. 7); εἰς πέρας 'at the end' Hb 2.3, εἰς τέλος 'in the end' Ge 46.4; εἰς τὸ πρωΐ 'in the morning' Ex 34.2, Am 8.4; εἰς τὸ ἑσπέρας 'in the evening' Ge 49.27; εἰς αὔριον 'tomorrow' Ex 8.10 (a reply to πότε 'when?'); εἰς πεντήκοντα δύο ἡμέρας 'in 52 days' Ne 6.15; 'at the place of' – ἠρεύνησεν εἰς τὸν οἶκον Ιακωβ καὶ ἐν τῷ οἴκῳ τῶν δύο παιδισκῶν 'he searched the dwelling of Jacob and the dwelling of the two maids' Ge 31.33; αἱ πόλεις, εἰς ἃς οὗτοι κατοικοῦσιν ἐν αὐταῖς Nu 13.20; παρενέβαλον εἰς τὴν ἔρημον Φαραν 33.36 (|| .. ἐν τῇ ἐρήμῳ Σιν); εἰς τὸν τόπον De 16.6 (|| ἐν vs. 5, 7); ἐκεῖ προφητεύσεις· εἰς δὲ Βαιθηλ οὐκέτι μὴ προσθῇς τοῦ προφητεῦσαι 'there you will prophesy, but in Bethel you will not prophesy again' Am 7.12f.; μισητὸς εἰς ἔθνη 'hated among the nations' Pr 24.24 (|| dat. pers.). Cf. BDAG, s.v. **1 a** δ and Soisalon-Soininen, *Studien* 139f.

9. with a num. or quantifier, *to the tune of, to the number of*: εἰς ἑξακοσίας χιλιάδας πεζῶν 'as many as 600,000 foot-soldiers' Ex 12.37; εἰς χιλιάδας 'up to thousands (of generations)' 20.6; 32.28, Jo 7.5, Ju 2.5; ἐπισιτισμὸν παντὶ ἀνδρὶ εἰς πλῆθος 'abundant provisions for everybody' Ju 2.18, ὡς ἡ ἄμμος ἡ ἐπὶ τῆς θαλάσσης εἰς πλῆθος 'as the sand on the beach ..' 2K 17.11; with a subst. preceding, εἰς ἄνδρας ὀκτακοσίους 'as many as 800 men' 1M 3.24. Cf. εἰς ἀριθμὸν τριάκοντα χιλιάδας 'up to as many as 30,000' 2C 35.7; 2M 8.1; τρεῖς σίκλοι εἰς τὸν ὀδόντα 'three shekels per tooth' 1K 13.21; εἰς φυλάς 'by tribes (?)' 10.21 (|| κατὰ τὰς φυλάς vs. 19).

Cf. ἐν.

εἷς, μία, ἕν; gen. ἑνός, μιᾶς, ἑνός. num.

If used adjectivally, the numeral usually follows a noun.

one: **a**. with some emphasis on oneness as against more than one, all, etc.: ἔσονται οἱ δύο εἰς σάρκα μίαν "the two shall become one flesh" Ge 2.24(*a*); χεῖλος ἕν, καὶ φωνὴ μία 'a single speech community and a single speech' 11.1(*a*); νόμος εἷς 'a single law' Le 6.37(*a*); εἶδον ἀμφότεροι ἐνύπνιον .. ἐν μιᾷ νυκτὶ .. 'they both saw a dream .. in one night ..' Ge 40.5(*a*); πατάξω .. ὡσεὶ ἄνθρωπον ἕνα 'strike down .. altogether, none excluded' Nu 14.15(*a*), sim. Ju 6.3; ὡς ἀνὴρ εἷς 2E 3.1(*a*); ὡσεὶ ἄνδρα ἑνά Jd 6.16(*a*); ὡσεὶ πορείαν ἡμέρας μιᾶς 'about a day's walk' Jn 3.4(*a*), ἀρχὴν μίαν 'a single authority' Ho 1.11(*a*), "on that day there shall be only one Lord (κύριος εἷς) and his name will be one (ἕν)" Zc 14.9(*a*bis), οὐχὶ θεὸς εἷς ἔκτισεν ἡμᾶς; οὐχὶ πατὴρ εἷς πάντων ἡμῶν; Ma 2.10(*a*bis) "two or three cities will come together εἰς πόλιν μίαν 'as one city'" Am 4.8(*a*), sim. πέντε πόλεις εἰς μίαν πόλιν Zc 8.21(*a*), opp. διπλοῦς 'double' Zc 9.12(-); "I will cut off three shepherds in one month (ἐν μηνὶ ἑνί)" Zc 11.8(*a*); opp. πάντες, "I will search out all the iniquity of that land in one day (ἐν ἡμέρᾳ μιᾷ)" Zc 3.9(*a*); with the art., ἐπὶ τὸν λίθον τὸν ἕνα ἑπτὰ ὀφθαλμοί εἰσιν 'there are seven eyes on the one stone' ib.(*a*). **b**. esp. with a negator, 'not even one': οὐδὲ εἷς *not even one* Zc 10.10(-), Si 42.20(*b*); εἷς λόγος Jo 23.14(*a*). The numeral either precedes or follows the noun nucleus without any functional opposition.

b. *a certain*, unspecified: μίαν ἡμέραν 'one day' Zc 14.7(*a*), μερὶς μία βραχήσεται, καὶ μερίς, ἐφ' ἣν οὐ βρέξω ἐπ' αὐτήν, ξηρανθήσεται 'one part will have rain, but the part on which I shall not send rain will dry up' Am 4.7(*a*).

c. with rather weak force, and approximating the indefinite article: μιᾶς ἐλατῆς 'a silver fir' Ge

21.15(*a*); καὶ ἰδοὺ βροῦχος εἷς 'and behold a locust' Am 7.1(*a*), μία γυνή Zc 5.7(*a*) (v.l. γ. μ.); 1E 4.18, 2M 8.33. Cf. *ND* 4.252; Kuhlmann, esp. 86f.

d. εἷς .. εἷς *one .. another* (or: *the one .. the other*), indicating random choice of any two members: ἐστήριζον τὰς χεῖρας αὐτοῦ, ἐντεῦθεν εἷς καὶ ἐντεῦθεν εἷς 'they were upholding his hands, one each on either side' Ex 17.12(*a*bis); δύο βάσεις τῷ στύλῳ τῷ ἑνὶ καὶ δύο βάσεις τῷ στύλῳ τῷ ἑνὶ εἰς ἀμφότερα τὰ μέρη αὐτοῦ 'two bases for each (of the four) columns on one side and two bases for each (of the four) columns on the other side, for both of its parts' 26.25(*a*bis); βρέξω ἐπὶ πόλιν μίαν, ἐπὶ δὲ πόλιν μίαν οὐ βρέξω 'I will send rain upon one city, but I shall not .. upon another' Am 4.7(*a*bis); "there are two olive-trees above it, one (μία) on the right of the bowl(?), another (μία) on the left" Zc 4.3(*a*bis); δύο δύο, ἓν κατέναντι τοῦ ἑνός Si 36.15 (-). Cf. εἷς εἷς 'one each' (?) 1C 24.7 (MT: אחד אחז .. אחז אחז); LSG s.v.

e. ὁ εἷς .. ὁ ἕτερος (*the*) *one .. the other*: "I will take for myself two rods, the one (τὴν μίαν) I called Beauty and the other (τὴν ἑτέραν) I called Line" Zc 11.7(*a*); ὁ ἕτερος elided, Ge 38.28(-); opp. δεύτερος (and other ordinals), ὄνομα τῷ ἑνὶ Φισων 'the name of one (of them) is P.' Ge 2.11(*a*); ὄνομα τῇ μιᾷ Αδα, καὶ ὄνομα τῇ δευτέρᾳ Σελλα 4.19(*a*); εἰς παρεμβολὴν μίαν .. ἡ παρεμβολὴ ἡ δευτέρα 32.8(*a*); ἐπὶ τὸ κλίτος τὸ ἓν .. ἐπὶ τὸ κλίτος τὸ δεύτερον 'on the one side .. on the other side' Ex 25.11(*a*); 25.31(*a*).

f. one out of several components: εἷς ἐξ αὐτῶν Ob 11(*a*); ἓν τῶν ὀρέων 'one of the mountains' Ge 22.2(*a*).

g. with the force of the ordinal πρῶτος: ἡμέρα μία Ge 1.5 (|| δευτέρα)(*a*), cf. Alexandre 100f.; w. ref. to the day of a month and ἡμέρα understood: μιᾷ τοῦ μηνός 'on the first of the month' Ge 8.13(*a*); in a compound numeral, μιᾷ καὶ εἰκάδι 'on the 21st' Hg 2.1(*a*). This is no Semitism: see BDAG, s.v. **4** b.

h. When used with an adj., the numeral may either precede or follow the adj., ἄρτον ἕνα ἄζυμον .. καὶ λάγανον ἄζυμον ἕνα 'one unleavened loaf .. and one unleavened cake' Nu 6.19(*a*); ἀμνὰς μία μικρά 'one tiny lamb' 2K 12.3(*a*); ἄγγος ἓν ὀστράκινον 'one earthen container' Ez.4.9(*a*); γυναῖκα μίαν καλήν 1E 4.18.

***i.** articular and attributive with distributive force: τὸ τρύβλιον τὸ ἓν .. ἡ φιάλη ἡ μία 'each of the cups .. each of the bowls' Nu 7.85(*a*); without a noun head - τέσσαρα πρόσωπα τῷ ἑνί 'each of them had four faces' Ez 1.6(*a*), 10.21(*a*).

Cf. ἕκαστος, μόνος.

a) אֶחָד, אַחַת; *b*) w. neg., כֹּל; *c*) Ar. חַד; *d*) זֶה.xʃ

εἰσάγω: fut.act. εἰσάξω; aor. εἰσήγαγον, subj. εἰσαγάγω, impv. ~άγαγε, inf. ~αγαγεῖν, ptc. ~αγαγών, pass. εἰσήχθην, inf. ~αχθῆναι; pf.2pl εἰσαγειόχατε.

to cause to move into a space: + acc., πρὸς ἑαυτὸν εἰς τὴν κιβωτόν Ge 8.9; πρὸς αὐτόν 'to his living quarters, tent' 29.23; εἰς τὸν οἶκον Φαραω 12.15; εἰς τὸν οἶκον αὐτοῦ 29.13 (as a guest); εἰς τὴν οἰκίαν 43.16; εἰς τὴν σκηνήν Ex 18.7; εἰς τὴν γῆν 13.5; De 26.9 (:: ἐξάγω vs. 8); Nu 14.3; εἰς τὸν Λίβανον εἰσάξω αὐτούς Zc 10.10; πρὸς τὴν θυγατέρα Φαραω Ex 2.10; τὸν τράχηλον αὐτοῦ ὑπὸ τὸν ζυγὸν βασιλέως 'his neck under the yoke of ..' Je 34.9 (|| ἐμβάλλω vs. 6), 10 (ὑπὸ τὸν ζυγόν understood); into the household, εἰσήγαγεν ἡμῖν παῖδα Ἑβραῖον Ge 39.14; τὰ εἰσαγόμενα 'the imports' Ez 27.15; σὸν πόδα πρὸς .. φίλον 'to (visit) a friend' Pr 25.17. **b.** = ἄγω: τινα ἐπὶ χειρός τινος 'to deliver to be executed by ..' 4K 10.24*L* (v.l. ἄγω). **c.** metaph., into a relationship: ἐν ἀρᾷ 'into (a covenant) with a curse attached in case of breach' Ez 17.13. Opp.: ἐξάγω Ex 3.8, 6.7, De 26.9.

Cf. ἄγω, ἐξάγω.

εἰσακούω: fut. ~ακούσομαι, pass. ~ακουσθήσομαι; aor. ~ήκουσα, subj. ~ακούσω, impv. ~άκουσον, inf. ~ακοῦσαι, ptc. ~ακούσας, pass. εἰσηκούσθην; pf. ~ακήκοα.

1. *to give ear* to sbd or sth: + acc. rei, στεναγμόν 'a sigh' Ex 2.24, 6.5; κραυγὴν πτωχῶν 'the cry of the poor' Jb 34.28¶, προσευχήν PSol 6.5; τὸν γογγυσμὸν ὑμῶν ἐπὶ τῷ θεῷ 'your grumble against God' Ex 16.7; τὴν ἀκοήν σου 'I have attentively listened to the report about you' Hb 3.2; respectfully or sympathetically, + gen. rei, φωνῆς Ge 21.17 (|| ἐπακούω); Zp 3.2 (|| δέχομαι παιδείαν); τῆς φωνῆς κυρίου Zc 6.15, τῶν λόγων .. τῶν προφητῶν Je 33.5; οὐκ εἰσήκουσεν κύριος τῆς φωνῆς ὑμῶν οὐδὲ προσέσχεν ὑμῖν '.. nor did he take notice of you' De 1.45; οἰκτίρησόν με καὶ εἰσάκουσον τῆς προσευχῆς μου 'Have pity on me and give my prayer a hearing' Ps 4.2, sim. 26.7, τῆς δεήσεώς μου 'my supplication' Ju 9.12; τῆς δικαιοσύνης μου 'my plea for justice' Ps 16.1; + dat. cogn., ἀκοῇ De 15.5; + acc. rei, τὴν ἐπιθυμίαν τῶν πενήτων 'the desire of the poor' Ps 9.38 (|| προσέχω); + both gen. and acc. rei, μὴ εἰσακούειν τοῦ νόμου μου καὶ τοὺς λόγους, οὓς ἐξαπέστειλε κύριος .. ἐν χερσὶ τῶν προφητῶν 'not to listen to my law and (hear) the words which the Lord sent .. through the prophets' Zc 7.12; + gen. pers., πρόσεχε σεαυτῷ καὶ εἰσάκουε αὐτοῦ καὶ μὴ ἀπείθει αὐτῷ 'make sure that you hearken unto him, and do not disobey him' Ex 23.21; + *εἰς– εἰς τὰ ἐπερχόμενα 'that which is about to happen' Is 42.23. **b.** to sbd crying for help: abs., κεκράξομαι καὶ οὐ μὴ εἰσακούσῃς Hb 1.2; προσέσχε κύριος καὶ εἰσήκουσε 'the Lord took notice of it ..' Ma 3.16; + gen. pers. οὐκ εἰσηκούσαμεν αὐτοῦ Ge 42.21 (ǁ ὑπερεῖδον); εἰσακούσεταί μου ὁ θεός μου Mi 7.7, sim. Zc 6.15, Mi 3.4, 7, Jn 2.3; ἐμοῦ τῆς χήρας 'me the widow' Ju 9.4; προσεύξασθε πρός με, καὶ εἰσακούσομαι ὑμῶν Je 36.12. **c**. pass. and *o* pers., ἐδεήθημεν τοῦ κυρίου καὶ εἰσηκούσθημεν 'we entreated the Lord and were heard' 2M 1.8, ἐν ἡμέρᾳ προσευχῆς αὐτοῦ Si 3.5; *o* rei, προσευχή To 3.16, δέησις Si 51.11, ῥῆμα Da 10.12 LXX.

2. *to act in accordance with the terms proposed* or *dictated by*: abs. Mi 5.15, Zc 7.13*a*; τὰ ὦτα αὐτῶν ἐβάρυναν τοῦ μὴ εἰσακούειν 'they hardened their ears not to listen' 7.11; + gen. pers. Ge 42.22, De 13.8 (ǁ συνθέλω τινί); Ho 9.17, Zc 1.4 (to God). **b**. + acc. rei, τὰς ἐντολάς μου καὶ τὸν νόμον μου Ex 16.28; εἰσακούσῃς τὰς ἐντολὰς κυρίου .. ἀγαπᾶν κύριον .. πορεύεσθαι ἐν ταῖς ὁδοῖς αὐτοῦ, φυλάσσεσθαι τὰ δικαιώματα αὐτοῦ .. De 30.16; κρίμα 3K 3.11. **c**. the terms indicated by an inf., μὴ εἰσακούσητε ἡμῶν τοῦ περιτέμνεσθαι Ge 34.17; Es 1.12 o'.

3. *to act obediently*: + inf., ποιεῖν πάντα τὰ ῥήματα τοῦ νόμου De 28.58.

Cf. ἀκούω, ἐπ~, ὑπακούω, προσέχω, συνθέλω: Barr 1980; Cox 1981; Spicq 1.439-41.

εἰσάπαξ. Read εἰς ἅπαξ.

εἰσβάλλω. aor.inf. ~βαλεῖν.ʃ

intr. *to move in*: *s* troops, 2M 13.13, 14.43 Del. 1E 6.20 v.l.

εἰσβλέπω: aor.impv. εἴσβλεψον, ptc. ~βλέψας.ʃ

to observe visually and carefully: abs. and ǁ εἰσακούω Is 37.17; + εἰς Jb 6.28, 21.5. Cf. βλέπω.

εἰσδεκτός. Read εἰς δεκτόν.

εἰσδέχομαι: fut. ~δέξομαι; aor.inf. ~δέξασθαι, ptc. ~δεξάμενος, pass. εἰσεδέχθην.

to admit, welcome: + acc. pers. τὴν ἐξωσμένην 'the rejected' Mi 4.6 (ǁ συνάγω), τὴν ἀπωσμένην 'the outcast' Zp 3.19 (so punctuated: *BA*); πρὸς αὐτὸν πάντας τοὺς λαούς Hb 2.5 (ǁ ἐπισυνάγω); as guest, βασιλεῖς Zp 3.8, ǁ προσδέχομαι Wi 19.16 (see vs. 15); fellow soldiers, 2M 10.36; into a city, 4.22, Ez 22.19; + a pred. adj., ἁγνόν 'as pure' 4M 5.37. Cf. δέχομαι.

εἰσδύω: 2aor. εἰσέδυν.ʃ

to move oneself into a space: εἰς τὰ σπήλαια 'into the caves' Je 4.29, ὑπὸ τὸν ἐλέφαντα 'under the elephant' 1M 6.46. Cf. εἰσέρχομαι, εἰσπορεύομαι.

εἰσεῖδον.ʃ

to gaze upon and study: εἰσήκουσεν κύριος τῆς φωνῆς αὐτῶν καὶ εἰσεῖδεν τὴν θλῖψιν αὐτῶν '.. their distress' Ju 4.13. Cf. εἶδον, ὁράω, βλέπω. Del. Ex 2.25 v.l.

εἴσειμι: inf. εἰσιέναι.

intr. *to move in*: *s* the high priest and εἰς τὸ ἅγιον 'into the sanctuary' Ex 28.23 (ǁ εἰσπορεύομαι vs. 26);:: ἔξειμι 28.31.

Cf. εἰσέρχομαι, ~πορεύομαι, ἔξειμι, εἶμι.

εἰσέρχομαι: fut. ~ελεύσομαι, inf. ~ελεύσεσθαι; aor. ~ῆλθον, 3pl. ~ήλθοσαν, subj. ~έλθω, impv. εἴσελθε, 3pl. ~ελθέτωσαν, inf. ~ελθεῖν, ptc. ~ελθών, opt. ~έλθοιμι; pf. ~ελήλυθα, inf. ~εληλυθέναι; plpf. ~εληλύθειν.

1. *to enter, make entry*: τὰ εἰσπορευόμενα .. εἰσῆλθεν Ge 7.16 (see Lee 87); *s* traveller, εἰς τὴν οἰκίαν αὐτοῦ 19.3; εἰς Αἴγυπτον 46.8; εἴσελθε 24.31 (said to one standing outdoors); ἐναντίον τινός Ex 7.10; 10.3 (ǁ πρός τινα vs. 1); πρός τινα Ge19.5 (as a guest), Ex 3.18, 5.1, 6.11 (for an audience); from outdoors, To 5.9; *s* servant into service, Ex 21.3 (:: ἐξέρχομαι); thief or robber, πρός τινα Ho 7.1, Ob 5, διὰ θυρίδων 'through windows' Jl 2.9; worshippers entering a temple, Hg 1.14, πρὸς τὸν Βεελφεγωρ Ho 9.10; πρὶν ἢ εἰσελθεῖν πρὸς αὐτὰς τὰς μαίας 'before the midwives come to them [= women in labour] Ex 1.19; theophany, τὴν νύκτα 'at night' Ge 20.3; εἰς τὴν κιβωτόν 6.18, εἰς Βαιθηλ Am 4.4; cultic functionaries, Jl 1.13, ἔσω εἰς τὸν οἶκον κυρίου 2C 29.16; invading foreign troops, Mi 4.8 (prec. by their arrival ἥκω), εἰς πύλας Ob 11, 13; conquerors, εἰς τὴν γῆν De 31.7; harvesters entering sbd's field, πρός τινα Ob 5; a lion's whelp entering its den, Na 2.12; offerings 'to be brought into' a temple, εἰς τὸν οἶκον τοῦ κυρίου Ho 9.4; fig. εἰσῆλθε τρόμος εἰς τὰ ὀστᾶ μου 'trembling entered my bones' Hb 3.16, cf. εἰς αὐτοὺς τὸ πνεῦμα 'the spirt entered them' Ez 37.10; a place into which entry is made indicated by εἰς, Ho 9.4, 11.9, ἐκεῖ Ge 19.22, ἐναντίον Ex 10.3, ὧδε Zc 7.3, πρός τινα 'to a place belonging to or owned by sbd' Ge 7.15, 39.14, Ho 9.10, Ob 5, acc., τὴν πόλιν 1K 9.13 (*L* εἰς ..), but not τὴν πύλην, ἣν εἰσελήλυθεν 'the gate by which he had entered' Ez 46.9; into a room or tent, Ge 20.3; ὑπὸ τὴν στέγην τῶν δοκῶν μου 'under the roof of my rafters' 19.8; ἑαυτῷ with centripetal force (see Muraoka 1978) Am 6.1; Zc 1.21 (v.l. ἐξήλθοσαν, ἐξῆλθον);:: ἐξέρχομαι Ge 43.30 (see vs. 31), Nu 27.17, 21; ǁ εἰσπορεύομαι Ez 46.10. **b**. with no indication of where into: ἐπ' αὐτόν '(into his quarters) to attack him' 2K 17.2*L* (B: ἐπέρχομαι). **c**. *to be admitted* as a member: εἰς ἐκκλησίαν κυρίου De 23.1, ἐν ἐκκλησίᾳ θεοῦ Ne 13.1. **d**. *to accept and agree to the terms* of (ἐν): ὁ λαὸς οἱ εἰσελθόντες ἐν τῇ διαθήκῃ Je 41.10, ἐν διαθήκῃ μετὰ σοῦ Ez 16.8, cf. CD 12.11 באו עִמּוֹ בברית אברהם. **e**. fig., *s* cry for help, εἰς τὰ ὦτα αὐτοῦ Ps 17.7, ἐνώπιόν σου ὁ στεναγμός 'the sigh' 78.11, προσευχή 'prayer'

87.3, ἀξίωμα 'request' 118.170; into a certain state, εἰς τὴν κατάπαυσιν ^τοῦ θεοῦ^ 'into the rest.' Ps 94.11, εἰς τὸ σκότος To 4.10 𝔊^I^. **f.** for an idiomatic collocation with ἐξέρχομαι as in 2C 1.10, see under εἰσπορεύομαι **b**.

2. *to begin* an action: εἰς κρίσιν Ps 142.2; 2M 3.18.

3. *to have sexual intercourse* (with πρός τινα): *s* alm. alw. male, εἰσῆλθεν πρὸς Αγαρ καὶ συνέλαβεν '.. and she became pregnant' Ge 16.4; 19.31, 29.21, Le 18.14. Thrice w. a woman as *s*, but without πρός: εἰσελθοῦσα ἡ πρεσβυτέρα ἐκοιμήθη μετὰ τοῦ πατρὸς αὐτῆς Ge 19.33; 19.34, 35: cf. 2K 11.4 εἰσῆλθεν πρὸς αὐτήν (MT /wattāvō' 'ēlāw/); with πρός, but the focus on entering a marriage relationship, Da 11.6 TH.

Cf. ἔρχομαι, συνεισέρχομαι, εἰσίημι, εἰσπορεύομαι, ἐμβαίνω, ἐξέρχομαι, παρεμπίπτω: Schneider, *TDNT* 2.676f. On a developing complementary distribution of εἰσέρχομαι and εἰσπορεύομαι and other pairs of related composita – the latter being usual in the pres. and impf., and the former rarely or not at all used in those tenses – see Lee 85-8.

εἰσκυκλέομαι.ʃ

to plunge into: metaph., + dat. (historical records to be studied) 2M 2.24.

εἰσκύπτω.ʃ

**to overhang*: *s* road, ἐπὶ Γαι 1K 13.18. Cf. κύπτω.

εἰσόδ(ε)ιος, α, ον. f.ʃ

pertaining to entry: subst.f., military *invasion*, Da TH 11.13. Cf. εἴσοδος.

εἰσοδιάζω: aor.ptc.pass. ~οδιασθείς.ʃ

pass. *to be collected and come in as revenue*: into a temple coffer, *s* ἀργύριον τῶν ἁγίων .. ἐν οἴκῳ κυρίου 4K 12.5 (|| εἰσφέρομαι 12.10, 22.4), εἰς οἶκον κυρίου 2C 34.14. Cf. ἐξοδιάζω.

εἴσοδος, ου. f.

1. *act of entering an arena of activities, arrival*: τῇ σῇ ~ῳ 'through your arrival' Ge 30.27; τίς ὑπομενεῖ ἡμέραν ~ου αὐτοῦ; 'who will abide the day of his arrival?' Ma 3.2; φυλάξει τὴν ~όν σου καὶ τὴν ἔξοδόν σου Ps 120.8; δόξης αὐτῆς Is 66.11; birth of hum., εἰς τὸν βίον Wi 7.6 (:: ἔξοδος).

2. *place where entrance is made*: τῆς θαλάσσης Ez 27.3 (w. ref. to the island city of Tyre), Si 14.22; entrance hall, 4K 23.11.

Cf. εἰσόδ(ε)ιος, ἔξοδος, εἰσέρχομαι, ἐξίημι, πάροδος: Talshir 114f. (on 1E 8.60).

εἰσπέμπω: aor. εἰσέπεμψα.ʃ

to send in: + dat. (com.) pers., τὰ δέοντα 'the necessary supplies' 2M 13.20. Cf. πέμπω.

εἰσπηδάω: aor. εἰσεπήδησα, subj. εἰσπηδήσω.ʃ

intr. *to move in rapidly*: ἡ ἄρκος 'a bear' .. εἰσπηδήσῃ εἰς τὸν οἶκον αὐτοῦ Am 5.19; διὰ τῆς πλαγίας θύρας 'through the side door' Su 26 TH. Cf. εἰσέρχομαι.

εἰσπλέω: aor.ptc. ~πλεύσας.ʃ

to sail into a space: 2M 14.1; τι 4M 13.6. Cf. πλέω.

εἰσπορεύομαι: aor. ~επορεύθην; pf. ~πεπόρευμαι, ptc. ~πεπορευμένος.

intr. *to move in*: abs. τὰ εἰσπορευόμενα .. εἰσῆλθεν Ge 7.16 (see Lee 87); Jl 3.11 (prob. into a battlefield), 13 (wine-vat), Jo 15.18 and Jd 1.14A (prob. a bride entering her husband's house or a bridal canopy); Zc 8.10 (opp. ἐκπ.); Ma 3.2 (|| εἴσοδος, q.v.); εἴς τι, Ge 23.10, Ex 33.8, Ho 4.15, Am 5.5, Hg 2.16; εἰς Αἴγυπτον Ex 1.1; ἐν ταῖς πύλαις 'through the gates' Je 17.20 (|| ταῖς πύλαις vs. 21, διὰ τῶν πύλων vs. 25), τὰς πύλας Ez 26.10; πρός τινα, esp. a woman, i.e. her quarters or dwelling in order to have sexual relationship, Ge 6.4, Am 2.7; not a woman, Ge 44.30; for an audience, πρὸς Φαραω Ex 5.23; + acc. loci, πύλας 'gates' Ez 44.17; || εἰσέρχομαι 46.10. ***b.** εἰσπορεύομαι καὶ ἐκπορεύομαι idiomatically indicates a whole gamut of activities and movements: εὐλογημένος σὺ ἐν τῷ εἰσπορεύεσθαί σε .. ἐν τῷ ἐκπορεύεσθαί σε De 28.6; οὐ δυνήσομαι ἔτι εἰσπορεύεσθαι καὶ ἐκπορεύεσθαι 31.2; To 5.18; the two (synonymous) verbs in the reverse order– ἐξελεύσεται πρὸ προσώπου αὐτῶν καὶ .. εἰσελεύσεται πρὸ προσώπου αὐτῶν Nu 27.17 (of leaders), ἐπὶ τῷ στόματι αὐτοῦ ἐξελεύσονται .. 27.21, cf. φυλάξει τὴν εἴσοδόν σου καὶ τὴν ἔξοδόν σου Ps 120.8, ἡ ἔξοδός σου καὶ ἡ εἴσοδός σου μετ' ἐμοῦ ἐν τῇ παρεμβολῇ 1K 18.6, and see also under εἰσέρχομαι **1f**.

Cf. εἰσέρχομαι, εἰσίημι, (ἐκ)πορεύομαι, παρεισπορεύομαι.

εἰσσπάω: aor.mid. εἰσεσπασάμην.ʃ *

to draw in: + acc. pers. πρὸς ἑαυτοὺς εἰς τὸν οἶκον Ge 19.10. Cf. σπάω.

εἰστρέχω: aor.ptc. ~δραμών.ʃ

to run inside: *s* hum., εἰς τὴν πόλιν 2M 5.26. Cf. τρέχω.

εἰσφέρω: fut. εἰσοίσω, pass. ~ενεχθήσομαι; aor.act. ~ήνεγκα, ptc. ~ενέγκας, impv. ~ένεγκε, ~ένεγκον, pass. εἰσηνέχθην, subj.act. ~ενέγχω, pass. ~ενεχθῶ, inf. ~ενεχθῆναι.

1. *to carry in, bring in* (into εἰς): + acc., τῷ πατρί σου Ge 27.10; αὐτῷ οἶνον 27.25; πᾶν τὸ ἀργύριον εἰς τὸν οἶκον Φαραω 47.14; τὰ καλὰ .. εἰς τοὺς ναοὺς ὑμῶν Jl 3.5; cultic offerings, εἰς τὸν οἶκον τοῦ κυρίου Ex 23.19, *o* δῶρα Je 40.11; ἐσώτερόν τινος Ex 26.33; Ma 1.13, 3.10; πόδας εἰς πέδας .. εἰς κλοιὸν τράχηλον 'feet into fetters .. neck into collar' Si 6.24, εἰς δουλείαν Ne 3.4; opp. ἐκφέρω

Ex 4.6; woman as wife from outside of one's own clan or tribe, Jd 12.9 B (A: εἰσάγω).

2. *to ingather, harvest* agricultural crop: + acc., σῖτον .. οἶνον .. ἔλαιον De 11.14, ἀμητοῦ εἰσφερομένου Is 23.3; ἐσπείρατε πολλὰ καὶ εἰσηνέγκατε ὀλίγα Hg 1.6, cf. 1.9 pass. and De 28.38 (:: ἐκφέρω).

3. pass. *to be subjected to*: κρίσιν 'trial' 2M 14.38, cf. Abel 1949 ad loc.

Cf. φέρω, εἰσφορά, ἐκφέρω.

εἰσφορά, ᾶς. f.

a legally imposed pecuniary contribution towards the maintenance of cultic activities: εἰ. κυρίῳ Ex 30.13 (to the amount of a drachm); δώσουσιν τὴν ~ὰν τῷ κυρίῳ 30.14; λήμψῃ τὸ ἀργύριον τῆς ~ᾶς παρὰ τῶν υἱῶν Ισραηλ 30.16. Cf. εἰσφέρω, ἀφαίρεμα.

εἶτα. adv.

should a certain condition be met, 'then,' mostly w. fut.: Jb 5.24; + pres., Pr 6.11.

εἴτε.

1. Repeated before each of two or more terms presented as equally possible or applicable: εἴτε δεξιὰ εἴτε ἀριστερά 'whether to the right or to the left' Is 30.21; εἴτε δέκα εἴτε ἑκατὸν εἴτε χίλια ἔτη 'whether it be ten or a hundred or a thousand years' Si 41.4; εἴτε τοῖς θεοῖς τῶν πατέρων ὑμῶν .. εἴτε τοῖς θεοῖς τῶν Αμορραίων Jo 24.15.

2. Following another conditional clause, 'if then; if, however': Jb 9.21, Wi 17.17, 18, 2M 12.45.

εἴτοι.

= εἴτε **1**: εἴτοι πτωχὸς εἴτοι πλούσιος 'whether poor or rich' Ru 3.10.

ἐκ. Prep. foll. by the genitive; before vowels, ἐξ.

1. indicates dissociation: with verbs of expelling, annihilating, removing, taking, receiving, rescuing, revenging, depletion of contents or resources, hanging, etc.– ἐξολεθρευθήσεται .. ἐκ τοῦ γένους αὐτῆς 'shall be exterminated out of its community' Ge 17.14; ἐκ τοῦ οἴκου μου ἐκβαλῶ αὐτούς Ho 9.15; ἀπολῶ σοφοὺς ἐκ τῆς Ἰδουμαίας Ob 8; ὅπως ἐξαρθῇ ἄνθρωπος ἐξ ὄρους Ησαυ 'to clear Esau's mountains of (fighting) men' Ob 9; ἐξ οἴκου θεοῦ σου ἐξολεθρεύσω τὰ γλυπτά '.. the graven images' Na 1.14; ἐξαιρούμενος ἐκ θλίψεως 'rescuing out of distress' 2.2; διέφθειραν .. ἐξ ἀνθρώπων 2.4; ἐτελεύτησεν οἱ βάτραχοι ἐκ τῶν οἰκιῶν 'the frogs perished ..' Ex 8.13; συνετρίβη ἐχθρὸς μέγας ἐξ Ισραηλ 'a great foe was crushed ..' 1M 13.51; ἀτεκνωθήσονται ἐξ ἀνθρώπων Ho 9.12; εἰς τὴν γῆν, ἐξ ἧς ἐλήμφθης 'into the ground, from which you were taken' Ge 3.19; δέξασθαι τὸ αἷμα .. ἐκ τῆς χειρός σου 'to receive the blood ..' 4.11, ἐκ χειρός μου ζήτησον αὐτόν 43.9; ἐξείλατο αὐτὸν ἐκ τῶν χειρῶν αὐτῶν 'rescued him ..' 37.21, cf. the sg. w. multiple persons– ἐξελεῖται ὑμᾶς ἐκ χειρὸς ἐχθρῶν ὑμῶν Ba 4.18, σώσει ὑμᾶς ἐκ χειρὸς ἐχθρῶν ἡμῶν 1K 4.3; ῥύσεται τὴν ψυχὴν αὐτοῦ ἐκ χειρὸς ᾅδου Ps 88.49; ἐκδεδίκηται ἐκ Καιν Ge 4.24; ἐξέλιπεν τὸ ὕδωρ ἐξ τοῦ ἀσκοῦ 'the water in the bag ran out' 21.15, sim. 47.15, 49.10; οὐκ ἐκλείψει ἐξ αὐτῶν πάντα 'nothing will be unattainable to them' 11.6, see below **11**; τούτων ἐκ μαστῶν κρεμάσαντες τὰ βρέφη 'making the babes hang at their breasts' 2M 6.10, ἡ ψυχὴ αὐτοῦ ἐκκρέμαται ἐκ τῆς τούτου ψυχῆς 'his soul is hanging on to the soul of this one' Ge 44.30. **b.** indicates distance, 'away from', = ἀπό: ἔστη ἡ θάλασσα ἐκ τοῦ σάλου αὐτῆς Jn 1.15; w. ἀποστρέφω 3.9; ἐξέρχομαι 4.5; ἐκκλίνω Ma 2.8; ἀνίημι 4.2; ἀνέχω (q.v.) Am 4.7. **c.** of waking up: ἐξεγείρων καθεύδοντα ἐκ βαθέος ὕπνου 'rousing a sleeper from deep sleep' Si 22.9; ἐκ τῆς νηστείας 'from the fast' 1E 8.70. **d.** ἐξ ἑαυτῆς ἐγένετο 'she got ecstatic, flabbergasted' 3K 10.5 || 2C 9.4.

2. indicates an entity out of which a component or part is singled out ("partitive"): οὐ λήμψῃ γυναῖκα ἐκ τῶν θυγατέρων Χανααν Ge 28.1 (|| ἀπό 27.46 and back to ἐκ 28.6); δέκα ἄνδρες ἐκ πασῶν τῶν γλωσσῶν τῶν ἐθνῶν 'ten men out of all the language communities' Zc 8.23; εἷς ἐξ ἡμῶν Ge 3.22, εἷς ἐκ τῶν ἑπτὰ .. ἀγγέλων To 12.12 𝔊^I (𝔊^II om. ἐκ); οὐ μὴ ὑπολειφθῇ ἐξ αὐτῶν ῥίζα Ma 4.1; the component not mentioned, οὐ σπαρήσεται ἐκ τοῦ ὀνόματός σου ἔτι 'there will not arise any more bearing your name' Na 1.14; w. superlative, τὰς κρατίστας ἐκ πασῶν τῶν βασιλειῶν τούτων 'the best of all these kingdoms' Am 6.2.

3. *some of, part of*, corresponding to the Heb. partitive מִן: ἔπιεν ἐκ τοῦ οἴνου 'he drank (a bit) of the wine' Ge 9.21; συγκόψεις ἐκ τούτων λεπτόν 'you shall crush some of them into powder' Ex 30.36; || ἀπό La 3.19. See ἀπό **3 b**.

4. *belonging to, affiliated to* a group: ἀδελφὴν ἐκ πατρὸς αὐτοῦ ἢ ἐκ μητρὸς αὐτοῦ Le 20.17, sim. De 13.6; Ζοροβαβελ τὸν τοῦ Σαλαθιηλ ἐκ φυλῆς Ιουδα Hg 2.21; 'characterised by' – Ταῦτα ἐκ κακοπαθείας ἐστί 'these are toilsome affairs' Ma 1.13.

5. indicates origin, point of departure, source: Τοῦτο νῦν ὀστοῦν ἐκ τῶν ὀστέων μου καὶ σὰρξ ἐκ τῆς σαρκός μου 'this is now a bone out of my bones ..' Ge 2.23, sim. 29.14; πόθεν ἔστε ὑμεῖς; .. Ἐκ Χαρραν ἐσμεν 29.4; οἱ ἄνθρωποι οἱ ἐκ τοῦ τόπου 'the local people' 38.22; ἐκ τούτων ἀφωρίσθησαν 'from these split off' 10.5; ἵνα τεκνοποιήσῃς ἐξ αὐτῆς 'so that you may produce a child through her' 16.2; δώσω σοι ἐξ αὐτῆς τέκνον 17.16; συνέλαβον .. ἐκ τοῦ πατρὸς αὐτῶν 'they became pregnant .. by their father' 19.36, ἐν γαστρὶ ἔλαβεν ἐξ αὐτοῦ 'she conceived by him' 38.18; ἀδελφή μού ἐστιν ἐκ πατρός 'she is a paternal sister of mine' 20.12; τῶν ἐξελθόντων ἐκ τῆς κιβωτοῦ '.. out of the ark' 9.10; πάντα τὰ ἀνατέλλοντα ἐκ τῆς γῆς 'all that sprouts out of the ground' 19.25; βασιλεῖς ἐκ σοῦ ἐξελεύσονται 17.6; ἐκπορευόμενα ἐκ μέσου δύο ὀρέων Zc 6.1; ὄξος ἐξ οἴνου 'vinegar made from wine' Nu 6.3; εἰσήκουσεν .. τῆς φωνῆς .. ἐκ τοῦ τόπου οὗ ἦν '.. from where he was' Ge 21.17; οὐδὲ μὴ ἀκούσθῃ ἐκ τοῦ στόματος ὑμῶν 'nor shall it be on your lips' Ex 23.13; πιεῖν ὕδωρ ἐκ τοῦ ποταμοῦ 'to drink water from the river' 7.21 (ǁ ἀπό vs. 18, 24); νίψεται Ααρων .. ἐξ αὐτοῦ (= τοῦ λουτῆρος 'wash-basin') τὰς χεῖρας 30.19; ǁ ἀπό – ὅσα γίνεται ἐξ ἀμπέλου, οἶνον ἀπὸ στεμφύλων 'that which comes from a vine, wine from pressed grapes' Nu 6.4; ἐξ αἱρέσεως αὐτῶν 'by their own choice' 1M 8.30. **b**. *from the inside of*: πηγὴ ἀνέβαινεν ἐκ τῆς γῆς 'a stream of water gushed up out of the ground' Ge 2.6; ἐκ τῆς κοιλίας τοῦ κήτους 'out of the belly of the giant fish' Jn 2.2, fig., τὸ σπέρμα σου μετὰ σέ, ὃς ἔσται ἐκ τῆς κοιλίας σου 2K 7.12 (of David's descendants); cf. προσδέχομαί τι ἐκ τῶν χειρῶν τινος 'to accept sth held in sbd's hands' Ma 1.10, 13; λαβεῖν .. ἐκ τῶν χειρῶν ὑμῶν 2.13.

6. *due to, caused by*: στεναγμῷ ἐκ κόπων 'with groaning caused by toil' Ma 2.13; ἐκ καρπῶν ἐπιτηδευμάτων αὐτῶν 'because of the fruits of their (mal)practices' Mi 7.13; γενομένου δέους .. φόβου τε ἐκ τῆς τοῦ τὰ πάντα ἐφορῶντος ἐπιφανείας 'dread and fear having come about due to the appearance of one who sees everything' 2M 12.22.

7. *by means of*: χρίσεις ἐξ αὐτοῦ τὴν σκηνὴν .. 'you shall anoint the tent with it [= ἔλαιον 'oil']' Ex 30.26; συνεχομένους ἐκ τῆς ὑακίνθου 'fastened with a string of blue' 36.29; Je 38.39.

8. *on the strength of, with the aid of*: ὁ δίκαιος ἐκ πίστεώς μου ζήσεται Hb 2.4.

9. with a passive verb marks the agent of an action: ἀδικοῦμαι ἐκ σοῦ 'I am being wronged by you' Ge 16.5, ἀνενεχθήσεται .. ἐκ λαοῦ Is 18.7 (ǁ ἀπό).

10. with nouns, often in the pl., indicating a position relative to a given point of reference: ἐκ δεξιῶν .. καὶ ἐξ εὐωνύμων 'on the right .. and on the left' Ex 14.22; ἐπορεύθη ἐκ τῶν ὄπισθεν .. ἔστη ἐκ τῶν ὀπίσω αὐτῶν 'moved at the back .. and stood behind them' 14.19; ἐξ ἀμφοτέρων τῶν κλιτῶν τοῦ ἱλαστηρίου 'at either side of the propitiatory' 25.17; γεγραμμέναι ἐξ ἀμφοτέρων τῶν μερῶν αὐτῶν 'inscribed on both their sides' 32.15; πῆχυν ἐκ τούτου καὶ πῆχυν ἐκ τούτου 'one cubit on one side and one cubit on the other' 26.13; ἐκ τῶν ἐμπροσθίων 'to the front' 28.14; ἐκ τοῦ πέραν 'on the other side' Nu 21.11; ἐκ δεξιῶν τῆς λυχνίας καὶ ἐξ εὐωνύμων 'to the right of the candlestick and to its left' Zc 4.11; ἐκ δεξιῶν τοῖς τέσσαρσι Ez 1.10; ὁ κλέπτης ἐκ τούτου 'the thief on this side' Zc 5.3; ἐξ ἀνατολῶν 'on the east' 14.4 (ǁ ἀπὸ ἀνατολῶν ἡλίου 'to the east' De 4.41). See ἀπό **8**.

11. *deprived of, lacking in*: ἡ γῆ ἀφανισθήσεται .. ἐκ διοδεύοντος 'the land will be devasted, with nobody passing through it' Zc 7.14; ἐξολεθρεύσει ἅρματα ἐξ Εφραιμ 'he will demolish chariots ..' 9.10; οὐκ ἐκλείψει ἐξ αὐτῶν πάντα 'nothing will be unattainable to them' Ge 11.6 (= ἀπό).

12. *beginning at the time of*: ἐκ παιδὸς ἕως τοῦ νῦν 'since our childhood till now' Ge 46.34, ἐκ παιδαρίου Je 31.11; ἐκ νεότητος αὐτοῦ 'since his youth' Ge 8.21; ἐκ νυκτός 'since when it was still night' Is 26.9; ἀπ' ἀρχῆς ἐξ ἡμερῶν αἰῶνος 'from the beginning since the earliest times' Mi 5.2; ἐκ πρωΐθεν ἕως δείλης 'from early morning till evening' 1M 10.30, cf. ἀπὸ πρωΐθεν ἕως μεσημβρίας 3K 18.26 and ἀπὸ τῶν χρόνων Σαμουηλ 1E 1.18. Cf. s.v. ἀπό **2 b**, and Renehan 1.145 s.v. νύξ. **b**. indicates a point of time in the past: ἐξ ἡμερῶν ἀρχῆς 'in the primaeval era' 4K 19.25*L*, ἐξ ἀρχαίων ἡμερῶν 'in primaeval times' Is 37.26 (opp. νῦν).

13. indicates material from which sth is fashioned: ποίησον σεαυτῷ κιβωτὸν ἐκ ξύλων τετραγώνων 'Make yourself an ark from square timber' Ge 6.14; ἐκ τῶν τοῦ πατρὸς ἡμῶν πεποίηκεν πᾶσαν τὴν δόξαν ταύτην 31.1; ἐποίησαν ἑαυτοῖς χώνευμα ἐκ τοῦ ἀργυρίου αὐτῶν 'they made themselves a molten image from their silver' Ho 13.2; Ez 16.17.

14. indicates close succession or proximity, with a noun repeated (the first noun in the acc.), alr. Classical, though not common, e.g. ἡμέραν ἐξ ἡμέρας Henioch. fragm. 5.13: ἡμέραν ἐξ ἡμέρας 'day in day out' Ge 39.10, cf. ἑκάστην ἡμέραν ἐξ ἡμέρας To 10.1 𝔊[II]; παρασιωπήσῃ αὐτῇ ἡμέραν ἐξ ἡμέρας 'keeps quiet to her for days on end' Nu 30.15; μισθωτὸς ἐνιαυτὸν ἐξ ἐνιαυτοῦ 'a labourer hired on yearly basis' Le 25.53; 'annually' De 15.20; μῆνα ἐκ μηνὸς καὶ σάββατον ἐκ σαββάτου 'month after m., and sabbath after sab.' Is 66.23; ὁλοκαύτωμα μῆνα ἐκ μηνός 'monthly burnt-offering' Nu 28.14; πόλιν ἐκ πόλεως φεύγων 'fleeing from city to city' 2M 5.8; εἰσελεύσεται ταμιεῖον ἐκ ταμιείου 'will enter room after room' 2C 18.24; πλανωμένη καὶ λάτρις τόπον ἐκ τόπου καὶ οἰκίαν ἐξ οἰκίας 'wandering around as a helpmaid from place to place and from home to home' Jb 2.9; πορεύσονται ἐκ δυνάμεως εἰς δύναμιν 'they will go from strength to strength' Ps 83.8. Cf. ἐξ ἀλλήλων συνεχόμεναι ἑτέρα ἐκ τῆς ἑτέρας 'joined with one another' Ex 26.3.

15. indicates a point of reference: ἀνακέκλημαι ἐξ ὀνόματος 'called by name' Ex 30.2, sim. 35.30; Nu 1.17; ἐξ ὀνομάτων αὐτῶν 'to mention them by name' 3.17; ἐξ ἀριθμοῦ ὀνομάτων 'in accordance with the number of names' 26.53.

16. *by paying as price*: ἐκ πάσης τιμῆς 'regardless of price' Ep Je 24.

17. *on having reached* a period of time: ἐκ τούτων Da 1.5 LXX (TH μετὰ ταῦτα).

18. Idiom: ἐκ δευτέρου 'for a second time' Hg 2.20, Zc 4.12; ἐξ ὑστέρου 'in the end' Ep Je 71. For ἐξ ἐναντίας and ἐκ προσώπου τινός, see under ἐναντίος and πρόσωπον respectively.

Cf. ἀπό: Johannessohn, *Präp.*, 284-93.

ἕκαστος, η, ον. pron.

each, separately and severally from the rest, 'on one's own,' emphasising individuality or independence: ἀναπαύσεται ἕκαστος ὑποκάτω ἀμπέλου αὐτοῦ 'each will take rest under his own vine' Mi 4.4; ἐφ' ἑκάστου πυλῶνος 'at each gate' 1E 1.15 (‖ πύλης καὶ πύλης 2C 35.15); ὑπέδειξε ~α 'told all things one by one' Da 2.17 LXX; ~α τούτων 'the full details of this information' 4M 4.4, cf. Renehan 2.62f.

There are a number of patterns for grammatical agreement between the pronoun – alw. in the sg. – on the one hand, and the verb and other associated adjuncts on the other.

a. the verb in the pl., but the adjuncts in the sg.: εἶπαν δὲ ἕκαστος πρὸς τὸν ἀδελφὸν αὐτοῦ 'they said to one another' Ge 37.19; ἕκαστος κατὰ τὸ αὐτοῦ ἐνύπνιον εἴδομεν 41.11; ἐξίσταντο οἱ ἄνθρωποι ἕκαστος πρὸς τὸν ἀδελφὸν αὐτοῦ 'the men kept exchanging looks of astonishment with one another' 43:33; πάντες οἱ λαοὶ πορεύσονται ἕκαστος τὴν ὁδὸν αὐτοῦ 'all the nations will go each its own way' Mi 4.5; ἕκαστος τὸν πλησίον αὐτοῦ ἐκθλίβουσιν 'each afflicting his own neighbour' 7.2; ὑμεῖς διώκετε ἕκαστος εἰς τὸν οἶκον αὐτοῦ 'you run each into his own house' Hg 1.9; Jl 2.7 +. Cf. Zc 10.1 (αὐτοῖς .. ἑκάστῳ); no adjunct, λαβέτωσαν ἕκαστος πρόβατον κατ' οἴκους πατριῶν Ex 12.3.

b. the verb in the sg.: ἕκαστος ἀπὸ τοῦ ἀδελφοῦ αὐτοῦ οὐκ ἀφέξεται Jl 2.8 (MT: pl.); no adjunct, αἰτησάτω ἕκαστος παρὰ τοῦ πλησίον καὶ γυνὴ παρὰ τῆς πλησίον Ex 11.2; ‖ a pl. construction w. a subsequent verb, ἔλαβεν ἕκαστος τὸ πυρεῖον αὐτοῦ, καὶ ἐπέθηκαν ἐπ' αὐτὰ πῦρ (MT: /wayyiqḥu .. wayyāśimu ../ Nu 16.18, see also Le 25.10.

c. the adjuncts also in the pl.: ἀφωρίσθησαν νῆσοι .. ἕκαστος κατὰ γλῶσσαν ἐν ταῖς φυλαῖς αὐτῶν 'islanders split .. each according to language in their tribes' Ge 10.5; ἀνεβόων ἕκαστος πρὸς τὸν θεὸν αὐτῶν 'they called aloud each to his own god' Jn 1.5 (MT: sg.); Ex 35.21.

d. the adjuncts partly in the sg. and partly in the pl.: κακίαν ἕκαστος τοῦ ἀδελφοῦ αὐτοῦ μὴ μνησικακείτω ἐν ταῖς καρδίαις ὑμῶν 'do not remember each his own brother's injury in his heart' Zc 7.10; ἐξαποστελῶ πάντας τοὺς ἀνθρώπους ἕκαστος ἐπὶ τὸν πλησίον αὐτοῦ 'I will send all the people each to his own neighbour' Zc 8.10, sim. 8.17.

e. The pronoun is often used in the form of ἕκαστος .. τὸν πλησίον (or ἀδελφὸν) αὐτοῦ (or some other appropriate case): e.g. διεχωρίσθησαν ἕκαστος ἀπὸ τοῦ ἀδελφοῦ αὐτοῦ 'they separated from each other' Ge 13.11; Zc 3.10, Hg 2.22.

f. εἷς is added to reinforce the notion of universal applicability: ἐξ ἑνὸς καὶ ~ου ὑμῶν 'from each one of you' Jd 15.7 A.

Cf. πᾶς: Schmidt 4.540-2, 547.

ἑκάτερος, α, ον.

each of the two already mentioned or *understood*: εἶδον ἀμφότεροι ἐνύπνιον, ἑκάτερος ἐνύπνιον 'they both saw a dream, each a dream' Ge 40.5, ἐξομολογήσαντο πρὸς ἀλλήλους ἑ. τὴν ὀδύνην αὐτοῦ 'they confessed to each other their agony' Su 14 LXX; ἐλάβομεν ἑ. ἕν 'we each took one' To 5.3 $\mathfrak{G}^{II}$, ~αις ταῖς χερσὶν αὐτοῦ 'with each of his hands' 11.13 $\mathfrak{G}^{II}$; τούτων ~ου 'of each of these two' Wi 15.7. **b**. more than two entities involved: Ez 37.7.

Cf. ἕκαστος, ἀμφότερος: Shipp 67.

ἑκατέρωθεν. adv.

on either side: w. ref. to both arms placed on hips, 4M 6.3.

ἑκατόν: indecl. num.

hundred: Ge 5.9; πεντήκοντα καὶ ἑ. '150' 8.3; ἑ. τριάκοντα ἓξ ἔτη '136 years' Ex 6.20. Cf. ἑκατοστεύω, ἑκατοντάς.

ἑκατονταετής, ές.ʃ

hundred years old: subst., Ge 17.17.

ἑκατονταπλασίων, ον.ʃ

hundredfold: subst.n.pl.acc. used adv., 2K 24.3B.

ἑκατονταπλασίως. adv.ʃ

hundredfold: 2K 24.3*L*, 1C 21.3.

ἑκατοντάρχης, ου. m.ʃ

= subs.: 4K 11.10, 15.

ἑκατόνταρχος, ου. m.

leader of hundred men: Ex 18.21; ‖ χιλίαρχος Nu 31.14, ‖ χιλίαρχος, πεντηκόνταρχος, δεκάδαρχος De 1.15. Cf. ἑκατόν, δεκάδαρχος, πεντηκόνταρχος, χιλίαρχος.

ἑκατοντάς, άδος. f.ʃ

assemblage comprising 100 members: of troops, + χιλιάς 1K 29.2, 2K 18.4, 1C 28.1. Cf. ἑκατόν.

ἑκατοστεύω.ʃ *

to yield a hundredfold (of crop): εὗρεν .. ἑκατοστεύουσαν κριθήν Ge 26.12.

ἑκατοστός, ή, όν.

hundredth: in order, 1M 1.10.

ἐκβαίνω: aor. ἐξέβην, inf. ~βῆναι, impv.2pl ~βητε.

1. *to move out on foot*: ἐκ τοῦ Ιορδάνου Jo 4.16, ἐκ τοῦ βοθύνου 'out of the pit' Is 24.18; from aboard a ship, 1M 15.4; fig., ἐξεβήσαν ἐξ ὁδοῦ τῶν πατέρων αὐτῶν 'parted with the ways of their forefathers' Ju 5.8.

2. *to result* in a certain way, 'turn out': "an unbroken horse turns out stubborn" Si 30.8; ἀπὸ λύπης ἐκβαίνει θάνατος 'death results from grief' 38.18, "what resulted was not what the king had commanded" 1M 4.27. Cf. χωρέω **2**.

Cf. ἔκβασις, ἐμβαίνω.

ἐκβάλλω: fut. ~βαλῶ; aor. ἐξέβαλον, impv. ἔκβαλε, subj. ~βάλω, inf. ~βαλεῖν, ptc. ~βαλών, pass. ἐξεβλήθην, impv.3pl ~βληθήτωσαν; pf.ptc.pass. ~βεβλημένος.

1. *to throw out*: physically, + acc. pers., εἰς τὴν θάλασσαν Jn 1.15; out of the belly of the fish, τὸν Ιωναν ἐπὶ τὴν ξηράν 'on to the dry land' 2.11; as useless, Le 1.16, τὰ βδελύγματα .. τὰ ἀργυρᾶ Is 2.20; εἰς γῆν Je 22.28 (+ ἐκρίπτω); as dangerous, αὐτοὺς ἔξω τῆς πόλεως εἰς τόπον ἀκάθαρτον Le 14.40; as street beggars, Ps 108.10.

2. *to sever a relationship* or *association by making move away*, 'expel': + acc. pers., Ge 21.10, Ex 2.17; 11.1 (+ cogn. dat. ἐκβολῇ); ἐκ τῆς γῆς 12.33; ἀπὸ προσώπου ὑμῶν τὸν Ἀμορραῖον καὶ Χαναναῖον .. 34.11, ἐχθρόν De 33.27; as punishment, ἐκ τοῦ οἴκου μου Ho 9.15: εἰς γῆν ἑτέραν De 29.28; εἰς τὰ ἔθνη 'among the (strange) peoples' Zc 7.14; ***o*** woman, w. ref. to divorce, Si 7.26, 28.15; along w. children, 1E 8.90; pass., ***o*** divorced woman, Le 21.7, χήραν καὶ ἐκβεβλημένην καὶ βεβηλωμένην καὶ πόρνην 'a widow .. a prostitute' 21.14, Ez 44.22 (not qualifying as a priest's wife); Nu 30.10.

3. *to make move out* or *depart*: + acc. pers., Ge 3.24 (|| ἐξαποστέλλω); ἀπὸ προσώπου τῆς γῆς 4.14, ἀπὸ προσώπου Φαραω Ex 10.11, ἐκ προσώπου τινος Jd 6.9; αὐτοὺς ἐκ τῆς γῆς αὐτοῦ Ex 6.1 (|| ἐξαποστέλλω). **b**. metaph.: τοὺς λόγους μου εἰς τὰ ὀπίσω '(to consign) my words to a rubbish-bin' Ps 49.17.

4. *to deploy*: + acc. pers. (ambush) 1M 11.68; 12.27.

Cf. βάλλω, ἐκβολή, ἐκσείω, ἐκτινάσσω, ἐξελαύνω, μετανοστεύω.

ἔκβασις, εως. f.ʃ

the end of an existence: of a hum. life, Wi 2.17; καιρῶν καὶ χρόνων 8.8. **b**. *that which happens in the course of an action*: pl., Wi 11.14.

Cf. ἐκβαίνω.

ἐκβιάζω: aor.mid. ἐξεβιασάμην, inf.act. ~βιάσαι.ʃ

1. act. *to force out*: + acc. pers., Jd 14.15B, mid., + acc. rei, ἑαυτοῦ τὴν ἀπώλειαν 'his own ruin' Pr 16.26.

2. mid. *to do violence to*: abs., Ps 37.13; + acc. pers., τὴν γυναῖκα Es 7.8 *L* (w. sexual overtones; οʹ βιάζομαι), sim. Su 19 LXX; + acc. rei, Wi 14.19.

ἐκβλαστάνω: fut. ~βλαστήσω; aor. inf. ~βλαστῆσαι, subj. ~βλαστήσω.ʃ

1. *to sprout*: *s* rod, Nu 17.5 (|| βλαστάνω vs. 8).

2. *to cause to grow*: abs. Is 55.10 (|| ἐκτίκτω); + acc., ἔξοδον χλοῆς 'a crop of green herbs' Jb 38.27¶.

Cf. βλαστάνω.

ἐκβλύζω.ʃ

intr. *to split open* due to excessive amount of liquid contained inside: + dat., οἴνῳ οἱ ληνοί 'the winepresses' Pr 3.10.

ἐκβοάω: aor. ἐξεβόησα.ʃ

to address sbd outside *in a loud voice*: πρός τινα 4K 4.36. Cf. βοάω, κράζω.

ἐκβολή, ῆς. f.ʃ

throwing out, jettisoning: ***o*** hum., σὺν παντὶ ἐκβαλεῖ ὑμᾶς ~ῇ 'he will throw you out with everything for good' Ex 11.1; cargo from ship, ~ὴν ἐποιήσαντο τῶν σκευῶν τῶν ἐν τῷ πλοίῳ Jn 1.5; metaph., 'rejection (by God)' Si 10.21¶ (:: πρόσληψις 'acceptance'). Cf. ἐκβάλλω.

ἔκβολος, ον.ʃ

frustrated: *s* hum., + ἄπρακτος 'unsuccessful' Ju 11.11.

ἐκβράζω: aor. ἐξέβρασα, pass. ~βράσθην.ʃ

to force to leave one's abode or *station*: + acc. pers., Ne 13.28, 2M 1.12; pass., εἰς Αἴγυπτον 5.8. Cf. ἐκβρασμός, ἀποικίζω.

ἐκβρασμός, οῦ. m.ʃ *

v.n. of prec.: ἐκτιναγμὸς καὶ ἀνατιναγμὸς καὶ ἐ. Na 2.11. Cf. ἀνα~, ἐκτιναγμός, ἐκβράζω, ἀποικισμός.

ἐκγελάω: fut. ~γελάσομαι; aor. ἐξεγέλασα.

*__1__. *to think of and treat with contempt*: τινα, Ps 2.4 (|| ἐκμυκτηρίζω), 58.9 (|| ἐξουδενόω), Wi 4.18 (|| ἐξουθενόω); + ἐπί τινι (pers.) Ne 4.1.

*__2__. *to make a laughing-stock of*: τινα 4K 4.16*L*.

Cf. γελάω, ἐκμυκτηρίζω, ἐδουδ/θενόω.

ἐκγεννάω: aor. ἐξεγέννησα.ʃ *

to bring out into existence: + acc., ἐκ γαστρός 'out of a belly' Ps 109.3. Cf. γεννάω.

ἔκγονος, ον.

1. *that which is born*: subst., 'offspring,' collective pl. and hum., τὰ ~α, ἃ ἐὰν γεννήσῃς Ge 48.6; τῆς κοιλίας σου De 7.13, 28.4 (not necessarily of a woman's belly), Is 48.19 (|| σπέρμα); domestic animals (cf. LSG s.v.), ἐπὶ τοῖς ~οις τῆς κοιλίας σου καὶ ἐπὶ τοῖς ~οις τῶν κτηνῶν σου καὶ ἐπὶ τοῖς γενήμασιν τῆς γῆς σου 28.11, sim. 28.51, 53 (of cannibalism in times of famine), 30.9; vipers, Is 11.8, 14.29.

2. *grandchild*: Si prol. II.

Cf. ἀπόγονος, σπέρμα, γεννάω, κλάδος, φυτόν **2**: Shipp 227.

ἐκγράφω: aor.mid. ἐξεγραψάμην.ʃ

to write out and copy sth that is already written: Cf. γράφω.

ἐκδαν(ε)ίζω: aor.subj. ~δανείσω.ʃ

to lend: + dat. pers. and acc. rei, ἀργύριον τῷ ἀδελφῷ Ex 22.25; anything, De 23.19. Cf. δαν(ε)ίζω.

ἐκδειματόω.ʃ

to frighten: pass., ***o*** hum., Wi 17.6. Cf. ἐκφοβέω.

ἐκδεκτέον.ʃ *

one must admit to the veracity of: ***s*** a proposition, ~ὸν ἢ νομιστέον ὅτι .. Ep Je 56. Cf. ἐκδέχομαι. Del. Ep Je 63 v.l.

ἐκδέρω: aor. ἐξέδειρα, ptc. ἐκδείρας.ʃ

1. *to strip off the skin from*: abs., 2C 35.11; + acc., ***o*** sacrificial animal, ὁλοκαύτωμα '(an animal offered as) a wholly burnt offering' Le 1.6.

2. *to remove* a thin, flat object off a surface: ***o*** τὴν δορὰν αὐτοῦ 'his skin' Mi 2.8; τὰ δέρματα αὐτῶν 'their skins' 3.3.

Cf. δείρω, δέρμα, δορά.

ἐκδέχομαι: fut. ἐκδέξομαι; aor.impv. ~δεξαι; pf. ἐκδέδεγμαι.

1. *to receive* (guest), *welcome*: τοὺς καταλοίπους Ισραηλ Mi 2.12, φίλους 3M 5.26; ἔκδεξαι τὸν δοῦλόν σου εἰς ἀγαθόν Ps 118.122.

2. *to be in store for*: + acc. pers., ***s*** disaster, ἡ καταστροφὴ αὐτῶν ἐκδέξεται αὐτά Ho 8.7, cf. 9.6.

3. *to take in charge*: τινα (a young boy), Ge 43.9; παρά τινος 44.32.

4. + τῇ καρδίᾳ *to pay attention to, take to heart*: abs., Is 57.1 (ǁ κατανοέω).

5. *to view mentally* in a certain way: τοὐναντίον 'in the opposite sense' 3M 3.22.

6. *to accept approvingly*: + acc., γνώμην μου 'my opinion' Si 6.23 (ǁ συμβουλία 'advice'), παιδείαν 18.14, 35.14. Cf. ἐκδεκτέον.

Cf. (ἐπι)δέχομαι, ἐκλαμβάνω: Lee 60.

ἐκδέω: fut. ~δήσω; aor. ἐξέδησα.ʃ

to bind so as to hang from: + acc., ἐκ τῆς ἄκρας 'from the citadel' 2M 15.35, εἰς τὴν θυρίδα 'into the window' Jo 2.18. Cf. δέω.

ἔκδηλος, ον.ʃ

clearly noticeable: ***s*** δυσμένεια 'ill will' 3M 3.19; God's power, 6.5. Cf. δῆλος **1**, ἐπιπολαίως.

ἐκδημία, ας. f.ʃ

going or *being away from home* or *out of town*: 3M 4.11. Cf. Spicq 1.453f.

ἐκδιαιτάω: aor. ἐξεδιῄτησα, inf.pass. ~τηθῆναι.ʃ

to cause to change one's way of life: + acc. pers., 4M 4.19; mid., + gen. (= abl.), τῶν πατριῶν ἐθῶν 'the ancestral customs' 18.5 (ǁ ἀλλοφυλέω). Cf. δίαιτα **1**.

ἐκδιδάσκω.ʃ

to teach: + acc. rei, σωφροσύνην καὶ φρόνησιν 'self-control and prudence' Wi 8.7, εὐσέβειαν 'piety' 4M 5.24 (ǁ παιδεύω); also + acc. pers., 4M 5.23 (ǁ ἐξασκέω 'to train').

Cf. διδάσκω.

ἐκδιδύσκω ʃ * (LSG s.v.)

to strip possessions off sbd: ***s*** highway robber, and abs., ἐκδιδύσκων λῃστὴς ἐν τῇ ὁδῷ αὐτοῦ Ho 7.1, 2K 23.10B (*L* σκυλεύω); τινα (dead soldiers) 1K 31.8 (*L* ἐκδύω); + double acc., αὐτὸν τὰ σκεύη αὐτοῦ 'his weapons' 31.9*L*. **b.** mid., *to remove* from one's own body: + acc., τὰ ἱμάτια αὐτοῦ Ne 4.23.

Cf. ἐκδύω.

ἐκδίδωμι: fut. ~δώσω, inf. ~δώσειν; aor.inf.act. ~δοῦναι, mid. ἐξεδόμην, inf. ~δόσθαι, impv.~δου, pass. ἐξεδόθην, subj. ~δοθῶ, 2aor.3pl ἐξέδοσαν; pf.mid. ἐκδέδομαι, ptc. ~δεδομένος.

I. act. *to bring into existence*: + acc., αὔλακας 'furrows' Si 38.26.

2. *to issue an official order*: + inf., 1E 1.30.

3. *to deliver*: ***o*** document, νόμος 1E 8.3; hum. for execution, Da 2.18 LXX.

4. *to surrender in submission*: + acc. and dat. pers., σοι ἑαυτούς Ju 2.10 (***s*** the vanquished), 8.11 (ǁ παρα~ vs. 9).

5. *to give out as expenditures*: + dat. pers., 4K 12.12 (*L* ἐξοδιάζω).

II. mid. *to give in marriage*: + acc. pers. (daughter) and dat. pers., ἐξέδοτο .. τὴν θυγατέρα αὐτοῦ Μωυσῇ γυναῖκα Ex 2.21; pass., ἀδελφῇ παρθένῳ .. τῇ μὴ ἐκδεδομένῃ ἀνδρί Le 21.3.

2. mid. *to publish*: + acc., βιβλίον 'book' Si prol. 33.

Cf. δίδωμ, ἀπεκδίδωμι.

ἐκδιηγέομαι: fut. ~γήσομαι; aor. inf. ~γήσασθαι, impv. ~διήγησαι

to recount, narrate: οὐ μὴ πιστεύσητε ἐάν τις ἐκδιηγῆται 'you would not believe it if someone told it' Hb 1.5; + acc., ἀνομίας Ez 12.16, τὰ ἔργα κυρίου Ps 117.17, σύνεσιν αὐτοῦ Si 1.24, ἐπαίνους 44.8; + dat., γῇ Jb 12.8. Cf. διηγέομαι.

ἐκδικάζω: fut.mid./pass. ~δικῶμαι. The impf.3ms. ἐξεδίκα and pres.subj.3ms. ἐκδικᾷ are from ἐκδικάω.ʃ

I. act. *to inflict retribution*: ***o*** pers. 1M 9.26, 2M 6.15; pass., Ju 11.10.

II. mid. *to avenge oneself, take vengeance for*: abs. Le 19.18; ***o*** (acc.) τὸ αἷμα τῶν υἱῶν αὐτοῦ De 32.43 (ǁ ἐκδικήσει καὶ ἀνταποδώσει δίκην).

Cf. ἐκδικέω.

ἐκδικάω. ⇒ ἐκδικάζω.

ἐκδικέω: fut. ~κήσω, inf. ~κήσειν, pass. ~κηθήσομαι; aor. ἐξεδίκησα, inf. ~κῆσαι, subj. ~κήσω, pass. ~κηθῆναι, impv. ~κησον, pass.3s ~κηθήτω, opt.act.3s ~κήσαι; pf.pass. ἐκδεδίκημαι.

1. *to requite, take action in response to a punishable deed* or *injustice*, often. w. God taking or instigating such action: μετὰ θυμοῦ 'indignantly' Na 1.2*b*, ἐν θλίψει 'by means of affliction' 1.9; an attribute of God, Θεὸς ζηλωτὴς καὶ ἐκδικῶν κύριος 1.2*a*; sword as instrument of divine punishment and with cogn. acc., δίκην Ez 25.12, μάχαιραν ἐκδικοῦσαν δίκην Le 26.25; ἐκδικήσει καὶ ἀνταποδώσει De 32.43. **b**. pass. with offender as grammatical subj., *to suffer vengeance*: Zc 5.3*bis*, Ez 19.12; substantivised, ἐκδικούμενα 'vengeance' Ge 4.15. **c**. impers. pass. with ἐκ + offender: ἑπτάκις ἐκδεδίκηται ἐκ Καιν 'Cain has been avenged sevenfold' Ge 4.24; *to be penalised*: δίκη ἐκδικηθήτω Ex 21.20.

The following constructions are attested: **a**. τινα (offender): Ob 21, Na 1.2*c*, Je 26.10. **b**. τι (offence): ἁμαρτίας Ho 8.13 (‖ μιμνήσκομαι ἀδικίας), τὸ αἷμα Jl 3.21; cogn. acc., δίκην Le 26.25; ἐκδίκησίν τινος Nu 31.2, 1M 9.42. **c**. τι ἐπί τινα: τὸ αἷμα τοῦ Ιεζραελ ἐπὶ τὸν οἶκον Ιηου Ho 1.4, πάντα ὅσα ἐξεδίκησα ἐπ' αὐτήν Zp 3.7; τὰς ἡμέρας τῶν Βααλιμ 'the period of Baal worship' Ho 2.13, τὰς ὁδοὺς 4.9 (‖ διαβούλια ἀποδίδωμι), ἁμαρτίας Am 3.2, ἀσεβείας 3.14*a*. **d**. τι (penalty) ἐπί τινα: ἐπ' αὐτοὺς τέσσαρα εἴδη '.. four kinds of punishment' Je 15.3. **e**. ἐπί τινα: τοὺς ἄρχοντας κτλ. Zp 1.8, τοὺς ἄνδρας 1.12; Je 28.44. **f**. ἐπί τινα κατά τι: ἐφ' ὑμᾶς κατὰ τὰ πονηρὰ ἐπιτηδεύματα ὑμῶν '.. in accordance with your evil practices' Je 23.2. **g**. τινα κατά τι: τὸν Ιακωβ κατὰ τὰς ὁδοὺς αὐτοῦ (‖ ἀνταποδίδωμι) Ho 12.2. **h**. ἔκ τινος (offender): Ge 4.24, Nu 31.2, De 18.19; τι ἐκ χειρός τινος– τὰ αἵματα ἐκ χειρὸς Ιεζαβελ 4K 9.7; με (*L* μοι dat. com.) ἐκ σοῦ 1K 24.13. **i**. ἐν τινι (offender): ἐν ἔθνει τῷ τοιούτῳ Je 5.9, 29, sim. 9.9; ἔν τινι (offence) 1K 3.13. **j**. εἴς τινα (offender): Ez 25.12, 1K 14.24*L*, 18.25. **k**. ἐπί τι: ἐπὶ πάντα ἐπιτηδεύματα αὐτῶν 'all their deeds' Ps 97.8; possibly ἐπὶ τὰ θυσιαστήρια Βαιθηλ Am 3.14*b*, δὶς ἐπὶ τὸ αὐτὸ 'for the same (offence)' [and not 'twice simultaneously'] Na 1.9, and cp. Ps 98.8. **l**. dat. (offence): ἁμαρτίαις To 3.3 𝔊[I] (𝔊[II] + ἔν τινι, cf. 3M 2.17, prob. dat. com.). **m**. περί τινος 1M 13.6. **n**. ἀντί τινος (offence) ἔκ τινος (offender) Jd 16.28 A (w. a cogn. obj., ἐκδίκησιν). The use of ἐπί τινα is most likely a Hebraism; see Helbing, *Kasus*., 37f., but cf. 1K 3.12 *L* ἐπί τινα, B: τινα for MT אֶת.

2. *to vindicate* sbd by taking up his cause: τινα 4M 17.10.

Cf. ἐκδίκησις, δίκη, ἐκδικάζω, ἀνταποδίδωμι.

ἐκδίκησις, εως. f.

v.n. of prec., act often to be carried out by God: μεγάλη Ex 7.4; αἱ ἡμέραι τῆς ~εως (‖ αἱ ἡ. τῆς ἀνταποδόσεως) Ho 9.7; ἐν πᾶσιν τοῖς θεοῖς τῶν Αἰγυπτίων ποιήσω ~ιν 'I will take vengeance upon all the gods of the Egyptians' Ex 12.12 (with Hebraistic ἐν; cf. Helbing, *Kasus*., 37), sim. Nu 33.4, Ez 16.49 (‖ κρίματα, q.v.), 1M 7.24, εἴς τινα Ez 25.11 (‖ ἐν vs. 17), ἔκ (B: ἀπό) τινος Jd 11.36 A, 2K 4.8; δώσω ~ίν μου ἐπὶ τὴν Ἰδουμαίαν Ez 25.14, sim. 25.17; λημψόμεθα τὴν ~ιν ἐξ αὐτοῦ Je 20.10; τὴν παρὰ σοῦ ~ιν ἐξ αὐτῶν '.. against them' 11.20, 20.12; παρὰ θεοῦ 27.15; Mi 5.15; αἱ ~εις σου 'your punishment' 7.4, motivated by anger, θυμοῦ Ez 5.15; αἵματος Ps 78.10. Cf. ἐκδικέω, ἀνταπόδωσις: *BA* 2.35.

ἐκδικητής, οῦ. m.∫

ag.n of ἐκδικέω: + ἐχθρός Ps 8.3. Cf. ἐκδικέω ..

ἔκδικος, ον.∫

subst.m. *he who defends the cause* of sbd else or sth: ἐναντίον ἐχθρῶν Si 30.6 (son on his father's behalf), κατὰ ἀδίκων ἀνθρώπων Wi 12.12; τοῦ νόμου 4M 15.29.

ἐκδιώκω: fut. ~διώξω, pass. ~διωχθήσομαι; aor. ἐξεδίωξα, inf. ~διῶξαι, pass. ἐξεδιώχθην.

to chase away: + acc. of an undesirable person, Ge 14.15 (enemies); πάντας τοὺς ἐχθρούς σου πρὸ προσώπου σου De 6.19 (*s* God); τὸν ἀπὸ βορρᾶ ἐκδιώξω ἀφ' ὑμῶν 'I shall chase the northerner away from you' Jl 2.20; ptc. subst. and + ἐχθρός Ps 43.17; ‖ ἐκθλίβω 118.157. Cf. διώκω and LSG s.v.

ἔκδοτος, ον.∫

subject to jurisdiction or discretion of: + dat. pers. and *s* Bel 22 TH.

ἐκδύνω. ⇒ subs.

ἐκδύω: fut.act. ~δύσω, mid. ~δύσομαι; 1aor. ἐξέδυσα, impv. ~δυσον, inf. ~δῦσαι, ptc. ~δύσας, mid. ἐξεδυσάμην, impv. ~δυσαι, subj.act. ~δύσω.

1. *to strip, take* sbd's clothes *off*: + acc. pers., 1K 31.8*L* (B: ἐκδιδύσκω); + acc. pers. and acc. of clothes, ἐξέδυσαν τὸν Ιωσηφ τὸν χιτῶνα Ge 37.23; ἔκδυσον Ααρων τὴν στολὴν αὐτοῦ Nu 20.26 (:: ἐνδύω); τὸν Ααρων τὰ ἱμάτια αὐτοῦ 20.28 (:: ἐνδύω); αὐτὴν γυμνὴν Ho 2.3; *+ acc. rei, gen. pers., 2M 8.27; fig., τὴν δόξαν ἀπ' ἐμοῦ Jb 19.9 (‖ ἀφαιρέω). **b**. mid., *take* one's own clothes *off*: abs. Is 32.11; + acc. rei, ἐκδύσεται τὴν στολὴν αὐτοῦ Le 6.11 (:: ἐνδύομαι); 16.23, ἱμάτια 'clothes' 1K 19.24, σκεύη 'weapons' 31.9B (*L* ἐκδιδύσκω, + acc. pers.); τὸν δεσμὸν τοῦ τραχήλου σου 'the chain round your neck' Is 52.2; metaph., ῥύπον 'filth' Jb 11.15.

*2. *to bare*: a female snake baring her breasts to feed her young, La 4.3.

3. *to escape* danger: *also in pres., ἐκ θήρας 'from being hunted and caught' Pr 11.8.

Cf. ἀπο~, ἐν~, περιδύω, ἐκδιδύσκω.

ἐκεῖ. adv.

1. *in that place already mentioned*, 'there': βάδιζε ἐκχώρησόν σοι εἰς γῆν Ιουδα καὶ ἐκεῖ καταβίου καὶ ἐ. προφητεύσεις 'Go, retire into the land of Juda, and live there and you shall prophesy there' Am 7.12.

2. with verbs of movement, *to* or *into that place*: εἰσελθεῖν ἐ. Ge 19.22; 24.6 (|| εἰς τὴν γῆν vs. 4); ἐγγίσῃ ἐ. Hg 2.14; κατήγαγον ἐ. Ge 39.1; κατάβητε ἐ. 42.2; εἰσάγω .. ἐ. Le 18.3; φυγεῖν ἐ. De 4.42.

3. pleonastically in a relative cl., referring back to an antecedent denoting a place: εἰς πάντα τόπον, οὗ ἐὰν εἰσέλθωμεν ἐ. Ge 20.13; ἐκ τοῦ τόπου, οὗ ἀπέδοσθε αὐτοῖς ἐ. 'from the place where you sold them' Jl 3.7.

Cf. ἐκεῖθεν, ἐκεῖσε, ὧδε: Shipp 227f.

ἐκεῖθεν

from there, thence: **a**. indicating a point from which a physical movement starts, Ge 2.10, Ob 4, Am 6.2, 9.2*bis*, 3. **b**. source of supply, Ho 2.15; out of danger, Mi 4.10*bis*. ***c**. pleonastically and Hebraistically in a relative clause: εἰς τὴν γῆν, ὅθεν ἐξῆλθες ἐκεῖθεν Ge 24.5.

Cf. ἐκεῖ.

ἐκεῖνος, η, ο.

Demonstrative pronoun referring to an entity considered relatively remote in terms of the discourse setting, 'that'.

A. subst. and || οὗτος: οὗτοι ἐκείνοις προσθήσονται 'these will be added to those' Zc 14.17; μετ' ἐκεῖνο 'thereafter' Ge 6.4, ἀπ' ἐκείνου μέχρι τοῦ νῦν 'since that time ..' 1E 6.19. **b**. w. ref. to an item mentioned earlier than the other, 'the former': To 14.10 𝔊[I].

B. adj., often in prophetic, eschatological sayings with ἐν τῇ ἡμέρᾳ ἐκείνῃ, ἐν ταῖς ἡμέραις ἐκείναις, or ἐν τῷ καιρῷ ἐκείνῳ, e.g. Ho 1.5, Jl 2.29, 3.1; otherwise, λάλησον πρὸς τὸν νεανίαν ἐκεῖνον Zc 2.4, παρατάξεται ἐν τοῖς ἔθνεσιν ἐκείνοις Zc 14.3. **b**. anaphoric: ἀπερίτμητος ἄρσην, .. ἡ ψυχὴ ἐκείνη .. Ge 17.14; resuming οὗτος– ἐν τῇ νυκτὶ ταύτῃ .. τὴν νύκτα ἐκείνην Ge 19.32f.

Both the prepositive and postpositive patterns are attested: ἐν ἐκείνῃ τῇ ἡμέρᾳ Ob 8 as against ἐν τῇ ἡμέρᾳ ἐκείνῃ Ho 1.5, the former 14 times in all, and the latter 199 times in the Pentateuch and the Twelve Prophets. Since the postpositive pattern became increasingly popular in Ptolemaic papyri, the usage in our corpus cannot be entirely attributed to Hebrew influence; see BDF, § 292, Mayser, II 2.79-82, Thack. 193. Note esp. Zc 12.8 with both the patterns in a single verse. On the other hand, the high frequency in our corpus of the adjectival use of the demonstrative with an articular noun is noteworthy in view of its marked infrequency in Ptolemaic papyri; see Mayser, II 2.79.

Cf. οὗτος.

ἐκεῖσε. adv.ʃ

thither: ἐ. ὢν ζητεῖ τὰ σῖτα 'going there he seeks food' Jb 39.29. Cf. ἐκεῖ.

ἐκζέω: aor. ἐξέζεσα, subj. ἐκζέσω.ʃ

I. tr. *to cause to boil over and come out*: ***s*** left-over food and ***o*** worms, ἐξέζεσεν σκώληκας καὶ ἐπώζεσεν 'it boiled out worms and stank' Ex 16.20; ***o*** mice, 1K 6.1 (***s*** land).

II. intr. *to be intensely and mentally agitated*, 'seethe': ***s*** pers., with illicit passions, Ge 49.4; κοιλία Jb 30.27.

2. *to burst out in large numbers*: ***s*** living organisms, Ez 47.9; 1K 5.6.

ἐκζητέω: fut. ~τήσω; aor. ἐξεζήτησα, opt.3s ~ζητήσαι, subj. ~ζητήσω, inf. ~ζητῆσαι, ptc. ~ζητήσας, impv. ~ζήτησον; pf.ptc.pass. ἐξεζητημένος.

1. *to look for, search* (sbd τινα or sth lost τι): abs. De 12.5; ***o*** God, .. ἐκζητῆσαι τὸν κύριον καὶ οὐ μὴ εὕρωσιν αὐτόν Ho 5.6; || ζητέω Le 10.16, De 4.29.

2. *to engage oneself earnestly and devotedly in* (+ acc.): τὸν κύριον Ho 10.12; ἐκζητήσατέ με καὶ ζήσεσθε Am 5.4, cf. ἐκζητῆσαι τὸ πρόσωπον κυρίου Zc 8.21 (|| δέομαι), 22; pagan gods, De 12.30, pagan idols, Am 5.5; + *dat. dei, 2E 4.2, 1C 22.19*L* (B: ζητέω); ***s*** guardian angels, τὰς ψυχὰς ὑμῶν Ep Je 6, cf. Ps 141.5 and Pr 29.10 (on the latter, cf. Evagrius p. 452). **b**. ***o*** sth abstract, τὰ δικαιώματά σου Ps 118.94; ἐκζητήσατε τὸ καλὸν καὶ μὴ τὸ πονηρόν, ὅπως ζήσητε Am 5.14; κρίσιν Is 1.17, κρίμα 16.5, διαθήκην .. μαρτύρια Ps 24.10; wisdom, Si 24.34; πονηρίαν 47.25, κακὰ .. γνῶσιν Pr 27.21a, αὐτῷ κακόν 1M 9.71, sim. 15.19; εἰρήνην 2E 9.12. **c**. + inf., De 12.30.

3. *to ask for* (sth τι) *as of right*: abs. and ***s*** God, παρὰ σοῦ De 23.21 (of a vow to be fulfilled); + acc. rei (shed blood of murder victim), Ge 9.5; κρίσιν παρὰ τοῦ θεοῦ 'judgement' Ex 18.15; τί ἐκζητεῖ παρὰ σοῦ ..; 'what does God require of you ..?' Mi 6.8; νόμον ἐκζητήσουσιν ἐκ στόματος αὐτοῦ 'they will demand a law from his mouth' Ma 2.7; ἐκ χειρός τινος Ge 9.5, Is 1.12, Ez 34.10.

4. *to demand an account of*: + acc., τὸ ὑμέτερον αἷμα τῶν ψυχῶν ὑμῶν Ge 9.5, τὸ αἷμα αὐτοῦ ἐκ χειρός σου Ez 3.18, 20; pass. τὸ αἷμα αὐτοῦ ἐκζητεῖται 'his murder is being revenged' Ge 42.22.

5. *to undertake an investigation*: ***s*** judge and abs., De 17.9. **b**. *to investigate and obtain a full understanding of*: abs., ἔν τινι (ventriloquist) 1K 28.7*L* (B: simp.); + acc. pers., 2K 11.3*L* (B: simp.); + acc. rei, ἔλεος καὶ ἀλήθειαν αὐτοῦ τίς ἐκζητήσει; Ps 60.8; τὸ ῥῆμα 'the case' 2E 10.16 (ll ἐτάζω 1E 9.16).

6. *to apply to sbd* (acc.) for guidance: of necromancy, divination etc., περὶ τῶν ζώντων τοὺς νεκροὺς Is 8.19 (ll ζητέω).

Cf. ζητέω, ἐκζητητής, δέομαι: LSG s.v.

ἐκζητητής, οῦ. m.*ʃ**

seeker: τῆς συνέσεως Ba 3.23. Cf. ἐκζητέω.

ἐκθαμβέω: fut. ~θαμβήσω.*ʃ*

to astonish: + acc. pers., Si 30.9. Cf. θαμβέω, ἔκθαμβος.

ἔκθαμβος, ον.*ʃ*

astonishing: ***s*** animal seen in a vision, + φοβερός, ἰσχυρός Da TH 7.7. Cf. ἐκθαμβέω. Del. Wi 10.19 v.l.

ἐκθαυμάζω: fut. ~θαυμάσω.*ʃ*

to marvel at: + acc., Si 43.18; ἐπὶ τῶν λόγων σου 27.23. Cf. θαυμάζω. Del. 4M 17.17 v.l.

ἔκθεμα, ατος. n.*ʃ*

public notice: advertisement, Ez 16.24; edict, Es 8.17 (ll πρόσταγμα). Cf. ἐκτίθημι: Passoni dell'Acqua 2002.58-60.

ἐκθερίζω: fut. ~θεριῶ; aor.inf. ~θερίσαι.*ʃ*

to harvest: + cogn. obj., θερισμόν Le 19.9*bis*; ***o*** τὰ αὐτόματα τὰ ἀναβαίνοντα 'that which grows by itself' 25.5. Cf. θερίζω.

ἔκθεσις, εως. f.*ʃ*

1. *exposure*: of child, Wi 11.14, cf. Huys.

2. *amount of food allocated regularly*: παρὰ τοῦ βασιλέως Da 1.5 LXX.

ἔκθεσμος, ον.*ʃ* *

contravening laws and regulations: ***s*** σακροφαγία 'eating of (ritually unclean) meat' 4M 5.14. Cf. ἄνομος, παράνομος.

ἐκθηλάζω: aor.ptc. ~θηλάσας.*ʃ* *

to suck out: abs., Is 66.11. Cf. θηλάζω.

ἐκθλιβή, ῆς. f.*ʃ*

v.n. of subs.: ἐκθλίβουσιν ~ῇ Mi 7.2. Cf. ἐκθλίβω.

ἐκθλίβω: fut. ~ίψω; aor. ἐξέθλιψα, impv. ~θλιψον; pf.ptc.pass. ~τεθλιμμένος.

1. *to squeeze, press*: τὴν σταφύλην εἰς τὸ ποτήριον 'the grapes into the cup' Ge 40.11; ***o*** testicles (understood), Le 22.24 (castrated animal unfit for offering and ll θλαδίας, ἐκτομίας, ἀπεσπασμένος), cf. LSG s.v.

2. *to cause* (sbd) *difficulties, harass*: + acc. pers., ὑμᾶς τοῦ μὴ εἰσελθεῖν .. 'to prevent you from entering ..' Am 6.14; Jd 2.18 (ll *L* κακόω); τὸν πλησίον αὐτοῦ .. ἐκθλιβῇ Mi 7.2, sim. Si 16.28; ll ἐκδιώκω Ps 118.157; pregnantly, εἰς τὸ ὄρος '(causing to move) into the mountains' Jd 1.34.

Cf. θλίβω and ἐκθλιβή.

ἔκθυμος, ον.

in violent mood: 'incensed' Es 7.9 *L*, 2M 7.3 (***s*** alw. king). Cf. θυμός.

ἐκκαθαίρω: aor. ἐξεκάθαρα, impv. ~κάθαρον.

to clear out: + acc., τὰ ἅγια ἐκ τῆς οἰκίας μου De 26.13; Jo 17.15 (ll ἐκκαθαρίζω vs. 18). Cf. ἐκκαθαρίζω.

ἐκκαθαρίζω: fut. ~ριῶ.*ʃ* *

1. *to cleanse morally and religiously*: ***s*** God, τὴν γῆν τοῦ λαοῦ αὐτοῦ De 32.43.

2. *to remove in order to make morally clean*: + acc., τὸ αἷμα .. ἐκ μέσου αὐτῶν Is 4.4 (ll ἐκπλύνω 'to wash out'), πονηρίαν Jd 20.13 B (A: ἐξαιρέω).

3. *to clear out undesirable objects or obstacles from and reclaim*: + acc., δρυμόν 'woodland' Jo 17.18 (ll ἐκκαθαίρω vs. 15).

Cf. ἐκκαθαίρω, καθαρίζω.

ἐκκαίδεκα. indecl. num.

sixteen: ἑ. ἐτῶν 4K 14.21 ll δέκα καὶ ἓξ ἐτῶν 2C 26.1.

ἐκκαιδέκατος, η, ον.

sixteenth: 1C 24.14.

ἐκκαίω: fut.act. ~καύσω, pass. ~καυθήσομαι, ~καήσομαι; aor. ἐξέκαυσα, ptc. ~καύσας, inf. ~καῦσαι, subj. ~καύσω, pass. ἐξεκαύθην, subj. ~καυθῶ, 2aor.3s ~καῇ, inf.pass. ~καῆναι, ptc.pass. ~καείς; pf.pass. ~κέκαυμαι, ptc. ~κεκαυμένος.

1. tr. *to burn*: + acc., as punitive action, ἐν καπνῷ πλῆθός σου '(I will burn) with smoke your plentiful wealth' Na 2.14, πόλιν Pr 29.8 (real ***s*** God). **b**. metaph. ἐξεκαύθη ἡ καρδία μου 'I had a burnout' Ps 72.21.

2. *to ignite*: pass., ἐν αὐτοῖς πῦρ παρὰ κυρίου Nu 11.1, 3; πῦρ ἐκκέκαυται ἐκ τοῦ θυμοῦ μου De 32.22 (ll καίω); Ob 18 εἴς τινα 'against sbd'; ***o*** spark (σπινθήρ) Si 28.12, ἄνθραξ 'coal' 8.10, φλόξ 'flame' Is 50.11, πῦρ Ex 22.6 (in an agricultural field), πῦρ ἐν ταῖς λαμπάσι 'fire to the torches' Jd 15.5B (A: ἐξάπτω). **b**. fig., *to cause to become active and intensify*, ***o*** ὀργὴ κυρίου De 29.20, ἡ ὀργή σου ὡς πῦρ Ps 88.47, θυμός 2.12, + ἔν τινι 'against sbd' 2C 34.21, ζῆλος ὡς πῦρ Ps 78.5, hum. anger Es 1.12 *L*, τὰ κακά Je 1.14, μάχη 'strife' Si 28.8; πῦρ, fig. of intense agitation, Ps 38.4; ψευδῆ 'lies' Pr 6.19 (ll ἐπιπέμπω), 14.25, κακίαν 19.9; θυμόν or ζῆλον understood with ref. to hot pursuit, ὀπίσω τινος (pers.) 1K 17.53 *L*, 3K 20.21.

3. *to heat intensely*: + acc., ὄρη Si 43.4 (***s*** sun); furnace, Da 3.19 TH.

Cf. καίω, ἀνα~, κατακαίω: Lee 1969.235f.

ἐκκαλέω: aor.mid.subj.2s ἐκκαλέσῃ.ʃ
mid. *to call out* for a talk or negotiation: + acc. pers., Ge 19.5; μετ' εἰρήνης De 20.10. Cf. καλέω.

ἐκκαλύπτω.ʃ
to disclose, to let slip out: inadvertently, + acc., τὰς ἑαυτοῦ ἁμαρτίας Pr 26.26. Cf. ἀποκαλύπτω.

ἐκκενόω: fut. ~κενώσω, pass. ~κενωθήσομαι; aor. ἐξεκένωσα, pass. ἐξεκενώθην, ptc. ~κενωθείς.
1. *to empty the contents of*: abs., Ἐκκενοῦτε .. ἕως ὁ θεμέλιος ἐν αὐτῇ 'Expose (it) as long as its foundation is there' Ps 136.7; + acc., τὴν ὑδρίαν εἰς τὸ ποτιστήριον 'the pitcher into the drinking-trough' Ge 24.20; + ἐκπίνω Is 51.17. **b.** mid., *to become empty*: λάκκος 'cistern' Ju 7.21; *to reach the end-point*: οἱ καιροὶ ἐκκενωθήσονται 'the appointed period will have elapsed' Da 9.25 TH.
2. *to remove* contents *completely*: ὁ τρυγίας αὐτοῦ οὐκ ἐξεκενώθη 'its dregs were not emptied out' Ps 74.9. ***b.** *to draw* a sword *out of its sheath and apply* to sbd: + acc., μάχαιραν ὀπίσω αὐτῶν Ez 5.2, ἐπὶ σέ 28.7, ῥομφαίαν 12.14, cf. ἐκχέω. **c.** *to remove and empty* the container: 'to decoy out,' + acc. pers. and + gen. rei, τῆς πόλεως 'out of the city' Jd 20.31 B, ἀπὸ τῆς πόλεως 20.32 B (A: ἐκσπάω).
3. *to pour out*: pass., *o* unguent (μύρον) Ct 1.3.
Cf. κενός.

ἐκκεντέω: aor. ἐξεκέντησα, impv. ~τησον; pf.ptc. pass. ~κεκεντημένος.
to stab: + acc. pers. and with a sword, Nu 22.29, 1K 31.4*L* (B: ἀπο~) ‖ 1C 10.4; pass. μαχαίραις Is 14.19, ἀπὸ γενημάτων ἀγρῶν 'robbed of produce of fields' (?) La 4.9, cf. Ol. PG 93.753 στερηθέντες; *o* snake, PSol 2.26. Cf. κέντρον, ἀπο~, (συνεκ)κεντέω.

ἐκκήρυκτος, ον.ʃ*
banished or *stripped of office by proclamation*: *s* hum., Je 22.30.

ἐκκινέω: aor.pass. ἐξεκινήθην.ʃ
to agitate emotionally: pass. *o* ψυχή and περί τινος 'over sth' 4K 6.11 (*L* ἐξίστημι).

ἐκκλάω: fut. ~κλάσω.ʃ
to slit: bird as sacrificial animal, ἐκ τῶν πτερύγων 'by its wings' Le 1.17.

ἐκκλησία, ας.
1. *act of congregating* for a public meeting: ἡ ἡμέρα τῆς ~ας De 4.10, 18.16. **b.** place for such a meeting: Ju 6.16, 21.
2. *large group of gathered people*: κυρίου Mi 2.5; ἁγιάσατε ~αν Jl 2.16 (‖ λαός), ὄχλου Si 26.5, προφητῶν 1K 19.20, πονηρευομένων Ps 25.5.
3. a social *organisation and body*: κυρίου De 23.1; Ἰσραηλ (gen.) 31.30, ἁγίων Ps 88.6, τῆς ἀποικίας 'of the (former) expatriates' 2E 10.8 (‖ πλῆθος 1E 9.4).
Cf. ἐκκλησιάζω, ἄθροισμα, συναγωγή, συνέδριον, σύνοδος: Deissmann 1923.90f.; Trench 1-6; Schmidt, *TDNT* 3.513-31; Harl 2001.871f.

ἐκκλησιάζω: aor.impv. ~κλησίασον, ptc. ~κλησιάσας.
to summon to an assembly, convene: + acc. (a group of individuals), πᾶσαν τὴν συναγωγὴν .. ἐπὶ τὴν θύραν Le 8.3; πρός με τὸν λαόν De 4.10; Ἰουδαίους Es 4.16. Cf. ἐκκλησία, ἐξεκλησιάζω, συνάγω.

ἐκκλησιαστής, οῦ. m.
convener of assembly (ἐκκλησία): Ec 1.1, see *BA* ad loc.

ἔκκλητος, ον.ʃ
summoned as defendant (?): Si 42.11.

ἐκκλίνω: fut. ~κλινῶ; aor. ἐξέκλινα, inf. ~κλῖναι, impv. ~κλινον, ptc. ~κλίνας, subj. ~κλίνω; pf. ~κέκλικα.
I. tr. **1.** *to bend, pervert*: *o* the right and just course of action, ὁδὸν ταπεινῶν Am 2.7, ὁδοὺς δικαιοσύνης Pr 17.23, τὸ δίκαιον ἐν κρίσει 18.5; κρίσιν Ex 23.2, De 16.19; κρίσιν προσηλύτου καὶ ὀρφανοῦ καὶ χήρας De 24.17, 27.19; Ma 3.7; κρίσιν πτωχῶν Is 10.2; δικαιώματα 1K 8.3.
2. *to wrong, do injustice to*: + acc. pers., πένητας 'the poor' Am 5.12, ἀδυνάτους Jb 34.20.
3. *to change, alter*: τὰς τρίβους 'the courses' Jl 2.7.
4. *to turn off* a current route: + acc., πρὸς αὐτὴν τὴν ὁδόν Ge 38.16.
***5.** *to cause to move away*: + acc., τὸν στῦλον τῆς νεφέλης .. ἀπ' αὐτῶν Ne 9.19; *o* divine blessings of nature and *s* one's sins, Je 5.25 (‖ ἀφίστημι). **b.** from a path: σε ἐκ τῆς ὁδοῦ σου Ez 16.27, ἐξ ὁδοῦ δικαίας Jb 24.4; Ps 43.19; τὸν πόδα σου ἐκ τῶν τρίβων αὐτῶν 'your foot from their paths' Pr 1.15, τὸ οὖς αὐτοῦ 'his ear (not to listen to the law)' 28.9; + gen., δεήσεως 'from a supplication' Jb 36.19. **c.** *to turn away and not accept*: + acc. rei, ἐκλεγμόν 'criticism' Si 35.17, ἐλέγχους Pr 5.12 (‖ μισέω).
6. *to direct wrongfully* in a certain direction: + acc., ἐπ' ἐμὲ ἀνομίαν Ps 54.4, τὴν καρδίαν μου εἰς λόγους πονηρίας 140.4.
***7.** *to be disposed to prefer*: + acc., *s* hum. heart, 1K 14.7 (*L* θέλω).
II. intr. *to turn away and shun* or *avoid*: + ἀπό cultic offerings, Ho 5.6; God, Zp 1.6 (‖ μὴ ζητεῖν τινα and μὴ ἀντέχεσθαί τινος); ἀπὸ προσώπου τινός (out of fear), De 20.3 (‖ φοβέομαι, θραύομαι), ‖ ἀπό τινος Nu 20.21, ἀπὸ παντὸς κακοῦ Pr 3.7, cf. ἀπεχόμενος ἀπὸ παντὸς πονηροῦ πράγματος Jb 1.1; ἐν ὀργῇ ἀπὸ τοῦ δούλου σου Ps 26.9; + ἐκ the right path, ἐκ τῆς ὁδοῦ Ma 2.8; ἐκ νόμου θεοῦ Ba

4.12; ἐκ τοῦ ᾅδου Pr 15.24; πρὸς τὸν παῖδά σου Ge 18.5; *s* ὀφθαλμός Jb 29.11.

2. *to deviate* from the set or right course: ἐξέκλιναν καὶ ἀπήλθοσαν Je 5.23; εἰς τὸν οἶκον τοῦ παιδὸς ὑμῶν Ge 19.2, εἰς κατάλυμα 'for a night's lodging' Je 14.8; + εἴς τινα (friendly gesture) Is 66.12, πρός τινα, Ge 19.3; ἐπ' αὐτήν 'towards her' Si 9.9; ὀπίσω τινός 'in pursuit of sth' 1K 8.3; δεξιὰ οὐδὲ εὐώνυμα 'to the right nor to the left' Nu 20.17; ἐν τῇ ὁδῷ πορεύσομαι, οὐκ ἐκκλινῶ δεξιὰ οὐδὲ ἀριστερά De 2.27, sim. 5.32; εἰς τὰ δεξιά Is 9.20, Pr 4.27 (but not an instance of the Deuteronomic phrase), εἰς δεξιὰ οὐδὲ εἰς ἀριστερά Jo 1.7; ἀπὸ τῶν ἐντολῶν σου Ps 118.21; τίνος ἡ διάνοια ἐξέκλινεν ἀπὸ κυρίου De 29.18. **b**. ἐκ τῆς ὁδοῦ Nu 22.23, De 31.29. **c**. *to decline*: *s* shadow on dial, Ps 108.23

3. *to take leave of a host*: ἐκκλίνας Μωυσῆς ἐξῆλθεν ἀπὸ Φαραω Ex 10.6.

Cf. κλίνω, ἀπέχω, ἐκνεύω, παραβαίνω.

ἐκκλύζω: fut. ~κλύσω.ʃ

to wash thoroughly to clean: ὕδατι Le 6.28. Cf. λούω, νίπτω.

ἐκκόλαμμα, ατος. n.ʃ *

figure or *letter carved* on stone: cogn. obj., λίθους .. γεγλυμμένους καὶ ἐκκεκολαμμένους ἐ. σφραγῖδος Ex 36.13. Cf. ἐκκολάπτω.

ἐκκολάπτω: pf.ptc.pass. ἐκκεκολαμμένος.ʃ See also under ἐγ- (so LSJ).

to carve on stone: + acc. and pass., λίθους .. γεγλυμμένους καὶ ἐκκεκολαμμένους ἐκκόλαμμα σφραγῖδος Ex 36.13. Cf. ἐκκόλαμμα.

ἐκκομιδή, ῆς. f.ʃ

act of removing: *o* funds, 2M 3.7.

ἐκκόπτω: fut. ~κόψω, pass. ~κοπήσομαι; aor. ἐξέκοψα, subj. ~κόψω, inf. ~κόψαι, impv. ~κοψον, ptc. ~κόψας, pass. ἐξεκόπην, subj. ~κοπῶ, opt.act. 2s ~κόψειας, 3pl ~κόψαισαν; pf.ptc.pass. ἐκκεκομμένος.

1. *to cut down*: + acc. τὰ ἄλση 'the sacred groves' Ex 34.13, De 7.5 (|| καθαιρέω, συντρίβω, κατακαίω), sim. 12.3 (also || ἀπόλλυμι), 4K 18.4*L* (B: ἐξολεθρεύω), δρυμόν 'thicket' Je 26.23; δένδρον De 20.19, ξύλον 20.20; Mi 5.14; ὥσπερ δένδρον τὴν ἐλπίδα μου Jb 19.10. **b**. an edifice or part of it: εἴδωλα Is 27.9, θύρας 'doors' Ps 73.6 (|| καταρράσσω).

2. *to destroy*: *o* residents and possessions in an encampment, Ge 32.8; city, Jb 42.17δε; enemy encampments, 1M 6.6; metaph., *o* ἐπιθυμίαν 4M 3.2 (|| ἐκριζωτής 'uprooter' vs. 4).

3. *to knock out*: + acc., ὀδόντα 'a tooth' Ex 21.27, ὀφθαλμούς Nu 16.14; Pr 30.17, ὄμματα 4M 5.30.

Cf. ἀφανίζω.

ἐκκρέμαμαι.ʃ.

to be dependent upon: ἔκ τινος– ἡ ψυχὴ αὐτοῦ ἐκκρέμαται ἐκ τῆς τούτου ψυχῆς 'his soul is hanging on to the soul of this one' Ge 44.30. Cf. Renehan 2.63.

ἐκκρούω: aor.pass.subj. ~κρουσθῶ.ʃ

to move forward with great force: *o* hand, De 19.5. Cf. Lee 1969.239; Hauspie 2004.116f.

ἐκκύπτω: aor. ἐξέκυψα; pf. ἐκκέκυφα.ʃ

1. *to peep out*: *s* hum., πρός τινα 4K 9.32*L* (B: κατα~); God, ἐξ ὕψους ἁγίου αὐτοῦ Ps 101.20 (|| ἐπιβλέπω); hum., διὰ τῶν δικτύων 'through the lattices' Ct 2.9 (|| παρακύπτω); a group of soldiers, 1M 4.19; ὄρθρος 'the rising sun (?)' Ct 6.10. Cf. διακύπτω.

2. *to emerge*: *s* κακὰ .. ἀπὸ βορρᾶ 'disasters' Je 6.1; hum., 1M 9.23 (|| ἀνατέλλω).

ἐκλαλέω: aor. ἐξελάλησα.ʃ

to divulge: παρά τινι (pers.) Ju 11.9. Cf. λαλέω.

ἐκλαμβάνω: aor.inf. ~λαβεῖν, ptc. ~λαβών, impv. ~λαβε, opt.3s ~λαβοι.ʃ

to receive approvingly: + acc., προφητείας γλώσσης 'prophecies (coming merely out of) tongue' Je 23.31 (v.l. ἐκβάλλω, cf. Ziegler 1958.45), παιδείαν 39.33 (v.l. ἐπι~, cf. ib. 52f.), ἐξηγορίαν Jb 22.22 (|| ἀνα~). **b**. *to welcome*: + acc., Jb 3.5.

Cf. λαμβάνω, ἐκδέχομαι.

ἔκλαμπρος, ον.ʃ *

emitting intense light and clearly visible: *s* flames of stars, Wi 17.5.

ἐκλάμπω: fut. ~λάμψω; aor. ἐξέλαμψα.ʃ

to shine, beam forth: *s* lamp, Si 26.17; the sun, and + acc., ἀκτῖνας 'rays' 43.4, ἐπὶ ναόν 50.7; the moon, 43.8; ἡ γῆ .. ὡς φέγγος Ez 43.2; Da 13.3 TH (LXX φαίνω). **b**. tr., *to cast light on and cause to become bright*: + acc., μοι τὸ σκότος μου 2K 22.29 (*L* ἀνα~).

Cf. ἔκλαμψις, λάμπω.

ἔκλαμψις, εως. f.ʃ

v.n. of prec.: χρυσέων κόσμων 'of golden ornaments' 3M 5.3.

ἐκλατομέω: aor. ἐξελατόμησα.ʃ

to dig soil or *rock out to make* a cavity in the ground: + acc. φρέαρ Nu 21.18 (|| ὀρύσσω); λάκκους λελατομημένους, οὓς οὐκ ἐξελατόμησας De 6.11. Cf. λατομέω, ὀρύσσω.

ἐκλέγω: fut.mid. ~λέξομαι; aor. ἐξέλεξα, mid. ἐξελεξάμην, subj. ~λέξωμαι, ptc. ~λεξάμενος, inf. ~λέξασθαι, impv. ἔκλεξαι, pass. ἐξελέγην, inf. ~λεγῆναι, ptc. ~λεγείς, subj. ~λεγῶ; pf.mid. ἐκλέλεγμαι, ptc.pass. ~λελεγμένος.

mid. *to pick, select* out of multiple alternatives: + acc., ἐξελέξατο ἑαυτῷ Λωτ πᾶσαν τὴν περίχωρον τοῦ Ἰορδάνου Ge 13.11; τὴν ζωήν De 30.19; ὑμῖν τόπον 1.33; τὴν Ιερουσαλημ Zc 3.2, πρεσβυτέρους Jl 2.16 v.l. (Zgl: ἐκδέξασθε, s.v. ἐκδέχομαι); με ὑπὲρ τὸν πατέρα σου '.. in preference to your father' 2K 6.21, ὑμᾶς παρὰ πάντα τὰ ἔθνη '.. over and above all the nations' De 7.7; + inf., "to be admitted into the house of God rather than (μᾶλλον ἤ) to dwell .." Ps 83.11; ἀπὸ πάντων τῶν ἐθνῶν De 14.2, ἐκ πασῶν φυλῶν Ισραηλ 3K 11.32; *+ ἐν (Hebraism), 1K 16.9, 10 (+ acc., vs. 8), 3K 8.16 (|| + acc.), Ne 9.7; || προαιρέω De 7.7, Is 7.15; || αἱρετίζομαι Ps 131.13; 2K 10.9*L* (B: ἐπιλέγω); for punishment, Ez 20.38; pass. 1C 16.41. **b.** *to confer unique status*: + dat. pers., Si 45.4.

Cf. ἐκλεκτός, ἐκλογή, ἐπιλέγω, αἱρέω, αἱρετίζω, προαιρέω: Schrenk, *TDNT* 4.168-70.

ἐκλείπω: fut. ~λείψω, inf. ~λείψειν; aor. ἐξέλιπον, subj. ~λίπω, ptc. ~λιπών, inf. ~λιπεῖν, opt.3s ~λίποι, 3pl ~λίποισαν; pf. ἐκλέλοιπα, inf. ~λελοιπέναι, ptc. ~λελοιπώς, pass. ~λελειμμένος.

I. tr. **1.** *to abandon, desert, neglect*: ὡς θημωνιὰ ἁλός 'like a heap of salt' Zp 2.9 (|| ἀφανίζω); πηγὴ ἣν ἐξέλιπεν ὕδωρ 'a fountain which never wanted in water' Is 58.11, cf. Ju 7.20, μὴ ἐκλίπωσίν σε αἱ πηγαί 'the fountains would not fail you' Pr 4.21; ἀπὸ τῶν ἔργων αὐτῶν 'none of their tasks' Si 16.27 (or: 'passed out under the weight of ..,' **II 3**).

2. *to part with*: + acc., τὸν βίον 2M 10.13 (w. ref. to suicide), ψυχήν Ju 7.27, φῶς Si 22.11 (*s* the deceased), ὑπομονήν 'patience' 17.24, σύνεσιν 22.11.

II. intr. **1.** *to cease to exist*: || ἀποθνήσκω, Zc 11.9*bis*; ἐξολεθρευθήσεται καὶ ἐκλείψει 13.8; ἐκλιπέτω ἀπὸ προσώπου τῆς γῆς Zp 1.2; λαοὶ ἱκανοὶ ἐν πυρί Hb 2.13 (|| ὀλιγοψυχέω), ἐν ῥομφαίᾳ καὶ ἐν λιμῷ Je 51.18; *s* flood water, ἐξέλιπεν τὸ ὕδωρ ἀπὸ προσώπου τῆς γῆς Ge 8.13; pillar of cloud and one of fire, Ex 13.22; cities, Zp 3.6 (v. s. παρά, **III 2**); mountains and highways with much traffic, Je 9.10; men and animals, Zp 1.3*a*; birds and fishes, 1.3*b*; fishes, Ho 4.3; sacrificial bulls, 13.2; grass, Is 15.6, flowers, Na 1.4; shadows, Je 6.4 (with the approaching night); sanctuary, 38.40 (|| καθαιρέομαι). **b.** 'to die': *s* hum., Ge 49.33 (natural death); violently and divine punishment, Is 29.20 (|| ἀπόλλυμι, ἐξολεθρεύομαι), Ps 72.19.

2. *to take leave of, become non-existent* for sbd (ἔκ/ἀπό τινος): ἐκλείψει ἀπὸ ^τῆς γῆς^ ἄνθρωπος καὶ κτήνη Je 43.29; οὐκ ἐκλείψει ἐξ αὐτῶν πάντα 'nothing will be unattainable to them' Ge 11.6; πρὶν ἢ ἐκλιπεῖν 'before (the meat) was finished off' Nu 11.33; οὐ μὴ ἐκλίπῃ ἐνδεὴς ἀπὸ τῆς γῆς 'the poor will never cease to be around in the land' De 15.11; ἐν τῷ ἐκλείπειν ἀπ' ἐμοῦ τὴν ψυχήν μου 'when my soul was failing me' Jn 2.8, ἐπὶ τῆς κλινῆς 'in his death-bed' To 14.11 𝔊^I; ἐν τῷ ἐκλείπειν ἐξ ἐμοῦ τὸ πνεῦμά μου Ps 141.4; + ἐκ, 54.12, Is 59.21, Ez 22.15; *s* φωνὴ εὐφροσύνης Ba 2.23. **b.** + dat. pers., ἐξέλειπεν Σάρρᾳ γίνεσθαι τὰ γυναικεῖα 'S. was missing her periods' Ge 18.11 (on the dat., see οὐκ ἐκλείψει σοι ἀνήρ 2 Ch 6.16).

3. *to lose strength* or *efficacy, fail to function properly*: physically, *s* hum. and in old age, ἐκλιπὼν ἀπέθανεν Ge 25.8, 35.29, cf. 49.33; ἦλθεν ἐκ τοῦ πεδίου ἐκλείπων 'came (home) from the field, exhausted' 25.29 (*s* famished hunter); ἐξέλιπεν ἡ γῆ Αἰγύπτου .. ἀπὸ τοῦ λιμοῦ '.. on account of the famine' 47.13; ἐν δίψει 'in thirst' Am 8.13, ἀπὸ τῆς δίψης Ju 7.22; *s* eyes, De 28.65 (|| σφακελίζω vs. 32), Ps 68.4, τοῦ βλέπειν Is 38.14, τοῦ πολεμεῖν Je 28.30; sheep, Ez 34.16 (|| ἀσθενέω vs. 4); river as source of drinking water, Is 19.5; ἡ δόξα τῶν υἱῶν Κεδαρ 21.16; "his appearance is ignoble and more morbid (ἐκλεῖπον) than that of all other men" 53.3; heavenly body failing to emit light, 60.20 (eclipse), Jb 31.26; *s* eyes, La 2.11, 4.17 (from vain expectation), 1K 2.33. **b.** mentally: ἐπιποθεῖ καὶ ἐκλείπει ἡ ψυχή μου εἰς τὰς αὐλὰς τοῦ κυρίου 'my soul faints with yearning after the courts of the Lord' Ps 83.3, εἰς τὸ σωτήριόν σου 118.81 (|| ἐπελπίζω), ἐπὶ τοῖς ἀνῃρημένοις 'over those slain' Je 4.31; ἐν ὀδύνῃ ἡ ζωή μου καὶ τὰ ἔτη μου ἐν στεναγμοῖς 'in sorrow .. my years with sighs' Ps 30.11; PSol 3.12. **c.** *to fail in one's undertaking*: "they harvested shame because they failed (ἐξελίποσαν)" Je 6.15.

***4.** *to run out of supply* of sth (ἀπό τινος): ἐξέλιπον ἀπὸ βρώσεως πρόβατα 'sheep ran out of food' Hb 3.17; ἀπὸ λαοῦ Is 7.8. For the syntax, see also Je 6.29.

5. *to become finished, exhausted*: ἐν τῷ ἐκλείπειν τὴν ἰσχύν μου 'as my strength fails' Ps 70.9, sim. Je 15.10; ἐξέλιπεν τὸ ὕδωρ ἐκ τοῦ ἀσκοῦ 'the water ran out from the skin bag' Ge 21.15; ἐξέλιπεν τὸ ἀργύριον ἐκ γῆς Αἰγύπτου 47.15, ἀπὸ τῶν θησαυρῶν 1M 3.29, οἱ ἄρτοι τῆς πόλεως Je 44.21, καρπός Ez 47.12; οἱ ὕμνοὶ Δαυιδ Ps 71.20; Ἐκλελοίπασιν τὰ παιδάρια; 'Are these all the kids you have?' 1K 16.11. Cf. ῥέω **2**.

6. *to leave off* doing, having completed what one set about doing: + ptc. pres., 2K 15.24*L* (B: παύομαι).

Cf. ἔκλειψις, ἀνεκλιπής, ἀμβλύνω, ἀπόλλυμι, ἀφανίζω, δαπανάω, ἐκλύω, ἐκψύχω, καταδαπανάω, κοπιάω, παραλύω, ὀλιγοψυχέω, παρεκλείπω, φθίνω.

ἐκλείχω: fut. ~λείξω; aor. ἐξέλιξα, opt.3s ~λείξαι.

to lick up: + acc., ἐκλείξει ἡ συναγωγὴ αὕτη πάντας τοὺς κύκλῳ ἡμῶν, ὡς ἐκλείξαι ὁ μόσχος τὰ χλωρὰ ἐκ τοῦ πεδίου 'this crowd is going to lick up all those round about us, as a calf might lick up the grass off the field' Nu 22.4; τὸ πρόσωπον τῆς γῆς πάσης Ju 7.4; "the pigs and the dogs licked the blood (of a fallen king)" 2K 22.38 (|| 20.19 simp.). Cf. λείχω.

ἔκλειψις, εως. f.

1. v.n. of ἐκλείπω (q.v.): ~ει ἐκλιπέτω ἀπὸ προσώπου τῆς γῆς 'let him indeed perish from the face of the earth' Zp 1.2; τῆς δόξης '(the decline) of the glory' Is 17.4.

2. *lack and want*: πάντων De 28.48 (:: πλῆθος πάντων 'abundance of ..'), λαοῦ 'diminution of the nation' Pr 14.28.

**3*. *cessation of a linear movement*, 'the far end': Ne 3.21.

Cf. ἐκλείπω: Tigner 196.

ἐκλεκτός, ή, όν.

chosen, selected for a task or a destiny: ταῖς πύλαις 'as gatekeepers' 1C 9.22; ποιέω τινα ~όν = ἐκλέγομαι, *o* πατέρας 'forefathers' 2M 1.25. **b**.. *of top quality*, 'choice': τὰ ~ὰ πάντων τῶν ἐθνῶν Hg 2.7; *s* things, μνημεῖον 'grave' Ge 23.6; cattle, βόες καλαὶ τῷ εἴδει καὶ ~αὶ ταῖς σαρξίν 41.2, 18 (fatness meant and :: λεπτός 'lean' vs. 3, 19); ἅρματα 'chariots' Ex 14.7; λίθος Is 28.16 (+ πολυτελής, ἔντιμος); κέδροι 'cedars' Je 22.7; δῶρα ~ά 'choice gifts' Am 5.11, cf. πᾶν ~ὸν τῶν δώρων ὑμῶν De 12.11; τὰ βρώματα αὐτοῦ ~ά Hb 1.16; τὰ κρέα τῶν ~ῶν Zc 11.16; ἔταξαν γῆν ~ὴν εἰς ἀφανισμόν 'they laid a choice land waste' 7.14; πόλις ἁγιάσματος 'holy city' Si 49.6; οἶκος Is 22.8, ἀργύριον Pr 8.19, χρυσίον Ba 3.30; hum., νεανίσκοι 'youths' Je 31.15, τὸ γένος μου τὸ ~όν Is 43.20; καρδία Pr 17.3; subst.m., God's chosen nation, Ps 104.6, || λαός 104.43, || ἔθνος 105.5, Is 65.9; an individual, Is 42.1 (=Jacob), Moses Ps 105.23; 'a notable figure' La 5.14 (|| πρεσβύτης); God, "with a decent fellow He is going to be decent" Ps 17.27.

Cf. ἐκλέγω, ἐπίλεκτος: Schrenk, *TDNT* 4.182f.

ἐκλευκαίνω: aor.subj.pass. ~λευκανθῶ.ʃ

to render rather white and free of stain: metaph., pass., *o* hum., Da 12.9 TH. Cf. ἔκλευκος.

ἔκλευκος, ον.ʃ

rather white: ὑποπυρρίζον ἢ ~ον 'reddish or rather white' Le 13.24. Cf. λευκός, ἐκλευκαίνω.

ἐκλικμάω: fut. ~μήσω; aor. ἐξελίκμησα.ʃ *

to winnow away: metaph. and + acc. (God's enemies) Wi 5.23; τὰ πεδία '(sweep all the crops of) the fields (and make off with them)' Ju 2.27.

ἐκλιμία, ας. f.ʃ *

exceeding hunger: divine punishment and || ἔνδεια, ἀνάλωσις 'deprivation, depletion' De 28.20. Cf. λιμός.

ἐκλιμπάνω.ʃ

to be missing: *s* sheep, Zc 11.16. Cf. ἐπισκέπτομαι **8b**.

ἐκλογή, ῆς. f.ʃ

act of choosing out of multiple options: PSol 9.4, ἡμέρα ~ῆς 'chosen day' 18.5. Cf. ἐκλέγω, αἵρεσις.

ἐκλογίζομαι.ʃ

**to call to account*: + acc. pers., 4K 12.16; also + acc. rei, αὐτοὺς τὸ ἀργύριον τὸ διδόμενον αὐτοῖς 22.7.

ἐκλογιστής, οῦ. m.ʃ*

officer charged with ἐκλογιστία (q.v.): To 1.22.

ἐκλογιστία, ας.ʃ*

task of inspecting revenue accounts: To 1.21.

ἐκλοχίζω: pf.ptc.pass. ~λελοχισμένος.ʃ *

to pick out of a cohort: pass., *o* hum., ἀπὸ μυριάδων 'out of myriads' Ct 5.10.

ἔκλυσις, εως. f.

loss of physical strength: χειρῶν Je 29.3; of loins, Is 21.3; + δειλία 'fear' 2M 3.24. Cf. ἐκλύω, ἐκλείπω.

ἐκλύτρωσις, εως. f.ʃ *

redemption: Nu 3.49. Cf. λύτρον, λυτρόομαι, ἀπολύτρωσις.

ἐκλύω: fut. ἐκλύσω, pass. ~λυθήσομαι; aor. ἐξέλυσα, subj. ἐκλύσω, impv. ἔκλυσον, pass. ἐξελύθην, subj. ~λυθῶ, impv.2pl ~λύθητε, ptc. ~λυθείς; pf.ptc. ~λελυκώς, pass. ~λέλυμαι, inf. ~λελύσθαι, ptc. ~λελυμένος.

1. *to remove pressure* or *tension on and allow free movement*, 'loosen, release': ἐκλύσεις τὸν ζυγὸν αὐτοῦ ἀπὸ τοῦ τραχήλου σου 'you will free his yoke from your neck' Ge 27.40; λύσατε, ἐκλύσατε ἄδικα δεσμά 'Loose, untie unjust bonds' 3M 6.27; ἐκλύειν με 'to free me' Jb 19.25; fig. οὐ μὴ ἐκλυθῶσιν ἐν φυλακαῖς αὐτῶν '(the heavenly bodies) will never be allowed to go lax in their watching duties' Si 43.10. **b**. of that which is to be held firmly together: ἐξελύθη τὰ νεῦρα βραχιόνων χειρῶν αὐτοῦ 'the sinews of the arms of his hands came loose' Ge 49.24; fig. ἐ. τὰς χεῖράς τινος *'to weaken' - τὰς χεῖρας τῶν ἀνθρώπων τῶν πολεμούντων 'to dishearten the warriors' Je 45.4, sim. 2E 4.4 and pass. Ἐκλυθήσονται αἱ χεῖρες αὐτῶν ἀπὸ τοῦ ἔργου τούτου Ne 6.9 (:: κραταιόω τὰς χεῖρας), ἀπό τινος 'abandoning sbd to his fate' Jo 10.6, || παρίεμαι 2K 4.1B; ἐξελύθη τὸ πνεῦμα αὐτοῦ 'his heart sank' Ju 14.6, μὴ ἐκλυέσθω ἡ καρδία ὑμῶν 'Don't let your heart fall' De 20.3 (|| φοβέομαι, θραύομαι). **c**. mid. *to be lax* to act: + *s* hum. and + inf., Jo 18.3. **d**. *to depart* in the course of military action: *s* pers., 2M 12.18, 13.16.

2. mid. *to suffer complete loss of strength*: physically, ἐκλελυμένῳ οὐκ ἰσχύοντι 'to one who is worn out, having no strength' Is 46.1, λιμῷ 'on account of famine' La 2.29; τοῦ πορεύεσθαι '(too exhausted) to march on' 1K 30.21 (cf. Tht 80.596

ἀτονήσαντας, but cf. *L* ἀπολειφθέντας 'exempted'); Jd 8.15A (B: ἐκλείπω); out of hunger, 1K 14.28; *s* voice of one in distress, Je 4.31, ἀσιτοῦντες 'having eaten nothing' 1M 3.17; mentally, Is 29.9 (|| ἐξίστημι), 1M 9.8, ἐπ' αὐτῷ 'over him' Ez 31.15, ἐπὶ τῷ ὁράματι 'over the vision' Da 8.27 LXX; Pr 3.11, 6.3; w. acc. of respect, τὰς χεῖρας 2K 17.2*L* (B: dat.) || *s* αἱ χεῖρες 4.1; mentally, + συγκεχυμένος καὶ ἐκλελυμένος 'upset and distraught' 3K 21.43. **b**. act. *to cause exhaustion*: + acc. pers., Je 12.5, cf. Aristot. *Rh*. 3.9.1409[b]. **c**. *to put out of action, disable*: + acc., 4M 15.24.

Cf. λύω, παραλύω, ἐκλείπω.

ἐκμαρτυρέω: aor. ἐξεμαρτύρησα.ʃ

to bear witness to sth (acc.) to sbd (dat.): 2M 3.36. Cf. μαρτυρέω.

ἐκμάσσω: aor.subj. ~μάξω; pf.ptc.act. ἐκμεμαχώς.ʃ

to clean sth *by wiping*: + acc., τὸ πρόσωπον αὐτῶν Ep Je 12, ἔσοπτρον 'mirror' Si 12.11. **b**. *to clean by wiping off* sth: + acc., ἰόν 'rust' Ep Je 23.

Cf. ἀπομάσσω.

ἐκμελετάω: pf.ptc. ~μεμελετηκώς.ʃ

to learn thoroughly: τι 2M 15.12.

ἐκμελίζω.*

to sever a limb from the body: 4M 10.5. Cf. (δια)μελίζω.

ἐκμετρέω: fut. ~μετρήσω, pass. ~ρηθήσομαι.ʃ

to measure completely: ἐπὶ τὰς πόλεις '(the distance) up to the cities' De 21.2; pass. ἡ ἄμμος τῆς θαλάσσης, ἣ οὐκ ἐκμετρηθήσεται 'the sand of the sea which cannot be completely measured' Ho 1.10 (|| ἐξαριθμέω). Cf. δια~, κατα~, μετρέω, μέτρον, ἐξαριθμέω.

ἐκμιαίνω: aor.inf.pass. ~μιανθῆναι.ʃ

1. *to defile thoroughly*: pass. Le 19.31.

2. pass. *to ejaculate*: πρὸς αὐτήν Le 18.20; 18.23. Cf. μιαίνω.

ἐκμυελίζω: fut. ~μυελιῶ.ʃ *

to suck the marrow out: + acc., τὰ πάχη αὐτῶν 'their thick marrows' Nu 24.8.

ἐκμυκτηρίζω: fut. ~ριῶ; aor. ἐξεμυκτήρισα.ʃ *

to turn the nose up at, 'sneer': + acc. pers., Ps 2.4 (|| ἐκγελάω), 21.8 (|| κινέω κεφαλήν), also + cogn. acc., με μυκτηρισμόν 34.16; + ἔν τινι (pers.) 1E 1.49. Cf. μυκτηρίζω, ἐκγελάω: Bertram, *TDNT* 4.796-8.

ἐκνεύω: fut. ἐκνεύσω; aor. ἐξένευσα, impv. ~νευσον.ʃ

1. *to turn one's head in another direction*: 4K 23.16.

2. *to move away*, leaving sbd unprotected: Mi 6.14 (*s*?); *s* hum. and from the (proper) course, εἰς τὸ φαῦλον 'to evil' 3M 3.22; ὀπίσω αὐτῶν 'to chase them' 4K 2.24 (*L* ἐπεστράφη).

3. intr. *to turn aside from the current course*: πρός με Jd 4.18A (B: ἐκκλίνω). **b**. *to leave a scene which is of concern to one*: resigned, Jd 18.26 A.

Cf. ἐκκλίνω: LSG s.v.

ἐκνήφω: fut. ~νήψω; aor. ἐξένηψα, impv. ~νηψον. * (but νήφω in Cl.Gk).

to become sober and mentally active again: Hb 2.7; *s* drunken person, ἐκνήψατε, οἱ μεθύοντες, ἐξ οἴνου αὐτῶν Jl 1.5; ἀπὸ τοῦ οἴνου Ge 9.24; ἔκνηψον ἐξεγέρθητι 'Sober up and get up on your feet' Hb 2.19. **b**. *tr. *to awaken*: + acc., ὕπνον '(keep) the sleeper awake' Si 34.2.

Cf. ἔκνηψις, μεθύω, μεθύσκω.

ἔκνηψις, εως. f.ʃ *

calming down following wild, drunken behaviour: μὴ δῷς ~ιν σεαυτῇ 'don't give rest to yourself' La 2.18; οὐ σιγήσομαι τοῦ μὴ εἶναι ~ιν 'I shall not keep quiet so that there will be no calm' 3.49. Cf. ἐκνήφω.

ἑκουσιάζομαι: aor. ἡκουσιασάμην, ἡκουσιάσθην, inf. ἑκουσιασθῆναι.ʃ*

to offer willingly: + acc., ἑκούσιον τῷ κυρίῳ 'a voluntary offering ..' 2E 3.5; 7.15; + inf., 7.13, Ne 11.2. **b**. *to offer oneself willingly*: abs. Jd 5.2B, 9B; εἰς οἶκον θεοῦ 'in the interest of ..' 2E 2.68, 7.16; τῷ νόμῳ 1M 2.42.

Cf. ἑκουσιασμός, ἑκούσιος.

ἑκουσιασμός, οῦ. m.ʃ *

willing spirit: 2E 7.16. Cf. ἑκουσιάζομαι.

ἑκούσιος, α, ον.

voluntary: *s* cultic offering, Le 7.6, δόματα Ju 4.14; βροχή ' (freely given) rain' Ps 67.10; subst.n., καθ' ~ον 'voluntarily' Nu 15.3, ἐν ~ῳ ἡμῶν Ne 5.8; pl. 'voluntary offerings' Le 23.38, Nu 29.39; ὁλοκαυτώματα .. θυσιάσματα .. ἀπαρχὰς .. εὐχὰς .. ~α .. πρωτότοκα De 12.6; τὰ ~α τοῦ στόματός μου 'my pledges made orally' Ps 118.108; φίλημα 'kiss' Pr 27.6. Often || εὐχή 'votive offering.' **b**. *wilful, wittingly done*: *s* ἁμάρτημα Si 20.8¶.

Cf. ἑκουσίως, ἑκών.

ἑκουσίως. adv.

willingly, of free will: ἑ. βουλομένους προσπορεύεσθαι Ex 36.2; ἑ. (Zgl: ἀ.) ἁμαρτὼν .. Jb 31.33; θύσω σοι Ps 53.8. Cf. ἑκούσιος, ἀκουσίως.

ἐκπαιδεύω: aor.inf. ~παιδεῦσαι.ʃ

to train thoroughly, 'groom': + acc. (youth) Da 1.5 LXX. Cf. παιδεύω.

ἐκπαίζω.ʃ

to mock: + acc. pers., 1E 1.49 (|| ἐκμυκτηρίζω).

ἐκπειράζω: fut. ~πειράσω; aor. ἐξεπείρασα, ἐξεπειρασάμην, subj. ~πειράσω.ʃ *

to put to a test to find out about sbd's quality: + acc. pers., *s* hum. and *o* God, De 6.16, Ps 77.18 (|| πειράζω Ex 17.2); *s* God and *o* person, ἐκπειράση σε καὶ διαγνωσθῇ τὰ ἐν τῇ καρδίᾳ σου De 8.2; 8.16. Cf. πειράζω.

ἐκπέμπω: aor. ἐξέπεμψα, inf. ~πέμψαι, impv.2pl ~πέμψατε, opt.3s ~πέμψαι.

1. *to allow to set out on a journey*: ἐκπέμψατέ με Ge 24.54, 56. ***b**. *to send off across*: αὐτὸν τὸν Ἰορδάνην 'him across the J.' 2K 19.32B (*L* προ~ ἐκ τοῦ 'I.).

2. *to send back*: + acc., 1E 4.44.

Cf. (προ)πέμπω, ἐξαποστέλλω **6**.

ἐκπεράω: aor. ἐξεπέρασα.ʃ

**to carry out*: + acc., ὀρτυγομήτραν 'quail' Nu 11.31.

ἐκπεριπορεύομαι.ʃ *

to move out, encircling: + acc. loci, Jo 15.3. Cf. περιπορεύομαι.

ἐκπετάζω: fut. ~πετάσω; aor. ἐξεπέτασα, impv. ~πέτασον, ptc. ~πετάσας, pass. ~πετάσθην, ptc. ~πετασθείς.*

I. tr. *to unfold*: + acc., τὰς χεῖράς μου πρὸς κύριον Ex 9.29, sim. Is 65.2 (an inviting gesture), Si 48.20 (in prayer), βιβλίον 1M 3.48, καταπετάσματα 'curtains' 4.51; in order to grab and + ἐπί τι, La 1.10, δίκτυον 'net' Ez 12.13; in order to cover and conceal, Jb 26.9¶. **b**. *to disclose the contents of*: *o* ἑαυτοῦ κακίαν Pr 13.16.

II. intr. (pass.) *to fly off*: of winged creatures, βροῦχος 'locust' Na 3.16; ὡς ὄρνεον Ho 9.11, ὥσπερ ἐνύπνιον 'as a dream' Jb 20.8 (|| πέτομαι).

Cf. subs., πετάννυμι.

ἐκπέτομαι: aor. ἐξέπτην.ʃ

to move swiftly away in the air: νεφέλαι ὡς πετεινά 'clouds like birds' Si 43.14. Cf. prec., πέτομαι, ἐξίπταμαι.

ἐκπηδάω: fut. ~δήσω; aor. ἐξεπήδησα, ptc. ~δήσας, subj. ~δήσω; pf.inf. ~πεπηδηκέναι

to leap out: *s* lion's whelp, ἐκ τοῦ Βασαν De 33.22; hum., escapee, 3K 21.39; law-breaker, Su 39 TH; crowd of hums., 2M 3.18. Cf. πηδάω.

ἐκπιάζω. ⇒ subs.

ἐκπιέζω: aor. ἐξεπίε/ασα; pf. ~πεπίακα, pass.ptc. ἐκπεπιεσμένος.

1. *to push out* as unwanted: + acc. pers., λαὸν .. ἀδικίᾳ Ez 22.29; pass. σώσω τὴν ἐκπεπιεσμένην Zp 3.19 (|| ἀπωθέω). **b**. + μυκτῆρας *to squeeze the nose and clear discharge out of the nostrils* Pr 30.33.

2. *to extract by force*: + obj. gen., θησαυροῦ Jd 18.7 B.

Cf. πιέζω, ἀπωθέω, ἐξωθέω.

ἐκπικραίνω: aor. ἐξεπίκρανα.ʃ

to irritate: + acc., *o* God, De 32.16 (|| παροξύνω). Cf. πικραίνω, παροξύνω.

ἐκπίνω: fut. ἐκπίομαι; aor. ἐξέπιον.ʃ

1. *to swallow*: + acc., κατέφαγεν πάντα καὶ ἐξέπιον Bel 15 TH (LXX: τὸν οἶνον); fig. of destruction, ὡς οἶνον Zc 9.15; ὁ θυμὸς αὐτῶν ἐκπίνει μου τὸ αἷμα Jb 6.4.

2. *to drink all the contents of*: + acc., τὸ κόνδυ τοῦ θυμοῦ 'the cup of wrath' Is 51.17 (|| ἐκκενόω 'to empty').

Cf. πίνω, καταπίνω, ἀφανίζω.

ἐκπίπτω: aor. ἐξέπεσα, subj. ~πέσω, ptc. ~πεσών, opt.3s ~πέσοι; pf.ptc. ~πεπτωκώς.

1. *to fall out* accidentally from a fixed position: *s* iron blade of an axe, De 19.5, 4K 6.5; a star, ἐκ τοῦ οὐρανοῦ Is 14.12; an acorn, ἀπὸ τῆς θήκης αὐτοῦ 'from its husk' 6.13.

2. *to fall*: *s* withering flower, Jb 14.2,15.30; metaph. of social dropouts, 24.9, ruining oneself Si 31.7.

3. *to suffer loss of*: + gen. and *s* a flower, τῆς ἐλπίδος τῆς δόξης Is 28.4, cf. ἐκ τῆς δόξης 28.1, so in Isoc. 5.64 and Aesch. *Prom.* 756f. τυραννίδος .. ἀρχῆς.

4. *to be publicly announced*: *s* edict, 2M 6.8.

Cf. πίπτω: Michaelis, *TDNT* 6.168.

ἐκπληρόω: fut.inf. ~πληρώσειν; aor.inf. ~πληρῶσαι.ʃ

to bring to full conclusion: + acc. rei, φόρον '(pay up) tribute' 2M 8.10; ἐπιβουλήν 'plot' 3M 1.2; πρόθεσις 'purpose' 1.22. Cf. πληρόω.

ἐκπλήρωσις, εως. f.ʃ

act of reaching the full measure: ἁμαρτιῶν 2M 6.14. Cf. πληρόω.

ἐκπλήσσω: aor.pass. ἐξεπλάγην, ptc. ~πλαγείς, subj. ~πλαγῶ.

pass., *to be astonished at, marvel at*: abs. Ec 7.16; + acc., τὴν ψυχήν 2M 7.12, δύναμιν 'their power' Wi 13.4; + gen., 4M 8.4. Cf. ἐξίστημι, θαμβέω, θαυμάζω.

ἐκπλύνω: fut. ~πλυνῶ.ʃ

to wash off: + acc., τὸν ῥύπον τῶν υἱῶν .. Σιων 'the filth of ..' Is 4.4 (|| ἐκκαθαρίζω). Cf. πλύνω.

ἐκποιέω: fut. ~ποιήσω; aor. ἐξεποίησα.ʃ

1. *to possess sufficient capacity* or *capability* for a given task: + inf., 2C 7.7 (*s* altar); + dat., 3K 21.10. **b**. impers.: + dat. and inf., οὐθενὶ ἐξεποίησεν ἐξαγγεῖλαι τὰ ἔργα αὐτοῦ 'nobody was good enough to recount his works' Si 18.4; 42.17. **c**. a partial Heb. calque (see under χείρ **1c**): καθὼς ἂν ἐκποιῇ ἡ χεὶρ αὐτοῦ 'to the best of his ability' Ez 46.7 (967: ἰσχύῃ), 11.

2. *to be sufficient with nothing more needed*: impers. and + dat. pers., Si 39.11.

ἐκπολεμέω: fut. ἐκπολεμήσω; aor. ἐξεπολέμησα, ptc. ~πολεμήσας, inf. ~πολεμῆσαι.

to go to war against: + acc. pers., Ex 1.10; ^πόλιν^ De 20.10, 19; *s* God, Jo 23.3. Cf. (συνεκ)-πολεμέω.

ἐκπολιορκέω: aor.impv.3pl ~κησάτωσαν.ʃ

to force to surrender or *capitulate*: τὴν πόλιν Jo 7.3; 10.5.

ἐκπολιτεύω: aor. ἐξεπολίτευσα.ʃ*

to change the system of a state and cause to degenerate: ἐπὶ πᾶσαν παρανομίαν 'to every manner of disregard of the law' 4M 4.19.

ἐκπορεύομαι: pf. ἐκπεπόρευμαι, ptc. ~πεπορευμένος.

to move out (intr.): ἐπὶ τὸ ὕδωρ 'to the river' Ex 7.15; εἰς τὴν σκηνήν 33.7; opp. εἰσπ., De 31.2, Zc 8.10; Ge 24.11 (|| ἐξέρχομαι vs. 43); opp. εἰσέρχομαι - ἀπὸ Φαραω Ex 5.20 (from an audience with him; see vs. 15); *s* river, Ge 2.10, De 8.7; branches of a lampstand jutting out from its sides - Ex 25.31; to perform some task, of enlisting as soldiers, Nu 1.3 (ἐν δυνάμει), 31.27 (εἰς τὴν παράταξιν 'into the battle-line'), Am 5.3, to draw water, Ge 24.13; words, τὰ ἐκπορευόμενα διὰ τῶν χειλέων σου De 23.23; curse, ἡ ἀρὰ ἐκπορευομένη ἐπὶ πρόσωπον πάσης τῆς γῆς Zc 5.3; divine message, ἐπὶ παντὶ ῥήματι τῷ ἐκπορευομένῳ διὰ στόματος θεοῦ De 8.3; of leaving one's usual abode, ἐκ τοῦ τόπου αὐτοῦ Mi 1.3; λαῖλαψ 'storm' Je 32.18; || ἐξέρχομαι Ez 46.10. **b**. *to emerge*: ἰδοὺ δύο γυναῖκες ἐκπορευόμεναι Zc 5.9; 6.1; ἐκ τῶν μηρῶν αὐτοῦ 'from his loins' (*s* offspring) Jd 8.30. **c**. + acc.: τὴν πύλην τῆς πόλεως Ge 34.24.

Cf. εἰσέρχομαι, εἰσ~, συνεκπορεύομαι, ἔξειμι, ἐξέρχομαι: Lee 91f.

ἐκπορθέω: aor.ptc. ~πορθήσας; pf. ~πεπόρθηκα.ʃ

1. *to pillage*: abs. 4M 17.24; *o* οἴκους Jb 12.5.

2. *to destroy*: + acc. pers., πολεμίους 'enemies' 4M 18.4.

Cf. ἀφανίζω.

ἐκπορνεύω: fut. ἐκπορνεύσω; aor. ἐξεπόρνευσα, inf. ~πορνεῦσαι, subj. ~πορνεύσω; pf. ἐκπεπόρνευκα. *

1. *to indulge in sexual immorality*: *s* woman, νύμφη Ge 38.24; μήτηρ Ho 2.5 (causing her children disgrace); θυγατέρες 4.13 (|| μοιχεύω); οὐκ ἐκπορνεύσει ἡ γῆ 'no prostitution shall be practised in the land' Le 19.29; εἰς τὰς θυγατέρας Μωαβ Nu 25.1; + ἔν τινι (pers.) Je 3.1; + ἐπί and acc., Ez 16.16 (|| ἐν vs. 17), 26; + pseudo-cogn. acc., ἔργα πόρνης 23.42. Cf. ἐκφύρομαι.

2. *to indulge in acts of unfaithfulness* in relation to God: ὀπίσω τῶν θεῶν αὐτῶν 'chasing their gods' Ex 34.15, ὀπίσω θεῶν ἀλλοτρίων De 31.16, ὀπίσω τῶν βδελυγμάτων αὐτῶν Ez 20.30; ἐκπορνεύσει ἡ γῆ ἀπὸ ὄπισθεν τοῦ κυρίου 'the land will indulge in acts of unfaithfulness behind the back of the Lord' Ho 1.2; ἀπὸ τοῦ θεοῦ αὐτῶν 4.12 (by practising idolatrous worship); 5.3 (|| μιαίνομαι); ἀπ' ἐμοῦ .. ὀπίσω τῶν ἐπιτηδευμάτων αὐτῶν Ez 6.9; *s* καρδία Si 40.11.

3. *to induce to do* ἐκπορνεύω: + acc. pers., τὴν θυγατέρα σου Le 19.29; Ez 16.33 ('pimp'), 2C 21.11. **b**. τοὺς υἱούς σου ὀπίσω τῶν θεῶν αὐτῶν Ex 34.16; αὐτοὺς εἰς τοὺς ἄρχοντας Le 20.5. **c**. τὸν οἶκον τοῦ πατρὸς αὐτῆς 'to implicate her family in fornication' De 22.21.

Cf. πορνεύω, μοιχεύω: LSG s.v.

ἔκπρακτος, ον.ʃ*

available for purchase: *s* ψυχή Si 10.8¶.

ἐκπρεπής, ές.ʃ

preeminent: τῇ ῥώμῃ 'in bodily strength' 2M 3.26 (|| κάλλιστος, διαπρεπής); *s* οἶκος 3K 8.53[a]; cultic offerings, + κάλλιστος 3M 3.17. Cf. διαπρεπής.

ἐκπρίαμαι.ʃ

to buy off and rescue: + acc. pers., *o* one who is sentenced to death, Pr 24.11 (|| ῥύομαι 'rescue'). Cf. λυτρόω.

ἐκπρίω: aor.ptc. ~πρίσας.ʃ

to saw: + acc., φυτόν 'tree' Wi 13.11. Cf. πρίζω, πρίων.

ἐκπυρόω: aor.ptc.pass. ~πυρωθείς.ʃ

to raise the temperature of: + acc. (pan), 2M 7.3.

ἐκρέω: fut. ~ρυήσομαι; aor. ἐξερρύην.ʃ

to fall off: *s* olive (ἐλαία), De 28.40; leaves (φύλλα) Is 64.6; fig. deserting soldiers, 1M 9.6.

ἔκρηγμα, ατος. n.ʃ

breach in a dam or suchlike (LSG): Ez 30.16. Cf. διακοπή.

ἐκρήγνυμι: aor.pass.opt.3s ~ραγείη.ʃ

to be taken away and unavailable: *s* cure, Jb 18.14.

ἐκριζόω: fut.pass. ~ριζωθήσομαι; aor. ἐξερρίζωσα, inf. ~ριζῶσαι, pass. ἐξερριζώθην. *

to pull out the roots of so as to destroy: acc. (tree), Da 4.11 LXX; root of a tree, 4.23 LXX. **b**. metaph., *to uproot* in order to cause destruction: + acc., ^τὴν πόλιν^ 1M 5.51, πολίτευμα 'community' 2M 12.7; pass., *o* pers. Zp 2.4 (|| ἐκρίπτω); + κατασκάπτω, ἀπολλύω Je 1.10; θεμέλια 'foundations' Si 3.9, οἶκος 21.4.

Cf. ῥίζα, ῥιζόω, ἐκριζωτής, ἀφανίζω.

ἐκριζωτής, οῦ. m.ʃ*

uprooter: *s* λογισμός 'rational will,' παθῶν 'of passions' 4M 3.5 (|| ἐκκόπτω 'to fell' vss. 2, 3, 4). Cf. ἐκριζόω.

ἐκριπτέω, ἐκρίπτω: fut.inf. ~ρίψειν, pass. ἐκριφήσομαι; aor. ἐξέρριψα, ptc. ~ρίψας, pass. ἐξερρίφην; pf.ptc.pass. ἐξερριμμένος, ἐκρεριμμένος.

1. *to throw out*: as ruined and *o* city, Zp 2.4 (|| ἐκριζόω 'to uproot'), σκεῦος 'vessel' as useless Je 22.28 (+ ἐκβάλλω); hum. Jd 6.13B (B: ἀπωθέω),

Pr 5.23, θηρίοις 'for beasts (as food)' 2M 9.15; weapons, 10.30; hum. bones dug out of their grave, τῷ καύματι τῆς ἡμέρας 'to be exposed to the heat of the day' Ba 2.25. **b.** *to set and place as a sacrificial offer*: + acc., τὴν ψυχὴν αὐτοῦ ἐξ ἐναντίας 'his own life in front of others' Jd 9.17 B (A: simp.).

*__2__. *to spread abroad*: "chaff that the wind spreads abroad off the surface of the earth" Ps 1.4. **b.** pass., intr. and *s* hums., *to spread out* Jd 15.9.

Cf. ῥίπτω, διασκορπίζω, σπείρω.

ἔκρυσις, εως.ʃ

outlet for sewage, excess fluid: Ez 40.38. Cf. ἔξοδος **5**.

ἐκσαρκίζω: pf.ptc.pass. ~σεσαρκισμένος.ʃ *

to separate flesh or *meat* from: "a leg and a shoulder with their flesh separated from the bones' Ez 24.4.

ἐκσείω: aor. ἐξέσεισα.ʃ

to drive out: τινα 4K 3.25*L*. Cf. ἐκβάλλω.

ἐκσιφωνίζω: opt.aor.pass.~νισθείην.ʃ*

to suck out: pass., ἡ ἰσχύς Jb 5.5.

ἐκσοβέω: pf.ptc.pass. ~σεσοβημένος.ʃ

to scare away: pass., *o* hum., ‖ φοβέω Wi 17.9. Cf. (ἐκ)φοβέω.

ἐκσπάω: fut. ~σπάσω, pass. ~σπασθήσομαι; aor. ἐξέσπασα, impv. ~σπασον, inf. ~σπάσαι, ptc. ~σπάσας, pass. ~σπασθῆναι, subj. ~σπάσω, pass. ~σπασθῶ, opt.3s ~σπάσαι; pf.ptc.pass. ἐξεσπασμένος.

to pull out: ἐκσπάσῃ ὁ ποιμὴν ἐκ στόματος τοῦ λέοντος δύο σκέλη 'a shepherd pulls out two legs from a lion's mouth' Am 3.12, sim. 1K 17.35; δαλὸς ἐξεσπασμένος ἐκ πυρός 'a fire-brand plucked out of fire' 4.11, Zc 3.2; οὐ μὴ ἐκσπασθῶσιν ἀπὸ τῆς γῆς αὐτῶν 'they (= plantations) will not be pulled out of their soil' Am 9.15, ἐκ ῥιζῶν Ez 17.9; ἐκ χειρὸς κακῶν 'from the hand of evil ones' Hb 2.9; *o* τὰ πρόβατα Zc 13.7, signet-ring Je 22.24; a sword from its sheath, Ez 21.3, 5, χόρτος 'grass' Ps 128.6. **b.** *to lure out*: acc. (enemy troops), Jd 20.32 A (B: ἐκκενόω), cf. Jo 8.6 (ἀποσπάω).

Cf. ἀποσπάω, ἐξέλκω.

ἐκσπερματίζω: fut. ~σπερματιῶ.ʃ *

to produce seed, i.e. offspring: *s* woman, Nu 5.28. Cf. σπερματίζω, σπέρμα.

ἐκσπονδυλίζω.ʃ

to break the vertebrae of: pass., *o* hum. under torture, 4M 11.18. Cf. σπόνδυλος.

ἔκστασις, εως. f.

loss of mental equilibrium, displacement of mind: ἔ. ἐπέπεσεν τῷ Αβραμ Ge 15.12; as cogn. acc., ἐξέστη Ισαακ ~ιν μεγάλην σφόδρα 27.33; caused by God, ἐπέβαλεν ὁ θεὸς ~ιν ἐπὶ τὸν Αδαμ 2.21 (leading to a state of coma; Alexandre 282f.), ἐπῆλθεν ἔ. κυρίου ἐπὶ τὸν λαόν 1K 11.7; ἐν ~ει 'with frenzy' Hb 3.14; Zc 12.4 (‖ ἐν παραφρονήσει); ἔ. κυρίου μεγάλη 14.13; παραπληξίᾳ καὶ ἀορασίᾳ καὶ ~ει διανοίας 'with derangement and loss of sight ..' De 28.28; + φρικτά 'dreadful things' Je 5.30, cf. 2.12; cogn. dat., Ez 26.16, 27.35, 32.10. **b.** a disconcerting report: τῆς γῆς 'concerning the land' Nu 13.33. **c.** in favourable sense, *great commotion and excitement*: κυρίου 'over the Lord' 2C 17.10; ἐξέστησας ἡμῖν πᾶσαν τὴν ἔκστασιν ταύτην 'you have gone to all this uncommon trouble for our sake' 4K 4.13 (*L* ἐξέταξας .. ἔκτακσιν).

Cf. ἐξίστημι, καταφορά, μανία, παραπληξία, παραφρόνησις.

ἐκστρατεύω.ʃ

to march out: as a group, *s* locusts, Pr 30.27.

ἐκστρέφω: fut. ~στρέψω; aor. ἐξέστρεψα; pf.ptc. pass. ἐξεστραμμένος.ʃ

1. tr. *to transform* (τι εἴς τι): Am 6.12. Cf. μεταστρέφω **3**.

2. *to put out of joint* (or: *to twist*): + acc. rei, τοὺς ἀστραγάλους 'the vertebrae (of a sheep's neck)' Zc 11.16. **b.** fig., + acc., ψυχάς Ez 13.20 (‖ συστρέφω); γενεὰ ἐξεστραμμένη 'a disjointed generation' De 32.20 (‖ διεστραμμένη vs. 5).

Cf. διαστρέφω, ἐκτρέπω.

ἐκσυρίζω: fut. ~συριῶ.ʃ

to hiss: in derision, ἐπ' ἀτιμίᾳ αὐτοῦ 'at his disgrace' Si 22.1. Cf. συρίζω.

ἐκσύρω: aor. ἐξέσυρα.ʃ

to sweep away: *s* river, *o* fallen soldier Jd 5.21 B. Cf. σύρω.

ἔκταξις, εως. f.ʃ

v.n. of ἐκτάσσω **4**: 4K 4.13*L* (B: ἐξέταξις). Cf. ἐκτάσσω.

ἐκταράσσω: aor. ἐξετάραξα.

to throw off balance mentally and cause anxiety: + acc. pers., *s* lawless acts Ps 17.5, threats by God 87.17; φαντασίαι 'apparitions' Wi 18.17, ἰνδάλμασιν 'with spectres' 17.3. Cf. ταράσσω. Del. Wi 17.4 v.l.

ἔκτασις, εως. f.ʃ

1. *act of stretching and extending*: Jd 16.14 A (or: *an instrument for the purpose).

2. *extent*: μακρὸς τῇ ~ει Ez 17.3 (of eagle with large wings).

Cf. ἀπέκτασις.

ἐκτάσσω: aor. ἐξέταξα, ptc. ~τάξας, pass. ~ταγείς; pf.ptc.pass. ~τεταγμένος.ʃ

1. *to draw out in battle-order*: pass., ἐνωπλισμένοι καὶ ἐκτεταγμένοι .. εἰς τὸν πόλεμον 'armed ..' Nu 32.27; 2M 15.20.

2. *to prescribe*: + acc., daily rations of food and drink, Da 1.10.

3. *to enlist* for military service: + acc. pers., 4K 25.19.

4. *to make provision* for a guest: + cogn. acc., ἡμῖν ἔκταξιν 4K 4.13*L* (B: ἐξίστημι).

Cf. ἔκταξις, ἐνοπλίζω: LSG s.v.

ἐκτείνω: fut.act. ἐκτενῶ, pass.~ταθήσομαι; aor. ἐξέτεινα, impv. ἔκτεινον, ptc.~τείνας, inf. ~τεῖναι, subj.~τείνω, pass. ἐξετάθην; pf. ~τέτακα, pass.ptc. ~τεταμένος.

1. *to spread* (a thin, flat object of considerable size): + obj. δίκτυον ἐκτεταμένον 'a net spread out' Ho 5.1; οἱ χερουβιμ ἐκτείνοντες τὰς πτέρυγας 'the cherubs spreading their wings' Ex 25.19; καταπέτασμα 'veil' 38.19; οὐρανόν, of God's creation of the universe, Zc 12.1, Is 44.24, Je 10.12, 28.15, Ps 103.2.

2. *to draw out* (a long object): ***o*** line of attacking troops understood, ἐπὶ τὴν πόλιν Jd 9.33, sim. 1K 27.8*L*; μέτρον ('a measure') La 2.8, ὑπόδημα 'sandal' Ps 59.10; pass. μέτρον ἐκταθήσεται ἐπὶ Ιερουσαλημ Zc 1.16, ῥομφαία 'sword' 1C 21.16.

3. *to put forth*: + acc., ἀναδενδράδα 'vine' Ez 17.6, κλάδους 'branches' Si 24.16. **b.** + χεῖρα in order to grasp sth, Ge 3.22, 8.9, 19.10 (pl. τὰς χεῖρας with pl. subj. as in Is 1.15, but w. sg. subj. at 1M 12.42), λαβεῖν τὴν μάχαιραν 22.10; καὶ ἐπιλαβοῦ τῆς κέρκου 'and grasp the tail' Ex 4.4 (:: εἰσφέρω vs. 6); in order to harm or attack, ἐκτείνας τὴν χεῖρα πατάξω .. 3.20, ἐπὶ Ιουδαν .. καὶ ἐξαρῶ .. Zp 1.4, ἐν ὑμῖν Ne 13.21; ἐκτενῶ τὴν χεῖρά μου καὶ διαφθερῶ σε Je 15.6, ἐν χειρὶ ἐκτεταμένῃ καὶ ἐν βραχίονι κραταιῷ '.. with a mighty arm' 21.5; ἐπὶ γῆν Αἰγύπτου Ex 10.12; Ho 7.5; τὴν δεξιάν σου Ex 15.12; in order to help, abs. Si 14.13, τῷ πτωχῷ 7.32; + acc. pers. 'to put forth a hand in order to support'(?) Ho 11.4 (cf. Cyr. I 229); in swearing, τὴν χεῖρά μου πρὸς τὸν θεόν Ge 14.22, εἰς τὸν οὐρανόν Ex 9.22, ***s*** God 6.8; in prayer, pl. χεῖρας πρός με Is 1.15, εἰς τὸν οὐρανόν 4M 4.11; to initiate an action, ἐν ἀνομίᾳ Ps 124.3; ***o*** ῥομφαίαν Ez 30.25 (or **2**), ῥάβδον Es 8.4 o', πόδα 'foot' (so as to start walking?) Jb 30.12¶. Cf. προφθάνω **4**.

4. *to prolong* an activity: abs., 1K 1.16; + acc., λόγους Pr 1.24. **b.** mid., + dat. rei, συμβολαῖς 'joint meals' Pr 23.20.

5. pass. and intr. *to extend*: ***s*** area, Es 7.32*L*. **b.** act. intr., *to spread out*: ***s*** troops, Jd 9.44B (:: ἐκχέομαι and A: so 20.37B), ἐπὶ τὰ .. ὄρη 1M 6.49. **c.** *to lie flat on the ground*: bitten by a venomous snake, Pr 23.32.

Cf. ἐκτενῶς, ἐν~ παρα~, παρεκτείνω, τείνω, τανύω: Caird 1968.469; LSG s.v.

ἐκτελέω: aor.opt.3s ~τελέσαι; pf.ptc. ~τετελεκώς.

to effect completely: abs. Da TH 3.40; + acc., ἀγῶνας 'struggles' 2M 15.9. Cf. τελέω.

ἐκτέμνω: aor. ἐξέτεμον, inf. ~τεμεῖν, ptc. ~τεμών.

to cut: ***s*** weaver and ***o*** web, Is 38.12; ***o*** tongue, 2M 15.33 (punishment).

ἐκτένεια, ας. f.ʃ

eagerness: ἀνεβόησαν .. πρὸς τὸν θεὸν ἐν ~ᾳ μεγάλῃ Ju 4.9, cf. ἐκτενῶς Jn 3.8; σῶμα καὶ ψυχὴν .. παραβεβλημένος μετὰ πάσης ~είας 'having risked body and soul ..' 2M 14.38; ἐπιστολὴν .. τὴν ~αν ἔχουσαν 'a letter .. couched in an earnest tone(?)' 3M 6.41. Cf. ἐκτενῶς.

ἐκτενής, ές.ʃ

indicative of maximum endeavour: πᾶν ~ὲς προσοίσεσθαι πρὸς ἀντίλημψιν 'to do the utmost to assist' 3M 3.10; ***s*** πρόθεσις 'purpose' 5.29.

ἐκτενῶς. adv.ʃ

earnestly, fervently: of a prayer to God, ἀνεβόησαν πρὸς θεὸν ἐ. Jn 3.8, cf. ἐν ἐκτενείᾳ μεγάλῃ Ju 4.9 and ὁμοθυμαδόν 'simultaneously' 4.12; κεκράξατε πρὸς κύριον ἐ. Jl 1.14; 3M 5.9; δεήθητε τοῦ θεοῦ ἐ. Es 4.11 *L*. Cf. ἐκτένεια, προθύμιος: Spicq 1.457-61.

ἐκτήκω: aor. ἐξέτηξα.ʃ

I. tr. *to cause to lose vitality*: ***o***, χήρας .. τὸν ὀφθαλμόν 'the eye(s) of a (needy) widow (yearning for help)' Jb 31.16, cf. ὀφθαλμούς Si 18.18; τὴν ψυχὴν αὐτοῦ Ps 38.12; ἐξέτηξέν με ὁ ζῆλος τοῦ οἴκου σου 'the zeal for your house has burned me out' 118.139; ἐκτήκει σάρκας 'saps one's bodily strength' Si 34.1. Cf. Renehan 2.65.

II. pass. *to lose vitality*, 'waste away, pine': ***s*** person, Ps 118.158; ἐπὶ τοῖς ἐχθροῖς σου 138.21; poss. act. in the same sense, ψυχή Le 26.16, cf. Ps 38.12.

ἐκτίθημι: fut. ~θήσω; aor. ἐξέθηκα, impv. ~θες, ptc. ~θείς, subj. ~θῶ, pass. ἐξετέθην, ptc. ~τεθείς, impv.3s ~τεθήτω.

1. *to put out*: ***o*** ἔκθεμα 'public notice' Es 8.17 o'; κρίμα πραέων '(publicly announce) the verdict concerning the meek' Jb 36.15, δόγμα 'edict' Da 3.96 TH, γραφήν 'written order' 6.8 TH, πρόσταγμα 5.7 LXX.

2. *to abandon and leave uncared for*: pass., ***o*** infant, Wi 18.5.

3. *to release and turn over*: + acc., corpses of criminals to be crucified, Es 9.14 o'.

4. *to expound*: abs., 2M 11.36.

Cf. ἔκθεμα.

ἐκτίκτω: aor.subj. ~τέκω.ʃ

to produce: ***s*** vegetation or crops, Is 55.10. Cf. ἐκφέρω.

ἐκτίλλω: fut.pass. ~τιλήσομαι; aor. ἐξέτιλα, subj. ~τίλω, inf. ~τῖλαι, impv. ~τιλον, opt.3s ~τίλαι, pass. ἐξετίλην.

to pluck out: ***o*** κλάδους 'branches' Da 4.11 TH, ῥίζας ἐθνῶν 'roots of ..' Si 10.15; nation, Je 24.6, sim. 49.10; opp. φυτεύω, 51.34, Ec 3.2, Si 10.15; pass., *o* ξύλα PSol 14.4, πτερά 'feathers' Da 7.4 TH.

ἐκτιναγμός, οῦ.ʃ*(ἐκτινάσσω: Homer +)

shaking out: of a destructive act, ἐ. καὶ ἀνατιναγμὸς καὶ ἐκβρασμὸς .. Na 2.11. Cf. ἐκτινάσσω, τίναγμα, ἀνατιναγμός.

ἐκτινάσσω: fut. ~τινάξω, pass. ~τιναχθήσομαι; aor. ἐξετίναξα, ptc. ~τινάξας, inf. ~τινάξαι, opt.3s ~τινάξαι, mid.impv. ~ναξαι, pass. ἐξετινάχθην; pf. ptc.pass. ~τετιναγμένος.

1. *to shake out*: + acc. pers., μέσον τῆς θαλάσσης 'into the midst of the sea' Ex 14.27, εἰς θάλασσαν Ps 135.15; Na 2.3, ὡς ἀκρίδες 'as locust' (of being treated as useless, obnoxious) Ps 108.23; pass., ἐκτετιναγμένος 'an outcast' 126.4. **b.** so as to get rid of things attached to it: + acc., χεῖρα Si 22.2; ἄμωμον τὴν ὁδόν μου 'in order to make my way impeccable' 2K 22.33B; Is 28.27. **c.** *to remove and destroy by shaking*: + acc. (leaves of a tree), Da 4.11 TH; water cans, Jd 7.19. **d.** mid. and + acc., ἐκτίναξαι τὸν χοῦν 'Shake the dust off yourself' Is 52.2.

2. *to force to move out* of a confined area: + acc. (flame), Da 3.49; 'to unload' (cargo) 3K 5.23; τὰς σχίζας εἰς τὸν λαόν '(fired) missiles into the people' 1M 10.80. **b.** *to break out by shaking off that which constrains one's freedom of movement*: Jd 16.20.

Cf. ἀποτινάσσω, ἐκ~, τιναγμός, ἐκβάλλω, κραδαίνω: Schmidt 3.133f.; Ziegler 1934.185.

ἐκτίνω: fut. ~τείσω.ʃ

to pay in full: ὑπὲρ τῆς ψυχῆς αὐτοῦ 'for his life' Jb 2.4.

ἐκτοκίζω: fut. ~τοκιῶ.ʃ

to demand and enforce payment of: + dat. pers. and cogn. acc., τῷ ἀδελφῷ σου τόκον ἀργυρίου καὶ τ. βρωμάτων καὶ τ. παντὸς πράγματος, οὗ ἂν ἐκδανείσῃς 'charge your brother interest on money, foods or anything which you might lend' De 23.19 (Syh *trabbe*); 23.20. Cf. τόκος: Lee 92f.; LSG s.v.

ἐκτομίας, ου. m.ʃ

a male whose testicles have been cut out: animal, Le 22.24 (unfit as offering). Cf. ἀποσπάω, θλαδίας, ἐκθλίβω.

ἐκτοπίζω.ʃ

to remove from a place: + acc. pers., ἑαυτούς 2M 8.13 (deserting soldiers). Cf. ἀποδιδράσκω.

ἐκτός. prep. c. gen.

1. *to the outside of*: ἐξῆλθεν .. ἐ. τῆς πόλεως Ex 9.33; οἱ ἐκτός 'the outsiders,' i.e. the non-Jews or laymen, Si prol. 5, cf. LSG s.v.

2. *not subject to, free from*: ἐ. ταραχῆς 'free from disquiet' 2M 11.25; ἀπωλείας 'perdition' Pr 24.22a.

3. *excepting*: ἐ. σου ἄλλον οὐκ οἴδαμεν Is 26.13; οὐθενὸς τῶν ἐ. αὐτοῦ εἰδότος 'nobody except him knowing about it' Bel 13 LXX; ἑτέροις ἐ. τούτων 'to others than these' 11.4 TH. **b.** *in addition to, not counting*, preceded by a numeral: ἑβδομήκοντα ἐ. γυναικῶν καὶ τέκνων Bel 10 TH; Jd 8.26B (|| πάρεξ and A: πλήν), 20.15B (A: χωρίς), 3K 4.23.

Cf. πλήν, χωρίς: Chadwick 100-5.

ἕκτος, η, ον.

sixth in order: ἐν τῷ μηνὶ τῷ ~ῳ 'in the sixth month' Hg 1.1. **b.** *sixth part*: τοῦ ιν 'of a hin' Ez 4.11.

Cf. ἕξ.

ἐκτρέπω.ʃ

1. *to order out of the way*: + acc. pers., ἐξ ὀφθαλμῶν αὐτοῦ '(to get) out of sight' Es 3.6 *L*.

2. *to transform* (τι εἴς τι): *s* God, εἰς τὸ πρωῒ σκιὰν θανάτου Am 5.8.

Cf. ἐκστρέφω and μετασκευάζω.

ἐκτρέφω: fut. ἐκθρέψω; aor. ἐξέθρεψα, subj. ἐκθρέψω, inf. ἐκθρέψαι, ptc. ~θρέψας, pass. ~τραφείς.

to rear, nurture (+ acc.): *o* κατάλειψιν 'survivors' Ge 45.7; τέκνα Ho 9.12, Zc 10.9, νεανίσκους Is 23.4 (|| ὑψόω); lamb 2K 12.3; plant Ez 31.4 (*s* water), Jn 4.10; ἐν ἄρτοις 'with foods' Ge 47.17; *s* hum. father, 1E 4.20, + ἄγω 'to lead' 1M 6.15. Cf. (συνεκ)τρέφω, τροφοφορέω.

ἐκτρέχω: aor. ἐξέδραμον.ʃ

to run out of a building: Jd 13.10 A (B: simp.), 3K 18.16. Cf. τρέχω.

ἐκτριβή, ῆς. f.ʃ

v.n. of subs.: ~ῇ ἐκτριβήσεσθε 'you will be totally destroyed' De 4.26. Cf. ἐκτρίβω, ἔκτριψις.

ἐκτρίβω: fut. ~τρίψω, pass. ~τριβήσομαι; aor. ἐξέτριψα, inf. ~τρῖψαι, impv. ~τριψον, subj. ~τρίψω, pass. ἐξετρίβην, subj. ~τριβῶ.

1. *to rub thoroughly*: + acc. *o* cooking vessel, Le 6.28; doorsteps, Si 6.36 (by frequent visits).

2. *to destroy completely*: *o* pers., ἐκτριβήσομαι ἐγὼ καὶ ὁ οἶκός μου Ge 34.30; τὴν πόλιν 19.14; οὐκ ἐκτριβήσεται ἡ γῆ ἐν τῷ λιμῷ '.. at the time of the famine' 41.36; ἀπὸ τοῦ κυρίου ἡμῶν 47.18 (resulting in permanent separation from him); men together with their belongings (τὰ ὑπάρχοντά σου) 45.11; ψυχή Nu 15.31, 19.13; ἐχθρός 32.21; *o* military strength, + ἐξαίρω 1M 3.35; ἀπὸ τῆς γῆς Ex 9.15 (as a result of πατάσσω), ἀπὸ γῆς ζώντων Je 11.19; ἐξ Ισραηλ Nu 19.13; ἀπὸ προσώπου τινός 32.21; De 2.12, 28.24, 52 (|| ἀπόλλυμι); called πληγή Ex 12.13; τρίβος 'path' Jb 30.13¶; ὑπερηφανίαν 'arrogance' PSol 17.23 (|| ἐξωθέω). **b.** *to harass and wear out*: + acc. pers., πένητα 'a poor person' Am 8.4 (|| καταδυναστεύω).

Cf. ἀφανίζω, ἐκτριβή, συνεκτρίβω.

ἔκτριψις, εως. f.ʃ

v.n. of prec.: cogn. dat., ~ει ἐκτριβήσεται 'shall be utterly destroyed' Nu 15.31. Cf. ἐκτρίβω, ἐκτριβή.

ἐκτρυγάω: fut. ~τρυγήσω.ʃ
to gather in the vintage (acc.): ***o*** σταφυλήν 'grapes' Le 25.5. Cf. τρυγάω.

ἐκτρώγω.ʃ
to devour, eat up: ***s*** σής 'moth' Mi 7.4. Cf. ἐσθίω and καταναλίσκω.

ἔκτρωμα, ατος. n.ʃ
stillborn child: ἔ. ἐκπορευόμενον ἐκ μήτρας μητρός Nu 12.12, Jb 3.16; fig. of misery, Ec 6.3. Cf. Schneider, *TDNT* 2.465f; Spicq 1.464-6; Muraoka 1973a.29f.

ἐκτυπόω: fut. ~τυπώσω; pf.ptc.pass. ~τετυπωμένος.
to work in relief: ***o*** cups of a lampstand and with double acc., καρυΐσκους 'nuts' Ex 25.32; metal leaf and + cogn. obj. ἐκτύπωμα, 28.32; γράμματα ἐκτετυπωμένα σφραγῖδος 'letters of a seal engraved in relief' 36.39. Cf. ἐκτύπωμα, ἐκτύπωσις.

ἐκτύπωμα, ατος. n.ʃ
figure in relief: σφραγῖδος 'of a seal' Ex 28.32, Si 45.12. Cf. ἐκτυπόω.

ἐκτύπωσις, εως. f.ʃ
v.n. of ἐκτυπόω (q.v.): 3K 6.35.

ἐκτυφλόω: fut.pass. ~τυφλωθήσομαι; aor. ἐξετύφλωσα, subj. ~τυφλώσω; pf.pass. ~τετύφλωμαι.
to make blind: abs. Ex 21.26; punishment, Je 52.11; pass. ὁ ὀφθαλμὸς ὁ δεξιὸς αὐτοῦ ἐκτυφλούμενος ἐκτυφλωθήσεται 'his right eye will be totally blinded' Zc 11.17; fig., τὰ δῶρα ἐκτυφλοῖ ὀφθαλμοὺς βλεπόντων 'gifts blind the eyes of beholders' Ex 23.8, .. σοφῶν De 16.19 (|| ἀποτυφλόω Si 20.29), intellectually Is 56.10. Cf. τυφλός, (ἀπο)τυφλόω.

ἐκφαίνω: fut.~φανῶ; aor.subj. ~φάνω, inf. ~φᾶναι, pass. ἐξεφάνην.
to disclose: + acc. rei and dat. pers., παντὶ ἀνθρώπῳ καρδίαν σου Si 8.19, παιδείαν 16.25, 24.27, κρίμα 19.25, μυστήρια Da 2.47 LXX (TH ἀποκαλύπτω), εὐσήμως 'clearly' Da 2.19 LXX, ***s*** ἀπέχθεια 'hostility' 3M 4.1; unintentionally, Si 14.7. **b.** *to display evidences of competence in and knowledge of*: + acc., παιδείαν καὶ κρίμα Si 38.33.
Cf. (ἀπο)φαίνω, ἀποκαλύπτω, γνωρίζω, μηνύω.

ἐκφαυλίζω: aor.ptc. ~φαυλίσας.ʃ
to hold in utter contempt, treat with utter disdain: + acc. pers., Ju 14.5. Cf. φαυλίζω.

ἐκφέρω: fut.act. ἐξοίσω, pass. ἐξενεχθήσομαι; aor. ἐξήνεγκα, ptc. ἐξενέγκας, pass. ἐξενεχθείς, inf. act. ἐξενέγκαι, pass. ἐξενεχθῆναι.
1. *to carry out, bring out* (*from* ἐκ): ἄρτους καὶ οἶνον Ge 14.18 (as a priest); αὐτοῖς ὕδωρ ἐκ τῆς πέτρας Nu 20.8; ἐξενεχθήσεσθε γυμναί 'you will be carried out (of the house) naked' Am 4.3; ἐκ τοῦ οἴκου 6.10; ἔξω Ex 12.46; ἔξω τῆς πόλεως εἰς τόπον ἀκάθαρτον Le 14.45; κλῆρον 'lot' Jo 18.6; ***o*** ἔξστασιν 'a disconcerting report,' πρός τινα Nu 13.33, cf. ῥήματα πονηρὰ περὶ τῆς γῆς 'unfavourable, critical report ..' 14.36, λοιδορίας 'abusive speech' Pr 10.18 (|| προφέρω vs. 13), ὅλον τὸν θυμὸν αὐτοῦ '(give) full vent to his anger' 29.11; ὡς φῶς τὴν δικαιοσύνην σου Ps 36.6; τὰ παρθένια τῆς παιδὸς πρὸς τὴν γερουσίαν 'the tokens of the child's virginity to the elders' De 22.15; seed, σπέρμα πολὺ .. εἰς τὸ πεδίον De 28.38. Opp. εἰσφέρω Ex 4.6, De 28.38.
2. *to produce*: ***o*** agricultural crop, βοτάνην χόρτου .. 'grassy plant ..' Ge 1.12, βλαστόν 'shoot' Nu 17.8; "a young bull growing horns and hooves" Ps 68.32; ὅσα ἐκφέρει ἡ γῆ Hg 1.11; ὄνομα πονηρὸν ἐπὶ παρθένον Ἰσραηλῖτιν 'a bad name against an Israelite virgin' De 22.19 (|| καταφέρω .. τινός vs. 14); κατὰ ἀριθμὸν τὸν κόσμον αὐτοῦ Is 40.26, σκεῦος εἰς ἔργον 'work tool' 54.16; justice through a judicial process, κρίσιν τοῖς ἔθνεσιν 42.1, κρίμα Je 28.10.
*__3__. *to exact*: τὸ ἀργύριον ἐπὶ πάντα Ισραηλ 4K 15.20.
Cf. ἐκτίκτω, ἐκφόριον, φέρω, εἰσφέρω.

ἐκφεύγω: fut. ~φεύξομαι, inf. ~φεύξεσθαι; aor. ἐξέφυγον, ptc. ~φυγών, inf. ~φυγεῖν; pf. ~πέφευγα, ptc. ἐκπεφευγώς.
1. *to escape* sth undesirable, unpleasant etc.: ***o*** (understood) pain of childbirth, Is 66.7; illness, 2M 9.22; violent death, 3M 6.29; assailants, τὰς χεῖρας ὑμῶν Su 22, δίκην 'divine justice' Es E 4, κρίσιν 2M 7.35, τὸ κρίμα κυρίου PSol 15.8, ἁμαρτίαν Pr 10.19; ***s*** plunderer, ἔν τινι 'making off with' Si 16.13; ἀπὸ προσώπου πολέμου 40.6 (deserter); ἐκ (B: ἀπὸ) προσώπου Μαδιαμ 'the watching eyes of Midianites' Jd 6.11 A.
2. *to fail to reach*: + acc. pers., "Let not proverbs of wisdom slip past you" Si 6.35. **b.** *to fail to attain*: τὸν τοῦ θεοῦ ἔπαινον 'God's praise' Wi 15.19.
3. *to emerge*: ***s*** baby out of a womb, Is 66.7.
Cf. ἐκφυγή, φεύγω: Schmidt 3.244-7; LSG s.v.

ἐκφλέγω.ʃ
to ignite: pass., ***o*** oven, πυρί 'with fire' 4M 16.3. Cf. φλέγω, καίω.

ἐκφοβέω: aor. ἐξεφόβησα, ptc. ~βήσας.
to scare: οὐκ ἦν ὁ ἐκφοβῶν 'there was none to scare (it) away' Na 2.12 (said of a lion); in a description of peace and security, οὐκ ἔσται ὁ ἐκφοβῶν Le 26.6, Mi 4.4, Zp 3.13; + acc. pers., ἐνυπνίοις 'with dreams' Jb 7.14 (|| καταπλήσσω), ἐν εἴδεσιν φόβου 'with frightening visions' 33.16. Cf. φοβέομαι, ἔκφοβος, ἐκδειματόω, καταπλήσσω, κατασείω.

ἔκφοβος, ον.ʃ
frightened: ***s*** hum., διὰ τὴν ὀργήν De 9.19; ἔντρομος καὶ ἔ. 'scared and ..' 1M 13.2. Cf. ἐκφοβέω, ἔντρομος, κατάφοβος, φόβος.

ἐκφορά, ᾶς. f.ʃ

funeral: 2C 16.14, 21.19.

ἐκφόριον, ου. n.ʃ

agricultural produce: δώσει ἡ γῆ τὰ ~α αὐτῆς Le 25.19; τὰ ~α τῆς γῆς σου De 28.33 (‖ πόνοι); ἡ γῆ ὑποστελεῖται τὰ ~α αὐτῆς 'the earth will hold back her products' Hg 1.10 (paraphrased as ὅσα ἐκφέρει ἡ γῆ, 11); εἰσηνέγκατε πάντα τὰ ~α εἰς τοὺς θησαυρούς Ma 3.10; Jd 6.4 A (B: καρπός). Cf. ἐκφέρω, καρπός, γένημα.

ἐκφυγή, ῆς. f.ʃ *

v.n. of ἐκφεύγω **1**: μηχανὴ ~ῆς 'a contrivance for escape' 3M 4.19.

ἐκφύρομαι: aor. ἐξεφύρθην.ʃ*

to have illicit sexual *dealings with*: Je 3.2. Cf. ἐκπορνεύω **1**.

ἐκφυσάω: aor. ἐξεφύσησα, inf. ~φυσῆσαι.ʃ

to blow away: + acc. rei, Hg 1.9, Ma 1.13. **b**. *to blow* at: ἐφ' ὑμᾶς ἐν πυρὶ ὀργῆς μου Ez 22.21; + acc., πῦρ 4M 5.32; εἰς αὐτὸ πῦρ Ez 22.20; ἀτμίδας πυρώδεις 'fiery vapours' Si 43.4 (*s* the sun).

Cf. ἀπο~, ἐμφυσάω.

ἐκφωνέω: aor.ptc. ~φωνήσας.ʃ

to speak out: abs., Da 2.20 LXX; ἐπί τινος 'in the presence of ..' 2.27 LXX, πρός τινα 2.47 LXX. Cf. φωνέω, λαλέω, λέγω.

ἐκχέω: fut. ~χεῶ, pass. ~χυθήσομαι; aor. ἐξέχεα, subj. ~χέω, inf. ~χέαι, impv. ~χεον, ~χεε, pass. ἐξεχύθην, ptc. ~χυθείς, subj. ~χυθῶ; pf. ~κέχυκα, ptc.pass. ἐκκεχυμένος.

1. *to pour out*: *o* αἷμα Ge 9.6a, 37.22, Nu 35.33 (of homicide); blood of a sacrificial animal, παρὰ τὴν βάσιν τοῦ θυσιαστηρίου 'beside the base of the altar' Ex 29.12, Le 4.7; σπονδάς 'libations' Is 57.6; εἰς αὐτὸν [= λουτήρ 'washing-tub'] ὕδωρ Ex 30.18; σποδιάν 'ashes (of burnt sacrificial animals)' Le 4.12; ὕδωρ ἐπὶ πρόσωπον τῆς γῆς Am 5.8, 9.6; χοῦν 'dust' Le 14.41; pass., λίθοι ἅγιοι La 4.1; poss. solid food rather than drinks, ἐπὶ στόματι Si 30.18, cf. τοὺς ἄρτους σου ἐπὶ τὸν τάφον ('the grave') τῶν δικαίων To 4.17 𝔊[I]. **b**. *to construct* a mound *by pouring out soil*: + acc., πρόσχωμα 2K 20.15, 4K 19.32B (*L* προσ~), Da 11.15 TH. **c**. *o* sth immaterial: spirit (πνεῦμα)– ἐκχεῶ ἀπὸ τοῦ πνεύματός μου ἐπὶ πᾶσαν σάρκα Jl 2.28, sim. 2.29; ἐπὶ τὸν οἶκον Δαυιδ .. πνεῦμα χάριτος καὶ οἰκτιρμοῦ Zc 12.10; καρδίαν La 2.19, Ps 61.9; ἐπ' ἐμὲ τὴν ψυχήν μου 41.5; "pour my heart out" 1K 1.15; ψυχὰς αὐτῶν εἰς κόλπον μητέρων αὐτῶν 'breathing their last in their mothers' bosom' La 2.12, καρδίαν 2.19; blessing, ὑμῖν τὴν εὐλογίαν μου Ma 3.10, λαλιάν Si 32.17; ἔλεος 18.11; wisdom, 1.9; teaching, 24.33; outrage, ὡς ὕδωρ τὸ ὅρμημά μου Ho 5.10; δέησιν 'request' Ps 101.1, λαλιάν 'talk' Si 35.4; ἐπ' αὐτοὺς πᾶσαν ὀργὴν θυμοῦ μου Zp 3.8, sim. La 4.11, εἰς ἡμᾶς PSol 2.24; τὰ κακὰ αὐτῶν 'their hardships' Je 14.16, honour or fame going down the drain, εἰς γῆν La 2.11; πορνείαν 'illicit sexual desires' Ez 16.15, 23.8; ἰσχύν Si 39.28; pass., χάρις Ps 44.3, χάριτες 'favours' Si 20.13. **d**. *to spill, shed*: abs. ἐξέχεεν ἐπὶ τὴν γῆν 'spilled (semen) on the ground (to prevent conception)' Ge 38.9; αἷμα δίκαιον 'innocent blood' Jl 3.19, cf. Zp 1.17 (but not of murder); αἷμα ἀναίτιον 'guiltless ..' De 19.10. **e**. *to send out in large numbers*: + acc., ἐπὶ Ιερουσαλημ δύναμιν '.. troops' Je 6.6; pass., *to launch a massive attack*: ἐπί τινα Jd 9.44 A (:: ἐκτείνομαι, and B: ἐκτείνω), Ju 15.3; πρός τινα Jd 20.37 A (B: abs.). **f**. ὡσεὶ ὕδωρ ἐξεχύθην 'I was poured out like water,' i.e. I have no strength left Ps 21.15.

*__2__. *to make lose equilibrium* or *direction*: pass., ἐξεχύθη τὰ διαβήματά μου 'my steps lost balance (or: direction)' Ps 72.2 (‖ σαλεύομαι), ἐκχυθέντες .. ἔφυγον Ju 15.2; pass., *o* ψυχή PSol 16.2. Cf. συγχέω.

*__3__. *to pull out*: + ῥομφαίαν Ps 34.3 (Heb. הֵרִיק), cf. ἐκκενόω, (ἐκ)σπάω.

4. pass. *to give oneself up* to sth: ἐπὶ ἐδεσμάτων 'to foods' Si 37.29.

Cf. ἔκχυσις, (συγ)χέω: Behm, *TDNT* 2.467f.

ἔκχυσις, εως.ʃ f.

act of pouring out: αἵματος (resulting in murder) Si 27.15, 'bleeding' 3K 18.28. **b**. *that which has been poured out*: ἔ. σποδίας 'ash dump' Le 4.12.

Cf. ἐκχέω.

ἐκχωρέω: aor. ἐξεχώρησα, impv. ~χώρησον.

to depart: ἐκ μέσου τῆς συναγωγῆς ταύτης Nu 16.45; + εἰς (destination), ἐκχώρησόν σοι εἰς γῆν Ιουδα 'Leave for the land of J.' Am 7.12. Cf. ἀναχωρέω, ἐξέρχομαι, ἐκπορεύομαι.

ἐκχωρίζω: aor. ἐξεχώρισα.ʃ

to set apart: + acc., 1E 4.44, 57. Cf. χωρίζω: LSG s.v.

ἐκψύχω: fut. ~ψύξω; aor. ἐξέψυξα.ʃ

1. *to lose strength*: ἐκψύξει πᾶσα σὰρξ καὶ πᾶν πνεῦμα Ez 21.7 (at a report of an imminent calamity); 2K 13.20*L*.

2. *to breathe one's last*, 'die': Jd 4.21A (B: ἀποθνήσκω).

Cf. ἐκλείπω, ἐκλύω.

ἑκών, οῦσα, όν.ʃ

witting, intentional: οὐχ ἑκών 'unintentionally' Ex 21.13; Jb 36.19. Cf. ἑκουσίως, ἄκων, αὐθαιρέτως: Schmidt 3.612f.

ἐλαία, ας. f.

1. *olive tree*: κατάκαρπος 'fruitful' Ho 14.7; ἔργον ~ας = ἔλαιον 'olive oil' Hb 3.17; Zc 4.3; τὸ ὄρος τῶν ~ῶν 'the Mount of Olives' 14.4.

2. *olive*: ἔλαιον ἐξ ~ῶν 'oil made from olives' Ex 27.20; πιέσεις ~αν 'you will press olives' Mi 6.15; τὰ ξύλα τῆς ~ας Hg 2.19; γῆ ~ας ἐλαίου De 8.8; ἐκρυήσεται ἡ ἐ. σου 'your olives will fall off' De 28.40.

Cf. ἐλάϊνος, ἔλαιον, ἐλαιών: Schnebel 302-11.

ἐλάϊνος, η, ον.ʃ

of olives: ἔλαιον ~ον καθαρόν 'pure olive oil' Le 24.2, see LSG s.v. Cf. ἔλαιον.

ἐλαιολογέω: aor.subj. ~γήσω.ʃ *

to pick olives at harvest-time: abs., De 24.20. Cf. ἔλαιον.

ἔλαιον, ου. n.

oil: agrarian produce, ἔ. ἐξ ἐλαιῶν 'oil made from olives' Ex 27.20; τὸν καρπὸν τῆς γῆς .., τὸν σῖτον .. τὸν οἶνον .. τὸ ἔ. De 7.13, 28.51; μέλι καὶ ἔ. 32.13; Ho 2.22, Hg 1.11; basic commodity for man's physical existence, τοὺς ἄρτους μου καὶ τὸ ὕδωρ μου καὶ τὰ ἱμάτιά μου καὶ τὰ ὀθόνιά μου καὶ τὸ ἔ. μου καὶ πάντα ὅσα μοι καθήκει Ho 2.5, sim Si 39.26; along w. σῖτος and οἶνος Ho 2.8, Jl 1.10, 2.19, 24; "the tubs will overflow with wine and olive oil" Jl 2.24; for nourishment, De 12.17, Ez 16.13, "bread or pottage or wine or olive oil or any food (βρῶμα)" Hg 2.12; commercial commodity, ἔ. εἰς Αἴγυπτον ἐνεπορεύετο Ho 12.1; specifically *olive oil*, Mi 6.15 (for anointing), ἅγιον Nu 35.25, Ps 88.21; poured on to the top of a stone pillar as a symbolic rite, Ge 28.18; used in kneading flour, Ex 29.2*a*; to smear cakes with, 29.2*b*; lamp-oil, φωτός 39.17; cultic offerings, οἴσεις τὰ ἐπιδέκατα τοῦ σίτου σου καὶ τοῦ οἴνου σου καὶ τοῦ ~ου σου De 14.22; medicinal, Is 1.6 (ǁ μάλαγμα 'emollient,' κατάδεσμος 'bandage'), cf. *ND* 4.248; used as body-lotion and + σμῆγμα 'soap', Da Su 17 TH. It is not always possible to say with certainty whether in a given occurrence ἔ. refers specifically to olive oil or any oily substance, except in Mi 6.15, cf. Brent Sandy 1984.

Cf. ἐλαία, ἐλάϊνος, ἐλαιών, ἐλαιολογέω, οἶνος, σῖτος: Trench 135-7; Schlier, *TDNT* 2.470-3.

ἐλαιών, ῶνος. m.

olive-yard: ǁ ἀμπελών Ex 23.11. De 6.11; ǁ κῆπος, ἀμπελών, and συκών, Am 4.9, Je 5.17. **b.** *fruits of olive-yard*: ǁ ἀμπελών Jo 24.13.

Cf. ἔλαιον, ἐλαία, ἀμπελών, κῆπος, παράδεισος, ῥών, συκών: Lee 108.

ἔλασμα, ατος. n.ʃ *

beaten-out metal: ἔ. χρυσίου καὶ ἀργυρίου Hb 2.19 (object of worship). Cf. ἐλαύνω, ἐλατός.

ἐλασσονόω. ⇒ ἐλαττονόω.

ἐλασσόω: ⇒ ἐλαττόω.

ἐλάσσων, ἔλασσον; super. ἐλάχιστος. Used as the comparative of μικρός. On the alternative spelling ἐλάττων, cf. BDF, § 34, 1.

1. *smaller*: in size, τὸν φωστῆρα τὸν ἐλάσσω 'the smaller light' Ge 1.16; in importance (?), ὁ μείζων δουλεύσει τῷ ἐλάσσονι 'the major shall serve the minor' 25.23; in age, 'younger', τὸν υἱὸν αὐτῆς τὸν ἐλάσσω 27.6 (:: πρεσβύτερος vs. 15); ἐλάχιστος 'the youngest' Jo 6.26 (:: πρωτότοκος 'the first-born').

2. *less* in quantity: συνέλεξαν, ὁ τὸ πολὺ καὶ ὁ τὸ ἔλαττον 'they collected, some much but others less' Ex 16.17. **b.** οὐκ ἐ. + gen., 'no fewer than, as many as': οὐκ ἐλάττους τῶν χιλίων 'no fewer than 1.000' 2M 5.5; subst.n.sg. and indec. 'the minimum of', ἔλαττον τῶν ἐνακισχιλίων 'at least 9.000' 10.18; 12.4

3. *of very small significance*: ἐν συνέσει 'in comprehension' Wi 9.6; *s* hum., PSol 17.20 (:: ἄρχων).

4. superl., ὁ ἐλάχιστος (ἔσται) εἰς ἔθνος μέγα Is 60.22.

Cf. ἐλαττονέω, ἐλαττονόω, ἥσσων, μείζων, μικρός, ὀλίγος, πολύς.

ἐλάτη, ῆς. f.

silver fir: growing in a desert, Ge 21.15. Cf. subs.

ἐλάτινος, η, ον.ʃ

made of fir or *pine-wood*: *s* ἱστός 'mast' Ez 27.5, cf. Hom. *Od.* 2.424.

ἐλατός, ή, όν.

beaten: *s* plate (λεπίς), Nu 16.38; σάλπιγξ, trumpet made of beaten metal, 10.2, Ps 97.6; metal weapon, 3K 10.16. Cf. ἐλαύνω, ἔλασμα, προσβλητός.

ἐλαττονέω: fut. ἐλαττονήσω; aor. ἠλαττόνησα. *

1. *to fail to reach an amount due* or *desired*: abs. and in the amount received, Ex 16.18 (:: πλεονάζω); in the amount given, οὐκ ἐλαττονήσει ἀπὸ τοῦ ἡμίσους τοῦ διδράχμου 'shall not be giving less than half a drachma' 30.15 (:: προστίθημι); 3K 17.14 (ǁ vs. 15 ἐλαττονόομαι and here:: ἐκλείπω).

2. mid. *to suffer from the lack of*: abs. Pr 11.24; τινι (rei), 3K 11.22.

Cf. ἐλαττονόω, ἐλαττόω, ἐλάσσων, πλεονάσω.

ἐλαττονόω: fut. ἐλαττονώσω; aor.mid.subj.2s ἐλαττονώσῃ, pass. ἐλαττονώθην, ἠλαττονώθην, subj. pass. ~νωθῶ, ptc. ~νωθείς. *

I. *to defeat, vanquish*: in war and pass., 2M 12.11; 13.19 (ǁ τροπόω 'put to flight').

2. *to take no notice of, omit*: To 14.4 𝔊[II].

3. *to lower the value* or *status of*: + acc., φυλάς Pr 14.34 (:: ὑψόω).

II. mid.tr. *to reduce* (+ acc.): ἔγκτησιν 'the acquisition price' Le 25.16 (:: πληθύνω).

III. mid.intr. **1**. *to decrease*: of flood water, Ge 8.3, 5; reserve of oil, 3K 17.16 (v.l. ἐλαττονέω, and ǁ vs. 14).

2. *to be smaller in quantity* (+ acc. *by* a certain quantity): ἐὰν δὲ ἐλαττονωθῶσιν οἱ πεντήκοντα δίκαιοι πέντε 'should the fifty righteous decrease by five' Ge 18.28. **b**. metaph.: καρδίᾳ 'to be heedless' Si 19.6; οὐθέν σοι οὐ μὴ ἐλαττονωθῇ 'you will suffer nothing' 19.7.

Cf. ἐλάσσων, ἐλαττονέω, ἐλαττόω, πληθύνω.

ἐλαττόω: fut. ἐλαττώσω, pass. ~ωθήσομαι; aor. ἠλάττωσα, subj. ἐλαττώσω, pass. ἠλαττώθην, subj. pass. ἐλαττωθῶ.

1. *to reduce the quantity of*: + acc., τὴν κληρονομίαν 'legacy' Nu 26.54 (:: πλεονάζω), τὴν κατάσχεσιν 'possessions' 33.54 (:: πληθύνω); ἰσχύν Si 34.30 (:: προσποιέω 'add'), ἡμέρας '(shortens) one's life' 30.24, ἁμαρτίας 28.8. **b**. pass. Je 37.19 (:: πλεονάζω), 51.18 (lowering of living standard); *to suffer reduction of* (τινος), οὐκ ἐλαττωθήσονται παντὸς ἀγαθοῦ Ps 33.11. **c**. mostly pass. pres. indic. or ptc., *to be wanting in* (τινι) - ἄρτοις 2K 3.29, συνέσει Si 25.2, 47.23, σοφίᾳ 19.23 (= ἄφρων), καρδίᾳ 'intellectually' 16.23 (|| ἄφρων); ἰσχύι 'physically' 41.2 (+ ἐπιδέομαι); πράξει '(spared the hassle of) business life' 38.24; ἀπό τινος 23.10; τινος 1K 21.16 (*L* προσδέομαι).

2. *to lower the status of*: + acc., ἠλάττωσας αὐτὸν βραχύ τι παρ' ἀγγέλους '.. a shade lower than ..' Ps 8.6; Si 39.18.

3. *to remove, take away*: pass., Si 42.21 (:: προστίθημι), Da 6.12a LXX.

Cf. ἐλαττονέω, ἐλαττονόω, ἐλάσσων, ἐλάττωμα, ὀλιγόω, πλεονάζω, πληθύνω.

ἐλάττωμα, ατος. n.ʃ

1. *defeat*: military, 2M 11.13.

2. *deficiency*: ἰσχύος 'physical weakness' Si 19.28.

Cf. ἐλαττόω.

ἐλάττων. ⇒ ἐλάσσων.

ἐλάττωσις, εως. f.

loss suffered: Si 20.3, 9; financial, 22.3 (brought about by the birth of a daughter); + ἔνδεια To 4.13 𝔊[I].

ἐλαύνω: fut. ἐλάσω.

1. *to beat out, forge*: + acc., ἐλάσεις αὐτῇ τέσσαρας δακτυλίους χρυσοῦς 'you shall beat out for it four golden rings' Ex 25.11.

2. *to make keep moving on*, 'drive': abs., 'chariot' as ***o*** understood, 2M 9.4; ***o*** cattle, Si 38.25.

3. intr. *to keep moving on*: ***s*** πλοῖον 'ship' Is 33.21; mariners, ναυτικοὺς ἐλαύνειν εἰδότας θάλασσαν 'seamen who know how to sail across the sea' 3K 9.27 (c. acc. loci, poss. ναῦν or πλοῖον understood as a dir. obj.).

4. *to plague, harass*: pass., ***o*** hum., Wi 16.18, 17.15.

Cf. ἀπελαύνω, ἐλατός, ἔλασμα: Shipp 233-5.

ἔλαφος, ου. m./f.

deer: as food and || δορκάς De 12.15 +; endearing appellation of one's wife, ἔ. φιλίας Pr 5.19.

ἐλαφρός, ά, όν.

1. *having little weight*, 'light': lit., Ez 1.7. **b**. in significance or difficulty, ***s*** ῥῆμα 'matter, issue' Ex 18.26 (:: ὑπέρογκος); ὁ βίος μού ἐστιν ἐλαφρότερος λαλιᾶς 'my life is lighter than a talk' Jb 7.6.

2. *light in moving*, 'swift, nimble': ὁ βίος μού ἐστιν ἐλαφρότερος δρομέως 'my life is swifter than a runner' Jb 9.25 (of fleeting life).

Cf. μικρός, ὀλίγος, κοῦφος, βραχύς, βαρύς, ὑπέρογχος.

ἐλάχιστος. ⇒ ἐλάσσων.

ἐλεάω. ⇒ ἐλεέω.

ἐλεγμός, οῦ. m.*

v.n. of ἐλέγχω (q.v.): as cogn. dat., Le 19.17; Nu 5.18; || κρίσις Ps 149.7; + θλῖΨις, παροργισμός 4K 19.3. Cf. Dorival 1995.261f. Cf. ἐλέγχω, ἔλεγχος, ἔλεγξις.

ἔλεγξις, εως. f.ʃ *

= ἐλεγμός (q.v.): Jb 21.4, 23.2. Cf. ἐλεγμός.

ἔλεγχος, ου. m; v.n. of ἐλέγχω.

1. *act of questioning*: ἐν ἡμέραις ~ου Ho 5.9; τί ἀποκριθῶ ἐπὶ τὸν ~όν μου; 'what ought I to answer on being questioned?' Hb 2.1; + παιδεία Pr 6.23.

2. v.n. of subs. **3**: ἐννοιῶν ἡμῶν 'on our thoughts' Wi 2.14.

3. *that which deserves open criticism*: Pr 28.13.

Cf. ἐλέγχω, ἐλεγμός, ὄνειδος, ψόγος.

ἐλέγχω: fut. ἐλέγξω, pass. ~γχθήσομαι; aor. ἤλεγξα, subj. ἐλέγξω, inf. ἐλέγξαι, impv. ἔλεγξον, 3pl ἐλεγξάτωσαν, pass.subj. ἐλεγχθῶ, ptc. ἐλεγχθείς, opt.3s ἐλέγξαι, mid. ἐλέγξαιτο.

1. *to question in public the morality of* (sbd's character or action): abs., Ho 4.4 (|| δικάζω); ἀνὰ μέσον τῶν δύο ἡμῶν Ge 31.37; τινα Wi 4.20; + τινά περί τινος, Ge 21.25; + ἐπί τινι Ps 49.8; ***o*** τὸν πλησίον σου Le 19.17; ἔθνη ἰσχυρά Mi 4.3 (|| κρίνω); subst. ptc., ἐμίσησαν ἐν πύλαις ἐλέγχοντα καὶ λόγον ὅσιον ἐβδελύξαντο Am 5.10, sim. Hg 2.14; + dat. cogn., ἐλεγμῷ Le 19.17; || παιδεύω Je 2.19, Ps 6.2; also || διδάσκω Si 18.13; ἐν μαλακίᾳ 'through an illness' Jb 33.19.

2. *to demonstrate verbally the virtue, justice* or *efficacy of*: + acc. rei, ἔπλασέ με τοῦ ἐλέγχειν παιδείαν αὐτοῦ Hb 1.12; + acc. pers., τοὺς ταπεινοὺς τῆς γῆς Is 11.4.

3. *to pass a negative judgment on* sbd or sth as: + acc., 2C 26.20, ἄχρηστον 'as useless' Wi 2.11.

Cf. ἔλεγχος, ἐλεγμός, ἔλεγξις, ἀπ~, δι~, ἐξελέγχω, ἀνεξέλεγκτος, κακίζω, κρίνω, μέμφομαι, ὀνειδίζω, παιδεύω, ψογίζω: Bertram, *TDNT* 2.473f.

ἐλεεινός, ή, όν.
**having received mercy*: from God, *s* hum., Da 9.23 LXX. Cf. ἔλεος.

ἐλεέω: fut. ἐλεήσω, ἐλεηθήσομαι, ptc.act. ἐλεήσων; aor. ἠλέησα, subj. ἐλεήσω, inf. ἐλεῆσαι, ptc. ἐλεήσας, impv. ἐλέησον, opt.3s ἐλεήσαι; pf.pass. ptc. ἠλεημένος. Also ἐλεάω.
to show mercy to, have pity on sbd in hardship: + acc. pers. De 7.2, Ho 1.6[2]; orphan, 14.4; children (τέκνα) 2.4; daughter, 1.6[1], 8; sister, 2.1; youth, De 28.50; virgins, 2C 36.17 (‖ φείδομαι); nation, Ho 1.7, 2.23*bis*, cf. Am 5.15, Zc 1.12, 17; + dat. instr., Ge 33.5; *s* God, Nu 6.26, De 30.3; by granting material wealth, Ge 33.11; to a growing youth, 43.29; ἐλεήσω ὃν ἂν ἐλεῶ Ex 33.19 (‖ οἰκτιρέω); ‖ δίδωμι ἔλεος De 13.17; αὐτὸς μαστιγοῖ καὶ ἐλεᾷ 'he whips ..' To 13.2; ἐλέησόν με, κύριε, ὅτι θλίβομαι Ps 30.10, ὅτι ἀσθενής εἰμι 6.3; ‖ οἰκτιρέω Is 27.11, 30.18, Si 36.17; *s* hum. and acc. rei, τὰ τοῦ γήρως αὐτοῦ 'his old age' 4M 6.13; ‖ κατοικτιρέω 8.19. **b**. with a pseudo double acc.: ἐλεήσει σε τὴν φωνὴν τῆς κραυγῆς σου Is 30.19 - on φωνήν, cf. ἐλέησόν αὐτῶν τὴν ὄπα 'have pity on their voice' Aristoph. *Pax* 400.
Cf. ἔλεος, ἐλεήμων, κατελέω, οἰκτιρέω, οἰκτιρμός: Spicq 1.473-9.

ἐλεημοποιός, όν.ʃ *
engaging oneself in acts of charity and compassion: *s* hum., + δίκαιος To 9.6 𝔊[II].

ἐλεημοσύνη, ης. f.
kindly, charitable disposition, compassion: **a**. hum. attribute and obj. of ποιέω – ποιήσεις ἐπ' ἐμὲ ~ην καὶ ἀλήθειαν Ge 47.29; To 4.7 𝔊[I]; πατρός 'towards an (elderly) father' Si 3.14. **b**. divine attitude, ἔσται σοι ἐ. ἐναντίον κυρίου 'the Lord will be favourably disposed towards you' De 24.13; 6.25; ‖ κρίμα Is 1.27, ‖ κρίσις 28.17. **c**. act of charity and compassion: God's, Ps 102.6; hum., Si 29.8, 34.11; ‖ οἰκτιρμοί Da 4.24 TH; principle of piety, + προσευχή, νηστεία To 12.8 𝔊[I], ποιοῦντες ~ας καὶ δικαιοσύνας 12.9 𝔊[I], alm. = 'alms-giving,' cf. BDAG, s.v.
Cf. ἔλεος.

ἐλεήμων, ον, gen. ~νος.
merciful: *s* God, ἐ. γάρ εἰμι Ex 22.27, οἰκτίρμων καὶ ἐ., μακρόθυμος καὶ πολυέλεος 34.6, ἐ. καὶ οἰκτίρμων ἐστί, μακρόθυμος καὶ πολυέλεος καὶ μετανοῶν ἐπὶ ταῖς κακίαις Jl 2.13, Jn 4.2, ἐ. ὁ κύριος καὶ δίκαιος Ps 114.5, + χρηστός PSol 5.2; hum. 2K 22.26 *L*, Pr 11.17. Cf. ἔλεος, ἐλεημοσύνη, πολυέλεος, φιλελεήμων, εὐίλατος, ἵλεως, οἰκτίρμων, ἀνελεήμων, ἀνηλεής: Schmidt 3.580f.

ἐλεηνός. ⇒ ἐλεεινός.

ἔλεος, έους; acc. also ἔλεον (cf. BDF, § 51; Thack. 158), m. / n.
1. *mercy, pity, compassion*: **a**. shown by God towards men, θελητὴς ~ους ἐστίν 'desirous of ..' Mi 7.18; ποίησον ἔ. μετὰ τοῦ κυρίου μου Αβρααμ Ge 24.12, ποιῶν ἔ. εἰς χιλιάδας τοῖς ἀγαπῶσίν με Ex 20.6; χρηστὸς κύριος, εἰς τὸν αἰῶνα τὸ ἔ. αὐτοῦ Ps 99.5; δώσεις .. ἔ. τῷ Αβρααμ Mi 7.20 (‖ ἀλήθεια); ἐν ~ει καὶ οἰκτιρμοῖς Ho 2.19 (‖ δικαιοσύνη and κρίμα), μνήσθητι τῶν οἰκτιρμῶν σου, κύριε, καὶ τὰ ἐλέη σου Ps 24.6; ἄφες τὴν ἁμαρτίαν τῷ λαῷ τούτῳ κατὰ τὸ μέγα ἔ. σου Nu 14.19; κατὰ τὸ ἔ. σου μνήσθητί μου .. ἕνεκα τῆς χρηστότητός σου Ps 24.7; κρεῖσσον τὸ ἔ. σου ὑπὲρ ζωάς '.. better than many lives over' 62.4; pl. 88.2, Si 18.5; opp. to ὀργή, Hb 3.2, Si 5.6, 16.11. **b**. shown by hum. towards hum.: Ho 6.4; Jn 2.9 (opp. μάταια καὶ ψευδῆ); κρίμα δίκαιον κρίνατε καὶ ἔ. καὶ οἰκτιρμὸν ποιεῖτε ἕκαστος πρὸς τὸν ἀδελφὸν αὐτοῦ Zc 7.9, ἐπί τινα Si 28.4; ἐπί τινι (rei) 4M 9.4; ‖ ἀλήθεια, Ho 4.1, + ἀλ. 2K 2.6, Ps 84.11, Pr 14.22; + πίστις ib.; ‖ ἐπίγνωσις θεοῦ Ho 4.1, 6.6; ‖ κρίμα, 12.6, Zc 7.9, cf. ποιεῖν κρίμα καὶ ἀγαπᾶν ἔ. Mi 6.8; shown by a superior, εὗρεν ὁ παῖς σου ἔ. ἐναντίον σου Ge 19.19, ποιήσεις ἔ. μετὰ τοῦ δούλου σου 1K 20.8.
***2**. *supplication for compassionate treatment*: πεσεῖται ἔ. αὐτῶν κατὰ πρόσωπον κυρίου 'their supplication may reach the Lord's presence' Je 43.7, sim. 44.20, 49.2, Ῥίπτω ἐγὼ τὸ ἔ. μου κατ' ὀφθαλμοὺς τοῦ βασιλέως 'I make my entreaty ..' 45.26, sim. Da 9.20 TH (LXX: δέομαι), καταβάλλομεν τὸν ~ον ἡμῶν κατὰ πρόσωπόν σου, κύριε Ba 2.19. Note the use of οἰκτιρμός in similar context at Da 9.18 TH.
Cf. ἐλεέω, ἐλεήμων, ἐλεημοσύνη, οἰκτιρμός, σπλάγχνα: Aristotle's definition in his *Rhetoric*, II.8.2 "a kind of pain (λύπη) excited by the sight of evil (κακόν), deadly or painful, which befalls one who does not deserve it" (ed. Loeb); Schmidt 3.572-80; Trench 166-71; Spicq 1.471-6; Joosten 2004.

ἐλέπολις, εως. f.ʃ
engine for sieges: 1M 13.43, 44.

ἐλευθερία, ας. f.
freedom from bondage or *slavery*: to be enjoyed by slaves, ἐ. οὐκ ἐδόθη αὐτῇ [= οἰκέτις 'slave girl'] Le 19.20, cf. Si 7.21, 30.34; by a nation, 1E 4.49, 53 (returnees from exile), 1M 14.26. Cf. ἐλεύθερος, δουλεία.

ἐλεύθερος, α, ον.
free from bondage or *slavery*: opp. παῖς Ex 21.2; οἰκέτης, θεράπαινα 21.26, 27; ἐξαπεστείλατε ~ους τῇ ψυχῇ αὐτῶν Je 41.16, cf. De 21.14; *s* οἶκος 'family' 1K 17.25; opp. δεσμώτης Je 36.2; subst. m., 'burger,' + πρεσβύτερος 'elder' 3K 20.8. Cf. ἐλευθερία, ἐλευθερόω, δουλεία.

ἐλευθερόω: aor.impv. ἐλευθέρωσον, inf. ~ρῶσαι.ʃ
to set free from bondage: + acc. pers., 2M 1.27, πόλιν 2.22. **b**. metaph.: *s* χάρις καὶ φιλία 'charm and friendship' Pr 25.10a.
Cf. ἐλεύθερος, ἀπελευθερόω, δουλεύω, καταδουλόω: LSG s.v.

ἐλευστέον.ʃ
one must go on: ἐπὶ τὴν διήγησιν 'to the discourse' 2M 6.17. Cf. ἔρχομαι.

ἐλεφαντάρχης, ου. m.
commander of a squadron of 16 elephants (LSJ): 2M 14.12. Cf. LSG s.v.

ἐλεφάντινος, η, ον.
1. *of elephant*: *s* ὀδούς 'ivory' Ez 27.15.
2. *made of ivory*: *s* house, Am 3.15; ἐπὶ κλινῶν ~ων 'on ivory couches' 6.4; throne, 3K 10.18; tablet, Ct 5.14; tower, 7.5.
Cf. ἐλέφας.

ἐλέφας, αντος. m.
1. *elephant*: on a military campaign, 1M 1.17.
2. *ivory*: material for handcraft, Ez 27.6.
Cf. ἐλεφάντινος.

ἑλικτός, ή, όν.ʃ
rolled: *s* some kind of baked cereal offering, Le 6.21; ἀνάβασις '(winding, spiral) staircase' 3K 6.8. Cf. ἑλίσσω.

ἕλιξ, κος. f.ʃ
tendril of the vine: Ge 49.11.

ἑλίσσω: fut.pass. ἑλιγήσομαι; aor.opt.pass.3s ἑλιχθείη.ʃ
1. *to roll up*: *o* βιβλίον 'scroll' and οὐρανός Is 34.4.
2. *to roll along*: *o* leg, ἐν δικτύῳ 'in a net' Jb 18.8.
Cf. ἑλικτός.

ἕλκος, ους. n.
festering wound, 'ulcer': a divine punishment affecting humans and animals, Ex 9.9, 10; of leprosy, Le 13.18; ἐν ταῖς ἕδραις 'in the buttocks' De 28.27 (to befall Israelites), πονηρὸν ἐπὶ τὰ γόνατα καὶ ἐπὶ τὰς κνήμας 'nasty .. on the knees and the legs' 28.35. Cf. τραῦμα: Schmidt 3.300.

ἕλκω: fut. ἑλκύσω; aor. εἵλκυσα, impv. ἕλκυσον, inf. ἑλκύσαι, subj. ἑλκύσω, opt.3s ἑλκύσαι, pass. εἱλκύσθην.
1. *to cause to move along* sth that is incapable of moving on its own: + acc. and *s* heifer, ζυγόν 'yoke' De 21.3; πρίων 'saw' Is 10.15; ἐν ἀμφιβλήστρῳ 'with a fishing-net' Hb 1.15 (ǁ σαγήνη); *o* sbd to be robbed, Ps 9.30; metaph. and + acc. pers., εἰς οἰκτίρημα 'to show compassion' Je 38.3, Ec 2.3; μετὰ βίας 'violently' 3M 4.7; 4M 15.11; ἐπ' αὐτοὺς ἔτη πολλά '(allowed) many years to elapse for their sake' Ne 9.30 (v.l. μακροθυμέω); *s* ἀπώλεια .. εἰς τέλος Jb 20.28. **b**. *to carry with one* a long object: + acc., sword, Jd 20.35 B (A: σπάω).
2. *to draw in*: + acc., ἄνεμον'(inhaled) air' Je 14.6, πνεῦμα Ps 118.131; γάλα 'milk (from mother's breast)' 3M 5.49.
3. *to make* furrows *by drawing a plough*: + acc., αὔλακας 'furrows' Jb 39.10.
4. fig., *to value highly*: + acc., σοφίαν ὑπὲρ τὰ ἐσώτατα 'wisdom more than the things deep inside the ground (?)' Jb 28.18¶.
5. intr. *to move a long way*: *s* the sun, εἰς τὸν τόπον αὐτοῦ Ec 1.5; stream of fire, Da 7.10 TH.
Cf. σπάω, σύρω: Schmidt 3.253-8; Trench 72-4.

Ἑλλάς, άδος. f.
Greece: Is 66.19.

ἐλλείπω.ʃ
to have a shortfall, be deficient: Si 42.24.

Ἑλληνικός, ή, όν.
Greek, Hellenic: Je 26.16; *s* βίος 'life' 4M 8.8.

Ἑλληνίς, ίδος. f. = Ἑλληνική.ʃ
Greek: *s* πόλις 2M 6.8.

ἐλλιπής, ές.ʃ
1. *sparing of provisions*: *s* miser, ἐπὶ τῆς τραπέζης 'at the dining-table' Si 14.10 (ǁ φθονερός).
2. *lacking*: *s* house, ἀπὸ πάντος 'everything' PSol 4.17.

ἕλος, ους. n.ʃ
marsh-meadow: of the Nile, Ex 2.3, 5; ǁ ποταμός and διῶρυξ 'canal' 7.19, 8.5; καλάμου καὶ παπύρου 'of reed and papyrus' Is 19.6; in a figure of rejuvenated nature, 35.7, 41.18; destruction of nature, ἕλη ξηρανῶ 'I shall dry up marshes' 42.15; of the Jordan Valley, 1M 9.42, 45. Cf. ποταμός, διῶρυξ, λίμνη: LSG s.v. **2**.

ἐλπίζω: fut. ἐλπιῶ; aor. ἤλπισα, impv. ἔλπισον.
1. *to put trust* (*in*), *to count* (*on*): + ἐν– ἐν τοῖς ἅρμασί σου 'in your chariots' Ho 10.13, ἐν ἀσπίδι .. 'in shields ..' Ju 9.7, ἐν τῷ ὀνόματι τῷ ἁγίῳ αὐτοῦ Ps 32.21; + ἐπί + acc., ἐπὶ τὸν θεόν 41.6, ἀγαθὸν ἐλπίζειν ἐπὶ κύριον ἢ ἐλπίζειν ἐπ' ἄρχοντας 117.9 (ǁ πεποιθέναι ἐπί τινα vs. 8), ἐπὶ (B: πρὸς) τὸ ἔνεδρον 'the troops in ambush' Jd 20.36A, ἐπ' ἀδικίαν Ps 61.11, ἐπὶ τὸ σωτήριον αὐτοῦ 77.22 (ǁ πιστεύω ἐν τῷ θεῷ), ἐπὶ τοὺς λόγους σου 118.42, ἐπὶ τὸ ἔλεος τοῦ θεοῦ 51.10, 146.11; + ἐπί τινι– ἐπὶ ἡγουμένοις 'leaders' Mi 7.5 (ǁ καταπιστεύω), ἐπὶ ψεύδει Is 30.12, ἐπὶ ψεύδεσι 'false gods' Je 13.25, ἐπὶ τῷ τόξῳ μου 'my bow' Ps 43.7, κύριε .. ἐπὶ σοὶ ἤλπισα 7.2, ἐπὶ τῷ ἐλέει σου 12.6 (ǁ ἐπὶ τὸ ἔλεος τοῦ θεοῦ 51.10, 146.11), ἐπὶ τῷ νόμῳ αὐτοῦ Is 42.4, ἐπὶ τῷ ὀνόματί σου 26.8; "dreams" Si 31.7; + πρός τινα (God) PSol 6.6.

*2. *to feel secure*: ἐν τῇ σκιᾷ τῶν πτερύγων σου ἐλπιῶ '.. in the shadow of your wings' Ps 56.2 (ll πέποιθα), ἐν σκέπῃ τῶν πτερύγων σου 'protected by ..' 35.8, ὑπὸ τὰς πτέρυγας αὐτοῦ 90.4.

3. *to entertain hope* for: abs., διὰ παντὸς ἐλπιῶ Ps 70.14, ἔθνος ἐλπίζον Is 18.7 (on which latter see van Menxel 244f.); + inf., ἐπικαλεῖσθαι τὸ ὄνομα τοῦ κυρίου Ge 4.26; in anticipation of assistance to come from (+ ἐπί τινα)– ἐξέλιπον οἱ ὀφθαλμοί μου ἀπὸ τοῦ ἐλπίζειν ἐπὶ τὸν θεόν μου 'my eyes became exhausted ..' Ps 68.4; + εἰς– οἱ ὀφθαλμοὶ πάντων εἰς σὲ ἐλπίζουσιν 144.15 (ll πρὸς σὲ προσδοκῶσιν 103.27), εἰς ἀγαθὰ καὶ εἰς εὐφροσύνην αἰῶνος καὶ ἔλεος Si 2.9, εἰς βοήθειαν .. τοῦ θεοῦ PSol 15.1, εἰς τὸν βραχίονά μου 'my arm' Is 51.5; + acc. rei, τὴν ἐλεημοσύνην σου 38.19, μισθὸν .. ὁσιότητος 'wages of piety (after death)' Wi 2.22; and + ἐπί τινι (pers.), ἤλπισα ἐπὶ τῷ αἰωνίῳ τὴν σωτηρίαν ὑμῶν 'I pinned my hope for your salvation on the Eternal' Ba 4.22; τῇ καρδίᾳ σου ὅτι .. Ju 6.9.

Cf. ἐλπίς, ἀνέλπιστος, ἀπ~, ἐπελπίζω, καταπιστεύω, πείθω, πιστεύω, προσδοκάω: Schmidt 3.584-7; Spicq 1.480-92; van Menxel 208-95; Bons 1994.

ἐλπίς, ίδος. f.

1. *confident expectation* of sth desirable: κατοικοῦσα ἐπ' ~ίδι Zp 3.1, cf. Ho 2.18; ἐν αὐτῷ ἔχει τὴν ~ίδα 'his hope for subsistence depends on it (= the wages)' De 24.15, τὴν ~ίδα ἔχει ἐπ' ἄνθρωπον Je 17.5; ἡ ἐ. ὑμῶν ἡ πρὸς τὸν ᾅδην 'the hope you are pinning on (your pact with) Hades' Is 28.18; + inf., 2M 9.22. **b**. *object of*, or *basis for*, *such expectation*: Κύριε .. ἐ. τῷ εὐσεβεῖ Is 24.16 (cf. *ND* 2.77); Noah's ark, Wi 14.6; immortality, 3.4; resurrection after death, and pl., 2M 7.14, cf. διὰ τὰς ἐπὶ κύριον ~ίδας 7.20; pl., Wi 13.10 (w. ref. to idols); ὁ στέφανος τῆς ~ός Is 28.5 (:: ὁ στ. τῆς ὕβρεως vs. 1, cf. van Menxel 267f.). **c**. sth undesirable, ominous premonition: ἐν νυκτὶ ἔσται ἐ. πονηρά Is 28.19.

2. *sense of security with no danger or attack in view*: κατασκηνώσει ἐπ' ~ίδι Ps 15.9, ἐπ' ~ίδι κατῴκισάς με 4.9 (ll ἐν εἰρήνῃ); ὡδήγησεν αὐτοὺς ἐν ~ίδι 'he led them ..' 77.53, κατοικήσουσιν ἐν ~ίδι, καὶ οὐκ ἔσται ὁ ἐκφοβῶν αὐτούς '.. and there will be none to scare them' Ez 34.28 (ll ἐν ~ίδι εἰρήνης vs. 27 and ἐπ' εἰρήνης 39.6); 28.26*bis* (ll ἐπ' εἰρήνης 38.8, 11, 14); τὸν λαὸν .. καθήμενον ἐν (B: ἐπ') ~ίδι Jd 18.7A; ll ἀφόβως Pr 1.33. This sense is also attested by Polybius: van Menxel 151.

Cf. ἐλπίζω, ἀσφάλεια: Bultmann, *TDNT* 2.521-3.

ἐμαυτοῦ, ~ῆς; ~ῷ, ~ῇ; ~όν, ~ήν.

Pronoun of reflexive reference, referring to the speaker; used only in oblique cases.

Κατ' ~οῦ ὤμοσα 'I swore by myself' Ge 22.16; ἔλαβον αὐτὴν ~ῷ 'I took her for myself' 12.19; ἐπάξω ἐπ' ~ὸν κατάραν 'I shall bring down a curse upon myself' 27.12. **b**. for ἐμός: τὴν ~οῦ ἐπιστήμην 'my knowledge' Jb 32.6.

ἐμβαίνω: aor. ἐνέβην, ptc. ἐμβάς, impv.2s ~βηθι, inf. ~βῆναι.ʃ

to enter on foot, 'step in': εἰς πλοῖον 1M 15.37; Jn 1.3; εἰς .. σκάφη 'boats' 2M 12.3; εἰς πηλόν 'into the clay' Na 3.14. Cf. ἐκβαίνω, εἰσέρχομαι, εἰσπορεύομαι, ἐμβολή.

ἐμβάλλω: fut. ~βαλῶ; aor. ἐνέβαλον, impv. ~βαλε, inf. ~βαλεῖν, ptc. ~βαλών, subj.act. ~βάλω, mid. ~βάλωμαι, pass. ἐνεβλήθην, inf. ~βληθῆναι; pf. pass. ἐμβέβλημαι.

1. *to throw in*: + acc. rei, εἰς τὰ σάγματα τῆς καμήλου 'into the saddle-bags of the camel' Ge 31.34; εἰς λέβητας ὑποκαιομένους 'into cauldrons which are being heated from underneath' Am 4.2; τριάκοντα ἀργυροῦς .. εἰς τὸ χωνευτήριον 'thirty pieces of silver .. into a smelting-furnace' Zc 11.13; ἐπὶ τοῦ στόματος τοῦ μαρσίππου 'into the top of the sack' Ge 44.1; "barley into the cornbin (κυψέλη)" Hg 2.16; + acc. pers., εἰς τὸν λάκκον 'into the cistern' Ge 37.22; εἰς τὸ ὀχύρωμα 'into the prison' 39.20; εἰς τὴν θάλασσαν Jn 1.12, εἰς τὴν κάμινον 'into the furnace' Da 3.21 LXX (ll TH βάλλω), εἰς χεῖρας τῶν ἀλλοφύλων 1K 18.25; metaph., εἰς ἐργασίαν 'put to work' Si 30.36.

2. *to place inside*: ἐνέβαλεν ὁ θεὸς ῥῆμα εἰς τὸ στόμα Βαλααμ Nu 23.5 (ll βάλλω 22.38), sim. 23.12, 16, ***o*** song, εἰς τὸ στόμα αὐτῶν De 31.19, Ps 39.4; recrimination (διαβολή) Si 28.9; εἰς τὴν κιβωτόν De 10.2; τὰ ῥήματα ταῦτα εἰς τὴν καρδίαν ὑμῶν καὶ εἰς τὴν ψυχὴν ὑμῶν 11.18; ***o*** neck, τὸν τράχηλον αὐτῶν ὑπὸ ζυγὸν βασιλέως .. '.. under the yoke of ..' Je 34.6 (ll εἰσάγω vs. 9), εἰς τὰ θεμέλια Σιων λίθον Is 28.16; foot, ἐν παγίδι 'in a trap' Jb 18.8; κλῆρον 'lot' Jo 18.10; χειρὶ χεῖρας 'to shake hands (to signal agreement)' Pr 11.21, 16.5.

3. *to cause to befall*: + acc., ἀμνηστίαν 'oblivion' Wi 19.4.

4. mid. *to tackle and assail*: + acc. pers., λόγοις Pr 7.5.

Cf. βάλλω.

ἐμβάπτω: aor. ἐνέβαψα.ʃ

to place into liquid or sth that contains liquidlike substance: + acc. rei, εἰς τὸ κηρίον 'into the honeycomb' 1K 14.27*L* (B: simp.). Cf. βάπτω.

ἐμβατεύω: aor.inf. ~βατεῦσαι.
1. *to take possession of*: + acc., τὴν γῆν Jo 19.49, 51.
2. *to set foot upon*: to invade, εἰς τὴν χώραν αὐτοῦ 1M 12.25. **b**. metaph. of a historian entering a field of data: 2M 2.30.
Cf. κατακληρονομέω: Preisker, *TDNT* 2.535.

ἐμβιβάζω.ʃ
to guide sbd (acc.) to (dat.): τροχιαῖς ὀρθαῖς 'to right paths' Pr 4.11(‖ διδάσκω). Cf. ὁδηγέω.

ἐμβίωσις, εως. f.ʃ *
1. *physical survival*: Si 38.14.
2. *way of living*: 3M 3.23.
3. *livelihood*: Si 31.26.
Cf. βίος.

ἐμβλέπω: fut. ~βλέψομαι; aor. ἐνέβλεψα, impv. ~βλεψον.
to observe with interest: visually and *s* hum., abs. Jb 2.10, Bel 40 TH; + dat., *to look in the face*, παντὶ ἀνθρώπῳ μὴ ἔμβλεπε ἐν κάλλει 'don't look anybody pretty straight in the face' Si 42.12 (mistaking H תתן 3fs for 2ms), Es 5.5 *L* (with anger); + εἰς– εἰς τὴν γῆν Is 5.30, ἀναβλέψονται εἰς τὸν οὐρανὸν ἄνω καὶ εἰς τὴν γῆν κάτω ἐμβλέψονται 8.21f., εἰς τοὺς ἐκλεκτοὺς οἴκους τῆς πόλεως '.. the top-class houses' .. 22.8, εἰς τὴν στερεὰν πέτραν 'the solid rock' 51.1; + πρός– ἐνέβλεπον ἕτερος πρὸς τὸν ἕτερον 'were eyeing one another' 1E 4.33; fig., εἰς χεῖρας υἱῶν σου Si 30.30 (with a begging look and cf. εἰς ἀντίλημψιν ἀνθρώπων 51.7); eyes and fig., οἱ ὀφθαλμοὶ αὐτοῦ εἰς τὸν ἅγιον τοῦ Ισραηλ ἐμβλέψονται Is 17.7. **b**. mentally, + acc., τὰ ἔργα κυρίου οὐκ ἐμβλέπουσι Is 5.12 (‖ κατανοέω and at Si 36.15 ‖ + εἰς); + εἰς– εἰς τὸν ἀπ' ἀρχῆς ποιήσαντα ^κολυμβήθραν^ καὶ τὸν κτίσαντα αὐτὴν οὐκ εἴδετε 22.11, εἰς Αβρααμ .. καὶ εἰς Σαρραν 51.2, εἰς ματαιότητας Ps 39.5, ἐμβλέψατε εἰς ἀρχαίας γενεὰς καὶ ἴδετε 'Look at the past generations and see' Si 2.10.
Cf. εἰσβλέπω, εἶδον, κατανοέω.

ἐμβολή, ῆς. f.ʃ
embarkation: εἰς τὸ πλοῖον 'aboard a boat' 3M 4.7. Cf. ἐμβαίνω.

ἐμβριμάομαι: fut. ~μήσομαι.ʃ
to speak sternly to: + dat. pers., Da 11.30 LXX. Cf. ἐμβρίμημα, προσεμβριμάομαι.

ἐμβρίμημα, ατος. n.ʃ*
intense emotional agitation: ὀργῆς (divine) La 2.6. Cf. ἐμβριμάομαι: Aitken 2007.153f.

ἔμετος, ου.ʃ
vomitted thing: Pr 26.11. Cf. ἐμέω.

ἐμέω: aor.impv. ἔμεσον.ʃ
to vomit: ὁ μεθύων καὶ ὁ ἐμῶν ἅμα 'one who gets drunk and vomits at the same time' Is 19.14; Si 34.21. Cf. ἔμετος, ἐξεμέω.

ἐμμανής, ές.ʃ
characterised by frenzy: *s* κῶμος 'revel' Wi 14.23. Cf. μανία.

ἐμμελέτημα, ατος. n.ʃ
that on which an art is practised: *s* idols, Wi 13.10.

ἐμμένω: fut. ~μενῶ; aor. ἐνέμεινα, subj. ~μείνω, impv. ~μεινον.
1. *to abide by*: abs., Nu 23.19; ἐν πᾶσιν τοῖς λόγοις τοῦ νόμου De 27.26, ἐν τῇ διαθήκῃ μου Je 38.32; ἐν ^θεῷ^ Is 30.18; + dat. rei, ἐντολαῖς Si 28.6, ταῖς ὁμολογίαις 'the promises' Je 51.25, τῇ φιλίᾳ ἡμῶν 'the friendly relationship with us' 1M 10.26. τῷ πόνῳ σου 'your work' Si 11.21; + dat. pers., 7.22; + inf., 1M 10.27.
2. *to stand the test, be valid*: *s* μάρτυς εἷς 'one witness' De 19.15; βουλή 'design, plan' Is 7.7, λόγος 8.10 (‖ βουλή), Je 51.29.
3. *to live long*: Si 39.11.
Cf. μένω, ἔμμονος.

ἐμμολύνω: fut.pass. ~λυνθήσομαι.ʃ*
to pollute: pass., Pr 24.9. Cf. μολύνω.

ἔμμονος, ον.ʃ
abiding, chronic: *s* disease, Le 13.51, 52, 14.44; ἀρρώστημα 'infirmity' Si 30.17. Cf. ἐμμένω.

ἐμός, ή, όν. poss. pron.
my, mine mostly with stressed notion of ownership, affiliation, or claim, often preceding the noun head: τῆς ἐμῆς φωνῆς Ge 22.18, Ex 19.5; τὰ δράγματα ὑμῶν προσεκύνησαν τὸ ἐμὸν δράγμα 'your sheaves ..' Ge 37.7, τὸν ἐμὸν λαόν 49.29; δώσω διαστολὴν ἀνὰ μέσον τοῦ ἐμοῦ λαοῦ καὶ ἀνὰ μέσον τοῦ σοῦ λαοῦ 'I shall discriminate between ..' Ex 8.23, τῷ ἐμῷ λαῷ Is 10.6, τῇ ἐμῇ βουλῇ .. τῷ ἐμῷ ῥήματι .. τὴν ἐμὴν λαλιάν Jb 29.21-3; τῆς γῆς τῆς ἐμῆς Is 14.25; anarthrous, ἐπ' ἐμῷ στεναγμῷ 'over my sigh' Jb 23.2, ἐμῆς κοιλίας ὠδῖνες καὶ πόνοι 'the pangs of my belly and pains' 2.9. **b**. a subst. understood: ἡ ψυχὴ ὑμῶν ἀντὶ τῆς ἐμῆς Jb 16.4. **c**. predicative, ἐμὴ ἐστιν πᾶσα ἡ γῆ Ex 19.5, ἐμὸν τὸ ἀργύριον καὶ ἐμὸν τὸ χρυσίον 'Mine is the silver and mine is the gold' Hg 2.8. Highly frequent in Pr, cf. Muraoka 2005a.306-8.
Cf. ἑαυτοῦ, σός, ἡμέτερος, ὑμέτερος.

ἔμπαιγμα, ατος. n.ʃ*
laughable, ridiculous object: w. ref. to idols, Is 66.4; μαγικῆς τέχνης 'of magic art' Wi 17.7. Cf. ἐμπαίζω.

ἐμπαιγμός, οῦ.*
v.n. of subs.: ἐ. καὶ ὀνειδισμός '.. abuse' Si 27.28 (typical of the arrogant); ‖ ὄνειδος Ez 22.4; αἱ ψύαι μου ἐπλήσθησαν ~ῶν 'mockeries penetrated even the muscles of my loins'(?) Ps 37.8. Cf. ἐμπαίζω: Harl, *Langue* 43-58.

ἐμπαίζω: fut. ~παίξω, ~παίξομαι; aor. ἐνέπαιξα, inf. ~παῖξαι, subj. ~παίξω; pf. ~πέπαιχα, ptc.pass. ~πεπαιγμένος.

1. *to sport jestfully*: + ἔν τινι – ἄνδρας δυνατοὺς ἐμπαίζοντας ἐν πυρί 'mighty men sporting with fire' Na 2.4; ἐν τοῖς ὀρνέοις 'with birds' Ba 3.17; of sexual maltreatment, ἔν τινι (woman) Jd 19.25 B (A: dat.).

2. *to mock*: abs. Zc 12.3; + dat. pers., Ge 39.14, 17, Ex 10.2, Nu 22.29, Is 33.4, 1M 9.26; sea-snake, Ps 103.26; + dat. rei, Pr 27.7; εἰς πᾶν ὀχύρωμα 'every fortress' Hb 1.10, cf. LSG s.v.; ἔν τινι Ez 22.5; + acc., 2M 7.10, pass. ἔργα ἐμπεπαιγμένα 'artefacts laughed out of court' Je 10.15 (of idols), 2M 8.17.

Cf. παίζω, ἔμπαιγμα, ἐμπαιγμός, ἐμπαίκτης, ἐντρυφάω: Harl, *Langue*, 47, 49.

ἐμπαίκτης, ου. m.ʃ *

mocker: Is 3.4. Cf. ἐμπαίζω.

ἐμπαραγίνομαι.ʃ *

to come along and befall: + dat. pers., *s* poverty Pr 6.11.

ἐμπάσσω: aor.impv. ἔμπασον.ʃ

to sprinkle into sth: + acc., εἰς τοὺς ὀφθαλμούς To 11.8 𝔊II. Cf. προσπάσσω.

ἐμπειρέω.ʃ *

to be well acquainted with: + gen. rei, τῆς ὁδοῦ To 5.4 𝔊II, 5.6 𝔊I; + ἐπίσταμαι 5.6 𝔊II. Cf. ἔμπειρος, ἐμπειρία.

ἐμπειρία, ας. f.ʃ

experience gained: of a craftsman, Wi 13.13. Cf. ἐμπειρέω. Del. Wi 13.18 v.l.

ἔμπειρος, ον.ʃ

well acquainted with: + gen. rei, τῶν τόπων To 5.5 𝔊I; *s* πολέμιος 'adversary' PSol 15.9. Cf. ἐμπειρέω.

ἐμπεριπατέω: fut. ~πατήσω; aor. ἐνεπεριπάτησα, ptc. ~πατήσας.

to walk about among (ἐν): *s* God, ἐν ὑμῖν Le 26.12; ἐν τῇ παρεμβολῇ σου De 23.14; Satan and + acc. loci, τὴν ὑπ' οὐρανόν Jb 1.7; hum., ἐν τῇ γῇ Jd 18.9A; cock, + dat., Pr 30.31 (lording it over?). Cf. περιπατέω.

ἐμπήγνυμι: aor. ἐνέπηξα, pass. ἐνεπάγην, inf. ~παγῆναι, subj. ~παγῶ; pf.ptc. ~πεπηγώς.ʃ

to place firmly into: + acc., αὐτὴν εἰς τὴν κοιλίαν Εγλωμ 'it [= sword] into E.'s belly' Jd 3.21A, arrows into sbd's heart 2K 18.14; pass. *to become firmly fixed*, *o* spear, 1K 26.7; city-gates (fallen to the ground), εἰς γῆν La 2.9, ἄκανθαν 'thorn' Ps 31.4, arrows 37.3; hum., ἐν διαφθορᾷ 9.16, εἰς ἰλὺν 'into a quagmire' 68.3. Cf. ἑδράζω.

ἐμπηδάω: aor. ἐνεπήδησα.ʃ

to leap into: εἰς τὸν Ἰορδάνην 1M 9.48. Cf. πηδάω.

ἐμπίμπλημι, ἐμπιμπλάω: fut. ἐμπλήσω, pass. ~πλησθήσομαι; impf.3pl ἐνεπίμπλασαν; aor. ἐνέπλησα; inf. ἐμπλῆσαι, ptc. ~πλήσας, subj. ~πλήσω, opt.1s ~πλήσαιμι, pass. ἐνεπλήσθην, subj. ἐμπλησθῶ, inf. ~πλησθῆναι, ptc. ~πλησθείς, impv. ~πλήσθητι, mid.2s ἐνεπίπλω, opt.pass.3s ~πλησθείη; pf.pass.3s ἐμπέπλησται.

1. act. *to have/take one's fill*: * + acc., ἰσχύν (|| gen.) Mi 3.8; τὸν πλοῦτον αὐτῶν ἀσεβείας 'their ungodly wealth' 6.12; τὸν χρόνον αὐτοῦ '(to live out) his natural life-span' Is 65.20.

2. *to fill*: + acc., οἰκίας De 6.11; ἡ δόξα κυρίου πᾶσαν τὴν γῆν Nu 14.21; and gen., τὰ ἀγγεῖα αὐτῶν σίτου 'their containers with grain' Ge 42.25, τοὺς θησαυροὺς αὐτῶν ἀγαθῶν 'their treasures with good things' Pr 8.21; + ἀπό τινος Si 1.17; metaph. τοῖς σοφοῖς .. οὓς ἐνέπλησα πνεύματος αἰσθήσεως Ex 28.3, αὐτοὺς σοφίας καὶ συνέσεως 35.35, τὴν γῆν πολέμων Is 14.21; ἀπὸ τοῦ αἵματός σου πᾶσαν τὴν γῆν Ez 32.5, φάραγγας ἀπὸ σοῦ [= your troops' corpses] 32.6; + double acc., αὐτὸν πνεῦμα θεῖον σοφίας Ex 31.3, αὐτὸν πνεῦμα φόβου θεοῦ Is 11.3; Ps 90.16; ἄρτον .. αὐτούς 104.40; + ἐν - ἐν ἀγαθοῖς 102.5; + dat., πνεύματι συνέσεως Si 39.6. **b**. *to give abundant food to*: + acc., θηρία Ez 32.4.

***3**. + τὰς χεῖράς τινος (Hebraism 'פ [sg.!] מִלֵּא יַד) 'to consecrate, install sbd as priest' Ex 28.37 (|| χρίω); τὴν χεῖρα Jd 17.5A, 12A (B: πληρόω). Cf. πληρῶσαι τὰς χεῖρας αὐτοῦ Nu 7.88, and the same Heb. idiom is rendered also with τελειόω (q.v.).

4. *to have* sth *maximalise its effect*: + acc., τὸν θυμόν μου Ez 24.13.

5. *to meet and satisfy the desire of*: τινά Pr 30.15; ψυχήν μου Ex 15.9, De 23.25, Is 58.10 (appetite), ψυχὴν πεινῶσαν 'a hungry soul' Je 38.25 (|| μεθύσκω).

6. pass. *to become sated*: lit., and w. gen. of food, Jl 2.19; of drink, Am 4.8; φάγεσθε καὶ οὐ μὴ ἐμπλησθῆτε Le 26.26, sim. Ho 4.10, Mi 6.14, Jl 2.26, cf. Hb 2.5; φαγὼν καὶ ἐμπλησθείς De 6.11, 11.16, φαγεῖν καὶ πιεῖν καὶ ἐμπλησθῆναι Is 23.18; ἐμπλησθέντες κορήσουσιν De 31.20; εἰς πλησμονήν added for reinforcement, Ho 13.6; + acc., εὐλογίαν De 33.23; ἐπὶ τὴν τραπέζην μου ἵππον .. Ez 39.20; || πληρόομαι 7.19; + ἀπό τινος Jb 19.22, Si 24.19. **b**. fig., + gen. ὕπνου 'to have sound sleep' Ho 7.6, cf. Pl. *Rep*. 503d and Xen. *Cyr*. 4.2.41; πνεύματος συνέσεως De 34.9; τοῦ γνῶναι = τῆς γνώσεως Hb 2.14, cf. Ec 5.11; emotion, πικρίας 'bitterness' Je 15.17, κοπετοῦ 'mourning' 3M 4.3; + μεθύσκω Je 26.10; ἐν τούτοις 'with these' Ez 16.29; ἀπό τινος Si 12.16; + dat., μερίδι 14.9.

7. pass.intr., *to fill up*: αἱ οἰκίαι ἤχου 'the houses .. with noise' Is 13.21; ἐμπέπλησται ἀνὰ μέσον μου καὶ θανάτου 'I am now on the brink of death' 1K 20.3 (*L* πεπλήρωται).

Cf. πίμπλημι, πληρόω, κορέννυμι, τελειόω.

ἐμπίμπρημι: impf.3s ἐνεπίμπρα, 3pl ~πίμπρων; fut. ἐμπρήσω, inf. ~πρήσειν; aor. ἐνέπρησα, inf. ~πρῆσαι, impv. ~πρησον, ptc. ~πρήσας, pass. ἐνεπρήσθην.

to set on fire: + acc., τὰς πόλεις αὐτῶν .. καὶ τὰς ἐπαύλεις αὐτῶν .. ἐν πυρί Nu 31.10; De 13.16; ἱεροὺς πυλῶνας 'sacred gates' 2M 8.33, πύργους 'towers' 10.36, τὸν λιμένα 'the harbour' 12.6; οἴκους Ez 16.41, σκηνώματα 'dwellings' Ju 2.26; ^κριθάς^ 'barley' 2K 14.30B (*L* ἐμπυρίζω); πάντα τὰ μισθώματα αὐτῆς .. ἐν πυρί 'all that she has hired .. with fire' Mi 1.7; Jd 9.49 A (B: ἐμπυρίζω), 15.6 B (A: ἐμπυρίζω). Cf. ἐμπυρίζω, καίω, ἀνάπτω.

ἐμπιπλάω. ⇒ ἐμπίμπλημι.

ἐμπίπτω: fut. ~πεσοῦμαι; aor. ἐνέπεσα, subj. ἐμπέσω, inf. ~πεσεῖν, ptc. ~πεσών, opt.3s ~πέσοι; pf.ptc. ἐμπεπτωκώς.

1. *to fall in*: ἐκεῖ and *s* hum., To 14.10 $\mathfrak{G}^{I}$ (into a trap [παγίς] and $\mathfrak{G}^{II}$ πίπτω), Ps 7.16 (into a pit [βόθρος]), sim. Is 24.18 (:: ἐκβαίνω) and Je 31.44 (:: ἀναβαίνω); μόσχος ἢ ὄνος Ex 21.33 (into a pit [λάκκος]); ἔνδον 'inside' Le 11.33; voluntarily, 'fling oneself in' Ge 14.10. **b**. *to penetrate* into a space: οἱ τέσσαρες ἄνεμοι τοῦ οὐρανοῦ .. εἰς μεγάλην θάλασσαν Da 7.2 LXX; εἰς οἰκίαν .. πῦρ Ep Je 54.

2. fig., *to fall into* a certain condition or state: ἐ. εἰς τὰς χεῖράς τινος 'to yield or submit to sbd's authority and will': voluntarily, Su 23; εἰς χεῖρας κυρίου καὶ οὐκ εἰς χεῖρας ἀνθρώπων Si 2.18, 1C 21.13 (‖ 2K 24.14*L*); involuntarily Si 38.15, Jd 15.18 (v.l. ἐν χειρί), εἰς ἐπαγωγήν 'into calamity' Is 10.4, εἰς ἐγγύην .. εἰς κρίσεις 'into surety .. into lawsuits' Si 29.19, εἰς βαθεῖαν .. λήθην 'into deep oblivion' Wi 16.11, εἰς ἀρρωστίαν 'fell sick' 1M 6.8, εἰς ἐνύπνια 'into dreams' Da 2.1 LXX; ὑπο τὴν εὔθυναν '(to incur) the punishment' 3M 3.28. **b**. + dat. pers., 2M 12.24.

3. *to fall upon, attack*, + dat.: *s* ἄρκος 'bear' Am 5.19; εἰς τὴν παρεμβολὴν Συρίας 4K 7.4; fig., μέριμνα 'angst' Pr 17.12, φόβος Da 10.7 LXX, μὴ ἔμπιπτε 'don't be pushy' Si 13.10.

4. *to move over* to sbd (πρός τινα) for protection: *s* soldier, 1K 29.3 (*L* εἰσέρχομαι); 'to defect' 4K 25.11 (*L* προσ~). See LSG s.v. **10**.

5. *to emerge*: κόπτειν .. τοὺς ἐμπίπτοντας 'to cut down those whom they run into' 2M 5.12, sim. 10.17, 35; 3M 7.14.

***6**. *to be alloted*: + dat. com. pers., *s* κληρονομία Jd 18.1 B (A: simp.).

Cf. πίπτω: Spicq 2.1f.

ἐμπιστεύω: fut. ~πιστεύσω, inf. ~πιστεύσειν, pass. ~πιστευθήσομαι; aor. ἐνεπίστευσα, impv. ~πίστευσον, subj. ~πιστεύσω, opt.3s ~πιστεύσαι, impv.pass.3pl ~πιστευθήτωσαν, ptc.pass. ~πιστευθείς.

1. *to trust in, give credence to* (τινι): τῷ θεῷ De 1.32, Jn 3.5; λόγῳ Si 36.3; εἰς χεῖρας 'manual skills' 38.31; ἐν κυρίῳ 2C 20.20; ἐπὶ σοί [= God] 2M 3.7; pass., Si 1.15. **b**. *to trust and accede to a request*: + dat. pers. and inf., Jd 11.20 B. **c**. pass. *to enjoy the confidence of*: *ἔν τινι (pers., Hebraism) 1K 27.12 (B simp.).

2. *to entrust*: + acc. rei, χρείας 'tasks' 2M 7.24; + acc. pers. and dat. pers., Si 7.26.

3**. *to demonstrate as reliable and trustworthy*: + acc., μεθ' ὑμῶν τὸ ἔλεος αὐτοῦ Si 50.24; + ***o hum. and pass., 36.21.

Cf. πιστεύω: LSG s.v.

ἐμπλατύνω: pres.subj. ~πλατύνω; aor.impv. ~πλάτυνον. *

to add to the area of, 'expand': + acc. τὰ ὅρια 'the territory' Ex 23.18, Am 1.13; ἐμπλάτυνον τὴν χηρείαν σου 'Extend your widowhood(?)' Mi 1.16; Γαδ, i.e. his territory, De 33.20. **b**. *to add to the prestige* or *standing of*: τινα Pr 18.16.

Cf. πλατύνω.

ἐμπλέκομαι: fut. ~πλακήσομαι; 1aor. ἐνεπλέχθην, 2aor.ptc. ~πλακείς.ʃ

1. *to get entangled and stuck*: Pr 28.18; + dat., metaph. τριβόλοις 'in prickles' Wi 5.7.

2. *to fight hand to hand*: 2M 15.17.

ἐμπληθύνω: aor.ptc.pass. ~θυνθείς.ʃ

to fill: ***o*** hum., + gen., ἀλογιστίας 'with madness' 3M 5.42. Cf. πληθύνω.

ἐμπλόκιον, ου. n.

accessory woven into hair: σφραγῖδας καὶ ἐνώτια καὶ δακτυλίους καὶ ~α καὶ περιδέξια Ex 35.22, sim. Nu 31.50, Is 3.20; made of pure gold, Ex 36.22.

ἔμπνευσις, εως.ʃ

act of blowing on sth or sbd: πνεύματος ὀργῆς Ps 17.16. Cf. ἐμπνέω.

ἐμπνέω: aor.ptc. ~πνεύσας.

1. *to breathe* as a sign of life: ptc.subst.n.sg., De 20.16, Jo 10.28+. **b**. *to breathe of*: + gen., πᾶν ἐμπνέον ζωῆς Jo 10.40.

2. *to blow a stream of air* at: ἐπί τινα 4K 4.35.

3. *to infuse*: ‖ ἐμφυσάω, *s* God, + dat. pers. and acc. rei, ψυχήν Wi 15.11.

Cf. πνέω, ἔμπνευσις, ἔμπνους, ἐμφυσάω, πνεῦμα: *ND* 4.147.

ἔμπνους, ουν.ʃ
breathing and alive: *s* hum., 2M 7.5, 14.45. Cf. ἐμπνέω.

ἐμποδίζω: aor.impv. ~πόδισον, subj.~δίσω, mid./pass. ἐνεποδίσθην, subj. ἐμποδισθῶ.ʃ
1. *to deprive freedom of movement* or *action*: + acc. and inf., αὐτοὺς τοῦ οἰκοδομεῖν 2E 4.4; pass., *o* the heels of a horse, Jd 5.22B, ὁ ἥλιος Si 46.4, τὰ ἔργα αὐτοῦ 1M 9.55. **b**. mid. *to fail deliberately to do* what one ought to do: + τοῦ inf., Si 18.22.
2. *to withhold and not give*: ἄρτους Si 12.5, μουσικά 'musical entertainments' 35.3.
Cf. ἐμποδιστικός, ἀνεμπόδιστος.

ἐμποδιστικός, ον.ʃ
acting as an impediment to: *s* passions, + gen., δικαιοσύνης .. ἀνδρείας 'justice .. courage' 4M 1.4 (ǁ vs. 3 κωλυτικός; ǁ vs. 5 ἐναντίος). Cf. ἐμποδίζω, κωλυτικός, ἐναντίος.

ἐμποδοστατέω: pf. ἐμπεποδοστάτηκα.ʃ
to present a difficult dilemma and impediment for: + acc. pers., Jd 11.35A. Cf. ἐμποδοστάτης.

ἐμποδοστάτης, ου. m.ʃ *
one who presents a difficult dilemma and impediment: 1C 2.7. Cf. ἐμποδοστατέω.

ἐμποιέω: aor. ἐνεποίησα.ʃ
to lay claim to: + gen., τοῦ λαοῦ μου Ex 9.17; ἱερωσύνης 'priesthood' 1E 5.38.

ἐμπολάω: fut. ~πολήσω.ʃ
to deal in: abs. Am 8.5. Cf. πωλέω and ἐμπορεύομαι.

ἔμπονος, ον.ʃ
requiring and occasioning much endeavour: *s* κραυγή 'outcry' 3M 1.28. Cf. πόνος.

ἐμπορεύομαι: fut. ἐμπορεύσομαι
1. *to conduct trade*: abs. οἱ ἐμπορευόμενοι 'tradesmen' 2C 9.14. **b**. 'to trade in (commodity)': + acc., wisdom (or: prudence) Pr 3.14; ἀπὸ παντὸς γενήματος 'every kind of product' Am 8.6; + ἐν - ἐν ψυχαῖς ἀνθρώπων Ez 27.13 (slave trade?); καμήλους .. ἐν οἷς ἐμπορεύονταί σε 27.21. **c**. 'to trade with (trading partner or sphere of trade)': ἐπ' αὐτῆς [= τῆς γῆς] Ge 34.10; *+ acc., καμήλους .. ἐν οἷς ἐμπορεύονταί σε Ez 27.21, ἐμπορευέσθωσαν αὐτήν (= τὴν γῆν) 'Let them make it an area for trading activities' Ge 34.21 ǁ τῇ γῇ 42.34; + dat. pers., σοι ἐν ψυχαῖς ἀνθρώπων Ez 27.13.
2. *to import* goods (τι) into (εἰς) another land: ἔλαιον εἰς Αἴγυπτον Ho 12.2.
Cf. ἐμπορία.

ἐμπορία, ας. f.
merchandise: ἐπλήθυνας τὰς ~ας σου ὑπὲρ τὰ ἄστρα τοῦ οὐρανοῦ 'you have increased your .. more than the stars in the sky' Na 3.16. Cf. ἐμπορεύομαι, ἔμπορος, ἐμπόριον.

ἐμπόριον, ου. n.ʃ
1. *centre for commercial activities*, 'mart, market town': of Tyre, πάσαις ταῖς βασιλείαις τῆς οἰκουμένης Is 23.17, τῶν λαῶν ἀπὸ νήσων πολλῶν Ez 27.3.
2. pl. *merchandise*: παράλιον κατοικούντων 'of residents along the seacoast' De 33.19.
Cf. ἐμπορία.

ἔμπορος, ου. m.
merchant, trader: τετρακόσια δίδραχμα ἀργυρίου δοκίμου ~οις '400 didrachms of silver current among merchants' Ge 23.16; οἱ Μαδιηναῖοι οἱ ~οι 37.28; Is 23.8 (ǁ μεταβόλος vs. 2f.). Cf. ἐμπορία, μεταβόλος: Drexhage.

ἐμπορπάω: pf.mid.ptc. ἐμπεπορπημένος.ʃ
mid. *to fasten one's garment* with a brooch: fig., + acc., ὠμότητα 'cruelty' 3M 7.5. Cf. πόρπη.

ἐμπορπόω.ʃ*
mid., = ἐμπορπάω: + acc. rei, πόρπην χρυσῆν 'with a golden brooch' 1M 14.44.

ἐμπρήθω. ⇒ ἐμπίμπρημι.

ἔμπροσθεν.
I. adv., of time, *previously, formerly*: καθὼς ἔ. 'as before' Jl 2.23; Mi 2.8. Used attributively: κατὰ τὰς ἡμέρας τὰς ἔ. 'as in olden days' Mi 7.20, κατὰ μῆνα ἔ. ἡμερῶν 'as the bygone month' Jb 29.2; κατὰ τὸ κήρυγμα τὸ ἔ. 'in the manner of the previous proclamation' Jn 3.2; sim. Hg 2.3, Zc 1.4, 7.7, 12, 8.11, Ma 3.4; τὰ ἔ. 'the former, past situation' Jb 42.12 (:: τὰ ἔσχατα).
2. *ahead*: τὰ ἔ. 'that which lies ahead, the future' Is 41.26 (:: τὰ ἐξ ἀρχῆς 'the past'); εἰς τὰ ὄπισθεν καὶ οὐκ εἰς τὰ ἔ. Je 7.24.
3. *situated in front of beholder*: τὰ ἔ. καὶ τὰ ὄπισθεν 'the obverse and the reverse (of a written document)' Ez 2.10. **b**. ἐκ τοῦ ἔ. τινος: ἀποξηράναντος κυρίου .. τὸ ὕδωρ .. ἐκ τοῦ ἔ. ὑμῶν 'the Lord having dried up the water .. (and thereby having cleared it) from before you' Jo 4.23, sim. 5.1. **c**. εἰς τὸ ἔ. 'to the front': 4M 8.12.
II. prep. c. gen., of place, *ahead of*: dynamic, ἔ. σου 'ahead of you, leading you' Ge 24.7; ἔ. αὐτοῦ 32.3, 46.28 (to pave his way); τὰς ἔ. αὐτῶν γεγενημένας ἀντιλήμψεις ἐξ οὐρανοῦ 'the helps which had presented themselves to them from heaven' 3M 5.50; static, τὰ ἔ. αὐτοῦ 'what lies ahead of them' (:: τὰ ὀπίσω αὐτοῦ) Jl 2.3, ἔ. καὶ ὄπισθεν αὐτῶν Ep Je 5. **b**. in status: ἔθηκεν τὸν Εφραιμ ἔ. τοῦ Μανασση Ge 48.20. **c**. of time: ἔ. τῆς τελευτῆς αὐτοῦ 'prior to his death' 1C 22.5.
Cf. ἐμπρόσθιος, ὀπίσω, ὄπισθεν: Sollamo, *Semiprep.*, 34-6, 319-25.

ἐμπρόσθιος, ον.ʃ
pertaining to the front: *s* ὁπλή 'hoof' 2M 3.25;

subst.n.pl. 'the front part' Ex 28.14, 1K 5.4. Cf. ἔμπροσθεν.

ἔμπτυσμα, ατος. n.ʃ

v.n. of ἐμπτύω, q.v.: τὸ πρόσωπόν μου οὐκ ἀπέστρεψα ἀπὸ αἰσχύνης ~άτων 'I did not turn my face away from the contempt of being spat at' Is 50.6. Cf. ἐμπτύω, προσσιελίζω.

ἐμπτύω: fut.mid. ἐμπτύσομαι; aor. ἐνέπτυσα.ʃ

to spit: εἰς τὸ πρόσωπόν τινος Nu 12.14; mid. De 25.9 (act of contempt). Cf. πτύω, ἔμπτυσμα.

ἐμπυρίζω: fut. ~ριῶ, pass. ~ρισθήσομαι; aor. ἐνεπύρισα, impv. ἐμπύρισον, subj. ἐμπυρίσω, pass. ἐνεπυρίσθην, ptc. ~ρισθείς, subj. ~ρισθῶ; pf. pass.3s ἐμπεπύρισται, ptc.pass. ἐμπεπυρισμένος; plpf.pass. ἐνεπεπυρίσμην.

to set on fire and burn: + acc. and of destruction, τὸν ἀμπελῶνα 'the vineyard' Is 3.14, πυρί Ps 79.17, ἐμπυρισμῷ Jo 6.24; as divine punishment and ***o*** hum., ὑπὸ κυρίου Le 10.6; young goat and pass., 10.16; cities, Je 4.26, gates 28.58, mountain 28.25, ἁγιαστήριον ἐν πυρί Ps 73.7. Cf. ἐμπυρισμός, ἐμπυριστής, ἐμπίμπρημι, (κατα)καίω: Ziegler 1934. 180f.

ἐμπυρισμός, οῦ. m.

act of catching fire and being burnt: leading to destruction as divine punishment, Le 10.6; poss. forest fire (?), 3K 8.37; as a place-name Nu 11.3 (with a folk-etymological gloss), De 9.22; παρέδωκαν τὸ σῶμα αὐτῶν εἰς ~όν Da 3.95 LXX (TH πῦρ). Cf. ἐμπυρίζω, πύρωσις: Lee 1969.239.

ἐμπυριστής, ου.ʃ

one who sets on fire: adj., ***s*** ἄγγελος 4M 7.11. Cf. ἐμπυρίζω.

ἔμπυρος, ον.ʃ

possessing fire: ~οι λοιμοί 'fiery destroyers' Am 4.2; subst., δι' ~ων 'through burning objects' Ez 23.37. Cf. πῦρ.

ἐμφαίνω: aor.pass.impv. ~φάνηθι.ʃ

to render visible: + acc., ἀγωνίαν 'anguish' 2M 3.16. **b**. pass. *to make appearance*: ***s*** God, Ps 79.2. Cf. ἐμφανίζω, δείκνυμι.

ἐμφανής, ές.ʃ

1. *belonging to public knowledge*, 'open': ~ὲς γέγονεν τὸ ῥῆμα 'the matter has come into the open' Ex 2.14; ~ὴς ἐγενόμην τοῖς ἐμὲ μὴ ζητοῦσιν (|| εὑρέθην) Is 65.1; θήσω εἰς τὸ ~ὲς τὴν γνῶσιν αὐτῆς 'I shall bring its knowledge into the open' (:: ἀποκρύψω) Wi 6.22; ὅσα τέ ἐστιν κρυπτὰ καὶ ~ῆ ἔγνων 7.21.

2. *physically visible*: ~ὲς τὸ ὄρος τοῦ κυρίου 'visible is the mountain of the Lord' Mi 4.1, sim. Is 2.2; ~ῆ εἰκόνα τοῦ τιμωμένου βασιλέως ἐποίησαν 'they made a visible image of the king being honoured' Wi 14.17.

Cf. ἐμφανῶς, γνωστός, κρυπτός, ἐμφαίνω, ἐμφανίζω: Schmidt 3.426f.

ἐμφανίζω: aor. ἐνεφάνισα, impv. ἐμφάνισον.ʃ

1. *to make visible*: + acc. and dat. pers., ἐμφάνισόν μοι σεαυτόν Ex 33.13.

2. *to make known, reveal*: + acc. rei, Wi 16.21; ἁμαρτίαν Is 3.9 (|| ἀναγγέλλω); ὁ καπνὸς ὁ θεωρούμενος ἐνεφάνιζε τὸ γεγονός 'the smoke they were watching revealed what had happened' 1M 4.20.

3. *to let be known, inform*: 'to apprise' and περί τινος 2M 3.7; + dat. pers. and inf., 11.29; + subordinate cl., δι' ἣν αἰτίαν 'for what reason' Wi18.18; τὰ τῆς ἐπιβουλῆς 'the matter of the conspiracy' Es 2.22 o'.

4. mid. *to manifest oneself, reveal one's nature*: + dat. pers. and ***s*** the Lord, Wi 1.2 (|| εὑρίσκομαι); ***s*** φάσματα 'phantoms' 17.4.

Cf. ἐμ~, ἐπιφαίνω, ἐμφανισμός, γνωρίζω.

ἐμφανισμός, οῦ. m.ʃ

v.n. of ἐμφανίζω **2**: 2M 3.9. Cf. ἐμφανίζω.

ἐμφανῶς. adv.ʃ

in full view of people round about: ὁ θεὸς ἐ. ἥξει 'God will arrive openly' Ps 49.2; ἐν πλατείαις 'in the streets' Pr 9.14. Cf. ἐμφανής.

ἔμφασις, εως. f.ʃ

pretext contradictory to true intention: + ὡς + inf., and opp. πρᾶγμα 2M 3.8.

ἐμφέρομαι.ʃ

to move in so as to assault: ***s*** troops, 2M 15.17.

ἔμφοβος, ον.ʃ

fearful: of committing a sin, Si 19.24. Del. 1M 13.2 v.l. (> ἔκ~).

ἐμφραγμός, οῦ. m.ʃ *

barring of passage: as cogn. dat., Mi 5.1; ὠτίων 'of ears' Si 27.14. Cf. ἐμφράσσω, φράσσω, φραγμός.

ἐμφράσσω: fut. ~φράξω, pass. ~φραχθήσομαι; aor. ἐνέφραξα, impv. ἔμφραξον, inf. ~φράξαι, pass. ἐνεφράγην, opt.3s ἐμφραχθείη; pf.ptc.pass. ἐμφραγμένος.

1. *to deny passage*: pass., + cogn. dat., ἐμφραχθήσεται θυγάτηρ ἐμφραγμῷ Mi 5.1. **b**. *to deny access to*: + acc., τοὺς λόγους Da 12.4 TH, + σφραγίζω 12.9 TH; ὕδατα 2C 32.3.

2. *to block up, close up* that which is open: + acc. rei, φρέατα .. ἐνέφραξαν καὶ ἔπλησαν αὐτὰ γῆς 'blocked up wells and filled them with earth' Ge 26.15; ***o*** πύλας 'gates' Is 22.7, τὴν ἔξοδον τοῦ ὕδατος 'the water canal' 2C 32.30, θύραν 'door' 2M 2.5, λίθοις 1M 5.47; pass., φάραγξ ὀρέων ἐμφραχθήσεται καθὼς ἐνεφράγη ἐν ταῖς ἡμέραις τοῦ σεισμοῦ 'the valley at the base of the mountains will be closed up as it was closed up at the time of the earthquake' Zc 14.5; στόμα Ps 62.12, 106.42, Jb 5.16; lions' mouths, Da 6.20 TH (|| ἀποκλείω 18 LXX).

Cf. ἐμφραγμός, φράσσω.

ἐμφυσάω: fut. ~φυσήσω; aor. ἐνεφύσησα, impv. ~φύσησον, inf. ~φυσῆσαι, ptc. ~φυσήσας.

to breathe at: + acc. rei, πνεῦμα ζωτικόν 'life-giving spirit' Wi 15.11 (|| ἐμπνέω 'infuse'); and + εἰς— εἰς τὸ πρόσωπον αὐτοῦ πνοὴν ζωῆς Ge 2.7; abs. and with hostile intent, εἰς πρόσωπόν σου Na 2.2, ἐπὶ σέ Ez 21.31, ἐπὶ ^τοὺς ὀφθαλμούς^ To 6.9 𝔊[II]; + dat., 3K 17.21, Jb 4.21. Cf. ἀπο~, ἐκφυσάω, ἐμπνέω.

ἐμφυσιόω: aor.pass. ἐνεφυσιώθην.ʃ

**to infuse life into*: + acc., τὴν ἀνάγνωσιν 'the recitation' 1E 9.48; *o* hum. and pass., ἐν τοῖς ῥήμασιν 9.55.

ἔμφυτος, ον.ʃ

inborn, innate: *s* κακία 'wickedness' Wi 12.10.

ἐν. Prep. foll. by the dat.

1. indicates a place: **a**. in which some object is found or placed: κύριος ὁ θεός σου ἐν σοί Zp 3.17; Θέσθε ἐν ταῖς καρδίαις ὑμῶν Hg 2.18; of an intangible object, ἀγαθὸν οὐκ ἔστιν ἐν αὐτοῖς 'they [= the idols] have nothing good about them' Je 10.5[b]. Difficult is κρέας ἐν αἵματι ψυχῆς 'meat (soaked) in the blood of life' Ge 9.4. **b**. in which some action takes place or some state prevails: σφάξῃ .. ἐν τῇ παρεμβολῇ 'slaughters .. in the camp' Le 16.3 (:: ἔξω τῆς παρεμβολῆς); ἐν τῇ ὁδῷ αὐτοῦ πορεύσονται Jl 2.7; λαλήσει ἐν ἐμοί Hb 2.1 (of God's inner communication); ἐγέλασεν .. ἐν ἑαυτῇ 'laughed to herself, i.e. not openly' Ge 18.12, φησὶν .. ἐν ἑαυτῷ (= /b-qerev libbō/); ἐροῦσιν ἐν ἑαυτοῖς 'will think aloud' (or: 'say among themselves') Wi 5.3, οἶδεν ἐν ἑαυτῷ ὅτι .. 'he is conscious that ..' Jb 15.23; ἐν θλίψει Jn 2.3; ἡ καρδία αὐτῶν ἡττηθήσεται ἐν αὐτοῖς 'they will feel depressed' Is 19.1, ταραχθήσεται τὸ πνεῦμα τῶν Αἰγύπτων ἐν αὐτοῖς 'the spirit of the Egyptians will be shaken' 19.3.

2. *amongst* a group of individuals: not physically, ἐν τοῖς ἔθνεσιν Ob 2; Ma 1.11; physically, βασιλεὺς παρὰ θεοῦ εἶ σὺ ἐν ἡμῖν Ge 23.6; τῶν Χαναναίων, μεθ' ὧν ἐγὼ οἰκῶ ἐν αὐτοῖς 24.3 (|| μετά); κατοικήσομεν ἐν ὑμῖν 34.15 (|| οἰκεῖν μεθ' ἡμῶν vs. 22); οὐκ ἦν ὁ ἐπικαλούμενος ἐν αὐτοῖς πρός με 'there was none amongst them who called unto me' Ho 7.7; ἐν τοῖς ἔθνεσιν ἐν μέσῳ λαῶν πολλῶν ὡς λέων ἐν κτήνεσιν '.. a lion among the cattle' Mi 5.8. Note the contrast with μετά: μετὰ σοῦ κατοικήσει, ἐν ὑμῖν κατοικήσει ἐν παντὶ τόπῳ De 23.16. **b**. "partitive": ἐν υἱοῖς ἀνθρώπων 'none amongst men' Mi 5.7.

3. indicates a point in time when something takes place: ἐν τῇ ἡμέρᾳ τῇ ἕκτῃ 'on the sixth day' Ge 2.2; ἐν ἐκείνῃ τῇ ἡμέρᾳ Ob 8; ἐν τῷ δευτέρῳ ἔτει Hg 1.1; ἐν τῇ ἐπισκοπῇ αὐτῶν 'when their census is taken' Ex 30.12; ἐν τῇ ὀπτασίᾳ αὐτοῦ 'on his appearance' Ma 3.2; ἐν ὕπνῳ 'in sleep' Ge 20.3. **b**. + τῷ + inf.: pres., ἐν τῷ παλαίειν αὐτὸν μετ' αὐτοῦ 'as he wrestled with him' Ge 32.25; ἐν τῷ ἐπιστρέφειν με Zp 3.20; Jn 2.8 (v.l. aor.), Hb 3.3*a*, Zc 13.4, Ma 1.7, 12; aor., Nu 35.21 (|| ὅταν + subj. aor. vs. 19), Ge 24.52, 39.15, 44.31, Hb 3.3*c*. Cf. Soisalon-Soininen, *Infinitive*, 80ff. **c**. *in the course of*: ἐν χρόνῳ 'with the passage of time' Wi 14.16, ἐν πλήθει τῶν ἡμερῶν 'after many days' Ec 11.1.

***4**. *in return for, for the price of*: ἐδούλευσά σοι δέκα τέσσαρα ἔτη <u>ἀντὶ</u> τῶν δύο θυγατέρων σου καὶ ἓξ ἔτη <u>ἐν</u> τοῖς προβάτοις σου Ge 31.41; ἐδούλευσεν .. ἐν γυναικὶ καὶ ἐν γυναικὶ ἐφυλάξατο '.. worked as (cattle-)watcher for a wife' Ho 12.12; || ἕνεκεν Si 7.18. Cf. μόνον ἐν τούτῳ ὁμοιωθήσονται .. ἐν τῷ περιτέμνεσθαι ἡμῶν πᾶν ἀρσενικόν 'only under the following condition they would consent .., (namely) that every male amongst us be circumcised' Ge 34.22; La 1.11, Ct 8.7. **b**. *as a retribution for*: ἐν αἵμασιν υἱοῦ Ιωδαε 2C 24.25.

5. *in the manner of*: ἐν τίνι 'in what way?' Ma 1.2, 6, 7; ἐν ἀπειλῇ .. ἐν θυμῷ Hb 3.12; ἐν ἀληθείᾳ καὶ ἐν δικαιοσύνῃ Zc 8.8.

6. *by means of, by using as instrument*: ἐν χαλάζῃ 'with hail' Hg 2.17; ἐμπαίζοντες ἐν πυρί 'playing with fire' Na 2.4; ἐν τούτῳ γνώσομαι 'I shall conclude from that' Ge 24.44; ἐν ᾧ πίνει ὁ κύριός μου 'from which my lordship drinks' 44.5, πίνειν ἐν χρυσώμασι 'to drink from gold cups' 1M 11.58. **b**. hum. agent (*pace* Soisalon-Soininen 1987.126): ἐνευλογηθήσονται ἐν σοὶ πᾶσαι αἱ φυλαὶ τῆς γῆς Ge 12.3, sim. 22.18; σώσω αὐτοὺς ἐν κυρίῳ .. οὐ .. ἐν τόξῳ Ho 1.7; ἐν προφήτῃ ἀνήγαγε κύριος τὸν Ισραηλ ἐξ Αἰγύπτου 12.13; Ἀρχὴ λόγου κυρίου ἐν Ωσηε 1.2; 2K 23.2. Cf. ἐν βασιλεῦσιν ἐντρυφήσει 'he will poke fun at kings' Hb 1.10 and συνετοὶ ἐν ἑαυτοῖς 'intelligent by their own judgement' Is 5.21 (|| ἐνώπιον ἑαυτῶν), cf. τί εὐθὲς ἐν ἐντολαῖς σου 'what is right according to your laws' Wi 9.9. **c**. *aided by* sbd: ἐν τῷ θεῷ ἐνδοξασθήσονται Is 45.25 (|| ἀπὸ κυρίου), ἐν σοὶ ῥυσθήσομαι '.. I shall escape' Ps 17.30, ἐν τῷ θεῷ ποιήσομεν δύναμιν 59.14; 43.6, 55.5, cf. BDAG, s.v. ἐν, **4 c**. **d**. || διά + gen.: Nu 5.8. **e**. || dat.: ἐλιθοβόλησαν αὐτὸν ἐν λίθοις 'they stoned him' 3K 12.18 (λίθοις || 2C 10.18 [*L* ἐν ..]). **f**. ἐν τούτῳ 'on this condition': ἐν τούτῳ ὁμοιωθησόμεθα ὑμῖν, ὅτι .. 'we shall consent to you on the following condition ..' Ge 34.15, cf. ἐν ταύτῃ διαθήσομαι ὑμῖν διαθήκην, ἐν τῷ ἐξορύξαι .. 'I shall make a covenant with you on condition that you all pluck out ..' 1K 11.2.

7. *equipped with*: ἐν τῇ ῥάβδῳ μου διέβην τὸν Ἰορδάνην τοῦτον 'with my staff I crossed this Jordan' Ge 32.10; ἐν ῥομφαίᾳ Hg 2.22; τὴν στολὴν τὴν ἁγίαν .. ἐν ᾗ ἱερατεύσει μοι 'the sacerdotal garments .. wearing which he shall serve me as priest' Ex 28.3; χρισθῆναι ἐν αὐτοῖς 'to be anointed (and consecrated) wearing them' 29.29; κατεπένθησαν ἐν πενθικοῖς 'bewailed, wearing mourning dress' 33.4; εἶναι ἐν πορφύρᾳ 'to dress in purple' 1M 11.58, τῶν ἱερέων ἐν πάσαις ταῖς ἐσθήσεσι 'the priests in all their vestments' 3M 1.16, sim. ἄνδρες δύο .. ἐν ἐσθῆτι ἀστραπούσῃ 'wearing a flashing robe' Lk 24.4; ἐν ὅπλοις πολεμικοῖς Ez 32.27 (or: **8**). Does ἔσται ἐν σημείῳ διαθήκης Ge 17.11 belong here, or is this akin to the so-called Beth essentiae? Cf. **14** below.

8. *carrying* or *taking with* one, esp. with verbs of movement: εἰσελεύσεται εἰς τὸ ἅγιον· ἐν μόσχῳ '.., having a calf' Le 16.3, cf. Ps 65.13 and Mi 6.6; ἀνέβη .. εἰς Σηλω ἐν μόσχῳ τριετίζοντι 'with a three-year-old calf' 1K 1.24; ἐν ἑβδομήκοντα ψυχαῖς κατέβησαν οἱ πατέρες σου εἰς Αἴγυπτον De 10.22, cf. ἐξήγαγεν αὐτοὺς ἐν ἀργυρίῳ καὶ χρυσίῳ Ps 104.37; Si 16.13, Jd 15.1 B, 1C 12.20. **b**. *accompanied by*: "an angel was sent with troops (ἐν ἰσχύι)" Da 4.10 LXX, sim. 20 LXX.

9. indicates an object to which some emotion or thought is directed: θέλημα ἐν ὑμῖν 'satisfaction with you' Ma 1.10; τὰ ἅγια κυρίου, ἐν οἷς ἠγάπησε 'the holy objects of the Lord, which he loved' 2.11; οὐκ εὐδοκεῖ ἡ ψυχή μου ἐν αὐτῷ Hb 2.4; ἐν ποταμοῖς ὠργίσθης 3.8, ἐθυμώθη κύριος ἐν τῷ Ισραηλ 4K 17.18; ἐν τῷ κυρίῳ ἀγαλλιάσομαι Hb 3.18; + αἰσχύνομαι Ho 10.6; + ἐλπίζω 10.13; + ἐκλέγομαι 'to select' 1K 16.9, 10.

10. indicates a person to whom sth is done: ποιήσεις ἐν ἐμοὶ ἔλεος Ge 40.14; ἐν πᾶσιν τοῖς θεοῖς τῶν Αἰγυπτίων ποιήσω τὴν ἐκδίκησιν Ex 12.12, sim. Nu 33.4, Mi 5.15, Ez 16.41, 30.14 (|| εἴς τινα 25.11), 1M 3.15; ποιήσω ἐν σοὶ κρίματα Ez 5.10, sim. 5.15, 11.9, 28.22, 26, 30.19; δολιοῦσθαι ἐν τοῖς δούλοις αὐτοῦ 'to deal treacherously ..' Ps 104.25. See also s.v. ποιέω **I 6a**. Maybe belongs here ἐν ἐμοὶ ἐπέστρεψε χεῖρα αὐτοῦ La 3.3, if not a Hebrew calque (/bi/). See also under verbs denoting contest, hostility and the like such as δικάζομαι, μάχομαι, πολεμέω, ἐκμυκτηρίζω.

11. *on account of, due to*: ἐπικατάρατος ἡ γῆ ἐν τοῖς ἔργοις σου 'the earth is accursed because of your works' Ge 3.17; ἕκαστος ἐν τῇ ἑαυτοῦ ἁμαρτίᾳ ἀποθανεῖται De 24.16, sim. Je 38.30; κρίμα καὶ δικαιοσύνην ἐποίησεν, ἐν αὐτοῖς ζήσεται Ez 33.16; ἀσθενήσουσιν ἐν ταῖς ἀδικίαις αὐτῶν 'they will languish in their iniquities' Ho 5.5; 'by having regard to,' ἕκαστον ἐν ταῖς ὁδοῖς αὐτοῦ κρινῶ Ez 33.20. **b**. ἐν τῷ + inf., ἐν τῷ φείσασθαι κύριον αὐτοῦ 'because the Lord had pity on him' Ge 19.16.

12. *in the character, function, role of*: δέδωκα πᾶν ἐπιδέκατον .. ἐν κλήρῳ 'I have given every tithe .. as a share' Nu 18.21, sim. 26; ἐν κλήρῳ δέδωκα τῷ Ησαυ τὸ ὄρος τὸ Σηιρ 'as a possession I have given Esau the mount Seir' De 2.5; ἐν δόματι Εφραιμ δέξεται Ho 10.6 (the obj. missing); Jo 13.6, 16.10. Perh. belongs here ἔσῃ .. ἐν αἰνίγματι .. De 28.37, cf. **13** below.

13. *while undergoing, experiencing*: ἐν λύπαις τέξῃ τέκνα 'you will bear children in pain' Ge 3.16; ἐν ἱδρῶτι τοῦ προσώπου σου φάγῃ τὸν ἄρτον σου 'you shall eat your bread with sweat of your face' 3.19; ἐν ὀδύνῃ 'in a situation of hardship (due to famine?)' De 26.14; θυγατέρες ἐν ἐλπίδι Is 32.9, ἐν ὀδύνῃ μετ' ἐλπίδος 32.10; ἐν κλαυθμῷ ἐξῆλθον, καὶ ἐν παρακλήσει ἀνάξω αὐτούς 'they went out weeping, and I shall lead them back with comfort' Je 38.9. Cf. ἐν οὐ θεῷ ἀληθινῷ 'with no true god' 2C 15.3.

14. *being found in* a certain state or condition, 'in spite of': ἐν τῷ λόγῳ τούτῳ οὐκ ἐνεπιστεύσατε κυρίῳ De 1.32; ἐν ταύτῃ ἐγὼ ἐλπίζω 'even in that situation I keep on hoping' Ps 26.3; ἐν τῇ φαρμακείᾳ σου 'even with your witchcraft' Is 47.9; 43.24. **b**. often with πᾶς: οὐ πιστεύουσίν μοι ἐν πᾶσιν τοῖς σημείοις Nu 14.11; ἐν πᾶσι τούτοις οὐκ ἀπεστράφη ὁ θυμός 'despite all this the anger is not turned away' Is 5.25 (|| ἐπί .. 9.12, 17, 21, 10.4: see under ἐπί **II 11**); ἐν πᾶσιν τούτοις ἥμαρτον ἔτι καὶ οὐκ ἐπίστευσαν ἐν τοῖς θαυμασίοις αὐτοῦ Ps 77.32; μὴ ἀτιμάσῃς αὐτὸν ἐν πάσῃ ἰσχύι σου Si 3.13, ἀτιμασθήσεται .. ἐν παντὶ τῷ πλούτῳ τῷ πολλῷ Is 16.14, cf. Ps 65.3.

15. marks the object of a discourse or thought: λαλήσεις ἐν ^τοῖς ῥήμασιν^ ('the matters') De 6.7; διηγήσασθε ἐν τοῖς πύργοις αὐτῆς 'Narrate about her towers' Ps 47.13, ἐν ταῖς ἐντολαῖς σου ἀδολεσχήσω '.. I shall ponder' 118.15, ἐν τῷ νόμῳ αὐτοῦ μελετήσει 1.2, διενοοῦ ἐν τοῖς προστάγμασιν κυρίου Si 6.37; τοὺς διαλογισμοὺς αὐτῶν ἐν ἐμοί 'their designs ..' La 2.60 (|| κατ' ἐμοῦ ib. 61); Ct 8.8, Da TH 10.11.

16. *as regards, in respect of*: ὡμοιώθη λέοντι ἐν τοῖς ἔργοις αὐτοῦ 'he was like a lion in his deeds' 1M 3.4, ἱκανοὶ ἐν τοῖς ἔτεσι 'mature in age' 16.3, ἐν τοῖς λοιποῖς ὠφελήσειν αὐτούς 'to be of assistance to them in other respects' 2M 12.11.

17. = εἰς, *into* (of movement or transformation): ἔσται ἐν σημείῳ διαθήκης Ge 17.11, ἔσται τὸ αἷμα ὑμῖν ἐν σημείῳ 'the blood will be for you a sign' Ex 12.13 (see **7** above); τὰ παιδία .. ἐν διαρπαγῇ ἔσεσθαι Nu 14.31 (‖ εἰς 14.3); ἐγενήθησαν ἐν σημείῳ 26.10; ἔρριψεν αὐτὴν ἐν μέσῳ .. 'he threw it into the midst of ..' Zc 5.8 (‖ εἰς), ἔσται εἰς σκιὰν .. καὶ ἐν σκέπῃ Is 4.6, ἐν Ῥάγοις To 9.2 𝔊^I^ (𝔊^II^ εἰς ~ας), cf. Johannessohn, *Kasus* 4 and Soisalon-Soininen 1987.131-40.

***18**. ἐν ἐμοί, κύριε (μου), a calque on Heb. בִּי אֲדֹנִי or בִּי אֲדֹנָי Jd 6.13, 13.8 (for the more idiomatic δέομαι or δεόμεθα κύριε, e.g. Ge 44.18), 1K 1.26, 3K 3.17.

Cf. εἰς: Johannessohn, *Präp*. 324-36.

ἐναγκαλίζομαι.ʃ

to take in one's arms: + acc., χερσὶν στήθη '(fold) your arms over your breast' Pr 6.10 (posture of inactivity). Cf. ἐναγκάλισμα.

ἐναγκάλισμα, ατος. n.ʃ*

v.n. of prec.: w. ref. to mother's loving care, 4M 13.21. Cf. ἐναγκαλίζομαι.

ἐναγωνίζομαι: aor.impv.2pl ἐναγωνίσασθε.ʃ

to compete in a contest: metaph., 4M 16.16. Cf. ἀγωνίζομαι.

ἐναθλέω.ʃ

to enter a contest: 4M 17.13. Cf. ἀθλητής.

ἐνακισχίλιοι, αι, α. num.ʃ

nine thousand: 2M 8.24, 10.18.

ἐνακόσιοι, αι, α. num.

nine hundred: Ge 5.5.

ἐνακούω: fut.pass. ~κουσθήσομαι.

1. *to hear*: ἡ ἀκοή σου οὐκ ἐνακουσθήσεται ἔτι 'the report of you will not be heard any more' Na 1.12.

2. *to hear and heed*: + acc. rei, 1E 4.3.

Cf. ἀκούω.

ἐναλλαγή, ῆς. f.ʃ

interchange: Wi 14.26.

ἐναλλάξ adv.ʃ

crosswise: Ge 48.14.

ἐνάλλομαι: fut. ~λοῦμαι; aor. ἐνηλάμην.ʃ

to jump on: to assail, ἐπὶ φίλῳ Jb 6.26. **b**. *to assail*: + εἰς 1M 3.23, 4M 6.8; verbally, + dat. pers., ῥήμασιν Jb 16.4, μοι ὀνείδει 'with an insult' 19.5, ἀκίσιν ὀφθαλμῶν 'with darts of the eyes' 16.10.

Cf. ἅλλομαι.

ἔναντι. prep. w. gen.*

1. *in front of and facing, in full view of*: στήσεται τὸ κτῆνος ἔ. τοῦ ἱερέως 'the beast shall be set before the priest' Le 27.11; De 25.2 (‖ ἐναντίον); ἐποίησεν ἔ. παντὸς Ισραηλ 34.12.

2. *mentally in the presence of*, esp. in descriptions of cultic rites with ἔ. κυρίου, cf. ἐναντίος **II 1b**: καύσει αὐτὸ Ααρων .. ἔ. κυρίου 'A. shall burn it .. in the presence of the Lord' Ex 27.21; εἰσιόντι εἰς τὸ ἅγιον .. ἔ. τοῦ θεοῦ 'as he enters the sanctuary ..' 28.23; σφάξεις τὸν μόσχον ἔ. κυρίου παρὰ τὰς θύρας .. 'you shall slaughter the bull before the Lord by the doors ..' 29.11; τῶν ἀζύμων τῶν προτεθειμένων ἔ. κυρίου 'the unleavened breads set before the Lord' 29.23; ‖ ἐνώπιον Le 4.4.

3. *in the estimation of*: δεκτὸν .. ἔ. κυρίου 'acceptable .. to the Lord' Ex 28.34; ἔ. Μωυσῇ ἦν πονηρόν 'M. was not amused' Nu 11.10.

Cf. ἐναντίος **II**, ἐνώπιον, ἀπέναντι, κατέναντι: Johannessohn, *Präp.* 193; Sollamo, *Semiprep.* 25-8, 131-3, 151f., 317; Wevers 1992.214f.

ἐναντίος, α, ον. adj.

I. **1**. *opposed, hostile*: + gen., τῆς δικαιοσύνης 4M 1.6 (‖ κωλυστικός vs. 3; ἐμποδιστικός vs. 4); subst. n.pl., πονηρὰ βουλευόμενος ~ία 'planning evil in opposition' Na 1.11, ποιῶν ~ία Ez 17.15, 18.18. **b**. sg.f. gen. ἐναντίας w. prep. ἐκ, *opposite, facing*: ἐξῆλθεν ἐξ ~ίας 'came out to meet (an invading army)' Jd 1.10; ἀντέστης ἐξ ~ίας 'you stood opposite' Ob 11; εἰς ἀσεβεῖς .. ἀνθεστηκότας .. ἐξ ~ίας Hb 1.9; + gen., ἐξ ἐναντίας Βεελσεπφων Ex 14.2; ἐξ ~ίας μου 'in my presence, in front of me' Hb 1.3. On the substantival use, see BDF, § 241.1. **c**. *opposite, reverse* (with no connotation of hostility): Wi 15.7.

2. *over against, facing*: Nu 1.53.

II. ἐναντίον as prep., + gen. pers.: **1**. *in front of, in the eyesight of*: καὶ νῦν ἰδοὺ ἡ γυνή σου ~ίον σου Ge 12.19; De 25.2 (‖ ἔναντι); with a nuance of daring, "should we offer as sacrifices what is abominable to the Egyptians under their nose (~ίον), we would be stoned" Ex 8.26; with a nuance of public humiliation, "to be put to public shame in front of kings" Ez 27.17, "in front of all your on-lookers" 27.18. **b**. not physically in the presence of, but mentally conscious of being in the presence of, cf. ἔναντι, **2**: εὐλογήσω σε ἐ. κυρίου Ge 27.7, sim. Da 6.10 TH; συμφαγεῖν ἄρτον .. ἐ. τοῦ θεοῦ Ex 18.12; ἁμαρτάνων ἐ. τοῦ ποιήσαντος αὐτόν '.. his maker' Si 38.15. **c**. *facing and in the direction of*: ἐ. Ιερουσαλημ 1E 4.58.

2. *in the estimation of*, εὗρεν χάριν ἐ. κυρίου τοῦ θεοῦ 'found favour in the eyes of ..' Ge 6.8; δίκαιον ἐ. ^τοῦ θεοῦ^ 7.1, ἁμαρτωλοὶ ἐ. τοῦ θεοῦ 13.13; ἠτιμάσθην ἐ. αὐτῆς 'I lost face in relation to her' 16.5; σκληρὸν ἐφάνη τὸ ῥῆμα σφόδρα ἐ. Αβρααμ 21.11; μικρὰ ἦν .. ἐ. ἐμοῦ 30.30 (hardly temporal, *pace* Wevers, *Notes*: see Sollamo, *Semiprep.*, 23, 76); Ἤρεσεν τὰ ῥήματα ἐ. Φαραω 'the words pleased Ph.' 41.37; μέγας ἐγενήθη σφόδρα ἐ. τῶν Αἰγυπτίων Ex 11.3; δεκτὸν ἔ. κυρίου 'acceptable to the Lord' Le 1.3; οὐδὲν ἥμαρτεν .. ἐ. τοῦ κυρίου Jb 1.22, ἡμάρτηκα ἐ. κυρίου .. καὶ εἰς ὑμᾶς Ex 10.16, cf. ἥμαρτον εἰς τὸν οὐρανὸν καὶ ἐνώπιόν σου Lk 15.18.

Cf. ἔναντι, ἀντιπρόσωπος, ἐχθρός, δυσμενής: Schmidt 3.500f.; Johannessohn, *Präp.* 190-3; Sollamo, *Semiprep.* 21-5, 27f., 98f., 109, 116f., 131-3, 151f., 313-7; Sollamo 2005; Joosten 2006.

ἐναντιόω: fut.ptc.mid./pass. ἐναντιωθησόμενος.ʃ

mid. *to contest in opposition to*: + dat. pers., τῷ κυρίῳ 1E 1.25; 8.51; + dat. rei, τοῖς ἔργοις ἡμῶν 'our actions' Wi 2.12; *s* rei, οὐκ ἐναντιοῦται ἐν ὀφθαλμοῖς αὐτοῦ πᾶν πονηρόν 'he will not entertain opposition of any evil' Pr 20.8; 4M 5.26, 7.20. **b**. *to become hostile*: + dat. pers., 3M 3.1; ‖ δυσμενής 3.7.

Cf. ἐναντίος.

ἐναπερείδομαι: aor.inf. ~ρείσασθαι.ʃ

to place firmly: τὴν κακίαν εἴς τινα 'to take out the misfortune suffered upon sbd' 2M 9.4.

ἐναποθνῄσκω: aor. ἐναπέθανον.

to die inside: *s* hum. heart, 1K 25.37; hum., following a torture, 4M 11.1. Cf. ἀποθνῄσκω.

ἐναποσφραγίζω.ʃ *

to impress in or *on*: τι εἴς τι 4M 15.4.

ἐνάρετος, ον.ʃ

conducive to virtue: *s* νόμος 4M 11.5.

ἐναρίθμιος, ον.ʃ

esteemed: *s* artefact, Si 38.29.

ἐναρμόζω: aor.mid.impv.2pl ἐναρμόσασθε, ptc. ~μοσάμενος.ʃ

to render suitable: in singing, + acc., ^τῷ κυρίῳ^ ψαλμόν Ju 16.1, σιδῆρας .. χεῖρας '(fitting themselves) with iron gauntlets' 4M 9.26.

ἐναρμόνιος, ον.ʃ

orderly, coherent: *s* σύνταγμα 'literary composition' Si prol. II. Cf. τεταγμένως.

ἐνάρχομαι: aor. ἐνηρξάμην, impv. ἔναρξαι; plpf. dep.3s ἐνῆρκτο.ʃ

I. intr., *to take a beginning*: ἐναρχομένου τῇ τεσσαρεσδεκάτῃ ἡμέρᾳ τοῦ μηνός 'beginning on the fourteenth day of the month' Ex 12.18, Nu 9.5, see *BA* ad Nu 9.5; ἤδη ἐνῆρκτο ἡ θραῦσις 'the plague had already begun' Nu 16.47 (‖ ἄρχομαι vs. 46).

II. tr., *to begin* an action: + inf., κληρονομεῖν De 2.24; aor.inf., 2.25; 2.31 (‖ ἄρχομαι); + τοῦ inf., 1M 9.54. **b**. + gen. of verbal noun, κτήσεως 'acquisition' Si 36.29, θρήνου 'mourning' 38.16, πολέμου Jo 10.24. ***c**. + ptc.: Pr 13.12; for ἄρχομαι + ptc., see LSJ, s.v. **I 5**.

Cf. ἄρχω: Lee 70f.

ἐνατενίζω: aor.ptc. ~νίσας.ʃ

to stare intently: abs., 3M 5.30. Cf. ἀτενίζω.

ἔνατος, η, ον.

ninth in order: τοῦ ~ου μηνός 'of the ninth month' Hg 2.10. Cf. ἐννέα.

ἐναφίημι: fut. ἐναφήσω.ʃ

to let loose, 'to give vent to': + acc., θυμόν Ez 21.17.

ἐνδεής, ές.

needy: To 2.2 $\mathfrak{G}^{I}$ ($\mathfrak{G}^{II}$ πτωχός); subst. and opp. 'well-off', De 15.4, 7 (‖ ἐπιδέομαι), 11 (dit.); ‖ πένης 24.14, ‖ πτωχός Is 41.17; + gen., ἄρτου καὶ ὕδατος Ez 4.17, προσόδων 'revenues' Pr 28.16, φρενῶν 'brains' 7.7. Cf. ἔνδεια, ἐνδέω, πένης, πτωχός, ἀπροσδεής.

ἔνδεια, ας. f.

want, lack: divine punishment, ~αν καὶ ἐκλιμίαν 'deprivation and hunger' De 28.20; + gen., πάντων 28.57, ἄρτων Am 4.6; + λιμός 'famine' Jb 30.3¶; + πτωχεία Si 18.25 (:: πλοῦτος); ‖ πενία Pr 6.11. Cf. ἐνδέω, ἐνδεής.

ἐνδείκνυμι: fut.ptc. ~δειξόμενος; aor. ἐνεδειξάμην, subj. ~δείξωμαι, pass. ἐνεδείχθην, subj. ~δειχθῶ.

1. *to cause to see*: + acc., τὴν ἰσχύν μου 'my strength' Ex 9.16. **b**. *to convince of fault* or *guilt*: pass., *o* pers., Jo 7.15-18. **c**. mid. *to show* the quality of sth: + dat. pers. and double acc., φανερὰν τοῦ θεοῦ πᾶσι τὴν δύναμιν 2M 9.8.

2. *to subject to, treat with*: + dat. pers., πάντα τὰ κακά, ἃ ἐνεδειξάμεθα αὐτῷ Ge 50.15, πονηρά σοι ἐνεδείξαντο 50.17; Da 3.44; 2M 13.9.

Cf. ἀπο~, δείκνυμι, ἀποφαίνω, γνωρίζω, ποιέω: Schmidt 3.407f.

ἐνδείκτης, ου. m.ʃ

informer: + gen., 2M 4.1.

ἕνδεκα. indecl. num.

eleven: ἕ. παιδία Ge 32.22 +.

ἑνδέκατος, η, ον.

eleventh: Ge 8.5, Zc 1.7. Cf. δέκατος.

ἐνδελεχέω.⇒ ἐνδελεχίζω.

ἐνδελεχής, ές.ʃ

continuous, unbroken: ἐπιθύουσιν διὰ πυρὸς ~οῦς 'they offer sacrifices with continually burning fire' 1E 6.23; οἱ ὀφθαλμοὶ αὐτοῦ ~εῖς ἐπὶ τὰς ὁδοὺς αὐτῶν 'his eyes are constantly on their paths' Si 17.19. Cf. ἐνδελεχῶς.

ἐνδελεχίζω: fut. ἐνδελεχίσω, ~χιῶ, ~χισθήσομαι. Only in Si, 9 times.

1. *to apply frequently*: + acc. rei, ὁ ἀγαπῶν τὸν υἱὸν αὐτοῦ ἐνδελεχίσει μάστιγας αὐτῷ 'he who loves his son whips him often' Si 30.1.

2. *to continue to exist*, 'persist': *s* ὄνειδος 'ill-repute' Si 41.6; μῦθος ἄκαιρος 'an ill-timed story' 20.19; ψεῦδος 'a lie' 20.24; hum., μετὰ ψαλλούσης 'with a geisha girl' 9.4; εἰς κακά 'in evil' 12.3; ὁ ἐνδελεχίζων ψεύδει 'a habitual liar' 20.25; εἰς μέσον διανοουμένων ἐνδελέχιζε 'Linger on among the thoughtful' 27.12.

Cf. ἐνδελεχῶς.

ἐνδελεχισμός, οῦ. m.

continuousness: κάρπωμα ~οῦ 'continuous offer' Ex 29.38; θυσία ~οῦ εἰς τὰς γενεὰς ὑμῶν 29.42; further glossed, θυμίαμα ~οῦ διὰ παντὸς .. εἰς τὰς γενεὰς αὐτῶν 30.8; ὁλοκαύτωμα ~οῦ Nu 28.6, 23; προσφορὰς ~οῦ 1E 5.51; ἐ. ^ψεύδους^ 'to get into the habit of lying' Si 7.13. At Da TH 11.31 and 12.11 'daily sacrifices' is elliptically meant; cf. θυσία Da LXX ad loc. Cf. ἐνδελεχῶς.

ἐνδελεχιστός. ⇒ ἐνδελεχισμός.

ἐνδελεχῶς. adv.

continuously: of daily sacrifices, Ex 29.38, Nu 28.3; θυσίαι .. καθ' ἡμέραν ἐ. δίς 'sacrifices .. twice daily without fail' Si 45.14; of a lamp in a sanctuary, ἀπὸ ἑσπέρας ἕως πρωῒ .. ἐ. Le 24.3 (|| διὰ παντός vs. 2); ἐ. κατ' ἐνιαυτόν 'yearly' 1E 6.29; ἡ αἰσχύνη αὐτοῦ μετ' αὐτοῦ ἐ. 'his shame stays with him for ever' Si 20.26; λατρεύεις ἐ. 'you serve perpetually' Da 6.16, 20. Cf. ἐνδελεχής, ~χίζω, ~χισμός.

ἔνδεσμος, ου. m.ʃ

1. *bag*: to hold stones, Ez 13.11; ἀργυρίου Pr 7.22.

2. *bonding* in a building: 3K 6.10.

Cf. LSG s.v. Del. 3M 3.25 > δεσμός.

ἐνδέχομαι.ʃ

impers. *to be feasible, practicable*: ἃ ἦν ἐνδεχόμενα 2M 11.18; + inf., οὐκ ἐνδέχεται γενέσθαι καθάπερ οἴει 'it cannot be done, as you think (it can)' Da LXX 2.11.

ἐνδεχομένως. adv.ʃ

as best as possible: 2M 13.26.

I ἐνδέω: pf.mid. ἐνδέδεμαι, ptc.pass. ἐνδεδεμένος.ʃ

to fasten inside: + acc. rei, gem stone stitched on a robe, Ez 28.13; φυράματα .. ἐνδεδεμένα ἐν τοῖς ἱματίοις 'doughs .. fastened inside the clothes' Ex 12.34; ἱμάντωσις .. ἐνδεδεμένη εἰς οἰκοδομήν 'a beam .. bonded into a building' Si 22.16, ἀναβαθμοὶ .. ἐνδεδεμένοι χρυσίῳ 'six steps .. riveted with gold' 2C 9.18; metaph., ἡ ψυχὴ κυρίου μου ἐνδεδεμένη ἐν δεσμῷ τῆς ζωῆς .. '.. bound with a bond of life ..' 1K 25.29. Cf. δέω.

II ἐνδέω: fut. ἐνδεηθήσομαι.ʃ

mid. *to lack, need*: abs. Pr 28.27; + acc., οὐδέν De 8.9, καθ' ὅσον ἐνδεεῖται 'in accordance with his needs' 15.8 (|| ἐπιδέομαι). Cf. ἐνδεής, ἐπιδέω, σπανίζω, ὑστερέω.

ἐνδιαβάλλω: aor.inf. ἐνδιαβαλεῖν.

1. *to calumniate, speak ill of*: + acc. pers., Ps 108.4 (opp. ἀγαπάω); τὴν ψυχήν μου 70.13.

2. *to dissuade* from a course of action: + acc. pers., Nu 22.22, see Caird 1968.471 and *BA* ad loc.

Cf. διαβάλλω. κακολογέω.

ἐνδιατρίβω: aor.subj. ~τρίψω.ʃ

to continue engaging oneself in sth with pleasure: + dat. rei, λόγοις 'conversation' Pr 23.16.

ἐνδιδύσκω.ʃ *

to clothe: pass., ***o*** hum., Pr 31.21; w. double acc., ὑμᾶς κόκκινα 'you with a scarlet robe' 2K 1.24. **b**. mid. *to put on*: + acc. of garment, Si 50.11 (|| ἀναβάλλω), 2K 13.18.

Cf. ἐνδύω.

ἐνδίδωμι: impf. ἐνεδίδουν; fut. ~δώσω; aor.subj. ἐνδῶ.ʃ

1. *to lose strength, and flag*: ***s*** flood-water, Ge 8.3*bis*; hum., Pr 10.30. Cf. Renehan 2.66.

2. *to give in* to a request, persuasion: || ἀκούω Ez 3.11.

Cf. ἀνίημι, χαλάω: Schmidt 3.266.

ἐνδογενής, ές.ʃ

born in the house: ***s*** half-sister and opp. γεγεννημένη ἔξω 'born outside' Le 18.9.

ἔνδοθεν. adv.ʃ

within: τὸ ἔ. τοῦ καταπετάσματος 'that which is within the screen' Nu 18.7. **b**. mentally: Wi 17.13; adj., τῶν ἔ. πόνων 'of the sufferings from within' 4M 18.2 (poss. physical, || ἔξωθεν).

Cf. ἔνδον, ἔξωθεν.

ἔνδον. adv.

into a space inside: ἐμπέσῃ .. ἔ. 'should fall inside' Le 11.33; εἰσάξεις ἔ. εἰς τὴν οἰκίαν σου De 21.12; 2M 6.4; τὰ ἔ. 'the internal organs (of body)' 9.5; οἱ ἔ. 'the people inside' 10.34. **b**. *in a space inside*: Es 1.5 *L*.

Cf. ἔνδοθεν.

ἐνδοξάζομαι: fut. ἐνδοξασθήσομαι; aor.impv. ἐνδοξάσθητι. *(ἔνδοξος: Plato +)

to attain fame and esteem: ***s*** God, ἐνδοξασθήσομαι ἐν Φαραω καὶ ἐν πάσῃ τῇ στρατιᾷ αὐτοῦ Ex 14.4 (|| δοξάζω 15.1); Hg 1.8; + μεγαλύνομαι, ἁγιάζομαι Ez 38.23; hum., Ex 33.16. Cf. δοξάζω, ἔνδοξος, δόξα: Kittel, *TDNT* 2.254.

ἔνδοξος, ον.

1. *highly esteemed* or *valued*: ***s*** pers., Ge 34.19, οἱ ~οι καὶ οἱ μεγάλοι καὶ οἱ πλούσιοι καὶ οἱ λοιμοί Is 5.14, God 60.9; things, ἐπὶ πάντα τὰ ~α αὐτῆς βαλοῦσι κλήρους 'they will cast lots over all its valuable objects' Na 3.1; stream in a parched land, Is 32.2.

2. *generally acclaimed, highly regarded*, 'glorious, splendid': ***s*** hum., merchants Is 23.8, ὁ ἅγιος τοῦ Ισραηλ 60.9, τὸ ὄνομα κυρίου 24.15, 59.19; ἔνδοξος ἐν γήρει 'of respectable age' Da LXX 6.1; πλούτῳ 'for wealth' 1M 6.1; opp. ταπεινός 'humble' 1K 18.23 (*L* ἔντιμος); σοφία Si 1.10¶; θρόνος

40.3. **b**. subst. m. 'notable' Is 22.24, τὴν ὕβριν τῶν ~ων 23.9, ‖ δυνάστης Si 11.6; subst. n.pl., ποιήσω ~α Ex 34.10 (God's deeds), sim. ἐποίησεν ἐν σοὶ τὰ μεγάλα καὶ τὰ ~α ταῦτα De 10.21; τὰ ~α ἀρχόντων 'of chieftains' Nu 23.21, excellent facilities of Jerusalem 1E 1.53.

Cf. ἐνδοξάζομαι, ἐνδόξως, δόξα, ἐπίδοξος, ὑπερένδοξος, ἔντιμος: Kittel, *TDNT* 2.254.

ἐνδόξως. adv.

in a manner which brings honour, 'honourably, gloriously': ἐ. δεδόξασται Ex 15.1; ἐτάφη ἐ. 'was buried with honour' To 14.1 𝔊II; ἀπέθανεν ἐ. To 14.14 𝔊II; ἀπήντησαν αὐτῷ .. ἐ. 'they met him and paid him honour' 1M 11.60; ἐπεδέξατο .. ἐ. 'welcomed .. with honour' 12.8. Cf. δόξα, ἐντίμως.

ἐνδόσθιος, ον. *

Alw. n.pl. used subst., *inwards, entrails*: κεφαλὴν σὺν τοῖς ποσὶν καὶ τοῖς ~ίοις 'the head with the legs and the entrails' Ex 12.9 (of sacrificial sheep to be consumed); Le 4.8. Cf. κοιλία.

ἔνδυμα, ατος. n.

clothing, garment: ἐνδεδυμένους ~ατα ἀλλότρια 'wearing alien garments' Zp 1.8; priest's uniform, Ps 132.2; commoner's, 2K 1.24B (*L* ἱματισμόν). Cf. ἐνδύω, ἔνδυσις, ἱμάτιον, στολή.

ἐνδυναμόω: aor. ἐνεδυνάμωσα.ʃ

to give power to: for a difficult mission, + acc. pers., Jd 6.34 B.

ἔνδυσις, εως. f.ʃ

= ἔνδυμα: Jb 41.5, Es D 4.

ἐνδύω: fut. ~δύσω, mid. ~δύσομαι; aor.act. ἐνέδυσα, impv. ἔνδυσον, mid. ἐνεδυσάμην, subj. ~δύσωμαι, inf. ~δύσασθαι, impv. ~δυσαι, opt. 3pl ~δύσαιντο; pf. ἐνδέδυκα, ptc. ~δεδυκώς, mid. ~δεδυμένος; plpf.act. ἐνδεδύκειν.

1. mid., *to put on* clothes: + acc., στολήν Le 6.11, De 22.5, 2K 6.14*L* (B: act.); σάκκους Jn 3.5; ἱμάτια χηρεύσεως 'clothes of widowhood' Ge 38.19; De 22.11 (‖ ἐπιβάλλομαι Le 19.19); χιτῶνα .. περὶ τὸ σῶμα αὐτοῦ 6.10; ἱμάτια ῥυπαρά 'filthy clothes' Zc 3.3; δέρριν τριχίνην 'hairy leather garment' 13.4; πορφύραν 'purple' Da 6.3 LXX; w. ref. to rams growing abundant hair (?), Ps 64.14. **b**. fig. of conferring a quality, κατάραν ὡς ἱμάτιον Ps 108.18, ἰσχὺν καὶ εὐπρέπειαν Pr 31.26, εὐπρέπειαν .. δύναμιν Ps 92.1, δικαιοσύνην 131.9; 'coat of mail (θῶραξ)' Is 59.17, Je 26.4, θώρακα δικαιοσύνην Wi 5.18, cf. Eph 4.24, 6.14; Is 49.18, 59.17 (‖ περιτίθημι); ἰσχύν 51.9, δόξαν 52.1, σωτηρίαν 2C 6.41, ἀφανισμόν 'devastation' Ez 7.27, αἰσχύνην Ps 34.26, Jb 8.22, 1M 1.28, ἐντροπήν Ps 108.29 (‖ περιβάλλομαι), φόβον Jb 39.19.

2. act., *to clothe*: + acc. rei (clothes) Ge 27.15; + acc. pers., Nu 20.26 (:: ἐκδύω); + double acc., αὐτὸν στολὴν βυσσίνην '.. a robe of fine linen' Ge 41.42; αὐτοὺς χιτῶνας Ex 29.8; ἐνδύσατε αὐτὸν ποδήρη 'clothe him with a long robe' Zc 3.4; Nu 20.28, μανδύαν καὶ περικεφαλαίαν 'woolen cloak and helmet' 1K 17.38; + dat. and acc., Jb 39.19. **b**. fig., "I shall clothe his enemies with shame" Ps 131.18, σωτηρίαν ib. 16; τὸν οὐρανὸν σκότος Is 50.3, ^ἀνθρώπους^ ἰσχύν Si 17.3; *s* divine spirit, *o* hum. Jd 6.34 A (B: ἐνδυναμέω 'empower'), 1C 12.19, 2C 24.20. **c**. pf. and plpf. act. in the sense of mid.: + acc. (clothes), Le 16.23 (:: ἐκδύομαι), 1K 17.5, 2K 6.14, Ez 9.2, Ju 9.1; ἐνδύματα ἀλλότρια 'alien clothes' Zp 1.8; δικαιοσύνην Jb 29.14; rarely also aor., 2K 14.2B.

Cf. ἔνδυμα, ἐνδιδύσκω, ἀνα~, ἐπι~, περιβάλλω, περιτίθημι, στολίζω, ἀπο~, ἐκδύω.

ἐνέδρα, ας. f. ʃ

ambush: Jo 8.7, 9, ἐγκάθηται ~ᾳ Ps 9.29. Cf. ἔνεδρον, ἐνεδρεύω.

ἐνεδρεύω: fut. ἐνεδρεύσω; aor. ἐνήδρευσα, subj. ἐνεδρεύσω, impv. ἐνέδρευσον.

1. *to lie in ambush for*: abs. and *s* ἄρκος 'bear' La 3.10 (‖ ἐν κρυφαίοις), ὡς λέων 'like a lion' Ps 9.30 (‖ ἐγκάθημαι), ἐν στενοῖς 'in narrow places' Jb 24.11, γλώσσῃ 'with a tongue' Si 5.14; + acc. pers., De 19.11, La 4.19; τὸν δίκαιον Wi 2.12; εἰς αἷμα Si 11.32; θήραν 'prey' Si 27.10. **b**. tr. *to position troops in ambush*: + acc., ἐπὶ Σικιμα τέσσαρας ἀρχάς (B: dat.) 'four detachments on Sichem' Jd 9.34 A.

2. *to conceive an insidious plan*: + ἵνα Su 28 LXX.

Cf. ἐνέδρα, ἔνεδρον, ἐγκάθημαι, ἐγκαθίζω, λοχάω.

ἔνεδρον, ου. n. *(syn. ἐνέδρα: Thucydides +)

1. *treachery*: ἐξ ~ου 'by treacherous means' Nu 35.20, 22.

2. *snare*: ἔθηκαν ~α ὑποκάτω σου 'they (i.e. your enemies) laid snares underneath you' Ob 7.

3. *place where a party in ambush lies*: 1M 9.40.

4. *men laid in ambush*: Jd 9.36; 20.30 A (ἔ. understood), 1M 11.68.

Cf. ἐνεδρεύω, ἐνέδρα.

ἐνεῖδον: ptc. ἐνιδών.ʃ

to remark, observe: Τί ἐνιδὼν ἐποίησας τοῦτο; 'what have you seen that you have done this?' Ge 20.10. Cf. εἶδον and γινώσκω.

ἐνειλέω: pf.ptc.pass. ἐνειλημένος.ʃ

to wrap in sth else: ^ῥομφαία^ ἐνειλημένη ἐν ἱματίῳ 'a sword wrapped in a garment' 1K 21.9 (*L* μάχαιρα .. εἰλημένη). Cf. εἰλέω.

ἔνειμι: pres. 3s ἔνι.

1. *to be present* in a place: τῆς πνοῆς μου ἐνούσης 'my breath being within me' Jb 27.3; τὴν ὑπ' οὐρανὸν καὶ τὰ ἐνόντα πάντα 'the world and all that is in it' 34.13.

2. *to be possible*: ὡς ἔνι μάλιστα 'as much as possible (= very much)' 4M 4.22.
Cf. εἰμί.

ἐνείρω: aor. ἐνεῖρα.ʃ
to thread: + acc., ὀστέοις δὲ καὶ νεύροις με ἐνεῖρας 'you threaded me with bones and sinews' Jo 10.11.

ἕνεκα, ἕνεκεν, εἵνεκεν (cf. Thack. 135): prep. c. gen., also postposition, esp. with pronouns.
1. indicates a reason, cause or ground: ἕνεκα τούτου 'because of this, therefore' Ho 13.6(*a*), ἕνεκεν τούτου Ge 2.24(*a*), Mi 1.8(*a*), Hb 1.4(*a*: ‖ διὰ τοῦτο); ἕ. ἀκαθαρσίας Mi 2.10(*d*); ἕ. τῆς γυναικός μου Ge 20.11(*i*); the interrogative in the gen. preceding, τίνος ἕ. 'on whose account?' Jn 1.7(*g*), 8(*i*), 'why?' Ju 11.3, but ἕ. τίνος 'on what account?' Ma 2.14(*a*); Jn 1.14(*f*); τίνος ἕ. αἰτίας 'for what reason?' 3M 5.18; the rel. pron. preceding and the main clause preceding, οὗ εἵνεκεν 'on the ground that ..' Ge 19.8(*j*), 22.16(*o*), 38.26(*b*), Nu 14.43(*b*); + τοῦ inf., Ex 20.20(*j*), Am 1.6(*a* ‖ ἀνθ' ὧν vs. 3), 11(*a* ‖ ἀνθ' ὧν vs. 9, 13). **b.** οὗ εἵνεκεν conj. 'because': Nu 10.31(*b*). **c.** *thanks to*: pers., ἕ. σοῦ Ge 12.13(*h*, ‖ διὰ σέ), 18.24(*k*) (‖ vs. 26 διά + acc.).
2. *for the sake of, for the benefit of*: Ex 18.8(*i*), Zp 3.19(*k*).
3. indicates a purpose or goal w. τοῦ inf.: ἕ. τοῦ μὴ ὀνομάσαι τὸ ὄνομα κυρίου 'in order that nobody will mention the Lord's name' Am 6.10(*j*); Ez 40.4(*k*), 1E 6.11(*q*).
*4. *in return for, in exchange for*: ἀπέδοντο ἀργυρίου δίκαιον καὶ πένητα ἕνεκεν ὑποδημάτων 'they sold a righteous man for silver and a poor man for shoes' Am 2.6(*d*); ἕνεκεν δώρων 'in return for gifts' Is 5.23(*p*).
Cf. διά, **II**.
a) עַל; *b*) οὗ εἵνεκεν כִּי עַל כֵּן; *c*) עַל דְּבַר; *d*) בַּעֲבוּר; *e*) לְבַעֲבוּר; *f*) -בְּ; *g*) בְּשֶׁל; *h*) בִּגְלָל; *i*) בַּאֲשֶׁר לְ־; *j*) כִּי; *k*) לְמַעַן [Zp 3.19, word div.]; *l*) תַּחַת; *m*) אוֹדוֹת; *n*) עַל אוֹדוֹת; *o*) כִּי יַעַן; *p*) עֵקֶב; *q*) לְ.

ἐνενήκοντα. indecl. num.
ninety: Ge 5.9.

ἐνενηκονταετής, ές.ʃ
ninety years old: ***s*** hum., 2M 6.24.

ἐνεξουσιάζομαι: aor.pass. ἐνεξουσιάσθην.ʃ
1. *to bring to submission*: pass., ***o*** hum., through carnal lust, Si 47.19.
2. *to pretend to authority*: Si 20.8, cf. Ryssel ad loc.
Cf. ἐξουσία, ἐξουσιάζω: Caird 1968.472.

ἐνεός, ά, όν.ʃ
incapable of speaking: ***s*** dog, Is 56.10; Ep Je 40, Pr 17.28. Cf. ἄλαλος.

ἐνεργάζομαι: aor.inf. ~γάσασθαι.ʃ
to effect among: + dat.pers., acc. rei, συμφοράν 'calamity' 2M 14.40. Cf. ἐργάζομαι.

ἐνέργεια, ας. f.ʃ
activity, operation: στοιχείων 'of the elements (of the universe)' Wi 7.17; δύναμιν καὶ ~αν 13.4; ὅπλων 'of weapons' 18.22; τοῦ θεοῦ 7.26, 3M 5.28, τοῦ δεσπότου 5.12; θεία 2M 3.29; προνοίας 'of providence' 3M 4.21. Cf. ἐνεργέω, ἐνέργημα.

ἐνεργέω: aor. ἐνήργησα.ʃ
to execute a task: abs., ἐν τῇ σκηνῇ τοῦ μαρτυρίου Nu 8.24, τίς ἐνήργησε καὶ ἐποίησε ταῦτα; Is 41.4, ψυχὴν ἐνεργοῦσαν Wi 15.11, ***s*** πῦρ 16.17; pass., ***o*** τὰ κατὰ τὸν ναόν 'the construction works around the temple' 1E 2.18. **b.** *to work on*: + acc., θησαυρίσματα 'fortunes' Pr 21.6, τῷ ἀνδρὶ ἀγαθά 31.12.
Cf. ἔργον, ἐργάζομαι, ἐνέργημα.

ἐνέργημα, ατος. n.ʃ
that which is executed and performed: by God, Si 16.15¶; w. ref. to the five senses, 17.5¶. Cf. ἐνεργέω, ἐνέργεια.

ἐνεργός, όν.ʃ
appointed for work: ***s*** ἡμέρα '(working) day' Ez 46.1. Cf. ἔργον.

ἐνευλογέομαι: fut.pass. ἐνευλογήθησομαι; aor.inf. ~γηθῆναι.*
1. *to make happy*: ***o*** hum. and pass., also with an indication of a third party (always Abraham and/or his offspring) becoming a catalyst and instrument, ἐνευλογηθήσονται ἐν σοι πᾶσαι αἱ φυλαὶ τῆς γῆς Ge 12.3, ἐνευλογηθήσονται ἐν τῷ σπέρματί σου πάντα τὰ ἔθνη τῆς γῆς 22.18; Si 44.21; ‖ ἐπαινέω Ps 9.24.
2. *to enjoy the benefit of*: + gen. rei, ἀπαρχῆς (*L* ~ήν) 'first-fruits' 1K 2.29.
Cf. εὐλογέω.

ἐνευφραίνω.ʃʃ
mid. *to rejoice* in: ἔν τινι Pr 8.31 (‖ εὐφραίνομαι). Cf. εὐφραίνω.

ἐνεχυράζω: fut. ἐνεχυράσω; aor. ἠνεχύρασα, subj. ἐνεχυράσω, inf. ἐνεχυράσαι.
to take in pledge as pawn: + acc. rei, μύλον .. ἐπιμύλιον 'a mill .. an upper millstone' De 24.6; + acc. cogn., ἐνεχύρασμα ἐνεχυράσῃς τὸ ἱματίον τοῦ πλησίον 'you take the neighbour's garment in pledge' Ex 22.26; ἐνεχυρασμόν Ez 18.16 (‖ καταδυναστεύω); ψυχήν 'life' De 24.6; ἐνέχυρον 'pledge' 24.10; μὴ ἐνεχυράζετε τὰς βουλὰς κυρίου 'Stop putting a deadline on the Lord's intentions' Ju 8.16; + acc. pers., Jb 22.6. Cf. ἐνεχύρασμα, ἐνεχυρασμός, ἐνέχυρον.

ἐνεχύρασμα, ατος. n.ʃ *
security taken: cogn. obj., ἐ. ἐνεχυράσῃς τὸ ἱματίον 'take the garment as security' Ex 22.26; ἐ.

ἀποδῷ 'return the security' Ez 33.15 (967 ~μον, || ἅρπαγμα). Cf. ἐνεχυράζω.

ἐνεχυρασμός, οῦ.ʃ

security taken: ὀφείλοντος 'of a debtor' Ez 18.7; ~ὸν οὐκ ἀπέδωκε 'did not return the pledge' 18.12 (|| καταδυναστεύω); ~ὸν οὐκ ἐνεχύρασε 'did not take pledge' 18.16. Cf. ἐνεχυράζω and LSG s.v.

ἐνέχυρον, ου. n.

security taken: cogn. obj. of ἐνεχυράζω De 24.10. Cf. ἐνεχυράζω.

ἐνέχω: pf.pass. ἐνέσχημαι.ʃ

1. *to have a grudge against*: + dat. pers., || λοιδορεύω Ge 49.23.

2. *to keep held, entangled, involved*: pass. and + ἐν, *o* thought Ez 14.4, pers. 14.7; life, + dat. rei, ἀσεβείαις 3M 6.10.

Cf. ἐγκοτέω, μνησικακέω: Spicq 2.3-5.

ἐνῆλιξ, ικος. m./f.ʃ

one who is in the prime of his or her life: 4M 18.9. Cf. ἀκμή.

ἔνθα. adv.ʃ

1. *in that just-mentioned place*: 4M 6.25.

2. ἔ. καὶ ἔ. 'on either side': 4K 2.8, 14, 1M 6.45. **b**. οὐ .. ἔ. καὶ ἔ. 'not .. to any place' 4K 5.25. Cf. ἔνθεν.

ἐνθάδε. adv.ʃ

at this place: 2M 12.27. **b**. *to this place*: 3M 6.25. Cf. ὧδε, αὐτοῦ.

ἔνθεμα, ατος. n.ʃ

**ornament*: round the neck of a woman, Ct 4.9.

ἐνθέμιον, ου. n.ʃ

socket of a lampstand: Ex 38.16*bis*.

ἔνθεν. adv.

1. ἔ. καὶ ἔ. 'on either side': Ex 26.13; τρεῖς ἔ. καὶ τρεῖς ἔ. 'three on either side' Ez 40.10; || ἐξ ἀμφοτέρων τῶν μέρων 'on both sides' Ex 32.15; 37.13; "the water divided to right and left" 4K 2.8. Cf. ἔνθα.

2. + gen., *on this side of* (from the speaker's perspective): ἔ. τοῦ ποταμοῦ Da 12.5 LXX (TH ἐντεῦθεν).

ἔνθεσμος, ον.ʃ*

lawful: *s* supplication, 3M 2.21.

ἐνθουσιάζω.ʃ

to be madly taken up by: + dat. (money), Si 34.7.

ἐνθρονίζω: aor. ἐνεθρόνισα.ʃ

to enthrone: + acc., ἐπὶ πάντων τὸν .. νοῦν 'the .. intellect over all' 4M 2.22. Cf. θρόνος.

ἐνθρύπτω: aor. ἐνέθρυψα; pf.ptc.pass. ἐντεθρυμμένος.ʃ

to crumble and put into liquid: + acc., bread, Bel 33.

ἐνθυμέομαι: fut. ~μηθήσομαι; aor. ἐνεθυμήθην, subj. ἐνθυμηθῶ, ptc. ~μηθείς, inf. ~μηθῆναι, impv. ~μήθητι; pf.ptc.pass. ἐντεθυμημένος.

1. *to give serious thought to*: *s* hum., ἀξίως 'worthily of ..' Wi 7.15, ἐν τῇ καρδίᾳ ὅπως μὴ ἀλισγηθῇ .. '.. so that he would not be defiled ..' Da 1.8 LXX (TH ἔθετο ἐπὶ τὴν καρδίαν); + acc., τὴν τρίβον αὐτῆς 'its path' Ba 3.31, τὰς ὁδοὺς αὐτοῦ Si 16.20 (|| διανοέομαι); + inf., βουλεύσασθαι .. εἰσελθεῖν 'whether he should enter ..' 3M 1.10; *s* God and + ὅτι, Ge 6.6, or possibly **4**; *s* hum. and a ὡς clause, 4M 5.13; + a ὅτι clause, 8.21.

*2. *to conceive mentally*: + acc., ἐποίησε κύριος ἃ ἐνεθυμήθη La 2.17; πονηρόν 'evil things' Si 17.31, κατὰ τοῦ κυρίου πονηρά Wi 3.14, cf. καθὼς ἐνεθυμεῖτο 'the way he was planning' 1M 6.8; pass., τῆς ἐντεθυμημένης βουλῆς 'the conceived plan' 3M 1.25.

3. *to infer, conclude*: τί θέλει ὁ κύριος 'what the Lord's will is' Wi 9.13 (|| γινώσκω); + περί τινος 6.15.

4. *to take to heart, feel irritated*. + ὅτι, Ge 6.6 (*s* God), cf. 6.7.

*5. *to take a liking* to: abs., ὅσοι ἐνθυμοῦνται 'as many as are so minded' 1E 8.11, οὕτως Is 10.7 (|| λογίζομαι); + gen. pers. (female), ἐνθυμηθῇς αὐτῆς καὶ λάβῃς αὐτὴν σεαυτῷ γυναῖκα De 21.11.

Cf. ἐνθύμημα, ἐνθύμιος, διανοέομαι, λογίζομαι, φρονέω, ἀρέσκω: Schmidt 3.642-4.

ἐνθύμημα, ατος. n.

that to which one's heart is inclined: πονηρὸν ἐ. Si 37.3; ἐ. διανοιῶν 1C 28.9 *L*; πορεύσονται ὀπίσω τῶν ~άτων τῆς καρδίας αὐτῶν τῆς πονηρᾶς Je 3.17, sim. Ez 20.16; || ὁδοί Ez 14.22, 24.14, || αἵματα ib.; w. ref. to objects of idolatry, 23.37, a word very frequent in Ez (19x), and alw. pl. Cf. ἐνθυμέομαι.

ἐνθύμιος, ον.ʃ

subst. n., *that which is on one's mind*, 'thought, idea': Ps 75.11. Cf. ἐνθυμέομαι.

ἐνιαύσιος, α, ον.

one-year-old: *s* cultic animals, πρόβατον Ex 12.5; ἀμνός 29.38, Nu 28.3; πρόβατον Le 14.10; ἐν μόσχοις ~οις 'with one-year-old bulls' Mi 6.6. Cf. ἐνιαυτός.

ἐνιαυτός, οῦ. m.

year: || ἡμέρα Ge 1.14; || ἔτος 47.17 (see vs. 18), Le 25.53 (|| ἔτος vs. 50); αἱ ἡμέραι Ιακωβ ~ῶν τῆς ζωῆς αὐτοῦ ἑκατὸν τεσσαράκοντα ἑπτὰ ἔτη Ge 47.28, ἁγιάσετε τὸ ἔτος τὸ πεντηκοστὸν ~όν '.. for a year' Le 25.10 (ἐνιαυτός "with the focus upon duration" LN 67.168), 25.15; ~ὸν κατ' ~όν. 'year in year out' De 14.21, see further s.v. κατά **II 8 b-c**; κατ' ~όν 'every year' Zc 14.16; ἐ. ἡμερῶν 'a full year' Le 25.29 (|| ἐ. ὅλος vs. 30).

Cf. ἐνιαύσιος and ἔτος.

ἐνίημι: aor. ἐνῆκα.ʃ

to infuse gradually: + acc. rei, αὐτοῖς φόβον 4M

4.10, τὸν θυμόν σου καὶ τὴν ὀργῆν σου εἰς ἡμᾶς Ba 2.20.

ἔνιοι, αι, α.ʃ

some out of a group: subst.m., 3M 2.31, 3.4.

ἐνίοτε. adv.ʃ

sometimes: Si 37.14.

ἐνίστημι: 2aor. ἐνέστην, ptc. ἐνστάς; pf.act. ἐνεστηκώς, ἐνεστώς.ʃ

1. intr. (pres.mid., 2aor., pf.act.) *to begin*: *s* a particular period of time, 3K 12.24[x], 1E 5.46, 9.6, 4M 2.8. Cf. Renehan 2.66.

2. *to be proceeding at the moment of speech or writing*: τὸ ἐνεστὸς ἔτος 'the present year' Es B 6 o'.

3. *to be present* or *come on*: *s* war and + dat. pers., 1M 8.24, 12.44; angst, 2M 3.17; misery, 6.9; ἐνέστη κρίσις πρὸς τὸν M. 'a case was opened against M.' 4.43; δυσμένεια 'animosity' 12.3, ταραχή 'disturbance' 3M 3.24; τὰ ἐνεστῶτα 'the current situation' 1.16.

ἐνισχύω: fut. ~χύσω; aor. ἐνίσχυσα, impv. ~ίσχυσον, 3s ~χυσάτω, ptc. ~χύσας, inf. ~χῦσαι, subj. ~χύσω.

I. tr. *to strengthen, give strength to*: + acc. pers., ἐνισχύσει κύριος τοὺς υἱοὺς Ισραηλ Jl 3.16, ἐπί τινα 'against sbd' Jd 3.12, + βοηθέω 'to help' Is 41.10; τοὺς βραχίονας Ez 30.25 (|| κατισχύω vs. 24); + acc., τὸ ἠσθενηκός 'the weakened (sheep)' 34.4, πόλιν ἐν πολιορκήσει '.. by fortification' Si 50.4; metaph., τὴν βουλήν σου '(backing up) your decision' Ez 27.9; ὁρισμόν '(to take) a resolute decision' Da 6.7 TH; τὴν ψυχήν μου PSol 16.12 (*s* God); τὰς χεῖράς τινος 'to give sbd a hand' Jd 9.24B (A: κατισχύω), cf. ἐν χερσὶν αὐτῶν 2E 1.6 (|| βοηθέω 1E 2.8).

II. intr. ***1**. *to show oneself to be stronger than* (τινι): ἐνισχύσει αὐτῷ Ιακωβ Ho 10.11.

***2**. *to display strength*: μετὰ θεοῦ Ge 32.28 (|| πρὸς θεόν 'vis-à-vis God' Ho 12.3); μετὰ ἀγγέλου 'in contest against an angel' 12.4. **b**. *to exert strong pressure*: ἐπί τινα Da 11.5 TH (LXX κατισχύω τινα), Ne 10.29.

***3**. *to grow in intensity and severity, gain strength*: *s* famine (λιμός), Ge 12.10, 43.1, 47.13, cf. 41.31; pers. 33.14; ψεῦδος καὶ οὐ πίστις Je 9.3. Cf. στερεόω **3**.

***4**. *to exert oneself, make physical effort*: ἐνισχύσας .. ἐκάθισεν ἐπὶ τὴν κλίνην Ge 48.2; Is 57.10; ἐνισχῦσαι καὶ ἀνδρίζεσθαι Da 11.1 LXX.

***5**. *to hold firmly and devotedly to*: abs. 3M 2.32; αὐτῷ De 32.43 (|| προσκυνέω); ἐν ὁδοῖς Δαυιδ Si 48.22.

Cf. ἰσχύς, κατισχύω, βοηθέω, δύναμαι.

ἐννακόσιοι, αι, α. num.

nine hundred: ἔτη ἐννακόσια καὶ τριάκοντα '930 years' Ge 5.5; ἐννακόσια πεντήκοντα ἔτη '950 years' 9.29.

ἐννέα. indecl. num.

nine: Ge 5.27; ἐννέα καὶ εἴκοσι 'twenty-nine' Ex 39.1.

ἐννεακαίδεκα: indecl. num.ʃ

nineteen: ἐ. ἄνδρες 2K 2.30.

ἐννεακαιδέκατος, η, ον.

nineteenth: 1C 24.16.

ἐννέμω.ʃ

mid. *to live amongst*: *s* hum., 3M 3.25. Cf. κατοικέω.

ἔννευμα, ατος. n.ʃ

signal made: δακτύλων 'with fingers' Pr 6.13. Cf. ἐννεύω.

ἐννεύω.ʃ

to signal: by the eye, ὀφθαλμῷ Pr 6.13 (|| σημαίνω), ὀφθαλμοῖς 10.10. Cf. ἔννευμα, διανεύω, σημαίνω.

ἐννοέω: fut.pass. ~νοηθήσομαι; aor. ἐνενόησα, impv. ~νόησον, pass. ~ενοήθην, ~νοήθητι, subj. pass. ~νοηθῶ.

1. *to ponder*: act. εἴς τινα Ba 2.16; mid. Is 41.20, + acc. rei, Ju 9.5, ἔν τινι (subject matter) Si 14.21 (|| διανοέομαι); + ὅτι 4M 1.24.

2. *to conceive in mind, hatch an idea of*: + acc., κακὰ πρὸς θεόν Jb 1.5; + inf. 2K 20.15 *L* (B: simp.).

Cf. ἐννόημα, διανοέομαι, λογίζομαι, φρονέω.

ἐννόημα, ατος. n.ʃ

that which results from pondering: Si 21.11. Cf. διανόημα.

ἔννοια, ας. f.

1. *that which is on one's mind*, 'thought; design': pl., σῆς καρδίας Pr 23.19, ἔλεγχος ~ῶν ἡμῶν 'a reproof of our thoughts' Wi 2.14; + κατά τινος Su 28 TH.

2. *ability to think*: + αἴσθησις Pr 1.4, || αἴ. 18.15, + γνῶσις 8.12.

Cf. διάνοια.

ἔννομος, ον.ʃ

conforming to the law: *s* life, Si prol. 14. Cf. ἐννόμως, νόμος: Wagner 123.

ἐννόμως. adv.ʃ .

in conformity with the law: βιοτεύειν 'to live' Si prol. 36; + προσεχόντως 'carefully, attentively' Pr 31.25 (|| νομοθέσμως vs. 28). Cf. ἔννομος.

ἐννοσεύω.ʃ

to build a nest: ἐν ταῖς κέδροις 'among the cedars' Je 22.23; περιστεραὶ .. ἐν πέτραις 'pigeons .. among rocks' 31.28; Ps 103.17. Cf. νοσσεύω, νοσσιά.

ἐννοσσοποιέω: aor.mid.ptc. ~ποιησάμενος.ʃ*
mid. *to make oneself a nest on*: *s* bird, τὰς τούτων ἄκρας 'the tops of them [= trees]' 4M 14.16. Cf. νοσσοποιέω, νοσσεύω.

ἔννυχος, ον.ʃ
nocturnal: *s* ἀσφάλεια 'guard' 3M 5.5. Cf. νύξ.

ἐνοικειόω.ʃ
pass. *to be related*: + dat. pers., Es 8.1 o'.

ἐνοικέω: fut. ~κήσω, aor. subj. ~κήσω.
to dwell in: ἐν ^τῇ γῇ^ Le 26.32, ἐπὶ τῆς γῆς Is 24.17, οἱ ἐνοικοῦντες ἐν Ιερουσαλημ 5.3; ‖ κατοικέω 32.18, καθίζω Je 29.19, κάθημαι Jd 6.10; + acc., ^τὸν τόπον^ 4K 22.16 (*L* κατοικέω ἐν αὐτῷ), 19 (*L* ἐν αὐτῷ), ^τὴν γῆν^ PSol 17.11. Cf. οἰκέω, ἔνοικος, καθίζω: Casevitz 1985.139-42.

ἐνοικίζω: aor.impv. ἐνοίκισον.ʃ
to allow in as co-resident: τινα Si 11.34.

ἔνοικος, ον.
subst., *inhabitant*: Jd 5.23A (B: κατοικῶν), Je 31.9, 51.2. Cf. ἐνοικέω.

ἐνοπλίζω: aor.ptc.mid. ~λισάμενος; pf.ptc.pass. ἐνωπλισμένος.
to arm: mid. 'to arm oneself' Nu 32.17, De 3.18; pass. εἰς παράταξιν Nu 31.5, εἰς πόλεμον 32.29, ἐνωπλισμένοι καὶ ἐκτεταγμένοι 32.27. Cf. ἐξοπλίζω, καθοπλίζω, ὅπλον.

ἔνοπλος, ον.
equipped with arms: *s* δύναμις 'army' 3M 5.48; subst.m., 2M 14.22. Cf. ὅπλον.

ἐνόρκιος, ον. n.ʃ
subst.n., *oath*: Nu 5.21. Cf. ὅρκος, ἔνορκος.

ἔνορκος, ον.ʃ
bound by oath: + dat. pers., Ne 6.18. Cf. ὅρκος, ἐνόρκως: LSG s.v.

ἐνόρκως. adv.ʃ
on oath: εἶπεν .. ἐ. To 8.20 𝔊ᴵ. Cf. ἔνορκος.

ἐνοχλέω: aor.inf. ἐνοχλῆσαι, pass. ἠνωχλήθην.
1. *to annoy*: + acc. pers., βασιλεῖς καὶ πόλεις 1E 2.19 (‖ κακοποιέω 2E 4.15). Cf. *ND* 3.67.
2. pass. *to suffer from physical ailment*: *s* hum., Ge 48.1 (aged Jacob), "to be indisposed" 1K 19.14; sacrificial animals, Ma 1.13 (‖ χωλός). **b**. *to suffer damage* or *loss* in general: Da 6.2 TH.
Cf. ἄρρωστος, ἀσθενέω, μαλακίζω: Lee 66; LSG s.v.

ἔνοχος, ον.
1. *deserving of punishment* or *penalty*: abs., Ex 22.3, Nu 35.27, Is 54.17, subst. ~ους ἠφίεις 'you forgave the guilty' Su 53 LXX (TH αἴτιος); οὐ καθαριεῖ τὸν ~ον Ex 34.7, Nu 14.18; + dat., θανάτῳ Ge 26.11 (on the dative case, see, Wilcken 13.11, Diodor S. 27.4 and cf. θανάτου Es 4.7 *L*, Mt 26.66); αἵματι 'capital punishment' De 19.10; + inf., ἀναιρεθῆναι Nu 35.31. **b**. + dat. of ground: ῥήμασι στόματός σου 'for your utterances' Jb 15.5. **c**. + dat. of the punished: ἔ. ἑαυτῷ ἔσται 'shall have only himself to blame' Jo 2.19*a*.
2. *liable to the imputation of*: ἱεροσυλίας 'of temple-robbery' 2M 13.6.
*__3__. *having become captivated and fascinated*, 'hooked on': τούτων 'by them' Si prol. 13.
Cf. αἴτιος, ἀναίτιος: Preisigke I 496.

ἐνσείω: fut. ~σείσω; aor. ἐνέσεισα, ptc. ~σείσας.
to cause to move swiftly and forcefully: + acc. and dat. (aim), 2M 14.46; so as to assail sbd (dat.), *s* horse, τὰς ὁπλάς 'the hooves' 2M 3.25. **b**. intr.: + dat., θηριωδῶς τῷ τείχει 'wildly at the wall' 2M 12.15.

ἐνσιτέομαι.ʃ*
to feed oneself: ἔν τινι Jb 40.30. Cf. σῖτος.

ἐνσκολιεύομαι.ʃ*
to twist and turn oneself: Jb 40.24¶, see Caird 1968.471 and cf. Walters 76.

ἔνταλμα, ατος.ʃ n.
= ἐντολή, q.v.: ~ατα ἀνθρώπων καὶ διδασκαλίας Is 29.13; divine, 55.11, Jb 23.11f. Alw. pl. Cf. ἐντολή.

ἐντάσσω: aor. ἐνέταξα, impv. ~ταξον, pass. ἐνετάγην; pf.ptc.pass. ~τεταγμένος
1. *to place* (in a certain location): + acc., ἀδάμαντα ἐν μέσῳ λαοῦ μου Am 7.8; ἐν βιβλίῳ 2E 7.17, ἐν γραφῇ Da 10.21 TH.
2. *to put down in writing*: + acc., γραφήν Da 5.24 TH, δόγμα 6.10 TH.
Cf. τάσσω, τίθημι.

ἐνταῦθα. adv.
1. *in this place*, 'here': Οὐκ ἦν ἐ. πόρνη 'there was no harlot here' Ge 38.21 (‖ vs. 22 ὧδε).
2. *to this place*: Ps 72.10.
3. *soon or immediately after that*: w. ref. to the past, 3M 2.21.
Cf. ὧδε, ἐντεῦθεν, αὐτοῦ (s.v. αὐτός **4**), ἐκεῖ.

ἐνταφιάζω: aor. ἐνεταφίασα, inf. ἐνταφιάσαι.ʃ *
to prepare for burial, 'lay out': + acc. pers. (dead person), Ge 50.2 (embalming included? See Harl ad loc.). Cf. ἐνταφιαστής, τάφος, θάπτω.

ἐνταφιαστής, οῦ. m.ʃ *
one who prepares for burial, 'undertaker': Ge 50.2. Cf. ἐνταφιάζω: Morenz 257; LSG s.v.

ἐντείνω: fut.act. ἐντενῶ; aor.act. ἐνέτεινα, impv. ἔντεινον; pf.pass.ptc. ἐντεταμένος.
to stretch tight: obj. τόξον 'a bow', Ho 7.16, Hb 3.9, Is 5.28, Je 4.29, cf. Zc 9.13 and τὴν γλῶσσαν αὐτῶν ὡς τόξον Je 9.3; ἐντείνοντες καὶ βάλλοντες τόξον Ps 77.9; τόξον understood, 44.5. Cf. ἐκτείνω, τείνω.

ἐντέλλομαι: fut. ~τελοῦμαι; aor. ἐνετειλάμην, subj. ἐντείλωμαι, impv. ἔντειλαι, inf. ~τείλασθαι; pf. ἐντέταλμαι.

1. *to issue an order* or *instruction, enjoin*: + dat. pers., καθὰ ἐνετείλατο αὐτῷ ὁ θεός Ge 21.4; Nu 27.22 (‖ συντάσσω vs. 23), 36.2 (‖ συντάσσω); πρός τινα (recipient of an order) 2C 19.9 (*L* dat. pers.); and also + acc. rei, πάντα ὅσα ἐγὼ ἐντέλλομαί σοι Ex 34.11; τοὺς λόγους μου καὶ τὰ νόμιμά μου .. ὅσα ἐγὼ ἐντέλλομαι .. τοῖς προφήταις Zc 1.6; the content of the order is expressed in the foll. co-ordinate clause with a verb in a finite tense, κύριος ἐντέλλεται καὶ πατάξει τὸν οἶκον .. Am 6.11; τῷ δράκοντι καὶ δήξεται αὐτούς '(I will command) the serpent, which will bite them' 9.3, sim. 9.4, 9, Na 1.14; περί τινος 'concerning sbd / sth' Ge 12.20, Nu 8.20; πρός + acc., 'with reference to, regarding,' Ex 12.50, 25.21, πρὸς λαὸν αὐτοῦ '(commands) meant for his people' Si 45.3; + cogn. obj., ἐντολαί, ἃς ἐνετείλατο κύριος τῷ Μωυσῇ πρὸς τοὺς υἱοὺς Ισραηλ Le 27.34, cf. Renehan 2.66; αὐτῷ ἐν Χωρεβ πρὸς πάντα τὸν Ισραηλ προστάγματα καὶ δικαιώματα Ma 4.6; ὑπέρ τινος 'concerning sbd' Na 1.14; by direct speech introduced by a pres. ptc. nom. of λέγω – ἐνετείλατο .. λέγων Ἀπὸ παντὸς ξύλου .. φάγῃ 'he commanded.. "From every tree.. you may eat"' Ge 2.16, 28.1, 32.4; with an inf., ταῖς νεφέλαις ἐντελοῦμαι τοῦ μὴ βρέξαι .. ὑετόν 'I shall command the clouds not to rain ..' Is 5.6, μὴ φαγεῖν Ge 3.11; συμπροπέμψαι 'to send off' 12.20; ἔντειλαι ταῦτα, λαβεῖν αὐτοῖς ἁμάξας .. 'Command thus, for them to get wagons..' 45.19; + ὅπως and subj., 1M 12.23, 15.39; + ἵνα 2M 2.2.

2. *to prescribe, charge with the execution of* or *adherence to*: + acc. rei and dat. pers., πάντα τὰ σημεῖα, ἃ ἐνετείλατο αὐτῷ Ex 4.28; παρέβησαν .. ἐκ τῆς ὁδοῦ, ἧς ἐνετείλω αὐτοῖς 'they have departed from the way which you commanded them' 32.8, sim. De 11.28, PSol 18.10. **b**. *to prescribe and pronounce with authority*: τῇ οἰκουμένῃ ὅλῃ κακὰ καὶ τοῖς ἀσεβέσι τὰς ἁμαρτίας αὐτῶν 'the whole world calamities and the impious the deserts of their sins' Is 13.11, τὴν εὐλογίαν καὶ ζωήν Ps 132.3; *o* διαθήκη 110.9, Jd 2.20, Je 11.4, πρόσταγμα Ps 7.7, νόμος Si 24.23.

3. *to transfer the authority to and place under the charge of*: pass., + acc. pers., εἰς χεῖρας σιδήρου 'to the power of the sword' Jb 15.22. **b**. *to authorise* sbd *to act* as: + dat. pers., εἰς ἄρχοντα 'as ruler' 1K 13.14, εἰς ἡγούμενον 'as leader' 25.30.

Cf. ἐντολή, κελεύω, ἐνυπο~, ἐπι~, προσ~, συντάσσω: Pelletier 1982; Lee 2003.517-23; Muraoka 2006.

ἔντερον, ου. n.ʃ

piece of the guts or *intestines*: συνεστρέφετο τὰ ~α αὐτοῦ ἐπὶ τῷ ἀδελφῷ αὐτοῦ 'his intestines were contracting over his brother' Ge 43.30; προβαλὼν τὰ ~α 'having plucked out his entrails' 2M 14.46; ὕπνος ὑγιείας ἐπὶ ~ῳ μετρίῳ 'healthy sleep depends on moderate eating' Si 34.20. Cf. ἔγκατον.

ἐντεῦθεν adv.

1. *from here*: ἀπήρκασιν ἐ. 'they have left here' Ge 37.17. **b**. *at this place*: To 7.11 𝔊ᴵᴵ. **c**. metaph., *in view of this*: 1E 4.22.

2. *on this side*: ἐ. εἷς καὶ ἐ. εἷς 'the one on this side and the other on the other side, one each on either side' Ex 17.12; φραγμὸς ἐ. καὶ φραγμὸς ἐ. 'a fence on either side' Nu 22.24; 1K 17.3*L* (B: ἐνταῦθα).

3. + gen., *on the side of*: Da 12.5 TH (LXX ἔνθεν).

Cf. ὧδε, ἐνταῦθα, ἐκεῖθεν.

ἔντευξις, εως. f.ʃ

private conversation with a high-ranking personage, 'audience': 2M 4.8. Cf. ἐντυγχάνω.

ἐντήκω: fut.pass. ~τακήσομαι; pf. ἐντέτηκα.ʃ

1. intr. *to flow into*: metaph., ἡμῖν .. φιλονεικία '.. a contentious spirit' 4M 8.26.

2. pass. *to melt* or *crumble and disappear*: *s* hum., ἐν ταῖς ἀδικίαις ὑμῶν Ez 24.23 (‖ τήκομαι 4.17).

Cf. τήκω.

ἐντίθημι: aor.ptc. ~θείς, mid.impv.2pl ~θεσθε; pf. ptc. ~τεθεικώς.ʃ

to place inside: + acc., 2M 3.27; λήθην κατὰ διάνοιαν 'forgetfulness in his mind' 3M 5.28; pass., 2E 5.8; mid., + acc. rei, καρδίαν 'intelligence' Pr 8.5 (‖ νοέω). Cf. τίθημι.

ἔντιμος, ον.

1. *in honour, of high rank*: *s* hum., ἄρχοντας .. ἐντιμοτέρους Nu 22.15; opp. ταπεινός 'humble' 1K 18.23*L* (B: ἔνδοξος); divine name, τὸ ὄνομα τὸ ~ον καὶ τὸ θαυμαστὸν τοῦτο De 28.58; kingship, Da 2.37 TH.

2. *valuable*: *s* pers., "more valuable than unsmeltered gold" Is 13.12; rei, λίθον πολυτελῆ ἐκλεκτὸν ἀκρογωνιαῖον ~ον 'costly, choice, corner-stone' 28.16; a pers.'s name, Ps 71.14.

Cf. ἐντίμως, τιμή, ἐντιμόω.

ἐντιμόω: aor.impv.pass.3s ἐντιμωθήτω.ʃ *

to regard valuable: pass., *o* hum. life, 4K 1.13, 14. Cf. ἔντιμος.

ἐντίμως. adv.ʃ

in such a manner as to display much respect, 'respectfully': of reception of guests, ἐ. τιμήσω σε Nu 22.17; ἐ. ὑποδεικνύοντες 'declaring with fitting honour' To 12.6 𝔊ᴵ, sim. 12.7 𝔊ᴵᴵ (𝔊ᴵ ἐνδόξως); οἰκοδομήσουσιν 14.5; ἐγήρασεν ἐ. 'was treated with much respect in his old age' 14.13 𝔊ᴵ. Cf. ἔντιμος, ἐνδόξως.

ἐντιναγμός, οῦ. m.ʃ*

colliding: Si 22.13. See Blomqvist 1985.38f.

ἐντινάσσω: aor. ἐνετίναξα, ptc. ~τινάξας.ʃ

to hurl against: + acc. and dat., λίθον αὐτοῖς 1M

2.36; εἴς τινα 2M 4.41. **b.** *to hurl oneself*: in military attack, λεοντηδόν 'like lions' 2M 11.11.

ἐντολή, ῆς. f.

1. *command, order*: issued by God to sbd (πρός τινα) – ἡ ἐ. αὕτη πρὸς ὑμᾶς, οἱ ἱερεῖς 'this command is meant for you, O priests!' Ma 2.1; 2.4; ἐφύλαξεν .. τὰ προστάγματά μου καὶ τὰς ~άς μου καὶ τὰ δικαιώματά μου καὶ τὰ νόμινά μου Ge 26.5; φυλάξῃ τὰ φυλάγματα αὐτοῦ καὶ τὰ δικαιώματα .. καὶ τὰς ~ὰς .. καὶ τὰς κρίσεις .. De 11.1; αἱ ~αὶ καὶ τὰ δικαιώματα καὶ τὰ κρίματα, ἃ ἐνετείλατο κύριος ἐν χειρὶ Μωυσῆ Nu 36.13; ἐ. νόμου Pr 6.23; as cogn. obj., ἐντολάς, ἃς ἐνετείλατο κύριος τῷ Μωυσῇ πρὸς τοὺς υἱοὺς Ισραηλ Le 27.34; issued by king, 2C 24.21, Ne 11.24, αἰνεῖν ἐν ~ῇ Δαυιδ 12.24.

2. *prescribed entitlement*: τῶν Λευιτῶν Ne 13.5.

Cf. ἐντέλλομαι, δια~, συνταγή, δικαίωμα, κέλευσμα, κρίμα, κρίσις, μαρτύριον, νόμιμον, πρόσταγμα, σύνταξις **3**, φύλαγμα: Schrenk, *TDNT* 2.546f.

ἐντομίς, ίδος. f.ʃ *

incision, gash: ἐπὶ ψυχῇ .. ἐν τῷ σώματι Le 19.28 (pagan practice), Je 16.6; ἐπὶ τὰς σάρκας αὐτῶν οὐ κατατεμοῦσιν ~ίδας Le 21.5. Cf. κατατέμνω: LSG s.v.

ἐντός. prep.

within, inside of: + gen., ὁ ἐ. τῶν πυλῶν σου 'within your gates' De 5.14; Ps 38.4, 108.22; τὰ ἐντός μου 'my entrails' 102.1 (ǁ ἡ ψυχή μου), Is 16.11 (ǁ κοιλία), Da 10.16 TH; τὰ ἐ. αὐτοῦ πλήρης δόλου '.. full of sorrow' Si 19.26; τὰ ἐ. τοῦ οἴκου 1M 4.48.

ἐντρέπομαι: fut.pass. ἐντραπήσομαι; aor.pass. ἐνετράπην, inf. ἐντραπῆναι, impv. ἐντράπηθι, subj. ~πῶ, opt.3pl ~πείησαν; pf.pass. ἐντέτραμμαι.

1. *to show respect to*: + acc. God, Ex 10.3; woman to her husband, Si 26.24¶; to the elderly, Wi 2.10 (ǁ φείδομαι); ἐπί τινι - ἐπὶ τῷ κρίματί μου 'my admonition' Si 41.16; ἀπὸ τῶν λόγων 1E 1.45; ἀπὸ προσώπου Ιερεμιου .. καὶ ἐκ στόματος κυρίου 2C 36.12, cf. τὸ πρόσωπόν σου 1K 25.35*L* (B: αἱρετίζω).

2. *to feel overawed by*: + acc. pers., Jb 32.21 (ǁ αἰσχύνομαι); + acc. rei, μέγεθος Wi 6.7, + ἀπὸ προσώπου τινός 1M 1.18. **b.** *to feel humiliated*: defeated on a battlefield, ἐνώπιόν τινος Jd 8.28 A (B: συστέλλομαι), ἀπὸ προσώπου τινός (victor's) 11.33 A (ditto).

3. *to feel shame* for wrongdoing: *s* hum., Nu 12.14; ἡ καρδία αὐτῶν ἡ ἀπερίτμητος 'their uncircumcised heart' Le 26.41; + αἰσχύνομαι Is 41.11, 44.11, 45.16, Ez 36.32 (last + ἔκ τινος), ǁ αἰσχύνομαι Ps 68.7 (ἐπί τινι [pers.]); + περί τινος Si 4.25.

4. *to feel diffident about and hesitate* to do: + inf., 2E 9.6.

Cf. ἐντροπή, αἰδέομαι, αἰσχύνω: Anz 13f.

ἐντρεχής, ές.ʃ

skilful: *s* hum., Si 34.22.

ἔντριτος, ον.ʃ *

of three strands: *s* σπαρτίον 'triple cord' Ec 4.12.

ἔντρομος, ον.

trembling: out of fear and *s* γῆ Ps 17.8, 76.19 (ǁ σαλεύομαι); *s* hum., Da 10.11 TH (LXX τρέμων), + ἔκφοβος 1M 13.2. Cf. τρέμω.

ἐντροπή, ῆς. f.

sense of shame: + αἰσχύνη Ps 34.26; ǁ αἰσχύνη 43.16, ὀνειδισμός 68.8. Cf. ἐντρέπω, αἰδώς, αἰσχύνη: Trench 66-9.

ἐντρυφάω: fut. ~τρυφήσω; aor. ἐνετρύφησα, impv. ~τρύφησον.ʃ

1. *to poke fun, derive* malicious *pleasure* from the misery of: ἐν βασιλεῦσιν 'kings' Hb 1.10.

2. *to experience delight*: ἐν ἀγαθοῖς ἡ ψυχὴ ὑμῶν Is 55.2; lustful, 57.4. At Je 38.20 παιδίον ἐντρυφῶν the sense expected is "(my) darling" ǁ υἱὸς ἀγαπητός; + dat., νεότησιν 'youthfulness' 4M 8.8.

Cf. τρυφερός, κατατρυφάω, ἐμπαίζω. On the Hebraising ἐν instead of the dat., see Helbing, *Kasus.*, 275f.

ἐντρύφημα, ατος. n.ʃ *

thing to take pleasure in: pl., Ec 2.8.

ἐντυγχάνω: aor. ἐνέτυχον, subj. ~τύχω, inf. ~τυχεῖν.

1. *to obtain an audience in order to raise some issue*: abs. 2M 4.36; + dat., τῷ βασιλεῖ Da 6.12 LXX.

2. *to put in a petition*: ἐντύγχανον 2M 6.2 (Hanhart: simp.; see Habicht ad loc.); κατά τινος '(to plead) *against sbd*' Es 7.19 *L*, 1M 8.32, 10.61; + dat. pers., τῷ βασιλεῖ 3M 6.37, τῷ κυρίῳ Wi 8.21 (ǁ δέομαι).

3. *to chance upon*: historical records, books, οἱ ἐντυγχάνοντες 'the readers' 2M 2.25; + dat. rei, τῇδε τῇ βίβλῳ 'this book' 6.12, sim. 15.39.

Cf. ἐντυχία, ἔντευξις, δέομαι: Spicq 2.6-10.

ἐντυχία, ας. f.ʃ

act of petitioning: περί τινος 3M 6.40. Cf. ἐντυγχάνω.

ἔνυδρος, ον.ʃ

having its habitat in water: subst.n., Wi 19.10, 19 (ref. to aquatic animals), sim. 19.19; + birds and quadrupeds, 4M 1.38.

ἐνυπνιάζομαι: fut. ἐνυπνιασθήσομαι; aor.mid. ἐ/ἠνυπνιασάμην, pass. ἐ/ἠνυπνιάσθην, ptc. ἐνυπνιασθείς.

1. *to see an extraordinary vision*: at night, Ge 28.12; + cogn. obj. ἐνύπνιον– οἱ πρεσβύτεροι ὑμῶν ἐνύπνια ~ασθήσονται 'your old men will see visions' Jl 2.28, sim. Da 2.1 TH; Ge 37.5, 9 (|| εἶδον, also 40.8, 41.11, 15, 42.9 – all of dreams seen by Egyptians, see Bickermann 1.188, "a touch of exoticism"), 37.10; De 13.1 (|| προφήτης); ἐν ὕπνῳ Is 29.7. **b**. + dat. pers., *to communicate an extraordinary vision*: illicit and + ψευδοπροφήτης, μαντευόμενος, οἰώνισμα, φάρμακος Je 34.7.

2. *to dream of*: + acc., κοίτην Is 56.10.

Cf. ἐνύπνιον, ἐνυπνιαστής, εἶδον, ὁράω.

ἐνυπνιαστής, οῦ. m.ʃ *

man given to dreaming, 'dreamer': Ge 37.19. Cf. ἐνύπνιον.

ἐνύπνιον, ου. n.

extraordinary vision, 'dream': cogn. obj. of ἐνυπνιάζομαι– οἱ πρεσβύτεροι ὑμῶν ~α ἐνυπνιασθήσονται 'your old men will see visions' Jl 2.28; Ge 37.5; εἶδεν ἐ. 37.9, 40.5, 41.1; ἐ. ἑώρακα 41.15; De 13.1; οἱ ὁρῶντες τὰ ~α Mi 3.7 (|| μάντις); seen at night, Ge 40.5; || ὅραμα Jb 7.14; + μαντεία, οἰωνισμός Si 31.5. Cf. ἐνυπνιάζομαι, ἐνυπνιαστής, ὕπνος, ὄνειρος, ὅραμα, ὅρασις: *ND* 4.136.

ἐνυποτάσσω: fut.pass. ~ταγήσομαι.ʃ*

to give a command: impers. pass., + dat. pers. and inf., To 14.8f. 𝔊II. Cf. συντάσσω.

ἔνυστρον, ου. n.ʃ

fourth stomach of ruminating animals: portion of a sacrifice due to priests De 18.3; ἔ. ἑορτῶν ὑμῶν '.. of your feasts' Ma 2.3.

ἐνώπιος, ον.

I. *found in full view of the public*: ἄρτοι 'shewbread' Ex 25.29(*q*), cf. Pelletier 1967a.366 and *BA* ad loc.

2. *in person, face to face*: ~ον εἶδον ὀφθέντα μοι 'I saw in person the one who appeared to me' Ge 16.13(*r*); ἐλάλησεν κύριος πρὸς Μωυσῆν ~ος ~ίῳ 'the Lord spoke to Moses face to face' Ex 33.11(*q*).

3. *evident*: Pr 8.9(*t*); n.sg. used adverbially, *evidently, manifestly*: Le 13.37(*c*).

II. n. ἐνώπιον as prep. used w. gen., unattested in 2-4M.

1. *in the presence of, in full view of*: ἀπέθανεν .. ἐ... τοῦ πατρὸς αὐτοὺ Ge 11.28(*d*); ἀναστῆναι ἐ. σου 31.35(*g*); "I shall expose her uncleanness before her lovers" Ho 2.10(*a*); Hg 2.3(*c*); 2.14(*b*); mentally and in a description of cultic practices, σφάξει τὸν μόσχον ἐ. κυρίου Le 4.4(*b*) (|| ἔναντι κυρίου). Cf. ἐ. τῶν ὀφθαλμῶν ὑμῶν Je 16.9(*m*). **b**. w. a verb of movement such as διέρχομαι, (δια)πορεύομα, περιπατέω, *s* public figure: "I have been active in your community since my youth until this day" 1K 12.2 (*L* ἀναστρέφομαι), cf. *BA* ad loc.

*__2__. *in the view, judgement of* (Hebraism): μὴ καὶ ~ον ἐμοῦ ἀδυνατήσει Zc 8.6²(*c*); καθὼς οὐχ ὑπάρχοντα ἐ. ὑμῶν 'virtually non-existent so far as you can see' Hg 2.3(*c*); καλὸν ἐ. κυρίου Ma 2.17(*c*); ἐ. ἑαυτῶν ἐπιστήμονες 'wise in their own judgement' Is 5.21 (|| ἐν ἑαυτοῖς)(*p*); "as far as they are concerned, God does not exist" Ps 9.25(-).

Cf. ἔμπροσθεν, ἐναντίος, κατέναντι: Wickenhauser 1910; Johannessohn, *Präp*. 194-6; Sollamo, *Semiprep*., 18-21, 128-30, 311-3.

a) לְעֵינֵי; *b*) לִפְנֵי [+ 1K 2.21 4Q51 for MT עִם]; *c*) בְּעֵינֵי; *d*) עַל־פְּנֵי; *e*) οὗ ἐνώπιον לַחַי; *f*) לְנֹכַח; *g*) מִפְּנֵי; *h*) אֶל; *i*) נֹכַח; *j*) עַד; *k*) פְּנֵי; *l*) אֶל־פְּנֵי; *m*) לְ; *n*) נֶגֶד; *o*) אֶת־פְּנֵי; *p*) נֶגֶד פְּנֵי; *q*) פָּנִים; *r*) הֲלוֹם; *s*) Ar. קֳדָם [To 6.8]; *t*) נָכֹחַ.

ἐνωτίζομαι: fut. ~τιοῦμαι, ~τισθήσομαι; aor. ἐ/ἠνωτισάμην, subj. ἐνωτίσωμαι, impv. ἐνώτισαι, 2pl ἐνωτίσασθε.*

to give ear, listen: abs., || ἀκούω Nu 23.18, Ho 5.1, Jl 1.2, ἐνωτίσατο καὶ ἤκουσεν Je 23.18; + acc. rei, μου τοὺς λόγους Ge 4.23 (|| ἀκούω), τὴν δέησίν μου Ps 142.1 (|| εἰσακούω, ἐπακούω); + dat. rei, ταῖς ἐντολαῖς αὐτοῦ Ex 15.26; πρός με Is 51.4; + gen. rei, προσευχῆς Ps 16.1 (|| εἰσακούω, προσέχω), δεήσεώς μου 38.13. Cf. εἰσ~, ἐπ~, ἀκούω, προσέχω.

ἐνώτιον, ου. n. Mostly in pl.

ear-ring: pl., woman's accessory, χρυσᾶ 'golden' Ge 24.22; τὰ ~α τὰ ἐν τοῖς ὠσὶν αὐτῶν 35.4; τὰ ~α τὰ ἐν τοῖς ὠσὶν τῶν γυναικῶν ὑμῶν καὶ θυγατέρων Ex 32.2; σφραγῖδας καὶ ~α καὶ δακτυλίους καὶ ἐμπλόκια καὶ περιδέξια 35.22; Ho 2.13 (|| καθόρμιον). **b**. sg. and for nose-ring, Ez 16.12, ἐν ῥινί 'on a nose' Pr 11.22.

Cf. κόσμος **3**: Russo 23-59.

ἕξ. num.

six: Gn 30.20+.

ἐξαγγέλλω: fut. ἐξαγγελῶ; aor. ἐξήγγειλα, subj. ἐξαγγείλω, inf. ~γγεῖλαι, impv. ~γειλον.

to give public, vocal expression to: + acc. rei, αἰνέσεις σου 'your praises' Ps 9.15, τὴν δικαιοσύνην σου 70.15 (*s* mouth), τὰ ἔργα αὐτοῦ 106.22, κρίματα 118.13, τὰς ὁδούς μου 118.26; + dat. pers., 55.9; opp. κρύπτω Pr 12.16; || διηγέομαι Si 39.10 (*o* ἔπαινον). Cf. ἀναγγέλλω: Schniewind, *TDNT* 1.69f.

ἐξαγοράζω.ʃ

to gain: + acc., καιρόν Da 2.8 (by delaying tactics).

ἐξαγορεύω: fut. ἐξαγορεύσω; aor. ἐξηγόρευσα, inf. ~ρεῦσαι, subj. ~ρεύσω.

to admit publicly to sth wrongful *having been committed*: abs., ἐν οἴκῳ κυρίου Ba 1.14; + acc., ἁμαρτίαν Le 5.5, Nu 5.7; ἀνομίας .. ἀδικίας .. ἁμαρτίας Le 16.21, sim. Da 9.20 TH (LXX ἐξομολογέομαι); ἐπὶ ἁμαρτίαις Ne 1.6; also + dat. pers., Ps 31.5. Cf. ἐξομολογέομαι.

ἐξαγορία, ας. f.ʃ
*v.n. of prec.: || ἐξομολόγησις PSol 9.6. Cf. ἐξαγορεύω, ἐξομολόγησις.

ἐξαγριαίνω: aor.pass. ἐξηγριάνθην.ʃ
to make savage: pass. *to become savage*, ***s*** animal, πρός τινα Da 8.7 TH (LXX θυμοῦμαι). Cf. ἀγριόω.

ἐξάγω: fut.act. ἐξάξω, pass. ἐξαχθήσομαι; aor. ἐξήγαγον, inf. ἐξαγαγεῖν, ptc. ~γών, impv. ἐξάγαγε, subj. ~γω, opt.3s ~γάγοι.

1. *to cause to move outside*: as a process of the primaeval creation, Ἐξαγαγέτω τὰ ὕδατα ἑρπετά 'Let the waters bring out creeping things' Ge 1.20; Ἐξαγαγέτω ἡ γῆ ψυχὴν ζῶσαν 1.24; + acc. pers., ἐκ τῆς χώρας τῶν Χαλδαίων 11.31; ἐκ τοῦ οἴκου τοῦ πατρός μου 20.13; ἐκ τοῦ τόπου τούτου 19.12; ἔξω 15.5, 19.17; εἰς τὴν ἔρημον ταύτην Ex 16.3; ἐξάξει με εἰς τὸ φῶς 'he will bring me out into the light' Mi 7.9; πρός τινα Ge 19.5, 43.23; for public execution, 'to take out' 38.24, De 17.5, 22.21, Da 2.12 LXX (TH ἀπολέσαι; ἀποκτεῖναι, συναπολέσθαι vs. 13 LXX), εἰς ἐκκλησίαν Si 23.24 (for public enquiry); ἐπὶ τὴν γερουσίαν De 21.19; from detention, Le 24.14; a prisoner set free, ἐκ τοῦ ὀχυρώματος Ge 40.14, 41.14; ἀπὸ τῆς δυναστείας τῶν Αἰγυπτίων 'from the domination by the Egyptians' Ex 6.6 (|| δουλεία ib.; καταδυναστεία vs. 7); ἐγώ εἰμι κύριος ὁ θεὸς ὑμῶν ὁ ἐξαγαγών ὑμᾶς ἐκ γῆς Αἰγύπτου Le 19.36 +; ἐκ μέσου αὐτῶν Ex 7.5; ***o*** animals, τὸν σκνῖφα 'the gnats' Ex 8.18; water, Nu 20.10. Opp. εἰσάγω Ex 3.8, 6.7, Nu 27.17, De 26.8. **b**. metaph., *to remove* from where one would rather remain: + acc. pers. and gen., ἑαυτοὺς τοῦ ἡδίστου βίου 'ourselves from the most delicious life' 4M 8.23 (|| ἀποστερέω 'to deprive'). **c**. intr. *to move out and lead to*: εἴς τι (loci) Jo 15.9.

2. *to bring into existence*: + acc., τίμιον ἀπὸ ἀναξίου 'sth valuable out of sth worthless' Je 15.19, ἄρτον ἐκ τῆς γῆς Ps 103.14; τὸ κρίμα μου Jb 23.7.
Cf. ἄγω, εἰσάγω.

ἐξάδελφος, ου. m.ʃ
nephew: To 1.22, 11.18.

ἔξαιμος, ον.ʃ
drained of blood: ***s*** hum., 2M 14.46.

ἐξαίρετος, ον.ʃ
1. *distinguished, excellent*: δίδωμί σοι Σικιμα ~ον ὑπὲρ τοὺς ἀδελφούς σου I give you Sichem as something unique far above that given to your brothers' Ge 48.22.

2. *taken out of, delivered*: ἐκ κακῶν 'out of hardships' Jb 5.5. Cf. ἐξαιρέω **II 2**.

ἐξαιρέω: fut. ἐξελῶ, mid. ἐξελοῦμαι; aor. ἐξεῖλον, inf. ἐξελεῖν, impv. ἔξελε, mid. ἐξειλάμην, subj. ἐξέλωμαι, opt.3s ἐξέλοιτο, inf. ἐξελέσθαι, impv. ἐξελοῦ, 3pl ἐξελέσθωσαν; pf.mid. ἐξήρημαι.

I. act. *to take out*: + acc. rei, internal organs of a fish cut up, To 6.5 𝔊[II]; honey, Jd 14.9.

2. *to move* from a fixed position, 'remove': + acc. rei, Le 14.40 (followed by ἐκβάλλω).

II. mid. *to carry off* for one's own benefit: τὰ ἀγαθά 'the goods' Mi 7.3.

2. *to free, rescue* from a state of danger, distress or being under sbd else's control (+ acc. and ἔκ τινος): ἐξελοῦ με ἐκ χειρός τοῦ ἀδελφοῦ Ησαυ Ge 32.11; ἐκ τῶν χειρῶν αὐτῶν 37.21, 22; ἐκ χειρὸς Φαραω Ex 18.4, ἐξαιρεῖσθαι ὑμᾶς καὶ σῴζειν ὑμᾶς ἐκ χειρὸς αὐτοῦ Je 49.11; ἐκ θλίψεως Na 2.2, ἐκ καιροῦ πονηροῦ Si 51.12 (|| σῴζω), ἐκ καμίνου πτωχείας 'out of the oven of poverty' Is 48.10, ἐξ ἀναγκῶν 'out of tight corners' Jb 5.19, ἐκ θανάτου Ps 114.8; ἐκ παραπτώματος 'from transgression' Wi 10.1, ἐξ ἁμαρτωλῶν Ps 36.40; ἀπό τινος Nu 35.25, ἀπὸ φόβου ἐχθροῦ ἐξελοῦ τὴν ψυχήν μου Ps 63.2; || ῥύομαι 30.2, 81.4, || λυτρόομαι 58.2, || σῴζω Si 58.8. Cf. ἐξαίρετος **2**. **b**. *to keep oneself free* or *stay clear* from: ἀπὸ πλημμελείας 'from blunders' Si 26.29; + acc. rei, τιμωρίαν 'punishment' 2M 6.26.

3. *to retrieve, restore* that which is unlawfully or violently taken: + acc., ἅρπαγμα Is 42.22.

Cf. ἀφαιρέω, ῥύομαι, σῴζω: Spicq 2.14-7; Buscemi esp. 295-304.

ἐξαίρω: fut. ἐξαρῶ, pass. ἐξαρθήσομαι; aor. ἐξῆρα, inf. ἐξᾶραι, ptc. ἐξάρας, impv. ἔξαρον, 2pl ἐξάρατε, subj. ἐξάρω, pass. ἐξήρθην, inf. ἐξαρθῆναι, subj. ἐξαρθῶ, opt.act.3s ἐξάραι; pf.pass. ἐξῆρμαι, ptc.pass. ἐξηρμένος.

A. tr. **1**. *to lift off*: τοὺς πόδας 'the feet (off the ground to set out on a journey)' Ge 29.1 (|| αἴρω τὸν πόδα Is 58.13), ἐπὶ τὴν κλίνην 49.33 (***s*** a dying man); τάλαντον μολίβου ἐξαιρόμενον 'a talent weight of lead (was) lifted off' Zc 5.7. **b**. *to sweep up and carry off*: abs. and ***s*** πνεῦμα 'wind' Ez 1.4, 13.11, πνοή 13.12.

2. *to raise*: + acc., ἄνευ σοῦ οὐκ ἐξαρεῖ οὐθεὶς τὴν χεῖρα αὐτοῦ ἐπὶ πάσῃ γῇ Αἰγύπτου Ge 41.44 (to initiate an action?); τοὺς ὀφθαλμοὺς αὐτοῦ Nu 24.2; τοὺς υἱοὺς Ισραηλ ἀπὸ θαλάσσης ἐρυθρᾶς Ex 15.22; to take an oath, ἐξῆρα τὴν χεῖρά μου ἐπ' αὐτοὺς .. τοῦ μὴ εἰσαγαγεῖν αὐτοὺς εἰς τὴν γῆν Ez 20.15, sim. 20.23; to bless (with pl.), ἐξάρας Ααρων τὰς χεῖρας ἐπὶ τὸν λαὸν εὐλόγησεν Le 9.22.

3. *to extol*: + acc., βουλήν 'advice offered' Si 37.7.

4. *to remove, get rid of, efface, obliterate*, often of objects considered undesirable: ***o*** the house of Jacob, Am 9.8; fortifications, Mi 5.10 (|| ἐξολεθρεύω); city, Am 6.8; fruits, 2.9*b*; household name, 1K 20.16

Ra; hum., Jd 2.3B (A: μετοικίζω), Je 18.7 (ll ἀπόλλυμι), Am 2.9*a*, Ob 9, 10, Na 2.1 (ll συντελέομαι), Zp 1.3 (v.l. ἀνόμους and ll ἐκλείπω), Zc 10.2; ψυχήν 'life' Ps 39.15; enemies, ἔθνη μεγάλα καὶ πολλά De 7.1; hostile nations Zc 12.9; shepherds, 11.8; false prophets and an unclean spirit, 13.2; τὸν πονηρόν De 17.7; ἁμαρτήματα Ex 28.34, ἐπιτηδεύματα '(evil) practices' Ez 20.39, καταδυναστείαν (ll ἀφαιρέω); fornication, Ho 2.2; τὸ αἷμα αὐτῶν ἐκ στόματος αὐτῶν καὶ τὰ βδελύγματα αὐτῶν ἐκ μέσου ὀδόντων αὐτῶν Zc 9.7; objects associated with idolatry, σκοπιαί .. στῆλαι 'high-places .. stelae' Nu 33.52, βωμοὶ Ων Ho 10.8, τὰ ὀνόματα τῆς Βααλ κτλ. Zp 1.4, sim. Ho 2.17, φάρμακα 'drugs' or 'charms' Mi 5.12 (v.l. ἐξολεθρεύσω); εἴδωλα Is 30.11; ὑπερηφανίαν 'arrogance' 16.6, ὀνειδισμόν 'disgrace' Si 47.4; kingdom of sinners, Am 9.8; tribe, 1.8 (ll ἐξολεθρεύω); pass. θυσία καὶ σπονδή Jl 1.9, εὐφροσύνη καὶ χαρά ib., τέρψις 'enjoyment' 1M 3.45; ἀδικίας from one's consciousness, 'to overlook, take no notice of' Mi 7.18 (ll ὑπερβαίνω 'to pass over'); χρεμετισμὸς ἵππων 'neighing of horses' Am 6.7; ὁ ζῆλός μου 'my zeal' Ez 16.42. **b**. *to make naught of*: λόγους δικαίων De 16.19.

5. *to keep away* from, 'withhold': + acc., τὴν μάχαιραν αὐτοῦ ἀφ' αἵματος Je 31.10; με .. ἀπὸ κληρονομίας θεοῦ 2K 14.16B (*L* ἐξολεθρεύω).

The sphere from which an object is to be removed is expressed variously: ἀπὸ τῆς γῆς Zc 13.2; ἀπὸ προσώπου σου De 7.1, ἀπὸ προσώπου τῆς γῆς Am 9.8, Zp 1.3; ἐκ προσώπου τινός Ho 2.2, Am 2.9; ἐκ στόματός τινος Ho 2.17, Jl 1.5, Zc 5.7; ἐκ τοῦ τόπου Zp 1.4; ἐξ οἴκου τινός Jl 1.9; ἐκ τῶν χειρῶν τινος Mi 5.12; ἐκ μέσου τινός Zc 9.7.

B. intr. *to start moving out*: on a journey: ἐξῆρεν Ισραηλ ἐκ Σικίμων Ge 35.5; Ex 13.20; ἐξῆρεν .. ἀπὸ προσώπου αὐτῶν καὶ ἔστη ἐκ τῶν ὀπίσω αὐτῶν 'moved .. from before them and stood behind them' 14.19; *s* ἡ σκηνὴ τοῦ μαρτυρίου Nu 1.51 (opp. παρεμβάλλω); παρεμβολή 4.5; troops, 2.9; a lion leaving his lair, Je 4.7 (+ ἐξέρχομαι); κρίμα 28.9.

Cf. αἴρω, ἀπαίρω, ἀφανίζω, ἐξολεθρεύω, συντελέω, ἔξαρσις, ἐξοδεύω: Anz 14f.

ἐξαίσιος, ον. Only in Jb (9x).

extraordinary: *s* θάνατος Jb 9.23, πτῶμα 18.12, πόλεμος 22.10; subst.n.pl., 4.12, ἔνδοξά τε καὶ ~α 5.9.

ἐξαίφνης. adv.

1. *suddenly, unexpectedly*: *s* some undesirable event, ἥξει ἐ. 'will suddenly come' Ma 3.1, Is 47.9.

2. *after the elapse of only a short while*, 'immediately': Mi 2.3.

Cf. αἰφνίδιος, ἐξάπινα, ἐξαπίνης. *Pace* Shipp 241, not confined to Jb, Pr and 3M; Schmidt 2.164-7; Spicq 3.10-2.

ἑξάκις. adv.

six times: Jo 6.15, Jb 5.19.

ἑξακισχίλιοι, αι, α: num.

six thousand: Nu 2.9.

ἐξακολουθέω: aor. ἐξηκολούθησα, inf. ~λουθῆσαι.ʃ

1. *to conform to*: + dat., τῷ ἁγίῳ Ισραηλ Je 2.2, γυναικὶ ἀνδρὸς ἑτέρου Jb 31.9, τῇ ψυχῇ σου καὶ τῇ ἰσχύι σου Si 5.2, ll φοβέομαι Da 3.41; and ὀπίσω τινός– τὰ μάταια αὐτῶν .. οἷς ἐξηκολούθησαν .. ὀπίσω αὐτῶν Am 2.4; ἐν ταῖς ὁδοῖς αὐτῶν '(pursue) their own paths' Is 56.11.

2. *to go after* sth attractive: + dat., γυναικί Jb 31.9 (*s* καρδία).

ἐξακονάω: aor.pass. ἐξηκόνθην.ʃ *

to sharpen: *o* sword, Ez 21.11. Cf. ἀκονάω, ὀξύνω.

ἑξακόσιοι, αι, α. num.

six hundred: Ex 12.37.

ἑξακοσιοστός, ή, όν. num.

six-hundredth: ἐν τῷ ἑνὶ καὶ ~ῷ ἔτει 'in the six hunderd and first year' Ge 8.13.

ἐξακριβάζω: aor.mid. ἐξηκριβασάμην, inf. ~βάσασθαι.ʃ *

to get to know accurately: mid. + acc., τὸ σπέρμα Ιακωβ Nu 23.10; πᾶν πέρας 'every limit' Jb 28.3 ¶; περί τινος Da 7.19 LXX. Cf. ἀκριβάζω, ἀκριβής.

ἐξάλειπτρον, ου. n.ʃ

unguent-box: Jb 41.23.

ἐξαλείφω: fut. ἐξαλείψω, pass. ~φθήσομαι; aor. ἐξήλειψα, impv. ἐξάλειψον, inf. ~λεῖψαι, subj. ~λείψω, pass. ἐξηλείφθην, inf. ἐξαλειφθῆναι, impv. ~λείφθητι, subj. ~λειφθῶ, opt.3s ~λειφθείη.

1. *to plaster over*: + acc., οἰκίαν Le 14.42, τοίχους 'walls' 1C 29.4.

2. *to obliterate*: *s* pers. Ho 11.9; + acc. ἐξαλείψω πᾶσαν τὴν ἐξανάστασιν, ἣν ἐποίησα, ἀπὸ προσώπου τῆς γῆς 'I shall wipe out everything that I made, from the surface of the earth' Ge 7.4 (ll ἀπαλείφω 6.7); *o* ἀνάστημα 7.23; πᾶσαν σάρκα 9.15 (ll vs. 11 καταφθείρω); ἐξάλειψόν με ἐκ τῆς βιβλίου σου Ex 32.32; memory, ἀλοιφῇ ἐξαλείψω τὸ μνημόσυνον Αμαληκ ἐκ τῆς ὑπὸ τὸν οὐρανόν 'I shall totally efface the memory of A. from under the heaven' Ex 17.14; a writing, 'to erase' Nu 5.23; sbd's name 27.4; τὸ ὄνομα αὐτῶν ὑποκάτωθεν τοῦ οὐρανοῦ De 9.14, ἐξ Ισραηλ 25.6 (:: ἀνίστημι vs. 7), ἐκ τῆς ὑπὸ τὸν οὐρανόν 25.19, 29.20; τὰς ἀνομίας σου Is 43.25, τὰς ἁμαρτίας αὐτῶν ἀπὸ προσώπου οσυ 'cancel out ..' Je 18.23 (ll ἀθῳόω), παραπτώματα 'transgressions' PSol 13.10; ὄνειδος 'disgrace' Pr 6.33.

Cf. ἀφανίζω, ἀλείφω, ἀπαλείφω.

ἐξάλειψις, εως. f.∫
v.n. of prec. **2**: ἀποκτείνατε εἰς ~ιν Ez 9.6; *o* pers., Mi 7.11.

ἐξαλλάσσω: pf.ptc.pass. ἐξηλλαγμένος.∫
ptc., *extraordinary, unusual*: complimentary, ἐξαλλασσούσας στολάς 'exceptionally (fine) robes' Ge 45.22; neutral or pejorative, ἐξηλλαγμέναι αἱ τρίβοι αὐτοῦ 'his ways are weird' Wi 2.15 (ǁ ἀνόμοιος 'unusual'). Cf. ἔξαλλος.

ἐξαλλοιόω: aor.inf. ἐξαλλοιῶσαι.∫
to effect changes: 3M 3.21. Cf. ἀλλοιόω.

ἐξάλλομαι: fut. ἐξαλοῦμαι; aor. ἐξηλάμην.∫
1. *to leap*: *s* horse, Hb 1.8, calf 2K 22.30*L*; chariots, Jl 2.5.
2. *to leap out*: *s* sheep, Mi 2.12; mountains and hills, Is 55.12; the besieged, 1M 13.44.
3. *to hop off*: ὡς ἀττέλεβος 'like locust' Na 3.17.
Cf. ἅλλομαι.

ἔξαλλος, ον.
extraordinary, substantially different from the normal and common: *s* νόμος Es 3.8 o' (*L* νόμιμα), στολή 'robe' 2K 6.14; subst.n., w. negative connotation, ~α λαλήσει Da 11.36 LXX (TH ὑπέρογκα). Cf. ἐξαλλάσσω.

ἐξαλλοτριόω: aor.inf.pass. ~τριωθῆναι.∫
pass. *to become estranged from*: + gen. pers. 1M 12.10. Cf. ἀλλοτριόω.

ἐξαλλοτρίωσις, εως. f.∫
domain under a different regime: Es 7.26 *L*.

ἐξαμαρτάνω: aor. ἐξήμαρτον, inf. ~μαρτῆσαι.
1. *to miss the aim*: *s* slinger, Jd 20.16 B (A: δι~). Cf. διασφάλλω, διαψεύδομαι.
2. *to do wrong, commit sin* (against sbd τινι): abs., *s* ψυχή Hb 2.10; τῷ κυρίῳ Zp 1.17; ǁ ἁμαρτάνω, ἀνομέω Da 3.29. **b**. caus.: τὴν σάρκά σου Ec 5.5, τὸν Ισραηλ 3K 15.26, Si 47.23; and + cogn. acc., αὐτοὺς ἁμαρτίαν μεγάλην 4K 17.21.
Cf. ἐφ~, ἁμαρτάνω, ἐπιτυγχάνω.

ἑξάμηνος, ον.∫
lasting six months: adv., ~ον 'six months long' 4K 15.8, 1C 3.4.

ἐξαναλίσκω: fut. ~αναλώσω, pass. ~λωθήσομαι; aor. ἐξανήλωσα, subj. ἐξαναλώσω, inf. ~λῶσαι, pass. ἐξανηλώθην; pf.pass. ἐξανήλωμαι.
to destroy utterly: + acc. pers., *s* God, ἀπὸ τῆς γῆς Ex 32.12 (preceded by ἀποκτείνω), De 28.21; ἐκ τῆς παρεμβολῆς 2.15; πρὸ προσώπου τινός 9.4 (ǁ ἐξολεθρεύω); sword as instrument of divine punishment, Le 26.33; rust in corn, De 28.42; pass., Nu 14.35 (ǁ ἀποθνήσκω), 17.12 (ǁ ἀπόλλυμι, παραναλίσκω); wild beasts and *o* domestic cattle, Le 26.22 (ǁ κατεσθίω); *o* trees and crops De 28.42, cultic offerings Ju 11.13. Cf. (παρ)αναλίσκω, ἀφανίζω, κατεσθίω.

ἐξανάστασις, εως. f.∫
substance that came into existence: ἐξαλείψω πᾶσαν τὴν ~ιν, ἣν ἐποίησα 'I shall wipe out everything that I made' Ge 7.4 (ǁ ἀνάστημα vs. 23), cf. ἐξανίστημι **II**. Cf. ἐξανίστημι and ἀνάστημα.

ἐξανατέλλω: fut. ~τελῶ; aor. ἐξανέτειλα.∫
I. tr. *to cause* sth (τι) *to spring up*: *s* God, *o* sprouting plant, ἐξανέτειλεν ὁ θεὸς .. ἐκ τῆς γῆς πᾶν ξύλον Ge 2.9; χόρτον τοῖς κτήνεσιν 'vegetation for cattle' Ps 103.14, sim. 146.8; κέρας τῷ Δαυιδ 'a horn for D.' 131.17.
II. intr. ἐξανέτειλεν ἐν σκότει φῶς τοῖς εὐθέσιν 'there sprang up in the darkness a light for the upright' Ps 111.4.
Cf. ἀνατέλλω.

ἐξανθέω: fut. ἐξανθήσω; aor. ἐξήνθησα, subj. ἐξανθήσω.
I. intr. *to sprout*: *s* ῥόα 'pomegranate-tree' Ex 28.29; πολιαί 'grey hair' Ho 7.9, cf. 2C 26.19 *L* ἀνέτειλεν ǁ Chrysostom ἐξήνθησεν; τὰ ἐξανθοῦντα τοῦ Λιβάνου ἐξέλιπε 'the vegetation of Lebanon died out' Na 1.4; fig. ἐξανθήσει ὡς ἄμπελος τὸ μνημόσυνον αὐτοῦ 'his memory will bloom like a vine' Ho 14.8, ὡσεὶ χόρτος 'as grass' Ps 71.16, τὸ ἁγίασμά μου [= God's] 131.18; *s* hum. and + βλαστάνω Is 27.6.
2. *to make flowers blossom*: *s* the wilderness, Is 35.2.
3. *to make appearance with force*, 'break out, burst out': *s* leprosy, Le 13.12.
II. tr. *to cause* flowers *to come out blooming*: + acc., ἄνθη 'flowers' Nu 17.8.
Cf. ἄνθος.

ἐξανίστημι: pres.mid.impv. ~ανίστασο; fut.act. ~αναστήσω, mid. ~αναστήσομαι; 1aor. ἐξανέστησα, subj. ἐξαναστήσω, 2aor. ἐξανέστην, subj. ἐξαναστῶ, ptc. ἐξαναστάς, opt.3s ἐξανίσταιτο; pf. ἐξανέστηκα.
I. intr. (fut.mid., 2aor., pf.) *to arise*: from a seated position, ἐκάθητο .. ἐξανίστη Ge 19.1; after a fall, 4M 6.8; ἀπὸ τοῦ ἐνέδρου 'from the ambush' 1M 9.40; ἐκ μέσου τῆς συναγωγῆς Nu 25.7; ἀπὸ τοῦ θρόνου αὐτοῦ Jn 3.6 (cf. ἐκ τοῦ θρόνου, Hdt. 5.72); out of bed, ἐκ τῆς κοίτης αὐτοῦ Ex 10.23; from a dream, Is 29.8; after illness, Ex 21.19; 'to emerge, take place,' ἀπώλεια ἐν τῷ λαῷ σου Ho 10.14, ὕβρις Ez 7.10 (ǁ ἀνθέω); with hostile intent, 'rise up in arms, challenge,' ἐξαναστῶμεν ἐπ' αὐτὴν εἰς πόλεμον Ob 1, cf. Je 28.29, 2K 14.7*L* (B: ἐπαν~); ἀπὸ προσώπου τινός 'in the presence of ..' Le 19.32. ***b**. w. weakened basic meaning, in signalling an action taken with clear intent - Hebraistic, cf. ἀνίστημι **II 1c**: ἐξαναστήσεται καὶ ἀνταποδώσει Si 17.23.

2. *to depart, set off* on a journey: ἐκεῖθεν Ge 18.16, ἀπὸ τοῦ συμποσίου Es 7.7 o'.

II. tr. (fut.act., 1aor.) *to bring into existence*: + acc., offspring, μοι ὁ θεὸς σπέρμα Ge 4.25; 19.32, 34; wastelands, Is 61.4. Cf. ἐξανάστασις.

2. *to perform*: + v.n., ἐκδίκησιν Ez 25.15.

3. *to help rise*: + acc. pers., ἀσθενοῦντας .. ῥήμασιν 'the enfeebled .. with words (of encouragement)' Jb 4.4.

Cf. ἀνίστημι, κάθημαι.

ἐξαντλέω: fut. ~λήσω; aor.inf. ~λῆσαι.ʃ

to draw out (liquid): ***o*** wine or olive oil from a vat, Hg 2.16; metaph., + acc., βουλήν Pr 20.5. Cf. ἀντλέω.

ἐξαπατάω: aor. ἐξηπάτησα, inf. ἐξαπατῆσαι.ʃ

to cheat, deceive: Ex 8.29; τὸ κάλλος ἐξηπάτησέ σε 'the good look deceived you' Su 56 TH. Cf. ἀπατάω.

ἐξάπινα. adv.

1. *accidentally*: ἀποθάνῃ ἐ. Nu 6.9.

*2. *with no premeditated intention*: Le 21.4, Nu 4.20; glossed as οὐ δι' ἔχθραν .. οὐκ ἐξ ἐνέδρου 'not with hostile intent .. not from an ambuscade' 35.22.

3. *all of a sudden, unexpectedly*: Ps 63.5.

Cf. ἐξαίφνης.

ἐξαπίνης. adv.

= ἐξαίφνης: Pr 6.15, 29.1.

ἐξαπόλλυμι.ʃ

to perish: ***s*** the ungodly, Wi 10.6. Cf. ἀπόλλυμι.

ἐξαπορέομαι: aor. ἐξηπορήθην.ʃ

to be in great material *†difficulty*: ***s*** hum., Ps 87.16 (‖ ἐν κόποις). Cf. ἀπορέω.

ἐξαποστέλλω: fut. ~στελῶ; aor. ἐξαπέστειλα, impv. ~στειλον, inf. ~στεῖλαι, ptc. ~στείλας, subj. ~στείλω, opt.3s ~στείλαι, ptc.pass. ~σταλείς; pf. ἐξαπέσταλκα, pass. ἐξαπέσταλμαι.

1. *to dispatch, send out*: ***o*** envoy, + πρός τινα, Hg 1.12, Zc 2.11, 4.9; envoy understood, Am 7.10, 1E 3.14, To 10.8 𝔊[I]; πρὸ προσώπου σου τὸν Μωυσῆν καὶ Ααρων καὶ Μαριαμ (as your leaders) Mi 6.4; εἰς + place, Zc 7.2; τὸν ἄγγελόν μου Ma 3.1; δρέπανον 'sickle' Jl 3.13; on an errand, Su 21 TH; pass., ἐξαποστελλόμενος 'envoy, emissary' Mi 1.14. **b**. ***o*** message: τοὺς λόγους .. ἐν χερσὶ τῶν προφητῶν Zc 7.12; a commandment, πρὸς ὑμᾶς τὴν ἐντολὴν ταύτην Ma 2.4. **c**. ***o*** hostile, threatening object: enemies, ἐπὶ σέ De 28.48; πῦρ εἴς τινα, 'set fire to' Ho 8.14, Am 1.4, 12; πῦρ ἐπὶ τὰ τείχη 1.7, 10; πῦρ ἐπί τινα Am 2.2, 5; θάνατον εἰς ὑμᾶς Le 26.25, sim. Am 4.10; σοι τὴν ἔνδειαν .. ἐπὶ πάντα '.. poverty' De 28.20 (‖ ἀποστείλαι κύριος ἐπὶ σὲ τὴν εὐλογίαν vs. 8); λιμὸν ἐπὶ τὴν γῆν 'famine ..' Am 8.11, λιμὸν καὶ θηρία πονηρά '.. and harmful beasts' Ez 5.17; βέλη 'arrows' Ps 143.6, but τὴν χεῖρά σου 'your (helping) hand' 143.7, cf. 17.17, 56.4 w. the obj. understood; ἡ δύναμίς μου ἡ μεγάλη 'my great army (of ravaging insects) .. εἰς ὑμᾶς Jl 2.25; περιοχήν ('a besieging army'[?; q.v.]) εἰς τὰ ἔθνη Ob 1; πάντας τοὺς ἀνθρώπους ἕκαστον ἐπι τὸν πλησίον αὐτοῦ 'set everybody on one another' Zc 8.10; ἐφ' ὑμᾶς τὴν κατάραν '.. the curse' Ma 2.2. **d**. ***o*** sth desirable: gifts (δῶρα) and + dat. pers., Ge 32.13, βοήθειαν 'help' Ps 19.3.

2. *to expel, drive out*: + acc. and ἐκ τοῦ παραδείσου τῆς τρυφῆς Ge 3.23 (‖ ἐκβάλλω), ἕως τῶν ὁρίων 'to the borders' Ob 7; ἀπό τινος Ge 25.6 (in order to break up a relationship), 45.1; πρὸ προσώπου τινός Le 18.24; ἔξω τῆς παρεμβολῆς 'outside of the encampment' Nu 5.3; μετ' εἰρήνης Ge 26.29; ἐν χειρί τινος (agency) Le 16.21. **b**. *to cast off*: as impediment, obstacle, χαλινόν 'bridle' Jb 30.11¶, ὠδῖνας 'birth-pangs' 39.3¶ (‖ λύω vs. 2).

3. *to cause to come out into the open*: τινα 4K 10.23*L*, 11.12B (*L* ἐξάγω; ‖ 2C 23.11).

4. *to divorce* (a wife), De 22.19; ἐκ τῆς οἰκίας αὐτοῦ 24.1; Ma 2.16, Is 50.1, Je 3.1, 8. **b**. *to marry off*: + acc. (daughter), Jd 12.9 (ref. to intertribal or interclan marriage).

5. *to release, set free, allow to depart*: ***o*** τὸν λαόν μου Ex 4.23; 6.1 (‖ ἐκβάλλω); ἐκ τῆς γῆς αὐτοῦ 6.11; δεσμίους 'prisoners' Zc 9.11, cf. τὸν Λωτ ἐκ μέσου τῆς καταστροφῆς Ge 19.29; exiles, Je 27.33; ἐλευθέρους 'as free persons' Ex 21.26, 27; μετ' εἰρήνης 3M 6.27; ἀπὸ σοῦ De 15.12; κενόν 'empty-handed' Ge 31.42, De15.13, cf. ἀποστέλλω κενόν Mk 12.3.

6. *to part with, give a send-off to*: + acc. pers., Ge 26.31; 31.27, Ex 18.27. Cf. προπέμπω **2**; συμπροπέμπω.

7. *to dispose of, do away with*: + acc., πόλεις ἐν πυρί '.. with fire' Jd 20.48 A (B: ἐμπίμπρημι).

Cf. ἀποστέλλω, προεξαποστέλλω, ἐκβάλλω, ἐξαποστολή, ἐκ~, προπέμπω: Rengstorf, *TDNT* 1.401, 406; Lee 93f.; ib. 2007.

ἐξαποστολή, ῆς. f.ʃ

expulsion, v.n. of prec. **2**: 3M 4.4. Cf. ἐξαποστέλλω.

ἐξάπτω: fut. ἐξάψω; aor. ἐξῆψα, pass. ἐξήφθην, ptc. ἐξαφθείς; pf.mid.3s ἐξῆπται.

1. *to set burning*: + acc. rei, λύχνους 'lamps' Ex 30.8, Nu 8.3, πῦρ ἐν ταῖς λαμπάσι '(he set) fire to the torches' Jd 15.5A (B: ἐκκαίω); *to inflame*, pass. ***o*** φλόξ 'flame' Ez 20.47, metaph. hum., La 4.19.

2. mid. *to fasten oneself to and gain a firm grip on*: metaph., + gen., "thoughtlessness has got hold of the heart of a youth" Pr 22.15.

Cf. ἅπτω, (ἐκ)καίω.

ἔξαρθρος, ον.ʃ *
with limbs dislocated: *s* hum. (under torture) 4M 9.13. Cf. ἐξαρθρόω.

ἐξαρθρόω.ʃ
to disjoint: + acc., hum. limbs (under torture), 4M 10.5. Cf. ἔξαρθρος.

ἐξαριθμέω: fut. ~μήσω, mid. ~ μήσομαι, pass. ~μηθήσομαι; aor. ἐξηρίθμησα, inf. ἐξαριθμῆσαι, mid. ~μήσασθαι.
1. *to count completely*: + acc., ἡ ἄμμος τῆς θαλάσσης, ἣ οὐκ ἐκμετρηθήσεται οὐδὲ ἐξαριθμηθήσεται 'the sand of the sea, which cannot be completely measured nor counted' Ho 1.10, sim. Ge 13.16; *o* stars, 15.5b; groups of people, Nu 23.10; πάντα τὰ διαβήματά μου 'all my steps' Jb 31.4¶; πάντα τὰ ὀστᾶ μου 'all my bones' Ps 21.18; ἡμέρας αἰῶνος Si 1.2.
2. *to size up, determine the size and extent completely*: + acc., τὴν δεξιάν σου 'your right hand' Ps 89.12; wisdom Si 1.9; κράτος 'might' 18.5.
3. *to go through* a period of time (acc.) *in full*: ἐξαριθμήσεις σεαυτῷ ἑπτὰ ἀναπαύσεως ἐτῶν Le 25.8; De 16.9, Ez 44.26 (αὑτῷ *pace* Zgl αὐτῷ).
Cf. ἀριθμός, ἀριθμέω, ἐκμετρέω.

ἐξαρκέω: fut. ἐξαρκέσω.ʃ
to suffice: Μὴ χεὶρ κυρίου οὐκ ἐξαρκέσει; Nu 11.23. Cf. ἀρκέω.

ἐξαρνέομαι: fut. ~αρνήσομαι.ʃ
to renounce personal relationship with: + acc. (priesthood), 4M 5.35 (|| ἐξομνύω vs. 34). Cf. ἀρνέομαι, ἐξομνύω.

ἐξαρπάζω: aor.inf. ἐξαρπάσαι.ʃ
to snatch away forcibly, 'kidnap': + acc. pers., 1M 7.29. Del. Jb 29.17 v.l.

ἔξαρσις, εως. f.ʃ
1. *setting out* on a journey or march: Nu 10.6, v.n. of ἐξαίρω **B**.
2. *destruction*: cogn. dat. of ἐξαίρω - ἐξάρσει καὶ ἀπωλείᾳ Je 12.17, v.n. of ἐξαίρω **A4**.
Cf. ἐξαίρω, ἀπώλεια.

ἐξαρτάω: pf.ptc.pass. ἐξηρτημένος.ʃ
to attach: ἐπὶ τοῖς δυσὶν μέρεσιν ἐξηρτημέναι 'attached to the two parts' Ex 28.7.

ἐξάρχω.
to act as leader of: in singing, abs. 1K 18.7, 21.12; + gen. pers., Ex 15.21; φωνὴ ἐξαρχόντων κατ' ἰσχὺν οὐδὲ φωνὴ ἐξαρχόντων τροπῆς, ἀλλὰ φωνὴ ἐξαρχόντων οἴνου 'the voice of those leading (an army) with strength, nor the voice of leaders in retreat, but the voice of wining and dining leaders' 32.18; κατ' αὐτῆς 'concerning (or: against) it' Is 27.2. **b**. + acc.: θρῆνον 'a lament' 3M 4.6, ἐξομολόγησιν Ju 15.14. **c**. + dat. pers., τῷ θεῷ μου ἐν τυμπάνοις Ju 16.1 (|| ᾄδω), τῷ κυρίῳ ἐν ἐξομολογήσει Ps 146.7; 1K 29.5.
Cf. ἄρχω.

ἐξασθενέω: aor. ἐξησθένησα; pf.ptc. ἐξησθενηκώς.ʃ
to become utterly weak: physically, *s* hum. tongue, Ps 63.9; hum., PSol 17.31. Cf. ἀσθενέω.

ἐξασκέω.ʃ
to provide training in: + acc. rei, ἀνδρείαν 'courage' 4M 5.23, ἀρετάς 'virtues' 13.24.

ἐξαστράπτω.ʃ*
to flash as with lightning: *s* weapons (ὅπλα) Na 3.3, fire (πῦρ) Ez 1.4; brass (χαλκός) 1.7, Da 10.6 LXX. Cf. στίλβω and ἀστραπή.

ἐξατιμόω: fut.pass. ~μωθήσομαι.ʃ *
to shame thoroughly: pass., *o* hum., Ez 16.61. Cf. ἀτιμόω.

ἐξαφίημι: aor.inf.act. ~φεῖναι.ʃ
to set free: + acc. pers. (POW), σῶον 'in safety' 2M 12.24 (|| ἀπολύω vs. 25). Cf. ἀφίημι, ἀπολύω.

ἐξεγείρω: pres.impv.pass. 3pl ἐξεγειρέσθωσαν; fut. pass. ἐξεγερθήσομαι; aor. ἐξήγειρα, impv. ~γειρον, pass. ἐξηγέρθην, subj. ἐξεγερθῶ, impv.s ἐξεγέρθητι; pf.pass.3s ἐξεγήγερται.
1. *to arouse, awake* from sleep: ἐξηγέρθη .. ἀπὸ τοῦ ὕπνου αὐτοῦ Ge 28.16; ἐξήγειρέ με ὃν τρόπον ὅταν ἐξεγερθῇ ἄνθρωπος ἐξ ὕπνου 'he woke me up as when one wakes up from sleep' Zc 4.1, cf. Ge 41.21; ἔκνηψον ἐξεγέρθητι 'sober up, wake up' Hb 2.19; *o* dead hum. still lying in bed, 4K 4.31*L* (B: simp.).
2. *to arouse, stir up from inactivity into action*: *o* μαχητάς 'warriors' Jl 3.9, Hb 1.6, cf. Jl 3.12 (mid.); ἀπολωλότας 'the lost' Jb 5.11; ἐπί τινα, 'to assail sbd' Zc 13.7; πνεῦμα 'wind' Jn 1.4, ἄνεμον καύσωνα διαφθείροντα 'destructive, scorching wind' Je 28.1; πνεῦμα 'human spirit' Hg 1.14, 2E 1.1, πνοήν 'breath' Is 38.16, δικαιοσύνην 41.2, θυμόν 'wrath' 2M 13.4; *s* sea, κλύδωνα 'wave' Jn 1.11; mid., ἐξηγείρετο .. ἐπ' αὐτούς '(the sea) stirred up against them' 1.13; ἐξεγήγερται ἐκ νεφελῶν ἁγίων αὐτοῦ 'he has awoken from the midst of his holy clouds' Zc 2.13; Jl 3.7.
3. *to raise, lift*: + acc., δόρυ ἐπί τινα 'a spear at sbd' 2K 23.18B; *o* δεσμοὺς ἕως τραχήλου 'fetters up to the neck' Hb 3.13.
4. *to cause to appear, bring into existence* (acc.): *o* ποιμένα 'shepherd' Zc 11.16, νέφη 'clouds' Pr 25.23.
5. mid. *to arouse oneself into action*: Jd 5.12, Is 51.9, Si 35.11.
Cf. ἐγείρω and ἐπεγείρω.

ἐξέγερσις, εως. f.ʃ
v.n. of ἐξεγείρω, *act of waking up from sleep*: opp. ὕπνος PSol 4.15.

ἐξέδρα, ας. f.
parlour: Ez 40.44. Cf. LSG s.v.

ἐξεικονίζω: pf.pass.ptc. ἐξεικονισμένος.ʃ
pass. *to be fully formed*: *o* foetus, ἐξέλθῃ τὸ παιδίον αὐτῆς μὴ ἐξεικονισμένον Ex 21.22; 21.23.

I **ἔξειμι**: inf. ἐξεῖναι, ptc.n.s ἐξόν; fut.3s ἐξέσται.
1, *to be allowed*, impers. ἔξεστι: + dat. pers. and inf., οὐκ ἔξεστιν ἡμῖν ἰδεῖν 'we are not allowed to see' 2E 4.14; οὐκ ἦν ἐξόν Es 4.2 o', sim. 4M 5.18; μοι understood, 1.12.
2. *to be possible*, impers., ἔξεστι: + inf., Es 7 o', ἐξὸν ἡμῖν ἦν 4M 17.7.
Cf. ἐξουσία, θεμιτός: Foerster, *TDNT* 2.560f.

II **ἔξειμι**.ʃ
intr. *to move out*: *s* the high priest from the sanctuary, Ex 28.31 (:: εἴσειμι); animals, 3M 5.48. Cf. ἐξέρχομαι, ἐκπορεύομαι, εἴσειμι.

ἐξεκλησιάζω: aor. ~κλησίασα, pass. ~κλησιάσθην. On the orthography, see Katz 85.
1. *to summon out to a meeting*: + acc., τὴν συναγωγὴν ἐπὶ τὴν θύραν Le 8.4 (|| vs. 3 ἐκκλησιάζω); Nu 20.10; τοὺς πρεσβυτέρους 'the elders' 2C 5.2.
2. pass. *to converge*: ἐπί τινα (with hostile intent) Je 33.9. Cf. συμφωνέω **2**.
Cf. ἐκκλησιάζω.

ἐξελαύνω. ʃ
tr. *to drive out, expel*: abs. Zc 9.8, 10.4. Cf. ἐκβάλλω.

ἐξελέγχω.ʃ
to blame: + acc., θράσυς 'audacity' Wi 12.17; τινα 4M 2.13. Cf. ἐλέγχω, μέμφομαι.

ἐξέλευσις, εως. f.ʃ *
act of exiting: 2K 15.20. Cf. ἐξέρχομαι, ἔξοδος.

ἐξελίσσω.ʃ
mid. *to extend and become connected to*: τινι 3K 7.45.

ἐξέλκω: fut. ἐξελκύσω; aor. ἐξείλκυσα, pass. ἐξειλκύσθην.
to pull out: ἐξείλκυσαν καὶ ἀνεβίβασαν τὸν Ιωσηφ ἐκ τοῦ λάκκου 'they pulled J. up out from the cistern' Ge 37.28; *o* enemy troops by stealth, Jd 20.31A. **b**. metaph., λόγους, *to engage in a verbal slinging match* Pr 30.33.
Cf. ἕλκω.

ἐξεμέω: fut. ~μέσω, pass. ~μεσθήσομαι; aor.impv. 2pl ἐξεμέσατε, subj. ~μέσω.ʃ
to vomit: abs., Je 32.2,13, Pr 25.16; + acc., ψωμόν 'morsel' Pr 23.8. **b**. in general, *to belch out*: pass. and *o* wealth, Jb 20.15.
Cf. ἐμέω.

ἐξεραυνάω: ⇒ ἐξερευνάω.

ἐξεργάζομαι: aor. ἐξειργασάμην, ptc. ἐξεργασάμενος.ʃ
to bring about through labour and efforts: 'to fashion,' *o* weapon Ps 7.14; kindness 30.20; deeds Es E 18. Cf. ποιέω, ἐργάζομαι.

ἐξεργαστικός, η, ον.ʃ
inclined to assiduity and diligence: subst.n.sg., τῆς πραγματείας 'exhaustive treatment (of a matter)' 2M 2.31.

ἐξερεύγομαι: fut. ἐξερεύξομαι; aor. ἐξηρευξάμην, opt.3pl ἐξερεύξαιντο.
to emit, 'spew out': + acc., ἐξερεύξεται ὁ ποταμὸς βατράχους 'the river will spew out frogs' Ex 8.3, cf. Wi 19.10; *o* good things, ἐξηρεύξατο ἡ καρδία μου λόγον ἀγαθόν Ps 44.2; ἐξερεύξαιντο τὰ χείλη μου ὕμνον 'may my lips bring forth a hymn' 118.171 (|| φθέγγομαι); μνήμην τοῦ πλήθους τῆς χρηστότητός σου 'memory of your abundant grace' 144.7. Cf. ἐξέρπω: LSG s.v.

ἐξερευνάω: fut. ~νήσω; aor. ἐξηρεύνησα, impv. ~νησον, subj. ~νήσω, pass. ~νήθην.
1. *to search out, search*: *o* hum., Ob 6; vine, Jl 1.7; discernment comparable to treasures, Pr 2.4 (|| ζητέω); from a place difficult of access, Am 9.3; a place being searched, Zp 1.12.
2. *to make enquiries into*: abs. ἐτάσεις καὶ ἐρωτήσεις καὶ ἐξερευνήσεις De 13.14; + acc. rei, ἀνομίας Ps 63.7, τὰ μαρτύρια αὐτοῦ 118.2 (|| ἐκζητέω), τὸν νόμον σου 118.34, τὰς ἐντολάς σου 118.69, τὰ ὁμοιώματα τῶν εἰδώλων αὐτῶν 'the likenesses of their idols' 1M 3.48; + dat. cogn., Ps 63.7; pass., ἐξηρευνήθη ἡ ὁδὸς ἡμῶν καὶ ἠτάσθη La 3.40. **b**. of military espionage: τὴν γῆν Jd 18.2 A (B: ἐξιχνιάζω), τὴν πόλιν 2K 10.3 (|| κατασκοπέ/εύω; || 1C 19.3 ἐξερευνάω).
Cf. ἐρευνάω, ἐτάζω, ἐρωτάω, ἐξερεύνησις: Passoni dell' Acqua 1983, esp. 213-5.

ἐξερεύνησις, εως. f.ʃ
v.n. of prec.: as dat. cogn., Ps 63.7. Cf. ἐξερευνάω.

ἐξερημόω: fut.act. ~μώσω, pass. ~μωθήσομαι; aor. ἐξηρήμωσα; pf.pass. ἐξερήμωμαι, ptc. ἐξηρημωμένος.
to leave destitute: + acc. and without indicating what is wanting, τὰς πηγάς '(to drain) the fountains' Ho 13.15 (|| ἀναξηραίνω), ποταμούς Na 1.4 + 4K 19.24*L* (|| ξηραίνω), θάλασσαν Is 50.2; αἱ τελεταὶ τοῦ Ισραηλ ἐξερημωθήσονται 'the mystic rites of Israel will be made destitute (of their practitioners?)' Am 7.9 (|| ἀφανίζομαι); τὰς ὁδοὺς .. τοῦ μὴ διοδεύειν Zp 3.6; τὰ ἅγια 'the sanctuary' Le 26.31; τὴν γῆν ὑμῶν 26.32, τὰς πόλεις Ez 19.7 (|| ἀφανίζω); ὁ οἶκος οὗτος ἐξερήμωται Hg 1.4; *o* hum., Je 25.9. Cf. ἐρημόω, ἔρημος, ἀναξηραίνω, ξηραίνω, ἀφανίζω.

ἐξέρπω: aor. ἐξῆρψα.∫
to become covered with crawling things: *s* ground, + acc., βατράχους 'frogs' Ps 104.30. Cf. ἕρπω, ἐξερεύγομαι: Caird 1968.472f.

ἐξέρχομαι: fut. ἐξελεύσομαι, inf. ἐξελεύσεσθαι; aor. ἐξῆλθον, ptc. ἐξελθών, subj. ἐξέλθω, impv. ἔξελθε, opt.3s ἐξέλθοι; pf. ἐξελήλυθα, ptc. ἐξεληλυθώς.

1. *to exit, depart* from a confined place: abs. Ex 16.4 ('outdoors'); to freedom, Ge 15.14; Ex 21.3 (:: εἰσέρχομαι); Ἔξελθε ἐκ τῆς γῆς σου καὶ ἐκ τῆς συγγενείας σου καὶ ἐκ τοῦ οἴκου τοῦ πατρός σου Ge12.1; ἐξῆλθεν .. ἀπὸ τοῦ φρέατος τοῦ ὅρκου καὶ ἐπορεύθη εἰς Χαρραν 'he left the well of the oath and set out for Haran' 28.10; ἀπὸ προσώπου τινός 4.16, 27.30; ἀπ' ἐμοῦ 'left me' 44.28; ἐξῆλθεν ἀπ' αὐτοῦ 'took leave of him' 47.10; for an outdoor activity, 24.43 (|| ἐκπορεύομαι vs. 11); ἐκ πόλεως Mi 4.10, Jn 4.5; ἐκ προσώπου τινός Ge 41.46; ἐκτὸς τῆς πόλεως Ex 9.33; ἐντεῦθεν Ge 42.15; ἔξω τῆς παρεμβολῆς De 23.10; for a battle, ἐν πολέμῳ .. εἰς συνάντησίν σοι Nu 20.18, εἰς πόλεμον 10.9, Jd 3.10B (A: ἐπὶ τὸν πόλεμον), εἰς πόλεμον ἐπὶ τοὺς ἐχθρούς σου De 20.1, 21.10, ἐξελεύσεται κύριος καὶ παρατάξεται ἐν τοῖς ἔθνεσι Zc 14.3; πρός σέ De 28.7; παρὰ κυρίου Nu 16.35; opp. εἰσέρχομαι πρός τινα Ex 8.12 (see vs. 1); δι' αὐτῆς 'through it (= gate)' Mi 2.13*a*; "you shall go forth and bound as young calves" Ma 4.2; εἰς τὸ πεδίον ἐκ τῆς κιβωτοῦ 'into the plain from the ark' Ge 8.19; ἐπὶ τὸ ὕδωρ 'to the river' Ex 8.20; πρός τινα Ge 34.6, Nu 10.9; in order to go into exile, ἐν αἰχμαλωσίᾳ Zc 14.2, Je 22.22, ἐκ τοῦ τόπου τούτου 22.11; + acc., τὴν πόλιν Ge 44.4, Ex 9.29; τὴν θύραν τοῦ οἴκου αὐτοῦ 12.22, sim. To 11.10 𝔊[II]; τὰ ὅρια τῆς πόλεως Nu 35.26; τοὺς διατεταγμένους '(walked out) past the personnel (?)' Jd 3.23B; *s* baby, Ge 38.28; foetus, Ex 21.22; bridegroom and his bride leaving their nuptial chamber, Jl 2.16; military leaders to a battlefield, Ge 14.8, 17; words uttered, πάντα, ὅσα ἂν ἐξέλθῃ ἐκ τοῦ στόματος αὐτοῦ Nu 30.3, ἐκ τῶν χειλέων αὐτῆς 'from her lips' 30.13; καταδεδικασμένος '(leave a court) with a 'guilty' verdict' Ps 108.7; κλῆρος 'lot (cast)' Jo 18.11; ἐξελθὸν πνεῦμα 'departed spirit (of the dead)' Wi 16.14. Opp. εἰσέρχομαι: Ge 43.31 (see vs. 30), and see on the idiomatic combination of the two verbs under εἰσέρχομαι.

2. *to emerge, appear*, usually w. ἐκ: *s* empire, ἐκ τῆς γῆς ἐκείνης ἐξῆλθεν Ασσουρ Ge 10.11; of sunrise, ὁ ἥλιος ἐξῆλθεν ἐπὶ τὴν γῆν 19.23; future leader, βασιλεῖς ἐκ τῆς ὀσφύος σου ἐξελεύσονται'.. out of your loins ..' 35.11; ἐκ σοῦ μοι ἐ. τοῦ εἶναι εἰς ἄρχοντα Mi 5.2; πηγή 'spring of water' Jl 3.18, ὕδωρ ζῶν Zc 14.8; evil design, Na 1.11; λῆμμα 'oracular pronouncement' Hb 1.7, λόγος 3.5 (|| πορεύομαι), ἐκ Σιων ἐ. νόμος καὶ λόγος κυρίου ἐξ Ιερουσαλημ Mi 4.2, Is 2.3, δικαιοσύνη 45.23, σωτήριον 51.5, ἀπὸ τῶν προφητῶν Ιερουσαλημ ἐξῆλθε μολυσμὸς ('defilement') πάσῃ τῇ γῇ (dat. incom.) Je 23.15, κρίμα Ps 16.2; βολίς 'arrow' Zc 9.14, ῥάβδος 'rod' Is 11.1 (|| ἀναβαίνω). **b**. as offspring, ἐκ σοῦ Ge 15.4; ἐκ τοῦ σπέρματος αὐτοῦ Nu 24.7; snakes, Is 14.29. **c**. in order to initiate some action: ὁ ἄγγελος .. καὶ εἶπε Zc 5.5; ἐξ αὐτοῦ .. πᾶς ὁ ἐξελαύνων 10.4. **d**. fire breaking out: Ex 22.6; παρὰ κυρίου Nu 16.35. **e**. fig.: ὀργὴ ἀπὸ προσώπου κυρίου Nu 16.46, ὀργὴ κυρίου Si 5.7, ὡς πῦρ ὁ θυμός μου Je 4.4; *s* ὡς φῶς ἡ δικαιοσύνη μου Is 62.1. **f**. *s* resulting boundaries determined by casting a lot: Jo 18.11.

3. of judgement, sentence, *to be announced and implemented*: τὸ κρίμα μου ὡς φῶς ἐ. Ho 6.5; Hb 1.4.

4. *to run the full course and come to an end*: *s* year (ἔτος) Ge 47.18; ἐξεληλυθυίας τῆς ἀφέσεως for τοῦ ἐνιαυτοῦ τῆς ἀφέσεως 'when the year of amnesty has run out' Le 27.21. Cf. ἐξελεύσεται τῇ ἀφέσει 'the alien ownership shall have elapsed in the year of release (or: through the release)' (?) Le 25.28 (|| ἐν τῇ ἀφέσει vs. 30).

Cf. ἔρχομαι, ἐκπορεύομαι, ἔξειμι, ἐξέλευσις, ἐξοδεύω, ἐξοδία, ἔξοδος, εἰσ~, συνεξέρχομαι: Schneider, *TDNT* 2.678f.

ἐξετάζω: fut. ἐξετάσω; aor. ἐξήτασα, subj. ἐξετάσω.
to examine well, scrutinise: *s* mostly sbd with superior knowledge or higher authority, judge, ἀκριβῶς 'accurately' De 19.18; + acc. pers., Si 13.11 (|| πειράζω), κύριον παντοκράτορα Ju 8.13 (in order to know him and *s* sbd putting himself in God's position); *s* king, τοὺς δύο εὐνούχους Es A 14 o' (*L* ἐτάζω), ὡς ἀπότομος βασιλεύς 'like a severe ..' Wi 11.10 (|| δοκιμάζω); God, κύριος ἐξετάζει τὸν δίκαιον καὶ τὸν ἀσεβῆ Ps 10.5, God's eyelids, τοὺς υἱοὺς τῶν ἀνθρώπων 10.4 (|| ἀποβλέπω); ***o*** οἰκέτης 'servant' Si 23.10; + acc. rei, ὑμῶν τὰ ἔργα Wi 6.3 (|| διερευνάω 'investigate'); ἰσχυρότερά σου 'matters beyond you' Si 3.21 (|| ζητέω), σεαυτόν 18.20 (|| ἐπισκοπή 'scrutiny'). Cf. ἐτάζω, ἐξέτασις, ἐξετασμός, ἐξεταστέον, (ἐξ)ερευνάω: *ND* 4.99.

ἐξέτασις, εως. f.∫
v.n. of prec.: eschatological, + gen. obj. Si 16.22¶; ἔν τινι '(enquiry) into ..' Wi 1.9; + ἀνάκρισις 3M 7.5. Cf. ἐξετάζω, ἀνάκρισις.

ἐξετασμός, οῦ.∫
v.n. of ἐξετάζω, *investigation*: juridical, Pr 1.32, Wi 4.6; καρδίας 'self-reflections' Jd 5.16B (A: ἐξιχνιασμός). Cf. ἐξετάζω, ἐξέτασις.

ἐξεταστέον.ʃ
one must enquire and investigate: 2M 2.29. Cf. ἐξετάζω.

ἐξευμενίζομαι.ʃ
to appease: + acc., heavenly army, 4M 4.11.

ἐξεύρεσις, εως.ʃ
v.n. of subs., *act of discovering the nature of*: οὐδὲ ἔστιν ἐ. τῆς φρονήσεως αὐτοῦ 'his prudence is not to be found out' Is 40.28; Ba 3.18.

ἐξευρίσκω: aor. ἐξεῦρον, ptc. ~ρών.ʃ
to discover after a search: + acc., prudence (φρόνησις) Ba 3.32, path 3.37; 2M 7.23. Cf. εὑρίσκω.

ἐξέχω.
to jut out, protrude: ἐκ τῶν καλαμίσκων οἱ βλαστοὶ ἐξέχοντες 'the buds protruding out of the branches' Ex 38.15; *s* a space of land, τὸ πέραν Αρνων .. τὸ ἐξέχον ἀπὸ τῶν ὁρίων τῶν Ἀμορραίων 'the area on the other side of Arnon .. jutting out from the territory of the Amorites' Nu 21.13; + gen., Ez 42.6.

ἐξηγέομαι: aor. ἐξηγησάμην, inf. ἐξηγήσασθαι.
1. *to interpret*: Le 14.57 (ǁ αὐγάζω).
2. *to narrate about* sbd or sth *at length*: + acc. rei, Pr 28.13; + acc. and dat. pers., τῷ πλησίον αὐτοῦ ἐνύπνιον Jd 7.13; Jb 28.27¶; + conj. ὡς 4K 8.5 (ǁ διηγέομαι vs. 4); περί τινος 1M 3.26; + τοῦ inf., Es A 12 *L*; in writing, pass., τὰ αὐτὰ .. καὶ ὡς .. ἐπισυνήγαγε .. 'the same things .. and the fact that he collected ..' 2M 2.13.
Cf. ἐξήγησις, ἐξηγητής, διηγέομαι, προσεξηγέομαι: Spicq 2.21-3.

ἐξήγησις, εως. f.ʃ
lengthy talk, 'chatter': μωροῦ 'of a fool' Si 21.16; with no negative connotation, ἐνυπνίου 'of a dream' Jd 7.15 B (A: διήγησις). Cf. ἐξηγέομαι, διήγησις.

ἐξηγητής, οῦ. m.
interpreter: of a dream, Ge 41.8 (+ σοφός), 24 (ǁ ἀπαγγέλλων). Cf. ἐξηγέομαι.

ἐξηγορία, ας. f.ʃ
utterance: Jb 22.22 (ǁ ῥήματα), 33.26.

ἑξήκοντα. indecl. num.
sixty: Ge 5.15.

ἑξηκονταετής, ές.ʃ
of sixty years in age: Le 27.3, 7.

ἑξηκοστός, ή, όν.
sixtieth: in order, 1M 10.1.

ἐξηλιάζω: aor. ἐξηλίασα, subj. ~λιάσω; pf.ptc.pass. ἐξηλιασμένος.*
to put out and expose to the heat of the sun: as a form of torture, τινα 2K 21.9. Cf. ἡλιάζω.

ἐξημερόω.ʃ
to reclaim for cultivation: metaph., + acc. (overgrown land), 4M 1.29.

ἑξῆς. adv.
1. *one after another in succession*: ἑ. ἐπέλθη τὰ σημεῖα ταῦτα Ex 10.1; ἐξωλεθρεύσαμεν πᾶσαν πόλιν ἑ. De 2.34, 3.6. Cf. Chadwick 107-11.
2. *thereafter*: τῇ ἑ., *on the following day*, Es 7.18; τὴν ἑ. 2M 7.8.
3. *properly belonging*: + dat., τῶν ἑ. τῷ τόπῳ 'that which befits the place' 3M 1.9.

ἐξηχέω: fut. ἐξηχήσω; aor. ἐξήχησα.ʃ *
to sound forth: ἦχοι ἐξήχησαν 'there rang out sounds' Jl 3.14; *s* βροντή 'thunder' Si 40.13; φήμη δυσμενής 'hostile rumour' 3M 3.2. **b.** *to cause to sound forth*: + acc. (hailstones?) 2K 22.15*L*.
Cf. ἠχέω, ἦχος, φωνέω.

ἐξικνέομαι.ʃ
to reach by way of enquiry: + acc., καρδίαν Jd 5.15B. Cf. ἀφικνέομαι.

ἐξίλασις, εως. f.ʃ
v.n. of subs.: Nu 29.11. Cf. ἐξιλάσκομαι, ἐξιλασμός.

ἐξιλάσκομαι: fut. ἐξιλάσομαι, pass. ἐξιλασθήσομαι; aor. ἐξιλασάμην, subj. ἐξιλάσωμαι, opt.3s ἐξιλάσαι, impv. ἐξίλασαι, inf. ἐξιλάσασθαι.
1. *to appease* sbd offended: abs. Hb 1.11, Ps 105.30 (ǁ περὶ τῶν υἱῶν Ισραηλ Nu 25.13 [cf. κατέπαυσεν τὸν θυμόν μου ἀπὸ τῶν υἱῶν Ισρ. vs. 11], Si 45.23); + acc., τὸν κύριον Zc 7.2; angry king, Pr 16.14; τὸ πρόσωπον κυρίου Zc 8.22; sim. Ma 1.9 (ǁ δέομαι); τὸ πρόσωπον αὐτοῦ (pers.) ἐν τοῖς δώροις 'with gifts' Ge 32.20; pass., ὑμῖν (dat. com.) 1K 6.3. Cf. *ND* 3.24f.
2. *to perform the rite of the atonement of sins*: *s* Aaron, and of the yearly day of atonement and performed by the high priest, ἅπαξ τοῦ ἐνιαυτοῦ 'once per year' Ex 30.10; + περί τινος 'with respect to', περὶ τῶν ψυχῶν ὑμῶν 30.15; περὶ τῆς οἰκίας 'over the house' Le 14.53; *s* Moses, περὶ τῆς ἁμαρτίας ὑμῶν Ex 32.30; περί τινος (hum.), Nu 8.12; περὶ αὐτοῦ ἀπὸ τῆς ἁμαρτίας αὐτοῦ Le 4.26, sim. 15.15; ἐν τῷ κριῷ τῆς πλημμελείας ἔναντι κυρίου 'by means of the ram of trespass offering before the Lord' 19.22, ἐν νηστείᾳ 'by fasting' PSol 3.8; + ὑπέρ τινος– ὑ. τοῦ οἴκου Ισραηλ Ez 45.17; + acc., τὸ ἅγιον ἀπὸ τῶν ἀκαθαρσιῶν τῶν υἱῶν Ισραηλ .. περὶ πασῶν τῶν ἁμαρτιῶν αὐτῶν 'the sanctuary ..' 16.16; 16.20; τὸ αἷμα 'with the blood' 2C 29.24 (Heb. calque).
3. *to effect atonement of sins*: τὸ αἷμα αὐτοῦ ἀντὶ τῆς ψυχῆς αὐτοῦ ἐξιλάσεται Le 17.11.
4. *to effect atonement for* a punishable deed (τι): ἐξιλασθήσεται αὐτοῖς τὸ αἷμα 'the bloodshed shall be atoned for them' De 21.8, cf. 1K 6.3; τὸ πλῆθος τῶν ἁμαρτιῶν μου 'the multitude of my sins' Si 5.6, σοι κατὰ πάντα ὅσα ἐποίησας Ez 16.63.

5. *to purge*: οὐκ ἐξιλασθήσεται ἡ γῆ ἀπὸ τοῦ αἵματος .. ἀλλ' ἐπὶ τοῦ αἵματος τοῦ ἐκχέοντος 'the land will not be purged from the blood .. except with the blood of one who sheds (it)' Nu 35.33; ***o*** altar and ‖ καθαρίζω Ez 43.26, sanctuary 45.18, temple 45.20.

*6. *to deal forgivingly* with sbd: + περί τινος and *s* God, περὶ τῶν ἀρχαίων γιγάντων 'the ancient giants' Si 16.7 (‖ φείδομαι vs. 8); ὑπέρ τινος 2C 30.18.

Cf. ἐξιλασμός, ἐξίλασμα, ἱλάσκομαι, ἱλασμός, δέομαι, φείδομαι: Dodd 1930f.; Hill 23-36; Grayston 640-56; Horsley at *ND* 3.24f.; *BA* 3.32f. On Da 3.40, see Koch1987.I 36f., II 55-7.

ἐξίλασμα, ατος. n.ʃ *

that which one gives to obtain appeasement: οὐ δώσει τῷ θεῷ ἐ. αὐτοῦ Ps 48.8 (λυτρόομαι); exacted by a person in authority, 1K 12.3. Cf. ἐξιλάσκομαι.

ἐξιλασμός, οῦ. m.

1. *atonement*: w. ref. to the yearly Day of Atonement, Ex 30.10; ἡμέρα ~οῦ Le 23.27, 28; ‖ ἱλασμοῦ 25.9; divine act, Si 17.29 (‖ ἐλεημοσύνη), 18.12 (‖ ἔλεος vs. 11).

2. *act of purging*: Ez 43.23.

Cf. ἐξιλάσκομαι, ἐξίλασις, ἱλασμός.

ἐξιππάζομαι: fut. ~άσομαι.ʃ *

to ride out on horse-back: *s* ἱππεῖς 'horsemen' Hb 1.8. Cf. ἱππάζομαι, ἵππος, and ἱππεύω.

ἐξίπταμαι.ʃ Later form of ἐκπετομαι, q.v.

to fly out: metaph., *s* mind, Pr 7.10 (of a lad seduced and taking leave of his senses).

ἕξις, εως. f.ʃ

1. *physical, bodily condition*: ὑγιὴς καὶ ἰσχύων τῇ ~ει 'healthy and going strong' Si 30.14 (‖ εὐεξία vs. 15); τοῦ σώματος Da 1.15 LXX; 7.28 LXX (TH μορφή); ἕ. μεγέθους 'large size' 1K 16.7. *b. *body*: λέοντος 'of a (dead) lion' Jd 14.9A; ὑποκάτωθέν μου ἐταράχθη ἡ ἕ. μου Hb 3.16, ἔφριξε τὸ πνεῦμά μου ἐν τῇ ~ει μου 'my mind shuddered ..' Da 7.15 TH.

2. *skill, expertise*: Si prol. 11.

Cf. διάθεσις, εὐεξία: Lee 1997.151-65, 2003a. 279-95.

ἐξισόω.ʃ

to make equal to: + dat. and pass., Ex 37.16, 38.15. Cf. ἴσος.

ἐξιστάνω.ʃ Later form of ἐξίστημι, q.v.*

to cause to dissociate oneself from: + gen., τῆς βουλῆς 'from the plan' 3M 1.25.

ἐξίστημι: impf.3pl ἐξίσταντο; fut.act. ἐκστήσω, mid. ἐκστήσομαι; 1aor. ἐξέστησα; 2aor. ἐξέστην, impv.2pl ἔκστητε, subj. ἐκστῶ, pass. ἐξεστάθην; pf.ptc. ἐξεστώς.

1. mid. and 2aor. *to become astonished, amazed, stunned*: out of admiration or awe: abs., Hb 3.2; + ἐπί τινι– ἐπὶ τῷ κυρίῳ καὶ ἐπὶ τοῖς ἀγαθοῖς αὐτοῦ Ho 3.5, cf. Ex 18.9; + ἐπί τινος– ἐπὶ τοῦ ὑετοῦ ^χιόνος^ 'at sleet' Si 43.18 (*s* καρδία and ‖ ἐκθαυμάζω); ‖ φοβέομαι Mi 7.17, Hb 3.2, Is 60.5 (last τῇ καρδίᾳ and w. a ὅτι-clause), Ez 2.6 (ἀπὸ προσώπου τινός); + ἐπί τι– ἐπὶ τὸ γεγονός 'at what had happened' Ju 15.1; ἐπὶ σέ Is 52.14; + dat., τῇ ἀπαντήσει αὐτοῦ 'at the encounter with him' 1K 16.4; with a sense of horror and shock, ἐξέστη Ισαακ ἔκστασιν μεγάλην σφόδρα Ge 27.33; ἕκαστος πρὸς τὸν ἀδελφὸν αὐτοῦ 43.33; ἐξέστη ἡ καρδία αὐτῶν 42.28, ἡ ψυχὴ αὐτοῦ Is 7.2, τὸ πνεῦμα αὐτοῦ Da 2.1 TH; + φοβέομαι 1K 28.5 (*s* καρδία), 17.11; astonishment, ἐξέστη ἡ διάνοια Ιακωβ Ge 45.26, ἐξέστη ὁ οὐρανὸς ἐπὶ τούτῳ καὶ ἔφριξεν 'the heaven was astounded at this and shuddered' Je 2.12 (cf. 5.30), ἀπολεῖται ἡ καρδία τοῦ βασιλέως .. οἱ ἱερεῖς ἐκστήσονται .. θαυμάσονται 4.9, ἐξέστησαν, ἐθυμώθησαν, ἀναπαύσασθαι οὐ μὴ δύνωνται 30.12; τῇ καρδίᾳ Jo 2.11; ἐκλύθητε καὶ ἔκστητε 'get exhausted ..' Is 29.9; + ταράσσομαι Ru 3.8; *s* birds and animals, Je 9.10. **b**. *to arouse intense desire* to act: ἐξέστη τὸ πνεῦμά μου τοῦ γνῶναι τὸ ἐνύπνιον '.. in order to find out about the dream' Da 2.3 TH (LXX ἐκινήθη 'was moved'); ἐξέστη ἡ καρδία Ὀλοφέρνου ἐπ' αὐτήν .. ἦν κατεπίθυμος σφόδρα τοῦ συγγενέσθαι μετ' αὐτῆς '.. longed intensely to get into bed with her' Ju 12.16.

2. *to take leave of one's senses*, 'go mad': ἐξέστησαν διὰ τὸν οἶνον Is 28.7 (‖ σείομαι, πλανάομαι). **b**. *to pass out, lose consciousness*: Jd 4.21B.

3. causative (fut.act., 1aor.act), *drive* one *out of one's senses*, 'astonish': + acc. pers., Ex 23.27, Is 41.2; + acc. rei, βουλὴν Jb 5.13; + cogn. acc., "you have gone to all this astounding length for our sake" 4K 4.13B.

4. act. *to take by surprise*: of surprise attack, τινα 2K 17.2 (‖ ἐκθαμβέω vs. 12*L*).

Cf. ἔκστασις, ἐκπλήσσω, θαυμάζω, μαίνομαι, παραφρονέω, παρεξίστημι: Spicq 2.24-9.

ἐξιχνεύω: aor. ἐξίχνευσα, impv. ~νευσον.ʃ

to track out: abs. Si 6.27; + acc., ἄβυσσον καὶ καρδίαν 42.18 (‖ διανοέομαι). Cf. ἐξιχνιάζω, ἰχνεύω.

ἐξιχνιάζω: fut. ~άσω, mid. ~άσομαι; aor. ἐξιχνίασα, impv. ~νίασον, inf. ~νιάσαι, subj. ~νιάσω.

= ἐξιχνεύω *to track out*: abs., Wi 6.22; + acc., τὴν τρίβον μου 'my track' Ps 138.3, τὴν γῆν Jd 18.2 (+ κατασκέπτω, A: also + ἐξεραυνάω), ἄβυσσον καὶ σοφίαν Si 1.3, τὰ μεγαλεῖα αὐτοῦ 18.4; δίκην Jb 29.16; ‖ ἐπερωτάω 8.8, ‖ ἀναζητέω 10.6 (***o*** ἁμαρτία); + acc. pers., 13.9; mid., + acc., κόσμιον παραβολῶν 'the beauty of parables' Ec 12.9.

Cf. ἐξιχνιασμός, ἐξιχνεύω, ἀναζητέω, ἐπερωτάω, ἀνεξιχνίαστος.

ἐξιχνιασμός, οῦ. m.ʃ

v.n. of prec.: καρδίας Jd 5.16A (B ἐξετασμός 'investigation'). Cf. ἐξιχνιάζω, ἐξετασμός.

ἐξοδεύω: aor.ptc. ~δεύσας, ptc.pass. ~δευθείς.

1. *to depart*: on a military mission, 1E 4.23. **b.** pass. 'to die': Jd 5.27B, cf. ἔξοδος **1c**, ἀπέρχομαι.

2. *to march along*: ***s*** army and + acc., ὁδούς 1M 15.41.

Cf. ἐξοδία, ἐξέρχομαι, ἐξαίρω.

ἐξοδία, ας. f.

exit, departure: ἐκ γῆς Αἰγύπτου De 16.3, ἐξ Αἰγύπτου Mi 7.15. **b.** for outdoor activities: De 33.18 (|| ἐν τοῖς σκηνώμασιν); military expedition, 2K 3.22.

Cf. ἐξέρχομαι, ἐξοδεύω, ἔξοδος.

ἐξοδιάζω: aor. ἐξωδίασα, pass. ἐξωδιάσθην.ʃ

to give out as expenses: τί τινι 4K 12.12*L* (B: ἐκδίδωμι); 12.13. Cf. εἰσοδιάζω.

ἐξόδιος, ον.

*subst.n.sg., *last day of a festival* (ἔξοδος **3**): Le 23.36, Nu 29.35, De 16.8; σκηνῆς 'of the (festival) of the tabernacle' Ps 28.1. Cf. ἔξοδος and *BA* 3.191.

ἔξοδος, ου. f.

1. *act of exiting*: as cogn. dat., ἐξόδῳ ἐξέλθῃ Nu 35.26; w. spec. ref. to the exodus from Egypt, Ex inscr. and subscr. (as the title of the book); τῶν υἱῶν Ισραηλ ἐκ γῆς Αἰγύπτου 19.1, Nu 33.38; opp. εἴσοδος– φυλάξει τὴν εἴσοδόν σου καὶ τὴν ~όν σου Ps 120.8; w. ref. to sunrise, Si 43.2, ἄστρων 'of stars (at the evening)' Ne 4.21; of snow falling out of the sky, Pr 25.13. **b.** military expedition: 2K 11.1 *L* (*B* ἐξοδία). **c.** fig. of human death: Wi 3.2 (|| τεθνάναι), 7.6 (:: εἴσοδος), cf. πνεύματος Si 38.23. **d.** *that which comes out*: vegetation, χλοής 'of young grass' Jb 38.27¶. **e.** *exit out of a womb*, 'delivery': ἐκ γαστρὸς μητρός 'from mother's womb' Si 40.1; Ps 143.13, cf. Euthymius Zig. PG 128.1288. ***f.** ἔξοδος καὶ εἴσοδος idiomatically indicates a whole gamut of activities and movements: ἡ ἔξοδός σου καὶ ἡ εἴσοδός σου μετ' ἐμοῦ ἐν τῇ παρεμβολῇ 1K 18.6, cf. φυλάξει τὴν εἴσοδόν σου καὶ τὴν ἔξοδόν σου Ps 120.8, and s.v. εἰσπορεύομαι and εἰσέρχομαι.

2. *origin, source*: αἱ ~οι αὐτοῦ ἀπ' ἀρχῆς ἐξ ἡμερῶν αἰῶνος Mi 5.2.

3. *coming to the end* of a period of time and entering the next phase: ἐπ' ~ου τοῦ ἐνιαυτοῦ 'at the end of the year' Ex 23.16; πρωίας καὶ ἑσπέρας 'of dawn and evening' Ps 64.9; τοῦ σαββάτου 2C 23.8 (:: ἀρχή).

4. *way leading out*: Is 51.20; || πλατεῖα 'street' Pr 1.20; La 2.21, 2K 22.43.

5. *place for exit*: ὑδάτων 'spring, fountain' Si 50.8. Cf. ἔκρυσις.

Cf. ἐξοδία, ἐξόδιος, ἐξέρχομαι, ἐξέλευσις, εἴσοδος, ὁδός: Michaelis, *TDNT* 5.104f.

ἐξοικοδομέω: aor. ἐξῳκοδόμησα.ʃ

= οἰκοδομέω: Ne 3.15.

ἔξοικος, ον.ʃ*

homeless: ***s*** hum., Jb 6.18.

ἐξοκέλλω: aor. ἐξώκειλα.ʃ

to cause to drift off the right course: metaph., Pr 7.21 (|| ἀποπλανάω 'to seduce away'). Cf. Renehan 2.68.

ἐξολέθρευμα, ατος. n.ʃ *

that which has been destroyed utterly: spoils taken in war, 1K 15.21 (*L* ἀνάθεμα).

Cf. ἐξολεθρεύω.

ἐξολέθρευσις, εως. f.*

v.n. of subs.: Ez 9.1; Jd 1.17A (B: ἀνάθεμα).

ἐξολεθρεύω: fut. ~εύσω, pass. ~ευθήσομαι; aor. ἐξωλέθρευσα, inf. ~λεθρεῦσαι, impv. ~λέθρευσον, subj. ~λεθρεύσω, opt.3s ~λεθρεύσαι, pass. ἐξωλεθρεύθην, subj. ἐξολεθρευθῶ, inf. ~ρευθῆναι, opt.3s ~ρευθείη. Also spelled ~λοθρεύω. *

to destroy utterly, mostly with God as the agent: abs. Ho 8.4; ***o*** life (ψυχή), Ge 17.14, Ex 12.15 (ἐξ Ισραηλ); sinner, 22.20 (pass. and θανάτῳ); offender, 30.33 (pass. || intr. mid. ἀπόλλυμι vs. 38), so De 28.20; people 1.27; Nu 19.20 (|| ἐκτρίβω vs. 13), Am 1.5 (|| συντρίβω), 8 (|| ἐξαίρω), 2.3, Na 3.15 (|| κατεσθίω, and with sword as the agent), Zp 1.11, 3.7, Ma 2.12; survivors of war Ob 14; remnants Zc 14.2; enemies Mi 5.9; military force, troops Hg 2.22 (|| καταστρέφω); cities Mi 5.11 (|| ἐξαίρω), De 2.34, 3.6; foreign gods Zp 2.11; names of idols Zc 13.2; μνημόσυνον 'that which reminds sbd's existence in the past' Ps 33.17; carved idols and stelae Mi 5.13 (|| ἐκκόπτω), cf. Na 1.14; horses Mi 5.10 (|| ἀπόλλυμι); chariots Zc 9.10; arrow, ib.; prey Na 2.14; land Ex 8.24 (ἀπὸ τῆς κυνομυίας 'on account of the dog-flies'); trees De 20.20 (|| ἐκκόπτω); food and joy Jl 1.16; deceitful lips Ps 11.4. **b.** results in severance of ties or affinity: ἀπ' ἐμοῦ 'away from my presence' Le 22.3; ἐκ μέσου τῆς συναγωγῆς Nu 19.20; ἀπὸ προσώπου τῆς γῆς De 6.15; ἀπὸ προσώπου τινός (pers.) 12.29. **c.** + gen. [= abl.] (victim) and acc., τοῦ Αχααβ οὐροῦντα πρὸς τοῖχον 'from Achab, one who pisses against the wall' 3K 20.21. **d.** *to suffer serious damage*: ἀπό τινος 'by losing sth' 3K 18.5.

Cf. ὀλεθρεύω, ἐξολέθρευμα, ἐξολέθρευσις, ἐξόλλυμι, ἀφανίζω.

ἐξόλλυμι, ἐξολλύω: fut.mid.2s ἐξολῇ, 3s ~λεῖται.ʃ

1. *to destroy utterly*: ***s*** and ***o*** hum., Pr 15.27; ***o*** his body, 11.17.

2. mid. *to perish utterly*: *s* hum., Si 5.7; hum. tongue, Pr 10.31.

Cf. ὄλλυμι, ἀφανίζω.

ἐξολοθρεύω. ⇒ ἐξολεθρεύω.

ἐξομβρέω: fut. ~βρήσω; aor. ἐξώμβρησα.ʃ

to cause to descend like rain: metaph., + acc., ἐπιστήμην καὶ γνῶσιν Si 1.19, βδέλυγμα 'abomination' 10.13. Cf. ὄμβρος, ἀνομβρέω.

ἐξόμνυμαι: fut. ~ομοῦμαι; aor.inf. ~ομνύναι, subj. mid. ~όσωμαι.ʃ

mid. *to renounce solemnly and publicly*: + acc. rei, τὸν Ἰουδαϊσμόν 'the Jewish faith' 4M 4.26; *o* virtue of self-control, 5.34 (‖ ἐξαρνέομαι vs. 35), brotherhood, 9.23, kinship, 10.3. Cf. ὀμνύω.

ἐξομοιόω.ʃ

pass. *to imitate and become alike*: 2M 4.16. Cf. ὁμοιόω.

ἐξομολογέομαι: fut. ~γήσομαι; aor.inf. ~γήσασθαι, impv.2pl ~γήσασθε, 3pl ~γησάσθωσαν.

to express recognition, acknowledge orally and in public, often appreciative and laudatory: + acc. rei, τὰς ἁμαρτίας μου Da 9.20 LXX (‖ TH ἐξαγορεύω), ἐξομολογήσονται οἱ οὐρανοὶ τὰ θαυμάσιά σου καὶ τὴν ἀλήθειάν σου ἐν ἐκκλησίᾳ ἁγίων Ps 88.6; + acc. rei and dat. pers., τοῦτο ἐξομολογήσομαι κυρίῳ Ge 29.35, τῷ κυρίῳ τὰ ἐλέη αὐτοῦ καὶ τὰ θαυμάσια αὐτοῦ τοῖς υἱοῖς τῶν ἀνθρώπων Ps 106.8, cf. ἐξομολογήσομαι τῷ ὀνόματί σου ἐπὶ τῷ ἐλέει σου .. 137.2; ^τῷ θεῷ^ ἐξομολογεῖσθε ἐνώπιον πάντων ζώντων ἃ [𝔊^{I} περὶ ὧν] ἐποίησεν μεθ' ὑμῶν ἀγαθά To 12.6 𝔊^{II}; ἐξωμολογοῦντο ⌜τὰ⌝ [𝔊^{II} ἐπὶ τὰ] ἔργα τὰ μεγάλα καὶ θαυμαστὰ τοῦ θεοῦ 12.22 𝔊^{I}; + πρός τινα Su 14 LXX; + ἐπί τι Ps 118.62; + ὅτι 2M 7.37. **b**. + dat. pers. only: τῷ κυρίῳ ἐν στόματί μου καὶ ἐν μέσῳ πολλῶν αἰνέσω αὐτόν Ps 108.30; σοί, κύριε, ἐν ἐκκλησίᾳ πολλῇ 34.18; Is 45.23, Je 40.11. ***c**. + dat. rei: τῇ μνήμῃ τῆς ἁγιωσύνης σου 'to the memory of your sanctity' Ps 29.5 (‖ ψάλλω), τῷ ὀνόματί σου, κύριε 53.8; expanded by a ὅτι-clause equivalent to an acc. rei, τῷ ὀνόματί σου τῷ μεγάλῳ, ὅτι φοβερὸν καὶ ἅγιόν ἐστιν 98.3. **d**. often ‖ αἰνέω, ὑμνέω, ψάλλω and the like: Ps 29.5, 34.18, 108.30, Si 51.1, ἐν κιθάρᾳ 'with a lyre' Ps 42.4; ‖ διηγέομαι 'narrate' 9.2.

The feature of thanks and gratitude cannot be established with certainty. The verb in ModGk means 'to confess, acknowledge,' but not 'to thank.' Cf. Helbing, *Kasus*. 243f.; Flashar 176-9; Tov 1990. 97-110.

Cf. ἐξομολόγησις, ὁμολογέω, ἐξαγορεύω, εὐχαριστέω.

ἐξομολόγησις, εως. f. *

v.n. of prec.: μετὰ φωνῆς αἰνέσεως καὶ ~εως θύσω σοι Jn 2.10, ἐ. καὶ φωνὴ αἰνέσεως Is 51.3; ‖ ἀνθομολόγησις, αἰνέω Si 17.28; ἔδωκεν ~ιν ἁγίῳ ὑψίστῳ ῥήματι δόξης 47.8. **b**. w. ref. to confession of sins: ‖ ἐξαγορία PSol 9.6. **c**. *that which is said in recognition and acknowledgement*: of God's nature and deeds, pl. + ὕμνος 2M 10.38; + ψαλμός 3M 6.35.

Cf. αἴνεσις and ὁμολογέω.

ἐξόπισθεν. prep.

1. *from behind*: + gen. (of sbd whose company one leaves), Ps 77.71, 3K 19.21, 4K 17.21, 1C 17.7.

2. *at the back of*, 'behind': opp. 'in front,' κατὰ πρόσωπον καὶ ἐ. 1C 19.10, ἐξ ἐναντίας ἡμῶν καὶ ἐ. ἡμῶν 'in front of us and behind us' 1M 9.45.

Cf. ὄπισθεν.

ἐξοπλίζω: aor.impv. ~όπλισον, subj.mid. ~ίσωμαι; pf.ptc.pass. ἐξωπλισμένος.ʃ

to arm fully: + acc. pers. Nu 31.3; mid. εἰς πόλεμον 32.20; pass. 2M 5.2. Cf. ὅπλον, ἐνοπλίζω, ἐξοπλισία.

ἐξοπλισία, ας. f.ʃ

armed parade: 2M 5.25.

ἐξορκίζω: fut. ~κιῶ; aor. ἐξώρκισα.ʃ

to charge (sbd τινα) *under oath*: abs., Jd 17.2 A (B: ἀράομαι); + double acc. and a ἵνα-clause, ἐξορκιῶ σε κύριον .. ἵνα μὴ λάβῃς γυναῖκα .. 'I shall adjure you by the Lord that you shall not take a wife ..' Ge 24.3. Cf. ὅρκος, ὁρκισμός, ὄμνυμι, ὁρκίζω: Aitken 2007.50.

ἐξορμάω: aor. ἐξώρμησα.

to dash out for an action: *s* hum., 3M 1.18; troops, 2M 11.7. Cf. ὁρμάω.

ἐξορύσσω: aor. ἐξώρυξα, inf. ἐξορύξαι.ʃ

1. *to gouge out*: + acc., ὀφθαλμούς Jd 16.21 A (B: ἐκκόπτω), sim. 1K 11.2.

2. *to cause to emerge in the open*: metaph., + acc. rei, ἁμαρτίας Pr 29.22 (‖ simp.).

Cf. ὀρύσσω.

ἐξουδενέω: aor. ἐξουδένησα. *

= ἐξουθενέω, q.v.: ‖ ἀπωθέω Ez 21.10; + acc., τὰ ἅγιά μου 22.8 (‖ βεβηλόω), τινα 4K 19.21 B (*L* φαυλίζω; ‖ μυκτηρίζω). Cf. ἐξουδένημα, ἐξουδενόω, μυκτηρίζω.

ἐξουδένημα, ατος. n.ʃ

that which is thought to be of no account and treated as such: *s* hum. and ‖ ὄνειδος Ps 21.7; Da 4.14 TH. Cf. ἐξουδενέω, ἐξουδένωμα.

ἐξουδενόω: fut. ~νώσω, pass. ~νωθήσομαι; aor. ἐξουδένωσα, subj. ~νώσω, ptc. ~νώσας; pf. ἐξουδένωκα, ptc.pass. ἐξουδενωμένος. *

to consider to be of no account and treat as such: abs. Zc 4.10; Τράπεζα κυρίου ἐξουδενωμένη ἐστί 'The table of the Lord is treated with contempt' Ma 1.7*a*; *o* cultic offerings, 1.7*b*, 12; of people, 2.9 (‖ παρίεμαι); ‖ προσοχθίζω Ps 21.25, + acc. pers., 1K 8.7 (‖ ἐξουθενέω), Jb 30.1¶, and ‖ ἐκγελάω Ps

58.9; + ἀτιμόω 1K 15.9B (*L* ἀπογινώσκω); + dat. pers. Ct 8.1.

Cf. ἐξουδ/θενέω, ἀδοξέω, ἀκυρόω, παρίημι, ὑπερφρονέω. On the spelling difference from ἐξουθενέω, see under οὐδείς.

ἐξουδένωμα, ατος. n.ʃ

= ἐξουδένημα, q.v.: Ps 89.5.

ἐξουδένωσις, εως. f. *

v.n. of ἐξουδενόω, directed at hum.: cogn. dat., Ct 8.7; + ὑπερηφανία 'arrogance' Ps 30.19, + ὄνειδος 118.22, 122.4. Cf. ἐξουδενόω.

ἐξουθενέω: fut.~νήσω; pf. ἐξουθένηκα. *

= ἐξουδενόω (q.v., and cf. Mayser I 2².117, I 3.216f.): Am 6.1; ἰῶντο .. ἐξουθενοῦντες 'performing a perfunctory treatment' Je 6.14; + gen. pers., Si 22.13¶; + acc. pers., 1K 8.7 (‖ ἐξουδενόω); + acc. rei, σοφίαν καὶ παιδείαν Pr 1.7. Cf. ἐξουδενόω, ἐξουθένωσις.

ἐξουθενόω: aor.pass. ἐξουθενώθην.

= prec.: ‖ ἀτιμόω PSol.2.5.

ἐξουθένωσις, εως. f.ʃ

= ἐξουδένωσις: 1M 1.39. Cf. ἐξουθενέω.

ἐξουσία, ας. f.

authoritative responsibility: ἐπὶ τὴν διοίκησιν 'for the administration' To 1.21 𝔊ᴵᴵ; + gen., τῆς γῆς Si 10.4, τῶν ἐπὶ ^τῆς γῆς^ 17.2, τὸν ἥλιον εἰς τὴν ~αν τῆς ἡμέρας Ps 135.8, cf. εἰς ἀρχὰς .. Ge 1.16; οἱ ἐπ' ~ῶν 'those holding positions of authority' Da 3.2. **b**. *absolute authority to deal with* sbd or sth *as one pleases*: God's, Da 4.34c LXX, + gen., πάντων τῶν ἐν τῷ οὐρανῷ 4.14 LXX; ἔν τινι 4.28 LXX **c**. *authority granted to take a certain action*: περὶ ^τῶν χρημάτων^ 'about these funds' 4M 4.5; τοῦ λέγειν 'to speak' 5.15; τῆς ἡγεμονίας 'to govern' 6.33; + inf., Si 9.13, To 2.13 (𝔊ᴵ θεμιτόν), 7.10 𝔊ᴵᴵ. **d**. *institution or individual invested with authority*: pl., Da 7.27 LXX (TH ἀρχαί).

Cf. ἐνεξουσιάζομαι, ἐξουσιάζομαι, I ἔξειμι: Foerster, *TDNT* 2.564f.

ἐξουσιάζω: fut. ~σιάσω; aor. ἐξουσίασα, mid. ἐξουσιασάμην.

1. *to have authority and permission*: + inf., 2E 7.24. ***b**. caus. *to grant permission*: + acc. pers. and inf., Ec 5.18, + dat. pers. 6.2.

2. *to wield power and exercise authority*: abs., βασιλεὺς ἐξουσιάζων Ec 8.4; ἐν πνεύματι 8.8, ἐπὶ τὰ σώματα ἡμῶν καὶ ἐν κτήνεσιν ἡμῶν ὡς ἀρεστὸν αὐτοῖς 'over our bodies and our cattle as he pleases' Ne 9.37. Cf. προστατέω **1**.

3. mid. *to swagger, behave in high-handed manner*: Si 35.9; ἐπί τινα Ne 5.15, 1M 10.70.

4. mid. *to exercise control over*: + ἐν Ec 2.19, 7.19, 8.9.

Cf. ἐνεξουσιάζομαι.

ἐξοχή, ῆς. f.ʃ

sth elevated and conspicuous: πέτρας 'of a rock' Jb 39.28¶.

ἐξόχως. adv.ʃ

exceedingly: 3M 5.31. Cf. σφόδρα.

ἐξυβρίζω: aor. ἐξύβρισα.ʃ

1. *to behave arrogantly*: βασάνισον τοὺς καταδυναστεύοντας καὶ ἐξυβρίζοντας ἐν ὑπερηφανίᾳ 'punish severely those who lord it over and behave arrogantly with insolence' 2M 1.28.

2. *to overflow violently*: ὡς ὕδωρ Ge 49.4 (metaph. of a reckless misdeed); ἐξύβριζε τὸ ὕδωρ ὡς ῥοῖζος χειμάρρου 'like a rushing wadi' Ez 47.5.

Cf. ὕβρις, ὑπερηφανία, αὐθάδης.

ἐξυμνέω: aor. ἐξύμνησα.ʃ

to sing a hymn: τῷ ὀνόματι τοῦ θεοῦ αὐτοῦ PSol 6.4. Cf. ὑμνέω.

ἐξυπνίζω: fut.pass. ~πνισθήσομαι; aor.pass. ἐξυπνίσθην.ʃ

pass. *to wake up* from sleep: ἐξ ὕπνου Jb 14.12¶; Jd 16.14B (A: ἐξεγείρομαι), 3K 3.15. Cf. ἔξυπνος, ἐξεγείρω.

ἔξυπνος, ον.ʃ *

awakened out of sleep: *s* hum., 1E 3.3. Cf. ἐξυπνίζω.

ἐξυπνόω: fut. ἐξυπνώσω.ʃ

intr. *to wake up* from a wrong mindframe: "from your (ἀπό) foolish philosophy" 4M 5.11. Cf. ἐξυπνίζω, ὑπνόω.

ἐξυψόω.ʃ *

to elevate: metaph., + acc., σεαυτόν Si 1.30, τὸν θεόν Da LXX 3.51 (+ ὑμνέω, δοξάζω, εὐλογέω). Cf. ὑψόω.

ἔξω: comp. ἐξώτερος, α, ον; adv. ἐξωτέρω; super. ἐξώτατος.

I. adv. *to the outside* of a building or room: ἐξήγαγεν αὐτὸν ἔξω Ge 15.5; ἐξῆλθεν ἔ. 39.13; οὐκ ἐξοίσετε ἐκ τῆς οἰκίας .. ἔξω 'you shall not take .. out of the house' Ex 12.46; outside of family circle, ἔ. ἀνδρὶ μὴ ἐγγίζοντι De 25.5. **b**. adj., αὐλὴ ἐξωτέρα 'outer court' Ez 10.5.

2. *in a space outside* of a building or room: ὅταν διακαθιζάνῃς ἔξω 'when you open the bowels outdoors' De 23.13; ἀνέγνωσαν ἔ. νόμον 'they read the law outdoors' Am 4.5. **b**. used attributively, τοῖς δυσὶν ἀδελφοῖς αὐτοῦ ἔξω Ge 9.22; τῆς ἐργασίας τῆς ἔ. 1C 26.29.

II. prep. *outside of*: + gen. ἔξω τῆς πόλεως Ge 24.11; ἔ. τῆς παρεμβολῆς Ex 33.7; ib. and opp. ἐν τῇ παρεμβολῇ Le 17.3; opp. εἰς τὴν παρεμβολήν De 23.10.

2. *without being affected by*: ἔξω φόβου Jb 39.3.

***3**. *in addition to and wilfully overlooking*: Jo 22.19.

III. comp. adj., αὐλὴ ἐξωτέρα 'outside court' Ez 40.17.

Cf. ἔξωθεν and ἔσω.

ἔξωθεν.

I. adv. **1**. *from the outside*: + gen. ἔκλεισεν .. ἔξ. αὐτοῦ τὴν κιβωτόν 'closed the ark on him from outside' Ge 7.16; 20.18; ‖ ἀπὸ τῶν πλατειῶν 'from the streets' Je 9.21. **b**. used adj.: τῶν ἔ. ἀλγηδόνων 'the external pains' 4M 6.34; opp. ἔνδοθεν 18.2.

2. *on the outside*: ἔσωθεν καὶ ἔ. Ge 6.14, Ex 25.10; De 32.25.

II. prep. *on the outside of*: + gen., Ex 26.35, 27.21, Le 24.3.

Cf. ἔξω, ἔνδοθεν, ἔσωθεν.

ἐξωθέω: fut. ἐξώσω, pass. ἐξωσθήσομαι; aor. ἐξῶσα, ἐξέωσα, inf. ἐξῶσαι, subj. ἐξώσω, impv. ἔξωσον, pass. ἐξώσθην; pf.pass.ptc. ἐξωσμένος.

1. *to eject*: + acc. pers. and ‖ ἀπορρίπτω Mi 2.9; ‖ ἀπωθέω 4.6; ἐκ τῶν ὁρίων αὐτῶν Jl 3.6. **b**. *to release*: ἐφ' ἡμᾶς τὴν κακίαν 'the calamity on us' 2K 15.14B.

2. *to expel, banish*: + acc. pers. αὐτὸν εἰς γῆν ἄνυδρον '.. into a waterless land' Jl 2.20, ἐκ γῆς Pr 2.22.

3. *to divert, lead away*: + acc. pers., ἐκ τῆς ὁδοῦ De 13.5; τὸν Ισραηλ ⸢ἀπὸ ὄπισθεν⸣ (B: ἐξόπισθεν) τοῦ κυρίου 4K 17.21.

Cf. ἔξωσμα, (ἀπ)ωθέω, ἀπορρίπτω, ἐκβάλλω.

ἔξωσμα, ατος. n.ʃ *

that which is to be rejected: + λήμματα μάταια 'meaningless messages' La 2.14. Cf. ἐξωθέω.

ἔοικα.ʃ

Impers., *it seems*: ὡς ἔοικεν 'as it seems' Jb 6.3, 25. Cf. δοκέω, φαίνω: Schmidt 1.324-6.

ἑορτάζω: fut. ἑορτάσω; aor.inf. ἑορτάσαι, impv. ἑόρτασον.

to celebrate (a religious festival): abs., ἵνα μοι ἑορτάσωσιν ἐν τῇ ἐρήμῳ Ex 5.1; ***o*** day, 12.14; w. ἑορτή as cogn. obj., Nu 29.12, Na 1.15, Zc 14.16; + dat. pers., αὐτὴν ἑορτὴν κυρίῳ Ex 12.14; De 16.15. Cf. ἑορτή, ποιέω **I 11**.

ἑόρτασμα, ατος. n.ʃ *

festive celebration: welcoming of foreign guests, Wi 19.16. Cf. ἑορτή.

ἑορτή, ῆς. f.

regular religious festival: ἑ. κυρίου τοῦ θεοῦ ἡμῶν Ex 10.9; ἐν ταῖς ἡμέραις τῆς εὐφροσύνης ὑμῶν καὶ ἐν ταῖς ~αῖς .. καὶ ἐν ταῖς νουμηνίαις .. Nu 10.10; μεταστρέψω τὰς ~ὰς ὑμῶν εἰς πένθος 'I will turn your festivities into sorrow' Am 8.10, cf. Zp 3.18, Zc 8.19; ‖ πανήγυρις Ho 2.11, 9.5, Am 5.21; ἑβδομάδων 'of weeks' Ex 34.22, De 16.16; τοῦ πάσχα Ex 34.25; τῶν σκηνῶν De 16.13; τῆς σκηνοπηγίας 'of the tabernacle' 16.16, Zc 14.16; τῶν ἀζύμων 'of the unleavened bread' Ex 23.15, De 16.16; as cogn. obj. of ἑορτάζω Na 1.15, Zc 14.16. Cf. ἑορτάζω, ἑόρτασμα, νουμηνία, πανήγυρις, σάββατον: Casarico.

ἐπαγγελία, ας. f.

1. *that which one has undertaken to produce*: Am 9.6; + τινι 1E 1.7; cogn. acc. of ἐπαγγέλλομαι Es 4.7.

2. *demand, request*: 4M 12.9, cf. *ND* 4.147.

Cf. ἐπαγγέλλομαι.

ἐπαγγέλλομαι: aor. ἐπηγγειλάμην, ptc. ~γγειλάμενος; pf.ptc.pass. ἐπηγγελμένος.

1. *to make profession of*: abs., .. μὴ ἐπαγγέλου 'Stop making an (unfounded) claim (of knowledge)' Si 3.25¶; + inf., Wi 2.13.

2. *to promise*: abs., Pr 13.12; + dat. pers., Si 20.23; τινί τι (money) 1M 11.28, 2M 4.27, 45; ἐπαγγελίαν as cogn. obj., Es 4.7 o'; + fut. inf. 3M 1.4; + διότι 2.10.

Cf. ἐπαγγελία, ὑπισχνέομαι, ὑπόσχεσις: Schniewind / Friedrich, *TDNT* 2.576-81.

ἐπάγω: fut. ἐπάξω, mid. ἐπάξομαι; aor. ἐπήγαγον, subj. ἐπαγάγω, ptc. ἐπαγαγών, inf. ἐπαγαγεῖν, ἐπάξαι, pass.subj. ἐπαχθῶ; pf.ptc.pass. ἐπηγμένος.

1. *to cause to move* over or on to sth, ἐπί τι/τινα: often w. hostile intent, ***o*** flood-water (κατακλυσμὸς ὕδωρ) Ge 6.17; ἐπ' αὐτοὺς .. τὸ ὕδωρ τῆς θαλάσσης Ex 15.19; rain (punitive) Ge 7.4 (‖ wind [πνεῦμα] 8.1); curse (κατάρα) 27.12, wrath (ὀργή) Is 26.21; blow (πληγή) Ex 11.1, 33.5; infirmity and blow (μαλακία, πληγή) De 28.61; hot wind Ho 13.15; southern wind which carries locusts, Ex 10.13; God's punitive hand, Am 1.8, Zc 13.7, Is 1.25; hostile nation, ἐπὶ σέ De 28.49, cf. Je 28.64; πρὸς ἑαυτοὺς ἁμαρτίαν Ex 28.39; ἐφ' ἑαυτοὺς ἀνομίαν Le 22.16; sword, ἐφ' ὑμᾶς μάχαιραν ἐκδικοῦσαν 26.25, ῥομφαίαν ἐπὶ τὴν γῆν Hg 1.11; calamity Am 5.9, κακά Je 25.17, 39.42; divine wrath, Is 42.25, Ps 7.12; ἐπ' ἐμὲ καὶ ἐπὶ τὴν βασιλείαν μου ἁμαρτίαν μεγάλην Ge 20.9, sim. Ex 32.21; ἐφ' ἡμᾶς ἄγνοιαν Ge 26.10, πένθος μέγα Ba 4.9, αἰχμαλωσίαν 4.10; φόβον καὶ δειλίαν Si 4.17; κραυγὴν πενήτων 'a cry of the poor' Jb 34.28¶; + dat. pers., πᾶσαν νόσον, ἣν ἐπήγαγον τοῖς Αἰγυπτίοις, οὐκ ἐπάξω ἐπὶ σέ Ex 15.26; Jb 22.17; τῇ ψυχῇ σου ἀτιμίαν '.. dishonour' Si 1.30; ἡμῖν καὶ ἐπὶ τὴν πόλιν σου Da 3.28. **b**. obj. = sth desirable: εὐφροσύνην Zp 3.17; w. no obj., ἡμῖν κατὰ τὸ ἔλεος αὐτοῦ Is 63.7. **c**. abs.: De 23.13 (perh. γῆ or σποδός 'soil' understood); ἐπ' αὐτὴν κατὰ πάσας τὰς κατάρας 29.27; a noun denoting a form of punishment or recompense understood (?), ἐπάξει ἐπὶ .. τὸν ἄρχοντα Is 10.12.

2. *to cause to bear punishment for* or *consequences of*, 'punish for': + ἐπί τινα + acc., ἐπάξω ἐπ' αὐτοὺς τὴν ἁμαρτίαν αὐτῶν Ex 32.34; ἐπάγων ἀνομίας πατέρων ἐπὶ τέκνα 34.7, ἐφ' ἡμᾶς ὅρκον '.. an oath' Ju 8.30; || (ἐπι)τίθημι Jd 9.24.

3. *to assail* with *s* God, prob. τὴν χεῖρα αὐτοῦ understood (see **1** above): ἐπήγαγες καὶ ἀπώλεσας καὶ ἦρας πᾶν ἄρσεν αὐτῶν 'you assailed, destroyed and took every male among them' Is 26.14.

4. *to cause to come true*: ἐπὶ Αβρααμ πάντα, ὅσα ἐλάλησεν πρὸς αὐτόν Ge 18.19, ἐπὶ τὴν γῆν ἐκείνην πάντας τοὺς λόγους Je 25.13.

5. *to set in motion*: + acc., πόλεμον '(wage) a war' Si 46.3.

6. mid. *to bring with one*: + acc., as companion, Pr 6.22.

*__7__. idiom., ἐπάγω χεῖρά μου πρὸς χεῖρά μου *to take resolute action*: ἐπί τινι 'over sth' Ez 22.13, cf. κροτέω.

Cf. ἄγω, ἐπαγωγή.

ἐπαγωγή, ης. f.

1. *calamity*: ἐκλελοιπότας ἐν ~ῇ 'exhausted ..' De 32.36; ἐν καιρῷ ~ῆς Si 2.2; ἐν ἡμέρᾳ ~ῆς 5.8; || ἐκδίκησις 25.14; pl. 10.13, 23.11; ~αί, λιμὸς καὶ σύντριμμα καὶ μάστιξ 'famine, destruction and scourge' 40.9.

2. v.n. of ἐπάγω **1** or **3**: ἐθνῶν 'of gentiles' PSol 2.22.

Cf. ἐπάγω.

ἐπαγωγός, ον.ʃ

alluring: subst.n.pl., *alluring offers*, 4M 8.15.

ἐπᾴδω: aor.inf. ἐπᾷσαι.

to act as enchanter: + cogn. acc., ἐπαοιδήν De 18.11; snake-charmer, Ps 57.6 (|| σοφός); + dat. (snake) Je 8.17. Cf. ἐπαοιδή.

ἐπαινετός, ή, όν.ʃ

deserving warm approbation: *s* πόλις Ez 26.17. Cf. ἐπαινέω.

ἐπαινέω: fut. ~νέσω, mid. ~νεσθήσομαι; aor. ἐπήνεσα, subj. ~νέσω, pass. ἐπηνέθην.

1. *to speak in warm approbation of*, 'to praise': abs., Ps 43.9 (|| ἐξομολογέομαι); *o* woman for her beauty and + πρός τινα– ἐπήνεσεν αὐτὴν πρὸς Φαραω Ge 12.15; hum., Ju 6.20, Si 27.7; God, τοὺς θεοὺς τῶν ἐθνῶν Da 5 praef. LXX, τὸν κύριον Ps 116.1, 147.1 (both || αἰνέω), and *s* lips, 62.4; pass. ἐπαινεῖται ὁ ἁμαρτωλὸς ἐν ταῖς ἐπιθυμίαις τῆς ψυχῆς αὐτοῦ 'over his heart's desires' 9.24 (|| ἐνευλογέω); + acc. rei, τοὺς λόγους μου 55.5, τὰ ἔργα σου 144.4; idols, 3M 4.16; + τινά τινος– τὸν Ισραηλ παιδείας καὶ σοφίας 'Israel for its good education and wisdom' Si prol. 3; 4M 1.10, 4.4, cf. Renehan 2.69 for the rection with the gen.

*__2__. mid. *to speak with pride of*: ἔν τινι– ἐν τῷ κυρίῳ ἐπαινεσθήσεται ἡ ψυχή μου Ps 33.3 (|| μεγαλύνω, ὑψόω vs. 4), ἐν τῷ θεῷ 43.9 (|| ἐξομολογέομαι), ἐν τῷ ὀνόματι τῷ ἁγίῳ 104.3; || εὐφραίνω 62.12, 63.11, 104.3, 105.5. The government by ἐν is Hebraistic.

Cf. αἰνέω, ἐπαινετός, ἔπαινος: Aejmelaeus 2003. 510f.

ἔπαινος, ου. m.

1. *approbation, public recognition of achievements* or *desirable qualities*: + obj. gen. and approbation of hum. by hum., τὸν ~ον αὐτοῦ ἐξαγγελεῖ ἐκκλησία Si 39.10, 44.15; pl. 44.8; by God, τὸν τοῦ θεοῦ (subj. gen.) ~ον καὶ τὴν εὐλογίαν αὐτοῦ Wi 15.19; + obj. gen., παρὰ σοῦ ὁ ἔ. μου ἐν ἐκκλησίᾳ Ps 21.26; ἐπορεύθη (*L* ἀπέθανεν) ἐν οὐκ ~ῳ 'he died in disgrace' 2C 21.20; + δόξα 1C 16.27 (ascribable to God).

2. *object deserving approbation*: = God, ὁ ἔ. Ισραηλ Ps 21.4.

Cf. ἐπαινέω, ψόγος: Preisker, *TDNT* 2.586f.

ἐπαίρω: fut.pass. ἐπαρθήσομαι; aor. ἐπῆρα, impv. ἔπαρον, ptc. ἐπάρας, inf. ἐπᾶραι, subj. ἐπάρω, opt. 3s ἐπάραι, mid. ἐπηράμην, ptc. ἐπαράμενος, pass. ἐπήρθην, impv. ἐπάρθητι, inf. ἐπαρθῆναι, ptc. ἐπαρθείς; pf.pass. ἐπῆρμαι, ptc. ἐπηρμένος.

1. *to raise, lift up*: *o* ship (κιβωτός) Ge 7.17 (*s* rising flood water); ῥάβδον εἰς τὸν οὐρανόν 'staff' Ex 10.13; hands of a military leader, Ex 17.11 (:: καθήκω), Si 46.2; with hostile intent, χεῖρα ἐπί τινα 2K 18.28*L*, 20.21 (*L* ἀνταίρω), 2M 7.34 (mid.); horn, τὰ ἔθνη τὰ ἐπαιρόμενα (mid.) κέρας ἐπὶ τὴν γῆν κυρίου 'the nations raising a horn against ..' Zc 1.21, εἰς ὕψος τὸ κέρας Ps 74.5 (|| ὑψόω); eyes in order to have a good look, ἐπάρας .. τοὺς ὀφθαλμοὺς αὐτοῦ εἶδεν .. Ge 13.10, πρὸς τὰ ἐνθυμήματα Ez 18.6; *face (of favourable attention), ἐπάραι κύριος τὸ πρόσωπον αὐτοῦ ἐπὶ σὲ καὶ δώῃ σοι εἰρήνην Nu 6.27; head with dignity Zc 1.21; hand for an action Nu 20.11, so as to attack Jb 31.21 (+ dat. of victim), of a worshipper Ps 133.2; pass., of sunrise, ἐπήρθη ὁ ἥλιος Hb 3.11; ἐπὶ θρόνου ὑψηλοῦ καὶ ἐπηρμένου 'on a high and raised throne' Is 6.1; metaph., pass., *o* God's magnificence, Ps 8.2; hum. promoted in rank, Es 3.1 *L*, ἐπηρμένος δυνάμει 'outstanding in physical strength' Jd 11.1 B. **b**. fig. of a shepherd carrying sheep on his shoulders (?): Ps 27.9. **c**. φωνήν: 1K 24.17*L* (B: simp.), Ps 92.3, Jd 2.4; Ru 1.9.

2. *to puff up, exalt*: of arrogant person, ὑπερηφανία τῆς καρδίας σου ἐπῆρέ σε Ob 3, σεαυτόν Si 6.1; οἱ ἐπηρμένοι ἀργυρίῳ 'those who are puffed up on account of silver' Zp 1.11; ἐπῆρέν σε ἡ καρδία σου 4K 14.10, ὑψώθη καὶ ἐπήρθη ἡ καρδία αὐτοῦ 1M 1.3, θυμῷ 'with rage' 2M 9.4; with no pejorative overtone, οἱ τίμιοι οἱ ἐπηρμένοι ἐν χρυσίῳ 'the honourable ..' La 4.2; mid., εἰς ὕβριν μὴ ἐπαίρου τῇ ψυχῇ σου 'don't get worked up into an arrogant attitude' Pr 19.18, ὕβρει καὶ θράσει 'in arrogance and audacity' 3M 2.21; ὡς τὰς κέδρους τοῦ Λιβάνου Ps 36.35 (ὑπερυψοῦμαι); to assert political independence, Ez 17.14, ἐπὶ βασιλεῖς 2E 4.19, sim. 1M 8.5, ἐπὶ τὴν βασιλείαν 3K 12.24b, ἐπὶ σῇ σοφίᾳ Pr 3.5.

3. intr. *to rise up*: Ez 10.15.

Cf. αἴρω, ὑπερηφανεύομαι: Jeremias, *TDNT* 1.186.

ἐπαισχύνω: fut. ~χυνθήσομαι; aor.pass. ἐπησχύνθην, subj. ~χυνθῶ.ʃ

1. pass. *to feel shame, lose face*: with a sense of disappointment at one's hope and trust betrayed: + ἐπί τινι– ἐπὶ τοῖς κήποις αὐτῶν, ἃ ἐπεθύμησαν 'over their gardens, which they desired very much' Is 1.29 (ǁ καταισχύνομαι).

***2**. *to feel diffident, shy towards*: abs., ἐν τῷ με ἐπιβλέπειν ἐπὶ πάσας τὰς ἐντολάς σου 'as I look at all of your commandments' Ps 118.6 (guilty conscience); + acc., οὐκ ἐπησχύνθη πρόσωπον ἐντίμου 'looked a notable straight in the face' Jb 34.19.

Cf. αἰσχύνω, καταισχύνω.

ἐπαιτέω: aor.impv.3pl ~τησάτωσαν.ʃ

to live by alms, 'beg': κρεῖσσον ἀποθανεῖν ἢ ἐπαιτεῖν 'better to die than to be a beggar' Si 40.28; Ps 108.10. Cf. ἐπαίτησις.

ἐπαίτησις, εως. f.ʃ

v.n. of prec.: ζωὴ ~εως 'life of begging' Si 40.28; 40.30.

ἐπακολουθέω: fut. ~ακολουθήσω; aor. ἐπηκολούθησα, inf. ~θῆσαι, impv. ~θησον, subj. ~θήσω, ptc. ~θήσας.

1. *to follow behind*: abs., Jo 6.8, Es D 4 o'; in pursuit, Ju 14.4; + dat. pers., Pr 7.22.

2. *to follow* sbd or sth *as having authority*: + dat. pers., εἰδώλοις Le 19.4, ἐγγαστριμύθοις 'ventriloquists' 19.31 (ǁ προσκολλάομαι), 20.6; God Nu 14.24, pagans De 12.30; τῷ προστάγματι κυρίου Jo 14.14, ταῖς ὁδοῖς μου Is 55.3; τῷ ὀφθαλμῷ Jb 31.7; ὀπίσω κυρίου Jo 14.9 (ǁ κυρίῳ vs. 8), ὀπίσω δυνάστου Si 46.6.

Cf. (συνεπ)ακολουθέω, προσκολλάω: Schmidt 3.240f.

ἐπακουστός, όν.ʃ

**entitled to compliance*: *s* king, 1E 4.12.

ἐπακούω: fut. ~κούσομαι; aor. ἐπήκουσα, inf. ἐπακοῦσαι, impv. ~κουσον, opt.3s ~κούσαι; pf. ἐπακήκοα.

1. *to give ear, listen*: + dat. pers. (see Helbing, *Kasus*. 155), τῷ οὐρανῷ .. τῇ γῇ (both personified as supplicants) Ho 2.21; 2.22b, Zc 10.6; αὐτὸς ἐπικαλέσεται τὸ ὄνομά μου, καὶ ἐγὼ ἐπακούσομαι αὐτῷ 13.9; ἐπακούσεταί μοι ἡ δικαιοσύνη μου 'my integrity will be my advocate' Ge 30.33. **b**. + gen. pers.: *s* God, 1K 28.15*L* (B: dat.). **c**. + gen. rei, τῆς φωνῆς τοῦ παιδίου Ge 21.17 (in distress and ǁ εἰσακούω), τῆς δεήσεως αὐτοῦ 'his entreaty' Si 4.6. **d**. *+ ἐπί τι - ἐπὶ τὰς δεήσεις μου Da 9.17 LXX (ǁ gen. rei; TH εἰσακούω). **e**. *εἴς τι: εἰς δέησιν πτωχοῦ 'to an entreaty by the poor' PSol 18.2. **f**. *ἔμπροσθέν τινος: Is 45.1.

2. *to take sympathetic note of*: + dat. rei, ἐπήκουσεν ὁ κύριος τῇ ταπεινώσει σου '.. your humiliating situation' Ge 16.11, εὐχαῖς Pr 15.29 'prayers'; + gen. pers., ἐπήκουσεν αὐτῆς ὁ θεὸς Ge 30.22; Is 49.8 (ǁ βοηθέω), Ps 142.1 (ǁ εἰσακούω, ἐνωτίζομαι), αὐτοῦ ἐν λίθοις χαλάζης 'with hailstones Si 46.5; + dat. pers., τῷ θεῷ τῷ ἐπακούσαντί μοι ἐν ἡμέρᾳ θλίψεως Ge 35.3.

3. *to accede to a request made orally by*: + gen. pers., *s* God, Ge 25.21; περὶ Ισμαηλ .. ἐπήκουσά σου 17.20.

***4**. *to grant* sth in response to a request: + acc., ἡ γῆ ἐπακούσεται τὸν σῖτον καὶ τὸν οἶνον καὶ τὸ ἔλαιον Ho 2.22a (so Cyr. I 78 ἐκδώσει, and Th 17 παρέξεται, and cf. Helbing, *Kasus*. 155); τοῦ ἀργυρίου ἐπακούσεται σὺν τὰ πάντα 'it [= wine], when paid for, would meet all the requests' Ec 10.19.

5. *to react* to oral message: orally, 'respond,' but not to a question asked– φωνῇ μεγάλῃ Da 6.21 LXX; Ju 14.15; not orally, ὁ θεός, ὃς ἐὰν ἐπακούσῃ ἐν πυρί 3K 18.24; *s* snake and + acc., φωνὴν ἐπᾳδόντων 'the voice of charmers' Ps 57.6.

Cf. (εἰσ)ακούω, ἐπακουστός, ἐπήκοος: Barr 1980; Cox 1981.

ἐπακρόασις, εως. f.ʃ

act of listening attentively: ǁ ἀκοή 1K 15.22. Cf. ἀκρόασις.

ἐπαλγής, ές.ʃ

painful: *s* torture, 4M 14.10.

ἔπαλξις, εως. f.

1. *battlements*: pl. φυλάσσετε ~εις Is 21.12; 54.12 (ǁ πύλαι); ἔπεσαν αἱ ~εις αὐτῆς [= of Babylon] Je 27.15, πόλεως Si 9.13; τὴν ἄκραν καὶ τὰς ~εις αὐτῆς 'the citadel ..' 3K 2.35[f].

2. *parapet*: τοῦ τείχους Ju 14.1.

ἐπαμύνω: aor.inf. ~μῦναι.ʃ

to come to aid: + dat., 3M 1.27. **b**. mid. *to assail and ward off*: + acc., τοὺς προσιόντας 'the intruders' 4M 14.19a.

Cf. ἀμύνω, ἀπαμύνω. Del. 4M 14.19b, v.l.

ἐπάν. conj.; = ἐπεὶ ἄν.ʃ

when: ref. to future, + subj. aor., Bel 11 LXX.

ἐπανάγω: aor.ptc.pass. ~ναχθείς.

1. *to cause to move up*: + acc. τὰς ἐπαρυστρίδας τὰς χρυσᾶς 'the golden funnels' Zc 4.12. **b.** *to cause to move out to sea*: pass. and ***o*** hum., 2M 12.4.

2. intr. *to return*: "from the region of Persia" 2M 9.21. **b**. metaph., ἐπὶ ὕψιστον 'to the Most High' Si 17.26; ἀπὸ δικαιοσύνης ἐπὶ ἁμαρτίαν .

Cf. ἄγω.

ἐπαναιρέω: aor.mid. inf. ~ελέσθαι, ptc. ~ελόμενος.ʃ

to make away with: τινα 2M 14.1. Cf. ἀφανίζω.

ἐπανακαινίζω.ʃ *

to do again, resume: + acc. rei, ἔτασιν μου 'torture against me' Jb 10.17. Cf. καινίζω.

ἐπαναπαύω: fut.mid. ~παύσομαι; aor.mid. ~νεπαυσάμην, impv.act. ~παυσον; pf.mid. ~πέπαυμαι.ʃ *

1. act. *to allow freedom of movement*: + acc. pers. (prisoner), Jd 16.26 A (B: ἀφίημι).

2. *to stop moving and come to rest*: τὸ πνεῦμα ἐπ' αὐτούς Nu 11.25, 26, cf. ἀναπαύσεται ἐπ' αὐτὸν πνεῦμα τοῦ θεοῦ Is 11.2, τὸ πνεῦμα Ηλιου ἐπὶ Ελισαιε 4K 2.15.

3. *to lean*: + ἐπὶ τῆς χειρός μου 4K 5.18; ἐπὶ τὴν χεῖρα αὐτοῦ [= of a trusted counselor] 7.2 (ǁ ἐπὶ τῇ χειρὶ αὐτοῦ and *L* .. χειρὸς .. vs. 17). **b**. metaph., *to rest assured and unworried*: ἐπὶ τὸν κύριον 'relying upon the Lord' Mi 3.11; ἐπὶ σέ Ez 29.7; + dat. pers., 1M 8.11.

Cf. πείθω, ἀναπαύω, ἐπ~, ἐρείδω, καθίζω.

ἐπανάστασις, εως. f.ʃ

act of rising up in rebellion: 4K 3.4 (?). Cf. ἐπανίστημι. Del. 3K 6.18.

ἐπαναστρέφω: fut. ~στρέψω, ~στραφήσομαι; aor. ptc. ~στρέψας, pass.n.s ~στραφέν.ʃ

to return to the same place: Ἐπαναστρέφων ἥξω πρὸς σέ 'I shall come back to you' Ge 18.10; ἐπαναστραφὲν τὸ ὕδωρ ἐκάλυψεν τὰ ἅρματα 'the water came back and covered the chariots' Ex 14.28; ***s*** widow, ἐπαναστρέψει ἐπὶ τὸν οἶκον τὸν πατρικόν 'shall return to her parental home' Le 22.13; murderer, ὁ φονεύσας εἰς τὴν γῆν τῆς κατασχέσεως αὐτοῦ 'to his land of inheritance' Nu 35.28; De 3.20; a harvester who forgot a sheaf in the field, οὐκ ἐπαναστραφήσῃ λαβεῖν αὐτό 24.19, sim. ib. 20; mortal man, ὁδῷ, ᾗ οὐκ ἐπαναστραφήσομαι, πορεύσομαι 'I shall go by the way by which I shall not return' Jb 16.22. **b**. fig., to the same, previous state of affairs: ***s*** husband who divorced a woman: ἐπαναστρέψας λαβεῖν αὐτὴν ἑαυτῷ γυναῖκα De 24.4.

Cf. ἀνα~, ἐπιστρέφω, ἐπανέρχομαι.

ἐπανατρυγάω: fut. ~τρυγήσω.ʃ *

to glean after the vintage: τὸν ἀμπελῶνά σου 'your vineyard' Le 19.10; ǁ τρυγάω and double acc., ^τὸν ἀμπελῶνά σου^ τὰ ὀπίσω σου 'that which you leave behind in your vineyard' De 24.21. Cf. τρυγάω.

ἐπανδρόω: aor.inf. ~δρῶσαι.ʃ *

to cause to become brave: τινα (soldiers), 2M 15.17. Cf. ἀνδρεῖος, θρασύς.

ἐπανέρχομαι: fut. ἐπανελεύσομαι; aor.ptc. ~νελθών.

1. *to return to the point of origin*: ἀναβὰς θάψω τὸν πατέρα μου καὶ ἐπανελεύσομαι Ge 50.5; εἰς τὴν κτῆσιν αὐτοῦ Le 25.13 (ǁ ἀπέρχομαι vs. 10).

2. *to do again* what was done before: + inf., Jb 7.7.

Cf. ἀναστρέφω.

ἐπανήκω: fut. ἐπανήξω.

to move back to the point of origin: Le 14.39; ἀλήθεια πρὸς τοὺς ἐργαζομένους αὐτὴν ἐπανήξει Si 27.9; εἰς τὸν οἶκον αὐτοῦ Pr 7.20; ǁ ἐπανέρχομαι 3.28. Cf. ἀπο~, ἐπιστρέφω, ἥκω.

ἐπανθέω: fut. ~θήσω.ʃ

to be in flower: ***s*** tree, Jb 14.7. Cf. ἀνθέω.

ἐπανίστημι: impf.mid.3s ἐπανίστατο; fut.mid. ~αναστήσομαι; 2aor. ἐπανέστην, inf. ἐπαναστῆναι, subj. ἐπαναστῶ, opt.3s ~ανασταίη; pf.ptc. ἐπανεστηκώς.

1. *to rise up*: to attack, abs. ἐπανεστηκότων ἐχθρῶν 'of enemies launching an attack' De 33.11; + ἐπί τινα 19.11, 22.26; + πρός τινα 2K 14.7B (*L* ἐξαν~); in rebellion: θυγάτηρ ἐπὶ τὴν μητέρα Mi 7.6; + dat. pers., PSol 17.5 (ǁ ἐπιτίθημι), Ps 26.12, ***s*** earth (accusing witness) Jb 20.27; mid. Ps 43.6, 108.28, Is 14.22.

2. *to be launched*: ***s*** πόλεμος ἐπί τινα Ps 26.3.

3. medical t.t. *to swell*: ***s*** eyes, 1K 4.15 B (*L* βαρύνομαι).

Cf. ἵστημι, ἐπιτίθημι, ἐπανάστασις.

ἐπάνοδος, ου. f.ʃ

moving back: to God in repentance, Si 17.24; 22.21; resurrection after death, 38.21. Cf. ἀποστροφή.

ἐπανορθόω: aor.inf. ~θῶσαι, pass. ἐπανωρθώθην.ʃ

to restore to former or *better conditions*: + acc., νόμους 2M 2.22; 5.20. Cf. ἐπανόρθωσις. Del. 2M 15.17.

ἐπανόρθωσις, εως. f.ʃ

v. n. of prec.: ***o*** cities, 1M 14.34; 1E 8.52. Cf. *ND* 2.84.

ἐπάνω.

I. adv. *above* a certain surface not mentioned but understood from the context: δέκα πέντε πήχεις ἐπάνω ὑψώθη τὸ ὕδωρ 'the flood rose 15 cubits above (the ground level)' Ge 7.20. **b**. fig. of superiority, ἔσῃ τότε ἐ. καὶ οὐκ ἔσῃ ὑποκάτω De 28.13. **c**. used attributively: ἐν τῷ κανῷ τῷ ἐ. 'in the basket above' Ge 40.17; τὰς ἐ. χώρας 'the inland regions' 1M 3.37, 6.1, cf. εἰς τοὺς ἄνω τόπους 2M 9.23 and LSG s.v.

2. *above and more than* in quantity: ἀπὸ εἰκοσαετοῦς καὶ ἐ. 'from twenty years old and upward' Ex 30.14.

3. *farther forward*: ἀπὸ τῆς ἡμέρας ἐκείνης καὶ ἐ. 'from that day forward' 1K 16.13 (*L* ἐπέκεινα).

II. prep. + gen. **1**. *above* and touching the surface underneath: σκότος ἐ. τῆς ἀβύσσου, καὶ πνεῦμα θεοῦ ἐπεφέρετο ἐ. τοῦ ὕδατος Ge 1.2, τοῦ ὕδατος τοῦ ἐ. τοῦ στερεώματος 1.7 (:: ὑποκάτω); ἐπεφέρετο ἡ κιβωτὸς ἐπάνω τοῦ ὕδατος 'the ark kept moving along on the water' 7.18; λυχνία .. λαμπαδεῖον ἐ. αὐτῆς .. λύχνοι ἐ. αὐτῆς .. τοῖς λύχνοις τοῖς ἐ. αὐτῆς Zc 4.2.

2. *higher than, but not directly above*: εἱστήκεισαν ἐπάνω αὐτοῦ 'stood over him' (he being seated καθημένου) Ge 18.2; ὁ ἐ. βροτῶν 'he who is above mortals' Jb 33.12. **b**. metaph., in estimation: Je 52.33; εἶναι ἐ. τοῦ λαοῦ 'as the ruler of ..' 2C 6.6.

3. *in the close vicinity of, beside*: δύο ἐλαῖαι ἐ. αὐτῆς Zc 4.3; Is 10.9.

*4. *situated to the north of*: Is 10.9, cf. ὑπεράνω **I 4**.

Cf. ἄνω, ἐπάνωθεν, ὑπεράνω, ὑποκάτω.

ἐπάνωθεν.

I. adv., *above*: Ex 25.19; ἐξῆρα τὸν καρπὸν αὐτοῦ ἐ. 'I dried up his fruits above' Am 2.9 (opp. ὑποκάτωθεν).

II. prep., *from above*: + gen., τοῦ ἅρματος 'the chariot' Jd 4.15B, τοῦ θυσιαστηρίου 'the altar' 13.20 A (B: ἐπάνω). **b**. of an undesirable situation affecting sbd: 2K 24.25B (*L* ἀπό).

2. *away from the vicinity of*: + gen., 2K 13.9[1]; with a redundant ἀπό prefixed, 9[2].

Cf. ἐπάνω and ὑποκάτωθεν.

ἐπαξονέω.∫*

**to enrol in tablets, register*: abs. Nu 1.18, see *BA* 4.161f. and Dorival 1996.534f.

ἐπαοιδή, ῆς. f.∫

act of enchanting: cogn. acc. of ἐπᾴδω De 18.11. Cf. ἐπᾴδω.

ἐπαοιδός, οῦ. n.

enchanter, charmer: τῶν Αἰγυπτίων Ex 7.11 (by means of their φαρμακεία and || σοφιστής, φάρμακος), ὀφιόδηκτος 'bitten by a snake' Si 12.13; + μάγος Da 1.20 TH. Cf. ἐγγαστρίμυθος, σοφιστής, φάρμακος.

ἐπαποστέλλω: fut. ~στελῶ, pass. ~σταλήσομαι; aor. ἐπαπέστειλα, opt.3s ~στείλαι; pf.ptc.pass. ἐπαπεσταλμένος.*

to cause to come: + acc. and ἐπί τινα– ἐπὶ σὲ .. κυνόμυιαν '.. dog-fly' (as punitive irritation) Ex 8.21; enemies, De 28.48; μάχαιραν 'sword' Je 9.16, 25.17, θυμόν Jb 20.23; + dat., Wi 11.15. **b**. mid., *to jump on*: to attack, + dat. pers. and *s* lion, Si 28.23.

Cf. ἀποστέλλω, ἐξαποστέλλω.

ἐπάρδω.∫

to turn the water on from the main irrigating ditch (Townshend): + acc. (plant), 4M 1.29.

ἐπαρήγω.∫

to come to aid: *s* God's protection (σκέπη), 2M 13.17. Cf. βοηθέω.

ἐπαρκέω: fut. ~κέσω.∫

to supply: + dat. pers. and acc. rei, σῖτον, ὅπλα .. 'food, weapons ..' 1M 8.26; by way of concession and exemption of levies, 11.35.

ἔπαρμα, ατος. n.∫

raised bank or *platform*: of a building, 2E 6.3. See also Caird 1968.473; Renehan 1.87, 2.69.

ἔπαρσις, εως. f.∫

1. *act of moving* sth *upwards*: hands in prayer, Ps 140.2.

2. *arrogance*: || καύχημα Zc 12.7. **b**. object of one's arrogance or pride: τὴν ~ιν τῆς καυχήσεως .. τὴν ~ιν ψυχῆς αὐτῶν Ez 24.25.

*3. *devastation*: + συντριβή La 3.47; pl., *heaps of ruins*, 4K 19.25.

Cf. ἐπαίρω, καύχημα, ὑπερηφανία.

ἐπαρυστήρ, ῆρος. m. ∫ *

vessel for pouring oil into a lamp (LSJ): Ex 25.38. Cf. ἐπαρυστρίς.

ἐπαρυστρίς, ίδος. f.∫ *

channel for pouring oil into a lamp, 'funnel': golden, Ex 38.17, Zc 4.12; Nu 4.9; τοῖς λύχνοις 'for the lamps' Zc 4.2; 3K 7.35. Cf. ἐπαρυστήρ.

ἔπαρχος, ου. m.

one who has the authority to rule and govern: governor of a province, 1E 6.3; captain of citadel, 2M 4.28. Cf. ἐπάρχω.

ἐπάρχω: aor.ptc. ἐπάρξας.∫

to gain the power to rule: + gen., πολλῶν ἐθνῶν Es B 2 o'. Cf. ἄρχω.

ἐπασθμαίνω.∫

to breathe hard: under torture, 4M 6.11.

ἔπαυλις, εως. f.

temporary or *modest living-quarters*: || σκηνή Ge 25.16; || οἰκία Ex 8.11, οἶκος Pr 3.33; || αὐλή Is 34.13; || πόλις Nu 31.10, 32.24, Jo 13.23, || κώμη Ju 15.7; οἰκίαι ἐν ἐπαύλεσιν Le 25.31 (as against those within a walled settlement– αἷς οὐκ ἔστιν αὐταῖς τεῖχος κύκλῳ 'around which there is no wall'); πόλις ~εων Nu 22.39; for cattle, προβάτων Nu 32.16, 36, Is 65.10, κτήνη 32.24. Cf. μάνδρα, σκηνή, φάτνη: *BA* 6.60.

ἐπαύξω.∫

to add to the quantity of: + acc. rei, 3M 2.25. Cf. αὐξάνω.

ἐπαύριον. Indeclinable noun.

the following day in the past: τῇ ἐ. Ge 19.34, Jn 4.7; τῇ ἐ. τοῦ πάσχα 'on the day after the passover'

Nu 33.3; corresponding to ἐν τῇ αὔριον 'tomorrow' Ex 9.6 (see vs. 5); μετὰ τὴν ἐ. 18.13; ὅλην τὴν ἡμέραν τὴν ἐ. 'the whole of the following day' Nu 11.32. Cf. αὔριον, ἐχθές, σήμερον.

ἐπαφίημι: fut. ἐπαφήσω; aor.subj. ἐπαφῶ.

to let loose: w. hostile intent, τὸν θυμόν μου ἐπί σε Ez 16.42, ἐπ' αὐτὸν τὰ ῥήματά μου Jb 10.1. **b**. *to entrust*: αὐτῷ τὰ ἔργα σου Jb 39.11. Cf. LSG s.v.

ἐπεγγελάω: aor.subj. ἐπεγγελάσω.ʃ

to look on and mock about: + dat. rei, 4M 5.27. Cf. καταγελάω.

ἐπεγείρω: fut. ἐπεγερῶ, pass. ἐπεγερθήσομαι; aor. ἐπήγειρα, inf.pass. ~γερθῆναι.

1. *to make rise, to raise*: abs. and ἐπί τινα, Is 10.26; ***o*** hostile entity, ἐφ' ὑμᾶς .. ἔθνος 'set a nation against you' Am 6.14, sim. Zc 9.13, εἰς ἔχθρον 'as an enemy' 1K 22.8; + dat. pers., Is 13.17. **b**. mid., *to rise with hostile intent as adversary*: Na 1.8; ἐπί τινα, Mi 5.5, Is 19.2; ***s*** ἐχθρός Si 46.1.

2. fig. *to arouse, awaken* an emotion, sentiment: + acc., ζῆλον Is 42.13; ***o*** hum., 2M 4.40.

3. *to cause to befall*: + acc. rei (punitive calamities), ἐπί τινα 1K 3.12.

Cf. ἐγείρω.

ἐπεί. conj.

1. *when*: ἐπεὶ ἐγίνετο ὁ ἥλιος πρὸς δυσμαῖς 'when the sun was just setting' Ge 15.17.

2. *for the reason that, seeing that*: ἐ. ἑώρακα τὸ πρόσωπόν σου Ge 46.30 (possibly temporal– *now that*); Ez 34.21, 1E 2.18, Ju 11.12.

Cf. ἐπειδή, ἐπάν, ὅτε, ὅτι, ὡς.

ἐπείγω.ʃ

1. *to exert great pressure on to act* in a certain way: + acc. pers., Bel TH 30.

2. intr. *to be executed with speed and urgency*: ***s*** royal edict, Da 3.22 LXX (TH ὑπερισχύω).

3. *to call for urgent attention*: ***s*** location, 2M 10.19.

Cf. κατεπείγω.

ἐπειδή. conj.

1. *for the reason that*: following the main clause and interrupted by a direct speech marker (καὶ εἶπεν Αβραμ), Ge 15.3 (*pace* Wevers ad loc., the foll. ὁ δὲ οἰκογενής μου κληρονομήσει με is no apodosis, but an independent clause.). **b**. Preceding the main clause: Ge 19.19, 23.13, 41.39, Ex 1.21, Ez 28.6, Jb 9.29; with the main clause introduced by τοιγαροῦν Pr 1.24f. **c**. Main clause wanting: Ge 18.31.

2. *after that*: + ind.aor., ἐ. κατέπαυσεν λαλῶν 'when he had finished speaking' Ex 34.33; 4M 8.2.

3. *during the time when*, 'while': + impf., 4M 3.20.

Cf. ἐπεί, ὅτε, ὅτι, ὡς.

ἐπεῖδον: aor. ἐπεῖδον, ptc. ἐπιδών, subj. ἐπίδω, inf. ἐπιδεῖν, impv. ἔπιδε, opt. 3s ἐπίδοι. For the present, ἐφοράω is used.

to look upon: + ἐπί + *dat., approvingly, Ge 4.4 (one who offers sacrifices and his sacrifices; ‖ vs. 5 προσέχω); + acc., ***o*** person in difficulties and ***s*** God, 16.13; ἐπεῖδεν ὁ θεὸς τοὺς υἱοὺς Ισραηλ Ex 2.25, τὴν ταπείνωσίν μου 'my humiliation' Ps 30.8; ἀνὰ μέσον ἐμοῦ καὶ σοῦ 'our mutual relationship' Ge 31.49; ***s*** hum., μὴ ἐπίδῃς ἡμέραν ἀδελφοῦ σου ἐν ἡμέρᾳ ἀλλοτρίων Ob 12; μηδὲ ἐπίδῃς .. τὴν συναγωγὴν αὐτῶν ἐν ἡμέρᾳ ὀλέθρου αὐτῶν ib. 13; ***s*** ὀφθαλμός, *+ ἐν (with malicious joy), ἐν τοῖς ἐχθροῖς μου Ps 53.9, 91.12 ‖ ἐπὶ τοὺς ἐχθροὺς αὐτοῦ 111.8; ἐπὶ τὰ κακὰ τοῦ ἔθνους ἡμῶν 1M 3.59 (helplessly). Cf. ἐφοράω and εἶδον.

I. ἔπειμι: impf.3pl ἐπῆσαν.

1. *to be present*: in an area, τὴν γῆν .., ἐφ' ἧς ὁ λαός μου ἔπεστιν Ex 8.22 (‖ vs. 21 ἐφ' ἧς εἰσίν).

***2**. impers. *to be incumbent upon*: + dat. pers. and inf., 4M 1.10.

II. ἔπειμι

to come later in time: τὸν ἐπιόντα χρόνον 'the future' De 32.29, ἐν τῷ ἐπιόντι ἔτει 'in the following year' 1C 20.1; ἡ ἐπιοῦσα (scil. ἡμέρα) Pr 3.28, 27.1. Cf. εἰσφέρω.

ἐπεισέρχομαι: aor. 3pl ἐπεισήλθοσαν.ʃ

to enter aiming at: to assail, + dat. pers., εἰς τὸ συμπόσιον 1M 16.16. Cf. εἰσέρχομαι.

ἐπεισφέρω: aor. ἐπεισήνεγκα.ʃ

to cause to move inwards: + acc., λαβήν 'haft (of a dagger)' Jd 3.22.

ἔπειτα ..ʃ

1. *thereafter*: 4M 6.3.

2. *that being so*, 'then, therefore': Is 16.2.

Del. Nu 19.19 v.l.

ἐπέκεινα.

1. + gen., *in the part beyond*: ἐ. τοῦ πύργου Γαδερ Ge 35.16; μετοικιῶ ὑμᾶς ἐ. Δαμασκοῦ 'I shall move you beyond D.' Am 5.27.

2. καὶ ἐ., *and farther, and beyond* the point indicated by the prec. noun of time or place: τῇ ἡμέρᾳ τῇ ὀγδόῃ καὶ ἐ. Le 22.27; ἀπὸ τῆς ἡμέρας .. καὶ ἐ. εἰς τὰς γενεὰς ὑμῶν Nu 15.23; εἰς τὸν αἰῶνα καὶ ἐ. 'for ever and even further' Mi 4.5; ἀπὸ τῆς ἡμέρας ταύτης καὶ ἐ. 'from this day onwards' Hg 2.18, cf. 2.15 (καὶ ὑπεράνω), sim. 1K 16.13*L* (B: καὶ ἐπάνω).

Cf. ὑπεράνω.

ἐπεκχέω: aor.subj.pass. ~χυθῶ.ʃ

mid. *to launch a massive attack upon*: + dat. pers., Ju 15.4.

ἐπελπίζω: aor. ἐπήλπισα.

1. *to pin one's hopes* on: ἐπὶ τὸ πλῆθος τοῦ πλούτου 'on the abundance of wealth' Ps 51.9, ἐπὶ τὰ κρίματά σου 118.43; + εἰς— εἰς τοὺς λόγους σου 118.74.

2. *to buoy up with hope*: + acc. pers., Ps 118.49; Μὴ ἐπελπιζέτω ὑμᾶς .. πρὸς (*L* ἐπὶ) κύριον 'Don't let him talk you into pinning your hopes on the Lord' 4K 18.30.

Cf. ἐλπίζω.

ἐπενδύτης, ου. m.ʃ

upper garment: + μάνδυα, worn by a prince, 1K 18.4; by princesses, 2K 13.18. Cf. στολή.

ἐπεξέρχομαι: aor. ἐπεξῆλθον.ʃ

1. *to march out to deal with*: τῷ πτώματι ἡμῶν 'to avert our fall' Ju 13.20; + acc., τὴν .. παράβασιν 'against the transgression ..' Wi 14.31.

2. *to carry out*: + acc., τὴν ἑαυτῶν πρᾶξιν 'their own business' Jb 24.5 (scripsit TM).

ἐπερείδω.ʃ

mid. *to lean on* for support: + dat. pers., Es D 3, ἐπί τινα Pr 3.18 (ǁ ἀντέχομαι). Cf. ἐρείδω, ἐπαναπαύω.

ἐπέρχομαι: fut. ἐπελεύσομαι, inf. ἐπελεύσεσθαι; aor. ἐπῆλθον, subj. ἐπέλθω, inf. ἐπελθεῖν, ptc. ἐπελθών, opt.3s ἐπέλθοι; plpf. ἐπεληλύθειν.

1. *to move on to*, 'to mount,' + ἐπί τι: ἐπὶ τὸ κάλλιστον τοῦ τραχήλου αὐτῆς 'the fairest part of her neck' Ho 10.11 (ǁ ἐπιβιβάζω). **b**. *to walk on*: + acc., ὁδοὺς ἀσεβῶν 'the ways of the impious' Pr 4.14; 5.6.

2. *to go* or *come to visit* out of interest: ἐκεῖ Pr 4.14.

3. *to come upon, befall*, *s* undesirable thing, καταιγίς 'desert storm' Is 28.18; + ἐπί + acc., θλῖψις 'hardship' Ge 42.21; ἁφή 'infection' Le 14.43; κακά Mi 3.11, κακία Na 3.19, κατάρα 'curse' Jd 9.57; πόλεμος καὶ κακά Ep Je 48; ῥομφαία Ez 33.4; ὀργὴ κυρίου .. ἡμέρα θυμοῦ κυρίου Zp 2.2, ὁ θυμὸς ^τοῦ θεοῦ^ Is 13.13, ἡ τοῦ θεοῦ κρίσις 2M 9.18, ἀδικία Wi 1.5; + dat. pers., ἐπέλθῃ αὐτῷ πνεῦμα ζηλώσεως 'a spirit of jealousy' Nu 5.14 ǁ ἐπ' αὐτόν 5.30, but sth desirable, πνεῦμα 'a (heavenly) spirit' Is 32.15; τὰ κακὰ πάντα τὰ ἐπελθόντα αὐτῷ Jb 2.11, καταστροφή 21.17, ἡμέρα ὀργῆς 20.28, ἡμέρα ἀνταποδώσεως 'the day of retribution' Is 63.4, τιμωρίαι 'punishments' Wi 19.13; πῦρ Ba 4.35; αὐτῶν ἐπὶ τὴν καρδίαν Is 65.17 (ǁ ἀναβαίνω, μιμνήσκω); "'descended' on the building" Bel 21 LXX. **b**. *to attack*, + ἐπί and acc.: *s* enemy Mi 5.5, 6 (ǁ ἐπιβαίνω); ἐξελαύνων 'one who drives away' Zc 9.8; τὰ ἔθνη .. ἐπὶ Ιερουσαλημ 12.9; ἐπὶ τὰς θύρας αὐτῶν 1E 4.49 (so as to force entry); God so as to punish, Jo 24.20. **c**. *to come to visit*: with no hostile intention, + acc. (place), τόπον 2M 9.17; 3M 1.6. **d**. *to happen*: τὰ ἐπερχόμενα ἐπ' ἐσχάτου 'future events' Is 41.23, Ju 9.5; *to become a reality*, 'come true,' + dat. pers. - *s* σύγκρισις / ~μα '(a dream) as interpreted' Da 4.16 LXX, 5.30 LXX.

4. *to come by chance*: τὸν χίμαρον, ἐφ' ὃν ἐπῆλθεν ἐπ' αὐτὸν ὁ κλῆρος 'the goat, upon which the lot fell' Le 16.9.

5. *to come after* another: ἡ ἐπερχομένη ἡμέρα 'the following day' 3M 5.2; not necessarily the day after, but some future day, Je 29.4.

6. tr. *to carry into effect*: + acc., βίᾳ πᾶν τὸ ἔργον αὐτοῦ 'his entire (military) operation strenuously' Da 11.17 LXX.

Cf. ἔρχομαι, εἰσέρχομαι, ἐπιβαίνω, ἐπιβιβάζω: Schneider, *TDNT* 2.680f.

ἐπερωτάω: fut. ~ρωτήσω; aor. ἐπηρώτησα, inf. ~ερωτῆσαι, impv. ~ερώτησον, subj. ~ερωτήσω, ptc.pass. ἐπερωτηθείς, subj.pass. ~τηθῶ.

1. *to put a question* to sbd about sth: abs. Zc 4.4, 12; + acc. rei, ἡμέρας προτέρας 'former times' De 4.32 (cf. Hex /ʿal yawmāṯā qaḏmāyē/), γενεὰν πρώτην Jb 8.8 (ǁ ἐξιχνιάζω), ὁ λόγος, ὃν .. ἐπερωτᾷ Da 2.11 TH; περί τινος 'concerning' Ge 26.7; + acc. pers., 24.23, 38.21; ἐρωτῶν ἐπηρώτησεν ἡμᾶς 'he questioned us doggedly' 43.7; τὸν θεόν Nu 23.3, 15, τὸν κύριον περὶ ἡμῶν '.. on our behalf' Je 21.2; τινά τι– ἐπηρώτησεν ἡμᾶς .. τὴν γενεὰν ἡμῶν '.. about our family' Ge 43.7 (:: ἀπαγγέλλω); αὐτὸν τὴν κρίσιν τῶν δήλων Nu 27.21; ἐπερώτησον τοὺς ἱερεῖς νόμον 'Ask the priests about law' Hg 2.11; + (indir.) question, Su 40; + εἰ-clause, 2M 15.3; of divination, νεκρούς De 18.11, "their gods, their idols, those who speak out of the ground and the ventriloquists" Is 19.3, διὰ τοῦ θεοῦ 1K 22.10*L* (B: simp.), sim. 1K 23.2, 4K 1.2; *ἔν τινι [= God] Jd 1.1A (B: διά τινος), 2K 2.1B (*L* διά τινος), Jd 18.5 A (B: simp.), Ez 14.7 (the preceding αὐτόν being prob. the *s* of ἐπερωτῆσαι); ἐν τῷ ἐγγαστριμύθῳ 'the ventriloquist' 1C 10.13; ἐν συμβόλοις (Zgl: ~βούλοις) ἐπηρώτων 'they would consult portents' Ho 4.12 (opp. ἀπαγγέλλω; see Muraoka 1983.44), ἐν τοῖς γλυπτοῖς 'the graven images' Ez 21.21; ἐπερώτησον .. ἀναγγελεῖ 'Ask .. he will tell ..' De 32.7.

2. *to ask after* about sbd's well-being: Je 37.14. ***b**. + εἰς εἰρήνην τινος 2K 10.7.

3. *to request* sbd to do sth: ἐὰν ἐπερωτηθῇς 'if you are asked to (speak)' Si 35.7.

***4**. *to ask for*: + double acc., ἡμᾶς ὕμνον Ps 136.3, cf. Mt 16.1.

Cf. ἐρωτάω, ἐπερώτησις, ἐπερώτημα, ἐξιχνιάζω, πυνθάνομαι, ἀποκρίνομαι, ἀπαγγέλλω.

ἐπερώτημα, ατος. n.ʃ

answer to a question put: Da 4.14 TH. Cf. ἐπερωτάω, ἐρώτημα: Spicq 2.32f.

ἐπερώτησις, εως. f.ʃ

v.n. of ἐπερωτάω, *questioning, interrogation*: ἀπηγγείλαμεν αὐτῷ κατὰ τὴν ~ιν ταύτην 'we told him in response to this questioning' Ge 43.7.

ἐπέτειος, ον.ʃ

lasting for one year: *s* μίσθιος 'labourer hired for one year' Si 37.11. Cf. ἐφέτειος.

ἐπευθυμέω: aor.subj. ~μήσω.ʃ *

to rejoice at sth: τινι Wi 18.6. Cf. εὐφραίνω.

ἐπευκτός, ή, όν.ʃ *

longed for: *s* day, Je 20.14 (:: ἐπικατάρατος); ἡ ὁδός σου 'You are welcome!' PSol 8.16. Cf. εὐλογητός.

ἐπεύχομαι.ʃ

to pray: ἐπὶ τῷ ὀνόματι αὐτοῦ 'invoking his [= God's] name' De 10.8 (|| εὐλογέω 18.5), 1C 23.13. Cf. προσεύχομαι.

ἐπέχω: fut. ἐφέξω; aor. ἐπέσχον, ptc. ἐπισχών, impv. ἐπίσχες, subj. ἐπίσχω.

1. *to wait without proceeding to next action*: ἐπισχὼν ἔτι ἡμέρας ἑπτὰ ἑτέρας 'having waited another seven days' Ge 8.10, 12; 1K 15.27*L* (B om.).

2. *to wait for*: + dat., τοῖς καιροῖς 'the propitious moments' 2M 9.25.

3. *to count on, depend on for help*: + dat., ἐνυπνίοις 'dreams' Si 31.2, τίνι 'on whom?' 31.18 (|| στήριγμα); + ἐπί τινι– μὴ ἔπεχε ἐπὶ χρήμασιν ἀδίκοις 'don't rely on dishonest monies' 5.8; + ἐπί τινος 15.4; ἐπί τι 16.3 (|| ἐμπιστεύω).

4. *to restrain from going into action*, 'hold back': abs., Je 6.11, 3K 22.6; Jd 20.28 B (A: κοπάζω); dat. pers. and τοῦ inf., 4K 4.24.

5. *to stop doing what one is doing*: *s* slaughter, 2K 24.21*L*, 25*L* (B: συνέχομαι).

6. *to have as one's purpose*: + inf., Si 13.11.

ἐπήκοος, (α,) ον.ʃ

willing to listen to: *s* God's ears, εἰς δέησιν 2C 6.40, προσευχῇ 7.15. Cf. ἐπακούω.

ἐπήλυτος, ον.ʃ

having arrived from outside: subst., 'stranger,' Jb 20.26. Cf. προσήλυτος.

ἐπί. Prep.

I. + gen. **1**. *in* or *at the time of*: καὶ ἐ. τοῦ καιροῦ τούτου 'on this occasion also' Ex 8.32; ἐπ' ἐξόδου τοῦ ἐνιαυτοῦ 'at the end of the year' 23.16; ἐ. καιροῦ αὐτοῦ 'in its time, season' De 28.12; ἐπ' ἐσχάτων τῶν ἡμερῶν 'in the last days' Ge 49.1, Ho 3.5, cf. ἐπ' ἐσχάτῳ τῶν ἡμερῶν 'at the end of the days' De 4.30; τί ἔσται αὐτοῖς ἐπ' ἐσχάτων; 'what is going to happen to them in the end?' 32.20; ἐπ' ἐσχάτων (|| ἐπ' ἐσχάτῳ 13.9) 'at the last' 17.7 (|| ἐν πρώτοις); ἐπὶ τοῦ παρόντος 'for the moment' 2M 6.25. Cf. **II 3** below. **b**. *during the reign of* a ruler already deceased: ἐν τῷ δευτέρῳ ἔτει ἐ. Δαρείου τοῦ βασιλέως 'in the second year under Darius the king' Hg 1.1; Zc 1.1, Si prol. 27; τὰ χείριστα τῶν ἐ. τοῦ πατρὸς αὐτοῦ γεγονότων 'things worse than that which had happened during his father's reign' 2M 13.9; To 1.22 $\mathfrak{G}^{II}$.

2. situated, moving, happening or performed *on the surface of*: ἕρποντι ἐ. τῆς γῆς 'crawling upon the earth' Ge 1.30; κατάρξει ἐ. τοῦ θρόνου αὐτοῦ 'he will rule upon his throne' Zc 6.13; κυλίονται ἐ. τῆς γῆς 'roll upon the land' 9.16; μάχαιρα ἐ. τοῦ βραχίονος αὐτοῦ 11.17; καθεύδοντες ἐ. κλινῶν ἐλεφαντίνων 'sleeping on ivory couches' Am 6.4; ἐ. τῶν τειχέων δραμοῦνται καὶ ἐ. τὰς οἰκίας ἀναβήσονται 'they will run on the walls and get up on to the houses' Jl 2.9; ἐγένετο λιμὸς ἐ. τῆς γῆς .. ἐνίσχυσεν ὁ λιμὸς ἐ. τῆς γῆς Ge 12.10 (a famine affecting people and animals living on the land); κατῴκησεν ἐν γῇ Αἰγύπτῳ ἐ. γῆς Γεσεμ 47.27; τὴν γῆν, ἐφ' ἧς κατοικεῖτε .., ἐφ' ἧς ἐγὼ κατασκηνώσω ἐν ὑμῖν Nu 35.34; περιπατήσῃ ἐ. ῥάβδου 'walk with a stick, i.e. leaning on it' Ex 21.19, cf. ὀρθωθεὶς .. ἐπ' ἀγκῶνος 'leaning on the elbow' Hom. *Il*. 10.80.

3. *close by*: (ἑστηκότος ἐ. τῶν καμήλων) ἐ. τῆς πηγῆς Ge 24.30; ἑστάναι ἐ. τοῦ ποταμοῦ 41.1 (|| παρὰ τὸ χεῖλος τοῦ ποταμοῦ 41.17), Χαρκαμυς ἐ. τοῦ Εὐφράτου 'Ch. on the Euph.' 1E 1.23, cf. Xen., *An*. 2.5.18 ποταμοὶ ἐφ' ὧν ..; ὄντας ἐ. τῆς θύρας 'being near the door' Ge 19.11; τρία ποίμνια προβάτων ἀναπαυόμενα ἐπ' αὐτοῦ 'three flocks of sheep resting by it [= φρέαρ 'well') 29.2; ἐκαθίσαμεν ἐ. τῶν λεβήτων τῶν κρεῶν 'we sat by the flesh-pots' Ex 16.3; Nu 20.24 (or: 'over, in the matter of'); Da 10.4 LXX (TH ἐχόμενα); ἐφ' ἑαυτῶν ἦσαν 'they had huddled together' 2M 10.27; ἐ. τοῦ τάφου 'at the grave' 2K 3.32B (*L* dat.). **b**. *in the presence of*: συμπόσια ἐ. πάντων τῶν εἰδώλων συνιστάμενος 'holding banquets in the presence of all the idols' 3M 4.16; and addressing sbd, ἀπεκρίθησαν .. ἐ. τοῦ βασιλέως Da 2.10 LXX (|| TH ἐνώπιον), δηλώσῃ πάντα ἐ. τοῦ βασιλέως 'explain ..' 2.16 (|| TH τῷ βασιλεῖ); ἐ. συναγωγῆς μεγάλης τῶν ἱερέων .. ἐγνώρισεν ἡμῖν 'declared to us .. at a large gathering of the priests ..' 1M 14.28; 2M 4.47.

4. *above the surface of*: πετεινὰ πετόμενα ἐ. τῆς γῆς 'birds flying above the earth' Ge 1.20; φαίνειν ἐ. τῆς γῆς 'to shine above the earth' ib.17.

5. *in charge of*: κατέστησεν αὐτὸν ἐ. τοῦ οἴκου αὐτοῦ Ge 39.4 (|| ἀποκαταστήσει σε ἐ. τὴν ἀρχιοινοχοΐαν σου 40.13); εἶπεν τῷ ἐ. τῆς οἰκίας αὐτοῦ 'said to his butler' 43.16; ἐ. τῆς φυλακῆς μου στήσομαι 'I shall stand upon my watch' Hb 2.1; τοῖς τεταγμένοις ἐ. πραγμάτων 'those charged with affairs (of the kingdom)' 3M 7.1; ἐ. τόπου μενεῖ 'will be on hand' Zc 14.10; ὁ ἄρχων ὁ ἐ. τῶν ἀρχόντων τῶν Λευιτῶν 'the leader over the leaders of Levites' Nu 3.32; 10.14 +; βασιλέα ἐφ' ὑμῶν Is 8.6; ἐ. τοῦ δακτυλίου 'keeper of the signet ring' To 1.22.

*6. *in combination with, together with* (= ἐπί τινι) in cultic terminology: ἄζυμα ἐ. πικρίδων ἔδονται 'one shall eat unleavend bread together with chicory' Ex 12.8 (|| κεφαλὴν σὺν τοῖς ποσίν 'the head with the legs' vs. 9); ἐπ' ἀζύμων καὶ πικρίδων φάγονται αὐτό Nu 9.11; οἶνον .. ἐ. τῆς δλοκαυτώσεως 15.5; οὐ φάγῃ ἐπ' αὐτοῦ (= τοῦ πάσχα) ζύμην De 16.3, but outside of the Pentateuch, ἤσθιεν .. σὺν τῷ αἵματι 1K 14.32; τὸν βραχίονα .. ἐ. τῶν καρπωμάτων .. προσοίσουσιν 'one shall offer the arm .. together with ..' Le 10.15; Ἕσπερον ἐ. κόμης αὐτοῦ 'Venus together with its luminous tails' Jb 38.32. Is this an extension of **1**: "at the same time as" > "together with"? See **II.5**, **III.9** below.

7. *in respect of*: πεπονηρεῦσθαι ἐφ' ὅλης τῆς παρακαταθήκης τοῦ πλησίον 'to have done anything wrong in respect of the neighbour's deposit' Ex 22.8 (|| καθ' ὅλης .. 22.11); De 32.51; ἐπὶ τῶν λόγων σου ἐκθαυμάσει 'marvel at what you say' Si 27.23, cf. below **II 4**. Cf. ἐπί τινων δεῖ ἐγκρατεύεσθαι 'in certain matters one ought to practise temperance' Hermas, *Mandate* 8.1: cf. BDAG, s.v. ἐπί 8 ad fin.

8. *on the basis of*: ἐ. τῶν λόγων τούτων τέθειμαί σοι διαθήκην 'on the basis of these terms I have instituted a covenant for you' Ex 34.27; οὐκ ἐξιλασθήσεται ἡ γῆ ἀπὸ τοῦ αἵματος .. ἀλλ' ἐ. τοῦ αἵματος τοῦ ἐκχέοντος 'the land will not be purged from the blood .. except with the blood of one who sheds (it)' Nu 35.33; ἐ. στόματος δύο μαρτύρων 'on the basis of a testimony of two witnesses' De 19.15; ἐπ' ἀληθείας 22.20, Je 23.28, Da LXX 8.26, To 8.7; ἐπ' εἰρήνης 'peacefully' Is 14.30, Ez 38.8; ἐ. συντελείας 'in masterly fashion' Si 38.28. Cf. ἐξαγορεύσει ἐπ' αὐτοῦ [= scapegoat] πάσας τὰς ἀνομίας .. Le 16.21.

9. *as a price for*: δώσεις τὸ ἀργύριον ἐ. παντός .. ἐ. βουσίν ἢ ἐ. προβάτοις .. ἢ ἐ. παντός De 14.25 (|| + dat., ib.).

*10. *at the expense of, to the disadvantage of*: ἐπὶ πτωχοῦ Si 32.16; Da 2.9 LXX.

II. + dat. **1.** *next to, beside* (of location): ἐ. τῷ φρέατι 'beside the well' Ge 21.33, οὐχ ὑπάρχουσιν βόες ἐ. φάτναις 'no oxen are to be found at mangers' Hb 3.17; καθήσῃ ἐπ' ἐμοί Ho 3.3 (of a woman and her husband); cf. ὑπομενῶ ἐ. τῷ θεῷ Mi 7.7; ἔστησαν ἀνὴρ ἐφ' ἑαυτῷ 'each man stood his own' Jd 7.21 B (A: καθ' ἑαυτόν).

2. *on the surface of*: moving along, ἐ. τῷ στήθει σου .. πορεύσῃ 'you shall walk on your chest' Ge 3.14; resting upon, ὁ τρόμος ὑμῶν .. ἔσται ἐ. πᾶσιν τοῖς θηρίοις τῆς γῆς καὶ ἐ. πάντα τὰ ὀρνέα .. 9.2 (|| ἐπί + acc.); λίθος ἦν μέγας ἐ. τῷ στόματι τοῦ φρέατος 'there was a large stone on the mouth of the well' 29.2; ἡ χεὶρ τοῦ θεοῦ ἦν ἐπ' αὐτοῖς (v.l. ἐπ' αὐτούς) ἐξαναλῶσαι αὐτοὺς .. '.. to annihilate them' De 2.15. **b**. intangible thing profoundly affecting: ἡ ἀκαθαρσία ἐπ' αὐτῷ Le 22.3; ὀργὴ θυμοῦ κυρίου ἐπ' αὐτοῖς Nu 12.9; κατὰ τὴν ἀκακίαν μου ἐπ' ἐμοί Ps 7.9.

3. indicates a point in time reached: ἐπ' ἐσχάτῳ τῶν ἡμερῶν 'at the end of the days' De 4.30 (|| ἐπ' ἐσχάτου τῶν ἡμερῶν Nu 24.14); ἐ. συντελείᾳ 'at the end' Si 22.10; + inf., 2K 15.5*L* (B: ἐν). Cf. **I 1** above.

4. *in the matter of, regarding*: ἐθαύμασα .. ἐ. τῷ ῥήματι τούτῳ 'in this matter' Ge 19.21; συνεστρέφετο τὰ ἔντερα αὐτοῦ ἐ. τῷ ἀδελφῷ αὐτοῦ 'his intestines were contracting over his brother' 43.30; + κλαίω 'to weep' 45.14, 15, Mi 2.6 (+ dat. pers.), Jb 30.25; ἐ. νεκρῷ Si 22.11; + λυπέω Jn 4.9, + πενθέω Je 4.28, ὀδύνη ἐπ' ἐμοί 'grief over me' To 6.15; εὐφρανθήσεσθε ἐ. πᾶσιν De 12.7 (|| ἐ. πάντα vs. 18); χαρήσομαι ἐ. τῷ θεῷ Hb 3.18, sim. Jn 4.6, Is 39.2; ᾐσχύνθη ἐ. τῷ παραπτώματι αὐτῆς Zc 9.5; οὐκ ἔπασχον .. ἐπ' αὐτοῖς 'did not grieve for them' 11.5; ἐκστήσονται ἐ. τῷ κυρίῳ 'they will be amazed at the Lord' Ho 3.5, Mi 7.17; ἐξέστη 'was astonished' Ex 18.9; ὠργίσθη 'was infuriated' Ge 40.2, ἐπικράνθη 'was embittered' Ex 16.20, παρώξυναν 'irritated' De 32.16, παρακληθήσεται 'will be comforted' 32.36; ἵλεως γενοῦ ἐ. τῇ κακίᾳ τοῦ λαοῦ σου 'Be forgiving of the wickedness of your people' Ex 32.12; φόβος ἐ. αὐτοῖς [= pagan gods] Ep Je 4; δίκαιος ἐ. πᾶσιν Da 2.27.

5. *adding to*: εἰ λήμψῃ γυναῖκας ἐ. ταῖς θυγατράσιν μου 'should you take wives in addition to my daughters' Ge 31.50 (cp. ἔλαβεν τὴν Μαελεθ .. πρὸς ταῖς γυναιξὶν γυναῖκα 28.9); Le 18.18; Δῶρον δέδοταί μοι ἐ. τῷ μισθῷ 'over and above my wages' To 2.14 𝔊[I]; προσθεῖναι ἁμαρτίας ἐφ' ἁμαρτίαις 'to add sins upon sins' Is 30.1; αἵματα ἐφ' αἵμασι μίσγουσι 'they mix blood with blood' Ho 4.2; τόκος ἐ. τόκῳ, δόλος ἐ. δόλῳ 'usury upon u., deceipt upon d.' Je 9.6; μητέρα ἐ. τέκνοις ἠδάφισαν 'smashed mothers along with their children' Ho 10.14; Ge 32.11, cf. μητέρα μετὰ τῶν τέκνων De 22.6; οὐ θύσεις ἐ. ζύμῃ αἷμα θυσιάματός μου 'you shall not offer the blood of my sacrifice together with leaven' Ex 23.18, sim. 34.25 (hardly 'in the vicinity of'); Ju 9.3; ἐπί σοι Jd 12.1 *L* (B: ἐπὶ σέ, on which see below, **III 7**). See Johannessohn, *Präp.*, 313, and **I.6** above and **III.9** below.

6. *on account of* ("cause," "ground"): μιανθήσονται .. ἐ. πατρὶ .. Le 21.2f.; μεμιαμμένος ἐ. ψυχῇ 'defiled on account of a corpse' Hg 2.13; ἀκάθαρτος ἐ. ψυχῇ Nu 5.2, 9.6; παιδεῦσαι ὑμᾶς .. ἐ. ταῖς ἁμαρτίαις ὑμῶν 'to chastise ..' Le 26.18; ἐ. ταῖς τρισὶν ἀσεβείαις Δαμασκοῦ .. οὐκ ἀποστραφήσομαι αὐτόν 'On account of the three godless acts of D. I shall not let it go unpunished' Am 1.3.

7. *guided by the principle of, on the basis of*: ἐ. τῇ μαχαίρᾳ σου ζήσῃ 'you shall live by your sword' Ge 27.40; οὐκ ἐπ' ἄρτῳ μόνῳ ζήσεται ὁ ἄνθρωπος, ἀλλ' ἐ. παντὶ ῥήματι τῷ ἐκπορευομένῳ διὰ στόματος θεοῦ ζήσεται ὁ ἄνθρωπος De 8.3; οὐκ ἀποθανεῖται ἐφ' ἑνὶ μάρτυρι 'he shall not die on the strength of one witness alone' 17.6; ἐ. ματαίῳ '.. in an irreverent, frivolous fashion' Ex 20.7; ἐπ' ἀδίκῳ 'falsely' Le 19.12, ἐπ' ἀδικίαις Jb 36.18, cf. Je 34.12 (|| ἄδικα προφητεύω vs. 11), ἐ. πᾶσι τοῖς δικαίοις 'with due respect to every rightful demand' 2M 11.14; ἐ. ψεύδει 'dishonestly' Zc 5.4, Ma 3.5; Je 3.10 (:: ἐξ ὅλης τῆς καρδίας); ἐ. δόλῳ 'by treachery; by deception' Ps 23.4, 2M 4.34; ἐφ' ὕβρει καὶ ὑψηλῇ καρδίᾳ 'in haughtiness and with an arrogant mind' Is 9.9; ἐπ' ἐλπίδι Ho 2.18.

8. *modelled on, by invoking, taking as authority*: ἐπωνόμασεν .. ἐ. τῷ ὀνόματι τοῦ υἱοῦ αὐτοῦ 'named .. after his son' Ge 4.17; ὀμνύοντας ἐ. τῷ ὀνόματί μου 'swearing ..' Ma 3.5. Cf. λαλῆσαι ἐ. τῷ σῷ ὀνόματι 'to speak in your name, i.e. as sent by you' Ex 5.23; λειτουργεῖν ἐ. τῷ ὀνόματι κυρίου De 17.12 (without ἐπί 18.7); λειτουργεῖν καὶ εὐλογεῖν ἐ. τῷ ὀνόματι αὐτοῦ 18.5; λειτουργεῖν καὶ ἐπεύχεσθαι ἐ. τῷ ὀνόματι αὐτοῦ 'to minister and pray by invoking his name' 10.8; ἐπὶ ταῖς δικαιοσύναις ἡμῶν .. δεόμεθα 'we entreat, appealing to our righteousnesses' Da 9.18 LXX; ἐπόρνευσας ἐπὶ τῷ ὀνόματί σου 'you prostituted, relying on your fame' Ez 16.15; Si prol. II.

9. *aiming at*: οὐκ ἔσῃ μετὰ πλειόνων ἐ. κακίᾳ 'thou shalt not side with the majority to achieve an evil cause' Ex 23.2; ἀνομοῦντες ἐ. κακίᾳ Is 29.20; Ge 31.52, Le 25.37; αἱ χεῖρές σου ἔσονται ἐπ' αὐτῷ .. ἀποκτεῖναι αὐτόν De 13.9; δύναμις ἐ. σωτηρίᾳ 3M 6.13; ἐφ' ἑστίᾳ 'for (a meal) at home' To 2.12 𝔊[II]. This perh. belongs under **6**, but not ἐ. πάσῃ ψυχῇ τετελευτηκυίᾳ οὐκ εἰσελεύσεται 'he shall not enter (the tent or house where the corpse is lying) in order to have dealings with it' Le 21.11, cf. Rashi and Ibn Ezra ad loc.

10. indicates one with whom responsibility or obligation lies: εὐχὴ αὐτοῦ ἐπ' αὐτῷ 'he is bound by his vow' Ma 1.13; αἱ πλάναι ἡμῶν καὶ αἱ ἀνομίαι ἡμῶν ἐφ' ἡμῖν εἰσι Ez 33.10; ὁ κύριος ἐδόξασεν πατέρα ἐπὶ τέκνοις 'the Lord has imposed a duty on chidren to honour their father' Si 3.2.

11. *being found in* a certain state or condition: ἐ. τούτοις ἐὰν μὴ παιδευθῆτε 'if you have not learned a lesson despite going through all this' Le 26.23; 26.27; ἐ. πᾶσι τούτοις ἀνέσχου 'for all this you restrained yourself' Is 64.12; ἐ. τῇ ὠδῖνι αὐτῆς ἐκέκραξεν 'cried out in her labour' 26.17; ἐ. ἁμαρτήμασιν 'engaged in sinful acts' Wi 17.3; ἐ. τέκνου σπλάγχνοις 'faced with pity for his child' 10.5 (w. ref. to Abraham in Ge 22); τὴν ἐ. ταῖς βασάνοις .. ὑπομονήν 'the perseverance under torture' 4M 17.23.

12. *as a price for*: δώσεις τὸ ἀργύριον ἐ. παντός .. ἐ. βουσίν De 14.25 (|| + gen., ib.); δῶρα ἐπ' ἀθῴοις οὐκ ἔλαβεν 'he did not take bribes for, i.e. in return for incriminating, the innocent' Ps 14.5; δόξαν ἐπ' αὐτῷ 'reputation won for ..' 4M 6.18; ἐπ' ἐλάσσονι 'for a poor return (or: gain)' Pr 22.16. **b.** *by paying as a price*: θυγάτηρ ἐπ' ἐλαττώσει γίνεται 'a daughter born means a financial loss' Si 22.4; ἐπὶ τῇ ἰδίᾳ τιμωρίᾳ 'at the cost of your own punishment' 4M 5.10.

13. *in respect of*: πληθυνεῖ σε .. ἐ. τοῖς ἐκγόνοις τῆς κοιλίας σου 'he shall help you prosper .. in respect of the fruits of your belly' De 28.11; χωρισμὸν ἐποίουν ἐ. τῷ κατὰ τὰς τροφάς 'they kept to themselves in respect of culinary matters' 3M 3.4; Ne 9.33. See Johannessohn, *Präp.* 316.

*__14__. indicates an action which should already have been performed or an (undesirable) state which should already have been dealt with: ἐὰν δὲ ἀνατείλῃ ὁ ἥλιος ἐπ' αὐτῷ 'should the sun rise while he was still at it [= διόρυγμα vs. 2 '(boring a) tunnel'] Ex 22.3; οὐκ ἐπιδύσεται ὁ ἥλιος ἐπ' αὐτῷ [= μισθῷ] 'the sun shall not set with the wage outstanding' De 24.15, cf. ὁ ἥλιος μὴ ἐπιδυέτω ἐπὶ παροργισμῷ ὑμῶν Eph 4.26. Cf. Hom., *Il.* 4.175 ἀτελευτήτῳ ἐ. ἔργῳ and LSJ, s.v. ἐπί, **II 1 i**.

*__15__. Hebraism: ἐ. τῷ στόματί σου [= /'al piḇā/] ὑπακούσεται 'will obey your orders' Ge 41.40; ἐ. τῷ στόματι αὐτοῦ ἐξελεύσονται .. καὶ .. εἰσελεύσονται 'shall act in accordance with his instruction' Nu 27.21.

16. marks a term required to be fulfilled: διατιθεμένους τὴν διαθήκην αὐτοῦ ἐ. θυσίαις 'making a covenant with Him by offering sacrifices' Ps 49.5; ἐ. τούτοις 'on these conditions' 1M 6.61.

17. Marks a personal entity who is or could be affected by a given utterance or deed: ἐφ' ὑμῖν ἀγαθόν 'acceptable to you' 1C 13.2. Cf. below **III 11**.

III. + acc. **1**. indicates a movement *on to the surface of*: ἐξέβαλε τὸν Ιωναν ἐ. τὴν ξηράν 'threw out J. on to the dry land' Jn 2.11; θεῖναι λίθον ἐ. λίθον Hg 2.15; ἐπιβήσομαι ἐ. πέτραν Hb 2.1; ἐπιβήσῃ ἐ. τοὺς ἵππους 'you shall mount the horses' 3.8; Zc 1.16*b*; ἐκπορευομένη ἐ. πρόσωπον πάσης τῆς γῆς 5.3; + ἐπάγω Hg 1.11; σπεύσουσιν ἐ. τὰ τείχη Na 2.6; Γράψον .. ἐ. πυξίον 'Write .. on a tablet' Hb 2.2 (|| γράψω ἐ. τῶν πλακῶν τὰ ῥήματα 'I shall write the words on the tablets' Ex 34.1; see Johannessohn, *Präp.* 308). Pregnantly: διαθρέψαι σπέρμα ἐ. πᾶσαν τὴν γῆν 'to feed (their) descendants regularly (in order for them eventually to be spread) over the entire face of the earth' Ge 7.3. **b**. indicates a movement from a higher position on to sth, descending on to sth: + κατάγω Ob 4; + πίπτω Jn 1.7; here also of divine revelation - λῆμμα λόγου κυρίου ἐ. τὸν Ισραηλ Ma 1.1. **c**. indicates a movement from a lower position to an object situated higher up: ἐ. τὴν δρῦν τὴν ὑψηλήν 'to the tall oak-tree' Ge 12.6; ἀνάβητε ἐ. τὸ ὄρος Hg 1.8; ἀπῆρεν .. ἐ. τὰ ὄρη Na 3.18; ἐ. τὰ ὑψηλὰ ἐπιβιβᾷ με Hb 3.19. **d**. emphasises that the whole of a surface or expanse is affected: γενηθήτω κονιορτὸς ἐ. πᾶσαν γῆν Αἰγύπτου 'Let there be dust over the whole of Egypt' Ex 9.9; ἐγένετο φόβος θεοῦ ἐ. τὰς πόλεις τὰς κύκλῳ αὐτῶν Ge 35.5.

2. indicates a movement towards, or aimed at, an object: ἔσπευσεν .. ἐ. τὴν σκηνὴν πρὸς Σαρραν 'sped .. to the tent to S.' Ge 18.6; πλατυνθήσεται ἐ. θάλασσαν .. 'will expand westwards ..' 28.14; ἐκμετρήσουσιν ἐ. τὰς πόλεις 'shall measure the distance up to the cities' De 21.2, "from one wall .. to the other wall" Ez 40.13; ἐπιστρέψω ἐ. Ιερουσαλημ ἐν οἰκτιρμῷ 'I shall return to J. with compassion' Zc 1.16; καταφεύξονται .. ἐ. τὸν κύριον 'flee ..' 2.11; ἐξελεύσεται ἐ. τὸ ὕδωρ 'he will go out to the river' Ex 8.20; ἐπάξει ἐ. σὲ εὐφροσύνην Zp 3.17. **b**. pregnant?: παρενέβαλον ἐ. θάλασσαν ἐρυθράν '(marched) towards the Red Sea and encamped there' Nu 33.10; ἐ. τὰ ὄρη 33.47.

3. indicates a surface on which some action takes place: προσκυνοῦντας ἐ. τὰ δώματα 'to worship on the roof-tops', unless pregnantly 'to go up to the roof-tops to worship there' Zp 1.5; ἐ. τὰς κορυφὰς τῶν ὀρέων ἐθυσίαζον 'they sacrificed on the mountain-tops' Ho 4.13; Σαλπίσατε .. ἐ. τοὺς βουνούς, ἠχήσατε ἐ. τῶν ὑψηλῶν 'Blow the horn on the hills, and sound on the high places' 5.8; 9.1; ἔπιες ἐ. τὸ ὄρος Ob 16, Am 3.14, 4.13, Mi 1.3 (note the sequence: καταβήσεται καὶ ἐπιβήσεται ἐ. τὰ ὑψηλὰ τῆς γῆς), Zp 1.9 (see under ἐκδικέω); τὰ κύματά σου ἐπ' ἐμὲ διῆλθον Jn 2.4. **b**. indicates a surface on which some object is situated: εἶδεν .. τὰ ψέλια ἐ. τὰς χεῖρας τῆς ἀδελφῆς αὐτοῦ 'he saw .. the armlets on his sister's hands' Ge 24.30; ἐ. τὸν λίθον τὸν ἕνα ἑπτὰ ὀφθαλμοί εἰσιν Zc 3.9; ἑστηκότων αὐτῶν ἐ. τοὺς πόδας αὐτῶν 'with them standing on their feet' 14.12; ἔσονται ἐ. κεφαλὴν Ιωσηφ καὶ ἐ. κορυφῆς (gen.!) ὧν ἡγήσατο ἀδελφῶν Ge 49.26.

4. indicates one to whom or that to which action, attention, thought, emotion, utterance, etc. are directed. **a**. of hostile action: ἐξαναστῶμεν ἐπ' αὐτὴν εἰς πόλεμον Ob 1; + συνεπιτίθημι 13; μετεστράφη ἡ καρδία Φαραω .. ἐ. τὸν λαόν 'Ph.'s .. attention turned to the people' Ex 14.5; οὐ λήμψεται ἔτι ἔθνος ἐπ' ἔθνος μάχαιραν Is 2.4, sim. Mi 4.3; ὠδῖνες ἐ. πᾶσαν ὀσφῦν 'pains of labour affecting the loin of every woman' Na 2.11; ἡ θάλασσα .. ἐξηγείρετο ἐπ' αὐτούς Jn 1.13; μὴ δῷς ἐφ' ἡμᾶς αἷμα δίκαιον 1.14; ἐπάταξεν ὁ ἥλιος ἐ. τὴν κεφαλὴν Ιωνας 4.8, cf. Πάταξον ἐ. τὸ ἱλαστήριον Am 9.1; ἐξαποστελῶ ἐφ' ὑμᾶς τὴν κατάραν Ma 2.2; ἐπελθεῖν ἐφ' ὑμᾶς ὀργὴν κυρίου Zp 2.2; ἐπιφέρω τὴν χεῖρα μου ἐπ' αὐτούς Zc 2.8. **b**. of hostile attitude or disposition: αἱ χεῖρες αὐτοῦ ἐ. πάντας Ge 16.12, αἱ χεῖρες ἡμῶν μὴ ἔστωσαν ἐπ' αὐτόν 37.27; ἐγγὺς ἡμέρα κυρίου ἐ. πάντα τὰ ἔθνη Ob 15; ὁ κλύδων .. ἐφ' ὑμᾶς ἐστι Jn 1.12; ἐγὼ ἐ. σέ Na 2.14, Ez 5.8. **c**. attention, thought, attitude, effort: διανοεῖται .. ἐ. τὰ πονηρά Ge 6.5, ἔγκειται ἡ διάνοια τοῦ ἀνθρώπου ἐπιμελῶς ἐ. τὰ πονηρά 'man's mind is intensely occupied with evil things' 8.21; .. τὴν δικαιοσύνην σου, ὃ ποιεῖς ἐπ' ἐμέ 19.19, ποιήσεις ἐπ' ἐμὲ ἐλεημοσύνην καὶ ἀλήθειαν 47.29, sim. 2K 2.5; τί ἀποκριθῶ ἐ. τὸν ἔλεγχόν μου; 'what should I answer to the reproach against me?' Hb 2.1; τί λογίζεσθε ἐ. τὸν κύριον; 'what are you scheming against the Lord?' Na 1.9; ἐπιβλέπειν ἐ. πόνους Hb 1.13; οὐκ ἐκακοπάθησας ἐπ' αὐτήν Jn 4.10; + βασιλεύω Mi 4.7; + πείθω (q.v.) Am 6.1; ἐλπίζω 1M 2.61. Cf. ἐ. ὀργήν μου καὶ ἐ. θυμόν μου ἦν ἡ πόλις αὕτη 'this city has been out to provoke me to anger' Je 39.31. **d**. speech: διεγόγγυζον ἐ. Μωυσῆν 'murmured .. ' Ex 15.24 (v.l. κατά, πρός), Nu 14.2; τὸν λόγον τοῦτον, ὃν ἐλάλησε κύριος ἐφ' ὑμᾶς Am 3.1; || dat. 3.9; λαλήσω ἐ. τὴν καρδίαν αὐτῆς Ho 2.14; cf. ἐπικέκληται τὸ ὄνομά μου ἐπ' αὐτούς 'my name is invoked and applied to them, i.e. I being their master' Am 9.12; κηρύσσοντας ἐπ' αὐτὸν [= τὸν λαόν μου] εἰρήνην Mi 3.5; ἐβαρύνετε ἐπ' ἐμὲ τοὺς λόγους ὑμῶν Ma 3.13; cf. εἶναι μάρτυς Ma 3.5, μαρτυρήσει ἐ. ψυχήν 'against ..' Nu 35.30, but ἐφ' ἡμᾶς 'in our favour' 1M 2.37; + λέγω Je 11.21, + εἶπον 39.36; ἔδωκεν ἐπ' ἐμὲ τὴν φωνὴν αὐτῆς 12.8. **e**. emotion, attitude: + ἐπιχαίρω 'to rejoice' Ho 10.5, Ob 12; + εὐφραίνομαι De 12.18 (|| ἐπί τινι vs. 7), Zp 3.17; θρηνέω Jl 1.8; θυμοῦμαι Ex 4.14, Ho 11.7; κροτέω χεῖρας 'to clap hands' Na 3.19;

μετανοέω Jn 3.10, 4.2; ὀργίζομαι Zc 1.2, 15; φείδομαι 'to take pity' 11.6. Cf. εἰ ἐ. τὸν βασιλέα ἀγαθόν 'Should the king please' 2E 5.17; 7.18. **f.** target, aim: καταβαίνοντες εἰς Αἴγυπτον ἐ. βοήθειαν '.. to seek help' Is 31.1, ἐ. σφαγὴν ἤχθη 'was led away to be slaughtered' 53.7 (|| εἰς θάνατον vs. 8); "the city has been out to provoke me to anger" Je 39.31, cf. Ol. PG 93.692; παραγεγονότων ἐ. τὸν ἀγορασμόν 'having come to buy' 2M 8.25, sim. 8.34.

5. *by having regard to*: προσλογιεῖται αὐτῷ .. τὸ ἀργύριον ἐ. τὰ ἔτη τὰ ἐπίλοιπα 'shall calculate for him the money for the remaining years' Le 27.18; La 1.5, 2.11, To 13.9.

6. indicates a matter over which there is a dispute, contention or deliberation: ἐ. πάντα τὰ ἔνδοξα αὐτῆς βαλοῦσι κλήρους 'they will cast lots over all her splendid objects' Na 3.10; Jl 3.3; ἐ. Ιερουσαλημ Ob 11. Cf. "the Lord is right over all the deeds (ἐ. πάντα τὰ ἔργα αὐτοῦ) that he commanded us" Ba 2.9. Perh. this belongs under **4**.

*__7__. *to the disadvantage of* sbd: τὰ πρόβατα καὶ αἱ βόες λοχεύονται ἐπ' ἐμέ 'the sheep and cows are giving birth' Ge 33.13 (adding to my hassle); ἐπ' ἐμὲ ἐγένετο πάντα ταῦτα 42.36; πολλὰ γένηται ἐ. σὲ τὰ θηρία τῆς γῆς 'the wild animals become too many for you' Ex 23.29, sim. De 7.22; κλαίουσιν ἐπ' ἐμὲ .. 'weep to my annoyance ..' Nu 11.13 (*pace* Wevers ad loc.: ἐπ' ἐμοὶ 'besides me'?), cf. Jd 14.16A, 17A ἔκλαυσεν ἐπ' αὐτόν (B: πρὸς αὐτόν); δύσεται ὁ ἥλιος ἐ. τοὺς προφήτας καὶ συσκοτάσει ἐπ' αὐτοὺς ἡ ἡμέρα 'the sun will set upon the prophets and the day will darken upon them' Mi 3.6, sim. Ez 32.8, σκότος καὶ γνόφος καλύψει γῆν ἐπ' ἔθνη Is 60.2, cf. ἐπέδυ ὁ ἥλιος αὐτῇ ἔτι μεσούσης τῆς ἡμέρας 'the sun set on her still in the prime of her life' Je 15.9, "the earth shook on its inhabitants" 1M 1.28; καταδολεσχήσει ἐπ' ἐμὲ ἡ ψυχή 'my soul will carry on a depressive chatter ..' La 3.20; αἱ ἀνομίαι μου .. ὡσεὶ φορτίον βαρὺ ἐβαρύνθησαν ἐπ' ἐμέ 'my lawlessness weighed heavy on me like a heavy burden' Ps 37.5; Jd 9.31, 12.1 B. Cf. Σίγα ἀπ' ἐμοῦ 'Shut up, and leave me alone' To 10.7 𝔊^II.

8. *facing, parallel with*: τὸ μῆκος τῆς αὐλῆς ἑκατὸν ἐφ' ἑκατόν, καὶ εὖρος πεντήκοντα ἐ. πεντήκοντα 'the length of the courtyard (shall be) 100 on either side, and its width 50 on either side (?)' Ex 27.18.

9. *in addition to, along with*: πατάξω τὸν οἶκον τὸν περίπτερον ἐ. τὸν οἶκον τὸν θερινόν 'I shall strike the colonnaded house along with the summer house' Am 3.15. **b**. same noun repeated: οὐαὶ ἐ. οὐαὶ ἔσται καὶ ἀγγελία ἐ. ἀγγελίαν ἔσται Ez 7.26; θλῖψιν ἐ. θλῖψιν προσδέχου Is 28.10 (|| ἐλπίδα ἐ. ἐλπίδι), εἰρήνην ἐπ' εἰρήνην 'limitless peace' 57.19, πρόσθες ἀνομίαν ἐ. τὴν ἀνομίαν αὐτῶν Ps 68.28, ἁμαρτία ἐφ' ἁμαρτίαν PSol 3.6, cf. λύπην ἐ. λύπην σχῶ Phil 2.27. See **I.6**, **II.5** above. **c**. ἐνιαυτὸν ἐπ' ἐνιαυτόν 'every year' Is 29.1.

10. *up to, as far as, to the extent of*: ἐ. πῆχυν τὸ ὕΨος 'their height comes up to one cubit' Ez 40.42; "he will generously (ἐπὶ πολύ) forgive your sins" Is 55.7, ἐ. πλεῖον σφόδρα Je 2.12, λυπουμένη ἐ. τὸ μέγεθος 'sorely grieving' Ba 2.18, cf. ἐ. μέγα ἐχώρησαν δυνάμεως 'gained considerable power' Thuc. 1.118; 2M 7.42. **b**. extent of time: ἐποίησεν .. πότον .. ἐ. ἑπτὰ ἡμέρας '.. a banquet lasting as long as seven days' Es 2.18 o'; ἐ. τὰς ἑπτὰ ἡμέρας 'throughout those seven days' Jd 14.17 (*L*: ἐν ..), ἐ. τέσσαρας ἡμέρας Jd 11.40 B (A*L* om. ἐ.); ἐ. πλεῖον 'over a long period of time' Si prol. 7, Ju 13.1; ἐ. πολύ 'for a long time to come' Si 49.13.

11. Marks a personal entity who is or could be affected by a given utterance or deed: εἰ ἐπὶ τὸν βασιλέα ἀγαθόν 'if the King pleases' Ne 2.5; Es 5.18 *L*; for dat. com., κουφιεῖς ἐφ' ἡμᾶς 'you lighten (the burden) for us' 3K 12.24^p. See above **7** and **II 17**.

12. Idiom. ἐπὶ τὸ αὐτό: *at the same time* De 22.10, Am 1.15, Na 1.9; ἐν εἰρήνῃ ἐ. τὸ αὐτὸ κοιμηθήσομαι καὶ ὑπνώσω 'the moment I hit the bed I shall fall asleep peacefully' Ps 4.9; *at the same place* or *together* De 25.5, Ho 1.11, Am 3.3; συνήχθησαν ἐ. τὸ αὐτό 'they banded together' Ps 2.2; μάχωνται ἐ. τὸ αὐτό 'fight each other' De 25.11 (glossed as ἄνθρωπος μετὰ τοῦ ἀδελφοῦ αὐτοῦ); *together* so as to form a single whole, συνάψεις τὰς πέντε δέρρεις ἐ. τὸ αὐτό 'you shall join the five curtains together' Ex 26.9; 'indiscriminately,' ὁ ἀκάθαρτος ἐν σοὶ καὶ ὁ καθαρὸς ἐ. τὸ αὐτὸ .. 'the impure among you and the pure alike ..' De 12.15 (|| ὡσαύτως vs. 22), cf. τὰ ἐπὶ τὸ αὐτό Ec 11.6. The idiom possibly originates in the use of ἐπί + acc. to indicate a static position and a point in time, the latter unattested in the LXX. It may ultimately be derived from the local or temporal application of ἐπί. **b**. ἐπ' εὐθεῖαν: πορευσόμεθα ἐπ' εὐθεῖαν 'we shall proceed by direct route' Ge 33.12.

Cf. ἐπάνω, ὑπέρ, ἅμα, ὁμοθυμαδόν: Johannessohn, *Präp*. 305-24.

ἐπιβάθρα, ας. f.ʃ

means for reaching sth: εὐσεβείας '(price for maintaining) religion' 3M 2.31.

ἐπιβαίνω: fut. ~βήσομαι; aor. ἐπέβην, subj. ~βῶ, inf. ~βῆναι, impv. ~βηθι, 2pl ~βητε; pf.ptc. ~βεβηκώς; plpf. ~βεβήκειν.

1. *to tread* upon, *walk* over (ἐπί τι): τὴν γῆν, ἐφ' ἣν ἐπέβη De 1.36; *s* God, ἐπὶ τὰ ὕψη τῆς γῆς 'the high places of the earth' Am 4.13, Mi 1.3; || καταπατέω Ps 90.13; + acc., τρίβους 'paths' Je 18.15 || ἐπι δύο τρίβους Si 2.12; *s* hum. foot, 51.15.

2. *to fall upon* with hostile intent: *s* enemy army, ἐπέλθη ἐπὶ τὴν γῆν ἡμῶν καὶ ὅταν ἐπιβῇ ἐπὶ τὴν χώραν ἡμῶν '.. our land' Mi 5.5; ἐπὶ τὰ ὅρια ἡμῶν 'our territories' 5.6, *pace* Orlinsky in 1937.367; ἐπὶ τὸν τράχηλον αὐτῶν 'on their necks' De 33.29, sim. Ba 4.26 (pl.); metaph., ἐπὶ τὴν ἰσχύν σου '(to gain) full control of your resources' Si 9.2; + dat. pers., Jb 6.21. **b**. *to assail and conquer*: + acc., πόλεις ὀχυράς 'fortified cities' Pr 21.22 (|| καθαιρέω 'overthrow').

3. *to light upon* (ἐπί τι): ὡς ἀκρὶς ~βεβηκυῖα ἐπὶ φραγμόν 'like a grasshopper which has alighted upon a fence' Na 3.17.

4. *to get on, mount* (ἐπί τι): *s* watchman, ἐπὶ πέτραν 'on a rock, cliff' Hb 2.1; ἐπὶ καμήλους Ge 24.61; horseman Je 26.4, ἐφ' ἵππους Hb 3.8, sim. Zc 1.8, ἐπὶ ὑποζύγιον καὶ πῶλον 'donkey and foal' 9.9; on a pack-saddle (ἐπίσαγμα) Le 15.9; ἐπὶ τὸν οὐρανόν De 33.26; idols on a wagon, Je 10.5^b. **b**. ἐπί τινος: ἐπὶ τῆς ὄνου Nu 22.22, ἐφ' ἁρμάτων καὶ ἵππων Je 22.4. **c**. ἐπί τινι: ἐφ' ἅρμασι καὶ ἵπποις 'on chariots and horses' Je 17.25 (|| κάθημαι). **d**. + acc.: ἵππους Ps 75.7. **e**. *to board a ship and set sail*: abs., Wi 14.4.

5. *to proceed further* to: *s* τὰ ὅρια 'the borers', ἐπὶ Βαιθαγλα 'on to B.' Jo 1.6.

Cf. ἀναβαίνω, ἐπιβιβάζω, ἐπικάθημαι, ἐπίβασις.

ἐπιβάλλω: fut. ~βαλῶ, pass. ~βληθήσομαι; aor. ἐπέβαλον, subj. ~βάλω, inf. ~βαλεῖν, ptc. ~βαλών, impv. ~βαλε, pass. ἐπεβλήθην, subj. ~βληθῶ; pf. ~βέβληκα.

1. *to cast* sth over sth: τὰς χεῖρας ἐπὶ τοὺς ὀφθαλμούς σου Ge 46.4 (at death); ἐπ' αὐτοὺς τὸ δίκτυόν μου 'my net over them' Ho 7.12; in order to harm, Μὴ ἐπιβάλῃς τὴν χεῖρά σου ἐπὶ τὸ παιδάριον Ge 22.12; Ex 7.4, Is 5.25 (latter: + πατάσσω), + dat. pers., 19.16, τροχόν 'wheel (of torture)' Pr 20.26, τὰς χεῖράς τινι Es A 13 o'; τὰς χεῖρας understood, Ju 11.12; for enjoyment, De 12.7; ἐν πᾶσιν, οὗ ἂν ἐπιβάλῃς τὴν χεῖρά σου 'whatsoever you might turn your hand to' 15.10, 28.8, glossed by ὅσα ἂν ποιήσῃς 28.20; with no hostile intention, ἐπὶ τὴν κεφαλὴν Εφραιμ Ge 48.14; χοῦν ἐπὶ τὰς κεφαλὰς αὐτῶν Jo 7.6 (as a gesture of remorse); ***o*** a stone-cutting tool, Ex 20.25; fire on to a censer, Le 10.1; sickle, De 23.24; garment, ἱμάτιον .. οὐκ ἐπιβαλεῖς σεαυτῷ Le 19.19 (|| ἐνδύω De 22.11). **b**. ***o*** κλήρους 'lots' Is 34.17, see under βάλλω.

2. *to place* sth on sth: ἐπίβαλε ἐπ' αὐτὸ θυμίαμα 'Put on it [= censer] incense' Nu 16.46; ἐπεβλήθη ἐπ' αὐτὴν ζυγός '.. a yoke' 19.2; Is 11.8. **b**. sth intangible: ἐπέβαλεν ὁ θεὸς ἔκστασιν ἐπὶ τὸν Αδαμ 'God cast ecstasy upon Adam' Ge 2.21, τὸν φόβον σου ἐπὶ πάντα τὰ ἔθνη Si 33.2.

3. *to impose* a task, obligation, fine: Ex 21.22; + dat. pers. and acc., τὴν σύνταξιν τῆς πλινθείας .. ἐπιβαλεῖς αὐτοῖς 'the quota of brick production' Ex 5.8; 1E 8.22; ***o*** λύτρον 'ransom' Ex 21.30; φόρον 'tribute' 4K 23.33 || 2C 36.3; λέπραν 'leprosy' 4K 15.5 *L*; οὐδὲν πρᾶγμα De 24.5.

4. *to direct*: ἐπέβαλεν ἡ γυνὴ .. τοὺς ὀφθαλμοὺς αὐτῆς ἐπὶ Ιωσηφ 'the woman set her eyes on J.' Ge 39.7.

*__5__. idiom. calqued on Heb. /nātan yād/, *to pledge*: + inf., τὰς χεῖρας 1E 9.20 (|| δίδωμι 2E 10.19).

6. *to come as entitlement*: + dat pers., *s* ἡ κληρονομία αὐτῆς 'to claim her (as your wife)' To 6.12 𝔊^I; + inf., 1M 10.30. **b**. impers. + dat. pers. and inf. *sbd is entitled to*: To 3.17.

7. *to belong* to: πρὸς τὰς λειτουργίας .. ἐπιβάλλοντα δαπανήματα 'expenses associated with the services ..' 2M 3.3, sim. 9.16.

8. *to mount an attack on*: abs. and in a law-court, Pr 18.17; + dat., 2M 12.9, 15.1; + ἐπί acc., πόλιν 12.13, Jd 9.33*L*; mid., 3M 1.16.

9. *to be about to arrive*: *s* a specific day, 2M 12.38.

Cf. βάλλω, ἐπιβολή, ἐνδύω.

ἐπίβασις, εως. f.ʃ

1. *that which one stands on*: 'steps' Ps 103.3, Ct 3.10.

2. *act of entering a space*: Wi 5.11 (|| δίοδος vs. 12).

3. *act of setting foot and advancing*: Wi 15.15.

Cf. ἐπιβαίνω.

ἐπιβάτης, ου. m.

one who gets on sth for the purpose of moving: sailor, Ez 27.29; horseman, 2M 3.25, ἵππων 4K 7.14.

ἐπιβιβάζω: fut. ἐπιβιβῶ; aor. ἐπεβίβασα, impv. ~βίβασον.

1. *to cause to ascend*: + acc. pers., ἐπὶ τὰ ὑψηλὰ ἐπιβιβᾷ με 'he will cause me to mount the high places' Hb 3.19; ἀνθρώπους ἐπὶ τὰς κεφαλὰς ἡμῶν Ps 65.12, ἐπὶ τὴν ἡμίονον 'on the mule' 3K 1.33; ἐπὶ τὸ ἅρμα 'on to the carriage' 4K 9.28B.

*__2__. *to ascend* to ride on: + acc. ἐπιβιβῶ Εφραιμ 'I shall mount E. (which is compared to a heifer)' Ho 10.11; ἵππους Hb 3.15.

Cf. ἐπιβαίνω, ἀναβιβάζω: LSG s.v.

ἐπιβιόω: fut. ~ βιώσω.ʃ

to survive longer than one is destined to: ὀλίγον χρόνον 'a little longer' 4M 6.20. Cf. βιόω, ἐπιζάω.

ἐπιβλέπω: fut. ~βλέψω, ~βλέψομαι; aor. ἐπέβλεψα, subj. ~βλέψω, inf. ~βλέψαι, impv. ~βλεψον, ptc. ~βλέψας.

1. *to look* or *watch attentively*: caringly, with affection or interest, abs. Na 2.9, Hb 1.5, 3.6, Zc 6.7, 10.4; ‖ προσνοέω Is 63.5; ἐπίβλεψον καὶ ἴδε .. La 5.1. **b**. + acc. ὁδόν Ma 3.1; approvingly, σωτηρίου ἐπιφανείας ὑμῶν 'your ostentatious thank-offering for deliverance' Am 5.22. **c**. εἰς– εἰς τὰ ὀπίσω 'backwards' Ge 19.26; Si 16.19 (‖ ἐπισκοπή vs. 18). **d**. ἐπί + acc.: ἐπὶ πρόσωπον Σοδόμων .. Ge 19.28; ἐφ' ὑμᾶς Le 26.9, Ez 36.9 (*s* God); ἐπὶ πᾶσαν τὴν γῆν Zc 4.10; ἐπὶ τὸν κύριον Mi 7.7; ἐπὶ καταφρονοῦντας Hb 1.13*b*; ἐπὶ τὴν προσευχὴν τῶν ταπεινῶν Ps 101.18; ἐπὶ πόνους Hb 1.13*a*; ἐπὶ τὰ σπήλαια αὐτῶν 'their privy parts' 2.15; 1K 16.7 (*L* προσέχω 'to pay attention'), ‖ εἶδον Nu 21.9 (cf. 8). **e**. πρός + acc. Nu 12.10, Ho 11.4, Zc 12.10, Jn 2.5. **f**. + dat. pers., La 4.16; αὐτῷ εἰς ἀγαθά Si 11.12; εἰς καταφθοράν Es C 8 o' (*L* ἐπιτίθημι mid.). **g**. + an indir. question: La 2.20. **h**. with unfavourable and inquisitive attention: ἐπὶ τὴν σκληρότητα τοῦ λαοῦ τούτου καὶ τὰ ἀσεβήματα .. De 9.27. **i**. ἐπιβλεπόμενον ἔταξεν αὐτό 'it placed it [= a shoot, growth] at a conspicuous spot' or 'it made it attractive' Ez 17.5, cf. Syh /meṯhazyānīṯā'/. **j**. mentally: εἰς τὴν διαθήκην σου Ps 73.20; ἐπὶ τὸ θυμίαμά μου καὶ εἰς τὴν θυσίαν μου ἀναιδεῖ ὀφθαλμῷ 'upon my incense and my sacrifice with an unashamed look' 1K 2.29; + ἔν τινι Ec 2.11.

2. *to stare at, be confronted by*: + acc. ταλαιπωρίαν καὶ ἀσέβειαν Hb 1.3.

3. *to look forward to, anticipate*: + εἰς- ἐπεβλέψατε εἰς πολλά, καὶ ἐγένετο ὀλίγα 'you looked forward to abundance, but it ended up with little' Hg 1.9; εἰς θυσίαν Ma 2.13; + acc. rei, πτῶσιν Si 11.30.

4. *to weigh carefully the possibility of*: + inf., Pr 24.32.

Cf. βλέπω, ἐπεῖδον, ἐφοράω, προσνοέω: LSG s.v.

ἐπίβλημα, ατος. n.ʃ

mantle: κατὰ τὴν οἰκίαν 'domestic, i.e. worn at home (or poss. "tailor-made")' Is 3.21. Cf. ἐπενδύτης, στολή: Caird 1968.473; LSG s.v.

ἐπιβοάω.ʃ

to address and shout to: *s* herald, 4M 6.4; mid., asking for help, Wi 14.1. Cf. βοάω.

ἐπιβοηθέω.

to come to the aid of: + dat. pers., 1M 7.7, 2M 11.7; + dat. rei, 8.8.

ἐπιβόλαιον, ου. n.ʃ *

processed fabric to cover part or the whole body: head-scarf, Ez 13.18; loose garment, Jd 4.18B. Cf. ἱμάτιον: Renehan 1.88.

ἐπιβολή, ῆς. f.ʃ

1. *assault*: military, 2M 8.7.

2. *imposition* of payment: 1E 8.22.

Cf. ἐπιβάλλω.

ἐπιβουλεύω: aor. ἐπεβούλευσα, ptc. ~βουλεύσας; pf.ptc. ~βεβουλευκώς.

to plot against: + dat. pers., Es E 23 (:: εὐνοέω), Pr 17.26 (‖ ζημιόω), 4K 21.23*L*. Cf. ἐπιβουλή.

ἐπιβουλή, ῆς. f.

plot: + δημαγωγία, ἐπισύστασις 1E 5.70; 4K 17.4*L*. Cf. ἐπιβουλεύω.

ἐπίβουλος, ον.

plotting against, having a design on (sbd τινος): τῆς ἰδίας ζωῆς Si 18.33¶; subst., ~οί σου Hb 2.7. Cf. ἐπιβουλή, βουλεύω.

ἐπιβρέχω: fut. ~βρέξω.ʃ

to cause to descend: ἐπὶ ἁμαρτωλοὺς παγίδας '.. traps' Ps 10.6. Cf. βρέχω.

ἐπιβρίθω.ʃ

to outweigh others: ὁδοῖς 'in (one's) affairs' Jb 29.4.

ἐπιγαμβρεύω: fut. ~γαμβρεύσω; aor.inf. ~γαμβρεῦσαι, impv. ~γάμβρευσον, mid. ἐπεγαμβρευσάμην, impv.2pl ~γαμβρεύσασθε.

mid. *to form connections by intermarriage*: + dat. pers., ἐπιγαμβρεύσασθε ἡμῖν· τὰς θυγατέρας ὑμῶν δότε ἡμῖν καὶ τὰς θυγατέρας ἡμῶν λάβετε τοῖς υἱοῖς ὑμῶν Ge 34.9; ἐν οἴκῳ Αχααβ 2C 18.1. **b**. act. = mid., σοι 1M 10.54, 56, τῷ βασιλεῖ 1K 18.22.

Cf. γαμβρός, γαμβρεύω, γάμος.

ἐπιγαμία, ας. f.ʃ

relationship formed through marriage: ~αν ποιέω πρός τινα 'to form kinship through marriage with sbd (= bride's father or head of household)' Jo 23.12. Cf. γάμος.

ἐπιγελάω: fut. ~γελάσομαι.ʃ

to laugh at and jeer: abs. To 2.8 𝔊^I (𝔊^II κατα~); malicious glee, + dat. rei ('over sth'), ‖ καταχαίρω Pr 1.26. Cf. (ἐπεγ)γελάω.

ἐπιγεμίζω.ʃ *

to lay a load: + acc., ἐπὶ τούς ὄνους .. οἶνον .. 'wine .. on to the donkeys' Ne 13.15. Cf. ἐπισάσσω.

ἐπιγίνομαι.ʃ

to come into being after: οἱ ἐπιγινόμενοι 'descendants, offspring' Ep Je 47, 3M 2.5. Cf. ἐπιγονή.

ἐπιγινώσκω: fut. ~γνώσομαι, pass. ~γνωσθήσομαι; aor. ἐπέγνων, impv. ἐπίγνωθι, inf. ~γνῶναι, ptc., ~γνούς, subj. ~γνῶ, pass. ἐπεγνώσθην; pf. ἐπέγνωκα, ptc. ἐπεγνωκώς.

1. *to come to know character and nature of*: + acc., God, τὸν κύριον Ho 2.20 (or poss. *to acknowledge sbd's authority over oneself*), τὴν αἰχμαλωσίαν Zc 6.10, sim. 6.14; such knowledge unattainable because of religious prostitution, Ho 5.4; 14.10 (‖ συνίημι); + ptc., ὃν ἂν ἐπιγνῷς συντηροῦντα ἐντολάς Si

37.12; pass., ἐν τῷ ἐγγίζειν τὰ ἔτη ἐπιγνωσθήσῃ 'your true character will be known with the approach of the years' Hb 3.2 (|| γινώσκομαι); ἀπό τινος 'on the basis of ..' Si 19.29. **b**. the content of the knowledge obtained is indicated by a ὅτι-clause: ἐπιγνώσεται αὐτούς, ὅτι οὗτοί εἰσι σπέρμα .. Is 61.9.

2. *to recognise* sbd or sth as having a certain familiar property or character: οὐκ ἐπέγνω αὐτόν 'he did not recognise him' Ge 27.23; ἰδὼν δὲ Ιωσηφ τοὺς ἀδελφοὺς αὐτοῦ ἐπέγνω 42.7; + acc. rei, 31.32*b*, 37.33; τὴν φωνὴν τοῦ Δαυιδ 1K 26.17; Ru 3.14; pass. Hg 2.19. **b**. the content of the recognition is elaborated through a ὅτι-clause: αὐτὸν ὅτι ἐκ τῶν προφητῶν οὗτος 'him that he was one of the prophets' 3K 21.41. **c**. *to distinguish* A from (ἀπό) B: 2E 3.13.

3. *to recognise as having a certain status, authority* or *privilege*: + acc. pers., τὸν πρωτότοκον υἱὸν .. δοῦναι αὐτῷ διπλᾶ '.. to give him a double portion' De 21.17; τοὺς ἀδελφοὺς αὐτοῦ 33.9 (+ neg. || ἀπογινώσκω); + acc. rei, divine laws, Jb 34.27. **b**. *to acknowledge the value of* and give preference to: + acc., 4M 15.27.

4. *to realise, recognise as a fact*: + ὅτι Jl 2.27, Zc 2.11; + διότι Jl 3.17, Zc 4.9, 6.15, Ma 2.4 (on the interchangeability of the two conjunctions, v. s. διότι); ἐπίγνωθι τοῦτο σεαυτῷ 2K 19.8*L*. Cf. διαλαμβάνω.

5. *to find out through inquiry or examination*: + indir. question, τί ἐστιν τῶν σῶν παρ' ἐμοί Ge 31.32*a*; τίνος ὁ δακτύλιος .. 'whose the signet-ring .. is' 38.25; τίνος ἕνεκεν 'on whose account ..?' Jn 1.7; εἰ χιτὼν τοῦ υἱοῦ σού ἐστιν ἢ οὔ 'whether it is the tunic of your son or not' Ge 37.32; + ὅτι 1E 5.64. **b**. + acc. rei: τὸ συντελούμενον 'that which was being done' Es 4.1 o' (*L* τὰ γεγονότα).

6. *to acquire an ability or skill* for doing sth: + inf., τὸ καλῶς ποιῆσαι Je 4.22. **b**. *having acquired the ability*: + inf., Ne 13.24.

7. *to notice the presence of*: pass. οὐκ ἐπιγνωσθήσεται ἡ εὐθηνία ἐπὶ τῆς γῆς 'the prosperity of the land would not be recognisable' Ge 41.31.

*8. ἐ. πρόσωπον 'to take the social standing of the person concerned into consideration in judging his case' for Heb. /hikkir pānim/: οὐκ ἐπιγνώσῃ πρόσωπον ἐν κρίσει De 1.17, 16.19 (the latter || λαμβάνω δῶρα 'take gifts').

Cf. ἐπίγνωσις and γινώσκω.

ἐπιγλύφω: pf.ptc.pass. ~γεγλυμμένος.ʃ

to mark carvings on: + acc., πλοῖα 'ships' 1M 13.29. Cf. γλύφω.

ἐπιγνωμοσύνη, ης. f.ʃ *

prudence: Pr 16.23. Cf. ἐπιγνώμων, σωφροσύνη.

ἐπιγνώμων, ονος. m./f.ʃ

1. *arbiter*: Pr 12.26, 13.10.

2. *prudent*: *s* hum., Pr 17.27.

3. *capable of comprehension*: *s* νοῦς 'mind' Pr 29.7.

Cf. ἐπιγνωμοσύνη.

ἐπίγνωσις, εως. f.

1. v.n. of ἐπιγινώσκω, sense **1**: ἐ. θεοῦ Ho 4.1 (|| ἀλήθεια and ἔλεος), 6.6 (|| ἔλεος, and opp. ὁλοκαυτώματα), Pr 2.5 (|| φόβος κυρίου); ~ιν ἀπώσω 'you have rejected ..' Ho 4.6 (|| γνῶσις).

2. *expert knowledge*: πεπληρωμένος τῆς τέχνης καὶ συνέσεως καὶ ~εως τοῦ ποιεῖν πᾶν ἔργον ἐν χαλκῷ 'full of skill, understanding and knowledge for manufacturing anything with copper' 3K 7.2.

Cf. ἐπιγινώσκω and γνῶσις.

ἐπίγνωστος, ον.ʃ*

known, recognisable: *s* hum., "among his folk" Jb 18.19. Cf. γνωστός.

ἐπιγονή, ῆς. f.

offspring: ἀκρίδων 'of locusts' Am 7.1; υἱῶν καὶ θυγατέρων 2C 31.18. Cf. ἐπιγίνομαι, σπέρμα, τέκνον.

ἐπιγράφω: fut. ~γράψω; aor. ἐπέγραψα, impv. ἐπίγραψον.

to write on sth: ἑκάστου τὸ ὄνομα αὐτοῦ ἐπίγραψον ἐπὶ τῆς ῥάβδου αὐτοῦ 'Write each his name on his staff' Nu 17.2, 3. Cf. γράφω.

ἐπιδεής, ές.ʃ

needy: *s* ὀφθαλμός 'the eyes of the needy' Si 4.1; || πτωχός 34.4. Cf. ἐνδεής.

ἐπιδείκνυμι: aor. ἐπέδειξα, mid. subj. ~δείξωμαι, inf. ~δείξασθαι, ptc. ~δειξάμενος, inf.act. ~δεῖξαι, pass. ~δειχθῆναι; pf.ptc.mid. ~δεδεγμένος.

1. *to demonstrate*: Is 37.26; by action, mid. and + acc. rei, τὴν ἑαουτοῦ ἀνδρείαν 'his own courage' Ep Je 58, κακοπάθειαν 'hard work' 2M 2.26; by argument, ἐπιδεικνυμένη πίστις 'trust that underpins one's argument' Pr 12.17, + ὅτι 4M 1.7.

2. *to point out* a fact: + dat. pers. and ὅτι, To 11.15 𝔊II; + inf., Es B 4 o' (*L* ὑπο~); + acc. rei, 4M 14.18.

3. *to point to* sth *in order to draw attention* to it: + dat. pers. and acc. rei, Bel 21 LXX. **b**. mid., mentally, *to present for discussion*: + εἰ introducing an indirect question, 4M 1.1.

Cf. ἀπο~, παρεπιδείκνυμι, ἐπίδειξις: Schmidt 3.409-11.

ἐπίδειξις, εως. f.ʃ

act of publicly demonstrating: εὐσεβείας 'of piety' 4M 13.10. Cf. ἐπιδείκνυμι.

ἐπιδέκατος, η, ον.

one of ten equal parts, tithe to be offered in a temple: subst. n.sg. Nu 18.21; σίτου .. καὶ ἐλαίου De 12.17; pl. οἴσετε .. ὁλοκαυτώματα .. θυσιάσματα .. ~α .. ἀπαρχὰς .. δόματα .. 12.11; ἠνέγκατε .. τὰ ~α ὑμῶν Am 4.4; τὰ ~α καὶ αἱ ἀπαρχαί 'the tithes and first-fruits' Ma 3.8. **b**. subst. n.sg.: of population, Is 6.13. Cf. δέκα.

ἐπιδέξιος, ον.ʃ

1. *smoothly and skilfully executed*: "this work proceeds smoothly" 2E 5.8.

2. *auspicious*: *s* the north wind, Pr 27.16.

ἐπιδέχομαι: aor. ἐπεδεξάμην, impv. ~δεξαι, inf. ~δέξασθαι, ptc. ~δεξάμενος; pf.ptc. ~δεδεγμένος.

to accept willingly and approvingly: abs., 2M 12.4; κατὰ ταῦτα '(accepted) those terms' 1E 9.14, sim. 1M 1.42; + acc. rei, παιδείαν Si 6.18, 51.26, τρυφήν 41.1, ἥγησιν 'leadership' 1M 9.31, κινδύνους 'dangers' 3M 6.26; + inf., ἀποθανεῖν 1M 1.63 (|| τὸν θάνατον 2M 7.29), 7.26. Cf. ἐκδέχομαι.

I **ἐπιδέω**: pres. subj. ~δέωμαι; fut. ~δεήσω; aor. ἐπεδεήθην.

1. *to need*: + dat. Si 30.39.

2. mid. *to lack*: abs. ὁ ἐπιδεόμενος 'the needy' Si 31.25 (|| πτωχός); τοῦ ἀδελφοῦ σου τοῦ ἐπιδεομένου 'your needy brother' De 15.7 (|| ἐνδεής); 15.11 (|| πένης, ἐνδεής); 'to need,' + gen., ῥήματος 'anything' 2.7, τῆς παρ' ὑμῶν ἰσχύος 'your strength' Jb 6.22; + adv(?). acc., ὅσον ἂν ἐπιδέηται 'whatever he might need' De 15.8.

Cf. δέομαι, ἐνδέω, πένης.

II **ἐπιδέω**: fut. ~δήσω; aor. ἐπέδησα.ʃ

1. *to tie fast*: To 8.3𝔊II; + acc. pers., ἐν πέδαις χαλκαῖς 'with brass chains' Jd 16.21B (A: ἔδησαν).

2. *to place* in order to tie: ἐπ' αὐτὸ [= βιβλίον 'a document'] λίθον Je 28.63.

Cf. I δέω.

ἐπίδηλος, ον.ʃ

seen clearly: *s* rei, πᾶσιν 'for everybody to see' 2M 15.35 (|| φανερός). Cf. φανερός: Schmidt 3.433.

ἐπιδιαιρέω: aor. ἐπιδιεῖλον.ʃ

to divide and assign to (ἐπί): + acc. pers., τὰ παιδία ἐπὶ Λείαν καὶ Ραχηλ καὶ τὰς δύο παιδίσκας Ge 33.1. Cf. διαιρέω.

ἐπιδίδωμι: fut. ~δώσω; aor. ἐπέδωκα, ptc. ~δούς, impv.2pl ἐπίδοτε, subj. ~δῶ, pass. ἐπεδόθην.

1. *to supply necessities*: + dat. pers., Ἐπίδοτε ἡμῖν ὅπως πίωμεν 'See to the supply of our wine' Am 4.1.

2. *to confer*: *s* trunk (στέλεχος)– ἐν τῷ γενήματι κάλλος Ge 49.21.

3. *to dedicate*: + acc., τὴν ψυχήν σου 'put your mind (to it)' Si 6.32; καρδίαν .. συντελέσαι '.. so as to complete' 38.30, sim. 39.5, τὸν νοῦν εἰς τὸν νόμον 1E 9.41, τὴν ψυχήν μου εἰς δέησιν '.. to supplication' Da 4.30a LXX.

4. *to pass on as information*, 'report': + acc. rei, χρηματισμόν 'communication' 2M 11.17; ***o*** number of casualties, + dat. pers. Es 9.11; 'convey, communicate (in writing),' also + acc. rei and περί τινος 2M 11.15.

5. intr. *to advance*: on battlefield, ὀπίσω τινός 'in sbd's footsteps' 1K 14.13.

Cf. δίδωμι: ἐπέδωκεν To 11.11 𝔊II corrupt for ἐπεδάκη 'it smarted'?

ἐπιδιπλόω: fut. ~διπλώσω.ʃ *

to make double: + acc., τὴν δέρριν τὴν ἕκτην 'the sixth curtain' Ex 26.9. Cf. διπλοῦς.

ἐπιδιώκω: aor.impv. ~δίωξον, ptc. ~διώξας.ʃ

to chase with hostile intent: abs., 3M 2.7; + ὀπίσω τινός Ge 44.4. Cf. διώκω.

ἐπίδοξος, ον.ʃ

highly regarded: *s* hum., in social rank, ὑψηλοὶ καὶ ~οι Si 3.19; subject matter, Da 2.11 LXX (+ βαρύς 'weighty'); bee, + ποθεινός 'sought-after' Pr 6.8*b*. Cf. δόξα, ἔνδοξος, ἐπιδόξως.

ἐπιδόξως. adv.ʃ*

in a manner deserving of high regard: "sat in front of all (assembled)" 1E 9.46. Cf. ἔνδοξος.

ἐπιδύ(ν)ω: fut. ~δύσομαι; aor. ἐπέδυν.

to descend: *s* the sun, οὐκ ἐπιδύσεται ὁ ἥλιος ἐπ' αὐτῷ [= τῷ μισθῷ] De 24.15 (the day's wage still unpaid), cf. ἐπί **II 14**; ἐπέδυ ὁ ἥλιος αὐτῇ 'the sun set on her' Je 15.9 (dat. incom.). Cf. δύνω, δύω.

ἐπιείκεια, ας. f.ʃ

fairness of personal character: of God as judge, Ba 2.27 (|| οἰκτιρμός 'clemency'), Da 3.42 (|| ἔλεος), Wi 12.18, 2M 10.4; hum. character, Wi 2.19 (|| ἀνεξικακία 'ability to endure wrongdoings against oneself'); 3M 3.15 (+ φιλανθρωπία). **b**. in a juridical sense, *equity*: ἵνα ἐ. δοθῇ σοι Da 4.24 LXX.

Cf. ἐπιεικής, ἐπιεικεύομαι: Preisker, *TDNT* 2.588f.; Spicq 1947.333-7; id. 2.34-8.

ἐπιεικεύομαι: aor. ἐπιεικευσάμην.ʃ*

to be fair-minded, reasonable of disposition: *s* God, ἡμῖν 2E 9.8. Cf. ἐπιείκεια, ἀνεπιεικής.

ἐπιεικέως. ⇒ ἐπιεικῶς.

ἐπιεικής, ές.ʃ

1. *befitting*: *s* ἀπάντησις 'reception' Es E 9 o'.

2. *morally fair, reasonable*: *s* God, + χρηστός Ps 85.5, PSol 5.12; hum. ruler, Es B 2.

Cf. ἐπιείκεια, ἐπιεικῶς.

ἐπιεικῶς. adv.ʃ

1. *kindly*: 4K 5.23*L*; ἐ. αὐλίσθητι 'Please, do stay overnight!' Jd 19.6 *L*.

2. *with fairness*: + φιλανθρώπως 2M 9.27.

Cf. ἐπιεικής.

ἐπιζάω: aor. ἐπέζησα, ptc. ~ζήσας.ʃ

**to live further* beyond a point reached in one's life: ἐπέζησεν .. δέκα ἑπτὰ ἔτη 'he lived on another seventeen years' Ge 47.28; + acc., βίον 4M 18.9. Cf. ζάω, ἐπιβιόω.

ἐπιζεύγνυμι: aor.ptc. ~ζεύξας.ʃ

to add on: + acc. and dat., τοῖς προειρημένοις τοσοῦτον 'just this much to what has already been said' 2M 2.32. Cf. προστίθημι.

ἐπιζήμιος, ον.ʃ

subst. n., *a fine*: ~ον ζημιωθήσεται 'he shall be made to pay a fine' Ex 21.22. Cf. ζημιόω.

ἐπιζητέω: fut. ~τήσω; aor.inf. ~ζητῆσαι, pass. ἐπεζητήθην.

1. *to pursue*: as object of devotion or care and + acc., κύριον τὸν θεὸν αὐτῶν καὶ Δαυιδ τὸν βασιλέα αὐτῶν Ho 3.5; τὸ πρόσωπόν μου (= God's) 5.15; opp. ἐγκαταλείπω Is 62.12.

2. *to seek after*: abs., in order to punish, Ep Je 34; + acc., βοήθειαν Si 40.26.

3. *to seek to obtain*: παρ' αὐτῶν εἰρήνην 1M 7.13.

4. *to initiate an enquiry and ask questions*: ˹ἐπ' ἐμὲ˺ (*L* om.) περὶ ἀδικίας γυναικός 2K 3.8. **b**. w. ref. to oracular enquiry: ἐν τῇ Βααλ 'through Baal,' but foll. by an acc., μυῖαν θεὸν Ακκαρων 'a mouse god of Ekronites' 4K 1.2, 3 (both *L* ἐπερωτάω), 6 (*L* ἐκζητέω) ‖ simp. 16 (*L* ἐπερωτάω).

Cf. ζητέω, ἐκζητέω, ἐπερωτάω.

ἐπιθανάτιος, ον.ʃ

sentenced to death: subst.m., Bel 31-32 LXX. Cf. θάνατος.

ἐπίθεμα, ατος. n.

1. *that which is put on and covers that which is underneath*, 'cover': explanatory gloss of ἱλαστήριον Ex 25.16; capital of a column, 3K 7.4.

2. *that which is placed on* (the altar as offering): Le 7.24, cf. vs. 20; δράγμα ἐπιθέματος 'a sheaf ..' 23.15.

Cf. ἐπιτίθημι, ἐπικάλυμμα.

ἐπίθεσις, εως. f.ʃ

1. military *assault*: 2M 4.41, ἐπὶ τὴν πόλιν 5.5; as cogn. obj., 2C 25.27.

2. *act of engaging oneself in a certain activity*, 'endeavour': Ez 23.11, 2M 14.14.

Cf. ἐπιτίθημι: Spicq 2.39f.

ἐπιθεωρέω.ʃ

to observe mentally and take note of a fact: + ὅτι 4M 1.30. Del. Si 42.22 v.l.

ἐπιθυμέω: fut. ~θυμήσω; aor. ἐπεθύμησα, subj. ~μήσω, inf. ~μῆσαι, impv. ~μησον, ptc. ~μήσας, pass. ~μηθείς.

to aim at obtaining or achieving: abs., 2K 23.15; + cogn. acc., ἐπεθύμησαν ἐπιθυμίαν Nu 11.4, ἐπιθυμίας κακάς Pr 21.26; + inf., 24.1 (‖ ζηλόω), Is 58.2; and cogn. dat., ἐπιθυμίᾳ ἐπεθύμησας ἀπελθεῖν .. Ge 31.30, cf. ἐν πάσῃ ἐπιθυμίᾳ τῆς ψυχῆς σου De 12.20; + acc. (cf. LSG s.v.), τὸ καλόν Ge 49.14, τὸ στέαρ τῶν θυσιῶν σου 'the fat of your sacrifices' Is 43.24, τροφήν 'food' Wi 16.3; αὐτήν Ju 16.22 (for a wife); τὴν ἡμέραν κυρίου Am 5.18; τὰ κρίματά σου Ps 118.20, σοφίαν Si 1.26, χάριν καὶ κάλλος 'charm and beauty' 40.22 (*s* ὀφθαλμός); + gen., τῆς γῆς σου Ex 34.24, τοῦ κάλλους σου 'your beauty' Ps 44.12, ἐδεσμάτων 'foods' Pr 23.3, τῶν σκύλων 'the spoils of war' 1M 4.17, τῶν λόγων μου and ‖ ποθέω 'to yearn' Wi 6.11; *s* soul, De 18.6, ἐὰν ἐπιθυμήσῃ ἡ ψυχή σου ὥστε φαγεῖν κρέα 12.20; 14.25, Is 26.9; βρῶσιν 'food' Jb 33.20¶. **b**. *o* = that which belongs to sbd else or is forbidden or imprudent, often with a negator: τὴν γυναῖκα τοῦ πλησίον σου .. τὴν οἰκίαν .. τὸν ἀγρὸν αὐτοῦ .. Ex 20.17, De 5.21 (‖ + gen. rei, τοῦ βοός αὐτοῦ .. ib.), ἀπ' αὐτῶν 7.25, τῆς βασιλείας αὐτοῦ 'his kingdom' 1M 11.11; foods, 4M 1.34, ἀγρούς Mi 2.2, gardens as sites of illicit cult, Is 1.29 (‖ βούλομαι); multitude of useless children, Si 16.1. For the rection, see also Renehan 1.89.

Cf. ἐπιθύμημα, ἐπιθυμία, ἐπιθυμητής, ἐπιθυμητός, κατεπίθυμος, βούλομαι, ἐπιποθέω, θέλω: Schmidt 3.594-6; Büchsel, *TDNT* 3.168-70.

ἐπιθύμημα, ατος. n.

1. *desired object*: οὐκ ἐ. οὐδενὸς αὐτῶν εἴληφα 'I haven't taken anything dear to any of them' Nu 16.15; ἐ. κοιλίας (subj. gen.) αὐτῶν Ho 9.16; ὀφθαλμῶν 'visually attractive objects' 3K 21.6, Si 45.12.

2. *desire, yearning*: + inf., Is 27.2.

Cf. ἐπιθυμέω.

ἐπιθυμητής, οῦ. m.ʃ

one who has intense desire: used attrib. and of appetite, *s* λαός Nu 11.34; + gen., τῆς ὕβρεως Pr 1.22. Cf. ἐπιθυμέω.

ἐπιθυμητός, ή, όν.

desirable: *s* σκεῦος Ho 13.15, Na 2.10; ἀμπελών Am 5.11, οἶκος Is 32.14, γῆ Ps 105.24 [= Canaan], μερίς Je 12.10, τὰ κρίματα κυρίου .. ὑπὲρ χρυσίον '.. more than gold' Ps 18.11, κτῆμα 'possession' Wi 8.5, θησαυρός 'treasure' Pr 21.20. Cf. ἐπιθυμέω, ποθεινός.

ἐπιθυμία, ας. f.

desire: as cogn. dat., ἐπιθυμίᾳ ἐπεθύμησας ἀπελθεῖν .. 'you strongly desired to go away ..' Ge 31.30; as cogn. acc., Nu 11.4; ‖ θυμός Ge 49.6; ἐν πάσῃ ~ίᾳ τῆς ψυχῆς σου φάγῃ 'eat to your heart's content' De 12.20 (‖ κατὰ τὴν ~ίαν τῆς ψυχῆς σου vs. 21 and ἐν πάσῃ ~ίᾳ σου 15); ‖ θέλησις Ps 20.3; ἀνὴρ ~ῶν 'a person much desired' Da 9.23 TH, ἄρτος ~ῶν 10.3; + gen. obj., παιδείας Wi 6.17, κάλλους '(of woman's) beauty' Pr 6.25; πρὸς τὴν τοῦ κάλλους μετουσίαν 'after the enjoyment of beauty' 4M 2.1; to be checked and kept under control 4M 1.31. **b**. carnal with sexual overtone: ἐγένοντο ἐν ~ίᾳ αὐτῆς 'they became desirous of her' Su 8 TH;

4M 1.3. **c.** *that which is desired*: Ps 77.29; pl. Si 18.30 (ll ὄρεξις).

Cf. ἐπιθυμέω, θέλησις, οἶστρος, ὄρεξις: Trench 324f.

ἐπιθύω: aor.inf. ~θῦσαι.

to offer (heathen, cultic) animal sacrifice: + dat. of a divinity, Ho 2.13; Ἰωσίας .. θύσει ἐπὶ σὲ [= θυσιαστήριον] τοὺς ἱερεῖς τῶν ὑψηλῶν τοὺς ἐπιθύοντας ἐπὶ σὲ .. 3K 13.2, cf. 1E 5.66. Cf. θύω: Renehan 2.70; Kilpatrick 1983.

ἐπικάθημαι.ʃ

= subs.: *s* birds, Ep Je 70; horse-rider, 2M 3.25 (ll ἐπιβάτης), Si 36.6; 2K 16.2 (*L* ἐπιβαίνω); commander of a besieging army, ἐπὶ ^τὴν πόλιν^ 4K 24.11*L*. Cf. ἐπιβαίνω.

ἐπικαθίζω: fut. ~καθιῶ; aor. ἐπεκάθισα, subj. ~καθίσω.

to sit on: + dat. rei, Ge 31.34 (idols in a camel's pack-saddle); + ἐπί τι, Le 15.20 (ll κοιτάζομαι), ἐπὶ ἡμίονον 'on a mule' 2K 13.29. **b.** caus., *to set*: + acc., ἐπὶ σέ Ez 32.4, ἐπὶ ἡμίονον 3K 1.38, ἐν ἅρματι 'in a chariot' 4K 10.16.

Cf. καθίζω.

ἐπικαινίζω: aor.inf.pass. ~καινισθῆναι.ʃ *

to renovate: pass., *o* temple, 1M 10.44.

ἐπίκαιρος, ον.

advantageous: strategically, *s* τόπος 2M 8.6, ὀχυρώματα 'fortifications' 10.15.

ἐπικαλέω: fut.mid. ~καλέσομαι, pass. ~κληθήσομαι; aor.mid. ἐπεκαλεσάμην, subj. ~καλέσωμαι, impv. ~κάλεσαι, ptc. ~καλεσάμενος, inf. ~καλέσασθαι, pass. ἐπεκλήθην, inf. ~κληθῆναι; pf.pass. ἐπικέκλημαι, ptc. ἐπικεκλημένος; plpf.pass.3s ἐπεκέκλητο.

A. act. *to nickname, give sbd* (dat.) *an additional title* (acc.) to emphasise a certain character of his: impers. pass., *o* name, ἐπικληθήσεται αὐτοῖς ὅρια ἀνομίας 'they will be nicknamed "realm of injustice"' Ma 1.4; 2K 2.16, Ez 10.13, Si 47.18. **b.** pass., *o* (entity to be renamed), + a new name 1K 23.28 (*L* simp.), Si 47.18; Δανιηλ, ὃς ἐπεκλήθη τὸ ὄνομα Βαλτασαρ Da 10.1 LXX, cf. Σίμωνα τὸν ἐπικαλούμενον Πέτρον 'Simon alias Peter' Acts 11.13. **c.** *o* τὸ ὄνομά τινος + a new name: Nu 21.3; pass., Da 10.1 TH.

2. *to address and utter*: + acc. rei, λόγους 4K 23.17, τὸ ὄνομα κυρίου PSol 6.1 (ll μνημονεύω); pass., φωνὴ κυρίου τῇ πόλει ἐπικληθήσεται 'the voice of the Lord will be addressed to the city' Mi 6.9.

***3.** in the phrase ἐ. τὸ ὄνομά τινος ἐπί τι (or τινα), *to call sth* or *sbd after sbd, to attach his name to it*, indicating his claim on, ownership of or protection of it: πάντα τὰ ἔθνη, ἐφ' οὓς ἐπικέκληται τὸ ὄνομά μου ἐπ' αὐτούς 'all the nations which have been called by my name' Am 9.12 (most prob. a Hebraism reflecting /qārā' šēm yhwh ʿal/), τὸ ὄνομά σου ἐπεκλήθη ἐπὶ Ισραηλ καὶ ἐπὶ τὸ γένος αὐτοῦ Ba 2.15; + ἐπί τινος– ἐξελέξω τὸν οἶκον τοῦτον ἐπικληθῆναι τὸ ὄνομά σου ἐπ' αὐτοῦ 1M 7.37; + ἐπί τινι– ἐν τῷ οἴκῳ οὗ ἐπικέκληται τὸ ὄνομά μου ἐπ' αὐτῷ Je 7.10, ἐπικέκληται τὸ ὄνομά σου ἐπ' ἐμοί 15.16; + ἔν τινι, Ge 48.16; + dat. pers., τὸ ὄνομα κυρίου ἐπικέκληταί σοι De 28.10. **b.** πάντας ὅσοι ἐπικέκληνται τῷ ὀνόματί μου 'all those who have been called by my name' Is 43.7.

4.** *to proclaim* an official event: pass. and ***o ἄφεσις 'remission' De 15.2.

B. mid., **1.a.** *to call upon*: + πρός τινα, a divinity, Ho 7.7. **b.** + acc. pers., *to call on, appeal to* sbd *for help*, ^κύριον^ De 4.7; Αἴγυπτον Ho 7.11 (ll πορεύεσθαι εἴς τινα), τὸν θεόν σου Am 4.12, Jn 1.6; Je 4.20 (Zgl 1958.40); εἰς βοήθειαν Ju 6.21; + περί τινος Wi 13.17 (ll ἀξιόω); also + acc. rei, πάντα, ὅσα ἂν ἐπικαλέσηταί σε 'whatever he might call upon you for' 3K 8.43; ἐν ὀνόματι ^κυρίου^ 1C 16.8; + inf. specifying the nature of help, Jb 17.14, Si 51.10, 2M 3.15. **c.** + acc. rei, *to invoke*, τὸ ὄνομα κυρίου Ge 4.26, 13.4, 21.33 (*pace* Wevers ad loc.); πᾶς ὃς ἂν ~καλέσηται τὸ ὄνομα κυρίου, σωθήσεται 'all who call the Lord's name will be saved' Jl 2.32, "he will invoke my name and I will hearken unto him" Zc 13.9; Zp 3.9, Je 10.25; τὴν σοφίαν Pr 2.3. **d.** same meaning as **c.** but + ἐπὶ τῷ ὀνόματί τινος– .. κυρίου Ge 12.8. **e.** *to address, accost*: + acc., Ps 41.8.

2. *to call for* some action: + acc., ὁμολογίας 'confessions' Am 4.5.

***3.** *to complain about, protest against*: + acc., Je 20.8, cf. Lampe, s.v. **4.**

4. pass. of **B 1b.**: ***o*** God, ἐπικληθήσομαι ἐν τοῖς υἱοῖς Ισραηλ Ex 29.45; ἐπικληθῆναι αὐτοῖς 29.46.

Cf. ἀγορεύω, καλέω, ἐπίκλητος, ὄνομα, ὀνομάζω: Spicq 2.41-6 and *ND* 1.89-96.

ἐπικάλυμμα, ατος. n.

that which is placed over sth else and covers it: Ex 26.14; 39.21 (ll κάλυμμα). **b.** metaph. *deception* (?): Jb 19.29.

Cf. (ἐπι)καλύπτω, (κατα)κάλυμμα, ἐπίθεμα.

ἐπικαλύπτω: aor. ἐπεκάλυψα, impv.3s ~καλυψάτω, pass. ἐπεκαλύφθην; pf.ptc.pass. ~κεκαλυμμένος.

1. *to place oneself over* sth else so that the latter becomes invisible, 'to cover': ἐπεκάλυψεν πάντα τὰ ὄρη τὰ ὑψηλά '(the flood-water) covered all the high mountains' Ge 7.19; + acc. or + ἐπί and acc., ἐπικαλυψάτω τοὺς Αἰγυπτίους, ἐπί τε τὰ ἅρματα καὶ τοὺς ἀναβάτας 'let it [= the sea water] cover the Egyptians as well as the chariots and the riders' Ex 14.26 (ll καλύπτω vs. 28).

2. *to place a cover over* sth else so that the contents of the latter are not allowed to come out or become visible: pass., ἐπεκαλύφθησαν αἱ πηγαὶ τῆς ἀβύσσου 'the fountains of the deep were sealed' Ge 8.2, metaph. ***o*** ἁμαρτίαι Ps 31.1 (ǁ ἀφίημι), ἀσέβειαν ἑαυτοῦ Pr 28.13; "they covered their heads" Je 14.4 (a gesture of shame), 2K 15.30.

3. *to affect deeply*: + acc. pers. and ***s*** ἀτιμία 'ignominy' Je 3.25 (ǁ αἰσχύνη), σκιὰ θανάτου Ps 43.20.

4. *to spread oneself* over an area: ἐπάνω τοῦ σώματος αὐτῶν Ez 1.11; ***s*** river in a fig. of all-pervasive divine blessing, Si 39.22 (ǁ μεθύσκω), + acc. γῆν 47.14 (ǁ ἐμπίμπλημι).

Cf. ἀποκαλύπτω, καλύπτω, ἐπικάλυμμα.

ἐπικαρπολογέομαι.ʃ *

to overdo in gathering: + acc., ἀμητούς 'crops' 4M 2.9.

ἐπικαταλαμβάνω: fut. ~λήμψομαι.ʃ

to reach out to in order to assist: + acc. pers., ἐπικαταλήμψεταί σε ὁ λόγος μου Nu 11.23.

ἐπικαταράομαι: fut. ~ράσομαι; aor. ~κατηρασάμην, impv. ~κατάρασαι.*

to pronounce curse upon, utter words consigning sbd or sth *to divine punishment*: ***s*** God, τὴν εὐλογίαν ὑμῶν Ma 2.2 (ǁ καταράομαι); hum. and + acc. pers., μοι τὸν λαὸν τοῦτον Nu 22.17; ǁ ἀράομαι 23.7; Ps 151.6; τὸ ὕδωρ τοῦ ἐλεγμοῦ τοῦ ἐπικαταρωμένου 'the water of this damning accusation' Nu 5.18; τὸ ὕδωρ τὸ ἐπικαταρώμενον 5.22; τὸ ὕδωρ τὸ ἐπικαταρώμενον τοῦ ἐλεγμοῦ 5.24; τὸ ὕδωρ τοῦ ἐλεγμοῦ τὸ ἐπικαταρώμενον 5.27.

Cf. ἀράομαι, καταράομαι, ἐπικατάρατος.

ἐπικατάρατος, ον. *

deserving to be cursed, accursed: ***s*** hum., Ge 9.25, ἁμαρτωλός Is 65.20; ὁ καταρώμενός σε ~ος 'he who curses you is accursed' Ge 27.29 (:: εὐλογημένος); ἀπὸ τῆς γῆς 4.11; De 27.15; ἀποθῆκαι 'stored food' 28.17; serpent Ge 3.14; anger (θυμός) 49.7; birthday Je 20.14 (ǁ ἐπευκτός). **b**. *liable to prompt one to utter curses*, 'ill-fated, damned': ***s*** the earth, ἐ. ἡ γῆ ἐν τοῖς ἔργοις σου 'you are likely to curse the earth as you toil on it' Ge 3.17.

Cf. κατάρατος, ἐπικαταράομαι, εὐλογητός: Deissmann 1923.74f.

ἐπίκειμαι.ʃ

1. *to be placed and lie* in a certain place: Ex 36.40; 2M 1.21.

2. *to take a hostile action, attack*: + dat. pers., Jb 19.3; τόλμῃ 'boldly' 21.27.

3. *to exert constant pressure on, press on*: τέλειον 'to its very end' 3M 1.22; + dat. pers., ἐπίκειται ἡμῖν τὰ τῆς βασιλείας 'the affairs of the kingdom press upon us' 1M 6.57.

ἐπικερδής, ές.ʃ

conducive to profit-making: ***s*** πανηγυρισμός 'festive celebration' Wi 15.12.

ἐπικίνδυνος, ον.ʃ

dangerous: ***s*** ἀπειλή 'threat' 3M 5.33. Cf. κίνδυνος.

ἐπικινέω: ʃ.

to move and arouse: emotionally or mentally, pass., ***o*** hum., ἐπὶ τῷ ῥήματι κυρίου 'on hearing ..' 1E 8.69 (ǁ διώκω λόγον θεοῦ 2E 9.3).

ἐπίκλησις, εως. f.ʃ

1. v.n. of ἐπικαλέω, **A 3**: ἕνεκα τῆς ἐπ' αὐτοὺς ~εως τοῦ σεμνοῦ .. ὀνόματος αὐτοῦ 'because they had been called by his holy .. name' 2M 8.15.

2. v.n. of ἐπικαλέω, **B 1 b**: μετ' ~εως καὶ εὐχῶν 'by means of invocation (of God's name) and prayers' 2M 15.26.

Cf. ἐπικαλέω: Connolly, esp. 359.

ἐπίκλητος, ον.

1. *bearing the name of*: λαὸς Συρίας ἐ. Am 1.5.

2. *invoked*: for help, ***s*** fountain, Jd 15.19 A (or: fountain 'nicknamed' "Of donkey").

3. *appointed* for a function: τῆς συναγωγῆς Nu 1.16, 26.9; ***s*** towns designated as refuge for murderers, Jo 20.9.

4. subst.f., *convocation, assembly*: ἐ. ἁγία Nu 28.18 (ǁ κλητὴ ἁγία vs. 25), 29.1, 7, 12.

Cf. ἐπικαλέω, ἐπίκλησις, κλητός: Tyrer; Harl 2001.886.

ἐπικλίνω: aor. inf. ~κλῖναι, impv. ἐπίκλινον, opt.3s ~κλίναι.ʃ

to cause to incline: + acc., Ἐπίκλινόν μοι τὴν ὑδρίαν σου Ge 24.14; metaph., τὴν καρδίαν ἡμῶν πρὸς αὐτόν 3K 8.58.

ἐπικλύζω: aor. ἐπέκλυσα.ʃ

1. *to bring in great quantities*, 'flood': ***o*** water, ἐπέκλυσεν τὸ ὕδωρ τῆς θαλάσσης .. ἐπὶ πρόσωπον αὐτῶν De 11.4; war victims, βάθει θαλάσσης 3M 2.7; χειμάρρους ἐπικλύζων δόξαν ἐθνῶν Is 66.12.

2. *to come in great quantities*: ποταμὸς ἐπικλύζων τοῖς νεκροῖς αὐτῶν 'a river overflowing with their dead' Ju 2.8.

ἐπικοιμάομαι: fut. ~μηθήσομαι; aor. ἐπεκοιμήθην.ʃ

1. *to spend the night*: ***s*** the corpse of a criminal hanged on a tree, De 21.23.

2. *to sleep on top of*: ἐπί τινα (baby) 3K 3.19.

3. *to make a nuisance of oneself*: + dat. pers. 1E 5.69.

Cf. κοιμάομαι.

ἐπικοινωνέω.ʃ

to be common property: + dat., πᾶσιν 'typical of all' Si 26.6; τοῖς ἱεροῖς 'meant for the temple needs' 4M 4.3.

ἐπικοπή, ῆς. f.∫
**person cut down* on a battlefield: δώῃ σε κύριος ~ὴν ἐναντίον τῶν ἐχθρῶν σου 'may the Lord make you fall before your enemies' De 28.25.
Cf. κοπή.

ἐπικοσμέω: aor.inf.pass. ~κοσμηθῆναι.∫
to add ornaments to sth defective: + acc., διεστραμμένον 'sth distorted or deformed' Ec 1.15.

ἐπικουρία, ας. f.∫
aid: Wi 13.18.
Cf. βοήθεια: Schmidt 4.153-7; *ND* 3.67f.

ἐπικουφίζω.∫
to lighten a burden *by carrying* for sbd else: + acc., τὴν ἔνδυμα αὐτῆς 'her robes' Es 5.2 *L* (o' κουφίζω). **b**. mid. + acc. rei, πόνον 'pain' 4M 9.31.
Cf. βαρύνω, κοῦφος.

ἐπικραταιόω: aor.subj.pass. ~ταιωθῶ.∫ *
to overpower physically: *o* hum., Ec 4.12, cf. Jarick 99. Cf. κραταιόω.

ἐπικράτεια, ας. f.
1. = ἐπικράτησις: Es 7.26 *L* (o' ἐπικράτησις).
2. *act of gaining and maintaining control of* sth: + gen., ἐπιθυμιῶν 'of desires' 4M 1.31; executed by λογισμός 'rational will' 1.34.

ἐπικρατέω: aor. ἐπεκράτησα, inf. ~κρατῆσαι, ptc. ~κρατήσας, impv. ~κράτησον.
to gain strength, become powerful: *s* flood-water, Ge 7.18; τὸ ὕδωρ ἐπεκράτει σφόδρα σφοδρῶς 'the water kept gaining strength very mightily' 7.19; famine (λιμός) 41.57; ταῖς χερσὶν αὐτῶν 'to (approve an idea and) give a hand' Je 5.31, cf. Thdt. PG 81.541 συγκατάθεσις, and cp. 1E 2.8 ἐβοήθησαν || 2E 1.6 ἐνίσχυσαν ἐν χερσὶν αὐτῶν, see under ἐνισχύω and κατισχύω. **b**. *to overpower*: + gen. pers., ἐπεκράτησεν αὐτῶν ὁ λιμός 'the famine got on top of them' Ge 47.20; + ἐπί τινα Ez 29.7; *to gain* or *hold control over*, + gen., πάσης οἰκουμένης 'the entire world' Es B 2, πάσης ἀρχῆς C 23 o', ἀπὸ ἁμαρτίας 'so as to keep (me) away from sin' PSol 16.7, ὀρέξεων 'proclinations' 4M 1.33, φιλίας 'affection' 2.11 (|| κυριεύω vs. 12; || δεσπόζω vs. 13); τινα 4M 17.20. **c**. *to exercise power and authority*: ptc. pres., 'ruler, sovereign' Es E 6.
Cf. κράτος, κατισχύω, ἐπικράτησις, κυριεύω, δεσπόζω.

ἐπικράτησις, εως. f.∫
domain: Es E 14 o' (*L* ἐπικράτεια). Cf. ἐπικράτεια.

ἐπικρεμάννυμι: pres.ptc.pass. ~μάμενος.∫
to hang on to: ἐκ τῆς κατοικίας αὐτοῦ Ho 11.7; + dat. and of trust, Is 22.24 (|| πεποιθώς). Cf. πείθω.

ἐπικρίνω: aor. ἐπέκρινα, ptc.pass. ἐπικριθείς.∫
to pronounce false verdict of: + acc. rei and dat. pers., τούτοις θάνατον 2M 4.47, τὴν .. ἐξαίφνης αὐτοῖς ἐπικριθεῖσαν ὀλεθρίαν 'the destruction that had been suddenly decreed against them' 3M 4.2. Cf. κρίνω: Kilpatrick 1983b.152f.

ἐπίκρισις, εως. f.∫
interpretation: of a dream, Es A 11 *L*. Cf. σύγκρισις.

ἐπικροτέω: fut. ~κροτήσω.∫
to strike with a rattling sound: 'to clap hands, applaud,' La 2.22 (Zgl: ~κρατέω, see Albrektson 125f.), πρὸς τὴν φωνὴν τῶν ὀργάνων 'at the sound of the instruments' Am 6.5, + ἐπιχαίρω Pr 17.18; ταῖς χερσίν '(to snap) the hands' Si 12.18 (a gesture of disdain); τοῖς κλάδοις 'with their boughs' Is 55.12 (a welcoming gesture). Cf. ἐπικρούω.

ἐπικρούω: fut. ~κρούσω.∫
to clap: ἐν χειρί Je 31.26. Cf. ἐπικροτέω.

ἐπίκτητος, ον.∫
acquired in addition: *s* grey hair, 2M 6.23.

ἐπικυλίω: aor. ἐπεκύλισα.∫
to roll on to: λίθους ἐπὶ τὸ σπήλαιον 'stones on to the cave' Jo 10.27. Cf. κυλίω.

ἐπικύπτω: aor. ἐπέκυψα.∫
to bow down: nearly fainting, ἐπὶ τὴν κεφαλήν (of an accompanying person) Es 5.6 *L* (o' προσεπι~). Cf. subs.

ἐπίκυφος, ον.∫ *
not standing erect but stooping: *s* old people, 3M 4.5. Cf. prec.

ἐπιλαμβάνομαι: fut. ~λήμψομαι; aor. ἐπέλαβον, mid. ~λαβόμην, ptc. ~λαβόμενος, subj. ~λάβωμαι, impv. ~λαβοῦ; pf.ptc. ἐπειλημμένος.
1. *to seize, lay hold of*: abs., Is 5.29; + gen., τῆς πτέρνης Ησαυ 'Esau's heel' Ge 25.26; τῆς κέρκου 'the tail (of a snake)' Ex 4.4; τοῦ ἀδελφοῦ αὐτοῦ Is 3.6; μαχαίρας Ez 30.21, ὅπλου Ps 34.2; τοῦ κρασπέδου ἀνδρὸς Ιουδαίου 'the hem of (the robe of) a Jew' Zc 8.23*bis*, τῆς χειρός 14.13; τοῦ Αμβακουμ τῆς κόμης τῆς κεφαλῆς 'Habakkuk by the hair of his head' Bel 36 LXX; τῇ χειρὶ αὐτῶν 'with their hand' Ez 29.7. **b**. metaph., *s* τρόμος .. ὠδῖνες 'trembling .. pangs of childbirth' Ps 47.7, sim. Je 30.13; κακά 51.23; + gen., ἐμῆς παιδείας '(hold fast) to my teaching' Pr 4.13 (|| φυλάσσω, and:: ἀφίημι 'let go of'). **c**. in order to help: Si 4.11, see LSG s.v. **III 1 b**.
2. *to reach:* + gen. τῆς πόλεως Jl 2.9 (MT: / yāšōqqu/).
Cf. λαμβάνω, κρατέω **1**.

ἐπιλάμπω: fut. ~λάμψω.∫
to shine: ἐπιλάμψει ὁ θεὸς ἐν βούλῃ μετὰ δόξης ἐπὶ τῆς γῆς Is 4.2. Cf. λάμπω, φαίνω.

ἐπιλανθάνω: fut. ~λήσομαι, ~λησθήσομαι; aor. ἐπελαθόμην, inf. ~λαθέσθαι, impv. ~λαθου, subj. ~λάθωμαι, opt.3s ~λάθοιτο, pass. ἐπελήσθην, subj.

~λησθῶ, opt.3s ~λησθείη; pf. ~λέλησμαι, ptc.pass. ~λελησμένος.

1. *to refuse to retain in memory, and disregard* or *neglect to act in accordance with one's knowledge of*: abs., De 25.19; + gen., ***o*** God, De 32.18 (ǁ ἐγκαταλείπω); κυρίου τοῦ θεοῦ σου 6.12, 8.11; ἐμοῦ [= God] Ho 2.13, μοῦ 13.6; τοῦ ποιήσαντος αὐτόν 8.14; Zion and sbd's right hand, Ps 136.5 (:: μιμνήσκομαι vs. 6); + gen. hum. and *s* God, Ps 41.10, τῶν πενήτων 9.33; + gen. rei, πάντων τῶν πόνων μου 'all my miseries' Ge 41.51, τῆς κραυγῆς τῶν πενήτων 'the cry of the poor' Ps 9.13; τοῦ ὀνόματός μου Je 23.27; + τοῦ inf., Ps 76.10, 101.5; + ptc. pres., Jb 9.27; + acc., θεόν Is 51.13, τοὺς λόγους De 4.9; τὴν διαθήκην κυρίου 4.23, διαθήκην Pr 2.17 (dep., ǁ ἀπολείπω); πάντα τὰ ἔργα ὑμῶν Am 8.7; νόμον θεοῦ σου Ho 4.6; opp. μιμνήσκομαι– μνήσθητι μὴ ἐπιλάθῃ De 9.7; pass. οὐ μὴ ἐπιλησθῇ ἀπὸ στόματος τοῦ σπέρματος αὐτῶν 'will never cease to be sung by their descendants' 31.21; pass. πόρνη ἐπιλελησμένη 'forgotten whore' Is 23.16 (:: μνεία γίνεται), ὁ πτωχός Ps 9.19; ἀπὸ καρδίας 30.13 (ǁ ἀπόλλυμι), γῆ ἐπιλελησμένη 87.13. On the use of the acc., see also Renehan 1.90. **b**. *to fail* to do what one ought to: + ptc. pres., 4M 18.18.

2. *to omit inadvertently to bring*: δράγμα ἐν τῷ ἀγρῷ σου 'a sheaf in your field' De 24.19.

3. *to be unable to recollect*: + gen. pers., οὐκ ἐμνήσθη .. τοῦ Ιωσηφ, ἀλλα' ἐπελάθετο αὐτοῦ Ge 40.23; + gen. rei, ἐπιλήσονται τῆς πλησμονῆς 'would not be able to recollect the abundance' 41.30; + acc. rei, ἃ πεποίηκας αὐτῷ Ge 27.45, ἀγαθά La 3.17; pass. οὐκ ἐπιλησθήσεται 'shall be unforgettable' Je 23.40; Si 32.9.

On the case, see Helbing 110f. Cf. μιμνήσκομαι, ἐπιλησμονή, ἀμνημονέω: Renehan 1.90 (s. ἐπιλήθω).

ἐπιλέγω: aor. ἐπέλεξα, impv. ἐπίλεξον, 3pl ~λεξάτωσαν, mid. ~λεξαι; pf.ptc.pass. ~λελεγμένος.

to pick out, select: + acc. pers., Ἐπίλεξον σεαυτῷ ἄνδρας δυνατούς Ex 17.9, cf. mid., ἐπίλεξαι σεαυτῷ ἄνδρας 1M 12.44; .. ἀπὸ παντὸς Ισραηλ Ex 18.25; De 21.5; + με ὑπὲρ τὸν πατέρα σου '(chose) me in preference to your father' 2K 6.21; + gen., τῶν πρεσβυτέρων 'some of the elders' 1M 11.23. Cf. ἐπίλεκτος, ἐκλέγω.

ἐπίλεκτος, ον.

1. *singled out, chosen*: subst., τῶν ~ων τοῦ Ισραηλ Ex 24.11.

2. *of choice quality*: ἀναβάτας 'riders' Ex 15.4; subst. and temple offerings, τὰ ~ά μου καὶ τὰ καλά Jl 3.5.

Cf. ἐκλεκτός and ἐπιλέγω.

ἐπιλημπτεύομαι.ʃ *

to suffer from epilepsy or psychiatric disorder: *s* hum., 1K 21.16. Cf. ἐπίλημπτος.

ἐπίλη(μ)πτος, ον.ʃ

suffering from epilepsy or psychotic disorder: *s* hum., 1K 21.15; subst.m., 1K 21.16, 4K 9.11. Cf. ἐπιλημπτεύομαι.

ἐπιλησμονή, ῆς.ʃ

act of forgetting: + gen. obj., Si 11.27. Cf. ἀμνησία, λήθη, ἐπιλανθάνω.

ἐπιλογίζομαι: aor.inf. ~λογίσασθαι, impv.2pl ~λογίσασθε.ʃ

1. *to take into account, reckon with*: + acc., τὸ τοῦ θεοῦ κράτος 'God's power' 2M 14.4, τοῦτο, ὅτι .. 'the following fact that ..' 4M 16.5.

2. *to present as conclusion*: + acc., τοῦτο 'this thesis' 4M 3.6.

Cf. λογίζομαι.

ἐπίλοιπος, ον.

1. *left remaining, surviving*: τῶν ~ων σκεύων 'some of the remaining vessels' Je 34.16; subst., 1E 1.53; sg. referring to multiple individuals, ὁ ~ος (B: κατάλοιπος) τοῦ λαοῦ Jd 7.6 A, τὸ ~ον Ἀζώτου 'the remnant of A.' Je 32.6; οἱ ~οι τῶν ἀδελφῶν αὐτῶν Mi 5.3.

2. *residual*: *s* ἔτη '(the remaining) years' Le 27.18, Is 38.10; χρόνος 'time' 3M 3.26; subst. n., τὸ ~ον τῆς ζωῆς μου 'the rest of my life' Is 38.12.

3. *another or others belonging to the same group but not explicitly mentioned so far*: subst., De 19.20, 21.21, 1E 2.17.

Cf. λοιπός, κατά~, περί~ ὑπόλοιπος: Schmidt 4.569.

ἐπιλυπέω: aor.subj. ~λυπήσω, ptc.pass. ~λυπηθείς; pf.ptc. ~λελυπηκώς.

to cause sbd (acc.) *grief*: 2M 8.32; pass., ψυχικῶς 'at heart' 4.37. Cf. λυπέω.

ἐπιμαίνομαι.ʃ

to rage madly: *s* billows, 4M 7.5. Cf. μαίνομαι.

ἐπιμαρτύρομαι: aor. ἐπεμαρτυράμην, impv.pl. ~μαρτύρασθε, inf. ~μαρτύρασθαι.

1. *to witness, testify*: + dat. pers. τῷ οἴκῳ Ιακωβ Am 3.13; ἔναντι κυρίου Si 46.19.

2. *to call as witness*: + acc. pers., μάρτυρας Je 39.25 (ǁ διαμαρτύρομαι vs. 10).

3. *to admonish sternly*: abs., 1M 2.56, Ne 13.15; + dat. pers., 9.29.

Cf. δια~, μαρτύρομαι.

ἐπίμεικτος. ⇒ ἐπίμικτος.

ἐπιμέλεια, ας. f.

1. *care and attention*: ~ᾳ συντελούμενα 'being executed with care' 1E 6.9 (construction work), ἔγλυψεν ἐν ~ᾳ ἀργίας αὐτοῦ 'carved in his leisure time' Wi 13.13; τὰ τῆς ~ας αὐτῶν 'the affairs pertaining to their interests' 1M 16.14, τὴν τῶν ἰδίων ~αν 'going about their own business' 2M 11.23; ἐλεφάντων 'of elephants' 3M 5.1; ἐν ~ᾳ Pr 13.4.

*2. *items needed for bodily care of women*, 'toiletries': σμῆγμα καὶ ἡ λοιπὴ ἐ. 'soap and the rest of toiletries' Es 2.3.

Cf. ἐπιμελέομαι.

ἐπιμελέομαι, ~μέλομαι: fut. ~μελήσομαι; aor.inf., ~μεληθῆναι.

1. *to take care of*: + gen. pers. Ge 44.21.

2. *to take care* to act in a certain way: + inf., ἀπέχεσθαι τοῦ τόπου 'to keep away from the place' 1E 6.26; τοῦ ποιῆσαι 1M 11.37.

3. *to pay eager attention to, show active interest in*: + gen. rei, βρωμάτων 'foods' Si 33.13b.

Cf. ἐπιμελῶς, ἐπιμέλεια, μέλω, ἀμελέω, φροντίζω: Schmidt 2.630; Spicq 2.47-53.

ἐπιμελῶς. comp. ~μελέστερον. adv.

with concentration of mind: διανοεῖται ἐν τῇ καρδίᾳ αὐτοῦ ἐ. ἐπὶ τὰ πονηρά Ge 6.5, cf. 8.21. Cf. ἐπιμελέομαι, ἀμελῶς.

ἐπιμένω: aor.inf. ~μεῖναι.ʃ

to stay on without departing: οὐκ ἠδυνήθησαν ἐπιμεῖναι 'they could not tarry' Ex 12.39. Cf. (ὑπο)μένω.

ἐπιμήκης, ες.ʃ

extensive: *s* τόπος Ba 3.24 (‖ μέγας). Cf. μέγας.

ἐπιμίγνυμι: aor.pass. ἐπεμ(ε)ίγην, inf. ~μιγῆναι.ʃ

1. pass. *to mingle oneself* with: ἐπεμίγη τὸ σπέρμα τὸ ἅγιον εἰς τὰ ἀλλογενῆ ἔθνη 'the holy seed got mixed up among the foreign nations' 1E 8.67.

2. *to have dealings* with: + ἔν τινι (pers.), Ez 16.37; + dat., τῇ ἀκαθαρσίᾳ τῶν ἐθνῶν τῆς γῆς 1E 8.84; Pr 14.10.

Cf. ἐπίμικτος.

ἐπίμικτος, ον.ʃ

having attached oneself to the dominant or main group: subst., ἐ. πολύς Ex 12.38; Nu 11.4 (apart from the Israelites); Ne 13.3 (Israelites with foreign wives and their children); Ez 30.5 (apart from Israelites and other nationals); Ju 2.20 (mercenaries?). Alw. (except Ez 30.5) in sg. used collectively. See *BA* 4 ad Nu 11.4.

ἐπιμιμνῄσκομαι: aor. ἐπεμνήσθην.ʃ

to think of: + gen. rei (past event), 1M 10.46. Cf. μιμνῄσκομαι.

ἐπιμίξ. adv.ʃ

confusedly, indiscriminately: Wi 14.25. Cf. μίγνυμι.

ἐπιμονή, ῆς. f.ʃ

steadfastness: + inf. (in some activity) Si 38.27.

ἐπίμοχθος, ον.ʃ

making strenuous efforts: subst.n.sg. adv., Wi 15.7. Cf. μόχθος, κόπος.

ἐπιμύλιον, ου. n.ʃ

upper millstone: ‖ μύλος De 24.6; Jd 9.53B. Cf. μύλος.

ἐπινεύω: aor. ἐπένευσα, ptc. ~νεύσας.

1. *to issue a command*: + inf., 1M 6.57.

2. *to consent*: 2M 4.10; ἐπί τινι (over sth) 11.15; + dat. rei, ταῖς συνθήκαις 'the terms of the agreement' 14.20. Cf. νεύω, ἐπιχωρέω, εὐδοκέω **3b**.

ἐπινεφής, ές.ʃ

clouded: *s* sun, 2M 1.21.

ἐπινίκιος, ον.ʃ

pertaining to victory: subst.n.pl., *prize of victory*, 1E 3.5 (speech contest); *victory*, 2M 8.33. Cf. νίκη.

ἐπινοέω: aor. ἐπενόησα, pass. ἐπενοήθην.ʃ

1. *to conceive mentally*: + obj. rei, sth intangible, Jb 4.18, Wi 14.14, 4M 10.16; sth tangible, Wi 14.2.

2. *to perceive, notice*: + acc., Si 51.19.

Cf. ἐπίνοια.

ἐπίνοια, ας. f.

that which one mentally conceives: purpose, design Wi 9.14 (‖ διαλογισμός), τὰς κακὰς ~ας αὐτοῦ 'his evil designs' 4M 17.2; Je 20.10; ἐ. προσδοκίας 'one's thought on future' Si 40.2 (‖ διαλογισμός); act of mentally producing, εἰδώλων Wi 14.12 (‖ εὕρησις).

ἐπινυστάζω: aor.subj. ~στάξω.ʃ *

to slumber, doze: Pr 6.4. Cf. νυστάζω, ὑπνόω.

ἐπιξενόομαι: fut. ~ξενωθήσομαι; aor.ptc. ~ξενωθείς; pf. ἐπεξένωμαι.ʃ

to be on a visit as guest of sbd (dat.): Si 29.27, Es E 10, Pr 21.7. Cf. ξενίζω.

ἐπιορκέω: aor.ptc. ~ορκήσας.ʃ

1. *to swear falsely*: Wi 14.28.

*2. *to act against the terms of a sworn oath*: abs., 1E 1.46.

Cf. ἐπιορκία, ἐπίορκος: *GI* s.v.

ἐπιορκία, ας. f.ʃ

perjury: Wi 14.25. Cf. ἐπιορκέω.

ἐπίορκος, ον.ʃ

perjurious, swearing falsely: subst., Zc 5.3 (‖ κλέπτης and paraphrased as ὀμνύων τῷ ὀνόματί μου [i.e. τοῦ θεοῦ] ἐπὶ ψεύδει 5.4). Cf. ὅρκος, ἐπιορκέω.

ἐπιπαραγίνομαι: aor. ἐπιπαρεγενόμην.ʃ

to arrive to assail: *s* military commander, ἐπί τινα Jo 10.9.

ἐπίπεμπτος, ον.

subst.n.sg., *one fifth*: τὸ ~ον προσθήσει ἐπ' αὐτό 'he shall add one fifth (of it) to it' Le 5.16; τὸ ~ον τοῦ ἀργυρίου 27.15; Nu 5.7. Cf. πέμπτος: Lee 1969.236.

ἐπιπέμπω: aor.inf. ~πέμψαι, ptc. ~πέμψας.ʃ

to cause to go against sbd: + acc., κρίσεις ἀνὰ μέσον ἀδελφῶν 'wranglings among brothers' Pr 6.19 (‖ ἐκκαίω); + dat. (incom.), πλῆθος ἄρκων 'a host of bears' Wi 11.17, φλόγα 'flame' 3M 6.6. Cf. πέμπω.

ἐπιπίπτω: fut. ~πεσοῦμαι; aor. ἐπέπεσον, ptc. ~πεσών, subj. ~πέσω, opt.3s. ~πέσοι; pf. ἐπιπέπτωκα; plpf. ~πεπτώκειν.

1. *to thrust oneself*: ἐπιπεσὼν ἐπὶ τὸν τράχηλον .. τοῦ ἀδελφοῦ αὐτοῦ ἔκλαυσεν ἐπ' αὐτῷ Ge 45.14 (|| προσπίπτω 33.4), sim. 46.29, To 11.9, 13; ἐπιπεσὼν Ιωσηφ ἐπὶ πρόσωπον τοῦ πατρὸς αὐτοῦ ἔκλαυσεν ἐπ' αὐτόν Ge 50.1 (of dead father); ἐπὶ ^τὴν ῥομφαίαν^ 1K 31.4 (suicide).

2. *to launch a (surprise) attack*: ἐπί τινα– τὴν νύκτα 'by night' Ge 14.15; + ἐπί τινι (pers.), Jb 6.27; + dat. (incom.) pers., Jb 6.16, Ju 15.6.

3. *to happen* with overwhelming force: + dat. pers., *s* sth undesirable or unpleasant, ἔκστασις .. φόβος σκοτεινὸς μέγας 'trance .. great, dark fear' Ge 15.12, ἔκστασις ἐπ' αὐτούς Da 10.7 TH; ἐπιπέσοι ἐπ' αὐτοὺς φόβος καὶ τρόμος 'fear and trembling ..' Ex 15.16, εἰς πάντα τὸν λαόν 1M 7.18, δειλία θανάτου 'fear of death' Ps 54.5; ἀγάπησις 2K 1.26; ὄλεθρος 'destruction' Je 31.32; + dat. incom., κλῆρος ἁμαρτωλοῦ 'the lot of sinners' Si 25.19.

4. *to fall accidentally*: ἐπί + acc. Le 11.32; Nu 35.23; *s* measuring cords, Ps 15.6; birds, εἰς μέσον τινος 77.27.

Cf. πίπτω, ἐμπίπτω, συμβαίνω.

ἐπίπληξις, εως. f.ʃ

act of rebuking: divine, 2M 7.33 (+ παιδεία 'discipline'), cf. Caird 1968.474; LSG s.v.

ἐπιπληρόω.ʃ

to fill up: pass., *o* temple, + gen. rei, ἀσωτίας καὶ κώμων 'with debauchery and revelries' 2M 6.4. Cf. πληρόω.

ἐπιποθέω: fut. ~ποθήσω; aor. ἐπεπόθησα, inf. ~ποθῆσαι.ʃ

1. *to yearn* after: abs. Wi 15.19; + acc., τὰς ἐντολάς σου Ps 118.131, τὸ σωτήριόν σου 118.174, γυναῖκα Si 25.21; *ἐπί or *πρός + acc., ὃν τρόπον ἡ ἔλαφος ἐπὶ τὰς πηγὰς τῶν ὑδάτων .. ἐπιποθεῖ ἡ ψυχή μου πρός σε, ὁ θεός 'as a hart yearns after the springs of water ..' Ps 41.2, cf. ὡς ἀρτιγέννητα βρέφη .. γάλα ἐπιποθήσατε 'like newborn babies ..' 1Pet 2.2; ἐπὶ ἅρπαγμα 'after robbed objects' Ps 61.11 (|| ἐλπίζω); ἐπιποθεῖ καὶ ἐκλείπει ἡ ψυχή μου εἰς τὰς αὐλὰς τοῦ κυρίου 'my soul yearns and swoons for the courts of the Lord' 83.3; *+ inf., τοῦ ἐπιθυμῆσαι τὰ κρίματά σου 'to desire your judgments' 118.20.

2. *to display* protective, caring *affection*: *s* animate and abs. Je 13.14 (|| φείδομαι, οἰκτιρέω); *ἐπί τινι, De 13.8 (|| φείδομαι, σκεπάζω), ὡς ἀετὸς σκεπάσαι νοσσιὰν αὐτοῦ καὶ ἐπὶ τοῖς νεοσσοῖς αὐτοῦ ἐπεπόθησεν 'as an eagle might shield its brood and displayed its affection towards its young' 32.11.

Cf. βούλομαι, ἐπιθυμέω, ἐλπίζω, θέλω, οἰκτιρέω, ὁμείρομαι, σκεπάζω, φείδομαι: Schmidt 3.596-601; Spicq 1957; id. 2.58-60.

ἐπίποκος, ον.ʃ*

covered with wool: *s* ram, 4K 3.4 *L*. Cf. πόκος.

ἐπιπολάζω: aor. ἐπεπόλασα.ʃ

to come up to the surface: *s* thehead of an axe fallen into a river, 4K 6.6.

ἐπιπολαίως. adv.ʃ

in a way that all can see that a certain condition prevails, 'obviously, manifestly': 3M 2.31. Cf. ἔκδηλος.

ἐπίπονος, ον.ʃ

toilsome: *s* ἐργασία 'labour' Si 7.15, καταστροφή 'destruction' 3M 5.47. Cf. πόνος.

ἐπιπορεύομαι: aor.ptc. ~πορευσάμενος.ʃ

1. *to traverse*: *s* destructive sword, Le 26.33; clouds, ἐφ' ὅλην τὴν οἰκουμένην Ep Je 61; + acc. loci, τὴν γῆν Ez 39.14; τὰς δυνάμεις 'the troops' 3M 1.4.

2. *to adhere to*: + dat., τοῖς ὑπογραμμοῖς τῆς ἐπιτομῆς 'the guidelines for the abridgement' 2M 2.28.

Cf. (δια)πορεύομαι, διέρχομαι: Lee 88f.

ἐπιπροστίθημι: aor.subj.pass., ~προσθῶ.ʃ

mid. *to gain in addition*: πολλῷ μᾶλλον 'very much more' Si prol. 14. Cf. προστίθημι. Del. To 5.15 v.l.

ἐπιρραίνω: aor.inf. ~ρρᾶναι.ʃ

to besprinkle: τῷ ὕδατι τά τε ξύλα 2M 1.21. Cf. ῥαίνω, ἐπιρραντίζω.

ἐπιρραντίζω: aor.subj.pass. ~ρραντισθῶ.ʃ

to sprinkle on: + dat., ᾧ ἂν ἐπιρραντισθῇ ἀπὸ τοῦ αἵματος αὐτῆς ἐπὶ τὸ ἱμάτιον 'whoever is besprinkled from its blood on his garment' Le 6.27 (|| ῥαντίζω). Cf. ῥαντίζω, ἐπιρραίνω.

ἐπιρρέω.ʃ

to keep on flowing: *s* river, Jb 22.16¶. Cf. ῥέω.

ἐπιρρίπτω: fut.act. ~ρρίψω; aor. ἐπέρριψα, subj. ~ρρίψω, impv. ~ρριψον, pass. ἐπερρίφην; pf. ἐπέρριφα.

1. *to cast* over or on to a surface: + acc. rei, ἐπ' αὐτὸν πᾶν σκεῦος Nu 35.20, 22; σιωπήν 'silence' Am 8.3; ἐπὶ σὲ βδελυγμόν 'abominable thing' Na 3.6; ἐπὶ κύριον τὴν μέριμνάν σου 'your worry' Ps 54.22; ἐπ' αὐτὴν τρόμον 'a trembling' Je 15.8; αὐτῷ πληγάς '.. blows' 2M 3.26; of sprinkling of salt on a sacrifice, Ez 43.24; τί τινι (pers.) - αὐτοῖς λίθους χαλάζης 'hailstones' Jo 10.11.

***2**. *to allot by lot*: + dat. (com.) pers. and acc., Jo 23.4.

Cf. ῥίπτω.

ἐπιρρωγολογέομαι.ʃ *
to overdo in harvesting grapes of: + acc., ἀμπελῶνας 'vineyards' 4M 2.9.

ἐπιρρώνυμι: aor.pass. ἐπερρώσθην.ʃ
to strengthen: pass., *o* hum., + inf., ταῖς ψυχαῖς 'mentally' 2M 11.9. Cf. ῥώννυμι, κραταιόω.

ἐπίσαγμα, ατος. n.ʃ *
pack-saddle: ὄνου 'of donkey' Le 15.9. Cf. ἐπισάσσω.

ἐπισάσσω: aor. ἐπέσαξα, impv. ἐπίσαξον; pf.ptc. pass. ~σεσαγμένος.

1. *to pile a load upon*: + acc., τὴν ὄνον αὐτοῦ 'his ass' Ge 22.3, Nu 22.21; mid. and metaph., ὑμᾶς κλοιῷ βαρεῖ '.. with a heavy collar (of bondage)' 3K 12.11.

2. *to place a saddle upon the back of* for action: + acc., ἵππους '(war) horses' Je 26.4, 'donkey' Jd 19.10.

Cf. ἀποσάσσω, ἐπίσαγμα, ἐπιγεμίζω.

ἐπισείω: aor. ἐπέσεισα; pf.ptc. ~σεσεικώς.ʃ
to incite: + acc. pers., 2M 4.1; also + inf., Jd 1.14, 1C 21.1; + ἐπί τινα 1K 26.19; ἔν τινι (pers.) 2K 24.1 (*L* εἴς τινα). Cf. ἐποτρύνω.

ἐπισημαίνω: aor.mid. 2s ἐπεσημήνω, inf. ~μάνασθαι.ʃ
**to recognise by means of a distinct feature*: abs., Jb 14.17; + acc., τὴν ὁδόν 2M 2.6.

ἐπίσημος, ον.ʃ
distinguishable from others: *s* πρόβατα, Ge 30.42 (bearing distinguishing marks); ἡμέρα ἐ. 'a notable day' Es 5.4, cf. ἔχειν ~ον 'to celebrate (as a special day)' 2M 15.36 and see LSG s.v.; ἐν τόπῳ ~ῳ 'in a conspicuous place' 1M 11.37; ἀνήρ 'a distinguished man' 3M 6.1. **b**. subst.n., *distinguishing mark*: || σφραγίς PSol 2.6.

Cf. ἄσημος, ἀπαρασήμαντος, διάδηλος.

ἐπισιτίζω: aor.mid. ἐπεσιτισάμην.ʃ
to get ready foods and drinks to be taken on a journey: mid., + ἑτοιμάζομαι Jo 9.4. Cf. ἐφοδιάζω.

ἐπισιτισμός, οῦ. m.
foods and drinks to be taken on a journey: ἐ. εἰς τὴν ὁδόν Ge 42.25, 45.21; οὐδὲ ~ὸν ἐποίησαν ἑαυτοῖς εἰς τὴν ὁδόν Ex 12.39. Cf. σῖτος, ἐπισιτίζω, ἐφόδιον.

ἐπισκάζω.*ʃ
to limp upon: + dat., τῷ μηρῷ αὐτοῦ 'on his thigh' Ge 32.31.

ἐπισκεπάζω: aor. ἐπεσκέπασα.ʃ* (ἐπισκεπής in Aristot.)

1. *to cover over*: in order to hit or crush(?), abs., La 3.43; + acc., σκότος ἐπισκεπάσει με Ps 138.11 Sym (LXX: καταπατέω).

2. *to place* sth *over to cover entirely*: + acc., νεφέλην La 3.44.

Cf. σκεπάζω.

ἐπισκέπτομαι: fut. ~σκέψομαι, pass. ~σκεφθήσομαι, ~σκεπήσομαι; aor. ἐπεσκεψάμην, impv. ἐπίσκεψαι, 3s ~σκεψάσθω, inf. ~σκέψασθαι, ptc. ~σκεψάμενος, subj. ~σκέψωμαι, pass. ἐπεσκέπην, subj. ~σκεφθῶ, impv.3s ~σκεπήτω, inf. ~σκεπῆναι; pf. ἐπέσκεμμαι, ptc.pass. ἐπεσκεμμένος.

1. *to take interest in, concern oneself with*: abs., *s* God, and with a punitive intent, Ex 32.34, Si 2.14, ἐν κρίματι αὐτοῦ PSol 15.12; || ἐκδικέω and + ἐπί τινι (ground or occasion) Je 5.9; + τινα - ἐν μαχαίρᾳ καὶ ἐν λιμῷ 34.6; + ἐπί τινα 36.32, 43.31 (|| ἐπάγω πάντα τὰ κακά), ἐν ῥομφαίᾳ καὶ ἐν λιμῷ καὶ ἐν θανάτῳ 51.13, εἰς πονηρά 51.29; + τι (offence), ἐν ῥάβδῳ τὰς ἀνομίας αὐτῶν καὶ ἐν μάστιξιν τὰς ἁμαρτίας αὐτῶν 'with the rod their iniquities and with the whips their sins' Ps 88.33. **b**. + τινα– ἐπεσκέψατο ὁ θεὸς τοὺς υἱοὺς Ισραηλ .. εἶδεν αὐτῶν τὴν θλῖψιν Ex 4.31, πάντα τὰ ἔθνη Ps 58.6; || μιμνήσκομαι 8.5, 105.4, Je 15.15; παρακαλέσαι καὶ ἐπισκέψασθαι αὐτόν 'to comfort and show concern about him' Jb 2.11; Ez 34.11 (|| ἐκζητέω); τοῦ ἀγαθῶσαι αὐτούς 'in their favour' Je 39.41; *s* shepherd and *o* sheep, 23.2, Zc 11.16; Si 7.22; + dat. cogn., ἐπισκοπῇ ἐπισκέψεται ὑμᾶς ὁ θεός Ge 50.24; 50.25, Ex 3.16 (ὑμᾶς καὶ ὅσα συμβέβηκεν ὑμῖν ἐν Αἰγύπτῳ 'you and that which has befallen you ..'); εἰς εἰρήνην '(to make sure that they are) all right' 1K 17.18. **c**. + ἐπί τινα, with a view to helping, οὐ μὴ ἐπισκέψωμαι ἐπὶ τὰς θυγατέρας ὑμῶν, ὅταν πορνεύωσι Ho 4.14; Zc 10.3*a*; + inf. (task commissioned) 2E 1.2. **d**. + acc. rei and pass., τὰ ὀστᾶ αὐτοῦ ἐπεσκέπησαν 'his bones were taken care of' Si 49.15.

2. *to consider, ponder, give thought to*: ἐπέσκεπται καὶ ἔγνω 'has considered and found out' Nu 16.5; + acc., τὸν ναὸν αὐτοῦ 'His temple' Ps 26.4 (|| θεωρέω); + ἔν τινι– ἐπισκέψασθε δὴ ἐν τούτῳ Ma 3.10.

3. *to visit*: + τινα, and benevolent, κύριος ἐπεσκέψατο τὴν Σάρραν Ge 21.1, τὴν γυναῖκα αὐτοῦ Jd 15.1, ἄρρωστον 'a sick person' Si 7.35.

4. *to count in a census*: τῶν ἐπεσκεμμένων ἀνδρῶν 'of the numbered men' Ex 39.2; + acc. pers. Nu 1.3; with ἐπίσκεψις as cogn. obj. Nu 1.44.

5. *to pass under review*: military t.t., 1K 15.4, pass., Nu 1.19; δύναμιν Si 17.32. **b**. *to call up for military duties*: *o* troops, Jd 20.15.

***6**. *to assess the quality of and appoint*: as overseer (?), + acc. pers., ἄνθρωπον ἐπὶ τῆς συναγωγῆς Nu 27.16; pass., Ne 7.1.

7. *to investigate*: abs., Ps 16.3 (|| δοκιμάζω, πυρόω), 1E 2.22; τινα PSol 9.4, τι Nu 14.34, Ju 7.7; + περί τινος Le 13.36, 2C 24.6 (*L* ἐκζητέω); ἐν βιβλίῳ 2E 4.15; "we have investigated and found out that .." 4.19. ***b**. *to discover as a result of investigation*: + ὅτι, Ju 5.20.

***8**. *to look for, search*: mid., + acc. pers., 1K 20.6; pass., ἐπεσκέπησαν, καὶ εὑρέθη 1C 26.31; οὐκ ἐπισκεφθήσεται 'nobody will miss it' Je 3.16. **b**. pass., *to be missing*: ἐπεσκέπη ὁ τόπος Δαυιδ 'David's seat was vacant' 1K 20.25; *s* hum., Jd 21.3 (*L* ἀφαιρεθῆναι), 2K 2.30, 4K 10.19B (*L* ἀπολείπομαι), cf. ἐκλιμπάνω.

Cf. ἐπίσκεψις, ἐπίσκοπος, ἐπισκοπή, ἐπισκοπέω, συνεπισκέπτω, ἐφοδεύω, κατασκοπεύω: Beyer, *TDNT* 2.600-3.

ἐπισκευάζω: aor.inf. ~σκευάσαι, pass. ~σκευασθῆναι.

to make ready for use: + acc. rei, λύχνους '(to trim) lamps' Ex 30.7; 1K 3.3B; τὸν οἶκον κυρίου 2C 24.4. Cf. ἑτοιμάζω.

ἐπίσκεψις, εως. f.

1. *numbering, census-taking*: παραπορεύομαι ~ιν 'undergo a census' Ex 39.3; cogn. obj. of ἐπισκέπτω Nu 1.44. **b**. *a number obtained by census-taking*: Nu 1.21 +.

***2**. *enquiry, investigation*: eschatological, Nu 16.29 (? and ‖ ἐπισκοπή); 2M 3.14, 14.20.

3. v.n. of ἐπισκεπτω, **1**: divine and punitive, Je 11.23, 23.12, 28.18, 31.44.

4. v.n. of ἐπισκέπτω, **4**: 1C 23.11.

5. *inspection*: 3M 7.12.

Cf. ἐπισκέπτω, ἐπισκοπή: LSG s.v.

ἐπισκιάζω: fut. ~σκιάσω; aor. ἐπεσκίασα.

to overshadow in order to create darkness: ἐπεσκίαζεν ἐπὶ ^τὴν σκηνήν^ ἡ νεφέλη Ex 40.29 (‖ σκιάζω Nu 9.18). **b**. *to provide protective shade*: ἐπὶ τὴν κεφαλήν μου ἐν ἡμέρᾳ πολέμου Ps 139.8; + dat. 90.4.

Cf. σκιά.

ἐπισκοπέω.ʃ

1. *to concern oneself with interest and attention*: *s* God, + acc., γῆν De 11.12; caring patron, Es 2.11.

2. *to look for*: pass., οὐκ ἐπισκοπεῖται γνῶσις 'no interest is shown in knowledge' Pr 19.23.

3. *to oversee*: abs., 2C 34.12 (*L* ἐπισπουδάζω).

Cf. ἐπισκέπτω, ἐπισκοπή, (παν)επίσκοπος.

ἐπισκοπή, ῆς. f. *

V.n. of ἐπισκοπέω.

1. *act of taking interest, concerning oneself*: divine intervention, ~ῇ ἐπισκέψεται ὑμᾶς ὁ θεός Ge 50.24; 50.25, Ex 3.16; ~ῆς γενομένης ἐπὶ τὴν αἰχμαλωσίαν παρὰ τοῦ κυρίου 1E 6.5; ἐ. κυρίου ὑπερεῖδέν με '.. passed by me' Jb 6.14; ἡ ἐ. σου ἐφύλαξέν μου τὸ πνεῦμα 10.12; ὁ θεὸς ~ὴν ἐποιεῖτο τοῦ οἴκου μου 29.4; providential overseeing, ἐ. ἐν τοῖς ἐκλεκτοῖς αὐτοῦ Wi 3.9 (‖ χάρις καὶ ἔλεος). **b**. hum. concern: πρὸς ~ὴν τῶν Ἰουδαίων 'in the interests of the Jews' 3M 5.42; ἔσται αὐτοῦ ἐ. ἐκ λόγων αὐτοῦ 'his interests will be served by what he himself has said' Wi 2.20; Si 31.6. **c**. punitive: αὐτὸς διὰ τί τούτων ~ὴν οὐ πεποίηται; Jb 24.12; ἐν καιρῷ ~ῆς αὐτῶν ἀπολοῦνται Je 10.15; ἐν εἰδώλοις ἐθνῶν ἐ. ἔσται Wi 14.11 (‖ κολάζω 'punish' vs. 10); Si 23.24; + gen. obj., Jb 7.18 (‖ κρίνω).

2. *numbering, census-taking*: Ex 30.12 (‖ ἐπίσκεψις vs. 13).

***3**. *enquiry, investigation*: Le 19.20 (or: 'punitive, divine visitation' Harl 2001.906); Jb 31.14 (‖ ἔτασις 'examination'); Οὐκ ἔσται ἐ. ἀνδρός· καὶ ἐ. αὐτῷ παρὰ κυρίου 34.9 (dat. also at Le 19.20), cf. Si 16.18 (‖ ἐπιβλέπω vs. 19); eschatological, ἐν καιρῷ ~ῆς αὐτῶν ἀναλάμψουσιν '.. will shine' Wi 3.7, ἐν ὥρᾳ ~ῆς Si 18.20 (‖ κρίσις); ψυχῶν Wi 3.13; Nu 16.29 (? and ‖ ἐπίσκεψις); reviewing of a (punitive) measure taken earlier, Is 24.22.

4. *act of overseeing*: ὅλης τῆς σκηνῆς Nu 4.16.

5. *public office* (of ἐπίσκοπος?): τὴν ~ὴν αὐτοῦ λάβοι ἕτερος Ps 108.8.

***6**. *that which has been entrusted for care*: μιανοῦσιν τὴν ~ήν μου 'they will defile my charge' Ez 7.22.

Cf. ἐπισκέπτω, ἐπίσκεψις, ἐπισκοπέω: Beyer, *TDNT* 2.606f.

ἐπίσκοπος, ου. m.

1. *overseer*: with cultic duties, Nu 4.16; military, τῆς δυνάμεως 31.14; ‖ ἄρχων Is 60.17; ἐπί τινα 1M 1.51; *s* God, Jb 20.29.

2. *investigator*: of human hearts, *s* God, ‖ μάρτυς Wi 1.6.

Cf. ἐπισκοπέω, ἐπόπτης: Beyer, *TDNT* 2.608-15.

ἔπισος. ⇒ ἔφισος.

ἐπίσπαστρον, ου. n.ʃ

curtain, hanging: Ex 26.36. Cf. καταπέτασμα.

ἐπισπάω: fut. ~σπάσομαι; aor.mid. ἐπεσπασάμην, impv. ἐπίσπασαι, inf. ~σπάσασθαι, ptc. ~σπασάμενος, subj. ~σπάσωμαι.

1. mid. *to draw* towards oneself: for one's own use, + acc., ὕδωρ περιοχῆς ἐπίσπασαι σεαυτῇ 'Draw in water (in large quantities) for yourself for a time of siege' Na 3.14; ***o*** woman, Ju 12.12, hearer, πρὸς τὴν μελέτην 'to the study' Si prol. II; fig., ὄλεθρον 'ruin' Wi 1.12, λογισμὸν ἀνοίας '(took recourse to) a silly notion' 19.3, τὰς ἁμαρτίας ὡς σχοινίῳ μακρῷ 'sins as with a long string' Is 5.18, βοήθειαν 'help' 1M 14.1; and + gen., ἐπεσπάσατο αὐτὸν τῶν ἱματίων 'she pulled him by the robes' Ge 39.12. **b**. *to draw out* enemies in order to attack: + acc., 2K 17.13*L*

2. *to protect*: τινα 3M 3.10.

Cf. σπάω.

ἐπισπεύδω.ʃ

1. *to urge on*: abs., 1E 1.25.

2. *to encourage to move with haste*: τινα ἐπὶ τὸν πότον Es 6.14 (*L* σπεύδω). **b.** intr. *to hurry*: *s* feet, κακοποιεῖν Pr 6.18.

Cf. σπεύδω, ἐπισπουδάζω, ἐποξύνω.

ἐπισπλαγχνίζομαι.ʃ *

to have compassion: Pr 17.5. Cf. οἰκτιρέω.

ἐπισπουδάζω.ʃ

tr. *to hurry up*: + acc. pers., ἐπεσπούδαζον οἱ ἄγγελοι τὸν Λωτ Ge 19.15; pass., ὕπαρξις ἐπισπουδαζομένη 'possessions accumulated in haste' Pr 13.11, sim. 20.9b.

Cf. (ἐπι)σπεύδω, σπουδάζω, σπουδή, ἐπισπουδαστής: LSG s.v.

ἐπισπουδαστής, οῦ. m. *ʃ

hard taskmaster (Ottley ad loc.): Is 14.4. Cf. ἐπισπουδάζω.

ἐπίσταμαι: impf. ἠπιστάμην, 2s ἠπίστω. Only in the pres. and impf.

1. *to find out, realise after an enquiry or investigation*: + ὅτι Ge 47.5; οὔτε ἔγνως οὔτε ἠπίστω Is 48.8.

2. pres. and impf., *to know for sure, be convinced*: + ὅτι Ex 4.14, 9.30, Nu 22.34; + cogn. obj., ἐπιστήμην ὑψίστου 24.16, σύνεσιν καὶ ἐπιστήμην 2C 2.11.

3. *to be well and fully acquainted with*: + acc. rei, τὸν μόχθον τὸν εὑρόντα ἡμᾶς 'the hardship which befell us' Nu 20.14; τὸ κακὸν καὶ τὸ ἀγαθόν 32.11; τὸν ἐρεθισμόν σου καὶ τὸν τράχηλόν σου τὸν σκληρόν 'your rebelliousness and your stiff neck' De 31.27; γράμματα Is 29.11, κρίματα PSol 5.1, τὴν ὁδόν To 5.5 𝔊II; + acc. pers., De 22.2, 28.33; 28.64 (foreign gods), Is 55.5 (|| οἶδα), οἱ ἐπιστάμενοί σε 'your acquaintances' Ez 28.19; *s* God and *o* hum., Je 1.5.

4. *to possess the necessary skill and ability* to do: + inf., λαλεῖν Je 1.6, γλύψαι 'to engrave' 2C 2.6 (|| οἶδα), ψάλλειν 'to play music' 1K 16.18*L* (B+: εἰδότα ψαλμόν), κρίνειν Jb 29.7 (|| συνίημι).

Cf. (ἐπι)γινώσκω, συνίημι, συνεπίσταμαι, ἐπιστήμη, ἐπιστήμων: Schmidt 1.290-3.

ἐπίστασις, εως. f.ʃ

v.n. of ἐφίστημι *to come upon suddenly*, 'onset': τῆς κακίας 2M 6.3.

ἐπιστατέω.ʃ

to be in charge of: + gen., τῶν ἱερῶν ἔργων 1E 7.2.

ἐπιστάτης, ου. m.

one who is assigned to oversee a task, 'overseer, foreman': ἐπέστησεν αὐτοῖς ~άτας τῶν ἔργων 'he appointed over them overseers of the works' Ex 1.11; τοῦ Φαραω 5.14; ἐν οἴκῳ κυρίου Je 36.26; τοῦ ἱεροῦ 1E 1.8 (|| ἄρχων 2C 35.8); army officer, + στρατηγός Ju 2.14. Cf. ἐφίστημι, ἐπόπτης, ἐργοδιώκτης: Oepke, *TDNT* 2.622f.

ἐπιστήμη, ης. f.

body of knowledge: a divine gift, and of practical and technical matters, πνεῦμα θεῖον σοφίας καὶ συνέσεως καὶ ~ης Ex 31.3, 35.31, σοφία καὶ ἐ. ἐν αὐτοῖς συνιέναι ποιεῖν πάντα τὰ ἔργα 36.1, ἔδωκεν ὁ θεὸς ~ην ἐν τῇ καρδίᾳ 36.2 (all of architecture); general knowledge, ἐπιστάμενος ~ην ὑψίστου Nu 24.16; || βουλή De 32.28; Jb 28.12 (|| σύνεσις vs. 20); σοφία καὶ ἐ. καὶ εὐσέβεια Is 33.6; || φρόνησις Ez 28.4; ἐ. συνέσεως Si 17.7; + γνῶσις 1.19, || παιδεία 16.25. Cf. ἐπίσταμαι.

ἐπιστήμων, ον, gen. ονος.

1. *prudent*: *s* person: leader, ἄνδρας σοφοὺς καὶ ~ονας καὶ συνετοὺς .. De 1.13 (to be appointed as ἡγούμενοι 'leaders'), 15, ἡγουμένους καὶ ~ονας 1E 8.43, ἀνὴρ ἐ. καὶ πεπαιδευμένος '.. well-educated' Si 40.29, Solomon 47.12; nation observant of divine ordinances, λαὸς σοφὸς καὶ ἐ. De 4.6.

2. *intellectually capable of comprehending profound matters*: *s* reader of the Scriptures, Si prol. 4; ~ονας ἐν πάσῃ σοφίᾳ καὶ γραμματικοὺς καὶ σοφοὺς .. Da LXX 1.4 (|| συνιέντας ib. TH). Cf. σοφιστής.

Cf. ἐπίσταμαι, ἐπιστήμη, συνετός, σοφός.

ἐπιστήριγμα, ατος. n.ʃ *

firm support: *s* God, 2K 22.19. Cf. ἐπιστηρίζω, στήριγμα.

ἐπιστηρίζω: fut. ~ριῶ, mid. ~ρίσομαι; aor. ἐπεστήρισα, mid. ~ρισάμην, pass. ~ρίχθην, subj. ~ρισθῶ; pf.pass.3s ἐπεστήρικται; plpf.mid.3s ἐπεστήρικτο.

to position firmly on sth: *o* one's eyes, ἐπὶ σὲ τοὺς ὀφθαλμούς μου Ps 31.8; harming hand, 37.3; mid. ὁ κύριος ἐπεστήρικτο ἐπ' αὐτῆς 'the Lord had stationed himself firmly on it [= the ladder]' Ge 28.13; pass. w. intransitive force, ἐπὶ ^ῥάβδον καλαμίνην^ ['reed staff'] ἐπιστηρισθῇ 'would clutch on to it' Is 36.6; ἐπὶ σὲ ἐπεστηρίχθην Ps 70.6; ὁ θυμός σου 87.8; ἐπί τινι Ju 8.24 (|| κρεμάζομαι), ἐπεστηρίσατο ἐπὶ ^τοὺς στύλους^ 'he gripped the columns firmly' Jd 16.29 A (B: ἐπεστηρίχθη ἐπ' αὐτούς); *s* edifice, ἐπὶ ^στύλων^ 'on columns' Jd 16.26 A (B:: στήκω).

Cf. στηρίζω, ἐρείδω, ἐφίστημι.

ἐπιστοιβάζω: fut. ~βάσω; aor.subj. ~βάσω.ʃ *

tr. *to pile up*: ξύλα ἐπὶ τὸ πῦρ Le 1.7, fig. Si 8.3; pieces of sacrificial animals, Le 1.8, 12. Cf. στοιβάζω.

ἐπιστολή, ῆς. f.

1. *missive, letter* containing a message: ὅμηρα καὶ ~ὰς βυβλίνας 'hostages and letters of papyrus' Is 18.2, .. ~ὰς καὶ πρέσβεις '.. and envoys' 39.1.

2. *command communicated by a messenger*: Es 7.16 *L*.

Cf. γράμμα: Deissmann 1923.193-6.

ἐπιστρατεία, ας. f.ʃ
military campaign: 3M 3.14.

ἐπιστρατεύω: aor. ἐπεστράτευσα, inf. ~τεῦσαι, ptc. ~τεύσας.
to make war (against ἐπί): ἐπὶ Ιερουσαλημ Zc 14.12; ἐπὶ τὸ ὄρος Σιων Is 29.8; 2M 12.27. Cf. στρατιά, στρατεύω, πολεμέω.

ἐπιστράτηγος, ου. m.ʃ
viceroy: 1M 15.38.

ἐπιστρατοπεδεύω: aor. ἐπεστρατοπέδευσα.ʃ
to encamp over against: ἀπὸ Βεκτιλεθ Ju 2.21. Cf. καταστρατοπεδεύω.

ἐπιστρέφω: fut. ~στρέψω, pass. ~στραφήσομαι; aor. ἐπέστρεψα, inf. ~στρέψαι, impv. ~στρεψον, ptc. ~στρέψας, subj. ~στρέψω, pass. ἐπεστράφην, subj. ~στραφῶ, ptc. ~στραφείς, impv. ~στράφητι, inf. ~στραφῆναι.

I. tr. *to bring back* to the point of origin or home: + acc., Nu 10.35; Je 35.6 (‖ ἀποστρέφω vs. 3); τὴν αἰχμαλωσίαν Ho 6.11, Am 9.14, Jl 3.1, Zp 3.20; stray sheep Ez 34.4; τινα Zc 10.10; τοὺς πόδας μου εἰς τὰ μαρτύριά σου Ps 118.59; εἰς τὸν νόμον σου Ne 9.29; caus. of ἀναστρέφω 2K 12.23. **b**. *to turn back*: πολλοὺς ἐ. ἀπὸ ἀδικίας 'turned many back from wrong-doing' Ma 2.6; Je 2.24; ἐπιστρέψατε τὰ πρόσωπα ὑμῶν 'Change your outlook' Ez 14.6, πρὸς αὐτὸν καρδίαν Ps 84.9; καρδίαν πατρὸς πρὸς υἱόν Ma 3.23, Si 48.10; τὸν ὀνειδισμὸν αὐτῶν εἰς τὴν κεφαλὴν αὐτῶν 'their taunt on to their own heads' Ne 3.36, κακίαν Jd 9.57 A (B: πονηρίαν), 1K 25.39 *L* (B: ἀπο~); ἑκάστῳ τὰς δικαιοσύνας αὐτοῦ 26.23, εὐλογίαν εἰς τὸν οἶκόν μου 2K 6.12*L*, τὸ ἔλεός σου ἐφ' ἡμᾶς PSol 8.27. **c**. *to revive, restore to strength*: ψυχήν La 1.11, Ps 18.8, 22.3, Ru 4.15. ***d**. τινι (pers.) λόγον / ῥῆμα, calqued on /hēšiv dāvār/, *to reply*: Ne 2.20, 3K 21.9; 'to report' 4K 22.9, 20.

2. *to cause to come back*: + acc., ἐπὶ σὲ πᾶσαν τὴν ὀδύνην Αἰγύπτου '.. all of the suffering in Egypt' De 28.60.

3. *to direct backwards*: + acc., face, Jd 18.23 (so as to address sbd); the face of a person spoken to in order to have his attention, 3K 13.11; τὴν χεῖρα αὐτοῦ εἰς τὸ στόμα αὐτοῦ 1K 14.26, 27 (after having dipped one's hand into a honeycomb).

4. *to transform*: + acc., τὴν κατάραν εἰς εὐλογίαν 'the curse into a blessing' Ne 13.2, τὸ ὄνομα αὐτοῦ Ιωακιμ 'renamed him Joachim' 3K 23.34B.

II. intr. *to reverse the direction of movement and return* to the point of origin: abs. Nu 14.25, De 1.7, Ho 11.5, Zc 10.9; πορευόμενον καὶ οὐκ ἐπιστρέφον Ps 77.39; εἰς τὴν πόλιν Ge 44.13; εἰς τὸν τόπον μου Ho 5.15, εἰς τὸν χοῦν αὐτῶν 'back to the soil' Ps 103.29 (upon death); ἐπί τινα Mi 5.3, Zc 1.16, 8.3; πρός τινα Ge 8.12, cf. Ho 2.7 ("to the former husband"); πρός τι Jn 1.13 ("to the land," *s* a ship and its passengers); Da 11.9 LXX (TH ἀνα~); in submission following military defeat, Ez 26.2, εἰς τὰ ὀπίσω Ps 55.10; ‖ ἀποστρέφω Ex 4.20 (vs. 21), Nu 23.5 (vs. 6); Da 4.33 TH (‖ pass.); of yearly cycle, *s* ἐνιαυτός 2K 11.1, 3K 21.22, 26. **b**. esp. as a result of change of heart: abs. Ho 12.6, Ma 3.7; ἐπὶ κύριον De 4.30, 30.2; ἐπιστράφητε πρός με ἐξ ὅλης τῆς καρδίας ὑμῶν Jl 2.12, ἐπὶ ψεύδει Je 3.10; ἐπιστρέψατε πρός με, καὶ ἐπιστραφήσομαι πρὸς ὑμᾶς Zc 1.3, Ma 3.7, sim. To 13.6; πρὸς τὸν θεὸν αὐτῶν Ho 5.4, sim. 6.1, 7.10, 14.2, 3, Am 4.6, 8, 9, 10, 11, Jl 2.13, Hg 2.17; τῇ διανοίᾳ De 4.39, τῇ καρδίᾳ Is 46.8, ἐπιστρέψουσιν ἐπὶ καρδίαν αὐτῶν 'they will come to their senses' Ba 2.30; opp. ἀποστρέφω Je 8.4; ἀπὸ τῶν κακῶν αὐτῶν 18.8; *s* God, Ps 6.5. **c**. *to renege*: 4K 24.1, Je 41.10.

2. *to turn round and head in a different direction*: εἰς δεξιὰν ἢ εἰς ἀριστεράν 'to the right or to the left' Ge 24.49; εἰς τὴν ἔρημον Ex 16.10; πρὸς κύριον 5.22; Nu 14.25, 21.33; mid., *to turn round, facing backwards*: Ez 1.9; ἐπορεύοντο καὶ οὐκ ἐπέστρεφον 'they kept going, without turning back' 1.12.

3. *to turn* towards *and focus one's attention and efforts* on: abs. 1K 22.18 (mid.; *L* act.); ἐπί + acc., ἐπὶ θεοὺς ἀλλοτρίους De 31.18, .. καὶ λατρεύσουσιν αὐτοῖς 31.20, ἐπὶ τὰς ἀδικίας τῶν πατέρων αὐτῶν τῶν πρότερον 'to the lawless practices of their forefathers' Je 11.10; *s* ὠδῖνες 'pains of labour,' ἐπ' αὐτήν 1K 4.19 (*L* simpl.); gen., "could not care less about the pains" 4M 13.5.

4. Followed by καί and another verb: **a**. underlining a change of heart or course of action, ἐπιστρέψω καὶ κομιοῦμαι τὸν σῖτόν μου 'I will now take away my corn' Ho 2.9; ἐπιστρέψει καὶ μετανοήσει καὶ ὑπολείψεται ὀπίσω αὐτοῦ εὐλογίαν 'He will change His mind and leave a blessing behind Him' Jl 2.14; ~ καὶ ἐκζητήσουσι κύριον Ho 3.5; Mi 7.19; τοῦ μὴ καταδιώκειν (B: simp.) 2K 18.15*L*, cf. ἀναστρέφω. **b**. indicates doing once again what one did or used to do, reverting to the former state of affairs: "they will sit under His shadow as before" Ho 14.8; ἐπιστρέψωμεν καὶ ἀνοικοδομήσωμεν τὰς ἐρήμους 'let us rebuild the desolate places' Ma 1.4 (ἐπι. is redundant); cf. Zc 4.1, 5.1, 6.1; + inf., ἐπιστρέψει κύριος .. εὐφρανθῆναι .., καθότι εὐφράνθη .. 'the Lord will again rejoice .. as he used to rejoice ..' De 30.9; La 2.8[1], Ps 103.9; ἐ. as a ptc. and without καί - ἐπιστρέψας ἐζωοποίησάς με 'he revived me again' 70.20 (‖ πάλιν); 70.21, 84.7, 3K 19.6.

N.B. The pass. fut. and aor. forms appear to be deponent: cp. ἐπιστραφήσονται ἐπι θεοὺς ἀλλοτρίους De 31.20 w. ἐπέστρεψαν ἐπὶ θεοὺς ἀλλοτρίους vs. 18, and see Ἐπιστρέψατε πρός με, καὶ ἐπιστραφήσομαι πρὸς ὑμᾶς Zc 1.3.

Cf. ἀνα~, ἀπο~, μετα~, ὑποστρέφω, στρέφω, ἀπο~, ἐπιστροφή, ἀνακάμπτω, ~κομίζω: Bertram, *TDNT* 7.722-5; Aubin 33-47.

ἐπιστροφή, ῆς. f.ʃ

1. *revolving door* (?): Ez 42.11.

2. *act of returning to the point of origin*: Ez 47.7, Jd 8.9B, Si 40.1; morally, 'repentance' 18.21, 49.2; with interest and concern, ἐπ' ἐμέ Ct 7.11, cf. Ge 3.16 (ἀποστροφή). **b.** *place for such an act to take place*: Ez 47.11.

ἐπισυνάγω: fut. ~άξω, pass. ~αχθήσομαι; aor. ἐπισυνήγαγον, inf. ~αγαγεῖν, impv. ~άγαγε, pass. ἐπισυνήχθην, inf. ~ναχθῆναι, ptc. ~ναχθείς; pf. pass. ~συνῆγμαι, ptc. ~συνηγμένος, inf. ~συνῆχθαι.

1. *to collect and bring*: + acc. rei, χεῖρα Ge 38.29 (*s* a baby at the time of delivery who put out a hand and closes it again so that the fingers attach themselves to one another); + acc. pers. and ἐπί τινα (of hostility), ἐπισυνάξω πάντα τὰ ἔθνη ἐπὶ Ιερουσαλημ εἰς πόλεμον Zc 14.2; for a convocation, Da 3.2 LXX; τὴν διασπορὰν ἡμῶν 2M 1.27; pass. βιβλία 2M 2.13.

2. *to narrow, straiten*: ***o*** part of an edifice, Ge 6.16; Ez 40.12.

3. pass. *to betake oneself together*: πρός με '(they came) to me altogether' 1E 8.69; + dat. pers., 5.49; ἐπί τινα Ju 7.23 (in protest); for a battle - Mi 4.11, 1M 3.59, ἅμα ἐπ' ἐμέ Ps 30.14; ἐπισυνῆκται ἐπ' αὐτὸν τὰ κακά 'the troubles have converged on him' 1M 15.12.

Cf. ἄγω, συνάγω, ἐπισυναγωγή.

ἐπισυναγωγή, ῆς. f.ʃ

group of individuals brought together: as cogn. obj., συναγάγη ὁ θεὸς ~ὴν τοῦ λαοῦ 2M 2.7. Cf. ἐπισυνάγω, συναγωγή: Deissmann 1923.81f.; Spicq 2.63f.

ἐπισυνέχω.ʃ*

to have as wife: + acc., woman, 1E 9.17,2E 10.14; Jd 20.38A (B: σημεῖον '[prescribed] signal').

ἐπισυνίστημι: fut.act. ~συστήσω, mid. ~συστήσομαι; 1aor.act. ~συνέστησα; 2aor.act.ptc. ~συστάς, impv.2pl ~σύστητε, subj. ~συστῶ; pf.mid. ~συνεσταμένος.ʃ

I. tr. (fut.act., 1aor.) *to incite to rebel*: + acc. pers. and ἐπί τινα, Nu 16.19.

2**. *to cause to happen to*: + τι ἐπί τινα and ***o distressful situation, ἐφ' ὑμᾶς τὴν ἀπορίαν '.. discomfort' Le 26.16.

II. intr. (fut.mid., 2aor., pf.mid.) *to conspire*: ἐφ' αἷμα τοῦ πλησίον σου 'for the life ..' Le 19.16; ἐπ' ἐμέ Nu 14.35, ἐπὶ Μωυσῆν 26.9; ἐπὶ σὲ κύκλῳ Ez 2.6; ἔναντι κυρίου Nu 27.3; + dat. pers., Jd 9.25*L*, Si 45.18, Je 20.10. Cf. συμφρονέω.

Cf. ἵστημι, ἐπισύστασις.

ἐπισύστασις, εως. f.ʃ

act of inciting to rebel (v.n. of ἐπισυνίστημι): Nu 16.40, cf. 14.35; + obj. gen., κυρίου 26.9; ἐπιβουλὰς καὶ δημαγωγίας καὶ ~εις ποιούμενοι 1E 5.70. Cf. ἐπισυνίστημι.

ἐπισυστρέφω: aor.inf. ~στρέψαι.ʃ

1. mid. *to gang up*: ἐπί τινα, Nu 16.42.

2. act. *to bring together, convene*: + acc., συστροφήν 'assembly' 1M 14.44.

Cf. συνάγω, ἐπισυνάγω, συστροφή.

ἐπισφαλής, ές.ʃ

precarious: ***s*** hum. thoughts, Wi 9.14. Cf. ἐπισφαλῶς, σφάλλω.

ἐπισφαλῶς. adv.ʃ

precariously: Wi 4.4. Cf. ἐπισφαλής.

ἐπισφραγίζω: aor.impv. ~σφράγισον, inf. ~σφραγίσαι.ʃ

1. *to put a seal* to an official document as a mark of ratification: abs., Ne 9.38. **b.** to entrance door (?) in order to close off the area inside: τῷ δακτυλίῳ Bel 14 LXX.

2. *to use in order to close securely*: + acc., κλεῖδας 'keys' Bel 11 LXX.

Cf. σφραγίζω.

ἐπισχύω: aor. ἐπίσχυσα.ʃ

1. *to grow strong*: militarily, 1M 6.6.

2. *to lend military support*: Es 7.29 *L* (o' συνεπι~).

3. τῇ χειρί τινος 'to lend (financial) support to sbd' τῇ χειρὶ αὐτοῦ Si 29.1 (a mistranslation for χεῖρας αὐτοῦ, cf. κραταιόω **1**.

Cf. ἰσχύω.

ἐπιταγή, ῆς. f.

that which has been enjoined, 'order, directive' (of no moral or ethical import): βασιλέως 1E 1.16 (|| ἐντολή 2C 35.16), 3M 7.20, τυράννων 'of monarchs' Wi 14.16; God's, 19.6. Cf. ἐπιτάσσω, ἐπίταγμα, ἐντολή: *ND* 2.86.

ἐπίταγμα, ατος. n.ʃ

= prec.: royal, 4M 8.5. Cf. ἐπιτάσσω, πρόσταγμα, ἐντολή.

ἐπιταράσσω.ʃ

to deprive sbd *of peace of mind*: pass., ***o*** hum., 2M 9.24. Cf. ταράσσω, συγχέω.

ἐπίτασις, εως. f.ʃ

intensified involvement: + gen., θρησκείας 'in worship' Wi 14.18.

ἐπιτάσσω: aor. ἐπέταξα, impv. ἐπίταξον, ptc. ~τάξας, subj. ~τάξω, mid. ἐπεταξάμην, pass. ἐπετάγην, subj. ~ταγῶ; pf. ἐπιτέταχα, pass.3s ~τέτακται.

1. *to enjoin, give orders*: + dat., Ps 106.29; + inf., 1E 2.22; orally at one's deathbed, Ge 49.33; pass. Ep Je inscr., ἐν τῷ νόμῳ 1E 5.50

2. impv. ἐπίταξον + inf., *please* do so and so: ἐπίταξον ἀναλαβεῖν τὸ πνεῦμά μου 'Please take my spirit' To 3.6, ἐπιβλέψαι ἐπ' ἐμέ 'to look upon me' 3.15 𝔊I, ἐλεῆσαί με 'to pity me' 8.7: Shipp 419.

Cf. ἐντέλλομαι, κελεύω, προσ~, συντάσσω, ἐπιταγή: Muraoka 2006.

ἐπιτάφιος, ον. n.ʃ

subst.n., *decorated tombstone*: 4M 17.8, see Deissmann 1921 ad loc. Cf. τάφος.

ἐπιτείνω: aor. ἐπέτεινα; plpf.mid./pass.3s ἐπετέτατο.

1. *to subject to intense pain*: pass., ταῖς ἀλγηδόσιν 'pains' 2M 9.11. **b**. *to exert intense mental pressure on*: + acc., *s* yearning 4M 3.11; 15.23.

2. *to add to the intensity of*: + acc., εὔνοιαν 'goodwill' 4M 13.25.

3. mid. *to put oneself out, exert oneself*: εἰς κόλασιν 'so as to punish' Wi 16.24.

4. mid. *to spread oneself widely and cover*: *s* darkness of night, Wi 17.21.

ἐπιτελέω: fut. ~τελέσω, pass. ~τελεσθήσομαι; aor. ἐπετέλεσα, inf. ~τελέσαι, impv. ~τέλεσον, pass. ἐπετελέσθην, subj. ~τελεσθῶ, inf. ~τελεσθῆναι, impv.3s ~τελεσθήτω.

1. *to bring to completion*: *o* building Zc 4.9; deed in general, ἐν ταῖς χερσὶν αὐτοῦ Da 11.16 LXX (TH συντελέω); punitive action 1K 3.12 B (ἄρχομαι ‖ *L* συντελέω).

2. *to celebrate*: *o* acc. (festivals), μνημόσυνον ἐπιτελούμενον 'a commemorative festival being celebrated' Es 9.27, γάμος To 12.1 𝔊II (poss. **1**).

3. *to discharge* a religious duty: in the form of offering, + acc. and dat. pers., θυσίας καὶ σπονδάς Da 2.46 LXX.

4. *to carry into effect*: abs. καθότι προστέταχά σοι 'as I have commanded you' Ju 2.13, κατὰ τὸ θέλημα τοῦ θεοῦ σου 'in accordance with the will ..' 1E 8.16; retribution, τινί (offender) κατά τι (punishable offence) Jd 20.10 A (B: ποιέω), cf. 1M 12.8; *o* a command, Es 8.14 o'; cultic duties, Le 6.22, εὐχήν 'vow' Jd 11.39 A (B: ποιέω); τί Nu 23.23; purpose 2M 3.8; αἴτημα 'request' PSol 6.6. **b**. *to be engaged in*: + acc. rei, 1E 6.4.

Cf. (συν)τελέω: Schmidt 4.503; Grundmann, *TDNT* 8.61.

ἐπιτέλλω.ʃ

to begin to appear: *s* new day, 3M 5.20.

ἐπιτέμνω: aor.inf. ~τεμεῖν.ʃ

to abridge: + acc. (a written account), 2M 2.23, ἱστορίαν 2.32. Cf. ἐπιτομή.

ἐπιτερπής, ές.ʃ

conducive to enjoyment: *s* χάρις 'attractiveness' 2M 15.39. Cf. τέρπω.

ἐπιτήδειος, α, ον.

made for a purpose, 'suitable': *s* τόπος 1M 4.46; + inf. 10.19; hum., 13.40; subst.n.pl., 1C 28.2. **b**. *useful*: πρὸς τῇ .. ἐπανορθώσει 'for the work of restoration ..' 1M 14.34, + πρός τι 2M 2.29, 3M 6.30; εἰς οὐθέν '(good) for nothing' Wi 4.5.

Del. 1M 11.37 v.l.

ἐπιτήδευμα, ατος. n.

1. *that in which one usually engages with devotion and eagerness*, alw. pl.: human deeds and evil in nature, κατὰ τὰ ~ατα γῆς Αἰγύπτου .. οὐ ποιήσετε Le 18.3; διὰ τὰς κακίας τῶν ~άτων αὐτῶν Ho 9.15; τὴν πονηρίαν τῶν ~άτων αὐτῶν Ps 27.4, sim. Je 4.4; ἐκ καρπῶν ~άτων Mi 7.13, sim. Je 17.10; Ho 12.2, Zc 1.6 (‖ ὁδοί); πονηρὰ ~ατα De 28.20, Mi 2.9, Zc 1.4, Je 23.2, 22, 25.5, 33.3, cf. Mi 3.4, Ne 9.35; ‖ ἁμαρτίαι Jb 14.16; ἀσεβεῖαι Ez 14.6, 21.24; Αἰγύπτου 20.7 (‖ βδέλυγμα); ἐβδελύχθησαν ἐν ~ασιν 'they made themselves abominable ..' Ps 13.1; ‖ ἔργα 27.4, 76.13, 105.39; ‖ ὁδοί Je 4.18, 7.3, 5, 18.11, 25.5, 42.15, Ez 20.43; "your depraved (διεφθαρμένα) practices" 20.44; τὰ μὴ ἀγαθά 36.31. **b**. God's good deeds: Ps 9.12; ‖ ἔργα 76.13.

***2**. *that which one intends to do*: τελειῶσαι τὰ ~ατά σου 'may he bring your design to conclusion' Ju 10.8; 11.6; ποιῆσαι τὸ ἐ. μου 'to carry out my design' 13.5.

Cf. ἐπιτηδεύω, ἔργον, πρᾶγμα.

ἐπιτηδεύω: fut. ~δεύσω; aor. ἐπετήδευσα.ʃ

to devote oneself to, busy oneself with (εἰς): εἰς θεοὺς ἀλλοτρίους 'alien gods' Ma 2.11; + inf. τῆς ἀρχῆς στερῆσαι ἡμᾶς 'to deprive us of the dominion' Es E 12 o'; καθυβρίσαι 3M 2.14; + acc. καλόν Je 2.33, μισοξενίαν 'hatred of aliens' Wi 19.13. Cf. ἐπιτήδευμα.

ἐπιτηρέω.ʃ

to wait for vigilantly: + acc. rei, τὴν ἔξοδον αὐτῆς 'for her to come out' Ju 13.3.

ἐπιτίθημι: pres.ptc.pass. ~τιθέμενος, subj. ~τιθῶ; fut. ~θήσω, inf. ~θήσειν; 1aor.act. ἐπέθηκα, inf. ~θεῖναι, impv.2s ἐπίθες, pl. ἐπίθετε, ptc. ~θείς, subj. ~θῶ; 2aor.mid. ἐπεθέμην, inf. ~θέσθαι, ptc. ~θέμενος, impv. ~θοῦ, subj. ~θῶμαι, pass. ἐπετέθην; pf.mid.3pl ~τέθεινται.

1. *to place* on sth: + ἐπί τινα / τι and acc., σάκκον ἐπὶ τὴν ὀσφῦν αὐτοῦ 'a sackcloth on his loins' Ge 37.34; τὸν σῖτον ἐπὶ τοὺς ὄνους αὐτῶν 42:26; τὴν δεξιάν σου ἐπὶ τὴν κεφαλὴν αὐτοῦ 48.18; τὴν χεῖρα ἐπὶ τὴν κεφαλὴν τοῦ καρπώματος '.. on the head of the offering' Le 1.4 (cultic symbolism?); τὰς χεῖράς σου ἐπ' αὐτόν Nu 27.18 (to appoint to an office), De 34.9; ἐπιθήσουσι χεῖρας ἐπὶ τὸ στόμα αὐτῶν 'they will put hands on their mouth (to keep silent)' Mi 7.16, sim. Wi 8.12, δάκτυλον ἐπιθέντες ἐπὶ στόματι Jb 29.9; in order to steal, Je 29.10; in order to harm, αὐτῇ χεῖρας 4K 11.16 (*L* ἐπιβάλλω); ἐπίθετε κίδαριν καθαρὰν ἐπὶ τὴν κεφαλὴν αὐτοῦ 'Put a pure turban on his head' Zc 3.5*a*, cf. 6.11 and Ex 3.22 (the latter w. ref. to clothes?), διάδημα 'diadem' 1M 1.9; ***o*** cultic offerings, θυμίαμα .. ἐπὶ τὸ θυσιαστήριόν σου De 33.10; τὰ ἐπιτιθέμενα βρώματα ἐξουδενωμένα 'the (cultic) foods set (upon the altar) are despicable' Ma 1.7; opp. περιαιρέω Ex 34.34. **b**. sth undesirable: τόκον 'interest' Ex 22.25; νόσους 'ailments' De 7.15; τὸν τρόμον ὑμῶν καὶ τὸν φόβον ὑμῶν .. ἐπὶ πρόσωπον πάσης τῆς γῆς 11.25; ἐπιθήσει κλοιὸν σιδηροῦν ἐπὶ τὸν τράχηλόν σου 'will place an iron collar on your neck' 28.48; μῶμον 'blame' Si 11.31; τὸ αἷμα αὐτῶν .. ἐπί τινα 'blame sbd for their death' Jd 9.24 A*L* (B: simp.). **c**. 'to impose': + dat. pers. and acc. αὐτῇ προφασιστικοὺς λόγους '(bring) against her false allegations' De 22.14, 17; αὐτοῖς .. ὀνόματα Da 1.7 (additional name). **d**. *to confer*: + acc., δόξαν Si 10.5; + dat. pers., αὐτοῖς κληρονομίαν Es 4.20 *L*; τέλον τῷ προειρημένῳ '(to bring) the aforesaid plan to a conclusion' 3M 1.26; τὸ ὄνομα αὐτοῦ Αβιμελεχ Jd 8.31 A (B: simp.), αὐτῷ ὄνομα Ιωακειμ 4K 23.34*L*, sim. 24.17*L*.

2. *to load a burden on* sbd else (i.e. his back or shoulder): + dat. ἐπέθηκεν .. τῷ υἱῷ αὐτοῦ Ge 22.6 (τὰ ξύλα as obj. understood); ἡμῖν ἔργα σκληρά De 26.6.

3. *to put in place, set up*: + acc. λύχνους 'lamps' Nu 8.2, cf. στήλην λίθου 'stone-pillar' Hdt 7.183.

4. *to try one's hand, attempt*: + inf., ὅσα ἂν ἐπιθῶνται ποιεῖν Ge 11.6.

5. *to lay hands on* to apprehend, arrest: + dat. pers. Ge 43.18.

6. mid. *to assail, attack*: abs., 2C 23.13; + dat. pers. Ex 18.11, 21.14, Je 27.24 (ἁλίσκομαι as a result), PSol 17.5 (‖ ἐπανίστημι), Es E 20, εἰς καταφθοράν 4.16 *L* (o' ἐπιβλέπω); + ἐπί τινα Ps 58.4 (‖ θηρεύω), 1K 23.27, 27.8, 2C 24.26; + cogn. acc., αὐτῷ ἐπίθεσιν 2C 25.27. Cf. συνεπιτίθημι.

7. *to turn one's attention to* in seeking a relationship with or involvement in: + acc., συμπλοκήν 'close engagement with idolatrous practice'; ἐπὶ τοὺς ἐραστὰς αὐτῆς 'her lovers' Ez 23.5, sim. 23.7, 9, 12, 16, 20.

Cf. τίθημι, ἐπι~, προσβάλλω, ἐπίθεσις.

ἐπιτιμάω: fut. ~τιμήσω; aor. ἐπετίμησα, impv. ~τίμησον, subj. ~τιμήσω, opt.3ms ἐπιτιμήσαι, ptc. pass. ~τιμηθείς.

to censure, rebuke: + dat. pers., ***s*** father to son, Ge 37.10; God, τῇ θαλάσσῃ Ps 105.9 (cf. Mt 8.26), ἐν ὀργῇ σου PSol 2.23; + ἔν τινι– Ἐπιτιμήσαι κύριος ἐν σοί 'May the Lord rebuke you!' Zc 3.2; ‖ μέμφομαι Si 11.7; pass., ***o*** hum., 3M 2.24. The combination with ἐν + dat. pers. is apparently a Hebraism: see Helbing, *Kasus*., 286. Cf. ἐπιτίμησις, προσεπιτιμάω, ἐλέγχω, μέμφομαι, ὀνειδίζω: Schmidt 1.147; Stauffer, *TDNT* 2.423-5.

ἐπιτίμησις, εως.

v.n. of prec.: God's, Ps 17.16, ‖ φωνὴ βροντῆς 'thundering noise' 103.7; σοφοῦ Ec 7.5.

ἐπιτιμία, ας. f.ʃ

punishment: Wi 3.10. Cf. ἐπιτίμιον.

ἐπιτίμιον, ου. n.ʃ

punishment: 2M 6.13. **b**. *fine* to be paid: pl., Si 9.5. Cf. ἐπιτιμία.

ἐπίτιμος, ον.ʃ

liable to punishment: subst.m., Si 8.5.

ἐπιτομή, ῆς. f.ʃ

v.n. of ἐπιτέμνω: 2M 2.26, 28. Cf. ἐπιτέμνω.

ἐπιτρέπω: aor. ἐπέτρεψα, ptc. ~τρέψας, opt.3s ~τρέψειεν.ʃ

1. *to entrust*: + acc. πάντα, ὅσα ἦν αὐτῷ, εἰς χεῖρας Ιωσηφ Ge 39.6; ***o*** task or responsibility, + dat. pers. and inf., Jb 32.14, 4M 4.18.

2. *to turn over to*: + dat. and acc., αὐτῷ τὴν ἀρχήν 'the leading position to him' 4M 4.17.

3. *to permit*: + inf., Es 9.14 o' (*L* συγχωρέω), Wi 19.2, 4M 5.26 (:: κωλύω 'to prevent'); and + dat. pers., 1M 15.6. Cf. ἀφίημι **3**, δίδωμι **16**, συγχωρέω.

ἐπιτρέχω: 2aor. ἐπέδραμον.

to run towards: ἐπέδραμεν ὁ παῖς εἰς συνάντησιν αὐτῇ 'the servant ran to meet her' Ge 24.17; + dat., αὐτῇ (victim of rape) Su 19 TH; so as to attack, ***s*** wild animals, PSol 13.3. Cf. τρέχω.

ἐπιτροπή, ῆς. f.ʃ

power to decide: 2M 13.14.

ἐπίτροπος, ου.

guardian: τοῦ βασιλέως 2M 11.1 (+ συγγενής).

ἐπιτυγχάνω: fut. ~τεύξομαι.ʃ

1. *to attain* what one is after: + gen., θῆρας 'game' Pr 12.27.

2. *to be successful*: ἀνὴρ ἐπιτυγχάνων Ge 39.2.

Cf. τυγχάνω, κατατυγχάνω, τύχη, ἐπιτυχία, εὐοδόω, ἐξαμαρτάνω.

ἐπιτυχία, ας. f.ʃ

success: χειρῶν 'of hands' Wi 13.19. Cf. ἐπιτυγχάνω.

ἐπιφαίνω: fut. ~φανήσομαι, ~φανοῦμαι; 1aor. ἐπέφανα, opt.3s ~φάναι, impv. ἐπίφανον, ptc. ~φάνας, 2aor. pass. ἐπεφάνην, subj. ~φανῶ, inf. ~φανῆναι, impv. ~φάνηθι, ptc. ~φανείς.

1. intr. (2aor. pass.) *to make appearance*: ***s*** God, ἐπεφάνη αὐτῷ ὁ θεὸς .. Ge 35.7, ὑμῖν Je 36.14; with hostile intent, ἐπιφανήσεται κύριος ἐπ' αὐτοὺς καὶ ἐξολεθρεύσει .. 'the Lord will appear unto them and annihilate ..' Zp 2.11; troops, 2M 12.22, ἐπιφανῆναι ἄνδρα πολιᾷ καὶ δόξῃ διαφέροντα 'a man distinguished by grey hair and dignity' 15.13; ἀστραπή 'lightning' Ep Je 60; supernatural beings, ἐξ οὐρανοῦ ἐφ' ἵππων .. ἄνδρες 2M 10.29, ἔφιππος ἐν λευκῇ ἐσθῆτι 'on horseback, wearing a white robe' 11.8. **b**. mid. ἐπιφάνηθι τοῖς ἀπὸ Ισραηλ γένους 'Reveal yourself to those of the nation of Is.' 3M 6.9; *to present oneself, assuming that one posseses some worthy quality*, ***s*** vine, μικρὰν τῷ μεγέθει τοῦ ἐπιφαίνεσθαι αὐτήν 'too small in size to show' Ez 17.6.

2. tr. (1aor.) *to cause to make appearance*: ***o*** (favourable) face, ἐπιφάναι κύριος τὸ πρόσωπον αὐτοῦ ἐπὶ σέ 'may the Lord show his face upon you' Nu 6.26; Ps 30.17, 66.2, 79.4, 8, 20, 118.135, Da TH 9.17; ἐπίφανον τὸ ἔλεός σου 'Reveal your mercy' 3M 2.19, φέγγος ἐπιφάνας ἐλέους Ισραηλ γένει 'showing the ray of mercy to the race of Israel' 6.4, τὸ ἅγιον αὐτοῦ πρόσωπον 'his holy countenance' 6.18. **b**. intr. *to make appearance*: ***s*** God, ἐπέφανεν ἐκ Σηιρ ἡμῖν 'he appeared ..' De 33.2 (|| ἥκω); κύριος .. ἡμῖν Ps 117.27, cf. ἐπιφανῆναι, πρότερον οὐχ ὁρώμενον 'to appear, formerly having been invisible' Didymus (Mühlenberg II 277) and BDAG s.v.

Cf. ἐπιφανής, ἐπιφάνεια, φαίνω, ἐμφαίνω, ἐμφανίζω, ὁράω: Renehan 1.92; Pax 159-70; Lührmann 1971; Spicq 2.65-7.

ἐπιφάνεια, ας. f.ʃ

1. *act of appearing, manifesting oneself*: of a divine saviour or some supernatural phenomenon, τὰς ἐξ οὐρανοῦ γενομένας ~ας 2M 2.21, τοῦ θεοῦ 15.27; 14.15; ῥύσασθαι αὐτοὺς μετὰ μεγαλομεροῦς ~ας ἐκ τοῦ παρὰ πόδας ἐν ἑτοίμῳ μόρου 'to rescue them with a glorious manifestation from the imminent fate' 3M 5.8, οἰκτῖραι μετὰ ~ας αὐτοὺς ἤδη πρὸς πύλας ᾅδου καθεστῶτας 'to show mercy to them with an epiphany as they stood already at the threshhold of Hades' 5.51; supernatural apparition, 2M 5.4 (|| φαίνεσθαι vs. 2).

2. *outward show*: σωτηρίου ~ας 'ostentatious deliverance-offering (?)' Am 5.22; στολὴ τῆς ~ας 'gorgeous (royal) robe' Es D 6 o'; ἐν ~ᾳ μεγαλοπρεπεῖ 'with a grandiose show' 3M 2.9; not pejorative, τοῦ ποιῆσαι μεγαλωσύνην καὶ ~αν 2K 7.23 (|| ὄνομα μέγα καὶ ἐπιφανές 1C 17.21), ~αν μεγάλην ἐποίησεν 2M 3.24 (*s* God).

Cf. ἐπιφανής, ὀπτασία, ὅρασις: Trench 355; Deissmann 1923.320f.; Spicq 2.67; Lührmann 1971.

ἐπιφανής, ές.

1. *remarkable, notable, distinguished*: ***s*** a day of theophany, ἡμέραν κυρίου τὴν μεγάλην καὶ ~ῆ Jl 2.31, Ma 4.4, sim. Jl 2.11 and cf. τὸν ~ῆ κύριον 2M 15.34, τὸν ~ῆ θεὸν κύριον 3M 5.35; city, ἡ ἐ. καὶ ἀπολελυτρωμένη Zp 3.2; hostile army, + φοβερός Hb 1.7; 'glorious (in outward appearance),' περιεβάλετο τὴν δόξαν αὐτῆς καὶ γενηθεῖσα ἐ. Es D 2 LXX (*s* Esther), ἄξιον .. ~οῦς πολιᾶς 'worthy of .. grey hairs' 2M 6.23, ἱερόν 14.33; *s* ὅρασις 'appearance, look' Jd 13.6B (A: φοβερός).

2. *renowned*: τὸ ὄνομά μου ~ὲς ἐν τοῖς ἔθνεσιν 'my name is well known among the nations' Ma 1.14, ὄνομα μέγα καὶ ~ές 21C 17.21.

3. *visually manifest*: ***s*** wind, clouds and rain, Pr 25.14.

Cf. ἐπιφαίνω ἐπιφάνεια: Schmidt 3.433f.; Tov 1990.110-8; *ND* 4.148; Spicq 2.68; Dogniez 2001. 248-51.

ἐπιφανῶς. adv.ʃ

1. *officially charged and commissioned*: Es A 16 *L*.

2. *in style*: ἤγαγεν .. τὸν γάμον 'celebrated the wedding' Es 2.18 *L*.

ἐπιφαύσκω.ʃ

to emit light and be bright: ***s*** moon, Jb 25.5; sun, 31.26 (opp. ἐπιλείπω); φέγγος 41.10. Cf. φαίνω.

ἐπιφέρω: fut. ἐποίσω; aor. ἐπήνεγκα, subj. ἐπενέγκω, inf. ἐπενέγκαι, ἐπενεγκεῖν, ptc.pass. ἐπενεχθείς.

1. *to bring* (over some object): τι ἐπί + acc., ἐπιφέρω τὴν χεῖρά μου ἐπ' αὐτούς 'I bring my (assailing) hand upon them' Zc 2.9; + dat. incom., χεῖρα δὲ μὴ ἐπενέγκητε αὐτῷ Ge 37.22; + acc., ῥῆμα πονηρόν 'ill repute' Ju 8.8. **b**. metaph., *to bring about as a consequence*: κρίσεις θάνατον ἐπιφέρουσαι 'cases ending in a death sentence' Su 53 LXX.

2. *to aim at*: w. hostile intent, + acc., Jb 15.12 (*s* eyes). **b**. pass. = act., + dat. pers., 2M 12.35.

3. pass. *to be borne along*, or mid. *to move along* over some surface: πνεῦμα θεοῦ ἐπεφέρετο ἐπάνω τοῦ ὕδατος Ge 1.2; ἐπεφέρετο ἡ κιβωτὸς ἐπάνω τοῦ ὕδατος 'the ark kept moving along on the water' 7.18. Cf. Alexandre 86.

Cf. φέρω.

ἐπιφημίζω: aor.mid.subj. ~μίσωμαι.ʃ

1. *to ascribe*: dat. pers. and acc., ἡμῖν ἁμαρτήματα 'us failings' Wi 2.12.

2. mid. *to state explicitly*: ἐν τῇ καρδίᾳ αὐτοῦ λέγων .. De 29.19 (cf. Syh *nṭabbev* or *naṭbev*).

ἐπιφυλλίζω: fut. ~φυλλίσω, ~φυλλιῶ; aor. ἐπεφύλλισα, impv. ~φύλλισον, pass. ἐπεφυλλίσθην.ʃ*

1. *to glean* grapes in a vineyard: De 24.21 Aq, Th (LXX: ἐπανατρυγάω, q.v.), Je 6.9 Sym (LXX: καλαμάομαι).

*2. *to cause severe damage to, ravage*: + dat. pers., La 1.22, 2.20; ἐπί + acc., ὁ ὀφθαλμός μου ἐπιφυλλιεῖ ἐπὶ τὴν ψυχήν μου 3.51; pass. 1.12 Sym.

Cf. ἐπιφυλλίς, ἐπανατρυγάω.

ἐπιφυλλίς, ίδος. f.ʃ

1. *small grapes left for gleaners*: ἐν τρυγήτῳ and ǁ καλάμη, 'stalk' stripped of grain, or mere 'stubble,' Mi 7.1; οὐκ ἂν ὑπελίποντο ~ίδα; Ob 5; διέφθαρται πᾶσα ἡ ἐ. αὐτῶν Zp 3.7; ǁ τρυγητός Jd 8.2.

2. v.n. of ἐπιφυλλίζω **2**: ποιέω ~ίδα La 1.22, 2.20.

Cf. ἐπιφυλλίζω.

ἐπιφύομαι.ʃ

to persist in: + dat., τῇ κακίᾳ 2M 4.50.

ἐπιφυτεύω.ʃ

to plant over or *on*: pass. and + a second acc., φιλοστοργίαν 'tender love and affection' 4M 15.6. Cf. φυτεύω.

ἐπιφωνέω: aor. ἐπεφώνησα, ptc. ~νήσας.ʃ

to utter in response: abs., 2M 1.23; ***o*** Αμην 1E 9.47, τὸ αλληλουια 3M 7.13.

ἐπιχαίρω: fut.pass. ~χαροῦμαι; aor.pass. ἐπεχάρην, also 2s ἐπέχαρας, ptc.pl ~χάραντες, subj. ~χαρῶ, opt.3pl ~χαρείησαν. Pass. in act. sense.

to rejoice, exult over, mostly of malicious joy: abs. Mi 4.11; + dat. pers. μὴ ἐπίχαιρέ μοι 7.8, dat. rei, τῇ σῇ πτώσει 'your fall' Ba 4.31 (ǁ χαίρω ἐπί τινι vs. 33); + ἐπί τινι Si 8.7; + ἐπί + acc., ἐπὶ τοὺς υἱοὺς Ιουδα Ob 12, ἐπὶ τὴν γῆν τοῦ Ισραηλ Ez 25.6; in good sense, ἐπὶ τὴν δόξαν αὐτοῦ Ho 10.5.

Cf. χαίρω, ἐπιχαρής, ἐπίχαρμα, ἐπίχαρτος, ἀγαλλιάομαι.

ἐπιχαρής, ές.ʃ

1. *capable of causing joy, agreeable*: πόρνη καλὴ καὶ ἐ. 'a good-looking and pleasant harlot' Na 3.4.

2. *rejoiced*: ***s*** hum., + dat., πτώματι ἐχθρῶν 'at the fall of enemies' Jb 31.29, cf. ἐπιχάρματα 'malicious joy' Eur. *Phoen.* 1555.

Cf. ἐπιχαίρω and χαίρω.

ἐπίχαρμα, ατος. n.

malicious *joy*: τοῖς ὑπεναντίοις αὐτῶν Ex 32.25; τοῖς ἔθνεσιν Ju 4.12; ἐχθρῶν Si 6.4; ἐχθροῖς 42.11. Cf. ἐπιχαίρω, ἐπίχαρτος.

ἐπίχαρτος, ον.ʃ

occasioning malicious *joy*: ***s*** sbd's death, Pr 11.3. Cf. χαρά, ἐπιχαρής.

ἐπιχειρέω: aor. ἐπεχείρησα, subj. ~ρήσω, ptc. ~ρήσας.

to attempt: + inf., 1E 1.26; an attack, + εἰς 2E 7.23, ἐφ' ἡμᾶς 2C 20.11. Cf. ἐγχειρέω, πειράζω.

ἐπιχείρημα, ατος. n.ʃ

arts used by harlots: pl., Si 9.4.

ἐπίχειρον, ου. n.ʃ

1. *arm*: Je 29.11; ***o*** of συντρίβω 31.25; divine and raised (ὑψηλός) 34.4.

2. punitive *reward*: pl., τῆς ἀνοίας 'for the folly' 2M 15.33.

Cf. βραχίων, μισθός: Pietersma 2002.

ἐπιχέω: fut. ~χεῶ, pass. ~χυθήσομαι; aor. ἐπέχεα, pass. ἐπεχύθην, subj. ἐπιχυθῶ; pf.ptc.pass. ~κεχυμένος.

to pour out upon sth: ***s*** abs., Zc 4.12 (part of a candlestick); + acc., ἔλαιον ἐπὶ τὸ ἄκρον αὐτῆς 'oil on its [= stone pillar's] top' Ge 28.18; ἐπ' αὐτὴν (= στήλην) ἔλαιον 35.14 (ǁ σπένδω); oil for consecration of priests, ἐπὶ τὴν κεφαλὴν αὐτοῦ καὶ χρίσεις αὐτόν Ex 29.7; on flour as cultic offering, Le 2.1, Nu 5.15; ***o*** ὕδωρ Le 11.38; drops of rain, Jb 36.27¶; olive-oil *into* a container, 4K 4.5B (*L* ἐγ~). **b.** metaph., pass., ***o*** dread, Wi 17.15.

Cf. ἐπίχυσις, (ὑπερ)χέω, κατασκεδάννυμι.

ἐπιχορηγέω: aor.subj.pass. ~χορηγηθῶ.ʃ

to provide monetary needs: for one's spouse - wife for husband, Si 25.22; 2M 4.9. Cf. χορηγέω.

ἐπίχυσις, εως. f.ʃ

v.n. of ἐπιχέω, *act of pouring out* metal into a furnace: ὅρασις ~εως 'molten mirror' Jb 37.18¶. Cf. ἐπιχέω.

ἐπιχωρέω: aor. ἐπεχώρησα.ʃ

to consent: somewhat grudgingly, + inf., 2M 12.12. Cf. εὐδοκέω **3b**, ἐπινεύω **2**.

ἐπιχώρησις, εως. f.ʃ*

permission: κατ' ~ιν Κύρου .. ἐπ' αὐτούς 'with the permission of Cyrus .. granted to them' 2E 3.7. Cf. ἄφεσις **4**.

ἐπιψάλλω.ʃ

**to sing*: + acc., ὕμνους 2M 1.30. Cf. ψάλλω, ὑμνέω.

ἐπιψοφέω: aor. ἐπεψόφησα.ʃ

to indicate approval loudly: τῷ ποδί 'by stamping with foot' Ez 25.6 (ǁ κροτέω χεῖρα), sim. 6.11. Cf. ψοφέω.

ἐπόζω: fut. ἐποζέσω; aor. ἐπώζεσα.

to become stinking: ***s*** river, Ex 7.18; rotten food, 16.20, 24. Cf. ὄζω.

ἐποίκιον, ου. n.ʃ

outlying settlement: ǁ κώμη 1C 27.25. Cf. κώμη.

ἕπομαι.ʃ

to act in conformity with: + dat., τῇ ἐκείνου θελήσει 'his will' 3M 2.26. Cf. ἀκολουθέω, συνέπομαι: Schmidt 3.235-7.

ἐπονείδιστος, ον.

subjected to disgrace or *reproach*: ***s*** hum., 3M 6.31; Pr 19.26 (καταισχύνομαι). **b.** *deserving reproach*: ***s*** hum., Pr 18.1; words, 27.11.

Cf. ὄνειδος.

ἐπονομάζω: fut.pass. ~μασθήσομαι; aor. ἐπωνόμασα, subj. ~μάσω, inf. ~μάσαι, pass. ἐπωνομάσθην.

1. *to give a name to*: + acc., τὴν πόλιν ἐπὶ τῷ ὀνόματι τοῦ υἱοῦ αὐτοῦ 'he named the city after his son' Ge 4.17; + dat. and ὄνομα– ἐπωνόμασεν αὐτοῖς ὀνόματα κατὰ τὰ ὀνόματα, ἃ ὠνόμασεν ὁ πατὴρ αὐτοῦ 'he gave them names after the names which his father had given' 26.18.

2. *to determine* sbd's name as: + acc. rei, τὸ ὄνομα αὐτοῦ Σηθ Ge 4.25; 21.31, 25.25; 26.21 (|| καλέω vs. 20), Ex 2.10; κατὰ τὸ ὄνομά τινος Nu 32.38; ἐκ τοῦ ὀνόματός τινος 32.42; + acc. pers. vel rei and name, Nu 13.17, Jo 7.26; pass. Ex 15.23.

3. *to utter* a name: τὸ ὄνομά μου Ex 20.24; Le 24.11; De 12.5; ***o*** names of heathen gods, Jo 23.7.

Cf. ὀνομάζω, ὄνομα, καλέω, ἐπικαλέω: Schmidt 1.123.

ἐποξύνω.ʃ

to increase the speed of: + acc., τὴν πορείαν 'the march' 2M 9.7. Cf. ἐπισπεύδω, ταχύνω.

ἐπόπτης, ου. m.ʃ

overseer: ***s*** God, + gen. obj., τὸν πάντων ~ην θεόν Es D 2 ο' (*L* γνώστην), 3M 2.21, + βοηθός 2M 3.39, + παντοκράτωρ 7.35. Cf. ἐφοράω, ἐποπτικός, ἐπίσκοπος, ἐργοδιώκτης: Michaelis, *TDNT* 5.373-5.

ἐποπτικός, ή, όν.ʃ

acting as overseer, watching over: ***s*** δύναμις, + gen., 4M 5.13. Cf. ἐπόπτης.

ἐποργίζομαι: fut. ~γισθήσομαι; pf.3s ἐπώργισται.ʃ*

to react angrily to: ***s*** hum., + dat. pers., ἐν ἅρμασι 'with chariots' Da 11.40 LXX; God, 2M 7.33.

Cf. ὀργίζομαι.

ἔπος, ους. n.ʃ

text to be sung to a tune: διηγούμενοι ἔπη ἐν γραφῇ 'putting a text down in writing' (:: μέλη 'tunes') Si 44.5. Cf. λόγος, ῥῆμα.

ἐποτρύνω.ʃ

to egg on to do sth: ἐπί τι (action) 4M 5.14; also + τινα 14.1. Cf. ἐπισείω.

ἐπουράνιος, ον.ʃ

heavenly: ***s*** κατοικία 'dwelling' 2M 3.39, θεός 3M 6.28, 7.6, cf. *ND* 4.149; subst.m.sg., = God, Ps 67.15. Cf. οὐρανός, οὐράνιος.

ἔποψ, πος. m.ʃ

hoopoe, Upupa epops (LSJ): Le 11.19, De 14.16; πτέρυγας ἔποπος 'a hoopoe's wings' Zc 5.9.

ἑπτά. indecl. num.

seven: ἑ. ποιμένες 'seven shepherds' Mi 5.5 +. Cf. ἑβδομήκοντα, ἑβδομηκοστός, ἕβδομος, ἑπτάκις, ἑπτακισχίλιοι.

ἑπταετής, ές.ʃ

seven-year-old: ***s*** calf for cultic sacrifice, Jd 6.25 A.

ἑπτακαίδεκα: indecl. num.

seventeen: ἑ. ἔτη 4K 13.1 || δέκα ἑπτὰ ἔτη 3K 14.21.

ἑπτακαιδέκατος, η, ον.

seventeeth: Ju 1.13.

ἑπτάκι(ς). adv.

seven times: Ge 4.24, 33.3, Le 4.6. **b**. Multiplicative w. another numeral: ἑπτὰ ἔτη ἑπτακίς 'seven times seven years' Le 25.8; ἑ. μύριαι '70,000' 2M 10.20, cf. *ND* 4.149.

Cf. ἑπταπλασίως.

ἑπτακισχίλιοι, αι, α.

Mostly pl., *seven thousand*: Nu 3.22 +; sg., 1M 3.39.

ἑπτακόσιοι, αι, α. num.

seven hundred: ἔτη ~α '700 years' Ge 5.4.

ἑπτάμηνος, ον.ʃ

subst.f., *period of seven months*: Ez 39.12, 14.

ἑπταμήτωρ, τορος. f.ʃ *

mother of seven children: 4M 16.24.

ἑπταπλάσιος, α, ον.

seven times as much or *many*: Is 30.26, Si 20.12; ἐπὶ ἁμαρτωλῶν ~α πρὸς ταῦτα 'on sinners seven times more than on those' 40.8. Cf. ἑπταπλασίως, ~σίων.

ἑπταπλασίων, ον.

= ἑπταπλάσιος: subst.n.pl., *seven times as much* Ps 78.12.

ἑπταπλασίως. adv.

seven times: frequency, Ps 11.7, Si 7.3; *seven times as much* Da 3.19. Cf. ἑπταπλάσιος, ἑπτάκις.

ἑπτάπυργος, ον.ʃ

equipped with seven towers: ***s*** εὐλογιστία 'sound reason' 4M 13.7. Cf. πύργος.

ἐπωθέω: aor. subj.mid. ἐπώσωμαι.ʃ

to thrust sth upon sbd: ἐφ' ἡμᾶς τὴν πόλιν 'force us (to defend and fight for) the city' 2K 15.14*L*. Cf. ὠθέω.

ἐπωμίς, ίδος. f.

*__1__. *the ephod* worn by the high priest: Ex 25.6, 28.4.

2. *shoulder-strap* of an ephod: Ex 28.7.

3. *side-piece*: of a door, Ez 40.48; of a gate, 41.2.

Cf. εφουδ.

ἐπώνυμος, ον.ʃ

named after sth: ***s*** ἑορτή '(commemorative) festival' Es E 22.

ἐπωρύομαι.ʃ

to howl: from sadness, αἱ ψυχαὶ αὐτῶν ἐπωρύοντο ἐπ' ἐμέ 'their souls howled over me' Zc 11.8, cf. Wolters 688-90. Cf. ὠρύομαι.

ἔραμαι: aor. ἠράσθην, impv. ἐράσθητι.ʃ

to desire intensely: ***s*** man and ***o*** woman, τῇ ἐρωμένῃ 'to his lover' 1E 4.24; Es 2.17; ***o*** (gen.) ῥῆσις 'words (of counsel)' Pr 4.6; ***s*** ἡ ψυχή μου and *+ ἐν, Si 25.1 (on ἐν, see under θέλω; ***o*** harmonious human relationships). Cf. ἐραστής, ἔρως, ἀγαπάω, ἐπιποθέω, φιλέω: Schmidt 3.475f.; Steinmueller 406-13; Casanova.

ἐραστής, οῦ. m.

1. *woman's partner for relationship of love*, 'lover': illicit, Πορεύσομαι ὀπίσω τῶν ~ῶν μου 'I will chase my lovers' Ho 2.5; opp. to 'husband,' πρὸς τὸν ἄνδρα μου τὸν πρότερον 2.7. **b.** fig. of unfaithful Israel's partner: Je 4.30, 22.20, La 1.19, Ez 16.33.

2. *person deeply attached to and attracted by*: + gen., ἐ. ἐγενόμην τοῦ κάλλους αὐτῆς 'I became enamoured of her [= wisdom's] beauty' Wi 8.2, κακῶν 'of evil things' 15.6.

Cf. ἀγαπάω, ἔραμαι, ἀνήρ.

ἐργάζομαι: (Attic) fut. ἐργῶμαι, 2s ἐργᾷ, pass. ἐργασθήσομαι; aor. ἠ/εἰργασάμην, subj. ἐργάσωμαι, inf. ἐργάσασθαι, impv. ἔργασαι, ptc. ἐργασάμενος; pf.pass. εἴργασμαι, ptc. εἰργασμένος.

1. *to perform* a certain deed: ***o*** ἀνομίαν Ps 13.4, 140.4, μάταια Ho 6.8, ψευδῆ 7.1, κακά Mi 2.1 (opp. λογίζομαι), εἰς σὲ .. κακόν Pr 3.30, κρίμα Zp 2.3, δικαιοσύνην Ps 14.2, σωτηρίαν 73.12; ἐργασία as cogn. obj., ἀντὶ τῆς ἐργασίας, ἧς ἐργᾷ παρ' ἐμοί 'in return for the labour you are going to perform with me' Ge 29.27 (ǁ δουλεύω vs. 25 with Jacob speaking and vs. 30 with the narrator concurring); πάντα (n.pl.) Ex 35.9; ἔργον as cogn. obj. Hb 1.5, cultic Ex 36.4, Nu 3.7; τὰ ἔργα κυρίου 8.11.

2. *to expend energies and efforts on*: ***s*** farmer and + acc., τὴν γῆν '(to till) the land' Ge 2.5, 3.23, Zc 13.5, Is 28.24; φάραγξ .., ἥτις οὐκ εἴργασται οὐδὲ σπείρεται 'a wadi which has never been cultivated or sown' De 21.4; oxen, Is 30.24; builder, τὸ χρυσίον καὶ τὸ ἀργύριον .. τὴν ὑάκινθον 'gold and silver .. hyacinth-coloured fabric' Ex 31.4; εἰς θεούς '(fashioned) gods (out of timber)' Is 44.15 (ǁ ποιέω εἰς vs. 17, 19); τὴν πόλιν Ez 48.18, 19, cf. τὴν θάλασσαν Rev 18.17 w. ref. to seamen; λίνον σχιτόν 'torn, flax fishing-net' Is 19.9 (***s*** fishermen mending their nets); σίδηρος εἰργασμένος 'processed iron' Ez 27.19. Cf. τεκταίνω. **b.** intr. *to work, labour*: ἓξ ἡμέρας ἐργᾷ 'thou shalt work six days' Ex 20.9, 34.21; ***s*** oxen in a field, Is 5.10; heifer, De 21.3; + ἐν, *to work by using as tool*: ἐν μόσχῳ 'calf' De 15.19; Si 24.22; *to have sbd else to work for oneself* - ἐν σοί 13.4, see also 30.13; ἐν παιδείᾳ 'by discipline' 30.34.

3. *to fashion, produce*: σκεῦος εἰργασμένον 'wrought implement' Nu 31.51; εἰς βόθρον, ὃν εἰργάσατο 'a pit which he made' Ps 7.16; ***o*** ἔργον 'artefact' Si 14.19.

4. *to serve, work for* sbd (dat.): τῷ βασιλεῖ Je 34.7, sim. 34.5 (ǁ δουλεύω); ^μόσχῳ^ 'calf' 41.18; θεοῖς ἑτέροις Ba 1.22. See LSG s.v.

Cf. ἔργον, ἐργασία, ἐργάτης, ἐργατεύομαι, ἐν~, συνεργέω, δουλεύω, ποιέω: Schmidt 1.397-423; Shipp 244; Ziegler 1934.182; Lindhagen 5-26; Harl 2001.901.

ἐργαλεῖον, ου. n.

tool, instrument: used for cultic purposes, πᾶσα ἡ κατασκευὴ καὶ πάντα τὰ ~εῖα Ex 27.19; ǁ σκεύη 39.21*a*; πάντα τὰ ~εῖα τὰ εἰς τὰ ἔργα τῆς σκηνῆς τοῦ μαρτυρίου 'all the instruments for the works in the tent of the testimony' 39.21*b*. Cf. ἔργον, σκεῦος.

ἐργασία, ας. f.

1. *labour*: cogn. obj. of ἐργάζομαι– ἀντὶ τῆς ~ας, ἧς ἐργᾷ παρ' ἐμοί 'in return for the labour you are going to perform with me' Ge 29.27, τὴν ~αν αὐτοῦ ἕως ἑσπέρας Ps 103.23 (ǁ ἔργον), ἐ. τέχνης 'pursuit of craftsmanship' Si 38.34.

2. *what one is habitually engaged in*, 'occupation': τίς σου ἡ ἐ. ἐστί; 'what is your trade?' Jn 1.8, cf. ἔργον **6**.

3. *technique, skill of a workman*, 'workmanship': ἐ. ὑφάντου 'weaver's skill' Ex 26.1 (ǁ ἔργον ὑφαντόν vs. 31); τῶν ἁγίων 'of the sacred vessels' 39.1.

4. *that which has been manufactured*, 'artefact': ἐξ αἰγείας 'from goat's hair' Nu 31.20.

Cf. ἔργον, ἐργατεία and ἐργάζομαι.

ἐργάσιμος, η, ον.ʃ

1. *that can be worked*: ***s*** δέρμα 'hide' Le 13.48; σκεῦος ~ον δέρματος 13.49.

2. *pertaining to work*: ***s*** ἡμέρα ~η 'working day' 1K 20.19 (*L* ἐργασίας).

Cf. ἔργον.

ἐργατεία, ας. f.ʃ *

act of working and labouring: Wi 7.16. Cf. ἐργασία.

ἐργατεύομαι.ʃ*

to work hard: To 5.5 𝔊[II]. Cf. ἐργάζομαι.

ἐργάτης, ου. m.ʃ

labourer: μέθυσος 'given to drinking' Si 19.1; opp. αὐτάρκης 'self-employed' 40.18; subject to hard work, Wi 17.17. **b.** *he who is habitually engaged in* a certain activity: τῆς ἀνομίας 1M 3.6.

Cf. ἐργάζομαι.

ἐργάτις, ιδος. f.ʃ

f. of prec.: used adj., *hard working*, ***s*** bees, Pr 6.8*a*.

ἐργοδιωκτέω.ʃ *

to oversee work: 2C 8.10. Cf. ἐργοδιώκτης.

ἐργοδιώκτης, ου. m.

overseer, foreman: appointed out of one's own group, Ex 3.7, 5.6, 10, 13, 1E 5.56. Cf. ἔργον, ἐργοδιωκτέω, ἐπόπτης: LSG s.v.

ἐργολαβία, ας. f.ʃ

act of profiteering: Si 29.19.

ἔργον, ου. n.

1. *that which is done*, 'deed,' esp. with ref. to its moral character: καταράσασθαι τὴν γῆν διὰ τὰ ~α τῶν ἀνθρώπων 'to curse the earth on account of man's deeds' Ge 8.21, πάσης σαρκός Si 39.19; ~α τῆς δικαιοσύνης Is 32.17, δικαίων Pr 10.16; ἔ., ὃ οὐδεὶς ποιήσει, πεποίηκάς μοι Ge 20.9; Am 8.7, Mi 6.16, Jn 3.10; ~α τῶν χειρῶν De 24.19, God's Pr 21.8. **b**. *that which can be performed only with much effort*: Pr 20.6.

2. *action*: ἐμεγάλυνε τὰ ἔ. αὐτοῦ 'he did great things' Jl 2.20; κατενόησα τὰ ἔ. σου 'I considered your actions' Hb 3.2; ἐποίουν ~α (w. ref. to the temple cult) Hg 1.14; as cogn. obj. ἔργον ἐργάζομαι Hb 1.5; Na 2.14; manual labour, πᾶν ἔ. οὐ ποιήσετε Le 16.29, cf. Ge 2.2, 3; 3.17, Ex 23.16 (agricultural); ǁ λύπαι τῶν χειρῶν Ge 5.29; ἐπιστάτης ~ων 'overseer of works' Ex 1.11; πᾶσιν τοῖς ~οις τοῖς ἐν τοῖς πεδίοις 'all the outdoor works' 1.14; one's daily labour, ἐξελεύσεται ἄνθρωπος ἐπὶ τὸ ἔ. αὐτοῦ Ps 103.23 (ǁ ἐργασία); ἱερὰ ~α 'construction works on the temple' 1E 7.3; ǁ πρᾶξις Si 37.16, ἐν ~ῳ καὶ λόγῳ 'by deed and word' 3.8; ǁ λόγοι 'words (and deeds)' 4M 16.14, cf. ~α λόγων αὐτοῦ 'His words translated into actions' Jl 2.11; military operation, Da 11.17 LXX.

*3. *cultic activity*: πάντα τὰ ~α τῆς σκηνῆς τοῦ μαρτυρίου Ex 35.21 (ǁ κάτεργον, q.v.); τοῦ ἁγίου 'of the sanctuary' 35.35, 36.3; ἐργάζεσθαι τὰ ~α τῆς σκηνῆς Nu 3.7; κυρίου 8.11.

4. *that which is manufactured*, 'artefact; product': σιτοποιοῦ 'of chief baker' Ge 40.17; θεοῦ Ex 32.16; πλίνθου 'brickwork' 24.10; ἔ. ὑφαντόν 'a woven thing' 26.31; τεκτόνων 'of craftsmen' Ho 13.2; idols, χειρῶν 14.4, Mi 5.13, Hg 2.14, 17, θεοῖς ἑτέροις, ~οις χειρῶν ἀνθρώπων, ξύλοις καὶ λίθοις De 4.28, sim. Is 37.19, but God's creation, τὰ ~α τῶν χειρῶν αὐτοῦ 5.12, ~α τῶν δακτύλων σου '.. of your fingers' Ps 8.4, τεχνίτης as agent Wi 13.1, "we all are clay, product of your hands" Is 64.8; abstract notions or their manifestations, ~α χειρῶν αὐτοῦ ἀλήθεια καὶ κρίσις Ps 110.7; of agricultural produce, συναγωγὴ τῶν ~ων σου ἐκ τοῦ ἀγροῦ σου Ex 23.16, τὰ ~α τῆς γῆς Je 14.3; ἔ. ἐλαίας 'olive crop' Hb 3.17.

5. *that which is effected*, 'effect': ἰσχυρὰ ~α λόγων αὐτοῦ 'the effect of his words is powerful' Jl 2.11.

6. *that which one habitually does*, 'occupation, profession': Τί τὸ ἔ. ὑμῶν ἐστιν; Ge 46.33, cf. ἐργασία **2**; administrative activities, Da 2.49 TH (LXX πράγματα).

7. *farm*: Jb 1.3. **b**. *property*: livestock in particular, 1K 15.9.

Cf. ἐργάζομαι, ἐργασία, ἐργοδιώκτης, ἐπιτήδευμα, κάτεργον, πρᾶγμα, πρᾶξις: Bertram, *TDNT* 2.635-52.

ἐρεθίζω: fut.pass. ἐρεθισθήσομαι; aor.pass.ptc. ἐρεθισθείς.

1. *to be quarrelsome*: abs. ὁ υἱὸς ἡμῶν ἀπειθεῖ καὶ ἐρεθίζει '.. disobedient and ..' De 21.20.

2. *to provoke* to a fight: + acc. pers. and pass. Da 11.10 LXX; εἰς πόλεμον 11.25.

3. *to render provocative*: + acc. rei, λόγους 'to say provocative things' Pr 19.7.

Cf. ἐρίζω, ἐρεθισμός, ἐρεθιστής: Spicq 2.69-72.

ἐρεθισμός, οῦ. m.ʃ

irritation: De 28.22 (divine punishment); ǁ τράχηλος σκληρός 'stiff neck' 31.27; ǁ ἀντίπτωμα 'quarrel' Si 34.29. Cf. ἐρεθιστής, ἐρίζω, ἐρεθίζω.

ἐρεθιστής, οῦ. m.ʃ

Used attr. *quarrelsome*: *s* υἱός De 21.18. Cf. ἐρίζω, ἐρεθίζω, ἐρεθισμός.

ἐρείδω: fut. ἐρείσω; aor. ἤρεισα, opt.3s ἐρείσαι.ʃ

1. *to fix and position firmly*: + acc., σὸν πόδα 'your foot' Pr 3.26 (so as to prevent a fall). **b**. intr. ὁ ἡμέτερος λόγος εἰς σὴν καρδίαν 'Let our word (take root) in your heart' Pr 4.4. **c**. mid.: + neg., *s* harlot's unstable, unreliable path followed by her undiscriminating client, Pr 5.5.

2. *to cause to move forward with vigour*: + acc. rei, τοὺς βραχίονας αὐτῆς εἰς ἔργον '(set) her arms to work (with determination)' Pr 31.17, sim. vs. 19 (ǁ ἐκτείνω 'to stretch out').

3. *to render support, prop*: + acc. pers., δόξῃ 'with honour' Pr 29.23. **b**. mid., metaph. *to lean upon as reliable*: ἐπὶ ψεύδεσιν 'on lies' Pr 9.12a; + dat., πλούτῳ 'wealth (to fall back on' 11.16; 30.28. ***c**. act. = mid.: ἐπὶ τῇ συστάσει αὐτῶν 'on their plot' Ge 49.6.

4. intr. *to strive in argument*, 'contest': abs. Jb 17.10.

Cf. ἔρεισμα, ἐπιστηρίζω.

ἐρεικτός, ή, όν.ʃ

pounded: πεφρυγμένα χῖδρα ~ά 'parched, pounded, unripe, wheaten-groats' Le 2.14. On the spelling, see Walters 30.

ἔρεισμα, ατος. n.ʃ

reliable support: Pr 14.26. Cf. ἐρείδω.

ἐρεοῦς, ᾶ, οῦν.ʃ

of wool, woolen: *s* ἱμάτιον Le 13.47; subst.n. and ǁ λινοῦς 'linen' 13.48, 52, Ez 44.17; ǁ στιππύινος 'made of tow' Le 13.47, 59.

Cf. ἔριον.

I **ἐρεύγομαι**: fut. ἐρεύξομαι.ʃ

to roar: of lion, λέων ἐρεύξεται, καὶ τίς οὐ φοβηθήσεται; 'a lion roars, and who would not be scared?' Am 3.8; 3.4, Ho 11.10; ὡς σκύμνος ἐρευγόμενος εἰς θήραν 'like a lion's whelp roaring for prey' 1M 3.4. Cf. ὠρύομαι.

II **ἐρεύγομαι**.ʃ

to eject from inside, 'to disgorge, belch out': + acc., ὕδατα Le 11.10; 'to blurt out, utter,' ἡμέρα τῇ ἡμέρᾳ ἐρεύγεται ῥῆμα Ps 18.3 (‖ ἀναγγέλλω). Cf. Shipp 245.

ἔρευνα, ης. f.ʃ

investigation, enquiry: τοῖς κραταιοῖς ἰσχυρὰ ἐφίσταται ἔ. 'for the powerful there awaits a thorough investigation' Wi 6.8. Cf. ἐρευνάω.

ἐρευνάω: fut. ἐρευνήσω; aor. ἠρεύνησα, impv. ἐρεύνησον, subj. ἐρευνήσω.

1. *to conduct a search*: abs. Ge 44.12; ἐρευνῶν ἐξερεύνησεν 'he made a thorough search' Jl 1.7; εἰς τὸν οἶκον Ιακωβ καὶ ἐν τῷ οἴκῳ .. Ge 31.33.

2. *to investigate, explore* in order to obtain information on or searching sth: abs. and + ἐπιζητέω Jd 6.29; + acc., ἠρεύνησας πάντα τὰ σκεύη μου Ge 31.37; a land, Je 27.26, + κατασκέπτομαι 2K 10.3 (*L* ~σκοπεύω).

Cf. δι~, ἐξ~, κατερευνάω, ἔρευνα, ἐξετάζω, σκάλλω, ζητέω: Passoni Dell'Acqua 1988, esp. 211-3.

ἐρημία, ας. f.

state of being desolate: Ba 4.33; cogn. dat. of ἐρημόω Is 60.12; ~αν ποιήσω 'I shall bring about desolation' Ez 35.4. **b**. *wilderness*: ‖ πεδίον 4M 18.8. Cf. ἔρημος.

ἐρημικός, ή, όν.ʃ*

native to a desert: *s* bird, Ps 101.7; stone, 119.4. Cf. ἔρημος, ἐρημίτης.

ἐρημίτης, ου. m.ʃ

inhabitant of desert: used adj., ὄνος ἐ. 'desert ass, wild ass' Jb 11.12. Cf. ἔρημος, ἐρημικός.

ἔρημος, ον.

1. *desolate*: *s* land and cities, Le 26.33; building, ὁ οἶκός μού ἐστιν ~ος Hg 1.9; unaccompanied hum., 2M 8.35. **b**. + ἀπό, 'emptied of': *s* land, ἀπὸ ἀνθρώπων καὶ κτηνῶν Je 40.10 (‖ ἄβατος 39.43), ἀπὸ κατοικούντων 41.22. **c**. subst. ~ος treated as f. *uninhabited desolate land, wilderness*: Ge 12.9, Ho 2.3, Ps 106.35 (‖ γῆ ἄνυδρος); ἀφανισμὸν ἄνυδρον ὡς ~ον Zp 2.13; ἐγὼ ἐποίμαινόν σε ἐν τῇ ~ῳ ἐν γῇ ἀοικήτῳ Ho 13.5; where the Israelites journeyed forty years, Am 2.10, cf. 5.25 v.l.; ‖ ἀγρός Jl 1.19; πεδία τῆς ~ου 2.22; also n.pl. Is 35.2, 2E 9.9; dried-up area of a river-bed, 4K 2.8B (*L* ξηρά).

2. *bereft of*: + gen., πάσης σκέπης 'of every protection' 3M 5.6.

Cf. ἐρημόω, ἐρημία, ἐρημικός, ἐρημίτης, ἀγρός, μόνος, χέρσος, πόλις: Schmidt 4.537-9.

ἐρημόω: fut. ἐρημώσω, pass. ἐρημωθήσομαι; aor. ἠρήμωσα, ptc. ~μώσας, inf. ~μῶσαι, pass. ἠρημώθην, inf. ἐρημωθῆναι, subj. ~μωθῶ, ptc. ~μωθείς; pf.pass. ἠρήμωμαι, ptc. ἠρημωκώς, pass. ἠρημωμένος.

1. *to lay waste*: *o* pillar as object of worship, Le 26.30 (‖ ἐξολεθρεύω); τὴν οἰκουμένην Is 24.1 (‖ καταφθείρω), θρόνον PSol 17.6; land, pass., ἡ γῆ ἐρημωθῇ Ge 47.19; sanctuary, Da 8.11; cities and houses because of depopulation, Is 6.11; sea, 11.15, ὕδατα 37.25, river Jb 14.11; ἔθνη Is 60.12; pasture, Je 10.25; wealth, Si 21.4; ὁδοὺς ^πόλεως^ 49.6.

2. *to strip of contents*: *o* road and pass., ἐρημωθήσονται αἱ ὁδοὶ ὑμῶν 'your roads will be deserted (with no travellers)' Le 26.22, cities Je 40.10 (‖ ἔρημος ἀπὸ ἀνθρώπων καὶ κτηνῶν).

3. *to deprive*: + acc. and ἀπό τινος– ἀπὸ τῶν θυγατέρων τὴν μόνην ἠρήμωσαν 'they bereaved the lonely (widow) of her daughters' Ba 4.16; Is 23.13, Je 33.9. **b**. *to deprive of company*, 'desert': κορώνη ἐρημουμένη 'deserted crow' Je 3.2.

*__4__. *to remove moist*: pass., *o* cord, Jd 16.7 A (*L* μὴ ἐξηραμμένος 'not dried' [*o* twig]; B: ὑγρός 'moist').

Cf. ἐξερημόω, ἐρήμωσις, ἔρημος.

ἐρήμωσις, εως. f.

state of lying waste: of land, Le 26.34, Je 7.34; ‖ ἄβατος 32.4; pl., manifestations of such a state, Da 9.27. Cf. ἐρημόω.

ἐρίζω: aor. ἤρισα, ptc. ἐρίσας, subj. ἐρίσω.

to quarrel: abs. and + μάχομαι, 4K 3.23*L*; + dat. pers., Ge 26.35; μετά τινος Si 8.2 (‖ διαμάχομαι vs. 1); περί τινος 'over sth' 11.9; τῷ στόματι κυρίου 1K 12.14f. Cf. ἐρεθιστής, ἐρεθίζω, ἔρις, μάχομαι: Schmidt 4.197-202.

ἐριθεύομαι.ʃ

to be gainfully employed: ἐν τοῖς ἔργοις τοῖς γυναικείοις 'in women's work' To 2.11 𝔊[II].

ἔριθος, ου. f.ʃ

weaver: Is 38.12.

ἐρικτός ⇒ ἐρεικτός.

ἔριον, ου. n.

wool: ἔρια καὶ λίνον 'wool and linen' De 22.11; symbol of whiteness, Is 1.18 (‖ χιών and:: φοινικοῦς, κόκκινος). Cf. ἐπίποκος, ἐρεοῦς.

ἔρις, ιδος. f.ʃ

quarrel, strife: κατασπευδομένη 'hasty' Si 28.11 (‖ μάχη); universal lot, but esp. of sinners, 40.5 and 9. Cf. ἐρίζω.

ἐρίφιον, ου. n.ʃ

young of goat: To 2.13𝔊[I]. Cf. ἔριφος.

ἔριφος, ου. m.

young of goat, 'kid': for cultic use, Ex 12.5 (+ ἀμνός); ἔσθοντες ~ους ἐκ ποιμνίων 'eating kids from flocks' Am 6.4 (describing a life of great comfort); αἰγῶν 'of goats' Jd 6.19.

Cf. ἐρίφιον, αἴξ: Shipp 245.

ἑρμηνεία, ας. f.ʃ

1. *act of translating* from one language into another: Si prol. 20.

2. *exposition* of difficult sayings: pl. Si 47.17; Da 5 pr. LXX.
Cf. ἑρμηνεύω.

ἑρμηνεύς, έως. m.ʃ
interpreter: τῶν ἐνεργημάτων ^τοῦ κυρίου^ 'of the Lord's activities' Si 17.5¶ (= λόγος). Cf. ἑρμηνευτής.

ἑρμηνευτής, οῦ. m.ʃ
translator: oral and between two languages, Ge 42.23. Cf. ἑρμηνεύω, ἑρμηνεύς.

ἑρμηνεύω: pf.inf. ἑρμηνευκέναι, ptc.pass. ἡρμηνευμένος.ʃ
to put into another language: ἔγραψεν .. Συριστὶ καὶ ἡρμηνευμένην 'wrote a document .. in Aramaic and translated' 2E 4.7; Es 10.11 F o'; οὗτος ἑρμηνεύεται ἐκ τῆς Συριακῆς βίβλου Jb 42.17bα. Cf. ἑρμηνευτής, ἑρμηνεία, διερμηνεύω, μεθερμηνεύω: Spicq 1.312-7.

ἑρπετόν, οῦ. n.
creeping animal: aquatic, Ge 1.20 (ǁ πετεινά 'birds'); τὰ ~ὰ τῆς γῆς Ho 2.12, 18 (in a tripartite division of the animal kingdom excepting aquatic species, and ǁ τὰ θηρία τοῦ ἀγροῦ and τὰ πετεινὰ τοῦ οὐρανοῦ); οἱ ἰχθύες τῆς θαλάσσης added, 4.3; coupled only with the latter, Hb 1.14 (τὰ ~ὰ τὰ οὐκ ἔχοντα ἡγούμενον 'which have no leader'); ἀπὸ πάντων τῶν ~ῶν τῶν ἑρπόντων ἐπὶ τῆς γῆς, and ǁ ὀρνέα and κτήνη Ge 6.20; τετράποδα καὶ ~ὰ καὶ θηρία τῆς γῆς 1.24; πᾶν ~ὸν κινούμενον ἐπὶ τῆς γῆς 7.14; food for humans, 9.3; winged, τὰ ~ὰ τῶν πετεινῶν 'flying insects' Le 11.20, De 14.18. Cf. ἕρπω, θηρίον, ἰχθῦς.

ἕρπω.
to move slowly: of animals on the surface of the earth (ἐπὶ τῆς γῆς), Ge 1.26, De 4.18, Ez 38.20; οἱ οὐρανοὶ καὶ ἡ γῆ, θάλασσα καὶ πάντα τὰ ἕρποντα ἐν αὐτοῖς Ps 68.35; ǁ κινοῦμαι Ge 7.14, 21, 8.17, 19. Cf. ἑρπετόν, ἐξέρπω: Schmidt 1.477-504; LSG s.v.

ἐρυθαίνω: aor.ptc. ἐρυθήνας.ʃ
to dye red: φύκει .. χρόαν αὐτοῦ 'its colour .. with orchil' Wi 13.14. Cf. ἐρυθρός.

ἐρύθημα, ατος. n.ʃ
redness: ἐ. ἱματίων 'red garments' Is 63.1.

ἐρυθριάω.ʃ
to blush: *s* woman, Es D 5; πρός τινα '(with anger) at sbd' To 2.14 𝔊[I] (𝔊[II] προσερυθριάω). Cf. προσερυθριάω.

ἐρυθροδανόω: pf.ptc.pass. ἠρυθροδανωμένος. *
to dye red: ***o*** animal skin, δέρματα κριῶν ἠρυθροδανωμένα 'skins of rams dyed red' Ex 25.5.

ἐρυθρός, ά, όν.
red in colour: ἡ ~ὰ θάλασσα which in Hdt. referred to the Indian Ocean, which sometimes included the Red Sea (LSJ) Ex 10.19, 13.18 + (ǁ θ. ἐ. 15.22 +); θάλασσα understood, De 1.1; *s* clothes, Is 63.2; pers. w. ref. to angry face, Es 3.3 *L*. Cf. ἐρυθαίνω, ἐρύθημα, ἐρυθριάω, ἐρυθροδανόω, κόκκινος, πυρράκης, πυρρός, φοινικοῦς: Schmidt 3.39-42.

ἐρυμνός, ή, όν.ʃ
strongly fortified: *s* χωρίον 'spot' 2M 11.5. Cf. ἐρυμνότης, ὀχυρός.

ἐρυμνότης, ητος. f.
state of being strongly fortified: of citadel, 2M 10.34; τῶν τειχέων 'of the walls' 12.14. Cf. ἐρυμνός.

ἐρυσίβη, ης. f.
rust in corn: destructive of trees and crops, ἐξαναλώσει De 28.42; καταφάγεται αὐτοὺς ἡ ἐ. 'the rust will eat them up' Ho 5.7; natural disaster mentioned with varieties of locust, Jl 1.4, 2.25. See Casevitz 1996.

ἔρχομαι: fut. ἐλεύσομαι; aor. ἦλθον, inf. ἐλθεῖν, ptc. ἐλθών, subj. ἔλθω, opt. 3s ἔλθοι; pf. ἐλήλυθα, ptc. ἐληλυθώς.

1. *to come* to or *arrive* at a focal point, whether the speaker himself or what looms large in his mind: abs. and subst. ptc., ἐρχόμενος ἥξει 'one who is to come will arrive' Hb 2.3; + dat. pers. = dat. com. *to become available for use* or *enjoyment*, ἕως τοῦ ἐλθεῖν γενήματα δικαιοσύνης ὑμῖν Ho 10.12; ἐπὶ τὸν τόπον Ge 22.3; so as to assist, Zc 9.9; + εἴς τι (place), εἰς γῆν Χανααν Ge 12.5, εἰς τὸ ὄρος Χωρηβ Ex 3.1; ἐκ τῆς Μεσοποταμίας Ge 33.18; + ἐπί τινα, with hostile intent, Am 4.2, Zc 14.16; w. friendly intent, *s* βοήθεια Ju 7.31; a danger implied, Ge 44.12; ἐπί τι (place), ἦλθεν ἐπὶ τὸ φρέαρ 46.1, ἐπὶ τὴν συναγωγήν Su 28 LXX; + πρός τινα, Ge 32.6, 37.23; + place-name with no prep., Hebraism?– ἐλθεῖν Εφραθα 48.7; of coming home from work outdoors, 34.7; τὰ ὑπὸ τὴν ὄψιν ἐρχόμενα 'what comes into our purview' Es E 10; ἦλθεν (*L* ἐγένετο) ἐπὶ τὴν καρδίαν σου τοῦ οἰκοδομῆσαι οἶκον 3K 8.18. Opp. πορεύομαι– πόθεν ἔρχῃ καὶ ποῦ πορεύῃ; 'where do you come from and where are you going to?' Ge 16.8, γενεὰ πορεύεται καὶ γ. ἔρχεται Ec 1.4. **b**. of a specific time or era, esp. in eschatological pronouncements: ἰδοὺ ἡμέραι ἔρχονται Am 4.2, 8.11, 9.13; sg. ἡμέρα Ma 4.1*bis*; ἡμέρα κυρίου Jl 2.31, Zc 14.1, Ma 4.4; καιρός 2C 21.19. **c**. of a prayer, *to reach*, + πρός τινα, Jn 2.8, cf. τὴν κραυγὴν αὐτῶν τὴν ἐρχομένην πρός με Ge 18.21, also Ps 101.2; εἰς τὸν οὐρανόν 2C 30.27. **d**. *to originate*: πόθεν ἔρχῃ; 'where are you from?' Jn 1.8. **e**. *to come to face* a certain condition: εἰς συνοχήν 'siege' 4L 25.2*L* (ǁ ἐν περιοχῇ 24.10*L*), Je 52.5, εἰς κρίσιν '(to go) to court' Jb 9.32, εἰς ἐπίγνωσιν 'recognition' 2M 9.11; εἰς αἷμα ἀθῷον '(end up) murdering sbd innocent' 1K 25.26, cf. Mt 6.13. **f.** *to move forward and advance*: ἐληλυθὼς ἐν ἔτεσιν 'advanced in age' 1K 17.11*L*, cf. προβαίνω.

2. *to befall*: ἐλεύσονται ἐπὶ σὲ πᾶσαι αἱ κατάραι αὗται 'all these curses will befall you' De 28.15, 45 (‖ ἥκω vs. 2), 30.1; *s* sth desirable, ἔλθοι ἐπ' ἐμὲ τὸ ἔλεός σου Ps 118.41, μοι οἱ οἰκτιρμοί σου 118.77.

*__3__. *to come to pass, happen and become a reality*: *s* τὸ σημεῖον ἢ τὸ τέρας, ὃ ἐλάλησεν 'the sign or the portent, which he spoke about' De 13.2, sim. 1K 10.9; ἐλθέτω ἡ βουλὴ τοῦ ἁγίου Ισραηλ Is 5.19; Je 35.9; μου ἡ αἴτησις 'my request' Jb 6.8; τὸ ῥῆμά (B: ὁ λόγος) σου Jd 13.12 A, 17.

4. *to come after, follow*: γενεὰ ἡ ἐρχομένη 'the future generaiton' Ps 21.31 (‖ σπέρμα).

N.B. The pres. is sometimes used with fut. force: ἰδοὺ ἐγὼ ἔρχομαι καὶ κατασκηνώσω ἐν μέσῳ σου Zc 2.10 (so many exs. in **1.b.** above), and cf. ἥξει .. ἰδοὺ ἔρχεται Ma 3.1.

ἥξω may be used as fut. of ἔρχομαι, cp. Ge 41.30 with 41.29.

Cf. ἐλευστέον, δι~, εἰσ~, ἐξ~, ἐπ~, παρ~, προσ~, συν~, συνεξέρχομαι, πορεύομαι, ἀναβαίνω, βαδίζω, εἶμι, ἥκω: Schmidt 1.477-504; Schneider, *TDNT* 2.666-8; Lee 85f.

ἐρωδιός, οῦ. m.ʃ On the spelling see Walters 70.

heron: forbidden as food, Le 11.19, De 14.15; inhabiting ruins, Ps 103.17 (‖ στρουθίον).

ἔρως, ωτος.ʃ

sexual passion: with an adulteress, Pr 7.18 (‖ φιλία); γυναικός 30.16. Cf. ἔραμαι, φιλία.

ἐρωτάω: fut. ἐρωτήσω; impf. ἠρώτων; aor. ἠρώτησα, impv. ἐρώτησον, inf. ἐρωτῆσαι, subj. ἐρωτήσω, pass. ἠρωτήθην; pf.ptc.pass. ἠρωτημένος.

to put a question, 'ask': abs., ἐτάσεις καὶ ἐρωτήσεις καὶ ἐξερευνήσεις De 13.14, ἐρωτᾶν καὶ μανθάνειν 'to ask and learn' 2M 7.2; + acc. pers. Ge 24.47; τὸ στόμα αὐτῆς 'her personally' 24.57; and + a question, Πῶς ἔχετε; 'How are you?' 43.27; λέγων Εἰ ἔχετε πατέρα .. Ge 44.19; + λέγων and direct speech, 32.17, 37.15, Ex 13.14; εἰπεῖν εἰ .. Je 44.17; + acc. rei, 'about sth,' τὸ ὄνομά μου Ge 32.29; τρίβους κυρίου αἰωνίους Je 6.16, ὁδόν 27.5; + double acc., τινά τι Ps 34.11, 2E 5.10, σε λόγον Je 45.14; περί τινος Is 45.11; to reinforce ἐπερωτάω– ἐρωτῶν ἐπερώτησεν ἡμᾶς 'he questioned us doggedly' Ge 43.7. *__b__. divination: ἔν τινι [= God], Jd 18.5 A (B: ἐπ~); διὰ τοῦ θεοῦ 1K 22.10 (*L* ἐπερωτάω). *__c__. idiom, τινα εἰς εἰρήνην 'how sbd was doing (out of concern for his wellbeing)' Jd 18.15B (*AL*: ἀσπάζομαί τινα), 1K 25.5 (*L* ἀσπάζομαί τινα εἰς εἰρήνην); τινα τὰ εἰς εἰρήνην 1K 10.4, 30.21; + εὐλογέω 2K 8.10; perh. Ps 121.6, see under ὁ **III c**.

Cf. ἐρώτημα, ἐπερωτάω, ἐτάζω, ἐξερευνάω, πυνθάνομαι, ἀποκρίνομαι: Greeven, *TDNT* 2.685-7.

ἐρώτημα, ατος. n.ʃ

answer obtained by asking: w. ref. to oracle, δήλων Si 36.4. Cf. ἐρωτάω, ἐπερώτημα.

ἐσθής, ῆτος. f.

garment: good-looking, ἱερά 1E 8.68, 70 (‖ ἱμάτιον), δοξική 'magnificent' 2M 8.35, βασιλική Es 7.39 *L* (ο' στολή). Cf. ἔσθησις, ἱμάτιον, στολή.

ἔσθησις, εως. f.ʃ

= prec.: 2M 3.33, 3M 1.16 ..

ἐσθίω, ἔσθω [the latter common in ptc., though not obligatory]: fut. ἔδομαι, φάγομαι; aor. ἔφαγον, inf. φαγεῖν, impv. φάγε, subj. φάγω, φάγωμαι, opt.3pl φάγοισαν. For the fut.pass., aor.pass. and pf., βιβρώσκω is used.

1. *to eat* as food and nourishment: abs. φαγεῖν καὶ πιεῖν Ex 32.6, πίετε, φάγετε Is 21.5; φάγονται καὶ οὐ μὴ ἐμπλησθῶσιν 'they will eat but not be satiated' Ho 4.10, sim. Mi 6.14, cf. φάγεσθε ἐσθίοντες καὶ ἐμπλησθήσεσθε Jl 2.26; εἰς στόμα ἔσθοντος Na 3.12; ἔφαγον καὶ ἔπιον 'had a meal' Ge 24.54, 31.46; of a cultic meal, Ex 24.11, 29.32; ***o*** ἄρτον Ge 28.20; Ex 2.20, Je 48.1 (to dine as guest); ζύμην 'leaven(ed bread)' 12.15; αἷμα Le 17.10, De 12.16; γῆν 'dust' Ge 3.14 (*s* snake, a figurative expression for a beast of the ground: see Wevers ad loc.); βρώματα 6.21; κρέα 'meat' Ho 8.13, κρέα υἱῶν σου καὶ θυγατέρων σου De 28.53; καρπὸν ψευδῆ Ho 10.13; ἐρήμους '(grass in) wilderness' Is 5.17; + partitive gen., Ge 3.17, Ex 34.15, Si 6.19, Pr 9.5, Jd 13.16 A (B: + ἀπό); + ἀπό indicating the source from which food is derived, ἀπὸ παντὸς ξύλου .. βρώσει φάγῃ 'you may indeed eat off any tree' Ge 2.16, sim. 3.1, De 20.19; and food itself, ἀπὸ καρποῦ ξύλου .. φαγόμεθα Ge 3.2, ἀπὸ τῶν ἄρτων τῆς γῆς Nu 15.19; ‖ πίνειν, Hg 1.6, Zc 7.6; + gen., φάγε τῆς θήρας μου 'Eat some of my game' Ge 27.19 (‖ φάγομαι ἀπὸ τῆς θήρας σου vs. 25). **b.** fig., 'to benefit from, enjoy': + acc., τὰ σκῦλα τῶν ἐθνῶν 'the spoils of the nations' De 7.16; ***o*** Wisdom personified, Si 24.21; + ἐκ, ἐκ τῶν διαβουλίων 'the fruits of their plan' Ho 11.6. **c.** fig., to *be forced to eat*, 'bear (the consequences of)': τῆς ἑαυτοῦ ὁδοῦ τοὺς καρποὺς Pr 1.31, τὰ γεννήματα τῶν ἔργων αὐτῶν 'the produce of ..' Is 3.10.

2. *to destroy*: + acc., φάγεται ὡσεὶ χόρτον τὴν ὕλην '.. like grass the woods' Is 10.17, ἀρὰ ἔδεται τὴν γῆν 'a curse ..' 24.6, ἀ. ἔδεται ταύτην τὴν βουλήν 28.8, πῦρ τοὺς ὑπεναντίους ἔδεται

26.11; τὸν λαόν μου Ps 52.5; *s* ἡ ὀργὴ .. ὡς πῦρ Is 30.27.

Cf. κατ~, συνεσθίω, ἀναλίσκω, ἀπογεύομαι, βιβρώσκω, βόσκω, γεύομαι, ἐκτρώγω, κατανέμομαι, σιτέομαι, πίνω, ἔδεσμα, νηστεύω, παντοφαγία: Behm, *TDNT* 2.689-92.

ἔσοπτρον, ου. n.ʃ

looking-glass, mirror: Si 12.11, Wi 7.26. Cf. κάτοπτρον: Kittel, *TDNT* 1.178-80; Spicq 2.73-6; *ND* 4.149f.

ἑσπέρα, ας. f.

evening: opp. πρωΐ and preceding it, 'morning' Ge 1.5, ἀφ' ~ας ἕως πρωί Ex 27.21, but ἀπὸ π. ἕως ~ας 3K 22.35, τὸ π. καὶ εἰς ~αν 2E 3.3, see also ἀπὸ πρωίθεν ἕως ~ας Ex 18.13, 1M 9.13, Jb 4.20, Si 18.26; καθ' ~αν 'in the evening' 1K 23.24; πρὸς ~αν 'towards the evening' Ge 8.11, Zc 14.7; τὸ πρὸς ~αν De 23.11; adverbial gen. ἑσπέρας 'in the evening' Ge 19.1; τὸ ~ας De 16.4 (‖ without τό vs. 6), 28.67 (:: τὸ πρωΐ); εἰς τὸ ~ας 'towards the evening' Ge 49.27 (‖ τὸ πρωϊνόν 'in the morning'); mistranslation of Ar. עֲבַר 'area on the other side' 2E 4.20. Cf. ἑσπερινός, ὀψέ, ὀψία: Shipp 246-8.

ἑσπερινός, ή, όν.

towards the evening: ἀνὰ μέσον τῶν ~ῶν 'sometime during the evening hours (?)' Le 23.5 (MT /bēn hāʻarbāyim/); *s* θυσία 'sacrifice' 4K 16.15 (:: πρωϊνός), Ps 140.2, Da LXX 9.21; σκότος 'darkness' Pr 7.9. Cf. ἑσπέρα.

Ἕσπερος, ου. m.ʃ

evening-star, *Hesperus*: Jb 9.9, 38.32¶.

ἑστία, ας. f.ʃ

home: To 2.12 𝔊^II^. Cf. οἰκία, οἶκος.

ἑστιατορία, ας. f.*

1. *allowance of food*: 4K 25.30.

2. *feast*: Da 5.1 LXX (TH δεῖπνον).

ἐσχάρα, ας. f.

1. *hearth*: ἐ. πυρός 'fire-place' Je 43.22, Jb 41.11; ἐ. ἄνθραξιν 'for coals' Pr 26.21.

2. *grid* or *lattice-work* forming the base of various structures (LSG s.v. **II 2**): of altar, Ex 27.4, Si 50.12, 2C 4.11; Le 2.7; 6.39 (‖ τήγανον 'frying-pan'). Cf. Chadwick 111-5.

Cf. ἐσχαρίτης: Shipp 232, 250; LSG s.v.

ἐσχαρίτης, ου.ʃ*

that which is baked over the fire: + κολλυρίς, λάγανον 2K 6.19. Cf. ἐσχάρα.

ἐσχατίζω: aor. ἠσχάτισα.ʃ

to lag behind: on battlefield, Jd 5.28A (‖ χρονίζω), 1M 5.53.

ἐσχατογήρως, ων.ʃ*

very far advanced in age: *s* hum. Si 41.2, 42.8. Cf. πρεσβύτερος.

ἔσχατος, η, ον.

1. of time, *later in future*, often w. ref. to a momentous event to happen, ἐν ταῖς ~αις ἡμέραις Is 2.2, cf. **2 b**; μεγάλη ἔσται ἡ δόξα .. ἡ ~η ὑπὲρ τὴν πρώτην 'the future glory will surpass the past one' Hg 2.9; subst., τὰ ~α Is 41.22 'the future events' (:: τὰ πρότερα and ‖ τὰ ἐπερχόμενα), 46.10, ~α αὐτῆς 'her destiny' La 1.9, 'the more recent situation' Jb 42.12 (:: τὰ ἔμπροσθεν); τὰ ἐπέρχομενα ἐπ' ~ου Is 41.23; τὰ ~α καὶ τὰ ἀρχαῖα Ps 138.5; τὰ ~α αὐτοῦ 'his posterity' Da 11.4 TH. **b**. *relatively later*, involving two terms: ἐν πρώτοις .. ἐπ' ~ῳ De 13.9 (‖ .. ἐπ' ~ων 17.7; cf. 2K 24.25, 3K 17.13*L* as at De 13.9), ἐπ' ~ων σου 'later in your life' Pr 19.20. **c**. *last in order or sequence*, involving more than two terms, 'last': predicatively used, Nu 10.25 (:: πρῶτος vs. 14); ἐπ' ~ων w. ref. to death, Si 1.13. **d**. n. used adverbially, ~ον 'subsequently, later on': Le 27.18, Pr 29.21. ***e**. n. used as prep. with a gen., 'after': ~ον τοῦ θανάτου μου 'after my death' De 31.27, ~ον τῆς τελευτῆς μου 31.29; ~ον τῶν ἡμερῶν 'at the end-time' 31.29, cf. ~η τῶν υἱῶν ἡ μήτηρ ἐτελεύτησεν 'after the sons their mother died' 2M 7.41.

2. *remotest, farthest removed*: physically, ἄβυσσος 'the deepest abyss' Jn 2.6; θάλασσα w. ref. to the Mediterranean Sea as seen from the East - De 34.2, Jo 1.4; Jl 2.20 (‖ πρῶτος), Zc 14.8 (ditto; see Tht PG 81.1953). **b**. subst. n. sg. and anarth. 'end-point': ἐπ' ~ου τῶν ἡμερῶν 'at the end of the days' Nu 24.14, cf. **1**; ἐπ' ~ῳ τῶν ἡμερῶν De 4.30; μακρόθεν ἀπ' ~ου τῆς γῆς Ge 28.49, ἕως ~ου τῆς γῆς Is 8.9; pl. ἐπ' ἐσχάτων 'at the end' 32.20; ἐπ' ~ων σου 'in your latter days' 8.16, ἐπ' ~ων αὐτοῦ 'at the end of his life' Je 17.11; ἐπ' ~ων τῶν ἡμερῶν 'in the last days' Ge 49.1, Ho 3.5; τὰ ~α τῆς θαλάσσης Ps 138.9; ἀπ' ου βορρᾶ 'from the extreme north' Ez 38.6; ἕως ~ου 'utterly' Wi 4.19, ἕως ~ων 'thoroughly (search)' Si 51.14; m.pl., 'the rear (of an army)' 1M 4.15.

3. of relative order, *last-mentioned*: τοῦ σημείου τοῦ ~ου Ex 4.8 (:: τοῦ πρώτου); De 24.3 (:: πρότερος vs. 4).

Cf. πρῶτος, τελευταῖος: Schmidt 4.526-8; Troxel 1992.

ἔσω: comp. ἐσώτερος, super. ἐσώτατος.

I. adv. situated *inside*: οὐθεὶς ἦν τῶν ἐν τῇ οἰκίᾳ ἔ. 'there was none of the staff in' Ge 39.11. **b**. *into the interior*: εἰσήχθη Le 10.18 (*pace* Wevers).

II. prep., ἐσώτερον 'farther inside than, beyond': + gen., τοῦ καταπετάσματος 'inside beyond the veil' Ex 26.33, Le 16.2, τοῦ σπηλαίου 'the cave' 1K 24.4.

III. adj. αὐλὴ ἐσωτέρα 'inner court' Ez 8.16, Es 4.11 o'; pred., 1K 24.4*L*; subst.n., τὰ ἐσώτατα 'the things far deep inside (the ground) (?)' Jb 28.18.

Cf. ἔσωθεν, ἔξω.

ἔσωθεν.
on the inside: ἔ. καὶ ἔξωθεν Ge 6.14, Ex 25.10. Cf. ἔσω and ἔξωθεν.

ἐτάζω: aor. ἤτασα, impv. ἔτασον, inf. ἐτάσαι, subj. ἐτάσω, pass. ἠτάσθην.

1. *to test*: ἐτάσεις καὶ ἐρωτήσεις καὶ ἐξερευνήσεις De 13.14; ‖ δοκιμάζω Wi 2.19.

2. *to subject to a trying experience*: + acc. pers. and cogn. dat., ἤτασεν ὁ θεὸς τὸν Φαραω ἐτασμοῖς μεγάλοις καὶ πονηροῖς Ge 12.17.

3. *to make enquiries into*: *o* καρδίας Je 17.10 (‖ δοκιμάζω), αὐτοῦ τὰ ἔργα 'his deeds' Jb 36.23; hum. suspects, Es 2.23 o'; pass., ἐξηρευνήθη ἡ ὁδὸς ἡμῶν καὶ ἠτάσθη La 3.40.

Cf. ἐτασμός, ἔτασις, ἀν~, ἐξετάζω, δοκιμάζω, ἐρωτάω, ἐξερευνάω, πειράζω, ἀνακρίνω: Korn 10, n. 6.

ἑταιρίζομαι.ʃ
to prostitute oneself: *s* γυνή Si 9.3. Cf. πορνεύω, ἑταῖρος: Wagner 207f.

ἑταῖρος, α, ον.

1. subst. m., *one who belongs to and moves round in the same circle or class as oneself*: Jd 4.17B, 14.11A, 20A, 2K 13.3; Daniel's 3M 6.6; τοῦ βασιλέως 'close companion of the king' 3K 4.5, sim. Da 5.1 LXX (TH μεγιστάν 'courtier'), + συμπότης 'drinking-mate' 3M 2.25; Ec 4.4; ἑ. καὶ φίλος, opp. enemy, Si 37.2, φ. καὶ ἑ. 40.23; not every ἑ. is φ., 37.4, 5; applied to wild animals, ‖ ἀδελφός Jb 30.29.

2. subst.f. *man's extra-marital female companion in bed*: 2M 6.4, Pr 19.13. **b**. adj.: *s* γυνὴ ἑ. 'a woman of the streets' Si 41.20, Jd 11.2 (‖ πόρνη vs. 1).

Cf. συνήθης, φίλος, γυνή, παλλακή, συνεταιρίς, συνέταιρος: Schmidt 2.415-7, 3.464-8; Rengstorf, *TDNT* 2.699-701; Spicq 2.77-9.

ἔτασις, εως. f.ʃ
V.n. of ἐτάζω:

1. *investigation*: Jb 31.14 (‖ ἐπισκοπή), 12.6.

2. *act of subjecting to a trying experience*: Jb 10.17.

Cf. ἐτάζω, ἐτασμός.

ἐτασμός, οῦ. m.ʃ
trying experience: ἤτασεν ὁ θεὸς τὸν Φαραω ~οῖς μεγάλοις καὶ πονηροῖς Ge 12.17; τῆς καρδίας Ju 8.27; μετὰ ~ῶν καὶ μαστίγων 'with trials and scourges' 2M 7.37. Cf. ἐτάζω and πειρασμός.

ἑτερόζυγος, ον.ʃ
heterogeneous: *s* animal, Le 19.19, cf. Spicq 2.80f.

ἑτεροκλινῶς. adv.ʃ
in a double-minded fashion: 1C 12.34.

ἕτερος, α, ον.

1. *the other* of two: .. δύο ῥάβδους, τὴν μίαν .. καὶ τὴν ~αν .. '.. two rods, the one .. the other ..' Zc 11.7; Ge 42.13; ὁ ἕτερος 'the other party (in a dialogue)' 2M 3.13, 15.5.

2. *not the same as one already mentioned* or *implied*, 'other': φρέαρ ἕτερον 'another well' Ge 26.21; οἶκοι ~οι πολλοί 'many other houses' Am 3.15; τὰ τέκνα ὑμῶν τοῖς τέκνοις αὐτῶν, καὶ τὰ τέκνα αὐτῶν εἰς γενεὰν ~αν Jl 1.3; ἄγγελος ἕ. 'another angel' Zc 2.3; *other than intended* ἀγρὸν ~ον Ex 22.5. **b**. with a negative nuance of *not properly belonging, and thus foreign, alien, and unacceptable*: οὐκ ἀνοίσεις .. θυμίαμα ~ον 'thou shalt not offer .. incense' Ex 30.9, οὐ μὴ προσκυνήσητε θεῷ ~ῳ 34.14, cf. πῦρ ἀλλότριον Le 10.1, γλῶσσα ~α Is 28.11 (= ἀλλοιοτέρα γλ. Eus. 182).

3. *additional, extra*: ~ος υἱός 'another son' Ge 30.24; ἀργύριον ~ον 43.22; + numeral and the notion of addition reinforced by ἔτι– ἐπισχὼν ἔτι ἑπτὰ ἡμέρας ~ας 'having waited another seven days' 8.10; ἔτι ἑπτὰ ἔτη ~α 'seven more years' 29.27; ἑπτὰ βόες ~αι 41.19 (‖ vs. 3 ἄλλαι ἑπτὰ βόες); θεοὶ ~οι πλὴν ἐμοῦ Ex 20.3; ὀπίσω θεῶν ~ων ἀπὸ τῶν θεῶν τῶν ἐθνῶν τῶν περικύκλῳ ὑμῶν 'behind alien gods out of the gods of the nations around you' De 6.14.

4. *the following*, articular: ἐν τῷ ἐνιαυτῷ τῷ ~ῳ 'next year' Ge 17.21, ἡ γενεὰ ἡ ~α 'the next generaiton' De 29.21, cf. τῆς ~ας 'tomorrow' Pl., *Cr.* 44a.

***5**. in an expression of reciprocity: ἀποστησόμεθα ~ος ἀπὸ τοῦ ~ου 'we shall be removed from each other' Ge 31.49; εἶπαν ~ος τῷ ~ῳ 'they said to one another' Ex 16.15, Nu 14.4; ~ος πρὸς τὸν ~ον Is 13.8. Cf. ἐξ ἀλλήλων συνεχόμεναι ἑτέρα ἐκ τῆς ~ας 'joined with one another' Ex 26.3.

Cf. ἄλλος, ἀλλότριος. Under sense **2** is the word used as a synonym of ἄλλος (q.v.): see Schmidt 4.559-62, 564-7; Trench 357-61; Shipp 251-3.

ἑτέρωθεν. adv.ʃ
from the opposite side: 4M 6.4.

ἔτι

1. indicates recurrence, *again*: συνέλαβεν ἔ. 'she conceived again' Ge 29.34, Ho 1.6. **b**. indicates persistence of a condition, *still*: Ἔ. ὁ λαὸς πολύς Jd 7.4; τί αὐτῷ ἔ. καὶ εἰδώλοις; 'what has he got to do any more with idols?' Ho 14.9; esp. with a gen. abs., ἔ. ὄντος μου ἐν τῇ γῇ μου 'while I was still in my country' Jn 4.2; foll. by an apodotic καί— ἔ. αὐτοῦ λαλοῦντος καὶ Ραχηλ .. ἤρχετο 'while he was still talking, there was R. coming along' Ge 29.9; Ps 77.30f.; ἔ. ἐξ αἰῶνος 'already a long time now' 1E 2.19. **c**. w. neg.: οὐκ ἀποθανεῖται πᾶσα σὰρξ ἔτι 'no flesh will ever die again' Ge 9.11; οὐ καλέσει με ἔ. Βααλιμ 'she will no longer call me B.' Ho 2.16; Am 8.14, "will now be beyond repair" Je 19.11. **d**. reinforced by the following καί: οὐκ εἶδον αὐτὸν ἔ. καὶ νῦν 'I haven't seen him once ever since' Ge 44.28, ἔ. καὶ ἕως νυκτός 'even far into the night' Ps 15.7, ἔ. καὶ ἡ σάρξ μου 'my body (even after my death' 15.9.

2. w. a fut. verb, indicates that sth has not yet happened and will yet happen in future: ἔ. κατοικιῶ σε ἐν σκηναῖς 'I shall yet settle thee in tents' Ho 12.9, ἔτι κριθήσομαι Je 2.9; cf. ἔ. ὅρασις εἰς καιρὸν καὶ ἀνατελεῖ εἰς πέρας Hb 2.3; Ez 8.6, 13, 15.

3. w. a numeral or quantifier, denotes an additional amount: ἔ. ἑπτὰ ἔτη ἕτερα 'seven more years' Ge 29.27; ἔ. ἅπαξ 'yet again' Hg 2.6; *Hebraistically foll. by καί, e.g. ἔ. μικρὸν καὶ ἐκδικήσω 'yet a little while, and I will avenge' Ho 1.4, sim. Ex 17.4, Is 10.25, Je 28.33, 35.3, Ps 36.10 (last: ὀλίγον); ἔ. τρεῖς ἡμέραι καὶ μνησθήσεται Φαραω .. 'yet three days, and Ph. will remember ..' Ge 40.13; Jn 3.4; without καί and with a noun in the gen., ἔ. ἡμερῶν ἑπτὰ ἐγὼ ἐπάγω ὑετόν 'in another seven days I am going to bring water down' Ge 7.4, ἔ. τριῶν ἡμερῶν ἀφελεῖ .. 'in another three days he will behead ..' 40.19; Is 7.8. **b**. without a quantifier: ἐξανέτειλεν ὁ θεὸς ἔτι .. πᾶν ξύλον ὡραῖον 'God has also (i.e. in addition to other vegetation already created, 1.12) caused every kind of beautiful tree to sprout' Ge 2.9; εἰ ἔ. ὑπάρχει παρὰ σοί; 'do you have anything more?' Am 6.10; οὐκ ἔστιν ἔ. πλὴν ἐμοῦ 'there is none other than me' Jl 2.27; οὐκ ἔστι μετ' ἐμὲ ἔτι 'there is no more to come after me' Zp 3.1. **c**. with a sg. noun: οὐκ ἀνέστη ἔτι προφήτης .. ὡς Μωυσῆς 'there arose no more ..' De 34.10.

Cf. οὐκέτι, μηκέτι, ἄλλος.

ἑτοιμάζω: fut. ἑτοιμάσω, pass. ἑτοιμασθήσομαι; aor. ἡτοίμασα, subj. ἑτοιμάσω, impv. ἑτοίμασον, inf. ἑτοιμάσαι, mid. ἡτοιμασάμην, impv. ἑτοίμασαι, pass. ἡτοιμάσθην, impv. ἑτοιμάσθητι, subj. ἑτοιμασθῶ; pf.act. ἡτοίμακα, pass.3s ἡτοίμασται, ptc.pass. ἡτοιμασμένος, inf. act. ἑτοιμακέναι, pass. ἡτοιμάσθαι; plpf.mid./pass.3s ἡτοίμαστο.

I. **1**. *to prepare, get ready* for use or for a certain purpose: abs. Ge 43.16 (preparation of a dinner), for a battle Je 26.14; + acc. pers., ταύτην ἡτοίμασας τῷ παιδὶ σου Ισαακ Ge 24.14, αὐτὸν εἰς βασιλέα 2K 5.12, οὐχ ἑτοιμασθήσῃ σὺ (asking) οὐδὲ ἡ βασιλεία σου 1K 20.31*L*; food, Ex 16.5, τροφήν Ps 64.10; τὴν οἰκίαν καὶ τόπον ταῖς καμήλοις Ge 24.31, τράπεζαν 'table' Is 21.5, Ps 22.5; ἁγίασμα 'sanctuary' Ex 15.17; βωμούς Nu 23.4, θρόνον Ps 9.8; δῶρα 'gifts' Ge 43.25; ἐπὶ τὸ κακὸν τὰς χεῖρας αὐτῶν Mi 7.3; προφυλακάς 'outposts' Na 2.6; θυρεούς 'shields' Is 21.5, ὅπλα 'weapons' Je 28.12, τόξον .. σκεύη θανάτου 'bow .. deadly instruments' Ps 7.13; πόλιν Hb 2.12; γῆν Ez 20.6; θυσίαν Zp 1.7; τὴν ὁδὸν κυρίου Is 40.3; πτῶμα 'downfall' Jb 18.12; ***o*** sth incorporeal, τὰς καρδίας ὑμῶν πρὸς κύριον 1K 7.3, τὴν ψυχήν σου εἰς πειρασμόν Si 2.1. **b**. abs., *to make provisions for*: + dat., τῷ πτωχῷ Ps 67.11. **c**. *to store up* for future use: + acc. rei, χρυσίον Jb 27.16.

2. *to bring into existence, fashion*: + acc., τὴν γῆν, ἣν ἡτοίμασά σοι Ex 23.20, τὸν οὐρανόν Pr 8.27; οἰκουμένην ἐν τῇ σοφίᾳ αὐτοῦ Je 28.15 (|| ποιέω), ὄρη Ps 64.7, τῇ γῇ ὑετόν 146.8; || θεμελιόω 23.2, || οἰκοδομέω 88.3 (***o*** ἀλήθεια), Si 49.12 (***o*** ναός); + acc. pers., τὸ σπέρμα σου Ps 88.5, σεαυτῷ τὸν λαόν σου Ισραηλ 2K 7.24; ***o*** sth incorporeal, εὐθύτητας 'deeds of integrity' Ps 98.4 (|| ποιέω), θέλησις 'desire' Pr 8.35.

3. *to execute* a task: ***o*** temple cult, 2C 35.16.

***4**. calque of /hēḵin pnē/ *to prepare oneself firmly* to confront: ^ἐπὶ τὴν πόλιν^ Ez 4.3, εἰς τὸν συγκλεισμὸν Ιερουσαλημ 'the siege of J.' 4.7.

II. mid. **1**. *to make oneself ready, become ready* for action: ἑτοιμάζου ὄρθρισον 'Make yourself ready eagerly' Zp 3.7; + inf., ἑτοιμάζου τοῦ ἐπικαλεῖσθαι τὸν θεόν σου 'Get ready to invoke your god' Am 4.12; ἑτοιμάσθητι καὶ ἑτοίμασον σεαυτόν Ez 38.7.

2. *to make ready* for one's own use: + acc. μερίδα 'a portion' Na 3.8. **b**. *to store up* for one's own use: + acc., τροφήν 'foods' Pr 6.8, 30.25; ἐπισιτισμόν 'provisions' Jo 1.11.

Cf. ἕτοιμος, προετοιμάζω, ἑτοιμασία, εὐτρεπίζω, ἐπι~, παρασκευάζω, ποιέω **3**: Grundmann, *TDNT* 2.704-6.

ἑτοιμασία, ας. f.

1. *preparation*: ἐπὶ τὴν ~αν αὐτοῦ 'in preparation for it' Zc 5.11; τροφῆς 'of a meal' Wi 13.12.

***2**. *that which has been prepared and produced*: thought, wish, etc., τῆς καρδίας Ps 9.38 (|| ἐπιθυμία), 88.15; w. ref. to begotten offspring (?), Da 11.7 TH. **b**. a site for a building: 2E 2.68, 3.3. **c**. office of rulership: Da 11.21 TH (LXX τόπος).

Cf. ἑτοιμάζω, ἕτοιμος, παρασκευή.

ἕτοιμος, η [also -ος, e.g. Ju 9.6], ον.

prepared, ready: ***s*** pers., ὡς ὄρθρον ~ον εὑρήσομεν αὐτόν 'we shall find him as dawn about to break' Ho 6.3; εἰς τὴν ἡμέραν τὴν τρίτην Ex 19.11, εἰς θήραν '(to pounce) upon a game' Ps 16.12, εἰς μάστιγας 'to be whipped' 37.18; + inf. τοῦ πορεύεσθαι Mi 6.8, ἐλπίζειν Ps 111.7; ***s*** hum. heart, Ps 56.8; τὸ ὄρος Mi 4.1; ~ον κατοικητήριόν σου 'your ready dwelling' Ex 15.17, cf. οἶκον .. ἅγιόν σοι καὶ ~ον τοῦ κατασκηνῶσαι 2C 6.2 (*L*: κατοικῆσαι). **b**. subst.n., ἐν ~ῳ κεῖμαι 'to stand ready' 3M 5.26.

Cf. ἑτοιμάζω, ἑτοιμασία, ἑτοίμως.

ἑτοίμως. adv.

readily: 2E 7.17; ἑ. ἔχω + inf., 'am ready to do' Da 3.15 LXX (TH: + ἵνα). Cf. ἕτοιμος.

ἔτος, ους. n.

year: **a.** a period of time in which an event occurs, ἐν τῷ δευτέρῳ ἔτει 'in the second year' Hg 1.1; καθὼς τὰ ἔτη τὰ ἔμπροσθεν 'as in the former years' Ma 3.4. **b.** a length of time: τὰ ἔτη ἡμερῶν ζωῆς τινος 'the length of sbd's life' Ge 25.7; αἱ ἡμέραι τῶν ἐτῶν τῆς ζωῆς μου 'the total number of years of my life (up to now)' 47.9 (|| ἔτη ἡμερῶν τῆς ζωῆς σου vs. 8); || ἐνιαυτός– αἱ ἡμέραι Ιακωβ ἐνιαυτῶν τῆς ζωῆς αὐτοῦ ἑκατὸν τεσσαράκοντα ἑπτὰ ἔτη 47.28, ἔ. ἐξ ἔτους 'from year to year' Le 25.50 (|| ἐνιαυτὸν ἐξ ἐνιαυτοῦ vs. 53), τὸ ἔ. τὸ πεντηκοστὸν ἐνιαυτόν 25.10, ἔ. ἀφέσεως 25.13 (|| ἐνιαυτὸς ἀφέσεως vs. 10); ἱκανὰ ἔτη 'a good number of years' Zc 7.3. **c.** indicates one's age: εἶναι + gen., Νῶε ἦν ἐτῶν ἑξακοσίων 'Noah was 600 years old' Ge 7.6; ἑκατὸν καὶ εἴκοσι ἐτῶν ἐγώ εἰμι 'I am 120 years old' De 31.2; γίνομαι + gen., Ἐγένετο Αβραμ ἐτῶν ἐνενήκοντα ἐννέα '.. 99 years old' Ge 17.1.

Cf. ἐνιαυτός: Shipp 253f.

εὖ

advantageously: ὅπως ἂν εὖ μοι γένηται 'so that it would work out to my advantage' Ge 12.13, sim. De 4.40; ὅταν εὖ σοι γένηται 'when things begin to look up for you' Ge 40.14; ἵνα εὖ σοι ᾖ De 10.13; εὖ ᾖ ὑμῖν Je 7.23 (opp. κακῶς εἶναι ὑμῖν vs.10)); εὖ σε ποιήσω 'I will do you good' Ge 32.9, sim. Nu 10.29, De 30.5; καλῶς εὖ σε ποιήσω Ge 32.12; εὖ ἐποίει ὁ θεὸς ταῖς μαίαις 'God dealt well with the midwives' Ex 1.20, sim. De 28.63.

Cf. καλός, καλῶς, κακῶς

εὐαγγελία, ας. f. *

good news: 2K 18.20B.

εὐαγγελίζω: fut. εὐαγγελιῶ, εὐαγγελιοῦμαι; aor. εὐηγγελισάμην, inf. εὐαγγελίσασθαι, ptc. ~ισάμενος, impv.mid. ~ισαι, pass.3s~ισθήτω, subj. ~ίσωμαι.

1. mid. *to announce good news*: subst. ptc. || ἀνασῳζόμενος Jl 2.32; οἱ πόδες ~ζομένου (|| ἀπαγγέλλοντος εἰρήνην) Na 1.15; + dat. pers. and λέγων announcing the birth of a baby boy, Je 20.15. **b.** + dat. (recipient of message), πτωχοῖς 'to the poor' Is 61.1; and + ὅτι, 2K 18.19. **c.** + pseudo-acc. pers.: pass., Εὐαγγελισθήτω ὁ κύριος 'Congratulations, sir' 2K 18.31 (*L* Εὐαγγέλια, κύριέ μου). **d.** orally: ὁ εὐαγγελιζόμενος Σιων· ὕψωσον .. τὴν φωνήν σου Is 40.9; Ps 67.12.

2. *to announce*: abs., || ἀναγγέλλω 2K 1.20 (*L* ἀπα~); + acc. (message), ἀκοὴν εἰρήνης .. ἀγαθά Is 52.7, τὸ σωτήριον κυρίου 60.6, sim. Ps 95.2, δικαιοσύνην ἐν ἐκκλησίᾳ μεγάλῃ 39.10.

No clear distinction is identifiable between the act. and mid., cf. 1K 31.9 B act., *L* mid.

Cf. εὐαγγέλιον, ἀπαγγέλλω: Friedrich, *TDNT* 2.710-4; *ND* 3.12-5; Spicq 2.82-92.

εὐαγγέλιον, ου. n.ʃ

reward of good news received given to the messenger: pl., 2K 4.10. Cf. Deissmann 1923.312-4.

εὐαγγελισμός, οῦ. m. *

good news: 2K 18.20*L* (B: εὐαγγελία); ἡμέρα ~οῦ 4K 7.9*L* (B: εὐαγγελίας). Cf. εὐαγγελία.

εὐάλωτος, ον.ʃ

easy to be caught: Pr 30.28. Cf. ἁλίσκομαι.

εὐανδρία, ας. f.ʃ

valour: on battlefield, 2M 8.7, 15.17.

εὐαπάντητος, ον.ʃ

affable: *s* φιλανθρωπία, 2M 14.9.

εὐαρεστέω: fut. ~τήσω; aor. εὐηρέστησα, inf. ~ρεστῆσαι, ptc. ~ρεστήσας.*(?)

1. *to conduct oneself to the satisfaction of*: abs., Ps 34.14; ἐναντίον κυρίου 114.9; + dat., Ενωχ τῷ θεῷ Ge 5.22, Si 44.16; || χάριν εὑρίσκω Ge 6.9; dat. = hum. master, 39.4, Ex 21.8; + ἐναντίον τινός (= God), Ge 17.1 = + dat. *and* ἐναντίον τινός, 48.15; ἐνώπιον τοῦ θεοῦ Ps 55.14.

2. intr. *to be satisfied*: *s* God, *+ ἐν Jd 10.16 A.

Cf. εὐάρεστος, ἀρέσκω, εὐδοκέω.

εὐάρεστος, ον.ʃ

acceptable: *s* hum., θεῷ Wi 4.10; τί ~όν ἐστιν παρὰ σοί [= God] 9.10. Cf. εὐαρεστέω, δεκτός.

εὐάρμοστος, ον.

harmonious: *s* harp, Ez 33.32; human relationship, 4M 14.3.

εὖγε interj.

Indicates the speaker's assessment that sth is justly or well executed: Jb 39.25; often a triumphant cry of malicious joy, 'Serves you right!,' Εὖγε 31.29, and repeated, Εὖγε εὖγε Ps 34.21, 39.16, 69.4; Εὖγε εὖγε τῇ ψυχῇ ἡμῶν 'we're justly saved' 34.25; Εὖγε εὖγε τοῖς βδελύγμασιν οἴκου Ισραηλ 'Serves the house of Is. right for their abominations' Ez 6.11. **b.** adv.: εὖ. γέγονεν εἰς σφαγήν 'they have been rightly doomed to a slaughter' Ez 21.15; 26.2, 36.2.

εὐγένεια, ας. f.

noble birth: Si 22.8¶ (:: δυσγένεια vs.7), 26.20¶, Wi 8.3. **b.** *gait and appearance typical of noble birth*: 4M 8.4.

Cf. εὐγενής, εὐγενίζω, δυσγένεια.

εὐγενής, ές.

1. *noble of birth*: *s* hum., Jb 1.3; + μεγαλόφρων 'courageous' 4M 6.5; συγγένεια 'kinship' 10.3, ἀδελφότης 'family ties' 10.15.

2. *typical of noble, lofty ideals*: *s* στρατεία 'battle' 4M 9.24, γνώμη 'decision' 9.27.

Cf. εὐγένεια, εὐγενῶς, μεγαλόφρων: Spicq 2.93-6.

εὐγενίζω: aor.ptc. εὐγενίσας.ʃ

to ennoble: + double acc., εὐγενῆ τὴν ἐξουσίαν 'command the respect due to his high office' 2M 10.13. Cf. εὐγένεια.

εὐγενῶς, adv.

nobly: to die, 2M 14.42, 4M 6.22; to bear torture, 9.22. Cf. εὐγενής.

εὔγεως, ων.ʃ

of good soil: *s* κλῆρος 'plot of land' Si 26.20¶.

εὐγνωμοσύνη, ης. f.ʃ

goodwill, good and benevolent intention: Es E 6. Cf. εὐμένεια.

εὔγνωστος, ον.

well-known: *s* σοφία, + dat. pers., Pr 3.15; hum., 26.26. Cf. γνωστός, ἄγνωστος, ὀνομαστός.

εὐδία, ας. f.ʃ

fine weather: Si 3.15. Cf. Shipp 255.

εὐδοκέω: fut. εὐδοκήσω; aor. εὐδόκησα, inf. ~δοκῆσαι, subj. εὐδοκήσω, impv. εὐδόκησον, pass. εὐδοκήθην. *(?). The augment is sometimes ηὐ-.

1. *to be favourably disposed, pleased*: abs., Ps 76.8; * ἔν τινι – οὐκ εὐδοκεῖ ἡ ψυχή μου ἐν αὐτῷ Hb 2.4, cf. ὁ ἀγαπητός μου εἰς ὃν εὐδόκησεν ἡ ψυχή μου Mt 12.18, apparently alluding to ὁ ἐκλεκτός μου, προσεδέξατο αὐτὸν ἡ ψ. μου Is 42.1; Hg 1.8, Ma 2.17, 1M 8.1; ἐξείλατό με, ὅτι εὐδόκησεν ἐν ἐμοί 'you rescued me, because ..' 2K 22.20 (*L* ἠθέλησέ με), sim. Ps 43.4. The construction w. ἐν is likely a Hebraism; cf. Helbing, *Kasus.*, 263f. **b**. + ἐπί τινι (pers.): Ju 15.10, Je 2.19. **c**. + dat., τοῖς ἔργοις αὐτῆς 'with its effects' 1E 4.39; τῇ λατρείᾳ αὐτοῦ 'his religion' 1M 1.43.

2. *to be satisfied, happy* about a situation: abs., Ge 24.26, 48, Si 45.19. **b**. + acc. rei, τὸν βίον Jb 14.6.

3. *to accept favourably* or *approvingly*: εὐδόκησεν ὁ βασιλεύς 'the king consented' 1M 11.29, εὐδόκησαν οὕτως 'they agreed thereto' To 5.17 𝔊[I]; + acc. pers., εὐδοκήσεις με Ge 33.10; εὐδοκήσει ἡ γῆ τὰ σάββατα 'the land will welcome its sabbaths' Le 26.34 (|| προσδέχομαι 26.43), sim. 1E 1.55; τὴν γῆν Ps 84.2; + acc. rei, τὰς ἁμαρτίας αὐτῶν 'their penalties' Le 26.41 (*s* hum., and see Milgrom 2001. 2333); ὁλοκαυτώματα οὐκ εὐδοκήσεις Ps 50.18 (|| θέλω), θυσίαν δικαιοσύνης 50.21; τὴν δόξαν σου '(consented to confer) your glory' 3M 2.16. **b**. *to consent* to do: abs., Jd 11.17B (|| ἀκούω; A θέλω); + inf., ηὐδόκουν φιλεῖν πέλματα ποδῶν αὐτοῦ 'I would have consented to kiss the soles of his feet' Es C 6, αὐλισθῆναι 'to spend the night' Jd 19.10 B (A: θέλω), εὐδόκησον .. τοῦ ῥύσασθαί με 'please, rescue me' Ps 39.14, δουλεύειν τῷ πατρί σου 1M 6.23; εὐδόκησαν τοῦ εἶναι αὐτῶν Σίμωνα ἡγούμενον 'they agreed that S. should be their leader' 14.41 (|| ὅπως + subj., vs. 42f.), ηὐδόκησας ναὸν .. ἐν ἡμῖν γενέσθαι 'you accepted the idea that there should be a temple .. among us' 2M 14.35. Cf. ἐπινεύω **2**, ἐπιχωρέω. **c**. *to be accommodating*: *s* ruler to his subjects, 2C 10.7. **d**. *to choose as preferable*: + acc., Si 15.17; + inf., ἤ 'rather than' 25.16.

4. pass., *to prosper*: *s* pers., 1C 29.23.

Cf. εὐδοκία, δέχομαι, θέλω, προσδέχομαι: MM, s.v.; Schrenk, *TDNT* 2.738-40; Lee 97; Spicq 2.99-103.

εὐδοκία, ας. f.*

1. *favourable estimation*: ὅπλον ~ας 'weapon conferred as a mark of favour' Ps 5.13; in God's eyes, 1C 16.10; Ποιήσατε μετ' ἐμοῦ ~αν (B: εὐλογίαν) 4K 18.31*L*. **b**. *that which wins sbd's favourable estimation*: God's, Si 1.27, 32.5, Ps 140.5. **c**. *choosing a course of action one favours*: Si 15.15.

2. *state of being satisfied*: καιρὸς ~ας 'the time of (my) contentment' Ps 68.14; 105.4; ~αν ἐπιθυμίας 'satisfaction of desire' Si 18.31; ἐπὶ μικρῷ καὶ μεγάλῳ 'whether with little or much' 29.23.

Cf. εὐδοκέω: Spicq 2.103-6.

εὐδοκιμέω: fut.pass. ~μηθήσομαι; aor.ptc. ~μήσας.ʃ

1, *to be genuine and authentic*, not counterfeit: *s* silver (ἀργύριον) Ge 43.23.

2. *to appreciate as valuable*: pass., πάντα ἐν καιρῷ εὐδοκιμηθήσεται 'everything will prove its value in its time' Si 39.34; ὑπὲρ ἀμφότερα 'above both, more than both' 40.25; 41.16.

3. *to be of good repute, distinguish oneself*: περὶ τὴν σοφίαν Si prol. II.

Cf. εὐδόκιμος.

εὐδόκιμος, ον.ʃ

in good repute: ~οι καθειστήκεισαν 'stood in good repute' 3M 3.5. Cf. εὐδοκιμέω.

εὐδράνεια, ας. f.ʃ *

bodily strength: Wi 13.19. Cf. ἀδράνης, κράτος.

εὐειδής, ές.ʃ

good-looking, 'handsome': *s* youth, Da 1.3 LXX (TH καλὸς τῇ ὄψει). Cf. καλός, αἰσχρός: Schmidt 4.354f.

εὐεκτέω.ʃ

to be of sound condition: physically, Pr 17.22.

εὔελπις, ι; gen. ~ιδος. adj.ʃ

full of hope: *s* hum., Wi 12.19, + inf., 3M 2.33. **b**. *offering good prospect*, 'promising': *s* hum., Pr 19.18.

εὐεξία, ας. f.ʃ

good physical condition: + ὑγίεια Si 30.15, cf. Pl. *es*. 444d, 559a. Cf. ἕξις.

εὐεργεσία, ας. f.
kind nature: God's, Wi 16.11, ‖ ἔλεος Si 51.8; hum., 2M 6.13; pl., *kind deeds* (by God) Ps 77.11, Si prol. II (:: κακά), 2M 9.26 (by king). Cf. εὐεργετέω, φιλανθρωπία: Spicq 2.107f.

εὐεργετέω: fut.pass. εὐεργετηθήσομαι; aor. εὐηργέτησα, ptc. εὐεργετήσας, pass. εὐεργετήθην.
to show kindness to: + acc. pers. and *s* God, Ps 12.6, 56.3, 2M 10.38; *s* hum. ruler, Es E 2; opp. κολάζω 'to punish' 4M 8.6. Cf. εὐεργεσία, εὐεργέτημα, ἀγαθύνω: Spicq 2.108f.

εὐεργέτημα, ατος. n.ʃ
deed beneficial to sbd else: done out of goodwill and kindness: Es 6.4 *L*; opp. δυσπέτημα 'misfortune' 2M 6.20. Cf. εὐεργετέω, δυσπέτημα.

εὐεργέτης, ου. m.
benefactor: hum., Es E 3, + σωτήρ 13; τῆς πόλεως 2M 4.2 (+ κηδεμών 'guardian'); + βασιλεύς 3M 3.19. Cf. εὐεργετικός: Spicq 2.109-13; Passoni dell'Acqua 1976.

εὐεργετικός, ή, όν.ʃ
beneficent: *s* spirit of Wisdom, Wi 7.22. Cf. εὐεργέτης.

εὔζωνος, ον.
well-girdled: *s* robber, Si 36.31; soldier, εἰς μάχην Jo 4.13, cf. *BA* ad loc. and *BA* 6.55.

εὐήθης, ες.ʃ
absurd: *s* act, 2M 2.32. Cf. μωρός: Schmidt 3.648-50.

εὐήκοος, ον.ʃ
willing to give ear, 'obedient': *s* heavenly bodies, Ep Je 59; hum. ears, Pr 25.12; hum. soul, PSol 18.4. Cf. Naumann 38.

εὐημερέω: aor.ptc. εὐημερήσας; pf.ptc. εὐημερηκώς.ʃ
1. *to be in good cheer*: 2M 13.16.
2. *to be successful* in sth: abs. 2M 12.11; ἐπὶ τῇ .. διαφθορᾷ 'in the destruction' 8.35.

εὐημερία, ας. f.ʃ
success: military, 2M 5.6 (:: δυσημερία); pl. 8.8; + νίκη 'victory' 10.28. **b**. *general welfare*: 2M 14.14 (:: ἀτυχίαι καὶ συμφοραaί 'misfortunes and calamities'), 3M 3.11.
Cf. εὐοδία.

εὔηχος, ον.ʃ
emitting agreeable sound: *s* cymbal, Ps 150.5; subst.n.pl., Jb 30.7¶.

εὐθαλέω.ʃ
to bloom, thrive: materially and *s* king, Da 4.1 TH (‖ εὐθηνέω and LXX εὐθηνέω). Cf. εὐθαλής, εὐδοκέω, εὐθηνέω, θάλλω.

εὐθαλής, ές.ʃ
full of vitality: *s* τὰ φύλλα αὐτῆς 'its leaves' Da 4.18 TH. Cf. εὐθαλέω, εὐθηνέω.

εὐθαρσής, ές.
feeling encouraged: *s* hum., 1E 8.27 (‖ κραταιοῦμαι 2E 7.28). Cf. θαρσέω.

εὐθαρσῶς. adv.ʃ
courageously: 2M 7.10.

εὔθετος, ον.ʃ
well-suited: *s* καιρός '(opportune) moment' Ps 31.6, ἡμέρα Su 15 TH.

εὐθέως. adv.
shortly after the main event: Jb 5.3. Mostly w. ref. to a past event exc. Wi 5.12, 2M 6.13. Cf. II εὐθύς, αὐθωρί, αὐτίκα, συντόμως.

εὐθηνέω: aor. εὐθήνησα, inf. εὐθηνῆσαι.
to thrive, flourish: materially, ἦν Ιερουσαλημ κατοικουμένη καὶ εὐθηνοῦσα 'Jerusalem was inhabited and thriving' Zc 7.7; *s* king, ἐπὶ τοῦ θρόνου μου Da 4.1 LXX (‖ εἰρηνεύω; TH εὐθαλέω); the wicked, Je 12.1; fruit, ὁ καρπὸς εὐθηνῶν αὐτῇ 'its fruits being plentiful' Ho 10.1; ἄμπελος 'vine' Ps 127.3; ξύλον εὐθηνοῦν παρ' ὕδατα 'a tree thriving by waters' Je 17.8.
Cf. εὐθηνία, ἀνοικοδομέω, εὐθαλέω, εὐπαθέω, θάλλω, κατορθόω, κατευθύνω.

εὐθηνία, ας. f.
material *prosperity*: of a country, πολλή Ge 41.29 (‖ πλησμονή vs. 30); τὰ ἑπτὰ ἔτη τῆς ~ας, ἃ ἐγένοντο ἐν γῇ Αἰγύπτῳ 41.53; ‖ πλησμονὴ ἄρτων 'abundance of foods' Ez 16.49; ‖ πίονες χῶραι 'fat lands' Da 11.24 TH; personal, ἐν ~ίᾳ μου Ps 29.7; ‖ εἰρήνη 121.6, 7. Cf. εὐθηνέω, εἰρήνη, εὐοδία, μακάριος, πίων, πλησμονή: Schmidt 4.406f.

εὐθής, ές. Some declined forms are indistinguishable from those of εὐθύς, an older and standard form, see Thack. § 12.7. *
1, *not given to or characterised by devious acts*, 'morally upright': *s* God, χρηστὸς καὶ εὐ. ὁ κύριος 'Gracious ..' Ps 24.8; God's words, ὁ λόγος τοῦ κυρίου 32.4 (‖ ἐν πίστει); man's spirit, πνεῦμα εὐθές 50.12 (‖ καρδία καθαρά); God's judgement (κρίσις) 118.137; hum., καρδίᾳ Ps 7.11, 31.11, μετ' αὐτοῦ [= God] 77.37; hum. deeds, ποιῆσαι τὸ ~ές Je 41.15; Jd 17.6 B (A: ἀγαθός); τί ~ὲς ἐν ἐντολαῖς σου 'what is right according to ..' Wi 9.9.
2. *conforming to well-grounded assessment and sound judgement*: οὐκ εὐ. ὁ λόγος ὑμῶν, ὃν ἐλαλήσατε .. Ju 8.11; *s* potential wife, Jd 14.3 B (A: ἀρέσκω).
3. *without curve or bend*: *s* τρίβος Ps 26.11; δι' εὐθείας (sc. ὁδοῦ) Is 59.14, opp. σκολιός 'rugged (terrain)' 40.4, 42.16; ἐπ' εὐθείας 'by taking the direct route' Jo 8.14.
Cf. εὐθύς, σκολιός. Del. Ju 10.16, Es 8.5 v.l.

εὐθίκτως. adv.ʃ *
to the point: τῇ συντάξει 'of this (written) work' 2M 15.38.

εὔθραυστος, ον.ʃ
easily broken, 'fragile': *s* clay idols, Wi 15.13. Cf. θραύω.

εὔθυμος, ον.ʃ
feeling reassured and hopeful: *s* hum., 2M 11.26. Cf. Spicq 2.114-7.

εὔθυνα, ας. f.ʃ
punishment: 3M 2.23, 3.28. Cf. εὐθύνω, κόλασις, τιμωρία.

εὐθύνω: fut. ~θυνῶ; aor.inf. εὐθῦναι, impv. εὔθυνον, subj. εὐθύνω, pass. εὐ/ηὐθύνθην.

1. *to cause to move on a straight line*: *o* ass, Nu 22.23; metaph., τὴν καρδίαν ὑμῶν πρὸς κύριον Jo 24.23, χεῖρας Si 38.10, τὰς ὁδούς σου 2.6, διαβήματα 'steps' Pr 20.24, τὴν φιλίαν 'the friendly relationship' Si 6.17.

2. *to punish*: + acc. pers., 3M 2.17 (|| ἐκδικέω), περί τινος (offence) PSol 9.7.

*__3__. pass. *to be considered acceptable, to be approved*: *s* state of affairs, ἐν ὀφθαλμοῖς αὐτοῦ 1K 18.20 (*L*: ἀρέσκω), || ὁ λόγος vs. 26; potential wife, ἐν ὀφθαλμοῖς τινος Jd 14.7 B (A: ἀρέσκω).

Cf. εὐθύς, κατευθύνω, εὔθυνα, κολάζω, τιμωρέω.

εὐθύς, εῖα, ύ.

I. *having no curves* or *undulations*, 'straight': *s* way, εὐθεῖαι αἱ ὁδοὶ τοῦ κυρίου 'the ways of the Lord are straight' Ho 14.10; ὁδὸς εὐσεβῶν εὐθεῖα ἐγένετο 'the way of the god-fearing has become plain sailing' Is 26.7, ~ας ποιεῖτε τὰς τρίβους τοῦ θεοῦ 40.3; sc. ὁδόν– ἐπορεύθη ~εῖαν 'moved straight' Nu 23.3, ἀπάγαγέ με ~εῖαν πρὸς .. 'Take me straight to ..' To 7.1 𝔊[II]; πορευσόμεθα ἐπ' ~εῖαν 'we shall take a direct route' Ge 33.12, κατ' εὐθεῖαν 'straight, by a straight route' Si 4.18, ἆρον εἰς ~εῖαν τοὺς ὀφθαλμούς σου 'raise your eyes straight' Je 3.2; opp. σκολιός Is 40.4, 42.16; κατ' εὐθύ 'on level ground' (as against in mountains) 3K 21.23, 25; κατ' εὐθὺ αὐτῆς by (the gate) lying straight ahead of it' Ez 46.9. **b**. fig. *in order, well arranged*: ~εῖα πάντα μετ' αὐτοῦ ποιήσει 'will straighten out everything with him' Da 11.17 TH.

2. *not given to devious acts*, 'morally upright': οἱ εὐθεῖς τῇ καρδίᾳ 'the upright of heart' Ps 63.11 +. **b**. 'fair': *s* ἡ ὁδὸς τοῦ κυρίου Ez 33.18, δικαιώματα κυρίου Ps 18.9.

II. adv., καὶ εὐθύς, *immediately thereafter*, marking a new turning-point in a narrative and foll. by an aorist: καὶ ~ὺς φωνὴ θεοῦ ἐγένετο πρὸς αὐτόν Ge 15.4; following the main clause, 38.29, cf. Jb 3.11. Cf. Muraoka - Porten, p. 310, n. 1210.

b. without καί and foll. by an impf.: ~ὺς Ῥεβέκκα ἐξεπορεύετο .. Ge 24.45.

Cf. εὐθύνω, κατευθύνω, εὐθέως, εὐθής, καμπύλος, σκαμβός, σκολιός, ὀρθός, παραχρῆμα.

εὐθύτης, ητος. f.

1. *straight gait without curves*: ἐπιβαίνω ἐν ~ητι 'to walk straight' Si 51.15; in same sense, εἰς ~ητα Ct 7.10.

2. moral *integrity*: of a judge, Ps 9.9 (|| δικαιοσύνη), of God as judge, 66.5; of the pious, 25.12; καρδίας 3K 3.6, PSol 2.15; pl., deeds of integrity, Ps 98.4 (|| κρίσις καὶ δικαιοσύνη).

Cf. εὐθύς.

εὐιλατεύω: fut. ~τεύσω; aor.inf. ~τεῦσαι.ʃ *
to be very merciful: *s* God and + dat. hum. De 29.20, + dat. rei, ταῖς ἀνομίαις σου Ps 102.3. Cf. εὐίλατος, ἐλεέω.

εὐίλατος, ον.ʃ
very merciful: *s* God and subst., εὐιλάτου ἐτύχομεν 'we won his mercies' 1E 8.53; ὁ θεός, σὺ εὐ. ἐγίνου αὐτοῖς Ps 98.8. Cf. εὐιλατεύω, ἵλεως, οἰκτίρμων.

εὐκαιρία, ας. f.
opportune moment for action: Ps 9.10; ἐὰν ~ας τύχω 'if I find an opportunity' 1M 11.42; σχολῆς 'free time essential (for intellectual development)' Si 38.24. Cf. εὔκαιρος: Spicq 2.118-20.

εὔκαιρος, ον.

1. *timely*: *s* feeding, Ps 103.27. **b**. subst.n.sg. = εὐκαιρία 2M 14.29.

2. *well suited*: *s* μέρος 'advantageous spot' 2M 15.20, τόπος 3M 5.44.

Cf. εὐκαιρία, εὐκαίρως, ἄκαιρος.

εὐκαίρως. adv.ʃ
in good time: Si 18.22. Cf. εὔκαιρος, ἀκαίρως.

εὐκατάλλακτος, ον.ʃ
easily appeased: *s* God, 3M 5.13. Cf. καταλλάσσω.

εὐκαταφρόνητος, ον.ʃ
despicable, little thought of: *s* hum. and || μικρός Je 29.16; Da 11.21 LXX (TH: ἐξουδενοῦμαι). Cf. καταφρονέω.

εὐκίνητος, ον.ʃ
agile: *s* spirit of Wisdom, Wi 7.22. **b**. adv. subst. n., *with agility*: of carpenter, || εὐμαθῶς 'skilfully' Wi 13.11, cf. Pesh. /ḥfiṭā'iṯ/ 'with zeal.'

εὐκλεής, ές.ʃ
having attained good reputation: *s* βακτηρία 'staff' Je 31.17, καρπός Wi 3.15. Cf. εὔκλεια, ἀκλεής, δυσκλεής, κλέος.

εὔκλεια, ας. f.
good reputation, 'fame': Wi 8.18; μετ' ~ας 'honourably' 2M 6.19. Cf. εὐκλεής.

εὐκληματέω.ʃ *
to have vigorously growing branches: *s* vine, ἄμπελος εὐκληματοῦσα Ho 10.1. Cf. κλῆμα.

εὔκολος, ον.ʃ
easy to understand: *s* λόγοι 2K 15.3B.

εὐκοπία, ας. f.ʃ
easiness of execution: 2M 2.25. Cf. εὔκοπος.

εὔκοπος, ον.ʃ
easy: *s* task, Si 22.15, 1M 3.18. Cf. εὐκοπία, εὐχερής, χαλεπός.

εὐκοσμέω.ʃ*
to behave in orderly manner: 1M 8.15. Cf. εὐκοσμία.

εὐκοσμία, ας. f.ʃ
orderly behaviour, good conduct in public: Si 35.2; ἐν ~ᾳ 'with decorum' 45.7. Cf. εὐκοσμέω.

εὔκυκλος, ον.ʃ
bent well and skilfully: *s* bow, Wi 5.21.

εὐλάβεια, ας. f.ʃ
1. *discretion*: Jo 22.24, Pr 28.14.
2. *dread and anxiety*: || δεῖμα 'dread' Wi 17.8.
Cf. εὐλαβέομαι, φόβος: Trench 36f.

εὐλαβέομαι: fut. εὐλαβηθήσομαι; aor. εὐλαβήθην, ptc. εὐλαβηθείς, impv. εὐλαβήθητι.
1. *to treat with reverent regard and awe*: + acc. pers., De 2.4 (|| φοβέομαι); + acc. dei, Na 1.7, Je 5.22; τίνα εὐλαβηθεῖσα ἐφοβήθης ἀπὸ ἀνθρώπου; Is 51.12, sim. 57.11; τὸ ὄνομα αὐτοῦ Ma 3.16 (|| φοβέομαι τὸν κύριον); + ἀπό - ἀπὸ προσώπου κυρίου Zp 1.7, ἀπὸ τοῦ ὀνόματος κυρίου 3.12.
2. *not to venture* (to do), *to refrain from* (doing) *out of a sense of awe*: + inf., εὐλαβεῖτο κατεμβλέψαι ἐνώπιον τοῦ θεοῦ 'he dared not look God straight' Ex 3.6; out of fear, Si 29.7, 1M 12.42.
3. *to act cautiously* not to do sth: Si 18.27; + μή and subj., Ep Je 4.
***4**. *to feel anxious and fearful*: *s* hum., "as a leaf shaken by the wind" Jb 13.25; Si 22.22; *s* καρδία 26.5 (|| φοβέομαι); μὴ οὐκ ἔχῃ 'that he might not have' 1M 3.30, μήποτε οὐκ ἐάσῃ 'that he might not allow' 12.40; + acc. rei, πολυπλήθειαν 'great numbers' 2M 8.16, οὐδέν (or: adv., 'in no way') Si 31.16 (|| δειλιάω); ἀπὸ προσώπου τινός (pers.), 1K 18.15, 29, Je 22.25, Si 7.6.
Cf. εὐλάβεια, εὐλαβής, δι~, ὑπερευλαβέομαι, δειλιάω, σέβομαι, φοβέομαι, φυλάσσω: van Herten 28-55; Bultmann, *TDNT* 2.751-4; Naumann 38f.; Kilpatrick 1990.27.

εὐλαβής, ές.ʃ
1. *cautious*: ἀπὸ τῶν ἀκαθαρσιῶν 'about the impurities' Le 15.31.
2. *devout*: ἀπόλωλεν εὐ. ἀπὸ τῆς γῆς Mi 7.2 (εὐσεβής v.l., || κατορθῶν).
Cf. εὐλαβέομαι, εὐσεβής: Trench 172-80; Spicq 1985.230f.

εὐλαβῶς. adv.ʃ
cautiously: διὰ τὸ εὐ. ἔχειν ἑαυτοῖς βοηθῆσαι 'for being hesitant about defending themselves' 2M 6.11.

εὔλαλος, ον.ʃ
eloquent: *s* hum., Jb 11.2; tongue, Si 6.5. Cf. ἰσχνόφωνος, μογιλάλος.

εὐλογέω: fut. ~ήσω, pass. ~γηθήσομαι; aor. εὐλόγησα, subj. εὐλογήσω, impv. εὐλόγησον, opt.3s. εὐλογήσαι, pass. ~θείη, inf. εὐλογηθῆναι; pf. εὐλόγηκα, pass. εὐλόγημαι, ptc. εὐλογημένος, ηὐλο~.
1. *to pronounce words held to confer special favour or well-being upon* (+ acc.): *s* God, Ge 1.22, 28; εὐλογήσω τοὺς εὐλογοῦντάς σε 12.3 (:: καταράομαι); + acc. cogn., εὐλόγησέν σε εὐλογίαν οὐρανοῦ ἄνωθεν 49.25; priest, εὐλόγησεν τὸν Αβραμ καὶ εἶπεν Εὐλογημένος Αβραμ τῷ θεῷ τῷ ὑψίστῳ 14.19, ὑπὸ κυρίου PSol 8.34; aged father to son, εὐλογήσῃ σε ὁ ψυχή μου Ge 27.4; ἐπὶ τῷ ὀνόματι ^τοῦ θεοῦ^ De 21.5; *o* τὴν ἡμέραν τὴν ἑβδόμην 'the seventh day (of the creation)' and + ἁγιάζω Ge 2.3, Ex 20.11; ἀγρός 'agricultural field' Ge 27.27; ἄρτον .. οἶνον .. ὕδωρ Ex 23.25; τὴν ἰσχὺν αὐτοῦ De 33.11; ἔτη δικαίου 'the years of a righteous person' 1K 2.9; pers., Ge 9.1, 12.3; soul, Ps 48.19; name, Is 65.15; *s* animals, Is 43.20. **b**. with dat. pers. of sbd capable of conferring a favour – Εὐλογημένος Αβραμ τῷ θεῷ τῷ ὑψίστῳ 14.19 (|| vs. 20 εὐλογητός *s* God); Jd 17.2, Ru 3.10, 1K 23.21, Ps 113.23.
2. *to say words of praise for*: abs., Hg 2.19; + acc., κύριον τὸν θεόν Ge 24.48, De 8.10, τὸ ὄνομα αὐτοῦ [= God's] Ps 95.2, sim. 144.21, but τῷ ὀνόματι κυρίου 'by invoking .. (?)' PSol 6.4; + dat., τῷ θεῷ Si 50.22, τοῖς ματαίοις ἐπὶ τῇ .. ἀπωλείᾳ 'to the vain gods over the destruction of ..' 3M 6.11, τῷ ὀνόματι κυρίου Si 51.12; εὐλογημένος κύριος Je 38.23, sim. Da 3.53 TH (LXX εὐλογητός); || αἰνέω Is 38.18, Je 4.2, Ps 144.2; + ὑμνέω To 12.6 𝔊II. **b**. sarcastic and effectively = *to curse*: acc. (God), Jb 1.11, toned down to εἶπόν τι ῥῆμα εἰς κύριον 2.9e; 3K 20.10.
3. *to make successful* or *well-off*: + acc. pers. and *s* God - ποιήσω σε εἰς ἔθνος μέγα καὶ εὐλογήσω σε καὶ μεγαλυνῶ τὸ ὄνομά σου Ge 12.2; εὐλογῶν εὐλογήσω σε καὶ πληθύνων πληθυνῶ τὸ σπέρμα σου .. καὶ κληρονομήσει τὸ σπέρμα σου τὰς πόλεις τῶν ὑπεναντίων 22.17; ὁ θεός μου εὐλογήσαι σε καὶ αὐξήσαι σε καὶ πληθύναι σε, καὶ ἔσῃ εἰς συναγωγὰς ἐθνῶν 28.3; ἔσομαι μετὰ σοῦ καὶ εὐλογήσω σε 26.3; by giving a farmer abundant

crop, 26.12; τῇ σῇ εἰσόδῳ 'through your arrival' 30.27.

4. *to make happy*: + acc. pers. and *s* God, in enabling an old woman to bear a child, Ge 17.16.

Cf. εὐλογία, εὐλογητός, ἐνευλογέω, κατευλογέω, αἰνέω, κακολογέω, καταράομαι, ἐπικαταράομαι: Bickerman 1962.524-32; Ledogar 1967. 50-5; *ND* 4.151; Van den Eynde; Aitken 2007 104; Tomson 2007.35-40.

εὐλογητός, ή, όν.*

1. *praiseworthy, worthy of adoration*: *s* God and in spontaneous exclamation, ~ὸς κύριος Ge 9.26; κύριος ὁ θεός 24.27; ὁ θεὸς ὁ ὕψιστος 14.20 (ǁ vs. 19 εὐλογημένος said of man); Zc 11.5; *s* hum., Ge 12.2, τῷ κυρίῳ 1K 15.13 (*L* εὐλογημένος, see Brock 1996.276), Ru 2.20.

2. *happy, well-off*: *s* hum., ποιήσω σε εἰς ἔθνος μέγα καὶ εὐλογήσω σε καὶ μεγαλυνῶ τὸ ὄνομά σου, καὶ ἔσῃ ~ός Ge 12.2; ὑπὸ κυρίου 26.29; τῷ θεῷ 43.28; παρὰ πάντα τὰ ἔθνη 'more than all the nations' De 7.14.

Cf. εὐλογέω, ἐπευκτός, μακάριος.

εὐλογία, ας. f.

1. *words of adoration*: directed to God, Jl 2.14; + αἴνεσις Ne 9.5.

2. *pronouncement of well-being* made for other persons: De 23.5 (:: κατάρα), πατρός Si 3.9.

3. *blissful state*: κατάραν καὶ οὐκ ~αν Ge 27.12; ἐγενήθη εὐ. κυρίου ἐν πᾶσιν τοῖς ὑπάρχουσιν αὐτῷ 39.5; οὐρανοῦ .. γῆς .. μαστῶν καὶ μήτρας 49.25; πατρός σου καὶ μητρός σου 49.26; ἔσεσθε ἐν ~ᾳ Zc 8.13 (:: κατάρα); ἐπικαταράσομαι τὴν ~αν ὑμῶν 'I will turn your bliss into a curse' Ma 2.2. **b**. Obj. of δίδωμι Ex 32.29; De 11.26 (:: κατάρα); λαμβάνω, φέρω Ge 33.11; ἐκχέω Ma 3.10; ἀποστέλλω Le 25.21; εὐλογέω Ge 49.25, Nu 23.11. **c**. granted by God: κυρίου De 33.13, παρὰ κυρίου 33.23; Le 25.21.

4. *that which makes for well-being*: "if I will not open the torrents of heaven and pour out for you my blessing (ἐκχεῶ ὑμῖν τὴν ~αν μου)" Ma 3.10; gifts, λάβε τὰς ~ας μου, ἃς ἤνεγκά σοι Ge 33.11.

Cf. εὐλογέω, ἀρά, κατάρα: Renehan 2.73f.; Aitken 2007.126f.

εὐλογιστία, ας. f.

1. *sound and thorough consideration*: 4M 5.22.

2. *eloquence*: 4M 8.15, but poss. **1**.

εὐμαθῶς. adv.ʃ

by using good, professional skills: Wi 13.11.

εὐμεγέθης, ες.ʃ

of good size: *s* hum. 1K 9.2, giants Ba 3.26. Cf. μέγας, ἐπιμήκης.

εὐμελής, ές.ʃ

melodious: *s* sound of birds, Wi 17.18. Cf. μέλος.

εὐμένεια, ας. f.ʃ

goodwill, favourable disposition: 2M 6.29 (:: δυσμένεια). Cf. εὐμενής, εὐμενῶς, εὐγνωμοσύνη, δυσμένεια.

εὐμενής, ές.ʃ

favourably disposed: *s* hum., πρός τινα 2M 12.31; 13.26. Cf. εὐμένεια, δυσμενής.

εὐμενῶς. adv.ʃ

showing favourable disposition: Wi 6.16. Cf. εὐμενής, δυσμενῶς.

εὐμετάβολος, ον.ʃ

changeable: γλῶσσῃ 'of speech' Pr 17.20.

εὐμήκης, ες.ʃ

tall: *s* hum., λαὸν μέγαν καὶ πολὺν καὶ ~ήκη De 9.1; 1C 11.23 *L* (B: ὁρατός). Cf. μῆκος, μέγας, ὑψηλός.

εὐμορφία, ας. f.ʃ

goodly physical shape: + ὑγίεια 'good health' Wi 7.10; of young men, 4M 8.10 (+ ἡλικία 'youth'). Cf. εὔμορφος.

εὔμορφος, ον.ʃ

of goodly shape: *s* woman, Si 9.8. Cf. εὐμορφία, εὐειδής, καλός: Schmidt 4.355f.; Shipp 256.

εὐνοέω: fut.inf. ~νοήσειν.ʃ

to be kindly disposed towards: abs., Es E 23; + dat., Da 2.43 LXX, 3M 7.11. Cf. δυσνοέω.

εὔνοια, ας. f.

goodwill: Si prol. 16, Es 2.23 o'; πρός τινα 2M 12.30, 4M 2.10, pl., 'tokens of goodwill' 1M 11.53. Cf. εὐνοέω: Spicq 2.123-8; Mitchell.

εὐνομία, ας. f.

way of life which conforms to the law: 4M 3.20, 4.24. Cf. παρανομία.

εὔνους, ν.ʃ

well-disposed: + dat., 4M 4.3.

εὐνοῦχος, ου. m.

eunuch: high-ranking courtier, Ge 39.1 (Pharaoh's chief-cook); 40.2, 7 (his chief butler and chief baker); socially discriminated against, Is 56.3 (ǁ ἀλλογενής); mentioned after βασιλεύς and βασίλισσα Je 36.2. For an application of the word to a faithful wife, see *ND* 3.41. Cf. ἀρχιευνοῦχος, θλαδίας, σπάδων: Schmidt 4.35-7; Schneider, *TDNT* 2.765-8; Guyot.

εὐοδία, ας. f.ʃ

1. *prosperity*: ἀσεβῶν 'of the impious' Si 9.12, 10.5; pl., To 4.6 𝔊[I].

2. *favourable development*, 'good turn': Si 20.9; recovery from illness, 38.13; safe journey, 1E 8.50 (ǁ ὁδὸς εὐθεῖα 2E 8.21), 1E 8.6.

Cf. εὔοδος, εὐημερία, εὐθηνία, ὄλβος.

εὔοδος, ον.ʃ

prosperous: οὐκ ~α ἔσται ὑμῖν Nu 14.41; ~α ἐγίνετο τὰ ἱερὰ ἔργα 'the sacred services went well' 1E 7.3. **b.** *conducive to prosperity*: *s* αἴσθησις 'understanding' Pr 11.9, πράξεις 'doings' 13.13a.

Cf. εὐοδόω.

εὐοδόω: fut. εὐοδώσω, pass. εὐοδωθήσομαι; aor. εὐόδωσα, impv. εὐόδωσον, pass. εὐοδώθην, subj. εὐοδωθῶ, opt.act. εὐοδώσαι, pass. εὐοδωθείην; pf. εὐόδωκα.

1. *to lead safely and without hindrance* to a destination: + acc. pers., ἐμὲ εὐόδωκεν κύριος εἰς οἶκον τοῦ ἀδελφοῦ τοῦ κυρίου μου Ge 24.27; pass. εὐοδωθείητε To 5.17 𝔊[I].

2. *to ensure trouble-free completion of* a passage, *success* of a mission or task: abs. 1C 22.11; + acc., σὺ εὐοδοῖς τὴν ὁδόν μου Ge 24.42, sim. 24.40, 56; οὐκ εὐοδώσει τὰς ὁδούς σου De 28.29 (like a blind man); + dat. com., εὐόδωσέν μοι ἐν ὁδῷ ἀληθείας Ge 24.48, τῷ παιδί σου 2E 11.11; 1M 4.55; εὐόδωσον ἐναντίον μου Ge 24.12 (guiding me?); ἐπὶ σὲ οὐκ εὐοδώσω Is 54.17; ὅσα ἂν ποιῇ, κύριος εὐοδοῖ ἐν ταῖς χερσὶν αὐτοῦ Ge 39.3, sim. 23; ***o*** praise (αἶνος) Si 15.10; pass., πᾶσαι αἱ τρίβοι καὶ βουλαὶ εὐοδωθῶσιν To 4.19 𝔊[I]; ἄγγελος ἀγαθὸς συμπορεύσεται αὐτῷ, καὶ εὐοδωθήσεται ἡ ὁδὸς αὐτοῦ, καὶ ὑποστρέψει ὑγιαίνων 'a good angel will accompany him, and his journey will be complete without a hitch and he will return safely' 5.22 𝔊[I]; Jd 15.18B ευδοκησας < ευοδωσας. Does ὦ κύριε, εὐόδωσον δή Ps 117.25 (ǁ σῶσον δή) belong here?

3. *to grant as a favour*: + acc., ὁ ἐλεήμων θεὸς εὐοδώσει ὑμῖν τὰ κάλλιστα '.. the best' To 7.11 𝔊[I]; ὁ θεὸς τοῦ οὐρανοῦ εὐοδώσαι ὑμῖν εἰρήνην 'may the god of heaven grant you peace' 7.12 𝔊[II]; impersonal pass. + inf., εὐοδώθη σοι τιμᾶν αὐτοὺς τὰς πάσας ἡμέρας τῆς ζωῆς αὐτῶν 'it was granted to you to honour them all their lifetime' 10.13 𝔊[II], cf. εὐοδώσαντι καθαρισθῆναι τὸν ἑαυτοῦ τόπον 'to the one who enabled successful purification of his own place' 2M 10.7; ἵνα εὐοδώσῃ αὐτοῖς ἀνάπαυσιν 'that he may grant them rest (of their patient?)' Si 38.14. **b.** impers. pass. *to be approved*: παρὰ κυρίου 1C 13.2.

4. pass. *to prosper, be successful*: ἀνδρὶ ἀπερισπάστῳ καὶ εὐοδουμένῳ 'for a man free from cares and prosperous' Si 41.1; Je 2.37; *s* ἔργον– τὰ ἔργα ἐκεῖνα ἐπὶ σπουδῆς γινόμενα καὶ εὐοδούμενον τὸ ἔργον ἐν ταῖς χερσὶν αὐτῶν 1E 6.9; ὁδὸς ἀσεβῶν Je 12.1, ψεῦδος Da LXX 8.25; σωτηρία 1M 3.6; εὐδοκία Si 11.17; person, οἱ ποιοῦντες ἀλήθειαν εὐοδωθήσονται ἐν τοῖς ἔργοις αὐτῶν To 4.6 𝔊[II]; ἐν ταῖς πραγματείαις τοῦ βασιλέως 'in the king's affairs' Da LXX 6.3; 8.11, 12, 11.36 (ǁ TH κατευθύνω); impers. + inf. subject, εὐοδώθη ἐν ταῖς χερσὶν αὐτοῦ τοῦ ἐξαρθῆναι τὰ ἔθνη 'through him they succeeded in ejecting the gentiles' 1M 14.36, sim. 16.2.

Cf. εὐοδία, εὔοδος, κατευοδόω, εὐθύνω: Anz 34f.

εὐόδως. adv.ʃ

by experiencing no difficulty: in moving along, Pr 30.29 (ǁ καλῶς).

εὔοπτος, ον.ʃ

clearly visible: *s* ἀστραπή 'lightning' Ep Je 60. Cf. Naumann 39f.

εὐπαθέω.ʃ

to enjoy onself, live comfortably: Ps 91.15; ǁ εὐθηνέω Jb 21.23¶. Cf. εὐθηνέω.

εὐπάρυφος, ον.ʃ

having a fine purple border: subst.n.pl., such a garment, Ez 23.12.

εὐπείθεια, ας.

meticulous adherence to: πρὸς τόν νόμον 4M 5.16, τοῦ νόμου 9.2. Cf. εὐπειθέω: Spicq 2.129f.; *ND* 4.152.

εὐπειθέω.ʃ

to obey willingly: + dat. pers., 4M 8.5 (:: ἀπειθέω). Cf. ἀπειθέω, πείθω.

εὐπορέω: aor. εὐπόρησα, ptc.pass. εὐπορηθείς, subj. εὐπορηθῶ.ʃ

1. *to have requisite means* for dealing with a difficulty: + τῇ χειρί Le 25.26, 49 (latter: ταῖς χερσίν, w. ref. to one person).

2. *to provide abundant means necessary* for dealing with a difficulty: + acc. pers., ἐν μόχθοις 'in hardships' Wi 10.10.

Cf. ἀπορία: Schmidt 4.385-7; Renehan 2.74; Spicq 2.134f.; Shipp 257.

εὐπραξία, ας. f.ʃ

good, commendable conduct: δικαίων 'of the righteous' 3M 3.5.

εὐπρέπεια, ας. f.

splendid look: δόξης ^κυρίου^ Je 23.9; παρὰ τοῦ θεοῦ δόξης Ba 5.1; ǁ δόξα Ps 25.8; ὡραιότητος 49.2; of woman, Ez 16.14 (ǁ ὡραιότης), + ἰσχύς Pr 31.26, of temple 3M 1.9; pl. and w. ref. to comfortable life-style, Jb 36.11¶ (ǁ ἀγαθά). Cf. εὐπρεπής, δόξα: Spicq 2.136.

εὐπρεπής, ές.

good-looking, comely: *s* horse, Zc 10.3; olive-tree, Si 24.14; wisdom more than the sun, Wi 7.29; hum., ǁ ὡραῖος 2K 1.23B; subst.n.pl., Jb 18.15¶. Cf. εὐπρέπεια, ~πῶς, καλός, ὡραῖος: Schmidt 4.356.

εὐπρεπῶς. adv.ʃ

in attractive manner, in style: 1E 1.10, Wi 13.11.

εὐπροσήγορος, ον.ʃ

courteous in speech: subst.n.pl., 'courteous response' Si 6.5.

εὐπρόσωπος, ον.ʃ

fair of face: *s* woman, Ge 12.11. Cf. καλός, ὡραῖος.

εὕρεμα, ατος. n.

1. *unexpected good fortune*: ἔσται ἡ ψυχή σου εἰς εὕ. Je 45.2, 46.18; δώσω τὴν ψυχήν σου εἰς εὕ. 51.35; *windfall*, Si 20.9, 29.4.

2. *that which one is capable of, can afford*: καθ' εὕ. χειρός 'to your best ability' Si 32.12, cf. εὑρίσκω **7 iv**.

Cf. εὑρίσκω.

εὕρεσις, εως. f.ʃ

1. *act of finding that which one is searching*: + gen. obj., Si 13.26 (good parables).

2. *act of devising*: + gen. obj. Wi 14.12 (idols).

Cf. εὑρίσκω.

εὑρετής, οῦ. m.ʃ

one who has designed and brought about: τῆς κακίας 'of the hardship' 2M 7.31; ἀγαθῶν Pr 16.20. Cf. εὑρίσκω.

εὑρετός, ή, όν.ʃ

discoverable: *s* tree, Jd 9.6B.

εὑρίσκω: fut. εὑρήσω, pass. εὑρεθήσομαι; aor. εὗρον, 3pl ~ροσαν, inf. εὑρεῖν, ptc. εὑρών, subj. εὕρω, opt.1s εὕροιμι, 3s εὕροι, pass. εὑρέθην, ptc. εὑρεθείς, subj. εὑρεθῶ, opt.3s εὑρεθείη, impv.3s εὑρεθήτω, mid.opt.3s εὕροιτο; pf. εὕρηκα, inf. εὑρηκέναι, pass. εὕρημαι.

1. *to find* after search: ζητήσετε .. καὶ εὑρήσετε De 4.29, sim. Je 36.13 w. ἐκζητέω and *o* God, Wi 13.6; ζητήσει αὐτοὺς καὶ οὐ μὴ εὕρῃ αὐτούς 'he will search for them, but will not find them' Ho 2.7, sim. 5.6, Am 8.12, Ps 36.36, Is 55.6; τὴν τρίβον 'the path' Ho 2.6, τὴν ὁδόν Is 48.17; ἀναψυχήν 'refreshment' 12.8*a*; pass., *o* σοφία Jb 28.12, God Is 65.1.

2. *to come upon*: + acc. and by chance, πᾶς ὁ εὑρίσκων με ἀποκτενεῖ με 'everyone who comes upon me will kill me' Ge 4.14; 4.15, 16.7, 32.19. Usually an undesirable situation or event as *s*: τὰ κακά, ἃ εὑρήσει τὸν πατέρα μου 'the evil (i.e. death) that is going to befall my father' Ge 44.34; εὑρήσουσιν αὐτὸν κακὰ πολλὰ καὶ θλίψεις De 31.17; ἐξελθὸν πῦρ εὕρῃ ἀκάνθας 'a fire, after having broken out, finds thorns in its way' Ex 22.6; πάντα τὸν μόχθον τὸν εὑρόντα ἡμᾶς 'all the hardship that befell us' Nu 20.14; κίνδυνοι ᾅδου 'dangers of Hades' Ps 114.3; De 4.30, 24.1, Ps 45.2. **b**. *s* a favourable circumstance, ἥξουσιν ἐπὶ σὲ πᾶσαι αἱ εὐλογίαι αὗται καὶ εὑρήσουσίν σε De 28.2 (‖ καταλαμβάνω vs. 15).

*__3__. *to undergo and experience*: + acc., θλῖψιν καὶ ὀδύνην 'hardship and sorrow' Ps 114.3, θάνατον Wi 19.5, ἐκδίκησιν 'vengeance' Si 28.1, ἀπώλειαν 33.11, ἐξιλασμόν 18.20.

4. *to find, encounter* sbd or sth in a certain location or state: παρ' ᾧ ἂν εὑρεθῇ τὸ κόνδυ τῶν παίδων σου 'whoever of your servants the drinking-vessel might be found with' Ge 44.9; Ho 12.4. **b**. in a certain condition: + adj., τὰ σώματα νεκρά Is 37.36; "found Israel as grapes in the wilderness" Ho 9.10; Am 2.16; "the inhabitants of Jerusalem (trusting) in their Lord" Zc 12.5; + ptc., εὗρεν αὐτὸν ἄνθρωπος πλανώμενον ἐν τῷ πεδίῳ '.. wandering in the field' Ge 37.15; ἄνδρα συλλέγοντα ξύλα 'gathering wood' Nu 15.32; πλοῖον βαδίζον εἰς Θαρσις 'a boat bound for Tarshish' Jn 1.3 (poss. after searching); pass., εὑρεθῇ ἄνθρωπος κοιμώμενος μετὰ γυναικὸς .. 'a man be found lying with a woman ..' De 22.22, Νωε εὑρέθη τέλειος δίκαιος Si 44.17; 44.20, 20.6, πιστός 1M 2.52; 4M 16.14, 1C 20.2.

5. *to discover* a fact after an examination: εὑρέθη ὅτι ἐστὶν ἡ πόλις ἐκείνη .. 1E 2.22; + ptc., ἐὰν εὑρίσκηται .. γενομένην τὴν οἰκοδομὴν .. 'should it turn out that the construction had taken place ..' 1E 6.21; + double acc., αὐτοὺς ἀξίους ἑαυτοῦ 'them to be worthy of Himself' Wi 3.5; pass., + ὅτι 2M 2.1 (‖ + ὡς vs. 2); 1C 20.2. **b**. *to discover a solution of*: + acc. rei, πρόβλημα 'riddle' Jd 14.18 A (B: γινώσκω).

6. pass. *to be available, at one's disposal*: πάντες οἱ πόνοι αὐτοῦ οὐχ εὑρεθήσονται αὐτῷ 'no fruit of his toil will be there for his enjoyment' Ho 12.8*b*, cf. 14.9; PSol 15.11. **b**. *to exist, to be present*, often with a negator: οὐχ ηὑρίσκετο 'he was not to be found' Ge 5.24; τῷ δὲ Αδαμ οὐχ εὑρέθη βοηθὸς .. 'for Adam, however, there was no helper' 2.20; ἀδικία οὐχ εὑρέθη ἐν χείλεσιν αὐτοῦ Ma 2.6 (‖ εἰμί); ἐν σοὶ εὑρέθησαν ἀσέβειαι Mi 1.13; ἐν τῷ στόματι αὐτῶν γλῶσσα δολία Zp 3.13; ‖ ὑπάρχω Je 27.20; τῷ λαῷ τῷ εὑρεθέντι 'to the people present (at a festival) 1E 1.7. **c**. *to present* or *reveal oneself*: εὑρέθην τοῖς ἐμὲ μὴ ἐπερωτῶσιν Is 65.1 (‖ ἐμφανὴς γίνομαι); Ps 20.9.

*__7__. Idiom: **i**. εὑρίσκω χάριν. **a**. *to win ethically / morally positive and favourable estimation*:–with (ἐναντίον) sbd (God), Νωε εὗρεν χάριν ἐναντίον κυρίου τοῦ θεοῦ Ge 6.8; εἰ εὗρον χάριν ἐναντίον σου 30.27 (speaking to a hum.); 32.5; no ethics or moral involved, 39.4, 50.4 (vis-à-vis a superior), 47.29 (an ageing and dying father to a son of his), De 24.1 (a woman to her husband); παρά τινι Ex 33.16, παρά τινος Es 2.15 o'. **b**. Added to a request as a mark of deference on the part of the speaker, 'if you please': εἰ ἄρα εὗρον χάριν ἐναντίον σου, μὴ παρέλθῃς τὸν παῖδά σου '.. do not pass by thy servant' Ge 18.3; ἐνώπιόν σου Nu 32.5. **ii**. εὑρίσκω ἔλεος 'to win the compassion', εὗρεν ὁ παῖς σου ἔλεος ἐναντίον σου Ge 19.19; παρὰ σοί Nu 11.15.

iii. εὑρίσκω χάριν καὶ ἔλεον: κατὰ πρόσωπόν τινος Es 2.9, 17 *L*. **iv**. εὑρίσκει ἡ χείρ τινος 'is capable of, can afford': ἐὰν μὴ εὑρίσκῃ αὐτοῦ ἡ χεὶρ ζεῦγος τρυγόνων 'should he not be able to afford a pair of turtle doves' Le 5.11 (slightly more idiomatically || Ἐὰν μὴ ἰσχύῃ ἡ χεὶρ αὐτοῦ τὸ ἱκανὸν εἰς πρόβατον 'should he not be able to afford a sheep' 5.7), cf. ἐὰν μὴ εὑρίσκῃ ἡ χεὶρ αὐτοῦ τὸ ἱκανὸν εἰς ἀμνόν 12.8 and τοῦ μὴ εὑρίσκοντος τῇ χειρὶ εἰς τὸν καθαρισμὸν αὐτοῦ 'incapable of providing for his own cleansing' 14.32; ἐὰν πένηται καὶ ἡ χεὶρ αὐτοῦ μὴ εὑρίσκῃ 'should he be poor and not be able to afford' 14.21, cf. εὕρεμα **2**; Jd 9.33 (*L* δύναμαι) **v**. εὑρίσκω τὴν καρδίαν μου: + inf., 'to find courage enough to do ..' 2K 7.27 (|| 1C 17.25 without καρδίαν).

***8**. mid./pass. *to be able to find one's way about, capable of coping with*: ἐν παραβολαῖς '(be comfortable) with proverbs' Si 38.34, cf. MH /māṣā'/, and Jewish Ar. /'immṣi/ *to succeed*.

Cf. εὕρεμα, εὕρεσις, εὑρετής, ἀν~, ἐξευρίσκω, ζητέω, ἥκω: Shipp 258; Preisker, *TDNT* 2.769; LSG s.v.

εὖρος, ους. n.

breadth, width: of table, Ex 25.22 (|| μῆκος, ὕψος); of curtain, 26.2 (|| μῆκος); of altar, 30.2 (|| μῆκος), θαλάσσης Jb 11.9; || πλάτος Ez 40.11. Cf. εὐρύς, μῆκος, πλάτος, ὕψος.

εὔρυθμος, ον.ʃ

rhythmical: *s* λόγος Es C 24.

εὐρύς, εῖα, ύ.

broad: *s* ring (δακτύλιος) Ex 38.4. Cf. εὖρος, εὐρυχωρία, εὐρύχωρος, πλατύς: Schmidt 4.465-7.

εὐρυχωρία, ας.ʃ

spaciousness: Ge 26.22. Cf. εὐρύς, εὐρύχωρος, στενοχωρία.

εὐρύχωρος, ον.

roomy, spacious: subst. 'spacious place' Ho 4.16, Ps 30.9; *s* land, Jd 18.10 A (B: πλατύς), grazing ground, Is 30.23, διῶρυξ 'canal' and + πλατύς 33.21; sea and + μέγας Ps 103.25. Cf. εὐρύς.

εὔρωστος, ον.ʃ

stout: *s* hum. spirit, Si 30.15. Cf. εὐρώστως.

εὐρώστως. adv.

with vigour: of military action, 2M 10.17, 12.27; Wi 8.1. Cf. εὔρωστος.

εὐρωτιάω.ʃ

to be or *become mouldy*: *s* food, Jo 9.5.

εὐσέβεια, ας. f.

reverence towards God: πνεῦμα γνώσεως καὶ ~ας Is 11.2; πρὸς τὸν κύριον 33.6, εἰς θεόν Pr 1.7 (|| φόβος θεοῦ); + μισοπονηρία 'hatred of evil' 2M 3.1. Cf. εὐσεβής, εὐσεβέω, θεοσέβεια, φόβος, δυσσέβεια: Foerster, *TDNT* 7.179; Spicq 1985, esp. 219-21.

εὐσεβέω: fut. ~βήσω; aor. εὐσέβησα, ptc. εὐσεβήσας.

to practise εὐσέβεια: abs., Su 62[b] LXX; + acc., τὸν πάντων κτίστην 'the creator of all' 4M 11.5. Cf. ἀσεβέω.

εὐσεβής, ές.

characterised by εὐσέβεια, q.v.: *s* hum., Is 24.16; purpose, + ὅσιος 2M 12.45; λογισμός 'reason' 4M 1.1+, ἐπιστήμη 11.21; subst. m. pl. Is 32.8; || συντηρῶν ἐντολάς 'observer of the law' Si 37.12; opp. ἁμαρτωλός Si 12.4, 13.17, 16.13, 36.14, πονηροί Is 32.7f., ἀθετοῦντες 'the disobedient' 24.16, ἀσεβεῖς 'the ungodly' Pr 12.12. Cf. εὐσέβεια, δυσσεβής, εὐλαβής, θεοσεβής, σέβομαι, ὅσιος: Trench 172-80.

εὔσημος, ον.ʃ

promising good luck: *s* festival, Ps 80.4.

εὐσήμως. adv.ʃ

distinctly: + ἐκφαίνω 'to disclose' Da 2.19 LXX.

εὔσκιος, ον.ʃ

**offering comfortable shade*: *s* olive-tree, Je 11.16. Cf. σκιά.

εὔσπλαγχνος, ον.ʃ

**compassionate*: *s* God, + μακρόθυμος, πολυέλεος Od 12.7. Cf. σπλάγχνα.

εὐστάθεια, ας. f.

tranquility and stability: political, πρὸς τὸ μὴ τὴν βασιλείαν ~ας τυγχάνειν 'so that the kingdom shall not attain ..' Es B 3.16 *L* (ο' συναρχία), sim. 2M 14.6, δήμου Wi 6.24; personal, PSol 4.9, καρδίας 6.4.

εὐσταθέω: fut.inf. ~θήσειν; aor. εὐστάθησα, subj. ~σταθήσω.

to enjoy tranquility and stability: *s* ἔθνος Je 30.9; hum., εὐ. καὶ τὰ τῆς ἡσυχίας ἄγειν '.. to live in peace' 2M 12.2; τὰ πράγματα ἡμῶν 'our political state of affairs' 3M 7.4; euphemism for eternal rest of death, Es 3.18 *L*. Cf. εὐσταθής.

εὐσταθής, ές.ʃ

tranquil and stable: *s* ~ῆ καὶ ἀτάραχα .. τὰ πράγματα 'our political state of affairs .. stable and untroubled' Es B 7. Cf. εὐσταθέω. Del. Si 26.18, 2M 12.2 v.l.

εὔσταθμος, ον.ʃ

having right measures and sizes: *s* πτέρνη 'heel (of a good-looking woman)' Si 26.18.

εὔστοχος, ον.ʃ

hitting the mark successfully: *s* flying missile, Wi 5.21. Cf. εὐστόχως.

εὐστόχως. adv.ʃ

aiming well: of archery, 3K 22.34B (|| 2C 18.33), but *L* ἀφελῶς. Cf. εὔστοχος.

εὐστροφία, ας.ʃ
compliant disposition: Pr 14.35.
εὐσυναλλάκτως.ʃ
in submissive and docile manner: Pr 25.10a.
εὐσχημοσύνη, ης. f.ʃ
gracefulness: ἐγκοσμούμενον τῇ περὶ τὴν εὐσέβειαν εὐσχημοσύνῃ 'trying to put on the best of the decency appropriate to the piety' (poss. ref. to an attempt to cover his privy parts) 4M 6.2. Cf. Spicq 2.139-42.
εὐσχήμων, ον.ʃ
modest in attitude: *s* hum. Pr 11.25; woman, and opp. ἀσχήμων Si 26.24¶ (poss. ref. to a woman who would not expose herself even in front of her husband). Cf. ἀσχήμων: Schmidt 4.356f.; Greeven, *TDNT* 2.771f.
εὐτακτέω.ʃ
to pay regularly: acc. rei (money owed), 2M 4.27.
εὐτάκτως. adv.ʃ
in orderly fashion: Pr 30.27. Cf. εὐταξία.
εὐταξία, ας. f.ʃ
orderliness: of a temple, 3M 1.10; ref. to hum. character, + σωφροσύνη 2M 4.37. Cf. εὐτάκτως, ἀταξία.
εὐτεκνία, ας. f.ʃ
state of being blessed with children: 4M 18.9 (:: ἀτεκνία). Cf. τέκνον, ἀτεκνία, πολύπαις, πολυτόκος.
εὐτελής, ές.
poor in quality: *s* timber, Wi 10.4; animals, 11.15. Cf. LSG s.v.
εὐτελῶς. adv.ʃ
poorly in quality: author's performance, 2M 15.38 (|| καλῶς and + μετρίως 'in mediocre fashion'). Cf. καλῶς.
εὔτηκτος, ον.ʃ
easily melting: Wi 19.21. Cf. τήκω.
εὐτολμία, ας. f.ʃ
daring attitude or *instance thereof*: 2M 13.18. Cf. τολμάω.
εὐτονία, ας. f.ʃ
ability to act strenuously: mental, Ec 7.7.
εὔτονος, ον.ʃ
exceedingly fit for strenuous activity, 'energetic': *s* soldiers, 2M 12.23, πυρός '(more so than) fire' 4M 7.10. Cf. εὐτόνως.
εὐτόνως. adv.ʃ
vigorously: sounding a trumpet, Jo 6.8. Cf. εὔτονος.
εὐτρεπίζω.ʃ
to make ready: + acc., τροχούς'(torturing) wheels' 4M 5.32. Cf. ἑτοιμάζω.
εὐφημέω.ʃ
to laud, praise: abs., 1M 5.64. Cf. αἰνέω, εὐλογέω, βλασφημέω, δυσφημέω.

εὔφθαρτος, ον.ʃ
perishable: *s* living creatures, Wi 19.21. Cf. φθαρτός, ἀφθαρτός.
εὐφραίνω: fut. εὐφρανῶ, pass. εὐφρανθήσομαι; aor. εὔφρανα, ηὔφρανα, inf. εὐφρᾶναι, opt.3s εὐφράναι, pass. εὐφράνθην, inf. εὐφρανθῆναι, ptc. εὐφρανθείς, impv. εὐφράνθητι, 3s ~θήτω, 2pl ~θητε, subj. ~θῶ, opt.3s ~θείη, 2pl ~θείητε.

I. act. *to gladden, cheer*: + acc. pers., wife, De 24.5; Ho 7.3; καρδίαν Ps 103.15 (*s* οἶνος), 18.9, τὴν ψυχήν μου 85.4; ἐπί σε ἐχθρόν La 2.17, sim. Ps 29.2; + acc. rei, τὴν νεότητά μου 42.4. **b**. *to raise the morale* of: + acc., soldiers, 2M 15.11.

II. pass. *to rejoice, be glad*: abs. Zc 8.19; opp. αἰσχύνομαι Is 65.13; Ho 9.1, Jl 2.21, Zc 10.7 (|| χαίρω); Zp 3.14 (|| χαίρω and κατατέρπομαι); Zc 2.10 (|| τέρπομαι), Is 12.6 (|| ἀγαλλιάομαι); + dat., πτώσει εὐσεβῶν 'at the downfall of the godly' Si 27.29; + ἐπί τινι – οἱ εὐφραινόμενοι ἐπ' οὐδενὶ λόγῳ 'those who rejoice over what is of no consequence' Am 6.13; ἐπὶ τῷ κυρίῳ Jl 2.23 (|| χαίρω), Ps 39.17, 96.12; over sacrificial meal, De 12.7 (|| ἐπί τι vs. 18); + ἐπί τινα – εὐφρανθήσεται ἐπὶ σὲ ἐν τέρψει ὡς ἐν ἡμέρᾳ ἑορτῆς 'he will rejoice over you with delight as in a day of festival' Zp 3.17, ἐπὶ κύριον Ps 31.11 (|| ἀγαλλιάομαι); + ἔκ τινος De 20.6, 28.39; + ἔν τινι – ἐν πᾶσιν τοῖς ἀγαθοῖς 26.11, ἐν ἀμήτῳ 'in harvesting' Is 9.3, ἐν τῷ οἴνῳ Es 1.10 *L*; κατ' ἐμοῦ Ps 35.15 (malicious joy); + cogn. acc., εὐφροσύνην μεγάλην 1M 14.11; *s* heart: Zc 10.7 (|| χαίρω), Ps 15.9 (|| ἀγαλλιάομαι), and + ἕνεκεν τούτου Hb 1.16 (|| χαίρω); God, De 28.63 (with an inf. indicating wherein the joy lies), 30.9 (ἐπί + dat. and acc. pers.); *s* trees, Is 14.8; heaven, 44.23, Ps 95.11, islands 96.1; opp. λυπέομαι Si 30.5.

Cf. ἐν~, συνευφραίνομαι, εὐφροσύνη, ἀγαλλιάομαι, ἐπιχαίρω, ἐπευθυμέω, σκυθρωπάζω, (κατα)τέρπομαι, φαιδρός, χαίρω: Aejmelaeus 2003.501-3.
εὐφροσύνη, ης. f.

1. *joy*: Zp 3.17; expressed verbally, εὐ. καὶ χαρά Jl 1.5, Je 15.16, εὐ. καὶ ἀγαλλίαμα Is 51.3; εὐ. καρδίας Si 50.23; + αἴνεσις, μεγαλειότης Je 40.9; ἀντὶ πένθους 'instead of sorrow' Is 61.3. **b**. *object of joy*: Is 32.14.

2. *merry-making*, esp. on festivals: μετ' ~ης καὶ μετὰ μουσικῶν Ge 31.27, τυμπάνων 'of tambourines' Is 24.8; ἐν ταῖς ἡμέραις τῆς ~ης ὑμῶν καὶ ἐν ταῖς ἑορταῖς ὑμῶν Nu 10.10; ἀποστρέψω πάσας τὰς ~ας (note pl.) αὐτῆς, ἑορτὰς αὐτῆς .. Ho 2.11, cf. Zc 8.19; secular, εὐ. καὶ ἀγαλλίαμα Is 22.13.

Cf. εὐφραίνω, γέλως, ἡδονή, ἱλαρότης, τέρψις, χαρμοσύνη, χαρά, πένθος: Schmidt 2.556f., 571f.; *ND* 4.152-4.

εὐφρόσυνος, η, ον, also ~ος, ον.ʃ
indicative of cheerfulness: *s* φωνή Ju 14.9, ἡμέρα Es 9.19 (+ ἀγαθός), 3M 6.36, 7.19. Del. Si 50.23 v.l.

εὐφυής, ές.ʃ
1. *naturally gifted*: *s* γραμματεύς 1E 8.3, παῖς 'child' Wi 8.19.
2. *well-suited*: *s* καιρός '(opportune) moment' 2M 4.32.

εὔχαρις, ι.ʃ
charming: subst.n., τὸ εὔχαρι 'the charm' Wi 14.20. Cf. χάρις.

εὐχαριστέω: aor.subj. εὐχαριστήσω, ptc. ~τήσας.ʃ
to give thanks: abs., 2M 12.31 (to humans by implication), the ground of thanks indicated by a ὅτι-clause, Wi 18.2; + dat. pers., κυρίῳ Ju 8.25, τῷ θεῳ 3M 7.16, μεγάλως εὐχαριστοῦμεν αὐτῷ 2M 1.11. Cf. εὐχαριστία, χάρις, ἐξομολογέομαι, εὐλογέω: Schermann 375-80, 83f.; *ND* 4.128; Tomson 2007. 40-7. Del. 2M 10.7 v.l.

εὐχαριστία, ας. f.ʃ
1. *sentiment of gratefulness*: Es E 4, Si 37.11; τῶν πολλῶν 'borne by many' 2M 2.27.
2. *act of giving thanks*: σου 'to you' Wi 16.28.
Cf. εὐχαριστέω: Schermann 380-2.

εὐχάριστος, ον.ʃ
gracious of personal character: Pr 11.16. Cf. χάρις.

εὐχερής, ες.ʃ
easy of execution: *s* task Ju 7.10, 2M 2.27, αἴσθησις Pr 14.6. Cf. εὐχερῶς, εὔκοπος, δυσχερής, χαλεπός.

εὐχερῶς. adv.
without difficulty, easily: Ju 4.7. Cf. εὐχερής.

εὐχή, ῆς. f.
1. *vow*: ἀπόδος τὰς ~άς σου 'pay your vows' Na 1.15; εὐ. αὐτοῦ ἐπ' αὐτῷ 'is bound by his vow' Ma 1.14; αἰνέσεως 'of praise' Ps 55.13; cog. obj. of εὔχομαι, Ge 31.13, Jn 1.16 +. **b**. *offering that has been vowed*: οἴσετε .. ὁλοκαυτώματα .. θυσιάσματα .. ἀπαρχὰς .. εὐχὰς .. ἑκούσια .. πρωτότοκα De 12.6; 1E 8.57, Pr 19.13. **c**. elliptical for κεφαλὴ ~ῆς 'a head shaven as a sign of a vow taken': Nu 6.19, cf. vs. 9.
2. *prayer of entreaty*: on one's own behalf, εὐ. μου Jb 16.17; μετ' ἐπικλήσεως καὶ ~ῶν 'with invocation and prayers' 2M 15.26. **b**. *that which is asked for through prayer*: 1K 2.9.
Cf. εὔχομαι, προσευχή: Spicq 2.152-4; LSG s.v.

εὔχομαι: fut. εὔξομαι; aor. ηὐξάμην, inf. εὔξασθαι, impv. εὖξαι, ptc. εὐξάμενος, subj. εὔξωμαι; pf.ptc. mid. ηὐγμένος.
1. *to utter a vow*: + acc. rei and dat. pers./dei, ηὔξω μοι .. εὐχήν Ge 31.13, κυρίῳ δῶρον Nu 6.21, κυρίῳ .. δόμα De 23.23; ὅσα ηὐξάμην, ἀποδώσω .. τῷ κυρίῳ Jn 2.10, εὔξονται εὐχὰς τῷ κυρίῳ καὶ ἀποδώσουσι Is 19.21; πρός τινα (= God) 2M 9.13; + cogn. obj. εὐχήν Ge 31.13, Jn 1.16 +; ηὔξατο .. εὐχὴν λέγων .. Ge 28.20; εἰς ἡμέραν κακήν, of those who religiously make vows but can only expect a day of misfortune(?) Am 6.3 (v.l. ἐρχόμενοι for MT *hmndym*); + inf., 1E 4.43, 44. **b**. *to pledge by a vow*: + acc. rei, νηστείαν τοῖς νεανίσκοις ἔναντι τοῦ κυρίου '(I declared) to the youth that I had vowed to fast before the Lord ..' 1Es 8.49.
2. *to pray*: on behalf of sbd else, 'intercede': abs., Da 6.11 LXX (ǁ προσεύχομαι 6.10 TH); περὶ ἐμοῦ πρὸς κύριον Ex 8.8 (with the burden of the prayer indicated by an inf., ἀφανίσαι τοὺς βατράχους 'to get the frogs removed'); 9.28, Nu 21.7 (foll. by καί and a 3rd pers. impv.); πρὸς τὸν θεόν De 9.26; ὑπὲρ νεκρῶν 2M 12.44. **b**. on one's own behalf, 'supplicate': εὐξαμένου σου πρὸς αὐτὸν εἰσακούσεταί σου 'when you pray to him, he will hear you' Jb 22.27, εὖξαι κυρίῳ, καὶ αὐτὸς ἰάσεταί σε 'Pray to the Lord, and then he will heal you' Si 38.9; ἐναντίον κυρίου Ba 1.5 (ǁ κλαίω, νηστεύω). **c**. *to utter by way of prayer*: + acc. rei, χάριν 'thanks' 2M 9.20.
3. *to wish for*: + acc. and dat., τὴν γῆν .. ταῖς ψυχαῖς αὐτῶν Je 22.27.
4. *to entreat*: + cogn. acc., εὐχήν and ἀπὸ .. θεοῦ .. παρὰ Δαρείου Da 6.5 LXX.
Cf. κατ~, προσεύχομαι, εὐχή, δέομαι, ἱκετεύω, λίσσομαι: Greeven, *TDNT* 2.775-8; Cimosa 1985. 31-6; Spicq 1.147-51.

εὐχρηστία, ας. f.ʃ
ready access to services and facilities: 3M 2.33.

εὔχρηστος, ον.ʃ
useful: ἀπόβλημα εἰς οὐθέν 'cast-off, which is (good) for nothing' Wi 13.13; fabric, Pr 31.13. Cf. χρήσιμος, ἄχρηστος.

εὐψυχία, ας. f.
stoutness of heart, good courage: ἐν τοῖς ἀγῶσιν 'in the (military) struggles' 2M 14.18; of those being tortured, 4M 6.11. Cf. εὔψυχος, θράσος.

εὔψυχος, ον.ʃ
stout of heart: *s* hum., τῇ καρδίᾳ 1M 9.14; cock, Pr 30.31. Cf. εὐψυχία, εὐψύχως, ἀνδρεῖος, θρασύς: Spicq 2.155f.

εὐψύχως. adv.ʃ
1. *with stout heart, courageously*: 2M 7.20.
2. *willingly*: 3M 7.18.
Cf. εὔψυχος.

εὐώδης, ες.ʃ
fragrant: *s* cinnammon and reed, Ex 30.23; εὐωδεστάτοις πόμασιν οἴνῳ λελιβανωμένῳ 'by most fragrant draughts of wine mixed with frankincense' 3M 5.45; flower, 7.16. Cf. εὐωδία, δυσώδης.

εὐωδία, ας. f.
fragrance: ὀσμὴ ~ας Ge 8.21, Ex 29.18, Le 17.4, Nu 28.2, cf. Daniel 175-99; ξύλον ~ας Ba 5.8; ^προσφορᾶς^ 'of a (cultic) offering' Si 32.8; + θυμίαμα 'incense' 45.16; fragrant libation, Da 2.46 TH. Cf. εὐωδιάζω, εὐώδης, ὀσμή.
εὐωδιάζω: aor.impv. εὐωδίασον.ʃ
to have a sweet smell: *s* wine, Zc 9.17; fig. of frankincense, ὡς λίβανος εὐωδιάσατε ὀσμήν 'Give out sweet savour as frankincense' Si 39.14. Cf. εὐωδία.
εὐώνυμος, ον.
of the left-hand side (opp. right): subst.f., χείρ understood, Ct 2.6; n.pl., ἐξ ~ων 'on the left' Ex 14.22, Zc 4.3, 11, 12.6 (opp. ἐκ δεξιῶν), *'to the north' Ez 16.46; οὐκ ἐκκλινοῦμεν δεξιὰ οὐδὲ ~α Nu 20.17. Cf. ἀριστερός and δεξιός.
εὐωχέομαι.ʃ
to wine and dine: *s* king, Es 7.6 *L*; + ῥαθυμέω 'to have fun in leisure' Ju 1.16; entirely at the king's expenses, 3M 6.40. Cf. εὐωχία.
εὐωχία, ας.
wining and dining: 1E 3.19 (+ εὐφροσύνη 'pleasure'); opp. πένθος Es C 10 o' (*L* εὐφροσύνη). Cf. εὐωχέω.
ἐφάλλομαι: fut. ἐφαλοῦμαι; aor. ἐφηλάμην.
to spring on to (ἐπί + acc.): *s* divine spirit of prophecy, 1K 10.6 (|| simp. vs. 10 B); with hostile intent, ἐπὶ τὰ πρόπυλα 'on to the porches' Zp 1.9 (Zgl ἐμφανῶς; for the emendation to ἐφαλλομένους, see Walters 137). Cf. ἀφάλλομαι, ἅλλομαι.
ἐφαμαρτάνω: aor.inf. ~αμαρτεῖν.ʃ*
to seduce to sin: + acc. pers., Je 39.35. Cf. ἐξ~, ἁμαρτάνω.
ἐφάπτομαι: pf.mid.3s ἐφῆπται.ʃ
1. *to hold fast to*: + gen., τῆς γῆς Am 9.5.
2. *to apply oneself to*: + gen., σαββάτων ψευδῶν Am 6.3.
3. *to partake of* food: ἀπὸ τῶν ἀθεμίτων ὑείων κρεῶν 'some of the unlawful pork' 2M 7.1.
4. mid. *to gain complete control over*: + gen. pers., *s* κακία 'disaster' Jd 20.34*L* (A: ἅπτομαι, B: φθάνω).
Cf. ἅπτομαι, ἀφάπτω.
ἐφαρμόζω: aor.ptc. ἐφαρμόσας.ʃ
to place and cause to fit to sth: + acc., knees to a catapult in order to torture, 4M 11.10.
ἐφελκύω.⇒ ἐφέλκω.
ἐφέλκω: pres.subj. ἐφέλκωμαι; aor. ἐφείλκυσα, ptc.pass. ~κυσθείς.ʃ
1. *to drag away*: pass., *s* hum., Ep Je 43. **b**. mentally *to attract*: + acc. pers., 4M 15.21, pass. Wi 14.20.
2. *to allow to drag on*, 'prolong': + acc., τὸν χρόνον Jo 24.31; mid. *to be stationary* when the subj. should be moving on: ὅταν ἐφέλκηται ἡ νεφέλη .. ἡμέρας πλείους 'when the cloud stayed .. for days on end' Nu 9.19.
ἐφέτειος, ον.ʃ
pertaining to one year: μισθός 'annual wages' De 15.18. Cf. ἐπέτειος.
ἐφηβία, ας. f.ʃ
youth club: + γυμνάσιον 2M 4.9.
ἔφηβος, ου. m.ʃ
male adolescent 18 years of age or older: 2M 4.12. Cf. μειράκιον, νεανίας, νιανίσκος: Schmidt 4.32f.
ἔφηλος, ον.ʃ
having a white speck on the eyes: *s* hum., τοὺς ὀφθαλμούς Le 21.20.
ἐφημερία, ας. f.
division of the priests for the daily temple service: 1C 9.33; στήσας τοὺς ἱερεῖς κατ' ~ας 'having placed the priests according to their daily divisions' 1E 1.2 (|| φυλακήν 2C 35.2).
ἐφθός, ή, όν.ʃ
boiled: *s* sacrificial animal, Nu 6.19; subst., 1K 2.15 (v.l. κρέας ~όν). Cf. ἕψω, ἡμίεφθος.
ἐφικτός, ή, όν.ʃ
lying within one's capability: τοῦτο ~όν ἦν μοι 'that was the best I could do' 2M 15.38.
ἔφιππος, ον.ʃ
mounted on horse: hum., 2M 12.35; angel, 11.8, 4M 4.10. Cf. ἀναβάτης.
ἐφίπτομαι.ʃ
to stop flying and descend on to sth: *s* bird, ἐπί τι Ep Je 21. Cf. πέτομαι, πίπτω.
ἔφισος, ον.ʃ
of same worth as: + dat., *s* φίλος Si 9.10; + gen., *s* wine, ζωῆς 'as valuable as life' 34.27. On the spelling ἔπισος, see Thack. § 8,3(5). Cf. ἴσος.
ἐφίστημι: fut. ἐπιστήσω, mid. ἐπιστήσομαι; 1aor. ἐπέστησα, subj. ἐπιστήσω, inf. ἐπιστῆσαι, impv. ἐπίστησον, 2aor. ἐπέστην, impv. ἐπίστηθι, subj. ἐπιστῶ; 1pf.act. ἐφέστηκα; 2pf.ptc. ἐφεστώς = || ἐφεστηκώς (cp. Zc 1.10 and 11), pass. ἐφεσταμένος; plpf. ἐφειστήκειν.
I. tr. fut.act., 1aor. **1**. *to appoint, put in charge*: + acc. pers. and dat. pers., αὐτοῖς ἐπιστάτας τῶν ἔργων 'the overseers of works' Ex 1.11; κριτάς .. συμβούλους 'judges .. counsellors' Is 1.26, μάστιγας 'whips' Si 23.2; double acc., νεανίσκους ἄρχοντας αὐτῶν Is 3.4; + ἐπί + acc., τοὺς Λευίτας ἐπὶ τὴν σκηνὴν τοῦ μαρτυρίου Nu 1.50.
2. *to place firmly*, mostly metaph.: οὐκ ἐπέστησεν τὸν νοῦν αὐτοῦ οὐδὲ ἐπὶ τούτῳ 'he did not direct his attention to this matter, either' Ex 7.23,

καρδίαν σου σαῖς ἀγέλαις 'your mind to your herds' Pr 27.23; νοῦν or καρδίαν understood, πρὸς πάντας τοὺς λόγους τοῦ νόμου Ne 8.13; τὸ πρόσωπόν μου ἐπὶ τὴν ψυχὴν Le 17.10, ἐπὶ τὸν ἄνθρωπον ἐκεῖνον 20.3, ἐφ' ὑμᾶς 26.17; τὸ σὸν ὄμμα πρὸς αὐτήν Pr 9.18a, sim. 23.5; + *o* πρόσωπον 'to fix one's stance': Jb 14.20, cf. στηρίζω; + inf. of intention, Je 51.11 (|| δίδωμι Da 11.17 LXX, TH: τάσσω), cf. s.v. δίδωμι **17 b**; + πόδα 'to secure one's position' Si 40.25; + χεῖρα 'to attack' 2K 8.3.

3. *to set up ready to function*: + acc., φαρέτρας 'quivers' Je 28.12, βελοστάσεις 'batteries of war-engines' 28.27, λέβητα 'cauldron' Ez 24.3; θύρας καὶ μοχλούς 'doors fitted with bolts' 1M 12.38, πύλας 'gates' Jo 6.26; τὴν ψυχήν σου Si 12.11, τὴν σὴν καρδίαν Pr 22.17; pass., παγὶς ἐφεσταμένη πλήρης πετεινῶν 'a trap set up full of (caught) fowl' Je 5.27.

***4**. *to cause to become reality*: ἐπιστήσω τοὺς λόγους μου ἐφ' ὑμᾶς Je 36.10.

5. *to interrupt activity of*, 'halt, check': + acc., ποταμούς Ez 31.15 (|| κωλύω).

II. intr. impf.mid., fut.mid., 2aor., pf., plpf. **1**. *to move up to and stand by*: ἐπὶ τὴν κοίτην αὐτῆς 'by her bed' Si 41.22; w. hostile intent, ἐπί + acc., διεκβολή 'a way-out' Ob 14. **b**. *to position oneself in order to attack*: ἐπίστηθι καὶ ἑτοίμασον Je 26.14; + dat., τοῖς ἀσεβέσιν .. θυμὸς ἐπέστη 'wrath confronted the ungodly' Wi 19.1, cf. Is 63.5.

2. *to be present, located, in position*: ἀνὰ μέσον τῶν ὀρέων Zc 1.10, 11 (syn. with ἵστημι [|| ib. 8 εἱστήκει]); *ἐπί + gen., well Ge 24.43, altar Am 9.1, sim. Nu 23.6; with friendly intention, ἡ νεφέλη σου Nu 14.14 (to guide); τὸ πνεῦμά μου ἐφέστηκεν ἐν μέσῳ ὑμῶν 'my spirit is present in your midst' Hg 2.5, ἡ ψυχή μου ἐφέστηκεν εἰς φόβον 'my soul is staring fear in the face' Is 21.4, or **1 b** above; ἐφ' ἡμᾶς 'to attack us' Je 21.2; ἐπὶ κρίσιν αἵματος ἐπιστήσονται 'they shall sit on a murder case' Ez 44.24; *s* φόβοι 'fears' Wi 18.17; hum., ἐπ' αὐτόν 'as his servant' Jd 3.19B (A: παρ~).

3. *to function as having authority over* or *responsibility for*: *s* foreman, ἐπί τινα [= a gang of harvesters] Ju 8.3; bodyguard, ἐπὶ ^τὸν βασιλέα^ 1K 22.17; + dat., πᾶσιν τοῖς ὑπάρχουσιν αὐτῇ 'all her properties' 8.10.

Cf. ἐπίστασις, ἐπιστάτης, ἵστημι, καθίστημι, ἐρείδω, στηρίζω.

ἐφοδεύω: aor. ἐφώδευσα, impv.3pl ἐφοδευσάτωσαν, inf. ἐφοδεῦσαι.ʃ

to explore as a spy: + acc. τὴν γῆν De 1.22; τὰς πηγὰς τῶν ὑδάτων 'the springs of water' Ju 7.7 (|| ἐπισκέπτω); πόλεις 1M 16.14, 2M 3.8. Cf. ἐπισκέπτω, κατασκοπεύω.

ἐφοδιάζω: fut. ἐφοδιάσω; aor.pass. ἐφωδιάσθην.ʃ

to furnish with supplies for a journey: + cogn. obj. and acc. pers., ἐφόδιον ἐφοδιάσεις αὐτὸν ἀπὸ τῶν προβάτων σου De 15.14. **b**. mid.: + acc. rei, ^ἄρτους^ Jo 9.12.

Cf. ἐφόδιον, ἐπισιτίζω.

ἐφόδιον, ου. n.ʃ

provisions for a journey: sg.coll., De 15.14. Cf. ἐφοδιάζω, ἐπισιτισμός.

ἔφοδος, ου. f.

1. *plan for action*: + βουλή 1M 9.68.

2. *arrival*: 1M 11.44, 14.21.

3. *act of setting out*: on military expedition, 2M 5.1.

4. *attack*: military, 2M 13.26 (:: ἀναζυγή 'retreat').

ἐφοράω; fut. ἐπόψομαι.

1. *to behold, watch*: gloatingly, ἐπὶ Σιων οἱ ὀφθαλμοὶ ἡμῶν Mi 4.11; + acc., οἱ ὀφθαλμοί μου ἐ. αὐτήν 7.10, τοὺς ἐχθρούς μου Ps 117.7; attentively, *o* ἔργα ἀσεβῶν Jb 21.16. **b**. *to watch over, oversee*: abs., Ez 9.9 (|| ὁράω 8.12), *s* God, 2M 7.6; + acc., κύριος ἐ. ἀνθρώπους καὶ πάσας φυλὰς τοῦ Ισραηλ Zc 9.1. **c**. abs. *to look upon the subject's conduct favourably*: τῷ πλήθει τῶν δώρων μου 'on account of my abundant offerings' Si 7.9.

2. *to survey the whole of* sth *from a higher position*: + acc., τὴν ὑπ' οὐρανὸν πᾶσαν Jb 28.24, τὰ πάντα (*s* God) 2M 12.22.

Cf. ὁράω, ἐπιβλέπω, ἐπόπτης.

εφουδ, ἐφωδ.

Transliteration of Heb. /'ēfōd/, 'priestly vestment,' + θεραφιν Jd 17.5; worn by an apprentice priest, 1K 2.18; used by an oracle-seeker, 30.7. Cf. ἐπωμίς: *BA* 9.1, pp. 89-93.

Ἐφραθαῖος, α, ον.

of Ephrath: Ru 1.2.

ἐφύβριστος, ον.ʃ

indicative of contempt: *s* reproach, Wi 17.7. Cf. Caird 1968.474.

ἐχθές. adv. On the frequent variant spelling χθές, see Thack., 97.

yesterday: ἐ. εἶπεν πρός με 'said yesterday to me' Ge 31.29; ἡ ἡμέρα ἡ ἐ. Ps 89.4; idiom, ὡς ἐ. καὶ τρίτην ἡμέραν 'as previously, as before' Ge 31.2, 5 = καθάπερ ἐ... Ex 5.7, 14, καθὼς ἐ. καὶ τρίτης ἡμέρας Su 15 TH, καθὰ ἐ. καὶ τρίτην ἡμέραν Jo 4.18; ἐ. καὶ τρίτην 1K 10.11 B (*L* .. τρίτης); * Hebraistically, πρὸ τῆς ἐ. οὐδὲ πρὸ τῆς τρίτης ἡμέρας 'not in the recent nor remote past' Ex 4.10; πρὸ τῆς ἐ. καὶ πρὸ τῆς τρίτης 'in the past, previously' 21.29, De 19.4, 6; πρὸ τῆς ἐ. καὶ τρίτης 4.42; ἀπ' ἐ. καὶ τρίτης ἡμέρας Jo 2.4, ἀπὸ τῆς ἐ... 1K 21.6*L* (B: ἐ. καὶ τρίτην ἡμέραν), see also under τρίτος **1**.

Cf. ἐπαύριον, σήμερον, πρώην.

ἔχθιστος. ⇒ ἐχθρός.

ἔχθρα, ας. f.

hostility: δι' ~αν 'with hostile intent' Nu 35.20 (‖ διὰ μῆνιν vs. 21), 35.22 (:: ἐξάπινα 'accidentally'); εἰς ~αν 'to display hostility' Mi 2.8, Si 6.9; ἐν ~ᾳ ἦσαν 1E 5.49; ἀνὰ μέσον σου καὶ ἀνὰ μέσον τῆς γυναικός 'between you and the woman' Ge 3.15; ἔ. αἰώνιος Ez 35.5. Cf. ἐχθρός, ἐχθρία, φιλεχθρέω, δυσμένεια.

ἐχθραίνω: aor. ἤχθρανα.

to confront as enemy: + dat. pers., Nu 25.17, 18, De 2.9, 19, 1K 18.29*L* (A: ἐχθρεύω), Ps 3.8, 1M 7.26; + cogn. acc., ἔχθραν 11.40. Cf. ἐχθρός, ἐχθρεύω.

ἐχθρεύω: fut. ἐχθρεύσω; aor.inf. ἐχθρεῦσαι.

to confront as enemy: Nu 33.55; + dat. pers., τοῖς ἐχθροῖς σου Ex 23.22 (‖ ἀντίκειμαι); + acc. pers., 1K 18.29A. Cf. ἐχθρός, ἐχθραίνω, ἀντίκειμαι.

ἐχθρία, ας. f.ʃ

hostility: Ge 26.21. Cf. ἔχθρα: Shipp 259.

ἐχθρός, ά, όν; superl. ἔχθιστος. Used mostly subst.

hostile, inimical: subst.m.sg., 2E 8.31 (+ πολέμιος), Ps 60.4; pl. 'enemy,' ἐκ χειρὸς ~ῶν σου Mi 4.10; 5.9 (‖ οἱ θλίβοντές σου 'your tormentors'); Ex 15.6, Na 1.2 (‖ ὑπεναντίος), 8 (‖ οἱ ἐπεγειρόμενοι 'the rebels'), De 30.7 (‖ τοὺς μισοῦντάς σε), sim. 32.41; the ungodly, οἱ ~οὶ τοῦ κυρίου Ps 36.20; the righteous as opponents of sinners, 9.26; opp. φίλος Si 6.1, Pr 6.1; n. ~ὸν κατεδίωξαν 'they pursued what is hateful (to me)' Ho 8.3 (opp. ἀγαθά); δίκης 'of justice' 4M 9.15. **b.** adj.: *s* μιαροφαγία 'eating of defiling food' 4M 5.27.

Cf. ἔχθρα, ἐχθρία, ἐχθραίνω, ἐχθρεύω, ἀντίπαλος, πολέμιος, πολεμόω, σατανᾶς, ὑπεναντίος, φίλος: Schmidt 3.496--8, 501-3; Foerster, *TDNT* 2.811f.

ἐχῖνος, ου. m.

hedgehog: Zp 2.14; inhabits wilderness, Is 34.11. Cf. Shipp 259.

ἔχις, εως. m.ʃ

viper: Si 39.30.

ἐχομένως. adv.ʃ

immediately thereafter: 2M 7.15. Cf. ἔχω **II 2**.

ἔχω: fut. ἕξω, inf. ἕξειν; impf. εἶχον; aor. ἔσχον, 3pl ἔσχοσαν, opt.3s σχοίη; pf. ἔσχηκα, ptc. ἐσχηκώς.

I. act. *to possess as appendage, part, quality*, etc.: + acc. συκαῖ σκοποὺς ἔχουσαι 'fig-trees having watchmen to protect' Na 3.12; γνῶσιν Ho 4.6; περιστερὰ ἄνους οὐκ ἔχουσα καρδίαν 'a silly pigeon with no brain' 7.11; γνόφος οὐκ ἔχων φέγγος αὐτῇ 'darkness having no light' Am 5.20; εἶχον πτέρυγας ὡς ἔποπος 'they had wings like those of a hoopoe' Zc 5.9; ἐκ λάκκου οὐκ ἔχοντος ὕδωρ 'from a cistern with no water in it' 9.11, sim. Ge 37.24; ἰσχύν Ho 8.7. **b**. idiom: ἐν γαστρὶ ἔχω 'to be pregnant' Ho 14.1, Am 1.3.

2. *to be* in a certain relationship w. sbd else, the exact nature of the relationship with whom is indicated by the following acc. noun: ἔχετε πατέρα ἢ ἀδελφόν Ge 44.19 (‖ εἰμί + dat. pers., vs. 20: ἔστιν ἡμῖν πατήρ). **b**. *to maintain* or *establish firm relationship with*: μέχρι θανάτου τὸν θεόν 3M 7.16.

3. *to hold in possession*: + acc., ἕξει υἱὸν Σάρρα Ge 18.10; τὰ ἑρπετὰ τὰ οὐκ ἔχοντα ἡγούμενον 'the reptiles which have no leader' Hb 1.14; ἕκαστος τὴν ῥάβδον αὐτοῦ ἐν τῇ χειρὶ αὐτοῦ 'each holding his staff in his hand' Zc 8.4.

4. *to hold and carry*: ἔχουσα τὴν ὑδρίαν ἐπὶ τῶν ὤμων 'carrying the pitcher on her shoulders' Ge 24.15. **b**. *to hold* in a certain condition: διερρηγμένα ἔχων τὰ ἱμάτια 'holding my clothes torn' 1E 8.70.

5. + inf., *to have authority to* do: λαλῆσαι Ge 18.31; ἕξει λαοὺς .. δουλεύειν αὐτῷ PSol 17.30 (or: **11**). **b**. *to be capable of* doing: Pr 3.27, 4M 1.7. **c**. *to have an option available to determine*: + interr. adv. and a deliberative subj., Jo 8.20.

6. *to be in a certain condition*: of health, Πῶς ἔχετε; 'How are you?' Ge 43.27; κακῶς '(to be) sickly' Ez 34.4. **b**. mental disposition: ἑτοίμως '(to be) ready (to act)' Da 3.15; εὖ .. ἐν τῷ οἴνῳ 2K 13.28*L*; τὸν τρόπον βαρβαρώτερον ἔχοντα 'being more barbarous in character' 2M 5.22; εὐλαβῶς 'cautious' 6.11, ἀπεχθῶς 'in hating mood' 3M 5.4; ἐπιμίξ 'in confusion' Wi 14.25, poss. **10**; συμπαθέστερον ἔσχον πρὸς ἀλλήλους 'they felt very much mutually bonded' 4M 13.23. **c**. *to hold in a certain state*: + a pred. adj., οὐδὲ πάντες φρόνιμον ἔχουσιν τὸν λογισμόν 'nor is the rational will possessed by everybody sound' 4M 7.18; 2M 14.30, 4M 9.21, 11.27, 15.9, 17.4, 24.

7. *to claim as one's own*: as wife, ἔσχεν αὐτήν Ex 2.1.

***8**. impers. and + dat. pers., 'the state of affairs is so and so for sbd': ἐχέτω ὑμῖν ὅτι πᾶσα ἡ συναγωγὴ πάντες ἅγιοι 'this whole congregation is entirely holy and you ought to keep it that way' (?) Nu 16.3. **b**. without dat. pers.: καλῶς ἔχειν ὑπολαμβάνομεν .. 'we consider it appropriate that ..' 1E 2.18; ἀκολούθως ᾧ ἔχει ἐν τῷ νόμῳ κυρίου 8.13.

9. *to look upon as*: + εἰς– ὃν ἔσχομέν ποτε εἰς γέλωτα 'whom we once thought to be a joke' Wi 5.4 (‖ λογίζομαι); + acc., φίλον 2M 7.24. Cf. λογίζομαι. **6**.

10. *to have firm control over*: + acc., ὠδῖνες αὐτοὺς ἕξουσιν 'acute pains will grip them' Is 13.8, Jb 21.17; *s* ἀνάγκη 'distress' 18.14, ὀδύναι 'sorrows' 21.6; θαῦμα ἔσχηεν ἀληθινούς 'amazement seized true men' 17.8, sim. 18.20; 17.9; pass., 19.20; τὸ κακόν 'the distressful plight' Su 10 LXX (TH ὀδύνη); poss.Wi 14.25 (reading πάντας for πάντα), see **6** above.

11. *to take into possession*: by force, τὰς γυναῖκας αὐτῶν Is 13.16 (ǁ προνομεύω).

12. *to have as content*: ***s*** document, + acc. rei, ταῦτα Es 7.35 *L*, οὕτως 36 *L*; circumstances, οὕτως 2M 10.9, 11.34, cf. περιέχω.

II. mid. *to hold fast to*: + gen. pers., ^κυρίου^ De 30.20, physically, 2M 12.35; metaph., + gen. rei, ἀκακίας Jb 2.3, δικαιοσύνης Pr 1.22.

2. pres.ptc. ἐχόμενος, *neighbouring*, *adjacent to* (+ gen.): ἐχόμενοι αὐτῶν Ge 41.23 (ǁ μετά + acc., vs. 6); παραπετάσματα ἐποίουν ἐχόμενα τοῦ θυσιαστηρίου 'they made curtains next to the altar' Am 2.8; ἐνιαυτὸς ἔχομενος ἐνιαυτοῦ 'year after year' 2K 21.1; οἶκον ἐχόμενον αὐτῆς Mi 1.11, cf. Husson, 204; with no gen., ἕκαστος ἐχόμενος 'keeping close to one another' Nu 2.17; w. indeclinable ἐχόμενα, 1K 4.18 B (*L* ~ος), Jd 4.11, 6.19 B, Ps 140.6, Ez 48.21, Da 10.4 TH (LXX ἐπί τινος), Ne 3.23. **b**. *coming next in order*: οἱ παρεμβάλλοντες ἐχόμενοι 'those who encamp next' Nu 2.5 (:: πρῶτοι 2.3); ἐν τῷ ἐχομένῳ ἐνιαυτῷ 'in the following year' 1M 4.28; ἡμέρᾳ understood, τῇ ἐχομένῃ 1C 10.8 (ǁ τῇ ἐπαύριον 1K 30.8), 2M 12.39. Cf. LSG s.v., **C I 3**; ἐχομένως, ἐγγύς, σύνεγγυς.

3. *to have to do with*: + gen., ζωῆς ψευδοῦς 'a false life' Pr 23.3.

Cf. εἰμί, ὑπάρχω, πέλας: Soisalon-Soininen 1987. 181-8.

ἔψεμα, ατος. n.

boiled food: ἥψεν ἔ. Ge 25.29; πυρρόν 'red' 25.30; φακοῦ 'of lentil' 25.34; as cultic offering, ἄρτου ἢ ~ατος ἢ οἴνου ἢ ἐλαίου ἢ παντὸς βρώματος Hg 2.12. Cf. ἔψω, ἔψημα.

ἔψημα, ατος. n.ʃ

= prec.: Bel 33 LXX (TH ἔψεμα).

ἔψω: impf.3pl ἥψουν; fut. ἑψήσω; aor. ἥψησα, impv.2pl ἑψήσατε, pass. ἡψήθην, subj. ἑψηθῶ; pf.pass. ἥψημαι, ptc. ἡψημένος. All forms other than the pres. are derived from either ἑψέω or ἑψάω.

to boil food: ***o*** ἔψεμα 'boiled food' Ge 25.29; κρέα (animal) meat Ex 29.31; ἐν ὕδατι 12.9; ἄρνα ἐν γάλακτι μητρός 'lamb in mother's milk' 23.19, De 14.20; ἐν τῇ χύτρᾳ 'in the pot' Nu 11.8; cultic offering, Zc 14.21, ἐν λέβησιν 'in cauldrons' 1E 1.11; hum. (cannibalism), La 4.10. Cf. ἔψεμα, ἑφθός, ἡμίεφθος.

ἑωθινός, ή, όν.

of very early morning, daybreak: φυλακὴ ~ή 'early morning watch' Ex 14.24; ἐπιγονὴ ἀκρίδων ἀρχομένη ~ή 'a breed of locusts getting into action early in the morning' Am 7.1; σκώληκι ~ῇ 'a worm active early in the morning' Jn 4.7; ***s*** ἀστήρ 'star' Si 50.6. **b**. adv. ~ῇ: 1M 5.30.

Cf. πρωϊνός.

ἔωλος, ον.ʃ

a day old: ***s*** κρέας 'meat' Ez 4.14.

I. **ἕως**, ἕω (gen. and acc.) f.ʃ

dawn: 3M 5.45. Cf. ἑωθινός, ἑωσφόρος.

II. **ἕως**

A. prep. w. gen., *up to, as far as*, giving the end-point or limit of movement, either local or temporal: ἦλθεν ἕως Χαρραν, καὶ κατῴκησεν ἐκεῖ Ge 11.31.

a. ἕ. ἄκρων τῆς γῆς 'to the far ends of the earth' Mi 5.3, μετὰ αὐτὸν οὐ προστεθήσεται ἕ. ἐτῶν εἰς γενεὰς γενεῶν 'after it there will not be again for many generations of years to come' Jl 2.2; ἕ. ψυχῆς Jn 2.6; ἕ. θεμελίου 'even to the foundation, thoroughly' Na 1.10; ἕ. τραχήλου Hb 3.13; Zc 9.10, 14.5; ἕ. τοῦ δεκάτου μηνός 'till the tenth month' Ge 8.5; ἕ. τοῦ νῦν 'up to now, so far' 15.16, 32.4; ἕ. καιροῦ 'for the time being' Is 8.22; ἕ. ἡμερῶν τριάκοντα 'for the (coming) 30 days' Da 6.5 LXX. Pregnantly ἕ. τῆς σήμερον ἡμέρας as in ἐκάλεσεν ὄνομα τῇ πόλει Φρέαρ ὅρκου ἕ. τῆς σήμερον ἡμέρας 'one named the city .., which is still its name today' Ge 26.33; 47.26; "you did signs and wonders in Egypt, ἕως τῆς ἡμέρας ταύτης 'as we remember even this day' Je 39.20. Also marks a point in time till when an activity continued and when it finished: 1E 7.5; ἕ τοῦ νῦν 'The time is up!, Enough of this!' 1M 2.33.

b. w. verbs of movement: ἥκω Mi 4.10, ἐξαποστέλλω Ob 7, εἰσέρχομαι Am 6.14, ἔρχομαι Ge 11.31, Mi 1.9*ter*.

c. *at some point in the period leading up to*, 'prior to': ἡτοίμασαν τὰ δῶρα αὐτῶν ἕ. τοῦ ἐλθεῖν Ιωσηφ Ge 43.25.

d. w. the two extreme points given: ἀπὸ βορρᾶ ἕ. ἀνατολῶν Am 8.12b; ἀπὸ τοῦ νῦν καὶ ἕ. εἰς τὸν αἰῶνα Mi 4.7 (*with a Hebraistically pleonastic καί: also De 11.12, 24); 6.5, 7.12; ἀπὸ μεγάλου αὐτῶν ἕ. μικροῦ αὐτῶν Jn 3.5; Zc 14.10*bis*; ἀπὸ ἀνθρώπου ἕ. κτήνους 'both humans and animals' Ge 6.7; ἀπὸ πρωΐθεν καὶ ἕ. ἑσπέρας 1M 9.13; ἐκ παιδὸς ἕ. τοῦ νῦν 'since our childhood till now' Ge 46.34; ἐκ νεότητος ἕ. τῆς ἡμέρας ταύτης 48.15; ἕ. repeated, ἀπὸ .. ἕ… καὶ ἕ… Ex 12.29.

e. ἕως τίνος 'until when, how long?, how much longer?' Ex 10.3, Nu 14.11; Ho 8.5, Hb 1.2, Zc 1.12; ἕ. τίνος ἔτι Je 13.27; ἕ. πότε Ps 12.3 (ǁ ἕ. τίνος), Is 6.11, Je 4.14. All these phrases often indicate impatience, frustration or protest.

f. ἕως τοῦ + inf.: Ge 3.19; 24.33, 33.3, 42.16, Ex 33.8, Ho 7.4, 10.12; with nuance of result, De 3.3, Mi 7.9. **b**. ἕως οὗ + inf.: Ru 3.3.

*g. ἕως (τοῦ) ἐλθεῖν, indicating an extremity as a partly literal rendering of Heb /'ad bō'ăḇā/: ἀπὸ Σιδῶνος ἕ. ἐλθεῖν εἰς Γεραρα 'from Sidon up to Gerara' Ge 10.19; ἕ. ἐλθεῖν πρὸς Ἀσσυρίους 25.18; Ju 1.10, 2.24.

h. conj. ἕως οὗ: ἕ. οὗ μέγας ἐγένετο σφόδρα 'in the end he became exceedingly great' Ge 26.13, ἕ. οὗ ἔδυ ὁ ἥλιος 'until the sun set' To 2.4 𝔊[I] (|| μέχρι τοῦ τὸν ἥλιον δύειν 𝔊[II]); + subj.aor., ἕ. οὗ ἀφανισθῶσι καὶ ἐπιζητήσουσι (fut.!) 'in the end they will be annihilated and start seeking ..' Ho 5.15, ἕ. οὗ ἀπίδῃ ..'waiting for the moment to see ..' Jn 4.5; Is 33.23; + opt. aor., Ps 122.2. **b**. = ἕως ὅτου: + subj. aor., Ez 39.15, 1K 22.3, Ne 4.11, Ec 12.6. **c**. *so long as*, partly calqued on Heb. /'ad še-/: Ct 1.12.

i. ἕως σφόδρα 'exceedingly, very much': ἐπένθησαν 'grieved' 1M 2.39, μεθύων '(utterly) drunk' 1K 25.36, καλή 3K 1.4 (*L* at both latter: om. ἕως).

j. w. another prep.: ἕ. εἰς μακράν Mi 4.3, ἕ. εἰς τὸν αἰῶνα Mi 4.7; ἀφίκετο ἕ. πρὸς ἄνθρωπον .. Ge 38.1; ἕ. εἰς αὐτὴν τὴν ἡμέραν ταύτην 'until this very day included' Le 23.14; 27.18; ἕ. εἰς τέλος Nu 17.13, De 31.24, 30; ἐκ μέρους τῆς γῆς ἕ. εἰς μέρος τῆς γῆς 'from one part of the earth to ..' Je 32.19; ἕ. ἐπὶ τὴν θάλασσαν Ez 47.8.

k. marks an extreme case: οὐκ ἔστιν ἕ. ἑνός 'there is not even one' Ps 13.1, 52.4; ἕ. θανάτου, distressed 'to the point of death' Jn 4.9, ἕ. θανάτου ἐκδικηθήσεται Zc 5.3, ἕ. θανάτου Si 4.27 (|| μέχρι θανάτου 2M 13.14), 4M 1.9; ἕ. ἀπὸ μακρόθεν 'even from far off' 2E 3.13; ἕ. χιλίων ψυχῶν ἀνθρώπων 1M 2.38, ἕ. τοῦ ἡμίσους τῆς βασιλείας μου 'even as much as half of my kingdom' Es D 3, cf. Mk 6.23 and *ND* 4.154; reinforced by καί— ἕ. καὶ ταῦτα ἐποίησάν μοι 'they did to me even these things' Ez 23.38.

l. ἕως + neg. A -- B, 'B is completed before A has not yet taken place': + inf., "when the matter became known (ἕ. τοῦ μὴ ἀποκαλυφθῆναι τὸν λόγον), they had already crossed the river" 2K 17.22*L*; 4K 4.24*L*. **b**. ἕως ὅτου μὴ ἔλθωσιν 'yet before they have arrived' Ec 12.1, sim. 12.6. **c**. ἕως οὗ μὴ σκοτισθῇ 'yet before (the sun) has darkened' Ec 12.2. Cf. BDB, s.v. עַד **II 2 d**; Azar 1995.119. **d**. neg. + A - ἕως B: To 1.21.

m. marks a point in future by which time a certain thing must have happened: ἀποθανεῖται ἕως πρωΐ 'he shall die by morning' Jd 6.31A, στρατεύθητι ἕως οὗ παρέλθῃ ἡ ἡμέρα 'Set out on a difficult journey by the time the day passes' 19.8*L*.

B. conj. **a**. w. subj. or fut., *until* or *whilst*: ἕως ἀγάγω .. καὶ ἥξει Mi 1.15.

b. *until*: + ind.aor. Ge 24.18; + subj.aor. and ἄν Ge 24.14, 19, Ex 15.16, 33.22, 34.35, Le 16.17, 23.14, Is 6.11; without ἄν and foll. an inf., ἕως τοῦ ἀποστρέψαι .. καὶ ἐπιλάθηται .. Ge 27.44f.

c. *whilst*: + impf., ἕως ἐλάλουν .. καὶ ἔτι λαλοῦντός μου .. Da 9.20f. LXX (|| TH ἔτι μου λαλοῦντος .. καὶ ἔτι μου λαλοῦντος ..).

d. *as long as*: + pres., ἕως ὑπάρχω 'as long as I live' Ps 103.33, 145.2; + nom. cl., ἕως ὁ θεμέλιος ἐν αὐτῇ 'as long as its foundation is there' 136.7.

Cf. μέχρι.

ἑωσφόρος, ου. m.

1. *the morning-star*: πρωὶ ἀνατέλλων Is 14.12; Jb 3.9.

2. *the time of appearance of the morning-star*, 'dawn': ἀπὸ ~ου ἕως δείλης 'from dawn to evening' 1K 30.17.

Cf. I ἕως.

Z

ζάω (contracted to ζῶ): pres.inf. ζῆν, impv. ζῆθι, 3s ζήτω; fut. ζήσομαι; aor. ἔζησα, ptc. ζήσας, impv. ζῆσον, opt.3s. ζήσαι.

1. physically *to live, be alive*: opp. "dead" or "die," ἵνα ζῶμεν καὶ μὴ ἀποθάνωμεν Ge 42.2, 43.8; γῆ ζώντων Je 11.19; καλὸν τὸ ἀποθανεῖν με ἢ ζῆν με Jn 4.3, sim. 8; οὐκ ἐπ' ἄρτῳ μόνῳ ζήσεται 'shall not live on bread alone' De 8.3; τὸν αἰῶνα ζήσονται 'live for ever' Zc 1.5, more commonly, εἰς τὸν αἰ., e.g. Ge 3.22; οὐ ζήσῃ, pronounced by the parents, Zc 13.3; ζῶ καὶ ἐπιβλέπω 'to live long enough to see' Si 25.7; w. indication of length, πᾶσαι αἱ ἡμέραι Αδαμ, ἃς ἔζησεν Ge 5.5; ἔζησεν .. ἔτη πεντακόσια 'lived 500 years' 11.11; *s* ψυχή 2.7, 12.13, 19.19; escaping a divine punishment of death, 20.7 (:: ἀποθνήσκω and ‖ being healed [ἰάσατο ὁ θεός 20.17]); χρώς 'skin (with open wound)' Le 13.14 (‖ ὑγιής vs. 15), cf. *ND* 9.37f.

2. *to be alive, full of life*, but not merely in physical sense: ψυχὴ ζῶσα 'living soul' Ge 1.24; *s* καρδία Ps 21.27; σὰρξ ζῶσα 'living being' Ge 8.21; θεὸς ζῶν De 4.33, Ho 1.10; ζῶν κύριος 4.15; in marking an oath, ζῶ ἐγὼ καὶ ζῶν τὸ ὄνομά μου Nu 14.21; ζῶ ἐγώ, λέγει κύριος Zp 2.9, Je 26.18, Ez 16.48, see s.v. εἰ **4** and ἐάν **III b**; ζῇ ὁ θεός σου Am 8.14*bis*; ὕδωρ ζῶν, of spring water as against stagnant (νεκρόν) cistern water, Ge 21.19, 26.19, Nu 5.17, Zc 14.8. ***b.** caus.: *s* God, *o* hum., Ps 40.3, 118.25, 37, 137.7, *s* divine message 118.50. On the oath formula, see Hauspie 2003a.4-12.

3. *to regain life, become alive*: ἀναστησόμεθα καὶ ζησόμεθα Ho 6.2; 14.8.

4. *to escape death against one's will and survive*: ἃ ποιήσας .. ζήσεται ἐν αὐτοῖς Le 18.5; ὁ δίκαιος ἐκ πίστεώς μου ζήσεται Hb 2.4; ἐκζητήσατέ με καὶ ζήσεσθε Am 5.4, sim. 5.6, 14.

5. *to lead a certain way of life*: ἐπὶ τῇ μαχαίρᾳ σου ζήσῃ 'you shall live by your sword' Ge 27.40; ἐν ἀγαθοῖς 'in comfort' Is 55.3, To 14.2 𝔊[II]; + acc., βίον 4M 6.18.

Cf. ζωή, ζῷον, δια~, ἐπιζάω, βιόω, ζωγρίας, ἀποθνήσκω: Lee 1980b; Kilpatrick 1990.195-200.

ζέα, ας. f.ʃ

one-seeded wheat, Triticum monococcum (LSJ): Is 28.25 (+ πυρός, κριθή), cf. Ziegler 1934.184.

ζειά, ᾶς.ʃ

one-seeded wheat: pl., 2K 21.9*L* (‖ κριθή), cf. LSG s.v. Cf. κριθή.

ζευγίζω: aor.pass. ἐζευγίσθην.ʃ

mid. *to become allied with*: + dat. pers., τοῖς ἔθνεσι 1M 1.15. Cf. ζεύγνυμι.

ζεύγνυμι: aor. ἔζευξα, impv. ζεῦξον, ptc. ζεύξας, pass. ἐζευγίσθην.

1. *to ready*: *o* vehicle for transport by land, ἅρμα 'carriage' Ge 46.29, Ex 14.6, ἅμαξα 'wagon, cart' Ju 15.11.

2. *to couple and fasten by means of a yoke* to: τὰς βόας ἐν τῇ ἁμάξῃ 'the oxen to the cart' 1K 6.7. **b.** *to fasten* to sth: *o* sword, ἐπὶ τῆς ὀσφύος 'to the waist' 2K 20.8B.

Cf. ζευγίζω, ζυγός, συζεύγνυμι.

ζεῦγος, ους. n.

1. *a pair* of two: δέκα ~η βοῶν 'ten pairs of oxen (coupled)' Is 5.10.

2. *two*: ζ. τρυγόνων 'two turtle doves' Le 5.11 (‖ δύο τρυγόνας 5.7).

Cf. δύο.

Ζεύς, Διός. m.

Zeus: 2M 6.2, 11.21.

ζέω: aor. ἔζεσα.ʃ

1. *to be cooked by boiling*: *s* meat, Ez 24.5.

2. *to boil with contents about to spill out*: *s* ἀσκός 'skin bag' Jb 32.19; metaph., *s* θυμός 'rage' 4M 18.20.

Cf. ἀνα~, ἐκζέω: Oepke, *TDNT* 2.875f.

ζῆλος, ου. m. or ους. n.

1. *sense of attachment and possessiveness, ardour, zeal*: ἐν πυρὶ ~ους αὐτοῦ καταναλωθήσεται πᾶσα ἡ γῆ 'the whole earth will be consumed by the fire of his (i.e. God's) ardour' Zp 1.18 (‖ ὀργή), sim. 3.8 (‖ ὀργὴ θυμοῦ), μου 'for me' Nu 25.11 (‖ ὀργή); as cogn. obj. Ἐζήλωκα .. ~ον μέγαν Zc 1.14 (‖ ὀργή), 8.2 + Ez 36.6 (‖ θυμός); Nu 25.11; firm determination, ὁ ζ. κυρίου σαβαωθ ποιήσει ταῦτα Is 9.7; ‖ ἀγάπη Ct 8.5 (poss. sense **2**); for God's cause, PSol 2.24 (:: wanton desire), τοῦ οἴκου σου Ps 68.10.

2. *jealousy*: Pr 27.4.

Cf. ζηλόω, ζήλωσις, ζηλωτής, ζηλωτός, ζηλοτυπία, ὁμοζηλία, θυμός, ὀργή, φθόνος: Trench 86-90; Stumpff, *TDNT* 2.878f., 883f.; Chadwick 119-23.

ζηλοτυπία, ας. f.

jealousy: felt by a husband suspecting his wife of adultery, θυσία ~ας Nu 5.15; νόμος ~ας 5.29. Cf. ζῆλος, ζήλωσις.

ζηλόω: fut. ζηλώσω; aor. ἐζήλωσα, subj. ζηλώσω, inf. ζηλῶσαι, impv. ζήλωσον, ptc. ζηλώσας; pf. ἐζήλωκα.

1. *to be filled with jealousy towards*: + acc. pers., Ge 26.14, 30.1, 37.11, Nu 5.14, 30; τὴν γυναῖκα τοῦ κόλπου σου 'the wife of your bosom' Si 9.1; ἐπί τινι– τοῖς ἀνόμοις Ps 72.3; *s* God and abs. De 32.19 (|| παροξύνω pass.), Jo 24.19.

2. *to show* ζῆλος **1**. *for* (acc.): abs. 1M 2.24; ἐζήλωσε κύριος τὴν γῆν αὐτοῦ Jl 2.18; θυμῷ μεγάλῳ ἐζήλωκα αὐτήν Zc 8.2*b*; ***o*** τὸ καταλειφθὲν ὑπόλειπον τοῦ λαοῦ Is 11.11; θάνατον Wi 1.12; + cogn. obj. Ἐζήλωκα τὴν Ιερουσαλημ .. ζῆλον μέγαν Zc 1.14, 8.2*a*.

3. *to act out of devotion to and concern for*: + dat. pers. Nu 11.29; τῷ θεῷ αὐτοῦ 25.13; + dat. rei, τῷ νόμῳ 1M 2.26; + cogn. acc., μου τὸν ζῆλον 25.11; ἐν φόβῳ κυρίου Si 45.23. Cf. μαιμάω.

4. *to envy*: + acc. pers., Ps 36.1 (|| παρα~ ἔν τινι); + acc. rei, δόξαν ἁμαρτωλοῦ Si 9.11.

5. *to emulate*: abs., Pr 6.6.

Cf. ζῆλος, ζήλωσις, παραζηλόω, πρόσκειμαι **2**.

ζήλωσις, εως. f.ʃ

jealousy: of a husband suspecting his wife of adultery, πνεῦμα ~εως Nu 5.14, 30; οὖς ~εως ἀκροᾶται τὰ πάντα 'a jealous ear hears everything' Wi 1.10. Cf. ζῆλος, ζηλοτυπία.

ζηλωτής, οῦ. m.ʃ

ardent person: divine attribute and adj., θεὸς ζ. Ex 20.5, 34.14, De 4.24, 6.15 (who does not countenance rival gods); zealous of justice, θεὸς ζ. καὶ ἐκδικῶν κύριος Na 1.2; De 5.9; ζ. τῶν νόμων 2M 4.2.

Cf. ζῆλος, ζηλόω, ζηλωτός.

ζηλωτός, ή, όν.ʃ

1. *enviable*: υἱὸς ηὐξημένος ζ. 'a fully grown-up, enviable son' Ge 49.22.

2. *liable to arouse jealousy*: *s* ὄνομα Ex 34.14.

Cf. ζηλωτής.

ζημία, ας. f.ʃ

1. *loss*: βίου 'of livelihood' 2E 7.25.

2. punitive *fine*: 1E 8.24, Pr 27.12, ἄδικος 2M 4.48; paid as tribute, 4K 23.33B (*L* φόρος).

Cf. ζημιόω, τιμωρία: Schmidt 4.172f., 177f.

ζημιόω: fut. ζημιώσω, pass. ζημιωθήσομαι; aor. ἐζημίωσα, pass. ἐζημιώθην.

1. *to make pay a fine*: + double acc., ζημιώσουσιν αὐτὸν ἑκατὸν σίκλους 'they shall impose upon him a fine of 100 shekels' De 22.19; + dat. (fine), χρυσίου ταλάντῳ ἑνί '1 talent of gold' 1E 1.34; pass. ἐπιζήμιον ζημιωθήσεται 'he shall be made to pay a fine' Ex 21.22.

2. *to penalise*: + acc. pers., δίκαιον Pr 17.26.

Cf. ἐπιζήμιος.

ζητέω: fut. ζητήσω, pass. ζητηθήσομαι; aor. ἐζήτησα, impv. ζήτησον, pass.3s ζητηθήτω, inf. ζητῆσαι, subj. ~ήσω, pass. ἐζητήθην, ptc. ζητηθείς.

1. *to look for, search* (what is lost): acc. pers., ζητήσετε κύριον .. καὶ εὑρήσετε De 4.29; ζητήσει αὐτοὺς καὶ οὐ μὴ εὕρῃ αὐτούς 'she will search them, but will not find them' Ho 2.7 (|| καταδιώκω); acc. rei, ζητοῦντες τὸν λόγον κυρίου καὶ οὐ μὴ εὕρωσιν Am 8.12; τὸ διεσκορπισμένον 'the scattered sheep' Na 3.11; *+ ὀπίσω τινός Jb 39.8¶; + dat. com. πόθεν ζητήσω παράκλησιν αὐτῇ; 'where shall I seek consolation for her?' Na 3.7; || ἐκζητέω Le 10.16; + ἔκ τινος (pers.) Ez 7.26; ***o*** how to do sth, πῶς .. Is 40.20.

2. *to pursue as desirable* (+ acc.): οἱ μισοῦντες τὰ καλὰ καὶ ζητοῦντες τὰ πονηρά Mi 3.2; ὁ ζητῶν κύριον Ex 33.7; τὸν κύριον Zp 1.6 (|| ἀντέχομαι), 2.3*a*, Ma 3.1 (|| θέλω), τὸν θεόν Is 55.6; τὸ πρόσωπον τοῦ θεοῦ Ps 23.6; δικαιοσύνην Zp 2.3*b*; τὰ κακά μοι Ps 70.13, sim. 1K 25.26; τὴν ψυχήν σου 'your life' 2K 4.8; ζητηθήσεται 'will be sought after, much in demand' Si 21.17, 39.17, εἰς βουλὴν λαοῦ 'to be a councillor' 38.32; *+ dat., τῷ κυρίῳ 1C 22.19. ***b**. idiom., ζ. τὸ πρόσωπόν τινος *to pursue and value the company of*: king, 3K 10.24; God, Ps 23.6 (|| τινα), 104.4.

3. *to aim to achieve* (+ inf.): κλαῦσαι 'to weep' Ge 43.30; αὐτὸν ἀποκτεῖναι 'to kill him' Ex 4.24; τοῦ ἐξᾶραι πάντα τὰ ἔθνη 'to obliterate all the peoples' Zc 12.9; Es E 3 (|| ἐπιχειρέω).

4. *to ask after* (sth [acc.] desirable or essential): Τί ἄλλο ἀλλ' ἢ σπέρμα ζητεῖ ὁ θεός; 'what else does God seek other than offspring?' Ma 2.15.

5. *to claim* as entitlement: + acc., ἐκ χειρός μου ζήτησον αὐτόν 'claim him from me' Ge 43.9; De 22.2.

6. *to apply to sbd* (acc.) for guidance: of necromancy, divination etc., τοὺς ἀπὸ τῆς γῆς φωνοῦντας 'those who speak out of the ground' Is 8.19 (|| ἐκζητέω; || ἐπερωτάω 19.3, De 18.11); ἐν αὐτῇ 'through her' 1K 28.7 (*L* ἐκζητέω). Prob. belongs here ζητήσατε εἰς εἰρήνην τῆς γῆς Je 36.7 with κύριον or suchlike understood, cf. || προσεύξασθηε .. πρὸς κύριον.

7. *to approach with a request*: pass. and + inf., τοῦτο ζητηθήσομαι .. τοῦ ποιῆσαι αὐτοῖς Ez 36.37.

8. *to inquire into* sth as obj. of intellectual pursuit: Si 3.21 (|| ἐξετάζω); ***o*** γενικὴ γραφή 'genealogy' 1E 5.39. **b**. *to seek to inform oneself about*: τινα 2K 11.3 (*L* ἐκ~), + acc. rei, παρ' αὐτῶν 'from them (informants)' Da 1.20; περί τινος 7.19 TH; a question introduced by εἰ 'whether' 4M 1.13.

Cf. ἀνα~, ἐπι~, ἐκ~, ζητέω, ζήτησις, διώκω, δέομαι, εὑρίσκω, καταδιώκω, σκάλλω, σκέπτομαι.

ζήτησις, εως. f.ʃ

v.n. of prec., *act of seeking*: κυρίου Si 20.32¶.

ζιβύνη, ης. f. Also spelled σ~.ʃ
spear as a weapon: ‖ μάχαιρα Is 2.4 (‖ Mi 4.3 δόρυ), τόξον Je 6.23 (‖ ἐγχειρίδιον 27.42); Ju 1.15. Cf. δόρυ.

ζυγός, οῦ. m. On the gender of the word, see Thack. 154, and Shipp 261f.
1. *yoke*: lit., Nu 19.2, De 21.3; in a fig. of servitude, ἐκλύσεις τὸν ~ὸν αὐτοῦ ἀπὸ τοῦ τραχήλου σου 'you will free his yoke from your neck' Ge 27.40, of religious allegiance Je 2.20, 5.5, Ps 2.3 (‖ δεσμοί), ‖ μάστιξ 'whip' PSol 7.9; on the shoulder, Is 10.27; δουλεύειν .. ὑπὸ ~ὸν ἕνα Zp 3.9; ἐμβάλωσι τὸν τράχηλον αὐτῶν ὑπὸ ζυγὸν βασιλέως .. '.. under the yoke of ..' Je 34.6 (‖ εἰσάγω vs. 9); τῶν ἁμαρτωλῶν .. τῶν ἀρχόντων Is 14.5; ζ. βαρύς 'heavy ..' w. ref. to hum. existence, Si 40.1, restraining influence of wisdom 51.26 (on one's neck), cf. La 3.27.
2. *pair of scales, balance* for weighing: ~ὰ δίκαια Le 19.36 (‖ στάθμια δίκαια, χοῦς δίκαιος), ~ὸς δίκαιος Ez 45.10 (most MSS including 967: ~ὸν ~ον); ζ. ἀδικίας 'false scales' Ho 12.7, ζ. ἄδικον Am 8.5 (‖ μέτρον and στάθμιον); ἐστάθη ἐν ~ῷ 'was put on the scales' Da 5.27 TH; ‖ σταθμός Is 40.12, 46.6, Si 28.25.
3. *oarsmen's benches joining* the opposite sides of a boat: 3M 4.9.
Cf. ζυγόω, βοοζύγιον, μέτρον, στάθμιον, ζεύγνυμι: Bertram, *TDNT* 2.896-8.

ζυγόω: pf.ptc.pass. ἐζυγωμένος.ʃ
to join together: pass., *o* porch, 3K 7.43; the sides of a house, Ez 41.26.

ζῦθος. ⇒ ζῦτος.

ζύμη, ης. f.
leaven: ἀφανιεῖτε ~ην ἐκ τῶν οἰκιῶν ὑμῶν 'you shall get rid of leaven from your houses' Ex 12.15; φάγῃ ~ην 'eats leaven(ed bread)' ib. (‖ ζυμωτός vs. 19); ζ. καὶ μέλι '.. and honey' Le 2.11. Cf. ζυμίτης, ζυμόομαι, ζυμωτός, ἄζυμος: Windisch, *TDNT* 2.902-6.

ζυμίτης, ου. m.ʃ
Used adj. (so alr. in Cl.), *leavened*: ἄρτος Le 7.13. Cf. ζύμη, ζυμωτός.

ζυμόω: aor.pass. ἐζυμώθην, inf. ζυμωθῆναι; pf.pass. ptc. ἐζυμωμένος.
pass. *to ferment*: τὸ σταῖς πρὸ τοῦ ζυμωθῆναι 'dough before fermentation' Ex 12.34; Ho 7.4. Cf. ζύμη.

ζυμωτός, ή, όν.
leavened: subst.n. 'leavened bread', φάγῃ ~όν 'eats leavened bread' Ex 12.19 (‖ ζύμη vs. 15). Cf. ζύμη, ζυμίτης.

ζῦτος, ου. m. Also ζῦθος: see Walters 113.
beer: Is 19.10. Cf. Wiedemann 327-9.

ζωγραφέω: aor. ἐζωγράφησα, inf. ~φῆσαι; pf.ptc. pass. ἐζωγραφημένος.ʃ
to portray in colours, 'paint': + acc., ἐπὶ τῶν χειρῶν μου .. τείχη 'walls .. on my hands' Is 49.16, ἄνδρας ἐζωγραφημένους ἐπὶ τοῦ τοίχου 'men painted on the wall' Ez 23.14*a*, ἐν γραφίδι ib. *b*; τῆς εὐσεβείας σου ἱστορίαν 'the history of your religion' 4M 17.7; + ἐγκαίω 2M 2.29. Cf. ζωγραφία, ἐγκαίω.

ζωγραφία, ας. f.ʃ
sth portrayed in colours: Si 38.27. Cf. ζωγραφέω.

ζωγρέω: fut. ζωγρήσω, aor. ἐζώγρησα, inf. ζωγρῆσαι, impv. ζώγρησον.
to keep the defeated *alive*, 'spare sbd death': + acc. pers. Nu 31.15, 18 (:: ἀποκτείνω), De 20.16; ‖ περιποιέομαι Jo 9.20; only to be killed soon after, 'to capture alive' 2C 25.12.
Cf. ζωγρίας, ζωογονέω, ζωόω, περιποιέω, ἀποκτείνω: Spicq 2.161-3.

ζωγρίας, ου. m.ʃ
one kept alive after defeat in a battle: μὴ καταλιπεῖν αὐτοῦ ~αν 'not to leave any one of them alive' Nu 21.35, sim. De 2.34; λαβεῖν ~αν 2M 12.35. Cf. ζωγρέω, ζάω.

ζωή, ῆς. f.
1. *state of being alive*, 'life': τὴν ~ὴν καὶ τὸν θάνατον, τὸ ἀγαθὸν καὶ τὸ κακόν De 30.15, προστάγματα ~ῆς 'instructions (observance of which secures) life' Ez 33.15; opp. φθορά, Jn 2.7, cf. καταφθεῖραι πᾶσαν σάρκα, ἐν ᾗ ἐστιν πνεῦμα ~ῆς Ge 6.17; ἐνεφύσησεν .. πνοὴν ~ῆς 'breathed a breath of life' 2.7 (of a human being); πάντα, ὅσα ἔχει πνοὴν ~ῆς 7.22 (of animals); καρπὸν ~ῆς Ho 10.12 (‖ δικαιοσύνη); ζ. καὶ εἰρήνη Ma 2.5; γῆ ~ῆς as against Hades, Ez 26.20, 32.23, 24, cf. γῆ ζώντων Je 11.19, Ps 26.13.
2. *period of time when one is alive, life-span*: ἐν τῷ ἑξακοσιοστῷ ἔτει ἐν τῇ ~ῇ τοῦ Νωε 'in the 600th year of Noah's life' Ge 7.11; ἐγένετο ἡ ~ὴ Σάρρας ἔτη ἑκατὸν εἴκοσι ἑπτά 'S.'s life-span came to 127 years' 23.1; Πόσα ἔτη ἡμερῶν τῆς ~ῆς σου; 'What is your age?' 47.8; αἱ ἡμέραι τῶν ἐτῶν τῆς ~ῆς μου 'the total number of years of my life (up to now)' 47.9; τὰ ἔτη τῆς ~ῆς Λευι 'L.'s life-span' Ex 6.16; πάσας τὰς ἡμέρας τῆς ~ῆς ὑμῶν De 16.3; pl., κρεῖσσον τὸ ἔλεός σου ὑπὲρ ζωάς 'your mercy is better than a life many times over' Ps 62.3. **b**. w. ref. to life hereafter: ζ. αἰώνιος following a resurrection: ἀναστήσονται [TH ἐξεγερθήσονται] .. εἰς ~ὴν αἰώνιον Da 12.2 LXX, εἰς αἰώνιον ἀναβίωσιν ~ῆς ἡμᾶς ajnasthvsei 2M 7.9, cf. [Akoue ejntola;" ~h'" Ba 3.9, makrobivwsi" kai; z. 3.14; To 12.9.

3. *a way of conducting one's life*: κατωδύνων αὐτῶν τὴν ~ήν 'they made their life miserable' Ex 1.14; ἐπαιτήσεως 'beggar's' Si 40.28, *o* of βιόω; ‖ βίος Wi 15.12.

4. *a means of living*: Si 4.1; ‖ βίος Pr 5.9.

Cf. ζάω, ζωτικός, βίος, ψυχή, θάνατος: Schmidt 4.41-51; Trench 91-5; Bertram, *TDNT* 2.851-4; Hill 1967.171-5.

ζωμός, οῦ. m.

soup or *sauce* to go with meat, fish etc.: θυσιῶν Is 65.4; Ez 24.10.

ζώνη, ης. f.

girdle: worn by persons, De 23.13; by high priest, Ex 28.4; ~η λινῇ ζώσεται 'he shall put on a linen girdle' Le 16.4. **b**. worn around the waist (ὀσφῦς): λύσουσι τὰς ~ὰς αὐτῶν ἀπὸ τῆς ὀσφύος αὐτῶν Is 5.27, ζ. σαπφίρου ἐπὶ τῆς ὀσφύος αὐτοῦ 'sapphire belt ..' Ez 9.2, ζ., ἣν .. περιζώννυται '.. which he puts on round (his waist)' Ps 108.19, περιέδησεν ~η ὀσφύας αὐτῶν 'fastened their waists with a belt' Jb 12.18¶.

Cf. ζώννυμι, παραζώνη, περίζωμα.

ζώννυμι: fut. ζώσω, mid. ζώσομαι; aor. ἔζωσα, ptc. ζώσας, mid. ἐζωσάμην, impv. ζῶσαι; pf.ptc.mid./pass. ἐζωσμένος.ʃ

I. act. *to fasten* sth *round* sbd or sth, mostly sbd's waist: + acc. pers. and dat. rei, ζώσεις αὐτοὺς ζώναις Ex 29.9, ἔζωσά σε βύσσῳ '.. with a linen garment' Ez 16.10 (‖ ἐνδύω, ὑποδέω, περιβάλλω); + acc. rei and dat. rei, τὰς ὀσφύας σάκκοις 'the waists [= their own waists!] with sackcloths' 2M 10.25; + acc. rei and pass., πύργοι ξύλινοι .. ἐφ' ἑκάστου θηρίου ἐζωσμένοι .. μηχαναῖς 'wooden towers fastened on to each beast with some devices' 1M 6.37; + acc. pers. and acc. rei, αὐτὸν τὴν ζώνην Le 8.7, αὐτοὺς ζώνας 8.13, ἔζωσεν τὸν Δαυιδ τὴν ῥομφαίαν αὐτοῦ ἐπάνω τοῦ μανδύου αὐτοῦ '.. above his cloak' 1K 17.39B.

II. mid. *to fasten* securely round the middle of one's body: + acc. rei, ζώσασθε ἕκαστος τὴν ῥομφαίαν αὐτοῦ 1K 25.13, ἄνδρες ἐζωσμένοι (B: περι~) σκεύη παρατάξεως '.. weapons' Jd 18.11A; ἐζώσατο σάκκον ἐπὶ τὸ σῶμα αὐτοῦ 3K 20.27, ἀνὴρ ῥομφαίαν αὐτοῦ ἐζωσμένος ἐπὶ τὴν ὀσφῦν αὐτοῦ Ne 4.18, ἄνδρας .. ἐζωσμένους ποικίλματα ἐπὶ τὰς ὀσφύας αὐτῶν 'girt with colourful embroidered work round their waists' Ez 23.14f. **b**. *to secure by fastening sth round*: + acc. (part of body), ζῶσαι ὥσπερ ἀνὴρ τὴν ὀσφῦν σου Jb 38.3, 40.7 (typical of men), sim. 4K 4.29, 9.1; + dat. rei, ἀνὴρ .. ἐζωσμένος τῇ ζώνῃ τὴν ὀσφῦν αὐτοῦ 'having put on the belt round his waist' Ez 9.11, metaph., ἔσται δικαιοσύνῃ ἐζωσμένος τὴν ὀσφῦν αὐτοῦ Is 11.5; acc. rei (part of body) understood, ζώνῃ λίνῃ ζώσεται 'he shall put on a linen girdle' Le 16.4, ἀντὶ ζώνης σχοινίῳ ζώσῃ 'with a cord instead of a belt' Is 3.24.

Cf. ζώνη, ἀνα~, παρα~, περι~, ὑποζώννυμι: Oepke, *TDNT* 5.302-8.

ζωογονέω: fut. ~γονήσω; aor.inf. ~γονῆσαι, subj. ~γονήσω; plpf. ἐζωγονήκειν.

1. *to engender*: *s* fauna, τῶν ζωογονούντων τὰ ἐσθιόμενα 'those which engender the edible' Le 11.47, cf. Frankel, *Vorstudien* 189.

*__2__. *to preserve alive without killing*: *o* hum. babes, Ex 1.17; ἄνδρα καὶ γυναῖκα 1K 27.9.

3. *to grant* or *confer physical life*: κύριος θανατοῖ καὶ ζωογονεῖ 1K 2.6.

Cf. ζωή, ζωγρέω, περιποιέω, θανατόω.

ζῷον, ου. n.

living entity: ψυχὴ ~ων ἑρπετῶν 'life of creeping animals' Ge 1.21; inhabiting the waters, Ps 103.25, Si 43.25, Ez 47.9; land animals, Jb 38.14; ‖ θηρίον Wi 7.20, 17.19; ‖ ἄνθρωπος Si 13.15, possessed of soul and most likely ref. to hums. 16.30, ‖ σάρξ Da 4.9 TH; mysterious, Ez 1.5. Very often in the pl. Cf. ζάω, ζωή, θηρίον, κνώδαλον, κτῆνος: Trench 308-10.

ζωοποιέω: fut. ~ποιήσω; aor. ἐζῳοποίησα, inf. ~ποιῆσαι.

= ζωόω: + acc. pers. and *s* God, Ps 70.20, Jb 36.6¶, opp. θανατόω 4K 5.7. Cf. ζωοποίησις, ζωπυρέω: Bultmann, *TDNT* 2.874.

ζῳοποίησις, εως.

v.n. of ζωοποιέω: ζ. μικρά 'brief relief' 2E 9.8. Cf. ζῳοποιέω.

ζωόω: fut. ζωώσω.ʃ

to keep alive without causing to perish: + acc. pers. and *s* God, Ps 79.19, 84.7. Cf. ζωγρέω, ζῳοποιέω.

ζωπυρέω: aor. ἐζωπύρησα.

to fill with power: w. ref. to resuscitation, υἱὸν τεθνηκότα 4K 8.5. Cf. ζωοποιέω.

ζώπυρον, ου. n.ʃ

bellow: pl., πυρός, used as an instrument of torture, 4M 8.13. Cf. βασανιστήριον.

ζῶσις, εως. f.ʃ

v.n. of ζώννυμι, q.v.: σάκκων and + κλαυθμός, κοπετός, ξύρησις Is 22.12 (a gesture of mourning and sorrow).

ζωτικός, ή, όν.ʃ

life-giving: *s* πνεῦμα Wi 15.11. Cf. ζωή.

H

ἤ

1. *or*: only the essential part(s) is given after ἤ: εἰ κλέπται εἰσῆλθον πρὸς σὲ ἢ λησταὶ νυκτός Ob 5(*b*); Am 3.12(*c*), Zc 11.12(*h*), Jl 1.2(*f*), Jn 4.11b(*g*), Zc 7.5(*d*)*bis*. **b**. introducing a disjunctive and complete interr. sentence, τοῦ γνῶναι εἰ .. ἢ οὐ 'in order to find out whether .. or not' Ge 24.21(*b*); Ho 14.10 (-), Mi 4.9(*b*), 6.3(*d*), Jl 3.4(*f*), but with no choice or selection intended, introducing a sentence of synonymous import, 'or again', εἰ προσδέξεταί σε, ἢ (only in Arm and Eth with MT!) εἰ λήμψεται πρόσωπόν σου Ma 1.8(*c*), καὶ τίς ὑπομενεῖ ἡμέραν εἰσόδου αὐτοῦ; ἢ (καὶ A Eth Arm with MT!) τίς ὑποστήσεται ἐν τῇ ὀπτασίᾳ αὐτοῦ; ib.3.2(*d*), a usage distinct from what is discussed in BDAG, s.v. **1.d.**β. **c**. juxtaposes two subordinate clauses: ὅταν .. ἢ ὅταν .. Ex 30.20(*c*). **d**. introduces alternative options with ἤ repeated: μάρτυς ἢ ἑώρακεν ἢ σύνοιδεν 'a witness whether he has seen or is acquainted (with the matter)' Le 5.1(*c*); repeated four times, 5.2(*c*); Le 6.2(*c*), 1M 4.35.

2. in comparison of degree, *than*: καλῶς .. τότε ἢ νῦν 'better then than now' Ho 2.7(*a*); κρεῖσσον ἡμᾶς δουλεύειν τοῖς Αἰγυπτίοις ἢ ἀποθανεῖν ἐν τῇ ἐρήμῳ τούτῳ 'it's better for us to serve the Egyptians than to die in this wilderness' Ex 14.12(*a*); an adjective or adverb understood, θέλω .. ἐπιγνῶσιν θεοῦ ἢ ὁλοκαυτώματα 'I prefer.. knowledge of God to a burnt-offering' Ho 6.6(*a*); καλὸν τὸ ἀποθανεῖν με ἢ ζῆν με Jn 4.3(*a*), 8(*a*); with a quantifying expression, πλείους ἢ δώδεκα μυριάδες ἀνθρώπων 'more than twelve myriad people' Jn 4.11(*a*); with an adjectival verb, ἰσχύει οὗτος ἢ ἡμεῖς Nu 22.6(*a*); ‖ ὑπέρ + acc., Si 30.17(*a*). **b**. resulting in the exclusion of one of the options: σὲ κακώσομεν μᾶλλον ἢ ἐκείνους 'we shall harm you rather than them' Ge 19.9(*i*); δεδικαίωται Θαμαρ ἢ ἐγώ 'T. has turned out to be right rather than I' 38.26(*a*); εἵλοντο τὸν θάνατον ἢ τὴν ζωήν 'they chose death rather than life' Je 8.3(*a*), "we are ready to die rather than transgress .." 2M 7.2, 4M 9.1. **c**. On the combination πρὶν ἤ 'prior to, earlier than,' see under πρίν **B II**. **d**. with a redundant ὅτι: ἢ ὅτι Ec 7.2 (*a*).

3. ἀλλ' ἤ, *except*: τί ἄλλο ἀλλ' ἢ σπέρμα ζητεῖ ὁ θεός; 'what else other than a seed does God seek?' Ma 2.15(-); in τί κύριος ἐκζητεῖ παρὰ σοῦ ἀλλ' ἢ τοῦ ποιεῖν κρίμα .. 'what does the Lord require of you other than for you to practise justice ..?' Mi 6.8b(*e*) and τί καλὸν .. ἀλλ' ἢ τὸ κατοικεῖν ..; Ps 132.1(-), ἄλλο may be understood or a negative may be implied as in 1Clem. 13.4 ἐπὶ τίνα ἐπιβλέψω ἀλλ' ἢ ἐπὶ τὸν πραΰν καὶ ἡσύχιον καὶ τρέμοντά μου τὰ λόγια;. See BDF, § 448.8. **b**. *but*, foll. a negative: De 4.26(*j*); "Not in great strength nor in power, ἀλλ' ἢ ἐν πνεύματί μου" Zc 4.6(*e*). **c**. ἀλλ' ἢ ὅτι: introduces a serious qualification and an expression of reservation, 'Mark, mind you', ἀλλ' ἢ ὅτι θρασὺ τὸ ἔθνος 'The people, however, are rather bold' Nu 13.29(*k*).

Cf. ἤπερ, ἤτοι: Margolis 1909; Chadwick 123-33.

a) מִן; *b*) אִם; *c*) also Ar. אוֹ; *d*) -ו; *e*) ἀλλ' ἤ כִּי אִם; *f*) וְאִם; *g*) בֵּין לְ־; *h*) וְאִם לא; *i*) μᾶλλον ἤ מִן; *j*) ἀλλ' ἤ כִּי; *k*) ἀλλ' ἢ ὅτι אֶפֶס כִּי. x∫

ἦ

Asseverative particle mostly as part of the phrase ἦ μήν. Variant spellings: εἰ μήν, εἶ μήν - cf. Thack. 83.

of truth, indeed, assuredly: in an oath, ὤμοσα .. ἦ μὴν εὐλογῶν εὐλογήσω σε 'I shall certainly bless you' Ge 22.17; ὀμεῖται, ἦ μὴν μὴ αὐτὸς πεπονηρεῦσθαι Ex 22.8, sim.11; in a solemn affirmation, νὴ τὴν ὑγιείαν Φαραω, ἦ μὴν κατάσκοποί ἐστε 'by the health of Pharaoh, you are surely spies' Ge 42.16; ζῶ ἐγὼ .. ἦ μὴν οὐκ ὄψονται τὴν γῆν Nu 14.21-23 (God speaking), sim. 14.28; 14.35, Is 45.23. **b**. introduces a rhetorical question: ἦ οὐκ ἐπ' αὐτῷ ἐπεποίθειν; 'I certainly trusted in him, didn't I?' Jb 6.13; 10.3; Jd 14.15, 2K 3.25. **c**. sometimes spelled and printed as εἰ: Εἰ ἄρα ἔστιν καρπὸς τῷ δικαίῳ Ps 57.12, "Chase them, you will surely catch up with them (εἰ καταλήμψεσθε αὐτούς)" Jo 2.5; Is 40.15, cf. Coleman 160-4.

Cf. Chadwick 123-33; Hauspie 2003a.12-5.

ἡγεμονία, ας. f.

1. *a place where one may exercise authority*: Ge 36.30; ‖ καθέδρα δόξης Si 7.4. **b**. *governing institution* or *manner and style of government*: Si 10.1.

2. *rank in a hierarchy*: Nu 1.52 (‖ τάξις).

3. *act of governing or ruling with authority*: 4M 6.33.

Cf. ἡγεμών and τάξις.

ἡγεμονικός, ή, όν.∫

pertaining to leading: *s* πνεῦμα Ps 50.14; ἀρχή 'office vested with authority' 4M 8.7. Cf. ἡγέομαι.

ἡγεμών, όνος. m.

chieftain: Ge 36.15 +; as title, ἡγεμὼν Θαιμαν ib.+; ~όνες Εδωμ καὶ ἄρχοντες Μωαβιτῶν Ex 15.15; military, + στρατηγός Je 28.23; βασιλέως

46.3; metaph., *s* λογισμός 'rational will,' ἀρετῶν 'of virtues' 4M 1.30 (|| αὐτοκράτωρ), νοῦς 'mind' 2.22. Cf. ἡγέομαι, καθηγεμών, ἁδρός, ἄρχων, δεσπότης.

ἡγέομαι: fut. ἡγήσομαι; aor. ἡγησάμην; pf. (with the force of the pres.) ἥγημαι.

1. *to direct* (organisation, group of individuals): || ἄρχων Ge 49.10; + gen. pers., ὁ δὲ θεὸς ἡγεῖτο αὐτῶν, ἡμέρας μὲν ἐν στύλῳ νεφέλης δεῖξαι αὐτοῖς τὴν ὁδόν, τὴν δὲ νύκτα ἐν στύλῳ πυρός 'but God led them, by day with a pillar of cloud to show them the way and by night with a pillar of fire' Ex 13.21; Mi 2.13; divine angel, Ex 23.23; *+ ἐν - ἐν Ισραηλ 2C 7.18, ἐν παντὶ λαῷ καὶ ἔθνει Si 24.6; *+ ἐπί τινος De 1.15, 1K 22.2, 1C 9.20; *+ ἐπί τινα 1C 17.7, 2C 16.5; subst. pres. ptc. ἡγούμενος, *s* governor, ruler or leader, ἡγούμενοι || γερουσία De 5.23; λαοῦ μου Mi 2.9, τοῦ οἴκου Ισραηλ 3.9, λαοῦ καὶ ἱερέων '.. of priests' 1E 1.47 (|| ἔνδοξοι 2C 36.14); τῆς πόλεως Si 10.2, ἐκκλησίας 30.27 (|| μεγιστᾶν), || δυνάστης 41.17, + στρατηγός Ez 23.6; οἴκου κυρίου Je 20.1; τὰ ἑρπετὰ τὰ οὐκ ἔχοντα ἡγούμενον 'the reptiles which have no guide' Hb 1.14; classified as χιλίαρχος, ἑκατόνταρχος, πεντηκόνταρχος, δεκάδαρχος 'leader of 1,000, 100, 50, 10 men' 1M 3.55, cf. 'commander-in-chief' ἡγούμενος πάντων υἱῶν Ἀμμών Ju 5.5. Cf. ποιμήν **2**.

2. *to claim control* (over sth τινος); subst. ptc., φαρμάκων Na 3.4.

3. *to move ahead of*: + gen., καὶ τὸν φόβον ἀποστελῶ ἡγούμενόν σου 'I shall send the fear ahead of you' Ex 23.27 (|| πρότερος vs. 28); πασῶν τῶν γυναικῶν Ju 15.13; τῶν πρώτων φίλων ἡγεῖσθαι 'to be Number One among his closest friends' 1M 11.27 (or: **4** 'to consider him to be one of his ..'); + πρό τινος Pr 16.18.

4. *to consider, regard* as: + acc., ἥγηται τὴν θάλασσαν ὥσπερ ἐξάλειπτρον 'he considers the sea as a pot of ointment' Jb 41.23 (|| λογίζομαι vs. 24); and + adj. pred., με ὑπεναντίον σοι 'me as hostile to you' 13.24, τὰς Ἑλληνικὰς δόξας καλλίστας ἡγούμενοι 'thinking the Hellenic status symbols the most beautiful' 2M 4.15; + inf. and adj., 9.21; and + nom. pred., ἐμαυτὸν γῆν καὶ σποδόν Jb 42.6; + acc. and a clause, δόξαν ἡγεῖται ὅτι .. 'counts it a glorious thing that ..' Wi 15.9.

Cf. ἄρχω, καθοδηγέω, προ~, προκαθηγέομαι, κατάρχω, κυριεύω, λογίζομαι, ὁδηγέω, ἡγεμών, ἡγεμονικός, ἡγητέον: Schmidt 1.333-47; Spicq 2.166-70.

ἥγημα, ατος. n.ʃ

**guidance, instruction*: + inf., Ez 17.3, cf. Thdt PG 81.960.

ἥγησις, εως.f.ʃ *

leadership position: 1M 9.31; σκῆπτρον ἐνισχύοντος ~εως 'sceptre of a victorious leader' Jd 5.14A (B: διή~).

ἡγητέον.ʃ

one must consider as: Pr 26.23. Cf. ἡγέομαι.

ἡδέως. adv.

in cheerful and merry mood: ἡ. γίνομαι Es 1.10 o' (*L* εὐφραίνομαι), To 7.10, πάσχω 'endure' 2M 6.30, ὑπνόω 'sleep' Pr 3.24. Cf. ἱλαρῶς.

ἤδη. adv.

1. *before this time*, 'already': καθότι ἐποίησα ἤδη ἱκανὰ ἔτη 'as I have already been doing many years' Zc 7.3.

2. *very soon after now*: + fut. Ἤδη ὄψει 'you will see very shortly' Ex 6.1; Nu 11.23.

ἥδομαι: aor.3s ἥσθετο.ʃ

to enjoy oneself: φίλου ἐν εὐφροσύνῃ 'when a friend is happy' Si 37.4; ἐπὶ θρόνοις καὶ σκήπτροις '(delight) in thrones and sceptres' Wi 6.21; ἐπ' αὐτοῖς (pers.) 4M 8.4. Cf. ἡδύνω.

ἡδονή, ῆς. f.

1. *pleasure*: + πόνος 'pain' 4M 1.20; of copulation, Wi 7.2.

2. *taste, flavour*: of food, Nu 11.8.

Cf. ἡδύνω, ἥδομαι, ἡδύς, ἀηδία: Schmidt 2.561-3; Stählin, *TDNT* 2.909-26; Renehan 1.100.

ἡδύνω: aor. ἥδυνα, pass. ἡδύνθην, opt.3s ἡδυνθείη.ʃ

to please, to be found likable by: + acc., *o* ψυχήν Pr 13.19; + dat. pers., οὐχ ἥδυναν αὐτῷ αἱ θυσίαι αὐτῶν 'their sacrifices did not meet with his pleasure' Ho 9.4 (*pace* Zgl's punctuation with αὐτῷ·), sim. Je 6.20. **b**. pass. = act., *s* ἄρτος Jb 24.5¶, ἡ διαλογή μου Ps 103.34 (|| εὐφραίνομαι), τὰ ῥήματά μου 140.6, αἴνεσις 146.1; woman, || ὡραιόομαι Ct 7.7. **c**. *to render pleasant and delightful*: *s* flute and harp, + acc., μέλη 'melodies' Si 40.21. Cf. ἀρέσκω, ἥδυσμα, ἡδονή.

ἡδυπάθεια, ας. f.ʃ

enjoyable living: w. carnal overtones, 4M 2.2, 4. Cf. ἡδύς.

ἡδύς, εῖα, ύ; comp. ἡδίων, ον; superl. ἥδιστος, η, ον.

pleasant, agreeable: *s* οἶνος Si 35.6, γλῶσσα 40.21, ὀσμή 'smell' Is 3.24; state of affairs, ὅτι ἐθερμάνθην 'that I became warm' 44.16, ὕπνος 'sleep' Je 38.26, 3M 5.12, cf. Hom. *Il*. 4.131; πᾶς θανάτου τρόπος 'every manner of death' 4M 9.29. **b**. *feeling pleased and happy*: *s* hum., in pubs, Pr 12.11a. **c**. *pleasure-seeking, hedonistic*: Pr 14.23.

Cf. ἡδέως, ἡδυπάθεια, τερπνός, λυπηρός: Schmidt 2.557f.; Spicq 2.171-3.

ἥδυσμα, ατος. n.

pl. *spices, aromatics*: for cultic use, Ex 30.23, 34; 3K 10.2; sg., of cooking oil, Ec 10.1. Cf. ἡδύνω, ὀσμή.

ἡδυσμός, οῦ. m.ʃ*
sweetness: of cultic spice offering, Ex 30.34.

ἡδύφωνος, ον.ʃ
having or *producing sweet voice*: *s* harp, Ez 33.32.

ἠδώ.ʃ
rainbow: Jb 36.30, see Ol. ad loc.

ἠθολογέω: aor.opt. ἠθολογήσαιμι.ʃ *
to verbalise the character of: + acc. rei, 4M 15.4. Cf. λέγω.

ἦθος, ους. n.
1. *custom*: Si prol. 35. **b**. *that which normally befalls* sbd: Si 20.26. **c**. τὸ ἦθος used adv., *habitually*: 4M 2.7. Cf. ἐθισμός.
2. *moral character or disposition*: πάθη καὶ ~η 'passions and ..' 4M 2.21.

ἥκω: 3pl ἥκασι (cf. Helbing, *Gram*., 103f), impv. ἧκε; fut. ἥξω, ptc. ἥξων.
The pres. is used with the force of the pf., whereas the fut. means "will come, arrive."
1. *to have come, arrived*: ἥκει τὸ πέρας ἐπὶ τὸν λαόν μου 'the end of my people has arrived' Am 8.2; *s* hum. Ge 18.10; 42.9 (‖ ἦλθον vs. 10, 12), Hg 2.7; God, Ho 6.3; days, Ho 9.7*bis*, Jl 1.15; ἑπτὰ ἔτη λιμοῦ 'seven years of famine' Ge 41.30; καιρός (for the annihilation of mankind) 6.13, τὸ πέρας 'the end' Je 28.13, Ez 7.2, ὥρα τῆς συντελείας 'the hour of the end' Da 11.45 LXX; εὐλογίαι De 28.2 (‖ εὑρίσκω τινά; ‖ ἔρχομαι vs. 15, 45), ῥήματα καλά Jo 23.15, βοήθεια 'help' Ps 120.1, ἐκδίκησις 'retribution' Mi 7.4, λιμός 'famine' Is 8.21, στεναγμός 'sigh' Jb 3.24, πόνος 'pain' 4.5; συντέλεια 'end' Hb 1.9, συντριβή 'destruction' Is 13.6, ὠδίν 'pain of labour' 37.3, κακά 'calamities' Je 28.60, μάχαιρα Ez 30.4; + dat. pers. Ho 13.13, Ez 32.11; + ἐπί τινα De 28.2, Mi 4.8, Am 8.2; + ἐπί τι Is 2.2; + εἰς of destination, συντέλεια εἰς ἀσεβεῖς ἥξει 'an end will befall the infidel' Hb 1.9; purpose of action, Is 3.14, 1K 29.9; + ἕως Mi 1.15, 4.10; ἐναντίον τινός Ge 6.13; πρός τινα 18.10, 46.31, Ex 20.24, To 13.11 $\mathfrak{G}^{I}$ ($\mathfrak{G}^{II}$ + dat.); opp. ἔσομαι Ez 39.8; ἥκων εἰς ἡμέρας 'advanced in age' 3K 1.1 (B: προβεβηκὼς ἡμέραις); *s* δικαιοσύνη καὶ δόξα Is 45.24.
2. fig. *to reach* a certain point: + εἰς– οὐ ἥκατε .. εἰς τὴν κατάπαυσιν 'you have not attained .. the rest' De 12.9; εἰς ὁμαλισμόν '(your cities) will eventually be levelled' Mi 7.12; εἰς χεῖρας κακῶν Pr 6.3.
In contrast to ἔρχομαι, the verb emphasises the end-point of the process of physical movement, thus 'to arrive': see esp. ἐρχόμενος ἥξει (not ἐλεύσεται) 'one who is to come will arrive' Hb 2.3.
Cf. ἔρχομαι, εὑρίσκω, I πάρειμι: Schneider, *TDNT* 2.926-8.

ἤλεκτρον, ου. n.
alloy of silver and gold: Ez 1.4, see Hauspie 2003 ad loc.

ἡλιάζω: aor.ptc.pass. ἡλιασθείς.ʃ
to expose to the heat of the sun: pass., *o* corpses, 2K 21.14B (*L* ἐξ~). Cf. ἐξηλιάζω: Shipp 263.

ἡλικία, ας. f.
1. *length of life reached*, 'age': προβεβηκὼς τὴν ~αν 'advanced in age' 2M 4.40, τὴν ~αν προήκων 4M 5.4. Cf. συνῆλιξ.
2. *manhood*: Si 26.19¶; οἱ ἐν ~ᾳ 'adult men' 2M 5.24.
3. *size*: κεφαλὴ πάσης ~ας Ez 13.18; stature of a woman, Si 26.17.
Cf. ἡλικιώτης: Shipp 264; Schneider, *TDNT* 2.941-3.

ἡλικιώτης, ου. m.ʃ
equal of age: *s* hum., 4M 11,14. Cf. ἡλικία.

ἥλιος, ου. m.
1. *the sun*: ἐπήρθη ὁ. ἥ. 'the sun was exalted' Hb 3.11 (‖ σελήνη); of its scorching heat, ἐπάταξεν ὁ ἥ. ἐπὶ τὴν κεφαλὴν Ιωνας Jn 4.8[2], ἡμέρας ὁ ἥ. οὐ συγκαύσει σε 'by day the sun will not burn you up' Ps 120.6; ὁ ἥ. καὶ ἡ σελήνη, as sources of light, Jl 2.10, sim. 2.31, 3.15; ὁ ἥ. καὶ ἡ σελήνη καὶ ἕνδεκα ἀστέρες Ge 37.9, sim. De 4.19; + δύω to suggest the loss of light, Am 8.9, Mi 3.6; + ἀνατέλλω, of sunrise Jn 4.8[1], Na 3.17, cf. Ma 1.11; ἐξέρχομαι Ge 19.23; + δύω, of sunset Ge 28.11, ἐπιδύω De 24.15; περὶ ~ου δυσμάς 'about the time of sunset' Ge 15.12; fig. ἀνατελεῖ .. ἥ. δικαιοσύνης Ma 4.2; fig. of permanency, Ps 88.37, revealing all Si 17.19, κατέναντι τοῦ ~ου 'in broad daylight' PSol 2.11 (ἀπέναντι .. vs. 12, Nu 25.4).
2. In the place-name Ἡλίου πόλις 'Heliopolis' Ge 46.20.
Cf. σελήνη, ἀστήρ, and ἄστρον.

ἧλος, ου. m.
nail, stud: Is 41.7, + σφῦρα 'hammer' Je 10.4; ἐν ταῖς πτέρναις 'in the heels' Jo 23.13 (impeding freedom of movement). Cf. διηλόω.

ἡμεῖς; ἡμῶν; ἡμῖν; ἡμᾶς.
Speakers' reference to themselves: 'we, our, us.' On the contrastive, emphatic nominative, see under ἐγώ, **I 1**. There exists no distinct enclitic form as με in contrast with ἐμέ.

ἡμέρα, ας. f.
1. *a period of time extending from one sunset to the following*, 'day': ἡ. δευτέρα 'a second day' Ge 1.8; μῆνα ἡμερῶν 'for the duration of one month' 29.14; ὡσεὶ πορείας ὁδοῦ ἡμερῶν τριῶν 'at a distance of about three days' journey' Jn 3.3; ἡμέρας μιᾶς 3.4. Mostly without the express connotation of 'full day': ἀφ' ἧς ~ας ἀνέστης ἐξ ἐναντίας 'since the day you

stood up in opposition' Ob 11*a*; esp. w. ref. to the eschatological day, ἐν ἐκείνῃ τῇ ~ᾳ, λέγει κύριος, ἀπολῶ σοφούς Ob 8, ~αν εἰσόσου αὐτοῦ 'the day of his entry' Ma 3.2, ἰδοὺ ἡ. ἔρχεται .. ἡ ἡ. ἐρχομένη 4.1, ἐγγὺς ἡ. κυρίου Ob 15; characterised by some event, θλίψεως 12, 14, ἡ. πόνων .. ἡ. ὀλεθροῦ .. ἡ. ἀπωλείας 13; πάγους 'frosty' Na 3.17; καθαρισμοῦ 'of purification' Ex 29.36; ἡ. ἀλλοτρίων 'the day when foreigners triumph' Ob 12; ἡ ἡ. σου καὶ καιρὸς ἐκδικήσεώς σου 'the day of your doom and time of vengeance against you' Je 27.31, sim. 27.27; an event expressed by means of a gen. abs., ἐν ~ᾳ ἐπιλαβομένου μου τῆς χειρὸς αὐτῶν .. 'on the day when I took hold of their hand ..' Je 38.32. **b.** "this day" = 'today': ἀπὸ τῆς ~ας ταύτης Hg 2.19. **c.** πάσας τὰς ~ας 'all the days, always, all the time' Ge 6.5. **d.** ~αν ἐξ ~ας 'day in, day out' Ge 39.10, Ps 60.9; ~αν ἐν ~ᾳ 2E 3.4, 6.9; ἐξ ~ας εἰς ~αν 1C 16.23 (‖ Ps 95.2 ~αν ἐξ ~ας), Je 52.34ʃ, sim. τὸ τῆς ~ας εἰς ~αν 1C 16.37. **e.** τὴν ἡμέραν 'daily, every day': Nu 28.24, slightly different from δύο τὴν ~αν 'two per day,' on which see under ὁ **VII a**. **f.** ἕως τῆς ~ας ταύτης 'even these days' De 34.6.

2. *the period of day from sunrise to sunset* as opposed to nighttime: ἡμέραν καὶ νύκτα 'day and night' Ge 8.22, Le 8.35; τῆς ~ας .. καὶ τῆς νυκτός 'by day .. by night' Ge 31.40; νυκτός .. ἡμέρας 'at night .. by day' De 1.33; ἡμέρας καὶ νυκτός 'day and night' 28.66, νυκτὸς καὶ ἡμέρας Is 34.10; ἡμέρας .. τὴν νύκτα Ps 120.6, Wi 10.17; ~ας .. ἐν νυκτί Is 28.19; Ἔτι ἐστὶν ἡ. πολλή 'it is yet high day' Ge 29.7; τρεῖς ἡμέρας καὶ τρεῖς νύκτας Jn 2.1; φεύξονται ~ας 'will flee by day' Na 2.6; Zc 14.7; Am 8.9.

3. pl. *a period of time of considerable length*, 'era, period': πᾶσαι αἱ ~αι Νωε Ge 9.29; αἱ ~αι τῆς ζωῆς 'life-time' 3.14; αἱ ~αι τῶν ἐτῶν τῆς ζωῆς μου 'the total number of years of my life (up to now)' 47.9 (‖ ἔτη ἡμερῶν τῆς ζωῆς σου vs. 8); πένθους 'of mourning' 27.41; 8.22; ἐν ~αις θερισμοῦ 'during a harvest season' 30.14; αἱ ~αι τοῦ αἰῶνος 'the olden days' Ma 3.4 (‖ τὰ ἔτη τὰ ἔμπροσθεν), ~αι πρότεραι 'former times' De 4.32, sim. ἀρχαῖαι .. Is 37.26; ἐσχάται ~αι 2.2; ἐν ταῖς ~αις ὑμῶν Hb 1.5; ἐν ἡμίσει ~ῶν αὐτοῦ 'half-way through his life' Je 17.11; ἐν ταῖς ~αις ἐκείναις Zc 8.6; ἐν ~αις πολέμου Ho 10.14; προβεβηκὼς ~ῶν 'advanced in age' Ge 18.11, 24.1, πρεσβύτεροι ~αις 'older in age' Jb 32.4¶; ἡμέρας τινάς 'for some time' Ge 27.44; πάσας τὰς ~ας 'for ever (thereafter)' 43.9, 'always' De 11.1; πάσας τὰς ~ας σου εἰς τὸν αἰῶνα 23.6; αἱ ~αι .. τοῦ ἀποθανεῖν Ge 47.29 (the closing days of life); ‖ καιρός Je 3.16. **b.** with another noun denoting greater length: μετὰ δύο ἔτη ~ῶν Ge 41.1, 1M 1.29; μῆνα ~ῶν 'for a month' Ge 29.14, sim. Nu 11.20; τρεῖς ἑβδομάδας ~ῶν 'for three weeks' Da 10.2 TH; ἡμέρας τοῦτο δεύτερον ἔτος 'quite a while, now already into a second year' 1K 29.2 (*L* ἤδη δ. ἔ. ~ῶν). ***c.** εἰς ~αν *for one year* counting from today: Jd 17.10 B (A: pl., MT *layyāmim*, see Rashi ad loc., ≠ 'situation carrying an annual emolument of ..'), εἰς ~αν ἀπὸ τῆς ἡμέρας ταύτης Ez 24.2. ***f.** ἐξ ἡμερῶν εἰς ἡμέρας (= מִיָּמִים יָמִימָה) 'year in year out': Jd 11.40 A (B: ἀπὸ .., so Ex 13.10, Jd 21.19), 1K 1.3.

4. *length of past existence*, 'age': ἀπὸ πλήθους ~ῶν 'on account of old age' Zc 8.4.

Cf. αἰών, καιρός, νύξ, μονοήμερος: Delling, *TDNT* 2.947f.

ἥμερος, α, ον.ʃ

1. *cultivated*: *s* φυτά 'plants' 4M 2.14.

2. *cultivated and suited to human habitation*: *s* βασιλεία Es B 2.

3. *tame* in character: *s* birds, 4M 14.15.

4. *civil* in attitude: *s* ἀπάντησις 'reception' 2M 12.30.

Cf. ἡμερόω: Schmidt 3.76-8, 79-82.

ἡμερόω.ʃ

to make tame: mid., *s* (intensity of) flame, Wi 16.18.

ἡμέτερος, α, ον.

belonging to us, appertaining to us, 'our,' with stressed notion of ownership and claim, and pl. of ἐμός, q.v.: κατ' εἰκόνα ἡμετέραν 'according to our own image' Ge 1.26. Cf. ἐμός, ἡμεῖς.

ἡμίεφθος, ον.ʃ

half-boiled: *s* σευτλίον 'beet' Is 51.20. Cf. ἕψω, ἑφθός.

ἡμιθανής, ές.ʃ

half-dead: *s* hum., 4M 4.11. Cf. ἡμίθνητος.

ἡμίθνητος, ον.ʃ

half-dead: Wi 18.18. Cf. ἡμιθανής.

ἡμίονος, ου. m./f.

mule: part of a nomad's possessions, ἐγένετο αὐτῷ πρόβατα καὶ μόσχοι καὶ ὄνοι, παῖδες καὶ παιδίσκαι, ~οι καὶ κάμηλοι Ge 12.16; beast of burden, 45.23 (‖ ὄνος); used in war as beast of burden, Zc 14.15 (‖ ἵππος, κάμηλος, and ὄνος), Ju 2.17; with poor intelligence, Ps 31.9.

ἡμίσευμα, ατος. n.ʃ *

a half: Nu 31.36, 42, 43, 47. Cf. ἥμισυς.

ἡμισεύω: aor.subj. ἡμισεύσω.ʃ*

to consume half of: *o* life-span, Ps 54.24. Cf. ἥμισυ.

ἥμισυς, εια, υ.

a half: subst.n.sg., τὸ ~υ τοῦ αἵματος 'half of the blood' Ex 24.6; πήχεος καὶ ~ους τὸ πλάτος 'with the width of one and a half cubit' 25.9; τὸ ~υ τῆς πόλεως 'half of the city' Zc 14.2; τὸ ~υ φύλης Μανασση 'the half-tribe M.' Nu 32.33 +; τὸ ~υ τῆς ἡμέρας 'midday' Ne 8.3; τὸ ~υ .. τὸ ~υ 'one half .. the other half' Zc 14.4; anarthrous and adv., *partly* Ne 13.24. Cf. ὁλόκληρος.

ἡνία, ας.
bridle, rein: αἱ ~αι τῶν ἁρμάτων '.. of chariots' Na 2.4; οἱ ἐπὶ τῶν ~ῶν 'those in authority' 1M 6.28. Cf. ἡνίοχος, κημός, χαλινός.

ἡνίκα. conj.
at the time when: of a past event and + aor. Ge 6.1, 16.16, 19.17, 24.30 (ǁ ὅτε), 27.34. 30.42, 43.2, Ex 12.27, 13.15, Nu 9.17; + impf. Ge 19.15, 38.27, 39.10, 45.1, 48.7, Ex 16.21, 32.19; following the main clause and + aor. Ge 21.5, Ex 7.7; + impf. Ge 45.1, Le 26.35; + pres. Ge 24.11. **b**. w. ref. to future, ἡ. ἄν or ἐάν + subj.pres., ἡ. ἂν εἰσπορεύησθε Le 10.9; + subj. aor. ἡ. ἂν ἔλθῃς Ge 24.41; 27.40; ἡ. ἂν συμβῇ Ex 1.10; ἡ. ἂν εἰσαγάγῃ 13.5; 33.22; Le 6.4, De 7.12, 25.19, Ez 32.9; Pr 1.26 (ǁ ὡς ἄν vs. 27). **c**. w. ref. to past and frequentative or habitual: ἡ. ἄν + impf. ἡ. ἂν εἰσεπορεύετο Ex 33.8; + aor. ἡ. ἂν ἀνέβη 40.30 (ǁ εἰ δὲ μὴ ἀνέβη vs. 31). **c**. generic time reference: ἡ. δεῖ εἰπεῖν λόγον Is 50.4.
Cf. ὅτε, ὅταν, ὡς.

ἡνίοχος, ου. m.ʃ
one who holds the reins, 'charioteer': 3K 22.34 (ǁ 2C 18.33). Cf. ἡνία.

ἧπαρ, ατος. n.
liver: Ge 49.6; λοβὸς τοῦ ἥπατος 'lobe of ..' Ex 29.13; of fish, To 6.5.

ἡπατοσκοπέομαι: aor.inf. ~σκοπήσασθαι.ʃ *
to examine livers: divination, ǁ μαντεύομαι Ez 21.21.

ἤπερ.ʃ
1. *than* in comparison: κρείσσων .. ἤ... 'better .. than ..' Si 18.29¶; 4M 15.16.
2. introduces a less likely alternative: ἐν τῇ Μηδίᾳ .. μᾶλλον ἤ. ἐν Ἀσσυρίοις '.. rather than in ..' To 14.4𝔊II; 2M 14.42.
Cf. ἤ.

ἠπιότης, τος. f.ʃ
gentleness: hum. character, Es B 2. Cf. Spicq 2.174-7.

ἠρεμάζω.ʃ*
to be still without moving: from grief, ἐκαθήμην ἠρεμάζων 2E 9.3, 4. Cf. κινέω, μένω: Shipp 90.

ἥρως, ωος. m.ʃ
hero: in a place-name, Ἡρώων πόλις 'Heroonpolis' Ge 46.28, 29 (= גֹּשֶׁן).

ἥσσων, ον. Also spelled ἥττων.
1. *inferior*: in force, 'weaker,' Is 23.8 (militarily and ǁ οὐκ ἰσχύω); Da 2.39 TH (LXX ἐλάττων); ἥ. γίνομαι 'to be defeated' 2M 13.23 (ǁ ἐλαττονόω vs. 19); opp. ἰσχυρός Ep Je 35; in importance, *s* μέρος 2M 15.18.
2. *less*: οὐθὲν ἧττον 'no less' Jb 13.10.
Cf. ἡττάω, κακός, χείρων, κρείσσων: Schmidt 4.314f.

ἡσυχάζω: fut. ἡσυχάσω; aor. ἡσύχασα, impv. ἡσύχασον, inf. ἡσυχάσαι, subj. ἡσυχάσω.
1. *to be* or *become restful, free from turbulance*: *s* pers., Ge 4.7, Ex 24.14, ἐν ἡσυχίᾳ Ez 38.11; free from war, ἡ γῆ κατοικεῖται καὶ ἡσυχάζει Zc 1.11, cf. ἡσύχασεν ἡ γῆ ἔτη πεντήκοντα Jd 3.11 and ἡσύχασεν ἡ γῆ ἐνώπιον αὐτοῦ 'the land was peaceful during his reign' 1M 11.38; the billows of the sea after a storm, Ps 106.30 (ǁ σιγάω), ὕδατα Ez 32.14, wild animals, ἐπὶ κοίτης 'in their lair' Jb 37.8, sword (μάχαιρα) in action, Je 29.6; μάχη 'strife' Pr 26.20. **b**. w. ref. to peace of mind: οὔτε εἰρήνευσα οὔτε ἡσύχασα οὔτε ἀνεπαυσάμην Jb 3.26; τοῦ ἡσυχάσαι καὶ μὴ φοβοῦ Is 7.4, ἡσυχάσει καὶ ὑπνώσει '.. and will sleep' Je 26.27, ὑπομενεῖ καὶ ἡσυχάσει εἰς τὸ σωτήριον κυρίου 'quietly waits for salvation from the Lord' La 3.26; gained after death, κοιμηθεὶς ἡσύχασα Jb 3.13 (ǁ ἀναπαύομαι); ἀφόβως ἀπὸ παντὸς κακοῦ Pr 1.33. Cf. Pr 7.11. ***c**. pass.impers., ἡσυχάζεται ἐπὶ τῆς γῆς 'it is all quiet and peaceful upon the earth' Jb 37.17.
2. *to fall silent*: γῆ ἐφοβήθη καὶ ἡσύχασεν Ps 75.9.
3. *to refrain from speaking*, 'keep quiet': ἡσύχασα φοβηθεὶς '.. out of diffidence' Jb 32.6.
4. *to refrain* from doing: + inf., Jb 32.1, 6.
Cf. ἡσυχῇ, ἡσυχία, ἡσύχιος, ἥσυχος, ἀναπαύομαι, εἰρηνεύω, σιγάω: Schmidt 1.222-4, 4.250-5; Spicq 2.178-83.

ἡσυχῇ. adv.ʃ
without making much noise, 'quietly, still': τὸ ὕδωρ .. τὸ πορευόμενον ἡ. Is 8.6, ἡ. μειδιάσει 'smiles ..' Si 21.20; Jd 4.21A (B: ἐν κρυφῇ). Cf. ἡσυχάζω.

ἡσυχία, ας.f.
1. *absence of excessive noise* or *movement*: ~αν ἔσχε 'he kept quiet' 2M 14.4; ἐν ἡμέραις ἡσυχίας μου 'when I am not on duty' Es C 27 o'; ~αν παρέξει 'will give quiet' Jb 34.29¶.
2. *peace of mind*: Si 28.16 (ǁ ἀνάπαυσις); ἐπὶ ἡσυχάζοντας ἐν ~ᾳ 'on those relaxing quietly' Ez 38.11 (ǁ ἐπ' εἰρήνης), ἐν ~ᾳ κατοικοῦσι πεποιθότες 'live quietly and feeling secure' 1M 9.58; εὐσταθεῖν καὶ τὰ τῆς ~ας ἄγειν 'to live in peace and quietly' 2M 12.2.
Cf. ἡσυχιάζω, ἀνάπαυσις.

ἡσύχιος, ον.ʃ
1. *making no excessive noise*, 'quiet': *s* hum., penitent and silenced?, τὸν ταπιενὸν καὶ ~ον Is 66.2.

2. *not suffering from disturbance* or *turbulance*: inner, *s* the soul of the innocent and pious, PSol 12.5.

Cf. ἡσυχιάζω.

ἥσυχος, ον.ʃ

= ἡσύχιος: ~ου σιγῆς 'dead silence' Wi 18.14; γυνὴ γλωσσώδης ἀνδρὶ ~ῳ 'a talkative wife to a quiet husband' Si 25.20. Cf. ἡσυχιάζω.

ἤτοι. conj.ʃ

= ἤ 'or': Wi 11.18 (‖ ἤ). Cf. ἤ.

ἡττάω: fut. ἡττήσω, pass. ἡττηθήσομαι; aor.subj. ἡττήσω, pass. ἡττήθην, ptc. ἡττηθείς, subj. ἡττηθῶ; pf.ptc.pass. ἡττημένος. Mostly in the pass.

1. *to defeat*: + acc. pers., Is 54.17 (in court), ἐναντίον τοῦ βασιλέως Da 6.5 LXX. **b**. pass. *to be defeated*: ἐὰν πάλιν ἰσχύσητε, πάλιν ἡττηθήσεσθε 'should you again get the upper hand, you would again be defeated' Is 8.9[3]. **c**. pass. *to surrender as inferior* or *defeated*: Is 8.9[1, 2] (:: ἰσχύω); τῷ φαυλισμῷ αὐτῶν 51.7 (‖ φοβέομαι); *s* καρδία 19.1 (‖ σείομαι 'shiver').

2. pass. *to be deficient*: ἐν συνέσει Si 19.24 (:: περισσεύω).

Cf. ἥττημα, ἥσσων, νικάω: Ziegler 1934.197.

ἥττημα, ατος. n.ʃ*

defeat in battle: Is 31.8. Cf. ἡττάω, νίκη.

ἥττων. ⇒ ἥσσων.

ἠχέω: fut. ἠχήσω; aor. ἤχησα, impv. ἤχησον, inf. ἠχῆσαι.

1. *to make sound*: φωνὴ τῆς σάλπιγγος ἤχει μέγα Ex 19.16; *s* hum. and ‖ σαλπίζω Ho 5.8, ἐν σάλπιγξιν ἐλαταῖς 'with trumpets of hammered metal' Si 50.16; in jubilation, πᾶσα ἡ πόλις Ru 1.19; a human belly, Is 16.11; a great mass of people, 17.12; billows of the sea, Je 5.22, 28.55; human ears tingling, 19.3, 1K 3.11; the ground with ecstatic people, κραυγήν 'loudly' 3K 1.45*L*, τὰ τείχη καὶ τὸ πᾶν ἔδαφος 'the walls and the entire ground' 3M 1.29, τὸ ἁγίασμα 'the sanctuary' Si 47.10. **b**. *to emit sound calling for*: + acc., *s* trumpet, σφαγὴν καὶ ὄλεθρον 'slaughter and destruction' PSol 8.1.

2. *to cause to make sound*: + acc., τὰ κύματα ^τῆς θαλάσσης^ 'the waves of the sea' Is 51.15, cf. *o* φωνήν Si 49.5.

Cf. ἐξ~, συνηχέω, ἦχος, βροντάω, γρύζω, κροτέω, ὀλολύζω, περικομπέω, σαλπίζω, φωνέω: Schneider, *TDNT* 2.954f.

ἦχος, ου. m.

sound: ᾠδῶν 'of songs' Am 5.23; ἑορτάζοντος Ps 41.5; of wild beasts (?), Is 13.21, of birds, εὐμελής 'melodious' Wi 17.18; κυμάτων 'of billows' Ps 64.8, Je 28.42, ἦ. ὕδατος 28.16; ἀσφαλείας 'that which sounds like, and smacks of, firm, confident counsel' (?) Pr 11.15. Cf. ἠχέω, ἦχος (subs.), ἠχώ, θόρυβος, κτύπος, κυδοιμός, λάβρος, μεγαλωστί, ὀλολυγμός, φωνή, ψόφος: Schmidt 3.315f.

ἦχος, ους. n.ʃ

= prec.: of a bewailing crowd, ἡ φωνὴ τοῦ ἤχους τούτου 1K 4.16 (‖ βοή vs. 14); sound of an edifice crashing, μετ' ἤχους 'with a thud' Ps 9.7; πλῆθος ~ους ὑδάτων 76.17.

ἠχώ, οῦς. f.

1. *echo*: Wi 17.19.

2. *ringing sound, loud noise*: nocturnal, Jb 4.13.

Cf. ἦχος, φωνή.

Θ

θάλαμος, ου. m.ʃ

chamber: for unmarried young women, 3M 1.18. Cf. κοιτών, παστός.

θάλασσα, ης. f.

1. *sea*: τὰ συστήματα τῶν ὑδάτων ἐκάλεσε ~ας 'he called the congregation of waters seas' Ge 1.10; Am 8.12; opp. ὁ οὐρανός and ἡ γῆ Zp 1.3; opp. ἡ γῆ, ὁ ἀγρός, and ὁ οὐρανός Ho 4.3; opp. ὁ οὐρανός, ἡ γῆ, and ἡ ξηρά Hg 2.6, 21; opp. ἡ ξηρά 'the dry land' made by God, Jn 1.9, cf. Na 1.4; || ποταμός 'river' Hb 3.8, Zc 9.10, 10.11; πρὸς ~αν 'towards the sea,' i.e. 'towards the west' opp. πρὸς ἀνατολάς 'towards the east'14.4; τὴν ~αν τὴν πρώτην .. τὴν ~αν τὴν ἐσχάτην 'the former sea .. the latter sea' Jl 2.20, Zc 14.8 (Cyr. seems to understand them as ref. to the Indian Ocean / Persian Gulf and the Mediterranean Sea [II. 524f] and Tht = στρατιά 'army' [PG 81.1649]); (ἡ) ἐρυθρὰ θ. 'the Red Sea' Ex 10.19 + (|| θ. ἐ. 15.22 +); "fishes of the sea" Ge 1.26, Ho 4.3, Hb 1.14, Zp 1.3; ἡ ἄμμος τῆς ~ης 'the sands of the sea' Ho 1.10; βάθη καρδίας ~ης 'the deep of the midst of the sea' Jn 2.4, sim. Am 9.3, Mi 7.19; ~η στενῇ 'a narrow sea' Zc 10.11*a*; τὸ ὕδωρ τῆς ~ης Am 5.8, 9.6; θ. καὶ ὕδωρ Na 3.8. **b**. w. ref. to lakes: Kinnereth, Jo 12.3, the Dead Sea (θ. Αρβα .. θ. τῶν ἁλῶν) ib. **c**. w. ref. to the great basin in the temple-court, filled with water for ritual ablution: 3K 7.10, 13, Je 52.17.

*2. *west*: κατὰ ~αν 'to the west' Ge 12.8; πρὸς βορρᾶν καὶ λίβα καὶ ἀνατολὰς καὶ ~αν 'towards the north, south, east and west' 13.14; ἐπὶ ~αν καὶ ἐπὶ λίβα καὶ ἐπὶ βορρᾶν καὶ ἐπ' ἀνατολάς 28.14; κατὰ ~αν καὶ βορρᾶν καὶ λίβα καὶ ἀνατολάς De 3.27. **b**. with no prep.: ~αν προνομεύουσιν καὶ τοὺς ἀφ' ἡλίου ἀνατολῶν 'they will plunder the west and those of the east' Is 11.14.

Cf. θαλάσσιος, ποταμός, πέλαγος, πόντος, ἀνατολή, βορρᾶς, λίψ: Schmidt 1.641-50; Trench 45f.; Chadwick 138-40; Caird 1968.474; Bogaert 1981; LSG s.v.

θαλάσσιος, α, ον.ʃ

originating from the sea: *s* πόρφυρα 'purple' 1M 4.23.

θαλλός, οῦ.ʃ

gift: pl., 2M 14.4 (poss. in the form of olive branches). Cf. δῶρον.

θάλλω.

1. *to grow vigorously*: *s* vine, θάλλουσα ἀνενηνοχυῖα βλαστούς '.. having grown shoots' Ge 40.10; papyrus, Jb 8.11; fire, Pr 26.20.

2. *to be cheerful*: *s* hum. face, Pr 15.13 (:: σκυθρωπάζω 'be gloomy').

Cf. ἀνα~, εὐθαλέω, εὐθηνέω, βλαστάνω: Schmidt 2.492f.

θάλπω: fut. θάλψω.ʃ

to keep warm: *s* a bird by sitting over eggs or young birds, ἡ μήτηρ θάλπῃ ἐπὶ τῶν νοσσῶν ἢ ἐπὶ τῶν ᾠῶν 'the mother sits over her young birds or eggs' De 22.6; Jb 39.14¶; + acc. pers., of a maiden sleeping next to an old man, 3K 1.2; 1.4 (*L*: σύγκοιτος). Cf. θερμαίνω **2**.

θαμβέω: aor. ἐθάμβησα, pass. ἐθαμβήθην.

1. pass. *to be astonished*: abs., Da 8.17 TH (LXX θορυβοῦμαι); + σαλεύομαι 1M 6.8. **b**. act. in the sense of the passive: *s* ἡ γῆ 1K 14.15 (*L* pass.).

2. *to alarm*: τινα 2K 22.5B (|| ἐκταράσσω Ps 17.5).

*3. pass. *to be feared*: θαμβούμενοι Jd 9.4A (ref. to hardy skinheads; *L* ἐπανίσταμαι 'to rebel').

Cf. θάμβος, ἐκθαμβέω, θαυμάζω, θορυβέω, ἐκπλήσσω, ἐξίστημι: Shipp 265; Bertram, *TDNT* 3.4f.

θάμβος, ου, m.; ους, n.

astonishment tinged with alarm and a sense of shock: Ez 7.18 (|| αἰσχύνη); causing mental exhaustion and deep sleep, θ. κυρίου 1K 26.12; close to dread, ἐν νυξίν Ct 3.8. **b**. sense of awe: at female beauty, Ct 6.4.

Cf. θαμβέω, ἔκθαμβος, θαῦμα, ἔκστασις: Schmidt 4.183f.

θανατηφόρος, ον.

death-bringing: *s* ἁμαρτία Nu 18.22, ἀπείθεια 'disobedience' 4M 8.18 (|| ὀλεθροφόρος 'leading to perdition'); ἄγγελος Jb 33.23; ψῆφος 'ballot' 4M 15.26. Cf. θάνατος, ὀλεθροφόρος.

θάνατος, ου. m.

permanent end of physical existence, 'death': τὴν ζωὴν καὶ τὸν ~ον, τὸ ἀγαθὸν καὶ τὸ κακόν De 30.15; 31.27 (|| τελευτή vs. 29); ἐκ ~ου λυτρώσομαι αὐτούς 'I shall redeem them from death' Ho 13.14 (|| ᾄδης); ἕως ~ου 'to the point of death, to the utmost limit' Jn 4.9; ὡς θ. οὐκ ἐμπιπλάμενος 'insatiable as death' Hb 2.5 (|| ᾄδης); personified, ποῦ ἡ δίκη, θάνατε Ho 13.14 (|| ᾄδης), ἡ ἀπώλεια καὶ ὁ θ. εἶπαν Jb 28.22; as punishment, θανάτῳ θανατωθήσεται 'he shall certainly be put to death' Ex 31.14, Le 20.2; ἔβαλες εἰς κεφαλὰς ἀνόμων ~ον Hb 3.13; πᾶς ὁ κλέπτης .. ἕως ~ου ἐκδικηθήσεται 'every thief will be liable to a penalty including death' Zc

5.3; πονηρός 'violent (or: miserable) death' Ps 33.22; as distinct from violent death (θ. αἱμάτων 2K 21.1), θ. καὶ αἷμα Si 40.9. **b.** *fatal illness*: θάνατος ἢ φόνος Ex 5.3; as divine punishment, ἐν ῥομφαίᾳ καὶ ἐν ~ῳ καὶ ἐν λιμῷ Ez 6.11, ἐν μαχαίρᾳ καὶ ἐν λιμῷ καὶ ἐν ~ῳ Je 14.12.

Cf. ἀποθνήσκω, θνητός, ᾅδης, ἀθανασία, ζωή.

θανατόω: fut. θανατώσω, inf. ~τώσειν, pass. ~τωθήσομαι; aor. ἐθανάτωσα, inf. ~τῶσαι, impv. ~τωσον, subj. ~τώσω, pass. ἐθανατώθην; pf. τεθανάτωκα, pass. τεθανάτωμαι, ptc.pass. τεθανατωμένος.

to cause to die, 'kill': + acc. pers. Ge 38.10 (divine punishment and ‖ ἀποκτείνω vs. 7); τὰς ψυχὰς ἡμῶν 4M 9.7; Ex 14.11 (‖ ἀποθνήσκω vs. 12), κύριος θανατοῖ καὶ ζωογονεῖ 1K 2.6; pass. and punishment, Ex 21.12, 15, Le 20.2 (+ dat. cogn. θανάτῳ), Ex 21.14; 31.15 (‖ τελευτάω 35.2); by stoning (λιθοβολέω) Nu 15.35, De 17.7; ὄφις θανατῶν 'killer snake' Nu 21.6, μυῖαι '(deadly) flies' Ec 10.1; *o* life, ἐν λάκκῳ ζωήν μου 'in a pit ..' La 3.53; *s* ζῆτος 'zeal, passion' Jb 5.2. Cf. θάνατος, θανατηφόρος, θανάτωσις, ἀποκτείνω, ἀφανίζω, ζωογονέω: Anz 35f.

θανάτωσις, εως. f.ʃ

act of putting to death: υἱὸς ~εως 'deserving of capital punishment' 1K 26.16. Cf. θανατόω.

θάπτω: fut.act. θάψω, pass. ταφήσομαι; aor. ἔθαψα, inf. θάψαι, impv. θάψον, ptc. θάψας, subj. θάψω, pass. ἐτάφην, ptc. ταφείς; pf.pass. 3s τέθαπται.

to bury (dead person): + acc. pers. Ge 50.5, Nu 11.34; εἰς τὸ σπήλαιον 'into the cave' Ge 25.9, ἐν τῷ σπηλαίῳ 49.29, ἐν τῷ τάφῳ 2K 19.38*L*; pass. ἐν γήρει καλῷ 'in good old age' Ge 15.15 (v.l. τραφείς 'having been nourished'), Je 8.2 (‖ κόπτομαι 'be mourned'); *o* corpse, Si 44.14; + cogn. dat., ταφῇ De 21.23, + cogn. acc., ταφὴν ὄνου 'ass's burial' Je 22.19. Cf. ταφή, τάφος, ἐγκεκηδεύω, ἐνταφιάζω, ἄταφος, ὀρύσσω.

θαρραλέος, α, ον.ʃ

courageous, undaunted: *s* hum., + φαιδρός 'beaming with joy' 4M 13.13. Cf. ἀνδρεῖος, θαρραλέως, θρασύς.

θαρραλέως. adv.

courageously: of soldiers, 3M 1.4.

θαρρέω.⇒ θαρσέω.

θαρσέω: aor.impv. θάρσησον Ju 11.1, pl. θαρσήσατε Ba 4.27; ptc. θαρσήσας. Alm. alw. in the impv., mostly pres. On the rare Attic spellings with -ρρ-, see Thack. 123 and Shipp 265f.

1. *to be of good cheer, not be afraid*: said to encourage and cheer up by a midwife to a woman in difficult labour, Ge 35.17; Jl 2.21 (‖ χαίρω and εὐφραίνομαι); Θάρσει, Σιων, μὴ παρείσθωσαν αἱ χεῖρές σου 'Be of good courage, Zion, let not your hands slack' Zp 3.16, cf. θαρσεῖτε καὶ κατισχύνετε ἐν ταῖς χερσὶν ὑμῶν Zc 8.13; aor., Θάρσησον, γύναι, μὴ φοβηθῇς Ju 11.1.

2. *to be trusting*, 'to count (on)': θαρσεῖ ἐπ' αὐτῇ ἡ καρδία τοῦ ἀνδρὸς αὐτῆς Pr 31.11

The only three exceptions, which are not impv., are: θαρροῦσα λέγει 'boldly says' Pr 1.21; 31.11; θαρσήσασα 'having plucked up courage' Es 7.8 *L*.

Cf. ἀθυμέω, θάρσος, θαρσύνω, εὐθαρσής, καταθαρσέω, θρασύνω, κατισχύνω, παραθαρσύνω, φοβέομαι: Grundmann, *TDNT* 3.25-7; Spicq 2.188-92.

θάρσος, ους. n.

courage: Jb 4.4; of armed forces, Ju 16.10 (‖ τόλμη), 2C 16.8, 1M 4.35. Cf. θαρσέω, θαρσύνω: Schmidt 3.543-7; Shipp 265f.

θαρσύνω: aor.impv. θάρσυνον.ʃ

to encourage in face of difficulties: + acc. pers., Es C 23 o'. Cf. θαρσέω.

θᾶττον. ⇒ ταχύς.

θαῦμα, ατος. n.ʃ

astonishment, amazement: sense of horror, Jb 17.8, 18.20. Cf. θαυμάζω, θάμβος.

θαυμάζω: fut.act. θαυμάσω, mid ~μάσομαι, pass. ~μασθήσομαι; aor. ἐθαύμασα, impv. θαύμασον, inf. ~μάσαι, ptc. ~μάσας, subj. ~μάσω, pass.inf. ~μασθῆναι, ptc. ~μασθείς, opt.act.2s ~μάσειας; pf. τεθαύμακα, ptc.pass. τεθαυμασμένος.

1. *to express surprise* at: τι 3M 1.10; ἐπί τινι, Le 26.32, Is 14.16 (mid. and a sense of shock); + dat. rei, ἀκοαῖς ὠτίων ἡμῶν 'at what our ears hear' Si 43.24; c. acc. cogn. θαυμάσια Hb 1.5; ἔν τινι Si 11.21. **b.** favourably, *marvel at*: + acc., 4M 9.26.

2. *to show respect to*: + acc. pers., τοὺς ἱερεῖς Si 7.29; κατά τινος (pers.) 4M 8.5 (‖ ὑπερτιμάω). ***b.** θ. πρόσωπόν τινος: by acceding to a request or demand, καὶ ἐπὶ τῷ ῥήματι τούτῳ τοῦ μὴ καταστρέψαι τὴν πόλιν 'also on this matter of not destroying the city' Ge 19.21; οὐ λήμψῃ πρόσωπον πτωχοῦ οὐδὲ θαυμάσεις πρόσωπον δυνάστου Le 19.15 (effectively favouritism); οὐ θαυμάζει πρόσωπον οὐδὲ μὴ λάβῃ δῶρον De 10.17; οὐ θαυμάσει πρόσωπον πρεσβυτέρου καὶ νέον οὐκ ἐλεήσει 28.50, πρεσβύτην καὶ τοὺς τὰ πρόσωπα θαυμάζοντας Is 9.14 (the latter prob. referring to corrupt judges, cf. Cyr. δωροδοκοῦντες ἀπλήστως 'taking bribes insatiably' PG 70.269 or people whose favour is curried and sought after, cf. αἰδέσιμος 'venerable' Eus. 70); ‖ αἰσχύνομαι, ἐντρέπομαι Jb 32.22; ‖ ἐπαισυχύνομαι, τιμὴν τίθεμαι 34.19; τεθαυμασμένος προσώπῳ 'highly thought of' 4K 5.1. See *BA* ad Ge 19.21 and Le 19.15.

3. mid. *to marvel at, admire*: + acc., βασιλέα σάρκινον 'king of flesh and blood' Es C 21. **b.** pass.

to be marvelled at: Is 61.6; *o* hum., ἐπὶ τῇ ἀνδρείᾳ 'on account of the courage' 4M 1.11, sim. 6.11. Cf. Renehan 1.103f.

4. mid. *to be shocked*: Je 4.9 (|| ἐξίστημι).

Cf. θαῦμα, θαυμάσιος, θαυμασμός, θαυμαστός, ἀπο~, ἐκθαυμάζω, θαμβέω, ἐκπλήσσω, ἐξίστημι, ταράσσω: Bertram, *TDNT* 3.27-36.

θαυμάσιος, α, ον.

amazing: *s* hum. face, Ju 10.14; subst. ~α Ex 3.20, Jl 2.26 (divine actions), μεγάλα De 34.12, Ps 135.4; || μεγάλα 130.1;|| σημεῖον Si 33.6; cogn. obj. θαυμάσατε ~α Hb 1.5. Cf. θαυμάζω, θαυμαστός.

θαυμασμός, οῦ. m.∫

act of being astonished: 2M 7.18, 4M 6.13. Cf. θαυμάζω.

θαυμαστός, ή, όν.

astonishing: *s* God, ἐν δόξαις Ex 15.11; τὰ ἔργα κυρίου 34.10; τὸ ὄνομα τὸ ἔντιμον καὶ τὸ ~ὸν τοῦτο, κύριον τὸν θεόν σου De 28.58; πληγὰς μεγάλας καὶ ~άς '.. blows' 28.59; σύμβουλος 'counsellor' Is 3.3; subst. ὄψεσθε ~ά 'you will witness astonishing things' Mi 7.15; with negative connotation, Am 3.9. Cf. θαυμάζω, θαυμάσιος, τέρας: Schmidt 4.184-6.

θαυμαστόω: aor. ἐθαυμάστωσα, impv. ~μάστωσον.

to render admirable: + acc. pers., Ps 4.4; + acc. rei, ἔλεος 16.7, 30.22; γνῶσις 138.6, ἀγάπησις 2K 1.26, τοῦ βοηθηθῆναι 'by being helped' 2C 26.15.

θαυμαστῶς. adv.

in astonishing manner: Ps 44.5.

θέα, ας. f.∫

that which is seen: πλοίων κάλλους 'of beautiful ships' Is 2.16. **b**. a performance in a theatre: γυναῖκες ἐρχόμεναι ἀπὸ ~ας Is 27.11.

Cf. θεάομαι, θεωρία, ὄψις, ὅραμα.

θεάομαι: aor. ἐθεασάμην, impv.2pl θεάσασθε, ptc. θεασάμενος, inf. θεάσασθαι; pf.ptc. τεθεαμένος.∫

to observe and study visually: + acc., ὄψα πολλά 'abundant foods' To 2.2 𝔊^{I}, ἃ ποιήσει μεθ' ὑμῶν 13.6 𝔊^{I}; πᾶσαν τὴν δόξαν σου 13.16 𝔊^{I} (𝔊^{II} ὄψονται); τὰ ἀγαθά Ju 15.8, τὴν τοῦ θεοῦ κληρονομίαν 2M 2.4, ὑπ' ὄψιν .. ἔργα τοῦ μεγίστου θεοῦ 'with his own eyes ..' 3.36; κόραις ὀφθαλμῶν 'personally and at close range' 3M 5.47; on a visit with sbd sick, 2C 22.6. Cf. θέα, βλέπω, ὁράω: Schmidt 1.265-9.

θεε, pl. also θειμ. n.

= תָּא 'chamber': 3K 14.28, Ez 40.6+.

θεῖον, ου. n.∫

brimstone, sulphur: punitive inflammatory instrument of destruction sent down by God, κύριος ἔβρεξεν ἐπὶ Σόδομα καὶ Γομόρρα θεῖον καὶ πῦρ .. ἐκ τοῦ οὐρανοῦ '.. brimstone and fire' Ge 19.24; πῦρ καὶ θ. βρέξω ἐπ' αὐτόν Ez 38.22; θ. καὶ ἅλα κατακεκαυμένον 'brimstone and burnt salt' De 29.23 (|| πληγὰς .. καὶ νόσους 'blows .. and diseases' vs. 22); a form of inflammatory disease(?), κατασπαρήσονται τὰ εὐπρεπῆ αὐτοῦ θείῳ 'his comeliness will be sown with brimstone all over' Jb 18.15¶; πῦρ καὶ θ. καὶ πνεῦμα καταιγίδος ἡ μερὶς τοῦ ποτηρίου αὐτῶν '.. a storm wind shall be the portion of their drink' Ps 10.6; ὁ θυμὸς κυρίου ὡς φάραγξ ὑπὸ ~ου καιομένη 'the wrath of the Lord is like a valley burning with sulphur' Is 30.33; στραφήσονται .. καὶ ἡ γῆ αὐτῆς εἰς ~ον '.. and its land will be turned into brimstone' 34.9 (|| πίσσα 'pitch'); τοὺς .. Σοδομίτας .. πυρὶ καὶ ~ῳ κατέφλεξας 'you consumed the Sodomites with ..' 3M 2.5. Cf. πῦρ.

θεῖος, α, ον.

pertaining to a divine being or *God*, 'divine': πνεῦμα θεῖον σοφίας Ex 31.3, 35.31; *s* ἐνέργεια 'activity' 2M 3.29, βίος '(godly) life' 4M 7.7, νόμος 5.16, προστάγματα 'commandments' 3M 7.11, διαθήκη Pr 2.17; πρᾶγμα 'matter', opp. ἀνθρώπινος 4M 1.16; δίκη 'justice' 8.22. Cf. θεός, θειότης, ἀνθρώπινος: Kleinknecht, *TDNT* 3.122f.

θειότης, ητος. f.∫

divine nature: ~ητος νόμος 'divine law' Wi 18.8. Cf. θεῖος.

θέλημα, ατος. n.

desire, interest: οὐκ ἔστι μοι θ. ἐν ὑμῖν 'I am not interested in you' Ma 1.10, ἐν τῷ νόμῳ κυρίου τὸ θ. αὐτοῦ Ps 1.2, ἐν τούτοις τὸ θ. μου Je 9.24; Jb 21.21¶; τῆς καρδίας αὐτῶν Je 23.26; || ὁδός Ps 102.7; λόγοι ~ατος 'attractive (or: acceptable) ideas' Ec 12.10. Cf. θέλω, εὐδοκία, ἐπιθυμία: Segalla 1965.

θέλησις, εως. f.

1. v.n. of θέλω: as cogn. dat., Ez 18.23; τοῦ θεοῦ 2M 12.16.

2. *that which is desired*: τῶν χειλέων 'expressed verbally' Ps 20.3 (|| ἐπιθυμία), cf. Wi 16.25; τὸ ὄρος τῆς ~εως τὸ ἅγιον Da 11.45 LXX.

Cf. θέλω, ὄρεξις, ἐπιθυμία.

θελητής, οῦ. m.∫ *

1. *one who desires, is desirous*: + gen. ἐλέους Mi 7.18 (*s* God); attr. ἱερεῖς ἀμώμους ~ὰς νόμου 'innocent priests ..' 1M 4.42.

2. a kind of pagan idol, an etymologising rendering of אוֹב < אבה 'to desire': 4K 21.6, + γνωριστής, θεραφιν, εἴδωλον 23.24 (*L* ἐγγαστρίμυθος).

Cf. θέλω.

θελητός, ή, όν.∫ *

wished for, desirable: "are burnt-offerings and sacrifices as desirable to the Lord as hearkening to the voice of the Lord?" 1K 15.22 (*L* θέλει), cf. Rowley; γῆ ~ή Ma 3.12. Cf. θέλω.

θέλω: impf. ἤθελον; fut. θελήσω; aor. ἠθέλησα, subj. θελήσω; pf. τεθέληκα, ἠθέληκα, inf. τεθεληκέναι.

1. *to want earnestly*: abs., ἕως οὗ θελήσῃ 'until he desires (it)' Ct 2.7, sim. 3.5, 8.4, εἰ μὴ σὺ ἠθέλησας 'if you yourself had not desired it' Wi 11.25, see also Si 39.6; an object inf. can be supplied from the context — ἐὰν θέλῃς, συντηρήσεις ἐντολάς 'if you so wish, observe the commandments' 15.15, ἐποίει ὡς ἤθελε 'he would do as he wished' Da 8.4 LXX, with which cp. ὅσα ἂν θέλῃ, ποιεῖν 'whatsoever he pleases he is to do' 4.14 LXX; + acc. rei ἔλεος .. θέλω καὶ οὐ θυσίαν Ho 6.6, τί θέλεις .. τί σού ἐστιν τὸ ἀξίωμα; 'what do you want to have .. what is your request?' Es 5.3 o', 3K 10.13 (|| αἰτέομαι), τὸν θάνατον τοῦ ἀνόμου Ez 18.23, τὸν νόμον Is 5.24, ἀνομίαν Ps 5.5, μοι κακά 39.15; *+ ἐν - ἐν ταῖς ἐντολαῖς αὐτοῦ 111.1, also 146.10 (|| εὐδοκέω); + inf. ἀνελεῖν Ex 2.14, φοβεῖσθαι Ne 1.11, καταλῦσαι 4M 17.9, τοῦ ποιῆσαι 2C 7.11; + acc. (= *s*) and inf., Wi 14.5, θέλω δικαιωθῆναί σε Jb 33.32; + a finite verb, subj. aor. in a person different from that of θέλω (see Renehan 1.76; BDAG s.v. **1**, LSG s.v. **I 7**), θέλεις καλέσω σοι γυναῖκα .. 'Do you wish me to call a woman for you ..?' Ex 2.7; *s* hum. heart, 1K 14.7 *L* (B: ἐκκλίνω); foll. by a syndetic clause—τί ὑμεῖς θέλετε (B: λέγετε), καὶ ποιήσω ὑμῖν; '(Tell me) what you want. I shall do it for you' 2K 21.4*L*. **b**. θελήσεις εἰ μὴ ἐγεννήθης 'you might come to wish that you had not been born' Si 23.14, εἰ ἐγενήθησαν πυρίκαυστοι 'that they had been burned with fire' Is 9.5.

*__2__. *to be favourably disposed towards*: + acc. pers., *s* God, Ps 17.20 (|| εὐδοκέω ἔν τινι 2K 22.20B), Ps 21.9, 40.12, To 13.6 𝔊[I], 1M 4.10, 3M 5.11; *s* hum., ἐὰν μὴ θέλῃς αὐτήν De 21.14, ὁ ἄγγελος τῆς διαθήκης, ὃν ὑμεῖς θέλετε Ma 3.1 (|| ζητέω); *s* God, + dat. pers., 2C 9.8 (*L* εὐδοκέω); *s* hum., ἐν σοί 2K 15.26 (*L* σε), 1K 18.22 (|| ἀγαπάω), 3K 10.9; ἐν ἐμοὶ ἠθέλησεν τοῦ γενέσθαι με βασιλέα 'he was in favour of me becoming king' 1C 28.4 (|| ἐκλέγομαι 'to choose').

3. *to be willing* to obey: Is 1.19f.; ἐν ψυχῇ θελούσῃ 'in a willing spirit' 1C 28.9. **b**. c. neg., *to refuse* to do: mostly with an indicative preterital form of θέλω - οὐκ ἤθελεν παρακαλεῖσθαι 'she would refuse to be comforted' Ge 37.35, οὐκ ἠθέλησεν ἐξαποστεῖλαι Ex 8.32 (cf. || βούλομαι vs. 5), οὐκ ἠθελήσατε ἀναβῆναι καὶ ἠπειθήσατε τῷ ῥήματι κυρίου 'you refused to go up, disobeying the word of the Lord' De 1.26, οὐκ ἠθέλησεν (*L* ἐβούλετο) φαγεῖν 2K 13.19; foll. a command, πάταξον .. καὶ οὐκ ἠθέλησεν .. πατάξαι 'Strike .., but he refused to strike' 3K 21.35, sim. Ge 39.8, 48.19, cf. μὴ ἀκούσῃς καὶ μὴ θελήσῃς 3K 21.8; || βούλομαι Ge 24.8 (see vs. 5), De 25.7; ἐὰν μὴ θέλητε μηδὲ εἰσακούσητέ μου Is 1.20, cf. οὐκ ἤθελον εἰσακοῦσαι Je 11.10. **c**. + neg., *to refuse to grant a request*: + an inf. clause, οὐκ ἠθέλησεν Σηων .. παρελθεῖν ἡμᾶς .. De 2.30, sim. Jd 11.20A (B: ἐμπιστεύω). **d**. + neg. and abs., *to refuse to react*, 'switch off': Ge 39.8, 2K 12.17 (*L* βούλομαι).

Cf. θέλημα, θέλησις, θελητής, θελητός, συνθέλω, βούλομαι, ἐπιθυμέω, ἐπιποθέω, εὐδοκέω, προσδέχομαι. On possible distinctions between θέλω and βούλομαι, see Schmidt 3.602-10, 617f.; Schrenk, *TDNT* 1.629-32; BDAG, s.v. βούλομαι; Shipp 166f.; Rödiger.

θέμα, ατος. n.

1. *that which is placed*: as an offering on an altar Le 24.6, 7; at a grave, Si 30.18. **b**. sth laid aside for future use: θ. ἀγαθὸν θησαυρίζεις σεαυτῷ εἰς ἡμέραν ἀνάγκης '.. for a day of emergency' To 4.9 𝔊[I].

2. *that in whch sth is placed*: coffer, 1K 6.8.

Cf. τίθημι.

θεμέλιον, ου. n. Used mostly in the pl. On the fluctuation between ~ος and ~ον, see Thack. 154f.

sth solid which lies at the base, supporting that which is above it: 'foundation' of a building, καταφάγεται ~α τειχέων αὐτῆς' (the fire) will completely destroy the foundations of its walls' Am 1.12, sim. 1.4; τὰ ~α αὐτῆς ἀποκαλύψω 'I shall expose its foundations' Mi 1.6; ἔδωκεν ~ους τοῦ οἴκου 'laid the foundations ..' 2E 5.16. **b**. ~α τῆς γῆς Mi 6.2, Ps 81.5, Si 16.19, τῆς οἰκουμένης 2K 22.16; opp. οὐρανός Is 14.15 (|| ᾄδης); φλέξει ~α ὀρέων 'will burn the foundations of the mountains' De 32.22; sg. ἕως ~ου Na 1.10. **c**. θ. τοῦ οὐρανοῦ = ἡ γῆ: ἀπ' ἄκρου ~ου τοῦ οὐρανοῦ 'from the end of ..' Is 13.5.

Cf. θεμελιόω, κρηπίς, ὑπόθεμα, ὑπόστασις **2**: Husson 8-90.

θεμελιόω: fut. θεμελιώσω; aor. ἐθεμελίωσα, ptc. θεμελιώσας, pass. ἐθεμελιώθην; pf.pass. τεθεμελίωμαι, ptc. τεθεμελιωμένος.

to set up on firm basis, + τι: ***o*** building, Hg 2.18, Zc 4.9, 8.9 (|| οἰκοδομέω), cf. θεμελιῶν γῆν 12.1 (|| πλάσσω), Is 48.13 (|| στερεόω), 51.13 (|| ποιέω), τὴν γῆν ἐπὶ τὴν ἀσφάλειαν Ps 103.5; Zion, Is 14.32; the sky, moon and stars, Ps 8.4; τὴν ἐπαγγελίαν αὐτοῦ ἐπὶ τῆς γῆς θ. 'establishing upon the earth what he promised' Am 9.6 (|| οἰκοδομέω); || ἑτοιμάζω Ps 23.2, Pr 3.19; τὴν ἀνάβασιν 'made a good start of the journey up to (Jerusalem)(?)' 2E 7.9. Cf. θεμέλιον, θεμελίωσις, ἱδρύω, οἰκοδομέω.

θεμελίωσις, εως. f.ʃ *

v.n. of prec.: 2E 3.11, 12. Cf. θεμελιόω.

θέμις, ιστος. f.ʃ
Used adj., *legally permitted*: *s* inf., 2M 6.20; + inf. to be supplied (λαλῆσαι) 12.14. Cf. θεμιτός: Schmidt 1.348-60.

θεμιτός, ή, όν.ʃ
permitted: *s* inf., To 2.13 𝔊ᴵ (𝔊ᴵᴵ ἐξουσίαν ἔχω). Cf. θέμις, ἀθέμιτος, I ἔξειμι.

θεόκτιστος, ον.ʃ
established by God: *s* νομοθεσία, ‖ ἅγιος 2M 6.23.

θεομαχέω.ʃ
to fight God: 2M 7.19. Cf. Renehan 1.104.

θεός, οῦ. m.
god. **a**. God of Israel: ὁ θ. Jn 3.3; κύριος ὁ θ. 2.2; κύριον τὸν ~ὸν τοῦ οὐρανοῦ καὶ τὸν θεὸν τῆς γῆς Ge 24.3; anarthrous, ἐξ οἴκου ~οῦ Na 1.14, ὁ δουλεύων ~ῷ Ma 3.14; God of an individual member of Israel, ὁ θ. μου Ge 28.3, 43.14, 48.3, ὁ. θ. ὁ ἐμός 49.25, ὁ θ. σου 17.1, 35.11, ὁ θ. ὁ ἅγιός μου Hb 1.12; τῆς ζωῆς μου Ps 41.9; ἱερεὺς τοῦ ~οῦ τοῦ ὑψίστου Ge 14.18; in the mouth of a non-Israelite, ὁ θ. σου Jn 1.6, ὁ ὕψιστος μέγιστος ζῶν θ. 'the highest, greatest and living God' Es E 16 o' (*L* ὁ μόνος θ. καὶ ἀληθινός); opp. hum., εἰ πτερνιεῖ ἄνθρωπος θεόν; Ma 3.8; θεὸς ἐγώ εἰμι καὶ οὐκ ἄνθρωπος Ho 11.9, ἄνθρωπον καὶ οὐ θεόν Is 31.3; θ. τῶν θεῶν De 10.17, Ps 135.2; υἱοὶ ~οῦ 88.7; τοῦ οὐρανοῦ 135.26, Jn 1.9, 2E 1.2, Ne 1.4, 2C 36.23. **b**. pagan deity: sg. τὸν ~ὸν αὐτῶν Jn 1.5; ὁ θ. Σοδομα καὶ Γομορρα Am 4.11; pl. ~οὺς ἀλλοτρίους Ma 2.11; πάντας τοὺς ~οὺς τῶν ἐθνῶν τῆς γῆς Zp 2.11. **c**. in general and anarthrous: πνεῦμα ~οῦ Ge 1.2; θ. μέγας καὶ κραταιός De 7.21; pl. and ‖ ἄρχων Ex 22.28; ~οί ἐστε Ps 81.6 (:: ἄνθρωπος vs. 7); υἱοὶ ~οῦ ζῶντος Ho 1.10; θ. ζηλωτὴς καὶ ἐκδικῶν κύριος Na 1.2; θ. εἷς '(the) only god' Ma 2.10. **d**. image of god, idol: ἔκλεψας τοὺς ~ούς μου 'you stole my gods' Ge 31.30, cf. LSG s.v. **I 1 g**. ***e**. calque of Heb. nouns for *god*: ὡσεὶ ὄρη ~οῦ 'as exceedingly high mountains' Ps 35.7, τὰς κέδρους τοῦ ~οῦ 'the very high (or: stately) cedar trees' 79.11; poss. πόλις μεγάλη τῷ ~ῷ Jn 3.3, cf. JM § 141 *n*.
Cf. κύριος, θεῖος: Schmidt 4.1-5; Frankel, *Einfl.* 26-9.

θεοσέβεια, ας.
fear of God: οὐκ ἔστιν θ. ἐν τῷ τόπῳ τούτῳ Ge 20.11; ἡ θ. ἐστιν σοφία Jb 28.28, disliked by sinners, Si 1.25; δόξα ~ας as Jerusalem's eternal name, Ba 5.4; + καθαρισμός 4M 7.6. Cf. θεοσεβής, σέβομαι, εὐσέβεια, φοβέομα: Bertram, *TDNT* 3.123-6; Spicq 1985.228-30.

θεοσεβής, ές.ʃ
god-fearing, pious: *s* leader, Ex 18.21 (‖ δίκαιος); Job, ἀληθινός, ἄμεμπτος, δίκαιος, θ., ἀπεχόμενος ἀπὸ παντὸς πονηροῦ πράγματος Jb 1.1, sim. 1.8, 2.3; Abraham, 4M 15.28; ἱερὰ καὶ θ. μήτηρ 16.12; of self-estimation, θ… θεραπεύουσα νυκτὸς καὶ ἡμέρας τὸν θεὸν τοῦ οὐρανοῦ Ju 11.17. Cf. θεοσέβεια: Trench 172-80; Spicq 2.196-9; *ND* 9.77-9.

θεοφιλής, ές.ʃ
dear to the gods: *s* story, Si prol. II.

θεράπαινα, ας. f.
female slave: παρὰ τὸν μύλον 'at the handmill' Ex 11.5 (:: Pharaoh); female counterpart of οἰκέτης Ex 21.26, 27;:: mistress and fem. counterpart of παῖς– ὁ παῖς ὡς ὁ κύριος καὶ ἡ θ. ὡς ἡ κυρία Is 24.2; ‖ θεράπων Jb 31.13. Cf. θεράπων, θεραπεία, κυρία, οἰκέτης, παῖς.

θεραπεία, ας. f.ʃ
1. *worship service*: κηρύξατε ~αν 'Announce ..' Jl 1.14, 2.15 (‖ νηστεία); τοῦ Βααλ 4K 10.20*L* (B: ἱερεία); Es 4.11*L*.
2. *a body of attendants* (θεράπων): Ge 45.16, Es D 16.
3. *being in sbd's service*: Es 2.12 o', ἱματία τῆς ~ας 'uniforms' D 1.
Cf. θεράπων.

θεραπεύω: fut. θεραπεύσω; aor. ἐθεράπευσα, ptc. ~πεύσας, inf.pass. ~πευθῆναι.
1. *to serve devotedly*: *s* a high-ranking courtier, ἄνθρωπος μέγας θεραπεύων ἐν τῇ αὐλῇ τοῦ βασιλέως Es A 2 o'; 6.10 o' (‖ *L* τῷ καθημένῳ ἐν τῷ πυλῶνι); temple functionaries, τοῖς υἱοῖς Λευι τοῖς θεραπεύουσιν εἰς Ιερουσαλημ To 1.7, + acc. pers., τὸ ἔθνος 1E 1.4 (‖ λατρεύω); a pious (θεοσεβής) individual, νυκτὸς καὶ ἡμέρας τὸν θεὸν τοῦ οὐρανοῦ Ju 11.17, κύριον Is 54.17, cf. Da 7.10 LXX (‖ TH λειτουργέω), Ep Je 25 (idols), Si 32.20; *o* wisdom personified, σοφία τοὺς θεραπεύοντας αὐτὴν .. Wi 10.9; fig., θύρας δικαίων Pr 14.19, πρόσωπα βασιλέων 19.6 (flattery), sim. 29.26.
2. *to restore to normal, proper state*, 'repair': + acc. rei, τὰ τείχη 'the (city) walls' 1E 2.17, τοὺς πόδας αὐτοῦ 'his legs' 2K 19.25 (washing [TrgJon] or shaving). **b**. *to cure medically*: *s* hum. and abs., Si 38.7; + acc. pers., To 2.10 𝔊ᴵᴵ (pass. and by doctors), 12.3*bis*, οὔτε βοτάνη οὔτε μάλαγμα ἐθεράπευσεν αὐτούς 'neither herbs nor plaster cured ..' Wi 16.12 (‖ ἰάομαι *s* God's word); ἐθεραπεύετο .. ἀπὸ τῶν τοξευμάτων 'was recovering .. from the arrow-wounds' 4K 9.16 (‖ ἱερατεύομαι vs. 15). **c**. mid., *to take good care of one's health*: Si 18.19.
Cf. θεράπων, θεραπεία, δουλεύω, λειτουργέω, λατρεύω, ἰάομαι: Schmidt 3.442f., 4.138-41; Wells 1998.109-12.

θεράπων, ονος. m.
one devoted to sbd else's service: to God's service, Ge 24.44 (w. ref. to Isaac and ‖ παῖς, vs. 14), Ex 4.10,

14.31, Nu 12.7, De 3.24 (Moses, but || οἰκέτης De 34.5), 9.27 (Abraham, Isaac and Jacob), Jb 2.3 (|| παῖς 1.8); to Pharaoh, Ex 5.21, De 29.2; distinct from the common folk and mentioned before the latter and in the pl.– εἰς τοὺς οἴκους τῶν ~όντων σου καὶ τοῦ λαοῦ σου Ex 8.3, sim. 8.4, 9, 11, 21, 29, 31+; to Moses, 33.11 (Joshua, || δοῦλος Jo 24.30), to Nebuchadnezzar, Ju 2.2; opp. ὁ κύριος (= Moses) Nu 32.31 (|| παῖς vss. 4, 25, 27), Jb 7.2. Cf. διάκονος, δοῦλος, θεράπαινα, θεραπεία, λειτουργός, παῖς, ὑπηρέτης ὑπουργός: Trench 30-2; Spicq 1978.214-6; *BA* ad Ex 5.21; Harl 2001.902; Renehan 1.104f.

θερίζω: fut. θεριῶ, θερίσω; aor. ἐθέρισα, impv.2pl θερίσατε, ptc. θερίσας, subj.pass. θερισθῶ; pf.ptc. pass. τεθερισμένος.

to harvest: + cogn. acc. θερισμόν Le 23.10, 22[1], θερισμὸν πυρῶν '.. of wheat' 1K 6.13; σπείρατε .. θερίσατε 'sow ..' Je 12.13; metaph., + acc. rei, κακά Pr 22.8. **b.** *to harvest crops of* a cultivated land: + acc., ἀγρόν 'field' Jb 24.6, πεδίον Ju 4.5.

Cf. θερισμός, ἐκ~, προθερίζω, θεριστής, ἀμάω, σπείρω.

θερινός, ή, όν.ʃ

intended for summer use: *s* house, Am 3.15; terrace or penthouse, Jd 3.20; threshing-floor, Da 2.35 TH. Cf. θέρος.

θερισμός, οῦ. m.

1. v.n. of θερίζω: σπέρμα καὶ θ. 'sowing and harvesting' Ge 8.22; ἐν ἡμέραις ~οῦ πυρῶν 'during a season of wheat harvest' 30.14; ἑορτὴ ~οῦ πρωτογενημάτων Ex 23.16; cogn. obj. of ἐκθερίζω, τῆς γῆς Le 19.9; τοῦ ἀγροῦ ib.

2. *that which has been harvested*, 'crop': || τρυγητός Is 16.9; Je 5.16.

Cf. θερίζω, τρύγητος, τρυγητός.

θεριστήριον, ου.ʃ

reaping-hook: 1K 13.20*L*. Cf. θέριστρον.

θεριστής, οῦ. m.ʃ

harvester: Bel 33. Cf. θερίζω.

θέριστρον, ου. n.ʃ

1. *light summer garment* or *veil*: λαβοῦσα τὸ θ. περιεβάλετο 'wrapped .. around' Ge 24.65; περιεβάλετο ~ῳ 38.14; περιείλατο τὸ θ. ἀφ' ἑαυτῆς 'took the veil off' 38.19, cf. Ct 5.7; κατάκλιτα 'flowing-down' Is 3.23 and van der Meer 2008.592-6.

2. *reaping-hook*: 1K 13.20, see *BA* ad loc.

Cf. θεριστήριον, (κατα)κάλυμμα, σιώπησις.

θερμαίνω: fut.pass. θερμανθήσομαι; aor.impv. θέρμανον, pass. ἐθερμάνθην, ptc. θερμανθείς, subj. θερμανθῶ.

1. *to add enthusiasm to* an act: + acc., κοπετόν 'beating one's chest over the deceased' Si 38.17.

2. pass. *to get warm*: *s* old man with a maiden sleeping beside him, 3K 1.2; by putting on clothes, 1.1, Hg 1.6, Jb 31.20, at fireside, Is 44.15; fig. of zeal and enthusiasm, ὡς κλίβανος Ho 7.7 (|| ἀνακαίομαι), of frustration and *s* καρδία Ps 38.4. Cf. θάλπω.

Cf. θερμασία, ψύχω: Shipp 267f.

θερμασία, ας. f.ʃ

state of being hot: Je 28.39; Da 3.46 LXX. Cf. θερμαίνω.

θέρμαστρις, εως. f.ʃ

kettle or *pot for boiling water* (LSJ): 3K 7.26, 31. Cf. Caird 1968.474.

θέρμη, ης. f.

high temperature, 'heat': of the sun, Ps 18.7; καμίνου 'of furnace' Si 38.28; of human body, Ec 4.11. Cf. θερμός, θερμότης, ῥῖγος.

θερμός, ή, όν.

having high temperature: *s* fresh droppings of a bird, To 2.10, στολή 'robe' Jb 37.17, ἄρτοι Jo 9.12; metaph. ψυχὴ ~ὴ ὡς πῦρ καιόμενον '.. like a burning fire' Si 23.16; subst., Je 38.2. Cf. θερμότης, πυρώδης, ψυχρός: Caird 1968.475.

θερμῶς. adv.ʃ

eagerly: Jd 5.26 *L*.

Cf. προθύμως.

θερμότης, ητος. f.ʃ

high temperature: of the sun, Wi 2.4. Cf. θερμός, θέρμη.

θέρος, ους. n.

summer: Ge 8.22, Zc 14.8 (|| ἔαρ 'spring'), Je 8.20 (|| θέρος 'summer'); θέρους 'in summer' Pr 6.8. Cf. θερινός, χειμών.

θέσις, εως. f.ʃ

1. v.n. of τίθημι, *act of placing, depositing*: τῆς ἁγίας κιβωτοῦ 'of the sacred ark' 1E 1.3.

2. *fixed position*: ἄστρων 'of stars' Wi 7.19, 29. **b.** *office*: of kingship, 3K 11.36 (*L* θέλησις).

Cf. τίθημι, πρόθεσις.

θεσμός, οῦ. m.ʃ

that which is laid down as rules of conduct: μητρός Pr 1.8 (|| παιδεία), 6.20 (|| νόμος). **b.** *officially established rite*: Wi 14.23, κοινός 'public' 3M 6.36, πάτριος 'ancestral' 4M 8.7.

Cf. θέμις, ἐντολή, νόμος.

θεωρέω: fut.pass. θεωρηθήσομαι; aor.inf. θεωρῆσαι, pass. ἐθεωρήθην. In the past, mostly impf.

1. *to observe visually*: abs., Jd 13.19, 20 A (B: βλέπω), 3M 6.17, οἱ θεωροῦντες 'the spectators' 4M 17.7; + acc., Ps 21.8; *+ ἐν marking sustained interest and concern, ἐν παιγνίαις Σαμψων Ju 16.27B; in a nocturnal vision, Da 4.10, ὅρασιν To 12.19[2] 𝔊[I]; + a ptc. cl., Jo 8.20; || ὁράω 4M 17.7; Da 8.15 LXX (TH εἶδον). **b.** *to notice visually*: + ptc. cl., To 1.17, 11.16 𝔊[I] (𝔊[II] εἶδον); + a ὅτι-clause, ἐθεωρεῖτέ με ὅτι οὐκ ἔφαγον 'you were watching me not eating' To 12.19[1] 𝔊[II] (𝔊[I] ὀπτάνομαι), sim. Da

3.94; + an indir. interr. cl., 4M 14.13. **c**. *to notice mentally*, 'mark': + acc. rei, ἀδικίαν Ps 65.18; + ὅτι 2M 9.23; + an indir. interr. cl., To 9.3f. 𝔊II; pass., *o* σοφία Wi 6.12, hum. 13.5. **d**. pass. *to become visible, appear to*: *s* ὅρασις and + dat. pers., To 12.19² 𝔊II.

2. *to deem* as: + ὡς Si 26.27¶.

Cf. βλέπω, εἶδον, θεάομαι, θεωρία, ἀθεώρητος, κατανοέω, ὁράω.

θεωρία, ας. f.

sth unusual which is visually observed, 'spectacle': Da 5.7 LXX, 2M 5.26. Cf. θέα.

θεωρός, οῦ.ʃ

official *spectator*: at athletic games, 2M 4.19.

θήκη, ης. f.ʃ

that inside of which sth lies deposited, 'sheath': Ex 25.26; κόσμου 'of cosmetics' Is 3.26; the ground in which the roots of a tree lie (?) or a husk of acorns, 6.13.

θηλάζω: fut. θηλάσω; aor. ἐθήλασα, impv. θήλασον, inf. θηλάσαι, ptc. θηλάσας, subj. θηλάσω, opt.3s θηλάσειεν.

1. *to suck and apply pressure to* breasts in order to draw milk: Nu 11.12; *s* babe and *o* breast, νήπια θηλάζοντα μαστούς Jl 2.16, cf. Ps 8.3.

2. *to give milk to*, 'suckle': *s* mother, *o* babe, θηλάζει παιδίον Σάρρα Ge 21.7; 3 years, 2M 7.27; animal, καμήλους θηλαζούσας Ge 32.15; + dat. com. Ex 2.7, 9.

3. *to suck*: **s** σκύμνοι 'snakes' young' La 4.3; opp. an elderly person De 32.25; *o* μέλι καὶ ἔλαιον 'honey and oil' 32.13, γάλα Is 60.15 (|| ἐσθίω); θυμὸν δρακόντων Jb 20.16.

Cf. ἐκθηλάζω.

θηλυκός, ή, όν.

female: *s* hum. and opp. ἀρσενικός 'male' Nu 5.3, De 4.16. Cf. θῆλυς, ἀρσενικός.

θηλυμανής, ές.ʃ

mad about women, 'womanising': *s* horse in a fig. of womanisers, Je 5.8.

θῆλυς, θήλεια, θῆλυ.

female: *s* hum., Ex 1.16 (:: ἄρσην); animal, Am 6.12, ὄνοι Jb 1.14, λογισμός 'womanlike way of reasoning' 2M 8.21; subst. n., but meaning women, Nu 31.15, cf. LSG s.v. **I 1 c**; subst.f., Ju 9.10. Cf. ἄρσην, θηλυκός, γυνή: Schmidt 2.401f.

θημωνιά, ᾶς. f.ʃ *(synon. θημών: Homer +)

heap: of dead frogs, Ex 8.14, pl. and of corpses, 1M 11.4; ἁλός 'of salt' Zp 2.9; σίτου 'of wheat' Ct 7.3, ἅλωνος 'of grain on a threshing-floor' Jb 5.26, cf. Si 20.28; pool of water, 39.17 (|| ἀποδοχεῖον; w. ref. to Jo 3.13-16). Cf. Renehan 1.105, and on the spelling, Walters 65f. and Shipp 268-70.

θήρ, ρός. m.

beast of prey: ἄγριος 'wild' Jb 5.23, 2M 11.9, βάρβαρος 4.25. Cf. θηρίον: Schmidt 2.432f.

θήρα, ας. f.

1. *animal as object of hunting* or *caught by hunting*, 'game': ἡ θ. αὐτοῦ βρῶσις αὐτῷ Ge 25.28; οἱ ἀγρεύοντες τὴν ~αν 'game-catchers' Ho 5.2; ἐρεύξεται λέων .. ~αν οὐκ ἔχων 'a lion roars .. not having any prey' Am 3.4; λέων .. ἔπλησε θήρας νοσσιὰν αὐτοῦ 'a lion stacked its lair with prey' Na 2.13; φάγῃ ~αν Nu 23.24.

2. *hunting of wild animals*: ἦλθεν ἀπὸ τῆς ~ας 'returned from the hunting' Ge 27.30; metaph. w. hum. target, Ho 9.3 (|| ἀποκέντησις 'piercing through'), Pr 11.8, 12.27.

Cf. θήρ, θήρευμα, θηρεύω, θηρίον: Schmidt 2.443f.

θήρευμα, ατος. n.ʃ .

animal caught by hunting: θηρεύσῃ θ. θηρίον ἢ πετεινόν 'hunts an animal or a bird as game' Le 17.13; fig., Je 37.17, Ec 7.26. Cf. θήρα.

θηρευτής, οῦ. m.ʃ

hunter: παγὶς ~ῶν 'hunters' snare' Ps 90.3; || ἁλεεύς 'fisherman' Je 16.16; πέρδιξ θ. 'decoy partridge' Si 11.30.

Cf. θηρεύω, ἰχνευτής: Schmidt 2.442f.

θηρεύω: fut. θηρεύσω, pass. θηρευθήσομαι; aor. ἐθήρευσα, impv. θήρευσον, inf. θηρεῦσαι, ptc. θηρεύσας, subj. θηρεύσω, opt.3pl θηρεύσαισαν, pass. ἐθηρεύθην.

to hunt game: + acc., θήρευσόν μοι θήραν 'hunt game for me' Ge 27.3; θηρεύσῃ θήρευμα θηρίον ἢ πετεινόν 'hunts an animal or a bird as game' Le 17.13; *o* fish, Ec 9.12; bird, ἐν παγίδι 'with a net' ib.; food, Jb 38.39; sbd else's possessions, 18.7; τὴν ψυχήν μου Ps 58.4 (|| ἐπιτίθεμαι); obj. hum., La 3.52 (ὡς στρουθίον .. δωρεάν 'like a sparrow .. for no good reason'), Je 5.6, || ἁλίσκομαι 28.41; ἄνδρα ἄδικον κακὰ θηρεύσει εἰς διαφθοράν 'calamity will hunt an unrighteous man into ruin' Ps 139.12; not with hostile intent Je 16.16 (|| ἁλιεύω). Cf. θήρα, θηρευτής, ἀγρεύω, κυνηγέω.

θηριάλωτος, ον.*

caught and torn by wild beasts: *s* cattle, Ex 22.13; considered ἀκάθαρτος Le 5.2; subst. n. Ge 31.39; often + θνησιμαῖος Le 5.2, 7.14, 17.15, 22.8, Ez 4.14, 44.31. Cf. θηρίον and θηριόβρωτος.

θηριόβρωτος, ον.ʃ.

eaten by wild beasts: *s* hum., Ge 44.28. Cf. θηρίον and θηριάλωτος.

θηρίον, ου. n.

undomesticated land animal, beast: constituting, together with κτήνη, the animal kingdom on the earth, Ge 3.14; καλά 1.25; fearful of humans, 9.2 (τρόμος καὶ φόβος); ταλαιπωρία ~ων 'misery of beasts' Hb 2.17; θηρία ἄγρια 'wild ..' Ex 23.11, τὰ ~α τοῦ ἀγροῦ 'wild animals' Ho 2.12, 18, 4.3 (|| τὰ πετεινὰ τοῦ οὐρανοῦ καὶ τὰ ἑρπετὰ τῆς γῆς) τοῦ πεδίου Ez 38.20; predators, Le 26.22, Ho 13.8; τὰ πετεινὰ τοῦ οὐρανοῦ καὶ ~α τῆς γῆς Is 18.6, ~α καὶ κτήνη 46.1; πονηρόν 'harmful' Ge 37.20, Le 26.6, Ez 5.17; νεμήσονται .. ποίμνια καὶ πάντα τὰ ~α τῆς γῆς Zp 2.14 (including reptiles Ge 3.1, cf. LSG s.v. **I 2**), cf. ἀφανισμόν, νομὴ ~ων Zp 3.1. Cf. θήρ, θήρα, θηριάλωτος, θηριόβρωτος, ζῷον, κνώδαλον, κτῆνος: Schmidt 2.433-5; Trench 308-10; Foerster, *TDNT* 3.133-5.

θηριόω: pf.ptc.pass. τεθηριωμένος.ʃ

pass. *to become wild*: τῇ ψυχῇ 'emotionally' 2M 5.11. Cf. θηριώδης.

θηριώδης, ες.ʃ

wild and harmful in effect: ***s*** θυμός 'fury' 2M 10.35; hum., 4M 12.13. Cf. θηριωδῶς, θηριόω: Renehan 2.79.

θηριωδῶς. adv.ʃ

in a manner to be characterised as θηριώδης: 2M 12.15. Cf. θηριώδης.

θησαυρίζω: aor. ἐθησαύρισα, inf. ~ρίσαι; pf.inf. pass. τεθησαυρίσθαι.

to store, hoard: obj. silver and gold, Zc 9.3; ἐν γαζοφυλακίοις 'in treasuries' 4M 4.3; fig. ἀδικίαν Am 3.10, κακά '(future) disasters' Pr 1.18; ζωὴν αὐτῷ παρὰ κυρίῳ PSol 9.5. Cf. θησαυρός, θησαύρισμα, ἀποθησαυρίζω.

θησαύρισμα, ατος. n.ʃ

accumulated possessions: Pr 21.6. Cf. θησαυρός, θησαυρίζω.

θησαυρός, οῦ. m. Used often in the pl.

1. *space for storing*: ἐσφράγισται ἐν τοῖς ~οῖς μου De 32.34; royal treasury, ~οὶ τοῦ οἴκου τοῦ βασιλέως 3K 15.18; temple treasury, ~οὶ οἴκου κυρίου 7.37; 'granary' for agricultural produce, Ma 3.10; || ληνός 'wine-vat' Jl 1.17; chamber of light, Je 28.16, of clouds Ps 134.7, of snow Jb 38.22.

2. *that which is stored as valuable*, 'treasure': ὁ θεὸς ὑμῶν .. ἔδωκεν ὑμῖν ~οὺς ἐν τοῖς μαρσίπποις ὑμῶν Ge 43.23; material wealth, Is 2.7; not material, Pr 21.20 (wisdom).

Cf. θησαυρίζω: Husson 91-3.

θησαυροφύλαξ, ακος. m.ʃ*

treasurer: 2E 5.14.

θίασος, ου. m.ʃ

banquet with heathen associations: Je 16.5, Wi 12.5.

θῖβις, εως. f.ʃ

basket plaited from papyrus: Ex 2.3, 5, 6. Cf. ἄγγος, κανοῦν, κόφινος.

θιγγάνω: fut. θίξω; 2aor. inf. θιγεῖν.ʃ

to touch: + gen., τῆς φιλιᾶς 'the lintel' Ex 12.22; θιγεῖν τι αὐτοῦ 'to touch it at all' (*pace* Wevers: 'any of it') 19.12 (|| ἅπτομαι). Cf. ἅπτομαι: Schmidt 1.227-32; Trench 58-60.

θιμωνία. ⇒ θημωνία.

θίς, νός. m. Alw. in pl.

hill: || ὄρος Ge 49.26, θῖνας ἀενάους 'everlasting ..' Ba 5.7; De 12.2 (site of cult); primaeval creation Jb 15.7. Cf. βουνός, ὄρος: Schmidt 3.107f.; Shipp 270-2.

θλαδίας, ου. m.ʃ *

castrated male: ***s*** animal, Le 22.24 (unfit as an offering); hum. De 23.1. Cf. ἀποσπάω, ἐκθλίβω, ἐκτομία, εὐνοῦχος.

θλάσμα, ατος. n.ʃ

bruise: πατάξει .. ~ασι 'he will smite .. with bruises' Am 6.11 (|| ῥάγμα). Cf. ῥάγμα and συνθλάω.

θλάω: fut. θλάσω; aor. ἔθλασα, impv. θλάσον, pass. ἐθλάσθην; pf.ptc.pass. τεθλασμένος.

1. *to crush*: ***o*** ῥάβδος καλαμίνη 'staff of reed' 4K 18.21 || Is 36.6, κάλαμος 'reed' 42.3, οἴκους Jb 20.19; bones of hum. victim, Da 6.24 LXX (TH λεπτύνω), κρανίον 'skull' Jd 9.53 B (A: συν~). **b**. metaph., by oppression and exploitation: τινα 1K 12.4 (+ ἀδικέω, καταδυναστεύω).

2. *to hit hard*: + acc., πλευράς 'sides of body' Si 30.12.

Cf. ἀφανίζω, συνθλάω, λεπτύνω, συντρίβω.

θλίβω: fut. θλίψω, pass. θλιβήσομαι; aor. ἔθλιψα, inf. θλῖψαι, ptc. θλίψας, subj. θλίψω, pass. ἐθλίβην, inf. θλιβῆναι; pf.ptc. τεθλιμμένος.

1. *to squeeze*: ***s*** potter, ***o*** earth, Wi 15.7; ἔθλιψαν ἀπ' αὐτῶν τὸ ὅριον τῆς μερίδος αὐτῶν 'they squeezed off them the area out of their share' Jo 19.47a.

2. *to cause* sbd *distress, oppress*: + acc., ὑψωθήσεται ἡ χείρ σου ἐπὶ τοὺς θλίβοντάς σε 'your hand will be lifted up against your oppressors,' but possibly 'you will gain the upper hand ..' Mi 5.9 (|| ἐχθρός), and see Th 221 and Cyr. I 639; + cogn. acc., τὸν θλιμμόν, ὃν οἱ Αἰγύπτιοι θλίβουσιν αὐτούς Ex 3.9; ***o*** προσήλυτος 'resident alien' 22.21 (|| κακόω), Le 19.33; σιτοδείᾳ ἄρτων 'through shortage of food' 26.26; ἱκέτης 'suppliant' Si 4.4; ***s*** ἐχθρός 'enemy' De 28.53, 55, 57; pass. Is 18.7, mentally La 1.20, 1K 30.6; through military operation, 2M 11.5.

Cf. ἀπο~, ἐκ~, προσθλίβω, θλῖψις, θλιμμός: Schlier, *TDNT* 3.140-3.

θλιμμός, οῦ. m.ʃ *

oppression: + obj.gen., ἡμῶν De 26.7 (|| ταπείνωσις and μόχθος), cf. τὸν ~όν, ὃν οἱ Αἰγύπτιοι θλίβουσιν αὐτούς Ex 3.9. Cf. θλίβω, θλῖψις, μόχθος, ταπείνωσις.

θλῖψις, εως. f.

1. *oppressive, distressful circumstance*: ψυχῆς 'inner agony' Ge 42.21; ἐν τῇ ~ει σου 'when you are in dire straits' De 4.29; Ho 6.1, Jn 2.3, Na 1.7; πρόβατα ἐν ~ει 'sheep in trouble' Mi 2.12; ἐν ἡμέρᾳ ~εως 'on the day of distress' Ob 12, 14, Hb 3.16; ἡμέρα ~εως καὶ ἀνάγκης 'a day of affliction and distress' Zp 1.15; θ. καὶ στενοχωρία Is 8.22; ἐν τῇ ἀκοῇ τῆς ~εως αὐτῶν 'through the rumour of their suffering' Ho 7.12; ἐν ~ει 'by means of affliction' Na 1.9; ἐξαιρούμενος ἐκ ~εως 'delivered from trouble' Na 2.2; || κακά Je 15.11, pl. κακὰ πολλὰ καὶ ~εις De 31.17; + πτωχεία Ps 43.25; opp. εἰρήνη– οὐκ ἔσται εἰρήνη ἀπὸ τῆς ~εως 'he will have no respite from the distress' Zc 8.10; βάσανος καὶ θ. Ez 12.18 (|| ὀδύνη).

2. *forced reduction*: ἄρτος ~εως καὶ ὕδωρ στενόν 'bread on reduced rations and scanty water' Is 30.20, ἄ. ~εως καὶ ὕ. ~εως 1K 22.27.

Cf. θλίβω, ἀωρία, στενοχωρία, ἀνάγκη: Trench 202f.

θνησιμαῖος, α, ον. *

subst.n., *dead body*: carcase of an animal, considered ἀκάθαρτος, Le 5.2, De 14.8; || θηριάλωτα 'cattle or animals caught and torn by wild beasts' Le 7.14, 17.15, Ez 4.14; corpse of hum., Ps 78.2 (|| σάρκες); of fallen soldiers, Is 5.25.

Cf. θνήσκω, σῶμα.

θνήσκω: fut. θανοῦμαι; fut.pf. τεθνήξομαι; aor.inf. θανεῖν, ptc. θανών, opt.3pl θάνοιεν; pf. τέθνηκα, 3pl τεθνᾶσιν, ptc. τεθνηκώς, τεθνεώς, inf. τεθνάναι, τεθνηκέναι; plpf. τεθνήκειν; fut.pf. τεθνήξομαι. Mostly in the pf. and plpf. with fut. and aor. θαν- in the higher register (Jb, 2M, 4M); in other tenses ἀποθνήσκω is the norm.

to die: ***s*** hum. Ge 50.15; Wi 3.2 (|| ἔξοδος); τῶν τεθνηκότων καὶ τῶν ζώντων Nu 16.48; De 25.5 || τελευτάω vs. 6); fallen on a battlefield, Nu 33.4; animal, Le 11.31. Cf. ἀπο~, ἐναπο~, προαπο~, συναποθνήσκω, θάνατος, τελευτάω.

θνητός, ή, όν.

subject to death, 'mortal': ***s*** ἄνθρωπος Is 51.12 (|| υἱὸς ἀνθρώπου), Wi 7.1; ~ὴ φύσις 'mortal creature' 3M 3.29; subst. m. Pr 3.13 (|| ἄνθρωπος), Jb 9.14, 30.23. See also Renehan 1.105. Cf. θάνατος, ἀθάνατος: Bultmann, *TDNT* 3.21f.

θοῖνα, ας. f.ʃ

meal: 3M 5.31; ἀνθρωπίνων σαρκῶν θ. καὶ αἵματος '.. of human flesh and blood' Wi 12.5.

θολερός, ά, όν.ʃ

turbid, muddy: ὁ ποτίζων τὸν πλησίον αὐτοῦ ἀνατροπῇ ~ᾷ 'one who makes one's neighbour drink unclear intoxicating drink (?)' Hb 2.15.

θορυβέω: fut.pass. θορυβηθήσομα; aor.ptc. θορυνβήσας, pass. ἐθορυβήθην; pf.ptc.pass. τεθορυβημένος.ʃ

to throw into disarray: on battlefield and pass. οἱ ἱππεῖς θορυβηθήσονται Na 2.4 (|| συγχέομαι); mentally, Wi 18.19 (***s*** dreams), Da 8.17 LXX (TH θαμβέομαι), Jd 3.26, Si 40.6. Cf. θόρυβος, συγχέω.

θόρυβος, ου. m.

1. *the confused noise of a crowded assembly* (LSJ): ἀκουτιῶ .. ~ον πολέμων Je 30.2; φωνὴ ~ου Da 10.6 LXX (TH: φ. ὄχλου), τῶν ἀνδρῶν Ju 6.1; φωναὶ καὶ ~ος Es A 4; || οὐαί Pr 23.29, || ὠδίν Ez 7.4, βαρυνηχῇ ~ον ἀκούσαντες 'having heard a loud, tumultuous noise' 3M 5.48.

2. *disarray* on battlefield: ἡμέρα ὕδατος καὶ ~ου Mi 7.12. **b**. *disconcerting situation*: Pr 1.27 (|| καταστροφή).

3. *confusion*: ἀγαθῶν 'over what is good' Wi 14.26.

Cf. θορυβέω, ἦχος, φωνή, ἡσυχία: Schmidt 3.375-7.

θράσος, ους. n.

courage: Ez 19.7; sensu malo, *audacity* 2M 2.2 (+ σθένος), + ὕβρις 3M 2.21, ἄνομον 6.4, + κόμπος 'boast' Es E 4 o', ἐξουσίας B 2. Cf. θρασύνω, θρασύς, εὐψυχία.

θρασυκάρδιος, ον.ʃ

excessively bold of heart: ***s*** hum. Pr 14.14, 21.4. Cf. θρασύς.

θρασύνω: aor.ptc.pass. θρασυνθείς.ʃ

to embolden: ***o*** hum., 3M 1.22, 26. Cf. θράσος, θαρσέω.

θρασύς, εῖα, ύ.

bold, fearless: ***s*** hum. Nu 13.29, ἐν γλώσσῃ σου Si 4.29; lion, Wi 11.17. **b**. in pejorative sense, *excessively bold, audacious*: ***s*** hum., Pr 9.13 (+ ἄφρων 'silly'), + αὐθάδης 'self-willed,' ἀλαζών 'boastful' 21.24.

Cf. θράσος, θρασυκάρδιος, εὔψυχος, δειλός.

θραῦσις, εως. f.

v.n. of θραύω, 'devastation': through a plague, Nu 16.47 (|| θραύειν vs. 46), 2K 24.15; on a battlefield, 17.9 (*L* πτῶσις), Ps 105.30 (vs. 29 πτῶσις). Cf. θραύω.

θραῦσμα, ατος. n.

1. *scab* in leprosy: Le 13.30 +.

2. military *loss and damage sustained*: Ju 7.9.

θραυσμός, οῦ. m.ʃ *

shattering: fig. of shattering experience, καρδίας θ. Na 2.11. Cf. θραύω.

θραύω: fut. θραύσω, pass. θραυσθήσομαι; aor. ἔθραυσα, inf. θραῦσαι, subj. θραύσω, impv. θραῦσον, pass. ἐθραύσθην, subj. θραυσθῶ; pf.ptc.pass. τεθραυσμένος.

1. *to crush*: + acc. and in a battle, ἐχθρούς Ex 15.6 (ll συντρίβω vs. 7); τὸν λαόν Nu 16.46; 24.17 (ll προνομεύω); τὴν γῆν Is 2.19; pass. δυναστεία Je 28.30.

2. *to treat very harshly*: pass. ἀδικούμενος καὶ τεθραυσμένος 'wronged and battered' De 28.33; causing illness, 2K 12.15B (*L* πατάσσω).

3. pass. *to feel devastated and daunted*: in face of overwhelming enemies, De 20.3 (ll φοβέομαι, ἐκκλίνω), καρδία Ez 21.7, heavily in debt, Is 58.6; ἐπὶ τὸν Δαυιδ 1K 20.34.

Cf. θραῦσις, θραῦσμα, θραυσμός, εὔθραυστος, συντρίβω: Schmidt 3.311f.

θρεπτός, ή, όν.ʃ

bred and raised in non-parental house: *s* brother's orphan daughter, παῖς Es 2.7 o'.

θρηνέω: fut.act. θρηνήσω, pass. θρηνηθήσομαι; aor. ἐθρήνησα, impv. θρήνησον.

1. *to express grief vocally* over some sad event, esp. death, 'wail': Zp 1.11; ll κόπτω Mi 1.8; θρηνοῦσα, professional female mourner, Je 9.17, cf. Ez 32.16; opp. revelling and merry-making, Jl 1.5, χαίρω Ez 7.12; θρήνησον πρός με ὑπὲρ νύμφην περιεζωσμένην σάκκον ἐπὶ τὸν ἄνδρα αὐτῆς τὸν παρθενικόν 'lament to me more (bitterly) than a bride girded with a sackcloth would do over the husband of her youth' Jl 1.8; ὑπέρ τινος 'over sth', of poor harvest, 1.11; ll περιζώννυμι καὶ κόπτω, 1.13; ll ὠρύομαι 'to howl', φωνὴ θρηνούντων ποιμένων 'a voice of wailing shepherds' Zc 11.3; + acc. pers., Je 22.10 (ll κλαίω), Ez 8.14, 32.16; and + ἐπί τι 32.16, ὑπέρ τινος (pers.) 1E 1.30 (ll πενθέω); + acc. cogn., τὸν θρῆνον τοῦτον ἐπὶ Ιερουσαλημ La ins.; pass., *o* dead children, Wi 18.10.

2. *to sing a dirge*, pass., + cogn. subj. θρηνηθήσεται θρῆνος 'a sorrowful song will be sung' Mi 2.4.

Cf. θρῆνος, θρήνημα, ἀποδύρομαι, κλαίω, λυπέω, κόπτω, ὀδύρομαι, ὀλολύζω, οἰμώζω, ὀλοφύρομαι, πενθέω, συμφοράζω: Schmidt 3.396; Trench 238f.; Stählin, *TDNT* 3.150f.

θρήνημα, ατος. n.ʃ

= subs.: θρῆνος καὶ θ. Ez 27.32. Cf. θρῆνος, ὀδυρμός.

θρῆνος, ου. m. (n. To 2.6 𝔊II)

lamentation over some sad event, esp. death, *a dirge* sung on such an occasion: τὸν λόγον .. ὃν ἐγὼ λαμβάνω ἐφ' ὑμᾶς ~ον '.. I take up as a dirge over you' Am 5.1; ll οἶκτος Je 9.20; ll πένθος καὶ κοπετός, Am 5.16; ll πένθος and opp. ᾠδή 'a joyous, festive song' 8.10; φωνὴ ~ου καὶ κλαυθμοῦ Je 38.15; as cogn. subj. θρηνηθήσεται θ. 'a mournful song will be sung' Mi 2.4; opp. ὑμέναιος 3M 4.6. Cf. θρήνημα, πολύθρηνος, γόος, κλαυθμός, κοπετός, λύπη, οἶκτος, ὀλολυγμός, πένθος.

θρησκεία, ας. f.

1. *worship expressed through cultic rites*: Wi 14.27 (pagan), cf. van Herten 2-27, Robert 1938.226-35, and Spicq 1985.232-4.

2. *religion*: Ἰουδαίων 4M 5.7.

Cf. θρησκεύω: Schmidt, *TDNT* 3.155-9. Del. Si 22.5 v.l.

θρησκεύω.ʃ

to render religious service to, 'worship': + acc., ἄλογα ἑρπετά 'irrational serpents' Wi 11.15; pass., *o* τὰ γλυπτά 'the graven idols' 14.16. Cf. θρησκεία, δουλεύω, λειτουργέω.

θρίξ, τριχός. f.

1. *hair*: αἰγεία 'of goat' Ex 25.4, 35.6 (sth valuable); of human skin, Le 13.3; κεφαλῆς Nu 6.5, fig. of great number - Ps 68.5; pubic hair, Ez 16.7.

2. *hair-like, thin, longish object*: ἐτμήθη τὰ πέταλα χρυσίου τρίχες 'the leaves of gold were cut into thin threads' Ex 36.10.

Cf. βόστρυχος, τρίχωμα, κόμη, μύσταξ, πλόκαμος, πώγων: Schmidt 1.379-83.

θροέω: aor.pass. ἐθροήθην.ʃ

to agitate intensely: pass., *o* ἡ κοιλία μου .. ἐπ' αὐτόν 'my stomach ..' Ct 5.4.

θρονίζομαι: aor. ἐθρονίσθην.ʃ*

to ascend the throne: Es 1.2 o' (*L* κάθημαι ἐπὶ τοῦ θρόνου). Cf. θρόνος.

θρόνος, ου. m.

chair of distinction: δόξης 1K 2.8; royal throne, πλὴν τὸν ~ον ὑπερέξω σου ἐγώ 'only with respect to the throne shall I have an edge over you' Ge 41.40, τῆς βασιλείας 3K 9.5; Jn 3.6, Hg 2.22; κατάρξει ἐπὶ τοῦ ~ου αὐτοῦ 'he will rule on his throne' Zc 6.13; καθήμενον ἐπὶ ~ου ὑψηλοῦ 'seated on a high ..' Is 6.1; judge's, εἰς κρίσιν Ps 121.5, also 9.5 + σκῆπτρον 'sceptre' Wi 7.8. **b**. by metonymy, *rule, reign*: Pr 25.5.

Cf. δίφρος, καθέδρα, (ἐν)θρονίζω: Schmitz, *TDNT* 3.160f.

θροῦς, οῦ. m.ʃ

great noise, 'din': of moving caravan, 1M 9.39; γογγυσμῶν 'of grumbles' Wi 1.10.

θρυλέω: aor.opt.pass. θρυληθείην.

to chatter about: + acc. rei, 3M 6.7; pass. *to be* or *become common talk*: ὑπὸ λαοῦ μου Jb 31.30. Cf. θρύλημα.

θρύλημα, ατος. n.ʃ*

topic of common talk, byword: ἐν ἔθνεσιν Jb 17.6 (ll γέλως); 30.9. Cf. θρυλέω.

θυγάτηρ, τρός, voc. θύγατερ. f.

1. *female child in relation to her parents*, 'daughter': ἔτεκε ~έρα 'she gave birth to a daughter' Ho 1.6; θ. ἐπαναστήσεται ἐπὶ τὴν μητέρα αὐτῆς 'a daughter will rise up against her mother' Mi 7.6; τὴν

~έρα σου οὐ δώσεις τῷ υἱῷ αὐτοῦ καὶ τὴν ~έρα αὐτοῦ οὐ λήμψῃ τῷ υἱῷ σου De 7.3 (in marriage); opp. υἱός and following it, ἐγέννησεν υἱοὺς καὶ ~έρας Ge 5.4; οἱ υἱοὶ .. καὶ αἱ ~έρες .. καὶ οἱ πρεσβύτεροι Jl 2.28; virgin, θυγατέρες, αἳ οὐκ ἔγνωσαν ἄνδρα 'daughters who have not yet had sex with a man' Ge 19.8. **b**. applied to daughter-in-law: Ru 2.2. **c**. applied to a female relation in an endearing address: Ru 2.8. **d**. w. God as father: υἱοῖς αὐτοῦ καὶ ~ράσι Si 17.22¶. **e**. applied to young animals: στρουθῶν 'of sparrows' Is 43.20.

*__2__. *inhabitant* (of a city or land): θ. Σιων .. θ. Ιερουσαλημ Mi 4.8, τοῦ γένους μου 'of my race' Is 22.4, Σιδῶνος 23.12; Βαβυλῶνος Zc 2.7; τῆς Ιουδαίας Ps 47.12. In this Hebraistic use, θ. is sg., though it refers collectively to 'inhabitants.' **b**. *members* of a nation: θύγατερ λαοῦ μου Je 6.26.

3. *female member of a community*, mostly pl.: γυνὴ ἀπὸ τῶν ~έρων τῆς γῆς ταύτης Ge 27.46; ἔλαβεν τῶν ~έρων Λευι 'took one of the women of the Levite tribe' Ex 2.1; ~έρας Μωαβ Nu 25.1 (illicit sexual partners); ἀπὸ τῶν ~έρων Ισραηλ De 23.17 (:: ἀπὸ υἱῶν Ισραηλ); Pr 31.29, Ct 2.2.

*__4__. *female person characterised by a certain property*: θ. ἀτιμίας 'ignominious woman' Je 30.4, cf. υἱός **4**. **b**. w. ref. to wife: Si 26.24¶.

5. *minor population centre adjoining and dependent on* a major one: Βαιθσαν .. τὰς ~ρας αὐτῆς Jd 1.27; 1M 5.8, 5.65.

Cf. υἱός, μήτηρ, and νυμφίος.

θυεία, ας. f.ʃ

mortar: ἔτριβον ἐν τῇ ~είᾳ 'pounded with the mortar' Nu 11.8.

θύελλα, ας. f.ʃ

hurricane, squall: juxtaposition of three nouns, σκότος γνόφος θ. 'pitch-dark stormy cloud(?)' Ex 10.22, De 4.11, 5.22. Cf. καταιγίς, λαῖλαψ: Trench 277f.

***θυΐσκη**, ης. f.*

censer: fixture of a ritual table, Ex 25.28; τὰ σκεύη τῆς τραπέζης, τά τε τρυβλία καὶ τὰς ~ας 38.12; silver, 1E 2.12; golden and silver, 2C 24.14; + φιάλη 4.21.

θυλάκιον, ου. n.ʃ

(small) *sack*: money-bag, To 9.5; not so small for two talents of silver, 4K 4.23*L*. Cf. θύλακος.

θύλακος, ou. m.ʃ

sack: money-bag, 4K 4.23B. Cf. θυλάκιον.

θῦμα, ατος. n.

slaughtered animal: for a meal, σφάξον ~ατα Ge 43.16; as cultic sacrifices, τῶν σωτηρίων 'of thank-offering for deliverance' Ex 29.28; ἑορτῆς τοῦ πάσχα 'of the Passover feast' 34.25; consisting of μόσχου καὶ ἀρνός 'calf and lamb' 2K 6.13*L*. Cf. θύω, θυσία.

θυμήρης, ες.ʃ

delightful: *s* God's reward, Wi 3.14.

θυμιάω. ⇒ θυμιάζω.

θυμιάζω and θυμιάω: fut. θυμιάσω; impf.3pl ἐθυμιῶσαν; aor. ἐθυμίασα, inf. θυμιάσαι, pass. θυμιαθῆναι, impv.3s θυμιαθήτω; pf.ptc.pass. τεθυμιαμένος. Also spelled θυμιάω.

1. *to burn so as to produce smoke*: ***o*** incense, + cogn. obj., θυμίαμα Ex 30.7; ἐπὶ ^θυσιαστηρίου^ 40.25; + dat. of a divinity, τοῖς γλυπτοῖς 'to the graven idols' Ho 11.2 (|| θύω), θεοῖς ἀλλοτρίοις 'to foreign gods' Je 19.4, τῷ ἀμφιβλήστρῳ 'to the casting net' (deified for its success) Hb 1.16 (|| θύω); ἐπὶ ταῖς πλίνθοις τοῖς δαιμονίοις 'over a brick altar to demons' Is 65.3, ἐπὶ τοῖς ὑψηλοῖς 'at the high places' 3K 3.2; ἐπὶ τῶν ὀρέων Is 65.7, ἐπὶ τῶν δωμάτων .. τῇ Βααλ 'on the rooftops to B.' Je 39.29; + θύω 3K 3.3. **b**. ***o*** sacrificial meat: 1K 2.15.

2. *to apply to one's own body*: + acc., σμύρναν 'myrrh' Ct 3.6.

Cf. θύω, θυμιάω, and θυμίαμα.

θυμίαμα, ατος. n.

1. *spice*: + ῥητίνη 'resin,' στακτή 'myrrh' Ge 37.25, 43.11.

2. *incense*: σύνθετον λεπτόν 'compounded, powdery' Ex 30.7; θ. προσάγεται τῷ ὀνόματί μου Ma 1.11 (|| θυσία); + εὐωδία Si 45.16.

Cf. θυμιάζω, θυμιατήριον: Nielsen 52f.

θυμιατήριον, ου. n.

altar on which incense is burned: Ez 8.11, 4M 7.11. Cf. θυμίαμα: *ND* 3.69.

θυμός, οῦ. m.

1. *anger, fury*, often. of God's indignation exc. Ge 49.6, Ex 32.19, Am 6.12, Is 14.3, Pr 20.2 (last: a lion's), 2M 14.4+: παρωξύνθη ὁ θ. μου ἐπ' αὐτούς 'my anger intensified against them' Ho 8.5, sim. Zc 10.3; || πικρία 'bitterness' Am 6.12, || ζῆλος Zc 8.2, Ez 36.6, 18, || ὀργή Ex 15.8 (see vs. 7), Ho 13.11, Is 34.2; θ. καὶ ὀργή Ge 27.45, De 29.23, Is 10.5; ὀ. καὶ θ. De 9.19; ἐν ~ῷ καὶ ὀργῇ καὶ παροξυσμῷ μεγάλῳ σφόδρα 29.28; causes destruction, ὁ θ. αὐτοῦ τήκει ἀρχάς 'his wrath brings dominions to nothing' Na 1.6*b*; ἡμέρα ~οῦ κυρίου Zp 2.2; ὀργίζομαι ~ῷ Ex 22.24, 32.19; ἐν ~ῷ 'angrily' Mi 5.15, Ho 13.11; Hb 3.12 (|| ἐν ἀπειλῇ 'threateningly'), Zc 10.4; μετὰ ~οῦ Ex 11.8, Na 1.2; combined w. ὀργή in a genitive relationship for emphasis, τὸν ~ὸν τῆς ὀργῆς μου Nu 14.34, ὀργὴ ~οῦ κυρίου 25.4, κατὰ τὴν ὀργὴν τοῦ ~οῦ μου Ho 11.9, cf. also Jn 3.9, Na 1.6*a*, Zp 3.8; ἰσχυρὸν καὶ σκληρὸν ὁ θ. κυρίου 'sth powerful and harsh ..' Is 28.2; w. ἐν to indicate an object against which anger is directed, οὐκ ἔσται θ. ἐν τοῖς υἱοῖς Ισραηλ Nu 18.5, ἐν ποταμοῖς ὁ θ. σου 'your anger is directed against rivers' Hb 3.8

(|| ὅρμημα), ἐν τοῖς ὑπεναντίοις 'against the opponents' Is 1.24; ἐπί τινα 34.2. **b.** of poisonous reptiles: δρακόντων .. ἀσπίδων De 32.33, cf. συρόντων ἐπὶ γῆς 'of those which creep on the ground' and ἰὸς ἀσπίδων 'vipers' venom' Ps 13.3, 139.4, cf. 57.5 and χόλος (LSG s.v.). **c.** occasions a murder: ἐν τῷ ~ῷ αὐτῶν ἀπέκτειναν ἀνθρώπους Ge 49.6 (|| ἐπιθυμία). **d.** *indignation* against injustice, maltreatment and the like: Is 14.3 (|| ὀδύνη), but cf. παίδευσον ἡμᾶς, πλὴν ἐν κρίσει καὶ μὴ ἐν ~ῷ Je 10.24.

2. *mental disposition*, 'temper': πλάγιος 'unfriendly, uncharitable' Le 26.24, 41, ἄρσην 'manly' 2M 7.21; ^γλώσσης^ 'powerful drive of a (slanderous) tongue' Si 28.19; Pr 6.34; ~οῦ περισπασμός 'what occupies his mind' Ec 2.23; pl., || ὀργή 2M 4.25.

Cf. θυμόω, θυμώδης, ἔκθυμος, ὀξύθυμος, ὀργή, θολερός, ζῆλος, μῆνις, ὅρμημα, παροξυσμός: Schmidt 3.551-8, 566f.; Trench 130-4; Chadwick 143-50; Muraoka 2001b.37-9, 2005.59f., 2005b.104f. On the synonymity with ὀργή, see under the latter, and Büchsel, *TDNT* 3.167f. Acc. to Irmscher 3ff., θ. is not used of god in secular literature.

θυμόω: fut.pass. θυμωθήσομαι, inf. ~μωθήσεσθαι; aor. ἐθύμωσα, pass. ἐθυμώθην, inf. θυμωθῆναι, ptc. θυμωθείς, impv. θυμώθητι.

to excite to anger, irritate: abs. Ho 12.14 (v.l., + με, and || παροργίζω); pass. (= intr.) ἤρξαντο οἱ ἄρχοντες θυμοῦσθαι ἐξ οἴνου 'the rulers began to become irritable by wine' 7.5; ὀργῇ Ge 39.19, Ex 4.14, 1K 11.6 (Ra: θυμός); ***o*** God, θυμωθεὶς ὀργῇ κύριος ἐπὶ Μωυσῆν Ex 4.14, cf. θυμωθεὶς ὀργισθῇ De 11.17; εἴς τινα Ex 32.10, 11, Nu 11.33; ἔν τινι 2K 24.1*L*; ἐπί τινα Le 10.16, Nu 24.10 (*s* hum.); ὁ θεὸς ἐπὶ τὰ τίμια αὐτοῦ θυμωθήσεται 'God will become angry over his precious things' Ho 11.7; ἐπί τινα 2K 12.5 *L* (B: + dat.); ἐπί τινι (pers.) De 9.8, Is 54.9; + dat. pers., τῇ Ραχηλ 'against R.' Ge 30.2; δι' ὑμᾶς 'on account of you' De 1.37; περὶ τῶν λεγομένων ὑφ' ὑμῶν 'over what was said by you' 4.21; + ὅτι Ge 6.7; *s* hum., κατά τινα 4M 2.16, 2K 11.22 πρὸς (*L* ἐπὶ) Ιωαβ, Ge 39.19; heaven, Is 13.13; sword, Ez 21.9; + acc. cogn., ὁ θυμός σου, ὃν ἐθυμώθης 37.29, cf. ἐθυμώθη ὀργὴ αὐτοῦ Jb 32.5¶.

Cf. θυμός, ἀγανακτέω, ἀγριαίνω, δεινάζω, (δι)οργίζομαι, παροργίζω, παροξύνω, χολάω.

θυμώδης, ες.

agitated by or *given to anger*: *s* hum., Pr 11.25; typical of a man in authority, 31.4; ὀργὴ κυρίου Je 37.23. Cf. θυμός, ὀργίλος.

θύρα, ας. f.

1. *door*: of ship Ge 6.16; Διάνοιξον .. τὰς ~ας σου 'Open your doors' Zc 11.1; of house, οἰκίας Le 14.38; συγκλεισθήσονται ~αι 'doors will be closed' Ma 1.10; of city-gates, Is 45.2, τῆς πύλης 2K 11.23B (*L* τῆς πόλεως); οὐρανοῦ Ps 77.23.

2. *a place where one makes entry* into a building or some confined space, 'entrance': σκηνῆς 'of a tent' Ge 18.1; τῆς σκηνῆς τοῦ μαρτυρίου Le 8.35; 2K 11.9 (*L* πυλών 'gate-house'). Cf. προσκήνιον.

Cf. θυρίς, θυρόω, θύρωμα, θυρωρός, πρόθυρον, πύλη: Husson 93-107.

θυρεός, οῦ. m.

oblong shield: Is 21.5, + πέλτη Ez 23.24, + ὅπλον Ps 34.2, + λόγχη, τόξον, θώραξ Ne 4.16. Cf. θυρεοφόρος, ἀσπίς: Oepke, *TDNT* 5.312-14.

θυρεοφόρος, ον.ʃ *

armed with a θυρεός (q.v.): *s* hum., + δορατοφόρος 1C 12.25.

θυρίς, ίδος. f.

window: τῆς κιβωτοῦ 'of the ark' Ge 8.6; διὰ ~ίδων εἰσελεύσονται ὡς κλέπται 'they will enter through windows like thieves' Jl 2.9; of being let downwards through a window, Jo 2.15, 1K 19.12, cf. 2Cor 11.33. Cf. θύρα, ψευδοθυρίς: Husson 109-18; id. 1983.155-62.

θυρόω: aor. ἐθύρωσα.ʃ

to fit with doors: + acc. (room) 1M 4.57.

θύρσος, ου. m.ʃ

wand wreathed in ivy and vine-leaves with a pine cone at the top (LSJ; but associated with the Dionysian cult!): Ju 15.12, 2M 10.7.

θύρωμα, ατος. n.

door: Ep Je 17, Ez 41.3. **b.** *doorway*: 3K 6.31.

Cf. θύρα: Caird 1968.475.

θυρωρός, οῦ. m.

gate-keeper, porter: 2K 4.6; of the temple, Ez 44.11, 1E 1.15 (|| πυλωρός 2C 35.15). Cf. θύρα, πυλωρός.

θυσία, ας. f.

1, *animal sacrifice offered as part of cultic institution*: Ho 3.4; 6.6, Ex 10.25 (|| ὁλοκαύτωμα), Ma 1.8; Zc 9.1; κυρίου Zp 1.8, cf. 1.7, 3.10; cogn. obj. of θύω, Ge 31.54, Ex 24.5, De 27.7, Ho 8.13; pl. Ho 9.4 (|| οἶνος), Am 4.4; σωτηρίου Ex 24.5, 32.6, De 27.7; as obj. of φέρω Ge 4.3; Am 5.22 (+ ὁλοκαύτωμα), Ma 1.13, ἀναφέρω Is 57.6; προσφέρω Ge 4.5; Am 4.4, 5.25 (|| σφάγιον); προσάγω Le 3.1, Ma 2.12, 3.3; προσδέχομαι Ma 1.10; δίδωμι Ex 10.25; ποιέω 'to prepare' Le 6.39, Is 19.21; ἀναποιέω Le 6.40; σφάζω Le 17.5; ἐπιβλέπειν εἰς ~αν Ma 2.13; καθαρὰ θ. Ma 1.11 (|| θυμίαμα); ἀρέσει τῷ κυρίῳ θ. Ιουδα καὶ Ιερουσαλημ Ma 3.4; || σπονδή Nu 28.9, Jl 1.9, 13, 2.14, Is 57.6; || σφαγή Is 34.6; μοσχάρια 'calves' Ex 24.5; + προσφορά Ps 39.7.

2. *cultic offering in general*: of products of the soil, ἀπὸ τῶν καρπῶν τῆς γῆς ~αν τῷ κυρίῳ Ge 4.3;

|| δῶρον 4.5; ἐνδεδελεχισμοῦ 'continual, daily' Ex 29.42; σεμιδάλεως 'of fine flour' Nu 15.4. **b**. metaph. θ. δικαιοσύνης Ps 4.6, 50.21, αἰνέσεως 49.14, 106.22, θ. αἰνέσεως σωτηρίου Le 7.3, 5.

Cf. θύω, θυσιάζω, σφαγή: Behm, *TDNT* 3.181f.; Wevers 1993.52, 1997.484-7; Rösel 102f.; Casabona 127; *BA* 3.35; Daniel 28f., 203, 209f.; Muraoka 1990a:46; id. 1993 s.v.

θυσιάζω: aor. ἐθυσίασα, subj. θυσιάσω.

1. *to perform the cultic task of offering sacrifices*: + dat. θεοῖς 'to (foreign) gods' Ex 22.20; τῷ κυρίῳ Le 24.9; "on the summits of the mountains" Ho 4.13 (|| θύω); ἄρχοντες θυσιάζοντες 12.11; Zc 14.21.

2. *to offer as cultic offering*: + acc. rei, δῶρον Le 7.6, σωτήριον Si 32.2, αἴνεσις 32.4.

3. *to slaughter*: τινα (with no cultic significance), ἱερεῖς (!) 4K 23.20 (*L* θύω).

Cf. θύω, θυσία, θυσίαμα and θυσιαστήριον.

θυσίασμα, ματος. n.

animal sacrifice: αἷμα ~ατος Ex 23.18, .. άτων 34.25; κυρίῳ 29.18; ὁλοκαυτώματα .. ~ατα .. ἀπαρχὰς .. εὐχὰς .. ἑκούσια .. πρωτότοκα De 12.6, sim. 12.11. Cf. θύω.

θυσιαστήριον, ου. n. * (Daniel 27)

altar to which cultic offerings are brought: Ho 3.4 (|| θυσία, ἱερατεία); 4.19; κατασκάψει 'will demolish ..' 10.2 (|| στήλη); λειτουργοῦντες ~ῳ Jl 1.9, 13; κυρίου Ma 2.13, cf. ᾠκοδόμησεν ἐκεῖ Αβραμ θ. κυρίῳ τῷ ὀφθέντι αὐτῷ Ge 12.7; ἐκ γῆς 'made of earth' Ex 20.24, ἐκ λίθων 20.25, θυμιάματος ἐκ ξύλων ἀσήπτων 'of incense made of incorruptible timber' 30.1; τῶν ὁλοκαυτωμάτων Le 4.25, τῆς ὁλοκαυτώσεως 4.34; κέρατα τοῦ ~ου 'the horns of ..' Am 3.14*b*. **b**. Applied to sites of idolatrous cults practised by Israelites: Ho 8.11, 10.1 (|| στήλη), 2, 8, 12.12, Am 2.8, 3.14*a*, Ez 6.4 (|| τέμενος), 5, 13.

Cf. βωμός, θυσία, θυσιάζω, στήλη: Daniel 15-32; Klauck 274-7; Hanhart 1992.346f.

θύω: fut. θύσω; aor. ἔθυσα, ptc. θύσας, impv. θύσον, subj. θύσω, pass. τυθῶ; pf. τέθυκα.

1. *to offer* (cultic) animal sacrifice: abs. ἐπὶ τοὺς βουνούς Ho 4.13 (|| θυσιάζω); μετὰ τῶν τετελεσμένων 'with the initiates' 4.14; + cogn. obj. θυσίαν Ge 31.54, De 27.7; θυσίαν τῷ θεῷ Ge 46.1; θυσίαν καὶ φάγωσι κρέα Ho 8.13, cf. θυσίαν τῷ κυρίῳ Jn 1.16 and διεφθαρμένον τῷ κυρίῳ Ma 1.14; αἷμα θυσιάματος Ex 23.18; + dat. of a divinity, 3.18, alien gods 34.15; Ho 11.2 (|| θυμιάω), Jn 2.10, cf. τῇ σαγήνῃ (successful fishing-net deified) Hb 1.16 (|| θυμιάω); τοῖς ματαίοις 'to the idols' Le 17.7; + acc. of victim, θύσατε ἀνθρώπους, μόσχοι γὰρ ἐκλελοίπασι 'sacrifice humans, for bulls have died out' Ho 13.2, υἱοὺς .. καὶ θυγατέρας .. τοῖς δαιμονίοις Ps 105.37; + θυμιάω 3K 3.3.

2. *to slaughter*: ***o*** a sacrificial animal, πάσχα 'paschal lamb' Ex 12.21; 20.24; μόσχον Is 66.3 (|| ἀποκτέννω); hum., υἱὸν ἔναντι τοῦ πατρὸς αὐτοῦ Si 31.24, ἔθυσεν αὐτοὺς εἰς τὸ φρέαρ τὸ μέγα '.., (throwing them) into the large pit' 1M 7.19; 4K 23.20*L* (B: θυσιάζω); in battle, Jd12.6 B(A: σφάζω); no cultic significance, πρόβατα Is 22.13 (|| σφάζω), θύματα 1K 25.11.

Cf. θυμιάω / θυμιάζω, ἐπιθύω, θυσιάζω, ἄθυτος, σφάζω, εἰδωλόθυτος: Shipp 274; Behm, *TDNT* 3.180f.; Kilpatrick 1990.201-4. On the distinction between θύω and θυμιάω / θυμιάζω on the one hand, and θύω and θυσιάζω on the other, see Muraoka 1983.48f.

θωρακίζω: pf.ptc.pass. τεθωρακισμένος.ʃ

to make ready for battle: pass. and ***o*** παρεμβολὴν .. ἰσχυρὰν τεθωρακισμένην 1M 4.7; troops, ἐν ἁλυσιδωτοῖς 'with coats of mail' 6.35; elephant, θώραξι 'with armour' 6.43. Cf. θώραξ.

θωρακισμός, οῦ. m.ʃ*

breast-armour: 2M 5.3. Cf. θώραξ.

θώραξ, ακος. m.

coat of mail: Is 59.17; ***o*** of ἐνδύομαι 1K 17.38*L*, Ez 38.4, 1M 3.3; w. ref. to crocodile's (?) scales, Jb 41.5.

Cf. θωρακίζω, θωρακισμός: Oepke, *TDNT* 5.308-10.

I

ἴαμα, ατος. n.

restoration of health, 'cure': fig., ἡ δρόσος ἡ παρὰ σοῦ ἴ. αὐτοῖς ἐστιν Is 26.19; 2C 36.16. **b**. *treatment aimed at restoring health* or *means used to that end*: Je 26.11, Wi 16.9. **c**. *cured tissue* (?): ἀνάξω τὸ ἴ. σου Je 37.17, sim. 40.6.

Cf. ἰάομαι, ἴασις, συνούλωσις.

ἰάομαι: fut. ἰάσομαι, pass. ἰαθήσομαι; aor. ἰασάμην, inf. ἰάσασθαι, impv. ἴασαι, subj. ἰάσωμαι; pass. ἰάθην, inf. ἰαθῆναι; pf. ἴαμαι.

1. *to treat bodily, psychic dysfunction or damage and restore health*: abs., De 32.39; + acc. of patient, Ex 15.26, Le 14.3; Ho 5.13; ἀσθενής Ps 6.3; τὸ συντετριμμένον 'the bruised' Zc 11.16; τοὺς συντετριμμένους τὴν καρδίαν 'the brokenhearted' Ps 146.3, Is 61.1; ‖ μοτόω Ho 6.1 (‖ ὑγιάζω vs. 2); acc. of disease or bodily weakness, νόσους 'illnesses' Ps 102.3 (‖ ἀνομίας), σύντριμμα .. ὀδύνην 'bruise .. pain' Is 30.26, Je 6.14, δίψαν 'thirst' 4M 3.10; + dat. cogn., ἰάσει Je 19.22; pass., ἰάθη ἡ ἁφή 'the infection has been cured' Le 14.48; metaph., ἁμαρτίας σου De 30.3, τὴν ψυχήν μου, ὅτι ἥμαρτόν σοι Ps 40.5; hurt feelings Pr 12.18 (*s* speech of the wise and:: τιτρώσκω 'to injure'); *s* usually God, if explicitly indicated, e.g., Ge 20.17 (‖ ζάω vs. 7; cure of temporary sterility) Ex 15.26, De 30.3; Je 17.14 (‖ σῴζω); an angel, To 3.17; 12.14; divine word, οὔτε βοτάνη οὔτε μάλαγμα ἐθεράπευσεν .. ὁ σὸς .. λόγος ὁ πάντα ἰώμενος 'neither herbs nor plaster cured ..' Wi 16.12; hum., Je 6.14.

2. *to restore to a well-functioning state*, 'to repair': *s* Elijah and + acc., τὸ θυσιαστήριον τὸ κατεσκαμμένον 'the altar which had been razed to the ground' 3K 18.32; God through Elisha and ***o*** polluted water (ὕδατα) 4K 2.21f., earthen vessel Je 19.11; *s* God, κατοικίας 'dwellings' Ho 14.5.

Cf. ἴασις, ἀνίατος, ἰατρεῖον, ἰατής, ἰατρεία, ἰατρεύω, ἰατρός, θεραπεύω, σῴζω, ὑγιάζω: Schmidt 4.108-10, 112-4; Oepke, *TDNT* 3.201-3; Wells 103-12.

ἴασις, εως. f.

healing: ἴ. τῇ συντριβῇ σου 'a cure for your bruise' Na 3.19; cogn. dat., Is 19.22; ὑγιεία ~εως as 'health restored through healing' Si 1.18; ζωῆς 31.20 (+ εὐλογία), ‖ ζωή Pr 4.22. **b**. relief from calamity, i.e. not necessarily medical, Si 3.28, from the intense heat of the summer, 43.22; Ps 37.4, Zc 10.2, Je 14.19.

Cf. ἰάομαι, ἴαμα.

ἴασπις, ιδος; acc. ἴασπιν. f.

jasper: Ex 28.18; precious stone, Is 54.12.

ἰατής, οῦ. m.ʃ

= ἰατρός 'physician': κακῶν Jb 13.4.

ἰατρεία, ας. f.ʃ

effective *medical treatment*: Je 31.2, 2C 21.18. Cf. ἰάομαι.

ἰατρεῖον, ου. n.ʃ

pl., *medical costs*: ἀποτείσει καὶ τὰ ~α 'he shall also pay the medical costs' Ex 21.19.

ἰατρεύω: fut. ἰατρεύσω; aor. ἰάτρευσα, pass. ἰατρεύθην, inf. ἰατρευθῆναι.

to treat medically: + acc. pers., unsuccessfully, Je 28.9; ἀπὸ πληγῆς ὀδυνηρᾶς 'for a painful blow' 37.17. Cf. ἰάομαι.

ἰατρός, οῦ. m.

physician: Is 26.14, Je 8.22. Cf. ἰατής.

ἶβις, ἴβιος/~εως, acc. ἶβιν. m.ʃ

ibis, an Egyptian bird: forbidden as food, Le 11.17, De 14.15; Is 34.11. Cf. Morenz 253f. and Görg 118f.

ἰγνύα, ας. f.ʃ

the part behind the thigh and knee: 3K 18.21.

ἰδέα, ας. f.

outward appearance, 'form': ἐγέννησεν κατὰ τὴν ~αν αὐτοῦ καὶ κατὰ τὴν εἰκόνα αὐτοῦ Ge 5.3; Ep Je 62; Da 1.13 TH (LXX ὄψις), 2M 3.16 (‖ ὄψις). **b**. not necessarily visible, but *manifestation recognisable as such*: παθῶν 'of passions' 4M 1.14, σοφίας 1.18.

Cf. εἶδος, εἰκών, μορφή, ὁμοίωμα, ὄψις, σχῆμα: Schmidt 4.348f.; Trench 261f., 266f.

ἰδιόγραφος ον.ʃ

written with one's own hand: ***s*** ψαλμός Ps 151.1. Del. Ps 151 subscr. v.l.

ἰδιοποιέω.ʃ

mid. *to win over*: τὴν καρδίαν τινός 2K 15.6.

ἴδιος, α, ον.ʃ

belonging to oneself and not shared by others: τοὺς ~ους οἰκογενεῖς αὐτοῦ 'his own home-born servants' Ge 14.14, cf. ταῖς ~αις αὐτῶν πονηρίαις 'because of their own wicked acts' Wi 19.13 (also with a poss. pron.); ἐν γῇ οὐκ ~ᾳ 'in a land not their own' Ge 15.13, πᾶν χρέος ~ον 'every private debt' De 15.2, ἕκαστον εἰς τὸν ~ον τόπον 'each to his home town' 1M 11.38, κόμμα ~ον 'own coin' 15.6, τῶν πολιτῶν τῶν ~ων 'of his compatriots' 2M 5.6, τὸν ἑαυτοῦ πατέρα ἐγκαταλείπει .. καὶ τὴν ~αν χώραν καὶ πρὸς τὴν ~αν γυναῖκα κολλᾶται 'leaves his own father .. and his own country and attaches himself to his own wife' 1E 4.20. **b.** subst.: *m.pl.* 'one's own circle', ὑπὸ τῶν ~ων βλάπτεσθαι 'to be injured by their fellow-soldiers' 2M 12.22, ἀπαλλοτριώσει σε τῶν ἰδίων σου 'he will make you a stranger to your own folk' Si 11.34; *n.pl.* 'one's own affairs; one's home,' τὰ ἴδια 'your own affairs' 2M 9.20, τὴν τῶν ~ων ἐπιμέλειαν 'attending to their own affairs' 11.23, ὄντων τῶν υἱῶν Ισραηλ ἑκάστου ἐν τοῖς ~οις 'every one of their Israelites being in his own home' 1E 5.46, ἐκ τῶν ~ων αὐτοῦ 'from his house' 6.31 (‖ οἰκία 2E 6.11), εἰσελθὼν εἰς τὰ ~α 'entering his home' Es 5.10 o' (*L* οἶκος), sim. 6.12 o' (*L* πρὸς ἑαυτόν), εἰς τὰ ~α ἐξαποστείλατε 'Send them back to their homes' 3M 6.27 (cf. εἰς τὰ ~α ἦλθεν Joh 1.11); *f.sg.* εἰς τὴν ~αν 3M 7.20 (‖ εἰς τὴν ~αν οἰκίαν 7.18). Cf. Neirynck 1979. **c.** κατ' ἰδίαν 'private': τὸ σύμφορον κοινῇ καὶ κατ' ~αν 'the interest, both public and private' 2M 4.5, κατ' ~αν παρεκάλουν 'privately encouraged' 6.21, κατ' ~αν ἥξουσιν εἰς τὸ αὐτό 'they would get together in private' 14.21, cf. λαβὼν ~ᾳ τὸν Ἀνδρόνικον 'taking A. aside' 4.34, ἀνοίσω πρὸς ἐμαυτὸν ~ᾳ λόγον Jb 7.13. **d.** virtually equivalent to a poss. pron.: ‖ poss. pron., τὸ ~ον σῶμα καὶ ἡ γῆ ἡμῶν 'our own bodies and our land' Ge 47.18; τῆς ἰδίας ἀνοίας 'of his folly' 2M 14.5; with some emphasis on close ties, πλεῖον ἀγαπᾷ ἄνθρωπος τὴν ~αν γυναῖκα μᾶλλον ἢ τὸν πατέρα καὶ τὴν μητέρα 'one loves one's wife rather better than one's ..' 1E 4.25, κινδυνεύσω τῷ ~ῳ τραχήλῳ 'I shall be risking my own neck' Da LXX 1.10, τῇ ~ᾳ ψυχῇ .. ἄχρηστος 'useless to himself' Si 37.19.

Cf. κοινός: Schmidt 3.471f.; Shipp 277f.; Spicq 2.205-11.

ἰδιότης, ητος. f.ʃ

characteristic feature or *property*: 3M 7.17; εἰκὼν τῆς ἰδίας ~ητος 'a reflection of his own character' Wi 2.23.

ἰδίως. adv.ʃ

by itself: Wi 17.11. Del. 3K 5.6 v.l.

ἰδιώτης, ου. m.ʃ

commoner: "kings and .." Pr 6.8*b*. Cf. ἰδιωτικός: Trench 302-4; Schlier, *TDNT* 3.215-7; Spicq 2.212-4; Kraus.

ἰδιωτικός, ή, όν.ʃ

belonging to private persons or *meant for private use*: *s* χρήματα 'monies, funds' 4M 4.3, 6. Cf. ἰδιώτης.

ἰδού.

A presentative particle used to draw the hearer's or reader's attention to what follows, 'Now look!, Pay attention!, Behold!':

a. foll. by a noun or noun phrase, Ἰδοὺ ἡ παιδίσκη μου Ge 30.3; Ἰ. ἀνήρ Zc 6.12; by a nominal clause, ἰ. ἐπὶ τὰ ὄρη οἱ πόδες εὐαγγελιζομένου 'Look! Here on the mountains are the feet of one who brings good news' Na 1.15; καὶ νῦν ἰ. ἡ γυνή σου ἐναντίον σου Ge 12.19; Ποῦ Σάρρα ἡ γυνή σου; .. Ἰδοὺ ἐν τῇ σκηνῇ 18.9; by a verbal clause mostly with a present tense verb, ἰ. ἐγὼ ἀφορίζω Ma 2.3, or a ptc., ἰ. ἐγὼ στερεῶν βροντὴν .. Am 4.13, but also an aor., ἰ. ἐκάλεσε Am 7.4, a pf., ἰ. γεγήρακα Ge 27.2, ἰ. ὀλιγοστὸν δέδωκα Ob 2; not clause-initial, Καὶ ἐγὼ ἰδοὺ ἡ διαθήκη μου μετὰ σοῦ Ge 17.4, Καὶ ἐγὼ ἰ. δέδωκα .. Nu 18.8; Ge 17.20, 34.10 +. In a respectful reply to a call: καὶ εἶπεν πρὸς αὐτόν Αβρααμ, Αβρααμ· ὁ δὲ εἶπεν Ἰδοὺ ἐγώ Ge 22.1, 11; 27.1, 18, 37.13; Ἰ. εἰμι ἐγώ 'Here I am (ready to act)' Is 6.8; Ἰδοὺ ὁ δοῦλός σου 2K 9.6, but cf. Ἰ. εἰμι (God speaking spontaneously) Is 65.1.

b. introduces an eschatological pronouncement: Καιρὸς παντὸς ἀνθρώπου ἥκει .. καὶ ἰ. ἐγὼ καταφθείρω αὐτοὺς .. Ge 6.13; ἰ. ἡμέρα ἔρχεται .. Ma 4.1. Not clause-initial: ἐγὼ δὲ ἰ. ἐπάγω .. Ge 6.17; ἐγὼ ἰ. ἀνίστημι .. 9.9; περὶ δὲ Ισμαηλ ἰ. ἐπήκουσα .. 17.20 (≠ MT).

c. following a verb of seeing or showing in the past tense, and introducing a report of the vision or sight, usually consisting merely of a noun with or without its qualifier (adj., ptc., etc.), and preceded by καί: ἀναβλέψας .. εἶδεν, καὶ ἰ. τρεῖς ἄνδρες εἱστήκεισαν .. 'looking up .. saw, and behold there were three men standing ..' Ge 18.2, sim. 22.13; ἐνυπνιάσθη, καὶ ἰ. κλῖμαξ ἐστηριγμένη ἐν τῇ γῇ 'he had a dream, and behold a ladder fixed on the ground ..' 28.12; ἐπέβλεψα .. καὶ ἰ. λεπρῶσα Nu 12.10; Ἑώρακα τὴν νύκτα καὶ ἰ. ἀνὴρ ἐπιβεβηκὼς ἐπὶ ἵππον .. 'I saw at night, and behold there was a man mounted on a horse ..' Zc 1.8; Οὕτως ἔδειξέ μοι κύριος καὶ ἰ. ἑστηκὼς ἐπὶ τείχους .. 'Thus the Lord showed me and behold, he was standing upon a wall ..' Am 7.7. Followed by a nominal clause: καὶ ὁρᾷ καὶ ἰ. φρέαρ ἐν τῷ πεδίῳ Ge 29.2; by a verbal clause, ἐγένετο δὲ πρωΐ, καὶ ἰ. ἦν Λεία 29.25.

d. introduces a parenthetical gloss: ἰ. ἀνὰ μέσον Καδης καὶ ἀνὰ μέσον Βαραδ 'Now (this place is) between ..' Ge 16.14.

e. marks surprise on the part of the speaker: "I have summoned you to have my enemies cursed, καὶ ἰ. εὐλογῶν εὐλόγησας τρίτον τοῦτο" Nu 24.10.

f. functions as a presentative drawing to the reader's attention an interesting or important message: ἰ. δέδωκα ὑμῖν πάντα χόρτον Ge 1.29, ἰ. ἐγὼ συντρίβω .. Ez 4.16. In such cases the immediately following pers. pron. nom. is not marked.

g. highlights a newly emerged situation introduced by καὶ ἰδοὺ, whilst another was on-going: "whilst (ἔτι) the letters were being read, there arrived other envoys (καὶ ἰδοὺ ἄγγελοι ..)" 1M 5.14; 1K 1.42, 4K 6.33.

h. not clause-initial: καὶ ἐγὼ ἰ. ἑόρακα Je 7.11, διὰ τοῦτο ἰ. ἐγὼ ἐπὶ σὲ συνάγω .. Ez 16.37; 2C 35.27, 36.8, Ec 1.16.

Cf. Johannessohn 1939-40, and for further literature, see BDAG, s.v. end.

Ἰδουμαῖος, α, ον.

Edomite: γῆ ~αία Ge 36.16; subst., De 23.7; f.sg., *Edom* Is 11.14.

ἱδρόω.ʃ

to sweat: *s* hum., 4M 3.8; τὸ πρόσωπον 'over the whole face' 6.11. Cf. ἱδρώς.

ἱδρύω: pf.ptc.pass.f. ἱδρυμένη.ʃ

to set firmly and found: στέγη ἐπὶ τοὺς στύλους .. ἱδρυμένη 'a roof founded on the pillars ..' 4M 17.3. Cf. καθιδρύω, θεμελιόω.

ἱδρώς, ῶτος. m.

sweat: a sign of hard labour, ἐν ~ῶτι τοῦ προσώπου σου φάγῃ τὸν ἄρτον σου 'you shall eat your bread with sweat of your face' Ge 3.19; + ἀγρυπνία 'lost sleep' 2M 2.26; symptom of angst, Es 5.12 *L*. Cf. ἱδρόω, κάθιδρος.

ἱέραξ, ακος. m.ʃ

hawk, falcon: forbidden as food, Le 11.16, De 14.14; Jb 39.26.

ἱερατεία, ας. f.

1. *priestly office*: Ex 29.9; τοὺς χιτῶνας τοῖς υἱοῖς Ααρων τῆς ~ας 35.19; Ho 3.4 (‖ δῆλοι).

2. *duties and tasks incumbent on priest*: Nu 3.10.

Cf. ἱερεύς, ἱερωσύνη, and ἱερατεύω.

ἱεράτευμα, ατος. n. *ʃ

1. *body of priests*: ὑμεῖς ἔσεσθέ μοι βασίλειον ἱ. 'royal p.' Ex 19.6 (of the Israelites).

2. *office of priest*, 'priesthood': τὸ βασίλειον καὶ τὸ ἱ. καὶ τὸν ἁγιασμόν 2M 2.17 (as divinely instituted).

Cf. ἱερεύς: Schrenk, *TDNT* 3.249f.

ἱερατεύω: fut. ἱερατεύσω, ptc. ἱερατεύσων; aor. ἱεράτευσα, subj. ἱερατεύσω* (but alr. in 2c. BCE inscriptions).

to serve as priest: + dat.(God), Ex 28.1, Ho 4.6; as high priest, 1M 7.5. Cf. ἱερατεία, ἱερεύς: MM, s.v.; *ND* 4.156.

ἱερατικός, ή, όν.ʃ

pertaining to priest: *s* στολή 'garment' 1E 4.54, 5.44, 2M 3.15. Cf. ἱερεύς.

ἱερεία, ας. f.ʃ

sacred worship service: 4K 10.20 (*L* θεραπεία).

ἱερεύς, έως; voc. ἱερεῦ. m.

priest: engaged in cultic activities, οἱ ~εῖς οἱ λειτουργοῦντες θυσιαστηρίῳ Jl 1.9, 13, cf. λειτουργοῦντες κυρίῳ 2.17; ἑστῶτα πρὸ προσώπου ἀγγέλου κυρίου Zc 3.1; τοὺς ~εῖς τοὺς ἐν τῷ οἴκῳ κυρίου 7.3 (‖ προφῆται); serving pagan gods, Zp 1.4; in Pharaoh's service, Ge 47.22; τοῦ θεοῦ τοῦ ὑψίστου 14.18; ἱ. μέγας 'high priest' Nu 35.25, Hg 1.1; has colleagues, ὁ. ἱ. ὁ μέγας, σὺ καὶ οἱ πλησίον σου οἱ καθήμενοι πρὸ προσώπου σου Zc 3.8; presides beside a messianic figure, Zc 6.13. Opp. to λαός 'the laity,' ἔσται καθὼς ὁ λαὸς οὕτως καὶ ὁ ἱ. 'it will be "Like people like priest"' Ho 4.9, cf. 4.4. Forms part of the elite of a nation, Ho 5.1 (‖ ὁ οἶκος τοῦ βασιλέως), Am 1.15 (‖ οἱ βασιλεῖς and οἱ ἄρχοντες), Mi 3.11 (‖ οἱ ἡγούμενοι and οἱ προφῆται), cf. Zp 3.4 (‖ προφήτης). Knowledgeable about the divine law, Hg 2.11; χείλη ~έως φυλάξει γνῶσιν, καὶ νόμον ἐκζητήσουσιν ἐκ στόματος αὐτοῦ 'the lips of a priest shall preserve knowledge, and they will seek out law from his mouth' Ma 2.7; Je 18.18 (‖ συνετός, προφήτης). Descended from Aaron: τοῖς ~εῦσιν τοῖς υἱοῖς Ααρων Le 21.1; from Zadok, Ez 43.19. Cf. ἀρχιερεύς, ἱεράτευμα, ἱερατεία, ἱερατικός, ἱερωσύνη, and ἱερατεύω.

ἱερόδουλος, ου. m.

temple staff: = Levite, 1E 1.3, cf. Scholl 1984.

ἱεροπρεπής, ές.ʃ

befitting a sacred person or *task*: *s* hum., 4M 9.25; struggle, 11.20. Cf. Spicq 2.215f.; Schrenk, *TDNT* 3.253f.

ἱερός, ά, όν.

dedicated to cult: ἱερὰ σκεύη 1E 1.43; subst.n., *temple*, τοὺς τοίχους τοῦ ~οῦ 'the walls of ..' 1C 29.4, τὸ ~ὸν τοῦ κυρίου τὸ ἐν Ιερουσαλημ 1E 2.6, τὸ ὄρος τοῦ ~οῦ 'the temple mount' 1M 13.52. τὸ μέγιστον καὶ ἅγιον ~όν 'the greatest and sacred ..' 2M 14.31; a pagan temple, Bel 8 LXX, 1M 6.2, τὸ ~ὸν Δαγων 10.84, cf. Pelletier 1967b.180; pl., utensils for cultic use, Ez 27.7, Ju 4.1. **b**. *dedicated to one's god and religion*: *s* hum. (ψυχή), 4M 7.4, ἀνήρ 6.30, μήτηρ 16.12 (+ θεοσεβής), εὐσεβείας .. χορός 'chorus of piety' 13.8; hum. teeth, 7.6; στρατεία 'battle' 9.24 (+ εὐγενής 'noble'); σάλπιγξ 'trumpet' Jo 6.8, τὰ ~ὰ σκεύη τοῦ οἴκου κυρίου 'the sacred vessels ..' 1E 6.25, γαζοφυλάκιον 'treasury' 5.44, θησαυρός 4M 4.7, ἔργα 'ministries' 1E 7.3, ἐσθής 'uniform' 8.70, βίβλον 'book' 2M 8.23.

Cf. ἱεροπρεπής, ἅγιος, μιαρός, ναός, τέμενος: Schmidt 4.322-36; Trench 10-5, 327-30, 348f.; Schrenk, *TDNT* 3.221-6, 232f.; Barr 1961.282-7; Renehan 1.108f.

Ἱεροσολυμίτης, ου. m.ʃ

resident of Jerusalem: Si 50.27, 4M 4.22, 18.5. Del. 2M 4.39 v.l.

ἱεροστάτης, ου. m.ʃ *

governor of the temple: 1E 7.2.

ἱεροσυλέω.ʃ
to commit sacrilege: 2M 9.2. Cf. Schrenk, *TDNT* 3.255f.

ἱεροσύλημα, ατος. n.ʃ*
sacrilegious plunder: 2M 4.39. Cf. ἱεροσυλία, ἱερόσυλος.

ἱεροσυλία, ς. f.ʃ
= ἱεροσύλημα: 2M 13.6.

ἱερόσυλος, ου. m.ʃ
subst.m. *one guilty of* ἱεροσύλημα, 'temple robber': 2M 4.42. Cf. ἱεροσύλημα.

ἱερουργία, ας. f.ʃ
temple services: 4M 3.20.

ἱεροψάλτης, ου. m ..
temple musician: 1E 1.14.

ἱερόψυχος, ον.ʃ *
having a holy, pious soul: *s* hum., 4M 17.4.

ἱέρωμα, ατος. n.ʃ
sacred token: talisman (?), 2M 12.40, cf. Robert 1989.751-3; LSG s.v.

ἱερωσύνη, ης. f.
institution or *office of priesthood*: held by Zadok, 1C 29.22, by Phinehas, ~ης μεγαλεῖον 'the splendour of priesthood' Si 45.24, 1E 5.38. Cf. ἱερατεία, ἱεράτευμα: Schrenk, *TDNT* 3.247f.

ἱκανός, ή, όν.
1. *sufficient, enough*: + dat. pers. 'for one's needs,' Ob 5, Na 2.13; + ὅτι-, οὐχ ~όν σοι ὅτι ἔλαβες τὸν ἄνδρα μου; Ge 30.15; 33.15, Ez 34.18; ~οὺς .. εἰς πρόβατον 'numerous enough for one sheep' Ex 12.4; εἰς καῦσιν 'for burning' Is 40.16; πρὸς τό + inf., 'for the purpose of' Wi 18.12. **b**. subst. m.sg. 'the Self-sufficient' as a divine title: anarth., κληρονομία ~οῦ 'an inheritance from ..' Jb 31.2¶ (|| θεός), see also 21.15, 40.2; articular, ὁ ἱ. ἐκάκωσέν με Ru 1.21, see also 1.20, and cf. Bertram 1958.
2. *having adequate strength*: οὐκ ἱ. εἰμι 'I am not up to it' Ex 4.10 (|| δυνάμενος vs. 13); + dat. τίς ἔσται ἱ. αὐτῇ; 'who will be equal to it?' Jl 2.11 (cf. Thdt ἀντιστῆναι τοῖς ἐπαγομένοις ὑπὸ θεοῦ κακοῖς οὐδεὶς ἀνθρώπων δυνήσεται, PG 81.1644); οὐδὲ πρὸς τὸ θάψαι οἱ ζῶντες ἦσαν ~οί 'the survivors were not able to cope with the task of burial' Wi 18.12 (there were too many dead to bury).
3. *considerable* in quantity: λαοὶ ~οί 'a good many people' Hb 2.13 (|| πολύς); ~ὰ ἔτη 'a good number of years' Zc 7.3, δύναμιν ~ήν 'a sizeable army' 1M 13.11, ἱκανοὶ ἐν τοῖς ἔτεσι 'mature in age' 16.3, χρήματα ~ά 'quite a sum of money' 2M 4.45; συνδιώξαντες αὐτοὺς ἐφ' ~όν 'having chased them quite a while' 8.25; subst. ἐξ αὐτῶν ~οί 'quite a few of them' 1M 13.49.
***4**. in a mechanical rendition of Heb. מִדֵּי 'every time that ..': ἀπὸ ~οῦ 1K 1.7*L*, 18.30, 4K 4.8, ἐφ' ~οῦ 1K 7.16, see Brock 1996.151.
Cf. ἱκανόω: Spicq 2.217-22.

ἱκανόω: pres.impv.3s ἱκανούσθω; aor.impv. ἱκάνωσον, pass. ἱκανώθην, inf. ἱκανωθῆναι. *
Pass. *to be sufficiently provided*: + dat., ἱκανοῦταί μοι ἀπὸ πάσης δικαιοσύνης .. 'I have mightily benefited from your justice' Ge 32.10; ἐκχεῶ ὑμῖν τὴν εὐλογίαν μου ἕως τοῦ ἱκανωθῆναι 'I shall pour out my blessing for you until you are sated' Ma 3.10; impers., ἱκανούσθω ὑμῖν 'you ought to be happy with that' Nu 16.7; sarcastic reprimand, Ἱκανούσθω ὑμῖν 'Enough of that!' Ez 45.9; + inf., ἱκανούσθω ὑμῖν κατοικεῖν ἐν τῷ ὄρει τούτῳ 'you ought to think that you've lived long enough in this mount' De 1.6; ἱκανούσθω ὑμῖν κυκλοῦν τὸ ὄρος τοῦτο 2.3; ἀπὸ πασῶν τῶν ἀνομιῶν ὑμῶν Ez 45.7; + ἐν 'with' Es C 19 o'; act. in the same sense and + inf., PSol 2.22. Cf. ἱκανός, ἱκανῶς.

ἱκανῶς. adv.ʃ
to considerable measure: Jb 9.31, 3M 1.4. Cf. ἱκανός.

ἱκετεία, ας. f.
entreaty: ὀρφανοῦ 'by an orphan' Si 32.17 (|| δέησις), πολύδακρυς 'tearful' 3M 5.25. Cf. ἱκετεύω, λιτανεία.

ἱκετεύω: aor.impv. ἱκέτευσον, ptc. ~τεύσας.
to entreat: abs. 4M 16.13; + acc. pers., Ps 36.7 (+ ὑποτάσσομαι), μετὰ δακρύων .. τὸν κύριον 'with tears ..' 2M 11.6, || προσκαλέομαι, δέομαι Jb 19.17; + περί τινος Wi 13.18 (ἐπικαλέομαι, ἀξιόω); + inf., 3M 5.51. Cf. ἱκετηρία, ἱκέτης, ἱκετεία, αἰτέω, δέομαι, εὔχομαι, λίσσομαι, λιτανεύω: Schmidt 1.184f.

ἱκετηρία, ας. f.ʃ
v.n. of prec.: || δέησις Jb 40.27; ἐπιστολὴ ~ας 2M 9.18. Cf. δέησις.

ἱκέτης, ου. m.
suppliant: ἐπορεύθημεν ~ται πρὸ προσώπου κυρίου 'we have gone into the presence of the Lord as suppliants' Ma 3.14, φωνὴ τῶν ~ῶν Ps 73.23, θλιβόμενος 'oppressed' Si 4.4 (approaching a hum. for help; || πτωχός). Cf. ἱκετεύω: van Herten 56-94.

ἰκμάς, άδος. f.ʃ
sth moist: fluid, Je 17.8. **b**. fig., sth vital and invigorating, λόγου 'of what is said' Jb 26.14¶, cf. Aristoph. *Nub*. 233 φροντίδος 'of thought.'

ἴκτερος, ου. m.
rust (LSJ Sup., of plant disease): || ἀπορία 'discomfort,' ψώρα 'itch' Le 26.16; ἐπάταξα ὑμᾶς ἐν πυρώσει καὶ ~ῳ Am 4.9. The usual meaning 'jaundice' is not impossible: cf. Eth *bedbed* 'pestilence,

rust,' and Cyr. I 447, Th 127, and Thdt PG 81.1685 ad Am 4.9. Cf. LSG s.v.

ἰκτίν, ῖνος. m.ʃ
kite: forbidden as food, Le 11.14, De 14.13.

ἱλαρός, ά, όν.ʃ
cheerful: *s* hum., Pr 22.8a; πρόσωπον Si 13.26, 26.4, Es D 5; ἐξομολόγησις 3M 3.35; subst.n., τὸ ~όν 'cheerfulness, good mood' Pr 19.12. Cf. ἱλαρότης: Bultmann, *TDNT* 3.207-300.

ἱλαρότης, ητος. f.ʃ
cheerfulness: Pr 18.22, PSol 4.5, 16.12. Cf. ἱλαρός, εὐφροσύνη.

ἱλαρόω: fut., ἱλαρώσω; aor.subj. ἱλαρώσω, impv. ~ρωσον, pass. ἱλαρώθην.ʃ
= ἱλαρύνω: abs. Si 43.22; + acc., πρόσωπον 32.11; μὴ ἱλαρώσῃς πρὸς αὐτὰς τὸ πρόσωπόν σου 'don't be too much of a darling father to them' 7.24. Cf. ἱλαρύνω, ἱλαρῶς.

ἱλαρύνω: aor.inf. ἱλαρῦναι.ʃ*
to brighten up, adding to a sense of joy: + acc., πρόσωπον ἐν ἐλαίῳ Ps 103.15, *s* pretty woman, Si 36.27. Cf. εὐφραίνω, ἱλαρόω.

ἱλαρῶς. adv.ʃ
cheerfully: Jb 22.26. Cf. ἱλαρόω, ἡδέως.

ἱλάσκομαι: fut. ἱλάσομαι; aor. ἱλάσθην, impv. ἱλάσθητι, inf. ~θῆναι.ʃ

1. *to be forgiving*: *s* God, abs. κύριε, ἱλάσθητι Da TH 9.19 (cf. ὁ θεὸς, ἱλάσθητί μοι τῷ ἁμαρτωλῷ Lk 18.13), οὐχ ἱλάσθης La 3.42; 4K 24.4, 2C 6.30; περὶ τῆς κακίας 'over the (punitive) disaster' Ex 32.14 (ǁ ἵλεως γίνομαι ἐπὶ τῇ κακίᾳ vs. 12); + dat. rei, ἁμαρτίᾳ μου Ps 24.11; 77.38 (ǁ οἰκτίρμων), 78.9 (ῥύομαι); + acc. rei, ἀσεβείας 64.4.

2. *to be favourably disposed*: *s* God, + dat. pers., ἐπάκουσον τῆς δεήσεώς μου καὶ ἱλάσθητι τῷ κλήρῳ σου 'Hearken to my entreaty and be favourable to your inheritance' Es C 10 o' (*L* + gen.; a plea over people in danger), τῷ δούλῳ σου 4K 5.18.

Cf. ἱλασμός, ἱλαστήριον, ἐξιλάσκομαι, ἱλατεύω, ἀφίημι, ἵλεως: Dodd 1930f.; Büchsel, *TDNT* 3.315; Grayston; Hill 27; Ysebaert 1-8; Harl 2001. 868-70.

ἱλασμός, οῦ. m.

1. *atonement* of sins: ἡ ἡμέρα τοῦ ~οῦ Le 25.9 ǁ .. τοῦ ἐξιλασμοῦ 23.27, 28; τοῦ κριοῦ τοῦ ~οῦ 'the ram for ..' Nu 5.8 (or apposition and sense **2**); ποιουμένου τοῦ ἀρχιερέως τὸν ~όν 2M 3.33.

2. *cultic object used as a means of appeasing*: κατὰ τοῦ ~οῦ Σαμαρείας Am 8.14; προσοίσουσιν ~όν 'they shall offer ..' Ez 44.27.

3. *act of allowing oneself to be appeased* or *inclination towards such*: τῷ κυρίῳ θεῷ ἡμῶν οἱ οἰκτιρμοὶ καὶ οἱ ~οί Da TH 9.9. **b**. *favourable, friendly attitude*: Es 7.6 *L*.

Cf. ἱλαστήριον, ἱλάσκομαι, ἐξιλασμός: Büchsel, *TDNT* 3.317f.; Hill 36f.

ἱλαστήριον, ου. n.*
place where cultic rites for appeasing a divine being are performed with an appropriate building attached: ἱ. ἐπίθεμα '.. a covering (of sins)' Ex 25.16; Πάταξον ἐπὶ τὸ ἱ. Am 9.1; positioned on the ark of the covenant, Ex 31.7; of two different sizes, Ez 43.14; ǁ θυσιαστήριον, 43.20, 45.19. **b**. *propitiatory offering*: θανάτου '(martyrs') death' 4M 17.22.

Cf. ἱλασμός: Deissmann 1903.193-212; Büchsel and Herrmann, *TDNT* 3.319f.; Manson; BDAG, s.v.; Harl, *Langue* 107.

ἱλατεύω: aor.impv. ἱλάτευσον.ʃ
to be forgivingly disposed: abs., Da 9.18 LXX. Cf. ἱλάσκομαι. Del. Ju 16.15 v.l.

ἵλεως, ων.
forgivingly disposed, 'propitious, gracious': *s* God, ἵ. γενοῦ ἐπὶ τῇ κακίᾳ τοῦ λαοῦ σου 'Be forgiving of the evilness of your people' Ex 32.12; Am 7.2; + dat. pers. ἵ. αὐτοῖς εἰμι Nu 14.20; τῷ λαῷ σου Ισραηλ De 21.8; Nu 14.19, 2M 2.22; + dat. rei, ἵ. ἔσομαι ταῖς ἀδικίαις αὐτῶν καὶ τῶν ἁμαρτιῶν αὐτῶν οὐ μὴ μνησθῶ ἔτι '.. I shall not remember ..' Je 38.34, ταῖς ἀδικίαις αὐτῶν καὶ ταῖς ἁμαρτίαις αὐτῶν 43.3; predicatively, εἶπε κύριος Ἵ. σοι Is 54.10; + dat. rei and dat. pers., ποίᾳ τούτων ἵ. γένωμαί σοι; 'which of these (offences) am I supposed to be forgiving you?' Je 5.7. **b**. Apparently elliptical: ἵ. ὑμῖν Ge 43.23 = ἵ ὑ. εἴη ὁ θεός, cf. ἵ. μοι ὁ θεὸς τοῦ ποιῆσαι τὸ ῥῆμα τοῦτο 1C 11.19, and see BD § 128.5, BDAG s.v., but cf. BDF ib., BDR ib., Jacobson 2000, and Joosten 2007. Likewise in expressions of strong wish against sth happening indicated by an εἰ-clause or an inf.: ἵ., ζῇ Κύριος, εἰ πεσεῖται .. 1K 14.45*L*, ἵ. μοι, ἵ. μοι, εἰ .. 2K 20.20 (*L* Μή μοι γένοιτο εἰ ..), ἵ. μοι, κύριε; τοῦ ποιῆσαι τοῦτο 23.17 (*L* Μή μοι γένοιτο παρὰ Κυρίου ποιῆσαι τοῦτο), sim. 1C 11.19; ἵ. ἡμῖν καταλιπεῖν νόμον 1M 2.21.

Cf. ἵλεως, ἱλάσκομαι, ἐλεήμων, εὐίλατος, καλός: Büchsel, *TDNT* 3.300f.; Jacobson.

ἴλη, ης. f.ʃ
organised military group: ἵππων 'of horses' 2M 5.3.

ἰλύς, ύος. f.ʃ
mud, slime: πηλοῦ 'of clay' Ps 39.3, βυθοῦ 'of the deep' 68.3.

ἱμάντωσις, εως.f.ʃ
piece of timber used instead of a bond-stone (LSJ): Si 22.16, see Lieberman 1934.54-6.

ἱμάς, άντος. m.ʃ
leather strap: ζυγοῦ 'of a yoke' Is 5.18 (ǁ σχοινίον and cf. Jb 39.10), ὑποδημάτων 'of sandals' Is

5.27; ζυγὸς καὶ ἱ. Si 30.35; used to bind captives, 4M 9.11.

ἱμάτιον, ου. n.

garment, clothing: τὸ ἄκρον τοῦ ~ου αὐτοῦ 'the skirt of his garment' Hg 2.12; ἐνδεδυμένος ~α ῥυπαρά 'clothed in filthy clothes' Zc 3.3; περιέβαλον αὐτὸν ~α 3.5; δῷ μοι ἄρτον φαγεῖν καὶ ἱ. περιβαλέσθαι 'gives me bread to eat and clothes to put on' Ge 28.20 (basic needs for human subsistence), sim. De 10.18 (provided by God); Ho 2.5, 9 (|| ὀθόνια); torn as mark of remorse, Jl 2.13; || ἱματισμός Ps 21.19. Often pl. Cf. ἀμφίασις, ἔνδυμα, ἐπι~, περιβόλαιον, ἐσθής, ἔσθησις, ἱματισμός, ποδήρης, σκεῦος, στολή, χιτών: Shipp 279.

ἱματιοφύλαξ, ακος. m.ʃ *

keeper of the wardrobe: in temple, 4K 22.14. Cf. φύλαξ.

ἱματισμός, οῦ. m.

Alw. sg., used collectively.

garment, clothing, 'vesture': σκεύη ἀργυρᾶ καὶ χρυσᾶ καὶ ἱ. 'silver and golden implements ..' Ge 24.53; χρυσίον καὶ ἀργύριον καὶ ἱ. Zc 14.14; τὰ δέοντα καὶ τὸν ~όν 'the necessities and ..' Ex 21.10; || ἱμάτια Ps 21.19. Cf. ἱμάτιον: Trench 184f.; *ND* 3.69f.

ἵν, νός. n.

an Egyptian and Jewish liquid measure: τὸ τέταρτον τοῦ ἵν οἴνου 'the fourth part of a hin of wine' Ex 29.40 (undeclined).

ἵνα conj.

1. indicates a purpose, 'in order that': + subj.aor. ἵνα μὴ ἀποθάνητε 'so that you may not die' Ge 3.3; ἵνα γνῶ 'in order to find out' 18.21; || ὅπως 27.4, Ex 9.16, 33.13, De 4.40; + subj.pres. Ex 33.13. **b**. || ὥστε + inf.: ἵνα νίπτωνται Ex 38.27 || ὥστε νίπτεσθαι 30.18. **c**. purpose of the speaker, not that of the subj. of the lead verb: "Prepare your children for slaughter .., for I do not wish them to arise and inherit .. (ἵνα μὴ ἀναστῶσι ..)" Is 14.21, see below, **5a**. **d**. introduces a clause with a negator, indicating apprehension and fear: ἀγωνιῶ ἵνα μὴ .. Da 1.10 LXX (TH μήποτε).

2. indicates a result: + subj.aor. ἵνα εἴπωσιν σήμερον 'as a result they say today' Ge 22.14; Je 43.3.

3. ἵνα τί *for what reason* or *purpose* .. ?, *why* .. ?, usually with an overtone of discontent, displeasure, incredulity, and the like: ἵνα τί περίλυπος ἐγένου; 'why have you become sad?' Ge 4.6; 12.19, Ex 2.20, Nu 14.3; ἵνα τί μοι ζῆν; 'what's my life for?' Ge 27.46, To 3.15 𝔊[I]; "why on earth should you die?" Ez 33.11; || διὰ τί Nu 11.11.

4. introduces an object clause: ἐξορκιῶ σε .. ἵνα μὴ λάβῃς γυναῖκα τῷ υἱῷ μου .. 'I adjure you .. that you shall not take a wife to my son ..' Ge 24.3; ὤμοσεν ἵνα μὴ διαβῶ .. 'swore that I would not cross ..' De 4.21; προστάξαι ἵνα .. 'to order that ..' 1E 6.31.

5. + subj., indicates a speaker's wish: equivalent to an impv.: 2M 1.9. See BDAG s.v. **2** η g; Mandilaras §§ 585-9. **b**. ἵνα θάψωμεν αὐτὸν καὶ μηδεὶς γνῷ 'let's bury him and let nobody know of it' To 8.12 𝔊[I] (𝔊[II] ὅπως).

Cf. διά, ἕνεκα, ὅπως, παρά.

ἴνδαλμα, ατος. n.ʃ

haunting, ghostly entity, 'spectre': inhabiting a wilderness, Je 27.39 (|| θυγατέρες σειρήνων); Wi 17.3. Cf. Renehan 2.81.

Ἰνδική, ῆς. f.

India: 1E 3.2.

ἰξευτής, οῦ. m.ʃ

fowler, bird-catcher: εἰ πεσεῖται ὄρνεον ἐπὶ τὴν γῆν ἄνευ ~οῦ; 'would a bird fall on to the ground without a fowler?' Am 3.5; ἄγγος ~οῦ 'a fowler's basket' 8.1*bis*.

ἰοβόλος, ον.ʃ

shedding venom: *s* serpent, Wi 16.10. Cf. II ἰός.

ἰόομαι: aor.impv.pass.3s ἰωθήτω.ʃ

to become rusty: *s* metal Si 12.10, 29.10. Cf. I ἰός.

Ἰορδάνης, ου. m.

the Jordan River: Ge 13.10.

I **ἰός**, οῦ. m.

rust on metal: Ez 24.6, Ep Je 11.

II **ἰός**, οῦ. m.

venom: of snake, Pr 23.32; ἀσπίδων 'of vipers' Ps 13.3.

III **ἰός**, οῦ. m.ʃ

arrow: φαρέτρας 'of quiver' La 3.13 (v.l. υἱός = MT). Cf. βέλος.

ἰουδαΐζω.ʃ*

to side with or *imitate the Jews* (LSJ): Es 8.17 o'. Cf. Ἰουδαῖος.

Ἰουδαῖος, α, ον.

Jewish: ἡ χώρα τῶν Ἰουδαίων Is 19.17; subst.f., *Jewess* Su 22 LXX. Cf. ἰουδαΐζω.

Ἰουδαϊσμός, οῦ. m.

Jewish religion and way of life: 2M 2.21, 4M 4.26.

Ἰουδαϊστί. adv.

in the language of Judaea: λαλέω Is 36.11, 13, Ne 13.24.

ἱππάζομαι: fut. ἱππάσομαι.ʃ

to ride a horse: *s* troops, ἐφ' ἵπποις Je 27.42, ἐφ' ἵππων Ez 23.6, 12. Cf. ἵππος, ἐξιππάζομαι.

ἱππάρχης, ου. m.ʃ

commander of cavalry: 2K 1.6.

ἱππασία, ας. f.ʃ

1. *cavalry*: ἡ ἱ. σου σωτηρία Hb 3.8.

2. *horses of cavalry*: ἀπὸ φωνῆς χρεμετισμοῦ ~ας '.. neighing of ..' Je 8.16.

Cf. ἵππος, ἱππικός.

ἱππεύς, έως. m.

1. *person on horse-back*: soldier, Ge 49.17; οὐδὲ ἐν ἵπποις οὐδὲ ἐν ~εῦσι Ho 1.7; ‖ τοξότης 'archer' Am 2.15; ἐξιππάσονται οἱ ~εῖς αὐτοῦ 'his horsemen will ride out' Hb 1.8; ἀναβάτας ~εῖς Is 21.7; ~εῖς ἱππαζόμενοι εφ' ἵππων Ez 23.6. **b**. postman: Es 8.14 o'.

2. *driver of horse-driven chariot*: Na 2.4; ἅρματα καὶ ~εῖς Ge 50.9; φωνὴ .. ἅρματος ἀναβράσσοντος καὶ ~έως ἀναβαίνοντος 'sound of .. bouncing chariot and mounting horsemen' Na 3.3.

Cf. ἵππος.

ἱππεύω: aor. ἵππευσα.ʃ

to ride a horse: 4K 9.16 (*L* ἐπιβαίνω); subst.ptc. ψόφος ἁρμάτων καὶ ἱππευόντων 'noise of chariots and soldiers on horse-back' Mi 1.13; ἐφ' ἵππων Ez 23.23. Cf. ἵππος and ἐξιππάομαι.

ἱππικός, ή, όν.ʃ

pertaining to cavalry: *s* δύναμις 'army' 1M 15.38, 3M 1.1 (+ πεζικός 'infantry'). Cf. ἱππασία.

ἱππόδρομος, ου. m.

hippodrome: ἐγγίζοντός μου κατὰ τὸν ~ον 'as I was approaching the h.' Ge 48.7; κατὰ τὸν ~ον παρῆγεν 'arrived at the ..' 3M 6.16. Cf. ἵππος.

ἵππος, ου. c.

I. *horse*: δάκνων πτέρναν ~ου 'biting a horse's heel' Ge 49.17; χρεμετισμὸς ~ων 'neighing of horses' Am 6.7; ὁ χαλινὸς τοῦ ~ου 'the bridle of ..' Zc 14.20; of various colours, Zc 1.8*b*, 6.2, 3, 6; εἰ διώξονται ἐν πέτραις ~οι; 'will horses race on rocks?' Am 6.12; ἐξαλοῦνται 'will bound' Hb 1.8; ἐπιβεβηκὼς ἐπὶ ~ον πυρρόν 'mounted on a red horse' Zc 1.8*a*; livestock and ‖ κτῆνος, ὑποζύγιον, κάμηλος, βοῦς, πρόβατον Ex 9.3. **b**. of horses in battlefield, οὐδὲ ἐν πολέμῳ οὐδὲ ἐν ἅρμασιν οὐδὲ ἐν ~οις οὐδὲ ἐν ἱππεῦσι Ho 1.7; ὡς ~ον εὐπρεπῆ αὐτοῦ ἐν πολέμῳ 'like his splendid horse in war' Zc 10.3; αἰχμαλωσία ~ων 'captured horses' Am 4.10; ἐφ' ~ον οὐκ ἀναβησόμεθα Ho 14.4; ἐπιβήσῃ ἐπὶ τοὺς ~ους σου Hb 3.8; ~ον καὶ ἀναβάτην '.. and rider' Ex 15.21, sim. Hg 2.22, Zc 12.4*a*, ἀναβάται ~ων Zc 10.5. **c**. ‖ ἅρμα: Ex 14.9, Mi 5.10, Na 3.2, Zc 9.10.

II. sg.f. used collectively, *cavalry*: τὴν ~ον πᾶσαν τὴν Σοδόμων καὶ Γομόρρας 'the entire cavalry of Sodomites and Gomorrans' Ge 14.11; Ex 14.7; τὴν δύναμιν τῶν Αἰγυπτίων, τὰ ἅρματα αὐτῶν καὶ τὴν ~ον αὐτῶν De 11.4; 3K 16.9.

Cf. ἱππεύς, ἱππεύω, ἱππασία, ἱππόδρομος, συνωρίς.

ἶρις, εως. f.ʃ

iris: for cultic use, Ex 30.24.

Ἰσάκιος, η, ον.ʃ *

typical of Isaac: *s* λογισμός 4M 7.14.

ἰσάστερος, ον.ʃ *

like a star: in brightness, *s* hum., 4M 17.5. Cf. ἀστήρ.

ἰσηγορέομαι.ʃ *

to talk as equals: μετά τινος Si 13.11.

ἰσοδυναμέω.ʃ

to be equivalent to or *capable of producing same effect as* sth else: + acc., Si prol. 21. Cf. δυναμέω: Wagner 125.

ἰσοδύναμος, ον.ʃ

capable of producing same effect or consequence: + dat., *s* water, 4M 3.15; deed, 5.20.

ἰσόμοιρος, ον.ʃ

sharing equally: w. ref. to division of spoils of war, 2M 8.30.

ἰσονομέω.ʃ

*act. *to apply the law impartially* or *keep the right balance*: 4M 5.24. Hardly derived from νέμω.

ἰσοπέδος, ον.ʃ

level with the ground: *s* building flattened, 2M 8.3; city, 9.14; region, 3M 5.43.

ἰσοπολίτης, ου.ʃ

adj. *having same civic standing as*: + dat. pers., 2M 2.30. Cf. πολίτης.

ἰσοπολῖτις, ιδος. f. of ἰσοπολίτης.ʃ

of equal or *comparable political significance*: *s* κάμινος 'oven' 4M 13.9. Cf. ἰσοπολίτης: Renehan 1.112f.

ἴσος, η, ον.

1. *equal* in amount, measure or value: Ex 26.24*b*; ἐκ ~ου 'arranged in pairs' (?) 26.24*a*; ἴσον ἴσῳ ἔσται 'they shall be in equal proportions' 30.34 (Lee 1983.35), ἐν ~ῳ 'in equal measure' Wi 14.9; ἑκάστῳ τὸ ~ον 'an equal amount to each one' Le 6.40; ἔθηκας ἴσα τῇ γῇ τὰ μετάφρενά σου 'you lay flat on the ground on your back' Is 51.23; λόγον δυνάμεως .. τὸν ~ον αὐτοῦ 'the word of might .. which befits him' Jb 41.4¶. **b**. *having a claim to same rights as*: *s* hum., + dat., Ἀθηναίοις 2M 9.15, cf. ἰσοπόλιτης.

2. *similar, comparable*: + dat. ἴσον θανάτῳ 'something like death' Nu 12.12; + gen. ὁ φίλος ὁ ~ος τῆς ψυχῆς σου '.. as valuable as your own life' De 13.6 (v.l. τῇ); + πρός τι Ez 45.11; θνητὸς ~ος ἅπασιν 'mortal like anyone else' Wi 7.1; ‖ εἷς 7.6. **b**. n.pl. + dat. used adverbially, *similarly to*, a classical use frequent (12x) in Jb: ψηλαφήσαισαν ~α νυκτί 'let them grope as in the night' Jb 5.14, χόρτον ~α βουσὶν ἐσθίει 'it eats grass like oxen' 40.15; πᾶσιν ~α 'like anyone else' Wi 7.3 (‖ κοινός).

Cf. ἰσότης, ἰσόω, ἐξισόω, ὅμοιος, διαφέρω: Schmidt 4.471-4, 482f.; Shipp 281f.; Stählin, *TDNT* 3.343-52.

ἰσότης, ητος. f.ʃ

1. *equality*: manifestation of justice, PSol 17.41.

2. *that which amounts to,* 'embodiment (?)': ἰ. χάριτος Zc 4.7.

3. *dimension, size*: σκηνῆς Jb 36.29¶.

Cf. ἴσος.

ἰσόψυχος, ον.ʃ

of like mind: *s* ἄνθρωπος Ps 54.14, cf. Fridrichsen.

ἰσόω: fut. ἰσώσω, pass. ἰσωθήσομαιʃ

to consider equal to: + dat. τίνι με ὡμοιώσατε καὶ ἰσωθήσομαι; 'to what did you liken me and (to what) would I be comparable?' Is 40.25; La 2.13 (ǁ ὁμοιόω); and pass. οὐκ ἰσωθήσεται αὐτῇ χρυσίον καὶ ὕαλος 'gold and crystal shall not be considered comparable with it' Jb 28.17¶; 28.19¶ (ǁ συμβαστάζω 'to compare'), Ps 88.7. Cf. ἴσος, ὁμοιόω, ἐξισόω, συμβαστάζω.

Ἰσραηλίτης, ου. m.

Israelite: Le 24.10 +.

Ἰσραηλῖτις, ιδος. f.ʃ

Israelite woman: Le 24.10, 11; adj., παρθένον ~ῖτιν De 22.19.

ἱστάνω, ἱστάω. ⇒ ἵστημι.

ἵστημι: pres.act.inf. ἱστάνειν, ptc. ἱστῶν, opt.3s ἱσταίη; fut. act. στήσω, mid. στήσομαι, pass. σταθήσομαι, inf.act. στήσειν; impf.act.3s ἵστα, mid. ἵστατο; 1aor. ἔστησα, 3pl ἔστησαν, subj. στήσω, inf. στῆσαι, impv. στῆσον, ptc. στήσας, opt.3s στήσαι, pass. ἐστάθην, ptc. σταθείς, subj. σταθῶ; 2aor. ἔστην, 3pl ἔστησαν, impv. στῆθι, στῆτε, στήτω, inf. στῆναι, ptc. στάς, subj. 2s στῇς, 3s στῇ; pf. ἕστηκα, ἕστακα, inf. ἑστάναι, impv.2pl ἑστήκατε, ptc. ἑστώς/ἑστηκώς, pass. ἕσταμαι, ptc. ἑστάμενος; plpf. εἱστήκειν.

I. intr. (fut.mid., 2aor., pf.[with the pres. sense], plpf.[with the impf. sense]) **1**. *to stand firm*: abs. Mi 5.4, Hb 3.6, Zc 2.3, 3.5, 7; Ho 10.9; ἐναντίον κυρίου Ge 19.27; ἐπάνω αὐτοῦ 'over him' 18.2; ἐπὶ τείχους 'on a wall' Am 7.7; ἐπὶ τῆς πηγῆς τοῦ ὕδατος 'by the spring of water' Ge 24.13; ἐπὶ τῆς φυλακῆς μου 'on my watch' Hb 2.1; ἐπὶ τὸ ὄρος Zc 14.4; ἐπὶ τοὺς πόδας αὐτῶν 14.12; ἀνὰ μέσον τινός 1.8; ἐκ δεξιῶν τινος 'at the right of sbd' 3.1*b*; ἐν συναγωγῇ θεῶν 'in an assembly of gods' Ps 81.1; ἔναντί τινος Nu 27.21, De 29.10; παρὰ τὰς θύρας 31.14; πρὸ προσώπου τινός Zc 3.1*a*, 3, 4; *s* standing, i.e. not yet reaped, grain Jd 15.5 A (B: ὀρθός). **b**. *to hold out* against assailants: in battle, μετά τινος (enemy) Da 11.15 LXX (ǁ ἀνθίστημι); κατὰ πρόσωπόν τινος 4K 10.4. **c**. *to observe allegiance to*, 'stand by': ἐν διαθήκαις Si 44.12. **d**. *to be permanent, enduring*: ἑστῶτα 'sth permanent' Am 6.5 (:: φεύγοντα 'fleeting, ephemeral'); ǁ μένω Is 66.22; ἡ γῆ εἰς τὸν αἰῶνα ἕστηκεν Ec 1.4, ἡ βασιλεία σου 1K 13.14. **e**. *to be present, to be found*: *s* ἰσχύς Da 10.17, πνεῦμα. Cf. στήκω.

2. *to stand still*: *s* hum., μηδὲ στῇς ἐν πάσῃ τῇ περιχώρῳ 'Nor stop anywhere in the surrounding area' Ge 19.17; στῆτε αὐτοῦ 'Stay here!' Nu 9.8; νεφέλη 'cloud' 9.17, 10.12; ἔστη ὁ ἥλιος καὶ ἡ σελήνη ἐν στάσει 'the sun and the moon came to a halt' Jo 10.13, ἡ σελήνη ἔστη ἐν τῇ τάξει αὐτῆς 'the moon stood still in its position' Hb 3.11; tempest, εἰς αὔραν '(turning) into a breeze' Ps 106.29; animals Ez 1.21 (:: πορεύομαι); οὐ στήσεται οὐδὲ χρονιεῖ 'he will not stand still nor be delayed' Is 51.14; πορεύεσθε καὶ μὴ ἵστασθε 'keep moving, don't stop' Je 28.50; Jb 32.16. **b**. *to stay put* without running away: Je 26.21. **c**. *to remain without disappearing*: ἔστη γεῦμα αὐτοῦ 'its taste remained' Je 31.11 (ǁ οὐκ ἐκλείπω).

3. *to stand up*: as a mark of respect and *s* hum., Jb 29.8, ἐν πλήθει πρεσβυτέρων 'in the company of old people' Si 6.34.

4. *to stop* doing: + inf.*, ἔστη τοῦ τίκτειν 'she stopped bearing' Ge 29.35, 30.9; Es 2.1 *L*; + ptc. pres., Jo 10.19, cf. ἀδικῶν Demosth. 10.10, and s.v. καταπαύω **A 4**.

5. *to stop flowing*, 'staunch': *s* blood, Ex 4.25 (after circumcision); river water, Si 39.17; olive-oil, 4K 4.6.

6. *legally to become property of* (sbd τινι): ὁ ἀγρός .. τῷ Αβρααμ εἰς κτῆσιν Ge 23.17-18 (ǁ ἐκυρώθη vs. 20).

7. *to enter sbd's service*: ἐναντίον Φαραω Ge 41.46, ἐν τῷ οἴκῳ τοῦ βασιλέως Da 1.4 TH.

8. *to present oneself* in sbd's presence: ἐναντίον Ιωσηφ Ge 43.15; Ex 9.11, Le 27.8; ἔναντί τινος Nu 27.2, κατὰ πρόσωπόν τινος Je 47.10, ἐπί τινα (as opponent) Jd 6.31 A (B: ἐπανίστημί τινι); in a court, εἰς κρίσιν Nu 35.12, ἔναντι τῶν κριτῶν De 19.17.

9. *to be set in motion*: *s* πνεῦμα καταιγίδος 'tempestuous wind' Ps 106.25; Jd 20.2 A.

10. *to be* or *become legally established and binding*: Le 27.12, Nu 30.5; κατ' αὐτῆς '(possibly) to her disadvantage' 30.12; + dat. pers., Da 6.12a LXX.

11. *to stand by to assist, protect or serve*: + ἐπί τινα, *s* angel, Da 12.1 LXX; πρὸ προσώπου μου Je 15.19.

II. tr. (pres.act., impf.act., 1aor., fut.act., pass.) **1**. *to help stand up*: acc. pers. (sbd fallen asleep on the ground), ἐπὶ πόδας 'on my feet' Da 8.18 LXX (TH ἐγείρω).

2. *to cause to stand*: in a legal court and + acc. pers., εἰς κρίσιν Is 3.13.

3. *to erect*: + acc. rei, σκηνήν 'tent' Ge 12.8, Ex 40.2; Nu 10.21 (ǁ ἀνίστημι 1.51), Da 11.45 LXX (TH πήγνυμι), οἶκον Si 47.13, πύλας καὶ μοχλούς 'gates fitted with bolts' 49.13 (|| ἐγείρω); παγίδας 'traps' Je 5.26; pass. Ex 40.15; ἔστησεν αὐτὸν στήλην 'he put it [= a stone] up as a stela' Ge 28.18, 31.45, θυσιαστήριον 'altar' 33.20, λίθους μεγάλους De 27.2, βδελύγματα 'abominable objects of idolatry' Od 12.10. Cf. στηλόω.

4. *to place in the balance, weigh*: + acc. rei, τριάκοντα ἀργυροῦς Zc 11.12, 3K 21.39; and + dat. pers., *to weigh and hand* to, 1E 8.55; pass. and *o* ἀργύριον, Jb 28.15, 1E 8.61; τὸ ἀργύριον ἐν ζυγῷ Je 39.10; pass., ἐστάθη ἐν ζυγῷ Da 5.27 TH. **b**. metaph., *to determine the intensity of*: + acc., μου τὴν ὀργήν 'my anger' Jb 6.2.

5. *to bring about, cause*: πνεῦμα ἔστησε ψεῦδος Mi 2.11; "his arm will not bring its strength (ἰσχύν) into full play" Da 11.6 LXX.

6. *to establish, bring into existence*: + acc. rei, διαθήκην and + πρός τινα Ge 6.18, 17.19 (|| + dat. pers.), Ex 6.4 (on the significance of πρός τινα, see Wevers ad Ge 6.18); ὅρκον 'oath' Ju 8.11; πρὸς ἑαυτοὺς φιλίαν 1M 10.54; + μετά τινος Le 26.9; + dat. pers., De 29.1 (|| διατίθημι ib.), Si 45.24; αὐτοῖς φιλίαν 1M 8.1, φιλίαν καὶ συμμαχίαν 'friendship and military alliance' 8.17, μεθ' ὑμῶν συμμαχίαν καὶ εἰρήνην 8.20; αὐτῷ ἐλευθερίαν 14.26; + acc. pers., αὐτὸν διαθήκην Si 45.7.

7. *to execute the terms provided in*: + acc., τὸν ὅρκον μου 'my oath' Ge 26.3, Je 11.5, cf. στῆσαι τὸν λόγον σου 'may He make your message come true' 35.6, cf. 1K 1.23; διαθήκην Je 41.18, Ez 17.14, Si 44.20, ῥῆμα Je 42.14, ἐντολήν 42.16, τοὺς λόγους τοῦ νόμου 2C 35.19[a], βουλήν Ps 20.12, Si 37.13, ὅρασιν Da 11.14 TH (LXX ἀναστῆσαι προφητείαν).

8. *to place and present*, 'to stand': + acc., ἑπτὰ ἀμνάδας προβάτων 'seven lambs' Ge 21.28; στήσω αὐτὸν ἐναντίον σου 43.9, 44.32; ἐναντίον τινός Nu 27.21 (|| ἔναντι vs. 19), ἔμπροσθεν τοῦ βασιλέως Da 1.5 LXX, cf. 2C 34.32.

9. *to station*: + acc. pers., τοὺς ἀδελφοὺς αὐτοῦ ἐν τῷ ὄρει Ge 31.25, σεαυτῷ στῆσον σκοπόν '.. a sentinel' Is 21.6, αὐτὸν ἄρχοντα '.. as leader' 22.23, ψαλτῳδούς 'singers' Si 47.9, ἱερεῖς 'priests' 1E 1.2, αὐτὸν τῇ ἱερωσύνῃ 1M 7.9, ἐπί τινα 'so as to oversee .., in charge of' 2E 3.8; ὄχλον πολύν 'a large army' Da 11.11 TH.

10. *to establish as legally applicable and binding*: + dat. pers. Nu 30.14 (:: περιαιρέω), 15; αὐτῷ τὴν ἀρχιερωσύνην '.. the high priesthood' 1M 11.27; ὅρια 'boundaries' De 19.14, 32.8; festivals to be celebrated, Es 9.21 o'; || ἀληθεύω Is 44.26; pass. Le 27.14, De 19.15. **b**. + inf. (pledge), Si 44.21, cf. 22; + inf. (concession), 1M 6.59; + inf. (directive), 2K 21.2*L*; + ἵνα 1M 4.59; + acc., τὸν ὁρισμόν, ὃν ἔστησαν κατ' αὐτοῦ 'the decree, which they had established against him' Da 6.10 LXX.

11. *to fix by agreement*: abs., "my affairs" understood, To 7.11 𝔊[I]; *to settle a legal case or a commercial transaction*, τὸν λόγον Ru 4.7. **b**. pass. *to come to firm agreement*: πρός με 'concerning my affairs' To 7.11 𝔊[I].

12. *to establish a relationship with*: + acc. pers., ἵνα στήσῃ σε ἑαυτῷ εἰς λαόν De 29.13.

13. *to hold firmly established*: pass., *o* the law and the sanctuary, 1M 14.29.

14. *to bring to a standstill, cause to stop*: acc. (God's anger), 2M 7.38.

Cf. ἀνθ~, ἀν~, ἀντικαθ~, ἐξαν~, ἐπαν~, ἐφ~, παρ~, προ~, προϋφ~, ὑφίστημι, κυρόω (**I 3**): Shipp 513f.

ἱστίον, ου. n.

large, thin, hanging fabric, 'curtain': τῆς αὐλῆς 'of a courtyard' shielding a tabernacle, Ex 27.9; sail of ship, Is 33.23. Cf. δέρρις.

ἱστορέω: aor.ptc.pass. ἱστορηθείς; pf.pass.3s ἱστόρηται.

to record as history: ἐν τῇ βιβλίῳ τῶν ἱστορουμένων περὶ τῶν βασιλέων 1E 1.31. Cf. γράφω: Büchsel, *TDNT* 3.391-6.

ἱστορία, ας. f.

history of past events: ἐκ τῶν παλαιοτέρων .. ~ῶν 'from the ancient records' Es E 7; 2M 2.24; ~ας ἀρχηγέτης 'original historian' 2.32.

ἱστός, οῦ. m.

1. *pole* standing erect: ἐπ' ὄρους Is 30.17 (for hoisting a flag). **b**. *mast*: ὁ ἱ. σου ἔκλινεν '.. bent' 33.23.

2. *web* cut from the loom: Is 38.12, To 2.12𝔊[II]; spider's, Is 59.5.

ἰσχίον, ου. n.ʃ

hip-joint: of hum. body, 2K 10.4.

ἰσχνόφωνος, ον.ʃ

having impediment in one's speech: ἰ. καὶ βραδύγλωσσος Ex 4.10; 6.30 (|| ἄλογος vs. 12). Cf. *BA* ad Ex 4.10. Cf. ἄλογος, βαθύχειλος, βραδύγλωσσος, μογιλάλος, ψελλίζω, εὔλαλος: Schmidt 3.369f.; LSG s.v.

ἰσχυρός, ά, όν.

1. *strong*: *s* nation, ἔθνη ~ά Ge 14.5; ἔθνος .. ~ὸν καὶ ἀναρίθμητον Jl 1.6; λαὸς πολὺς καὶ ἰ. 2.5 (of military might), ὄχλος ~ός Is 43.17, ἐν ὄχλῳ βαρεῖ καὶ ἐν χειρὶ ~ᾷ 'with a host of heavily-armed powerful troops' Nu 20.20; opp. ἀσθενής 13.19, *s* sheep Ez 34.20; voice, Da 6.20 TH (LXX μεγάλη), Ex 19.19, βοή 3M 7.16. **b**. *resistant to breakage*: ὡς δρῦς 'as an oak' Am 2.9. **c**. *difficult*: intellectually, ἰσχυρότερά σου 'things which are beyond you' Si 3.21;

physically, ref. to a stone heavy to lift, 6.21; *s* ἄγων 'race' Wi 10.12.

2. *grave, serious*: ἁμαρτία Am 5.12.

3. *characterised by powerful effect*: *s* λιμός 'famine' Ge 41.31, so Thuc. 3.85.2, Lk 15.14; κοπετὸν μέγαν καὶ ~όν Ge 50.10; flood water, Is 8.7; ~ὰ ἔργα λόγων αὐτοῦ 'the effect of his words is powerful' Jl 2.11, ῥῆσις Pr 27.27; φόβος Da 10.7 LXX; παγίς 'trap' Pr 6.2; ἔρευνα '(strict) examination' Wi 6.8 (ǁ ἀπότομος'ruthless' vs. 5).

Cf. ἰσχύς, ἰσχυρῶς, ἰσχύω, δυνατός, κραταιός, στερεός, σκληρός, χαλεπός, ἄνισχυς, ἀσθενής: Chadwick 165-70.

ἰσχυρόω: aor. ἰσχύρωσα.ʃ

to fasten: + acc.rei, ἐν ἥλοις 'with nails' Is 41.7 (ǁ στερεόω Je 10.4).

ἰσχυρῶς. adv.ʃ

1. *by applying considerable physical force*: to gird up the loins, Pr 31.17. **b**. not physical: heated argument, Jd 8.1B (A: κραταιῶς).

2. *exceedingly*: πρόσεχε ἰ. De 12.23; c. adj., Pr 14.29. Cf. *mighty* in colloquial English.

Cf. ἰσχυρός, βιαίως, κραταιῶς, λίαν, σφόδρα.

ἰσχύς, ύος. f.

1. *strength*: **a**. in general, ἔθετο ἀγάπησιν κραταιὰν ~ύος αὐτοῦ Hb 3.4; ἐν τῇ ~ύι ἡμῶν 'with our own strength,' i.e. unaided Am 6.13; see also Hb 1.11; μετὰ ~ύος 'forcefully' Is 42.13, ἀναβόησον ἐν ~ύι 58.1; ǁ κράτος De 8.17, Da 11.1 TH, cf. ἐν ~ύι κράτους μου 4.27 LXX (TH ἐν τῷ κράτει τῆς ~ύος μου); God's strength, τὴν ~ύν σου καὶ τὴν δύναμίν σου καὶ τὴν χεῖρα τὴν κραταιάν De 3.24; ἐν ('relying on') ~ύι κυρίου Mi 5.4, μεγάλη ἡ ἰ. αὐτοῦ (i.e. κυρίου) Na 1.3; Mi 3.8; God Himself, Je 16.19 (ǁ βοήθεια, καταφυγή 'help, refuge'), Ps 17.2; ἡ ἰ. τῆς θαλάσσης 'the mighty sea' Is 23.4; economic, 23.11 (see also **3** below); verbal, ῥημάτων Jb 4.2. **b**. *physical, bodily strength*: ἐν πάσῃ τῇ ~ύι μου δεδούλευκα τῷ πατρὶ ὑμῶν Ge 31.6; βραχιόνων 'of arms' De 33.27; ἡ ἰ. σου ἀνδρὸς πειρατοῦ 'your strength is that of a brigand' Ho 6.9; ἀνδρίσαι τῇ ~ύι σφόδρα 'play the man well' Na 2.2; ǁ δύναμις, and opp. a divine spirit, Zc 4.6; ǁ ὀχύρωμα 'fortress' and opp. συντριμμός 'ruin' Am 5.9; Mi 7.16 (ǁ θαυμαστά 'marvels, wonders' vs. 15); ὁ κραταιὸς οὐ μὴ κρατήσῃ ~ύος αὐτοῦ 'the strong will not maintain his strength' Am 2.14; expended in tilling the land, ἔσται εἰς κενὸν ἡ ἰ. ὑμῶν 'your toil will be in vain' Le 26.20; εἰς οὐθὲν ἔδωκα τὴν ~ύν μου 'my efforts were for nothing' Is 49.4. **c**. *military might*, 'armed forces': Ex 32.18; Αἰθιοπία ἡ ἰ. αὐτῆς Na 3.9; Ez 31.18; 2K 24.2 (ǁ *L*, 1C 21.2 δύναμις). **d**. *politically or socially influential position*: χρήματα καὶ ἰ. 'wealth and ..' Si 40.26. ***e**. w. ref. to agricultural produce, fruit as manifestation of power inherent in the soil or plants: ἐργᾷ τὴν γῆν, καὶ οὐ προσθήσει τὴν ~ὺν αὐτῆς δοῦναί σοι 'you till the land, and yet it shall no longer provide you with its fruit' Ge 4.12; Ez 34.27; ἄμπελος καὶ συκῆ ἔδωκαν τὴν ~ὺν αὐτῶν 'the vine and fig-tree have yielded their fruits' Jl 2.22 (ǁ καρπός). Cf. ἀνεβίβασεν αὐτοὺς ἐπὶ τὴν ~ὺν τῆς γῆς '.. the most fertile part of the land (?)' De 32.13 (ǁ ἀναβιβάσει σε ἐπὶ τὰ ἀγαθὰ τῆς γῆς Is 58.14); Jb 31.39. **f**. financial magnates who control food and water supply, ἰ. ἄρτου καὶ ἰ. ὕδατος Is 3.1. **g**. ἐν ~ύι *forcibly*: 1M 2.46.

2. *innate ability* to do sth: δράγμα οὐκ ἔχον ~ὺν τοῦ ποιῆσαι ἄλευρον 'a sheaf of corn which does not have the capability of yielding meal' Ho 8.7.

3**. *wealth, material possessions* as indication of one's strength (cf. s.v. δύναμις, **4**): consisting in a vast quantity of gold, silver and robes, Zc 14.14; ǁ πλῆθος 'abundance' Mi 4.13; κατέφαγον ἀλλότριοι τὴν ~ὺν αὐτοῦ 'strangers devoured his wealth' Ho 7.9; αὐτῆς ἡ ἰσχὺς καὶ ὁ πλοῦτος Is 29.2, cf. 61.6; Pr 5.10 (ǁ πόνοι); κατάξει ἐκ σου ~ύν σου Am 3.11 (of wealth laid up in an elevated fortress? Or possibly of troops high up in a fortress, cf. Cyr. I 432); + θησαυροί Je 20.5; ***o of προνομεύω 'plunder' Is 10.13; ǁ καλλονή Ps 77.61 (or: the cream or elite of society).

Cf. ἰσχυρός, ἰσχύω, ἐνισχύω, κατισχύω, ἀλκή, δύναμαι, δύναμις, δυναστεία, κυριεία, κράτος, ῥώμη, σθένος: Schmidt 3.660-2.

ἴσχυσις, εως. f.ʃ *

strength: pl., manifestations of it, ǁ δυνάμεις Ct 2.7.

ἰσχύω: fut. ἰσχύσω; aor. ἴσχυσα, subj. ἰσχύσω, inf. ἰσχῦσαι, ptc. ἰσχύσας, impv. ἴσχυσον; pf.ptc. ἰσχυκώς.

1. *to be* or *become strong*: physically, ἀνδρίζου καὶ ἴσχυε De 31.6, 7, 23 (perh. also morally, see Rashi ad Jo 1.6); ἰσχύει ὑπὲρ ἡμᾶς 'is stronger than we' Ex 1.9, ἐπὶ πάντας Es C 30 o' (*L* δυνατός); ὁ ἀδύνατος λεγέτω ὅτι Ἰσχύω ἐγώ 'Let the weak say– "I am strong"' Jl 3.10, ἐκλελυμένῳ καὶ οὐκ ἰσχύοντι 'to one who is exhausted ..' Is 46.2; ἴσχυσα πρὸς αὐτόν 'I overpowered him' Ps 12.5, cf. Si 50.29, PSol 7.6; *s* chains, fetters, Is 28.22; warrior Je 20.11, εἰς τὰ πολεμικά 31.14 (ǁ ἰσχυρός); 'to be strong enough, capable' + inf. 1E 9.11 (ǁ ἔστιν δύναμις 2E 10.13), Si 41.1, 3M 4.17; χείρ, ready to act, Jd 7.11. **b**. politically: οἱ ἰσχύοντες Ισραηλ 'the powerful men of Is.' Is 1.24; ἰσχύοντα καὶ ἰσχύουσαν 3.1, ǁ δυνάστης 5.22. **c**. mentally or morally: ἰσχύσατε, μὴ φοβεῖσθε Is 35.4; 2C 19.11 (*L* ἀνδρίζομαι).

2. *s* ἡ χείρ τινος 'to be capable, competent'*: οὐκ ἰσχύσει ἡ χείρ σου 'you will be powerless' De 28.32; + inf., ἰσχύει ἡ χείρ μου κακοποιῆσαί σε 'I am capable of harming you' Ge 31.29; 'having sufficient financial means'—Ἐὰν δὲ μὴ ἰσχύῃ ἡ χεὶρ αὐτοῦ τὸ ἱκανὸν εἰς πρόβατον 'should he not be able to afford a sheep' Le 5.7 (‖ εὑρίσκῃ αὐτοῦ ἡ χείρ 5.11); καθάπερ ἰσχύει ἡ χεὶρ τοῦ εὐξαμένου 'according as one making a vow can afford' Le 27.8; καθότι ἰσχύει ἡ χείρ σου De 16.10, sim. Ez 46. 7 (967: Zgl ἐκποιέω). **b.** without χείρ: + inf., 2C 2.5, Si 7.6, 17.16¶, Wi 13.1, 9, 4M 4.1, cf. LSG s.v. and κατισχύω **II 2a**.

*__3__. *to make strenuous efforts, endeavour*: + inf., τοῦ φυλάξασθαι τὰς ἐντολάς μου 1C 28.7; ἐν ταῖς ἀποστροφαῖς αὐτῶν 'in their deviations' Je 5.6. Cf. κατισχύω **4**.

4. tr. *to make strong*: ***o*** νεφέλας 'clouds' Si 43.15, ἄρτον .. πᾶσαν ἡδονὴν ἰσχύοντα 'bread .. that magnifies every pleasure' Wi 16.20; θεὸν ἰσχύοντα Is 10.21.

Cf. ἰσχύς, ἐπ~, κατισχύω, ἀνδρίζομαι, δύναμαι, κραταιόω, σθένω, ἡττάω.

ἴσως. adv.

perhaps: clause-initial, Ge 32.20, Je 33.3, 4M 1.5. Cf. τάχα: Schmidt 1.329-32.

ἰταμία, ας. f.ʃ *

recklessness: καρδίας Je 29.17. Cf. ἰταμός.

ἰταμός, ή, όν.ʃ

having no regard to consequences, 'reckless': ***s*** enemy troops, Je 6.23, 27.42. Cf. τολμηρός: Schmidt 3.548.

ἰτέα, ας. f.ʃ

willow: Le 23.40, Ps 136.2; growing by a stream, Is 44.4.

ἰχθυηρός, ά, όν.ʃ

pertaining to fish: ***s*** πύλη, one of the walls of Jerusalem, Ne 3.3, 12.39.

ἰχθῦς, ύος. m. On the accent, see Walters 96f.

fish: ~ύες τῆς θαλάσσης Ge 9.2 (‖ τὰ θηρία τῆς γῆς .. τὰ ὄρνεα τοῦ οὐρανοῦ .. πάντα τὰ κινούμενα ἐπὶ τῆς γῆς), Ho 4.3 (‖ τὰ πετεινὰ τοῦ οὐρανοῦ and τὰ ἑρπετὰ τῆς γῆς); also + τῶν κτηνῶν Ge 1.26; ἐν τῷ ποταμῷ Ex 7.18; as food, Nu 11.5. Cf. κῆτος.

ἰχνευτής, οῦ. m.ʃ

hunter: Si 14.22. Cf. θηρευτής, ἰχνεύω.

ἰχνεύω.ʃ

to search to find: + acc., ^σοφίαν^ Si 51.15; + an indirect question, ποῦ πότοι γίνονται 'where could drinks be had?' Pr 23.30. Cf. ἐξιχνεύω.

ἴχνος, ους. n.

1. *the hard sole* of foot: οὗ ἂν πατήσῃ τὸ ἴ. τοῦ ποδὸς ὑμῶν 'wherever the sole of your foot might tread' De 11.24; the lowest part of a human body, ἀπὸ ~ους τῶν ποδῶν σου ἕως τῆς κορυφῆς σου 'from the sole of your feet to the crown of your head' De 28.35; that on which one stands, οὐδὲ μὴ γένηται στάσις τῷ ~ει τοῦ ποδός σου 'nor shall the sole of your foot stand firmly' 28.65. ***b**. flat object looking similar to the sole of a foot: τὰ ~η χειρῶν 'the palms of hands' 1K 5.4 (*L* correcting to .. ποδῶν), doublet of καρπός 'wrist.'

*__2__. *route* for travelling: κατανοῆσαι τὰ ~η τῆς χώρας ἥκατε 'you have come to study the routes of the land' Ge 42.9, sim. 42.12; Si 50.29. Cf. LSG s.v.

3. *trace left on a surface by a moving object*: 'wake (left by a sailing ship' Jb 9.26, Wi 5.10 (‖ τεκμήριον vs. 11); footprint, Bel 19 LXX; trace in general, ~η νεφέλης 'of clouds' Wi 2.4 **b**. *tell-tale mark, symptom*: καρδίας 'of inner mood' Si 13.26.

Cf. ἀτραπός, ὁδός, πούς, τεκμήριον: Stumpff, *TDNT* 3.402-6.

ἰχώρ, ρος. m.

1. *serous* or *sero-purulent discharge*: Jb 2.8.

2. *gore* of blood: 4M 9.20.

Cf. Shipp 285f.

K

κάδιον, ου. n.ʃ Dim. of κάδος.

small container for liquid: carried by shepherds, 1K 17.40, 49. Cf. κάδος.

κάδος, ου. m.ʃ

1. *container for liquid*, 'jar, pitcher': σταγὼν ἀπὸ ~ου 'a drop ..' Is 40.15.

2. a liquid measure: 2C 2.9 v.l.

Cf. κάδιον, ἀσκός, ὑδρία.

καθά conj.

as, just as of similarity or identity: + a clause, καθὰ ἐνετείλατο αὐτῷ ὁ θεός 'just as God had commanded him' Ge 7.9(*b*) (cf. 6.22 with ὅσα); καθὰ (v.l. [= BSV+] for καθώς) ἐλάλησε κύριος Jn 3.3(*a*); + ἄν and subj., καθὰ ἂν ἀρέσκῃ ὑμῖν 'as it pleases you' Ge 19.8(*a*), 1K 8.7B (*b*, so 4Q51?); with a preceding cataphoric οὕτως, Οὕτως ποίησον, κ. εἴρηκας 18.5(*b*); Ex 39.11(*d*); Nu 27.22(*b*) (ǁ καθάπερ vs. 23). **b**. + a non-clausal component and with a reinforcing καί– καθὰ καὶ τὸ πρῶτον 'like the first one' Le 9.15(*a*); κ. καὶ τὰ λοιπὰ ἔθνη De 17.14(*a*); Jo 23.14 (-); 1K 8.5(*a*) (*L* καθώς).

Cf. καθάπερ, καθό, καθότι, καθώς, ὡς, τρόπος.

a) כְּ; *b*) כַּאֲשֶׁר; *c*) אֲשֶׁר; *d*) לַאֲשֶׁר; *e*) אֵת כָּל. xʃ

καθαγιάζω: fut. ~γιάσω; aor.impv. ~γίασον, pass. subj. ~γιασθῶ; pf.ptc.pass. καθηγιασμένος. *

to render ἅγιος (q.v.): + acc. and with a pleonastic ἅγιος – τὸ πέταλον .. τὸ καθηγιασμένον ἅγιον 'the leaf .. rendered sacred' Le 8.9; acc. pers., 2M 1.26, ***o*** temple 15.18. Cf. ἁγιάζω.

καθαίρεσις, εως. f.ʃ

1. v.n. of καθαιρέω **4**: ***o*** stone pillars as objects of pagan worship, Ex 23.24; of sth intangible, τῆς δόξης σου Es 3.8 *L*.

2. *that which has been destroyed*: ἀναστήσωμεν τὴν ~ιν τοῦ λαοῦ ἡμῶν 'let us restore what has been destroyed of our people' 1M 3.43.

Cf. καθαιρέω.

καθαιρέω: fut.act. καθελῶ, pass. καθαιρεθήσομαι; aor. καθεῖλον, subj. καθέλω, inf. καθελεῖν, ptc. καθελών, pass. καθῃρέθην, subj. καθαιρεθῶ; pf.ptc.pass. καθῃρημένος; plpf.pass. 3s καθῄρητο.

1. tr. *to cause to shift position downwards*: + acc., καθεῖλεν τὴν ὑδρίαν ἐπὶ τὸν βραχίονα αὐτῆς 'took the pitcher down on to her arm' Ge 24.18; ἀφ' ἑαυτῆς 24.46; τὸν μάρσιππον αὐτοῦ ἐπὶ τὴν γῆν 'his bag on to the ground' 44.11; Jerusalem, To 13.12 $\mathfrak{G}^{II}$. **b**. of pulling down a tabernacle on decampment: ***o*** σκηνήν and opp. ἀνίστημι Nu 1.51, 10.17. **c**. *to remove that which was placed on a relatively high position*: pass., ἀπὸ κεφαλῆς ὑμῶν στέφανος '(royal) crown ..' Je 13.18; 2E 6.11.

2. *to obliterate*: + acc. rei, ὕβριν ἀλλοφύλων 'the arrogance of foreigners' Zc 9.6.

3. *to overthrow, defeat*: abs., Ge 27.40 (obj. pers. understood). Cf. LSG s.v. **II 1 b**.

4. *to destroy, demolish* esp. sth erect: + acc. rei, οἰκίαν 'house' Le 14.45, οἴκους Is 22.10; τείχη 'walls' De 28.52, Is 5.5 (ǁ ἀφαιρέω), ὀχύρωμα 'fortification' Pr 21.22; βωμούς 'altars' (sites of heathen cult) Ex 34.13, De 7.5 (ǁ συντρίβω, ἐκκόπτω, κατακαίω), θυσιαστήριον 3K 19.14 (ǁ vs. 10 κατασκάπτω), ἁγίασμα Je 38.40 (ǁ ἐκλείπω), πόλεις Ez 36.36 (:: οἰκοδομέω, ǁ ἀφανίζω), Is 14.17, θρόνους 'seats' Si 10.14; temple, 1E 6.15 (ǁ καταλύω 2E 5.12); + acc. pers., Ps 59.3; + dat. cogn., καθαιρέσει καθελεῖς Ex 23.24 (ǁ συντρίβω); opp. οἰκοδομέω Ps 27.5, Si 31.28. Cf. LSG s.v. **II 3**.

Cf. καθαίρεσις, ἀφαιρέω, ἀφανίζω, κατασκάπτω, ἀνίστημι, οἰκοδομέω: Schneider, *TDNT* 3.411f.

καθαίρω: pf.pass. κεκάθαρμαι.ʃ

to improve the quality of by removing undesirable things from: pass. and ***o*** μελάνθιον 'black cummin' Is 28.27, πυρούς 'wheat' 2K 4.6; ***o*** hum. 1K 20.26*L* (B: καθαρίζω). Cf. ἀποκαθαίρω: Ziegler 1934. 184f.

καθάπερ.

I. conj. *in accordance with that which*: κ. ἐλάλησεν αὐτῷ κύριος Ge 12.4; κ. ὥρκισέν σε 50.6; Le 27.8; correlated with a following οὕτως, Ex 7.6; with a cataphoric οὕτως 7.10; Nu 27.23 (ǁ καθά vs. 22); ὡσαύτως following, 2M 15.39. **b**. introduces a gen. abs.: 4M 1.28.

II. prep. marking analogy or similarity: **a**. + a subordinate clause, κ. καὶ ὅτε .. 'as even when ..' Ex 5.13. **b**. + an adverbial, κ. ἐχθὲς καὶ τρίτην ἡμέραν 'as before, as formerly' Ex 5.14. **c**. + a nominal: κ. καὶ αἱ πρῶται Ex 34.4 (ǁ καθώς vs. 1); Le 15.25; κ. καὶ τὸ πρότερον 'as on the first occasion' De 9.18.

Cf. καθά, καθό, καθότι.

καθαρειότης, ητος. f.

purity: of precious stones, Ex 24.10; στερέωμα ~ητος 'clear sky' Si 43.1; moral, τῶν χειρῶν μου Ps 17.21 (ǁ δικαιοσύνη). Cf. καθαρός, καθαρειόω.

καθαρειόω: aor.pass. ἐκαθαρειώθην.ʃ *

to purify: morally and ***s*** hum., ναζιραῖοι αὐτῆς ὑπὲρ χιόνα '.. whiter than snow' La 4.7. Cf. καθαρειότης, καθαρίζω.

καθαρίζω: fut. καθαρίσω, ~ριῶ, pass. ~ρισθήσομαι; aor. ἐκαθάρισα, inf. ~ρίσαι, ptc. ~ρίσας, impv. ~ρισον, pass. ἐκαθαρίσθην, inf. ~ρισθῆναι, ptc. ~ρισθείς, impv.mid. ~ρίσασθε, pass. ~ρίσθητι, subj. ~ρίσω, pass. ~ρισθῶ, opt.act.3s καθαρίσαι; pf.pass. κεκαθάρισμαι, ptc.pass. κεκαθαρισμένος.

1. *to make clean, remove* dirt or impure substance *from*: of metal refining, ὡς τὸ ἀργύριον καὶ ὡς τὸ χρυσίον Ma 3.3*a*, Pr 25.4, ‖ πυρόω Ps 11.7; πυρούς 'wheat' (by winnowing) 2K 4.6; κάμινον 'furnace' Si 38.30, τὸν νεώ 'the temple' 2M 10.3, ὁδούς Is 57.14; Ιερουσαλημ ἀπὸ ἐθνῶν PSol 17.22; fig. + acc. pers. Ma 3.3*b*; + gen. rei, αὐτὸν τῆς πληγῆς Is 53.10.

2. *to render ritually or morally clean and acceptable*: ritual and + acc. rei, altar, Ex 30.10, Le 8.15; innocent blood, De 19.13; by fire, Nu 31.23; + acc. pers. αὐτὴν ἀπὸ τῆς πηγῆς τοῦ αἵματος αὐτῆς Le 12.7 (*o* menstruating woman); ἐκ τῆς ῥύσεως 'from the discharge (of semen)' Le 15.13; + ἁγιάζω 16.19. **b**. morally: + acc. pers., ἀπὸ πασῶν τῶν ἁμαρτιῶν Le 16.30, ἀπὸ .. ἀδικιῶν Je 40.8, ἀπὸ ἀκαθαρισμῶν .. εἰδώλων Ez 36.25, ἀπὸ ἀνομιῶν 36.33, ἐκ τῶν κρυφίων μου 'from my hidden transgressions' Ps 18.13; + acc. rei, ἀπὸ ἁμαρτίας .. καρδίαν Si 38.10; τὸ ἅγιον 'the sanctuary' Da 8.14.

3. *to perform the ritual of purgation*: περὶ τῶν ἱερέων Le 16.20.

4. *to judge as morally pure*: + acc. pers. and *s* God, Ex 20.7; τὸν ἔνοχον 'the guilty' 34.7; and + καθαρισμῷ Nu 14.18.

5. *to declare ritually clean*: + acc. pers. and *s* priest, Le 13.6 (:: μιαίνω vs. 3).

6. mid. *to make oneself clean ritually and religiously*: by removing objects of paganism, Ge 35.2; Is 66.17 (+ ἁγνίζομαι).

Cf. καθαρισμός, ἀποκαθαρίζω, καθαρός, καθαρειόω, καθάρσιος, ἁγιάζω, μιαίνω: Shipp 287.

καθαριότης. ⇒ καθαρειότης.

καθαριόω. ⇒ καθαρειόω.

καθαρισμός, οῦ. m.

1. *purification*: Ex 29.36, Le 14.32; τοῦ ἱεροῦ 'of the temple' 2M 1.18, τοῦ ναοῦ 10.5.

2. v.n. of καθαρίζω **4**: ~ῷ οὐ καθαριεῖ τὸν ἔνοχον Nu 14.18.

3. *purity*: Si 51.20.

Cf. καθαρός, καθαρίζω.

καθαρός, ά, όν.

1. *containing no foreign mixture*, 'pure, genuine': *s* metal, χρυσίον 'gold' Ex 25.10, Pr 8.10, cf. Is 1.25.

2. *free from dirt*, 'clean,' or *clear of objects*, 'empty': *s* φάτνη 'manger' Pr 14.4.

3. *pure* (in religious, moral or cultic sense): ἐν ~ᾷ καρδίᾳ 'with a clear conscience' Ge 20.5; ~ὸς ὀφθαλμὸς τοῦ μὴ ὁρᾶν πονηρά 'an eye too pure to watch evil things' Hb 1.13; ἐκ ῥύσεως αὐτοῦ νυκτός 'from his nocturnal discharge (of semen)' De 23.10; ἀπὸ ῥύπου 'from filth' Jb 14.4; ἀπὸ ἁμαρτίας PSol 17.36, ἀπὸ πάσης ἀκαθαρσίας ἀνδρός 'from every illicit contact with a male' To 3.14 𝔊II; *s* ὁδός Is 35.8 (‖ ἅγιος); κ. χεῖρας 'pure of hands' Jb 17.9; hum., 8.6 (‖ ἀληθινός), οὐχ ἁμαρτών 'having not sinned' 33.9. **b**. in cultic, ritual sense, *s* animals (κτήνη) Ge 7.2; birds (πετεινά) 8.20; head-dress (κίδαρις) Zc 3.5; sacrifice (θυσία) Ma 1.11; subst.n. and opp. ἀκάθαρτος and ‖ ἅγιος Le 10.10, Ez 22.26. Cf. LSG s.v. **I 2**.

4. *released from the power of* (+ ἀπό): ἀπὸ τοῦ ὅρκου 'from (the terms of) the oath' Ge 24.8 (‖ ἀθῷος vs. 41).

5. *free of guilt*, 'innocent': *s* hum., Ge 44.10, τῇ καρδίᾳ Ps 23.4 (‖ ἀθῷος).

Cf. καθαρῶς, καθαρίζω, καθαρισμός, κάθαρσις, ἁγνός, εἰλικρινής, ἄτρυγος, ἀκάθαρτος, ἀκαθαρσία, ῥυπαρός: Trench 320-2; Shipp 288.

καθάρσιος, ον.ʃ

capable of cleansing and purifying: morally, *s* martyr's blood, 4M 6.29. Cf. καθαρίζω.

κάθαρσις, εως. f.

1. v.n. of καθαρίζω **4**: of menstruating woman, Le 12.4; cogn. dat. of καθαρίζω Je 32.15.

2. *pruned wood, prunings*: burned yearly, Ez 15.4 (Cf. LSG s.v. **III**).

Cf. καθαρίζω, καθαρισμός.

καθαρῶς. adv.ʃ

in a state of moral integrity: 2M 7.40. Cf. καθαρός.

καθέδρα, ας. f.

1. *act of sitting*: opp. ἀνάστασις La 3.63, ἔγερσις Ps 138.2.

2. *act of settling and living* somewhere: 4K 17.25.

3. *seat*: ἐπὶ ~αν .. ἐκάθισεν Ps 1.1, πρεσβυτέρων 'of elders' 106.32, δόξης Si 7.4.

4. *sitting posture*: of hum., ‖ στάσις 'standing posture' 3K 10.5.

Cf. καθίημι, κάθημαι, θρόνος, στάσις.

καθέζομαι: fut. καθεδοῦμαι, καθεσθήσομαι; aor. ptc. καθεσθείς.

1. *to remain in a certain situation without any action* or *movement*: *s* menstruating woman, ἐν αἵματι ἀκαθάρτῳ αὐτῆς Le 12.4; γὺψ .. ἐπὶ νοσσιᾶς αὐτοῦ 'a vulture on its nest' Jb 39.27.

2. *to remain seated*: ἐπὶ τὴν γῆν Ez 26.16.

3. *to remain built and established*: *s* temple, Je 37.18.

Cf. κάθημαι, καθίζομαι.

καθεῖς. ⇒ κατά **8 f**.

κάθεμα, ατος. n.ʃ

necklace, collar: women's accessory, Is 3.19; περὶ τὸν τράχηλόν σου 'round your neck' Ez 16.11. Cf. καθόρμιον, μηνίσκος: LSG s.v.; Russo 75-8.

καθεύδω. Used only in pres. or impf.

to be lying asleep: ἡ γῆ, ἐφ' ἧς σὺ καθεύδεις ἐπ' αὐτῆς Ge 28.13; ἐπὶ κλινῶν ἐλεφαντίνων 'on ivory beds' Am 6.4; ἐκάθευδε καὶ ἔρρεγχε '.. and was snoring' Jn 1.5; 1K 3.2 (‖ vs. 9 κοιμάομαι); *s* a male with a female, μετ' αὐτῆς τοῦ συγγενέσθαι αὐτῇ Ge 39.10; dead hum., Da 12.2. Cf. κοιμάομαι, παρακαθεύδω: Schmidt 1.442-70.

καθηγεμών, όνος. m.ʃ

leader: driving force on battlefield, *s* θυμός 'rage' 2M 10.28. Cf. ἡγεμών, ἀρχηγός.

καθήκω.ʃ

to be meet, proper, fitting: ἔργα καθήκοντα 'prescribed jobs' Ex 5.13, τὰ ἔργα κατὰ τὰ ἅγια καθήκοντα 'the works prescribed as proper for the sanctuary' 36.1 (*pace* Mortari: *secondo gli uffici santi*), ἐν .. ταῖς λοιπαῖς καθηκούσαις ἡμέραις 'on the other appropriate days' 1M 12.11; + dat., τὸ καθῆκον τῇ ἡμέρᾳ 'the daily quota' Ex 5.19; τὸ καθῆκον αὐτῷ 'the amount due to him' 16.21; τούτῳ καθήκει τὰ πρωτοτοκεῖα 'he is entitled to the rights of the firstborn' De 21.17; σοὶ κληρονομία καθήκει λαβεῖν τὴν θυγατέρα αὐτοῦ 'it is an inheritance due to you, to take his daughter' To 6.13 𝔊ᴵᴵ; ἄρτους .. ὕδωρ .. καὶ πάντα ὅσα μοι καθήκει '.. all that is due to me' or '.. requisite, needed' (cf. Syh /ḥāšḥān/) Ho 2.5; τὰ μὴ καθήκοντα 'inappropriate things' 2M 6.4, 3M 4.16; + inf., τὸ ἐμβατεύειν .. τῷ τῆς ἱστορίας ἀρχηγέτῃ καθήκει 'to occupy the ground .. is the original historian's duty' 2M 2.30. **b.** pres.ptc., *kinsman, relative*: οἱ καθήκοντες 'those qualified who meet the condition(?)' Ex 16.16, 18, cf. Syh /hānon d-zādqin lwāteh/ and Lampe s.v. **c.** impersonally: ὡς καθήκει πάσῃ τῇ γῇ 'as it ought to happen in the whole land' Ge 19.31; ὡς καθήκει 'as it is/was proper' Le 5.10, 9.16, 1E 1.11; ἐδίδουν οἷς καθήκει 'I gave to those who were entitled to it' To 1.8 𝔊ᴵ; + inf., οὐ καθήκει δοξάσαι ἄνδρα ἁμαρτωλόν Si 10.23 (‖ οὐ δίκαιον); and + dat. pers., τὴν κληρονομίαν σοὶ καθήκει λαβεῖν 'you are entitled to take this inheritance' To 6.13 𝔊ᴵ.

Cf. προσκαθήκω, δέω, προσήκω, πρέπω.

καθηλόω: aor.impv. καθήλωσον.ʃ

to nail down: + acc. rei, Ps 118.120.

κάθημαι: impv. κάθου, κάθησο; fut. καθήσομαι; impf. ἐκαθήμην. Occurs only in the pres., impf., and fut. Note 1K 20.5 ἐγὼ καθίσας οὐ καθήσομαι.

1. *to be seated*: ἀπέναντι αὐτοῦ 'over against it' Ge 21.16 (‖ καθίζω); ἐπὶ τῆς θύρας τῆς σκηνῆς 'at the entrance to the tent' 18.1; ἐπὶ ^τοῦ λίθου^ Ex 17.12, ἐπὶ θρόνου 'on a throne' Is 6.1; ἐν μέσῳ τινός Zc 5.7; παρὰ τὴν πύλην Σοδόμων 'beside the gate of S.' Ge 19.1 (:: ἐξανίστημι); ὑποκάτω αὐτῆς ἐν σκιᾷ Jn 4.5 (‖ καθίζω); ἐν οἴκῳ De 6.7, 11.19 (:: πορεύομαι, κοιτάζομαι, διανίστημι); at a royal dining-table, 1K 20.5 (‖ καθίζω). **b.** in some official status: next to the high priest, οἱ πλησίον σου οἱ καθήμενοι πρὸ προσώπου σου Zc 3.8; *s* elders, 8.4; ruler, Φαραω, ὃς κάθηται ἐπὶ τοῦ θρόνου Ex 11.5; judge, 18.14; priest, 1K 1.9.

2. *to remain, and not move away* or *abandon*: ἐν τῷ ὄρει Ge 19.30; χήρα 'as a widow' 38.11; ἡμέρας πολλὰς καθήσῃ ἐπ' ἐμοί 'you will stay with me many days' Ho 3.3, cf. 3.4; pregnantly with εἰς– καθήσεσθε ἕκαστος εἰς τοὺς οἴκους ὑμῶν 'each of you shall retire indoors and sit there' Ex 16.29. **b.** movement contrasted with lack of it: Οἱ ἀδελφοὶ ὑμῶν πορεύσονται εἰς πόλεμον, καὶ ὑμεῖς καθήσεσθε αὐτοῦ '.. you stay here' Nu 32.6; ἐν περιοχῇ 'besieged' Je 28.30; "I shall retire to relaxed lifestyle (in my old age)" 1K 12.2.

3. *to dwell*: ἐν ὀχυρώμασι 'in fortified places' Zc 9.12; *s* temporary lodger, 3K 17.19 (‖ vs. 20 κατοικέω).

Cf. καθίζω, ἐξανίστημι, ἀπο~, ἐγ~, παρα~, προ~, συγκάθημαι, διακαθιζάνω, διφρεύω.

καθημερινός, ή, όν.ʃ *

happening daily: *s* δίαιτα 'way of living' Ju 12.15.

κάθιδρος, ον.ʃ *

sweating profusely: *s* ἵππος Je 8.6. Cf. ἱδρώς.

καθιδρύω: aor. καθίδρυσα, ptc. ~ιδρύσας.ʃ

to position permanently to perform a function: *o* idols, ἐν τοῖς οἴκοις Ep Je 16. **b.** *to found* an institution: + acc., γυμνάσιον 2M 4.12, prayer-house 3M 7.20.

Cf. ἱδρύω: Naumann 40.

καθιζάνω.ʃ

to seat: + acc. pers., βασιλεῖς ἐπὶ θρόνους Jb 12.18; Pr 18.16. Cf. καθίζω.

καθίζω: fut.act. καθιῶ, καθίσω, mid. ~ιοῦμαι, also spelled ~ίομαι [apparently not different in sense from act.]; aor. ἐκάθισα, inf. καθίσαι, impv. κάθισον, ptc. καθίσας, subj. καθίσω; pf. κεκάθικα. On the unlikely fut. such as καθίεται Ps 28.10 (v.l. καθιεῖται), see Walters 306, 10. Attested only in the fut. or aor.

1. a. *to seat oneself*: ἀπέναντι αὐτοῦ 'over against it' Ge 21.16 (‖ κάθημαι); ἐναντίον + gen. pers., Ge 43.33 (for a meal), Ex 32.6 (for a sacrificial meal); having interrupted a journey, αὐτοῦ 'here' Ge 22.5; for a meal, φαγεῖν ἄρτον 37.25, ἐπὶ τραπέζης 'at a dining-table' Si 34.12, ἐπὶ τῶν λεβήτων τῶν κρεῶν 'by the flesh-pots' Ex 16.3; for comfort, Ho 14.8, cf.

ἐν τῷ σκότει Mi 7.8 and ἐπὶ σποδοῦ 'on ashes' Jn 3.6; to do writing, Is 30.8; ἐπί τι Le 15.4; εἰς γῆν La 2.10. **b**. 'to sit up' (?): ἀναστὰς κάθισον καὶ φάγε Ge 27.19; ἐπὶ τὴν κλίνην 48.2. **c**. engaged in some activity: ***s*** judge, Jl 3.12, ἐπὶ καθέδραν Ps 1.1, ἐπὶ θρόνου 9.5; ruler Zc 6.13, king Ps 28.10, Je 13.18, εἰς βασιλέα 'as king' Ne 6.7; councillor Je 15.17; discussing and planning, μετὰ συνεδρίου Ps 25.4, ἐν συνεδρίῳ Pr 31.23; harlot Ge 38.14; widow Is 47.8; metalsmith at work, Ma 3.3.

2. *to cease moving and come to rest*: ***s*** ark (κιβωτός), Ge 8.4; bird's falling excrement, εἰς τοὺς ὀφθαλμούς μου To 2.10 𝔊II.

*__3__. *to reside*: ἐπὶ τοῦ φρέατος 'beside the well' Ex 2.15 (following κατῴκησεν); ‖ ἐνοικέω Je 29.19, κατοικέω 30.11; + acc., παραλίαν 'seashore' Jd 5.17 B; ἐν Ιερουσαλημ 2K 11.1 (‖ *L* κατοικέω). **b**. *to stay as a guest for a brief period*: μετά τινος Jd 19.4 (*L* μένω πρός τινα).

4. *to become established*: ***s*** cities, ὀχυραὶ ἐκάθισαν 'firmly ..' Ez 36.35.

5. *to make sit*, 'seat': + acc. pers., a defendant in a court, ἔναντι τῶν κριτῶν 'before the judges' De 25.2; μετὰ δυναστῶν 'with powerful people' 1K 2.8, ἐν μέσῳ μεγιστάνων καθίσει αὐτόν 'will win him a seat among the great people' Si 11.1; ***o*** ruler, 10.14, με ἐπὶ τοῦ θρόνου 3K 8.20 *L* (B: intr., ἐκάθισα), sim. 4K 11.19, εἰς νῖκος 'as a triumphant king' Jb 36.7¶.

6. *to make settle and dwell permanently*: + acc. pers., Je 39.37. **b**. w. ref. to interconfessional marriage: ***o*** women, 2E 10.2 (‖ συνοικίζω 1E 8.89), Ne 13.23.

Cf. κάθημαι, καθιζάνω, ἀντι~, δια~, παρα~, προκαθίζω, ἐνοικέω, συνεδρεύω: *ND* 1.9.

καθίημι: aor. καθῆκα, impv. κάθες.ʃ

tr. *to cause to move downwards*: ***o*** weary, drooping hands, Ex 17.11 (:: ἐπαίρω); Κάθες αὐτοὺς εἰς τὸ χωνευτήριον 'Drop them into the furnace' Zc 11.13, cf. 1K 2.14 *L*.

καθίπταμαι.ʃ *

to fly downwards: ***s*** bird, Si 43.17. Cf. πέτομαι.

κάθισις, εως. f.ʃ

v.n. of κάθημαι, **3**: Je 29.9, 30.8.

καθίστημι: pres.ptc.act. καθιστῶν; fut. καταστήσω, inf. ~στήσειν, mid. ~στήσομαι, pass. ~σταθήσομαι, inf. ~σταθήσεσθαι; 1aor. κατέστησα, inf. ~στῆσαι, impv. ~στησον, ptc. ~στήσας, subj. ~στήσω, opt.3s ~στήσαι, pass. κατεστάθην, inf. ~σταθῆναι, ptc. ~σταθείς; 2aor. κατέστην, 3pl ~στησαν, subj. ~στῶ, inf. ~στῆναι, impv.2pl ~στητε, ptc. ~στάς; pf. καθέστα/ηκα, inf. καθεστάναι, ptc.act. καθεστηκώς, ~τώς, pass. καθεσταμένος; plpf. καθειστήκειν.

I. tr. (pres.act./pass., 1aor., fut.act./pass., pf.act./pass.), *to put in charge*, 'appoint': + acc. pers., αὐτὸν ἐπὶ τοῦ οἴκου αὐτοῦ Ge 39.4; ἐπὶ γῆς Αἰγύπτου 41.33; ἐπὶ τῆς σκηνῆς τοῦ μαρτυρίου Nu 3.10; + ἐπί τινα De 28.36, Je 1.10; + ἐπί τι Ps 8.7; εἰς ἔργα Si 30.38, cf. ἐπὶ τὰ ἔργα τοῦ Σαλωμων 3K 3.35h; + dat. pers., ἑκάστῳ ἔθνῳ .. ἡγούμενον Si 17.17; pass., κατασταθῆναι αὐτὸν ἐπὶ τοῦ οἴκου αὐτοῦ καὶ ἐπὶ πάντα, ὅσα ἦν αὐτῷ Ge 39.5, καθεσταμένος φυλάσσειν .. Nu 3.32; ἡμῖν .. προφήτας Je 36.15.

2. *to put under the charge of* (τινι): + acc., τὴν χώραν 'the region' 1M 7.20.

3. *to station*: + acc., ἐν μέσῳ τοῦ λαοῦ 1K 10.23; ἐπὶ τῶν τειχέων σου .. κατέστησα φύλακας 'on your walls .. I stationed sentinels' Is 62.6, ἔνεδρα 'troops in ambush' Jo 8.2; ἐν τοῖς ὀχυρώμασιν .. ἐπὶ τῶν χρειῶν 'in the fortresses .. over tasks' 1M 10.37.

4. *to establish an office of*: τοπάρχας ἐπὶ τῆς γῆς Ge 41.34, κριτὰς καὶ γραμματοεισαγωγεῖς 'judges ..' De 16.18, ἐπ' ἐμαυτὸν ἄρχοντα 17.14, ἐφ' ὑμᾶς σκοπούς '.. watchmen' Je 6.17, νομοθέτην 'lawgiver' Ps 9.21. Cf. τίθημι **II 6**. **b**. *to appoint* to an office: εἰς τὰς χιλιαρχίας 'to the post of χιλίαρχος' Nu 31.48; εἰς κεφαλήν De 28.13, εἰς κεφαλὴν ἐθνῶν Ps 17.44, εἰς βασιλέα 'as king' 2C 36.1 (‖ ἀναδείκνυμι 1E 1.32); + double acc., αὐτοὺς ἄρχοντας Ge 47.5, 1C 12.19; σε ἄρχοντα καὶ δικαστὴν ἐφ' ἡμῶν Ex 2.14, σε ἀρχιερέα 1M 10.20; opp. ἀφαιρέομαι 'depose' Ep Je 33; pass. οἱ γραμματεῖς .. οἱ κατασταθέντες ἐπ' αὐτοὺς ὑπὸ τῶν ἐπιστατῶν τοῦ Φαραω 'the recorders who had been appointed over them by Ph.'s supervisors' Ex 5.14, καθεσταμένος ἡγούμενος 'appointed as leader' Je 20.1, κατεστάθην βασιλεύς Ps 2.6.

5. *to act on* sbd that he *assumes* a certain character: + double acc., πολλοὺς τῶν .. μετόχους 'making many of .. partakers' Es E 5 o' (*L* αἰτίους 'responsible'); pass. E 24 o'.

6. *to bring into being*: + acc., χειμάρρους 'wadis' Nu 21.15; ἐκ τοῦ ὀνόματος τοῦ τετελευτηκότος 'after the name of the deceased' De 25.6; ἐγχείρημα καρδίας 'that which one has willed to try' Je 37.24; calm life, Es B 2, sim. 3M 3.26.

7. *to bring back*: + acc., εἰς τὴν νομὴν αὐτῶν 'into their pasturage' Je 23.3. **b**. *to restore*: + acc., φυλὰς Ιακωβ Si 48.10.

8. *to demonstrate to be so and so*: + double acc., αὐτοὺς .. ψευδομάρτυρας Su 61; 3M 3.19.

9. *to ready*: + acc., τὸν ναὸν σποδῷ 'the temple (by besprinkling it) with ashes' Bel 14 LXX.

10. *to establish as legally applicable and binding*: + inf., σε .. φίλον βασιλέως καλεῖσθαι 1M 10.20.

11. *to transform and cause to be*: + double acc., προθυμοτέρους αὐτούς '(made) them more enthusiastic' 2M 15.9; 3M 1.7; 2nd acc. understood, 2.5.

II. intr. (fut.mid., 2aor., pf. and plpf. act.): *to stand straight up*: Es D 8 o'.

2. *to stand against, oppose*: in court, μάρτυς ἄδικος κατὰ ἀνθρώπου De 19.16.

3. *to acquire the quality of*: + adj., αἴτιος 'responsible' 4M 1.11. **b**. pf., plpf. *to have acquired the quality of*, 'be': + adj., μετὰ καθεστηκότος πρεσβύτου 'with one who has aged' De 32.25; 2M 3.28, 4.1, 50, 14.5; θεοῦ '(to be) of divine origin' or 'to be a business of God' 4M 5.25 ..

4. *to take charge*: as judge, καταστήσεται εἰς κρίσιν Is 3.13; as leader ἐπὶ ^προφητῶν^ 1K 19.20; ἐπὶ τὴν βασιλείαν 2C 21.5; *s* soldier on horse-back, ἐν περικεφαλαίαις 'with helmets on' Je 26.4, "before the walls" 2M 12.27; as a worshipper 1K 1.9. **b**. pf. *to be in charge*: ἐπὶ τὰς ἡμιόνους 'of the mules' 1K 22.9 (*L* καθεσταμένος).

5. *to come forward in response to a call*: 1E 2.7 (|| ἀνίστημι 2E 1.5), ἐνώπιον τοῦ βασιλέως Es D 6 o' (*L* ἵστημι), ἐνώπιον κυρίου 1K 10.19, cf. 1.9; as a defendant, εἰς κρίσιν Jo 20.6, 9.

6. *to cease to move*: καθεστηκὸς ὕδωρ 'stagnant water' Ez 34.18; *to stay put*, παροικῆσαι ἐκεῖ Je 51.28.

7. *to become quiet*: *s* πύλαι '(it became quiet) around the gates' Ne 13.19, cf. La *quieverunt*; metaph., *s* τὸ πνεῦμα αὐτοῦ 1K 30.12, cf. Aristot. *Ph*. 248ᵃ2 [ἡ ψυχὴ] καθίσταται καὶ ἠρεμίζεται.

Cf. ἀνθ~, ἀν~, ἐφ~, προσκαθίστημι, ἀναδείκνυμι, κατατάσσω.

καθό. conj.ʃ

as, just as of similarity and comparison: κ. ἐνετείλατο Μωυσῆς 'as Moses commanded' Le 9.5; Ju 3.3 (|| καθὼς 3.2). Cf. καθά, καθάπερ, καθότι, καθώς, ὡς.

καθοδηγέω: fut. ~γήσω; aor.ptc. ~γήσας.ʃ *

to lead as a guide: + acc. pers., ἐν τῇ ἐρήμῳ Je 2.6; Ez 39.2; false guide, Jb 12,23 ¶. Cf. ὁδηγέω.

κάθοδος, ου. f.

1. *passage downwards* (i.e. to the south): 1E 2.20.

2. *recurrence*: χιλίων ἐτῶν ~ους 'thousands of years many times over' Ec 6.6; ~ους πολλάς 'many times' 7.22 (|| πολλάκις); τρεῖς ~ους 'three times' 3K 9.25 v.l.

καθόλου. adv.ʃ

in any way, if ever: εἰ δώσει σκύμνος φωνὴν αὐτοῦ ἐκ τῆς μάνδρας αὐτοῦ κ. ἐὰν μὴ ἁρπάσῃ τι; 'would a lion roar out of his thicket at all unless he has caught something?' Am 3.4; 3.3; τὸ κ. w. neg. and preceding the verb, 'in no way whatsoever', τὸ κ. μὴ βλέπουσιν Ez 13.3, sim. vs. 22, 17.14; following the verb, οὐχ ἥψατο αὐτῶν τὸ κ. τὸ πῦρ 'the fire did not touch them at all' Da 3.50.

καθομολογέω: aor.mid. καθωμολογησάμην, subj. ~γήσωμαι.ʃ

to promise to give in marriage: *s* father and + acc. pers. (daughter) and dat. pers.(male), ἣν αὐτῷ καθωμολογήσατο 'whom he [= the girl's father] had betrothed to him' Ex 21.8; 21.9.

καθοπλίζω: aor.mid. καθωπλισάμην, ptc.act., ~οπλίσας, impv. ~όπλισον, subj. ~οπλίσωμαι; pf.ptc. ~ωπλικώς, pass. ~ωπλισμένος.

to arm fully: + acc.pers., 2M 4.40; pass., ὅπλοις 'with arms' Je 26.9; + double acc., ἕκαστον .. οὐ τὴν ἀσπίδων .. ἀσφαλείαν '(arming) each .. not so much with the safety of shields' 2M 15.11; *o* animals, 3M 5.23, 38; mid., + acc. (arms), 4M 3.12; pass., *o* army, 4M 4.10; priest, θυμιατηρίῳ 'with an incense-burner' 7.11; metaph., *o* παθοκρατείαν 'control of passions' 13.16. Cf. ἐνοπλίζω.

καθοράω.ʃ

1. *to look down upon* from a higher position: + acc. and ptc., Nu 24.2.

2. *to observe and visually investigate*: abs. and || ὁράω, βλέπω Jb 10.4; + acc., τὰ πρὸς νότον 'what lies in the north' 39.26.

3. *to contemplate mentally*: + acc., τὸ τοῦ μεγίστου θεοῦ κράτος 'the power of the supreme God' 3M 3.11.

Cf. ὁράω.

καθόρμιον, ου. n.ʃ

necklace: woman's accessory, Ho 2.13 (|| ἐνώτιον). Cf. κάθεμα.

καθότι. conj.

1. *as, just as* of similarity: μὴ ποιήσειν μεθ' ἡμῶν κακόν, κ. ἡμεῖς σε οὐκ ἐβδελυξάμεθα Ge 26.29(*b*)(|| ὃν τρόπον); κ. ὤμοσας 'as you swore' Mi 7.20(*a*); κ. εἶπε κύριος 'as the Lord said' Jl 2.32(*b*); κ. ἐνετειλάμην αὐτῷ Ma 4.6(*a*); κ. ἐξαπέστειλεν αὐτὸν κύριος πρὸς αὐτούς 'in accordance with the message the Lord sent them through him' Hg 1.12(*b*); sim. Zc 7.3(*b*); πληθυνθήσονται κ. ἦσαν πολλοί 'they will multiply to their former number' ib. 10.8(*j*). **b**. with ἄν: καθότι ἂν ἐπιβάλῃ 'as much as he might impose' Ex 21.22(*b*). **c**. with coordinating οὕτως: κ. ἂν δῷ μῶμον τῷ ἀνθρώπῳ, οὕτως δοθήσεται αὐτῷ Le 24.20(*b*); 27.12(*h*)(|| ὡς vs. 14). **d**. *to the extent that, as much as*: κ. ἰσχύει ἡ χείρ σου .. κ. εὐλόγησέν σε κύριος 'as much as lies in you .. as much as the Lord blessed you' De 16.10(*l*) (|| κατὰ δύναμιν τῶν χειρῶν ὑμῶν κατὰ τὴν εὐλογίαν κυρίου vs. 17).

2. *in so far as*: ἠγνοήσαμεν κ. ἡμάρτομεν 'we were ignorant in so far as our having sinned was concerned' Nu 12.11(*g*).

3. *for the reason that*: 1E 1.48 (|| 2C 36.15 ὅτι), 2K 20.12B (*L* ὅτι)(*b*), Ec 7.2(*p*).

Cf. καθά, καθάπερ, καθό, καθώς, ὡς.

a) אֲשֶׁר; *b*) כַּאֲשֶׁר; *c*) כָּל־אֲשֶׁר; *d*) כְּכֹל אֲשֶׁר; *e*) וְכָל־אֲשֶׁר; *f*) מֵאֲשֶׁר; *g*) וַאֲשֶׁר; *h*) כְּ; *i*) כְּכָל־ [De 18.6 (MT בכל)]; *j*) כְּמוֹ; *k*) לְפִי; *l*) מִסַּת; *m*) אֵת כָּל אֲשֶׁר; *n*) כִּי; *o*) fr; *p*) בַּאֲשֶׁר. x∫

καθυβρίζω: fut. ~ρίσω; aor.inf. ~ρίσαι.∫

to insult: + acc. pers., Je 28.2; τὸν ἅγιον τόπον 3M 2.14; δικαίωμα Pr 19.28. Cf. ὑβρίζω.

καθυμνέω.∫

to sing a song of praise: τῷ κυρίῳ 2C 30.21. Cf. ὑμνέω.

καθύπερθε. adv.∫

over above: "with a thick deck lying over above them" 3M 4.9.

καθυπνόω.∫

to fall fast asleep: || νυστάζω 'to doze' Pr 24.33. Cf. ὑπνόω.

καθυστερέω: fut. καθυστερήσω; aor.inf. ~ρῆσαι.∫

1. *to be late*: in coming true, *s* ὑπομονή 'that which one is hoping for' Si 16.13. **b**. *to be late*: in offering, + acc., ἀπαρχὰς ἅλωνος καὶ ληνοῦ 'the first-fruits of threshing floor and winepress' Ex 22.29.

2. *to fail to obtain*: + gen. rei, Si 37.20. **b**. *to lack what is needed*: abs., 1C 26.27.

Cf. ὑστερέω and χρονίζω.

καθυφαίνω: fut. ~φανῶ; pf.ptc.pass. ~φασμένος.*∫

to interweave, weave in: + acc., ὕφασμα κατάλιθον 'a texture holding stones' Ex 28.17; ἐκ .. λίθων πολυτελῶν καθυφασμένων 'from interwoven precious stones' Ju 10.21. Cf. ὑφαίνω.

καθώς. conj.

1. *as, just as* of similarity and comparison: **a**. elliptically, followed by a word or word-group; κ. ἡμέρα γενέσεως αὐτῆς 'as in the day of her birth' Ho 2.3(*a*), for the omission of the prep. ἐν, which is added in Lucianic MSS, see also ib. 12.9(*a*) κ. ἡμέρα ἑορτῆς; κ. αἱ ἡμέραι τοῦ αἰῶνος Am 9.11(*a*), Mi 7.14(*a*), Ma 3.4a(*a*); κ. ἡμέρα παρατάξεως Zc 14.3(*a*); κ. τὰ ἔτη τὰ ἔμπροσθεν Ma 3.4b(*a*); κ. τὰ πετεινὰ τοῦ οὐρανοῦ Ho 7.12b(*a*); same term repeated in both members of the comparison, κ. ὕψος κέδρου τὸ ὕψος αὐτοῦ 'his height was like the height of a cedar' Am 2.9(*a*), τὴν ὕβριν Ιακωβ κ. ὕβριν τοῦ Ισραηλ Na 2.3(*a*); κ. ἔμπροσθεν Jl 2.23(*a*); κ. ἀπ' ἀρχῆς Zc 12.7(*a*). **b**. The following noun may be case-neutral and syntactically equivalent with ὡς: Λάξευσον .. δύο πλάκας λιθίνας κ. καὶ αἱ πρῶται 'Cut .. two stone tablets similar to the first' Ex 34.1(*a*) (|| καθάπερ vs. 4); κ. ἡ ἀνατολὴ τοῦ ἀγροῦ δέδωκά σε Ez 16.7(*a*); 42.6(*a*). **c**. Followed by a clause: κ. ἐποίησα Ge 8.21(*b*); κ. ἀγαπᾷ ὁ θεὸς τοὺς .. Ho 3.1(*a*); ib. 10.5(*a*), Am 4.11(*a*), Jn 3.3(*a*) (v.l. καθά, καθάπερ), Zc 14.5(*b*). This use of καθώς is more frequent than that of ὡς. **d**. Correlated with οὕτως(= MT *k*- .. *k*-, a Heb. idiom signifying "completeness of correspondency between two objects" [BDB, s.v. *k*-, **2**, p. 454a]) and reinforced by καί: ἐγενήθη δὲ καθὼς συνέκρινεν ἡμῖν, οὕ. καὶ συνέβη Ge 41.13(*b*); ἔσται κ. ὁ λαὸς οὕ. καὶ ὁ ἱερεύς 'Like priest like nation' Ho 4.9(*a*); Zc 1.6(*b*); without οὕτως- Κ. ἡ μήτηρ, καὶ ἡ θυγάτηρ 'Like mother like daughter' Ez 16.44f.(*a*). **e**. As part of the predicate of εἰμί: ἔσονται κ. οὐχ ὑπάρχοντες (/klō' hāyu/) Ob 16(*a*) (Am 5.5 ἔσται ὡς οὐχ ὑπάρχουσα), cf. Hg 2.3(*a*); w. γίνομαι– μὴ γίνεσθε κ. οἱ πατέρες ὑμῶν Zc 1.4(*a*).

2. Temporal, *when*: with ἄν and pres.subj., κ. ἂν πορεύωνται 'whenever they go' Ho 7.12a(*b*). In all cases mentioned at BDAG, s.v. **4**, the verb is in the indicative, mostly aorist; this use of καθώς is not recognised by Mayser, II 3.77. **b**. + impf., Es 2.20 o'.

Cf. καθά, καθότι, and ὡς.

a) כְּ [Jl 2.23, Zc 12.7 MT *b*-]; *b*) כַּאֲשֶׁר; *c*) אֲשֶׁר; *d*) לְפִי; *e*) (-). x∫

καί. Crasis is sometimes observed: καὶ ἐάν > κἄν, καὶ ἐγώ > κἀγώ, καὶ ἐκεῖ > κἀκεῖ, καὶ ἐκείνοις > κἀκεῖνοις etc.

1. Marks coordinate relationship between two or more terms (single words, phrases, and clauses), 'and': πρὸς βορρᾶν καὶ λίβα καὶ ἀνατολὰς καὶ θάλασσαν 'towards the north, south, east and west' Ge 13.14; ἐν ἡμέραις Οζίου καὶ Ιωαθαμ καὶ Αχαζ καὶ Εζεκίου βασιλέων Ιουδα καὶ ἐν ἡμέραις Ιεροβοαμ υἱοῦ Ιωας βασιλέως Ισραηλ 'in the era of Uzziah and Jotham and Ahaz and Hezekiah the kings of Judah and in the era of Jeroboam the son of Joash king of Israel' Ho 1.1. **b**. The relationship can be between two or more independent clauses: ἀπέρριψάς με εἰς βάθη καρδίας θαλάσσης, καὶ ποταμοί με ἐκύκλωσαν 'you cast me into the depths of the midst of the sea, and currents encircled me' Jn 2.4. **c**. The particle can be left out, resulting in asyndetic construction: Βάδιζε κατάβηθι 'Now, go down' Ex 19.24, ἀνάσθητι πορεύθητι 'Up and go!' Jn 3.2; ἑτοιμάζου ὄρθρισον 'prepare yourself eagerly' Zp 3.7. **d**. The particle may join two verbs the first of which has only a weakened meaning: ἀνάστητε καὶ ἐξαναστῶμεν ἐπ' αὐτὴν εἰς πόλεμον 'Now, let us set out to make war against her' Ob 1. For further examples, see under ἀνίστημι and βαδίζω. **e**. Often joins two or more co-terminous, synonymous terms: μὴ ἐπίδῃς ἡμέραν ἀδελφοῦ σου .. καὶ μὴ ἐπιχαρῇς ἐπὶ τοὺς υἱοὺς Ιουδα Ob 12. **f**. Joins two or more components of a compound numeral: τὰ λύτρα τριῶν καὶ ἑβδομήκοντα καὶ διακοσίων 'the ransoms of the 273' Nu 3.46; τῇ τετράδι καὶ εἰκάδι 'on the twenty-fourth' Hg 2.1; without καί - ἐνενήκοντα ἕξ '96' Je 52.23; ἑκατὸν ὀγδοήκοντα '180' Es 1.4 o' (*L* ὀ. καὶ ἑ.). **g**. The phrase or clause preceded by καί may not be affected by a negative used with the verb in the preceding clause: ὅπως μὴ λάβητε ἀδικίαν καὶ λάβητε ἀγαθά Ho 14.3, but cp. οὐκ ἐκπορνεύσει ἡ γῆ καὶ ἡ γῆ πλησθήσεται ἀνομίας Le 19.29; οὐδὲ ὁ ἱππεὺς οὐ μὴ σώσῃ τὴν ψυχὴν αὐτοῦ, καὶ εὑρήσει τὴν καρδίαν αὐτοῦ ἐν δυναστείαις Am 2.15f., οὐ μὴ οἰκοδομήσουσι καὶ ἄλλοι ἐνοικήσουσι Is 65.22; μὴ ἐλθεῖν εἰς αἵματα καὶ σῶσαι .. 1K 25.33 ǁ *L* μὴ ἐλθεῖν .. καὶ μὴ σῶσαι .. **h**. Even at the start of an utterance or a book: Καὶ ἀκούσεται .. Nu 14.13; Καὶ ἀνεκάλεσεν Μωυσῆν .. Le 1.1; Nu 1.1, Ho1.2, Jn 1.1. ***i**. Hebraistic pleonasm: ἀπ' ἀρχῆς τοῦ ἐνιαυτοῦ καὶ ἕως συντελείας τοῦ ἐνιαυτοῦ 'from the beginning of the year till its end' De 11.12, ἀπὸ τοῦ νῦν καὶ ἕως εἰς τὸν αἰῶνα Mi 4.7; De 11.24, see under ἕως **d**. **j**. indicates an approximate quantity by joining two consecutive cardinal numerals: δύο καὶ τρεῖς πόλεις 'two or three cities' Am 4.8 (MT: no Waw); two numerals separated - τρεῖς σελίδας καὶ τέσσαρας 'three or four columns' Je 43.23 (MT: with a Waw), cf. ἅπαξ καὶ δίς 'once or twice' Ne 13.20 (MT: with a Waw) and ῥῶγες ἐλαίας δύο ἢ τρεῖς 'two or three olive-berries' Is 17.6. **k**. joins two antonymous terms, as an equivalent of ἀλλά or ἀλλ' ἤ: εἰς κακὰ καὶ οὐκ εἰς ἀγαθά Je 46.16, Am 9.4; εἰς σκότος καὶ οὐ φῶς La 3.2.

2. marks addition, 'also, likewise,' placed immediately before the term so to be qualified: ἔδωκεν καὶ τῷ ἀνδρὶ αὐτῆς 'gave also to her husband' Ge 3.6; καθὰ καὶ αὐτοὶ περιτέτμηνται 'just as they also are circumcised' 34.22; ἐγενήθη δὲ καθὼς συνέκρινεν ἡμῖν, οὕτως καὶ συνέβη 41.13; πίε καὶ σύ 'Drink, you, too!' Hb 2.16. **b**. with repetition of καί, 'both .. and': ἔλαβεν δὲ καὶ τὸ πῦρ .. καὶ τὴν μάχαιραν '.. both the fire .. and the knife' Ge 22.6; καὶ ἐὰν ἀγαθὸν καὶ ἐὰν κακόν 'whether good or bad' Je 49.5; καὶ πλούτῳ καὶ σοφίᾳ 'in wealth and wisdom alike' 2C 9.22; πολυμαθὴς ἀληθῶς καὶ ὢν καὶ καλούμενος 'truly erudite, both actually and so reputed' Si prol. II; with a single καί - ἐκ στόματος ὑψίστου οὐκ ἐξελεύσεται τὰ κακὰ καὶ τὸ ἀγαθόν; La 3.38; with more than two terms, 2M 15.17; 1K 2.26. **c**. often reinforcing in comparisons: καθὼς καὶ αἱ πρῶται 'like the first' Ex 34.1; καθάπερ καὶ αἱ πρῶται 'like the first' Ex 34.4; καθὰ καὶ τὸ πρῶτον 'like the first one' Le 9.15; καθὼς ἡ μήτηρ, καὶ ἡ θυγάτηρ 'Like mother like daughter' Ez 16.44; τὰ δέοντά σοι ὡς καὶ τῷ υἱῷ μου 'the expenses for you as well as for my son' To 5.15 𝔊I (𝔊II .. σοι ὁμοίως τῷ ..). **d**. Repeated also before the corresponding term in a coordinate expression: ὡς καὶ παρεμβάλλουσιν, οὕτως καὶ ἐξαροῦσιν 'just as they encamp, so will they set off' Nu 2.17. **e**. κἀγώ etc. does not mark mere addition (A and B), but 'A, B also,' hence it can be clause-initial, e.g. Jb 1.9dα, 16.4, 42.4, Ps 87.14.

3. *together with*: prefixed to the second and any subsequent nominal of multiple subjects agreeing with a verb in the sg., εἰσελεύσῃ εἰς τὴν κιβωτόν, σὺ καὶ οἱ υἱοί σου καὶ ἡ γυνή σου καὶ αἱ γυναῖκες τῶν υἱῶν σου μετὰ σοῦ Ge 6.18. See also ποιμένες προβάτων οἱ παῖδές σου .. καὶ ἡμεῖς καὶ οἱ πατέρες ἡμῶν 'your servants are shepherds, both we and our forefathers' Ge 47.3. **b**. The first constituent plays a dominant role, the subsequent relegated to the status of attachments, ἐσόμεθα ἡμεῖς καὶ ἡ γῆ ἡμῶν παῖδες Φαραω Ge 47.19. **c**. hendiadys: πύλας καὶ μοχλούς 'gates fitted with bolts' Si 49.13.

4. indicates contrast: ἐργᾷ τὴν γῆν, καὶ οὐ προσθήσει τὴν ἰσχὺν αὐτῆς δοῦναί σοι 'you till the land, and yet it no longer provides you with its fruit' Ge 4.12; "you may take a wife, but (καὶ) another man is going to have her. You may build a house, but (καὶ) you are not going to get to live in it. You may plant a vineyard, but (καὶ) you are not going to harvest it" De 28.30; "they might run, even so they wouldn't get worn out (καὶ οὐ κοπιάσουσι)" Is 40.31; ἐσπείρατε πολλὰ καὶ εἰσηνέγκατε ὀλίγα, ἐφάγετε καὶ οὐκ εἰς πλησμονήν, ἐπίετε καὶ οὐκ εἰς μέθην Hg 1.6; Zp 1.13*b*; "I loved you, says the Lord, but (καί) you said, With what did you love us?" Ma 1.2; ἀντέσθησαν θεῷ καὶ ἐσώθησαν 'they rebelled against God, but they were saved none the less' 3.15; De 28.38, 1K 29.6, Am 5.11, Mi 6.14, 15.

5. introduces an element of surprise or something unexpected: "they were both naked, καὶ οὐκ ᾐσχύνοντο ('and yet they did not feel ashamed')" Ge 3.1; καὶ αὐτὴ κοινωνός σου 'and yet she is your partner' Ma 2.14; "Would a trumpet sound in a city without (καὶ λαὸς οὐ πτοηθήσεται) scaring the folk?" Am 3.6; καὶ αὐτό ἐστι φαντασία Hb 2.19; καὶ σύ ἦς ὡς εἷς ἐξ αὐτῶν 'and you [not: you also, like some others] behaved like one of them' Ob 11; Hb 1.2; Zc 1.4*c*.

6. highlights a logical contradiction with what precedes: ἵνα τί αὕτη ὑμῖν ἡ ἡμέρα τοῦ κυρίου; καὶ αὐτή ἐστι σκότος καὶ οὐ φῶς 'what is this all of your concern about the Lord's day when it is darkness and not light at all?' Am 5.18; "The ark and Israel .. reside in tents .. and my lord Joab .. are encamped καὶ ἐγὼ [*L*: καὶ πῶς ἐγὼ] εἰσελεύσομαι εἰς τὸν οἶκόν μου ..;" 2K 11.11, εἶπας Οὐχ οὕτως ἔσται, καὶ ἐποίησαν 'You said, 'That shall not happen, and yet they did it all the same' Ju 9.2; μέλαινά εἰμι καὶ καλή 'I am black and yet pretty' Ct 1.5; "I did not send the prophets, and yet (καί) they were running about, and I did not speak to them, and yet (καί) they were prophesying" Je 23.21; Ez 13.10, 33.17, To 5.2, most likely Semitism, see Blomqvist 1979.46f.

7. gives parenthetical, supplementary information, 'and that' (Germ. *und zwar*): Γράψον ὅρασιν καὶ σαφῶς ἐπὶ πυξίον 'Write down a vision, and that clearly on a tablet' Hb 2.2; Δείξω αὐτῷ, καὶ οὐχὶ νῦν, μακαρίζω, καὶ οὐκ ἐγγίζει 'I shall show him, but not now; I bless (him), but not very soon' Nu 24.17. Poss. also καταφιλῆσαι τὰ παιδία μου καὶ τὰς θυγατέρας 'to kiss my children good-bye, and that the daughters in particular' Ge 31.28; δύο καὶ πονηρά 'two things, and wicked things at that' Je 2.13.

8. introduces an extreme case or invites comparison of the assertion, negation etc. with a less plausible one that might have been made: "Even his life on the earth were a mere day (καὶ μία ἡμέρα)" Jb 14.5, cf. τιμὴ πόρνης ὅση καὶ ἑνὸς ἄρτου 'the value of a whore is just as much as that of one loaf of bread' Pr 6.26; "they wounded many, even killed some (τινὰς δὲ καὶ κατέβαλον) 2M 4.42; βαρὺς ἡμῖν ἐστιν καὶ βλεπόμενος 'his sight alone is unbearable to us' Wi 2.14. **b**. καὶ ἐάν 'even if': καὶ ἐὰν ἐκθρέψωσι .. 'even if they should bring up' Ho 9.12; 9.16. **c**. εἰ καὶ 'even if': εἰ δὲ καὶ ἐπιλάθοιτο 'even if she forgot' Is 49.15.

9. introduces a consequence which would ensue if what is denoted by the preceding clause is realised: μήποτε ἐκτείνῃ τὴν χεῖρα καὶ λάβῃ τοῦ ξύλου τῆς ζωῆς καὶ φάγῃ καὶ ζήσεται εἰς τὸν αἰῶνα Ge 3.22 (note the shift of mood and tense in ζήσεται, ind.fut.); Τί σοι ποιήσωμεν καὶ κοπάσει ἡ θάλασσα ..; 'what shall we do to you to get the sea to calm down ..?' Jn 1.11; "Keep away (impv. ἀπόστηθι) from lawlessness, then (καί) it will move away (fut. ἐκκλινεῖ) from you" Si 7.2.

10. introduces an apodosis and indicates a consequence to follow when a request or command is acted upon: τὸν ἀδελφὸν ὑμῶν .. ἀγάγετε πρός με, καὶ πιστευθήσονται τὰ ῥήματα ὑμῶν 'Bring your brother to me, and then your words would become credible' Ge 42.20; Ἐκζητήσατέ με καὶ ζήσεσθε Am 5.4 (|| ἐκζητήσατε τὸν κύριον καὶ ζήσατε vs. 6); Ἐπιστρέψατε πρός με, καὶ ἐπιστραφήσομαι πρὸς ὑμᾶς 'Return to me, and then I shall return to you' Zc 1.3.

***11**. Hebraistically introduces an apodosis—Waw apodoseos—where the protasis itself is introduced by a conjunction or is in the form of a temporal adjunct: Εἰ ὁ κύριός μου οὐ γινώσκει .. καὶ πῶς ποιήσω .. Ge 39.8f.; Ἐὰν .. προσφέρῃ .. καὶ προσοίσει .. Le 1.14; ἡνίκα ἐὰν ἔλθῃς .. καὶ μή σοι δῶσιν, καὶ ἔσῃ ἀθῷος .. 'if you go .. and they do not give you, then you shall be immune ..' Ge 24.41; ἔτι αὐτοῦ λαλοῦντος καὶ Ραχηλ .. ἤρχετο 'while he was still speaking, there came R. along' 29.9; ὅτε ἐνεβάλλετε εἰς κυψέλην κριθῆς εἴκοσι σάτα, καὶ ἐγένετο κριθῆς δέκα σάτα 'when you cast into a barley container twenty measures, there came out ten measures of barley' Hg 2.16*a*, sim. 2.16*b*; ὡς δὲ ἐπισυνήγαγεν .. καὶ εὐθὺς ἐξῆλθεν Ge 38.29; ἔτι τρεῖς ἡμέραι καὶ μνησθήσεται .. 40.13; ἔτι μικρὸν καὶ καταλιθοβολήσουσίν με 'A while yet, and then they are going to stone me' Ex 17.4; Ho 1.4; ἰδὼν .. ὅτι .., καὶ ἐνεθυμήθη .. 'Having seen .. that .., then he took to heart ..' Ge 6.5f.; καὶ ἔσται ἐὰν ὑπολειφθῶσι δέκα ἄνδρες .. καὶ ἀποθανοῦνται 'should there be ten men left over, they should die' Am 6.9; 8.9; καὶ ἄνθρωπος ἄνθρωπος .. ὃς ἂν φάγῃ πᾶν αἷμα, καὶ ἐπιστήσω τὸ πρόσωπόν μου ἐπὶ τὴν ψυχὴν .. Le 17.10; Ἀνθ' ὧν ἐξέχεας .. καὶ ἀποκαλυφθήσεται .. 'because you poured out .., it will be laid bare ..' Ez 16.36; ἐν τῷ ἀποστρέψαι δίκαιον .. καὶ ἀποθανεῖται .. 33.18. See BDAG, s.v. **1 b δ**, and Aejmelaeus (1982.128-38). **b**. preceded by a non-temporal adjunct: Ἀνθ' ὧν ὑψώθησαν .., καὶ ταπεινώσει .. Is 3.16f.; sim. Je 7.13f. **c**. Very often reflecting the Hebrew Waw "consecutive," marking the progression of a narrative consisting of a series of actions or events occurring in succession: καὶ ἀνέστη Ιωνας .. καὶ κατέβη .. καὶ εὗρε .. καὶ ἔδωκε .. καὶ ἀνέβη Jn 1.3.

***12**. Hebraistically καὶ ἔσται introduces an utterance indicating that which may or ought to happen, with an adverbial clause or phrase intervening: καὶ ἔσται ἐὰν μὴ θέλῃς αὐτήν, ἐξαποστελεῖς αὐτὴν .. 'should you not like her, you shall send her away ..' De 21.14; καὶ ἔσται ἡνίκα ἂν καταπαύσῃ .. ἐξαλείψεις .. 'when he gives you rest .. you shall obliterate ..' 25.19; καὶ ἔσται ἐν τῇ ἡμέρᾳ ἐκείνῃ .. καλέσει με 'on that day .. it shall call me' Ho 2.16; καὶ ἔσται ἐν πάσῃ τῇ γῇ .. τὰ δύο μέρη ἐξολεθρευθήσεται 'in the whole land the two parts shall be annihilated' Zc 13.8; with its apodosis likewise introduced by καί: καὶ ἔσονται .. γυναῖκες, καὶ ἀφαιρεθήσεται ὁ κλῆρος 'should they become wives .., the inheritance shall be taken away' Nu 36.3. For further details, see s.v. εἰμί **5**.

13. introduces a phrase or clause which explicates what precedes: εὐλογῶν εὐλογήσω σε καὶ πληθύνων πληθυνῶ τὸ σπέρμα σου .. καὶ κληρονομήσει τὸ σπέρμα σου τὰς πόλεις τῶν ὑπεραντίων 'I shall surely bless you by multiplying ..' Ge 22.17; ὑπήκουσεν .. τῆς ἐμῆς φωνῆς, καὶ ἐφύλαξεν τὰ προστάγματά μου καὶ τὰς ἐντολάς μου .. 26.5; Ταπεινώθητε καὶ καθίσατε 'Humble yourselves and sit (on the ground)' Je 13.18.

14. reinforces an argument, 'and besides; after all': Μὴ κατέχετέ με, καὶ κύριος εὐόδωσεν τὴν ὁδόν μου 'Don't hold me up. After all, the Lord has prospered my journey' Ge 24.56.

15. singles out one member for special mention: αὐτοὺς καὶ τὸν Βενιαμιν 'them, Benjamin among them included' Ge 43.16; ἴδετε τὴν γῆν καὶ τὴν Ιερειχω Jo 2.1, δέκα ἄνδρες καὶ Ασαηλ 2K 2.30, ἔλαβεν γυναῖκας ἀλλοτρίας καὶ τὴν θυγατέρα Φαραω 3K 11.1, πᾶς Ιουδα καὶ Ιερουσαλημ 2C 35.24, sim. Mk 16.7 (BDAG s.v. **1aγ**) and cf. Rashi ad Jo 2.1.

16. introduces an emotionally charged question: καὶ ἵνα τί παρελογίσω με; 'And why have you cheated me?' Ge 29.25; Καὶ ποῦ ἐστιν; 'And so where is he?' Ex 2.20; καὶ διὰ τί οὐκ ἐφοβήθητε ..; 'and why did you not fear ..?' Nu 12.8; καὶ ἵνα τί .. καὶ ἵνα τί .. 20.4f.; καὶ σὺ τί ποιήσεις .. Je 4.30; 1K 15.14, Ju 6.2. Cf. JM § 177 *m*.

17. 'namely, more specifically': ἐν τοῖς ὕδασιν καὶ ἐν ταῖς θαλάσσαις καὶ ἐν τοῖς χειμάρροις Le 11.9, cf. 11.10 where καί is replaced by ἤ.

***18**. Hebraistically introduces a circumstantial clause loosely hanging to the preceding main clause and is either in the indic. present tense, pf./plpf. or ptc.: **a**. pres.: "they placed a cover on the naked body of their father καὶ τὸ πρόσωπον αὐτῶν ὀπισθοφανές, 'with their face facing backwards'" Ge 9.23; .. καὶ αἱ δύο πλάκες ἐπὶ τῶν χειρῶν Μωυσῆς 'with the two tablets on M.'s hands' Ex 34.29 (no apodosis *pace* Wevers ad loc.); .. καὶ δύο παῖδες μετ' αὐτοῦ Nu 22.22. **b**. pf. or plpf.: ἀνέστη ὁ ἄγγελος .. καὶ αὐτὸς ἐπιβεβήκει ἐπὶ τῆς ὄνου 'the angel stood up .. when he was already seated on the ass' Nu 22.22; ἐξῆλθεν ὁ ἀδελφὸς αὐτοῦ, καὶ ἡ χεὶρ αὐτοῦ ἐπειλημμένη τῆς πτέρνης Ησαυ '.. with his hand having caught Esau's heel' Ge 25.26.

19. In a series of verbal clauses linked by καί, their linear sequence does not necessarily agree with their strictly chronological one: "I shall give you a new heart, and a new spirit I shall plant in you, and I shall remove the stony heart from your flesh and give you a heart of flesh" Ez 36.26.

20. otiose: φρουρὰν .. καὶ μάλα ὀχυράν 'a very strong garrison' 2M 12.18.

21. On καί γε, see under γέ.

Cf. τέ.

καινίζω: fut. καινιῶ.

1. *to make new, rejuvenate*: + acc. pers. Zp 3.17, + acc. rei, πόλεις ἐρήμους 'cities in ruins' Is 61.4; *s* wisdom, τὰ πάντα Wi 7.27.

2. *to introduce for the first time*: + acc., παρανόμους ἐθισμούς 'unlawful customs' 2M 4.11.

Cf. καινός, ἐγ~, ἐπανακαινίζω, παλαιόω.

καινός, ή, όν.

brand new: *s* οἰκία 'house' De 20.5, ἀσκός 'skin bag' Jo 9.13, ἅμαξα 'chariot' 1K 6.7, ἱματίον 3K 11.29, θυσιαστήριον 1M 4.47; ὄνομα Is 65.15; heaven and earth, 65.17; gods, ~οὶ πρόσφατοι 'new, not previously known' De 32.17; καρδίαν ~ὴν καὶ πνεῦμα ~όν Ez 18.31, cf. καρδίαν ἑτέραν καὶ πνεῦμα ~όν 11.19; διαθήκη Je 38.31; ᾆσμα 'song' Ps 32.3, ὕμνος PSol 3.1; subst.n., ~ά 'new things' Is 42.9. Cf. καινότης, καινίζω, καινουργός, νέος, παλαιός: Trench 219-25.

καινότης, ητος.ʃ

newness: Ez 47.12; ἐπὶ ~ητος 'anew' 3K 8.53[a]. Cf. καινός.

καινουργός, όν.ʃ

inventing sth new: subst.m., βασάνων 'torturing instruments or methods' 4M 11.23. Cf. καινός.

καίπερ. conj.

1. *although*: + adding an explanatory gloss, 2M 4.34; Pr 6.8*c*, 4M 3.10; + ptc., 4M 12.2; + gen. abs., 3M 4.18, 4M 4.27.

2. *not only that which has been just said*: 3M 5.32.

καίριος, α, ον.ʃ

occurring at the right time, 'well-timed': *s* remark, Pr 15.23. Cf. καιρός, ἄκαιρος.

καιρός, οῦ. m.

1. *major division of the year*, 'season': signalled by the sun and the moon, and pl. Ge 1.14 (|| 'days' and 'years'); εἰς τὸν ~ὸν τοῦτον ἐν τῷ ἐνιαυτῷ τῷ ἑτέρῳ 'at this time next year' Ge 17.21; ὁ κ. χειμερινός '.. wintry' 2E 10.13.

2. *season when something regularly happens*: δώσω ὑετὸν ὑμῖν ἐν ~ῷ αὐτοῦ Le 26.4, ἐν ~ῷ τῆς ἀφέδρου αὐτῆς 'at the time of her menstruation' 15.25; τὸν οἶνόν μου ἐν ~ῷ αὐτοῦ 'my wine in its season' (|| καθ' ὥραν αὐτοῦ) Ho 2.9.

3. *historical, chronological period associated with particular events* or *circumstances*: ἐν τῷ ~ῷ ἐκείνῳ, alw. w. ref. to future, Am 5.13, Zp 3.16, 19, 20; Jl 3.1 + Jer 27.4 (|| ἐν ταῖς ἡμέραις ἐκείναις); κ. πονηρός 'evil era' Am 5.13, Mi 2.3; εἰς ~ὸν γήρους 'in old age' Ps 70.9.

4. *point in time suitable for something to happen* or *when it is expected to happen, right moment*: ἔτεκεν .. υἱὸν .. εἰς τὸν ~όν, καθὰ ἐλάλησεν αὐτῷ κύριος Ge 21.2, ἀπόδος .. εἰς ~όν 'repay .. on time' Si 29.2; καὶ ἐπὶ τοῦ ~οῦ τούτου 'on this occasion also' Ex

8.32; ἕως ~οῦ τικτούσης 'until the time when a woman gives birth' Mi 5.3; ἕως ~οῦ 'until an opportune moment' Si 1.22, 'for the time being' To 14.4 𝔊[I]; κ. τῷ παντὶ πράγματι Ec 3.1; ὅρασις εἰς ~όν 'the vision is meant for some future time' Hb 2.3; ἔσται ταῦτα εἰς ἡμέρας ~ῶν 'they have a message with long-term implications' Is 30.8 (|| ἕως εἰς τὸν αἰῶνα); ἐν τῷ παρεῖναι τὸν ~όν 'when the time comes' Hb 3.2; foll. by ὅταν, De 32.35 (|| ἡμέρα), Zp 3.20; κατὰ ~οὺς ὡρῶν 'at appropriate times(?)' Ex 13.10; κατὰ ~όν 'at the opportune moment' Jb 5.26 (|| καθ' ὥραν), Nu 23.23; οὐκ ἐπὶ ~οῦ 'not opportune' Jb 19.4; πρὸ ~οῦ 'in advance' 1M 6.36; πρὸ ~οῦ .. ἐν ~ῷ αὐτοῦ Si 51.30; τοῖς ~οῖς αὐτῶν 'in their time' To 14.4 𝔊[II]; ἀπὸ ~οῦ ἕως ~οῦ 'at regular intervals, i.e. once at a fixed time every day' Ez 4.10, 11, ἀπὸ ~οῦ εἰς ~όν 1C 9.25 (once at a fixed time every week); τρεῖς ~οὺς τοῦ ἐνιαυτοῦ 'on three occasions per year' Ex 23.14, 17, 34.23, 24, De 16.16, 3K 9.25, 2C 8.13ʃ, ~οὺς τρεῖς τῆς ἡμέρας Da 6.10 TH (LXX τρίς ..), cf. τρὶς τῆς ἡμέρας Rosetta Stone 40, ἐν ἡμέραις ~οῦ 'in festal seasons' Ba 1.14 (|| ἐν ἡμέρᾳ ἑορτῆς); + inf., οὐχ ἥκει ὁ κ. τοῦ οἰκοδομῆσαι .. 'the time for building .. has not come yet' Hg 1.2; εἰ κ. ὑμῖν μέν ἐστι τοῦ οἰκεῖν ἐν οἴκοις .. 'is it time for you to dwell ..' 1.4; ἐτήρει ~ὸν τοῦ ἀπατῆσαι αὐτήν 'he kept watching for a chance to seduce her' Ju 12.16; κ. τοῦ τεκεῖν καὶ κ. τοῦ ἀποθανεῖν Ec 3.2. **b**. What is going to happen is stated in a following, separate clause: κ. παντὸς ἀνθρώπου ἥκει .. καὶ ἰδοὺ ἐγὼ καταφθείρω αὐτοὺς .. Ge 6.13; with a v.n., ἐκδικήσεως 'for punishment' Je 27.27, 31. **c**. The foll. gen. (pers.) refers to his/her destiny: τοῦ ἐλθεῖν ~ὸν αὐτῆς Ez 22.3; αὐτῆς 'for her (to die)' 1K 4.20. **d**. gen.,= χρόνος, *a period of time*: πρὸς ~όν 'for now' Pr 5.3 (:: ὕστερον 'subsequently'), Wi 4.4, cf. πρόσκαιρος. **e**. || χρόνος (**2b**) sg. Ec 3.1, + χ. Da 7.12; pl., || χ. Wi 7.18, + χ. 8.8, Da 2.21.

Cf. χρόνος, ὅρος, ὥρα, ἀνοχή, ἄκαιρος, καίριος: Trench 209-12; Delling, *TDNT* 3.458f.; Barr 1962.32-44; Shipp 290-2; Trédé; Wilson; Eynikel and Hauspie 1997; Harl 2001.886.

καίτοι. adv.ʃ

and further: 4M 2.6, 5.18.

καίω: fut. καύσω, mid. καύσομαι, pass. καυθήσομαι, καήσομαι; aor.inf. καῦσαι, ptc. καύσας, pass. ἐκάην, inf. καῆναι, ptc. καυθείς.

1. *to start fire by igniting*, 'kindle': ***o*** ἔλαιον 'oil' Ex 27.21; ξύλα Le 6.12; λύχνος 24.3. **b**. ἐν ^ὅπλοις^ πῦρ '(by using the fallen enemy's) weapons (as firewood)' Ez 39.9², cf. ib.¹ without πῦρ. **c**. pass. and intr. 'to burn', ὁ βάτος καίεται πυρί, ὁ δὲ βάτος οὐ κατακαίεται 'the bramble is aflame, but the bramble is not burning out' Ex 3.2; ***s*** λύχνος 'lamp' 27.20; πῦρ Le 6.9, Is 4.5, 9.18*bis*, ἐφ' ὑμᾶς Je 15.14; λαμπάς Is 62.1; κάμινος 'furnace' Da 3.6, κλίβανος 'oven' Ho 7.4, ἡμέρα ἔρχεται καιομένη ὡς κλίβανος Ma 4.1; τὸ ὄρος ἐκαίετο πυρί De 4.11, 5.23, 9.15; φλόξ 'flame' Is 10.18, πῦρ 65.5; fig. θυμός 'wrath' 30.27, ὁ λόγος αὐτοῦ ὡς λαμπάς '.. as a torch' Si 48.1; fig., ***s*** hum. *to be on fire with vile passions*: Ps 7.14, cf. Ho 7.4, Si 23.17, Euth. ad loc. (PG 128.125), and BDAG s.v. πυρόω.

2. *to ignite*: ***o*** πῦρ Ex 35.3 (domestic fire), De 32.22 (|| ἐκκαίω), Je 7.18 (cultic); military action, πῦρ ἐν τείχει 30.16; λύχνους 'lamps' Ep Je 18.

3. *to set on fire*: + acc., human bones, 3K 13.2; pass., Je 7.20; ***o*** temple, To 14.4 𝔊[II].

4. *to raise the temperature of*, 'heat': ***o*** furnace, Da 3.19 LXX.

5. *to destroy by burning*: ***o*** καυθήσεται καλάμη ὑπὸ ἄνθρακος 'stubble is burnt off by coal' Is 5.24 (|| συγκαίω).

Cf. ἀνα~, ἀπο~, δια~, ἐγ~, κατα~, προσ~, συγ~, ὑποκαίω, καῦμα, πρόσκαυμα, καύσων, καῦσις, καυστικός, πυρίκαυστος, ἀνάπτω, πυρόω, πυρσεύω, φλέγω, φλογίζω, ἐμπρήθω.

κακηγορέω.ʃ

to speak evil of sbd: abs., 4M 9.14. Cf. κακο~, καταλογέω.

κακία, ας. f.

1. *moral evilness, vice*, alm. alw. pertaining to humans as indicated by a gen. pers. attached: || ἀδικία and manifested in treachery and falsehood (ψευδῆ, cf. Ho 7.3) 7.1; Jn 1.2; Na 3.19; Zc 7.10, 8.17 (c. gen. obj.); pl., *evil deeds*: αἱ ~αι τῶν ἀνθρώπων Ge 6.5, πάσας τὰς ~ας, ἃς ἐποίησαν De 31.18; Ho 7.2, 3 (|| ψεῦδος), 9.15*a*, 10.15; τὰς ~ας τῶν ἐπιτηδευμάτων αὐτῶν 'their malpractices' 9.15*b*.

***2**. *physically* or *materially hard* or *distressful circumstance*: cogn. dat., κακίᾳ κακώσητε αὐτούς 'you treat them harshly' Ex 22.23; τίνος ἕνεκεν ἡ κακία αὕτη ἐστὶν ἐν ἡμῖν; 'on whose account are we in these dire straits?' Jn 1.7; brought about by God as punishment, περὶ τῆς ~ας, ἧς εἶπεν ποιῆσαι τὸν λαὸν αὐτοῦ Ex 32.14; κ... ἣν κύριος οὐκ ἐποίησε Am 3.6; μετενόησεν ὁ θεὸς ἐπὶ τῇ ~ᾳ, ᾗ ἐλάλησε τοῦ ποιῆσαι αὐτοῖς 'God had a change of heart over the trouble he had said that he would cause them' Jn 3.10; μετανοῶν ἐπὶ ταῖς ~αις Jl 2.13, Jn 4.2; opp. ἀγαθωσύνη Ec 7.14.

3. *unpleasant, undesirable state*: κ. προσώπου 'stern, not cheerful look' Ec 7.3.

Cf. κακός, πονηρία, ἀγαθωσύνη: Trench 37-40.

κακίζω: aor.ptc.pass. κακισθείς.ʃ

to criticise: pass., ***o*** hum., 4M 12.2. Cf. ἐλέγχω.

κακοήθεια, ας. f.ʃ
wicked disposition: Es E 6 o' (*L* κακοποιΐα); hostile attitude, 3M 3.22, 7.3, 4M 1.4; ‖ θυμός 3.4. Cf. κακοήθης, κακία: Trench 37-40; Spicq 2.236f.

κακοήθης, ες.ʃ
malevolent: *s* διάθεσις 'disposition' 4M 1.25, πάθος 'passion' 2.16.

κακολογέω: fut. κακολογήσω.
to speak evil of: abs. 2K 16.5*L* (‖ καταράομαι vs. 7 and B here); + acc., πατέρα αὐτοῦ ἢ μητέρα αὐτοῦ Ex 21.16; θεούς 22.28 (‖ κακῶς λέγω); also + ὡς 2M 4.1. Cf. *ND* 2.88: διαβάλλω, δυσφημέω, κακηγορέω, καταλαλέω, λοιδορέω, εὐλογέω.

κακόμοχθος, ον.ʃ *
toiling for wrong purposes: *s* hum., Wi 15.8.

κακοπάθεια, ας. f.ʃ On the orthography, see Walters 45.
laborious, arduous toil: Ma 1.13; involved in compilation of a history, 2M 2.26; religious martyrdom, 4M 9.8. Cf. κακοπαθέω, μόχθος: Spicq 2.238-40.

κακοπαθέω: aor. ἐκακοπάθησα.ʃ
to strain oneself, suffer difficulties: ἐπί τι 'over sth', Jn 4.10. Cf. κακοπάθεια and κακός: Michaelis, *TDNT* 5.936f.

κακοποιέω: fut. ~ποιήσω; aor. ἐκακοποίησα, inf. ~ποιῆσαι, ptc. ~ποιήσας, subj. ~ποιήσω.
to cause harm to: abs., Is 11.9, Si 19.28; + acc. pers. Ge 31.7, 29, 1K 25.34 (:: ἀγαθόω, *L* καλῶς ποιέω); not material, Ge 43.6; financial loss, 2E 4.13; 4.15 (‖ ἐνοχλέω 1E 2.19); τοῖς χείλεσιν 'with the lips' Le 5.4 (of careless oaths and:: καλῶς ποιῆσαι, see also Je 4.22); Nu 35.23. Cf. κακός, κακοποιός, κακοποίησις, ἀγαθοποιέω.

κακοποίησις, εως. f.ʃ
v.n. of prec.: + dat. incom., 2E 4.22 (‖ ἐνοχλέω 1E 2.22), 3M 3.2.

κακοποιΐα, ας. f.ʃ
evil-doing: Es 7.23 *L* (o' κακοήθεια). Cf. κακοπραγία.

κακοποιός, όν.ʃ
doing ill: *s* hum., Pr 12.4; subst.m., ‖ ἁμαρτωλός 24.19. Cf. κακοποιέω and ἀγαθοποιός.

κακοπραγία, ας. f.ʃ
evil-doing: Wi 5.23. Cf. κακοποιΐα.

κακός, ή, όν.
1. *bad in effect*: ἡμέρα ~ή 'day of misfortune' Am 6.3. **b**. subst. n. pl. *misfortune, misery*: ~ὰ πολλὰ καὶ θλίψεις De 31.17, sim. Je 15.11; Am 9.4 (opp. ἀγαθά), 9.10, Mi 3.11; γινώσκω 'to experience' Mi 4.9; βλέπω Zp 3.15, cf. ἑώρων .. ἑαυτοὺς ἐν ~οῖς 'they realised that they were in trouble' Ex 5.19, sim. Es 7.7 o'; μὴ καταλάβῃ με τὰ ~ὰ καὶ ἀποθάνω Ge 19.19; euphemism for death, τὰ ~ὰ, ἃ εὑρήσει τὸν πατέρα μου 44.34, ποιήσει ~ά 'he might commit suicide' 2K 12.18, cf. μηδὲν πράξῃς σεαυτῷ ~όν Acts 16.28; brought about by God, κατέβη ~ὰ παρὰ κυρίου Mi 1.12; λογίζομαι κ. ἐπί τινα 2.3; *physical hardship*, Jn 4.6; εἰς ~ά 'to sbd's disadvantage, aiming at his misery' Zc 1.15; sg., τὴν ζωὴν καὶ τὸν θάνατον, τὸ ἀγαθὸν καὶ τὸ ~όν De 30.15.
2. *morally bad*: *s* πλεονεξία 'greed' Hb 2.9*a*, ἐπιθυμία 'desire' Pr 12.12 (:: ἀγαθή 11.23), καρδία Je 7.24; subst.n.sg., οὐκ οἴδασιν ἀγαθὸν οὐδὲ κακόν Nu 14.23, sim. De 1.39, Ps 33.15; m.pl. *evildoers, wicked people*, ἐκ χειρὸς ~ῶν Hb 2.9*b*; n.pl. subst. *evil deeds*, ἐργάζεσθαι Mi 2.1 (‖ κόποι), τὴν δικαιοσύνην μου καὶ τὰ ~ά σου Is 57.12; Jl 3.13. **b**. of action, *improper, unacceptable*: Ge 50.15 (‖ πονηρά vs. 17), Ma 1.8*bis*.
Cf. κακία, κακοπαθέω, κακοποιέω, κακόω, κάκωσις, μνησικακέω, πονηρός, φαῦλος, ἥσσων, χείρων, ἀγαθός, καλός: Schmidt 4.315f.; Trench 315-7.

κακοτεχνέω.ʃ
to use base tactics: κατὰ τούτων (pers.) .. τι .. πονηρόν 3M 7.9. Cf. κακότεχνος.

κακότεχνος, ον.ʃ
associated with base tactics: *s* ψυχή Wi 1.4; man's purpose, 15.4, ὄργανον '(torturing) device' 4M 6.25. Cf. κακοτεχνέω.

κακουργία, ας. f.
malice: Ps 34.17. **b**. *malicious deed*: 2M 3.32. Cf. κακοῦργος.

κακοῦργος, ον.ʃ
given to malpractices: *s* hum.,:: law-abiding, Es E 15, οἰκέτης 'servant' deserving torture and trial, Si 30.35; subst.m., 11.33; opp. δίκαιος, ὅσιος Pr 21.15. Cf. κακουργία.

κακουχέω: aor.pass. ἐκακουχήθην.ʃ
to maltreat: pass., *o* hum., 3K 2.26.

κακοφροσύνη, ης. f.ʃ *
ill will: Pr 16.18. Cf. κακόφρων.

κακόφρων, ον, gen. ονος.ʃ
bearing ill will: *s* hum., Pr 11.22, 19.19. Cf. δυσμενής, κακοφροσύνη.

κακόω: fut.act. κακώσω, pass. κακωθήσομαι; aor. ἐκάκωσα, subj. κακώσω, inf. κακῶσαι, ptc. κακώσας, opt.3s κακώσαι, pass. ἐκακώθην, inf. κακωθῆναι; pf. κεκάκωκα, inf.pass. κεκακῶσθαι.
to treat harshly, cause difficulty, harm: abs. Is 41.23 (:: εὖ ποιέω); + acc. pers. and *s* God, Ex 5.22, Nu 11.11 (‖ κάκωσις vs. 15), Zp 1.12 (:: ἀγαθοποιέω), Je 51.27 (:: ἀγαθόω), Zc 8.14 (:: καλῶς ποιέω); foreign masters, Ge 15.13 (‖ δουλόω, ταπεινόω), ἐν ἔργοις Ex 1.11, cf. De 26.6; harsh mistress, Ge 16.6; pass. Ps 105.32 (Moses' exclusion from Canaan), Ho 9.7, Zc 10.2; *o* προσήλυτον 'resident alien' Ex 22.21 (‖ θλίβω); χήραν καὶ ὀρφανόν

'a widow and an orphan' 22.22; + cogn. dat., κακίᾳ κακώσητε αὐτούς 22.23; ψυχήν w. ref. to a fast, Nu 29.7 (ǁ w. ταπεινόω Le 23.27), cf. Da 10.12 TH (LXX ταπεινοῦμαι); τὸν οἶκον αὐτοῦ Jb 20.26; by gossipping, 31.30, by calumny 4M 4.1. **b**. not unjustly, De 8.2.

Cf. κάκωσις, κακός, κακοποιέω, προκακόω, θλίβω, ἀγαθόω, ἀγαθοποιέω.

κακῶς. adv.

1. *in an offensive* or *hurtful manner*: κ. λέγω τινά 'to speak evil of sbd' Ex 22.28 (ǁ κακολογέω), Is 8.21; Le 19.14, 20.9; λαλέω 1M 7.42, ὀμνύω 'to swear' Wi 14.29, φρονέω 'to think' 14.30.

2. *in a distressful, painful way*: τοῦ κ. εἶναι ὑμῖν 'to end up in a bad way yourselves' Je 7.10 (opp. εὖ ᾖ ὑμῖν 7.23), τὸ κακῶς ἔχον '(sheep) which are sickly' Ez 34.4, κ. πάσχουσιν 'suffer badly' Wi 18.19, οἰμώξεις 'you regret (bitterly)' 4M 12.14.

3. *in a dishonourable way*: φρονέω 'to think' 4M 6.17.

Cf. κακός.

κάκωσις, εως. f.

1. *maltreatment*: + obj. gen., τοῦ λαοῦ μου τοῦ ἐν Αἰγύπτῳ Ex 3.7 (ǁ ὀδύνη); μου Nu 11.15 (ǁ ἐκάκωσας τὸν θεράποντά σου vs. 11); + subj. gen., τῶν Αἰγυπτίων Ex 3.17; ἄρτον ~εως De 16.3; + πόνος, πληγή Is 53.4. **b**. v.n. of κακόω, q.v., *causing hardships* (κακά): Je 11.14.

2. *distress felt and suffered*: ǁ πένθος Ba 5.1; opp. τρυφή 'pleasure' Si 11.27.

Cf. κακόω, ὀδύνη.

καλαβώτης, ου. m.ʃ *

spotted lizard, gecko: ritually unclean, Le 11.30, Pr 30.28.

κάλαθος, ου. m.ʃ

basket narrow at the base (LSJ): συκῶν 'for figs' Je 24.1, 2. Cf. ἄγγος.

καλαμάομαι: fut. ~μήσομαι; aor.inf. ~μήσασθαι.ʃ

to gather up left-overs after harvest: abs. ὀπίσω τρυγητῶν 'behind harvesters' Si 30.25; + acc. rei, τὰ ὀπίσω σου 'what you left behind' De 24.20, ἐλαίαν Is 24.13[1], ὡς ἄμπελον τὰ κατάλοιπα τοῦ Ισραηλ Je 6.9; *o* enemy troops still left to be destroyed, Jd 20.45. **b**. *to rob* sbd *of everything*: + acc. pers., Is 3.12 (*s* bailiffs), 24.13[2].

Cf. καλάμη.

καλάμη, ης. f.

1. *cut stalks of cereal plants left sticking up after harvest*, 'stubble': συναγαγεῖν ~ην εἰς ἄχυρα 'to gather stubble for straw' Ex 5.12 (as material for bricks); συνάγων ~ην ἐν ἀμήτῳ, of the hungry poor who are reduced to gathering mere stubble, ǁ ἐπιφυλλίδα ἐν τρυγήτῳ, Mi 7.1; inflammable, Jl 2.5, Ob 18, ὡς λαμπάδα πυρὸς ἐν ~η (ǁ ἐν ξύλοις) 'like a torch of fire in stubble' Zc 12.6; to be destroyed like stubble in fire as punishment, Ex 15.7, Ma 4.1; ~ στιππύου as a figure of sth frail, Is 1.31.

2. *straw*: Am 2.13.

Cf. καλαμάομα, καλάμημαι, καλάμινος: Schnebel 116-9.

καλάμημα, ατος. n.ʃ

gleanings: Je 29.10. Cf. καλάμη.

καλάμινος, η, ον.ʃ

of καλάμη (q.v.): *s* ῥάβδος 'staff' in a fig. of unreliable support, 4K 18.21 ǁ Is 36.6, Ez 29.6.

καλαμίσκος, ου. m.

**small, tube-shaped object*: branch of a lampstand, Ex 25.30; λυχνίας 25.31. Cf. κάλαμος, λυχνία.

κάλαμος, ου. m.

reed: εὐώδης 'fragrant' Ex 30.23; ἕλος ~ου καὶ παπύρου 'marsh of .. and papyrus' Is 19.6; μέτρου 'of measuring-line' Ez 40.3; reed-pen, Ps 44.2, + χαρτηρία 'papyrus' 3M 4.20. Cf. καλαμίσκος: Schnebel 115f.

καλέω: fut. καλέσω, pass. κληθήσομαι and κεκλήσομαι (the latter at Le 13.45, Ho 11.12 and alr. Homer); aor. ἐκάλεσα, subj. καλέσω, ptc. καλέσας, impv. κάλεσον, inf. καλέσαι, pass. ἐκλήθην, inf. κληθῆναι, ptc. κληθείς, subj. κληθῶ, opt.3pl κληθείησαν; pf. κέκληκα, pass. κέκλημαι, impv. pass.3s κεκλήσθω, ptc. κεκληκώς, pass. κεκλημένος.

1. *to give a name to, name* sbd or sth so and so with two acc.'s: ἐκάλεσεν ὁ θεὸς τὴν ξηρὰν γῆν 'God called the dry land earth' Ge 1.10. **b**. καλέω τὸ ὄνομά τινός τι 'to determine sbd's name as so and so': κ. τὸ ὄνομα αὐτοῦ Ισμαηλ 'name him Ishmael' Ge 16.11, sim. Ho 1.6, 9; Ge 26.20 (ǁ ἐπονομάζω vs. 21), ἐκάλεσά σε τὸ ὄνομά σου Is 43.1; pass., ἐκλήθη τὸ ὄνομα αὐτῆς Σύγχυσις 'its name was called Confusion' Ge 11.9. **c**. καλέω ὄνομα + dat., 'give a name to', ὀνόματα πᾶσιν τοῖς κτήνεσιν 'to all the animals' Ge 2.20, sim. Ps 146.4; ἐκάλεσεν ὄνομα τῇ πόλει Φρέαρ ὅρκου Ge 26.33; without ὄνομα and pass., σοὶ κληθήσεται Θέλημα ἐμόν 'you shall be called "My desire"' Is 62.4; 65.15, Jd 18.12 A. **d**. + ἐν 'after': ἐν Ισαακ κληθήσεταί σοι σπέρμα 'your offspring will be called after Isaac' Ge 21.12; ἐπὶ τῷ ὀνόματί τινος 48.6, Si 36.17.

2. *to refer to sbd verbally as* sth (w. double objs): ἀκάθαρτος κεκλήσεται Le 13.45; κληθήσονται .. υἱοὶ θεοῦ ζῶντος 'will be called sons of the living God' Ho 1.10, sim. 2.16, 11.12, Zc 8.3, 11.7*bis*; ὁ οἶκός μου οἶκος προσευχῆς κληθήσεται πᾶσιν τοῖς ἔθνεσιν 'my house will be known to all the nations as a house of prayer' Is 56.7; τῷ ὀνόματι Ισραηλ 48.1. **b**. w. ref. to a nickname: 1M 2.3 (ǁ vs. ἐπι~ 2). Cf. προσαγορεύω **2**.

3. *to call upon, summon* sbd or sth (acc.): so as to perform some task, εἰς πένθος 'for mourning' Am 5.16, εἰς γυμνασίαν 4M 11.20, ἐπὶ βοήθειαν 'for help' 1M 11.47; πρὸς τὴν ἔξοδον 'to march out' 3M 5.26; τὴν δίκην ἐν πυρί 'the judgement by means of fire' Am 7.4; for questioning, Ge 12.18, 24.57, 26.9; for making an announcement, 20.8 (τοὺς παῖδας); πάντας τοὺς ἐξηγητὰς Αἰγύπτου καὶ πάντας σοφοὺς αὐτῆς 41.8; πᾶσαν γερουσίαν Ισραηλ Ex 12.21; ὀνόματι 'by name' Es 2.14 o'; + dat. com., θέλεις καλέσω σοι γυναῖκα .. 'Do you wish me to call a woman for you ..?' Ex 2.7; To 5.9 𝔊[II]; καταρᾶσθαι τὸν ἐχθρόν μου 'in order to have my enemies cursed' Nu 24.10; for help, πρὸς ἐμέ Is 21.12, ἐπί τινα (so as to attack) Ez 38.21; ἔμπροσθεν ἐμοῦ 2E 4.18.

4. *to accost, address* sbd (acc.): ἐκάλεσεν κύριος .. τὸν Αδαμ Ge 3.9; ἐκάλεσεν ἄγγελος τοῦ θεοῦ τὴν Αγαρ ἐκ τοῦ οὐρανοῦ 21.17; πρὶν ἢ γνῶναι τὸ παιδίον καλεῖν πατέρα ἢ μητέρα 'before the child has learned to address his father or mother' Is 8.4; πάντας ἐπ' ὀνόματι καλέσει 'he will call everyone by name' 40.26; εἰς εἰρήνην 'to make peace' Jd 21.13; μάχαιραν .. ἐπὶ τοὺς καθημένους ἐπὶ τῆς γῆς Je 32.15. **b**. the acc. pers. understood: ἐπὶ τῷ ὀνόματί μου Κύριος ἐναντίον σου 'as one bearing the name "the Lord" ..' Ex 33.19; τῷ ὀνόματι κυρίου 34.5. **c**. with double acc.: καλέσει σε τὸ ὄνομα σου τὸ καινόν Is 62.2.

5. *to proclaim publicly as*: κληθήσεται ἁγία Ex 12.16.

6. *to invite as guest*: + acc. pers. Ex 34.15; ἐπὶ τὰς θυσίας Nu 25.2 (cf. BDAG s.v. καλέω **2**, ἐπὶ θυσίαν ὑπὸ τῶν μαθητῶν κληθῆναι), εἰς τὸν γάμον 'to the wedding' To 9.5 𝔊[II], cf. ἐπὶ τὴν ἀπόδειξιν τῆς ἱστορίας 'to the exposition of the story' 4M 3.19.

*__7__. *to proclaim* a public event: abs.(?) Le 23.21 (cf. *BA* and Wevers ad loc.); + acc., κληταὶ ἅγίαι, ἃς καλέσετε αὐτὰς ἐν τοῖς καιροῖς αὐτῶν 'holy convocations which you shall convene in their seasons' 23.4; κλαυθμὸν καὶ κοπετὸν καὶ ξύρησιν καὶ ζῶσιν σάκκων 'weeping, mourning, shaving and wearing of sackcloths' Is 22.12; νηστείαν 'fast' 58.5, 3K 20.12 (|| κηρύσσω 2C 20.3, Jn 3.5), ἐνιαυτὸν κυρίου δεκτόν Is 61.2; ἄφεσιν 'emancipation (of slaves)' Je 41.8. Cf. καλέσατε ἐπ' αὐτοὺς ἀπώλειαν Je 30.7, λιμὸν ἐπὶ τὴν γῆν 'a famine ..' 4K 8.1, and ἐκάλεσεν ἐπ' ἐμὲ καιρὸν συντρῖψαι .. 'a time for crushing ..' La 1.15. Cf. κηρύσσω **2**. A Hebraism for קָרָא qal?

8. *to invoke*: + acc., ὄνομα κυρίου De 32.3.

*__9__. in the phrase κ. τὸ ὄνομά τινος ἐπί τι (or τινα), *to call sth* or *sbd after sbd, to attach his name to it*, indicating his claim on, ownership or protection of it: τὸ ὄνομα τὸ σόν κεκλήσθω ἐφ' ἡμᾶς Is 4.1, κληθῇ τὸ ὄνομά μου ἐπὶ ^τὴν πόλιν^ 2K 12.28. Cf. ἐπικαλέω and ὀνομάζω.

10. *to call out* sbd's name to identify with him: + acc., τὸ ὄνομά σου Is 45.4.

Cf. ἐπικαλέω, ἐπίκλητος, κλητός, μετακαλέω, μεταπέμπομαι, προσκαλέομαι, συγκαλέω, ὄνομα, (ἐπ)ονομάζω, φωνέω: Cerunda 1975, esp. 450-2.

καλλιόω: aor.pass. ἐκαλλιώσθην.ʃ *

to make more beautiful: pass., ***o*** woman's breasts, Ct 4.10. Cf. καλός.

καλλίπαις, δος.m./f.ʃ

one who is blessed with beautiful children: ***s*** mother, 4M 16.10.

κάλλιστος: ⇒ καλός.

καλλονή, ῆς. f.

1. = κάλλος: Ps 77.61; applied to Israel, 46.5; || κάλλος Wi 13.3; μέγεθος καὶ κ. κτισμάτων 'magnitude and .. of creatures' 13.5; w. ref. to the Jerusalem Temple, 1M 2.12 (|| δόξα).

2. *generosity*: Si 34.23.

3. *good manners*: Si 4.23¶.

Cf. κάλλος, ὡραιότης.

κάλλος, ους. n.

1. *beauty*, 'good looks': of sth, Ge 49.21; θέα πλοίων ~ους 'sight of beautiful ships' Is 2.16, στέφανος ~ους 'crown ..' 62.3; κυπαρίσσου 'of cypresses' 37.24; of a hum. Ps 44.4 (+ ὡραιότης), De 33.17; of woman, Ez 16.14, καλὴ τῷ εἴδει καὶ τῷ ~ει 1E 4.18; κ. ἀλλότριον 'sbd else's pretty wife' Si 9.8b. **b**. *beautiful costume*: Ez 27.3.

2. *delight, pleasure*: symbolic name of a staff, Zc 11.7.

Cf. καλός and ὡραιότης.

κάλλυνθρον, ου. n.ʃ *

palm-*frond* (LSG s.v.): φοινίκων Le 23.40.

καλλωπίζω: aor.mid. ἐκαλλωπισάμην; pf.ptc.pass. κεκαλλωπισμένος.ʃ

to make look beautiful: mid. ***s*** woman, Ge 38.14 (harlot); εἰς ἀπάντησιν ὀφθαλμῶν ἀνδρῶν 'to catch the eye of men' Ju 10.4. **b**. pass.: ***o*** girls, Ps 143.12 (|| κοσμέω); idols, ἀργυρίῳ καὶ χρυσίῳ Je 10.4; heifer (δάμαλις) 26.20.

Cf. καλός, κοσμέω: Schmidt 4.221-4.

καλοκἀγαθία, ας. f.

perfect nobleness of character: the highest ideal of human existence, 4M 1.10, cf. καλὸν καὶ ἀγαθὸν ἄνδρα 4.1.

κάλος, ου. m.ʃ

cord: Nu 3.37, 4.32.

καλός, ή, όν. Comp. καλλίων; superl. κάλλιστος.

1. *advantageous, beneficial, desirable*: ἐν γήρει ~ῷ 'in good old age' Ge 15.15; δῶρον ~όν 30.20; ἔτος 'year (of good harvest)' 41.35; οἱ λόγοι αὐτοῦ εἰσι ~οί Mi 2.7, ῥήματα ~ά Zc 1.13, cf. Mi 3.2; *s* temple fixtures, Jl 3.5 (|| ἐπίλεκτος 'choice'); εἴ τι ~ὸν αὐτοῦ Zc 9.17 (|| ἀγαθός); + εἰς 'for the purpose of,' καλὸν τὸ ξύλον εἰς βρῶσιν Ge 3.6. **b**. neuter: εἰ ~ὸν ἐνώπιον ὑμῶν ἐστι 'if you please, if it meets your approval' Zc 11.12; w. inf. as subj., Οὐ ~ὸν εἶναι τὸν ἄνθρωπον μόνον Ge 2.18, ~ὸν τὸ ἀποθανεῖν με ἢ ζῆν με 'it is better for me to die than to stay alive' Jn 4.3, sim. 4.8; ~ὸν σκέπη 'a shade is good' Ho 4.13 (w. lack of concord); πᾶς ποιῶν πονηρόν, ~ὸν ἐνώπιον κυρίου Ma 2.17; πονηρὰ ἀντὶ ~ῶν Ge 44.4. **c**. *of good quality*: *s* offering to God and opp. πονηρός, Le 27.10, 12, 14; ἡ γῆ .. εἰ ~ή ἐστιν ἢ πονηρά Nu 13.20; meal, To 2.1.

2. *morally good and acceptable*: γνωστὸν ~οῦ καὶ πονηροῦ 'knowable of good and evil' Ge 2.9; γινώσκοντες ~ὸν καὶ πονηρόν 3.5; ποιῆσαι .. ~ὸν ἢ κακόν Nu 24.13; ἐκζητήσατε τὸ ~ὸν καὶ μὴ τὸ πονηρόν Am 5.14, μεμισήκαμεν τὰ πονηρὰ καὶ ἠγαπήκαμεν τὰ ~ά 5.15, cf. Mi 3.2; τί ~όν; 6.8; τὸ ἀρεστὸν καὶ τὸ ~ὸν ἔναντι κυρίου De 6.18 (|| τὸ κ. καὶ τὸ ἀ. 12.25, 28, 13.18); καλὸν καὶ ἀγαθὸν ἄνδρα 4M 4.1, cf. καλοκἀγαθία. **b**. subst.m. καλὸς καὶ ἀγαθός: perfect gentleman or person of impeccable character To 9.6 𝔊[II], cf. 5.14, 7.6, 2M 15.12. **c**. w. inf. as subj., καλόν ἐστιν ἔναντι κυρίου εὐλογεῖν Nu 24.1.

3. *good and pleasing in appearance, beautiful*: *s* heavenly luminaries, Ge 1.4 (cf. Alexandre 92f.), ῥάβδος 'staff' Zc 11.10; τὸ κάλλιστον τοῦ τραχήλου αὐτῆς 'the fairest part of her neck' Ho 10.11; a female, αἱ παρθένοι αἱ ~αί Am 8.13, πόρνη ~ή Na 3.4; Ge 12.14 (|| εὐπρόσωπος, vs. 11); ~ὴ τῇ ὄψει 'good-looking' 24.16, τῷ εἴδει καὶ τῷ κάλλει 1E 4.18; a male, καλὸς τῷ εἴδει καὶ ὡραῖος τῇ ὄψει Ge 39.6; animals, βόες ~αὶ τῷ εἴδει 41.2 (:: αἰσχρός 'ugly' vs. 3).

4. *conducive to pleasure and enjoyment*, 'delightful, pleasant': *s* fellowship Ps 132.1 (|| τερπνός).

Cf. καλῶς, κάλλος, καλλιόω, ἀγαθός, ἐλεήμων, χρηστός, εὐειδής, εὔμορφος, εὐπρεπής, ὡραῖος, καλλωκακός, συμφέρω, αἰσχρός, κακός, πονηρός: Shipp 296; Grundmann, *TDNT* 3.543f.

κάλπη, ης. f.ʃ *

pitcher: for carrying water in, 4M 3.12. Cf. ἀσκός, ὑδρία.

κάλυμμα, ατος. n.

that which makes invisible what lies behind or *inside*, 'screen, curtain, veil': τῇ πύλῃ τῆς αὐλῆς κ. 'for the gate of the courtyard ..' Ex 27.16; ἐπὶ τὸ πρόσωπον αὐτοῦ κ. 34.33; κ. καὶ κατακάλυμμα Nu 3.25; δερμάτινον ὑακίνθινον 'leather, blue-coloured' 4.8; 'armour' 1M 4.6, + θώραξ, ὅπλα 6.2. Cf. κατακάλυμμα, καλύπτω, θέριστρον, σιώπησις.

κάλυξ, υκος. f.ʃ

cup or *calyx of a flower*: ῥόδου 'rosebud' Wi 2.8.

καλυπτήρ, ῆρος. m.ʃ

that which covers sth, 'cover': of altar, Ex 27.3; τὸν ~ῆρα ἐπιθήσει ἐπὶ τὸ θυσιαστήριον Nu 4.13; 4.14. Cf. καλύπτω: Frankel *Einfl*. 97, 185; Gooding 60f.

καλύπτω: fut. καλύψω, pass. καλυφθήσομαι; aor. ἐκάλυψα, inf. καλύψαι, impv. κάλυψον, subj. καλύψω; pf.3s. κεκάλυφεν (!) Nu 22.11.

1. *to place* sth *over the entire surface of*: πόντῳ ἐκάλυψεν αὐτούς 'covered them with the ocean' Ex 15.5, καλύψουσιν ^τὴν τράπεζαν^ καλύμματι δερματίνῳ '.. with a covering of hide' Nu 4.8, αὐτὰ χαλκῷ 'them [= the horns of an altar] with copper' Ex 27.2, δάκρυσι τὸ θυσιαστήριον κυρίου καὶ κλαυθμῷ καὶ στεναγμῷ 'to cover the Lord's altar with tears and wailing and groans' Ma 2.13; πᾶν τὸ πρόσωπον τῆς γῆς ἐν τοῖς ποσὶν τῆς δυνάμεώς μου '.. with the feet of my soldiers' Ju 2.7, ἐν ἅρμασιν καὶ ἱππεῦσιν καὶ πεζοῖς ἐπιλέκτοις 'with chariots, cavalry, and picked foot soldiers' 2.19, τὴν ξηρὰν ἐν δολιότητι 'the dry land with deception' Si 37.3, ψυχῇ παντὸς ζῴου τὸ πρόσωπον ^τῆς γῆς^ '.. with the soul of every kind of living being' 16.30; στόμα ἀσεβῶν 'the mouth(s) of the impious' (to make them speechless)' Pr 10.6. **b**. in order to hide an obj. (underneath): ἀσχημοσύνην 'private parts' Ex 28.38; τοῦ μὴ καλύπτειν τὴν ἀσχημοσύνην αὐτῆς 'so that she will not cover up her pudenda' Ho 2.9, ἱμάτιον .. καλύπτων ἀσχημοσύνην Si 29.21 (the ptc. concording with the immediately prec. οἶκος); καλύψατε ἡμᾶς Ho 10.8, cf. Hom., *Il*. 10.29; ἥλιον ἐν νεφέλῃ καλύψω Ez 32.7; τοῦ μὴ καλύψαι αὐτό [= τὸ αἷμα] 24.8, but cf. τοῦ καλύψαι ἐπ' αὐτὸ γῆν 'to spread soil on it' vs. 7, ἐκάλυψεν (sc. ἡ γῆ) ἐπὶ τὴν συναγωγὴν Αβιρων Ps 105.17; obj. understood and fig. μὴ καλύψῃς ἐπὶ ἀνομίαν 'don't overlook iniquity' Ne 4.6; τὴν ἀνομίαν μου οὐκ ἐκάλυψε Ps 31.5 (|| ἐγνώρισα), cf. ἐκάλυψας πάσας τὰς ἁμαρτίας αὐτῶν 84.3 (|| ἀφῆκας 'you forgave,' cf. 31.1); κάλυψον τὰ προστάγματα καὶ σφράγισον .. '.. and seal ..' Da 12.4 LXX; ἔχθραν 'hostility,' opp. ἐκφέρω 'bring into the open' Pr 10.18. **c**. in order to ensure safe passage over the surface: + λάκκον (into which a human or animal might fall) Ex 21.33. **d**. so as to protect: ἀπὸ τοῦ ὑετοῦ 'against rain' Ez 40.43; Si 40.27.

2. *to extend over* an entire surface: καλύψει τὴν ὄψιν τῆς γῆς 'it [= the locusts] will cover the surface of the earth' Ex 10.5, sim. Nu 22.11 (|| κατακαλύπτω vs. 5), ἐκάλυψεν ἡ νεφέλη τὸ ὄρος 'the cloud covered the mount' Ex 24.15, ἐκάλυψεν ἡ νεφέλη τὴν σκηνήν '.. the tent' Nu 9.15, ἐκάλυψεν ὄρη ἡ σκιὰ αὐτῆς 'its shade ..' Ps 79.11; ἐκάλυψεν αὐτοὺς θάλασσα Ex 15.10, cf. Ps 105.11; καλύψῃ ἡ λέπρα πᾶν τὸ δέρμα 'the leprosy covers the entire skin' Le 13.12. **b.** *to spread, to affect* - mostly not favourably - *altogether*: ὁ βάτραχος .. ἐκάλυψεν τὴν γῆν Αἰγύπτου 'the frogs ..' Ex 8.6, ἐκάλυψεν τὸ πρόσωπον τῆς γῆς Χαναan λιμός 'a famine ..' Ju 5.10; σκότος καὶ γνόφος καλύψει γῆν ἐπ' ἔθνη Is 60.2 (on the force of ἐπί, see s.v. **III 7**), fig. ἐκάλυψέν με σκότος Ps 54.6; ἀσέβεια τοῦ Λιβάνου καλύψει σε 'you will be wholly tainted by the ungodliness of Lebanon,' but, without ref. to the Heb., the meaning could be 'the ungodliness perpetrated against Lebanon will overwhelm you, cover you' (cf. Th and Thdt ad loc) Hb 2.17; ἐκάλυψεν οὐρανοὺς ἡ ἀρετὴ αὐτοῦ (|| πλήρης) 3.3; * + ἐπί τι (Hebraism?; so Ps 105.17), καλύψει ἀσέβεια ἐπὶ τὰ ἐνδύματα αὐτοῦ 'ungodliness will fasten itself to all his clothing' Ma 2.16; fig. καλύψει σε αἰσχύνη 'a sense of shame will overwhelm you' Ob 10, ἐκάλυψεν ἐντροπὴ τὸ πρόσωπόν μου 'shame ..' Ps 68.8, καλύψει αὐτοὺς θάμβος 'astonishment ..' Ez 7.18.

Cf. ἀνα~, ἀπο~, ἐπι~, κατα~, συγ~, ὑποκαλύπτω, κάλυμμα, καλυπτήρ, σκιάζω, σκεπάζω: Anz 15f.; Spicq 2.224-50.

καλῴδιον, ου. n. On the spelling, see Katz 70.

(small) cord: for tying, Jd 15.13.

καλῶς. adv.

1. *in a manner beneficial and pleasing* to the other party: ἐχρησάμεθά σοι κ. 'we treated you well' Ge 26.29, cf. Est 2.9; κακοποιῆσαι ἢ κ. ποιῆσαι Le 5.4; Je 4.22. **b.** κ. ἐστί τινι 'sbd is well-off, is doing well': κ. ἔσται ὑμῖν 4K 25.24, μακάριος εἶ καὶ κ. σοι ἔσται Ps 127.2, κ. μοι ἦν τότε ἢ νῦν 'I was better off then than now' Ho 2.7; κ. ἔχειν 'to be in your best interest' 1E 2.18; ingressive, κ. γένοιτο Ῥωμαίοις 1M 8.23; caus., κ. ὑμῖν ποιήσω 'I shall deal with you well' Zp 3.20, cf. κ. ποιῆσαι τὴν Ιερουσαλημ Zc 8.15. **c.** to one's own advantage: ἔπραττον καλῶς 'were thriving' 4M 3.20; κατοικοῦσα κ. τὰς πόλεις αὐτῆς '.. in comfort' Mi 1.11; σφόδρα κ. ἀκούων 'being very well spoken-of' 2M 14.37.

2. *in a manner meeting the speaker's approval*: θάψον με κ. 'Give me a proper burial' To 4.3 $\mathfrak{G}^{II}$; κ. ἑόρακας Je 1.12, κ. ἐλάλησας Es 6.10 o'. **b.** κ. ποιέω in this sequence and nothing intervening except a particle in between: κ. ἐποίησας ὅτι ἐγενήθη ἐπὶ τὴν καρδίαν σου 'you did well to consider such a thing' 3K 8.18; esp. + ptc., κ. ποιήσετε ἀντιφωνήσαντες 'you will do well to respond' 1M 12.18, sim. 12.22, 2M 2.16, κ. οὖν ποιήσετε μὴ προσχρησάμενοι (*L* .. ποιήσατε μὴ προσέχοντες) '.. not to implement (heed)' Es E 17 o'; w. πράττω - , κ. καὶ ἀστείως πράττων 'acting well and properly' 2M 12.43. **c.** elliptically, poss. for κ. εἶπας or suchlike, 'Done!, Agreed!': 3K 2.18; κ. ἐγὼ ⌈B: ἐ. κ.⌉ διαθήσομαι .. 2K 3.13 *L*, so poss. Ge 32.13. **d.** the other party's approval: κ. πεπεισμένοι 'convinced' 3M 3.24.

3. *in an aesthetically or artistically pleasing manner and conducive to pleasure*: κ. ψάλατε 'Sing well' Ps 32.3, κιθάρισον 'play the lyre' Is 23.16, διαβαίνει 'walks (gracefully)' Pr 30.29.

Cf. καλός, εὐτελῶς, κακῶς.

κάμαξ, ακος.f.ʃ

shaft of a spear: 2M 5.3.

καμάρα, ας. f.ʃ

vaulted ceiling: στήσας ὡς ~αν τὸν οὐρανόν Is 40.22. Cf. LSG s.v.

καμηλοπάρδαλις, εως. f.ʃ

camelopard, giraffe: ritually clean food, De 14.5.

κάμηλος, ου. m./f.

camel: part of nomad's possessions, ἐγένετο αὐτῷ πρόβατα καὶ μόσχοι καὶ ὄνοι, παῖδες καὶ παιδίσκαι, ἡμίονοι καὶ ~οι Ge 12.16; 24.35 (also "silver and gold"); || κτῆνος, ἵππος, ὑποζύγιον, βοῦς, πρόβατον Ex 9.3; used in war as beast of burden, Zc 14.15 (|| ἵππος, ἡμίονος, and ὄνος), Ju 2.17; used for transport in a desert and + ὄνος Is 30.6; as a mount, 21.6 (|| ὄνος); its meat forbidden as food, Le 11.4.

καμιναία, ας. f.ʃ *

furnace: αἰθάλη ~ας 'soot of furnace' Ex 9.8 (unlikely an adj.), 10. Cf. κάμινος.

κάμινος, ου. f.

furnace: ἀτμὶς ~ου 'steam out of a furnace' Ge 19.28, Si 22.24; καπνὸς ~ου 'smoke ..' Ex 19.18; ἐκ τῆς ~ου τῆς σιδηρᾶς 'out of the iron furnace' De 4.20 (of the bondage of Egypt), sim. Je 11.4, πυρός Da 3.6; fig. of harship and distress, πτωχείας 'of poverty' Is 48.10, ταπεινώσεως Si 2.5. Cf. καμιναία.

καμμύω: fut. καμμύσω; aor. ἐκάμμυσα, inf. καμμύσαι.ʃ *

to close the eyes in order not to see: ***o*** eyes, μήποτε ἴδωσι τοῖς ὀφθαλμοῖς Is 6.10, sim. 33.15; sbd else's eyes, 29.10. **b.** *to close the eyes of*: + acc. hum., La 3.45 (Zgl κάμψαι).

Cf. ἀνοίγω: Shipp 297.

κάμνω: aor.ptc. καμών; pf.ptc. κεκμηκως.

1. *to be* or *grow weary*: τῇ ψυχῇ Jb 10.1 (|| στένω); 17.2, Wi 15.9; *s* sinews, 4M 6.13.

2. *to die*: aor., *s* hum., Wi 4.16; pres., 15.9.

Cf. κοπιάω, ἀποθνήσκω: Schmidt 2.615-20, 3.698f.; Spicq 2.251-3.

κάμπη, ης. f.∫
caterpillar: natural calamity, ἀμπελῶνας ὑμῶν .. κατέφαγεν ἡ κ. 'your vineyards were eaten by caterpillars' Am 4.9; ‖ ἀκρίς Jl 1.4; ‖ ἀκρίς, βροῦχος, ἐρυσίβη 2.25. Cf. ἀκρίς: Shipp 297.

καμπή, ῆς. f.∫
bend of a road: Ne 3.24, 31.

κάμπτω: fut. κάμψω; aor. ἔκαμψα, subj. κάμψω, inf. κάμψαι, ptc. κάμψας, impv. κάμψον, pass. ἐκάμφθην, inf. καμφθῆναι.
to bend: + acc., τὰ γόνατα 1E 8.70 (worshipping posture); τὰ γ. understood, 2C 29.29; τράχηλον 'neck' Is 58.5, Si 7.23, 30.12¶ (fig. of submission). **b**. metaph. *to suppress the will to assert itself*: + acc., ἰσχύν Si 38.18, 30. **c**. *to bring to submission, subjugate*: τινα 2K 22.40 B, La 3.45, Jb 9.13. **d**. *to bend oneself* or *itself*: powerless and defeated, Jd 5.27 A (‖ συγ~), 4K 9.24; ἐπὶ τὰ γόνατα '(to go down) on one's knees (to drink water from a river)' Jd 7.5 A (B: κλίνω); honorific salutation, 4K 1.13; κάμπτων ἐπὶ τὰ γόνατα αὐτοῦ καὶ προσευχόμενος 'was down on his knees, praying' Da TH 6.10; pass. in the same sense, + προσκυνέω Es 3.1 *L*; metaph., τῇ κακοηθείᾳ 'to malice' 4M 3.4 (‖ δουλεύομαι vs. 2); *s* γόνυ - ἐμοὶ κάμψει πᾶν γόνυ 'every knee shall bow to me' Is 45.23; κ. γόνυ as a phrasal verb, γόνατα, ἃ οὐκ ἔκαμψαν (B: ὤκλασαν) γόνυ τῇ Βααλ 3K 19.18*L*.
Cf. δια~, κατα~, συγκάμπτω, κλίνω, ὀκλάζω: Schmidt 3.267-76; Schlier, *TDNT* 3.594f.

καμπύλος, η, ον.∫
curved: ‖ σκολιός 'crooked,' *s* τροχιά 'path' Pr 2.15. Cf. σκαμβός, σκολιός, εὐθύς, ὀρθός: Schmidt 4.461f.

κἄν: crasis for καὶ ἄν or καὶ ἐάν, q.v.

κάνθαρος, ου. m.∫
dung-beetle (LSJ): ~ος ἐκ ξύλου φθέγξεται αὐτά '.. will speak out of the timber' Hb 2.11. See Muraoka 1991.213f.; Lee 1969.240.

κανθός, οῦ. m.∫
corner of the eye: To 11.13.

κανοῦν, νοῦ. < κάνεον; dat.sg., κανῷ, pl.nom./ acc. κανᾶ. n.
basket of reed or *cane*: containing food, χονδριτῶν 'of bread made of coarse meal' Ge 40.16; ἀζύμων 'of unleavened bread' Le 8.2, Nu 6.15; Jd 6.19 A (B: κόφινος). Cf. ἄγγος, θῖβις, κόφινος.

κανών, όνος. m.∫
1. *a piece of squared timber of fair length*, 'beam': σὴς ἐκτρώγων καὶ βαδίζων ἐπὶ ~όνος 'a moth eating away and walking on a beam (?)' Mi 7.4; κ. κλίνης 'bedpost' Ju 13.6.
2. *set of principles and rules*: τῆς φιλοσοφίας 4M 7.21. Cf. *ND* 1.44f.

κάπηλος, ου. m.∫
1. *tradesman*: Si 26.29 (‖ ἔμπορος).
2. *proprietor of a pub* or *wine merchant*: Is 1.22. Cf. καπηλεῖον 'tavern, pub.'
Cf. ἔμπορος: Windisch, *TDNT* 3.603-5; Spicq 2.254-7; Drexhage.

καπνίζω: fut. καπνίσω, pass. καπνισθήσομαι; aor. inf. καπνίσαι, impv. κάπνισον.
1. *to emit smoke*: pass., *s* κλίβανος 'furnace' Ge 15.17; Mount Sinai, Ex 19.18 ‖ act. τὸ ὄρος τὸ καπνίζον 20.18; pass., τῶν ξύλων τῶν δαλῶν τῶν καπνιζομένων 'the burning, smoking wooden sticks' Is 7.4.
2. *to burn so as to cause to emit smoke*: + acc. (organs of fish), To 6.8.
Cf. καπνός: Anz 16.

καπνός, οῦ. m.
smoke: ἀνέβαινεν ὁ κ. ὡς κ. καμίνου 'like the smoke of a furnace' Ex 19.18; ἀτμίδα ~οῦ 'steamy smoke (?)' Jl 2.30; ἐκκαύσω ἐν ~ῷ .. 'I will burn up .. in the smoke' Na 2.14; of a signal-fire or of conquered, burning cities, Is 14.31; symb. of anger, θυμοῦ 65.5, ἐν ὀργῇ Ps 17.9, of fleeting existence, 36.20, 101.4, Wi 2.2. Cf. καπνίζω.

κάππαρις, εως. f.∫
caper-plant: Ec 12.5.

καρδία, ας. f.
1. 'heart' *as an internal organ of a living organism*: of fish, To 6.5; of hum., ἡ ῥομφαία αὐτῶν εἰσέλθοι εἰς τὴν ~αν αὐτῶν 'May their sword penetrate their hearts' Ps 36.15; διαρρήξω συγκλεισμὸν ~ας αὐτῶν 'I will tear apart the joints of their hearts' Ho 13.8, cf. διαρρήξατε τὰς ~ας ὑμῶν καὶ μὴ τὰ ἱμάτια ὑμῶν 'Rend your hearts, and not your clothes' Jl 2.13; ἐτάζων ~ας καὶ νεφροὺς ὁ θεός 'God scrutinises hearts and kidneys' Ps 7.10; κύριε κρίνων δίκαια δοκιμάζων νεφροὺς καὶ ~ας Je 11.20, 20.12, sim. 12.3, Ps 16.3. **b**. partly metaph.: "I shall pull out the stony heart from their flesh (σάρξ) and give them heart of flesh (~αν σαρκίνην)" Ez 11.19.
2. *centre, midst*: βάθη ~ας θαλάσσης 'the depths of the midst of the sea' Jn 2.4; Pr 23.34; δένδρου '(thick foliage) of a tree' 2K 18.14*L*. Cf. κόλπος, μέσος.
3. *seat where human thoughts, intentions and attitudes are generated and take shape*: διανοεῖται ἐν τῇ ~ᾳ αὐτοῦ Ge 6.5, ἡ κ. αὐτοῦ μάταια νοήσει Is 32.6, νοῆσαι τῇ ~ᾳ 44.18; ἀπὸ καρδίας αὐτῶν λαλοῦσιν 'they speak their own thoughts' Je 23.16, sim. Ez 13.3; ἐν καθαρᾷ ~ᾳ 'with clear conscience' Ge 20.5; οἱ εὐθεῖς τῇ ~ᾳ 'the upright of heart' Ps 63.11 +; παντὶ συνετῷ ~ᾳ δέδωκα σύνεσιν 'I have given understanding to everyone intelligent of mind'

Ex 31.6; ᾧ ἔδωκεν ὁ θεὸς ἐπιστήμην ἐν τῇ ~ᾳ 36.2, ἀσύνετοι τῇ ~ᾳ 'wanting in understanding' Ps 75.6, περιστερὰ ἄνους οὐκ ἔχουσα ~αν 'a silly dove wanting in intelligence' Ho 7.11, ἀπολωλεκότες τὴν ~αν Is 46.12, cf. μωρὸς καὶ ἀκάρδιος Je 5.21; οὐκ ἔδωκεν κύριος .. ὑμῖν ~αν εἰδέναι De 29.4, τῇ ~ᾳ συνῶσι Is 6.10; θέσθε δὴ ἐπὶ τὰς ~ας ὑμῶν 'Do lay (the matter) to your heart' Ma 1.1; θέσθε ἐν ταῖς ~αις ὑμῶν Hg 2.18; ἐὰν μὴ θῆσθε εἰς τὴν ~αν ὑμῶν τοῦ δοῦναι δόξαν τῷ ὀνόματί μου 'unless you are considering showing respect for my name' Ma 2.2, sim. Hg 1.7, 2.15, 19, Ma 1.1; τάξατε δὴ τὰς ~ας ὑμῶν εἰς τοὺς ὁδούς Hg 1.5; μὴ λογίζεσθε ἐν ταῖς ~αις ὑμῶν Zc 8.17, ἐλογίσατο ἐν τῇ ~ᾳ αὐτοῦ Is 44.19 (|| ψυχή); ὑπερηφανία τῆς ~ας Ob 3; ἀποκαταστήσει ~αν πατρὸς πρὸς υἱόν 'will redirect the heart of a father towards his son' Ma 4.5; Ἐπιστράφητε πρός με ἐξ ὅλης τῆς ~ας ὑμῶν Jl 2.12; ἐξ ὅλης τῆς ~ας σου καὶ ἐξ ὅλης τῆς ψυχῆς σου De 4.29 (+ ἐκζητέω), 30.2 (+ ὑπακούω), 30.6 (+ ἀγαπάω), 30.10 (+ ἐπιστρέφομαι); ~ᾳ πλήρει 'wholeheartedly' 1M 8.25 (|| ἐκ ψυχῆς vs. 27), ~ᾳ μεγάλῃ καὶ ψυχῇ βουλομένῃ 'with an eager heart and a willing soul' 2M 1.3 (cf. 1C 28.9); τὰ αἰτήματα τῆς ~ας σου 'the desires of your heart' Ps 36.4. **b.** || ψυχή: Ex 35.21, De 4.29, 6.6, 13.3, Si 34.28; || διάνοια Je 38.33, Ex 35.29, with which cp. 35.21. **c.** opp. σῶμα: Pr 25.20, Jb 36.28. **d.** λέγω ἐν ~ᾳ = 'to think': Ob 3, Zp 3.1; φθεγγόμεναι ἐν ~αις αὐτῶν 'thinking aloud' Na 2.8. **e.** of God: Je 39.41 where, however, the omission of μου is poss. deliberate, and cf. Ge 6.6 and 8.21 with לִבּוֹ 'His heart' left untranslated, but Je 19.5 with μου.

4. *seat of emotions*: ἐξέστη ἡ κ. αὐτῶν 'they were inwardly shocked' Ge 42.28; εὐφραίνου καὶ κατατέρπου ἐξ ὅλης τῆς καρδίας σου Zp 3.14; Hb 1.16; ἡ κ… βοᾷ ἐν ἑαυτῇ Is 15.5; ἡ κ. μου ἐντός μου '.. inside me' Ps 38.4.

5. *moral strength*: εὑρήσει τὴν ~αν αὐτοῦ ἐν δυναστείαις 'find his confidence in power' Am 2.16, τοῦ προσεύξασθαι '(enough courage) to pray' 2K 7.27; Ps 26.14.

Cf. νοῦς, πνεῦμα, ψυχή, καρδιόω, ἀκάρδιος.

καρδιόω: aor. ἐκαρδίωσα.ʃ *

to hearten: τινα Ct 4.9. Cf. καρδία.

καρόω: aor.subj.pass. καρωθῶ.ʃ

to plunge into deep sleep: pass., ***o*** hum., out of intoxication, Je 28.39 (+ ὑπνόω). Cf. ὑπνόω.

καρπάσινος, ον.ʃ *

made of κάρπασος 'flax': + βύσσινος Es 1.6.

καρπίζω: fut.mid. καρπιοῦμαι; aor. ἐκαρπισάμην.ʃ

mid. *to enjoy the fruits of*: abs. Pr 8.19; ἀθανασίας δένδρον Si 19.19¶, χώραν Jo 5.12.

κάρπιμος, ον.ʃ

fruit-bearing: ***s*** tree, ξύλον κ. ποιοῦν καρπόν Ge 1.11, 12. Cf. καρπός.

καρπόβρωτος, ον.ʃ *

with edible fruit: ***s*** ξύλον De 20.20.

I **καρπός**, οῦ. m.

1. *fruit* which grows on a plant: κ. ξυλινός 1M 10.30; ἐξῆρα τὸν ~ὸν αὐτοῦ ἐπάνωθεν 'I cut off its fruits above' Am 2.9; ξύλον ἤνεγκε τὸν ~ὸν αὐτοῦ 'a tree bore its fruits' Jl 2.22, τὰ ξύλα τῆς ἐλαίας τὰ οὐ φέροντα ~όν 'unproductive olive-trees' Hg 2.19; for consumption as food, φάγονται τὸν ~ὸν Am 9.14. **b.** fig.: κ. κοιλίας μου 'the fruit of my belly, i.e. baby' Mi 6.7, κ. τῆς γαστρός Ps 126.3 (|| υἱοί), just καρπός 20.11 (|| σπέρμα); κ. ζωῆς Ho 10.12; κ. ψευδῆ 10.13; δικαιοσύνης Am 6.12; ~οὶ χειρῶν 'manual labour' Pr 31.16; ~οὶ στόματος 12.14, χειλέων 'of lips,' i.e. words of prayer offered, Ho 14.3, religious song PSol 15.3; ~ῶν ἐπιτηδευμάτων 'consequences of practices' Mi 7.13 (sim. Je 17.10 || ὁδοί), κακὰ, τὸν ~ὸν ἀποστροφῆς αὐτῶν '.. of their apostasy' Je 6.19. **c.** The sg. is often used collectively: τὸν ~όν || τὰ γενήματα αὐτοῦ Le 19.25; Nu 13.27, De 1.25.

2. *produce*: agricultural produce, τῆς γῆς Ge 43.11, Ma 3.11; ἡ γῆ οὐ δώσει τὸν ~ὸν αὐτῆς De 11.17; specified, σῖτον .. οἶνον .. ἔλαιον .. βουκόλια .. ποίμνια 7.13 (|| γένημα 28.4); as cultic offering, ἀπὸ τῶν ~ῶν τῆς γῆς Ge 4.3 (including animals, Rösel 106), κατὰ τὸ πλῆθος τῶν ~ῶν ἐπλήθυνε τὰ θυσιαστήρια 'he increased the (number of) altars in accordance with the abundance of crops' Ho 10.1; grapes, Zc 8.12.

Cf. καρποφορέω, κατάκαρπος, γένημα, ἀκρόδρυα, ἄκαρπος: Renehan 1.116.

II **καρπός**, οῦ. m.ʃ

1. *wrist*: οἱ ~οὶ τῶν χειρῶν αὐτοῦ 1K 5.4 (doublet of ἴχνος).

2. *hand*: τοὺς πόνους τῶν καρπῶν σου 'the fruits of the toil of your hands' Ps 127.2, ~ὸν ἐξέτεινεν πτωχῷ 'she extended her hand to the poor' Pr 31.20 (|| χείρ).

Cf. χείρ, καρπωτός: Rahlfs 1930.105; Seeligmann 1990.217.

καρποφορέω: fut. ~φορήσω.ʃ

to bear fruit: ***s*** fruit-tree, συκῆ οὐ καρποφορήσει Hb 3.17 (|| γίνομαι γενήματα); καρποφοροῦντα φυτά 'fruit-bearing plants' Wi 10.7. Cf. καρποφόρος, καρπός, φέρω.

καρποφόρος, ον.ʃ

producing fruit, 'fruitful': ***s*** γῆ 'fertile land' Ps 106.34 (:: ἅλμη 'saltiness'), ξύλα 148.9, ἄμπελος 'vine' Je 2.21. Cf. καρποφορέω, κατάκαρπος, ἄκαρπος: Robert 1960.290-6.

καρπόω: aor. ἐκάρπωσα, inf. καρπῶσαι.ʃ
1. *to offer* κάρπωμα: + dat. dei, Le 2.11; ἐναντίον σου Da 3.38 TH (LXX ἐνώπιόν σου); pass., ἐπὶ τὸ θυσιαστήριον ὁλοκαυτώματα καρποῦσθαι 1E 4.52.
2. t*o enjoy, have the pleasure of*: ἀπ' αὐτῶν De 26.14.
Cf. κάρπωμα, κάρπωσις.

κάρπωμα, ατος. n.
cultic offering of any kind: κ. ἐστιν κυρίῳ Ex 29.25; ἐνδελεχισμοῦ 'perpetual' 29.38; ‖ θυμίαμα, θυσία 30.9; θυσιαστήριον ~άτων 40.6; κ... ὁλοκαύτωμα ἢ θυσίαν Nu 15.3; animals, Le 1.4; τὰ δῶρά μου δόματά μου ~ατά μου εἰς ὀσμὴν εὐωδίας Nu 28.2; the Levites' share, De 18.1. Cf. κάρπωσις, καρπόω: LSG s.v.

κάρπωσις, εως. f.ʃ
1. *act of presenting cultic offerings* of all kinds to be enjoyed by cultic functionaries: θυσιαστήριον ~εως Le 4.10 (‖ θ. καρπωμάτων Ex 40.6), θ. ~εων 4.18; εἰς ~ιν οὐ δώσετε 22.22; ποιήσει ~εις περὶ ὑμῶν Jb 42.8.
2. *cultic offering*: προσαγαγεῖν ~ιν, θυμίαμα καὶ εὐωδίαν Si 45.16.
Cf. κάρπωμα.

καρπωτός, όν.ʃ *
reaching down to the wrist: *s* χιτών 'coat' (worn by princesses) 2K 13.18B, 19B. Cf. II καρπός.

κάρρον, ου. n.ʃ
cart: 1E 5.53, see Hanhart 1974.64-7.

κάρταλλος, ου. m.ʃ *
a kind of *basket*: container of fruits and vegetables for cultic use, De 26.2, 4; for carrying heads of dead humans in, 4K 10.7; for a vintager, Je 6.9; a carrier of birds, Si 11.30. Cf. ἄγγος: Lee 115f.

καρτερέω: fut. καρτερήσω; aor. ἐκαρτέρησα, ptc. ~τερήσας, impv. ~τέρησον, subj. ~τερήσω.
to bear patiently: ὡς ἡ τίκτουσα Is 42.14, εὐγενῶς 'nobly' 4M 13.11, μέχρι τίνος 'how much longer' Jb 2.9; ‖ διαμένω Si 12.15; + acc., βάσανον 'torture' 4M 9.9, ἀλγεδῶνα 'suffering' 9.28, θάνατον 10.1. Cf. προσκαρτερέω, δια~, ὑπομένω, ὑπο~, φέρω.

καρτερία, ας. f.
v.n. of prec.: 4M 6.13; εἰς τὸν νόμον 11.12. **b**. w. negative connotation, 'obstinacy': 4M 8.26. Cf. Renehan 2.83.

καρτερός, ά, όν.
= κρατερός, *strong*: in intensity, *s* μάχη '(fierce) battle' 2M 10.29; soldier, 12.35, 4M 3.12; wind, 15.32. Cf. καρτερῶς.

καρτεροψυχία, ας. f.ʃ *
strength and resoluteness of spirit: 4M 9.26.

καρτερῶς. adv.ʃ
by showing strength of body and will: to endure, 4M 15.31. Cf. καρτερός.

καρύα, ας. f.ʃ
nut-bearing tree of various kinds (LSJ): Ct 6.11. Cf. κάρυον.

καρύϊνος, η, ον.ʃ
made of nut-wood: *s* ῥάβδος 'rod' Ge 30.37; βακτηρία 'rod' Je 1.11. Cf. κάρυον.

καρυΐσκος, ου.* m.ʃ
Dim. of κάρυον: Ex 25.32, 33. Cf. κάρυον.

κάρυον, ου. n.ʃ
any kind of *nut*: agricultural produce and gift, Ge 43.11; ἐβλάστησεν ~α 'it produced almonds' Nu 17.8. Cf. καρύα, καρύϊνος, καρυΐσκος, καρυωτός: Shipp 305.

καρυωτός, ή, όν.ʃ
adorned with a nut-shaped boss: *s* bowl of lamp, λαμπάδιον Ex 38.16. Cf. κάρυον.

κάρφος, ους. n.ʃ
dry twig: of olive-tree, Ge 8.11.

Καρχηδών, όνος. f. GN.
Carthage: Is 23.6 +.

κασία, ας.
cassia: Ez 27.17.

κασσιτέρινος, η, ον.ʃ *(?)
made of tin: λίθος κ. 'tin plummet' Zc 4.10. Cf. κασσίτερος.

κασσίτερος, ου. m.
tin (kind of metal): ‖ χρυσίον, ἀργύριον, χαλκός, σίδηρος, and μόλιβος Nu 31.22; less valuable than gold and ‖ μόλιβος Si 47.18; needing refining Ez 22.20; imported from Carthage, 27.12. Cf. κασσιτέρινος.

κατά. Prep.
I. + gen. **1**. *displaying hostile attitude to and to the disadvantage of*: ὑμεῖς ἐβουλεύσασθε κατ' ἐμοῦ εἰς πονηρά, ὁ δὲ θεὸς ἐβουλεύσατο περὶ ἐμοῦ εἰς ἀγαθά 'you resolved to my disadvantage, whereas God resolved in my favour' Ge 50.20, λογισμὸς κ. τοῦ κυρίου πονηρὰ βουλευόμενος Na 1.11; οὐ ψευδομαρτυρήσεις κ. τοῦ πλησίον σου 'giving a false testimony against your neighbour' Ex 20.16; πεπονηρεῦσθαι καθ' ὅλης τῆς παρακαταθήκης τοῦ πλησίον 'to have done anything wrong to the detriment of his neighbour's deposit' 22.11 (‖ ἐφ' ὅλης .. 22.8); κ. Μωυσῆ Nu 12.1; Ma 3.13; συνήχθησαν .. κ. τοῦ κυρίου 'banded together .. ' Ps 2.2; w. προφητεύω (prophecy of doom) Je 33.11 (‖ ἐπί τινα vs. 12). Cf. κ. παίδων αὐτοῦ οὐ πιστεύει 'he does not trust his servants' Jb 4.18.
2. *by invoking* (in swearing): ὀμνύοντας κ. τοῦ κυρίου Zp 1.5; ἃ ὥρκισεν αὐτὸν κ. τοῦ θεοῦ 'that which he had made him swear by God' 2C 36.13.

3. *in respect of, concerning*: ἡμάρτηκεν κατ' αὐτῆς Le 5.5; Is 27.2, Jb 1.8, 4M 8.5.

4. *downwards from*: κ. τοῦ τείχου ἐκρήμνισαν 'hurled down from the wall' 2M 6.10. **b**. λυπούμενος κ. κεφαλῆς 'mourning downcast, crest-fallen' Es 6.12 o'.

5. *downwards on to*: κ. γῆς ῥιφέντα 'thrown down to the bottom (of the pit)' 3M 6.7, cf. 2.22; "the fat closed in on the blade underneath it" Jd 3.22.

6. *behind, in the rear of*: ἀπέκλεισεν τὰς θύρας .. κατ' αὐτοῦ 'he closed the doors .. behind him [= himself] (or: on him [= on Eglon])' Jd 3.23B (A: ἐπ' αὐτόν = ἐπ' αὐτόν [= on Eglon](?), see 4K 4.4*L* ἐπὶ σεαυτήν || B: κατὰ σοῦ); "she closed (the door) on him" 4K 4.21B (*L* ἐπ' αὐτόν), 4.33*L*; κ. νώτου τῶν πυλῶν 'behind the gates' Ez 40.18.

II. + acc. **1**. *under the surface of*: κ. τὸ στερέωμα τοῦ οὐρανοῦ 'under the firmament of the sky' Ge 1.20, hardly sense **4** below, and cf. Alexandre 150f.

2. *towards the direction of*: κ. ἀνατολάς 'towards the east' Ge 2.8, 12.8; κ. θάλασσαν 'to the west' 12.8; κ. λίβα 'to the south' Nu 3.29 (|| vs. 35 πρὸς βορρᾶν); ἀναβλέψας τοῖς ὀφθαλμοῖς κ. θάλασσαν καὶ βορρᾶν καὶ λίβα καὶ ἀνατολάς De 3.27; κυκλῶν πᾶσαν τὴν γῆν κ. τὴν ἔρημον 'going through the entire land towards the wilderness' Zc 14.10; ἀπέστειλεν .. καθ' Ἡρώων πόλιν Ge 46.2; κ. πρόσωπον 'in front' Ex 28.25, 36.26; ἤγαγέ με κ. νότον 'he led me to the south' Ez 40.24; ἐκάλεσεν αὐτὴν κ. πόδας αὐτοῦ Is 41.2, cf. Jd 4.10 and Shipp 306; κ. χεῖρας αὐτῆς 'near her' Si 14.25. On the combination with πρόσωπον, see also under πρόσωπον **6g**.

3. *facing, over against*: ἥ ἐστιν κ. πρόσωπον Αἰγύπτου 'which is opposite Egypt' Ge 25.18; παρενέβαλεν κ. πρόσωπον τῆς πόλεως 'encamped ..' 33.18, see s.v. πρόσωπον **6g**. **b**. κατ' ὀφθαλμούς τινος 'in the sight of', πατάξει αὐτοὺς κατ' ~οὺς ὑμῶν 'he will smite them ..' Je 36.21, εἶπέν μοι .. κατ' ~οὺς τῶν ἱερέων .. 35.1; with a nuance of defiance or challenge, ποιοῦντες τὸ πονηρὸν κατ' ~ούς μου 39.30, ποιῆσαι τὰ κακὰ κατ' ~οὺς τοῦ κυρίου Ba 1.22, see under ὀφθαλμός; στῆθι κατ' ἐμὲ καὶ ἐγὼ κατὰ σέ Jb 33.5; Da 11.7 LXX.

4. *throughout* a space or surface: κ. πᾶσαν γῆν Αἰγύπτου Ex 11.6; κ. τὸ ξηρόν 'through the dry ground' 14.16, cf. ἀφεθήσεται κ. πᾶσαν συναγωγὴν υἱῶν Ισραηλ καὶ τῷ προσηλύτῳ Nu 15.26; κατοικῶν κ. τὴν ἔρημον 21.1; τοῖς κ. Αἴγυπτον Ἰουδαίοις 2M 1.1 (|| ἐν vs. 10); indicating a part of the body attacked, πειρατεύσει αὐτῶν κ. πόδας 'he will raid them at the feet,' cf. νύξε κ. δεξιὸν ὦμον 'stabbed his right shoulder' Hom. *Il*. 5.46. **b**. *throughout the period of*: κ. τὸν καιρὸν αὐτῆς 'throughout the rest of her life' Ju 16.21; κ. τὸν βίον 3M 6.1.

5. *along* (of extension in space): Ex 27.7, 28.14, Le 4.6; κ. πᾶσην τὴν ὁδόν De 1.31, 5.33, 1M 5.53; κ. τὴν ὁδὸν Ἀσσυρίων Ho 13.7.

6. *at the time of*: κ. τὸν καιρὸν τοῦτον 'around this time' Ge 18.10 (|| εἰς τὸν καιρὸν τοῦτον vs. 14), sim. Nu 22.4; κ. τὸ παρόν 'at the present time' 3M 3.11; κ. καιρόν 'in due course, when time comes' Is 60.22; κ. τὴν ἡμέραν ταύτην De 10.15; κ. τὸν καιρόν τοῦ μηνὸς τῶν νέων 'at the time of the new moon' Ex 23.15 (|| εἰς τὸν καιρόν ἐν μηνὶ τῶν νέων 34.18); κ. τὸν καιρὸν αὐτοῦ Nu 9.13; καθ' ὥραν αὐτοῦ 'at its appointed time' 9.2, De 11.14, "when its season arrives" Ho 2.9 (|| ἐν); κ. καιρούς Nu 9.3; καθ' ὕπνον 'in sleep' Ge 20.6, 31.24; κατ' ὄρθρον 'at dawn' Ps 138.9, κ. νύκτα 91.3; κατ' ἀρχάς 'at the beginning' 101.26, 118.152.

7. indicates a pattern, model, norm or criterion to be followed or adopted: Ποιήσωμεν ἄνθρωπον κατ' εἰκόνα ἡμετέραν 'Let us make man according to our own image' Ge 1.26, cf. βοηθὸν κατ' αὐτόν 'a helper as cut out for him' 2.18, || ὅμοιος αὐτῷ vs. 20, To 8.6, and οὐ εἶ ἄνθρωπος κατ' ἐμέ 'you are not human as me' Jb 9.32; οὐκ ἔστιν κατ' αὐτόν 'his like is not to be found' 1.8, κατ' αὐτὸν δυνάστης 'as powerful as he is' 36.22; ποιήσεις κ. τὸν τύπον τὸν δεδειγνυμένον σοι '.. the model shown to you' Ex 25.40; ποιμὴν κ. τὴν καρδίαν μου 'a shepherd (leader) of my choice' Je 3.14, sim. 1K 13.14, δώῃ σοι κ. τὴν καρδίαν σου 'may He give you what (or: as much as) your heart desires'; κ. σχολὴν τῆς πορεύσεως κ. πόδα τῶν παιδαρίων 'with a leisurely pace of the march as suited to the pace of the children' Ge 33.14; πορεύεται κ. χεῖράς σου 'follows your lead' Si 25.26; κ. τὸ κήρυγμα τὸ ἔμπροσθεν 'in the manner of the previous proclamation' Jn 3.2; κ. τὰς ἡμέρας τὰς ἔμπροσθεν Zc 8.11; ἀπηγγείλαμεν αὐτῷ κ. τὴν ἐπερώτησιν ταύτην 'we told him in response to this questioning' Ge 43.7; τὰ κατ' ἐθισμὸν τῶν γυναικῶν 'that which is customary with women' 31.35; τὰ κ. ἀλήθειαν 'the true facts' To 5.12 $\mathfrak{G}^{II}$; ἐγένετο κ. τὸ ὄνομα αὐτοῦ μέγας ἐπὶ σωτηρίᾳ .. 'became great, true to his name, in saving ..' Si 46.1, sim. 6.22; εἰ ἔστιν ἄλγος κ. ἄλγος μου 'if there is pain comparable to my pain' La 1.12; λαλήσω καθ' ὑμᾶς 'I shall speak just as you do' Jb 16.4; ἔσομαι κ. πάντας τοὺς ἀνθρώπους Jd 16.17 (B: ὡς and see also vss. 7, 11, 13); καθ' αὐτόν 'measured by his own yardstick' 2M 8.35. **b**. *in proportion to*: κ. τὸν ἀριθμὸν τῶν ἡμερῶν 'as many as the number of the days' Nu 14.34, κ. ἀριθμὸν τῶν πόλεών σου ἦσαν θεοί σου 'your gods were as many as your cities' Je 11.13, cf. κατὰ σῶμα 'according to the number of persons' Ge 47.12; κ. τὸ πλῆθος αὐτῶν οὕτως ἥμαρτόν μοι 'they sinned against me in proportion to their large number' Ho 4.7; 10.1; κ. τὰς ἡμίσεις τῶν ἁμαρτιῶν σου οὐχ ἥμαρτε 'it did not sin half as much as you' Ez 16.51; αἰνεῖτε αὐτὸν κ. τὸ πλῆθος τῆς μεγαλωσύνης αὐτοῦ 'Praise him as matches his greatness' Ps 150.2, cf. φωνὴ ἐξαρχόντων κατ' ἰσχὺν οὐδὲ φωνὴ ἐξαρχόντων τροπῆς, ἀλλὰ φωνὴ ἐξαρχόντων οἴνου 'the voice of those leading (an army) with strength, nor the voice of leaders in retreat, but the voice of wining leaders' Ex 32.18, κ. κράτος 'by resorting to their (military) might' Jd 4.3; κ. μικρόν 'little by little, by degrees' Si 19.1, κ. ὀλίγον Wi 12.2. **c.** *by taking as a criterion*: ἀφωρίσθησαν .. κ. γλῶσσαν 'they split .. according to language' Ge 10.5; ποιῆσαι κ. τὰς ὁδοὺς ἡμῶν 'to act by having regard to our life-style' Zc 1.6; κ. τὴν θλῖψιν αὐτῆς 'in view of her distress' 1K 1.6. **d.** *on the ground of, in the light of*: κ. τί γνώσομαι, ὅτι ..; 'what evidence is there to convince me that ..?' Ge 15.8, cf. κ. τί γνώσομαι τοῦτο; Lk 1.18. **e.** *in accordance with, in line with, in agreement with*: εἰ κ. τὴν κραυγὴν αὐτῶν .. συντελοῦνται 'whether they are practising .. matching the outcry against them' Ge 18.21; κ. τὰ εἰρημένα ὑπὸ Φαραω 'in conformity with that which has been told by Ph.' 45.21; κ. πάντα, ὅσα ἐνετειλάμην σοι 'precisely in accordance with what I have commanded you' Ex 29.35; κ. στόμα Ααρων 'as instructed by A.' Nu 4.27; ἐποίησαν κ. τὸ γεγραμμένον 2E 3.4; ἐγενήθη κ. τὸ ῥῆμα Ιωσηφ, καθὼς εἶπεν Ge 44.2; Ἔστω κ. τὸ ῥῆμά σου 'Let it be as you say' 30.34 (cf. ποιήσεις ὡς τὸ ῥῆμα τοῦτο 18.25); κ. τὸ αὐτό 'likewise' Ex 26.24, 'in the same manner' 2K 12.3 *L* (B: ἐπὶ τὸ αὐτό). **f.** *with respect to*: εὐλόγησεν τὸν Αβρααμ κ. πάντα '.. in every respect' Ge 24.1, κ. πάντα εὐλογητὸς ἡμῶν ὁ θεός 2M 1.17; καθ' ἅπαν 15.30; ὑπακούσῃ τῆς φωνῆς αὐτοῦ κ. πάντα .. De 30.2; κ. πᾶν ἄχρηστος 'altogether unusable' 3M 3.29; ἡ χείρ σου οὐκέτι ἰσχύει κ. θάλασσαν 'your strength as a maritime nation is no longer there' Is 23.11; κ. σῶμα .. κ. ψυχήν 'bodily .. spiritually' 2M 6.30. **g.** *pertaining to*: πάντα τὰ κ. τὸν βωμόν 'all that is concerned with the altar' Nu 3.10; 1E 1.22, 2.18; τὰ κ. σέ To 10.8 𝔊ᴵ (𝔊ᴵᴵ περὶ σοῦ); 2M 15.37. **h.** *authored by*: ἐν τοῖς ὑπομνηματισμοῖς τοῖς κ. τὸν Νεεμίαν 'in the memoranda drawn up by N.' 2M 2.13. **i.** κ. σπουδήν 'with speed, without delay', κ. σ. ἔρχεται Si 21.5. **j.** κ. τὴν ὁδὸν .. *using as the route*, 'by the way of': ἤρχετο κ. τὴν ὁδὸν τῆς πύλης 'came by the way of the gate' Ez 43.2; 43.4, 44.1+, cf. κατ' εὐθεῖαν 'straight, by a straight route' Si 4.18. **k.** κατ' ὄνομα 'individually, personally' 1E 9.16, cf. *ND* 1.56, 2.63, 3.77.

8. "distributive," indicating repetition of same process with multiple entities (mostly with a sg. noun, and alw. anarthrous with no further addition, cf. κ. παρεμβολὰς αὐτῶν 'according to their encampments' Ex 17.1 and ἔκρυψεν αὐτοὺς [= ἑκατὸν προφήτας] κ. (*L* ἀνὰ, so unanimously at vs. 13) πεντήκοντα ἐν σπηλαίῳ 'hid them by fifty in a cave' 3K 18.4): σπεῖρον σπέρμα κ. γένος καὶ καθ' ὁμοιότητα 'engendering seed per genus and per species' Ge 1.11; γομορ κατὰ κεφαλὴν κατὰ ἀριθμὸν ψυχῶν ὑμῶν 'an omer per head according to the number of your persons' Ex 16.16; ἄνδρα ἕνα κ. φυλήν 'one man per tribe' Nu 13.3; δώδεκα ἄνδρας, ἄνδρα ἕνα κ. φυλήν 'twelve men, one man per tribe' De 1.23; πρόβατον κατ' οἰκίαν 'one sheep per household' Ex 12.3; πέντε σίκλους κ. κεφαλήν 'five shekels per head' Nu 3.47 (cf. δραχμὴ μία τῇ κεφαλῇ 'one drachm per head' Ex 39.2). Cf. the pl. in τὸν κρίον διχοτομήσεις κ. μέλη 'thou shalt cut the ram up into pieces' Ex 29.17, τὸ σῶμα κ. μέλος 'your body, limb by limb' 2M 7.7, sim. 15.33; τὰ κ. μέρος 'the pertinent details' 11.20, κατὰ μ. 'bit by bit' Pr 29.11, πλανήσουσιν Αἴγυπτον κ. φυλάς 'they will mislead Eg. tribe after tribe' Is 19.13. **b.** *every single*: τὰ ἔργα τὰ καθήκοντα καθ' ἡμέραν 'the daily quota' Ex 5.13; κατ' ἐνιαυτόν 'every year' Zc 14.16, 1M 7.49 +; κ. μῆνα 'monthly' 2M 6.7; ἡ θυσία ἡ καθ' ἡμέραν 'the daily offering' Nu 4.16, cf. καθ' ἡμέραν εἰς ἡμέραν 'day after day, daily' Ex 16.5 = with τό, Le 23.37. ***c.** same noun repeated with κατά in-between: ἐνιαυτὸν κατ' ἐνιαυτόν De 14.21, 1M 4.59, 1K 1.7 (|| 7.16 κατ' ~ον ~ον and ἱκανοῦ ~ον κατ' ~ον at both in *L*), ἡμέραν καθ' ἡμέραν Ps 67.20; ἄνδρα κατ' ἄνδρα 'every single man' Nu 4.49; πρόσωπον κ. πρόσωπον ἐλάλησεν κύριος πρὸς ἡμᾶς 'the Lord spoke to us personally' De 5.4, ἔγνω κύριος αὐτὸν πρόσωπον κ. πρόσωπον '.. knew him personally' 34.10; στόμα κ. στόμα λαλήσω αὐτῷ 'I shall speak to him tête-à-tête' Nu 12.8; with a pl. noun, prob. due to its meaning, ὀφθαλμοῖς κατ' ὀφθαλμοὺς ὀπτάζῃ 'you appear personally' Nu 14.14. ***d.** same noun repeated after κατά, prob. a variant on κατά with a single noun (cf. κ. μικρόν 2M 8.8 = κ. μικρὸν μικρόν 'little by little,' see below and ἵνα αὐτοὺς κ. βραχὺ ἐξολεθρεύσωσιν 'in order to destroy them piecemeal' Wi 12.8 and κρίνων κ. βραχύ 'judging little by little' 12.10): τὸ κ. ἐνιαυτὸν ἐνιαυτόν 3K 10.25; κόψεται ἡ γῆ κ. φυλὰς φυλάς 'the land shall mourn, each tribe separately' Zc 12.12 (pl. and foll. by φυλὴ οἴκου Δαυιδ καθ' ἑαυτὴν καὶ αἱ γυναῖκες αὐτῶν καθ' ἑαυτάς .., see below **9**), συναγάγετε τοὺς υἱοὺς Ισραηλ κ. ἕνα ἕνα 'gather .. one by one' Is 27.12; κ. μικρὸν μικρόν 'by degrees, little by little' Ex 23.30, De 7.22 (latter:: τὸ τάχος). Cf. ἑκατὸν εἴκοσι ἑπτὰ σατραπείαις κ. χώραν καὶ χώραν, κ.

τὴν ἑαυτῶν λέξιν 'to 127 satrapies to each region in its own respective language' Es 8.9, ἐνετείλατο ταῖς πόλεσιν Ἰούδα θυσιάζειν κ. πόλιν καὶ πόλιν 'ordered the Judaean cities to offer a sacrifice in every city' 1M 1.51. Note the intervening καί in most of the examples above. **e.** reinforced by ἕκαστος: καθ' ἑκάστην ἡμέραν Ex 5.8, Ps 7.12, cf. δύο μνέαι τεταγμέναι κατ' ἄνδρα αἰχμάλωτον 'two minas allocated for each male POW' Hdt. 6.79; by πᾶς– κ. πᾶσαν ἀπώλειαν De 22.3. **f.** καθ' ἕνα etc. = πᾶς 'every single':; καθ' ἕνα παῖδα 'each child' 4M 15.12; τὸ καθ' ἓν πραχθὲν τῆς πράξεως Ἰωσίου 'every single one of J.'s deeds' 1E 1.31; spelled as one word, ὁ καθεῖς τῶν φίλων 'every one of the friends' 3M 5.34, καθένα στρεβλούμενον 'each of them tortured' 4M 15.14. Cf. ἀνά **II**; Shipp 289.

9. indicates, esp. w. a refl.pron., separation, dissociation or seclusion: διεχώρισεν ἑαυτῷ ποίμνια καθ' ἑαυτόν 'he separated flocks for himself alone' Ge 30.40; τῶν καθ' αὑτὸν οὐδέν 'nothing of his own affairs' 39.6; παρέθηκαν αὐτῷ μόνῳ καὶ αὐτοῖς καθ' ἑαυτοὺς καὶ τοῖς Αἰγυπτίοις .. καθ' ἑαυτούς 'they set (foods) to him alone and to them apart and to the Egyptians .. apart' Ge 43.32; εἴη μοι καρδία καθ' ἑαυτὴν ἐφ' ὑμᾶς 'may my heart be entirely dedicated to you' 1C 12.18; κατοικήσει ἔτι καθ' ἑαυτήν 'will still live by herself' Zc 12.6; 12.12-14, Mi 7.14, 1K 26.11B, 2M 13.13. Cf. μόνος **3**.

See Johannessohn, *Präp*. 245-59.

καταβαίνω: fut. ~βήσομαι; aor. κατέβην, impv. 2s κατάβηθι, 2pl ~βητε, 3s ~βήτω, inf. ~βῆναι, ptc. ~βάς, subj. ~βῶ; pf. ~βέβηκα, inf. ~βεβηκέναι.

1. *to descend* from a higher to a lower place: from the plateau of the Judeaen Desert to Sodom and Gomorrah, Ge 18.21 (or of God from heaven as at Ex 3.8); ἀπὸ τοῦ ὄρους Ex 32.15; ἐκ τοῦ ὄρους πρὸς τὸν λαόν 19.14; to a fountain (ἐπὶ τὴν πηγήν) to draw water, Ge 24.16 (:: ἀναβαίνω); οἱ ἄγγελοι τοῦ θεοῦ ἀνέβαινον καὶ κατέβαινον ἐπ' αὐτῆς 28.12; from the river bank to the river (ἐπὶ τὸν ποταμόν) to bathe, Ex 2.5; from the Holy Mount, Ob 16; from the land of Israel to Egypt (εἰς Αἴγυπτον) Ge 12.10, 26.2, 43.4 (:: ἀναβαίνω 44.24), De 10.22; from Jerusalem or Judaea (?) to Joppa or from the inland to the coast, Jn 1.3; *s* birds, Ge 15.11, manna Nu 11.9, hail Is 32.19, δρόσος 'dew' 2K 1.21B (*L* πίπτω), ὑετὸς ἢ χιὼν ἐκ τοῦ οὐρανοῦ 'rain or snow ..' Is 55.10, δάκρυα .. ἐπὶ σιαγόνα 'tears .. on the cheeks' Si 32.18, cf. vs. 19 with κατάγω; seamen, οἱ καταβαίνοντες εἰς τὴν θάλασσαν Is 42.10, ἐν πλοίοις 'in boats' Ps 106.23; God, ἐπὶ τὸ ὄρος τὸ Σινα Ex 19.11; God's glory, 24.16; column of cloud, 33.9. **b.** with the indication of destination by εἰς Ge 12.10, Am 6.2, Jn 1.3; εἰς τὴν κοίλην τοῦ πλοίου 'into the hold of the ship' 1.5; εἰς ᾅδου Ge 37.35, Nu 16.30, 33, Is 14.11 (last: *s* δόξα, εὐφροσύνη); εἰς (τὴν) γῆν 'to Hades' Ps 21.30, (so Cyr. I 582 and Thph 126.937) Jn 2.7, εἰς βόθρον Ez 26.20; εἰς λάκκον Ps 27.1; ἐπὶ πύλας Mi 1.12; πρός τινα Ge 43.13, 45.9, Ex 11.8, + acc., πεδία 'fields' Ps 103.8 (*s* flood waters), ὄρος Ju 10.10. **c.** of a mythological descent of God from his abode above: Ge 11.5, 7, Mi 1.3. **d.** of a calamity brought down by God: κατέβη κακὰ παρὰ κυρίου ἐπὶ πύλας Ιερουσαλημ 'calamities descended from the Lord upon the gates of J.' Mi 1.12; χοῦς 'dust' ἐκ τοῦ οὐρανοῦ καταβήσεται ἐπὶ σέ De 28.24. **e.** of the level of a river, *to come down*: Am 8.8, 9.5 (:: ἀναβαίνω). **f.** *to come down* defeated (?): καταβήσονται ἵπποι καὶ ἀναβάται αὐτῶν ἕκαστος ἐν ῥομφαίᾳ πρὸς τὸν ἀδελφὸν αὐτοῦ 'horses and their riders will come down ..' Hg 2.22, but possibly this is a shorthand for 'horses will fall and their riders (as a consequence) will be thrown off to the ground'; καταβήσεται ἕως τοῦ ἐδάφους '(the wall) will be razed to the ground' Is 25.12.

2. *to suffer deterioration on socio-economic ladder*: κάτω κάτω De 28.43 (:: ἀναβαίνω); *s* οἱ ἔνδοξοι καὶ οἱ μεγάλοι καὶ οἱ πλούσιοι καὶ οἱ λοιμοί Is 5.14, cf. καταβήσεται ἡ ὕβρις .. αὐτῆς Ez 30.6 (|| ἀπόλλυμι vs. 18).

3. *to step back*: ἀπὸ σοῦ Na 3.7 (cf. Thph PG 126.1029: = ἀποπηδήσει 'to turn away [in horror]').

*__4__. *to cause to descend*: + acc., διεξόδους ὑδάτων 'streams of water [= tears]' Ps 118.136. **b.** *to apply* sth to a surface: ***o*** gold, 3K 6.31 (|| B: κατάγω).

Cf. ἀνα~, συγκαταβαίνω, κατάβασις, καταβάσιος, καταβιβάζω, καταδύω, κατέρχομαι.

καταβάλλω: fut. ~βαλῶ; aor. κατέβαλον, inf. ~βαλεῖν, ptc.pass. ~βληθείς, subj.act. ~βάλω; pf. καταβέβληκα.

1. *to cast downwards*: + acc., τὰ δένδρα σου Is 16.9, τὴν μαχαίραν αὐτοῦ ἐκ τῆς χειρὸς αὐτοῦ Ez 30.22, σπέρμα '(to sow) seeds' Ps 105.27; pass., εἰς λέβητα 'into a cauldron' 4M 12.1. **b.** intr. *to fall, drop*: *s* leaves on a tree, Si 14.18 (:: φύω).

2. *to bring low* that which is standing erect and destroy it: + acc., πόλεις ὀχυράς καὶ κατάξεις ἕως ἐδάφους '.. and raze to the ground' Is 26.5; τὰ τείχη Σορ .. τοὺς πύργους σου 'the walls of Tyre .. your towers' Ez 26.4; 2K 20.15; trees, 4K 3.19. **b.** metaph. 'to humiliate': + acc. pers., ἐν μέσῳ συναγωγῆς 'in public' Si 1.30, σεαυτὸν ἐν ὄχλῳ 7.7; γαυρίαμα τοῦ Γολιαθ 'G.'s hubris' 47.4; 'to ruin,' ***o*** hum., Pr 7.26.

3. *to cause to fall defeated*: in battle and + acc. pers., ἐν μαχαίρᾳ ἐναντίον τῶν ἐχθρῶν αὐτῶν 'with a sword in front of their foes' Je 19.7, ἐν ῥομφαίᾳ Ez 23.25, ῥομφαίᾳ 1M 4.33; mortally, 2M 4.42.

4. *to bring under notice*: τὸν ἔλεον ἡμῶν κατὰ πρόσωπόν σου '(we present) to you a plea for merciful consideration of our predicament' Ba 2.19. Note an analogous use of πίπτω **4** and ῥίπτω **2**.

5. mid. *to found*: + acc., βιβλιοθήκην 2M 2.13, τρόπαια 'monuments' 5.6 (|| συνίστημι 15.6).

Cf. καταβολή, κατακρημνίζω, καταράσσω, καταρίπτω, ἀφανίζω.

καταβαρύνω: aor.pass. κατεβαρύνθην, subj. ~βαρυνθῶ.ʃ

tr. *to weigh down*: pass. καταβαρυνόμενοι ἐν τοῖς ὅπλοις αὐτῶν 'weighed down by their (own) arms' Jl 2.8. **b**. pass. *to become heavy*: *s* hair on one's head, 2K 14.26; metaph., *to become unbearable*: *s* arrows shot by enemies, ἐπί τινα 2K 11.24*L*; *to impose oneself and become a burden*, 13.25 (*L* simp.).

Cf. βαρύς.

καταβάσιος, ον.ʃ *

descending: *s* punitive fire, Wi 10.6. Cf. καταβαίνω.

κατάβασις, εως. f.

1. v.n. of καταβαίνω, 'descent': of snow, Si 43.17b.

2. *downward slope, declivity*: ὕδωρ καταφερόμενον ἐν ~ει 'water running down a slope' Mi 1.4.

Cf. καταβαίνω, καταφερής.

καταβιάζομαι: aor. κατεβιασάμην.ʃ

to request forcefully, 'entreat, press': + acc. pers. Ge 19.3, Ex 12.33, 2K 13.25*L*. Cf. παραβιάζομαι.

καταβιβάζω: fut. ~βιβάσω; aor. κατεβίβασα, impv. ~βίβασον, pass. ~βιβάσθητι.

1. *to cause to move down*: + acc., τὴν δάμαλιν εἰς φάραγγα 'the heifer into a wadi' De 21.4, εἰς ᾅδου Ez 31.16 (|| καταβαίνω); πρός τινα 26.20; Jd 7.5 A (|| κατάγω vs. 4); Jo 2.18 (|| καταχαλάω vs. 15).

2. *to lead away* to an undesirable destination: + acc., ὡς ἄρνας εἰς σφαγήν 'like lambs to be slaughtered' Je 28.40.

*__3__. intr. *to move down*: κατεβίβασεν ὑπέρογκα 'she had a rather bad fall, she fell with a heavy thud' (?) La 1.9.

Cf. καταβαίνω, ἐπιβρέχω, (κατα)χαλάω.

καταβιβρώσκω: aor.pass. κατεβρώθην, subj. ~βρωθῶ, impv.3s ~βρωθήτω.

1. *to eat up* and destroy: *o* hum., Bel LXX 31f. (TH: κατεσθίω).

2. *to ruin completely*: *o* hum., ἐν ὀργῇ πυρός Si 33.11; gates, ἐν πυρί Ne 2.3, πυρί 2.13.

Cf. βιβρώσκω, κατάβρωμα, κατάβρωσις, ἀφανίζω, κατεσθίω.

καταβιόω: pres.impv. ~βίου.ʃ

to pass one's life: Am 7.12. Cf. βιόω.

καταβλάπτω.ʃ

to hurt gravely: τινα 3M 7.8. Cf. βλάπτω.

καταβλέπω: aor. κατέβλεψα.ʃ

to look down from a higher position: ἐπὶ πρόσωπον Σοδόμων καὶ Γομόρρας Ge 18.16. Cf. βλέπω, κατεῖδον.

καταβοάω: fut. ~βοήσομαι; aor. κατεβόησα, subj. ~βοήσω.ʃ

to appeal for help out of distress to sbd in a position of authority: πρὸς Φαραω Ex 5.15; to God, 22.23 (κεκράξαντες), 27, 2M 8.3 (*s* victims' blood); κατὰ σοῦ πρὸς κύριον 'against you ..' De 24.15. Cf. καταβόησις, βοάω, κράζω.

καταβόησις, εως. f.ʃ

v.n. of prec.: *s* widow and + ἐπί ('against') τινι, Si 32.19.

καταβολή, ῆς. f.ʃ

act of building (v.n. of καταβάλλω **5**): καινῆς οἰκίας 2M 2.29. Cf. καταβάλλω, οἰκοδομέω: Hauck, *TDNT* 3.620f.

καταβόσκω: aor.subj. ~βοσκήσω, inf. ~βοσκῆσαι.ʃ

to feed flocks upon or *in* a place: + acc., ἀγρὸν ἢ ἀμπέλωνα 'a field or a vineyard' Ex 22.5. Cf. βόσκω.

κατάβρωμα, ατος. n.

food: fig. of a conquered people, Nu 14.9, Ju 10.12; ἐν πυρὶ ἔσῃ κ. Ez 21.32; cadaver, οἱ νεκροὶ ὑμῶν κ. τοῖς πετεινοῖς De 28.26; τοῖς θηρίοις .. καὶ τοῖς πετεινοῖς '.. to the beasts .. and the birds' Ez 29.5. Cf. κατάβρωσις, βρῶμα, βρῶσις.

κατάβρωσις, εως. f.ʃ *

v.n. of καταβιβρώσκω: cogn. dat., κατέφαγεν ~ει τὸ ἀργύριον ἡμῶν 'ate our silver up rapaciously' Ge 31.15; ἔσονται εἰς ~ιν πάσης τῆς στρατιᾶς σου 'they will be devoured by your entire army' Ju 5.24. Cf. κατάβρωμα, κατεσθίω.

κατάγαιος, ον.ʃ

situated below or *at the ground* or *lowest level*: subst., pl.n. 'lower cabins' (of boat) Ge 6.16 (|| διώροφα and τριώροφα); ἐν ~οις κρυφίοις '.. secret places' PSol 8.9. Cf. διώροφος and τριώροφος.

καταγγέλλω: aor. κατήγγειλα.ʃ

to state solemnly and publicly the veracity or reality of: + inf., 2M 8.36; + acc. rei, τὸ τοῦ θεοῦ κράτος 'God's power' 9.17. Cf. Schniewind, *TDNT* 1.70f.

καταγέλαστος, ον.ʃ

laughable, ridiculous: *s* dread, Wi 17.8. Cf. καταγελάω, γελοῖος: Schmidt 4.190f.

καταγελάω: fut. ~γελάσω, mid. ~γελάσομαι, pass. ~γελασθήσομαι; aor. κατεγέλασα, impv.3pl ~γελασάτωσαν, subj.pass. ~γελασθῶ.

to deride: abs. To 2.8 $\mathfrak{G}^{II}$ ($\mathfrak{G}^{I}$ ἐπι~); + gen., Ps 24.2, Jb 41.21; + gen. pers., πτωχοῦ 'the poor' Pr

17.5, πατρός (|| ἀτιμάζω); + καταμωκάομαι 2C 30.10; + acc. pers., Si 7.11; pass. καταγελασθήσονται οἱ μάντεις 'the diviners shall be laughed at' Mi 3.7 (|| καταισχύνομαι); Ge 38.23; * + ἔν τινι - ἐν τῇ πτώσει ἡμῶν Es C 22 o', cf. Aes. *Ch.* 222 ἐν κακοῖς τοῖσι ἐμοῖς γελᾶν; pass., ἐπὶ δειλίᾳ 'on account of (our) cowardice' 4M 6.20; mid., abs., Pr 29.9. Cf. καταγέλως, ἐπεγ~, ἐπι(γελάω), ἀτιμάζω, καταισχύνω, κολαβρίζω, ὀνειδίζω: Schmidt 4.189.

καταγέλως, ωτος. m.ʃ

object of derision, 'laughing-stock': μὴ οἰκοδομεῖτε ἐξ οἴκου ~τα, γῆν καταπάσασθε ~τα ὑμῶν 'Do not rebuild a house into a laughing-stock, sprinkle earth on your laughing-stock(?)' Mi 1.10; + ὀνειδισμός To 8.10 𝔊[II], 1M 10.70; || ὄνειδος and μυκτηρισμός Ps 43.14; + μυκτηρισμός PSol 4.7. Cf. καταγελάω, μυκτηρισμός, ὄνειδος, ὀνειδισμός.

καταγηράσκω: aor.subj. ~ράσω.ʃ

to grow old: Is 46.4. Cf. γηράω.

καταγίνομαι ʃ

to dwell: Ex 10.23; in tents, Nu 5.3; in a mountain, De 9.9; in a house, Bel 21 LXX. Cf. κατοικέω.

καταγινώσκω: fut.mid. ~γνώσομαι, pass. ~γνωσθήσομαι; aor. κατέγνων, subj. καταγνῶ.ʃ

1. *to pronounce* sbd (gen.) *guilty*: τοῦ ἀσεβοῦς (:: δικαιόω) De 25.1; οὐ κατέγνω ἡ ψυχὴ αὐτοῦ (Zgl: αὐτοῦ, cf. Acta Thomae 94, p. 207, 11f.) 'his conscience was not pricked' Si 14.2. Cf. καταδικάζω **1**.

2. *to observe closely and form an unfavourable opinion of*, 'despise': + gen. pers., Pr 28.11; pass., ***o*** hum., Si 19.5.

Cf. κατάγνωσις, κατακρίνω, καταφρονέω, δικαιόω.

κατάγνυμι: fut. κατάξω; aor. κατέαξα, impv. κάταξον, ptc.~άξας.ʃ

to break in pieces: + acc. rei, ὀσφῦν .. ἐχθρῶν 'the loins of .. enemies' De 33.11, τόξον 'bow' 2K 22.35, τὸ κράτος αὐτῶν Ju 9.8 (|| ῥάσσω); pers. ἐν θυμῷ κατάξεις ἔθνη Hb 3.12; Zc 1.21. Cf. ῥάσσω, ῥήγνυμι, συντρίβω: Schmidt 3.305-7.

κατάγνωσις, εως. f.ʃ

denunciation: Si 5.14. Cf. καταγινώσκω.

καταγογγύζω.ʃ

to express discontent: κατά τινος (pers.) 1M 11.39. Cf. γογγύζω.

καταγράφω: fut. ~γράψω; aor. κατέγραψα, impv. κατάγραψον, ptc.pass. ~γραφείς; pf.ptc.pass. ~γεγραμμένος.

1. *to put down in writing*: + acc., εἰς μνημόσυνον ἐν βιβλίῳ 'for a memorial in a book' Ex 17.14; καταγράψω αὐτῷ πλῆθος 'I shall write down many things for him' Ho 8.12. **b**. *to record in writing* about sbd or sth as being so and so: abs., on brass tablets, 1M 14.26; pass., ἕτοιμος 'as ready' Si 48.10. **c**. *to correspond by letter*: + dat. pers., κατά τινα 'against' 1E 2.15.

2. *to record in a list, register*: ***o*** pers., Nu 11.26.

3. *to produce by writing*: + acc., βιβλίον 'a book' 2C 20.34.

Cf. γράφω.

κατάγω: fut. κατάξω; aor. κατήγαγον, inf. ~αγαγεῖν, impv. ~άγαγε, 3pl ~γαγέτωσαν, ptc. ~αγαγών, pass. κατήχθην, κατεάχθην, ptc. καταχθείς, opt.3pl ~αχθείησαν.

1. tr. *to move* sth or sbd (acc.) *from a higher to a lower position, bring down*: εἰς Αἴγυπτον Ge 37.25; 39.1*a* (pass.); caus. of καταβαίνω, 45.13 (|| κατάβηθι vs. 9); πρός με 44.21; κατάξετέ μου τὸ γῆρας μετὰ λύπης εἰς ᾅδου 42.38, 44.29, sim. 44.31 and To 3.10, 6.15, κατάγει εἰς ᾅδου καὶ ἀνάγει 1K 2.6, sim. To 13.2, Wi 16.13, cf. κατάξεις αὐτοὺς εἰς φρέαρ διαφθορᾶς '.. into a well of perdition' Ps 54.24, εἰς χοῦν θανάτου 'into dust of death' 21.16; ἐπὶ τὴν γῆν Ob 3; in a simile of a hunter bringing birds down with a net, Ho 7.12; ἐκεῖθεν = ἐκ τοῦ οὐρανοῦ Am 9.2; an urban settlement considered as higher ground, εἰς ἔρημον Ho 2.14; ἐκ σοῦ ἰσχύν (cf. Arab. /tazūlu/; Cyr. I 432 συνθραυθήσεται) Am 3.11 (see also under ἰσχύς); καταγαγέτωσαν οἱ ὀφθαλμοὶ ἡμῶν δάκρυα '.. tears' Je 9.18, sim. 13.17, cf. καταγάγετε ἐπ' ὀφθαλμοὺς ὑμῶν δάκρυα 14.17; ὁ ὀφθαλμός μου κατήγαγεν ὕδωρ La 1.16, sim. 3.48; ***s*** pers. and ***o*** δάκρυα Si 22.19, 32.19, cf. vs. 18 with καταβαίνω; ἐπὶ νεκρῷ κατάγαγε δάκρυα 38.16; τὸ αἷμα αὐτῶν εἰς γῆν Is 63.3, 6; ἕως ἐδάφους '(raze cities) to the ground' 26.5; εἰς γῆν La 2.10 (burial?); τινα ἐν ῥομφαίᾳ 'with a sword' 2C 32.21. **b**. pass. *to disembark*: 3M 7.19. **c**. *to apply* sth to a surface: pass., ***o*** gold, 3K 6.35 (|| *L* καταβαίνω vs. 31).

2. *to bring back*: 'to recall from banishment,' + acc. pers., Is 9.3.

3. fig. *to destroy*: + acc., ἐν θυμῷ κατάξεις ἔθνη 'you will destroy nations' Hb 3.12, sim. Ps 55.8.

4. *to lead to an inferior, undesirable destination*: + acc. pers., εἰς ἀπώλειαν Si 48.6.

Cf. ἄγω, ἀνάγω, καταβαίνω, ἀφανίζω: Spicq 2.258-61.

καταδαμάζω: aor. κατεδάμασα.ʃ *

to subdue: + acc., δάμαλιν 'heifer' Jd 14.18A. Cf. δαμάζω.

καταδαπανάω: aor.pass. κατεδαπανήθην.ʃ

metaph. *to exhaust the energy and vitality of*, 'wear out': pass., ***o*** hum., Wi 5.13. Cf. δαπανάω, ἐκλείπω.

καταδείκνυμι: aor. κατέδειξα, ptc. ~δείξας.ʃ

to invent, bring into existence (+ acc.): ***o*** musical instruments, ψαλτήριον καὶ κιθάραν Ge 4.21; the universe and ***s*** God, τίς κατέδειξε πάντα ταῦτα; Is

40.26, cf. 41.20 (|| ποιέω); τὴν γῆν 45.18 (|| ποιέω); Ισραηλ βασιλέα ὑμῶν 'Israel as your king' 43.15 (cf. Seeligman 112). Cf. ἑτοιμάζω, κτίζω, πλάσσω, ποιέω: Renehan 1.117, 2.83f.

καταδέομαι: impf.3s κατεδέετο; aor. κατεδεήθην.ʃ

to implore out of distress: + gen. pers. from whom help is sought, Ge 42.21, Is 57.10. Cf. δέομαι.

καταδεσμεύω: fut., aor.subj. ~μεύσω.ʃ *

to put a bandage around as medical treatment: + acc., τραύματα 'wounds' Si 30.7. **b**. metaph. *to deal with painful consequences of*: + acc., ἁμαρτίαν Si 7.8. Cf. δεσμεύω.

κατάδεσμος, ου. m.ʃ

bandage (for wounds): Is 1.6 (|| μάλαγμα 'emollient,' ἔλαιον 'oil'). Cf. καταδέω.

καταδέχομαι: aor.impv.3pl ~δεξάσθωσαν.ʃ

to submit oneself to instruction or *direction*: abs. τῇ καρδίᾳ Ex 35.5; De 32.29.

καταδέω: fut. ~δήσω; aor.inf. ~δῆσαι, impv. ~δησον, mid. ~εδησάμην, pass. κατεδέθην; pf.pass. ~δέδεμαι.

to bind fast: + acc. and pass., ὅσα οὐχὶ δεσμὸν καταδέδεται ἐπ' αὐτῷ 'on which no tie is securely bound' Nu 19.15; ***o*** wounded person, Ez 30.21, sheep 34.4; eyes with a bandage 3K 21.38, a wound with a bandage, Si 27.21, gold and silver pieces, 28.24. Cf. δέω, κατάδεσμος.

καταδιαιρέω: aor.impv. καταδίελε, ptc. ~διελών, mid. κατεδιειλάμην, impv.2pl ~διέλεσθε.ʃ

I. act. *to divide into two, dissect, cut apart*: + acc., γλῶσσαν 'tongue' Ps 54.10 (punishment); τὴν ἐρυθρὰν θάλασσαν εἰς διαιρέσεις 'the Red Sea into parts' 135.13.

II. mid. **1**. *to divide* in order to take possession of: ***s*** conqueror, τὴν γῆν μου Jl 3.2.

2. *to examine in detail*: + acc., βάρεις 'tower-houses (of Jerusalem)' Ps 47.14.

Cf. διαιρέω, μερίζω.

καταδικάζω: fut.mid. ~κάσομαι; aor.subj. ~κάσω, inf. ~κάσαι, mid. ~κάσωμαι; pf.ptc.pass. ~δεδικασμένος.

1. *to pass a 'Guilty' sentence against*: + acc. pers., La 3.36; ***s*** a merciless king, Wi 11.10; + dat. (penalty), θανάτῳ καταδικάσωμεν αὐτόν 'let us condemn him to death' 2.20; pass., ἐξέλθοι καταδεδικασμένος 'may he come out declared guilty' Ps 108.7; mid., *to get a 'Guilty' sentence passed against*, abs. Jb 34.29, + acc., αἷμα ἀθῷον 'sbd innocent of murder' Ps 93.21. Cf. καταγινώσκω **1**.

2. *to make a statement to the disadvantage of*: + acc. and dat. pers., τὴν κεφαλήν μου τῷ βασιλεῖ Da 1.10 TH.

Cf. κατακρίνω, καταδίκη, δικάζω: Schrenk, *TDNT* 3.621f.

καταδίκη, ης. f.ʃ

judgement or *sentence pronounced against*: Wi 12.27. Cf. καταδικάζω.

καταδιώκω: fut. ~διώξω, mid. ~διώξομαι; aor. κατεδίωξα, subj. ~διώξω, opt.3s ~διώξαι, impv. ~δίωξον, pass. κατεδιώχθην.

1. *to search eagerly, hunt*: abs. ***s*** horsemen, Jl 2.4; + acc. pers. "she will eagerly search for her lovers, but will not find them" Ho 2.7; pass. κατεδιώχθητε οὐδενὸς διώκοντος Mi 2.11; with hostile intent, τὴν ψυχήν μου Ps 7.6, με 30.16 (|| ἐχθροί).

2. *to seek after, aim at*: ἀπεστρέψατο ἀγαθά, ἐχθρὸν κατεδίωξαν 'they rejected good things, and pursued what is inimical (to them)' Ho 8.3.

3. *to chase* sbd who has wronged, an enemy or an escapee, 'hunt down': + ὀπίσω τινός– ἕως Δαν Ge 14.14; 31.23, 36; Ex 14.4; ***s*** κατάραι 'curses' De 28.45, κακά 'calamities' Pr 12.26 (***o*** sinners); ***o*** acc. (enemy), ὡς εἰ ποιήσαισαν αἱ μέλισσαι 'as bees might do' De 1.44; τὴν ψυχήν μου Ps 7.6.

4. *to force to move on*, 'overdrive': ***o*** cattle, Ge 33.13.

5. *to accompany permanently*: + acc. pers. and ***s*** divine mercy, Ps 22.6.

Cf. διώκω, ζητέω.

καταδολεσχέω: fut. ~χήσω.ʃ *

to chatter so as to annoy or depress: ἐπ' ἐμέ La 3.20 (on the force of ἐπί, see s.v. **III 7**). Cf. ἀδολεσχέω.

καταδουλόω: fut.act. ~δουλώσω; aor.mid. κατεδουλωσάμην, ptc. ~ωσάμενος.

to enslave: + acc. pers., πάντα τὰ ἔργα, ὧν κατεδουλοῦντο αὐτοὺς μετὰ βίας 'all the works, with which they made forced slaves of them' Ex 1.14 (on the difficult gen. ὧν, see *BA* ad loc.); ἐξελοῦμαι αὐτοὺς ἐκ χειρὸς τῶν καταδουλωσαμένων αὐτούς 'I shall set them free from the hand of those who have enslaved them' Ez 34.27; and dat.(refl.) pers. com., τὸν λαὸν κατεδουλώσατο αὐτῷ εἰς παῖδας 'he enslaved the people to himself as slaves' Ge 47.21; + cogn. dat., δουλείᾳ μεγάλῃ Ez 29.18; + cogn. acc., τὸν Ισραηλ δουλείαν 1M 8.18; ***o*** losers in a war, 1M 8.10. Alw. in the mid. exc. καταδουλώσω σε κύκλῳ τοῖς ἐχθροῖς σου 'I shall enslave you to all your enemies around' Je 15.14 where the subj. gains no benefit from the obj.'s slavery. Cf. δοῦλος, δουλεύω, ἐλευθερόω.

καταδρομή, ῆς. f.ʃ

charge of troops in battle: 2M 5.3 (+ προσβολή).

καταδυναστεία, ας. f. *

v.n. of subs.: ὁ θεὸς ὑμῶν ὁ ἐξαγαγὼν ὑμᾶς ἐκ τῆς ~ας τῶν Αἰγυπτίων Ex 6.7; Am 3.9, Ez 22.12.

καταδυναστεύω: fut. ~δυναστεύσω; aor. κατεδυνάστευσα, ptc. ~τεύσας, subj. ~τεύσω, inf.pass. ~τευθῆναι; pf. ~δεδυνάστευκα, pass. ~δεδυνάστευμαι.

1. *to cause* (sbd τινα) *unjust hardship*, often from a position of power: τὸν ἀντίδικον αὐτοῦ Ho 5.11 (|| καταπατέω κρίμα); πτωχοὺς .. πένητας Am 4.1; sim. 8.4 (|| ἐκτρίβω πένητα); || διαρπάζω Mi 2.2; ἀσεβὴς .. τὸν δίκαιον Hb 1.4; χήραν καὶ ὀρφανὸν καὶ προσήλυτον καὶ πένητα μὴ καταδυναστεύετε 'Stop oppressing widows, orphans, foreigners, and poor people' Zc 7.10; χήραν Ma 3.5; βίᾳ Ex 1.13 (|| μετὰ βίας vs. 14); εἰς δούλους 'to be put out or sold as slaves' Ne 5.5; pass. and ***o*** exiles, Je 27.33.

2. *to cause to submit to one's power and authority*: τινα Ex 21.17 (forcibly), Si 48.12. **b**. *to overpower, defeat*: on battlefield, + gen. pers., 1K 17.9*L*, 2K 8.11.

Cf. καταδυναστεία.

κατάδυσις, εως. f.ʃ

haunt for secret meetings: 3K 15.13.

καταδύω: fut. ~δύσω, δύσομαι; aor. κατέδυσα, subj. ~δύσω.ʃ

1. intr., *to sink, plunge*: ***s*** vanquished enemies, κατέδυσαν εἰς βυθὸν 'they went down into the bottom' Ex 15.5; of political demise, καταδύσεται Βαβυλὼν καὶ οὐ μὴ ἀναστῇ Je 28.64.

2. *to slink away and lie hidden*: εἰς τὰ βάθη τῆς θαλάσσης 'into the depths ..' Am 9.3.

3. *to cause to sink* or *go down*: + acc., ἀδικίας Mi 7.19; ἐν ὀλισθήματι πόδας σου 'your feet with a slip' Je 45.22.

Cf. δύω, καταβαίνω.

καταθαρσέω: aor. κατεθάρσησα.ʃ

to feel encouraged in face of a perilous situation: ἐπὶ τοῖς λόγοις Εζεκιου 'by Hezekiah's words' 2C 32.8. Cf. θαρσέω.

καταθλάω: aor. κατέθλασα; inf. ~θλάσαι.ʃ *

to crush into small pieces with the implication of violence and hostility: ***o*** τὰ ὀστᾶ μου 'my bones' Ps 41.11; αὐτοὺς [= τὰ ἔθνη] ὡς γῆν 'like dust' Is 63.3 (|| καταπατέω 'to trample'). Cf. θλάσμα, καταλόαω, συνθλάω.

καταθύμιος, ον.ʃ

being in accordance with one's mind: subst., ποιοῦντες τὰ ~α αὐτῶν 'doing what they please' Is 44.9; ~ον ψυχῆς αὐτοῦ Mi 7.3. Cf. ἀρέσκω: LSG s.v.

καταιγίς, ίδος. f.

sudden blast of wind: || ἄνεμος Is 17.13, 57.13; πνεῦμα ~ίδος Ps 10.6; desert storm, Is 21.1; destructive, κ. φερομένη 'rushing ..' 28.15, 18, κ. φερομένη καὶ φλὸξ πυρὸς κατεσθίουσα '.. and a consuming fire' 29.6; διασπερεῖ αὐτούς 'will scatter them abroad' 41.16 (|| ἄνεμος), ἀποίσει κ. 'will carry off' 57.13; fig. of fast-turning wheels 5.28, 66.15; of sudden onslaughts of famine, La 5.10. **b**. sea storm: κατεπόντισέν με '.. drowned me into the ocean' Ps 68.3, ὕδατος 68.16.

Cf. ἄνεμος, θύελλα, λαῖλαψ.

καταιδέομαι: aor.ptc.pass. ~ιδεσθείς.ʃ

to pay due respect for and honour: + acc., τὴν τοῦ βασιλέως ἐπιθυμίαν 'the king's desire' 4M 3.12. Cf. αἰδέομαι.

καταικίζω: aor.inf. ~κίσαι, ptc. ~κίσας, pass. ~κισθείς.

to torture hard: abs., + dat. rei, with whips, 4M 6.3, βασάνοις 'with tortures' 11.1; with verbal threats, 7.2; τινα 9.15. Cf. αἰκίζομαι.

καταισχύνω: fut. ~χυνῶ, pass. ~χυνθήσομαι; aor. κατῄσχυνα, subj. καταισχύνω, pass. κατῃσχύνθην, subj. ~χυνθῶ, impv.3pl ~χυνθήτωσαν, opt. ~χυνθείην; pf.ptc.pass. κατῃσχυμμένος.

to make feel shame, make lose face: obj. understood, Ho 2.5; + ἐκ 'on account of' (sinful acts) - ἐκ τῶν θυσιαστηρίων 4.19; ἐκ πάντων τῶν ἐπιτηδευμάτων σου 'of all your practices' Zp 3.11; 'humiliated' in the face of failure, ἐκ πάσης τῆς ἰσχύος αὐτῶν 'on account of all their might (, which has failed them) Mi 7.16, sim. Zp 3.20; public humiliation, ***o*** τὸ πρόσωπον τῶν πτωχῶν Is 3.15, sim. Je 7.19, + ὀνειδίζω 15.9; philosophical reason, 4M 5.35. **b**. with a sense of disappointment and disillusionment at one's hope and trust betrayed: + ἐπί τινι - ἐπὶ τοῖς εἰδώλοις αὐτῶν 'over their idols' Is 1.29 (|| ἐπαισχύνω), ἐπὶ τοῖς γλυπτοῖς 'over the carved (images)' Je 10.14; ἐπὶ σοὶ πέποιθα· μὴ καταισχυνθείην 'I trust in you. May I not be disappointed' Ps 24.2, cf. 21.6; + ἀπό τινος Je 2.36, 31.13, ἀπὸ τῆς προσδοκίας μου 'in my expectation' Ps 118.116. **c**. *to make look foolish* by preventing sth achieving its aim: + acc., βουλὴν πτωχοῦ Ps 13.6. **d**. + neg. and acc. rei: λόγον 'in no way whatsoever' (? or a mechanical rendition of MT דָּבָר) Jd 18.7 B.

Cf. αἰσχύνη: Muraoka 1983.60f.

κατακαίω: fut. ~καύσω, pass. ~καυθήσομαι, ~καήσομαι; aor. ~έκαυσα, impv. ~καυσον, subj. ~καύσω, opt.3s ~καύσαι, subj.pass. ~καυθῶ, impv.3s ~καυθήτω; pf.pass. ~κέκαυμαι, ptc. ~κεκαυμένος, ~κεκαομένος.

tr. *to burn*: ***o*** hum., Ge 38.24, Le 20.14 (as punishment); human sacrifice, ἐν πυρί De 12.31, Je 7.31, 19.5; human bones, Am 2.1; corpse, 1K 30.12; metal calf (object of worship), πυρί (|| ἐν πυρί De 9.21) Ex 32.20; τὰ γλυπτά 'the carved idols' 34.13, De 7.5 (|| καθαιρέω, συντρίβω, ἐκκόπτω), sim. 12.3; pagan altars (βωμοί) Je 30.2; pass. and ***o*** vegetation, 'to burn out, be consumed', ὁ βάτος καίεται πυρί, ὁ δὲ βάτος οὐ κατακαίεται 'the bramble is burning, but the bramble is not burning out' Ex 3.2; left-overs of sacrificial animals, ἐν πυρί 12.10; πυρί 29.14; sacrificial animals, ἐπὶ ξύλων ἐν πυρί Le 4.12 (|| καίω); ἐπὶ πυρός 21.9; temple, To 14.4 𝔊[I], temple gates, 1M 4.38; ashes, Nu 19.17; garment affected by disease, Le 13.52; κρέα .. καὶ αἷμα .. σὺν τῇ κόπρῳ αὐτῆς 'meat .. blood .. together with its excrement' Nu 19.5; salt, De 29.23; words written on a papyrus-scroll, Je 43.32; fig., hum., οἱ ἄνομοι καὶ οἱ ἁμαρτωλοί Is 1.31, ὡς ὑπὸ πυρός 9.19; *s* φλόξ 'flame' 43.2, quoted at 4M 18.14. **b**. *to destroy*: + acc., ἑορτάς 'festivals' Ps 73.8.

Cf. καίω, ἐκκαίω, κατάκαυμα, συμφλογίζω.

κατακάλυμμα, ατος. n. *

that which covers sth else: for a tabernacle, Ex 26.14 (|| ἐπικάλυμμα); for an entrance to a sacred space, κάλυμμα καὶ κ. Nu 3.25; bed-covering, 'blanket' Is 14.11; veil worn by ladies, 47.2. Cf. ἐπικάλυμμα, κάλυμμα, κατακαλύπτω, θέριστρον, σιώπησις.

κατακαλύπτω: fut. ~καλύψω; aor. κατεκάλυψα, inf. ~καλύψαι, opt.3s ~καλύψαι, mid. κατεκαλυψάμην, pass. κατεκαλύφθην; pf.ptc.pass. ~κεκαλυμμένος.

1. *to place a cover and make invisible*: + acc., τῷ καταπετάσματι τὴν κιβωτὸν τοῦ μαρτυρίου 'with the veil ..' Ex 26.34, cf. ἐν ^τῷ καταπετάσματι^ Nu 4.5; mid., κατεκαλύψατο τὸ πρόσωπον αὐτῆς καὶ οὐκ ἐπέγνω αὐτήν 'she had a veil on her face, so he did not recognise her' Ge 38.15, abs. Su 32 TH (:: ἀποκαλύπτω); pass., a land submerging under the sea, Je 28.42; divine ordinances, Da 12.9 LXX (+ σφραγίζω 'to seal'). **b**. mid. *to cover oneself up*: in order to disguise oneself, 2C 18.29 (|| 3K 22.30 συγ~).

2. *to be situated over the entire surface of*: τὸ στέαρ τὸ κατακαλύπτον τὴν κοιλίαν 'the fat covering the intestines' Ex 29.22, Le 3.14; κατεκάλυψεν τὴν ὄψιν τῆς γῆς Nu 22.5 (|| καλύπτω vs. 11); ὡς ὕδωρ κατακαλύψει αὐτούς 'as water covers them' Hb 2.14, sim. Is 11.9, Je 26.8, *s* ὁμίχλη 'mist' Si 24.3; fig. "shame covered our faces" Je 28.51.

3. *to envelop completely*: + acc., "their [= of the horses] dust will cover you" Ez 26.10.

Cf. κατακάλυμμα, συγ~, καλύπτω.

κατακάμπτω: aor. κατέκαμψα, pass. ~κάμφθην.

tr. *to bend down*: + acc., τὴν ψυχήν μου Ps 56.7, pass. *o* hum. 37.7 (depressed); under the burden of sins, Od 12.10, cf. Ryssel ad loc. Cf. κάμπτω.

κατάκαρπος, ον.ʃ *

bearing abundant fruit: *s* ἐλαία 'olive-tree' Ho 14.7, Ps 51.10. Cf. ἔγκαρπος, καρποφόρος, καρπός.

κατακάρπως. adv.ʃ *

to a large extent: κ. κατοικηθήσεται Ιερουσαλημ 'J. will be densely populated' Zc 2.4.

κατακάρπωσις, εως. f.ʃ *

ashes of a burnt sacrifice: Le 6.10, 11.

κατάκαυμα, ματος. n.

1. *a burn* as a form of injury: Ex 21.25 (|| τραῦμα); κ. πυρός Le 13.24 (or: 'fiery inflammation').

2. *part of a body which suffered a burn*: Le 13.25.

3. *act of burning*: δαμάλεως 'of a heifer' Nu 19.6; Je 31.34.

Cf. κατακαίω.

κατακαυχάομαι: fut. ~καυχήσομαι.ʃ *

to exult, glory: ἐν τῷ ὀνόματι ^τοῦ κυρίου^ Zc 10.12; || εὐφραίνομαι Je 27.11. Cf. καύχημα, αἰσχύνω.

κατάκειμαι: fut. ~κείσομαι.

1. *to lie in bed*: idly, *s* hum., Pr 6.9.

2. *to lie in store*: *s* scorn and reproach, Wi 17.7.

κατακενόω.ʃ

to remove the contents of, 'empty': abs. 2K 13.9; + acc., σάκκους 'bags' Ge 42.35. Cf. κενόω, κενός, ἀποχέω, ἐμπίμπλημι.

κατακεντέω: aor. κατεκέντησα; pf.ptc.pass. ~κεκεντημένος.

pierce through: *o* soldier, Je 28.4, ἐν ξίφοις 'with swords' Ez 23.47. Cf. κεντέω.

κατακλάω: aor.pass. κατεκλάσθην.ʃ

to sap the energy of, 'exhaust': Ez 19.12.

κατάκλειστος, ον.ʃ

shut up, confined: *s* maiden confined indoors, 2M 3.19, 3M 1.18; Wi 18.4. Cf. subs.

κατακλείω: aor. κατέκλεισα, pass. κατεκλείσθην, ptc. ~κλεισθείς; pf.ptc.pass. κατακεκλεισμένος.

1. *to shut up, confine*: + acc. pers., Je 39.3; pass., 2M 13.21, εἰς τὴν ἀσίδηρον εἱρκτήν 'into a prison not made of iron' Wi 17.16, ὀρόφοις 'under roofs' 17.2. Cf. κατάκλειστος.

2. *to bind fast and securely*: pass., *o* hum., ἐν δεσμοῖς σιδηροῖς πάντοθεν 'with iron fetters on all sides' 3M 3.25.

κατακληροδοτέω: aor.inf. ~δοτῆσαι.ʃ

to parcel out by lot: + acc., τὴν γῆν αὐτῶν 1M 3.36. Del. De 1.38, 21.16 v.l.

κατακληρονομέω: fut. ~ήσω; aor. κατεκληρονόμησα, inf. ~μῆσαι, ptc. ~μήσας, impv. ~μησον, subj. ~μήσω, pass. κατεκληρονομήθην, impv. ~μήθητι. *

1. *to take possession of*, following a successful military operation, + acc. rei: land or part of it, Nu 13.31, Am 2.10, Ob 19*bis*; σκηνώματα Hb 1.6; ἐν κλήρῳ Nu 33.54; ^σοφίαν^ Si 4.16.

2. *to dispossess*: + acc. pers. De 18.14, 19.1, 31.3; κατακληρονομήσουσιν ὁ οἶκος Ιακωβ τοὺς ~μήσαντας αὐτούς Ob 17*bis*; + ἔν τινι, Hebraism, Ez 22.16.

3. *to appoint as heir*: ~ κύριος τὸν Ιουδαν τὴν μερίδα αὐτοῦ ἐπὶ τὴν γῆν τὴν ἁγίαν 'the Lord will appoint Judah His portion as heir over (= of) the holy land' Zc 2.12 (but cf. Th 339: ὅς τῷ τε Ιουδα τὴν παλαιὰν αὐτῷ μερίδα τῆς γῆς ἀποδώσει).

4. *to give as possession*: τινί τι– ὑμῖν τὴν γῆν Nu 34.18 (|| simp. vs. 17), αὐτοῖς τὴν γῆν De 3.28, αὐτὴν αὐτοῖς 31.7; τοῖς υἱοῖς τὰ ὑπάρχοντα αὐτοῦ 'to the sons his possessions' 21.16; τοῖς καταλοίποις τοῦ λαοῦ μου πάντα ταῦτα '.. all these things [= natural resources]' Zc 8.12; Jd 11.24A*L* (B: simp.); τινά τι Je 3.18; τινι ἔκ τινος Ez 46.18; θρόνον δόξης 'a glorious throne' 1K 2.8; without dir. obj., κύκλῳ ἀπὸ πάντων τῶν ἐχθρῶν 'by eliminating all the enemies around' 2K 7.1B (MT הניח לו > הנחילו).

5. pass. *to settle as legal owner* of a land *and resident*: ἐν τῇ κληρονομίᾳ, ᾗ κατεκληρονομήθης De 19.14, ἐν Ισραηλ Si 24.8 (|| κατασκηνόω).

Cf. κληρονομέω, ἐμβατεύω.

κατακληρόω: aor.subj.mid. ~ρώσωμαι.

to determine as the best or the right by casting the lot: pass., ***o*** hum., 1K 10.20; mid., τινα 14.42, cf. vs. 40; ἔργον ἐπὶ Ισραηλ '(allocate and impose) tasks on Israel' 14.47. Cf. κλῆρος, κληρόω.

κατακλίνω: aor. κατέκλινα, pass. κατεκλίθην, impv. ~κλίθητι, ptc. ~κλιθείς, subj. ~κλιθῶ.

to cause to lie down: to sleep, τινα ἐν τῇ σκηνῇ 3M 1.3. **b.** pass., *to lie down*: ***s*** the injured, ἐπὶ τὴν κοίτην 'on the bed' Ex 21.18, ἐπὶ τῆς κλίνης Da 2.29 LXX; defeated, Jd 5.27 B; lion, κατακλιθεὶς ἀνεπαύσατο '.. rested' Nu 24.9; for a meal, 1K 16.11 (*L* ἀνα~).

Cf. κλίνω, ἀνακλίνω, ἀνάκειμαι.

κατάκλιτος, ον.ʃ *

flowing down (?): ***s*** θέριστρα 'veils (worn by women)' Is 3.23.

κατακλύζω: fut. ~κλύσω, pass. ~κλυσθήσομαι; aor. κατέκλυσα, pass. κατεκλύσθην ..

to inundate: abs., ***s*** a massive army, Da 11.10 TH, χείμαρρος 'wadi' Je 29.2, ὕδωρ Jb 14.19¶, ὑετός Ez 13.11 (divine punishment); + acc., γῆν Je 29.2, wadi Ps 77.20 (pass.), enemies Wi 10.19, troops Da 11.26 TH, ***s*** also troops Ju 6.4. Cf. κατακλυσμός and συγκατακλύζω.

κατακλυσμός, οῦ. m.

flood, inundation: κ. ὕδωρ 'flood-water' Ge 6.17; κ… ὕδατος 7.6, 9.11; διὰ τὸ ὕδωρ τοῦ ~οῦ 7.7, 9.11; ἐν ~ῷ πορείας 'by flooding the route' Na 1.8. Cf. κατακλύζω and πλήμμυρα.

κατακολουθέω: aor.ptc. ~θήσας, subj. ~θήσω, inf. ~θῆσαι.

1. *to follow closely*: + ὀπίσω τινός (pers.), Je 17.16.

2. *to act in accordance with*: + dat. rei, τοῖς λόγοις τῆς παιδίσκης σου Ju 11.6, τῷ νόμῳ σου Da 9.10 LXX.

Cf. ἀκολουθέω.

κατακονδυλίζω ʃ

to maltreat: + acc. pers. πτωχούς Am 5.11, cf. κονδυλίζω ὀρφανούς Ma 2.5. Cf. κονδυλίζω, ἀδικέω: Muraoka 1991.209.

κατακοντίζω: aor. κατηκόντισα.ʃ

to hurl a weapon *and wound*: + acc. pers., βέλεσιν 'with arrows' Jb 30.14; ἐν ζιβύναις 'with spears' Ju 1.15. Cf. ἀκοντίζω.

κατάκοπος, ον. *

very weary: ***s*** hum., τῷ σώματι Jb 3.17; subst. m., Jd 5.26A. Cf. κόπος.

κατακόπτω: fut. ~κόψω; aor. κατέκοψα, pass. κατεκόπην; pf.pass.ptc. ~κεκομμένος.

1. *to cut to pieces*: ***o*** idols, Mi 1.7; weapon, 4.3 (|| συγκόπτω Is 2.4); "the stones of pagan altars broken up like fine dust" 27.9.

2. *to destroy*: acc. pers., γίγαντας Ge 14.5, ἄρχοντας ib. 7; Am 1.5 (|| συντρίβω and ἐξολεθρεύω), Zc 11.6; ἐν μαχαίραις Je 20.4.

3. *to cut away*, 'prune': ***o*** κληματίδας 'vine-branches' Is 18.5.

Cf. κόπτω, ἀφανίζω, συντρίβω.

κατακοσμέω: aor. κατεκόσμησα.ʃ

to adorn: acc., στύλους 'pillars' Ex 39.6; νύμφην .. κόσμῳ 'bride ..' Is 61.10; τὸ κατὰ πρόσωπον τοῦ ναοῦ στεφάνοις χρυσοῖς 'the façade of the temple with golden crowns' 1M 4.57. Cf. κόσμος.

κατακρατέω: aor.act. κατεκράτησα; ptc. ~κρατήσας, impv. ~κράτησον, pass. ~κρατήθην. A favourite word of 1M (15 out of 29).

I. tr. **1.** *to intensify, strengthen*: ὑπὲρ πλίνθον 'more than bricks' Na 3.14^2 (πηλόν 'clay' understood as ***o***); pass., ***o*** ruler, 2C 12.1.

2. *to gain or maintain mastery over* (or: *control of*): + acc., πόλεις Je 47.10, τὴν γῆν καὶ τὴν θάλασσαν 1E 4.2. **b.** + gen., ***s*** birth pangs, κατεκράτησάν σου ὠδῖνες 'birth pangs have overwhelmed you' Mi 4.9, θλῖψις 'distress' like birth pangs Je 27.43 (cf. 6.24, 13.21 with κατέχω), food shortage 1M 6.54; enemy troops in battlefield, ἐφ' ἡμᾶς 2K 11.23*L*; τῶν πόλεων τῶν ὀχυρωμάτων'the fortified cities' 2C 12.4, ὀχυρωμάτων 'fortifications' Na 3.14^1; material resources, τῶν μετάλλων τοῦ χρυσίου καὶ τοῦ ἀργυρίου 'of the metalls of gold and silver' 1M 8.3; ἐννοήματος 'thought' Si 21.11, τῆς ἐπιβουλῆς 'the plot' 3M 1.6. **c.** *to win an argument against*: + gen. pers., 1K 14.42, cf. τὸ ῥῆμα τὸ τοῦ βασιλέως ὑπὲρ Ιωαβ 'the king's argument carried the day as against J.' 2K 24.4*L* (B: ὑπερισχύω; || 1C 21.4 κραταιοῦμαι). **d.** pass. *to be* *taken away by force*: ***o*** land, 1M 15.33 (|| λαμβάνω, κρατέω).

II. intr. **1**. *to intensify*: ***s*** πληγή 'plague' Mi 1.9.

2. *to hold on to* an attitude, opinion etc.: "he put his foot down" 3K 12.24[u]; pass., ἐν τῇ προαιρέσει αὐτῶν 'to their preference' Je 8.5.

Cf. κρατέω, (κατ~, ὑπερ)ισχύω.

κατακρημνίζω: aor. ~εκρήμνισα, ptc. ~νίσας, inf. pass. ~νισθῆναι.

to cause to fall: + acc., ἀπὸ τοῦ ἄκρου 'from the pinnacle' 2C 25.12; ἑαυτὸν .. εἰς τοὺς ὄχλους 2M 14.43; defeated, + acc., τὴν Ιεριχω 12.15. Cf. καταβάλλω.

κατακρίνω: fut. ~κρινῶ; aor. κατέκρινα.

to pronounce guilty: + acc. pers., τὸν ἀθῷον 'the innocent' Su 53 (:: ἀπολύω 'let go as innocent'); ἀποθανεῖν 41 TH, θανάτῳ Da 4.34[a] LXX. Cf. κρίνω, καταγινώσκω, καταδικάζω, ἀπολύω.

κατακροτέω: aor.impv.pl. ~τήσατε.ʃ *

to applaud excessively: triumphantly, ἐπ' αὐτήν 'at her' Je 27.15. Cf. κροτέω.

κατακρούω: aor. κατέκρουσα.ʃ

to beat and hammer in: ***o*** woven locks of hair understood, ἐν τοῖς πασσάλοις 'with pegs (or: pins)' Jd 16.14 A (B: πήγνυμι), πάσσαλον 4.21 *L*. Cf. (ἐγ)κρούω.

κατακρύπτω: fut. ~κρύψω; aor. κατέκρυψα, impv. ~κρυψον, inf. ~κρύψαι, pass. ~κρύβην, subj. ~κρυβῶ, impv. ~κρύβηθι; pf.ptc.pass. ~κεκρυμμένος.

1. *to bury and make invisible*: + acc. rei, ὑπὸ τὴν τερέμινθον 'under the terebinth' Ge 35.4; in the crack of a rock, Je 13.4; in order to protect, Ps 30.21 (|| σκεπάζω); pass. = mid., Je 43.19. **b**. *to store in secret*: + acc. rei, 2M 1.19.

2. intr. *to conceal oneself, lie hidden*: w. hostile intent, Ps 55.7. **b**. pass. in the same sense: εἰς τὸ σπήλαιον 'into the cave' Jo 10.16.

Cf. κρύπτω.

κατακτάομαι: fut.inf. ~κτήσεσθαι; aor.subj. ~κτήσωμαι.ʃ

to get for oneself: + acc. pers., εἰς δούλους 'as slaves' 2C 28.10; + acc. rei, μύσος καὶ κηλῖδα 'defilement and blemish' 2M 6.25. Cf. κτάομαι.

κατακτείνω: aor.inf. ~κτεῖναι, ptc. ~κτείνας.ʃ

to kill: unjustly, τινα 4M 11.3. Cf. ἀποκτείνω.

κατακυλίω: fut. ~κυλιῶ, pass. ~κυλισθήσομαι; aor. pass. κατεκυλίσθην.ʃ

1. *to roll down*: + acc., Je 28.25.

2. pass. *to lie flat in one mass*: ***s*** hum., beaten, Jd 5.27 B.

3. pass. *to slide downwards*: down a slope, 1K 14.8.

κατακύπτω: aor. κατέκυψα.ʃ

to peep downwards: πρός τινα 4K 9.32 (*L* ἐκ~). Cf. ἐκκύπτω.

κατακυριεύω: fut. ~ριεύσω; aor. κατεκυρίευσα, impv. ~ρίευσον, subj. ~ριεύσω, pass. ~ριευθῶ.

1. *to gain dominion over*: + gen., τῆς γῆς αὐτοῦ Nu 21.24; Ge 1.28 (|| ἄρχω), || θηρίων καὶ πετεινῶν 'wild animals and birds' Si 17.4; pass. κατακυριευθῇ ἡ γῆ ἔναντι κυρίου Nu 32.22.

2. *to exercise absolute authority over*: ***s*** God and abs., Ps 71.8; + gen. pers., Je 3.14.

Cf. ἄρχω, κυριεύω, (κατα)κρατέω.

καταλαλέω: fut. ~λαλήσω; aor. κατελάλησα, inf. ~λαλῆσαι.

to speak in hostile or *unfavourable manner*: κατά τινος (hum.) Nu 12.8 (|| simp. vs. 1), πρὸς τὸν θεὸν καὶ κατὰ Μωυσῆ 21.5 (protest and complaint; || κατὰ τοῦ κυρίου καὶ κατὰ σοῦ vs. 7), κατ' ἐμοῦ Ps 118.23; + gen. pers., τοῦ θεοῦ 77.19, λάθρᾳ τοῦ πλησίον 'against the neighbour behind his back' 100.5; + acc. rei, κατ' ἐμοῦ ψευδῆ Ho 7.13; ταῦτα .. πρὸς τὸν πλησίον αὐτοῦ Ma 3.16. Cf. καταλαλιά, λαλέω, κατεῖπον, καταλέγω, κακολογέω, διαβάλλω.

καταλαλιά, ᾶς. f.ʃ

slander: Wi 1.11 (|| γογγυσμός).

καταλαμβάνω; fut. ~λήμψομαι, pass. ~λημφθήσομαι; aor.act. κατέλαβον, impv.2pl ~λάβετε, mid. κατελαβόμην, inf. ~λαβέσθαι, subj.act. ~λάβω, mid. ~λάβωμαι, opt.act.3s ~λάβοι, pass. κατελήμφθην, subj. ~λημφθῶ; pf.ptc.pass. κατειλημμένος

1. *to lay hold of*, 'seize': pass. and ***o*** burglar caught red-handed, Ex 22.4; κατελήμφθη αὐτοῦ τὰ κεκρυμμένα 'his hidden treasures were seized' Ob 6; fig. of a human attempt to win divine favour, ἐν τίνι καταλάβω τὸν κύριον .. εἰ καταλήμψομαι αὐτὸν ἐν ὁλοκαυτώμασιν ..; 'with what would I secure the Lord? .. Shall I secure him with burnt offerings ..?' Mi 6.6 (|| ἀντιλαμβάνω, q.v.); ***s*** sword, ***o*** hum., Ez 33.4. **b**. fig.: εὐφροσύνη καταλήμψεται αὐτούς 'joy will grip them' Is 35.10, 51.11; Es C 12 o'; ***s*** divine anger, Ps 68.25; gluttony and sexual drive, Si 23.6; sin, Ju 11.11; κακὴ βουλή Pr 2.17, cf. **6** below.

2. *to conquer and capture* by military operation: mid. and ***o*** (acc.) city, land etc., Nu 21.32, Ju 2.25; τὴν οἰκουμένην ὅλην 'the entire world' Is 10.14 (|| αἴρω).

3. *to catch up with, overtake*: + acc. pers., after a pursuit, καταδιώξεται τοὺς ἐραστὰς αὐτῆς καὶ οὐ μὴ καταλάβῃ αὐτούς 'she will chase her lovers, but will never catch them' Ho 2.7 (|| εὑρίσκω); ***o*** escapee, Ge 31.23; after a hot chase (ἐπιδιώκω), 44.4, Si 11.10 (διώκω), Jo 2.5, Je 52.8, La 1.3; διώξας καταλήμψομαι Ex 15.9, sim. De 19.6; καταδιώξονταί σε καὶ καταλήμψονταί σε 28.45, cf. Jd 1.5B (A: εὑρίσκω), PSol 15.8. **b**. *to reach a target*: + acc., "If you pursue (διώκῃς) righteousness, you will attain it" Si 27.8, ^σοφίαν^ 15.7; ***s*** divine message, τοὺς λόγους μου καὶ τὰ νόμιμά μου .. οὐ κατελάβοσαν τοὺς πατέρας ὑμῶν; Zc 1.6; mid., φιλίαν τοῖς Ἰουδαίοις 'to conclude a friendship treaty with ..' 1M 10.23.

4. *to reach* a stage: κ. ὁ ἀλόητος τὸν τρύγητον 'the threshing will last up to the harvesting (of grapes)' Le 26.5, Am 9.13.

5. *to befall*: τινα, *s* sth undesirable, μὴ καταλάβῃ με τὰ κακὰ καὶ ἀποθάνω Ge 19.19, στενοχωρία 'distress' 3M 2.10, τραῦμα 'a wound' Je 10.19, οὐ μὴ καταλάβῃ αὐτοὺς ἐν τῷ βουνῷ πόλεμος 'a war will never befall them ..'(?) Ho 10.9 (read, *pace* Zgl, ἦλθεν and construe ἐπὶ τὰ τέκνα ἀδικίας with it).

6. *to extend its effect to and affect*: + acc., *s* "my deeds of lawlessness" Ps 39.13, κατάραι 'curses' De 28.15 (ǁ εὑρίσκω vs. 2), οὐ μὴ καταλάβῃ αὐτοὺς δικαιοσύνη Is 59.9, cf. τοὺς δικαίους καταλήμψεται ἀγαθά Pr 13.21 (ǁ καταδιώκω), cf. **1b** above.

7. *to find* to be in a certain state or in action: + acc. and ptc., πολιορκοῦντα τὸν βασιλέα Λομνα 'the king besieging L.' Is 37.8; 1E 6.8, Su 58, Da 6.11 LXX (TH εὑρίσκω and vs. 13 LXX); + adj. and ptc., 1.20 LXX.

8. *to grasp with the mind, comprehend*: + acc., ἀνεξιχνίαστα 'inscrutable things' Jb 34.24, τρίβους εὐθείας 'straight paths' Pr 2.19. Cf. συνίημι: Shipp 306.

Cf. ἀντι~, προκατα~, λαμβάνω, κατάλημψις, κρατέω, ἁλίσκομαι.

καταλάμπω.ʃ

mid. *to become bright and illuminated*: *s* the world, φωτί 'with light' Wi 17.20. Cf. λάμπω.

καταλεαίνω: fut. ~λεανῶ.ʃ *

to grind down, smash up into pieces: + acc., ^πᾶσαν τὴν γῆν^ Da 7.23 LXX. Cf. καταλέω, συντρίβω.

καταλέγω.ʃ

to accuse: + gen. pers. and acc. rei, αὐτοῦ ἀσέβειαν De 19.16. Cf. κατεῖπον, καταλαλέω.

κατάλειμμα, ματος. n.

that which has remained unharmed, survived: ὑπολείπεσθαι ὑμῶν κ. ἐπὶ τῆς γῆς Ge 45.7; αὐτῶν ὄνομα καὶ κατάλειμμα καὶ σπέρμα Is 14.22; 1M 3.35; w. ref. to a semi-autonomous area within an occupied land, Je 47.11. **b**. *that which has remained unconsumed*: Is 37.30. **c**. *the remaining part(s) or individuals*: τοῦ λαοῦ 1K 13.15.

Cf. καταλείπω, κατάλειψις, λεῖμμα, ὑπόλειμμα.

καταλείπω: fut.act. ~λείψω, pass. ~λειφθήσομαι; aor. κατέλιπον, impv.3s ~λιπέτω, ptc. ~λιπών, inf. ~λιπεῖν, subj. ~λίπω, pass. κατελείφθην, subj. ~λειφθῶ, ptc. ~λειφθείς, inf. ~λειφθῆναι; pf. ~λέλοιπα, pass. καταλέλειμμαι, inf. ~λελεῖφθαι, ptc.act. ~λελοιπώς, pass. ~λελειμμένος.

1. *to leave neglected and uncared for*: + acc. pers., ἐν τῇ ἐρήμῳ Nu 32.15; *s* shepherd, οἱ καταλελοιπότες τὰ πρόβατα Zc 11.17; *o* benefactor, Ex 2.20; *s* God and *o* hum., καταλείψω αὐτοὺς καὶ ἀποστρέψω τὸ πρόσωπόν μου ἀπ' αὐτῶν '.. and shall turn my face away from them' De 31.17; *o* God, Is 17.10 (ǁ οὐκ μιμνήσκομαι); pass., ἀπὸ τοῦ ἀνδρὸς αὐτῆς 'by her husband' Ru 1.5; *o* land, Is 6.11, καταλελειμμένη εἰς τὸν αἰῶνα 'forsaken for ever' 17.2; flock 27.10 (ǁ ἀνίημι).

2. *to leave unharmed*: pass. κατελείφθη μόνος Νωε 'Noah only was spared' Ge 7.23; αὐτὸς μόνος καταλέλειπται 'he alone has been left' 42.38; τὸ περισσὸν τὸ καταλειφθέν, ὃ κατέλιπεν ὑμῖν ἡ χάλαζα 'the residue left over for you by the hail' Ex 10.5 (ǁ ὑπολείπω vs. 12); οἱ καταλειφθέντες 'the survivors' Ge 14.10, Le 26.36, Is 10.19, τὸ καταλειφθὲν τοῦ Ισραηλ 4.2, 10.20 (ǁ οἱ σωθεντὲς τοῦ Ιακωβ) τὸ ὑπολειφθὲν ἐν Σιων καὶ τὸ καταλειφθὲν ἐν Ιερουσαλημ 4.3; ὅσοι ἐὰν καταλειφθῶσιν 'whosoever might be spared' Zc 14.16; ἀπὸ τοῦ θανάτου καὶ ἀπὸ τοῦ λιμοῦ .. Je 21.7; "these survived among the cities of Judaea, being fortified cities (πόλεις ὀχυραί)" 41.7; opp. ἀπόλλυμι Nu 33.55; unused, Ex 39.13 (ǁ λοιπός vs. 12), Le 5.13, 19.10; unconsumed and + dat. pers., De 28.51.

3. *to sever ties with* (acc.): + acc. pers., καταλείψει ἄνθρωπος τὸν πατέρα αὐτοῦ καὶ τὴν μητέρα αὐτοῦ Ge 2.24; Οὐ δυνήσεται τὸ παιδάριον καταλιπεῖν τὸν πατέρα 44.22, τὸν ἄνδρα 'the husband' Si 23.22; + acc. rei, τὴν διαθήκην κυρίου De 29.25; opp. κρατέω Ba 4.1.

4. *to cause to remain behind*: + acc., καταλιπὼν τὰ ἱμάτια ἐν ταῖς χερσὶν αὐτῆς 'leaving the clothes in her hands' Ge 39.12; Καταλείψω μετὰ σοῦ ἀπὸ τοῦ λαοῦ 'Let me leave with you some of the folk' 33.15; ὑπόδειγμα 'example' 2M 6.28; τὰ καταλειπόμενα ἀπ' αὐτοῦ 'what is left over unconsumed of it [= sacrificial sheep]' Ex 12.10; 16.19, 20; Si 23.26; καταλειφθῇ .. καλάμη 'there will remain (nothing but) stubble' Is 17.6. **b**. to be looked after by sbd remaining behind: + acc. rei, ἀλλοτρίοις τὸν πλοῦτον αὐτῶν 'their wealth to strangers (upon their death)' Ps 48.11; pass., *o* τὰ πράγματα 'the state affairs' 2M 9.24.

5. *to leave* in a certain state after a certain process is gone through: often pass., καταλειφθήσονται ἄνθρωποι ὀλίγοι Is 24.6, πόλεις ἔρημοι 24.12.

Cf. κατάλοιπος, ἐκ~, ἐγκατα~, περι~, προσκατα~, ὑπολείπω, κατάλειμμα, κατάλειψις, λοιπός, καταλιμπάνω.

κατάλειψις, εως. f.ʃ

one who has survived a danger or crisis: sg.coll., 'survivors,' Ge 45.7. Cf. καταλείπω.

καταλέω: aor. κατήλεσα, ptc. καταλέσας.ʃ
to grind: *o* a metal object, λεπτόν (ǁ σφόδρα De 9.21) 'into small particles' Ex 32.20; De 9.21, cf. Anz 16. Cf. ἀλέω, καταλεαίνω, συντρίβω.

καταλήγω: aor.ptc. ~λήξας.ʃ
to leave off speaking: abs., "as she was about to stop speaking" 2M 7.30; + acc., τὸν λόγον 9.5; *+ gen., θρήνων 'dirges' 3M 6.32. Cf. λήγω, παύω.

κατάλημψις, εως. f.ʃ
v.n. of καταλαμβάνω, **2**: αὐτῆς [= πόλεως] De 20.19.

καταλιθοβολέω: fut. ~λήσω; aor.inf. ~λῆσαι.ʃ
to kill by stoning: + acc. pers., Ex 17.4, ἐν λίθοις Nu14.10. Cf. λιθοβολέω.

κατάλιθος, ον.ʃ *
set with precious stones: ὕφασμα ~ον τετράστιχον 'a woven piece set with four rows of precious stones' Ex 28.17, 36.17.

καταλιμπάνω.ʃ
1. *to cause to remain* without going elsewhere: + acc., καταλιμπάνει τὰ ἱμάτια παρ' ἑαυτῇ Ge 39.16; 2K 5.21.
2. *to desert as an act of betrayal*: + acc., τὸν κύριον θεόν 3K 18.18.
Cf. καταλείπω.

καταλλαγή, ῆς. f.
1. *interest* accrued: Is 9.5, cf. Cyr. (PG 70.253 προσθήκη); Ziegler 1934.195; Seeligmann 1948.50.
2. *reconciliation*: between God and humans, 2M 5.20.
Cf. καταλλάσσω, διαλλαγή: Spicq 2.262-6.

καταλλάσσω: fut.pass. ~λλαγήσομαι; aor.inf.pass. ~λλαγῆναι; opt.pass.3s ~λλαγείη.ʃ
mid. *to reconcile oneself w.* after a period of enmity: *s* God, + dat. pers., 2M 1.5, 7.33, 8.29. Cf. καταλλαγή, διαλλάσσω, εὐκατάλλατος.

καταλοάω: aor. κατηλόησα.ʃ
to crush into pieces: + acc. rei, Da 2.34 LXX (ǁ συν~ 2.45). Cf. (συν)αλοάω, καταθλάω, καταξαίνω, λεπτύνω.

καταλογίζω: aor.pass. κατελογίσθην.ʃ
1. *to regard and treat as belonging* to: ἐν ἡμῖν κατελογίσθης '.. like one of us' Is 14.10, ἐν υἱοῖς θεοῦ Wi 5.5 (ǁ λογίζομαι vs. 4).
2. *to determine the nature of*: pass., αὕτη ἡ γραφὴ .. κατελογίσθη Da 5.17 LXX.

κατάλοιπος, ον.
Often used substantivally with the article and followed by a genitive.
left remaining untouched, unharmed or not mentioned, often with a nuance of inferior quality or lesser importance: τὸ ~ον τοῦ αἵματος Le 5.9; τὰ ~α τῆς κάμπης .. τῆς ἀκρίδος .. τοῦ βρούχου 'what has been left over by the caterpillar .. of the locust .. of the palmerworm' Jl 1.4; τὰ ~α πάντων τῶν ἔργων αὐτοῦ 'the rest of all its works' Nu 3.26; τὰ ~α τῆς νομῆς 'the remainder of the pasture,' following ἡ καλὴ νομή Ez 34.18 (ǁ λοιπός). **b**. of survivors, those spared, often w. ref. to the post-exilic community: ἀπολοῦνται οἱ ~οι τῶν ἀλλοφύλων Am 1.8; τοῖς ~οις τῆς κληρονομίας αὐτοῦ Mi 7.18; οἱ ~οι τοῦ λαοῦ μου Zp 2.9 (*DJD* 8: ἐπι~); subst. n. s. coll. Is 15.9 (ǁ σπέρμα), τὸ ~ον τοῦ Ισραηλ 46.3. **c**. adj.: οἱ ~οι λόγοι Σαλωμων 2C 9.29 ǁ τὰ ~α τῶν λόγων Εζεκίου 32.32; οἱ ~οι σύνδουλοι 2E 4.9, τοῖς ~οις ἔθνεσι Ez 36.3.
Cf. καταλείπω, ἐπί~, περίλοιπος, περισσός.

καταλοχία, ας. f.ʃ *
= καταλοχισμός: 2C 31.18.

καταλοχισμός, οῦ. m.
register: of population, 1E 5.39, τῶν ἱερέων 2C 31.17, κατὰ γενέσεις 1C 5.7; of residential areas, 4.33. Cf. καταλοχία.

κατάλυμα, ατος. n.
1. *place where a traveller lodges on his way*: Ex 4.24, Je 14.8; + σκηνή 2K 7.6 ǁ 1C 17.5; w. ref. to brothel, Ez 23.21.
2. *more or less permanent dwelling-place*: κ. ἅγιόν σου Ex 15.13, εἰρήνης 'peaceful' Je 32.23; lions' lair, 32.24.
Cf. καταλύω: *BA* ad Ex 4.25, 15.13.

κατάλυσις, εως. f.ʃ
1. = κατάλυμα **2**: for animals, Je 29.21.
2. *act of dismantling and breaking up*: τῆς προγονικῆς πολιτείας 'of the ancestral way of life' 2M 8.17; σου 'your (ruin)' 4M 11.25. **b**. *act of disentangling*: *o* mysteries, Da 2.22 LXX.
3. *cessation of existence*: κ. σου 'your end' 4M 11.25.
Cf. κατάλυμα, καταλύω.

καταλύτης, ου.ʃ
guest staying a short period: μονοήμερος 'for just a day' Wi 5.14. Cf. καταλύω.

καταλύω: fut. ~λύσω; aor. κατέλυσα; inf. ~λῦσαι, ptc. ~λύσας, subj. ~λύσω, impv. ~λυσον, pass.inf. ~λυθῆναι; pf. ~λέλυκα.
1. *to have rest* after the day's work: δείλης 'in the evening' Zp 2.7. **b**. caus.: τὸν λαόν 'the army' 2K 17.8B (*L* ~παύω).
2. *to take up one's quarters*: ἐν μέσῳ τοῦ οἴκου αὐτοῦ Zc 5.4; ǁ κατοικέω Je 28.43.
3. *to lodge*: during a journey, ἐκκλίνατε εἰς τὸν οἶκον τοῦ παιδὸς ὑμῶν καὶ καταλύσατε Ge 19.2; τόπος ἡμῖν καταλῦσαι 'room for us to stay' 24.23; αὐτοῦ τὴν νύκτα 'here tonight' Nu 22.8 (ǁ καταμένω here and ὑπομένω vs. 19). **b**. *to stay temporarily* at sbd else's: ἐν οἴκοις πορνῶν 'at brothels' Je 5.7, cf. καιρὸς καταλυόντων 'time for receiving lodgers [=

clients at a brothel] Ez 16.8, κοίτη καταλυόντων 23.17; παρά τινι Je 44.13; of locusts alighting, Si 43.17; ice settling on water, 43.20; πρός τινα 27.9.

4. *to break up* what is neatly constructed or set up: + acc., σκηνήν Is 38.12, οἶκον 2E 5.12; τρυμαλιὰς πετρῶν 'caves of rocks' Je 29.17; ἐφημερίας '(dismiss the) daily order of services' 2C 23.8. **b.** *to tear apart by argument and demolish*: + acc., τυραννίδα 'tyranny' 4M 8.15.

5. *to cause to disappear*: + acc., ἐκ πόλεων Ιουδα .. φωνὴν εὐφραινομένων .., Je 7.34, sim. 16.9; τὸ πλῆθος τῶν μουσικῶν 'a lot of music' Ez 26.13; city, 26.17; passions, 4M 1.6; tyranny, 1.11; fear, 14.8; tyrannical force, 17.2 (|| ἀκυρόω) + pers., ἐχθρόν Ps 8.3, ἀγχιστέα Ru 4.14.

6. *to depose*: + acc. pers., τῆς ἀρχιερωσύνης 'from the office of high priest' 4M 4.16; ἀπὸ καθαρισμοῦ αὐτόν 'withheld a chance of purification from him' Ps 88.45.

7. *to abolish*: + acc., νόμους 2M 2.22, νομίμους πολιτείας 'lawful ways of living' 4.11; maintenance (?) of the temple, 4M 4.20; against one's will, 5.33.

Cf. κατάλυμα, κατάλυσις, καταλύτης, ὑπομένω.

καταμανθάνω: aor. κατέμαθον, inf. καταμαθεῖν, impv. ~μαθε.

to watch and observe to investigate: + acc. pers., a marriageable woman, Ge 24.21; τὰς θυγατέρας τῶν ἐγχωρίων 'the daughters of the locals' 34.1 (*s* woman); οἰκίαν 'house' Le 14.36; + an exclam. cl., Jb 35.5. **b.** *to become* unduly *curious about*: + acc. pers., παρθένον 'virgin' Si 9.5.

Cf. μανθάνω.

καταμαρτυρέω: fut. ~ρήσω; aor. ~εμαρτύρησα, impv. ~μαρτύρησον, ptc. ~μαρτυρήσας.

to testify against: + gen. pers., Jb 15.6. **b.** *to say as witness against*: + gen. pers. and acc. rei, μαρτυρίαν ψευδῆ Pr 25.18. ψευδῆ μου 'falsehoods against me' Su 43 TH; + ὅτι 21 TH.

Cf. μαρτυρέω.

καταμένω: aor. κατέμεινα, subj. ~μείνω.

to remain in a certain place: Οὐ μὴ καταμείνῃ τὸ πνεῦμά μου ἐν τοῖς ἀνθρώποις τούτοις Ge 6.3; *s* hum., κατέμεινεν ὁ λαὸς ἐν Καδης Nu 20.1; guests, παρὰ Βαλααμ 22.8 (|| καταλύω here and ὑπομένω vs. 19). Cf. μένω, ὑπομένω, καταλύω.

καταμερίζω: fut. ~μεριῶ, ~μερίσω; aor. κατεμέρισα, inf. ~μερίσαι, mid. κατεμερισάμην, subj. pass. ~μερισθῶ.

1. *to divide into multiple parts or groups*: + acc. pers., ἐν ταῖς φυλαῖς αὐτῶν 'by tribe' PSol 17.28.

2. *to divide and give out*, 'portion out': + dat. pers., Nu 34.29; also + acc., Le 25.46.

3. *to divide sth and cause to take possession* of that which has been apportioned: + acc. pers. and pass., καταμερισθῶσιν οἱ υἱοὶ Ισραηλ ἕκαστος εἰς τὴν κληρονομίαν αὐτοῦ Nu 32.18; + dat. pers., τὰ ὅρια τῆς γῆς, ἣν καταμερίζει σοι κύριος De 19.3; mid. and + double acc., 3M 6.31.

Cf. διαιρέω, κατακληρονομέω, καταμερισμός.

καταμερισμός, οῦ. m.ʃ

act of dividing and alloting: *o* land, Jo 13.14. Cf. καταμερίζω.

καταμεστόομαι: pf.ptc.~μεμεστωμένος.ʃ

to become full: τινι 3M 5.46. Cf. μεστόω, πληρόω.

καταμετρέω: fut. ~ρήσω, pass. ~ρηθήσομαι; aor. pass. κατεμετρήθην.ʃ

to measure (+ τι): of a land to be taken by conquerors, Nu 34.7; mid., τὴν γῆν ἐν κληρονομίᾳ Ez 45.1; pass., ἡ γῆ σου ἐν σχοινίῳ καταμετρηθήσεται 'your land will be measured up with a measuring-line' Am 7.17, sim. Mi 2.4; Ez 48.14. Cf. δια~, ἐκμετρέω, μέτρον.

καταμήνιος, ον.ʃ

subst.n.pl., *menses*: ῥάκος ~ων, rags worn by a woman segregated during menstruation Es C 27.

καταμηνύω: aor. κατεμήνυσα.ʃ

to give some previously unknown information about: τι 4M 4.4. Cf. μηνύω.

καταμίγνυμι: pf.ptc.pass. ~μεμιγμένος.ʃ

to intermix: by sewing in, κροσσωτὰ .. καταμεμιγμένα ἐν ἄνθεσιν 'tassels .. intermixed with flowers' Ex 28.14. Cf. μίγνυμι.

καταμιμνήσκομαι: aor.ptc. ~μνησθείς.ʃ

to recall to mind: abs., 4M 13.12. Cf. μιμνήσκομαι.

καταμωκάομαι: fut. ~κήσομαι.

to mock at, make a fool of: + gen. pers., Je 45.19; + καταγελάω 2C 30.10. Cf. καταγελάω.

καταναγκάζω.ʃ

to enforce: + acc. rei, ἀπόστασιν 'apostasy' 1M 2.15. Cf. ἀναγκάζω.

καταναλίσκω: fut. ~λώσω; pass. ~λωθήσομαι; aor. ~λωσα, subj. ~λώσω, inf. ~λῶσαι, pass. κατανα-λώθην.

1. *to spend*: + acc., εἰς ἑαυτούς '(to put) to their own use' Ep Je 9.

2. *to devour*: *s* the fire of altar, Le 6.10; destructive fire, κύριος ὁ θεός σου πῦρ καταναλίσκον ἐστίν De 4.24; God and *o* hum., τὰ ἔθνη ταῦτα ἀπὸ προσώπου σου 7.22 (|| ἐξαναλίσκω), ἐν πυρί Si 45.19, δόρατι καὶ πυρί 'with spear ..' Es E 24; *o* μόχθους 'fruits of toil' Je 3.24; pass. ἐν πυρὶ ζήλους αὐτοῦ καταναλωθήσεται πᾶσα ἡ γῆ 'the whole earth shall be consumed with the fire of his zeal' Zp 1.18; metaph. and *s* truth, Is 59.14; worries, Da 11.26 LXX (TH ἐσθίω), sorrow Si 27.29.

Cf. (ἐξ)αναλίσκω, ἀφανίζω, ἐσθίω.

κατανέμομαι: aor. κατενεμησάμην.ʃ
to feed on: + acc., grape-vine, Ps 79.14. Cf. νέμω, βόσκω, ἐσθίω.

κατανίσταμαι.ʃ
to lord it over sbd (ἐπί τινα): ἐπὶ τὴν συναγωγὴν κυρίου Nu 16.3.

κατανοέω: fut. ~νοήσω; aor. κατενόησα, inf. ~νοῆσαι, part. ~νοήσας.
1. *to observe closely to find out about*: abs., Is 59.16 (ll εἶδον), Ex 19.21, 33.8; + acc. rei, ξύλον, ὡραῖόν ἐστιν τοῦ κατανοῆσαι Ge 3.6; τὰ ἴχνη τῆς χώρας 'the routes of the land' 42.9 (*s* spies and ll εἶδον vs. 12); τὴν γῆν Nu 32.8, 9 (ll κατασκοπεύω De 1.24); πόνον 'hardship' Ex 2.11, Ps 9.35; τὰ ἔργα σου Hb 3.2 (ll εἰσακούω), τὰ ἔργα ^κυρίου^ Is 5.12 (ll ἐμβλέπω), τὰς ὁδούς σου Ps 118.15 (ll ἀδολεσχέω, μελετάω); εἰς ἀπόκρυφα μέρη 'into hidden corners' Si 23.19 (ll ἐπιβλέπω); w. evil design, + acc. pers., Ps 36.32; τοῖς ὀφθαλμοῖς σου 90.8; + ὅτι Si 30.26; + ptc. clause, τὸ κέρας .. πόλεμον συνιστάμενον 'the horn .. waging a war' Da 7.21 LXX (TH θεωρέω); 2M 9.25.
2. *to comprehend*: τὸν λόγον αὐτοῦ 'his thought' Ju 8.14.
Cf. κατανόησις, ἀτενίζω, διανοέομαι, εἶδον, θεάομαι, θεωρέω, κατοπτεύω, ὁράω, συνίημι: Schmidt 3.645-7; Behm, *TDNT* 4.973f.

κατανόησις, εως. f.ʃ
v.n. of κατανοέω **1**: γυναικός Si 41.21.

καταντάω: aor. κατήντησα, ptc. καταντήσας, impv. ~τησον.ʃ
1. *to arrive* at: εἰς Ἱεροσόλυμα 2M 4.21; fig., + πρός and acc., 6.14; *s* sin and its consequences, ἐπὶ κεφαλὴν Ιωαβ καὶ ἐπι πάντα τὸν οἶκον τοῦ πατρὸς αὐτοῦ 2K 3.29B.
*__2__. caus. of **1**: metaph., εἰς ἑαυτὸν κατήντησε τὴν ἀρχιερωσύνην 'made the high priesthood land at his own door' 2M 4.24.
Cf. ἀφικνέομαι, κατάντημα: Spicq 2.269f.

κατάντημα, ατος. n.ʃ *
goal of movement: Ps 18.7. Cf. καταντάω.

καταντλέω.ʃ
to pour liquid over sbd or sth *and to cause to move downwards*: metaph., pass., *o* hum. under torture, τρικυμίαις 'with billows' 4M 7.2. Cf. καταχέω.

κατάνυξις, εως. f.ʃ *
act of benumbing the senses: ἐπότισας ἡμᾶς οἶνον ~εως 'you made us drink stunning wine' Ps 59.5 (of deeply hurtful experiences; ll ἔδειξας τῷ λαῷ σκληρά 'you showed the people harsh things'); πεπότικεν ὑμᾶς κύριος πνεύματι ~εως 'the Lord intoxicated you with a stupefying spirit' Is 29.10 (ll ἐκλύθητε καὶ ἔκστητε καὶ κραπαλήσατε 'faint and be astonished and become dizzy'). Cf. κατανύσσω.

κατανύσσω: fut.pass. ~νυγήσομαι; aor.pass. κατενύχθην, ~νύγην, ptc. ~νυχθείς, impv. ~νύγητι, inf. ~νυγῆναι, subj. ~νυγῶ; pf.pass. ~νένυγμαι, ptc. ~νενυγμένος. Alw. pass. *
to affect mentally and profoundly, 'to cut to the heart': *o* pers., Ge 27.38 (reacting to a deeply painful situation), 34.7 (resulting in λυπηρόν τινί ἐστι σφόδρα), Le 10.3, "even if you said it in private, you might grind your teeth in bed with vexation" Ps 4.5; κατανενυγμένος τῇ καρδίᾳ 108.16 (cf. τὴν καρδίαν Acts 2.37), ἐπὶ τῶν ῥημάτων μου 'by what I said' Si 12.12, ἐπὶ τῇ ἀφροσύνῃ σου 'over your folly' 47.20, ἐν λύπῃ ἁμαρτιῶν 'with sorrow for sins' 14.1, περὶ αὐτῆς 'over her' Su 10, ὑπὲρ τοῦ λόγου 3K 20.27. Cf. κατάνυξις: *BA* ad Ge 27.38 and Harl, *Langue* 77-95.

κατανύω.ʃ
to complete: + acc., τὴν πορείαν 'the journey' 2M 9.4. Cf. συντελέω.

κατανωτίζομαι: aor. κατενωτισάμην.ʃ
to ignore a command: τοῦ μὴ ἐλθεῖν Ju 5.4.

καταξαίνω: fut. ~ξανῶ; aor. κατέξανα.ʃ
to tear up in pieces: + acc., σάρκας '(their) flesh' Jd 8.7 A (B: ἀλοάω); + acc. pers., 8.16 A (B: ἀλοάω). Cf. καταλοάω.

καταξηραίνω: fut. ~ξηρανῶ; aor. κατεξήρανα.ʃ
tr. *to dry up*: τὴν γῆν αὐτοῦ καὶ πάντα τὰ σκεύη τὰ ἐπιθυμητὰ αὐτοῦ Ho 13.15 (ll ἀναξηραίνω and ἐρημόω); τὴν ἐρυθρὰν θάλασσαν Jo 2.10, Ju 5.13. Cf. (ἀνα)ξηραίνω, κατάξηρος.

κατάξηρος, ον.ʃ
very dry, parched: fig., ἡ ψυχὴ ἡμῶν κ. 'we are distraught' Nu 11.6. Cf. καταξηραίνω.

κατάξιος, α, ον. f.ʃ
fitting: *s* κρίσις 'penalty' Es E 18 o' (*L* δίκη).

καταξιόω: aor.ptc. ~ξιώσας, inf. ~ξιῶσαι, pass. κατηξιώθην.
1. *to implore earnestly*: + acc. pers., τὸν κύριον μετὰ κλαυθμοῦ καὶ νηστειῶν 'the Lord with crying and fasts' 2M 13.12.
2. *to consider deserving*: + acc. pers. and gen. rei, 3M 3.21; pass., 4M 18.3. Cf. ἀξιόω.

καταξύω: pf.ptc.pass. κατεξυσμένος.ʃ
to smooth, plane down: *o* wooden pagan idol, ὑπὸ τέκτονος 'by a carpenter' Ep Je 7.

καταπαίζω: fut. ~παίξομαι.ʃ
to deal with sbd *not seriously* or *with sincerity*: 'to make fun of,' + gen. pers., 4K 2.23 (verbally); in general and + gen. pers., Je 2.15; + κατά τινος (pers.) 9.5 (ll οὐ λαλέω ἀλήθειαν).

καταπαλαίω: aor.inf. ~παλαῖσαι.ʃ
to defeat in a combat: + acc., ἀλγηδόνας 'pains' 4M 3.18.

καταπανουργεύομαι: aor. κατεπανουργευσάμην.ʃ * *to devise villainously*: + ἐπὶ τὸν λαόν σου .. γνώμην Ps 82.4.

καταπάσσω: aor.ptc. ~πάσας, mid. κατεπασάμην, impv. ~πασαι, pl. ~πάσασθε, ptc. ~πασάμενος.ʃ

mid. *to besprinkle*: sth (acc.) with sth (acc.), γῆν καταπάσασθε καταγέλωτα ὑμῶν 'Besprinkle your laughable object with dust' Mi 1.10; ἐπί τι - γῆν ἐπὶ τὴν κεφαλῆν αὐτοῦ Jb 1.20 v.l., 2.12 (only γῆν, so also 2M 14.15), an expression of distress or remorse, cf. ἐν σποδῷ 'with ashes' Je 6.26, σποδόν Es 4.1, and act. γῇ 'dust' τὰς κεφαλὰς καταπάσαντες 2M 10.25. Cf. ῥαίνω.

καταπατέω: fut. ~πατήσω, pass. ~πατηθήσομαι; aor. act. κατεπάτησα, impv. ~πάτησον, subj. ~πατήσω, opt.3s ~πατήσαι, pass. κατεπατήθην; pf.pass. ~πεπάτημαι, ptc. ~πεπατημένος.

1. *to tread under foot*: abs., ὁ ἄρχων καταπατῶν ἐπὶ τῆς γῆς Is 16.4; + acc. κεραμεὺς καταπατῶν τὸν πηλόν 'a potter .. his clay' 41.25, τοὺς ἅλω 'the threshing-floors' 1K 23.1; λίθον ~τούμενον 'a trampled stone' Zc 12.3; ***o*** Jerusalem, ib., the Jerusalem sanctuary 1M 3.45 (pass.), πόλεις Is 10.6 (***s*** army), ἐν ταῖς ὁπλαῖς τῶν ἵππων .. τὰς πλατείας 'with the hooves of the horses .. the streets' Ez 26.11; ποταμούς 32.2, ὕδωρ 32.13 (***s*** ἴχνος); grazing ground, 34.18; ἀνόμους 'the lawless' Ma 4.3, ἀμπέλους 'grape-vines' Is 16.8; + ἐπί τινι 16.9; fig. and ***o*** ὁ στέφανος τῆς ὕβρεως 'the crown of arrogance' 28.3, εἰς γὴν τὴν ζωήν μου Ps 7.6.

2. *to deal harshly and oppressively with*: + acc. pers. πένητας 'the poor' Am 4.1 (ǁ καταδυναστεύω); δίκαιον 5.12.

3. *to show no regard for*: + acc. rei, κρίμα Ho 5.11 (ǁ καταδυναστεύω).

Cf. καταπάτημα, ~σις, πατέω, καταδυναστεύω: Passoni dell'Acqua 1984, 1986.

καταπάτημα, ατος. n. *

1. *that which is trampled under foot*: ἔσται εἰς κ. ὡς πηλὸς ἐν ταῖς ὁδοῖς 'will become an object to be trampled like mire on roads' Mi 7.10, sim. Is 5.5, Ez 36.4.

2. *act of trampling under foot*: destructive, ἡμέρα ταραχῆς καὶ ἀπωλείας καὶ ~ατος 'a day of turmoil, perdition and ..' Is 22.5; 22.18, 28.18.

Cf. καταπατέω.

καταπάτησις, εως. f.ʃ *

v.n. of καταπατέω **1**: PSol 2.19. Cf. καταπατέω.

κατάπαυμα, ατος. m.ʃ

1. *rest*: Ιερουσαλημ τόπον ~ατός σου Si 36.18, cf. τόπος τῆς καταπαύσεως μου Is 66.1.

2. *sabbath rest* (?): εἰς πέψιν ~ατος 'for the baking of sabbath bread (?)' Ho 7.4 Zgl (*pace* ~καυματος, on which see *BA* ad loc.).

Cf. κατάπαυσις.

κατάπαυσις, εως. f.

1. v.n. of καταπαύω **A 1**: Ex 35.2. Cf. στάσις **1**.

2. *rest* following toil: De 12.9; ἡμέρα ~εως w. ref. to Sabbath, 2M 15.1.

3. *resting-place*: Ps 131.14, τὸ σκήνωμα τῆς ~εως τοῦ ὀνόματος τῆς δόξης σου Ju 9.8.

Cf. καταπαύω, κατάπαυμα.

καταπαύω: fut. ~παύσω; aor. κατέπαυσα, subj. ~παύσω, impv. ~παυσον, inf. ~παῦσαι, mid. ~παύσασθαι.

A. intr. **1**. *to leave off* some activity (ἀπό τινος) *and rest*: ***s*** God resting on completion of the creation of the universe, ἀπὸ πάντων τῶν ἔργων αὐτοῦ Ge 2.2, 3; abs. τῇ ἡμέρᾳ τῇ ἑβδόμῃ Ex 20.11; τῇ ἡμέρᾳ τῇ ἑβδόμῃ ἐπαύσατο καὶ κατέπαυσεν 'on the seventh day He stopped and rested' 31.17.

2. *to become idle, cease to work*: ***s*** ῥομφαία Ho 11.6 (ǁ ἀσθενέω); ἔργον Ne 6.3; "the commotion died out" Ju 6.1.

3. *to cease to exist*: ***s*** the order of nature such as seasons, Ge 8.22; mid. and ***s*** δρόσος 'dew' Ex 16.13 (Katz 1946.320-2 *pace BA* ad loc.), χαρά La 5.15.

4. *to stop* doing sth: + pres.ptc., οἰκοδομοῦντες 'building' Ge 11.8, ἐπιτάσσων 'charging' 49.33, λαλῶν Ex 31.18, 34.33; + inf., 3K 12.24, cf. ἵστημι **I 4**.

5. *to stop moving and come to settle* at a certain place: ***s*** locusts, ἐπὶ πάντα τὰ ὅρια Αἰγύπτου Ex 10.14 (ǁ ἀναπαύομαι Is 7.19); divine anger, Si 5.6; hum., De 33.12, scouts Jd 18.2A (B: αὐλίζομαι; *L* καταλύω); birds on a rock, 2K 21.10B.

6. mid., *to be free from harassment*: ἀφ' ὑμῶν Jb 21.34.

B. tr. **1**. *to allow to enjoy rest and quiet*: + acc. pers. 2K 17.8*L* (***o*** troops; B: ~λύω); and ἀπό τινος– μὴ καταπαύσωμεν αὐτοὺς ἀπὸ τῶν ἔργων Ex 5.5; ἀπὸ τῶν ἐχθρῶν De 12.10, 25.19; κυκλόθεν Jo 21.44; + dat. pers., 2C 14.5 (ǁ vs. 6 τινα), 15.15. **b**. *to grant a restful existence*: Si 47.13.

2. *to cause to stop affecting*: τὸν θυμόν μου ἀπὸ υἱῶν Ισραηλ Nu 25.11; Ps 84.4; τὸ μνημόσυνον αὐτοῦ Si 38.23; ἁμαρτίας μεγάλας Ec 10.4.

3. caus. of **A 5**: + acc. pers. and ***s*** God, Ex 33.14, De 3.20, τὴν θάλασσαν Jb 26.12. **b**. *to cause to position itself*: εὐλογίαν .. ἐπὶ κεφαλὴν Ιακωβ Si 44.23.

4. caus. of **A 3**, *to efface*: + acc., ἀπὸ γῆς τὸ μνημόσυνον αὐτῶν '.. their memory' Si 10.17.

5. caus. of **A 2**: + acc., τὸ ἔργον Ne 4.11, τὸν λόγον 'my account' 2M 15.37.

6. *to relieve of an office or function*: + acc., χωμαριμ 'priests' 4K 23.5Ra, 11Ra.

Cf. παύω, κατάπαυμα, ~παυσις, δυσκατάπαυτος, λήγω.

καταπειράζω: aor. κατεπείρασα.ʃ
to make an attempt on: + acc., τοὺς τόπους 'the (military) positions' 2M 13.18.

καταπελματόω: pf.ptc.pass. ~πεπελματωμένος.ʃ *
to mend with patch: pass., ***o*** shoes, Jo 9.5.

καταπέλτης, ου. m.
catapult: used as an instrument of torture, 4M 8.13. Cf. βασανιστήριον.

καταπενθέω: aor. κατεπένθησα.ʃ
to bewail: ἐν πενθικοῖς 'wearing mourning dress' Ex 33.4. Cf. πενθέω.

καταπέτασμα, ατος. n. *
piece of hanging material serving to conceal what is behind it, 'veil': of the tabernacle, of blue and purple and scarlet woven (κεκλωσμένος) and fine linen spun (νενησμένος)' Ex 26.31; οἶκος ~ατος '.. furnished with a curtain' Si 50.5. Cf. ἐπίσπαστρον: Deissmann 1923.80; Gurtner.

καταπέτομαι: aor.subj.pass. ~πετασθῶ.ʃ
to fly downwards: ***s*** bird, Pr 27.8. Cf. πέτομαι.

καταπήγνυμι: aor. κατέπηξα.ʃ
to plant firmly: acc., corpse of a fallen soldier, ἐν τῷ τείχει 'in the wall' 1K 31.10; net (δίκτυον), Ho 5.2; fig. μανίαν ἐν οἴκῳ θεοῦ κατέπηξαν 'they firmly established madness in the house of God' 9.8. Cf. πήγνυμι.

καταπηδάω: aor. κατεπήδησα.ʃ
to alight: ἀπὸ τῆς καμήλου Ge 24.64 (mark of respect), ἀπὸ τῆς ὄνου 'from the mule' 1K 25.23 (*L* καταβαίνω); ἀπὸ τοῦ ἅρματος 'from the carriage' 4K 5.26*L*; astonished or panicked, ***o*** hum., ἀπὸ τοῦ θρόνου αὐτοῦ Es 5.8 *L* (o' ἀνα~). Cf. καταβαίνω.

κατάπικρος, ον.ʃ *
very bitter: ***s*** hum., τῇ ψυχῇ 2K 17.8B (*L* simp.). Cf. πικρός.

καταπίνω: fut. ~πίομαι; aor. κατέπιον, inf. ~πιεῖν, subj. ~πίω, opt.3s ~πίοι, impv.3s ~πιέτω, pass. ~επόθην, subj. ~ποθῶ.

1. *to swallow down, gulp*: + acc. pers. Jn 2.1, To 6.3 (***s*** fish), early fig Is 28.4. **b**. fig. *to swallow up, engulf, absorb, make away with*: ***o*** pers., κατεπόθη Ισραηλ (|| κατεσθίω, also Nu 21.28) Ho 8.8; κληρονομίαν Κυρίου 2K 20.19*L* (|| διαφθείρω vs. 20; B: ~ποντίζω here); καταπίνειν ἀσεβῆ τὸν δίκαιον Hb 1.13; Is 9.16, Ps 106.27; + acc. rei, κρίσεις Pr 19.28.

2. *to make away with by absorbing inside oneself*: ***s*** and ***o*** ears of corn (στάχυες), Ge 41.7 (|| vs. 4 κατεσθίω); one staff (ῥάβδος) swallowing another, Ex 7.12, cf. κατέπιεν αὐτοὺς γῆ 15.12, sim. Nu 16.30, 32, 34, 26.10, De 11.6, Ps 105.17; ***s*** death, Is 25.8, δράκων 'snake' Je 28.34 (|| κατεσθίω); + acc. pers., ὥσπερ ᾅδης Pr 1.12.

Cf. (ἐκ)πίνω, καταποντίζω, κατεσθίω, ἀφανίζω: Renehan 2.84.

καταπίπτω: aor. κατέπεσον, subj. ~πέσω, ptc. ~πεσών; pf.ptc. ~πεπτωκώς.
to fall down: ἐπὶ τὴν γῆν Wi 7.3 (of a baby born); ***s*** a handmade idol, 13.16; hum. and sign of weakness, Ps 144.14; mentally downcast, Ne 8.11, 3M 2.20. Cf. πίπτω, κατάπτωμα, ~πτωσις: Michaelis, *TDNT* 6.169; LSG s.v.

καταπιστεύω.ʃ *
to put trust (in ἐν): ἐν φίλοις Mi 7.5 (|| ἐλπίζω). Cf. πιστεύω.

καταπλάσσω: aor.impv.mid. ~πλασαι.ʃ
to plaster over: thus concealing what is underneath, ἐκλεκτὸν καταπλάσσει νεφέλη 'clouds cover what is dear (to him)' Jb 37.11¶; mid., abs., Is 38.21.

καταπληγμός, οῦ. m.ʃ *
bullying, intimidation: Si 21.4. Cf. καταπλήσσω.

κατάπληξις, εως. f.ʃ
= καταπληγμός, q.v.: ἐπί τινα 2E 3.3.

καταπλήσσω: aor.pass. ~επλάγην, inf. ~πλαγῆναι, ptc. ~πλαγείς, opt.3pl ~πλαγείησαν; pf.ptc.pass. ~πεπληγμένος.

to terrify: + acc. pers., ἐν ὁράμασιν 'with visions' Jb 7.14 (|| ἐκφοβέω); ***o*** hum. heart, Jo 5.1; pass., τοῖς πολεμίοις 'by the enemies' 2M 8.16. **b**. pass. *to be deeply impressed*: + dat., τῇ σπουδαιότητι 'by the excellence' 3M 1.9, φόβῳ 2.23; + acc. of respect or ground, τὰς βασάνους 'by the tortures' 4M 16.17; + ἐπί τινι 3M 5.27.

Cf. ἐκπλήσσω, καταπληγμός, κατάπληξις, ἐκφοβέω.

κατάπλους, ου. m.ʃ
act of sailing: 3M 4.10 (|| παράπλους vs. 11). Cf. παράπλους, πλέω.

καταπολεμέω.ʃ
to wage war against: τινα Jo 10.25. Cf. πολεμέω ..

κατάπολις, ιδος, dat.pl. εσιν.ʃ
situated in city: ***s*** temple, 3M 3.16.

καταπονέω: aor.pass. κατεπονήθην.ʃ
to wear out, exhaust: by harsh treatment, pass. and ***o*** hum., 2M 8.2, 3M 2.2, 13; hum. eyes, La 3.49 (v.l. καταπίνω). Cf. κατάπονος.

κατάπονος, ον.ʃ
very tiring, back-breaking: ***s*** λατρεία 3M 4.14.

καταποντίζω: fut. ~ποντιῶ; aor. κατεπόντισα, impv. ~πόντισον.

1. *to throw into the sea*: + acc., ἐπιλέκτους ἀναβάτας .. ἐν ἐρυθρᾷ θαλάσσῃ 'top riders .. into the Red Sea' Ex 15.4 (|| ῥίπτω); ***s*** καταιγίς Ps 68.3; 68.16 (|| καταπίνω), ὕδωρ 123.4.

2. *to obliterate, annihilate*: abs. 2K 20.20B (+ διαφθείρω: *L* καταπίνω), Ps 54.10; + acc., κληρονομίαν κυρίου [= cities] 2K 20.19B (*L* καταπίνω), sim. La 2.5 (|| διαφθείρω); *s* χείλη ἄφρονος 'a fool's lips' Ec 10.12.

Cf. καταποντισμός, καταπίνω, ῥίπτω, ἀφανίζω.

καταπόντισμα, ατος. n.ʃ *

= καταποντισμός, q.v.: La 2.8 (v.l. καταπάτημα).

καταποντισμός, οῦ. m.ʃ

v.n. of καταποντίζω: τὰ ῥήματα τοῦ ~οῦ, γλῶσσαν δολίαν 'talk of drowning (innocent) people, deceitful tongue' Ps 51.6. Cf. καταποντίζω.

καταπορεύομαι.ʃ

to return home: 2M 11.30; εἰς τὴν πόλιν 3M 4.11.

καταπραΰνω: aor. κατεπράϋνα, subj. ~πραΰνω.ʃ

to reduce the intensity of: emotions, 'to appease': abs., Ps 82.2, 2M 13.26; contention, Pr 15.18; the violent force of waves, Ps 88.10. Cf. πραΰνω.

καταπρί(ζ)ω: aor.subj. ~πρίσω.ʃ

to cut down with a saw: + acc. pers., Da Su 58 LXX. Cf. πρίζω.

καταπροδίδωμι.ʃ

to abandon allegiance and loyalty to: + acc., ἀρετήν 'virtue' 4M 2.10. Cf. παραδίδωμι.

καταπρονομεύω: aor. κατεπρονόμευσα.ʃ *

1. *to carry off as booty*: + acc., αἰχμαλωσίαν 'prisoners of war' Nu 21.1.

2. *to take booty from*: τινα Jd 2.14B (A: simp.). Cf. προνομεύω.

καταπτήσσω: fut. ~πτήξω; pf. κατέπτηκα.ʃ

to cower beneath out of fear: abs., δι' εὐλάβειαν 'with discretion' Pr 28.14 (with adverbial πάντα 'wholly'); + acc., φόβον Si 35.18; κτῆνος 'animal' Pr 30.30; *+ ἀπό τινος (pers.) Jo 2.24.

κατάπτωμα, ατος. n.ʃ *

act of falling down or *collapsing*: φραγμοῦ 'of a fence' Ps 143.14. Cf. καταπίπτω.

κατάπτωσις, εως. f.ʃ

act of falling down defeated: 3M 2.14. Cf. καταπίπτω.

κατάρα, ας. f.

1. *pronouncement of curse*: De 23.5 (:: εὐλογία), by a hum., Si 3.9.

2. *accursed, odious state*: ~αν καὶ οὐκ εὐλογίαν Ge 27.12; εὐλογίαν καὶ ~αν De 11.26; ἦτε ἐν ~ᾳ Zc 8.13 (:: εὐλογία); ἐξαποστελῶ ἐφ' ὑμᾶς τὴν ~αν Ma 2.2 (:: εὐλογία); + μῖσος 'hate' Je 24.9, + ὀνειδισμός 51.12; θεοῦ (subj. gen.) Pr 3.33; cogn. dat., Nu 23.25.

Cf. ἀρά, καταράομαι, εὐλογία.

καταράκτη, ης. f.ʃ Etymologically related to καταρράκτης.

a kind of bird, sea-bird known for its swift downward swoop (?): Le 11.17, De 14.17.

καταράομαι: fut. ~άσομαι; aor. κατηρασάμην, inf. ~ράσασθαι, ptc. ~ρασάμενος, impv. ~ρασαι, subj. ~ράσωμαι, opt.3s ~ράσαιτο, pass.opt.3s ~ραθείη; pf.pass. κεκατήραμαι, ptc. (κε)κατηραμένος.

to pronounce curse upon, utter words consigning man or object to odious state: abs., Le 24.11; + *acc. pers., ὁ καταρώμενός σε ἐπικατάρατος 'he who curses you is accursed' Ge 27.29 (:: εὐλογέω), sim. Nu 24.9; *s* God and *o* the earth, Ge 5.29; θεόν Le 24.15, sim. Ps 36.22; καταράσομαι ^τὴν εὐλογίαν ὑμῶν^ Ma 2.2 (|| ἐπικαταράομαι); both *s* and *o* pers., τοὺς καταρωμένους σε (καταράσομαι) Ge 12.3 (|| εὐλογέω), De 23.4; *o* own birthday, Jb 3.2, PSol 3.9; + acc. pers. and cogn. acc., 3K 2.8; + cogn. dat., Nu 23.25, Jd 5.23 A; + dat. pers., Ep Je 65, 2K 16.10*L* (|| acc., vs. 9), 4K 2.24B (*L* acc.); ἔν τινι (divinity invoked), ἐν τοῖς θεοῖς αὐτοῦ 1K 17.43. **b**. *to bind under a curse*: + acc. pers., Ne 10.29.

Cf. κατάρα, κατάρασις, κατάρατος, ἐπικαταράομαι, ἀράομαι, (κατ)εὐλογέω: Naumann 41.

κατάρασις, εως. f.ʃ //s *

v.n. of prec., q.v.: + obj. gen. Nu 23.11 (:: εὐλογία); cogn. dat. 23.25, Jd 5.23 A; εἰς ὀνειδισμὸν καὶ εἰς ~ιν ἔσῃ Je 29.14. Cf. καταράομαι and εὐλογία.

καταράσσω: fut.pass. ~ραχθήσομαι; aor. κατέρραξα; pf.ptc.pass. κατερραγμένος.ʃ

1. *to break in pieces*: + acc., ἐν πελέκει καὶ λαξευτηρίῳ 'with an axe and a stonemason's tool' Ps 73.6 (|| ἐκκόπτω); ἦχοι καταράσσοντες 'deafening sounds' (emitted by a crashing object?) Wi 17.4; fig. of mental agitation (?), Ho 7.6.

2. *to hurl forcefully downwards*: with hostile intent, τὸν θρόνον αὐτοῦ εἰς τὴν γῆν 'his throne to the ground' Ps 88.45; acc. pers. and opp. ἐπαίρω 'to lift,' 101.11; pass. 'to fall (involuntarily)' - ἀνορθοῖ πάντας τοὺς κατερραγμένους 'he raises all that have fallen' Ps 144.14 (|| καταπίπτω), 145.8; ὅταν πέσῃ, οὐ καταραχθήσεται 'even when he slips, he will not fall headlong' 36.24. **b**. *to cause to befall*: + acc. rei, ἐπ' ἔθνος πόλεμον 'he thrust a battle against the nation' Si 46.6.

Cf. Shipp 90f., s.v. ἀράσσω, καταβάλλω, καταρίπτω.

κατάρατος, ον.ʃ

deserving to be cursed, 'accursed': *s* hum. and subst., 2M 12.35; 4M 4.5. Cf. καταράομαι.

καταργέω: aor. κατήργησα, inf. ~αργῆσαι, pass. ~αργηθῆναι.

to force sbd *to stop doing what he is doing*: + acc., 2E 4.21 (|| ἀποκωλύω 1E 2.24), 2E 4.23 (|| κωλύω 1E 2.25). Cf. ἀργέω, εἴργω, (ἀπο)κωλύω, παύω: Delling, *TDNT* 1.452-4.

καταργυρόω: pf.ptc.pass. κατηργυρωμένος.ʃ

to cover with silver: *o* columns of an edifice, ἀργύρῳ Ex 27.17. Cf. περιαργυρόω, ἀργύριον, καταχρυσόω.

καταριθμέω: pf.ptc.pass. κατηριθμημένος.

1. *to count*: pass., Nu 14.29.

2. pass. *to amount to* in number: οὕτως καταριθμοῦνται αἱ ἡμέραι τῆς ταφῆς 'that is the number of the burial days' Ge 50.3.

Cf. ἀριθμέω.

καταρράκτης, ου. m. Etymologically related to καταράκτη.

gate through which a large quantity of water rushes downwards: οἱ ~ται τοῦ οὐρανοῦ ἠνεῴχθησαν 'the heavenly sluices opened' Ge 7.11 (‖ αἱ πηγαὶ τῆς ἀβύσσου); 8.2, Ma 3.10. **b**. a shaft leading to an underground water-channel (?): Je 20.2, 36.26 (serving as a dungeon: at latter ‖ ἀπόκλεισμα).

Cf. Shipp 307; LSG s.v.

καταρρεμβεύω: aor. κατερρέμβευσα.ʃ *

to cause to roam about: + acc. pers., αὐτοὺς ἐν τῇ ἐρήμῳ Nu 32.13. Cf. ῥέμβω.

καταρρέω: pf. κατερρύηκα.ʃ

1. *to stream down*: *s* spittle, ἐπὶ τῶν πώγωνα αὐτοῦ 'on to his beard' 1K 21.14. **b**. *to have one's body streaming down with*: + dat., αἵματι 'with blood' 4M 6.6.

2. *to drop off*: *s* leaves of a tree, Je 8.13; fig., soul, 1K 2.33.

Cf. ῥέω, κατάρρυτος.

καταρρήγνυμι: pf.ptc. κατερρωγώς.ʃ

intr. *to split into parts and be no longer in one piece*: *s* skin for wine, Jo 9.4; pass. and metaph .. *s* ψυχή Pr 27.8 (tormented), cf. Si 19.10. Cf. ῥήγνυμι.

καταρρίπτω: aor. κατέρριψα.ʃ

to hurl down: + acc., ἐξ οὐρανοῦ εἰς γῆν δόξασμα La 2.1; *o* rocks, Wi 17.19. Cf. ῥίπτω, καταβάλλω, καταρράσσω.

κατάρρυτος, ον.ʃ

having sth flowing along over the surface, 'awash': + dat., *s* lake, αἵματι 2M 12.16. Cf. καταρρέω.

καταρτίζω: aor.mid. κατηρτισάμην, impv. κατάρτισαι, inf. ~τίσασθαι, pass.subj. ~τισθῶ; pf.ptc.pass. κατηρτισμένος. Alw. mid./pass.

1. *to put various* or *multiple components together and produce*: *o* κατοικητήριον 'dwelling' Ex 15.17 v.l., ὃ κατηρτίσω, καθεῖλον 'what you put together, they demolished' Ps 10.3, αἶνον 'praise' 8.3, διαβήματα 'steps' 16.5, πόδας 'feet' 17.34, moon 88.38, sim. 73.16.

2. *to restore to sound condition*: *o* grape-vine, Ps 79.16, βροχήν '(diminished) rainfall' 67.10, walls lying in ruins 2E 4.12, temple furniture (χορηγία) 5.3; abs., + ἀνοικοδομέω 6.14, cf. + οἰκοδομέω 5.11; ὠτία '(attentive) ears' Ps 39.7, τὰ διαβήματά μου 'my steps' 16.5. **b**. *to give requisite strength and make ready*: *s* God, + acc., ἐλάφους 'deer (about to give birth)' Ps 28.9.

Cf. Spicq 2.18-20, 271-4.

κατάρχω: fut. κατάρξω; aor. κατῆρξα, inf. κατάρξαι mid. κατηρξάμην, ptc. καταρξάμενος.

1. *to rule, govern*: ἐπὶ τοῦ θρόνου αὐτοῦ 'on his throne' Zc 6.13; + gen. pers., κατάρχεις ἡμῶν ἄρχων Nu 16.13; Jl 2.17; + gen. rei, κύριος κ. ὑδάτων πολλῶν Na 1.12; ὑδάτων Zc 9.10; ἐπὶ τὸν λαόν μου 1K 9.17 *L* (B: ἄρχω ἐν ..).

2. mid. *to begin*: τι 2M 12.37. **b**. *to play a leading role*: abs., 2M 1.23.

Cf. ἄρχω, ἡγέομαι, κυριεύω: Gooding 1965.333; Caird 1969.21.

κατασβέννυμι: fut. ~σβέσω; aor. κατέσβεσα.ʃ

to stifle and suppress that which is flaring up: metaph., + acc. rei, κρίσεις 'litigations' Pr 15.18a, 28.2, πάθη 'intense emotions' 4M 16.4. Cf. σβέννυμι.

κατασείω.ʃ

to frighten: abs., 1M 6.38. Cf. ἐκφοβέω.

κατασήθω: aor. κατέσησα, inf. ~σῆσαι.ʃ

to strew: τὸν ναὸν σποδῷ 'the temple (floor) with ashes' Da Bel LXX 14; ib. TH. Cf. στρώννυμι.

κατασιωπάω: aor. κατεσιώπησα, subj. ~σιωπήσω.ʃ

1. *to make stop speaking*: + acc. pers., τὸν λαὸν πρὸς Μωυσῆν Nu 13.31; κατεσιώπων πάντα τὸν λαὸν λέγοντες Σιωπᾶτε Ne 8.11; Jb 37.20.

2. *to withhold from*: αὐτῇ .. σοφίαν Jb 39.17¶.

Cf. σιωπάω.

κατασκάπτω: fut.act. ~σκάψω, pass. ~σκαφήσομαι; aor. ~έσκαψα, impv. ~σκαψον, pass. ~εσκάφην; pf.ptc.pass. κατεσκαμμένος.

to raze to the ground: + acc.(edifice), βωμούς De 12.3 (‖ συντρίβω, ἐκκόπτω, κατακαίω, ἀπόλλυμι); θυσιαστήρια Ho 10.2, Jd 2.2 Ra (B: καθαιρέω), πορνεῖον 'brothel' Ez 16.39 (‖ καθαιρέω), city 1C 20.1; + ἐκριζόω 'uproot,' ἀπολλύω Je 1.10, + ἀφανίζω Ez 36.35 (*o* cities); opp. ἀνίστημι 'establish' Pr 29.4; pass. τὰ κέρατα (the horns) τοῦ θυσιαστηρίου Am 3.14; parts of a tent, 9.11, ληνοί 'winepresses' Jl 1.17, τεῖχος 'city-wall' Je 27.15, τοῖχος 'wall' Ez 13.14; πόλις Pr 11.11, οἴκους (understood) 14.1 (:: οἰκοδομέω). Cf. ἀφανίζω, ἐξαίρω, ἐξολεθρεύω, κατασπάω, καταστρέφω.

κατασκεδάννυμι: aor. κατεσκέδασα.ʃ

to pour liquid *over*: + gen., (τὸ αἷμα) .. κατεσκέδασεν τοῦ λαοῦ 'poured (the blood) over the people' Ex 24.8. Cf. ἐπιχέω.

κατασκέπτομαι: fut. ~σκέψομαι; aor. κατεσκεψάμην, ptc. ~σκεψάμενος, inf. ~σκέψασθαι, impv.2pl ~σκέψασθε.

1. *to look out for*: + acc. αὐτοῖς ἀνάπαυσιν 'a resting-place for them' Nu 10.33.

2. *to spy out, reconnoitre*: + acc., τῆν γῆν τῶν Χαναναίων Nu 13.3; Jd 1.23B, 18.2 (+ ἐξιχνιάζω). **b**. *to enquire into, investigate*: περὶ πάντων Ec 1.13 (‖ ἐκζητέω), + ζητέω 7.25.

Cf. (ἐκ)ζητέω, κατασκοπεύω.

κατασκευάζω: aor. κατεσκεύασα, inf. ~σκευάσαι, ptc. ~σκευάσας, pass. ~σκευασθείς, subj.pass. ~σκευασθῶ; pf.pass. κατεσκεύασμαι, ptc.pass. κατεσκευασμένος.

to construct: ***o*** city, ἵνα οἰκοδομηθῇ καὶ κατασκευασθῇ πόλις Σηων 'so that the city of Sihon may be built and constructed' Nu 21.27; the universe and ***s*** God, τὰ ἄκρα τῆς γῆς Is 40.28, τὴν γῆν Ba 3.32, ***o*** mankind, Is 43.7 (‖ πλάσσω, ποιέω), Wi 9.2 (‖ ποιέω), cf. ἀκατασκεύαστος Ge 1.1; φῶς Is 45.7 (‖ ποιέω), crown, Ep Je 8; lectern, 1E 9.42, gymnasium 4M 4.20; πληγή 'disaster' 1M 3.29; + double acc., ὁμοίωμα .. αὐτόν 'him as an image' Is 40.19. **b**. *to endeavour to give the quality of*: + acc. and pred. adj., 4M 13.26.

Cf. προκατασκευάζω, κατασκευή, κατασκεύασμα, οἰκοδομέω, πλάσσω, ποιέω.

κατασκεύασμα, ατος. n.ʃ

fittings, furniture: sg. collectively, ἐν ~ατι χρυσῷ 'among golden furniture' Si 35.6. Cf. κατασκευάζω, κατασκευή, σκεῦος.

κατασκευή, ῆς. f.

1. v.n. of κατασκευάζω, 'constructing, fabricating': τὰ ἔργα τῆς ~ῆς Ex 35.24; αὕτη ἡ κ. τῆς λυχνίας 'this is how the lamp is to be made' Nu 8.4; τοῦ λόγου 'the composition of the story' 2M 15.39.

2. *fittings, furniture*: sg. collectively and for cultic use, Ex 27.19; pl., 'implements for warfare' 3M 5.45. Cf. σκεῦος **1c**, χορηγία **3**.

Cf. κατασκευάζω, κατασκεύασμα, σκεῦος.

κατασκηνόω: fut. ~νώσω; aor. κατεσκήνωσα, inf. ~σκηνῶσαι, impv. ~σκήνωσον, ptc. ~σκηνώσας, opt.3s ~σκηνώσαι.

1. *to dwell*, not in a house, but not specifically in encampment or tent: ***s*** hum., ἐν ταῖς ὀπαῖς τῶν πετρῶν 'in cracks of rock-faces' Ob 3; ἐν πεδίῳ 'in the field' after having moved out of a city, Mi 4.10; birds, Ps 103.12, wild animals under a tree Da 4.9 TH (‖ κατοικέω; LXX σκιάζω 'to seek shade'); God dwelling in Zion his holy mount, Jl 3.17, 21; God coming to dwell amongst his people, τὴν γῆν, ἐφ' ἧς κατοικεῖτε ἐπ' αὐτῆς, ἐφ' ἧς ἐγὼ κατασκηνώσω ἐν ὑμῖν· ἐγὼ γάρ εἰμι κύριος κατασκηνῶν ἐν μέσῳ τῶν υἱῶν Ισραηλ Nu 35.34; Zc 2.10; ἡ σκηνὴ κυρίου Jo 22.19; God's name, Ez 43.7; in Jerusalem, Zc 8.3, 8; of nations doing the same, 2.11; ἐν τῷ ὄρει τῷ ἁγίῳ σου Ps 14.1 (‖ παροικέω). **b**. + acc. loci, *to inhabit*: δρυμόν 'a thicket' Mi 7.14; τὴν γῆν Ps 36.3.

***2**. *to make dwell, settle*: εἰς τὴν γῆν .. κατασκηνῶσαι ὑμᾶς ἐπ' αὐτῆς Nu 14.30; εἰσάξω αὐτοὺς καὶ κατασκηνώσω ἐν μέσῳ Ιερουσαλημ 'I will bring them in and settle (them) in J.' Zc 8.8, cf. Th 360 οὓς ἀποδώσω τῇ οἰκήσει τῆς γῆς τῆς οἰκείας, and Eth /ʾāḫadderomu/ and Arb /ʾuskinuhum/. The causative use is assured by Je 7.12 κατεσκήνωσα τὸ ὄνομά μου ἐκεῖ and Ps 22.2 ἐκεῖ με κατεσκήνωσεν, cf. BDAG, s.v.; metaph., τὴν δόξαν μου εἰς χοῦν 'into the dust' Ps 7.6, βουλήν Pr 8.12.

Cf. σκηνή, κατασκήνωσις, κατοικέω, κατοικίζω, οἰκέω.

κατασκήνωσις, εως. f.ʃ

v.n. of prec. **1**: God's Ez 37.27, ὁ ναὸς τῆς ~ως τοῦ θεοῦ To 1.4 𝔊II, πόλις ~εως Wi 9.8; 1C 28.2. Cf. σκηνόω.

κατάσκιος, ον.ʃ

situated in shade: ***s*** mountain, ἐξ ὄρους ~ίου δασέος '.. thickly wooded ..' Hb 3.3; Zc 1.8; tree, Je 2.20, Ez 20.28 (a site for pagan cult). Cf. σκιά.

κατασκοπεύω: aor. κατεσκόπευσα, inf. ~πεῦσαι, ptc. ~πεύσας, subj. ~πεύσω. *

to observe closely: abs. κατεσκόπευεν ἡ ἀδελφὴ αὐτοῦ μακρόθεν μαθεῖν τί τὸ ἀποβησόμενον αὐτῷ 'his sister was watching from a distance to find out what was going to happen to him' Ex 2.4. **b**. *to reconnoitre*: abs. Jo 2.1; + acc., τὴν γῆν Ge 42.30 (‖ κατάσκοπος vs. 31); De 1.24; τὴν πόλιν 2K 10.3*L* (B: ~σκοπέω; ‖ ἐξερευνάω), τὴν παρεμβολήν 1M 5.38.

Cf. κατασκέπτομαι, κατάσκοπος, κατασκοπέω, ἐπισκέπτω, καταμανθάνω, κατανοέω, ἐφοδεύω, φυλάσσω.

κατασκοπέω: aor.subj. ~σκοπήσω.ʃ

= κατασκοπεύω: + acc., ^τὴν πόλιν^ 2K 10.3 (‖ ἐξερευνάω), τὴν γῆν 1C 19.3. Cf. σκοπέω.

κατάσκοπος, ου. m.

spy: Ge 42.11, 31, 34 (:: εἰρηνικός 'man of peaceful intention'); ὡς ὁ κ. ἐπιβλέπει πτῶσιν 'like spies he feasts his eyes upon your downfall' Si 11.30; ἀπέστειλε ~ους εἰς τὴν παρεμβολὴν αὐτῶν 1M 12.26. Cf. κατασκοπεύω.

κατασμικρύνω: aor.pass. κατεσμικρύνθην; pf.pass. 3pl κατεσμίκρυνται.ʃ

to hold or express a low view of, 'to belittle': pass., ***o*** hum., reinforced by μικρόν added, 2K 7.19B, ***o*** deeds or matters, ib. *L*. Cf. μικρός, ἐξουδενέ/όω.

κατασοφίζομαι: aor. κατεσοφισάμην, subj. ~σοφίσωμαι, inf. ~σοφίσασθαι.ʃ

to outwit: + acc. pers., Ex 1.10; ἐν πόνῳ καὶ πλίνθῳ 'cunningly talked them into hard labour and making of bricks' Ju 5.11; πᾶσαν τὴν γῆν 10.19.

κατασπαταλάω.ʃ *

to live in excessive comfort: ἐπὶ ταῖς στρωμναῖς 'on beds' Am 6.4; Pr 29.21. Cf. σπαταλάω, τρυφάω.

καταστράω: fut. ~σπάσω; aor.act. κατέσπασα, inf. ~σπάσαι, impv. ~σπασον, pass. κατεσπάσθην.

to force to move downwards: τινα 'Hurl her down' 4K 9.33*L* (B: κυλίω; ‖ ῥίπτω); pass., τὸ κάλλος ἀπὸ θρόνου δόξης 'the beauty ..' PSol 2.19. **b**. *to demolish, pull down*: ***o*** stones of a building, Mi 1.6; Jerusalem, La 3.11 (‖ ἀφανίζω), its walls To 13.12 𝔊II; ὑπερηφάνους 'arrogant people' Zp 3.6 (ditt.); idol, Bel 28 (‖ καταστρέφω 22); pass. κατεσπάσθη ὁ δρυμὸς ὁ σύμφυτος 'the thickly planted forest has been torn down' Zc 11.2. **c**. *to bring sbd's morale low, devastate*: abs., 2C 32.18.

Cf. ἀφανίζω, ἐκσπάω, καταστρέφω, ῥίπτω.

κατασπείρω: fut. ~σπερῶ, pass. ~σπαρήσομαι.ʃ

1. *to plant by sowing*: ***o*** vineyard, Le 19.19, De 22.9.

2. *to spread abroad*: ***o*** sun-beams at daybreak, 3M 5.26.

3. *to cause to cover thoroughly and entirely*: pass. Jb 18.15¶ (θείῳ 'with brimstone').

Cf. σπείρω.

κατασπεύδω: aor. κατέσπευσα, impv. ~σπευσον.

I. tr. *to egg on* to an action: + acc. pers., ***s*** ἐργοδιῶκται 'taskmasters' Ex 5.10, 13; 2C 35.21; + inf., 1M 13.21.

2. *to accelerate*: + acc., ἔρις 'strife' Si 28.11, ἴασιν πάντων κατασπεύδει ὁμίχλη 'a mist hastens universal healing' 43.22; πορείαν 'movement' 43.5; ‖ ταχύνω 43.13; σημεῖα '(performed) signs (in quick succession)' 45.3.

3. *to cause to move with speed*: αὐτὸν ἐκεῖθεν 2C 26.20.

4**. *to unsettle mentally*: + acc. pers., ***s ὑπόνοιαι 'suspicions' Da 5.6 LXX (TH συνταράσσω), cf. ὑπονοίᾳ κατασπευθείς Da 4.16 LXX, φοβῆσαι αὐτοὺς καὶ κατασπεῦσαι (so Walters 144) 2C 32.18. Cf. Caird 1969.21.

II. intr. *to move with speed*: ἐξ ὄρους Φαραν De 33.2; eagerly, ἐπὶ τὰ κρίματα αὐτοῦ 'to obtain his precepts' Si 18.14; ***s*** μάχη 28.11, ἀστραπή 'lightning' 35.10.

2. *to act with speed*: + inf., συναγαγεῖν τὰ κτήνη σου 'to round up your cattle' Ex 9.19; κατέσπευσεν Φαραω καλέσαι Μωυσῆν 'Ph. lost no time in summoning M.' 10.16; syndetically with another verb, Si 50.17; + καί and a vb., 1M 6.57.

Cf. σπεύδω, καταταχύνω, ἐξίστημι, συγχέω.

κατασπουδάζομαι: aor.subj. ~σπουδασθῶ.ʃ

to be diffident, act with diffidence: ἀπὸ προσώπου αὐτοῦ Jb 23.15¶ (‖ πτοέω, σπουδάζω).

καταστασιάζω: aor.ptc. ~στασιάσας.ʃ

to agitate against the authority: Ex 38.22.

κατάστασις, εως. f.ʃ

pleading of a case: τίς εἰς ~ίν σοι ἐλεύσεται ἔκδικος ..; 'Who would come to you as an advocate to plead ..?' Wi 12.12.

καταστέλλω: aor.inf. ~στεῖλαι, ptc. ~στείλας.ʃ

1. *to restore order to*: + acc. rei, τὰ πράγματα 'the affairs' 2M 4.31.

2. *to restrain* sbd (acc.) to do: + inf., 3M 6.1.

κατάστεμα, ατος.ʃ

mental or physical *condition*: μανιῶδες 'mad' 3M 5.45.

καταστενάζω: fut. ~στενάξω; aor. ~εστέναξα, impv. ~στέναξον ʃ*

to sigh, groan under hardship: ***s*** hum., ἀπὸ τῶν ἔργων Ex 2.23; ἐν τῷ ἐλθεῖν σοι ὀδύνας, ὠδῖνας ὡς τικτούσης 'when pains come upon you, travails like those of a woman in labour' Je 22.23; out of hunger, La 1.11; spiritual or mental distress, καταστεναζόντων καὶ κατοδυνωμένων ἐπὶ πάσαις ταῖς ἀνομίαις Ez 9.4; 21.6 (foll. by καὶ ἐν ὀδύναις στενάξεις); 3M 6.34. Cf. στενάζω.

καταστέφω: pf.ptc.pass. κατεστεμμένος.ʃ

to deck with crown (of flowers): pass., ***o*** hum., 3M 7.16. Cf. στέφανος.

καταστηρίζω: pf.inf.pass. ~εστηρίχθαι.ʃ

to establish firmly: ***o*** hum., Jb 20.7. Cf. στηρίζω.

καταστολή, ῆς. f.ʃ

clothes: δόξης 'glorious' Is 61.3. Cf. ἱμάτιον, στολή.

καταστραγγίζω: fut. ~στραγγιῶ.ʃ *

to squeeze out: ***o*** blood of sacrificial animal, Le 5.9.

καταστρατοπεδεύω: aor. κατεστρατοπέδευσα.ʃ

1. *to encamp*: Jo 4.19, Ju 3.10.

2. *to march off and arrive* at: εἰς τὴν Φοινίκην 2M 4.22.

Cf. ἐπιστρατοπεδεύω: Caird 1969.21; LSG s.v.

καταστρέφω: fut. ~στρέψω, pass. ~στραφήσομαι; aor. ~έστρεψα, inf. ~στρέψαι, subj. ~στρέψω, opt. 3s ~στρέψαι, pass. κατεστράφην; pf.pass. κατέστραμμαι, ptc. κατεστραμμένος.

1. *to overturn, turn upside down*: + acc. rei, θρόνους βασιλέων (‖ ἐξολεθρεύω) .. ἅρματα καὶ ἀναβάτας Hg 2.22; ἐπὶ πρόσωπον αὐτοῦ 'on its head' 4K 21.13. Cf. περιτρέπω.

2. *to upset* what is set and stable for the moment: + acc., τὰ πράγματα 'the way the state is run' 3M 3.23.

3. *to ruin, destroy*: ***o*** (acc.) city, πρὸ τοῦ καταστρέψαι τὸν θεὸν Σοδομα καὶ Γομορρα Ge 13.10; 19.29 (‖ ἐκτρίβω); including its inhabitants and the flora in the area, 19.25; group of people, κατέστρεψα ὑμᾶς, καθὼς κατέστρεψεν ὁ θεὸς Σοδομα καὶ Γομορρα Am 4.11, sim. Je 27.40, cf. pass. Νινευη καταστραφήσεται Jn 3.4 (cf. La 4.6), χώρας ἐθνῶν Si 10.16 (‖ ἀπόλλυμι); opp. (ἀν)οικοδομέω, Ma 1.4*bis*.; ***o*** τὴν διαθήκην Ps 88.40; house or home, Si 27.3; idol, Bel 22 LXX (TH his temple).

4. *to bring to an end*: + acc., τὸν βίον '(own) life' 2M 9.28.

Cf. καταστροφή, ἀφανίζω, ἐκτρίβω, (ἀν)οικοδομέω, καταστπάω.

καταστροφή, ῆς. f.

1. *ruin, state of being ruined*: ἐκ μέσου τῆς ~ῆς Ge 19.29; + subj.gen. Ho 8.7, cf. Meadowcroft; ‖ ὠδῖνες Jb 21.17.

2. *end, close*: Da 7.27 LXX (TH πέρας), τοῦ βίου 'of life' 3M 4.4; Pr 1.18.

Cf. καταστρέφω, πέρας.

καταστρώννυμι, ~στρωννύω: fut.pass. ~στρωθήσομαι; aor. κατέστρωσα, imp. ~στρωσον, inf. ~στρῶσαι, pass. ~στρωθῆναι.

1. *to disperse*: ***o*** a group of people in helpless condition, αὐτοὺς ἐν τῇ ἐρήμῳ Nu 14.16 or sense **2**; pass. Ju 7.14.

2. *to lay low*: ***o*** a group of people, Ju 14.4; ἔθνη Jb 12.23¶; 2M 5.26.

3. *to set a dinner-table*: pass., Ju 12.1.

κατασύρω: fut. ~συρῶ; aor. κατέσυρα.ʃ

to lay waste: abs. Da 11.10, 26 LXX (TH: κατακλύζω 'inundate'); + acc. pers., Je 29.11.

κατασφάζω: fut. ~σφάξω; aor. κατέσφαξα, inf. ~σφάξαι.*

to slaughter: ***o*** sheep, Zc 11.5; hum., ἐν ξίφοις Ez 16.40, + κόπτω 'to cut down' 2M 5.12. Cf. σφαγή, σφάζω.

κατασφαλίζω: aor.mid. κατησφαλισάμην; pf.ptc. pass. κατησφαλισμένος.ʃ

1. mid. *to take precautions*: 2M 1.19.

2. mid. *to make fast, secure*: + acc. rei, τοὺς πόδας .. πέδαις 'the feet .. with fetters' 3M 4.9.

κατασφραγίζω: aor.pass. κατεσφραγίσθην.ʃ

to seal up securely: ***o*** death, Wi 2.5; *+ κατά τινος Jb 9.7; *+ ἔν τινι 37.7¶. Cf. σφραγίζω.

κατάσχεσις, εως. f.

1. *act of holding in possession*: δοθήτω ἡ γῆ .. ἐν ~ει Nu 32.5; εἰς ~ιν De 32.49.

***2**. *that which one possesses*: αἰώνιος Ge 17.8, 48.4 (of the promised land); a plot of land or estate granted by a ruler, 47.11; γῆ ~εως Le 25.24, ἀγρὸς ~εως 27.16, πόλις ~εως 1C 13.2, σκήνωμα ~εως 2C 11.14, οἶκος ~εως Ju 9.13; διασκεδάσαι ~ιν 'to scatter the possession' Zc 11.14; patrimony inherited from forefathers, not purchased, Le 27.22; κ. κληρονομίας Nu 27.7; ‖ κληρονομία Ps 2.8.

Cf. κτῆμα, κατέχω.

κατασχίζω: aor. κατέσχισα, ptc. ~σχίσας.ʃ

to break forcibly into parts: + acc., τὸ ὕδωρ Is 63.12 (at the Red Sea); books, 1M 1.56.

κατατάσσω: fut. ~τάξω; aor. κατέταξα; pf.pass. ~τέταγμαι.ʃ

1. *to consign* to the (undesirable) fate of (εἰς): + acc., τὴν πόλιν ταύτην εἰς ἀφανισμὸν καὶ εἰς συριγμόν '.. to obliteration and (derision of) being whistled at' Je 19.8; Jb 15.23.

2. *to appoint*: + sbd (τινα) charged with a task, Ez 44.14.; ἐπ' ἐμὲ φυλακήν 'a watch over me' Jb 7.12; 35.10.

Cf. καθίστημι.

καταταχύνω: aor. κατετάχυνα.ʃ *

to cause to lose one's mental equilibrium, 'upset': τινα 1C 21.6*L*. Cf. (κατα)σπεύδω.

κατατείνω: fut. ~τενῶ.ʃ

1. *to stretch out*: pass., ***o*** hum., on a torturing rack, 4M 9.13, 11.18.

2. *to impose strenuous work on*, 'overwork': + acc. pers., ἐν μόχθῳ 'with hard labour' Le 25.43, 46, 53. Cf. Lee 71f.

κατατέμνω: fut. ~τεμῶ; pf.ptc.pass. ~τετμημένος.ʃ

to make incision, lacerate (one's own body): ἐπὶ τὰς σάρκας αὐτῶν οὐ κατατεμοῦσιν ἐντομίδας Le 21.5, pass. βραχίονες κατατετμημένοι Is 15.2; mid. ἐπὶ σίτῳ καὶ οἴνῳ κατετέμνοντο 'they lacerated themselves over corn and wine' Ho 7.14, ἐν μαχαίραις 3K 18.28. Cf. ἐντομίς, τέμνω.

κατατέρπω.ʃ *

mid. *to enjoy thoroughly*: εὐφραίνου καὶ κατατέρπου ἐξ ὅλης τῆς καρδίας σου Zp 3.14. Cf. τέρπω, εὐφραίνω, χαίρω.

κατατήκω: fut. ~τήξω.ʃ

to cause to vanish, 'liquidate': + acc. pers. λαοὺς πολλούς Mi 4.13. Cf. ἀφανίζω.

κατατίθημι: 1aor. κατέθηκα; 2aor.mid. κατεθέμην, inf. ~θέσθαι.ʃ

I. act. **1**. *to set down*: + acc., ῥομφαίαν εἰς τὸν κολεόν 'a sword in the sheath' 1C 21.27.

2. *to realise* a goal: pass. and + acc., Es B 4.

3. *to expend*: pass. and + acc. (money) 2M 4.19; time, εἰς εὐφροσύνην 'for merriment' 3M 5.17.

II. mid. **1**. *to lay up for memory*: + acc., ἐν τῇ καρδίᾳ σου Ju 11.10.

2. *to assert, aver* in court: + acc., λόγον παράνομον κατ' ἐμοῦ Ps 40.9.

κατατίλλω: aor. κατέτιλον.ʃ

to pull off, pluck out: + gen., hair 1E 8.68. Cf. τίλλω.

κατατιτρώσκω.ʃ

to wound: pass., ***o*** the sides of a hum. body, 4M 6.6. Cf. τιτρώσκω.

κατατολμάω: aor. κατετόλμησα, ptc. ~μήσας.ʃ
to be reckless enough to do: + inf., 2M 3.24, 5.15. Cf. τολμάω.

κατατοξεύω: fut. ~τοξεύσω, pass. ~τοξευθήσομαι; aor. κατετόξευσα, inf. ~τοξεῦσαι.ʃ
to shoot dead: + acc. pers., τοὺς εὐθεῖς τῇ καρδίᾳ 'the upright in heart' Ps 10.2, ἐν ἀποκρύφοις ἄμωμον, ἐξάπινα .. 'in secret an innocent person, all of a sudden ..' 63.5; ταῖς βολίσιν αὐτοῦ κατατοξεύσει ἐχθρόν 'will shoot an enemy dead with his missiles' Nu 24.8; and + cogn. acc., τόξευμα 4K 9.16; pass., βολίδι Ex 19.13. Cf. τοξεύω.

κατατρέχω: aor. κατέδραμον.ʃ
to pursue: abs. and with hostile intent, Le 26.37 (|| διώκω vs. 36), ἐπ' ἐμοί Jb 16.10, ἐπὶ σέ Da 4.21 LXX; ὀπίσω αὐτοῦ Jd 1.6B (A: ~διώκω), 3K 19.20 (no hostility implied; *L* τρέχω); + acc. pers., 2M 8.26. Cf. τρέχω, διώκω.

κατατρίβω: fut. ~τρίψω; aor.pass. κατετρίβην, subj. ~τριβῶ.
1. *to wear out by much use*: pass. and ***o*** clothes, τὰ ἱμάτιά σου οὐ κατετρίβη ἀπὸ σοῦ De 8.4 (|| παλαιόω 29.5); footwear, τὰ ὑποδήματα ὑμῶν οὐ κατετρίβη ἀπὸ τῶν ποδῶν ὑμῶν 29.5.
2. *to have to do with* sth *very frequently*: + acc. rei, ἀτιμίαν 'disgrace' Si 26.24¶.

κατατρυφάω: fut. ~τρυφήσω; aor.impv. ~τρύφησον.ʃ
**to obtain delight from*, 'enjoy': + gen. pers., τοῦ κυρίου Ps 36.4; ἐπί τινι– ἐπὶ πλήθει εἰρήνης 36.11. On the rection, see Helbing, *Kasus*. 135. Cf. (ἐν)τρυφάω.

κατατρώγω.ʃ
to eat up: metaph., ***s*** hum. bones, Pr 24.22e (|| ἀναλίσκω vs. 22d).

κατατυγχάνω: aor.subj. ~τύχω.ʃ
to attain that which one has been after: abs., Jb 3.22. Cf. τυγχάνω, ἐπιτυγχάνω.

καταυγάζω.ʃ
1. intr. *to shine brightly*: ***s*** mountains, ὡς λαμπάδες πυρός 'like torches' 1M 6.39.
2. tr. *to illumine*: ***s*** shining stars, + acc., νύκτα Wi 17.5.
Cf. αὐγάζω.

καταφαίνω: 2aor. κατεφάνην.ʃ
to be adjudged as, 'seem; look like': βαρὺ αὐτῷ κατεφάνη 'it appeared to him unbearable' Ge 48.17. Cf. δοκέω, φαίνω.

καταφερής, ές.ʃ
going down: subst.n. 'downhill road' Jo 7.5. Cf. καταφέρω, κατάβασις.

καταφέρω: aor. κατήνεγκα, subj. κατενέγκω, pass. κατηνέχθην.
1. *to bring to a lower place*: πρὸς ἡμᾶς De 1.25; ἀπὸ τοῦ θρόνου Da 5.20 TH; pass., ***o*** hum., εἰς τὴν γῆν To 14.10 𝔊[II] (of attempted murder). Cf. συγκαταφέρω.
2. *to bring* to sbd's disadvantage: ψόγον πονηρὸν πρὸς Ισραηλ 'malicious criticism' Ge 37.2; + gen. pers., αὐτῆς ὄνομα πονηρόν 'a reputation unfavourable against her' De 22.14 (|| ἐκφέρω .. ἐπί τινα vs. 19).
3. mid. intr. *to move downwards*: ὡς ὕδωρ καταφερόμενον ἐν καταβάσει 'like water running down a slope' Mi 1.4; ὕδατος πολλοῦ βίᾳ καταφερομένου 'a great mass of water violently cascading' Is 17.13, χάλαζα .. βίᾳ καταφερομένη 'hail ..' 28.2; Ez 47.2 (***s*** water, || ~βαίνω vs. 1).
Cf. φέρω.

καταφεύγω: fut. ~φεύξομαι; aor. κατέφυγον, inf. ~φυγεῖν, ptc. ~φυγών, subj. ~φύγω.
to go to seek protection or *shelter*: ἡ πόλις αὕτη ἐγγὺς τοῦ καταφυγεῖν με ἐκεῖ Ge 19.20; ὀχυρὰ τοῦ καταφυγεῖν 'fortresses ..' Is 17.3, cf. τὸ ὀχύρωμα εἰς ὃ κατεφύγομεν 1M 5.11; εἰς τὰς πόλεις ὑμῶν Le 26.25; + ἐπί τινα/τι, ***s*** gentiles embracing the religion of Israel, Zc 2.11, Is 54.15, 55.5; ἐπὶ τὸν κύριον ἐν ἀγῶνι θανάτου '.. in a life-or-death struggle' Es C 12; ἐπὶ σχεδίας 'raft' (w. ref. to Noah's ark) Wi 14.6; + πρός τινα– πρὸς τίνα καταφεύξεσθε τοῦ βοηθηθῆναι; '.. to be helped' Is 10.3, sim. Je 27.5, Ps 142.9; ***s*** murderer seeking refuge at an altar, Ex 21.14; εἰς τὴν πόλιν τοῦ φυγαδευτηρίου 'into the city of refuge' Nu 35.25; De 4.42, 19.5. Cf. φεύγω, καταφυγή: Schmidt 3.248f.; Spicq 2.275-7.

καταφθάνω: aor. κατέφθανα.ʃ *
to befall unexpectedly: ***s*** war, + τινα Jd 20.42 A (B: simp.). Cf. φθάνω.

καταφθείρω: fut.pass. ~φθαρήσομαι; aor. κατέφθειρα, inf. ~φθεῖραι, impv. ~φθειρον, subj. ~φθείρω, pass. κατεφθάρην, subj. ~φθαρῶ; pf. κατέφθαρκα, ptc. ~φθαρκώς, pass. κατεφθαρμένος.
to ruin, devastate: physically, ***s*** God, ***o*** His creation, ἐγὼ καταφθείρω ^ἀνθρώπους^ καὶ τὴν γῆν Ge 6.13 (as punishment for their ruining of the earth morally), πᾶσαν σάρκα 6.17 (through flooding || ἐξαλείφω 9.15); kingdoms and islands, κατέφθειραν καὶ ἐδούλωσαν 1M 8.11, τὴν καταφθειρομένην πόλιν καὶ μέλλουσαν ἰσόπεδον γίνεσθαι 'the city being destroyed and about to be levelled to the ground' 2M 8.3, τὴν οἰκουμένην ὅλην Is 13.5, τὴν χώραν ἡμῶν 1M 15.4, τοὺς καρποὺς .. κατέφθειρεν πῦρ Wi 16.22, δένδρον Da LXX 4.14; || ἐρημόω Is 24.1; ***o*** hum., 2C 35.21 (individual). **b**. pass.: διὰ τὰς ἁμαρτίας Le 26.39 (|| τήκομαι 'to melt away'); out of exhaustion from a demanding task, φθορᾷ καταφθαρήσῃ ἀνυπομο-

νήτῳ ('unbearable') Ex 18.18; *o* ζυγός 'yoke' Is 10.27. **c**. morally: *o* γῆ Ge 6.12 (|| φθείρω vs. 11); ὁδός 'way of life' ib.

Cf. καταφθορά, ἀφανίζω, ἐξαλείφω, φθείρω; on a possible difference from which last see Rösel 166. See also Spicq 2.278f.

καταφθορά, ᾶς. f.

decaying and dying: Ps 48.10 (|| ἀποθνήσκω), + θάνατος Si 28.6. Cf. prec.

καταφιλέω: aor. κατεφίλησα, inf. ~φιλῆσαι.

to kiss: + acc. pers., as a gesture of courtesy on meeting, ἀλλήλους Ex 4.27; at parting from kinsmen, τὰ παιδία μου καὶ τὰς θυγατέρας Ge 31.28, τοὺς υἱούς 31.55, τὸν πατέρα μου 3K 19.20; from a friend, 1K 20.41; + acc. rei, financial supporter's hands Si 29.5 (condescending gesture). **b**. metaph.: reciprocal, δικαιοσύνη καὶ ἀλήθεια κατεφίλησαν Ps 84.11 (|| συναντάω).

Cf. φιλέω.

καταφλέγω: aor. κατέφλεξα, subj. ~φλέξω.

1. tr. *to burn*: + acc., φλὸξ .. ἁμαρτωλούς 'a flame ..' Ps 105.18, σκάφη 'boats' 2M 12.6, πυρὶ καὶ θείῳ 'with fire and sulphur' 3M 2.5.

2. *intr. *to burn*: *s* πῦρ Ps 104.32.

Cf. φλέγω, καίω.

καταφλογίζω: aor. κατεφλόγισα.ʃ *

intr. *to burn*: *s* πῦρ Ps 17.9. Cf. φλογίζω.

κατάφοβος, ον.ʃ

struck with fear: *s* hum., Pr 29.16. Cf. δειλός, ἔκφοβος, φόβος.

καταφορά, ᾶς. f.ʃ

act of falling into a comatose condition: ὑπνούντων 'of sleepers' PSol 16.1. Cf. ἔκστασις, ὕπνος.

καταφράσσω.ʃ *

to fortify and protect: pass., *o* elephants, 1M 6.38.

καταφρονέω: fut. ~νήσω, pass. ~νηθήσομαι; aor. κατεφρόνησα, ptc. ~νήσας, subj. ~νήσω, pass. ~νηθῶ.

to despise, belittle, treat with contempt: abs. Ge 27.12, Hb 1.13; + gen., God, Ho 6.7, ὁσιότητος 'piety' Wi 14.30, τοῦ νεώ 'the temple' 2M 4.14 (|| ἀμελέω); hum., Ju 10.19; + ἐπί τινι Zp 1.12, To 4.18 𝔊[I]; pass., *o* δόγματα 'decrees' 4M 4.26. Cf. καταφρόνησις, ~νητής, ~νητέον, εὐκαταφρόνητος, περι~, ὑπερφρονέω, ἐξουδενέω, καταγινώσκω, σκυβαλίζω: Spicq 2.280-4.

καταφρόνησις, εως. f.ʃ

contemptuous attitude: Si 22.8¶. **b**. *contempt suffered*: 2M 3.18. Cf. καταφρονέω.

καταφρονητέον.ʃ

deserving of contempt: Si 22.23¶. Cf. καταφρονέω.

καταφρονητής, οῦ. m. *(but see καταφρονέω).

he who despises, is contemptuous, scorner: κ. ἀνήρ Hb 2.5 (|| κατοινωμένος and ἀλαζών). Cf. καταφρονέω.

καταφυγή, ῆς. f.

place where one seeks safety from danger, 'refuge, shelter': Κύριός μου κ. Ex 17.15, sim. Je 16.19 (|| ἰσχύς, βοήθεια 'strength, help'), || κραταίωμα Ps 30.3; πόλις ~ῆς Nu 35.27, 28; οἶκος ~ῆς Ps 30.3; φονευτῇ 'for a murderer' De 19.3; τὸ ὕψος τῆς ~ῆς τοῦ τοίχου 'the high defence wall' Is 25.12; shelter for the poor, Ps 9.10 (|| βοηθός); || στερέωμα, ῥύστης 17.3; ἀπὸ θλίψεως 31.7; || ἀντιλήμπτωρ 90.2; τοῦ πτώχου 'for the poor' PSol 5.2. **b**. *act of* or *possibility of seeking refuge*: ἐπὶ τὸν κύριον 2M 10.28.

Cf. καταφεύγω, φυγαδευτήριον: Schmidt 3.250.

καταφύτευσις, εως. f.ʃ *

act of planting: Je 38.22. Cf. καταφυτεύω.

καταφυτεύω: fut. ~τεύσω; aor. ~εφύτευσα, subj. ~τεύσω, impv. ~τευσον, ptc. ~τεύσας.

1. *to place into ground* or *soil so that it may take root and grow*: + acc. *o* ξύλον βρώσιμον 'fruit-tree' Le 19.23; fig., a nation, Je 24.6, 2M 1.29.

2. *to plant, establish* (vineyard, orchard etc.): + acc., ἀμπελῶνας Am 9.14, || φυτεύω Is 65.21, ἀμπελῶνας καὶ ἐλαιῶνας '.. olive groves' De 6.11; ἐπὶ τῆς γῆς Am 9.15 (*o* κῆποι 'orchards'); fig., ^τὸν λαόν σου^ εἰς ὄρος κληρονομίας σου Ex 15.17, βασιλείαν Je 18.9 (+ ἀνοικοδομέω); + οἰκοδομέω 38.28, Si 49.7; πόλεις (|| οἰκοδομέω, :: ἀφανίζω) Ez 36.36.

Cf. φυτεύω, καταφύτευσις, οἰκοδομέω: Lee 57f.; LSG s.v.

καταχαίρω: fut.~χαροῦμαι.ʃ

to exult with malicious joy: abs., || ἐπιγελάω Pr 1.26.

καταχαλάω: aor. κατεχάλασα.ʃ *

to cause to descend: αὐτοὺς (pers.) διὰ θυρίδος '.. through the window' Jo 2.15 (|| καταβιβάζω vs. 18). Cf. χαλάω, καταβιβάζω.

καταχαλκόω: pf.ptc.pass. ~κεχαλκωμένος.ʃ

to cover with bronze: pass., *o* door, 2C 4.9. Cf. χαλκός.

καταχέω: impf. (so Helbing, *Gram.* 110) 3s κατέχεεν; aor. κατέχεα.ʃ

to pour from above: ἐπ' αὐτόν Jb 41.15¶; εἰς μυκτῆρας 'into nostrils' 4M 6.25; *s* God and + gen. pers. and acc. rei, κατέχεεν αὐτοῦ ἔλεος 'kept pouring mercy to him from above' Ge 39.21; κατέχεας αὐτοῦ αἰσχύνην Ps 88.46 - on the gen., see Helbing, *Kasus.* 185; + double acc., τὸ ὕδωρ .. λίθους 'the water on to the stones' 2M 1.31. Cf. κατάχυσις, χέω, καταντλέω.

καταχράομαι: aor. κατεχρησάμην.ʃ

to use up: abs., Ep Je 27 (proceeds of sale understood as *o*); + acc., τὴν νωθρότητα .. ποδῶν .. πρὸς ὀξεῖαν .. πορείαν 'the sluggish feet .. for a swift march' 3M 4.5, εἰς ὕπνον .. τὸν χρόνον 'the time .. for sleep' 5.22. Cf. χράω: Naumann 41.

κατάχρεος, ον; also ~εως, ~εων.ʃ
subjugated to, under the control of: + gen., ἁμαρτίας Wi 1.4.
καταχρίω: aor. κατέχρισα, ptc. ~χρίσας.ʃ
to smear sticky substance: + acc., αὐτὴν ἀσφαλτοπίσσῃ '(coated) it [= basket] with bitumen' Ex 2.3, μίλτῳ 'with red paint' Wi 13.14. Cf. χρίω.
καταχρυσόω: fut. ~χρυσώσω; aor. κατεχρύσωσα; pf.ptc.pass. ~κεχρυσωμένος.
to cover with gold-leaf, gild: τι, the ark of testimony, χρυσίῳ καθαρῷ 'with pure gold' Ex 25.10 (|| χρυσόω), 38.2; || κατακοσμέω 39.6; temple, 2C 3.5; throne, 9.17. Cf. χρυσόω, καταργυρόω, καταχαλκόω.
κατάχυσις, εως. f.ʃ
that which pours down, 'torrent' (?): Jb 36.16¶. Cf. καταχέω.
καταχώννυμι: fut. ~χώσω.ʃ
to bury under a heap of objects and destroy: + acc. pers. αὐτοὺς ἐν λίθοις Zc 9.15 (|| καταναλίσκω).
καταχωρίζω: aor.inf. ~χωρίσαι, pass. κατεχωρίσθην.ʃ
1. *to record*: εἰς μνημόσυνον ἐν .. βιβλιοθήκῃ ὑπὲρ τῆς εὐνοίας Μαρδοχαίου '.. about M.'s good offices' Es 2.23 o'; ***o*** ἀριθμός 1C 27.24.
2. *to set apart and assign* to (εἰς) a certain category: + acc. pers., 3M 2.29.
καταψεύδομαι.ʃ
to speak lies: ***s*** στόμα Wi 1.11.
Cf. ψεύδομαι, καταψευσμός.
καταψευσμός, οῦ. m.ʃ *
calumny: Si 26.5. Cf. καταψεύδομαι.
καταψύχω: aor.impv.2pl ~ψύξατε.ʃ
to cool off temporarily during a journey in hot weather: ὑπὸ τὸ δένδρον 'under the tree' Ge 18.4. Cf. ἀναψύχω, ψῦχος.
κατεγχειρέω.ʃ
to do in underhanded manner: pass., 3M 1.21.
κατεῖδον (aor.): inf. κατιδεῖν, impv. κάτιδε.ʃ
1. *to look down* from a higher position: ***s*** God, ἐκ τοῦ οἴκου τοῦ ἁγίου σου ἐκ τοῦ οὐρανοῦ De 26.15, sim. Ba 2.16; Κύριε ὁ θεὸς τοῦ οὐρανοῦ, κάτιδε ἐπὶ τὰς ὑπερηφανίας αὐτῶν '.. their insolences' Ju 6.19.
2. *to recognise visually, catch sight of*: + acc., τὴν γῆν 'the ground' Ex 10.5.
Cf. καταβλέπω.
κατεῖπον (aor.): ptc. κατείπας.ʃ
to speak ill of (κατά τινος): + acc. rei, κατὰ τῆς γῆς πονηρά Nu 14.37.
Cf. καταλέγω, καταλαλέω.
κατελεέω: aor.impv. κατελέησον.ʃ
to treat with compassion: + acc. pers., ἑαυτούς 4M 8.10. Cf. ἐλεέω.
κατεμβλέπω: aor.inf. κατεμβλέψαι.ʃ *
to look in the face: εὐλαβεῖτο κατεμβλέψαι ἐνώπιον τοῦ θεοῦ 'he dared not look God straight in the face' Ex 3.6. Cf. βλέπω and ἐμβλέπω.
κατέναντι. prep. w. gen.
1. *facing* (of geographical or physical position), *opposite to*: Ge 2.14(*e*), 4.16(*e*), 50.13(*c*), Ex 19.2(*b*), 32.5(*d*), Nu 17.4(*d*); τὸ ὄρος τῶν ἐλαιῶν τὸ κ. Ιερουσαλημ Zc 14.4(*c*).
2. *before* (of place), *in the presence of*: ἐδεήθη .. κ. κυρίου 'he supplicated .. before the Lord' Ex 32.11(*f*); in describing some outrageous or humiliating action, "you will be brought forth naked in front of one another (κ. ἀλλήλων)" Am 4.3(*b*); κ. τῶν ὀφθαλμῶν ἡμῶν Jl 1.16(*b*); κ. προσώπου ὑψίστου La 3.35(*b*); κ. τοῦ ἡλίου 'in broad daylight' PSol 2.11 (ἀπέναντι .. vs. 12).
3. *in opposition to, faced with*: κ. τῆς εἰρήνης αὐτοῦ Mi 2.8(*a*).
Cf. ἀπέναντι, ἐναντίος, κατόπισθεν: Sollamo, *Semiprep.*, 107f., 317-9.
a) מִמּוּל; *b*) נֶגֶד; *c*) עַל פְּנֵי; *d*) לִפְנֵי; *e*) קִדְמַת; *f*) אֶת־פְּנֵי; *g*) עַל; *h*)?[Am 3.12]. xʃ
κατεντευκτής, οῦ. m.ʃ *
accuser: Jb 7.20.
κατενώπιον. prep. + gen.*
1. *right opposite*: Lv 4.17(*a*), in order to challenge, Jo 1.5(*b*), 21.42(*c*), 23.9(*c*).
2. κ. οὗ 'in spite of the fact that': Da 5.22 TH(*e*).
3. *in the estimation of*: + gen. pers., Jo 3.7(*d*).
a) אֶת פְּנֵי; *b*) לִפְנֵי; *c*) בִּפְנֵי; *d*) בְּעֵינֵי; *e*) Ar. כָּל־קֳבֵל .ʃ
κατεπείγω.ʃ
to press hard mentally: ***s*** creditor, Ex 22.25. Cf. ἐπείγω.
κατεπίθυμος, ον.ʃ *
intensely desirous: + τοῦ inf., Ju 12.16. Cf. ἐπιθυμέω.
κατεπικύπτω: aor. κατεπέκυψα.ʃ *
to bow down upon: ἐπὶ τὴν κεφαλήν (of an accompanying companion) Es D 7 o'. Cf. κύπτω.
κατεργάζομαι: fut.mid. κατεργῶμαι, pass. ~γασθήσομαι; aor.mid. κατειργασάμην, pass. κατειργάσθην; pf.ptc.pass. κατεργασμένος.
1. *to effect by labour*: + acc., κατοικητήριον 'dwelling-place' Ex 15.17; ὅσα κατεργάζεται ἐκ σταφυλῆς οὐ πίεται 'whatever is manufactured from grapes he shall not drink' Nu 6.3.
2. *to work at, process*: + acc., ξύλα 'wood, timber' Ex 35.33; pass., τὸ χρυσίον, ὃ κατειργάσθη εἰς τὰ ἔργα 39.1.
3. *to cultivate* (of agricultural activity): ἀμπελῶνα φυτεύσεις καὶ κατεργᾷ 'you shall plant a vineyard and cultivate (it)' De 28.39; + σπείρω Ez 36.9.

4. *to apply intense pressure*, 'harass': mentally and + acc. pers., τοῖς λόγοις αὐτῆς ὅλην τὴν νύκτα Jd 16.16A (+ παρενοχλέω; ‖ B: ἐκθλίβω); physically and *s* shepherd, τὸ ἰσχυρὸν κατηργάσασθε μόχθῳ 'made the (still) strong (sheep) work hard' Ez 34.4.

5. *to conquer*: + acc., *s* army, 1E 4.4.

6. *to transform and cause to be*, a causative transform of εἶμι/γίνομαι: w. double acc., αὐτὸν δυνατόν PSol 17.37.

Cf. κατεργασία, ἐργάζομαι, ἑτοιμάζω, ποιέω: Bertram, *TDNT* 3.634f.

κατεργασία, ας. f.ʃ

v.n. of κατεργάζομαι **1**: τοῦ παραδείγματος '(drawing up) of the blueprint' 1C 28.19. Cf. κατεργάζομαι.

κάτεργον, ου. n.ʃ

operating costs (Wevers ad Ex 30.16): δώσεις αὐτὸ εἰς κ. τῆς σκηνῆς τοῦ μαρτυρίου 'you shall allocate it towards the operating costs of the tent of testimony' Ex 30.16; ἤνεγκαν ἀφαίρεμα κυρίῳ εἰς πάντα τὰ ἔργα τῆς σκηνῆς τοῦ μαρτυρίου καὶ εἰς πάντα τὰ ~α αὐτῆς 35.21.

κατέρχομαι: aor. κατῆλθον ptc. κατελθών.ʃ

1. *to descend*: εἰς τὸν ᾅδην Es B 7 o'; *s* dew falling on the ground, Wi 11.22.

2. *to come back* after a long absence: to one's usual place of residence To 1.22 𝔊II (𝔊I ἔρχομαι); home, 2.1, 2M 11.29.

Cf. καταβαίνω, ἀνα~, ἐπιστρέφω.

κατεσθίω, ~έσθω [on the latter, see under ἐσθίω]: fut. καταφάγομαι, κατέδομαι; aor. κατέφαγον, inf. ~φαγεῖν, impv. ~φαγε, 3s. ~φαγέτω, opt.act.3s ~φάγοι.

1. *to eat up, devour* (+ acc.): *s* animals of prey, θηρίον πονηρὸν κατέφαγεν αὐτόν Ge 37.20 (*o* hum.), Le 26.22 (dit. and ‖ ἐξαναλίσκω); Ge 41.4 (both *s* and *o* animals); Ho 2.12, 13.8, Am 4.9; birds, Ge 40.17; locusts, περισσὸν καταλειφθέν .. πᾶν ξύλον τὸ φυόμενον ὑμῖν ἐπὶ τῆς γῆς Ex 10.5 (vegetation left over after damage by hail); πᾶσαν βοτάνην τῆς γῆς 10.12; τὸν χόρτον τῆς γῆς Am 7.2, cf. 4.9, Jl 1.4*ter*, 2.25; *s* cankerworm, Ho 5.7; leprosy, τὸ ἥμισυ τῶν σαρκῶν αὐτῆς Nu 12.12; *o* foodstuff, σῖτος Ge 43.2; cattle and agricultural produce, De 28.51; γάλα 'milk' Ez 34.3 (967: ἐκπίνω); κεφαλίδα '(written) scroll' 3.1.

*2. fig., *to consume, destroy* (+ acc.): κατέδεται ὑμᾶς ἡ γῆ τῶν ἐχθρῶν ὑμῶν Le 26.38; γῆ κατέσθουσα τοὺς κατοικοῦντας ἐπ' αὐτῆς Nu 13.33; τὴν χώραν ὑμῶν Is 1.7; κατέφαγεν αὐτοὺς ὡς καλάμην Ex 15.7 (*s* ὀργή); κατέφαγον ἀλλότριοι τὴν ἰσχὺν αὐτοῦ 'strangers devoured his wealth' Ho 7.9; *s* ὁ ζῆλος τοῦ οἴκου σου 'the passion for your house' Ps 68.10; *o* τὸ ἀργύριον ἡμῶν Ge 31.15 (+ cogn. dat. καταβρώσει); τὰς σάρκας τοῦ λαοῦ μου Mi 3.3, but prob. lit. κατεσθιέτωσαν ἕκαστος τὰς σάρκας τοῦ πλησίον αὐτοῦ Zc 11.9. **b.** freq. *s* πῦρ, ῥομφαία or μάχαιρα: Le 9.24 (*o* cultic offerings upon an altar); γῆν καὶ τὰ γενήματα αὐτῆς De 32.22 (‖ φλέγω); καταφάγεταί σε πῦρ, ἐξολεθρεύσει σε ῥομφαία, καταφάγεταί σε ὡς ἀκρίς 'a fire will consume you, a sword will destroy you, it will consume you like locusts' Na 3.15; καταφαγέτω πῦρ τὰς κέδρους σου (addressed to Lebanon) Zc 11.1; so καταφάγεται (πῦρ) τὰ θεμέλια αὐτῶν 'will destroy their foundations' Ho 8.14, sim. Am 1.4, 7, 10, 12, 14, 2.2, 5, 7.4*bis*, Na 3.13, cf. Am 5.6, Ob 18, Zc 12.6; ὡραῖα τῆς ἐρήμου Jl 1.20; φωνὴ φλογός πυρὸς κατεσθιούσης καλάμην Jl 2.5; *s* sword, τοὺς λέοντάς σου καταφάγεται ῥομφαία Na 2.14 (‖ ἐξολεθρεύω); μάχαιρα Je 12.12, and *o* hum., Is 1.20; ‖ καταπίνω Nu 21.28; *o* ὄρη, ‖ ἐκκαίω Si 43.21.

Cf. ἐσθίω, (ἐξ)αναλίσκω, καταπίνω, καταβιβρώσκω, κατάβρωσις, ἀφανίζω: Schmidt 2.368-70, 76-8.

κατευθικτέω: aor.ptc. ~κτήσας.ʃ

to hit with precision: abs., 2M 14.43.

κατευθύνω: fut. κατευθυνῶ, pass. ~θυνθήσομαι; aor. κατεύθυνα, κατηύθυνα, subj. κατευθύνω, ptc. ~θύνας, inf. ~θῦναι, impv. ~θυνον, 2pl ~θύνατε, opt.3s ~θύναι, pass. κατευθύνθην, impv.3s ~θυνθήτω, opt.3pl ~θυνθείησαν.

I. intr. *to move in a straight line*: κατευθύνων ἐπορεύθη μετ' ἐμοῦ 'he walked straight along with me' Ma 2.6; ἔδραμον καὶ κατεύθυναν 'they ran straight' Ps 58.5; Pr 9.15; a divine spirit's descent, ἐπ' αὐτόν Jd 14.6A, 19A (B: ἅλλομαι'to leap'); πρός τινα 4K 4.27; + acc. loci, τὸν Ἰορδάνην 2K 19.18B. **b.** metaph., Je 21.12 (*pace* Ziegler 1958.95), Pr 15.8 (:: ἀσεβής), 21; *s* heart – ὑπὲρ πάσης καρδίας κατευθυνούσης ἐκζητῆσαι κύριον 'for every heart seeking the Lord single-mindedly' 2C 30.19; οἱ λόγοι σου καλοὶ καὶ κατευθύνοντες 'your argument is good and on the right track' 2K 15.3*L*.

2. *to prosper*: Ho 4.10, Je 15.11, Ps 100.7; *s* ὁδός Ez 18.25 (‖ κατορθόω vs. 29), Pr 29.27. **b.** = pass., αἱ ὁδοί μου Ps 118.5.

3. *to succeed in* doing sth: + τοῦ inf., Jd 12.6.

4. pass. *to achieve the end*: κατευθυνθήτω ἡ προσευχή μου 'my prayer' Ps 140.2.

II.tr. *to lead straight*: + acc., *s* shepherd, Zc 11.16; *o* pers., δίκαιον Ps 7.10, ἐν ἔργοις δικαιοσύνης PSol 18.8; ^ὕδατα^ 2C 32.30.

2. *to render straight*: + acc., ὁδόν Ps 5.9 (‖ ὁδηγέω), διαβήματα 'steps' 36.23, 39.3; metaph. τὴν καρδίαν 77.8, πρὸς κύριον τὴν καρδίαν αὐτοῦ Si

49.3, εἰς ^σοφίαν^ 51.20, βουλὴν καὶ ἐπιστήμην 39.7, κρίμα Pr 1.3, ἐννοίας 'thoughts' 23.19.

3. *to cause to prosper*: + acc. pers., PSol 12.5, Da 3.97 TH, + acc. rei, τὰ ἔργα τῶν χειρῶν ἡμῶν Ps 89.17, τὴν ὁδὸν αὐτῆς Ju 12.8, τὰ πράγματα 'the government' 3M 7.2.

Cf. εὐθύς, εὐθηνέω, εὐθύνω, κατορθόω, (κατ)ευοδόω.

κατευλογέω: aor. κατευλόγησα.ʃ

to pronounce words held to bring special favour upon: ***s o*** hum., To 10.13𝔊[I], 11.17 𝔊[I](𝔊[II] simp.). Cf. εὐλογέω, καταράομαι.

κατευοδόω: fut. ~οδώσω, pass. ~οδωθήσομαι; aor. pass. ~οδώθην. *

1. *to lead safely and without hindrance*: abs., ***s*** ruler, Ps 44.5.

2. *to ensure trouble-free completion of* a passage, *success* of a mission or task: + dat. pers. (com.), ***s*** God, Ps 67.20.

3. pass. *to prosper, be successful*: ***s*** action, Ps 1.3, ὁδός 'way of life' Pr 17.23, κατευοδώθη τὸ ἔργον ἐν χειρὶ αὐτοῦ 1M 2.47; pers., ἐν τῇ ὁδῷ αὐτοῦ Ps 36.7. **b**. impers.: + dat. pers., Da 8.11 TH (LXX εὐοδώθη). **c**. act. = pass.: ***s*** ὁδός Jd. 18.5A (B: εὐοδόομαι).

Cf. εὐοδόω, κατευθύνω.

κατευφημέω: aor.ptc.~μήσας.ʃ *

to applaud: τινα 3M 7.13. Cf. αἰνέω.

κατεύχομαι: aor.ptc. ~ευξάμενος.ʃ

to pray earnestly: τινι (on behalf of) 2M 15.12. **b**. *to imprecate*: τι 4M 12.19. Cf. (προσ)εύχομαι.

κατέχω: fut. καθέξω, pass. κατασχεθήσομαι; aor. κατέσχον, subj. κατάσχω, inf. κατασχεῖν, impv. ~σχε, pass. κατεσχέθην, impv.3s κατασχεθήτω.

1. *to hold fast and not let go*: + acc., Μὴ κατέχετέ με 'Do not hold me up' Ge 24.56; Jd 13.16B (A: βιάζομαι, *L*: παρα~); ῥομφαίαν 'sword' Ct 3.8; + gen. rei, 3K 1.51; ***o*** prisoner (δεσμώτης) Ge 39.20; ἐν τῇ φυλακῇ 42.19; pass. and + gen., κριὸς εἷς κατεχόμενος ἐν φυτῷ .. τῶν κεράτων 'a ram caught in a plant .. by its horns' 22.13; ***o*** tool, δρέπανον 'sickle' Je 27.16. **b**. *to detain* a visitor *to stay on*: Jd 13.16B (*L* παραβιάζομαι; A: simp.). **c**. the continual aspect of the action not emphasised, *to apprehend*: aor., τινα 2K 4.10. **d**. fig. with emotions as ***s***: + acc. pers., ἀθυμία κατέσχεν με 'despondency gripped me' Ps 118.53, ἀνάγκη καὶ θλῖψις 'distress and anguish' Jb 15.24; ὠδῖνες καθέξουσί σε .. ὡς γυναῖκα τίκτουσαν 'pangs .. like a woman in labour' Je 13.21, ὠδῖνες ὡς τικτούσης 6.24, cf. 27.43 with κατακρατέω.

2. *to keep in possession and not lose*: ***o*** land, καθέξουσιν αὐτὴν εἰς τὸν αἰῶνα Ex 32.13, τὴν γῆν Ez 33.24, τὴν βασιλείαν ἕως αἰῶνος Da LXX 7.18, κληρονομίαν 'inheritance' Si 46.9, χρήματα 'money' Jb 27.17; + gen., πλούτου 'wealth' Ps 72.12.

3. *to gain possession of*: + acc., city, Ju 5.19, γῆν Jo 1.11.

4. *to restrain and not allow to go into action*: + gen., οὐ δυνήσῃ τοῦ κατασχεῖν αὐτῶν 'you will not be able to hold them off' 1M 6.27; ***s*** fear, Pr 19.15. **b**. pass. = refl.: αὐτοῖς 'for their sake' Ru 1.13.

***5**. *to have an area assigned to be responsible for*: 4K 12.13, Ne 3.4, 5.

***6**. *to succeed in* doing sth: + inf., 2M 15.5.

Cf. κατάσχεσις, κατόχιμος, κάτοχος, κατακρατέω: Spicq 2.285-90.

κατηγορέω: fut. ~ρήσω; aor. κατηγόρησα; pf. κατηγόρηκα.

to accuse: + gen. pers., περί τινος πρός τινα Da 6.4 LXX; + acc. rei (contents of accusation), αὐτῶν πονηρά 1M 7.25; + ὡς-clause, 2M 10.21. Cf. προηγορέω.

κατήγορος, ου. m.ʃ

accuser: + gen. pers., Pr 18.17, 2M 4.5. Cf. προήγορος.

κατηφής, ές.ʃ

inspiring only gloomy prospects: ***s*** φάσματα 'sombre sights' Wi 17.4. Cf. Shipp 308.

κατιόω: aor. κατίωσα.ʃ *

to become rusty: metaph., ***s*** hum., Si 12.11. Cf. ἰόομαι.

κατισχύω: fut. ~ισχύσω; aor. κατίσχυσα, impv. ~ίσχυσον, inf. ~ισχῦσαι, ptc. ~ισχύσας, subj. ~ισχύσω, opt. 3s ~ισχύσαι.

I. tr. **to strengthen, give strength to*: + acc. pers. Ex 18.23, Ho 14.9, Zc 10.6; + acc. rei, τοὺς βραχίονας αὐτοῦ Ez 31.24 (|| ἐνισχύω vs. 25), sim. Ho 7.15; part of a building in bad repair, 4K 22.5 (|| vs. 6 κραταιόω); τὴν καρδίαν De 2.30 ('the determination' and || σκληρύνω τὸ πνεῦμα ib. and ἀποστέργω 15.7), and + inf., Jo 11.20; χεῖρας ἀνόμου 'to support and help a lawless person' Ez 13.22, sim. Jd 9.24A (B: ἐνισχύω), cf. κραταιόω **1b**; εὐσέβειαν Si 49.3; by providing military training (?), Jd 7.8 B.

2. *to overpower*: + acc. pers., κατίσχυσεν αὐτοὺς πόλεμος Is 42.25; ***s*** ἀπορία .. ὠδῖνες 'helplessness .. pains' Je 8.21; + gen., βασιλείας Da 11.21 TH; οἱ κατισχύοντες 'the taskmasters' PSol 2.7. **b**. *to be more powerful than*: + acc. pers., 1E 5.49, cf. ὑπερισχύω.

***3**. *to have good understanding of*: + acc., τοὺς λόγους μου Da 13.3 LXX (|| συνίημι).

II. intr. **1**. *to take courage, find encouragement*: Hg 2.5*ter* (|| θαρσέω); ***s*** hand, κατισχυέτωσαν αἱ χεῖρες ὑμῶν Zc 8.9, cf. κατισχύετε ἐν ταῖς χερσὶν ὑμῶν 8.13.

2. *to become powerful*: *s* population, κατίσχυον σφόδρα σφόδρα Ex 1.7; an army, 17.11; + ἐπί τινος– κατίσχυσε ἐπὶ ^τῆς γῆς^ ἡ ἀνομία 'the lawlessness gained the upper hand of the land' Is 24.20; king, ἐπί τινα 2C 17.1(*L* ἐν~); + gen. of comparison, Je 15.18; πρός σέ 'challenging you' 2C 14.10; + inf., 'to be powerful enough to ..' Wi 17.5, cf. ἰσχύω **2b**. **b**. *to overpower*: *s* sword, + ἐπί τινα Ju 11.10; χείρ Jd 6.2 A [B: simp.] (the enemy gaining the upper hand).

3. *to become insensitive, unsusceptible, irresponsive*: *s* human heart, Ex 7.13 (|| σκληρύνω vs. 3 and βαρύνω vs. 14).

*4. *to make strenuous efforts, endeavour*: 1C 11.10 (*L* ἀντέχομαι); + inf., Is 22.4, σφόδρα Jo 23.6; ἐν τῇ λειτουργίᾳ 2C 31.4; obstinately, 36.13. Cf. ἰσχύω **3**.

Cf. ἰσχύς, ἐν(ισχύω), ἐπι~, κατακρατέω, βαρύνω, ἐπιρρωνύω, σκληρύνω, θαρσέω.

κατοδυνάω: pf.ptc.pass. κατωδυνωμένος.ʃ *

1. *to make grievously painful*: + acc., τὴν ζωὴν αὐτῶν ἐν τοῖς ἔργοις τοῖς σκληροῖς 'their life with hard works' Ex 1.14.

2. *to cause grievous hardship*: ***o*** mind, εὐφρανεῖς τὴν ψυχὴν τῆς θυγατρός μου τὴν κατωδυνωμένην 'you shall cheer up the downcast spirit of my daughter' To 8.20 𝔊II.

3. *to cause deep grief*: + ***o*** pers. and ἐπί τινι –τῶν ἀνδρῶν τῶν στεναζόντων καὶ τῶν κατοδυνωμένων ἐπὶ πάσαις ταῖς ἀνομίαις 'of the men who are sighing and deeply grieved over all the unlawfulnesses' Ez 9.4.

Cf. ὀδύνη, ὀδυνάω.

κατοικεσία, ας. f.ʃ *

1. *area inhabited*: La 1.7.

2. *inhabitation*: πόλις ~ας Ps 106.36.

Cf. κατοίκησις.

κατοικέω: pres.subj. ~κῶ; fut. ~κήσω, pass. ~κηθήσομαι, ptc. ~κηθησόμενος; aor. κατῴκησα, subj. ~κήσω, pass. ~κηθῶ, impv. ~κησον, inf. ~κῆσαι, ptc. ~κήσας; pf. κατῴκηκα.

1. *to dwell, live as permanent resident*: abs. (but with the notion of dwelling-place understood) Zp 1.13, 3.6; κατοικήσει Ιερουσαλημ ἔτι καθ' ἑαυτήν 'J. will again dwell by herself, i.e. without foreign co-residents' Zc 12.6; + ἐν τοῖς οἴκοις Ge 9.27, Am 5.11; ἐν τῇ ἐρήμῳ Ge 21.20; ἐν ταῖς πόλεσιν αὐτῶν καὶ ἐν ταῖς οἴκοις αὐτῶν De 19.1; ἐν γῇ Αἰγύπτῳ ἐπὶ γῆς Γεσεμ Ge 47.27; ἐν τῇ γῇ τοῦ κυρίου Ho 9.3a; ἐν οἴκῳ κυρίου Ps 22.6; ἐν ποταμοῖς Na 3.8; μετὰ ἀσφαλείας 'with a sense of security' Le 26.5; ἐπ' ἐλπίδι 'on hope' Zp 3.1; || καταλύω Je 28.43, || καθίζω 30.11, sim. 2K 11.1. **b**. The pl. ptc. pres. is often used substantivally, *inhabitants*: καὶ πάντας τοὺς κατοικοῦντας ἐν ταῖς πόλεσιν Ge 19.25; ἐξολεθρεύσω ~οῦντας ἐκ πεδίου Ων 'I will obliterate inhabitants from the plain of On' Am 1.5; 1.8. The gen. is not used, even in cases like Mi 7.13 /yōšvehā/ or Jl 1.2 /yōšvē hā'āreṣ/ , but acc., cf. τῷ κυρίῳ τῷ κατοικοῦντι ἐν Σιων Ps 9.12. **c**. + acc. of place: γῆν Ge 12.6, Le 26.35, Ho 4.1, 3, Am 9.5; Σαμάρειαν Ho 10.5 (cp. ἐν Σ~ᾳ Am 3.12); city (πόλιν) Am 1.5, Mi 1.11*bis*, 6.16(?), Hb 2.8(?), 17(?), Zc 13.1 v.l.; τὴν κατακεκομμένην 'the struck down' (sc. πόλιν) Zp 1.11; κατοικοῦντες πόλεις πολλάς Zc 8.20; 8.21; τὸ σχοίνισμα τῆς θαλάσσης 'the coastal strip' Zp 2.5; οἰκίας πηλίνας 'houses of clay' Jb 4.19; fig. ὀδύνας 'sorrows' Mi 1.12. **d**. οἱ κατοικοῦντες ἔναντι κυρίου: priests and temple functionaries, Is 23.18.

2. *to settle (in) new land* as colonist: ἐν γῇ Χανααν Ge 13.12; εἰς Αἴγυπτον 'moved into Egypt and settled there' Ho 9.3*b* (so prob. different from κατῴκησεν Εφραιμ ἐν Αἰγύπτῳ ib. 11.5); ἐπὶ ^τῆς γῆς^ De 17.14; παρὰ τὴν δρῦν τὴν Μαμβρη 'beside the oak of M.' Ge 13.18; *s* returnees from abroad, Am 9.14.

3. *to come to be present* or *inherent*: δικαιοσύνη ἐν τῷ Καρμήλῳ κατοικήσει Is 32.16 (|| ἀναπαύομαι).

4. pass. *to be settled, populated*, as opp. to being in an uninhabited, desolate state (ἀφανισμός): ἡ Ιουδα εἰς τὸν αἰῶνα κατοικηθήσεται Jl 3.20; πᾶσα ἡ γῆ κατοικεῖται καὶ ἡσυχάζει Zc 1.11; κατακάρπως κατοικηθήσεται Ιερουσαλημ ἀπὸ πλήθους ἀνθρώπων καὶ κτήνων ἐν μέσῳ αὐτῆς 'J. will be heavily populated by plenty of men and animals therein' 2.4; "when Jerusalem was populated and thriving (εὐθηνοῦσα), and the cities around her, the hilly area and the low-lying area were populated" 7.7; οὐ μὴ κατοικηθῇ 9.5, Je 27.39; ἄβατον γῆν ἥτις οὐ κατοικηθήσεται 6.8.

Cf. κατοικίζω, κατοικεσία, κατοίκησις, κατοικητήριον, οἰκέω, ναίω, πρόσκειμαι, ἐννέμω: Casevitz 1985.161-3.

κατοίκησις, εως. f.

1. *area inhabited*: Ge 10.30.

2. *inhabitation*: Ge 27.39; ἡ κ. τῶν υἱῶν Ισραηλ, ἣν κατῴκησαν ἐν γῇ Αἰγύπτῳ .. 'the sojourning of the children of Is. which they made in the land of E...' Ex 12.40; γῆ ~εως Nu 15.2.

3. *people living together*: τοῦ οἴκου Σιβα 2K 9.12 (*L* κατοικία).

Cf. κατοικέω, κατοικεσία: Casevitz 1985.165.

κατοικητήριον, ου. n.

dwelling-place: of hum., Ex 12.20, 15.17; God's, Ps 32.14, Da 2.11 LXX (TH κατοικία), glossed as ὁ οὐρανός 2C 30.27; lions' lair, Na 2.12, 13; of snakes, Je 9.11. Cf. κατοικία and οἴκησις.

κατοικία, ας. f.

1. *habitation, dwelling-place*: Le 3.17; ὑψῶν ~αν αὐτοῦ 'building his house high up' Ob 3; Ho 11.7, 14.5, Zp 2.5.

2. coll. *inhabitants, population*: τοῦ Ισραηλ Je 3.6.

Cf. κατοικητήριον, οἰκεία: Casevitz 1985.164.

κατοικίζω: fut. κατοικιῶ; aor. κατῴκισα, impv. κατοίκισον, inf. κατοικίσαι, pass. κατῳκίσθην, inf. κατοικισθῆναι; pf.pass.3s κατῴκισται.

1. Causative of κατοικέω, thus *to make dwell*: + acc. pers., Ge 3.24; 47.6 (|| κατοικέω 47.4); in tents and on festivals, Le 23.43, Ho 12.9; κ. σε ἐπ' ἐλπίδι Ho 2.18; παρά τινι and pass. with middle force, Ex 2.21, De 2.12, 21, 22, 23, ἐν τῇ ὀρεινῇ 'in the mountainous region' Ju 5.19.

2. *to settle*: *o* land, Ps 92.1; κατακλυσμόν 'inundated area(?)' 28.10; πόλεις ἠρημωμένας 'depopulated cities' Is 54.3.

Cf. κατοικέω, κατοικοδομέω: Casevitz 1985. 165-73.

κατοικοδομέω: pf.ptc.pass. κατῳκοδομημένος.ʃ

to use as a dwelling-place: subst.ptc.f. ἐν ταῖς κατῳκοδομημέναις 'in the dwelling-places' Ge 36. 43. Cf. κατοικέω, κατοικίζω, οἰκέω.

κάτοικος, ου. m.

one who lives, 'inhabitant': τῆς γῆς Χανααν Ge 50.11. Cf. κατοικέω: Casevitz 1985.163.

κατοικτίρω: aor.ptc. ~τίρας, subj. ~τίρω.ʃ

to take pity on: + acc., old age, 4M 8.20 (|| ἐλεέω), τινα 12.2. Cf. οἰκτιρέω, ἐλεέω.

κατοινόομαι: pf.ptc. κατοινωμένος.ʃ

to become inebriated with wine: κατοινωμένος καὶ καταφρονητὴς ἀνήρ .. Hb 2.5 (Zgl: cf. *BA* ad loc.).

κατόπισθεν. prep. w. gen.

behind (of place): ἐπορεύθη .. κ. τῶν ἀδελφῶν αὐτοῦ Ge 37.17; ἐξεπορεύοντο κ. αὐτῶν Zc 6.6; 7.14. Cf. ὄπισθεν, subs., κατέναντι.

κατοπίσω. prep.ʃ *

= κατόπισθεν, q.v.: Jd 18.22A.

κατοπτεύω.ʃ

to observe closely: *s* God, Es E 4 o', 7.28 *L*. Cf. κατανοέω.

κάτοπτρον, ου. n.ʃ

mirror: used by women, Ex 38.26. Cf. ἔσοπτρον.

κατορθόω: fut. ~θώσω; aor. ~ώρθωσα, subj. ~ορθώσω, inf. ~ορθῶσαι, impv. ~όρθωσον, mid. ~θώσασθαι, pass. κατωρθώθην, impv.3s ~ορθωθήτω.

*__1__. *to conduct oneself in an upright, virtuous manner*: κατορθῶν ἐν ἀνθρώποις οὐχ ὑπάρχει Mi 7.2 (|| εὐλαβής); Pr 2.7.

2. *to prosper*: Zc 4.7; Ez 18.29 (|| κατευθύνω vs. 25); *s* πόλις Pr 11.10 (:: κατασκάπτομαι 'to be ruined'); θρόνος 'royal rule' Pr 25.5; hum. Ez 12.3.

3. *to erect, establish firmly*: + *o* acc., altar, 2C 33.16; βασιλείαν Is 9.7, 1C 28.7; τὴν οἰκουμένην, ἥτις οὐ σαλευθήσεται 'the world, which will not be shaken' Ps 95.10; φόρον '(ensure payment of) tributes' (?) 2M 8.36; pass., *o* ἡ γῆ 1C 16.30 (:: σαλεύομαι).

4. *to keep straight*: fig. and + acc., πορείαν Je 10.23, ὁδόν Ps 118.9, ἄξονας 'paths' Pr 2.9.

5. *to execute properly*: *o* cultic service, 2C 35.10, 16; construction work, 29.35; σύνεσιν Pr 9.6. **b**. intr.: ἕως κατορθώσῃ ἡ ἡμέρα 'until the day has advanced quite a while' Pr 4.18.

6. *to rectify errors* or *defects*, 'to repair': + acc., βούκεντρον 'ox-goad' 1K 13.21 *L*.

Cf. κατόρθωσις, ὀρθός, εὐλαβέομαι, εὐθηνέω, κατευθύνω. On sense **1**, cf. LSJ, s.v. κατόρθωμα, 2. *virtuous action*.

κατόρθωσις, εως. f.ʃ

1. *firm basis*: Ps 96.2; || ἰσχύς 2C 3.17.

2. *secure subsistence*: πάσης ψυχῆς Ju 11.7.

κατορύσσω: fut. ~ορύξω; aor. κατώρυξα; pass. κατωρύγην, subj. κατορυγῶ. On the form (for earlier κατορυχθῶ), see Thack. 236f.

to bury and put out of reach: *o* a dead pers., ἐν τῇ ὁδῷ Ge 48.7; Ez 39.12; εἰς ᾅδου Am 9.2; *o* εἴδωλα To 14.6 𝔊I (𝔊II ἀφίημι). Cf. κρύπτω and ὀρύσσω.

κατορχέομαι: aor. κατωρχησάμην.ʃ

to dance triumphantly: Zc 12.10. Cf. ὀρχέομαι.

κατοχεύω: fut. κατοχεύσω.ʃ *

to make a mating male animal (acc.) *cover* a female (dat.): τὰ κτήνη σου οὐ κατοχεύσεις ἑτεροζύγῳ '.. a heterogeneous animal' Le 19.19.

κατόχιμος, η, ον.ʃ

held in possession: *s* slave, εἰς τὸν αἰῶνα Le 25.46. Cf. κατέχω.

κάτοχος, ον.ʃ

detaining, holding back: subst. and of bars on a door, ~οι αἰώνιοι Jn 2.7. Cf. κατέχω.

κάτω, comp. κατώτερον, super. κατώτατος, adv. κατωτάτω.

I. adv. *at a point low down*: abs., ἀπὸ εἰκοσαετοῦς καὶ κ. 'from 20 years old and below' 1C 27.23; + gen., κατώτερον Βαιθηλ Ge 35.8; ἕως ᾅδου κατωτάτω τῆς γῆς To 13.2 𝔊II.

2. *down below*: ἐν τῷ οὐρανῷ ἄνω καὶ .. ἐν τῇ γῇ κάτω Ex 20.4, De 5.8, .. ἐπὶ τῆς γῆς κάτω 4.39.

3. *downwards*: καταβήσῃ κάτω κάτω De 28.43; ἕως ᾅδου κάτω 32.22, .. κατωτάτω To 4.19 𝔊II.

4. *relatively late in history*: ἐν χρόνοις κάτω Si prol. II.

II. adj. *situated very low*: ἐκ λάκκου κατωτάτου 'out of a pit very deep down' La 3.55, ἐξ ᾅδου κατωτάτου Ps 85.13; subst.n.pl., τὰ κατώτατα 'the lowest parts,' ἐν τοῖς κατωτάτοις τῆς γῆς 138.15, Od 12.13; Ne 4.13.

Cf. κάτωθεν, ὑποκάτω, ἄνω.

κατώδυνος, ον.

exceedingly distressed: *s* hum., ψυχῇ Jd 18.25 Ra (AB: πικρός), 1K 1.10; ψυχή 1K 30.6, 4K 4.27. Cf. ὀδύνη.

κάτωθεν.

1. adv. *in* or *at the lower part*: Ex 26.24 (Wevers ad loc.: 'from the bottom up'), 28.29. **b.** ὁ ᾅδης κ. Is 14.9; ἐκ τῶν κ. ἀναβαίνωσιν 'arise from the lower parts' Ez 41.7.

2. prep. + gen. *underneath, below*: Ex 36.28.

Cf. κάτω.

καυλός, οῦ. m.ʃ

tubular structure: stem or shaft of lampstand, Ex 25.30, 38.14, Nu 8.4.

καῦμα, ατος. n.

condition of being hot: ‖ ψῦχος 'cold' Ge 8.22; endured by labourer outdoors in the daytime and ‖ παγετός 'frost' 31.40, sim. Je 43.30; causing thirst, ἐν δίψει ~ατος ἐν ἀνύδρῳ 'in thirst from heat in waterless land' De 32.10; σκιὰ ἀπὸ ~ατος 'shade against heat' Is 4.6; φῶς ~ατος μεσημβρίας 'blazing midday heat' 18.4; ἐν τῷ ~ατι τῆς ἡμέρας 'about the heat of the day' 2K 4.5; ^ἡλίου^ Si 43.3. Cf. καύσων, ψῦχος.

καῦσις, εως. f.ʃ

1. *act of being consumed by fire*: λύχνοι τῆς ~εως 'lamps for burning' Ex 39.17, 2C 13.11.

2. *act of consuming by fire*: Le 6.9; τὸ σῶμα αὐτοῦ ἐδόθη εἰς ~ιν πυρός Da 7.11; of sacrificial animals, Is 40.16, of firewood, 44.15; gets rid of filth as a consequence, 4.4.

Cf. καίω.

καυστικός, ή, όν.ʃ

capable of burning sth or sbd: *s* fire, 4M 10.14. **b.** *executed through burning*: *s* βάσανος 'torture' 4M 6.27. Cf. καίω.

καύσων, ωνος. m. *

1. *sun heat*: sunstroke, Ju 8.3.

2. *hot wind*: ‖ πονηρὸν πνεῦμα, Ho 12.1; harmful and ‖ ὁ ἥλιος Is 49.10; as a qualifier, ~ωνα ἄνεμον 'a hot wind (from the desert to the east of Israel)' Ho 13.15 (cf. ἄνεμος κ. Je 18.17), ἄνεμον καύσωνα διαφθείροντα 'destructive, scorching wind' Je 28.1, πνεύματι ~ωνος συγκαίοντι Jn 4.8; *s* of ξηραίνω 'to dry' Ez 19.12.

Cf. καίω.

καυτήριον, ου. n.ʃ

branding iron: instrument of torture, 4M 15.22. Cf. βασανιστήριον.

καυχάομαι: fut. καυχήσομαι; aor.subj. καυχήσωμαι, inf. καυχήσασθαι.

to take pride in (ἐν, ἐπί): Μὴ καυχάσθω ὁ σοφὸς ἐν τῇ σοφίᾳ αὐτοῦ .. ἀλλ' ἢ ἐν τούτῳ καυχάσθω ὁ καυχώμενος, συνίειν καὶ γινώσκειν ὅτι ἐγώ εἰμι κύριος .. Je 9.23f. **b.** w. positive connotation, abs. Ps 31.11 (‖ εὐφραίνομαι, ἀγαλλιάομαι), *s* ὅσιοι 'the pious' 149.5 (‖ ἀγαλλιάομαι), Si 24.1 (‖ αἰνέω); ἐν σοί [= ἐν κυρίῳ], ἐν δόρατι κέντρου 'the shaft of a goad' 38.25 (farmer's professional pride), ἐν νόμῳ διαθήκης κυρίου 39.8; ἐπὶ τοῖς θαυμασίοις αὐτοῦ 'his marvellous deeds' 17.8, ἐπ' αὐτῷ 30.2 [= one's well-disciplined son]; ἔναντι δυναμέως αὐτοῦ 'faced with His might' 24.2. **c.** with negative connotation, *to boast, brag*, abs. ἕως πότε ἁμαρτωλοὶ καυχήσονται Ps 93.3, καυχώμενος ἐπήνεσε πάντας τοὺς θεοὺς τῶν ἐθνῶν .. Da LXX 5.1 praef.; + acc. rei, τὰ εἰς αὔιρον 'about tomorrow' Pr 27.1; ἔν τινι – ἐν τῇ φρονήσει αὐτοῦ .. ἐν τῇ δυνάμει αὐτοῦ .. ἐν τῷ πλούτῳ αὐτοῦ 'in his sagacity .. in his might .. in his wealth' 1K 2.10, ἐν περιβολῇ ἱματίων 'wearing (fine) clothes' Si 11.4; ἐπί τινι – ἐπὶ τῷ πλήθει τοῦ πλούτου 'in the abundance of riches' Ps 48.7; ἐπ' ἐμέ 'at my expense' Jd 7.2; + inf., Pr 20.9 (‖ παρρησιάζομαι); ‖ ἀγαλλιάομαι 3M 2.17.

Cf. καύχημα, καύχησις, ἐγκαυχάομαι, ἀγαυριάομαι, γαυριάω, μεγαλαυχέω, μεγαλύνω: Fuchs 1977.

καύχημα, ατος. n.

that which makes one proud, object of pride: ^κύριος^ κ. σου De 10.21, τὸ κ. τῆς δυνάμεως αὐτῶν εἶ σύ Ps 88.18, κ. μου σὺ εἶ Je 17.14; ἡ μάχαιρα κ. σου De 33.29, ἐποίησέν σε ὀνομαστὸν καὶ κ. καὶ δοξαστόν 26.19; θήσομαι αὐτοὺς εἰς κ. καὶ ὀνομαστούς 'I shall make them objects of pride and of fame' Zp 3.19, τὸ κ. πάσης τῆς γῆς Je 28.41 (Babylon in her glory); ἐν φόβῳ κυρίου ἔστω τὸ κ. σου Si 9.16, sim. 10.22; w. ref. to a pers., σὺ [= Judith] κ. μέγα τοῦ γένους ἡμῶν Ju 15.9 (‖ γαυρίαμα), εἰς λαὸν ὀνομαστὸν καὶ εἰς κ. καὶ εἰς δόξαν 'a famous people ..' Je 13.11. Cf. (κατα)-καυχάομαι, καύχησις, ἀγαυρίαμα. See *BA* ad Zp 3.20 on the positive sense of the noun in the LXX as against its negative one in Cl. Gk, which also applies to the verb, καυχάομαι; also Spicq 2.295-302.

καύχησις, εως. f.

1. *act of taking pride* in: Je 12.13; τὴν ἔπαρσιν τῆς ~εως αὐτῶν 'the pride of their boasting' Ez 24.25 (sc. their children).

2. *ground for pride*: Si 34.10; στέφανος ~εως 'crown ..' Pr 16.31 (old age), Ez 16.12; σκεύη ~εως

Ez 16.17; αἰνοῦμαι τὸ ὄνομα τῆς ~εώς σου 1C 29.13.

Cf. καυχάομαι.

καψάκης, ου. f.

flask: for oil, Ju 10.5, 3K 17.12; for water, 19.6.

κέγχρος, ου. m.ʃ

millet: Ez 4.9.

κέδρινος, η, ον.

of cedar (κέδρος): *s* ξύλον Le 14.4 +, Nu 19.6. Cf. κέδρος.

κέδρος, ου. f.

cedar: known for its great height, ὕψος ~ου Am 2.9; Lebanon famed for it, Zc 11.1, ~ον τοῦ Λιβάνου τῶν ὑψηλῶν καὶ μετεώρων Is 2.13; παρ' ὕδατα Nu 24.6, || κυπάρισσος 'cypress' Si 24.13; building material, + συκάμινος Is 9.10. Cf. κέδρινος.

κεῖμαι

1. *to be present*: σημεῖον κείμενον διὰ παντός 'a token permanently there' Jo 4.6; τὰ κείμενα .. φιλάνθρωπα 'the currently existing privileges' 2M 4.11; κίνδυνος .. κεῖμενός τινι 'a danger .. awaiting sbd' 4M 13.15. **b**. *to be present and situated* somewhere: ὁ ζυγὸς ὁ ἐπ' αὐτῶν κείμενος 'the yoke lying on them' Is 9.4, ἐπὶ στόματος Αβεσσαλωμ ἦν κείμενος 'A. never stopped mentioning it' 2K 13.32; 1E 6.22, 25 (|| τίθημι pass.), 3M 4.8, Si 22.18, Je 24.1

2. *to be found* in a certain state: ἐν ἀντιπαραγωγῇ 'in opposition' Es B 5 o'; ἐν ὑπεροχῇ 'in good standing' 2M 3.11, ἐν ἐσχάτῃ πνοῇ 'about to breathe his last' 3.31, ἐν ἀξιώματι 'dignitary' 4.31, ἐν ὑποψίᾳ 'in suspicion' 4.34, ἐν ἥττονι μέρει 'carrying less weight' 15.18, ἐν ἑτοίμῳ 'ready' 3M 5.26, ἐν τῷ σκότει To 5.10 𝔊[II], ἐν μερίμνῃ 'worrying' Si 38.29; φυγάδες .. ἔκειντο 'they were there like fugitives' Wi 17.2.

Cf. εἰμί, εὑρίσκω.

κειρία, ας. f.ʃ

bedspread: Pr 7.16.

κείρω: aor.act.inf. κεῖραι, subj. κείρω, mid. ἐκειράμην, impv. κεῖραι; pf.ptc.pass. κεκαρμένος.

1. *to cut the hair of*, 'shear': + acc., πρόβατα Ge 31.19, De 15.19; ποίμνιον 1K 25.2, ἀγέλαι τῶν κεκαρμένων 'flocks of shorn (sheep)' Ct 4.2, 6.6. **b**. *to cut, shear* in general: ***o*** πόαν 'grass' Pr 27.25.

2. mid. *to cut one's own hair* or *to have it cut* as a sign of mourning: Mi 1.16 (|| ξυράω); + acc., τὴν κεφαλήν σου '(shave) your (own) head' Je 7.29, cf. 30.10; τὴν κόμην τῆς κεφαλῆς αὐτοῦ 'the hair of his head' Jb 1.20.

Cf. περικείρω, κουρά, κουρεύς, ξυράω.

κεκρυμμένως. adv.ʃ *

away from public attention: κ. κλαύσεται 'will weep secretly' Je 13.17. Cf. κρυπτῶς.

κέλευσμα, ατος. n.ʃ

order for an action: Pr 30.27. Cf. κελεύω, ἐντολή.

κελεύω: aor. ἐκέλευσα, impv. κέλευσον, ptc. κελεύσας, pass. κελευσθείς. Mostly confined to 1-4M.

to issue a command: + acc. pers. and inf., Bel 14 LXX (TH ἐπιτάσσω), 2M 1.21; + inf. alone, ib., Es 7.12 *L*; + dat. pers., Ju 2.15 (v.l. προστάσσω); + dat. pers. and inf., To 8.18, 2M 5.12; + dat. pers. and λέγων 1E 9.53; pass., ***o*** hum., 4M 9.11. Cf. ἐντέλλομαι, παραγγέλλω, ἐπι~, προσ~, συντάσσω, τάσσω, κέλευσμα: Schmidt 1.203f.; Shipp 310f.; Pelletier 1962.277-88; Lee 2003.517-23; Muraoka 2006.

κενεών, ῶνος. m.ʃ

hollow place: 2M 14.44. **b**. between ribs and hip: 4M 6.8.

κενοδοξέω: aor.subj. ~δοξήσω.ʃ

to indulge in vainglory: περί τι 'over sth' 4M 5.10, ἐπί τινι 8.24. Cf. κενοδοξία.

κενοδοξία, ας. f.ʃ

vainglory: Wi 14.14, 2M 4.15, 8.19. Cf. κενοδοξέω.

κενολογέω.ʃ

to utter meaningless things: of pagan divination, Is 8.19 (|| other forms of divination).

κενός, ή, όν.

1. *containing nothing*, 'empty': ὁ λάκκος κ., ὕδωρ οὐκ εἶχεν 'the cistern was empty, having no water (in it)' Ge 37.24; εἴδοσαν .. τὰς τραπέζας ~άς 'they saw .. the tables empty' Da LXX Bel 17, ἐκτετιναγμένος καὶ κ. 'shaken out and ..' Ne 5.13; κ. χερσίν 'empty-handed' PSol 4.17. **b**. *with desire unsatisfied, need not met*: τὰς ψυχὰς τὰς διψώσας ~ὰς ποιῆσαι 'to leave the thirsty souls unsatisfied' Is 32.6, ἐχόρτασεν ψυχὴν ~ήν 'he sated ..' Ps 106.9; *s* hum., 'disgruntled' Jd 9.4.

2. *having nothing with one*, 'empty-handed': νῦν ἂν ~όν με ἐξαπέστειλας 'you would have sent me off empty-handed' Ge 31.42, χήρας ἐξαπέστειλας ~άς 'you sent widows away ..' Jb 22.9, ἀνέστρεψαν τοὺς ἀγγέλους αὐτοῦ ~οὺς ἐν ἀτιμίᾳ 'they sent back his envoys empty-handed in disgrace' Ju 1.11; οὐκ ἀπελεύσεσθε ~οί 'you are not going to leave ..' Ex 3.21; οὐκ ὀφθήσῃ ἐνώπιόν μου ~ός 'you shall not appear in my presence empty-handed,' i.e. without sacrifices 23.15, 34.20, sim. De 16.16, Si 32.6; βολὶς μαχητοῦ συνετοῦ οὐκ ἐπιστρέψει ~ή 'the arrow of an intelligent warrior shall not come back just like that' Je 27.9, ῥομφαία Σαουλ οὐκ ἀνέκαμψε (*L* ἀπέστρεψε) ~ή 2K 1.22.

3. *meaningless, devoid of substance*: *s* λόγοι Ex 5.9, λόγος De 32.47; ῥήματα Jb 6.6, ~αὶ ἐλπίδες καὶ ψευδεῖς 'vain and false hopes' Si 31.1, cf. εἰς ~ὸν ἤλπισεν Is 29.8 and ~ὴ ἡ ἐλπὶς αὐτῶν Wi 3.11 (:: ἐλ... ἀθανασίας πλήρης 3.4); subst.n.pl., λαλοῦσι ~ά Is 59.4 (|| μάταια), ἐμελέτησαν ~ά Ps 2.1, ~ὰ καὶ μάταια Ho 12.1, μάταια καὶ κενά Is 30.7; εἰς ~ὰ ἐγένοντο Mi 1.14. **b**. subst. f., διὰ κενῆς *for no justifiable reason, with no justifiable motive*: διὰ ~ῆς ὤμοσεν 'swore frivolously' Si 23.11; τὰ ὑπάρχοντα αὐτοῦ διὰ ~ῆς ἀπολέσαι 'to destroy his possessions for no good reason' Jb 2.3; Ps 24.3.

4. *without effect or result, serving no good purpose*: *s* φθέγμα λαθραῖον 'words spoken in secret' Wi 1.11; κ. μου ὁ βίος Jb 7.16. **b**. Mostly subst. n. and with εἰς.: Jb 9.17; ἔσται εἰς ~ὸν ἡ ἰσχὺς ὑμῶν 'your efforts will be of no avail' 26.20; οὐκ εἰς ~όν 'not in vain' Hb 2.3, οὐκ εἰς ~ὸν ἐποιήσεν αὐτὴν ἀλλὰ κατοικεῖσθαι 'he did not make it (i.e. the earth) for nothing, but to be inhabited' Is 45.18, εἰς ~ὸν ἐθυμίασαν 'they burned incense ..' Je 18.15, οὐ κοπιάσουσι .. εἰς ~όν 'shall not toil in vain' 28.58, Is 65.23; Je 26.11, Jb 39.16¶, 1M 9.68; εἰς κενὰ καὶ μάταια ἐκοπίασεν Jb 20.18. **c**. without a prep. and adv., παρακαλεῖτε ~ά 'comfort ..' Jb 21.34, poss. under **3**.

Cf. κενόω, κατακενόω, κενῶς, μάταιος: Trench 180-4; Spicq 2.303-10.

κενοτάφιον, ου. n.ʃ

empty tomb or *coffin*: w. ref. to pagan objects of worship and divination (תְּרָפִים), a compromise rendering (instead of εἴδωλον Ge 31.19 or θεραφιν 1K 15.23, 4K 23.24) out of respect for the future king of Israel(?) 1K 19.13, 16, cf. *BA* 9.1: 93-6; Muraoka 2008b.226f.

κενόω: aor.pass. ἐκενώθην.ʃ

to empty the contents of, strip the possesions of, 'to deplete': pass., αἱ πύλαι αὐτῆς ἐκενώθησαν 'her gates were emptied out' (or: were abandoned, deserted?) Je 14.2, ἐκενώθη ἡ τίκτουσα ἑπτά 'the woman who bore seven (lost all her children?)' 15.9. Cf. κενός, κατακενόω: LSG s.v.

κεντέω.ʃ

to prick, stab: *s* arrows and *o* hum. (acc.) Jb 6.4. Cf. ἀπο~, ἐκ~, κατα~, συνεκ~, συγκεντέω.

κέντρον, ου. n.

any sharp point: goad, Ho 5.12 (|| ταραχή 'upheaval'); ὄνῳ 'for an ass' Pr 26.3 (|| μάστιξ 'whip,' ῥάβδος 'rod'); sting of bees, 4M 14.19. **b**. metaph.: ποῦ τὸ κ. σου, ᾅδη; 'where is your goad, o Hades?' Ho 13.14.

Cf. βούκεντρον: Schmid, *TDNT* 3.663-6; Muraoka 1986a:133f.; *ND* 4.157.

κενῶς. adv.ʃ

to no good purpose: κ. ἐκοπίασα καὶ εἰς μάταιαν καὶ εἰς οὐθὲν ἔδωκα τὴν ἰσχύν μου 'I toiled .. and in vain and for nothing I expended my energy' Is 49.4. Cf. κενός.

κεπφόω: aor.ptc.pass. κεπφωθείς.ʃ

to delude easily: pass., Pr 7.22. Cf. ἀπατάω, πλανάω: *GI* s.v.; *BA* 17.104f.; Caird 1968.21f.

κεραμεύς, έως. m.

potter: πηλὸς ~έως 'potter's clay' Is 29.16, Je 18.6; σκεύη ~έως 'vessels made by ..' Si 27.5, fig. of trivial objects PSol 17.23.

κεραμικός, ή, όν.ʃ

ceramic: *s* ὄστρακον Da 2.41 LXX.

κεράμιον, ου. n.ʃ

1. *earthenware vessel, jar*: ἐκ ~ου λεπτά 'thin pieces of ..' Is 30.14; οἴνου Je 42.5.

2. a dry measure amounting to what can be contained in an earthenware vessel: minuscular quantity, Is 5.10.

κέραμος, ου. m.ʃ

potter's clay: σκεύη ~ου 'earthenware' 2K 17.28.

κεράννυμι: aor. ἐκέρασα, ptc. κεράσας, pass. κερασθείς; pf.ptc.pass. κεκερασμένος, κεκραμένος.

1. *dilute* wine *with water for a drink*: + acc., σικερα Is 5.22; οἶνος Da LXX Bel 11 (pass.; TH act.), Pr 9.5.

2. *to prepare as a drink*: fig. and + acc., αὐτοῖς πνεῦμα πλανήσεως '.. a misguiding spirit' Is 19.14, PSol 8.14. **b**. *to pour* a drink: εἰς κρατῆρα .. οἶνον 'wine .. into a bowl' Pr 9.2 (or εἰς = ἐν, then **1**).

Cf. συγκεράννυμι, ἄκρατος, μίσγω: Schmidt 4.650-6; Shipp 312.

κέρας, ατος. n.

1. *horn* of an animal: Ge 22.13; symbol of might, De 33.17, Ez 29.21, Si 47.7, || δόξα 49.5; οὐκ ἔδωκεν κ. τῷ ἁμαρτωλῷ 'did not allow the sinner to triumph' 1M 2.48; Οὐκ ἐν ἰσχύι ἡμῶν ἔσχομεν ~ατα; 'Surely we shall have horns in our might?' Am 6.13; τὰ ~ατά σου θήσομαι σιδηρᾶ 'I shall make your horns iron' Mi 4.13; instrument of destruction, τὰ ἔθνη τὰ ἐπαιρόμενα κ. ἐπὶ τὴν γῆν κυρίου τοῦ διασκορπίσαι αὐτήν 'the nations which raised the horn against the land of the Lord to scatter it' Zc 1.21; fig. of protector and *s* God, κ. σωτηρίας Ps 17.3; *o* of ὑψόω 'to raise high' 1K 2.1, of ἐπαίρω Ps 74.6.

2. *horn-shaped object*: of corners of altar (θυσιαστήριον), Ex 27.2, Le 4.7, Am 3.14; drinking-horn, Je 31.12 (Zgl: κεράσματα); summit of a hill or a mount as suitable for vineyard, Is 5.1.

3. *wing of an army*: δεχιόν 1M 9.12, κατὰ κ. 'on either flank' 2M 15.20.

Cf. κερατίζω, κερατίνος.

κέρασμα, ατος. n.ʃ

alcoholic substance as a drink: ποτήριον .. οἴνου ἀκράτου πλῆρες ~ατος 'a cup .. of neat wine, full of a drink' Ps 74.9; πληροῦντες τῇ τύχῃ κ. 'filling (a cup of) mingled drink to Fortune' Is 65.11.

κεράστης, ου. m.ʃ

horned serpent: ‖ ὄφις 'snake' Pr 23.32. Cf. ὄφις.

κερατίζω: fut. κερατιῶ; aor.subj. κερατίσω.

1. *to gore with horns*: ***s*** ταῦρος 'bull' and + acc. pers., Ex 21.28; ***o*** another bull, 21.35; ***s*** ram Da 8.4; κέρασιν 'with horns' Ez 34.21, ἐν κέρασιν τὴν Συρίαν 3K 22.11 (***s*** hum.).

2. *to assault*: τοῖς ποταμοῖς σου 'with your rivers' Ez 32.2; + acc., ἐχθρούς Ps 43.6.

Cf. κέρας, κερατιστής: LSG s.v.

κεράτινος, η, ον.

made of horn: ***s*** σάλπιγξ 'trumpet' Ps 97.6; subst. f., 'trumpet made of horn' Jd 3.27, 2K 16.10B (*L* σάλπιγξ). Cf. κέρας, σάλπιγξ: Barthélemy 1963. 60-3; LSG s.v.

κερατιστής, οῦ. m.ʃ *

one that is prone to goring with horns: bull, Ex 21.29, 36. Cf. κερατίζω.

κεραυνός, οῦ. m.

thunderbolt: Jb 38.35; weapon, + τοξεύματα 'arrows' 2M 10.30. Cf. κεραυνόω.

κεραυνόω: fut. ~νώσω.ʃ

to strike with thunderbolts: ***s*** God, βιαίως Is 30.30. Cf. κεραυνός.

κέρκος, ου. f.ʃ

tail: of a snake, Ex 4.4*bis*; of a dog, Pr 26.17; of a fox, Jd 15.4. Cf. οὐρά.

κέρκωψ, πος. m.ʃ

teller of false tales: Pr 26.22. Cf. LSG s.v.

κεφάλαιον, ου. n.ʃ

1. *principal, capital*: Le 6.5, Nu 5.7. Cf. *ND* 3.70.

2. *sum total*: Λάβε τὸ κ. τῶν υἱῶν Καα θ 'Work out the total of ..' Nu 4.2; 31.26, 49. Cf. ἀρχή **1 g**.

3. *main division of a book*, 'chapter': ἔγραψεν εἰς ~α λόγων 'wrote (the matter) in chapters' Da LXX 7.1.

Cf. κεφαλαιόω.

κεφαλαιόω: aor.impv. κεφαλαίωσον.ʃ

to summarise: λόγον, ἐν ὀλίγοις πολλά Si 35.8.

κεφαλή, ῆς. f.

1. *head* as the highest part of a human or animal body: ἀπὸ ~ῆς ἕως ποδῶν 'from head to foot' Le 13.12, ἀπὸ ποδῶν ἕως ~ῆς Jb 2.7; of the sun beating down on one's head, Jn 4.8; 2.6, 4.6 *bis*; it may go bald, Am 8.10; where a head-dress (κίδαρις) is worn, Zc 3.5 *bis*; a crown (στέφανος) is placed there, 6.12; αἴρω ~ήν 'to raise one's head,' of one who has been humiliated, 1.21; λυπούμενος κατὰ ~ῆς 'mourning downcast, crest-fallen' Es 6.12 o'. Esp. as an object of physical violence and as a vulnerable spot and a vital organ: αὐτός σου τηρήσει ~ήν 'he will watch your head' Ge 3.15; ἐκονδύλιζον ~ὰς πτωχῶν Am 2.7, διάκοψον εἰς ~ὰς πάντων 9.1, διέκοψας ~ὰς δυναστῶν Hb 3.14, ἔβαλες εἰς ~ὰς ἀνόμων θάνατον 'you have sent death upon the heads of the unlawful' 3.13, τὸ αἷμά σου ἐπὶ τὴν ~ν σου; a place upon which a punitive action is brought down, ἀνταποδώσω τὸ ἀνταπόδομα ὑμῶν εἰς ~ὰς ὑμῶν Jl 3.7, sim. Ob 15.

2. *the uppermost part*: αἱ ~αὶ τῶν ὀρέων 'the mountain tops' Ge 8.5; of tower (πύργος), 11.4; of ladder (κλῖμαξ), 28.12 (reaching the sky); of stone pillar (στύλη) 3K 7.16.

3. *person* as a unit of counting: γόμορ κατὰ ~ήν 'gomor per head' Ex 16.16, δραχμὴ μία τῇ ~ῇ 'one drachm per head' 39.2. Cf. LSG s.v. **I 2 b**.

4. *he who or that which plays a leading role*: in a societal group (?), Nu 1.2, 20; De 28.13, 44 (:: οὐρά 'tail'); ~ὴν καὶ οὐράν, μέγαν καὶ μικρόν Is 9.14 (‖ ἀρχή); ~ὴν καὶ οὐράν, ἀρχὴν καὶ τέλος 19.15; κ. ἐθνῶν Ps 17.44, κ. γωνίας 'corner-stone' 117.22. **b**. principal city: Is 7.8. **c**. principal nation: Je 38.7.

5. *advancing troops* as against those in ambush or reserve soldiers: Jb 1.17, cf. Wissemann; GLS s.v. **V 4**.

Cf. κορυφή, πολυκέφαλος, προτομή: Schmidt 1.361-9; Chadwick 177-83.

κεφαλίς, ίδος. f.

1. *rounded top end*, 'capital': of a column, Ex 26.32, 37.4 (:: βάσις 'base'); of a tent, Nu 3.36.

*__2__. *scroll* of a document, βιβλίου Ez 2.9, Ps 39.8, 2E 6.2.

Cf. κεφαλή, βάσις.

κηδεία, ας. f.ʃ

funeral: 2M 4.49, 5.10.

κηδεμονία, ας. f.ʃ

interest and concern about sbd else's safety, welfare etc.: εἰς τὸν βασιλέα 4K 4.4; τοῦ ἱεροῦ 'the servicing of the temple' 4.20.

κηδεμών, όνος. m.ʃ

protector, guardian: + gen., 2M 4.2 (+ εὐεργέτης). Cf. Schmidt 2.631f.

κηλιδόω: fut.pass. κηλιδωθήσομαι; pf.pass. κεκηλίδωμαι.ʃ

to soil: morally, pass. ἐν ταῖς ἀδικίαις σου Je 2.22. Cf. μολύνω.

κηλίς, ῖδος. f.ʃ

stain: Wi 13.14; moral, + μύσος 'defilement' 2M 6.25.

κημός, οῦ.m.

muzzle: applied to a caught lion in transport, Ez 19.4; to horses and mules, Ps 31.9 (+ χαλινός 'bridle'). Cf. ἡνία, χαλινός.

κῆπος, ου. m.

orchard: κ. λαχανείας 'garden of herbs' De 11.10; ‖ ἀμπελών, συκών, ἐλαιών Am 4.9; φυτεύσουσι ~ους 'they will plant orchards' 9.14 (|| ἀμπελών), where a luxurious private home with a garden may be meant, cf. Husson 147-50; || παράδεισος Si 24.31; royal, Ec 2.5 (+ παράδεισος), Es 7.7 o'. **b.** a site for illicit cult: Is 1.29, 65.3, 66.17.

Cf. ἀμπελών, ἐλαιών, παράδεισος, συκών, φυτεῖα **2**: Alexandre 244-6.

κηρίον, ου. n.

honeycomb: fig. of sth choice and pleasant, παρὰ πᾶσαν τὴν γῆν 'superior to the whole earth' Ez 20.6, 15 (w. ref. to the promised land); μέλι καὶ κ. 'honey and ..' Ps 18.11; κ. μέλιτος Jd 14.8*L* (AB: μέλι), μέλιτος κ. 1K 14.27, Si 24.20, Pr 16.24. Cf. μέλι, κηρογονία.

κηρογονία, ας.f.ʃ *

making of honeycomb: 4M 14.19. Cf. κηρίον.

κηρός, οῦ. m.

wax: melts, τακήσονται ὡς κ. Mi 1.4; ὡς τήκεται κ. ἀπὸ προσώπου πυρός 'as wax would melt before fire' Ps 67.3, sim. Is 64.1.

κήρυγμα, ατος. n.

public proclamation: 1E 9.3; contents of such, τὸ κ. τὸ ἔμπροσθεν 'the previous proclamation' Jn 3.2. Cf. κηρύσσω.

κῆρυξ, υκος. m.

one who makes public proclamation, 'herald': ἐκήρυξεν .. κ. Ge 41.43; Si 20.15. Cf. κηρύσσω and στρατοκῆρυξ.

κηρύσσω: fut. κηρύξω; aor. ἐκήρυξα, impv. κήρυξον, inf. κηρύξαι, pass. ἐκηρύχθην.

1. *to make public proclamation*: abs. *s* κῆρυξ Ge 41.43; χαῖρε .. κήρυσσε .. εὐφραίνου καὶ κατατέρπου, perh. referring to verbal or oral expression of joy, Zp 3.14, sim. Zc 9.9; of Jonah's mission, Jn 1.2, 3.2; the contents of the proclamation introduced by λέγω or εἶπον 3.4, 7 (pass.); λέγων Ex 36.6; ἐν γραπτῷ 'in writing' 2C 36.22; + dat. pers., Da 3.4 LXX; + inf., 5.29 TH, 1M 10.63. **b.** accompanied by noise aimed at attracting attention: σαλπίσατε .. ἠχήσατε .. καὶ κηρύξατε 'blow a trumpet .. shout ..' Ho 5.8, sim. Jl 2.1 (in order to call a meeting), 15. **c.** *to make heard publicly*: + acc. ταῦτα Jl 3.9, φωνήν PSol 10.1; + dat. and acc., αἰχμαλώτοις ἄφεσιν 'release to the captives' Is 61.1.

2. *to announce in public the holding of*: + acc. rei, νηστείαν 'fasting' Jn 3.5, θεραπείαν 'worship service' Jl 1.14, 2.15. Cf. καλέω **7**.

3. *to speak in public, advocating* sth (τι): *s* false prophets, ^ἐπὶ τὸν λαόν^ εἰρήνην Mi 3.5, σοφίαν Pr 8.1.

Cf. κήρυγμα, κῆρυξ, ἀνακηρύσσω.

κῆτος, ους. n.

huge sea-fish: one of the primaeval creatures made by God, τὰ ~η τὰ μεγάλα Ge 1.21; κ. μέγα Jn 2.1*a*; 2.1*b*, 11; without μέγα, Jb 9.13, 26.12, Si 43.25, Da 3.79. Cf. ἰχθῦς δράκων: Schmidt 2.439; Alexandre 151-4.

κίβδηλος, ον.ʃ

not genuine, 'spurious, counterfeit, suspect': *s* garment woven from two diverse fabrics, Le 19.19; ~ον, ἔρια καὶ λίνον, ἐν τῷ αὐτῷ '.. woolen and linen in one and the same (garment)' De 22.11; *s* hum. and subst., Wi 2.16; n.pl., *s* pagan idols 15.9. Cf. Renehan 2.88.

κιβωτός, οῦ. f.

enclosed container as depository usually for valuable objects: wooden, ἐκ ξύλων τετραγώνων 'from square wooden (planks)' Ge 6.14 (of Noah's ark); μαρτυρίου 'of testimony' Ex 25.9; τῶν μαρτυρίων 30.6, διαθήκης ἁγίου Ισραηλ Je 3.16, τοῦ ἁγιάσματός σου [= God's]' Ps 131.8. Cf. Chamberlain 27; Harl, *Langue* 97-125.

κίδαρις, εως. f.

turban: of the high priest, Ex 28.4; βυσσίνη 'made of linen' 28.35; ἐπίθετε ~ιν καθαρὰν ἐπὶ τὴν κεφαλὴν αὐτοῦ Zc 3.5; ~ιν λινῆν περιθήσεται 'shall wear a linen turban' Le 16.4. Cf. μίτρα, τίαρα.

κιθάρα, ας. f.

lyre: ψαλτήριον καὶ ~αν Ge 4.21; used on festive occasions, 31.27 (|| τύμπανον), μετὰ ~ας καὶ ψαλτηρίου καὶ τυμπάνων καὶ αὐλῶν Is 5.12; on battlefield, μετὰ ~ῶν καὶ κιθάρας πολεμήσουσιν 30.32; produces a mournful tune, 16.11. Cf. κιθαρίζω.

κιθαρίζω: aor.impv. κιθάρισον.ʃ

to play the lyre: Is 23.16. Cf. κιθάρα.

κινδυνεύω: fut. ~νεύσω; aor. ἐκινδύνευσα, subj. ~νεύσω.

1. *to face a dangerous situation*: abs., κινδυνεύσουσι καὶ συντριβήσονται '.. and will be smashed' Is 28.13; ἕως θανάτου Si 31.13, cf. τῆς γῆς .. εἰς ἄσπορον κινδυνευούσης 'the land threatens to degenerate into an uncultivated land' *P. BGU* 1821; κινδυνεύσω τῷ ἰδίῳ τραχήλῳ 'to risk my own neck' Da LXX 1.10, cf. Hdt 2.120 τῷ σώματι and *P. Teb* 44 τῷ ζῆν; 2M 15.17.

2. *to be in danger of*: + inf. τὸ πλοῖον ἐκινδύνευε συντριβῆναι 'the boat looked like going to pieces' or '.. was in danger of ..' Jn 1.4; διαρπασθῆναι 'to be plundered' 3M 5.41.

Cf. κίνδυνος, διακινδυνεύω: Wollentin, esp. 13-8.

κίνδυνος, ου. m.

danger: ~οι ᾅδου Ps 114.3 (|| ὠδῖνες θανάτου). Cf. (δια)κινδυνεύω, ἐπικίνδυνος.

κινέω: fut. κινήσω, pass. κινηθήσομαι; aor. ἐκίνησα, inf. κινῆσαι, impv. κίνησον, ptc. κινήσας, pass. ἐκινήθην, subj. κινηθῶ; ptc. κινηθείς. For instances of the fut.act. in Cl. Gk, see Renehan, 1.122.

A. act. tr. *to set in motion*, 'move': + acc., Nu 14.44; τὰς χεῖρας αὐτοῦ Zp 3.1 (ǁ συριεῖ; expression of astonishment, cf. Th 294), πόδας 'legs' Je 14.10; tent pegs which should not move, Is 33.20 (ǁ σείω); κ. κεφαλήν ἐπί τινα / τινι (pers.), an expression of disdain, Ps 21.8, Is 37.22 (ǁ φαυλίζω, [ἐκ]μυκτηρίζω), an expression of astonishment Je 18.16 (+ ἐξίστημι), La 2.15 (+ συρίζω), ἐπί τινι Si 13.7; καθ' ὑμῶν Jb 16.4; κεφαλήν understood and an expression of mourning, Je 31.17. **b**. *to arouse mentally, agitate*: pass., ***o*** μου τὸ πνεῦμα Da LXX 2.3; pers., Es 3.6*L*, τῇ διανοίᾳ 1M 10.74; πρός τι '(to feel attracted) to sth' 4M 1.33. Cf. Renehan 2.88. **c**. *to remove* from office, 'dismiss, fire': pass., ***o*** ὁ ἄνθρωπος ὁ ἐστηριγμένος ἐν τόπῳ πιστῷ 'the person established in a secure position' Is 22.25 (ǁ πίπτω). **d**. intr.: looking for a place to settle, Ge 11.2; ἐκεῖθεν .. εἰς γῆν πρὸς λίβα '.. to the southern region' 20.1, cf. Polyb. 2.54.2.

B. mid. intr. *to set oneself* or *itself in motion*, 'move': ***s*** animals πᾶσα σὰρξ κινουμένη ἐπὶ τῆς γῆς τῶν πετεινῶν καὶ τῶν κτηνῶν καὶ τῶν θηρίων, καὶ πᾶν ἑρπετὸν κινούμενον ἐπὶ τῆς γῆς Ge 7.21 (ǁ ἕρπω 6.20); πάντα τὰ κινούμενα ἐπὶ τῆς γῆς 9.2. **b**. *to move away*: ἐντεῦθεν '(to leave) here' To 8.20 𝔊[II] (𝔊[I] ἐξέρχομαι), Jd 6.18A (B: χωρίζομαι); ***s*** κακά Pr 17.13. **c**. *to move away from* (ἀπό) *and neglect*: ἀπὸ τῆς λειτουργίας ἁγίων 'from the sacred liturgical duties' 2C 35.15 (ǁ παραβαίνω 1E 1.15).

Cf. δια~, μετακινέω, κίνημα, κίνησις, κινητικός, ἠρεμάζω, σείω, τινάσσω: Schmidt 3.128-32; Renehan 2.88; Chadwick 183-8.

κίνημα, ατος. n.ʃ

commotion: κ. μέγα ἐν τῇ πόλει 1M 13.44; τοῦ σώματος 'of the body' 4M 1.35. Cf. κινέω.

κίνησις, εως. f.

v.n. of κινέω: κεφαλῆς Ps 43.15, cf. κινέω, **A a**; χειλέων 'of lips [as an organ of speech]' Jb 16.5; καρδίας Wi 2.2 (w. ref. to heartbeat). Cf. κινέω.

κινητικός, ή, όν.ʃ

mobile: ***s*** σοφία Wi 7.24. Cf. κινέω.

κιννάμωμον, ου. n. < Heb. קִנָּמוֹן+

"*a superior kind of* cassia, Cinnamomum Cassia" (LSJ): aromatic for cultic use, εὐώδης Ex 30.23; ǁ λίβανος 'frankincense' Je 6.20; ǁ κρόκος 'saffron' Pr 7.17.

κινύρα, ας. f. < Heb. כִּנּוֹר+

string instrument: Si 39.15; + αὐλός 1M 3.45, + κιθάρα, κύμβαλον 4.54. See *BA* 9.1, pp. 86-8.

κιρνάω.ʃ

to mix: + acc., τὸ πόμα μου μετὰ κλαυθμοῦ 'my drink with crying' Ps 101.10. Cf. μίγνυμι.

κισσάω: aor. ἐκίσσησα.ʃ

to desire to conceive: με Ps 50.7 (ǁ συλλαμβάνω).

κισσός, οῦ. m.ʃ

ivy: carried in celebration, 2M 6.7.

κισσόφυλλον, ου. n.ʃ

ivy-leaf: 3M 2.29.

Κιτιεύς, έως. GN.

m.pl. Κιτιεῖς 'Cyprus': Is 23.1.

κιχράω. *

to put at sbd else's disposal: abs., 'to lend' and + οἰκτιρέω Ps 111.5, Pr 13.11; + acc. (one's own child and life-long), τῷ κυρίῳ 1K 1.28 (*L* κίχρημι). Cf. δανείζω, χρήσις, χράω, κίχρημι.

κίχρημι.ʃ

= κιχράω: ***s*** mother, αὐτὸν [= a just weaned son] τῷ κυρίῳ 1K 1.28*L*.

κίων, όνος. m.

pillar: of a building, Jd 16.25 B (A: στῦλος). Cf. στῦλος.

κλάδος, ου. m.

1. *branch*: of tree, ~ους ξύλου δασεῖς 'thick boughs of trees' Le 23.40; τῶν ἐλαίων Zc 4.12; πορεύσονται οἱ ~οι αὐτοῦ 'its branches will grow' Ho 14.7.

2. *that which grows and results*:'offshoot,' ^τῆς σοφίας^ Si 1.20; hum. offspring, 23.25 (ǁ τέκνα), 40.15 (ǁ ῥίζα).

Cf. κλῆμα, κλών, ῥάβδος, ἔκγονος, ῥάδαμνος, σπέρμα: Schmidt 2.468-70.

κλαίω: fut.mid. κλαύσομαι (κλαύσω does not occur in LXX), pass. κλαυσθήσομαι; aor. ἔκλαυσα, inf. κλαῦσαι, impv. κλαῦσον, subj. κλαύσω, pass. κλαυσθῶ.

1. *to weep*: Ge 42.24; for help, + δέω 'implore' Ho 12.4; Jl 2.17; for sorrow, ǁ λυπέομαι, ὀλολύζω Is 15.2, ǁ στενάζω 'groan' Jb 31.38 (***s*** furrows of exploited land); πικρῶς 'bitterly' Is 22.4, 33.7; ǁ νηστεύω, εὔχομαι Ba 1.5; ***s*** a babe, Ex 2.6; cattle for lack of pasture, Jl 1.18; with tears, μὴ κλαίετε δάκρυσι (ǁ δακρύω) Mi 2.6; κλαυθμῷ πλείονι 'with much weeping' Ge 46.29, κλαυθμῷ μεγάλῳ Is 38.4; opp. revelling and ǁ θρηνέω, Jl 1.5, opp. γελάω Ec 3.4; + ἀναβοάω, Ge 21.16; 27.38 (hurt and mortified); βοήσας τῇ φωνῇ αὐτοῦ ἔκλαυσεν 'crying aloud, he wept' 29.11. **b**. + ἐπί τινι (pers.): Ge 45.14, 15, Si 22.11. **c**. + ἐπί τινα (deceased): Ge 50.1 (v.l. τινα), Nu 11.13 (Wevers: ἐπ' ἐμοί); + ἐπί τι: Jd 11.37, 38. **c**. + ἀπὸ προσώπου τινος: ὕβρεως 'pride' Je 13.17. **d**. + acc. pers. (deceased), Ge 37.35, Nu 20.29, De 21.13, 34.8; τὸν τεθνηκότα Je 41.5; 22.18, 1M 9.20 (both last ǁ κόπτω). **e**. + περί τινος To 7.16 𝔊[II]. **f**. πρός τινα: Jd 14.16, 17 (*L* ἐπ' αὐτόν). **g**. + dat. pers.: ἔκλαυσεν ἕκαστος τῷ [*L* ἐπὶ τὸν] πλησίον αὐτοῦ 1K 20.41. **h**. + cogn. acc.: κλαυθμὸν μέγαν Jd 21.2.

2. *to bemoan*: + acc. rei, τὸν ἐμπυρισμόν Le 10.6, τὴν παρθενίαν αὐτῆς Jd 11.38 *L* (ǁ ἐπὶ τὴν ~αν μου vs. 37), + acc. pers. (dead), κλαυθμῷ Je 22.10; + ἐπί τινι (rei), ἐπὶ παντὶ ἀδυνάτῳ Jb 30.25, ἐπὶ τούτοις 'about these matters' La 1.16; pass., Ps 77.64.

Cf. θρηνέω, λυπέω, πενθέω, κλαυθμός, κλαυθμών, ὀλολύζω, στενάζω: Schmidt 1.471-6; Muraoka 2005b.106-8.

κλάσμα, ατος. n.

fragment: morsel of cake, διαθρύψεις αὐτὰ ~ατα 'you shall break them into morsels' Le 2.6; 6.21; of bread, Ez 13.19, Jd 19.5A; of a hand-mill, 9.53. Cf. κλάω.

κλαυθμός, οῦ. m.

weeping: ἀφῆκεν φωνὴν μετὰ ~οῦ Ge 45.2, ὀλολύζετε μετὰ ~οῦ Is 15.3; Mi 7.4; ἔκλαυσεν ~ῷ πλείονι Ge 46.29, ~ῷ μεγάλῳ Is 38.4; ἐκ κόπων 'because of troubles' and ‖ στεναγμός 'groaning' Ma 2.13, ‖ κραυγή Is 65.19, + κρ. 1E 5.60, ‖ δάκρυα Je 38.16; + θρῆνος, ὀδυρμός 38.15; as a sign of sincere repentance, ἐν νηστείᾳ καὶ ἐν ~ῷ καὶ ἐν κοπετῷ 'with fasting, weeping and breast-beating' Jl 2.12, sim. Is 22.12; αἱ ἡμέραι πένθους ~οῦ Μωυσῆ De 34.8. Cf. θρῆνος, κοπετός, λύπη, πένθος, ὀδυρμός, κλαίω, κλαυθμών, κωκυτός: Schmidt 1.471-6.

κλαυθμών, ῶνος. m. *

place for weeping: Jd 5.5, Ps 83.7.

κλάω: aor.subj.pass. κλασθῶ.

to break into small parts: pass., *o* bread, Je 16.7, hum. skull Jd 9.53 B (A: συνθλάω). Cf. κλάσμα, ἀπο~, διακλάω, διαθρύπτω, συντρίβω.

κλεῖθρον, ου. n.

bar: for closing a door and + μοχλός Ep Je 17; οὐρανοῦ Jb 26.13; + πύλη 'gate' 38.10. Cf. μοχλός.

κλείς, δός. f.

1. *key*: Jd 3.25.

2. *collar-bone*: Jb 31.22.

κλείω: fut. κλείσω, pass. κλεισθήσομαι; aor. ἔκλεισα, subj. κλείσω, pass. ἐκλείσθην, subj. κλεισθῶ, ptc.act. κλείσας, impv. κλεῖσον, pass.3pl κλειέσθωσαν; pf. κέκλεικα, pass. κέκλειμαι, ptc.pass. κεκλεισμένος.

1. *to shut, close*: *o* boat (κιβωτός) Ge 7.16, οἰκίαν τοῦ μὴ εἰσελθεῖν Is 24.10, τὴν ἄβυσσον Od 12.3 (‖ πεδάω, σφραγίζομαι), θύρας 'doors' Ne 6.10, πύλας 'gates' 13.19; pass., *o* πύλαι (:: ἀνοίγω) Is 60.11, στόμα 'mouth (of the dead)' Si 30.18, κῆπος 'orchard' Ct 4.12; opp. ἀνοίγω Jb 12.14.

2. *to confine and deprive freedom of movement*: τινα εἰς τὰς χεῖράς τινος 1K 23.20 (*L* ἀποκλείομαι), cf. Caird 1969.22; LSG s.v.

Cf. ἀνοίγω, προσοίγω, ἀπο~, ἐγ~, κατα~, παρα~, συγκλείω, σφηνόω.

κλέμμα, ατος. n.

a stolen thing: κλέμματα ἡμέρας καὶ ~ατα νυκτός 'things stolen by day and things stolen by night' Ge 31.39; εὑρεθῇ ἐν τῇ χειρὶ αὐτοῦ τὸ κ. 'the stolen article should be found in his hand' Ex 22.4. Cf. κλέπτω.

κλέος, ους. n.ʃ

good repute, 'fame': αὐτῆς 'about it' Jb 28.22 (or simply 'report about it'), κ. ἐσβεσμένον ἀπὸ γῆς '.. vanished from the earth' 30.8 (‖ ὄνομα). Cf. ἀ~, εὐ~, δυσκλεής, κῦδος, ὄνομα: Shipp 317.

κλέπτης, ου. m.

burglar: Ex 22.2, Zc 5.3, 4; εἰσέρχεσθαι πρός τινα, Ho 7.1, Ob 5 (‖ λῃστής); διὰ θυρίδων 'through windows' Jl 2.9 (in a description of a swarm of locusts). Cf. κλέπτω, λῃστής: Trench 157-60.

κλέπτω: fut. κλέψω; aor. ἔκλεψα, subj. κλέψω, ptc. κλέψας, opt.1pl κλέψαιμεν, aor.pass. ἐκλάπην, subj. κλαπῶ; pf.ptc.pass. κεκλεμμένος.

1. *to steal*: abs., Ex 20.14, Le 19.11; *s* thief or robber, Ob 5; + acc. rei, Ge 31.19, 30; pass., ἐκ τῆς οἰκίας Ex 22.7; παρ' αὐτοῦ 22.12. **b**. + acc. pers., 'to kidnap' Ex 21.17; pass. with a cognate noun, κλοπῇ ἐκλάπην ἐκ γῆς Ἐβραίων Ge 40.15.

2. *to avoid being seen by*: + acc. pers., ἀλλήλους Su 12 LXX. Cf. λανθάνω.

Cf. κλοπή, κλέμμα, κλέπτης, κλεψιμαῖον, λῃστεύω, νοσφίζομαι.

κλεψιμαῖον, ου. n.ʃ *

stolen good: To 2.13.

κληδονίζομαι. *

to act as diviner: ‖ μαντεύομαι, οἰωνίζομαι, φάρμακος etc. De 18.10, 4K 21.6. Cf. κληδονισμός, κληδών.

κληδονισμός, οῦ. m.ʃ *

message communicated by diviner: Is 2.6. Cf. κληδονίζομαι.

κληδών, όνος. f.ʃ

= prec.: ‖ μαντεία De 18.14. Cf. κληδονίζομαι.

κλῆμα, ατος. n.

branch of plant: of vine, βότρυος Nu 13.24, ἀμπέλου Ps 79.12, Je 31.32, Ez 17.6, 7, 19.11; of fig-tree, Jl 1.7; of cedar (κέδρος) Ez 17.23; fig. of family members, Na 2.3; ‖ ῥίζα Ma 4.1. Cf. κλάδος, εὐκληματέω, κληματίς: Schmidt 2.471f.; Shipp 318.

κληματίς, ίδος. f.ʃ. Dim. of κλῆμα.

vine-branch: De 32.32 (‖ ἄμπελος, σταφύλη); fuel, Da 3.46; pl. Is 18.5. Cf. κλῆμα.

κληροδοσία, ας.f. *

1. *distribution of land*: σχοινίον ~ας 'a measure ..' Ps 77.55.

2. *wealth* or *property that has been distributed*: Ec 7.11, Da 11.21, 1M 10.89.

κληροδοτέω: aor. ἐκληροδότησα, subj. ~δοτήσω.ʃ *

1. *to cause to settle on the land*: + acc. pers., Ps 77.55.

2. *to bequeath*: + dat. pers., 2E 9.12; and acc. rei, νόμον ζωῆς Si 17.11.

Cf. κληροδοσία.

κληρονομέω: fut. ~μήσω; aor. ἐκληρονόμησα, inf. ~μῆσαι, ptc. ~μήσας, subj. ~μήσω, impv.3s ~μησάτω, opt. 3pl ~μήσαισαν.

1. *to take possession of*: abs. Ge 47.27; + acc. rei, τὴν γῆν ταύτην 15.7; τὴν γῆν τῆς παροικήσεώς σου 28.4; τὰς πόλεις τῶν ὑπεναντίων 'the cities of the enemies' 22.17, 24.60; ἀμπελῶνα 'vineyard' 3K 20.15 (illegally); τὸ ἀργύριον αὐτῶν ὄλεθρος 'destruction [= hostile, destructive troops?] will inherit their silver' Ho 9.6; acc. cogn., κληρονομίαν Nu 18.23 (κλῆρος ‖ vs. 24); + acc. pers. (as wife), To 3.17, 6.12 𝔊II. **b**. *to attain*, 'land': ***o*** shame and reproach, Si 6.1, perdition 20.25, ὀργήν '(God's) wrath' 39.23, ἄνεμον 'wind, i.e. of no value' Pr 11.29; ***o*** sth of value, τὰ μαρτύριά σου εἰς τὸν αἰῶνα Ps 118.111, δόξαν Si 4.13, Pr 3.35, cf. λαγχάνω.

2. *to become heir to*: abs. ***s*** a female servant's child fathered by her mistress's husband potentially being co-heir with (μέτα) his own son, Ge 21.10; + acc. pers., 15.3, ***o*** vanquished people, ἐπὶ σοῦ 'to your own advantage (?)' Jd 11.23, father To 3.15,.

***3**. *to dispossess*: + acc. pers., ἔθνη De 9.1, 11.23; Zp 2.9 (‖ διαρπάζειν 'to plunder'), Zc 9.4; Is 17.14 (‖ προνομεύω).

4**. *to give an inheritance to*: + acc. pers. and ***s pers., τὸν Ισραηλ Si 46.1, υἱοὺς υἱῶν Pr 13.22; ‖ μερίζω Is 53.12; double acc., ἡμᾶς κλῆρον ἕνα '.. one portion of inheritance' Jo 17.14.

***5**. *to give as possession*: τινί τι - ὑμῖν τὴν γῆν Nu 34.17 (‖ κατα~ vs.18), ὅσα κατεκληρονόμησέν ⌜B: simp.⌝ σοι Χαμως .., αὐτὰ κληρονομήσεις Jd 11.24A*L*.

Cf. κατα~, συγ~, συγκατακληρονομέω, κλῆρος, κληρονομία, κληρονόμος. On the fact that the word group κληρονόμος in the LXX often signifies, no doubt under Hebrew influence, violent appropriation rather than peaceful transfer of property upon someone's natural death, see esp. Foerster in Kittel 3.776-9, and also Dalman, 102f. Note, for instance, the use of κληρονομέω with ref. to Ahab's appropriation of Naboth's vineyard on the latter's "death" (3K 20.15-9).

κληρονομία, ας. f.

possession, thing possessed: Israel is referred to as God's κληρονομία, Mi 7.18, Jl 2.17, τοῦ λαοῦ μου καὶ τῆς ~ας μου Ισραηλ 3.2, sim. Ps 27.9, τὰς φυλὰς τῆς ~ας σου Is 63.17, cf. De 9.26 (‖ κλῆρος vs. 29), κ. Ιακωβ Si 23.12; λίθον ~ας 'inherited stone'(?) Zc 4.7; ἄνδρα καὶ ~αν αὐτοῦ Mi 2.2 (‖ οἶκος); πρόβατα ~ας σου 7.14; esp. of landed property that comes into one's possession, μερὶς ἢ κ. Ge 31.14; Mi 1.14, 15; "I turned his ~ into desert gifts" Ma 1.3; ὄρος ~ας σου Ex 15.17; κατάσχεσις ~ας Nu 27.7; ‖ μερίς 2K 20.1, Is 17.14, κατάσχεσις Ps 2.8. **b**. w. ref. to God allotted to Israel: Je 10.16; to the Levites and priests, Ez 44.28 (‖ κατάσχεσις). **c**. v.n. of κληρονομέω **1**: To 6.12 𝔊I.

Cf. κλῆρος, κληρονόμος, κατάσχεσις, μερίς.

κληρονόμος, ου. m.

one who is entitled to inherit an estate: δώσω .. τοὺς ἀγροὺς αὐτῶν τοῖς ~οις Je 8.10; Mi 1.15. Cf. κληρονομία: LSG s.v.

κλῆρος, ου. m.

1. *lot* used for decision-making, such as pebble, small stick, and rope: idiom. βάλλω ~ους ἐπί τι/τινα 'to cast lots over sth' to settle ownership, τὴν γῆν μου καταδιείλαντο [3]καὶ ἐπὶ τὸν λαόν μου ἔβαλον ~ους 'they divided my land and cast lots for my people' Jl 3.2f.; Ob 11, Na 3.10; περί τινος 'concerning sth' Ne 10.34[1]; in order to reach decision, βάλωμεν ~ους καὶ ἐπιγνῶμεν τίνος ἕνεκεν ἡ κακία αὕτη ἐστὶν ἐν ἡμῖν. καὶ ἔβαλον ~ους 'let us cast lots and find out who is the cause of this trouble amongst us ..' Jn 1.7*a*,*b* [used w. βάλλω, the noun is alw. (and so mostly in LXX irrespective of the number of the Heb. equivalent) pl.] — sg.ʃ, Jo 18.10 (ἐμβάλλω), 1K 14.42*L* (B abs.), Ps 21.19, Pr 1.14, Si 37.8 (ἐπὶ σοί); a decision is thus reached, ἔπεσεν ὁ κ. (sg.) ἐπὶ Ιωναν 'the lot fell on Jonah,' Jn 1.7*c*; + εἴς τι Es 3.7 o'; + ψήφισμα 9.24 o'; ***o*** of ἐπιβάλλω Is 34.17.

2. *dividing of possessions by lot*: οὐκ ἔσται σοι βάλλων σχοινίον ἐν ~ῳ 'you will have nobody casting lots by a rope for you' Mi 2.5.

3. *what is allotted, allotment*: land, farm, estate, Ge 48.6; δώσω ὑμῖν αὐτὴν ἐν ~ῳ Ex 6.8; ἔδωκας ἡμῖν ~ον ἀγροῦ Nu 16.14; καταφάγεται αὐτοὺς ἡ ἐρυσίβη καὶ τοὺς ~ους αὐτῶν 'rust will consume them and their estates' Ho 5.7; μερὶς καὶ κ. De 10.9; οὐκ ἔστιν αὐτῷ μερὶς οὐδὲ κ. μεθ' ὑμῶν 12.12, sim. 14.26, 28; as acc. cogn., οὐ κληρονομήσουσιν ~ον Nu 18.24 (‖ κληρονομία vs. 23); ~οι κατασχέσεως 35.2; people, λαός σου καὶ κ. σου De 9.29 (‖ κληρονομία vs. 26); Es C 3.10 o' (‖ κληρονομία 8, μερίς 9); state of affairs, Je 13.25; assignment, task Ne 10.34[2]; status attained, ἐν ἁγίοις ὁ κ. αὐτοῦ ἐστιν Wi 5.5.

Cf. κληρονομία, κληρονομέω, ἔγκληρος, μερίς: Dorival 1996.538.

κληρόω: fut.mid.2s κληρώσῃ; aor.subj.mid.2s κληρώσῃ.ʃ

1. impers. pass .. *lots cast indicate* sbd: ***o*** hum., κληροῦνται Ιωναθαν καὶ Σαουλ 1K 14.41 (*L* κατακληροῦται; see also vs. 42).

2. mid. *to obtain* landed property: abs. Is 17.11.

Cf. κλῆρος, κατακληρόω.

κληρωτί. adv.*
by lot (κλῆρος): Jo 21.4. Cf. κλῆρος.

κλῆσις, εως. f.ʃ
1. v.n. of καλέω, q.v. - *act of publicly addressing*: Je 38.6.
*2. *public event*, 'reception, party': Ju 12.10; ὁ πρὸς ταῖς ~σεσι τεταγμένοις 'the master of ceremonies, the master of the revels' 3M 5.14, or poss. 1, 'the one charged with dispatching formal invitations.'
Cf. καλέω.

κλητέος, α, ον.ʃ
one must call by a certain name: νομιστέον ἢ κλητέον αὐτοὺς ὑπάρχειν θεούς 'one must consider them or call them gods' Ep Je 39, sim. 44, 63.

κλητός, ή, όν.
summoned to perform a certain task: subst. ἡγίακε τοὺς ~οὺς αὐτοῦ 'he consecrated his appointees' Zp 1.7. **b**. *guest invited*: for a wedding, Jd 14.11 B. *c. subst. f., *a day when people are called upon to attend a public gathering*: ἁγία Ex 12.16, Le 23.2, Nu 28.25 (|| ἐπίκλητος ἁγία vs. 18); sabbaths included, Le 23.3.
Cf. καλέω, ἄκλητος: Harl 2001.886.

κλίβανος, ου. m.
oven: καπνιζόμενος 'smoking' Ge 15.17; in similes of heat, ὡς κ. καιόμενος 'like a burning oven' Ho 7.4, sim. Ma 4.1; ἀνεκαύθησαν ὡς κ. Ho 7.6; ἐθερμάνθησαν ὡς κ. 7.7; ὡς ~ον πυρὸς Ps 20.10; livid in colour, La 5.10. Cf. Shipp 319.

κλίμα, ατος. n.ʃ
a great mass moving in a certain direction: ἔστη τὸ κ. παντὸς τοῦ λαοῦ 'the whole nation started moving en masse' Jd 20.2 A.

κλιμακτήρ, ῆρος. m.
stair on a flight of stairs: pl., Ez 40.22 (|| ἀναβαθμός vs. 6). Cf. κλῖμαξ.

κλῖμαξ, ακος. f.ʃ
1. *ladder*: ἐστηριγμένη ἐν τῇ γῇ 'firmly fixed on the ground' Ge 28.12 (seen in a vision and reaching the sky); αἴροντες ~ακας καὶ μηχανάς 1M 5.30 (battle equipment).
2. *flight of stairs, stairway*: ἕως τῶν ~άκων τῶν καταβαινουσῶν ἀπὸ πόλεως Δαυιδ 'up to the stairways descending from the city of David' Ne 3.15; ἀνέβησαν ἐπὶ ~ακας πόλεως Δαυιδ 12.37; ἀπὸ τῆς ~ακος Τύρου 'from the stairway of Tyre' 1M 11.59.
Cf. κλιμακτήρ.

κλίνη, ης. f.
bed: ἐκάθισεν ἐπὶ τὴν ~ην Ge 48.2; σιδηρᾶ 'iron' De 3.11; οἱ καθεύδοντες ἐπὶ ~ῶν ἐλεφαντίνων 'those who sleep in ivory beds' Am 6.4; ἐστρωμένη 'spread' Ez 23.41; || στρωμνή Ps 6.7, || κοίτη 40.4. **b**. for the dead, 'bier': 2K 3.31.
Cf. κοίτη, στρῶμα.

κλίνω: fut. κλινῶ, pass. κλιθήσομαι; aor. ἔκλινα, subj. κλίνω, impv. κλῖνον, inf. κλῖναι, pass. ἐκλίθην, subj. κλιθῶ; pf. κέκλικα, ptc. κεκλικώς, pass. κεκλιμένος.
I. intr. *to incline* (towards πρός): abs., Jd 16.30A; πρὸς βορρᾶν 'northwards' Zc 14.4; fig., *s* καρδία Jd 9.3 (ὀπίσω τινός), hum. 3K 2.28; pass., Ps 103.5, *s* hum. εἰς τὰ σκῦλα 'into the (storage-area of) spoils' 1K 14.32 (*L* ὁρμάω).
2. *to lean from the vertical position*: ἐπὶ τὰ γόνατα '(to go down) on the knees' 2E 9.5; *s* the earth, Is 24.20, ἱστός 'mast' 33.23; threatening to fall, Si 15.4.
3. *to draw near to the end-point*: κέκλικεν ἡ ἡμέρα Je 6.4, Jd 19.11A (B: προβαίνω), *s* πόλεμος 1K 4.3; metaph., αἱ ἡμέραι μου ὡσεὶ σκιὰ ἐκλίθησαν Ps 101.12, cf. τὴν σκιὰν κλῖναι δέκα βαθμούς '.. ten degrees' 4K 20.10.
II. tr. *to pour out* [= to tip sth containing liquid]: ἐκ τούτου εἰς τοῦτον Ps 74.9; + acc. rei, εἰς σὲ κακά 20.12, οὐρανὸν εἰς γῆν Jb 38.37.
2. *to incline*: + acc., τὸ οὖς 'the ear(s)' Je 17.22, Si 6.33 (|| ἀκούω), Da 9.18 TH (LXX προσέχω), ἐμοί Ps 16.6 + 114.2 (|| εἰσακούω), πρός με 30.3, εἰς τὰ ῥήματα 77.1, εἰς τὴν δέησίν μου 87.3; τὴν καρδίαν μου 118.112; τὸν ὦμον ὑμῶν 'your shoulder (in submission)' Ba 2.21; οὐρανόν Ps 17.10, οὐρανούς σου 143.5; τοίχῳ κεκλιμένῳ καὶ φραγμῷ ὠσμένῳ 'with a leaning wall and a tottering fence' 61.4 (sth life-threatening); γόνυ καρδίας 'the knee(s) of (my) heart (in entreaty)' Od 12.11.
3. *to cause to turn aside* from the right path: + acc. pers., Je 31.12.
4. *to turn* in a certain direction: + acc., ἐπ' ἐμὲ .. ἔλεος 2E 7.28; εἰς σὲ κακά Ps 20.12.
5. *to make subservient, subjugate* (ἐπὶ γόνυ 'on one's knees' understood?): pass., ***o*** πᾶσα ἡ Ἰουδαία Ju 8.21.
Cf. ἐκκλίνω, κλίνη, κάμπτω: Schmidt 3.267-76; Katz 1946.322-4.

κλισία, ας. f.ʃ
**company of people sitting at meals*: 3M 6.31.

κλίτος, ους. n.
*1. *side*: of an architectural structure, Ex 25.11; of a lampstand, 25.31; ἐκ τοῦ ~ους τοῦ πρὸς βορρᾶν 'on the north side' 26.18 (|| μέρος vs. 22); of an incense altar, 30.4.
*2. *corner off the centre*: Ex 30.4, τῆς οἰκίας Ps 127.3.
Cf. πλευρόν.

κλοιός, οῦ. m.
collar: ~ὸν χρυσοῦν περὶ τὸν τράχηλον αὐτοῦ Ge 41.42 (|| στολὴ βυσσίνη and worn by a man in high office), cf. Pr 1.9; an instrument of bondage, ἐπιθήσει ~ὸν σιδηροῦν ἐπὶ τὸν τράχηλόν σου 'will place an iron collar on your neck' De 28.48; εἰσένεγκον .. εἰς τὸν ~ὸν αὐτῆς τὸν τράχηλόν σου 'Put your neck ..' Si 6.24 (|| πέδη 'fetter'; fig. of discipline); Hb 2.6; pl., ἔλαβεν .. τοὺς ~οὺς ἀπὸ τοῦ τραχήλου Ιερεμίου Je 35.10 (|| ζυγόν); + δεσμοί 34.1; ζυγὸς ~οῦ Da 8.25 TH; 1C 18.7 (|| χλίδων 2K 8.7). Cf. ζυγός, ἐγκλοιόω: Russo 79.

κλοπή, ῆς. f.
stealing, theft: as dat. cogn., κλοπῇ ἐκλάπην 'I was really stolen' Ge 40.15; in a catalogue of vices, Ho 4.2, Wi 14.25. Cf. κλέπτω.

κλοποφορέω: aor. ἐκλοποφόρησα.ʃ *
to plunder: + acc. pers., Ge 31.26. Cf. κλέπτω, διαρπάζω, προνομεύω: Munnich 1986.

κλύδων, ωνος. m.
wave of the sea: Jn 1.11; μέγας 1.4, 12. **b**. metaph., *dire straits*: μέγας 1M 6.11. Cf. κλυδωνίζω, κῦμα.

κλυδωνίζω: fut.pass. ~νισθήσομαι.ʃ
to toss about: *o* hum. and fig., Is 57.20. Cf. κλύδων.

κλώθω: pf.pass.ptc. κεκλωσμένος.
to twist by spinning, 'spin': βύσσον κεκλωσμένην 'spun linen' Ex 25.4; as material for a tabernacle curtain, 26.1; κοκκίνου κεκλωσμένου '.. crimson yarn' ib.; || κλωστός Le 14.6; κεκλωσμένη κόκκῳ, ἔργῳ τεχνίτου 'with twisted crimson, the work of an artisan' Si 45.11 (of the high priest's robe). Cf. κλῶσμα, κλωστός.

κλών, νός. m.ʃ
twig: ἄγνου 'of chaste-tree' Jb 40.22; Wi 4.5; ποδός 'toe' 18.13. Cf. κλάδος.

κλῶσμα, ατος. n.ʃ
thread: κ. ὑακίνθινον 'blue cord' Nu 15.38 (on the fringe of a garment), Si 6.30; Jd 16.9A. Cf. κλώθω.

κλωστός, ή, όν.ʃ
spun: *s* κόκκινον 'scarlet' Le 14.6 (|| κεκλωσμένον vs. 4). Cf. κλώθω.

κνήμη, ης. f.
part between knee and ankle, 'leg': De 28.35; || πούς Da 2.33 TH (|| LXX σκέλος).

κνημίς, ίδος. f.ʃ
greave: made of bronze, 1K 17.6.

κνήφη, ης. f.ʃ *
itch: divine punishment, De 28.27.

κνίδη, ης. f.ʃ
nettle: Jb 31.40 (|| βάτος 'bramble'). Cf. Shipp 322.

κνίζω ʃ
to scratch: *o* συκάμινα 'mulberries' Am 7.14. Cf. Muraoka 1991.212; LSG s.v.

κνώδαλον, ου. n.
wild creature: as object of worship, Wi 11.15 (|| ζῷον); || ἑρπετά 'snakes' 17.9. Cf. ζῷον, θηρίον.

κοιλάς, άδος. f.
deep-lying space, depression: valley, ἡ κ. ἡ ἁλυκή w. ref. to the basin of the Dead Sea, Ge 14.10 (|| ἡ φάραγξ 14.3); || ὄρος Mi 1.4. **b**. *low-lying plain* bordered by a mountainous region: Jd 1.19 (w. ref. to the Coastal Plain). **c**. *cavity* in the wall of a house infected by fungi: Le 14.37.
Cf. αὐλών, φάραγξ, χάος.

κοίλασμα, ατος. n.ʃ *
hollow place: ἐν ~ατι ἐγκαθήμενοι 'lying in ambush ..' Is 8.14 (|| παγίς 'trap'). Cf. κοῖλας.

κοιλία, ας. f.
1. *belly*: τοῦ κήτους 'of the fish' Jn 2.1, 2; of a snake crawling on it, Ge 3.14 (|| στῆθος); of cows, 41.21; πεσόντες ἐπὶ ~αν 'prostrating themselves' 2M 10.4; of a hum. and as a seat of emotions, ἐπτοήθη ἡ κ. μου 'my belly was terrified' Hb 3.16, ἡ κ. μου ἐταράχθη '.. was upset' La 1.20, τὴν ~αν μου καὶ τὰ σπλάγχνα μου πονῶ PSol 2.14; emits a mournful sound, Is 16.11 (|| τὰ ἐντός).

2. *womb*: τὰ ἐπιθυμήματα ~ας αὐτῶν'the desirable fruits of their womb' Ho 9.16; 12.3; καρπὸν ~ας μου Mi 6.7 ("my" being most likely gender-neutral; τὰ ἔκγονα τῆς ~ας σου 'the offspring ..' ("your" being gender-neutral) De 7.13, 28.4, cf. τὸ σπέρμα σου μετὰ σέ, ὃς ἔσται ἐκ τῆς κοιλίας σου 2K 7.12 (of David's descendants; sim. Ps 131.11), οἱ ἐξελθόντες ἐκ ~ας αὐτοῦ 'his own children' 2C 32.21); || γαστήρ Ge 25.23. **b**. ἐκ κοιλίας 'from the time of pregnancy': ὁ πλάσας σε ἐκ ~ας 'one who formed you ..' Is 44.2, αἰρόμενοι ἐκ ~ας καὶ παιδευόμενοι ἐκ παιδίου 'carried .. and educated ..' 46.3; || ἀπὸ γαστρός, ἐκ νεότητος Ps 70.6.

3. *entrails, intestines* of sacrificial animals: τὸ στέαρ τὸ ἐπὶ τῆς ~ας 'the fat on the surface of the intestines' Ex 29.13.

4. *any cavity* or *inner chamber which holds objects in it*: ᾅδου 'of Hades' Jn 2.3. **b**. metaph.: τὸν νόμον σου ἐν μέσῳ τῆς ~ας μου Ps 39.9; λόγος ἐν ~ᾳ 'concealed within oneself' Si 19.12.

Cf. ἐγκοίλιος, ἔγκοιλος, γαστήρ, μήτρα, ὑποχόνδριος.

κοῖλος, η, ον.
1. *empty and hollow inside*: *s* the bottom part of altar, Ex 27.8; leprous skin, Le 13.32, 34.

2. subst.: f., *hold* of ship: τὴν ~ην τοῦ πλοίου Jn 1.5. **b**. n. 'sole of footwear': pl., Jo 9.5.

3. Κοίλη Συρία 1E 2.16+.

Cf. κοιλότης, κοίλασμα, κοίλωμα.

κοιλοσταθμέω: aor. ἐκοιλοστάθμησα.ʃ *

to fit with a panel: τὸν οἶκον κέδροις '.. with cedar' 3K 6.9; 6.15. Cf. κοιλόσταθμος.

κοιλόσταθμος, ον.ʃ

panelled, provided with a coffered ceiling: ἐν οἴκοις .. ~οις Hg 1.4. Cf. κοιλοσταθμέω: LSG s.v.

κοιλότης, ητος. f.ʃ

hollow space or *area*: of or in mountains, Wi 17.19. Cf. κοῖλος.

κοίλωμα, ατος. n.ʃ

1. *hollow, low-lying place*: Ge 23.2; the bottom of an altar, Ez 43.14; Ct 2.17, 2M 1.19.

2. *groove*: in an altar, Ez 43.14; in a pillar, 3K 7.3.

κοιμάομαι: fut. κοιμηθήσομαι; aor. ἐκοιμήθην, inf. κοιμηθῆναι, ptc. κοιμηθείς, impv.2s κοιμήθητι, 3s κοιμηθήτω, subj. κοιμηθῶ; pf. κεκοίμημαι, ptc. κεκοιμημένος.

1. *to lie (down)*: in order to sleep, Ge 19.3, 24.54, 31.54 (after a meal), also Nu 23.24; Ge 28.11 (after sunset); τὴν νύκτα ἐκείνην 32.13; ἐκοιμήθην καὶ ὕπνωσα '.. and slept' Ps 3.6; ἐκοιμήθησαν καὶ οὐκ ἀναστήσονται Is 43.17; *s* wild animal, Ge 49.9, ἐπὶ φάτνης 'at a manger' Jb 39.9; ἐπὶ ^κοίτης^ Le 15.4; 1K 4.9 (|| καθεύδω vs. 2); as mourner, ἐπὶ τὴν γῆν 2K 13.31B.

2. *to sleep*: + acc. cogn., ὕπνον Wi 17.14. **b**. *to rest*: "his heart does not rest even at night" Ec 2.23.

3. *to have sexual intercourse*: *s* woman, ἐκοιμήθη μετὰ τοῦ πατρὸς αὐτῆς Ge 19.33 (for procreation); man, μετὰ τῆς γυναικός σου 26.10; 30.15, 39.7, 12, 14; premarital, 34.2, and punishable, Ex 22.16; adulterous, μετὰ γυναικὸς συνῳκισμένης ἀνδρί 'with a woman wedded to a man' De 22.22; illicit, μετὰ γυναικὸς τοῦ πατρὸς αὐτοῦ 27.20, μετὰ ἀδελφῆς 27.22, μετὰ πενθερᾶς 'mother-in-law' 27.23, μετὰ κτήνους 'animal' Ex 22.19, De 27.21; + cogn. obj., κοιμηθῇ μετ' αὐτῆς κοίτην σπέρματος Le 15.18, sim. 19.20; μετὰ ἄρσενος οὐ κοιμηθήσῃ κοίτην γυναικός 'with a man you shall not have intercourse (which you would have) with a woman' 18.22.

4. *to remain during the night*: μὴ κοιμηθῇ στέαρ .. ἕως πρωΐ 'fat shall not remain .. till morning' Ex 23.18; οὐ κοιμηθήσεται ἀπὸ τῶν κρεῶν 'of the meat' De 16.4; οὐ κοιμηθήσεται ὁ μισθὸς τοῦ μισθωτοῦ παρὰ σοὶ ἕως πρωΐ 'the wage of the hireling shall not remain with you (unpaid) till morning' Le 19.13.

5. *to join one's ancestors on one's death*: μετὰ τῶν πατέρων μου Ge 47.30; De 31.16. **b**. 'to die': Si 48.11, Is 14.8; ἐν τιμῇ 14.18; Jb 14.12 (:: ἀνίστημι).

6. *to be* or *become a permanent, integral part of sth*: πόλις .., ἐν ᾗ δικαιοσύνη ἐκοιμήθη Is 1.21.

Cf. καθεύδω, κοιμίζω, κοίτη, κοίμησις, κοιτάζομαι, ἐπι~, συγκοιμάομαι: Schmidt 1.442-70.

κοίμησις, εως. f.ʃ

v.n. of κοιμάομαι **5**: πρὸ καιροῦ ~εως αἰῶνος 'prior to the time of his eternal sleep' Si 46.19 (|| ὕπνόω vs. 20); 18.9¶, 48.13. Cf. κοιμάομαι.

κοιμίζω: aor. ἐκοίμισα, ptc. κοιμίσας; pf.ptc.pass. κεκοιμισμένος.On the confusion between ι and η, see Walters 119.

1. *to put to sleep*: + acc., καμήλους Ge 24.11, ἐν τῷ κόλπῳ αὐτῆς 'in her bosom' 3K 3.20, ἐπὶ τῆς κλίνης αὐτοῦ 'on his bed' 17.19; not necessarily at night, Jd 16.19; fig. of temporarily putting out of action, τοὺς δυνάστους σου Na 3.18 (|| νυστάζω).

2. *to cause to lie down*: + acc. pers., ἐπὶ τὴν γῆν 2K 8.2, ἐπὶ τὴν κλίνην 'on the bed' 4K 4.21; metaph., εἰς ἀπώλειαν PSol 2.31.

Cf. κοιμάομαι: Walters 119.

κοινολογέομαι: fut.ptc. ~γησόμενος.ʃ

to discuss: περί τινος 1M 14.9; + dat. pers., 15.28. Cf. κοινολογία.

κοινολογία, ας. f.ʃ

oral discussion: 2M 14.22. Cf. κοινολογέω.

κοινός, ή, όν.

A adj. 1. *jointly done*: *s* ἱκετεία 'supplication' 2M 8.29, τῆς πόλεως ψήφισμα '(public) vote by the city' 12.4. **b**. *shared with others*: *s* οἶκος Pr 21.9, βαλλάντιον 'purse' 1.14, ἀήρ 'air' Wi 7.3. **c**. subst. n. *public body*: w. ref. to council or whole community, Pr 15.23, cf. Tréheux.

2. *universally applicable*: *s* ἀσφάλεια '(general) security' 2M 9.21, πρόσταγμα '(public) edict' 10.8.

*3. ritually *profane*: *s* κτήνη '(sacrificial) animals' 1M 1.47.

B. adv. κοινῇ *with all constituents involved*: ἔκτισεν τὰ πάντα κ. Si 18.1, πᾶς ὁ λαὸς κ. 50.17. **b**. *public* as against individual and private: κ. καὶ κατ' ἰδίαν 2M 4.5, 9.26.

Cf. ἀκοινώνητος, κοινόω, ἴδιος, πάνδημος, βέβηλος: Trench 374-7; Hauck, *TDNT* 3.790f.

κοινόω: aor. ἐκοίνωσα.ʃ

to render ritually profane: + acc., hum. stomach, 4M 7.6. Cf. κοινός.

κοινωνέω: fut. ~νήσω, ptc. ~νήσων; aor. ἐκοινώνησα, ptc. ~νήσας, impv. ~νησον.

to have or *do in common with*: + gen. rei, ὁδοῦ .. μετὰ ποιούντων τὰ ἄνομα Jb 34.8; ἐλθὲ μεθ' ἡμῶν, κοινώνησον αἵματος 'Come with us, join us as murderer' Pr 1.11; βίου 2M 14.25; εὐκλείας 'reputation' 3M 3.21, εὐεργετημάτων 'good fortunes' 2M 5.20 (|| συμμετέχω); + dat pers., Si 13.17 (|| πρός τινα), 1, 2; + *πρός acc. (cf. κοινώνημα πρὸς ἀλλήλους Plut. 2.158c), "How can a clay pot get along with an iron kettle?" Si 13.2; 2C 20.35, Ec 9.4. Cf. συμμετέχω.

κοινωνία, ας. f.ʃ

1. *joint ownership*: Le 6.2.

2. *act of forming close association with and involving oneself with*: κ. λόγων αὐτῆς [= σοφίας] Wi 8.18; γαμικός 'marital' 3M 4.6.

Cf. κοινωνός, μετοχή.

κοινωνός, οῦ. m. and f.ʃ

partner: spouse, Ma 2.14; ~οἱ κλεπτῶν 'fellow thieves' Is 1.23, ἀνδρὸς ἀσεβοῦς 'of a godless man' Pr 28.24; βασιλείας κ. 'royal consort' Es E 13 o'; κ. τραπεζῶν 'fellow-guest at dinner-table' Si 6.10; ‖ ὁδοιπόρος 'fellow-traveller' 42.3; + φίλος 41.18; 4K 17.11. Cf. μέτοχος: *ND* 3.19, 153.

κοινῶς. adv.ʃ

jointly, together: to act, μετ' ἐμοῦ To 2.2 𝔊[II]; 9.6

κοιτάζομαι: fut. κοιτασθήσομαι.

I. act. *to cause to lie down for sleep*: *o* πρόβατα Je 40.12; ἐν μεσημβρίᾳ 'at midday' Ct 1.7, ἐν μάνδραις 'in pens' Ps 103.22.

II. mid. *to go to sleep*: *s* hum., Le 15.20; De 6.7, 11.19 (:: κάθημαι, πορεύομαι, διανίστημι); animals, Zp 2.14.

Cf. κοιμάομαι, καθεύδω: Shipp 324f.

κοιτασία, ας. f.ʃ *

sexual intercourse, copulation: δῷ ~αν αὐτοῦ ἐν τετράποδι Le 20.15 (‖ κοίτην 18.23 and with instrumental ἐν here). Cf. κοίτη, κοιμάομαι.

κοίτη, ης. f.

1. *bed*: for sleeping, Ge 49.4, Mi 2.1; sick-bed, Ex 21.18, Jb 33.19; κοιμηθῇ ἐπ' αὐτῆς [= κοίτης] Le 15.4; lair of the young of vipers, Is 11.8; sparrows' nest Je 10.22.

2. *pen, fold* for domestic animals: for sheep, Mi 2.12, Is 17.2; for cattle, Jb 36.28.

3. *sexual intercourse*: as cogn. obj., μετὰ ἄρσενος οὐ κοιμηθήσῃ ~ην γυναικός Le 18.22, sim. 20.13; ἄρσενος 'with a male' Nu 31.17 (‖ κ. ἀνδρός vs. 35); ἐν παραπτώματι 'illicit' Wi 3.13 (‖ παράνομος vs. 16).

4. κοίτη σπέρματος 'ejaculated semen': Le 15.16. **b**. 'sexual intercourse': γυνή, ἐὰν κοιμηθῇ ἀνὴρ μετ' αὐτῆς ~ην σπέρματος Le 15.18; πρὸς τὴν γυναῖκα τοῦ πλησίον σου οὐ δώσεις ~ην σπέρματός σου 18.20. **c**. elliptically 'semen': πρὸς πᾶν τετράπουν οὐ δώσεις τὴν ~ην σου εἰς σπερματισμόν 'with no quadruped should you have intercourse ..' Le 18.23; ἔδωκεν τὴν ~ην αὐτοῦ ἐν σοί Nu 5.20.

Cf. κοιτών, κοιμάομαι, κοιτασία, κλίνη, μάνδρα, στρωμνή.

κοιτών, ῶνος. m.

bedroom: ταμιεῖα τῶν κοιτώνων 'recesses of bed-chambers' Ex 8.3; of a bridegroom, ἐξελθάτω νυμφίος ἐκ τοῦ ~ῶνος αὐτοῦ Jl 2.16 (‖ παστός for bride); 2K 13.10B (‖ ταμιεῖον), 4.7, 1E 3.3; Jd 3.24A, 15.1A (B: ταμιεῖον); ταμιεῖον κοιτῶνος 4K 6.12. **b**. *private chamber* in general: secluded, Ez 8.12; w. ref. to toilet, Jd 3.24A.

Cf. κοίτη, θάλαμος, παστός: Husson 151-4 ("typical of urban life-style," 152).

κόκκινος, η, ον.

scarlet in colour: subst. *sth scarlet*, Ge 38.28 (a piece of cloth bound round a new-born baby's hand for identification?); διπλοῦν 'doubly (scarlet)' Ex 25.4 (‖ πορφύρα); valuable fabric used for a tabernacle curtain, κ. κεκλωσμένος 'spun' 26.1 (‖ βύσσος, ὑάκινθος, πορφύρα); material for a veil of the tabernacle, 26.31; κλωστόν 'spun' Le 14.6 (‖ κεκλωσμένον vs. 4); subst. ~α (sc. ἱμάτια) Is 3.23 (+ βύσσινα, ὑακίνθια); Je 4.30 (‖ κόσμος), μετὰ κόσμου 2K 1.24. **b**. *s* sins, Is 1.18 (‖ φοινικοῦς and::λευκός).

Cf. κόκκος, ἐρυθρός, φοινικοῦς: Shipp 325; Michel, *TDNT* 3.812-4.

κόκκος, ου. m.ʃ

scarlet product: priest's uniform Si 45.11, bedding La 4.5. Cf. κόκκινος: LSG s.v.

κολαβρίζω: fut. pass. ~ρισθήσομαι.ʃ

**to deride*: *o* hum., Jb 5.4. Shipp 326. Cf. καταγελάω.

κολάζω: fut.pass. κολασθήσομαι; aor. ἐκόλασα, inf. κολάσαι, subj. κολάσω, impv.3s κολασάτω, inf. mid. κολάσασθαι, pass. ἐκολάσθην, inf. κολασθῆναι, ptc. κολασθείς, subj. κολασθῶ.

to penalise: + acc. pers., 1M 7.7; 4M 2.12 (‖ ἀπελέγχω vs. 11, ‖ ἐξελέγχω vs. 13), opp. εὐεργετέω 8.6; pass., "whether by death, punishment or expulsion" 1E 8.24; φόνῳ Es 7.18 *L*, τιμωρίαις 'with punishments' 3M 7.3; mid. = act., 7.14, Wi 11.16 (*s* God; cf. Gilbert 1985); pass. *o* hum., ‖ βασανίζω 'torment' 16.1. Cf. κόλασις, ἀκόλαστος, τιμωρέω, τίνω: Schmidt 4.172-7; Shipp 326.

κολακεύω.ʃ

to flatter: + acc. pers., Jb 19.17, king Wi 14.17; so as to appease sbd disgruntled, 1E 4.31; + τὸ πρόσωπόν τινος ὑπέρ τινος 'on behalf of sbd' Es 4.4*L*. Cf. Schmidt 3.438-42; Spicq 2.319-21.

κολάπτω: aor. ἐκόλαψα; pf.ptc.pass. κεκολαμμένος.

to engrave: *o* γραφή 'writing,' ἐν ταῖς πλαξίν 'on the tablets' Ex 32.16; ἐν γραφῇ Si 45.11; ἐκόλαψεν γραφὴν 3M 2.27 (written on a stele). Cf. ἐγκολάπτω, γλύφω, γράφω.

κόλασις, εως. f.

punishment: Je 18.20; τῶν ἀδικιῶν Ez 14.3; *o* of λαμβάνω 43.11, of ἀποδίδωμι 2M 4.38, of κομίζομαι 3M 1.3. Cf. κολάζω, τιμωρία: Trench 24-6.

κολεός, οῦ. m.

sheath: for sword, Je 29.6; for ἐγχειρίδιον 'hand-weapon' Ez 21.3.

κόλλα, ης. f.∫

glue, adhesive: Is 44.13.

κολλάω: fut.pass. κολληθήσομαι; aor. ἐκόλλησα, pass. ἐκολλήθην, impv. κολλήθητι, opt.3s κολληθείη; pf. κεκόλληκα, pass. κεκόλλημαι.

to attach firmly, fasten: + acc., τὸ περίζωμα περὶ τὴν ὀσφῦν .. πρὸς ἐμαυτὸν τὸν οἶκον Ισραηλ 'the girdle round the waist ..' Je 13.11; εἰς τὴν γῆν '(raze) to the ground' La 2.2, Ps 43.26. **b.** pass. *to attach oneself* or *itself* to, *cleave* to: *s* person, πρός τινα, to God, De 6.13, 10.20, πρὸς τὴν ἰδιάν γυναῖκα 1E 4.20 (marital union, cf. Ge 2.24 with προσ~), ὀπίσω σου Ps 62.9; + ἔν τινι - ἐν ταῖς ἁμαρτίαις 4K 1.21, 3.3; painful, hateful things and + ἔν τινι– ἐν σοί De 28.60; ἐν αὐτῷ πᾶσαι αἱ ἀραί 29.20; ἡ χεὶρ .. ἐπὶ τὴν ῥομφαίαν 'the hand .. to the sword' 2K 23.10*L* (B: πρὸς τὴν μάχαιραν); + dat., ἡ γλῶσσά μου τῷ λάρυγγί μου Ps 21.16, 136.6, || πρὸς φάρυγγα 'throat' La 4.4; αὐτῷ [= κυρίῳ; opp. ἀφίστημι] Si 2.2, τοῖς μαρτυρίοις σου Ps 118.31, as likeminded colleague, 1M 3.2; mental union, ἡ ψυχὴ αὐτοῦ ἐκολλήθη αὐτῇ To 6.18 𝔊[II] (𝔊[I] καρδία .. εἰς αὐτήν); πόρναις 'harlots' Si 19.2; of deserting and going over to the other party, 1M 6.21, 2K 20.2B (*L* προσχωρέω); ἐκολλήθη ἡμῖν τὰ κακά Ba 3.4 || εἰς ἡμᾶς τὰ κ. καὶ ἡ ἀρά 1.20; + gen., Jb 41.8¶, see Helbing, *Kasus.*, 249; μετά τινος (pers.) Ru 2.8.

Cf. προσκολλάω, κόλλησις, προσγίνομαι.

κόλλησις, εως. f.∫

v.n. of κολλάω: Si 25.12¶.

κολλυρίζω: aor. ἐκολλύρισα, impv.3s κολλυρισάτω.∫

to bake cakes: + acc., κολλυρίδας 2K 13.6, 8(9). Cf. κολλυρίς.

κολλύριον, ου. n.∫

Dim. of κολλυρίς (q.v.): present for children, 3K 12.24[h].

κολλυρίς, ίδος. f. *

some sort of baked food: breadlike, ἄρτου 2K 6.19; *o* of κολλυρίζω 13.6, of ἕψω 13.8; + ἄρτος 3K 14.3 v.l. Cf. κολλυρίζω, κολλύριον, λάγανον: Shipp 328.

κολοβόκερκος, ον.∫ *

with a docked tail: *s* unacceptable sacrificial animal, Le 22.23.

κολοβόριν, ινος. m./f.∫

slit-nosed person: disqualified for priesthood, Le 21.18.

κολοβόω: aor. ἐκολόβωσα.∫

to mutilate: + acc., hands and feets of a dead hum., 2K 4.12.

κολόκυνθα, ης. f. On the ending with η, see LSJ, s.v.

round gourd, Cucurbita maxima (LSJ): Jn 4.6. Cf. τολύπη: Shipp 329.

κόλπος, ου. m.

1. *bosom*: where a male embraces a woman— δέδωκα τὴν παιδίσκην μου εἰς τὸν ~ον σου 'I've placed my maidservant into your bosom' Ge 16.5; ἡ γυνὴ ἡ ἐν ~ῳ σου De 13.6; the other way round, τὸν ἄνδρα αὐτῆς τὸν ἐν τῷ ~ῳ αὐτῆς De 28.56, γυνὴ ~ου σου Si 9.1; of a nurse looking after a babe, Λάβε αὐτοὺς εἰς τὸν ~ον σου, ὡσεὶ ἄραι τιθηνὸς τὸν θηλάζοντα '.. just as a foster-father would pick up his babe' Nu 11.12; an infant in mother's bosom, 3K 3.20; as depository for personal small articles, Ex 4.6, κ. κενός 'empty ..' Jb 31.34, for crops Ps 128.7; ἀποδῶ εἰς τὸν ~ν αὐτῶν τὰς ἁμαρτίας αὐτῶν 'requite their sins into their lap' Is 65.6, sim. Je 39.18, Ps 78.12, cf. 34.13, Pr 16.33. **b.** *hollow space*: of a chariot, 3K 22.35. **c.** metaph. of personal, inner being: "the humiliation .., which I bore close to my heart (ἐν τῷ ~ῳ μου)" Ps 88.51; Jb 19.27.

2. *midst*: εἰς ~ον αὐτῶν 'into their midst' Ho 8.1. Cf. καρδία.

Cf. μέσος: Lee 1969.237, f.n. 4; *ND* 3.106f.

κόλπωμα, ατος. n.∫

cavity: drain round an altar, κ. βάθος 'dug round' Ez 43.13.

κολυμβήθρα, ας.

1. *swimming-bath*: Na 2.9 (in a simile on Nineveh).

*__2__. *water reservoir*: Is 7.3; ὑδάτων Ec 2.6.

κόμη, ης. f.

1. *hair* of a human's head: κεφαλῆς Le 19.27; ~ην τρίχα κεφαλῆς Nu 6.5; ἐκείρατο τὴν ~ην .. 'shaved ..' Jb 1.20; ~ας .. ψιλώσουσι 'will pluck off' Ez 44.20; without κεφαλή, Jb 16.12; pl., Ez 24.23, 44.20; λαβών με τῆς ~ης 'taking me by the hair' Jb 16.12, cf. Da LXX Bel 36.

2. *luminous tail of a comet* (LSJ): Jb 38.32¶.

Cf. θρίξ: Schmidt 1.379-83.

κομιδῇ. adv.∫

in every respect: γελοῖος '(entirely) ridiculous' 4M 3.1.

κομίζω: fut.mid. κομιοῦμαι, ptc.act. κομιῶν; aor. act. ἐκόμισα, inf. κομίσαι, mid. ἐκομισάμην, subj. κομίσωμαι, inf. κομίσασθαι, impv. κόμισαι, pass. subj. κομισθῶ; pf.mid. κεκόμισμαι.

1. *to carry off*: *o* spoils of war, τῷ βασιλεῖ πάντα 1E 4.5; + acc. and mid. for one's own use, τὸν σῖτόν μου Ho 2.9 (|| ἀφαιρεῖσθαι); αὐτὴν κατὰ τὴν κρίσιν 'her as duly (wedded wife)' To 7.11 𝔊[I].

2. *to go and bring*, 'fetch': + acc., τὸν νόμον '(the copy of) the law' 1E 9.39 (|| φέρω Ne 8.1), μοι τὸ ἀργύριον To 9.2 𝔊[I].

3. *to sustain*: + acc., ἁμαρτίαν 'the penalty of sin' Le 20.17 (|| ἀποφέρομαι vs. 19), βάσανον 'torture' Ez 16.52 (|| λαμβάνω 32.24), αἰσχύνην 'shame' Ps

39.16, κόλασιν 'punishment' 3M 1.3, θάνατον 2M 13.8. **b**. *to attain*: μισθόν 'recompense' 8.33.

4. *to recover*: + acc. rei, τὸν ἀρραβῶνα παρὰ τῆς γυναῖκος 'to retrieve the pledge from the woman' Ge 38.20; 2M 7.11; τὸ ἱερόν καὶ τὴν πόλιν 'the temple and the city' 10.1; τὰ ἑαυτῶν 'one's own property' 3M 7.22; + acc. pers., 7.29.

5. *to receive and accept*: + acc. (gift), 1M 13.37.

Cf. ἀφαιρέομαι, φέρω: Schmidt 3.189-92.

κόμμα, ατος. n.ʃ

coinage: ‖ νόμισμα 1M 15.6.

κόμπος, ου. m.ʃ

boast: Es E 4; + θράσος 'audacity' 3M 6.5. Cf. ἀλαζονεία.

κόνδυ, υος. n.

drinking-vessel: ἀργυροῦν 'silver' Ge 44.2; fig. τοῦ θυμοῦ Is 51.17, 22 (‖ ποτήριον). Cf. ποτήριον: Cunen; Caird 1969.22.

κονδυλίζω.ʃ

to hit with the fist, thereby causing unjust suffering: ἐκονδύλιζον εἰς κεφαλὰς πτωχῶν 'they boxed the poor on the head' Am 2.7; + acc. ὀρφανούς Ma 3.5 (‖ καταδυναστεύω χήραν and ἐκκλίνω κρίσιν; κατα~ πτωχούς Am 5.11). Cf. κονδυλισμός, κατακονδυλίζω, πυγμή.

κονδυλισμός, οῦ. m.ʃ *

v.n. of prec.: Zp 2.8 (‖ ὀνειδισμός), the reference here being prob. not to physical blows, but to hurting, verbal abuses.

κονία, ας. f.ʃ

1. *plaster, stucco*: κονιάσεις .. ~ᾳ De 27.2, 4; made by burning human bodies, Am 2.1; the chalk of the Jordan River (?), Jb 28.4¶.

2. *dust*: λεπτή 'fine' Is 27.9.

Cf. κονίαμα, κονιάω, κονιορτός.

κονίαμα, ατος. n.

= prec. **1**: Da 5.1 LXX; τοῦ τοίχου τοῦ οἴκου 5.5 TH. Cf. κονία.

κονιάω: fut. ~άσω.ʃ

to spread plaster over: ^λίθους μεγάλους^ κονίᾳ De 27.2, 4; Pr 21.9. Cf. κονία, κονίαμα.

κονιορτός, οῦ. m.

dust: originally furnace soot (αἰθάλη) sprinkled and fallen on the ground, Ex 9.9; powdery, De 9.21; νεφέλαι κ. ποδῶν αὐτοῦ 'clouds are dust raised by His feet' Na 1.3, τροχοῦ 'of a wheel' Is 17.13, ἀπὸ τροχοῦ 29.5 (fig. of sth ephemeral); cities turned to rubbles and dust, 10.6; fig. of sth valueless and unattractive, 5.24 (:: ἄνθος 'flower'). Cf. κονία, κόνις, σποδός: Shipp 331.

κόνις, εως. f.ʃ

dust: sprinkled on the head as a sign of mourning, 3M 1.18. Cf. κονιορτός, σποδός.

κοντός, οῦ. m.ʃ

pole: as weapon, Ez 39.9, δόρατος 'of spear' 1K 17.7.

κόνυζα, ης. f.ʃ

"name of various species of Inula, fleabane" (LSJ): Is 55.13.

κοπάζω: fut. κοπάσω; aor. ἐκόπασα, impv. κόπασον, inf. κοπάσαι, subj. κοπάσω; pf. κεκόπακα.

1. *to lose strength and cease to be troublesome* or *noxious*: *s* the flood water, Ge 8.1; + ἀπό τινος (victim), κεκόπακεν τὸ ὕδωρ ἀπὸ τῆς γῆς 8.11, cf. ἀπὸ προσώπου τῆς γῆς '(had weakened and receded) from the surface of the earth' 8.8; the sea, κοπάσει ἡ θάλασσα ἀφ' ἡμῶν 'the sea will become calm to relieve us (of anxiety)' Jn 1.11, 12; fire, Nu 11.2; destructive plague (θραῦσις), 16.48, 50 (‖ Ps 105.30); "the king had no mental strength to go (τοῦ ἐξελθεῖν) after Abshalom" 2K 13.39. ***b**. tr. *to curb, moderate*: + acc., θυμόν 'anger' Si 39.28, ὀργήν 48.10, ἄβυσσον 'the deep' 43.23, γογγυσμὸν πονηρίας 'secret plotting of wickedness' 46.7.

2. *to cease, stop what one is doing*: abs. Ho 8.10, Am 7.5, Si 23.17, Ps 48.10; Je 14.21 (or: **1b** with θυμόν or ὀργήν understood), Jd 20.28 A (B: ἐπέχω); + gen., ἡ γῆ ἐκόπασε τοῦ πολέμου Jo 14.15; τοῦ θυμοῦ Es 2.1 o'; + ἀπό τινος - ἀπὸ τῶν ἁμαρτιῶν αὐτῶν Ez 43.10; + inf., τοῦ λαλῆσαι Ru 1.18.

Cf. κόπος, κοπιάω, παύω: LSG s.v.

κοπανίζω: pf.ptc.pass. κεκοπανισμένος. *

to bray, pound: pass., *o* ἄλευρον 'wheat-meal' 3K 2.46[e]. Cf. τρίβω: Shipp 332f.

κοπετός, οῦ. m.

mourning over some lamentable situation, esp. for the dead: Am 5.16*a*, 17, Zc 12.11*a*; accompanied by highly audible noise, ποιήσεται ~ὸν ὡς δρακόντων Mi 1.8 (see Cyr. I 614); + πένθος Mi 1.8; + πένθος and θρῆνος Am 5.16*b*; + νηστεία and κλαυθμός, as a sign of sincere repentance, Jl 2.12, sim. Is 22.12; as a cogn. obj. ἐκόψαντο αὐτὸν ~ὸν μέγαν καὶ ἰσχυρὸν σφόδρα Ge 50.10; κόψονται ἐπ' αὐτὸν ~όν 'they will mourn for him' Zc 12.10, ἐπὶ τὰ ὄρη λάβετε ~όν Je 9.10 (‖ θρῆνος); τινος 'for sth', Zc 12.11b; opp. χορός Ps 29.12.

The noun is derived from κόπτω, q.v. **4**. Cf. θρῆνος.

κοπή, ῆς. f.ʃ

military strike: against sbd (τινος), τοῦ Χοδολλογομορ καὶ τῶν βασιλέων τῶν μετ' αὐτοῦ Ge 14.17; Ju 15.7; cogn. acc. of κόπτω Jo 10.20. Cf. κόπτω, ἐπικοπή.

κοπιάω: fut. κοπιάσω; impf.2s ἐκοπίας; aor. ἐκοπίασα, inf. κοπιᾶσαι, subj. κοπιάσω; pf. κεκοπίακα.

1. *to become exhausted*: physically, De 25.18*a*; ἐπείνας καὶ ἐκοπίας 'you were famished and exhausted' 25.18*b*, κοπιῶν καὶ ἐκλελυμένος χερσίν (*L* τὰς χεῖρας) 'exhausted and worn-out' 2K 17.2, φορτίον κοπιῶντι καὶ πεινῶντι καὶ ἐκλελυμένῳ οὐκ ἰσχύοντι 'a burden for ..' Is 46.1f., οὐ πεινάσουσιν οὐδὲ κοπιάσουσιν 'they will not go hungry nor ..' 5.27, sim. 40.28; 40.30 (‖ πεινάω, ἄνισχύς εἰμι), δραμοῦνται καὶ οὐ κοπιάσουσι 'even if they ran, ..' 40.31, ἐκοπιάσαμεν, οὐκ ἀνεπαύθημεν '.. we did not relax' La 5.5, sim. Si 16.27; κοπιῶν καὶ πονῶν καὶ σπεύδων 'tires himself out, toils and presses on' 11.11; will perish in the end (ἀπολοῦνται) Is 31.3; πολυοδίαις 'with many journeys' 57.10, ἐν στεναγμῷ 'sighing' Ps 6.7, κράζων 'crying' 68.4; *s* military horses, 1M 10.81. **b**. mentally: ἐν ταῖς βουλαῖς σου '(got tired) of counsels you received' Is 47.13, ἐν τῇ μεταβολῇ 'with business transactions [or: migration]' 47.15.

2. *to work hard, toil*: ἐκοπίασεν πλούσιος ἐν συναγωγῇ χρημάτων 'the rich worked hard amassing money' Si 34.3 (:: ἀνάπαυσις), 6.19. **b**. *to work hard in order to attain*: + acc. rei, εἰς κενὰ καὶ μάταια ἐκοπίασεν πλοῦτον 'absolutely for nothing he toiled for wealth (which he would not enjoy)' Jb 20.18, ὠδῖνες καὶ πόνοι, οὓς εἰς τὸ κενὸν ἐκοπίασα μετὰ μόχθων 2.9b; of wasted efforts, εἰς μάτην 'in vain' Ps 126.1, μάτην Is 30.5, κενῶς 49.4, εἰς κενόν Jb 39.16¶, Is 65.23, cf. 1Cor 15.10, Joh 4.38.

Cf. κόπος, κοπάζω, κοπόω, ἐκλείπω, κάμνω, μοχθέω.

κόπος, ου. m.ʃ

hardship: physical, κ. τῶν χειρῶν μου 'my harsh manual labour' Ge 31.42; φέρειν τὸν ~ον ὑμῶν 'to bear your burden' De 1.12; Hb 3.7; leading to tears and groans, Ma 2.13; ἐν ~οις αὐτοῦ ἐνίσχυσε πρὸς θεόν 'in his struggles he defeated God' Ho 12.3; λογιζόμενοι ~ους καὶ ἐργαζόμενοι κακὰ ἐν ταῖς κοίταις αὐτῶν 'thinking out troubles and working out evil things in their beds' Mi 2.1; ἐλάλησαν ~ους .. ὁράσεις ψευδεῖς .. μάταια παρεκάλουν Zc 10.2; μισθὸς ~ων 'a reward of ..' Wi 10.17. **b**. mental: 'annoyance, nuisance, pain in the neck': ἵνα μὴ ~ον ἔχῃς 'so that you may be spared a burden' Si 22.13; 29.4; 'strenuous mental, intellectual efforts,' διαλογισμοὶ μετὰ ~ων 'hard thinking' 13.26; 'depression, misery (?)' Jb 4.2. **c**. *suffering, distressful situation*: ἴδε τὴν ταπείνωσιν καὶ τὸν ~ον μου 'Look at my degradation and ..' Ps 24.18, πτωχός εἰμι ἐγὼ καὶ ἐν ~οις ἐκ νεότητός μου 87.16, ~ους καὶ πόνους Hb 1.3, cf. προσέθηκε κύριος ~ον ἐπὶ πόνον μου 'the Lord added hardship to my pain' Je 51.33, ὑπὸ τὴν γλῶσσαν αὐτοῦ κόπος καὶ πόνος Ps 9.28 (to be inflicted on others: ‖ πικρία καὶ δόλος and cf. ἀνομία καὶ κ... καὶ ἀδικία 54.11 and πλάσσων ~ον 93.20 [‖ ἀνομία]), ἐταπεινώθη ἐν ~οις ἡ καρδία αὐτῶν 'they were depressed ..' 106.12; on battlefield, τοὺς ~ους, οὓς ἔσχοσαν 1M 10.15; destined for human existence, "why did I come out from the womb to see sufferings and pains (~ους καὶ πόνους)?" Je 20.18, τὸ πλεῖον αὐτῶν κ. καὶ πόνος 'most of it [= man's life] is ..' Ps 89.10, ἄνθρωπος γεννᾶται ~ῳ 'man is born for hardship' Jb 5.7. **d**. pl. *product of toil*: οὐχὶ .. καταλείψεις .. τοὺς ~ους σου εἰς διαίρεσιν κλήρου; 'you are surely not going to leave .. to be divided by lot?' Si 14.15 (‖ πόνος), cf. Joh 4.38; also sg., χειλέων 'of lips (of conspirators)' Ps 139.10. Cf. Dresher 1970. 142-5.

Cf. κοπιάω, ἀκοπιάτως, ἔγκοπος, κόπωσις, λύπη, μόχθος, πόνος, ὀδύνη, ἀνάλγητος: Lightfoot 26; Spicq 2.322-9.

κοπόω: fut. κοπώσω; pf.ptc.pass. κεκοπωμένος.*

to make tired: ***o*** hum., Ec 10.15, pass. Ju 13.1. Cf. κοπιάω.

κοπρία, ας. f.

1. *rubbish-heap*: ἐκάθητο ἐπὶ τῆς ~ας ἔξω τῆς πόλεως Jb 2.8, ἀπὸ ~ας ἀνύψων πένητα 'raising the poor out of ..' Ps 112.7 (sim. 1K 2.8 and ‖ γῆ), βόλβιτον ~ων 'filth of ..' Si 22.1; in the name of a gate of Jerusalem, ἡ πύλη τῆς ~ας Ne 2.13; of a section of the wall, 12.32; of human corpses, Is 5.25.

*__2__. *rubbish, refuse*: Si 27.4 (‖ σκύβαλα 'crap'); fig., περιεβάλοντο ~ας 'wore rags' La 4.5.

Cf. κόπριον, κόπρος, περίκαθαρμα, σκύβαλον.

κόπριον, ου. n.ʃ

excrement: fig. of sth despised and pl., ἐπὶ προσώπου τῆς γῆς Je 32.19, ἡ δόξα αὐτοῦ εἰς ~α καὶ εἰς σκώληκας '.. worms' 1M 2.62; Si 22.2. Cf. κόπρος.

κόπρος, ου. f.

excrement: of animals and to be burned with other parts outside of the camp, Ex 29.14, Le 4.11, Nu 19.5; fig. of sth useless to be thrown out, Is 30.22, of pigeons 4K 6.25. Cf. κοπρία, κόπριον, ἀφόδευμα, βόλβιτον, οὖρον, προχώρημα.

κοπρών, ῶνος.m.ʃ

place for dung: 4K 10.27*L* (B: λυτρών).

κόπτω: fut.act. κόψω, mid. κόψομαι, pass. κοπήσομαι; aor. ἔκοψα, impv. κόψον, inf. κόψαι, subj. κόψω, mid. ἐκοψάμην, inf. κόψασθαι, subj. κόψωμαι, impv.2pl κόψασθε, pass.subj. κοπῶ, impv.3s κοπήτω; pf.ptc.pass. κεκομμένος.

1. act. *to cut*: + acc., κλῆμα 'branch' Nu 13.24; βότρυν 'bunch of grapes' 13.25; with axe or mallet, κόψατε ξύλα 'fell trees (for building a house)' Hg 1.8, sim. De 19.5, firewood Ez 39.10; *s* sword, Je 29.6. **b**. *to cut off*: + acc. and ἀπό τινος Je 31.2.

2. *to hit, strike*: + dpin;e acc/. πτῶσις, ἣν κόψει κύριος πάντας τοὺς λαούς 'the overthrow with which the Lord will smite all the peoples' Zc 14.12. **b**. ἔλαιον κεκομμένον 'olive-oil made by beating olives' (fine and costly kind) Ex 27.20, 29.40; lamp oil, ἔλαιον καθαρὸν κεκομμένον εἰς φῶς Le 24.2. **c**. on battlefield and slaying implied: abs., ἐν τῷ πολέμῳ 2K 5.24 (ll *L* τύπτω); + acc. pers., Jd 1.4B (A: πατάσσω).

3. *to tire out*: + acc. pers., 1M 12.44.

4. mid. *to mourn death of* sbd *by beating one's breast*: abs. κόψεται ἡ γῆ κατὰ φυλὰς φυλάς 'the land will mourn, each tribe by itself' Zc 12.12; + θρηνέω Mi 1.8, + νηστεύω Zc 7.5, + περιζώννυμι and θρηνέω Jl 1.13; + acc. pers. 'for sbd deceased,' κόψασθαι Σάρραν καὶ πενθῆσαι Ge 23.2, ll κλαίω Je 22.18, 41.5, 1M 9.20; + cogn. obj. and acc. pers., Ge 50.10, 1M 2.70, 9.20; *ἐπί τινα – κόψονται ἐπ' αὐτὸν κοπετὸν ὡς ἐπ' ἀγαπητόν and ll ὀδυνάω, Zc 12.10 (the combination with ἐπί τινα occurs only here, 2K 1.12, 11.26*L* (B: acc.), and Rev 1.7, 18.9, most likely a Hebraism); pass., οὐ κοπήσονται 'no mourning ceremony will be conducted for them' Je 8.2 (ll οὐ ταφήσονται), 16.4; opp. ὀρχέομαι 'to dance' Ec 3.4. **b**. same meaning with acc. πρόσωπον: Ez 6.9, 20.43. On the sense **4**, see κοπετός.

Cf. ἀπο~, δια~, κατα~, συγκόπτω, ξυλοκόπος, κοπή, θρηνέω, κρούω, λυπέω, παίω, πατάσσω, πενθέω, πλήσσω, προσοδύρομαι, τύπτω: Schmidt 3.284-92; Trench 239.

κόπωσις, εως. f.ʃ *

hard, physical labour: *s* writing of books, σαρκός Ec 12.12. Cf. κόπος.

κόραξ, κος. m.

raven: Ge 8.7, Zp 2.14; forbidden as food, Le 11.14, De 14.14; inhabits wilderness, Is 34.11. Cf. κορώνη: Shipp 333.

κοράσιον, ου. n.

young female child, 'girl': playing with boys on a street, Zc 8.5; ll παιδάριον and sold for wine, Jl 3.3. **b**. of working age: farm-hand, Ru 2.8; fit as king's consort, Es 2.1 o' (*L* παρθένος), παρθενικόν 'virgin' 2.3 o'.

Cf. ἅβρα, νεᾶνις, παιδίσκη, παιδάριον, παρθένος: Spicq 1978.201-8; Shipp 431f.

κορέννυμι: fut. κορήσω.ʃ

to get sated: ἐμπλησθέντες κορήσουσιν De 31.20. Cf. ἐμπίμπλημι.

κόρη, ης. f. On the alternative spelling ~α, see Thack. § 10.3.

pupil of the eye: ὀμμάτων Pr 7.2, 4M 18.21; fig. of a carefully guarded object of value, κ. τοῦ ὀφθαλμοῦ Zc 2.8, cf. διεφύλαξεν αὐτὸν ὡς ~ην ὀφθαλμοῦ De 32.10; Ps 16.8; elliptically, ὡς ~ην συντηρήσει Si 17.22 (ll σφραγίς), sim. 3.25¶; κόραις ὀφθαλμῶν θεάσασθαι 'to observe personally and at close range' 3M 5.47.

κόριον, ου. n.ʃ

coriander, Coriandrum sativum (LSJ): ὡσεὶ κ. λευκὸν ὡσεὶ πάγος ἐπὶ τῆς γῆς 'like white coriander like frost on the ground' Ex 16.14; ὡς σπέρμα ~ου λευκόν 16.31; Nu 11.7, all describing "manna."

I **κόρος**, ου. m. < Heb. כֹּר+

a dry measure, 'homer': Le 27.16 (of barley); Nu 11.32 (of quails).

II **κόρος**, ου. m.ʃ

satiety, overabundance: Es E 3. Cf. κόρος.

κορύνη, ης. f.ʃ

club as weapon: 2K 21.16B. Cf. ῥάβδος.

κόρυς, θος.f.ʃ

helmet: Wi 5.18. Cf. περικεφάλαιος.

κορυφή, ῆς. f.

highest spot: βουνοῦ 'of a hill' Ex 17.9 (of strategic importance); τοῦ ὄρους 'of the mountain' 19.20, Nu 14.40, τοῦ Καρμήλου Am 1.2; difficult of access, 9.3; ὀρέων Nu 23.9; site for pagan cultic practices, ἐπὶ τὰς ~ὰς τῶν ὀρέων ἐθυσίαζον καὶ ἐπὶ τοὺς βουνοὺς ἔθυον 'they sacrificed on the mountain tops and on the hills ..' Ho 4.13; of hum. body, ἀπὸ ἴχνους τῶν ποδῶν σου ἕως τῆς ~ῆς σου 'from the sole of your feet to the crown of your head' De 28.35, cf. 33.16 (ll κεφαλή), Ez 8.3; τριχός 'hairy (crown)' Ps 67.22 (ll κεφαλή); κεφαλῆς understood, Pr 1.9 (ll κ. 4.9). **b**. *the farthest end*: δακτύλου 'fingertip,' reinforced with ἄκρος 4M 10.7.

Cf. κεφαλή, ὕψος: Schmidt 1.361-9.

κορώνη, ης. f.ʃ

crow: Je 3.2, Ep Je 54. Cf. κόραξ.

κόσκινον, ου. n.ʃ

sieve: Si 27.4.

κοσμέω: fut. κοσμήσω, inf. κοσμήσειν; aor. ἐκόσμησα, inf. κοσμῆσαι, impv. κόσμησον, pass. ἐκοσμήθην, subj.mid. κοσμήσωμαι; pf.ptc.pass. κεκοσμημένος.

1. *to adorn, beautify*: τίς κοσμήσω πόλιν; Mi 6.9; *s* woman, τὴν κεφαλὴν αὐτῆς 4K 9.30*L* (B: ἀγαθύνω); ***o*** woman and pass., τῷ ἱματισμῷ καὶ παντὶ τῷ κόσμῳ τῷ γυναικείῳ Ju 12.15, χρυσίῳ καὶ ἀργυρίῳ Ez 16.13; idols, ἐνδύμασι 'with garments' Ep Je 10; dining-table (τράπεζα) Ez 23.41, cf. κόσμησον τράπεζαν Si 29.26; temple, τὸν οἶκον λίθοις τιμίοις εἰς δόξαν 2C 3.6, καλλίστοις ἀναθήμασι 'with most beautiful offerings' 2M 9.16; banquet hall, βυσσίνοις 'with linen fabrics' Es 1.6 o'; καιρούς 'festival days' Si 47.10 (with music and other events: Segal ad loc.); a priest's turban, ἐπιθυμήματα ὀφθαλμῶν κοσμούμενα 'adorned as a delight to the eyes' 45.12, cf. κεκοσμημένον παντὶ λίθῳ πολυτελεῖ 'with every precious stone' 50.9; of craftsmanship, 38.28; the created universe, 16.27; *o* συναναστροφήν 'life-style' 3M 3.5. **b.** mid.: *s* woman, κόσμῳ χρυσῷ Je 4.30; Ez 23.40.

2. *to set and arrange in orderly manner*: *o* God's creative work, τὰ ἔργα αὐτοῦ Si 16.27, τὰ μεγάλαια τῆς σοφίας αὐτοῦ 42.21, προσφορὰν ὑψίστου 'the offering to the Most High' 50.14.

Cf. κόσμος, δια~, περικοσμέω: Spicq 2.330-5.

κόσμιον, ου. n.ʃ

exquisite set: παραβολῶν 'of parables' Ec 12.9.

κοσμοπληθής, ές.ʃ *

affecting the whole world: *s* κατακλυσμός 'flood' 4M 15.31.

κοσμοποιΐα, ας. f.ʃ

making of the universe: 4M 14.7.

κόσμος, ου. m.

1. *ordered whole consisting of multiple units*: physical universe, πᾶς ὁ κ. αὐτῶν 'the entire universe comprised by them [= ὁ οὐρανὸς καὶ ἡ γῆ) Ge 2.1, cf. Alexandre 212-4; subsidiary components of the universe beside the heaven and the earth, Od 12.2; object of worship, τὸν ἥλιον καὶ τὴν σελήνην καὶ τοὺς ἀστέρας καὶ πάντα τὸν ~ον τοῦ οὐρανοῦ De 4.19, sim. 17.3; ὅλος ὁ κ. τῶν χρημάτων 'the whole lot of material resources around' Pr 17.6a. **b.** *the created world*: θάνατος εἰσῆλθεν εἰς τὸν ~ον Wi 2.24; most likely focused on humans, 2M 3.12. **c.** *set order of liturgy*: Si 50.19. Cf. δύναμις **3** and στρατιά.

2. *act of adorning, decorating*: κ. αὐτῆς Na 2.10. **b.** *that which adorns*: ‖ δόξα Pr 20.29.

3. sg. coll. *ornaments* such as jewellery: τὰς στολὰς τῶν δοξῶν καὶ τὸν ~ον 'the stately robes and ornaments' Ex 33.5; κ. προσώπων 'cosmetics (for women's make-up)' Is 3.19, τοῦ ~ου τῆς κεφαλῆς τοῦ χρυσίου 3.24, σύνθεσις τοῦ ~ου τῆς δόξης 'a wardrobe of glorious dresses (for ladies)' or 'an assortment of glorious cosmetic accessories' 3.20, νύμφης 'of a bride' 49.18, χρύσεος Si 6.30, ἐκλεκτὰ ~ου 'choice ornaments' Ez 7.20; as cogn. dat., ἐκόσμου ~ῳ 23.40, ~ῳ χρυσῷ Je 4.30; glorious cityscape, Ju 1.14 (:: ὄνειδος 'disgrace'). **b.** pl.: τὴν δόξαν τοῦ ἱματισμοῦ αὐτῶν καὶ τοὺς ~ους αὐτῶν Is 3.18; χρυσέων ~ων 'of golden ..' 2M 5.3. Cf. δακτύλιος, ἐνώτιον, φιλόκοσμος, χλιδών, ψέλιον.

Cf. κοσμέω, κοσμοπληθής, κοσμοφορέω: Sasse, *TDNT* 3.880-3; Finkelberg; Görg 123f.

κοσμοφορέω.ʃ *

to carry the world: *s* Noah's ark, 4M 15.31. Cf. κόσμος.

κόσυμβος, ου. m.ʃ *

fringe: decorative part of a garment, τῶν χιτώνων ἐκ βύσσου 'of the linen tunics' Ex 28.35; Is 3.18. Cf. κροσσωτός, λῶμα.

κοσυμβωτός, ή, όν.ʃ *

tasselled: *s* χιτών 'tunic' (priestly garment) Ex 28.4. Cf. κόσυμβος, κροσσωτός.

κοτύλη, ης. f.

liquid measure, ca. 0.5 litre: ἐλαίου Le 14.10; δέκα ~αι εἰσι γόμορ Ez 45.14.

κουρά, ᾶς. f.

wool shorn, 'fleece': a cultic offering, προβάτων De 18.4, ἀμνῶν Jb 31.20. Cf. κείρω, πρωτοκουρά.

κουρεύς, έως. m.

barber: Ez 5.1. Cf. κείρω.

κουφίζω: fut. κουφιῶ; aor.subj. κουφίσω, impv. κούφισον, pass.inf. ~ισθῆναι.

to lighten of load: abs., ἀπὸ τῆς δουλείας .. τῆς σκληρᾶς 'of the heavy bondage' 3K 12.4 (‖ 2C 10.4 ἀφίημι), ἀπὸ τοῦ κλοιοῦ 'the collar (of bondage)' 3K 12.9; ἀφ' ἡμῶν 12.10, ἐφ' ἡμᾶς 12.24pB; pass. κουφισθῆναι ἀπ' αὐτῶν 'so as to be lightened of them, i.e. cargo' Jn 1.5; pass., εἰς ἡμέραν ἀπωλείας Jb 21.30 (so that he may hasten ..?). **b.** *to lighten* a burden *by carrying* for sbd else: + acc., τὴν ἔνδυσιν αὐτῆς 'her robes' Es D 4 o'. **c.** metaph., *to lighten* a burden *by lifting and removing*: abs., ἀπό σου 'lighten your burden' Ex 18.22; + acc., τὰς ἁμαρτίας ἡμῶν 1E 8.83; τὴν χεῖρα αὐτοῦ ἀφ' ὑμῶν 1K 6.5, cf. βαρύνω **2 b**.

Cf. κοῦφος, ἐπικουφίζω, βαρύνω.

κοῦφος, η, ον.

1. *light-footed, nimble*: *s* hum., Is 18.2, τοῖς ποσίν 2K 2.18; fast-moving animals, 30.16[1] (‖ ἵππος), eagles, La 4.19; gazelles, 1C 12.9; subst., soldier and ‖ ἰσχυρός Je 26.6. **b.** καρδίᾳ 'thoughtless' Si 19.3.

2. *light in weight*: *s* νεφέλη 'cloud' Is 19.1, πνεῦμα 'air' Wi 5.11.

3. *easy for execution*: 4K 3.18, Si 11.21.

4. *of little consequence, trivial*: 1K 18.23.

Cf. κουφίζω, subs., χαῦνος, βαρύς, σκληρός, χαλεπός: Shipp 338.

κούφως.ʃ

nimbly and unencumbered: of movement, ταχὺ κ. ἔρχονται Is 5.26. Cf. prec., βαρέως: Chadwick 67.

κόφινος, ου. m.

basket: Ps 80.7; Jd 6.19B (A: κανοῦν). Cf. ἄγγος, θῖβις, κανοῦν.

κόχλαξ, ηκος. m.ʃ *

pebble in river-bed: + λίθος 1K 14.14, 1M 10.73. Cf. λίθος, ψῆφος.

κραδαίνω: aor.ptc. κραδάνας.ʃ

to hold and move vigorously in various directions: + acc., weapons, 2M 11.8; ἔνθεν καὶ ἔνθεν .. ὡς κάλαμον 'on this side and that .. as a reed' 3M 2.22. Cf. ἐκτινάσσω: Schmidt 3.135f.

κράζω: impf. ἐκέκραγον Is 6.3 (‖ ἔλεγον) (poss. aor.: Thack. 273); fut. κεκράξομαι (κράξομαι v.l.:

cf. Helbing, *Gram.* 90f.); aor. ἐκέκραξα v.l. ἔκραξα (cf. Helbing, ib.), impv. κέκραξον, ptc. κεκράξας, subj. κεκράξω; pf. κέκραγα, inf. κεκραγέναι, ptc. κεκραγώς.

to emit loud vocal sound, 'shout': appealing for help, abs. Ex 22.23, Hb 1.2, Zc 7.13; * + acc. pers. (= God), Ho 8.2, Ps 118.146, 129.1; πρὸς Φαραω περὶ ἄρτων Ge 41.55; πρὸς κύριον Mi 3.4, Jl 1.14; ἐν ὅλῃ καρδίᾳ μου Ps 118.145; φωνῇ μου 141.2 (‖ δέομαι), cf. τῆς φωνῆς μου, ἧς ἐκέκραξα 26.7; μέγα Je 4.5, πικρόν 'bitterly' Ez 27.31; contents given by οὕτως, Mi 3.4; by direct speech, Jl 1.14; διὰ τοὺς θλίβοντας αὐτούς 'on account of their oppressors' Is 19.20; for pain, 65.14 (‖ ὀλολύζω), *s* πόλις 14.31 (‖ ὀλολύζω), ‖ βοάω, δίδωμι φωνήν Je 22.20, ‖ ἀλαλάζω 29.2, 30.3; lions beside their prey, 31.4; donkey, Jb 6.5; crow at the dawn, 3M 5.23. Cf. βοάω, θρηνέω, ὀλολύζω, ἀνακράζω, κραυγή, κραυγάζω: Schmidt 1.129f.; Stauffer, *TDNT* 1.625-8, Grundmann ib. 3.898-900.

κραιπαλάω: aor.impv. ~πάλησον; pf.ptc. κεκραιπαληκώς.ʃ

to be intoxicated: *s* hum., μεθύων καὶ κραπαλῶν Is 24.20, οὐκ ἀπὸ σικερα οὐδ' ἀπὸ οἴνου 29.9; Ps 77.65. Cf. μεθύω, μεθύσκω, οἰνοφλυγέω: Trench 227.

κρᾶμα, ατος. n.ʃ

mixed drink: wine, Ct 7.3.

κρανίον, ου. n.ʃ

skull: Jd 9.53, 4K 9.35.

κράσπεδον, ου. n.

tassel on the four corners of an outer garment: ποιησάτωσαν ἑαυτοῖς ~α ἐπὶ τὰ πτερύγια τῶν ἱματίων αὐτῶν 'Let them make themselves tassels on the hems of their garments' Nu 15.38; ἐπιλάβωνται τοῦ ~ου ἀνδρὸς Ἰουδαίου 'Take hold of the tassel of a Jew' Zc 8.23. Cf. LSG s.v. Cf. κρασσός.

κραταιός, ά, όν.

1. *possessed with might*: ἐὰν μὴ μετὰ χειρὸς ~ᾶς 'unless with brute force' Ex 3.19; ἐν χειρὶ ~ᾷ .. καὶ ἐν βραχίονι ὑψηλῷ 6.1 (of Pharaoh's action); divine power, ἐν χειρὶ ~ᾷ ἐξήγαγέν σε κύριος ἐξ Αἰγύπτου 13.9; τὴν ἰσχύν σου καὶ τὴν δύναμίν σου καὶ τὴν χεῖρα τὴν ~ὰν καὶ τὸν βραχίονα τὸν ὑψηλόν De 3.24; *s* βασιλεύς Ps 135.18, βοηθός 70.7; σκέπη 'protection' Si 6.14 (‖ ἰσχύος vs. 29), δύναμις 46.5; + δυνατός Ps 23.8; ἐν πολέμῳ Si 46.1; subst. ὁ κ. οὐ μὴ κρατήσῃ τῆς ἰσχύος αὐτοῦ Am 2.14 (‖ μαχητής).

2. *intense in effect*: ἀγάπησιν ~ὰν ἰσχύος αὐτοῦ 'intense love of his power' Hb 3.4, ~ὰ ὡς θάνατος ἀγάπη Ct 8.6; *s* ἀρρωστία 'illness' 3K 12.24g, λιμός 'famine' 18.2, πόλεμος 'battle' 2K 11.15; God's word, 22.31.

Cf. δυνατός, ἰσχυρός, κραταιότης, κραταιῶς, παντοκράτωρ: Passoni Dell'Acqua 1982.192-4.

κραταιότης, ητος. f.ʃ *

physical *strength*: ἐταράχθησαν τὰ ὄρη ἐν τῇ ~ητι αὐτοῦ 'the mountains shook in his might' Ps 45.4. Cf. κραταιός, κράτος, δύναμις, ἰσχύς.

κραταιόω: fut. κραταιώσω; aor. ἐκραταίωσα, inf. κραταιῶσαι, impv. κραταίωσον, subj. κραταιώσω, pass. ἐκραταιώθην, subj. κραταιωθῶ, impv.3s κραταιωθήτω; pf.pass. κεκραταίωμαι.*

1. *to make strong*: *o* τὴν θάλασσαν Ps 73.13; pers. and pass., La 1.16, Ps 37.20; hum. heart, 26.14, 30.25, cf. κατισχύω **I 1**. **b**. *to lend support to*, moral or material: τινα Si 24.24¶, 2K 11.25B; βεδεκ 'part of a building in bad repair' 4K 12.6, 22.6 (‖ vs. 5 κατισχύω); pass. Ps 9.20, Da 5.20 TH. **c**. pass. *to prove to be (too) strong*: abs. κραταιούμενα 'very difficult questions' Da 5.12 TH (LXX ὑπέρογκα), ἐν πολέμῳ Ju 1.13; ἐπί τινα Jd 3.10, ὑπέρ τινα 1K 17.50*L* (B: act.), 2K 10.11 (*L* κρατέω) (poss. **2**). **d**. *to add to the intensity of*: + acc., ἔλεος Ps 102.11, πόλεμον 2K 11.25. **e**. idiom., τὰς χεῖράς τινος 'to help and support sbd' 1K 23.16, 2E 6.12, pass. "they felt encouraged" Ne 2.18, cf. ἐπισχύω.

2. *to commit oneself firmly* to a course of action: abs. and foll. by καί and a verb. fin., 2C 23.1; + acc. rei, ἑαυτοῖς λόγον πονηρόν Ps 63.6. **b**. mid., + inf., κραταιοῦται .. τοῦ πορεύεσθαι 'insists on going (or: is determined to go)' Ru 1.18, 2C 35.22; syndetically, κραταιοῦ καὶ ποίησον 'Take a firm action' 2E 10.4 (‖ ἰσχὺν ποιέω 1E 8.91); + ὀχυροῦμαι 1M 1.62.

3. *to establish a firm relationship with*: + acc. pers., σεαυτῷ Ps 79.16, 18.

4. *to have* or *gain the upper hand*: Jb 36.22¶; militarily, ἐφ' ἡμᾶς 2K 11.23B (*L*: κατακρατέω), ὑπὲρ ἡμᾶς 3K 21.23. **b**. pass.: τὸ ῥῆμα τὸ τοῦ βασιλέως ἐκραταιώθη ἐπὶ τῷ Ιωαβ 'the king's argument carried the day as against J.' 1C 21.4 (‖ 2K 24.4*L* κατακρατέω, B: ὑπερισχύω); "the battle had gone against him for him to handle it (ὑπὲρ αὐτόν)" 4K 3.26*L* (B: act.).

Cf. ἐπικραταιόω, κρατέω, ἐπιρρωνύω.

κραταίωμα, ατος. n.

strength: *s* κύριος Ps 24.14; ‖ ὑπερασπιστής 27.8, + καταφυγή 30.4. Cf. κράτος.

κραταιῶς. adv.ʃ

by applying considerable force: to punish, Pr 22.3. **b**. w. ref. to heated dispute: Jd 8.1A (B: ἰσχυρῶς); unilateral action, 1K 2.16; παίω 'hitting (hard on battlefield)' PSol 8.15. Cf. κράτος, βιαίως, ἰσχυρῶς.

κραταίωσις, εως.f ʃ *

strength: *s* people, Ps 59.9; divine gift, + δύναμις 67.36; bodily, Ju 7.22. Cf. κράτος.

κρατέω: fut.act. κρατήσω; aor. ἐκράτησα, inf. κρατῆσαι, ptc. κρατήσας, impv. κράτησον, subj. κρατήσω, pass. ἐκρατήθην, ptc. κρατηθείς; pf. κεκράτηκα, inf. κεκρατηκέναι, ptc.pass. κεκρατημένος; plpf.3s κεκρατήκει.

1. *to lay hold of, grasp*: + gen., τῆς χειρὸς αὐτοῦ Ge 19.16, ὀσφύος 'waist' Na 2.2; σκυτάλης 'staff' (to lean on for support) 2K 3.29; + acc., κράτησον τῇ χειρί σου αὐτό 'with your hand' Ge 21.18, τόξον 'bow' Je 6.23, γνῶσιν Si 21.14 (*s* ἀγγεῖον 'container'); ‖ ἐπιλαμβάνομαι To 6.4, Jd 16.21. **b**. fig.: κρατήσει ἡ δικαιοσύνη ἀνάπαυσιν 'righteousness will gain permanency' Is 32.17.

2. *to have at one's disposal*: + gen. ὁ κραταιὸς οὐ μὴ κρατήσῃ τῆς ἰσχύος αὐτοῦ 'the mighty will not have use of his (own) strength' Am 2.14; Hb 1.10.

3. *to have* or *gain control over*: following a military action and + gen., πόλεων De 2.34, 3.4 (cities which they had captured [ἐλάβομεν]), Da 11.43 LXX (TH κυριεύω), γῆς Pr 8.16, ὀργῆς 'anger' 16.32, ^γλώσσης^ 18.21, ‖ λαμβάνω, κατακρατέω 1M 15.33; pass. *o* cities, Ju 5.18, sim. Jo 18.1; + acc., χώραν 1E 4.50; metaph., "arrogance dominated them" Ps 72.6; ἀγνωσίᾳ κεκρατημένος 'overcome by ignorance' 3M 5.27. **b**. *to gain possession of, acquire*: + gen., αἰσθήσεως 'comprehension' Pr 14.18. **c**. *to lord it over*: + gen. pers., Ne 5.16; ὁ κρατῶν 'one who is in power' 2M 4.50, Wi 14.19. **d**. *to gain the upper hand*: on battlefield, ὑπέρ τινα 'over..' 1C 19.12 ‖ 2K 10.11*L* (B: κραταιόομαι); ὑπὲρ αὐτήν 'overpowered her' 2K 13.14*L* (B: κραταιόω) (of a rape). **e**. *to compel*: τινα + inf., 4K 4.8.

4. *to hold fast to* as valuable: + acc., the book of divine rules, Ba 4.1 (:: καταλείπω); of attitude, + *ἐν - ἐν φόβῳ κυρίου Si 27.3. **b**. *to retain without letting go of*: + gen., Jd 7.8 A.

5. *to remain strong, retain strength* or *gain strength*: *s* χεῖρες Ez 22.14 (‖ ὑφίστημι), 2K 16.21*L* (B: ἐνισχύω), Pr 12.24.

6. *to lend support to*, 'to shore up': + acc. rei, βεδεκ 'part of a building in bad repair' 4K 12.6 (*L* κραταιόω); Ne 3.6.

Cf. κατα~, περικρατέω, κράτησις, κραταιόω, δράσσομαι, λαμβάνω, ἐπιλαμβάνομαι **1**. Sense **1**. is poss. *; see LSJ, s.v. **IV**; Shipp 339f.

κρατήρ, ῆρος. m.

hollow bowl: as receptacle of blood of sacrificial animals, Ex 24.6; component of lampstand, Ex 25.30, 32, 33. **b**. vessel for mixing wine with water: Pr 9.2; by metonymy, *drinking party* 9.3. **c**. *object resembling hollow bowl*: w. ref. to a woman's navel, Ct 7.3

Cf. ἀναλημπτήρ, ὁλκεῖον, σκάφη, τρύβλιον, φιάλη.

κράτησις, εως. f.ʃ *

being possessed of supreme political and military *power*: of rulers and kings, Wi 6.3 (‖ δυναστεία). Cf. κρατέω.

κράτιστος.⇒ κρείσσων.

κράτος, ους. n.

1. *physical force*: συνετρίβη μετὰ ~ους Ge 49.24; τῆς χειρός μου De 8.17 (‖ ἰσχύς); + ἰσχύς Jb 12.16, Pr 27.24 (hum.), Da 11.1 TH. **b**. hostile: κ. ^τοῦ θεοῦ^ καὶ θυμὸς αὐτοῦ 2E 8.22.

2. *authority*: κ. καὶ οἰκονομία '.. and stewardship' Is 22.21; βασιλεὺς πάντων ~ῶν, a title of God, Es C 2 o' (*L* παντοκράτωρ).

Cf. κραταιός, κρατέω, κραταίωμα, κραταιῶς, κραταίωσις, δύναμις, εὐδράνεια, ἰσχύς, ῥώμη, σθένος, ἀσθένεια, ἀκρατής: Schmidt 3.667-70.

κρατύνω: aor.ptc.pass. κρατυνθείς.ʃ

to confirm the validity or *veracity of*: pass., *o* τὸ ἀσεβὲς ἔθος 'the ungodly custom' Wi 14.16.

κραυγάζω: aor. ἐκραύγασα.ʃ

to shout: *s* hum. (crowd), φωνῇ μεγάλῃ 2E 3.13; animal, To 2.13 𝔊^{I} (𝔊^{II} κράζω). Cf. κράζω.

κραυγή, ῆς. f.

emission of loud sound: of hum. voice, κ. Σοδόμων καὶ Γομόρρας 'against S. and G.' Ge 18.20 (cf. Harl ad loc.); κακίας (gen.) Jn 1.2; ‖ φωνή, and for help out of distress, 2.3, ‖ κλαυθμός Is 65.19, + κλ. 1E 5.60; of war-cry, μετὰ ~ῆς 'amid war-cry' Am 1.14; 2.2 (‖ μετὰ φωνῆς σάλπιγγος); of soldiers assailing cities, ἡμέρα σάλπιγγος καὶ ~ῆς ἐπὶ τὰς πόλεις Zp 1.16; φωνὴ ~ῆς 1.10; πολέμου Je 4.19; μεγάλη Ex 11.6, 12.30; demanding justice, Is 5.7; ‖ ἀλαλαγμός Je 20.16; of waves of the sea, 38.36; + κοπετός, πένθος 'chest-beating, mourning' Es 4.3 o'. Cf. κράζω, βοή, ἀλάλαγμα, ἀλαλαγμός, ὀλολυγμός.

κρέαγρα, ας. f.

flesh-hook for picking meat out of a pot: Ex 27.3; made of copper, 38.23; three-pronged, 1K 2.13.

κρεανομέω: aor. ἐκρεανόμησα.ʃ

to divide the flesh of: + acc. (sacrificial animal), κατὰ μέλη 'limb by limb' Le 8.20.

κρέας, n., pl. κρέα, gen. κρεῶν.

1. *meat*: **a**. as food, κ. εἰς χύτραν Mi 3.3 (‖ σάρξ); τὰ κρέα τῶν ἐκλεκτῶν καταφάγεται 'he will devour the meat of choice sheep' Zc 11.16; θηριάλωτον 'caught by wild beasts' Ex 22.31; + ἄρτος 16.3. **b**. as cultic offering: of sacrificial animals, Ex 29.14, Ho 8.13, ταύρων 'of bulls' Ps 49.13; κ. ἅγιον Hg 2.12, Je 11.15. **c**. exceptionally w. ref. to human flesh of soldiers fallen in a battlefield, but as food for swords, cf. Engl. *cannon-fodder*: ἡ μάχαιρά μου καταφάγεται κρέα De 32.42 (‖ αἷμα); κ. ὁσίων σου καὶ αἷμα αὐτῶν 1M 7.17.

2. *flesh as a component of human body*: + δέρμα 'skin' Jb 10.11.

Cf. σάρξ, σῶμα: Scharbert 1972.121-4.

κρείσσων, ον, spelled also ~ττ~: pl.m.nom., ~ους, n.pl. nom., ~ω, superl. κράτιστος. Extremely frequent in the wisdom literature (Pr and Si).

1. *superior* or *the best* in quality: τὰς κρατίστας ἐκ πασῶν τῶν βασιλειῶν τούτων 'the best of all these kingdoms' Am 6.2; *s* military leader, Jd 11.25A (B: ἀγαθώτερος); drinking glass, Ps 23.5; gift, 2M 3.2; weapon, 3M 1.2.

2. *more* or *the most advantageous*: κρεῖσσον ἡμᾶς δουλεύειν τοῖς Αἰγυπτίοις ἢ ἀποθανεῖν ἐν τῇ ἐρήμῳ ταύτῃ 'it's better for us to serve the Egyptians than to die in this wilderness' Ex 14.12; + dat. comm., κρεῖσσον ἡμῖν γενηθῆναι ... 'it is better for us to become ..' Ju 7.27; || βελτίων Pr 8.19.

3. *more* or *the most preferable*: Pr 12.9; κρεῖσσον τὸ ἔλεός σου ὑπὲρ ζωάς 'your mercy is better than a life many times over' Ps 62.3; κρεῖσσον εἷς ἢ χίλιοι 'one is better than a thousand' Si 16.3; οὐθὲν κρεῖττον φόβου κυρίου 'nothing is better than the fear of the Lord' 23.27.

Cf. ἀγαθός, καλός, βελτίων, ἄριστος, χείρων: Schmidt 4.294-6, 304f.

κρείττων.⇒ κρείσσων.

κρεμάζω, κρεμάω: pres.pass.3s κρέμαται, ptc. κρεμάμενος; fut. κρεμάσω; aor. ἐκρέμασα, subj. κρεμάσω, inf. κρεμάσαι, ptc. κρεμάσας, impv. κρέμασον, pass. ἐκρεμάσθην, inf. κρεμασθῆναι, impv.3s κρεμασθήτω; pf.inf.pass. κεκρεμάσθαι.

tr. *to hang, suspend*: + acc. pers. and as punishment, κρεμάσει σε ἐπὶ ξύλου Ge 40.19, corpse of a criminal sentenced to death De 21.22; pass. κεκατηραμένος ὑπὸ θεοῦ πᾶς κρεμάμενος ἐπὶ ξύλου 'everyone hanged on a tree is accursed by God' 21.23; + acc. rei, πέλτας καὶ περικεφαλαίας 'shields and helmets' Ez 27.10; *o* musical instrument, Ps 136.2 (ἐπί τινι); τούτων ἐκ μαστῶν κρεμάσαντες τὰ βρέφη 'making the babes hang at their breasts' 2M 6.10, ἐν χερσίν 'with hands tied or nailed' La 5.12; fig. ἔσται ἡ ζωή σου κρεμαμένη ἀπέναντι τῶν ὀφθαλμῶν σου De 28.66 (of a precarious existence), ἐξ ἡμῶν κρέμαται ἡ ψυχὴ αὐτῶν 'their lives depend on us' Ju 8.24. **b**. pass. *to become suspended*: up in a branch above the ground, 2K 18.9B (*L* ἀνα~), ἐπὶ τῷ δένδρῳ 10*L* (B: ἐν τῇ δρυί).

Cf. ἀνακρεμάζω, κρεμαστός: Bertram, *TDNT* 3.915f.

κρεμαστός, ή, όν.

hanging: *s* piece of a building, 3K 7.6. **b**. subst.n., *fortress*: Jd 6.2 B(?).

Cf. κρεμάζω.

κρημνίζω: aor. ἐκρήμνισα.ʃ *

to hurl: + acc., κατὰ τοῦ τείχους 'down the wall' 2M 6.10. Cf. βάλλω.

κρημνός, οῦ.ʃ

cliff: 2C 25.12.

κρήνη, ης. f.

storage facility for water built in the ground, 'cistern': 3K 2.35[e], Si 48.17. Cf. λάκκος, πηγή, φρέαρ: Schmidt 1.628-32; Renehan 1.164f.

κρηπίς, ῖδος. f.

1. *foundation* of built structure: of altar, ἀνὰ μέσον τῆς ~ῖδος καὶ τοῦ θυσιαστηρίου 'between the foundation and the altar' Jl 2.17; 2M 10.26.

2. *bank* of a river: τοῦ Ἰορδάνου 1M 9.43, sim. Jo 3.15. Cf. LSG s.v.

Cf. θεμέλιον: Hauspie 2004.115f.

κριθή, ῆς. f.

barley: γομορ ~ῶν Ho 3.2 (|| οἶνος); κυψέλη ~ῆς 'container for barley' Hg 2.16*a*; || πυρός 'wheat' De 8.8; as cattle food, Jl 1.11, Is 30.24. Cf. κρίθινος, πυρός, σῖτος.

κρίθινος, η, ον.

made from barley: ἄλευρον ~ον 'barley meal' Nu 5.15; *s* ἐγκρυφία 'cake' Ez 4.12, ἄρτος Jd 5.8A. Cf. κριθή.

κρίκος, ου. m.

ring: used to join curtains, Ex 26.6; of a pillar, 27.10; ~ους τῆς σκηνῆς χρυσοῦς 'rings of the tabernacle golden' 38.19; αὐλῆς 'of a court' ib.; of the earth, ἐπὶ τίνος οἱ ~οι αὐτῆς πεπήγασι; 'on what are its rings fastened?' Jb 38.6; serpent's (δράκων) nose-ring, 40.26; κάμψῃς ὡς ~ον τὸν τράχηλόν σου 'you bend your neck like a ring' Is 58.5. Cf. Shipp 342f.

κρίμα, ατος. n.

1. *law-suit, forensic process in law court*: πρὸς ὑμᾶς ἐστι τὸ κ. 'the law-suit is against you' Ho 5.1; ἀποκαταστήσατε ἐν πύλαις κ. 'Reestablish a court at the gate' Am 5.15; Hb 1.4*a* (|| κρίσις 1.3); δικαίωμα ~ατος 'decision reached through juridical process' Nu 35.29 (|| δ. κρίσεως 27.11); κ. δίκαιον κρίνατε καὶ ἔλεος καὶ οἰκτιρμὸν ποιεῖτε Zc 7.9; κ. εἰρηνικὸν κρίνατε 8.16.

2. *sentence* handed down in court: κ. θανάτου 'capital sentence' De 21.22 (|| κρίσις θ. 19.6). **b**. *just, fair decision*: given by God, δώσει κ. αὐτοῦ 'will give out his just decision' Zp 3.5 (opp. ἀδικία), κ. πτωχῶν Jb 36.6¶; ποιέω κ. / ~ατα ἔν τινι 'mete out justice to sbd' Ez 5.10, 15, 11.9, 28.22, 26 (|| ἐκδικήσεις 16.41). **c**. *destiny*: Si 38.22; θανάτου '(sentence) of death' 41.3.

3. *justice as moral quality* or *principle*: ἐν δικαιοσύνῃ καὶ ἐν ~ατι καὶ ἐν ἐλέει καὶ οἰκτιρμοῖς Ho 2.19; μετὰ ~ατος σωθήσεται .. καὶ μετὰ ἐλεημοσύνης Is 1.27, μετὰ δικαιοσύνης .. ἐν ~ατι Je 22.13; ἔλεον καὶ κ. Ho 12.6; ποιεῖν κ. Mi 6.8 (|| ἔλεος), Pr 21.15; κ. ἐργάζεσθε Zp 2.3 (|| δικαιοσύνη); κατεπάτησε κ. 'he trampled justice' Ho 5.11; βδελυσσόμενοι κ. 'loathe justice' Mi 3.9 (|| τὰ ὀρθά); divine, Ps 71.1 (|| δικαιοσύνη), τὸ κ. μου ὡς φῶς ἐξελεύσεται 'my justice will go forth like a light' Ho 6.5; κύριος ὁ ποιῶν .. κ. 'the Lord who acts justly' Am 5.7 (|| δικαιοσύνη); cf. ἐν πνεύματι κυρίου καὶ ~ατος Mi 3.8; ποιήσει τὸ κ. μου 'will act justly for me' 7.9; *s* hum., Je 5.1 (|| ζητέω πίστιν). **b.** *instance conforming to the principle of justice*: statements made in a court, ~ατα λαλήσω Je 12.1.

4. *injunction to be observed*: divine, φυλάξεσθε πάντα τὰ προστάγματά μου καὶ πάντα τὰ ~ατά μου καὶ ποιήσετε αὐτά Le 18.5; αἱ ἐντολαὶ καὶ τὰ δικαιώματα καὶ τὰ ~ατα, ἃ ἐνετείλατο κύριος ἐν χειρὶ Μωυσῆ Nu 36.13; τὰ μαρτύρια καὶ τὰ δικαιώματα καὶ τὰ κ. De 4.45, 6.20, sim. 6.17; Jd 13.12 A (B: κρίσις). **b.** *firm advice to be followed*: Si 41.16.

5. *that which rightfully belongs to sbd*: κρίμα πενήτων 'the just share of the poor' Is 10.2.

6. *fair claim*: σοὶ κ. παραλαβεῖν εἰς κτῆσιν 'you are entitled to take it into possession' Je 39.7, sim. 39.8.

7. *rule of conduct and practice accepted as generally applicable*: κατὰ τὸ κρίμα 'as it should happen' 4K 11.14; 2C 30.16.

Cf. κρίσις, κρίνω, and δικαιοσύνη.

κρίνον, ου. n.

1. *white lily*: ἀνθήσει ὡς κ. 'it will blossom as a lily' Ho 14.6; Ct 2.1.

2. *lily-shaped* (?) *architectural ornament*: Ex 25.30, 3K 7.8.

κρίνω: fut. κρινῶ, pass. κριθήσομαι, ptc. κριθησόμενος; aor. ἔκρινα, 3pl ἐκρίνοσαν, pass. ἐκρίθην, subj.act. κρίνω, inf. κρῖναι, pass. κριθῆναι, ptc. κρίνας, impv.act. κρῖνον, pass. κρίθητι, opt. 3s κρίναι; pf. κέκρικα, pass. κέκριμαι, ptc. κεκριμένος; plpf. ἐκεκρίκειν.

1. act. *to act as judge over*: *s* hum., μετὰ δώρων 'taking gifts' Mi 3.11; + acc. pers., πᾶσαν τὴν γῆν Ge 18.25; τὸν λαόν Ex 18.13, 22; ἐν δικαιοσύνῃ κρινεῖς τὸν πλησίον σου Le 19.15; τοὺς πτωχοὺς ἐν κρίσει Ps 71.2; ἀνὰ μέσον ἡμῶν Ge 31.53; ἀνὰ μέσον λαῶν πολλῶν 'between many peoples' Mi 4.3 (|| ἐλέγχω), sim. Is 2.4; also + cogn. obj., τὸν λαὸν κρίσιν δικαίαν De 16.18; *s* God, ἀνὰ μέσον ἐμοῦ καὶ σοῦ Ge 16.5, πρὸς τοὺς ἀντιδίκους αὐτοῦ 'against His adversaries' Je 27.34, ἀνὰ μέσον κριοῦ πρὸς κριόν Ez 34.22. The collocation with ἀνὰ μέσον is most likely a Heb. calque. **b.** *to act as just judge in the interest of*: + dat. com. μοι Ge 30.6, δικαίοις Si 32.22; and *s* hum., ὀρφανῷ Is 1.17 (|| δικαιόω), ὀρφανῷ καὶ ταπεινῷ Ps 9.39; also + cogn. obj., ταπεινῷ κρίσιν Is 11.4, τὴν κρίσιν τοῦ λαοῦ αὐτοῦ Si 32.25. **c.** problematic cases of conflation of syntagms: κρίνατε ἐν ἐμοὶ καὶ ἀνὰ μέσον τοῦ ἀμπελῶνός μου for 'judge between me and my grape-vine' Is 5.3; κρινῶ ἀνὰ μέσον κριοῦ πρὸς κριόν 'between a ram and a ram' Ez 34.22.

2. *to take up a legal case for*: + acc. pers., *s* God, De 32.36 (|| παρακαλέω pass.), ὀρφανὸν καὶ πτωχόν 'orphans and the poor' Ps 81.3 (|| δικαιόω).

3. *to determine* or *pronounce as a verdict*: + acc. rei, εὐθύτητας 'just decisions' Ps 74.3, εὐθεῖα 57.1, δικαιοσύνην 9.5, ἀδικίαν 81.2, δίκαια Je 11.20; + cogn. obj. κρίμα δίκαιον Zc 7.9; κρίμα εἰρηνικόν 8.16; τὰ κρίματά μου 'verdicts acceptable to me [= God]' Ez 44.24; κρίσιν Ge 19.9, κρίσιν ὀρφανοῦ Je 5.28, κρίσιν ταπεινῷ οὐδὲ κρίσιν πένητος 22.16; κρίσεις ἀδίκους Su 53 TH; + ἐπί τινα Da 9.24 LXX; + ὅτι 1E 3.9, + ἵνα Da 3.96 LXX. **b.** impers. pass.: ὅταν κρίνηται αὐτῷ 'when a verdict over him is pronounced' Ps 36.33. **c.** *to come to a conclusion and present as such*: not juridical, 2E 4.9, πρὸς ταῦτα 'over these matters' Da 2.7 LXX; + an adj. predicate, 2M 13.15, δίκαιον κρίνει τὸν ἄδικον Pr 17.15, sim. 30.12, ὡς πολεμίους .. ἔκρινον 'they began to regard them as hostile' 3M 2.33; impers., ἐὰν .. κρίνηται τῷ κυρίῳ βασιλεῖ 'should his majesty the king so please' 1E 6.21 (|| εἰ κρίνετα, βασιλεῦ vs. 20), ὡς ἐκρίθη σοι 'as it seemed right to you' 8.90, cf. εἰ δοκεῖ τῷ βασιλεῖ καὶ ἀγαθὴ ἡ κρίσις ἐν τῇ καρδίᾳ αὐτοῦ Es 3.9 *L*.

4. *to decide in favour of*: + acc. rei, τὰ φιλάνθρωπα 'humane policy' 1E 8.10; Wi 2.22.

5. *to execute judgement on*: + acc. pers. and pass., "with the fire of the Lord the whole earth will be executed" Is 66.16; + dat. (of punishment), αὐτὸν θανάτῳ καὶ αἵματι καὶ ὑετῷ .. καὶ λίθοις .. Ez 38.22.

6. *to decide*: + inf., Is 41.6, Ju 2.3, 1M 11.33, 2M 6.14, 11.25, 3M 6.30. See LSG s.v. **II 8**. **b.** *to take a decision over*: + acc., τὰ πράγματα 'the businesses of the state' 2M 13.13.

7. *to resolve* a military conflict *by winning it*: + acc., τὸν πόλεμον PSol 8.15.

8. *to interpret*: abs., Da 2.6 LXX, + acc. rei, τὰ ἐνύπνια 'the dreams' 4.15 LXX. **b.** *to assess and form a judgement of*: τινα, *s* God, Jb 7.18; pass., περὶ πορνείας 'over sexual immorality' Si 42.8.

9. mid. *to contest a legal case*: πρός τινα– κρίθητε πρὸς τὴν μητέρα ὑμῶν 'against your mother' Ho 2.2; πρὸς τὰ ὄρη Mi 6.1; + dat., Is 50.8, Jb 9.3; περὶ ἐκείνου 'over that' Ge 26.21. **b.** not necessarily in a court: πρός τινα Jd 21.22.

10. mid. *to debate*: abs., 2K 19.10B, μετά τινος (pers.) Jd 8.1A (B: διαλέγομαι).

Cf. κρίμα, κρίσις, κριτής, κριτήριον, δια~, κατα~, προκρίνω: Schmidt 1.348-60.

κριός, οῦ. m.

1. *uncastrated male sheep*, 'ram': κ. τριετίζοντα 'a three-year-old ram' Ge 15.9; κ. προβάτων 31.38; as food, στέαρ ἀρνῶν καὶ ~ῶν, υἱῶν ταύρων καὶ τράγων 'fat of lambs and rams, of calves and kids' De 32.14, + μόσχος, τράγος Ez 39.18; cultic offering, εἰς ὁλοκαύτωμα Le 16.3; τοῦ ἱλασμοῦ Nu 5.8; Mi 6.7 (ǁ πίων 'fat'), cf. Ge 22.13; ἄμωμος Ex 29.1; κ. πλημμελείας Le 19.21.

2. *battering-ram*: + μηχανή 2M 12.15.

Cf. πρόβατον.

κρίσις, εως. f.

1. *acting as judge*: of God as judge, κ. τῷ κυρίῳ πρὸς τοὺς κατοικοῦντας τὴν γῆν 'the Lord has a case against those who dwell in the land' Ho 4.1, sim. 12.2, Mi 6.2*b*, cf. Ma 3.5*a*; of human judge, Hb 1.3; κ. προσηλύτου 'judgement of an immigrant' Ma 3.5*b*, χηρῶν 'of widows' Is 1.23; as cogn. obj., κρίσιν κρίνειν Ge 19.9; ~ιν ἐκ τῶν ἐχθρῶν μου ποιήσω Is 1.24, sim. Ps 118.84, αἱ ~εις σου ποιῆσαι ἐξ ἐμοῦ περὶ τῶν ἁμαρτιῶν μου To 3.5 𝔊[II], οὐκ ἔκριναν ~ιν ταπεινῷ οὐδὲ ~ιν πένητος Je 22.16, ἐποίησας τὴν ~ιν μου καὶ τὴν δίκην μου Ps 9.5, sim. 139.13.

2. *sentence* handed down in court: κ. θανάτου 'capital sentence' De 19.6 (ǁ κρίμα θ. 21.22); of God's, ἀκούσατε .. τὴν ~ιν τοῦ κυρίου 'Hear the judgement of the Lord' Mi 6.2*a*, θεοῦ Es E 18 o' (*L* δίκη); δικαιώματα καὶ ~εις Ex 15.25, De 4.5; κ. τῶν δήλων 'decision reached by means of ..' Nu 27.21; φυλάξῃ τὰ φυλάγματα αὐτοῦ καὶ τὰ δικαιώματα .. καὶ τὰς ἐντολὰς .. καὶ τὰς ~εις .. De 11.1.

3. *a decision taken* setting out what is to be done: αὕτη ἡ κ. τῶν ἱερέων '.. concerning the priests' De 18.3; Jd 13.12 B (A: κρίμα).

4. *an act of uprightness* or *such a conduct*: ποιεῖν δικαιοσύνην καὶ ~ιν Ge 18.19; *s* God, πᾶσαι αἱ ὁδοὶ αὐτοῦ ~εις De 32.4; social justice, ποιῶν ~ιν προσηλύτῳ .. 10.18; hum., Is 1.17.

5. *moral, ethical integrity*: Is 1.21; + δικαιοσύνη 33.5, + ἀλήθεια 'loyalty' 1M 7.18.

6. *a court proceeding*: ἐνωπίον τοῦ θεοῦ ἐλεύσεται ἡ κ. ἀμφοτέρων 'the case of the two parties shall proceed into the presence of God' Ex 22.9; προσήγαγεν .. τὴν ~ιν αὐτῶν ἔναντι κυρίου 'presented their case to the Lord' Nu 27.5; Ex 23.3; ἐάν τινι συμβῇ κ. 'should someone have a legal case' 24.14; ἡ κ. καθίσεται Da 7.26 LXX (ǁ TH κριτήριον); εἰς ~εις καὶ μάχας 'for the sake of court actions and wrangles' Is 58.4; ἐλάλησεν αὐτῷ μετὰ ~εως 'he arraigned him in a court' Je 52.9.

7. *standing in society*: κατὰ τὴν ~ιν αὐτοῦ 'as befits his status' Si 38.16, cf. κατὰ τὴν ἀξίαν αὐτοῦ vs. 17 and LSG s.v.

8. *interpretation*: ^ἐνυπνίου^ 'of a deram' Da 2.5, 45 LXX (TH σύγκρισις); Ἀνάγγειλον δή μοι τὴν κρίσιν ταύτην 'Tell me, please, what you make of this.' Cf. λύσις.

9. *decisive settling of an issue*: δι' αἱμάτων 'through bloodshed (accompanying armed contests)' 2M 14.18; decisive battle, 15.20.

10. *contention and dispute* calling for a resolutoin: Pr 28.2; + μάχη 'strife' 30.33, Is 58.4; + ἀντιλογία 2K 13.4B (*L* om. ἀ.).

Cf. κρίνω, κρίμα, κριτής, βουλή, μάχη, σύγκρισις.

κριτήριον, ου. n.

court of justice: τοῦ θεοῦ Ex 21.6; κ. ἐκάθισε 'a court sat' Da 7.10; 7.26 TH (ǁ LXX κρίσις), Su 49. Cf. κρίνω.

κριτής, οῦ. m.

one who decides after having considered evidences and data: Wi 15.7. **b.** *judge* in juridical sense: hum., De 16.18 (ǁ γραμματοεισαγωγεύς), Am 2.3, Mi 7.3 (ǁ ὁ ἄρχων); ǁ σύμβουλος Is 1.26; "Judges" - Jd 2.16, 17 (Ra), 18, 19, Ru 1.1, Si 46.11; *s* God, 33.22 (ǁ ἄρχων, βασιλεύς), κ. χηρῶν 'of widows' Ps 67.6, ὁ δίκαιος κ. θεός 2M 12.6; + δικαστής 1K 24.16. **c**. w. ref. to rulers: ἀπὸ ~οῦ καὶ ἄρχοντος Si 41.18, cf. 10.1; ǁ ἡγούμενος 10.2, ǁ βασιλεύς vs. 3.

Cf. κρίνω, δικαστής, δικαιοκρίτης.

κρόκη, ης. f.

woof: Le 13.48. Cf. στήμων.

κροκόδιλος, ου. m.∫

lizard: ritually unclean, Le 11.29.

κρόκος, ου. m.∫ < Heb. כַּרְכֹּם+

saffron: + νάρδος, ǁ κιννάμωμον Ct 4.14; sprinkled on a bed, Pr 7.17.

κρόμμυον, ου. n. On the spelling, see Walters 82.∫

onion: as food, Nu 11.5.

κροσσός, οῦ. m.

tassel, fringe of the high priest's breastplate: συμπεπλεγμένοι 'woven' Ex 28.22. Cf. κροσσωτός, κράσπεδον.

κροσσωτός, ή, όν.∫

tasselled: subst. n.pl. 'tasselled part of a garment' Ex 28.14*a*; πεπλεγμένα 'braided fringes' 28.14*b*; ἐν ~οῖς χρυσοῖς περιβεβλημένη πεποικιλμένη 'wearing a robe decorated with golden tassels and embroidered' Ps 44.14. Cf. κοσυμβωτός.

κρόταφος, ου. m.

side of the forehead, 'temple': Ps 131.4; sg., Jd 4.21B (*AL*: γνάθος). Cf. γνάθος.

κροτέω: fut.act. κροτήσω; aor. ἐκρότησα, impv. κρότησον.

to clap: χεῖρας ἐπὶ σέ 'hands against you (out of malicious joy)' Na 3.19 (a gesture of contempt); and || συρίζω 'to hiss' La 2.15, Jb 27.23¶; out of joy, κροτήσατε χεῖρας Ps 46.2 (|| ἀλαλάζω); χειρί 97.8 (|| ἀγαλλιάομαι), χερσίν 4K 11.12*L*, in both with pl. *s*; malicious joy, τῇ χειρί Ez 6.11, τὴν χεῖρά σου 25.6 (both || [ἐπι]ψοφέω ποδί); *out of grief, κρότησον ἐπὶ τὴν χεῖρά σου 21.12; *indicative of resolve and readiness to act, χεῖρα ἐπὶ χεῖρα 21.14, χεῖρά μου πρὸς χεῖρά μου 21.17, cf. ἐπάγω χεῖρά μου πρὸς χεῖρά μου 22.13. Cf. ἠχέω, ψοφέω, κατα~, συγκροτέω: Schmidt 3.325f.

κρουνηδόν. adv.ʃ *

like a spring, 'gushing forth': *s* blood, 2M 14.45.

κρούω: aor. ἔκρουσα.ʃ

to strike and knock: + acc. rei, αὐλαίαν 'curtain' Ju 14.14, τὴν θύραν 'door' Jd 19.22A, ἐπὶ τὴν θύραν 'the door' ib. B, Ct 5.2. Cf. ἐγ~, κατα~, προσκρούω, κόπτω: Schmidt 3.289-92.

κρυβῇ. adv.ʃ

= κρυπτῶς, κρυφῇ (q.v.): 1K 19.2 (*L* κρυφῇ); 2K 12.12 (:: "in front of all Israel and before this sun"); 3M 4.12. Cf. κρυπτῶς, κρυφῇ.

κρυπτός, ή, όν.

hidden, concealed: ῥῆμα ~ὸν ἐν τῇ καρδίᾳ σου De 15.9; κυρίῳ 29.29 (:: φανερός); opp. ἐμφανής Wi 7.21; subst.s.n. ἐν ~ῷ 'in secret' 2K 12.12*L* (B: κρυβῇ); pl.n. τὰ κρυπτά 'the hidden treasures' Is 22.9, *'hide-outs' Je 29.11, 'esoteric, abstruse matters' Si 3.22 (|| μυστήρια vs. 19). Cf. κρύπτω, κρυπτῶς, κρυφαῖος, μυστήριον, φανερός.

κρύπτω: fut. κρύψω, pass. κρυβήσομαι; aor. ἔκρυψα, subj. κρύψω, impv. κρύψον, inf. κρύψαι, ptc. κρύψας, pass. ἐκρύβην, inf. κρυβῆναι, ptc. κρυβόμενος, impv. κρύβηθι, subj. κρυβῶ; pf. pass. κέκρυμμαι, ptc. κεκρυμμένος.

1. *to hide, conceal*: abs. Nu 5.13; + acc. αἷμα Ge 37.26, ἀδικήματα 'keep a lid on sbd else's deeds of injustice' Pr 17.9; ὁδόν Ho 6.9; ἀπὸ Αβρααμ .. ἃ ἐγὼ ποιῶ Ge 18.17; ears, μὴ κρύψῃς τὰ ὦτά σου εἰς τὴν δέησίν μου 'to my entreaty' La 3.56; face, τὸ πρόσωπον αὐτοῦ ἀφ' ὑμῶν To 13.6; + double acc., σε βουλήν Jb 42.3. **b**. pass., mostly not hidden deliberately, but *to be invisible, unknowable*: παράκλησις κέκρυπται ἀπὸ ὀφθαλμῶν μου 'consolation is hidden from my eyes' Ho 13.14, "his hidden treasures (τὰ κεκρυμμένα) were seized" Ob 6, ἀπὸ πετεινῶν τοῦ οὐρανοῦ ἐκρύβη Jb 28.21¶ (*s* wisdom, || λανθάνω), αἱ πλημμέλειαί μου ἀπὸ σοῦ οὐκ ἐκρύβησαν 'my wrongdoings did not go unnoticed by you' Ps 68.6; ἀπὸ τῆς γνώσεως σου 'from your knowledge' PSol 9.3; ἀπέναντι τῶν ὀφθαλμῶν μου Je 16.17. **c**. pass. also used as mid. with reflexive force, *to go into hiding, be in hiding*: ἀπὸ προσώπου τοῦ κυρίου .. ἐν μέσῳ τοῦ ξύλου Ge 3.8, ἀπὸ τοῦ προσώπου σου '(to disappear) from your sight' Si 6.12; ἀπὸ σοῦ De 7.20; εἰς τὴν γῆν ἀπὸ προσώπου τοῦ φόβου κυρίου Is 2.10, τόπος τοῦ κρυβῆναι τοὺς ποιοῦντας τὰ ἄνομα 'a hiding-place for those who do unlawful things' Jb 34.22.

2. *to keep in the dark* by withholding information: + acc. pers., Jb 38.2; and an epexegetical inf., ἔκρυψεν Ιακωβ Λαβαν .. τοῦ μὴ ἀναγγεῖλαι αὐτῷ .. Ge 31.20; ἀναγγείλατε .. ἀκουστὰ ποιήσατε καὶ μὴ κρύψητε Je 27.2; + τινά τι, Jb 15.18.

3. *to store* as valuable: + acc., ἐν τῇ καρδίᾳ μου .. τὰ λόγιά σου Ps 118.11.

Cf. ἀποκαλύπτω, ἀπο~, ἐγ~, κατα~, συγ~, συναποκρύπτω, κρυφαῖος, κρυπτός, κρυπτῶς, κρυφός, κατορύσσω, λανθάνω, στέγω: Shipp 343; Oepke, *TDNT* 3.958f.

κρυπτῶς. adv.ʃ

in secret, unnoticed by others: ἐκάλεσεν .. κ. 'summoned ..' To 12.6; 1M 10.79. Cf. κρυβῇ, κρυπτός, κρυφαίως, κεκρυμμένως, λάθρᾳ, μυστικῶς.

κρυσταλλοειδής, ές.ʃ

crystal-like: Wi 19.21. Cf. κρύσταλλος.

κρύσταλλος, ου. m.

1. *ice*: κ. πεπηγώς 'congealed ice' Jb 6.16, cf. Si 43.20; cold, Ps 147.6, cf. Wi 16.22; χάλαζα, χιών, κ. 'hail, snow, ice' 148.8.

2. *rock-crystal*: Nu 11.7; λίθους ~ου Is 54.12.

Cf. κρυσταλλοείδης.

κρυφαῖος, α, ον.ʃ

hidden and not observable: ἐν ~ᾳ χειρί Ex 17.16; *s* ἁμαρτήματα 'sins' Wi 17.3. **b**. subst.n.pl. 'hidden place(s)': εἰ κρυβήσεταί τις ἐν ~οις, καὶ ἐγὼ οὐκ ὄψομαι αὐτόν 'if someone hides in secret places ..' Je 23.24, ἄρκος ἐνεδρεύουσα .. λέων ἐν ~οις 'a bear lying in ambush .. a lion in secret places' La 3.10. Cf. κρύπτω, κρυπτός, κρυφαίως.

κρυφαίως. adv.ʃ

in secret, unnoticed by others: ἠρώτα 'asked' Je 44.17; 47.15. Cf. κρύπτω, κρυφαῖος, κρυφῇ, κρυπτῶς, λάθρᾳ, λεληθότως.

κρυφῇ. adv.

avoiding the key person's attention, 'secretly, by stealth': κ. ἀπέδρας 'you ran away ..' Ge 31.26; λάλησον κ. εἰς τὰ ὦτα τοῦ λαοῦ Ex 11.2; καταφάγεται .. κ. De 28.57. *Also ἐν ~ῇ Is 29.15, 45.19; Jd 4.21 B (A: ἡσυχῇ), Ps.138.15. Cf. κρύπτω, κρυφαίως, λάθρᾳ, παρρησία.

κρύφιος, α, ον.

hidden: *s* ἄρτοι Pr 9.17; λόγος 'matter' Jd 3.19; subst.m. ~ε 'Mr so and so!' Ru 4.1; n.pl., *secrets* Ps

9 tit., τῆς καρδίας 43.22; hidden transgressions, 18.13; τῆς σοφίας 50.8 (+ ἄδηλος).

κρυφός, οῦ. m.

hiding-place: 1M 1.53; ἐν τῇ ἐρήμῳ 2.31. Cf. κρύπτω.

κτάομαι: fut. κτήσομαι, pass. κτηθήσομαι; aor. ἐκτησάμην, impv. κτῆσαι, ptc. κτησάμενος, subj. κτήσωμαι, impv. κτῆσαι, inf. κτήσασθαι; pf. κέκτημαι, ptc. κεκτημένος.

1. *to procure for oneself, acquire*: abs. Ru 4.4; + acc. *o* pers. ἄνθρωπον Ge 4.1 (by giving birth to, so in Eur. *Iph. T.* 696); ἡμᾶς καὶ τὴν γῆν ἡμῶν ἀντὶ ἄρτων 'in return for food' Ge 47.19; wife, Ru 4.5; ὁ λαός σου Ex 15.16; παῖδα 'domestic servant' 21.2; δοῦλον καὶ δούλην Le 25.44; ἐν ἀργυρίῳ πτωχοὺς καὶ ταπεινὸν ἀντὶ ὑποδημάτων Am 8.6; φίλον Si 6.7; τὰ ὑπάρχοντα 'possessions' Ge 12.5; σπήλαιον 'cave' 25.10 (as burial ground); τὴν μερίδα τοῦ ἀγροῦ .. παρὰ Εμμωρ 'the portion of the field .. from Hamor' 33.19; ψυχήν 'domestic staff(?)' ib.; sheep, Zc 11.5, ox Is 1.3 (|| κύριος); ἐκ χειρός τινος Ge 39.1; παρά τινος 49.30; cogn. obj., πᾶσαν τὴν κτῆσιν, ἣν ἐκτήσατο Ge 46.6; + dat. com.pers., 47.20, 23, σεαυτῷ περίζωμα '.. a girdle' Je 13.1; for payment, 39.9, ἐν ἀλλάγματι 2K 24.24; + gen. pretii, ἀργυρίου Le 22.11, Je 39.25; opp. selling (πιπράσκω, πρᾶσις), Le 25.14, De 28.68; Ez 7.12 (:: πωλέω); || κομίζομαι 2M 7.11; + περιποιέομαι 2K 12.3; *o* sth incorporeal, αἴσθησιν 'understanding' Pr 18.15; πίστιν μετά τινος 'sbd's trust' Si 22.23.

2. *to bring upon oneself*: κακῶν ἀνδρῶν ὀνείδη 'reproaches by evil people' Pr 3.31.

3. *to bring* into a certain state of mind: + acc. pers. and adj., ἐκτήσατο αὐτὸν ἐχθρόν δωρεάν 'made an enemy out of him for nothing' Si 20.23, 29.6.

Cf. κτῆμα, κτῆσις, ἐγ~, κατακτάομαι, περιποιοῦμαι, λαμβάνω.

κτείνω: aor.inf. κτεῖναι.

to kill: τινα 3M 1.2. Cf. ἀποκτείνω, ἀφανίζω.

κτῆμα, ατος. n.

pl. *landed property*, esp. *farm, estate*: Ho 2.15 (or: 'possessions'); θρηνεῖτε, ~ατα, ὑπὲρ πυροῦ καὶ κριθῆς 'Mourn, O farms, over wheat and barley' Jl 1.11; possibly 'acquisition' Jb 20.29. Cf. κτάομαι, κτῆσις, ὕπαρξις: Shipp 344; MM, s.v.; Renehan 1.127.

κτῆνος, ους. n. Mostly in pl.

1. *livestock*: as prey of lion, Mi 5.8 (|| ποίμνια προβάτων); τοῦ πεδίου 'in pasture' Jl 1.20, 2.22.

2. *domestic animals in general*: constituting, together with θηρία, the animal kingdom on the earth, Ge 3.14, Is 46.1; ἑρπετά 'reptiles' added, Ge 6.19; summing up a list consisting of horses, mules, camels, and asses, καὶ πάντων τῶν ~ῶν Zc 14.15. || ἄνθρωπος Ge 6.7 and 7.23 (also foll. by ἑρπετά, πετεινά); || ἄνθρωποι Jn 3.7 (also foll. by οἱ βόες καὶ τὰ πρόβατα), 8, 4.11, Hg 1.11, Zc 2.4, 8.10; ἐάν τε κ. ἐάν τε ἄνθρωπος, οὐ ζήσεται 'whether it be an animal or a human, it shall not live' Ex 19.13; Zp 1.3 (also || τὰ πετεινὰ τοῦ οὐρανοῦ καὶ οἱ ἰχθύες τῆς θαλάσσης); domesticated as against wild animals (θηρία τὰ ἐν τῇ γῇ) Le 25.7; ἀποσκευὴ .. γυναῖκες .. καὶ ~η Nu 32.26; ~εσιν .. τετράποσιν '.. and quadrupeds' 35.3. **b**. as possessions: πλούσιος σφόδρα ~εσιν καὶ ἀργυρίῳ καὶ χρυσίῳ 'very rich in cattle and silver and gold' Ge 13.2; ~η προβάτων καὶ ~η βοῶν καὶ γεώργια πολλά '.. and many fields' 26.14; ~η πολλὰ καὶ βόες καὶ παῖδες καὶ παιδίσκαι καὶ κάμηλοι καὶ ὄνοι 30.43; specified as ἵπποι, πρόβατα, βόες, and ὄνοι 47.17. **c**. as food for human consumption: Le 11.2. **d**. as cultic offerings: ~η Le 1.2 (further specified as βόες καὶ πρόβατα).

3. *large animal* in general whether domesticated or not: coll. and distinct from humans, reptiles and birds, πᾶν τὸ ἀνάστημα (living creature) .. ἀπὸ ἀνθρώπου ἕως ~ους καὶ ἑρπετῶν καὶ τῶν πετεινῶν τοῦ οὐρανοῦ Ge 7.23, sim. 8.17. **b**. w. ref. to wild beasts: ~ατα ἐν τῷ δρυμῷ 'in thickets' Mi 5.8, τοῦ πεδίου Ps 8.8 (+ sheep, cattle, birds, fishes); distinct from birds and predatory, ~ατα τῆς γῆς 1K 17.44 (*L*: θηρία).

Cf. ζῷον, θηρίον, κτηνοτρόφος, κτηνώδης: Shipp 344.

κτηνοτρόφος, ον.ʃ *

pertaining to stock-farming: ἄνδρες ~οι 'stockmen' Ge 46.32 (|| ποιμήν), 34; γῆ κ. 'pastoral land' Nu 32.4; subst., ἐν σκηναῖς ~ων 'in stockmen's tents' Ge 4.20. Cf. κτῆνος, ποιμήν: LSG s.v.

κτηνώδης, ες.ʃ *

beastly: *s* hum., Ps 72.22. Cf. κτῆνος.

κτῆσις, εως. f.

1. *that which is* or *has been acquired*, 'possession': πᾶσαν τὴν ~ιν, ἣν ἐκτήσατο Ge 46.6 (|| τὰ ὑπάρχοντα). **b**. landed property: τάφου 'for a grave' Ge 23.4; μνημείου 23.9; ἐν τῇ γῇ τῆς ~εως αὐτῶν 'in the land of their acquisition' 36.43; παρά τινος 49.32; ἀγροῦ 'of a piece of land' 49.32; δίδωμί τινι ἐν ~ει Le 14.34. **c**. livestock: pl., Jd 6.5 B (A: κτήνη).

2. v.n. of κτάομαι, q.v.: παραλαβεῖν εἰς ~ιν 'take into possession' Je 39.7; βιβλίον ~εως 'bill of purchase' 39.11, πολλῶν 'of much' Pr 8.18; Ba 3.17, Si 36.29.

Cf. κτάομαι, κτῆμα, ὕπαρξις.

κτίζω: fut.pass. κτισθήσομαι; aor. ἔκτισα, inf. κτίσαι, ptc. κτίσας, impv. κτίσον, pass. ἐκτίσθην, inf.

κτισθῆναι, ptc. κτισθείς; pf.pass. ἔκτισμαι, ptc. ἐκτισμένος.

to bring into being (+ acc.): abs. and *s* non-divine, architect or builder, παντὶ τῷ κτίζοντι Hg 2.9 (see Th 313: τὸ ἔργον τῆς οἰκοδομῆς), cf. Le 16.16 and 1E 4.53; *o* a particular land or country, ἀφ' ἧς ἡμέρας ἔκτισται 'since the day it (= Egypt) was founded' Ex 9.18; pool Is 22.11; city (Tyre) Ez 28.14, Jerusalem 1E 4.53; σοφία Si 1.4. **b**. *s* divine act: τῷ θεῷ τῷ ὑψίστῳ, ὃς ἔκτισεν τὸν οὐρανὸν καὶ τὴν γῆν Ge 14.19, sim. 22; only γῆν Ho 13.4[1] (ǁ στερεόω); οὗ αἱ χεῖρες ἔκτισαν πᾶσαν τὴν στρατιὰν τοῦ οὐρανοῦ 'whose hands created the entire host of heaven' 13.4[2]; πνεῦμα Am 4.13 (ǁ στερεόω), καρδίαν καθαράν Ps 50.12; σωτηρίαν Je 38.22; God as creator of mankind, ἔκτισεν ὁ θεὸς ἄνθρωπον ἐπὶ τῆς γῆς De 4.32, σε Ec 12.1; Ma 2.10; ǁ ποιεῖν De 32.6 (*s* God the father), ὁ ποιῶν εἰρήνην καὶ κτίζων κακά Is 45.7, ἔκτισα καὶ ἐποίησα 46.11; ǁ γίνεσθαι Ps 32.9, 148.5; *o* agriculture, Si 7.15, arrogance 10.18.

Cf. ἑτοιμάζω, θεμελιόω, οἰκίζω, πλάσσω, ποιέω, καταδείκνυμι, κτίσις, κτίστης, νεόκτιστος, συγκτίζω, στερεόω: Foerster, *TDNT* 3.1023-8; Bons 2007.

κτίσις, εως. f.

that which has been brought into being: the universe, sg. εὐλογησάτωσάν σε οἱ οὐρανοὶ καὶ πᾶσα ἡ κ. σου 'Let the heavens and all your creation praise you' To 8.5 𝔊[II] (ǁ pl. 𝔊[I]), βασιλεῦ πάσης ~εώς σου Ju 9.12, δέσποτα πάσης τῆς ~εως 3M 2.2; ǁ ἡ ὑπ' οὐρανόν Si 16.15¶; pl. οἱ ἅγιοί σου καὶ πᾶσαι αἱ ~εις σου καὶ πάντες οἱ ἄγγελοί σου καὶ οἱ ἐκλεκτοί σου 'your saints and all your creatures and all your angels and your elect' To 𝔊[II] 8.15. Cf. κτίζω, κτίσμα, ποίησις: Casevitz 1985.54f., 232.

κτίσμα, ατος. n.

that which has been created: by God, Si 36.20, 38.34, Wi 9.2. Cf. κτίσις.

κτίστης, ου, voc. ~α. m.

creator: ἁπάντων 'of all' Si 24.8 (ǁ ὁ κτίσας), τῶν ὑδάτων Ju 9.12, τοῦ κόσμου 2M 7.23, 4M 5.25, πάντων 11.5; *s* God, 2K 22.32. Cf. κτίζω.

κτύπος, ου. m.ʃ

loud sound of sth violently breaking or falling: of falling stones, Wi 17.19. Cf. ἦχος, φωνή: Schmidt 3.319-21; Shipp 344f.

κύαθος, ου. m.

ladle for drawing wine: Ex 25.28; Je 52.19.

κύαμος, ου. m.ʃ

bean: food, Ez 4.9, 2K 17.28.

κυβερνάω: aor.ptc. ~νήσας, pass. ~νηθείς.

to serve as leader of: + acc. pers., τὸν λαόν Su 5; + acc. rei, δόλους 'deceptions' Pr 12.5; κυβερνηθεῖσα τῇ σῇ χειρί 'guided by your hand' Wi 14.6. Cf. κυβέρνησις, κυβερνήτης, διακυβερνάω, ἡγέομαι, ὁδηγέω, πηδαλιουχέω.

κυβέρνησις, εως. f.

skill and ability to serve as leader: Pr 1.5; of military commander, 24.6. Cf. κυβερνάω: Beyer, *TDNT* 3.1035-7.

κυβερνήτης, ου. m.

steersman, pilot of ship: Ez 27.8; fig. of leader, 4M 7.1. Cf. κυβερνάω, πρῳρεύς: *ND* 4.116f.

κύβος, ου. m.ʃ

1. *block*: of stone, Jb 38.38.

2. *anything of cubic shape*: golden and silver ring for a hanging, Es 1.6.

κυδοιμός, οῦ. m.ʃ

exceedingly loud noise: of stormy shower (?), Jb 38.25. Cf. ἦχος, φωνή.

κῦδος, ους. n.ʃ

fame: Is 14.25. Cf. κλέος, ὄνομα.

κύησις, εως. f.ʃ

v.n. of κύω: lit., becoming pregnant, Ru 4.13.

κύθρα, ας. f.⇒ χύτρα.

κυθρόπους, ποδος. m.ʃ See also χυτρόπους.

vessel for cooking food and boiling in, 'pot, cauldron': κλίβανος καὶ κ. 'oven and ..' Le 11.35.

κυκλεύω. ⇒ κυκλόω, and cf. Walters 119.

κυκλόθεν. adv.

round about: Τύρος καὶ κ. 'Tyre and the area round about' Am 3.11; παροικεῖ κ. Je 6.25; κ. κύκλῳ 'all round' Ez 37.2. **b**. following a noun: τὰ ἔθνη κ. 'the nations round about' Jl 3.11, 12; τεῖχος πυρὸς κ. 'a fiery wall round about' Zc 2.5; 7.7, 12.6, 14.14. **c**. prep. + gen.: 4M 14.17.

Cf. κύκλος and κυκλόω.

κύκλος, ου. m.

I. *circuit*: of the wind, Ec 1.7; of the sun, 1E 4.34.

2. *pattern of periodical alterations*, 'cycle': ἐνιαυτοῦ 'of the year' Wi 7.19.

II. κύκλῳ **a**. as prep. *around*: + gen., τὰς πόλεις τὰς κ. αὐτῶν Ge 35.5; ὕδωρ κ. αὐτῆς 'water around her' Na 3.8; used attr., τὰς κύκλῳ πόλεις 2M 4.32; following a noun (cf. κυκλόθεν), τοῖς λαοῖς κύκλῳ 'the peoples around' Zc 12.2. **b**. as adv.: ἐν τοῖς ὁρίοις αὐτοῦ κ. 'in its area all round' Ge 23.17; πρὸς τὸ θυσιαστήριον κύκλῳ 'on to the altar all round' Ex 29.16.

Cf. κυκλόθεν, κυκλόω, περικύκλῳ.

κυκλόω: fut. κυκλώσω; aor. ἐκύκλωσα, subj. κυκλώσω, inf. κυκλῶσαι, ptc. κυκλώσας, impv. κύκλωσον, pass. ἐκυκλώθην.

I. intr. *to come round*: ἐκύκλωσεν ἐπὶ σὲ ποτήριον δεξιᾶς κυρίου 'the cup of the right hand of the Lord came round to you' Hb 2.16; ἐπὶ σέ 'to besiege you' Is 29.3, ἐπὶ τὸν βασιλέα κύκλῳ 4K 11.8 (in order to protect him); mid. and + dat., Ez 43.17.

2. *to move round and go to various places* within a space: ἐν τῇ πόλει Ct 3.2.

II. tr. **1**. *to go round*: + acc., πᾶσαν τὴν γῆν Ge 2.11; ὑμᾶς Nu 34.4; τὸ ὄρος τὸ Σηιρ De 2.1; γῦρον οὐρανοῦ Si 24.5.

2. *to encircle*: + acc. pers., Ps 7.8 (not with hostile intent), 21.17 (with hostile intent and ‖ περιέχω); pass., ἀπὸ ὁδοῦ πονηρᾶς '(so as to protect) from an evil way' PSol 10.1. **2**. tr. *to position in the form of a circle*: + acc., 2K 18.15*L* (or: intr. with παιδάρια as *s*).

3. *to surround and affect the entirety of*: + acc. pers. and to protect, *s* God, De 32.10; God's mercy, Ps 31.10; God's fidelity, 90.4 (ὅπλῳ); with hostile intent, Ho 7.2, Jn 2.4, 6; *s* θλίψεις καὶ πόλεμοι 1M 12.13, ὠδῖνες θανάτου 'deadly pangs' 2K 22.6B.

4. *to encircle with*: + acc. rei, ἐπ' αὐτὴν [= city] χάρακα 'a palisade ..' Is 37.33.

5. *to do* sbd (τινα) the ultimate of (ἔν τινι): ἐκύκλωσέ με ἐν ψεύδει .. καὶ ἐν ἀσεβείαις Ho 11.12.

6. *to lead by a roundabout way*: + acc. pers., τὸν λαὸν ὁδὸν τὴν εἰς τὴν ἔρημον '.. along the way into the desert' Ex 13.18. **b**. *to deal with in a roundabout way*: + acc., τὸ πρόσωπον τοῦ λόγου τούτου 'this state of affairs' 2K 14.20*L*, cf. Proc., PG 87I. 1136

Cf. κύκλος, κυκλόθεν, κύκλωσις, γυρόω, περιέχω, περιλαμβάνω, περιπορεύομαι.

κύκλωμα, ατος. n.

1. *that which goes round*, 'circumference': Ez 43.17, 48.35.

2. *a circle or group* of people formed for a particular purpose: Ps 139.10.

3. *disc*: Jb 37.12¶.

Cf. LSG, s.v.

κύκλωσις, εως. f.ʃ

act of going round sth or in some space: Si 43.12. Cf. κυκλόω.

κύκνειος, ον.ʃ

of κύκνος (q.v.): *s* melody, + σειρήνιος 4M 15.21.

κύκνος, ου. m.ʃ

swan, Cycnus olor (LSJ): forbidden as food, Le 11.18, De 14.15.

κυλικεῖον, ου. n.ʃ

stand for drinking cups: 1M 15.32.

κυλίκιον, ου. n.ʃ

small cup: Es 1.7 o'. Cf. ποτήριον.

κυλίω: fut. κυλισθήσομαι; aor.impv. κύλισον.

1. intr. *to move by rolling*: ἐγὼ κυλίω ὑποκάτω ὑμῶν, ὃν τρόπον κυλίεται ἡ ἅμαξα ἡ γέμουσα καλάμης 'I roll under you as a cart fully laden with straw will roll' Am 2.13; λίθοι ἅγιοι κυλίονται ἐπὶ τῆς γῆς αὐτοῦ 'sacred stones roll on his land' Zc 9.16. **b**. mid.: Jd 7.13 A (B: στρέφομαι). **c**. tr.: + acc., λίθον Pr 26.27, ἐπὶ τὸ στόμα τοῦ σπηλαίου 'on to the entrance of the cave' Jo 10.18; τινα 4K 9.33B (*L* κατασπάω).

2. *to flow along with great speed*: of water, fig., κυλισθήσεται ὡς ὕδωρ κρίμα Am 5.24.

Cf. ἐπι~, κατακυλίω.

κῦμα, ατα. n.

wave of the sea: κ. θαλάσσης Is 48.18; pl. Ex 15.8; and + μετεωρισμοί 'billow' Jn 2.4; πατάξουσιν ἐν θαλάσσῃ ~ατα Zc 10.11. Cf. κυμαίνω, κλύδων, μετεωρισμός, τρικυμία.

κυμαίνω.ʃ

1. intr., *to rise in waves*: θάλασσα κυμαίνουσα Is 17.12 (of great agitation), Je 6.23 (of a roaring sea), sim. Is 5.30; ναῦς διερχομένη κυμαινόμενον ὕδωρ 'a ship sailing through the raging water' Wi 5.10.

2. tr., *to agitate*: ὡς ποταμοὶ κυμαίνουσιν ὕδωρ Je 26.7.

Cf. κῦμα.

κυμάτιον, ου. n.ʃ

small wavy moulding: ~ια στρεπτὰ χρυσᾶ 'twisted, golden ..' Ex 25.10 (engraved on the ark of testimony); 25.23 (on a table); 25.24 (on a capital of a pillar).

κυμβαλίζω.ʃ

to play the cymbals: Ne 12.27. Cf. subs.

κύμβαλον, ου. n.

cymbal: Ps 150.5; ‖ σάλπιγξ 2E 3.10, ‖ τύμπανον 1K 18.6, Ju 16.1; + κιθάρα, κινύρα 1M 4.54. See *BA* 9.1, pp. 83f.

κύμινον, ου. n.ʃ < Heb. כַּמֹּן+

cummin: Is 28.25, 27. Cf. Ziegler 1934.183f.

κυνηγέω.ʃ

to hunt game: εἰδὼς κυνηγεῖν Ge 25.27. Cf. κυνηγός, ἀγρεύω, θηρεύω: Schmidt 2.444f.

κυνήγιον, ου. n.ʃ

**animal as food for wild beasts*: Si 13.19.

κυνηγός, οῦ. m.ʃ

huntsman: γίγας κ. 'giant hunter' Ge 10.9 (of Nimrud [Νεβρωδ]) ‖ 1C 1.10. Cf. κυνηγέω: Shipp 346.

κυνικός, ή, όν.ʃ

surly: *s* hum., 1K 25.3.

κυνόμυια, ας. f. Before the LXX, spelled κυνάμυια.

dog-fly: noisome and irritating, Ex 8.21; destructive, 8.24; Ps 77.45 (‖ βάτραχος 'frog'); κ. καὶ σκνῖπες '.. and gnats' 104.31.

κυοφορέω.ʃ

to be pregnant: *s* hum. fem., Ec 11.5. Cf. κυοφορία, γεννάω, γαστήρ, συλλαμβάνω.

κυοφορία, ας. f.ʃ *
pregnancy: 4M 15.6, 16.7. Cf. κυοφορέω, γέννησις.

κυπαρίσσινος, ον.ʃ
of cypress-wood: *s* ξύλον Ne 8.15; subst.n.pl., artifices made of such, Ez 27.24. Cf. κυπάρισσος.

κυπάρισσος, ου.f.
cypress: Is 37.24 (of Lebanon); fig. of tall, straight tail, Jb 40.17.

κυπρίζω.ʃ *
to bloom: *s* vine, Ct 2.13, 15. Cf. κυπρισμός, ἀνθέω.

Κύπριος, α, ον.ʃ
of Cyprus: 2M 4.29.

κυπρισμός, οῦ. m.ʃ *
bloom of the olive or vine (LSJ): Ct 7.13. Cf. κυπρίζω.

κύπρος, ου.ʃ < Heb. כֹּפֶר.
henna: Ct 1.14, 4.13.

κύπτω: fut. κύψω; aor.act. ἔκυψα, ptc. κύψας, impv. κύψον.
to bend forward: κύψαντες προσεκύνησαν αὐτῷ Ge 43.28 (a mark of humble respect), κύψας ἐπὶ τὴν γῆν προσεκύνησεν Ex 34.8, ἐπὶ πρόσωπον αὐτοῦ ἐπὶ τὴν γῆν καὶ προσεκύνησεν 1K 24.9; to heathen idols, Is 2.9 (ǁ ταπεινοῦμαι), 46.6 (cf. Ge 43.28); 'to stoop on the ground' Is 51.23; βαδίζει κύπτον Ba 1.18 (in sorrow); κύψει καὶ πεσεῖται Ps 9.31. Cf. ἐγ~, εἰσ~, κατεπι~, προσ~, συγκύπτω, κύφω.

I **κυρία**, ας. f.
one (female) who owns and controls (possessions): in relation to maidservant, Ge 16.4, 8, 9; opp. παιδίσκη Ps 122.2; οἴκου 'landlady' 3K 17.17. Cf. κύριος: Shipp 347.

II **κυρία**, ας. f.
area under one's control, 'dominion': 1M 8.24.

κυριεία, ας.ʃ
authority: divine, Is 40.10 (ǁ ἰσχύς), Da 6.26 TH (ǁ βασιλεία), 11.5 TH (ǁ LXX δυναστεία); hum., 4.19 TH; + obj. gen., πάσης σαρκός Bel 5 TH.

κυρίευσις, εως. f.ʃ * (?)
domination: αἰώνιος 'eternal' Es 7.56 *L*. Cf. κυριεύω.

κυριεύω: fut. κυριεύσω, pass. κυριευθήσομαι; aor. ἐκυρίευσα, inf. κυριεῦσαι.
1. *to conduct oneself as master over, dominate*, often with hostile connotation: + gen., αὐτός σου κυριεύει Ge 3.16; 37.8 (ǁ βασιλεύω); Nu 21.18 (ǁ βασιλεία); ǁ ἄρχω Jd 9.2 A, 15.11 A; ἐκυρίευσεν αὐτῶν οἱ λέοντες 'the lions overmastered them' Da TH 6.24; *o* land, Je 37.3, Is 7.18; *s* king, τῆς θαλάσσης καὶ τῆς γῆς 1E 4.3 (ǁ δεσπόζω), 15; *o* hum., 4.14 (ǁ δεσπόζω; *s* women); *s* tongue with pervasive influence, Si 37.18, powers to be, ἐν ταῖς βασιλείαις αὐτῶν 44.3, τῶν θηρίων ἐπὶ τῆς γῆς Ba 3.16 (ǁ ἄρχοντες); conquerors and rulers, πόλεων Ju 1.14 and 1M 11.8, πάσης τῆς ὀρεινῆς 'the entire mountain region' 10.13; hand and abs., Ex 15.9; δοῦλος La 5.8; + ἐν (Hebraism?), ἐν τοῖς ἀποκρύφοις τοῦ χρυσοῦ 'gain control of the hidden gold' Da TH 11.43 (LXX κρατέω); pass. κυριευθήσονται οἱ κυριεύσαντες αὐτῶν Is 14.2. **b**. metaph., *s* λογισμός 'rational will,' + gen., παθῶν 'passions' 4M 1.4 (ǁ ἐπικρατέω vs. 3).
2. *to gain possession of*: + gen., κυριείας πολλῆς 'much power' Da 11.3.
Cf. κυρίευσις, κύριος, κατακυριεύω, ἄρχω, βασιλεύω, δεσπόζω, ἡγέομαι: Spicq 2.351f.

κύριος, ου. m. Originally adj. (~ος, α, ον), but used mostly as subst. m.
1. *one who owns and controls* (possessions): opp. δοῦλος 'slave' Ma 1.6, οἰκέτης Ge 27.37, παῖς Ex 21.4, οἰκέτις 21.8; ǁ ὁ κτησάμενος 'one who procured' Is 1.3; ταύρου 'of bull' Ex 21.28, λάκκου 'of cistern' 21.34; of a slave, 21.4; τῆς γῆς Pr 31.39.
2. *a person addressed or perceived as being of higher societal situation*: in voc., 'sir', Κύριε Ge 18.3 (the speaker calling himself ὁ παῖς σου), 19.18 (addressing more than one person), Nu 12.11; a daughter to her father, 31.35; ~οι .. τοῦ παιδὸς ὑμῶν 19.2; of husband, ὁ κ. μου 18.12 (said by his wife); of an estranged elder brother, τῷ ~ῳ μου 32.4, 5 (the speaker referring to himself as ὁ παῖς σου); Aaron to Moses, Ex 32.22, sim. Nu 36.2; Hannah to Eli the priest, 1K 1.15, 26; ~ε βασιλεῦ 1K 26.17, Je 44.20, Da LXX 3.9; in officialese, τῷ κυρίῳ βασιλεῖ 'to his majesty the king' 1E 2.17, 18.
3. *one who exercises absolute authority* over sbd else or sth: applied to the God of Israel, κ. ὄνομα αὐτῷ Ps 67.5; ἐγώ εἰμι κ. Ex 14.4, κ. εἷς De 6.4, εἷς κ. ἡμῶν Da 3.17 LXX; κύριε πάτερ Si 23.1, κύριε κύριε Ps 139.8; κ. ὁ ὕψιστος 96.9; κ. παντοκράτωρ Hg 1.6 (see under π.); ~ε τῆς σωτηρίας μου Is 38.20; δέσποτα ~ε Jn 4.3, Da LXX 9.15; ὁ κ. πάσης τῆς γῆς Ex 8.22, Zc 6.5, Mi 4.13 (cf. its application to Nebuchadnezzar, Ju 2.5, 6.4), τοῦ οὐρανοῦ To 618 $\mathfrak{G}^{II}$; κ. ὁ θεός Ge 2.8 +; ὁ κ. θεός Jn 1.9; κ. τῶν κυρίων De 10.17, Ps 135.3; κ. σαβαωθ Is 1.9 +; ἡμέρα ~ου 'the day (for punishment) of the Lord' Ob 15; λόγος ~ου Jn 1.1; δοῦλος ~ου 1.9; ἄγγελος ~ου Hg 1.13; ὁ ναὸς ~ου 2.15, 18; often in the phrase λέγει κ. foll. by a quote, Hg 1.13; ὁ κ. without any qualifier, even the definite article, Ob 21; Jn 1.16*bis*, 2.8, 10, Zp 2.3, note esp. Εὐλογητὸς κ. ὁ θεὸς τοῦ ~ου μου Αβρααμ Ge 24.27 (on the use or non-use of the article w. κ., see Debrunner 1925; Ziegler 1956. 133-6; Solà; Kilpatrick 1990.216-22. Cf. Ὁ πάντων

κύριος (applied to Zeus) Pindar, *Isthm.* 5.53 and see Spicq 2.344f. **b.** hum.: ὁ κ. τῆς γῆς Ge 42.30 (Joseph and ‖ ἄρχων τῆς γῆς vs. 6, cf. Ps 104.21), Αἰγύπτου 1M 2.53; τῆς οἰκίας 'the head of the household' Ex 22.8; γίνου κ. τοῦ ἀδελφοῦ σου Ge 27.29; employer and provider of work, To 2.12.

4. *having the authority* or *right* to act in a certain way: + inf., οὐ κύριός ἐστιν πωλεῖν αὐτήν 'has no right to sell her' Ex 21.8 (‖ ἀποδίδωμι vs. 7). **b.** *valid*: *s* matters, 1M 8.30.

*__5.__ = בַּעַל: κ. τοξευμάτων 'archer' Ge 49.23.

6. adj., *being in absolute control over*: *s* λογισμός 'rational will,' + gen., παθῶν 'passions' 4M 2.7 (‖ αὐτοκράτωρ, αὐτοδέσποτος 1.30), φρόνησις 'prudence,' πάντων 'over everything' 1.19.

Cf. δεσπότης, ἡγεμών, θεός, παντοκράτωρ, δοῦλος, παῖς: Schmidt 4.122-4; Trench 96-8; Cerfaux 1931a, b; Foerster and Quell, *TDNT* 3.1041-85; Spicq 2.341-50; Hagedorn & Worp; Harl in *BA* 1.51f.

κυρίως. adv.ʃ

in accordance with law: 3K 22.17*L*.

κυρόω: fut.pass. κυρωθήσομαι; aor. ἐκύρωσα, pass. ἐκυρώθην.ʃ

1. *legally to confirm as property of* (sbd τινι): pass. ἐκυρώθη ὁ ἀγρὸς .. τῷ Αβρααμ Ge 23.20; κυρωθήσεται ἡ οἰκία .. τῷ κτησαμένῳ αὐτήν 'the house shall legally become property of .. its purchaser' Le 25.30.

2. *to establish the truthfulness of*: + acc., εὐνομίαν 'the adherence to the law' 4M 7.9.

3. *to ratify* an official agreement or treaty: abs. and *s* king, ἔστησε καὶ ἐκύρωσε 'established and ..' Da 6.9 LXX (*o* ὁρισμός 'decree, edict' understood).

Cf. ἵστημι, ἀκυρόω: Behm, *TDNT* 3.1098f.; Preisigke I 855f.

κυρτός, ή, όν.ʃ

hunchbacked (ellipsis for κ. τοὺς ὤμους): *s* hum., Le 21.20; opp. ὀρθός (*L*: ὄρθιος) 'standing erect' 3K 21.11.

κύτος, ους. n.

hollow space or cavity: τῆς θαλάσσης Ps 64.8; hollow trunk of a gigantic tree, Da 4.8.

κύφω.ʃ

= κύπτω: ὀφθαλμοῖς 'with downcast eyes' Jb 22.29¶.

κυψέλη, ης. f.ʃ

hollow container: for grain, κ. κριθῆς Hg 2.16. Cf. Carden 178, n. 13.

κύω.ʃ

to conceive in mind: abs., Is 59.13 (+ μελετάω); + acc., πόνον 59.4 (‖ τίκτω). Cf. LSG s.v.

κύων, νός. m.

dog: οὐ γρύξει κ. τῇ γλώσσῃ αὐτοῦ 'no dog will growl with its tongue' Ex 11.7; contemptible, τῷ ~νὶ ἀπορρίψατε αὐτό 'throw it to a dog' 22.31; ἀναιδεῖς τῇ ψυχῇ 'shameless ..' Is 56.11; ἄλλαγμα ~νός 'dog's fee' De 23.18 [w. ref. to male temple prostitute]; fig. of hostile hum., Ps 21.17. Cf. LSG s.v.

κῴδιον, ου. n.ʃ On the spelling, see Walters 70.

sheepskin, fleece: Ne 3.15, Ju 12.15.

κώδων, ωνος. m.

ornamental *bell* on the hem of a robe: Ex 28.29; golden, 36.33, 2C 4.13, Si 45.9.

κώθων, ωνος. m.ʃ

drinking bout: + εὐφροσύνη Es 8.17, 3M 6.31. Cf. κωθωνίζομαι: Shipp 348; LSG s.v.

κωθωνίζομαι.ʃ

to drink hard: Es 3.15 ο', μετὰ μουσικῶν καὶ χαρᾶς 1E 4.63. Cf. κώθων.

κωκυτός, οῦ. m.ʃ

act of wailing loudly: + οἰμωγή 3M 6.32. Cf. κλαίω, κλαυθμός, οἰμωγή: Schmidt 3.387-93.

κωλέα, ας. f.ʃ

thigh-bone with the flesh on it (LSJ): 1K 9.24.

κῶλον, ου. n.

limb, member of a body: of humans and idols, Le 26.30; of humans, Nu 14.29, Is 66.24; of fallen soldiers, 1K 17.46 (‖ σάρκες vs. 44). Alw. in pl. Cf. μέλος, σῶμα; Schmidt 4.623-5.

κώλυμα, ατος. n.ʃ

that which impedes: 'shackles' for feet, Jb 13.27. Cf. κωλύω.

κωλυτικός, ή, όν.

acting as a hindrance to: *s* passions, + gen., σωφροσύνης 'prudence' 4M 1.3 (‖ vs.4 ἐμποδιστικός). Cf. ἐμποδιστικός.

κωλύω: fut.act. κωλύσω, ptc. κωλύσων, pass. κωλυθήσομαι; aor. ἐκώλυσα, subj. κωλύσω, impv. κώλυσον, inf. κωλῦσαι, pass. ἐκωλύθην, subj. κωλυθῶ.

1. *to prevent, stay the hand of*: abs., To 8.3 $\mathfrak{G}^{II}$; + acc., κώλυσον αὐτούς 'Stop them!' Nu 11.28; πλῆθος ὕδατος Ez 31.15 (‖ tr. ἐφίστημι), 1E 2.25 (‖ καταργέω 2E 4.23); τὰ χείλη μου 'hold silence' Ps 39.10, λόγον Si 4.23; ὁλοκαυτώματα ἐκ τοῦ ἁγιάσματος 'burnt offerings in the temple' 1M 1.45; + inf., Is 28.6, ὁ κωλύσων αὐτὸν τοῦ ἀποστρέψαι 'one willing to stop him in order to turn him back' (or: '.. prevent him from coming back') Mi 2.4; + τοῦ μή inf., 1K 25.26 (‖ ἀπο~ vs. 33); pass., ἐκωλύθη ὁ λαὸς ἔτι προσφέρειν 'the people were prevented from bringing any more' Ex 36.6; + gen., τῆς οἰκοδομῆς 'from the construction work' 1E 6.6; + ἀπό - ἀπὸ ἁμαρτίας Si 46.7; 3M 3.2.

2. *to deny access to, withhold*: + acc. and ἀπό τινος (pers.), τὸ μνημεῖον αὐτοῦ ἀπὸ σοῦ 'withhold his grave from you' Ge 23.6; ἐκ πάσης ὁδοῦ πονηρᾶς .. τοὺς πόδας μου Ps 118.101; To 6.13 $\mathfrak{G}^{II}$. **b.** mid. *to deny oneself, abstain* from (ἀπό): Si 18.30.

c. pass. *to be spared* undesirable consequences: ἀπὸ ἐλαττώσεως 'loss' Si 20.3.

Cf. κώλυμα, κωλυτικός, ἀποκωλύω, ἀκώλυτος, εἴργω.

κωμάρχης, ου. f.ʃ

village chief: Es 2.3 o'.

κώμη, ης. f.

unwalled village: adjacent to a walled city, κατελάβοντο αὐτὴν [= Jazer] καὶ τὰς ~ας αὐτῆς Nu 21.32, sim. 32.42; + πόλις Je 19.15, 2M 8.6. Cf. πόλις, ἐποίκιον.

κῶμος, ου. m.ʃ

revel, merry-making: pl., Wi 14.23, + ἀσωτία 'profligacy' 2M 6.4. Cf. Trench 226f.

κωνώπιον, ου. n.

couch with mosquito-curtains: Ju 10.21.

κώπη, ης. f.ʃ

oar: Ez 27.6. Cf. κωπηλάτης.

κωπηλάτης, ου. m. *

rower, oarsman: Ez 27.8. Cf. κώπη.

κωφεύω: fut. κωφεύσω; aor. ἐκώφευσα, inf. κωφεῦσαι, impv. κώφευσον.

= κωφόομαι: Jb 6.24, 13.5,:: λαλέω 13.13, 2K 13.20B (*L* σιωπάω). Cf. κωφόω, σιωπάω.

κωφός, ή, όν.

1. *incapable of speaking* (or possibly hearing, or both): *s* δύσκωφον καὶ ~όν 'deaf and dumb' Ex 4.11; ἡ σοφία ἤνοιξε στόμα ~ῶν Wi 10.21; εἴδωλα Hb 2.18; subst. Le 19.14.

2. *incapable of hearing*, 'deaf': ὡσεὶ κ. οὐκ ἤκουον Ps 37.14, ὦτα ~ῶν ἀκούσονται Is 35.5, 43.8 (|| τυφλός); *s* ἀσπίς 'asp' Ps 57.5; idols, ~ὰ καὶ μὴ δυνάμενα αὐτοῖς λαλεῖν '.. and not capable of being spoken to' 3M 4.16.

Cf. (ἀπο)κωφόω, βραδύγλωσσος, ἰσχνόφωνος, ἄλαλος, ἀπενεόομαι, ἐθελοκωφέω: Shipp 349-51.

κωφόω: aor.pass. ἐκωφώθην.ʃ

pass. *to keep one's mouth shut*: Ps 38.3, 10. Cf. κωφός, κωφεύω.

Λ

λαβή, ῆς. f.ʃ

haft of a sword: Jd 3.22.

λαβίς, ίδος. f.ʃ

snuffer: Ex 38.17, Is 6.6, 2C 4.21; τοὺς λύχνους αὐτῆς καὶ τὰς ~ίδας αὐτῆς 'its lamps and its snuffers' Nu 4.9.

λάβρος, ον.ʃ

boisterous: ***s*** rain, Pr 28.3, Jb 38.25; τρόμος ὕδατος 'vibration of water' 38.34; fire, 4M 16.3.

λάγανον, ου. n.

thin broad cake, of meal and oil (LSJ): ~α ἄζυμα κεχρισμένα ἐν ἐλαίῳ 'unleavened cakes smeared with oil' Ex 29.2, Nu 6.15; ‖ ἄρτος Ex 29.23;.. διακεχρισμένα '.. thoroughly smeared..' Le 2.4; ἀπὸ τηγάνου '(fresh) from a frying-pan' and + κολλυρίς, ἐσχαρίτης 2K 6.19. Cf. ἐσχαρίτης, κολλυρίς, πέμμα: Shipp 352.

λαγχάνω: aor. ἔλαχον; pf.ptc. λελογχώς.ʃ

to attain: ***o*** (acc.) old age, 3M 6.1; + gen., ψυχῆς ἀγαθῆς Wi 8.19. Cf. κληρονομέω **1b**, τυγχάνω: Spicq 2.355-7.

λαγών, όνος. f.ʃ

the hollow on each side below the ribs: sg. 2K 20.10*L* (B: ψόα), pl. Si 47.19.

λάθρᾳ. adv.

out of public view: De 13.7; ὡς ἔσθων πτωχὸς λ. 'like a poor man eating in secret' Hb 3.14. **b**. with hostile intention: καταλαλοῦντα λ. τοῦ πλησίον αὐτοῦ Ps 100.5, ἠπατήθη λ. 'was secretly deceived' Jb 31.27¶, ἀπέστειλεν ἐπιστολὰς λ. 1M 9.60, λ. μηχανώμενοι 'secretly devising' 3M 6.24.

Cf. λανθάνω, λαθραίως, λεληθότως, κρυπτῶς, κρυφαίως, κρυφῇ. Cf. Spicq 2.358-61.

λαθραῖος, α, ον.ʃ

done in secret: ***s*** φθέγμα 'utterance' Wi 1.11. Cf. λάθριος.

λαθραίως. adv.ʃ

= λάθρᾳ: 1K 26.5*L* (B: λάθρᾳ), 24.5, 2M 1.19.

λάθριος, α, ον.ʃ

= λαθραῖος: ***s*** δόσις 'gift' Pr 21.14.

λαῖλαψ, απος. f.

furious rain-storm: Je 32.18; ‖ ἄνεμος Jb 21.18, ‖ πνεῦμα δυνάμεως 'powerful wind' Wi 5.23. Cf. ἄνεμος, θύελλα, καταιγίς, πνεῦμα, γαληνός: Schmidt 2.218f.; Trench 277; Shipp 353.

λαιμαργία, ας. f.ʃ

gluttony: + παντοφαγία 'indiscriminate eating' 4M 1.27.

λακάνη, ης. f.ʃ Hellenistic spelling for Attic λεκάνη, which is also found at Jd 5.25 B and 6.38.

relatively shallow, flat container: for butter, Jd 5.25; water 6.38.

λάκκος, ου. m.

1. *cavity in the ground*: cistern for storing water, ὁ λ. κενός, ὕδωρ οὐκ εἶχεν Ge 37.24; ἐκ ~ου οὐκ ἔχοντος ὕδωρ Zc 9.11; πλὴν πηγῶν ὑδάτων καὶ ~ου καὶ συναγωγῆς ὕδατος Le 11.36; βόθυνος ~ου Is 51.1; in a wilderness (ἔρημος) Ge 37.22; used as prison, Ex 12.29; fig. w. ref. to Hades, τοῖς καταβαίνουσιν εἰς ~ον Ps 27.1, 142.7.

2. *incision*: ἐν τῇ σιαγόνι 'in the (donkey's) jaw' Jd 15.19 B (A: τραῦμα 'wound').

Cf. βόθρος, κρήνη: LSG s.v.

Λακωνικός, ή, όν.ʃ

Laconian: ***s*** women's see-through clothes, Is 3.22.

λαλέω: fut.act. λαλήσω, pass. λαληθήσομαι; aor.act. ἐλάλησα, impv. λάλησον, inf. λαλῆσαι, ptc. λαλήσας, subj. λαλήσω, opt.3s λαλήσαι, 3pl λαλήσειν, pass. ἐλαλήθην, ptc. λαληθείς; pf. λελάληκα, inf. λελαληκέναι, pass. λελάλημαι.

1. *to speak*: abs. Ob 18, Jn 3.3; τῇ γλώσσῃ τῇ Χανανίτιδι Is 19.18; ἐν χειρί τινος 'through sbd' Hg 2.1; *ἐπὶ τὴν καρδίαν τινός 'to speak in a manner which touches his heart' Ho 2.14, ‖ διαλάσσω 'to reconcile' Jd 19.3A*L* (B: ‖ ἐπιστρέφω), in an attempt to persuade and win the heart over - 2C 30.22, 32.6; *εἰς τὴν καρδίαν τινός Ge 50.21 (reassuringly), Is 40.2 + Ru 2.13 (‖ παρακαλέω), cf. Dogniez 2002.6-10, but also = καταλαλέω Da 4.34a LXX; ἀπὸ καρδίας αὐτῶν 'their own thoughts' Je 23.16; περί τινος Ge 19.21; ὑπέρ τινος Je 18.20; *ἔν τινι 'about' De 6.7, Ez 39.8; ἐναντίον τινός Ex 6.11; μετά τινος Ez 3.10, 44.5; πρός τινα 'to address sbd' Ge 16.13, Ex 12.3; 20.19 (‖ + dat. pers.), Zc 2.4; ἀνεβόησε καὶ ἐλάλησε πρός με 6.8; + dat. pers., Ge 17.3, Ex 4.14; εἰς τὰ ὦτά τινος Ge 50.4, Ex 11.2, Nu 14.28; κύριος ἐλάλησεν in a formula concluding a divine pronouncement, Jl 3.8; + ἐν τῇ διανοίᾳ 'to verbalise one's thought without actually uttering it in sbd else's hearing' Ge 24.15, 45, sim. ἐν τῇ καρδίᾳ 1K 1.13, 27.1, cf. Ge 8.21; ἐπί τινα Ez 36.5 (aggressive), Da 9.6 LXX (TH πρός τινα; ‖ dat. pers.); κατὰ τὴν διανοίαν τινός 'by taking note of sbd's intention' Ge 34.3; κατά τινος 'to criticise' Nu 12.1; ***s*** human mouth (στόμα), Ge 45.12. **b**. pass. impers.: σοι λελάληται 'you were spoken to' Jb 4.2; ἐλαλήθη πρὸς αὐτόν Ho 12.4.

2. tr. *to utter*, + acc.: τὸ κήρυγμα .. ἐλάλησα πρός σέ Jn 3.2; ***o*** πάντα τὰ ῥήματα ταῦτα εἰς τὰ ὦτα αὐτῶν 'within their earshot' Ge 20.8, ^λόγους^ 1K 8.21, ἐν τοῖς ὠσὶν ὑμῶν De 5.1; + dat. pers., Ge 49.28; λάλησον πρὸς Φαραω .. ὅσα ἐγὼ λέγω πρὸς σέ Ex 6.29; λαλησάτω ὁ παῖς σου ῥῆμα ἐναντίον σου Ge 44.18; ῥήματα προφάσεις ψευδεῖς Ho 10.4; τὸ ῥῆμα, ὃ ἐλάλησας ποιῆσαι De 1.14; τὸν λόγον τοῦτον, ὃν ἐλάλησε κύριος ἐφ' ὑμᾶς Am 3.1; ταῦτα Mi 4.4; οὐκ ἐδύναντο λαλεῖν αὐτῷ οὐδὲν εἰρηνικόν Ge 37.4, εἰρηνικοὺς λόγους Mi 7.3, εἰρηνικὰ μετά τινος Ju 7.24, εἰρήνην 15.8; σκληρά 'harsh things' Ge 42.7; καλά Si 13.6; λαλεῖτε ἀλήθειαν ἕκαστος πρὸς τὸν πλησίον αὐτοῦ 'Speak truth to one another' Zc 8.16, ψευδῆ Je 9.5, ὑπερηφανίαν 1M 1.24, ἀνομίαν Ps 30.19, σοφίαν 48.4; εἴς τινα 'against sbd' Da 7.25 LXX (TH πρός τινα); ἐπί τινα 10.11 LXX.

3. *to talk about as sth important*: + acc., κόπους .. τὰ ἐνύπνια ψευδῆ Zc 10.2, κατὰ τοῦ θεοῦ ἀδικίαν Ps 74.6, ἀνομίαν 30.19, εἰρήνην Is 32.4; πλάνησιν 32.6; μωρά 'foolish things' ib. (ǁ μάταια); μάταια Zp 3.13; εὐθεῖαν ὁδόν Is 33.15, δίκαια 59.4.

4. *to declare* one's intention to do sth: τῇ κακίᾳ, ᾗ ἐλάλησε τοῦ ποιῆσαι αὐτοῖς 'the trouble he had said he would cause them' Jn 3.10, ἐπὶ σὲ κακὰ ἀντὶ τῆς κακίας .. '(the Lord pronounced) disasters against you for the wickedness ..' Je 11.17, sim. 16.10; 18.7, 9; ἐλάλησεν μετὰ Σεδεκίου κρίσιν 'pronounced a decision to S.' 4K 25.6 ..

5. *to mention verbally*: + acc., τὸ ἀργύριον, ὃ ἐλάλησεν Ge 23.16; τὸν λόγον τοῦτον 'this matter' De 3.26.

6. *to negotiate orally*: λαλήσω περὶ αὐτῆς τοῦ δοθῆναί σοι αὐτὴν εἰς γυναῖκα To 6.12 𝔊ᴵ.

Cf. ἐκ~, κατα~, προσ~, συλλαλέω, λάλημα, λαλητός, λαλιά, ἄλαλος, λέγω, σεμνολογέω, φθέγγομαι, ψελλίζω: Shipp 355f.

λάλημα, ατος. n.

favourite topic to be talked about: w. neg. connotation, εἰς γυναῖκας Ez 23.10, γλώσσῃ 36.3 (ǁ ὀνείδισμα), εἰς παραβολὴν καὶ λ. καὶ ὀνειδισμόν ἐν πᾶσιν τοῖς ἔθνεσιν To 3.4 𝔊ᴵᴵ. Cf. λαλέω, ὀνείδισμα.

λαλητός, ή, όν.ʃ *

capable of speech: Jb 38.14. Cf. λαλέω.

λαλιά, ᾶς. f.

1. v.n. of λαλέω: Si 5.13.

2. *that which people say in general*: κατὰ τὴν ~άν ἐλέγξει 'admonishes in accordance with the general opinion' Is 11.3 (ǁ κατὰ τὴν δόξαν); ψευδής 'false (rumour)' 2M 5.5; ǁ λόγος Ps 18.4; fig. of insignificance, Jb 7.6.

3. *topic of conversation*: ἐν πόλει 'the talk of the town' Si 42.11.

Cf. λαλέω.

λαμβάνω: fut. λή(μ)ψομαι (on variants without μ, see Thack. 108f.), pass. λη(μ)φθήσομαι, inf. λήμψεσθαι, ptc. λημψόμενος; aor. ἔλαβον, impv. λάβε, 3pl λαβέτωσαν, inf. λαβεῖν, subj. λάβω, ptc. λαβών, mid. λαβόμενος; pass. ἐλή(μ)φθην, inf. λημφθῆναι, impv. 3s λη(μ)φθήτω, ptc. λημφθείς, opt. 3s λάβοι; pf. εἴληφα, inf. εἰληφέναι, ptc.act. εἰληφώς, pass. εἰλημμένος.

I. actively: **1**. *to take*, *take hold of*: τινα Ge 8.9, Jn 1.15; τὸν ἄνδρα μου Ge 30.15; by force, Ho 5.14 (in a simile of a wild animal taking its prey); + ἀπό of origin, Ge 2.22; + gen., λαβοῦσα τοῦ καρποῦ αὐτοῦ 3.6 (partitive), τοῦ ξύλου 3.22; ἐν ταῖς χερσίν τινος 'to take with oneself (to a given place)' 43.12, 15 (things; see καὶ τὸν Βενιαμιν added parenthetically at 43.15); + acc. and gen., λαβών με τῆς κομῆς 'taking me by the hair' Jb 16.12. **b**. mid. and + gen. rei: Si prol. II; τῆς χειρὸς αὐτῆς To 7.12 𝔊ᴵᴵ (𝔊ᴵ act.); 2M 12.35.

2. *to assume possession of*, *avail oneself of* for some use or purpose: πάντα τὰ τοῦ πατρὸς ἡμῶν 'all possessions of our father' Ge 31.1; + dat. com., λαβεῖν αὐτοῖς ἁμάξας 'wagons' 45.19; by deception, μετὰ δόλου ἔλαβεν τὴν εὐλογίαν σου 27.35; 27.36; unjustly, Nu 16.15; possessions, Jl 3.5; treasures, Is 39.6; opp. δίδωμι – δὸς καὶ λάβε Si 14.16; pass. λημφθήτω δὴ ὕδωρ Ge 18.4. **b**. intangible obj.: "he did not exercise his mind (ψυχήν) in a futile manner" Ps 23.4, cf. Ehthymius ad loc. (PG 128. 300).

3. *to procure* through purchase: + acc., ὕδωρ .. ἀργυρίου '.. for silver' De 2.6 (ǁ ἀγοράζω), σῖτον 'grain' Ne 5.2, 3; 4K 5.26*L*.

4. *to fetch*: + acc., ἄρτον Ge 18.5; Τίς .. λήμψεται ἡμῖν αὐτήν; 'who is going to fetch it for us?' De 30.12, 13; 2K 11.4.

5. *to seize*: + acc. of hidden objects Am 9.3.

6. *to capture* or *conquer* (often) *by military operation*: + acc., ἐν ὅπλοις 'with weapons' Am 4.2; τὴν ἵππον πᾶσαν .. καὶ πάντα τὰ βρώματα αὐτῶν 'the entire cavalry .. and their foods' Ge 14.11; prey, Is 31.4; enemy territories, 36.1; τούτους ἄνεμος λήμψεται 57.13; πόλιν Da 11.15 LXX (TH συλλαμβάνω).

*7. *to take* (a woman) *in marriage*: abs., Le 18.17; ἔλαβεν ἑαυτῷ Λαμεχ δύο γυναῖκας Ge 4.19; ἔλαβον αὐτὴν ἐμαυτῷ εἰς γυναῖκα 12.19; ἔλαβεν τὴν Ελισαβε .. γυναῖκα Ex 6.23 (ǁ εἰς γυναῖκα vs. 20), λαβεῖν αὐτὴν ἑαυτῷ γυναῖκα De 24.4; τοὺς γαμβροὺς αὐτοῦ τοὺς εἰληφότας τὰς θυγατέρας αὐτοῦ 'his in-laws who had taken his daughters in marriage' Ge 19.14; τῶν θυγατέρων Λευι 'one of the women of the Levite tribe' Ex 2.1; *s* father, ἔλαβεν Ιουδας γυναῖκα Ηρ 'J. took a wife for Er' Ge 38.6; mother, ἔλαβεν αὐτῷ ἡ μήτηρ γυναῖκα 21.21; servant for his master's son, 24.3; arranged marriage 2C 24.3. Opp. δίδωμι: τὰς θυγατέρας ὑμῶν δότε ἡμῖν καὶ τὰς θυγατέρας ἡμῶν λάβετε τοῖς υἱοῖς ὑμῶν Ge 34.9, sim. Ex 34.16.

8. *to pick up, choose*: abs. and + ἐκ 'from among' Am 2.11 (‖ ἀνα~ 7.15); τινα Hg 2.23; τι Ge 9.23; χρόνον 1E 9.12.

9. *to cause to come* or *go with one, to carry*: εἰς τὴν γῆν, ἐξ ἧς ἐλήμφθης 'into the earth, from which you were taken' Ge 3.19; λάβε τὴν γυναῖκά σου .. καὶ ἔξελθε 19.15; ὅταν παρέλθῃ, λήμψεται ὑμᾶς 'when it [= storm] departs, it would take you along with it' Is 28.19; + dat. pers., Λάβε μοι δάμαλιν .. 'Fetch me a heifer ..' 15.9; fig. λάβετε μεθ' ἑαυτῶν λόγους Ho 14.3; εἰς τὸ αὐτό 'to the same destiny (?)' Ma 2.3.

*10. *to pronounce, utter*: + acc., Οὐ λήμψῃ τὸ ὄνομα κυρίου τοῦ θεοῦ σου ἐπὶ ματαίῳ '.. in an irreverent, frivolous fashion' Ex 20.7, De 5.11; τὸν λόγον κυρίου .. ἐφ' ὑμᾶς θρῆνον 'the word of the Lord, which I pronounce over you as a dirge' Am 5.1; θρῆνον ἐπί τινα, Is 14.4, Ez 19.1, 26.17, 27.2, 32 (θρῆνον καὶ θρήνημα Σορ), 28.12, 32.2, sim. Je 9.10 (‖ κοπετόν); λῆμμα 4K 9.25; παραβολὴν κατ' αὐτοῦ λήμψονται Hb 2.6; τίς ἔλαβεν ἐπ' αὐτὴν ὀνειδισμόν 'who uttered an insult against her?' Zp 3.18, ὀνειδισμὸν οὐκ ἔλαβεν ἐπὶ τοὺς ἔγγιστα αὐτοῦ Ps 14.3, ψαλμόν 80.3, λόγους προσευχῆς 4K 19.4*L* (B: προσευχήν); pass. λημφθήσεται ἐφ' ὑμᾶς παραβολή Mi 2.4. Cf. ἀναλαμβάνω **7**.

11. *to take control of, overpower*: + acc. pers. and *s* emotions, ὠδῖνες ἔλαβον κατοικοῦντας Φυλιστιιμ 'pains seized the inhabitants of Philistia' Ex 15.14, sim. Is 21.3; ἔλαβεν αὐτοὺς τρόμος 'a shiver' 15.15, sim. 33.14 (‖ κατέχω Je 13.21); φόβος Is 10.29, Ep Je 4, αἰσχύνη Is 19.9, ὀδύνη 23.5, λύπη 'sorrow' Wi 11.12 (‖ στεναγμός 'sigh'), ζῆλος Is 26.11, καταιγίς 40.24, ἀλγηδών 'acute pain' 2M 9.5.

12. *to consider and assess*: ἐὰν λάβῃς τὸν συλλογισμὸν τῶν υἱῶν Ισραηλ 'if you assess (the results of) the counting of ..' Ex 30.12; πρὸ ὀφθαλμῶν 'envisaging' 2M 8.17; 3M 4.4.

13. *to undertake* or *initiate* an action: periphrastically with a v.n. (acc.), παῦλαν λ. 'to cease' 2M 4.6; ἐκδίκησιν 'vengeance' Je 20.10; πεῖραν 'an attempt' + inf., De 28.56.

14. *to take away and remove*: ἐλήμφθη τὸ πνεῦμα αὐτῶν ἀπὸ τῶν σπλάγχνων αὐτῶν Ba 2.17.

II. passively: **1**. *to receive, to be given*: + acc. of gifts, δεκτὸν ἐκ τῶν χειρῶν ὑμῶν 'accept a tithe at your hands' Ma 2.13; τὸ ἀργύριον τοῦ ἀγροῦ λάβε παρ' ἐμοῦ Ge 23.13; cultic offering, παρὰ τῶν υἱῶν Ισραηλ Le 7.24; τὰς εὐλογίας μου .. ἐβιάσατο αὐτὸν καὶ ἔλαβεν '.. he urged him, and he accepted (them)' Ge 33.11 (‖ δέχομαι vs. 10); + acc. of bribe, Ex 23.8; ὁ κριτὴς λ. Hb 1.3 (an acc. understood, cf. Cyr. ad loc.); δικαιώματα Ho 13.1; of commercial transaction, ἄλλαγμα Am 5.12; ὅταν λάβω καιρόν 'when occasion arises' Ps 74.3. **b**. οὐκ ἔλαβεν συντέλειαν 'it has not been completed' 1E 6.19.

2. *to be subjected to*: + acc. of verbal abuse, ὀνείδη λαῶν Mi 6.16, ὀνειδισμόν Je 15.15, κατάραν 36.22; πληγὴν ὀδύνης 'a painful blow' Mi 1.11; ἀτιμία Ez 36.7, 39.26; αἰσχύνην 'humiliation' 2M 5.7.

3. *to undergo, experience*: + acc., γεῦμα εὐτολμίας 'a taste of (the enemies') daring' 2M 13.18; "visually confronted by the common object of pity" 3M 4.4.

4. *to take* consequences for by being punished: + acc., λήμψεται ἀνόμημα αὐτοῦ Le 17.16, κόλασιν 'punishment' Ez 43.11. See further under ἀδικία **b**, ἁμαρτία **4**, ἀνόμημα **2**, ἀνομία **2**.

5. *to attain*: distinction (ἀρετή), Zc 6.13; *s* construction work, συντέλειαν 'completion' 1E 6.19.

6. *to receive into one's care*: + acc. (married daughter), Ex 18.2.

***III**. Idioms: **1**. λ. τὴν ψυχήν μου ἔν τινι *to covet, have an eye on*: Ho 4.8; ἐπὶ ματαίῳ 'on vain things' Ps 23.4.

2. λ. πρόσωπόν τινος (pers.) *to treat favourably* or *approvingly* Ma 1.8, in same sense also λ. ἔκ τινος πρόσωπόν τινος 1.9; *with respect*, π. ἱερέων La 4.16. **b**. *to show partiality and favouritism*: οὐ λήμψῃ πρόσωπον πτωχοῦ Le 19.15 (‖ θαυμάζω πρόσωπόν τινος); ἐλαμβάνετε πρόσωπα ἐν νόμῳ 'you practised favouritism in court' Ma 2.9, κρίνετε ἀδικίαν καὶ πρόσωπα ἁμαρτωλῶν λαμβάνετε Ps 81.2; ‖ διάφορα (q.v.) 1E 4.39. Cf. δόξα προσώπου; Harl 1992.152f.; Dogniez 2002.10-3.

3. λ. ἐν γαστρί 'to conceive, become pregnant': Ge 25.21, Ex 2.2; *s* hum. male, Nu 11.12 (‖ τίκτω).

4. λ. τὴν κεφαλήν τινος: *to show favour to* sbd by pardoning his past wrongdoings: Je 52.31.

5. λ. δεξιάς 'to have terms of peace granted' 1M 11.66, 13.50, 2M 12.12, cf. δεξιός **IIa**.

The object of the verb is always in the acc., never gen.

Cf. ἀνα~, ἀπο~, ἐκ~, ἐπι~, κατα~, προ~, συλλαμβάνω, λῆμμα, λῆμψις, δέχομαι, νοσφίζομαι, δίδωμι.

λαμπαδεῖον, ου. n.ʃ On the spelling, see Walters, 50f.

**bowl* of a lamp: Ex 38.16; λ. ἐπάνω ^λυχνίας^ Zc 4.2; 4.3, 3K 7.35. Cf. λαμπάς, λυχνία, λύχνος: Boyd-Taylor 2001.78f.

λαμπάς, άδος. f.

that which gives out light: 'torch', λ. πυρός Ge 15.17 (κλίβανος καπνιζόμενος 'smoking furnace'),

Na 2.5 (ǁ ἀστραπή 'lightning'), Zc 12.6. **b**. 'flash(es) of lightning': Ex 20.18.

Cf. λαμπαδεῖον, λαμπτήρ.

λαμπήνη, ης. f.

covered chariot: 1K 26.5, Is 66.20. Cf. λαμπηνικός.

λαμπηνικός, ή, όν. *ʃ

resembling a λαμπήνη 'covered chariot': ἁμάξας 'chariots' Nu 7.3.

λαμπρός, ά, όν.ʃ

1. *emitting light*, 'bright, radiant': *s* heavenly bodies, Ep Je 59; φῶς ~ὸν λάμψει 'a bright light will shine ..' To 13.11 𝔊II; metaph. and *s* σοφία Wi 6.12.

2. *looking splendid*: ἐδέσματα ~ά '.. foods' Si 29.22.

3. *joyous*: ~ὰ καρδία καὶ ἀγαθή 'a joyous and contented heart' Si 33.13b.

4. *generous*, *munificent*: ἐπ' ἄρτοις 'in handing out foods' Si 34.23.

Cf. λαμπρότης, δοξαστός.

λαμπρότης, ητος. f.ʃ

1. *splendour*: μετὰ δόξης μεγάλης καὶ ~ητος τοῦ αἰωνίου '.. of the Everlasting' Ba 4.24; 5.3.

2. *bright light*: Is 60.3 (of a guiding lamp), κυρίου Ps 89.17, τῶν ἁγίων 109.3; ἐκλάμψουσιν ὡς ἡ λ. τοῦ στερεώματος Da 12.3 TH (LXX: φωστῆρες).

Cf. λαμπρός, δόξα.

λαμπτήρ, ῆρος. m.

that which shines and serves as a guide: ἀσεβῶν 'of the impious' Pr 21.4; δόλου 'deceptive' 16.28. Cf. λαμπάς.

λάμπω: fut. λάμψω; aor. ἔλαμψα, subj. λάμψω.ʃ

1. *to emit light*: φῶς λάμψει ἐφ' ὑμᾶς Is 9.2; *s* stars, Ba 3.34, the sun Ep Je 66 (ǁ φωτίζω); τὸ τῆς δικαιοσύνης φῶς Wi 5.6; εἰς πάντα τὰ πέρατα τῆς γῆς 'into all the corners of the earth' To 13.11 𝔊II.

2. *to be bright*, *glow*: *s* Nazirites, ὑπὲρ γάλα 'more than milk' La 4.7; the sun, Ep Je 66 (ǁ φωτίζω); αἱ ὁδοὶ τῶν δικαίων φωτὶ .. λάμπουσιν Pr 4.18. For a metaph. use, cf. προκοπαῖς λάμψας 'having attained dazzling successes' Aristoph. *Vesp*. 62 and *ND* 4.35f.

Cf. ἀνα~, ἀντι~, ἐπι~, καταλάμπω, λάμψις, αὐγάζω, φαίνω: Schmidt 1.563-98; Oepke, *TDNT* 4.16f., 22f.

λάμψις, εως. f.ʃ

shining, v.n. of prec.: metaph., of the divine law, Ba 4.2. Cf. λάμπω.

λανθάνω: fut. λήσομαι; aor. ἔλαθον, subj. λάθω, inf. λαθεῖν, ptc. λαθών; pf. λέληθα.

to escape notice of, mostly of inadvertent omission on the part of the beholder: + acc. pers., ἔλαθεν αὐτόν 'it escaped his notice' Le 5.3; λάθη αὐτὸν πρὸ ὀφθαλμῶν 5.4; ἐὰν λάθη αὐτὸν λήθη 'should it escape him because of oblivion' 5.15, sim. Nu 5.27; λάθη ῥῆμα ἐξ ὀφθαλμῶν τῆς συναγωγῆς 'a matter should go unnoticed by the congregation' Le 4.13, sim. Nu 5.13; λέληθεν αὐτὸν οὐδὲν ὧν πράσσουσιν 'none of their deeds has escaped him' Jb 34.21, sim. οὐδέν σε ἔλαθεν Is 40.26; λέληθεν πάντα ἄνθρωπον 'everybody has missed it' Jb 28.21; οὐκ ἔλαθές με ἀγαθοποιῶν 'I did not fail to notice your good deeds' To 12.13 𝔊I. **b**. + ἀπό τινος (pers.): 2K 18.13B. **c**. with no acc.: φθεγγόμενος ἄδικα οὐδεὶς μὴ λάθη 'nobody would be overlooked when uttering unrighteous things' Wi 1.8, λανθάνειν νομίζοντες ἐπὶ κρυφαίοις ἁμαρτημάτων 'thinking they would go unnoticed in their secret sins' 17.3, see also 10.8; ἕως ἑνὸς οὐκ ἔλαθεν ὃς οὐ διῆλθεν .. 'there was not even one who did not cross unnoticed' 2K 17.22B.

Cf. δια~, ἐπιλανθάνω, λήθη, λάθρᾳ, κλέπτω **2**, παροδεύω: Spicq 2.369f.

λάξ. adv.ʃ

with the foot: kicking, 4M 6.8.

λαξευτήριον, ου. n.ʃ *

stone-cutter's tool: + πέλεκυς 'axe' Ps 73.6. Cf. λαξεύω.

λαξευτής, οῦ. m.ʃ

stone-cutter: 4K 12.13*L* (B:). Cf. λαξεύω, λατόμος, λιθουργός.

λαξευτός, ή, όν.ʃ *

hewn out of rock: as an attribute of a place-name, De 4.49. Cf. λαξεύω.

λαξεύω: aor. ἐλάξευσα, impv. λάξευσον, subj. λαξεύσω; pf.ptc.pass. λελαξευμένος.*

to cut into shape, 'hew': + acc. rei, πλάκας λιθίνας 'stone tablets' Ex 34.1; τράπεζαι .. λίθιναι λελαξευμέναι 'hewn stone tables' Ez 40.42; Ju 1.2; as part of a construction work, Is 9.10. Cf. λαξευτήριον, λαξευτός, λατομέω.

λαογραφία, ας. f.ʃ *

national census-taking: 3M 2.28.

λαός, οῦ. m.

1. *a large body of humans*, 'people': ἀπέθανεν λ. πολὺς τῶν υἱῶν Ισραηλ Nu 21.6; ǁ χώρα 'country' Jn 1.8; ǁ ἔθνος Ge 25.23; pl. ǁ ἔθνη Hb 2.5, 8, 13, Ez 36.15; of army, λ. πολὺς καὶ ἰσχυρὸς παρατασσόμενος εἰς πόλεμον '.. being deployed for a war' Jl 2.5, ǁ ἄνθρωποι 4K 18.26 (cf. Is 36.11); household members other than kinsmen and spouses, Ge 14.16; ἅπας ὁ λαός 'the entire townsfolk' 19.4. **b**. ὁ λ. τῆς γῆς 'lay people' as against clerics: Le 4.27, cf. 'the local population' 2E 4.4, λαοὶ τῆς γῆς 10.2, 11, Ne 10.30, πᾶς ὁ λαὸς τῆς γῆς Je 40.9; opp. ἄρχων Ez 7.27. **c**. the entire mankind: διδοὺς πνοὴν τῷ λαῷ τῷ ἐπὶ ^τῆς γῆς^ 'gives breath to all the people who are on the earth' Is 42.5.

2. *a large body of people affiliated and defined along ethnic, racial, religious or political lines*, 'nation': τῆς γῆς 'the local population' Ge 23.7; members of a tribe, 49.16; πᾶς ὁ λ. μου 41.40; ὥστε εἶναι λαὸν ἕνα 34.22; ἐν πᾶσι τοῖς λαοῖς τῆς γῆς Zp 3.20; w. ref. to the Israelites, οἱ κατάλοιποι τοῦ ~οῦ Hg 1.12; God's people, πάντα, ὅσα ἐποίησεν κύριος Ισραηλ τῷ ἑαυτοῦ ~ῷ 'all that the Lord had done to Israel his own people' Ex 18.1, εἶναι αὐτῷ ~ον περιούσιον παρὰ πάντα τὰ ἔθνη 'to be a people of His distinct from all the nations' De 7.6; λαοῦ σου Hb 3.13; λ. ἅγιος κεκλήσεται θεοῦ 'they shall be called God's holy nation' Ho 11.12; || ἐκκλησία Jl 2.16; God speaking of his own people, λ. μου Is 51.4, οἱ κατάλοιποι ~οῦ μου Zp 2.9, λ. παροικίας μου Hb 3.16; Hg 2.14 (|| ἔθνος); as against the people of Israel, συναχθήσονται ἐπ' αὐτοὺς ~οί Ho 10.10; one's own forefathers, προσετέθη πρὸς τὸν ~ὸν αὐτοῦ 'joined his forbears (upon death)' Ge 25.8 (|| γένος vs. 17 w. ref. to non-Israelites, see Rösel 236f.). **b**. prob. distinct from ἔθνος: λ. σου τὸ ἔθνος τοῦτο Ex 33.13, λαοὶ τῶν ἐθνῶν 2E 9.11. **c**. the general body of people excluding leaders: οἱ ἱερεῖς καὶ ὁ λ. Ex 19.24.

Cf. ἔθνος, φυλή: Schmidt 4.573-5; Trench 367; Strathmann, *TDNT* 4.32-9; Spicq 2.371-4; Vandersleyen 1973.

λαπιστής, οῦ. m.ʃ

swaggerer: Si 20.7. Cf. Shipp 358.

λάπτω: aor.subj. λάψω, ptc. λάψας.

to lap with the tongue: *s* dog, τῇ γλώσσῃ ἐκ (B: ἀπὸ) τοῦ ὕδατος Jd 7.5 A, ἐν τῇ γλώσσῃ 7.6 A; ἐν χειρὶ αὐτῶν πρὸς τὸ στόμα αὐτῶν 7.6 B.

λάρος, ου. m.ʃ

sea-mew, gull (?): forbidden as food, Le 11.15, De 14.14. See Shipp 359.

λάρυγξ, υγγος. m.

larynx: Ps 5.10 (|| γλῶσσα). **b**. organ of speech, Ps 113.15; hence speech, λ. γλυκύς 'sweet manner of speech' Si 6.5 (|| γλῶσσα). **c**. digestive organ: *s* of γεύομαι 'to taste' Jb 12.11; γλυκὺς ἐν ~γι 'sweet ..' Ct 2.3.

Cf. φάρυγξ.

λατομέω: aor. ἐλατόμησα, inf. λατομῆσαι, subj. λατομήσω, pass. ἐλατομήθην; pf.ptc.pass. λελατομημένος.

1. *to dig in the ground and construct* (a cavity): + acc., λάκκον Ex 21.33; pass., λάκκους λελατομημένους De 6.11, Ne 9.25; μνημεῖον 'grave' Is 22.16 (|| γράφω); ἀποδοχεῖον ὑδάτων 'water reservoir' Si 50.3.

2. *to dig into*: + acc., πέτρα 'rock' Is 51.1.

3. *to dig out*: + acc., λίθους 1C 22.2; pass., χαλκὸς ἴσα λίθῳ λατομεῖται 'copper is dug out like stone' Jb 28.2; 4K 12.13*L*.

Cf. ἐκλατομέω, λάκκος, λατόμος, ὀρύσσω.

λατομητός, ή, όν.ʃ

quarried and hewn: *s* building stone, 4K 12.13B (*L* λελατομημένος), 22.6. Cf. λατομέω.

λατόμος, ου. m.

stone-cutter: 2E 3.7 (+ τέκτων). Cf. λαξευτής, λιθουργός.

λατρεία, ας.

1. *service rendered*: forced labour, 3M 4.14.

2. *religious rite*: *o* of φυλάσσομαι Ex 12.25; of ποιέω 13.5. **b**. *religion*: 1M 1.43 (heathen), 2.19 (Israelite).

Cf. λατρεύω, λειτουργία.

λατρευτός, ή, όν.

servile: *s* ἔργον – πᾶν ἔργον ~ὸν οὐ ποιήσεται Ex 12.16 (a ban on any servile work on the first day of the passover celebration), Le 23.7 (ποιήσετε), Nu 28.18. Cf. λατρεύω.

λατρεύω: fut. λατρεύσω, aor. ἐλάτρευσα, inf. λατρεῦσαι, impv. λάτρευσον, subj. λατρεύσω.

1. *to perform religious, cultic services*: abs. 1E 4.54; + dat., τῷ θεῷ ἐν τῷ ὄρει τούτῳ Ex 3.12; by offering sacrifices (θύω, see 3.18), 7.16; 20.5 (|| προσκυνέω); αὐτοῖς [= participants in a rite] Nu 16.9; to pagan gods, Ex 23.24, θεοῖς ἑτέροις De 4.28, 13.2, 17.3, + προσκυνέω Jd 2.19, ὡς τὰ ἔθνη καὶ ὡς αἱ φυλαὶ τῆς γῆς τοῦ λατρεύειν ξύλοις καὶ λίθοις Ez 20.32 (Pap. 967 δουλεύειν), εἰδώλῳ Da 3.12 LXX; to heavenly bodies, De 4.19, 17.3, 29.26 (|| προσκυνέω); || θεραπεύω 1E 1.4. **b**. w. focus on one's attitude: κυρίῳ .. ἐξ ὅλης τῆς καρδίας σου καὶ ἐξ ὅλης τῆς ψυχῆς σου De 10.12.

2. *to offer* in cultic services: + acc., τί λατρεύσωμεν κυρίῳ τῷ θεῷ ἡμῶν Ex 10.26.

3. *to dedicate oneself in service to*: + dat. pers., τοῖς ἐχθροῖς σου De 28.48 (|| κυρίῳ τῷ θεῷ σου 47); σοφία personified, Si 4.14 (|| λειτουργέω ἁγίῳ).

Cf. λατρεία, λατρευτός, λειτουργέω, δουλεύω: Schmidt 4.137f.; Trench 125-7.

λάτρις, ιος. f.ʃ

handmaid: Jb 2.9d. Cf. ἅβρα, δούλη, παιδίσκη: Schmidt 4.137.

λαφυρέω: aor. ἐλαφύρησα.ʃ

to take spoils from in war: + acc. (enemies), Ju 15.11. Cf. λάφυρον, ἁρπάζω.

λάφυρον, ου. n.ʃ

pl. *spoils taken in war*: Ju 15.7, 1C 26.27, 2M 8.30. Cf. λαφυρεύω, ἁρπαγή.

λαχανεία, ας. f.ʃ *

herbs: κῆπος ~ας 'garden of herbs' De 11.10. Cf. λάχανον.

λάχανον, ου. n.ʃ

garden-herbs as food for humans, 'vegetables': pl. (so usually in Cl. Gk) ~α χόρτου 'vegetables' Ge 9.3; ~α χλόης Ps 36.2 (‖ χόρτος); κῆπος ~ων 'vegetable garden' 3K 20.2; ξενισμὸς ~ων 'entertainment with ..' Pr 15.17 (fig. of humble meals). Cf. λαχανεία: Schnebel 210.

λέαινα, ης. f.

lioness: ‖ λέων Jb 4.10. Cf. λέων.

λεαίνω: fut. λεανῶ; aor. ἐλέανα.ʃ

1. *to smooth*: : + acc. rei, λίθους ἐλέαναν ὕδατα 'water smoothed stones' Jb 14.19.

2. *to grind down, crush*: + acc. pers., ὡς πηλὸν πλατειῶν 'as mud of streets' Ps 17.43, ὡς χοῦν γῆς 'as dust of the ground' 2K 22.43B (‖ λεπτύνω).

Cf. λεπτύνω.

λέβης, ητος. m.

cauldron: cooking utensil, κρεῶν 'for meat' Ex 16.3; ὡς σάρκας εἰς ~τα 'as meat into a cauldron' Mi 3.3 (‖ χύτρα); used to boil sacrificial meat, οἱ ~τες ἐν τῷ οἴκῳ κυρίου Zc 14.20; instrument of torture (cf. βασανιστήριον), εἰς ~τας ὑποκαιομένους 'into boiling cauldrons' Am 4.2, + τήγανον 2M 7.3.

λέγω: fut. ἐρῶ; aor. εἶπον (q.v.), ἔλεξα, ptc.pass. λεχθείς. Used mostly as pres.ptc. λέγων marking the onset of direct speech, except the prophetic formula λέγει κύριος.

1. *to utter*, 'say': foll. by direct speech, Jn 1.14, 2.3; introducing a divine oracle or message communicated through human agent, τάδε λέγει κύριος Ob 1, Na 1.12; at the conclusion of such, Ob 4, Hg 1.8, 13; placed in the middle of such, ἐν ἐκείνῃ τῇ ἡμέρᾳ, λέγει κύριος, ἀπολῶ σοφοὺς κ.τ.λ. Ob 8; Hg 2.14, Ma 1.2; often introducing a responding speech in Jb, ὑπολαβὼν .. λέγει 4.1+, see Woo 80f. **b**. foll. by an inf., λέγουσιν μὴ εἶναι ὧδε πόρνην 'they say that there is no harlot here' Ge 38.22; λεγόντων ἀκούσαντά σε ἐνύπνια συγκρῖναι αὐτά 41.15. **c**. The pres. ptc. nom., e.g. λέγων, following another verb of saying, marks the following as direct speech: καὶ ἐγένετο λόγος κυρίου πρὸς Ιωναν .. λέγων 'Ανάστηθι .. Jn 1.1f, 3.1; ἐλάλησε κύριος .. λέγων Hg 2.1; 2.20, 21; εἶπεν .. λέγουσα .. Ge 39.14; ὥρκισέν με λέγων .. 50.5. Indeclinable and following an impersonal verb: ἐκηρύχθη καὶ ἐρρέθη .. λέγων .. Jn 3.7; ἐγενήθη ῥῆμα κυρίου πρὸς Αβραμ .. λέγων .. Ge 15.1; with no agreement in number, διεβοήθη ἡ φωνὴ εἰς τὸν οἶκον Φαραω λέγοντες .. 45.16; ἀνηγγέλη Μωυσῇ λέγοντες 'Ἰδοὺ .. 'it was reported to Moses, "Behold .."' Ex 18.6. Even following a form of λέγω: ἔλεγον .. λέγοντες .. Ex 5.10. The lead verb does not have to be a verb of saying and its subject is not identical with that of λέγων: ἐμαστιγώθησαν .. λέγοντες .. 'they were whipped .. being told ..' Ex 5.14; so also 5.19. This is no Hebraism: see LSJ, s.v. **III 7**. **d**. in conjunction with another verb of saying and foll. by direct speech: ἀπήγγειλεν .. λέγων Ge 47.1, ἐβόησεν .. λέγων, Nu 12.13, ἀπεκρίθησαν καὶ εἶπαν .. Zc 1.6. **e**. + acc. rei, λέγε σὺ τὰς ἁμαρτίας σου 'confess your sins' Is 43.26, ψεύδη Je 47.16. **f**. in writing: λέγεται ἐν βιβλίῳ Nu 21.14. **g**. + acc. (topic) foll. by direct speech: Je 39.36.

2. *to direct oneself to* sbd *in speech*, 'to address': πρός τινα Jn 4.10, 11, Hg 2.2; ἐπί τινα Je 11.21, 22.18; + τινι - ὁ λέγων τῷ ξύλῳ Hb 2.19. Cf. εἰπὸν τῷ .. βασιλεῖ Ιουδα καὶ πρὸς πάντα οἶκον Ιουδα 3K 12.23.

3. *to give a command to*: + dat. pers. and inf., τὴν πλίνθον ἡμῖν λέγουσιν ποιεῖν 'they tell us to make bricks' Ex 5.16; ‖ impv., Is 49.9. See χαλᾶν λέγω σοι Soph. *OC* 840.

4. λ. ἐν τῇ καρδίᾳ τινός to hold the opinion or intention as follows, 'to think aloud': foll. by direct speech, οἱ λέγοντες ἐν ταῖς καρδίαις αὐτῶν Οὐ μὴ ἀγαθοποιήσῃ κύριος Zp 1.12; ἡ λέγουσα ἐν τῇ καρδίᾳ αὐτῆς 'Εγώ εἰμι .. 3.1, cf. εἶπον **1 d**. **b**. *to say things in private*: Ps 4.5.

5. *to designate as, categorise as*: + double acc., οἱ λέγοντες τὸ πονηρὸν καλὸν καὶ τὸ καλὸν πονηρόν Is 5.20 (‖ τίθημι); 2M 4.2. **b**. *to call by the name of*: double acc., pass., ἐπὶ τὸν λεγόμενον Θεραν ποταμόν 'to the river called Th.' 1E 8.41.

6. *to speak about* sbd or sth (acc.) in a certain way: κακῶς ἐρεῖτε τὸν ἄρχοντα 'you will speak ill of the ruler' Is 8.21; Ex 22.28; also + dat. pers., 4M 18.12 (‖ ἀναγινώσκω 'to recite'). Cf. Aesch. *Ag*. 445. **b**. *s* Bible scholar: Si prol. 6 (: : γράφω), cf. תורה שבעל פה 'oral teaching' vs. תורה שבכתב 'teaching in writing.'

7. *to wish to say*, 'mean, be referring to': + acc., 2M 14.7, 4M 1.2.

Cf. λόγος, λέξις, ἀναγγέλλω, βοάω, εἶπον, ἡθολογέω, κράζω, λαλέω, ῥητός, φάσκω, φημί, φθέγγομαι, φράζω, ἄλεκτος.

λεηλατέω.ʃ

to plunder: + acc., χώραν 'country' 2M 2.21. Cf. ἁρπάζω, προνομεύω.

λεῖα, ας. f.ʃ

crowd of people under one's absolute control: *s* captives, 4M 8.2. Cf. πλῆθος.

λεῖμμα, ατος. n.ʃ

that which has remained: without perishing, 2K 21.2B (*L* λοιποί), 4K 19.4. Cf. λείπω, λοιπός, κατά~, ὑπόλειμμα.

λειμών, ῶνος. m.ʃ

meadow: euphemism for fem. genitalia, Wi 2.9. See Busto Saiz 1991.

λειοπετρία, ας. f.
smooth rock: Ez 24.7 (w. ref. to the rocky island city of Tyre following devastation). Cf. πέτρα.

λεῖος, α, ον.
with no protrusion on the surface, 'smooth': *s* ἀνήρ 'a man with no thick body-hair' Ge 27.11 (:: δασύς), ὁδός Is 40.4, τρίβος Pr 2.20, λίθους 'stones' 1K 17.40. **b**. metaph.: *s* χείλη 'lips' Pr 26.23 (|| μαλακός 'soft'); subst.n.pl. adv., ὁ βλεπών λεῖα 'he who has gentle looks' 12.13a.
Cf. δασύς, τραχύς.

λ(ε)ιποτακτέω: aor.subj. ~τακτήσω.ʃ *
to desert one's post, not caring about: + acc., μου τὸν ἀγῶνα 'my struggle' 4M 9.23. Cf. λείπω.

λείπω: aor. ἔλιπον; pf.ptc.pass. λελειμμένος.ʃ
1. *to sever ties with and abandon*: + acc., ἀλλήλους Jb 4.10; pass., λελειμμένος 'forsaken (with no ally)' 2M 4.45; Pr 19.4.
2. *to leave unaffected by*: pass., + gen., τῆς ἡμετέρας ἀλκῆς '(spared the exercise) of our military strength' 3M 3.18, τιμωρίας 'punishment' 4.13.
3. *to leave behind*: + acc., μετάμελον 'a sense of loss' Pr 11.3.
4. intr. *to be absent and missing when it ought to be in possession of* sbd or sth (dat.): τὴν λείπουσαν ταῖς βασάνοις .. κόλασιν 'the punishment which their torments still lacked' Wi 19.4. Cf. Shipp 361.
Cf. λειποτακτέω, κατα~, περι~, ὑπολείπω, λεῖμμα, ὑστερέω: Spicq 2.375-7.

λειτουργέω: fut. λειτουργήσω; aor. ἐλειτούργησα, inf. λειτουργῆσαι.
to render service: *s* public, cultic functionary, Ex 28.39; λειτουργεῖν καὶ ἐπεύχεσθαι De 10.8; + dat. ('in deference to') τῷ προσώπῳ κυρίου 1K 2.11 (*L*: τῷ κυρίῳ), τῷ οἴκῳ 'the temple' Ez 44.11 (v.l. ἐν τῷ ..), 45.5, οἱ ἱερεῖς οἱ λειτουργοῦντες θυσιαστηρίῳ Jl 1.9; θεῷ ib.; κυρίῳ 2.17; ἁγίῳ Si 4.14 (|| λατρεύω σοφίᾳ); αὐτῷ [= Aaron] Nu 3.6; ἐν τοῖς ἁγίοις 'in the sanctuary' Ex 29.30; ἐν σκηνῇ ἁγίᾳ Si 24.10, ἐν τῇ σκηνῇ τοῦ μαρτυρίου Nu 4.37; ἐπὶ βωμῶν Si 50.14; ἐπὶ τῷ ὀνόματι 'on the authority of' De 17.12 (without ἐπί at 18.7); + acc. rei, τὰ ἔργα τῆς σκηνῆς τοῦ μαρτυρίου 'the services in the tent of testimony' Nu 4.30; + cogn. acc., λειτουργίαν 8.22, τὰς λειτουργίας τῆς σκηνῆς κυρίου 16.9; Aaron's twofold function is – λειτουργεῖν αὐτῷ ἅμα καὶ ἱερατεύειν Si 45.15, cf. τοῖς ἱερεῦσι τοῖς λειτουργοῦσι 1M 10.42. **b**. w. ref. to paganism: τῇ Ἀστάρτῃ 2C 15.16; αὐτοῖς (= Israelites) πρὸ προσώπου τῶν εἰδώλων αὐτῶν Ez 44.12 (|| proper religious service, vs. 11). **c**. neither cultic nor public: + dat. pers., Ps 100.6, 3K 1.4; μεγιστᾶσιν 'eminent people' Si 8.8.
Cf. λειτουργία, λειτουργός, λατρεύω, θεραπεύω: Trench 125-7; Daniel 93-117; Strathmann, *TDNT* 4.219-22; Spicq 2.378-84; *ND* 6.93-111.

λειτούργημα, ατος. n.ʃ
performance of religious, cultic ritual: Nu 4.32; τοῦ ἁγίου 'of the sanctuary' 7.9. Cf. λειτουργία.

λειτουργήσιμος, ον.ʃ *
pertaining to cultic service: *s* σκεύη 1C 28.13. Cf. λειτουργία.

λειτουργία, ας. f.
service: cultic, τῶν Λευιτῶν Ex 37.19, οἴκου θεοῦ 2E 7.19, ἁγίων 'sacred (service)' 2C 35.15, θυσιαστηρίου 2M 4.14; as cogn. acc. of λειτουργέω Nu 8.22, 16.9; περὶ τὰς τοῦ θυσιαστηρίου ~ας προθύμους εἶναι τοὺς ἱερούς 'for the priests to be enthusiastic about the services at the altar' 2M 4.14; general, occasional, ἐλειτούργησαν τὴν ~αν τοῦ διαβιβάσαι τὸν βασιλέα 'they rendered the service of getting the king across' 2K 19.19, ἀντὶ τῆς ~ας αὐτοῦ, ἧς ἐδούλευσεν .. Ez 29.20. Cf. λειτουργέω, λειτουργικός, λειτουργήσιμος, λειτούργημα: Romeo; Lewis.

λειτουργικός, ή, όν.
pertaining to religious service: *s* στολή 'garment' Ex 31.10; σκεῦος 'vessel' Nu 4.12; ἔργον ~όν 'cultic service' 7.5. Cf. λειτουργία.

λειτουργός, οῦ. m.
one who renders service: public, cultic, ὑμεῖς ἱερεῖς κυρίου κληθήσεσθε, ~οὶ θεοῦ Is 61.6, ~οὶ αὐτοῦ ποιοῦντες τὸ θέλημα αὐτοῦ Ps 102.21, cf. Si 7.30 (|| ἱερεῖς vs. 29), = πῦρ φλέγον 'a fire in flames' Ps 103.4 (|| ἄγγελοι); οἴκου θεοῦ 2E 7.24, Ne 10.39 (in a series of cultic functionaries); officials under a judge, Si 10.2; functionaries in a royal palace, πρὸς τούτους 'in charge of these people' 3M 5.5; || παιδάριον 4 Ki 6.15, || παῖς 3K 10.5; a prince's personal assistant, 2K 13.18, Elisha's 4K 4.43, judge's Si 10.2. Cf. λειτουργέω, διάκονος, θεράπων, παιδάριον, παῖς, ὑπηρέτης, ὑπουργός: Strathmann, *TDNT* 4.229f.

λειχήν, ῆνος. m.ʃ
lichen-like eruption on the skin (LSJ): bodily defect disqualifying its sufferer for priesthood, Le 21.20, 22.22.

λείχω: fut. λείξω; aor. ἔλειξα.ʃ
to lick: *s* pigs and dogs 3K 20.19 (*o* hum. blood); + acc. rei, χοῦν ὡς ὄφις 'dust like a snake' Mi 7.17 (indicative of obsequiousness and humiliation, and cf. γῆν φάγῃ 'thou shalt eat dust' Ge 3.14), ἐπὶ πρόσωπον τῆς γῆς προσκυνήσουσί σοι καὶ τὸν χοῦν τῶν ποδῶν σου λείξουσιν 'they will bow down to you on the face of the earth and lick the dust of your feet' Is 49.23; *s* enemies, Ps 71.9. Cf. ἐκλείχω.

λεκάνη. ⇒ λακάνη.

λεληθότως. adv.ʃ

secretly: 2M 6.11, 8.1. Cf. λανθάνω, λάθρᾳ, κρυφαίως.

λέξις, εως. f.

1. *act of saying*, v.n. of λέγω: Jb 36.2.

2. *single word or phrase*: Si prol. 20, cf. Wagner 118.

3. *manner of speech*: Si 23.12.

4. *set of sounds and words and the way they are used*, 'language': κατὰ τὴν ~ιν αὐτῶν 'in their respective language' Es 1.22 o'.

Cf. λέγω: Schmidt 1.100f.

λεοντηδόν. adv.ʃ*

like a lion: fig. of bravery, 2M 11.11. Cf. λέων.

λεπίζω: aor. ἐλέπισα, pass. ἐλεπίσθην.

to strip away, peel away: + cogn. obj., λεπίσματα λευκά 'white stripes' Ge 30.37; τὸ λευκόν, ὃ ἐλέπισεν 'the white part which he produced by stripping' ib.; obj., rod (ῥάβδος) 30.38; λευκώματα 'white parts' To 3.17 𝔊I (medical treatment); pass. 11.13 𝔊I. Cf. ἀπολεπίζω, λέπισμα, λεπίς.

λεπίς, ίδος. f.

fairly broad, thin flat object: pl., 'scales' of fish: πτερύγια καὶ ~δες 'fins and scales' Le 11.9 +. **b**. 'plate' of metal: ~δας ἐλατάς 'beaten plates' Nu 16.38.

Cf. λέπισμα, λεπίζω.

λέπισμα, ματος. n.ʃ *

that which has been peeled off: ~ατα λευκά Ge 30.37 (peeled off from a rod). Cf. λεπίζω, λεπίς.

λέπρα, ας. f.

leprosy: ἁφὴ ~ας 'infection of ..' Le 13.2; even affecting garments, 13.47 (in the form of mould or mildew?). Cf. λεπρός, λεπράω. See *BA* 3.45.

λεπράω ʃ

to suffer leprosy: ‖ γονορρυής Le 22.4; ὡσεὶ χιών 'like snow' Nu 12.10. Cf. λεπρός.

λεπρός, ά, όν.

suffering leprosy: *s* hum., Le 13.44; subst.m. 'leper' 13.45, 14.2; ‖ γονορρυής, ἀκάθαρτος Nu 5.2. Cf. λέπρα.

λεπρόω: pf.ptc.pass. λελεπρωμένος.

to afflict with leprosy: *o* hum., 4K 5.1B, 15.5B. Cf. λεπρός.

λεπτός, ή, όν.

1. *having a thin top-layer*: *s* cows (βόες), λεπταὶ ταῖς σαρξίν 'skinny' Ge 41.3 (:: ἐκλεκταὶ ταῖς σαρξίν vs. 2); ear of corn, στάχυες ~οὶ καὶ ἀνεμόφθοροι 'thin and wind-damaged ears of corn' 41.6 (:: πλήρεις vs. 7, 22, 24); hair, Le 13.30. **b**. subst.n. λεπτόν 'thin layer' Ex 16.14.

2. *in small particles*: θυμίαμα σύνθετον ~όν 'powdery, compound incense' Ex 30.7; subst. 'powder' 30.36. **b**. as a result of grinding: De 9.21, of crushing– κονία ~ή 'fine dust' Is 27.9, ἐκ κεραμίου ~ά 'tiny pieces of a smashed earthen vessel' Is 30.14; ~ὰ ποιέω 'to smash into tiny pieces, pulverise' 30.22.

3. *capable of discerning subtleties*: *s* spirit of Wisdom, Wi 7.22.

4. *gentle and not harsh to the eardrums*: *s* αὔρα 'breeze' 3K 19.12.

Cf. λεπτύνω.

λεπτύνω: fut. λεπτυνῶ; aor. ἐλέπτυνα, pass. ἐλεπτύνθην, inf. λεπτυνθῆναι.

to crush into small pieces: + acc., βουνούς 'hills' Is 41.15 (‖ ἀλοάω), σκεύη 'vessels' Je 31.12 (‖ συγκόπτω), κέρδους 'cedar trees' Ps 28.6, εἴδωλα 'idols' 2C 23.17 (‖ 4K 11.18 συντρίβω); *o* enemies, ὡς χοῦν 'as dust' 17.43. Cf. λεπτός, θλάω, καταλοάω, λεαίνω.

λέπυρον, ου. n.ʃ

bark of plant, 'rind': ῥόας 'of a rose' Ct 4.3, 6.7.

λέσχη, ης. f.ʃ

malicious gossip: from a victim's perspective, Pr 23.29.

Λευίτης, ου. m.

Levite: Ex 4.14 +.

λευκαθίζω: pf.ptc.pass. λελευκαθισμένος.ʃ

to be white: *s* spots on the skin of a human body, Le 13.38, 39 (‖ αὐγάζω); pass. λελευκαθισμένη 'clad in white' Ct 8.5. Cf. λευκός, λευκαίνω.

λευκαίνω: fut. λευκανῶ, pass. λευκανθήσομαι; aor. ἐλεύκανα.ʃ

1. *to become white*: of healed leprous skin, τηλαυγὴς λευκαίνουσα 'visibly growing white' Le 13.19 (‖ πυρρίζω).

2. *to make white*: pass. *o* snow, ὑπὲρ χιόνα λευκανθήσομαι 'I shall be made whiter than snow' Ps 50.9, cf. ὡς χιόνα λευκανῶ .. ὡς ἔριον ('wool') λευκανῶ Is 1.18; *o* κλήματα 'branches' (by peeling them) or **1** Jl 1.7.

Cf. λευκός, λευκαθίζω, ἐκλευκαίνω.

λευκανθίζω. ⇒ λευκαθίζω. See Walters, 87.

λεύκη, ης. f.ʃ

white poplar: Is 41.19; growing on a site of pagan cult, ἐπὶ τοὺς βουνοὺς ἔθυον, ὑποκάτω δρυὸς καὶ ~ης καὶ δένδρου συσκιάζοντος '.. under an oak-tree and a white poplar and a shady tree ..' Ho 4.13. Cf. λευκός.

λευκός, ή, όν.

white: λεπίσματα ~ά 'white peels (peeled away from a rod) Ge 30.37; *s* milk, 49.12; leprous skin, Le 13.3; horse, Zc 1.8; garment, Ec 9.8, 2M 11.8, compared to snow Da 7.9 TH; pure wool, 7.9 LXX 967. Cf. λεύκη, λευκαθίζω, λευκαίνω, λευκότης, λεύκωμα: Schmidt 3.10-4; Shipp 361f.; Passoni dell'Acqua 1998.95.

λευκότης, ητος. f.∫
whiteness: of snow and its beauty, Si 43.18. Cf. λευκός.

λεύκωμα, ατος. n.
white thing: produced in the eyes by a bird's droppings, To 2.10. Cf. λευκός.

λεχώ, όος. f.∫
woman at childbirth: Ep Je 28.

λέων, οντος, pl.dat. λέουσι. m.
lion: predator, Ho 5.14 (ǁ πανθήρ); ἐκ στόματος ~τος Am 3.12; life-threatening, 5.19 (ǁ ἄρκος 'bear'); ὡς λ. ἐν κτήνεσιν 'like a lion amongst cattle' Mi 5.8 (ǁ σκύμνος); οἱ ὀδόντες αὐτοῦ ὀδόντες ~τος 'its teeth are those of a lion' Jl 1.6 (ǁ σκύμνος); λ. ἥρπασε τὰ ἱκανὰ τοῖς σκύμνοις αὐτοῦ καὶ ἀπέπνιξε τοῖς λέουσιν αὐτοῦ 'a lion carried away enough prey for its whelps and strangled for its (young) lions' Na 2.13; roaring, ὡς λ. ἐρεύξεται Ho 11.10; Am 3.4 (ǁ σκύμνος); of its scaring effect, 3.8; ὠρυόμενοι 'howling' Zp 3.3 (ǁ λύκος); Zc 11.3; fig. of a poweful nation, λ. ἔθνων Ez 32.2. Cf. λέαινα, λεοντηδόν, μυρμηκολέων, πανθήρ and σκύμνος.

λήγω: aor. ἔληξα.∫
1. *to cease to take effect*: *s* pain abating, 2M 9.18.
2. *cease from, stop engaging in*: + gen., ἀγερωχίας 'arrogance' 2M 9.7, ὑπερηφανίας 'haughtiness' 9.11, ἀνοίας 'folly' 3M 3.16, προσευχῆς 'prayer' 6.16. **b**. *to stop speaking*: 2M 15.24.
Cf. καταλήγω, καταπαύω.

λήθη, ης. f.
act of overlooking: inadvertently and as an instr. dat. of (ἐπι)λανθάνω (q.v.), Ψυχὴ ἐὰν λάθῃ αὐτὸν ~ῃ καὶ ἁμάρτῃ ἀκουσίως 'should somebody act inadvertently, not being aware of the matter, and sin unintentionally' Le 5.15; Nu 5.27; ~ῃ ἐπιλάθῃ De 8.19; ἐν ~ῃ Si 14.7; deliberately, Jb 7.21. **b**. *act of inadvertently forgetting*: 3M 5.28.
Cf. λανθάνω, ἀμνησία, ἀμνηστία, ἐπιλησμονή.

λῆμμα, ατος. n.
1. *material gain, profit*: ἕνεκεν τῶν ~άτων αὐτῶν τῶν ὀρθρινῶν 'because of their gains made in the morning' Hg 2.14.
*__2__. *prophetic message*: λ. Νινευη 'message concerning Nineveh' Na 1.1; seen in a vision, τὸ λ., ὃ εἶδεν Αμβακουμ Hb 1.1. μάταιον 'meaningless' La 2.14. **b**. substance and contents of such message: λ. λόγου κυρίου ἐν γῇ Σεδραχ Zc 9.1; ἐπὶ τὸν Ισραηλ 12.1, Ma 1.1.
*__3__. oppressive *burden imposed* on one, whether physical or mental: Jb 31.23.
See Harl 1999.

λῆμψις, εως. f.
act of receiving: λ. καὶ δόσις Si 41.19, δόσις καὶ λ. 42.7, δώρων 'of bribes' Pr 15.27; of income or returns on invested capital or efforts, 15.29a. Cf. λαμβάνω, δόσις.

ληνός, οῦ. f.
1. *trough*: ἐν ταῖς ~οῖς τῶν ποτιστηρίων τοῦ ὕδατος Ge 30.38.
2. *walled space for treading and squeezing out oil or fluid*: ἅλων καὶ λ. 'threshing-floor and ..' De 16.13, Ho 9.2; κατεσκάφησαν ~οί '.. were razed to the ground' Jl 1.17, poss. meaning *entire winery, wine-producing installation*; ὑπερεκχυθήσονται αἱ ~οὶ οἴνου καὶ ἐλαίου '.. will overflow with wine and olive-oil' 2.24 (ǁ ἅλων); πλήρης ἡ λ. '.. is full' 3.13 (ǁ ὑπολήνιον); *o* of πατέω 'to tread' 3.13, La 1.15.
Cf. προλήνιον, ὑπολήνιον: Schnebel 285-92; Mayerson 2000.161f.

λῆρος, ου. m.∫
nonsense: ǁ φλύαρος 4M 5.11. Cf. ληρώδης: Spicq: 2.387f.

ληρώδης, ες.∫
frivolous: + περισσός 'redundant,' *s* prayer 2M 12.44. Cf. λῆρος.

ληστεύω.∫
to act as robber: ληστεύειν καὶ κλέπτειν 1E 4.23. Cf. ληστής, κλέπτω.

ληστήριον, ου. n.∫
band of robbers: 2C 22.1, 36.5[b].

ληστής, οῦ. m.
robber, brigand: highway robber, ἐν τῇ ὁδῷ Ho 7.1; active at night, Ob 5; ǁ κλέπτης Ho 7.1, Ob 5, Ep Je 56; murderous, Ez 22.9; nearly as damaging as war, Ep Je 14; highly mobile with no fixed address, Si 36.31. Cf. κλέπτης, πειρατής, ληστεύω: Trench 157-60; Spicq 2.389-95.

λίαν adv.
to a large extent, 'very': + adj., καλὰ λίαν 'very good' Ge 1.31; Je 24.3 (ǁ σφόδρα vs. 2); + verb, ἐλύπησεν τὸν Καιν λ. 'C. was much grieved' Ge 4.5; ἰσχυρὸς σφόδρα λ. Da 11.25 LXX; ὥστε λ. 2K 2.17. Cf. ἄγαν, πάνυ, σφόδρα, ὑπεράγαν.

I λίβανος, ου. f. < Heb. לְבֹנָה.
frankincense: λ. διαφανῆ 'translucent ..' Ex 30.34; Le 2.1; + σμύρνα Ct 3.6. Cf. λιβανόω, λιβανωτός: *ND* 4.129f.

II Λίβανος, ου. m. GN
Lebanon: Ho 14.6 +; famous for its forest, τὰ ξύλα τοῦ ~ου .. ἡ κέδρος τοῦ ~ου Is 14.8.

λιβανόω: pf.ptc.pass. λελιβανωμένος.∫
to scent with frankincense: *o* wine, 3M 5.45. Cf. I λίβανος.

λιβανωτός, οῦ. m.∫
frankincense: with intoxicating effect, + οἶνος 3M 5.2; cultic offering, + ἄρωμα 2C 9.29. Cf. I λίβανος.

λιγύριον, ου. n. *
a precious stone, 'stone of Ligurie' (*BA* ad Ex 28.19): Ex 28.19; Ez 28.13.

λιθάζω.ʃ
to hurl stones at: out of malice and + acc. pers. 4K 2.23*L*; and pleonastic ἐν λίθοις 2K 16.6, 13 (‖ *L* βάλλω λίθους ἐπί τινα). Cf. λιθάζω, λιθοβολέω.

λίθινος, η, ον.
made of stone: στήλη Ge 35.14; πυξία ~α 'stone tablets' Ex 24.12; πλάκες ~αι 'stone tablets' 32.15; καρδία Ez 11.19, Si 17.16¶ (:: σαρκίνη); δόμος 'course of stones' 1E 6.24 (‖ ξύλινος 'timber'), στῦλος 'pillar' Es 1.6 o'. Cf. λίθος, λιθώδης, πέτρινος.

λιθοβολέω: fut. ~βολήσω, pass. ~βοληθήσομαι; aor. ἐλιθοβόλησα, inf. ~βολῆσαι, impv. ~ βόλησον; pf.pass. λελιθοβόλημαι.*
to stone as capital punishment: ***s*** alw. hum. and ***o*** hum. (acc.), ἐν λίθοις Ex 19.13, Le 20.2, De 13.10, λίθοις Ex 21.28, Nu 15.35, ἐπ' αὐτὰς λίθοις ὄχλων Ez 23.47; to kill, καὶ τελευτήσουσιν De 17.5; pass., Ex 8.26 (non-Israelite practice); ***o*** bull, 21.28. Cf. λίθος, βάλλω, λιθάζω, λιθοβόλος, καταλιθοβολέω: Casevitz 1995.

λιθοβόλος, ον.ʃ
subst.n., *engine for hurling stones* in war: πυροβόλα καὶ ~α 1M 6.51. Cf. λιθοβολέω, πυροβόλος.

λίθος, ου. m.
1. *stone* as substance: Zc 3.9; τὸν λ. τῆς κληρονομίας 4.7; λ. σφενδόνης 'sling-stone' 9.15; ~οι ἅγιοι 9.16; λ. καταπατούμενος 'stone trampled upon' 12.3; building material, Le 14.45, Hg 2.15; less valuable than iron, Is 60.17; Zc 5.4 (‖ ξύλον); εἰς τὰ θεμέλια Σιων ~ον πολυτελῆ ἐκλεκτὸν ἀκρογωνιαῖον ἔντιμον 'into the foundations of Zion a costly, choice, valued corner-stone' Is 28.16; λ. ἐκ τοῦ τοίχου βοήσεται 'a stone shall cry out of the wall' Hb 2.11; ‖ θεμέλιον Mi 1.6; material used for sculpting idols Hb 2.19 (‖ ξύλον); object of worship, λατρεύσεις .. θεοῖς ἑτέροις, ξύλοις καὶ ~οις De 28.36; λίθοι χαλάζης 'hailstones' Jo 10.11, Si 43.15. **b**. precious stone: ἐκ Σουφιρ Is 13.12; used on a robe for decoration, Ez 28.13. **c**. fig. of lack of life, ***s*** hum. heart, 1K 25.37.
2. *weight, heavy body*: builder's tool, τὸν λ. τὸν κασσιτέρινον 'the plummet of tin' Zc 4.10; λ. τοῦ μολίβου 'weight of lead' 5.8.
Cf. λίθινος, λιθοβολέω, λιθώδης, κόχλαξ, πέτρα, πέτρος, χάλιξ, ψῆφος.

λιθόστρωτον, ου. n.ʃ
paved area: floor, Es 1.6, 2C 7.3, Ct 3.10, see Bruneau, esp. 443-6; Spicq 2.399f.

λιθουργέω: aor.inf. λιθουργῆσαι.ʃ
to work stone: + acc., τὸν λίθον καὶ κατεργάζεσθαι τὰ ξύλα Ex 35.33. Cf. λιθουργός.

λιθουργικός, ή, όν.ʃ
pertaining to λιθουργός, q.v.: ἔργον ~ῆς τέχνης 'work of stonecutter' Ex 28.11; subst. τὰ ~ὰ καὶ εἰς τὰ τεκτονικά '.. into carpenters' work' 31.5. Cf. λιθουργός, τεκτονικός.

λιθουργός, οῦ. m.ʃ
stone-cutter: ἔργον ~οῦ Si 45.11 (‖ τεχνίτης). Cf. λίθος, λιθουργέω, λιθουργικός, λαξευτής, λατόμος.

λιθώδης, ες.ʃ
stony: ***s*** road full of stones, Si 35.20. Cf. λίθος, λίθινος.

λικμάω: fut. λικμήσω; aor. ἐλίκμησα, ptc. λικμήσας, pass. λικμηθείς; pf.ptc.pass. λελικμημένος.ʃ
1. *to winnow*: ὡς χνοῦν ἀχύρου λικμώντων ἀπέναντι ἀνέμου 'like the dust of chaff of winnowers before the wind' Is 17.13; fig. μὴ λίκμα ἐν παντὶ ἀνέμῳ 'Seize the right moment' Si 5.9 (cf. Segal ad loc. and see Je 30.10); pass. λικμᾶται ἐν τῷ λικμῷ 'as (grain) is sifted with a winnow' Am 9.9b, ἄχυρα .. λελικμημένα 'winnowed chaff' Is 30.24. **b**. **to engage in winnowing at*: + acc., τὸν ἅλωνα τῶν κριθῶν 'the threshing-floor for wheat' Ru 3.2.
2. *to disperse*: abs. Is 41.16; + acc., βρόμον .. καπνοῦ 'foul-smelling smoke' Wi 11.18 (mid.); as undesirable or worthless: ὡς ὕδωρ ἀποκαθημένης 'like fluid of a menstruating woman' Is 30.22 (***o*** εἴδωλα understood); + acc., αὐτοὺς παντὶ πνεύματι 'at the first opportunity, by all means' Je 30.10, ὁ λικμήσας τὸν Ισραηλ 'he who winnowed Israel away' 38.10, λικμήσω τὸν χοῦν αὐτῆς ἀπ' αὐτῆς 'I shall blast her [= Tyre] earth off her' Ez 26.4; εἰς τὰς χώρας 29.12, 30.23, 26, 36.19 (‖ διασπείρω); λεπτυνεῖ καὶ λικμήσει πάσας τὰς βασιλείας 'he will pulverise ..' Da 2.44 TH (LXX ἀφανίσει), λικμήσει αὐτὸν ἐκ τοῦ τόπου αὐτοῦ 'will blast him out of his spot' Jb 27.21¶; pass., λικμηθέντες ὑπὸ πνεύματος δυνάμεώς σου 'scattered by the breath of your power' Wi 11.20. Cf. διασπείρω.
Cf. λικμίζω, λικμήτωρ, λικμός: Shipp 365f.; Spicq 2.401f.

λικμήτωρ, ορος. m.ʃ
one who winnows: metaph., ἀσεβῶν 'of the impious' Pr 20.26. Cf. λικμάω.

λικμίζω: fut. λικμιῶ (v.l. λικμήσω).ʃ *
= λικμάω: fig. and ***o*** τὸν οἶκον Ισραηλ Am 9.9*a*; on the fig. use, destruction, see Shipp 366. Cf. λικμάω and ἀφανίζω.

λικμός, οῦ. m.ʃ *
winnowing-fan: λικμᾶται ἐν τῷ ~ῷ '(grain) is sifted with a winnow' Am 9.9. Cf. λικμάω: Shipp 363-8.

λιμαγχονέω: aor. ἐλιμαγχόνησα.ʃ
to weaken by low diet: + acc. pers., De 8.3. Cf. λιμός: Shipp 368.

λιμήν, ένος.m.
harbour: εἰς τὸν Ἰόππης ~ένα 1E 5.53; ἐπὶ ~ένα θελήματος αὐτῶν 'to the haven of their desire' Ps 106.30, ἐπὶ τὸν τῆς ἀθανάτου νίκης ~ένα 'into the port of immortal victory' 4M 7.3, εὐσεβείας 'of religion' 13.7.

λίμνη, ης. f.
marshy lake: ὑδάτων Ps 106.35 (ǁ διέξοδος). **b**. ἁλός 'salt (pond)' at the Dead Sea, 1M 11.35.
Cf. ἕλος.

λιμοκτονέω: fut. ~νήσω.ʃ
to starve to death: + acc. pers., Pr 10.3 (ǁ ἀνατρέπω 'to overthrow'). Cf. λιμός, ἀποκτείνω.

λιμός, οῦ. m.
prolonged and widespread lack of food, 'famine': ἐγένετο λ. ἐπὶ τῆς γῆς Ge 12.10; ἰσχυρός 'severe' 41.31; ἐνίσχυσεν 43.1; ἀποκτεῖναι .. ἐν ~ῷ Ex 16.3; ἐν ~ῷ καὶ ἐν δίψει καὶ ἐν γυμνότητι καὶ ἐν ἐκλείψει πάντων 'in hunger, thirst, nakedness and lack of everything' De 28.48; ἐξαποστελῶ ~ὸν ἐπὶ τὴν γῆν, οὐ ~ὸν ἄρτου οὐδὲ δίψαν ὕδατος, ἀλλὰ ~ὸν τοῦ ἀκοῦσαι λόγον κυρίου 'I shall send famine upon the earth, not shortage of bread nor that of water, but of the word of the Lord to be heard' Am 8.11; + μάχαιρα Is 51.19, Je 5.12, 34.6; opp. πλησμονή, ǁ πτωχεία καὶ ἔνδεια 'abundance' Si 18.25. Cf. λιμαγχονέω, λιμώσσω, ἐκλιμία, δίψα, ἔνδεια, πεινάω, σιτοδεία.

λιμώσσω: fut. λιμώξω.ʃ*
to be famished: *s* hum. ὡς κύων 'as a dog' Ps 58.7, 15. Cf. λιμός.

λινοκαλάμη, ης. f.ʃ
flax-straw: Jo 2.6.

λίνον, ου. n.
flax: + κριθή 'barley' Ex 9.31(*bis*); + ἔριον 'wool' De 22.11; fig. of sth fragile and easily shaken about, PSol 8.5. **b**. *fishing-net made from flax*: σχιστόν 'torn' Is 19.9. **c**. *wick made from flax*: Is 42.3.
Cf. λινοῦς.

λινοῦς, ῆ, οῦν.
made from flax, linen: περισκελῆ ~ᾶ 'linen drawers' Ex 28.38 (ἐκ βύσσου κεκλωσμένης 'made from spun flax' ǁ 36.36); *s* χιτών 'tunic' Le 6.10; ζώνη 'girdle' 16.4; κίδαρις 'turban' ib.; στολή 'robe' 16.23 (priestly), Ju 16.8 (worn by a woman to beguile a man); περίζωμα 'girdle' Je 13.1; ǁ ἐρεοῦς 'woolen' Le 13.48; subst.n.pl. λινῆ 'linen fabric' 13.48. Cf. βύσσος, λίνον, ὀθόνιον.

λιπαίνω: aor. ἐλίπανα, impv. λίπανον, pass. ἐλιπάνθην.ʃ
1. *to smear with oil*, 'anoint': ***o*** hum. and pass., De 32.15; body - ἐν ἐλαίῳ τὴν κεφαλήν μου Ps 22.5; cultic offering - προσφοράν Si 38.11; altar - προσφορὰ δικαίου λιπαίνει θυσιαστήριον 32.8; σὸν φάρυγγα 'your palate (by kissing)' Pr 5.3; *s* oil - ἔλαιον .. μὴ λιπανάτω τὴν κεφαλήν μου Ps 140.5; fig. of luxury, Ne 9.25 (ǁ τρυφάω).
2. *to enhance the value of*: + acc. μερίδα αὐτοῦ 'his portion' Hb 1.16.
Cf. χρίω, ἀλείφω, τρυφάω: Schmidt 4.681f.

λιπαρός, ά, όν.ʃ
1. *looking splendid*: *s* ἄρτος Is 30.23; n. (!), able-bodied soldier, Jd 3.29 B.
2. *fertile, rich*: *s* ἐν τῇ γῇ πλατείᾳ καὶ ~ᾷ 'in the spacious and fertile land' Ne 9.35.
Cf. λίπασμα, πίων: Schmidt 4.677-80.

λίπασμα, ατος. n.ʃ
fat, rich food: 1E 9.51 ǁ Ne 8.10 (+ γλύκασμα).

λιποθυμέω.ʃ
to breathe one's last: 4M 6.27.

λίσσομαι.ʃ
to entreat: κάμνων 'kneeling' Jb 17.2 (ǁ δέομαι vs. 1). Cf. δέομαι, εὔχομαι, ἱκετεύω.

λιτανεία, ας. f.
entreaty: in prayer to God, 2M 10.16 (ǁ ἀξιόω), 3.20; 3M 5.9. Cf. λιτανεύω, ἱκετεία.

λιτανεύω: fut. λιτανεύσω.ʃ
to entreat: ***o*** τὸ πρόσωπόν σου Ps 44.13; God, 2M 14.15. Cf. λιτανεία, ἱκετεύω.

λιτός, ή, όν.ʃ
financially destitute: *s* hum., Jd 11.3A. Cf. πτωχός.

λιχνεία, ας. f.ʃ
gluttony: + πότος 3M 6.36.

λίψ, βός. f.
***1**. *south*: πρὸς βορρᾶν καὶ λίβα καὶ ἀνατολὰς καὶ θάλασσαν 'towards the north, south, east and west' Ge 13.14; κατὰ θάλασσαν καὶ βορρᾶν καὶ λίβα καὶ ἀνατολάς De 3.27; εἰς γῆν πρὸς λίβα Ge 20.1; θάλασσαν καὶ λίβα De 33.23.
2. *west*: πρὸς λίβα Ex 27.9, 2C 32.30; ἀπὸ λιβός 33.14, Da 8.5 TH (LXX: ἀπὸ δυσμῶν), see Bogaert 1981.
***3**. *west wind*: opp. νότος Ps 77.26.
Cf. ἀνατολή, βορρᾶς, νότος, θάλασσα: Boyd-Taylor 2004.

λοβός, οῦ. m.
lobe: of the liver, ἥπατος Ex 29.13, τὸν ~ὸν τὸν ἐπὶ τοῦ ἥπατος Le 3.4; of a hum. ear, ὠτός Ex 29.20; of an animal's ear, ὠτίου Am 3.12.

λογεία, ας. f.ʃ
act of collecting: of funds, 2M 12.43. Cf. Deissmann 1923.81-5; Kittel, *TDNT* 4.282f.

λογίζομαι: fut. λογισθήσομαι, λογιοῦμαι; aor. ἐλογισάμην, subj. λογίσωμαι, ptc. λογισάμενος, impv. λόγισαι, pass. ἐλογίσθην, inf. λογισθῆναι, impv.3pl λογισθήτωσαν, opt. λογισθείην; pf.pass. λελόγισμαι.

1. *to calculate and determine the quantity of*: pass., *o* sacrificial animals, + ἀριθμέω 2C 5.6.

2. *to devise, scheme* with hostile intent: + acc., εἰς ἐμὲ ἐλογίσαντο πονηρά 'devised evils against me' Ho 7.15; κόπους 'troubles (for others)' Mi 2.1 (ǁ ἐργάζομαι κακά); + ἐπί τινα - ἐπὶ τὴν φυλὴν ταύτην κακά 2.3, ἐπ' ἐμὲ ἐλογίσαντο λογισμὸν πονηρόν Je 11.19 (also + λογισμόν 18.11, 18, 27.45, 29.21, 30.8 (ǁ βουλεύομαι), 36.11, Ez 38.10, Da TH 11.24, 25; μάταια 'senseless things' Ez 11.2 (ǁ βουλεύομαι); τί λογίζεσθε ἐπὶ τὸν κύριον; 'what are you scheming against the Lord?' Na 1.9; ἕκαστος τὴν κακίαν τοῦ πλησίον αὐτοῦ μὴ λογίζεσθε ἐν ταῖς καρδίαις ὑμῶν 'Stop scheming the evil against one another in your hearts' Zc 8.17; + inf., λογιζόμενοί μοι ποιῆσαι πονηρίαν Ne 6.2, ἀποστατῆσαι 'to rebel' 6.6, τῶν κακῶν, ὧν ἐλογισάμην τοῦ ποιῆσαι αὐτοῖς Je 18.8; + inf. fut., 2M 11.2; + dat. incom., μοι κακά Ps 34.4, κατ' ἐμοῦ .. κακά μοι 40.8; *s* hum. tongue, 51.4; τῇ ψυχῇ and ǁ ἐνθυμέομαι Is 10.7 (both verbs often joined by Demosthenes).

3. *to excercise the mind and consider* an issue or situation: πάλιν ἐλογίσατο 'she thought it over' To 3.10 𝔊[II]; ἐν πόσαις πορεύσεται 'in how many days he could go' 10.1 𝔊[II]; οὐκ ὀρθῶς 'unsoundly' Wi 2.1; + indir. question, 4M 8.16.

4. *to give thought to and take notice of*: + acc., τί ἐστιν .. υἱὸς ἀνθρώπου, ὅτι λογίζῃ αὐτόν; Ps 143.3; οὐ λογίζονται ἀργύριον οὐδὲ χρυσίου χρείαν ἔχουσι 'they think nothing of silver nor could care less for gold' Is 13.17; τὴν ἄδηλον τοῦ βίου καταστροφήν 'the unforeseeable end of life' 3M 4.4; ἠτιμάσθη καὶ οὐκ ἐλογίσθη 'he was belittled and was not taken notice of' Is 53.3.

5. *to reason, consider*: + acc., ταῦτα ἐλογίσαντο 'thus they reasoned' Wi 2.21; ταῦτα λογισάμενος ἐν ἐμαυτῷ καὶ φροντίσας ἐν καρδίᾳ μου 8.17; οὐκ ἐλογίσατο τῇ καρδίᾳ αὐτοῦ οὐδὲ ἀνελογίσατο ἐν τῇ ψυχῇ αὐτοῦ οὐδὲ ἔγνω τῇ φρονήσει ὅτι .. Is 44.19; καθὰ ἐλογίσαντο Wi 3.10.

6. *to deem, consider*: + acc. and predicate, παραβαίνοντας ἐλογισάμην πάντας τοὺς ἁμαρτωλοὺς .. 'I considered all the sinners transgressors ..' Ps 118.119, οὐ μὴ λογίσησθε αὐτοὺς ἀνθρώπους 'you will not consider them to be human' Is 33.8; ǁ ἔχω + acc. + εἰς + acc., Wi 5.4 (ǁ καταλογίζομαι vs. 5), ǁ τιμάω 14.20; pass., γῆ Ραφαιν λογισθήσεται 'it shall be considered to be the land of R.' De 2.20, πιστοὶ ἐλογίσθησαν 'they were considered to be reliable' Ne 13.13; Wi 3.2 (ǁ δοκέω), ὑπὲρ ἀμφότερα γυνὴ ἄμωμος λογίζεται 'an impeccable wife is considered worth more than either' Si 40.19; + dat., λογισθήσεται τῷ ἀνθρώπῳ ἐκείνῳ αἷμα Le 17.4; ἐναντίον αὐτῆς Wi 7.9 (ǁ ἐν ὄψει αὐτῆς); + ὡς - ὡς ἑστῶτα ἐλογίσαντο 'considered them to be permanent' Am 6.5; Si 29.6 (ǁ νομίζω vs. 4); pass. ὡς αἱ ἀλλότριαι λελογίσμεθα αὐτῷ Ge 31.15; ὡς ἀλλότρια ἐλογίσθησαν 'were regarded as foreign' Ho 8.12; + ὥσπερ De 2.11; + εἰς - αὐτὴν εἰς μεθύουσαν 1K 1.13, ἄβυσσον εἰς περίπατον 'the abyss as (his) beat' Jb 41.24 (ǁ vs. 23 ἡγέομαι), πάντα τὰ ἔθνη ὡς οὐδέν εἰσι καὶ εἰς οὐθὲν ἐλογίσθησαν Is 40.17, ǁ pass. τίθεμαι ὡς 29.17; + dat. pers. and pass., εἰς κίβδηλον ἐλογίσθημεν αὐτῷ 'we were considered by him as suspect' Wi 2.16; + inf., ἐλογίσατο παίγνιον εἶναι τὴν ζωὴν ἡμῶν 'he considered our life to be a mere game' 15.12; αὐτὸν εἶναι ἐν πόνῳ Is 53.4; 1M 10.38. Cf. ἔχω **9**.

7. *to come to the realisation, conclusion*: + ὅτι, 1M 6.9; + inf., 2M 6.12.

8. *to put down* (τινι 'to sbd's account'): + acc. and dat. pers., μακάριος ἀνήρ, ᾧ (v.l. οὗ Ra) οὐ μὴ λογίσηται κύριος ἁμαρτίαν Ps 31.2; and pass., τοῦτό μοι .. ἀνομία ἡ μεγίστη λογισθείη 'let this be reckoned as the greatest injustice towards me' Jb 31.28 (ǁ ἐφ' ἡμῖν 34.37); to his credit, Le 7.8; and + εἰς 'as having the value of,' ἐλογίσθη αὐτῷ εἰς δικαιοσύνην Ge 15.6, Ps 105.31, 1M 2.52.

9. *to regard and treat as belonging to the category of*: + dat. pers., σοι λελογίσμεθα 'we have been declared to be yours' Wi 15.2 (ǁ σοί ἐσμεν); + πρός + acc., πρὸς τὸν ἀγρὸν τῆς γῆς λογισθήτωσαν 'let them be considered as belonging to the open country' Le 25.31; οὗτος ὁ θεὸς ἡμῶν, οὐ λογισθήσεται ἕτερος πρὸς αὐτόν 'This is our God; no other shall be reckoned to be of his class' Ba 3.36; λογιεῖται πρὸς αὐτὸν .. τὸ τέλος τῆς τιμῆς 'shall reckon for him the full amount of the assessment ..' Le 27.23; + ἐν - ἐν τοῖς ἀνόμοις ἐλογίσθη 'he was counted among the lawless' Is 53.12; μετά τινος- μετὰ τῶν ἁμαρτωλῶν εἰς ἀπώλειαν PSol 16.5. See BDAG and MM s.v.

Cf. λογισμός, λογιστής, ἀνα~, δια~, ἐπι~, προσλογίζομαι, βουλεύομαι, ἔχω, ἡγέομαι, τιμάω, φροντίζω: Heidland, esp. 38-57.

λόγιον, ου. n.

1. *oracle*: divine, θεοῦ Nu 24.4, 16 (ǁ ὅρασις θεοῦ), τὰ ~α κυρίου ~α ἁγνά Ps 11.6.

2. *that which is said by way of instruction*: ἐφύλαξεν τὰ ~ά σου De 33.9 (ǁ διαθήκη); ǁ τὸν νόμον κυρίου Is 5.24, ǁ λόγος Ps 147.4. **b**. in gen., *that which is said*: τὰ ~α τοῦ στόματός μου Ps 18.15.

3. woven piece of an ephod placed on the breast worn by a high priest and used to arrive at legal decisions by means of δήλωσις καὶ ἀλήθεια, 'oracle box': λ. τῶν κρίσεων Ex 28.15; τῆς κρίσεως 28.23, Si 45.10.

λογισμός, οῦ. m.

1. *that which is on one's mind*, 'thought': οὐκ ἔγνωσαν τὸν ~ὸν κυρίου 'they did not come to know the Lord's thinking' Mi 4.12 (ǁ βουλή); λ. κατὰ τοῦ κυρίου 'a plan against the Lord' Na 1.11; τῆς καρδίας Ps 32.11; cogn. acc. of λογίζομαι Je 18.11, 27.45.

2. *way of reasoning*: Si 27.4. **b**. *outcome of reasoning*, 'conclusion': Ec 7.27.

3. *category among which sbd or sth is reckoned*: οὐκ ἔστιν .. ἐν ~ῷ ζωῆς 'does not count as life' Si 40.29.

4. *settling of an account*: Si 42.3.

5. *that which is discussed about*: Es A 13 o'.

6. *rational will*: εὐσεβής 4M 1.1+; *s* νοῦς 1.15, cf. Lauer; 2.4 (ǁ διάνοια vs. 3).

Cf. λογίζομαι.

λογιστής, οῦ. m.ʃ

one who calculates and designs: of war-engines, 2C 26.15. Cf. λογίζομαι.

λόγος, ου. *m*.

1. *that which is said or uttered*: ἐνωτίσασθέ μου τοὺς ~ους 'listen to what I say' Ge 4.23, ὁ κριτὴς εἰρηνικοὺς ~ους ἐλάλησε Mi 7.3; ἐβαρύνατε ἐπ' ἐμὲ τοὺς ~ους ὑμῶν 'what you said was unbearable to me' Ma 3.13; κατὰ τὸν ~ον Εφραιμ 'in accordance with what was said by E.' Ho 13.1 (to be construed with the preceding as in Cyr, Th, Thdt, and Thph); ~ον ὅσιον ἐβδελύξαντο 'they loathed godly speech' Am 5.10; ǁ λαλιά Ps 18.4; ~ῳ .. πράγματι 'by word .. (but) in practice' 3M 3.17, ἐν ἔργῳ καὶ λόγῳ Si 3.8. **b**. of divine message communicated to a hum. or hums.: mediated by Moses, τοὺς ~ους κυρίου, οὓς ἀπέστειλεν '.. of the Lord, which He had entrusted' Ex 4.28, τοὺς δέκα ~ους 'the Decalogue' 34.28; by a prophet, τοὺς ~ους τούτους ἐκ στόματος τῶν προφητῶν Zc 8.9; ἐγένετο λ. κυρίου ἐν χειρὶ 'Αγγαίου τοῦ προφήτου Ag 1.1, 3; spoken by a prophet, ἀκούσατε τὸν ~ον κυρίου τοῦτον Am 5.1; often as part of the caption of divine oracle, λ. κυρίου Ho 1.1, Jl 1.1; with γίνομαι as in ἐγένετο λ. κυρίου πρὸς Ζαχαρίαν foll. by λέγων introducing an oracle, ἐγένετο λ. κυρίου πρὸς 'Αγγαῖον .. λέγων .. Hg 2.10 (sim. 1.1, 3, 2.20, Mi 1.1, Zc 1.1, Jn 1.1, 3.1); ἀρχὴ ~ου κυρίου ἐν Ωσηε Ho 1.2 (cf. ἀρχὴ τοῦ εὐαγγελίου 'Ιησοῦ Χριστοῦ Mk 1.1); λῆμμα ~ου κυρίου Zc 9.1, Ma 1.1; ǁ νόμος - νόμος καὶ λ. κυρίου Mi 4.2; τοὺς ~ους μου καὶ τὰ νόμιμά μου δέχεσθε Zc 1.6; angel speaking, τῷ ἀγγέλῳ τῷ λαλοῦντι ἐν ἐμοὶ ῥήματα καλὰ καὶ ~ους παρακλητικούς 'the angel saying to me sweet and comforting words' Zc 1.13. **c**. *written message*: ἴδε τοὺς ~ους Is 37.17. **d**. *communication*: ~ον οὐκ ἔχουσιν πρὸς ἄνθρωπον 'they would not have a word with anybody' Jd 18.7B. **e**. *proposal*: Bel 11 LXX.

2. *report, news, rumour*: ἤγγισεν ὁ λ. πρὸς τὸν βασιλέα Jn 3.6; πρὸ προσώπου αὐτοῦ πορεύεται λ. Hb 3.5. **b**. *act of presenting a report*: 3M 5.15.

3. esp. pl., *a chain of connected events*, 'a story, an account': διηγήσατο τῷ Λαβαν πάντας τοὺς ~ους τούτους 'recounted to L. this whole story' Ge 29.13; πάντας τοὺς ~ους, οὓς ἑωράκασιν οἱ ὀφθαλμοί σου De 4.9; οἱ ~οι Ιωσια 'the events pertaining to Josiah' 2C 35.26, βιβλίον ~ων τῶν ἡμερῶν τοῖς βασιλεῦσιν Ιουδα 'the book of the annals of the Judahite kings' 36.8.

4. *what is or may be a good reason*: οἱ εὐφραίνοντες ἐπ' οὐδενὶ ~ῳ 'those who are rejoicing over what amounts to nothing' Am 6.13.

***5**. *course of action, step to be taken*: τοῦτόν σοι τὸν ~ον, ὃν εἴρηκας, ποιήσω Ex 33.17; οὗτοι οἱ ~οι, οὓς ποιήσετε 'these are the things that you are going to do' Zc 8.16; Jd 21.11 A, Je 49.3, Si 48.13.

6. *matter under discussion*: ἐν τῷ ~ῳ τούτῳ 'in this matter' De 1.32, 1K 28.10; a legal case, De 22.20; ἐρωτήσω σε λόγον, καὶ μὴ κρύψῃς ἀπ' ἐμοῦ ῥῆμα 'I'm going to ask you about something. Don't hide from me anything' Je 45.14. **b**. *subject matter, topic*: Da 1.20 LXX; ἐν παντὶ ~ῳ 'in every respect' Es A 11 o'; φιλόσοφος 'philosophical' 4M 1.1.

7. *value* put on sth or sbd: in a phrase λόγον ἔχω τινος - ἔχω ~ον τῶν 'Ιουδαίων .. 'I had better keep in mind those Judaeans ..' Je 45.19; μὴ ~ον ἔχε 'Don't you worry!' To 5.21; τοῦ δαιμονίου μηδένα ~ον ἔχε 'Take no notice of the demon' 6.16 𝔊[I]; Je 49.16. Cf. οὐκ ἔστιν λ. 'there is nothing to worry about' 1K 20.21 (*L* λ. πονηρός).

8. *consideration*: τούτου ~ον ἐποιήσω 'you took such a person into account' Jb 14.3; 22.4.

9. *amount agreed and fixed*: λ. ἡμέρας 'daily amount' (of cultic offering) 2E 3.4, Ne 12.47; κατὰ τὸν ~ον ἡμέρας ἐν τῇ ἡμέρᾳ 'according to the daily roster' 2C 8.14, εἰς (B: om.) ~ον ἡμέρας ἐν ἡμέρᾳ αὐτοῦ 'as much as his daily ration' 4K 25.30*L*.

10. *reasonable expectation based on calculation and consideration*: κατὰ ~ον 'as expected' 3M 3.14; παρὰ ~ον 'unreasonable' 2M 4.36.

11. *intellectual faculty capable of reasoning and thinking*: of hums., Wi 2.2; φιλόσοφος 'philosophical' 4M 5.25.

12. *an account which may be credited or debited*: τοῦ βασιλέως 1M 10.40 (pl.), τῶν θυσίων 'earmarked for sacrifices' 2M 3.6, λαβεῖν τὰ χρήματα εἰς φερνῆς ~ον 'to take the money by way of a dowry' 2M 1.14; μὴ δότω ὁ βασιλεὺς κατὰ τοῦ δούλου αὐτοῦ ~ον 'May not the king put anything down to his servant's account' 1K 22.15.

13. administrative or financial *account* to be submitted to one's superior: ἀποδίδωμί τισιν λόγον Da 6.3 TH.

Cf. λαλέω, λέγω, ῥῆμα, πρᾶγμα: Schmidt 1.97-100.

λόγχη, ης. f.

oblong metal weapon to be thrown, 'spear, javelin, lance': Ez 26.8; + ἀσπίς 'shield' 2M 15.11; + θυρεός Jd 5.8B (A: σιρομάστης). Cf. ἀσπίς, σιρομάστης.

λοιδορέω: aor. ἐλοιδόρησα, pass. ἐλοιδορήθην.ʃ

1. *to speak in insulting manner and with disagreeable tone*: abs. 2M 12.14 (ǁ βλασφημέω) εἴς τινα 'against sbd' Ge 49.23; + acc. pers., Je 36.27.

2. mid. *to rail at*: + πρός τινα Ex 17.2 (ǁ + dat. pers.), Nu 20.3; = pass. and + ἔναντί τινος, 20.13 (ǁ act. + acc. pers., De 33.8).

3. mid. *to quarrel* with one another: Ex 21.18.

Cf. λοιδορία, λοιδόρησις, βλασφημέω, ἐρίζω, κακολογέω, κακῶς λέγω, καταλαλέω, μυκτηρίζω, ὑβρίζω: Schmidt 1.139f.

λοιδόρησις, εως. f.ʃ

railing, abuse: Ex 17.7 (ǁ λοιδορία). Cf. λοιδορέω, διαλοιδόρησις.

λοιδορία, ας. f.

= λοιδόρησις: Ex 17.7; w. ref. to the incident told in 17.1-6, ὕδωρ τῆς ~ας Nu 20.24; resulting in murder, Si 22.24, + κατάρα 29.6; ǁ ἔχθρα 'hostility' Pr 10.18. Cf. λοιδορέω.

λοίδορος, ον.ʃ

given to railing and abusive language: *s* γυνή 'wife' Pr 25.24, 27.15; ἀνήρ 26.21. **b**. subst.m. Si 23.8 (+ ὑπερήφανος).

Cf. λοιδορέω.

λοιμεύομαι.ʃ *

to conduct oneself as a pernicious person: *s* hum., Pr 19.19. Cf. subs.

λοιμός, ή, όν.

pernicious, dangerous: *s* hum., Pr 29.8, θυγάτηρ 1K 1.16; outrageous priests, 2.12; subst., ἔμπυροι ~οί 'fiery destroyers' Am 4.2; Ho 7.5; οἱ ἔνδοξοι καὶ οἱ μεγάλοι καὶ οἱ πλούσιοι καὶ οἱ ~οί Is 5.14; + πονηρός Je 15.21; ǁ ἀσεβής, ἁμαρτωλός Ps 1.1. Alw. *s* pers. exc. λόγον ~όν 1K 29.10. Cf. λοιμεύομαι, λοιμότης.

λοιμότης, ητος. f.ʃ *

pernicious, ruinous character: Es E 7o'. Cf. λοιμός.

λοιπός, ή, όν.

left and remaining out of a given number or quantity: ἔτι ~ὰ πέντε ἔτη 'another five, remaining years' Ge 45.6; ἓξ ὀνόματα .. καὶ τὰ ἓξ ὀνόματα τὰ ~ά Ex 28.10; 39.12 (ǁ καταλειφθείς vs. 13); subst., alw. articular, sg., τὸ ~ὸν τοῦ θερισμοῦ 'that remains after the harvest' Le 23.22, τὸ ~ὸν τῆς θυσίας 2.3, τὸ ~όν *the rest, residue*, Ez 34.18 (ǁ κατάλοιπος), Is 44.15, 17; "tonight and ever after (καὶ εἰς τὸ ~όν)" Ju 11.3, sim. 2M 11.19, καὶ εἰς τὰ ~ά 'also in the future' 12.30; pl., οἱ ~οί 1M 2.44, τὰ ~ὰ τῶν βιβλίων 'the rest of the books' Si prol. 25. Cf. λείπω, λεῖμμα, ἐπί~, κατά~, περί~, ὑπόλοιπος, καταλείπω, ἄλλος: Schmidt 4.559f., 569; LSG s.v.

λουτήρ, ῆρος. m.*

washing-tub for ritual use: Ποίησον ~ρα χαλκοῦν καὶ βάσιν αὐτῷ χαλκῆν ὥστε νίπτεσθαι 'Make a copper washing-tub with a copper base in order to wash (in it)' Ex 30.18; holds water, ib. Cf. λούω, νίπτω.

λουτρόν, οῦ. n.

v.n. of λούω: ritual washing, Si 31.30. **b**. place where livestock are washed, Ct 4.2. Cf. λούω: Spicq 2.410-4.

λούω: fut. λούσω, mid. λούσομαι; aor. ἔλουσα, mid. ἐλουσάμην, inf. λούσασθαι, impv. λοῦσαι, subj. λούσωμαι, pass. ἐλούσθην; pf.ptc.pass. λελουσμένος.

1. *to wash*: + acc. pers., ἐν ὕδατι Ex 29.4, ὕδατι 40.10.

2. *to drench*: + acc., κλίνην 'couch' Ps 6.7 (ǁ βρέχω).

3. mid. *to bathe*: in a river, Ex 2.5, 4K 5.13 (ǁ βαπτίζομαι vs. 14); ὕδατι Le 11.40, 17.15; ἐν ὕδατι 14.8; + acc. rei, τὸ σῶμα αὐτοῦ 'his (own) body' 14.9, Nu 19.7, ὕδατι De 23.11, ǁ νίπτω, πλύνω Le 15.11, ἐλούσαντο καὶ ἐνίψαντο To 7.9 𝔊II. **b**. fig., in order to become ethically clean (καθαρός): Is 1.16.

Cf. ἀπολούω, βαπτίζω, ἐκκλύζω, νίπτω, πλύνω, λουτήρ, λουτρόν: Trench 160-3; Lee 1983.36-40.

λοφιά, ᾶς. f.ʃ

a narrow protruding strip of land: on the SE shore of the Dead Sea, Jo 15.2; on its N shore, 15.5, 18.19.

λοχάω.ʃ

to ambush: abs., Wi 14.24. Cf. ἐνεδρεύω.

λοχεύομαι.ʃ

to give birth: *s* livestock, τὰ πρόβατα καὶ αἱ βόες Ge 33.13; Ps 77.71. Cf. γεννάω, ἀποκυέω, τίκτω: Schmidt 4.62f., 80-82.

λυθρώδης, ες.ʃ *

liable to defile with gore: *s* blood, Wi 11.6.

λύκος, ου. m.

wolf: predatory, λ. ἅρπαξ Ge 49.27; swift, ὀξύτεροι ὑπὲρ τοὺς ~ους τῆς 'Αραβίας 'swifter than. 'Hb 1.8; ǁ λέων Je 5.6; insatiable, οἱ κριταὶ αὐτῆς ὡς ~οι τῆς 'Αραβίας Zp 3.3, οἱ ἄρχοντες αὐτῆς .. ὡς ~οι ἁρπάζοντες Ez 22.27. Cf. Spicq 2.415f.

λυμαίνομαι: fut. λυμανοῦμαι; aor. ἐλυμηνάμην, subj. λυμήνωμαι.

to cause or inflict serious harm and damage to: abs., 2C 16.10; + acc., *s* leopard, Si 28.23, "a wild boar ruined it [= grape-vine]" Ps 79.14, various wild beasts Is 65.25, lions Da 6.23 TH; *o* ὀχύρωμά σου 'your stronghold' Je 31.18, τὰ ἀλλότρια 'sbd else's possessions' Pr 27.13; morally, + acc., *s* bribe, ῥήματα δίκαια 'course of justice' Ex 23.8, τὰς ὁδοὺς αὐτοῦ Pr 19.3, λόγους καλούς 'delightful speech' 23.8, μου τὰ ἁγνὰ τῆς παρθενίας 'the purity of my virginity' 4M 18.8. Cf. subs.

λυμεών, ῶνος. m.ʃ

corrupter: of moral corruption, 4M 18.8a (‖ φθορεύς). Cf. λυμαίνομαι, φθορεύς.

λυπέω: fut. λυπήσω, pass. λυπηθήσομαι; aor. act. ἐλύπησα, subj. λυπήσω, pass. ἐλυπήθην, ptc. λυπηθείς, impv. λυπήθητι; pf.mid. λελύπημαι.

The party affected is hum., exc. Ez 16.43.

1. act. *to grieve, cause grief*: + acc. pers. Mi 6.3; *o* one's mother, To 4.3 𝔊[I] (𝔊[II] τὸ πνεῦμα αὐτῆς), one's father, 9.4 𝔊[II]; God, Es 7.4 *L*; + acc. rei, καρδίαν Pr 25.20, πνεῦμα 2K 13.21; impers. and + τινα Ge 4.5. **b**. mid. *to be grieved, grieve, feel grief and sorrow*: Ge 45.5, μὴ λυπεῖσθε 1E 9.52, 53; λίαν To 10.3 𝔊[I], σφόδρα Jn 4.4; + cogn. obj. λυπὴν μεγάλην 4.1; ἐπί τινι 'over sth' 4.9, Si 26.28 (at latter: *s* καρδία), ἐφ' ἑαυτοῖς Is 15.2 (‖ κλαίω, ὀλολύζω), περὶ ἐμοῦ To 2.10 𝔊[II]; could drive one to suicide, 3.10, ἕως θανάτου 'so much so that I wish for death' Jn 4.9; τῇ καρδίᾳ σου De 15.10, λυπηθεὶς ἔκλαυσα To 3.1 𝔊[I]; over sbd's death, Si 30.5 (:: εὐφραίνομαι), ὡς οὐδ' ἀποθνησκόντων ἐλυπήθη 4M 16.12.

2. *to displease*: οὐκ ἐλύπησεν τὸ πνεῦμα Αμνων 'he did not rub A. the wrong way' 2K 13.21. **b**. pass. *to be displeased, take offence*: ἐλυπήθη ὁ βασιλεὺς καὶ ὠργίσθη Es 1.12 o', cf. Si 26.28 (‖ θυμός), Es 2.21, Is 8.21 and περιβλεψάμενος αὐτοὺς μετ' ὀργῆς, συλλυπούμενος .. Mk 3.5; ἐπ' αὐτῷ 'over him' 1K 29.4 (*L* θυμόομαι).

Cf. θρηνέω, κλαίω, κόπτω, ἐπι~, συλλυπέω, λύπη, λυπηρός, ὀδυνάω, πενθέω, πονέω: Spicq 2.417-22.

λύπη, ης. f.

1. *grief, sadness*: μετὰ ~ης Ge 42.38 (‖ μετ' ὀδύνης 44.31); as cogn. obj. ἐλυπήθη Ιωνας ~ην μεγάλην 'Jonah grieved sorely' Jn 4.1; πᾶσα καρδία εἰς ~ην Is 1.5 (‖ πόνος); ἀπέδρα ὀδύνη καὶ λ. καὶ στεναγμός 'pain .. groaning departed' 35.10 (:: αἴνεσις, ἀγαλλίαμα, εὐφροσύνη); could be fatal and sap one's bodily strength, Si 38.18; causes illness, 1M 6.8; ἀπόλλυμαι ~ῃ μεγάλῃ 'I am dying of deep grief' 6.13, cf. πολλοὺς ἀπώλεσεν ἡ λ. 'the grief ruined many' Si 30.23; at sbd's death, 38.17; caused to one's father, 22.4.

2. *physical pain*: pl. and experienced by woman in childbirth, Ge 3.16 (‖ στεναγμός 'groaning'); agricultural toil, αἱ ~αι τῶν χειρῶν 5.29.

Cf. κλαυθμός, κοπετός, κόπος, λυπέω, ὀδύνη, πένθος, πόνος, ὠδίν: Schmidt 2.588-91.

λυπηρός, ά, όν.

causing grief, distressful: ~ὸν ἦν αὐτοῖς σφόδρα Ge 34.7 (an understatement for 'shocking, offensive'?); ὀλίγος ἐστὶν καὶ λ. ὁ βίος ἡμῶν 'our life is brief and sorrowful' Wi 2.1; *s* λόγος 'speech' Pr 15.1. **b**. *feeling or liable to distress and pain*: *s* ψυχή Pr 14.10 (‖ αἰσθητικός).

Cf. λύπη, λυπέω, ἡδύς, τερπνός.

λύσις, εως. f.

interpretation: τοῦ λόγου τούτου Da 12.8 LXX, αἰνιγμάτων Wi 8.8. Cf. κρίσις, σύγκρισις.

λυσιτέλεια, ας. f.ʃ

quality of being profitable and beneficial: *s* invitation to banquet, 2M 2.27. Cf. λυσιτελής, ὠφέλεια.

λυσιτελέω: fut. ~λήσω.

to be advantageous, profitable: *s* gift, + dat. com., σοι Si 20.10, 14; *s* inf., To 3.6. Cf. λυσιτελής, συμφέρω, ὠφελέω.

λυσιτελής, ές.ʃ

advantageous, profitable: *s* Hades, Si 28.21. Cf. λυσιτελέω, συμφορός: Schmidt 4.162-7.

λύτρον, ου. n.

Mostly pl., *sum payable as ransom*: ~α ἐπιβληθῇ αὐτῷ Ex 21.30; τῆς ψυχῆς αὐτοῦ 'a sum required in order to obtain one's own freedom' 30.12; περὶ ψυχῆς Nu 35.31; ~οις οὐ λελύτρωται Le 19.20, sim. Nu 18.15; ~α δώσετε τῆς γῆς Le 25.24; οὐ μετὰ ~ων οὐδὲ μετὰ δώρων Is 45.13. Cf. λυτρόομαι, ἐλευθερία: *ND* 2.90, 3.72-5.

λυτρόομαι: pres.subj. λυτρῶμαι; fut. λυτρώσομαι, pass. λυτρωθήσομαι; aor. ἐλυτρωσάμην, impv. λύτρωσαι, inf. λυτρώσασθαι, ptc. λυτρωσάμενος, subj. λυτρώσωμαι, pass. λυτρωθῶ; pf. λελύτρωμαι, ptc.pass. λελυτρωμένος.

1. *to procure* for sbd or sth *release from bondage*: + acc. pers. Ex 6.6, 15.13; *o* an animal, τῷ προβάτῳ 'by (offering instead) a sheep' 34.20 (‖ ἀλλάσσω 13.13), slave girl - λύτροις οὐ λελύτρωται Le 19.20; a nation, ἐξ οἴκου δουλείας Mi 6.4 (w. ref. to the Exodus), ἐκ τῆς δουλείας De 13.5, ἐκ χειρὸς Φαραω 7.8; τὸν λαόν σου καὶ τὴν κληρονομίαν σου, ἣν ἐλυτρώσω 9.26, τὴν μερίδα σου, ἣν σεαυτῷ ἐλυτρώσω ἐκ γῆς Αἰγύπτου Es C 9 (the mid. voice reinforced with a refl. pron.); with no money changing hands, δωρεὰν ἐπράθητε καὶ οὐ μετὰ ἀργυρίου λυτρωθήσεσθε 'For nothing you were sold and for no money you will be set free!' Is 52.3.

*__2__. *to rescue* from a state of danger, discomfort, confinement etc.: + acc. pers., ἐγένου βοηθὸς καὶ ἐλυτρώσω με Si 51.2f., ἔστιν ὁ λυτρούμενος καὶ σῴζων τὸν Ισραηλ 1M 4.11 (cf. μὴ ὄντος λυτρουμένου μηδὲ σῴζοντος Ps 7.3 [from a lion]); ἐκ θανάτου Ho 13.14 (‖ ἐκ χειρὸς ᾅδου ῥύομαι), ἐκεῖθεν Mi 4.10 (‖ ῥύομαι); λελύτρωταί σε ἐκ χειρὸς ἐχθρῶν σου 'he has rescued you from the clutch of your enemies' Zp 3.15, ἐκ τῶν ἐπανιστανομένων ἐπ' ἐμέ 'from those who rise up against me' Ps 58.2 (‖ ἐξαιρέω), ἐκ τόκου καὶ ἐξ ἀδικίας .. τὰς ψυχὰς αὐτῶν 'from usury ..' 71.14, ἐκ φθορᾶς τὴν ζωήν μου 102.4; τὸ σῶμά μου ἐκ ἀπωλείας Si 51.2; + ῥύομαι Is 51.11. **b**. from sins, their power and consequences: ἐκ ἀνομιῶν Ps 129.8.

3. *to buy back*: + acc., Ex 13.13; πρᾶσιν 'that which has been sold' Le 25.25.

***4**. *to atone for*: + acc. rei, τὰς ἁμαρτίας [LXX ἀδικίας] σου ἐν ἐλεημοσύναις 'your sins with acts of charity' Da 4.24 TH.

Cf. ἀπολυτρόω, ἐκλύτρωσις, ἐκπρίαμαι, ἐξαιρέω, ῥύομαι, σῴζω, λύτρον, λυτρωτός, λύτρωσις, λυτρωτής, ἀπελευθερόω: Hill 58-64; Spicq 2.423-9.

λυτρών, ῶνος. m.ʃ *

latrine: 4K 10.27B (*L* κοπρών).

λύτρωσις, εως. f.*

act of procuring release from bondage, 'redemption': human, juridical process, Le 25.29, Nu 18.16; τιμὴν τῆς ~εως τῆς ψυχῆς αὐτοῦ Ps 48.9; provided by God, πολλὴ παρ' αὐτῷ λ. 129.7, ~ιν ἀπέστειλεν τῷ λαῷ αὐτοῦ 110.9, ἐνιαυτὸς ~εως Is 63.4. **b**. *claim on that which is currently not in one's possession*: Jd 1.15.

Cf. λυτρόομαι, ἀπολύτρωσις.

λυτρωτής, οῦ, voc. ~ά. m.ʃ*

he who procures release from bondage: God of Israel, κύριε, βοηθέ μου καὶ ~τά μου Ps 18.14; 77.35 (‖ βοηθός). Cf. λυτρόομαι.

λυτρωτός, ή, όν.ʃ *

redeemable: ***s*** dwelling, Le 25.31f. Cf. λυτρόομαι.

λυχνία, ας. f.

lampstand: ἐκ χρυσίου καθαροῦ 'of pure gold' Ex 25.30; τοῦ φωτός 35.16; φωτίζουσα 'giving out light' Nu 4.9; χρυσῆ 'golden' Zc 4.2. Cf. λύχνος, λαμπαδεῖον, καλαμίσκος.

λύχνος, ου. m.

lamp: in a tabernacle, Ex 25.37; ἑπτὰ ~οι ἐπάνω αὐτῆς (i.e. λυχνίας 'lampstand') καὶ ἑπτὰ ἐπαρυστρίδες ('funnels') τοῖς ~οις τοῖς ἐπάνω αὐτῆς Zc 4.2; used in searching a dark place, Zp 1.12; for pedestrians, τοῖς ποσίν μου Ps 118.105 (‖ φῶς); ***o*** of καίω Ep Je 18. Cf. λυχνία.

λύω: fut. λύσω, pass. λυθήσομαι; aor. ἔλυσα, ptc. λύσας, inf. λῦσαι, impv.act. λῦσον, mid. λῦσαι, ptc.pass. λυθείς; pf.pass. λέλυμαι, ptc. λελυμένος.

1. *to untie*: + acc. rei, μάρσιππον 'bag' Ge 42.27, μήτραν παρθένου Ju 9.2 (of deflowering), ζώνας 'girdles' Is 5.27, σύνδεσμον ἀδικίας 'a bond of wickedness' 58.6 (‖ διαλύω); leading to loss of one's self-control and will power, 'debilitating' 4M 3.11; mid. τὸ ὑπόδημα ἐκ τῶν ποδῶν σου 'the sandal from your (own) feet' Ex 3.5, Jo 5.15, πλοκάμους 'locks of hair' 3M 1.4; pass., ***o*** sinews, 4M 7.13 (‖ περιχαλάω). **b**. *to unscroll* a book: + acc., τὸν νόμον 1E 9.46.

2. *to remove the grip of*: + acc., ὠδῖνας 'birthpangs' Jb 39.2 (‖ ἐξαποστέλλω vs. 3), δεσμούς 39.5, + dat. com., ἔλυσεν τὴν ἁμαρτίαν αὐτοῖς 42.9 (‖ ἀφίημι vs. 10); pass., λέλυται ἡ ἁμαρτία αὐτῆς Is 40.2, sim. Si 28.2; τὴν ὀργὴν τοῦ κυρίου ἀφ' ἡμῶν 1E 9.13; + ἀπό τινος To 3.17 𝔊II.

3. *to set free*: + acc. pers., ἀπὸ τῶν χειροπέδων 'from the handcuffs' Je 47.4; pass., 3M 6.29.

4. *to destroy*: + acc., τὰ τείχη 'the walls' 1E 1.52 (‖ 2C 36.19 κατασκάπτω).

Cf. δέω, ἐλευθερόω, δια~, περι~, ὑπολύω, ἀφανίζω.

λῶμα, ατος. n.*

hem, fringe, border of a robe: ὑποδύτου 'of an undergarment' Ex 28.29. Cf. κόσυμβος, περιστόμιον.

λωποδυτέω.ʃ

to rob, plunder: 1E 4.24 (+ κλέπτω, ἁρπάζω). Cf. ἁρπάζω, κλέπτω, προνομεύω.

M

μά.ʃ
Marks an entity by which an oath is made: μὰ τὸν μακάριον .. θάνατον 'by the blessed death ..' 4M 10.15, μὰ τὴν ζωήν σου 'upon your life' 2K 11.11 *L*. Cf. νή.

μαγειρεῖον, ου.ʃ
kitchen: Ez 46.23.

μαγειρεύω: aor. ἐμαγείρευσα.ʃ
to butcher, massacre: abs., La 2.21. Cf. μάγειρος, ἀφανίζω.

μαγείρισσα, ας. f.ʃ *
female cook: + perfumer and baker, 1K 8.13.

μάγειρος, ου. m.
butcher: 1K 9.24, La 2.20, Ez 46.24. Cf. μαγειρεύω: Berthiaume.

μαγικός, ή, όν.ʃ
magical: ***s*** τέχνη 'magic art' Wi 17.7.

μαγίς, ίδος. f.ʃ
kneaded mass: ἄρτου Jd 7.13.

μάγος, ου. m.ʃ
priestly sage capable of interpreting dreams: + ἐπάοιδος Da 1.20 TH, 2.2, 10. Cf. Delling, *TDNT* 4.356-9; Rigsby; LSG s.v.

μαδαρόω: aor. ἐμαδάρωσα.ʃ
to shave the head of: to humiliate and + acc. pers., Ne 13.25. Cf. μαδάω, ξυράω: Renehan 2.97.

μαδάω: aor.subj. μαδήσω.ʃ
to lose hair, become bald: ***s*** head, Le 13.40, 41; shoulder, Ez 29.18 (result of physical exhaustion and || bald head). Cf. μαδαρόω, φαλακρός.

Μαδιανίτης, ου. m.ʃ
Midianite man: Nu 10.29, 31.2.

Μαδιανῖτις, ~ίτιδος. f.
Midianite woman: Nu 25.6.

μάζα, ης. f.ʃ
kind of cake: Bel 27.

μάθημα, ατος. n.ʃ
that which is learnt, 'lesson': ἐδίδαξας αὐτοὺς .. ~ατα 'you taught them lessons' Je 13.21. Cf. μανθάνω.

μαῖα, ας. f.
midwife: Ge 35.17, Ex 1.15. Cf. μαιόομαι.

μαιμάω. Also spelled μαιμάσσω.ʃ
to be very eager: ***s*** ψυχή Je 4.19; *+ ptc. Jb 38.8. Cf. ζηλόω **3**.

μαίνομαι: fut. μανήσομαι; aor.inf. μανῆναι, subj. μανῶ; pf. (w. pres. sense) μέμηνα.
to be beside oneself: ***s*** hum. and + ἀπὸ προσώπου τινός Je 32.2. **b**. *to act and behave as if one has taken leave of one's senses*: + cogn. acc., μανίαν 4M 8.5, 10.13.
Cf. μανία, ἀπο~, ἐπιμαίνομαι, (παρ)εξίστημι: Schmidt 4.239-45; Preisker, *TDNT* 4.360f.; Spicq 2.430f.

μαιόομαι: fut. pass. μαιωθήσομαι.ʃ
1. *to act as midwife for*, 'deliver': + acc. pers., τὰς Ἐβραίας Ex 1.16.
2. *to bring forth into existence*: pass. γίγαντες μαιωθήσονται 'giants will be brought forth' Jb 26.5¶.
Cf. μαῖα, γεννάω, τίκτω.

μακαρίζω: fut. μακαριῶ, pass. ~ρισθήσομαι; aor. ἐμακάρισα, opt. ~ρίσαιμι.
to declare or consider fortunate, congratulate: + acc. pers. Ge 30.13, Ma 3.12, 15; not sincerely, but with ulterior motive, Is 3.12, 9.16; + gen., 'on account of,' 4M 1.10. **b**. *to make fortunate*: ***s*** God, ***o*** hum., Ps 40.3; ***s*** hum., Si 25.23. Cf. μακάριος, τύχη.

μακάριος, α, ον.
found in a desirable, agreeable condition, 'fortunate': ***s*** hum., Μακαρία ἐγώ Ge 30.13 (a mother of many children); a nation saved by God, De 33.29; wives and servants of a wise king, 3K 10.8; Ps 136.8f., Si 25.8, Is 32.20; old age, 4M 7.15.

With a limited number of exceptions [see below], μ. opens, as in the Beatitudes (Mt 5.3-10), a generic, typological statement in the form of a nominal clause without a copula with the fortunate character of the subject–a human, never a divinity–formulated by means of a relative clause or a participial clause: e.g., μακάριος ἀνὴρ, ὃς οὐκ ἐπορεύθη ἐν βουλῇ ἀσεβῶν Ps 1.1, ~οι ὧν ἀφέθησαν αἱ ἀνομίαι 'Blessed are those whose iniquities have been forgiven' 31.1; ~οι πάντες οἱ φοβούμενοι τὸν κύριον 127.1.

With a subj. pers. pron. in the second position: ~α ἐγώ, ὅτι .. Ge 30.13, so also De 33.29, Ec 10.17ʃ; with εἰμί in the 1st or 2nd pers. but with no pers. pron., μ. ἔσομαι To 13.16 𝔊II, μ. εἶ, καὶ καλῶς σοι ἔσται Ps 127.2, Ba 4.4 ~οί ἐσμεν, Ισραηλʃ; μ. in a non-initial position, γυναικὸς ἀγαθῆς μ. ὁ ἀνήρ Si 26.1, φοβουμένου τὸν κύριον ~α ἡ ψυχή 31.17ʃ; a variety of other structures (in Pr and 4M), ~ους τοὺς παῖδας αὐτοῦ καταλείψει 'will leave his servants happy' Pr 20.7, ὦ ~ου γήρως .. 'O man of blessed old age ..' 4M 7.15, τὸν ~ον βιοῦσιν αἰῶνα 'they live the life of blessed eternity' 17.18, πάντα πόνον ὑπομένειν ~όν ἐστιν 'to endure every suffering is blessed' 7.22 (*s* action!), μὰ τὸν ~ον .. θάνατον 'by the blessed death ..' 10.15 (*s* inanimate obj.!)ʃ.

Cf. μακαρίζω, μακαριστός, μακαρίως, εὐθηνία, εὐλογητός, ταλαίπωρος: Schmidt 4.402-6; Shipp 3375f.; Spicq 2.432-41.

μακαριότης, ητος. f.ʃ

blissful state: τοῦ ἱεροῦ τόπου 'of the holy place' 4M 4.12.

μακαριστός, ή, όν.

to be deemed fortunate: πλουτιεῖν καὶ ~ὸν ποιήσειν 'to make him rich and enviable' 2M 7.24. Cf. μακάριος.

μακαρίως. adv.ʃ

in blessed fashion: to die, 4M 12.1. Cf. μακάριος.

μακράν. adv.

far-off: οὐ μακρὰν ἀποτενεῖτε πορευθῆναι 'don't go too far away' Ex 8.28; ~ὰν ἀπὸ τῆς παρεμβολῆς 'far away from the camp' 33.7; ἔθνος ~ὰν ἀπέχον 'a nation located far away' Jl 3.8; οἱ ~ὰν ἀπ' αὐτῶν 'those who are far away from them' Zc 6.15, sim. 10.9; τῶν ἐγγιζόντων σοι ἢ τῶν μακρὰν ἀπὸ σοῦ De 13.7; ἕως εἰς ~άν Si 24.32; + gen., 15.8, 23.3¶, Pr 19.7; τοῖς ~ὰν καὶ τοῖς ἐγγὺς οὖσι Is 57.19; attr. δρυμὸς μ. 'a forest far off' 27.9. Cf. μακρός.

μακρόβιος, ον.ʃ

having lived long: *s* hum., Wi 3.17; σπέρμα ~ον 'long-living offspring' Is 53.10. Cf. μακροήμερος.

μακροβίωσις, εως. f.ʃ *

longevity: hum., μ. καὶ ζωή Ba 3.14. Cf. μακρόβιος, μακροημέρευσις.

μακροημέρευσις, εως. f.ʃ *

longevity: divine blessing, φόβος κυρίου .. δώσει εὐφροσύνην καὶ χαρὰν καὶ ~ιν Si 1.12; 1.20; ‖ ζωή 30.22. Cf. μακροημερεύω, μακροβίωσις.

μακροημερεύω: fut. ~εύσω; aor. ἐμακροημέρευσα, subj. ~εύσω.*

to enjoy longevity: divine blessing in the promised land, De 5.33, 6.2, 11.9, 32.47. Cf. μακροήμερος, ~μέρευσις, πολυημερεύω.

μακροήμερος, ον.ʃ *

enjoying longevity: ὅπως ~οι γένησθε De 4.40. Cf. μακροχρόνιος, μακροημερεύω, μακρόβιος.

μακρόθεν. adv.

1. *from afar*: Ex 2.4; ὁρμήσουσιν μ. 'they will rush from afar' Hb 1.8. **b**. in time: ‖ ἐξ ἡμερῶν ἀρχῆς 4K 19.25*L*.

2. *at a distance, at a remove*: ἐκάθητο .. μ. ὡσεὶ τόξου βολήν 'sat .. at some distance about a bowshot' Ge 21.16; εἶδεν τὸν τόπον μ. 22.4; προεῖδον αὐτὸν μ. 37.18; φοβηθέντες .. ἔστησαν μ. Ex 20.18. **b**. attr. adj.: ἐκ γῆς μ. 'from a far-off land' Je 4.16, Pr 25.25. **c**. with a redundant ἀπό: ἕως ἀπὸ μ. 'even from far off' 2E 3.13.

Cf. μακρός, πόρρωθεν, ἐγγύθεν.

μακροθυμέω: aor. ἐμακροθύμησα, impv. ~μησον, subj. ~μήσω. *

to maintain same attitude long, to bear up long without breaking down or being provoked into retaliation: abs., οὐ εἰς τὸν αἰῶνα ζήσομαι, ἵνα μακροθυμήσω 'I am not going to live for ever and persevere' Jb 7.16, ἐν ἀλλάγμασιν ταπεινώσεώς σου μακροθύμησον 'when you've fallen on the hard times, hold it out' Si 2.4, ἀναμένει μακροθυμῶν 'bides the time patiently' 2M 6.14; ἐπὶ ταπεινῷ 'the underprivileged' Si 29.8 (even when he is a shade too demanding). **b**. *to take long to act and respond to*: + ἐπί τινι [= pers.], ἐμακροθύμησεν κύριος ἐπ' αὐτοῖς 'the Lord bore with them [= mankind with a short life-span] generously' Si 18.11; to make keep waiting, ὁ κύριος οὐ μὴ βραδύνῃ οὐδὲ μὴ μακροθυμήσῃ ἐπ' αὐτοῖς '.. will not tarry nor keep them [= the entreating poor] waiting' 32.22, cf. Lk 18.7; + acc. rei, τὴν ὀργήν 'the (divine) wrath' Ba 4.25.

Cf. μακροθυμία, ἀνέχω, ἀντέχω, βραδύνω, χρονίζω: Trench 195-9; Riesenfeld; Wifstrand; Rogland.

μακροθυμία, ας. f.

1. *ability to bear up without giving up*: κύριος .. ὀλιγοψύχοις διδοὺς ~αν Is 57.15.

2. *taking time in action*: ἐν ~ίᾳ φθέγγου ἀπόκρισιν 'take time in giving an answer' Si 5.11 (:: γίνομαι ταχύς 'to be quick'); 1M 8.4.

Cf. μακρόθυμος, ὑπομονή.

μακρόθυμος, ον.

able to bear up under provocation (BDAG): *s* God, Ex 34.6 (‖ οἰκτίρμων, ἐλεήμων, πολυέλεος); κύριος μ. Na 1.3; μ. καὶ πολυέλεος Jl 2.13; τοῖς παραπτώμασίν σου 'your transgressions' Da 4.24 TH; hum., Pr 16.32 (glossed as κρατῶν ὀργῆς 'controlling one's anger'); opp. ὀλιγόψυχος 14.29, ὑψηλὸς πνεύματι 'haughty in spirit' Ec 7.8. Cf. μακροθυμέω, ὀλιγόψυχος, ὀξύθυμος.

μακρός, ά, όν. adj.

1. *extending over a long distance*: ἐὰν μακροτέρα ᾖν ἡ ὁδός De 19.6; σχοινίον 'cord' Is 5.18. **b**. temporal: χρόνον ~όν Ep Je 2, εἰς ἡμέρας μακράς 'for many days to come' Ba 4.35 (‖ τὸν πλείονα χρόνον and cf. ἰς μακροὺς χρόνους 'for a very long time' *CPR* V 19.5); *s* illness, Si 10.10.

2. *situated at a long distance away*: a subst. (e.g. χώρα) understood, ἐλέγξει ἔθνη ἰσχυρὰ ἕως εἰς ~άν 'he will chastise mighty nations up to a great distance, i.e. the chastisement will affect even far-away places' Mi 4.3; ἐκ ~ῶν 'from afar' (?) 1C 17.17. **b**. μακράν (acc.) used adverbially and of place, far-off: see under **μακράν**. **c**. μακρότερον adv., and almost with the force of the positive degree: ἐὰν μακρότερον ἀπέχῃ σου ὁ τόπος 'should the place be removed from you' De 12.21.

3. *large in size*: Jb 11.9.

Cf. μακρότης, μακρόθεν, ἐγγύς.

μακρότης, ητος. f.

long duration, 'prolongation': τῶν ἡμερῶν 'longevity' as divine gift De 30.20, sim. Ps 20.5, 90.16; τῆς ζωῆς Da TH 7.12; εἰς ~τα ἡμερῶν 'for a long time' Ps 22.6, 92.5; ‖ εἰς νῖκος La 5.20. Cf. μακρός, μακροήμερος.

μακροτονέω: aor. ἐμακροτόνησα.ʃ

to prolong an activity: + ptc. pres., 2M 8.26.

μακροχρονίζω: aor.subj. μακροχρονίσω.ʃ *.

to live a long time, enjoy longevity: De 32.27. Cf. μακροχρόνιος, πολυχρονίζω.

μακροχρόνιος, ον.

being a long time: *s* hum., ἵνα μ. γένῃ ἐπὶ τῆς γῆς τῆς ἀγαθῆς Ex 20.12; ἐπὶ τῆς ἀρχῆς αὐτοῦ 'in his office' De 17.20. Cf. μακροήμερος, μακροχρονίζω, πολυχρόνιος.

μάκρυμμα, ατος. n.*

that which is put far away: 2E 9.1, 11 (‖ ἀκαθαρσία 1E 8.66).

μακρύνω: fut. μακρυνῶ, pass. ~ρυνθήσομαι; aor. ἐμάκρυνα, inf. μακρῦναι, impv. μάκρυνον, subj. μακρύνω, opt.3s μακρύναι, pass. ἐμακρύνθην, subj. μακρυνθῶ, inf. μακρυνθῆναι, ptc. μακρυνθείς; pf.ptc. μεμακρυγκώς, pass. μεμακρυμμένος.*

1. *to make large*, 'enlarge': + acc., σχοινίσματα 'allotments' Is 54.2 (‖ πλατύνω). **b**. *to add to the extent of*: + acc. rei, ἀνομίαν Ps 128.3.

2. *to keep at a distance*: + acc. pers., Is 6.12 (care neglected and ‖ καταλείπω), ἑαυτοὺς ἀπὸ σοῦ Ps 72.27; +acc. rei, βοήθειαν 21.20, "your mercies" 39.12; + ἀπό τινος Je 34.8, ἀπὸ ἀκάκων χείλη παρανόμων 'lips of the lawless from the innocent' PSol 12.4; intr. pass., La 1.16, Ps 108.17, 1M 8.23.

3. *to delay an action*: + τοῦ inf., Ju 2.13.

4. intr. *to move a long distance*: Ps 54.8; Jd 18.22 (*L*: pass.).

5. intr. *to remain at a distance*: indifferently, ἀπ' ἐμοῦ Ps 70.12; ἀπὸ περιλήμψεως '(refrain) from embracing' Ec 3.5.

Cf. μεγαλύνω.

μάλα. adv.

1. An asseverative particle, 'in truth': εὖ μ. 2M 10.32; often following καί, 2K 14.5 (*L* ὄντως), 4K 4.14, Da 10.21 LXX, To 7.10 𝔊II.

2. Intensifies an adj. or adv., *exceedingly*: 4M 13.13; preceded by an otiose καί - φρουρὰν .. καὶ μ. ὀχυράν 'a very strong garrison' 2M 12.18. **b**. εὖ μ.: postpositive, 2M 8.30, 10.18.

μάλαγμα, ατος. n.ʃ

agent that soothes pain: ἐπιθεῖναι 'to put on' Is 1.6 (‖ ἔλαιον 'oil', κατάδεσμος 'bandage'); μ. ἐθεράπευσεν αὐτούς Wi 16.12 (‖ βοτάνη 'herb'); Ez 30.21.

μαλακία, ας. f.

physical weakness, illness: Μήποτε συμβῇ αὐτῷ μ. 'I fear he may fall ill' Ge 42.4, sim. 44.29; ἀποστρέψω ~αν ἀφ' ὑμῶν 'I shall ward illness off you' Ex 23.25, sim. De 7.15 (‖ νόσος); ‖ πληγή 28.61 (divine punishment). Cf. ἀρρωστία, ἀσθενής, μαλακίζομαι, νόσος, ὑγίεια.

μαλακίζομαι: aor. ἐμαλακίσθην, inf. μαλακισθῆναι, impv. ~κίσθητι, ptc. ~κισθείς; pf. μεμαλάκισμαι.

to fall ill: συμβήσεται αὐτὸν μαλακισθῆναι ἐν τῇ ὁδῷ Ge 42.38 (‖ συμβῇ αὐτῷ μαλακία ἐν τῇ ὁδῷ 44.29); ‖ τραυματίζομαι 'to be wounded' Is 53.5, ἕως θανάτου 38.1; opp. ὑγιάζομαι; τοὺς πόδας αὐτοῦ 'in his feet' 2C 16.12 (‖ 3K 15.23 πονέω). Cf. μαλακία, ἀσθενέω, ἐνοχλέω.

μαλακός, ή, όν.ʃ

gentle, not harsh: *s* γλῶσσα Pr 25.15, λόγοι 26.22. Cf. μαλακύνω, μαλακῶς, σκληρός: Schmidt 4.671-3.

μαλακοψυχέω: aor.ptc. ~ψυχήσας.ʃ *

to be cowardly or *act cowardly*: 4M 6.17.

μαλακύνω: aor. ἐμαλάκυνα.ʃ

to soften: + acc., τὴν καρδίαν μου Jb 23.16. Cf. μαλακός.

μαλακῶς. adv.ʃ

gently: attitude of supliant, Jb 40.27. Cf. μαλακός.

μάλιστα: ⇒ μᾶλλον.

μᾶλλον adv.

I. *more*: with a comparative, ἰσχυρότερόν ἐστιν ἡμῶν μ. Nu 13.32; ἔθνη μεγάλη καὶ ἰσχυρότερα μ. ἢ ὑμεῖς De 9.1. **b**. with an adj. / adv. in the positive degree: ἔθνος μέγα καὶ πολὺ μ. ἢ τοῦτο Nu 14.12, sim. De 9.14; Is 13.12, 54.1. **c**. with a verb, ἐξήγειρε μ. κλύδωνα 'raised up billows ever more' Jn 1.11; 1.13; ἠγάπησεν Ραχηλ μ. ἢ Λείαν 'he loved R. better than L.' Ge 29.30. **d**. with a noun: ἔσται εἰρήνη μᾶλλον To 14.4 𝔊I (𝔊II + ἤπερ ἐν 'Ασσυρίους).

2. *by preference*: σὲ κακώσομεν μ. ἢ ἐκείνους 'we shall harm you rather than them' Ge 19.9; Si 20.18.

3. *otherwise than expected or hoped for*, 'rather': Jb 30.26, Pr 15.18a.

4. μ. δε 'to be more precise,' introducing a qualification of an earlier statement: Wi 8.18.

II. μάλιστα *most of all*: "especially advantageous" 2M 8.7; 4M 15.4. **b**. ὡς μ., *exceedingly*: διψῶν 'thirsty' 4M 3.10; ὡς ἔνι μ. χαίροιεν 'they were ecstatic' 4.22.

μάμμη, ης.ʃ

grandmother: 4M 16.9. Cf. μήτηρ, πάππος.

μάν. n., indecl.; see also under μάννα.
manna: Ex 16.31.

μάνδρα, ας. f.
enclosed space for animals, 'pen, fold': for lion's cubs (σκύμνος) Am 3.4; for sheep, νομὴ ποιμνίων καὶ μ. προβάτων Zp 2.6, || φάτνη 'stall' 2C 32.28; lion's lair, Je 4.7, place of ambush Ps 9.30; shelter Jd 6.2 A. Cf. ἔπαυλις, νομή, κοίτη, φάτνη: Shipp 380; Schnebel 348; Gagliano.

μανδραγόρας, ου. m.
mandrake: Ge 30.15; μῆλα ~ου 'mandrake fruits' 30.14.

μανδύας, ου. m. *
woolen cloak: Jd 3.16; warrior's outfit, 1K 17.38.

μανθάνω: fut. μαθήσομαι; aor. ἔμαθον, subj. μάθω, inf. μαθεῖν, impv. μάθε, ptc. μαθών; pf. μεμάθηκα, inf. μεμαθηκέναι, ptc. μεμαθηκώς.

1. *to learn* (a skill, art, habit): abs., || συνίημι Wi 6.1; κατὰ τὰς ὁδῶν τῶν ἐθνῶν Je 10.2 (|| τὴν ὁδὸν τοῦ λαοῦ μου 12.16), *+ gen, rei, τῶν ὁδῶν αὐτοῦ Pr 22.25; + inf. πολεμεῖν Mi 4.3 (|| Is 2.4); attitude, φοβεῖσθαί με De 4.10, sim. 14.22, 17.19, 31.12, 13; καλὸν ποιεῖν Is 1.17, ἀκούειν 28.19Q, ὑπακούειν 29.24; + acc. rei, δικαιώματα καὶ κρίματα De 5.1, δικαιοσύνην Is 26.9, τὴν ὁδὸν τοῦ λαοῦ μου Je 12.16, τὰ κακά 13.23, ἐπιστήμην Si 16.24; + an indir. question, Ba 3.14; and + παρά τινος (pers.), παρ' αὐτῶν μαθήσῃ παιδείαν Si 8.8; + gen. pers., ἐρωτᾶν καὶ μανθάνειν ἡμῶν (v.l. παρ' ἡμῶν) 2M 7.2.

2. *to find out by observation or by asking around*: + interr., τί τὸ ἀποβησόμενον αὐτῷ 'what was going to happen to him' Ex 2.4; + ὅτι Es A 13 o'; + acc. rei, παρὰ τοῦ Μορδοχαίου τὸ ἀκριβές 'from M. the exact details' 4.5 o'.

Cf. μάθημα, πολυ~, φιλομαθής, σχολάζω, διδάσκω, ἀμαθία.

μανία, ας. f.
madness: ἐπληθύνθη μ. σου Ho 9.7; 9.8; ψευδής 'derived from falsehood' Ps 39.5; as cogn. obj. of μαίνομαι 4M 8.5, 10.13. Cf. μαίνομαι, ἐμμανής, μανιώδης, ἔκστασις, ἀπόνοια, παραφρόνησις.

μανιάκης, ου. m.
necklace: 1E 3.6; golden, Da LXX 5.7 (+ πορφύρα). Cf. μηνίσκος, ὁρμίσκος: Russo 80-5.

μανιώδης, ες.ʃ
mentally deranged: *s* κατάστεμα 'condition' 3M 5.45. Cf. μανία.

μαννα. n. indecl.; see also under μάν.
manna: Nu 11.6, De 8.3.

μαντεία, ας. f.
divination: σκοτία ὑμῖν ἔσται ἐκ ~ας 'divination will lead you into darkness' Mi 3.6 (|| ὅρασις); || οἰωνισμός Nu 23.23, sim. De 18.10; + οἰωνισμός, ἐνύπνιον Si 31.5; ~ῶν ἀκούσονται De 18.14. Cf. μάντις, μαντεύομαι, μαντεῖος, οἰωνισμός, ὅρασις.

μαντεῖος, α, ον.ʃ
pertaining to μαντεία: subst.n.sg. 'divination' Ez 21.22, Pr 16.10; n.pl. 'fees for divination' Nu 22.7 (or: pl. of μαντεῖον). Cf. μαντεία.

μαντεύομαι: aor.subj. μαντεύσωμαι, inf. μαντεύσασθαι, impv. μάντευσαι.
to practise divination: pagan practice and + cogn. acc., μαντείαν De 18.10, μαντείαις 4K 17.17*L* (B: acc.; + οἰωνίζομαι); + acc. rei, ψεύδη 'lies' Ez 21.29; *s* prophet, μετὰ ἀργυρίου 'in return for payment of silver' Mi 3.11. **b**. + dat. pers., *to communicate a message of divination*: + ψευδοπροφήτης, ἐνυπνιαζόμενος, οἰώνισμα, φάρμακος Je 34.7.

Cf. μάντις, μαντεία: Trench 19-24.

μάντις, εως. m.
diviner: οἱ ~εις ὁράσεις ψευδεῖς 'the diviners (pronounced) false visions' Zc 10.2 (|| ἐνύπνιον); || ὁρῶν 'seer' Mi 3.7; || ψευδοπροφήτης Je 36.8; || ἐπαοιδός 1K 6.2. Cf. μαντεία, μαντεύομαι, ἐπαοιδός, ὁράω, προφήτης, στοχαστής, ψευδοπροφήτης, and ἀποφθέγγομαι.

μαραίνω: aor.opt.3s μαράναι, pass. ἐμαράνθην, inf. μαρανθῆναι.
to cause to wither: + acc., βλαστόν 'bud' Jb 15.30. **b**. *to cause to lose suppleness* or *vitality*: + acc., flesh, Wi 19.21. **c**. pass. *to wither*: fig., *s* hum. and plant, ἐν καύματι 'in heat' Jb 24.24.

Cf. ἀμάραντος: Spicq 2.445f.

μαρμάρινος, η, ον.ʃ
made from marble: *s* column, Ct 5.15. Cf. subs.

μάρμαρος, ου. m./f.ʃ
marble: Ep Je 71. Cf. prec.

μαρσίππιον, ου. n. dim. of μάρσιππος.ʃ
small bag: for money, οὐδέν σοι ἐστιν ἐν ~ίῳ 'you have not a penny in your purse' Si 18.33; χρυσίον ἐκ ~ίου 'a piece of gold out of the purse' Is 46.6; || βαλλάντιον Pr 1.14. Cf. μάρσιππος, βαλλάντιον, δεσμός **2**.

μάρσιππος, ου. m.
bag: container for corn, λύσας .. τὸν ~ον Ge 42.27; ἠνοίξαμεν τοὺς μαρσίππους ἡμῶν 'we opened ..' 43.21; Πλήσατε .. 'Fill up ..' 44.1; τὸ στόμα τοῦ μ. 44.1; καθεῖλαν .. ἐπὶ τὴν γῆν 'put down on the ground' 44.11; used for measuring grain for sale, Mi 6.11 (|| ζυγόν). Cf. σάκκος and μαρσίππιον: Lee 117.

μαρτυρέω: fut. μαρτυρήσω; aor. ἐμαρτύρησα, inf. μαρτυρῆσαι.

1. *to serve as witness*: *s* cairn, Ὁ βουνὸς οὗτος μαρτυρεῖ ἀνὰ μέσον ἐμοῦ καὶ σοῦ Ge 31.46; στήλη 31.48; + dat. dei, 2C 28.10 (*L* aliter); ἐπί τινα 'against sbd' Nu 35.30, but ἐφ' ἡμᾶς ὁ οὐρανὸς καὶ ἡ γῆ 'in our favour' 1M 2, 37; κατὰ πρόσωπον μαρτυροῦσα 'as a personal witness' De 31.21.

2. *to say as witness*: + acc. rei, ἄδικα De 19.18; Wi 17.11.

3. *to say solemnly*: + dat. pers. and acc. rei, La 2.13.

Cf. μάρτυς, μαρτύρομαι, ἀντι~, ἀπο~, ἐκ~, προσμαρτυρέω, ἐπι~, διαμαρτύρομαι.

μαρτυρία, ας.

1. *something which serves as witness*: βουνὸς ~ας 'a cairn of ..' Ge 31.47.

2. *act of bearing witness, testifying*: οὐ ψευδομαρτυρήσεις .. ~αν ψευδῆ Ex 20.16, De 5.20; ~αν ἀποδίδωμι 'to testify, admit solemnly' 4M 6.32.

Cf. μάρτυς.

μαρτύριον, ου. n.

1. *something which or someone who serves as witness*: ἔσται εἰς μ. ἀνὰ μέσον ἐμοῦ καὶ σοῦ Ge 31.44 (*s* διαθήκη); κιβωτὸς ~ου 'ark of testimony' Ex 25.9; ἔσται κύριος ἐν ὑμῖν εἰς μ. 'the Lord will be a witness amongst you' Mi 1.2. **b**. w. ref. to the Decalogue as a reminder of the relationship between Israel and their God: τὰ ~α, ἃ ἂν δῶ σοι Ex 25.15, 20; τὰς δύο πλάκας τοῦ ~ου 31.18, sim. 32.15; κιβωτὸς ~ου 25.9.

2. *testimony*: οὐ συνέσχεν εἰς μ. ὀργὴν αὐτοῦ 'he has not retained his anger for a testimony' Mi 7.18.

3. *evidence*: ἵνα ὦσίν μοι εἰς μ., ὅτι .. 'so that they may serve me as evidence that ..' Ge 21.30.

4. elliptically for ἡ κιβωτὸς τοῦ ~ου 'the ark of the covenant': Ex 16.34; ἡ σκηνὴ τοῦ ~ου 27.21.

***5**. Hebraism for עֵדוּת and pl., *binding, legal stipulations*: ‖ δικαιώματα, κρίματα, ἐντολαί De 4.45, 6.17, 20, 4K 23.3, cf. Fitzmyer 1995.58 w. n. 6 there.

***6**. *strict instruction*: 1K 13.8 (w. ref. to a designated date, מוֹעֵד).

Cf. μάρτυς, ἐντολή: Harl 2001.904.

μαρτύρομαι: aor.inf. μαρτύρασθαι.ʃ

1. *to invite to serve as witness*: + acc., ὑμῖν τὸν οὐρανὸν καὶ τὴν γῆν 'against you ..' Ju 7.28.

2. *to remind forcefully*: Es A 6*L*.

Cf. μαρτυρέω, ἐπιμαρτύρομαι: Strathmann, *TDNT* 4.510f. Del. 1M 2.56 v.l.

μάρτυς, υρος. m.

1. *person bearing witness*: ὁ θεὸς μ. ἀνὰ μέσον ἐμοῦ καὶ σοῦ Ge 31.44; ἔσομαι μ. ταχὺς ἐπὶ τὰς φαρμάκους .. 'I shall be a swift witness against the witches ..' Ma 3.5; βουνὸς ('cairn') μ. Ge 31.47; ἄδικος De 19.16; εἰς ~ρα δίκαιον καὶ πιστόν Je 49.5; μάρτυρες ὑμεῖς .. ὅτι .. 'you are witnesses for the fact that ..' Ru 4.9.

2. *person who was present at event*, whether seeing or hearing: μ. ἢ ἑώρακεν ἢ σύνοιδεν Le 5.1; μ. μὴ ᾖ μετ' αὐτῆς Nu 5.13; w. ref. to God, Jb 16.19 (‖ συνίστωρ).

Cf. μαρτυρέω, μαρτυρία, μαρτύριον, συνίστωρ, ψευδομάρτυς: Spicq 2.447-52.

μαρυκάομαι.ʃ *

= μηρυκάομαι: μηρυκισμὸν οὐ μαρυκᾶται 'does not chew the cud' Le 11.26, De 14.8 and ‖ ἀνάγω μηρυκισμόν. Cf. μηρυκισμός, μασάομαι.

μασάομαι.ʃ

to chew: + acc., roots of trees as food, Jb 30.4. Cf. διαμασάομαι, ἀμάσητος, μαρυκάομαι.

μαστιγόω: fut.~γώσω, pass. ~γωθήσομαι; aor. ἐμαστίγωσα, inf. ~γῶσαι, pass. ἐμαστιγώθην, ptc. ~γωθείς, subj. ~γωθῶ; pf.pass. μεμαστίγωμαι, ptc. μεμαστιγωμένος.

to beat with a whip, 'to flog': as punishment and ***o*** hum., Ex 5.14, De 25.2, Ps 72.14, Wi 16.16, σκληρὰς ὑποφέρω κατὰ σῶμα ἀλγηδόνας μαστιγούμενος 'I endure severe bodily sufferings under this beating' 2M 6.30; applied to servants, To 3.9; μαστιγῶσαι αὐτὸν ὑπὲρ ταύτας τὰς πληγὰς πλείους 'to flog him over and above these beatings' De 25.3; with good intention to discipline and ***s*** God, To 11.15 𝔊[I], εἰς νουθέτησιν 'for admonition' Ju 8.27, μαστιγοῖ καὶ ἐλεᾷ To 13.2, ἐπὶ τὰ ἔργα 'over the deeds' 13.9 𝔊[I]; υἱόν Pr 3.12 (‖ παιδεύω). **b**. metaph.: εἰς σῶμα Si 30.14 (w. ref. to illness).

Cf. μάστιξ, μαστίζω.

μαστίζω: aor. ἐμάστιξα, inf. μαστίξαι.ʃ

to beat with a whip: as punishment and ***o*** ass, Nu 22.25, hum., 3M 2.21 (*s* God); fig. πληγῇ ταρσῶν μαστιζόμενον πνεῦμα κοῦφον 'the light air lashed by the beat of its pinions' Wi 5.11. Cf. μάστιξ, μαστιγόω.

μάστιξ, γος. f.

whip: applied to horses pulling a chariot, φωνὴ ~ίγων Na 3.2; to discipline, ~γες καὶ παιδεία Si 22.6; applied to a child, 30.1; πόνῳ καὶ ~γι παιδευθήσῃ Je 6.7; punitive, μάστιγες τοῦ ἁμαρτωλοῦ Ps 31.10, ‖ τιμωρίαι 'punishments' Pr 19.29; instrument of discipline, παιδείας PSol 7.9 (‖ ζυγός). **b**. w. ref. to assailant (not necessarily physical): Ps 34.15. **c**. metaph., θεία μ. 'divine scourge': in the form of bodily suffering, 2M 9.11, cf. μ. παρὰ κυρίου οὐκ ἔστιν ἐπ' αὐτοῖς Jb 21.9, ἀπόστησον ἀπ' ἐμοῦ τὰς ~άς σου 'Remove ..' Ps 38.11; γλώσσης Jb 5.21.

Cf. μαστιγόω, μαστίζω: Spicq 2.539-42.

μαστός, οῦ. m. Mostly in pl.

breast: of woman Ho 2.2, of man Ct 1.2, of female snake La 4.3; source of milk, νήπια θηλάζοντα ~ούς 'breast-sucking babes' Jl 2.16; μ. ξηρός 'dry, i.e. not producing milk' Ho 9.14 (|| μήτρα ἀτεκνοῦσα 'infertile womb'); εὐλογίαι ~ῶν καὶ μήτρας Ge 49.25. Cf. μήτρα, ὑπομαστίδιος: Shipp 383.

μάταιος, α, ον.

1. *meaningless, worthless*: οἴκους ~ους Mi 1.14 (|| κενός); μ. ὁ δουλεύων θεῷ Ma 3.14; *s* action, Is 1.13; κενῶς ἐκοπίασα καὶ εἰς μάταιαν καὶ εἰς οὐθὲν ἔδωκα τὴν ἰσχύν μου 'I toiled to no good purpose and in vain and for nothing I expended my energy' 49.4; fem. beauty, Pr 31.30 (|| ψευδής). **b**. subst. n. pl.: πόλις ἐργαζομένη μάταια Ho 6.8 (Cyr. I 145 and Thph PG 126.681 take this as 'manufacturing images for worship'); κενὰ καὶ ~α 12.1, ~α καὶ κενά Is 30.7; ~α παρεκάλουν Zc 10.2 (|| ψευδῆ). Esp. w. ref. to idols and images for heathen worship: θύσουσιν .. τοῖς ~οις Le 17.7; πορεύεσθαι ὀπίσω τῶν ~ων Ho 5.11, Je 2.5; ἐπλάνησεν αὐτοὺς τὰ μ. αὐτῶν, ἃ ἐποίησαν Am 2.4; ποιμαίνοντες τὰ μ. Zc 11.17; ~α ἀλλότρια Je 8.19 (|| γλυπτά).

2. *lacking in substance, counterfeit, false*: *s* ἀκοή 'baseless hearsay' Ex 23.1, ἰσχύς Is 30.15, ἐλπίς 'hope' 31.2, μαντεία 'divination' Ez 13.7, ἀρά 'curse' Pr 26.2; subst. μάταια καὶ ψευδῆ Jn 2.9; οὐ λαλήσουσιν ~α Zp 3.13 (|| γλῶσσα δολία), μαντευόμενοι ~α Ez 13.6, ἀποφθεγγόμενοι ~α 13.9.

3. *irreverent, frivolous*: ἐπὶ ματαίῳ '.. in an irreverent, frivolous fashion' Ex 20.7, De 5.11.

Cf. ματαιότης, ματαιόφρων, κενός, ψευδής: Trench 180-4.

ματαιότης, ητος. f.*

that which lacks substance: || ψεῦδος Ps 4.3; *s* mankind, 143.4; μ. ματαιοτήτων Ec 1.1. Cf. μάταιος: Bauernfeind, *TDNT* 4.523.

ματαιόφρων, ον; gen. ονος.∫ *

tending to vain thoughts: *s* heathens, 3M 6.11.

ματαιόω: fut.pass. ματαιωθήσομαι; aor.impv. ματαίωσον, pass. ἐματαιώθην; pf.pass. μεματαίωμαι.

1. *to engage oneself senselessly in*: + acc., ὅρασιν 'vision' Je 23.16.

2. *to prevent successful conclusion of*, 'thwart, jeopardise': + acc., βουλήν 'plan' 2K 15.31*L* (|| διασκεδάζω vs. 34 and B here).

3. dep. *to act senselessly*: by following senseless things (τὰ μάταια) Je 2.5, ἀπὸ γνώσεως 'because of (false?) knowledge' 28.17; || ἁμαρτάνω 1C 21.8 (*L* ἀφρονέω). **b**. *to turn out to be baseless*: *s* assertion, Ju 6.4. **c**. impers.: μεματαίωταί σοι 'you have acted senselessly' 1K 13.13, cf. μεματαίωμαι 26.21.

Cf. ἀφρονέω, διασκεδάζω: Bauernfeind, *TDNT* 4.523.

ματαίως. adv.

for no good, justifiable reason: ἐχθραίνω 'to show hostility' Ps 3.8; 72.13, 88.48, Jb 35.16¶.

μάτην. adv.

1. *with no chance of achieving desired effect*: Is 27.3; πεποιθότες μ. ψεύδει 'trusting in a lie in vain' 28.17; Ps 126.2. **b**. *without having achieved desired effect*: Je 2.30; εἰς μ. Ps 126.1, Da 11.24 LXX.

2. *for no good, justifiable reason*: || δωρεάν Ps 34.7.

μάχαιρα, ας. f.

1. *sword*: destructive weapon, Ge 48.22 (|| τόξον 'bow'), Le 26.25, Zc 11.17; Nu 22.31 (|| ῥομφαία vs. 23), De 32.25, Is 2.4 (|| ῥομφαία Mi 4.3), ~αν ἁγίαν καὶ μεγάλην καὶ ἰσχυράν Is 27.1, ~αν ὀξεῖαν 'sharp ..' 49.2; ἐν φόνῳ ~ας 'by killing with a sword' De 13.15, 20.13, εἰς σφαγήν 'for slaughtering' Je 15.3; κυρίου 12.12; + λιμός 'famine' Je 5.12, 34.6, Is 51.19; sg. coll. τὸ πλῆθος τῆς μαχαίρας 21.15. **b**. meton., *army*: Ἑλληνική Je 26.16.

2. *large knife*: sacrificial knife, Ge 22.6.

Cf. ἀκινάκης, ῥομφαία, ξίφος.

μάχη, ης. f.

strife arising out of conflicting interests: ἀνὰ μέσον τῶν ποιμένων τῶν κτηνῶν τοῦ Αβραμ καὶ ἀνὰ μέσον τῶν ποιμένων τῶν κτηνῶν τοῦ Λωτ Ge 13.7; ἀνὰ μέσον ἐμοῦ καὶ σοῦ ib. 8; εἰς κρίσεις καὶ ~ας 'for the sake of court actions and wrangles' Is 58.4; *o* of ποιέω Si 8.16; + στάσις 'sedition' Pr 17.14, + ἔχθρα 'enmity' 25.10, || ἔ. Si 6.9, + κρίσις 'dispute' Is 58.4, || ἔρις 'quarrel' Si 28.11. **b**. military battle: + πόλεμος Jb 38.23, || π. Jo 4.13, Jd 11.25A.

Cf. μαχητής, μάχομαι, μάχιμος, πεζομαχία, πόλεμος, στράτευμα, ἀμάχως: Trench 322f.

μαχητής, οῦ. m.

fighter: Am 2.14, Jl 3.11; πτοηθήσονται οἱ ~αί σου Ob 9; Zc 10.5 (cf. Th and Tht ad loc.); *o* of ἐξεγείρω 'to arouse,' Jl 3.9, Hb 1.6; ῥομφαία ~οῦ Zc 9.13; || πολεμιστής Jl 2.7, 3.9. Cf. μάχη, μάχομαι, ὁπλόμαχος, πολεμιστής, στρατιώτης.

μάχιμος, η, ον.

1. *trained to engage in a battle*: subst.m., soldier, Jo 5.6.

2. *quarrelsome*: *s* γυνή, + γλωσσώδης 'talkative' Pr 21.19.

Cf. μάχη, μαχητής.

μάχομαι: aor. ἐμαχεσάμην.

1. *to get involved in a strife and dispute*: μετά τινος Ge 26.20; πρός τινα Ne 5.7; περί τινος 'over sth' Ge 26.22 (|| κρίνομαι vs. 21). **b**. *to assail verbally*: + dat. pers., ὠργίσθη .. καὶ ἐμαχέσατο τῷ Λαβαν 'he became enraged .. and retorted to L.' Ge 31.36; .. καὶ εἶπα .. Ne 13.11, 17.

2. *to fight physically*: μάχωνται δύο ἄνδρες Ex 21.22; De 25.11; military and πρός τινα Je 40.5, μετά τινος Jd 11.25 (|| πολεμέω); τινι (pers.) Jo

9.18; not military, and reciprocal, 2K 14.6B (*L* δια~); *ἔν τινι (pers.) Ct 1.6. Cf. συμβάλλω **4**.
Cf. μάχη, κρίνομαι, μάχομαι, προ~, μονο~, ὑπομαχέω, ἀνταγωνίζομαι.

μεγαλαυχέω: aor. ἐμεγαλαύχησα, inf. ~χῆσαι.ʃ
to brag, boast: abs. Ps 9.39, Ez 16.50; ἐν ὑπερηφανίᾳ 'with arrogance' Si 48.18; ἐπὶ τὸ ὄρος τὸ ἅγιόν μου 'over against my holy mount' Zp 3.11, sim. 2M 15.32. Cf. μεγαλύνω, μεγαλαυχία, καυχάομαι, μεγαλορρημονέω.

μεγαλαυχία, ας. f.ʃ
boastfulness: + κενοδοξία, ἀλαζονεία 4M 2.15. Cf. μεγαλαυχέω.

μεγαλεῖος, α, ον.
magnificent, splendid: n.subst. and *s* divine actions, De 11.2, cf. ἐποίησας ~εῖα Ps 70.19 and τὰ ~εῖα τοῦ θεοῦ Acts 2.11; God's power, 2M 3.34; God's creation, τὰ ~εῖα τῆς σοφίας αὐτοῦ Si 42.21; τὰ ~εῖα τὰ γενόμενα αὐτῷ '.. that had happened to him' To 11.15 𝔊[I]; ἱερωσύνης ~εῖον 'the splendour of priesthood' Si 45.24, ~εῖον δόξης 17.13, τὸ ~εῖον τῶν ἔργων αὐτοῦ 17.8 (|| τὰ ~εῖα τῶν ἔργων αὐτοῦ w. ref. to manifestations of the splendour, vs. 9). Cf. μέγας, μεγαλειότης, μεγαλομερής: Spicq 2.457-61

μεγαλειότης, ητος. f.ʃ*
1. *magnificence*: μ. πάντων τῶν αἰώνων 1E 4.40 (an attribute of Truth), μ. πάντων τῶν ὑπὸ τὸν οὐρανὸν βασιλέων Da 7.27 LXX (|| ἐξουσία, βασιλεία and TH μεγαλωσύνη). **b**. *sth that is laudable*: || εὐφροσύνη, αἴνεσις Je 40.9
2. *bounty, generous provision*: κατὰ τὴν ~τα Σαλωμων 1E 1.4.
Cf. μεγάλειος, μεγαλωσύνη: Grundmann, *TDNT* 4.541f.

μεγαλόδοξος, ον.ʃ
very glorious: *s* God, 3M 6.18. Cf. μεγαλοδόξως.

μεγαλοδόξως. adv.ʃ *
in very glorious manner: 3M 6.39. Cf. μεγαλόδοξος.

μεγαλοκράτωρ, ορος. m.ʃ*
one possessed of mighty power: *s* God, βασιλεῦ μ. 3M 6.2 (παντοκράτωρ).

μεγαλομερής, ές.ʃ
magnificent: *s* ἐπιφάνεια '(divine) epiphany' 3M 5.8. Cf. μεγαλεῖος.

μεγαλομερῶς. adv.ʃ
in grandiose fashion, 'in style': reception of guests, 2M 4.22; funeral, 4.49; thanks to God, 3M 6.33. Cf. μεγαλομερής.

μεγαλοπρέπεια, ας. f.ʃ
state befitting a great person, 'magnificence': divine quality, Ps 8.1; 28.4 (|| ἰσχύς), 67.35 (|| δύναμις), 70.8 (|| δόξα), 95.6 (|| ἁγιωσύνη), τὴν ~αν τῆς δόξης τῆς ἁγιωσύνης σου 144.5 (|| θαυμάσια), τὴν δόξαν τῆς ~ας τῆς βασιλείας σου 144.12, cf. μ. τὸ ἔργον αὐτοῦ 110.3; τῆς δόξης σου [= God's] Od 12.5; human quality, Ps 20.6 (|| δόξα). Cf. μεγαλοπρεπής.

μεγαλοπρεπής, ές.ʃ
befitting a great person, 'magnificent': *s* name, τοῦ σεμνοῦ καὶ ~οῦς ὀνόματος αὐτοῦ 'of his holy and glorious name' 2M 8.15, ὑπεροχή 'authority, dignity' 15.13 (|| θαυμαστός), ἐπιφανεία '(divine) epiphany' 3M 2.9; subst. and a person himself, God, ὁ μ. τοῦ στερεώματος '.. of the firmament' De 33.26. Cf. μεγαλοπρέπεια, μεγαλοπρεπῶς: Spicq 2.458f.

μεγαλοπρεπῶς. adv.ʃ
in a manner befitting a great person: befitting God, 4M 5.24. Cf. μεγαλοπρεπής.

μεγαλοπτέρυγος, ον.ʃ*
having great wings: *s* eagle, Ez 17.3,7. Cf. πτέρυξ.

μεγαλορρημονέω: aor. ἐμεγαλορρημόνησα, subj. ~νήσω.ʃ*
to boast, talk boastfully, mostly an unfriendly gesture: abs., Ob 12; + acc. rei, ὅσα .. εἰς τὸν οἶκον Ισραηλ; + ἐπί τινα, Ps 34.26, 37.17, 54.13, Ez 35.13 (last with τῷ στόματι). Cf. μεγαλορρημοσύνη, μεγαλορρήμων, μεγαλαυχέω.

μεγαλορρημοσύνη, ης. f.ʃ *
boastful talk: 2K 2.3. Cf. μεγαλορρήμων.

μεγαλορρήμων, ον, gen. ονος.ʃ*
given to boasting, 'boastful': *s* γλῶσσα Ps 11.4 (|| δόλιος), 3M 6.4. Cf. μεγαλορρημονέω, μεγαλορρημοσύνη.

μεγαλόσαρκος, ον.ʃ*
having great phallus: w. ref. to Egyptians, Ez 16.26, cf. 23.20 and see Rashi and Qimhi ad loc.

μεγαλοσθενής, ές.ʃ
possessed of great strength: *s* God's hand, 3M 5.12. Cf. σθένος.

μεγαλοφρονέω.ʃ
to be high-minded: πρὸς τὰς ἀνάγκας 'over against the tortures' 4M 6.24. Cf. μεγαλόφρων.

μεγαλόφρων, ονος. m./f.ʃ
1. *high-minded*: *s* hum., + εὐγενής 'noble' 4M 6.5; 9.21.
2. *arrogant*: ἐφ' ὕβρει Pr 21.4 (|| θρασυκάρδιος 'bold').
Cf. εὐγενής, ὑπερήφανος.

μεγαλόφωνος, ον.ʃ
speaking loudly: *s* hum., Si 26.27¶ (+ γλωσσώδης 'talkative').

μεγαλόψυχος, ον.ʃ
magnanimous: *s* hum., 4M 15.10. Cf. μεγαλοψύχως.

μεγαλοψύχως. adv.ʃ
magnanimously: 3M 6.41. Cf. μεγαλόψυχος.

μεγαλύνω: fut.act. ~λυνῶ, pass. ~λυνθήσομαι; aor. act. ἐμεγάλυνα, inf. ~λῦναι, impv. μεγάλυνον, ptc. μεγαλύνας, opt.3s ~λύναι, pass. ἐμεγαλύνθην, impv. ~λύνθητι, inf. ~λυνθῆναι, ptc. ~λυνθείς, opt. 3s ~λυνθείη; pf.pass. μεμεγάλυμμαι.

I. act., *to enlarge, make great*: lit. of weight of a balance - Am 8.5 (of fraudulent trading practice). **b**. metaph.: + acc., fig. μεγαλυνῶ τὸ ὄνομά σου (|| εὐλογήσω σε and *s* God) Ge 12.2; δικαιοσύνην 19.19; εὐχήν '(to vow) a major vow' Nu 15.3, 8 (see *BA* ad loc., and cf. μεγάλως εὔξηται εὐχήν 6.2); αἴνεσιν Is 42.21; ἐμεγάλυνε κύριος τὰ ἔργα αὐτοῦ 'the Lord wrought great things' Jl 2.20; αὐτὸν (pers.) εἰς ὕψος 2C 1.1; + epexegetical inf., ἐμεγάλυνε κύριος τοῦ ποιῆσαι 2.21, Ps 125.2, 3 (without ποιῆσαι 1K 12.24). **c**. *to increase the intensity of* an activity: + acc., πτερνισμόν Ps 40.10.

2. *to declare or consider great*: ***o*** God, Ps 33.4, ἐν αἰνέσει 'through praise' 68.31, καθώς ἐστιν '(adequately) as he is' Si 43.31; + acc. pers., 45.2, Es 3.1*L* (o' δοξάζω); τὴν γλῶσσαν ἡμῶν Ps 11.5, τὰς σωτηρίας 17.51; pass., ***o*** pers., Mi 5.4. **II 2** may belong here.

II. mid. **1**. *to be or become great*: ***s*** share, ἐμεγαλύνθη ἡ μερὶς Βενιαμιν παρὰ τὰς μερίδας πάντων πενταπλασίως πρὸς τὰς ἐκείνων 'B.'s share was greater than those of everybody, five times as much as theirs' Ge 43.34; lamentation, Zc 12.11; τὸ ἔλεός σου Ps 56.11. **b**. *to become grave*: ***s*** ἀδικία Ez 9.9, ἕως εἰς οὐρανόν '(reaching) even the sky in dimension' 2E 9.6.

2. *to gain eminence, to have eminence acknowledged*: ***s*** God, Ez 38.23 (+ ἁγιάζομαι, ἐνδοξάζομαι), Ma 1.5, Ps 39.17; God's works, 91.6; God's name, 2K 7.26; hum. and + πλουτέω 'to become rich' Je 5.27; || κρατέω Pr 8.16.

3. *to consider oneself great*, 'boast': Mi 1.10; + ἐπί 'against' + acc. Zp 2.8, 10, Zc 12.7, ἐπὶ κύριον Je 31.26; Da 11.36 TH (LXX ὑψόομαι); + ἐπί τινι (pers.) Jb 19.5.

Cf. μέγας, μεγαλωσύνη, μεγαλαυχέω, μακρύνω: Spicq 2.459f.

μεγάλωμα, ατος. n.ʃ*
greatness in importance, 'pre-eminence': ῥάβδος ~ατος 'outstanding staff' Je 31.17. Cf. μέγας.

μεγαλώνυμος, ον.ʃ
bearing a great name or *title*: ***s*** κύριος Je 39.19. Cf. μέγας.

μεγάλως. adv.
to a great extent: μ. εὔξηται εὐχήν 'makes a major vow' Nu 6.2, cf. μεγαλύνω εὐχήν 15.3, 8; μ. μεγιστᾶνες ἐταλαιπώρησεν 'mighty men suffered great misery' Zc 11.2, μ. ἐγήρασεν 'he aged much' To 14.3 𝔊[I], εὐφρανθῆναι μ. 'to rejoice ..' 1E 9.54; + εὐχαριστέω 'thank' 2M 1.11; + ἀγωνιάω 'to agonise' 2M 3.21. Cf. μέγας, μικρῶς.

μεγαλωστί. adv.ʃ
loudly: σαλπίζω 1E 5.62. Cf. μέγας **2b**, ἦχος.

μεγαλωσύνη, ης. f.*
greatness: δότε ~ην τῷ θεῷ ἡμῶν 'Ascribe ..', i.e. 'Declare him great!' De 32.3, τῆς ~ης αὐτοῦ οὐκ ἔστιν πέρας '.. is infinite' Ps 144.3; μ. τοῦ βραχίονός σου 'of your arm, i.e. power' 78.11 (|| μέγεθος Ex 15.16), μ. ἰσχύος Pr 18.10, Ep. Arist. 192; τεταλαιπώρηκεν ἡ μ. αὐτῶν 'their greatness suffered miserably' Zc 11.3. Cf. μέγας, μεγαλύνω, μέγεθος: Spicq 2.460.

μέγας, ~γάλη, ~γα; comp. μείζων, μεῖζον; superl. μέγιστος, η, ον.

1. *large in size*: ***s*** adult (:: child), μέγας γένηται Ge 38.11; πόλις 10.12, Jn 1.2; κλύδων 'wave' 1.4; κῆτος 'fish' 2.1; ὄρος Zc 4.7; opp. μικρός Jn 3.5; κατάλειψις μεγάλη 'a large group of survivors' Ge 45.7.

2. *great in degree, intensity*: ***s*** ἐτασμός 'trying experience' Ge 12.17; φόβος Jn 1.10, 16; λύπη 'distress' 4.1; χαρά 4.6; δόξα Hg 2.9; ἰσχύς Na 1.3; συντριμμός 'crushing' Zp 1.10, συντριβή Je 6.1, θάνατος 21.6; κακά 39.42; ὀργή Zc 1.2; ζῆλος 1.14; δύναμις 4.6; φωνή Ge 39.14, Pr 2.3. **b**. adv. κεκράξατε μέγα 'Shout loud' Je 4.5; 3M 6.17; μεγάλα Wi 3.5 (:: ὀλίγα).

3. *great in importance, high-ranking, of far-reaching consequences*: ὁ μείζων δουλεύσει τῷ ἐλάσσονι 'the major shall serve the minor' Ge 25.23; προβαίνων μείζων ἐγίνετο 'achieving progress, he grew in importance' 26.13; ἔθνος μέγα καὶ πολύ Nu 14.12, De 26.5; ὁ ἱερεὺς ὁ μ. Hg 1.1, Zc 3.1; ***s*** God's name (ὄνομα) Ma 1.11; βασιλεύς 1.14; ἡμέρα κυρίου ἡ μεγάλη καὶ ἐπιφανής 4.4, Zp 1.14; ἡμέρα μεγάλη 'an important feast-day' Is 1.13; οἶκος Am 6.11 (opp. μικρός); ῥῆμα μέγα ἢ μικρόν 1K 20.2; νοῦς μέγας 'self-aggrandising mind' Is 10.12, βουλή 'counsel, design' 9.6, ἀρχή 'rule; authority' 9.7; τράπεζα 'dinner-table' Si 34.12; n., μέγα μοί ἐστιν, εἰ ἔτι ὁ υἱός μου ζῇ Ge 45.28; λαλοῦν μεγάλα 'speaking arrogantly' Da 7.8. **b**. *wealthy*: ***s*** hum., 2K 19.33,4K 4.8.

4. *grave in seriousness*: μείζων ἡ αἰτία μου 'my guilt ..' Ge 4.13, ἀνομίαι Ez 8.6.

5. *senior in age*: ὄνομα τῇ μείζονι Ge 29.16 (:: νεώτερος).

6. Juxtaposed with μικρός, marks the whole gamut: μικρὸν ἢ μέγα 'whether significant or trivial' Nu 22.18; κατὰ τὸν μικρὸν καὶ κατὰ τὸν μέγαν κρινεῖς De 1.17; ἀπὸ μικροῦ ἕως μεγάλου Ge

19.11, sim. Je 6.13, 38.34, ἀπὸ μικροῦ καὶ ἕως μεγάλου 49.1, Jn 3.5.

Cf. μικρός, μεγαλεῖος, μεγαλύνω, μεγάλωμα, μεγαλώνυμος, μεγάλως, μεγαλωσύνη, μέγεθος, ὑπερμεγέθης, ἐπιμήκης, πολύς, πρεσβύτερος.

μέγεθος, ους. n.

1. *being large in size*, 'magnitude': βραχίονος 'of (God's rescuing) arm' Ex 15.16, 2M 15.24 (|| μεγαλωσύνη Ps 78.11); μ. κέδρου 'huge cedar-trees' 4K 19.23; ἐκ ~ους καὶ καλλονῆς κτισμάτων 'from the greatness and beauty of created things' Wi 13.5; λυπουμένη ἐπὶ τὸ μ. 'sorely grieving' Ba 2.18.

2. *size*: Ez 31.5; μέγας τῷ ~ει 31.10, cf. ἕξιν μεγέθους 'large size' 1K 16.7; μικρὰν τῷ ~ει 'small in size' Ez 17.6, ὑψηλὸς τῷ ~ει 'tall ..' 31.3.

Cf. μέγας, μεγαλωσύνη, ὑπερμεγέθης: Spicq 2.461.

μεγιστάν, ᾶνος. m. Alm. alw. in pl.

courtier, nobleman: παρὰ τοῦ βασιλέως καὶ παρὰ τῶν ~άνων αὐτοῦ Jn 3.7; οἱ ~ᾶνες .. ἀσθενήσουσιν Na 2.6; .. δεθήσονται χειροπέδαις 'will be bound in chains' 3.10; || βασιλεύς, ἄρχων Is 34.12, βασιλέα καὶ τοὺς ~ᾶνας αὐτοῦ Je 24.8; + κριτής, δυνάστης Si 10.24; || ἡγούμενος 39.4, || τύραννος Pr 8.16. Cf. μέγας.

μέγιστος, η, ον. ⇒ μέγας.

μεθαρμόζω.ʃ

mid. *to adapt oneself* to a new order: Wi 19.18.

μεθερμηνεύω: aor.inf. μεθερμηνεῦσαι.ʃ

to put into another language, 'translate': τοῦ μεθερμηνεῦσαι τήνδε τὴν βίβλον Si prol. 30 (|| μετάγω εἰς ἑτέραν γλῶσσαν 22). Cf. ἑρμηνεύω, μετάγω: Wagner 126f.

μέθη, ης. f.

1. *strong drink*: Pr 20.1 (|| οἶνος).

2. *drunkenness, intoxication*: πίνοντες οἶνον εἰς ~ην '.. till they get drunk' Jl 1.5; Hg 1.6; πίεσθε αἷμα εἰς ~ην ἀπὸ τῆς θυσίας μου Ez 39.19 (|| εἰς πλησμονήν); pl., heavy intoxication, Ju 13.15. Cf. μεθύω, μεθύσκω.

μεθίστημι: pres.inf.act. μεθιστᾶν; fut.act. ~στήσω, mid. μεταστήσομαι, inf. μεταστήσεσθαι (*pace* Zgl at Is 54.10 -σα-); 1aor.act. μετέστησα, impv. μετάστησον, ptc. ~στήσας, inf. ~στῆσαι, pass. μετεστάθην; 2aor. μετέστην, impv.2pl ~στήτε, ptc. ~στάς, subj. μεταστῶ.

I. tr. (pres./fut.act., 1aor.) *to remove*: μετάστησον ἀπ' ἐμοῦ ἦχον ᾠδῶν σου 'Move the sound of your songs away from me' Am 5.23; τὴν διάνοιαν τοῦ συνιέναι 'the mind to comprehend' Is 59.15; ***o*** βασιλεῖς Da 2.21 LXX (|| καθίστημι), ἐξουσία 7.12 TH; pagan idols, Jd 10.16 A (B: ἐκκλίνω).

2. *to deprive*: + acc. pers. and gen. rei, Es 7.26 L (o' στερέω), τῆς χρείας '(to relieve him) of office' 1M 11.63, τοῦ μὴ εἶναι ἡγουμένην 3K 15.13, τοῦ ζῆν 3M 2.28, 3.1, 6.12.

3. *to cause to shift positions*: + acc. pers., ἐπὶ τὸν Ἑλληνικὸν χαρακτῆρα 'to the Hellenic life-style' 2M 4.10.

4. *to change the nature of*: for worse, τὴν καρδίαν τινός Jo 14.8.

II. intr. (fut.mid., 2aor.) *to go over to another party, revolt*: of apostasy and ***s*** καρδία De 17.17, 30.17.

2. *to shift positions*: ***s*** τὰ ὄρη Is 54.10*a* (|| μετακινέομαι); δεξιὰ οὐδὲ ἀριστερά 'neither to the right nor to the left' 1K 6.12 (*L* ἐκκλίνω 'to deviate').

3. *to move away, vanish*: ***s*** ἡ διαθήκη τῆς εἰρήνης Is 54.10b; upon death, εἰς θεούς 2M 11.23.

Cf. μετάθεσις.

μεθοδεύω: aor. μεθώδευσα.ʃ

to take recourse to a ruse against sbd (ἔν τινι): πρός τινα '(by informing) sbd' 2K 19.28B (*L* κατηγορέω).

μέθοδος, ου. f.ʃ

devious method of pursuing and achieving an aim, 'trick, ruse': Es E 13, 2M 13.18.

μεθόριον, ου. n.ʃ

border area: Jo 19.27A.

μεθύσκω: fut. μεθύσω, pass. μεθυσθήσομαι; aor. ἐμέθυσα, subj. μεθύσω, impv. μέθυσον, pass. ἐμεθύσθην, impv.2pl μεθύσθητε; pf.ptc.pass. μεμεθυσμένος.

I. act. *to cause to become intoxicated*: abs., ποτίζων .. καὶ μεθύσκων Hb 2.15; + acc. pers., μέθη Je 28.57; fig. μεθύσω τὰ βέλη μου ἀφ' αἵματος 'I shall make my arrows drunk with blood' De 32.42, cf. ***o*** μάχαιρα Is 34.5 and || ἐμπίμπλημι 34.7, Je 38.25; μεθύσω τὴν ψυχὴν τῶν ἱερέων 38.14 (|| ἐμπίμπλημι); + gen. rei, με χολῆς 'with gall' La 3.15 (|| χορτάζω); ***s*** drinking-cup with its content, Ps 22.5; + τινα ἀπό τινος (rei), Si 1.16, 35.13. **b**. *to irrigate well*: + acc., πρασιάν 'garden-plot' Si 24.31, ξηράν 'dry land' 39.22 (***s*** flood and || ἐπικαλύπτω), τὴν γῆν Is 55.10 (of rain or snow moistening the soil), αὔλακας 'furrows' Ps 64.11.

II. pass. **1**. *to be or get drunk*: ἔπιεν ἐκ τοῦ οἴνου καὶ ἐμεθύσθη Ge 9.21; 43.34, Na 3.11; οἴνῳ Pr 4.17; fig., ἀπὸ τοῦ αἵματος αὐτῶν Je 26.10 (|| ἐμπίμπλημι).

2. *to become satiated*: σίτῳ 'with grain' Ho 14.8; ἀπὸ πιότητος 'with the abundance' Ps 35.9; ***s*** razor (ξυρός) which has shaven many victims, Is 7.20, mountains with fallen soldiers' blood Ju 6.4.

Cf. μεθύω, μέθη, μέθυσμα, ἐμπίμπλημι, κατοινόομαι, κραιπαλάω, οἰνοφλυγέω.

μέθυσμα, ατος. n.ʃ *
intoxicating drink: οἶνον καὶ μ. 1K 1.11, 15, Ho 4.11, Mi 2.11; Je 13.13. Cf. μεθύω, μεθύσκω, μέθη, and σίκερα.

μέθυσος, η, ον.ʃ
given to heavy drinking: *s* hum. Si 19.1, woman 26.8; + πορνοκόπος 'patron of brothel' Pr 23.21, ‖ ἄφρων 'the silly' 26.9; ‖ γαστρίμαργος 'glutton' 4M 2.7. Cf. μεθύω.

μεθύω (only pres. and impf.: fut., aor. and pf. under μεθύσκω).
to be drunk: ἐκνήψατε, οἱ μεθύοντες, ἐξ οἴνου 'Awake, O drunkards, from wine' Jl 1.5, οὐκ ἀπὸ οἴνου Is 51.21; ὁ μεθύων καὶ ὁ ἐμῶν '.. vomits' Is 19.14, ἄνευ οἴνου 28.1; κῆπος μεθύων 'well-watered orchard' 58.11. Cf. μεθύσκω, μέθυσμα, μέθυσος, and μέθη.

μεῖγμα, ατος. n.ʃ
mixed compound: medicinal, Si 38.8.

μείγνυμι. ⇒ μίγνυμι.

μειδιάω: fut. μειδιάσω.ʃ
to smile: ἡσυχῇ 'quietly' Si 21.20. Cf. γελάω, ἀμείδητος, προσμειδιάω: Schmidt 4.192f.

μείζων. ⇒ μέγας.

μειόω.ʃ
pass. *to become smaller*: *s* moon, Si 43.7. Cf. μικρός.

μειράκιον, ου. ν.
lad: 2M 7.25 (‖ νεανίας); 4M 8.14. Cf. μειρακίσκος, ἔφηβος, νεανίας, μεῖραξ: Schmidt 4.26f.

μειρακίσκος, ου.ʃ
= μειράκιον: 4M 8.1, 11.13.

μεῖραξ, άκος. m.ʃ
= μειράκιον: 4M 14.6, 8. Cf. μειράκιον.

μέλαθρον, ου. n.
beam: 3K 6.5. Cf. μελαθρόω.

μελαθρόω: pf.ptc.pass. μεμελαθρωμένος.ʃ
to connect by beams: 3K 7.42. Cf. μέλαθρον.

μελάνθιον, ου. n.ʃ
black cummin: Is 28.25, 27. Cf. Ziegler 1934.183f.

μελανία, ας. f.ʃ
gloomy look: Si 19.26. Cf. σκυθρωπός.

μελανόω: pf.ptc.pass. μεμελανωμένος.ʃ
to make black in colour: pass., *o* face from smoke, Ep Je 20; sun-burnt, Ct 1.6. Cf. μέλας.

μέλας, μέλαινα, μέλαν.ʃ
black-coloured: *s* hair, Le 13.37; horse, Zc 6.2, 6; good-looking woman, Ct 1.5; locks of hair, ὡς κόραξ 'like a raven' 5.11. Cf. μελανόω: Schmidt 3.14-6.

μέλεος, α, ον.ʃ
unhappy: *s* hum., ‖ τρισάθλιος 'miserable' 4M 16.6. Cf. τρισάθλιος, τάλας, μακάριος: Schmidt 4.434-6.

μελετάω: fut. μελετήσω; aor. ἐμελέτησα.
1. *to apply one's mind to*, 'ponder, contemplate, study': abs., ἔτη αἰώνια ἐμνήσθην καὶ ἐμελέτησα 'I recalled the years long past and pondered' Ps 76.6 (‖ διαλογίζομαι); + acc., τὸν νόμον σου 118.70, τὰ λόγιά σου 118.148; κενά 'meaningless things' 2.1, δολιότητας 'deceptions' 37.13; φόβον Is 33.18; + ἐν – μελετήσεις ἐν ^τῷ νόμῳ^ Jo 1.8, sim. Ps 1.2, ἐν τοῖς δικαιώμασίν σου 118.16, 117, ἐν ταῖς ἐντολαῖς σου 118.47 (sim. Si 6.37 and ‖ διανοέομαι), ἐν πᾶσιν τοῖς ἔργοις σου Ps 76.13 (‖ ἀδολεσχέω), ‖ also κατανοέω 118.16, ἐν σοφίᾳ Si 14.20; εἰς σε [= God] Ps 62.7 (‖ μνημονεύω); + inf., τῷ πνεύματι τῷ σκληρῷ ἀνελεῖν αὐτοὺς .. 'to destroy them with your hard spirit' Is 27.8; *s* ψυχή Jb 27.4, Is 33.18.
*2 *to recite constantly in order to ponder over*: + acc. and *s* tongue, ἡ γλῶσσά μου μελετήσει τὴν δικαιοσύνην σου, ὅλην τὴν ἡμέραν τὸν ἔπαινόν σου '.. the whole day your praise' Ps 34.28, ἡ γλῶσσα ὑμῶν ἀδικίαν μελετᾷ Is 59.3 (‖ λαλέω); *s* στόμα δικαίου μελετήσει σοφίαν Ps 36.30, λάρυγξ Jb 6.30, φάρυγξ Pr 8.7; *s* hum., λόγους ἀδίκους Is 59.13.
*3. *to raise gentle voice*: ὡς περιστερά 'like a pigeon' Is 38.14 (‖ φωνέω); 'to address sbd (τινι)' 16.7.
Cf. ἀδολεσχέω,ἀνα~, διαλογίζομαι, διανοέω, μνημονεύω, μελέτη, ἐπιμελέομαι, μεριμνάω, φροντίζω: Schmidt 2.631.

μελέτη, ης. f.
1. *act of pondering over* sth: ἐν ~ῃ νυκτερινῇ 'nocturnal ..' Jb 33.15 (‖ ἐνύπνιον 'dream' vs. 34); τῆς βίβλου Si prol. II.
2. *object of pondering*: τὰ μαρτύριά σου μ. μού ἐστιν Ps 118.24, ὁ νόμος σου .. 118.77, αἱ ἐντολαί σου .. 118.143.
3. *thought resulting from pondering*: Ἤκουσας .. τοὺς διαλογισμοὺς αὐτῶν .. καὶ μελέτας αὐτῶν κατ' ἐμοῦ La 3.61f.; ἡ μ. τῆς καρδίας μου ἐνώπιόν σου διὰ παντός Ps 18.15 (‖ λόγια); Jb 37.2 (‖ ἀκοή).
Cf. μελετάω.

μέλι, ιτος. n.
honey: apiarian product, Ge 43.11 (as gift); γῆν ῥέουσαν γάλα καὶ μέλι 'a land flowing with milk and honey' Ex 3.8, De 6.3 +; γῆ ἐλαίας ἐλαίου καὶ μέλιτος 8.8. Cf. μέλισσα, μελισσών, κηρίον.

μελίζω: fut. μελιῶ; aor. ἐμέλισα, impv.3pl μελισάτωσαν.
to dismember, cut in pieces: *o* sacrificial animals, κατὰ μέλη 'limb by limb' Le 1.6 (‖ διαιρέω vs. 12, διχοτομέω Ex 29.17); σάρξ (?) – ὡς σάρκα εἰς λέβητα 'as pieces of meat to go into a cauldron' Mi 3.3; hum. (corpse), εἰς δώδεκα μερίδας 'into twelve parts' Jd 19.29 A (B: .. μέλη). Cf. δια~, ἐκαμελίζω,

διαιρέω, καταδιαιρέω, διχοτομέω, μερίζω, κρεονομέω, μέλος.

μέλισσα, ας. f.

bee: De 1.44; ~αι κηρίον '.. a honeycomb' Ps 117.12; coll. sg., Is 7.18, winged insects - μικρὰ ἐν πετεινοῖς μ. '.. small among flying insects' Si 11.3; model of industry, Pr 6.8*a*. Cf. μέλι.

μελισσών, ῶνος. m.ʃ *

bee-house: 1K 14.25f. Cf. μέλι, μέλισσα.

μέλλω

1. Indicates the high probability of something happening: + inf. pres., Εἰ οὕτως μοι μέλλει γίνεσθαι 'if it is going to be like this to me' Ge 25.22; ἐκεῖ μέλλει ἀριστᾶν 'he was going to dine there' 43.25; + inf. aor. ἃ μέλλεις λαλῆσαι 'what you are going to speak' Ex 4.12, μὴ καὶ οὕτως μέλλει σωθῆναι; 'even so is there any chance for her to survive?' Is 15.7. **b**. indicates a likely logical consequence: + inf. pres.: πῶς τε δὴ μέλλει .. εἶναι θεοί; 'how on earth could they .. be gods?' Ep Je 47.

2. Indicates the imminency of an event: + inf. pres., ὅταν μέλλῃς γίνεσθαι μετ' αὐτῆς 'when you are about to join her in bed' To 6.18 𝔊II; "I am not going to ask to be spared .." 4M 11.2; + inf. aor., Jb 3.8, Is 59.5, 2M 14.41; + inf. fut., 8.11. **b**. an inf. such as γίνεσθαι understood: τὰ μέλλοντα 'the things to come' Wi 8.8 (:: τὰ ἀρχαῖα 'the things foregone'), cf. τὰ καινὰ ἀπὸ τοῦ νῦν, ἃ μέλλει γίνεσθαι Is 48.6.

3. *to delay*: τί μέλλετε; 'What's the matter with you? Come on, do it now!' 4M 6.23; 9.1.

Cf. Basset; Evans 2001.227-9.

μέλος, ους. n.

1. *constituent part of an animate body with distinct features*, arm and leg in particular, 'limb': σείομαι πᾶσιν τοῖς ~εσιν 'I shake with all my limbs' Jb 9.28, ~η ποιήσαντες 'dismembering them' 2M 1.16, πρὸ τοῦ τιμωρηθῆναι τὸ σῶμα κατὰ μ. 'before his body is punished limb by limb' 7.7, τοῖς μέλεσιν ἀναπήρους 'maimed' 8.24, τοῖς ~εσιν παραλελυμένον 'paralysed in his limbs' 3M 2.22, πάντα τὰ μέλη τοῦ σώματος 2M 9.7; of sacrificial animals, διχοτομήσεις κατὰ μέλη 'you shall cut (it) up into pieces limb by limb' Ex 29.17; μελιοῦσιν αὐτὸ κατὰ μέλη 'they shall dismember it ..' Le 1.6; τὴν κεφαλὴν καὶ τὰ ~η καὶ τὸ στέαρ 'the head and the limbs and the fat' 8.20.

2. *musical tune*: θρηνηθήσεται θρῆνος ἐν ~ει 'a mournful tune will be sung' Mi 2.4 (|| παραβολή), ἐν ~εσι γοεροῖς 'with mournful tunes' 3M 5.25, θρήνων πανόδυρτον μ. 'chants of a most lamentable dirge' 6.32; θρῆνος καὶ μ. καὶ οὐαί Ez 2.10; μ. μουσικῶν Si 35.6, 44.5; 40.21.

Cf. εὐμελής, μελίζω, μελῳδία, μελῳδός, παμμελής, κῶλον, ᾠδή: Schmidt 4.628.

μέλω.

Impers. *to matter*: + dat. pers., οὐ μέλει μοι 'it doesn't matter to me' To 10.5𝔊I; ᾧ μέλει περὶ πάντων 'he is concerned about everybody' Wi 12.13. Cf. ἀμελέω, ἐπιμελέομαι.

μελῳδέω.ʃ

to sing: acc. pers., i.e. songs written by him, 4M 18.15. Cf. μέλος, μελῳδός, ᾄδω, ψάλλω.

μελῳδία, ας. f.ʃ

musical tune: 4M 15.21. Cf. μέλος.

μελῳδός, ον.ʃ

fond of music: *s* γλῶττα 4M 10.21. Cf. μελῳδέω. Del. 4M 15.21 v.l.

μέμφομαι: fut. μέμψομαι; aor.subj. μέμψωμαι, ptc. μεμψάμενος.ʃ

to rebuke, blame: abs. Si 11.7 (|| ἐπιτιμάω); + dat. pers., 41.7, 2M 2.7. Cf. μέμψις, ἄμεμπτος, ἀπομέμφομαι, (ἐξ)ελέγχω, ἐπιτιμάω: Schmidt 1.145-7.

μέμψις, εως. f.

occasion for blame: κατά τινος Jb 33.10, ἐπί τινι Wi 13.6. **b**. *act of blaming*: Jb 39.7. Cf. μέμφομαι.

μέν.

A particle, never clause-initial, underlines logical contrast with what is stated in the following clause, which contains δέ: Ἡ μὲν φωνὴ φωνὴ Ιακωβ, αἱ δὲ χεῖρες χεῖρες Ησαυ Ge 27.22; ἐὰν μὲν ἄρσεν ᾖ, ἀποκτείνατε αὐτό, ἐὰν δὲ θῆλυ, περιποιεῖσθε αὐτό 'if it be male, kill it, but if female, let it live' Ex 1.16; εἰ μὲν .. εἰ δὲ μή, .. 32.32; Εἰ καιρὸς ὑμῖν μέν ἐστι τοῦ οἰκεῖν .., ὁ δὲ οἶκος οὗτος ἐξηρήμωται; 'Is it the right time for you to be dwelling in your panelled houses at the time when this house is in ruins?' Hg 1.4; Zc 1.15. **b**. without a matching δέ: Ex 9.2, Is 6.2.

Cf. δέ: Naumann 44; Lee 1985.1-11.

μέντοι. conj. Not clause-initial.

1. *in contradiction* or *contrast to what has just been stated*, 'nevertheless': Pr 5.4, 16.25.

2. marks irritation: 4M 7.16.

Del. Le 7.2 v.l.

μέντοιγε.ʃ

Particle which expresses one's agreement with the preceding utterance, 'yes, indeed': Ps 38.7, cf. Blomqvist 1969.28f.

μένω: fut. μενῶ; aor. ἔμεινα, impv. μεῖνον, 3s μεινάτω, subj. μείνω, inf. μεῖναι, ptc. μείνας; pf.ptc. μεμενηκώς.

1. *to stay put without moving away*: Μεινάτω ἡ παρθένος μεθ' ἡμῶν ἡμέρας ὡσεὶ δέκα Ge 24.55 (:: ἀπέρχομαι), πρὸς αὐτόν 'at his' Jd 19.4 (AB: καθίζω μετ' αὐτοῦ); ἐπὶ τόπου μενεῖ 'will be on hand' Zc 14.10; τὸ ὀψέ 'far into the evening' Is 5.11.

b. + ἐπί τινος '(to remain a widow content) with ..' Ju 8.7.

2. *to adhere to and not contravene* (ἐν): Da 6.12a LXX, 2M 8.1.

3. *to remain in force*: μενοῦσιν αὐτῇ 'she shall remain bound by them [= commitments made]' Nu 30.5; ὁρισμός 'decision' Da 6.12 LXX.

4. *to wait for*: sth (acc.), αὐγήν 'daybreak' Is 59.9; sth to happen, + inf., τοῦ ποιῆσαι σταφυλήν '(for the vine) to produce a cluster of grapes' 5.2, τοῦ ποιῆσαι κρίσιν '(for them) to practise justice' 5.7; for a chance to act, τοῦ οἰκτιρῆσαι ὑμᾶς 'to show mercy on you' 30.18; sbd (acc.) To 2.2 𝔊I (𝔊II προσ~), 6.7 𝔊II; for assistance, τὸν θεόν Is 8.16 (‖ πεποιθὼς εἰμι 'to be trustful').

5. *to bear with, endure*: + acc., "Bear with me a while yet" Jb 36.2, cf. Hom., *Il* 15.620; ἀνάγκην Wi17.17.

Cf. ἀνα~, προσ~, ὑπομένω, μονή, ἠρεμάζω.

μεριδάρχης, ου. m.ʃ

governor of a province: 1M 10.65.

μεριδαρχία, ας. f. *

division of a nation: πατρική 'in accordance with parental lineage' 1E 1.5 (‖ διαίρεσις 2C 35.5) ‖ τῶν πατέρων 1E 1.10; ‖ πατριά 8.28.

μερίζω: fut. μεριῶ, mid. μεριοῦμαι, pass. μερισθήσομαι; aor. ἐμέρισα, impv. μέρισον, ptc. μερίσας, mid. ἐμερισάμην, pass. ἐμερίσθην, ptc.pass. μερισθείς; pf.ptc.pass. μεμερισμένος.

1. *to divide into parts*: ***o*** σκῦλα 'spoils' Ex 15.9; μερίς De 18.8; ἐμέρισε καρδίας αὐτῶν Ho 10.2. **b**. + double acc.: τὴν γῆν ἑπτὰ μερίδας 'the land into seven parts' Jo 18.6.

2. *to divide and give*, 'allot, portion out': + dat. pers. and acc. rei, Si 45.20, οἶκον καὶ ὕπαρξιν .. παισίν 'house and possessions .. to children' Pr 19.14; Τούτοις μερισθήσεται ἡ γῆ κληρονομεῖν Nu 26.53, ἐν κληρονομίᾳ Jo 13.7, οὐκ ἐμέρισεν αὐτῇ ἐν τῇ συνέσει 'did not give her a share in intelligence' Jb 39.17¶; διὰ κλήρων 'by lots' Nu 26.55, κληρονομίαν ἐκ τοῦ κλήρου 26.56; + dat. pers. and ἀπό τινος 2M 8.28.

3. *to give as a gift*: ***o*** sth incorporeal and dat. pers., μετάνοιαν Si 17.22¶; woman as wife, To 6.18 𝔊II.

4. *to assign* to a certain class: pass., εἰς κατάραν Si 41.9.

5. mid. *to obtain as one's share*: + acc., κακίαν Pr 14.18. **b**. + dat. pers., κλέπτῃ 'with a thief' Pr 29.24.

Cf. μερίς, ἀποδιαστέλλω, ἀπο~, διαμερίζω, (κατα)διαιρέω, μελίζω, ταμείω, ἀμερής: Schmidt 4.607f.

μερικός, ή, όν.ʃ

concerned with individual items, 'specific, particular': ***s*** story, Si prol. II.

μέριμνα, ας. f.

care and concern: + φροντίς Jb 11.18 (opp. εἰρήνη), so Aristeas 271; ^πλούτου^ 'about wealth' Si 34.1 (‖ ἀγρυπνία 'vigilance'). **b**. *object of care and concern*: Ps 54.23; μ. ἀγρυπνίας 'sleepless worry' Si 34.2.

Cf. ἀμέριμνος, μεριμνάω.

μεριμνάω: aor.subj. ~νήσω, impv.3pl μεριμνάτωσαν.

to focus one's mind on: abs., οἱ τὸ ἀργύριον τεκταίνοντες καὶ μεριμνῶντες 'those who work at silver ..' Ba 3.18, ἀναπαύσομαι καὶ οὐ μὴ μεριμνήσω οὐκέτι 'I shall relax and not worry any more' Ez 16.42; + acc. (assigned work) Ex 5.9; σου τὴν ἀγαθότητα 'your goodness' Wi 12.22; + ἐν – ἐν λόγοις κενοῖς 'meaningless chatter' Ex 5.9; ὑπὲρ τῆς ἁμαρτίας μου Ps 37.19; + indir. question, Es A 9 L (‖ ἀναζητέω vs. 10). Cf. μερίμνα, ἐπιμελέομαι, μελετάω, φροντίζω: Schmidt 2.628-30.

μερίς, ίδος. f.

1. *part of a whole*: Nu 31.36, Am 4.7.

2. *that part which has been* or *is to be allotted and to which one is entitled*, 'share': οὗτοι λήμψονται ~ίδα Ge 14.24; μ. ἢ κληρονομία ἐν τῷ οἴκῳ τοῦ πατρὸς ἡμῶν 31.14, sim. Nu 18.20; μ. κληρονομίας Ps 15.4; μ. καὶ κλῆρος De 10.9; οὐκ ἔστιν αὐτῷ μ. οὐδὲ κλῆρος μεθ' ὑμῶν 12.12, sim. 14.26, 28; μ. λαοῦ μου κατεμετρήθη ἐν σχοινίῳ 'the share of my people has been measured out with a line' Mi 2.4; ἐλίπανε ~ίδα αὐτοῦ 'he has made his portion fat' Hb 1.16; τὸν Ιουδαν τὴν ~ίδα αὐτοῦ Zc 2.12; ἔσται σοι ἐν ~ίδι 'shall be your share' Ex 29.26; ἐγένετο Μωυσῇ ἐν ~ίδι Le 8.29; De 32.9 (‖ σχοίνισμα κληρονομίας); ‖ κληρονομία 2K 20.1, Is 17.14, Je 28.19; Israel as what God claims as his share, 12.10 (‖ vs. κληρονομία 9), Si 17.17; Es C 9 o' (‖ κλῆρος vs. 10). **b**. w. ref. to one's offspring or members of household: ‖ υἱοί Jb 17.5, cf. Jul. ad loc. (τέκνα). **c**. retribution: μ. ἀνθρώπου ἀσεβοῦς παρὰ κυρίου '.. of an impious man from ..' Jb 20.29, τῶν ἁμαρτωλῶν PSol 3.12. **d**. *present, gift*: Es 9.19 o'. **e**. *common cause*: μετὰ μοιχῶν τὴν ~δα σου ἐτίθεις 'you would cast your lot in with adulterers' Ps 49.18; Wi 1.16.

Cf. μέρος, (δια)μερίζω, κλῆρος, μεριτεύομαι: Schmidt 4.497-9.

μερισμός, οῦ. m.ʃ

1. *act of dividing*: ἐθνῶν '(the world population) into peoples' Si 17.17¶; Jo 11.23.

2. *group of people divided for joint activities*: 2E 6.18 (ǁ διαίρεσις).

Cf. μερίζω.

μεριτεύομαι.ʃ

to share w. sbd else: + acc., Jb 40.30. Cf. μερίς.

μέρος, ους. n.

1. *part of a whole*: μ. τοῦ ἀγροῦ αὐτοῦ 'part of his field' Ge 23.9; πέμπτον μ... τέσσαρα μέρη 'fifth part .. four parts' 47.24; Zc 13.8; κατὰ μ. 'bit by bit' Pr 29.11. **b**. part of a geopolitical entity, 'region, district': τῆς Φοινίκης Ex 16.35, τὰ ~η τῆς Ιουδαίας Is 9.1.

2. 'side': ἐκ μέρους 'at the side' Nu 8.2, 22.36; ἀπὸ ~ους 'separately' 4K 17.32*L*; ἀπὸ ~ους τῆς θαλάσσης 'from the side of the sea' Nu 34.3; κατὰ τὸ μ. τὸ πρὸς θάλασσαν 'to the west side' Ex 26.22 (ǁ κλίτος vs. 20); τὸ ἓν μ. 'on one side' Je 52.23, ἐπὶ τὰ τέσσαρα ~η αὐτῶν 'on their four sides' Ez 1.8, cf. Lee 72-6 and *ND* 3.75.

3. *the periphery of an area*: ὅ ἐστι μ. τι τῆς ἐρήμου 'which is just at the edge of the desert' Nu 33.6; τῆς παρεμβολῆς 'of the camp' Jd 7.19 A (B: ἀρχή). **b**. *end*: of one's life, Da 11.45 TH (LXX συντέλεια).

4. *one's turn*: ἐν μέρει 'in turn' Jb 30.1.

5. *class to be assigned to*: ἐν ἥττονι ~ει κείμενος αὐτοῖς 'being of lesser category to them' 2M 15.18.

Cf. μερίς, κλίτος, πλευρόν, ὅλος, πολυμερής: Schmidt 4.599-604; LSG s.v.

μεσάζω.ʃ

to be found in the middle on a linear course: μεσαζούσης νυκτός 'it being midnight' Wi 18.14.

μέσακλον, ου. n.ʃ *

heddle-rod: ὑφαινόντων 'of weavers' 1K 17.7. Cf. LSG s.v.

μεσημβρία, ας. f.

1. *midday*: gen. of time, Ge 18.1, Jd 5.10B, δύσεται ὁ ἥλιος ~ας 'the sun will set at midday' Am 8.9; acc. of time, Ge 43.16; opp. σκότος Is 58.10, μεσονύκτιον 59.10; τὸ πρωί Je 20.16; fig. of openness and visibility, Ps 36.6.

2. *the south*: Da 8.4 LXX (TH νότος).

Cf. μεσημβρινός, μεσονύκτιος.

μεσημβρινός, ή, όν.ʃ

pertaining to midday: *s* σκοτία 'darkness' Is 16.3, δαιμόνιον Ps 90.6 (:: νυκτερινός vs. 5); subst. n.sg., *midday*, ἕως ~οῦ 1E 9.41; adv., τὸ ~όν Jb 5.14 (ǁ ἡμέρας), 2K 4.5*L*. Cf. μεσημβρία: Shipp 386.

μεσίτης, ου. m.ʃ

arbiter: + ἐλέγχων Jb 9.33. Cf. Oepke, *TDNT* 4.598-624; Spicq 2.465-8.

μεσόγειος, ον.ʃ

inland: subst., ὁδός understood, 2M 8.35.

μεσονύκτιος, ον.

subst.n., *midnight*: opp. μεσημβρία Is 59.10; adv., at midnight Ps 118.62. Cf. μεσημβρία, ἀωρία: Shipp 387.

μεσοπόρφυρος, ον.ʃ

mixed or *shot with purple*: ~α, prob. ἱμάτια understood, Is 3.21 (+ περιπόρφυρα); *s* χιτών 3.24. Cf. πορφύρα.

Μεσοποταμία, ας. f.

Mesopotamia: Ge 24.10.

μέσος, η, ον.

I. adj., *situated well inside of an enclosed space* or *far into a period of time*: ἔσται τὸ περιστόμιον ἐξ αὐτοῦ μέσον 'its opening shall be in the middle' Ex 28.28; περὶ μέσας νύκτας 'about midnight' Ex 11.4 (on the pl., see Hdt 4.181). **b**. Used predicatively preceding an articular noun and concording with it – Δίελθε μέσην τὴν Ιερουσαλημ 'Go through the middle of Jerusalem' Ez 9.4.

2. *situated between two objects on either side* - ὁ μοχλὸς ὁ μ. 'the middle bar' Ex 26.28; ἐν πύλῃ τῇ μέσῃ 'in the middle gate' Je 46.3; δοκοὶ μέσοι 'middle bearing-beams' Ep Je 54. **b**. Pred., διεῖλεν αὐτὰ μέσα 'he divided them in half' Ge 15.10; σχίσει σε μέσον 'shall cut you apart in the middle' Da TH Su 55; πρίσαι σε μέσον 'split ..' ib. 59; οἱ δύο καὶ τὸν Μακκαβαῖον μέσον λαβόντες 'two of them took M. round the waist' 2M 10.30.

II. subst., *inside space* or *expanse marked off from the outside*, very often preceded by a preposition. Except for the combination with ἀνά, the μέσο-, when combined with one of the other prepositions, serves largely to underline the notion that something well inside of a circumscribed space or expanse is affected. Thus εἰς μέσον τινός is but slightly different from εἴς τι: see, e.g., ἐβλήθησαν εἰς μέσον τῆς καμίνου Da 3.21 TH ǁ .. εἰς τὴν κάμινον LXX ib. and ἐκ μέσου πυρὸς ἐρρύσατο ἡμᾶς Da 3.88 TH ǁ ἐκ τοῦ πυρὸς ἐλυτρώσατο ἡμᾶς LXX ib. The μέσο- form can be followed by either an articular or anarthrous substantive (cf. BDF, § 264, 4). When the following genitive subst. or pron. is sg., what is inside of the expanse is perceived as a single whole – *inside, in the middle of*; if pl. or sg. collective subst., it is perceived as consisting of multiple units or entities – *amongst*.

A. n.sg., τὸ μέσον τῆς καμίνου 'the inside of the furnace' Da 3.50; ἐν τῷ μέσῳ αὐτοῦ Ez 1.4; without a gen., ἐν τῷ μέσῳ ὡς ὁμοίωμα τεσσάρων ζῴων 'in (its) midst something shaped like four animals' 1.5; pl. and vertically, τὰ μέσα 'the middle part': ǁ τὰ ὑπερῷα 'the floor above' and τὰ τριώροφα 'the third floor' Ez 41.7; ǁ τὰ ὑποκάτωθεν 'the lower part' 42.6. Cf. Renehan 2.99.

B. ἀνὰ μέσον 'between'; see under ἀνά.

C. διὰ μέσου marks a flat space to be traversed from end to end: ἄξω σε διὰ ~ου τῆς Ἰουδαίας 'I shall take you through Judaea' Ju 11.19; Ps 135.14; ἦλθε καὶ διῆλθε διὰ ~ου τῆς πόλεως Je 44.4; διελεύσομαι διὰ ~ου σου 'I shall pass through you [= Israel]' Am 5.17. **b.** to mark a space to be traversed from end to end and among which multiple entities are found: ἔρριψε πῦρ διὰ ~ου αὐτῶν 'cast a fire to go through their [= captives'] midst' Da LXX Su 62.

D. εἰς μέσον, *right into, into the middle of*: + gen., εἰσπορεύομαι εἰς ~ον Αἰγύπτου Ex 11.4; εἰς ~ον αὐτῶν 'into their midst' Ne 4.11; εἰς ~ον τοῦ Εὐφράτου Je 28.63; εἰς ~ον καμίνου 'into the midst of a furnace' Ez 22.20; w. the art., εἰς τὸ μέσον τῆς νεφέλης '.. of the cloud' Ex 24.18; εἰς τὸ ~ον τῆς πόλεως ταύτης Je 21.4; Ez 10.2. **b.** = ἐν μέσῳ Si 27.12*bis*.

E. ἐκ μέσου, *from inside*: ἦρται ἐκ τοῦ ~ου 'he has been taken away from (their) midst' Is 57.2; ἐκ μέσου τῆς καταστροφῆς 'from the midst of the destruction' Ge 19.29; ἐκ μέσου τῆς νεφέλης '.. the cloud' Ex 24.16; pred. concording w. a foll. gen. noun, ἀνέβη δόξα κυρίου ἐκ μέσης τῆς πόλεως Ez 11.23. **b.** ἐκ μέσου *from amongst* more than one object: ἐκ ~ου ὑμῶν Ge 35.2; ἐκ ~ου μαστῶν αὐτῆς 'from between her breasts' Ho 2.2; μοσχάρια ἐκ ~ου βουκολίων 'calves from amongst stalls' Am 6.4; ἐκ στόματος αὐτῶν .. ἐκ ~ου ὀδόντων αὐτῶν '.. their teeth' Zc 9.7; Ἐκ ~ου 'Leave us alone, Everybody out' Jd 3.19A (|| *L* εἶπεν πάντας ἐκ μέσου γενέσθαι).

F. ἐν μέσῳ *in the midst of, within, deep inside*: ἐν τῷ μέσῳ 'in the middle' Ex 36.31; ὁ θεὸς ἔστη ἐν συναγωγῇ θεῶν, ἐν μέσῳ δὲ θεοὺς διακρίνει 'God stood in an assembly of gods, and he judges gods in their midst' Ps 81.1; ἐν ~ῳ λαοῦ μου Am 7.8; ἐν ~ῳ τοῦ Καρμήλου Mi 7.14; ἐν ~ῳ τοῦ Ισραηλ ἐγώ εἰμι Jl 2.27; κατασκηνώσω ἐν ~ῳ σου Zc 2.10; ἔρριψεν αὐτὴν ἐν ~ῳ τοῦ μέτρου 'he cast it into the midst of the measure' 5.8; || ἐν Ez 22.9. **b.** pred. concording with a foll. dat. noun, ἐν μέσῳ τῷ παραδείσῳ 'right in the midst of the garden' Ge 2.9; ἐν ~ῳ τῷ πεδίῳ 'in the middle of the plain' 37.7, To 5.6 $\mathfrak{G}^{II}$; ἐν μέσῃ τῇ πόλει Ez 5.2; ἐν μέσῳ τῷ πυρί Da LXX 3.25; ἐν μέσῳ τῷ λαῷ Su 34 TH. **c.** *amongst* multiple entities, ἐπὶ πάσαις ταῖς ἀνομίαις ταῖς γινομέναις ἐν μέσῳ αὐτῶν 'over all the lawless deeds taking place amongst them' Ez 9.4. **d.** *in the middle of* a still on-going process or state: ἐν ~ῳ τῆς ζωῆς αὐτῶν 'in the prime of their lives' Ez 31.17

G. κατὰ μέσον and pred.: ἦλθε κατὰ μέσον τὸν κενεῶνα 'he came down into the middle of the empty space' 2M 14.44.

III. prep. μέσον *well inside the circumscribed space of*: + gen., ἐξετίναξεν .. μέσον τῆς θαλάσσης 'threw out ..' Ex 14.27, Nu 33.8; μέσον τοῦ χειμάρρου ὅριον 'in the middle of the torrent a border' De 3.16; temporally, μέσον ἡμέρας 'at noon' Su 7 TH; *amongst* – μέσον τῶν παρεμβολῶν Nu 2.17. See Sollamo, *Semiprep*. 256.

Cf. ἀνά, ἐντός, μεσόω, μετά + gen., μεταξύ, καρδία, κόλπος, ἀμεσσαῖος: Sollamo, *Semiprep*., 236-9, 251-7, 267-9, 343-8.

μεσότης, ητος.f.ʃ

middle point on a linear scale of time: "the beginning, and the end, and the middle point (μ. χρόνων)" Wi 7.18. Cf. ἀρχή, τέλος.

μεσόω.ʃ

to reach far into a period of time: μεσούσης τῆς νυκτός 'the night was far advanced' Ex 12.29; ὕπνωσεν μέχρι μεσούσης τῆς νυκτός 'slept till midnight' Ju 12.5; μεσοῦντος τοῦ ἐνιαυτοῦ 'in midyear' Ex 34.22; ἐπέδυ ὁ ἥλιος αὐτῇ ἔτι μεσούσης τῆς ἡμέρας 'the sun set on her still in the prime of her life' Je 15.9; μεσούσης ἤδη δεκάτης ὥρας 3M 5.14. Except Jd 7.19A alw. as a temporal adjunct in the form of a genitive absolute, though not quite so at Ju 12.5. Cf. μέσος.

μεστός, ή, όν.

full of (sth τινος): ξηρασίας 'dryness' Na 1.10, ζήλου 'jealousy' Pr 6.34. Cf. πλήρης, (κατα)μεστόω.

μεστόω: pf.ptc.pass. μεμεστωμένος.ʃ

to fill: pass. and ***o*** hum., ὀργῇ καὶ χόλῳ 'with anger and fury' 3M 5.1; + gen., λιβάνου 'with frankincense' 5.10 (|| πληρόω). Cf. μεστός, καταμεστόω, πίμπλημι, πληρόω.

μετά. prep.

I. + gen., far more frequent than σύν + dat. (Johannessohn, *Präp*., 202).

1. *in company of* sbd as associate, companion, helper etc.: ἡ γυνή, ἣν ἔδωκας μετ' ἐμοῦ Ge 3.12; ἦν ὁ θεὸς μ. τοῦ παιδίου 21.20; πάροικος καὶ παρεπίδημος ἐγώ εἰμι μεθ' ὑμῶν 'I am an alien and sojourner among you' 23.4 (|| παρά τινι Ps 38.13); .. τῶν Χαναναίων, μεθ' ὧν ἐγὼ οἰκῶ ἐν αὐτοῖς Ge 24.3 (|| ἐν); ἐγώ εἰμι μ. σοῦ 'in your service' 31.38; "God is with you" Zc 8.23[2]; 10.5; μ. σοῦ εἰμι τοῦ σῴζειν σε Je 15.20; τοὺς μεθ' ὑμῶν Am 4.2, sim. 8.10; "to sail with them to Tarshish" Jn 1.3; Ho 5.6, 9.8; "to walk with the Lord your God" Mi 6.8; Zc 8.23[1]; Ma 2.6; τρέφεσθαι μ. σοῦ 'to be fed under your care' Ge 6.20; ὅσα ἦν κτήνη σου μετ' ἐμοῦ 'all that which was your livestock entrusted to me' 30.29; ἐκοιμήθην .. μ. τοῦ πατρὸς 'I slept ..' 19.34; παρέλαβεν μεθ' ἑαυτοῦ δύο παῖδας καὶ Ισαακ 22.3, ἔλαβεν Μωυσῆς τὰ ὀστᾶ Ιωσηφ μεθ' ἑαυτοῦ

Ex 13.19; μ. τοῦ προσώπου σου 'in your personal presence' Ps 15.11; Jd 7.4 [3, 4] B (:: σύν [1, 2]). **b**. *taking, carrying* or *having brought* with one: συναντῆσαι .. ὑμῖν μ. ἄρτων καὶ ὕδατος 'to receive you ..' De 23.4 (‖ ἐν ἄρτῳ καὶ ὕδατι Ne 13.2). **c**. *present with, in possession of*: ἐστιν φόβος κυρίου μετ' αὐτῶν Si 16.2; λύπη πολλὴ μετ' ἐμοῦ To 3.6 𝔊[II] (𝔊[I] ἐν ἐμοί), ἀφροσύνη μετ' αὐτοῦ 1K 25.25.

2. *accompanied by*, indicating a trait, or an accompanying action which characterises an action: **a**. an action, μ. φωνῆς αἰνέσεως καὶ ἐξομολογήσεως θύσω σοι Jn 2.10; ἀφῆκεν φωνὴν μ. κλαυθμοῦ Ge 45.2; μ. κραυγῆς Am 1.14; μ. ᾠδῆς Hb 3.1, cf. μ. κιθάρας καὶ ψαλτηρίου .. τὸν οἶνον πίνουσι Is 5.12; μεθ' ὅρκου 'by oath' Le 5.4, Nu 30.11; μ. τῆς τοῦ Μενελάου γνώμης 'with the connivance of M.' 2M 4.39, μ. κοινοῦ προστάγματος 'by public decree' 10.8. **b**. an accompanying sentiment, emotion or attitude: μ. δόλου 'by deception' Ge 27.35, μ. λύπης 'in sorrow' 42.38, 44.29 (‖ μ. ὀδύνης vs. 31), μ. εὐφροσύνης 'with joy' Is 12.3, μ. κράτους 'forcefully' Ge 49.24, μ. βίας 'by force' Ex 1.14, μ. θυμοῦ 'in rage' 11.8, Na 1.2; μ. πονηρίας ἐξήγαγεν 'brought out with an evil design' Ex 32.12; μ. ἀληθείας ἐν καρδίᾳ ἀληθινῇ Is 38.3; μ. σωτηρίας 'safely' Ge 26.31, μ. ἀσφαλείας 'securely' Le 26.5. Cf. σύν **4**.

*3. *possessing, possessed of* (to indicate that sth has sth else as attachment or component): φιλοῦσιν πέμματα μ. σταφίδων 'cakes stuffed with raisins' Ho 3.1 (MT /ʾăšišē ʿănāvim/); λαμπῆναι .. μ. σκιαδίων 'carriages .. with sunshades' Is 66.20.

4. indicates a relationship which is forged: διαθησόμεθα μ. σου διαθήκην Ge 26.28; Ho 2.18; "they got entangled with a harlot" 4.14[3]; καὶ αὐτοὶ μ. τῶν πορνῶν συνεφύροντο 4.14[1]; ἔσται οὕτως μεθ' ὑμῶν κύριος 'the Lord will be with you on such terms' Am 5.14.

5. indicates common fate or lot: "Judaea also will languish along with them" Ho 5.5; Am 2.3, 4.10; θηλάζων μ. καθεστηκότος πρεσβύτου 'a suckling with an elderly' De 32.25 (‖ σύν), ἡμάρτομεν μ. τῶν πατέρων ἡμῶν Ps 105.6.

6. *in concert with, jointly with*: "he stretched out his hands with rogues" Ho 7.5; Zc 14.5.

7. *in opposition to, in antagonism to*: ἐμαχέσαντο .. μ. τῶν ποιμένων Ισαακ 'fought .. with Is.'s shepherds' Ge 26.20, ἐπάλαιεν μετ' αὐτοῦ 'wrestled with him' 32.24, ἐποίησαν πόλεμον μ. Βαλλα 14.2; ἐνίσχυσε μ. ἀγγέλου 'he matched his strength with an angel' Ho 12.4; "he will argue with Israel" Mi 6.2; μὴ ἔριζε μ. ἀνθρώπου πλησίου 'Stop quarelling with a neighbour' Si 8.2.

8. *in the presence of, beside*: λάβετε μεθ' ἑαυτῶν λόγους Ho 14.3; "the tithes and first-fruits are with you" Ma 3.8; To 6.4 𝔊[II].

***9**. *in the estimation of, in the opinion of*: οὐχ οἱ λόγοι αὐτοῦ εἰσι καλοὶ μ. αὐτοῦ 'surely what he is saying is acceptable to him?' Mi 2.7.

***10**. *in return for, in exchange for*: "her prophets gave oracles in return for payment of silver" Mi 3.11; Is 52.3.

11. *in dealings with*: ποίησον ἔλεος μ. τοῦ κυρίου μου Αβρααμ Ge 24.12 (‖ dat., vs. 14); τὴν δικαιοσύνην, ἣν ἐποίησα μ. σοῦ 21.23; μὴ ποιήσειν μεθ' ἡμῶν κακόν 26.28; πορεύσομαι μεθ' ὑμῶν θυμῷ πλαγίῳ 'I shall conduct myself towards you with an unkindly attitude' Le 26.24, sim. 26.41; "what He has done to you" Jl 2.26; ποίησον μετ' ἐμοῦ .. εἰς ἀγαθόν Ps 85.17; μ. Ιωας ἐποίησεν κρίματα 2C 24.24; Is 3.14, 4K 4.28. **b**. in oral communication: λαλῆσαι μ. Ιακωβ πονηρά Ge 31.24, 29; ἐλάλησεν μετ' αὐτῶν εἰρηνικοὺς λόγους 1M 7.15.

12. *by using*: "conduct a thorough search of Jerusalem with a candle" Zp 1.12; παιδεύων μ. συμφορᾶς 'disciplining with calamities' 2M 6.16.

13. *in accordance with, in line with*: δώσει μ. ἀξιώματος 'he shall pay in accordance with the assessment' Ex 21.22, cf. μ. τοῦ νόμου καὶ τοῦ δικαίου Plato, *Apologia* 32b.

14. marks a person whose concern sth is: ἴδε ταῦτα μ. σοῦ γνωστά ἐστιν 'Look, I now know what these deeds of yours were all about' To 2.14 𝔊[II]; ἐγένετο ταῦτα μ. σου 'you have engaged yourself in these things' 3K 11.11.

II. + acc.

1. *after, following, subsequently to*: μεθ' ἡμέρας 'after several days' Ge 4.3, Ju 14.8; μ. τριετῆ χρόνον 'after a lapse of three years' 2M 4.23, μετ' οὐ πολὺν χρόνον 6.1, μ. χρόνον 'after a while' Is 27.11; μ. ταῦτα, w. ref. to the future, 'thereafter, then; henceforward, from now on' Ge 24.55, Ho 3.5, Is 1.26; μ. τὰ ῥήματα ταῦτα Ge 15.1; τί εἴπωμεν .. μ. τοῦτο; 'What shall we say .. with all this behind us?' 2E 9.10; πρὸ ἑορτῆς .. μ. ἑορτήν 1M 10.34; qualifying a noun phrase: τῷ σπέρματι ὑμῶν μεθ' ὑμᾶς 'your offspring (to come) after you' Ge 9.9; 41.3 ‖ ὀπίσω 41.19; μετ' αὐτόν 'after his death' Jb 21.21; + inf., μ. τὸ γεννῆσαι αὐτὸν τὸν Σηθ 'after he begot Seth' Ge 5.4; μ. τὸ ἀποθανεῖν Αβρααμ 26.18. **b**. in rank or priority order: Ru 4.4.

***2**. *in addition to, apart from*: οὐκ ἔστι μετ' ἐμὲ ἔτι 'there is none beside me' (an assertion of the uniqueness) Zp 3.1; 2C 17.15.

3. *into the midst of*: ἔλαβεν .. μ. χεῖρας (*pace* Wevers: χεῖρα) Ge 22.6; To 11.4𝔊[II] (𝔊[I] παρὰ χεῖρα), cf. ἔχων μετὰ χῖρας ξοίλιον 'having in his hands a stick' *POxy*. 901.9. An example of μ. χεῖρα mentioned at LSG s.v. **C IV** does not belong here, as it is not about the hand(s) of the subject of the verb. See Muraoka 2001a.21f.

Cf. σύν, ὕστερον, πρό: Johannessohn, *Präp*. 202-16.

μεταβαίνω: pf.inf. ~βεβηκέναι.∫

1. *to leave one's usual place and move* to: εἰς ὁσίας ψυχάς Wi 7.27; ἐπὶ γῆς 19.19.

2. *to change one's stance by distancing oneself*: ἀπὸ τῶν πατρίων νόμων 'from the ancestral laws' 2M 6.1; ἐπὶ τὰ Ἑλληνικά 'towards the Greek customs' 6.9, εἰς ἀλλοφυλισμόν 'to an alien culture' 6.24.

μεταβάλλω: fut. ~βαλῶ; aor. μετέβαλον, subj. ~βάλω, ptc. ~βαλών, mid. ~βαλόμενος, opt.mid.1pl ~βαλοίμεθα; pf.ptc. ~βεβληκώς.

I. tr. *to change the course of movement of*: ***o*** wind (ἄνεμος), Ex 10.19; τὸ πνεῦμα Hb 1.11, poss. intr. 'to change one's course'; αὐχένα ἀπέναντι τοῦ ἐχθροῦ αὐτοῦ 'neck,' i.e. 'to take to heels in the face of their enemies' Jo 7.8 (|| ἐπιστρέφω vs. 12).

2. *to change the nature of*: + acc., τὸ πρόσωπον αὐτῶν ὡς φλόξ '(the colour of) their faces like a flame' Is 13.8, cf. Eus. 97; τὸ πρόσωπον αὐτοῦ Is 29.22; τὰ νόμιμα 'the customs' 3M 1.3.

II. intr. *to have the nature changed*: abs. Si 18.26 μεταβαλεῖ εἰς αἷμα 'it [= the water of the river] will change to blood' Ex 7.17 (|| ἔσται αἷμα vs. 19), 20; μεταβαλοῦσα μεταπέσῃ 'change distinctly' Le 13.7; + adj., λευκή 'white' 13.3; + acc. noun, ἡ θρὶξ αὐτοῦ οὐ μετέβαλεν τρίχα λευκήν 'its hair has not turned to white hair' 13.4; + εἰς– εἰς λευκήν 13.20; ***s*** πνεῦμα Es 6.13 *L*.

2. *to change one's direction of movement*: abs. Jo 8.21; εἰς σέ Is 60.5; metaph., εἰς δυσμένειαν 'to illwill' 2M 6.29. **b**. metaph. 'to change one's mind': abs., Jb 10.8, 16; mid., 4M 6.18, 15.14.

Cf. μεταβολή, μεταπίπτω.

μεταβολή, ῆς. f.

change: of state or nature Es E 9 o', καιρῶν 'of seasons' Wi 7.18 (|| ἀλλαγή); of domicile, Es C 29, Is 47.15; ψυχῆς 'of mood' 3M 5.42; ἐκ~ῆς 'otherwise than customary, for a change' Is 30.32. Cf. μεταβάλλω.

μεταβολία, ας. f.∫*

commercial business: Si 37.11. Cf. μεταβόλος.

μεταβόλος, ου. m.∫

agent promoting production and subsequent distribution or marketing of a product: Φοινίκης Is 23.2; σπέρμα ~ων .. ~οι τῶν ἐθνῶν 'descendants of .. international traders' 23.3 (|| ἔμπορος vs. 8). Cf. ἔμπορος, μεταβολία: van der Kooij 1998.52; Armoni.

μεταγενής, ές.∫

of later time: comp. ~γενέστερος τούτων 'subsequent to this' 1E 8.1.

μεταγίνομαι: aor.ptc. ~γενόμενος.∫ *

to migrate: involuntarily, 2M 2.1, 2. Cf. ἀπ~, μετοικίζω, μεταίρω.

μετάγω: aor. μετήγαγον, inf. μετάξαι, pass. μετήχθην, subj. μεταχθῶ, ptc. ~χθείς.

to transfer: + acc. pers., εἰς Βαβυλῶνα 1E 1.43; ἀπὸ ἔθνος εἰς ἔθνος Si 10.8. **b**. 'to translate': εἰς ἑτέραν γλῶσσαν 'into a different language' Si prol. 22, cf. μεθερμηνεύω.

μεταδιαιτάω: aor.ptc.pass. ~διαιτηθείς.∫ *

pass. *to change one's way of life*: 4M 8.8.

μεταδίδωμι: aor. μετέδωκα

1. *to give part of* sth (acc.) *to share*: + dat. pers. only, ὀρφανῷ Jb 31.17, πτωχῷ Ep Je 27; abs., πολλὰ διάφορα ἐλάμβανε καὶ μετεδίδου 'he exchanged many various things' 2M 1.35.

2. *to communicate a message about*: + acc. rei, παρουσίαν 'arrival' 2M 8.12; + dat. pers., τὸν λόγον τῷ Ραγουηλ To 7.10 𝔊[I].

Cf. δίδωμι, ἀπαγγέλλω.

μεταδιώκω.∫

to pursue and cultivate: ***o*** way of conducting oneself, 2M 2.31. Cf. διώκω.

μετάθεσις, εως.∫

v.n. of μετατίθημι **1b**: ἐπὶ τὰ Ἑλληνικά '(conversion) to Hellenism' 2M 11.24.

μεταίρω: aor. μετῆρα.

to cause to move elsewhere: + acc., ἄμπελον ἐξ Αἰγύπτου Ps 79.9; ***o*** population, 4K 25.11B (*L*: μετοικίζω), ὅρια 'boundaries' Pr 22.28 (|| μετατίθημι 23.10). Cf. μεταγίνομαι, μετοικίζω, μετατίθημι.

μετακαλέω: aor. μετεκάλεσα, inf. ~καλέσαι.∫

to summon to come over from a distance: + acc. pers., ἐξ Αἰγύπτου μ. τὰ τέκνα αὐτοῦ 'I recalled his children from Egypt' Ho 11.1, sim. 11.2; 1E 1.48. Cf. καλέω, μεταπέμπομαι.

μετακινέω: fut. ~κινήσω, pass. ~κινηθήσομαι; aor. μετεκίνησα.

1. *to shift the position of*: + acc., ὅρια 'boundaries' De 19.14 (|| μετατίθημι 27.17); βουνοί 'hills' Is 54.10 (|| μεθίστημι); pass. *defeat and remove from the stage*, δύο μετακινήσουσιν μυριάδας De 32.30.

2. *to transform, alter*: pass., γῆ μετακινουμένη ἐν μετακινήσει 'a land going through various changes' 2E 9.11.

Cf. μετακίνησις, κινέω, μετατίθημι, μεθίστημι.

μετακίνησις, εως. f.∫

v.n. of μετακινέω **2**: γῆ μετακινουμένη ἐν ~ει λαῶν τῶν ἐθνῶν 'a land going through various changes brought about by the different ethnic communities' or '.. the large-scale ethnic population movements' 2E 9.11. Cf. μετακινέω.

μετακιρνάω.ʃ *

mid. *to change one's nature*: + πρός acc., 'so as to fit sth' Wi 16.21.

μεταλαμβάνω: fut.inf.mid. ~λήμψεσθαι; aor. ~έλαβον, ptc. ~λαβών.

1. *to receive information about and realise*: + inf., 2M 4.21, 13.23; + ptc. (acc.) clause, 11.6, 12.8, 15.1; + acc. rei, 12.5, 21.

2. *to be given as a substitute*: τι ἀντί τινος 3M 4.6.

3. *to have a share of*: τινος "both blessings and dangers" Wi 18.9; sth desirable, 4M 8.8, 16.18.

μεταλλάσσω: aor. μετήλλαξα., inf. ~λλάξαι, ptc. ~λλάξας; pf.ptc. μετηλλαχώς.

1. *to alter*: + acc., ἀγωγήν 'life-style' Es 2.20 o'.

2. *to quit*: + acc., τὸν βίον αὐτοῦ 1E1.29. **b**. abs., *to decease*: *s* hum., 2M 6.31, Es 2.7 o'.

Cf. Spicq 2.469f.

μεταλλεύω: fut. μεταλλεύσω.ʃ

1. *to dig in the ground and extract*: + acc., ἐκ τῶν ὀρέων αὐτῆς .. χαλκόν De 8.9.

2. *to transform* (?) (poss. infl. by μεταλλοιόω or μεταλλάσσω): + acc. and for the worse, 'pervert,' νοῦν ἄκακον 'innocent mind' Wi 4.12; mid., εἰς πάντα 'into all sorts of form' 16.25. Cf. LSG s.v.

μέταλλον, ου. n.ʃ

mine, quarry: gold and silver, 1M 8.3.

μεταμέλεια, ας. f.ʃ

sense of regret: on the part of God, Ho 11.8; on a hum.'s part, PSol 9.7. Cf. μεταμέλομαι, μετάμελος.

μεταμέλομαι: fut. ~μεληθήσομαι; aor. μετεμελήθην, ptc. ~μεληθείς, subj. ~μελήσω, pass. ~μεληθῶ; pf. ~μεμέλημαι.

to regret one's action and change one's mind: abs. ἐν τῷ ποιῆσαί σε μὴ μεταμελοῦ 'once you've started acting, stop having second thoughts' Si 35.19; Zc 11.5 (|| πάσχω), Wi 19.2, Si 30.28; ἐπὶ τὰ κακά 'over the hardships' Ez 14.22; + ptc., δοὺς αὐτῷ τὴν θυγατέρα μου 'that I gave ..' 1M 11.10; ἐπ' ἐσχάτων 'in the end, afterwards' Pr 25.8; *s* God, 1K 15.35 (+ ὅτι), Ps 109.4, Je 20.16, ἐπὶ τῇ κακίᾳ 1C 21.15; κατὰ τὸ πλῆθος τοῦ ἐλέους αὐτοῦ Ps 105.45. **b**. act. and impers. + dat. pers.: Μήποτε μεταμελήσῃ τῷ λαῷ ἰδόντι πόλεμον 'in case the people regret, having seen a war' Ex 13.17.

Cf. πάσχω, μεταμέλεια, μετάμελος, μετανοέω: Trench 255-61.

μετάμελος, ου. m.ʃ

disquiet over what has happened or has been done: over one's wrongdoing, οὐδαμῶς εἰς ~ον ἦλθεν 'he has never got to repenting' 3M 2.24; a sense of loss of sth or sbd valuable, Pr 11.3; a sense of shock over a calamity (?), 4K 3.17. Cf. μεταμέλεια, μεταμέλομαι.

μεταναστεύω: aor.inf. ~στεῦσαι subj. ~στεύσω, opt. 3s ~στεύσαι.*

act. *to cause to depart*: as punishment, + acc. pers., ἀπὸ σκηνώματος Ps 51.8 (+ ἐκτίλλω); = mid., 61.7; mid. *to depart*: to flee from danger, ἐπὶ τὰ ὄρη 10.1. Cf. ἐκβάλλω.

μετανίστημι: fut.act. ~αναστήσω; 2aor.act.impv.3pl ~αναστήτωσαν.ʃ

1. tr. (fut.act.) *to make to move from usual place of residence*: + acc., τὸν τόπον σου 2K 15.20B.

2. intr. (2aor.act.): *to move out from usual place of residence*: Ps 108.10 (|| ἐκβάλλομαι).

Cf. μετοικίζω.

μετανοέω: fut. ~νοήσω; aor. μετενόησα, impv. ~νόησον.

to change one's mind, revise one's previous view or design: *s* God, Jl 2.14 (+ ἐπιστρέφω), Jn 3.9 (+ ἀποστρέφω), Zc 8.14; ἐλάλησα καὶ οὐ μετανοήσω Je 4.28 (|| ἀποστρέφω); ἐπὶ τούτῳ 'over this matter' Am 7.3, 6; ἐπὶ ταῖς κακίαις 'over the planned (or: executed) disasters' Jl 2.13, Jn 4.2 (at both movitated by His mercies), sim. ib. 3.10, περὶ τῶν κακῶν, ὧν ἐλογισάμην τοῦ ποιῆσαι αὐτοῖς Je 18.8, περὶ τῶν ἀγαθῶν 18.10; hum., Wi 5.3, Si 17.24; eventually leading to abandoning one's previous view and practice, οὐ μετενόησεν .. οὐκ ἀπέστησαν ἀπὸ τῶν ἁμαρτιῶν αὐτῶν Si 48.15, ἀπὸ τῆς κακίας αὐτοῦ Je 8.6, μετανοήσατε, οἱ πεπλανημένοι, ἐπιστρέψατε τῇ καρδίᾳ 'O those who have gone astray, repent, change your hearts' Is 46.8.

μετανοέω and μετάνοια do not necessarily imply admission of guilt or error, cf. Behm, *TDNT* 4.976f.

Cf. μετάνοια, ἐπιστρέφω, μεταμέλομαι: Trench 255-61; Spicq 3.471-77; Harl, *Langue*, 142.

μετάνοια, ας. f.

v.n. of μετανοέω, deciding to change one's attitude: ἁμαρτήματα .. εἰς ~αν Wi 11.23; 12.10, 19, Si 44.16. For the use of the lexeme with no theological import, see *ND* 4.160. Cf. μετανοέω.

μεταξύ.ʃ

1. prep. + gen., *mingled among*: ζῶν μ. ἁμαρτωλῶν 'though living among sinners' Wi 4.10; μ. τοῦ ὕδατος 16.19.

2. *between* two parties: prep., μ. ποδῶν αὐτῆς 'between her legs' Jd 5.27 A (B: ἀνὰ μέσον). **b**. adv., μ. στάς 'having positioned himself in between' Wi 18.23.

Cf. μέσος.

μεταπαιδεύω.ʃ *

to reform by education: pass., ***o*** hum., 4M 2.7. Cf. παιδεύω.

μεταπείθω: aor.inf. ~πεῖσαι.ʃ

to persuade and change the view of: + acc., τὸν λογισμὸν ἡμῶν 4M 11.25.

μεταπέμπομαι: fut. ~πέμψομαι; aor. μετεπεμψάμην.
to summon: + acc. pers., μεταπέμψομαί σε ἐκεῖθεν Ge 27.45; ἐκ Μεσοποταμίας μ. με Nu 23.7. Cf. πέμπω, ἀποστέλλω, (μετα)καλέω.

μεταπίπτω: fut.mid.inf. ~πεσεῖσθαι; aor. μετέπεσον, subj. ~πέσω, inf. ~πεσεῖν.
to undergo change: *s* medical condition and for the better, ἁφή 'infection' Le 13.5; + a synonym, μεταβαλοῦσα μεταπέσῃ ἡ σημασία 'should the symbol undergo change' 13.7; mid. and *s* general situation, 3M 3.8. **b**. *to change sides*: Es 7.4 *L*.
Cf. ἀλλοιόω, μεταβάλλω, ~στρέφω.

μετασκευάζω.ʃ
to transform: *s* God and + acc. ποιῶν πάντα καὶ μετασκευάζων Am 5.8. Cf. ἐκτρέπω, ἀλλοιόω, μετασχηματίζω, ~τίθημι.

μεταστρέφω: fut. ~στρέψω, pass. ~στραφήσομαι; aor. μετέστρεψα, inf. ~στρέψαι, pass. μετεστράφην.
1. tr. *to turn over*: ἐγκρυφίας οὐ μεταστρεφόμενος 'a loaf not turned over' Ho 7.8.
2. *to change, alter the nature of* sth: γλῶσσαν Zp 3.9; εἰς, so as to pursue, 1E 3.19. **b**. pregnantly: καρδίαν ἄλλην '(changed his) heart (and gave) something different' 1K 10.9.
3. *to change, convert* sth to (εἰς) sth else: κατάρας εἰς εὐλογίας 'curses to blessings' De 23.5; τὰς ἑορτὰς ὑμῶν εἰς πένθος 'your festivals to a mourning' Am 8.10, τὰ ἀγαθὰ εἰς κακά Si11.31; without εἰς, 2C 36.4. Cf. ἐκστρέφω **1**.
4. *to cause to revert*: + acc., Je 21.4. **b**. *to avert, ward off*: + acc., βουλὴν ἀνοσίαν 'wicked design' 3M 5.8.
5. *to direct into a certain direction*: + acc., τὴν βουλὴν τοῦ βασιλέως ἐπ' αὐτούς 1E 7.14 (‖ ἐπιστρέφω 2E 6.22).
6. pass. *to direct oneself* in a certain direction: μετεστράφη ἡ καρδία Φαραω .. ἐπὶ τὸν λαόν 'Ph.'s .. attention turned to the people' Ex 14.5; μεταστραφήσονται αἱ οἰκίαι αὐτῶν εἰς ἑτέρους 'their houses will pass into foreign hands' Je 6.12; "our inheritance fell into the hands of (μετεστράφη) aliens" La 5.2. **b**. *to return from a battlefield*: Jd 5.28 A.
7. intr. pass. *to change*: μετεστράφη ἡ καρδία μου 'my mind has changed' Ho 11.8; to (εἰς) sth else, ὁ ἥλιος μεταστραφήσεται εἰς σκότος καὶ ἡ σελήνη εἰς αἷμα Jl 2.31.
Cf. ἐπιστρέφω, ἀλλοιόω.

μεταστροφή, ῆς. f.ʃ
new direction: 3K 12.15 ‖ 10.15.

μετασχηματίζω.ʃ
to transform: pass., *o* hum., εἰς ἀφθαρσίαν 'into immortality' 4M 9.22. Cf. ἀλλοιόω, μετασκευάζω, ~τίθημι.

μετατίθημι: pres.act.ptc. ~τιθείς; fut. ~θήσω, pass. ~τεθήσομαι; 1aor. μετέθηκα, 2aor.subj. ~θῶ, inf. ~θεῖναι, impv. ~θες, pass. μετετέθην.
1. *to shift* from one place to another: *o* pers., Ge 5.24, Si 44.16, Wi 4.10, all of Enoch (and his death?); ὅρια 'boundaries' De 27.17 (‖ μετακινέω 19.14), Ho 5.10, ὅρια αἰώνια 'long-standing ..' Pr 23.10 (‖ μεταίρω 22.28); 'to avert,' + acc., ὁρμήν 3M 1.16. **b**. mid. *to distance oneself*: in attitude, ἀπό τινος 'away from ..' 2M 7.24.
2. *to change the nature of*: + acc., τὸν λαὸν τοῦτον Is 29.14; τὸν βασιλέα 'the king's mind' 2M 4.46, cf. 3K 20.25. **b**. *to transform so as to become*: + ὡς and pass., Is 29.17 (‖ λογίζομαι εἰς), φίλος μετατιθέμενος εἰς ἔχθραν Si 6.9.
Cf. τίθημι, μετακινέω, μετάθεσις, ἀμετάθετος, μεταίρω.

μετατρέπω: aor. μετέτρεψα, inf. ~τρέψαι, pass. μετετράπην.
mid. *to turn round and change course*: moral decision, 4M 6.5; + acc. of respect, τὸν λογισμόν 7.12 ‖ act., τὸν λογισμόν 15.11, τινα 15.18.

μεταφέρω: aor.subj. μετενέγκω.ʃ
to shift: + acc., ἀπὸ τοῦ Λιβάνου εἰς Ιερυσαλημ 1E 4.48 (*o* timber), πρὸς ἡμᾶς 1C 13.3 (God's ark). Cf. φέρω.

μετάφρασις, εως. f.ʃ *
act of recasting a story: 2M 2.31.

μετάφρενον, ου. n.
the back of a body: of a bird carrying its young on it, De 32.11; secure place, Ps 90.4 (both ‖ πτέρυγες 'wings'); of a hum., Is 51.23. Alw. pl. (so already in Hom., *Il*. 12.428). Cf. νῶτος.

μεταχέω.ʃ *
to pour on sth *from a vessel*: + acc. (plant), 4M 1.29. Cf. χέω.

μετέπειτα. adv.
afterwards: εἰς τὸν μ. χρόνον 'hereafter' Es B 7 ο' (*L* εἰς τὰ μ.), 7.24 *L* (ο' τὰ μετὰ ταῦτα); τὰ μ. 'subsequent things' Ju 9.5.

μετέρχομαι: fut. ~ελεύσομαι; aor. μετῆλθον, inf. ~ελθεῖν, impv.3s ~ελθέτω, subj. ~έλθω.
1. *to leave and move* elsewhere: εἰς Γεθθα 'into Gath' 1K 5.8 (*L* + πρὸς ἡμᾶς).
2. *to pursue, go after*: with hostile intent, + acc. pers., Wi 14.30, 1M 15.4; *s* God, 4M 10.21; divine justice, 18.22. Cf. διώκω.
Cf. ἔρχομαι.

μετέχω: aor. μετέσχον, subj. μετάσχω, impv.2pl μετάσχετε, inf. μετασχεῖν; pf.ptc. μετεσχηκώς.
1. *to partake of* sth desirable, usually in common with others: + gen. rei, τῶν ἁγίων 'sacred meals' 1E 5.40, γεύσεως 'food' Wi 16.3; δικαίων 'the rights' 19.16, παιδείας 'education' Si 51.28, κηδείας οὐδ'

ἡστινοσοῦν 'no funeral whatsoever' 2M 5.10; + dat. pers., μηδεὶς ἀλλότριος μετασχήτω σοι Pr 5.17 (one's wife and ‖ ἔστω σοι μόνῳ).

2. *to do and practise* sth *in common with others*: + gen. rei, τῆς ἀνομίας ταύτης 1E 8.67, παρανόμου χορηγίας 'unlawful event' 2M 4.14, μολυσμοῦ 'defilement' 5.27, φόνου 'murder' Pr 1.18.

Cf. μετοχή, μέτοχος, συμμετέχω, κοινοῦν.

μετεωρίζω: fut.pass. ~ρισθήσομαι; aor. ἐμετεωρίσθην, impv. μετεώρισον, ptc. ~ρισθείς, subj. ~ρισθῶ.ʃ

to raise to a height: ***o*** the mountain of the Lord, ὑπεράνω τῶν βουνῶν 'above the hills' Mi 4.1; of bringing up to the surface sth sunken in a river 4K 6.7*L* (B: ὑψόω); pass. with the force of mid., of an eagle, ἐὰν μετεωρισθῇς ὡς ἀετός 'even if you soared like an eagle' Ob 4 (‖ ὑψόω Je 29.17); cherubs' wings, ἀπὸ τῆς γῆς Ez 10.16; ἐμετεωρίσθησαν οἱ ὀφθαλμοί μου Ps 130.1 (‖ ὑψόω), ἐμετεωρίζετο τὴν διάνοιαν 'was elated in spirit' 2M 5.17, μὴ μάτην μετεωρίζου φρυαττόμενος .. 'Don't be elated in vain, puffed up ..' 7.34, ἐπὶ τὴν ἁγίαν σου πόλιν 3M 6.5. Cf. μετεωρισμός, μετέωρος, ὑψόω, φρυάττω: Spicq 2.483-5.

μετεωρισμός, οῦ. m.ʃ

1. **billow*, often symbolic of hostile forces: + κῦματα, Jn 2.4, Ps 41.8; τῆς θαλάσσης 92.4.

2. *act of lifting high*: fig. of arrogance, ὀφθαλμῶν 'haughty look' Si 23.4, 26.9 (see under μετέωρος); τῆς καρδίας 2M 5.21 (‖ ὑπερηφανία).

Cf. μετεωρίζω, κῦμα, and κλύδων.

μετέωρος, ον.

1. *lifted into mid-air*: ***s*** hum., Ez 3.15 (or: 'elated; in suspense': MT תֵּל > תָּלִי, cf. Schleusner s.v.).

2. *lifted high off the ground*, 'high, tall': ***s*** mountain, Ez 17.23, ὄρος ὑψηλὸν καὶ ~ον Is 57.7; hill, 30.25 (‖ ὑψηλός); ἐπ' ἄκρου ~ου 'on the top end (of an olive tree)' 17.6; cedars of Lebanon 2.13 (+ ὑψηλός); subst.n., 'high spot' Si 22.18, σκόποι ἐπὶ ~ου 'sentinels high up there' 37.14; ὑψωθῇ .. εἰς τὸ ~ον Je 38.35 (:: ταπεινωθῇ κάτω), pl. 'high places (for pagan cult)' 4K 12.4*L* (B: ὑψηλά), 15.4 *L* ‖ ὑψηλά; n.pl. ~α 'the things in heaven above' or '.. in high mountains' Jb 28.18¶ (:: τὰ ἐσώτατα 'the things deep in the ground [?]'); (water resources in a) hilly area, Jd 1.15 (:: ταπεινά).

3. *haughty, proud*: ***s*** hum., ὑψηλὸν καὶ ~ον Is 2.12, ἔθνος 18.2; human eyes, 5.15 (see under μετεωρισμός).

Cf. ὑψηλός.

μετοικεσία, ας.f. *

1. *act of residing in a place other than one's normal or present place of residence*: εἰς ~αν πορεύσεται αἰχμάλωτος 'will go as captives to live in exile' Na 3.10; Jd 18.30 A (B: ἀποικία).

2. *colony of expatriates*: Ob 20*a*; μ. Ιερουσαλημ, consisting of former residents of Jerusalem, 20*b*; ἐν ~ᾳ καὶ ἐν αἰχμαλωσίᾳ Ez 12.11.

Cf. μετοικίζω, μετοικία, αἰχμαλωσία.

μετοικέω: pf. μετῴκηκα.ʃ

to move to a new abode than one's normal or present place of residence: ἐκ τοῦ τόπου σου 2K 15.19.

μετοικία, ας. f.

act of moving to a new abode, resettling: δώσω τὴν Ιερουσαλημ εἰς ~αν Je 9.11; 20.4 (‖ μετοικίζω); γῆ μετοικίας (*L* μετοικεσίας) 'land of deportation' 3K 8.47. Cf. μέτοικος, μετοικεσία, μετοικίζω, αἰχμαλωσία.

μετοικίζω: fut. ~ιῶ; aor. μετῴκισα, pass. ~ῳκίσθην.

to cause to move to a new abode, resettle: + acc. pers. μετοικιῶ ὑμᾶς ἐπέκεινα Δαμασκοῦ 'I will move you beyond D.' Am 5.27, εἰς Βαβυλῶνα 1E 5.7; by force, Jd 2.3A (B: ἐξαίρω), intr. pass. μετῳκίσθη ἀπ' αὐτοῦ 'moved away from it' Ho 10.5.

Cf. μετοικεσία, μετοικία, μέτοικος, μεταίρω, μετανίστημι, ἀποικίζω: Casevitz 1985.181f.

μέτοικος, ου. m.ʃ

actor noun of μετοικίζω: used as a PN, Je 20.3. Cf. μετοικίζω.

μετουσία, ας. f.ʃ

act of enjoying: + gen., κάλλους 'of beauty' 4M 2.1. Cf. ἀπόλαυσις.

μετοχή, ῆς. f.ʃ

act of sharing and taking part in: + gen., Ps 121.3, ἁμαρτίας PSol 14.6. Cf. μέτοχος, μετέχω, κοινωνία and Caird 1969.22.

μέτοχος, ον.ʃ

1. *implicated in* (sth τινος): μ. εἰδώλων 'idol worship' Ho 4.17; αἱμάτων ἀθῴων 'murder of the innocent' Es E 5 o', ἄνδρες αἱμάτων ~οι Pr 29.10.

2. subst., *one who is closely associated in outlook, purpose* etc.: μ. ἐγώ εἰμι πάντων τῶν φοβουμένων σε '.. of all those who fear you' Ps 118.63, τοὺς ~ους σου 44.8; τῶν ἀεὶ ἱερέων 'of the regular priests' 3M 3.21; τινι (pers.), 1K 20.30. **b.** *another member in same group*: ἐὰν πέσωσιν, ὁ εἷς ἐγερεῖ τὸν ~ον αὐτοῦ 'should they fall, the one would raise his associate' Ec 4.10 (‖ δεύτερος).

Cf. μετοχή, μετέχω, κοινωνός: Spicq 2.478-82 and *ND* 1.84f., 9.47f.

μετρέω: fut. μετρήσω; aor. ἐμέτρησα, ptc. μετρήσας; pf.pass. μεμέτρημαι.ʃ

1, *to determine the quantity of*, 'measure': solid food, τῷ γομορ 'by an omer' Ex 16.18; + acc., part of a building, τὸ κλίτος τὸ πρὸς ἀνατολάς 'the eastern side' Nu 35.5; τῇ χειρὶ τὸ ὕδωρ Is 40.12, τὴν βασιλείαν σου Da 5.26 TH; pass., ἀριθμῷ ἐτῶν 'with the number of years (lived)' Wi 4.8.

2. *to measure and separate a certain quantity from the rest*: + acc. rei, "six measures of barley" Ru 3.15.

Cf. μέτρησις, μετρητής, μέτρον, δια~, ἐκ~, καταμετρέω.

μέτρησις, εως. f.ʃ

yardstick for measurement: 3K 7.24. Cf. μετρέω.

μετρητής, οῦ. m.

a certain liquid measure: ἐξαντλῆσαι πεντήκοντα ~άς 'to draw out 50 measures' Hg 2.16; οἴνου 1E 8.20, ἐλαίου Bel 3 LXX. **b**. a certain dry measure: σπέρματος 'of seeds' 3K 18.32.

Cf. μέτρον.

μετριάζω.ʃ

to be reasonably well: of health condition, Ne 2.2. Cf. μέτριος.

μέτριος, α, ον.ʃ

within measure, not excessive: *s* ἔντερον 'belly,' i.e. 'moderate consumption of food' Si 34.20. Cf. μετρίως, μετρίζω, μέτρον, συμμετρία.

μετρίως. adv.ʃ

in a mediocre fashion: εὐτελῶς καὶ μ. 'in a perfunctory and mediocre fashion' 2M 15.38. Cf. μέτριος.

μέτρον, ου. n.

1. *that by which anything is measured*: ἐν ~οις καὶ ἐν σταθμίοις καὶ ἐν ζυγοῖς Le 19.35; μ. ἀληθινὸν καὶ δίκαιον (|| στάθμιον ἀ. καὶ δ.) De 25.15; Mi 6.10; μ. καὶ μ. 'unequal measures' De 25.14 (|| στάθμιον vs. 13); ποιῆσαι μικρὸν μ., of unethical trade-practice, Am 8.5; measuring line, Zc 1.16; ὕδωρ ~ῳ λήμψεσθε .. ἀργυρίου De 2.6 (or: 'within due limits, moderately'); ὕδωρ ἐν ~ῳ πίεσαι 'thou shalt drink water by measuring (carefully a certain quantity)' Ez 4.11 (ἐν σταθμῷ vs. 16); κάλαμος ~ου 'reed ..' 40.3; || ἀριθμός 'number,' σταθμός 'weight' Wi 11.20.

2. *measured-out quantity*: in the midst of which one can sit, Zc 5.7, cf. 5.8, 9, 10; μ. τὸ αὐτὸ ἔσται πάσαις ταῖς αὐλαίαις 'all the curtains shall have the same measurement' Ex 26.2; || σταθμός Jb 28.25.

3. *a fixed amount*, 'measure': unspecified amount, τρία ~α σεμιδάλεως '.. of fine flour' Ge 18.6, τὸ δέκατον τῶν τριῶν ~ων 'one tenth of three measures' Ex 16.36.

Cf. δια~, ἐκ~, καταμετρέω, μετρητής, ζυγός, ἀριθμός, στάθμιον, σταθμός, σχοινίον, γεωμετρικός, μέτριος, δίμετρον, ἀμέτρητος.

μέτωπον, ου. n.

the space between the eyes, 'forehead': Ex 28.34, Ez 9.4; fig., τὸ μ. σου χαλκοῦν 'your forehead is brazen' Is 48.4 (|| τράχηλος); critical spot when injured, 1K 17.49.

μέχρι(ς): the longer form is supposed to be used when foll. by a vowel: cf. BDAG s.v.

up to, as far as, giving the end-point or limit of movement or state which continues or will have continued, either local or temporal.

I. prep. + gen.

A. Temporal–

1. + τοῦ inf.aor.: μέχρι τοῦ βασιλεῦσαι Πέρσας 1E 1.54(*a*), μ. τοῦ οἰκοδομηθῆναι 4.51; 6.6(*a*) (ἕως || 2E 5.5), 27; μ. τοῦ σε ἐλθεῖν To 2.2 𝔊II; 2.4 𝔊II (|| ἕως οὗ 𝔊I), Ps 104.19(*c*), 1M 4.46, 2M 6.14.

2. + gen.: μέχρι τοῦ δευτέρου ἔτους 1E 2.25(*a*) (ἕως || 2E 4.24), μ. τοῦ νῦν 3M 6.28, ἀπ' ἐκείνου μ. τοῦ νῦν 1E 6.19 (ἕως || 2E 5.16), ἀπὸ φυλακῆς πρωΐας μ. νυκτός 'from the early watch till night' Ps 129.6(-), μ. τῆς σήμερον ἡμέρας 1E 8.74(†)(ὡς || 2E 9.7); μ. χρόνου 'for a while to come' To 14.4 (|| ἕως καιροῦ); μ. τίνος; 'how much longer?' Jb 2.9(*d*), 8.2(*a*), 3M 5.40, cf. τέο μέχρις; Hom. *Il*. 24.128 and Renehan 2.101; μ. τέλους 'thoroughly in execution' Wi 16.5, 19.1, cf. μ. συντελείας Si 47.10(†). **b**. with an indeclinable word: μ. νῦν Es C 29, Ps 70.17(*a*). **c**. + a participial phrase in the gen.: ὕπνωσεν μ. μεσούσης τῆς νυκτός 'slept till it was midnight' Ju 12.5, cf. μ. ἡλίου δύοντος *IG* 1^2.188.4. **d**. indicates a point in time prior to which sth may or should happen, 'by': τοῖς καταπορευομένοις μ. τριακάδος 'those returning by the 30th' 2M 11.30.

3. μέχρι ὅτου + subj.aor.: To 5.7 𝔊II. **b**. μέχρις οὗ + inf.aor.: To 11.1 𝔊I. **c**. μέχρις οὗ + indic. aor.: Ju 12.9; + subj. aor. Da 11.36 TH(*a*) (LXX ἕως ἄν).

4. indicates the continuation of a state or action indicated by the verb in the subordinate phrase or clause, 'so long as': μέχρις οὗ διετράφησαν 'so long as they were provided with food' Ju 5.10.

B. Local–

+ gen.: ἀπὸ τῆς Ἰνδίκης μ. τῆς Αἰθιοπίας 1E 3.2, μ. περάτων Es B 2, μ. τούτου Jb 38.11(*a*), μ. τῶν περάτων τῆς γῆς 'to the ends of the earth' Ps 45.10(*a*). **b**. with a pleonastic καί: ἀπὸ ἀνατολῶν ἡλίου καὶ μ. δυσμῶν Ps 49.1.

C. Logical–

ἀπὸ γεραιοῦ μ. νηπίου 'from the elderly to the infants' 3M 3.27. **b**. marks the extreme case: ἐρρύσω μ. τριχός 'you rescued .. even to a hair, i.e. preventing the loss of even a single hair' 3M 6.6, cf. "I don't have anyone who could give me as much as a cup of water (μ. ποτηρίου ὕδατ[ο]ς)" P.Oxy 3314.10f. **c**. indicates the extent or degree, 'as far as, so much as, to the point of': τοσούτῳ μᾶλλον ἐξετυφλοῦντο .. μ. τοῦ ἀποτυφλωθῆναι 'my sight became all the worse .. and in the end I became completely blind' To 2.10 𝔊II, γενναίως ἀγωνίσασθαι μ. θανάτου περὶ νόμων 'to fight gallantly even to the point of death for the sake of the laws' 2M 13.14, μ. θανάτου τὸν θεὸν ἐσχηκότες 'have held on to God, risking even death' 3M 7.16, cf. γενόμενος ὑπήκοος μ. θανάτου, θανάτου δὲ σταυροῦ 'having become obedient ..' Phil 2.8 (in both Ma passages the subject[s] eventually escaped death in action).

II. conj., μ. ἄν + subj.aor.: μ. ἂν συντελεσθῇ τοῦτο 'until this has been accomplished' 3M 7.4.

Cf. ἕως, ἄχρι.

a) עַד also Ar.; *b*) וְעַד Ar.; *c*) עַד־עֵת; *d*) עֹד.

μή. Negative particle.

I. Usually placed immediately before a verb and thus negativing the entire statement. The verb, if not inf., impv. or ptc., is mostly in the subj. mood (cf. BDF, § 426).

1. ὅπως μὴ λάβητε ἀδικίαν Ho 14.3(*l*); ἐὰν μὴ γνωρίσωσιν ἑαυτούς Am 3.3(*g*); 3.4(*g*), 7(*h*), 5.6 (*m*), Mi 3.8(*i*), 5.7(*b*), Jl 2.17(*n*), Zc 12.7(*b*), 14.17(*b*), 18(*b*bis), 19(*b*), Ma 2.2(*j*bis). **b**. Occasionally w. indic.: εἰ μὴ βούλει ἐξαποστεῖλαι Ex 4.23(*p*), 9.2(*p*) (|| ἐὰν μὴ βούλῃ .. 8.21); Εἰ μὴ κεκοίμηταί τις μετὰ σοῦ Nu 5.19(*b*); εἰ μή σοι ἀρέσκει 'if it does not please you' 22.34(*q*); 22.33(*r*) (unreal condition, so also Ge 31.42[*s*], 43.10[*s*]). Here does not belong μή when it is part of a compound particle εἰ μή 'unless' (see BDF, § 428.3): εἰ μὴ Γαλααδ ἐστιν Ho 12.11(*k*). **c**. elliptically εἰ δὲ μή 'if not' with εἰ + indic. in the preceding full clause, Ge 24.49(*j*).

2. Indicates a prohibition or a negative wish of the speaker: **a**. w. a verb in the 2nd pers.: μὴ θυμωθῇς Ge 44.18(*a*); μὴ ἐπίδῃς .. μὴ ἐπιχαρῇς .. μὴ μεγαλορρημονήσῃς Ob 12(*a*ter), μὴ δῷς Jl 2.17(*a*); Jn 1.14[2](*a*), Ma 2.15(*a*). **b**. w. a verb in the 1st pers. μὴ ἀπολώμεθα 'let us not perish' Jn 1.14[1](*a*). **c**. w. a verb in the third pers. μὴ περάνῃ 'let him not finish' Hb 2.5(*b*). **d**. + pres.impv. μὴ φοβοῦ 'Fear not!' Ge 21.17(*a*); μὴ ἀγνόει .. μὴ εἰσπορεύεσθε .. μὴ ἀναβαίνετε .. μὴ ὀμνύετε Ho 4.15 (*a* quat); 9.1(*a*), Am 5.5(*a*, *b*bis), 7.16(*b*), Mi 1.10(*a*bis), 2.6(*a*), 7.5(*a*bis), 8(*a*), Zc 1.4(*a*), 7.10(*a*bis), 8.17(*a*bis); + aor. impv. μὴ γευσάσθωσαν 'let them not taste' Jn 3.7(*a*); Zp 3.16(*a*).

3. τοῦ μὴ + inf. of purpose: τοῦ μὴ καλύπτειν 'in order (for her) not to cover' Ho 2.9(*w*); Am 6.10(*b*), 14(*c*), Zp 3.6(*e*); "they made their ears heavy in order not to listen (τοῦ μὴ εἰσακούειν) and made their heart disobedient in order not to listen (τοῦ μὴ εἰσακούειν) to my law" Zc 7.11f(*c*bis). **b**. after a verb of negative nuance such as verbs of withholding, preventing etc. (BDF, § 400.4): ἀπώσομαί σε τοῦ μὴ (v.l.) ἱερατεύειν μοι 'I will reject you (and not allow you) to serve me as a priest' Ho 4.6(*c*)(see Muraoka 1983.35); "I will set up a defence for my house so that they may not pass through (τοῦ μὴ διαπορεύεσθαι)" Zc 9.8(*d*). See Soisalon-Soininen, *Infinitive*, 75-80. **c**. after an adj.: καθαρὸς ὀφθαλμὸς τοῦ μὴ ὁρᾶν πονηρά 'an eye too pure to behold wicked things' Hb 1.13(*c*). **d**. without τοῦ: ὥστε μὴ ἱκανοὺς εἶναι Ex 12.4(*w*), 14.11(*e*).

4. + ptc.: τοῦ παιδίου μὴ ὄντος μεθ' ἡμῶν Ge 44.34(*k*); τὰ μὴ ἐσθιόμενα 'the inedible' Le 11.47 (*b*); τοὺς μὴ ζητήσαντας .. τοὺς μὴ ἀντεχομένους Zp 1.6(*b*bis); Ma 3.5(*b*), 18(*b*). See BDF, § 426.

5. + subj. indicating a negative purpose, 'in order that .. not' (= ἵνα μή, ὅπως μή), μὴ ἔλθω καὶ πατάξω 'so that I may not come and strike ..' Ma 4.5(*f*).

6. in a relative clause of general application with an indic.: πᾶσα ψυχή, ἥτις μὴ ταπεινωθήσεται 'every soul that shall not be humbled' Le 23.29(*b*); πηγὴ ἣν μὴ ἐξέλιπεν ὕδωρ 'a fountain which never wanted in water' Is 58.11 (*b*). See KG 2.185.

7. with another negator: εἰς τοὺς ἄνδρας τούτους μὴ ποιήσητε μηδὲν ἄδικον 'Only to these men do not do anything unjust' Ge 19.8(*a*).

8. elliptically: εἰ δὲ μή 'if not, otherwise' Ge 30.1(*u*); not negativing the intention implicit in a threat, 'if you don't do as told' Je 11.21.

9. at considerable remove from the verb: De 22.1(*b*).

II. Negatives part of a sentence which gives a command: ἐκζητήσατε τὸ καλὸν καὶ μὴ τὸ πονηρόν 'Seek the good and not the evil' Am 5.14(*a*); sim. Jl 2.13(*a*).

III. Introduces a rhetorical question to which a negative answer is expected: μὴ φύλαξ τοῦ ἀδελφοῦ μού εἰμι ἐγώ; Ge 4.9(*d*); μὴ ἀντὶ θεοῦ ἐγώ εἰμι ..; 'surely I cannot act in God's place ..?' 30.2(*d*); μὴ σφάγια καὶ θυσίας προσηνέγκατέ μοι; 'Surely you have not offered me victims and sacrifices?' Am 5.25(*d*); μὴ βασιλεὺς οὐκ ἦν σοι; 'surely you had a king?' Mi 4.9(*d*); Μὴ χεὶρ κυρίου οὐκ ἐξαρκέσει; Nu 11.23(*d*); Am 2.11(*d*) (on the double negative, which expects an affirmative answer, see BDAG, s.v. **3 a** end); ib. 6.10(*d*), Jl 3.4(*d*), Hb 3.8(*d*). Also Zc 8.6(*w*). Perh. under the Heb. influence, the μή may be found in the middle of the question: οἱ προφῆται μὴ τὸν αἰῶνα ζήσονται; Zc 1.5(*d*), sim. 7.5(*d*).

IV. Negatives an adjective: ἀπὸ τῶν κτηνῶν τῶν μὴ καθαρῶν Ge 7.2(*b*); Ez 36.31(*b*).

V. Elliptical negation: Μή τι, κύριε, ἐὰν λαλήσω Ge 18.30(*t*), 32(*t*).

VI. Signals dissent: Μή, κύριε· 'No, sir' Ge 23.6(*b*).

VII. Introduces a clause expressing apprehension, 'I fear': + ind., μή τίς ἐστιν ἐν ὑμῖν .. De 29.18(*m*) (replace the semicolons in ed. Wevers with a full stop); Je 45.19(*f*), Si 7.6(*v*). Cf. Bel 15-17 LXX. **b**. a sense of apprehension made explicit by φοβέομαι preceding: φοβοῦμαι .. μὴ ἀποθάνω To 6.15. **c**. introduces a clause of fear: εὐλαβήθη μὴ οὐκ ἔχῃ 'he feared that he might not have' 1M 3.30. Cf. LSG s.v. **C II 1**.

On οὐ μή, οὐδὲ μή, οὐδὲ οὐ μή, οὐκέτι μή, and οὐκέτι οὐ μή, see under οὐ.

a) אַל; *b*) לֹא; *c*) מִן; *d*) -הֲ; *e*) מִבְּלִי; *f*) פֶּן; *g*) ἐὰν μή בִּלְתִּי; *h*) ἐὰν μή כִּי אִם; *i*) ἐὰν μή אוּלָם; *j*) ἐὰν μή אם לֹא; *k*) μή εἶμι אֵין; *l*) בַּל [Ho 14.3 *k* > *b*]; *m*) ὅπως μή פֶּן; *n*) ὅπως μή לָמָּה; *o*) וְלֹא; *p*) μὴ βούλομαι מָאַן pi.; *q*) רַע בְּעֵינֵי; *r*) εἰ μή אוּלַי; *s*) εἰ μή לוּלֵי, לוּלֵא ; *t*) אַל נָא יִחַר; *u*) אַיִן; *v*) אִם; *w*) (-). x∫

μηδαμόθεν. adv.∫

by no means: Wi 17.10.

μηδαμῶς.

certainly not, oh no, expressing strong negative reaction and protest: abs., μ., κύριε Jn 1.14; Ge 18.25, 19.7; negating a verb, μ. σὺ ποιήσεις .. 18.25. **b**. μ. μοι/ἐμοί (or in reverse order) *I absolutely reject the notion implied* or *proposition*: + inf., 1K 12.23 (*L* ἐμοὶ μὴ γένοιτο), 26.11 (idem), παρὰ κυρίου 24.7; σοι 20.2

Cf. μή and οὐδαμῶς.

μηδέ

nor, attached to a second (and subsequent) negatived element in a series of negations introduced by μή: w. pres. impv., μὴ χαῖρε .. μηδὲ εὐφραίνου Ho 9.1(*a*); Mi 2.6 (*b*); w. a mixture of pres. and aor. impv., Jn 3.7(*a*bis); w. impv. and subj., De 31.6(*a*); w. aor. subj. μὴ περιβλέψῃς .. μηδὲ στῇς .. Ge 19.17(*a*); ὅπως μὴ συναχθῇ μηδεὶς μηδὲ ὑποστῇ Mi 5.7(*b*); Ob 13(*a*tres), 14(*a*bis); Zc 14.18(*b*); in a series of elliptical phrases with the leading nucleus not repeated – μὴ ἀδικήσειν με μηδὲ τὸ σπέρμα μου μηδὲ τὸ ὄνομά μου Ge 21.23(*e*). The use of μηδέ is not compulsory, but may be replaced by καὶ μή: μὴ ἐπίδῃς .. καὶ μὴ ἐπιχαρῇς .. καὶ μὴ μεγαλορρημονήσῃς .. μηδὲ εἰσέλθῃς .. μηδὲ ἐπίδῃς .. μηδὲ συνεπιθῇ .. μηδὲ ἐπιστῇς .. μηδὲ συγκλείσῃς Ob 12-14.

On the simultaneous use of another negative pronoun or adverbial, see under the latter.

a) אַל; *b*) לֹא; *c*) אֵין; *d*) מִן; *e*)(-). x∫

μηδείς, μηδεμία, μηδέν. Also spelled with θ instead of δ.

A syntactically conditioned equivalent of οὐδείς.

I. subst. **a**. m./f., *nobody, not even one person*: παρὰ (q.v.) τὸ μηδένα ὑπάρχειν Zp 3.6; after ὅπως – ὅπως μηδεὶς μήτε δικάζηται μήτε ἐλέγχῃ μηδείς, so also Mi 5.7. **b**. n., *nothing, not a thing*: μὴ γευσάσθωσαν μηδέν Jn 3.7; adv., 'in no respect' 2M 14.28.

II. pseudo-attributive: εἰς τοὺς ἄνδρας τούτους μὴ ποιήσητε μηδὲν ἄδικον 'Only to these men do not do anything unjust' Ge 19.8. **b**. w. def. article: ἐν τῷ μηδένι 'in no time; swiftly' Ps 80.15.

Cf. οὐδείς.

μηδέποτε

never: μ. δευτερώσῃ λόγον 'Never repeat what you've heard' Si 19.7; + ptc., 3M 3.16; + fut. inf., 7.11. Del. 3M 7.4 v.l.

Μηδία, ας. f.

Media: 1E 3.1.

Μῆδοι. m.pl.

Media: Is 13.17; Medes Ju 16.10.

μηθέτερος, α, ον.∫

neither of the two mentioned: Pr 24.21 (|| ἀμφότεροι vs. 22).

μηκέτι.

not .. any longer: + impv.pres., Ex 36.6, 1M 13.39, with another negator, To 3.13 𝔊[II] (aor. 𝔊[I]); + subj. aor., To 14.10 𝔊[I]; with another negator, ἥμαρτες, μὴ προσθῇς μ. 'you have sinned. Don't do so again' Si 21.1; + ptc.pres., οἱ νεκροὶ οἱ μ. θεωροῦντες τὸ φῶς To 5.10 𝔊[II]; + inf.pres., 2M 4.14, 3M 4.17; + inf.aor., 2M 10.4. Cf. ἔτι.

μῆκος, ους. n.

measurement from end to end, 'length': of boat, Ge 6.15 (|| πλάτος 'width' and ὕψος 'height'); of city, Zc 2.2 (|| πλάτος); of sickle, 5.2 (id.); of land and along the north-south axis, διώδευσεν Αβραμ τὴν γῆν εἰς τὸ μ. αὐτῆς 'A. travelled through the land through its length' Ge 12.6; || πλάτος 13.17; of curtain, Ex 26.2 (|| εὖρος); of altar, 30.2 (|| εὖρος); of bed or sarcophagus, De 3.11 (|| εὖρος); βίου 'of life' Pr 3.2. **b**. *great length*: βίου 'longevity' Pr 16.17; ἀνέβη μ. τῶν ἔργων 'the (building) works made quite a progress' 2C 24.13.

Cf. εὖρος, πλάτος, ὕψος: Shipp 377.

μηκύνω: aor. ἐμήκυνα, subj. μηκύνω.∫

1. *to help grow in height*: + acc. (tree) and ***s*** rain, Is 44.14.

2. *to speak at length*: ***s*** God Ez 12.25. **b**. *to be prolonged*: ***s*** οἱ λόγοι μου Ez 12.28.

μῆλον, ου. n.

1. any *tree-fruit*: μ. μανδραγόρου 'of mandrake' Ge 30.14, χρυσοῦν 'golden' Pr 25.11 (part of a necklace).

2. specifically *apple-tree*: ῥόα καὶ φοίνιξ καὶ μ. Jl 1.12. Cf. Shipp 379; Schnebel 314.

3. *cheek*: Ct 4.6, 6.7.

μηλωτή, ῆς. f.

rough wooly skin: as mantle, 3K 19.13.

I **μήν**, νός. m.

month: ἐν τῷ μηνὶ τῷ ἕκτῳ 'in the sixth month' Hg 1.1; ἐν μηνὶ τῷ ἑβδόμῳ 'in the seventh month'

Ge 8.4; μῆνα ἡμερῶν 'for one month' 29.14, Nu 11.21 (|| ἕως μηνὸς ἡμερῶν 'up to a full month' vs. 20); μηνὸς ἡμέρας (pl. acc.) 'for a full month' De 21.13; ἀρχὴ μηνῶν 'the first month (of a year)' Ex 12.2; ἐν τοῖς μησὶν τοῦ ἐνιαυτοῦ ib.; μ. τῶν νέων 'the month of Abib' 13.4; πρὸ τριῶν μηνῶν τοῦ τρυγήτου 'three months before the harvest' Am 4.7. Cf. μηνιαῖος, νουμηνία.

II **μήν**. Asseverative particle, not clause-initial. See also under ἦ.

οὐ μ. δὲ ἀλλά Jb 2.5, 5.8, 12.6, 4M 15.9; οὐδὲ μ. ἄλλως Es 9.27 o'. Cf. Blonqvist 1969.53f., 60.

μηνιαῖος, α, ον.

of one month in age: Le 27.6, Nu 3.15. Cf. μήν.

μηνίαμα, ατος. n.ʃ

fury: μ. καὶ ἔρις '.. and strife' Si 40.5. Cf. μῆνις.

μηνιάω: aor.subj. μηνιάσω.ʃ

to act with wrath against: *s* hum., + dat. pers. Si 28.7; and ἐπί τινι ('over sth'), 10.6. Cf. μηνίω, μῆνις.

μῆνις, ιος / ιδος. f.

anger, rage: human and || θυμός Ge 49.7; || ἔχθρα Nu 35.21; + ὀργή Si 27.30. Cf. θυμός, μηνίαμα, μήνισις, ὀργή: Schmidt 3.566; Shipp 388.

μήνισις, εως. f.ʃ *

= μῆνις: ἐν ὀργῇ καὶ θυμῷ μετὰ ~εως PSol 2.23.

μηνίσκος, ου. m.ʃ

crescent-shaped neck-ornament: of women, Is 3.18; of camels, Jd 8.21; of kings, 8.26B. Cf. κάθεμα, μανιάκης: Russo 211-5.

μηνίω: fut. μηνιῶ; aor.ptc. μηνίσας.ʃ

to act with wrath against: abs. and *s* God, Ps 102.9 (|| ὀργίζομαι), Od 12.13; + dat. pers. Je 3.12 (+ neg., because He is ἐλεήμων); *s* hum., Le 19.18. Cf. μηνιάω, μῆνις, ὀργίζομαι.

μηνύω: aor.pass. ἐμηνύθην, ptc. μηνυθείς.ʃ

1. *to supply not generally known information about*, 'to tip': abs., 3M 3.28; + inf. clause, 4M 4.3, Es 7.37 *L*; pass., + dat. pers., περὶ τῶν αὐτῷ μηνυθέντων χρημάτων 'about the funds about which he had been informed' 2M 3.7. **b**. pass., *o* sbd whose secret whereabouts is betrayed: + dat. pers., 2M 6.11.

2. *to supply injurious, unfavourable information about*, 'denounce': pass., + dat. pers. and predicate, ἐμηνίθη Νικάνορι ἀνὴρ φιλοπολίτης 'he was denounced to N. as being a patriotic man' 2M 14.37.

Cf. γνωρίζω, κατα~, προμηνύω, ἀποκαλύπτω.

μήποτε

1. *in order that .. not*, expressing apprehension: + subj.aor., μήποτε συμπαραλημφθῇς 'lest you be taken along together (to destruction)' Ge 19.17; with the main clause suppressed, μ. ἐκτείνῃ τὴν χεῖρα 'he shall never stretch his hand' 3.22; Φύλαξαι σεαυτόν, μ. λαλήσῃς μετὰ Ιακωβ πονηρά 'Beware not to speak wrong things to J.' 31.24, 29; μ. συναντήσῃ ἡμῖν θάνατος ἢ φόνος Ex 5.3; || μή Si 12.12.

2. *out of the fear that, fearing*: + subj., ἐφοβήθη γὰρ εἰπεῖν ὅτι Γυνή μού ἐστιν, μ. ἀποκτείνωσιν αὐτὸν .. 'for he was too scared to say "she is my wife," fearing that they might kill him ..' Ge 20.2, 26.7.

3. introduces a clause expressing apprehension, 'I fear': + ind., Μ. οὐ βούλεται ἡ γυνὴ πορευθῆναι μετ' ἐμοῦ 'the woman may not wish to come with me, I fear' Ge 24.5; + subj., Μ. ἀποθάνω δι' αὐτήν 26.9; 31.31, 42.4, 47.18, 50.15, Ex 19.21, 32.12, 34.15, Nu 16.34. **b**. indicates a fear which might become a reality: + subj., μ. ἐπὶ τὴν γῆν πέσῃ 'should they, Heaven forbid, fall to the ground' Ep Je 26. **c**. introduces a subordinate clause of fear: εὐλαβήθη, μ. οὐκ ἐάσῃ αὐτὸν .. 'he feared that he might not allow him to ..' 1M 12.40.

4. introduces a noun clause giving contents of a negative wish or command: γνώμη ἐτέθη μ... 'a command was issued that ..' 2E 6.8.

5. *perhaps, perchance*: μ. ἀγνόημά ἐστιν 'perhaps it's a mistake' Ge 43.12; Jd 3.24, Jb 1.5.

μήπως.ʃ

to avert the eventuality that: πρόσεχε μήπως ὀλίσθῃς 'Watch out in case you slip' Si 28.26. Cf. μή.

μηρίον, ου. n. Alw. pl.

thigh: of sacrificial animal, Le 3.4; Jb 15.17. Cf. μηρός.

μηρός, οῦ. m.

1. *thigh*: θὲς τὴν χεῖρά σου ὑπὸ τὸν ~όν μου Ge 24.2 (in a ritual of swearing an oath); πλάτος ~οῦ 'hip joint(?)' 32.25; ἀπὸ ὀσφύος ἕως ~ῶν 'from the hips down to the thighs' Ex 28.38; involved in sexual intercourse, Nu 5.21.

2. pl., *loins*: as seat of procreative power, οἱ ἐξελθόντες ἐκ τῶν ~ῶν αὐτοῦ 'his offspring' Ge 46.26, with ἐκπορεύομαι Jd 8.30; ἐτέχθησαν ἐπὶ ~ῶν Ιωσηφ 'were born ..' Ge 50.23; mother's, De 28.57. **b**. where a sword is worn: Ps 44.4. ***c**. *an area that lies deep inside* or *at the base of*: ὄρους 'of mountain(s)' Jd 19.1; ἐπὶ ~ὸν τοῦ θυσιαστηρίου 4K 16.14.

Cf. μηρίον.

μηρυκισμός, οῦ. m. *

cud: κτῆνος .. ἀνάγον ~όν 'animal .. chewing the cud' Le 11.3; ~ὸν οὐ μαρυκᾶται 'does not chew the cud' 11.26, sim. De 14.8. Cf. μαρυκάομαι.

μηρύομαι.ʃ

wind off thread of: + acc., ἔρια 'wool' Pr 31.13.

μήτε.ʃ

Shows that the negation applies equally to both coterminous constituents, and is repeated: ὅπως μηδεὶς μήτε δικάζηται μήτε ἐλέγχῃ μηδείς 'so that nobody either pleads or reproaches' Ho 4.4, ὅπως μ. ἀγοράζωσι μ. πωλῶσι 'so that it could neither buy nor sell' 1M 12.36; w. a single μ., 2M 10.13. Cf. μή and οὐτέ.

μήτηρ, τρός, voc. μῆτερ. f.

female parent, 'mother': one who gives birth to a child, Ho 2.5 (|| τεκοῦσα); || τέκνον, 10.14; deserving of respect, Ex 20.12 (|| πατήρ), Mi 7.6 (|| θυγάτηρ); ὁ πατὴρ αὐτοῦ καὶ ἡ μ. αὐτοῦ οἱ γεννήσαντες αὐτόν 'his father and his mother who produced him' Zc 13.3; not necessarily sbd's wife, Ho 2.2; of an animal, Ex 34.26. **b**. *ultimate origin*: ὅτι αὕτη μ. πάντων τῶν ζώντων 'because this is the mother of all living beings' Ge 3.20, cf. μ. πάντων Si 40.1 w. ref. to the earth; τῆς ἀγαπήσεως .. φόβου .. γνώσεως .. ἐλπίδος 24.18¶. **c**. *leading female figure and patron*: w. ref. to Deborah, Jd 5.7.

Cf. πατήρ, πολυμήτωρ.

μήτρα, ας. f.

womb: female reproductive organ, συνέκλεισαν .. πᾶσαν ~αν 'closed every womb' Ge 20.18; ἤνοιξεν τὴν ~αν αὐτῆς 29.31 (resulting in pregnancy); εὐλογίαι μαστῶν καὶ ~ας 'blessings of breasts and ..' 49.25; πρωτογενὲς διανοῖγον πᾶσαν ~αν Ex 13.2; ἔκτρωμα ἐκπορευόμενον ἐκ ~ας μητρός 'an aborted foetus ..' Nu 12.12, Jb 3.16; ~αν ἀτεκνοῦσαν 'infertile womb' Ho 9.14 (|| μαστοὶ ξηροί); || κοιλία μητρός Ps 21.11; || γαστήρ 57.4. **b**. seat of emotions: ἐταράχθη ἡ μήτρα αὐτῆς 'she was emotionally agitated' 3K 3.26.

Cf. κοιλία, μαστός.

μητρόπολις, εως. f.

chief city of a region: Jo 14.15, μ. πιστὴ Σιων 'a loyal metropolis, Zion' Is 1.26 (|| πόλις vs. 21); pl. Es 9.19 o' (|| χώρα ἔξω 'the outlying countryside'). Cf. πόλις.

μητρῷος, α, ον.ʃ

having to do with mother: *s* γαστήρ 'belly' 4M 13.19. Cf. πατρῷος.

μηχανάομαι; pf.ptc.pass. μεμηχανημένος.

1. *to plot*: + dat.pers.incom., Es E 3.

2. *to devise means and plans to achieve* an end: + acc. rei, ἀσφάλειαν 'secure custody' 3M 5.5.

Cf. μηχανή, μηχανεύω.

μηχανεύω: pf.ptc.pass. μεμηχανευμένος.ʃ

to devise means and plans to achieve an end: + cogn. acc., μηχανήν 'engine of war' 2C 26.15; 3M 6.22. Cf. μηχανάομαι, μηχανή: Renehan 2.102.

μηχανή, ῆς. f.

1. *engine of war*: 1M 5.30 (+ κλίμαξ 'ladder'), 6.20 (+ βελόστασις 'siege tower').

2. *mechanical device*: 1M 6.37.

3. *plan designed to achieve sth*: ἐκφυγῆς 'for escape' 3M 4.19.

Cf. μηχανάομαι, μηχανεύω.

μηχάνημα, ατος. n.ʃ

elaborate construction: attached to funerary pyramids, 1M 13.29 (or foundation to build on, Abel 1948.190f.); engine of war, 4M 7.4.

μιαίνω: fut. μιανῶ, pass. μιανθήσομαι; aor. ἐμίανα, inf. μιᾶναι, impv. μίανον, pass. ἐμιάνθην, subj.act. μιάνω, pass. μιανθῶ, inf. μιανθῆναι; pf.pass. μεμίαμμαι, ptc. μεμιαμμένος.

1. *to taint, defile*: of religious, ceremonial or cultic pollution, Ho 9.4; opp. ἁγιάζω Hg 2.13*ter*; 2.14; and || βδελύσσω Le 11.43; and || βεβηλόω 20.3; ἐν αὐτοῖς 'through them' 22.8; ***o*** stone altar, Ex 20.25; τὰς ψυχὰς ὑμῶν Le 11.44; τὴν σκηνὴν κυρίου Nu 19.13; τὸν ναὸν τὸν ἅγιόν σου Ps 78.1, τὸ ἱερόν 1E 1.47, τὰ ἅγιά μου Is 43.28, τὴν κληρονομίαν μου 47.6; τὴν γῆν Nu 35.34, De 21.23, 24.4; temple, Je 7.30; pagan temple, 4K 23.13; sites of pagan cult, 23.8, 10; τὸ στόμα μου (which might utter words of infidelity) 4M 5.36. **b**. religious disloyalty compared to marital infidelity, || ἐκπορνεύω Ho 5.3, || πορνεία 6.10; humans and pass., Le 18.24. **c**. of illicit sexual intercourse, Nu 5.13; sleeping with sbd else's unbetrothed daughter: τὴν θυγατέρα αὐτοῦ Ge 34.5, νύμφην .. ἐν ἀσεβείᾳ 'daughter-in-law illicitly' Ez 22.11, ἀνδρὸς γυναῖκα Jb 31.11; στρωμνήν 'bed' Ge 49.4 (with father's concubine); pass. and of a remarried divorcee, De 24.4.

2. *to declare defiled*: ritually and + dat. cogn., μιάνσει μιανεῖ αὐτὸν ὁ ἱερεύς 'the priest shall surely pronounce him [= a leper] defiled' Le 13.44 (:: καθαρίζω vs. 6), 59; pass. 13.14.

Cf. μίανσις, μίασμα, μιασμός, ἐκ~, συμμιαίνω, βεβηλόω, ἁγιάζω: Trench 110f.

μιαιόω: aor. ἐμιαίωσα.ʃ

= μιαίνω **1**: + acc. pers., PSol 2.13.

μιαιφονία, ας.ʃ

murderousness: 4M 10.11 (+ ἀσέβεια 'impiety'), 9.9. Cf. μιαιφόνος.

μιαιφόνος, ον.ʃ

murderous: subst.m., *s* hum., 2M 4.38, 12.6. Cf. φονεύς, μιαιφονία.

μίανσις, εως. f.ʃ *

v.n. of μιαίνω **1**: μιάνσει μιανεῖ αὐτὸν ὁ ἱερεύς 'the priest shall surely pronounce him defiled' Le 13.44. Cf. μιαίνω, μίασμα, μιασμός.

μιαρός: ⇒ μιερός.

μιαροφαγέω: aor. ἐμιαροφάγησα, inf. ~φαγῆσαι, opt.1pl ~φαγήσαιμεν.*

to eat ritually unclean food: abs., 4M 5.3, 25.

μιαροφαγία, ας. f.

v.n. of μιαροφαγέω: 4M 5.27.

μίασμα, ατος. n.ʃ

1. v.n. of μιαίνω **1**: in cultic sense, Le 7.8; sexually violating a woman, Ju 9.2, εἰς μ. καὶ αἰσχύνην 13.16; religious, μ. αἵματος 9.4.

2. *that which defiles*: religious, Je 39.34, Ez 33.31; ἐκαθάρισεν τὴν ἄκραν ἀπὸ τῶν ~άτων 1M 13.50.

Cf. μιαίνω, μιασμός.

μιασμός, οῦ. m.ʃ *

v.n. of μιαίνω **1**: ψυχῶν Wi 14.26; λίθοι τοῦ ~οῦ (placed in a temple) 1M 4.43. Cf. μιαίνω.

μίγμα.⇒ μεῖγμα.

μίγνυμι: aor. ἔμιξα, pass. ἐμίγην, impv.2pl μ(ε)ίχθητε; pf.ptc.pass. μεμιγμένος.

to mix: + acc. οὐκ ἔμιξεν αὐτὰ εἰς τὰ πρόβατα Λαβαν 'he did not mix them with L.'s flock' Ge 30.40; θυμίαμα .. μεμιγμένον 'incense .. consisting of multiple ingredients' Ex 30.35. **b**. pass. as mid., *to mingle oneself, associate oneself*: ἐν τοῖς ἔθνεσιν Ps 105.35; μείχθητε τῷ κυρίῳ μου τῷ βασιλεῖ Ἀσσυρίων 'Join the side of my lord, the ..' 4K 18.23 (= Is 36.8); + dat. pers., ἀνόμῳ 'the lawless' Pr 14.16 (pres., cf. Renehan 1.135).

Cf. ἀνα~, κατα~, παρα~, προσ~, συμμίγνυμι, μίσγω, ἐπιμίξ, παμμιγής, κιρνάω, συγκεράννυμι, σύνθεσις, φύρω, ἀμιξία: Schmidt 4.650-6; Denooz.

μιερός, ά, όν. Later form of μιαρός.

abominable, repulsive: morally, *s* hum., 2M 4.19; hum. hand, 5.16 (‖ βέβηλος); ritually, foods 4M 4.26. Cf. παμμίαρος.

μικρολόγος, ον.ʃ

concerned about petty details of book-keeping: *s* hum., Si 14.3.

μικρός, ά, όν.

small: *s* amount, ~ὰ βρώματα Ge 42.2; ~ὸν μέτρον 'a small measure' Am 8.5, ἐν ~ῷ θυμῷ 'with slight anger' Is 54.8; ἡμέρας ~άς 'few days' Zc 4.10, χρόνον ~όν 'for a while' Is 54.7; of time and used subst., ἔτι ~όν 'yet in a while' Ho 1.4, κοπάσουσιν ~όν 'they will stop a while' 8.10, ~ὸν ὅσον ὅσον 'only just a while' Is 26.20 (cf. LSJ s.v. ὅσος **IV 2**), πρὸ ~οῦ 'a short while ago' Wi 15.8 (:: μετ' ὀλίγon), = ~ῷ πρότερον 2M 3.30, 6.29, 9.10; size, πόλις Ge 19.20; οἶκος Am 6.11 (:: μέγας); social standing, ἀπὸ μεγάλου αὐτῶν ἕως ~οῦ αὐτῶν Jn 3.5; importance, 'insignificant, of little consequence' Nu 16.9, 13; Je 29.16 (‖ ὀλιγοστός Ob 2), Ez 16.20, *s* ἁμαρτία 4M 5.19; subst. n.(?) pl. ἐπὶ ~οῖς καὶ μεγάλοις 'in matters whether minor or major' 5.20; μικροῦ adv., 'by a small margin, nearly', μικροῦ ἐκοιμήθη τις τοῦ γένους μου .. 'one of my household has nearly lain ..' Ge 26.10; κατὰ ~όν Si 19.1, κατὰ ~ὸν ~όν 'little by little, by degrees' Ex 23.30, De 7.22 (latter:: τὸ τάχος); παρὰ ~όν 'almost' Ps 72.2 (‖ παρ' ὀλίγον), PSol 16.1 (ditt. vs. 2). **b**. juxtaposed with μέγας, marks the whole gamut: μικρὸν ἢ μέγα 'whether significant or trivial' Nu 22.18, see further under μέγας; ἀπὸ μεγάλου αὐτῶν ἕως ~οῦ αὐτῶν Jn 3.5.

Cf. μικρῶς, μικρότης, μέγας, μειόω, ὀλίγος, ἐλάσσων, ἐλαφρός: Shipp 388-90.

μικρότης, ητος. f.

**small object*: w. ref. to small finger (?), 3K 12.10, 24[r] (‖ 2C 10.10 μικρὸς δάκτυλος). Cf. μικρός.

μικρύνω.⇒ σμικρύνω.

μικρῶς. adv.ʃ

to a small degree: οὐ μ. 'in no small degree' 2M 14.8. Cf. μικρός, μεγάλως.

μίλτος, ου. m.ʃ

red earth, red ochre: χρίω ἐν ~ῳ Je 22.14; καταχρίω ~ῳ Wi 13.14 (‖ φῦκος'orchil').

μιμέομαι: aor.impv.2pl μιμήσασθε, subj. μιμήσωμαι.

to emulate: + acc., (moral) virtue Wi 4.2; τινα 4M 9.23. Cf. μίμημα.

μίμημα, ατος. n.ʃ

that which is made as imitation of: + gen., Wi 9.8. Cf. μιμέομαι, ἀπείκασμα.

μιμνῄσκομαι: fut. μνησθήσομαι; aor. ἐμνήσθην, ptc. μνησθείς, sub. μνησθῶ, inf. μνησθῆναι, impv. μνήσθητι, opt.3s μνησθείη; pf. μέμνημαι, ptc. μεμνημένος; plpf.mid. ἐμεμνήμην.

1. *to recall to mind, to remind oneself*, often followed by an action whether favourable or unfavourable to a person so remembered: abs. De 9.7 (:: ἐπιλανθάνω), Na 2.6; + gen. rei vel pers., ἐμνήσθη ὁ θεὸς τοῦ Νωε Ge 8.1; ἐμνήσθη ὁ θεὸς τῆς Ραχηλ, καὶ ἐπήκουσεν αὐτῆς ὁ θεός, καὶ ἀνέῳξεν αὐτῆς τὴν μήτραν 'God remembered R., God paid attention to her, and opened her womb' 30.22, μνήσθητί μου, ὁ θεὸς ἡμῶν, εἰς ἀγαθωσύνην Ne 13.31; κύριος ἐμνήσθη ἡμῶν καὶ εὐλόγησεν ἡμᾶς Ps 113.20; τῆς διαθήκης μου Ge 9.15; τῆς διαθήκης ὑμῶν Ex 6.5; ἐλέους Hb 3.2, and + dat. com., τοῦ ἐλέους αὐτοῦ τῷ Ιακωβ Ps 97.3; τοῦ κυρίου Jn 2.8, ἐν θλίψει ἐμνήσθην σου Is 26.16, οὐ μὴ μνησθήσομαι ἁμαρτιῶν αὐτῶν Je 40.8 (Heb: "I shall forgive .."); + acc. rei, διαθήκην αἰώνιον Ge 9.16, sim. Si 28.7 (‖ + gen.); πάσας τὰς κακίας αὐτῶν Ho 7.2; τὰς ἀδικίας αὐτῶν 8.13, 9.9 (foll. by punitive action), ἁμαρτίας .. καὶ ἀγνοίας μου μὴ μνησθῇς Ps 24.7, τὰ ἐλέη σου 24.6; καιρόν Si 18.24, 25. **b**. evocation of the past, ὅσα ἐποίησεν De 7.18, Ju 8.26; ἡμέρας αἰῶνος 'days of old' 32.7, τοὺς ἰχθύας Nu 11.5, Αἰγύπτου Ez 23.27; τῆς Σιων Ps 136.1; + gen. pers. and acc. rei, τῶν υἱῶν Εδωμ τὴν ἡμέραν Ιερουσαλημ 'the Edomites in connection with the day of J.' 136.7, μου εἰς ἀγαθὸν πάντα, ὅσα ἐποίησα .. Ne 5.19, cf. μου .. ἐν ταύτῃ, .. ὃ ἐποίησα .. 13.14; + gen. pers. and gen. rei, ἡμῶν ἀνομιῶν ἀρχαίων Ps 78.8; + ptc., μνήσθητι ἑστηκότος μου .. 'my standing ..' Je 18.20; + dat. (incom.?). pers. + ἐπί τινι – ἐπὶ ἀγχιστείᾳ τῆς ἱερατείας καὶ διαθήκῃ τῆς ἱερατείας 'over their dismissal from priesthood and the covenant of ..' Ne 13.29 (+ τοὺς Λευίτας[!]), τῷ Τωβίᾳ .. ὡς τὰ ποιήματα αὐτοῦ 6.14; + περί τινος, To 4.1 𝔊[I] (|| 𝔊[II] + gen.); || ἀναβαίνει ἐπέρχεται ἐπὶ τὴν καρδίαν τινος Is 65.17; pass., Ez 3.20. **c**. + indir. question: Mi 6.5, Jb 4.7. **d**. + ὅτι - μνήσθητι ὅτι μεγάλα ἐστὶν αὐτοῦ τὰ ἔργα Jb 36.24, ὅτι σάρξ εἰσιν Ps 77.39; 77.35. **e**. what is to be remembered is indicated by a syndetic verb structure: μνησθῆτε καὶ ποιήσητε πάσας τὰς ἐντολάς μου Nu 15.40 || μνησθήσεσθε πασῶν τῶν ἐντολῶν κυρίου καὶ ποιήσετε αὐτάς 15.39. **f**. + inf., Is 64.7; + τοῦ inf., Ps 108.16. **g**. That some action is expected of the person addressed (i.e. the subject of an impv.) or implicitly requested is clear in πρὸς ταῦτα μνήσθητί μου, ὁ θεός 'Remember me (and reward me) accordingly, O God' Ne 13.22; on πρὸς ταῦτα, see under πρός **III 9**. So poss. in Ne 5.19, 13.14, 29, 31 mentioned above under **a** and **b**; κατὰ τὸ ἔλεός σου μνήσθητί μου Ps 24.7, μνήσθητι, κύριε, ὡς ἐπορεύθην ἐνώπιόν σου Is 38.3.

2. *to keep in mind so as not to forget, heed*: + acc., τὴν ἡμέραν τῶν σαββάτων Ex 20.8, μνήσθητι ταῦτα .. μὴ ἐπιλανθάνου μου Is 44.21; + gen., διαθήκης Am 1.9; νόμου Ma 4.6; μου Zc 10.9; opp. ἐπιλανθάνω 'to forget' Ps 136.6; + ὅτι, De 5.15, 16.12. **b**. pass., poss. **3**: ὄνομα αὐτοῦ οὐ μὴ μνησθῇ οὐκέτι Je 11.19, sim. Ho 2.17, Ps 82.5; Ez 18.22, 24, PSol 3.11.

3. *to make mention*: + acc. rei and dat. pers., Ps 118.49; + περί τινος πρός τινα - μνησθήσῃ περὶ ἐμοῦ πρὸς Φαραω 'you shall make mention of me to Pharaoh' Ge 40.14, ἐμνήσθη πρὸς αὐτὸν περὶ τοῦ Δανιηλ Da LXX 5.10; + gen., ἐν παντὶ καιρῷ ἀδιαλείπτως .. μιμνῃσκόμεθα ὑμῶν .. ὡς δέον ἐστὶ καὶ πρέπον μνημονεύειν ἀδελφῶν 'on every occasion we mention you incessantly .. as it is obligatory and appropriate to remember brothers' 1M 12.11, cf. 1Thes 1.2f.; οὐ σιωπήσονται μιμνῃσκόμενοι κυρίου 'will not cease ..' Is 62.6, τῆς δικαιοσύνης σου Ps 70.16, μὴ μνησθῶ τῶν ὀνομάτων αὐτῶν διὰ χειλέων μου 15.4; + dat. pers., 86.4; + ὅτι, Is 12.4 (|| ἀναγγέλλω: or **1d**).

4. *to take notice of and show interest in* or *care about*: + gen., οὐκέτι ἐμνήσθη τῆς Αστιν μνημονεύων οἷα ἐλάλησεν 'he no longer showed interest in A., remembering what she had said' Es 2.1 o'; Ps 8.5, Je 15.15 (|| ἐπισκέπτομαι), Si 16.17.

5. *to take into consideration*: εἰς τὰ μετὰ ταῦτα 'what might be in store (for him)' Si 3.31; + acc., οὐ μέμνηται βασιλέα 1E 3.20, τὸν πατέρα 4.21; τὰ ἔσχατα 'the end' Si 7.36.

6. *to be able to call back into memory, not having forgotten*: οὐκ ἐμνήσθη .. τοῦ Ιωσηφ, ἀλλ' ἐπελάθετο αὐτοῦ '.., but had forgotten about him' Ge 40.23, ἐμνήσθην περὶ τοῦ ἐνυπνίου 'I still remember the dream' Es F 2; + acc., τὰς τρίβους ^τῆς σοφίας^ 'the paths of ..' Ba 3.23.

On the case, see BDF § 175, Helbing, *Kasus.*, 107-9, and Mayser, II 2.209ff.

Cf. μνεία, μνήμη, μνημόσυνον, ἀνα~, ἐπι~, κατα~, ὑπομιμνήσκομαι, προσυπομιμνήσκω, ἀμνησία, ἀμνημονέω, ἐπιλανθάνω: Spicq 2.489-501.

μισάνθρωπος, ον.ʃ

hating mankind: subst.m., *s* hum., 4M 11.4.

μισάρετος, ον.ʃ

hating virtue: subst.m., *s* hum., 4M 11.4. Cf. ἀρέτη.

μίσγω. On the spelling, see BDF § 23 and Walters 31.ʃ

to put together: two liquid substances τί τινι - οἱ κάπηλοί σου μίσγουσι τὸν οἶνον ὕδατι 'your pubkeepers add water to wine' Is 1.22. **b**. by placing sth on sth else (τι ἐπί τινι): αἵματα ἐφ' αἵμασι μίσγουσι Ho 4.2 (i.e. perpetrate repeated murders); see Helbing, *Kasus.*, 251.

Cf. συναναμίσγω, σύμμικτος, (συνανα)μίγνυμι, κεράννυμι.

μισέω: fut. μισήσω, pass. μισηθήσομαι; aor. ἐμίσησα, subj. μισήσω, impv. μίσησον, ptc. μισήσας, pass. μισηθείς, inf. μισῆσαι, pass. μισηθῆναι, subj. μισηθῶ; pf. μεμίσηκα, ptc.pass. μεμισημένος.

1. *to have strong dislike of*: + τινα– ἠγάπησα τὸν Ιακωβ, τὸν δὲ Ησαυ ἐμίσησα Ma 1.2f., + ἐπί τινι 'on account of sth' Wi 12.4; and + a cogn. obj., μῖσος ἄδικον ἐμίσησάν με Ps 24.19, sim. 2K 13.15; *s* enemies – Le 26.17, ἐπὶ τοὺς ἐχθρούς σου καὶ ἐπὶ τοὺς μισοῦντάς σε, οἳ ἐδίωξάν σε De 30.7; *o* wife, μισήσῃ αὐτὴν .. ἐξαποστελεῖ αὐτήν 'should he have developed intense dislike of her, he should divorce her' De 24.3 (|| μὴ εὕρῃ χάριν ἐναντίον αὐτοῦ vs. 1); Ma 2.16; God, Ex 20.5, De 5.9 (:: ἀγαπάω), Nu 10.34, De 32.41 (|| ἐχθρός); pass. μισεῖται 'is disliked' Ge 29.31, + ἐγκαταλείπω Is 60.15; + acc. rei, μεμισήκαμεν τὰ πονηρὰ καὶ ἠγαπήκαμεν τὰ καλά Am 5.15; τὰ καλά Mi 3.2 (:: ζητέω); Am 5.21 (|| ἀπωθέω); τὰς χώρας αὐτῶν 6.8; ὑπερηφανίαν 'haughtiness' Ex 18.21; hollow religiosity, Is 1.14, νόμον Si 36.2; + inf., Pr 17.9; *s* God, διὰ τὸ μισεῖν κύριος ἡμᾶς De 1.27; ἡ ψυχή μου Is 1.14.

2. *to neglect to further the interests of*: τὴν ἑαυτοῦ ψυχὴν Ps 10.5; τὸν υἱὸν αὐτοῦ Pr 13.24 (:: ἀγαπάω). Cf. Mt 6.24, Joh 12.25.

Cf. μισητός, μῖσος, μισάνθροπος, μισάρετος, μισοξενία, μισοπονηρία, ἀγαπάω, ἀπωθέω, ἀπεχθάνομαι, βδελύσσω, στυγέω, φιλέω: Schmidt 3.492-6; Michel, *TDNT* 4.685f.

μισητός, ή, όν.

disliked, hateful: *s* hum., Μισητόν με πεποιήκατε ὥστε πονηρόν με εἶναι πᾶσιν τοῖς κατοικοῦσιν τὴν γῆν Ge 34.30; ἔναντι κυρίου καὶ ἀνθρώπων ὑπερηφανία Si 10.7; θεῷ καὶ ὁ ἀσεβῶν καὶ ἡ ἀσέβεια αὐτοῦ Wi 14.9. Cf. μισέω, ἀπεχθής, στυγνός.

μίσθιος, α, ον.

hired for a pay: subst., pers. 'hireling, hired labourer' - Le 25.50, To 5.12 𝔊I; μ. αὐθημερινός 'day-labourer' Jb 7.1 (|| μισθωτός 7.2), ἐπέτειος 'hired for a year' Si 37.11; || οἰκέτης 7.20; γυνή 'whore' 26.22¶. Cf. μισθός, μισθωτός.

μισθός, οῦ. m.

1. *that which is paid for service rendered*, 'wages': τὸν ~όν μου τρίακοντα ἀργυροῦς Zc 11.12b; μετὰ ~οῦ 'in return for pay' Mi 3.11 (|| μετὰ δώρων and μετὰ ἀργυρίου); ~οὺς συνάγων 'collect pay' Hg 1.6; w. gen. of person to whom payment is due, διάστειλον τὸν ~όν σου πρός με 'State your rate of hire to me' Ge 30.28, εἶπον τίνα σοι ἔσομαι ~ὸν διδόναι To 5.15 𝔊I, ~ὸν τὴν ἡμέραν δραχμήν '.. one drachm per day' ib. 𝔊II; ἀποστεροῦντας ~ὸν μισθωτοῦ 'robbing a hired labourer of his pay' Ma 3.5; due even to beasts, τῶν κτηνῶν Zc 8.10; ἀντὶ τῶν λειτουργιῶν ὑμῶν 'for your services' Nu 18.31; opp. δῶρον To 2.14; ἔστι μ. τοῖς ἔργοις σου Je 38.16; ἐφέτειον ~ὸν τοῦ μισθωτοῦ 'annual wages of the hired labourer' De 15.18. **b**. *profits made from commerce*: ἐμπορία καὶ μ. 'merchandise ..' Is 23.18.

2. *recompense for good moral conduct and loyalty*: given by God, ὁ μισθός σου πολὺς ἔσται σφόδρα Ge 15.1, cf. ὁ μ. σου πλήρης παρὰ κυρίου Ru 2.12 and ὁ μ. ὑμῶν πολὺς ἐν τοῖς οὐρανοῖς Mt 5.12, ἐν κυρίῳ ὁ μ. αὐτῶν [= δίκαιοι] Wi 5.15, εὐσεβοῦς 'of the godly' Si 11.22; Ἔδωκεν ὁ θεὸς τὸν ~όν μου ἀνθ' ὧν ἔδωκα τὴν παιδίσκην μου τῷ ἀνδρί μου Ge 30.18; result of a hard military operation, Ez 29.18, 19; τοῖς σοῖς ἔργοις Je 38.16.

Cf. μισθόω, μίσθωμα, μίσθιος, μισθωτός, ἀμισθί, ἐπίχειρον, ὀψώνιον: Will 1975; Spicq 2.502-15.

μισθόω: aor.mid. ἐμισθωσάμην, ptc. ~θωσάμενος, inf. ~θώσασθαι; pf.mid. μεμίσθωμαι, ptc. μεμισθωμένος.

mid. *to hire for a pay*: + acc., μεμίσθωμαι γάρ σε ἀντὶ τῶν μανδραγορῶν 'for I have hired you in return for the mandrakes' Ge 30.16; ἐπὶ σὲ τὸν Βαλααμ 'B. against you' De 23.4, sim. 2E 4.5 with an obj. understood; + gen. of price, ἐμισθωσάμην ἐμαυτῷ πεντεκαίδεκα ἀργυρίου 'I hired (her) to myself for fifteen (pieces) of silver' Ho 3.2; εἰς βοήθειαν αὐτοῖς 'to assist them' 1M 5.39. **b**. mostly + acc. pers., but ἅρματα 'chariots' 1C 19.6f.

Cf. μισθός, μίσθωμα, μισθωτός: Spicq 2.513-55.

μίσθωμα, ατος. n.

amount of payment agreed on for services to be rendered: paid to a woman for provision of sexual favour (so alw. in the LXX), μ. πόρνης De 23.18 (|| ἄλλαγμα κυνός), ἑταίρας 'of a courtesan' Pr 19.13; pl., μ. πορνείας Mi 1.7; συνάγουσα ~ατα 'collecting fees' Ez 16.31 (*s* harlot), λαμβάνουσα .. 16.32, "gave away what she [= a harlot] had earned" or "paid (her client lovers) an incentive for the bother of coming to please her" 16.33. Cf. μισθός: Mealand 1990.583-7.

μισθωτής. ⇒ μισθωτός.

μισθωτός, ή, όν. m.

hired: δυνάμεις ~αί 'mercenary forces' 1M 6.29. Mostly subst., person hired for pay: μ. ἀναμένων τὸν μισθὸν αὐτοῦ '.. waiting for his pay' Jb 7.2 (|| θεράπων μίσθιος αὐθημερινός 'day-labourer' vs. 1); vulnerable to exploitation, μισθὸς ~οῦ Le 19.13; 22.10 (|| πάροικος), 25.6 (|| παῖς, παιδίσκη, πάροικος); Ma 3.5 (|| χήρα, ὀρφανός, and προσήλυτος); of lowly and humble societal position, Is 16.14, 21.16; mercenary, Je 26.21, Ju 6.2; an expression of contempt, Αχιωρ ~ὲ τοῦ Αμμων 6.5, see Heltzer. Cf. μισθός, μίσθιος: Spicq 1.385f.

μισοξενία, ας.ʃ *

hatred towards alien residents: Wi 19.13.

μισοπονηρέω: aor.inf. ~ρῆσαι, ptc. ~ρήσας.

to hate the wicked or wickedness: Es 7.6 *L*, 2M 4.49. Cf. μισοπονηρία.

μισοπονηρία, ας. f.ʃ

v.n. of μισοπονηρέω: + εὐσέβεια 2M 3.1. Cf. μισοπονηρέω, μισοπόνηρος.

μισοπόνηρος, ον.ʃ

hateful of the wicked or wickedness: *s* God's justice, Es E 4. Cf. μισοπονηρία and φιλάγαθος.

μῖσος, ους. n.

act or attitude of hating: ἐν μίσει 'with hatred' (attitude) Ez 23.29; as cogn. acc., μ. ἄδικον ἐμίσησάν με 'hated me unjustly' Ps 24.19, τέλειον μ. ἐμίσουν αὐτούς 'hated them utterly' 138.22; λόγοι ~ους 'words expressive of hatred' 108.3; + κατάρα 'curse' Je 24.9; opp. ἀγάπησις Ps 108.5; + obj. gen., τοῦ πολεμοῦντος 'warrior' Es C 24; opp. φιλία Pr 10.12. **b**. passively, *hatred borne*: Je 24.9 (|| κατάρα 'curse').

Cf. μισέω, ἀγάπησις, ἀπέχθεια, φιλία.

μίσυβρις, ιος. m./f.ʃ *

hater of ὕβρις (q.v.): *s* God, 3M 6.9. Cf. ὕβρις.

μίτρα, ας. f.

head-dress: of the high priest, Ex 28.33; made of fine linen, 36.36; ἐπέθηκεν τὴν ~αν ἐπὶ τὴν κεφαλὴν αὐτοῦ Le 8.9; Ju 10.3; of a bride-groom, Is 61.10; symbol of dignity and distinction, Ba 5.2, Ez 26.16.

μνᾶ, ᾶς. f. < Heb. מָנֶה.

1. monetary unit, *mina*: = 100 drachmae, 2E 2.69.

2. unit of weight: = 50 shekels, Ez 45.12.

μνεία, ας. f.

1. *being able to call back into memory, not having forgotten*: οὐκέτι ἔσται αὐτῶν μ. 'nobody will remember them any longer' or 'no mention of them will be made any longer' Zc 13.2, sim. Is 23.16, Ez 21.32, 25.10.

2. *act of mentioning*: ~αν ἐποιήσατο τῶν θαυμασίων αὐτοῦ '.. his wonderful deeds' Ps 110.4.

3. *act of calling back into memory, reminding oneself*: ἡμέρας ἐνιαυτοῦ ~αν ποιήσασθε ἐν ὀδυνῇ 'the seasons (of the agricultural calendar) ..' Is 32.10; as dat. cogn., ~ᾳ De 7.18, Je 38.20; as acc. cogn., ~αν μου ποιήσῃ Jb 14.13. **b**. such an act is translated into some reaction: beneficial, Ba 4.27, see vs. 29; χαίροντας τῇ τοῦ θεοῦ ~ᾳ 'rejoicing at having been remembered by God' 5.5.

4. *that which is held in one's memory from the past*: ἠλπίσαμεν .. ἐπὶ τῇ ~ᾳ, ᾗ ἐπιθυμεῖ ἡ ψυχὴ ἡμῶν 'we have pinned our hope .. on the reminiscences which our souls cherish so' Is 26.8, καταλύτου μονοημέρου 'of a guest who stayed but a while' Wi 5.14.

Cf. μιμνήσκομαι, μνήμη, λήθη.

μνῆμα, ατος. n.

grave, tomb: Ex 14.11, Nu 11.34; site of divination, Is 65.4 (+ σπήλαιον 'cave'); Ez 37.12 (|| τάφος vs. 13). Cf. μνημεῖον and τάφος.

μνημεῖον, ου. n.

1. *sth that reminds one of a past event*, 'monument': + obj.gen., ἀπιστούσης ψυχῆς μ. ἑστηκυῖα στήλη ἁλός 'a stele of salt standing as a reminder of an incredulous soul' Wi 10.7 (|| μνημόσυνον vs. 8).

2. **tomb, grave*: ἔστησεν Ιακωβ στήλην ἐπὶ τοῦ ~ου αὐτῆς 'J. erected a pillar upon her tomb' Ge 35.20; στήλη ~ου ib.; privately purchased and owned, κτῆσις ~ου 23.9, 49.30; made by excavating (ὀρύσσω), 50.5; a cave (σπήλαιον), 49.30, 50.13; οἶκος ~ων πατέρων μου 'the site of my ancestral graves' Ne 2.3; 2.5 (with πόλις for οἶκος); ἐλατόμησας σεαυτῷ .. μ. καὶ ἐποίησας .. ἐν ὑψηλῷ μ. 'you have hewn yourself a grave .. and .. high up ..' Is 22.16; ἐγερθήσονται οἱ ἐν τοῖς ~οις 'those who are in graves will rise up' 26.19; τόπον ὀνομαστόν, μνημεῖον 'a well-known place, ..' Ez 39.11.

Cf. μνῆμα, πολυανδρεῖον, τρόπαιον, τάφος, ταφή.

μνήμη, ης. f.

1. *that which is remembered from the past*: + obj. gen., τῆς ἁγιωσύνης αὐτοῦ Ps 29.5, 96.12; μ. τοῦ πλήθους τῆς χρηστότητός σου 'the memory of the abundance of your kindness' 144.7; ἡ μ. αὐτῶν ἀπολεῖται 'that which reminds them will vanish' Wi 4.19, αἰώνιος 'eternal' 8.13, τῶν παρελθόντων 'of what happened' 11.12.

2. *capacity to memorise*: 2M 2.25.

3. *being retained in memory*: μνήμης ἀγαθῆς ἀξία 'deserving of fond memory' 2M 7.20; + gen. obj., σου PSol 16.6.

Cf. μιμνήσκω.

μνημονεύω: fut. μνημονεύσω; aor.impv.3s μνημονευσάτω.

1. *to call to one's mind*: ***o*** (acc.) a memorable day, τὴν ἡμέραν ταύτην Ex 13.3; τὰ πρῶτα 'the former things' Is 43.18 (|| συλλογίζομαι); ὑμῶν τε τιμὴν καὶ τὴν εὔνοιαν 'your esteem and goodwill alike' 2M 9.21; τὸν κύριον 2K 14.11B; also + gen., τοῦ κυρίου .. καὶ τὰ κρίματα αὐτοῦ PSol 3.3; + ὡς 'that' 2M 10.6.

2. *to call to sbd else's mind*, 'make mention of': + acc., ἐδεήθη κυρίου μνημονεύων πάντα τὰ ἔργα κυρίου 'implored the Lord ..' Es C 1 o'; + gen., σου Ps 6.6 (|| ἐξομολογέομαι), σου ἐπὶ τῆς στρωμνῆς μου '.. in my bed' 62.7.

3. *to retain in memory without forgetting*: + gen., κυρίου τοῦ θεοῦ To 4.5, μνημόνευε τῶν ἐντολῶν μου καὶ μὴ ἐξαλειφθήτωσαν ἐκ τῆς καρδίας σου 'Remember my laws and let them not be erased from your mind' 4.19 $\mathfrak{G}^{I}$ (|| τὰς ἐντολάς $\mathfrak{G}^{II}$), τῶν ἔργων ἡμῶν Wi 2.4 (|| ἐπιλανθάνω 'to forget'); διαθήκης αὐτοῦ .. λόγον αὐτοῦ 1C 16.15; + acc., ἰσχὺν θεοῦ ἕως αἰῶνος Ju 13.19, οὐκέτι ἐμνήσθη τῆς Αστιν μνημονεύων οἷα ἐλάλησεν 'he no longer showed interest in A., remembering what she had said' Es 2.1 o', ἐν παντὶ καιρῷ ἀδιαλείπτως .. μιμνησκόμεθα ὑμῶν .. ὡς δέον ἐστὶ καὶ πρέπον μνημονεύειν ἀδελφῶν 'on every occasion we mention you incessantly .. as it is obligatory and appropriate to remember brothers' 1M 12.11.

Cf. μιμνήσκομαι, μνημόσυνον.

μνημόσυνος, η, ον.

likely to remain in one's memory: τοῦτό μού ἐστιν ὄνομα αἰώνιον καὶ ~ον γενεῶν γενεαῖς 'this is my eternal and memorable name for many generations to come' Ex 3.15; εἰς ~ον αἰώνιον ἔσται δίκαιος 'the righteous will be remembered for ever' Ps 111.6. **b**. subst., *that which awakens or preserves memory of sth*, 'reminder': ἔσται ἡ ἡμέρα αὕτη ὑμῖν μ. Ex 12.14; || σημεῖον 13.9 (not necessarily phylacteries, see *BA* ad loc.); λίθοι ~ου 28.12; μ. περὶ αὐτῶν 'a reminder of them' ib.; θυσία ~ου ἀναμιμνήσκουσα ἁμαρτίαν 'an offering of remembrance that reminds of a sin' Nu 5.15; ὁ κύριος ὁ θεὸς ὁ παντοκράτωρ ἔσται μ. αὐτοῦ Ho 12.5; ἐξανθήσει ὡς ἄμπελος τὸ μ. αὐτοῦ (obj. gen.) 14.8; βιβλίον ~ου 'a book of memoranda, notebook' Ma 3.16; μ. ἐπιτελούμενον 'a commemorative festival being celebrated' Es 9.27; one's children, Jb 2.9b; prayer, To 12.12; Μωυσῆς, οὗ τὸ μ. ἐν εὐλογίαις 'Moses of blessed memory' Si 45.1, cf. 46.11; pl. γράμματα ~α τῶν ἡμερῶν 'books of historical records' or 'books reminiscent of the past [μ. as adj.]' Es 6.1; Wi 10.8 (|| μνημεῖον vs. 7).

Cf. μιμνήσκομαι, μνημόσυνος, μνημεῖον: Spicq 2.500f.; Daniel 229-37; LSG s.v.

μνησικακέω: aor. ἐμνησικάκησα, subj. μνησικακήσω.

to bear sbd (*ἐπί τινι = Heb. /ʿal/) *a grudge for* sth (τι): abs., ἐμνησικάκησαν καὶ ἐξεδίκησαν δίκην 'they have exacted recompense out of a grudge' Ez 25.12; + acc. rei, κακίαν ἕκαστος τοῦ ἀδελφοῦ μὴ μνησικακείτω 'let not each one bear a grudge against his fellow-man for his evil deed' Zc 7.10; ἐπ' ἐμοί Jl 3.4; + dat. pers., Ge 50.15. Cf. μιμνήσκω, μνησίκακος, ἐνέχω, and κακός.

μνησίκακος, ον.ʃ

revengeful: *s* hum., Pr 12.28. Cf. μνησικακέω.

μνηστεύομαι: fut. ~τεύσομαι; pf. μεμνήστευμαι, ptc. pass. μεμνηστευμένος.

1. *to betroth* (τινά τινι): *s* male person and + acc. pers. (woman), γυναῖκα De 20.7, σοὶ αὐτήν To 6.13 𝔊II; pass. παρθένος μεμνηστευμένη ἀνδρί De 22.23.

2. *to court, seek in marriage*: + acc. (woman), μνηστεύσομαί σε ἐμαυτῷ Ho 2.19; γυναῖκας 1M 3.56.

μογιλάλος, ον.ʃ

having an impediment in one's speech: Is 35.6. Cf. ἰσχνόφωνος.

μόγις. ⇒ μόλις.

μοιχαλίς, ίδος, acc. ~λίν. f.*

adulteress: Ma 3.5 (|| "sorcerers and those who swear by the name of the Lord"); Ho 3.1; of Israel unfaithful to her God, Ez 16.38. Cf. μοιχεία, μοιχεύω, μοιχός.

μοιχάομαι. Alw. pres. or impf.

= μοιχεύω (q.v.): + acts of theft, murder, false testimony etc., Je 7.9; + acc. pers., τὰς γυναῖκας 36.23; *s* woman, Ez 16.32. **b.** fig. of moral depravity: Je 9.2 (|| ἀθετέω); 23.14.

Cf. μοιχεύω.

μοιχεία, ας.ʃ

act of adultery: Ho 2.2 (|| πορνεία); ἀρὰ καὶ ψεῦδος καὶ φόνος καὶ κλοπὴ καὶ μ. 4.2; γάμων ἀταξία, μ. καὶ ἀσέλγεια 'marriage irregularities, .. debauchery' Wi 14.26. Cf. μοιχαλίς.

μοιχεύω: fut. μοιχεύσω; aor. ἐμοίχευσα, pass. ἐμοιχεύθην, subj. mid. μοιχεύσωμαι.

to commit adultery: abs., οὐ μοιχεύσεις Ex 20.13, αἱ νύμφαι ὑμῶν μοιχεύσουσιν 'your daughters-in-law will commit adultery' Ho 4.13 (|| ἐκπορνεύω), ὁ μοιχεύων καὶ ἡ μοιχευομένη Le 20.10, adulterer compared to a hot-glowing baking oven, Ho 7.4; ἐν πορνείᾳ 'in whoredom' Si 23.23; + acc. (partner), γυναῖκα ἀνδρός, ἢ .. γυναῖκα τοῦ πλησίον Le 20.10, τὸ ξύλον καὶ τὸν λίθον Je 3.9 (of pagan cultic practices). Cf. μοιχάομαι, μοιχαλίς, μοιχεία, νοθεύω: Bogner 1941.

μοιχός, οῦ. m.

adulterer: + πόρνη 'harlot' Is 57.3. Cf. μοιχαλίς.

μόλιβος, ου. m. See Shipp 393.

lead (as metal): τοῦ χρυσίου καὶ τοῦ ἀργυρίου καὶ χαλκοῦ καὶ σιδήρου καὶ ~ου καὶ κασσιτέρου Nu 31.22, sim. Ez 22.18, 20, 27.12; ἐν γραφείῳ σιδηρῷ καὶ ~ῳ 'with an iron pen and lead' Jb 19.24¶; τὸν λίθον τοῦ ~ου 'the weight of lead' Zc 5.8; heavy metal, ὑπὲρ ~ον τί βαρυνθήσεται; 'what would be heavier than lead?' Si 22.14, cf. ἔδυσαν ὡσεὶ μ. 'sank like lead' Ex 15.10; comparatively abundant metal, Si 47.18 (|| κασσίτερος 'tin'). Cf. Shipp 393.

μόλις. adv.

only just, scarcely: Pr 11.31, Si 21.20, 26.29. Cf. Barr 1975.

μολόχη, ης. f.ʃ

mallow: Jb 24.24. Cf. Shipp 378; Renehan 2.103.

μόλυνσις, εως. f.ʃ*

v.n. of μολύνω: in religious sense, Je 51.4. Cf. μολύνω, μολυσμός.

μολύνω: fut. μολυνῶ, pass. μολυνθήσομαι; aor. ἐμόλυνα, inf. μολῦναι, pass. ἐμολύνθην, subj. μολυνθῶ; pf.ptc.pass. μεμολυμμένος.

1. *to make physically dirty*, 'stain': τὸν χιτῶνα τῷ αἵματι 'the tunic with the blood' Ge 37.31; by touching pitch, Si 13.1.

2. *to violate* (a woman sexually): αἱ γυναῖκες μολυνθήσονται Zc 14.2.

3. *to defile*: + acc. and morally, γῆ μεμολυμμένη μολυσμῷ τῶν ἀλλογενῶν τῆς γῆς 'a land defiled by defilement through the alien nations of the land' 1E 8.80; ***o*** ὄνομα To 3.15; the temple in Jerusalem, 2M 6.2; τὴν ἑαυτοῦ ψυχήν Si 21.28; αἱ χεῖρες ὑμῶν μεμολυμμέναι αἵματι Is 59.3, ἐν αἵματι La 4.14 (***o*** hum.); Je 12.10 (|| διαφθείρω). **b.** in a cultic sense: ***o*** σκεύη 'vessels' Is 65.4.

Cf. ἀλισγέω, βεβηλόω, κηλιδόω, μιαίνω, ἐμ~, συμμολύνω, μόλυνσις, μολυσμός, ἀμόλυντος, διαφθείρω: Trench 110f.

μολυσμός, οῦ. m.ʃ*
v.n. of μολύνω: γῆ μεμολυμμένη μολυσμῷ 'a land defiled by defilement' 1E 8.80; occasioned by Jerusalem prophets, Je 23.15; 2M 5.27. Cf. μολύνω, μόλυνσις.

μονάζω.ʃ
to be alone: Ps 101.8. Cf. μονή.

μοναρχία, ας. f.ʃ
government by a single ruler: Es 3.17 *L* (o' συναρχία).

μόναρχος, ου. m.ʃ
sole ruler: *s* God, 3M 2.2.

μονή, ῆς. f.ʃ
act of remaining alive: 1M 7.38. Cf. μένω, μονάζω, μονιός.

μόνιμος, η, ον.ʃ
1. *lasting, stable*: *s* mountain, Ge 49.26.
2. subst. n., *fixed abode*: μ. τοῖς σοῖς τέκνοις Je 38.17.

μονιός, όν.ʃ
solitary: subst., μ. ἄγριος 'solitary wild boar' Ps 79.14 (ǁ σῦς). Cf. μόνος, μονή: Shipp 393.

μονογενής, ές.
being the only representative of the kind: *s* the only child, τῷ πατρί μου To 6.15𝔊[II] (𝔊[I] μόνος), + πτωχός Ps 24.16; dear and valuable, + ἀγαπητός Jd 11.34 A; δύο ~εῖς To 8.17; spirit (πνεῦμα) Wi 7.22; subst. f.sg. w. ref. to one's soul and ǁ ψυχή, Ps 21.21, 34.17. Cf. Büchsel, *TDNT* 4.737-9; Pendrick.

μονόζωνος, ον. *
lightly armed: *s* soldier, Jb 29.25¶; 2K 22.30B (*L* πεφραγμένος), 4K 6.23B (*L* πειρατής). Cf. Barthélemy 1963.81f.

μονοήμερος, ον.ʃ
lasting only one day: *s* καταλύτης 'guest' Wi 5.14. Cf. ἡμέρα.

μονόκερως, ωτος. m.
one-horned: *s* wild animal, Nu 23.22; κέρατα ~τος 'horns (pl.!) of..' De 33.17, Ps 21.22. Cf. κέρας: Caird 1969.22f.; LSG s.v.

μονομαχέω: fut. ~χήσω; aor. ἐμονομάχησα.ʃ
battle single-handedly or unaided: 1K 17.10 (duel), Ps 151.1. Cf. μάχομαι.

μόνον. adv.
a. Introduces an additional, qualifying statement: μόνον εἰς τοὺς ἄνδρας τούτους μὴ ποιήσητε μηδὲν ἄδικον 'Only to these men do not do anything unjust' Ge 19.8, μ. τὸν υἱόν μου μὴ ἀποστρέψῃς ἐκεῖ 'only, however, do not take my son back there' 24.8; stressing the most important matter, μ. ὑπάκουσον τῆς φωνῆς μου 27.13, μ. τὴν ψυχὴν αὐτοῦ διαφύλαξον 'only preserve his life' Jb 2.6; μ. μὴ χρονίσῃς 'Don't take too long, though' To 5.8.
b. Attached to an exclusion constituent: at the tail, χωρὶς τῆς γῆς τῶν ἱερέων μόνον 'with the exception of .. only' Ge 47.22, 26; οὐκ ἐνεδύσατο ἀλλογενὴς πλὴν τῶν υἱῶν αὐτοῦ μόνον 'no outsider has worn it except his sons only' Si 45.13; τοῦτο μ. 'this alone' Ex 12.16; De 22.25; τούτοις μ. Wi 16.4; ἔστιν φίλος ὀνόματι μ. φίλος 'there is a friend in name only' Si 37.1; preceding but only in an expression for "not only, .. but also"– οὐ μ. ἄνθρωποι .., ἀλλὰ καὶ τὰ θηρία τοῦ ἀγροῦ 'not only humans .., but also the wild beasts' Ju 11.7, but οὐ τὸν βασιλέα μ... ἀλλὰ καὶ πάντας .. Es 1.16; elliptically, οὐ μ., ἀλλ' ἢ .. 'not only so, but also ..' Wi 19.15; οὐ ταῦτα μ..., ἀλλ' ἢ .. 1M 11.42; μὴ μ... ἀλλὰ καὶ .., 3M 1.29, cf. μόνος **1**.
Cf. μόνος.

μόνορχις, εως. m.ʃ *
having one testicle: hum., Le 21.20.

μόνος, η, ον.
Used mostly predicatively or adverbially–
1. *with the exclusion of any other than*: concording with the preceding noun or pronoun of the entity singled out – nom., σωθεὶς ἐγὼ μόνος 'I as the sole survivor' Jb 1.15, 16; σὺ εἶ ὁ θεὸς μόνος ὁ μέγας Ps 85.10; other cases, τούτου μόνου μὴ φαγεῖν 'not to eat from this alone' Ge 3.17; τῆς δικαιοσύνης σου μόνου Ps 70.16; παρέθηκεν αὐτῷ μόνῳ καὶ καθ' ἑαυτούς 'they set (the meal) for him alone and for them by themsleves' Ge 43.32; ἐπ' ἄρτῳ μόνῳ 'on bread alone' De 8.3; πλὴν κυρίῳ μόνῳ 'except to the Lord alone' Ex 22.20, but cf. οὐκ ἐνεδύσατο ἀλλογενὴς πλὴν τῶν υἱῶν αὐτοῦ μόνον 'no outsider has worn it except his sons only' Si 45.13 (with a genitive-governing preposition πλήν); in an expression "not only .., but also .." – οὐχ ὑμῖν μόνοις ἀλλὰ καὶ τοῖς ὧδε οὖσιν μεθ' ἡμῶν 29.14 (cf. μόνον [indeclinable] **b**). **b**. μόνος preceding: μόνοις δὲ ἐκείνοις Wi 17.21; ἦν μόνη ἡ πεῖρα τῆς ὀργῆς ἱκανή 'only to test the anger sufficed' 18.25; μετὰ δύο μόνων κορασίων 'with only two lasses' Su 15 TH, μόνος αὐτὸς θεός ἐστιν 2M 7.37; μόνον τὸν ὄντα θεόν 'the only one that is God' 4M 5.24 (poss. 'only the God who exists'); 3M 1.11. **c**. the notion of exclusion is reinforced: by the superlative: τόδε τὸ ἔθνος μονώτατον 'this nation, and it alone' Es B 5 o'; μονώτατος ἐπαίρῃ ἐφ' ἡμᾶς 'you are the only one to rise up against us' 1M 10.70; 2K 13.32B, 3M 3.19. **d**. exceptionally (and erroneously?) for a postpositive μόνον (so one MS): ἦσαν υἱοὶ Ισραηλ .. μόνοι ποιοῦντες τὸ πονηρὸν .. '.. were practising only wicked things ..' Je 39.30.
2. *alone, unaccompanied, unaided*: οὐ καλὸν εἶναι τὸν ἄνθρωπον μόνον 'it is not good for the

man to be alone' Ge 2.18; βοήθησόν μοι τῇ μόνῃ καὶ μὴ ἐχούσῃ βοηθὸν εἰ μὴ σέ 'Help me who am alone and have no helper but for you' Es C 14 o'; αὐτὴν δυνήσονται εὑρεῖν μόνην 'they would be able to find her alone' Su 14 TH; κατελείφθη μόνος Νωε 'Noah remained alone' Ge 7.23; ὑπελείφθη Ιακωβ μόνος 32.24; αὐτὸς μόνος καταλέλειπται 'he alone has been left' 42.38; ἔστησεν .. ἑπτὰ ἀμνάδας προβάτων μόνας 'set seven female lambs by themselves' 21.28; κάθησαι μόνος 'you sit alone' Ex 18.14, οὐ δυνήσομαι ἐγὼ μόνος φέρειν 'I could not bear (them) single-handed' Nu 11.14; σωθήσῃ μόνη 'you can save your skin on your own' Es 4.13; μόνος κτεῖναι αὐτόν 'to kill him single-handed' 3M 1.2; ἐγὼ μόνος εἰμὶ τῷ πατρί 'I am the only child of my father' To 6.15 𝔊I (𝔊II μονογενής); σὺ εἶ μόνος Es C 14 o' (*L* μόνος βοηθός); super., "all alone" Jd 3.20. **b**. only rarely attributively: λαὸς μόνος 'a lone people' Nu 23.9; ὁ μόνος βασιλεύς .. ὁ μόνος χορηγός, ὁ μόνος δίκαιος 'the sole king, the only bountiful ..' 2M 1.24f.; τὴν μόνην 'the solitary (widow)' Ba 4.16.

3. κατὰ μόνας 'separately': ἔδωκεν .. ποίμνιον κατὰ μόνας 'positioned flocks in separate groups' Ge 32.16; ὑψῶσαι ὕψος μέγα ἀνὰ μέσον τῆς ἄκρας καὶ τῆς πόλεως εἰς τὸ διαχωρίσαι αὐτὴν τῆς πόλεως, ἵνα ᾖ αὐτὴ κατὰ μόνας 'to raise a high partition between the citadel and the city in order to separate it from the city so that the latter might be isolated' 1M 12.36; κ. μ. ἐπ' ἐλπίδι κατῴκισάς με 'you allowed me to dwell alone [i.e. secluded away from enemies] and in hope' Ps 4.9, cf. κ. μ. εἰμὶ ἐγώ 140.10, κ. μ. ἐκαθήμην Je 15.17, καθήσεται κ. μ. La 3.28; ὁ πλάσας κ. μ. τὰς καρδίας αὐτῶν 'one who moulded in solitude their hearts' (or: 'one by one' –Vulg. *sigillatim*) Ps 32.15; οἶνον κ. μ. πίνειν 'to drink wine neat (!), i.e. not mixed with water' 2M 15.39. Cf. κατά **II 9**.

Cf. μόνον, μόνωσις, μονάζω, μονιός, εἷς, ἔρημος: Schmidt 4.535; Delling 473f.

μονότροπος, ον.ʃ

living alone: *s* hum., Ps 67.7.

μονοφαγία, ας. f.ʃ *

act of eating alone (without sharing with others?): 4M 1.27. Cf. μονοφάγος.

μονοφάγος, ον.ʃ *

given to μονοφαγία (q.v.): 4M 2.7. Cf. μονοφαγία.

μόνωσις, εως. f.ʃ

state of being alone: ἀτεκνίας 'of childlessness' PSol 4.18. Cf. μόνος.

μόρον, ου. n.ʃ

black mulberry: 1M 6.34.

μόρος, ου. m.

1. *fate*: 2M 9.28.

2. violent *death*: 3M 3.1, 5.2.

Cf. τύχη.

μορφή, ῆς. f.

1. *shape, form*: ἀνδρός Is 44.13; ὡς εἶδος ~ῆς υἱῶν βασιλέων 'having the features of princes' Jd 8.18A; almost = 'body,' + ψυχή 4M 15.4.

2. *a way sth or sbd looks*, 'appearance': ἡ μ. τοῦ προσώπου αὐτοῦ ἠλλοιώθη 'the appearance of his face changed' Da 3.19 LXX (TH: ὄψις).

***3**. *favourable estimation* on the part of sbd else: χάρις καὶ μ. 'favour and good standing' To 1.13.

Cf. εἶδος, εἰκών, ἰδέα, ὄψις, ἄμορφος, ῥυθμός, σχῆμα: Schmidt 4.349-54; Trench 262-6; Wallace; Behm, *TDNT* 4.742-6; Spicq 1973; ibid. 2.52-5.

μοσχάριον, ου. n.

little (?) *calf*: one of βόεις, and slaughtered for meat – μ. ἁπαλὸν καὶ καλόν 'tender and good' Ge 18.7; as sacrificial offering, Ex 24.5; μ. ἐκ βοῶν 29.1; ~α ἐκ δεσμῶν ἀνειμένα 'calves let loose from tethers' Ma 4.2; || ἔριφος 'kid' Am 6.4; μ. καὶ ταῦρος καὶ λέων '.. and a bull and a lion' Is 11.6. Cf. μόσχος, βοῦς: Lee 108f.

μόσχευμα, ατος. n.ʃ

seedling taken off and planted (LSJ): Wi 4.3.

μόσχος, ου. m. or f.

the young of cattle, calf: sacrificial animal and || πρόβατον Ho 5.6; || αἴξ, πρόβατον Le 17.3; ἐν τοῖς ἐνιαυσίοις 'with one-year-old calves' Mi 6.6 (|| ὁλοκαυτώματα); μ. ἐκ βοῶν Le 16.3, Nu 28.11, De 14.4; object of idolatrous worship, μ. χωνευτός 'molten ..' Ex 32.4; Ho 8.5, 6, 10.5, 13.2; part of nomad's possessions, ἐγένετο αὐτῷ πρόβατα καὶ ~οι καὶ ὄνοι Ge 12.16 (along with παῖδες καὶ παιδίσκαι, ἡμίονοι καὶ κάμηλοι); food, + κριός, τράγος Ez 39.18; three years old, 1K 1.24. The term can refer to six to seven years olds: Scherer 580. Cf. μοσχάριον and βοῦς.

μοτόω: fut. μοτώσω.ʃ

to plug a wound with lint (LSJ): + acc. pers. Ho 6.1 (|| ἰάομαι). See LSG s.v.

μουσικός, ή, όν. Alw. subst.

Subs.n.pl., *music*: as a form of entertainment, μετ' εὐφροσύνης καὶ μετὰ ~ῶν, τυμπάνων καὶ κιθάρας Ge 31.27; ἐκωθωνίζοντο μετὰ ~ῶν καὶ χαρᾶς 'kept drinking hard with music and joy' 1E 4.63; μετὰ ~ῶν, τυμπάνων καὶ αὐλῶν '.. timbrels and flutes' (or: 'musical instruments, [such as] ..') 5.2; μουσικὰ ἐν πένθει 'music in time of mourning' Si 22.6 (sth incongruous); σύγκριμα ~ῶν 'music concert' 35.5, μέλος ~ῶν 'melody of ..' 35.6, οἶνος καὶ ~ὰ εὐφραίνουσιν καρδίαν '.. make for a cheerful heart' 40.20, ὡς ~ὰ ἐν συμποσίῳ οἴνου '.. in a drinking party' 49.1; || ψαλτήρια Ez 26.13; παντὸς ἤχους ~ῶν 'every kind of musical sound' Da LXX 3.7. **b**. musical instruments used in cultic service, οἱ ἱερεῖς ἐστολισμένοι μετὰ

~ῶν καὶ σαλπίγγων 'the priests dressed in a uniform with .. trumpets' 1E 5.57; μετὰ τυμπάνων καὶ ~ῶν 1M 9.39; μετεστράφη .. φωνὴ ~ῶν αὐτῶν εἰς θρῆνον 'their musical sound turned into a dirge' 9.41.

μοχθέω: aor. ἐμόχθησα, subj. μοχθήσω.
to toil, work hard: πονεῖτε καὶ μοχθεῖτε 1E 4.22; τὸν οἶνόν σου ἐφ' ᾧ ἐμόχθησας 'your wine, on which you laboured so hard' Is 62.8; La 3.5. Cf. μόχθος, κοπιάω, πονέω.

μοχθηρός, ά, όν.ʃ
liable to cause severe mental distress: Si 26.5; ἀκοὴ ~ά 'distressful to listen to' 27.15. Cf. μόχθος.

μόχθος, ου. m.
physical hardship, hard work, often pl.: πάντα τὸν ~ον τὸν γενόμενον αὐτοῖς ἐν τῇ ὁδῷ 'all the hardship that had befallen them on the way' Ex 18.8; πάντα τὸν ~ον τὸν εὑρόντα ἡμᾶς Nu 20.14, sim. Ne 9.32; ‖ πόνος Nu 23.21, Wi 10.10; ‖ ταπείνωσις, θλιμμός De 26.7; κατατείνω τινα ἐν ~ῳ 'overwork sbd' Le 25.43, 46, 53, cf. τὸ ἰσχυρὸν κατειργάσασθε ~ῳ 'you worked the strong hard' Ez 34.4; ἐκοπίασα μετὰ ~ων .. ἵνα ἀναπαύσωμαι τῶν ~ων καὶ τῶν ὀδυνῶν 'I toiled hard .. so that I might have respite from the toil and agony' Jb 2.9; τῶν κατ' ἐρημίαν ἐργάτης ~ων 'a labourer toiling away alone' Wi 17.17; ‖ ταλαιπωρία 'misery' Je 28.35. Often with πᾶς or σύμπας. ***b**. *fruits of hard work*: δώσω τὸν ~ον αὐτῶν δικαίως Is 61.8; in the form of agricultural produce and offspring, ἡ Αἰσχύνη κατανάλωσε τοὺς ~ους τῶν πατέρων ἡμῶν 'the Shame has consumed ..' Je 3.24; λήμψονται πάντας τοὺς πόνους σου καὶ τοὺς ~ους σου Ez 23.29; Ec 2.19.
Cf. κόπος, κακοπάθεια, πόνος, μοχθέω, μοχθηρός, ἐπί~, κακόμοχθος: Lightfoot 1895.26; Schmidt 2.624; Spicq 2.526f.

μοχλός, οῦ. m.
long piece of hard material placed across: made from acacia wood and joining two columns securely, Ex 26.26; on a door, serving to keep intruders out, Jn 2.7; Am 1.5, Na 3.13; iron bolts, Is 45.2; πύλαι καὶ ~οί 'gates and bolts' De 3.5, θύρα καὶ μ. Si 28.25, τῶν πυλῶν Ps 147.2. Cf. κλεῖθρον.

μυαλόω: pf.ptc.pass. μεμυαλωμένος.ʃ*
to stuff with marrow: ὁλοκαυτώματα μεμυαλωμένα 'whole burnt-offerings stuffed with marrow' Ps 65.15. Cf. μυελός.

μυγαλῆ, ῆς. f.ʃ
shrew-mouse: ceremonially unclean, Le 11.30.

μυελός, οῦ. m.ʃ
marrow: ‖ ἔγκατα 'inwards' Jb 21.24; τὰ ὀστᾶ αὐτοῦ ἐμπλήσει ~οῦ 'his bones he will fill with marrow' 33.24. **b**. fig., *choice food*: φάγεσθε τὸν ~ὸν τῆς γῆς Ge 45.18.
Cf. μυαλόω.

μυέω: pf.ptc.pass. μεμυημένος.ʃ
to initiate into the mysteries: κατὰ τὰς τελετάς 'in accordance with the mystic rites' 3M 2.30.

μυθολόγος, ου. m.ʃ
story-teller: Ba 3.23. Cf. μῦθος.

μῦθος, ου. m.ʃ
story told for entertainment: Si 20.19. Cf. μυθολόγος: Trench 337-9; Stählin, *TDNT* 4.765-9; Spicq 2.528-33.

μυῖα, ας. f.
fly: buzzing, Is 7.18 (‖ μέλισσα 'bee'); delivers a deadly sting, Wi 16.9 (‖ ἀκρίς 'locust'). Cf. Shipp 394.

μυκτήρ, ῆρος. m.
nostril: ἕως ἂν ἐξέλθῃ ἐκ τῶν ~ῶν ὑμῶν 'until it [= meat] pops out of your nostrils' Nu 11.20.

μυκτηρίζω: aor. ἐμυκτήρισα, subj. ~ρίσω.
to turn the nose up at, 'sneer at': + acc. pers., 4K 19.21 (‖ ἐξουδενέω, *L* φαυλίζω) ‖ Is 37.22 (‖ φαυλίζω, κεφαλὴν κινέω), Jb 22.19 (‖ γελάω), 1M 7.34 (+ καταγελάω), μητέρα αὐτοῦ Pr 15.20, ‖ ἐξουδενέω, ἐμπαίζω 2C 36.16; + acc. rei, ἐμοὺς ἐλέγχους 'my admonitions' Pr 1.30; pass. 12.8 (:: ἐγκωμιάζω), Je 20.7. Cf. φαυλίζω, ἐξουδενέω, ἐκμυκτηρίζω, μυκτηρισμός, σκυβαρίζω: Preisker, *TDNT* 4.796; Spicq 2.534f.

μυκτηρισμός, οῦ. m.
1. v.n. of μυκτηρίζω: as cogn. acc. of ἐκμυκτηρίζω Ps 34.16; + καταγέλως 43.14. Cf. σκορακισμός.
2. *target of sneering*: Ne 4.4, 5.
Cf. μυκτηρίζω.

μύλη. f. Alw. pl.
**back tooth*, 'molar': σκύμνου 'of a young lion' Jl 1.6 (‖ ὀδούς); τὰς ~ας τῶν λεόντων συνέθλασεν 'he broke ..' Ps 57.7; συνέτριψα ~ας ἀδίκων 'I smashed ..' Jb 29.17. Cf. ὀδούς: Shipp 395.

μύλος, ου. m.
mill, hand-mill: τῆς θεραπαίνης τῆς παρὰ τὸν ~ον 'of the female slave at the handmill' Ex 11.5; ἤληθον αὐτὸ ἐν τῷ ~ῳ 'ground it with the mill' Nu 11.8; + ἐπιμύλιον 'upper millstone' De 24.6; Is 47.2, La 5.13. Cf. ἐπιμύλιον, μυλών: Shipp 395.

μυλών, ῶνος.ʃ
millhouse: οἰκία ~ῶνος Je 52.11. Cf. μύλος.

μυξωτήρ, ~τῆρος. m.ʃ
**pipe* as conduit for fluid: attachment of candlestick, τῶν δύο ~τήρων τῶν χρυσῶν Zc 4.12.

μυρεψικός, ή, όν.ʃ
manufactured by perfumer (μυρεψός): μύρον ~όν 'unguent manufactured by ..' Ex 30.25; 30.35; subst.n. 'perfume' Ct 5.13, οἶνος ~οῦ 'spiced wine' 8.2. Cf. μύρον, μυρεψός.

μυρεψός, οῦ. m.
one who boils and prepares unguents: τέχνη ~οῦ 'craft of perfumer' Ex 30.25; ἔργον ~οῦ 30.35, 38.25, Si 49.1; 38.8, *s* fem., + cooks and bakers, 1K 8.13; μύρου 'of ointment' 1C 9.30. Cf. μύρον, μυρεψικός.

μυριάς, άδος. f.
myriad, number of 10,000: δώδεκα ~άδες Jn 4.11; De 33.17, Mi 6.7 (|| χιλιάς); γίνου εἰς χιλιάδας μυριάδων 'Grow to thousands of myriads' Ge 24.60. Cf. χιλιάς, μύριοι, μυριοπλάσιος, ~ίως, μυριότης.

μύριοι, αι, α.
ten thousand: πρόβατα ~α τετρακισχίλια '40.000 sheep' Jb 42.12; μύριαι μυριάδες 'hundreds of thousands' Da 7.10. Cf. μυριάς. Del. Ne 7.71, Si 16.3 v.l.

μυριοπλάσιος, ον.ʃ
immense in number: *s* τὸ ἅρμα τοῦ θεοῦ 'God's carriages' Ps 67.18. Cf. μυριάς, ἀναρίθμητος.

μυριοπλασίως. adv.ʃ*
in immense measure: μ. ἡλίου φωτεινότεροι 'immensely brighter than the sun' Si 23.19. Cf. μυριάς.

μυριότης, ητος. f.ʃ*
ten thousand: ἐν ~ητι 'ten thousand times' Wi 12.22. On a conjecture ἐν μετριότητι 'moderately,' cf. Gilbert 1976. Cf. μυριάς.

μυρισμός, οῦ. m.ʃ
ointment: for female's face, Ju 16.7.

μυρμηκιάω.ʃ *
to be afflicted with warts: *s* sacrificial animal, not acceptable, Le 22.22.

μυρμηκολέων, οντος. m.ʃ*
ant-lion: Jb 4.11. Cf. λέων: Gerhardt; LSG s.v.

μύρμηξ, ηκος. m.ʃ
ant: model of industry, Pr 6.6; 30.25.

μυροβρεχής, ές.ʃ *
wet with unguent: *s* bride's hair, 3M 4.6. Cf. μύρον.

μύρον, ου. n.
ointment: for anointing the body, μύρον μυρεψικόν 'unguent manufactured by perfumer' Ex 30.25; τὰ πρῶτα ~α χριόμενοι 'anointing themselves with the first-rate ointment' Am 6.6; + ἄρωμα 2C 16.14, see *ND* 4.130f. Cf. μυροβρεχής, ἔλαιον: Trench 135-7.

μυρσίνη, ης. f.
myrtle: Is 41.19. Cf. subs.: Shipp 396.

μυρσιών, ῶνος. m.ʃ
myrtle-grove: Jd 1.35. Cf. prec.

μῦς, ός. m; pl.nom. μῦς, μύες.
mouse, rat: ceremonially unclean, Le 11.29; ἔσθοντες κρέας ὕειον καὶ τὰ βδελύγματα καὶ τὸν μῦν 'eating pork and abominable things and mouse' Is 66.17. See *BA* 9.1, pp. 100-2.

μυσερός, ά, όν.ʃ
loathsome: *s* deed, Le 18.23.

μύσος, ους. n.
uncleanness, defilement: cultic, religious, 2M 6.19.

μύσταξ, ακος. m.ʃ
moustache: 2K 19.25. Cf. θρίξ, πώγων: Shipp 396f.

μυστήριον, ου. n.
carefully guarded, important matter: divine, Si 3.19¶ (|| τὰ κρυπτά vs. 22), θεοῦ Wi 2.22; βασιλέως To 12.7; pl. *a system of esoteric teaching*, τελετὰς ἢ κρύφια ~α 'mystic rites or ..' Wi 14.23, κρυπτά 'hidden' Da 2.47 LXX. **b**. *secret*: τὸ μ. τῆς βουλῆς αὐτοῦ 'his secret decision' Ju 2.2; ~ου ἀποκάλυψις 'disclosure of ..' Si 22.22; military, 2M 13.21.
Cf. κρυπτός, κρύφιος: Bornkamm, *TDNT* 4.813-7.

μύστης, ου. m.ʃ
one who is initiate: Wi 12.5. Cf. μύστις.

μυστικῶς. adv.ʃ *
in secret: 3M 3.10. Cf. κρυπτῶς.

μύστις, ίδος. f.ʃ
f. of μύστης: *s* Wisdom, τῆς τοῦ θεοῦ ἐπιστήμης 'of the knowledge of God' Wi 8.4. Cf. μύστης.

μυχός, οῦ. m.ʃ
inmost part: of a house, Wi 17.4; of Hades, 17.14.

Μωαβίτης, ου.
a Moabite: Ge 19.37.

Μωαβῖτις, ιδος. f.
1. *the land of Moab*: Is 15.1, cf. Ottley ad loc., or the capital city of M.
2. *Moabite woman*: Ru 1.4.

μωκάομαι: pf.ptc.pass. μεμωκημένος.ʃ
to do or *make in jest*: ἔργα μεμωκημένα 'works of jest' Je 28.18 (w. ref. to idols). Cf. μωκός, γελοιάζω: Schmidt 3.459. Del. Si 31.21 v.l.

μωκός, οῦ. m.ʃ
mocker: as adj., φίλος μ. Si 36.6. Cf. μωκάομαι: Shipp 397.

μώλωψ, ωπος. m.
bruise, weal: caused by the blow of a whip, πληγὴ μάστιγος ποιεῖ ~πα Si 28.17; || τραῦμα Ge 4.23, Ex 21.25, Ju 9.13, Is 1.6; ἐσάπησαν οἱ ~πές μου 'my bruises became putrid' Ps 37.6. Cf. πληγή and τραῦμα.

μωμάομαι: fut. μωμήσομαι; aor.ptc. μωμησάμενος; pf.ptc.pass. μεμωμημένος.ʃ
to judge to be blemished or reproachable: **o** hum., Wi 10.14; ἑαυτόν Pr 9.7 (|| λαμβάνω ἀτιμίαν); cultic offering, προσφορά Si 31.21. Cf. μῶμος: Schmidt 3.458f.

μωμητός, ή, όν.ʃ
deserving of reproach: *s* τέκνα De 32.5. Cf. μῶμος.

μῶμος, ου. m.
1. *public reproach*: || λύπη λόγων 'painful, stinging remark' Si 18.15; of a lying habit, 20.24; μὴ δῷς

~ον ἐν τῇ δόξῃ σου 'don't risk a reproach and mar your honour' 30.31, sim. 47.20.

2. **defect*: bodily - οὐκ ἔστιν ἐν αὐτοῖς μ. 'they are impeccable' Da 1.4 TH (ib. LXX ἄμωμος), Ct 4.7, 2K 14.25 (all:: καλός); and disqualifying one for priesthood, Le 21.17; specified as 'lame, blind, slit-nosed or with slit ears' 21.18; De 15.21; *s* sacrificial animal, δάμαλιν ἄμωμον, ἥτις οὐκ ἔχει ἐν αὐτῇ ~ον 'an impeccable heifer ..' Nu 19.2.

Cf. ἄμωμος, μωμητός.

μωραίνω: fut.pass. μωρανθήσομαι; aor.pass. ἐμωράνθην, subj. μωρανθῶ.

1. *to declare foolish*: ***o*** βουλή 'advice, counsel' and pass., Is 19.11; hum., ἐμωράνθη πᾶς ἄνθρωπος ἀπὸ γνώσεως 'as wanting in knowledge' Je 10.14 (ǁ καταισχύνομαι; also in connection with the folly of idol worship at Rom 1.10), τῷ ἐθισμῷ 'on account of some (bad) habit' Si 23.14.

2. pass. *to act foolishly*: ἐμωράνθην σφόδρα 2K 24.10 (*L* ἐματαιώθην). Perh. Si 23.14 also belongs here.

Cf. μωρός.

μωρεύω.ʃ *

= μωραίνω, q.v.: τὴν βουλὴν αὐτῶν Is 44.25.

μωρία, ας. f.ʃ

stupidity: ἀποκρύπτων τὴν ~αν αὐτοῦ 'hiding ..' Si 20.31, 41.15 (:: σοφία). Cf. μωρός.

μωρός, ά, όν.

stupid: ***s*** hum., λαὸς μ. καὶ οὐχὶ σοφός De 32.6; ἄρχοντες Is 19.11 (:: σοφός), cf. 32.5; subst. m., Ps 93.8 (ǁ ἄφρων), περὶ παιδείας ἀνοήτου καὶ ~οῦ Si 42.8, n.pl. 16.23. Cf. μωρία, ἀνόητος, ἄνους, ἀσύνετος, ἄφρων, εὐήθης, φλύαρος, σοφός: Shipp 398; Bertram, *TDNT* 4.832-6; Spicq 2.536-41.

Μωυσῆς, ῆ, ῇ, ῆν.

Moses: Ex 2.10 +. See Morenz 252.

N

νάβλα, ας. f. < Heb. נֵבֶל.

musical instrument of twelve strings: + τύμπανον, αὐλός, κινύρα 1K 10.5, + κινύρα, κύμβαλον 1M 13.51. See *BA* 9.1, p. 88f.

ναζιραῖος, α, ον.ʃ < Heb. נָזִיר.

subst., *Nazirite* consecrated by Nazirite vows: Jd 13.5, 7, La 4.7, 1M 3.49; θεοῦ Jd 16.17 A (B: ἅγιος θεοῦ).

ναί.ʃ

1. gives an affirmative answer to a yes-or-no question, 'yes, indeed': Ge 17.19, To 5.6 $\mathfrak{G}^{\mathrm{II}}$.

2. affirms a thought which was at the back of one's mind as a possibility: Ge 42.21; reinforced by δή – ναὶ δὴ ἐπ' ἀληθείας ἐγὼ ἐπλανήθην 'Yes, indeed, in truth I have erred' Jb 19.4.

3. forcefully affirms one's own thought: Ju 9.12.

4. contradicts a negative statement made by another person, 'no, the contrary is true': Is 48.7.

Cf. οὐ.

ναίω.ʃ

to inhabit: + acc. loci, τὰ ὑψηλά Jb 22.12. Cf. (κατ)οικέω: Schmidt 2.543f.

νᾶμα, ατος. n.ʃ

anything flowing, 'juice': Ct 8.2.

ναός, οῦ. m.

1. *temple, shrine*: τὰ φατνώματα ('coffers') τοῦ ~οῦ Am 8.3; of the Jerusalem temple, Hg 2.9; τὸν ~ὸν τὸν ἅγιόν σου Ps 27.2, Jn 2.5, sim. 2.8, Hb 2.20; κυρίου Hg 2.15, 18; ‖ ὁ οἶκος κυρίου Zc 8.9, cf. Ma 3.1.

2. *palace*: βασιλέως Ps 44.16.

Cf. ἅγιος, ἱερός, νεώς, σηκός, τέμενος: Trench 10-5.

νάπη, ης. f.

woodland vale, glen: Nu 21.20; ~αι σκιάζουσαι 'shady glens' 24.6; De 3.29; ‖ ὄρη, βουνοί, φάραγγες Ez 6.3. Cf. φάραγξ: Shipp 399f.

νάρδος, ου.f. < Heb. נֵרְדְּ.

spikenard: Ct 1.12. Cf. LSG s.v.

ναρκάω: fut. ναρκήσω; aor. ἐνάρκησα.ʃ

to grow stiff, numb resulting in dysfunction of a limb: *s* πλάτος μηροῦ (hip joint?) Ge 32.25; sinew (νεῦρον) 32.32; bones (ὀστέα) Jb 33.19¶; arm (βραχίων) Da 11.6 LXX.

ναῦλος, ου. n. (on the gender, see Walters, 172f., 328).ʃ

passage money, fare for travel by boat: διδόναι ~ον 'to pay a fare' Jn 1.3.

ναῦς, νηός. f.

ship: Jb 9.26; warship, Da 11.40 TH (LXX πλοῖον); ship in general, Wi 5.10. Cf. πλοῖον, σκάφος.

ναυτικός, οῦ. m.ʃ

sailor, seaman: Jn 1.5; ἀνὴρ ν. 3K 9.27.

νάφθα, ας. f.ʃ < Heb./Aram. נֵפְט.

naphtha: fuel, Da 3.46.

νεάζω.ʃ

to act with youthful vigour: *s* λογισμός 'rational will' 4M 5.31. Cf. νέος, ἀνανεάζω.

νεανίας, ου; voc. ~νία. m.

young man: Ru 3.10, Zc 2.4. Cf. νεανίσκος, νέος, νεότητος, μειράκιον: Schmidt 4.31f.

νεανικός, ή, όν.ʃ

pertaining to young age: + ἀκμαῖος, *s* ἡλικία 'age' 3M 4.8.

νεᾶνις, ιδος, acc. νεᾶνιν, νεάνιδα. f.

young woman, 'girl': also called ἅβρα, a companion of Pharaoh's princess, Ex 2.8; married woman whose virginity was disputed, De 22.19; betrothed young woman (παῖς παρθένος) who was subsequently raped, 22.24, 26; virgin, 3K 1.2 B (virginity emphasised by the preposed παρθένος; ‖ παῖς 1.3 *L*). Cf. κοράσιον, παρθένος, subs.

νεανίσκος, ου. m.

young man, lad: De 32.25, Am 8.13, Zc 9.17 (‖ παρθένος); Ge 19.4; Ex 10.9, Jl 2.28 (‖ πρεσβύτερος); of recruit for cultic service, Ex 24.5; Am 2.11 (‖ υἱός); ‖ ἀνήρ Ge 4.23; ‖ νεώτερος Is 40.30; ‖ νήπιος Je 9.21; 1K 20.22B (*L* νεανίας) (‖ παιδάριον vs. 21); ν. στρατιώτης 'young soldier' 4M 3.12. Cf. νέος, νεανίας, πρεσβύτερος: Schmidt 4.29-31.

νεβελ.ʃ < Heb. נֵבֶל.

a definite liquid measure: ν. οἴνου 1K 1.24, 2K 16.1, Ho 3.2.

νεβρός, οῦ. m.

young deer: ἐλάφων 'of deer' Ct 2.9. Cf. ἔλαφος.

νεῖκος, ους. n.

quarrel, contention: ἀγαπᾶν ν. 'quarrelsome' Ho 10.11; Ez 3.8, 9. Cf. ἔρις, φιλονεικία: Schmidt 4.200-2.

νεκρός, ά, όν.

1. *dead*: subst., hum. ἐπερωτῶν τοὺς ~ούς 'enquiring of the dead' De 18.11; ~οὶ πολέμου Is 22.2.

2. *subject to death*, 'mortal': *s* ἄνθρωπος Wi 14.15.

3. subst.m., *corpse, cadaver*: θάψω τὸν ~όν μου 'I shall bury ..' Ge 23.4; ἅψηται .. τραυματίου ἢ

~οῦ ἢ ὀστέου ἀνθρωπίνου 'touches .. a mortally wounded person or a corpse or a human bone' Nu 19.16 (|| τεθνηκότος 'a dead person's' vs. 18); ἔσονται οἱ ~οὶ ὑμῶν κατάβρωμα τοῖς πετεινοῖς 'your corpses shall be food for the birds' De 28.26.

Cf. ζάω.

νέμω: fut.act. νεμήσω, mid. νεμήσομαι; aor.pass. ἐνεμήθην.

I. act.tr. *to tend in the open*: abs. Ge 36.24 (ἐν τῇ ἐρήμῳ); + acc., ἡμιόνους 'mules' 1K 21.8; + acc. pers. and fig. νεμήσει αὐτοὺς κύριος ὡς ἀμνὸν ἐν εὐρυχώρῳ Ho 4.16.

II. mid.intr. 1. *to live in the open which provides grass and water*: *s* flock, τὰ πρόβατα καὶ αἱ βόες Ex 34.3; Jn 3.7 (|| γεύω and πίνω ὕδωρ), ποίμνια Zp 2.14; + acc. of land, τὴν Βασανῖτιν Mi 7.14, καλὴν νομήν Ez 34.18; cows (βόες)– παρὰ τὸ χεῖλος τοῦ ποταμοῦ 'by the river-bank' Ge 41.3 (|| βόσκω vs. 2); ἐν τῷ ἄχει 'among the reed-grass' 41.18.

2. *to roam about*: like sheep or cattle looking for grass and water, ἔσονται νεμόμενοι ἐν τῇ ἐρήμῳ τεσσαράκοντα ἔτη Nu 14.33 (cf. Vulg. *erunt vagi*); ἐν τοῖς ὄρεσι καὶ ἐν τοῖς σπηλαίοις θηρίων τρόπον ἦσαν νεόμενοι 'they were roaming about in the mountains and in the caves like beasts' 2M 10.6; *s* horses, Wi 19.9 (|| διασκιρτάω 'skip around').

3. *to feed on*: + acc., χόρτον 'grass' Da 4.12 LXX (*s* cows).

Cf. νομή, βόσκω, ποιμαίνω: Schmidt 4.578-83; Chadwick 198-207.

νεογνός, ή, όν.ʃ

new-born: *s* hum. child, 3M 1.20; πρὸς μαστούς 'at the breasts' 5.49.

νεόκτιστος, ον.ʃ

just recently created: *s* animal, Wi 11.18. Cf. κτίζω.

νεομηνία: ⇒ νουμηνία.

νέος, α, ον.

young in age: ὁ υἱὸς αὐτοῦ ὁ νεώτερος 'his younger son' Ge 9.24; νεώτερος 'younger' 29.16 (:: μείζων); νεώτερος ἄπειρος 'inexperienced younger one' Nu 14.23; παιδίον νέον De 1.39; πῶλος ν. 'a young foal' Zc 9.9; opp. παλαιός, Le 26.10, || νεανίσκος Is 40.30; commanding respect, De 28.50, Wi 8.10 (:: πρεσβύτερος). **b**. νεώτερος relatively young in age: νεώτερος ἐγενόμην 'I grew up to be a young man' Ps 36.25 (opp. γηράω); τῷ χρόνῳ and opp. πρεσβύτερος Jb 32.6; Je 1.7; wanting in ἐπιστήμη, Ba 3.20. **c**. ὁ μὴν τῶν νέων 'the month of Abiv' Ex 13.4, De 16.1; ἡ ἡμέρα τῶν νέων 'the day of the new growths' Nu 28.26, ἡμέραι νέων 'season of new fruits' Si 24.25, 50.8.

Cf. καινός, ἀνανεόω, ἀνα~, νεάζω, νεότητος, νεανίσκος, νεωστί, πρεσβύτερος: Trench 219-25.

νεοσσιά ⇒ νοσσία.

νεοσσός, νεοττός. ⇒ νοσσός.

νεότης, τος. f.

1. *state of being young*: γυνὴ ~τός σου 'the wife of your youth, i.e. whom you married when you were young' Ma 2.14, 15. **b**. *manifestation or trait typical of youth*: 4M 8.8.

2. *a period in one's life when one is young*: ἐκ ~τος 'since youth' Ge 8.21, 48.15; κατὰ τὴν ~τα αὐτῆς 'as when she was young' Le 22.13; ἐν τῇ ~τι αὐτῆς Nu 30.4; opp. τελείωσις 'maturity' Je 2.2, γῆρας 'old age' Si 25.3.

Cf. νέος.

νεόφυτος, ον.ʃ

newly planted: subst.n., *young plant* Is 5.7, Jb 14.9; οἱ υἱοί σου ὡς ~α ἐλαιῶν '.. young olive trees' (full of vitality) Ps 127.3, sim. 143.12. Cf. φυτόν.

νεόω: aor.impv.2pl νεώσατε.ʃ

to plough up: + cogn. acc., νεώματα Je 4.3. Cf. νέωμα.

νεῦμα, ατος. n.ʃ

bodily signal indicating one's desire or consent: ~ασιν ὀφθαλμῶν 'with winks' Is 3.16; ἑνὶ ~ατι καταβαλεῖν 'to strike down with a single nod' 2M 8.18. Cf. νεύω.

νευρά, ᾶς; pl.acc. also νευρέας. f.

cord made of sinews of animals: used to tie up an obj., Jd 16.7; torturing instrument, 2M 7.1 (+ μάστιξ 'whip'). Cf. Caird 1969.23.

νευροκοπέω: fut. ~πήσω; aor. ἐνευροκόπησα; pf. pass.ptc. νενευροκοπημένος.ʃ

to cut the sinews of, hamstring: + acc., ταῦρον 'bull' Ge 49.6; δάμαλιν 'heifer' De 21.4, 6; ἵππους 'horses' Jo 11.6, 9. Cf. νεῦρον.

νεῦρον, ου. n.

sinew: of a thigh (μηρός), Ge 32.32; of an arm (βραχίων), 49.24; ν. σιδηροῦν 'iron-hard' Is 48.4; + ὀστοῦν 'bone' Jb 10.11; || τόνος 4M 7.13. Cf. νευροκοπέω, τόνος.

νεύω: aor.subj. νεύσω.ʃ

to signal, by beckoning, approval of and consent to: *s* hum. and abs., Pr 21.1; eyelids, + acc., δίκαια 'right things' 4.25. Cf. νεῦμα, ἀνα~, δια~, ἐπινεύω, (συν)ευδοκέω, ὁμολογέω, συμφωνέω, συνθέλω.

νεφέλη, ης. f.

cloud in the sky: Ge 9.13; στῦλος ~ης 'column of ..' Ex 13.21; ν. πρωινή 'morning c.' (of sth fleeting, evanescent) Ho 6.4, 13.3 (|| δρόσος ὀρθρινή 'morning dew'); || ὁμίχλη 'fog, mist' Jl 2.2, Zp 1.15, || γνόφος 'dark clouds' Is 44.22; + γ. Ez 34.12 (ref. to thick fog?); ~αι κονιορτὸς ποδῶν αὐτοῦ 'clouds are the dust of His feet' Na 1.3; ~ῶν ἁγίων αὐτοῦ 'His holy clouds' Zc 2.13; containing moisture for rain, Is 5.6, v. δρόσου 'cloud saturated with dew' 18.4, ὑετοῦ 'bringing rain' Si 32.26; pl., ἕως τῶν ~ῶν 'very extensive' Ps 35.6, ἐν ~αις 'in heaven' 88.7. Cf. νέφος, ὀμίχλη: Schmidt 1.616-22.

νέφος, ους. n.

cloud: Ps 103.3, Wi 5.21. Cf. νεφέλη.

νεφρός, οῦ. m. Alw. in pl.

kidney: of sacrificial animals, δύο ~ούς Ex 29.13; ἀμφοτέρους τοὺς νεφρούς Le 3.10; rich food, μετὰ στέατος ~ῶν πυροῦ 'with the fat of the kidneys of wheat' [= the very best wheat, Wevers] De 32.14; of nephromancy, ἐτάζων καρδίας καὶ ~οὺς ὁ θεός 'God is one who examines hearts and kidneys' Ps 7.10, sim. 25.2, Je 11.20, 17.10. **b**. metaph. for a centre of attitudes and intentions, Wi 1.6, Je 12.2 (|| καρδία vs. 3), *s* of παιδεύω Ps 15.7.

νέωμα, ατος. n.ʃ*

fallowed land: Je 4.3. Cf. νεόω.

νεώς, gen. and acc. νεώ. m.

Attic form occurring only in 2M alongside ναός, q.v.: 2M 4.14 +.

νεωστί. adv.ʃ

only a short while ago: Ju 4.3 (|| προσφάτως). Cf. (προσ)αρτίως, προσφάτως.

νεωτερίζω: aor.ptc. ~ρίσας.ʃ

to launch radical reform: πρός τι 'aimed at ..' 4M 3.21.

νεωτερικός, ή, όν.ʃ

typical of young people: *s* ῥαθυμία 'revelry' 3M 4.8.

νή, particle of strong affirmation.ʃ

+ acc.: νὴ τὴν ὑγιείαν Φαραω 'by the health of Ph.' Ge 42.15, 16. Cf. μά.

νήθω: pf.ptc.pass. νενησμένος.

to spin: ταῖς χερσίν Ex 35.25; *o* fine linen (βύσσος) 26.31; τρίχας αἰγείας 'goat-hair' 35.26. Cf. διανήθω, νηστός.

νηκτός, ή, όν.ʃ

capable of swimming: subst.n.pl., aquatic animals as against land animals (χερσαῖα), Wi 19.19. Cf. νήχομαι.

νηπιοκτόνος, ον.ʃ *

infanticidal: *s* διάταγμα 'command' Wi 11.7.

νήπιος, α, ον.

infant: παιδίον ~ον 'infant child' Is 11.8; subst. τὰ ~α αὐτῆς ἐδαφιοῦσιν 'they will dash her infants' Na 3.10; ~α θηλάζοντα μαστούς 'infants sucking the breasts' Jl 2.16, cf. ἐκ στόματος ~ων καὶ θηλαζόντων Ps 8.3; || νεανίσκος Je 9.21; in need of divine protection, φυλάσσων τὰ ~α ὁ κύριος Ps 114.6. **b**. fig., *mentally or morally still undeveloped*: *s* Ισραηλ Ho 11.1; subst. νήπιον παιδεύειν 'to educate ..' Pr 23.13, ἡ μαρτυρία κυρίου .. σοφίζουσα ~α Ps 18.8, ἡ δήλωσις τῶν λόγων σου .. συνετιεῖ ~ους 118.130, ~ων δίκην ἀφρόνων 'in the manner of silly ..' Wi 12.24, sim. 15.14. **c**. *morally innocent*: ἠδίκουν ~ους Pr 1.32.

Cf. νηπιότης, βρέφος, παῖς, παιδάριον, παιδίον, τέκνον, ὑποτίτθιος, ἄκακος, ἄφρων: Shipp 402; Bertram, *TDNT* 4.912-7; Dupont 1967; *ND* 1.117.

νηπιότης, τος. f.

state of being infant, 'infancy': κατὰ τὰς ἡμέρας ~τος αὐτῆς Ho 2.15. Cf. νήπιος.

νῆσος, ου. f.

1. *island*: Is 20.6; τῆς θαλάσσης 24.15.

2. *inhabitant of island*: νῆσοι τῶν ἐθνῶν 'islanders of the nations' Ge 10.5, Zp 2.11.

νηστεία, ας. f.

v.n. of νηστεύω: ἁγιάσατε ~αν 'declare a religious fast' Jl 1.14, 2.15; ἐκήρυξαν ~αν Jn 3.5; as cogn. obj., μὴ ~αν νενηστεύκατέ μοι Zc 7.5; || κλαυθμός and κοπετός, Jl 2.12, sim. Is 22.12; a principle of piety, + προσευχή, ἐλεημοσύνη, δικαιοσύνη 'almsgiving' To 12.8 𝔊[I]. Cf. νηστεύω, νήστης.

νηστεύω: aor. ἐνήστευσα, subj. νηστεύσω, impv.2pl νηστεύσατε, ptc.f.pl.gen. νηστευσασῶν; pf. νενήστευκα.

to abstain from food: Ex 38.26, Zc 7.5a; || κόπτω 7.5b, || καλίω, εὔχομαι Ba 1.5; || ἀσιτέω Es 4.16 o'; ἐπὶ ἁμαρτιῶν 'over sins' Si 31.31; + cogn. acc., νηστείαν 2K 12.16, Zc 7.5. Cf. νηστεία, ἀσιτέω, ἐσθίω.

νήστης, ου. m.ʃ

one who is fasting: Da 6.18 LXX (TH ἄδειπνος). Cf. νηστεία.

νηστός, ή, όν.ʃ *

spun: κόκκινον ~όν 'spun scarlet thread' Ex 31.4. Cf. νήθω.

νήχομαι.ʃ

to swim: metaph., Jb 11.12. Cf. νηκτός.

νικάω: aor. ἐνίκησα, inf. νικῆσαι, ptc. νικήσας, subj. νικήσω; pf.inf.pass. νενικῆσθαι.

to win victory against, *defeat*: Hb 3.19; ὑπὲρ πάντα 1E 3.12; + acc. pers., 2M 3.5; metaph, Pr 6.25, *o* παθήματα 'passions' 4M 6.33. **b**. *to win victory in*: + acc., ἀγῶνα '(moral) struggle' Wi 4.2. ***c**. *to succeed in an effort*: + inf., PSol 4.10.

Cf. νίκη, νῖκος, ἡττάω.

νίκη, ης. f.

victory: on battlefield, πολέμου 1M 3.19, + εὐημερία 'success' 2M 10.28. Cf. νῖκος, ἐπινίκιος, ἀνίκητος, ἥττημα.

νῖκος, ους. n.

victory: δώσει κρίμα αὐτοῦ καὶ οὐκ εἰς ν. ἀδικίαν 'he will hand down his sentence, and will not allow injustice to prevail (?)' Zp 3.5 (cf. La, Syh, Eth,

Co, 1E 3.9, 2M 10.38), 1E 4.59. On the idiom εἰς νῖκος, see Caird 1969.24 and cp. Kraft 1972a.153-6. But note that already at 2K 2.26 where it could mean "to the bitter end, i.e. till one has defeated the other," La and Arm understood the phrase to mean 'for ever,' and likewise Tht PG 81.1853 μέχρι τέλους, but Cyr. II 219 εἰς ἐκνίκησιν or εἰς ἅπαν; ‖ εἰς τὸν αἰῶνα Je 3.5, εἰς μακρότητα ἡμερῶν La 5.19. **b.** *prize for the winner*: 4M 17.12.

Cf. νικάω, νίκη: LSG s.v.

νίπτω: fut.mid. νίψομαι, pass. νιφήσομαι; aor.mid. ἐνιψάμην, inf.act. νίψαι, mid. νίψασθαι, impv. νίψαι, 2pl νίψασθε, 3pl νιψάτωσαν, ptc.mid. νιψάμενος, opt.act.3s νίψαι; pf.mid. νένιμμαι.

to wash clean (+ acc.): act. and with water, νιψάτωσαν τοὺς πόδας ὑμῶν Ge 18.4 (to be done by servants). **b.** mid. νίψασθε τοὺς πόδας ὑμῶν Ge 19.2 (the guests doing it themselves); νίψεται Ααρον καὶ οἱ υἱοὶ αὐτοῦ ἐξ αὐτοῦ [= λουτήρ 'washing-tub'] τὰς χεῖρας καὶ τὰς πόδας ὕδατι Ex 30.19; ‖ λούω, πλύνω Le 15.11, ἐλούσαντο καὶ ἐνίψαντο To 7.9 𝔊II. **c.** pass. and *o* wooden vessel: ὕδατι Le 15.12. **d.** *to remove* sth undesirable: ἐπ' αὐτὸν ὀδύνας 'sorrows on to him' Jb 20.23.

Cf. ἐκκλύζω, λούω, πλύνω, ἀπο~, περινίπτω: Trench 160-3; Anz 17; Shipp 404.

νίτρον, ου.ʃ

sodium carbonate: used as detergent, Je 2.22.

νιφετός, οῦ. m.ʃ

snowstorm or drizzle: De 32.2 (‖ ὑετός, δρόσος, ὄμβρος); pl. δρόσοι καὶ ~οί Da 3.68.

νοερός, ά, όν.ʃ

having intellectual abilities: *s* πνεῦμα possessed by Wisdom, Wi 7.22; by varieties of spirts, 7.23. Cf. νοῦς.

νοέω: fut. νοήσω; aor. ἐνόησα, inf. νοῆσαι, ptc. νοήσας, impv. νόησον, subj. νοήσω, opt.3s νοήσαι.

1. *to direct one's mind to*, 'to consider, ponder': abs., Si 11.7 (:: act), *s* flocks, Je 10.21; καρδία 1K 4.20; + acc., ἡ καρδία αὐτοῦ μάταια νοήσει Is 32.6, τῇ καρδίᾳ 44.18, ἐν τῇ καρδίᾳ σου 47.7 (‖ μιμνήσκομαι); λόγους φρονήσεως 'matters concerning wisdom' Pr 1.2 (‖ γινώσκω), δικαιοσύνην 1.3; ‖ τίθεμαι καρδίαν 8.5, ‖ ἐπιγινώσκω 30.18, ‖ τίθημι ἐπὶ διανοίᾳ 'take to heart' Wi 4.14, ‖ διανοέω Si 34.15, ἐξετάζω 'investigate' 11.7; + ὅτι 17.11¶; + indir. question, Wi 4.17, 13.4. **b.** + inf., *to contemplate a plan* to do: 2K 20.15 (*L* ἐν~), Jb 33.23.

2. *to notice and realise*: + acc. rei, κρίμα Pr 28.5 (‖ συνίημι); + ὅτι 2K 12.19 (*L* αἰσθάνομαι); + inf. clause, 2M 14.30 (‖ συνεῖδον).

Cf. νόημα, νοήμων, νοητῶς, προνοέω, αἰσθάνομαι, λογίζομαι, συνεῖδον, συνίημι, φρονέω: Schmidt 3.634-6; Behm, *TDNT* 4.948-50.

νόημα, ατος. n.ʃ

that which one thinks, 'thought': τῆς καρδίας Ba 2.8; 3M 5.30. Cf. ἐννόημα, νοέω, πρόνοια. Del. Si 21.11.

νοήμων, ονος.

thoughtful, prudent: *s* hum., Si 19.29; opp. ἄφρων 'foolish' Pr 17.2, 12; subst.m., ‖ σοφός 1.5. Cf. σοφός, ἄφρων.

νοητῶς. adv.ʃ

by giving much thought: Pr 23.1. Cf. νοέω.

νοθεύω.ʃ

to commit adultery: Wi 14.24. Cf. μοιχεύω.

νόθος, η, ον.ʃ

cross-bred: *s* μόσχευμα Wi 4.3. Cf. γνήσιος.

νόθως. adv.ʃ

insincerely: 3M 3.17.

νομάς, άδος. c.

nomad: Jb 20.17, 30.1; Arabs, 2M 12.11. **b.** used as adj., *roaming freely and grazing, not confined to a stall*, 'free-ranging': *s* ὄνος 'ass' Jb 1.3, δάμαλις 'calf' 1K 28.24B, βοῦς 'ox' 3K 2.46[e], cf. Caird 1969.24.

νομή, ῆς. f.

1. *pasture-land, grazing/feeding ground*: οὐ γάρ ἐστιν ν. τοῖς κτήνεσιν Ge 47.4; αἱ ~αὶ τῶν ποιμένων Am 1.2; ν. ποιμνίων καὶ μάνδρα ('pen') προβάτων Zp 2.6; ἡ ν. ἡ οὖσα τοῖς σκύμνοις Na 2.12; ν. θηρίων Zp 3.1, καμηλῶν .. προβάτων Ez 25.5; τῆς ἐρήμου 'in the wilderness' Je 23.10; metaph., Si 13.19.

*__2.__ *flock or herd feeding in a pasture-land*: fig. w. ref. to a religious community under a leader, Je 10.21, τὰ πρόβατα τῆς ~ης αὐτῶν 23.1.

3. *nourishment, food*: Da 4.29 LXX.

4. χειρῶν νομή 'hand-to-hand fight': 2M 5.14, cf. χειρονομία 3M 1.5.

Cf. νέμω, ποιμαίνω, βόσκημα.

νομίζω: aor. ἐνόμισα, impv. νόμισον, ptc. νομίσας, subj. νομίσω, opt.3s νομίσειεν.

1. *to adjudge as*: + acc., ὡς εὕρεμα 'as a windfall' Si 29.4 (‖ λογίζομαι vs. 6); + double acc., Wi 13.2; + inf., 2M 4.32, 4M 4.7, 9.4.

2. pass. *to be customary*: τῶν νομιζομένων θαλλῶν 'some of the customary gifts' 2M 14.4.

Cf. δοκέω: Schmidt 1.333-47.

νομικός, ή, όν.ʃ

**learned in the Jewish law*: subst.m., 4M 5.4. Cf. νόμος.

νόμιμος, η, ον. Mostly subst., and then alw. used in the n. and mostly pl.

1. *individual statute prescribing man's conduct*: ~α λαοῦ μου Mi 6.15; of God, τοὺς λόγους μου καὶ τὰ ~ά μου δέχεσθε, ὅσα ἐγὼ ἐντέλλομαι 'you accept my words and my statutes that I command' Zc 1.6;

ἐφύλαξεν .. τὰ προστάγματά μου καὶ τὰς ἐντολάς μου καὶ τὰ δικαιώματά μου καὶ τὰ ~ά μου Ge 26.5; ἐξεκλίνατε ~ά μου 'you have perverted ..' Ma 3.7; βασιλέως 'royal mandate' 2E 8.36. **b**. sg.: ~ον αἰώνιον Ex 13.12, 27.21, 28.39, 29.28. **c**. *that which one is entitled to*, 'due': τοῖς υἱοῖς σου Le 10.13.

2. *customary*: subst. ~α ἐβδελυγμένα 'detestable customs' Le 18.30 (of sexual immoralities), Ez 20.18; 3M 1.3. Cf. ἐθισμός.

3. *conforming to the law*: ~ους πολιτείας 'lawful ways of life' 2M 4.11 (:: παράνομος), βίος 4M 5.36.

Cf. νομίμως, νόμος, ἐντολή, δικαίωμα, πρόσταγμα, παράνομος: Harl 2001.893; LSG s.v.

νομίμως. adv.ʃ

in conformity with the law: 4M 6.18. Cf. νόμιμος, νομοθέσμως.

νόμισμα, ατος. n.ʃ

1. *mandate*: royal, 2E 8.36.

2. *current coin*: ‖ κόμμα 1M 15.6.

νομιστέος, α, ον.ʃ

n., *one must take the view*: + inf. clause, αὐτοὺς ὑπάρχειν θεούς 'that they are gods' Ep Je 39, sim. 63 (‖ ὥστε θεοὺς αὐτοὺς ὑπάρχειν vs. 44, ὅτι εἰσὶ θεοί vs. 56). Cf. νομίζω.

νομοθεσία, ας. f.

entire code of laws: θεόκτιστος 'established by God' 2M 6.23, θεία 'divine' 4M 17.16. Cf. νόμος.

νομοθέσμως. adv.ʃʃ *

in conformity with law: Pr 31.28 (‖ ἐννόμως vs. 25). Cf. νομίμως.

νομοθετέω: fut. ~τήσω; aor. ἐνομοθέτησα, inf. ~τῆσαι, impv. ~τησον, ptc. ~τήσας, subj.pass. ~τηθῶ.

1. *to frame laws*: *s* God and + dat. pers., Ex 24.12, De 17.10, Ps 118.102; αὐτῷ ἐν ὁδῷ, ᾗ ᾑρετίσατο 'in the way he has chosen' 24.12; abs., 83.7; τὸν περὶ παρακαταθήκης νομοθετήσαντα 'one who had legislated about deposits' 2M 3.15.

2. *to instruct in moral matters*: *s* God and + acc. pers., ἁμαρτάνοντας ἐν ὁδῷ 'those who sin ..' Ps 24.8 (‖ ὁδηγέω, διδάσκω), με τῇ ὁδῷ σου 26.11 (‖ ὁδηγέω); + acc. pers. and acc. rei, με τὴν ὁδὸν τῶν δικαιωμάτων σου 118.33.

Cf. νόμος: Flashar 180f.; Munnich 1979.342-6.

νομοθέτης, ου. m.ʃ

legislator or *law-enforcement officer*: Ps 9.21.

νόμος, ου. m. Alm. alw. in the sg.

1. *body of normative rules prescribing man's conduct*: derived from God, ν. θεοῦ σου Ho 4.6; ν. κυρίου Ex 13.9; τὰς ἐντολάς μου καὶ τὸν ~ον μου 16.28 (in the reverse order, 24.12); τὰ προστάγματα τοῦ θεοῦ καὶ τὸν ~ον αὐτοῦ 18.16; κρίματα .. προστάγματα .. ον. Le 26.46; τὸν ~ον μου φυλάξεσθε 19.19; διασαφῆσαι τὸν ~ον 'to expound the meaning of ..' De 1.5; originates in Zion, Mi 4.2 (‖ λόγος κυρίου); πάντας τοὺς λόγους τοῦ ~ου τούτου De 27.3 (‖ πάντα τὰ ῥήματα τοῦ ~ου τούτου 28.58, 29.29); τὸ βιβλίον τοῦ ~ου τούτου 28.61, 29.20, 21, 27, 30.10, 31.26; transmitted through Moses, Le 26.46, Ma 4.6, Μωυσέως ν. 1E 8.3; recorded by Moses, De 31.9; to be publicly recited, 31.11; κατὰ τὸν ~ον μου ἠσέβησαν Ho 8.1 (‖ διαθήκη); ἀσεβοῦσι ~ον Zp 3.4; well-known to priests, Hg 2.11, Ma 2.7; ν. ἀληθείας Ma 2.6 (opp. ἀδικία), ν. ζωῆς Si 17.11; anarthrous though referring to the law, that of the God of Israel, Am 4.5, Mi 4.2, Hb 1.4 (‖ κρίμα), Zp 3.4, Ma 2.6, 7, 8, 9. **b**.'the basic law, constitution': τὸ δικαίωμα τοῦ ~ου 'the decision based on the law' Nu 31.21; δικαιώματα καὶ κρίματα δίκαια κατὰ πάντα τὸν ~ον τοῦτον De 4.8. **c**. rare examples of pl.: κρίματα εὐθεῖα καὶ ~ους ἀληθείας καὶ προστάγματα καὶ ἐντολὰς ἀγαθάς Ne 9.13 (given at Sinai, but תּוֹרוֹת), δώσω ~ους μου Je 38.33 (תּוֹרָתִי); 38.37 (חֻקִּים); 2M 2.22; ἀπὸ τῶν πατρίων ~ων καὶ τοῖς τοῦ θεοῦ ~οις 6.1; 8.36; said by a gentile, Es B 4. Cf. Blank 279f. **c**. of hum. origin and pl., ~ους πατρός σου Pr 6.20 (‖ θεσμοί [MT: תּוֹרָה] 'rules of conduct [as laid down by mother!]').

2. *binding regulation and rule* pertaining to a specific matter: τοῦ πάσχα 'concerning the passover' Ex 12.43, τῆς ὁλοκαυτώσεως 'concerning the whole burnt-offering' Le 6.9, τῆς θυσίας 6.14, τῆς ἁμαρτίας 'concerning the sin-offering' 6.25; περὶ τῶν κτηνῶν 'concerning the beasts' 11.46; κατὰ πᾶσαν ἁφὴν λέπρας 'concerning every type of leprous infection' 14.54; τοῦ εὐξαμένου 'concerning one who takes a vow' Nu 6.13; κατὰ τὸν ~ον αὐτοῦ καὶ τὴν σύγκρισιν αὐτοῦ 9.3; κατὰ τὸν ~ον καὶ κατὰ τὴν κρίσιν De 17.11; κατὰ τὸν ~ον τοῦ πάσχα καὶ κατὰ τὴν σύνταξιν αὐτοῦ Nu 9.14; ν. εἷς 'common' Ex 12.49, Nu 15.15, Le 6.37; ν. αἰώνιος 6.22, Nu 15.15. **b** .οἷς οὐκ ἦν ν. πιεῖν 'those who were not permitted to drink' Je 29.13.

3. *the Pentateuch*: 4M 1.34, see Redditt 250; + οἱ προφῆται Si prol 1, 8, 2M 15.9, 4M 18.10.

Cf. ἀνομέω, ἀνομία, ἄνομος, νομοθεσία, νομικός, νόμιμος, παράνομος, ἐντολή, πρόσταγμα: Schmidt 1.348-60; Gutbrod, *TDNT* 4.1046f.; Dodd 1935.25ff.; Monsengwo Pasinya, esp. 139f.; Harl 2001.891f.

νομός, οῦ. m.

district: of Egypt and ‖ πόλις Is 19.2, 3M 4.3; in general, 1M 10.30.

νομοφύλαξ, ακος. m./f.ʃ

**observer of the law*: 4M 15.32.

νοσερός, ά, όν.ʃ

pertaining to bodily disease: *s* θάνατος Je 14.15. 16.4. Cf. νόσος: Schmidt 3.700f.

νοσέω.ʃ
to be ill: ***s*** hum., ψυχή Wi 17.8; + acc. (ailment), εὐλάβειαν 'dread' ib. Cf. νόσημα, νόσος.

νόσημα, ατος. n.ʃ
disease: moral, Su 57 TH. Cf. νοσέω, νόσος.

νόσος, ου. f.
sickness, disease: Ex 15.26; ‖ μαλακία De 7.15; ‖ πληγή 29.22; ‖ ὀδύνη Ho 5.13.
Cf. ἀσθένεια, ἀσθενέω, μαλακία, νοσερός, νοσέω, νόσημα, and ὀδύνη. For a distinction between νόσος and ἀσθένεια on the one hand (the former denoting a more serious condition), and a possible difference in their usage between the New Testament and papyri on the other, see *ND* 4.248f.; Schmidt 3.697-9.

νοσσεύω: aor. ἐνόσσευσα.
1. *to make nest*: ***s*** hedgehog, Is 34.15; birds, Da 4.9, 18 LXX (TH: κατασκηνόω).
2. *to build a dwelling*: ***o*** θεμέλιον αἰῶνος 'an eternal foundation' Si 1.15.
Cf. ἐννοσσεύω, νοσσοποιέω, νοσσιά.

νοσσιά, ᾶς. f.
1. *nest*: of birds, to build (***o*** of τίθημι) Nu 24.21, Ob 4 (τάσσω), Hb 2.9; ὀρνέων De 22.6; 32.11; honeycomb, 4M 14.19; to be taken by force in a fig. of military conquest, Is 10.14.
2. *space provided for rest and protection*: cabin of ship, Ge 6.14; man's home, Si 36.31.
3. *lion's den*: Na 2.13.
Cf. νοσσός, ἐννοσσεύω, νοσσοποιέω: Shipp 404f.

νοσσίον, ου. n.ʃ
nestling: young bird, Ps 83.4. Cf. νοσσός.

νοσσοποιέω.ʃ*
to build a nest: ***s*** ἐχῖνοι 'hedgehogs' Is 13.22. Cf. ἐννοσσεύω, ἐννοσσοποιέω, νοσσιά, νοσσεύω.

νοσσός, οῦ. m. Also νεοσσός, νεοττός.
young bird: περιστερῶν 'young dove' as cultic offering, Le 5.7, 14.22; νοσσοῖς ἢ ᾠοῖς '.. or eggs' De 22.6; 32.11. Cf. νοσσιά, νοσσίον: Shipp 404f.

νοσφίζω: aor.mid. ἐνοσφισάμην, ptc. ~φισάμενος.ʃ
to purloin: abs., Jo 7.1 (‖ κλέπτω 'steal' vs. 11); + acc., temple funds, 2M 4.32. Cf. κλέπτω, λαμβάνω: Spicq 2.546f.

νότος, ου. m.
1. *south wind*: appositionally, ἄνεμος ν. Ex 10.13, 14.21; opp. λίψ Ps 77.26.
2. *south*: ἐπὶ γῆν ~ου Zc 6.6; ἐν τῇ γῇ τῇ πρὸς ~ον Nu 13.30.
Cf. ἀνατολή, βορρᾶς, θάλασσα, λίψ, δυσμή.

νουθεσία, ας. f.ʃ
warning issued: Wi 16.6. Cf. νουθετέω, νουθέτημα.

νουθετέω: fut. νουθετήσω; aor. ἐνουθέτησα, ptc. pass. νουθετηθείς; pf.pass. νενουθέτημαι.
1. *to give counsel to*: + acc. pers., Jb 4.3. **b**. *to admonish*: ***s*** father Wi 11.10, God ὡς υἱὸν ἀγαπήσεως PSol 13.9.
2. *to let know*: pass., ***o*** hum., + acc. rei, εὖρος 'breadth' Jb 38.18.
3. *to reprimand*: + acc. pers. (offender), 1K 3.13, Jb 30.1; pass., 23.15, 36.12, 40.4.
4. mid. *to heed counsel concerning*: abs., Jb 34.16; + acc. rei, 37.14.
Cf. νουθεσία, νουθέτημα, νουθέτησις: Behm, *TDNT* 4.1019-21; Spicq 2.548-51.

νουθέτημα, ατος. n.ʃ
warning issued: Jb 5.17. Cf. νουθετέω, νουθεσία.

νουθέτησις, εως. f.ʃ
v.n. of νουθετέω, act of warning: from God, Ju 8.27; from hum., τῷ υἱῷ σου Pr 2.2. Cf. νουθετέω.

νουμηνία, ας. f.
the first day of a month: ἐν ἡμέρᾳ μιᾷ τοῦ μηνὸς .. ~ᾳ Ex 40.2; festival to be celebrated, ἐν ταῖς ἡμέραις τῆς εὐφροσύνης ὑμῶν καὶ ἐν ταῖς ἑορταῖς .. καὶ ἐν ταῖς ~αις .. Nu 10.10; Ho 2.11 (‖ ἑορτή and σάββατον). Cf. μήν, ἑορτή, προνουμηνία, σάββατον: *ND* 3.76f.

νοῦς, νοός. m.
1. *mind possessed of perceiving and thinking faculty*: ν. ἐπιγνώμων 'intelligent ..' Pr 29.7; οὐκ ἐπέστησεν τὸν νοῦν αὐτοῦ οὐδὲ ἐπὶ τούτῳ 'he did not direct his attention to this matter, either' Ex 7.23; ‖ ψυχή Is 10.7; κυρίου 40.13; besides the five senses, Si 17.5¶ (‖ λόγος); ἔχω κατὰ νοῦν 'bear in mind' 2M 15.8, ἐπιδίδωμι τὸν νοῦν εἰς 'direct one's mind to ..' 1E 9.41; conceives a plan, 3M 1.25; ***s*** λογισμός 4M 1.15.
2. *that which is on one's mind*: κατὰ τὸν νοῦν αὐτοῦ 'as he intended (me to do)' Jo 14.7; τίς ἔγνω νοῦν κυρίου; Is 40.13, sim. Ju 8.14.
Cf. καρδία, διάνοια, νοερός, φρήν, ψυχή: Schmidt 3.622-8, 633f., 636-8; Behm, *TDNT* 4.952f.; Krischer 1984.

νυκτερινός, ή, όν.ʃ
nocturnal: ***s*** φόβος Ps 90.5 (:: ἡμέρα), φ. καὶ ἠχώ '.. noise' Jb 4.13, φάσμα 'vision' 20.8, μελέτη 'meditation' 33.15, φυλακή 'watch' 35.10, ἡσυχία 'quiet' Pr 7.9. Cf. νύξ.

νυκτερίς, ίδος. f.ʃ
bat: forbidden as food, Le 11.19, De 14.17; Is 2.20, Ep Je 21.

νυκτικόραξ, κος. m.ʃ
long-eared owl: forbidden as food, Le 11.17, De 14.16; solitude-loving, Ps 101.7 (‖ πελεκάν); active at night, 1K 26.20.

νύκτωρ. adv.
by night: ν. ὡς ἡμέρας Si 38.27; 2M 12.6. Cf. νύξ.

νυμφαγωγός, οῦ. m.ʃ

one who leads the bride to the bridegroom's house: Ge 21.22, 32, 26.26, cf. ἑταῖρος Jd 14.11A, συνέταιρος 15.2, 6A (B: φίλος); 14.20A (B: φίλος). Cf. νύμφη: Caird 1969.24f.

νύμφευσις, εως. f.ʃ *

wedding: Ct 3.11. Cf. νύμφη, γάμος.

νύμφη, ης. f.

1. *daughter-in-law*: τὴν Σαρραν τὴν ~ην αὐτοῦ, γυναῖκα Αβρααμ τοῦ υἱοῦ αὐτοῦ Ge 11.31; αἱ ~αι ὑμῶν μοιχεύσουσι 'your daughters-in-law will commit adultery' Ho 4.13 (ǁ θυγάτηρ); ἐπαναστήσεται .. ν. ἐπὶ τὴν πενθερὰν αὐτῆς 'a daughter-in-law will rebel against her mother-in-law' Mi 7.6 (ǁ θυγάτηρ); defined as γυνὴ υἱοῦ σου Le 18.15.

2. *newly wed wife*: ~ην περιεζωσμένην σάκκον ἐπὶ τὸν ἄνδρα αὐτῆς τὸν παρθενικόν '.. with a sackcloth wrapped around for the sake of her husband of youth' Jl 1.8; newly wed, ἐξελθάτω .. ν. ἐκ τοῦ παστοῦ αὐτῆς '.. come out of her closet' 2.16 (ǁ νυμφίος), sim. Ps 18.5.

Cf. νυμφίος, νύμφευσις, θυγάτηρ, πενθερά.

νυμφίος, ου. m.

1. *newly wed husband*, 'bridegroom': ἐξελθάτω ν. ἐκ τοῦ κοιτῶνος αὐτοῦ 'Let a bridegroom come out of his chamber' Jl 2.16 (ǁ νύμφη), ἐκ παστοῦ αὐτοῦ 'out of his chamber' Ps 18.6; applied to a man aged about 30, *ND* 4.223 (on an Egyptian papyrus of no date), and also ib. 4.226f for implications of both ἄγαμος and νυμφίος applied to same man.

*__2__. *son-in-law*: Ne 13.28.

Cf. νύμφη, σύννυμφος, and ἀνήρ.

νυμφών, ῶνος.ʃ*

bridal chamber: To 6.14, 17.

νῦν. adv.

When used as a pure adverb usually placed as close as possible to the beginning of a clause.

1. *now, at the present time*: καλῶς μοι ἦν τότε ἢ νῦν 'it was better for me then than now' Ho 2.7; καὶ νῦν τάδε λέγει κύριος Hg 1.5; + art., τὸ νῦν – ἡμάρτηκα τὸ νῦν Ex 9.27; ἕως τοῦ νῦν Ge 46.34, Nu 14.19, De 12.9; ἀπὸ τοῦ νῦν καὶ ἕως εἰς τὸν αἰῶνα Mi 4.7. As a noun qualifier: ἐν τῷ νῦν καιρῷ Ge 29.34, 30.20, Ex 9.14. **b**. adv. τὰ νῦν 'now': 2M 15.8.

2. Emphasises the contemporaneity: "I will take away the raiment I provided her with .. and by so doing / in that process (καὶ νῦν) I shall expose her uncleanness" Ho 2.10.

3. καὶ νῦν: marks a new phase or turn in discourse: Ex 32.32, Am 7.16, Mi 4.9, Jn 4.3, Is 2.5. Cf. Jeremias 119f.

4. νῦν οὖν: introduces a proposal resulting from consideration of the present circumstances – νῦν οὖν ὄμοσον .. 'now then, swear ..' Ge 21.23; νῦν οὖν σκέψαι ἄνθρωπον φρόνιμον '.. look for a prudent man' 41.33; νῦν οὖν ἄκουσόν μου Ex 18.19.

5. *under the present circumstances, this being the case*: Ho 4.16, 5.7, Ma 1.9.

6. w. ref. to a recent event: + aor., νῦν ἐξεπόρνευσεν Εφραιμ Ho 5.3; + pf., Jb 6.16.

Cf. νυνί, ἄρτι, τότε: Laurentin; Brongers.

νυνί. adv.

Mostly foll. by δέ.

now, at the present time: Ex 32.34; in contrast to the past, Nu 11.6, De 10.22; with no δέ following, Ps 16.11; ǁ νῦν Jb 30.1. **b**. marks a new phase in a course of development: 4M 6.33. **c**, w. ref. to a recent event: + aor., ν. δὲ κατεγέλασάν μου 'they have mocked at me' Jb 30.1.

Cf. νῦν.

νύξ, κτός. f.

night: ǁ ἡμέρα Ge 1.14, ἡμέραν καὶ νύκτα 8.22; τρεῖς ἡμέρας καὶ τρεῖς νύκτας 'for three days and three nights' Jn 2.1, cf. Am 5.8, Zc 14.7; νὺξ ὑμῖν ἔσται ἐξ ὁράσεως 'it will be night for you on account of vision' Mi 3.6; νυκτός 'at night' when thieves and robbers are about, Ob 5; νυκτός .. ἡμέρας 'at night .. by day' De 1.33; ἡμέρας καὶ νυκτός 'day and night' 28.66, νυκτὸς καὶ ἡμέρας Is 34.10; time for sleep, Ho 7.6; τὴν νύκτα 'by night' when a vision appears, Zc 1.8, but 'tonight' Ge 19.5; propitious for military attack, 14.15; ἐκ νύκτων 'at night' Pr 31.15; ὑπὸ νύκτα 'by night' Jn 4.10. **b**. symbol of intellectual and moral darkness and ignorance, νυκτὶ ὡμοίωσα τὴν μητέρα σου Ho 4.5; when darkness prevails, Am 5.8.

Cf. ἡμέρα, ἑσπέρα, ἔννυχος, νυκτερινός.

νύσσω: aor. ἔνυξα.ʃ

to touch with a sharp point: + acc., 'to pierce,' ὀφθαλμὸν .. καρδίαν Si 22.19; 'to nudge' 3M 5.14; so as to awaken, ***s*** κέντρον 'goad,' ***o*** hum. PSol 16.4.

νύσταγμα, ατος. n.ʃ *

(*period of*) *short or light sleep*: ἐπὶ ~άτων ἐπὶ κοίτης 'whilst dozing off in bed' Jb 33.15. Cf. νυστάζω, νυσταγμός: Caird 1969.25; LSG s.v.

νυσταγμός, οῦ. m.

short or light sleep: εἰ δώσω ὕπνον τοῖς ὀφθαλμοῖς μου, καὶ τοῖς βλεφάροις μου ~όν 'I shall not give sleep to my eyes and slumber to my eyelids' Ps 131.4; as cogn. obj., Je 23.31. Cf. νύσταγμα, νυστάζω, and ὕπνος.

νυστάζω: fut. ~τάξω; aor.act. ἐνύσταξα, inf. ~τάξαι, subj. ~τάξω.

to doze: ***s*** shepherds, Na 3.18, ὁ φυλάσσων 'the guard' Ps 120.3; indefatigable troops, οὐδὲ νυστάξουσιν οὐδὲ κοιμηθήσονται Is 5.27; κύνες .. φιλοῦντες νυστάξαι 'dogs ..' 56.10; οὐ νυστάξει οὐδὲ ὑπνώσει Ps 120.4; + cogn. acc., νυσταγμόν Je 23.31; *s* ψυχή Ps 118.28. Cf. ἐπινυστάζω, νύσταγμα, νυσταγμός, καθεύδω, ὑπνόω: Schmidt 1.442-70.

νωθροκάρδιος, ον.ʃ *

slow on the uptake: *s* hum., Pr 12.8 (:: συνετός). Cf. νωθρός.

νωθρός, ά, όν.ʃ

sluggish: *s* hum., Pr 22.29 (:: ὀξὺς ἐν τοῖς ἔργοις), καὶ παρειμένος ἐν τοῖς ἔργοις σου 'and lax in your deeds' Si 4.29; not necessarily a vice, 11.12. Cf. νωθρότης, νωθροκάρδιος: Spicq 2.550-2.

νωθρότης, ητος. f.ʃ

sluggishness: typical of advanced age, ποδῶν 'of feet' 3M 4.5. Cf. νωθρός.

νῶτος, ου m., ~τον, ου, n. Mostly m.:Thack. 155.

1. *hinder surface of body*, 'back': of hum., ἐπὶ τὰ δύο ~α αὐτῶν 'on their two backs' Ge 9.23; vulnerable for attack, αἱ χεῖρές σου ἐπὶ ~ου τῶν ἐχθρῶν σου 'your hands are on the back of your enemies' 49.8, cf. ~ον εἰς μάστιγας 'for whips' Is 50.6; κατὰ ~ου ἔχωμεν πολεμίους 'have behind our backs as enemies' 3M 3.24; of animals, esp. donkeys on whose back a restraining yoke is to be placed, ἔδωκαν ~ον παραφρονοῦντα 'turned a (rebellious) senseless back' Zc 7.11, ἀπειθοῦντα 'disobedient' Ne 9.29; ἐπέστρεψαν πρός με ~ον καὶ οὐ πρόσωπον 'they turned the back to me, and not face' Je 39.33; where a burden is carried, Ps 65.11. **b**. κατὰ ~ου *behind, at the back of*: Ez 40.18, 46.18. ***c**. δίδωμί τινα ~ον *to put sbd to flight*: + dat. (com.) pers., Ps 17.41, θήσεις αὐτοὺς ~ον 20.13, cf. Or ad loc. (PG 12.1252. θῇ αὐτοὺς φεύγοντας νῶτον) and σὺ μὴ δῷς ~ον μηδενί 'don't run away from anybody' *PTeb*. 21.8.

2. *flank*: of a tabernacle, Ex 37.11, 13.

3. *flat, wide surface* of a horizontally lying body: surface of a lake, θαλάσσης Χενερεθ Nu 34.11; a fig. of a great mass of people (?), ν. ἐθνῶν πολλῶν Is 17.12.

Cf. μετάφρενον: Caird 1969.25.

νωτοφόρος, ου. m.ʃ

porter: 2C 2.17, 34.13.

Ξ

ξανθίζωʃ
to be yellow (ξανθός): *s* hair, Le 13.30, 31, 32. Cf. ξανθός.

Ξανθικός, οῦ. m.
name of a month in the Macedonian calendar: Es A 1*L*, 2M 11.30.

ξανθός, ή, όν.ʃ
yellow: *s* hair, Le 13.36. Cf. ξανθίζω: Schmidt 3.34-6.

ξενίζω: fut. ξενιῶ.
1. *to serve and entertain*: ***o*** master of the house Si 29.25.
2. *to be strange* or *extraordinary*: *s* διαγωγή 'life-style' Es B 5 o' (*L* παραγωγή); mode of punishment, 3M 7.3.
Cf. ἐπιξενόομαι, ξενισμός.

ξένιος, α, ον.
1. *hospitable*: Ζεὺς ~ς, so called as protector of the rights of hospitality, 2M 6.2.
2. subst.n.pl., *gift*: of war prisoners to be presented to a victorious ruler, Ho 10.6; ~α καὶ δῶρα Si 20.29; for those about to set out on a journey, 2E 1.6. **b**. *provisions for sustenance*: for soldiers sent on a military expedition, 1M 10.36. **c**. *tribute* given by the vanquished: 2K 8.2.
Cf. δόμα and δῶρον: Spicq 2.597.

ξενισμός, οῦ. m.ʃ
entertainment: λαχάνων 'with vegetables' Pr 15. 17. Cf. ξενίζω.

ξενιτεία, ας. f.ʃ *
act of living abroad: Wi 18.3. Cf. παροικία.

ξενολογέω: aor. ἐξενολόγησα.ʃ
to enlist as mercenary: abs. 1M 4.35; + acc. pers., 11.38, 15.3.

ξένος, η, ον.
1. *not belonging to and being outside of* a company of people: *s* hum., τοῖς υἱοῖς τῆς μητρός μου Ps 68.9 (ǁ ἀπηλλοτριωμένος); + προσήλυτος, πτωχός Si 10.22; traveller, 2K 12.4, Jb 31.32; newly arrived immigrant, Ru 2.10; ~αι δυνάμεις 'mercenary troops' 2M 10.24.
2. *unfamiliar*: *s* hum., λαός Is 18.2; ǁ ἀλλότριος La 5.2; γεῦσις 'meal' Wi 16.2, ὑετός 'rain,' θάνατος 19.5; subst.f., χώρα, γῆ or suchlike understood, 2M 9.28, cf. Renehan 1.145.
3. subst.m./f., *invitee*: for a sacrificial meal, 1K 9.13 (ǁ κεκλημένος vs. 22).
Cf. ἀλλότριος: Spicq 2.555-60.

ξενοτροφέω.ʃ
to maintain mercenary troops: 2M 10.14.

ξεστός, ή, όν.ʃ
1. *built of hewn stone*: of luxurious house, οἴκους ~ούς Am 5.11.
2. *planed, polished*: *s* τοῖχος 'wall' Si 22.17; λίθος 1M 13.27.
Cf. ξυστός.

ξηραίνω: fut. ξηρανῶ, pass. ξηρανθήσομαι, aor. ἐξήρανα, pass. ἐξηράνθην, inf. ξηρανθῆναι, opt.3s ξηρανθείη.
1. act. *to dry, to cause to lose moisture*: ***o*** the sea, Na 1.4 (ǁ ἐξερημόω, ὀλιγόω), ἕλη 'marshes' Is 42.15, πηγή 'well' Je 28.36, ποταμούς 'rivers' Ps 73.15, cf. Si 40.13 (fig. of wrongfully acquired possessions), ξύλον χλωρόν 'green tree' Ez 17.24 (:: ἀναθάλλω), τὴν γῆν Jb 12.15; *s* καύσων 'hot wind' Ez 19.12.
2. pass. *to become dry, lose moisture*: *s* the flooded earth, Ge 8.14; trees, Jl 1.12, grape-vine, ib.; roots, ἐξηράνθη τὰς ῥίζας αὐτοῦ 'it dried up at its roots' Ho 9.16; χόρτος 'grass' Je 12.4; arm, Zc 11.17*bis*; land, as a result of drought, Am 4.7, νομή 'pasture' Je 23.10; 'the summit of Carmel' Am 1.2; fishes, Is 50.2, ὀστᾶ 'bones' Pr 17.22. **b**. *s* normally moist place: ἀφέσεις ὑδάτων Jl 1.20, πάντα τὰ βάθη ποταμῶν Zc 10.11, ποταμός Is 19.5, συναγωγὴ ὕδατος 'water reservoir' 19.6. **c**. *s* moist, fluid object, *to run dry, to run out of supply*: water, ἕως ξηρανθῆναι τὸ ὕδωρ ἀπὸ τῆς γῆς 'until the water dried up from the earth' Ge 8.7; wine, Jl 1.10 (ǁ ὀλιγόομαι); then by extension also of solid objects, ἐξηράνθη σῖτος Jl 1.17, and even ἐξηράνθησαν οἱ γεωργοί 'the farmers ran out of supply of their agricultural produce, became impoverished' Jl 1.11; ὡς ὄστρακον ἡ ἰσχύς μου 'my strength as a potsherd' Ps 21.16, ὡς χόρτος .. ἡ καρδία μου 'my heart .. as grass' 101.5. **d**. mid. *to become stiff and immobile*: *s* hum. hand, 3K 13.4, cf. Mk 3.1 and Renehan 1.145f.
Cf. ἀνα~, ἀπο~, καταξηραίνω, ξηρός: Schmidt 2.329-31.

ξηρασία, ας. f.
dryness: καλάμη ~ας μεστή 'stubble fully dry' Na 1.10; cogn. dat., Ez 17.10; opp. ὑετός 40.43, opp. δρόσος 'dew' Jd 6.37. **b**. *dry area*: Ne 9.11.
Cf. ξηρός.

ξηρός, ά, όν. adj.

lacking fluid and moisture, 'dry': ἐποίησεν τὴν θάλασσαν ~άν 'he made the sea dry' Ex 14.21; *s* χόρτος 'grass' Is 37.27, μαστοί 'breasts' which have run out of milk, Ho 9.14, ἄγρωστις 'dog's-tooth grass' Is 9.18, ξυλὸν ~όν 'dry wood' Is 56.3 (of eunuchs). **b**. subst. ἡ ξηρά *dry (land)*: Ge 1.9; ἐπορεύθησαν διὰ ~ᾶς ἐν μέσῳ τῆς θαλάσσης Ex 15.19; opp. the sea, Jn 2.11, Ps 65.6; + ἡ θάλασσα Jn 1.9, Hg 2.6, 21, 1M 8.23; ‖ ἡ θάλασσα Ps 94.5; dried-up area of a river-bed, 4K 2.8 (B: ἔρημος). **c**. τὸ ξηρόν *dry ground* Ex 4.9 (:: river), 14.16 (:: sea). Cf. γῆ, ξηρασία, αὐχμώδης, χέρσος, ὑγρός: Schmidt 2.324f.

ξιφηφόρος, ον.ʃ

carrying a sword: *s* hum. hand, 4M 16.20. Cf. ξίφος.

ξίφος, ους. n.

sword: destructive weapon, Ez 16.40; ἐν στόματι ~ους 'with the blade of ..' Jo 10.28; ὀξύ 'sharp' Wi 18.16; ἀκμὴ ~ους 'point of ..' 2M 12.22. Cf. μάχαιρα, ῥομφαία, ξιφηφόρος.

ξυλάριον, ου. n.ʃ

Dim. of ξύλον, *small piece of wood*: 3K 17.14. Cf. ξύλον.

ξύλινος, η, ον.

1. *pertaining to tree*: καρπὸς ~ος 'fruit(s) growing on a tree' Le 27.30; ‖ δερμάτινος 'of leather' Nu 31.20. **b**. subst.: ξύλινα = ξύλα De 28.42.

2. *made of wood* or *timber*: σκεῦος ~ον 'wooden vessel' Le 11.32, 15.12; ~α χειροποίητα 'wooden, hand-made idols' 26.30, θεοὺς ἀργυροῦς καὶ χρυσοῦς καὶ ~ους Ep Je 3; *s* κιβωτός 'chest' De 10.1; κλοιοί 'collars' Je 35.13; πύργος 'tower' on the back of an elephant 1M 6.37; δόμος 'course of timber' 1E 6.24 (‖ λίθινος); ἱμάντωσις 'beam' Si 22.16.

Cf. ξύλον.

ξυλοκόπος, ον. m.ʃ

subst. *wood-feller*: ‖ ὑδροφόρος De 29.11, Jo 9.21, 27; ‖ δοῦλος 9.23.

ξύλον, ου. n.

1. *timber, wood*: material used to construct a building, Hb 2.11, Zc 5.4 (‖ λίθος); vessel, ἐξ ~ων τετραγώνων Ge 6.14; of idols for worship, Hb 2.19 (‖ λίθος); of firewood, Zc 12.6, Je 5.14; used to kindle a sacrifice, ξύλα ὁλοκαρπώσεως Ge 22.6; τέκτων τῶν ~ων 'carpenter' 4K 12.12; less valuable than copper, Is 60.17. **b**. *piece of wood*: poisonous, Je 11.19. **c**. anything made of wood: cudgel (for punishment) or stocks, La 5.13, Jb 33.11; handle of an axe, De 19.5, cf. LSG s.v. **II 3 b**.

2. *live wood, standing tree* (so alr. in Xen. *An.* 6.4.5): τὰ ~α ἐν τοῖς πεδίοις Ex 9.25; τοῦ ἀγροῦ Jl 1.12, 19; fruit-bearing, ξύλον .. καλὸν εἰς βρῶσιν .. τὸ ξ. τῆς ζωῆς .. καὶ τὸ ξ. τοῦ εἰδέναι γνωστὸν καλοῦ καὶ πονηροῦ 'plant (the fruit of which is) good for eating .. the tree of life .. and the tree for knowing what is knowable of good and bad' Gn 2.9, cf. Is 65.22; κάρπινον 'fruit-bearing' Ge 1.11, καρποφόρον Ps 148.9, βρώσιμον Le 19.23, τὸ ξ. τοῦ ἀγροῦ ὑμῶν οὐ δώσει τὸν καρπὸν αὐτοῦ Le 26.20; Jl 2.22, τῆς ἐλαίας 'olive-trees' Hg 2.19; building materials, κόψατε ~α 1.8; object of worship, λατρεύσεις .. θεοῖς ἑτέροις, ξύλοις καὶ λίθοις De 28.36 (‖ δουλεύσεις vs. 64); 29.17.

Cf. δένδρον, ξυλοκόπος: Shipp 408; on sense **1**, see Husson 180-2.

ξυλοφορία, ας. f.ʃ

**wood-offering*: Ne 10.34.

ξυλοφόρος, ου. m.ʃ

wood-bearer or *wood-offerer*: Ne 13.31.

ξυλόω: aor. ἐξύλωσα; pf.ptc.pass. ἐξυλωμένος.ʃ

to cover the wall of a building or room *with wooden panel*: *o* house, ξύλοις κεδρίνοις 2C 3.5; room, ἐν κέδρῳ 'with cedar timber' Je 22.14.

ξυράω: fut.act. ξυρήσω, mid. ξυρήσομαι, ξυρηθήσομαι; aor. ἐξύρησα, mid.impv. ξύρησαι, inf. ξυρήσασθαι, subj. ξυρήσωμαι, pass. ἐξυρήθην, ξυρηθῆναι; pf.ptc.mid. ἐξυρημένος.

I. act. *to shave*: *hair of the head* or *part of the body of*: + acc. pers. Ge 41.14 (*o* freed prisoner), leper Le 13.34; + acc. of part of sbd else's body - *o* head, De 21.12; hair and part of body, πᾶσαν τὴν τρίχα αὐτοῦ, τὴν κεφαλὴν αὐτοῦ καὶ τὸν πώγωνα καὶ τὰς ὀφρύας καὶ πᾶσαν τὴν τρίχα αὐτοῦ 'his entire hair, his head, his chin, the eyebrows and his entire hair' 14.9; ξυρῷ 'with a razor' Is 17.20; pass. and double acc. [= pers., and hair of part of his body or part of his body] (see ξυρήσας μιν τὰς τρίχας Hdt. 5.35), ξυρηθήσεται αὐτοῦ πᾶσαν τὴν τρίχα 'he shall have his entire hair cut' Le 14.8, *o* skin 13.33[1], scabs on it 13.33[2], φαλάκρωμα οὐ ξυρηθήσεσθε τὴν κεφαλὴν .. 'one shall not cut the hair of your head bald ..' 21.5[1].

II. mid. *to shave oneself* or *to have sbd else shave*: abs. Mi 1.16 (‖ κείρω); *o* part of one's own body - head, Nu 6.9 (mid. ‖ 'passive'), 18, Ez 44.20 (last: ‖ ψιλόω), κεφαλὰς καὶ πώγωνας '.. and beards' Ep Je 30; *o* hair of part of one's own body, τὴν ὄψιν τοῦ πώγωνος οὐ ξυρήσονται 'they shall not cut their beard, leading to a changed look' Le 21.5[2], cf. *BA* ad loc.

Cf. ξύρησις, ξυρόν, κείρω, μαδαρόω.

ξύρησις, εως. f.ʃ

v.n. of ξυράω: + κλαυθμός, κοπετός, ζῶσις σάκκων as a gesture of mourning and repentance, Is 22.12, cf. LSG s.v.

ξυρόν, οῦ. n.
razor: ξ. οὐ ἐπελεύσεται ἐπὶ τὴν κεφαλὴν αὐτοῦ 'no razor shall be applied to his head' Nu 6.5; to shave the entire body, ἐπὶ πᾶν τὸ σῶμα 8.7; οὐκ ἀναβήσεται Jd 16.17A (|| B σίδηρος); ξυρήσει .. τῷ ~ῷ τῷ μεγάλῳ καὶ τῷ μεμεθυσμένῳ 'with the large and drunken ..' Is 7.20; scribe's penknife, Je 43.23; κουρέως 'of a barber' Ez 5.1; ἠκονημένον 'sharpened' Ps 51.4. Cf. ξυράω.

ξύστης, ου. m.∫
polisher: λίθων 4K 12.13*L*. Cf. ξύω.

ξυστός, ή, όν.
smoothed: ***s*** stone as building material, 1E 6.8, δόμος λίθινος 'course of planed stone' 6.24. Cf. ξεστός, ξύω.

ξύω.∫
to scrape away: Jb 2.8, 7.5. Cf. ξύστης, ξυστός, περιξύω.

O

ὁ, ἡ, τό.

I. A reference to an entity, event or state clearly identifiable from the linguistic or extra-linguistic context. **a.** "Anaphoric": Ἑώρακα .. καὶ ἰδοὺ ἀνὴρ ἐπιβεβηκὼς ἐπὶ ἵππον .. ἀπεκρίθη ὁ ἀνὴρ ὁ ἐφεστηκὼς .. 'I saw .. and behold there was a man mounted on a horse .. that mounted man answered ..' Zc 1.8, 10. **b.** with unique entities: Ἐν ἀρχῇ ἐποίησεν ὁ θεὸς τὸν οὐρανὸν καὶ τὴν γῆν Ge 1.1; τῆς καρδίας σου Ob 3 ‖ ἐν καρδίᾳ (v.l. pr. τῇ) αὐτοῦ ib.; ἡ γῆ 'the earth' Ob 3; τὴν θάλασσαν καὶ τὴν ξηράν Jn 1.9. **c.** familiarity determined by the general context: ἔπιεν ἐκ τοῦ οἴνου 'he drank (a bit) of the wine (produced in the vineyard mentioned in the preceding verse) Ge 9.21; περιοχὴν εἰς τὰ ἔθνη ἐξαπέστειλεν 'he has sent a circular to the peoples concerned' Ob 1; ὁ νεανίσκος Nu 11.27, ἡ παιδίσκη 2K 17.17. **d.** with personal or place names: τῇ Ἰδουμαίᾳ Ob 1; ἡ Βασανῖτις Na 1.4; ὁ Κάρμηλος ib.; τὸν Ιωναν Jn 1.15; ἐπὶ τὸν Ισραηλ Ma 1.1. Cf. BDF, § 260. Used w. indeclinable names to make the syntactic relationship clear (BDF, § 260.2): εἶπεν ὁ θεὸς τῷ Νωε Ge 9.8; οὐκ ἀδελφὸς ἦν Ησαυ τῷ Ιακωβ; 'Wasn't Esau Jacob's brother?' Ma 1.2; the gen. in genealogy, πρὸς Σοφονίαν τὸν τοῦ Χουσι υἱὸν Γοδολίου τοῦ Αμαρίου τοῦ Εζεκίου 'to Z. the son of C., son of G., son of A., son of H.' Zp 1.1. **e.** w. ref. to a species rather than a particular representative of it, so-called "generic" article: ἔγκειται ἡ διάνοια τοῦ ἀνθρώπου ἐπιμελῶς ἐπὶ τὰ πονηρά 'man's mind is intensely occupied with evil things' Ge 8.21. ***f.** Semitistically added to a noun indicating a person addressed in speech, but not formally in the vocative: Ἀκούσατε, οἱ ἱερεῖς, .. Ho 5.1; Ma 2.1; Ὁ θεός 'O God!' Ho 8.2 (see BDF, § 147.3). **g.** added only to the first of multiple coordinate terms: τῷ Αβρααμ καὶ Ισαακ καὶ Ιακωβ Ex 6.8, 33.1, Nu 32.11, De 1.8, 6.10; τὸν Ἀμορραῖον καὶ Χαναναῖον καὶ Χετταῖον .. Ex 34.11, sim. 23.23, 33.2, πάντα τὰ ἔθνη καὶ φυλὰς καὶ γλώσσας Da 3.2 LXX, but the article is repeated at Ge 10.15-8 where individual mention is important.

II. Added to a qualifier following an articular nominal nucleus. **a.** + adj.: τὸν ἄνδρα μου τὸν πρότερον 'my previous husband' Ho 2.7; more than once, ἡ βόμβησις ἡ μεγάλη ἡ πολλὴ αὕτη Ba 2.29. **b.** + ptc.: ὁ θεὸς ὁ ἐξαγαγών σε .. Ge 15.7; τὰ ξύλα τῆς ἐλαίας τὰ οὐ φέροντα καρπόν 'the olive-trees which do not bear fruits' Hg 2.19. **c.** + adv.: τοῦ λοιμοῦ τοῦ πρότερον 'the earlier famine' Ge 26.1; ἐν τῇ ἡμέρᾳ τῇ αὔριον 'on the following day' 30.33; τὰς ἡμέρας τὰς ἔμπροσθεν 'the former era' Mi 7.20; Zc 8.11; τὰ ἔμπροσθεν αὐτοῦ 'what lies ahead of them' Jl 2.3; τὰ ὀπίσω σου Na 3.5. **d.** + prepositional phrase: τοῦ ὕδατος τοῦ ἐπάνω τοῦ στερεώματος 'the water over the firmament' Ge 1.7; τὴν ἄμμον τὴν παρὰ τὸ χεῖλος τῆς θαλάσσης 'the sand along the seashore' 22.17; τὸν χιτῶνα τὸν ποικίλον τὸν περὶ αὐτόν 'the multicoloured tunic on him' 37.23; ἡ χήρα ἡ ἐν ὑμῖν 'the widow amongst you' De 16.11 (‖ ἡ χ. ἡ οὖσα ἐν ταῖς πόλεσίν σου vs. 14); τῆς ἀδικίας τῆς ἐν χερσὶν αὐτῶν 'the iniquity which is on their hands' Jn 3.8; τὴν ἀσέβειαν τὴν εἰς τὸν ἀδελφόν σου (v.l. τὴν ἀσ. ἀδελφοῦ σοῦ) Ob 10. See Johannessohn, *Präp.* 366-9. **e.** + πᾶς + noun, πάσῃ ψυχῇ τῇ ζώσῃ μεθ' ὑμῶν 'every living being living with you' Ge 9.10; πᾶν ξύλον τὸ φυόμενον ὑμῖν ἐπὶ τῆς γῆς 'every tree growing for you on the ground' Ex 10.5; πάσας νόσους Αἰγύπτου τὰς πονηράς, ἃς ἑώρακας καὶ ὅσα ἔγνως De 7.15. **f.** + an anarthrous noun head: ἐν πόλει τῇ ἐχούσῃ τεῖχος Le 25.30, οἴκου ἀποτεταγμένου τοῦ ὑπερῴου 'the upper, special house' Je 20.2, γῆ ἡ οὐ βρεχομένη Ez 22.24, ἔθνη τὰ μὴ γινώσκοντά σε Ps 78.6; 111.5; εἰς εἰρήνην τὴν Ιερουσαλημ 'for the peace of J.' 121.6; Pr 7.5, 21.

III. Substantivizing, i.e. with a nucleus noun understood. **a.** + adj.: τὰ ἱκανά 'enough, a sufficient amount' Ob 5; τοὺς ἀλλοφύλους 'foreigners' 19; approaches the force of the superlative, ὁ ἁπαλὸς ἐν σοί 'the most delicate among you' De 28.54 (‖ σφόδρα), ἡ καλὴ ἐν γυναιξίν 'the prettiest among women' Ct 1.8, 6.1, τὸν ἀγαθὸν .. ἐν τοῖς υἱοῖς τοῦ κυρίου ὑμῶν 'the best .. among the sons of your master' 4K 10.3, cf. ὁ μικρότατος (v.l. νεώτερος) τῶν υἱῶν αὐτοῦ 2C 21.17 and JM § 141 *j*. **b.** + ptc.: τοὺς κατακληρονομήσαντας αὐτούς 'those who dispossessed them' Ob 17; τὰ οὐκ ὄντα αὐτοῦ 'that which is not his own' Hb 2.6. **c.** + prep. phrase: τῷ ἐπὶ τῆς οἰκίας αὐτοῦ 'to the one who is in charge of his household' Ge 44.4 (‖ τῷ ὄντι .. vs. 1); οἱ ἐν Ναγεβ .. οἱ ἐν τῇ Σεφηλα Ob 19; τὰ εἰς εἰρήνην Ps 121.6; ἡ ὑπ' οὐρανόν 'the world' Jb 18.4, 19 28.24 (scil. οἰκουμένη or γῆ), ‖ κτίσις Si 16.15¶; τὰ μετὰ ταῦτα 'the future' Si 3.30; ἡ πρὸ τοῦ σαββάτου 'the day before the sabbath' 2M 8.26. **d.** + gen., esp. of proper nouns: Εφρων τῷ τοῦ Σααρ 'to E. the (son) of S.' Ge 23.8; πρὸς Ιωναν τὸν τοῦ Αμαθι 'to Jonah the (son) of Amittai' Jn 1.1; πρὸς Ζοροβαβελ τὸν τοῦ Σαλαθιηλ Hg 1.1, 2.21, cf. τὸ ὄρος τὸ Ησαυ 'the mountain(s) of Esau' Ob 19; πάντων τῶν αὐτοῦ 'all his affairs' Ge 24.2; the gen. understood, ἐν τῷ χρόνῳ τῷ Αβρααμ 'at the time of A.' 26.1; ἐν τῇ ἐρήμῳ τῇ Σινα 'in the wilderness of Sin' Nu 1.1; τὰ εἰς εἰρήνην τὴν Ιερουσαλημ Ps 121.6, but see under ἐρωτάω; τὰ αὐτοῦ 'his estate, premises' or οἱ αὐτοῦ 'his household' Jb 18.19. **e.** + numeral: οἱ δύο 'the two (mentioned earlier)' Ge 2.24, 3.1. **f.** + adv.: ἕως τοῦ νῦν 'until now' Ge 32.4; τὸ νῦν Ex 9.27, To 7.11 𝔊[I] (𝔊[II] > τό); τὸ ἑσπέρας (gen.) Nu 9.15. **g.** + adverbial prep. phrase: τὸ πρὸς ἑσπέραν 'towards the evening' Ge 8.11, Nu 9.11 (|| without τὸ at 9.3); τὸ καθ' ἡμέραν εἰς ἡμέραν 'day in day out' Ex 16.5, Le 23.37; τὸ πρὸς ἑσπέραν .. τὸ πρωΐ Ex 16.12, sim. Nu 28.4, and cf. πρὸς ἑσπέραν (without τό) Zc 14.7; τὸ ἀπ' ἀχρῆς 'formerly' Jo 24.2, ὡς τὸ ἀπ' ἀρχῆς 'as in former times' Is 63.19; τὰ πρὸς κύριον 'as regards the Lord' De 1.36, Is 3.8, τὰ πρὸς τὸν θεόν De 31.27; εἰς τὰ ὄπισθεν καὶ οὐκ εἰς τὰ ἔμπροσθεν Je 7.24. **h.** + an antecedentless rel. pron.: τὰ ὅσα .. 'all that ..' Ec 2.12, 8.9.

IV. As a dem. pronoun immediately followed by δέ or μέν: ὁ δὲ ἀποκριθεὶς εἶπεν .. Ge 18.9; ἡ δὲ εἶπεν 38.16, Jd 11.36 B; οἱ δὲ εἶπαν 'thereupon they said' Ge 29.5, 6, 8; foll. by a noun phrase, ἡ δὲ εἶπεν αὐτῇ ἡ θυγάτηρ Φαραω Ex 2.8; οἱ μὲν .. ἡμεῖς δὲ .. 'they .. but we ..' 2M 8.18; in obl. case, τῶν δὲ .. 2M 14.44, 15.4, 3M 1.11. **b.** + prep.: ἀπὸ τοῦ 'since that time' Jb 20.4, cf. LSJ s.v. **A VIII 5**.

V. In juxtaposition: 'the one .. the other,' 'some .. others'– συνέλεξαν, ὁ τὸ πολὺ καὶ ὁ τὸ ἔλαττον 'they collected, some much but others a little' Ex 16.17; τὰ μὲν καταβάλλει, ἄλλα δὲ φύει .. ἡ μὲν τελευτᾷ, ἑτέρα δὲ γεννᾶται 'Some (leaves) fall off, others grow .. one generation dies, then another is born' Si 14.18; 2M 3.19, 4M 14.15f. **b.** adv., τὰ μὲν .. τὰ δὲ .. 'partly .. partly ..' 4M 6.12f.

VI. + infinitive: **a**. the case of the article determined by the preceding prep. – διὰ τὸ λαὸν σκληροτράχηλόν σε εἶναι 'because you are a stiff-necked people' Ex 33.3 (see under διά **II 1b**); ἐν τῷ ἐκλείπειν Jn 2.8 (see under ἐν **3b**); ἕως τοῦ ἐλθεῖν (see under II ἕως **Af**); πρὸ τοῦ ἐπελθεῖν Zp 2.2 (see under πρό **Ic**); **b**. τοῦ inf.: **i**. qualifying a noun, ἀπὸ τοῦ ξύλου τοῦ γινώσκειν καλὸν καὶ πονηρόν 'from the tree of knowledge of good and evil' Ge 2.17; ὁ καιρὸς τοῦ οἰκοδομῆσαι 'the time for building' Hg 1.2. **ii**. final, i.e. indicating a purpose, mostly with an aor. inf. (BDF, § 400), τοῦ ἰδεῖν 'in order to see' Ge 8.7; ἀνέστη Ιωνας τοῦ φυγεῖν 'Jonas got up to run away' Jn 1.3; pres. ἐξαπέσταλκα πρὸς ὑμᾶς τὴν ἐντολὴν ταύτην τοῦ εἶναι τὴν διαθήκην μου 'I sent you this commandment in order for it to become my covenant' Ma 2.4. **iii**. merely replacing a bare inf.: μηδαμῶς σὺ ποιήσεις ὡς τὸ ῥῆμα τοῦτο, τοῦ ἀποκτεῖναι δίκαιον μετὰ ἀσεβοῦς 'surely you are not going to act like that, killing the righteous along with the godless' Ge 18.25; ἤρξατο Ιωνας τοῦ εἰσελθεῖν 'Jonas began to enter' Jn 3.4; ἐλάλησε τοῦ ποιῆσαι 'he said that he would do' 3.10; προέφθασα τοῦ φυγεῖν 'with foresight I fled' 4.2; οὐ μὴ προσθήσω τοῦ ἀγαπῆσαι αὐτούς 'I shall not love them again' Ho 9.15; ἕτοιμον εἶναι τοῦ πορεύεσθαι 'to be ready to walk' Mi 6.8. **iv**. with the "ablative" force of separation, derivation etc.: ἠμβλύνθησαν οἱ ὀφθαλμοὶ αὐτοῦ τοῦ ὁρᾶν 'his eyes became too dim to see' Ge 27.1; ἔστη τοῦ τίκτειν 'she stopped bearing' 29.35; ἦν γὰρ αὐτῶν τὰ ὑπάρχοντα πολλὰ τοῦ οἰκεῖν ἅμα 'for their possessions were too much for them to live together' 36.7; ἀποκωλῦσαι τοὺς ἀνθρώπους .. τοῦ οἰκοδομῆσαι τὴν πόλιν 'to stop the people rebuilding the city' 1E 2.24; καθαρὸς ὀφθαλμὸς τοῦ μὴ ὁρᾶν πονηρά 'an eye too pure to watch evil things' Hb 1.13 (with μή!). **v**. with a comparative: μείζων ἡ αἰτία μου τοῦ ἀφεθῆναί με; 'Is my guilt too grave for me to be forgiven?' Ge 4.13. **c**. an inf. understood: πρὸ τοῦ ὑμᾶς Le 18.30 (cf. v.l. πρὸ τοῦ ὑμᾶς γενέσθαι) and πρὸ τοῦ σέ Ex 17.6 v.l. Cf. Hauspie 2006.

VII. Special usages: acc.sg. with distributive force, ἀμνοὺς δύο .. τὴν ἡμέραν 'two .. lambs a day' Ex 29.38, τὴν ἡμέραν δύο σώματα 'two cadavers per day' Bel TH 32 (LXX: καθ' ἑκάστην ἡμέραν), cf. τὴν ἡμέραν εἰς τὰς ἑπτὰ ἡμέρας 'daily during the seven days' Nu 28.24. **b**. also w. gen. sg.: δραχμὴν τῆς ἡμέρας 'a drachma per day' To 5.15 𝔊[I] (𝔊[II] τὴν ~αν), τρίς τῆς ἡμέρας 'thrice a day' Da 6.5 LXX; ἄρτον ἕνα τῆς ἡμέρας 'one piece of bread a day' Je 44.21, cf. πρὸς ἀνατολὰς ἓξ τὴν ἡμέραν, βορρᾶ τῆς (*L*: τὴν) ἡμέρας τέσσαρες 'on the east six (Levites) each day, on the north ..' 1C 26.17.

On the definite article as a whole, see BDF, § 252-76.

ὀβελίσκος, ου. m.∫

nail, stud: ὀξύς 'sharp' Jb 41.22, 4M 11.19 (instrument of torture). Cf. βασανιστήριον.

ὀβολός, οῦ. m.

obol, a weight: εἴκοσι ~οὶ τὸ δίδραχμον Ex 30.13, see *BA* ad loc.; a fig. of modest quantity, ἀργυρίου 'of silver' 1K 2.36.

ὀγδοήκοντα. indecl. num.

eighty: ὀγδοήκοντα ἓξ ἐτῶν '86 years old' Ge 16.16.

ὀγδοηκοστός, ή, όν.ʃ
eightieth: 2M 1.10.

ὄγδοος, η, ον.
eighth in order: τῇ ἡμέρᾳ τῇ ~όῃ 'on the eighth day' Ge 17.14; τῇ ὀγδόῃ ἡμέρᾳ 21.4.

ὅδε, ἥδε, τόδε.
1. attributively used and preceding the nominal, *this which is present before the person(s) being spoken to*: τόδε τὸ ἀργύριον Ge 43.21; οἵδε ἡμεῖς σοι οἰκέται 50.18; Nu 14.40; ὅδε ἐγώ Ex 8.29, 17.6, Da 3.92 TH; poss. pointing to a map, 4K 6.8. **b.** following: τὴν ἐπιστολὴν τήνδε 'this letter' 3M 3.25. **c.** substantivally: τίνες οἵδε .. 'Who are these ..?' Is 60.8.
2. substantivally, *this* with ref. to what is immediately to follow, and often in the standing phrase τάδε λέγει κύριος 'thus says the Lord' (e.g. Ex 4.22), which introduces a divine message conveyed through a prophet or God's messenger, except in Τάδε λέγει Φαραω Ex 5.10 and τάδε λέγει Αμως Am 7.11; with indication of the person spoken to, Τάδε ἐρεῖς τῷ οἴκῳ Ιακωβ Ex 20.22; πρὸς τὸν οἶκον Ισραηλ Am 5.4, τῇ Ιδουμαίᾳ Ob 1; followed immediately by direct speech of message, Hg 1.9, Is 1.24 +, except in Hg 1.2 and Zc 7.9 with λέγων intervening; τάδε εἶπεν κύριος 1K 2.30. **b.** anaphorically referring to what has just been mentioned, Le 10.16; τήνδε ἐκάλυψεν αὐτὴν ἡ νεφέλη 'the cloud covered this' Nu 16.42; 2M 12.40; κατὰ τάδε 'in this way' 1K 2.14.
3. equivalent of a pers. pron.: τῇδε (= αὐτῇ) ἦν δίδυμα ἐν τῇ κοιλίᾳ αὐτῆς 'she had twins in her belly' Ge 25.24 (or: adverbial, 'thus there were'), sim. 38.27.
Cf. οὗτος: Humbert, § 32-34. On the distinction between οὗτος and ὅδε, see also Abel, § 34 *a*.

ὁδεύω.ʃ
to journey: *s* hum., To 6.6 𝔊[I] (𝔊[II] πορεύομαι). Cf. πορεύομαι, συνοδεύω.

ὁδηγέω: fut. ὁδηγήσω; aor. ὡδήγησα, impv. ὁδήγησον.
to lead along a certain route: *s* mostly God, + acc. pers., τὸν λαόν σου τοῦτον Ex 15.13; εἰς τὸν τόπον 32.34 (*s* hum.); ὁδὸν γῆς Φυλιστιιμ 'along the way of the land of the Philistines' 13.17; ἐξ Αἰγύπτου Nu 24.8; ἐπὶ τρίβους δικαιοσύνης Ps 22.3, ἐπὶ λιμένα θελήματος αὐτῶν 'to a haven of their desire' 106.30; ὁδηγῶν ὑμᾶς ἐν πυρὶ νυκτός, δεικνύων ὑμῖν τὴν ὁδόν 'leading you by fire at night, showing you the way' De 1.33, με ἐν τῇ δικαιοσύνῃ σου Ps 5.9, + ἄγω 42.3; *o* children, Jb 31.18¶ (*s* hum.; ∥ ἐκτρέφω 'nourish'); *s* καρδία μου ἐν σοφίᾳ Ec 2.3, σοφία Wi 9.11, ἐν τρίβοις εὐθείας 'on paths of integrity' 10.10. Cf. ἡγέομαι, καθοδηγέω, ὁδηγός, ὁδοποιέω, ἐμβιβάζω, οἰακίζω: Michaelis, *TDNT* 5.97f.

ὁδηγός, οῦ. m.
1. *leader*: 2E 8.1.
2. *guide*: ∥ διορθωτής Wi 7.15; 1M 4.2.
Cf. ὁδηγέω, προοδηγός, διορθωτής ἡγέομαι.

ὁδοιπορία, ας. f.
journey: ὁδηγὸν μὲν ἀγνώστου ~ας 'a guide for an unknown journey' Wi 18.3; τοῦ πλήθους 'of the multitude' 1M 6.41. Cf. ὁδοιπόρος.

ὁδοιπόρος, ου. m.
wayfarer, traveller: ~οι Ἰσμαηλῖται Ge 37.25; κακός 'highway bandit' Pr 6.11; ∥ ξένος 'stranger' 2K 12.4*L* (B: πάροδος); Jd 19.17 A (B: ὁ. ἀνήρ). Cf. ὁδοιπορία, ὁδός, πάροδος.

ὁδοποιέω: aor. ὡδοποίησα, impv. ~ποίησον.
to serve as a guide: + dat.pers., Is 62.10; ἔμπροσθεν αὐτῆς Ps 79.10. **b.** *to point* a way to follow: ἐπ' ἐμὲ τρίβους ἀπωλείας 'to me paths of perdition' Jb 30.12.
Cf. ὁδηγέω.

ὁδός, οῦ. f.
1. *road, way* for travel: ἀπελεύσεσθε εἰς τὴν ὁδόν Ge 19.2; ἐν τῇ ὁδῷ αὐτοῦ πορεύσονται Jl 2.7; ἐν ταῖς ~οῖς Na 2.5; πηλὸν ~ῶν 'dust of roads' Zc 9.3; βασιλική 'royal' Nu 20.17; ∥ πλατεῖα 'street' Am 5.16, Je 5.1; ∥ τρίβος Ge 49.17, Is 40.3; ἐν θαλάσσῃ Wi 14.3, cf. Beentjes 1992. ***b.** acc. ὁδόν 'along (the route)': foll. by a gen., ὡδήγησεν .. ~ὸν γῆς Φυλιστιιμ 'led .. along the way of the land of the Philistines' Ex 13.17, ἡ γῆ Νεφθαλιμ ~ὸν θαλάσσης Is 9.1; foll. by an acc., ἐκύκλωσεν .. ~ὸν τὴν εἰς τὴν ἔρημον 'led .. by the roundabout way into the desert' Ex 13.18, ἀνέβησαν ~ὸν τὴν εἰς Βασαν Nu 21.33; De 1.40, 3.1; 'in the direction of' - + gen., ὁδὸν γῆς αὐτῶν .. τῆς πόλεως .. καὶ τοῦ οἴκου 3K 8.48.
2. *way, path* leading to some object or location: τοῦ ξύλου τῆς ζωῆς Ge 3.24; Σουρ 16.7 (?); Jb 28.13; metaph., ὁ. πάσης τῆς γῆς 'universal human destiny' (ref. to approaching death) 3K 2.1.
3. *way in which one conducts oneself, life-style*, often pl.: κατέφθειρεν πᾶσα σὰρξ τὴν ὁδὸν αὐτοῦ ἐπὶ τῆς γῆς Ge 6.12; ἀπὸ τῆς ~οῦ αὐτοῦ τῆς πονηρᾶς Jn 3.8, sim. 3.10; ∥ ἐπιτήδευμα Ho 12.2, Zc 1.4, 6; ∥ διαβούλιον Ho 4.9; ~οὶ καὶ ἔργα Je 33.13; πάντες οἱ λαοὶ πορεύσονται ἕκαστος τὴν ~ὸν αὐτοῦ Mi 4.5; as divinely prescribed, Ἐὰν ἐν ταῖς ~οῖς μου πορεύῃ καὶ ἐὰν τὰ προστάγματά μου φυλάξῃς Zc 3.7; Ma 2.9; Na 1.3.
4. *journey*: ἐν τῇ ὁδῷ 'during the journey' Ge 44.29; ἐν ὁδῷ μακρὰν 'in the middle of a journey far (away from home)' Nu 9.10; ἐπισιτισμὸν .. εἰς τὴν ὁδόν 'provisions .. for the journey' Ex 12.39; *o* of ποιέω Jd 17.8.

5. *distance* capable of being covered in: + gen., ὁ. τριῶν ἡμερῶν Ge 30.36, Ex 3.18, Nu 10.33; ὡσεὶ πορείας ~οῦ ἡμερῶν τριῶν 'at a distance of about three days' journey' Jn 3.3; ὁδὸν ἡμέρας Nu 11.31.
Cf. ἀτραπός, εἴσοδος, ἔξοδος, ἴχνος, πλατεῖα, τρίβος, τροχιά, ὁδοιπόρος, πολυοδία: Schmidt 4.632f.

ὀδούς, όντος, pl.dat. ὀδοῦσιν. m.
tooth: Ex 21.24; part of digestive system, τὰ κρέα .. ἐν τοῖς ὀδοῦσιν αὐτῶν 'the meat ..' Nu 11.33; ἐξαρῶ .. τὰ βδελύγματα αὐτῶν ἐκ μέσου ὀδόντων αὐτῶν 'I shall move their abominable foods from between their teeth' Zc 9.7 (|| στόμα); γομφιασμὸν ~των 'idleness of their teeth (i.e. shortage of food)' Am 4.6; δάκνοντας ἐν τοῖς ὀδοῦσιν αὐτῶν 'biting with their teeth' Mi 3.5; of predatory animal, θηρίων De 32.24, λέοντος Jl 1.6 (|| μύλαι 'molars'); of venomous snakes, Wi 16.10; biting, hence destructive, Pr 30.14 (|| μύλη 'molar'). **b.** *pointed object or part of it*, 'prong': of an agricultural tool, 1K 13.21.
Cf. μύλη and στόμα.

ὀδυνάω: fut.pass. ὀδυνηθήσομαι; aor.pass. ὠδυνήθην.
to cause pain: mental, + acc. pers., Wi 14.24. **b.** pass. *to feel agony*: || φοβέομαι Zc 9.5; ἀπὸ προσώπου τινός 'on account of sth' Hg 2.14; + cogn. obj. and ἐπί τινι– ὀδύνην ὡς ἐπὶ πρωτοτόκῳ 'they will feel agony as over a first-born child' Zc 12.10, ἐφ' ἑαυτῷ 'one's own lot' Pr 29.21; + acc. (of time, rather than dir. obj.?), ἀτεκνίας καιρόν 'time of childlessness' 4M 18.9; + περί τινος (pers.) 2K 19.3*L* (B: λυπέομαι), Is 53.4. Cf. ὀδύνη, συνοδυνάομαι, θρηνέω, κλαίω, λυπέω, πενθέω, and πονέω.

ὀδύνη, ης. f.
pain, suffering: physical, υἱὸς ~ης μου 'a son of my suffering' Ge 35.18 (so named by a mother after difficult delivery), cf. Je 22.23; Αἰγύπτου 'experienced in Egypt' De 28.60; || νόσος, Ho 5.13*a*; πληγὴ ~ης 'a painful blow' Mi 1.11, ὀ. πληγῆς 'pain of blow' Is 30.26; mental, μετ' ~ης Ge 44.31 (|| μετὰ λύπης 42.38, 44.29); ἐν ~ῃ 'in a situation of hardship (due to famine?)' De 26.14; || πένθος, Am 8.10; ὀ. καὶ λύπη καὶ στεναγμός Is 51.11, || βάσανος, θλῖψις Ez 12.18, || κακά Ps 106.39, + μόχθος Jb 2.9d; κατοικοῦσα ~ας 'one who dwells amongst sufferings' Mi 1.12; as cogn. obj. of ὀδυνάω, Zc 12.10. Cf. ἀλγηδών, ὀδυνηρός, κατώδυνος, κλαυθμός, κόπος, κάκωσις, λύπη, νόσος, ὀδυνάω, πένθος, πόνος: Schmidt 2.598-603; *BA* ad Ge 42.38.

ὀδυνηρός, ά, όν.
liable to cause pain, 'grievous, painful': *s* πληγή 'blow' Je 14.17, 37.16; κατάρα 'curse' 3K 2.8. **b.** *suffering pain*: *s* καρδία La 5.17.
Cf. ὀδύνη, ἐπαλγής: Schmidt 2.607f.

ὀδυρμός, οῦ. m.ʃ
lamentation: φωνὴ .. θρήνου καὶ κλαυθμοῦ καὶ ~οῦ Je 38.15; μετὰ ~ῶν καὶ δακρύων ἱκέτευον 'entreated with .. and tears' 2M 11.6. Cf. ὀδύρομαι, γόος, θρῆνος.

ὀδύρομαι.ʃ
to lament: Je 38.18. Cf. ὀδυρμός, πανόδυρτος, προσοδύρομαι, θρηνέω, ὀλολύζω, στενάζω: Schmidt 3.384f.

ὄζος, ου. m.ʃ
knot or *eye* from which a branch or leaf springs (LSJ): Wi 13.13. Cf. κλάδος: Schmidt 2.469f.

ὄζω: aor. ὤζεσα.ʃ
to give out smell: unpleasant, 'stink', ὤζεσεν ἡ γῆ Ex 8.14 (of the ground that was littered with dead frogs). Cf. ἐπ~, προσόζω, ὀσμή.

ὅθεν
whence, from where: εἰς τὴν γῆν, ὅθεν ἐξῆλθεν ἐκεῖθεν 'into the land whence he came' Ge 24.5; συλλέγετε ἑαυτοῖς ἄχυρα ὅ. ἂν εὕρητε 'Gather straw for yourselves wherever you may find it from' Ex 5.11. Elliptically: ἐπορεύθη ὅ. ἦλθεν εἰς τὴν ἔρημον, ἕως Βαιθηλ .. 'he travelled (to the place) whence he had gone, into the desert, up to Bethel ..' Ge 13.3. **b.** in indirect question: ὅθεν δή 'never mind where (it comes) from' Wi 15.12. **c.** not local: πεποίθατε ἐπὶ λόγοις ψευδέσιν, ὅ. οὐκ ὠφεληθήσεσθε 'you trust in false things from which you would derive no benefit' Je 7.8. **c.** *therefore, hence*: To 12.18 𝔊[I], 2M 14.7, 4M 3.12.

ὀθόνιον, ου. n.ʃ
1. *linen cloth*: essential for human subsistence along with ἄρτος, ὕδωρ, ἱμάτια and ἔλαιον, Ho 2.5; for covering one's body, 2.9 (|| ἱμάτια).
2. *linen garment*: Jd 14.13B (A: σινδών).
Cf. ἱμάτιον, βύσσινος, λινοῦς: Bartina 1965; Spicq 2.564-67.

οἰακίζω.ʃ
to steer, guide: + acc., Jb 37.10; τὸν κόσμον Si 18.3¶. Cf. ὁδηγέω.

οἴαξ, ακος. m.ʃ
handle of ship's rudder: metaph., τῆς εὐσεβείας 'of piety' 4M 7.3. Cf. Shipp 410.

οἶδα (pf.): ptc. εἰδώς, subj. εἰδῶ / εἴδω, inf. εἰδέναι; plpf. ᾔδειν; fut. εἰδήσω; aor.inf. εἰδῆσαι.
Pf. with force of the pres., and plpf. with that of the impf.
1. *to have learnt, be able to recall*: + indir. question opening with εἰ, Ge 43.7, Jl 2.14, Jn 3.9; w. an interrogative, οὐκ οἴδαμεν, τίς ἐνέβαλεν τὸ ἀργύριον .. Ge 43.22; Οὐκ οἶδας τί ἐστι ταῦτα; Zc 4.13; + ὅτι Ge 3.5, 18.19; + ὡς De 29.16.
2. *to have knowledge of* sth (τι) *through experience* or *learning*: τὴν ὀδύνην αὐτῶν 'their suffering' Ex

3.7; τὴν ψυχὴν τοῦ προσηλύτου 23.9; εἰδότας θρῆνον w. ref. to professional crying women, Am 5.16; τὸ ὅρμημα τοῦ λαοῦ τούτου 'the impulse of this people' Ex 32.22; οὐκ οἴδασιν ἀγαθὸν οὐδὲ κακόν Nu 14.23; πόλεμον 1M 6.30; εἰδώς (ptc.) + inf., κυνηγεῖν 'to hunt' Ge 25.27, ξύλα κόπτειν 'to fell trees' 3K 5.20, τοῦ ποιῆσαι ἐν τῷ χρυσίῳ 'to work in gold' 2C 2.6, ψάλλειν 'to play music' 1K 16.16, τοῦ ποιῆσαι κακόν Ec 4.17, φέρειν μαλακίαν 'to bear infirmity' Is 53.3; τιμὴν θέσθαι ἁδροῖς 'to show respect to the great' Jb 34.19.

3. *to be aware, conscious*: οὐκ ᾔδει ἐν τῷ κοιμηθῆναι αὐτήν 'he was not aware of it when she lay' Ge 19.33; Ἔστιν κύριος ἐν τῷ τόπῳ τούτῳ, ἐγὼ δὲ οὐκ ᾔδειν 28.16; φονεύσῃ .. οὐκ εἰδώς De 4.42; + inf., Ec 4.17.

4. *to take interest in, concern oneself with*: + acc., οὐκ ᾔδει τῶν καθ' αὐτὸν οὐδέν 'he did not concern himself with any of his affairs' Ge 39.6 (‖ vs. 8 γινώσκει); τὸν κύριον Jb 36.12, sim. Wi 12.27, 16.16; κακίαν PSol 17.27.

5. *to be acquainted with*: + acc. pers., οὐκ ᾔδει τὸν Ιωσηφ Ex 1.8; οὐκ οἶδα τὸν κύριον 5.2; Οἶδά σε παρὰ πάντας 'I know you better than anybody else' 33.12; γνωστῶς εἴδω σε 'Let me know you fully' 33.13; θεοῖς ἑτέροις, οὓς οὐκ οἴδατε De 13.2; acc. rei, κοίτην ἄρσενος 'sleeping with a male' Nu 31.18 (‖ γινώσκω vs. 17); τὸ παιδάριον οὐκ ἔγνω οὐδέν, πλὴν Ιωναθαν και Δαυιδ ᾔδεισαν τὸ ῥῆμα 'the boy didn't notice anything, but J. and D. knew about the matter' 1K 20.39. **b**. with a ὅτι-clause indicating what one knows about the object: οὓς .. οἶδας ὅτι οὗτοί εἰσιν πρεσβύτεροι .. Nu 11.16, οἶδα ὑμᾶς ὅτι .. ἐπίκεισθέ μοι 'I know you, that you are going to attack me' Jb 21.27.

6. *to come to know, learn, find out by observation* or *enquiry* (= γινώσκω **1**): εἰδέναι εἰ ἀγαπᾶτε 'to find out whether you love' De 13.3; οὐκ ἔδωκεν κύριος .. ὑμῖν καρδίαν εἰδέναι 29.4; τὸ ξύλον τοῦ εἰδέναι γνωστὸν καλοῦ καὶ πονηροῦ 'the tree that enables one to know what is knowable of good and evil' Ge 2.9, 2.17.

*7. Calqued on Heb. מִי יוֹדֵעַ אִם *Who knows? Perhaps* ..: Τίς οἶδεν εἰ ἐλεήσει ..; 'Who knows? Perhaps he will pity ..' 2K 12.22, τίς οἶδεν εἰ εἰς τὸν καιρὸν τοῦτον ἐβασίλευσας; '.. you have become ruler for this time' Es 4.14; Jl 2.14, Jn 3.9.

Cf. γινώσκω, ἐπίσταμαι, σύνοιδα: Schmidt 1.289f.

οἰκεῖος, α, ον.

subst. *family member, kinsman*: οἰκεία πατρός Le 18.12; οἱ. ἔγγιστα 'the nearest of kin' 21.2; Am 6.10; + φίλος Pr 17.9; neut. but with personal referent, πάντα οἰκεῖα σαρκός 'every kinsman' Le 18.6. **b**. subst.n., *that which properly belongs to*: πάντα τῆς ἀρετῆς ~α 'all that properly belongs to excellence' 2M 15.12.

Cf. οἶκος, οἰκέτης, οἰκειότης: Spicq 1.216f.

οἰκειότης, ητος. f.ʃ

female member of same household: Le 20.19 (w. ref. to sister, full or half). Cf. οἰκεῖος.

οἰκειόω: fut.ptc.pass. οἰκειωθησόμενος.ʃ

to make suitable to: + dat., ἡμῶν ταῖς ψυχαῖς, ***o*** foods, 4M 5.26.

οἰκέτης, ου. m.

1. *male domestic employee*: ἰδού ἐσμεν ~έται τῷ κυρίῳ ἡμῶν Ge 44.16 (‖ ἐσόμεθα παῖδες .. vs. 9, cf. also vs. 33); παῖς οἱ. ἔσται τοῖς ἀδελφοῖς αὐτοῦ 9.25; opp. κύριος 27.37, δεσπότης Pr 22.7, ἐλεύθερος 1E 3.18. **b**. in the service of a ruler: Pharaoh, Ex 5.15 (‖ παῖς vs. 16); τῷ Φαραω De 6.21. **c**. male counterpart of θεράπαινα: Ex 21.26.

2. submissive designation in relation to God: "Abraham, Isaac, and Jacob your servants (τῶν σῶν οἰκετῶν)" Ex 32.13; Le 25.42, 55 (at latter ‖ παῖς), De 34.5. **b**. "your servant(s)" = "I (we)" as a submissive self-designation: τοῖς ~έταις σου [= ἡμῖν] Nu 32.5.

Cf. δοῦλος, παῖς, παιδίσκη, δεσπότης, κύριος, οἰκεῖος, οἰκέτις: Schmidt 4.127-9; Trench 33; Spicq 1978.218-20.

οἰκετικός, ή, όν.ʃ

pertaining to slaves: ***s*** διάθεσις 'status (as slave)' 3M 2.28. Cf. δοῦλος.

οἰκέτις, ιδος. f.ʃ

female domestic employee: Ex 21.7, Le 19.20; opp. κυρία Pr 30.23. Apparently of a higher status than δούλη: see Ex 21.7, Frankel, *Einfl.* 91, and *BA* ad loc. Cf. οἰκέτης, δούλη.

οἰκέω: fut. οἰκήσω; aor. ᾤκησα, impv. οἴκησον, inf. οἰκῆσαι.

to dwell: ἐν σκηναῖς κτηνοτρόφων 'in cattle-keepers' tents' Ge 4.20; .. τῶν Χαναναίων, μεθ' ὧν ἐγὼ οἰκῶ ἐν (‖ μετά) αὐτοῖς 24.3; + acc. rei, αἱ θυγατέρες τῶν οἰκούντων τὴν πόλιν 'the daughters of the residents of the town' 24.13; οἰκῶν οἰκίαν 'living indoors' 25.27; τὸν τόπον 'the local (residents)' 2M 6.2; ἐν οἴκοις .. κοιλοστάθμοις 'in panelled houses' Hg 1.4. **b**. pass.: γῆ οἰκουμένη 'inhabited land' Ex 16.35 (as against ἔρημος). **c**. ἡ οἰκουμένη *the world*: physically, τὰ θεμέλια τῆς ~ης 'the foundation of the world' Ps 17.16, εἰς τὰ πέρατα τῆς ~ης 'to the ends of ..' 18.5, ἡ οἱ. καὶ πάντες οἱ κατοικοῦντες ἐν αὐτῇ 23.1; its human inhabitants, αὐτὸς κρινεῖ τὴν ~ην ἐν δικαιοσύνῃ 'he will judge the world with justice' 9.9; τὸ περιβόητον καθ' ὅλην τὴν ~ην ἱερόν 'the world-famous temple' 2M 2.22. Cf. Renehan 2.106.

Cf. ἐν~, κατ~, συνοικέω, οἰκήτωρ, οἰκία, κατοικία, ναίω, ἀοίκητος.

οἴκημα, ατος. n.

house: Wi 13.15; οἴ. πορνικόν 'brothel' Ez 16.24. Cf. οἶκος: Schmidt 2.522-4.

οἴκησις, εως. f.

edifice for dwelling: 2C 17.12 (*L* βᾶρις); within a walled city, To 13.12 𝔊[II]. Cf. οἶκος: Schmidt 2.521f.

οἰκητήριον, ου. n.ʃ

residential area: *s* city, 2M 11.2; heaven as God's abode, 3M 2.15. Cf. οἶκος.

οἰκητός, ή, όν.ʃ

inhabited: οἰκία ~ή 'dwelling-house' Le 25.29; τόπος 2M 9.17, 3M 4.3. Cf. οἶκος, οἰκέω.

οἰκήτωρ, ορος. m.ʃ

inhabitant: γῆς Wi 12.3, Pr 2.21. Cf. οἰκέω.

οἰκία, ας. f.

1. *building for dwelling*, 'house': εἰσῆλθον εἰς τὴν οἰκίαν αὐτοῦ Ge 19.3, cf. 43.16 (|| οἶκος vs. 17); οἰκῶν ~αν 'living indoors' 25.27; οἰκοδομήσας ~αν καινήν De 20.5; Zp 1.13; τρυφῆς 'luxury home' Mi 2.9; διαρπαγήσονται αἱ ~αι 'the houses will be ransacked' Zc 14.2; || ἀγρός 'agricultural field' Ex 20.17. **b**. *tower on the back of an elephant for its riders*: 2M 13.15, cf. οἰκίδιον in the same sense.

2. *indoor space*: shelter from danger, εἰσέλθῃ εἰς ~αν Ex 9.19 (|| οἶκος vs. 20); οἰ. φυλακῆς 'prison' Je 44.15, οἰ. λάκκου 'dungeon' 44.16.

3. *household, family*: τῷ παιδὶ αὐτοῦ τῷ πρεσβυτέρῳ τῆς ~ας αὐτοῦ 'to his elderly servant of his household' Ge 24.2; ἐὰν ὑπολειφθῶσι δέκα ἄνδρες ἐν ~ᾳ μιᾷ 'if ten men were left in one household' Am 6.9; pl. Ge 50.21.

Cf. οἶκος, οἰκίδιον, ἑστία: on sense **1**., see Husson 191-206; Schmidt 2.515-8.

οἰκίδιον, ου. n.ʃ

small house: To 2.4 𝔊[II], 2M 8.33. Cf. οἶκος οἰκία **1b**.

οἰκίζω: fut.pass. οἰκισθήσομαι; aor. ᾤκισα.ʃ

1. *to build and establish*: pass., *o* city, Si 10.3, 38.32.

2. *to allow to settle as colonist*: + acc. pers., ἐπὶ τῆς γῆς 'in the land' Jb 22.8.

Cf. κτίζω, οἰκοδομέω.

οἰκογενής, ές.

Alw. used substantivally.

1. *born in the house*, 'homegrown,' not applied to one's own children: as soldier engaged by the head of a household, τοὺς ἰδίους ~νεῖς Ge 14.14 (|| vs. 15 παῖδες); of slave, υἱὸς .. τῆς ~νοῦς μου 15.2, cf. δοῦλον .. οἰκογενὴν ἐκ δούλης Θαήσιος 'a slave .. house-born from the slave Thaesis' *P.Oxy. Hels.* 26.10 and μὴ δοῦλός ἐστιν Ισραηλ ἢ οἰ. ἐστιν; Je 2.14; opp. slaves bought with money, πάντες οἱ ἄνδρες τοῦ οἴκου αὐτοῦ καὶ οἱ ~νεῖς καὶ οἱ ἀργυρώνητοι 'all the men of his household and the homegrown slaves and those bought with money' Ge 17.27. Cf. Wodke 1977.68.

2. *belonging to the (royal) household*: princes, aristocrats, etc., 1E 3.1, cf. Rundgren 1957.

Cf. δοῦλος, παῖς, παιδίσκη.

οἰκοδομέω: fut. ~μήσω, pass. ~μηθήσομαι; aor. ᾠκοδόμησα, impv. οἰκοδόμησον, inf. ~μῆσαι, ptc. ~μήσας, subj. ~μήσω, pass. ᾠκοδομήθην, subj. ~μηθῶ, impv.3s ~μηθήτω, inf. ~μηθῆναι; pf.pass. ᾠκοδόμημαι, ptc. ᾠκοδομημένος.

1. *to build, construct* a building or some edifice: *o* θυσιαστήριον τῷ θεῷ Ge 8.20, θυσιαστήριον κυρίῳ 13.18; πόλιν 4.17, πόλεις Am 9.14, cf. Ge 10.11 (Nineveh), Mi 3.10, Hb 2.12; πόλιν καὶ πύργον '.. tower' Ge 11.4; τείχη '(city-)walls' Ps 50.20; πύργον Is 5.2 (in a vineyard); βωμούς 'altars' Nu 23.1; τεμένη 'sacred precincts' Ho 8.14; στήλας 'monuments' 10.1; οἶκον κυρίου Hg 1.2, Zc 6.12; ὁ ναὸς ἀφ' οὗ ᾠκοδόμηται 8.9 (|| θεμελιόω); οἴκους ξεστούς 'houses built of hewn stones' Am 5.11; οἰκίας Zp 1.13; ἀνάβασιν 'upward passage' Am 9.6; w. dat. com., αὐτῷ οἰκίαν Zc 5.11; Τύρος ὀχυρώματα ἑαυτῷ 9.3; ἵνα οἰκοδομηθῇ καὶ κατασκευασθῇ πόλις Σηων 'so that the city of Sihon may be built and constructed' Nu 21.27. Cf. ᾠκοδόμησεν .. τὴν πλευράν .. εἰς γυναῖκα 'formed.. the rib into a woman' Ge 2.22, cf. 4M 18.7. **b**. + double acc.: λίθους ὁλοκλήρους οἰκοδομήσεις τὸ θυσιαστήριον 'you shall process perfect stones into the altar' De 27.6. **c**. *to work on and transform into sth useful*: + acc., ἐρήμους αἰωνίας 'eternal wastelands' Is 61.4 (|| ἐξανίστημι), Ez 36.33. **d**. *to be engaged in construction works*: abs., ἐν τῷ τείχῳ 'on the wall' Ne 4.10, ἐν τῷ οἴκῳ κυρίου Zc 6.15, Ne 4.10, cf. 2C 27.3*b*; opp. καταστρέφω Ma 1.4 (|| ἀνοικοδομέω). **e**. *to expand* or *rebuild* an existing city: τὴν πόλιν Jo 19.50, cf. LSG s.v.

2. *to use as building material*: οὐκ οἰκοδομήσεις αὐτοὺς τμητούς 'thou shalt not use them [= λίθους 'stones'] in cut form' Ex 20.25; κέδρος .. ᾠκοδομήθη σοι 'cedar ..' Ez 27.4.

3. *to bring into being and sustain*: + acc. rei, οἶκον 'home, family' De 25.9 (ref. to levirate marriage); *s* God *o* Israel, Je 38.4, 40.8; ὑμᾶς 49.10 (:: καθαιρέω); *o* ἔλεος Ps 88.3, εἰς γενεὰν καὶ γενεὰν τὸν θρόνον σου 88.5.

4. *to incorporate into an already existing structure*: *o* hum. and pass., ἐν μέσῳ τοῦ λαοῦ μου Je 12.16.

Cf. οἶκος, οἰκία, οἰκοδόμος, ἀν~, δι~, ἐξ~, προσαν~, συνοικοδομέω, οἰκίζω, καταβάλλω, καταλύω **4**, κατασκευάζω, καταστρέφω: Schmidt 2.520f.

οἰκοδομή, ῆς. f.

that which has been built: as dwelling, Ez 16.61. **b**. *act of building*: πόλεως Si 40.19, τοῦ ἱεροῦ 1E 4.51.

οἰκοδόμος, ου. m.

builder: Is 58.12; τοίχων 'of walls' 1C 14.1.

οἰκονομέω: fut. ~μήσω, ptc. ~μήσων.

to see to good progress or execution of: + acc., τοὺς λόγους αὐτοῦ ἐν κρίσει Ps 111.5, τὴν περὶ τούτων ἐπίσκεψιν 'the inspection of these (monies)' 2M 3.14.

οἰκονομία, ας. f.ʃ

office of steward: Is 22.19; + κράτος 'authority' 22.21.

οἰκονόμος, ου. m.

steward: 3K 16.9; ‖ γραμματεύς, ὑπομνηματογράφος (‖ 4K 18.18 ἀναμιμνήσκων) Is 36.3, 22; ‖ τοπάρχης, στρατηγός, σατράπης 1E 4.47; βασιλικοὶ ~οι 8.64 (‖ ἔπαρχος), ‖ οἱ ἄρχοντες τῶν σατραπῶν Es 8.9; τοῦ βασιλέως 1C 29,6. Cf. Reumann; *ND* 4.160f.; Spicq 2.568-75.

οἰκόπεδον, ου. n.ʃ

site where a house once stood, 'ruins': a haunt of owls, Si 49.13, Ps 101.7; of beggars, 108.10. Cf. οἶκος.

οἶκος, ου. m.

1. *permanent* or *semi-permanent edifice*: for dwelling, accommodating or depositing, Hg 1.9; ἐν ~οις ὑμῶν κοιλοστάθμοις 'in your panelled houses' 1.4; ‖ κληρονομία Mi 2.2. **b**. w. ref. to the temple in Jerusalem, God's dwelling-place: οἶ. κυρίου Hg 1.2; οἶ. κυρίου τοῦ θεοῦ Zp 1.9; οἶ. θεοῦ 1C 9.13, Na 1.14; simply ὁ οἶ. Hg 1.8; ὁ οἶ. μου 1.9, Ma 3.10. **c**. opp. land and fields, ἐν πᾶσιν τοῖς ὑπάρχουσιν αὐτῷ ἐν τῷ ~ῳ καὶ ἐν τῷ ἀγρῷ Ge 39.5. **d**. place where one leads one's life with no emphasis on buildings: ἐκ γῆς Αἰγύπτου, ἐξ οἴκου δουλείας Ex 20.2, cf. LSG s.v. **I 1**. **e**. edifice used for purposes other than dwelling: τὴν σκηνήν, τὸν ~ον τοῦ μαρτυρίου Nu 9.15; also ‖ σκηνή 24.5; πότου 'a pub' Ec 7.2. **f**. indoor space: shelter from danger, Ex 9.20 (‖ οἰκία vs. 19).

2. *the entirety of one's close kinsfolk*, 'family': πᾶς ὁ οἶ. σου Ge 7.1 = οἱ υἱοί σου καὶ ἡ γυνή σου καὶ αἱ γυναῖκες τῶν υἱῶν σου 6.18; τοῦ πατρός σου (‖ συγγένεια) 12.1; ἐχθροὶ ἀνδρὸς οἱ ἄνδρες οἱ ἐν τῷ ~ῳ 'one's enemies are one's own family members' Mi 7.6. Possibly including highly placed courtiers, but not necessarily blood relations, 'royal household': Φαραω .. καὶ τὸν ~ον αὐτοῦ Ge 12.17; 41.40 (*pace* Wodke 85, not the whole of Egypt).

3. *domestic establishment*, 'household': πότε ποιήσω κἀγὼ ἐμαυτῷ ~ον; 'whe can I set up a household of my own?' Ge 30.30; royal court, 39.2. **b**. where one is not one's own master: δουλείας Ex 13.3, Mi 6.4.

4. *group of people descended from and named after* prominent ancestor: ὁ οἶ. Ιακωβ Ob 17, Is 2.5; ὁ οἶ. Ιωσηφ Ob 18; ὁ οἶ. Ιουδα Zp 2.7; ὁ οἶ. Ισραηλ Zc 8.13. **b**. ὁ οἶ. Δαυιδ w. ref. to the royal household of the southern kingdom, Zc 12.8, Is 7.2.

5. *community of residents in a certain locality*: Βηθλεεμ οἶ. τοῦ Εφραθα Mi 5.2.

Cf. οἰκία, οἰκεῖος, οἴκημα, οἰκητός, οἰκίδιον, οἰκητήριον, οἰκοδομέω, ἑστία, συγγένεια: on senses **1**. and **2**., see Husson 211-5; Schmidt 2.513-5; Wodke.

οἰκουμένη. ⇒ οἰκέω.

οἰκτείρω. ⇒ οἰκτιρέω.

οἰκτιρέω, οἰκτίρω: fut. οἰκτιρήσω; aor. οἰκτίρησα, inf. οἰκτιρῆσαι, οἰκτεῖραι, subj. οἰκτιρήσω, impv. οἰκτίρησον, opt.3s ~ρήσαι. See Thack., pp. 278f.

to have pity on, act out of compassion towards: abs., *s* hum. Ps 36.21 (giving alms), + κιχράω 'to lend' 111.5, Pr 13.11, ψυχὰς κτηνῶν αὐτοῦ 12.10; + acc. rei, "your own old age" 4M 5.12, ‖ + gen. rei, τῆς ἡλικίας '(young) age' 8.10 (‖ ἐλεέω vs. 20); *s* God and + acc. hum., Mi 7.19, ‖ ἐλεέω Ex 33.19, Is 27.11, 30.18, Si 36.18, ‖ φείδομαι, ἐπιποθέω and + ἀπὸ διαφθορᾶς αὐτῶν 'to be deterred from destroying them' Je 13.14, κατὰ τὸ πλῆθος τοῦ ἐλέους αὐτοῦ La 3.32; + acc. rei, τὸν ναόν 2M 8.2 (‖ ἐλεέω). Cf. οἰκτιρμός, κατοικτιρέω, (κατ)ελεέω, ἔλεος, ἐπισπλαγχνίζομαι, οἶκτος, φείδομαι, ἐπιποθέω.

οἰκτίρημα, ατος. n.ʃ

deed of compassion: Je 38.3 (God's).

οἰκτιρμός, οῦ. m.

1. *mercy, compassion*: of God to men, ἐν ἐλέει καὶ ἐν ~οῖς Ho 2.19; ἐν ~ῷ Zc 1.16, ἐν ~οῖς 3M 6.2; πνεῦμα χάριτος καὶ ~οῦ Zc 12.10; of deed by man to man, ἔλεος καὶ ~ὸν ποιεῖτε ἕκαστος πρὸς τὸν ἀδελφὸν αὐτοῦ 7.9; πενητῶν 'towards the poor' Da 4.24 TH (‖ ἐλημοσύναι 'alms'); εἰμὶ ἐν ~οῖς ἐναντί τινος 'I am in sbd's good books' 2C 30.9.

2. *supplication for compassionate treatment*: ῥιπτοῦμεν τὸν ~ὸν ἡμῶν ἐνώπιόν σου 'we are presenting to you a humble plea for compassionate consideration of our predicament' Da 9.18 TH (LXX δεόμεθα ἐν ταῖς προσευχαῖς ἡμῶν ..). See an analogous use of ἔλεος **2**.

The word is mostly used in the plural in the LXX. Cf. οἰκτίρμων, οἰκτιρέω, οἶκτος, ἔλεος.

οἰκτίρμων, ον, gen. ~ονος.

merciful, compassionate: *s* God, ἐλεήμων καὶ οἰ. Ex 34.6, Jl 2.13, Jn 4.2 (|| μακρόθυμος, πολυέλεος); De 4.31; hum. mother, La 4.10. Cf. οἰκτιρμός, ἐλεήμων, εὐίλατος, μακρόθυμος, πολυέλεος.

οἰκτίρω. ⇒ οἰκτιρέω.

οἶκτος, ου. m.ʃ

1. *compassion*: ἄνευ παντὸς ~ου καὶ φειδοῦς 'without any pity or sparing' Es B o' 6; + δάκρυα 3M 6.22.

2. *lamentation*: φωνὴ ~ου Je 9.19; 9.20 (|| θρῆνος); μετὰ ~ου καὶ δακρύων 'with .. tears' 3M 1.4; + γόος 'groan' 5.49.

Cf. οἰκτιρέω, οἰκτρός, ἔλεος, σπλάγχνα, θρῆνος, οἰμωγή, φειδώ.

οἰκτρός, ά, όν; superl. οἴκτιστος, η, ον; οἰκτρότατος, η, ον.ʃ

liable to evoke pity: *s* κοπετός 'mourning' Je 6.26, μόρος 'fate' 2M 9.28; θεωρία 'sight' 3M 5.24, φωνή Wi 18.10. **b**. subst.n. adv., *with pity*: to look on sbd., 4M 15.18.

Cf. οἶκτος: Schmidt 3.581f.

οἶμαι: shorter form of οἴομαι, q.v.

οἴμμοι.

An expression of a sense of horror: Jd 11.35A (B: ἆ ἆ), Je 22.8; the ground for such a sentiment indicated by a ὅτι-clause, Mi 7.1*a*; 7.1*b* with an intervening vocative (ψυχή); repeated three times and followed by εἰς to indicate that *over* which the sentiment is expressed – Οἴ. οἴ. οἴ. εἰς ἡμέραν, ὅτι ἐγγὺς ἡμέρα κυρίου 'O how fateful is the day, for the day of the Lord is near!' Jl 1.15; foll. by a nom., Οἴ. ἐγώ, ὅτι .. Je 4.31, οἴ. οἴ., ὅτι .. 51.33; foll. by a question, Je 15.10, 1M 2.7; in an apodosis, Jb 10.15, Ez 11.13. On the spelling with double μ, see Walters 83f., 229f.

Cf. ἆ, οὐαί Kraft 1972.169.

οἰμωγή, ῆς. f.ʃ

lamentation: + κωκυτός 3M 6.32. Cf. οἰμώζω, οἶκτος, θρῆνος. Del. 3M 6.17 v.l.

οἰμώζω: fut. οἰμώξω.ʃ

to lament: 4M 12.14. Cf. οἰμωγή, θρηνέω.

οἰνοποτέω.ʃ *

to drink wine: Pr 31.4. Cf. πίνω, οἰνοπότης.

οἰνοπότης, ου. m.ʃ

heavy drinker: Pr 23.20. Cf. οἰνοποτέω.

οἶνος, ου. m.

wine. Specifically of a drink produced from grapes by planting a vineyard (ἀμπελών), Ge 9.21, Am 5.11, 9.14, Zp 1.13. Mentioned with other agricultural products: ἐπὶ τὸν σῖτον καὶ ἐπὶ τὸν ~ον καὶ ἐπὶ τὸ ἔλαιον καὶ ὅσα ἐκφέρει ἡ γῆ 'the grain, wine, oil and all that the earth produces' Hg 1.11; see also De 7.13, 28.51, Ho 2.8, 22, 7.14, Zc 9.17, Jl 1.10, 2.24. As provisions made by God, + σῖτος, ἱμάτιον, and ὀθόνιον Ho 2.9; + σῖτος and ἔλαιον Jl 2.19. In a list of drinks and foods: ἄρτου ἢ ἑψέματος ἢ ~ου ἢ ἐλαίου ἢ παντὸς βρώματος Hg 2.12; origin specified: οἶ. Λιβάνου 'of Lebanon' Ho 14.8; ἐξηράνθη '(supply of) wine has dried up' Jl 1.10; ὑπερεκχυνθήσονται αἱ ληνοὶ ~ου καὶ ἐλαίου 'the vats of wine and oil will overflow' Jl 2.24; || ἅλων καὶ ληνός 'threshing floor and wine-vat' Ho 9.2; ***o*** of πίνω Ge 9.21, Am 2.8, Mi 6.15, πίνω εἰς μέθην 'to drink and get drunk' Jl 1.5*b*; ἐκπίνω 'to gulp' Zc 9.15; ποτίζω Am 2.12. Strained (διυλισμένος) wine as drink of the rich, Am 6.6; sweet-smelling (εὐωδιάζων) wine suited to young girls, Zc 9.17; drunk for pleasure, Jd 9.13, Jl 3.3; cultic offerings, οἴσεις τὰ ἐπιδέκατα τοῦ σίτου σου καὶ τοῦ οἴνου σου καὶ τοῦ ἐλαίου σου De 14.22; ἄρτους καὶ οἶνον Ge 14.18; poured (σπένδω) as libation to God, Ho 9.4; εἰς σπονδήν Nu 15.5; sacrilegious drinking carousals on the Temple Mount, Ob 16; a whore's pay, w. ἀργύριον and κριθή 'barley' Ho 3.2. Effects of wine: χαίρω ἐν ~ῳ 'under its effect' Zc 10.7; ἔπιεν .. καὶ ἐμεθύσθη Ge 9.21; μεθύω ἐξ ~ου 'to get drunk from wine' Jl 1.5*a*; θυμόομαι ἐξ ~ου 'to burst into rage ..' Ho 7.5; πίνω ~ον εἰς μέθην Jl 1.5*b*; οἶ. καὶ μέθυσμα 'wine and intoxicating drink' Mi 2.11 (see Muraoka 1983.43f.).

Cf. οἰνοχοέω, οἰνοφλυγέω, σῖτος, ἔλαιον.

οἰνοφλυγέω.ʃ * (οἰνοφλυγία: Xen. +)

to be drunken: De 21.20. Cf. μεθύω: Trench 226.

οἰνοχοέω: aor.inf. οἰνοχοῆσαι.ʃ

to pour wine: Ge 40.13; + dat. pers. and ἐν (instr.), οἰνοχοῆσαι ἐν αὐτοῖς τοῖς ἑταίροις αὐτοῦ 'to pour wine with them to his associates' Da 5.2 LXX. Cf. οἶνος, ἀρχιοινοχόος, ἀρχιοινοχοΐα, οἰνοχόος: Anz 17f.

οἰνοχόη, ης. f.ʃ

female cupbearer: Ec 2.8. Cf. οἰνοχόος, οἰνοχοέω.

οἰνοχόος: ~ου. m.

male cupbearer: τῷ βασιλεῖ Ne 1.11. Cf. οἰνοχόη.

οἴομαι: impf. ᾤμην; aor.pass. ᾠήθην.

to assume as probable though not absolutely certain: abs., ἐγὼ μέν οἶμαι 'that's my opinion, at least' 4M 1.33; + inf., ᾤμην ἡμᾶς δεσμεύειν δράγματα 'it seemed to me that we were binding sheaves' Ge 37.7; ᾤετο ἑστάναι ἐπὶ τοῦ ποταμοῦ 'he imagined that he was standing by the river' 41.1; Jb 34.12; + ὅτι Is 57.8; + indir. question, πῶς Es 9.12 o'; + inf. 1M 5.61, 2M 5.21, 13.3 Cf. δοκέω, ἡγέομαι, νομίζω, ὑπολαμβάνω: Schmidt 1.333-47.

οἷος, α, ον.

1. *such as*: ἄνθρωπος οἷος ἐγώ 'a person such as I' Ge 44.15, οὐχ οἷος ὁ πρότερος 'not like the former one' To 14.5 𝔊[I] (𝔊[II] ὡς). **b.** with a correlative and often with a negator: βόες .. πονηραὶ .., οἵας οὐκ εἶδον τοιαύτας .. 'bad cows .. the like of which I have never seen ..' Ge 41.19, cf. θλῖψις οἷα οὐ γέγονεν τοιαύτη ἀπ' ἀρχῆς κτίσεως .. ἕως τοῦ νῦν καὶ οὐ μὴ γένηται Mk 13.19; πάσχα τοιοῦτο, οἷον ἤγαγεν Ιωσιας 'a (splendid) passover such as that which J. celebrated' 1E 1.19; οὐδεὶς .. τοιοῦτος οἷος Ενωχ Si 49.14. **c.** introduces an illustrative case: οἷον κακοηθείας 'such as malice' 4M 1.4; an example in the form of a clause with a finite verb, 3.2.

2. = ὅς: τὴν ὁδὸν ἔξω, οἵας ἀπῆλθαν 'the road outside, along which they had departed' To 10.7 𝔊[I]. **b.** with an indefinite antecedent, 'the like of which': κακὰ μεγάλα, οἷα οὐκ ἐγενήθη ὑπὸ τὸν οὐρανόν Da 9.12 LXX, ἡ ἡμέρα θλίψεως, οἷα οὐκ ἐγενήθη .. ἕως τῆς ἡμέρας ἐκείνης 12.1. **c.** antecedentless rel. pron.: μνημονεύων οἷα ἐλάλησεν '(he no longer showed interest in A.), remembering what she had said' Es 2.1 o'; οὐχ οἷα ἤθελε, τοιαῦτα ἐγεγόνει 'the sorts of things which he wished for had not happened' 1M 4.27; 5.56.

3. *what sort of ..!*, in an exclamatory utterance: Οἷα συνετέλουν 'what sort of things have I done!' Jb 33.27.

4. *practicable*: n., ὡς οἷόν τε ἦν 'as much as they could' 4M 4.7.

Cf. ὡς.

οἰστρηλασία, ας. f.ʃ *

vehemently passionate driving force: w. carnal overtones, 4M 2.4. Cf. οἶστρος.

οἶστρος, ου. m.ʃ

vehement desire: w. carnal overtones, 4M 2.3; 3.17. Cf. ἐπιθυμία: Schmidt 4.233-6.

οἰφί. indecl.

ephah: τὸ δέκατον τοῦ οἰ. σεμίδαλιν 'the tenth part of an ephah, fine flour' Le 5.11, Nu 28.5 (|| .. σεμιδάλεως Le 6.20).

οἴχομαι: fut. οἰχήσομαι; impf. ᾠχόμην. Always (in the LXX) impf. except Ho 10.14, and not in plpf., but aor. sense.

1. *to leave a place and go off*: ᾤχετο μετ' αὐτοῦ Λωτ Ge 12.4 (|| ἐπορεύθη); ἀναστὰς ᾤχετο 25.34; ᾤχετο κεῖραι τὰ πρόβατα αὐτοῦ 'to shear his sheep' 31.19; ὀπίσω θεῶν ἀλλοτρίων 'after foreign gods' Je 16.11; on death, Jb 14.10, ἐξ ἀνθρώπων Si prol. II.

2. *to disappear*: *s* fortifications, Ho 10.14; σοφία Je 29.8 (|| ἀπόλλυμι).

Cf. II ἄπειμι, ἀπέρχομαι, ἀποίχομαι, ἀπόλλυμι, πορεύομαι, ὑπάγω.

οἰωνίζομαι: fut. οἰωνιοῦμαι; aor. οἰωνισάμην.

1. *to practise divination*: ἐν αὐτῷ [= 'with a drinking-vessel'] Ge 44.5; + dat. cogn., οἰωνισμῷ 44.15; abs. and forbidden, οὐκ οἰωνιεῖσθε οὐδὲ ὀρνιθοσκοπήσεσθε '.. nor shalt thou divine by inspection of birds' Le 19.26; οὐχ εὑρεθήσεται ἐν σοι .. οἰωνιζόμενος, φάρμακος 'there shall not be found amongst you .. a diviner, magician' De 18.10; + μαντεύομαι 4K 17.17.

2. *to guess*: Εἰ εὗρον χάριν ἐναντίον σου, οἰωνισάμην ἄν 'If I were favourably regarded by you, I would have guessed' Ge 30.27.

Cf. οἰώνισμα, οἰωνισμός, οἰωνός.

οἰώνισμα, ματος. n.ʃ

omen obtained by observing the flight and cries of birds: ὁράσεις ψευδεῖς καὶ μαντείας καὶ ~ματα καὶ προαιρέσεις καρδίας αὐτῶν 'false visions and oracles and .. and what their minds fancy' Je 14.14 (practised by false prophets); μὴ ἀκούετε τῶν ψευδοπροφητῶν ὑμῶν καὶ τῶν μαντευομένων ὑμῖν καὶ τῶν ἐνυπνιαζομένων ὑμῖν καὶ τῶν οἰωνισμάτων ὑμῶν καὶ τῶν φαρμάκων ὑμῶν 34.7; condemned as ἁμαρτία 1K 15.23. Cf. οἰωνίζομαι, οἰωνισμός.

οἰωνισμός, οῦ. m.ʃ *

practice of οἰωνίζομαι (q.v.): used as cogn. dat., ~ῷ οἰωνίζεται Ge 44.5; 44.15; forbidden, οὐ γὰρ οἰ. ἐν Ιακωβ, οὐδὲ μαντεία ἐν Ισραηλ Nu 23.23, cf. μαντεῖαι καὶ ~οὶ καὶ ἐνύπνια μάταιά ἐστιν 'sorceries and .. and dreams are futile' Si 31.5. Cf. οἰωνίζομαι, μαντεία.

οἰωνόβρωτος, ον.ʃ

to be eaten as food by birds: *s* hum. corpse, 2M 9.15, 3M 6.34. Cf. βιβρώσκω.

οἰωνός, οῦ.ʃ

portent, presage: Nu 24.1. Cf. οἰωνίζομαι: Schmidt 2.448.

ὀκλάζω: aor. ὤκλασα; pf.ptc. ὀκλακώς.ʃ

to go down on one's knees: *s* woman in labour, 1K 4.19; worshipper, ἐπὶ τὰ γόνατα αὐτοῦ 3K 8.54 (*L* κάμπτω), + acc., but also γόνυ as *s* (!), γόνυ τῷ Βααλ 19.18 (*L* κλίνω). Cf. κάμπτω.

ὀκνέω: aor. ὤκνησα, subj. ὀκνήσω, impv.3s ὀκνησάτω.

to hesitate: + inf., Nu 22.16; Ju 12.13 (or: * + ptc. ἐλθοῦσα .. δοξασθῆναι); πρὸς τὸν θάνατον ὤκνησεν 'recoiled from death' 4M 14.4.

ὀκνηρία,, ας. f.ʃ *

sloth, laziness: || ἀργία χειρῶν Ec 10.18. Cf. ὀκνηρός, ἀργία.

ὀκνηρός, ά, όν.

habitually disinclined to work, 'lazy, idle': subst. and *s* hum., Ἴθι πρὸς τὸν μύρμηκα, ὦ ~έ 'O sluggard, visit the ants' Pr 6.6, ἕως τίνος, ~έ, κατάκεισαι; 'how much longer, O lazy-bones, are you going to hang round?' 6.9, μὴ βουλεύου .. μετὰ ~οῦ περὶ παντὸς ἔργου 'don't consult .. the idler about any work whatsoever' Si 37.10f.; food not obtained by hard work, Pr 31.27. Cf. ἄοκνος, ἀεργός, ἀργός, ὀκνηρία: Spicq 2.576f.

ὀκτακισχίλιοι, αι, α: num.
eight thousand: Nu 4.48.

ὀκτακόσιοι, αι, α. num.
eight hundred: Ge 5.17.

ὀκτάπηχυς, υ.∫
of eight cubits in length: *s* stone, 3K 7.47.

ὀκτώ. indecl. num.
eight: Ge 5.28+. Cf. ὀγδοήκοντα, ὄγδοος, ὀκτακόσιοι, ὀκτακισχίλιοι.

ὀκτωκαίδεκα. indecl. num.
eighteen: ὀ. ἔτη Jd 10.8A (B: δέκα ὀκτὼ ἔτη).

ὀκτωκαιδέκατος, η, ον.
eighteenth: 1E 1.20.

ὄλβος, ου. m.∫
worldly happiness: Si 30.15. Cf. εὐοδία: Schmidt 4.377f., 383f.

ὀλεθρεύω: fut. ~ρεύσω, pass. ~ρευθήσομαι; aor. ὠλέθρευσα, subj. ~ρεύσω, inf. ~ρεῦσαι; plpf.pass. 3s ὠλέθρευτο.* (but ὄλεθρος 'destruction' alr. in Hom. *Iliad*).
to destroy: abs., Ex 12.23; + acc. pers., Nu 4.18, ‖ συντρίβω PSol 17.24; *o* sacred grove, Jd 6.25 B (A: ἐκκόπτω); *s* lion, Je 2.30; wolf, 5.6.
Cf. ὄλεθρος, ὀλεθρία, ἐξολεθρεύω, ἀφανίζω.

ὀλεθρία, ας. f.∫
v.n. of ὀλεθρεύω: genocide, Es E 21 o', 3M 4.2, 5.5. Cf. ὀλεθρεύω, ὄλεθρος.

ὀλέθριος, ον.∫
pertaining to destruction: ἡμέρα ὀ. 'day of d.' Es 5.23*L*; *s* hum., 3K 21.42; γῆ (doomed to perish) Wi 18.15. Cf. ὄλεθρος.

ὄλεθρος, ου. m.
destruction: ἐν ἡμέρᾳ ~ου αὐτῶν Ob 13; τὸ ἀργύριον αὐτῶν ὀ. κληρονομήσει 'destruction will inherit their silver' Ho 9.6; of hum., Pr 1.26 (‖ ἀπώλεια), 4M 10.15 (‖ θάνατος). Cf. ὀλεθρεύω, ὀλέθριος, ὀλεθρία: Schmidt 4.83-5.

ὀλεθροφόρος, ον.∫
bound to lead to ruin: *s* ἀλαζονεία 'boastfulness' 4M 8.18 (‖ θανατοφόρος). Cf. ὄλεθρος, θανατοφόρος.

ὀλέκω.∫ Only in Jb, see Ziegler 1985.111.
to cause severe distress, harass: + acc. pers., Jb 10.16, 32.18; pass., *o* hum., 17.1.

ὀλιγόβιος, ον.∫
short-lived: Jb 11.2, 14.1. Cf. πολυήμερος, ὀλιγοχρόνιος.

ὀλιγοποιέω: aor. ὠλιγοποίησα.∫
to reduce the quantity of: + acc. hum., Si 48.2. Cf. ὀλιγόω, ἐλαττόω, πληθύνω.

ὀλίγος, η, ον.
little or *few* in quantity: ἡμέραι ~αι 'just a few days' Ge 29.20. ἔθνη οὐκ ~α Is 10.7; *s* βίος '(short) life' Wi 2.1; opp. πολύς– εἰ ~οι εἰσὶν ἢ πολλοί Nu 13.19, ~οι ἀπὸ πολλῶν Je 49.2; ἐσπείρατε πολλὰ καὶ εἰσηνέγκατε ~α 'you sowed much but gathered in little' Hg 1.6, cf. 1.9; ~οι ἀριθμῷ 'few in number' De 4.27, Je 51.28. **b**. subst.n.: καὶ ἔτι ὀλίγον 'and yet a while' Ps 36.10 (‖ μικρόν Ex 17.4 +: see under ἔτι **3a**), δι' ~ων 'in few words, i.e. after this brief digression' 2M 6.17, κατ' ~ον 'little by little' Wi 12.2, μετ' ~ον 'shortly later' 15.8 (‖ πρὸ μικροῦ), πρὸ ~ου 'a short while ago' 14.20; of degree and opp. μέγας - ὀργὴν μεγάλην ὀργίζομαι .. ὠργίσθην ~α Zc 1.15; ~ον σοφίας 'a bit of wisdom' Ec 10.1; adv., Wi 3.5 (:: μεγάλα).
Cf. ὀλιγοστός, ὀλιγόω, μικρός, ἐλαφρός, πολύς.

ὀλιγοστός, ή, όν.
very small in number: *s* hum. (so alw. in the LXX), ἐγὼ δὲ ὀ. εἰμι ἐν ἀριθμῷ Ge 34.30, ὀ. ἀριθμῷ 1C 16.19; Le 26.22, Am 7.2, 5, Mi 5.2; ~ὸν δέδωκά σε ἐν τοῖς ἔθνεσιν Ob 2 (perh. with the superlative force; ‖ μικρός Je 29.16). Cf. ὀλίγος: Cacciari.

ὀλιγότης, ητος. f.∫
being small in number: τῶν ἡμερῶν μου Ps 101.24; 2K 22.37*L*. Cf. ὀλιγός.

ὀλιγοχρόνιος, ον.∫
capable of existing only a short while: *s* hum., ‖ ἀσθενής 'frail' Wi 9.5. Cf. ὀλιγόβιος.

ὀλιγοψυχέω: aor. ὠλιγοψύχησα, subj. ὀλιγοψυχήσω.
1. *to become disheartened*: Nu 21.4, Jn 4.8, Hb 2.13; *s* πνεῦμα '(hum.) spirit' Ps 76.4, Ju 7.19; ἐπὶ τῇ σπάνει τῶν ὑδάτων 'over the scarcity of water' 8.9; God, + ἐν Jd 10.16 A (B: ὀλιγόομαι).
2. *to be infirm of will and purpose*: *s* judge, Si 4.9.
3. *to become mentally worn-out*: *s* hum., ἕως εἰς θάνατον 'was nearly as good as dead' Jd 16.16 A.
Cf. ὀλιγοψυχία and Lee 176.

ὀλιγοψυχία, ας. f.∫
faint-heartedness: Ex 6.9, Ps 54.9, PSol 16.11. Cf. ὀλιγοψυχέω.

ὀλιγόψυχος, ον.
1. *faint-hearted*: *s* hum., Is 25.5; τῇ διανοίᾳ 'mentally' 35.4; ‖ συντετριμμένοι τὴν καρδίαν 'the broken-hearted' 57.15.
2. *short-tempered*: opp. μακρόθυμος Pr 14.29, 18.14.
Cf. μακρόθυμος.

ὀλιγόω: fut. ὀλιγώσω, pass. ~γωθήσομαι; aor.subj. ὀλιγώσω, pass. ὠλιγώθην, impv.3s ὀλιγωθήτω.*
1. tr. *to reduce, diminish the quantity or size of*: abs. 4K 4.3; + acc. and in size, ἐν ἀπειλῇ ὀλιγώ-

σεις γῆν 'with a threat you will cut the land down to size' Hb 3.12, cf. Na 1.4 (pass.); in quantity, ἐξηράνθη οἶνος, ὠλιγώθη ἔλαιον Jl 1.10; αἱ συκαῖ 1.12. **b**. pass., *to diminish*: in number, Pr 10.27 (:: προστίθημι), Ps 11.2, 106.39; in will power, *s* ἡ ψυχὴ ^τοῦ κυρίου^ Jd 10.16 B (A: ὀλιγοψυχέω).

2. *to belittle*: pass. and *o* μόχθος Ne 9.32.

Cf. ὀλίγος, ὀλιγοποίεω, ἐλαττόω, σμικρύνω, προστίθημι.

ὀλιγωρέω: fut. ὀλιγωρήσω.ʃ

1. *to belittle*: *+ gen., παιδείας Pr 3.11.

2. *to take no heed, remain unconcerned*: + ptc., παιδευόμενος 'when remonstrated' PSol 3.4.

Cf. πολυωρέω, παροράω, ὑπεροράω, ἀμελέω.

ὀλισθάνω: fut. ὀλισθήσω; aor. ὠλίσθησα, subj. ὀλίσθω.

to cause to slip: metaph., + acc., διανοίας 'minds' Si 3.24; εἰς ἀπώλειαν 9.9. **b**. intr., *to slip*: metaph., ἐν στόματι 'in speech' Si 14.1, ἐν γλώσσῃ 25.8. Cf. ὀλίσθημα.

ὀλίσθημα, ατος. n.

act of slipping: ἀπὸ ἐδάφους 'on the pavement' Si 20.18. **b**. *cause of slipping*: ἐν γνόφῳ 'in darkness' Je 23.12; 45.22; σκότος καὶ ὀ. Ps 34.6.

Cf. ὀλισθάνω, ὀλίσθρημα, πλημμέλεια.

ὀλίσθρημα, ατος. n.ʃ

tactics designed to cause a fall: pl., Da 11.21 TH. Cf. ὀλίσθημα.

ὁλκεῖον, ου. n.ʃ

large bowl: + other valuable furniture, Ju 15.11. Cf. κρατήρ.

ὁλκή, ῆς. f.

weight: ἐνώτια χρυσᾶ ἀνὰ δραχμὴν ~ῆς 'golden ear-rings each a drachm in weight' Ge 24.22; τρύβλιον ἀργυροῦν ἕν, τριάκοντα καὶ ἑκατὸν ὁ. αὐτοῦ 'one silver dish, its weight being 130' Nu 7.13; δόρυ ~ῆς 'heavy spear' Si 29.13; ‖ σταθμός 1C 28.16. **b**. heavy weapon: pl., 2M 12.28 (v.l. ἀλκή 'strength').

Cf. σταθμός: Lee 62f.

ὄλλυμι: fut.act. ὀλῶ, mid. ὀλοῦμαι; aor.act.subj. ὀλέσω, opt.3pl ὀλέσαισαν, mid. ὠλόμην; pf.ptc. ὀλωλώς.

mid. *to perish*: *s* hum., Je 30.3; ἐπίχειρα 'arms' 29.11; ἐν μαχαίρᾳ 38.2; lion, Jb 4.11 (starvation); ways of the godless, Pr 2.22; hope, 11.7; teeth and feet of the wicked, 25.19. **b**. act.caus., *to cause to perish*: + acc. pers., Je 38.2, Jb 18.11; τοὺς πονηρούς 34.17, ἀσεβεῖς 'the godless' Pr 1.32.

Cf. ἀπ~, δι~, ἐξόλλυμι: Schmidt 4.83-6.

ὅλμος, ου. m.ʃ

round, smooth stone: σιαγόνος 'of jaw' Jd 15.19 *L* (ref. to the Adam's apple?; A τραῦμα 'wound,' B: λάκκος 'cavity').

ὁλοκαρπόω: fut.pass. ~πωθήσομαι.ʃ*

to present as a whole burnt-offering: pass., *o* θυσία Si 45.14; Isaac and Joseph, 4M 18.11. Cf. ὁλοκάρπωμα.

ὁλοκάρπωμα, ατος. n.ʃ *

whole burnt-offering: ποιήσει ὁ. Le 16.24; ὁ. θυσίας Wi 3.6. Cf. ὁλοκαρπόω, ὁλοκάρπωσις, ὁλοκαύτωμα.

ὁλοκάρπωσις, εως. f.*

whole burnt-offering: ἀνήνεγκεν ~εις ἐπὶ τὸ θυσιαστήριον Ge 8.20; human sacrifice, 22.2; ξύλα ~εως 22.6 (used to kindle a sacrifice), πρόβατα ~εως Is 43.23. Cf. θυσία, ὁλοκάρπωμα: Rösel 191.

ὁλόκαυτος, ον.ʃ

burnt entirely: *s* cultic offering (θυσία), Le 6.23. Cf. ὁλοκαύτωμα.

ὁλοκαύτωμα, ατος. n.*(ὁλοκαυτέω: Xen. +)

In the Pentateuch more often than not in the pl.

wholly burnt offering: ‖ θυσία Ex 10.25, Ho 6.6, Am 5.22 (ἐὰν ἐνέγκητέ μοι ~ατα καὶ θυσίας ὑμῶν); ‖ θυσίασμα Ex 29.18; ὁλοκαύτωμα ἢ θυσίαν Nu 15.3; ‖ μόσχος Mi 6.6; ~ατα .. καὶ σωτήρια, πρόβατα καὶ μόσχους Ex 20.24; τὸ θυσιαστήριον τῶν ~άτων 30.28, Le 1.2; of an animal sacrifice, 1.3; κριῶν 'of rams' Is 1.11; Nu 23.6 (‖ ὁλοκαύτωσις 23.17); ~ματα .. θυσιάσματα .. ἀπαρχὰς .. εὐχὰς .. ἑκούσια .. πρωτότοκα De 12.6; ‖ περὶ ἁμαρτίας 'sin-offering' Ps 39.7. Cf. θυσία, ὁλόκαυτος, ὁλοκαύτωσις: Daniel 239-58.

ὁλοκαύτωσις, εως. f. *

In the Pentateuch never in the pl.

= (?) ὁλοκαύτωμα: τὸ θυσιαστήριον τῆς ~εως Ex 29.25, Le 4.34; ἐπὶ τῆς ~εως ἢ ἐπὶ τῆς θυσίας Nu 15.5 ‖ ὁλοκαύτωμα ἢ θυσίαν 15.3, 6, 8; pl. 2E 3.2. Cf. Daniel 249-54.

ὁλόκληρος, ον.ʃ

1. *not curtailed, and complete*: ἑπτὰ ἑβδομάδας ~ους 'seven full weeks' Le 23.15, De 16.9; 'intact, natural,' *s* building-stone, 27.6, Jo 9.2b, 1M 4.47; wood, Ez 15.5; ὁ. δικαιοσύνη 'the entirety of righteousness' Wi 15.3.

2. *sound in all parts and having no defect*: *s* sheep, Zc 11.16; εὐσέβεια 'piety' 4M 15.17.

Cf. ὅλος, παντελής, ἥμισυς: Trench 74-7; Foerster, *TDNT* 3.766f.; Spicq 2.578f.

ὀλολυγμός, οῦ. m.ʃ

loud cry of sorrow: of mourners, Zp 1.10 (‖ φωνὴ κραυγῆς and συντριμμός); Is 15.8 (‖ βοή). Cf. ὀλολύζω, βοή, ἦχος, and κραυγή.

ὀλολύζω: fut. ~λύξω; aor. ὠλόλυξα, impv. ~λυξον. Often impv.

to cry loud, 'howl': out of sorrow, ‖ βοάω Ho 7.14, ‖ κράζω Is 65.14, + ἐπί and ‖ κλαίω, λυπέομαι 15.2, μετὰ κλαυθμοῦ 15.3, περὶ τοῦ οἴνου 24.11; *s* coffers in ceiling, Am 8.3; trees, Zc 11.2; idols, Is 10.10; city gates, 14.31 (|| κράζω); φωνή Je 2.23. Cf. ὀλολυγμός, ἀλαλάζω, ἠχέω, θρηνέω, κράζω, στενάζω: Schmidt 3.395f.

ὁλοπόρφυρος, ον.ʃ
all purple: *s* ἱμάτιον Nu 4.7, 13. Cf. πορφύρα.

ὁλορριζεί. adv.ʃ *
together with the entire root: ἀπολέσαι 'to destroy' Es B 6 o'. Cf. ὁλόρριζος.

ὁλόρριζος, ον.ʃ
together with the entire root: ~οι ἀπώλοντο 'perished with the roots and all' Jb 4.7, sim. Pr 15.6; Es 3.18 *L*. Cf. ὁλορριζεί, ῥίζα.

ὅλος, η, ον. Mostly in sg.
entire, whole (of a complete, undiminished unit): **a**. preceding an articular subst., ἐν ὅλῳ τῷ οἴκῳ Ge 31.35; ~ην τὴν ἡμέραν ἐκείνην καὶ ~ην τὴν νύκτα Ex 10.13; ἐξ ~ης τῆς καρδίας σου καὶ ἐξ ~ης τῆς ψυχῆς σου De 4.29, 30.2; Jl 2.12. **b**. following an articular subst., τὸν κριὸν ~ον 'the ram in its entirety' Ex 29.18; τὸν μόσχον ~ον Le 4.21; τὴν νύκτα ~ην 'all night' To 10.7 𝔊[II]. **c**. with an anarthrous subst., ἐν ~ῃ γῇ Αἰγύπτῳ Ge 41.19, 30 (|| ἐν πάσῃ γῇ Αἰγύπτῳ vs. 29, cp. also vs. 41 and 43); ἐνιαυτὸς ~ος 'a full year' Le 25.30 (|| ἐνιαυτὸς ἡμερῶν vs. 29); ἐν ~ῃ [+ τῇ 𝔊[II]] καρδίᾳ ὑμῶν καὶ ἐν ~ῃ τῇ ψυχῇ To 13.6 𝔊[I]. **d**. predicatively foll. a subst., 'in its / their entirety'– ἔργον ὑφαντὸν ~ον ὑακίνθινον 'a woven work entirely of ὑ. [q.v.]' Ex 36.30, cf. ἱμάτιον ὁλοπόρφυρον 'a cloth wholly purple' Nu 4.6; πόλις αἱμάτων ~η ψευδής 'a bloody city, deceitful through and through' Na 3.1; λυχνία χρυσῆ ~η 'a lampstand of pure gold' Zc 4.2; στερεὰ ~η 'entirely solid' Nu 8.4; ~ος ὡσεὶ δορὰ δασύς 'entirely like a shaggy hide' Ge 25.25; at a remove from the subst., τὸ ὄρος τὸ Σινα ἐκαπνίζετο ~ον 'the entire Mount Sinai kept smoking' Ex 19.18, cf. ὅλη καταδυναστεία ἐν αὐτῇ 'there is oppression in it everywhere' Je 6.6; Ct 5.16, cf. Joh 13.10. **e**. adv. τοῖς ὅλοις = ὅλως *by all accounts, altogether*: 2M 6.3, 7.5. **f**. subst. and + negator, 'nothing': τῶν ὅλων ἀπροσδεής 'in need of nothing' 2M 14.35; with no negator, τῶν ὅλων ἐπικρατῶν 'controlling all' 3M 2.3 (|| τὰ πάντα); δι' ~ου 'continually' 3K 10.8 (*L* διὰ παντός), 'entirely' Ez 38.8. Cf. Renehan 2.107.

Cf. ὁλόκληρος, πᾶς, σύνολος, μέρος: Schmidt 4.540-2, 553f.; Shipp 414.

ὁλοσφύρητος, ον.ʃ
made of solid beaten metal: *s* σκεῦος 'vessel' Si 50.9.

ὁλοσχερής, ες.ʃ
complete and lacking nothing: *s* πίστις 'loyalty' 3M 5.31. Cf. ὁλοσχερῶς. Del. Ez 22.30 v.l.

ὁλοσχερῶς. adv.ʃ
completely and lacking nothing: οἰκοδομῆσαι 'to build' 1E 6.27; morally, Ez 22.30. Cf. ὁλοσχερής.

ὁλοφύρομαι.ʃ
to lament over: + acc. rei, ὀλεθρίαν 'ruin' 3M 4.2; + acc. pers., 4M 16.12 || ἐπί τινι (pers.) 16.5. Cf. θρηνέω.

ὄλυνθος, ου. m.ʃ
edible fruit of the wild fig: Ct 2.13. Cf. συκῆ: Shipp 415.

ὄλυρα, ας. f.ʃ
one-seeded wheat, Triticum monococcum (LSJ): + πυρός 'wheat' Ex 9.32, Ez 4.9. Cf. πυρός, ὀλυρίτης.

ὀλυρίτης, ου. m.ʃ *
food made of ὄλυρα 'one-seeded wheat; rice-wheat': in apposition to ἐγκρυφίας 'cake' 3K 19.6.

ὁμαλίζω: fut. ~λιῶ; aor. ὡμάλισα, subj. ~λίσω; pf.ptc.pass. ὡμαλισμένος.ʃ
to make level: + acc., αὐτῆς τὸ πρόσωπον 'the surface of it [= agricultural field]' Is 28.25; ὄρη ὁμαλιῶ 'I shall flatten mountains' 45.2; ὁδοὺς τραχείας 'uneven roads' PSol 8.17; "the way of sinners is paved with stones, i.e. with no pot-holes" Si 21.10. Cf. ὁμαλισμός: Ziegler 1934.183.

ὁμαλισμός, οῦ. m.ʃ * (~λίζω: Xen. +)
being levelled, razed to the ground: of cities, Mi 7.12 (|| διαμερισμός 'being divided up'); φάραγγας πληροῦσθαι εἰς ~ὸν τῆς γῆς 'valleys to fill up to become flat ground' Ba 5.7; PSol 11.4.

ὄμβρημα, ατος. n.ʃ*
rain-water: Ps 77.44. Cf. ὄμβρος, ὑετός.

ὄμβρος, ου. m.ʃ
storm of rain: De 32.2 (|| ὑετός, δρόσος, νιφετός); pl. and divine punishment (|| ὑετός, χάλαζα) Wi 16.16, Si 49.9; ὄ. καὶ δρόσος Da 3.64, ~οι καὶ πηγαί LXX 3.77. Cf. δρόσος, ὄμβρημα, ὑετός, ἐξομβρέω: Schmidt 1.623-7.

ὀμείρομαι.ʃ*
to desire, long for: + gen., θανάτου Jb 3.21. Cf. βούλομαι, ἐπιθυμέω, ἐπιποθέω, θέλω.

ὅμηρος, ου. m. In the LXX, alw. n.pl.
hostage: ἀποστέλλων ἐν θαλάσσῃ ~α Is 18.2; even of one person, ὃς ἦν ~α ἐν Ῥώμῃ 1M 1.10, διδόναι .. φόρον μέγαν καὶ διδόναι ~α 8.7, ἔλαβε τοὺς υἱοὺς .. ~α 9.53 (|| εἰς ~α 11.62), τὰ ~α τὰ ἐν τῇ ἄκρᾳ .. παραδοῦναι 10.6. Cf. Renehan 2.107.

ὁμιλέω: fut. ὁμιλήσω; aor. ὡμίλησα, ptc. ὁμιλήσας.

1. *to busy oneself with*: ἐν ^διαθήκῃ^ Si 11.20; + dat., ἀλλήλοις 'with each other' Su 37 LXX (w. sexual overtone), sim. αὐτῇ Ju 12.12; σοι [= husband] Pr 5.19. **b**. *to have frequent dealings with*: μετὰ σοφῶν 'with the wise' Pr 15.12.

2. *to converse with*: + dat. pers., Da 1.19 LXX (TH λαλέω).

Cf. ὁμιλία.

ὁμιλία, ας. f.ʃ

1. *social gathering*: at a party, 3M 5.18.

2. *intimate, close contact*: συγγιμνασία ~ας ^τῆς σοφίας^ 'gaining more experience under the close tutelage of Wisdom' Wi 8.18; sexual intercourse as a conjugal right, Ex 21.10. Cf. Shipp 415.

3. *conversation*: Pr 7.21.

Cf. ὁμιλέω.

ὁμίχλη, ης. f.ʃ

mist: of poor visibility, Jl 2.2, Zp 1.15 (ǁ σκότος, γνόφος and νεφέλη); of the blind, οἱ ἐν τῇ ~ῃ ὀφθαλμοί (ǁ σκότος) Is 29.18; created by God, Am 4.13 (ǁ ὄρθρος 'dawn'); fig. of ephemeral nature, ὁ. δρόσου 'of dew' Jb 24.20, cf. ὁ. καὶ δ. Aristoph., *Nu.* 330; ǁ νέφος Jb 38.9, ǁ νεφέλη Wi 2.4; ὡς σποδόν 'like ashes' Ps 147.5; affecting a wide area, ὡς ὁ. κατεκάλυψα γῆν Si 24.3 (of Wisdom); soaked with beneficial moisture, 43.22 (ǁ δρόσος). Cf. νεφέλη: Schmidt 1.611-5.

ὄμμα, ατος. n. Only in Pr, Wi, and 4M.

eye: Pr 6.4 (ǁ βλέφαρος 'eyelid'), 9.18a; an organ for visual perception, Wi 15.15 (ǁ ῥίς 'nostril'). Cf. ὀφθαλμός: Schmidt 1.370-8; Shipp 415.

ὀμνύω: fut.mid. ὀμοῦμαι, 2s ὀμῇ; aor. ὤμοσα, impv. ὄμοσον, subj. ὀμόσω, ptc. ὀμόσας; pf. ὀμώμοκα.

1. *to make solemn, affirmatory statement*: by invoking God (acc.), τὸν θεόν Ge 21.23, ζῶντα κύριον Ho 4.15; Da 12.7 LXX (TH ἐν τῷ ζῶντι); + acc. rei, τὴν δεξιάν μου 'my right hand' De 32.40, cf. LSG s.v. **III**; addressed to (dat. pers.), στήσω τὸν ὅρκον μου, ὃν ὤμοσα .. τῷ πατρί σου 'I shall discharge the terms of my oath, which I swore .. to your father' Ge 26.3; ὤμοσαν ἄνθρωπος τῷ πλησίον 'they swore to each other' 26.31; τοῖς πατράσιν ἡμῶν Mi 7.20; + acc. and dat., ὄμοσόν μοι τὸν θεὸν .. 'Swear to me by God ..' Ge 21.23; + κατά τινος 'by invoking so and so'– κατὰ τοῦ κυρίου .. κατὰ τοῦ βασιλέως Zp 1.5, κατὰ τῶν ἁγίων αὐτοῦ 'His saints (or: sacred objects, cf. Cyr. I 438)' Am 4.2, κατὰ τοῦ ἱλασμοῦ Σαμαρείας 'the propitiation effected by the gods of S.' 8.14; *s* God, Ex 33.1, Nu 32.10; of God invoking Himself, καθ' ἑαυτοῦ Am 6.8, κατ' ἐμαυτοῦ Ge 22.16, Is 45.23, Je 22.5, κατὰ σεαυτοῦ De 9.27, κατὰ τῆς δεξιᾶς αὐτοῦ καὶ κατὰ τῆς ἰσχύος τοῦ βραχίονος αὐτοῦ 'by His right hand and by the might of His arm' Is 62.8; also + dat. pers., Ex 32.13, Ps 14.4, τῷ κυρίῳ 131.2 (ǁ εὔχομαι); τῇ καρδίᾳ αὐτῶν .. καὶ τοῖς ὀφθαλμοῖς αὐτῶν Ez 6.9; + dat. inst., τῷ ὀνόματί μου ἐπ' ἀδίκῳ 'by wrongfully invoking my name' Le 19.12, τῷ ὀνόματι κυρίου Is 19.18; *+ ἔν τινι - ἐν κυρίῳ Jd 21.7, ἐν τῷ ζῶντι τὸν αἰῶνα Da TH 12.7 (LXX acc.), ἐν ὀνόματι κυρίου 1K 20.42; ἐπὶ ψεύδει 'dishonestly' Zc 5.4, Ma 3.5, ἐπὶ ψεύδεσιν Je 5.2. **b**. the content of an oath given in an infinitival clause, ὄμοσόν μοι τὸν θεὸν μὴ ἀδικήσειν με 'Swear to me by God not to wrong me' Ge 21.23; ἦ μὴν μὴ αὐτὸς πεπονηρεῦσθαι Ex 22.8, sim.11; Le 5.4; with λέγων and direct speech, Nu 32.10; in a ἵνα-clause, ἵνα μὴ διαβῶ .. De 4.21; in a μήποτε clause, μήποτε συναντήσητε Jd 15.12 B; in an εἰ-clause (q.v.) and not necessarily in public, *to resolve and pledge firmly*: 1K 3.14, Is 62.8; + an inf., Ps 118.106 (+ ἵστημι 'to execute'); in a διότι-clause, Je 28.14; in a ὅτι-clause, 2K 19.8, Bel 7 LXX; + acc. rei, τῷ Δαυιδ ἀλήθειαν ib. 11. **c**. + περί: ὤμοσεν αὐτῷ περὶ τοῦ ῥήματος τούτου 'about this matter' Ge 24.9; Le 6.3. **d**. + ὅρκον: Nu 30.3, 1M 7.18; + dat. pers. Ge 26.3, De 7.8.

2. *to promise to give by an oath*: + acc. rei and dat. pers., τὴν γῆν, ἣν ὤμοσεν ὁ θεὸς τοῖς πατράσιν ἡμῶν Ge 50.24, cf. τὴν γῆν .., ἣν ὤμοσεν τοῖς πατράσιν σου δοῦναί σοι Ex 13.5; Nu 32.11, De 1.8.

3. *to conclude solemnly by an oath*: + dat. pers. and acc., διαθήκην De 4.31, 8.18, 9.5.

4. *to impose an oath* on sbd to do sth: + inf., Es 7.7 *L*, To 9.3 𝔊[I].

5. *to lash out verbally at, denounce* (κατά τινος): κατὰ τῆς ὑπερηφανίας Ιακωβ 'against the arrogance of J.' Am 8.7.

Cf. ὁρκίζω, ἐξομνύω, ἐπιορκέω.

ὁμοεθνής, ές.

belonging to same ἔθνος: subst.m. 2M 4.2. Cf. ὁμόφυλος.

ὁμοζηλία, ας. f.ʃ *

common, shared enthusiasm: τῆς καλοκἀγαθίας 'for the highest moral ideal' 4M 13.25. Cf. ζῆλος.

ὁμοθυμαδόν. adv.ʃ

1. *acting in unison as one person*: αὐτὸς καὶ οἱ υἱοὶ Ισραηλ ὁ. καὶ πᾶσα ἡ συναγωγή Nu 27.21; συνήχθησαν 'assembled ..' 1E 5.46, ἔφυγον Ju 15.2, πάντες ὁ. ἐπέπεσον ἐπ' αὐτούς '.. attacked them' 15.5, παρεγένοντο πρὸς αὐτὸν ὁ. 'came to him ..' Jb 2.11. **b**. c. verba dicendi: ἀπεκρίθη πᾶς ὁ λαὸς ὁ. Ex 19.8, ἔκλαυσαν Jb 31.38, ἐβόησαν Ju 4.12, cf. ἐγένετο κλαυθμὸς μέγας ἐν μέσῳ τῆς ἐκκλησίας ὁ. 7.29, εὐλόγησαν 15.9, θρῆνον .. ὁ. ἐξῆρχον 'were leading a chorus of lament' 3M 4.7, ᾔνεσαν Wi 10.20.

2. *acting in same manner as members of other group*, 'likewise': καὶ αὐτοὶ ὁ. ἀπολοῦνται 'they shall likewise perish' Nu 24.24, ὁ. συνέτριψαν ζυγόν 'they [= the rich] also broke the yoke (just like the poor)' Je 5.5, ἐπένθησε τὸ προτείχισμα,

καὶ τεῖχος ὁ. ἠσθένησεν 'the outer wall grieved, and the (inner) wall likewise pained' La 2.8. Cf. Jb 6.2.

3. *affecting all*: ὁ. τὸ πρωὶ αὐτοῖς σκιὰ θανάτου 'the morning is a shadow of death to all of them' Jb 24.17¶, τελευτήσεται πᾶσα σὰρξ ὁ. 'death is the common lot of mankind' 34.15, ὁ. πάντες ἐν ἑνὶ ὀνόματι θανάτου 'they altogether, under the common denominator of death' Wi 18.12, αὐτοὺς ἐρρύσατο ὁ. 'he rescued them all' 3M 6.39. **b**. *in identical location*: ὁ. ἐκρύβησαν 'they hid together' Jb 24.4, sim. 40.13.

NB. Actors or entities ultimately affected by an action qualified with ὁ. are invariably human.

Cf. ἅμα, ἐπὶ τὸ αὐτό, ὁμοῦ, συμφώνως: Spicq 2.580-2.

ὁμοιοπαθής, ές.ʃ

having like feelings or *passions* (LSJ): *s* γῆ Wi 7.3; subst.m., hum., 4M 12.13. Cf. συμπαθεία.

ὅμοιος, α, ον.

similar (to sbd/sth τινι), *resembling*: βοηθὸς ὅ. αὐτῷ Ge 2.20 (‖ βοηθὸν κατ' αὐτόν 2.18, Si 36.29), Jl 2.2; τίς ὅμοιός σοι ἐν θεοῖς ..; 'who is like unto you among gods ..?' Ex 15.11; ὁμοία ἐθνῶν πολλῶν Is 13.4 (brachylogy for ὁ. τῇ [φωνῇ] ἐ. π.). **b**. subst., *sbd* or *sth that reminds of* sbd or sth else: τῷ ὁμοίῳ αὐτοῦ 'his kind, his like' Si 13.16 (‖ γένος; and αὐτῷ vs. 15), Jb 35.8¶; n. pl. adv., οὐχ ~α δικαίοις 'differently from the righteous' Wi 11.14.

Cf. ὁμοιόω, ἀνόμοιος, ὁμοιότης, ἴσος, κατά + acc., ὡς: Schmidt 4.471f., 475f., 483.

ὁμοιότης, ητος. f.

1. *being similar*, 'similarity, likeness': Ge 1.11.

2. *mental image of sbd or sth formed by observation*: 4M 15.4.

Cf. ὅμοιος.

ὁμοιότροπος, ον.ʃ

similar in nature: *s* ψυχή Si 26.27¶.

ὁμοιόψηφος, ον.ʃ*

indicative of unity of view, 'unanimous': 2M 14.20 (v.l. ὁμόψηφος).

ὁμοιόω: fut.pass. ὁμοιωθήσομαι; aor. ὡμοίωσα, inf. ὁμοιῶσαι, pass. ὡμοιώθην, impv. ὁμοιώθητι, subj. ὁμοιωθῶ; pf.ptc.pass. ὡμοιωμένος.

1. *to make similar* (to sth τινι): + acc., νυκτὶ ὡμοίωσα τὴν μητέρα σου 'I rendered your mother similar to night' Ho 4.5 (fig. of ignorance - Th 22); pass., ἐν χερσὶ προφήτων ὡμοιώθην 12.10 (cf. Thph PG 126.783, and Harl in Harl et al. 1988.307f); + ὡς– ὡμοιώθη ὁ λαός μου ὡς οὐκ ἔχων γνῶσιν 'my people became similar to those who lack knowledge' 4.6; Is 1.9. **b**. *to produce a reproduction of*: + acc., Si 38.27.

2. *to consider to be similar to, compare with*: + acc. and dat., τίνι ὡμοιώσατε κύριον ..; Is 40.18; 46.5, Ps 39.6; pass., 48.13 (‖ παρασυμβάλλομαι).

***3**. *to consent*: pass./mid. and + dat. pers., ὁμοιωθησόμεθα ὑμῖν καὶ κατοικήσομεν ἐν ὑμῖν Ge 34.15; + inf., ὁμοιωθήσονται ἡμῖν οἱ ἄνθρωποι τοῦ οἰκεῖν μεθ' ἡμῶν 34.22. This sense is likely an Aramaism: cf. Syr. *'eštwi* and Palest. Trg. (Cairo Genizah) at Ge 34.15, 23 נִשְׁתְּוֵה; see also Egypt. Ar. at *TAD* B2.11:2 אשתוין כחדה 'we have reached agreement.' See Muraoka 2005b.106.

Cf. ὅμοιος, ἐξομοιόω, ἀπεικάζω, παρασυμβάλλω, προσδέχομαι **3**, συναινέω, συνεῖπον.

ὁμοίωμα, ατος. n.

sth visible and tangible which resembles sth else, 'image, effigy': an object of worship, οὐδὲ παντὸς ὁ. 'not an image of anything' Ex 20.4; μὴ .. ποιήσητε ὑμῖν αὐτοῖς γλυπτὸν ὁ., πᾶσαν εἰκόνα, ὁ. ἀρσενικοῦ ἢ θηλυκοῦ .. 'you shall not make yourselves any graven image, any symbol, anything resembling a masculine or feminine (creature)' De 4.16; ὁ. οὐκ εἴδετε, ἀλλ' φωνήν 'you did not see anything except (hearing) a voice' 4.12; Ez 1.5 (‖ ὅρασις vs. 4); drawing or miniature of an altar, 4K 16.10B (*L* ὁμοίωσις). Cf. ὅμοιος, ὁμοίωσις, εἰκών, ἀπείκασμα: Trench 49-53.

ὁμοίως. adv.

similarly: + dat., Ez 14.10, 1E 5.66. Cf. ἀναλόγως.

ὁμοίωσις, εως. f.

Mostly foll. by a gen.

1. *being similar, resemblance*: ἄλλο θηρίον ~ιν ἔχον ἄρκου 'another animal bearing resemblance to a bear' Da 7.5 LXX (= TH ὅμοιον ἄρκῳ); κατ' εἰκόνα ἡμετέραν καὶ καθ' ~ιν 'in accordance with our own image and so that it would resemble (us)' Ge 1.26; θυμὸς αὐτοῖς κατὰ τὴν ~ιν τοῦ ὄφεως 'they have a venom like a snake' Ps 57.5; ἀποσφράγισμα ~εως 'seal of duplication (?)' Ez 28.12, cf. Thdt PG 81.1093 ..

2. *that which is similar*: ὁ. τῶν προσώπων αὐτῶν 'something similar to their faces' Ez 1.10; with redundant ὡς– ὡς ὁ. χειρὸς ἀνθρώπου 'something like a human hand' Da 10.16 LXX; ὡς ὁ. υἱοῦ ἀνθρώπου ib. TH; drawing or miniature of an altar, 4K 16.10*L* (B: ὁμοίωμα).

Cf. ὅμοιος and ὡς.

ὁμολογέω: fut. ~γήσω; aor. ὡμολόγησα, inf. ~γῆσαι, ptc. ~γήσας.

1. *to admit to*: abs., Es A 14 (wrongdoing), ἐφ' ἁμαρτίαις σου Si 4.26; σοι 1E 4.60; + acc., τὴν ἐπιθυμίαν αὐτῶν 'their lust' Su TH 14.

2. *to accept as true*: + ὅτι, Jb 40.14, τῷ κυρίῳ 1E 5.58; + inf. clause, Wi 18.13, 2M 6.6, 4M 6.34.

3. *to promise publicly*: + cogn. acc., ὁμολογίας Je 51.25.

4. *to consent* to do: + inf., 4M 9.16. Cf. συναινέω, νεύω.

Cf. ὁμολογία, ὁμόλογος, ὁμολογουμένως, ἐξομολογέομαι, συνομολογέω, ἀρνέομαι: *ND* 6.32.

ὁμολογία, ας. f.ʃ

1. *acknowledgement, confession* of sin or error: ἐπεκαλέσαντο ~ας 'they called for confessions' Am 4.5; δότε ~αν δόξαν τῷ κυρίῳ 1E 9.8.

***2**. *solemn promise* in the form of an oath to a divine being: || αἵρεσις 'free choice' Le 22.18; ποιήσομεν τὰς ~ας ἡμῶν, ἅς ὡμολογήσαμεν Je 51.25.

***3**. *cultic offering in accordance with solemn promise*: φαγεῖν .. τὰς ~ας ὑμῶν De 12.17; ὁ. ὁλοκαύτωμα σωτηρίου '.. in the form of a whole burnt-offering for salvation' Ez 46.12.

Cf. ὁμολόγως, ὁμολογέω, ἐξομολόγησις: Tov 1990.97-110.

ὁμόλογος, ον.ʃ

admitting to wrongdoing, 'confessing': Su 61 LXX.

ὁμολογουμένως. adv.

by common admission, as everyone would agree: 4M 6.31. Cf. ὁμολογέω: Spicq 2.583f.

ὁμολόγως. adv.ʃ

willingly: ἀγαπήσω αὐτοὺς ὁ. Ho 14.5. Cf. ὁμολογία: Tov 1990.98, 109.

ὁμομήτριος, ον.ʃ

born from same mother: *s* brother, Ge 43.29. Cf. ὁμοπάτριος.

ὁμονοέω:ʃ

to hold same or *similar view*: + dat. pers., Le 20.5, Es C 24, Da LXX 2.43. Cf. ὁμόνοια.

ὁμόνοια, ας. f.

likemindedness: ἐβουλεύσαντο ἐν ~ᾳ ἐπὶ τὸ αὐτό 'we jointly arrived at the same decision' Ps 82.6; || φιλία Si 25.1. Cf. ὁμονοέω, ὁμόψυχος.

ὁμοπάτριος, α, ον.ʃ

born from same father: *s* sister, Le 18.11. Cf. ὁμομήτριος.

ὁμορέω.

to border upon: + dat., Σοδομα καὶ Γομορρα καὶ τὰς ὁμορούσας αὐταῖς Je 27.40; τοὺς ὁμοροῦντάς σοι 'your neighbours' Ez 16.26. Cf. ὅμορος, προσκυρέω.

ὅμορος, ον.ʃ

having same borders with: pl., τὰ ~α τῶν πόλεων Nu 35.5 (|| τὰ προάστια τῶν πόλεων vs. 2; τὰ συγκυροῦντα τῶν πόλεων vs. 4); 2C 21.16. Cf. προάστιον, προσ~, συγκυρέω, ὁμορέω.

ὁμόσπονδος, ον.ʃ

bound by treaty: *s* hum., τῷ βασιλεῖ 3M 3.7.

ὁμοῦ. adv.

1. *in a manner similarly applicable to two or more entities*: κατὰ ἔθνους καὶ κατὰ ἀνθρώπου ὁ. 'against a nation and against an individual alike' Jb 34.29; ἵνα ὁ... πλησθῇς 'that you may share the pleasure ..' Si 22.23; καὶ τούτοις ὁ. τὸν αὐτὸν τρόπον ἐπιμελῶς ὡς ἐκείνοις ποιῆσαι 'to deal with these people precisely in the same fashion as those' 3M 4.13.

2. *acting or happening at the same time*: ἐπώλουν .. ὁ. δὲ τὸν κύριον ἠξίουν 'they started selling, .. at the same time imploring the Lord' 2M 8.14; ὁ. δὲ πάντες εὐλόγησαν 'they all praised unanimously' 11.9; 11.7, 13.12, 3M 5.21, Wi 7.11.

3. + dat., *in addition to, besides*: ὁ. τούτῳ 2M 10.15.

Cf. ἅμα, ὁμοθυμαδόν.

ὁμόφυλος, ον.ʃ

belonging to same φυλή: subst.m., 2M 4.10, 3M 3.21. Cf. ὁμοεθνής, ἀλλόφυλος.

ὁμόψυχος, ον.ʃ *

same-minded: *s* hum., + dat., 4M 14.20. Cf. ὁμόνοια.

ὀμφακίζω.ʃ

to bear sour grapes: Is 18.5. Cf. ὄμφαξ.

ὀμφαλός, οῦ. m.ʃ

1. *navel*: Ct 7.3.

2. *centre*: γαστρός 'of belly' Jb 40.16; τῆς γῆς Jd 9.37, Ez 38.12.

ὄμφαξ, ακος. f.ʃ

unripe grape: ὄ. ἀνθήσῃ ἄνθος ὀμφακίζουσα '.. blossoms as a blossom bearing sour grapes' Is 18.5; causing the teeth to be set on edge, Je 38.29, 30, Ez 18.2; ὀδοῦσι βλαβερόν 'injurious to the teeth' Pr 10.26; πρὸ ὥρας 'before the season' Jb 15.33.

ὁμώνυμος, ον.ʃ

bearing the same name: *s* hum., + dat. pers., Si prol. II.

ὅμως. adv.

all the same, having said that: 2M 2.27.

ὄναγρος, ου. m.ʃ *

wild ass: Ps 103.11, ἐν ἐρήμῳ Si 13.19. Cf. ὄνος.

ὀνειδίζω: fut. ὀνειδιῶ, pass. ~δισθήσομαι; aor. ὠνείδισα, subj. ὀνειδίσω, ptc. ~δίσας, pass. ὠνειδίσθην, inf. ~δισθῆναι.

1. *to censure, criticise*: + dat. pers. and acc. rei, ἡμῖν ἁμαρτήματα Wi 2.12; + acc. pers., ἄνθρωπον ἀποστρέφοντα ἀπὸ ἁμαρτίας '.. turning away from sin' Si 8.5; ὀνειδισμοὺς .. ἐν οἷς ὠνείδιζον τὸν λαόν μου Zp 2.8; || μεγαλύνω 'to boast' 2.10; + cogn. and acc. pers., ὀνειδισμὸν .., ὃν ὠνείδισάν με Ps 78.12.

2. *to insult*: verbally, θεὸν ζῶντα Is 37.4, κύριον 37.24; τίνα ὠνείδισας καὶ παρώξυνας; 'whom have you insulted and provoked?' 37.23. **b**. *to utter so as to insult*: + double acc., τῶν λόγων .., οὓς ὠνείδισάν με Is 37.6, cf. Ps 78.12 under **1** above.

3. *to cause and subject to public humiliation*: *o* hum., PSol 2.19; pass., *o* hum., κατῃσχύνθη καὶ ὠνειδίσθη Je 15.9.

Cf. ὀνειδισμός, ἐλέγχω, μέμφομαι: Schmidt 1.137-9; Spicq 2.585-7; Renehan 2.108.

ὀνείδισμα, ατος. n.ʃ

target of verbal abuse: Ez 36.3 (ǁ λάλημα). Cf. ὀνειδισμός.

ὀνειδισμός, οῦ. m. * (ὄνειδος: Hom. +)

1. *bad reputation, disgrace*: suffered by a group, οὐ δώσω ὑμᾶς οὐκέτι εἰς ~ὸν ἐν τοῖς ἔθνεσι 'I shall not disgrace you again among the foreign nations' Jl 2.19, cf. ἀπὸ τῆς αἰχμαλωσίας ἐκεῖ ἐν τῷ χώρᾳ ἐν πονηρίᾳ μεγάλῃ καὶ ἐν ~ῷ Ne 1.3; ǁ κονδυλισμός (q.v.) Zp 2.8; divine punishment, ὀ. αἰώνιον καὶ ἀτιμίαν αἰώνιον Je 23.40, εἰς ~ὸν καὶ εἰς παραβολὴν καὶ εἰς μῖσος καὶ εἰς κατάραν 24.9; suffered by the pious, ἕνεκά σου ὑπήνεγκα ~όν 'for your sake I bore ..' Ps 68.8, ὡς ἔλαβον περὶ σοῦ ~όν 'I became the butt of insult for your sake' Je 15.5, see also Ps 68.10, Je 20.8, but λαμβάνω ~ὸν ἐπί τινα 'to utter insult against sbd' Ps 14.2; ǁ ἀτιμία Ez 36.15, + ἀτιμία Ps 23.40, + ἀρά Je 49.18, κατάρα 51.12.

2. *act of insulting*: τῶν ἐθνῶν τῶν ἐχθρῶν ὑμῶν 'by your enemy nations' Ne 5.9. **b**. *insulting utterance*: ἠκούσαμεν ~ὸν ἡμῶν '.. against us' Je 28.51, ἀκοῦσαι ~ούς To 3.7 𝔊II. **c**. *target of insult*: τὸ ῥῆμα κυρίου ἐγένετο αὐτοῖς εἰς ~όν Je 6.10, ἐστράφησαν .. τὰ σάββατα αὐτῆς εἰς ~όν 1M 1.39.

3. *fault deserving denunciation*: ἔναντι κυρίου Je 12.13.

Cf. ὀνειδίζω, ὄνειδος, ὀνείδισμα, καταγέλως.

ὄνειδος, ους. n.

1. *being disgraced, humiliated*: Ἀφεῖλεν ὁ θεός μου τὸ ὄ. 'God took away my disgrace' Ge 30.23; ~η λαῶν λήμψεσθε 'you will suffer disgrace at the hands of nations' Mi 6.16; μὴ δῷς τὴν κληρονομίαν σου εἰς ὄ. τοῦ κατάρξαι αὐτῶν ἔθνη 'Do not subject your inheritance to the humiliation of being ruled over by gentile nations' Jl 2.17; + αἰσχύνη Si 6.1, Is 30.3, and τῆς χηρείας 'of widowhood' 54.4. **b**. *target of humiliation*: ἀνθρώπου Ps 21.7 (ǁ ἐξουδένημα).

2. *reproach, criticism*: 4M 5.9. **b**. *that which is reproachable*: *s* behaviour, Le 20.17.

Cf. ὀνειδισμός, ὀνειδίζω, ἔλεγχος, καταγελάω, καταισχύνω, ψόγος.

ὄνειρος, ου. m.ʃ

dream: 2M 15.11; disturbing, 4M 6.5, Wi 18.17, 19. Cf. ἐνύπνιον.

ὄνησις, εως. f.ʃ

enjoyment: ὁ μισθὸς τῶν ἀνθρώπων οὐκ ἔσται εἰς ~ιν Zc 8.10. Cf. ὀνίνημι, ἀπόλαυσις.

ὀνίνημι: fut.mid. ὀνήσομαι; aor.pass. ὠνάσθην.ʃ

1. *to have advantage* from: + gen. pers., To 3.8𝔊I.

2. *to have delight* from:*ἐπί τινι Si 30.2.

Cf. ὄνησις, ἀνόνητος, συμφέρω: Schmidt 4.167-9.

ὀνοκένταυρος, ου. m.ʃ*

a kind of *demon* haunting wild places (LSJ): Is 13.22 (ǁ δαιμόνια, ἐχῖνοι), 34.11, 14.

ὄνομα, ατος. n.

1. *that by which a person* or *object is called and whose identity is known*, 'name': Κάλεσον τὸ ὄ. αὐτοῦ Ιεζραηλ 'Name him Jezreel' Ho 1.4; identifies one's family ties, Na 1.14; to be borne by descendants, ἀπόλω αὐτῶν ὄ. καὶ κατάλειμμα καὶ σπέρμα Is 14.22; an entity exists only as long as it has a name – ἐξολεθρεύσω τὰ ~τα τῶν εἰδώλων ἀπὸ τῆς γῆς Zc 13.2, cf. Pr 10.7 (ǁ μνήμη); ~τι μόνον φίλος 'friend by name only' Si 37.1; God's name, τὸ ὄ. τοῦ θεοῦ Am 2.7, ὁ θεὸς ὁ παντοκράτωρ ὄ. αὐτῷ '"God the almighty" is his name' 5.27, cf. 4.13, 5.8, 9.6, and τοῦτο ὄ. αὐτῷ 'that was its name' Ge 2.19; ἔσται κύριος εἷς καὶ τὸ ὄ. αὐτοῦ ἕν Zc 14.9; φοβούμενοι τὸ ὄ. αὐτοῦ Mi 6.9, cf. Zp 3.12; ὄ. αἰώνιον Ex 3.15; object of glorification or reverence, τὸ ὄ. μου δεδόξασται Ma 1.11, cf. 2.2; τοῖς φοβουμένοις τὸν κύριον καὶ εὐλαβουμένοις τὸ ὄ. αὐτοῦ 3.16; αἰνέσετε τὸ ὄ. κυρίου Jl 2.26, cf. Ma 1.6 (w. φαυλίζω 'to show contempt for'); invoked for help, πᾶς, ὃς ἂν ἐπικαλέσηται τὸ ὄ. κυρίου, σωθήσεται Jl 2.32; in oath, ὀμνύοντας ἐπὶ τῷ ~τί μου Ma 3.5; λαλῆσαι ἐπὶ τῷ σῷ ~τι 'as sent by you' Ex 5.23; a letter written ἐπὶ τῷ ~ατι Αχααβ 3K 20.8; Ma 1.11 (when offering sacrifices); as a sign of submission, τοῦ ἐπικαλεῖσθαι πάντας τὸ ὄ. κυρίου τοῦ δουλεύειν αὐτῷ Zp 3.9; of idols and foreign gods, τὰ ~τα τῆς Βααλ Zp 1.4; mark of ownership or allegiance, οἱ κατάλοιποι τῶν ἀνθρώπων καὶ πάντα τὰ ἔθνη, ἐφ' οὓς ἐπικέκληται τὸ ὄ. μου Am 9.12; αὐτὸς ἐπικαλέσεται τὸ ὄ. μου .. καὶ ἐρῶ Λαός μου οὗτός ἐστι, καὶ αὐτὸς ἐρεῖ Κύριος ὁ θεός μου Zc 13.9; cf. πορευσόμεθα ἐν ~τι κυρίου 'we shall walk in such a way as would show our allegiance to the Lord' Mi 4.5; confers authority - ψευδῆ ἐλάλησας ἐν ~τι κυρίου 'you told lies on the authority of the Lord (by invoking His name)' Zc 13.3, ἐπροφήτευσας τῷ ~τι κυρίου Je 33.9. **b**. A standing formula for indicating the name of a person or place mentioned in a narrative is: ὄνομά τινι ..: e.g. καὶ ὄ. τῷ ἀδελφῷ αὐτοῦ Ιουβαλ 'the name of his brother was J.' Ge 4.21; ὄ. τῇ γυναικὶ Αβραμ Σαρα 11.29; outside of a narrative, κύριος ὄ. αὐτῷ Ex 15.3, Ἀνατολὴ ὄ. αὐτῷ Zc 6.12; also with the dat. of a rel. pron., ἡ παλλακὴ αὐτοῦ, ᾗ ὄ. Ρεημα 'his concubine by the name of R.' Ge 22.24; ἀδελφὸς ἦν, ᾧ ὄ. Λαβαν 24.29, cf. παῖς .. ᾧ ὄ. Ἥρμων *P.Par.* 10.2f., the acc. in Cl. Gk, e.g. Ποταμός, Κύδνος ὄ. Xen. *Anab.* 1.2.28 (so 2M 12.13) and dat. preceding a name, δοῦλον ὀνόματι Σαρμάτην 'a slave by the name of S.' *P.Oxy. Hels.* 26.10, so νεωτέρῳ ὀνόματι Δανιηλ 'to a lad called D.' Su 45 LXX, sim. 4M 5.4. **c.** ἐξ ὀνόματος / ὀνομάτων 'by name'– ἀνακληθέντας ἐξ ~τος 'called by name' Nu 1.17. **d.** πάντας ἐπ' ὀνόματι καλέσει Is 40.26. **e.** ἐπ' ὀνόματος Da 3.93 LXX; ἐκλεγέντες ἐπ' ~τος 'chosen by name' 1C 16.41. **f.** ὁμοθυμαδὸν πάντες ἐν ἑνὶ ~ατι θανάτου 'they altogether, under the common denominator of death' Wi 18.12 (*pace* LSG s.v. **IV 1**).

2. *fame*: ποιήσωμεν ἑαυτοῖς ὄ. 'let us win fame' Ge 11.4; μεγαλυνῶ τὸ ὄ. σου 12.2; ἐξῆλθέ σοι ὄ. ἐν τοῖς ἔθνεσιν Ez 16.14; ἐπὶ τῷ ~τί σου 'with your fame as a selling point' 16.15.

3. *reputation*: of one's father, Le 21.9; πονηρόν 'unfavourable' De 22.14, Si 6.1; 1M 8.1.

4. *news*: αὐτῶν 'about them' 1M 3.41.

Cf. ὀνομάζω, ὀνομασία, ὀνομαστός, ἐπονομάζω, καλέω, ἀνώνυμος, ὁμώνυμος, κλέος, κῦδος: Shipp 416.

ὀνομάζω: fut. ὀνομάσω, pass. ~μασθήσομαι; aor. ὠνόμασα, inf. ~μάσαι, ptc. ~μάσας, pass. ὠνομάσθην, inf. ὀνομασθῆναι.

1. *to utter* (a name): + acc. (ὄνομα) Ge 26.18 (|| ἐπονομάζω); ὀνομάσαι τὸ ὄνομα κυρίου Le 24.16 (|| ἐπονομάζω vs. 11), Am 6.10; τὸ ὄνομα κυρίου understood, ὁ ὀμνύων καὶ ὀνομάζων Si 23.10, see Lieberman 1965.34. **b.** ἐν πόλει, ἐν ᾗ ὠνομάσθη τὸ ὄνομά σου ἐπ' αὐτήν Je 32.15, τὸ ἱερὸν .. ἐπ' αὐτῷ 1E 4.63, see under ἐπικαλέω **B 1c** and καλέω **9**.

2. *to call by the name of*: + double acc., person named and name, De 2.20, Wi 2.13; name understood, Ba 4.30.

3. *to mention*: + acc. and pass., Je 3.16; + acc. and dat. pers., Is 19.17. **b.** *to give publicity to*: *o* royal decree, Es 9.4 o'. **c.** psss. *to gain fame*: + δοξάζω 1M 11.51.

Cf. ὄνομα, ἐπ~, προσονομάζω, καλέω: Schmidt 1.120-2.

ὀνομασία, ας. f.ʃ

act of naming: ~ᾳ τοῦ ἁγίου μὴ συνεθισθῇς 'Do not acquire the habit of invoking the name of the Holy One' Si 23.9. Cf. ὄνομα, ὀνομάζω, καλέω.

ὀνομαστός, ή, όν.

famed, widely known: *s* pers., ἄνθρωποι Ge 6.4; ἄνδρες Nu 16.2, λαός Je 13.11; || καύχημα, δοξαστός De 26.19; || καύχημα Zp 3.19, 20; τόπον ~όν, μνημεῖον '.. a monument' Ez 39.11, τόπος understood, 39.13; *infamous* 24.14. Cf. ὄνομα, γνωστός, εὔγνωστος, περιβόητος.

ὀνοματογραφία, ας. f.ʃ *

act of writing names: τὴν ~αν ᾐτοῦμεν αὐτοὺς τῶν προκαθηγουμένων 'we asked them to write down the leaders' names' 1E 6.11; 8.48.

ὄνος, ου. m./f.

ass: used as a mount, Ge 22.3, Nu 22.21; used in war as beast of burden, Zc 14.15 (|| ἵππος, κάμηλος, and ἡμίονος), Ju 2.17; Is 1.3 (|| βοῦς); used for transport in a desert, and + κάμηλος 30.6; part of nomad's possessions, ἐγένετο αὐτῷ πρόβατα καὶ μόσχοι καὶ ὄνοι Ge 12.16 (along with παῖδες καὶ παιδίσκαι, ἡμίονοι καὶ κάμηλοι); 24.35 (silver and gold also included); Ex 13.13 (|| ὑποζύγιον 34.20), || ἱμάτιον De 22.3. **b.** ὄ. ἄγριος 'wild ass': Is 32.14, Jb 39.5.

Cf. ὄναγρος, ὑποζύγιον: Lee 140-3; Spicq 3.588-90.

ὄντως. adv.

Indicates agreement, *really, truly*: to a proposition, and clause-initial, Nu 22.37, Je 3.23, 10.19; designed to impress on the hearer the veracity of one's statement, 2K 14.5*L* (B: καὶ μάλα); not clause-initial and w. ref. to part of a proposition, ἀδύνατον ὄ.'truly impossible' Wi 17.15. Cf. ἀληθῶς, ἀληθινῶς.

ὄνυξ, υχος. m.ʃ

1. *claw* of beast of prey: Da 7.19; of lion, 4.30[b] LXX; of vulture, 4.30 TH; of eagle, Ez 17.3, 7. **b.** *claw-shaped object*: 4M 9.26.

2. *hoof*: of swine, ὁπλῆς Le 11.7, De 14.8.

3. a precious stone, 'onyx': ἐν ~χι τιμίῳ Jb 28.16¶ (|| σάπφιρος).

4. an aromatic substance, 'onycha': Ex 30.34, Si 24.15 (|| χαλβάνη, στακτή).

Cf. ὀνύχιον, ὀνυχίζω, ὁπλή.

ὀνυχίζω.

1. ὀ. ὀνυχιστῆρας 'to have a cloven foot': *s* animal, δύο χηλῶν 'into two claws' Le 11.3 +; ὄνυχας ὁπλῆς 11.7, De 14.8.

2. *to pare the nails of*: mid., τὰς χεῖρας αὐτοῦ 'his own hands' 2K 19.25*L* (B: abs.).

Cf. ὄνυξ, ὀνυχιστήρ, περιονυχίζω, διχηλέω.

ὀνύχιον, ου. n, dim. of ὄνυξ.ʃ

onyx: Ex 28.20, 36.20, Ez 28.13.

ὀνυχιστήρ, ῆρος. m.*

hoof: κτῆνος .. ~ας ὀνυχίζον 'animal with a split hoof' Le 11.3 (|| διχηλοῦν ὁπλήν). Cf. ὁπλή, ὀνυχίζω.

ὀξέως. adv.

speedily: ἐὰν ὀ. τελευτήσωσιν 'if they die quickly' Wi 3.18; || ταχέως Is 8.3; ὀ. καὶ ταχέως (*contra* Zgl: ὀ.) Jl 3.4. Cf. ὀξύς, ταχέως, σπουδή.

ὄξος, ους. n.ʃ

vinegar: ἐξ οἴνου 'made from wine' Nu 6.3; drink, Ps 68.22; with which to moisten bread, Ru 2.14; bad when applied to a sore, Pr 25.20.

ὀξυγράφος, ον.ʃ *
capable of writing fast: *s* γραμματεύς Ps 44.2.

ὀξύθυμος, ον.ʃ
quick to anger: *s* hum. Pr 14.17. Cf. θυμός, μακρόθυμος, ὀλιγόψυχος.

ὀξύνω: fut. ὀξυνῶ; aor. ὤξυνα, inf. ὀξῦναι, subj.pass. ὀξυνθῶ.
to make sharp (ὀξύς): *o* horn (κέρας) as weapon, Zc 1.21, iron (σίδηρος) Is 44.12, σίδηρος σίδηρον Pr 27.17 (|| παροξύνω, play on words); metaph., ὀργήν 'wrath' Wi 5.20. **b**. mid. *to become sharp*: *s* sword, Ez 21.9, 10; metaph., θυμός Pr 24.22d.
Cf. ὀξύς, ἀκονάω.

ὀξύς, εῖα, ύ. Comp. ὀξύτερος.
1. *swift in movement*: *s* wolf and horse, Hb 1.8; soldier, ὀ. τοῖς ποσίν 'quick-footed' Am 2.15; opp. νωθρός 'sluggish' Pr 22.29; foot, Ps 13.3; march, 3M 4.5; in effect, δύναμις 4M 14.10.
2. *pointed, not blunt*: *s* βέλος 'arrow' Is 5.28, μάχαιρα 'sword' 49.2, ῥομφαία Ez 5.1, ὀβελίσκος 'spit' 4M 11.19; subst.n., *sharp object*, Jb 16.10. **b**. metaph. *poignant, painfully sharp*: *s* punishment, 3M 2.23.
3. *capable of keen and penetrating discernment*: *s* spirit of Wisdom, Wi 7.22; hum., ἐν κρίσει 'in judgement' 8.11; ἐν ἔργων Pr 22.29 (|| ὁρατικός 'observant').
Cf. ὀξύνω, ὀξέως, ταχύς, ταχινός, νωθρός: Schmidt 2.152; Chadwick 211-7.

ὀξύτης, ητος. f.ʃ
sharpness of sound: φωνὴ ~ητος ἵππων 'the sharp sound of horses' Je 8.16.

ὀπαδός, οῦ. m.ʃ
he who does the same as a predecessor: τοῦ Σολομῶντος Si prol. II.

ὀπή, ῆς. f.
aperture: πέτρας 'of a rock' Ex 33.22; τῶν πετρῶν on rock face and used for human habitation, Ob 3 (|| τρυμαλιά Je 29.17); of socket of eye, Zc 14.12; window, Ec 12.3; δένδρων 'of trees' 4M 14.16.

ὁπηνίκα. conj.ʃ
at the time when: + ind. aor., 4M 2.21; + ἄν subj., Ju 11.11. Cf. ὅτε.

ὀπήτιον, ου. n.ʃ
awl: used to bore an ear, Ex 21.6, De 15.17.

ὄπισθεν.
prep. c. gen., *behind* (of place): οὖσα ὄ. αὐτοῦ 'being behind him' Ge 18.10; τὰ ὄ. αὐτοῦ (opp. τὰ ἔμπροσθεν αὐτοῦ) 'what lies behind them' Jl 2.3, ἔμπροσθεν καὶ ὄ. αὐτῶν Ep Je 5; ἐπορεύθη ἐκ τῶν ὄ. 'moved behind' Ex 14.19 (|| ἐκ τῶν ὀπίσω τινός); εἰς τὰ ὄ. καὶ οὐκ εἰς τὰ ἔμπροσθεν Je 7.24. **b**. ἀπὸ ὄ. τινος: ἐκπορνεύσει .. ἀπὸ ὄ. τοῦ κυρίου 'will engage in prostitution (and cease) from closely following the Lord' Ho 1.2 (on the duplication of ablative notion, cf. Hom. *Il*. 8.365 ἀπ' οὐρανόθεν, 24.492 ἀπὸ Τροίηθεν), ἀπέστημεν ἀπὸ ὄ. τοῦ θεοῦ 'rebelled ..' Is 59.13, μὴ ἐκκλίνητε ἀπὸ ὄ. κυρίου 1K 12.20, ἀπέστρεψεν ἀπὸ ὄ. μου 15.11, + ἀναστρέφω 'to turn back' 24.2, ἀπὸ ὄ. Δαυιδ ὀπίσω Σαβεε 'abandoning David, following S.' 2K 20.2. **b**. adv. *behind, at the back* of sth: τὰ ἔμπροσθεν καὶ τὰ ὄ. 'the obverse and the reverse (of a written document)' Ez 2.10.
Cf. ὀπίσω, ὀπίσθιος, ἐξόπισθεν, κατόπισθεν, and ἔμπροσθεν.

ὀπίσθιος, α, ον.
belonging to the hinder part: Ex 26.27; subst.n.pl. τὰ ~ια 'the hinder part,' ἐκ τῶν ~ίων 'at the back' 26.23; 'the buttocks' Je 13.22, τὰ ~ια αὐτῶν πρὸς τὸν ναόν 'with their buttocks turned towards the temple' Ez 8.16 (:: πρόσωπον). Cf. ὀπίσω: Shipp 417.

ὀπισθίως. adv.ʃ
backwards: ἔπεσεν 'he fell' 1K 4.18 (*L* εἰς τὰ ὄπισθεν).

ὀπισθότονος, ον.ʃ
suffering from a disease in which the body is drawn back and stiffens (cf. LSJ): ὀ. ἀνίατος '.. beyond cure' De 32.24.

ὀπισθοφανής, ές.ʃ
looking backwards: τὸ πρόσωπον αὐτῶν ~ές 'their face was facing backwards' Ge 9.23. Cf. ὀπισθοφανῶς.

ὀπισθοφανῶς. adv.ʃ *
looking backwards: ἐπορεύθησαν ὀ. 'walked ..' Ge 9.23. Cf. ὄπισθεν and ὀπισθοφανής.

ὀπίσω.
I. prep. c. gen., **1**. *behind* (of place): Ge 32.18; 41.19 (|| μετά + acc., 41.3); Jl 2.14, Zc 1.8; the gen. noun indicating an object of attachment and devotion: πορεύεσθαι ὀ. ἐραστῶν Ho 2.5, 13, τῶν ματαίων 5.11, κυρίου De 13.4, Ho 11.10, Δαυιδ 2K 2.10; ἐξακολουθεῖν ὀ. αὐτῶν (= τῶν ματαίων) Am 2.4; ἀποστέλλειν ὀ. δόξης Zc 2.8, cf. ὀ. τῶν ἐνθυμημάτων τῶν πατέρων αὐτῶν ἦσαν οἱ ὀφθαλμοὶ αὐτῶν Ez 20.24; hot pursuit, ἐπιδίωξον ὀ. τῶν ἀνθρώπων Ge 44.4. **b**. of time: ἕως ὀ. τοῦ σαββάτου 'until the sabbath is over' Ne 13.19; ὀ. αὐτοῦ 'after his death' Ec 10.14; 12.2.
2. *close behind* in time: Ge 8.8.
3. τὰ ὀπίσω 'the space behind': μὴ περιβλέψῃς εἰς τὰ ὀπίσω 'don't look round backwards' Ge 19.17; ἔστη ἐκ τῶν ὀ. αὐτῶν 'stood behind them' Ex 14.19 (|| ἐκ τῶν ὄπισθεν); τὰ ὀ. μου 33.23 (|| τὸ πρόσωπόν μου); τὰ ὀ. αὐτοῦ (opp. τὰ ἔμπροσθεν αὐτοῦ) 'what lies behind them' Jl 2.3, 20; τὰ ὀπίσω σου 'your buttocks' Na 3.5, cf. Shipp 417.

II. adv. *close behind*: πορευθῆναι μετ' ἐμοῦ ὀ. 'to follow me closely' Ge 24.5; De 11.30.

2. *backwards*: τῶν ὀ. σε πλανησάντων 'of those who made you wander backwards' Is 30. 21; abandoning following and moving forwards, Je 15.6.

Cf. ὄπισθεν, ὀπίσθιος: Johannessohn, *Präp.* 215f.; Balode & Blomqvist.

ὁπλή, ῆς. f.

hoof: Ex 10.26; κτῆνος διχηλοῦν ~ήν 'animal with a split hoof' Le 11.3; pl. ‖ κέρας 'horn' Mi 4.13; ὑπὲρ μόσχον νέον κέρατα ἐκφέροντα καὶ ~άς 'more than a young calf growing horns and hooves' Ps 68.32; of horse and threatening to trample down, Je 29.3, Ez 26.11; ἐμπρόσθιος 'front' 2M 3.25. Cf. χήλη, διχλέω, ὄνυξ, ὀνυχιστήρ.

ὁπλίτης, ου. m.ʃ

heavily armed foot-soldier: Nu 32.21. Cf. πολεμιστής.

ὁπλοδοτέω: aor. ὡπλοδότησα.ʃ

to equip with weapons: + acc. pers. (soldiers), 1M 14.32.

ὁπλοθήκη, ης. f.ʃ

arsenal: 2C 32.27.

ὁπλολογέω: aor.ptc. ~γήσας.ʃ*

collect arms from: + acc. pers. (defeated enemy troops), 2M 8.27, 31. Cf. ὅπλον.

ὁπλομάχος, ον.ʃ

fighting with heavy arms: *s* ἔθνος Is 13.4; subst. m., Is 13.15. Cf. μαχητής, πολεμιστής: LSG s.v.

ὅπλον, ου. n. Mostly in pl.

1. *implement of warfare*, 'arms, weapon': ὅ. δυναστείας Na 2.4, ~α πολεμικά Je 21.4, Ez 32.27; foll. by a list of weapons, 39.9.

2. *large shield*: ἐξαστραπόντων ~ων 'gleaming arms' Na 3.3 (‖ ῥομφαία), cf. Hb 3.11; ἀναλάβετε ὅπλα καὶ ἀσπίδας 'pick up small and large shields' Je 26.3.

3. *armed men*: 2M 5.26.

Cf. ἐνοπλίζω, ἔνοπλος, ἐξοπλίζω, ὁπλίτης, ὁπλολογέω, ~ποιέω, ἀσπίς.

ὁπλοποιέω: fut. ~ποιήσω.ʃ

to use as weapon: + acc., τὴν κτίσιν 'the creation' Wi 5.17. Cf. ὅπλον.

ὁπλοφόρος, ον.ʃ

bearing arms: subst.m., troops, 2C 14.7.

ὁποῖος, α, ον.ʃ

of what kind?: indir. interr., 2M 11.37.

ὁπόταν. conj.ʃ

every time when: + *impf. Jb 29.22.

ὁπότε. conj.ʃ

when: w. ref. to the past, + impf. To 6.14 𝔊[II], 7.11 (𝔊[I] + ἐάν), Ps 3.1; aor., Is 16.13, Ps 33.1, 55.1, 58.1, 59.1; w. ref. to the fut., + fut. Jb 26.14.

ὅπου.

where: Is 42.22; ὅ. οὐκ ἔστιν βοήθεια 'where no help is to be had' Si 8.16. **b**. *in a case such as*: 4M 2.14, 14.11.

ὀπτάζομαι ʃ *

to be seen: ὀφθαλμοῖς κατ' ὀφθαλμούς 'eye to eye' Nu 14.14. Cf. ὀπτασία, βλέπω, εἶδον, θεωρέω, ὁράω.

ὀπτάνομαι*

= ὀπτάζομαι: *s* God, Si 1.10¶; hum., To 12.19 𝔊[I] (𝔊[II] θεωρέω).

ὀπτασία, ας. f.

1. *act of appearing*: ἐν ~ᾳ αὐτοῦ Ma 3.2 (‖ εἴσοδος); *s* sun, Si 43.2.

2. *sth extraordinary which has been visually revealed*, 'vision': Da 9.23 TH, 10.8 (LXX ὅρασις).

Cf. ὁράω, ὀπτάζομαι, ὅρασις, ἐπιφάνεια, φαίνω.

ὀπτάω: fut. ὀπτήσω; aor. ὤπτησα, inf. ὀπτῆσαι, subj. ὀπτήσω, ptc. ὀπτήσας.

to place in, and treat with, fire: + obj.acc., ὀπτήσωμεν αὐτὰς πυρί 'let's heat them [= πλίνθους 'bricks'] with fire' Ge 11.3; ἑψήσεις καὶ ὀπτήσεις 'thou shalt boil and roast [sc. Passover meat]' De 16.7, ὤπτησαν τὸ πάσχα πυρί 1E 1.11 (‖ ἐν πυρί 2C 35.13); meat, κρέας ὀπτήσας ἔφαγε Is 44.16; ἰχθὺν 'fish' To 6.6 𝔊[I] (𝔊[II] τοῦ ἰχθύος). Cf. ὀπτός, ἕψω: Rösel 215f.; Shipp 417f.

ὀπτός, ή, όν.ʃ

placed in, and treated with, fire: of cooked meat, κρέα .. ὀπτὰ πυρί Ex 12.8; 12.9. Cf. ὀπτάω.

ὀπώρα, ας. f.

fruit: Je 31.32 (‖ τρυγητής), συναγάγετε οἶνον καὶ ~αν καὶ ἔλαιον 47.10, sim. 12. Cf. καρπός.

ὀπωροφυλάκιον, ου. n.ʃ *

orchard-guard's shed as a symbol of ruin and desolation: Mi 1.6, 3.12, Is 1.8; a tottering, unstable structure, 24.20; a shabby hut, formerly a temple, Ps 78.1. Cf. φυλάσσω: Lee 1969.242.

ὅπως. conj.

1. modal. **a**. *in such a manner as*: + ἄν + subj. aor. (see BDF, § 369.6), ὅ. ἂν ἐκδύσω αὐτὴν γυμνήν 'by stripping her naked' Ho 2.3(*a*). **b**. + subj. pres. *so much so that, to such an extent that*: ὅ. μηδεὶς μήτε δικάζηται μήτε ἐλέγχῃ μηδείς '(the land will mourn .. the fish of the sea shall fail) so that neither any one may plead, nor any one reprove' Ho 4.4(*b*).

2. resultative. **a**. *as a consequence of which*: + subj.pres., ὅ. συνᾴδωσιν (v.l. ~δουσιν) Ho 7.2(*c*); + subj.aor. Mi 5.7(*g*). **b**. to indicate a result which was not necessarily intended by the subject marked by the verb in the main clause, but was bound to ensue: + subj. aor. ὅ. ἐξολεθρευθῶσιν Ho 8.4(*d*); Am 2.7(*d*), Mi 6.16(v.l. fut.)(*d*).

3. introduces a noun clause of command, instruction, decision and suchlike, *that*: + subj. aor. εἴπατε αὐτῷ ὅ. μὴ λάβητε ἀδικίαν 'promise him not to take up any unrighteous practice' Ho 14.3(*c*), ὑμῖν λέγεται ὅ... γίγνηται 1E 8.22(*n*), γεγραμμένον .. ὅ. μὴ εἰσέλθωσιν .. Ne 13.1(*c*); ὁρισμόν 'decision' Da 6.7 TH(*n*); ἐνετείλατο 'he commanded' 1M 15.39 (‖ + inf.); εὐδόκησαν 'they agreed' 14.42 (‖ + inf., vs. 41); συμβουλεύσαιμι 'I would advise' 4M 1.1 (opt.), παρακαλούμενος 'being urged' 10.1. **b**. without a lead verb: ὅ. ἂν θάψωμεν αὐτὸν, ὅ. μηδεὶς γνῷ 'let's bury him, let nobody know of it' To 8.12 𝔊[II] (𝔊[I] ἵνα).

4. final, purposive, *in order that*: + subj. pres. ὅ. ἐμπλατύνωσι τὰ ὅρια αὐτῶν 'in order to extend their borders' Am 1.13(*d*), ὅ. διώκῃ Hb 2.2(*d*), 15(*d*); + subj. aor. ὅ. εὐλογήσῃ Ge 27.4 (‖ ἵνα)(*e*), 29.21(*h*); ἐπίδοτε ἡμῖν ὅ. πίωμεν Am 4.1(*e*); 5.6(*a*), 14(*d*), 15(v.l. fut.)(*f*), Mi 6.5(*d*), Jl 2.17(*h*), 3.6(*d*), Ob 9(*d*), Jn 1.6 (close to **3**., foll. ἐπικαλέομαι 'to invoke')(*f*), Zp 2.3(*f*), Zc 12.7(*d*), Si 23.3 (‖ fut.); ‖ ἵνα Ex 9.16 (*e*), De 4.40(*k*). **b**. + ἄν: + sub. aor., ὅπως ἂν εὖ μοι γένηται Ge 12.13(*d*), 50.20(*d*); Ex 13.9(*d*), De 8.2(*d*); + ἄν + subj. pres., ὅ. ἂν ὦ εὑρηκὼς .. Ex 33.13(*d*) (‖ ἵνα). **c**. + opt. aor.: 4M 4.6, 23, 6.8.

5. in indirect questions, *in what way*: 2M 7.22.

On the tense and mood of the verb following ὅ., see BDF § 369, Mayser, II 1.247-61.

Cf. ἵνα and ὡς.

a) אוּלַי; *b*) אַךְ; *c*) אֲשֶׁר; *d*) בַּל [+ Ho 14.3]; *e*) בַּעֲבוּר; *f*) לְבַעֲבוּר; *g*) בַּעֲבוּר אֲשֶׁר *h*) ?? following an impv.; following a cohortative; *i*) לְ; *j*) לָמָּה; *k*) לְמַעַן; *l*) לְמַעַן אֲשֶׁר; *m*) פֶּן; *n*) Ar. דִּי; *o*) שֶׁ. x∫

ὅραμα, ματος. n.

what is seen, usually with an extraordinary message, 'vision': ἐγενήθη ῥῆμα κυρίου πρὸς Αβραμ ἐν ~ατι 'a word of the Lord was conveyed to Abram in a vision' Ge 15.1; ἐν ὁράματι τῆς νυκτός 46.2; τὸ ὅ. τὸ μέγα τοῦτο 'this great sight' Ex 3.3; ἐν ~ασιν μεγάλοις 'with great spectacles' De 4.34, 26.8 (‖ σημεῖα, τέρατα); ἐν ~ατι .. ἐν ὕπνῳ Nu 12.6; τὰ ~ατα τῶν ὀφθαλμῶν, ἃ βλέψῃ De 28.34 (‖ ὄψῃ vs. 67); τοῖς τὰ ~ατα ὁρῶσι 'the visionaries' Is 30.10 (‖ τοῖς προφήταις); ‖ ἐνύπνιον Jb 7.14; κεφαλῆς 'mental vision' Da 2.28 LXX. Cf. ὅρασις, θέα.

ὅρασις, εως. f.

1. *prophetic vision conveying a divine message*: transmitted through prophet, Ho 12.10, Hb 2.3, and ‖ νόμος, βουλή Ez 7.26; to be seen, ὅρασιν θεοῦ εἶδεν Nu 24.4; ~εις ὄψονται Jl 2.28; committed by prophet to writing, γράψον ~ιν Hb 2.2; ‖ μαντεία Mi 3.6; transmitted by μάντις – οἱ μάντεις (ἐλάλησαν) ~εις ψευδεῖς (‖ κόπους) Zc 10.2, sim. Je 14.14; κατὰ Βαβυλῶνος 'against B.' Is 13.1; ‖ ὀπτασία Da 10.8 LXX; title of entire book, Ob 1, cf. βιβλίον ~εως Ναουμ Na 1.1 and ἐκ τῆς ~εως ἐν τῷ προφητεύειν αὐτόν Zc 13.4. **b**. generally *that which one sees*: καρδίας 'mental vision; imagination' Si 40.6, ἐνυπνίου '(that which was seen) in a dream' Da 4.6 TH.

2. *outward appearance, look*: ὡς ὅ. ἵππων ἡ ὅ. αὐτῶν Jl 2.4, sim. Na 2.5; ὡς ὅ. ἠλέκτρου Ez 1.4 (‖ ὡς ὁμοίωμα .. vs. 5).

3. v.n. of ὁράω, *act of beholding, visually observing*: ξύλον ὡραῖον εἰς ~ιν 'a tree beautiful to gaze at' Ge 2.9; ὅ. τοῦ ἐνυπνίου 40.5; medical examination, Le 13.12; ἔσονται εἰς ~ιν πάσῃ σαρκί 'will become a general spectacle' Is 66.24; ὀφθαλμῶν Ez 23.16.

4. *act of appearing*: divine epiphany, τὸ φρέαρ τῆς ~εως Ge 24.62 (= φ. οὗ ἐνώπιον εἶδον 16.14).

Cf. ὁράω, θέα, ὀπτασία, ἐπιφάνεια, μαντεία.

ὁρατής, οῦ. m.∫ *

he who visually observes: ἔργων ἀνθρώπων Jb 34.21 (*s* God), τῶν συντελούντων τὰ ἄνομα 'of perpetrators of unlawful deeds' 35.13f. Cf. ὁράω, παντεπόπτης.

ὁρατικός, ή, όν.∫

able to see: *s* hum., metaph. of keen observation and perception, Pr 22.29. Cf. ὁράω, βλέπω.

ὁρατός, ή, όν.∫

being observed, visible: *s* hum., Jb 34.26; light and + dat., 37.21. **b**. *conspicuous, standing out* (?): *s* hum., 2K 23.21 ‖ 1C 11.23 (*L* εὐμήκης 'tall').

Cf. ὁράω, ἀόρατος.

ὁράω: pres.impv. ὅρα; impf.3s ἑώρα; fut. ὄψομαι, inf. ὄψεσθαι, pass. ὀφθήσομαι, ὁραθήσομαι; aor. pass. ὡράθην, ὤφθην, ptc. ὀφθείς, inf. ὀφθῆναι, ὁραθῆναι, impv. 3s ὀφθήτω, subj. ὀφθῶ, ὁραθῶ, opt.3s ὀφθείη; pf. ἑώρακα (on the variant [Attic] spelling ἑό~, e.g. in Zc 1.8, see Helbing, *Gram.*, 78, Mayser I 2.103, BDF § 68, and Walters 73), pass.3s ὦπται, ἑώραται. For the aor., εἶδον (q.v.) is used: ὁρᾷς Ge 13.15 ‖ ἴδε ib. 14, ἑόρακα Je 23.14 ‖ εἶδον ib. 13.

I 1. *to perceive visually*, 'see, notice': abs. οὐκ ὄψονται οὐδὲ μὴ ἀκούσωσιν De 4.28; ἠμβλύνθησαν οἱ ὀφθαλμοὶ αὐτοῦ τοῦ ὁρᾶν 'his eyes became too dim to see' Ge 27.1; + acc., οὐχ ὁρᾷ οὐδένα Ex 2.12; τί σὺ ὁρᾷς; Am 7.8 (‖ τί σὺ βλέπεις; ib. 8.2, cf. Zc 5.2); ἐνύπνιον Ge 41.15; θλιμμόν 'oppression' Ex 3.9 (‖ εἶδον vs. 7); θαυμαστά Mi 7.15; σέ Na 3.7, Hb 3.10; ἐν τοῖς ὀφθαλμοῖς μου Zc 9.8; *s* οἱ ὀφθαλμοί σου De 4.9; Ma 1.5. A following ὅτι-clause indicates what one notices of sbd or sth: ὁρῶ ἐγὼ τὸ πρόσωπον τοῦ πατρὸς ὑμῶν ὅτι οὐκ ἔστιν πρὸς ἐμοῦ ὡς ἐχθὲς καὶ τρίτην ἡμέραν Ge 31.5; ὄψεται .. τὰ ἔργα κυρίου ὅτι θαυμαστά ἐστιν Ex 34.10; ὄψονταί σε .. ὅτι τὸ ὄνομα κυρίου ἐπικέκληταί σοι De 28.10; + ptc., ὁρᾷ παιδίον κλαῖον Ex 2.6; 2.11, 13, Jb 2.13, 4M 4.24.

2. *to observe, look at*: abs. and *s* shepherd, στήσεται καὶ ὄψεται καὶ ποιμανεῖ Mi 5.4; + acc., οἱ ὁρῶντες τὰ ἐνύπνια 3.7 (ǁ μάντεις), τὰ κρυπτά Is 29.10; ὁράσεις Jl 2.28, ὁράματα Is 30.10 (ǁ προφήτης); πονηρά 'evil things' Hb 1.13 (ǁ ἐπιβλέπω); ἀστέρας 'stars' Is 47.13; "they will behold their children and their hearts will rejoice" Zc 10.7; ἀνὰ μέσον δικαίου καὶ ἀνὰ μέσον ἀνόμου Ma 3.18; + πρός τινα / τι– ὀφθαλμοὶ πρὸς ὀφθαλμοὺς ὄψονται 'they will eye one another' Is 52.8; + εἰ clause, 'if, whether' Ge 18.21; τί ἔσται τὰ ἐνύπνια αὐτοῦ 'how his dreams are going to turn out' 37.20; ὄψεσθε τὴν γῆν τίς ἐστιν .. καὶ τὸν λαὸν .. εἰ ἰσχυρότερός ἐστιν .. Nu 13.19; ***o*** τὸ πρόσωπόν τινος 'to meet him' Ge 43.3 (ǁ εἶδον 44.23), 46.30; τὸ ὅραμα τὸ μέγα τοῦτο 'this great sight' Ex 3.3; ἁφήν 'infection' Le 13.3; *+ ἔν marking sustained interest and concern: ἐν πᾶσιν τοῖς κακοῖς 2C 34.28 (*L* acc.). **b.** *to observe mentally and form a judgement by considering* (+ εἰς): εἰς πρόσωπον .. εἰς καρδίαν 1K 16.7; + double acc., Jb 6.7. **c.** ὁρῶν 'seer' ὁρῶν 'seer,' prophetic figure endowed with mystic, visionary abilities: Am 7.12, Mi 7.10, Zc 1.8; ǁ προφήτης 2C 9.29, ⸢τὸν προφήτην⸣ (om. *L*) τὸν ὁρῶντα 2K 24.11 (in David the king's service), sim. 4K 17.13, and cf. ὁ βλέπων (Samuel) 1K 9.9; 2C 33.18, 19. ***c.** ὁρῶν τὸ πρόσωπον βασιλέως < רֹאֵה פְּנֵי מֶלֶךְ 'king's privy councillor': 4K 25.19, cf. ὁ βλέπων, s.v. βλέπω **1b**.

3. *to come to the conclusion through observation*: + ὅτι Ge 26.28 (ǁ εἶδον); cf. ἑώρων .. ἑαυτοὺς ἐν κακοῖς 'they realised that they were in trouble' Ex 5.19; + inf. clause and ptc. clause, 2M 4.6. Cf. σοφίζω **4**.

4. *to witness, experience*: τὴν δόξαν μου καὶ τὰ σημεῖα Nu 14.22; οὐκ ὄψῃ κακὰ οὐκέτι Zp 3.15, τὴν δικαιοσύνην αὐτοῦ Mi 7.9; μάχαιραν καὶ λιμὸν οὐκ ὀψόμεθα Je 5.12; θάνατον Ps 88.49; κινδύνους 'dangers' To 4.4.

5. *to see to it that sth* (acc.) *is provided*: + dat. com. Ὁ θεὸς ὄψεται ἑαυτῷ πρόβατον εἰς ὁλοκάρπωσιν Ge 22.8, Ὅρα μισθὸν τῷ ἀνθρώπῳ To 12.1 𝔊ᴵ.

6. *to take note of mentally*: ὅρα 'Mark!' Ge 31.50; + an asyndetic clause, ὅρα οὖν ἀποκτενῶ τὸν υἱόν σου .. Ex 4.23; + acc., τὴν φωνὴν καὶ τὰς λαμπάδας 'the sound and the lights' 20.18.

II. intr. **1.** *to see to* it that sth happens or does not happen, *take care*: pres. impv. + an asyndetic clause with a fut., ὅρα ποιήσεις κατὰ τὸν τύπον 'Make sure that you construct in accordance with the pattern' Ex 25.40; perh. also ὅρα πάντα τὰ τέρατα .. ποιήσεις αὐτὰ .. 4.21 (though in the MT πάντα .. is a direct object of רְאֵה); ὅρα .. οὐ συνεπισκέψῃ Nu 1.49. **b.** + μή and subj.: ὁρᾶτε μὴ πληγὴν ἄλλην ἐπαγάγω ἐφ' ὑμᾶς 'Take care so that I shall not bring down upon you another blow' Ex 33.5. **c.** + a syndetic clause: Ὁρᾶτε καὶ τὰ σάββατά μου φυλάξεσθε Ex 31.13. **d.** + inf.: ὅρα δοῦναι .. To 12.1 𝔊ᴵᴵ.

2. pass., *to become visible, make appearance, present oneself*: *s* the earth, ὤφθη ἡ ξηρά 'the dry land appeared' Ge 1.9; rainbow, 9.14, αἱ πηγαὶ τῶν ὑδάτων 'the fountains ..' Ps 17.16 (ǁ ἀνεκαλύφθη); God (of theophany) and + dat. pers., ὤφθη κύριος τῷ Αβραμ Ge 12.7; ἐν τῇ νυκτὶ ἐκείνῃ 26.24; ὁ θεὸς ὁ ὀφθείς σοι 31.13; 35.1 (ǁ ἐπιφαίνομαι vs. 7); ἄγγελος κυρίου Ex 3.2; κύριος ὁ θεὸς .. ὦπταί μοι 3.16; οὐκ ὀφθήσεταί σοι ζυμωτόν 'leavened bread is not to be seen around your place' 13.7, sim. De 16.4; + ἐπί τινα Is 60.2; + πρός τινα, Ex 6.3, Jd 13.3, ἡ δόξα κυρίου πρὸς αὐτούς Nu 20.6; ἐν ὑμῖν 'among you' Le 9.4; + dat., τῷ προσώπῳ σου Ps 16.15; *s* hum., οὐκέτι ὀφθήσομαί σοι εἰς πρόσωπον 'I shall not turn up in your presence any more' Ex 10.29; in God's presence, i.e. in a sanctuary– οὐκ ὀφθήσῃ ἐνώπιόν μου κενός 'you shall not appear in my presence empty-handed' 23.15, 34.20, ἐν προσώπῳ κυρίου Si 32.6, τῷ προσώπῳ κυρίου 1K 1.22; ὀφθῶμεν ⸌ἐν⸍ (om. B) προσώποις 'Let's meet each other personally' 4K 14.8, sim. 14.11, 2C 15.27 ǁ vs. 21 ὤφθησαν ἀλλήλοις; ἐν τῷ τόπῳ τοῦ θεοῦ Ex 24.11; ἐναντίον κυρίου De 16.16 (at festivals and ǁ ἐνώπιον), ἐνώπιον κυρίου 31.11; nonhuman, horse 2M 3.25.

Cf. ὅρασις, ὁρατής, ὁρατός, ἀόρατος, ὀπτασία, ὀπτάζομαι, βλέπω, θεάομαι, δι~, καθ~, προ~, συνοράω, εἶδον, ἐπι~, προ~, φαίνω, ἀναφαίνομαι, φαντάζομαι: Schmidt 1.253-60; Michaelis, *TDNT* 5.329f.

ὀργανικός, ή, όν.ʃ

serving as instrument: of war, *s* μηχανή 'war-engine' 2M 12.15.

ὄργανον, ου. n.

1. *instrument*: for music making, ψαλμὸν ~ων σου 'a psalm made by your musical instruments' Am 5.23, τὴν φωνὴν τῶν ~ων 6.5; for torturing, 4M 6.25.

2. *part of the body*: 4M 10.7; φωνῆς ὄ., = γλῶσσα 10.18.

ὀργή, ῆς. f.

indignation, wrath: mostly of God's wrath, which is implied also in Zp 1.15 and Hb 3.2. Thus ὁ. κυρίου

Mi 7.9, Zp 1.18, 2.2; ἐγένετο ὀ. μεγάλη παρὰ τοῦ κυρίου Zc 7.12; ‖ θυμός Ex 15.7 (see vs. 8), De 9.19, 29.23, Ho 13.11, Mi 5.15, Na 1.6, Zp 2.2; often combined w. θυμός for the effect of intensification as in ὁ θ. τῆς ~ῆς μου Nu 14.34, De 29.24, ὀ. θυμοῦ κυρίου Nu 25.4, κατὰ τὴν ~ὴν τοῦ θυμοῦ μου Ho 11.9, sim. Jn 3.9, Na 1.6*b*, Zp 3.8; ‖ ζῆλος Zp 1.18, 3.8, Zc 1.15; ‖ θυμός and παροξυσμός De 29.28; opp. to an attitude of love and care, Ho 14.5; opp. ἔλεος, Hb 3.2, Si 5.6; results in perdition, destruction, Ho 11.9, Am 4.10, Jn 3.9; in punishment, Mi 5.15; provoked by sins and disobedience, ~ὴν κυρίου ὑποίσω, ὅτι ἥμαρτον αὐτῷ Mi 7.9; Zc 7.12; w. obj.gen. in ἐν τῇ ~ῇ ὑμῶν Am 4.10; + εἴς τινα 1E 8.21 (‖ ἐπί τινα 2E 7.23); as cogn. obj. Ὠργίσθη κύριος .. ~ὴν μεγάλην Zc 1.2, so 15; ἡμέρα ~ῆς Zp 1.15 (‖ ἡ. θλίψεως καὶ ἀνάγκης, ἡ. ἀωρίας καὶ ἀφανισμοῦ), 18, 2.3; as adverbial adjunct, θυμωθεὶς ~ῇ κύριος ἐπὶ Μωυσῆν Ex 4.14; 32.10. **b**. hum. anger: ἐθυμώθη ~ῇ Ge 39.19; royal, ~ῃ καὶ χόλῳ 3M 5.1. **c**. w. no moral connotation: pl. and of raging wild animals, 2M 4.25.

Cf. ὀργίζομαι, ὀργίλος, θυμός, ζῆλος, μῆνις, ὅρμημα, παροξυσμός, χόλος. For a discussion on possible contrast with θυμός, see Schmidt 3.551-8; Trench 130-4. See also Kleinknecht, *TDNT* 5.383-92, Grether / Fichtner, ib. 409-12, but the distinction between the two does not seem to be maintained in the LXX; cf. Grether/Fichtner, op. cit., 409f.; Muraoka 1986a:130f.

ὀργίζομαι: fut. ὀργισθήσομαι; aor. ὠργίσθην, ptc. ὀργισθείς, subj. ὀργισθῶ, inf. ὀργισθῆναι.

to get angry: *s* God, abs. Zc 1.15*b*; θυμῷ Ex 22.24, 32.19, Nu 22.22, De 29.27; *s* θυμός Ps 73.1 (+ ἐπί τινα); against (ἐν), Hb 3.8, 4K 23.26; εἴς τινα De 7.4; ἐπί τινα, Nu 32.13, De 29.27; and w. cogn. acc., Ὠργίσθη κύριος ἐπὶ τοὺς πατέρας ὑμῶν ὀργὴν μεγάλην Zc 1.2, sim. 15*a*; ἐπί τι Ps 79.5; ἐπί τινι Is 57.6, θυμωθεὶς ὀργισθῇ ἐφ᾽ ὑμῖν De 11.17; + dat. pers., Nu 25.3, De 31.17, Jd 2.14A (B: ἔν τινι), Ps 17.8. **b**. *s* hum., Ge 31.36, 45.24, Pr 29.9; ἐπί τινι (pers.) Ge 40.2; + dat. pers., 41.10, Nu 31.14, κατά τινος (pers.) Jb 32.3; *s* θυμός Ps 123.3.

Cf. ὀργή, ἀπ~, δι~, ἐπ~, παροργίζομαι, ἀγριαίνω, θυμόω, μηνιάω, μηνίω, παραθερμαίνω, χαλεπαίνω.

ὀργίλος, η, ον.ʃ

irascible: *s* hum., Ps 17.49, Pr 21.19; ‖ θυμώδης 22.24, 29.22. Cf. θυμώδης, ὀργή.

ὀργίλως. adv.ʃ

in a manner likely to awaken anger and infuriate: 4M 8.9. Cf. ὀργίλος.

ὀρεινός, ή, όν.

situated in ὄρος 'mountain, hilly land': sc. γῆ 'mountainous area' Ge 14.10, Nu 13.30, De 2.37, Je 40.13, cf. πᾶσαν τὴν γῆν τῆς ~ῆς Jo 10.40; *s* γῆ - γῆ ~ὴ καὶ πεδινή De 11.11, πόλις Zc 7.7 (‖ πεδινή), χόρτος 'grass' Pr 27.25. Cf. ὄρος, πεδινός.

ὄρεξις, εως. f.

yearning: κοιλίας 'of stomach' Si 23.6; πορισμῶν 'for gain' Wi 14.2; ἐπιθυμία ~εως 16.2. **b**. *that which one years for*: pl., Si 18.30, 4M 1.33.

Cf. ἐπιθυμία, θέλησις: Spicq 2.591f.

ὄρθιος, α, ον.ʃ

standing erect: *s* hum., 1K 28.14; opp. κυρτός 'hunchbacked' 3K 21.11*L* (B: ὀρθός). Cf. ὀρθός.

ὀρθός, ή, όν.

1. *without curves* or *bends*, 'straight': *s* ὁδός Je 38.9. **b**. vertically, οὐ μὴ πορευθῆτε ~οί 'you shall not walk upright' Mi 2.3; ἔστησαν ~οί 1E 9.46; *s* στάχυς 'ear of corn (still) standing upright' Jd 15.5 B (A: ἑστώς).

2. *honest of character*: ~οὶ πεπόρευνται 'they have conducted themselves honestly' Mi 2.7. **b**. adv. n.pl. ὀρθά = ὀρθῶς: κρῖναι 'to judge' Pr 31.5.

3. *morally correct and proper*: οἱ βδελυσσόμενοι κρίμα καὶ πάντα τὰ ~ὰ διαστρέφοντες 'those who loathe justice and distort everything that is straight' Mi 3.9; *s* τροχιά 'path' Pr 4.11, καρδία 15.14.

Cf. ὀρθόω, ὄρθιος, κατορθόω, ὀρθῶς, εὐθύς, καμπύλος, σκολιός.

ὀρθοτομέω.ʃ

to cut in a straight line so that one can reach the destination without unnecessary detour: + acc., ὁδούς Pr 3.6, 11.5. Cf. Köster, *TDNT* 8.111f.; Spicq 2.595.

ὀρθόω: fut. ὀρθώσω, pass. ὀρθωθήσομαι; aor.pass. ὠρθώθην, subj. ὀρθωθῶ; pf.pass. ὤρθωμαι, ptc. ὠρθωμένος. Mostly pass.ʃ

1. *to make stand upright*: ἀνέστη τὸ ἐμὸν δράγμα καὶ ὠρθώθη 'my sheaf stood up straight' Ge 37.7; ὠρθωμένος παγήσεται ἐπ᾽ αὐτοῦ 'will be impaled upright on it' 2E 6.11; ὤρθωται .. ξύλον 'a stake .. has been erected' Es 7.9 LXX; Je Ep 27.

2. *to make straight*: morally, + acc. rei, ὁδοὺς δικαίων PSol 10.3 (:: διαστρέφω 'to twist, bend').

3. *to consider morally right*: ὠρθώθη τὰ ἔργα Ιωσίου ἐνώπιον τοῦ κυρίου αὐτοῦ 1E 1.21; μαρτύρια Je 37.20.

Cf. ἀνίστημι, κλίνω, ὀρθός.

ὀρθρεύω: aor. ὤρθρευσα.ʃ

to leave bed in the morning after the night's sleep: ὤρθρευσαν ($\mathfrak{G}^{II}$ ὤρθρισαν) κοινῶς καὶ ἦλθοσαν εἰς τὸν γάμον 'they got up together in the morning and went to the wedding' To 9.6 $\mathfrak{G}^{I}$. Cf. ὀρθρίζω.

ὀρθρίζω: fut. ὀρθριῶ; aor. ὤρθρισα, inf. ὀρθρίσαι, impv. ὄρθρισον, ptc. ὀρθρίσας; plpf. ὠρθρίκειν. *(but see Lee 46).

1. *to rise from bed in the morning*: ὀρθρίσαντες ἀπελεύσεσθε Ge 19.2; τὸ πρωῒ 19.27, Ex 8.20, 9.13, Nu 14.40, 1M 4.52; ὀρθρίζων οὐκέτι εἰμί 'I shall be no early riser any more' Jb 7.21. **b**. *to act in the morning*: + ὀψίζω 1K 17.16 *L*.

*2. *to seek and turn in eager anticipation* (to sbd, πρός τινα): ἐν θλίψει αὐτῶν ὀρθριοῦσι πρός με 'in their distress they will eagerly look to me' Ho 6.1, ὁ θεός μου, πρὸς σὲ ὀρθρίζω Ps 62.2; ἐκ νυκτὸς ὀρθρίζει τὸ πνεῦμά μου πρὸς σέ Is 26.9; πρὸς ^σοφίαν^ Si 4.12, cf. ἐπ' αὐτήν Wi 6.14.

*3. *to act eagerly*: in hendiadys, ἑτοιμάζου ὄρθρισον 'prepare yourself eagerly' Zp 3.7 (see Th 297: μετὰ πάσης ἐπιμελείας τε καὶ σπουδῆς), ἐλάλησα πρὸς ὑμᾶς ὀρθρίζων Je 25.3 (|| ὄρθρου vs. 4), ἐξαπέστειλεν .. ὀρθρίζων καὶ ἀποστέλλων 2C 36.15.

Cf. ὄρθρος, ὀρθρινός, ὀψίζω, προθύμως: *ND* 1.86; Tov 1990.118-25; LSG s.v.; Muraoka 2007.

ὀρθρινός, ή, όν.ʃ *

of early morning: δρόσος ὀ. 'morning dew' Ho 6.4, 13.3; ῥανὶς δρόσου ~ή 'an early drop of dew' Wi 11.22; Hg 2.14 (indicative of eagerness: cf. Th 315 μετὰ πάσης .. τῆς σπουδῆς). Cf. ὄρθρος, ὄρθριος, and ὀρθρίζω.

ὄρθριος, α, ον.ʃ

acting in the morning: *s* hum., Jb 29.7, 3M 5.10, 23. Cf. ὀρθρινός.

ὄρθρος, ου. m.

1. *the period preceding daybreak while it is still dark* (LSG s.v.), 'dawn': ἡνίκα ὄ. ἐγίνετο 'as it was dawning' Ge 19.15; ἀνέβη ὁ ὄ. 'it has dawned' 32.26; πρὸς ~ον 'towards dawn' Ex 19.16; ὡς ὄ. ἕτοιμον 'ready as dawn' Ho 6.3; || ὁμίχλη 'mist' Am 4.13; *s* of διαφαύσκω 'to become light' Ju 14.2.

2. adv. gen. ὄρθρου, *in the morning*: Es 5.14 o'. ***b**. *with eagerness*: with repetition of same or synonymous verb, ὄρθρου ἀπερρίφησαν, ἀπερρίφη Ho 11.1, ἀπέστελλον .. ὄρθρου ἀποστέλλων Je 25.4 (sim. 33.5, 51.4), ἐλάλησα πρὸς ὑμᾶς ~ου (|| ὀρθρίζων 25.3) καὶ ἐλάλησα 42.14; ἐδίδαξα αὐτοὺς ~ου καὶ ἐδίδαξα 39.33; with reinforcing καί– ἡμέρας καὶ ὄρθρου 7.25.

Cf. I ἕως, ὀρθρινός and ὀρθρίζω: Renehan 1.153.

ὀρθῶς adv.

in correct way, in accordance with the rule: of cult, ἐὰν ὀ. προσενέγκῃς, ὀ. δὲ μὴ διέλῃς 'should you correctly offer, but not correctly divide' Ge 4.7; ὀ. συνέκρινεν 'he interpreted correctly' 40.16; οὐκ ὀ. σὺ ποιεῖς τὸ ῥῆμα τοῦτο Ex 18.17; ὀ... λελαλήκασιν Nu 27.7; general ethical standards, Es 6.4 *L*; συμβουλεύσαιμι ὀ. 'it would be right for me to advise' 4M 1.1. Cf. ὀρθός.

ὁρίζω: fut. ὁριῶ; aor. mid. ὡρισάμην, ptc. ὁρισάμενος, subj. ὁρίσωμαι.

1. *to form boundary*: ἡ θάλασσα ἡ μεγάλη ὁριεῖ Nu 34.6, Jo 13.7.

2. mid. *to determine clearly* what and how it ought to be done: + cogn. dat., ὁρισμῷ περὶ τῆς ψυχῆς αὐτοῦ Nu 30.3; + cogn. acc., ὁρισμόν 30.4; ὁρισμὸν κατὰ τῆς ψυχῆς αὐτῆς 30.5, 6, 7, 8, 9, 12; + ὅρκον 'oath' and inf., 3M 5.42, θεσμόν 'rule' + inf., 6.36; + ἵνα Da 6.12 LXX. **b**. also act.: Pr 16.30, 18.18.

Cf. ὁρισμός, διαστέλλω: Shipp 418-20.

ὅριον, ου. n. Alm. alw. pl.

1. *limit, boundary*: ἔστησεν ~α ἐθνῶν 'he set the boundaries of the nations' De 32.8, ἀφελῶ ~α ἐθνῶν 'I shall dismantle..' Is 10.13; μετατιθέναι ~α. 'to shift landmarks' Ho 5.10; ἕως τῶν ~ων ἐξαπέστειλέν σε 'they expelled you to the sparsely populated frontiers (as against cities and towns)' Ob 7. **b**. sg.: πρὸς τὸ ὅ. αὐτῆς 'at its border' Is 19.19, ὅ., ὃ οὐ παρελεύσονται '.. which they shall not cross' Ps 103.9; τῆς εἰρήνης αὐτοῦ οὐκ ἔστιν ὅ. 'his peace is unlimited' Is 9.6, cf. Cyr. (PG 70.257 τέλος).

2. sg. *area adjoining a main population centre*: τὴν Γάζαν καὶ τὸ ὅ. αὐτῆς Jd 1.18 (|| περισπόρια). **b**. pl. *area circumscribed by border*, 'territory, domain': ἐγένοντο τὰ ~α τῶν Χαναναίων ἀπὸ Σιδῶνος ἕως ἐλθεῖν εἰς Γεραρα .. 'the territory of the Chaldaeans became from Sidon up to the entry of Gerara ..' Ge 10.19; ἀπ' ἄκρων ~ων Αἰγύπτου ἕως ἄκρων 'from one end of the territory of Egypt to the other' 47.21; ἐν πᾶσιν τοῖς ~οις σου 'on all your premises' De 16.4; πλείονα τὰ ὅ. αὐτῶν ἐστι τῶν ὑμετέρων 'their territories are larger than yours' Am 6.2; ἐξώσητε αὐτοὺς ἐκ τῶν ~ων αὐτῶν 'eject them out of their territories' Jl 3.6; ὑπεράνω τῶν ~ων τοῦ Ισραηλ 'all over the territories of Israel' Ma 1.5; ἐμπλατύνειν ὅ. 'to expand ..' Am 1.13; || γῆ Mi 5.6; || λαός Zp 2.8; ὅ. ἀνομίας 'domain of lawlessness' Ma 1.4; ἐν τοῖς ~οις σου 'in your own (agricultural) land' Is 28.25.

Cf. θυγάτηρ, ὁρισμός, περισπόριον.

ὁρισμός, οῦ. m.

1. *the act of delimiting a territory*: τῶν βατράχων Ex 8.12 (the frogs should be confined to the rivers).

2. *clear determination* as to what and how it ought to be done: cogn. dat. of ὁρίζω, Nu 30.3, cogn. acc. of id., 30.4, Da LXX 6.12; || εὐχή, ὅρκος Nu 30.3; || εὐχή 30.4 +; κατὰ τῆς ψυχῆς αὐτῆς 30.13; μεθ' ὅρκου 'made with an oath' 30.11; τοὺς ~οὺς τοὺς ἐπ' αὐτῆς στήσει αὐτῇ 'shall make the determinations over her' 30.15; ἐξᾶραι ~ὸν στόματός σου 'to make naught of your decree' Es C 20; μνήσθητι ~οῦ 'Remember ..' Si 33.10; στήσωμεν ~ὸν καθ' ἑαυτῶν 'Let's agree among ourselves' Da LXX 6.5; ~ὸν καὶ στάσιν ἐστήσαμεν 6.7; μενεῖ ὁ ὁ. 6.12;

οὐκ ἔμεινεν ἐν τῷ ~ῷ τούτῳ 'did not adhere to this decree' 6.12[a]; ἐνισχῦσαι ~όν 'to establish firmly ..' Da TH 6.7; ~ὸν ἔταξας 'you established ..' 6.12; πιστώσαντος .. τὸν ~όν 'having confirmed the promise' 2M 12.25.

Cf. ὅριον, ὁρίζω, διαστολή.

ὁρκίζω: fut. ὁρκιῶ; aor. ὥρκισα, ptc. ὁρκίσας, pass. ὁρκισθείς.

to make swear: abs. Ge 50.16; + acc. pers., 24.37, ἃ ὥρκισεν αὐτὸν κατὰ τοῦ θεοῦ 'that which he had made him swear by God' 2C 36.13, ἐν τῷ θεῷ Ne 13.25; with a cogn. dat., ὅρκῳ ὥρκισεν Ιωσηφ τοὺς υἱοὺς Ισραηλ λέγων .. Ex 13.19, cf. τοῖς Μήδων καὶ Περσῶν δόγμασιν Da 6.12a LXX; ἐν τοῖς ὅρκοις τῆς ἀρᾶς ταύτης Nu 5.21; before death, Ge 50.16, 25; + inf., Ne 5.12; *s* master Ge 24.37, father 50.6, Ex 13.19, Joseph to his brothers Ge 50.25, priest Nu 5.19; the content of an oath follows with a ὅπως-clause, 3K 22.16 (|| 2C 18.15 ἵνα). ***b**. that which one pledges not to do is Hebraistically introduced with a conditional clause: ἐὰν ἐγείρητε 'you shall not awaken' Ct 2.7, 8.4.

Cf. ὅρκος, ὁρκισμός.

ὁρκισμός, οῦ. m.ʃ

1. *making of oath*: φρέαρ ~οῦ 'well of ..' Ge 21.31, 32 || φρέαρ ὅρκου 21.14, 22.19.

2. *oath*: ἀθῷος ἀπὸ τοῦ ~οῦ μου 'released from the oath I made (you) swear' Ge 24.41 (|| ἀρά); φωνὴ ~οῦ Le 5.1; ἠθέτησε τὸν ὁρκισμόν, ὃν ὤμοσε 'annulled the oath, which he had sworn' 1M 6.62.

Cf. ὅρκος, ἀρά.

ὅρκος, ου. m.

oath: τὸ φρέαρ τοῦ ~ου 'the well of the oath' Ge 21.14 (formally named φ. ὁρκισμοῦ vs. 31), Am 4.5; καθαρὸς ἀπὸ τοῦ ~ου τούτου 'exempt from this oath' Ge 24.8 (|| ἀρά), ἀρὰ καὶ ὅ. Ne 10.29; ~ον ψευδῆ 'a fraudulent oath' Zc 8.17; στήσω τὸν ~ον μου, ὃν ὤμοσα .. τῷ πατρί σου 'I shall discharge the terms of my oath, which I swore .. to your father' Ge 26.3; τοῦ θεοῦ, made by invoking God, Ex 22.11. **b**. ὀμνύω ~ον: Ge 26.3, Nu 30.3. **c**. διατηρέω ~ον, ὃν ὤμοσα τοῖς πατράσιν ὑμῶν De 7.8. **d**. ἵστημι ~ον Ju 8.11. **e**. || εὐχή– ὅ. δεσμοῦ 'a binding oath' Nu 30.14.

Cf. ὀμνύω, ὁρκισμός, πολύορκος, ἀρά, ἐπίορκος, ἐνόρκιος, ἔνορκος, συνθήκη.

ὁρκωμοσία, ας. f.ʃ

oath: Ez 17.18, || διαθήκη 19, πρὸς τὸν κύριον 1E 8.90. Cf. ὅρκος, διαθήκη.

ὁρμάω: fut.act. ὁρμήσω; aor. ὥρμησα, ptc. ὁρμήσας.

to put oneself in (*swift*) *motion*: βροῦχος ὥρμησε 'locusts started moving' Na 3.16; *s* ἱππεῖς 'horsemen' Hb 1.8; troops, ὡς λέοντες 'like lions' Is 5.29; to reach a destination (εἴς τι), εἰς τὸ ὄρος Ge 31.21, cf. εἰς φυγήν 2M 12.22; ἐπὶ τὴν σκηνήν 'made for the tent' Nu 16.42, ἐπὶ τὰ σκῦλα 'for the spoils' 1K 14.32*L* (B: κλίνομαι); ἐπὶ τὴν βοηθείαν 'to aid' 2M 9.2; + inf., 2K 15.19B (*L* om.). **b**. *to set some plan into action*: Je 4.28.

Cf. ὅρμημα, ὁρμή, ἐξορμάω, κινέω.

ὁρμή, ῆς. f.ʃ

1. *rapid, forward movement*: military, Je 29.3; ἐπὶ τὰ ὅπλα ποιεῖσθαι 'to make for the arms quickly' 3M 1.23; ὕδατος Pr 21.1. **b**. *hostile move*: Pr 3.25.

2. *overwhelming, overzealous demand*: ἐπιθεῖναι τὴν ~ὴν τοῦ λαοῦ τούτου ἐπ' ἐμέ Nu 11.11; 11.17.

3. *impulse*: 3M 1.16.

Cf. ὅρμημα, ὁρμάω: Trench 325-7.

ὅρμημα, ατος. n.

1. *outburst of anger, indignation*: ἐκχεῶ ὡς ὕδωρ τὸ ὅ. μου 'I will pour out my outrage like water' Ho 5.10; τὸ ὅ. αὐτοῦ ἐφύλαξεν εἰς νῖκος Am 1.11; || θυμός Hb 3.8.

2. *tendency to violent and impetuous outburst of emotions*: τοῦ λαοῦ τούτου Ex 32.22.

3. *sudden rush and movement*: ἀετοῦ 'of an eagle' De 28.49; τοῦ ποταμοῦ τὰ ~ατα Ps 45.5, cf. ὁρμὴ ὕδατος Pr 21.1; of troops, 1M 4.8, 6.33, τοῦ δυνατοῦ 4.30 (ref. to Goliath).

Cf. θυμός, ὀργή, ὁρμάω, ὁρμή: LSG s.v.

ὁρμίσκος, ου. m.

1. *small necklace*: Pr 25.11. Cf. μανιάκης.

2. *signet-cord*: Ge 38.18, 25.

ὅρμος, ου. m.ʃ

1. *the inner part of a harbour where ships lie*: πλοίων Ge 49.13, 4M 13.6.

2. *surrounding wall* (?): Ez 27.11.

Cf. τεῖχος: Shipp 421.

ὄρνεον, ου. n.

bird: qualified by πετεινός and || κτήνη .. ἑρπετά Ge 6.20; ~εα τοῦ οὐρανοῦ (|| θηρία τῆς γῆς .. ἰχθύες τῆς θαλάσσης) 9.2; 40.19 (|| τὰ πετεινὰ τοῦ οὐρανοῦ vs. 17); ὁμοίωμα παντὸς ~έου πτερωτοῦ 'image of any winged bird' De 4.17; sacrificial animals τρυγών 'turtle dove' and περιστερά 'pigeon' Ge 15.10; predatory, κατέβη ~εα ἐπὶ τὰ σώματα, τὰ διχοτομήματα 'birds (of prey) descended on to the carcasses, the cloven pieces' 15.11; timid creature, Ho 11.11 (|| περιστερά); food, De 14.11; plaything, Jb 40.29 (|| στρουθίον); game, Am 3.5; *s* of ἐκπετάζω 'to fly away' Ho 9.11, πέτομαι 'to fly' Pr 9.12a, of καταβαίνω 'to descend' Ge 15.11, ἐσθίω 40.19. Cf. ὀρνίθιον, ὄρνις, πετεινός, στρουθίον: Schmidt 2.448f.; Shipp 422f.; MM, s.v.

ὀρνίθιον, ου. n., dim. of ὄρνις.

small bird as cultic offering: ζῶντα καθαρά Le 14.4. Cf. ὄρνεον, ὄρνις.

ὀρνιθοσκοπέομαι: fut. ~πήσομαι.ʃ*
to practise divination by inspection of birds: οὐκ οἰωνιεῖσθε οὐδὲ ὀρνιθοσκοπήσεσθε '.. nor shalt thou divine by inspection of birds' Le 19.26. Cf. οἰωνίζομαι.

ὄρνις, ιθος. m./f.ʃ
bird: 3K 2.46[e], 5.3. Cf. ὄρνεον.

ὄρος, ους. n: pl. ὄρη, gen. ὀρέων.
mountain. **a**. τὰ ὄρη τὰ ὑψηλά, ἃ ἦν ὑποκάτω τοῦ οὐρανοῦ 'the high mountains that were under the sky' Ge 7.19; φάραγξ ὀρέων 'a valley surrounded by mountains' Zc 14.5*bis*; τῶν ἐλαιῶν 'the Mount of Olives' 14.4*a*, *b*; vineyards planted on its slopes produce sweet wine, Am 9.13, Jl 3.18; where timber for building can be had, Hg 1.8; from where a message can be audibly announced, Na 1.15; where refuge is sought, Na 3.18 (see Th, 257); normally solid and immovable, but shaken in an eschatological age, Mi 1.4, Na 1.5, Hb 3.6; χαλκοῦς 'brazen' Zc 6.1c; symbol of strength perh. because a fortress is often located there, τοῖς πεποιθόσιν ἐπὶ τὸ ὄ. Σαμαρείας 'those who rely on ..' Am 6.1; its summit, κορυφὴ ὄρους Ho 4.13, Mi 4.1; σχισμαὶ ~ων 'mountain clefts' Jn 2.6; audience to hear litigations between God and His people, Mi 6.1; path of a marching army, Jl 2.2, 5; ‖ γῆ Hg 1.11; ‖ βουνός Ho 4.13, 10.8, Mi 6.1, and higher than the latter, Mi 4.1, Is 2.2; τὰ ὄρη καὶ οἱ βουνοὶ καὶ οἱ δρυμοί '.. valleys and thickets' 10.18. **b**. sg. used collectively, *mountains, mountainous region*: ὄ. Σαμαρείας Am 3.9 (MT: pl.), 4.1, 6.1, ~ Ησαυ w. ref. to the plateau of Edom, Ob 8, 9, sim. τὸ ~ τὸ Ησαυ 19*a*, τὸ ~ Ησαυ 21, cf. Ma 1.3; pl. τὰ ὄρη τὰ Αραρατ 'the Ararat mountain range' Ge 8.4, To 1.21. **c**. in apocalyptic descriptions: Zc 6.1*c*, 14.5. **d**. hilly area as opposed to plains, ὄρος καὶ πεδίον De 1.7, sim. 8.7. **e**. elevated sacred site as a scene of cultic activity and religious significance: Μὴ ἔσθετε ἐπὶ τῶν ὀρέων Le 19.26; Ho 4.13, 10.8; τὸ ~ τοῦ οἴκου 'the Temple Mount' Mi 3.12, 1M 4.46, cf. ἤρξατο Σαλωμων τοῦ οἰκοδομῆσαι τὸν οἶκον κυρίου ἐν ὄρει Αμορια, οὗ ὤφθη κύριος τῷ Δαυιδ 2C 3.1 and οἰκοδομῆσαι ναὸν ἐν ὄρει ἁγίῳ Wi 9.8; τοῦ θεοῦ Ex 24.13; τοῦ κυρίου Mi 4.1, 2; τὸ ~ τὸ ἅγιόν μου Ob 16, Zp 3.11, ἐν ὄρει ἁγίῳ μου Jl 2.1; ~ Σιων Mi 4.7, Jl 2.32; ἐξ ~ους κατασκίου δασέος 'from a dark shady mount' Hb 3.3. **f**. The name of a mountain is expressed in a variety of ways: τὸ ὄ. τὸ Σινα Ex 19.11; ἐπ' ὄρους Σ. 19.16; ἐν τῷ ὄρει Σ. Le 7.28 and Nu 28.6, ἐν ὄρει Σ. 3.1; τὸ ὄρος Ησαυ (the latter apparently in the gen. as in ~ Σαμαρείας Am 3.9) Ob 21, τὸ ὄρος τὸ Ησαυ 19*a*, ὄρος Η. 8, 9.

Cf. βουνός, ὀρεινός, πεδίον: Spicq 2.597-9; Cadell and Rémondon 1967.

ὅρος, ου. m.ʃ
a point or *period of time specified for something to take place*: ἔδωκεν ὁ θεὸς ~ον 'God set a time' Ex 9.5; Ne 2.6. Cf. καιρός.

ὀροφοιτέω.ʃ
to roam the mountains: ***s*** birds, 4M 14.15.

ὄροφος, ου. m.ʃ
roof of a house: Wi 17.2. Cf. ὀρόφωμα, στέγη.

ὀρόφωμα, ατος. n.ʃ
= ὄροφος: Ez 41.26, 2C 3.7. Cf. ὄροφος.

ὀρτυγομήτρα, ας. f.ʃ
a bird which migrates with quails, perh. *corncrake, landrail, Rallus crex* (LSJ and cf. LSG s.v. 'giant quail'): food divinely provided in the desert, Ex 16.13, Nu 11.31, 32, Ps 104.40; τροφὴν ἡτοίμασας ~αν 'you provided .. as nourishment' Wi 16.2; 19.12.

ὄρυξ, γος. m.ʃ
"a kind of *gazelle* or *antelope*, in Egypt and Libya, *Oryx leucoryx*" (LSJ): ritually clean food, De 14.5.

ὀρύσσω: fut. ὀρύξω; aor. ὤρυξα, impv. ὄρυξον, ptc. ὀρύξας, subj.pass. ὀρυγῶ.

1. *to excavate the ground*: Ex 7.24; De 23.13 (to relieve oneself); to take out sth hidden, Je 13.7; ὀρύξας ἔθαψα αὐτόν To 2.7; horizontally through a wall, Ez 8.8. **b**. *to excavate under*: + acc., ἀκρότομον 'a rock' Si 48.17. **c**. *to form by excavating the ground*: ***o*** φρέαρ 'well' Ge 21.30, 26.15; φρέαρ ὕδατος 26.18, μνημεῖον 'tomb' 50.5, τάφον 'tomb' Ju 8.9, βόθρον 'a pit (in the ground)' Zc 3.9 and Ps 56.7, προλήνιον 'wine-vat' Is 5.2, λάκκους 'cisterns' Je 2.13, 'pit' Ps 7.16. **c**. metaph., *to bring about*: κακά 'calamities' Pr 16.27, νεῖκος 'quarrel' 29.22.

2. *to perforate*: χεῖράς μου καὶ πόδας '(they gouged) my hands and feet' Ps 21.17.

Cf. ἐξ~, κατορύσσω, (ἐκ)λατομέω, σκάπτω.

ὀρφαν(ε)ία, ας. f.ʃ
state of being an orphan: Is 47.8, PSol 4.10.

ὀρφανός, οῦ. m.
child without one or both of the parents: vulnerable member of society mentioned along with χήρα 'widow,' προσήλυτος 'resident alien,' and πένης 'poor person' Ex 22.22, Zc 7.10, sim. De 10.18, 14.28; πατὴρ ~ῶν Ps 67.6 (= God); ***o*** of ἐλεέω Ho 14.4, διαρπάζω Mi 2.2, καταδυναστεύω Zc 7.10, κονδυλίζω Ma 3.5, cf. ~ὸν εἰς προνομὴν '.. as a target of plundering' Is 10.2; κρίνατε ὀρφανὸν καὶ πτωχόν Ps 81.3; + dat., ποιέω κρίσιν De 10.18. Cf. *ND* 4.162-4; Shipp 424.

ὀρχέομαι: fut. ὀρχήσομαι; aor.inf. ὀρχήσασθαι.
to dance: ***s*** pers., 2K 6.16, δαιμόνια Is 13.21; + παίζω 2K 6.21, 1C 15.29. Cf. κατορχέομαι.

ὅς, ἥ, ὅ.
Relative pronoun: λόγος κυρίου, ὃς ἐγενήθη πρὸς Ωσηε 'the word of the Lord, which was com-

municated to Hosea' Ho 1.1. **a**. An antecedent may be incorporated in the relative clause: the antecedent positioned immediately after the relative – ᾗ ἡμέρᾳ ἐποίησεν ὁ θεὸς .. 'on the day when God made ..' Ge 2.4; ἀφ' ἧς ἡμέρας .. 'from the day when ..' Ex 9.18, Ob 11, Is 7.17; δι' ἣν αἰτίαν 'for which reason' 1E 2.19; σωτηρίαν .. ἐν ᾗ σωτηρίᾳ .. Je 38.22; ὃν τρόπον .. 'in the manner as ..' Ho 9.13, Ob 16, Jn 1.14, Ma 3.17; at some remove - ἣν ἂν βουλεύσησθε βουλήν 'a plan that you might make' Is 8.10; δι' ἣν ἐποίησεν ἀνομίαν Je 36.23; ἐφ' ὧν προσφέρομεν θυσιῶν 'at the time of sacrifices which we offer' 1M 12.11, cf. αἰνέσετε τὸ ὄνομα κυρίου .., ἃ ἐποίησε μεθ' ὑμῶν εἰς θαυμάσια Jl 2.26. See BDF, § 294.5; BDAG, s.v. I, **e**. **b**. with a pleonastic pronoun referring back to the antecedent: εἰς γῆν, ἧς οἱ μοχλοὶ αὐτῆς .. Jn 2.7, ὑπὲρ τῆς κολοκύνθης, ὑπὲρ ἧς οὐκ ἐκακοπάθησας ἐπ' αὐτήν Jn 4.10, σκεῦος, οὗ οὐκ ἔστι χρεία αὐτοῦ 'an instrument of which there is no need' Je 22.28. Cf. Margolis 1912-13; Bakker; Sollamo 1991. **c**. The pleonastic deictic element or an appropriate prep. before the rel. pron. may be left out: ἐν τῷ τόπῳ, ᾧ ἐλάλησεν μετ' αὐτοῦ Ge 35.14 (with ἐκεῖ understood or instead of ἐν ᾧ), ἐν τῇ γῇ, ᾗ ἐγενήθη 11.28, ἐκ τῆς γῆς, ἧς ἐγενήθην 24.7, ἐν τῇ ὁδῷ, ᾗ ἂν πορευήσθε 42.38, τοῦ ἔτους, οὗ ἀπέθανεν 'in the year in which he died' Is 14.28 (rather than οὗ 'when'). **d**. The prep. of the antecedent may be repeated in the relative cl.: ἀπὸ τῆς ἡμέρας, ἀφ' ἧς .. Ez 24.2. **e**. with particles: ἕως οὗ 'until' (see under ἕως) – Ge 26.13, Jo 4.5, Ho 5.15; ἀφ' οὗ 'since the time of'– ἀφ' οὗ ἤρξω λαλεῖν 'since you have begun to speak' Ex 4.10; ἀφ' οὗ οἱ βουνοί 'since the time the hills were there' Ho 10.9; ἀφ' ἧς ἐχωρίσθημεν ἀπ' αὐτῶν 'since we cut our ties with them' 1M 1.11, cf. Renehan 1.36f.; causal, ἀφ' οὗ ἔντιμος ἐγένου 'since you became precious' Is 43.4; ἀνθ' ὧν 'because,' indicating a ground for a remuneration or retribution Ge 22.18, Am 1.3 (see under ἀντί); οὗ εἵνεκεν = ὅτι 'because' Ge 18.5, see further under ἕνεκα; ὑπὲρ οὗ 'over the fact that' 2K 6.8, 8.10, 4K 22.13B (*L* διότι), sim. περὶ οὗ 21.1B. **f**. + ἐάν (q.v., **II**) or ἄν (q.v., **2b**), in a generalising nominalised rel. clause without an antecedent – ὃς ἐὰν ἐγγίσῃ ἐκεῖ, μιανθήσεται .. Hg 2.14. **g**. The case of the rel. pron., which is usually determined by its syntactic function in the rel. clause, may be assimilated to that of the antecedent: περὶ τῆς γυναικός, ἧς (for ἣν) ἔλαβες Ge 20.3, ἀπὸ τῆς ἡμέρας, ἧς (instead of ἐν ᾗ or ᾗ) ἐθεμελιώθη ὁ ναὸς κυρίου 'from the day when the Lord's temple was founded' Hg 2.18, προσεκύνησαν, οἷς ἐποίησαν οἱ δάκτυλοι αὐτῶν 'they worshiped what their fingers made' Is 2.8; a prep. attached to the antecedent may also be carried over - ἐκ τοῦ χρυσίου .. καὶ ἐκ τοῦ ἀργυρίου .., ἐξ ὧν ἔδωκά σοι Ez 16.17. **h**. Very occasionally the case of the antecedent may be attracted to that of the rel. pron.: παντός, οὗ ἂν ἅψηται αὐτοῦ 'anything that he might touch ..' Nu 19.22, λόγον [= λόγος], ὃν ἂν λαλήσητε Is 8.10; νόμον [= νόμος], ὃν ἐνετείλατο ἡμῖν Μωυσῆς Si 24.23. **i**. Antecedentless: ὃς ἐξελεύσεται ἐκ σοῦ .. 'he who will proceed from you ..' Ge 15.4; παρ' ᾧ ἂν εὑρεθῇ τὸ κόνδυ 'whoever the drinking-vessel may be found with' 44.10 (|| ὁ ἄνθρωπος, παρ' ᾧ εὑρέθη τὸ κόνδυ vs. 17); ἃ μέλλεις λαλῆσαι 'what you are going to speak about' Ex 4.12; τί ἀράσομαι ὃν μὴ ἀρᾶται κύριος; 'How am I going to curse one whom the Lord would not curse?' Nu 23.8; ᾧ λόγος στόματος κυρίου πρὸς αὐτόν 'one to whom a divine message is communicated' Je 9.12; 50.11; ἀπὸ προσώπου ὧν ἐθυμιᾶτε 'because of what you burn as incense' 51.23; Μνήσθητι .. ὅ τι ἐγενήθη ἡμῖν 'Remember .. that which has befallen us' La 5.1. **j**. non-restrictive: ὃς δὲ προήνεγκεν 'thereupon he produced' To 9.5 𝔊I; "they came to Jerusalem, the rebellious and evil city, which they are rebuilding" (εἰς .. τὴν πόλιν .., ἣν οἰκοδομοῦσιν) 2E 4.12; δι' ἣν αἰτίαν 'for which reason' 1E 2.19, 2M 4.28; 4.34. **k**. The case of the resumptive pronoun may be attracted to that of the antecedent: ἕως πάντων, ὧν ἔλαβον αὐτῶν (for αὐτά)

Cf. ὅσος and ὅστις.

ὅσιος, α, ον.

1. *sanctioned by divine law*: Ὅσιά μοι γένοιτο ὅτι .. 'May I be allowed to ..' De 29.19; τὰ ~α Δαυιδ τὰ πιστά 'that which was firmly sanctioned by God in David's interest' Is 55.3, cf. Dupont 1961.96-105, 108-11.

2. *pious*: *s* hum., De 33.8; ψάλατε τῷ κυρίῳ οἱ ~οι αὐτοῦ Ps 29.5; 2K 22.24*L* (B: ἄμωμος); καρδία PSol 15.3 (+ δίκαιος), Pr 22.11; thing, λόγον ~ον ἐβδελύξαντο 'they abhorred words of piety' Am 5.10; hope, Si 24.18¶; deed, + εὐσεβής 2M 12.45.

3. *holy*: *s* God, δίκαιος καὶ ὅ. κύριος De 32.4, sim. ἐν πᾶσιν τοῖς ἔργοις αὐτοῦ Ps 144.17; ἡ ὁδὸς ^κυρίου^ 2K 22.31*L* (B: ἄμωμος) On this divine attribute, see Orphica, *Hymni* 77.2, θεοῖς ~οις καὶ δικαίοις *CIG* 3830, and Bolkestein 188-92.

Cf. ὁσιότης, ὁσίως, ἅγιος, δίκαιος, ἄμωμος, ἀνόσιος, ὁσιόω, εὐσεβής: Schmidt 4.330-6, 344f.; Trench 329-31; Bolkestein; Chadwick 221-6.

ὁσιότης, ητος. f.

piety: of human character, τῆς καρδίας σου De 9.5 (|| δικαιοσύνη), + ἀλήθεια Jd 9.16*L* (AB: τελειότης), + εὐθύτης 3K 9.4; divine attribute, Wi

9.3 (+ δικαιοσύνη). **b.** *symbol certifying piety*: 1K 14.41 (|| δῆλοι).

Cf. ὅσιος, δικαιοσύνη.

ὁσιόω: fut.pass. ὁσιωθήσομαι.

to regard as ὅσιος: *o* hum. and pass., Wi 6.10. **b.** mid. *to conduct oneself as* ὅσιος: *s* God, Ps 17.26.

Cf. ὅσιος.

ὁσίως. adv.ʃ

adv. of ὅσιος: ὁ. πορεύεσθαι .. καὶ φυλάσσειν ἐντολὰς αὐτοῦ 3K 8.61, φυλάξοντες ὁ. τὰ ὅσια Wi 6.10. Cf. ὅσιος.

ὀσμή, ῆς. f.

smell: ὠσφράνθη κύριος ὁ θεὸς ~ὴν εὐωδίας '.. inhaled fragrant smell (of sacrifices offered)' Ge 8.21; ἱματίων 'of clothes' 27.27; τοῦ υἱοῦ μου ib.; ἀγροῦ πλήρους 'of a fertile field' ib.; of corpses unburied, Is 34.3, μύρου 'of ointment' Je 25.10; fig., ἐβδελύξατε τὴν ὀσμὴν ἡμῶν ἐναντίον Φαραω 'you made personae non gratae of us with Ph.' Ex 5.21; as cogn. obj., οὐ μὴ ὀσφρανθῶ τῆς ~ῆς τῶν θυσιῶν ὑμῶν Le 26.31. **b.** *perfume*: ἡδεῖα 'sweet-smelling' Is 3.24.

Cf. ὀσφρασία, εὐωδία, ἥδυσμα, βρόμος, σαπρία.

ὅσος, η, ον.

Relative pronoun, *all who* .., *all that* .., used mostly in the pl.

1. ὅσοι 'all those who ..': ὅσοι ἐὰν καταλειφθῶσιν 'all those who may survive' Zc 14.16, sim. 17, 18, 19, Mi 6.14. **b.** ὅσα 'all that which': ἔδωκεν αὐτῷ ὅσα ἦν αὐτῷ 'he gave him all that he had' Ge 24.36; ὅσα ἦν κτήνη σου 'all that which was your livestock' 30.29; ὅσα εὐξάμην, ἀποδώσω 'all that I vowed I will pay' Jn 2.10; often with πάντα preceding– πάντα ὅσα ἐποίησεν 'all that he had made' Ge 1.31; πάντα ὅσα ἐξεδίκησα 'all that I meted out as punishment' Zp 3.7; πάντα ὅσα μοι καθήκει 'all that I need' Ho 2.5; in apposition, ἄμπελον αὐτῆς καὶ τὰς συκᾶς αὐτῆς, ὅσα εἶπα .. 'her grape .. and her figs, all that about which she said ..' Ho 2.12, sim. Zc 1.6; 2M 11.18 (|| ἅ). **c.** with a nominal clause lacking a copula– πάντα τὰ ἔθνη, ὅσα ἐπὶ προσώπου τῆς γῆς De 7.6. **d.** || ὅς: ἕκαστος ὧν ἔφερεν ἡ καρδία αὐτῶν καὶ ὅσοις ἔδοξεν τῇ ψυχῇ αὐτῶν Ex 35.21; τὰς ἐντολὰς κυρίου .., ὅσας (B: ἃς) ἐγὼ ἐντέλλομαι ὑμῖν .. De 11.27, see Wevers 1978.106. **e.** coordinated with οὕτως– ὅσα συνέταξεν κύριος .. οὕτως ἐποίησαν .. Ex 39.22 (|| ὃν τρόπον vs. 23); with τοσοῦτος— ὅσῳ μέγας εἶ, τοσούτῳ ταπείνου σεαυτόν 'the greater you are, humble yourself the more' Si 3.18, ὅσῳ .. τοσούτῳ μᾶλλον To 2.10 𝔊ᴵᴵ. **f.** ὅσα = ὅτι: μὴ ἐπιλάθῃ ὅσα παρώξυνας .. 'do not forget that you provoked ..' De 9.7; 4K 14.28; 20.3 (*L* ὡς). **g.** + inf. *so much as is enough for*: φάγῃ σταφυλὴν ὅσον ψυχήν σου ἐμπλησθῆναι 'eat as many grapes as would satisfy your appetite' De 23.25; Wi 15.19. **h.** + a subst.: ὅσον χρόνον 'so long as' Jo 4.14, Pr 1.22.

2. Unlike in Cl. Gk. no instance is attested with a correlative: ἐπὶ τὸν σῖτον καὶ ἐπὶ τὸν οἶνον καὶ ἐπὶ τὸ ἔλαιον καὶ ὅσα ἐκφέρει ἡ γῆ Hg 1.11 (note also the omission of ἐπί before the rel. pron. despite MT *'al*).

3. With an antecedent prefixed by πᾶς: πάντας τοὺς λαούς, ὅσοι ἐπεστράτευσαν Zc 14.12; De 7.6 (see **1c** above).

4. Idiom: μικρὸν ὅσον ὅσον 'just a little while' Is 26.20, cf. LSJ s.v. ὅσος IV 2.

5. Virtually equivalent to πόσος 'how many, how much?': Si 20.17.

6. *as much as*: τιμὴ πόρνης ὅση καὶ ἑνὸς ἄρτου 'the value of a whore is just as much as that of one loaf of bread' Pr 6.26; ὅσον δρὰξ ἀλεύρου 'just a handful of flour' 3K 17.12. **b.** ὅσον *nearly, approximately*: distance, ὅσον δισχιλίους πήχεις 'about 2,000 cubits' Jo 3.4.

Cf. ὅς and ὅστις.

ὅσπερ, ἥπερ, ὅπερ.ʃ

1. rel. pron., *the very person who, the very thing which*: 2M 3.36. **b.** non-restrictive rel pron., ὅπερ εἴωθα ποιεῖν 'which is exactly my custom' 4M 1.12; 13.19, Wi 19.18.

***2**, interr. pron., *exactly what*: indir. question, ὅπερ ἦν Jb 6.17.

ὄσπριον, ου. n.ʃ

edible seed, 'pulse': Da 1.12, 16 LXX (TH σπέρμα).

ὀστέον.⇒ ὀστοῦν.

ὅστις, ἥτις, ὅ τι.

Rel. pron. of general reference, though the classical distinction between ὅς and ὅστις is no longer strictly maintained in the Koiné, and the latter is far less common, occurring only about 130 times in the entire LXX (BDF, § 293): χάλαζαν πολλὴν σφόδρα, ἥτις τοιαύτη οὐ γέγονεν ἐν Αἰγύπτῳ 'an exceeding amount of hail, the like of which has never been in Egypt' Ex 9.18; κραυγὴ μεγάλη .. ἥτις τοιαύτη οὐ γέγονεν 'a great cry .. the like of which had never occurred' 11.6; ψυχή, ἥτις ἂν ἅψηται .. Le 5.2; πᾶσαν γυναῖκα, ἥτις .. Nu 31.17; .. ἀνθρώπων, οἵτινες οὐκ ἔγνωσαν .. 'people such as who did not know ..' Jn 4.11. **b.** with a definite antecedent and with non-restrictive force: Ἐγώ εἰμι κύριος ὁ θεός σου, ὅστις ἐξήγαγόν σε ἐκ γῆς Αἰγύπτου .. Ex 20.2; 32.4, Ps 89.4, 95.10. **c.** antecedentless: Is 13.15 (|| ὃς ἐάν), Jb 6.16. **d.** ἕως ὅτου + sub. aor. indicates that a period of time has to elapse before an intended event takes place: the lead verb indicates a temporary measure, Ez 39.15; that which is indicated by the lead verb takes place only when that which is indicated by the subordinate verb takes place, To 5.3 𝔊II. **e.** ἕως ὅτου + ind. impf./ aor. = ἕως or ἕως οὗ 'until': 3K11.16B (*L* ἕως οὗ), 4K 2.17B (*L* ἕως). **f.** ‖ ὅς: Jo 1.18.

Cf. ὅς and ὅσος.

ὁστισοῦν, ἡτισοῦν, ὁτιοῦν.ʃ

anybody (*anything*) *whosoever* (*whatsoever*): predicatively, ὀφείλημα ὁτιοῦν τι 'whatever debt' De 24.10. **b.** attributively, κηδείας ἡστινοσοῦν 'of any kind of funeral' 2M 5.10; καθ' ὁντιναοῦν τρόπον 'in any way whatsoever' 14.3; 3M 7.7.

ὀστοῦν, έον; pl.nom./acc. ὀστᾶ, gen. ὀστέων, ὀστῶν, dat. ὀστέοις. n.

bone: together with "flesh" as essential component of human body – ὀστοῦν ἐκ τῶν ~έων μου καὶ σὰρξ ἐκ τῆς σαρκός μου Ge 2.23; ἐκ τῶν ὀστῶν μου καὶ ἐκ τῆς σαρκός μου εἶ σύ 'you are a very close relation of me' 29.14; Am 2.1 (burned); ἁρπάζοντες .. τὰς σάρκας αὐτῶν ἀπὸ τῶν ~έων αὐτῶν Mi 3.2; 3.3 (deliberately broken); the inner part of human body– εἰσῆλθε τρόμος εἰς τὰ ~ᾶ μου 'trembling penetrated my bones' Hb 3.16; of corpse, Am 6.10; of sacrificial animal, Ex 12.10; ἀνθρώπινον 'human' Nu 19.16, 18 (of a corpse).

ὀστράκινος, η, ον.

made of clay, 'earthen': *s* σκεῦος 'vessel, instrument' Le 6.28 (:: χαλκοῦς); ἀγγεῖον 'container' 14.5, Is 30.14; βῖκος 'jar' Je 19.1; ἄγγος 'container' 19.11; ἀγγεῖα ~α, ἔργα χειρῶν κεραμέως 'earthen jars, potter's handmade artefacts' La 4.2; opp., iron (σιδηροῦς) Da 2.33 TH (LXX ὄστρακον). Cf. ὄστρακον.

ὄστρακον, ου. n.

fragment of earthen vessel, potsherd: Jb 2.8. Cf. ὀστράκινος.

ὀστρακώδης, ες.ʃ

full of potsherds: *s* mountain, Jd 1.35B.

ὀσφραίνομαι: fut. ὀσφρανθήσομαι; aor. ὠσφράνθην, subj. ὀσφρανθῶ, inf. ~ρανθῆναι, opt.3s ὀσφρανθείη.

I. tr. *to inhale smell of*: abs. To 6.18; *o*, + acc. ὀσμὴν εὐωδίας 'fragrant smell' Ge 8.21 (*s* God); ὀσμὴν ἱματίων 27.27; obj. (prob. θυσίας, so v.l.) understood– οὐ μὴ ὀσφρανθῶ ἐν ταῖς πανηγύρεσιν ὑμῶν '.. in your festive assemblies' Am 5.21; +gen. τῆς ὀσμῆς τῶν θυσιῶν Le 26.31, πολέμου Jb 39.25; *Hebraism with ἐν, Ex 30.38; *o* θυσία 1K 26.19.

***2.** *to offer* sth for its fragrant smell: pass., *o* θυσία 1K 26.19*L*.

II. intr. *to be capable of perceiving smell*: "they are not capable of seeing, nor hearing nor eating nor smelling (οὐδὲ μὴ ὀσφρανθῶσιν)" De 4.28 (a description of pagan idols), cf. Ps 134.17.

Cf. ὀσφρασία and ὀσμή.

ὀσφρασία, ας. f.ʃ

odour, scent of agreeable kind: ἡ ὀ. αὐτοῦ ὡς Λιβάνου 'its odour will be as that of Lebanon' Ho 14.7. Cf. ὀσμή, ὀσφραίνομαι.

ὀσφῦς, ύος. f. On the accent, see Walters 96f.

waist, loins: where a mourner's sackcloth (σάκκος) is worn, Am 8.10, στεναγμὸς ὀσφύος 'sighing of ..' Ez 24.17; κράτησον ~ύος 'lay hold of loins' (to be ready for a fight) Na 2.2 (‖ ἀνδρίζεσθαι); where birth pangs are felt, 2.11; where the male procreatory organs are located – βασιλεῖς ἐκ τῆς ~ύος σου ἐξελεύσονται 'kings will come out of your loins' Ge 35.11; ἀπὸ ~ύος ἕως μηρῶν 'from the hips down to the thighs' Ex 28.38; περιεζωσμέναι 'girded round' 12.11, λύσουσι τὰς ζώνας αὐτῶν ἀπὸ τῆς ~ύος αὐτῶν 'will loosen their girdles ..' Is 5.27; of sacrificial animal, Le 3.9; seat of strength, συνετρίβη ἡ ὀ. μου 'my hips collapsed' (out of fear) PSol 8.5.

ὅταν. conj.

at the time when, when. **1.** + impf. ὅταν εἰσήρχετο Ge 38.9(*a*); + aor.indic., ὅτ. ἐκαθίσαμεν Ex 16.3(*c*) (foll. by impf.); + pres. subj. without the idea of repetition: ὅτ. ἀποτρέχητε Ex 3.21(*g*), ὅτ. πορνεύωσι .. ὅτ. μοιχεύωσι Ho 4.14 (*a*bis), PSol 3.11; with a subst. denoting a period of time, ἐν τῇ ἡμέρᾳ, ὅτ. ἐκδικῶ Am 3.14(-); ἐν τῷ καιρῷ ἐκείνῳ, ὅτ. εἰσδέχωμαι Zp 3.20*b*(-). **b.** precedes the main clause: Ex 30.20(*c*), Ps 77.34(*a*).

2. + aor. subj.: where a ὅταν-clause follows the main clause– μνήσθητί μου .. ὅτ. εὖ σοι γένηται Ge 40.14(*e*); De 4.29(*f*); Mi 5.5(*a*bis), 6(*a*bis); ἐν τῷ καιρῷ ἐκείνῳ, ὅτ. ἐπιστρέψω Jl 3.1(*d*); ἐν τῷ καιρῷ ἐκείνῳ, ὅτ. ποιήσω (fut.?) Zp 3.20*a*(-); Ez 42.14(-). **b.** precedes the main clause: Ex 11.1(*d*), 18.16(*f*), 19.13(*c*), Le 19.23(*f*), 23.10(*f*), Nu 10.7(*c*), 11.9(*c*); Is 1.15(*c* and ‖ ἐάν). **c.** preceded by ὃν τρόπον and almost pleonastic: ὃν τρόπον ὅτ. ἐκσπάσῃ Am 3.12(*b*), where ὅτ. is possibly a doublet or an equivalent of ἐὰν or ἄν as in Am 5.19 v.l., cf. Mi 5.8(*c*), Zc 4.1(*b*).

Cf. ὅτε, ἡνίκα.

a) אִם; *b*) אֲשֶׁר; *c*) -בְּ + inf.; *d*) -כְּ + inf.; *e*) כַּאֲשֶׁר; *f*) כִּי; *g*) הָיָה כִּי *h*) לְעֵת.xʃ

ὅτε. conj.

1. *during the time when, while*: + impf. ὅτε ἐνεβάλλετε (v.l. aor.) Hg 2.17(*b*); Zc 7.7(*a*); ὅτε ἀπέθνῃσκεν 'when he was about to die' To 14.3 𝔊II.

2. *at the time when*: + aor., ὅτε ἐγένετο 'when it happened' Ge 2.4(*a*); 24.30(*b*) (‖ ἡνίκα), To 6.10 𝔊II(*f*); + impf., Nu 33.39(*a*), 40(*a*); De 32.8(*a*) (‖ ὡς and precedes the main clause).

Cf. ὅταν, ἡνίκα, ὁπηνίκα, ὡς.

a) -בְּ; *b*) -כְּ; *c*) -וְ; *d*) -כ; *e*) אֲשֶׁר; *f*) Ar. כְּדִי [To 6.10]. x∫.

ὅτι

1. introduces a causal clause, 'because, for': normally follows the main clause – Jn 1.2, 11, 14, Ma 2.2; preceding, Ge 3.14, 29.15, Le 10.17, Nu 20.12, De 7.7, 1K 30.22B (*L* διότι), Ez 33.16, but hardly so at Ge 6.13; the main clause introduced by a coordinating διὰ τοῦτο, Is 30.12f. **b**. Answers a 'why'-question marked by ἕνεκα τίνος, Ma 2.14; marked by ἐν τίνι, 3.8. **c**. ‖ ἀνθ' ὧν De 22.29 (see 22.24). Cf. Aejmelaeus 1985.

2. introduces a substantival clause: obj. of verbs of verbal communication, sense perception, etc.– οὐκ ἔγνωσαν ὅτι ἴαμαι αὐτούς 'they did not realise that I was healing them' Ho 11.3; Jn 1.10, 12, 4.2; ἰδόντες .. ὅτι καλὴ ἦν σφόδρα 'having seen .. that she was exceedingly beautiful' Ge 12.14; the subj. of the main verb in the ὅτι clause, being identical with the obj. of the preceding verb, is supressed (also in Cl. Gk., LSJ s.v. **A III 2**)– εἶδεν ὁ θεὸς τὸ φῶς ὅτι καλόν Ge 1.4, cf. 6.2 and ἄνδρας .., οὓς .. οἶδας ὅτι οὗτοί εἰσιν πρεσβύτεροι Nu 11.16; ἰδὼν τὴν ἀνάπαυσιν ὅτι καλή, καὶ τὴν γῆν ὅτι πίων Ge 49.15; To 6.13 𝔊[I]. **b**. introduces a subject clause: Ἡδύ μοι ὅτι ἐθερμάνθην 'it is nice that I became warm' Is 44.16. **c**. introduces direct (!) speech –ὅτι *recitativum* (also in Cl. Gk, LSJ s.v. **A II 1**): εἰπὸν οὖν ὅτι Ἀδελφὴ αὐτοῦ εἰμί 'Say, therefore, "I am his sister"' Ge 12.13; 14.23, 18.28, 20.13, 26.7; 45.26, 48.1. On **c**, cf. Préaux; Aejmelaeus 1990.

3. introduces a clause which explains what is meant by the preceding clause: εἶδεν ὁ θεὸς τὰ ἔργα αὐτῶν, ὅτι ἀπέστρεψαν ἀπὸ τῶν ὁδῶν τῶν πονηρῶν 'God took note of their works, which indicated that they had turned away from the wicked ways' Jn 3.10. **b**. introduces a demonstration of the truthfulness of the preceding statement: ὅτι ἐργᾷ τὴν γῆν, καὶ οὐ προσθήσει τὴν ἰσχὺν αὐτῆς δοῦναί σοι 'that is why you till the land, and yet it no longer provides you with its fruit' Ge 4.12.

*__4__. τί ὅτι 'why?': see under τίς **II f**.

*__5__. *seeing that*, introducing an extraordinary or remarkable circumstance which calls for an explanation and has prompted the preceding question: Τί τοῦτο ἐποίησάς μοι, ὅτι οὐκ ἀπήγγειλάς μοι ὅτι .. 'What on earth have you done to me in that you did not inform me that ..?' Ge 12.18; μή τι ἡμάρτομεν εἰς σέ, ὅτι ἐπήγαγες ἐπ' ἐμὲ καὶ ἐπὶ τὴν βασιλείαν μου ἁμαρτίαν μεγάλην; 'Have we wronged you in any way, seeing that you have gravely wronged us and my royal household?' 20.9; τί τὸ ἀδίκημά μου καὶ τί τὸ ἁμάρτημά μου, ὅτι κατεδίωξας ὀπίσω μου, [37]καὶ ὅτι ἠρεύνησας πάντα τὰ σκεύη μου; 31.36f.; Τίς εἰμι, ὅτι πορεύσομαι πρὸς Φαραω ..; 'What am I that I should go to Ph…?' Ex 3.11; ἡμεῖς δὲ τί ἐσμεν ὅτι διαγογγύζετε καθ' ἡμῶν; 'but what are we that you should grumble at us?' 16.7; 32.21, sim. Nu 16.11; Τί ὠφελεῖ γλυπτόν, ὅτι ἔγλυψεν αὐτό; 'They have made a graven image, but what is its use?' Hb 2.18; τί ἐστιν ἄνθρωπος, ὅτι μιμνῄσκῃ αὐτοῦ; 'What is man that you should remember him?' Ps 8.5. See also Nu 11.12, Jd 14.3, 1K 17.43, 20.1, 3K 18.9, 4K 5.7, Is 22.1, 36.5, Jb 6.11, 7.17. Cf. LSJ s.v. **B 2**; Monro, § 269, (2); Baumert; Perri 81-94.

6. explicates the preceding noun: τοῦτό σοι τὸ σημεῖον ὅτι ἐγώ σε ἀποστέλλω 'this is the sign showing that I am the one who is sending you' Ex 3.12.

7. indicates elative force w. a superlative adv.: ὅτι κάλλιστα 'as best as could have been possible' 2M 3.1.

*__8__. redundant under Heb. infl. (כִּי): 2K 2.27*L* (B διότι), 3.9[2]B (*L* om.), 4K 23.9 (*L* om.), 23, Ec 8.15. **b**. with no Heb. infl.: ἢ ὅτι 'more than' Ec 7.2.

*__9__. ὅτι ἐάν 'unless,' calqued on Heb. כִּי אִם 4K 4.24B.

Cf. διότι, ἐπεί, ἐπειδή, ὡς.

ὀτρύνω.∫

to urge to attend to: τινα πρός τι 3M 5.46.

οὐ; before a vowel with a smooth accent οὐκ; before a vowel with a rough accent οὐχ.

a. Negates an indicative verb: οὐκ ἔστιν ἀλήθεια 'there is no truth' Ho 4.1. The negation relates to the entire, following clause: οὐκ ἀπελεύσεται ὥσπερ ἀποτρέχουσιν αἱ δοῦλαι Ex 21.7 signifies that the manner of her departure as οἰκέτις shall be different from that of δοῦλαι. **b**. positioned immediately before a word or phrase to be negatived: οὐκ ὀρθῶς σὺ ποιεῖς τὸ ῥῆμα τοῦτο Ex 18.17; Οὐκ ἐγὼ ἡ ὄνος σου ..; Nu 22.30; οὐχ οὗτοι οἱ λόγοι μου; 'is this not what I said?' Jn 4.2; ἔλεος θέλω καὶ οὐ θυσίαν 'I want mercy, not sacrifice' Ho 6.6. **c**. negates a participle: ἐκ λάκκου οὐκ ἔχοντος ὕδωρ 'out of a cistern lacking water' Zc 9.11; ἐν τοῖς οὐκ οὖσι θεοῖς 'by those which are no real gods' Je 5.7, οὐκ ὄντες θεοί Ep Je 14. See BDF, § 426. **d**. in a rhetorical question anticipating an affirmative answer: οὐκ ἰδοὺ πᾶσα ἡ γῆ ἐναντίον σού ἐστιν; 'Behold, isn't all the land before you?' Ge 13.9; ἐγὼ δὲ οὐ φείσομαι ὑπὲρ Νινευη ..; "Would I not have pity on Nineveh ..?' Jn 4.11; at the beginning of a clause– οὐ ταῦτά ἐστι παρὰ κυρίου ..; 'Surely these are from the Lord ..? Hb 2.13; Ma 1.2. **e**. used as an elliptical negative answer to a Yes/No question: Hg 2.12. **f**. negates a segment of a clause: ἐν γῇ οὐκ ἰδίᾳ 'in a land not their own' Ge 15.13; σκηνώματα οὐκ αὐτοῦ 'settlements not his' Hb 1.6; οὐ κατὰ τὰς ἡμέρας τὰς ἔμπροσθεν ἐγὼ ποιῶ Zc 8.11; οὐ πάντες 'not everyone' 4M 7.17. **g**. somewhat forceful and made to sound solemn by the immediately following μή: w. subj. Οὐ μὴ φάγητε .. Ge 3.1; οὐ μὴ ἀπολέσω 18.29; Οὐ μή σε ἀποστείλω 32.26; τοῦτο οὐκ ἔσται .. τοῦτο οὐ μὴ γένηται Am 7.3-6; οὐ μὴ ἐμπλησθῶσιν 'they will never be sated' Ho 4.10, see BDB, § 365, and Lee 1985.18-23; w. fut. 2K 18.12*L*, Is 16.10, Ez 33.31 (at latter, 967: subj.), Si 19.10; a coordinate, following verb in the fut.: Ex 33.20. **h**. conjoined to another negator: οὐκ ἐποίησα οὐδέν Ge 40.15; οὐκ εἴληφας ἐκ χειρὸς οὐδενὸς οὐδέν 'you did not take from anybody anything' 1K 12.4. **i**. negates a categorical injunction in the future: Οὐ μοιχεύσεις. οὐ κλέψεις. οὐ φονεύσεις. οὐ ψευδομαρτυρήσεις .. Ex 20.13-16. **j**. negates a noun, 'non-': ἐπ' οὐ θεῷ 'over that which is no god' De 32.21 (poss. also 32.17, and ‖ εἴδωλα), ἐπ' οὐκ ἔθνει 'over that which is no nation' 32.21, ἐν οὐκ ἰσχύι 'powerless' La 1.6, ψεῦδος καὶ οὐ πίστις 'falsehood and disloyalty' Je 9.3, cf. ὤμνυον ἐν τοῖς οὐκ οὖσι θεοῖς 'swore by what is no gods' Je 5.7 (see **c** above); τοῦ ἀσεβοῦς καὶ οὐκ ἀρχιερέως Ἰάσονος 'of the ungodly, false high priest Jason' 2M 4.13. Slightly different is: ἐν οὐ θεῷ ἀληθινῷ .. καὶ ἐν οὐ νόμῳ 'without having a true god ..' 2C 15.3. Cf. ἐν οὐ καιρῷ 'at an untimely moment' Eur. *Bac.* 1287. **k**. double-duty negator: οὐ κοπιάσουσι .. καὶ .. ἐκλείψουσιν [= οὐδὲ ἐκλείψουσιν] Je 28.58, see Ol. PG 93.676.

Cf. οὐδέ, μή, and οὐχί: Shipp 424f.

οὗ

place where: οὗ ἄν σοι ἀρέσκῃ, κατοίκει 'dwell wherever you like!' Ge 20.15; ἐν τῇ ὁδῷ πάσῃ, οὗ ἂν πορευθῇς 28.15; ἐν τῷ τόπῳ, οὗ ἐρρέθη αὐτοῖς 'at the place where they were told' Ho 1.10; with a Semiticising ἐκεῖ– ἐκ τοῦ τόπου, οὗ ἀπέδοσθε αὐτοὺς ἐκεῖ 'from the place where you sold them' Jl 3.7; ἡ νομὴ .. οὗ ἐπορεύθη λέων τοῦ εἰσελθεῖν ἐκεῖ 'the grazing-ground where a lion went to enter' Na 2.12; ἐκεῖ preceding – ἐκεῖ οὗ ἐστιν τὸ χρυσίον 'where gold is' Ge 2.11. At Is 5.10 οὗ ἐργῶνται δέκα ζεύγη βοῶν, the particle most likely means 'one whose ..'

οὐαί *

I. An expression of grief or sense of horror: abs., ἐν πάσαις ὁδοῖς ῥηθήσεται Οὐαὶ οὐαί Am 5.16; Mi 7.4; Zp 3.18. **b**. foll. by a dat. pers. over whose condition the utterance is made: οὐαί σοι, Μωαβ Nu 21.29, οὐαὶ ὑμῖν, ἄνδρες ἀσεβεῖς Si 41.8; οὐαὶ τοῖς ἐξουθενοῦσι Σιων Am 6.1; the reason indicated by a ὅτι- or διότι-clause – οὐαὶ αὐτοῖς, ὅτι ἀπεπήδησαν ἀπ' ἐμοῦ 'What a disaster for them that they should have walked away from me!' Ho 7.13 (‖ δείλαιος 'wretched'); Is 3.9 (διότι). **c**. + voc.: Οὐαὶ ἀδελφέ 3K 13.30. **d**. + ἐπί: οὐαὶ ἐπὶ συντρίμματί σου Je 10.19; ἐπὶ τὸν ἄνδρα τοῦτον 22.18, οὐαὶ ἐπὶ Βαβυλῶνα 28.2. **e**. foll. by a nom.: Οὐαὶ οἱ ἐπιθυμοῦντες τὴν ἡμέραν κυρίου Am 5.18; with the added nuance of denunciation – Οὐαὶ ὁ πληθύνων ἑαυτῷ τὰ οὐκ ὄντα αὐτοῦ Hb 2.6; 2.12; οὐαὶ ἔθνος ἁμαρτωλόν Is 1.4.

II. indeclinable subst., *woeful state*: θρῆνος καὶ μέλος καὶ οὐ. Ez 2.10, οὐ. ἐπὶ οὐ. ἔσται 7.26; οὐαὶ αὐτοῖς ἐστι Ho 9.12.

Cf. οἴμμοι: Lowe; Kraft 1972b.170-2; BDR, § 4; Spicq 2.442-4.

οὐδαμοῦ. adv.

nowhere: Jb 19.7. **b**. *not .. to any place*: 3K 2.36.

οὐδέ

Marks negation immediately following another negation, 'nor.'

a. following οὐ: introduces an independent clause – Οὐκ ἔγνων, τίς ἐποίησεν .. οὐδὲ σύ μοι ἀπήγγειλας, οὐδὲ ἐγὼ ἤκουσα .. Ge 21.26; with ellipsis, οὐ σώσω αὐτοὺς ἐν τόξῳ οὐδὲ ἐν ῥομφαίᾳ οὐδὲ ἐν πολέμῳ οὐδὲ ἐν ἅρμασιν οὐδὲ ἐν ἵπποις οὐδὲ ἐν ἱππεῦσι Ho 1.7; οὐδὲ μή De 31.8 (‖ οὔτε μή vs. 6). **b**. following οὐ μή: οὐ μὴ ὑπολειφθῇ ἐξ αὐτῶν ῥίζα οὐδὲ κλῆμα 'no root will remain of them nor branch' Ma 4.1. **c**. following a negator *and* preceding μή – Οὐ φάγεσθε .. οὐδὲ μὴ ἅψησθε αὐτοῦ Ge 3.3; Ex 23.13, De 13.8, 22.5. **d**. preceded *and* followed by another negative: οὐ μὴ ἀγαθοποιήσῃ κύριος οὐδὲ οὐ μὴ κακώσῃ Zp 1.12; Jb 7.10. **e**. makes the least likely element stand out, 'not even': Οὐ φάγεσθε .. οὐδὲ μὴ ἅψησθε αὐτοῦ 'do not even touch it, let alone eat of it' Ge 3.3; οὐ κατελείφθη ἐξ αὐτῶν οὐδὲ εἷς 'Not even one of them survived' Ex 14.28; Nu 31.49; οὐ μὴ δῶ ὑμῖν ἀπὸ τῆς γῆς αὐτῶν οὐδὲ βῆμα ποδός 'I shall never give any of their land, not even a piece to set foot upon' De 2.5; Zc 10.10. **f**. in conjunction with οὕτως the preceding negator is understood: οὐδ' οὕτως ἐνεπλήσθης 'Even with that you were not satisfied' Ez 16.28; Is 58.6, cf. ὥς. **g**. with a redundant καί: οὐχὶ ἐμόλυνά μου τὸ ὄνομα καὶ οὐδὲ τὸ ὄνομα τοῦ πατρός μου 'I haven't besmirched my name nor ..' To 3.15 𝔊[II]. **h**. negates a segment of a phrase: οὐ πάντες .. οὐδὲ πάντες .. 'not everyone .. nor everyone ..' 4M 7.17.

Cf. οὐ, οὔτε, μηδέ.

οὐδείς m., οὐδεμία f., οὐδέν n.; gen. οὐδενός, οὐδεμίας, οὐδενός. On the spelling with θ., also applicable to μηδείς, see Thack. 58-62, BDF, § 33, and Gignac, I, 97.

I. subst. **a**. m./f. *nobody*: οὐθενὸς διώκοντος 'with nobody chasing' Le 26.17, 36, Mi 2.11; οὐδεὶς αὐτῶν 'none of them' Zc 1.21; w. οὐ μὴ negativing a verb, Ho 2.10; **b**. impersonal, ἐν οὐδεμιᾷ τῶν πόλεών σου 'in none of your cities' De 16.5; **c**. n. *nothing*: οὐ δώσεις μοι οὐθέν 'you are not going to give me anything' Ge 30.31; οὐκ ἔπασχον οὐδέν 'they suffered nothing' Am 6.6, Zc 11.5; Hb 2.5 (w. μή before a verb); *thing of no account* – τὸ πρᾶγμα οὐδέν ἐστιν 'the action in question should be no concern to you' Nu 20.19; ἀπεστράφησαν εἰς οὐθέν Ho 7.16. **c**. οὐδέν / οὐθέν *in no regard*: οὐθὲν ἧττον 'no less' Jb 13.10, οὐδὲν ἥμαρτεν 1.22, οἷς οὐδὲν ὄφελος 'which have no merit' 15.3, οὐδὲν ἠδικημένοι 3M 3.8, almost = οὐ, cf. Psichari 203f.

II. adj.: εὐφραινόμενοι ἐπ' οὐδενὶ λόγῳ 'rejoice over what amounts to nothing, for no apparent reason' Am 6.13. **b**. reinforcing negation with another negator: οὐ ἐξουσίαν ἔχομεν .. φαγεῖν οὐδὲν κλεψιμαῖον 'we are not permitted to eat any stolen thing at all' To 2.13 𝔊[II].

Cf. μηδείς.

οὐδέποτε. adv.

never: in the past, οὐδέποτε ἑωράκασιν 'they have never seen before' Ex 10.6; in the future, 2M 6.16. Cf. οὐδέπω, οὔπω, μηδέποτε.

οὐδέπω ʃ

never before: οὐ. πεφόβησθε τὸν κύριον 'you have never before feared the Lord' Ex 9.30. Cf. οὐδέποτε.

οὐκέτι

Indicates that a certain condition does *not* prevail or repeat itself *any longer*, mostly w. ref. to future: οὐ. ἔσται κατακλυσμὸς ὕδατος 'there will be no more flooding' Ge 9.11; οὐ μὴ μνησθῶσιν οὐ. τὰ ὀνόματα αὐτῶν 'they will no longer remember their names' Ho 2.17; οὐ. μὴ εἴπωμεν 14.4; οὐ. μὴ προσθῶ τοῦ παρελθεῖν αὐτόν 'I will not pass beside it any more' Am 8.2; οὐ μὴ κατοικηθῇ οὐκέτι εἰς τὸν αἰῶνα 'it shall never again be inhabited' Je 27.39. In reply to ἔτι: Εἰ ἔτι ὑπάρχει παρὰ σοί; καὶ ἐρεῖ Οὐκέτι Am 6.10. With a redundant double negative: οὐ δώσω ὑμᾶς οὐ. εἰς ὀνειδισμόν Jl 2.19; 2.27, Ho 2.17, Na 2.14. Cf. ἔτι.

οὐλή, ῆς. f.

scar: Le 13.2; λευκή 'white' (of leper) 13.10.

οὖν

in view of what has been just stated or *observed*, 'hence, therefore': ποίησον οὖν .. 'Make therefore ..' Ge 6.14; εἰπὸν οὖν ὅτι .. 'Say, therefore, that .. ' 12.13; τίς οὖν ὁ θηρεύσας μοι θήραν ..; 'Who is then one who has procured game for me ..?' 27.33; καλέσατε οὖν αὐτόν 'Call him then' Ex 2.20; νῦν οὖν Nu 14.3.

The particle is never clause-initial. Cf. τοιγαροῦν.

οὗπερ. conj.

to the very spot where: 2M 4.38.

οὔπω ʃ

not yet: + pf., Ge 15.16, 18.12, Is 7.17, 1E 5.52, 2M 7.35; + impf. 3M 5.26; + aor. Ec 4.3; + nominal clause, οὔπω ὥρα συναχθῆναι τὰ κτήνη 'it is not yet the time for the cattle to be gathered together' Ge 29.7.

οὐρά, ᾶς. f.

1. *tail*: lit., of an animal, ὡς κυπάρισσον 'like a cypress' Jb 40.17, of a snake 40.31.

2. *a person* or *group playing a subordinate role in a society*: opp. κεφαλή – καταστῆσαι σε κύριος .. εἰς κεφαλὴν καὶ μὴ εἰς ~άν De 28.13; 28.44, cf. Is 9.14f. See further s.v. κεφαλή, **4**.

Cf. κεφαλή, κέρκος, οὐραγία.

οὐραγέω.ʃ

to be the last in moving on to the next stage: *s* departing guest, Si 35.11; ὀπίσω τῆς κιβωτοῦ 'behind the ark' Jo 6.9.

οὐραγία, ας. f.ʃ *

rearguard: ἔκοψεν σου τὴν ~αν De 25.18; Jo 10.19. Cf. οὐρά.

οὐράνιος, ον.

heavenly: *s* κύριος (= God) 1E 6.14, παῖς 'God's servant' 2M 7.34, ἐξουσία Da 4.23 TH; ἄστρα 'stars' 2M 9.10, πύλαι 'gates' 3M 6.18, στρατός 'army' 4M 4.11.

οὐρανόθεν. adv.ʃ

from the direction of heaven: 4M 4.10. Cf. οὐρανός.

οὐρανός, οῦ. m.

space far above the earth, 'sky, heaven': τὸν οὐρανὸν καὶ τὴν γῆν Ge 1.1; ἐποίησεν κύριος τὸν ~ὸν καὶ τὴν γῆν καὶ τὴν θάλασσαν καὶ πάντα τὰ ἐν αὐτοῖς Ex 20.11; πύργος, οὗ ἡ κεφαλὴ ἔσται ἕως τοῦ ~οῦ 'a tower the top of which will be up to the sky' Ge 11.4; ἀνὰ μέσον τῆς γῆς καὶ ἀνὰ μέσον τοῦ ~οῦ Zc 5.9; τὰ ἄστρα τοῦ ~οῦ Na 3.16; ἡ στρατιὰ τοῦ ~οῦ Ho 13.4; οἱ τέσσαρες ἄνεμοι τοῦ ~οῦ 'the four directions' Zc 6.5; constituting, together with γῆ, the whole material universe, Hg 2.6, 21, Hb 3.3; τὰ θηρία τοῦ ἀγροῦ καὶ τὰ πετεινὰ τοῦ ~οῦ καὶ τὰ ἑρπετὰ τῆς γῆς 'the beasts of the field and the birds of the sky and the reptiles of the earth' Ho 2.12. **b**. *pl., much less frequent than the sg. (ca. 8%), stylistically marked (common in poetry), mostly no genuine pl.: ἐκάλυψεν ~οὺς ἡ ἀρετὴ αὐτοῦ Hb 3.3, Οἱ ~οὶ διηγοῦνται δόξαν θεοῦ Ps 18.2, οἱ ~οὶ καὶ ἡ γῆ 68.35, δέσποτα τῶν ~ῶν καὶ τῆς γῆς Ju 9.12, τῷ ποιήσαντι τοὺς ~οὺς Ps 135.5, τὸ ὕδωρ ὑπεράνω τῶν ~ῶν 148.4; for the use of the pl. in a non-Jewish / Christian religious document of monotheistic character, see *ND* 3.31f. See also Torm;

Pennington. **c**. ὁ οὐ. καὶ ὁ οὐ. τοῦ ~οῦ De 10.14, Si 16.18; οἱ ~οὶ τῶν ~ῶν Ps 148.4. **d**. symbolising eternal existence: Ba 1.11, ὡς τὰς ἡμέρας τοῦ οὐρανοῦ Ps 88.30 (‖ εἰς τὸν αἰῶνα τοῦ αἰῶνος). **e**. a substitute for ὁ θεός: 2M 7.11, 8.20 (‖ θεός vs. 18), but *pace* LEH, s.v., not Jb 22.26; cf. οὐράνιος and BDAG, s.v. **3**.

Cf. οὐράνιος, οὐρανόθεν, ἐπουράνιος, γῆ: Traub, *TDNT* 5.509-11.

οὐρέω.

to urinate: οὐρῶν πρὸς τοῖχον 'he who pisses against a wall' 1K 25.22 + (w. ref. to a male member of a society). Cf. οὖρον.

οὔριος, α, ον.ʃ

subst.n., for ~ον ᾠὸν 'wind-egg' (full of wind and produces no chicken) Is 59.5.

οὖρον, ου. n.ʃ

urine:+ κόπρος 'excrement' Is 36.12, 4K 18.27. Cf. οὐρέω, ὕδωρ, κόπρος.

οὖς, ὠτός, pl.gen. ὤτων, dat. ὠσίν. n.

organ of hearing, 'ear': οὖς ἀκούει Pr 20.12 (‖ ὀφθαλμός); καρδίαν εἰδέναι καὶ ὀφθαλμοὺς βλέπειν καὶ ὦτα ἀκούειν De 29.4; ἐλάλησεν εἰς τὰ ὦτα αὐτῶν Ge 20.8 (addressed them); εἶπεν τῷ Εφρων εἰς τὰ ὦτα τοῦ λαοῦ τῆς γῆς 23.13 (in their earshot); διηγήσησθε εἰς τὰ ὦτα τῶν τέκνων ὑμῶν Ex 10.2; ἀνέγνω εἰς τὰ ὦτα τοῦ λαοῦ 'he read .. as the people listened' 24.7, ἐν ὠσὶν τοῦ λαοῦ Ne 13.1; ἡ κραυγή μου .. εἰσελεύσεται εἰς τὰ ὦτα αὐτοῦ 'my cry .. will reach his ears' Ps 17.7; τὰ ὦτα αὐτῶν ἀποκωφωθήσονται 'their ears will be deafened' Mi 7.16; τὰ ὦτα αὐτῶν ἐβάρυναν τοῦ μὴ ἀκούειν 'they made their ears heavy in order not to hear' Zc 7.11; τὰ ὦτα δώσουσιν ἀκούειν 'they will lend their ears to listen' Is 32.3. Cf. ὠτίον: Shipp 425.

οὐσία, ας. f.ʃ

property owned: Da 3.96 LXX, To 14.13 𝔊I (𝔊II οἰκία), 3M 3.28.

οὔτε

nor: following οὐ or a derivative of it and may be repeated more than once – οὐ μή σε ἀνῇ οὔτε μή σε ἐγκαταλίπῃ De 31.6 (‖ οὐκ .. οὐδὲ μή vs. 8); οὐκ ἐπιθυμήσεις τὴν οἰκίαν τοῦ πλησίον σου οὔτε τὸν ἀγρὸν αὐτοῦ οὔτε τὸν παῖδα αὐτοῦ οὔτε .. οὔτε .. Ex 20.17, sim. De 5.21. **b**. repeated with each term and followed by a negator, 'neither .. nor'– Οὔτε κατάραις καταράσῃ .. οὔτε εὐλογῶν μὴ εὐλογήσῃς αὐτόν Nu 23.25; Si 30.19. **c**. repeated with each term, but with no further negator: οὔτε εἰρήνευσα οὔτε ἡσύχασα οὔτε ἀνεπαυσάμην Jb 3.26, οὔτε ἔγνως οὔτε ἠπίστω Is 48.8.

Cf. οὐ, οὐδέ, μήτε.

οὗτος m., αὕτη f., τοῦτο n.

1. Demonstrative pronoun referring to an entity considered relatively close in terms of the discourse setting, 'this'. **a**. referring to an entity physically close: αὕτη 'this (woman)' standing next to me Ge 2.23; τὸν οἶκον τοῦτον 'the temple in front of you' Hg 2.3; ταῦτα in a reply to a question with οὗτοι, Zc 1.9; strengthened by -ί — ὁ ψευστὴς οὑτοσί 'this liar here' Es 7.8 *L*. **b**. ref. to what is presently prominent in the speaker's mind: ἐν τῇ γενεᾷ ταύτῃ 'in the current generation' Ge 7.1; ἐν τῇ νυκτὶ ταύτῃ 'in that night' 19.33; ἡ κακία αὕτη 'this trouble, the present trouble' Jn 1.7; ἡ ἡμέρα αὕτη 'this day, today' Hg 2.15, 19. **c**. ref. to that which is about to be mentioned ("cataphoric"), 'the following': μόνον ἐν τούτῳ ὁμοιωθήσονται .. ἐν τῷ περιτέμνεσθαι ἡμῶν πᾶν ἀρσενικόν 'only under the following condition they would consent .., (namely) that every male amongst us be circumcised' Ge 34.22; Ob 20, Je 9.24. **d**. ref. to that which has just been mentioned ("anaphoric"): Οὐ κληρονομήσει σε οὗτος 'that one shall not inherit you' Ge 15.4; Αὕτη ἡ βίβλος γενέσεως οὐρανοῦ καὶ γῆς 'the above is the chapter concerning the emergence of heaven and earth' Ge 2.4; ἑβδόμῃ καὶ εἰκάδι τοῦ μηνός, τῇ ἡμέρᾳ ταύτῃ .. 'on the 16th (day) of the month, on that day ..' 7.11; τὸ ῥῆμα, ὃ ἂν λαλήσω πρὸς σέ, τοῦτο ποιήσεις Nu 22.20; ἰδοὺ δύο γυναῖκες .. καὶ αὗται εἶχον πτέρυγας .. Zc 5.9; w. ref. to a general thought mentioned before – διὰ τοῦτο Jn 4.2; ἕνεκεν τούτου Hb 1.16; 'the latter, the other' parallel to αὐτός 'the former, the one' – Hb 2.19; resumptively, ὃς ἐξελεύσεται ἐκ σοῦ, οὗτος κληρονομήσει σε Ge 15.4, Pr 28.24 (‖ ὁ τοιοῦτος vs. 21, 26), κύριος ὁ θεός σου, οὗτος θεὸς ἐν τῷ οὐρανῷ ἄνω .. De 4.39; Ps 100.5f.; in a gloss-like expression, 'that is to say, namely'– Βαλα (αὕτη ἐστὶν Σηγωρ) 'B., namely S.' Ge 14.2; τῷ ἑνδεκάτῳ μηνί, οὗτός ἐστιν ὁ μὴν Σαβατ 'in the eleventh month, i.e. the month of Shebat' Zc 1.7, sim. Je 39.1; in appositional resumption, χήραν καὶ ἐκβεβλημένην .. καὶ πόρνην, ταύτας οὐ λήμψεται 'a widow, a divorcee, .. a prostitute, these he shall not marry' Le 21.14; Ez 44.15. ***e**. Hebraistically following an interrogative and emphasising the latter: τί τοῦτο ἐποίησας; 'what on earth have you done?' Ge 3.13, 12.18, 20.9, 26.10, 29.25; ἵνα τί τοῦτο .. Ex 17.3, Nu 20.5, Je 20.18; τί τοῦτο 'what on earth?' Jn 1.10, τίς οὗτος ποιμήν, ὃς .. Je 27.44, but cf. τί τοῦτο ἔλεξας; Soph., *Philoctetes* 1173. ***f**. adv. to indicate how often a given thing has already occurred, including the present occurrence, or how long a given situation has prevailed up to the moment of speaking, often tinged with a sense of irritation, astonishment, exasperation and the like: **i**. frequency: with n.sg. τοῦτο and a n.sg. ordinal ἐπτέρνικεν γάρ με ἤδη δεύτερον τοῦτο 'this is already a second time that he has cheated me' Ge 27.36; πέπαικάς με τοῦτο τρίτον 'this is already a third time that you've hit me' Nu 22.28, 32; 14.22; εὐλόγησας τρίτον τοῦτο 24.10; **ii** length: an appropriately declined form of a dem. pron. with a noun of duration– ταῦτά μοι εἴκοσι ἔτη ἐγώ εἰμι μετὰ σοῦ 'already 20 years I have been with you' Ge 31.38, 41; **iii**. mixed structure: τοῦτο δεύτερον ἔτος λιμὸς .. 'this is already second year of the famine ..' 45.6; τοῦτο ἑβδομηκοστὸν ἔτος Zc 1.12; 1K 29.3; **iv** with an indeclinable, fossilised τοῦτο: ⸢τοῦτο⸣ (*L* om.) ἡμέρας πολλάς 2K 14.2.

2. May be used substantivally: οὐχ οὗτοι οἱ λόγοι μου .. 'Wasn't that what I said ..?' Jn 4.2; ἕως τούτου 'up to this moment' Ex 7.16; ἐν τούτῳ γνώσῃ ὅτι .. 'through this you shall find out that ..' 7.17; n.pl. ταῦτα: 'this situation, plight' Hb 2.13, Ma 1.9. **b.** τοῦτο cataphorically elaborated by the following ὅτι-clause: ἕνεκεν τούτου ὅτι .. 'on account of the fact that ..' Ex 18.11; 4M 2.9. **c**. opposed to "you": οὗτος δανιεῖ σοι, σὺ δὲ τούτῳ οὐ δανιεῖς 'he will lend to you, but you will not lend to him' De 28.44. **d.** may resume a preceding noun: λίθον, ὃν .., οὗτος ἐγενήθη .. 'a stone, which .., that one became ..' Ps 117.22.

3. When used attributively, it mostly follows the noun nucleus with the pattern ὁ λόγος οὗτος, even when an attributive adjective is further added – ὁ κλύδων ὁ μέγας οὗτος 'this enormous wave' Jn 1.12; anarthrous – ἑπτὰ οὗτοι 'these seven' Zc 4.10, ἐν παγίδι ταύτῃ Ps 9.16, ἐν ὁδῷ ταύτῃ 141.4, δόξα αὕτη 149.9. Exc. τὸ ὄρος τοῦτο τὸ ἀγαθόν De 3.25, αὕτη ἡ ἰσχύς 'this power' Hb 1.11, τὴν πολλὴν ταύτην ὕβριν 'this great arrogance' Je 13.10. **b.** οὗτος ὁ πρωτότοκος 'This is the firstborn' Ge 48.18 is theoretically ambiguous. See under ἐκεῖνος. **c.** ταύτῃ 'in this way': 4M 2.2.

4. When used substantivally, it may or may not concord with the following predicate noun: Αὕτη ἡ σύγκρισις αὐτοῦ 'This is its interpretation' Ge 40.18 ǁ Τοῦτο ἡ σ. αὐτοῦ vs. 12.

***5.** οὗτος .. δεύτερος 'one .. the other': ἐκ τοῦ κλίτους τούτου .. ἐκ τοῦ κλίτους τοῦ δευτέρου 'on one side .. on the other side' Ex 25.18.

6. repeated to indicate reciprocity – πῆχυν ἐκ τούτου καὶ πῆχυν ἐκ τούτου 'one cubit on one side and one cubit on the other' Ex 26.13 (ǁ ἔνθεν καὶ ἔνθεν); τοῦτον ταπεινοῖ καὶ τοῦτον ὑψοῖ 'he humbles one and exalts another' Ps 74.8; ἔκλινεν ἐκ τούτου εἰς τοῦτο 'inclined from one to the other' 74.9; οὗτοι .. οὗτοι .. 'some .. others ..' Da 12.2 TH (LXX οἱ μὲν .. οἱ δὲ ..); ἐὰν .. βουλεύσωνται οὗτοι καὶ οὗτοι .. 'should either party decide ..' 1M 8.30; 9.17.

Cf. οὕτως and ἐκεῖνος.

οὕτως, adv. Rarely (e.g. Jb 27.2) οὕτω: cf. Thack. 136.

thus, in this way, underlining the notion of comparability and analogy.

A. anaphoric, w. ref. to what precedes: **a.** οὕτως ἔσται τὸ σπέρμα σου Ge 15.5 ("so numerous"); οὕτως λελάληκεν 24.30; οὕ. ποιήσω σοι Am 4.12*bis*; Na 1.12; as predicate of εἰμί, which, however, may be understood, ἔσται οὕ. Zc 14.8, οὕ. ὁ λαὸς οὗτος καὶ οὕ. τὸ ἔθνος τοῦτο .. οὕ. πάντα τὰ ἔργα τῶν χειρῶν αὐτῶν Hg 2.14; οὐχ οὕ. 'that is not true' Ge 4.15. **b.** w. correlative force, *so much, accordingly*: ἐγενήθη καθὼς συνέκρινεν ἡμῖν, οὕ. καὶ συνέβη Ge 41.13; κατὰ τὸ πλῆθος αὐτῶν οὕ. ἥμαρτόν μοι 'according to their multitude they sinned against me' Ho 4.7; ἔσται καθὼς ὁ λαὸς οὕ. καὶ ὁ ἱερεύς 'it will be *Like nation like priest*' 4.9; w. correlative κατά τι – κατὰ τὸ παραδειχθέν σοι .. οὕ. ποιήσεις 'in accordance with what was shown to you .., so shall you do' Ex 27.8; with ὡς 10.14f, De 8.5, Jl 2.4, with καθώς, Ho 11.2, Zc 1.6, with καθάπερ, Ex 7.6, 2M 2.29; with καθότι, Le 24.20; with ὃν τρόπον Am 3.12, 5.14, Mi 3.3f, Zc 7.13, 8.13, 14f; the relationship between the two members can be that of antithetical contrast, "as (καθώς) I called them, so (οὕτως) they departed from my presence' Ho 11.2, sim. Zc 8.13; οὐχ οὕ... ὡς .. 'not so much .. as ..' 3M 5.22; οὐχ οὕ... ὥστε + inf., 'not so .. as to' 4M 5.31, 9.17, 10.14. **c.** = τάδε, namely direct object: οὕ. ἔδειξέ μοι κύριος 'thus showed me the Lord' Am 7.1, 4, 7, 17. Perh. Am 4.12*bis* (see **a.** above) also belongs here. **d.** On the repeated καί in a formula such as ὡς καὶ .. οὕτως καὶ .., see under καί **2c**. **e.** οὕ. καὶ οὕ., without elaborating and going into details: Jo 7.20, Jd 18.4.

B. cataphoric, w. ref. to what follows: οὕ. ποιήσεις τὴν κιβωτόν 'this is how you ought to make the ark' Ge 6.15; οὕ. ποίησον, καθὰ εἴρηκας 18.5; Am 4.12*bis*, possibly 5.14, 7.1, 4, 7, 17; foll. by a καθάπερ clause, Ex 7.10.

Cf. οὗτος.

οὐχί.

1. *Surely it is the case that ..?*, positioned at the very beginning of a sentence which expects an affirmative answer: Οὐχὶ διὰ τοῦ θεοῦ ἡ διασάφησις αὐτῶν ἐστιν; 'Surely the exposition of them is through God?' Ge 40.8; οὐχὶ θεὸς εἷς ἔκτισεν ἡμᾶς; 'surely one god created us?' Ma 2.10*a*; 2.10*b*; Hb 2.6; Nu 23.12.

2. 'No' as an answer to a question asking for confirmation: Nu 22.30; Οὐχί, κύριε 'No, sir' Zc 4.5, 13; to a suggestion or proposal, Ge 19.2 (ἀλλά introducing a counter-proposal).

3. disputing the other person's statement: Οὐχί, ἀλλὰ ἐγέλασας 'No, that is not true. You did laugh' Ge 18.15; 42.12.

4. signaling dissent: Οὐχί, κύριε Ge 23.15, 42.12; οὐχί, ἀλλὰ Nu 13.31.

5. equivalent to οὐ and negativing part of a clause: καὶ οὐχὶ νῦν Nu 24.17; De 4.26; οὐχι .. ἀλλ' ἢ .. 5.3; μωρὸς καὶ οὐχὶ σοφός 32.6; To 8.7 𝔊[II] (𝔊[I] οὐ).

Cf. οὐ and μή.

ὀφείλημα, ατος. n.ʃ

that which is owed: De 24.10 (|| τὸ δάνειον vs. 11), 1M 15.8; painful to recall, λύπην καὶ ὀ. 1E 3.19. Cf. ὀφείλω, δάνειον.

ὀφείλω: fut. ὀφειλήσω, inf. ὀφειλήσειν; unaugmented aor.(?) ὄφελον, on which see Schwyzer II 346.5, 554, but BDF § 67.2: ptc. with ἐστίν understood.

1. *to have an obligation to repay*, 'owe': + acc. rei and dat. pers., πᾶν χρέος ἴδιον, ὃ ὀφείλει σοι ὁ πλησίον 'every personal debt owed by your neighbour' De 15.2; ὁ ὀφείλων ὡς ᾧ ὀφείλει 'the debtor as the creditor' Is 24.2 (|| δανείζω); εἰς τὸ βασιλικόν 'the royal treasury' 1M 13.14. **b.** *to be obliged to execute*: + acc. rei (v.n.), καθαρισμόν 'purification' Pr 14.9.

2. *to make onself liable to* a penalty: + acc., θάνατον To 6.13, τιμωρίαν 'punishment' 4M 11.3, αἰσχύνην Jb 6.20; τῆς ὀφειλομένης κολάσεως 'the punishment they deserved' 3M 7.10; + dat., θανάτῳ Wi 12.20. **b.** + inf.: τὸν μὴ ὀφείλοντα κολασθῆναι 'one who does not deserve to be punished' Wi 12.15.

3. ὄφελον with a fin. verb* introduces an unreal or intense wish, 'would that ..': + indic. aor. with ref. to what did not happen in the past, Ὄφελον ἀπεθάνομεν πληγέντες ὑπὸ κυρίου 'Would that we had died, having been smitten by the Lord' Ex 16.3; Nu 14.2, 20.3, Jb 14.13. **b.** + opt. aor. with ref. to what one wishes would happen now or in the future, ὄ. κατευθυνθείησαν αἱ ὁδοί μου 'Would that my ways were straightened' Ps 118.5; εἰ γὰρ ὄ. δυναίμην .. Jb 30.24; 4K 5.3. See under εἰ.

On the morphology of ὄφελον, see BDAG s.v. See also Muraoka 2000.

Cf. δανείζω, ὀφείλημα.

ὄφελος, ους. n.ʃ

benefit, usefulness: Jb 15.3. Cf. ὠφέλεια **1**.

ὀφθαλμός, οῦ. m.

organ of sight, 'eye': ὀ. ὁρᾷ Pr 20.12 (|| οὖς), ἐπάρας .. τοὺς ~οὺς αὐτοῦ εἶδεν .. Ge 13.10; οἱ ~οὶ ὑμῶν βλέπουσιν .. Ge 45.12; οἱ ~οὶ ὑμῶν ὄψονται Ma 1.5; ὀ. τοῦ μὴ ὁρᾶν πονηρά Hb 1.13; ἦρα τοὺς ~ούς μου καὶ εἶδον καὶ ἰδοὺ .. Zc 1.18; ἡ κόρη τοῦ ~οῦ 'the pupil of the eye' 2.8; giving attention, οἱ ~οὶ κυρίου .. ἐπὶ ^τῆς γῆς^ De 11.12, θήσω ~ούς μου ἐπὶ σέ 'I shall look after you well' Je 47.4 (|| στηρίζω 24.6, Am 9.4); ἐπὶ τὸν οἶκον Ιουδα διανοίξω τοὺς ~ούς μου Zc 12.4; στηριῶ τοὺς ~ούς μου ἐπ' αὐτοὺς εἰς κακά Am 9.4 (see under στηρίζω); directed towards object of desire, "their eyes were after their fathers' objects of desire" Ez 20.24, ὀ. πονηρός 'greedy ..' Si 34.13, see also the idiom φείδεται ὁ ὀ. (s.v. φείδομαι) and opp. ἐν ἀγαθῷ ~ῷ 'generously, liberally' 32.10, 12. In prepositional phrases: ἐν ~οῖς '(a pleasure) to be looked at' Jb 21.8, cf. Or ad loc. (Hagedorn 1997. 2.352); θάνατος αὐτῶν ἐν ~οῖς αὐτῶν 'death was staring at them' Es C 11 o'; ἐξ ~ῶν τινος '(to be expelled or disappear) out of sbd's sight or view' Am 9.3, Jn 2.5, Zp 3.7; λάθῃ ῥῆμα ἐξ ~ῶν τῆς συναγωγῆς 'a matter should go unnoticed by the congregation' Le 4.13; ἐξ ~ῶν τῆς συναγωγῆς γενηθῇ 'should happen unnoticed by ..' Nu 15.24; κατ' ~ούς τινος 'before the eyes of, under the nose of sbd' 2K 13.5B + 4K 25.7B (*L* ἐνώπιον), Je 52.10: see under κατά **II 3b** and Sollamo, *Semiprep.*, 153-5, 332f. **b.** source of tears: Je 9.1, Si 34.13.

Cf. βλέπω, ὄμμα: Schmidt 1.370-8; Shipp 426f.

ὀφθαλμοφανῶς. adv.ʃ*

so that everyone can see: of a notice put out, Es 8.13 o'.

ὀφιόδηκτος, ον.ʃ*

bitten by a snake: *s* enchanter, Si 12.13.

ὀφιομάχης, ου. m.ʃ *

a kind of locust: allowed as food, Le 11.22 (|| βροῦχος, ἀττάκης, ἀκρίς). Cf. ἀκρίς.

ὄφις, εως. m.

serpent: said to be φρονιμώτατος πάντων τῶν θηρίων τῶν ἐπὶ τῆς γῆς 'the shrewdest of all the animals ..' Ge 3.1; ἐφ' ὁδοῦ 'at the roadside' 49.17; δάκῃ αὐτὸν ὁ ὄ. 'a serpent bites him' Am 5.19; λείξουσι χοῦν ὡς ὄ. 'they will lick dust as a serpent' Mi 7.17, cf. Je 26.22; θανατῶν 'deadly' Nu 21.6, Je 8.17; ὄφις δάκνων καὶ σκορπίος De 8.15. Cf. ἀσπίς, δράκων, ἔχις, κεράτης: Dafni 2000.

ὄφλησις, εως.ʃ *

penalty: Ba 3.8. Cf. τιμωρία.

ὀφρῦς, ύος. f.ʃ

eyebrow: to be shaved, Le 14.9.

ὀχεία, ας. f.ʃ

act of (male animals) *covering*: ἵππος εἰς ~αν Si 36.6.

ὀχλαγωγέω: aor.act.subj. ὀχλαγωγήσω.ʃ

to play the demagogue: ἐπὶ (s.v. **III 4d**) τὸν οἶκον Ιακωβ Am 7.16. Cf. δημαγωγία: Horsley 1994.111f.

ὀχλέω: aor.subj.pass. ὀχληθῶ.ʃ

to cause trouble to, annoy: abs., *o* 'general public' understood, 3M 5.41; + acc. pers., *s* δαιμόνιον ἢ πνεῦμα πονηρόν To 6.8 𝔊[I].

ὄχλος, ου. m.

mass of individuals: army, ἐν ~ῳ βαρεῖ καὶ ἐν χειρὶ ἰσχυρᾷ 'with a host of heavily-armed powerful troops' Nu 20.20, ὄ. ἰσχυρός Is 43.17, ~ων πλῆθος 3M 2.7, δυνάμεων πολλῶν 'consisting of many armies' Da 11.10 TH; nation, ὄ. πολύς Je 38.8, cf. ~οι ἐθνῶν 'masses of various nations' Wi 6.2; often w. πολύς, 2C 20.15, 1E 8.88, Ju 7.18, Je 38.8, Ez 17.17, Da 11.10 LXX, 13. **b**. a large crowd gathered, 1E 5.62, 2E 3.12; pl., Ez 16.40, Da 3.4 LXX (including dignitaries), 2M 4.40.

Cf. ἄθροισμα, λαός, πλῆθος, πολυοχλία, συναγωγή.

ὀχυρός, ά, όν.

firm, lasting: *s* πόλις Ex 1.11, Nu 32.36, De 3.5, Mi 7.12; ὀχυραὶ τετειχισμέναι '.. walled' Nu 13.29; τόπος Ps 70.3; τὰ τείχη τὰ ὑψηλὰ καὶ τὰ ~ά 'the high and solid walls' De 28.52; n.(?) pl. *securely fortified places* Is 37.26. Cf. ὀχύρωμα, ἐρυμνός.

ὀχυρόω: aor. ὠχύρωσα, inf. ὀχυρῶσαι, ptc. ὀχυρώσας, subj. ὀχυρώσω, pass. ὠχυρώθην; pf.ptc.pass. ὠχυρωμένος.

to strengthen structure of against attack, 'fortify': + acc., ὕψος ἰσχύος 'a powerful (fortress positioned) high up' Je 28.53, πόλιν Si 48.17, οἴκους Ep Je 17, ὄρος 1M 4.61, πύλας 'gates' 15.39; πρός ἀσφάλειαν 'for security' 14.37, τείχεσιν 'with walls' 2C 11.11. **b**. fig., ἐκραταιώθησαν καὶ ὠχυρώθησαν .. τοῦ μὴ φαγεῖν κοινά 'they were firmly determined .. not to eat profane things' 1M 1.62.

Cf. ὀχύρωμα, ὀχύρωσις, προσοχυρόω.

ὀχύρωμα, ατος. n.

1. *fortress*: ᾠκοδόμησε Τύρος ~ατα ἑαυτῇ 'Tyre built herself fortresses' Zc 9.3; ‖ ἰσχύς Am 5.9; ‖ πόλις Mi 5.11; ὀ. τοῦ τείχους 'walled f.' Is 22.10.

2. *prison*: εἰς τὸ ὀ. εἰς τὸν τόπον, ἐν ᾧ οἱ δεσμῶται τοῦ βασιλέως κατέχονται '.. where the king's prisoners are held' Ge 39.20.

Cf. ὀχυρός, ὀχυρωμάτιον, δεσμωτήριον, δυνάστευμα, πυργόβαρις.

ὀχυρωμάτιον, ου. n.ʃ *

dim. of ὀχύρωμα, q.v.: 1M 16.15.

ὀχύρωσις, εως. f.ʃ

act of fortifying: a city, 1M 10.11, 14.10. Cf. ὀχυρόω.

ὀψάριον, ου. n.ʃ

cooked food: πλεῖονα To 2.2 𝔊[II] (𝔊[I] ὄψον). Cf. ὄψον, ὄψος: Kallitsunakis; Shipp 427.

ὀψέ.ʃ

late in the day, in the evening: Ex 30.8, Je 2.23; *τὸ ὀψέ = ὀψέ Is 5.11; *τὸ πρὸς ὀψέ = ὀψέ Ge 24.11. On the redundant article, see BDF § 160 and Mayser II 2 § 104. Cf. ὄψιμος, ἑσπέρα, πρωΐ.

ὀψία, ας. f.ʃ

evening: Jd 13.1. Cf. ὀψέ, ἑσπέρα.

ὀψίζω: aor.subj. ὀψίσω.ʃ

to act late in the evening: + ὀρθρίζω 1K 17.16*L*. **b**. *to arrive late at night*: *s* hum., Si 36.31. Cf. ὀρθρίζω.

ὄψιμος, ον.

far on in time, 'late': *s* the spring rainfall, βρέξει ὑμῖν ὑετὸν πρόϊμον καὶ ~ον 'he will shower upon you the early and the later rain' Jl 2.23, sim. De 11.14, Je 5.24; wheat and spelt not yet ripened, Ex 9.32; rain cloud, Pr 16.15. Cf. ὀψέ, πρόϊμος: Shipp 427f.

ὄψις, εως. f.

1. *outward appearance, look*: ἡ παρθένος ἦν καλὴ τῇ ὄψει 'the maiden was good-looking' Ge 24.16; ὡραία τῇ ὄψει 26.7; καλὸς τῷ εἴδει καὶ ὡραῖος τῇ ὄψει 39.7, τοῦ προσώπου Da 3.19 TH (LXX: μορφή); pl., αἰσχραί 'ugly' Ge 41.21; ὡς ὄ. λαμπάδων 'something that looks like torches' Ez 1.13; ‖ ἰδέα 2M 3.16.

2. *that which is visible*: καλύψει τὴν ὄψιν τῆς γῆς καὶ οὐ δυνήσῃ κατιδεῖν τὴν γῆν 'it [= the locusts] will cover the surface of the earth and you will not be able to recognise it' Ex 10.5, sim. Nu 22.5; τῆς ἁφῆς 'the visible symptom of the infection' Le 13.3.

3. *act of visually perceiving*: ἔρχομαι ὑπὸ τὴν ~ιν 'come into view' Es E 9, τεθεαμένος ὑπὸ ~ιν 2M 3.36, ὑπὸ ~ιν ὁράω 'to see with one's own eyes' 12.42; ἐν ~ει ἀνθρώπων 'from human perspective' Wi 3.4.

4. *eyesight*: To 14.2 𝔊[I].

Cf. εἶδος, μορφή, πρόσοψις, ὅρασις, περιγραφή: Brunschwig 1973.

ὄψον, ου.ʃ

cooked food: πολλά To 2.2 𝔊[I] (𝔊[II] ὀψάριον); πλεῖονα 7.9 𝔊[I]. Cf. ὄψος, ὀψάριον, ἔδεσμα: Shipp 428; Kallitsunakis.

ὀψοποίημα, ατος. n.ʃ*

food: pl., Ju 12.1.

ὄψος, ους. n.ʃ

fish as food: τῆς θαλάσσης Nu 11.22. Cf. ἰχθῦς, ὄψον.

ὀψώνιον, ου. n.ʃ Alw. pl.

pay or more likely, *provisions or victuals, as remuneration for labour*: of guards, 1E 4.56; of soldiers, 1M 3.28, 14.32. Cf. μισθός: Heidland, *TDNT* 5.591f.; Shipp 429; Caragounis; Spicq 2.600-3; *ND* 2.93.

Π

παγγέωργος, ον.ʃ *
serving as master-gardener: metaph., *s* λογισμός 'rational will' 4M 1.29. Cf. γεωργός.

παγετός, οῦ. m.ʃ
frost: night frost indicative of severe climate, τῆς ἡμέρας συγκαιόμενος τῷ καύματι καὶ ~ῷ τῆς νυκτός Ge 31.40, sim. Je 43.30, Ba 2.25; εὐδία ἐπὶ ~ῷ 'fair weather with frost' Si 3.15. Cf. πάγος, ῥῖγος.

παγιδεύω.ʃ *
to trap: metaph., *s* hum., τὴν ψυχήν μου 1K 28.9; pass., *o* hum. in a metaph. of being overtaken by misfortune, ‖ θηρεύω Ec 9.12. Cf. παγίς: Schneider, *TDNT* 5.595f.

παγιόω: aor.impv.pass. παγιώθητι.ʃ
pass. *to hold fast* to sth: ἐν ^τῷ φόβῳ τοῦ θεοῦ^ Si 2.6¶. Cf. πήγνυμι: Auwers 41.

παγίς, ίδος. f.
trap: set on road, π. σκολιὰ ἐπὶ πάσας τὰς ὁδοὺς αὐτοῦ 'a crooked trap on all his ways' Ho 9.8; σχασθήσεται π. ἐπὶ τῆς γῆς ..; 'Would a trap on the ground spring ..?' Am 3.5, ~ας ἔστησαν .. συνελαμβάνοσαν Je 5.26, ~ας ἔκρυψαν 'set the traps concealed' 18.22; φόβος καὶ βόθυνος καὶ π. Is 24.17, sim. Je 31.43; θηρευτῶν 'of hunters' Ps 90.3, τῶμ θηρευόντων 123.7; verbal, π. διαβολῆς γλώσσης Si 51.2; *o* of τίθημι Ps 118.110, of πήγνυμι and π. θανάτου To 14.10; metaph., *that which occasions a mistaken conduct*, Pr 20.25. Cf. παγιδεύω, βρόχος, σκάνδαλον.

παγκρατής, ές.ʃ
capable of accomplishing anything, 'almighty': τὸν ~ῆ κύριον 2M 3.22. Cf. παντοκράτωρ.

πάγος, ους. n.(m.): see Thack. 159.
frost: π. ἐπὶ τῆς γῆς Ex 16.14; ἐν ἡμέραις ~ους 'in a frosty period' Na 3.17; ‖ ψῦχος Zc 14.6, Da 3.69. Cf. παγετός, πάχνη, ψῦχος: Schmidt 2.286-8.

παθεινός, ή, όν.ʃ*
mourning, grieving: subst.m., Jb 29.25¶. Cf. πένθος: LSG s.v.

παθοκράτεια, ας. f.ʃ *
act of bringing or *keeping under control*: 4M 13.5, 16. Cf. παθοκρατέω.

παθοκρατέω.ʃ *
pass. *to be governed by passion*: *s* hum., 4M 7.20. Cf. παθοκράτεια, πάθος.

πάθος, ους. n.
1. *misfortune*: Jb 30.31 (v.l. πένθος 'sorrow'; ‖ κλαυθμός). **b**. ἐν σώματι 'bodily complaint' Pr 25.20.
2. *that which one mentally or physically experiences and also dictates one's thoughts and actions*, 'passion' as a t.t. of the Stoic philosophy: manifested as gluttony, lust (4M 1.3), malice, anger, fear, pain (1.4), pleasure (1.21).

παιάν, ᾶνος. m.ʃ
battle-song: + σάλπιγξ 'trumpet' 2M 15.25.

παιγνία, ας. f.ʃ
play as amusement: Jd 16.27B. **b**. *jestful, contemptuous attitude* (?): Je 29.17, cf. Hb 1.10. Cf. παίζω.

παίγνιον, ου. n.ʃ
plaything, toy: τύραννοι ~α αὐτοῦ 'princes are his toys' Hb 1.10. **b**. *playful act*, 'game': ἐπιτιμήσεως 'of rebuke' Wi 12.26; ‖ πανηγυρισμός'festive celebration' 15.12.
Cf. παίζω.

παιδάριον, ου. n.
young male child, 'boy': Ge 22.5 (Abraham speaking of Isaac); ‖ παιδίον 44.22 (with intense affection?), To 6.3 𝔊[I] (‖ παιδίον 5.18); παιδαρίων καὶ κορασίων παιζόντων ἐν ταῖς πλατείαις αὐτῆς 'young boys and girls playing on its streets' Zc 8.5, Jl 3.3 (‖ κοράσιον); 1K 20.21 (‖ νεανίσκος vs. 22; *L* νεανίας); applied even to a foetus still in its mother's womb, *SIG*[3] 1163.5. **b**. *young male*: of working age - foreman, Ru 2.5, 6; general farm-hand, 2.9. **c**. *childhood*: ἐκ ~ου 'since childhood' Je 31.11.
Cf. παιδίον, νεανίσκος, τέκνον, κοράσιον: Schmidt 2.428f.; Shipp 433f; *ND* 1.87; Muraoka 2001a.18f.

παιδεία, ας. f.
1. *education, instruction* (in religion and morality): κυρίου De 11.2 (subj. gen.); οὐκ ἐδέξατο ~αν 'he refused to be educated' Zp 3.2, sim. 3.7, Je 5.3; οὐ μὴ λάβητε ~αν τοῦ ἀκούειν τοὺς λόγους μου; 'are you never going to take to heart what I say to you?' 42.13.
2. *body of knowledge to be inculcated*: ἀποκαλύψη ~αν πρὸς τοὺς δούλους αὐτοῦ Am 3.7; τοῦ ἐλέγχειν ~αν αὐτοῦ 'to scrutinize his teaching' Hb 1.12; + σοφία Si prol. 3, 1.27, Pr 1.2; στόματος 'on speech' 23.7; συνέσεως καὶ ἐπιστήμης 50.27; ‖ θεσμοί 'rules of conduct' Pr 1.8.
3. *lesson taught or learned by way of punishment or constructive criticism*: Je 37.14 (‖ πληγή); + ἐπίπληξις '(divine) rebuke' 2M 7.32; ‖ ἔλεγχος Pr 12.1.
Cf. παιδεύω, ἀνατροφή: Bertram 1932.

παιδευτής, οῦ; voc. ~ά. m.
educator, instructor: ***s*** God, ἐγὼ π. ὑμῶν Ho 5.2; hum., πολλῶν Si 37.19; divine law, 4M 5.34. Cf. παιδεύω, παιδεία: Spicq 3.1-3; LSG s.v.

παιδεύω: fut. ~δεύσω, pass. ~δευθήσομαι; aor. ἐπαίδευσα, inf. ~δεῦσαι, subj. ~δεύσω, impv. ~δευσον, opt.3s ~δεύσαι, pass. ἐπαιδεύθην, subj. ~δευθῶ, ptc. ~δευθείς, impv. ~δεύθητι; pf.ptc.pass. πεπαιδευμένος.
1. *to instruct*: ***s*** God + acc. pers., De 4.36; τῇ ἐπιστήμῃ αὐτῶν 'through their knowledge' Ez 28.3.
2. *to teach lesson by way of punishment, to discipline*: + acc. pers., ἐπὶ ταῖς ἁμαρτίαις ὑμῶν 'on account of ..' Le 26.18; πόνῳ καὶ μάστιγι Je 6.8, ζυγῷ βαρεῖ .. ἐν μάστιξιν 'with a heavy yoke .. and with whips' 2C 10.11; ***o*** rebellious, quarrelsome son, De 21.18; παιδεύσω αὐτοὺς ἐν τῇ ἀκοῇ τῆς θλίψεως αὐτῶν 'I shall discipline them through the rumour of their suffering' Ho 7.12; ἦλθον παιδεῦσαι αὐτοὺς .. ἐν τῷ παιδεύεσθαι αὐτοὺς ἐν ταῖς δυσὶν ἀδικίαις αὐτῶν '.. on account of their two injustices' 10.10; ***s*** ἀποστασία 'apostasy' Je 2.19 (|| ἐλέγχω); + ἐλέγχω, διδάσκω Si 18.13.
3. *to train and teach*: ***s*** God + acc. pers., ὡς εἴ τις παιδεύσαι τὸν υἱὸν αὐτοῦ, οὕτως κύριος ὁ θεός σου παιδεύσει σε De 8.5; 32.10; || σοφίζω Ps 104.22; || διδάσκω Si 30.2 (father > son); ***o*** hum., ἐπιστήμων καὶ πεπαιδευομένος 'sensible and well-educated' Si 40.29. **b.** *to train and teach in*: + acc. rei, δικαιοσύνην 'justice' 4M 5.24 (|| ἐκδιδάσκω). **c.** mid. *to submit oneself to instruction*: Ps 2.10 (|| συνίημι), Si 6.32.
Cf. παιδεία, παιδευτής, ἀπαίδευτος, μεταπαιδεύω, (ἐκ)διδάσκω, ἐλέγχω, μανθάνω, συνετίζω: Schmidt 4.100-02; Bertram, *TDNT* 5.608-12.

παιδίον, ου. n.
young child: male, π. ὀκτὼ ἡμερῶν περιτμηθήσεται ὑμῖν πᾶν ἀρσενικόν 'every male (child) of yours shall be circumcised when eight days old' Ge 17.12; θηλάζει π. Σάρρα 'S. is suckling a child' 21.7; ηὐξήθη τὸ π. καὶ ἀπεγαλακτίσθη 'the child grew and was weaned' 21.8; τὰς γυναῖκάς μου καὶ τὰ ~ία 30.26 (including teenagers); a few months old, Ex 2.6; π. μικρόν Is 11.6, π. νήπιον 11.8; opp. πρεσβύτης Ba 4.15. **b.** newly-wed son-in-law: To 8.21 𝔊II. **c.** female: old enough to marry, To 7.11 𝔊I (|| 𝔊II θυγάτηρ). **d.** includes girls, Ex 21.4, 5 (= υἱοὶ ἢ θυγατέρες); καταφιλῆσαι τὰ ~ία μου καὶ τὰς θυγατέρας Ge 31.28 (ref. to grandchildren). **e.** of animals: camel, Ge 32.15; calf and lamb, Le 22.28. **f.** foetus: ἐσκίρτων τὰ ~ία ἐν αὐτῇ 'the children skipped inside her' 25.22; Ex 21.22. **g.** *childhood*: ἐκ ~ου 'since ..' Is 46.3 (|| ἐκ κοιλίας).
The feature of endearment and affection appears to be present in some cases: e.g., Οὐ μὴ ἴδω τὸν θάνατον τοῦ ~ίου μου Ge 21.16; οὐκ ἠξιώθην καταφιλῆσαι τὰ ~ία μου καὶ τὰς θυγατέρας 31.28 (|| τέκνα 43 and υἱοί 55); To 6.3 𝔊I (|| παιδίον 5.18).
Cf. παῖς, παιδάριον, παιδίσκη, νήπιος, τέκνον, υἱός: Schmidt 2.426-8; Shipp 433; Muraoka 2001a. 18f.

παιδίσκη, ης. f.
female servant: part of nomad's possessions, ἐγένετο αὐτῷ πρόβατα καὶ μόσχοι καὶ ὄνοι, παῖδες καὶ ~αι, ἡμίονοι καὶ κάμηλοι Ge 12.16; owned by a wife, 16.1; with a child fathered by the mistress's husband, 21.10; one's own given away to a daughter on marriage, 29.24; sexually exploited by both father and son, Am 2.7 (cf. Tht PG 81.1673: παλλακίς 'concubine'); χωρὶς δούλων αὐτῶν καὶ ~ῶν αὐτῶν 2E 2.65, Ne 7.67. **b.** a female counterpart of παῖς: τὸν παῖδα αὐτοῦ ἢ τὴν ~ην αὐτοῦ Ex 21.20; 21.32, sim. Le 25.6 (|| μισθωτός, πάροικος), To 10.10 𝔊II; ranked higher than δοῦλος and δούλη Le 25.44; lower in rank than family members, ὁ παῖς σου καὶ ἡ π. σου ὥσπερ καὶ σύ De 5.14 (|| οἰκέτης vs. 15); same person called ἅβρα Ju 10.2, π. 10.10, δούλη 12.15; || δοῦλος Ps 122.2. **c.** self-effacing appellation: ἡ παιδίσκη σου = ἐγώ Ps 85.16.
Cf. ἅβρα, δούλη, κοράσιον, λάτρις, παῖς, οἰκέτης: Schmidt 2.429; Shipp 430; Spicq 1978.223f.; Heinen.

παιδοποιέω: aor.mid.inf. ~ποιήσασθαι.ʃ
mid. *to produce offspring*: ***s*** male, 2M 14.25. Cf. παιδοποιΐα.

παιδοποιΐα, ας. f.ʃ
v.n. of παιδοποιέω: 4M 17.6.

παίζω: fut. παίξομαι; aor. ἔπαιξα, impv.3s παιξάτω.
to engage in relaxed and lively activities, 'play, have fun': παίζοντα μετὰ Ισαακ Ge 21.9 (of two children); παῖζε καὶ ποίει τὰ ἐνθυμήματά σου 'have fun as you please' Si 35.12; of a dallying married couple, Ge 26.8; παιδαρίων καὶ κορασίων παιζόντων ἐν ταῖς πλατείαις αὐτῆς 'boys and girls playing in its streets' Zc 8.5; Ex 32.6; τοῖς ποσὶν παίζουσαι Is 3.16 (of women coquettishly dancing along?); ἐν συνεδρίῳ αὐτῶν παιζόντων 'their fun-making party' Je 15.17, μετὰ συναγωγῆς παιζόντων 38.4, ᾀδόντες καὶ φωνὴ παιζόντων 37.19; ἐν αὐτῷ ὡς ὀρνέῳ 'with it like with a bird' Jb 40.29, ἐν λέουσιν 'with lions' Si 47.3; of a show for public entertainment, Jd 16.25; + ὀρχέομαι 'to dance' 2K 6.21, 1C 15.29. Cf. ἐγκατα~, ἐμ~, προσ~, συμπαίζω, παιγνία, παίγνιον: Schmidt 3.449-51, 4.205f.; Shipp 435.

παῖς, δός. c.
1. *child*: ***s*** woman of marriagiable age, Ge 24.28; Λάβε μοι τὴν παῖδα ταύτην εἰς γυναῖκα 34.4; mar-

ried daughter, De 22.15; opp. parents, Pr 29.15, father 4.1. **b.** *descendant*: not only biologically, but also spiritually, Αβρααμ 'of Abraham' 4M 6.17, 22.

2. *person of servile status*: π. οἰκέτης 'domestic servant' Ge 9.25 (of Canaan condemned to such a status vis-à-vis his brothers); ‖ οἰκέτης 44.33, Ex 5.16 (see vs. 15); = οἰκογενεῖς engaged as fighting force, Ge 14.15; house-manager or butler, τῷ ~δὶ αὐτοῦ τῷ πρεσβυτέρῳ τῆς οἰκίας αὐτοῦ τῷ ἄρχοντι πάντων τῶν αὐτοῦ 24.2; ministers and courtiers, ἐναντίον Φαραω καὶ ἐναντίον πάντων τῶν ~δων αὐτοῦ 41.37; king's entourage, Je 52.8; part of nomad's possessions, ἐγένετο αὐτῷ πρόβατα καὶ μόσχοι καὶ ὄνοι, ~δες καὶ παιδίσκαι, ἡμίονοι καὶ κάμηλοι Ge 12.16, sim. 30.43; courteous self-designation, π. σου 18.3 ‖ God calling Abraham π. μου 18.17, Caleb Nu 14.24, Isaiah Is 20.3, Eljakim 22.20, Israel (Jacob) 41.8, Je 26.28; Israel as God's people, PSol 12.6; prophets, τῶν παίδων μου τῶν προφητῶν Je 33.5, 42.15, 51.4 (‖ δοῦλοι 7.25, Ez 38.17), Jb 1.8 (‖ θεράπων 2.3); κύριοι .. τοῦ ~δὸς ὑμῶν Ge 19.2 (Lot to guests); cooks for his master, 18.7; of βασιλεύς 20.8; ~δες καὶ παιδίσκαι 'male and female servants' 12.16, 20.14, To 10.10 𝔊[II]; ἓξ ἔτη δουλεύσει σοι Ex 21.2; vis-à-vis Moses, οἱ παῖδές σου Nu 32.4, 25, 27 (‖ θεράποντες vs. 31). **b.** opp. κύριος– οἰκέται τῷ κυρίῳ ἡμῶν Ge 44.16 (‖ παῖδες vs. 9); Is 24.2 (‖ θεράπαινα), Ex 21.4. **c.** 'your servant(s)' as polite substitute for 'I' (sg.) or 'we' (pl.) where the person of the verb, however, is often that of the speaker, i.e. first person, κτηνοτρόφοι ἐσμὲν οἱ ~δές σου 'your servants are cattlemen' Ge 46.34, but εἰρηνικοί ἐσμεν, οὐκ εἰσὶν οἱ ~δές σου κατάσκοποι 42.11; the sg. often prefers the 3rd pers., ἐπειδὴ εὗρεν ὁ π. σου χάριν 19.19, λαλησάτω ὁ π. σου ῥῆμα 44.18. **d.** a male counterpart of παιδίσκη: τὸν ~δα αὐτοῦ ἢ τὴν παιδίσκην αὐτοῦ Ex 21.20; 21.32, sim. Le 25.6 (‖ μισθωτός, πάροικος); higher positioned than δοῦλος and δούλη 25.44; lower in rank than family members, ὁ π. σου καὶ ἡ παιδίσκη σου ὥσπερ καὶ σύ De 5.14 (‖ οἰκέτης vs. 15).

3. *a period of life when one is a child*, 'childhood': ἐκ ~δὸς ἕως τοῦ νῦν 'since our childhood till now' Ge 46.34.

The primary meaning seems to be a person of minor status whether in terms of descent [son or daughter], **1.** age [child] or **2.** social status [servant]. Cf. Wodke 69f.; Heinen.

Cf. διάκονος, δοῦλος, θεράπων, λειτουργός, οἰκέτης, παιδίσκη, ὑπουργός, κύριος: Schmidt 2.423-6; Shipp 430-3; Zimmerli, *TDNT* 5.673-7, Jeremias ib. 682-700; Shipp 430; Spicq 1978.220f.; Wright; Harl 2001.902; LSG s.v. **I 1**, **II**.

παίω: aor. ἔπαισα, ptc. παίσας, subj. παίσω; pf. πέπαικα.

to smite: in order to harm, ἐν γῇ Αἰγύπτῳ Ex 12.13; + acc. pers., Nu 22.28, Jd 14.19 A (B: πατάσσω); με εἰς σιαγόνα 'me on the cheek' Jb 16.10; ψυχήν Jo 20.9 (‖ πατάσσω vs. 3); fatally, 3K 16.16 (‖ vs. 10 πατάσσω καὶ θανατόω); also + acc. cogn. ἔθνος πληγὴν θυμοῦ 'with an indignant blow' Is 14.6 (‖ πατάσσω), πληγὴν ἐχθροῦ Je 37.14; *s* wild beast, 5.6; on battlefield, 1K 13.4. Cf. κόπτω, πατάσσω, πλήσσω, τύπτω: Schmidt 3.278-80, 283f.

παλάθη, ης. f.

cake of preserved fruit (LSJ): 2K 16.1*L* (B: φοῖνιξ 'date'), Is 38.21 (made of figs), Ju 10.5.

πάλαι. adv.

long ago: + aor., Is 37.26 (‖ ἀρχαῖαι ἡμέραι), Wi 11.14; opp. νῦν Is 48.7; attrib. with the def. art., τὰ π. 'things of old' 48.5, οἱ π. καὶ νῦν Es B 7. **b.** *before now*, 'previously': + impf., Wi 12.27. **c.** *not long ago, recently*: Bel 28 LXX.

Cf. παλαιός, ἀρχαῖος, ἄρτι.

παλαιός, ά, όν.

old and not new: *s* agricultural produce, Le 25.22; φάγεσθε ~ὰ καὶ ~ὰ ~ῶν '.. exceedingly old' 26.10 (:: νέος); ῥάκη .. σχοινία 'rugs .. strings' Je 45.11; ἱστορία 'ancient record' Es E 7; χρόνοι 'times (gone-by)' 2M 6.21; hum., + πρεσβύτης Jb 15.10¶, inhabitant of long standing, Wi 12.3. Cf. πάλαι, παλαίωμα, ἀρχαῖος, πρεσβύτης, νέος, καινός: Schmidt 2.79-87; Trench 249-53.

παλαιόω: fut. παλαιώσω, pass. παλαιωθήσομαι; aor. ἐπαλαίωσα, pass. ἐπαλαιώθην, subj. παλαιωθῶ, impv. παλαιώθητι; pf.mid. πεπαλαίωμαι, ptc. πεπαλαιωμένος.

1. *to make old*: + acc., σάρκα μου La 3.4; hence useless and worthless, ***o*** argument, Jb 32.15.

2. *to make wear out*: + acc. pers., Da TH 7.25.

3. *to continue in existence for a long time*: *s* dwellings and orchards, Is 65.22; mid. λέπρα παλαιουμένη 'chronic leprosy' Le 13.11. **b.** mid. *to become old and worn-out*: *s* clothes, De 29.5, shoes ἀπὸ τῆς πολλῆς ὁδοῦ 'from the long journey' Jo 9.13, wine Si 9.10; hum., Ba 3.10, Ps 6.8; w. no negative connotation, but 'enjoy longevity' Jb 21.7, "keep working till you reach your old age" Si 11.20; hum. bones out of distress, Ps 31.3, garments 101.27; trees, Ez 47.12.

Cf. παλαιός, παλαίωσις, καινίζω.

παλαιστής, οῦ. m. Also spelled παλαστή, ῆς f.

four fingers' breadth as a measure of length, Ex 25.23, Ez 40.5; fig. of extreme brevity, Ps 38.6.

παλαίστρα, ης. f.ʃ

wrestling ring: 2M 4.14. Cf. παλαίω.

παλαίω.ʃ
to wrestle: abs. and *s* δράκων 'snake' Es A 5; μετά τινος [= opponent] Ge 32.24, 25; troops, Jd 20.33 A. Cf. παλαίστρα, ἀντίπαλος.

παλαίωμα, ατος. n.ʃ*
ancient part of the creation (?): alw. pl., Jb 36.28¶, 37.18¶, 21¶, see Ol. ad 36.28 and cf. Caird 1969.26. Cf. παλαιός.

παλαίωσις, εως. f.ʃ
decay: Na 1.15. Cf. παλαιόω.

παλαστή, ῆς. f.⇒ παλαιστής.

πάλιν. adv.
again: π. ἐξαπέστειλεν 'again sent out' Ge 8.10; π. συνάξει σε De 30.3. **b.** καὶ π. 'again and again' Si 36.1.

παλλακή, ῆς. f.
concubine: Ge 22.24 (bearing children); multiple, 25.6 (their children receiving gifts from their father), 35.21 (having intercourse with her father's legitimate son). Cf. γυνή, παλλακίς: Schmidt 2.413f.

παλλακίς, ίδος. f.ʃ
= παλλακή: Jb 19.17.

παλλακός, οῦ. m.ʃ
object of favourite attention and affection, 'minion': Ez 23.20, see Bewer 422.

πάλλομαι.ʃ
to swing oneself to and fro: as a mark of remorse, 2E 9.3, 5.

παμβασιλεύς, έως. m.
absolute monarch: w. ref. to God, Si 50.15. Cf. βασιλεύς: Renehan 2.112.

παμβότανον, ου.n.ʃ*
all the herbage: fig. of abundance, Jb 5.25.

παμμελής, ές.ʃ*
consisting of all kinds of melody: *s* ὕμνος 'hymn' 3M 7.16.

παμμίαρος, ον.ʃ
utterly abominable: *s* hum., 4M 10.17. Cf. μιερός.

παμμιγής, ές.ʃ
mixed of all sorts: *s* πρόπτωσις '(mass) prostration' 2M 3.21, ἔθνη 'all sorts of peoples' 12.13.

παμπληθής, ές.ʃ
very numerous: *s* troops, 2M 10.24. Cf. πολύς, πλῆθος.

παμποίκιλος, ον.ʃ
of all kinds and varieties: *s* torment, 4M 15.11.

παμπόνηρος, ον.ʃ
thoroughly depraved: *s* hum., 2M 14.27.

πάμφυλος, ον.ʃ
pertaining to mixed races or *tribes*: *s* πλῆθος 'population' 2M 12.27; area, 4M 4.11. **b.** subst.m.pl., 2M 8.9.

πανάγιος, α, ον.*
very holy: subst.m., *s* hum. 4M 7.4. Cf. ἅγιος.

πάνδεινος, ον.ʃ
capable of instilling extreme fear: *s* κίνδυνος 'danger' 4M 3.15; situation, 4.7. Cf. δεινός.

πανδημεί. adv.ʃ
wholly, en masse: reinforcing πᾶς – πάντα τὰ σκῦλα αὐτῆς π. 'all of its spoils altogether' De 13.16.

πάνδημος, ον.ʃ
done by all the people: *s* ἱκετεία 'supplication' 2M 3.18.

πανεθνεί. adv.ʃ
together as one nation: Wi 19.8.

πανεπίσκοπος, ον.ʃ
showing universal, beneficent concern: *s* spirit of Wisdom, 7.23.

πανηγυρίζω: aor.impv. ~γύρισον.ʃ
to celebrate a πανήγυρις (q.v.): Is 66.10. Cf. πανηγυρισμός.

πανήγυρις, εως. f.
public festival: of religious character, ἡμέρα ~εως Ho 9.5 (ǁ ἑορτή); joyous and ǁ ἑορτή, νουμηνία, and σάββατον, 2.11. Cf. ἑορτή: Spicq 3.4-8; Casarico; LSG s.v.

πανηγυρισμός, οῦ. m.ʃ
**festive celebration*: ǁ παίγνιον'pastime' Wi 15.12. Cf. πανηγυρίζω.

πάνθηρ, ηρος. m.ʃ
panther: ǁ λέων Ho 5.14; ǁ πάρδαλις 13.7.

πανόδυρτος, ον.ʃ
indicative of profound lament: *s* βοή 3M 4.2, μέλος 'tune' 6.32. Cf. ὀδύρομαι.

πανοικία, ας. f. *
the entire household: excluding immediate kinsmen such as brothers, πᾶσα ἡ π. Ιωσηφ καὶ οἱ ἀδελφοὶ αὐτοῦ καὶ ἡ οἰκία ἡ πατρικὴ αὐτοῦ Ge 50.8; αὐτὸς καὶ οἱ ἀδελφοὶ αὐτοῦ καὶ πᾶσα ἡ π. τοῦ πατρὸς αὐτοῦ 50.22; + κτῆσις 'possessions' Jd 18.21A (B: τέκνα; *L* ἀποσκευή); ~ᾳ 'along with their family' 3M 3.27. Cf. οἰκία.

πανοπλία, ας. f.
full armour: 2K 2.21, Jb 39.20, Si 46.6, 2M 10.30. Cf. ὅπλον: Oepke, *TDNT* 5.295-8.

πανούργευμα, ατος. n.
wonderful feat: pl., σοφίας Si 1.6, ǁ σοφία Ju 11.8. Cf. πανοῦργος: Caird 1969.26f.

πανουργεύομαι: aor.ptc. ~γευσάμενος, subj. ~γεύσωμαι.ʃ *
to play the knave: 1K 23.22. Cf. πανουργία.

πανουργία, ας. f.
1. *knavery*: Nu 24.22, Si 19.23.
2. *cleverness*: Si 21.12.
Cf. πανοῦργος.

πανοῦργος, ον.
1. *knavish*: subst.m., *rogue*, Jb 5.12.

2. *smart, clever*: *s* hum., Si 6.32; capable of being educated, 21.12; σφραγίς 'seal (on my lips)' 22.27; opp. ἄφρων Pr 12.16, 13.16, opp. ἄκακος 'simple-minded' 14.15.

Cf. πανουργία, πανούργευμα.

πάνσοφος, ον.ʃ

wise in every way: *s* God, 4M 1.12; hum., 2.19; divine providence, 13.19. Cf. σοφός.

πανταχῆ. adv.

everywhere: Is 24.11, 3K 2.3. Cf. πανταχοῦ, πάντῃ, πανταχόθεν, ἀλλαχῆ.

πανταχόθεν. adv.ʃ

from every direction: of consensus view, 4M 13.1; 15.32. Cf. πανταχῆ, πάντοθεν, ἀλλαχόθεν.

πανταχοῦ. adv.ʃ

everywhere: Is 42.22. Cf. πανταχῆ.

παντελής, ές.ʃ

complete with nothing missing: *s* ἀπόλαυσις 'enjoyment' 3M 7.16. Cf. ὁλόκληρος.

παντελῶς. adv.

without qualification: π. ἀμήχανον 'absolutely impossible' 2M 3.12, π. ἐν ἐσχάτῃ πνοῇ 'breathing the very last' 3.31, πεποιθώς 'relying' 7.40.

παντεπόπτης, ου. m.ʃ

one who sees all: π. κύριος 2M 9.5. Cf. ὁρατής.

παντευχία, ας.ʃ

= πανοπλία 'complete armour': 4M 3.12.

πάντῃ. adv.ʃ

everywhere: Si 50.22, 3M 4.1. Cf. πανταχῆ.

παντοδαπός, ή, όν.ʃ

of all sorts: *s* δένδρον Jb 40.21. Cf. παντοῖος: Schmidt 4.360f.

παντοδύναμος, ον.ʃ *

omnipotent: *s* spirit of Wisdom, 7.23; God's hand, 11.17; God's word, 17.15. Cf. παντοκράτωρ.

πάντοθεν. adv.

1. *from* or *on all sides*: Je 31.31; περιέσχον με π. 'they surrounded me ..' Si 51.7. Cf. πανταχόθεν.

2. *in every respect*: Je 20.9; στενά μοι π. 2K 24.14B.

παντοῖος, η, ον.

of all sorts: δόματα ~α 'all sorts of gifts' Da 2.6 LXX; 4M 1.34. Cf. παντοδαπός.

παντοκρατορία, ας. f.ʃ*

omnipotence: God's, Si 19.20¶. Cf. παντοκράτωρ.

παντοκράτωρ, ορος. m.

almighty, omnipotent being, as epithet of the God of Israel and often with κύριος: κύριος π. 2K 5.10 +; κύριε π. θεέ 7.25 +; (ὁ) κύριος ὁ θεὸς ὁ π. Ho 12.5 +; (ὁ) κύριος (ὁ) π. Mi 4.4 +; τῷ κυρίῳ ~ρι 3K 19.10 +; κύριος π. θεός τινος 2K 7.27, Hg 1.14 +; ὁ κύριος π. Zc 14.20 +; βασιλεὺς κύριος π. Zc 14.16 +; θεὸς π. ἐθνῶν Je 3.19; π. alone, 1C 29.12, Jb 5.17, 11.7, Wi 7.25, 2M 5.20 +. **b**. alm. attributive adj.: ὁ π. βοηθός '.. helper' Jb 22.25; παντοκράτορι θεῷ ὑψίστῳ Si 50.17; 2M 7.35, 3M 2.8 +.

Cf. παγκρατής, ~τορία, παντοδύναμος: Montevecchi; *ND* 3.118, 6.175, Dogniez 1997, and cf. LSG s.v.

πάντοτε. adv.ʃ

at all times: Wi 11.21, 19.18. Cf. ἀεί: Shipp 438f.; Renehan 2.112f.

παντοτρόφος, ον.ʃ

nurturing all: *s* God's gift, Wi 16.25.

παντοφαγία, ας. f.ʃ *

act of eating anything indiscriminately: + λαιμαργία 'gluttony' 4M 1.27.

πάντως. adv.ʃ

1. *wholly*: π. ἔσται 'it will all happen' To 14.8 𝔊ᴵ.

2. *at any rate*: 2M 3.13, 3M 1.15.

πάνυ. adv.

Indicates the fullest applicability of a given attribute: π. δικαίως 'very justly' 2M 9.6; π. καλῶς 'very well' 12.43; λογοῖς π. καλοῖς 'with very nice words' 15.17. Cf. λίαν, σφόδρα.

πανυπέρτατος, ον.ʃ

highest of all: *s* temple, 3M 1.20. Cf. ὑψηλός, ὑπερμήκης: Renehan 2.113.

πάππος, ου. m.ʃ

grandfather: Si prol. 7. Cf. πρόπαππος, μάμμη.

πάπυρος, ου. m./f.

papyrus: ἕλος καλάμου καὶ ~ου 'marsh of reed and ..' Is 19.6; μὴ θάλλει π. ἄνευ ὕδατος; 'papyrus does not thrive without water, does it?' Jb 8.11 (‖ βούτομον 'sedge'), παρὰ ~ον καὶ κάλαμον καὶ βούτομον 40.21.

παρά prep.

I. + gen. indicates origin, source, starting point of physical movement, 'from': w. αἴρω Ge 43.34, φέρω Ex 35.22, δέχομαι Am 5.11, λαμβάνω Ge 23.13, Zc 6.10*ter*, ἐκζητέω Ex 18.15, Mi 6.8, αἰτέω Ex 3.22, Zc 10.1, κτάομαι 'to acquire' Ge 25.10, κλέπτω 'to steal' Ex 22.12, κομίζω 'to carry off' Ge 38.20, 2M 7.11; ὡς δρόσος π. κυρίου πίπτουσα Mi 5.7; ἀναβάντες παρ' ὑμῶν πρὸς ἡμᾶς 'having come up ..' 1E 2.17; source of misfortune, κατέβη κακὰ π. κυρίου Mi 1.12, ἐγένετο ὀργὴ μεγάλη π. κυρίου Zc 7.12; οὐ ταῦτά ἐστι π. κυρίου; Hb 2.13; source of news, report, τὸ ῥῆμα π. τοῦ θεοῦ Ge 41.32, ὁ λόγος ὁ γενόμενος π. κυρίου πρὸς Ησαίαν Is 2.1; ἀκοὴν ἀκήκοα π. κυρίου Ob 1, ἐρρέθη π. βασιλέως καὶ π. τῶν μεγιστάνων αὐτοῦ Jn 3.7, πυθέσθαι π. κυρίου 'to enquire of the Lord' Ge 25.22, ἔμαθον π. τῶν πατέρων αὐτῶν 'learned from their parents' Si 8.9, cf. ἐρωτᾶν καὶ μανθάνειν ἡμῶν 2M 7.2 (v.l. pr. π.); source of potential and energy, μὴ ἀδυνατεῖ π. τοῦ θεοῦ ῥῆμα; Ge 18.14 (cf. οὐκ ἀδυνατεῖ [*L* ἔστι] π. σοὶ σῴζειν .. 2C 14.10 and Lk

1.37), τὴν σωτηρίαν τὴν π. τοῦ θεοῦ Ex 14.13, ἡ ἀντίληψις αὐτοῦ π. σοῦ 'his help ..' Ps 83.6, τὴν π. τοῦ θεοῦ βοήθειαν 2M 12.11; source of authority, π. κυρίου ἐξῆλθεν τὸ πρόσταγμα τοῦτο Ge 24.50; παρ' ἐμαυτοῦ 'at my discretion' Nu 24.13 (|| ἐν τῇ διανοίᾳ μου 22.18). Cf. βασιλεὺς π. θεοῦ εἶ σὺ ἐν ἡμῖν Ge 23.6.

2. marks the agent of an action analogously to ὑπό τινος: κληθήσεται σου τὸ ὄνομα παρὰ τοῦ θεοῦ .. Ba 5.4, π. κυρίου τὰ διαβήματα αὐτοῦ κατευθύνεται 'his steps are straightened by ..' Ps 36.23, Ἰωάννης καὶ Αβεσσαλωμ οἱ πεμφθέντες παρ' ὑμῶν '.. sent ..' 2M 11.17, cf. ἄνθρωπος ἀπεσταλμένος π. θεοῦ Joh 1.6. **b.** only seemingly so: πάντων τῶν ἡγιασμένων μοι π. τῶν υἱῶν Ισραηλ Nu 18.8, cf. τὸ ἐπιδέκατον, ὃ δέδωκα ὑμῖν παρ' αὐτῶν ἐν κλήρῳ 18.26 and καλεῖται π. τοῖς πολλοῖς νεφθαι 2M 1.36.

3. *in the presence of* [= παρά + dat.]: μοιχωμένη .. π. τοῦ ἀνδρὸς αὐτῆς 'indulging in adultery .. under the nose of her husband' Ez 16.32, but cf. ἀνήρ **1c**. **b.** *in the circle or company of*: τοὺς παρ' αὐτοῦ 'his subordinates' Bel 14 LXX (TH τοῖς παιδαρίοις αὐτοῦ); οἱ π. αὐτῆς 'the members of her household' Pr 31.21; ὁ παρ' αὐτῆς 'its possessor' Ec 5.10, 7.12, 8.8.

II. + dat., indicates proximity, 'beside, at': πάροικος ἐγώ εἰμι π. σοί Ps 38.13 (|| μετά τινος Ge 23.4); οἰκήσομεν παρ' ὑμῖν 34.16; κεκλεμμένον .. παρ' ἐμοί 'stolen property in my possession' 30.33; καταλιπὼν τὰ ἱμάτια αὐτοῦ παρ' ἐμοί 39.15 (|| vs. 12, 13 ἐν ταῖς χερσὶν αὐτῆς); ἔθετο αὐτοὺς ἐν φυλακῇ π. τῷ ἀρχιμαγείρῳ εἰς τὸ δεσμωτήριον 'he put them under house arrest at the chief cook's into the prison cell' 40.3 (|| ἐν τῷ οἴκῳ τοῦ ἀρχι. 41.10); παρὰ σοί 'at your place (Fr. *chez vous*)' Nu 22.9, Am 6.10; παρ' ἐμοὶ γενοῦ 'Come near me!' Ge 23.11; ἐργᾷ παρ' ἐμοί 'you will work with me' 29.27; ἐγένετο .. π. τῷ κυρίῳ τῷ Αἰγυπτίῳ 'he entered .. the Egyptian master's service' 39.2; ὅσα ἂν ᾖ σοι παρ' αὐτῷ 'whatever he might owe you' De 15.3. **b.** marks attitudinal proximity or affinity: οὐκ ἔστιν παρ' αὐτῷ δόξα προσώπου 'with him favouritism is not on' Si 32.15; οὐκ ἔστι παρ' αὐτῷ δόλος Bel 18 LXX; ἐγγὺς π. τῷ θεῷ ἰάσασθαί σε 'God is very much willing to cure you' To 5.10 𝔊II; Jb 10.12.

2. *in relation to*: χάριν ἔχεις παρ' ἐμοί 'you are a favourite of mine' Ex 33.12, cf. εὗρες χάριν π. τῷ θεῷ Lk 1.30; φοβερῷ π. τοῖς βασιλεῦσι τῆς γῆς 'feared by ..' Ps 75.13.

3. *in the estimation of*: μὴ ἴσθι φρόνιμος π. σεαυτῷ 'don't be a judge of your own prudence' Pr 3.7; 14.12 (|| dat. pers. 16.25), 21.15, 26.5.

III. + acc. **1.** indicates a place to the proximity of which one moves: ἐκόμισεν τὰς καμήλους .. π. τὸ φρέαρ 'moved the camels .. to the well' Ge 24.11; ἐκάθητο π. τὴν πύλην Σοδόμων 'sat (down and remained) beside the gate of Sodom' 19.1; στῆτε π. τὰς θύρας '(go and) stand by the doors' De 31.14; λάβε π. χεῖρα 'Take in hand' To 11.4 𝔊I (𝔊II μετὰ ~ας). **b.** no movement involved, but static: τὴν ἄμμον τὴν π. τὸ χεῖλος τῆς θαλάσσης 'the sand on the beach' Ge 22.17; ἐκ Ροωβωθ τῆς π. ποταμόν 36.37; ἐνέμοντο π. τὰς βόας π. τὸ χεῖλος τοῦ ποταμοῦ 'were grazing next to the cows by the edge of the river' 41.3; ἑστάναι π. τὸ χεῖλος τοῦ ποταμοῦ 41.17 (|| ἐπὶ τοῦ ποταμοῦ vs. 1); κέδροι παρ' ὕδατα Nu 24.6 (|| ἐπὶ ποταμῶν); τῆς θεραπαίνης τῆς π. τὸν μύλον 'of the female slave at the handmill' Ex 11.5; 12.22; π. θάλασσαν 'to the west' Nu 2.18 (|| πρὸς λίβα 'to the south' 2.10 and πρὸς βορρᾶν 'to the north' 2.25); π. πόδας ἤδη τὸν ᾅδην ὁρῶντες κείμενον 'already seeing the sheol lying just next to them' 3M 4.8, ἐκ τοῦ π. πόδας ἐν ἑτοίμῳ μόρου 'from the fate in store close by' 6.8; π. τοὺς ἐχθροὺς ἡμῶν 'in the presence of our enemies' Ps 43.11; To 5.6 𝔊I (𝔊II + dat.). **c.** *along*: π. τὸ ὄρος παρελευσόμεθα Nu 20.19.

2. *for the reason of*: + acc. and inf., ἦσαν ἐναντίον αὐτοῦ ὡς ἡμέραι ὀλίγαι π. τὸ ἀγαπᾶν αὐτὸν αὐτήν 'they [the seven years of service] appeared to him like just a few days because he was in love with her' Ge 29.20; π. τὸ μὴ ὑπάρχειν μνήματα 'because there are no graves' Ex 14.11; π. τὸ μὴ δύνασθαι .. καὶ π. τὸ μισῆσαι .. De 9.28; ἐξέλιπον αἱ πόλεις αὐτῶν π. (v.l. διὰ) τὸ μηδένα ὑπάρχειν μηδὲ κατοικεῖν 'their cities died out because there was nobody to live therein' Zp 3.6 where the v.l. suggests reason or cause (so Bo, and Johannessohn, *Präp.*, 234, and cf. Mayser, II 1.331 and Ba 3.28 || διά τι), but the consecutive force is also possible, though such is not attested elsewhere, cf. Th 297 ὥστε and Eth *wa'albo*; Ez 34.8 (|| διά + inf. vs. 5); Je 40.10. For a similar ex., see Je 2.15, 9.10. Cf. διά **II 1**.

3. *more than*, often with πᾶς, but not with a comparative: Ιακωβ ἠγάπα τὸν Ιωσηφ π. πάντας τοὺς υἱοὺς αὐτοῦ Ge 37.3; ἐμεγαλύνθη .. π. τὰς μερίδας πάντων πενταπλασίως 'was five times larger than everybody's portion' 43.34; μέγας κύριος π. πάντας τοὺς θεούς Ex 18.11; Οἶδά σε π. πάντας 'I know you better than anybody else' 33.12; πραῢς σφόδρα π. πάντας τοὺς ἀνθρώπους Nu 12.3; λαὸν περιούσιον π. πάντα τὰ ἔθνη 'dearer than ..' De 7.6 (|| ἀπό Ex 19.5), πολυπληθεῖτε π. πάντα τὰ ἔθνη 'more numerous than any other people' De 7.7, ὀλιγοστοὶ π. πάντα τὰ ἔθνη ib.

4. *in excess of, over and above, in addition to*: πλῆθος .. π. τὰ ἔργα, ὅσα συνέταξεν κύριος 'much .. more than the works that the Lord has charged' Ex 36.5; De 16.21.

5. indicates an amount by which sth could be or could have been accomplished, mostly w. an aor. ind.: π. μικρόν 'almost' Ps 72.2 (‖ παρ' ὀλίγον), Ez 16.47, π. ὀλίγον Pr 5.14; π. βραχὺ παρῴκησεν τῷ ᾅδῃ ἡ ψυχή μου 'my life would nearly have come to settle at the edge of the sheol' Ps 93.17; 118.87. Cf. "that (παρὰ τοῦτο) would not cut the tongue of our rational will off" 4M 10.19.

6. *as having the value of*: μεταβολὰς τῆς ψυχῆς παρ' οὐδὲν ἡγούμενος 'taking no account of the changes of the mood' 3M 5.42.

7. *in respect of*: προδότης π. ἕκαστα ἀκούων 'hearing himself called a traitor at every turn' 2M 10.13; 10.14, 3M 3.23. Cf. Polyb. 3.57.4.

8. *in opposition to, contrary to*: π. τὸν νόμον Es 4.16 o', π. τὴν γραφήν 2C 30.18; π. ταῦτα ποιήσῃ ἢ ἀθετήσῃ τι τούτων 'acts contrary to these terms or disregards ..' 1M 14.45, ὑπὲρ τοῦ π. λόγον τὸν Ὀνίαν ἀπεκτονῆσθαι 'over the unreasonable murder of O.' 2M 4.36, περὶ τῶν γεγενημένων π. λόγον 'the irrational things that had happened' 3M 7.8.

9. *as compared with*: πονηροτάτῳ π. πᾶσαν τὴν γῆν 'the worst in the whole world' Da 3.32; διαφέροντα ἓν π. τὸ ἕν 'different from one another' 7.3 LXX (TH ἀλλήλων); μόνη .. π. πάντας τοὺς Ἰουδαίους '(you) alone of all the Jews' Es 4.13 o'; διεστραμμένον π. τὰς γυναῖκας 'perverse as compared with the (normal) women (harlots)' Ez 16.34. **b**. *otherwise than, differently from*: Ju 5.4.

10. *throughout*: π. πᾶσαν τὴν γῆν Ju 11.23.

Cf. ἀπό, ἐκ: Johannessohn, *Präp*. 226-35.

παραβαίνω: fut. ~βήσομαι; aor. παρέβην, subj. ~βῶ, inf. ~βῆναι, ptc. ~βάς; pf. ~βέβηκα, ptc. ~βεβηκώς.ʃ

to move unjustly away from or off, 'transgress, overstep': *s* heavenly bodies, ἀπὸ ὁδοῦ 'the orbit' PSol 18.10. **b**. mostly fig.: abs. Le 26.40, De 11.16; ἐκ τῆς ὁδοῦ Ex 32.8, De 9.12 (‖ ἀπὸ .. vs. 16), ἀπὸ τῶν ἐντολῶν δεξιὰ ἢ ἀριστερά 17.20, sim. 28.14, ἀπὸ τῆς κλίνης αὐτοῦ 'against (the sanctity of) his wedlock' Si 23.18 (‖ abs. 42.10); + acc. rei, τὸ ῥῆμα κυρίου Nu 14.41, 22.18, 24.13, De 1.43, διαθήκην 'divine covenant' Jo 7.11, Ho 6.7, 8.1, '(a political) treaty' Ez 17.15, τὸν νόμον Is 24.5, νόμιμα 1E 1.46, κρίσιν Je 5.28, ἐντολάς To 4.5, τὸν ὅρκον 'the oath' 9.4 𝔊II, τὸν λόγον τοῦ βασιλέως 1E 4.5; + acc. pers., τὸν ἅγιον θεόν 3M 7.10 (‖ τοῦ θεοῦ τὸν νόμον); + ἔν τινι (pers.), Is 66.24 (*against God*); + epexegetical inf., Nu 5.19; ὀπίσω τινος 'in pursuit of ..' 1K 12.21 (*L* ἐκκλίνω). The rection with the prepositions mentioned here are most likely under Heb. influence; cf. Helbing, *Kasus*., 85f.

Cf. παρέρχομαι, ἐκκλίνω, παρανομέω, παράβασις.

παραβάλλω: fut.~βαλῶ; aor. παρέβαλον, impv. ~βαλε; pf.ptc.pass. ~βεβλημένος.

1. *to place* next to sbd *as a provision*: abs., *o* 'fodder' understood, ὑποζυγίοις 'to donkeys' Jd 19.20 A; Ru 2.16.

2. *to turn and direct attentively* towards: καρδίαν σου εἰς σύνεσιν .. ἐπὶ νουθέτησιν Pr 2.2; τοῖς ἐμοῖς λόγοις .. σὸν οὖς 'your ear .. to my words' 4.20, sim. 22.17.

3. mid. *to expose to danger or hazard*, 'devote entirely': + acc., σῶμα καὶ ψυχὴν ὑπὲρ τοῦ Ἰουδαϊσμοῦ 'body and soul for the cause of Judaism' 2M 14.38.

παραβασιλεύω.ʃ

to usurp rulership: 3M 6.24.

παράβασις, εως. f.ʃ

v.n. of παραβαίνω: ποιοῦντας ~εις Ps 100.3; τῶν ἀδίκων 'of the unrighteous' (subj. gen.) Wi 14.31, ὅρκων '(violation) of oaths' 2M 15.10. Cf. παραβαίνω: Trench 244f.; Renehan 2.113.

παραβιάζομαι: fut. ~βιῶμαι; aor. παρεβιασάμην, ptc. ~βιασάμενος, subj. ~βιάσωμαι.*

1. *to endeavour, strive*: + inf. τοῦ ἐξενέγκαι τὰ ὀστᾶ αὐτῶν 'to carry out their bones' Am 6.10, τοῦ ἐπιστρέψαι Jn 1.13.

2. *to put pressure on* (sbd τινα): Ge 19.9, 1K 28.23; + inf., 4K 5.16. **b**. *to detain* a visitor *to stay on*: Jd 13.16*L* (A: simp., B: κατέχω).

3. *to put one's foot down*: παραβιασάμενοι ἀνέβητε εἰς τὸ ὄρος 'you obstinately went up into the mountain' De 1.43.

Cf. βία, (κατα)βιάζομαι: Caird 1969.27; LSG s.v.

παραβιβάζω: aor. παρεβίβασα, impv. ~βίβασον.ʃ

to put aside: + acc., ἁμάρτημα 2K 12.13 (*L* ἀφαιρέω), ἀνομίαν 24.10 (*L* περιαιρέω); τὸν νόμον or suchlike understood?, Da TH 11.20.

παραβλέπω: aor. παρέβλεψα.ʃ

1. *to cast a glance at*: abs. Jb 20.9¶; + acc. and *s* ὀφθαλμός 28.7¶, the sun Ct 1.6.

2. *to look away and fail to act at once*: Si 38.9.

Cf. βλέπω.

παραβολή, ῆς. f.

***1**. *mocking or hurting speech*: ἔσῃ .. ἐν αἰνίγματι καὶ ἐν παραβολῇ .. De 28.37; π. ὀνειδισμοῦ To 3.4 𝔊I, Wi 5.4; *o* of λαμβάνω – λημφθήσεται ἐφ' ὑμᾶς π. 'a mocking speech will be made about you' Mi 2.4 (‖ θρῆνος); Hb 2.6 (‖ πρόβλημα), Je 24.9 (+ ὀνειδισμός); of ἀναλαμβάνω – ἀναλαβὼν τὴν ~ὴν αὐτοῦ εἶπεν .. Nu 23.7 +; π. θρήνου Ez 19.14. **b**. target of such a speech: Ps 68.12.

*2. *proverbial saying*: 1K 10.12, 3K 5.12; ἐν αἰνίγμασιν παραβολῶν Si 39.3, ἐν παραβολαῖς αἰνιγμάτων 47.15, cf. Si prol. II; Ps 48.5 (|| πρόβλημα); 2C 7.20 (+ διήγημα).

Cf. παροιμία: Wackernagel 1239-44; Hauck, *TDNT* 5.744-51; Dorival in *BA* 4.155.

παραγγέλλω: aor. παρήγγειλα, impv. ~γγειλον, ptc. ~γγείλας; pf.ptc.pass. ~ηγγελμένος.

1. *to issue an order* to act or do sth: abs., military, Je 26.14 (|| ἀναγγέλλω); + dat. pers., 1M 5.58, 9.63, cf. ἐπί τινα (to attack) Je 27.29, 28.27; + acc. of action, ἐξοπλισίαν 'to parade fully armed' 2M 5.25, θεραπείαν 'worship service' Es 4.16 *L*, pass. 3M 4.14, not military, + acc. ("fasting and supplication") and inf., Da 2.18 LXX; + inf., Ju 7.1, 2C 36.22, 2M 13.10, 1K 23.8. **b**. *to order to present oneself* at a certain place, 'summon' (inf. such as παραγενέσθαι understood?): + dat. pers., 1K 10.17 (*L* συνάγω), 15.4, 3K 15.22, Jd 4.10A.

2. *to transmit a message*: + φωνήν 2E 1.1.

Cf. ἐντέλλομαι, παράγγελμα, κελεύω: Schmidt 1.204-6; Spicq 3.9-11; Muraoka 2006.

παράγγελμα, ατος. n.ʃ

that which has been determined and given as an order: royal, 1K 22.14.

παραγίνομαι: aor. παρεγενόμην, ~γενήθην, subj. ~γένωμαι, ptc. ~γενόμενος, ~γενηθείς, inf. ~γενέσθαι, ~γενηθῆναι, impv.mid.~γενοῦ, pass.2pl ~γενήθητε; pf. ~γέγονα, ptc. ~γεγονώς.

1. *to come to be* in a place, 'to appear, turn up': παραγενόμενος τῶν ἀνασωθέντων τις 'one of the survivors appeared' Ge 14.13; παραγενόμενοι .. ἀπήγγειλαν 26.32; εἰς τοὺς οἴκους Φαραω Ex 8.24 (*s* dog-flies); ἐφ' ἅλωνα Αταδ 'to the threshing-floor of A.' Ge 50.10; πρός τινα 50.16, Ex 2.18, 18.6; εἰς τὴν συμποσίαν 'for the drinking-party' 3M 5.16; with hostile intention, ἐπί τινα 2M 15.24.

2. *to come to, present oneself to*: *s* God, πρὸς σὲ ἐν στύλῳ νεφέλης 'in a column of cloud' Ex 19.9; 20.20; workman, 36.4; troops to report for duties, 2M 13.12; saviour, + dat. pers., Is 62.11; on return from a mission, Nu 14.36; to confess, πρὸς Μωυσῆν 21.7.

3. *to reach, arrive*: εἰς μέρος τῆς Φοινίκης 'the region of Phoenicia, i.e. Canaan' Ex 16.35; εἰς Ωρ τὸ ὄρος Nu 20.22.

4. *to happen as expected*: *s* event, Si 48.25; Jo 21.45.

Cf. διανύω.

παράγω: aor. ~ήγαγον, inf. ~αγαγεῖν, impv. ~άγαγε, pass. παρήχθην.

A. tr. **1**. *to cause to move* to a certain destination: pass., 2E 9.2, πλησίον αὐτοῦ 4M 5.4.

2. *to cause to move past* sbd: + acc. pers., 1K 16.9; πονηρίαν ἀπὸ σαρκός σου Ec 11.10 (|| ἀφίστημι).

3. *to help move on*: + acc. pers., Ne 2.7.

B. intr. **1**. *to pass by*: οἱ παράγοντες 'passers-by' Ps 128.8; 3M 6.16.

2. *to move on and cease to exist*: *s* hum. life and shadow, Ps 143.4.

3. *to come over across the coast*: 1E 5.53.

Cf. ἄγω, παρέρχομαι.

παραγωγή, ῆς. f.ʃ

deviation: + gen. [= abl.], Es B 3.17.

παράδειγμα, τος. n.

1. *pattern* or *model* for the use of an architect: τῆς σκηνῆς Ex 25.8 (|| τύπος vs. 40); blueprint, 1C 28.11, cf. ὑπόδειγμα τοῦ οἴκου Ez 42.15.

2. *example* held up for public mockery: θήσομαί σε εἰς π. 'I shall make an example of you' Na 3.6.

Cf. παραδειγματίζω, παραδειγματισμός, παραδείκνυμι, τύπος, ὑπόδειγμα: Schmidt 3.416f.

παραδειγματίζω: fut.pass. ~τισθήσομαι; aor. παρεδειγμάτισα, impv. ~τισον, inf.pass. ~τισθῆναι.ʃ*

to subject to public disgrace: + acc. pers., Es C 22, Da LXX 2.5; and dat. pers., αὐτοὺς κυρίῳ ἀπέναντι τοῦ ἡλίου Nu 25.4; + acc. rei, τὰς πτέρνας σου 'your heels' (of an adulterous woman) Je 13.22 (|| ἀνακαλύπτω); ἐναντίον βασιλέων Ez 28.17; ἀπέναντι τοῦ ἡλίου .. ἀδικίας αὐτῶν PSol 2.12. Cf. παράδειγμα: Spicq 3.12.

παραδειγματισμός, οῦ. m.ʃ

v.n. of παραδειγματίζω: 3M 4.11; pl., 7.14. Cf. παράδειγμα.

παραδείκνυμι: aor. παρέδειξα, impv. ~δειξον, subj. ~δείξω, ptc.pass. ~δειχθείς.

to point to: + acc. and dat. pers. κατὰ τὸ παραδειχθέν σοι 'in accordance with what was shown to you' Ex 27.8 (|| δείκνυμι 26.30); οὐ παρέδειξά σοι αὐτά Ho 13.4; + ὅτι Bel 9 LXX (TH δείκνυμι). Cf. δείκνυμι and παράδειγμα.

παράδεισος, ου. m. < Heb. פַּרְדֵּס.

enclosed spacious plantation for cultivating fruits, 'orchard': ἐφύτευσεν .. ὁ θεὸς ~ον ἐν Εδεμ 'God planted a plantation in Eden' Ge 2.8, φυτεύσατε ~ους καὶ φάγετε τοὺς καρποὺς αὐτῶν Je 36.5; ὡς ὁ π. τοῦ θεοῦ Ge 13.10 (of Sodom and Gomorrah before their destruction); π. κυρίου (:: ἔρημος) Is 51.3; π. τρυφῆς 'luxuriant garden' Ge 3.23, 24, Jl 2.3, ἐν τῇ τρυφῇ τοῦ ~ου τοῦ θεοῦ Ez 28.13; τὰ ξύλα τοῦ ~ου τῆς τρυφῆς τοῦ θεοῦ 31.9; ἐπὶ ποταμῶν 'by rivers' Nu 24.6; π. ὕδωρ μὴ ἔχων Is 1.30; || κῆπος Si 24.30, Su 54 (|| 58). **b**. planted with trees for timber: Ne 2.9. **c**. adjoins a wealthy man's residence: Da TH Su 4.

Cf. κῆπος, φυτεία **2**: Lee 53-6; Husson 1988; Harl, *Langue* 148f.; Renehan 2.113; Alexandre 244-6.

παραδέχομαι: fut. ~δέξομαι; aor.ptc. ~δεξάμενος.ʃ

1. *to admit as true*: + acc., ἀκοὴν ματαίαν 'baseless hearsay' Ex 23.1; + inf., τἀληθὲς αὐτοὺς λέγειν 'that they are telling the truth' 3M 7.12.

2. *to embrace as being genuinely so*: πάντα υἱὸν ὃν παραδέχεται 'every son whom he [= the father] accepts as such' Pr 3.12 (ǁ ἀγαπάω).

Cf. προσδέχομαι.

παραδίδωμι: fut. ~δώσω, pass. ~δοθήσομαι, inf. ~δώσειν; aor.act. παρέδωκα, subj. ~δῶ, inf. ~δοῦναι, impv. ~δος, opt.3s ~δώη, pass. παρεδόθην, inf. ~δοθῆναι, ptc. ~δοθείς, subj. ~δοθῶ, impv.3pl ~δοθήτωσαν; pf. ~δέδωκα, pass. ~δέδομαι, ptc. ~δεδομένος.

1. *to give up and hand* or *turn over* to a third party to be handled as he pleases: + acc., De 32.30 (ǁ ἀποδίδωμι mid.); + acc. and dat. pers., 23.15, παραδίδωμί σοι αὐτόν 'I [=God] hand him [=Job] over to you [=the devil]' Jb 2.6, με τοῖς ἀδικοῦσίν με Ps 118.121, λέοντι 'to a lion' Is 38.13, ἁμαρτίαις 53.6; σὴν χεῖρα ἐχθρῷ 'your freedom of action to your enemy' (?) Pr 6.1; ***o*** the conquered and + εἰς (τὰς) χεῖράς τινος Ex 23.31, Le 26.25, Zc 11.6 (occasionally + ἐν χειρί τινος Is 36.15, 2E 9.7, 1M 5.50); a murderer to an avenger, εἰς χεῖρας τῷ ἀγχιστεύοντι τοῦ αἵματος De 19.12; + *ἐνώπιόν τινος 1.8 (ǁ πρὸ προσώπου τινός), 31.5, 2E 7.19; *ἐναντίον τινός Ge 27.20; with the aim of ἐξολεθρεῦσαι ἡμᾶς De 1.27; pass. παραδοθήσονται ἐν τοῖς ἔθνεσι 'they shall be abandoned among the nations' Ho 8.10; εἰς ῥομφαίαν Mi 6.14 (εἰς χεῖρας ῥομφαίας Ps 62.11), εἰς μάχαιραν Is 65.12, εἰς θάνατον 53.12, 2C 32.11, εἰς σφαγήν 'for slaughter' Is 34.2, εἰς προνομὴν 33.23, εἰς σφάγια ῥομφαίας Ez 21.15, εἰς ἀφανισμόν Mi 6.16, εἰς χάλαζαν 'to the hail' Ps 77.48 (ǁ τῷ πυρί); παρέδωκαν τὰ σώματα αὐτῶν εἰς πῦρ Da TH 3.95; + acc. pers. and pred. adj., ὁ θεὸς ὁ ὕψιστος, ὃς παρέδωκεν τοὺς ἐχθρούς σου ὑποχειρίους σοι '.. as subordinate to you' Ge 14.20, sim. Nu 21.2, 3. **b**. *to withdraw support, care and attention from*, poss. an extension through ellipsis of **a**: + acc., παρέδωκας ἡμᾶς διὰ τὰς ἁμαρτίας ἡμῶν 'you gave up on us because of ..' Is 64.7; pass. διὰ τὰς ἁμαρτίας αὐτῶν παρεδόθη 53.12 (ǁ ταῖς ἁμαρτίαις ἡμῶν vs. 6). The examples mentioned above under ἐν χειρί τινος may be subsumed here with the prep. phrase as marking an instrument. **c**. restitution of hostages: 1M 10.6, 9 (at latter ǁ ἀποδίδωμι w. ref. to subsequent returning to parents). **d**. pass., fig. *to abandon oneself, yield completely* to sth questionable: Je 2.24.

2. *to transmit*: ***o*** information, data etc. to sbd else, + dat. pers. and acc., τοῖς ὑποχειρίοις μυστήρια καὶ τελετάς 'secret rites and initiations to his subordinates' Wi 14.15, cf. BDAG s.v. **3**; pass., ἐκ τῶν παραδεδομένων ἡμῖν ἱστοριῶν 'out of the records handed down to us' Es E 7 o'. **b**. object: dart, 1K 20.36. **c**. ***o*** wealth or physical strength (?), ἐκ γενεᾶς εἰς γενεάν Pr 27.24.

3. *to entrust as deposit*: + acc., Si 42.7.

Cf. (ἀπο)δίδωμι, παράδοσις: Ziegler 1934.198; Spicq 3.13-23.

παραδοξάζω: fut. ~δοξάσω; aor. παρεδόξασα.ʃ*

The subj. is alw. the God of Israel.

1. *to act in discriminating fashion*: in favour of sbd (τινα), τὴν Γεσεμ Ex 8.22, cf. vs. 23 δώσω διαστολὴν 'I shall make a distinction'; τὸν ἑαυτοῦ τόπον 2M 3.30, sim. 3M 2.9 (w. ref. to the temple). **b**. without making it explicit who is being favoured, ἀνὰ μέσον τῶν Αἰγυπτίων καὶ τοῦ Ισραηλ Ex 11.7, sim. 9.4.

2. *to render extraordinary*: in severity and + acc., τὰς πληγάς σου 'your plagues' De 28.59; ἐπαγωγάς 'calamities' Si 10.13.

Cf. διαστέλλω, παράδοξος: *BA* II, p. 34.

παράδοξος, ον.

contrary to expectation: ***s*** ἔργα, + θαυμάσιος Si 43.25; σωτηρία 3M 6.33, ὁδοιπορία 'journey' Wi 19.5; subst.n., ~ον σωτηρίας 5.2.

παραδόξως. adv.ʃ

contrary to what one normally would expect: 4M 4.14.

παράδοσις, εως. f.ʃ

v.n. of παραδίδωμι **1c**: used as cogn. dat., Je 39.4, 41.2.

παραδρομή, ῆς. f.ʃ

1. *retinue*: 2M 3.28.

*__2__. *conduit, canal*: euphemism for female genitals (?), Ct 7.6, see Stoop - van Paridon 384.

παραζεύγνυμι: aor. παρέζευξα.ʃ

to cause to accompany sbd (dat.): Ju 10.17.

παραζηλόω: fut. παραζηλώσω; aor. παρεζήλωσα, ptc. ~ζηλώσας.*

1. *to provoke to jealousy*: + acc. pers., ***o*** God, De 32.21¹ (ǁ παροργίζω), Ps 77.58, hum. De 32.21² (ǁ παροργίζω), Si 30.3. **b**. *to become jealous*: abs., Es 3.6 *L*.

2. *to become envious*: + ἐν – ἐν πονηρευομένοις 'wrongdoers' Ps 36.1 (ǁ ζηλόω τινα), 7, alw. in a negative injunction.

Cf. ζηλόω, παροργίζω: LSG s.v.

παραζώνη, ης. f.ʃ *

girdle: 2K 18.11. Cf. ζώνη.

παραζώννυμι.ʃ

mid. *to fasten round one's waist*: ***s*** soldier, + acc., παραζώνην 'girdle' 4K 3.21*L* (B: περι~). Cf. ζώννυμι.

παραθαλάσσιος, ον.
situated along the coast: *s* πόλις Ez 25.9; subst. f., Je 29.7. Cf. *ND* 4.165.

παραθαρσύνω.ʃ
to encourage, cheer up: τινα (sbd. in difficulty), 4M 13.8. Cf. θαρσέω.

παράθεμα, ατος.* n.
appendage: Ex 38.24; τὸ π. τὸ χαλκοῦν τοῦ θυσιαστηρίου Ex 39.10.

παραθερμαίνω: pf.pass. ~τεθέρμαμαι.ʃ
to add to the heat: fig. παρατεθέρμανται τῇ καρδίᾳ 'has got incensed' De 19.6.

παράθεσις, εως. f.
1. *that which is stored for future use*: βρωμάτων 'of foods' 2C 11.11, 1M 9.52, 2M 12.14.
2. v.n. of παρατίθημι: Pr 6.8; μόσχων '(serving) of calves (as food)' 15.17 (|| ξενισμός 'entertainment'). **b**. *that which is set and offered to be taken*: foods and drinks, 4K 6.23.
Cf. παρατίθημι.

παραθήκη, ης. f.ʃ
state of being entrusted for safe-keeping: ἐν ~ῃ 'in trust' Le 6.2; παρατίθεμαί σοι τὴν θυγατέρα μου ἐν παραθήκῃ 'I give my daughter in your charge' To 10.12 𝕲[II]. **b**. *that which has been entrusted for safe-keeping*: π. ἥτις παρετέθη αὐτῷ Le 6.4.
Cf. παρακαταθήκη, παρατίθημι: Kiessling 1956; Spicq 3.24-7.

παραθλίβω: aor.impv. ~θλιψον.ʃ
to press close: αὐτὸν ἐν τῇ θύρᾳ 4K 6.32 (*L* ἐκ~). Cf. θλίβω.

παραίνεσις, εως. f.ʃ
advice: Wi 8.9. Cf. παραινέω.

παραινέω: aor.ptc. ~αινέσας.ʃ
to exhort: + inf., 2M 7.25, 3M 5.17. Cf. παραίνεσις.

παραιρέω: aor. παρειλάμην.ʃ
to take away, remove: ἀπὸ τοῦ πνεύματος 'some of the spirit' Nu 11.25 (|| ἀφαιρέω vs. 17). Cf. ἀφαιρέω.

παραιτέομαι: aor. παρῃτησάμην, inf. ~τήσασθαι, ptc. ~τησάμενος; pf. παρῄτημαι.
1. *to plead with*: abs., πρός τι 'concerning sth' 4M 11.2; + acc. pers., τὸν βασιλέα Es 4.8 o', τὴν βασίλισσαν 7.7 o'.
2. *to ask to be excused from*: + acc. rei, 2M 2.31. Cf. *ND* 3.78.
3. *to beg forgiveness for*: + acc. rei, 3M 6.27; ἀπό τινος (pers. = host) + inf., 1K 20.6, παρ' ἐμοῦ 20.28.
Cf. αἰτέω: Schmidt 1.195f.

παραίτιος, ον.ʃ
jointly responsible: + gen. rei, 2M 11.19.

παρακαθεύδω.ʃ*
to sleep beside to watch over: + dat. pers., Ju 10.20. Cf. καθεύδω.

παρακάθημαι.ʃ
to be seated beside in official function: *s* royal counsellor, + dat., τῷ βασιλεῖ Es 1.14 o'. Cf. κάθημαι.

παρακαθίζω: aor. παρεκάθισα.ʃ
*act. *to sit beside*: + dat. pers. (mourner), Jb 2.13. Cf. καθίζω.

παρακαλέω: fut. ~καλέσω, pass. ~κληθήσομαι, ptc. ~καλέσων; aor. παρεκάλεσα, subj. ~καλέσω, inf. ~καλέσαι, ptc. ~καλέσας, impv. ~κάλεσον; pass. παρεκλήθην, ptc. ~κληθείς, subj. ~κληθῶ, inf. ~κληθῆναι, impv. ~κλήθητι; pf.ptc.pass. ~κεκλημένος, impv.2pl ~κέκλησθε.
1. *to comfort, console*: *o* mourner, Ge 37.35, 38.12; ἐμαυτόν Is 21.2, τοὺς πενθοῦντας 61.2, τὴν καρδίαν σου Si 30.23; μάταια π. '(gave) vain comfort' Zc 10.2; pass., περί τινος 'in the matter of' Ge 24.67, ἐν χείλεσιν Ez 24.17, παρὰ στόματός τινος 24.22; παρακλήθητι 'receive condolences' Si 38.17, 23; ironically said, 1K 15.11, see *BA* ad loc.
2. *to encourage*: sbd (acc.) fearful and apprehensive, and following Μὴ φοβεῖσθε and foll. by ἐλάλησεν αὐτῶν εἰς τὴν καρδίαν Ge 50.21, τῇ χειρί 'by waving your hand' Is 13.2 (cf. προτρέχοντες Eus. 96); De 3.28 (|| κατισχύω); *o* pregnant sheep, Is 40.11; χεῖρας ἀσθενοῦς 'the hands of the feeble' Jb 4.3; to act in a certain way, De 13.6.
3. *to invite*: εἰς κατάλυμα ἅγιόν σου 'into your holy dwelling' Ex 15.13; for negotiation, τινα 2M 13.23.
4. *to plead for*: + acc. rei, εἰρήνην Is 33.7. **b**. + acc., τὸ πρόσωπον τοῦ βασιλέως 'an expression of favourable, friendly reception on the part of the king' 1K 22.4.
5. *to urge* to act in a certain way: abs., ἐπὶ τὰ εἴδωλα '(to go) to the idols (for help)' Is 57.5, cf. Cyr. ad loc. (PG 70.1260) and Xen., *An*. 3.1.24 τινα ἐπὶ τὰ κάλλιστρα ἔργα; + acc. pers., Pr 1.10, Es 1.16 *L*; + inf., 2M 9.26 (+ ἀξιόω), 2.3, 6.12, 12.3; + ὅπως and subj. aor., 4M 4.11. Cf. παράκειμαι **2**, προτρέπομαι.
***6**. pass. *to be touched and affected emotionally*: περί τινος (pers.) Jd 21.6A (B: πρός τινα). **b**. by a misfortune visited on: + dat. pers., Jd 21.15 A (B: ἐπί τινι); *s* God, ἐπὶ τῇ κακίᾳ 2K 24.16B (*L* μεταμέλομαι). **c**. *to allow oneself to be swayed* by a plea to help: ἀπὸ τοῦ στεναγμῶν αὐτῶν 'by their groan' Jd 2.18; ἐπί τινι (pers.) and *s* God, De 32.36 (cf. Eth. *yetnābbab* 'he will speak up on behalf of'), Ps 89.13, 134.14, Si 16.9¶, + inf. Si prol. 15, cf. Lat. juxta LXX

deprecabilis esto and Lampe, s.v. ad fin. "pass., '*be pleased to*' .. '*be so kind as to*'."

Cf. παράκλησις, παρακλήτωρ, παρακλητικός, παραμυθέομαι, παρηγορέω, προσπαρακαλέω: Lee 83.

παρακάλυμμα, ατος. n.ʃ

sth that conceals that which is inside or behind: metaph., ἀφεγγὲς λήθης π. 'a dark veil of oblivion' Wi 17.2. Cf. subs.

παρακαλύπτω.ʃ

1. act. *to cover by hanging sth beside*: + acc., ἀπὸ τῶν σαββάτων μου τοὺς ὀφθαλμοὺς αὐτῶν 'turned a blind eye to my sabbaths' Ez 22.26; *o* one's face as a gesture of grieving, 2K 19.5*L* (B: κρύπτω). Cf. prec.

2. mid., *to deceive oneself by ignoring reality*: Is 44.8.

παρακαταθήκη, ης. f.

1. *state of being entrusted to sbd else's care*: παρατίθεμαί σοι τὴν θυγατέρα μου ἐν ~η To 10.12 𝔊[I].

2. *deposit* of money or property *entrusted to one's care* (LSJ): τοῦ πλησίον Ex 22.8, 11, χηρῶν τε καὶ ὀρφανῶν 'for widows and orphans' 2M 3.10; τὸν περὶ ~ης νομοθετήσαντα τοῖς παρακαταθεμένοις ταῦτα σῷα διαφυλάξειν 'one who had legislated about the deposit to keep it safe for those who had deposited it' 3.15.

Cf. παραθήκη, παρακατατίθημι: Kiessling 1956.

παρακατατίθημι: 2aor.mid. παρεκατεθέμην.

to entrust sbd or sth (acc.) *with* sbd (dat.): αὐτῷ ἄνδρας καὶ γυναῖκας αὐτῶν Je 47.7; 2M 3.15. Cf. παρακαταθήκη.

παράκειμαι.

1. *to be at hand* to serve or be used: *s* hum., παρακείμεθα ἐνώπιόν σου, χρῆσαι ἡμῖν 'we are here in your presence, use us' Ju 3.2, sim. 3.3; foods offered at a grave, Si 30.18, τὰ παρακείμενά σοι 'what has been served to you' 34.16. **b**. in terms of physical location: *to be in the proximity of*: σποδός 'ashes (lying about there)' 2M 4.41; + dat., 2M 9.25 (|| γειτνιάω 'neighbouring'). Cf. πρόκειμαι **1**.

2. *to urge* to act in a certain way: + dat. pers., 3M 7.3. Cf. παρακαλέω **5**.

Cf. παραμένω, παραστήκω, παρίστημιι.

παρακελεύω.ʃ

to exhort to act in a certain way: act., + dat. pers. and + inf., 4M 5.2; mid., Pr 9.16.

παρακλείω: aor. παρέκλεισα.ʃ

to shut up out of public sight: euph. for murdering, + acc. pers., 2M 4.34, cf. de Bruyne 408f.

παράκλησις, εως. f.

1. v.n. of παρακαλέω **1**: πόθεν ζητήσω ~ιν αὐτῇ 'whence shall I seek comfort for her?' Na 3.7; Ho 13.14; μαστὸς ~εως 'breast of ..' Is 66.11; ἐπὶ τεθνηκότι 'over the dead' Je 16.7; shown by God, Ps 93.19.

2. v.n. of παρακαλέω **2**: λόγοι ~εως 1M 10.24, τὴν ἐν τοῖς ἀγαθοῖς λόγοις ~ιν 2M 15.11; w. ref. to the Holy Scripture, 1M 12.9.

3. v.n. of παρακαλέω **5**: διὰ λόγων ἐποιεῖτο τὴν ~ιν 2M 7.24.

Cf. παρακαλέω and παρακλητικός.

παρακλητικός, ή, όν.ʃ

providing comfort: λόγους ~ούς 'comforting words' Zc 1.13. Cf. παρακαλέω and παράκλησις.

παρακλήτωρ, ορος. m.ʃ *

comforter: Jb 16.2. Cf. παρακαλέω.

παρακμάζω: aor. ~κμάσω.ʃ

to go past the prime: *s* a girl missing the chance to marry, Si 42.9. Cf. ἀκμή.

παράκοιτος, ου. c.ʃ

one who shares bed: wife, παλλακὴ καὶ π. 'concubine..' Da 5.2, 3, 23 TH. Cf. γυνή.

παρακολουθέω: fut.inf. ~θήσειν.ʃ

to follow very closely behind: + dat. pers., *s* divine punishment (δίκη), 2M 8.11; + dat. rei, sbd's intention (προαίρεσις) 9.27. Cf. ἀκολουθέω: Schmidt 3.241; Kittel, *TDNT* 1.215f.

παρακομίζω.

1. *to carry with oneself* for delivery: + acc., money, 2M 4.19.

2. *to transport along* a way: + acc. pers., 2M 9.9; the body of the deceased, 9.29.

Cf. φέρω.

παρακούω: aor. παρήκουσα, subj. ~ακούσω.

to refuse to listen: Is 65.12 (|| οὐχ ὑπακούω), Es 4.14. **b**. *to disobey*: + gen. pers., 1E 4.11; + gen. rei, ἐντολῶν To 3.4, νόμων Es 3.8 o' (|| *L* οὐ προσέχω); + acc. rei, τὰ ὑπὸ τοῦ βασιλέως λεγόμενα 3.3 o' (|| *L* τοῦ βασιλέως).

Cf. ἀπειθέω, εἰσ~, ὑπακούω: Spicq 3.28f.

παρακρούομαι: aor. παρεκρουσάμην.ʃ

to cheat: + acc. pers., Ge 31.7. Cf. δολιόω, δολόω, πτερνίζω.

παρακύπτω: aor. παρέκυψα, ptc. ~κύψας.

to peep: διὰ τῆς θυρίδος 'through the window' Jd 5.28 B (A: δια~), Ge 26.8, Si 14.23, ἀπὸ θυρίδος Pr 7.6 (cf. Aristoph., *Pax* 980-83 ἅπερ αἱ μοιχευόμεναι δρῶσι γυναῖκες .. παρακλίνασαι τῆς αὐλείας παρακύπτουσιν 'what the adulterous women do .. open a bit of the half-door to peep out'; Albright 10), ἀπὸ θύρας εἰς οἰκίαν Si 21.23; θυρὶς παρακυπτομένη 'peeping window(?)' 3K 6.4; || ἐκ~ Ct 2.9. Cf. εἶδον, ὁράω, ἀνα~, ἐκ~, διακύπτω: Neirynck 1977.

παραλαλέω.ʃ

to talk falsehood: + ὀνειδίζω Ps 43.17. Cf. ψεύδομαι.

παραλαμβάνω: fut. ~λήμψομαι, ptc. ~λημψόμενος; aor. παρέλαβον, ptc. ~λαβών, pass. ~λημφθείς, inf.act. ~λαβεῖν, impv. ~λαβε, subj. ~λάβω; pf.pass. παρείλημμαι.

1. *to take over* from sbd that which belonged to him: abs. παραλημψόμενος 'successor, heir' Je 30.1; + acc., ib., τὴν ἀρχὴν αὐτοῦ 'his leadership' 30.2, τὸ βασίλειον 'kingship' 1E 4.43, τὴν βασιλείαν Bel 1 TH, τὰ τῶν πραγμάτων 'the management of the state affairs' 1M 6.56.

2. *to take along* to some place: + acc., μεθ' ἑαυτοῦ δύο παῖδας Ge 22.3; 31.23; Nu 23.14, pass., 23.20.

3. *to receive* that which has been handed: ***o*** offering, 1E 8.59 (|| δέχομαι 2E 8.30); pass., ***o*** the soul of the dead, Wi 16.14, cf. παραλημφθεὶς ὑπὸ θεῶν καταχθονίων '.. by subterranean gods' *IG* 14.1702.

4. *to go and bring with one*, 'fetch': + acc. pers., Jd 11.5 A (B: simp.).

Cf. λαμβάνω, συμπαραλαμβάνω.

παραλείπω: aor. παρέλιπον, inf. ~λιπεῖν.

to leave out: + acc., Παραλειπομένων 1C tit.; w. collateral notion of neglect, μηδέν 'nothing' 1E 8.7, αἰδῶ 'modesty' 3M 1.19.

παράλιος, α, ον.

by the sea: π. κατοικήσει Ge 49.13; subst. f.sg., πρὸς λίβα καὶ ~ίαν 'to the south and the seacoast' De 1.7, οἱ ἐν πάσῃ τῇ ~ίᾳ τῆς θαλάσσης Jo 9.1, οἱ τὴν ~ίαν κατοικοῦντες Is 9.1; Jd 5.17 B (A: αἰγιαλός); n.sg. ~ιον κατοικούντων De 33.19. Cf. αἰγιαλός.

παραλλαγή, ῆς. f.ʃ

haphazard, disorderly conduct: of military leader, 4K 9.20.

παράλλαξις, εως. f.ʃ

abrogation: ἐνδελεχισμοῦ 'of perpetual offering' Da 12.11 TH. Cf. παραλλάσσω.

παραλλάσσω: aor.inf. παραλλάξαι, impv. ~λλαξον; pf.ptc.pass. παρηλλαγμένος.ʃ

1. *to replace*: παρηλλαγμένα 'replacement (utensils)' 2E 1.9.

2. *to modify*: + acc. (decision once taken), Da 6.15 TH. **b**. mid., intr. *to change*: τὸ τῆς χρόας παρηλλαγμένον 'his changed colour' 2M 3.16.

3. *to differ*: + acc. of respect, Es B 5 o'.

4. *to overlook on purpose*: + acc., 3K 5.1.

5. *to turn off the course being followed and avoid* sth: abs., Pr 4.15.

Cf. παράλλαξις.

παραλογίζομαι: aor. παρελογισάμην, ptc. ~λογισάμενος.

1. *to handle fraudulently in respect of*, 'cheat': + acc. pers., Ge 29.25, Jd 16.10 A (B: πλανάω); + acc. rei, τὸν μισθόν μου 'my hire' Ge 31.41; sbd else's goodwill, Es E 6.

2. *to cause* sbd *to make false judgement*, 'deceive, delude': + acc. pers., Bel 7 LXX (TH: πλανάομαι).

Cf. δολιόω, παραλογισμός.

παραλογισμός, ου. m.ʃ

v.n. of παραλογίζομα **1**: ψευδὴς π. Es 7.23 o', πολύπλοκος 'intricate, involved' E 13 o', ἱερός 'involving religion' 2M 1.13. **b**. v.n. of παραλογίζομαι **2** or 'false reasoning': PSol 4.10.

παράλυσις, εως. f.ʃ

paralysing, weakening: physical, ἑτοίμη εἰς ~ιν Ez 21.10. Cf. παραλύω.

παραλύω: fut. ~λύσω, pass. ~λυθήσομαι; aor. παρέλυσα, inf. ~λῦσαι, pass. παρελύθην; pf.ptc.pass. ~λελυμένος.

*1. *to pay*: ἑπτὰ ἐκδικούμενα 'seven vengeances' Ge 4.15.

2. pass. *to be or become physically exhausted*: ***s*** hum., ζητοῦντες τὴν θύραν 'in an attempt to look for the door' Ge 19.11; De 32.36 (|| ἐκλείπω); Je 27.36, τοῖς μέλεσι 'in his limbs' 3M 2.22; ***s*** hands, Je 6.24, 27.15, Ez 21.7; knees, Is 35.3, Si 25.23 (|| slackened hands).

3. *to let hang loose*: ***o*** clothes, τὰ ἱμάτια αὐτοῦ ἔστω παραλελυμένα 'let his clothes hang loose' Le 13.45.

4. *to put an end to*: + acc., ὕβριν 'arrogance' or 'pride' Is 23.9.

5. *to render feeble and disable*: + acc., μόσχον Je 26.15; + acc. pers., Ju 16.4; chariots, 2K 8.4. **b**. *to paralyse*: out of dread, τινα Wi 17.19. Cf. παρίημι.

6. *to detach*: + acc. and ἀπό τινος Ez 25.9.

Cf. παράλυσις, ἐκλείπω, ἐκλύω: Caird 1969.27.

παραμένω: fut. ~μενῶ; aor. ~έμεινα, subj. ~μείνω.

1. *to stay beside* to serve: + dat. pers., παραμενῶ σοι παῖς Ge 44.33, cf. τῇ ἡμῶν ὑπηρεσίᾳ 'in our service' *P.Oxy. Hels*. 26.13; ἐν ἡμέρᾳ θλίψεως 'in time of trouble' Si 6.8.

2. *to hold on to and remain loyal to*: abs., Si 1.21¶.

3. *to remain long without going away*: ***s*** hum., Ju 12.7; sorrow, Si 38.19; design, plan, Da 11.17 TH.

Cf. (συμπαρα)μένω, παράκειμαι: Samuel 1965; *ND* 4.98f., 102.

παραμίγνυμι: pf.ptc.pass. ~μεμ(ε)ιγμένος.ʃ

to mix with: + dat. Da 2.43 LXX. Cf. μίγνυμι.

παραμυθέομαι.ʃ

to address so as to encourage and reassure: τινα (possibly fearful people) 2M 15.9 (|| vs. 8 παρακαλέω). Cf. παραμυθία, ~θιον, παρακαλέω: Stählin, *TDNT* 5.818-20; Spicq 3.30-5.

παραμυθία, ας. f.ʃ

1. *persuasion*: Es E 5 o'.

2. *relief from distressful situation*: Wi 19.12.

παραμύθιον, ου. n.ʃ
expression of encouragement: for the ill-fated, + ἐλπίς Wi 3.18. Cf. παραμυθέομαι: *ND* 4.166.

παραναγινώσκω: 2aor.ptc. ~γνούς, pass. ~γνωσθείς.ʃ
to read aloud publicly: + acc., Bible, 2M 8.23; pass., νόμος 3M 1.12. Cf. ἀναγινώσκω.

παρανακλίνω: aor. παρανέκλινα.ʃ*
to lay beside: τὰς λαγόνας σου γυναιξίν 'women at your side' Si 47.19.

παραναλίσκω: pf.pass. παρανήλωμαι.ʃ
to spend to no good purpose, 'squander': pass. and *o* hum., Nu 17.12 (ll ἀπόλλυμι, ἐξαναλίσκω). Cf. ἀφανίζω.

παρανομέω: aor.ptc. ~νομήσας.
to transgress the (divine) law: abs., PSol 16.8; ll ἀπὸ τοῦ νόμου ἐκκλίνω Ps 118.51, cf. 4M 5.16f.; + ἀδικέω Ps 70.4, ll ἁμαρτάνω 74.5. Cf. παράνομος, παρανομία, παραβαίνω.

παρανομία, ας. f.ʃ
attitude given to transgressing the (divine) law: ll ἀπείθεια 'disobedience,' ἁμαρτία PSol 17.20. Cf. παρανομέω, εὐνομία.

παράνομος, ον.
inclined to transgress the (divine) law: *s* hum. De 13.13, ἐθισμός 'custom' 2M 4.11; deed, ἀπώλεια 'destruction' 2M 8.4; subst. m., Ps 35.2, 1M 1.11. Cf. ἄδικος, ἀθέμιστος, ἄθεσμος, ἄνομος, ἔκθεσμος, νόμος, νόμιμος, παρανόμως.

παρανόμως. adv.
unlawfully: + χράομαι 'to deal with sbd' Jb 34.20. Cf. παράνομος, ἀδίκως.

παραξιφίς, ίδος. f.ʃ
knife worn beside the sword: 2K 5.8.

παράπαν. adv.
τὸ παράπαν *altogether, entirely*: ἐξερήμωσα τοὺς ὁδοὺς αὐτῶν τὸ π. 'I turned their roads into a total ruin' Zp 3.6; τὸ π. οὐκ ὠφελήσουσιν 'they will be totally useless' Je 7.4; Ez 20.9.

παραπέμπω: aor.ptc. ~πέμψας.ʃ
to disregard, pay no heed to: *o* royal command, Es B 4; 3M 1.26.

παραπέτασμα, ατος. n.ʃ
that which is spread before sth: 'curtain' in a temple, ~ατα ἐχόμενα τοῦ θυσιαστηρίου 'curtains next to the altar' Am 2.8.

παραπηδάω: aor. παρεπήδησα.ʃ
to spring forward: *s* hum., 4M 11.1. Cf. πηδάω.

παραπικραίνω: aor. παρεπίκρανα, inf. ~πικρᾶναι, ptc. ~πικράνας. *
1. *to invite harsh reaction of, infuriate*: abs. Ps 77.8, 105.7; + acc., τὰ πρὸς τὸν θεόν 'as regards what relates to God' De 31.27; *o* God, Ho 10.5, τὸν οἶκον τοῦ Ισραηλ τοὺς παραπικραίνοντάς με Ez 2.3, τὸ στόμα ^κυρίου^ La 1.18, ll παροργίζω Ps 77.40.
2. *to add to the harshness and bitterness of*: + acc., τοὺς λόγους αὐτοῦ '(provoked) his harsh words' Ps 104.28, τὰ λόγια τοὺ θεοῦ 106.11; based on a faulty analysis of the Heb. text, 3K 13.21, 26.
3. *to feel bitter* about sth: abs., La 1.20, Ps 67.7.
Cf. πικρός, ἐκπικραίνω, παραπικρασμός: Flashar 1912.186-8.

παραπικρασμός, οῦ. m.ʃ *
act of provoking: against God, Ps 94.8. Cf. παραπικραίνω.

παραπίπτω: aor. παρέπεσον, inf. ~πεσεῖν, subj. ~πέσω, impv.3s ~πεσάτω; pf. ~πέπτωκα.
1. *to go astray, err*: morally, + cogn. acc., παράπτωμα Ez 14.13 (ll παραπτώματι 15.8); εἰς ἐμέ [= God] 20.27; ll ἁμαρτάνω Wi 12.2.
2. *to fail to be acted upon*: *s* advice, proposal Es 6.10.
Cf. παράπτωμα, πλανάω.

παραπλαγιάζω.ʃ
to go obliquely: military manœuvre, 1K 23.26*L*.

παράπληκτος, ον.ʃ
deranged: divine punishment, διὰ τὰ ὁράματα .. ἃ βλέψῃ De 28.34. Cf. παραπληξία.

παραπληξία, ας. f.ʃ
**derangement*: divine punishment, De 28.28 (ll ἔκστασις διανοίας), cf. LSG s.v. Cf. ἔκστασις, μανία, παράπληκτος, παραφρόνησις.

παράπλους, ου. m.ʃ
voyage by boat along the coast: 3M 4.11 (ll κατάπλους vs. 10). Cf. κατάπλους, πλέω.

παραπομπή, ῆς. f.ʃ
convoy accompanying the chief traveller(s): 1M 9.37.

παραπορεύομαι: aor. παρεπορεύθην.
1. *to go past*: *s* caravan, κατὰ πρόσωπον αὐτοῦ 'in front of him' Ge 32.21; ἔμποροι 'merchants' 37.28; καταιγίς 'tempest' Pr 10.25; ἐπ' αὐτῆς 'by it [a city in ruins]' Je 19.8.
2. *to move along*: διὰ τῶν ὁρίων .. 'through the territory of ..' De 2.4; ἀπὸ Καδης Βαρνη 2.14; + acc., τὰ ὅρια Μωαβ 2.18.
3. *to walk along*: παρὰ τὸν ποταμόν 'by the river' Ex 2.5; + acc., ὁδόν Jb 21.29¶.
4. *to get over, cross*: τὴν φάραγγα Ζαρεδ 'the wadi Z.' De 2.13 (ll παρέρχομαι vs. 14).
**5*. *to submit oneself to and go through* a process: ἐπίσκεψιν 'census-taking' Ex 30.13, 39.3; εἰς τὴν ἐπίσκεψιν 30.14.
**6*. *to pass away and cease to exist*: ὡς ἄνθος παραπορευόμενον 'like a transient flower' Zp 2.2.
**7*. *to transgress*: + acc., τὰς ἐντολὰς κυρίου 2C 24.20.

Cf. πορεύομαι, παρέρχομαι, διοδεύω, εἰσέρχομαι: Lee 92.

παράπτωμα, ατος. n.

transgression, in moral, religious sense: Zc 9.5; as cogn. acc., Ez 14.13, as cogn. dat.,15.8; *o* of ποιέω 18.22, Da 6.22 TH. Cf. παράπτωσις, παραπίπτω, παράβασις: Trench 245-7; Michaelis, *TDNT* 6.170.

παράπτωσις, εως. f.

= παράπτωμα, q.v.: Je 22.21.

παραριθμέω: aor. ~ηρίθμησα.ʃ

to count and check contents: + acc., money-bags, To 9.5 𝔊[II]. Cf. ἀριθμέω.

παραρρέω: ~ρρυῇς aor.subj.2sʃ

1. *to flow by*: *s* ὕδωρ Is 44.4.

2. *to be careless*: Pr 3.21.

Cf. ῥέω.

παραρριπτέω. Variant of παραρρίπτω.

παραρρίπτω: aor. παρέρριψα, impv. ~ρρίψον.ʃ

1. *to toss*: 2M 1.16.

2. *to accept for membership* or *office*: + acc. pers., ἐπὶ ἱερατείαν 'for priesthood' 1K 2.36, pass. ἐν τῷ οἴκῳ τοῦ θεοῦ Ps 83.11.

Cf. παραρριπτέω, ῥίπτω.

παράρρυμα, ατος. n.ʃ

that which is drawn along or *over* sth: attached to a tabernacle (σκηνή), Ex 35.10.

παράσημον, ου. n.ʃ

distinguishing mark: branded on slave's body, 3M 2.29. Cf. σημεῖον.

παρασιωπάω: fut. ~πήσομαι, pass. ~πηθήσομαι; impf. παρεσιώπα; aor. παρεσιώπησα, subj. ~πήσω.

1. *to refrain from speaking*, 'keep quiet, keep secret': abs. Ge 24.21 (while engaged in an investigative watch), 34.5. **b**. in tacit approval: abs. Nu 30.5; + dat. pers., 30.8, 12 (:: ἀνανεύω), 15 (‖ σιωπάω).

2. *to pass over in silence, take no notice of, turn a deaf ear to*: + acc. pers. Ho 10.11; + acc. rei, ἀσέβειαν 10.13, τὴν κακίαν 1K 23.9, τὴν αἴνεσίν μου Ps 108.1; + ἀπό τινος– ἀπ' ἐμοῦ Ps 27.1, τοῦ μὴ (*L* om.) βοᾶν 1K 7.8; + gen., τῶν δακρύων μου 'my tears' Ps 38.13; + ἐν, Am 6.12; ἐν τῷ καταπίνειν ἀσεβῆ τὸν δίκαιον 'when a godless person swallows up a righteous man' Hb 1.13.

Cf. σιγάω and σιωπάω.

παρασκευάζω: fut.mid. ~κευάσομαι; aor.impv. 2pl ~σκευάσατε, mid. παρεσκευασάμην, impv.2pl ~σκευάσασθε, inf.act. ~σκευάσαι, mid. ~σκευάσασθαι, ptc.pass. ~σκευασθείς; pf.ptc.pass. παρεσκευασμένος.

1. *to get ready*: + acc., τὰ ἅρματα 'the chariots' Je 26.9, τοξεύματα 'arrows' 28.11; animal meat for food, To 8.19 𝔊[II]; συμπόσιον 'banquet' 2M 2.27; pass., παρεσκευασμένη ἡ ὁδὸς τῶν εὐσεβῶν 'the way of the god-fearing has been made ready' Is 26.7; as cultic offerings, τῷ Βηλ Bel 8 LXX; mid. εἰς πόλεμον Je 6.4, 27.42, εἰς τὸν ἀγρόν 'for the field' Pr 24.27.

2. *to occasion, bring about*: + acc., μάχας 'fights' Pr 15.18.

*2. mid. *to relieve oneself*: 1K 24.4, cf. OL *requiescere*, Joseph. *JA* 6.13.

Cf. παρασκευή, ἑτοιμάζω.

παρασκευή, ῆς. f.ʃ

1. *that which has been prepared*, 'equipage': Ex 39.22; military, 2M 15.21.

2. *food supply* for troops: Ju 2.17.

3. *act of getting ready*, 'preparation': πολέμου Ju 4.5.

Cf. παρασκευάζω, ἑτοιμασία.

παράστασις, εως. f.ʃ

impressive, pompous state: 1M 15.32.

παραστήκω.ʃ * See Thack. § 19,1.

to be present nearby to serve, 'wait on': + dat. pers., ψωμίζουσά με 'feeding me' 2K 13.5*L*; ὁ παραστήκων '(king's) servant' Jd 3.19A (B: ἐφεστηκώς). Cf. ἐφ~, παρίστημι, παράκειμαι.

παρασυμβάλλω: aor.pass. ~συνεβλήθην.ʃ *

pass., *to resemble*: + dat., Ps 48.13, 21 (‖ ὁμοιόω). Cf. ὁμοιόω.

παρασφαλίζω: aor.mid. παρησφαλισάμην.ʃ *

to fortify next in order: Ne 3.8, see Hanhart 2003. 397-402. Cf. ἀσφαλίζω.

παράταξις, εως. f.

1. *battle-line*: πολέμου Nu 31.14, 21.

2. *battle*: ἐνωπλισμένοι εἰς ~ιν 'armed for ..' Nu 31.5; ἐκπορεύομαι εἰς τὴν ~ιν 31.27, 28; συναγωγὴ ~εως 'troops deployed' Is 22.6, ὄχλος ~εως 1E 2.25; ‖ πόλεμος Ps 143.1; of holy war, καθὼς ἡμέρα ~εως αὐτοῦ ἐν ἡμέρᾳ πολέμου Zc 14.3; πρός τινα 2M 8.20.

3. *act of posting side by side*: ἐν τῇ ~ει 'in neat arrangement' Jd 6.26.

Cf. παρατάσσω, μάχη, πόλεμος, στρατεία.

παρατάσσω: fut. ~τάξομαι; aor.mid. παρεταξάμην, impv. παράταξαι, inf. ~τάξασθαι, ptc. ~ταξάμενος, subj. ~τάξωμαι; pf. mid. and pass. παρατέταγμαι.

1. *to draw up in battle-order*: pass. λαὸς πολὺς καὶ ἰσχυρὸς παρατασσόμενος εἰς πόλεμον 'a numerous and strong nation drawn up for a battle' Jl 2.5; mid., + dat. pers. (enemies), αὐτοῖς εἰς πόλεμον Ge 14.8; ἐπί τινα - ἐπὶ Μαδιαν Nu 31.3; λαὸς ἐφ' ὃν παρατέτακται κύριος 'a people against whom the Lord is lined up' Ma 1.4, *s* παρεμβολή 'encampment' Ps 26.3. Cf. συντάσσω **3**.

2. mid. *to do battle*: *s* troops, Zc 10.5; the God of Israel, + ἔν ('against') τινι 14.3, *s* hum., πρός τινα Jd 1.3 B (A: πολεμέω), τινι 9.38 B (:: πρός τινα vs. 39); περί τινος 'in the interest of' Ne 4.14; ἐν τῇ

δυνάμει αὐτοῦ πρὸς Αρφαξαδ 'with his army against A.' Ju 1.13; πολέμῳ 1K 17.8 (*L* εἰς πόλεμον).

3. mid. *to make preparations for*: + acc., πολέμους Ps 139.3, παράταξιν 1K 17.21.

4. pass. *to stand mentally prepared* to act: + final inf. Zc 1.6; παρατέταγμαι καὶ διανενόημαι .. τοῦ ποιῆσαι .. 8.15. Cf. *BA* ad Zc 1.6.

Cf. παράταξις, πολεμέω.

παρατείνω: fut. ~τενῶ; aor. παρέτεινα, impv. ~τεινον.

1. *to allow to last long*: + acc., τὸ ἔλεός σου Ps 35.11 (or: hold out, offer).

2. *to be continuous* from a certain point, 'extend, stretch': *s* an area, ἕως Σίδωνος Ge 49.13; εἰς τὴν ἔρημον Nu 23.28; Ἑλλὰς καὶ ἡ σύμπασα καὶ τὰ παρατείνοντα 'Greece, both the whole of the mainland and its peripheries (?: or its overseas colonies?)' Ez 27.13; ἡ παρατείνουσα 'the area extending beyond' 2K 2.29. **b**. *to position oneself over a wide area*: *s* army, Ju 7.3.

Cf. ἐκτείνω.

παρατηρέω: fut.mi. ~τηρήσομαι; aor.subj.mid.2s ~τηρήσῃ.ʃ

1. *to watch closely*: for an opportunity, Su 12 TH; + acc., ἡμέραν εὔθετον 'an opportune day' 15 TH, + acc. pers., 16 TH; with evil design, Da 6.11 TH (LXX τηρέω), τὸν δίκαιον Ps 36.12.

2. *to observe and study carefully*: +acc., ἀνομίας Ps 129.3.

Cf. τηρέω.

παρατίθημι: fut. ~θήσω, mid. ~θήσομαι; 1aor.act. παρέθηκα, impv. παράθες, mid. παρεθέμην, inf. ~θέσθαι, pass. παρετέθην, inf. ~τεθῆναι, ptc. ~τεθείς.

1. *to set beside*: + acc., ῥάβδους 'rods' Ge 30.38; *o* τράπεζα 'a (dinner-)table' To 2.2 𝔊II.

2. *to set and offer to be taken*: + acc. rei (food) and dat. pers., παρέθηκεν αὐτοῖς ἄρτους φαγεῖν Ge 24.33; Παράθετε ἄρτους 43.31; τράπεζα To 2.2 𝔊II; offerings to a divinity, Ep Je 26; ἐνώπιον τοῦ βασιλέως .. τῷ Βηλ Bel 11 LXX; + cogn. acc., παράθεσιν μεγάλην 4K 6.23.

3. *to present for consideration and attention*: + acc. rei and dat. pers., παρέθηκεν αὐτοῖς πάντας τοὺς λόγους τούτους Ex 19.7; δικαιώματα, ἃ παραθήσεις ἐνώπιον αὐτῶν 21.1, σοι πῦρ καὶ ὕδωρ Si 15.16; mid. De 4.44.

4. mid. *to give in charge, entrust*: + dat. pers. and acc., *o* money, To 4.1; παρατίθεμαί σοι τὴν θυγατέρα μου ἐν παραθήκῃ 'I place my daughter in your charge' To 10.12 𝔊II; εἰς χεῖράς σου .. τὸ πνεῦμά μου Ps 30.6, εἰς φυλακήν 'for imprisonment' 2C 16.10; pass. and + dat. pers., τὴν παραθήκην, ἥτις παρετέθη αὐτῷ Le 6.4.

5. mid. *to set aside and store up for future use*: + acc., ὅπλα καὶ τροφήν 'arms and food' 1M 1.35.

Cf. τίθημι, δίδωμι, παράθεσις, παραθήκη.

παρατρέχω.

1. *to run beside* sbd: as part of a king's bodyguard, 1K 22.17.

2. *to move by with speed on to next destination*: *s* ἀγγελία 'news; report' Wi 5.9; ὁ τῆς συμποσίας καιρός 'the hour of the banquet' 3M 5.15.

Cf. τρέχω.

παραυτίκα.ʃ adv.

straightaway: Ps 69.4, To 4.14. Cf. παραχρῆμα.

παραφέρω: aor. παρήνεγκα.ʃ

1. *to bring over*: + acc., Jd 6.5A, φωνήν 'a message' 2E 10.7.

2. mid. *to make confused gestures*: ἐν ταῖς χερσὶν αὐτοῦ 1K 21.14.

Cf. φέρω: Spicq 3.38f.

παραφρονέω ʃ

to be beside oneself, senseless: ἔδωκαν νῶτον παραφρονοῦντα 'they turned their backs senselessly' Zc 7.11. Cf. παραφρόνησις, παράφρων, ἐξίστημι, μαίνομαι, παρεξίστημι: Schmidt 4.245f.

παραφρόνησις, εως. f.ʃ

delirium: caused by God, πατάξω πάντα ἵππον ἐν ἐκστάσει .. καὶ ἐν ~σει Zc 12.4. Cf. παραφρονέω, παράφρων, ἔκστασις, παραπληξία, μανία.

παράφρων, ον.ʃ

wandering from reason, out of one's mind: subst. m., Wi 5.20. Cf. παραφρονέω.

παραφυάς, άδος. f.

that which grows from the main stem of a plant, 'branch; offshoot': φυτῶν .. ~άδες '.. of plants' 4M 1.28; of grape-vine, Ps 79.12; Ez 31.3; nesting place for birds, 31.6. Cf. κλάδος, φυτόν.

παραφυλακή, ῆς. f.ʃ

act of taking steps to safeguard: sbd else's life, Es 6.4*L*. Cf. φυλάσσω.

παραχρῆμα adv.

on the spot, forthwith: Nu 6.9, 12.4, Is 30.13, Ps 39.16, 2M 4.34. Cf. εὐθύς, παραυτίκα.

παραχωρέω: fut.inf. ~ρήσειν; aor.ptc. ~ρήσας.ʃ

to leave sth (acc.) *to the responsibility of* sbd (dat.): 2M 2.28. **b**. *to give away for sale*: ταλάντου 'for one talent' 2M 8.11.

παρδάλεος, ον.ʃ

leopard-like: *s* animal, 4M 9.28. Cf. πάρδαλις.

πάρδαλις, εως. f.

leopard: known for speed, Hb 1.8; ‖ πανθήρ Ho 13.7; predatory, Je 5.6 (‖ λέων, λύκος). Cf. παρδάλεος.

παρεδρεύω.ʃ

to be seated as advisor to judge: *s* wisdom, ἐπὶ

πύλαις δυναστῶν 'at the gates of notables' Pr 1.21 (|| παρὰ πύλαις 8.3). Cf. πάρεδρος.

πάρεδρος, ον.ʃ

seated as counsellor: + gen. loci, τῶν πυλῶν αὐτοῦ 'at his gates' Wi 6.14, τῶν σῶν θρόνων 'by your throne' 9.4. Cf. παρεδρεύω.

παρεῖδον (aor.): inf. παριδεῖν, ptc. παριδών, subj. παρίδω, impv. ~ιδε.

to disregard, intentionally overlook: + acc., τὰς ἐντολὰς κυρίου Le 6.2, ἄγνοιαν Si 28.7; || πλημμελέω Nu 5.6; παρίδῃ αὐτὸν ὑπεριδοῦσα 'disregard him, despising (him)' 5.12; || ἐπιλανθάνομαι 'forget' Pr 4.5; + inf., Si 7.10. Cf. ὑπεροράω.

I **πάρειμι** (< εἰμί): inf. παρεῖναι, ptc. παρών; impf.3s παρῆν; fut. παρέσομαι; aor.subj. παρῶ.

1. *to be alongside as companion of*: + dat. pers., Da 7.13 LXX. **b**. *to be present*: *s* hum., ἀπόντες καὶ παρόντες 'whether absent or present' Wi 11.11. Cf. συμπάρειμι.

2. *to have arrived*: πάρεστιν ἕτοιμα ὑμῖν 'they have arrived ready for you' De 32.35; ἤδη παρέσται 'he'll be here at any moment' To 10.6 $\mathfrak{G}^{II}$; πάρει 'you are there already' Ps 138.8 (|| εἶ ἐκεῖ), Πάρεσμεν 'Here we are, sir' Ba 3.35; || παραγέγονα Jb 1.7; ἐπί + acc. (place), 3M 1.23; πρός τινα 1E 6.3 (|| ἔρχομαι 2E 5.3); *s* inan., ἐν τῷ παρεῖναι τὸν καιρόν 'when the time comes' Hb 3.2 (|| ἐγγίζω), sim. La 4.19 (|| ἐγγίζω, πληρόομαι); πάρεστιν ἡμέρα κυρίου 'the day of the Lord has arrived' Jl 2.1, ἐνιαυτὸς λυτρώσεως 'the year of redemption' Is 63.4; ἡ κατὰ τὸ παρὸν εὐημερία 'the present success' 3M 3.11, ἐπὶ τοῦ παρόντος 'for the moment' 2M 6.26; πτῶμα 'collapse' Is 30.13; opp. ἀπέρχομαι Wi 4.2. **b**. *to have presented oneself*: to meet a visitor arrived, εἰς ἀπάντησίν τινος Jd 19.3 A.

3. impers., + inf., *to be possible*: 2M 6.9, + dat. pers. Wi 11.21, cf. πάρεστίν σοι .. τὸ δύνασθαι 12.18; παρόν μοι σῴζεσθαι 'though it is possible to rescue myself' 4M 6.27.

Cf. ἄπειμι, παρουσία, ἥκω.

II **πάρειμι** (< εἶμι): pres.ptc. παριών.ʃ

to chance to pass by: *s* pedestrian, Pr 9.15; 15.10.

παρεισπορεύομαι.ʃ *

to infiltrate: εἰς τὰς κώμας 'the villages' 2M 8.1. Cf. εἰσπορεύομαι: Caird 1969.27.

παρεκλείπω: aor. ~εξέλιπον.ʃ*

to fail to be available any more for sbd: *s* foods, + acc. pers., Ju 11.12. Cf. ἐκλείπω.

παρεκτείνω.ʃ

1. *to stretch out and reach*: ἐπὶ τὴν θάλασσαν Ez 47.19.

2. mid. *to measure oneself with*: + dat., Pr 23.4.

παρέλκυσις, εως. f.ʃ *

delay: of punishment, Jb 25.3. Cf. παρέλκω, χρονίζω.

παρέλκω: aor.subj. ~ελκύσω.ʃ

to keep in suspense: + acc., ὀφθαλμοὺς ἐπιδεεῖς 'the eyes of the needy' Si 4.1, ἐπ' ἐλημοσύνῃ .. αὐτόν '(keep) him (waiting) for your alms' 29.8; δόσιν 4.3; χρόνον 'to delay' 29.5. Cf. παρέλκυσις.

παρεμβάλλω: fut. ~βαλῶ; aor. παρενέβαλον, impv. ~έμβαλε, ptc. ~βαλών, inf. ~βαλεῖν, subj. ~βάλω; pf. ~βέβληκα, ptc. ~βεβληκώς; plpf. παρεμβεβλήκειν.

1. *to take up temporary quarters*: εἶδεν παρεμβολὴν θεοῦ παρεμβεβληκυῖαν Ge 32.1; *s* a large crowd on movement, παρὰ τὰ ὕδατα Ex 15.27; ἐπ' ὄρους τοῦ θεοῦ 18.5; troops, ἐπὶ τοὺς ἐχθρούς σου De 23.9, ἐπὶ τὴν ἄκραν 'against the citadel' 1M 6.26; εἰς αὐτούς Jd 6.5 B (A: ἐπ' αὐτούς); troops led by an angel (?), π. ἄγγελος κυρίου κύκλῳ τῶν φοβουμένων αὐτὸν καὶ ῥύσεται αὐτούς Ps 33.8.

2. *to force oneself* into: ἐν μέσῳ λόγων '(interrupt) when sbd else is speaking' Si 11.8.

Cf. παρεμβολή.

παρεμβολή, ῆς.

1. *place of encampment*: where soldiers are quartered, Jo 4.8 (|| στρατοπεδεία vs. 3), Zc 14.15; θεοῦ Ge 32.1; of nomads, 32.7; of temporary station on the Israelites' journey in the wilderness, Ex 29.14. Cf. στρατοπεδεία and ὑπόστημα **2**.

2. *company of soldiers ready for battle*: Am 4.10; Jl 2.11, 1M 3.17, 6.33.

3. *company of people travelling together*, 'convoy, caravan': μεγάλη Ge 50.9. Cf. συνοδία.

Cf. παρεμβάλλω.

παρεμπίπτω.ʃ

to undertake entry: εἴς τι Wi 7.25. Cf. εἰσέρχομαι.

παρενοχλέω: fut.pass. ~ληθήσομαι; aor. παρηνώχλησα. On the twofold augment, see Thack. 208.

to annoy: + dat. pers., Jd 14.17 B (A: acc.), Jb 16.3¶, + inf. (bother caused) 1K 28.15; *s* god, Mi 6.3 (|| λυπέω); + acc. pers., Je 26.27, Da 3.50; *s* lions, 6.18 LXX; pass. and + περί τινος 2M 11.31. On the fluctuation between the dat. and acc., see Helbing, *Kasus*., 99f. and *ND*, 4.167.

πάρεξ.

I. prep. w. gen., *beside, on a level with* (i.e. implying an equivalent or alternative), often with a negator: σῴζων οὐκ ἔστιν πάρεξ ἐμοῦ 'there is no saviour beside me' Ho 13.4 (|| πλήν), sim. Is 45.21; οὐκ ἔστιν ἑτέρα π. ⸢ταύτης ἐνταῦθα⸣ (*L*: αὐτῆς ὧδε) 'there is here none other than this' 1K 21.10; Ez 42.14. **b**. *in addition to, besides*: Ne 7.67 (|| χωρίς 2E 2.65), Jd 8.26 B (A: πλήν; || B: ἐκτός), 2E 1.6.

II. adversative adv.: "the boy did not notice anything of the matter, but (πάρεξ) Jonathan and David did" 1K 20.39 (*L* πλήν); "would they take of it a peg to hang on it every kind of tool? No (πάρεξ), it is only given to fire to be consumed' Ez 15.3f.

Cf. ἐκτός, πλήν, χωρίς.

παρεξίστημι: pf.ptc. παρεξεστηκώς.ʃ

to take leave of one's senses: *s* prophet and ‖ πνευματοφόρος, Ho 9.7. Cf. ἐξίστημι.

παρεπιδείκνυμι.ʃ *

to point out besides: + pleonastic ἅμα and acc. rei, 2M 15.10. Cf. ἐπιδείκνυμι.

παρεπίδημος, ον.ʃ

being a sojourner in a foreign land: subst., πάροικος καὶ π. ἐγώ εἰμι μεθ' ὑμῶν 'I am an alien and a sojourner among you' Ge 23.4; πάροικος ἐγώ εἰμι παρὰ σοὶ καὶ π. καθὼς πάντες οἱ πατέρες μου Ps 38.13, cf. 1Pet 1.11. Cf. πάροικος: Grundmann, *TDNT* 2.64f.; Spicq 3.41-3.

πάρεργος, ον.ʃ

trifling, of little consequence: *s* οὐ π. ἀγωνία 'no little anxiety' 2M 15.19.

παρέρχομαι: fut. παρελεύσομαι; aor. παρῆλθον, inf. παρελθεῖν, ptc. ~ελθών, impv. ~ελθε, subj. ~έλθω, opt.3s ~έλθοι; pf.ptc. παρεληλυθώς.

1. *to move past without taking notice of*: abs., ἐπὶ ^τῆς τρίβου^ Jb 28.8 (*s* lion and ‖ πατέω); + acc. pers., μὴ παρέλθῃς τὸν παῖδά σου Ge 18.3; Ex 23.5, De 2.8, Is 33.22; + acc. rei, τὸν λόγον αὐτοῦ 'what he said' Ju 11.10. **b**. *to fail to be noticed by*: *s* sins, Jb 14.16, "Don't give a miss to your share of hearty delight" Si 14.14, "no thought escaped Him" 42.20 (‖ κρύπτομαι); subject-matter, οὐ παρῆλθεν λόγος ἀπὸ Σαλωμων 'nothing escaped S.' 2C 9.2.

2. *to pass by beside*: abs. Ex 12.23*a*, 33.22; + acc., παρελθάτω τὰ πρόβατά σου Ge 30.32, τὴν θύραν Ex 12.23*b*; παρὰ τὸ ὄρος Nu 20.19; διὰ τῶν ὁρίων αὐτοῦ 20.21; διὰ τῆς γῆς σου 21.22; ‖ παραπορεύομαι Is 51.23; κατὰ πρόσωπόν τινος 'in front of sbd' 1K 16.8.

3. *to depart and move on to the next stage*: εἰς τὴν ὁδὸν ὑμῶν Ge 18.5; safely and unharmed, ὁ λαός σου οὗτος, ὃν ἐκτήσω 'this nation of yours, whom you have acquired' Ex 15.16; Is 10.29; ὅταν παρέλθῃ, λήμψεται ὑμᾶς 'when it [= storm] departs, it would take you along with it' 28.19; πρότερός σου 'ahead of you' 33.19; διὰ τῆς γῆς σου Nu 20.17, διὰ τῶν ὁρίων αὐτοῦ 21.23. **b**. *to depart and be gone*: *s* God's injunction, Ps 148.6; ἀνομία 56.2 (poss. **5b**); ἐξουσία Da 7.14 TH; ὡς σκιά 'like a shadow' Wi 5.9; τὰ παρελθόντα 'the past events' 11.12, τὰ παρηλυθότα καὶ τὰ ἐσόμενα 'the past and the future' Si 42.19.

4. *to traverse* en route to another destination: + acc., τὰ ὅριά σου Nu 20.17, 21.22; τὸν Ἰορδάνην 32.21 (‖ διαβαίνω vs. 29), φάραγγα 'valley' Is 10.29; ἐν μέσῳ τῶν ἐθνῶν, οὓς παρήλθετε De 29.16.

5. *to come to an end, glide by*: *s* a period of time, τὰ ἑπτὰ ἔτη τῆς εὐθηνίας 'the seven years of abundance' Ge 41.53; αἱ ἡμέραι τοῦ πένθους 'the mourning period' 50.4; ἕως οὗ παρέλθῃ ἡ ἡμέρα 'Set out on a difficult journey by the time the day passes' Jd 19.8*L*; ἕως ἂν παρέλθῃ ἡ ὀργὴ κυρίου Is 26.20; ἄμητος 'harvest' Je 8.20 (‖ διέρχομαι). **b**. *to lapse, become no longer binding*: *s* δόγμα 'decree' Da 6.12 TH.

6. *to come forward* for some business: 4M 11.3.

7. *to overlook, allow to go unpunished* or *unharmed*: + acc. pers., Am 7.8, 8.2; οὐ μὴ παρέλθῃ ὑμᾶς καταιγίς ('storm') Is 28.17.

8. *to move over* to an object: παρελθὼν ὄψομαι τὸ ὅραμα τὸ μέγα τοῦτο 'I shall go over and see this great sight' Ex 3.3; πάρελθε 'Come over here' Si 29.26.

9. *to contravene, transgress*: + acc., διαθήκην De 17.2, Je 41.18; ἐντολήν De 26.13; Da 9.5 LXX (TH ἐκκλίνω), τὴν λατρείαν ἡμῶν 'our religion' 1M 2.23, τὸν φόβον σου '(to fail to show) the respect due to you' Es *L* 7.5; ὅριον 'boundary limiting access' Ps 103.9; ἀπὸ ἐνταλμάτων αὐτοῦ 'from his commands' Jb 23.12. Cf. παραβαίνω.

10. *to enter a relationship*: ἐν διαθήκῃ De 29.11 (ἐν = εἰς), cf. a frequent QH collocation **עבר בברית** e.g., 1QS 1.16.

11. *to fail to come to pass*: Es F 2 o'.

Cf. ἔρχομαι, παράγω, παροδεύω, ἐκκλίνω.

παρέχω: fut.act. παρέξω, mid. παρέξομαι, ptc.mid. παρεξόμενος; aor.act. παρέσχον, mid. παρεσχόμην, inf. παρασχέσθαι.ʃ

1. *to cause, occasion*: + acc. rei, τὴν βάσανον 'the torment' Wi 17.13; and dat., ἀγῶνα παρέχειν ἀνθρώποις 'to present men with a struggle' Is 7.13; κόπον τοῖς βοηθήσασιν αὐτοῖς 'trouble to those who helped them' Si 29.4; παρέχωσιν ἡμῖν πράγματα 'cause us troubles' Es 3.18 *L*.

2. *to supply, furnish*: + acc. rei, ἡσυχίαν Jb 34.29¶, ἥλιον ἀβλαβῆ 'a harmless sun' Wi 18.3; and dat., ἕτοιμον ἄρτον .. παρέσχες αὐτοῖς 16.20; παρέσχου τῷ κάλλει μου δύναμιν 'you provided my beauty with strength' Ps 29.8; εὐστάθειαν .. τοῖς ἡμετέροις πράγμασιν 'our government with stability' 3M 6.28. **b**. *to supply means* for sth to become a reality: + an inf. clause, 4M 3.2, 11.12.

3. *to render* so and so: + acc. and pred. adj., εὐσταθῆ καὶ ἀτάραχα παρέχωσιν ἡμῖν .. τὰ πράγματα 'to make our government .. secure and trouble-free' Es B 7. **b**. mid. = act.: + acc. and pred. adj., τήν τε βασιλείαν ἥμερον .. παρεξόμενος 'making the kingdom peaceful ..' Es B 2. Cf. τίθημι **II 3**.

παρηγορέω.ʃ
to exhort: abs., 4M 12.2 (ll παρακαλέω vs. 6). Cf. παρηγορία, παρακαλέω.

παρηγορία, ας.ʃ
exhortation: from a king to a subject of his, 4M 5.12, 6.1. Cf. παρηγορέω.

παρθενία, ας. f.ʃ
state of being a virgin or *a phase in a woman's life when she is a virgin*: Jd 11.37f. *L*, Je 3.4; γυνὴ ~ας Si 15.2; 42.10 (ll νεότης vs. 9); τὰ ἁγνὰ τῆς ~ας 'the purity of virginity' 4M 18.8. Cf. παρθένος, νεότης.

παρθένια. n.pl.ʃ *
tokens of virginity: De 22.14, 15, 17, 20. **b**. *period* or *state of virginity*: Jd 11.37, 38 (*L* παρθενία). Cf. παρθένος.

παρθενικός, ή, όν.ʃ
pertaining to a period when one (fem.) *is young*: τὸν ἄνδρα αὐτῆς τὸν ~όν 'her husband whom she married when young' Jl 1.8; κοράσια ~ὰ καλὰ τῷ εἴδει 'good-looking young maidens' Es 2.3 o'. Cf. παρθένος.

παρθένος, ου. f.
young woman: marriageable, Ge 24.14; not yet touched by a man, π. ἦν, ἀνὴρ οὐκ ἔγνω αὐτήν 24.16 (sim. Jd 21.12), ἀμνήστευος 'not engaged' Ex 22.16, παῖς π. μεμνηστευμένη 'engaged' De 22.23; so called just after having been raped, Ge 34.3; so referred to by her brother and mother, 24.55 (ll παῖς vs. 57); ll νεανίσκος, Am 8.13, Zc 9.17, Je 28.22, La 1.18, Ps 77.63; applied to the Israelites - π. τοῦ Ισραηλ Am 5.2 (ll οἶκος Ισραηλ), π. Ισραηλ Je 18.13, π. θυγάτηρ Σιων Is 37.22, ~ῳ θυγατρὶ Ιουδα La 1.15; γυναῖκα ~ον Le 21.13; as distinct from widow and divorcée, Ez 44.22; conceives and gives birth, Is 7.14. Applied to a girl as young as five years old: *ND* 4.224, see also Plato, *Leg*. 794c, and cf. Renehan 2.114f. **b**. virginity stressed (?): π. νεᾶνις 3K 1.2 (MT: נַעֲרָה בְתוּלָה = *L*), cf. παῖς π. De 22.23, 28 (MT same as at 3K 1.2) and γηραιαὶ ~οι 'elderly virgins' Philo, *Contemp. Life* 68.

Cf. γυνή, παρθενικός, παρθένια, ἀποπαρθενόω, κοράσιον, νεανίσκος, παῖς: Spicq 3.44-52; Chadwick 226-9.

παρίημι: fut. παρήσω; aor. παρῆκα, impv. πάρες, subj. παρῶ, pass. παρείθην; pf.pass. παρεῖμαι, impv.3pl παρείσθωσαν, ptc. παρειμένος.

1. *to let fall*: ***o*** hand, Je 4.31 (***s*** a woman in labour out of despair). **b**. pass. *to become emasculated, enervate*: ***s*** hands Zp 3.16, Si 2.12 (ll καρδία δειλή 'fearful heart' ll κ. παρειμένη vs. 13), 25.23 (ll γόνατα παραλελυμένα 'paralysed knees'); hum., 4.29 (+ νωθρός 'sluggish'); ἐκλελοιπότας .. καὶ παρειμένους 'exhausted .. weakened' De 32.36, παντόθεν 'altogether' Je 20.9; ll ἐκλύομαι 2K 4.1B; 3M 2.13.

2. *to take no note of, disregard*: + acc., Ps 137.8, ἁμαρτήματα 'sins' Si 23.2, ἱεροὺς .. ὅρκους 'sacred oaths' 4M 5.29; pass. Ma 2.9 (ll ἐξουδενόω); γῆν '(stopped working) the ground' 1K 2.5; ***o*** soil, 'neglected,' hence 'lean' Nu 13.21 (:: πίων 'fertile'). Cf. παροράω.

3. *to give complete freedom of action and not interfere* or *bother*: + acc. pers., Πάρες ἡμᾶς, ὅπως δουλεύσωμεν .. 'Leave us alone so that we may serve ..' Ex 14.12; Ju 12.12. Cf. ἀφίημι.

Cf. ἐκλείπω, ἐκ~, παραλύω.

πάρινος, η, ον.ʃ*
of marble: ***s*** στῦλος 'pillar' Es 1.6, λίθος ib. o'.

πάριος, α, ον.ʃ
of (the island) Paros: ***s*** precious building stone, 1C 29.2.

παρίστημι: fut. παραστήσω, mid. ~στήσομαι; 1aor. ~έστησα, inf. ~στῆσαι, ptc. ~στήσας, subj. ~στήσω, 2aor. ~έστην, impv. παράστηθι, inf. ~στῆναι, ptc. ~στάς, pass. ~σταθείς; pf. ~έστηκα, 3pl ~κασι, ptc. παρεστηκώς, παραστήκων, inf. παρεστάναι, ~εστηκέναι; plpf. ~ειστήκειν.

I. tr.(pres.act., fut.act., 1aor.), *to stand next to* sbd or sth (dat.): + acc., "stationed 1,000 soldiers with each elephant' 1M 6.35, ἱερεῖς 'priests' 3K 12.32; παρὰ Δαγων '(the ark of the Lord) beside D.' 1K 5.2.

2. *to present, proffer*: abs., Ps 49.21 (***o*** prosecutor or witness?), Ex 19.17; εἰς θήραν .. τὰ τέκνα αὐτῶν 'their children for prey' Ho 9.13.

3. *to furnish, supply*: κληρονόμον 'heir' Si 23.22, τέκνα 23.23.

4. *to dispose* to a certain action: + acc. (elephants) εἰς τὸν πόλεμον 1M 6.34; + acc. pers. (soldiers), εὐθαρσεῖς .. καὶ ἑτοίμους .. ἀποθνῄσκειν 'bold .. and ready to die' 2M 8.21.

II. intr. (pres.mid., fut.mid., 2aor., pf. with the present force, plpf. with the impf. force), *to stand by* literally: + dat. pers., Ex 18.13 (watching the proceedings?); 34.5; ἐπὶ τῆς θυσίας Nu 23.3; ἐκ δεξιῶν σου 'at your right hand' Ps 44.10, ἐνώπιόν σου 3K 10.8 (ll dat. 2C 9.7); + dat. rei, θείῳ θρόνῳ 'divine throne' 4M 17.18. **b**. *to present oneself, appear*: Ju 9.6 (ll πάρειμι), πρός τινα 4K 5.25 *L* (B: dat.); as adversary Ps 2.2, Si 51.2; ***s*** lions' whelps, Is 5.29.

2. *to stand by to serve* or *assist*: + dat. pers., Ge 18.8, 40.4, 45.1, Ex 24.13, De 1.38; Da 7.10 LXX (ll θεραπεύω; TH λειτουργέω); τῷ κυρίῳ πάσης τῆς γῆς Zc 4.14, 6.5; Jd 3.19A (royal servant; B: ἐφίστημι); ἐκ δεξιῶν πένητος 'at the right hand of the poor' Ps 108.31; ἐνώπιον τοῦ κυρίου Jb 1.6, ᾧ

[= τῷ θεῷ] παρέστην ἐνώπιον αὐτοῦ 3K 17.1; ἐνώπιον ^τῆς κιβωτοῦ^ Jd 20.28; μετά τινος Nu 1.5; ἐπὶ τῆς ἐπισκοπῆς 'to oversee the census-taking' 7.2; as cultic functionary, ἔναντι τῆς συναγωγῆς λατρεύειν αὐτοῖς 16.9; ἔναντι κυρίου λειτουργεῖν De 10.8; 17.12, κατὰ πρόσωπόν μου [= τοῦ θεοῦ] Je 42.19; *s* God, Wi 19.22. **b**. *to render support*: to a cause (dat.), πάσῃ ὁδῷ οὐκ ἀγαθῇ Ps 35.5.

3. *to be ripe*: *s* crop, ἡ κριθὴ παρεστηκυῖα 'the barley was ripe' Ex 9.31; παρέστηκε τρυγητός 'the crop is ripe (for harvesting)' Jl 3.13, see Walters 226f. and Lee 56f.

4. *to hold one's own and function well*: Ex 18.23.

Cf. (συμπαρ)ίστημι, παραστήκω, διακονέω, θεραπεύω, λειτουργέω, παράκειμαι: Bertram, *TDNT* 5.838f.

παροδεύω: aor. παρώδευσα, subj. ~δεύσω, impv.3s ~δευσάτω, ptc. ~δεύσας.ʃ

to happen to pass by: *s* hum., Ez 36.34; memory, Wi 5.14. **b** *to fail to notice*: + acc., Wi 1.8 (ǁ λανθάνω); *to pass by without taking notice of*: + acc., 2.7, τὴν ἀλήθειαν 6.22, σοφίαν 10.8.

Cf. παρέρχομαι.

πάροδος, ου. m./f.

1. f. *way past* or *by* (?): Ge 38.14.

*__2__. m. *passer-by*: Ez 16.15; 2K 12.4 (*L* ὁδοιπόρος).

3. *act of passing on the way to elsewhere*: of a foreign army, 4K 25.24; of animals, Wi 17.9; fig. of evanescent human existence, 2.5.

Cf. ὁδός, ὁδοιπόρος.

παροικεσία, ας. f.ʃ * (παροικέω and πάροικος attested in Cl. Gk)

temporary stay as resident alien (πάροικος): ἀντὶ μιᾶς ἡμέρας ~ας σου 'your one-day stay as πάροικος' Zc 9.12; γῆ ~ας Ez 20.38. Cf. παροικέω.

παροικέω: fut. ~κήσω; aor. παρῴκησα, inf. ~οικῆσαι; pf. παρῴκηκα.

1. *to live in the proximity of* (τινι): τῷ μόσχῳ τοῦ οἴκου Ων 'next to the calf of the house of On' Ho 10.5; παρά τι Jd 5.17 A. **b**. *to be present nearby*: "enemies' swords are nearby all around you" Je 6.25.

2. *to stay as (short-term) resident alien*: of Abram in Egypt during a famine back home, Ge 12.10; μετὰ Λαβαν 32.4 (having lasted some 20 years); προσήλυτος ὁ παροικῶν ἐν σοί Ex 20.10; *s* fugitives, σοι Is 16.4. At Ge 47.9 Jacob is said to have lived (παροικῶ) already 130 (!) years: most likely a mechanical translation of מְגוּרַי rather than "j'ai passés sur terre" (*BA*).

3. *to live as new resident*: + acc., γῆν Ge 17.8, Ex 6.4 (ǁ ἐπὶ γῆς); ἐν τῇ γῇ 47.4 (ǁ κατοικεῖν 'to settle down').

4. *to dwell* in general: ἐν τῷ σκηνώματί σου Ps 14.1 (ǁ κατασκηνόω).

Cf. παροικεσία, παροικία, πάροικος, πρόσκειμαι: Casevitz 1985.184f.

παροίκησις, εως. f.ʃ

= παροικεσία, q.v.: κληρονομῆσαι τὴν γῆν τῆς ~εώς σου Ge 28.4; 36.7; ἐν ~ει μισηθήσεται 'will be hated as sojourner' Si 21.28. Cf. παροικεσία, παροικέω: Casevitz 1985.185.

παροικία, ας. f. * (⇒ παροικεσία).

1. *state of being* πάροικος (q.v.): λαὸς ~ας Hb 3.16; ἐπὶ τὸν τῆς ~ας αὐτῶν χρόνον 'during their time of transit' 3M 7.19. **b**. *act of living w. sbd else at his expense*: Si 29.23.

2. = πάροικος: La 2.22.

3. *dwelling-place*: Ps 54.16. **b**. coll., *residents in one's neighbourhood*: Si 16.8.; *residents as* πάροικοι, PSol 17.17.

Cf. παροικέω, ξενιτεία: Casevitz 1985.185.

πάροικος, ον.

1. *situated in the neighbourhood*: αἱ ~οι αὐτῆς 'its neighbouring (cities)' Je 29.19.

2. *being in the status of short-term resident alien*: ~ον ἔσται τὸ σπέρμα σου ἐν γῇ οὐκ ἰδίᾳ 'your offspring shall be resident aliens in a land not their own' Ge 15.13; ~ός εἰμι ἐν γῇ ἀλλοτρίᾳ Ex 2.22, sim. 18.3; π. καὶ παρεπίδημος ἐγώ εἰμι μεθ' ὑμῶν 'I am .. and a sojourner among you' Ge 23.4, cf. Ps 38.13; subst., π. ἢ μισθωτός '.. or a hireling' Ex 12.45 (unlike προσήλυτος [vs. 48] not allowed to partake of a passover meal), Le 22.10; ἀντιλήμψῃ αὐτοῦ ὡς προσηλύτου καὶ ~ου 'you shall assist him ..' 25.35; τῷ ~ῳ τῷ προσκειμένῳ πρὸς σέ 25.6; ~οι Κρητων Zp 2.5; ǁ ἀλλότριος De 14.20; + ἀλλογενής PSol 17.28.

Cf. παροικία, παροικέω, παρεπίδημος, προσήλυτος: *BA* ad Ex 2.22; Casevitz 1985.186f.

παροιμία, ας. f.

proverbial saying: συνέσεως Si 6.35; ǁ διήγημα 8.8; + ᾠδή, παραβολή 47.17; Pr 1.1. Cf. παραβολή.

παροιμιάζω.ʃ

cite proverbs written by: τινά τινι (audience) 4M 18.16.

παροινέω: fut. ~νήσω.ʃ

to revile, abuse: Is 41.12 (ǁ ἀντιπολεμέω).

παροιστράω: fut. παροιστρήσω; aor. παροίστρησα.ʃ *

to act in frenzy: ὡς δάμαλις παροιστρῶσα 'as a heifer hopping mad' Ho 4.16, ὥσπερ ἄρκοι 'as bears' 2K 17.8*L*; *s* hum. παροιστρήσουσι καὶ ἐπισυστήσονται ἐπὶ σὲ κύκλῳ 'they will go mad and gang up against you all around' Ez 2.6.

παροξύνω: fut. ~ξυνῶ, fut. ~ξυνθήσομαι; aor.act. παρώξυνα, inf. παροξῦναι, ptc. ~ξύνας, pass. παρωξύνθην, ptc. παροξυνθείς, subj. ~ξυνθῶ.

1. *to sharpen* and thus make glisten and shine: ***o*** metal weapon, ὡς ἀστραπὴν τὴν μάχαιράν μου 'my sword like a lightning' De 32.41.

2. *to provoke*: ἐπί + acc., παρωξύνθη ὁ θυμός μου ἐπ' αὐτούς 'my anger has been aroused against them' Ho 8.5, sim. Zc 10.3; ἐπί + dat., De 9.19, 32.16; ***o*** (acc.) God, Nu 14.11, 16.30, 20.24, De 31.20, 32.16 (last ‖ ἐκπικραίνω); ἐχθρούς 2K 12.14 (*L* παροργίζω 'to anger'); τὸν θεὸν ἐν τοῖς λόγοις ὑμῶν 'provoke God with your words' Ma 2.17*a* cf. ib. *b*; God's spirit, Is 63.10; τὸ ὄνομά σου Ps 73.10, πρόσωπον ἑταίρου (‖ ὀξύνω) Pr 27.17; βασιλεῖς Is 23.11; pass. De 1.34, 32.19, Ho 8.5; ***o*** τὰ ὄρη Is 5.25; + dat., τοῖς κατοικοῦσι Βαβυλῶνα Je 27.34; *+ ἔν τινι (pers.) Je 22.15, 2E 9.14.

3. *to go against the grain of, defy*: + acc. rei, τὸ λόγιον τοῦ ἁγίου Ισραηλ Is 5.24 (‖ οὐ θέλω), τὴν βουλὴν τοῦ ὑψίστου Ps 106.11.

Cf. παροργίζω, παροξυσμός, πικραίνω, θυμόω.

παροξυσμός, οῦ. m.ʃ

state of being irritated: ***s*** God, ἐν θυμῷ καὶ ὀργῇ καὶ ~ῷ μεγάλῳ σφόδρα De 29.28, sim. Je 39.37. Cf. παροξύνω, θυμός, ὀργή.

παρόρασις, εως. f.ʃ

v.n. of παροράω: ***s*** God, περὶ τὸν τόπον 2M 5.17. Cf. παροράω.

παροράω: fut. ~όψομαι, inf.pass. ~ραθήσεσθαι; pf. ptc.pass. παρωραμένος.

to overlook on purpose, disregard: + acc. pers., σε ἰδὼν παρορῶ Is 57.11; + acc. rei, ἁμαρτήματα 'sins' Wi 11.23. Cf. παρόρασις, παρεῖδον, παρίημι.

παροργίζω: fut. ~γιῶ; aor. παρώργισα, subj. ~γίσω, inf. ~γίσαι, pass. ~γισθῆναι; pf.ptc.pass. παρωργισμένος.

to anger: + acc., ***o*** God, De 4.25, τὸν ἅγιον τοῦ Ισραηλ Is 1.4; ἐν τοῖς εἰδώλοις 32.21a (‖ παραζηλόω); Ho 12.14 (v.l. με, and ‖ θυμόω), ἐν τῷ παροργίσαι με τοὺς πατέρας ὑμῶν Zc 8.14; ‖ παραπικραίνω Ps 77.40; πνεῦμα κυρίου Mi 2.7; + παροξύνω PSol 4.21; ***o*** hum., De 32.21[2] (‖ παραζηλόω), Si 4.2 (‖ λυπέω), καρδίαν 4.3, Ez 32.9. **b**. *to arouse*: + acc., θυμὸν ^τοῦ θεοῦ^ Od 12.10.

Cf. παρόργισμα, ὀργίζομαι, παροξυσμός, παροξύνω, θυμόω, παραζηλόω, παραπικραίνω.

παρόργισμα, ατος. n.

act which angers: ***o*** God, 2C 35.19[d] (‖ παροργισμός 4K 23.26). Cf. παροργίζω and subs.

παροργισμός, οῦ. m.

= prec.: 4K 23.26 (‖ παρόργισμα 2C 35.19[d]).

παρορμάω: aor.inf. ~μῆσαι, opt.3s ~μήσειεν.ʃ

to urge on: ἐπί τι 2M 15.17, 4M 12.6.

παρουσία, ας. f.ʃ

1. *arrival*: of the enemy, 2M 8.12; of sbd important: Ju 10.18. Cf. *ND* 4.167f.

2. *presence in the vicinity*: 2M 15.21, 3M 3.17.

Cf. I πάρειμι: Deissmann 1923.314-20; Spicq 3.53.

παρρησία, ας. f.

freedom of action: μετὰ ~ας 'openly' Le 26.13, Pr 10.10 (opp. winking), μ. π... χηρῆσθαι τοῖς ἑαυτῶν νομίμοις 'to practise their own laws freely' Es E o' 19; στήσεται ἐν ~ᾳ πολλῇ 'will take a truly fearless stance' Wi 5.1; 3M 4.1, 7.12, Si 18.29¶; εὐγενείας 'due to noble birth' 26.21¶. **b**. *candid and uninhibited manner of speech*: μὴ ἔχει τινα ~αν ἔναντι αὐτοῦ; 'he would probably not be allowed to speak up in his presence' Jb 27.10, ἐν πλατείαις ~αν ἄγει 'exercises freedom of speech on the streets' Pr 1.20 (‖ vs. 21 θαρροῦσα 'boldly'), ἐλέγχων μετὰ ~ας 'admonish candidly' 10.10 (instead of eyeing and winking); 'licence of tongue' Si 25.25; 1M 4.18.

Cf. παρρησιάζομαι: Schlier, *TDNT* 5.875-7; Shipp 441f.; Spicq 3.56-62; Drescher 1970.149-52.

παρρησιάζομαι: fut. ~σιάσομαι, ~σιασθήσομαι; aor. ἐπαρρησιασάμην.ʃ

to act with boldness: ἔναντι κυρίου Jb 22.26. **b**. in speech: παρρησιάσομαι ἐν αὐτῷ 'I shall speak boldly about it'(?) Ps 11.6; ἐπὶ τοὺς οἰκέτας σου παρρησιάσεται 'will speak boldly to your domestic staff' Si 6.11; τίς παρρησιάσεται καθαρὸς εἶναι ἀπὸ ἁμαρτιῶν; 'who would have the audacity of saying that he is free from sins?' Pr 20.9 (‖ καυχάομαι); Ps 93.1.

Cf. παρρησία.

παρωθέω: aor.ptc. παρώσας.ʃ

to set aside and ignore: + acc., φιλάνθρωπα '(royal) concessions' 2M 4.11.

παρωμίς, ίδος. f.ʃ *

shoulderstrap: Ex 28.14. Cf. ὦμος.

πάρωρος, ον.ʃ

untimely: occasioned by delay, 3M 5.17.

πᾶς, παντός m.; πᾶσα, πάσης f.; πᾶν, παντός n., on whose use as masc., see Thack. § 12,4.

I. Used absolutely: mostly pl., τὸ πρόσωπον πάντων 'everyone's face' Na 2.11; ποιῶν πάντα 'doing everything' Am 5.8; πάντα ὅσα μοι καθήκει 'all that I need' Ho 2.5, but πᾶς, ὃς ἦν ἐπὶ τῆς ξηρᾶς Ge 7.22, καὶ ἔσται πᾶς, ὃς ἂν ἐπικαλέσεται .. Jl 2.32 and διὰ παντός 'continually' Ex 25.29, Le 6.13, Na 3.19; foll. by pl., ἀπὸ παντὸς τούτων 'any of these' Hg 2.13. **b**. With a generalising τις: πᾶς τις διανοεῖται .. ἐπὶ τὰ πονηρά 'every single one that you may care to name is thinking of evil things' Ge 6.5. **c**. With the def. article: τὸ πᾶν 'everything' Si

42.17; τὰ πάντα, ὅσα ἐποίησεν 'all that he had made' Ge 1.31; τὰς πάσας (sc. πόλεις) παρέδωκεν De 2.36; τοῖς πᾶσι 'to everybody' 2M 12.40. **d.** τὰ πάντα, adv. *in every respect, totally*: Si 22.13¶.

II. Used appositionally with another noun. **a.** *every single* (w. an anarthrous sg. noun following): ἐν παντὶ τόπῳ 'in every single place' Ma 1.11; πᾶς ποιῶν πονηρόν 'every evil-doer' 2.17; exceptionally with the article, πᾶς ὁ κλέπτης .. πᾶς ὁ ἐπίορκος 'every thief .. every perjurious person' Zc 5.3; w. a substantivised ptc. πᾶς ὁ εὑρίσκων με Ge 4.14; πᾶς ὁ ἐκπορευόμενος ἐν (τῇ) δυνάμει Nu 1.3 +; παντὶ τῷ κτίζοντι 'everyone that builds' Hg 2.9, and πᾶς ὁ ὁρῶν σε Na 3.7; *no matter which,* ἄρτου ἢ οἴνου ἢ ἐλαίου ἢ παντὸς βρώματος Hg 2.12; Pr 19.6. ***b.** *no .. whatsoever*, reinforcing negation and with an anarthrous sg. noun following: οὐκ ἀποθανεῖται πᾶσα σὰρξ .. Ge 9.11; πᾶν πνεῦμα οὐκ ἔστιν ἐν αὐτῷ 'there is no breath whatsoever in it' Hb 2.19; perh. not at Si 10.6. See BDF, § 302.1 and Bruce 1952 ad Acts 10.14. Absolutely: οὐκ ἐκλείψει ἐξ αὐτῶν πάντα 'nothing will be unattainable to them' Ge 11.6. With an articular noun, Σῖτος δὲ οὐκ ἦν ἐν πάσῃ τῇ γῇ 'Grain was nowhere in the land' Ge 47.13. **c.** *any* with an anarthrous sg. noun: ὑποζύγιον ἢ πρόβατον ἢ μόσχον ἢ πᾶν κτῆνος 'an ass or a sheep or a bull or any animal' Ex 22.10, παντὸς πράγματος ἀκαθάρτου 'any unclean thing whatsoever' Le 5.2, παρὰ παντὸς θεοῦ 'from any god' Da 6.7. **d.** *the entire, whole*: w. an articular sg. noun following, πᾶσα ἡ γῆ Hb 2.20; following the article, τὸ λοιπὸν πᾶν αἷμα 'the whole of the remaining blood' Ex 29.12; τὸ πᾶν αἷμα αὐτοῦ Le 4.25 ‖ πᾶν τὸ αἷμα αὐτῆς 4.30, πᾶν αὐτοῦ τὸ αἷμα 4.34; τὸ πᾶν στέαρ 4.19 ‖ πᾶν τὸ στέαρ 4.31, πᾶν αὐτοῦ τὸ στέαρ 4.35; τὸν πάντα λαὸν τοῦτον Nu 11.12, τὴν πᾶσαν κακίαν ταύτην 1K 12.20; rarely without the article, πᾶσα συναγωγή Le 9.5; after a noun phrase, τὴν ἵππον πᾶσαν 'the entire cavalry' Ge 14.11, ἐν τῇ ὁδῷ πάσῃ, οὗ ἂν πορευθῇς 'along any route that you might take' 28.15, τῆς γῆς πάσης Ju 7.4, Si 17.17¶. **e.** w. an articular pl. noun or pron. following, 'all': πάντες οἱ ἄνδρες Ob 7; preceding a nominal, τὰ πάντα ἀγαθὰ Αἰγύπτου Ge 45.20, τοὺς πάντας ἄνδρας Jd 12.4 B; πάντων ἡμῶν Ma 2.10; ἐν πᾶσι τούτοις Ho 7.10, cf. ἡ γῆ καὶ οἱ πάντες ἐν αὐτῇ Mi 1.2, and τὸν πάντα Ισραηλ 2K 11.1 (*L* πάντα τὸν Ι.). **f.** articular and w. a num. to indicate a precise quantity: ἐπ' ἄνδρας τοὺς πάντας δύο 'for two men exactly, for two men at the most' Ju 4.7. **g.** w. an anarthrous pl. noun following (rather rare): ἐν πάσαις ὁδοῖς Am 5.17; πάντες ταπεινοὶ γῆς Zp 2.3; πάσας φυλὰς τοῦ Ισραηλ Zc 9.1, but cf. συναγάγετε πρεσβυτέρους πάντας κατοικοῦντας γῆν Jl 1.14. **h.** in apposition to the latent subject: προσήλθατέ μοι πάντες 'you all came up to me' De 1.22.

Cf. ἅπας, ἕκαστος, σύμπας and ὅλος.

πάσσαλος, ου.

oblong object used to fasten to sth more or less stationary, 'peg, pin': π. τοῦ κρεμάσαι ἐπ' αὐτὸν πᾶν σκεῦος '.. to hang on it every kind of tool' Ez 15.3; αὐλῆς 'of a courtyard' Ex 27.19; σκηνῆς 'of a tent' 38.21; ἐπὶ τῆς ζώνης σου 'on your girdle' De 23.13. **b.** euphemism for 'penis': Si 26.12.

πάσσω: aor. ἔπασα, impv.3s πασάτω, ptc.mid. πασάμενος; pf.ptc.pass. πεπασμένος.

to sprinkle solid particles: *o* furnace soot, εἰς τὸν οὐρανόν Ex 9.8, 10; ashes, Ps 147.5; snow-flakes, Si 43.17; roses, Es 1.6 o'; + dat., χοΐ 'soil' 2K 16.13. Cf. Shipp 443.

παστός, οῦ. m.

chamber of newly wed person: **a.** of bridegroom, νυμφίος ἐκπορευόμενος ἐκ ~οῦ αὐτοῦ Ps 18.6. **b.** of bride, νύμφη ἐκ τοῦ ~οῦ αὐτῆς Jl 2.16 (‖ κοιτών for bridegroom); καθημένη ἐν ~ῷ 1M 1.27; 3M 4.6.

Cf. θάλαμος, κοιτών: Drew-Bear 88; LSG s.v.

παστοφόριον, ου. n.

small chamber in a temple: Is 22.15, Je 42.4, Ez 40.17, 1M 4.38; Levites', 1C 9.26; storeroom for cultic objects, 1E 8.58. Cf. Passoni dell'Acqua 1981.

πάσχα. n. indecl., < Semitic פַּסְחָא. *

1. *Passover festival*: π. ἐστὶν κυρίῳ Ex 12.11, ποιῆσαι τὸ π. κυρίῳ 'to celebrate the Passover for the Lord' 12.48; De 16.1; ὁ νόμος τοῦ πάσχα Ex 12.43.

2. *paschal lamb*: θύσατε τὸ π. Ex 12.21; De 16.2.

πάσχω: fut. πείσομαι; aor.subj. πάθω, inf. παθεῖν, ptc. παθών; pf. πέπονθα; plpf. ἐπεπόνθεισα.

1. *to have* sth *done to oneself*: ἐὰν κακὸν πάθωσιν ὑπό τινος .. ἀγαθόν 'if they suffer evil .. or good at sbd's hands' Ep Je 33, κακῶς πάσχουσιν 'they suffer badly' Wi 18.19, τὰ χείριστα 'the worst imaginable' 2M 9.28; 4M 4.25.

2. *to grieve oneself* (over ἐπί τινι): οὐκ ἔπασχον οὐδὲν ἐπὶ τῇ συντριβῇ Ιωσηφ 'they did not grieve at all for the destruction of J.' Am 6.6; Zc 11.5 (‖ μεταμέλομαι); παθεῖν τι ἐπὶ σοί 'to grieve over you a little' Ez 16.5.

Cf. πάθος, μεταμέλομαι: Michaelis, *TDNT* 1.904-9; Chadwick 229-33.

πατάσσω: fut. πατάξω; aor. ἐπάταξα, impv. πάταξον, inf. πατάξαι, ptc. πατάξας, subj. πατάξω, opt. 3s πατάξαι. Never used in the present or impf.

1. *to hit* (mostly) *physically*: **a.** + acc. of victim, με καὶ μητέρα ἐπὶ τέκνοις Ge 32.11; πατάξει καὶ μοτώσει ἡμᾶς 'he will hit us and dress our wounds' Ho 6.1; λίθῳ ἢ πυγμῇ 'with a stone or a fist' Ex

21.18, πληγῇ ἀνιάτῳ 'with an incurable blow' Is 14.6 (|| παίω), πληγῇ μεγάλῃ 19.22; no harm intended, τὴν πέτραν τῇ ῥάβδῳ Nu 20.11; τὴν ὄνον τῇ ῥάβδῳ 22.23 (|| τύπτω vs. 27). **b**. usually w. obj. pers. or animate object, but of the surface of a river, Ex 7.20 (|| τύπτω vs. 17); dust of the earth (χῶμα τῆς γῆς) 8.16; plant, Jn 4.7. **c**. a fatal blow implied: πατάξας τὸν Αἰγύπτιον ἔκρυψεν ἐν τῇ ἄμμῳ 'having struck him, buried him in the sand' Ex 2.12; De 19.4; αὐτοῦ τὴν ψυχήν καὶ ἀποθάνῃ 19.6; || ἀποκτείνω Ps 135.17. **d**. in order to overpower: πατάξουσιν ἐν θαλάσσῃ κύματα, of a rough passage by sea, Zc 10.11. **e**. of military operation and slaying implied: φόνῳ μαχαίρας Nu 21.24; Jd 1.4A (B: κόπτω), πατάξει εἰς θάλασσαν δύναμιν αὐτῆς 'he will deal a blow to her force, which will plunge into the sea' Zc 9.4; + virtual cogn. acc., αὐτοὺς πληγὴν μεγάλην 1M 5.3, sim. 1.30, 1K 6.19, 4K 8.29. **f**. ἔν τινι indicating an instrument used: ἐν ῥάβδῳ πατάξουσιν ἐπὶ σιαγόνα τὰς φυλὰς τοῦ Ισραηλ 'they will hit the tribes of Israel on the cheek with a rod' Mi 5.1; ἐν γλώσσῃ 'with slanders' Je 18.18. **g**. ἔν τινι indicating harm done: "with parching and blight" Am 4.9, sim. Hg 2.17, Zc 12.4*bis*; dat. so used, πατάξει τὸν οἶκον τὸν μέγαν θλάσμασι καὶ τὸν οἶκον τὸν μικρὸν ῥάγμασιν 'he will hit the large house with breaches and the small house with fractures' Am 6.11; πατάξαι σε κύριος παραπληξίᾳ 'may the Lord smite you with derangement' De 28.28 (|| ἐν ἕλκει 'with an ulcer' vs. 27). ***h**. ἔν τινι, a Heb. calque marking a victim: ἐν χιλιάσιν αὐτοῦ 1K 18.7, ἐν τοῖς ἀλλοφύλοις ἑκατὸν ἄνδρας 18.27, τοὺς ἀλλοφύλους .. ἐν τοῖς ἀλλοφύλοις 23.2; also w. a sg. victim - ἐν Δαυιδ 18.11, but local, 'amongst,' ἐν αὐτοῖς ἄνδρας Ne 13.25. **i**. ἐπί τι indicating a place to be hit: πάταξον ἐπὶ τὸ ἱλαστήριον Am 9.1, τὴν εἰκόνα ἐπὶ τοὺς πόδας Da 2.34, cf. εἰς τὸν τράχηλον αὐτοῦ 'at his throat' Ju 13.8, ἐπὶ σιαγόνα 'on the cheek' Mi 5.1. **j**. morally or mentally: + acc., γῆν λόγῳ τοῦ στόματος αὐτοῦ Is 11.4; καρδία Δαυιδ αὐτόν 1K 24.6, 2K 24.10.

2. *to harm physically*: ἐπάταξεν ὁ ἥλιος ἐπὶ τὴν κεφαλὴν Ιωνα Jn 4.8; on ἐπί τι, see above, **1.i**; opp. ἰάομαι De 32.39. **b**. of divine punishment: πᾶσαν σάρκα ζῶσαν Ge 8.21; εἰς ψυχήν 'to kill' 37.21, cf. πατάξῃ ψυχὴν ἀνθρώπου Le 24.17; *o* humans and animals, Ex 9.25; cogn. obj., ἐπάταξεν κύριος ἐν τῷ λαῷ πληγὴν μεγάλην σφόδρα Nu 11.33. **c**. *s* hail (χάλαζα), Ex 9.25. **d**. w. acc. of victim and dat. of instrument, ἀορασίᾳ 'with blindness' Ge 19.11; θανάτῳ Ex 9.15; Nu 14.12 (|| ἀπόλλυμι); ἀπορίᾳ καὶ πυρετῷ καὶ ῥίγει καὶ ἐρεθισμῷ καὶ φόνῳ καὶ ἀνεμοφθορίᾳ καὶ τῇ ὤχρᾳ 'with discomfort, fever, chill, irritation, murder, blight and mildew' De 28.22. **e**. περί τινος (a ground for punishment): Ex 32.35; ἀντὶ τῶν ἁμαρτιῶν ὑμῶν Le 26.24. **f**. fatally: ψυχήν ἀκουσίως Nu 35.11 (manslaughter).

3. *to cause forcefully to move with speed*: + acc. rei, ^κρεάγραν^ εἰς τὸν λέβητα 'the flesh-hook into the cauldron' 1K 2.14, τὸ δόρυ εἰς Δαυιδ .. εἰς τὸν τοῖχον 'the spear at D… at the wall' 19.10 (*L* ἐν τῷ δόρατι τὸν Δ… τὸ δ. εἰς τὸν τ.).

Cf. πλήσσω, παίω, ῥαπίζω, τύπτω, κόπτω, ἀπόλλυμι, ἀφανίζω: Schmidt 3.280-2.

πάταχρον, ου. n.ʃ(< Ar. פִּתַכְרָא) *

idol: Is 8.21, 37.38. Cf. Walters 173-5.

πατέω: fut. πατήσω; aor. ἐπάτησα, subj. πατήσω, inf. πατῆσαι, impv.3s πατησάτω.

1. intr. *to set down one's foot, tread*: in a wine-vat, εἰσπορεύεσθε πατεῖτε Jl 3.13; *s* sole of foot, De 11.24; sandals, ἕνεκεν ὑποδημάτων, τὰ πατοῦντα ἐπὶ τὸν χοῦν τῆς γῆς 'for the sake of sandals with which one walks on the dust of the earth' Am 2.7; cattle and donkeys, Is 32.20.

2. tr. *to tread on*: + acc., μαχηταὶ πατοῦντες πηλὸν ἐν ταῖς ὁδοῖς 'soldiers walking on mire on roads' Zc 10.5; ληνόν 'trough' La 1.15; οἶνον εἰς τὰ ὑπολήνια 'wine into the vats' Is 16.10; ἅλωνα ἐν ἁμάξαις 'a threshing-floor with wagons' 25.10; ruined cities, 26.6; τὴν αὐλήν 'the temple-court' 1.12, τὴν γῆν 42.5; τρίβον 'path' Jb 22.15¶, θυσιαστήριον PSol 8.12; *s* foot, 7.2

Cf. ἐμπερι~, κατα~, περι~, συμπατέω, πατητός: Shipp 443; Bertram, *TDNT* 5.941-3.

πάτημα, ατος. n.ʃ

that which has been trodden on: 4K 19.26; grazing ground, τῶν ποδῶν Ez 34.19. Cf. πατέω.

πατήρ, τρός, voc. πάτερ. m.

1. *male parent*: vs. "son," υἱὸς δοξάζει ~έρα 'A son honours his father' Ma 1.6*a*; || πρεσβύτερος De 32.7; || μήτηρ, Ex 20.12, Mi 7.6; ὁ π. αὐτοῦ καὶ ἡ μήτηρ αὐτοῦ οἱ γεννήσαντες αὐτόν 'his father and mother who begot him' Zc 13.3; applied to God, De 32.6, Ma 1.6*b*, 2.10, Is 63.16, Je 3.19, Ps 88.27. **b**. vocative without a poss. pron.: πάτερ Ge 22.7; κύριε πάτερ καὶ θεὲ ζωῆς μου Si 23.4, but πάτερ μου Jd 11.36 A (B: om. μου). **c**. in collocation with μήτηρ, alw. placed first: even at Le 19.3 against MT. **d**. *he who has brought into being*: || ὁ τετοκώς Jb 38.28, cf. Renehan 1.160.

2. *ancestor, forefather*: ἀπελεύσῃ πρὸς τοὺς ~έρας σου μετ' εἰρήνης Ge 15.15 (of death); ἔσῃ π. πλήθους ἐθνῶν 'ancestor of a multitude of peoples' 17.4, Si 44.19; οὗτος π. Μωαβιτῶν Ge 19.37; καθότι ὤμοσας τοῖς ~άσιν ἡμῶν κατὰ τὰς ἡμέρας τὰς ἔμπροσθεν 'as you swore to our forefathers as in olden days' Mi 7.20; Jl 1.2; of grandfather, Ge 32.9;

+ πρόπαππος 'great-grandfather' Ex 10.6; opp. τέκνον 34.7.

3. honorific title: in official epistles, 1M 11.32; in an address to a prophet-master, 4K 2.12; to one's master, 5.13; a martyr-saint, 4M 7.9.

Cf. μήτηρ, υἱός, πατριά, πατρικός, πάτριος, πρόπαππος, πάππος, πατρῷος.

πατητός, ή, όν.ʃ*

trodden: *s* ληνός 'winepress' Is 63.2. Cf. πατέω.

πατράδελφος, ου. m.

paternal uncle: Jd 10.1. Cf. Renehan 2.115.

πατριά, ᾶς. f.

1. *parental home*: εἰς τὴν ~ὰν αὐτοῦ ἀπελεύσεσθε Le 25.10; ‖ φυλή De 29.18.

2. *group of individuals bound through paternal lineage*, 'clan': ἀρχηγοὶ οἴκων ~ῶν 'heads of households of paternal lineage' Ex 6.14, ἡγούμενοι ~ῶν 'leaders ..' 2C 5.2; τῶν ἐθνῶν Ps 21.28, 95.7; ‖ φυλή Ju 8.1, 2K 14.7B.

Cf. πατήρ: Bertram, *TDNT* 5.1016.

πατριάρχης, ου. m.

chief of a tribe: τῶν φυλῶν Ισραηλ 1C 27.22+. **b**. *remote ancestor*, 'patriarch': *s* Abraham, Isaac, Jacob, 4M 7.19, 16.25.

πατρικός, ή, όν.

pertaining to one's father: πᾶσα ἡ οἰκία ἡ ~ὴ αὐτοῦ Ge 50.8; *s* οἶκος 'parental home' Le 22.13, = ~ά Si 42.10; κατάσχεσις 'property' Le 25.41; κληρονομία 'inheritance' Nu 36.8. **b**. *pertaining to forefathers*: *s* βίβλος '(ancestral) book' Es C 20 *L*, cf. βιβλίον πάτριον Si prol. 10.

Cf. πατήρ, πάτριος, πατρῷος, προγονικός: Schmidt 4.38-40.

πάτριος, α, ον.

pertaining to forefathers: *s* βιβλίον '(ancestral) book' Si prol. 10, cf. πατρικὴ βίβλος Es C 20 *L*; ἐντολαί 4M 9.1, νόμοι 2M 6.1, φωνή 'language' 7.8, ᾠδή 'song' 3M 6.32; subst.n.pl. 2M 7.24. Cf. πατήρ, πατρικός, προγονικός.

πατρίς, ίδος. f.

one's place of origin: γῆ ~ίδος Je 22.10, Ez 23.15; 4M 1.11.

πατρῷος, ον.

1. = πάτριος: Es 7.14 *L*; ~οι τιμαὶ 'that which was valued by forefathers' 2M 4.15; *s* τάφος 'grave' 5.10, ἑορταί 'festivals' 6.6, νόμος 3M 1.23.

2. *of father*: *s* χείρ 4M 16.20.

Cf. πατήρ, πάτριος, μητρῷος: Schmidt 4.38-40.

παῦλα, ας. f.ʃ

cessation: + gen., τῆς ἀνοίας 'of the folly' 2M 4.5. Cf. παῦσις.

παῦσις, εως. f.ʃ *

stillstand: cogn. acc., Je 31.2. Cf. παύω, ἀνάπαυσις, παῦλα.

παύω: fut.act. παύσω, mid. παύσομαι; aor.act. impv. παῦσον, mid. ἐπαυσάμην, impv. παῦσαι, 3s παυσάσθω, inf. παύσασθαι, ptc. παυσάμενος, subj. παύσωμαι; pf. πέπαυμαι.

I. mid. *to stop* doing something, having finished that which one has set out to do: αἱ φωναὶ παύσονται Ex 9.29; τῇ ἡμέρᾳ τῇ ἑβδόμῃ ἐπαύσατο καὶ κατέπαυσεν 'on the seventh day He stopped and left off' 31.17; + gen., τῆς ὀργῆς τοῦ θυμοῦ σου 32.12, τῆς λέξεως 'speech' Jb 38.1; + ἀπό τινος - ἀπὸ τῶν κακῶν 'the harassments' Je 33.13, ἀπὸ πονηριῶν Is 1.16, ἀπὸ ὀργῆς Ps 36.8 (‖ ἐγκαταλείπω); + dat. rei, ῥήμασιν Jb 31.40; **s** rainfall and hail, Ex 9.34; God's anger (θυμός), Is 1.24; slaughter as divine punishment, ἀπὸ υἱῶν Ισραηλ Nu 25.8; complaining, παυσάσθω ὁ γογγυσμὸς .. ἀπ' ἐμοῦ 17.10; + pres. ptc., οἰκοδομοῦντες τὴν πόλιν 'building the city' Ge 11.8; λαλῶν 18.33, De 20.9, Nu 16.31, Jd 15.17 B (A: συντελέω), λέγοντες Jb 37.19, πίνουσαι Ge 24.14, εὐλογοῦντα 27.30; κλαίουσα To 6.1 𝔊[I] (𝔊[II] ἐσίγησεν); Si 28.6; + inf. aor., Je 38.37. **b**. impers. and + τοῦ inf., παυσάσθω τοῦ γενηθῆναι φωνὰς θεοῦ Ex 9.28; Je 28.63.

2. *to cease to be effective*: οὐ δύναται παύσασθαί μου ἡ ψυχή 'my soul cannot stop going' Jb 6.7; ἕως ἂν παύσηταί σου ἡ ὀργή 'until your anger abates' 14.13, sim. Is 10.25.

3. *to cease to exist*: πέπαυται εὐφροσύνη τυμπάνων 'the joy of tambourines is gone' Is 24.8; 16.10; ὁ ἀσεβής 26.10; καταλύματα εἰρήνης 'peaceful dwellings' Je 32.23.

II. act. *to cause to cease to exist*: + acc. rei, τὸ μνημόσυνον αὐτῶν 'their memory' De 32.26, ἀντιλογίας 'quarrels' Pr 18.18.

2. *to stop* sbd (acc.) *doing* sth (ἀπό τινος): παῦσον τὴν γλῶσσάν σου ἀπὸ κακοῦ 'Keep your tongue away from evil' Ps 33.14. **b**. *to suspend operation of*: *o* τρίβους 'roads' Is 58.12. **c**. *to silence*: ῥήμασίν με '.. with words' Jb 6.26.

Cf. ἀφανίζω, καταπαύω, παῦσις, διαλείπω, καταργέω, συντελέω, ἀποτείνω.

πάχνη, ης. f.

frost: harmful to crops, Ps 77.47 (‖ χάλαζα 'hail'), ἐν οὐρανῷ Jb 38.29, χιών 'snow' Da 3.70 LXX; fig. of sth light and evernescent, Wi 5.14, χειμέριος 'wintry' 16.29. Cf. πάγος: Schmidt 2.286-8.

πάχος, ους. n.

thickness: τῆς γῆς '(thick, sticky) soil, i.e. clay' or '(deep) in the ground' 2C 4.17; pl. w. ref. to thick, fatty marrow, Nu 24.8. **b**. *thick object*: ~η ξύλων 'blocks of wood' 2M 4.41.

Cf. παχύς.

παχύνω: aor. ἐπάχυνα, pass. ἐπαχύνθην, subj. παχυνθῶ.ʃ

1. *to fatten*: ***o*** hum. and pass., De 32.15; sword, ἀπὸ στέατος ἀρνῶν '(thickly coated) with the fat of lambs' Is 34.6. **b**. *to make thick*: ***o*** turbulent water (?) 2K 22.12. **c**. pass. *to multiply*: ***s*** grasshoppers, Ec 12.5.

2. metaph., *to make mentally dull*: ***o*** 'mind' (καρδία) Is 6.10.

Cf. πάχος, παχύς.

παχύς, εῖα, ύ.ʃ

1. *having a large quantity of components tightly packed*: ***s*** finger, 2C 10.10, well-fed animals with plump flesh, βόες Ps 143.14, subst.n.sg., Ez 34.3; liquid, ὕδωρ ~ύ 'thick liquid' 2M 1.21, myrrh Ju 10.3.

2. *fertile* (soil): ***s*** ὄρος Is 28.1.

Cf. παχύνω, πάχος, χαῦνος.

πεδάω: aor.ptc. πεδήσας, pass. ἐπεδήθην; pf.ptc. pass. πεπεδημένος.

to constrict: pass., ***o*** hum., Ps 67.7, τοὺς πεπηδημένους τῇ καρδίᾳ 'those with a blocked mind' 89.12, ἐν χειροπέδαις 'with handcuffs' Jb 36.8¶; τὴν θάλασσαν Od 12.3 (ǁ κλείω, σφραγίζομαι). Cf. πέδη, πεδήτης.

πέδη, ης. f.

fetter: Ps 104.18; metaph. of discipline, Si 6.24, ἐν ποσίν 'on feet' 21.19; made of copper, Jd 16.21. Cf. πεδάω, χειροπέδη.

πεδήτης, ου. m.ʃ

one who is incarcerated: metaph., μακρᾶς νυκτός 'of long night' Wi 17.2. Cf. πεδάω.

πέδιλον, ου. n.ʃ

sandal: ἐν ~οις οἱ πόδες αὐτοῦ 'his feet are shod with sandals' Hb 3.5. Cf. ὑπόδημα, σανδάλιον.

πεδινός, ή, όν.

situated in πεδίον 'low-lying land': ***s*** γῆ De 4.43, γῆ ὀρεινὴ καὶ ~ή 11.11; ὄρος Is 13.2; opp. δρυμός 'thicket' 32.19. **b**. subst.f., γῆ understood – αἱ πόλεις αὐτῆς κυκλόθεν καὶ ἡ ὀρεινὴ καὶ ἡ ~ὴ .. Zc 7.7; Je 17.26; ǁ αὐλών 'glen' 31.8.

Cf. πεδίον, ὀρεινός.

πεδίον, ου. m.

plain, *open land* or *field*: hunting ground, ἔξελθε εἰς τὸ π. καὶ θήρευσόν μοι θήραν Ge 27.3; Zc 12.11; w. gen. of particular plains (mostly sg.), π. Συρίας Ho 12.12, Σαμαρείας Ob 19 (ǁ τὸ ὄρος Εφραιμ); of countryside, "you will leave a city and take up your abode ἐν ~ῳ" Mi 4.10; κτήνη τοῦ ~ου 'wild animals' [or better: 'cattle of the field'?] Jl 1.20, 2.22*a*, cf. τοῖς κτήνεσίν σου τοῖς ἐν τοῖς ~οις Ex 9.3; π. ἀφανισμοῦ 'a desolate plain' Jl 3.19, opp. παράδεισος τρυφῆς 2.3; of agricultural land (in pl. and see Lee 58), βρώματα τῶν ~ων τῆς πόλεως τῶν κύκλῳ αὐτῆς 'foods (produced) in the fields around the city' Ge 41.48; τεταλαιπώρηκε τὰ π. 'the fields have suffered' Jl 1.10 (ǁ ἡ γῆ), βεβλάστηκε ~α τῆς ἐρήμου 'fields of the wilderness have come into bloom' 2.22, τὰ π. οὐ ποιήσει βρῶσιν Hb 3.17; opp. built-up area (πόλις), ὅσα τε ἦν ἐν τῇ πόλει καὶ ὅσα ἦν ἐν τῷ ~ῳ Ge 34.28; De 28.3, Je 14.18; difficult there for a victim of violence to call for help, De 22.25 (ǁ ἀγρός vs. 27); opp. temple, 2M 14.33; opp. indoors, πᾶσιν τοῖς ἔργοις τοῖς ἐν τοῖς ~οις 'all the outdoor works' Ex 1.14; Le 17.5; opp. hilly area, ὄρος καὶ π. De 1.7, sim. 8.7, see πεδινός.

Cf. ἀγρός, πεδινός, and ὄρος.

πεζικός, ή, όν.

pertaining to infantry: ***s*** δύναμις 'army' 1M 15.38, 3M 1.1 (+ ἱππικός 'cavalry'). Cf. πεζός.

πεζομαχία, ας. f.ʃ

infantry warfare: 4M 17.24, cf. Renehan 1.161, s.v. πεζομαχέω.

πεζός, ή, όν.

on foot, *walking*: subst. εἰς ἑξακοσίας χιλιάδας ~ῶν 'to the tune of 600,000 foot-soldiers' Ex 12.37; Nu 11.21; of captives being taken away abroad, Ba 5.6. **b**. adv. πεζῇ 'on foot.'

Cf. πεζικός.

πειθαρχέω: fut. ~χήσω.ʃ

to obey: abs., ***s*** servant, Si 30.38; + gen., τοῦ νόμου 1E 8.90; + dat. pers., Da 7.27 LXX (ǁ ὑποτάσσομαι; TH: ὑπακούω). Cf. ἀκολουθέω, πείθω, ὑπακούω, ὑποτάσσω: Schmidt 4.130f.; Spicq 3.63-5.

πείθω: fut.inf. πείσειν; old aor.act. ἔπεισα, impv. πεῖσον, inf. πεῖσαι, opt. πείσαιμι, pass. ἐπείσθην, ptc. πεισθείς, inf. πεισθῆναι, impv. πείσθητι, opt.1pl πεισθείημεν; new aor. ἐπεποίθησα; pf. πέποιθα, ptc.act. πεποιθώς, inf. πεποιθέναι, impv. 2pl πεποίθατε, 3s πεποιθέτω, pass. πέπεισμαι, ptc. πεπεισμένος; plpf.act. ἐπεποίθειν, 3pl ἐπεποίθεισαν. The pf. has the present meaning, and the plpf. the preterite.

1. new aor., pf./plpf. act. *to rely* on *and trust* in *with confidence*: ἐπί + acc., ἐπὶ κύριον Jb 27.8, Is 58.14, ἀγαθὸν πεποιθέναι ἐπὶ κύριον ἢ πεποιθέναι ἐπ' ἄνθρωπον Ps 117.8 (ǁ ἐλπίζειν ἐπί τινα vs. 9), ἐπὶ τὸ ὄρος Σαμαρείας Am 6.1; ἐπὶ τὸ πλάσμα αὐτοῦ 'his work' Hb 2.18; cavalry, 1M 10.77; ἐπὶ τὴν ῥάβδον Is 36.6; the middle notion reinforced, πέποιθας σαυτῷ ἐπὶ τὴν ῥάβδον 4K 18.21. **b**. ἐπί + dat., De 32.37, ἐπὶ τῷ κυρίῳ Zp 3.2, 2M 7.40, Da LXX Su 35, πεποιθὼς ἔσομαι ἐπ' αὐτῷ καὶ οὐ φοβήσομαι Is 12.2, ἐπὶ τῷ ὀνόματι κυρίου 50.10, ἐπ' αὐτῷ Da 3.95 TH (ǁ ἐλπίζω ib. LXX), "Blessed is the man who trusts in the Lord (πέποιθεν ἐπὶ τῷ κυρίῳ), and the Lord shall be his hope (ἐλπίς)" Je 17.7; city walls, De 28.52, ἐπὶ πόλεσιν καὶ χρήμασιν Jb 6.20, treasures, Je 30.4, glory,

31.11, spears, Ju 7.10, horses and chariots, Is 31.1, humans, 32.3, force, Ps 48.7 (ǁ καυχάομαι), pagan idols, 113.16, 134.18, ἐπὶ τίνι .. ἐπὶ τὴν ῥάβδον .. ἐπ' Αἴγυπτον .. ἐπ' αὐτῷ Is 36.5f., ἐπ' Αἰγυπτίοις εἰς ἵππον καὶ ἀναβάτην 'on Egyptians for horses and horsemen' 36.9, ἐπὶ ματαίοις 'on vain things' 59.4, ἐφ' ἑαυτοῖς ἐπὶ λόγοις ψεύδεσιν Je 7.4, ἐπ' ἀδελφοῖς αὐτῶν 9.4, ἐπὶ τῇ δικαιοσύνῃ αὐτοῦ 'his own righteousness' Ez 33.13. **c.** + dat., μάτην ψεύδει 'falsehood to no avail' Is 28.17, λίθῳ πολυτελεῖ 'a precious stone' Jb 31.24, ἀψύχοις .. εἰδώλοις 'soulless idols' Wi 14.29, κυρίῳ Si 35.24 (ǁ πιστεύω τινί), Οἱ μὲν ὅπλοις πεποίθασι ἅμα καὶ τόλμαις 'they rely on arms and bravados' 2M 8.18 (foll. by ἡμεῖς δὲ ἐπὶ τῷ παντοκράτορι θεῷ .. πεποίθαμεν 'we, however, rely on the almighty God'). ***d.** + ἐν (Hebraism): ἐν ἰσχύι αὐτῶν 'in their strength' Ju 2.5, ἐν ὀχυρώμασί σου 'in your fortresses' Je 31.7 (poss. local); ἐν (B: om.) σεαυτῷ ἐπὶ τὴν ῥάβδον 4K 18.21 *L*. On the rection, see Helbing, *Kasus.*, 197-200.

2. pf. (esp. ptc.act. πεποιθώς) *to feel confidence, secure and free from worries*: Is 32.11, 17, πεποιθώς τε ἔσῃ Jb 11.18; ἐν γῇ εἰρήνης σὺ πέποιθας Jer 12.5, ἐν τῷ κάλλει σου 'on your beauty' Ez 16.15; κατοικήσετε ἐπὶ τῆς γῆς πεποιθότες Le 25.18; De 33.12, 28; κατασκηνώσει πεποιθώς Si 4.15 and Je 23.6, ἐνοικήσει πεποιθώς Is 32.18, ἀνεπαύσατο πεποιθώς 14.6, ἐν ἡσυχίᾳ κατοικοῦσι πεποιθότες 1M 9.58, Τί πεποιθὼς εἶ; 'why are you feeling secure?' Is 36.4, ἡ τρυφερὰ ἡ καθημένη πεποιθυῖα 'one used to luxury and sitting secure' 47.8, καθιῶ αὐτοὺς πεποιθότας Je 39.37; + inf. μηδεὶς πεποιθέτω πονηρὸς ὢν ἀθῷος ἔσεσθαι 'let no evil man believe that he would be able to get away scot-free' Jb 12.6, μετὰ πάσης ἐλπίδος .. τεύξασθαι .. 'with every hope .. to obtain ..' 2M 15.7, τοῦ φυγεῖν εἰς αὐτοὺς εἰς βοήθειαν 'to flee to them for help' Is 20.6; + ὅτι 'with the knowledge that' Jb 31.21, 40.23.

3. pres./impf.mid., *to put trust in*: + dat. pers., οὐκ ἐπείθετο οὐδενί 'she wouldn't trust anybody' To 10.7 𝔊II; + dat. rei, πείθονται τῇ ὄψει 'give credence to what they see' Wi 13.7.

4. pf.pass., *to believe firmly, be certain of the veracity of*: + acc., πέπεισμαι ὅσα ἐλάλησεν Ἰωνᾶς 'I believe firmly what J. said' To 14.4 𝔊I (ǁ πιστεύω τῷ ῥήματι 𝔊II); + inf., 2M 9.27, 3M 3.24. **b.** *to believe in and uphold* a certain stance: + inf., 4M 5.16.

5. fut., old aor., **a.** *to persuade and get sbd to accept* a proposition: + acc. pers. and ὅτι, Wi 16.8, 4M 2.6, 9.18. **b.** *to persuade and get sbd to agree* to do or not to do sth: abs. οὐδαμῶς ἐπείθετο 'he would not agree' 3M 1.11; + inf., Πεῖσον .. τὴν γυναῖκα .. τοῦ ἐλθεῖν 'Persuade the woman .. to come' Ju 12.11, προελθεῖν 2M 4.34; 11.14[1]; ἐν λόγοις 1K 24.8. **c.** *to win over by persuasion* or *by pecuniary inducement*: + acc. pers., 2M 4.45, 7.26; pass. μὴ πεισθῇς 'don't be fooled' Pr 26.25; ἐπὶ δόλῳ 'by treachery' 4.34, ὑπό τινων .. ἐπείσθησαν ἀργυρίῳ 'were persuaded over by some .. with money as a bait' 10.20; περὶ τούτου 'concerning this' 3M 4.19.

6. old aor. pass. *to obey*: + dat., ἐντολαῖς 4M 6.4.

Cf. ἐλπίζω, ἐπαναπαύομαι, ἀ~, εὐπειθέω, συμπείθω, πεποίθησις, πεποιθότως, ἐρείδω: Schmidt 1.333-47, 4.129f.; Spicq 3.66-79.

πεινάω: fut. πεινάσω; aor. ἐπείνασα, subj. πεινάσω.

1. *to suffer from hunger*: πᾶσα ἡ γῆ Αἰγύπτου Ge 41.55; ἐπείνας καὶ ἐκοπίας 'you hungered and toiled' De 25.18; ǁ διψάω Is 32.6, 65.13, Si 24.21; ψυχὴ πεινῶσα 'the soul of the hungry' 4.2, Is 32.6.

2. *to suffer from loss of physical strength*, 'be exhausted': διδοὺς τοῖς πεινῶσιν ἰσχὺν 'giving strength to those ..' Is 40.29, πεινάσει καὶ ἀσθενήσει 44.12, βαδιοῦνται καὶ οὐ πεινάσουσιν 'they might march ..' 40.31 (ǁ κοπιάω), Si 16.27 (ditt.).

Cf. λιμός, λιμώσσω.

πεῖρα, ας. f.

1. *attempt*: οὐχὶ ~αν ἔλαβεν .. βαίνειν .. 'did not make an attempt to tread ..' De 28.56.

2. *testing*: ἐπείρασαν αὐτὸν ἐν πείρᾳ 'they put him to test' De 33.8; θανάτου 'through death' Wi 18.20; ὀργῆς 18.25.

3. *experience*: ἐν πολεμικαῖς χρείαις ~αν ἔχοντα 'having experience in military matters' 2M 8.9.

Cf. πειράζω, πειρασμός, II ἄπειρος: Spicq 3.80-90.

πειράζω: fut. πειράσω, mid. πειράσομαι; aor. ἐπείρασα, subj. πειράσω, inf. πειράσαι, impv. πείρασον, pass. ἐπειρά(σ)θην, subj. πειρασθῶ; pf.mid. πεπείραμαι. Syn. πειράω.

1. *to put to a test*: + acc. pers., ὃς οὐκ ἐπειράσθη, ὀλίγα οἶδεν 'one who has not been tried knows little' Si 31.10; and *s* God, ὁ θεὸς ἐπείραζεν τὸν Αβρααμ Ge 22.1, Ex 15.25; εἰδέναι εἰ ἀγαπᾶτε 'in order to find out whether you love' De 13.3, εἰ πορεύσονται τῷ νόμῳ '(to see) if they follow the law' Ex 16.4; δοκίμασόν με, κύριε, καὶ πείρασόν με Ps 25.2; ἐν πείρᾳ De 33.8; *s* divine wisdom, Si 4.17; hum., τὴν ψυχήν σου 'your life' 37.27; *o* God, Ex 17.2, Nu 14.2, Is 7.12; Wi 1.2 (ǁ ἀπιστέω); ǁ δοκιμάζω, Ps 94.9; provocative and irritating to God, 77.41, 56; part of educating and cleansing process, Da 12.9 LXX; *o* hum., 3K 10.1.

2. *to make an attempt, try*: pass., + inf., De 4.34, 1M 12.10; mid., + inf., 2M 2.23, 10.12, 11.19.

3. *to experience*: + acc., ἀγαθὰ καὶ κακά Si 39.4, ^θάνατον^ Wi 2.24, κρίσιν θεοῦ 12.26. **b.** mid.:

πεπείραμαι 'I am experienced' 1K 17.39 (*L*: + αὐτῶν '[I'm not used] to them').

Cf. πεῖρα, πειρασμός, ἀποπειράω, ἐκπειράζω, ἐγ~, ἐπιχειρέω, δοκιμάζω, ἐξετάζω: Trench 279-81; Shipp 444; Lyonnet 28-31.

πειρασμός, οῦ. m.ʃ*

putting of character to a test: directed at God, Ex 17.7; ἐν τῇ ἐρήμῳ Ps 94.8. **b**. an act performed by God and directed at hum.: De 4.34, μεγάλοι 7.19, 29.3 (ǁ σημεῖα καὶ τέρατα); ἐν ~ῷ εὑρέθη πιστός Si 44.20, 1M 2.52; τὴν ψυχήν σου εἰς ~όν Si 2.1, cf. 36.1; directed by hum. at hum.: ἐν ~ῷ κτῆσαι αὐτόν [= φίλον] 'gain him through testing' Si 6.7; 27.5. **c**. place-name based on Ex 17.1-6–17.7, De 6.16, 9.22.

Cf. πειράζω, πεῖρα.

πειρατεύω: fut. πειρατεύσω.ʃ

to raid: *s* a gang of pirates (πειρατήριον) and + acc. pers., Ge 49.19. Cf. πειρατής.

πειρατήριον, ου. n.

1. *gang of pirates*: π. πειρατεύσει αὐτόν Ge 49.19; raiders, ἦλθον .. ἐπ' ἐμοί Jb 19.12; ῥυσθήσομαι ἀπὸ ~ου 'I shall be rescued ..' Ps 17.30.

2. *hard, harsh experience*: *s* human life, Jb 7.1; 10.17 (ǁ ἔτασις).

Cf. πειρατής.

πειρατής, οῦ. m. *

brigand: βέλη ~ῶν 'the arrows of robbers' Jb 16.9; Ho 6.9. Cf. λῃστής, πειρατεύω, πειρατήριον.

πειράω: ⇒ πειράζω.

πέλαγος, ους. n.ʃ

sea: ǁ γῆ 2M 5.21; metaph., vast, perilous sphere, τῶν παθῶν 'of passions' 4M 7.1, cf. κακῶν Aes. *Pers*. 433 and Renehan 1.161f. Cf. θάλασσα, πόντος: Schmidt 1.641-50; Trench 45f.

πέλας. adv.ʃ

near by: ὁ π. 'the neighbour' Pr 27.2. Cf. πλησίον, ἐγγύς, μακρός.

πέλειος, α, ον.ʃ

livid in colour: *s* eyes, Pr 23.29. Cf. πελιόομαι: Shipp 445.

πελεκάν, ᾶνος. m.ʃ

pelican, Pelecanus onocrotalus (LSJ): forbidden as food, Le 11.18, De 14.17; solitude-loving and inhabiting wilderness, Ps 101.7 (ǁ νυκτικόραξ).

πελεκάω: aor. ἐπελέκησα.ʃ

to shape with an axe: + acc. (unwrought building stone), 3K 6.1[b]. Cf. ἀπελέκητος, πελεκητός, πέλεκυς.

πελεκητός, ή, όν.ʃ

hewn and already wrought: *s* stones as building materials, 3K 10.22. Cf. prec.

πέλεκυς, εως. m.ʃ

battle-axe: Ep Je 14. **b**. *two-edged axe*: cutting or felling instrument, + λαξευτήριον Ps 73.6; Je 22.7, 3K 6.7.

Cf. πέλυξ, πελεκάω.

πελιόομαι: aor.pass. ἐπελιώθην.ʃ

to become livid: *s* human skin, La 5.10. Cf. πέλειος.

πέλμα, ατος. n.ʃ

sole of the foot: Es 4.6.

πελταστής, ου. m.ʃ

one who bears πέλτη (q.v.): + τοξότης 'archer' 2C 14.7, 17.17. Cf. πέλτη.

πέλτη, ης. f.

small wooden or *wicker shield with covering of skin* (LSG s.v.): + θυρεός Ez 23.24, + περικεφαλαία 27.10, + κοντός etc. 39.9. Cf. θυρεός.

πέλυξ, υκος. m.ʃ

*a kind of *axe*: for stone-cutting, π. κόπτων πέτραν Je 23.29; used to slaughter hums., Ez 9.2. Cf. πέλεκυς.

πέμμα, ατος. n.

cake: offered to pagan god, φιλοῦσι ~ατα μετὰ σταφίδων 'they love cakes of dried grapes' Ho 3.1; Ez 45.24. Cf. πέσσω, ἐγκρίς, ἐγκρυφίας, χάγανον, μάζα, χαυών.

πέμπτος, η, ον.

fifth: in order, υἱὸς π. Ge 30.17; part (μέρος), 47.24; γενεά 'generation' Ex 13.18.

πέμπω: fut.inf. πέμψειν; aor. ἐπέμψα, impv. πέμψον, pass.3s πεμφθήτω, inf. πέμψαι, ptc.act.f. πέμψασα, pass. πεμφθείς; pf. πέπομφα.

to make go, 'send': *o* pers. (messenger) understood, πέμψασα ἐκάλεσεν .. τὸν υἱὸν αὐτῆς Ge 27.42; hum. delegate, παρά τινος 2M 11.17; letter, 2E 4.14, πρός με 1E 2.22; εἰς ᾅδην 3M 5.42; ǁ ἀποστέλλω Wi 9.10; *o* understood, 2E 5.17. Cf. ἀνα~, εἰσπέμπω, ἀποστέλλω: Schmidt 3.157f.; Chadwick 233-40.

πένης, ητος. m.

poor, indigent person: subjected to exploitation and oppression, Ex 23.6; μισθὸν ~τος καὶ ἐνδεοῦς 'wages of a poor and needy person' De 24.14 (ǁ προσήλυτος); καταδυναστεύουσαι πτωχοὺς καὶ καταπατοῦσαι ~τας Am 4.1; 2.6 (ǁ πτωχός and ταπεινός); ǁ ἐνδεής, ἐπιδεόμενος De 15.11; ǁ χήρα, ὀρφανός, and προσήλυτος Zc 7.10; ǁ ταπεινός Ps 81.3; π. καὶ πτωχός 81.4. **b**. unjustly favoured: Ex 23.3.

Cf. πτωχός, πενία, πένομαι, πενιχρός, ταπεινός, ἐπιδέω, ἐνδεής, πλούσιος. Difficult to establish any distinction between πένης and πτωχός, on which see Hatch 71-6; Schmidt 4.388-91; Trench 128-30; Shipp 446f.; Coin-Longeray.

πενθερά, ᾶς. f.
the mother of one's spouse: wife's, De 27.23; husband's, νύμφη ἐπὶ τὴν ~ὰν αὐτῆς 'a daughter-in-law against her mother-in-law' Mi 7.6; Ru 1.14. Cf. πενθερός, νύμφη, μήτηρ: LSG s.v.

πενθερός, οῦ. m.
the father of one's spouse: husband's, Ge 38.13, 25; wife's, 1K 4.19; pl., To 10.12 𝔊ᴵ. Cf. πενθερά, πατήρ.

πενθέω: fut. πενθήσω; aor. ἐπένθησα, inf. πενθῆσαι, impv. πένθησον, subj. πενθήσω, pass. ἐπενθήθην.
to grieve: Am 8.8, 9.5, Jl 1.9; *s* the earth as a consequence of the depravity of its inhabitants, Ho 4.3, Jl 1.10, Is 24.4, Je 12.4, 23.10; pastures because of a drought, Am 1.2; οἶνος, ἄμπελος Is 24.7 (‖ στενάζω), πεδία .. ἄμπελος 16.8; ἐπί τινος 66.10; ἐπὶ τῇ ἀνομίᾳ 1E 8.69; ὑπὲρ τῶν ἀνομιῶν 1E 9.2. **b.** tr. *to grieve the death of*: + acc. pers. (deceased), ἐπένθει τὸν υἱὸν αὐτοῦ ἡμέρας πολλάς Ge 37.34; ἑβδομήκοντα ἡμέρας '70 days' 50.3; accompanied by weeping, 37.35; σφόδρα Nu 14.39; κόψασθαι Σάρραν καὶ πενθῆσαι Ge 23.2; ‖ στενάζω Is 19.8, ‖ θρηνέω 1E 1.30, + κλαίω 2K 19.2; fig., *s* αἱ θῆκαι τοῦ κόσμου 'your chests of cosmetics' Is 3.26 (i.e. either you will have no occasions to use them or you will be using them as mourners), the streets of Zion La 1.4; *ἐπί τινα Ho 10.5 (usually + acc. or ἐπί τινι; ἐπί + acc. is found only here, 2K 13.37, 2C 35.24, 1M 2.39, and Rev 18.11); pass., *o* virgins, Ps 77.63.
Cf. θρηνέω, καταπενθέω, πένθος, ἀπένθητος, κλαίω, λυπέω, ὀδυνάω, πονέω: Trench 238.

πενθικός, ή, όν.ʃ *
pertaining to mourning: *s* ἱμάτιον 2K 14.2; subst. n.pl., πενθικά 'mourning dress' Ex 33.4. Cf. πένθος.

πένθος, ους. n.
grief, esp. over the dead: ‖ κοπετός, Am 5.16, Je 6.26; π. ὡς θυγατέρων σειρήνων 'grief like that shown by the daughters of sirens' Mi 1.8; ‖ θρῆνος - μεταστρέψω τὰς ἑορτὰς ὑμῶν εἰς πένθος 'I will turn your (joyous) festivals into doleful occasions' Am 8.10*a*; εὐφροσύνη ἀντὶ ~ους 'joy instead of ..' Is 61.3; + gen. pers. αἱ ἡμέραι τοῦ ~ους τοῦ πατρός μου 'the days of mourning for my father' Ge 27.41, αἱ ἡμέραι ~ους κλαυθμοῦ Μωυσῆ De 34.8, π. ἀγαπητοῦ 'mourning for a loved one' Am 8.10*b* (‖ ἡμέρα ὀδύνης), Je 6.26; μέγα 'large-scale' Ge 50.11; ἄρτος ~ους 'bread of grief,' i.e. bread offered to mourners who cannot find any pleasure in partaking thereof, Ho 9.4 (cf. Th 47). **b.** *funeral or mourning period*: obj. of ποιέω Ge 50.10, Si 22.6, 38.17; lasting seven days, 22.12.
Cf. πενθέω, πενθικός, κλαυθμός, κοπετός, κόπος, λύπη, ὀδύνη, παθεινός, πόνος: Schmidt 2.585.

πενία, ας. f.
lack of material means, 'poverty': Jb 36.8¶; + νόσος 'illness' Si 2.5¶, ‖ ἔνδεια 'neediness' Pr 6.11, + ἀτιμία 'disrepute' 13.18; opp. πλοῦτος 30.8, ‖ πόνοι 'toils' 31.7. Cf. πένης, πτωχεία.

πενιχρός, ά, όν.ʃ
possessing limited material resources, 'poor': *s* ἀδελφός 'fellow-brother' Ex 22.25; ‖ πτωχός Pr 28.15; 29.7. Cf. πένης, πτωχός: *ND* 3.80.

πένομαι: subj.pres. πένωμαι; aor.ptc. πενηθείς.
to live in poverty: Ex 30.15 (:: πλουτέω); πένηται .. καὶ ἀδυνατήσῃ ταῖς χερσίν '.. and is struggling (financially)' Le 25.35; might be forced to pawn one's own possessions, De 24.12. **b.** *to fall into poverty*, 'become poor': Pr 30.9.
Cf. πένης, πλουτέω.

πενταετηρικός, όν.ʃ
coming every fourth year, 'quinquennial': *s* ἀγών 'athletic games' 2M 4.18.

πενταετής, ές.ʃ
of five years in age: Le 27.5, 6.

πεντάκις. adv.ʃ
five times: 4K 13.19.

πεντακισχίλιοι, αι, α. num.
five thousand: 1E 1.9; Jd 20.45 B (A: πέντε χιλιάδες).

πεντακόσιοι, αι, α. num.
five hundred: Ge 5.30.

πεντάπηχυς, υ.ʃ
five-cubit-long: height, *s* hum., 1C 11.23.

πενταπλασίως. adv.ʃ
by five times: ἐμεγαλύνθη ἡ μερὶς Βενιαμιν παρὰ τὰς μερίδας πάντων πενταπλασίως πρὸς τὰς ἐκείνων 'B.'s share was greater than those of everybody, five times as much as theirs' Ge 43.34.

πενταπλοῦς, ῆ, οῦν.ʃ
five-fold: 3K 6.31.

Πεντάπολις, εως. f.ʃ
group of five cities: Wi 10.6.

πέντε. indecl.num.
five: ἔτη διακόσια πέντε '205 years' Ge 5.6. Cf. πέμπτος.

πεντεκαίδεκα. indecl.num.
fifteen: Le 27.7; π. ἔτη 4K 14.17 ‖ δέκα πέντε ἔτη Ge 5.10. Cf. πεντεκαιδέκατος.

πεντεκαιδέκατος, η, ον.
fifteenth: Ex 16.1 +. Cf. πεντεκαίδεκα.

πεντεκαιεικοσαετής, ές.
twenty-five-year-old: subst.m., ἀπὸ ~οῦς καὶ ἐπάνω 'people from 25 years and older' Nu 4.23.

πεντήκοντα. indecl.num.

fifty: ἡμέρας ἑκατὸν π. 'for 150 days' Ge 7.24; π. καὶ ἑκατόν '150' 8.3; π. δίκαιοι 18.24. Cf. πέντε, πεντηκοστός, πεντηκονταετής.

πεντηκονταετής, ές. num.

fifty-year-old: subst.m., Nu 4.23 +.

πεντηκόνταρχος, ου. m.

leader over fifty men: Ex 18.21, Is 3.3. Cf. ἑκατόνταρχος.

πεντηκοστός, ή, όν.

fiftieth in order: τὸ ἔτος τὸ ~όν Le 25.10, 11; ἡ πεντηκοστὴ τῆς ἑορτῆς .. ἁγία ἑβδομάδων 'the 50th (day) of the festival of weeks .. the holiday of the weeks' To 2.1 𝔊[II].

πέπειρος, ον.ʃ

ripe: ~οι οἱ βότρυες σταφυλῆς 'the bunches of grapes (were) ripe' Ge 40.10.

πεποίθησις, εως. f.ʃ *

confident hope: cogn. acc. of πείθω 4K 18.19. Cf. πείθω.

πεποιθότως. adv.ʃ *

with confident hope: κατοικήσει Ιερουσαλημ π. Zc 14.11. Cf. πείθω.

πέπων, ονος. m.ʃ

melon: as food, Nu 11.5.

περαίνω: fut. περανῶ; aor.subj. περάνω, ptc.pass. περανθείς.ʃ

to bring to an end, complete: οὐδὲν μὴ περάνῃ Hb 2.5; τοῦ παράπλου περανθέντος 'the coasting voyage having been completed' 3M 4.11. **b**. *to accomplish with success*: + acc. rei, οὐθέν 1K 12.21.

Cf. συντελέω.

πέραν.

I. prep. + gen., *on the other side of, beyond*: π. τοῦ Ἰορδάνου Ge 50.10, Nu 32.32, De 1.1; τῆς θαλάσσης 30.13, τοῦ ποταμοῦ 3K 5.4, cf. τὸ πέραν alone at 10.15; τὸ π. τῆς θ. Je 22.20; ἐκ παντὸς π. αὐτῶν 'from every quarter beyond them' 30.10.

II. adv. used as subst., *the other side, beyond*: τὸ ὄρος τὸ ἐν τῷ π. 'the mountain on the other side' Nu 27.12, ἐκ τοῦ π. 'on the other side' 21.11.

πέρας, ατος. n.

1. *end beyond which no further movement occurs* or *is possible, extreme limit*: οὐκ ἦν π. τοῦ κόσμου αὐτῆς 'there was no end of her adorning' Na 2.10; οὐκ ἦν π. τοῖς ἔθνεσιν αὐτῆς 'there was no end to her nations' 3.3; εἰς π. 'at the end' Hb 2.3; ἤχθη ἐπὶ π. '(the matter) was settled' 1E 9.17 (ǁ τελέω 2E 10.17); π. ἐπέθηκεν τῇ συμφορᾷ 'put a halt to the disaster' Wi 18.21. **b**. *end aimed at*, 'goal': Es B 3.

2. *end of existence, extinction*: Ἥκει τὸ π. ἐπὶ τὸν λαόν μου 'The end has come upon my people' Am 8.2; ǁ καιρός Ez 7.1, ǁ ἡμέρα 21.25.

3. *farthest spot* or *area*: ἐκ ~άτων ποταμῶν Αἰθιοπίας 'from the remotest reaches of Ethiopian rivers' Zp 3.10; τὰ ~τα τῆς γῆς 'the whole of the earth' Ps 2.8, τὰ ~τα τῶν ἐχθρῶν μου 'every corner where my enemies might be found' 7.7.

4. adv. *in the end, ultimately*: Je 18.7, 9, 2M 5.8, cf. τέλος.

Cf. καταστροφή, ὅριον, τέλος, τέρμα, I ἄπειρος, ἀπέραντος, περασμός: Schmidt 4.497f., 506f., 517-20.

περασμός, οῦ. m.*

exhausting and coming to the end of a process: + dat., τῷ μόχθῳ 'of the toil' Ec 4.8. Cf. πέρας, τέλος.

περάτης, ου. m.ʃ *

wanderer, emigrant: *s* Abram, Ge 14.13. Alternatively the word means 'one who has come from the other side (πέρας עֵבֶר) of Euphrates or Mesopotamia (עֵבֶר הַנָּהָר)': see Wevers and *BA* ad loc.

πέρδιξ, ικος. f.ʃ

partridge: Je 17.11, Si 11.30.

περί. prep.

I. + gen. **1**. *concerning*, to indicate a subject-matter of verbal communication: + λαλέω Ge 19.21, ἐπερωτάω 26.7, κράζω 41.55; εἶδον Mi 1.1 (vision and ǁ ὑπέρ); προσπεσόντων τῷ βασιλεῖ π. τῶν γεγονότων 'when the king got word of what had happened' 2M 5.11.

2. *in the matter of*: π. Σαρας 'in connection with S. [an occasion for, and ground of, divine punishment] Ge 12.17; σὺ ἀποθνήσκεις π. τῆς γυναικός 20.3; παρεκλήθη .. π. Σάρρας 'was comforted ..' 24.67; μήποτε ἀποκτείνωσιν αὐτὸν .. π. Ῥεβέκκας 26.7 (ǁ δι' αὐτήν 20.2, 26.9); ἐν ἁμαρτίᾳ ἐσμὲν π. τοῦ ἀδελφοῦ ἡμῶν 'we are guilty over our brother' 42.21; ἐδεῖτο .. κυρίου π. Ρεβεκκας 'pleaded .. the Lord over R.' 25.21; ἐκρίνοντο καὶ π. αὐτοῦ (sc. τοῦ φρέατος) 'had a dispute over the well, too' 26.21, οὐκ ἐμαχέσαντο π. αὐτοῦ 'did not fight ..' 26.22; ἤλεγξεν .. π. τῶν φρεάτων 'remonstrated .. over the wells' 21.25. **b**. with emotions and sentiments involved: ἐνεκότει .. π. τῆς εὐλογίας 'held a grudge .. over the blessing' Ge 27.41, ἐδυσφόρουν π. τῶν συνθηκῶν 'were indignant over the treaty' 2M 13.25; ὁ π. τοῦ καθηγιασμένου ναοῦ φόβος 'the fear over the consecrated sanctuary' 15.18.

3. *occasioned by and in order to deal with*: π. τῆς ποιήσεως τοῦ μόσχου Ex 32.35; προσάξει π. τῆς ἁμαρτίας αὐτοῦ .. μόσχον 'he shall offer a bull on account of his sin' Le 4.3; ἐξιλάσεται π. αὐτοῦ ὁ ἱερεὺς π. τῆς ἁμαρτίας αὐτοῦ 'the priest will perform a rite of atonement on his behalf ..' 5.6; Je 15.4; occasion for punishment, π. πασῶν τῶν πονηριῶν αὐτῶν 40.5; for reward, Es A 16 ο'. **b**. often without a head noun: τὸ π. ἁμαρτίας ὥσπερ τὸ π. τῆς πλημμελείας '(an offering) for sin as (an offering) for sinful error' Le 14.13; Ba 1.10.

4. *on behalf of, in furtherance of the interest of* sbd else: λαλήσατε π. ἐμοῦ Εφρων 'Speak on my behalf to E.' Ge 23.8; ἐβουλεύσατο π. ἐμοῦ εἰς ἀγαθά 'he has resolved in my favour' 50.20 (:: κατ' ἐμοῦ εἰς πονηρά); κύριος πολεμήσει π. ὑμῶν 'the Lord will fight for you' Ex 14.14; ἐξιλάσεται π. αὐτῶν ὁ ἱερεύς Le 4.20, τὰς ἁμαρτίας ἡμῶν φέρει καὶ π. ἡμῶν ὀδυνᾶται 'he bears our sins and suffers for our sake' Is 53.4; ἔλαβον π. σοῦ ὀνειδισμόν 'I became the butt of insult for your sake' Je 15.15; ᾧ μέλει π. πάντων 'who has everyone's interests close to his heart' Wi 12.13; προσεύξεται π. σου Ge 20.7, εὔξασθε π. ἐμοῦ πρὸς κύριον 'Pray for me ..' Ex 8.8.

5. *in return for*: δουλεύσω σοι ἑπτὰ ἔτη π. Ραχηλ 'I shall serve you for seven years for R.' Ge 29.18, π. ὧν δεδούλευκά σοι 'in return for my services to you' 30.26 (|| ἐδούλευσά σοι δέκα τέσσαρα ἔτη <u>ἀντὶ</u> τῶν δύο θυγατέρων σου καὶ ἓξ ἔτη <u>ἐν</u> τοῖς προβάτοις σου 31.41); δῶρα δοῦναι π. αὐτοῦ Is 8.20.

II. + acc. **1**. *in the vicinity of* [time]: π. ἡλίου δυσμάς 'about the time of sunset' Ge 15.12, so Lysias 1.39 and cf. π. δυσμὰς ἡλίου De 24.13 and πρὸς δυσμὰς ἡλίου 16.6; π. μέσας νύκτας 'about midnight' Ex 11.4, so Xen., *An*. 1.7.1; π. τὸν καιρὸν τοῦτον 'about this time' 2M 5.1, π. τὴν ἕω 'at about dawn' 3M 5.46. Cf. π. τὰς ὀκτὼ μυριάδας 'about 80 thousand' 2M 11.2.

2. *round*: τὸν χιτῶνα .. τὸν π. αὐτόν 'the tunic (wrapped) round him' Ge 37.23; ἐνδύσεται .. χιτῶνα .. π. τὸ σῶμα αὐτοῦ Le 6.10; περικαθίσῃς π. πόλιν 'besiege ..' De 20.19; πάντες οἱ π. αὐτόν 'all his court' 2K 15.18, cf. οἱ π. τὸν Μακκαβαῖον 'M.'s troops' 2M 10.16 (M. included, see Weierholt, Gorman and Radt; so Da LXX 3.20); οἱ π. αὐτὸν ὄντες 'those who were round him' 3M 1.27.

3. in place of gen., esp. in 2-4M: ἡ π. αὐτὸν .. δύναμις .. τῶν π. τὴν Ναναίαν ἱερέων 'his army .. the priests of N.' 2M 1.13, τὴν .. π. αὐτοὺς ἀσφάλειαν 'their custody' 3M 5.5. Cf. τὸ γεγονὸς π. αὐτὸν ἐλάττωμα 'the defeat which he had sustained' 2M 11.13.

4. marks an object or activity to attend to: π. τὴν γεωργίαν ἐγίνοντο 'were busy as farmers' 2M 12.1, π. τὸ σάββατον 8.27, συνετελέσατο πολλὰ π. τὸν βωμὸν ἁμαρτήματα 'committed many sins over the altar' 13.8, π. τὸν νόμον φυλακή 'adherence to the law' 4M 13.13, οὐκ ἐσπούδασαν εὐθέως π. τὴν ἄφοδον 'did not immediately set about preparing for departure' 3M 7.10; οἱ π. τινα 'sbd's bodyguard' 1M 13.40; 2M 4.14, cf. οἱ π. τὸ σῶμα τοῦ βασιλέως 1C 28.1.

5. *in respect of*: περὶ τὴν σοφίαν εὐδοκιμήσας 'having established fame for (his) wisdom' Si prol. II.

III. + dat. (only in Pr), *positioned round*: κλοιὸν χρυσέον π. σῷ τραχήλῳ 'a golden chain round your neck' Pr 1.9; 3.22.

Cf. ὑπέρ: Johannessohn, *Präp*. 219-26.

περιαγκωνίζω: aor.ptc. ~αγκωνίσας.ʃ *

to make place hands on hips with elbows turned outwards: abs., torturing position, 4M 6.3.

περιάγω: fut. ~άξω; aor.act. περιήγαγον.

1. *to cause to move round, led by sbd else*, in an area: + acc. pers., ὑμᾶς ἐν τῇ ἐρήμῳ Am 2.10; με ἐπ' αὐτὰ κυκλόθεν κύκλῳ 'me over them [= the bones] round round' Ez 37.2; + acc. loci, τὴν ὁδὸν ἔξωθεν 'along the outer way' 47.2, αὐτὰς τὴν πόλιν 2M 6.10; καθ' ὅλην τὴν πόλιν 'throughout the city' 4.38.

2. intr. *to move round in an area*: *s* τροχὸς ἁμάξης 'the wheel of a (threshing-)wagon' Is 28.27. Cf. ἄγω.

περιαιρέω: fut.act. ~ελῶ, mid. ~ελοῦμαι, pass. ~αιρεθήσομαι; aor.act. ~εῖλον, impv. ~ελε, 3s ~ελέτω, ptc. ~ελών, subj. ~έλω, mid. ~ειλάμην, impv. ~ελοῦ, ~έλεσθε, ptc. ~ελόμενος.

I. act. *to remove*, often some impediment: abs. 'to annul, abrogate' Nu 30.13, 14 (:: tr. ἵστημι); + acc. τοὺς βατράχους ἀπ' ἐμοῦ καὶ ἀπὸ τοῦ ἐμοῦ λαοῦ Ex 8.8 (|| ἀφανίζω vs. 9); θάνατον 10.17; μαλακίαν .. καὶ .. νόσους .. πονηράς 'infirmity .. and bad illnesses' De 7.15 (:: ἐπιτίθημι); ἀπ' ἐμοῦ ὄνειδος καὶ ἐξουδένωσιν Ps 118.22; ἀπὸ σοῦ τὰ φαυλίσματα τῆς ὕβρεώς σου Zp 3.11, τὰ ἀδικήματά σου 3.15, τὴν κακίαν (*L* ἀδικίαν) παιδός σου 1C 21.8; τὴν ἀκροβυστίαν τῆς καρδίας ὑμῶν '.. the foreskin ..' Je 4.4, βδελύγματα 'abominations' 4.1, τοὺς θεοὺς τοὺς ἀλλοτρίους ἐκ μέσου ὑμῶν 1K 7.3, ἐγγαστριμύθους "ventriloquists' 28.3 (*L* ἐξαίρω); ἀπ' ἐμοῦ τὸν γογγυσμόν Nu 17.5; ἱμάτια αἰχμαλωσίας 'garments of captivity' De 21.13; + gen. instead of + ἀπό τινος, Nu 30.16, Pr 4.24; pass., περιαιρεθήσονται οἱ βάτραχοι ('the frogs') ἀπὸ σοῦ καὶ ἐκ τῶν οἰκιῶν ὑμῶν Ex 8.11; τὴν κυνόμυιαν ἀπὸ Φαραω 'the dog-flies ..' 8.31; σκῆπτρον Αἰγύπτου περιαιρεθήσεται Zc 10.11. **b**. ***o*** sth desirable: ἀγαλλίαμα 'joy' Ba 4.34 (and + gen. abl.), ἐκ τοῦ στόματός μου λόγον ἀληθείας Ps 118.43.

2. *to detach*: + acc., πᾶν τὸ στέαρ .. περιελεῖ ἀπ' αὐτοῦ 'he shall remove .. all the fat from it' Le 4.8; 3.4, 9, 10, 15, 31, 35, 6.34.

II. mid. *to remove from oneself or sbd close to oneself*: + acc., τὰ ἱμάτια τῆς χηρεύσεως ἀφ' ἑαυτῆς 'having removed the garments of widowhood off herself' Ge 38.14 (:: περιβάλλομαι); περιείλατο τὴν στολὴν αὐτοῦ ἀφ' ἑαυτοῦ 'took off his robe' Jn 3.6;

τὴν θέριστρον ἀφ' ἑαυτῆς '.. the veil ..' Ge 38.19 (:: ἐνδύομαι); τὸν δακτύλιον ἀπὸ τῆς χειρὸς αὐτοῦ 'the signet ring from his (own) hand' 41.42 (:: περιτίθημι); Περιέλεσθε τὰ ἐνώτια τὰ χρυσᾶ τὰ ἐν τοῖς ὠσὶν τῶν γυναικῶν ὑμῶν 'Remove the golden earrings on the ears of your wives' Ex 32.2; 33.6 ‖ ἀφαιρέομαι vs. 5; κάλυμμα 'veil' 34.34 (:: ἐπιτίθημι vs. 33); οἶνον 'Sober up' 1K 1.14.

Cf. αἱρέω, ἐξαίρω, περιβάλλω, ἀφανίζω, ἀφαιρέω: Spicq 2.679f.

περιαντλέω.ʃ

to pour all over: pass., *o* hum., κατακλυσμῷ 'completely submerged under flood' 4M 15.32.

περιάπτω: aor. περίηψα.ʃ

to mark out for special attention by attaching: + dat., ψόγῳ 'reproach' 3M 3.7.

περιάργυρος, ον.

set in silver, plated with silver: *s* idols, περίχρυσα καὶ ~α Ep Je. 8; + ξύλινα 'wooden' 38; οἱ θεοὶ αὐτῶν εἰσι ξύλινοι καὶ περίχρυσοι καὶ ~οι 69. Cf. περιαργυρόω and περίχρυσος.

περιαργυρόω: aor. ~ηργύρωσα; pf.ptc.pass. ~ηργυρωμένος.

to plate with silver: + acc., *o* sockets of pillars, ἀργύρῳ Ex 27.11; capital of a column, 37.15; pillar of tabernacle, 38.18; wings of a dove, Ps 67.14; idols, τὰ εἴδωλα τὰ περιηργυρωμένα καὶ τὰ περικεχρυσωμένα 'the idols plated with silver or gold' Is 30.22. Cf. περιχαλκόω, ~χρυσόω, περιάργυρος, καταργυρόω.

περιαστράπτω.ʃ *

to flash all round: *s* angels, ὅπλοις 'by means of weapons' 4M 4.10. Cf. ἀστραπή.

περιβάλλω: fut. ~βαλῶ, mid. ~βαλοῦμαι; aor.act. ~έβαλον, subj. ~βάλω, impv. ~βαλε, inf. ~βαλεῖν, mid. ~εβαλόμην, subj. ~βάλωμαι, impv. ~βαλοῦ, 3s ~βαλέσθω, inf. ~βαλέσθαι, ptc. ~βαλόμενος, pass. ~βληθείς; pf.ptc.mid./pass. ~βεβλημένος.

I. act. *to put* sth flat *round or over*: ἐπὶ σὲ δίκτυα 'nets' Ez 32.3; ἐπὶ ^τὴν πόλιν^ χάρακα 'palisade' 4.2; δίκτυον τοῖς ἑαυτοῦ ποσίν '.. his own feet' Pr 29.5, ἑαυτοῖς τεῖχος 'wall' 28.4.

2. *to clothe*: abs. Is 58.7 (*o* the naked understood); τινά τι (clothing) - αὐτὸν ἱμάτια Zc 3.5, σε ὑάκινθον Ez 27.7; τινά τινι Jd 4.18B (A: συγκαλύπτω), σε τριχάπτῳ 'you with a fine veil of hair' Ez 16.10, cf. τὸ θυσιαστήριον σάκκῳ '(drape) the altar with a sackcloth' Ju 4.12; pass., σκότει 'with darkness' Wi 19.17.

3. *to cause to undergo much of*: τινά τινι - συμφοραῖς 'in calamities' Es E 5, αἰκίαις 'tortures' 3M 6.26.

II mid. *to throw round or over oneself* (w. sth.: τινι or τι): abs. περιεβάλεσθε καὶ οὐκ ἐθερμάνθητε 'you put on clothes but did not get warmth' Hg 1.6; Ge 24.65; ἱμάτιον 28.20; περὶ τὸ στόμα αὐτοῦ 'round his mouth' Le 13.45, κόκκινον 'scarlet garment' Je 4.30, σάκκον Jn 3.6, 8, διπλοΐδα 'double cloak' Ba 5.2; metaph., δόξαν Es 5.1 o' (*L*: ἱμάτια δόξης); not voluntarily — 'to sustain' αἰσχύνην Mi 7.10, αἰσχύνην καὶ ἐντροπήν Ps 70.1, αἰσχύνην ἐφ' ἑαυτοῖς 3M 6.34, ἱμάτιον ἐκδικήσεως καὶ τὸ περιβόλαιον Is 59.17, ἀδικίαν καὶ ἀσέβειαν Ps 72.6; + dat., θερίστρῳ 'veil' Le 38.14; *+ ἐν – τῶν περιβολαίων σου, ἃ ἂν περιβάλῃ ἐν αὐτοῖς 'of whatever garments with which you clothe yourself' De 22.12, ἐν σάκκοις 'with sackcloths' 1C 21.16.

2. *to place all around oneself*: + acc., πέτραν '(embraced) a rock' Jb 24.8.

Cf. βάλλω, περιαιρέω, περιβολή, περιβόλαιον, περίβλημα, περιστέλλω.

περιβιόω: pf.ptc. ~βεβιωκώς.ʃ

to survive unharmed: *s* hum., 3M 5.18.

περίβλεπτος, ον.ʃ

looked up by everyone: *s* hum. Pr 31.23.

περιβλέπω: fut.mid. ~βλέψομαι; aor.subj. ~βλέψω, ptc. ~βλέψας, mid. ~βλεψάμενος, impv.mid. ~βλεψαι.

1. *to look round* inquisitively: εἰς τὰ ὀπίσω 'backwards' Ge 19.17; περιβλεψάμενος ὧδε καὶ ὧδε οὐχ ὁρᾷ οὐδένα 'having looked all round, he spies nobody' Ex 2.12; πρὸς ἀνατολάς Ba 4.36.

2. *to look about for*: + acc., To 10.7 𝔊[II]; εἰς τὴν ὁδὸν τὸν παῖδα αὐτῆς 11.5 𝔊[I].

Cf. βλέπω.

περίβλημα, ατος. n.ʃ

garment: Nu 31.20. Cf. περιβάλλω, ἱμάτιον.

περιβόητος, ον.ʃ

renowned: *s* temple, 2M 2.22. Cf. γνωστός, ὀνομαστός.

περιβόλαιον, ου. n.

clothing: ‖ ἱμάτιον Ex 22.27, Is 59.17; ~ων σου, ἃ ἂν περιβάλῃ ἐν αὐτοῖς 'clothes with which you clothe yourself' De 22.12; π. χαλκοῦν 'copper ..' Je 15.12; ~α βύσσινα 'linen ..' Ez 16.13. Cf. ἱμάτιον, περιβάλλω, περίβλημα, and περιβολή.

περιβολή, ῆς. f.ʃ

1, *garment of good quality*: ‖ στολή Ge 49.11; ἁγιάσματος Si 50.11; Da LXX 7.9. 2M 3.26.

2. *act of wearing*: ἱματίων Si 11.4.

Cf. περιβόλαιον, ἱμάτιον, and στολή.

περίβολος, ον. Used as subst.m.

1. *enclosing wall*: of a city, Is 54.12, Ez 40.5.

2. *enclosed space*: temple precinct, π. ἱεροῦ Si 50.2, τοῦ ἱεροῦ 4M 4.11; Da 3.1 LXX, 3M 4.11, τεμένους 'of a precinct' 2M 1.15, ἱερός 6.4, τῶν ἁγίων 1M 14.48.

περιγίνομαι: aor. ~εγενόμην, ptc.pass. ~γενηθείς.ʃ
to be superior: κατὰ τὴν περιγενηθεῖσαν αὐτῷ σύνεσιν 'according to his uncommon intelligence' 1C 28.19; + gen., τῶν παθῶν '(prevailed) over the passions' 4M 13.3. Cf. I περίειμι **2**, ὑπερβάλλω.

περιγραφή, ῆς. f.ʃ
general, outward appearance: Si 22.23¶, cf. π. οὐρανοῦ 'circumference of ..' Jb 22.14 Sym. Cf. εἶδος and ὄψις.

περιδειπνέω: aor.inf. ~δειπνῆσαι.ʃ *
to cause to eat a funeral meal: τὸν Δαυιδ ἄρτοις 2K 3.35. Cf. περίδειπνον.

περίδειπνον, ου. n.ʃ
funeral feast: νεκροῦ Ep Je 31. Cf. περιδειπνέω.

περιδέξιον, ου. n.ʃ
armlet for the right arm: woman's accessory, σφραγῖδας καὶ ἐνώτια καὶ δακτυλίους καὶ ἐμπλόκια καὶ ~α Ex 35.22; Nu 31.50, Is 3.20.

περιδέω: aor. ~έδησα.ʃ
to tie around: + acc., ζωνῇ ὀσφύας αὐτῶν 'a girdle round their waist' Jb 12.18¶. Cf. I δέω.

περιδιπλόω: aor. ~εδίπλωσα.ʃ*
wrap up: + acc., ἀγγεῖα 'dishes' Ju 10.5.

περιδύω: aor. ~έδυσα.ʃ
to strip clothes off sbd: τινα 4M 6.2. Cf. ἀπο~, ἐκ~, ἐνδύω.

I **περίειμι**.
1. *to be still present*: having survived, Jb 27.3, 15, 2M 7.24; ἡ περιοῦσα ἡμέρα 'today' 3M 5.18.
2. *to be superior*: Jb 31.21; *to excel*, *s* hum., Si 26.21¶, cf. περιγίνομαι, ὑπερβάλλω.

II **περίειμι**: impf.1s ~ῄειν.ʃ
to move about in pursuit of some objective: + pres. ptc., Wi 8.18. Cf. εἶμι.

περιεκτικός, ον.ʃ
comprising: *s* φύσεις περιεκτικώταται 'all-embracing manifestations' 4M 1.20.

περιεργάζομαι.ʃ
to waste one's labour on: + ἔν τινι, Si 3.23. Cf. περιεργασία: *ND* 3.26.

περιεργία, ας. f.
act of busying oneself improperly: παιδίσκης αὐτοῦ '(having excessive dealings) with his maid' Si 41.22.

περιέρχομαι: fut. ~ελεύσομαι; aor.ptc. ~ελθών, impv.3 ~ελθέ.
to move around: Je 38.22; + acc. loci, τὴν γῆν Jb 1.7 (|| ἐμπεριπατέω), τὴν πόλιν Es 6.11 *L*; εἰς πάντα τὸν Ισραηλ 2K 24.2*L*. **b**. *to overcome by encircling*: metaph., τὸ πρόσωπον τοῦ ῥήματος (*L* λόγου) τούτου 'this state of affairs' 2K 14.20 B (*L* κυκλόω).

περιέχω: aor. ~έσχον.
1. *to surround*: + acc. pers. and w. hostile intent, "fat bulls surrounded me" Ps 21.13 (|| περικυκλόω), *s* ὠδῖνες θανάτου 'deadly pangs' 17.5, κακά 39.13; || κυκλόω 87.18; παντόθεν 'from all around' Si 51.7; pass., κυκλόθεν 'all around' Je 26.5; w. no hostility implied, 4M 8.4. **b**. metaph., + acc. pers., χαλεπὴ περίστασις 'harsh situation' 2M 4.16; pass., περιεχόμην ἐκστάσει 'I was deeply perturbed' Da 7.28 LXX.
2. *to have as contents*: *s* book and + acc., Si prol. II, Es 7.33 *L*, 1M 15.2, *s* letter οὕτως 2M 9.18 || ἔχω 11.34; λόγος 'discourse' 4M 1.2; *s* hum., ἐπιστήμην 1E 8.7.
Cf. περι~, κυκλόω.

περίζωμα, ατος. n.
loin-cloth: made of leaves of a fig-tree Ge 3.7. Cf. ζώνη, περιζώννυμι: Lee 95; LSG s.v.

περιζώννυμι, ~ζωννύω: fut.mid. ~ζώσομαι; aor.act. ~έζωσα, mid. ~εζωσάμην, impv. περίζωσαι, 2pl ~ζώσασθε; pf.mid./pass.ptc. περιεζωσμένος.
I. act. *to put* (garment) *round* sbd's body: + *double acc., αὐτὸν περιστολὴν δόξης '.. a glorious robe' Si 45.7; metaph., ὁ θεὸς ὁ περιζωννύων με δύναμιν εἰς πόλεμον Ps 17.40, με εὐφροσύνην 29.12. **b**. pass.: *o* (acc.) part of a body, αἱ ὀσφύες ὑμῶν περιεζωσμέναι Ex 12.11, τὴν ὀσφῦν .. χρυσίον Da KXX 10.5.
II. mid., *to gird up one's loins for action*: abs. and said to soldiers, Περιζώσασθε .. γίνεσθε ἕτοιμοι .. τοῦ πολεμῆσαι 1M 3.58.
2. *to put all round oneself*: + acc. rei, belt, ζώνη, ἣν .. περιζώννυται Ps 108.19; sash or sackcloth worn by a mourner, νύμφην περιεζωσμένην σάκκον 'a bride enwrapped in a sackcloth' Jl 1.8, περιζώσασθε σάκκους καὶ κόπτεσθε Is 15.3, Je 4.8; σάκκους understood, περιζώσασθε καὶ κόπτεσθε Jl 1.13. **b**. a sword fastened with a belt round one's body or part of it: τὴν ῥομφαίαν σου ἐπὶ τὸν μηρόν σου 'your sword on your thigh' Ps 44.4, ^μάχαιραν^ ὑπὸ τὸν μανδύαν '.. underneath the cloak' Jd 3.16; battle-gear in general, σκεύη πολεμικά 18.16 A (B: ἀνα~). **c**. + ἔν τινι: ἐν στολῇ 1C 15.27; metaph., ἐν δυναστείᾳ Ps 64.7 (|| ἑτοιμάζω). **d**. metaph., ἀγαλλίασιν οἱ βουνοὶ περιζώσονται Ps 64.13; δύναμιν 1K 2.4.
3. *to secure with belt*: + acc. of part of body, τὴν ὀσφῦν σου Je 1.17; pass. αἱ ὀσφύες ὑμῶν περιεζωσμέναι Ex 12.11, ἡ ὀσφῦς αὐτοῦ περιεζωσμένη ἐν χρυσίῳ Da TH 10.5.
4. *to put all round*: + *double acc., σάκκους τὰς ὀσφύας Is 32.11, sim. Ju 4.14; τὴν ὀσφῦν περιεζωσμένος χρυσίον Da LXX 10.5; 4K 1.8B (*L* ζώνην .. τὴν ὀσφῦν αὐτοῦ).
Cf. ζώννυμι, περίζωμα, περιτίθημι.

περίθεμα, ατος. n.ʃ *
1. *that which encloses*: τῷ θυσιαστηρίῳ Nu 16.38, 39.

2. *that which is put round* sth: ornament round a camel's neck, Jd 8.26 B.

Cf. περιτίθημι.

περιΐπταμαι.ʃ

to fly around: *s* bird, 4M 14.17. Cf. πέτομαι.

περιίστημι: 1aor.subj. ~στήσω, impv. στησον; pf. ptc. ~εστώς / εστηκώς; plpf. παρειστήκειν.ʃ

I. tr. (1aor.) *to bring round*: + acc. pers., ἄνθρωπον τυφλὸν εἰς ὅρασιν 'restore a blind man his sight' Ep Je 36.

2. *to encircle*: pass., τοῦ περιισταμένου γένους 'the beleagured nation' 2M 14.9.

3. *to position round*: αὐτῇ τοὺς μαχίμους κύκλῳ 'the warriors round it [= Jericho]' Jo 6.3.

II. intr. (pf.) *to stand round*: *s* hum., Ju 5.22; *s* subordinates, + dat. pers., 1K 4.15, 2K 13.31.

Cf. ἵστημι: Naumann 41f.

περικαθαίρω: aor. ~εκάθαρα.ʃ

to purify completely: + acc. pers. and of a pagan practice, τὸν υἱὸν .. ἐν πυρί De 18.10; through circumcision, Jo 5.4. **b**. by removing alien or undesirable growth all around: + acc. (plant) and + ἀποκνίζω 'to prune' 4M 1.29.

Cf. περικαθαρίζω, περικάθαρμα.

περικαθαρίζω: fut. ~καθαριῶ.ʃ* (but περικαθάρσεις τῶν ἀνωτάτων ῥιζῶν 'clearing round the upper roots' Theophrastus [iv/iii BCE] *CP* 5.9.11)

1. *to purge away*: + acc., τὴν ἀκαθαρσίαν Le 19.23 (of fruit-trees); *s* God, τὰς ἁμαρτίας σου Is 6.7 (‖ ἀφαιρέω).

2. *to clean morally*: *s* God, καρδίαν De 30.6.

Cf. καθαρίζω, περικαθαίρω, ἀφαιρέω, ἀπερικάθαρτος.

περικάθαρμα, ατος. n.ʃ*

that which is thrown away in cleansing, 'refuse, rubbish': metaph., *s* hum., Pr 21.18. Cf. περικαθαίρω, κοπρία, περίψημα, σκύβαλον: Spicq 3.93-5.

περικάθημαι:

1. *to pester*: + acc. pers., 1M 5.3 (with military attacks); ἐπὶ ^τὴν πόλιν^.1M 6.24.

2. *to besiege*: + acc., τὴν ἄκραν 'the citadel' 1M 11.21; τὴν πόλιν Jd 9.31 B (A: πολιορκέω), ἐπὶ τὴν πόλιν 2K 11.16 *L*.

Cf. πολιορκέω, περικαθίζω.

περικαθίζω: fut. ~καθιῶ; aor. ~εκάθισα, inf. ~καθίσαι, ptc. ~καθίσας, subj. ~καθίσω.

to besiege: + acc., De 20.12, τὴν Ραββα 1C 20.1 (‖ 2K 11.1 δια~; *L* περι~ ἐπί); + πολιορκέω Jo 10.31, 34; περὶ πόλιν 20.19, ἐπὶ ^τὴν πόλιν^ Jd 9.50 A (B: παρεμβάλλω ἔν τινι)), 1M 6.20, ἐπί τινας 6.19. **b**. *to hem in under siege*: τινα 2K 20.15*L*, 3K 15.27.

Cf. περιοχή, περικάθημαι, πολιορκέω, διακαθίζω.

περικαίω.ʃ

to add to the intensity of emotions of: τινα 4M 16.3.

περικαλύπτω: aor.inf. ~καλύψαι; pf.ptc.pass. ~κεκαλυμμένος.

to cover all round: *o* ornamental precious stones and χρυσίῳ 'with gold' Ex 28.20; 3K 7.5 (*L* ἐπι~). Cf. καλύπτω.

περικατάλημπτος, ον.ʃ *

hunted down and with enemies all round: *s* hum., 2M 14.41.

περίκειμαι.ʃ

to have or *put round oneself*: *o* gold as ornament (εἰς κάλλος) Ep Je 23; robe and pass. ib. 57; fetters, 4M 12.2.

περικείρω: pf.ptc.mid. ~κεκαρμένος.ʃ

mid. *to cut one's hair round*: + acc., τὰ κατὰ πρόσωπον αὐτοῦ '(shave) his face round about' Je 9.26, 32.23. Cf. κείρω.

περικεφάλαιος, α, ον.

subst.f. *helmet*: warrior's gear, Is 59.17, Je 26.4; + πέλτη 'light shield' Ez 38.4; χαλκή 'of copper' 1M 6.35; ἐπὶ κεφαλῆς 1K 17.5, περὶ κεφαλήν 17.38. Cf. κόρυς: Oepke, *TDNT* 5.314f.

περικλάω: fut.pass. ~κλασθήσομαι; aor. ~έκλασα.ʃ

1. *to break off, pluck*: + acc., ἅλιμα ἐπὶ ἠχοῦντι 'seaweed on the roaring beach' Jb 30.4¶; pass., κλῶνες 'branches' Wi 4.5.

2. *to break*: + acc., limbs, 4M 10.6 (torturing); metaph., κλύδωνας 'billows' 7.5 (or: to turn away).

περικλύζω: aor.mid. ~εκλυσάμην, inf. ~κλύσασθαι.ʃ

mid. *to wash all round*: in a river, To 6.3 𝔊[I] (𝔊[II] ~νίπτομαι); + acc. rei, τὸ σῶμα ὕδατι Ju 10.3. Cf. περινίπτω.

περικνημίς, ῖδος. f.ʃ

covering for the leg: Da 3.21 TH. Cf. κνημίς.

περικομπέω.ʃ *

to sound round about: *s* ἦχοι 'sounds' Wi 17.4. Cf. ἠχέω.

περικοσμέω: pf.ptc.pass. ~κεκοσμημένος.ʃ*

to adorn all round: *o* daughter, Ps 143.12. Cf. κοσμέω.

περικρατέω: aor. ~εκράτησα, opt.3s ~τήσειε.

to be in or *gain firm control of*: + gen., παθῶν 'passions' 4M 1.9 (‖ κρατέω vs. 5, 6), ἀνδρῶν 14.11. Cf. κρατέω.

περικυκλόω: fut. ~κυκλώσω, pass. ~κυκλωθήσομαι; aor. ~εκύκλωσα; pf.ptc.pass.~κεκυκλωμένος.

1. *to encircle*: + acc. rei, τὴν οἰκίαν 'the house' Ge 19.4; gem-stones, Ex 36.20 (‖ 28.20 περικαλύπτω); cities, Nu 32.38 (with walls? See Trg N ad loc. and Je 38.39), a column, *s* measuring cord giving a certain circumference, Je 52.21; enemies, *o* pers. Ps 16.11, *s* μόσχοι πολλοί 'many young bulls' 21.13 (‖ περιέχω); τὴν πόλιν Jo 6.13; w. no hostile intent, Ju 13.13.

2. *to hem in and overpower*: + acc. pers., "the tribulations of Hades got on top of me" Ps 17.6.

3. *to move along the periphery of*: acc. rei, τὴν γῆν Εδωμ Nu 21.4.

Cf. κυκλόω, περικύκλῳ, περιέχω.

περικύκλῳ.

I. adv. *round about*: Ex 28.29.

II. prep. + gen. *round about*: τῶν ἐθνῶν π. ὑμῶν 'of the peoples round you' De 6.14, 13.7; πάντα τὰ π. αὐτῆς 'all its surroundings' Is 4.5.

Cf. κύκλος, περικυκλόω.

περιλακίζω.ʃ*

to tear all round: pass., *o* flesh of sbd under torture, 4M 10.8.

περιλαμβάνω: fut.mid. ~λήμψομαι, pass. ~λημφθήσομαι; aor. περιέλαβον, subj. ~λάβω, inf. ~λαβεῖν, ptc. ~λαβών, impv. ~λαβε; pf.ptc. ~ειληφώς.

1. *to hold closely in the arms*, 'embrace, hug': + acc. pers., περιλαβὼν αὐτὸν ἐφίλησεν '.. and kissed' Ge 29.13 (a man and a nephew of his), 33.4 (reconciled brothers), ἐφίλησεν αὐτοὺς καὶ περιέλαβεν αὐτούς 'he kissed them and embraced them' 48.10 (an aged father and grandchildren), εὐνοῦχος περιλαμβάνων παρθένον Si 30.20; *s* a man's right-hand, Ct 2.6; + acc. rei (colums of a building) Jd 16.29. Cf. περιπλέκω **3**; συμπλέκω **1**.

2. *to surround*: + acc., κυκλώσατε καὶ περίλαβε αὐτήν [= Σιων] Ps 47.13; + acc. pers. and dat., pass. πέτρᾳ ὡς χάρακι 'with a rock as with a palisade' Is 31.9, cf. Polyb. 1.48.10.

3. *to place round* sth: + acc., τὰς χεῖρας αὐτοῦ '(to fold) his hands' (a fig. of lethargy) Ec 4.5.

Cf. κυκλόω, περίλημψις.

περιλείπω: pf.ptc.pass. ~λελειμμένος.

to leave untouched: pass., 2M 1.31; survivor, 4M 12.6. Cf. (κατα)λείπω: Spicq 3.96.

περίλημψις, εως. f.ʃ

v.n. of περιλαμβάνω **1**: Ec 3.5.

περίλοιπος, ον.ʃ

left remaining, surviving: τοὺς π. Ιωσηφ Am 5.15; ^κυρίου^ Ps 20.13. Cf. κατάλοιπος.

περίλυπος, ον.

very sad, deeply grieved: *s* pers., π. γίνομαι Ge 4.6 (ǁ λυπέω), ǁ στυγνός 'gloomy' Da LXX 2.12, ǁ σύννους 'grave-looking' 1E 8.68; π. γενόμενος τῇ ψυχῇ To 3.1 $\mathfrak{G}^{I}$; ψυχή Ps 41.6. Cf. λύπη, λυπηρός, στυγνός, and σύννους.

περιλύω: aor.ptc. ~λύσας.ʃ *

to loosen all round: + acc., ὄργανα 'parts of the body' 4M 10.7. Cf. λύω.

περιμένω: fut. ~μενῶ.ʃ

to wait expectantly for; + acc., τὴν σωτηρίαν .. κυρίου Ge 49.18; σιγῶντά με 'whilst I am silent' Wi 8.12. Cf. προσδοκάω, ὑπομένω.

περίμετρον, ου. n.

circumference: of cistern, Si 50.3. Cf. περιφερής.

περινίπτω: aor.inf. ~νίψασθαι.ʃ

mid. *to wash round*: + acc. rei, τοὺς πόδας εἰς τὸν Τίγριν ποταμόν 'to wash his (own) feet in the River Tigris' To 6.2 $\mathfrak{G}^{II}$. Cf. νίπτω, περικλύζω.

περιξύω: aor. περιέξυσα.ʃ

to scrape all round and remove: + acc., φλοιόν 'bark' Wi 13.11. Cf. ξύω.

περιοδεύω: aor. ~ώδευσα, impv. ~όδευσον, inf. ~οδεῦσαι; pf. περιώδευκα.ʃ

to go around, travel all over an area: + acc., τὴν γῆν Zc 1.10, 11, 6.7*ter*.; ἐν πάσῃ τῇ γῇ 2K 24.8B (*L* περιέρχομαι; ǁ 1C 21.4 διέρχομαι). Cf. ἔρχομαι, διοδεύω, δι~, περιέρχομαι, πορεύομαι.

περίοδος, ου. f.ʃ

a point in time when a certain thing happens periodically: τῇ ~ῳ τῇ ἑβδόμῃ 'on the seventh occasion' Jo 6.16. Cf. καιρός.

περιοικοδομέω: fut. ~οικοδομήσω; aor. ~ῳκόδομησα; pf.pass. ~ῳκοδόμημαι.

to build structures *round*: *o* city w. ref. to military installations, Je 52.4 (ǁ περιχαρακόω); κύκλῳ Jb 19.8; περὶ ^τὴν πόλιν^ τεῖχος κύκλῳ 4K 25.1*L*. Cf. οἰκοδομέω.

περίοικος, ον.

adjacent: subst.f., ἡ π. 'the adjacent area,' τὰς πόλεις ταύτας καὶ πᾶσαν τὴν ~ον Ge 19.25; 19.29; n.(?)sg., ἐν τῷ ~ῳ τοῦ Ἰορδάνου 3K 7.33; n.pl., Jd 1.27B (A: περισπόρια,:: θυγατέρες 'satellite cities'); m.pl. 'neighbours'– πάντας τοὺς ~ους Αραβα De 1.7. Cf. θυγάτηρ, περίχωρον, περισπόριον: Casevitz 1985.189.

περιονυχίζω: fut. ~χιῶ.ʃ *

to pare the nails of: + acc. (woman), De 21.12. Cf. ὀνυχίζω.

περιουσιασμός, οῦ. m.ʃ

specially dear and valuable possession: τὸν Ιακωβ ἐξελέξατο ἑαυτῷ ὁ κύριος .. εἰς ~ὸν αὐτοῦ Ps 134.4; Ec 2.8. Cf. περιούσιος.

περιούσιος, ον.ʃ *

selected as *specially dear and valuable*: Israelites as God's people, ἔσεσθέ μοι λαὸς π. ἀπὸ πάντων τῶν ἐθνῶν '.. (distinct) from all the nations' Ex 19.5; λαὸς ἅγιος εἶ κυρίῳ .. καὶ ἐξελέξατο κύριος .. γενέσθαι σε αὐτῷ λαὸν ~ον ἀπὸ πάντων τῶν ἐθνῶν τῶν ἐπὶ προσώπου τῆς γῆς De 14.2; σὲ προείλατο κύριος .. εἶναι αὐτῷ λαὸν ~ον παρὰ πάντα τὰ ἔθνη 7.6; 26.18. Cf. περιουσιασμός, ἐκλεκτός: Preisker, *TDNT* 6:57f.

περιοχή, ῆς. f.

act of enclosing from all sides or *state of being so enclosed*: ἔσται π. ἐπὶ Ιερουσαλημ Zc 12.2; ὕδωρ ~ῆς 'water supplies for a time of siege'(?) Na 3.14, cf. ποταμοὺς ~ῆς 4K 19.24B (Syh /d-'uššānā/); ~ὴν (MT *ṣir*) εἰς τὰ ἔθνη ἐξαπέστειλεν 'he dispatched a besieging army to the nations'(?) Ob 1 (so Th 161 and Cyr. I 549; ‖ ἄγγελοι Je 29.15); trapped in a net, Ez 17.20; + πολιορκία Je 19.9; πόλις ~ῆς Ps 30.22, θύρα ~ῆς 140.3. **b**. *place surrounded by a protective wall*: 1K 22.4. ***c**. *wall of circumvallation* (LSG s.v.): Ez 4.2.

Cf. συνοχή, περικαθίζω, πολιορκέω.

περιπαθῶς. adv.ʃ*

with violent emotion or indignation: 4M 8.2.

περιπατέω: fut. ~πατήσω; aor.~επάτησα, subj. ~πατήσω, ptc. ~πατήσας, opt.3pl ~πατήσαισαν.

1. *to walk about* over an area: τοῦ θεοῦ περιπατοῦντος ἐν τῷ παραδείσῳ Ge 3.8, ἐπὶ πᾶν τεῖχος 'over every wall' Is 8.7; ***s*** a person recovered from illness, ἔξω ἐπὶ ῥάβδου 'outdoors on a stick' Ex 21.19; lightnings, Jb 20.25; begging (?) Si 38.32. **b**. *to take a walk*: Pr 6.22.

***2**. *to conduct one's life*: ἐν ὁδοῖς δικαιοσύνης Pr 8.20 (‖ ἀναστρέφομαι), ἐνώπιόν σου (= God) ἐν ἀληθείᾳ 4K 20.3.

Cf. βαδίζω, (ἐμπερι)πατέω, subs., πορεύομαι: Bertram, *TDNT* 5.942f.

περίπατος, ου. m.

1. *place for walking*: in a temple court, Ez 42.4; "he considered the abyss his beat" Jb 41.24¶.

2. *discussion*: 2M 2.30.

περιπίπτω: fut. ~πεσοῦμαι; aor. ~έπεσον, inf. ~πεσεῖν, ptc. ~πεσών.ʃ

to encounter unintentionally: + dat. (sth undesirable, unpleasant), θανάτῳ Da LXX 2.9, ἐπιτιμίοις 'punishments' 2M 6.13, δυσχερεῖ πτώματι 'a hard fall' 9.7, ἀσθενείᾳ 'illness' 9.21, τοιούτοις κακοῖς 'such misfortunes' 10.4; ἀδικίᾳ Pr 11.5, ^θυμῷ^ 4M 1.24. **b**. generally: περιπτώματι τῇ μερίδι τοῦ ἀγροῦ Βοος 'by chance the part of the field belonging to B.' Ru 2.3; ἐν τῷ ὄρει 2K 1.6.

Cf. περίπτωμα: Michaelis, *TDNT* 6.173; Spicq 3.97-9.

περιπλέκω: aor.pass. ~επλάκην; pf.ptc.pass. ~πεπλεγμένος.

1. mid. *to entangle, intertwine*: σμῖλαξ περιπλεκομένη 'entangled bindwood' Na 1.10, ἄμπελος .. περιπεπλεγμένη πρὸς αὐτόν 'vine .. towards it' Ez 17.7; σχοινία Ps 118.61.

2. *to bind up*: + acc. (plant), 4M 1.29.

3. mid. *to hug, embrace*: + dat. pers., 3M 5.49. Cf. περιλαμβάνω **3**.

4. metaph. *to make up and compose*: + acc., δολιότητα 'deceptive story' Ps 49.19.

5. metaph. *to apply all over*: pass., δικαίᾳ περιπεπλεγμένος κρίσει 'roundly and justly punished' 3M 2.22.

Cf. (συμ)πλέκω.

περιπνίγω: aor. ~έπνιξα.ʃ

to cause to suffocate: τινα, by drowning, 2K 22.5*L*. Cf. ἀποπνίγω, πνιγμός.

περιποιέω: fut.act. ~ποιήσω, inf. ~ποιῆσαι, mid. ~ποιήσομαι; aor.inf.act. ~ποιῆσαι, mid. περιεποιησάμην, inf. ~ποιήσασθαι, impv. ~ποίησαι, ptc. ~ποιησάμενος, subj. ~ποιήσωμαι; pf.mid. ~πεποίημαι.

I. act. **1**. *to allow to survive without destroying*: + acc. pers., φαρμάκους οὐ περιποιήσετε 'Do not spare sorcerers' Ex 22.18; + acc. rei, τὸ ζῆν 2M 3.35.

2. *to obtain*: + acc., περιποιῆσαι ἑαυτῷ ὄνομα αἰώνιον 'to win himself eternal fame' 1M 6.44, ἀγάπησιν Si 19.18¶.

II. mid. **1**. *to let live without destroying* or *without letting perish, and for one's own benefit*: + acc., ἀποκτενοῦσίν με, σὲ δὲ περιποιήσονται 'they will kill me, but you they will spare' Ge 12.12; ἐὰν μὲν ἄρσεν ᾖ, ἀποκτείνατε αὐτό, ἐὰν δὲ θῆλυ, περιποιεῖσθε αὐτό 'if it be male, kill him, but if it be female, let it live' Ex 1.16 (note the tense differentiation); Nu 22.33 (:: ἀποκτείνω), Ez 13.19 (‖ ζάω and:: ἀποκτείνω), περιποίησαι τοὺς υἱοὺς τῶν τεθανατωμένων Ps 78.11; ἃ περιεποιήσατο, ἀπώλετο 'that which he saved perished' Je 38.36; ‖ ἐξαιρέω, σῴζω Is 31.5; ἐκ χειρὸς κακῶν 1K 25.39; 2K 21.7*L* (B: φείδομαι).

2. *to acquire*: + acc., πᾶσαν τὴν ἀποσκευὴν αὐτοῦ, ἣν περιεποιήσατο 'all his possessions that he had acquired' Ge 31.18; πάντα τὰ ὑπάρχοντα καὶ πάντα τὰ κτήνη καὶ πάντα, ὅσα ἐκτήσατο καὶ ὅσα περιεποιήσατο 'all the possessions and all the cattle and all that he had come to possess and that he had acquired' 36.6; λαόν μου, ὃν περιεποιησάμην .. Is 43.21; ἱκανὴν ἕξιν 'sufficient fluency' Si prol. 11; + κτάομαι Ge 36.6, 2K 12.3; + dat. com., τοῖς ἀξίοις περιποιεῖται τὴν νίκην 'he wins victory for the sake of those who deserve it' 2M 15.21, νίκην καὶ τιμήν 'victory and honour' Pr 22.9a (‖ κτάομαι); ***o*** sth undesirable, ἀπώλειαν 6.32.

Cf. ζωγρέω, ζωογονέω, ζωοποιέω, κτάομαι.

περιποίησις, εως. f.ʃ

1. *act of gaining possession of*: δώσω .. εἰρήνην ψυχῆς εἰς ~σιν 'I shall grant .. peace of mind to be possessed' Hg 2.9.

2. *that which is acquired*: ἔσονταί μοι .. εἰς ~σιν 'they will become mine .. to become my possession' Ma 3.17.

3. *survivors*: coll., ὥστε μὴ εἶναι ἐν αὐτοῖς ~ιν 2C 14.12.

Cf. περιποιέω: Spicq 3.100-2.

περιπόλιον, ου. n.ʃ

suburb: 1M 11.4, 61.

περιπορεύομαι.ʃ
to encircle: + acc. loci, Jo 15.3. Cf. ἐκπεριπορεύομαι, κυκλόω.

περιπόρφυρος, ον.ʃ
edged with purple: ~α, prob. ἱμάτια understood, Is 3.21 (+ μεσοπόρφυρα), cf. Passoni dell'Acqua 1998.97f.

περίπτερος, ον.ʃ
1. *flying about*: subst.n., πυρός 'fire-flake, spark,' glossed as φλόξ Ct 8.6.
2. *having a single row of columns all round it* (LSJ): *s* house, Am 3.15.

περίπτωμα, ατος. n.ʃ
accidental convergence: ~ατι περιπίπτω 'to encounter just by chance' 2K 1.6, Ru 2.3. Cf. περιπίπτω.

περιρραίνω: fut. ~ρρανῶ.ʃ
to besprinkle: ἐπί + acc., ἐπὶ τὸν καθαρισθέντα ἀπὸ τῆς λέπρας 'one who was purified from leprosy' Le 14.7; ἐν αὐτοῖς [= with things soaked in the blood of a sacrificial animal] ἐπὶ τὴν οἰκίαν 14.51; + acc. ὕδωρ ῥαντισμοῦ Nu 19.21; + double acc., ^τοὺς Λευίτας^ ὕδωρ ἁγνισμοῦ 8.7. Cf. ῥαίνω, περιρραντίζω.

περιρραντίζω: aor.pass. περιερραντίσθην.ʃ *
to besprinkle around: ὕδωρ ῥαντισμοῦ οὐ περιερραντίσθη ἐπ' αὐτόν Nu 19.13, 20. Cf. ῥαντίζω, περιρραίνω.

περιρρέω.ʃ
to fall all round: *s* pieces of hum. flesh, 4M 9.20.

περιρρήγνυμι: aor.ptc. ~ρρήξας.ʃ
to rend and tear off: + acc. (clothes), 2M 4.38. Cf. ῥήγνυμι.

περισιαλόομαι: pf.ptc.pass. ~σεσιαλωμένος.ʃ*
to embroider round the edge: *o* decorative stone and pass., χρυσίῳ 'with gold' Ex 36.13.

περισκελής, ές.
round the leg: subst.n.pl. ~ῆ *two-legged undergarment* worn by priests, 'drawers,' λινᾶ 'linen' Ex 28.38 (worn to cover the privy parts); ~ῆ καὶ ποδήρη καὶ ἐπωμίδα Si 45.8; ἐπὶ τὰς ὀσφύας 'on the loins' Ez 44.18; sg. περὶ τὸ σῶμα 'round the body' Le 6.10; ἐπὶ τοῦ χρωτός 'on the skin' 16.4. Cf. σκέλος.

περισκυθίζω: aor.ptc. ~σκυθίσας.ʃ*
to cut the hair of the head of sbd *all round*: + acc. pers., 2M 7.4.

περισπασμός, οῦ. m.
1. *act of wheeling round*: 2M 10.36.
2. *that which occupies one's mind*: To 10.6 𝔊II, Ec 1.13, θυμοῦ 2.23.
Cf. περισπάω: Caird 1969.27f.

περισπάω: aor. περιέσπασα.
1. *to cause* sbd or sth (acc.) *to come loose from his or its fixed position*: ark on a moving cart, 2K 6.6.
2. *to occupy the mind of*: + acc. pers., Ec 5.19. **b**. pass. *to have one's mind occupied* over various matters: περὶ πάντων Si 41.2; + ἔν τινι Ec 1.13.
Cf. περισπασμός: Caird 1969.28.

περισπόριον, ου. n.*
Alw. pl., *area surrounding a population centre*: πόλεις καὶ τὰ ~α Jo 21.2, τὴν Ἄζωτον καὶ τὰ ~α αὐτῆς Jd 1.18. Cf. θυγάτηρ, ὅριον, περίοικος: Caird 1969.28.

περισσεία, ας. f. *
advantage: Ec 1.3.

περίσσευμα, ατος. n.ʃ
superfluity: ἐκ ~ατος λαλεῖ 'he talks one minute too long' Ec 2.15. Cf. περισσός.

περισσεύω: aor. ἐπερίσσευσα, subj. ~σσεύσω.
1. *to have more than enough*: ἐν πᾶσιν Si 10.27, ἐν φρονήσει 'in prudence' 19.24; + dat., πτωχείᾳ 'poverty' 11.12 (:: ὑστερέω).
2. *to outdo*: + ὑπέρ τινα 1M 3.30; παρά τινα Ec 3.19. **b**. *to do more than enough* or *appropriate* 'go overboard': Si 30.38.
3. *to remain unused* or *unaffected* by calamity: *s* food, σοι To 4.16; hum., 1K 2.36B (*L*: ὑπολελειμμένος).
Cf. περισσός, ὑστερέω.

περισσός, ή, όν.
1. *more than enough*: τὸ ~ὸν τὸ καταλειφθέν 'the residue which was left over' Ex 10.5; Nu 4.26, see *BA* ad 3.26; Ez 48.21; *s* hum., ἐν λόγοις 'verbose' PSol 4.2; subst. n.pl. adverbially used, ~ά 'excessively' Ec 7.16. **b**. *other than normal*, 'uncommon, singular': *s* πνεῦμα 'intelligence' Da 5.12 TH, σοφία 5.14 TH. **c**. *redundant*: 2M 12.44; ~ὸν ὅτι .. 'it goes without saying that ..' Ec 12.9.
2. *additional*: ἐπί τινι '(additional) to, over and above' Ez 48.15. **b**. ἐκ περισσοῦ 'over and above the normal' Da 3.22 TH. **c**. subst. n. pl., τὰ ~α τῶν λόγων τινός 1M 9.22.
Cf. κατάλοιπος, λοιπός, περίσσευμα, περισσεύω.

περισσῶς. adv.ʃ
to an extensive degree: + vb, Ps 30.24, 2M 8.27, διαφέρον 'differing' Da 7.7 TH; ἰσχυρὸν π. 'exceedingly powerful' Da 7.7 TH. Cf. σφόδρα.

περίστασις, εως. f.ʃ
1. *installation situated round*: π. ὅπλων 'arsenal' Ez 26.8.
2. *situation*: χαλεπή 'grave' 2M 4.16.

περιστέλλω: fut. ~στελῶ; aor. ~έστειλα, impv. ~στειλον, subj.~στείλω, pass. ~σταλῶ.ʃ
to clothe, wrap up: + acc., the dead at his funeral,

To 12.13; a corpse, Si 38.16; pass., *o* hum., Ez 29.5; metaph., ἡ δόξα τοῦ θεοῦ περιστελεῖ σε Is 58.8, "my tongue and lips with words of truth" PSol 16.10. Cf. περιβάλλω.

περιστερά, ᾶς. f.
dove, pigeon: Ge 8.8; τρυγόνα καὶ ~άν 15.9, π. ἄνους 'silly dove' Ho 7.11; ‖ ὄρνιον 11.11; ἡ πόλις ἡ π. Zp 3.2. Cf. τρυγών.

περιστήθιον, ου. n.ʃ*
breastband worn by priests: Ex 28.4.

περιστολή, ῆς. f.ʃ
1. *ornamental garment*: ‖ κόσμος Ex 33.6 (‖ στολαὶ δοξῶν vs. 5, cf. π. δόξης, of Aaron's robe, Si 45.7).
*2. *tender care*: ἐν ~ῇ PSol 13.8, cf. LSJ, s.v. περιστέλλω **III 3**.
Cf. στολή.

περιστόμιον, ου. n.ʃ
that which lies all round the periphery of sth: collar of a garment, Ex 28.28; of an undergarment, 36.31; of a tunic, Jb 30.18¶; 15.27¶; edge of a ravine, Ez 39.11. Cf. λῶμα.

περιστρέφω: fut.pass. ~στραφήσομαι; aor.pass.ptc. ~στραφείς.ʃ
1. intr. *to turn round* to face sbd frontally and show him respect: mid. περιστραφέντα τὰ δράγματα ὑμῶν προσεκύνησεν τὸ ἐμὸν δράγμα 'your sheaves turned round and did obeisance to my sheaf' Ge 37.7.
2. intr. *to move on to another thing*: mid. οὐ περιστραφήσεται κλῆρος .. ἐκ φυλῆς ἐπὶ φυλὴν ἑτέραν 'no lot shall shift positions from one tribe to another' Nu 36.9, sim. 36.7 ἀπὸ φυλῆς ἐπὶ φυλήν.
Cf. περιστροφή.

περιστροφή, ῆς. f.ʃ
act of turning round: ναοῦ 'out of the temple (?)' Si 50.5. Cf. περιστρέφω.

περίστυλος, ον.
subst.n., *collonade* round an enclosed space: round a temple, Ez 40.17. **b**. *long row*: of elephants moving to a battlefield, 3M 5.23.

περισύρω: aor.pass. ~σύρας.ʃ
to tear off: + acc. rei, τὸ χλωρόν 'the green part (of a rod)' Ge 30.37, τὸ τῆς κεφαλῆς δέρμα 'the skin of the head' 2M 7.7.

περισχίζω.ʃ
to split oneself into two: Ez 47.15, 48.1. Cf. σχίζω.

περιτειχίζω: aor. ~ετείχισα; pf.ptc.pass. ~τετειχισμένος.ʃ
to build defence structure round (sth τι): πύργοις ὑψηλοῖς καὶ τείχεσι μεγάλοις .. 'with high towers and large walls ..' 1M 13.33; τὰ περιτετειχισμένα σου οἰχήσεται 'your surrounding walls shall disappear' Ho 10.14. Cf. περιτείχισμα, τεῖχος and τειχίζω.

περιτείχισμα, ατος. n.ʃ
surrounding wall: 2K 20.15*L* (B: προ~). Cf. περίτειχος, περιτειχίζω.

περίτειχος, ου. n.ʃ*
surrounding wall: τεῖχος καὶ π. Is 26.1; ᾠκοδόμησεν ἐπ' αὐτὴν [= Jerusalem] κύκλῳ 4K 25.1 (*L* τεῖχος). Cf. τεῖχος, περιτειχίζω, περιτείχισμα.

περιτέμνω: fut. ~τεμῶ, mid. ~τεμοῦμαι, pass. ~τμηθήσομαι; aor. περιέτεμον, mid. ~ετέμην, impv.act. ~τεμε, pass. ~ετμήθην, inf. ~τμηθῆναι, impv. ~τμήθητι, ptc. ~τμηθείς; pf.pass.3pl περιτέτμηνται, ptc.act. ~τετμηκώς, pass. ~τετμημένος.
to make an incision round, 'to circumcise': + acc., τὴν σάρκα τῆς ἀκροβυστίας 'the flesh of the foreskin' Ge 17.24 (one's own), τὴν ἀκροβυστίαν τοῦ υἱοῦ αὐτῆς Ex 4.25; mid. Ge 34.24 (one's own). **b**. *to perform circumcision on*: + acc. pers. (alw. hum. male other than *s*), Ge 17.27, Ex 12.44, τέκνα 1M 1.60 (*s* mother, so 2M 6.10, 4M 4.25), παιδάρια ἀπερίτμητα 1M 2.46; τῇ ὀγδόῃ ἡμέρᾳ 'on the eighth day' Ge 21.4; pass., περιτμηθήσεται ὑμῶν πᾶν ἀρσενικόν 'every male of yours ..' 17.10 (including adults); + 2nd obj., περιτμηθήσεται τὴν σάρκα τῆς ἀκροβυστίας 17.14 (mid. 34.24, of one's own foreskin); τὴν ἀκροβυστίαν understood, 34. 22*bis*. **b**. fig.: mid. and *o* σκληροκαρδία 'stubbornness of heart' De 10.16.
Cf. περιτομή, ἀπερίτμητος, ἀκροβυστία, τέμνω: *ND* 3.81.

περιτίθημι: fut. ~θήσω, mid. ~θήσομαι; impf.mid. ~ετιθέμην; aor. ~έθηκα, inf. ~θεῖναι, ptc. ~θείς, mid. ~εθέμην, impv. ~θου, 3sg ~θέσθω.
1. *to put* (bodily decorative accessories, acc.) *round* oneself or part of one's body [mid.] or sbd else's body [act.]: mid. κίδαριν 'turban' Le 16.4; ἐνώτια 'earrings' Ho 2.13; περὶ τὴν ὀσφῦν σου 'round your waist' Je 13.1 (‖ act. vs. 2) δεσμοὺς καὶ κλοιοὺς .. περὶ τὸν τράχηλόν σου 'chains and collars .. round your neck' 34.1; fig., περικεφαλαίαν σωτηρίου ἐπὶ τῆς κεφαλῆς 'helmet ..' Is 59.17 (‖ ἐνδύομαι, περιβάλλομαι), κόρυθα 'helmet' Wi 5.18, ὅπλα 'armour' Je 28.3; σοῖς δακτύλοις 'round your fingers (like a ring)' Pr 7.3. **b**. act.: τινί (pers.) τι - περιέθηκα αὐτῇ τὰ ἐνώτια καὶ τὰ ψέλια περὶ τὰς χεῖρας αὐτῆς Ge 24.47; περιθήσεις αὐτοῖς τὰς κιδάρεις 'you shall put the turbans upon them' Ex 29.9; αὐτῇ τὸ διάδημα '.. the diadem' Es 1.11 o'; τὰ δέρματα τῶν ἐρίφων περιέθηκεν ἐπὶ τοὺς βραχίονας αὐτοῦ καὶ ἐπὶ τὰ γυμνὰ τοῦ τραχήλου αὐτοῦ 'she put the hides of the goats round his arms and on the exposed parts of his neck' Ge 27.16; ^δακτύλιον^ ['signet-ring'] ἐπὶ τὴν χεῖρα Ιωσηφ 41.42 (:: περιαιρέομαι); κλοιὸν χρυσοῦν 'golden collar' ib.; ψέλια .. κάθεμα 'armlets .. necklace' Ez

16.11; φραγμόν 'a fence' Is 5.2; τιμὴν ἑαυτῷ '(put on) a pose of dignity (or: a glorious garment)' Pr 12.9. **c.** fig.: μοι νεότητος ἁμαρτίας '.. sins of (my) youth' Jb 13.26, μοι δύναμιν 2K 22.33*L*.

2. *to bestow, confer upon*: τί τινι– τὸν κλῆρον τοῦ πατρὸς αὐτῶν αὐταῖς 'their father's lot to them' Nu 27.7, σοι δόξαν Ez 27.7; τιμὴν τοῖς ἀνδράσιν ἑαυτῶν Es 1.20 o'; Jb 39.19.

Cf. τίθημι, περίθεμα, περιζώννυμι, περιαιρέομαι, ἐνδύω.

περιτομή, ῆς. f.ʃ

act of excising around: circumcision and as cogn. dat., Ge 17.13; τὸ αἷμα τῆς ~ῆς Ex 4.25, 26; lopping of a tree, Je 11.16. Cf. περιτέμνω.

περιτρέπω: fut. ~τρέψω.ʃ

overturn: + acc., θρόνους 'thrones' Wi 5.23. Cf. καταστρέφω **1**.

περιτρέχω: fut. ~δραμοῦμαι; aor.impv. περίδραμε.ʃ

to run about in search of sth: ζητοῦντες τὸν λόγον κυρίου Am 8.12; ἐν ταῖς ὁδοῖς Ιερουσαλημ .. ζητήσατε Je 5.1. Cf. τρέχω.

περιφανῶς. adv.ʃ

for all to see: 4M 8.2.

περιφέρεια, ας. f.ʃ

erroneous thinking: ἐν καρδίᾳ Ec 9.3; 10.13. Cf. περιφορά, περιφέρω: Caird 1969.28f.; LSG s.v.

περιφερής, ές.ʃ

1. *revolving*: *s* some torturing device (ὄργανον), 2M 13.5.

2. subst. n., *circumference*: Ez 41.10. Cf. περίμετρον.

περιφέρω: aor.ptc. ~ενέγκας.

1. *to carry with one always*: + acc. pers., a foetus in one's womb, 2M 7.27.

2. *to cause to move to and fro*: pass., 'be tossed about' Pr 10.24.

3. *to make dizzy*: τινα Ec 7.7 (ǁ ἀπόλλυμι καρδίαν). Cf. σκοτόω **2**.

Cf. περιφέρεια, περιφορά.

περιφορά, ᾶς. f.

1. *act of causing the loss of mental equilibrium*: *s* laughter, Ec 2.2, cf. Gregory 176.

2. *erroneous thinking*: Ec 7.25.

Cf. περιφέρεια: Caird 1969.28f.; LSG s.v.

περιφράσσω: aor. ~έφραξα, impv. ~φραξον, inf. ~φράξαι, ptc. ~φράξας; pf.ptc.pass. ~πεφραγμένος.

to build a fence around sth *to prevent entry into it*: + acc. rei, Jb 1.10, ἀκάνθαις 'with thorn-bushes' Si 28.24; + cogn. acc., τὸν φραγμὸν τῆς πόλεως 3K 10.22[a]; pass., *o* αὐλαί 'courtyards' Ep Je 17; city, τείχεσι 'with walls' 2M 12.13. Cf. φράσσω.

περιφρονέω: aor.inf. ~φρονῆσαι.ʃ.

to refuse to attach importance or value to, 'to contemn': + gen., τῆς ἀνάγκης 'the suffering (of torture)' 4M 6.9, βασάνων 'tortures' 7.13, ἀλγηδῶν 'pains' 14.1. Cf. καταφρονέω, περίφρων: Spicq 3.103f.

περίφρων, ον; gen. ~ονος.ʃ

contemptuous of: + gen., 4M 8.28. Cf. περιφρονέω.

περιφυτεύω: pf.ptc.pass. περιεφύτευσα.ʃ

to plant round about: τι 4M 2.21. Cf. φυτεύω.

περιχαλάω: pf.ptc.pass. περικεχαλασμένος.ʃ*

to relax all round: pass., *o* parts of hum. body, 4M 7.13 (ǁ λύω). Cf. λύω.

περιχαλκόω: fut. ~κώσω.ʃ

to overlay with copper: *o* poles of altar, Ex 27.6. Cf. χαλκός, περιαργυρόω, ~χρυσόω:LSG s.v.

περιχαρακόω: aor. ~εχαράκωσα, impv. ~κωσον.ʃ

to surround with a stockade: *o* city, Je 52.4 (ǁ περιοικοδομέω); metaph., mother's speech to be preserved, Pr 4.8. Cf. χαρακόω.

περιχαρής, ές.

very glad: Jb 3.22, 3M 5.44. Cf. χαρά.

περιχέω: aor. περιέχεα, pass. ~εχύθην, ptc. ~χυθείς; pf.ptc.pass. ~κεχυμένος; plpf.pass.3s ~εκέχυτο, ʃ

1. *to pour round* (+ acc.): τὸ αἷμα τῷ θυσιαστηρίῳ 2C 29.22; pass. περιεχύθη μοι ὕδωρ 'water was poured round me' Jn 2.6; οἶνος Ju 13.2.

2. *to affect thoroughly and profoundly*: περιεκέχυτο περὶ τὸν ἄνδρα δέος τι καὶ φρικασμὸς σώματος 'terror and bodily trembling had completely come over the man' 2M 3.17; πολλῷ σκότει περιχυθέντα 'thrown into much darkness' 3.27.

Cf. χέω.

περίχρυσος, ον.

set in gold, plated with gold: *s* pillar, Es 1.6 *L*; idols, ~α καὶ περιάργυρα Ep Je 7; + ξύλινα 'wooden' 38; οἱ θεοὶ αὐτῶν εἰσι ξύλινοι καὶ ~οι καὶ περιάργυροι 69. Cf. περιάργυρος and περιχρυσόω.

περιχρυσόω: aor. ~εχρύσωσα; pf.ptc.pass. ~κεχρυσωμένος.ʃ

to plate with gold: + acc., idols, τὰ εἴδωλα τὰ περιηργυρωμένα καὶ τὰ περικεχρυσωμένα 'the idols plated with silver and gold' Is 30.22; *o* image (εἰκών) 40.19, θρόνος 3K 10.18. Cf. περιαργυρόω, ~χαλκόω, περίχρυσος.

περίχωρος, ον.

situated round about: τῆς γῆς τῆς ~ου Ge 19.28. **b.** subst.: f.sg., area, πᾶσαν τὴν ~ον τοῦ Ἰορδάνου Ge 13.10; ἐν πάσῃ τῇ ~ῳ 19.17; πᾶσαν τὴν ~ον Αργοβ De 3.13, 14; n.pl., ἐν πόλει τῶν ~ων (sc. τοῦ Ἰορδάνου) Ge 13.12, ǁ sg. 2C 4.17; πάντα τὰ ~α Αργοβ De 3.4; πάντα τὰ ~α Ἰεριχώ 34.3.

Cf. περίοικος.

περίψημα, ατος. n.ʃ *
thing of no value (LSG): To 5.19. Cf. περικάθαρμα: Stählin, *TDNT* 6.84-90; Spicq 3.93-5.

περίψυκτος, ον.ʃ
very much loved: *s* hum., the only child (young, still unmarried) Jd 11.34 *L* (+ ἀγαπητός). Cf. περιψύχω.

περιψύχω.ʃ
to pamper: + acc. pers. (child), Si 30.7. Cf. περίψυκτος.

περκάζω: fut. περκάσω.ʃ
to turn dark (of grapes beginning to ripen): περκάσει ἡ σταφυλὴ ἐν τῷ σπόρῳ 'the grapes will turn black at seedtime' Am 9.13; ὡς περκαζούσης σταφυλῆς Si 51.15.

Πέρσης, ου.
Persian: pl., *Persia* 1E 1.54, *Persians* Ju 16.10.

Περσικός, ή, όν.
Persian: subst.f.sg., *Persia* 2M 1.19.

Περσίς, ίδος. f.
**Persia*: 1E 3.1.

πέσσω: fut. πέψω, pass. πεφθήσομαι; aor. ἔπεψα; pf.ptc.pass. πεπεμμένος.
to bake: + acc. rei, ἀζύμους ἔπεψεν αὐτοῖς 'he baked them unleavened loaves of bread' Ge 19.3; *o* σταῖς 'dough' Ex 12.39; ἄρτους ἐν κλιβάνῳ '.. in an oven' Le 26.26, ἐπὶ τῶν ἀνθράκων 'on the coals' Is 44.19; τὸ μαναα Ez 46.20, ἄζυμα 'unleavened bread' 1K 28.24. Cf. πέμμα, πέψις.

πέταλον, ου. n.
thin, more or less broad object: golden leaf of metal, Ex 28.32, Le 8.9. Cf. φύλλον.

πέταμαι. ⇒ πέτομαι.

πετάννυμι: aor.mid.pass. ἐπετάσθην.ʃ.
mid. *to spread oneself wide*: *s* celestial pillars having collapsed and fallen flat on the ground(?), Jb 26.11.

πέτασος, ου. m.ʃ
broad-brimmed felt hat worn by ἔφηβοι, hence used as their badge (LSJ): 2M 4.12.

πετεινός, ή, όν.
capable of flying in the air: subst.n., πᾶν ~ὸν πτερωτόν 'every winged bird' Ge 1.21; θηρίον ἢ πετεινόν Le 17.13; ~ὰ πετόμενα 'flying birds' Ge 1.20; τὰ ~ὰ τοῦ οὐρανοῦ 40.17 (‖ τὰ ὄρνεα τοῦ οὐ. vs. 19); τὰ θηρία τοῦ ἀγροῦ, τὰ ~ὰ τοῦ οὐρανοῦ καὶ τὰ ἑρπετὰ τῆς γῆς 'the wild beasts, the birds of the sky, and the reptiles of the earth' Ho 2.12, sim. 2.18, 4.3; Zp 1.3 (‖ οἱ ἰχθύες τῆς θαλάσσης); ‖ τὰ θηρία τῆς γῆς De 28.26, Is 18.6; cultic offerings, Le 1.14; 7.16 (‖ κτήνη). Cf. ὄρνεον, πετάννυμι, πέτομαι: Shipp 55f.

πέτευρον, ου. n.ʃ
springboard: fig. of imminent risk, Pr 9.18. Cf. Shipp 448; Caird 1969.29.

πέτομαι, πέταμαι: fut. πετασθήσομαι; impf.3pl ἐπέταντο; 2aor. 3s ἔπτη, 1aor. ἐπετάσθην, inf. πετασθῆναι.
intr. *to move in the air with speed*, 'fly': πετεινὰ πετόμενα ἐπὶ τῆς γῆς 'birds flying above the earth' Ge 1.20; ὀρνέου πτερωτοῦ, ὃ πέταται ὑπὸ τὸν οὐρανόν 'of a winged bird which flies under the sky' De 4.17; ταῖς δυσίν [sc. πτέρυξιν 'wings'] Is 6.2; ἐπὶ πτερύγων ἀνέμων 'on wings of winds' Ps 17.10; ὡς ἀετός 'like an eagle' Hb 1.8; *s* δρέπανον πετόμενον 'a flying sickle' Zc 5.1, 2; reptiles, Is 14.29, 30.6; arrows, Ps 90.5; sword, Ez 32.10; clouds, Is 60.8. **b.** *to fly away*: Ps 54.7. **c.** + acc. of space: τὰ ὑψηλά 'the high places' Jb 5.7. **d.** in general, *to move with speed*: ἐν πλοίοις 'in ships' Is 11.14.
Cf. πετάννυμι, ἀν~, δι~, περιΐπταμαι, ἐκπετάζω, πετεινός, ὄρνεον.

πέτρα, ας. f.
1. *rock*: Ex 17.6; αἱ ~αι διεθρύβησαν ἀπ' αὐτοῦ 'the rocks were pulverised by him' Na 1.6; στερεὰ π. 'solid rock' Is 5.28; where a bird makes a nest, Nu 24.21; unlikely place for a horse to run on, Am 6.12; of elevated rock citadel or observation point (?), Hb 2.1, cf. Cyr. ad loc.; difficult of access by assailants, Je 4.29, Ps 26.5, + ὀχύρωμα 'fortress' 2K 22.2.
2. *hollow rock*, 'cave': a dwelling-place, Je 31.28.
Cf. πέτρος, πέτρινος, λίθος, λειοπετρία: Schmidt 2.171-3.

πέτρινος, α, ον.
made from a piece of rock: *s* μάχαιρα 'knife' Jo 5.2. Cf. πέτρα, λίθινος.

πετροβόλος, ου. m.ʃ
instrument for throwing stones, 'catapult, slinger': Jb 41.20, Wi 5.22; λίθος π. 'stone thrown (as weapon)' Ez 13.11. **b.** *missile hurled*: of hailstones (?), 2K 22.15*L* (B: βέλος 'arrow').

πέτρος, ου. m.ʃ
stone: used as weapon and capable of being picked up with hands and thrown, 2M 1.16, 4.41. Cf. πέτρα, λίθος: Schmidt 2.171-3.

πεύκη, ης.ʃ
pine: building material from Lebanon, Is 60.13. Cf. πεύκινος, πίτυς.

πεύκινος, η, ον.
pertaining to πεύκη (q.v.): *s* ξύλον and + κέδρινος 'cedar' 3K 5.22. Cf. πεύκη.

πέψις, εως. f.ʃ
act of cooking: Ho 7.4. Cf. πέσσω.

πηγή, ῆς. f.
1. *source of stream of fluid*, 'spring, fountain': αἱ ~αὶ τῆς ἀβύσσου Ge 7.11 (‖ οἱ καταρράκται τοῦ οὐρανοῦ, so also 8.2), De 8.7, sim. 33.13; ἐπὶ τῆς ~ῆς τοῦ ὕδατος ἐν τῇ ἐρήμῳ Ge 16.7; ~αὶ ὑδάτων

Nu 33.9; + λάκκος, συναγωγὴ ὕδατος Le 11.36; τοῦ ὕδατος Ge 24.13 (ǁ φρέαρ vs. 11); ǁ λίμνη Ps 113.8; + ὄμβρος Da 3.64; source of water, Is 41.15 (ǁ ποταμός); δακρύων 'of tears' Je 9.1. **b**. female genital organ: Le 20.18. **c**. breast: 4M 13.21.

2. *stream of liquid*: of running water, π. ἀνέβαινεν ἐκ τῆς γῆς 'a stream of water would come up out of the ground' Ge 2.6; ἐξ οἴκου κυρίου ἐξελεύσεται Jl 3.18; αἵματος Le 12.7 (of menstruating woman).

3. fig. *source* of resources: σωτηρίου Is 12.3, ζωῆς Je 17.13, Si 21.13, Pr 10.11, σοφίας 1.5¶, Ba 3.12.

Cf. φλέψ, κρήνη, ῥύσις, φρέαρ: Schmidt 1.628-32; Shipp 449-51 and LSG s.v. **II 1**.

πῆγμα, ατος. n.ʃ

anything formed into solid mass: of water, Jo 3.16; ligaments of bones, 4M 9.21. Cf. πήγνυμι.

πήγνυμι: fut. πήξω, pass. παγήσομαι; aor. ἔπηξα, ptc., πήξας, impv. πῆξον, pass. ἐπάγην, ptc. παγείς; pf. πέπηγα, ptc. πεπηγώς - pf. used as pass.

1. *to position firmly*: abs., Is 54.2; + acc., tent - σκηνήν Ge 26.25, Ex 33.7; Da 11.45 TH (LXX ἵστημι); πάσσαλον 'tent-peg' Si 14.24, πασσάλῳ 'with a pin' Jd 16.14 B; trap (παγίς), To 14.10; the sky, Is 42.5 (ǁ στερέω); the surface of the abyss, Jb 38.30. **b**. pass., βέλος πεπηγὸς ἐν μηρῷ 'an arrow stuck in a thigh' Si 19.12; "their skin clove fast to their bones" La 4.8.

2. pass. *to become solid*: ἐπάγη ὡσεὶ τεῖχος τὰ ὕδατα, ἐπάγη τὰ κύματα ἐν μέσῳ τῆς θαλάσσης 'the waters became like a solid wall, the waves became still in the middle of the sea' Ex 15.8; *s* πάχνη 'frost' Si 43.19, κρύσταλλος πεπηγώς (act. in form) 'congealed ice' Jb 6.16; καρδία .. ὡς λίθος 41.16.

Cf. πῆγμα, πῆξις, καταπήγνυμι, παγιόω, στερεόω.

πηδαλιουχέω.ʃ

to steer: metaph., ὁ λογισμὸς .. τὴν τῆς εὐσεβείας ναῦν 'the rational will .. the ship of piety' 4M 7.1. Cf. κυβερνάω.

πηδάω.ʃ

to move leaping: *s* flying insects, ἐπὶ τῆς γῆς Le 11.21, ἐπὶ τὰ ὄρη Ct 2.8 (ǁ διάλλομαι). Cf. ἅλλομαι, ἀνα~, ἐμ~, ἐκ~, κατα~, παραπηδάω, σκιρτάω: Schmidt 1.536-46.

πηλίκος, η, ον. interr.ʃ

how large?: ~ον τὸ πλάτος αὐτῆς 'how large its breadth is' Zc 2.2; 4M 15.22.

πήλινος, η, ον.

of clay (πηλός): *s* house, Jb 4.19, σῶμα 13.12, ὄστρακον Da 2.41 LXX; idol, Bel 7 LXX. Cf. πηλός.

πηλός, οῦ. m.

clay: building material, ἄσφαλτος ἦν αὐτοῖς ὁ π. 'clay served them as pitch' Ge 11.3, cf. Ex 1.14 (ǁ πλινθεία); potter's material, π. κεραμέως Is 29.16, Je 18.6; substance to be trampled upon, καταπάτημα ὡς π. ἐν ταῖς ὁδοῖς Mi 7.10; ὡς ~ὸν ὁδῶν Zc 9.3 (ǁ χοῦς), πλατειῶν 'of streets' Ps 17.43; πατοῦντας ~ὸν ἐν ταῖς ὁδοῖς Zc 10.5, ἔμβηθι εἰς ~ὸν καὶ συμπατήθητι .. 'step into the clay and tread ..' Na 3.14; substance in which one could be trapped, Ps 68.15; fig. of sth easily available, hence not valuable, Jb 27.16. Cf. πήλινος, πηλουργός, πλινθεία, βόρβορος, χοῦς: Schmidt 2.191-3.

πηλουργός, όν.ʃ

working in clay: subst.m., ǁ κεραμεύς 'potter' Wi 15.7. Cf. πηλός.

πῆξις, εως. f.ʃ

v.n. of πήγνυμι **1**: ἀγκῶνος 'of the elbow' (w. ref. to leaning on it during meals) Si 41.19. Cf. πήγνυμι.

πήρα, ας. f.

leathern pouch: for victuals, Ju 10.5. Cf. Deissmann 1923.87f.; Michaelis, *TDNT* 6.119-21.

πηρόω: aor. ἐπήρωσα.ʃ

to mutilate: + acc. (pupils of martyr's eyes), 4M 18.21.

πῆχυς, χεος; pl. gen. ~χεων, ~χῶν. m.

1. *forearm*: ǁ χείρ Pr 31.19.

2. *cubit*: δέκα πέντε ~εις '15 cubits' Ge 7.20; ~εος καὶ ἡμίσους τὸ πλάτος 'with the width of one and a half cubits' Ex 25.9; ἀνδρός 'ordinary cubit' De 3.11; δρέπανον πετόμενον μῆκος ~εων εἴκοσι 'a flying sickle of twenty cubits in length' Zc 5.2.

Cf. βραχίων.

πιάζω: fut. πιέσω, pass. πιασθήσομα; aor.impv. πίασον.ʃ

1. *to press tight, squeeze*: in order to extract olive oil, *o* ἐλαίαν 'olives' Mi 6.15.

2. *to lay hold of*: + acc., ἀλώπεκας 'foxes' Ct 2.15; *o* hum. and pass., Si 23.21.

Cf. ἀπο~, ἐκπιέζω: Shipp 454f.

πιαίνω: fut. πιανῶ, pass. πιανθήσομαι; aor.impv.3s πιανάτω.

to nourish and make grow: *o* human bones, Is 58.11, Si 26.13, Pr 15.32 (in a fig. of contentment); vine, Ez 17.8; "let him regard your burnt-offering as fat (πιανάτω)" Ps 19.4; τὰ ὡραῖα τῆς ἐρήμου 'the beautiful parts of the wilderness' 64.13.

πιέζω:⇒ πιάζω.

πίθηκος, ου. m.ʃ

monkey: 2C 9.21.

πίθος, ου. m.ʃ

large jar for storing fermenting wine: *s* commodious house, Pr 23.27. Cf. Mayerson 2000.

πικραίνω: fut.pass. πικρανθήσομαι; aor. ἐπίκρανα, impv. πίκρανον, ptc. πικράνας, pass. ἐπικράνθην, subj. πικρανθῶ.ʃ

1. *to make bitterly felt*: + acc., κλαυθμόν 'crying (over the deceased)' Si 38.17. **b**. pass. *to conduct oneself in harsh manner*: *s* God, ἐν ἐμοί 'against me' Ru 1.20.

2. *to irritate, emotionally embitter*: + acc. pers., βασιλεῖς 1M 3.7 (:: εὐφραίνω), cf. τὴν ψυχήν μου Jb 27.2 (*s* God); pass. *to feel bitter*, abs. Is 14.9 (*s* Hades); + dat. pers., To 5.14 𝔊[II] (𝔊[I] ὀργίζομαι), ἐπί τινι (pers.) Ex 16.20, ἐπί τινα 1E 4.31, Je 44.15, περί τινος 40.9, ἐν ἑαυτῇ 'within herself, deep down' La 1.4; impers. μοι ὑπὲρ ὑμᾶς 'to me about you' Ru 1.13.

Cf. πικρός, ἐκ~, παραπικραίνω, ὀργίζω, παροξύνω: Schmidt 3.563f.; Shipp 455.

πικρασμός, οῦ. m.ʃ

bitterness and harshness: of experiences, δουλείας Es C 19 o'.

πικρία, ας. f.

1. *bitterness* of taste: of water, Ex 15.23; grapevine, Je 2.21.

2. *harshness, cruelty* (of character): Am 6.12 (|| θυμός), cf. ἐν χολῇ καὶ ~ίᾳ 'with gall ..' De 29.18, sim. La 3.20, χολῆς .. ~ας De 32.32; || ὀδύνη Wi 8.16.

3. *bitter feelings*: Je 15.17; ψυχῆς Jb 21.25 (fatal), Si 4.6, 7.11, 3M 4.4.

Cf. πικρός, χολή.

πικρίς, ίδος. f.ʃ

ox-tongue or *chicory*: to be eaten with unleavened bread, ἐπὶ ~ίδων ἔδονται Ex 12.8; with meat Nu 9.11.

πικρός, ά, όν.

1. *bitter to taste*: *s* water, Ex 15.23, σικερα Is 24.9; opp. γλυκύς Is 5.20.

2. *harsh, cruel*: *s* hum. ἔθνος Hb 1.6; φωνὴ ἡμέρας κυρίου Zp 1.14 (|| σκληρός); deed liable to bring about harsh consequences, Je 2.19, κακία 4.18, λόγος 20.8, ζωή Si 30.17, θάνατος 1K 15.32. **b**. *entertaining hard feelings*: *s* hum., ταῖς ψυχαῖς αὐτῶν 2K 17.8*L*.

3. *showing intense mental* or *emotional pain*: subst. n.pl. adverbially used, ἀνεστέναξεν ~ά 'he groaned bitterly' Si 25.18.

Cf. κατάπικρος, πικρία, πικραίνω, παραπικραίνω, πικρῶς.

πικρῶς. adv.

1. *bitterly*: + κλαίω 'to weep' Is 22.4, 33.7.

2. *harshly*: physical, bodily treatment or manhandling, Je 27.21, 4M 6.1.

Cf. πικρός.

πίμπλημι: fut.act. πλήσω, pass. πλησθήσομαι; aor. act. ἔπλησα, impv. πλῆσον, subj. πλήσω, pass. ἐπλήσθην, inf. πλησθῆναι, ptc. πλησθείς, subj. πλησθῶ.

1. act. *to fill*: + acc. of container and gen. of content, τὸν ἀσκὸν ὕδατος 'the skin bag with water' Ge 21.19; αὐτὰ γῆς '.. with soil' 26.15 (of water holes); ὑδρίαν 'water pitcher' 24.16; ἔπλησε θήρας τὴν νοσσιὰν αὐτοῦ 'filled its den with prey' Na 2.13; πλήσω τὸν οἶκον τοῦτον δόξης Hg 2.7, τὴν γῆν ἀνομίας Ez 8.17; bowl, Zc 9.15; *+ ἀπό τινος - τὴν κοιλίαν αὐτοῦ ἀπὸ τῆς τρυφῆς μου 'its belly with my delicacies' Je 28.34, ἀπὸ τῆς δόξης σου Si 36.19; + ἐν - ἐν ἀκαθαρσίαις 2E 9.11; + acc. of content, σοφίαν Si 24.25 (|| ἀναπληρόω).

*2. + τὰς χεῖράς τινος (Hebraism 'פ [sg.!] מִלֵּא יַד) 'to consecrate sbd as priest': Ez 43.26, but not Le 9.17 (see Wevers ad loc.). See s.v. ἐμπίμπλημι **3** and πληρόω **4**.

*3. *to allow to come to the full*: + acc., τὸν θυμόν μου ἔπλησα Je 6.11; θυμὸν ὀργῆς ^κυρίου^ ἐν Αμαληκ 'to vent the Lord's furious wrath at A.' 1K 28.18*L*.

4. pass. *to become full* of a large quantity of sth: + gen. πλησθήσονται οἱ ἅλωνες σίτου 'the threshing-floors will fill with grain' Jl 2.24 (|| ὑπερεκχέομαι); "the streets will fill with boys and girls" Zc 8.5; πλησθήσονται αἱ οἰκίαι .. τῆς κυνομυίας 'the houses will fill up .. with dog-flies' Ex 8.21; ἄρτων 16.12; δόξης κυρίου 40.28; αἵματος Is 15.9; ἀδικίας Ge 6.11, ἀνομίας Le 19.29; δικαιοσύνης PSol 1.2; κραυγῆς 'cry' Je 26.12; ἐκλύσεως 'paralysis' Ez 23.33, σου '(to become fed up) with you (a frequent visitor)' Pr 25.17; + ἐν - ἐν κλαυθμῷ Ez 31.5, ἐν τοῖς ἀγαθοῖς τοῦ οἴκου σου Ps 64.5; || χορτάζομαι 16.14; + ἀπό Pr 14.14 (|| + gen.). **b**. *to eat much food*, 'become sated': Pr 30.9.

4. pass. *to reach the ultimate*: *s* humiliation, Is 40.2.

Cf. γέμω, μεστόω, διεμ~, ἐμπίμπλημι, πλῆθος, πλήρης, πληρόω, and πλησμονή.

πίνινος, ου.ʃ*

π. λίθος 'mother of pearl': Es 1.6 o'.

πίνω: fut. πίομαι; aor. ἔπιον, 3pl ἐπίοσαν, inf. πιεῖν, subj. πίω, impv. πίε; pf. πέπωκα; plpf. πεπώκειν.

to drink: abs. Ge 24.14; φαγεῖν καὶ πιεῖν Ex 32.6, πίετε, φάγετε Is 21.5; + βιβρώσκω Bel 7 TH; *o* water, Ex 7.18, Jn 3.7, during drought, Am 4.8, *s* trees Ez 31.16; ***o*** wine, Ge 9.21, Ob 16*b*, Am 5.11; strained wine (διυλισμένος οἶνος) drunk by the rich, 6.6; for pleasure and merry-making, οἶνον εἰς μέθην 'to get drunk' Jl 1.5, sim. Hg 1.6; in a cultic feast, Ob 16*c*, αἷμα Ez 39.17, ἐπὶ τὸ ὄρος τὸ ἅγιόν μου Ob 16*a*, ἐν τῷ οἴκῳ τοῦ θεοῦ Am 2.8; τὸ ποτήριον 'out of the glass' Je 29.13; with partitive ἐκ: ἐκ τοῦ οἴνου Ge 9.21, ἀπὸ τοῦ οἴνου Je 28.7; + gen., τοῦ ὕδατός σου Nu 20.19, τοῦ οἴνου αὐτοῦ Ju 12.1, οἴνου καὶ στέαρ (acc.!) Is 55.1; + instrumental ἐν, Ge 44.5, 1E 3.6. **b**. fig. πλησμονὴν ἀτιμίας 'a fill of disgrace' Hb 2.16; with ἐσθίω, Zc 7.6*bis*; πίονται εὐφροσύνην, πίονται οἶνον Is 25.6.

Cf. ἐκ~, κατα~, συμπίνω, ποτίζω, πόμα, πόσις, ποτόν, πότος, ποτήριον.

πιότης, τος. f.

abundance: τῆς γῆς Ge 27.28, 39 (of rich crops); + στέαρ 'fat' Ps 62.6; υἱοὶ τῆς ~τος 'embodiments of abundance (?)' Zc 4.14; ***o*** of πίνω Ez 25.4. **b**. *rich food* or *drink*: τράπεζα πλήρης ~τος 'table laden with ..' Jb 36.16¶; of olive-oil, Jd 9.9, cultic oil on an altar, 3K 13.3.

Cf. πίων, πλησμονή.

πιπράσκω: fut.pass. πραθήσομαι; aor.pass. ἐπράθην, impv.3s πραθήτω, subj. πραθῶ, inf. πραθῆναι, ptc. πραθείς; pf. πέπρακα, ptc. πεπρακώς, pass. πέπραμαι, ptc. πεπραμένος.

to sell: + acc. pers., Ge 31.15; pass., Ex 22.3; ***o*** land, Le 25.23; cattle, 27.27; hum. and + dat. pers. (buyer), De 15.12, 28.68; and + gen. of price and cogn. dat., πράσει οὐ πραθήσεται ἀργυρίου De 21.14; εἰς δουλείαν Es 7.4 o'. **b**. *to abandon* to a certain destiny: ***s*** God, + acc. hum., εἰς τὰς χεῖρας αὐτῶν (= enemies) Ju 7.25; 1K 23.7. **c**. mid. *to sell one's soul*: τοῦ ποιῆσαι τὸ πονηρόν 1M 1.15, sim. 3K 20.20, 25, 4K 17.17.

Cf. ἀποπρατίζομαι, πρᾶσις, πρατός, πωλέω, ἀγοράζω.

πίπτω: fut. πεσοῦμαι; aor. ἔπεσον, subj. πέσω, ptc. πεσών, inf. πεσεῖν, impv.2pl πέσατε, opt. 3s πέσοι; pf. πέπτωκα, inf. πεπτωκέναι, ptc. πεπτωκώς.

Almost alw. involuntary action, whether the ***s*** be animate or inanimate.

1. intr. *to move downward*: ***s*** beast of burden, Ex 23.5; ἐν τῇ ὁδῷ De 22.4; a human from the roof of a dwelling, 22.8; corpses (κῶλα) Nu 14.32, εἰς τὴν παγίδα 'into the trap' To 14.10 𝔊[II] (𝔊[I] ἐμπίπτω), ἐν ἀμφιβλήστρῳ 'into a net' Ps 140.10; bird, ὄρνεον ἐπὶ τὴν γῆν 'a bird drops on to the ground' Am 3.5; οὐ μὴ πέσῃ σύντριμμα ἐπὶ τὴν γῆν 'no crushed grain ..' 9.9; hail (χάλαζα) Ex 9.19, dew (δρόσος), Mi 5.7, dew and rain 2K 1.21, stars Is 34.4; dice (κλῆρος), Jn 1.7; fruit Na 3.12, leaves Is 34.4, a drunken man 24.20 (:: ἀνίστημι), ἐπ' ἐμὲ πνεῦμα Ez 11.5; ἔπεσον οἱ μαστοὶ αὐτῶν 'their breasts drooped' 23.3; ***s*** φάραγγες 'valleys (caved-in)' 38.20. **b**. metaph. πεσεῖται ὕψος ἀνθρώπων Is 2.17 (‖ ταπεινόω pass., vs. 11); financially, Si 19.1 (:: πλουτίζομαι 'become rich'), morally 22.27. ***c**. Idiom: ἐπὶ πρόσωπον 'to prostrate, throw oneself down,' a gesture of reverence, Ge 17.3; without a poss. pron. coreferent with the subj. of the verb, ἔπεσαν ἐπὶ π. Le 9.24, sim. Nu 16.4, 20.6, Si 50.17, To 12.16 𝔊[I] (𝔊[II] w. pron.); w. a poss. pron., Da 6.10, 8.17 LXX; with a historic present, καὶ πίπτω ἐπὶ π. μου Ez 2.1, 3.23, 11.13, 43.3, 44.4, Da TH 8.17, 18– Hauspie 2001; suppliant, Nu 14.5 (or out of despair, Sforno); not very respectful, foll. by ἐγέλασεν Ge 17.17; ἐναντίον αὐτοῦ ἐπὶ τὴν γῆν 44.14, ἐπὶ τὴν γῆν ἐπὶ π. ἐναντίον κυρίου Jo 7.6, ἐπὶ π. αὐτῶν ἐπὶ τὴν γῆν Jd 13.20, ἐπὶ π. αὐτῆς καὶ προσεκύνησεν ἐπὶ τὴν γῆν Ru 2.10; ἐπὶ τοὺς πόδας αὐτοῦ ἔπεσεν 'she fell at his feet' 1K 25.24*L*; ἐπὶ κοιλίαν 'flat on the ground' 2M 10.4; πίπτω alone, but + προσκυνέω 2C 29.30 (‖ vs. 29 κάμπτω 'to kneel'). **d**. voluntary: ἔπεσεν ἐπὶ τὸν τράχηλον αὐτοῦ 'flung himself on his neck' To 11.13 𝔊[II] (𝔊[I] ἐπιπίπτω, which is the more common idiom, q.v.); πέσατε ἐφ' ἡμᾶς 'fall down upon us' so as to cover us and shield us from shame, Ho 10.8; 1K 28.20. **e**. metaph. *to fail to materialise*: ***s*** God's pledge, ἀπὸ τοῦ ῥήματος κυρίου εἰς τὴν γῆν 4K 10.10.

2. *to fall defeated* or *exhausted* in battle: ***s*** hum., πεσεῖται ὁ ἱππεὺς εἰς τὰ ὀπίσω 'the horseman will fall back' Ge 49.17 (with the heel of his horse bitten by a snake), cf. Is 28.13; μαχαίρᾳ Nu 14.43, Is 3.25; ἐν ῥομφαίᾳ 'by the sword' Ho 7.16, 14.1, Am 7.17, ἐν μαχαίρᾳ Je 16.4; Ho 7.7; ἐν τῷ πολέμῳ Is 21.15, μαχαίρᾳ ἐν πολέμῳ Je 18.21, ἐν σφαγῇ Is 65.12; opp. ἀνίστημι– πέπτωκα καὶ ἀναστήσομαι 'I have fallen but I will get up on my feet' Mi 7.8, sim. Am 5.2, 8.14; ***s*** casualties on battlefield, πολὺς ὁ πεπτωκώς (coll. sg.); soldiers weighed down by heavy weapons they carry, Jl 2.8; φόνῳ 'killed' Le 26.7 (‖ μαχαίρᾳ vs. 8); ἡ γῆ τῶν ἀσέβων Is 26.19; fig. πέπτωκε κέδρος 'a cedar has fallen' Zc 11.2. **b**. not specifically on a battlefield: Ex 19.21, 32.28; Nu 14.29; ἐπὶ τὴν κοίτην 1M 6.8 (sickbed), νόσῳ 'with illness' Jb 24.23; Πέπτωκε Βαβυλών Is 21.9; 'to drop dead' Jb 14.10; ἀπ' ἐλπίδος '(to fail to attain) what one has been hoping for' Si 14.2.

3. *to collapse*: ***s*** edifice or part of it, "the horns of the altar will .. collapse ἐπὶ τὴν γῆν" Am 3.14; 9.11*bis* (opp. ἀνίστημι and ἀνοικοδομέω), cf. Husson 200-3; city-wall, τεῖχος πῖπτον παραχρῆμα πόλεως ὀχυρᾶς Is 30.13, wall of house, τοῖχος Ez 13.10; defence-tower, Is 30.25; foundations of a city, 25.2.

***4**. *to win notice*: πεσεῖται ἔλεος αὐτῶν κατὰ πρόσωπον κυρίου 'their supplication may reach the Lord's presence' Je 43.7, sim. 44.20, 49.2, cf. an analogous use of καταβάλλω **4** (Ba 2.19) and ῥίπτω **2** (Je 45.26, Da 9.18, 20 TH).

5**. *to be alloted*: + dat. pers., πεσεῖται ἡ γῆ .. ὑμῖν ἐν κληρονομίᾳ Ez 47.14; ***s κληρονομία Jd 18.1A (B: ἐμ~); εἰς τὴν θυσίαν '(was earmarked) for the sacrifice' 2M 4.20.

***6**. *to turn out at the end of a process*, 'fall out, result': πῶς οὐ πεσεῖται ῥῆμα 'how a certain thing might not eventuate' Ru 3.18. Cf. ἔπεσεν αὐτοῖς βουλὴ ἀγαθή 'in the end a good plan occurred to them' 1M 4.45.

Cf. ἀπο~, δια~, ἐκ~, ἐμ~, περι~, προ~, προσ~, συμ~, ὑποπίπτω, παράπτωμα, πτῶμα, πτῶσις, πταίω, (ὑπο)σκελίζω, σφάλλω: Spicq 3.105-7.

πίσσα, ης. f.∫

pitch: inflammable, Is 34.9 (ǁ θεῖον 'sulphur'); dirty, Si 13.1; + νάφθα Da 3.46; ingredient for cakes, Bel 27.

πιστεύω: fut. πιστεύσω, pass. πιστευθήσομαι; aor. ἐπίστευσα, subj. ~τεύσω, pass. ἐπιστεύθην, ptc. ~τευθείς; pf.ptc. πεπιστευκώς, pass. πεπιστευμένος.

1. *to put trust in*, 'believe': abs., κατὰ ἁγίων Jb 15.15; + dat. pers., τῷ θεῷ Ge 15.6; dat. hum., μὴ πιστεύσωσίν μοι μηδὲ εἰσακούσωσιν τῆς φωνῆς μου Ex 4.1; πιστεύσωσίν σοι τῆς φωνῆς τοῦ σημείου τοῦ ἐσχάτου 4.8 (the gen. under the infl. of the preceding εἰσακούσωσιν τῆς φωνῆς ..); *with a double dative, σοι τοῖς δυσὶν σημείοις τούτοις Ex 4.9. **b**. *to accept that* sbd (dat.) *is speaking truth*: To 2.14. **c**. *to consider* sbd *worthy of trust and confidence*: pass., ***o*** hum., + inf., προφήτης γενέσθαι 1K 3.21. **d**. + dat. rei, τῇ ζωῇ σου De 28.66; 2M 3.12. **e**. + ἔν τινι (hum.), Je 12.6; ἐν τῷ θεῷ αὐτοῦ Da 6.23 TH; ἔν τινι (rei) Ps 77.32, Si 35.21. **f**. ἐπί τινα: Wi 12.2. **f**. pass. *to enjoy the confidence of*: *ἔν τινι (pers., Hebraism), 1K 27.12 (*L* ἐμ~).

2. *to admit the veracity of*: + acc. rei, ὃ οὐ μὴ πιστεύσητε Hb 1.5, pass., πιστευθήσονται τὰ ῥήματα ὑμῶν Ge 42.20; + dat. rei, τοῖς λόγοις ^τοῦ θεοῦ^ Je 25.8, τῷ ῥήματι τοῦ θεοῦ To 14.4 $\mathfrak{G}^{II}$; + ὅτι Jb 9.16, 39.12, La 4.12, 4M 7.19; + inf., Ps 26.13, 4M 5.25.

3. *to entrust*: pass. ***o*** hum. and + inf. (a task), Su 53 LXX, Es E 5 o' (*L* ἐμ~); + dat., ξύλῳ .. ψυχάς 'their own souls .. to a piece of wood' Wi 14.5; ***o*** funds, τῷ ἱερῷ θησαυρῷ 'to the temple treasury' 4M 4.7.

Cf. ἀπιστέω, ἐμ~, καταπιστεύω, πίστις, πιστός: Schmidt 1.333-47; Lührmann 1973; Barth, esp. 120-2.

πίστις, εως. f.

1. *loyalty*: De 32.20; πρὸς ἡμᾶς 1M 10.27, πρὸς τὸν θεόν 4M 16.22, sim. 15.24; βεβαία 'firm' and + εὐνοία 'goodwill' Es B 3.

2. *faith, trust* placed in sbd: ἐν πίστει 'trustingly' Ho 2.20, 'without betraying trust put in oneself' 4K 22.7; μετὰ ~εως 'confidently' 3M 5.44; ἐν τῇ ~ει ἐπὶ τὰ ἔργα 'were entrusted with the works' 1C 9.31; Si 27.16; w. obj. gen. π. μου 'faith put in me' Hb 2.4, cf. van Daalen. **b**. *behaviour, attitude or deed which inspires trust*: ψεῦδος καὶ οὐκ π. Je 9.3, cf. ὕδωρ ψευδὲς οὐκ ἔχον ~ιν 15.18; ποιήσω αὐτοῖς εἰρήνην καὶ ~ιν 40.6 (***s*** God); God's quality, ἡ πίστις σου PSol 8.28; concrete proof of it, ~τεις ἐδίδουν συνασπιεῖν 'they gave pledges to shelter' 3M 3.10; a formal agreement of mutual trust, 2E 19.38; pl. Pr 3.3, 12.22 (:: ψευδής 'deceitful'), 14.22, 15.27a.

Cf. πιστεύω.

πιστοποιέω: aor. ἐπιστοποίησα.∫

to enhance the credibility and validity of: τινα 4M 18.17; + acc., λόγους 7.9. Cf. πιστός.

πιστός, ή, όν.

1. *trustworthy*: ***s*** God, De 7.9, 32.4, + ἀληθινός 3M 2.11; μάρτυς δίκαιος καὶ π. Je 49.5, ἡ διαθήκη μου ~ὴ αὐτῷ Ps 88.29, ὁ νόμος αὐτῷ ~ός Si 36.3; hum., Is 8.2; subst. n.pl., ἔδειξα ~ά 'I demonstrated my trustworthiness, bona fide' Ho 5.9. **b**. *able to be believed to be true*: ***s*** μαρτυρία 'testimony' Si 34.23 (ǁ ἀκριβής 'accurate' vs. 24); π. ὁράσεως 'knowledgeable about visions' 46.15; κρίσις 'interpretation' Da 2.45 LXX. **c**. *reliable*: τὸ ὕδωρ αὐτοῦ ~όν 'his water supply is secured' Is 33.16, μισθός 'reward (certain to come)' Pr 11.21. **d**. *possessing certain efficacy*: ***s*** disciplinary disease, De 28.59, cf. Rashi ad loc. "to chastise you and achieve their mission." **e**. *reliable, secure*: ***s*** τόπος Is 22.23. **f**. *having won sbd else's confidence and trust*: ***s*** hum., ἱερεύς 1K 2.35, εἰς προφήτην 'as a prophet' 3.20.

2. *faithful, loyal*: ***s*** a city and its citizens to their God, Is 1.21; τῷ βασιλεῖ 1M 7.8.

Cf. πιστεύω, ἄπιστος, ἀξιόπιστος, πιστῶς, πιστοποιέω: *ND* 9.9-14.

πιστόω: aor.ptc. πιστώσας, impv. πίστωσον, opt.3s πιστώσαι, pass. ἐπιστώθην, impv. πιστώθητι.

1. act. *to pledge*: + inf., δι' ὅρκων 'with oaths' 2M 7.24. **b**. *to pledge to act on*: abs., 3K 1.36B (*L*: + τοὺς λόγους); + acc. rei, τὸ ῥῆμα, ὃ ἐλάλησας 2K 7.25B (*L*: πιστωθήτω).

2. *to confirm*: + acc. rei, διὰ πλειόνων τὸν ὁρισμόν 'the pledge with many words' 2M 12.25.

3. *to render secure*: pass. and ***o*** royal house, 2K 7.16; + acc. pers., αὐτὸν ἐν τῷ οἴκῳ μου 1C 17.14.

4. pass. *to act in a faithful manner*: μετὰ τοῦ θεοῦ 'towards God' Ps 77.8, ἐν τῇ διαθήκῃ 'in respect of ..' 77.37. **b**. *to prove to be true to its claim*: ***s*** God's teaching, Ps 92.5; 3K 8.26.

πιστῶς. adv.∫

in conformity with the trust placed by sbd else: piety, 4K 16.2 B; w. ref. to the bringing up of an adopted child, Es 2.7 *L*. Cf. πιστός.

πίτυρον, ου.∫

bran: burned as incense, Ep Je 42.

πίτυς, υος. f.∫

pine-tree: Zc 11.2 (ǁ κέδρος); Ez 31.8 (ǁ κυπάρισσος). Cf. πεύκη.

πίων, πῖον, ~ονος.

1. *made plump*: *s* sacrificial animal fattened for slaughter, ἐν μυριάσι χειμάρρων πιόνων 'with tens of thousands of lines of fattened animals' Mi 6.7; hum., Ps 21.30.

2. *fattening, rich*: ἄρτος Ge 49.20, ἔλαιον Ps 91.11.

3. *fertile*: *s* land, ἰδὼν .. τὴν γῆν ὅτι πίων Ge 49.15; Nu 13.21 (:: παρειμένη 'neglected'); τόπος 'spot, plot of land' Is 5.1, 30.23; νομή 'pasture' Ez 34.14; ὄρος Ps 67.16; χῶραι Da 11.24 TH; subst. n.pl., τὰ ~ονα τῆς δόξης αὐτοῦ Is 17.4. **b**. *well-provided*: *s* γῆρας 'old age' Ps 91.15.

Cf. πιότης: Schmidt 4.677f.

πλαγιάζω: aor. ἐπλαγίασα, subj. πλαγιάσω.ʃ

to make deviate from straight path, 'pervert': morally, ἐν ἀδίκοις δίκαιον 'the just person by unjust means' Is 29.21; ὅπως πλαγιάσῃ τὸν οἶκον τοῦ Ισραηλ κατὰ τὰς καρδίας αὐτῶν τὰς ἀπηλλοτριωμένας ἀπ' ἐμοῦ ἐν τοῖς ἐνθυμήμασιν αὐτῶν 'in order to lead the house of I. astray in accordance with their hearts alienated from me in their designs' Ez 14.5. Cf. πλάγιος, πλανάω.

πλάγιος, α, ον.

1. *positioned at the side*: ἐξῆλθαν κατὰ τὰς ~ας θύρας 'they went out by the side doors' Su TH 18.

2. *deviating from straight line*: figuratively and complement of πορεύομαι – πορεύησθε ~οι καὶ μὴ βούλησθε ὑπακούειν μου Le 26.21; ἐπορεύθησαν ἐναντίον μου ~οι 'they walked against me contrariwise' 26.40.

3. *unfavourably and hostilely disposed*: *s* θυμός – Ἐὰν .. μὴ ὑπακούσητέ μου ἀλλὰ πορεύησθε πρός με ~οι, πορεύσομαι κἀγὼ μεθ' ὑμῶν ἐν θυμῷ ~ίῳ, καὶ παιδεύσω ὑμᾶς Le 26.27f.; 26.41.

4. subst. τὰ πλάγια 'side(s)' as opp. to 'front' or 'back,' the pl. being used also with ref. to one side only: esp. ἐκ ~ων 'on the side'– τὴν θύραν ἐκ ~ων '(you shall make) the door on the side' Ge 6.16; ἐκ ~ων τοῦ θυσιαστηρίου 'at the side of the altar' Le 1.11; ἐκ ~ων τῆς σκηνῆς κατὰ λίβα 'at the side of the tent towards the south' Nu 3.29; συγκαλύπτον ἐπὶ τὰ ~α τῆς σκηνῆς ἔνθεν καὶ ἔνθεν 'covering the sides of the tabernacle on either side' Ex 26.13.

Cf. εὐθύς, ὀρθός, πλαγιάζω, σκολιός: Schmidt 4.488f.; Shipp 457f.

πλανάω: fut. ~νήσω, pass. ~νηθήσομαι; aor. ἐπλάνησα, inf. ~νῆσαι, ptc. ~νήσας, subj. ~νήσω, pass. ἐπλανήθην, ptc. ~νηθείς, subj. ~νηθῶ, inf. ~νηθῆναι, impv. ~νήθητι, opt.3pl πλανηθείησαν; pf. πεπλάνηκα, pass. πεπλάνημαι, ptc. πεπλανημένος.

1. *to lead away from the right path*, 'misguide, mislead': + acc. pers., τυφλὸν ἐν ὁδῷ De 27.18; Ho 2.14; μή με πλάνα 'Don't try to fool me' To 10.7 𝔊[II]; ἀπὸ κυρίου De 13.5, ἀπὸ τῆς ὁδοῦ σου Is 63.17; + double acc., πάντας τοὺς ἀνθρώπους .. τὴν διάνοιαν 1E 3.17 (*s* wine); pass. and fig. of pagan practices, πνεύματι πορνείας ἐπλανήθησαν 'they were misled by a spirit of fornication' Ho 4.12; πλανῶν ἦν ὁ μόσχος σου 8.6; Am 2.4; of false prophet, τοὺς προφήτας τοὺς πλανῶντας τὸν λαόν μου Mi 3.5, sim. De 13.5; οἴνῳ Is 28.7 (ǁ διὰ τὸ σικερα); τῶν ὀπίσω σε πλανησάντων 'of those who made you wander backwards' 30.21.

2. mid. *to wander about, not knowing whither heading*: + acc. loci, ἐπλανᾶτο τὴν ἔρημον Ge 21.14, sim. Is 16.8, Pr 9.12b, τόπον ἐκ τόπου Jb 2.9d; ἐν τῷ πεδίῳ Ge 37.15; *s* cattle, ἐν τῇ ὁδῷ De 22.1; sheep, Is 13.14; ὁ μεθύων 'the drunk' 19.14. Cf. ἀνὴρ πεπλανημένος 'a widely travelled man' Si 31.9. **b**. morally or religiously, τῇ καρδίᾳ Ps 94.10, τῷ πνεύματι Is 29.24, τῇ ὁδῷ αὐτοῦ 53.6; of pagan practices, 'to wander off' ἀπὸ τῆς ὁδοῦ De 11.28, ἀπὸ ὁδοῦ ἀληθείας Wi 5.6; ἀπὸ τοῦ θεοῦ Ba 4.28; ἐκ τῶν ἐντολῶν σου Ps 118.110; πόρρω τῆς ἀληθείας 'far from the truth' 3M 4.16 (*s* mind); πλανηθεὶς προσκυνήσῃς θεοῖς ἑτέροις De 30.17, sim. 4.19; κατόπισθεν τῶν ἐνθυμημάτων αὐτῶν Ez 44.10; + περί τι Wi 14.22; + cogn. dat., Ez 44.13, ἐν τῇ πλανήσει 48.11.

3. mid., *to make a false judgement*: Bel 7 TH, 2M 7.18.

Cf. διαπλανάω, πλανήτης, πλάνησις, πλάνος, πλαγιάζω, ἀπατάω, παραπίπτω: Schmidt 1.547-62; Braun, *TDNT* 6.233-6.

πλάνη, ης. f.ʃ

v.n. of πλανάω, q.v. **2**: Wi 1.12, ~ης ὁδός 'erroneous path' 12.24; pl., + ἀνομίαι Ez 33.10; as cogn. acc., To 5.14 𝔊[I]. Cf. πλανάω, πλάνησις.

πλάνησις, εως. f.

1. v.n. of πλανάω, q.v. **2**: πνεῦμα ~εως Is 19.14. Cf. Je 4.11, cf. πνεύματα πλάνα 1Tim 4.11; cogn. obj., To 14.6 𝔊[II].

2. *misleading message*: Μὴ ἀναγγέλλετε ἡμῖν ἑτέραν ~ιν Is 30.10. **b**. *that which is off the morally right track*: Is 32.6.

Cf. πλανάω, πλάνη.

πλανήτης, ου. m.ʃ

he who moves about without being able to stay in one place, 'wanderer': ~ται ἐν τοῖς ἔθνεσιν Ho 9.17. Cf. πλανάω.

πλάνος, ου. m.ʃ

1. *misleading, deceptive statement* or *teaching*: Je 23.32 (ǁ ψεῦδος), Jb 19.4.

2. *act of going astray, error*: Jb 19.4.

Cf. πλανάω.

πλάξ, ακός, pl.dat. πλαξίν. f.

flat stone: τὰς δύο πλάκας τοῦ μαρτυρίου, πλάκας λιθίνας γεγραμμένας (+ ἐν De 9.10) τῷ δακτύλῳ τοῦ θεοῦ 'the two tablets of the testimony, stone tablets inscribed by God's finger' Ex 31.18; τῆς διαθήκης 34.28, De 9.9; πλάκες λίθιναι 'stone tablets' Ex 32.15 (|| πυξία λίθινα 24.12). Cf. πυξίον: Shipp 458.

πλάσμα, ατος. n.ʃ

1. *that which has been moulded, fashioned physically, handiwork*: of images, πέποιθεν ὁ πλάσας ἐπὶ τὸ π. αὐτοῦ 'the maker trusts what he made' Hb 2.18; ***s*** animal, π. κυρίου Jb 40.19, cf. Si 17.21¶; || ποίημα Is 29.16.

2. *the nature of what has been fashioned*: ἔγνω τὸ π. ἡμῶν Ps 102.14; τὸ π. τῆς καρδίας σου Ju 8.29.

Cf. πλάσσω, ποίημα.

πλάσσω: fut.pass. πλασθήσομαι; aor. ἔπλασα, ptc. πλάσας, inf. πλάσαι, mid. ἐπλασάμην, pass. ἐπλάσθην, inf. πλασθῆναι, ptc. πλασθείς; pf.ptc.pass. πεπλασμένος.

1. *to form, fashion, mould*: ***s*** God - ὁ πλάσας τὰ πάντα Je 28.19; ***o*** hum., ἔπλασεν ὁ θεὸς τὸν ἄνθρωπον Ge 2.7 (|| ποιέω 1.26, cf. Alexandre 193f., 233-5), sim. Is 27.11, 43.1, πηλόν με ἔπλασας '.. clay' Jb 10.9; γῆν Je 40.2 (|| ποιέω), τὴν γῆν καὶ τὴν οἰκουμένην Ps 89.2; ὀφθαλμόν 93.9; ἐν κοιλίᾳ 'in (the) belly' Je 1.5; ***o*** animals, ἐκ τῆς γῆς πάντα τὰ θηρία τοῦ ἀγροῦ καὶ πάντα τὰ πετεινὰ τοῦ οὐρανοῦ Ge 2.19; cf. πνεῦμα ἀνθρώπου Zc 12.1; molten image, ἔπλασεν αὐτὸ χώνευμα .. ὁ πλάσας ἐπὶ τὸ πλάσμα Hb 2.18; ἐν γραφίδι 'with a graving tool' Ex 32.4; βῖκος 'jar' Je 19.1. **b**. mid. mentally, 'to devise': ἑορτήν 'feast' 3K 12.33.

2. *to cause to happen, bring about*: + acc. rei, ἐφ' ὑμᾶς κακά 'hardships against you' Je 18.11, ἀνθρώπου γένεσιν 2M 7.23.

Cf. πλάσμα, πλάστης, ἀναπλάσσω, πρωτόπλαστος, ἐργάζομαι, ἑτοιμάζω, κτίζω, ποιέω: Shipp 458.

πλάστης, ου. m.ʃ

one who fashions: ***s*** God, ***o*** hum., 2K 22.3*L*. Cf. πλάσσω.

πλάστιγξ, γγος. f.ʃ

scale of a balance: 2M 9.8, Wi 11.22.

πλάτανος, ου. f.ʃ

plane: famed for its great height, ἀνυψώθην ὡς π. Si 24.14 (|| φοῖνιξ); Ge 30.37.

πλατεῖα, ας. f.

street: as a passage way for transport, Na 2.5; outdoor open space - καθήσονται πρεσβύτεροι καὶ πρεσβύτεραι ἐν ταῖς ~αις Ιερουσαλημ 'elderly men and women will sit in the streets of J.' Zc 8.4; αἱ ~αι τῆς πόλεως 8.5 (where children play); as against indoor space, ἐν τῇ ~ᾳ καταλύσομεν Ge 19.2 (where travelers sleep rough); || ὁδός Je 5.1, Am 5.16; To 13.17 (|| ῥύμη 13.18 𝔊[I]); || ἔξοδος Pr 1.20, || ἔξωθεν Je 9.21. Cf. ἄγυια, ὁδός, ῥύμη.

πλάτος, ους. n.

1. *measurement from side to side*, 'width': of boat, Ge 6.15 (|| μῆκος 'length' and ὕψος 'height'); πηλίκον τὸ π. αὐτῆς ἐστι; 'what is its (i.e. of Jerusalem) width?" Zc 2.2 (|| μῆκος); π. πήχεων δέκα 'ten cubits in width' 5.2; πληρῶσαι τὸ π. τῆς χώρας σου 'to fill up your country from one end to the other' Is 8.8; || εὖρος Ez 40.11; γῆς Si 1.3 (|| ὕψος).

2. *wide area* or *surface*, 'expanse': τὰ ~η τῆς γῆς Hb 1.6; τοῦ μηροῦ 'of the thigh' Ge 32.25 (hip joint?); for a public gathering, Ne 8.1 (|| εὐρύχωρον 1E 9.38); ἐπίγραψον ἐπὶ τὸ π. τῆς καρδίας σου 'Write (them) large on your heart' Pr 7.3, sim. 22.20. See also Renehan 1.51, s.v. βάθος and 1.165, s.v. πλάτος.

3. *capacity to take in a great deal*: καρδίας 'intellectual' 3K 2.35[a] (|| 5.9 χύμα), cf. Gooding 1976: 35f.

Cf. πλατεῖα, πλατύς, πλατύνω, εὖορς, μῆκος, and ὕψος.

πλατύνω: fut.pass. ~τυνθήσομαι; aor. ἐπλάτυνα, impv. πλάτυνον, opt. 3s ~τύναι, pass. ἐπλατύνθην, subj. ~τυνθῶ.

1. *to make wide*, 'widen': ***o*** ways, Je 2.24 (in order to gain easy access), city-wall 28.58, διαβήματα Ps 17.37, στόμα 80.11, ἐπὶ ἐχθρούς (so as to devour them) 1K 2.1; *fig. and pass., πλατυνθῇ ἡ καρδία σου 'you become puffed up' De 11.16, cf. πλατὺς ψυχῇ 'arrogant' Pr 28.25 Aq. (Sym. πλατύψυχος MT /rḥav nefeš/), but with no negative connotation at "you have broadened my mind (καρδίαν)" or ".. freed my heart from constraints" Ps 118.32; ἐπλάτυνεν ὁ ᾅδης τὴν ψυχὴν αὐτοῦ καὶ διήνοιξε τὸ στόμα αὐτοῦ 'the H. enlarged its appetite and opened its mouth wide' Is 5.14, sim. Hb 2.5.

2. *to expand*: pass. and ***s*** people, πλατυνθήσεται ἐπὶ θάλασσαν καὶ ἐπὶ λίβα .. 'will expand westwards and southwards..' Ge 28.14; 'to grow (in size)' De 32.15 (of human body); fig., δόξαν 1M 3.3. **b**. intr. *to increase*: ***s*** καύχησις Si 1.18¶; pass., θλίψεις 'afflictions' Ps 24.17.

3. *to provide abundant space*: + dat. com. (pers.), πλατύναι ὁ θεὸς τῷ Ιαφεθ Ge 9.27; 26.22. **b**. metaph.: + dat.pers. (com.), ἐν θλίψει 'when I was in dire straits' Ps 4.2.

4. mid. *to brag*: σοῖς χείλεσιν 'with your own lips' Pr 24.28.

Cf. πλάτος.

πλατύς, εῖα, ύ.
1. *spacious*: ἡ γῆ ἰδοὺ ~εῖα ἐναντίον ὑμῶν Ge 34.10; 34.21; *s* πόλις Ne 7.4, διῶρυξ 'canal' and + εὐρύχωρος Is 33.21, ποτήριον 'cup' and + βαθύς 'deep' Ez 23.32.
2. *extensive*: *s* ἔργον Ne 4.19 (+ πολύς).
Cf. πλάτος, εὐρύς: Schmidt 4.467-71.

πλατυσμός, οῦ. m.
freedom from stress and distress: ἐξήγαγέ με εἰς ~όν Ps 17.20, ἐπορευόμην ἐν ~ῷ 118.45, κατέλυσεν ἐν ~ῷ 'lived in security' Si 47.12.

Πλειάς, άδος. f.
Pleias: Jb 9.9.

πλειστάκις. adv.ʃ
very often: ‖ καθόδους πολλάς 'many times over' Ec 7.22; Jd 15.7*L*. Cf. πλεονάκις, ποσάκις.

πλεῖστος. ⇒ πολύς.

πλείων. ⇒ πολύς.

πλέκω: aor.ptc.pass. πλακείς; pf.ptc.pass. πεπλεγμένος.ʃ
to braid, interweave: pass., τὰ κροσσωτὰ τὰ πεπλεγμένα 'the braided fringes' Ex 28.14. **b**. *to make by braiding*: pass., στέφανος .. πλακείς 'crown ..' Is 28.5.
Cf. πλοκή, πλόκιον, περι~, συμπλέκω.

πλεονάζω: fut. πλεονάσω; aor. ἐπλεόνασα, inf. ~νάσαι, subj. ~νάσω, pass. ἐπλεονάσθην.
I. intr. *to have in excess*: abs. Ex 16.18 (:: ἐλαττονέω).
2. *to be in excess*: Ex 16.23, 26.12; τὸ πλεονάζον 'the surplus' or 'the outstanding fund yet to be paid' 1M 10.41, cf. Dancy 1954.146.
3. *to exceed the proper bounds*: πλεοναζούσης τῆς νεφέλης 'the cloud overstaying' Nu 9.22; λόγῳ 'to talk too much' Si 20.8, cf. 2M 2.32.
4. *to grow in quantity*: *s* sins, Si 23.3 (‖ πληθύνομαι), ὑπὲρ τὰς κεφαλὰς ἡμῶν 'higher than our heads' 1E 8.72; righteousness, Pr 15.6. **b**. pass. in same meaning: 1C 5.23. **c**. *to do more*: ὑπέρ (+ acc.) 'than' 2K 18.8.
II. tr. *to add to the quantity of*: + acc., τὴν κληρονομίαν Nu 26.54 (:: ἐλαττόω), Je 37.19 (ditto), ἀπαρχήν 'first-fruits offered' 2C 31.5, κακίαν Ps 49.19; παρὰ τὸ κρίμα σου 'over and above that which you have determined' PSol 5.4.
Cf. πλεόνασμα, πλεονασμός, ἐλαττονέω, ἐλαττόω, πληθύνω, αὐξάνω, περισσεύω.

πλεονάκις. adv.
frequently: Is 42.20, Ps 105.43. Cf. πλειστάκις.

πλεόνασμα, ατος. n.ʃ*
excess amount, surplus: τῆς προνομῆς 'of plunder' Nu 31.32. Cf. πλεονασμός.

πλεονασμός, οῦ. m.
excessive added value: usurious interest, ἐπὶ ~ῷ οὐ δώσεις .. βρώματα 'you shall not lend food on condition that it be returned with ..' Le 25.37; ‖ τόκος Ez 18.8, 13, 17, + τόκος Pr 28.8. Cf. τόκος, πλεονάζω, πλεόνασμα.

πλεοναστός, ή, όν.ʃ*
numerous: **s** hum., ~όν σε ποιήσει ὑπὲρ τοὺς πατέρας σου 'make you more numerous than your forefathers' De 30.5; 1M 4.35. Cf. πολύς.

πλεονεκτέω.ʃ
to be greedy: Jd 4.11B; w. cogn. acc. πλεονεξίαν κακήν Hb 2.9; w. cogn. dat. Ez 22.27. Cf. πλεονεξία, πλεονέκτης.

πλεονέκτης, ου. m.ʃ
greedy person: Si 14.9 (‖ miser, vs. 8). Cf. πλεονεκτέω.

πλεονεξία, ας. f.
1. *greed*: as cogn. acc., πλεονεκτῶν ~αν κακήν Hb 2.9; as cogn. dat. Ez 22.27.
2. *gain derived*: ἀργυρίου 'of silver' Jd 5.19A (B: δῶρον).
Cf. πλεονεκτέω: Trench 81-4.

πλευρά, ᾶς. f.
1. *rib*: of a man, Ge 2.21 (used to create a woman).
2. *side*: pl., of hum. body, Nu 33.55, Is 11.5; of a hum. male as seat of virility, 3K 8.19 (‖ 2C 6.9 ὀσφῦς); of sheep, Ez 34.21; of wall, 41.5; of mountain, 2K 16.13B (*L* κλίτος).
3. *chamber on either side of a passage*: Ez 41.7.
Cf. πλευρόν.

πλευρόν, οῦ. n.
1, *side*: θυσιαστηρίου 'of altar' Ex 27.7; 30.4; of hum. body, Ez 4.4.
2. *chamber on either side* of a passage: Ez 41.6.
Cf. κλίτος, μέρος, πλευρά.

πλέω: aor. ἔπλευσα, inf. πλεῦσαι.
to travel by boat: *s* hum. and εἰς + destination, Jn 1.3; ἐπὶ λιμένα 'into a harbour' 4M 7.3; + acc., θάλασσαν Si 43.24, sim. Is 42.10, εἰς τὴν θάλασσαν .. καὶ ποταμούς 1E 4.23, cf. Renehan 2.118. Cf. πλωτός, παράπλους, εἰσ~, καταπλέω, πλοῦς, πλοῖον: Shipp 460.

πληγή, ῆς. f.
1. *blow* or *injury sustained* or *caused*: ἔτι μίαν ~ὴν ἐπάξω ἐπὶ Φαραω Ex 11.1, sim. 33.5 and Is 10.14; military and as cogn. acc. of πατάσσω Jd 11.33, 1M 5.3; resulting in annihilation (ἐκτρίβομαι) Ex 12.13; Mi 1.9; π. ὀδύνης 'painful blow' 1.11; τί αἱ ~αὶ αὗται ἀνὰ μέσον τῶν χειρῶν σου; Zc 13.6; divine punishment and as cogn. obj., ἐπάταξεν κύριος ἐν τῷ λαῷ ~ὴν μεγάλην σφόδρα Nu 11.33; ἀπέθανον .. ἐν τῇ ~ῇ ἔναντι κυρίου 14.37; ἔργων 'for deeds' Pr 22.8; ~ὰς μεγάλας καὶ θαυμαστάς De 28.59; ‖ νόσος 'disease' 29.22, ‖ τραῦμα, μώλωψ Is 1.6, ἐν πόνῳ καὶ ἐν ~ῇ καὶ ἐν

κακώσει εἶναι 53.4; cogn. dat. of πατάσσω 30.31; disciplinary, administered by hum. to hum., + ἔλεγχος 'reproach' Pr 29.15; metaph., π. καρδίας Si 25.13.

2. *act of hitting*: μάστιγος 'with a whip' Si 28.17; metaph., γλώσσης 'with a tongue' ib.

Cf. πλήσσω, σύντριμμα, and ὑπώπιον.

πλῆθος, ους. n.

1. *large quantity*, 'multitude': ηὐξήθη εἰς π. 'grew into a large number' Ge 30.30; εἰς π. πολύ 48.16; εἰς π., 'in a large quantity' 3K 1.19, Zc 14.14; ἐπὶ πλήθει 'with compound interest' or 'on a long-term (loan)' Le 25.36 (see *BA* ad loc.); μέγα π. Ex 1.9 (of a large ethnic group); ἔθνος μέγα καὶ π. πολὺ καὶ μέγα De 26.5; κατὰ τὸ π. αὐτῶν ἥμαρτόν μοι 'as they are numerous, so they have sinned greatly against me' Ho 4.7; ὡσεὶ τὰ ἄστρα τοῦ οὐρανοῦ τῷ ~ει '(as numerous) as the stars of the sky in multitude' Ex 32.13, De 1.10, 10.22, 28.62; + gen., ἐθνῶν Ge 17.4 (‖ πολλῶν ἐθνῶν vs. 5); τῶν ὑπαρχόντων 'of the possessions' 36.7 (‖ τὰ ὑπάρχοντα πολλά); σίτου καὶ οἴνου 'of grain and wine' 27.28; διὰ τὸ π. πάντων 'because of the abundance of everything' De 28.47 (:: ἐν ἐκλείψει ['shortage'] πάντων vs. 48); τῶν ἀδικιῶν Ho 9.7; τραυματιῶν Na 3.3; τῶν ἡμερῶν 'seniority' Zc 8.4; ὕδατος Je 10.13. **b**. adverbially: παρεγένετο ἡ κυνόμυια π. 'the dog-flies arrived en masse' Ex 8.24; κτήνη π. ἦν τοῖς υἱοῖς Ρουβην 'R.'s children had a huge number of cattle' Nu 32.1.

2. *large crowd*: "I will burn up your crowd in the smoke" Na 2.14, cf. Zc 9.10; Si 7.14. **b**. w. ref. to army of troops: Jd 4.7, Ez 31.2, πολέμου 'battle-ready' Ju 2.16; pl., 2M 13.1.

3. *majority*: οὐ προσθήσῃ μετὰ ~ους 'thou shalt not side with the majority' Ex 23.2 (‖ πλείονες).

4. *organised body of members*: πόλεως Si 7.7; τῆς αἰχμαλωσίας '(the community) of the former expatriates' 1E 9.4 (‖ ἐκκλησία 2E 10.8), τῶν Ἰουδαίων 'the Jewish (community)' 2M 11.16; the community at large as against its ruler, 14.20.

Cf. πληθύνω, πίμπλημι, ἐθνόπληθος.

πληθύνω: fut. πληθυνῶ, pass. ~θυνθήσομαι; aor. ἐπλήθυνα, subj. ~θύνω, inf. ~θῦναι, ptc. ~θύνας, opt. 3s ~θύναι, impv. πλήθυνον, pass. ἐπληθύνθην, inf. ~θυνθῆναι, ptc. ~θυνθείς, subj. ~θυνθῶ, opt. 3s ~θυνθείη; pf.pass. πεπλήθυμμαι, ptc. πεπληθυμμένος.

1. *to increase the quantity of*: + acc. λύπας 'pains' Ge 3.16 (associated with childbirth); σπέρμα 'offspring' 16.10; 17.20, 28.3 (‖ αὐξάνω), ὡς τοὺς ἀστέρας τοῦ οὐρανοῦ καὶ ὡς τὴν ἄμμον τὴν παρὰ τὸ χεῖλος τῆς θαλάσσης 22.17, sim. Da 3.36 TH (‖ LXX πολυπληθύνω); σέ De 28.11 (collectively); κραυγή 'outcry' Ge 18.20, δέησιν 'supplication' Is 1.15, πορνήν 'harlotry' 57.9, ἀσεβείας Je 5.6; ἔλεος Ps 35.8; φερνή 'bride's price' Ge 34.12; σημεῖα καὶ τέρατα Ex 7.3, 11.9; ἀργύριον ἐπλήθυνα αὐτῇ Ho 2.8; ὁ πληθύνων ἑαυτῷ τὰ οὐκ ὄντα αὐτοῦ Hb 2.6; opp. ἐλαττονόω Le 25.16, ἐλαττόω Nu 33.54. ***b**. 'to do sth frequently or over a long time,' + inf., τοῦ ἀσεβῆσαι '(you) frequently committed sin' Am 4.4; Ps 77.38, 4K 21.6, 2C 33.6, 36.14; + ptc., προσευχομένη 1K 1.12ʃ.

2. pass. intr. *to increase in quantity*: *s* living creatures, Ge 1.22 (‖ αὐξάνομαι), flock and herd Je 23.3 (ditto); including hum., Ge 8.17; hum., 9.1, 35.11, 47.27, Ex 1.7 (+ αὐξάνομαι), Je 36.6 (:: μικρύνομαι); εἰς πλῆθος πολύ 'into a great multitude' Ge 48.16; ὕδωρ 7.17; ἐπληθύνθη μανία σου 'your madness increased' Ho 9.7; ἁμαρτίαι Je 37.14; πληθυνθήσονται καθότι ἦσαν πολλοί 'they will regain their former number' Zc 10.8; wicked deeds, αἱ κακίαι τῶν ἀνθρώπων Ge 6.5, destruction 2E 4.22; πεπλήθυνται τὰ κακὰ αὐτῶν 'their evils have increased' Jl 3.13; a period of time, ἐπληθύνθησαν αἱ ἡμέραι 'a long time elapsed since' Ge 38.12. ***b**. + gen. (analogy of πίμπλημι, πληρόω etc.?, see 2E 9.11): ἡ πόλις ἡ πεπληθυμμένη λαῶν La 1.1; + ἐν - ἐν ἔθνεσιν ib.; *s* hum., + dat., χρυσίῳ .. καὶ ἐν κτήνεσιν πολλοῖς 'in gold .. and abundant cattle' Ju 5.9.

3. intr. *to distinguish oneself in quantity*: ὑπὲρ ἀκρίδα 'locusts' Je 26.23; ἐν ἰσχύι Si 43.30; ἅρμασιν 'in chariots' 3M 6.4, συστροφαῖς 'with gangs' 5.41. **b**. *to become numerous*: *s* hum., 2M 3.19; lawless acts, Od 12.9; humiliating experiences, 2K 22.36*L*. **c**. *to become intense*: *s* sound, 1K 14.19 (*L* mid.).

Cf. αὐξάνω, πλῆθος, (ἐμ)πληθύνω, πίμπλημι, πλατύνω, πλεονάζω, πολύς, πολυπληθύνω, προσποιέω **I**, ἐλαττονόω, ἐλαττόω, ὀλιγοποιέω.

πληθύς, ύος. f.ʃ

great quantity: of people, 3M 4.17. Cf. πλῆθος.

πληθύω.ʃ

intr. of πληθύνω: *to be* or *become full* of: τινι 3M 5.41. Cf. πληθύνω.

πλημμέλεια, ας. f.

sinful error: ἀνομία ~είας Le 22.16; τοῦ κριοῦ τοῦ περὶ τῆς ~είας 'of the ram which is for the sinful error' 6.31; in the gen. and with no head noun, but only the def. article, in the sense of 'trespass offering'– ὥσπερ τὸ τῆς ~είας 'like the trespass offering' 6.17; ἀπὸ τοῦ αἵματος τοῦ τῆς ~είας 'some of the blood of the trespass offering' 14.14; even without the def. article of the head noun, οἴσει τῆς ~είας αὐτοῦ 'he shall bring his trespass offering' 5.15; nor with the def. article of π.– εἰς ~ειαν 'as a trespass offering' 5.18, Nu 6.12; 2E 10.19. Cf. πλημμελέω, ἁμαρτία: Trench 248f.; Daniel 308-16, 321-3, 341-61; Harl 2001.884.

πλημμελέω: fut. ~λήσω; aor. ἐπλημμέλησα; subj. ~λήσω.

to commit a sinful error: against divine orders, abs. Le 4.13; ἁμάρτῃ καὶ πλημμελήσῃ 4.22; κυρίῳ 5.6; ἐπλημμέλησεν πλημμέλησιν ἔναντι κυρίου 5.19; πλημμέλειαν Si 49.4; + εἰς, Le 6.6, 14.21, Si 23.23; + acc., τὴν κληρονομίαν μου Je 16.18; *s* ψυχή Nu 5.6. **b**. no ethical aspect emphasised, 'faux pas, blunder': Si 9.13. **c**. *to miss one's goal* or *suffer a bad turn*: Ps 33.22, 23.

Cf. πλημμέλεια, ~μέλημα, ~μέλησις, ἁμαρτάνω.

πλημμέλημα, ατος. n.ʃ

1. moral *fault*: Je 2.5.

2. *that which is given* or *paid as compensation* for an offence or damage caused: Nu 5.8.

Cf. πλημμελέω.

πλημμελής, ές.ʃ

out of favour: *s* ἐξ ἀμφοτέρων ἀδικία 'with both parties ..' Si 10.7.

πλημμέλησις, εως. f.ʃ *

act of commiting an error: ἐπλημμέλησεν ~ιν ἔναντι κυρίου Le 5.19; 2E 10.19. Cf. πλημμέλεια.

πλήμυρα, ας. f.ʃ

flood: Jb 40.23. Cf. κατακλυσμός: on the spelling, see Walters 84.

πλήν.

A. **1**. At the beginning of a clause, and interrupting a discourse and emphasising what is important, 'but, anyway; mind you': Ge 9.4, Zp 3.7, Zc 1.6, Is 4.1.

2. 'but,' 'contrary to what one might expect': Ho 12.8, 1M 4.6.

3. 'solely, only': π. τὸν θρόνον ὑπερέξω σου ἐγώ 'only with respect to the throne shall I have an edge over you' Ge 41.40; Ex 8.9, De 3.11; π. ὑμᾶς ἔγνων 'I knew only you' Am 3.2; Je 3.23, 1M 5.48.

4. πλὴν ὅτι introducing a parenthetic after-thought, 'however': Am 9.8, 1K 8.9. **b**. without ὅτι: Le 21.23.

5. introduces a qualifying statement, Ge 9.4, Nu 18.3, 22.35, 36.6.

6. *other than*: reinforced by μόνος - θυσιάζων θεοῖς .. π. κυρίῳ μόνῳ 'offers sacrifices to gods .. other than the Lord alone' Ex 22.20.

B. prep. w. gen., mostly w. a negator: 'other than, except': τῶν καθ' αὐτὸν οὐδέν π. τοῦ ἄρτου 'nothing of his own affairs except the bread' Ge 39.6; οὐκ ἔστιν ἄλλος π. κυρίου 'there is none other than the Lord' Ex 8.10; οὐκ ἔσονται θεοὶ ἕτεροι π. ἐμοῦ 20.3; οὐκ ἔστιν ἔτι π. ἐμοῦ Jl 2.27, Is 46.9, sim. De 4.35, 39; θεὸν π. ἐμοῦ οὐ γνώσῃ 'you shall not recognise any god other than me' Ho 13.4 (ǁ πάρεξ), sim. Is 45.21; π. σοῦ 'except you' Es C *L* 19 (oʹ εἰ μὴ σέ); reinforced by μόνος - π. Σάρρας μόνης 'with the sole exception of S.' To 6.12 𝔊II, but with an indeclinable adv. μόνον - οὐκ ἐνεδύσατο ἀλλογενὴς π. τῶν υἱῶν αὐτοῦ μόνον 'no outsider has worn it except his sons only' Si 45.13. A negator is implied in the preceding εἰ .. λήμψομαι 'I shall not take' (vs. 23) at π. ὧν ἔφαγον οἱ νεανίσκοι .. καὶ τῆς μερίδος .. 'with the exception of that which the youths ate .. and the share of ..' Ge 14.24; also in a rhetorical question, τίς θεὸς π. τοῦ κυρίου; τίς θεὸς π. τοῦ θεοῦ ἡμῶν; Ps 17.32. With no negator: ἔδωκέν τις .. π. τοῦ ἀνδρός σου 'sbd other than your husband ..' Nu 5.20, cf. μάρτυρες ὑμεῖς ἐστε, εἰ ἔστι θεὸς π. ἐμοῦ 'you have witnessed it (and know) if there is ..' Is 44.8. **b**. *not counting together, exclusive of*: οἱ ἄνδρες π. τῆς ἀποσκευῆς 'the men, exclusive of the dependants' Ex 12.37. **c**. *in addition to*: π. τῆς ἀργίας 'in addition to (the loss of income arising from) unemployment' Ex 21.19; De 29.1. **d**. specifies a circumstance to which the preceding statement does not apply: "they shall be unclean .. In the case of wells of water, however (π. πηγῶν ὑδάτων ..), it shall be clean' Le 11.35f.; Jo 13.14, Ez 46.17.

Cf. ἀλλά, ἐκτός, πάρεξ, χωρίς: Thrall 20-5; Blomqvist 1969.75-100, esp. 92-100; Lee 2003a. 311-5.

πλήρης, ες.

1. *full*: + gen., Λάβετε ὑμεῖς ~εις τὰς χεῖρας αἰθάλης καμιναίας 'Take handfuls of furnace soot' Ex 9.8; π. ὁ ληνός 'the wine-press is full' Jl 3.13; ἀργυρίου καὶ χρυσίου 'of silver and gold' Nu 22.18; ἀδικίας π. 'full of injustice' Na 3.1, ἁμαρτιῶν Is 1.4; αἰνέσεως αὐτοῦ π. ἡ γῆ 'the earth is full of his praise' Hb 3.3; κρίσεως Is 1.21, δόξης 6.1, 3; πρεσβύτης καὶ π. ἡμερῶν 'elderly and advanced in age' Ge 25.8, 35.29, Jb 42.17¶, 1C 23.1, sim. 29.28, 2C 24.15 (all of sbd just deceased exc. Da LXX 6.1 where + doublet ἔνδοξος ἐν γήρει), πρεσβύτερος μετὰ ~ους ἡμερῶν '.. together with the dying' Je 6.11 (so Rashi ad loc., "lived out the life-span granted to him"). **b**. *to be sated, have too much of*: + gen., π. εἰμὶ ὁλοκαυτωμάτων κριῶν 'I am fed up with burnt-offerings of rams' Is 1.11 (ǁ οὐ βούλομαι), ἄρτων 1K 2.5. **c**. *not wanting in quantity*: φόροι ~εις 'tributes in full' 2E 4.20; καρδίᾳ ~ει 'whole-heartedly' 1M 8.25, ἐν καρδίᾳ πλήρει 2C 25.2, cf. ἐν καρδίᾳ τελείᾳ 1C 28.9.

2. *rich in content*: ὀσμὴ ἀγροῦ ~ους 'scent of a fertile field' Ge 27.27; *s* σταχύες 'ears of corn' (:: λεπτός 'thin') 41.7, ἡμέραι Ps 72.10.

Cf. πλῆθος, πληρόω, and πίμπλημι.

πληροφορέω: aor.pass. ἐπληροφορήθην.ʃ*
pass. *to be fully bent on*:*s* καρδία, + inf., Ec 8.11. Cf. Spicq 3.120-3.

πληρόω: fut. πληρώσω, pass. πληρωθήσομαι; aor. ἐπλήρωσα, subj. ~ρώσω, impv. ~ρωσον, inf. ~ρῶσαι, opt.3s ~ρώσαι, pass. ἐπληρώθην, subj. ~ρωθῶ, inf. ~ρωθῆναι, ptc.~ρωθείς, impv.3s ~ρωθήτω; pf. πεπλήρωκα, ptc. πεπληρωκώς, pass. πεπλήρωμαι, ptc. ~ρωμένος, inf. ~ρῶσθαι; plpf.pass.3s ἐπεπλήρωτο.

1. *to fill*: + acc., πληρώσατε τὰ ὕδατα Ge 1.22, τὴν γῆν ib. 28; τὸν οὐρανὸν καὶ τὴν γῆν '(permeate) the heaven ..' Je 23.24, φαρέτας 'quivers (with arrows)' 28.11, ληνόν 'wine press' Si 30.25, γαστέρα 'belly' Jb 20.23; *s* hum., Ge 1.28, 9.1; non-hum., 1.22; + acc. (sth) and gen. (with sth), τὸν οἶκον κυρίου .. ἀσεβείας καὶ δόλου Zp 1.9, pass., τὸ στόμα μου αἰνέσεως Ps 70.8, ταραχῆς 'confusion' 2M 10.30; + acc. pers., εὐφροσύνης Ps 15.11, τέχνης καὶ συνέσεως 'skill and understanding' 3K 7.2, ὑπερηφανίας 'arrogance' 2M 9.7; + dat., μεθύσματι 'intoxication' Je 13.13; pass., + acc. pers. and dat. rei, χαρᾷ πεπληρωμένος 'filled with joy' 3M 4.16, χόλῳ 'with rage' 5.30, γενναίῳ .. φρονήματι 'with a noble thought' 2M 7.21.

2. *to complete* a period of time: τεσσαράκοντα ἡμέρας Ge 50.3 (following the death of a person), τὰ ἔτη αὐτοῦ 'his full life-span' Si 26.2.

3. *to cause sth to come to full realisation*: ***o*** τὸν θυμόν μου Is 13.3, τὴν βουλήν σου .. τὰ αἰτήματά σου 'your decision .. your requests' Ps 19.5f.; God's prophecy, 2C 36.21 (‖ ἀναπλήρωσις 1E 1.54), 22 (‖ συντέλεια 1E 2.1); εὐσέβειαν 'piety' 4M 12.14.

*__4__. + τὰς χεῖράς τινος (Hebraism /millē' yad-[sg.!]/) *to consecrate* sbd *as priest*: Nu 7.88 (no corresponding Heb. text, and, *pace BA* 4.44, not applied to θυσιαστήριον, neuter noun, cf. Ez 43.26), Ex 32.29 nor to be confused with + ἐν ταῖς χερσίν τινος 'with one's own hands,' e.g. 3K 8.15, 24; τῷ κυρίῳ 2C 29.31. **b**. obj., own hands: ἐν τῷ τόξῳ 'do one's utmost' 4K 9.24*L* (B: πίμπλημι), τῷ κυρίῳ 'for the Lord's sake' 1C 29.5. See s.v. ἐμπίμπλημι, **3** and πίμπλημι **2**.

5. *to bring to completion that which was begun*: abs., ταῖς χερσίν ὑμῶν Je 51.25; ***o*** sins, Da 4.30c LXX, 8.23; ταῦτα 'words of a speech' 1M 4.19, τοὺς λόγους σου '(back up) what you say' 3K 1.14.

*__6__. *to increase the quantity of*, 'multiply': + acc., πτώματα 'corpses (of fallen soldiers)' Ps 109.6.

7. pass. *to reach the end* of a period: ἐπληρώθησαν αἱ ἡμέραι τοῦ τεκεῖν αὐτήν 'the (waiting) period for her to give birth was over' Ge 25.24; πεπλήρωνται αἱ ἡμέραι μου 29.21; Le 8.33; αἱ ἡμέραι καθάρσεως 12.4 (‖ ἀναπληροῦμαι); ἐνιαυτὸς ἡμερῶν 25.29; εἰς σφαγήν 'to be slaughtered' Je 32.20; ‖ ἐγγίζω, πάρειμι La 4.19; To 8.20 𝔊[I] (‖ συντελέομαι). Cf. συντελέω **11**.

8. *to bring the end of life and existence of*: + acc., βασιλείαν Da 5.26 TH (LXX ἀπολήγω).

9. pass. *to become full*, a gap or empty space vanishing: ***s*** φάραγξ 'chasm, cleft' Is 40.4; κοιλία 'belly' sated with food, Ez 7.19 (‖ ἐμπίμπλημι); impers., 1K 20.3*L*, see under ἐμπίμπλημι **7**. **b**. act. in the same sense: ***s*** river, Jo 3.15, 1C 12.16.

Cf. ἐκ~, ἐπιπληρόω, ἐκπλήρωσις, γέμω, μεστόω, πίμπλημι, πλήρης.

πλήρωμα, ατος. n.

the full content: ἡ γῆ καὶ τὸ π. αὐτῆς 'the earth and all that is in it' Je 8.16, 29.2, Ps 23.1, Ez 12.19; ἡ οἰκουμένη καὶ τὸ π. αὐτῆς Ps 49.12; ἡ θάλασσα καὶ τὸ π. αὐτῆς 95.11; opp. δράξ 'handful' Ec 4.6. **b**. *that which is completely filled*: ὑδάτων 'full water-pool' Ct 5.12. Cf. πληρής.

πλήρωσις, εως. f.

1. *act of filling in*: of gem stones, λίθοι ~εως Ex 35.27, 1C 29.2; λάκκων 'of cisterns' Ju 8.31.

2. *state of being full*, 'abundance': γῆ ~εως 'a land of plenty' De 33.16.

3. *act of bringing to realisation*: πνεῦμα ~εως Je 4.12 (full vengeance?); κατὰ καιρὸν ~εως προστάγματος θερισμοῦ 'at the time appointed for the expected harvest to be brought in' Je 5.24.

4. *complete elapse* of a period of time: ἐτῶν ἑβδομήκοντα 'of 70 years' 2C 36.21 *L* (B: συμ~), Ez 5.2.

5. *that which goes to fill*: ἡ γῆ σὺν τῇ ~ει αὐτῆς 'the land with all its resources' Ez 32.15.

Cf. πλήρης, πληρόω.

πλησιάζω.ʃ

to have intimate relationship with: + dat. pers. (whores), 2M 6.4.

πλησίον; comp. πλησιέστερος.

Indecl. except the comp. form, and mostly with the def. article, used substantivally.

1. *neighbour*, not necessarily next-door neighbour, but rather *fellow man, member of same community* or *group*: ποτίζων τὸν π. αὐτοῦ 'gives his neighbour to drink' Hb 2.15; Zc 14.13*b*; *colleague*, *work-mate*, σὺ καὶ οἱ π. σου 'you [who are a judge] and your colleagues' Zc 3.8; ‖ ὁ ἔγγιστα Ps 14.3, ‖ ἀδελφός 34.14; + φίλος 87.19; ‖ ὅμοιος Si 13.15. **b**. 'the other party present or involved': "if two men were quarrelling, καὶ πατάξῃ τις τὸν π. 'and one (of them) hit the other'" Ex 21.18.

*__2__. component of a Hebraistic expression of reciprocity, joined with ἕκαστος (q.v.) or ἄνθρωπος indicating individuality and separateness: ἵνα μὴ ἀκούσωσιν ἕκαστος τὴν φωνὴν τοῦ π. 'so that they would not comprehend one another's speech' Ge

11.7; ἕκαστος τὸν π. αὐτοῦ ἐκθλίβουσιν 'they harass each his own neighbour' Mi 7.2; applied to animals, Zc 11.9. **b**. with ἄνθρωπος: εἶπεν ἄνθρωπος τῷ π. 'they said to one another' Ge 11.3; ἄνθρωπος τὸν ἀδελφὸν αὐτοῦ καὶ ἄνθρωπος τὸν ~ον αὐτοῦ Is 19.2; Je 9.20. **c**. with γυνή: αἰτησάτω ἕκαστος παρὰ τοῦ π. καὶ γυνὴ παρὰ τῆς π. Ex 11.2. **d**. ǁ ὁ ἀδελφὸς αὐτοῦ, ὁ ἔγγιστα αὐτοῦ: Ex 32.27, cf. ἕκαστος τῷ π. καὶ τῷ ἀδελφῷ Is 41.6; Je 23.35.

4. πλησίον, adv., *nearer to oneself*: ~ον καλέσας 'having summoned nearer' 4M 8.4; 12.2. **b**. foll. by gen., *in the vicinity of*: π. τοῦ ὄρους 'in the vicinity of the mountain' Ex 34.3; τὸ ὄρος π. γῆς Εδωμ Nu 33.37; π. τῆς ἐρυθρᾶς 'in the vicinity of the Red (Sea)' De 1.1; 11.30. **c**. ὁ οἶκος καὶ τὰ π. 'the temple and the adjoining buildings' Ez 41.16.

Cf. πέλας: Fichtner, *TDNT* 6.311-5.

πλησμονή, ῆς. f.

1. *satiety*: lit. ἠσθίομεν ἄρτους εἰς ~ήν Ex 16.3, ἐφάγετε καὶ οὐκ εἰς ~ήν Hg 1.6; ἐνεπλήσθησαν εἰς ~ήν 'they (= the flock) were completely full up' Ho 13.6; εἰς ~ήν ǁ εἰς μέθην Ez 3919; fig. ~ὴν ἀτιμίας ἐκ δόξης πίε 'Drink a full measure of ignominy from glory (?)' Hb 2.16, cf. π. βίου in an epitaph of a man who died young, *ND* 4.25; plentiful rainfall, Je 14.22; ἄρτων Ez 16.49 (ǁ εὐθηνία); ἐγενήθητέ μοι εἰς ~ήν 'you have become too much for me' Is 1.14; π. σοφίας Si 1.16.

2. *abundant quantity*: σίτου 'of grains' Pr 3.10.

Cf. πίμπλημι, εὐθηνία, II κόρος, πιότης.

πλήσσω: fut.pass. πληγήσομαι; aor.impv.2pl πλήξατε, pass. ἐπλήγην, ptc. πληγείς, subj.pass. πληγῶ; pf.act. in passive sense, πέπληγα, ptc.act. πεπληγώς.

to hit physically in order to harm: pass., ***o*** hum., and resulting in death, ἀπεθάνομεν πληγέντες ὑπὸ κυρίου Ex 16.3; 22.2; on battlefield, Is 9.13, 2K 11.20; agricultural plant, λίνον καὶ κριθή 'flax and barley' Ex 9.31; + cogn. obj. (αἱ πληγαὶ) ἃς ἐπλήγην Zc 13.6; ǁ πατάσσω Is 27.7; πεπληγὼς τοὺς πόδας 'disabled in the feet' 2K 4.4, 9.3; μαχαίρᾳ 2C 29.9. **b**. *to attack*: biting snake, Pr 23.32; stinging bee, 4M 14.19. Cf. πληγή, πατάσσω, πταίω, κόπτω, τύπτω: Schmidt 3.280-4.

πλινθεία, ας. f.*

manufacturing of bricks: Ex 1.14; ἡ σύνταξις τῆς ~ας 'the quota of bricks to be baked' 5.8. Cf. πλινθεύω, πλινθεῖον, πλίνθος.

πλινθεῖον, ου. n.ʃ

brickworks: 2K 12.31B, 3K 2.46^h.

πλινθεύω: aor.subj. πλινθεύσω.ʃ

to manufacture bricks: δεῦτε πλινθεύσωμεν πλίνθους 'let's bake bricks' Ge 11.3. Cf. πλίνθος, πλινθεία.

πλινθίον, ου. n.ʃ

= πλινθεῖον, *brickworks*: 2K 20.23*L*.

πλίνθος, ου. f.

brick: ἡμέρας ἀλοιφῆς ~ου 'day of brick-making' Mi 7.11; material for altar, Is 65.3; symbol of strength, Na 3.14; as a cogn. obj., δεῦτε πλινθεύσωμεν ~ους 'let's bake bricks' Ge 11.3; sg. coll., Is 24.23 (of a city-wall). Cf. πλινθεία.

πλινθουργία, ας.ʃ *

manufacturing of bricks: Ex 5.7. Cf. πλίνθος, πλινθεία, πλινθεύω.

πλοῖον, ου. n.

boat: ὅρμον ~ων 'anchorage of boats' Ge 49.13; ocean-going, Jn 1.3, 4, 5*bis*, θαλάσσης Is 2.16, γῆ πλοίων 'a land of sea-farers' 18.1; ἁλιέων 'fishermen's' Jb 40.31¶; warship, Da 11.40 LXX (TH ναῦς). Cf. ναῦς, πλέω, πλωτός, σκάφος.

πλόκαμος, ου. m.ʃ

lock of hair: of woman, 3M 1.4. Cf. θρίξ.

πλοκή, ῆς. f.ʃ

act of braiding: ἔργον πλοκῆς Ex 28.14. Cf. πλέκω.

πλόκιον, ου. n.ʃ

braided or *curled hair*: of a woman, Ct 7.6.

πλοῦς, οῦ. m.ʃ

act of sailing: Wi 14.1. Cf. πλέω.

πλούσιος, α, ον.

having abundant possessions, 'rich, wealthy': *s* hum., οἱ ἔνδοξοι καὶ οἱ μεγάλοι καὶ οἱ ~οι καὶ οἱ λοιμοί Is 5.14; + dat. rei, κτήνεσιν καὶ ἀργυρίῳ καὶ χρυσίῳ 'in livestock and silver and gold' Ge 13.2; πόλις Is 33.20; subst. m. ǁ πονηρός 53.9.

Cf. πλοῦτος, πλουτέω, πλουτίζω, πένης, πτωχός: Schmidt 4.377f., 381-3.

πλουτέω: fut. ~τήσω; aor. ἐπλούτησα, inf. πλουτῆσαι, subj. ~τήσω; pf. πεπλούτηκα.

to become materially rich: *s* nomad, Ge 30.43; Ex 30.15 (:: πένομαι); through trade, Zc 11.5; through illegal trade practices, Ho 12.8. ***b**. c. cogn. acc.: πλοῦτον μέγαν Da 11.2.

Cf. πλουτίζω, πλοῦτος, πένομαι.

πλουτίζω: fut. πλουτίσω, ~ιῶ, pass. πλουτισθήσομαι, inf. πλουτιεῖν; aor. ἐπλούτισα, inf. πλουτίσαι, subj.pass. πλουτισθῶ.

to cause to become rich and wealthy: + acc. pers., τὸν Αβραμ Ge 14.23, πένητα 'the poor' Si 11.21; τὴν γῆν Ps 64.10; opp. πτωχίζω 1K 2.7; + cogn. acc., πλοῦτον μέγαν 17.25 v.l.; + ἑαυτόν 'to attain the recognition as the rich' Pr 13.7 (:: ταπεινόω ἐμαυτόν). **b**. pass. *to become rich*: Si 19.1.

Cf. πλουτέω, πτωχίζω: Schmidt 4.384-7.

πλοῦτος, ου. m., but n. at Is 29.2; see Thack. 158f.; Shipp 461.

material wealth, riches: πάντα τὸν ~ον καὶ τὴν δόξαν Ge 31.16; θαλάσσης 'gained by sea-trade' De 33.19, αὐτῆς [= pasture] Ps 36.3; τὸν ~ον αὐτῶν ἀσεβείας ἐνέπλησαν 'they have multiplied their ungodly wealth' Mi 6.12, π. ἀσεβῶν Is 24.8; opp. πτωχεία καὶ ἔνδεια Si 18.25 (ǁ πλησμονή). **b**. metaph.: of wisdom, Wi 7.13.

Cf. πλουτέω, πλουτίζω, πλούσιος, πτωχεία.

πλύνω: fut. πλυνῶ, pass. πλυθήσομαι; aor. ἔπλυνα, subj. πλύνω, impv. πλῦνον, 3pl πλυνάτωσαν, ptc. mid. πλυνάμενος, inf.pass. πλυθῆναι.

to wash: πόα πλυνόντων 'lye of cleaners' Ma 3.2; + acc. rei, ***o*** clothes, ἐν οἴνῳ τὴν στολὴν αὐτοῦ Ge 49.11, τὰ ἱμάτια Ex 19.10, πλυνάμενος τὰ ἱμάτια 'one's own clothes' Le 13.6 ǁ w. an active verb, Nu 8.7, 21; internal organs of sacrificial animals, τὰ ἐνδόσθια καὶ τοὺς πόδας ὕδατι 'intestines and feet with water' Ex 29.17, sim. Le 1.9, 8.21; person, 6.27; ǁ νίπτω, λούω 15.11; metaph., + acc. pers., με ἀπὸ τῆς ἀνομίας μου Ps 50.4 (ǁ καθαρίζω). Cf. ἀπο~, ἐκπλύνω, λούω, νίπτω: Trench 160-3.

πλωτός, ή, όν.ʃ

1. *floating*: subst.n., 'ship' Jb 40.31 (ǁ πλοῖον).

2. *navigable*: ***s*** land, 2M 5.21 (ǁ πορευτός 'walkable').

πνεῦμα, ατος. n.

1. *air in motion*, 'wind': Ge 8.1; τοῦ θυμοῦ σου 'of your anger' Ex 15.8, π. ὀργῆς Jb 4.9; ǁ βροντή 'thunder' Am 4.13; συστροφὴ ~ατος 'a blast of wind' Ho 4.19; blowing on the sea Jn 1.4; π. καύσωνος 'scorching wind' 4.8; Ez 13.11 (ǁ πνοή vs. 12); cool, refreshing wind, Is 25.4 (ǁ σκέπη); κοῦφον 'light' Wi 5.11; ἡ ὁδὸς τοῦ ~ατος 'the path of the wind' Ec 11.5. **b**. fig. of ephemeral existence, Jb 30.15 (ǁ νέφος 'cloud'), 7.7, ῥήματα ~ατος 16.3. **c**. *breath*: symbol and evidence of physical life, Ps 145.4, cf. **2b** below, and πνοή.

2. *animating principle* or *influence w. certain moral* or *religious propensity*: π. χάριτος καὶ οἰκτιρμοῦ Zc 12.10; τὸ π. τὸ ἀκάθαρτον 'the unclean spirit' 13.2; π. κρίσεως Is 28.6; ~ατι πορνείας ἐπλανήθησαν 'they were led astray by a spirit of fornication' Ho 4.12; sim. of such an inherent force, 5.4; ἐξήγειρε κύριος τὸ π. Ζοροβαβελ Hg 1.14; ὁ Εφραιμ πονηρὸν π. Zc 12.1 (cf. LSG s.v. **V**); π. ἔστησε ψεῦδος 'a spirit has brought about falsehood' Mi 2.11; φιλάνθρωπον π. σοφία 'wisdom is a spirit that loves man' Wi 1.6; δαιμόνιον ἢ π. πονηρόν To 6.8. **b**. *animating force* or *energy*: οὐκ ἔστι π. ἐν αὐτοῖς [= idols] Je 10.14; "I shall place my π. into them, and they shall live" Ez 37.14; ἐν ἐξόδῳ ~ατος αὐτοῦ 'on breathing his last' Si 38.23. **c**. *inner vigour and strength*: Jo 2.11.

3. *rational* or *intelligent being with no material existence*: **a**. conceived of as possessed by God, π. θεοῦ Ge 1.2; π. κυρίου Mi 2.7, 3.8, Hg 2.5, cf. Zc 1.6 and τὸ π. τὸ ἅγιόν σου Ps 50.13, τὸ ἅ. σου π. Wi 9.17, τὸ π. τὸ ἅ. αὐτοῦ Is 63.10; creative agent, Ju 16.14; source of wisdom, ἅγιον π. παιδείας Wi 1.5, π. συνέσεως De 34.9, Si 39.6; associated with prophetic activities, ἐκχεῶ ἀπὸ ~ατός μου Jl 2.28, 29, cf. Zc 7.12; θεὸς τῶν ~άτων καὶ πάσης σαρκός Nu 16.22, 27.16 (apparently w. ref. to some heavenly beings); πᾶν π. οὐκ ἔστιν ἐν αὐτῷ, said of a lifeless idol, Hb 2.19; opp. to human physical, military might, Zc 4.6; guiding spirit, ἀνθρώπων ἀδικουμένων 'of people being wronged' Is 25.4. **b**. conceived of as possessed by humans, πλάσσω π. ἀνθρώπου ἐν αὐτῷ 'fashioning a human spirit in him' Zc 12.1; divine gift, ἔχει π. θεοῦ ἐν αὐτῷ Ge 41.38 (= ἄνθρωπος φρόνιμος καὶ συνετός vs. 39); ἔχει π. ἐν ἑαυτῷ Nu 27.18; τοῖς σοφοῖς .. οὓς ἐνέπλησα ~ατος αἰσθήσεως Ex 28.3; ἐνέπλησα αὐτὸν π. θεῖον σοφίας 31.3; π. τοῦ θεοῦ, π. σοφίας καὶ συνέσεως, π. βουλῆς καὶ ἰσχύος, π. γνώσεως καὶ εὐσεβείας .. π. φόβου θεοῦ Is 11.2f.; directs actions, ἐκόπασεν τὸ π. τοῦ βασιλέως .. 'the king had no mental strength (to go after Absalom)' 2K 13.39. Cf. .. σῶμα νέρθεν, πνεῦμα καὶ ψυχὴ μένει 'the body of PN is below, but (his) spirit and soul remain' on an epitaph (*ND* 4.38). **c**. resides inside man's body (σπλάγχνα) and leaves it on his death: Ba 2.17. **d**. animating and possessed by every living being (σάρξ), π. ζωῆς Ge 6.17, 7.15, cf. πνοὴ ζωῆς 2.7, 7.22. **e**. personified: instrument of divine punishment, Si 39.28.

*4. *one of the four cardinal points*: ἐκ τῶν τεσσάρων ~άτων Ez 37.9, cf. ἄνεμος.

Cf. ἀήρ, ἄνεμος, αὔρα, πνοή, καρδία, ψυχή: Schmidt 2.232f.; Trench 276; BDAG, s.v.; Kleinknecht et al., *TDNT* 6.332-455, esp. 367-72; Hill 217-23; Scharbert 124f.; Alexandre 239-42.

πνευματοφορέω.ʃ*

to carry as by the wind: fig., ἐν ἐπιθυμίαις ψυχῆς αὐτῆς 'by desires ..' Je 2.24.

πνευματοφόρος, ον.ʃ *

carried away or *moved by evil spirit*: ***s*** man, Ho 9.7 (ǁ παρεξεστηκώς 'deranged'); οἱ προφῆται αὐτῆς ~οι, ἄνδρες καταφρονηταί Zp 3.4. Cf. πνευματοφορέω: Dafni 2001a.

πνεύμων, ονος. m.ʃ

the lungs: 3K 22.34 (ǁ 2C 18.33).

πνέω: fut. πνεύσω; aor. ἔπνευσα.ʃ

1. *to move along*, 'blow': ***s*** πνεῦμα 'wind' Ep Je 60, νότος 'south wind' Si 43.16, ψυχρὸς ἄνεμος 'cold wind' 43.20.

2. *to blow air*: *s* God, ἐπ' αὐτούς Is 40.24; + acc., τὸ πνεῦμα αὐτοῦ Ps 147.7; metaph., πῦρ θυμοῖς 'fire with rage' 2M 9.7.

Cf. πνοή, ἐμπνέω, ἄπνοος, πυριπνοῦς, πύρπνοος: Schmidt 2.219-22, 29f.

πνιγμός, οῦ. m.ʃ

suffocation: πυρᾶς 'of burning stuff' Si 51.4.

Cf. ἀπο~, περιπνίγω.

πνίγω.ʃ

to vex: acc. pers., *s* πνεῦμα πονηρόν 1K 16.14, 15.

πνοή, ῆς. f.

breath: ἐνεφύσησεν .. ~ὴν ζωῆς 'infused a breath of life' Ge 2.7 (of a hum.); πάντα, ὅσα ἔχει ~ὴν ζωῆς 7.22 (of animals and ‖ πνεῦμα ζωῆς 6.17, 7.15); ‖ πνεῦμα Is 42.5, 57.16, Ez 13.13 (see vs. 11), Jb 32.8 (God-given); οὐ κατελείφθη ἐν αὐτοῖς π. 'they were out of breath (from shock)' Ne 6.1; ἐν ἐσχάτῃ ~ῇ 'breathing his last' 2M 7.9; used in speech, Pr 1.23, ~ῇ κρύπτει 'does not breathe a word of ..' 11.13. **b**. *act of blowing*: ἀπὸ ~ῆς ⌜*L* om.⌝ πνεύματος θυμοῦ αὐτοῦ 'because the wind of his fury blew' 2K 22.16.

Cf. ἄσθμα, πνεῦμα: Trench 275f.; Lee 1969.239; Renehan 1.166.

πόα, ας (also ποία, ας). f.ʃ

1. *grass, herbage*: κερεῖς ~αν 'you will cut grass' Pr 27.25 (‖ χλωρά and χόρτος).

2. *lye, strong alkaline solution*: as detergent, Je 2.22 (‖ νίτρον); π. πλυνόντων Ma 3.2.

Cf. βοτάνη, λάχανον, χόρτος.

ποδάγρα, ας.ʃ

clamp for tying the feet: applied to knees, 4M 11.10.

ποδήρης, ες.

subst.m. *a long robe falling over the feet*: Ex 25.6 (‖ ἐπωμίς 'ephod'); ἐνδύσατε αὐτὸν ~ρη 'Clothe him with ..' Zc 3.4; also ‖ περιστήθιον 'breastband,' χιτών 'tunic,' κίδαρις 'headdress,' and ζώνη 'girdle' Ex 28.4; *s* ὑποδύτης 'undergarment' 28.27; poss. adj., ἐπὶ ~ους ἐνδύματος 'on (his) long robe' Wi 18.24. Cf. στολή: Trench 187.

ποδιστήρ, ῆρος. m.ʃ

*a kind of *tripod*: temple fixture, 2C 4.16.

ποθεινός, ή, όν.ʃ

sought after, desirable: *s* bees, + dat., Pr 6.8*b* (+ ἐπίδοξος); brotherly love, 4M 13.26; piety more desirable to a mother than her own children, 15.1. Cf. ποθέω, ἐπιθυμητός: Schmidt 3.596-601.

πόθεν.

whence?, where .. from?: π. ἔρχῃ 'where do you come from?, where is your home?' Jn 1.8(*a*); ‖ ποῦ - π. ἔρχῃ καὶ ποῦ πορεύῃ; 'where do you come from and where are you going to?' Ge 16.8(*b*); Πόθεν ἐστέ To 7.3(*c*); π. ἔστε ὑμεῖς; .. Ἐκ Χαρραν ἐσμεν 29.4(*a*); π. ἥκατε ..; .. Ἐκ γῆς Χανααν 42.7(*a*); π. μοι κρέα δοῦναι παντὶ τῷ λαῷ τούτῳ; 'where do I get meat from to give to all this people?' Nu 11.13(*a*); π. ζητήσω παράκλησιν αὐτῇ; 'whence shall I seek comfort for her?' Na 3.7(*a*). **b**. fig., π. ἰαθήσομαι; 'where shall I seek my cure?' Je 15.18.

Cf. ποῦ.

a) מֵאַיִן [+ Je 15.18 MT *m'nh*]; *b*) אֵי־מִזֶּה; *c*) Ar. מנאן [To 7.3].xʃ

ποθέω: aor.impv. πόθησον.

to desire: abs., ‖ ἐπιθυμέω Wi 6.11; + acc., εἰρήνην Es B 2, τὸ πρόσωπόν σου Pr 7.15, ^ἀρετήν^ 'virtue' Wi 4.2. Cf. ἐπιποθέω, ἐπιθυμέω, θέλω.

ποιέω: fut. ποιήσω, inf. ποιήσειν, mid. ποιήσομαι, pass. ποιηθήσομαι, ptc. ποιηθησόμενος; aor. ἐποίησα, opt. 3s ποιήσαι, 3pl ποιήσαισαν, subj. ποιήσω, ptc. ποιήσας, mid. ποιησάμενος, mid. ἐποιησάμην, inf.act. ποιῆσαι, mid. ποιήσασθαι, impv.act. ποίησον, mid. ποίησαι, pass. ἐποιήθην, subj. ποιηθῶ; pf. πεποίηκα, inf. πεποιηκέναι, ptc. πεποιηκώς; plpf. πεποιήκειν.

I. act. **1**. *to perform* actions: abs. 'to act'– ἰδοὺ ἐγὼ ποιῶ ἐν σοι Zp 3.19; ἐμεγάλυνε κύριος τοῦ ποιῆσαι 'the Lord has performed great things' Jl 2.21 (‖ ἐμεγάλυνε τὰ ἔργα αὐτοῦ 2.20); in a certain way, ὃν τρόπον ἐβούλου πεποίηκας 'you have done as you wished' Jn 1.14; οὐ μὴ ποιήσω κατὰ τὴν ὀργὴν τοῦ θυμοῦ μου Ho 11.9; τῇ ἰσχύι ποιήσω καὶ τῇ σοφίᾳ τῆς συνέσεως 'I shall act with might and intelligent wisdom' Is 10.13; + acc. rei, οὐ δυνήσομαι ποιῆσαι πρᾶγμα 'I shall not be able to do a thing' Ge 19.22; τίς ἐποίησεν τὸ πρᾶγμα τοῦτο; 21.26, θαυμαστὰ πράγματα Is 25.1; τὰ ἔργα αὐτοῦ Ge 39.11 (administrative tasks); τῆς πλινθείας, ἧς αὐτοὶ ποιοῦσιν 'the manufacturing of bricks ..' Ex 5.8; ῥῆμα Ge 41.32; σημεῖα Ex 4.17; τί τοῦτο ἐποίησας; 'what on earth have you done?' Jn 1.10; + τί τινι (dat. of the person affected by the action), Τί τοῦτο ἐποίησας ἡμῖν; Ge 20.8; τί σοι ποιήσω, Εφραιμ; 'what shall I do to you, E.?' Ho 6.4; τῇ κακίᾳ, ᾗ ἐλάλησε τοῦ ποιῆσαι αὐτοῖς 'the hardship, which He declared that He would cause them' Jn 3.10, cf. οὕτως ποιήσω ὑμῖν Ho 10.15; "your abandoning me has brought upon you all this" Je 2.16, sim. 4.18; καλῶς ὑμῖν ποιήσω 'act towards you kindly' Zp 3.20, ποιήσωμεν εἰρήνην αὐτῷ 'let's make peace with him' Is 27.5; + μετά τινος (see μετά **I 11**) - ἃ ἐποίησε μεθ' ὑμῶν εἰς θαυμάσια Jl 2.26, μετὰ Αβρααμ Ju 8.26; κατὰ τὸ ῥῆμα τοῦτο Ge 44.7; εἰς τὰ μετὰ ταῦτα 'with the future in view' Je 5.31; abs., ποίησον ἡμῖν ἕνεκεν σοῦ 'Do something for us for your own sake' 14.7; Da 9.19 LXX.

2. *to treat* sbd in a certain way: + acc. pers., εὖ σε ποιήσω Ge 32.9, sim. Nu 10.29, cf. εὖ ποιεῖν ἀνθρώποις Ep Je 63, εὖ ποίησον ταπεινῷ (w. ref. to financial help) Si 12.5; καλῶς εὖ σε ποιήσω Ge 32.12; οὕτως Ex 22.30, 23.11, De 22.3, Jd 15.7B; καθότι .. Nu 33.56; τοῦ καλῶς ποιῆσαι τὴν Ιερουσαλημ Zc 8.15; ποιήσεις τοὺς ἀνθρώπους ὡς τοὺς ἰχθύας τῆς θαλάσσης Hb 1.14; De 3.21 (|| + dat.), τὴν Χεβρων καὶ τῷ βασιλεῖ αὐτῆς .. τῇ Δαβιρ καὶ τῷ βασιλεῖ αὐτῆς Jo 10.39, cf. ποιήσω ὑμᾶς εἰς συντέλειαν Je 5.18, sim. Ne 9.31; εὖ ποίει σεαυτόν 'treat yourself well, enjoy yourself' Si 14.11; ἡμᾶς ἐν χάριτι 1E 8.77; with double acc., περὶ τῆς κακίας, ἧς εἶπεν ποιῆσαι τὸν λαὸν αὐτοῦ 'over the hardship which He said he would cause His people' Ex 32.14, cp. τῇ κακίᾳ, ᾗ ἐλάλησε τοῦ ποιῆσαι αὐτοῖς 'the hardship, which He declared that He would cause them' Jn 3.10; τί ποιήσωσιν αὐτόν Nu 15.34, τί ποιήσει ὁ λαὸς οὗτος τὸν λαόν σου 24.14, ὅσα ἐποίησεν τὴν δύναμιν τῶν Αἰγυπτίων De 11.4; συντέλειαν ποιήσεται πάντας τοὺς ἐπεγειρομένους Na 1.8, cf. Helbing, *Kasus*. 3f.; + double acc. rei, τί ποιήσεις τὸ ὄνομά σου ..: 'what are you going to do with your .. name?' Jo 7.9; + dat. pers., εὖ ποίει φίλῳ Si 14.13; + μετά τινος - μεθ' ἡμῶν κατὰ τὸ ἔλεος αὐτοῦ 50.22, sim. To 8.16. Cf. **1** above and χράω **II 1**.

3. *to fashion, construct, manufacture*: abs., ἐν τῷ χαλκῷ 'by using copper' 2C 2.6, cf. πᾶν ἔργον ἐν χαλκῷ 3K 7.2, ἐργάζεσθαι τὸν χαλκόν Ex 31.4, and ποιεῖν τὸν χαλκόν 35.32; + acc., ποιῆσαι μικρὸν μέτρον καὶ τοῦ μεγαλῦναι στάθμια καὶ ποιῆσαι ζυγὸν ἄδικον 'to make the measure small, enlarge the weight, and falsify the balance' Am 8.5; ποίησόν μοι ἐδέσματα 'make me food' Ge 27.4; θυσιαστήριον 35.1 (|| οἰκοδομέω vs. 7); οἰκίας 33.17; σκηνήν 'tent' Jn 4.5 (+ dat. com. ἑαυτῷ); θεοὺς χρυσοῦς Ex 32.31, εἴδωλα Hb 2.18; *s* God, τὸν οὐρανὸν καὶ τὴν γῆν Gn 1.1, cf. Frankel, *Einfl.* 35-7; ἐποίησεν ὁ θεὸς τὰ κήτη τὰ μεγάλα 'God made the large fishes' 1.21; ἄρσεν καὶ θῆλυ ἐποίησεν αὐτούς 'he made them, male and female' 1.27 (|| πλάσσω 2.7, Is 27.11); τὴν θάλασσαν καὶ τὴν ξηράν Jn 1.9; τὸν κόσμον Wi 9.9; τοῦ ποιήσαντος αὐτόν 'his Creator' Ho 8.14; || κτίζω Is 22.11 (pool), De 32.6; 32.15 (|| γεννάω vs. 18); *s* hum., acc. παιδία Is 38.19 (|| γεννάω 39.7), κτήσεις 'possessions' Ez 38.12. **b**. + ἐκ (of source or material): ἐκ τῶν τοῦ πατρὸς ἡμῶν πεποίηκεν πᾶσαν τὴν δόξαν ταύτην Ge 31.1. Cf. ἑτοιμάζω **I 2**.

4. *to fashion and provide with* (double acc.): κατάγαια, διώροφα καὶ τριώροφα ποιήσεις αὐτήν 'build ground-level, second-level and third-level cabins for it (the ark)' Ge 6.16.

5. *to produce, yield* (of agricultural produce, acc.): ξύλον .. ποιοῦν καρπόν Ge 1.11, τὰ πεδία οὐ ποιήσει βρῶσιν Hb 3.17, σταφυλήν .. ἀκάνθας 'a cluster of grapes .. thorns' Is 5.2; *s* farmer, 5.10; cattle, ποιεῖν γάλα 'milk' 7.22. Cf. φέρω **3**.

6. *to engage oneself in and effect*: + acc. rei, ἄδικον Zp 3.5; εἰς τοὺς ἄνδρας τούτους μὴ ποιήσητε μηδὲν ἄδικον 'to these men do not do anything unjust' Ge 19.8 (on εἰς, see s.v. **3** and Joh 15.21), ἐπ' ἐμέ Ge 19.19; ἀδικίαν Zp 3.13; ἁμαρτίαν De 9.21, cf. ἀπὸ τῶν ἁμαρτιῶν 'any of the sins' Nu 5.6; ἀνομίαν Ho 6.9; ἄνομα Ma 3.15, 4.1; κακόν Ge 26.29; πονηρά Nu 32.13, ~όν Ma 2.17; δικαιοσύνην καὶ κρίσιν Ge 18.19, sim. De 33.21, ἐπ' ἐμέ Ge 20.13, τὴν δικαιοσύνην, ἣν ἐποίησα μετὰ σοῦ 21.23, ἔλεος καὶ δικαιοσύνην πρὸς τὸν κύριόν μου 24.49; ἀπὸ πάσης δικαιοσύνης καὶ ἀπὸ πάσης ἀληθείας, ἧς ἐποίησας τῷ παιδί σου 32.10, cf. κατὰ τὴν δικαιοσύνην .. ποιήσεις μετ' ἐμοῦ καὶ τῇ γῇ 21.23; κρίμα Am 5.7; ἔλεος μετά τινος Ge 24.12 (|| τινι vs. 14), τοῖς ἀγαπῶσίν ^τὸν θεόν^ Ex 20.6, De 5.10; ἔλεος καὶ οἰκτιρμόν Zc 7.9; ἔλεος καὶ δικαιοσύνην Ge 24.49; ποιήσεις ἐν ἐμοὶ ἔλεος 40.14 (on ἐν, see s.v. **10**), εἰς ἐμὲ ἔλεος καὶ ἀλήθειαν Jo 2.14, cf. θυμὸν ὀργῆς ^κυρίου^ ἐν Αμαληκ 1K 28.18; ἐφ' ἡμᾶς ἔλεος καὶ σωτηρίαν To 8.4 𝔊[II], ἔλεος καὶ εἰρήνην 7.11 𝔊[II]; αὐτοῖς εἰρήνην καὶ πίστιν Je 40.6, ἀλήθειαν Is 26.10; σοφίαν Ps 110.10, Si 51.18; ἔργα (cultic practice) Hg 1.14; ἔργον (manual labour) De 5.13 (|| ἐργάζομαι), 5.14. Cf. τεκταίνω **2**. **b**. + action noun in the acc. (see **II**. below): συντέλειαν καὶ σπουδήν .. ἐπὶ πάντας τοὺς κατοικοῦντας τὴν γῆν Zp 1.18; τὴν ἀπώλειαν αὐτοῦ Ez 31.11; ἐκδίκησιν ἔν τινι (pers.) Ex 12.12, Nu 33.4, Mi 5.15, Ez 16.41 (967* sg.), 30.14, εἴς τινα 25.11, cf. ἐποίησας εἰς ἡμᾶς .. κατὰ πᾶσαν ἐπιείκειάν σου .. 'you have dealt with us .. in accordance with all your clemency ..' Ba 2.27; κρίμα / ~ατα ἔν τινι (pers.) Ez 5.10, 15, 11.9, 28.22, 26, 30.19, cf. πῶς ποιήσεις ἐν φρυάγματι τοῦ Ἰορδάνου; 'How are you going to handle the glory of the Jordan?' Je 12.5 and ἐν καιρῷ θυμοῦ σου ποίησον ἐν αὐτοῖς 18.23; πόλεμον Ge 14.2, πρὸς σὲ πόλεμον De 20.12, 20, μάχην Si 8.16; ἁγνισμόν Nu 8.7; φόνον De 22.8; ἐπιλησμονὴν τρυφῆς 'forgetfulness of pleasure' Si 11.27; λόγους ψευδεῖς ποιήσασθαι ἐπ' ἐμοῦ 'to play lies on me' Da 2.9 LXX; w. double acc., συντέλειαν τινά ποιέω = συντελέω Ez 11.13, see Na 1.8 under **II** below.

7. *to act upon and implement*: ποιήσει αὐτῇ .. πάντα τὸν νόμον τοῦτον 'shall apply to her this entire law' Nu 5.30; τὴν διαθήκην αὐτοῦ, ἣν ἐνετείλατο ὑμῖν ποιεῖν De 4.13; ἐν αὐτῇ τὴν εὐχὴν αὐτοῦ '.. his vow' Jd 11.39 B.

*8. *to process and work on*: an animal by slaughtering it for food or sacrificing (< Heb. עָשָׂה qal): αὐτό (= μοσχάριον 'calf') Ge 18.7, Ex 29.36, 38; Le 15.15, Nu 6.11, Jd 6.19. **b**. a 2nd acc. indicating a product: ποιήσω αὐτοὺς ἐδέσματα τῷ πατρί σου 'I shall cook them as food for your father' Ge 27.9; ἐποίησεν αὐτὰ μόσχον χωνευτόν 'he made them into a molten calf' Ex 32.4; πάντα, ὅσα ἂν ποιηθῇ δέρματα 'anything which skins might be worked up into' Le 13.51.

9. *to transform and cause to be*, a causative transform of εἰμί/γίνομαι: w. double acc., κύριον αὐτὸν ἐποίησά σου 'I have made him your master' Ge 27.37; Μισητόν με πεποιήκατε ὥστε πονηρόν με εἶναι πᾶσιν τοῖς κατοικοῦσιν τὴν γῆν 34.30. Perh. also ἐποίησεν τὰς δύο παιδίσκας καὶ τοὺς υἱοὺς αὐτῶν ἐν πρώτοις, καὶ Λείαν καὶ τὰ παιδία αὐτῆς ὀπίσω, καὶ Ραχηλ καὶ Ιωσηφ ἐσχάτους Ge 33.2. **b**. + acc. and εἴς τινα/τι– ποιήσω σε εἰς ἔθνος μέγα Ge 12.2, 46.3, Ex 32.10, sim. Nu 14.12, De 9.14 (|| γινόμενος .. εἰς ἔθνος μέγα Ge 18.18); εἰς συναγωγὰς ἐθνῶν Ge 48.4, εἰς ἄρτους Ez 4.9; + ὡς - ποιήσω τὸ σπέρμα σου ὡς τὴν ἄμμον τῆς γῆς 'I shall make your offspring like dust of the earth' Ge 13.16 (|| ἔσται .. 28.14); ἐποίησέν με ὡς πατέρα Φαραω 45.8. Cf. εἰμί **3**, γίνομαι **3b**, τίθημι **I 4**, **II 3, 4**.

10. *to arrange and stage*: + acc. rei, πότον 'drinking party' Ge 19.3, 40.20; γάμον 'wedding reception' 29.22, To 6.13, 10.7, χορούς 'dances' Jd 9.27 A, δοχήν 'reception' Da 5 pr. LXX; πένθος 'funeral' + dat. pers., Ge 50.10. Cf. συνίστημι **I 6**.

11. *to celebrate*: *o* religious festival, τὴν ἡμέραν ταύτην (the passover) Ex 12.17; ποιῆσαι τὸ πάσχα κυρίῳ 12.48; λατρείαν 13.5; τὰ σάββατα 31.16; ἑορτὴν ἑβδομάδων 'the feast of the weeks' De 16.10; ἑορτὴν τῶν σκηνῶν 16.13. Ποιέω πάσχα might belong under **8**, see esp. ποιήσουσιν αὐτό [= τὸ πάσχα] .. φάγονται αὐτό Nu 9.11. See s.v. ἄγω **2**, συντελέω **10**.

12. *to present as cultic offering*: + acc., ὁλοκαύτωμα ἢ θυσίαν Le 17.8; ποιῆσαι αὐτὸ τῷ κυρίῳ 17.9; ὀσμὴν εὐωδίας Nu 15.3, οἶνον εἰς σπονδήν 15.5, cf. Xen., *HG* 4.5.1-2.

13. *to occasion*: γέλωτά μοι ἐποίησεν κύριος 'the Lord gave me a cause for laughter' Ge 21.6.

14. *to cause, compel* to do: + inf., ζῆν De 32.39 (:: ἀποκτείνω); + acc. and inf. ἐπιλαθέσθαι με ἐποίησεν .. πάντων τῶν πόνων μου 'made me forget all my hardships' Ge 41.51; ἵνα μὴ ἁμαρτεῖν σε ποιήσωσιν πρός με 'so that they may not make you sin against me' Ex 23.33; ποιεῖ λαλεῖν 'it makes talk' 1E 3.20; Ps 103.32; + ἵνα - ποιήσω ἵνα ἐν τοῖς δικαιώμασίν μου πορεύησθε Ez 36.27.

15. *to forge and enter a relationship based on*: + συνθήκας Is 30.1, Da 11.6 TH (LXX: ποιήσασθαι), διαθήκην μετά τινος Is 28.15, κατὰ πρόσωπόν τινος Je 41.18.

16. *to spend* a period of time (acc.) engaged in some activity: δίκαιοι ποιήσουσιν ἐν πλούτῳ ἔτη πολλά 'the righteous will spend many a year in wealth' Pr 13.23; ^ἡμέρας^ Ec 6.12. See BDAG s.v. **5 c** and *ND* 4.66. **b**. abs.: ποῦ ἐποίησας; 'where have you worked?' Ru 2.19.

17. *to appoint*: + acc. pers., τὸν Μωυσήν 1K 12.6; θελητὴν καὶ γνώστας 4K 21.6, ἐπισκόπους 1M 1.51.

18. *to procure*: + acc., μοι ᾄδοντας 'singers for me' Ec 2.8.

19. *to set in order*, 'to trim, groom': + acc., μύστακα 'moustache' 2K 19.25.

II. mid. with a verbal noun as a periphrasis for the verb itself: ἐκβολὴν ἐποιήσαντο (= ἐξέβαλον) Jn 1.5, συντέλειαν ποιήσεται τοὺς ἐπεγειρομένους Na 1.8 (w. double acc.) (with which cp. Zp 1.18, see **6b** above), συστροφάς 'conspiracies' Am 7.10, κοπετόν Mi 1.8, μνείαν Ps 110.4, σύστασιν 3M 2.9, λήθην .. καθαρισμόν 'oblivion .. cleansing' Jb 7.21, ἐπισκοπήν 'visit' 29.4, ἀπόκρισιν 31.14, ἔτασιν 'enquiry' ib., ἀνάγνωσιν 'reading' Si prol. 17, εὐφροσύνην καὶ ἀγαλλίαμα Is 22.13, πένθος ἀγαπητοῦ ποίησαι σεαυτῇ Je 6.26, πορείαν 2M 12.10, πρεσβείαν 'mission' 4.11, ἐκκομιδήν 'removal' 3.7, ἀναζυγήν 'departure' 9.2, σφαγάς 'slaughter' 5.6, ἱλασμόν 'atonement' 3.33, λιτανείαν 'supplication' 10.16. See also 1E 5.70, and cf. χράω **II 3**. Cf. τίθημι **II 10**.

2. *to forge and enter a relationship based on*: + συνθήκας Da 11.6 LXX (TH act.), 17, more commonly in the active: see **I 15** above.

Cf. ποίημα, ποίησις, ποιητής, ἀνα~, συμποιέω, ἀνύω, δημιουργέω, διαρτίζω, δράω, ἑτοιμάζω, (ἐξ)-εργάζομαι, κατασκευάζω, κτίζω, πλάσσω, πράσσω, τάσσω, τίθημι: Schmidt 1.397-423; Trench 361-4; Shipp 461-8.

ποίημα, ατος. n.

1. *that which has been made*: || πλάσμα Is 29.16; God's and || ἔργον Ps 63.10; God's handiwork, ~ασι τῶν χειρῶν σου 142.5 (|| ἔργα).

2. *that which has been done*, 'deed': pl., Ne 6.14, ἐν ~ασιν ἡμῶν τοῖς πονηροῖς 2E 9.13; 1K 19.4 (*L* ἔργα).

Cf. ἔργον, πλάσμα, ποίησις, πρᾶξις.

ποίησις, εως. f.
1. *act of fabricating*: Ex 28.8; μόσχου 'of bull' 32.35; the creation of the universe, || κτίσις Si 16.26, χειρῶν 'by hands' Ps 18.1.
2. *the way sth is fabricated*: κατὰ τὴν ~ιν τῆς ἐπωμίδος Le 8.7.
3. *act of practising in conformity* w. sth: νόμου Si 19.20, 51.19.
Cf. ποιέω, κτίσις.

ποιητής, οῦ. m.ʃ
one who puts into practice: τοῦ νόμου 1M 2.67. Cf. ποιέω.

ποικιλία, ας. f.
1. *marking with various colours, embroidering*: κεκλωσμένης τῇ ~ᾳ τοῦ ῥαφιδευτοῦ 'spun with the embroiderer's multicoloured work' Ex 27.16; ἔργον ἀρχιτεκτονίας ~ας 'work of multicoloured architecture' 35.35; Jd 5.30.
2. *great variety*: π. παντὸς ζῴου Si 43.25; 4M 15.24.
Cf. ποικίλος, ποικίλλω, ποίκιλμα: Schmidt 4.361-63.

ποικίλλω: pf.ptc.pass. πεποικιλμένος.ʃ
to clothe elegantly: *o* queen, ἐν ἱματισμῷ διαχρύσῳ περιβεβλημένη πεποικιλμένη 'attired with a chic robe interwoven with gold' Ps 44.10, sim. 44.14. Cf. ποικίλος.

ποίκιλμα, ατος. n.ʃ
that which is multicoloured: alw. pl., εἰ ἀλλάξεται .. πάρδαλις τὰ ~ατα αὐτῆς; 'would .. the leopardess change her spots?' Je 13.23; ἐζωσμένους ~ατα ἐπὶ τὰς ὀσφύας αὐτῶν 'wearing embroidered girdles round their loins' Ez 23.15; 'embroidered stuff,' στακτὴν καὶ ~ατα ἐκ Θαρσις 'myrrh and .. from Tarsis' 27.16. Cf. ποικίλος.

ποικίλος, η, ον.
1. *multicoloured*: *s* sheep, Ge 30.40 (distinct from διάλευκος), tunic (χιτών) 37.3, horse Zc 1.8, 6.6 (distinct from ψαρός); 6.3 (explanatory of ψαρός); subst. n.pl. *multicoloured garments*, Ez 16.10, cf. Renehan 1.167.
2. *of diverse sorts*: *s* παρασκευή 'supply of arms' 2M 15.21, δέησις 'supplication' 3M 1.21.
Cf. ποικιλία, ποικίλλω, ποίκιλμα, ποικιλτής, ποικιλτικός, ποικιλτός, ποικίλως: Görg 124; LSG s.v. **II 1 b**.

ποικιλτής, οῦ. m.
embroiderer, pattern-weaver: ἔργον ~οῦ Ex 26.36; 28.6; Si 45.10 (|| τεχνίτης vs. 11). Cf. ποικίλος and ῥαφιδευτής.

ποικιλτικός, ή, όν.ʃ
pertaining to embroidery: τίς ἔδωκεν γυναιξὶν ὑφάσματος σοφίαν ἢ ~ὴν ἐπιστήμην; 'who gave women skill of weaving or knowledge of embroidery?' Jb 38.36. Cf. ποικίλος.

ποικιλτός, ή, όν.ʃ
embroidered: τὰ ὑφαντὰ καὶ τὰ ~ὰ ὑφᾶναι 'to weave woven and embroidered things' Ex 35.35; 37.21. Cf. ποικίλος.

ποικίλως. adv.ʃ
1. *by using various colours*: στρωμναὶ διαφανεῖς π. διηνθισμέναι 'transparent coverings embroidered with multicoloured flowers' Es 1.6.
2. *in various manners*: 4M 16.3.
Cf. ποικίλος.

ποιμαίνω: fut. ποιμανῶ, pass. ποιμανθήσομαι; aor. impv. ποίμανον.
1. *to tend* flocks: *o* ποίμνιον Mi 5.4; πρόβατα Ge 30.31, 36; 37.13 (|| vs. 12 βόσκω); *s* daughters, Ex 2.16. **b**. fig. *to look after devotedly, nurture*: οἱ ποιμαίνοντες τὰ μάταια καὶ οἱ καταλελοιπότες τὰ πρόβατα Zc 11.17; of God tending and looking after his people, Ho 13.5, Zc 11.9, λαόν σου ἐν ῥάβδῳ σου Mi 7.14, με Ps 22.1; *o* shepherd Je 22.22 (*s* [frivolous, unreliable] wind, and sarcasm?), πόρνας 'whores' Pr 29.3, ἀνέμους '(fleeting) winds' 9.12a (|| διώκω), ἀσωτίαν 'extravagant life" 28.7; *s* θάνατος Ps 48.15.
2. *to guide*: ποιμανοῦσι τὸν Ασσουρ ἐν ῥομφαίᾳ Mi 5.6.
Cf. ποιμήν, ποιμενικός, ποίμνιον, βόσκω, νέμω: Schmidt 4.585-8; Trench 84-6.

ποιμενικός, ή, όν.ʃ
pertaining to shepherd (ποιμήν): σκεύη ~ὰ ποιμένος ἀπείρου 'tools of an inexperienced shepherd' Zc 11.15; *s* κάδιον 'jar' 1K 17.40. Cf. ποιμήν.

ποιμήν, ένος. m.
1. *one who tends livestock*: π. προβάτων Ge 4.2, 46.34 (|| ποιμήν and κτηνοτρόφος vs. 32), fig. of Moses, Is 63.11; αἱ νομαὶ τῶν ~ένων Am 1.2; σκεύη ποιμενικὰ ~ένος ἀπείρου 'tools of an inexperienced shepherd' Zc 11.15; τῶν κτηνῶν Ge 13.7.
2. fig. *leader*: ἐνύσταξαν οἱ ~ένες σου 'your leaders have slumbered' Na 3.18 (|| δυνάσται), cf. Zc 10.3, 11.5; charged with care of vineyard (= God's people) Je 12.10. Cf. ἡγέομαι **1**.
Cf. ποιμαίνω, αἰπόλος: Schmidt 4.584f.; Caird 1969.29; Spicq 1.206-8.

ποίμνη, ης. f.ʃ
herd of small livestock: ἀνὰ μέσον ~ης καὶ ~ης 'between flocks' Ge 32.16. Cf. ποίμνιον, ἀγέλη.

ποίμνιον, ου. n.
flock, herd of small livestock: of goats, Am 6.4; of sheep (προβάτων) Ge 29.2, Mi 5.8; Jl 1.18 (|| βουκόλια); || πρόβατα Mi 2.12; τὸν καρπὸν τῆς γῆς .. τὰ βουκόλια τῶν βοῶν .. καὶ τὰ ~α τῶν προβάτων

De 7.13, τὰ γενήματα τῆς γῆς .. 28.4, 18, 51; consisting of goats (αἶξ, τράγος), sheep (πρόβατα, κριός), camels (κάμηλος), bovine cattle (βοῦς, ταῦρος), donkeys (ὄνος, πῶλος) Ge 32.14-16; νομὴ ~ων 'pasture for flocks of sheep' Zp 2.6; fig. of God's people, τὸ π. αὐτοῦ τὸν οἶκον Ιουδα Zc 10.3; πύργος ~ου Mi 4.8; ‖ θηρία Zp 2.14. *b. *sheep-fold*: Is 27.10.

The sg. is used mostly collectively. Cf. ποίμνη, ἀγέλη, βουκόλιον.

ποίμνιος, α, ον.ʃ

pertaining to ποίμνιον: subst. n., 'sheep-fold' Is 27.10*bis*.

ποῖος, α, ον.

Interr. pron. used to determine the nature or identity of an entity, 'of what kind?, which?'

I. adj., preceding the noun head: ποῖον ἔθνος μέγα .. De 4.7, 8, ἐκ ποίας χώρας καὶ ἐκ ποίου λαοῦ εἶ σύ; 'what country and what people are you from?' Jn 1.8, ἐκ ποίας φυλῆς καὶ ἐκ ποίας πατριᾶς σὺ εἶ; 'from which tribe and from which country are you?' To 5.11 𝔊[I].

II. subst.: ποίᾳ τούτων .. 'in response to which of these ..?' Je 5.7, ἴδετε, ποία ἐστὶν ἡ ὁδὸς ἡ ἀγαθή 'See which is the good way' 6.16; σπέρμα ἔντιμον ποῖον; σπέρμα ἀνθρώπων 'which is the worthy offspring? Human offspring' Si 10.19; ποῖός τις εἴη ἐπιτήδειος .. 'who might be a suitable person ..' 2M 3.37.

See BDF, § 298.2. Cf. ποταπός and τίς.

πόκος, ου. m.

fleece: Ps 71.6, ἐρίων 'of wool' Jd 6.37; of lambs and rams, 4K 3.4. Cf. ἐπίποκος.

πολεμέω: fut. ~μήσω, pass. ~μηθήσομαι; aor. ἐπολέμησα, subj. ~μήσω, inf. ~μῆσαι, impv. ~μησον; pf. πεπολέμηκα.

to make war: abs. De 1.42; οὐκέτι μὴ μάθωσι πολεμεῖν 'they will not learn to make war any more' Mi 4.3, sim. ‖ Is 2.4. **b**. + τινα 'against sbd': ὁ κύριος πολεμεῖ περὶ αὐτῶν τοὺς Αἰγυπτίους 'the Lord is fighting the Egyptians for them' Ex 14.25, βασιλέα Μωαβ Nu 21.26, τὴν Ιερουσαλημ Jd 1.8 AB (Ra: ἐν), and + μάχομαι, αὐτόν 11.25B (A: αὐτοῖς); + dat. pers., Jd 20.28*L*; also *+ ἔν τινι (pers.) 1.1 (B: πρός τινα), 2K 12.26 (*L* acc.), 1M 3.58; + ἐπί τινι (pers.), Ex 17.16 and + πρός τινα Nu 21.1, Je 15.20; + ἐπί τινα 39.29 (‖ + acc., vs. 24); + μετά τινος 1K 17.9*L* (B: πρός τινα), 33, Da 11.11; περί τινος (pers.) 'on the side of' - κύριος πολεμήσει περὶ ὑμῶν Ex 14.14; 14.25, De 3.22; ὑπὲρ σοῦ Si 4.28; + cogn. acc., *s* God, τὸν πόλεμον ἡμῶν 2C 32.8. **c**. pass. *to have war made upon* one: Jo 11.23.

Cf. μάχομαι, πόλεμος, πολεμιστής, ἐκ~, κατα~, συμ~, συνεκπολεμέω, συγκερατίζομαι, παρατάσσω.

πολεμικός, ή, όν.

pertaining to war: σκεύη ~ά 'weapons' De 1.41, ὅπλα ~ά Je 21.4; τόξον ~όν 'bow of war' Zc 9.10; subst.n.pl. ~ά = πόλεμος Je 31.14. Cf. πόλεμος.

πολέμιος, α, ον.

hostile: + τινος To 12.10, 4M 11.23; subst.m., mostly pl., *enemy* (mostly in public area) 1E 4.4, ‖ ἐχθρός Wi 11.3, Es 9.16 o' (‖ ἐχθ. 9.22 o'), + ἐχθρός 2E 8.31; f.sg. 'enemy land (or: city [πόλις, see Cyr, MG 70.596])' Is 27.4. **b**. *harmful*: *s* deed, 2M 15.39.

Cf. ἐχθρός.

πολεμιστής, οῦ. m.

warrior: τῶν ~ῶν τῶν ἐκπεπορευμένων εἰς τὴν παράταξιν Nu 31.27, 28; w. pleonastic ἀνήρ (q.v.) 31.32, 42, 49, 53, De 2.14, 16; and ‖ μαχητής, Jl 2.7 (ἀναβήσονται ἐπὶ τὰ τείχη), 3.9; ἄνδρες ~αί Jd 20.17 A (B: ~ παρατάξεως), Je 27.30. **b**. used adj.: λαὸς π. Jo 8.3, 11, 1K 13.15.

Cf. πολεμέω, πόλεμος, μαχητής, στρατιῶτις.

πόλεμος, ου. m.

war, battle: ἐν ἡμέραις ~ου Ho 10.14, Am 1.14, Zc 14.3; ‖ τόξον, ῥομφαία, ἅρμα, ἵππος, ἱππεύς Ho 1.7, sim. 2.18; ἐν ~ῳ 'in battlefield' Nu 14.3, Zc 10.3, 5; συντριμμὸς ~ου 'confrontation in war' Mi 2.8; συντρίβω ~ον 'to do away with war' Ho 2.18 (same phrase at Ex 15.3 means 'to come out victorious in war'); ποιέω ~ον μετά τινος 'to wage war against sbd' Ge 14.2, πρός τινα De 20.12, 20; συνάπτω ~ον πρός τινα De 2.5, 9, 24, τινι (pers.) εἰς ~ον 2.19; ἐγείρω ~ον ἐπί τινα 'to wage war against sbd' Mi 3.5 (:: εἰρήνη); παρατάσσομαι εἰς ~ον 'to line up for battle' Jl 2.5, παρετάξαντο αὐτοῖς εἰς ~ον '.. against them' Ge 14.8, cf. παρατάξεως ~ου Nu 31.14, 21; ἁγιάζω ~ον 'to declare a holy war' Jl 3.9; ἐξανίστημι ἐπί τινα εἰς ~ον 'to rise up against sbd for a battle' Ob 1; ἐπισυνάγω τινα εἰς ~ον 'to call up sbd for war' Zc 14.2; ἐξέρχομαι εἰς ~ον Nu 21.33, De 2.32, πορεύομαι εἰς ~ον Nu 32.6, De 20.3; ἐξοπλίζομαι εἰς ~ον Nu 32.20, ἐνοπλίζομαι 32.29; καταλαμβάνει π. τινα 'war overtakes sbd' Ho 10.9; ἡνίκα ἂν συμβῇ ἡμῖν π. 'whenever war befalls us' Ex 1.10; π. τοῦ κυρίου Nu 21.14; + μάχη Jb 38.23.

Cf. πολεμέω, πολεμικός, πολεμιστής, πολεμοτροφέω, μάχη, παράταξις, στρατεία: Trench 322f.

πολεμοτροφέω.*

to maintain warlike policy: + πρός τινα 2M 10.14; + στασιάζω 'stir up sedition' 14.6. Cf. πόλεμος.

πολεμόω: aor. ἐπολέμωσα.ʃ*

to make an enemy of: τινά τινι (both hum.), 4M 4.21. Cf. ἐχθρός.

πολιορκέω: fut. ~κήσω; aor. ἐπολιόρκησα, inf. ~κῆσαι; pf.pass. πεπολιόρκημαι.

to besiege: *o* πόλις Is 1.8, τὸν Ἰουδάν 9.21; ἐπ' (*L* om.) αὐτήν [= Samaria] 4K 18.9B. **b.** *to confine in a besieged city*: + acc. pers., Is 37.9, Je 19.9. **c.** *to deprive freedom of movement and action*: + acc. pers., Jd 2.18 (+ A: κακόω; B: ἐκθλίβω), Jb 17.7.

Cf. πολιορκία, περικαθίζω, δυσπολιόρκητος.

πολιόρκησις, εως. f.ʃ

v.n. of πολιορκέω: Si 50.4.

πολιορκία, ας. f.

1. *siege*: + περιοχή Je 19.9; 2M 10.18; + θλῖψις Pr 1.27.

2. *blockade*: 1E 2.19.

Cf. πολιορκέω, περιοχή.

πολιός, ά, όν.

subst. *grey hair* of head: f.pl. Is 47.2, ~αὶ ἐξήνθησαν αὐτῷ 'his hair turned grey' Ho 7.9; 'old age' Si 6.18, 25.4; sg. 2M 15.13 (+ δόξα), 4M 5.7 (+ ἡλικία 'age'), ἀγαθή 'respectable' Jd 8.32 A. **b.** m. 'elderly person' deserving respect, Le 19.32 (|| πρεσβύτερος).

Cf. θρίξ; Byl 443-5.

πολιόω: pf.pass. πεπολίωμαι.ʃ

*mid. *to get the hair of one's head turn grey in old age*: *s* elderly hum., + γηράσκω 1K 12.2 *L*. Cf. γηράσκω, πολιός.

πόλις, εως. f.

large population centre, 'town, city': ~ιν καὶ πύργον 'a city and (its) tower' Ge 11.4; αἱ πλατεῖαι τῆς ~εως πλησθήσονται παιδαρίων καὶ κορασίων 'the streets of the city will be full of boys and girls' Zc 8.5; π. μεγάλη Jn 1.2, 3.2, 4.11; ~ιν σὺν πᾶσι τοῖς κατοικοῦσιν αὐτήν Am 6.8; τοῦ Ναγεβ Ob 20; ~εις τετειχισμένας 'walled ..' Ho 8.14; θεμέλια τῶν ~εων 'the foundations of ..' Am 2.2; αἱ ~εις σου αἱ ὀχυραί 'your fortified cities' Mi 7.12; οἰκοδομῶν ~ιν Hb 2.12; opp. open (agricultural) field (πεδίον) - ὅσα τε ἦν ἐν τῇ ~ει καὶ ὅσα ἦν ἐν τῷ πεδίῳ Ge 34.28, ἐν ~ει .. καὶ ἐν ἀγρῷ De 28.3; Je 14.18; opp. private residences, διήρπασαν ὅσα τε ἦν ἐν τῇ ~ει καὶ ὅσα ἦν ἐν ταῖς οἰκίαις Ge 34.29. **b.** *inhabitants of large population centre*: sg. ἐργαζομένη μάταια Ho 6.8; π. αἱμάτων 'murderous ..' Na 3.1; ἐξελεύσεται τὸ ἥμισυ τῆς ~εως ἐν αἰχμαλωσίᾳ 'half of the city will leave as exiles' Zc 14.2.

Cf. πολίτης, μητρόπολις, κώμη: Schmidt 2.495-502; Strathmann, *TDNT* 6.516-27.

πολιτεία, ας.

1. *way of life*: 2M 4.11.

2. *conditions and rights of a citizen*: 3M 3.21.

Cf. πολίτης.

πολίτευμα, ατος. n.ʃ

body of citizens: 2M 12.7. Cf. πολίτης.

πολιτεύομαι.

to live as a citizen: νόμοις 'in accordance with laws' Es E 15, τοῖς τοῦ θεοῦ νόμοις 2M 6.1; κατὰ τὰ .. ἔθνη 'in accordance with the .. customs' 11.25. **b.** the feature of citizenship may be absent, *to live* in accordance with a certain philosophy of life: τῷ νόμῳ 4M 2.8, 4.23, 5.16.

Cf. πολίτης.

πολίτης, ου. m.

1. *fellow citizen*: Ge 23.11, Zc 13.7, Je 36.23; 38.34 (|| ἀδελφός).

2. *compatriot*: 2M 5.4 (|| συγγενής).

Cf. πόλις, πολίτευμα, ἰσοπολίτης, πολιτεύομαι, πολιτεία, φιλοπολίτης: Schmidt 2.502-4; Spicq 3.125-8.

πολλάκις. adv.

many times: Jb 4.2, Si 19.15. Cf. ἅπαξ, ποσάκις.

πολλαχόθεν. adv.ʃ

from many quarters: by adducing many sources in an argument, + ἀλλαχόθεν 4M 1.7.

πολλαχῶς. adv.ʃ

in many ways: Ez 16.26, 3M 1.25.

πολλοστός, ή, όν.ʃ

* = πολύς: *s* hum., ~ὸς ἔσῃ 'you will be much better off' Pr 5.19; ἀνὴρ .. ~ὸς ἔργοις 'a man .. of many deeds' 2K 23.20.

πολυανδρεῖον, ου. n.

common burial-place shared by non-family members: || μνημεῖον 'tomb' Ez 39.11; site for illicit sexual orgy, Je 2.23; for a public gathering, 19.2. Cf. μνημεῖον and τάφος.

πολυάνδριος, ον.ʃ

full of many people: *s* χωρίον 'spot' 4M 15.20.

πολύγονος, ον.ʃ

highly productive: *s* πλῆθος 'large group (of men)' Wi 4.3; mother, 4M 15.5.

πολύδακρυς, υ, gen. υος.ʃ

accompanied by many tears: *s* ἱκετεία 'supplication' 3M 5.25. Cf. δάκρυον.

πολυέλεος, ον.ʃ *

very merciful: **s** God, μακρόθυμος καὶ π. Ex 34.6, Nu 14.18, Ne 9.17, Jl 2.13, Jn 4.2, Ps 85.15, 102.8, 144.8; 85.5 (|| χρηστός, ἐπιεικής); μίσυβρι πολυέλεε τῶν ὅλων σκεπαστά 'very merciful hater of insolence, who watches over all' 3M 6.9; a property manifesting itself in forgiving of sins, Ne 9.17; in cancelling a punitive action, Jl 2.13, Jn 4.2. Cf. ἔλεος, ἐλεήμων, εὔσπλαγχνος, οἰκτίρμων, χρηστός, ἐπιεικής.

πολυετής, ές.ʃ

blessed with longevity: *s* γῆρας 'old age' Wi 4.16. Cf. πολυήμερος.

πολυημερεύω: aor.subj. ~εύσω.ʃ* (but πολυήμερος Hip.)

to attain longevity: *s* hum. and "days" - ἵνα πολυημερεύσητε καὶ αἱ ἡμέραι τῶν υἱῶν ὑμῶν De 11.21. Cf. πολυήμερος.

πολυήμερος, ον.ʃ

having attained longevity: *s* hum. and as divine blessing, ἵνα εὖ σοι γένηται καὶ π. ἔσῃ De 22.7; 25.15, 30.18, Da 4.24 LXX. Cf. πολυημερεύω, πολυετής, ὀλιγόβιος.

πολύθρηνος, ον.ʃ

much-lamenting: *s* mother, 4M 16.10. Cf. θρῆνος.

πολυκέφαλος, ον.ʃ

many-headed: *s* torturing instrument, 4M 7.14. Cf. κεφαλή.

πολυλογία, ας. f.ʃ

talkativeness: Pr 10.19. Cf. γλωσσώδης, πολυρ(ρ)ήμων.

πολυμαθής, ές.ʃ

erudite: Si prol. II. Cf. μανθάνω, διδακτός.

πολυμερής, ές.ʃ

consisting of many parts, 'composite': *s* intelligent spirit of Wisdom, Wi 7.22. Cf. μέρος.

πολυοδία, ας. f.ʃ*

long or *frequent journey*: Is 57.10. Cf. ὁδός.

πολύορκος, ον.ʃ*

swearing much: *s* hum., Si 23.11, 27.14. Cf. ὅρκος.

πολυοχλία, ας. f.

great number of population: Ba 4.34; πόλεως Jb 39.7. Cf. ὄχλος.

πολύπαις, παιδος. m./f.ʃ

one who has many children: *s* mother, 4M 16.10. Cf. εὐτεκνία, πολυτόκος, ἄτεκνος.

πολυπειρία, ας. f.

much experience: of wisdom, Si 1.7¶; of the elderly, 25.6. Cf. πολύπειρος.

πολύπειρος, ον.

much experienced: Si 21.22. Cf. πολυπειρία, II ἄπειρος, πεῖρα.

πολυπλασιάζω: aor.pass.subj. ~σιασθῶ.ʃ *

pass.intr. *to grow in quantity*, 'multiply': *s* group of people, De 8.1, 11.8. Cf. πολυπλάσιος, πληθύνω.

πολυπλάσιος, α, ον.ʃ

many times as many or *much*: 2M 9.16. Cf. πολυπλασιάζω.

πολυπλήθεια, ας. f.ʃ

large number, 'multitude': ἐθνῶν 2M 8.16, cf. LSG s.v. Cf. πολυπληθέω, πλῆθος.

πολυπληθέω.ʃ*

to be great in quantity: *s* hum., λαός Ex 5.5; παρὰ πάντα τὰ ἔθνη 'more than any other people' De 7.7; animals, ποσίν 'in respect of feet, multi-footed' Le 11.42. Cf. πολύς, πληθύνω, πολυπλήθεια

πολυπληθύνω: fut. ~πληθυνῶ; aor.inf. ~πληθῦναι.ʃ

tr. *to increase*: ***o*** hum., τὸ σπέρμα ὑμῶν ὡσεὶ τὰ ἄστρα τοῦ οὐρανοῦ τῷ πλήθει Ex 32.13, sim. Da 3.36 LXX (ǁ TH πληθύνω). Cf. πολυπληθέω, πληθύνω.

πολύπλοκος, ον.ʃ

1. *intricate*: *s* παραλογισμός 'design' Es E 13; mother's love, 4M 14.13, ποικιλία 'variety' 15.24.

2. *having a devious mind*: subst.m., βουλὴ ~ων Jb 5.13.

Cf. ἁπλοῦς.

πολυπραγμονέω.ʃ

to enquire closely: ἔν τινι 2M 2.30.

πολυρ(ρ)ήμων, ον.ʃ

talkative, garrulous: πνεῦμα ~ον τοῦ στόματός σου Jb 8.2. Cf. πολυλογία.

πολύς, πολλή, πολύ, pl. πολλοί, ~αί, ~ά Comp. πλείων, ~ονος, πλεῖον, pl. πλείους, πλείω; superl. πλεῖστος, η, ον. On the spelling πλέον for πλεῖον, see Thack. 81f.

great: **a**. in number or quantity, τοσούτῳ πλείους ἐγίνοντο 'they would become all the more numerous' Ex 1.12; πλείους ἢ δώδεκα μυριάδες 'more than twelve myriads' Jn 4.11; opp. ὀλίγος, Nu 13.19, 26.56, Hg 1.6, 9; θαυμαστὰ ~ά 'many wonders' Am 3.9; the sg. for the pl., πολὺς ὁ πεπτωκώς 'many will be the fallen' 8.3, ~ὺ ἔθνος 'populous nation' Pr 14.28; λαοὺς ~ούς 'many peoples' Mi 4.13 ǁ λαὸς π. 'populous people' Jl 2.5; ἔθνος μέγα καὶ πολύ Nu 14.12, De 26.5; τί πλέον .. 'what more is there to be gained ..?' Ma 3.14; π. ἐν ῥήμασιν 'talkative' Jb 11.3, cf. μὴ πολὺς ἴσθι πρὸς ἀλλοτρίαν '.. with a strange woman' Pr 5.20 (see Demosth. 40.51); ~ὴ ἐν ταῖς ἀνομίαις Ez 22.5 (Hebraism: = ~αῖς ἀνομίαις, sim. ~ὴ τοῦ παραπικραίνειν 24.14, π. ἐν φρονήσει Pr 14.29); μετ' οὐ πολύ 'before long' 1E 3.21; subst., οὐκ ἔσῃ μετὰ πλειόνων 'You shall not side with the majority' Ex 23.2 (ǁ πλῆθος), πολλοὶ ὑμεῖς 'you have the number' 3K 18.25; ~οὺς ἐπέστρεψεν ἀπὸ ἀδικίας 'he turned many away from iniquity' Ma 2.6; τὸ πλεῖστον αὐτῶν 'the majority of them (hums.)' 1C 12.30; opp. ἐλάσσων 'less' Ex 16.17. **b**. in size, εἰς γῆν ἀγαθὴν καὶ ~ήν Ex 3.8, De 8.7; ἄβυσσος Am 7.4. **c**. in extent: adv.n., πολύ Ec 7.16 (ǁ περισσά); πολὺ πλέον 'with much greater effect' 4M 1.8, "he will generously (ἐπὶ πολύ) forgive your sins" Is 55.7; w. the article, τὸ πολύ 'for the most part' 2M 9.11. **d**. The comparative is used elatively, 'very much, very many': ἔκλαυσεν κλαυθμῷ πλείονι 'wept very much' Ge 46.29; ἡμέρας πλείους 'for very many days' Nu 9.19 (:: ἡμέρας ἀριθμῷ 'only a few days' 9.20), De 20.19; Is 22.9; τὸν πλείονα χρόνον Ba 4.35 (ǁ εἰς ἡμέρας μακράς); τὸ πλεῖον αὐτῶν 'most of them' Ps 89.10, cf. τὸ πλεῖον μέρος τῆς .. στρατιᾶς 'the greatest part of the army ..' 2M 8.24; οἱ πλείονες αὐτῶν 'most of them' 2M 11.12. **e**. The superlative is used elatively, 'very much, very many': πλεῖστον ποιεῖν γάλα 'to produce very much milk' Is 7.22; Si 45.9; subst. n.sg., τὸ πλεῖστον τοῦ λαοῦ 'the multitude of ..' Is 9.3. **f**. superlative = comparative: πλείστην ἢ ἔμπροσθεν 'greater than before' 3M 7.21, πλεῖστα τούτων 'more than these' 2C 25.9. **g**. subst. pl. articular, 'the majority': τοῖς πλείστοις τοῦ ἔθνους 2M 6.31.

Syntax: where a noun is qualified by both πολύς and another adjective, the sequence is <noun–adj.–πολύς>, e.g. οἶκοι ἕτεροι πολλοί Am 3.15.

Cf. μέγας, βραχύς, ὀλίγος, μικρός, ἀμύθητος, πλεοναστός, παμπληθής, συχνός, χυδαῖος: Jeremias, *TDNT* 6.536-8.

πολυτελής, ές.

very expensive: in the LXX, *s* often λίθος - λίθον ~ῆ ἐκλεκτὸν .. ἔντιμον 'a .. choice .. valuable stone' Is 28.16, λίθων ξυστῶν 'hewn ..' 1E 6.8, χρυσοῦ καὶ λίθων ~ῶν Es D 6; κρείσσων σοφία λίθων ~ῶν Pr 8.11; οἴνου ~οῦς Wi 2.7.

Cf. ἔντιμος, τίμιος: Spicq 3.134f.

πολυτόκος, ον.ʃ

giving birth to more than one, 'highly productive': *s* sheep, Ps 143.13. Cf. πολύπαις.

πολύτροπος, ον.

showing diverse forms, 'varied': *s* διάθεσις 'disposition' 4M 1.25.

πολύφροντις, ιδος. m.ʃ

one who is full of thought, used. subst.: *s* νοῦς 'mind' Wi 9.15. Cf. φρονέω.

πολυχρονίζω: fut. ~ιῶ.ʃ *

to live long: ἡμέρας 'for days' De 4.26. Cf. πολυχρόνιος, πολυήμερος, μακροχρονίζω.

πολυχρόνιος, ον.ʃ

living or *lasting long*: of long-term sojourn, ἐγένετο π. ἐκεῖ 'his sojourn there lasted long' Ge 26.8; of longevity, οὐ μὴ γένωνται ~οι 'they (= craftsmen) shall not live long' Ep Je. 46; ‖ γέρων Jb 32.9; πρεσβύτου .. πολιὰς ~ους 'the ancient grey hairs of the elderly' Wi 2.10; *s* ζωή 4M 17.12; subst. n., τὸ ~ον 'longevity' Wi 4.8. Cf. πολυχρονίζω, πολυημερεύω, μακροχρόνιος.

πολυωρέω: fut. ~ωρήσω; aor. ἐπολυώρησα.ʃ

to care for sbd *well*: *s* God and *o* hum., σε κύριος De 30.9; Ps 11.9, 137.3. Cf. ὀλιγωρέω.

πόμα, ατος. n.

liquid as drink: Ps 101.10 (‖ ἄρτος), οἶνος ~ατος Da 1.16 TH. Cf. πίνω, πότημα, ποτόν.

πομπεύω.ʃ

to take part in a procession: τῷ Διονύσῳ 'in honour of Dionysus' 2M 6.7; Wi 4.2.

πονέω: fut. πονέσω; aor. ἐπόνεσα.

1. *to suffer, be afflicted*: τοὺς πόδας αὐτοῦ 'in his feet' 3K 15.23, ἐπόνεσε Εφραιμ, τὰς ῥίζας αὐτοῦ ἐξηράνθη Ho 9.16 (or: 'suffered at its roots,' cf. *BA* ad loc.), cf. Thph σαθρὰ γέγονε PG 126.736, and Theophrastus *Historia Plantarum* 3.7.1 ῥίζαι πεπονηκυῖαι; τόπος πονῶν 'sector (of a battlefield) in trouble' 2K 11.16*L*.

2. *to undertake hard labour*: ὑπόθηκεν τὸν ὦμον αὐτοῦ εἰς τὸ πονεῖν 'he put his shoulder to labour' Ge 49.15; πονεῖτε καὶ μοχθεῖτε 1E 4.22; περὶ ἐμοῦ 1K 23.21; + κοπιάω Si 11.11; 13.5. Cf. φιλοπονέω.

3. tr., *to cause distress and suffering*: + acc., ψυχάς Is 19.10; mentally, τὴν κοιλίαν μου καὶ τὰ σπλάγχνα μου ἐπὶ τούτοις '.. over these matters' PSol 2.14; οὐκ ἐπόνεσαν ἐν αὐτῇ χεῖρας 'with nobody (needing to) raise a finger at it' or 'nobody in it tiring (of wrongdoings) [cf. Olymp. PG 93.752]' La 4.6.

Cf. πόνος, συμπονέω, κοπιάω, μοχθέω: Shipp 470f.

πονηρεύομαι: fut. ~ρεύσομαι; aor. ἐπονηρευσάμην, subj. πονηρεύσωμαι; pf.inf. πεπονηρεῦσθαι.

1. *to conduct onself immorally*: w. ref. to sexual immorality, Ge 19.7; ἐπονηρεύσαντο ἐν τοῖς ἐπιτηδεύμασιν αὐτῶν Mi 3.4; w. explanatory inf., ἐπονηρεύοντο τοῦ ἀποκτεῖναι αὐτόν 'started to draw up an evil scheme to murder him' Ge 37.18; ‖ ἀσεβής Ps 25.5; *s* ὀφθαλμός – πονηρεύσηται ὁ ὀφθαλμός σου τῷ ἀδελφῷ σου τῷ ἐπιδεομένῳ 'you will be looking at your needy brother maliciously' De 15.9; + ἔν τινι (pers. harmed), Ps 104.15, ἃ πονηρεύονται .. ἐν ἐμοί 'what they wrongfully accuse me of' Su 35ª LXX, κατ' ἐμοῦ 43 TH, ἐπί τινα Es 4.29 *L*; + dat. pers., 61 TH (LXX κατά τινος).

2. *to slander*: τινα Ec 7.22.

Cf. πονηρός, κακολογέω.

πονηρία, ας. f.

1. *evil design and intention*: π. πρόκειται ὑμῖν 'you have some wicked idea up your sleeves' Ex 10.10; μετὰ ~ας .. ἀποκτεῖναι ἐν τοῖς ὄρεσιν 32.12; οἶδα τὴν ~αν αὐτῶν De 31.21; opp. τὸ ἀγαθόν Is 7.16. **b**. pl. *wicked, evil deeds*: Is 1.16.

2. *evilness, wickedness*: τῶν ἐπιτηδευμάτων 'of the practices' Ps 27.4.

3. *poor quality*: of fruits, Je 24.2, 3.

4. *painful, grievous situation*, 'calamity, disaster': Je 31.16, Ne 1.3; Jd 20.41 B (A: κακία); καρδίας 2.2.

Cf. πονηρός, κακία, ἀγαθός: Harder, *TDNT* 6.562-4.

πονηρός, ά, όν.

1. *morally* or *ethically wrong, evil*: ποιήσω τὸ ῥῆμα τὸ ~όν Ge 39.9; ~ὰ ἐπιτηδεύματα 'evil practices' Mi 2.9, sim. Zc 1.4*b*; ἀπὸ τῆς ὁδοῦ αὐτοῦ τῆς

~ᾶς Jn 3.8, sim. 3.10, Zc 1.4*a*; καιρὸς π. Am 5.13, Mi 2.3; π. πνεῦμα Ho 12.1. Subst. n., *evil things, immorality*: διανοεῖται .. ἐπὶ τὰ ~ά Ge 6.5; γυναῖκα ἀγαπῶσαν ~ά Ho 3.1; εἰς ἐμὲ ἐλογίσαντο ~ά 7.15, sim. Na 1.11; ὁρᾶν ~ά Hb 1.13; ποιῶν ~όν Ma 2.17; opp. καλός - γνωστὸν καλοῦ καὶ ~οῦ 'knowable of good and evil' Ge 2.9; 3.5; ποιῆσαι .. ~ὸν ἢ κακόν Nu 24.13; οἱ μισοῦντες τὰ καλὰ καὶ ζητοῦντες τὰ ~ά Mi 3.2, sim. Am 5.14, 15, Ma 2.17; ‖ κακός Ge 50.17 (see vs. 15); ‖ μὴ ἀγαθός Ez 36.31; + λοιμός Je 15.21; *s* hum. in relation to God, ~οὶ καὶ ἁμαρτωλοὶ ἐναντίον τοῦ θεοῦ Ge 13.13. **b**. w. special ref. to lack of generosity, i.e. miserliness: ὀφθαλμῷ Si 14.8, ὀφθαλμὸς ~ός 14.10, cf. 14.5 (:: ἀγαθός), 6.

2. *harmful and injurious*: ἐτασμοῖς μεγάλοις καὶ ~οῖς Ge 12.17; θηρίον ~ὸν κατέφαγεν αὐτόν 'a harmful beast ate him' 37.20; ~ὰ ἀντὶ καλῶν 44.4; opp. ἀγαθός 50.20; *s* ῥομφαία '(hostile) sword' Ps 144.10; by-gone years of one's life, Ge 47.9, ἡμέρα Je 17.17, Ps 40.2; ἐν καιρῷ ~ῷ 'in hard times' 36.19 (‖ λιμός 'famine'); utterance, τὸ ῥῆμα τὸ ~ὸν τοῦτο 'this harsh message' Ex 33.4, ἀκοή 'report' Je 30.12, ἀγγελία 'message' 4K 19.7*L*; ὄνομα ~όν 'bad reputation' De 22.14, 19; ἕλκος ~όν 'nasty ulcer' 28.35; ὀδύνη 'suffering' 28.60; ἐλπὶς ~ά 'ominous prospect' Is 28.19; ~ὰ ἐνύπνια 'nightmares' PSol 6.3; subst. n.pl. 'disaster, calamity' Je 45.4 (:: εἰρήνη). **b**. *dangerously serious in effect and extent*: νόσος 'disease' De 28.59, μαλακία 'illness' 2C 21.15; θάνατος Si 28.21, Ps 33.22.

3. *out of favour*: ~αί εἰσιν αἱ θυγατέρες Χαναan ἐναντίον Ισαακ Ge 28.8; Μισητόν με πεποιήκατε ὥστε ~όν με εἶναι πᾶσιν τοῖς κατοικοῦσιν τὴν γῆν 'you have made me hated so that I am a persona non grata to the local residents' 34.30; ~ὸν ἦν αὐτῷ 'he was not amused' Ne 4.1.

4. *deficient, of poor quality*: *s* offering to God and opp. καλός, Le 27.10, 12, 14; fruits, Je 24.2 (:: χρηστός); πρόσωπον Ne 2.2.

Cf. πονηρεύομαι, παμπόνηρος, κακός, φαῦλος, ἀγαθός, καλός: Trench 315-7; Harder, *TDNT* 6.546-52.

πόνος, ου. m. Mostly pl.

1. *toil, suffering, hardship*: ὀδυνηθήσονται ἀπὸ προσώπου ~ων αὐτῶν 'they will suffer on account of their toils' Hg 2.14; brought about by a victorious hostile army, ἐν ἡμέρᾳ ~ων αὐτῶν (‖ θλῖψις, ὄλεθρος) Ob 13; κόπους καὶ ~ους Hb 1.3; brought about by injustice done by sbd else, "your eye is (?) too pure to behold wickednesses (πονηρά) and you will not be able to gaze at sufferings (πόνους)" Hb 1.13; ‖ μόχθος Nu 23.21, Ez 23.29, Wi 10.10; + πληγή, κάκωσις Is 53.4; mental, ψυχῆς 53.10, καρδίας 65.14 (‖ συντριβὴ πνεύματος); divine punishment, ~ῳ καὶ μάστιγι παιδευθήσῃ 'you shall be disciplined by .. and whipping' Je 6.7f., ἀπεθάνοσαν ἐν ~οις πονηροῖς, ἐν λιμῷ καὶ ἐν ῥομφαίᾳ .. 'they died .. by famine and sword ..' Ba 2.25, cf. π. λιμοῦ Je 14.18; psychosomatic, π. ἀγρυπνίας καὶ χολέρας 'distress of insomnia and nausea' Si 34.20. **b**. wrongly inflicted on others: λογισμοὶ ~ων Je 4.14, συνέλαβεν ~ον Ps 7.15 (‖ ἀδικία, ἀνομία), 7.17 (‖ ἀδικία), κόπος καὶ π. 9.28 (‖ πικρία καὶ δόλος), Is 10.1 (‖ πονηρία), 59.4 (‖ ἀνομία), see under κόπος **c**.

2. *physical pain, ache*: ἦσαν ἐν τῷ ~ῳ Ge 34.25 (following an adult circumcision); Is 1.5 (‖ λύπη); of childbirth (ὠδίνων) 66.7.

3. pl. *product of toil*: πάντες οἱ π. αὐτοῦ οὐχ εὑρεθήσονται αὐτῷ 'none of the fruits of his toil will be available to him' Ho 12.8; πάντας τοὺς ~ους τῶν χειρῶν αὐτῶν Hg 1.11, cf. De 28.33; λήμψονται πάντας τοὺς ~ους σου καὶ τοὺς μόχθους σου Ez 23.29, οὐχὶ ἑτέρῳ καταλείψεις τοὺς ~ους σου 'you are surely not going to leave ..' Si 14.15 (‖ κόπους); agricultural produce and ‖ καρπός Ps 77.46, not necessarily agricultural Pr 3.9; ‖ θησαυρός Je 20.5; children, υἱοὶ καὶ θυγατέρες, ἐμῆς κοιλίας ὠδῖνες καὶ πόνοι Jb 2.9b, cf. ὁ ἐμὸς ὠδίνων π. ref. to a child (Eur. *Phoen.* 30) and ‖ πρωτότοκος Ps 77.51 (cf. sg. 104.36), but not at Is 66.7, on which see above, **2**; honey produced by bees, Pr 6.8b; ‖ ἰσχύς 5.10; Wi 10.10.

Cf. ἄπονος, ἔμπονος, ἀλγηδών, κόπος, λύπη, μόχθος, ὀδύνη: Spicq 3.136-40.

ποντόβροχος, ον.ʃ *

drowned in the sea: *s* troops, 3M 6.4.

ποντοπορέω.ʃ

to move in the ocean: *s* ship, Pr 30.19. Cf. πορεία.

πόντος, ου. m.ʃ

open sea, ocean: ~ῳ ἐκάλυψεν αὐτούς Ex 15.5. Cf. θάλασσα, καταποντίζω, πέλαγος: Schmidt 1.641-50.

πορεία, ας. f.

1. *walking*: ποδῶν 'by foot' Is 3.16.

2. *journey, going, marching*: σταθμοὶ τῆς ~ας 'stages of the journey' Nu 33.2; π. ὁδοῦ ἡμερῶν τριῶν 'three days' journey by road' Jn 3.3; π. ἡμέρας μιᾶς 3.4; ἐν τῇ ~ᾳ αὐτῶν 'on their way, as they go' Na 2.5; π. αἰωνία 'eternal march' Hb 3.6; ὁδὸς εἰς ~αν Je 18.15; military, 2M 12.10; ἀφ' ἡμῶν '(leaving) us (upon death)' Wi 3.3; bird's flight, 5.11. **b**. metaph., *conducting oneself* in a certain way: π. τῆς ὁδοῦ τοῦ λαοῦ τούτου Is 8.11.

3. *course* taken by sbd moving or journeying, 'route, passage': ἐν κατακλυσμῷ ~ας 'by flooding the route' Na 1.8; ὕδατα ~ας Hb 3.10.

Cf. πορεύομαι, ποντοπορέω, ὁδός.

πορεῖον, ου. n.ʃ
pl. *transport animals, beasts of burden*: γεμίσατε τὰ ~α ὑμῶν 'load your pack animals full' Ge 45.17, see LSG s.v.

πορεύομαι: fut. πορεύσομαι; aor. ἐπορεύθην, inf. πορευθῆναι, ptc. πορευθείς, subj. πορευθῶ, impv. πορεύθητι; pf. πεπόρευμαι, ptc. πεπορευμένος.

I. 1. *to leave a place and head for another*: abs. Ge 12.4 (in response to Ἔξελθε), Ho 1.3 (in response to βάδιζε); 6.4 ('to vanish'), 7.12, Am 3.3, Mi 4.2*a*; ἀνάστηθι καὶ πορεύου Mi 2.10; πορεύεσθε καὶ περιοδεύσατε τὴν γῆν Zc 6.7*b*; Πορευθῶμεν καὶ λατρεύσωμεν De 13.2; ἱκέται 'as suppliants' Ma 3.14; + final inf. τοῦ ἐκζητῆσαι τὸν κύριον Ho 5.6; + διά - ἐπορεύετο διὰ τῆς ἐρήμου 'walked through the wilderness' Ge 24.62; + εἰς of destination, Ge 11.31 (εἰς γῆν Χανααν), Ho 7.11, Jn 1.2, 3.2, Hb 3.11; εἰς μετοικεσίαν (q.v.) Na 3.10; μετά τινος Ge 24.58; ποῦ Zc 2.2; + πρός τινα, for a visit, Ge 26.26; for help, 41.55, Ho 5.13; ἐν αἰχμαλωσίᾳ 'as exiles' Am 1.15, 9.4; + ἐκ, *to move out of*, ἐκ ταλαιπωρίας 'out of misery' Ho 9.6; + κατά τι– τὴν ὁδόν, καθ' ἣν πορεύεσθε ἐν αὐτῇ De 1.33; + κατόπισθέν τινος 'after sbd' Ge 37.17; + acc. ὁδόν– τὴν ὁδὸν αὐτῶν 1K 1.19, τὴν ὁδόν, ἣν ἐπορεύθητε De 1.31, but cf. ὁδῷ βασιλικῇ πορευσόμεθα Nu 20.17, Ποίᾳ ὁδῷ πεπόρευται; .. τὴν ὁδὸν ⸢ἐν ᾗ⸣ (v.l. ἣν) ἀνῆλθεν 3K 13.12, ἐν τῇ ὁδῷ ᾗ ἐπορεύθης ἐν αὐτῇ vs. 9 (ἐν αὐτῇ > MT), ὁδῷ ἀληθινῇ Is 65.2, ἐν ᾗ πορεύσομαι Ps 142.8, and ἐπορεύθησαν ὁδὸν εἰς Αραβα Je 52.7, ὁδὸν μακράν Pr 7.19; To 5.17 𝔊[II]; τρίβους Jd 5.6A. With an anarthrous ὁδόν – πορευσώμεθα ὁδὸν τριῶν ἡμερῶν εἰς τὴν ἔρημον 'Let us go a distance of three days into the wilderness' Ex 3.18; 8.27. Opp. ἔρχομαι– πόθεν ἔρχῃ καὶ ποῦ πορεύῃ; 'where do you come from and where are you going to?' Ge 16.8, γενεὰ πορεύεται καὶ γ. ἔρχεται Ec 1.4. Indicates a journey undertaken to reach a certain location, with ἔρχομαι indicating the location reached: ἐξήλθοσαν πορευθῆναι εἰς γῆν Χανααν, καὶ ἦλθον εἰς γῆν Χ. Ge 12.5. **b**. *to go off* following some action: ἁρπῶμαι καὶ πορεύσομαι Ho 5.14. **c**. *to set out on a journey*: Am 3.3; asyndetically foll. by another verb of movement, πορεύου ἀνάβηθι Ex 33.1. **d**. *to go about in a certain state and manner*: ἀνυπόδετος καὶ γυμνή 'bare-footed and naked' Mi 1.8; ὀρθοί 'erect, upright' ib. 2.3; ὡς τυφλοί Zp 1.17. **e**. movement contrasted with lack of it: Οἱ ἀδελφοὶ ὑμῶν πορεύσονται εἰς πόλεμον, καὶ ὑμεῖς καθήσεσθε αὐτοῦ '.. you are sitting around here' Nu 32.6. **2**. *to march, move along*, emphasising continuous aspect: Ge 3.14, Hb 3.5, Ma 2.6; ἐν ὁδῷ De 6.7, 11.19 (:: κάθημαι, κοιτάζομαι, διανίστημι); w. military connotation, ἐν τῇ ὁδῷ αὐτοῦ Jl 2.7, 8 (of soldiers), Hb 1.6 (army), cf. Zc 9.14; ἐπὶ ὁδόν Ge 24.42; + acc., ὁδὸν ἣν ἐπορεύθης Je 38.21, *s* travellers To 6.2 𝔊[I]; *s* river flowing, Ge 2.14, ποταμοὶ ὡς ἔλαιον Ez 32.14, ἡσυχῇ 'quietly' Is 8.6, χείμαρροι εἰς τὴν θάλασσαν Ec 1.7; flood water receding, Ge 8.3; ship, Is 33.21; πᾶς ὁ πορευόμενος ἐπὶ κοιλίας '.. on its belly' Le 11.42 (|| ἐπὶ τεσσάρων 'on all its fours'); τῇ ὁδῷ 'by the road (without digressing)' Nu 21.22.

*__3__. Closely bound w. another verb, indicates a determined and deliberate action (Hebraism): πορεύεσθαι λατρεύειν τοῖς θεοῖς τῶν ἐθνῶν ἐκείνων De 29.18; πορευθέντες ἐλάτρευσαν θεοῖς ἑτέροις 29.26; πορεύθητι καὶ ἀγάπησον γυναῖκα .. Ho 3.1, 5.15.

*__4__. In hendiadys: π. καὶ ἐπιστρέφω, *to go back, revert in repentance*, Ho 2.7 (asyndesis in the Heb.), 6.1, but πνεῦμα πορευόμενον καὶ οὐκ ἐπιστρέφον 'a wind which departs, never to return' Ps 77.39, and not at 2K 3.16.

II. Fig. *__1__. *to grow, develop*: κλάδοι 'branches' Ho 14.7.

*__2__. in conj. with another verb, indicates a continuing process, a calque of Heb. הָלַךְ qal: τὸ ὕδωρ πορευόμενον ἠλαττοῦντο 'the water kept diminishing' Ge 8.5; ἡ θάλασσα ἐπορεύετο καὶ ἐξήγειρε μᾶλλον κλύδωνα 'the sea kept ever throwing up billows' Jn 1.11, sim. 1.13; ἐπορεύθη .. πορευόμενος καὶ ἐγγίζων 'kept coming closer' 1K 17.41*L*, cf. .. καὶ ἤγγιζεν 18.25*L* (B: ἐγγίζων); Jd 4.24, 2K 3.1, 15.12

3. *to conduct oneself, follow a certain moral lifestyle*: δίκαιοι π. ἐν ^ταῖς ὁδοῖς τοῦ κυρίου^ Ho 14.10, sim. Zc 3.7; ἐν πάσαις ταῖς ὁδοῖς αὐτοῦ De 19.9; ἐν ταῖς τρίβοις ^τοῦ κυρίου^ Mi 4.2*b*; ἐν ^τοῖς προστάγμασιν κυρίου^ Le 18.4; ἕκαστος τὴν ὁδὸν αὐτοῦ .. ἐν ὀνόματι κυρίου Mi 4.5; μετὰ κυρίου 6.8; ἐν ταῖς βουλῇ ἀσεβῶν Ps 1.1; ἐν ἐπιθυμίαις καρδίας σου Si 5.2; ἐν δικαιοσύνῃ Is 33.15; πλάγιος 'perverse' Le 26.21; μεθ' ὑμῶν θυμῷ πλαγίῳ 'towards you with unfriendly attitude' 26.24 (|| ἐν θ. π. vs. 27, 41); ἐναντίον ^τοῦ θεοῦ^ πλάγιοι 26.40; ἐνώπιόν σου μετὰ ἀληθείας Is 38.3; + dat., τῷ νόμῳ μου Ex 16.4, τοῖς νομίμοις αὐτῶν Le 18.3; οὐ πορεύσῃ δόλῳ ἐν τῷ ἔθνει σου 19.16; τοῖς προστάγμασίν μου πορεύησθε καὶ τὰς ἐντολάς μου φυλάσσησθε καὶ ποιήσητε αὐτάς Le 26.3; τῷ φωτὶ κυρίου Is 2.5, τῷ φωτὶ τοῦ πυρός .. καὶ τῇ φλογί 50.11; ὁδῷ ἀληθινῇ 65.2, τὴν ὁδόν, ᾗ πορευσόμεθα ἐν αὐτῇ Je 49.3, ὁδοῖς ἀληθείας .. καὶ δικαιοσύνης To 1.3 𝔊[I] (ἐν δικαιοσύναις 𝔊[II]); ταῖς ἐπιθυμήμασι τῆς καρδίας 'the heart's desires' Je 7.24, τοῖς θελήμασιν αὐτῶν 23.17, σοφίᾳ Pr 28.26; + acc., ὁδοὺς οὐκ ἀγαθάς 6.12.

4. *to function, work*: ὀρθοὶ π. 'the words of the Lord went right, functioned properly' Mi 2.7.

***5**. *to associate oneself* w. sbd or sth (ὀπίσω τινός) out of personal attachment (Hebraism): ὀπίσω Βεελφεγωρ De 4.3; ὀ. θεῶν ἑτέρων 6.14, 8.19, ὀ. θεῶν ἀλλοτρίων Je 7.6; ὀ. τῶν ἐραστῶν Ho 2.5, 13; ὀ. τῶν ματαίων 5.11; ὀ. κυρίου De 13.4, Ho 11.10, Si 46.10, ὀ. θεῶν ἑτέρων λατρεύειν αὐτοῖς De 28.14, ὀ. τῶν ἁμαρτιῶν αὐτῶν Is 65.2, ὀ. τῶν ἐνθυμημάτων τῶν καρδιῶν αὐτῶν Ez 20.16, sim. Si 18.30; ὀ. αὐτῶν (= heavenly bodies) Ho 13.4.

***6**. Mechanical translation of the Heb. הֹלֵךְ: ἐγὼ πορεύομαι τελευτᾶν /'ānōḵi hōlēḵ lāmut/, hardly = 'I am at the point of death' Ge 25.32; 1C 21.20 (*L* ἀποθνήσκω).

Cf. βαδίζω, ἔρχομαι, δια~, εἰσ~, ἐκ~, παρα~, συμπορεύομαι, πορεία, πόρευσις, πορευτός, περιπατέω, ὁδεύω, οἴχομαι: Schmidt 1.477-504; Lee 85f.

πόρευσις, εως. f.ʃ

journey: κατὰ σχολὴν τῆς ~εως Ge 33.14. Cf. πορεία, πορεύομαι.

πορευτός, ή, όν.ʃ

suited for travel: *s* road, Es B 2. **b**. suited for walking on: *s* πέλαγος 'ocean' 2M 5.21 (‖ πλωτός 'sailable').

Cf. πορεύομαι.

πορθέω: aor. ἐπόρθησα.ʃ

to kill and destroy: τινα 4M 4.23, 11.4. Cf. ἀφανίζω: Spicq 3.141f.

πορίζω.ʃ

to make pecuniary profit: Wi 15.12. Cf. πορισμός.

πορισμός, οῦ. m.ʃ

v.n. of πορίζω: Wi 13.19. **b**. *pecuniary gain made*: pl., Wi 14.2.

Cf. πορίζω: *ND* 4.169.

πορνεία, ας. f.

1. *sexual immorality*: of man To 4.12 𝔊[I]; of woman, γυναῖκα ~ας καὶ τέκνα ~ας 'an immoral woman and children born out of a relationship with her' Ho 1.2 (poss. metaph. [see *BA* ad loc.]); ‖ μοιχεία 2.2; + φόνος 'murder' Ez 43.7.

2. *unfaithfulness and apostasy* in relation to God: πνεύματι ~ας ἐπλανήθησαν Ho 4.12; πνεῦμα ~ας ἐν αὐτοῖς ἐστιν, τὸν δὲ κύριον οὐκ ἐπέγνωσαν 5.4; ἀπαλλοτρίωσις ~ας Je 13.27. **b**. consequences of such: Nu 14.33.

3. *activity and attitude indicative of lust and search for gratification* in general: πωλοῦσα ἔθνη ἐν τῇ ~ᾳ αὐτῆς Na 3.4 (‖ φάρμακα).

Cf. πορνεύω, πόρνη, and μοιχεία.

πορνεῖον, ου. n.ʃ

brothel: "you have built your brothels at every street-corner" Ez 16.25; ‖ βάσις 'high-place' 16.31, 39. Cf. πορνεύω.

πορνεύω: fut.act. πορνεύσω; aor. ἐπόρνευσα, subj. πορνεύσω; pf. πεπόρνευκα.

1. *to practise sexual immorality*: *s* woman, ἡ γυνή σου ἐν τῇ πόλει πορνεύσει Am 7.17; Ho 3.3 (‖ ἀνδρὶ γίνομαι); 4.14 (‖ μοιχεύω); male temple prostitute and further specified as τελισκόμενος, De 23.17 (:: πόρνη).

2. *to act unfaithfully* towards God and move away from him: abs. Jd 2.15A (B: ἐκπορεύομαι), ἐπόρνευσαν ἀπὸ τοῦ θεοῦ σου Ho 9.1; 4.10 (‖ μὴ κατευθύνω); Ps 72.27 (‖ μακρύνω ἀπό τινος); ὀπίσω θεῶν λαῶν τῆς γῆς 'following the gods of the local peoples' 1C 5.25.

Cf. πορνεία, πόρνη, πορνεῖον, ἐκπορνεύω, ἑταιρίζομαι, and μοιχεύω.

πόρνη, ης. f.

woman who regularly and/or professionally practises sexual immorality: Ge 38.15; γυναῖκα πόρνην Le 21.7; presumably 'prostitute' μετὰ τῶν ~ῶν συνεφύροντο .. ὁ λαὸς οὐ συνίων συνεπλέκετο μετὰ ~ης 'they associated with prostitutes .. the people, out of lack of understanding, became involved with prostitutes' Ho 4.14; ἔδωκαν τὰ παιδάρια ~αις Jl 3.3; symbol of lust and gratification, π. καλὴ καὶ ἐπιχαρὴς ἡγουμένη φαρμάκων 'a pretty and attractive harlot making masterly use of enchanted potions' Na 3.4; + μοιχός Is 57.3. **b**. temple prostitute: De 23.17 (specified as τελεσφόρος). **c**. metaph. w. ref. to a city and its citizens faithless to their God: Is 1.21 (previously πόλις πιστή).

Cf. πορνεία, πορνεύω, πόρνος, πορνικός, μοιχαλία, μοιχαλίς: Schmidt 2.417f.

πορνικός, ή, όν.ʃ

pertaining to πόρνη: *s* οἴκημα 'brothel' Ez 16.24; εἶδος 'look' Pr 7.10. Cf. πόρνη.

πορνοκόπος, ου. m.ʃ

frequent visitor to brothels: Pr 23.21, cf. Kindstrand 104.

πόρνος, ου. m.ʃ

male fornicator: Si 23.16, 17. Cf. πόρνη. Del. Si 23.18 v.l.

πόρος, ου. m.ʃ

means and way of achieving an end: + τοῦ inf., 1M 12.40.

πόρπη, ης. f.

brooch, buckle: worn as emblem of rank, and golden, 1M 10.89. Cf. ἐμπορπάω, ἐμπορπόω.

πόρρω. adv.

to a distance: + διώκω Is 17.13; π. πεφεύγασι 22.3; Π. ἀπ' ἐμοῦ, μὴ ἐγγίσῃς μου 'Be away from me!, Don't come near me!' 65.5; opp. ἐγγύς Je 12.2, 31.24; + gen., πεπλανημένη π. τῆς ἀληθείας 'having strayed far from the truth' 3M 4.16. **b.** used attrib.: νῆσοι π. 'distant isles' Si 47.16.

Cf. πόρρωθεν, μακρός, ἐγγύς, πέλας.

πόρρωθεν.

1. *from afar*: ἡ θλῖψις ὑμῖν π. ἥξει 'the tribulation will come to you ..' Is 10.3, ἐπάγω ἐφ' ὑμᾶς ἔθνος π. Je 5.15, κύριος π. ὤφθη αὐτῷ '.. appeared to him' 38.3; ἰδόντες αὐτὸν π. Jb 2.12.

2. *situated far away*: as attr. adj., ἔρχεσθαι ἐκ γῆς π. 'to come from a far-away land' Is 13.5, ἀπὸ γῆς π. .. ἀπ' ἄκρων τῆς γῆς '.. from the ends of the earth' 43.6, γῆν π. 33.17; θεὸς π. Je 23.23 (:: θεὸς ἐγγίζων); οἱ π. Is 33.13 (:: οἱ ἐγγίζοντες); π. ὄψιν 'appearance far-away' Wi 14.17.

Cf. πόρρω, μακρόθεν, ἐγγίζω.

πορφύρα, ας. f.

1. *purple stripe*: Ex 25.4.

2. valuable *purple fabric*: Ex 26.1, 28.5 (|| βύσσος, ὑάκινθος, κόκκινος); material for a veil of the tabernacle, 26.31. **b.** *robe made of purple fabric*: 1E 3.6; worn by dignitaries, 2M 4.38.

Cf. πορφυροῦς, μεσο~, ὁλο~, περιπόρφυρος, πορφυρίς, πορφυρίων.

πορφυρίς, ίδος. f.ʃ

purple garment: royal, Jd 8.26 B. Cf. πορφύρα.

πορφυρίων, ωνος. m.ʃ

purple coot or *water-hen, Fulica porphyrion* (LSJ): forbidden as food, Le 11.18, De14.17.

πορφυροῦς, ᾶ, οῦν.ʃ

purple-dyed: *s* ἱμάτιον Nu 4.14, ἱματισμός Ep Je 11, περιβόλαια 'cloaks' Jd 8.26A, σχοινία .. 'cords' Es 1.6^2 (+ βυσσίνος), διάδημα βύσσινον καὶ ~οῦν 'linen .. diadem' 8.15. **b.** *made of purple-dyed fabric*: ἐπίβασις 'steps' Ct 3.10.

Cf. πορφύρα: LSG s.v.

ποσάκις.

How often?, How many times?: π. παρεπίκραναν .. 'How often have they embittered ..?' Ps 77.40; Si 20.17, 3M 5.37. Cf. πόσος, πλειστάκις, ποσαπλῶς.

ποσαπλῶς.ʃ

How often!: Ps 62.2. Cf. πόσος, ποσαχῶς.

ποσαχῶς.ʃ

In how many more ways, how much more!: ὁ δεδοξασμένος ἐν πτωχείᾳ, καὶ ἐν πλούτῳ π.; 'One who is honoured in poverty, and how much more so in wealth!' Si 10.31*a*; 10.31*b*. Cf. πόσος, ποσαπλῶς.

πόσις, εως. f.ʃ

liquid as drink: + βρῶσις Da 1.10. Cf. πίνω, πόμα, βρῶσις.

πόσος, η, ον.

How many, how much?: attrib., Πόσα ἔτη ..; 'How many years..?' Ge 47.8; predic., πόσαι εἰσὶν αἱ ἁμαρτίαι μου ..; 'How many are my sins..?' Jb 13.23. **b.** exclamatory: μετὰ πόσης ἀκριβείας .. 'With hoch much accuracy..!' Wi 12.21; 4M 15.22.

Cf. ποσάκις, ποσαπλῶς, ποσαχῶς. Del. Si 11.11 v.l.

ποσός, ή, όν.

of some quantity or *extent*: κατὰ ποσόν τι 'to some extent' 1E 8.75.

ποταμός, οῦ.

river: Ge 2.10, Hb 3.8 (|| θάλασσα); anarth., w. ref. to Euphrates, Mi 7.12; ~ῶν γῆ, ref. to Mesopotamia (so Cyr. II 145 and Thph PG 126.887), Hb 3.9; πύλαι τῶν ~ῶν Na 2.7 (see s.v. πύλη); ἀναβήσεται ὡς π. συντέλεια, of a river level rising and causing destruction, Am 8.8*a*, 9.5; καταβήσεται ὡς π. Αἰγύπτου 'will subside as the Nile' Am 8.8*b*, 9.5; ξηρανθήσεται πάντα τὰ βάθη ~ῶν 'all the deep rivers will run dry' or 'will become dry down to the riverbed' Zc 10.11; τὸν Ἰορδάνην ~όν Nu 13.30, ἐπὶ τῷ ~ῷ Εὐφράτῃ Je 26.2; source of water, Is 41.15 (|| πηγή). Cf. θάλασσα, χειμάρρους: Schmidt 1.633-40.

ποταπός, ή, όν.ʃ

of what sort?: ~ῷ τοῦ παραδείσου τόπῳ Su 54 LXX (|| ποῖος vs. 58). Cf. ποῖος: Spicq 143f.

πότε. adv.

when?: Ge 30.30, Am 8.5; ἕως π. 'till when, how much longer' Ps 81.2; indir. question, Ex 8.9. Cf. ποτέ.

ποτέ.

at some unknown point of time: in the past, ἡμέρας πολλάς, ὅσας ποτὲ ἡμέρας ἐνεκάθησθε 'many days when you once stayed (there)' De 1.46, χρείαν, ἥν ποτε εἶχον 'a need which they ever had' Jb 31.16; where an exact year and/or date is not mentioned - 4M 4.1. **b.** not in the past, Is 41.7; "Think judiciously for once" Ps 93.8; π. καὶ ἄλλοτε 'any other time' 2M 13.10; π. μὲν .. καὶ π. ⌜δὲ⌝ (om. B) .. 'at one point or other' 2K 11.25*L*.

Cf. πότε, πώποτε, ἄλλοτε, τότε.

πότερον. Only in Jb.

1. an interr. asking which of two alternatives applies, the second alternative introduced by ἤ: π. θάλασσά εἰμι ἢ δράκων 'Am I a sea or a serpent?' Jb 7.12.

2. the second alternative suppressed, hence virtually equivalent to a question marker, mostly accompanied by a negator, οὐ, οὐχ, or οὐχί anticipating a positive reply: π. οὐχ ἡ κακία σού ἐστιν πολλή Jb 22.5.

πότημα, ατος. n.ʃ

something to drink: to soothe thirst in heat, Je 28.39. Cf. πίνω, πόμα.

ποτήριον, ου. n.

drinking-vessel: Ge 40.11, Hb 2.16; χρυσοῦν 'golden' Je 28.7; metaph. of a harsh fate, π. θυμοῦ ..

π. πτώσεως Is 51.17 (|| κόνδυ), συντριβῆς La 2.13, ἀφανισμοῦ Ez 23.33, cf. Mt 26.39 and μερὶς ~ου Ps 15.5 (|| κληρονομία), 10.6. **b**. *that which is drunk from a drinking-vessel*: Je 16.7, Ps 22.5; οἴνου PSol 8.14.

Cf. πίνω, κόνδυ, κυλίκιον.

ποτίζω: fut. ποτιῶ, pass. ποτισθήσομαι; aor. ἐπότισα, subj. ποτίσω, ptc. ποτίσας, inf. ποτίσαι; pf. πεπότικα.

to supply liquid *to drink*: + acc. pers., τὸ παιδίον 'the boy' Ge 21.19, τὸ γένος μου τὸ ἐκλεκτόν 'my chosen people' Is 43.20, ἐπότισεν αὐτοὺς ὡς ἐν ἀβύσσῳ πολλῇ 'he gave them to drink as in an abundant subterranean spring' Ps 77.15; ***o*** animals, πάντα τὰ θηρία τοῦ ἀγροῦ 'all the animals of the field' Ps 103.11 (***s*** πηγαί 'springs'); livestock, καμήλους Ge 24.14; ἐκ τοῦ φρέατος ἐκείνου ἐπότιζον τὰ ποίμνια 'from that well they would water the flocks' 29.2; πρόβατα 29.8, Ex 2.16; τὴν συναγωγὴν καὶ τὰ κτήνη αὐτῶν Nu 20.8; πόλιν Is 27.3; + acc. pers. and acc. rei, τὸν πατέρα ἡμῶν οἶνον Ge 19.32, με μικρὸν ὕδωρ 24.17, με ὄξος '(gave) me vinegar to drink' Ps 68.22, τὸν χειμάρρουν τῆς τρυφῆς σου ποτιεῖς αὐτούς 'you will give them to drink from the plentiful wadi' 35.9, οὐ ποτιοῦσιν αὐτὸν ποτήριον εἰς παράκλησιν 'they will not offer him a cup (of water) to comfort him' Je 16.7, ὕδωρ πικρόν 'bitter water' 23.15 (|| ψωμίζω); + acc. pers. and dat. rei, τὸν πλησίον αὐτοῦ ἀνατροπῇ θολερᾷ '.. unclear intoxicating drink (?)' Hb 2.15, πνεύματι κατανύξεως 'with a stupefying spirit' Is 29.10 (cf. οἶνον κατανύξεως Ps 59.5); + ἐν – ἡμᾶς ἐν δακρύσιν 'us with tears' 79.6 (|| ψωμίζω 'to feed'). **b**. forcibly, ποτιεῖ τὴν γυναῖκα τὸ ὕδωρ Nu 5.24. **c**. *to make drunk*: + acc. (elephants), οἴνῳ 'with wine' 3M 5.2. **d**. *to irrigate*: (πηγὴ) ἐπότιζεν πᾶν τὸ πρόσωπον τῆς γῆς '(a stream of water) watered the whole surface of the ground' Ge 2.6; πηγὴ .. ποτιεῖ τὸν χειμάρρουν 'a well will fill the wadi' Jl 3.18; ***s*** ποταμός and ***o*** παράδεισος, Ge 2.10, τοῖς ποσὶν ὡσεὶ κῆπον λαχανείας '(turning the irrigation-wheel?) by the feet like a garden of herbs' De 11.10 (cf. LSG s.v., Wevers 1995.192f., Cadell 1994.115f. and πότισον τὴν γῆν ἀπὸ χερός *SB* 6733, 3), κῆπον Si 24.31, πόλιν Is 27.3, ὄρη ἐκ τῶν ὑπερῴων αὐτοῦ 'mountains from his upper levels' Ps 103.13; pass. ποτισθήσεται ἡ γῆ ἀπὸ τῶν προχωρημάτων σου '.. with your excrements' Ez 32.6.

Cf. πίνω, ποτιστήριον: Spicq 3.145-8.

ποτιστήριον, ου. n.ʃ*

drinking-trough for livestock: ἐξεκένωσεν τὴν ὑδρίαν εἰς τὸ π. 'emptied the (contents of) the pitcher into the drinking-trough' Ge 24.20; ἐν ταῖς ληνοῖς τῶν ~ων τοῦ ὕδατος 30.38. Cf. ποτίζω.

ποτόν, οῦ. n. No example in the LXX of adjectival use: see esp. 2 Es 3.7 βρώματα καὶ ποτά.

that which one drinks, 'drink': πᾶν π., ὃ πίνεται ἐν παντὶ ἀγγείῳ 'every kind of drink that is drunk with any kind of vessel' Le 11.34 (|| βρῶμα); βρωτὰ καὶ ~ά 1E 5.53. Cf. πόμα, πότος, πίνω, and βρωτός.

πότος, ου. m.

1. *social occasion where drinks are served and had*: ἐποίησεν αὐτοῖς ~ον 'held a drinking party' Ge 19.3; πᾶσιν τοῖς παισὶν αὐτοῦ 40.20; οἰκία ~ου Je 16.8, οἶκος ~ου Ec 7.2; Es 1.3 *L* (o' δοχή).

2. *liquid* for nourishment: for plants, Jb 8.11 (|| ὕδωρ).

Cf. ποτόν, συμπόσιον, and πίνω.

που.

1. *somewhere* unspecified: Pr 31.21; w. negator, *nowhere* 3K 10.12.

2. tones down the veracity of an utterance: w. numerals, *approximately*, 2M 5.27.

Cf. ποῦ.

ποῦ.

where?: of location, and alw. in locational clauses, Ho 13.10(*a*), 14(*a*)*bis*, Mi 7.10(*a*), Jl 2.17(*b*), Ob 5(*b*), Na 2.12b(*a*), Ma 1.6(*b*)*bis*, 2.17(*a*); not at the head of a clause, Zc 1.5(*b*). **b**. of direction, *whither?, where .. to?*: ποῦ σὺ πορεύῃ; Zc 2.2(*d*); || πόθεν 'where .. from?' – πόθεν ἔρχῃ καὶ ποῦ πορεύῃ; 'where do you come from and where are you going to?' Ge 16.8(*d*).

Cf. που, πόθεν.

a) אֵי; *b*) אַיֵּה [+ Ho 13.10, 14, metath.; Ob 5, voc.]; *c*) אֵיפֹה; *d*) אָנָה. xʃ

πούς, ποδός, dat.pl. ποσίν. m.

1. *foot*: for moving on a surface – of birds, Ge 8.9; of humans, ὀξὺς τοῖς ποσίν 'quick-footed' Am 2.15; οἱ πόδες εὐαγγελιζομένου 'the feet of a bearer of good news' Na 1.15; ἐν πεδίλοις οἱ πόδες αὐτοῦ 'with sandals on his feet' Hb 3.5; τοῖς ποσίν τινος 'on foot' 2K 15.16B (*L* πεζός) || 17 πεζῇ; on which one stands – ἑστηκότων αὐτῶν ἐπὶ τοὺς πόδας αὐτῶν 'they standing on their feet' Zc 14.12, cf. 14.4; under which sth is trampled, Ma 4.3, cf. "you placed everthing under his feet (ὑποκάτω τῶν ποδῶν αὐτοῦ)" Ps 8.7; to be washed at the end of a journey, Ge 18.4, 19.2; κονιορτὸς τῶν ποδῶν αὐτοῦ 'dust of his feet,' anthropomorphically said of God, Na 1.3; || σκέλος Ez 1.7; ἐπὶ τῷ ποδί μου 'on account of my coming' (?) Ge 30.30 (MT: /l-ragli/); κατὰ πόδας 'without delay' 49.19, cf. Shipp 306. **b**. one end of human body: ἀπὸ ποδῶν ἕως κεφαλῆς Is 1.6. **c**. *the lower part* of hum. body: euphemism for anus (?), Jd 3.24B. **d**. *advance* made by a moving object: by a chariot, Jd 5.28B. ***e**. ὁ ἐν ποσίν τινος *soldier under sbd's command*, Hebraism: Jd 8.5 B (A: μετά τινος), cf. 4K 3.9.

2. *upright, oblong, supporting part* of a structure, 'leg': of table, Ex 25.25.

Cf. πεζός, σκέλος.

πρᾶγμα, ατος. n.

1. *deed, action*: οὐ δυνήσομαι ποιῆσαι π. 'I shall not be able to do a thing' Ge 19.22; οὐ μὴ ποιήσῃ κύριος .. π. 'the Lord would not take any action' Am 3.7; Τί ὅτι ἐποιήσατε τὸ π. τοῦτο ..; 'why have you done this ..?' Ex 1.18, ἐποίησας θαυμαστὰ ~ατα Is 25.1; 2K 11.11*L* (B: ῥῆμα); τὸ π. οὐδέν ἐστιν 'the action in question should be no concern to you' Nu 20.19; λόγῳ .. ~ατι 'by word .. (but) in practice' 3M 3.17. **b**. *proposed course of action*: Es 2.4 o'.

2. *object, tangible thing*: ἅψηται παντὸς ~ατος ἀκαθάρτου 'touches any unclean thing whatsoever' Le 5.2; Nu 31.23, Ps 90.6.

3. *matter of concern*: "Don't quarrel about a matter which is none of your business" Si 11.9.

4. pl., *running and managing of a state*: ἐν πάσῃ τῇ ἑαυτοῦ βασιλείᾳ Da 1.20 LXX, τῆς Βαβυλωνίας 4.48 LXX; 4.49 LXX (TH ἔργα). **b**. *state* as a polity: 2M 11.19.

5. mostly pl., *trouble, annoyance*: παρέχω τινι ~τα 'to cause sbd troubles' Es 3.18 *L*.

Cf. ποίημα, πράσσω, ἔργον.

πραγματεία, ας. f.

official task to be executed: king's, 3K 9.1, 1C 28.21; administrative, Da 6.3 LXX, 3K 10.22[a]; of a historian treating a subject, 2M 2.31.

Cf. πραγματεύομαι: Maurer, *TDNT* 6.640f.; Spicq 3.149-51.

πραγματεύομαι: aor. ἐπραγματευσάμην.ʃ

to busy oneself with and execute: + acc., βασιλικά 'business of kingdom' Da 8.27 LXX (TH ποιέω); + cogn. acc., πραγματείαν 3K 10.22[a]. Cf. συμπραγματεύομαι, πραγματεία.

πραγματικός, ή, όν.ʃ

subst.m. *staff* of an institution: administrative staff of the temple, 1E 8.22.

πράκτωρ, ορος. m.ʃ

bailiff: οἱ ~ες ὑμῶν καλαμῶνται ὑμᾶς 'your bailiffs fleece you of all' Is 3.12 (‖ ἀπαιτῶν 'creditor'). Cf. πρᾶξις **2**, πράσσω **5**: Spicq 3.152-9.

πρᾶξις, εως. f.

1. *that which one does*, 'action, deed': Jb 24.5, Si 11.10, 35.24; ‖ ἔργον 37.16. **b**. *that which one has done, achieved*: ruler's 2C 12.15, 1M 16.23. **c**. in the way of business: Si 38.24. **c**. v.n. of πράσσω **2**: PSol 4.10.

2. *exaction* of money, *recovery* of arrears: τῶν διαφόρων 'of the monies' 2M 4.28, cf. πράσσω **5**, πράκτωρ: *ND* 6.90-2.

Cf. ἔργον, πρᾶγμα, πράσσω, ποίημα: Maurer, *TDNT* 6.642f.

πρασιά, ᾶς. f.ʃ

garden-plot: Si 24.31; Jb 8.16 (Zgl. σαπρία), cf. Orlinsky 1962.133.

πράσινος, ον.ʃ

leek-green, light green: of the colour of a kind of precious stone – ὁ λίθος ὁ π. Ge 2.12 (‖ ἄνθραξ). Cf. πράσον, χλωρός.

πρᾶσις, εως. f.

1 *sale*: ἔστιν π. ἐν Αἰγύπτῳ Ge 42.1; + ἀγορασμός 'purchase' Si 27.2; cogn. obj. of ἀποδίδωμι mid., Le 25.14; cogn. dat. of πιπράσκω, De 21.14.

2. *that which has been* or *is to be sold*: Le 25.25, De 18.8; + ἀγορασμός Ne 10.31. **b**. *proceeds of sale*: 4K 12.6.

Cf. πιπράσκω, πριάομαι, διάπρασις, ἀγορασμός.

πράσον, ου. n.ʃ

leek: as food, Nu 11.5. Cf. πράσινος.

πράσσω: fut. πράξω; aor. ἔπραξα, ptc. πράξας, inf. act. πρᾶξαι, subj. πράξω, pass. ἐπράχθην, ptc. πραχθείς; pf.inf. πεπραχέναι. Also spelled πράττω: 2M 9.19.

1. *to act* in a certain manner: improperly, ἀφρόνως 'foolishly' Ge 31.28.

2. *to do*: + acc. rei, ἄτοπα 'wrong things' Jb 27.6, 36.21, ἄδικα 36.23, κακά Pr 13.10, ἔχθιστα 'utterly detestable things' Wi 12.4, μηδὲν ἐν ἔργοις ὕβρεως 'nothing to do with works of insolence' Si 10.6, ταῦτα Is 57.10; τὸ καθ' ἓν πραχθὲν τῆς πράξεως Ἰωσίου 'every single one of J.'s deeds' 1E 1.31.

3. *to take possession of*, 'win': + acc., δόξαν βασιλείας Da 11.20 TH.

4. *to experience one's life* in a certain way: ὑγιαίνειν καὶ εὖ πράττειν 'health and prosperity' 2M 9.19; ἔπραττον καλῶς 'were thriving' 4M 3.20.

5. *to exact payment*: abs., 1M 10.35. Cf. πράκτωρ.

Cf. ποιέω, πρᾶγμα, δια~, προπράσσω: Schmidt 1.397-423; Trench 361-4; Shipp 466-8.

πρατός, ή, όν.ʃ

put on sale: *s* office of high priest, 2M 11.3. Cf. πιπράσκω.

πράττω: ⇒ πράσσω.

πραΰθυμος, ον.ʃ *

of modest disposition: *s* hum., Pr 14.30, 16.19. Cf. πραΰς.

πραΰνω: aor.inf. πραῦναι.ʃ

to reduce the intensity of: αὐτῷ ἀφ' ἡμερῶν πονηρῶν 'some of his hard time' Ps 93.13; + acc., θυμόν 'anger' Pr 18.14. Cf. καταπραΰνω.

πραΰς, εῖα, ΰ.

modest, unassuming: *s* hum., Nu 12.3 (Moses); λαὸν πραῢν καὶ ταπεινόν Zp 3.12, πόδες ~έων καὶ ταπεινῶν 'the feet of the modest and lowly' Is 26.6, ~ν τὸν τρόπον 'gentle of manners' 2M 15.12 (Onias the high priest); ὁ π. ἔστω μαχητής Jl 3.11; messianic king, π. καὶ ἐπιβεβηκὼς ἐπὶ ὑποζύγιον καὶ πῶλον νέον '.. mounted on an ass and a young foal' Zc 9.9; of lowly humble social stratum, Si 10.14 (:: ἄρχοντες); subst. m. pl. ~εῖς γῆς 'the meek of the earth' Jb 24.4, διδάξει ~εῖς Ps 24.9 ('pliable'), thus obedient to God 146.6 (:: sinners), οἱ ~εῖς κληρονομήσουσιν τὴν γῆν 36.11; opp. ὑψηλός 2K 22.28*L*; voice, φωνῇ ~είᾳ 'in a subdued tone' Da LXX 4.16.

Cf. πραΰθυμος, πραΰτης, ταπεινός: Spicq 1947. 324-32; ib. 3.160-71, esp. 166-8; de Romilly.

πραΰτης, ητος. f. Also spelled πραότης (archaic spelling): Es D 7 *L*.

1. human *quality of being* πραΰς (q.v.): applied to Moses Si 45.4, to David Ps 131.1; a virtue pleasing to God, ἡ εὐδοκία αὐτοῦ πίστις καὶ πρ. Si 1.27; in one's relation to the poor, 4.8; ἔλεος καὶ π. 36.28 (as woman's desirable manners of speech).

2. *calm and soothing disposition*: transformed from rage, Es D 7 *L*.

Cf. πραΰς:Trench 148-53; *ND* 4.169f.

πρεπόντως. adv.ʃ

in fitting manner: of speech, 2M 15.12. Cf. πρέπω.

πρέπω

to be becoming, proper: + dat., τοῖς εὐθέσι πρέπει αἴνεσις 'praise befits the upright' Ps 32.1, τῷ οἴκῳ σου πρέπει ἁγίασμα 92.5; ἐν ταῖς πρεπούσαις ἐξομολογήσεσιν 'with appropriate thanksgivings' 3M 7.19. **b**. impers.: καθὼς πρέπει αὐτῷ Si 30.38, καθὼς ἔπρεπεν 3M 3.20; ὡς δέον ἐστὶ καὶ πρέπον 'as is necessary and proper' 1M 12.11.

Cf. πρεπόντως, (προσ)καθήκω.

πρεσβεία, ας. f.ʃ

official journey made on behalf of an individual or body in authority: 2M 4.11.

Cf. πρεσβευτής, πρέσβυς.

πρεσβεῖον, ου. n.ʃ

1. *privilege of seniority in age*: ὁ πρωτότοκος κατὰ τὰ ~α αὐτοῦ Ge 43.33 (:: νεότης); Su 50 TH.

2. *old age*: ἕως γήρους καὶ ~ου Ps 70.18; ἐν ~ῳ 3M 6.1.

Cf. πρεσβύτερος, γῆρας, νεότης: Katz 1960.

πρεσβευτής, οῦ. m.

envoy: 1M 13.21; τῶν Ἰουδαίων 15.17, Ῥωμαίων 2M 11.34, τῶν ἀρχόντων 2C 32.31. Cf. πρέσβυς, πρεσβεία: Spicq 3.172-6.

πρέσβυς, εως. m.

envoy: ἀπέστειλεν .. ~εις πρὸς Σηων βασιλέα Nu 21.21; Ho 5.13; βασιλέως Is 37.6; ‖ ἄγγελος 63.9; ambassador to peace talks, 1M 9.70. Cf. ἄγγελος, πρεσβευτής, πρεσβεία.

πρεσβύτερος, α, ον.

Often subst. **1**. absolutely *old of age*, 'elderly,' *s* alw. person: πατήρ Ge 44.20; glossed as προβεβηκότες ἡμερῶν 'advanced in age' Ge 18.11, 24.1; 19.4; Ex 10.9, De 32.7 (‖ πατήρ), Jl 2.28 (:: νεανίσκος); π. καὶ πλήρης ἡμερῶν Ge 35.29; in leadership position, καθήσονται ~οι καὶ ~αι ἐν ταῖς πλατείαις Ιερουσαλημ, ἕκαστος τὴν ῥάβδον αὐτοῦ ἔχων ἐν τῇ χειρὶ αὐτοῦ ἀπὸ πλήθους ἡμερῶν 'the senior men and women will seat themselves in the streets of J., each holding his own staff in his hand on account of his old age' Zc 8.4; τῷ παιδὶ αὐτοῦ τῷ ~ῳ τῆς οἰκίας αὐτοῦ τῷ ἄρχοντι πάντων τῶν αὐτοῦ 'to his elderly servant of his household in charge of all his affairs' Ge 24.2; πάντες οἱ παῖδες Φαραω καὶ οἱ ~οι τοῦ οἴκου αὐτοῦ καὶ πάντες οἱ ~οι γῆς Αἰγύπτου 50.7; ἐκάλεσεν τοὺς ~ους τοῦ λαοῦ Ex 19.7; τοῖς ἱερεῖς .. καὶ τοῖς ~οις τῶν υἱῶν Ισραηλ De 31.9; commanding respect, 28.50, Wi 8.10 (:: νέος); ‖ ἄρχων Ps 104.22.

2. relatively *older of age*: εἶπεν δὲ ἡ ~ρα πρὸς τὴν νεωτέραν 'the elder said to the younger' Ge 19.31; τὸν υἱὸν αὐτοῦ τὸν ~ον 27.1 (:: ἐλάσσων vs. 6 and νεώτερος 15), ἡμέραις 'in age' Jb 32.4¶; *s* ἀδελφή Ez 16.46 (:: νεώτερος).

Cf. γέρων, νεανίσκος, νέος, πρεσβύτης: Bornkamm, *TDNT* 6.652-4; Tomsin.

πρεσβύτης, ου, voc. ~βῦτα. m.

1. *old man*: ἀπέθανεν .. ἐν γήρει καλῷ π. καὶ πλήρης ἡμερῶν Ge 25.8; De 32.25; ‖ γέρων 4M 7.10; opp. παιδίον Ba 4.15, νεανίσκος Jb 29.8.

2. *person invested with authority*: Nu 10.31. **b**. *envoy*: 2C 32.31.

Cf. πρεσβύτερος, πρεσβῦτις, ἐσχατογήρως, παλαιός.

πρεσβῦτις, ιδος. f.ʃ

elderly woman: 4M 16.14. Cf. πρεσβύτης.

πρήθω: fut.pass. πρησθήσομαι; aor.inf. πρῆσαι; pf. ptc.pass. πεπρησμένος.ʃ

to cause to swell: ***o*** γαστήρ 'belly' Nu 5.22; and pass., κοιλία '(woman's) abdomen' 5.21; pers., πρησθήσεται τὴν κοιλίαν 'she will be swollen in her belly' 5.27.

πρηνής, ές.ʃ

falling forwards: ***s*** edifice, 3M 5.43; hum., prostrating, 5.50; defeated, Wi 4.19.

πρίαμαι: aor.inf. πριάσασθαι, impv.2pl πρίασθε.

to purchase: + dat. pers. and acc. rei, πρίασθε ἡμῖν μικρὰ βρώματα Ge 42.2 Cf. ἀγοράζω, πιπράσκω, πωλέω.

πρί(ζ)ω: aor.act.inf. πρίσαι.ʃ

to cut with saw: + acc. pers. πρίοσι σιδηροῖς τὰς ἐν γαστρὶ ἐχούσας 'pregnant women with iron saws' Am 1.3; with a sword, πρίσαι σε μέσον 'to cut you into halves' Su 59 TH; ὁ σίδηρος ὁ πρίζων πάντα 'an iron tool which saws everything' Da LXX

(967) 2.40 (v.l. δαμάζων). Cf. πρίων, δια~, κατα-πρίζω: *ND* 4.170.

πρίν.

A. adv., *previously*: τῶν πρὶν αὐτῷ μεμηχανημένων 'of the things which he had previously devised against him' 3M 5.28; 6.34. **b**. used attrib.: τὸν π. Αἰγύπτου ταύτης δυνάστην 'formerly the ruler of this Egypt' 3M 6.4; so τὸ π.– οἱ τὸ π. ἐπονείδιστοι 'those who were once considered to be disgraceful' 6.31.

B. *before, prior to*.

I. conj. w. subj. and preceding the main clause: Πρὶν ἐξετάσῃς, μὴ μέμψῃ 'Don't find fault, before you have investigated' Si 11.7 (|| πρὶν ἤ + inf. vs. 8). **b**. w. an inf. aor. πρὶν ἀποθανεῖν με 'before I die' Ge 27.4 (πρὸ τοῦ ἀ. με vs. 7), To 4.2, 14.16 𝔊[I] (πρὸ τοῦ ἀ. 𝔊[II]); πρὶν ἐλθεῖν ἡμέραν κυρίου 'before the day of the Lord comes' Jl 2.31, Ma 4.4; 2M 8.14; precedes the main clause - πρίν σε τελευτῆσαι εὖ ποίει φίλῳ 'Before you die, treat your friend well' Si 14.13.

II. conj. with ἤ: w. a noun – δοῦναι τὴν νεωτέραν π. ἢ τὴν πρεσβυτέραν 'to give (in marriage) a younger before an elder one' Ge 29.26. **b**. w. an inf. aor. - τίκτουσιν π. ἢ εἰσελθεῖν πρὸς αὐτὰς τὰς μαίας 'they deliver before the midwives have got to them' Ex 1.19; Nu 11.33, To 2.4, 3.8, Ju 7.14, Wi 2.8, Si 19.17, 1M 10.4; preceding the main clause - Si 11.8 (|| πρίν + subj., vs. 7), 18.19 (|| πρό), 21, 23, 23.20, Is 7.15, 16, 28.4, 48.5, 65.24; π. ἢ τὴν ὠδίνουσαν τεκεῖν, π. ἐλθεῖν τὸν πόνον τῶν ὠδίνων 'before the woman in labour gives birth, before the pain of labour comes' 66.7. **c**. with no verb following: π. ἢ πρωὶ .. 'before dawn ..' Is 17.14.

III. prep. + gen.: π. γενέσεως αὐτῶν 'before their happening' Su 35a LXX || TH 42.

Cf. πρό: Amigues; Chadwick 131f.

πρῖνος, ου. f.ʃ

holm-oak: Su 58.

πριστηροειδής, ές.ʃ*

resembling a saw: *s* threshing wheel, Is 41.15. Cf. πρίων.

πρίων, ονος. m.ʃ

saw: instrument of torture – ἔπριζον πρίοσι σιδηροῖς τὰς ἐν γαστρὶ ἐχούσας 'they sawed pregnant women with iron saws' Am 1.3; 2K 12.31 = 1C 20.3; *o* of ἕλκω 'to pull' Is 10.15. **b**. *serrated, ragged mountain ridge*: Ju 3.9.

Cf. πρίζω, δια~, ἐκπρίω, πριστηροειδής, βασανιστήριον.

πρό Prep. w. gen.

I. Of time *prior to, before*: **a**. π. τῆς τελευτῆς αὐτοῦ De 33.1(*a*); π. τῶν ἡμερῶν ἐκείνων Zc 8.10(*a*); π. αἰῶνος 'from time immemorial' Ps 73.12(*k*), π. τοῦ αἰῶνος ἀπ' ἀρχῆς ἔκτισέν με Si 24.9, εἷς ἐστιν π. τοῦ αἰῶνος καὶ εἰς τὸν αἰῶνα 42.21(*k*); ὁ θεὸς .. ὁ ὑπάρχων π. τῶν αἰώνων Ps 54.20(*l*); ἀγρὸν π. ὥρας .. ἐθέρισαν 'they harvested the field prematurely' Jb 24.6(†); π. καιροῦ γῆρας 'premature ageing' Si 30.24(*m*); π. ὀλίγου 'shortly before' Wi 14.20, π. μικροῦ 15.8, π. βραχέως 'a short while ago' 4M 9.5. **b**. followed by the genitive of a noun denoting a period of time at the end of which an event denoted by another, immediately following genitive takes place (see Turner, *Syntax*, 260): π. δύο ἐτῶν τοῦ σεισμοῦ 'two years before the earthquake' Am 1.1(*a*); π. τριῶν μηνῶν τοῦ τρυγήτου 'three months before the harvest' 4.7(*b*). **c**. + τοῦ inf. aor.: π. τοῦ γενέσθαι ἐπὶ τῆς γῆς 'before it appeared on the earth' Ge 2.5(*g*); π. τοῦ ἀποθανεῖν με 27.7(*a*) (|| πρὶν ἀποθανεῖν με vs. 4); π. τοῦ ἐπελθεῖν ἐφ' ὑμᾶς ὀργὴν κυρίου 'before the anger of the Lord came upon you' Zp 2.2b(*a*), sim. 2.2a(*e*), c(*d*), Hg 2.15(*f*).

II. Of place *in front of, ahead of*, often as *πρὸ προσώπου τινός, τινος alw. being gen. pers. exc. at Zc 14.20 and 2C 1.13 (v.l. ἀπὸ π.): ὁ ἄγγελός μου προπορεύσεται π. προσώπου σου Ex 32.34(*a*); πορευθῶσιν ἐν αἰχμαλωσίᾳ π. προσώπου τῶν ἐχθρῶν αὐτῶν 'go as captives in front of their enemies' Am 9.4(*c*); Mi 2.13*bis*(*c*), Jl 2.3(*c*), Hb 3.5(*c*), Zc 3.1(*c*), Ma 3.1(*c*); ἐν τῷ π. τοῦ ἱεροῦ πυλῶνος εὐρυχώρῳ 'in the open square before the gate of the temple' 1E 9.41(*a*). **b**. πρὸ ὀφθαλμῶν τινος: ἔσται σοι .. μνημόσυνον π. ὀφθαλμῶν σου Ex 13.9(*h*), ἔσται ἀσάλευτα π. ὀφθαλμῶν σου De 6.8(*h*); Ps 100.3(*j*), Jb 4.16(*j*); fig., ποιῆσαι τὸ εὐθὺς π. ὀφθαλμῶν μου 'to do the right things ..' Je 41.15(*i*), λάθῃ αὐτὸν π. ὀφθαλμῶν 'should escape his notice' Le 5.4(*k*); π. ὀφθαλμῶν λαβόντας τὴν .. ὕβριν 'having visualised .. the outrage' 2M 8.17, λαμβάνοντας π. τῶν ὀφθαλμῶν τὸν κοινὸν ἔλεον 'perceiving the common object of pity' 3M 4.4.

Cf. ἔμπροσθεν, πρίν, ὀπίσω: Sollamo, *Semiprep*., 321-4.

a) לִפְנֵי; *b*) בְּעוֹד; *c*) לִפְנֵי πρὸ προσώπου; *d*) בְּטֶרֶם לֹא; *e*) בְּטֶרֶם; *f*) מִטֶּרֶם; *g*) טֶרֶם; *h*) בֵּין עֵינֵי; *i*) בְּעֵינֵי *j*) לְנֶגֶד עֵינֵי *k*) מִן; *l*) קֶדֶם; *m*) בְּלֹא. xʃ

προάγω: fut. ~άξω; aor.pass. προήχθην, ptc. ~αχθείς.

1. tr. *to move forward* or *onward*: + acc., ἑαυτόν Si 20.27 (fig. of advance in society), Es 2.21 o'; τὰς πορείας σου 'your steps' Pr 4.27b.

2. intr. *to move ahead of*: + gen. pers., *s* lamps, Ju 10.22; + acc. pers., as leader and *s* God, 2M 10.1.

3. intr. *to move on to the next phase*: *s* an event, Es 7.1 *L*; troops, 2M 10.27; pass. = act., 3M 3.16.

4. *to induce* to do: + inf. and pass., Si prol. 12; ἐπιθυμίᾳ προαχθέντες 'led by desire' Wi 19.11.

5. pass. *to excel, distinguish oneself*: Pr 6.8*c*.

Cf. ἄγω, προβαίνω, προέρχομαι.

προαγωνίζομαι.ʃ

to precede sbd as a contestant: ***s*** hum., 4M 17.13. Cf. ἀγωνίζομαι.

προαδικέω: pf.ptc.pass. ~ηδικημένος.ʃ

to wrong previvously: pass., ***o*** hum., Wi 18.2. Cf. ἀδικέω.

προαίρεσις, εως. f.

that which one has selected as desirable, suited: Je 8.4; ~εις καρδίας αὐτῶν 'what their minds fancy' 14.14; 2M 9.27; πνεύματος Ec 1.14 +, cf. Jarick 21f. Cf. προαιρέω.

προαιρέω: aor.mid. προειλόμην, inf. ~ελέσθαι, ptc. act. ~ελών.

1. *to bring forth* sth that has been stored: + acc. rei, enemy's head, ἐκ τῆς πήρας 'out of the bag' Ju 13.15.

2. *to select out of multiple alternatives as desirable, suited*: + acc. pers., ὁ υἱός μου προείλατο τῇ ψυχῇ τὴν θυγατέρα ὑμῶν Ge 34.8; + double acc., με βασιλέα 'me as king' Wi 9.7; ***s*** God - σὲ προείλατο κύριος ὁ θεός σου εἶναι αὐτῷ λαὸν περιούσιον παρὰ πάντα τὰ ἔθνη De 7.6; 7.7 (‖ ἐκλέγομαι); τοὺς πατέρας ὑμῶν προείλατο κύριος ἀγαπᾶν αὐτούς 10.15 (‖ ἐκλέγομαι); ***s*** hum., ***o*** rei, πονηρά Is 7.15 (:: ἐκλέγομαι τὸ ἀγαθόν), τὸν φόβον τοῦ κυρίου Pr 1.29; + inf., 21.25, Wi 7.10, 2M 6.9, 3M 2.30.

Cf. προαίρεσις, ἐκλέγω.

προαλής, ές.ʃ

headstrong: ***s*** child, Si 30.8.

προαναμέλπω.ʃ *

to sing before sbd else does (out of eagerness?): + acc., αἴνους 'songs of praise' Wi 18.9.

Cf. ᾄδω, αἰνέω.

προανατάσσω: aor.mid.subj. ~τάξωμαι.ʃ*

give top priority to: + acc., Ps 136.6.

προανατέλλω.ʃ

to sprout afresh: ***s*** grape-vine, Ez 17.9. Cf. ἀνατέλλω.

προαπαγγελλω: aor.subj. ~γγείλω.ʃ

to draw attention verbally to: + dat.pers. and acc. rei., Ez 33.9 (προπαραγγέλλω 967).

προαποδείκνυμι: pf.ptc.pass. ~δεδειγμένος.ʃ

to mention previously: pass., ***o*** hum., 3M 2.25. Cf. προεῖπον, προδηλόω, προσημαίνω.

προαποθνῄσκω: aor.ptc. ~θανών.ʃ

to die before sbd: 4M 13.18. Cf. θνῄσκω.

προαποστέλλω: pf.ptc.pass. ~απεσταλμένος.ʃ

to send previously: ***o*** missive, Es 7.28 *L*. Cf. ἀποστέλλω.

προασπίζω: aor.opt.1pl ~ασπίσαιμεν.ʃ

to protect from danger: + gen., τῶν νεοττῶν 'the young birds' 4M 14.15; metaph., νόμου 9.15, ‖ νόμον 6.21. Cf. ἀσφαλίζω, προΐστημι, συνασπίζω.

προάστιον, ου. n.ʃ

land outside a town (LSG): pl. τὰ ~α τῶν πόλεων Nu 35.2 (‖ τὰ ὅμορα τῶν πόλεων vs. 5; τὰ συγκυροῦντα τῶν πόλεων vs. 4); 35.7. Cf. ὅμορος, συγκυρέω: Husson 1967.

προβαίνω: aor.subj. ~βῶ; pf. ~βέβηκα, ptc. ~βεβηκώς; plpf. ~βεβήκειν.

intr. *to move forward*: ἐγίνοντο αἱ φωναὶ τῆς σάλπιγγος προβαίνουσαι ἰσχυρότεραι σφόδρα 'the sound of the trumpet kept moving forward with increasing force' Ex 19.19; προβεβηκὼς ἡμερῶν 'advanced in age' Ge 18.11, 24.1 (gloss on πρεσβύτεροι; cf. τῇ ἡλικίᾳ 'in age' Lys. 24.16, τὴν ἡλικίαν 2M 4.40, 6.18, ἐν ταῖς ἡμέραις αὐτῶν Lk 1.7, ἐληλυθὼς ἐν ἔτεσιν 1K 17.12*L*), Jo 13.1, ταῖς ἡμέραις 23.2 (‖ γηράσκω), 3K 1.1 (*L* ἥκων εἰς ἡμέρας); fig. προβαίνων μείζων ἐγίνετο 'achieving progress, he grew in importance' Ge 26.13, sim. Ju 16.23, military 2M 8.8; sarcastically, τὴν ἄνοιαν 'in stupidity' 4.40; ***s*** time elapsing, χρόνος πολύς Jb 2.9, ἡμέρα Jd 19.11 B (A: κλίνω); an affair, 1E 2.24; banquet, 3M 5.18. Cf. προήκω.

προβάλλω: aor. ~έβαλον, impv.2pl ~βάλετε, mid. 2s ~βαλοῦ, ptc.act. ~βαλών.

1. *to place and hold in front of oneself*: + acc., δόρατα 'spears' Je 26.4, τὴν γλῶσσαν 2M 7.10.

2. *to present for consideration*: + dat. pers. and acc. rei, πρόβλημα 'riddle' Jd 14.12 A, λόγους Pr 26.18. **b**. mid. with same meaning: Jd 14.12 B, 13.

3. mid. *to challenge for a debate*: + dat. pers., Pr 22.21.

Cf. Spicq 3.177f.

προβασανίζω: aor.ptc.pass. ~βασανισθείς.ʃ

to torture earlier than sbd else: pass., ***o*** hum., 4M 8.5, 10.16. Cf. βασανίζω.

προβασκάνιον, ου. n.ʃ

scarecrow: in a cucumberfield, Ep Je 69. See Naumann 42.

προβατικός, ή, όν.

pertaining to sheep: ***s*** πύλη, one of the gates of Jerusalem, Ne 3.1. Cf. πρόβατον.

προβάτιον, ου. n.ʃ

dim. of πρόβατον: μικρὰ ~α 1K 17.28*L*.

πρόβατον, ου. n.; also f. w. ref. to mother - Le 22.28. Almost alw. in pl. [sg.: Ge 30.32].

1. *small livestock* as nomad's possessions and of unspecified species: πορευθεὶς εἰς τὰ ~α λάβε μοι ἐκεῖθεν δύο ἐρίφους 'Go into the flocks, get me from there two goats' Ge 27.9; consisting of ἄρνες 'lambs' and αἶγες 'goats' 30.32; ἔριφον αἰγῶν ἐκ τῶν ~ων 'a kid out of the flock' 38.17; cultic offerings and ἀπὸ τῶν ~ων specified as ἀπό τε τῶν ἀρνῶν καὶ τῶν ἐρίφων Le 1.10.

2. *sheep*: offered in cult, Ge 4.4; Ho 5.6 (|| μόσχοι); || αἴξ, μόσχος Le 17.3; τὰ ~α τῆς σφαγῆς Zc 11.4, τῆς νομῆς Je 23.1; part of nomad's possessions - ἐγένετο αὐτῷ ~α καὶ μόσχοι καὶ ὄνοι Ge 12.16 (along with παῖδες καὶ παιδίσκαι, ἡμίονοι καὶ κάμηλοι); ~α καὶ βόες καὶ σκηναί 13.5 (= τὰ ὑπάρχοντα vs. 6), 24.35 (along with silver and gold, male and female servants, camels and donkeys); κτήνη ~ων καὶ κτήνη βοῶν καὶ γεώργια πολλά '.. and many fields' 26.14; + κτῆνος, ἵππος, ὑποζύγιον, κάμηλος, βοῦς Ex 9.3; || ποίμνιον Mi 2.12, Zp 2.6, cf. ποίμνια ~ων Mi 5.8; De 7.13, Jl 1.18 (|| βουκόλια βοῶν); οἱ βόες καὶ τὰ ~α Jn 3.7, cf. Hb 3.17; fig. of people or nation - Ποίμαινε λαόν σου .. ~α κληρονομίας σου Mi 7.14; ὡς ~α λαὸν αὐτοῦ Zc 9.16.

Cf. ἀμνός, ἀρήν, βοῦς, ἵππος, κριός, κτῆνος, ποίμνιον, προβατικός, ὑποζύγιον: Shipp 474.

προβιβάζω: fut. ~βιβάσω; aor.inf. ~βιβάσαι.ʃ

**to teach, instruct*, 'to coach' (BDAG): abs. Ex 35.34; + acc. pers. and rei - αὐτὰ [= τὰ ῥήματα ταῦτα] τοὺς υἱούς σου De 6.7, cf. εἰς ἀρετήν, εἰς ἐγκρατείαν Pl. *Prot.* 328a. Cf. διδάσκω, συμβιβάζω: Caird 1969.29.

προβλέπω.ʃ *

to see beforehand, 'foresee': προβλέπει ὅτι ἥξει ἡ ἡμέρα αὐτοῦ Ps 36.13. Cf. βλέπω, προεῖδον, προοράω.

πρόβλημα, ατος. n.

riddle: Jd 14.12, Hb 2.6, Ps 48.5 (|| παραβολή); συνίων ~ατα Da TH 8.23.

προβλής, ῆτος. m./f.ʃ

Used adj., *jutting out*: *s* tower, 4M 13.6. Cf. πρόκρημνος.

προγίνομαι: pf.ptc. ~γεγονώς.ʃ

1. *to happen before* the event being spoken about: τὰ προγεγονότα αὐτοῖς 'their previous experiences' 2M 15.8; Wi 19.13.

2. *to become before* the event being spoken about: 2M 14.3.

Cf. γίνομαι, προηγέομαι, συμβαίνω.

προγινώσκω: aor.pass. ~εγνώσθην, inf. ~γνωσθῆναι.ʃ

to come to know beforehand: *s* Wisdom, τι Wi 8.8; pass., *o* pers., 6.13, 18.6. Cf. γινώσκω, πρόγνωσις.

πρόγνωσις, εως. f.ʃ *

foreknowledge: Ju 11.19; possessed by God, 9.6. Cf. προγινώσκω.

προγονικός, ή, όν.ʃ

originating from forefathers: *s* πολιτεία '(traditional) way of life' 2M 8.17, δόξα '(ancestral) glory' 14.7. Cf. πατρικός, πρόγονος.

πρόγονος, ον.

subst. *forefather, ancestor*: Si 8.4, 2M 11.25. Del. Si 9.6 v.l. Cf. πατήρ, προγονικός.

προγράφω: aor.impv.pass.3pl ~γραφήτωσαν; pf.ptc. pass. ~γεγραμμένος.ʃ

1. *to notify officially in writing*: 1E 6.31.

2. *to summon officially*: pass., *o* hum., Da LXX 3.3 (or: 'the aforementioned'). Cf. προσκαλέομαι **1**.

3. *to enlist*: for military service, 1M 10.36.

πρόδηλος, ον.ʃ

made manifest in public: *s* ἡ σοφία σου Ju 8.28; inner anguish, τοῖς θεωροῦσι 2M 3.17, enmity 14.39.

προδηλόω: pf.ptc.pass. ~δεδηλωμένος.ʃ

to mention beforehand: τι 3M 4.14. Cf. προαποδείκνυμι, προεῖπον.

προδίδωμι: fut.ptc. ~δώσων.

1. *to part with willingly*: + acc., "both my body and soul for the sake of (περὶ τῶν) the ancestral laws" 2M 7.37. Cf. φείδομαι.

2. *to give up treacherously*: + acc. pers., τὴν πατρίδα 'the fatherland' 4M 4.1; and dat. pers., 4K 6.11. Cf. προδοσία, προδότης, καταπροδίδωμι.

προδοσία, ας. f.ʃ

v.n. of προδίδωμι **1**: Wi 17.12. **b**. *act of refusing to remain associated* or *helpful*: Wi 17.15. Cf. παραδίδωμι.

προδότης, ου. m.

traitor: τῶν νόμων καὶ τῆς πατρίδος 2M 5.15; + πολέμιος 'enemy' 3M 3.24. Cf. προδίδωμι.

πρόδρομος, ον.ʃ

serving as harbinger: subst. ~οι σταφυλῆς 'early grapes' Nu 13.21; σύκου 'of figs' Is 28.4; π. τοῦ στρατοπέδου σου 'advance contingent of your army' Wi 12.8. Cf. LSG s.v. **I 2 c**.

προεῖδον. aor.ʃ

to perceive visually beforehand: προεῖδον αὐτὸν μακρόθεν πρὸ τοῦ ἐγγίσαι αὐτὸν πρὸς αὐτούς 'they had spied him from a distance before he came near to them' Ge 37.18; πάσας τὰς ὁδούς μου προεῖδες Ps 138.3. Cf. προβλέπω, προοράω, εἶδον.

προεῖπον: pf. ~είρηκα, ptc.pass. ~ειρημένος.

to say before: 2M 2.32, τὰ προειρημένα 'what has been said earlier' 14.8; by way of command, 1E 6.31. Cf. προδηλόω, ~λέγω, ~μηνύω, ~σημαίνω, προαποδείκνυμι.

προεκφέρω: aor. προεξήνεγκα.ʃ

to put out forward: *s* a baby leaving his mother's womb - προεξήνεγκεν τὴν χεῖρα Ge 38.28.

προενέχομαι.ʃ*

to be involved in before: + dat. rei, ἁμαρτήμασι 2M 5.18.

προεξαποστέλλω: aor. ~εξαπέστειλα.ʃ

to send out ahead of some major event: + acc. pers., 2M 12.21. Cf. ἐξαποστέλλω.

προέρχομαι: fut. ~ελεύσομαι; aor. προῆλθον, inf. ~ελθεῖν, impv.3s ~ελθέτω.

1. *to move ahead of*: + ἔμπροσθέν τινος – προελθέτω ὁ κύριός μου ἔμπροσθεν τοῦ παιδός Ge 33.14; 33.3; + gen. pers., Ju 2.19, 15.13.

2. *to move forward*: *s* snake, Es A 5. **b**. *to move forward and act*: ἐπὶ τοσοῦτον θράσους .. ὥστε .. 'as audaciously as ..' 3M 2.26.

3. *to move out and expose oneself*: ἐκ τοῦ ἀσύλου 'out of the sanctuary' 2M 4.34. **b**. *to come into view and make appearance*: *s* part of the universe at its creation, Pr 8.24.

Cf. προάγω, προπορεύομαι.

προετοιμάζω: fut. ~μάσω; aor. ~ητοίμασα.ʃ

to prepare beforehand: Is 28.24, Wi 9.8. Cf. ἑτοιμάζω.

προέχω.ʃ

to excel: προέχοντα χαλκᾶ 'top-quality copper-work' 3K 7.17*L*. Cf. ὑπεράγω and ὑπέρκειμαι.

προηγέομαι: aor.ptc. προηγησάμενος.

1. *to take the lead*: 2M 4.40; + gen. 8.23, 11.8; subst. ptc. 1E 8.28, 67; + gen., τοῦ λαοῦ De 20.9; 1E 5.8, 9.12, 2M 8.22; ǁ δυνάστης Si 41.17. **b**. + inf., συντηρεῖν 'in observing' 2M 10.12.

2. *to occur prior to*: + gen., Pr 17.14, cf. 16.18.

Cf. ἡγέομαι, προγίνομαι.

προηγορέω: aor.ptc. ~ηγορήσας.ʃ

speak in defence: + περί τινος 2M 4.48. Cf. προήγορος, κατηγορέω.

προήγορος, ου.ʃ *

one who speaks on behalf of others: 2M 7.2, 4. Cf. προηγορέω, κατήγορος.

προήκω. Pres. with pf. meaning.ʃ

to move forward: τὴν ἡλικίαν προήκων 'advanced in age' 4M 5.4. Cf. προβαίνω.

προθερίζω: pf.ptc.pass. ~τεθερισμένος.ʃ *

to harvest in advance: pass., Jd 15.5 A. Cf. θερίζω.

πρόθεσις, εως. f.

1. *that which is set before God as an offering*: τράπεζα τῆς ~εως *a table on which cultic offerings are set* Ex 39.18; προθήσεις τὴν ~ιν 40.4; προέθηκεν ἐπὶ ^τῆς τραπέζας^ ἄρτους τῆς ~εως ἔναντι κυρίου 40.21. Cf. Pelletier 1960.966-8.

2. *act of setting before God as an offering*: ἄρτων 2M 10.3.

3. *purpose*: 2M 3.8.

Cf. προτίθημι, θέσις.

προθυμέομαι: aor. προεθυμήθην, inf. ~μηθῆναι, ptc. ~μηθείς.

to become enthusiastic about an idea: abs., 1M 1.13; τῷ κυρίῳ 2C 17.16; + inf., 3M 1.8, 1C 29.5; + acc. rei, πάντα ταῦτα 29.17; + dat. pers., σοι (God), ib. Cf. προθυμία, πρόθυμος, ζηλόω, ὀρθρίζω: Rengstorff, *TDNT* 6.694f.

προθυμία, ας. f.ʃ

eagerness: ἐν ἀγαθότητι ~ας ψυχῆς αὐτοῦ 'with the goodness of his eager soul' Si 45.23 (enthusiastic priest). Cf. πρόθυμος, σπουδή: Rengstorff, *TDNT* 6.697f.

πρόθυμος, ον.

eager: ἀετὸς π. εἰς τὸ φαγεῖν 'an eagle eager to eat (its prey)' Hb 1.8; *s* priests, περὶ τὰς τοῦ θυσιαστηρίου λειτουργίας 'for the services at the altar' 2M 4.14; soldiers, 15.9; subst. m. π. τῇ καρδίᾳ 2C 29.31; subst. n., *that which one is eager for* – τὸ ~ον τοῦ βασιλέως κεῖσθαι ἐν ἑτοίμῳ 'what the king was keen on was ready' 3M 5.26. Cf. ἐκτενῶς, προθυμία, ~θύμως: Spicq 3.180-4.

προθύμως. adv.

with eagerness and ardour of attitude: π. καὶ γενναίως .. ἀπευθανατίζειν 'to die well, willingly and nobly' 2M 6.28; eager welcome extended, To 7.8𝔊[I]. Cf. πρόθυμος, θερμῶς, ὀρθρίζω.

πρόθυρον, ου. n.

doorway: with a door (θύρα) further behind it, Ge 19.6; ~α σαλευόμενα 'shaking d.' Zc 12.2; in the temple and ǁ φλιά Ez 43.8; τῶν πυλῶν Ιερουσαλημ Je 1.15. Cf. θύρα.

προΐημι: fut.mid. προήσομαι; 2aor.subj.mid. ~ῶμαι, 2s πρόῃ, ptc.mid. προέμενος.ʃ Alw. in the mid.

1. *to allow with indifference*: + acc. pers. and ǁ ἐάω Jb 7.19; + acc. pers. and inf., οὐ προήσεται ὑμᾶς Φαραω .. πορευθῆναι Ex 3.19.

2. *to give up* or *throw away* sth of value: abs., Jb 27.6 (:: προσέχω, ǁ ἀπαλλάσσω vs. 5); + dat. pers., acc. rei, ἄλλοις ζωήν σου Pr 5.9.

3. *to utter*: + acc., λόγους ἀθεμίτους 'ungodly words' 2M 10.34 (ǁ βλασφημέω), λαλιάν 15.12; + dat. pers., ῥῆσιν Pr 1.23, ῥῆμα 17.27, φωνήν 8.4.

4. *to yield completely* to sth: σεαυτὸν εἰς εὐφροσύνην Pr 30.32; διὰ τὴν εὐσέβειαν .. τὰ σώματα τοῖς πόνοις 'their bodies to the pains .. for the sake of piety' 4M 18.3.

Cf. ἀφίημι.

πρόϊμος, ον. On the spelling (with ο or ω, and with a diaeresis), see Walters 75f., 92f.

early: *s* autumnal rainfall – ὑετὸν .. ~ον καὶ ὄψιμον De 11.14, Je 5.24; Αἰτεῖσθε παρὰ κυρίου καθ' ὥραν ~ον καὶ ὄψιμον 'Ask the Lord in season for the early and late rain' Zc 10.1 (ὑετὸν understood); ὡς σκοπὸν .. ~ον 'like an early watchman' Ho 9.10; σῦκα 'figs' Je 24.2. **b**. n.subst. adv. 'early in the day, at early morn': Is 58.8.

Cf. πρωΐ, πρωϊνός, and ὄψιμος: Shipp 428.

προΐστημι: 2aor. ~έστην, impv.2pl ~στητε; pf. ~έστηκα, ptc.act. προεστηκώς, ~εστώς.

1. *to stand in front of*: as leader and + gen., τοῦ λαοῦ τούτου 1M 5.19; pf.ptc. subst. προεστηκώς 'leader, chief'– τοῦ οἴκου 'butler' 2K 13.17 (glossing παιδάριον, *L* παῖς; || λειτουργός vs. 18), τῆς οἰκίας 'of the household' Am 6.10, τοῦ ἱεροῦ Bel LXX 8, cf. *ND* 4.82.

2. *to guard and protect*: + gen. pers., Is 43.24, 4M 11.27; + gen. rei, ἀλλοτρίας κρίσεως so as to champion a cause not of his own, Pr 26.17; ὁ προεστηκὼς αὐτοῦ 'his patron' 23.5.

Cf. ἵστημι, προστάτης, προσασπίζω.

προκαθηγέομαι.ʃ

to be in a leadership position: 1E 6.11. Cf. ἡγέομαι.

προκάθημαι.

to sit in front: metaph., *s* leader, 1E 1.30 (|| ἄρχων 2C 35.25), elders 1E 9.4; ἐνώπιον πάντων 9.45. Cf. κάθημαι.

προκαθίζω: aor.ptc. ~καθίσας.ʃ

to sit in public: *s* king, 4M 5.1. Cf. καθίζω.

προκακόω: aor.ptc.pass. ~κακωθείς.ʃ *

to treat harshly before: pass., *o* hum., 4M 17.22. Cf. κακόω.

προκαταλαμβάνω: fut.mid. ~λήμψομαι; aor.impv. act.3pl ~λαβέτωσαν, mid. ~κατελαβόμην, subj. ~λάβωμαι, inf. ~λαβέσθαι, impv. ~λαβοῦ; pf.pass. ~κατείλημμαι.

1. *to seize in advance*: military operation, + acc., πᾶν ὅριον αὐτῶν 'all their territory' Ju 2.10; in anticipation of imminent attack, 4.5; τὴν πόλιν 1M 5.44; 2C 17.2. The notion of *in advance* is not always present, the meaning probably being just *to seize, capture*: e.g., *o* city, Jd 9.50A (B: κατα~), 4K 12.18, 1M 9.2, 2M 10.36; troops and horses, 2K 8.4, 1C 18.4.

2. *to act ahead of*: + acc. pers., φυλακάς '(waking up earlier than) night-watches' (?) Ps 76.5; preventively, 1M 6.27.

3. *to grasp securely*: + acc. pers., Ps 78.8 (*s* divine mercy), 3M 2.20.

Cf. κατα~, προ~, λαμβάνω.

προκατασκευάζω.ʃ

mid. *to prepare oneself beforehand*: + inf., Si prol. 35. Cf. κατασκευάζω.

προκατασκιρόομαι: pf.ptc.pass. προκατεσκιρωμένος.ʃ *

to become hardened beforehand: *s* enmity, 3M 4.1. Cf. σκληρύνω.

πρόκειμαι.

1. *to lie ready and set*: lit. τράπεζα προκειμένη Ex 38.9; ἄρτοι προκείμενοι 39.18 (shewbread); fig. πονηρία πρόκειται ὑμῖν 'you have an evil design ready' 10.10. Cf. παράκειμαι **1**.

2. *to be prescribed and applicable*: *s* νόμος Es 1.8 o'.

3. *to precede*: προκειμένη ἐπιστολή 'afore-mentioned letter' Es F 11 o' (or: 'made public').

4. *to be mentally close by*: τὸ προκείμενον 'the business at hand' 3M 5.46.

προκοπή, ῆς. f.ʃ

progress: moral and intellectual, Si 51.17 (economical, societal advance also included?); military, 2M 8.8. Cf. Stählin, *TDNT* 6.704f., 709; Spicq: 3.185-8; *ND* 4.36.

πρόκρημνος, ον.ʃ *

overhanging, jutting out: *s* citadel, 4M 7.5. Cf. προβλής.

προκρίνω: aor. προέκρινα.ʃ

to assess to be of greater value: + gen. and acc., ^σοφίαν^ σκήπτρων 'wisdom more valuable than sceptres' Wi 7.8. Cf. κρίνω.

προλαμβάνω: aor.ptc.pass. ~λημφθείς.ʃ

to seize in advance: prior to protective measures being taken (?), pass., *o* hum., Wi 17.17. Cf. λαμβάνω. Del. Wi 17.11 v.l.

προλέγω.ʃ

to foretell: Is 41.26. Cf. προεῖπον, ~σημαίνω.

προλήνιον, ου. n.ʃ*

vat in front of a winepress: π. ὤρυξα 'I dug ..' Is 5.2. Cf. ληνός: Ziegler 1934.179.

πρόλοβος, ου. m.ʃ

crop of birds for temporary storage of food prior to digestion: Le 1.16.

πρόλογος, ου. m.ʃ

prologue to a literary work: Si prol.

προμαχέω: aor. προεμάχησα.ʃ

to wage a proactive war: Wi 18.21. Cf. μάχομαι.

προμαχών, ῶνος. m. Alw. pl.ʃ

battlement: Je 5.10, 40.4, Ez 4.2, To 13.16.

προμηνύω: aor. προεμήνυσα.ʃ

to indicate beforehand: τι Wi 18.19. Cf. μηνύω, προεῖπον.

προνοέω: aor. προενόησα, pass.inf. ~νοηθῆναι, impv. ~νοήθητι, subj. ~νοηθῶ.ʃ

1. mid. *to take precaution* so as to prevent sth from happening: + ὅπως and a negator, 1E 2.24, + μή and subj., 3M 3.25.

2. mid. *to pay regard* to: ἐπὶ τοὺς θεούς Da 11.37 LXX; ἐν ἐπιθυμίᾳ γυναικός 'woman's desire' ib. **b**. *to give thought to*: τι Pr 3.4; act., περί τινος Wi 6.7; + gen., "to piety wholeheartedly" 4M 7.18. **c**. *to take thought for* sbd's difficulty or danger: + gen., 2M 14.9; act., + gen. and a ἵνα-clause, Wi 13.16.

Cf. πρόνοια, νοέω: Behm, *TDNT* 4.1009-11.

πρόνοια, ας. f.

thought taken for sbd *ahead of what might happen to him*: *s* God, *o* hum. (gen.), ~αν ποιησάμενος ^τοῦ Δανιηλ^ Da 6.18 LXX; divine providence, ἐξ οὐρανοῦ 3M 4.21, θεοῦ 5.30, θεία 4M 13.19, Wi 14.3, 17.2, cf. *ND* 3.143f. Cf. προνοέω.

προνομεύω: fut. ~μεύσω, pass. ~μευθήσομαι; aor. ἐπρονόμευσα, inf. ~μεῦσαι, ptc. ~μεύσας, subj. ~μεύσω, pass. ~μεύθην; pf.ptc.pass. πεπρονομευμένος.

1. *to take as spoils of war*, 'plunder': + acc. pers., Nu 24.17, 31.9; Is 17.14 (|| κληρονομέω), 42.22 (|| διαρπάζω); sheep, Nu 31.32; livestock De 2.35, livestock and spoils 3.7; houses, Is 13.16; τὴν ἰσχὺν αὐτῶν 'their wealth' 10.13, γῆ (+ cogn. dat.) 24.3; cogn. acc., προνομήν De 21.10, Ez 38.12, || σκυλεύω ib.; *s* warrior, Nu 31.32, 53.

2. *to take spoils of war from*: abs. Is 8.3 (|| σκυλεύω); τινα Jd 2.14A (B: κατα~).

Cf. προνομή, καταπρονομεύω, ἁρπάζω, διαρπάζω, λωποδέω, σκυλεύω.

προνομή, ῆς. f.

1. *that which is* or *has been plundered*: men and livestock, πᾶσαν τὴν ~ὴν καὶ πάντα τὰ σκῦλα αὐτῶν ἀπὸ ἀνθρώπων ἕως κτήνους Nu 31.11; αἰχμαλωσίαν .. καὶ σκῦλα .. καὶ ~ήν 31.12; π. σκύλων '.. of spoils' Is 8.1; φάγῃ πᾶσαν τὴν ~ὴν τῶν ἐχθρῶν σου De 20.14; cogn. acc. of προνομεύω, 21.10. **b**. w. ref. to labour force recruited not illegally or by force, but under much pressure, 3K 10.22[a], Caird 1969.30.

2. *act of plundering*: cogn. dat., Is 24.3; 33.23; of women as target, Ju 4.12.

Cf. προνομεύω.

προνουμηνία, ας. f.ʃ*

the day before a new moon: Ju 8.6. Cf. νουμηνία.

προοδηγός, οῦ.ʃ *

one who takes the lead in: *s* God, πολέμου 2M 12.36. Cf. ὁδηγός.

πρόοιδα: ptc. προειδώς.ʃ

to have foreknowledge of: + acc., Wi 19.1; + ὅτι 4M 4.25. Cf. οἶδα.

προοίμιον, ου. n.ʃ

1. *preamble*: Jb 27.1, 29.1.

2. *premonition*: || φόβος Jb 25.2.

προοράω: impf. mid. προωρώμην.ʃ

to look at in front of oneself: προωρώμην τὸν κύριον ἐνώπιόν μου Ps 15.8. Cf. ὁράω.

πρόπαππος, ου.ʃ

great-grandfather: οἱ πατέρες σου οὐδὲ οἱ ~οι αὐτῶν Ex 10.6. Cf. πάππος, πατήρ.

προπάτωρ, ορος. m.ʃ

primal founder: *s* God, 3M 2.21.

προπέμπω: fut. ~πέμψω; aor.subj. ~πέμψω, inf. ~πέμψαι, ptc. ~πέμψας.

1. *to send forth*: + acc. pers., Wi 19.2, εἰς τὸν ᾅδην 2M 6.23.

2. *to escort*: + acc. pers., 1E 4.47, μετ' εἰρήνης 1M 12.4. **b**. *to escort up to a certain point and farewell*, 'to send off': τινα 2K 19.32*L* (B: ἐκπέμπω). Cf. ἐξαποστέλλω **6** and συμπροπέμπω.

Cf. πέμπω, ἐκπέμπω **1b**, προπομπή.

προπέτεια, ας. f.ʃ

reckless attitude: 2K 6.7*L*. Cf. προπετής.

προπετής, ές.ʃ

ever too eager to act, 'reckless, rash': subst.m. ἐν λόγῳ Si 9.18, χείλεσι 'of lips' Pr 13.3, στόμα ~οῦς 10.14. Cf. Spicq 3.189f.

προπίπτω: fut. ~πεσοῦμαι; pf.ptc. ~πεπτωκώς.

1. *to fall prostrate*: *s* worshipper, ἐνώπιόν τινος Ps 21.30, 71.9.

2. *to throw oneself forward*: ἐπὶ τὴν κλίνην 'on to the bed' Ju 13.2.

3. *to fall before the rest*: in battle and *s* hum., 2M 12.39.

Cf. πίπτω, πρόπτωσις, προσκυνέω.

προπομπή, ῆς. f.ʃ

escort of troops for protection: 1E 8.51. Cf. προπέμπω.

προπορεύομαι: fut. ~πορεύσομαι.

1. *to move ahead of*: abs. Pr 4.18; ἔμπροσθέν μου Ge 32.16; προτέρα αὐτῶν 'ahead of them' Nu 10.33; *s* God's angel and + gen., τῆς παρεμβολῆς τῶν υἱῶν Ισραηλ Ex 14.19; Jo 3.6 (|| ἔμπροσθεν τοῦ λαοῦ); πρὸ προσώπου σου Ex 32.34; God, 33.14, De 1.30, 9.3, 31.3, μεθ' ὑμῶν 20.4, μεθ' ὑμῶν ἐν ὑμῖν 31.6; gods, Ex 32.1; hum. leader, 17.5; metaph., ἡ δικαιοσύνη σου Is 58.8.

2. *to move forward*: *s* the sun in its orbit, Jo 10.13.

Cf. προέρχομαι.

πρόποσις, εως. f.ʃ

public drinking-party: Es 7.1*L*. Cf. συμπόσιον, πότος.

προπράσσω: aor.ptc.pass. ~πραχθείς; pf.ptc.pass. ~πεπραγμένος.ʃ

to do before: τὰ προπραχθέντα 'the former deeds' 1E 1.31; 3M 6.27. Cf. πράσσω, ποιέω.

προπτύω: aor.ptc. ~πτύσας.ʃ*

to spit forth: abs., 2M 6.20. Cf. πτύω.

πρόπτωσις, εως. f.ʃ

prostration: 2M 3.21; + νηστεία, κλαυθμός 'fasting, wailing' 13.12. Cf. προπίπτω.

πρόπυλον, ου. n ..

threshold in the entrance, gateway of a building: pl. and of a temple - σεισθήσονται τὰ ~α Am 9.1. Cf. πυλών.

πρός. Prep.

I. with gen., *on the side of, in favour of*: π. ἐμοῦ εἶ Ge 23.13; π. ἐμοῦ ἔσται ὁ ἀνήρ μου 29.34; οὐκ ἔστιν (sc. τὸ πρόσωπον τοῦ πατρὸς ὑμῶν) π. ἐμοῦ ὡς ἐχθὲς καὶ τρίτην ἡμέραν 31.5 (|| π. αὐτόν vs. 2: Muraoka 2001a.20); τῆς διαθήκης .. π. .. τῶν δούλων αὐτοῦ 2M 1.1.

2. *with the approach of*, 'towards': *temporal - τὸ π. δείλης 'towards the evening' Ge 24.63, an extension of local use of similar sense, or possibly **I 3** with a fossilised, adverbial gen. δείλης: see Johannessohn, *Präp*. 259-61.

3. *in the vicinity of*: ἔθηκεν π. κεφαλῆς αὐτοῦ 'put (a stone) where his head would lie' Ge 28.11, sim. 18; γυνὴ κοιμᾶται π. ποδῶν αὐτοῦ 'a woman lay at his feet' Ru 3.8, ἀκαθαρσία αὐτῆς π. ποδῶν αὐτῆς La 1.9; ἀποκαλύψεις τὰ π. ποδῶν αὐτοῦ 'you shall uncover the area round his feet' Ru 3.4. See Johannessohn, *Präp*. 259.

4. marks an agent with a pass. verb: 4M 4.20.

II. with dat., *in close vicinity of*: local - κατῴκει π. τῇ δρυὶ .. 'lived close by the oak ..' Ge 14.13; π. τῇ θύρᾳ τῆς σκηνῆς 18.10. **b**. temporal: ἐπεὶ δὲ ἐγίνετο ὁ ἥλιος π. δυσμαῖς 'when the sun was about to set' Ge 15.17; + inf., ὦσιν π. τῷ τίκτειν 'are about to give birth' Ex 1.16.

2. *in an area in the direction of*: π. δυσμαῖς 'towards the west' De 1.1, Ju 1.7, 2.19.

3. *in addition to*: ἔλαβεν τὴν Μαελεθ .. π. ταῖς γυναιξὶν αὐτοῦ γυναῖκα 'took M. as a wife in addition to his wives (whom he already had)' Ge 28.9 (|| ἐπί τινι 31.50); π. τούτοις 'in addition to these things' 2M 4.9; ὅσα ἐπιτήδεια ἦν π. τῇ τούτων ἐπανορθώσει 'whatever was needed in addition to their reconstruction' 1M 14.34; ἑξήκοντα π. τοῖς τριακοσίοις '360' 2M 4.8.

4. indicates engagement, involvement: π. τῷ παρανόμῳ σπλαγχνισμῷ τεταγμένοι 'charged with the unlawful eating of intestines' 2M 6.21, π. ταῖς κλήσεσι τεταγμένος 'charged with the invitations' 3M 5.14; γίνεσθαι π. τοῖς ἰδίοις 'to busy yourselves with your own affairs' 2M 11.29, τὸν π. τῇ τῶν ἐλεφάντων ἐπιμελείᾳ 'who was in charge of the care of elephants' 3M 5.1.

III. with acc., *in the direction of, towards*: with verbs of physical movement such as coming, entering, approaching and mostly w. acc. pers., ἀποκαθίστημι Ma 4.5*bis*; ἀποστέλλω Ho 5.13; ἐγγίζω Ge 27.22 (|| + dat. vs. 21), Jn 3.6; εἰσάγω Ge 39.17 (|| + dat. vs. 14); εἰσδέχομαι Hb 2.5; εἰσέρχομαι Ge 6.20, Ho 7.1; ἐκκλίνω Ge 18.5; ἐξαποστέλλω 25.6, Hg 1.12; ἐξέρχομαι Ge 19.6; ἐπιστρέφω Ho 2.7, Am 4.8 +; ἐπισυνάγω Hb 2.5; ἔρχομαι Jn 2.8; καταβαίνω Hg 2.22; πορεύομαι Ho 5.13; προσάγω Ma 1.7 ('to bring'), 3.5 ('to draw near'); προσέρχομαι Jn 1.6; σπεύδω Mi 4.1; συνάγω Ge 6.21. See also π. τὸ ἀποτρέχειν ἐκ τοῦ ζῆν εἰμι 'I am about to take leave of this life' To 14.3 𝔊[I], γενόμενος π. τὸ (v.l. τῷ) τελευτᾶν 'having come near the time of death' 2M 7.14, and π. τὸν ἄνδρα σου ἡ ἀποστροφή σου Ge 3.16. Cf. δεσμεύων π. ἄμπελον τὸν πῶλον αὐτοῦ 'tying his colt to a vine' Ge 49.11 (|| + dat., τῇ ἕλικι 'to a tendril'); π. αὐτὸν ἰδών 'having cast his glance towards him' 2M 7.16. **b**. w. acc. rei, ἀπέρχομαι (+ π. τὰ ἔργα αὐτοῦ) Ex 5.4; πίπτω (+ π. τὴν γῆν) 2M 3.27; π. τέλος ἀφικομένων ἡμῶν τῶν ἁμαρτιῶν 'after our sins having reached their height' 6.15; fig., ἐτρέπετο π. τὴν εὐχωρίαν 'he turned to the feasting' 3M 5.3; γενέσθαι π. τὴν τῶν ἰδίων ἐπιμέλειαν 'get involved with their own affairs' 2M 11.23. **c**. with no movement implied - *situated in the direction of*: εἰς γῆν π. λίβα 'into the southern region' Ge 20.1, ἐν τῇ γῇ τῇ π. λίβα 24.62; ἐν τῇ γῇ τῇ π. νότον Nu 13.30, 1M 5.65; π. ἀνατολάς .. π. θάλασσαν .. π. βορρᾶν .. π. νότον Zc 14.4; Nu 2.10, 25 (|| παρὰ θάλασσαν 2.18); ἐκ τοῦ κλίτους τοῦ π. βορρᾶν 'on the north side' Ex 26.18, κατὰ τὸ μέρος τὸ π. θάλασσαν 'to the west side' 26.22; π. δίφρους κάθηται 'he is spending a penny' Jd 3.24A.

2. with verbs of speaking, addressing, etc.: + πρός τινα - ἀναβαίνει κραυγή Jn 1.2; ἀναβοάω 1.5; ἀποκαλύπτω Am 3.7; ἀποκρίνομαι Hb 2.2; βοάω Ho 7.14; γογγύζω Ex 17.3; γράφω 1M 11.31; διαμαρτύρομαι Zc 3.6; διαστέλλω 'to specify' Ge 30.28; ἐντέλλομαι Ex 12.50, Ma 4.6; ἐπαινέω Ge 12.15; αἰνεῖν ἐφημερίαν π. ἐφημερίαν Ne 12.24 (double chorus?); ἐπικαλέω Ho 7.7; εὔχομαι 2M 9.13; θρηνέω Jl 1.8; καταλαλέω Ma 3.16; κατηγορέω 1M 7.6; κράζω Mi 3.4, Jl 1.14; λαλέω Ge 23.8, Ho 12.4; λαλέω ἀλήθειαν Zc 8.16; λέγω Ho 1.2; λοιδορέω Ex 17.2; προσεύχομαι Jn 2.2; ἔρχεται προσευχή Jn 2.8, cf. οὐκ ἦραν π. τὸν θεὸν τὰς χεῖρας αὐτῶν 'they did not raise their hands to God' Mi 2.1; π. ἑαυτὸν ἀντιβάλλων τὸ γεγονὸς περὶ αὐτὸν ἐλάττωμα 'asking himself about the defeat sustained' 2M 11.13. **b**. Also belong here the standing formulae introducing divine communication: ἐγενήθη ῥῆμα κυρίου π. Αβραμ Ge 15.1; ἐγένετο (or ἐγενήθη) λόγος κυρίου πρός τινα, Ho 1.1 +. See also οὗτος ὁ λόγος κυρίου π. Ζοροβαβελ 'this is the word of the Lord addressed to Z.' Zc 4.6; ἡ ἐντολὴ αὕτη π. ὑμᾶς 'this commandment is addressed to you' Ma 2.1; of clapping hands in applause, Am 6.5.

3. with verbs of seeing and looking, *in the direction of, towards*: ἀναβλέπω Jl 1.20, ἐπιβλέπω Ho 11.4; hopefully, ἐλπίζω 12.6; ἴδε π. βορρᾶν καὶ λίβα .. Ge 13.14, εἶδον θεὸν πρόσωπον π. πρόσωπον 'I saw God face to face' 32.30, sim. Jd 6.22; ὀφθαλμοὶ π. ὀφθαλμοὺς ὄψονται Is 52.8, cf. ὀφθαλμοῖς κατ' ὀφθαλμοὺς ὀπτάζῃ 'you are seen, your eyes meeting ours' Nu 14.14, λαλήσει στόμα αὐτοῦ π. στόμα αὐτοῦ, καὶ ὀφθαλμοὶ αὐτοῦ τοὺς ὀφθαλμοὺς αὐτοῦ ὄψονται Je 39.4 and στόμα κατὰ στόμα λαλήσω αὐτῷ Nu 12.8. Cf. also the formula indicating an epiphany: ὤφθην π. Αβρααμ 'I appeared to A.' Ex 6.3 (‖ + dat. pers., Ge 12.7), ὀφθῆναι π. Μανωε καὶ π. τὴν γυναῖκα αὐτοῦ Jd 13.21, ὤφθη ἡ δόξα κυρίου π. αὐτούς Nu 20.6 (‖ + dat. pers., Le 9.23).

4. with verbs of contesting: ἰσχύω Ps 12.5, ἐνισχύω Ho 12.3; δύναμαι Ge 32.25, ἠδυνάσθησαν π. σὲ ἄνδρες εἰρηνικοί σου 'your allies prevailed against you' Ob 7 (sim. in Je 1.19, 15.20, 45.5); πρός τι - οὐ μὴ δύνωμαι π. αὐτήν [= γνῶσιν] 'I shall never be able to cope with it' Ps 138.6. Cf. οἱ τέσσαρες βασιλεῖς π. τοὺς πέντε 'the four kings against the five' Ge 14.9; πολεμέω 1M 3.10; συναθροίζω 1.52 (pass.); συνάγω 2.42 (pass.); συνάπτω πόλεμον 5.7; τὴν π. τοὺς Γαλάτας παράταξιν 2M 8.20; ἀσφαλεία π. τοὺς ἐναντιουμένους 'security against the enemies' 1E 8.51. Cf. μηχανὰς π. τὰς μηχανάς αὐτῶν 'engines to match theirs' 1M 6.52. **b**. juridical: συλλογιεῖται π. τὸν κεκτημένον αὐτόν 'he shall calculate with his purchaser' Le 25.50, cf. διαλογίζεσθαι πρός τινα 'to balance accounts with sbd' Demos. 52.3 and τί τὸ ἄχυρον π. τὸν σῖτον; 'how does straw compare with corn?' Je 23.28; διακρίνομαι Jl 3.2; κρίνομαι Ho 2.2, Mi 6.1; κρίμα πρός τινα Ho 5.1; κρίσις τινί πρός τινα 4.1, 12.2, Mi 6.2; τὰ π. τὸν θεόν '(legal) matters pertaining to God' Ex 18.19; of rising up against sbd, ἀνθίστημι Ho 14.1; of sinning against sbd, ἁμαρτάνω Ge 44.32, Ex 23.33.

5. marks a personal entity with which a relationship is established, maintained, etc.: διατίθημι διαθήκην 'to establish a covenant' Zc 11.10; στήσω τὴν διαθήκην μου π. σέ Ge 6.18; τοῦ εἶναι τὴν διαθήκην μου π. τοὺς Λευίτας 'that my covenant might be with the Levites' Ma 2.4; συμπλακήσεται ἡ χεὶρ αὐτοῦ π. χεῖρα τοῦ πλησίον αὐτοῦ 'his hand will be clasped with his neighbour's hand' Zc 14.13; συνθέσθαι π. αὐτὸν εἰρήνην 1M 9.70; συντηρεῖν φιλίας π. ἡμᾶς 10.20, συντηροῦσι τὰ π. ἡμᾶς δίκαια 'fulfil their obligations to us' 11.33; τὴν .. π. τὸν ἄνδρα γνῶσιν 'the .. acquaintance with him' 2M 6.21; ἡ ἐλπὶς ὑμῶν ἡ πρὸς τὸν ᾅδην 'the hope you are pinning on (your pact with) Hades' Is 28.18; κοπιάσουσι πρὸς λαόν 'will be working hard on a people (to get some benefit out of them)' 30.5.

6. *being disposed* or *acting towards* sbd in a certain way: Τίς π. κύριον; 'Who is for the Lord?' Ex 32.26; πορεύησθε πρός με πλάγιοι 'you behave perversely towards me' Le 26.23; ἔλεος καὶ οἰκτιρμὸν ποιεῖτε πρὸς τὸν ἀδελφὸν αὐτοῦ Zc 7.9, οὐκ ἦν π. αὐτόν ὡς ἐχθὲς καὶ τρίτην ἡμέραν 'it [= his countenance] was not like before towards him' Ge 31.2 (‖ π. ἐμοῦ 31.5); ἐξίσταντο οἱ ἄνθρωποι ἕκαστος π. τὸν ἀδελφὸν αὐτοῦ 'the men looked at one another in consternation' 43.33, ἐταράχθησαν π. ἀλλήλους 'they were disturbed ..' 42.28; ἔλπιζε πρὸς τὸν θεόν σου Ho 12.6; χάριν τῆς ἐξ αὐτῶν εὐνοίας π. ἡμᾶς 'on account of their goodwill towards us' 1M 11.33, διὰ τὴν ἀρχαίαν π. αὐτοὺς φιλίαν 'because of the old friendship towards them' 2M 6.22; ἀπεχθῆ π. τοὺς πολίτας Ἰουδαίους ἔχων διάθεσιν 'having a hostile attitude towards the Jewish citizens' 5.23. Cf. οὐκ ἔστιν ἡ ψυχή μου π. αὐτούς 'my heart is not with them' Je 15.1. **b**. unfavourably, hostility implied: "I am against (πρός) the prophets who prophesy false dreams' Je 23.32; 23.31.

7. *in comparison with*: ἐμεγαλύνθη .. πενταπλασίως π. τὰς ἐκείνων 'was five times larger .. in comparison with theirs' Ge 43.34; Si 25.19.

8. *in* numerical *proportion to*: π. ταῦτα ἀποδώσει 'he shall pay in proportion to (the number of) these (years)' Le 25.50, π. ταῦτα μνήσθητί μου Ne 13.22. Cf. π. τὴν ἀφροσύνην αὐτοῦ 'matching his folly' Pr 26.4 (‖ vs. 5 κατὰ τὴν ~ην αὐτοῦ).

9. *with regard to, concerning*: πάντα, ὅσα ἂν ἐντείλωμαί σοι π. τοὺς υἱοὺς Ισραηλ 'all that I might command you with regard to the children of Israel' Ex 25.21; τὰ π. τὸν πλησίον 'matters concerning the neighbour' Le 6.2; ἐντολάς, ἃς ἐνετείλατο κύριος τῷ Μωυσῇ π. τοὺς υἱοὺς Ισραηλ 27.34; τὰ π. κύριον De 9.7, 24, τὰ π. τὸν θεόν 31.27; Jo 23.14.

10. *for the purpose of*: μίσθωμα πόρνης .. π. πᾶσαν εὐχήν 'a harlot's fee.. towards any vow' De 23.18; ὠχύρωσεν αὐτὴν π. ἀσφάλειαν τῆς χώρας 'fortified it for the security of the area' 1M 14.37; + inf., π. τὸ πεῖσαι τὸν βασιλέα 'in order to persuade the king' 2M 4.45, οὐδὲ π. τὸ θάψαι οἱ ζῶντες ἦσαν ἱκανοί 'nor were the living present in sufficient numbers to bury them [= the casualties]' Wi 18.12; ἱκανοὺς π. τὴν τούτων πολιορκίαν 'sufficient for the purpose of besieging them' 10.19; τὰ λοιπὰ π. εὐωχίαν ἐπιτήδεια 'the other things necessary for the celebration' 3M 6.30. **b**. w. weakened final force, alm. epexegetical: "we followed.. Jonadab's instruction not to drink wine (π. τὸ μὴ πιεῖν οἶνον)" Je 42.8, sim. 42.14, 49.13, 51.5, Ba 1.19.

11. *meant for the duration of*: πρὸς καιρόν (for π. καιρὸν βραχύν or ὀλίγον?) 'for now' Pr 5.3 (‖ ὕστερον), Wi 4.4, cf. πρόσκαιρος; BDAG s.v. **1a** ad fin.

12. *in view of*: π. τὰς χρείας αὐτοῦ 'in view of the services rendered by him' Si 38.1; π. ταῦτα 4M 6.22.

13. *in accordance with*: π. ὃ ἀπέστειλεν .. οὕτως .. 'in accordance with what he had instructed through a message ..' 2E 6.13 (‖ κατακολουθέω 1E 7.1); π.

ἀλήθειαν 4M 6.18; 7.21. **b.** πρὸς καιρόν 'at the right moment, in due season' Ec 10.17, cf. εὐκαίρως Gregory ad loc. (Jarick 271).

14. *in the proximity* or *company of, at the home of*: π. τὸ ὅριον αὐτῆς 'near its border' Is 19.19, ἐπὶ Δάφνης τῆς π. Ἀντιόχειαν κειμένης 'at D. situated near A.' 2M 4.33; τὰ π. τὸν πλησίον ἐν παραθήκῃ 'things which are at the neighbour's in trust' Le 6.2; ἕτεραι νεογνὰ π. μαστοὺς ἔχουσαι βρέφη 'others having newborn babes at their breasts' 3M 5.49; "birds form a colony with those like themselves" Si 27.9.

15. *approximately, in the region of*: + a numeral, 2M 4.40.

16. *near the beginning* of a period of time, *shortly prior to* a point in time: π. ὄρθρον 'towards daybreak' Ex 19.16, π. τὸν ὄρθρον Jd 19.26B; π. ἡμέραν Ex 14.27, Es 2.14 o'; *τὸ π. ὀψέ = ὀψέ Ge 24.11; τὸ π. πρωί = πρωί Ps 45.6, Jd 19.26 A; π. ἑσπέραν 'towards evening' Ex 12.6 (‖ τὸ π. ἑσπέραν 16.12, De 23.11), Zc 14.7; π. ἡλίου δυσμάς 'towards the sunset' Jo 10.27.

17. marks an entity to which sth properly belongs: "the collection of monies was up to him" 2M 4.28.

IV. adv., *besides, over and above*: καὶ πρὸς ἐπὶ τούτοις πικρὰ ἀκούσῃ 'to cap it all, you end up hearing hard things said to you' Si 29.25; νέα π. παλαιά 'new ones as well as old ones' Ct 7.14; 1.16.

Cf. Johannessohn, *Präp.* 259-71.

προσάββατον, ου. n.ʃ *

pre-sabbath: ἡμέρα τοῦ ~ου Ps 92.1; Ju 8.6. Cf. σάββατον.

προσαγγέλλω: aor. ~ήγγειλα, inf. ~αγγεῖλαι, subj. pass. ~αγγελῶ, ptc.pass. ~αγγελείς.

to inform orally: + dat. pers., περί τινος Ju 10.18, 3M 5.10; + περὶ τοῦ inf., 2M 3.6; + acc. rei (military intelligence),13.21. Cf. ἀναγγέλλω.

προσαγορεύω: fut. ~ρεύσω; aor. προσηγόρευσα, pass.ptc. ~ρευθείς.ʃ

1. *to address* sbd *by saying*: + dat. pers. and acc. rei, εἰρηνικὰ αὐτοῖς καὶ συμφέροντα αὐτοῖς 'friendly and helpful words' De 23.6.

2. *to call by the name of*: + double acc.– τὰ τοσαῦτα κακὰ εἰρήνην προσαγορύουσιν 'they call such great evils peace' Wi 14.22; 2M 1.36, pass. 1M 14.40, 2M 4.7, 10.9.

Cf. προσλαλέω, φωνέω, καλέω **2**.

προσάγω: fut. ~άξω, pass. ~αχθήσομαι; aor. ~ήγαγον, impv. προσάγαγε, subj. ~αγάγω, inf. ~αγαγεῖν, mid. ~ηγαγόμην, impv. ~αγάγου, pass. ~ήχθην; pf.3pl προσαγειόχασιν (on the spelling, see under ἄγω).

1. tr. *to bring*: abs., + dat. pers., μοι Ge 27.25; + acc., Προσάγαγέ μοι αὐτούς 48.9; + πρός and acc., προσηγαγόμην ὑμᾶς πρὸς ἐμαυτόν Ex 19.4, also mid. with πρός and refl. pron. acc. - 28.1, Nu 16.5*bis*, 9, 18.2; πρὸς τὸ κριτήριον τοῦ θεοῦ Ex 21.6; ἐπὶ τὰς θύρας 29.3, 40.10; prayer to God, To 12.12; legal case (κρίσις), Nu 27.5; *o* cultic offering, Ma 1.7 (πρὸς τὸ θυσιαστήριον), 8, 3.3; τῷ κυρίῳ Le 19.21 (‖ φέρω 5.15), Ma 2.12; δῶρα τῷ κυρίῳ Le 1.2 (‖ προσφέρω, sim. Nu 28.3 ‖ vs. 2); ἔναντι κυρίου Le 10.19, ἐνώπιόν τινος (distinguished guest; 'foods' understood) 1K 28.25; pass. θυμίαμα προσάγεται τῷ ὀνόματί μου Ma 1.11. **b.** idiom. τὰς χεῖράς τινι 'to assail sbd' 1M 15.25, see LSJ s.v. χείρ **II 4 d**.

2. intr. *to draw near, come up to*: Ex 3.4 (‖ ἐγγίζω vs. 5), 2K 15.5*L* (B: ἐγγίζω), Ex 14.10 (with hostile intention), πρός με Ez 44.15 (cultic), Is 48.16; πρὸς τὴν πόλιν Jo 8.5; ἐπὶ τὸ τύμπανον 'to the rack' 2M 6.19; ἐγγύς τινος De 2.19; *s* soldiers, Jl 3.9, εἰς πόλεμον Je 26.3, ἐπὶ φρούριον 'fortress' 2M 13.19; God for a punitive action, πρὸς ὑμᾶς Ma 3.5; + dat., θηρίοις 'wild animals' Si 12.13 (‖ προσπορεύομαι); + dat. pers., αὐτῇ To 6.15 𝔊[I] (𝔊[II] ἐγγίσαι αὐτῆς: so as to have sexual intercourse); ὧδε 'hither' Jo 3.9.

Cf. κατάγω, προσφέρω, ἐγγίζω: Schmidt, *TDNT* 1.131-3.

προσαιτέω: fut. ~αιτήσω.ʃ

to beg as a beggar: abs., Jb 27.14. Cf. προσδέομαι.

προσαναβαίνω: fut. ~βήσομαι; aor. ~ανέβησα, inf. ~βῆναι, ptc. ~βάς.

to ascend towards: abs. 2M 10.36; + acc. loc., τὸ ὄρος Ju 13.10, cf. πρὸς τὸ ὄρος Ex 19.23; *s* τὰ ὅρια 'the boundaries' Jo 15.3. Cf. ἀναβαίνω, προσανάβασις.

προσανάβασις, εως. f.ʃ

ascending road: Jo 15.3, 7. Cf. προσαναβαίνω.

προσαναλέγομαι: aor.ptc. ~λεξάμενος.ʃ*

to recount in addition: + dat. pers. and acc. rei, 2M 8.19. Cf. διηγέομαι.

προσαναπαύω: fut.mid. ~παύσομαι.ʃ

mid. *to find rest in the company of*: inner rest, + dat., ^τῇ σοφίᾳ^ Wi 8.16. Cf. ἀναπαύομαι.

προσαναπληρόω: aor.subj. ~πληρώσω.ʃ

to add further to that which is already present: τινί τι Wi 19.4. Cf. προστίθημι.

προσανατρέπω: fut.~τρέψω.ʃ*

to give an extra push to: τινα Si 13.23.

προσαναφέρω: fut. ~ανοίσω; aor.pass.inf. ~ανενεχθῆναι.ʃ *

to bring sth to the attention of a higher authority: + acc., τὰς προσευχὰς τῶν ἁγίων To 12.15 𝔊[I]; + dat. pers., τῷ βασιλεῖ 2M 11.36; to a commander, Ju 11.36.

προσανοικοδομέω: fut.pass. ~μηθήσομαι.ʃ*
to add an extension to one's dwelling: metaph. and pass. Si 3.14, cf. Caird 1969.30. Cf. οἰκοδομέω.

προσαξιόω: aor. ~ηξίωσα.ʃ
to put a request to: τινα and inf., 3M 7.10. Cf. ἀξιόω.

προσαποθνήσκω: fut. ~θανοῦμαι.ʃ
to die in addition: *s* the owner of a bull together with the beast, Ex 21.29. Cf. ἀποθνήσκω.

προσαπόλλυμι: aor.inf. ~απολέσαι.ʃ
to cause to perish: abs., 2M 13.4. Cf. ἀπόλλυμι.

προσαποστέλλω: aor.ptc. ~στείλας.ʃ
to send emissary to sbd: dat. pers., 2M 11.13. Cf. ἀποστέλλω.

προσαπωθέω.ʃ *
to reject: + ***o*** hum. (in need) and pass., Si 13.21 (:: στηρίζω 'support'). Cf. ὠθέω.

προσαρτίως. adv.ʃ *
only recently: 3M 1.19. Cf. ἀρτίως, νεωστί, προσφάτως.

προσασπίζω: aor.opt.1pl ~ασπίσαιμεν.ʃ
to stand up in defence of: + acc., τὸν νόμον 4M 6.21. Cf. προΐστημι.

προσβαίνω: aor. ~έβην, inf. ~βῆναι.
to ascend: from Babylon to Jerusalem, 1E 8.1 (‖ ἀνα~ vs. 3), 4.53. **b**. *to ascend and approach*: + dat., ταῖς κορυφαῖς τῶν ὀρέων 'the mountain tops' Ju 7.10.
Cf. πρόσβασις, ἀναβαίνω.

προσβάλλω: aor.ptc. ~βαλών.
1. *to make go at and attack*: + acc. and dat., σοι .. ἀλάστορα '.. avenger' 4M 11.23.
2. *to mount an attack*: abs. and military 2M 10.28; + dat., 10.17, 35; *s* troops, + dat. pers., 12.10, 13.23; gale winds, + εἰς τὴν θάλασσαν Da TH 7.2.
Cf. προσβολή, ἐπιτίθημι.

πρόσβασις, εως. f.
1. *path for ascending*: Ju 4.7.
2. *rise and increase*: ἀλλοφυλισμοῦ (‖ Ἑλληνισμοῦ) 'of alien culture' 2M 4.13.
3. *act of moving towards the target*: 3M 1.26.
Cf. προσβαίνω, ἀνάβασις.

προσβλητός, ή, όν.ʃ *
beaten (?): *s* ἀργύριον 'silver' Je 10.9. Cf. ἐλατός.

προσβολή, ῆς. f.ʃ
military *attack*: 2M 5.3 (+ καταδρομή), 15.19. Cf. προσβάλλω.

προσγελάω: fut. ~λάσω; aor.subj. ~λάσω.
to laugh towards, smile at: + dat. pers., 1E 4.31 (‖ simp.), Si 13.6. Cf. γελάω.

προσγίνομαι: aor.subj. ~γένωμαι, ptc. ~γενόμενος; pf.mid.ptc. ~γεγενημένος.ʃ
to attach oneself to an existing community: προσήλυτος 'as a new member' Le 18.26 (:: ἐγχώριος), 20.2, Nu 15.14. Cf. προσέρχομαι, προσήλυτος, κολλάω.

προσδεκτός, ή, όν.ʃ *
deserving acceptance or *approval*: *s* hum., + dat. pers., Pr 11.20, 16.15; deeds, Wi 9.12. Cf. δεκτός, προσδέχομαι.

προσδέομαι: fut. ~δεηθήσομαι; aor. ~εδεήθην, subj. ~δεηθῶ.
1. *to be in need of*: material help and abs., Si 4.3; + gen., ἀντιλήμψεως 'help; support' 11.12, συμβούλου 'advisor' 42.21, ἄρτου Pr 12.9; 1K 21.16*L* (B: ἐλαττόομαι).
2. *to beg* for material help, abs. and *s* the poor, Si 13.3. **b**. pass. *to be reduced to begging*: Si 18.32.
Cf. δέομαι, προσαιτέω.

προσδέχομαι: fut. ~δέξομαι, pass. ~δεχθήσομαι; aor. ~εδεξάμην, impv. ~δέξαι, inf. ~δέξασθαι, opt. pass.1pl ~δεχθείημεν.
1. *to receive approvingly* or *favourably*: + acc. rei, cultic offerings, θυσίαν οὐ προσδέξομαι ἐκ τῶν χειρῶν ὑμῶν Ma 1.10, sim. Ho 8.13, Am 5.22, Ma 1.13; σάββατα Le 26.43; τὸ πρόσωπόν μου Ge 32.21; τὴν προσευχήν μου Ps 6.10; ***o*** one who offers cultic offerings, Ma 1.8 (‖ λαμβάνω πρόσωπόν τινος); guests, Is 55.12; food, Jb 33.20; *ἔν τινι, Mi 6.7 (Hebraism); not favourably, ἀπεχθῶς 'with hostility' Wi 19.15 (‖ εἰσδέχομαι vs. 16).
2. *to pardon*: ἁμαρτίαν Ex 10.17.
3. *to assent*: οὕτως προσδέξεται 'he shall assent thereto' Ex 22.11. Cf. ὁμοιόω **3**, συναινέω, συνάλλαγμα.
4. *to anticipate*: + acc. (undesirable event), Ez 32.10, 2M 8.11; + inf., Wi 14.29.
5. *to look forward to*: abs., Ps 103.11 (on the following εἰς δίψαν, see under δίψα); + acc., τὸν σῴζοντά με 54.9, τὸν ἥλιον Jb 2.9d, τὸν ὑετόν 'rain' 29.23, τινα 2K 15.28*L*; pass., ***o*** salvation, Wi 18.7; + inf., Da 7.25 LXX (TH ὑπονοέω); sarcastically (?), 2M 3.38.
Cf. βούλομαι, (παρα)δέχομαι, προσδοκάω, προσδεκτός, εὐδοκέω, θέλω, and λαμβάνω.

προσδέω: aor. προσέδησα.ʃ
to tie and fasten to: + acc., ὀργάνῳ 'to an instrument (of torture)' 4M 9.26. Cf. I δέω.

προσδίδωμι: impf. προσεδίδουν; aor. προσέδωκα, ptc. προσδούς.
to give in addition: προσέδωκέν μοι καὶ τοῦτον 'gave this also to me' Ge 29.33; προσδόντες καὶ ἔριφον 'giving also a kid' To 2.12 𝔊[I]; "she would even pay her pimps (a share of) what she collected as her fees" Ez 16.33. Cf. δίδωμι.

προσδοκάω: impf. προσεδόκα; aor. προσεδόκησα.ʃ
1. *to look forward to*: + acc. rei, τὸ σωτήριόν σου 'your salvation' Ps 118.166, ἔλεος Wi 12.22, ἡμέρα

(the day of victory) La 2.16, νίκη 'victory' 2M 15.8, πρωΐαν 'daybreak' 3M 5.24, ἐλπίς (of resurrection) 2M 7.14, τὸ ἀποβησόμενον 'what might happen' 9.25, τὴν ἐσομένην κρίσιν 'the imminent outcome' 15.20; + inf. τοὺς προπεπτωκότας ἀναστῆναι 'for the fallen to rise again' 12.44; πρός τινα and inf. - πρὸς σὲ προσδοκῶσιν δοῦναι τὴν τροφὴν αὐτοῖς 'for you to give them food' Ps 103.27; pass., *o* ὡς ὑετὸς τὸ ἀπόφθεγμά μου 'like rain my pronouncement' De 32.2.

2. *to anticipate*: *o* unfavourable circumstance – ὀνειδισμὸν .. καὶ ταλαιπωρίαν 'humiliation .. misery' Ps 68.21.

Cf. προσδοκία, προσδέχομαι, ἀπροσδόκητος: Schmidt 3.587-9; Harl, *Langue*, 129f.

προσδοκέω. ⇒ ~δοκάω.

προσδοκία, ας. f.

1. *what is expected, what one looks forward to*: Ge 49.10, Ps 118.116. **b**. *what one anticipates*: anxiously – ἐπίνοια ~ας, ἡμέρα τελευτῆς Si 40.2; 2M 3.21, 3M 5.41, 49.

2. *act of looking forward*: Wi 17.13.

Cf. προσδοκάω.

προσεγγίζω: fut. ~εγγιῶ; aor. προσήγγισα, inf. ~εγγίσαι, ptc. ~εγγίσας, subj. ~εγγίσω.

1. intr. *to move near to*: abs., Ge 33.6, De 20.2; πρὸς τὸ θυσιαστήριον Le 2.8; πρὸς τὰ ἅγια 'the sanctuary' Nu 8.19; πρός τινα Ez 18.6; + dat. pers., Da 9.21 LXX, + dat. loci, To 6.10 $\mathfrak{G}^{I}$; εἰς πόλεμον Jd 20.23 A.

2. tr. *to cause to move near to*: + acc. (food offered), Jd 5.25 A (B: προσφέρω).

Cf. ἐγγίζω, προσφέρω.

προσεδρεία, ας. f.ʃ

assiduity: 3M 4.15.

προσεδρεύω.ʃ

to badger sbd (dat.): + ὅπως 1M 11.40.

προσεῖδον: inf. ~ιδεῖν.ʃ

to look at with interest or *concern*: + acc., με Jb 6.15, ἀέρα 'air' Wi 17.10. Cf. εἶδον.

πρόσειμι: pres.ptc. ~ιών.

to move towards and approach: + dat. pers., 4M 6.13; w. hostile intent, 14.16, νοσσιᾷ 'hive' 14.19. Cf. εἶμι, προσέρχομαι.

προσεῖπον.ʃ

to say to sbd: abs., 2M 7.8; + dat. pers. Pr 7.13; ἐν ὠσί μου 'in my hearing' Jd 17.2B. Cf. εἶπον.

προσεκκαίω: aor. ~εξέκαυσα.ʃ

to set fire *to besides*: + acc. rei, πῦρ ἐπὶ Μωαβ Nu 21.30. Cf. καίω.

προσεμβριμάομαι: aor.~ενεβριμησάμην.ʃ*

to orally express indignant displeasure besides causing some other discomfort or injury: abs. Si 13.3. Cf. ἐμβριμάομαι.

προσεμπίμπρημι: aor.subj. ~πρήσω.ʃ

to set on fire besides: + acc., ἅλωνα .. 'threshing-floor ..' Ex 22.6. Cf. ἐμπίμπρημι.

προσεξηγέομαι: aor.ptc. ~γησάμενος.ʃ *

to narrate besides: + acc. rei, dream 2M 15.11. Cf. ἐξηγέομαι.

προσεπικατατείνω.ʃ *

to strain still further: + acc., τροχόν 'wheel (as an instrument of torture) 4M 9.19. Cf. τείνω.

προσεπιτιμάω: aor. προσεπετίμησα.ʃ

to rebuke besides, not only offering help: τινι (pers.) Si 13.22. Cf. ἐπιτιμάω.

προσερυθριάω.ʃ *

to blush: *s* hum., πρός τινα '(with anger) at sbd' To 2.14 $\mathfrak{G}^{II}$ ($\mathfrak{G}^{I}$ ἐρυθριάω). Cf. ἐρυθριάω.

προσέρχομαι: fut. ~ελεύσομαι; aor. ~ῆλθον, ptc. ~ελθών, impv.2s πρόσελθε, subj. ~έλθω.

1. *to go over to, approach*: πρός τινα/τι Ge 42.24, Jn 1.6; ἐναντίον τοῦ θεοῦ Ex 16.9; ἐνώπιον τοῦ θεοῦ 22.8 (|| ἔρχομαι vs. 9); ἔναντι τῆς γερουσίας De 25.9; + dat. pers., 1.22; in prayer, μοι περὶ αὐτῶν '.. on their account' Je 7.16; cultic service - προσφέρειν τὰ δῶρα τοῦ θεοῦ Le 21.17 (|| ἐγγίζω vs. 21), cf. δουλεύειν κυρίῳ Si 2.1; πρός τινα for sexual intercourse, Le 18.6 (|| εἰσέρχομαι vs. 14), 20.16 (*s* woman), Is 8.3, πρός με (= Wisdom for instruction) Si 24.19, *s* κακά Ps 90.10 (w. hostile intent; || ἐγγίζω); ἐπὶ τὸ βῆμα 'on to the lectern' 2M 13.26; + acc. pers., 3M 5.14. **b**. γυναικί 'a woman' (for sexual intercourse) Ex 19.15, De 22.14. **c**. εἰς κρίσιν '(to go) to court' De 25.1; ἐξελέσθαι τὸν ἄνδρα αὐτῆς 'in order to rescue her husband' 25.11; εἰς πόλεμον Jd 20.23*L*. **d**. *to change sides and go over* to: πρός τινα 1M 2.16, cf. προσχωρέω.

2. *to arrive*: εἰς τὴν πατρίδα ἡμῶν 'to our country' 4M 4.6; as resident alien with the intention of joining the local community: πρὸς ὑμᾶς προσήλυτος Ex 12.48, Nu 9.14; sim. Le 19.33 (|| προσπορεύομαι vs. 34), cf. προσήλυτοι προσελεύσονταί σοι δι' ἐμοῦ Is 54.15.

3. *to apply oneself to*: + dat. rei, φόβῳ κυρίου Si 1.30, ^τῇ σοφίᾳ^ 6.19.

Cf. ἔρχομαι, εἰσέρχομαι, προσήλυτος, προσπορεύομαι, ἐγγίζω, πρόσειμι.

προσέτι. adv.

moreover: Jb 36.16¶, καὶ π. 2M 16.14.

προσευχή, ῆς. f. * (προσεύχομαι: Aes. +)

prayer (offered): ἔλθοι πρός σε ἡ π. μου εἰς ναὸν ἅγιον σου 'may my prayer reach you, your holy temple' Jn 2.8; ἐν τῷ οἴκῳ τῆς προσευχῆς μου Is 56.7, οἶκος ~ῆς καὶ δεήσεως 1M 7.37; μετὰ ᾠδῆς 'accompanied by an ode' Hb 3.1; φωνὴ ~ῆς χειλέων μου 'voice of prayer of my lips' 3.16; Si 32.21 (|| δέησις vs. 20); a principle of piety, +

νηστεία, ἐλεημοσύνη, δικαιοσύνη To 12.8 𝔊ᴵ; ~ῆς = τόπος ~ῆς 3M 7.20 (v.l. ~ήν, cf. BDAG, s.v. 2). Cf. προσεύχομαι, δέησις, εὐχή.

προσεύχομαι: fut. ~εύξομαι; aor. ~ηυξάμην, impv. ~ευξαι, 2pl ~εύξασθε, inf. ~εύξασθαι, ptc. ~ευξάμενος, subj. ~εύξωμαι.

to pray: πρός τινα - πρὸς κύριον τὸν θεὸν αὐτοῦ Jn 2.2; sim. 4.2, Ge 20.17, Ex 10.17; a function of a prophet, περὶ σοῦ Ge 20.7, περὶ τοῦ λαοῦ τούτου Je 7.16, 11.14 (|| δέομαι), ὑπὲρ ὑμῶν 1K 7.5 *L* (B: περὶ ὑμῶν, see Brock 1996.245f.); || ἐπικαλέω, ἀξιόω, ἱκετεύω, αἰτέομαι Wi 13.17; + εἰς 2E 6.10; + cogn. acc., προσευχήν Ne 1.6. Results in a misfortune being averted: Ge 20.7, 17, Ex 10.17. **b**. *to say in prayer*: τι πρός τινα 4K 19.20. Alw. addressed to God.

Cf. αἰτέομαι, ἐπικαλέω, εὔχομαι, κατεύχομαι, ἀξιόω, δέομαι, ἱκετεύω, προσευχή: Trench 188f.; Cimosa 29-33.

προσεχόντως. adv.ʃ

cautiously: speak, Pr 31.25 (|| σοφῶς vs. 28). Cf. προσέχω.

προσέχω: fut. ~έξω; aor. προσέσχον, subj.2s προσσχῇς, impv. πρόσσχες. On the spelling with -σσ-, see Walters 83.

1. *to turn* sth *towards sbd or sth attentively*: + acc., οὐκ ἤκουσάν μου καὶ οὐ προσέσχον τὸ οὖς αὐτῶν '.. did not incline their ears' Je 7.24, sim. Da 9.18 LXX (TH κλίνω), Je 7.27; τὸν νοῦν εἰς αὐτόν 'your mind ..' Jb 7.17.

2. *to pay attention, give heed*: abs. and || ἀκούω De 32.1, Ho 5.1, Mi 1.2, Zc 7.11; τοῖς ὠσὶν ὑμῶν 'with your ears' Je 25.4, τῇ διανοίᾳ σου 'in your mind' Jb 1.8; προσέσχε κύριος καὶ εἰσήκουσε 'the Lord took notice of the matter and hearkened' Ma 3.16; οὐ προσέσχον τοῦ εἰσακοῦσαί μου Zc 1.4; + μήπως and subj. Si 28.26; *+ ἀπό with the notion of avoiding, προσεχέτωσαν ἀπὸ τῶν ἁγίων Le 22.2; Si 6.13 (|| διαχωρίζομαι), 2C 35.21; πρόσεχε σεαυτῷ ἀπὸ πάσης πορνείας 'against every form of fornication' To 4.12 𝔊ᴵ; + *ἐπί τινι, pers. and his cultic offerings, Ge 4.5 (|| vs. 4 ἐπεῖδον 'to look upon favourably'); + ἐπί τι - προσέχετε τῇ καρδίᾳ (= ἑαυτοῖς) ἐπὶ πάντας τοὺς λόγους τούτους De 32.46; ἐπί τινος Si 16.24; *+ ἐν - πρόσεχε σεαυτῷ ἐν τῇ ἁφῇ τῆς λέπρας 'Be careful about the infection of leprosy' De 24.8, ἐν τοῖς χείλεσίν σου 'about your lips' Si 1.29; *+ εἰς - μὴ προσέσχεν τῇ διανοίᾳ (= ἑαυτῷ) εἰς τὸ ῥῆμα κυρίου Ex 9.21 (|| φοβέομαι vs. 20), εἰς τὴν ὄψιν αὐτοῦ 'his looks' 1K 16.7*L* (B: ἐπιβλέπω), Μὴ προσσχῇς εἰς τὴν θυσίαν αὐτῶν 'Do not take notice of their sacrifice' Nu 16.15, but not εἰς τὴν βοήθειάν μου Ps 37.23 and 70.12 (cf. εἰς τὸ βοηθῆσαί μοι 39.14), εἰς τὴν ἀντίλημψίν μου 21.20, εἰς τὴν δίκην μου 34.23; + acc., πρόσεχε σὺ πάντα, ὅσα ἐγὼ ἐντέλλομαί σοι 'Heed you all that I charge you' Ex 34.11, νόμον θεοῦ Is 1.10, κρίσιν χηρῶν 1.23, *s* God's ears Ps 9.38, εἰς τὴν προσευχήν Ne 1.11; *+ gen., προσέσχεν τῇ ψυχῇ Δίνας 'paid personal attention to D.' Ge 34.3 (poss., + dat.), τῶν ἐντολῶν σου καὶ τὰ μαρτύριά σου Ne 9.34; + dat., οὐδὲ προσέσχεν ὑμῖν De 1.45 (|| εἰσακούω τῆς φωνῆς τινος), μοι Ps 21.1; τῇ φωνῇ τῆς δεήσεώς μου 5.3, τῇ δεήσει μου 16.1 (|| ἐνωτίζομαι), τῇ ψυχῇ μου 68.19; σοφίᾳ Si 4.15, ἐντολαῖς 32.2.

3. *to take care and ensure* that something happens or does not happen: esp. πρόσεχε σεαυτῷ, foll. by a negative command, μὴ ἀποστρέψῃς τὸν υἱόν μου ἐκεῖ Ge 24.6, μὴ ἐπιλάθῃς τοὺς λόγους De 4.9 'don't forget the words' (reinforced by καὶ φύλαξον τὴν ψυχήν σου σφόδρα), 6.12 +; by an inf. with negation understood, ἔτι προσθεῖναι ἰδεῖν μου τὸ πρόσωπον 'not to see my face yet again' Ex 10.28, τοῦ ἀναβῆναι εἰς τὸ ὄρος 19.12; with an explicit negator, πρόσεχε ἰσχυρῶς τοῦ μὴ φαγεῖν αἷμα De 12.23; by καί + an impv., καὶ εἰσάκουε αὐτοῦ Ex 23.21; by μήποτε + subj., μήποτε θῇς διαθήκην .. 34.12; with a nominative pron. instead of a refl., προσέχετε ὑμεῖς, μὴ ἐπιλάθησθε τὴν διαθήκην .. '.. don't forget the covenant ..' De 4.23. On the dat. refl. pron., cp. Aristoph. *Ec*. 294 and Pl., *Symp*. 174d, and Helbing, *Kasus*., 291 ("Dativ des Zieles"). **b**. + an inf. without any negation implied: πρόσσχες τοῦ ἐπισκέψασθαι πάντα τὰ ἔθνη 'Make sure to punish ..' Ps 58.6; Pr 4.1; + a negated inf., τοῦ μὴ διελθεῖν 4K 6.9*L* (B: φυλάσσομαι).

On τὰ προσέχοντα 3K 7.17, see Schleusner s.v. and *L* προέχοντα.

Cf. προσοχή, ἀκούω, εἰσακούω, ἀκροάομαι, συντηρέω, φυλάσσω.

προσηκόντως. adv.ʃ

as it should happen: 4M 6.33.

προσήκω.ʃ

1. *to belong* to (πρός + acc.): 2M 3.6. **b**. + dat. (owner): 4M 4.3.

2. impers. *to be proper*: ptc., ὡς προσῆκον ἦν 'as was proper' 1E 5.50.

Cf. (προσ)καθήκω, πρέπω: LSG s.v.

προσηλόω: pf.ptc.pass. ~ηλωμένος.ʃ

to fix securely: τινά τινι 3M 4.9 (τοὺς τραχήλους 'by the neck').

προσηλυτεύω.ʃ*

to live as προσήλυτος (q.v.): Ez 14.7.

προσήλυτος, ου. m. *

one who has arrived at a place as foreigner: ἐάν τις προσέλθῃ ⸢πρὸς ὑμᾶς⸣ [|| ὑμῖν Le 19.33] π. Ex 12.48 (opp. αὐτόχθων, with whom he may partake of a passover meal or any other cultic meal, but not πάροικος or μισθωτός vs. 45 and Le 22.10), ὁ π. ὁ προσπορευόμενος πρὸς ὑμᾶς Le 19.34; π. ὁ παροικῶν ἐν σοί Ex 20.10; ὁ αὐτόχθων καὶ ὁ π. ὁ προσκείμενος ἐν ὑμῖν Le 16.29; Ἄνθρωπος ἄνθρωπος τῶν υἱῶν Ισραηλ καὶ ἀπὸ τῶν υἱῶν τῶν ~ων τῶν προσκειμένων ἐν ὑμῖν 17.8; ὑμῖν [= Israelites] καὶ τῷ ~ῳ καὶ τῷ αὐτόχθονι Nu 9.14; || πάροικος 35.15; likely to be subjected to (social) injustice, ~ον οὐ κακώσετε οὐδὲ μὴ θλίψητε αὐτόν· ἦτε γὰρ ~οι ἐν γῇ Αἰγύπτῳ Ex 22.21 (applied to Israelites in Egypt), sim. 23.9, Le 19.34, De 10.19; χήραν καὶ ὀρφανὸν καὶ ~ον καὶ πένητα μὴ καταδυναστεύετε 'do not oppress a widow and an orphan and a foreign resident and a poor person' Zc 7.10; τοὺς ἐκκλίνοντας κρίσιν ~ου 'those who bend (the law of) justice for the sojourner' Ma 3.5 (|| μισθωτός, ὀρφανός, χήρα); object of special consideration, τῷ πτωχῷ καὶ τῷ ~ῳ Le 19.10, 23.22; ἀντιλήμψῃ αὐτοῦ ὡς ~ου καὶ παροίκου 'you shall assist him ..' 25.35; || πένης καὶ ἐνδεής De 24.14, || ὀρφανὸς καὶ χήρα 24.19; + ξένος, πτωχός Si 10.22.

In some cases, e.g. Ex 12.48, the person designated as π. prob. refers to a coreligionist, whether a recent immigrant or sbd in transit.

Cf. πάροικος, αὐτόχθων, ἐγχώριος, προσέρχομαι, ἐπήλυτος: Allen; Loader; Lee 1980a.112, n. 27; Muraoka 1986b.260f.; *BA* 2.51f.; Harl 2001.887f.

προσημαίνω: aor.ptc.pass. ~σημανθείς; pf.ptc.pass. ~σεσημαμμένος.

to mention previously: pass., 2M 4.23; "the foretold time" 3M 5.13. Cf. προεῖπον, προαποδείκνυμι.

προσημειόομαι.ʃ *

to signal imminent arrival of: + acc. rei, θάνατον '(one's own) death' 4M 15.19. Cf. σημαίνω.

προσηνής, ές.ʃ

soothing: *s* cool water to the thirsty compared to good news from afar, Pr 25.25.

πρόσθεμα, ατος. n.ʃ

that which is additional: extra crop, Le 19.25; part jutting out from a wall, Ez 41.7. Cf. προστίθημι, πρόσθεσις.

πρόσθεσις, εως. f.ʃ

that which has been added: Ez 47.13. Cf. πρόσθεμα.

προσθλίβω: aor. ~έθλιψα.ʃ

to press against: + acc., ἑαυτὴν πρὸς τὸν τοῖχον 'herself against the wall' Nu 22.25. Cf. θλίβω.

προσκαθήκω.ʃ

to be appropriate to: + dat., δαπάνη τοῖς ἁγίοις 'expenses duly associated with the sanctuary' 1M 10.39. Cf. καθήκω, πρέπω.

προσκαθίστημι: 1aor. ~κατέστησα.ʃ

to appoint in addition: extra bodyguards, τινά τινι (pers.) Jd 14.11A. Cf. καθίστημι.

πρόσκαιρος, ον.

of short duration only, 'temporary': *s* σωτηρία 4M 15.2. Cf. καιρός, πρός **III 11**: Delling, *TDNT* 3.463f.

προσκαίω: aor.subj.pass. ~καυθῶ.ʃ

to set on fire besides: Ez 24.11. Cf. καίω.

προσκαλέομαι: fut.mid. ~καλέσομαι; aor.mid. ~εκαλεσάμην, ptc. ~καλεσάμενος, pass. ~εκλήθην, ptc. ~κληθείς; pf.mid.~κέκλημαι.

1. mid. *to demand the presence of*, 'summon (for an interview)': + acc. pers. Ge 28.1, Ex 3.18, 5.3, Si 13.9; as a witness in court, τὸν οὐρανόν Ps 49.4; pass. Es 8.1, 2M 4.28, εἰς συνέδριον 14.5. Cf. προγράφω **2**. **b**. so as to charge with a task: τὸ ὕδωρ τῆς θαλάσσης Am 5.8, 9.6.

2. mid. *to speak to, address*: + acc. pers., 1K 26.14, Jb 19.17, Jl 2.32.

3. mid. *to induce* to undertake sth: ἐπ' ἀγορασμόν 'to buy' 2M 8.11. **b**. *to attempt to recruit as ally*: τινα πρὸς ἑαυτούς Jd 9.25*L*.

Cf. καλέω, πρόσκλησις.

προσκαρτερέω: aor.ptc. ~καρτερήσας.ʃ

1. *to make determined efforts*: προσκαρτερήσαντες λήμψεσθε 'Take painstakingly' Nu 13.21. **b**. *to persist in making appearances*: ἐν τῇ οἰκίᾳ τινός Su 6 TH.

2. *to wait patiently*: abs., To 5.8 𝔊[II].

Cf. καρτερέω: Grundmann, *TDNT* 3.618f.; Spicq 3.191-4; Renehan 1.171.

προσκαταλείπω: aor. ~κατέλιπον.ʃ

to leave over as surplus: abs. Ex 36.7. Cf. καταλείπω.

πρόσκαυμα, ατος. n.ʃ.*

marks of burning: πᾶν πρόσωπον ὡς ~ χύτρας 'every face like burnt earthenware' (w. ref. to the black or dark colour due to fear, cf. Thph PG 126. 1017 and Tht PG 81.1644) Jl 2.6, sim. Na 2.11. Cf. καίω: Dogniez 2001.251-3.

πρόσκειμαι.

1. *to reside alongside* native population: *s* alien, ὁ προσήλυτος ὁ προσκείμενος ἐν ὑμῖν Le 16.29 (:: αὐτόχθων), Nu 15.15, 16; πρὸς ὑμᾶς 15.26; Ἄνθρωπος ἄνθρωπος τῶν υἱῶν Ισραηλ καὶ ἀπὸ τῶν υἱῶν τῶν προσηλύτων τῶν προσκειμένων ἐν ὑμῖν Le 17.8; τῷ παροίκῳ τῷ προσκειμένῳ πρὸς σέ 25.6; + dat., τοῖς ὁρίοις Μωαβ Nu 21.15; ἐπί τινα Ez 37.16 (|| προστίθημι pass.). Cf. παροικέω.

2. *to act with dedication and devotion*: τὰ πρὸς κύριον 'in matters pertaining to the Lord' De 1.36 (on the syntax, see *BA* ad loc.); + dat., κυρίῳ τῷ θεῷ ὑμῶν 4.4, + λατρεύω Jo 22.5, || βοηθέω Jb 26.2; +

πρός τινα Is 56.3 (πρὸς κύριον || κυρίῳ δουλεύειν αὐτῷ vs. 6). Cf. ζηλόω **1**.

προσκεφάλαιον, ου. n.

1. *cushion for the head*, 'pillow': Ez 13.18.

2. royal *treasure-chamber*: 1E 3.8, see Hilhorst.

προσκήνιον, ου. n.ʃ *

**entrance of a tent*: Ju 10.22. Cf. θύρα.

πρόσκλησις, εως. f.ʃ

official summons: 2M 4.14. Cf. προσκαλέομαι: Caird 1969.30.

προσκλίνω: plpf.mid./pass. ~εκεκλίμην.ʃ

to attach oneself to sbd *in disposition and attitude*: τινι 2M 14.24. Cf. (προσ)κολλάω.

προσκολλάω: fut. ~κολλήσω, pass. ~κολληθήσομαι; aor.act.opt.3s ~κολλήσαι, pass.impv. ~κολλήθητι.

1. *to attach firmly*: + acc. rei, προσκολλήσαι κύριος εἰς σὲ τὸν θάνατον De 28.21, πρός τι Ez 29.4.

2. mid. *to enter into close association* with: + πρός τινα and *s* a man (husband), πρὸς τὴν γυναῖκα αὐτοῦ Ge 2.24, cf. 1E 4.20 (with simp.); + dat. pers., τοῖς ἐπαοιδοῖς 'enchanters' Le 19.31, κυρίῳ τῷ θεῷ ὑμῶν Jo 23.8, τῷ ὁμοίῳ αὐτοῦ 'his like' Si 13.16; + dat. rei, σοφίᾳ 6.34; with God, De 11.22, Ps 72.28; + ἐν – ἐν τῇ κληρονομίᾳ Nu 36.7, 9; + μετά τινος Da 2.43 TH; *s* spoils of war, ἐν τῇ χειρί σου De 13.17 (so that you are not able to part with them).

3. mid. *to attach closely* to one another: ἀνὴρ τῷ ἀδελφῷ αὐτοῦ Jb 41.9¶ (*s* scales of crocodile[?] and || συνέχομαι).

Cf. κολλάω, ἐπακολουθέω, προσκλίνω.

πρόσκομμα, ατος. n. *

1. *occasion for causing to stumble*: λίθου Is 8.14 (|| πτῶμα 'fall'), || πτῶσις Si 31.19, ξύλον ~ατος 'stumbling block' 34.7; metaph. of heathen people or their idols, Ex 23.33, 34.12; partner for illicit sexual relationship, Je 3.3.

2. *occasion for taking offence*: τοὺς ἐλέγχοντας ἐν πύλαις π. θήσουσι 'they will take offence at the moralists at city-gates' Is 29.21.

Cf. προσκόπτω, σκάνδαλον.

προσκόπτω: fut. ~κόψω; aor. προσέκοψα, inf. ~κόψαι, subj. ~κόψω.

*__I__. tr., *to strike* sth against sth: πρὸς λίθον τὸν πόδα σου Ps 90.12.

II. intr. *to collide* in hostile situation: τὸ παιδίον πρὸς τὸν πρεσβύτην Is 3.5.

2. *to make forceful contact*: πρὸ τοῦ προσκόψαι τοὺς πόδας ὑμῶν ἐπ' ὄρη σκοτεινά 'before your feet hit dark mountains' Je 13.16.

*__3__. *to stumble upon some impediment and fall*: ἐν λιθώδεσιν 'on stony roads' Si 35.20; προσκόψει καὶ πεσοῦται Da 11.19 LXX; + dat., ῥομφαίᾳ 11.33 (TH ἀσθενέω); τοῖς ποσίν To 11.10 𝔊II, cf. *s* πούς Pr 3.6; troops on battlefield, defeated Jd 20.32 A (B: πίπτω). **b**. fig.: in speech, Si 13.23; 30.13.

4. *to commit an offence*: abs., Si 34.17; PSol 3.5 (|| πίπτω), *s* sinner, 3.9.

Cf. πρόσκομμα, πίπτω, πταίω, σκανδαλίζω: Stählin, *TDNT* 6.745f.

προσκρούω: fut. ~κρούσω.ʃ

to strike against sth else: Si 13.2; military attack, 2M 13.19; *s* river-water, εἰς τὸ στόμα αὐτοῦ 'into its mouth' Jb 40.23¶. Cf. κρούω.

προσκυνέω: fut.act. ~νήσω; aor. προσεκύνησα, inf. act. ~νῆσαι, subj. ~νήσω, ptc. ~νήσας, impv. ~νησον; pf. ~κεκύνηκα.

1. *to do obeisance, prostrate oneself*: ἐπὶ τὴν γῆν Ge 18.2, 33.3; τῷ προσώπῳ Nu 22.31, τῷ προσώπῳ τινος [= sbd other than *s*] Ju 14.7; τῷ προσώπῳ ἐπὶ τὴν γῆν Ge 19.1; κύψας ἐπὶ τὴν γῆν 'stooping towards the ground' Ex 34.8; + *dat. pers., τῷ λαῷ τῆς γῆς Ge 23.7; τῷ κυρίῳ 24.48; αὐτῷ ἐπὶ πρόσωπον ἐπὶ τὴν γῆν 42.6, 43.26; 48.12 (ἐπὶ τῆς γῆς); τῷ βασιλεῖ κυρίῳ παντοκράτορι Zc 14.16, 17; ἐπὶ τὰ δώματα τῇ στρατιᾷ τοῦ οὐρανοῦ 'on the rooftops out of reverence for the heavenly host' Zp 1.5; προσκυνήσουσίν σοι ἄρχοντες Ge 27.29 (|| δουλεύω); + προσπίπτω Ps 94.6, Ju 14.7; ἔναντι κυρίου De 26.10; ἐνώπιόν μου [= God] Is 66.23, sim. Ps 21.28; ἐναντίον τοῦ λαοῦ Ge 23.12; idolatrous images, Ex 20.5 (|| λατρεύω), Is 2.8; pagan gods, τοῖς θεοῖς αὐτῶν Ex 23.24, sim. De 29.26, 30.17 (|| λατρεύω), + δουλεύω Je 13.10; a stone, Le 26.1; heavenly bodies, De 4.19, 17.3 (|| λατρεύω). **b**. + acc.: acc. rei, τὸ ἐμὸν δράγμα 'my sheaf' Ge 37.7; acc. pers., 49.8, Ex 11.8, Es 3.3 *L* (o': + dat.); + acc. dei, Jd 7.15 A (B: + dat.); carved images, Is 44.15 (|| + dat., vs. 17), Ep Je 5 (|| + dat.).

2. *to take part in worship*: ἐν οἴκῳ κυρίου Je 33.2, πρὸς ναὸν ἅγιόν σου 'facing your holy temple' Ps 5.8, 137.2; *s* hum. lip, τῷ (*L* τῇ) Βααλ 3K 19.18.

3. *to pay respectful regard to*: + acc., πανουργίαν 'exhortation' 4M 5.12.

Cf. προσκύνησις, προπίπτω, λατρεύω: Helbing, *Kasus*. 196-8; Naumann 42; Cimosa 53-62; Jobes 186f.

προσκύνησις, εως. f.ʃ

v.n. of προσκυνέω: Si 50.21, 3M 3.7. Cf. προσκυνέω, πρόπτωσις.

προσκύπτω: aor.ptc. ~κύψας.ʃ

to lean towards to address: + dat. pers., 2M 7.27. Cf. κύπτω.

προσκυρέω.ʃ

to adjoin: + dat., τὴν προσκυροῦσαν (scil. χώραν) αὐτῇ 'the area adjoining it' 1M 10.39. Cf. ἐγκολλάω, ὁμορέω, συγκυρέω.

προσλαλέω: fut. ~λαλήσω.ʃ
to speak to, 'address': πρὸς τὸν λαόν Ex 4.16; + dat., ἀψύχῳ 'a lifeless thing' Wi 13.17. Cf. λαλέω, προσαγορεύω.

προσλαμβάνω: aor.mid. ~ελαβόμην, ptc. ~λαβόμενος, inf.pass. ~λημφθῆναι; pf.act. προσείληφα.
I. act. *to add*: + acc. rei, τὰ χαλεπά '(exaggerate) the difficulties' Wi 17.11.
II. mid. *to accept in a welcoming and helpful manner*: pass., *o* hum., by God, Si 23.28¶. **b**. mid. + *acc. pers., Ps 64.5 (+ ἐκλέγομαι 'choose'), 26.10, ἐξ ὑδάτων πολλῶν 17.17, μετὰ δόξης 72.24; ὑμᾶς αὐτῷ εἰς λαόν 1K 12.22. Cf. ἀπο~, προσδέχομαι.
2. *to enlist* as soldier: + acc. pers., 2M 8.1.
Cf. πρόσληψις: Spicq 3.195-200.

πρόσληψις, εως. f.ʃ
v.n. of prec. **II**: by God, Si 10.21¶ (:: ἐκβολή 'rejection'), 19.18¶. Cf. προσλάμβανω, ἐκβολή.

προσλογίζομαι: fut. ~λογιοῦμαι; aor.pass. ~ελογίσθην.
1. *to calculate*: + dat. com. pers. and acc. rei, τὸ ἀργύριον ἐπὶ τὰ ἔτη τὰ ἐπίλοιπα 'the silver in proportion to the remaining years' Le 27.18.
2. *to regard as*: μετά τινος 'as belonging to the class of' Ba 3.11, Ps 87.5; ἐν πλήθει ἁμαρτωλῶν Si 7.16. **b**. *to regard as constituting*: pass., + dat., Jo 13.3.
Cf. λογίζομαι.

προσμαρτυρέω: aor.ptc.~ρησάς.ʃ
to give additional testimony in support of sbd: τινι 3M 5.19. Cf. μαρτυρέω.

προσμείγνυμι.ʃ
mid. *to become mingled*: ἐν εὐφροσύναις .. λύπη 'sorrow .. in joy' Pr 14.13. Cf. μίγνυμι.

προσμειδιάω: aor. ~εμειδίασα.ʃ
to smile at: + dat. pers., 4M 8.4. Cf. μειδιάω.

προσμένω: fut. ~μενῶ; aor. ~έμεινα.ʃ
1. *to remain attached to*: metaph., + dat. pers. (God), Wi 3.9.
2. *to wait in expectation*: abs., Jd 3.25 A (B: ὑπο~); + acc. pers., μέχρι .. To 2.2 𝔊[II]; 3M 7.17.
Cf. μένω, ὑπομένω.

προσνέμω.ʃ
to admit that A (acc.) *properly belongs to B* (dat.): ^τῷ λογισμῷ^ τὴν ἐξουσίαν 'the authority to the rational will' 4M 6.33.

προσνοέω: fut. ~νοήσω; aor. ~ενόησα.
to observe visually: abs., Is 63.5 (‖ ἐπιβλέπω); + acc., Nu 23.9 (‖ ὁράω), *s* eye, Jb 24.15 ¶; and + ptc., αὐτὸν ἐρχόμενον To 11.6; *+ dat., Jd 3.26, Da 7.8 TH. Cf. ἐπιβλέπω, ὁράω, κατανοέω.

πρόσοδος, ου. f.
1. *right or possibility of access*: πρὸς τὸ θυσιαστήριον 2M 14.3.
2. *revenue*: 2M 3.3, 4.8, 9.16; pl., Pr 28.16, 3M 3.16.

προσοδύρομαι.ʃ *
to lament beside: + dat., τάφοις 'graves' Wi 19.3. Cf. ὀδύρομαι, θρηνέω, κόπτομαι.

προσόζω: aor. ~ώζεσα.ʃ
to stink: *s* bruises, Ps 37.6. Cf. ὄζω, I βρόμος.

προσοίγω: aor. προσέῳξα.ʃ *
to shut: τὴν θύραν προσέῳξεν ὀπίσω αὐτοῦ Ge 19.6. Cf. κλείω.

προσονομάζω: aor.inf. ~μάσαι.ʃ
to rename: 1st acc. understood, Διὸς Ὀλυμπίου '(the temple) of Olympian Zeus' 2M 6.2. Cf. ὀνομάζω.

προσοχή, ῆς. f.
careful attention: Si prol. 16; 11.18 (in finance); + gen. obj., νόμων Wi 6.18 (‖ τήρησις). Cf. προσέχω.

προσοχθίζω: fut. ~οχθιῶ; aor. ~ώχθισα, subj. ~οχθίσω, pass. ~ωχθίσθην; pf. ~ώχθικα. *
to become weary of and dislike: + dat. rei, τῇ ζωῇ μου Ge 27.46; τοῖς κρίμασίν μου προσοχθίσῃ ἡ ψυχὴ ὑμῶν Le 26.15; τοῖς προστάγμασίν μου προσώχθισαν τῇ ψυχῇ αὐτῶν 26.43; + dat. pers., 18.25, 26.30; ὥστε ἐξαναλῶσαι αὐτούς 26.44; + cogn. dat., προσοχθίσματι προσοχθιεῖς 'you will become utterly disgusted' De 7.26 (+ βδελύσσομαι); + ἐν - ἡ ψυχὴ ἡμῶν προσώχθισεν ἐν τῷ ἄρτῳ τῷ διακένῳ τούτῳ '.. this worthless bread' Nu 21.5, ἐν ἀνομίαις Ez 36.31; + ἀπό - ἀπὸ προσώπου υἱῶν Ισραηλ Nu 22.3; + κατά - κατὰ πρόσωπον αὐτῶν Ez 36.31; ‖ ἐξουδενόω 'to belittle' Ps 21.25; pass., *o* weapon, 2K 1.21B (*L* ἐξαίρω). Cf. προσόχθισμα, βδελύσσω.

προσόχθισμα, ατος. n. *
v.n. of προσοχθίζω: as cogn. dat., ~ατι προσοχθιεῖς 'you will become utterly disgusted' De 7.26; disgustingly boring experience, Si 27.13. **b**. *object of intense dislike*: object of idolatry, 3K 11.33 ‖ βδέλυγμα 2C 15.16, so also Od 12.10.
Cf. προσοχθίζω, βδέλυγμα.

προσοχυρόω: aor. ~ωχύρωσα.ʃ *
to fortify more securely: + acc. (city), 1M 13.48; the Temple Mount, 13.52. Cf. ὀχυρόω.

πρόσοψις, εως. f.
what sbd or *sth looks like outwardly*: Da 2.31, 2M 6.18. Cf. ὄψις.

προσπαίζω.ʃ
1. *to pass time pleasantly with*: abs., Jb 21.11 (among themselves).
2. *to make fun of*: + dat. pers., Si 8.4.
Cf. παίζω.

προσπαρακαλέω: aor.ptc. ~καλέσας.ʃ
to turn to sbd *and urge* to do: + inf., 2M 12.31. Cf. παρακαλέω.

προσπάσσω: aor. προσέπασα.ʃ *
to sprinkle: + acc. rei, To 11.11 𝔊I. Cf. ἐμπάσσω, ῥαίνω.

προσπίπτω: aor. προσέπεσον, subj. ~πέσω, inf. ~πεσεῖν, ptc. ~πεσών.
1. *to fling oneself*: upon (ἐπί) - προσέπεσεν ἐπὶ τὸν τράχηλον αὐτοῦ 'flung himself on his neck' Ge 33.4 (ǁ ἐπιπίπτω 45.14, 46.29); πρὸς τοὺς πόδας 'at his feet' Ex 4.25, τοῖς ποσίν τινος Ju 14.7; αὐτῷ Ps 94.6 (+ προσκυνέω). **b**. metaph., with eagerness: ἐπὶ κάλλος γυναικός Si 25.21, εἰς μάχην ταχέως 'quickly into a fight' Pr 25.8.
2. *to happen, occur*: ὁ γράφων τὰ προσπίπτοντα 'secretary' 1E 2.21, without γράφων 16. Cf. συμβαίνω.
3. *to come one's way, arrive*: *s* written instruction, 1E 8.8, πρόσταγμα Es 9.4 o'; decree, 3M 4.1. **b**. *to reach*: *s* letter, 3M 3.25. **c**. as news: + dat. pers., τὰ κατὰ Νικάνορα .. γεγονότα 'what had happened to N…' 2M 9.3; the news as inf. cl., 13.1. **d**. impers.: περί τινος 2M 5.11, + dat. pers., 8.12.

προσποιέω: aor.mid. ~εποιησάμην.ʃ
I. act. tr. *to increase*: + acc. rei, Si 34.30. Cf. πληθύνω.
II. mid. **1**. *to admit kinship* or *affinity with*: + acc. pers., Jb 19.14.
2. *to admit to*: + acc. rei and dat. pers., τὸ κακόν 'the (mental) distress' Da Su 10 LXX (TH: ἀναγγέλλω).
3. *to pretend to be what one really is not*: abs., 1K 21.14; + inf., ἐνοχλεῖσθαι 'to be unwell' 2K 13.5*L*, 6*L*. **b**. + neg., *to pretend the contrary*: + inf., μὴ προσποίου .. λαλῆσαι 'to pretend not to have the intention of speaking ..' 2K 13.20*L*, cf. ὑποκρίνομαι: Renehan 2.122.

προσπορεύομαι: pres.subj. ~πορεύωμαι.
1. *to turn to*, *approach* with a request, seeking help, to officiate etc.: + dat. pers. (judge), Ex 24.14; αὐτῇ To 6.18 𝔊I (𝔊II γίνεσθαι μετ' αὐτῆς: for sexual intercourse); ǁ προσάγω Si 12.14; as proselyte, τῷ Ισραηλ Jo 9.2f.; πρὸς τὸ θυσιαστήριον Ex 28.39, 30.20; προσήλυτος ὁ προσπορευόμενος πρὸς ὑμᾶς Le 19.34; Nu 18.7 (ǁ προσέρχομαι vs. 4); of sth untoward befalling, Es 6.22 *L*. **b**. so as to engage in an activity: πρὸς τὰ ἔργα Ex 36.2, πρὸς τὸν νόμον τοῦ θεοῦ Ne 10.28; εἰς πόλεμον ἐπὶ τοὺς ἐχθροὺς ὑμῶν De 20.3.
2. *to come in* as revenue: 2E 7.17, see Hanhart 2003.379-81.
Cf. προσέρχομαι: Lee 89-91.

προσπυρόω: aor. ~επύρωσα.ʃ*
to incense still more: τινα 2M 14.11. Cf. πυρόω.

προσραίνω: fut. ~ρανῶ; aor. ~έρρανα.ʃ
to sprinkle: ἀπὸ τοῦ αἵματος 'some of the blood' Le 4.6 (ǁ ῥαίνω vs. 17); ἐπί + acc., 8.30. Cf. ῥαίνω, προσπάσσω.

προσσιελίζω: aor.subj. ~σιελίσω.ʃ *
to spit upon (ἐπί + acc.): ἐπὶ τὸν καθαρόν Le 15.8. Cf. (προ)πτύω.

προσταγή, ῆς. f.ʃ *
command: βασιλέως Da 3.95 LXX (TH ῥῆμα). Cf. προστάσσω, προσταγή, ἐντολή.

πρόσταγμα, ατος. n.
1. *command*: divine, τὰ ~ατα τοῦ θεοῦ καὶ τὸν νόμον αὐτοῦ Ex 18.16; ǁ κρίματα Le 18.5; ποιήσητε τὰ ~ατά μου Le 26.14; τὰ ~ατα αὐτοῦ οὐκ ἐφυλάξαντο (ǁ τὸν νόμον κυρίου) Am 2.4, sim. Zc 3.7; ἐφύλαξεν .. τὰ ~ατά μου καὶ τὰς ἐντολάς μου καὶ τὰ δικαιώματά μου καὶ τὰ νόμιμά μου Ge 26.5; ἀπὸ τῶν ~των, ὧν οὐ δεῖ ποιεῖν Le 4.2; ἐνετειλάμην αὐτῷ .. ~ατα καὶ δικαιώματα Ma 4.6. All in the pl., and mostly so in the LXX.
2. *instruction, directive*: divine, παρὰ κυρίου ἐξῆλθεν τὸ π. τοῦτο Ge 24.50; διὰ ~ατος κυρίου Nu 9.18; 9.20 (ǁ διὰ φωνῆς κυρίου); φονευτοῦ 'pertaining to murderer' De 19.4. **b**. human and issued by sbd in authority, Ge 47.26.
*__3__. *natural order, set pattern*: κατὰ καιρὸν πληρώσεως ~ατος θερισμοῦ 'at the time appointed for the expected harvest to be brought in' Je 5.24.
Cf. προστάσσω, δικαίωμα, ἐντολή, νόμιμον, νόμος: Preisigke II 412; Passoni Dell'Acqua 1988; Harl 2001.892f.

προσταράσσω: aor.subj. ~ταράξω.ʃ*
to trouble further: + acc., καρδίαν Si 4.3. Cf. ταράσσω.

προστάς, άδος. f.ʃ
vestibule, entrance hall (?): Jd 3.22B.

προστάσσω: fut. ~τάξω; aor. προσέταξα, impv. ~ταξον, inf. ~τάξαι, ptc. ~τάξας, pass. ~ετάγην, ptc. ~ταγείς, ~ταχθείς; pf. ~τέταχα, pass.3s ~τέτακται, ptc. ~τεταχώς, pass. ~τεταγμένος.
to issue a command, order: abs. Ex 36.6; + dat. pers., 1E 6.10 (ǁ συντάσσω vs. 4), Ge 47.11; and inf., Ge 50.2, κύριος κήτει μεγάλῳ καταπιεῖν τὸν Ιωναν Jn 2.1; + ἵνα and an inf.(!), 1E 6.31; impers. pass. + dat., προσετάγη τῷ κήτει Jn 2.11; the content of an order expressed as a result in the following clause in a finite tense, προστάξει ὁ ἱερεὺς καὶ σφάξουσιν .. 'the priest shall command and they shall slaughter ..' Le 14.5; προσέταξε κύριος .. κολοκύνθῃ καὶ ἀνέβη ὑπὲρ κεφαλῆς τοῦ Ιωνα Jn 4.6, sim. 2.11, 4.7, 8. **b**. *to issue* as an order: + acc., βασιλικόν 'royal decree' Es 1.19 o'; also + dat. pers., Jo 5.14 **c**. *to prescribe* in the form of an order: + dat. pers. and acc., πῦρ .., ὃ οὐ προσέταξεν κύριος αὐτοῖς Le 10.1; pass., with no dat., 2M 6.21.

Cf. πρόσταγμα, ἐντέλλομαι, ἐπι~, συντάσσω: Muraoka 2006.

προστατέω: aor.inf. ~στατῆσαι.ʃ

1. *to exercise authority over*: + gen., Si 45.24, 1M 14.47, Es 2.9 *L*. Cf. ἐξουσιάζω **2**.

2. *to place* under the guardianship of: ὑπὸ χεῖρα .. τοῦ εὐνούχου Es 2.3 *L*.

Cf. ἄρχω, ἡγέομαι.

προστάτης, ου. m.

ruler, governor: τῆς Ἰουδαίας 1E 2.11 (|| ἄρχων 2E 1.8), τοῦ ἱεροῦ 'of the temple' 2M 3.4; ὑπαρχόντων '(steward) of (royal) property' 1C 27.31, ἔργων 'of (royal) works' 29.6. Cf. προΐστημι: *ND* 4.241-4.

προστίθημι: fut.act. προσθήσω, mid. ~θήσομαι, pass. ~τεθήσομαι; 1aor.act. προσέθηκα, 2aor.ptc. προσθείς, impv. ~θες, 3s ~θέτω, inf. ~θεῖναι, subj. ~θῶ, opt. ~θείην, ~θείη, mid. προσεθέμην, ptc. ~θέμενος, subj. ~θῶμαι, pass. προσετέθην, ptc. ~τεθείς, impv.sg. ~τέθητι, 3s ~τεθήτω, pl. ~τεθήτωσαν, subj. ~τεθῶ, opt.3s ~τεθείη; pf. ~τέταχα, ~τέθεικα, mid. ~τέθειμαι, ptc.pass. ~τεθειμένος.

1. *to add*: abs., ὁ πλουτῶν οὐ προσθήσω 'the well-to-do shall not add (any more to his wealth)' Ex 30.15 (:: ἐλαττονέω), :: ἐλαττόω Si 18.6, 42.21, cf. Ec 2.9; + πρός τι De 4.2 (:: ἀφαιρέω); + acc., ἀνομίαν Is 1.5; + dat. and acc., Προσθέτω ὁ θεός μοι υἱὸν ἕτερον 'May God add to me another son' Ge 30.24; pass., σοι Nu 18.2 (|| πρὸς σέ vs. 4); οὗτοι ἐκείνοις προστεθήσονται Zc 14.17; + ἐπί c. acc., Le 5.16, 22.14; 27.13 (|| πρός τι vs. 15), Nu 32.14; De 12.32, 1M 8.30 (:: ἀφαιρέω); + ἐπί c. dat., Jb 34.37; σοφίαν ἐπὶ πᾶσιν '(I increased my) wisdom over and above that which was possessed by all (my predecessors)' Ec 1.16; pass. Am 3.15, Jl 2.2; μετά τινος (pers.) 1K 15.6; *ἐπί τινος (pers.), pass. Es 9.27; + πρός c. acc., προσετέθη πρὸς τὸν λαὸν αὐτοῦ 'was gathered to his forbears (upon death)' Ge 25.8, 17, 49.33, Ju 16.22, πρὸς τὸ γένος αὐτοῦ Ge 35.29, πρὸς τὸν λαόν σου Nu 31.2, || τελευτάω De 32.50, πρὸς τοὺς πατέρας αὐτῶν Jd 2.10, sim. 1M 2.69; the verb alone with the same meaning, Nu 20.26, 1K 12.25 (*L* ἀπόλλυμι), 15.6, 26.10, cf. εἰς χεῖρας Σαουλ 27.1; + εἰς– εἰς τὴν κληρονομίαν τῆς φυλῆς Nu 36.3 (|| ἐπί + acc., vs. 4), cf. Dogniez 2002.4-6. **b**. with ἔτι reinforcing: Nu 32.14, 15, Is 1.5.

*__2__. + inf. with (mostly) or without τοῦ, *still to do* sth *as formerly, do* sth *again* (most likely Hebraism; see BDF, § 435 and BDAG, s.v. **1c**): οὐ προσθήσει τὴν ἰσχὺν αὐτῆς δοῦναί σοι 'it no longer provides you with its fruit' Ge 4.12; οὐ μὴ προσθήσω τοῦ ἀγαπῆσαι αὐτούς Ho 9.15; 13.2; ἆρα προσθήσω τοῦ ἐπιβλέψαι πρὸς τὸν ναὸν τὸν ἅγιόν σου; 'will I indeed have another chance to look towards your holy temple?' Jn 2.5; the notion of "still" reinforced by the addition of ἔτι and often with a neg., οὐ προσέθετο ἐπιστρέψαι πρὸς αὐτὸν ἔτι Ge 8.12; οὐ μὴ προσθήσω ἔτι ἐλεῆσαι Ho 1.6; οὐκέτι μὴ προσθῇ τοῦ ἀναστῆναι 'will not rise any more' Am 5.2; 7.8, 13, 8.2, Na 1.15, Zp 3.11; in an affirmative clause, Nu 22.15; reinforced by πλείων, comparative of πολύς– προσθῶσιν μαστιγῶσαι .. ὑπὲρ ταύτας τὰς πληγὰς πλείους 'keep whipping more than these beatings' De 25.3. At προσέθηκεν τεκεῖν τὸν ἀδελφὸν αὐτοῦ Ge 4.2 what is affected by προσ. is συλλαβοῦσα in the preceding verse, or there is a pause after τεκεῖν. **b**. as conjunctive ptc.: προσθέμενος .. ἔλαβεν γυναῖκα Ge 25.1; καὶ προσθεῖσα ἔτι ἔτεκεν υἱόν 38.5; w. slightly different nuance, προσθεῖσα ἐλάλησεν 'she went on to speak' Es 8.3 o'. **c**. + καί and a verb. fin.: προσέθετο ὁ ἄγγελος .. καὶ ἀπελθὼν ὑπέστη .. Nu 22.26; 1K 3.6B (vs. 8B and vs. 6 *L*: + inf.). **d**. pass. and with or without inf., *to repeat itself, recur*: κραυγὴ μεγάλη .. ἥτις τοιαύτη οὐ γέγονεν καὶ τοιαύτη οὐ προστεθήσεται 'a great cry .. the like of which had never occurred and will not be repeated' Ex 11.6; μετ' αὐτὸν οὐ προστεθήσεται 'after it there will not be the like of it again' Jl 2.2; impers., οὐκέτι προστεθήσεται διδόναι 'one is no longer going to give' Ex 5.7. **e**. abs., Nu 11.25; elliptical and resumed by a vb. fin., Is 10.20.

3. mid. *to side* with, *choose the side of*: οὐ προστεθήσῃ μετὰ πλήθους 'thou shalt not side with the majority' Ex 23.2; αὐτῷ (pers.) De 13.4, Jo 23.12, Jb 13.9.

4. mid. *to come, seeking affiliation* or *protection*: *s* fugitive slave, προστέθειταί σοι παρὰ τοῦ κυρίου αὐτοῦ De 23.15; εἰς τὸν οἶκον Ισραηλ Ju 14.10.

5. mid. *to apply to oneself*: + καρδίαν '(pay) attention' Ps 61.11.

Cf. ἐπιπροστίθημι, πρόσθεμα, πρόσθεσις, ἐπιστρέφω, ἐπιζεύγνυμι, προσαναπληρόω.

πρόστιμον, ου. n.ʃ

penalty: meted out by God, δίκαιος 2M 7.36. Cf. τιμωρία.

προστρέχω: aor. προσέδραμον, ptc. ~δραμών.ʃ

to run towards eagerly, *s* being of a relatively lowly situation: abs. Nu 11.27, Pr 18.10, To 11.9 $\mathfrak{G}^{I}$ ($\mathfrak{G}^{II}$ ἀνατρέχω); εἰς συνάντησίν τινι 'to meet sbd as a guest and welcome him' Ge 18.2 (foll. by προσκυνέω), 33.4; + dat. pers. To 11.10 $\mathfrak{G}^{I}$. Cf. τρέχω.

προσυπομιμνήσκω: aor.ptc. ~μνήσας.ʃ

to remind besides: τινά τι 2M 15.9. Cf. μιμνήσκομαι.

προσυστέλλω: pf.ptc.pass.προσυνεσταλμένος.ʃ *
to restrict previously: ***o*** αὐθεντία 'autonomous district' 3M 2.29.

προσυψόω: aor.inf. ~υψῶσαι.ʃ *
to make higher still: + acc. (city walls), 1M 12.36. Cf. ὑψόω.

πρόσφατος, ον.ʃ
1. *unprocessed*, 'fresh': ***s*** σταφυλή 'grapes' Nu 6.3 (: : σταφίς 'dried grapes')
2. *not well-known*: ***s*** gods, καινοὶ ~οι De 32.17; || ἀλλότριος Ps 80.10; φίλος 'friend', opp. ἀρχαῖος and || νέος Si 9.10; subst.n., || καινόν Ec 1.9.
Cf. καινός, νέος, προσφάτως, and ἀρχαῖος.

προσφάτως. adv.ʃ
recently: Ἐὰν τις λάβῃ γυναῖκα π. 'if someone has married recently' De 24.5; Ju 4.3, 5, Ez 11.3, 2M 14.36. Cf. πρόσφατος, νεωστί, (προσ)αρτίως.

προσφέρω: fut. ~οίσω, inf.mid.~οίσεσθαι; aor.act. προσήνεγκα, inf. ~ενέγκαι, ~νεγκεῖν, subj. ~ενέγκω, mid. ~ηνεγκάμην, ptc. προσενεγκάμενος, inf. ~ενέγκασθαι, pass. προσηνέχθην, inf. ~ενεχθῆναι; pf.act.1pl προσενηνόχαμεν.
1. *to bring* (to sbd): abs. Ex 36.6 (|| φέρω vs. 5), Nu 7.2; + acc. rei and dat. pers., αὐτῷ τὰ δῶρα Ge 43.26; + acc. (cultic offering) θυσίαν σωτηρίου Ex 32.6; || προσάγω Le 1.2, 3, 16.9, Nu 28.2 (|| προσάγω vs. 3); + acc., δῶρα Le 22.18, Jd 3.18; μίσθωμα πόρνης .. ἄλλαγμα κυνὸς εἰς τὸν οἶκον κυρίου 'harlot's fee .. dog's [= male prostitute's] wages ..' De 23.18; and dat. dei, μὴ σφάγια καὶ θυσίας προσηνέγκατέ μοι; 'you didn't bring me slaughtered animals and sacrifices, did you?' Am 5.25; πρὸς τὴν θύραν τῆς σκηνῆς τοῦ μαρτυρίου Le 1.3, ἐπὶ ^θυσιαστήριον^ 1E 5.48; πῦρ ἀλλότριον ἔναντι κυρίου Nu 3.4, 26.61, cf. Le 10.1; ἐναντίον κυρίου Ez 43.24. **b**. orally: προσήγαγεν .. τὴν κρίσιν αὐτῶν ἔναντι κυρίου 'presented their case to the Lord' Nu 27.5, cf. LSG s.v. **A I 4**; + dat. pers., 2M 11.18, + inf. cl. 3M 4.17.
2. mid. *to bring to bear*, 'apply': + acc., σπουδὴν καὶ φιλοπονίαν 'zeal and devotion' Si prol. 30, ἀγρυπνίαν καὶ ἐπιστήμην 'alertness and erudition' 31.
3. mid. *to consume*: abs., Wi 16.21; + acc., τροφήν 'food' Ju 12.9; Pr 6.8*b*.
Cf. φέρω, προσάγω, ἀναφέρω, προσφορά.

προσφιλής, ές.
liked, well-thought of: ***s*** hum. and + dat., συναγωγῇ Si 4.7; hum. face, Es D 5. Cf. φιλέω, ἀγαπητός: *ND* 4.171.

προσφορά, ᾶς. f.
that which is presented: cultic offering, + θυσία Ps 39.7, || δώρημα Si 31.21; ***o*** of προσάγω 14.11. Cf. προσφέρω.

προσφύω: aor.ptc.pass. ~φυείς.ʃ
pass., *to grow in addition* to sth else: ***s*** horn, Da 7.20 LXX (TH ἀναβαίνω). Cf. φύω.

προσφωνέω: aor.inf. ~φωνῆσαι, pass. ~φωνηθῆναι, impv.3s ~φωνησάτω.ʃ
to address and communicate to: + dat. pers., in writing, 1E 2.18, περί τινος 6.21; + acc. rei, τάδε, orally, 2M 15.15.

προσχαίρω.ʃ *
to rejoice at: τινι Pr 8.30. Cf. χαίρω.

προσχέω: fut. ~χεῶ; aor. προσέχεα, inf. ~χέειν, subj. ~χέω.
to pour forth at: ***o*** blood of a sacrificial animal, πρὸς τὸ θυσιαστήριον Ex 24.6, 29.16, Nu 18.17; ἐπὶ τὸ θυσιαστήριον Le 1.5; ἐπὶ τὴν βάσιν τοῦ θυσιαστηρίου 6.32; τὸ αἷμα τοῦ σωτηρίου 7.4. **b**. *to construct* a mound *by pouring out soil*: + acc., πρόσχωμα 'mound' 4K 19.32*L* (B: ἐκ~).
Cf. χέω.

προσχράομαι: aor.ptc. ~χρησάμενος.ʃ
to implement: + dat., directive, Es E 17 o' (*L* προσέχω).

πρόσχωμα, ατος. n.
**mound raised for attacking a city* (LSJ): 2K 20.15 (*L* χάραξ), Da 11.15 TH.

προσχωρέω: aor. προσεχώρησα, inf. ~χωρῆσαι; pf. ptc. ~κεχωρηκώς.ʃ
to side with and support: πρός τινα Je 21.9; "they shifted their allegiance from (ἀπό) Manasseh to (πρός) David" 1C 12.20; 2K 20.2*L* (B: κολλάομαι); + dat. pers., αὐτῷ ἀπὸ Μανασση 1C 12.21; "you remained loyal friends and did not move over to our enemies' side" 1M 10.26. Cf. προσέρχομαι **1d**.

προσωθέω.ʃ
to push towards: εἰς ὄλεθρον 'to ruin' 2M 13.6. Cf. ὠθέω.

προσωπεῖον, ου. n.ʃ
mask: 4M 15.15.

πρόσωπον, ου. n.
1. *front of head*, 'face': σκορπιῶ ἔνυστρον ἐπὶ τὰ ~α ὑμῶν 'I shall spread cud on your faces' Ma 2.3; Na 2.2, 3.5, Jl 2.6*b*; God's, Ex 33.23 (: : τὰ ὀπίσω μου vs. 23). **b**. the focal point of personal contact: anthropomorphically, δεηθῆναι τοῦ ~ου κυρίου Zc 8.21; ἐπιζητήσουσι τὸ ~όν μου Ho 5.15; ἐκζητῆσαι τὸ π. κυρίου Zc 8.22; ἀποστρέψει τὸ π. αὐτοῦ ἀπ' αὐτῶν 'he will cease to pay attention to them' Mi 3.4; used pleonastically in idioms expressing personal relationship, ἐξιλάσκομαι τὸ π. τινος 'to appease sbd' (e.g. Zc 8.22, Ma 1.9) = ἐξιλάσκομαί τινα (e.g. Zc 7.2). Also with λαμβάνω (see under λ., **III 2**), εἶδον, and ὁράω. **b**. With ref. to facial expression of one's inner state, συνέπεσεν τῷ ~ῳ 'he became despondent' Ge 4.5, cf. 4.6; τί ὅτι

τὰ ~α ὑμῶν σκυθρωπὰ σήμερον; 'why are you looking gloomy today?' Ge 40.7; Διὰ τί τὸ π. σου πονηρὸν ..; Ne 2.2; ἀναιδὲς ~ῳ De 28.50 (|| τῇ ψυχῇ Is 56.11), Pr 7.13 || ψυχὴ ἀναιδής Si 23.6. Cf. **7**.

2. *surface*: ἐπὶ ~ου ὕδατος Ho 10.7; ἀπὸ ~ου τῆς γῆς Ge 6.7, De 6.15; ἐπὶ ~ον τῆς ἐρήμου Ex 16.14; ἐπὶ ~ου τοῦ πεδίου Nu 19.16; ἐπὶ ~ον πάσης τῆς γῆς Zc 5.3. Cf. below **6a, f**.

3. *foremost part* or *line of hostile army*: ἀνθεστηκότας ~οις αὐτῶν 'those who have taken up the position of frontal resistance' Hb 1.9.

4. *area facing* sth: ἐκ τοῦ ἑνὸς ~ου 'from one direction' Ex 25.37.

5. idiom, ἐπιγινώσκω / θαυμάζω / λαμβάνω / ὑποστέλλω π. τινος 'to show respect,' see under each of the respective verbs.

*6. under the infl. of Heb. פָּנִים, becomes a constituent of various compound prepositions. **a**. ἀπὸ ~ου τινός w. verbs of moving away or removing, ἀναστέλλω Na 1.5; ἀπαλείφω Ge 6.7; ἀποδιδράσκω 16.6, 8, 35.1; ἐκβάλλω 4.14, Ex 34.24, De 11.23; ἐκλείπω Zp 1.2; ἐξαίρω 1.3; ἐξέρχομαι Ge 27.30; ἐξολεθρεύω De 9.5, 31.3; κρύπτω 3.8; πορεύομαι 36.6; φεύγω Ex 14.25, De 28.7; w. verbs or nouns of fearing, δειλιάω, De 31.6; εὐλαβέομαι Zp 1.7, Hb 2.20; διευλαβέομαι De 28.60; πτοέω 31.6; φοβέομαι ib., Hg 1.12, φόβος καὶ τρόμος Is 19.16 (|| διά τι vs. 17); στέλλομαι Ma 2.5, σείομαι 'tremble' Ez 38.20; ἀπὸ ~ου πολιοῦ ἐξαναστήσῃ 'in the presence of an elderly person you shall stand up' Le 19.32; *on account of, because of* - ἀπὸ ~ου κακιῶν ὑμῶν Ho 10.15; Hg 2.14 (|| ἕνεκεν); *confronted by*, ἀπὸ ~ου ὀργῆς αὐτοῦ τίς ὑποστήσεται 'who could withstand His wrath?' Na 1.6; ἀπὸ ~ου αὐτοῦ συντριβήσονται λαοί 'nations will be crushed ..' Jl 2.6; τακήσονται ὡς κηρὸς ἀπὸ ~ου πυρός 'will melt as wax before the fire' Mi 1.4; κατακρύψω ἀπὸ ~ου τοῦ φόβου κυρίου Is 2.18f.; σεισθήσεται 'will shiver' 19.1: Sollamo, *Semiprep.*, 33f., 85f., 95-7, 114, 328f. **b**. ἀπέναντι τοῦ ~ου μου ἐγένοντο 'they came face to face with me' Ho 7.2. **c**. εἰς ~όν τινος– *in the face of*, indicating humiliation inflicted or suffered: ἐμπτύσεται εἰς τὸ ~ον αὐτοῦ 'she will spit at him' De 25.9 (poss. literal), ταπεινωθήσεται ἡ ὕβρις Ισραηλ εἰς ~ον αὐτοῦ 'Israel's hubris will be brought low in his face' Ho 7.10, cf. δώσω τὸν βάσανον εἰς τὸ ~ον αὐτοῦ 'I shall subject him to torments' Ez 3.20; without τινος - εἰς ~ον σε εὐλογήσει 'he will bless (!) you openly' Jb 1.11; *into the space directly opposite*: Le 16.2. **d**. ἐκ ~ου τινός, indicating movement *away from* w. verbs of fleeing, ἀποίχομαι Ho 11.2, φεύγω Jn 1.3*a*; departing, ἐξέρχομαι Ge 41.46, emerging Ps 16.2, sent by a king on a military expedition Ju 2.5; avoiding and shunning, Jn 1.3*b*, 10; removing, λάβητε 'take away' Ge 44.29; ἐξαρῶ τὴν πορνείαν αὐτῆς ἐκ ~ου μου 'I shall get her fornication out of my sight' Ho 2.2; of an edict issued by a king, Da 6.26 TH; *on account of*, 1K 8.18. **e**. ἐν ~ῳ τινός 'in the presence of': μὴ ὀφθῇς ἐν ~ῳ κυρίου κενός 'Do not appear .. empty-handed, i.e. with no offering' Si 32.6, cf. Ex 23.15 with ἐνώπιον; ἄνδρας ὀνομαστοὺς ἐν ~ῳ τοῦ βασιλέως 'renowned men from among the inner circle of the king' Je 52.25. **f**. ἐπὶ ~ου πάσης τῆς γῆς Ge 7.23, 41.56; ἐπὶ ~ου Ιεριχω 'facing, looking towards J.' De 34.1 (|| κατὰ Ι. vs. 8); ἐπέβλεψεν ἐπὶ ~ον Σοδόμων .. 'looked at the whole expanse of Sodom ..' Ge 19.28; ἐπὶ ~όν μου 'confronting me' Jb 19.8; hostile action, 29.5; ἐπὶ ~ον ἀνέμου 2K 22.43*L* (based on a faulty Heb. text על פני רוח for 4Q51 [על] פני ארח). **g**. κατὰ ~όν τινος 'facing, opposite': κ. π. πάντων τῶν ἀδελφῶν αὐτοῦ κατοικήσει Ge 16.12; κατὰ π. Μαμβρη 23.17 (|| ἀπέναντι Μ. vs. 19); "in his presence, under his personal supervision" 2C 34.4; '(folding over) at the front edge of ..' Ex 26.9; Εἰσέλθοι πᾶσα ἡ κακία αὐτῶν κ. π. σου 'Let all their wrongdoings come up before you (for judgement)!' La 1.22; ἐν τοῖς νομίμοις μου, οἷς ἔδωκα κ. π. ὑμῶν 'my statutes which I set before you' Je 33.4; metaph.,'vis-à-vis, in relation to' - δὸς ἡμῖν χάριν κατὰ π. τῶν ἀποικισάντων ἡμᾶς 'Grant us favour in the sight of those who have taken us into exile' Ba 2.14; κατὰ ~ον with no gen. following, meaning either 'in front' Ex 28.25, 36.26 or 'in person' or 'individually, i.e. not collectively' (*BA* ad De 7.10) – De 7.10, 31.21, Jo 6.5, Si 17.25, 45.5, see Sollamo, *Semiprep.*, 325-7; ἔγνω κύριος αὐτὸν π. κατὰ π. '.. knew him personally' De 34.10; π. κατὰ π. ἐλάλησεν κύριος πρὸς ὑμᾶς 5.4; λήμψεται αὐτοὺς κατὰ π. αὐτῶν 'he will confront them and capture them' Is 30.28. **h**. πρὸ ~ου τινός: *ahead of* – ἀποστέλλω τὸν ἄγγελόν μου πρὸ ~ου σου Ex 23.20; ἐξαπέστειλα πρὸ ~ου σου τὸν Μωυσῆν Mi 6.4 (as leader); εἰς τὴν γῆν De 31.7; κύριος δώσει φωνὴν αὐτοῦ πρὸ ~ου δυνάμεως αὐτοῦ Jl 2.11; πρὸ ~ου αὐτοῦ πορεύσεται λόγος Hb 3.5; *facing, opposite* – πεσεῖσθε πρὸ ~ου τῶν ἐχθρῶν ὑμῶν Nu 14.42; ὡς παράδεισος τρυφῆς ἡ γῆ πρὸ ~ου αὐτοῦ Jl 2.3; τὸν ἱερέα τὸν μέγαν ἑστῶτα πρὸ ~ου κυρίου ἀγγέλου Zc 3.1; καθήμενοι πρὸ ~ου σου 3.8; *in the sight of, before the eyes of, right in front of* - ἐξολεθρεῦσαι ἔθνη .. πρὸ ~ου σου De 4.38, sim. 9.4 (|| ἀπὸ ~ου σου 9.5, 18.12), ἐξαναλῶσαι κύριον .. τὰ ἔθνη ταῦτα πρὸ ~ου σου, cf. κύριος .. προπορεύεται πρὸ ~ου σου .. ἐξολεθρεύσει αὐτούς 9.3; 'in defiance of' – οὐκ ἔσονταί σοι θεοὶ ἕτεροι πρὸ ~ου μου De 5.7:

Sollamo, *Semiprep.*, 30f., 87f. **i.** σὺν τῷ ~ῳ τινός 'in the close proximity of ..' Ps 139.14ʃ. **j.** εἶδον θεὸν π. πρὸς π. 'he saw God face to face' Ge 32.30; Jd 6.22.

7. In some Hebraistic collocations, πρόσωπον denotes that part of a human body where one's inner feelings and attitudes may be read off and where one's whole person is represented, cf. **1 b** and Engl. *to lose/save face*: ʽΟρῶ ἐγὼ τὸ π. τοῦ πατρὸς ὑμῶν ὅτι οὐκ ἔστιν πρὸς ἐμοῦ ὡς ἐχθὲς καὶ τρίτην ἡμέραν Ge 31.5; Ἐξιλάσομαι τὸ π. αὐτοῦ .. ὄψομαι τὸ π. αὐτοῦ .. προσδέξεται τὸ π. μου 'I shall appease him ..' 32.20; τιμήσεις ~ον πρεσβυτέρου 'to show respect to an elderly person' Le 19.32; ἠρέτισα (*L* ἐνετράπην) τὸ π. σου 1K 25.35; μὴ ἱλαρώσῃς πρὸς αὐτὰς τὸ π. σου 'don't appear too accommodating towards them' Si 7.24, καρδία ἀνθρώπου ἀλλοιοῖ τὸ π. αὐτοῦ 'man's mood alters ..' 13.25; ἐφόβου .. τὸ π. τοῦ θυμοῦ .. Is 51.13; τὸ π. σου ζητήσω Ps 26.8; μετὰ αἰσχύνης ~ου 'shame-faced' 2C 32.21. Cf. τῷ ~ῳ τῆς ἐξουσίας 'with an air of authority' 2M 4.24.

***8**. mechanical rendition of Heb.: τὸ π. τοῦ ⌜λόγου⌝ (B: ῥήματος) = פְּנֵי הַדָּבָר 'the state of affairs' 2K 14.20*L*.

See, beside Sollamo, *Semiprep.*, also Ghiron-Bistagne.

προτάσσω: aor.subj. ~τάξω.ʃ

to estimate to be greater than: + acc. and gen., Es 4.15 *L*.

προτείνω: aor. ~έτεινα, ptc. ~τείνας.

to stretch forth: + acc., τὰς χεῖρας εἰς τὸν οὐρανόν 2M 3.20 (*s* suppliant), 7.10 (willing victim of torture). Cf. τείνω.

προτείχισμα, ατος. n.

structure in front of main line of defence: "between the wall and ..' Je 52.7; ‖ τεῖχος La 2.8; 2K 20.15B (*L* περι~). Cf. περιτείχισμα, τεῖχος.

προτέρημα, ατος. n.ʃ

advantage gained: military victory, Jd 4.9.

πρότερος, α, ον.

1. *former, prior to the present time*: τὴν ἀρχήν σου τὴν ~αν 'your earlier office' Ge 40.13; τὸν ἄνδρα μου τὸν ~ον 'my former husband' Ho 2.7; subst., τὰ ~α 'the past events' Is 41.22 (:: τὰ ἔσχατα). **b**. predicatively: οἱ Ομμιν ~οι ἐνεκάθηντο ἐπ' αὐτῆς 'the O. used to live there formerly' De 2.10. **c**. τὸ πρότερον: adv. 'formerly'– Ge 13.3, 28.19, Nu 21.26, De 2.20, Jd 1.10B (A: ἔμπροσθεν); without the article, 2M 10.24; ὡς τὸ ~ον .. ὡς τὸ ἀπ' ἀρχῆς Is 1.26; opp. νυνί Jb 42.5; opp. τὸ ἔσχατον 'thereafter' Jo 10.14; used as indecl. adj., ἐν ταῖς ~ον ἡμέραις Ju 8.18, τὴν .. συμμαχίαν τὴν ~ον 1M 12.16.

2. *earlier*: Οὗτος ἐξελεύσεται ~ος 'this shall come out first' Ge 38.28. **b**. + gen. and used predicatively, προτέρα αὐτῆς οὐ γέγονεν τοιαύτη ἀκρίς 'before these there had never been so many locusts' Ex 10.14; οἱ ὄντες ~οι ὑμῶν 'who were (there) before you, your predecessors' Le 18.27 (‖ τοῖς πρὸ ὑμῶν vs. 28); ἡμέρας ~έρας τὰς γενομένας ~έρας σου 'earlier days which preceded you' De 4.32; οἱ προφῆται οἱ γεγονότες ~οί μου 'the prophets who preceded me' Je 35.8. **c**. sg. n., adv. 'in advance': ἀναγγέλλων ~ον τὰ ἔσχατα πρὶν αὐτὰ γενέσθαι 'announcing the future events in advance before they happen' Is 46.10; *earlier than a point in the past* - 1M 1.1.

3. *further ahead*, predicatively + gen.: ἀποστελῶ τὰς σφηκιὰς ~ας σου 'I shall send the hornets ahead of you' Ex 23.28; παρελεύσομαι ~ός σου 33.2; 33.19.

Cf. πρῶτος, ἔσχατος, ὕστερος: Shipp 475.

προτίθημι: fut. ~θήσω, mid. ~θήσομαι; aor. ~έθηκα, ptc. ~θείς, mid. ~εθέμην, pass.ptc. ~τεθείς, 2aor. act.3pl ~ἔθεσαν; pf.ptc.pass. ~τεθειμένος.

to set before sbd: ***o*** an object dangerous to a pedestrian, ἀπέναντι τυφλοῦ οὐ προθήσεις σκάνδαλον Le 19.14; cultic offering, τῶν ἀζύμων τῶν προτεθειμένων ἔναντι κυρίου 'of the unleavened bread set before the Lord' Ex 29.23; πρόθεσιν 'offering' 40.4; ἐπὶ ^τῆς τραπέζης^ ἄρτους τῆς προθέσεως 40.21; + dat. pers., αὐτοῖς ἐπιστήμην Si 17.11; pass., ***o*** ὅρκος 'oath' Pr 29.24. **b**. mid., ***s*** the high priest Si 24.8, τὸν θεὸν ἐνώπιον αὐτῶν Ps 53.5 (to obey Him), sim. 85.14; ***o*** proposal, + inf., 3M 2.27.

Cf. τίθημι, προστίθημι, πρόθεσις.

προτιμάω: pf.ptc.pass. ~τετιμημένος.ʃ

to honour more than others: ***o*** day, 2M 15.2; + acc. rei, 4M 1.15. Cf. τιμάω.

προτομή, ῆς. f.ʃ

head and face of the decapitated: of bulls, 3K 10.19; of hum., 2M 15.35. Cf. κεφαλή.

προτρέπομαι: aor. ~ετρεψάμην, ptc. ~τρεψάμενος.ʃ

to urge to an action: + acc. pers., 4M 12.7; and inf., 2M 11.7; + εἴς τι Wi 14.18, + ἐπί τι 4M 15.12, 16.13. Cf. παρακαλέω **5**: Spicq 3.201-3.

προτρέχω: aor.subj. ~δράμω, ptc. ~δραμών.

to run ahead of sbd: τινος 1K 8.11, To 11.3 𝔊II (𝔊I ἔμπροσθέν τινος); πρὸ προσώπου τινος 2K 15.1*L*; ***s*** he-goat as leader, Je 27.8, see Ziegler 1958.25. Cf. τρέχω.

προϋπάρχω.ʃ

to be so and so *previously*: Jb 42.17bγ. Cf. εἰμί, ὑπάρχω, προϋφίστημι.

προυποτάσσω: pf.ptc.pass. ~τεταγμένος.ʃ *

to place earlier under the responsibility of: + dat. pers., ***o*** weapons, 3M 1.2. Cf. ὑποτάσσω.

προϋφίστημι: pf.ptc. ~ϋφεστώς.ʃ
= προϋπάρχω: *s* raging sea water, Wi 19.7.

προφαίνω: aor. προεφάνησα, προυφάνησα, on which latter see Thack. 138.ʃ
to come into view: 4M 4.10; of sbd. (dat.), 2M 3.26 (|| ὤφθη vs. 25). Cf. (ἐπι)φαίνω, ὁράομαι.

προφανῶς. adv.ʃ
openly, in public: Si 51.13.

προφασίζομαι.ʃ
1. *to offer excuses, attempt to justify oneself by deception*: w. cogn. acc., ἐν ἁμαρτίαις 'while sunken in sins' Ps 140.4; Pr 22.13.
2. *to seek an excuse for a quarrel against*: + acc. pers., 4K 5.7 (v.l. dat.).
Cf. πρόφασις.

πρόφασις, εως. f.
ostensible reason for an action, 'excuse, pretext': λαλῶν ῥήματα ~εις ψευδεῖς 'uttering words which amount to nothing but false excuses' Ho 10.4; cogn. acc. of προφασίζομαι Ps 140.4; ground for false allegation, ἐζήτουν εὑρεῖν ~ιν κατὰ Δανιηλ Da TH 6.4; + παράπτωμα 'slip, false step' ib.; + inf., Pr 18.1. Cf. προφασιστικός, προφασίζομαι: Spicq 3.204-6.

προφασιστικός, ή, όν.ʃ *
consisting of false allegations (LSG): *s* λόγοι De 22.14, 17. Cf. πρόφασις.

προφέρω: aor. προήνεγκα.
1. *to bring before, produce*: + acc., To 9.5; metaph., ἐκ χειλέων .. σοφίαν 'from lips ..' Pr 10.13 (|| ἐκφέρω vs. 18).
2. mid. *to insist on saying*: + inf., 3M 1.12, 4.17, 7.11; + acc. rei, τάδε 3M 5.39. Cf. LSG s.v.

προφητεία, ας. f.
that which has been said by προφήτης: ἐπ' ὀνόματί σου 'in your name' Si 36.20. **b**. pl., the second division of the tripartite Hebrew Bible: ὁ νόμος καὶ αἱ ~αι καὶ τὰ λοιπὰ τῶν βιβλίων Si pr 24 (|| προφῆται 1, 9). Cf. προφήτης.

προφητεύω: fut. ~φητεύσω; aor. ἐπροφήτευσα, impv. ~φήτευσον, inf. ~φητεῦσαι, subj. ~φητεύσω.
to prophesy: in response to God's utterance, Am 3.8; addressing sbd (ἐπί τινα), 7.15; following an outpouring of the divine spirit, Nu 11.25, Jl 2.28; + dat. (authority invoked), τῇ Βααλ Je 2.8 (|| διὰ τῆς Β. 23.13), τῷ ὀνόματι κυρίου 33.9; ἐπὶ τῷ ὀνόματι κυρίου 11.21; dat. (addressee) and + acc. rei, ὁράσεις ψευδεῖς καὶ μαντείας καὶ οἰωνίσματα καὶ προαιρέσεις καρδίας αὐτῶν .. ὑμῖν 'false visions and oracles and .. and what their minds fancy to you' 14.14, ψευδῆ 14.15, ἄδικα 36.9, τοὺς λόγους τούτους 20.1, τὰ θελήματα τῆς καρδίας αὐτῶν 23.26, ἐνύπνια ψευδῆ 'false dreams' 23.32; κατά τινος 33.11 (|| ἐπί τινα vs. 12), προφητείαν ἐπί τινα 2E 5.1; 'to play the prophet' 1K 18.10*L*. Cf. προφήτης, προφητεία.

προφήτης, ου. m.
1. *prophet*: named, Αγγαῖος ὁ π. Hg 1.12; called God's δοῦλος, Am 3.7, Zc 1.6; appointed by God, Am 2.11; || ἡγιασμένος Am 2.12; leader of a nation, Ho 12.13; Mi 3.11 (|| ἡγούμενος), + ἄρχοντες Is 29.10, + ἱερεύς 28.7, cf. τοὺς ~ας τοὺς πλανῶντας τὸν λαόν μου 'who lead my people astray' Mi 3.5; practises divination 3.11; conveys divine message, Hg 1.1, 3, Zc 1.4; divine vision (ὅρασις) 13.4; prays, Hb 3.1, on behalf of someone else (περί τινος) Ge 20.7; || ἐνυπνιαζόμενος ἐνύπνιον De 13.1, 3, 5; || ἱερεύς, συνετός Je 18.18. **b**. glossed as βλέπων 'seer' 1K 9.9, ὁρῶν 2K 24.11.
2. *spokesman*: for another person, Ααρων ὁ ἀδελφός σου ἔσται σου π. Ex 7.1.
3. *the books of the Prophets* including the historical books: + ὁ νόμος Si prol 1, 9.
Cf. προφητεία, προφητεύω, προφῆτις, ψευδοπροφήτης, ἐνυπνιάζομαι, μάντις: Frascher 1927. 102-52.

προφῆτις, εως. f.
prophetess: playing a leading role, Ex 15.20; Jd 4.4, Is 8.3. Cf. προφήτης.

προφθάνω: fut. ~φθάσω; aor. προέφθασα, impv. ~φθασον, subj. ~φθάσω; pf. ~έφθακα.
1. *to act with foresight and in anticipation*: + inf. προέφθασα τοῦ φυγεῖν 'with foresight I fled' Jn 4.2; Ps 118.148, 1M 10.4; ἐν ἀωρίᾳ 'in the dead of night' Ps 118.147.
2. *to act ahead of*: + acc. pers., Ps 16.13, Si 19.27; + inf., 1M 10.23; *s* God's mercy, Ps 58.11. **b**. abs., *to lead the way*: Ps 67.26.
3*. *to face, confront* sbd: + acc. pers., 1K 20.25; ***o* τὸ πρόσωπον αὐτοῦ ἐν ἐξομολογήσει Ps 94.2, ἐν εὐλογίαις 20.4; *s* σκληρότητες (*L*: παγίδες) θανάτου 'agonies of death' 2K 22.6, παγίδες Ps 17.6, ἡμέραι πτωχείας 'days of poverty' Jb 30.27¶, θυρεός 'shield' 4K 19.32 (*L*: θυρεῷ), προσευχή Ps 87.14.
***4**. *to stretch out*: χεῖρα αὐτῆς τῷ θεῷ Ps 67.32, cf. ἐκτείνω **3**.
Cf. φθάνω.

προφυλακή, ῆς. f.
1. *outpost for defence*: ἡμεῖς ἐνοπλισάμενοι π. πρότεροι τῶν υἱῶν Ισραηλ 'we, having armed ourselves, shall be the first line of defence ..' Nu 32.17; ἑτοιμάσουσι τὰς ~ὰς αὐτῶν Na 2.6; Ez 26.8; τῶν 'Ασσυρίων Ju 10.11.
2. *staying awake and alert* at night, 'vigil': ἐκείνη ἡ νὺξ αὕτη π. κυρίῳ Ex 12.42 (the paschal night); ἔστω ὑμῖν ἡ νὺξ ~ὴ καὶ ἡ ἡμέρα ἔργον 'Let your night be a time for vigil and the day a time for work' Ne 4.22.

3. *guard duty*, not necessarily at night: ἄνδρες τῆς ~ῆς Ne 4.23; ἀνὴρ ἐν ~ῇ αὐτοῦ 7.3; εἰς ~ὴν τοῦ μὴ ἐξελθεῖν ἐκ τῆς πόλεως ἄνδρα ἕνα '.. so that not a man would leave the city' Ju 7.13

Cf. προφύλαξ, (προ)φυλάσσω.

προφύλαξ, ακος. m.ʃ

advance guard: ἐστήσαμεν ~ακας ἐπ' αὐτοὺς ἡμέρας καὶ νυκτός 'we set guards against them day and night' Ne 4.9; 7.3; ἐξέβαλεν ~ακας κύκλῳ τῆς παρεμβολῆς 'stationed outposts around the camp' 1M 12.27.

Cf. προφυλακή.

προφυλάσσω: fut.mid.~φυλάξομαι.ʃ

to be on guard against sbd or sth: ἀπὸ τῆς ἀνομίας μου 2K 22.24B (*L* simp.).

Cf. φυλάσσω.

προχαλάω: pf.pass.3s ~κεχάλασται.ʃ

to cause to hang loose before sbd: pass., *o* one's tongue, 4M 10.19. Cf. χαλάω.

προχειρίζω: aor.impv.mid. ~χείρισαι, ptc.mid. ~χειρισάμενος, pass. ~χειρισθείς.

to choose for a task out of multiple alternatives: + acc. pers., δυνάμενον ἄλλον Ex 4.13, ὑμῖν δώδεκα ἄνδρας ἀπὸ τῶν υἱῶν Ισραηλ Jo 3.12; 2M 3.7, Da LXX 3.22. Cf. αἱρετίζω, ἐκλέγω, διακρίνω: Spicq 3.207-9; *ND* 3.82.

πρόχειρος, ον.ʃ

about to happen at any moment, 'round the corner': *s* sbd's death, Pr 11.3.

προχώρημα, ατος. n.ʃ

excrement: human, Ez 32.6. Cf. ἀφόδευμα.

πρύτανις, εως. m.ʃ

ruler: κόσμου Wi 13.2. Cf. ἄρχων.

πρώην. adv.ʃ

the day before yesterday: Jo 8.5. Cf. ἐχθές.

πρωΐ, n. (indeclinable) and adv.

I. *n. *morning*: καὶ ἐγένετο π. 'and it became morning' Ge 1.5, 8 (opp., and preceded by, ἑσπέρα); τὸ πρωῒ ἐγενήθη 'it dawned' Ex 10.13; τὸ π. διέφαυσεν 'the morning dawned' Ge 44.3.

II. adv. *in the morning*: opp. 'in the night' Ho 7.6; π. π. 'morning after morning' Ex 16.21, Zp 3.5, Is 28.19, Ez 46.13 (967); = τὸ π. π. Ex 30.7, 36.3, Le 6.12, 1C 9.27. **b**. τὸ π. = π.: ἀναστὰς τὸ πρωῒ 'rising early' Ge 21.14, 22.3; opp. τὸ δειλινόν Le 6.20; τὸ ἑσπέρας De 28.67; τὸ π. καὶ εἰς ἑσπέραν 2E 3.3. **c**. εἰς τὸ π. = π.: ἐκτρίβοντες εἰς τὸ π. πένητα 'oppress the poor in the morning' Am 8.4; 4.4; 'till the morning' Ex 16.19, Zp 3.3.

Cf. πρωϊνός, πρώϊος, δειλινός, ἑσπέρα, ἑωθινός, ὄρθρος, ὀψέ, and νύξ.

πρωΐθεν.

an early hour of the day: alw. + ἀπό or ἐκ, ἀπὸ π. ἕως ἑσπέρας 'from the morning till the evening' Ex 18.13 (‖ ἀπὸ πρωῒ ἕως δείλης vs. 14), Jb 4.20, Si 18.26; ἐκ π. ἕως δείλης 1M 10.80, .. ἕως μεσημβρίας '.. till midday' 3K 18.26B. Cf. πρωΐ, πρωϊνός, δείλη.

πρωϊνός, ή, όν.

occurring early in the day: *s* θυσία Ex 29.41, ὁλοκαύτωμα 'whole burnt offering' Le 9.17, ὁλοκαύτωσις 4K 16.15B (:: ἑσπερινός); νεφέλη ~ή 'morning cloud' Ho 6.4, 13.3; φέγγος 'light' Jb 38.12; φυλακή '(morning) watch' 1K 11.11. **b**. τὸ ~όν adv., Ge 49.27 (‖ εἰς τὸ ἑσπέρας 'towards the evening'), 1E 1.10; τὸ πρωϊνὸν καὶ τὸ δειλινόν 5.49.

Cf. δειλινός, ἑσπερινός, ἑωθινός, πρόϊμος, πρώϊος: Shipp 428.

πρώϊος, α, ον.

early in the day: ἀπὸ φυλακῆς ~ας μέχρι νυκτός 'from the morning watch till the night' Ps 129.6. **b**. subst. f., *morning*: sg., ἐξόδους ~ας καὶ ἑσπέρας Ps 64.9, προσδοκῶντα τὴν ~ΐαν 'looking forward to the dawn' 3M 5.24; Si 47.10; ἐν ~ΐᾳ Ec 10.16, 11.6 (:: εἰς ἑσπέραν), pl. εἰς τὰς ~ας 'till the morning' Ps 72.14, 100.8.

Cf. πρωΐ, ἑσπέρα, and νύξ.

πρῳρεύς, έως.ʃ

skipper, captain of ship: Jn 1.6; τῆς θαλάσσης Ez 27.29. On the spelling, see Walters, 69. Cf. κυβερνήτης.

πρωταγωνιστής, οῦ. m.

leader on battlefield: 1M 9.11. Cf. στρατηγός.

πρώταρχος, ον.ʃ

primal: *s* στρατηγός 'governor' 2M 10.11.

πρωτεύω.ʃ

to hold the leading position: *s* Haman and + ἡγέομαι τῆς βασιλείας Es 5.11 o'; γραμματεύς 2M 6.18; elephant as fighting force, 13.15.

Cf. ἡγέομαι, πρώταρχος: *ND* 4.172.

πρωτοβαθρέω.ʃ*

to place sbd's *seat in front of* others: + gen. pers., Es 3.1 o'.

πρωτοβολέω: fut. ~βολήσω.ʃ *

to produce new fruit: Ez 47.12.

πρωτογένημα, ατος. n.

first-fruit of labour: agricultural, ἑορτὴν θερισμοῦ ~άτων .. τῶν ἔργων Ex 23.16; τὰς ἀπαρχὰς τῶν ~άτων τῆς γῆς 23.19; as cultic offerings, Le 2.14, Nu 18.13. Cf. πρωτόγονος.

πρωτογενής, ές.ʃ

first-born: *s* both humans and animals, πρωτότοκον ~ές Ex 13.2; υἱός Pr 31.2.

Cf. πρωτόγονος.

πρωτόγονος, ον.ʃ

first to emerge: subst. as child, 'first-born'– Ισραηλ, ὃν ~ῳ ὡμοίωσας 'Israel, whom you compared to the first-born child' Si 36.17, sim. 17.18¶; 'first-fruits' Mi 7.1. Cf. πρωτότοκος, πρωτογένημα, πρωτογενής, πρωτότοκος.

πρωτοκλήσιον, ου. n.ʃ*
pl. *a festival on a king's coronation*: 2M 4.21.

πρωτοκουρία, ας. f.ʃ *
first-shearing: as cultic offering, To 1.6 𝔊I.

πρωτοκουρά, ᾶς. f.ʃ*
= πρωτοκουρία: as cultic offering, τῶν προβάτων To 1.6 𝔊II. Cf. κουρά.

πρωτολογία, ας. f.ʃ
act of speaking first in a law-court: Pr 18.17.

πρωτόπλαστος, ον.ʃ *
first-formed: *s* Adam, Wi 7.1, 10.1. Cf. πλάσσω.

πρῶτος, η, ον.
first in order: ἡ ἀρχὴ ἡ ~η Mi 4.8; || δεύτερος and τρίτος Zc 6.2, 14.10; among more than two terms, Nu 10.14 (opp. ἔσχατος 10.25); among two terms, ἐν πρώτοις .. ἐπ' ἐσχάτῳ De 13.9 (|| .. ἐπ' ἐσχάτων 17.7; cf. 3K 17.13 .. ἐπ' ἐσχάτου, but *L* as at De 13.9), 3K 21.17; ἐν ~οις 'at the beginning, initially' Si 4.17, 'as the first (to do)' 1C 11.6; δυνάμει ἰσχυρᾷ ἐν ~οις 'heading a strong army' 1M 6.6; adv. n., ~ον .. δεύτερον .. τὸ τρίτον 'firstly .. secondly ..' 23.23; παῦσαι π. 'be the first to finish' Si 34.17. **b.** of space, *found at the front, foremost*: w. ref. to the East, τὴν θάλασσαν τὴν ~ην Jl 2.20 and Zc 14.8 (see s.v. ἔσχατος); ἐποίησεν τὰς δύο παιδίσκας καὶ τοὺς υἱοὺς αὐτῶν ἐν ~οις 'he positioned the two maids and their sons up front' Ge 33.2, cf. 1K 9.22. **c.** *earlier* in time: "the past (πρώτη) glory will surpass the future (ἐσχάτη) one" Hg 2.9; τὰ πρῶτα Is 43.18 (|| τὰ ἀρχαῖα); ἐν ~οις 'in earlier times' 2K 20.18; ἐκ ~ου 'previously, before' Jb 42.11. **d.** of degree, *choice, of top quality*: ~α μύρα Am 6.6, ~ον μέλι καὶ ἔλαιον Ez 27.17. **e.** subst. n.sg. *before everything else*: Τοῦτο ~ον ποίει 'Do this first' Is 9.1.
Cf. πρότερος, πρωτότοκος, ἀρχαῖος, and ἔσχατος.

πρωτοστάτης, ου. m.ʃ
one who holds the highest office: used adj., στρατηγὸς π. Jb 15.24.

πρωτοτοκεύω: aor.inf. ~κεῦσαι.ʃ *
to invest with the privilege of primogeniture: + dat. pers., De 21.16. Cf. πρωτότοκος, πρωτοτόκια.

πρωτοτοκέω.ʃ *
to bear one's first-born: Je 4.31; *s* cow, 2K 6.7, 10. Cf. πρωτότοκος and τίκτω.

πρωτοτόκια. n.pl. *
rights of the first-born: τούτῳ (= τῷ πρωτοτόκῳ υἱῷ) καθήκει τὰ π. 'the rights of primogeniture are properly his' De 21.17; Ge 25.31, 33.
Cf. πρωτότοκος.

πρωτότοκος, ον.
**first-born*: υἱός defined as πρωτογενὲς διανοῖγον πᾶσαν μήτραν 'born first, opening every womb' Ex 13.2; Ge 25.25 (one of twins); υἱὸς π. Ισραηλ Ex 4.22; subst. and esp. valued, *s* sacrifical animals, Ge 4.4; child, 10.15, 27.19, Zc 12.10 (|| ἀγαπητός, cf. 2K 13.21, 2C 21.3); both humans and animals, Ex 12.29; opp. νεώτερος Ge 43.33; offered to God, Mi 6.7; || ἀπαρχή Ex 22.29 || ἀφαίρεμα, ἀπαρχή Ez 44.30; ~ον .. ὑψηλὸν παρὰ τοῖς βασιλεῦσιν τῆς γῆς Ps 88.28; ~ον μόσχου καὶ ~ον προβάτου Ex 34.19; ὁλοκαυτώματα .. θυσιάσματα .. ἀπαρχὰς .. εὐχὰς .. ἑκούσια .. ~α De 12.6; ταύρου 33.17. Cf. ἀπαρχή, πρῶτος, πρωτοτοκεύω, πρωτοτόκια, πρωτόγονος, πρωτογενής, τίκτω: Michaelis 1954. 313-20, esp. 314: Frey 1930.385-90; Spicq 3.210-2.

πταῖσμα, ατος. n.ʃ
failure to achieve an aim: on battlefield, euphemistically for defeat, 1K 6.4. Cf. πταίω, πτῶσις **2**.

πταίω: aor. ἔπταισα, inf. πταῖσαι, subj. πταίσω; pf. ἔπταικα, ptc. ἐπταικώς.
1. *to stumble, trip*: metaph., Si 37.12; morally, De 7.25; 'to sustain defeat (on battlefield)' 2K 10.15. **b.** tr. *to cause to sustain defeat*: on battlefield, τινα 1K 4.3.
2. *to fail to materialise*: *s* μισθός 'reward' Si 2.8.
Cf. πταῖσμα, προσκόπτω, πίπτω.

πταρμός, οῦ. m.ʃ
act of sneezing: Jb 41.10.

πτέρνα, ης. f.
heel, hoof: of hum., Ge 3.15; of horse, 49.17; ~η πτερνίζω 'cheat' Je 9.4; ἐν πτέρναις τινός 'closely following behind sbd' Ct 1.8. Cf. πτερνίζω.

πτερνίζω: fut. ~νιῶ; aor. ἐπτέρνισα; pf. ἐπτέρνικα.ʃ *
1. *to kick (with) the heel* with a view to throwing the opponent: + acc. pers., ἐπτέρνικε γάρ με Ge 27.36; ἐν τῇ κοιλίᾳ ἐπτέρνισε τὸν ἀδελφὸν αὐτοῦ 'he kicked his brother in the womb' Ho 12.3 (w. ref. to Jacob and Esau in Ge 25.22-26).
***2.** based on the reading of Ge 27 in the LXX version, *to cheat, defraud by withholding* or *robbing what is due to sbd else*: + acc. pers., εἰ πτερνιεῖ ἄνθρωπος θεόν; διότι ὑμεῖς πτερνίζετέ με. καὶ ἐρεῖτε Ἐν τίνι ἐπτερνίκαμέν σε; ὅτι τὰ ἐπιδέκατα καὶ αἱ ἀπαρχαὶ μεθ' ὑμῶν εἰσι· καὶ ἀποβλέποντες ὑμεῖς ἀποβλέπετε. καὶ ἐμὲ ὑμεῖς πτερνίζετε· 'Shall a man cheat God? for you are cheating me. Then you will say, "In what have we cheated you?" Because the tithes and the first-fruits are (still) with you. You are certainly disregarding me, and you are cheating me' Ma 3.8f; "Be on guard against one another; do not trust your own brothers, ὅτι πᾶς ἀδελφὸς πτέρνῃ πτερνιεῖ 'for every brother will

resort to treachery' and every friend will behave deceitfully" Je 9.4. See Caird 1969.31f., Stählin 1930. 133-5, and Muraoka 1986.265-8; cf. LSG s.v.

Cf. πτέρνα, πτερνισμός, παρακρούομαι, σκελίζω.

πτερνισμός, οῦ. m.ʃ *

**treachery, cunning*: Ιου ἐποίησεν ἐν ~ῷ 'Yehu acted with cunning' 4K 10.19; ὁ ἐσθίων ἄρτους μου ἐμεγάλυνεν ἐπ' ἐμὲ ~όν 'one who eats my bread has acted against me rather treacherously' Ps 40.10. Cf. πτερνίζω.

πτερόν, οῦ. n.

Mostly in pl., *feather*: of birds, Le 1.16; πετεινοῦ 'of a bird' Da 7.6.

πτεροφυέω: fut. ~φυήσω.ʃ

to grow wings: *s* eagle, Is 40.31. Cf. πτέρυξ.

πτερύγιον, ου. n.

1. pl., *fins* of fish: ~α καὶ λεπίδες 'fins and scales' Le 11.9.

2. *flap, fold*: ἱματίων Nu 15.38, cf. Ex 36.27.

3. *wing*: of a cherub, 3K 6.24.

πτέρυξ, υγος. f. Mostly pl.

1. *wing* of bird: ἀετῶν 'of eagles' Ex 19.4, ἔποπος 'of a hoopoe' Zc 5.9*b*, περιστερᾶς 'of a dove' (|| μετάφρενον 'the back'); ἀναλαμβάνω τὰς ~ας 'take the wings' Ps 138.9; *o* of ἀναπετάννυμι 'to spread out' Jb 39.26, of ἐκτείνω Je 29.23; of seraphs, Is 6.2; of cherubs, τῶν διαπεπετασμένων ταῖς ~υξιν 'with their wings spread out' 1C 28.18; where the movement of the wind is visible, πνεῦμα ἐν ταῖς ~υξιν Zc 5.9*a*, cf. Ho 4.19, and ἐπετάσθη ἐπὶ ~ύγων ἀνέμων 'he flew ..' Ps 17.11; fig. of the rays of the sun, Ma 4.2; shelter, ἐν σκέπῃ τῶν ~ύγων σου 'in the shelter of your wings' Ps 16.8, ἐν τῇ σκιᾷ τῶν ~ύγων σου ἐλπιῶ 56.2, ὑπὸ τὰς ~υγας αὐτοῦ 90.4 (|| μετάφρενον 'the back'); of the sails of a ship, πλοίων Is 18.1 (see Ottley ad loc.), cf. ~ες ἀνέμου 'of the wind' 2K 22.11. **b**. sg.: ἡ μία π. 'one of the wings (of the cherubs)' 2C 3.11. **c**. side(s) of snake: Ez 29.4.

***2**. calque on Heb. /kānāf/, the *extremity* of some expanse: pl. and of the earth, world, ἐπὶ ~ύγων τῆς γῆς Jb 37.3¶ (v.l. ἄκρων), συνάξει ἐκ τῶν τεσσάρων ~ύγων τῆς γῆς Is 11.12; Ez 7.2. See LSG s.v.

Cf. πτερύσσομαι, πτερωτός, πτεροφυέω, μεγαλοπτέρυγος: Schmidt 2.454.

πτερύσσομαι.ʃ *

to flutter and extend oneself so as to touch sth else: *s* wings, ἑτέρα τῇ ἑτέρᾳ Ez 1.23 (|| ἑτέρα πρὸς τὴν ἑτέραν 3.13). Cf. πτέρυξ: Schmidt 2.456.

πτερωτός, ή, όν.

having wings: of birds, πᾶν πετεινὸν ~όν 'every winged bird' Ge 1.21; ὁμοίωμα παντὸς ὀρνέου ~οῦ 'image of any winged bird' De 4.17; of mystic animals' feet, Ez 1.7; subst. n.pl. 'birds' Pr 1.17. Cf. πτέρυξ.

πτήσσω: aor. ἔπτηξα, subj. πτήξω, impv.3s πτηξάτω.

to crouch for fear: abs., μὴ πτήξητε μηδὲ φοβηθῆτε ἀπ' αὐτῶν De 1.29, ἐφοβήθησαν καὶ ἔπτηξαν τῇ καρδίᾳ αὐτῶν 1M 12.28; Jb 38.17; + acc., σὴν δύναμιν ἀνίκητον 'your invincible might' 3M 6.13. Cf. πτοέω, φοβέομαι.

πτίλος, η, ον.ʃ

suffering from πτίλωσις, "a disease of the eyelids in which their edges become swollen and inflamed, and the eyelashes fall off" (LSJ): *s* hum., τοὺς ὀφθαλμούς Le 21.20.

πτοέω: fut. πτοήσω, pass. πτοηθήσομαι; aor.pass. ἐπτοήθην, subj. πτοηθῶ, opt. πτοηθείην; pf.pass. ἐπτόημαι.

to move: emotionally, ταλαιπωρία θηρίων πτοήσει σε Hb 2.17; pass., πτοηθήσονται καὶ αἱ σκηναὶ γῆς Μαδιαμ 3.7; ἐπτοήθη ἡ κοιλία μου ἀπὸ φωνῆς προσευχῆς τῶν χειλέων μου 'my bowels were moved by the voice of prayer of my lips' 3.16; + ἔκ τινος (pers.) Jb 23.15¶. See Renehan 2.122f. **b**. *to frighten, scare*: pass., at manifestations of theophany, Ex 19.16; ἡ καρδία τοῦ λαοῦ Jo 7.5; at the sounding of a horn, λαὸς οὐ πτοηθήσεται Am 3.6; πτοηθήσονται οἱ μαχηταί σου Ob 9; ἀπὸ προσώπων αὐτῶν De 31.6 (|| φοβέομαι, δειλιάω, and opp. ἀνδρίζομαι, ἰσχύω), Ez 3.9 (|| φοβέομαι), + *ἀπό τινος (pers.) 1M 7.30, + ἐναντίον τινός Je 1.17; *+ acc.rei, τὸ πλῆθος τοῦ θυμοῦ 'at the extent of the wrath' Is 31.4 (see Helbing, *Kasus*. 27); *s* birds, Je 4.25, arrow 28.56. Cf. Renehan 2.122f.

Cf. δειλιάω, πτήσσω, πτόη, φοβέομαι, ἀνδρίζομαι, ἰσχύω, ἀπτόητος: Schmidt 3.517-20.

πτόη, ης. f.ʃ *

extreme fear: 1M 3.25 (|| φόβος), 3M 6.17. Cf. πτοέω, πτόησις, φόβος.

πτόησις, εως.ʃ

that which terrifies: Pr 3.25. Cf. πτόη.

πτύελος, ου. m.ʃ

saliva: Jb 7.19, 30.10. Cf. σίαλον, πτύω.

πτύξις, εως. f.ʃ

**fold*: of crocodile's (?) scales, Jb 41.5.

πτυχή, ῆς. f.ʃ

leaf of a folding door: 3K 6.34.

πτύω: aor.subj. πτύσω.ʃ

to spit: Nu 12.14; ἐπί τι Si 28.12. Cf. ἐμ~, προπτύω, πτύελος, σίαλον.

πτῶμα, ατος. n.

1. *act of falling*: πέτρας 'caused by a stone' Is 8.14 (|| πρόσκομμα 'stumbling,' accidental and harmful), cf. ἵππου 'from a horse' P.Oxy 3314.7; of a conquered city, Is 30.13, 14; falling out of a chariot, 2M

9.7; political, military, + σύντριμμα Is 51.19, Ju 8.19; Ba 4.33 (‖ πτῶσις). **b**. *downfall, ruin*: Jb 20.5, Si 34.6 (‖ ἀπώλεια), Pr 16.18 (‖ συντριβή 'defeat').

2. *whole remains of a living organism*: lion's carcass, Jd 14.8; hum., Wi 4.19, cf. *ND* 4.8.

Cf. πίπτω, πτῶσις, ὑποσκέλισμα: Michaelis, *TDNT* 6.166.

πτῶσις, εως. f.

1. *fall*: βαρεῖα 'heavy' Na 3.3; metaph., 'downfall' Si 1.22, 20.18, 25.7; ‖ πρόσκομμα 'stumbling' 31.19.

2. *defeat in battlefield* (v. s. πίπτω, **2**): virtual cogn. obj. of κόπτω 'to strike' Zc 14.12, of πατάσσω 14.18; "overthrow of horses, mules .." 14.15. Cf. πταῖσμα.

3. *loss of human life* or *damage*, 'calamity': as divine punishment, Ex 30.12 (or poss., 'there should be no dodging,' cf. ἐκ δρόμου πεσὼν τρέχω Aesch., *Agam.* 1245); Ba 4.31 (‖ πτῶμα vs. 33).

*__4__. *that which has fallen*: trunk of a felled tree, Ez 31.13.

5. *place where one lies prostrate* or *such a posture*: ἀνέστη ἀπὸ τῆς ~εως Ju 10.2.

Cf. πίπτω, πτῶμα, διάπτωσις.

πτωχεία, ας. f.

poverty: οὐ μετὰ ~ας φάγῃ τὸν ἄρτον σου '.. frugally' De 8.9; + θλῖψις Ps 43.25; + ἔνδεια and :: πλοῦτος Si 18.25. Cf. πτωχός, πενία, πλοῦτος.

πτωχεύω: fut. ~χεύσω; aor. ἐπτώχευσα, inf. ~χεῦσαι.

to become materially poor: "the rich became poor and hungry" Ps 33.11. Cf. πτωχός, προσδέομαι, πλουτέω.

πτωχίζω.ʃ *

to make poor: abs. and :: πλουτίζω 1K 2.7. Cf. πτωχός, πλουτίζω.

πτωχός, ή, όν.

materially poor, needy: subst., subjected to exploitation and oppression, Am 2.7 (‖ ταπεινός and πένης); καταδυναστεύουσαι ~ούς 4.1 (‖ πένης); κατεκονδυλίζετε ~ούς 5.11; κτᾶσθαι ἐν ἀργυρίῳ ~ούς 8.6 (‖ ταπεινός); ἐνδεής Is 41.17; opp. δυνάστης Le 19.15. **b**. object of special attention: τῷ ~ῷ καὶ τῷ προσηλύτῳ Le 19.10; κρίνατε ὀρφανὸν καὶ ~όν Ps 81.3, ἐξέλεσθε πένητα καὶ ~όν 'Rescue ..' 81.4.

Cf. πένης, ἐνδεής, λιτός, πτωχεία, πτωχεύω, πτωχίζω, ταπεινός, πλούσιος.

πύγαργος, ου. m.ʃ

white-rump: ritually clean food, De 14.5.

πυγμή, ῆς. f.ʃ

fist: a means of assailment, πατάξῃ .. λίθῳ ἢ ~ῇ Ex 21.18; τύπτετε ~αῖς Is 58.4. Cf. χείρ, κονδυλίζω: Schmidt 1.389-96.

πυθμήν, ένος. m.

1. *bottom*: ᾅδου Pr 14.12, 16.25. Cf. Renehan 2.123.

2. *stem* or *stalk* of a plant: of a vine, Ge 40.10 +. Cf. βυθός and ῥίζωμα **2**.

πυκάζω: aor.subj. πυκάσω; pf.ptc.pass. πεπυκασμένος.ʃ

to be thickly covered: with leaves and *s* tree, Ho 14.9, vine Jb 15.32; ἐν τοῖς πυκάζουσιν 'with thick boughs' (?) Ps 117.27; πολιᾷ 'with grey hair' 3M 4.5. Cf. συσκιάζω: Lee 1990.8-10.

πυκνός, ή, όν.

frequent: *s* cry, 3M 1.28; fire of punishment, 4M 12.12. **b**. comp. n. adv. used with elative force, 'very often': Es E 2, 2M 8.8, 3M 4.12.

Cf. σπάνιος.

πύλη, ης. f.

gate: τῆς αὐλῆς 'of the courtyard (of the tabernacle)' Ex 27.16; one of the gates in a city wall, Zp 1.10, Zc 14.10*ter*; πόλεων Is 14.31; οἴκου κυρίου Je 33.10; in a *pars pro toto* expression, κατέβη κακὰ παρὰ κυρίου ἐπὶ ~ας Ιερουσαλημ Mi 1.12, cf. ὁ Λευίτης ὁ ἐπὶ τῶν πυλῶν ὑμῶν 'the Levite within your cities' De 12.12; the first line of defence of city, ~αι καὶ μοχλοί 'gates and bolts' De 3.5; διῆλθον ~ην καὶ ἐξῆλθον δι' αὐτῆς, 'went through the gate,' i.e. breached it, thus gaining complete control over the access to the city, Mi 2.13; of invading enemy troops, εἰσέρχομαι εἰς ~ας Ob 11, 13; conceivably situated on the rivers encircling or flowing through a city (see Rashi, Cyr, and Delitzsch ad loc.), ~αι τῶν ποταμῶν (v.l. πόλεων) διηνοίχθησαν Na 2.7; reached by the enemy, ἥψατο ἕως ~ης λαοῦ μου Mi 1.9; ~αι τῆς γῆς σου 'the defensive gates on the border of your land' or 'the city gates found up and down your land' Na 3.13; τοῦ οὐρανοῦ Ge 28.17, ᾅδου 'of Hades' Is 38.10, 3M 5.51, cf. Mt 16.18; ~αι τοῦ θανάτου Ps 9.14, 106.18, Jb 38.17; ~αι προσώπου 'jaws'(?) 41.6. **b**. *a space round (the double wings of) the gate of a town* or *city which served as a forum for public gatherings, a public square*, often in pl. (so in Cl. Gk generally) even when the Heb. has the sg.: Ge 34.20; ἐν ~αις where a moralist taught, Am 5.10, Hg 2.14; a court is held, De 21.19, Am 5.12, 15, Zc 8.16; ἐπὶ τὴν ~ην ἐπὶ τὴν γερουσίαν De 25.7; καθήμενοι ἐν ~ῃ 'seated ..' Ps 68.13. **c**. *space through which entry is made*: γαστρὸς μητρός μου 'of my mother's womb' [= cervix] Jb 3.10.

Cf. θύρα, πυλωρός.

πυλών, ῶνος. m.

gate-tower, gate-house: ἐλάλησεν αὐτῷ ἐν τῷ ~ῶνι τοῦ οἴκου Ge 43.19; habitation of ravens, Zp 2.14; ἱεροί 'of temple' 2M 8.33. Cf. πρόπυλον: Lee

108; Husson 243-7 ("typical of luxurious residences," 244).

πυλωρός, οῦ. m.
gate-keeper: ᾅδου Jb 38.17; of the Jerusalem temple, 2C 35.15 (ǁ θυρωρός 1E 1.15), τῆς θύρας τῆς σκηνῆς τοῦ μαρτυρίου 'of the door to the tent of testimony' 1C 9.21. Cf. θυρωρός.

πυνθάνομαι: aor.inf. πυθέσθαι, ptc. πυθόμενος.
to enquire, seek information: from a divine being, παρὰ κυρίου Ge 25.22; + gen. pers.(hum.), πρεσβυτέρων 1E 6.10; Es B 3; + indir. inter. cl., τί τὸ πρᾶγμα 'what the matter was' 3M 5.27. **b.** *to learn about* sth (τι) *by asking* sbd: παρ' αὐτοῦ τὸ τέρας 2C 32.31.
Cf. (ἐπ)ερωτάω, ζητέω.

πυξίον, ου. n.
tablet as writing material: Hb 2.2; λίθινον 'stone tablet' Ex 24.12 (ǁ πλάκες λίθιναι 'stone tablets' 32.15); γράψον .. ἐπὶ ~ου .. καὶ εἰς βιβλίον Is 30.8. Cf. πλάξ.

πύξος, ου. m.ʃ
box: a kind of tree, Is 41.19.

πῦρ, πυρός. n.
1. *fire*: ἐν πυρὶ φλογός 'in the fire in the form of a flame' Ex 3.2; π. χωνευτηρίου 'of smeltering furnace' Ma 3.2, cf. Ge 11.3; λαμπάδες ~ός 'burning lamps' Na 2.5; ἐμπαίζοντες ἐν ~ί 'sporting with fire' 2.4; ἔσται π. 'will go up in flames (and be destroyed)' Ob 18 (ǁ φλόξ); destructive, ἐξέλιπον .. ἐν ~ί 'perished by fire' Hb 2.13; τεῖχος ~ός 'a (defensive) wall of fire' Zc 2.5; instrument of divine punishment, κύριος ἔβρεξεν ἐπὶ Σοδομα καὶ Γομορρα θεῖον καὶ πῦρ '.. brimstone and fire' Ge 19.24 (for a collocation with θεῖον, see under θεῖον); κύριος ὁ θεός σου πῦρ καταναλίσκον ἐστίν '.. consuming fire' De 4.24; καταφαγέτω π. τὰς κέδρους σου 'Let a fire consume your cedars' Zc 11.1; kindled to burn corpses, Is 66.24. **b.** cultic: ἀλλότριον Le 10.1, Nu 26.61; with cleansing power, Nu 31.23. **c.** in a fig. of intensity and severity of effect: ἐν ~ὶ ζήλους αὐτοῦ καταναλωθήσεται πᾶσα ἡ γῆ 'the whole earth will be consumed by the fire of his zeal' Zp 1.18; ἐν ~ὶ θυμοῦ Ez 36.5, ὀργῆς 38.19; π. καὶ ὕδωρ Ps 65.12 (fig. of trying experiences).
2. *a burning stick* or *live coal to kindle fire*: Ge 22.6.
Cf. ἔμπυρος, ἐμπρήθω, καίω, ὀπτάω, πυρά, πυρεῖον, πύρινος, πυρόω, πυριπνοῦς, πύρπνοος, πυρώδης, and φλόξ.

πυρά, ᾶς. f.
burning mass: Si 51.4, 2M 1.22; *o* of ἀνάπτω 'kindle' 10.36. Cf. πῦρ.

πυραμίς, ίδος. f.ʃ
pyramid: as sepulchral monument, 1M 13.28.

πυργόβαρις, εως. f.ʃ*
fortress: pl. and of Jerusalem, Ps 121.7, PSol 8.19. Cf. ὀχύρωμα.

πύργος, ου. m.
tower: οἰκοδομοῦντες τὴν πόλιν καὶ τὸν ~ον Ge 11.8; π. ποιμνίου 'flock-tower' Mi 4.8; attached to city-walls as a defensive structure, Zc 14.10, ᾠκοδόμησαν τὴν πόλιν Δαυιδ τείχει μεγάλῳ καὶ ὀχυρῷ, ~οις ὀχυροῖς '.. with a large and strong wall ..' 1M 1.33, destroyed by fire, 5.5 and 2M 10.36 (at latter: part of φρούριον 'fort'), ποιήσωμεν τείχη καὶ ~ους καὶ πύλας καὶ μοχλούς '.. bolts' 2C 14.6, π. ὑψηλός Is 2.15 (ǁ τεῖχος ὑψηλόν, sim. Ez 26.4, To 13.16 𝔊[I]); ἐξέχων ἐκ τοῦ οἴκου τοῦ βασιλέως 'jutting out from the royal palace' Ne 5.25f.; ξύλινος 'wooden' on the back of an elephant 1Mc 6.37. **b.** *movable tower* for storming cities: θήσω περὶ σὲ ~ους Is 29.3. **c.** watchtower in the countryside: ἐν τῇ ἐρήμῳ 2C 26.10; with sentinels, 4K 9.17; used as storage room, 1C 27.25. **d.** small fort in the countryside: 1M 16.10.
Cf. ἑπτάπυργος: Shipp 477-9; Spicq 2.213-8.

πυρεῖον, ου. n.
censer: used at an altar, Ex 27.3, Le 10.1, Nu 4.14, 2C 4.11; ἐπίθετε ἐπ' αὐτὰ πῦρ 16.7; χαλκοῦν 'bronze' 16.37; πῦρ καὶ λίβανος ἐπὶ ~ου 'fire and incense ..' Si 50.9. Cf. πῦρ.

πυρετός, οῦ. m.ʃ
disease with extremely high bodily temperature, 'fever': divine punishment, De 28.22.

πυρίκαυστος, ον.ʃ
destroyed by fire: *s* πόλις Is 1.7; glorious temple, 64.11; humans, 9.5. Cf. καίω.

πύρινος, η, ον.ʃ
of fire: *s* λίθος Ez 28.14, 16; ἵππος Si 48.9. Cf. πῦρ.

πυριπνοῦς, οῦν.ʃ
fire-breathing: *s* τόλμα 'audacity' 3M 6.34. Cf. πύρπνοος, πνέω: Walters 125.

πυριφλεγής, ές.ʃ
set ablaze: *s* edifice, 3M 3.29, Wi 18.3.
Cf. πῦρ, καίω, φλόξ.

πυροβόλος, ον.ʃ
subst.n.pl. *engine for hurling fire*: + λιθοβόλος 1M 6.51. Cf. βολή, λιθοβόλος: Walters 125.

πυρός, οῦ. m.
wheat: θερισμὸς ~ῶν 'wheat harvest' Ge 30.14; + ὄλυρα (q.v.) Ex 9.32; σεμίδαλις ἐκ ~ῶν 'the finest flour obtained from ..' 29.2; ǁ κριθή 'barley' De 8.8, Je 48.8; as fodder, Jl 1.11. Cf. κριθή, ὄλυρα, σῖτος: Cadelle 1973; Battaglia 42.

πυρόω: fut. πυρώσω; aor. ἐπύρωσα, inf. πυρῶσαι, ptc. πυρώσας, impv. πύρωσον, pass.subj. πυρωθῶ, ptc. πυρωθείς; pf.ptc.pass. πεπυρωμένος.

1. *to cause to become aflame*: + acc. rei, λίθους 'flint' 2M 10.3, σάρκας '(hum.) flesh' 4M 9.17 (torture). **b**. *to heat*: + acc., nails, 4M 11.19. **c**. metaph., *to inflame*: ***o*** hum. face, δόξῃ Es D 7; καρδία 3M 4.2; hum., θυμοῖς 'with emotions of fury' 2M 4.38, 10.35.

2. *to treat by fire* in a smelter so as to improve the purity of: ***o*** precious metal, πυροῦται τὸ ἀργύριον 'silver is refined by fire' Zc 13.9 and Ps 65.10 (‖ δοκιμάζω), ‖ καθαρίζω 11.7; ἀργύριον becoming καθαρόν as a result, Jb 22.25, cf. PSol 17.43.

3. metaph., *to cleanse and purify*: + acc., ***o*** νεφροὺς καὶ καρδίαν 'kidneys and heart' ‖ δοκιμάζω, πειράζω Ps 25.2; τὰ λόγια κυρίου πεπυρωμένα 'the Lord's utterances have been proven to be pure' 17.31, sim. Pr 30.5; + acc. pers., εἰς καθαρόν Is 1.25, εἰς ἐτασμὸν τῆς καρδίας αὐτῶν 'to try their hearts' Ju 8.27; ‖ δοκιμάζω Je 9.7, Ps 16.3; + ἐκλευκαίνω Da 12.10 TH.

Cf. πῦρ, πύρωσις, προσπυρόω, καίω, δοκιμάζω, καθαρίζω: Schmidt 2.382f.

πύρπνοος, ον.ʃ

fire-breathing: ***s*** ἄσθμα 'breath' Wi 11.18. Cf. πυριπνοῦς.

πυρπολέω.ʃ

to destroy: pass., ***o*** hum., αἰκισμοῖς τε καὶ στρέβλαις 'with torturing instruments' 4M 7.4. Cf. ἀφανίζω.

πυρράκης, ου.ʃ

red, ruddy: ***s*** newly-born baby boy, Ge 25.25; youth, 1K 16.12, 17.42. Cf. πυρρός, ἐρυθρός.

πυρρίζω

to become red: ***s*** leper's ulcerous skin, Le 13.19 (‖ λευκαίνω); ‖ χλωρίζω 'to become greenish' 13.49. Cf. ὑποπυρρίζω, πυρρός.

πυρρόομαι: aor. ἐπυρρώθην.ʃ

to become red: ***s*** stone, La 4.7. Cf. πυρρός.

πυρρός, ά, όν.

tawny of colour: ***s*** hum., Ct 5.10; heifer, Nu 19.2; horse, Zc 1.8; water and blood, 4K 3.22. Cf. ἐρυθρός, πυρράκης.

πυρσεύω: aor.opt.3pl ~σεύσαισαν.ʃ

to kindle: + acc., λαμπτῆρα 'torch' Pr 16.28; metaph., ὀδύνας 'sorrows' Jb 20.10. Cf. καίω.

πυρσός, οῦ. m.ʃ

signal-fire: καπνοῦ 'smoking' Jd 20.38 A (B: σύσσημον), glossed as στῦλος καπνοῦ 'column of smoke' 40 A (ditto); ἀρεῖτε ~ον εἰς τὸ ὕψος 20.28*L*.

πυρφόρος, ον.ʃ

subst. *fire-bearer*, as last person to perish, in proverbial expression implying total defeat (cf. LSJ, s.v. **II 2.b** and LSG ad loc.; J.E. Powell ad Hdt. 8.6): οὐκ ἔσται π. τῷ οἴκῳ Ησαυ, implying defeat, Ob 18. **b**. *firebrand*: σεισμοῦ ~ου 'brandishing of a firebrand' Jb 41.21

On the alternative spelling πυροφόρος of same meaning, see Walters 124f., and cf. Dogniez 2001. 253-5.

πυρώδης, ες.ʃ

fire-like: intensely hot, ***s*** ἀτμίς 'vapour' Si 43.4. Cf. πῦρ, θερμός.

πύρωσις, εως. f.ʃ

1. *forest fire* triggered by drought conditions: punitive natural calamity, ἐπάταξα ὑμᾶς ἐν ~ει καὶ ἰκτέρῳ (q.v.) Am 4.9. Alternatively the word may mean 'fever' as a form of human disease: cf. Eth *faṣant*.

2. *putting through fire to test the quality*: Pr 27.21. Cf. ἐμπυρισμός, πυρόω; Lee 1969.239.

πυρωτής, οῦ. m.ʃ*

one who works with fire, 'smith': Ne 3.8.

πώγων, ωνος. m.

1. *beard*: τὴν ὄψιν τοῦ ~νος ὑμῶν 'the look of your b.' Le 19.27, 21.5; τὰς τρίχας τῶν ποδῶν καὶ τὸν ~να 'the hairs of the legs ..' Is 7.20.

*2. *chin*: of a human, Le 13.29, 30, 14.9.

πωλέω.

to sell: ὁ ἀγοράζων ὡς ὁ πωλῶν Is 24.2; + dat. pers., Ge 41.56; 42.6 (:: ἀγοράζω vs. 5); + acc. pers., ***o*** daughter as slave, Ex 21.8 (‖ ἀποδίδωμι vs. 7); women and children, 2M 5.24; τὰ κοράσια .. ἀντὶ οἴνου 'the girls in exchange for wine' Jl 3.3; ***o*** ἔθνη .. καὶ φυλάς Na 3.4; sheep, Zc 11.5; opp. κτάομαι Ez 7.12. Cf. ἀποδίδωμι, ἀγοράζω, κτάομαι, πιπράσκω, ῥοποπώλης.

πῶλος, ου. m./f.

any young animal: of an ass, ὄνους εἴκοσι καὶ ~ους δέκα Ge 32.15; π. τῆς ὄνου 49.11; ἐπιβεβηκὼς ἐπὶ ὑποζύγιον καὶ ~ον νέον Zc 9.9. Cf. ὄνος and ὑποζύγιον.

πώποτε. adv.

ever once: + neg., *never* in the past, Su 27 TH; non-past, 1K 25.28. Cf. ποτέ.

πωρόω: pf.pass. πεπώρωμαι.ʃ

pass. *to harden and lose elasticity*: ***s*** eyes, Jb 17.7. Cf. σκληρός.

πως.

1. In a combination εἴ πως 'perhaps and hopefully': εἴ π. ἰαθήσεται '.. she might be cured' Je 28.8(*a*); + opt., 2K 16.12B(*a*). **b**. ἐάν πως + subj. aor.: 3K 18.5(*a*).

2. Nuances a conditional clause w. an opt.: εἴ π. πληρῶσαι 'should he perchance fill ..' Jb 20.23(-).

a) εἴ πως אוּלַי. Del. Si 28.26, Jn 1.6.

πῶς.

I. interr. 1. *In what manner?*: Π. ἔχετε; *How are you?* Ge 43.27(-); Hg 2.3(*d*). **b**. w. a potential opt.: π. ἂν εὕροις ..; 'how could you find ..?' Si 25.3.

2. in rhetorical questions, *How on earth could you suggest and imply that ..?* – π. ποιήσω τὸ ῥῆμα τοῦτο καὶ ἁμαρτήσομαι .. Ge 39.9(*a*); 44.8(*a*) (with ἄν and opt.). **b**. + a negator: *most certainly* – π. οὐχὶ καὶ ἔσχατον τοῦ θανάτου μου 'most certainly after my death, too' De 31.27(-), cf. BDAG s.v. δ. **c**. + a verbal adj. with ~τέον: πῶς οὖν νομιστέον ἢ κλητέον ..; 'how could they then be considered or called ..?' Ep Je 44. **d**. in a hypothetical question: π. δὲ διέμειναν ἄν τι, εἰ μὴ σὺ ἠθέλησας; 'how could they have endured at all, if you had not so willed? Wi 11.25.

3. introduces a substantival clause: Μνήσθητι ὅσα ἐποίησέν σοι .. π. ἀντέστη σοι ἐν τῇ ὁδῷ 'Recall what he did to you .. how he stood in your way' De 25.17f.(*c*); 29.16[1] v.l. (Wevers: ὡς).

4. deliberative, asking oneself or one's immediate company: π. μεγαλύνωμεν τὸν Ζοροβαβελ; 'how shall we extol Z.?' Si 49.11(*d*), π. εἴπωμεν ..; 2K 12.18(*a*).

II. *How!* in exclamation over incomprehensible events that have taken place: π. ἐξηρευνήθη Ησαυ καὶ κατελήμφθη αὐτοῦ τὰ κεκρυμμένα Ob 6(*a*); π. ἐγενήθη εἰς ἀφανισμόν Zp 3.1(*a*); La 1.1(*a*), Ez 26.17(*a*). **b**. w. a potential opt.: π. ἂν κλέψαιμεν ..; 'How on earth could we steal ..?" Ge 44.8(*a*); π. ἂν γένοιτο ἑσπέρα 'how could it become evening?' De 28.67(*f*); Jb 11.5(*f*).

Cf. Bauer 1957.

a) אֵיךְ; *b*) אֵיכָה; *c*) אֲשֶׁר; *d*) מָה; *e*) בַּמֶּה; *f*) מִי יִתֵּן.x∫

P

ῥαβδίζω: aor. ἐρράβδισα.ʃ

to beat with a rod or *stick* so as to extract the contents: + acc., πυρούς 'wheat' Jd 6.11 A (B: σῖτον 'grain'); Ru 2.17. Cf. ῥάβδος.

ῥάβδος, ου. f.

1. *rod*: Ge 30.37 (used collectively: cf. αὐτάς); used in divination, Ho 4.12 (|| σύμβολον), Ez 21.21; for hitting, Mi 5.1, ἐπὶ τοῦ τραχήλου αὐτῶν 'on their neck' Is 9.4 (|| ζυγός 'yoke'); instrument of punishment, ἡ ῥ. τοῦ θυμοῦ μου καὶ ὀργῆς 10.5, ἐν ~ῳ πατάξει σε 10.24, καλαμίνη 'of reed' Ez 29.6; || μάστιξ .. κέντρον 'whip .. goad' Pr 26.3; + ἁφή 2K 7.14; used by a scribe as a pointer, Jd 5.14B. **b**. metaph. w. ref. to God's people: ῥ. κληρονομίας σου Ps 73.2.

2. shepherd's *staff*, *crook*: Ποίμαινε λαόν σου ἐν ~ῳ σου Mi 7.14; Zc 11.7; σιδηρᾶ 'iron' Ps 2.9; fig. of leadership and authority, ὑπὸ τὴν ~ον μου Ez 20.37; Ps 44.7.

3. *walking-stick* for supporting oneself: held in hand by elderly people, Zc 8.4, cf. τὴν ~ον τὴν ἐν τῇ χειρί σου Ge 38.18; To 5.18; περιπατήσῃ ἔξω ἐπὶ ~ου Ex 21.19.

4. *young shoot* of some trees (LSJ): of grape-vine, Ez 19.11. Cf. στέλεχος **a**.

The primal meaning is "an object relatively thin and oblong, held or standing in upright position."

Cf. βακτηρία, κλάδος, κορύνη, ῥαβδίζω, ῥόπαλον, σκῆπτρον: Schmidt 2.473-5; LSG s.v. **I 1**.

ῥαγάς, άδος. f.ʃ

crevice, chink: where insects settle, Is 7.19 (|| τρώγλη, σπήλαιον). Cf. ῥάγμα.

ῥάγμα, ατος. n.(LSJ: ῥῆγμα).ʃ *

laceration: πατάξει .. ~ασιν Am 6.11 (|| θλάσμασι). Cf. ῥήγνυμι, ῥαγάς.

ῥάδαμνος, ου. m.

bough, branch: Jb 8.16. Cf. κλάδος.

ῥᾴδιος, α, ον.ʃ

easy of execution: 2M 2.26, 4.17. Cf. κοῦφος, χαλεπός.

ῥᾳθυμέω.ʃ On the spelling, see Walters 72.

1. *to behave with indifference*: Ἵνα τί ῥαθυμεῖτε; 'why are you being so indifferent?' Ge 42.1.

2. *to rest and have fun*: *s* army, ῥαθυμῶν καὶ εὐωχούμενος 'resting and entertaining themselves in style' Ju 1.16; ῥαθυμούντων μεθ' ἑταιρῶν 'dallying with prostitutes' 2M 6.4.

3. *to hang round with no clear purpose*: μὴ ῥαθύμει Si 35.11.

Cf. ῥαθυμία: Bain 131.

ῥᾳθυμία, ας. f.ʃ

having fun, having a good time: ἀντὶ εὐωχίας καὶ νεωτερικῆς ~ίας 'instead of feasting and youthful revelry' 3M 4.8; on the collocation of ῥαθυμέω with εὐωχέομαι, cf. Ju 1.16. Cf. ῥαθυμέω, εὐωχία.

ῥαίνω: fut. ῥανῶ; aor. ἔρρανα, impv.3pl ῥανάτωσαν.

to scatter liquid *in small drops* or *particles*, 'sprinkle': + acc. rei [= what is to be sprinkled] and ἐπί + acc. [where it is to be sprinkled], τὸ αἷμα αὐτοῦ ἐπὶ τὸ ἱλαστήριον 'its [= the bull's] blood on the lid of the ark of the covenant' Le 16.15, ῥανῶ ἐφ' ὑμᾶς ὕδωρ καθαρόν '.. pure water' Ez 36.25; the 1st acc. understood, ἐπὶ Ααρων καὶ ἐπὶ τὴν στολὴν αὐτοῦ Ex 29.21; fig. αἱ νεφέλαι ῥανάτωσαν δικαιοσύνην 'Let the clouds sprinkle righteousness!' Is 45.8. **b**. ἀπό τινος instead of acc., ῥανεῖ τῷ δακτύλῳ τῷ δεξιῷ ἀπὸ τοῦ ἐλαίου τοῦ ἐν τῇ χειρὶ αὐτοῦ 'sprinkle some of the oil in his hand with the right finger' Le 14.27.

Cf. δια~, περιρραίνω, προσραίνω, καταπάσσω, ῥαντίζω.

ῥάκος, ους. n.ʃ

tattered garment: worn by a woman segregated during menstruation, ῥ. ἀποκαθημένης Is 64.6, Es 4.26 *L*, cf. ῥ. καταμηνίων C 27 o'; παλαιὰ ~η 'old rags' Je 45.11. Cf. ῥακώδης.

ῥακώδης, ες.ʃ

ragged: subst.n. 'ragged clothes' Pr 23.21 (+ διερρηγμένα 'tattered clothes'). Cf. ῥήγνυμι, ῥάκος.

ῥάμμα, ατος. n.ʃ

thread: Jd 16.12 A (B: σπαρτίον).

ῥάμνος, ου. f.

a kind of *prickly shrub*: ἐν κήπῳ 'in a garden' Ep Je 70; Jd 9.14.

ῥανίς, ίδος. f.ʃ

round, pear-shaped portion of liquid of small quantity: δρόσου 'of dew' Wi 11.22. Cf. σταγών, σταλαγμός, ψεκάς.

ῥαντίζω: fut. ῥαντιῶ; aor.pass. ἐρραντίσθην, subj. ῥαντισθῶ.ʃ *

to sprinkle: + acc. ***o*** blood of sacrificial animal, ἐπ' αὐτό [= ἱμάτιον] Le 6.27 (|| ἐπιρραντίζω and πλύνω); person and + dat. rei [= means of cleansing], με ὑσσώπῳ Ps 50.9 (|| πλύνω); πρὸς τὸν τοῖχον 'against the wall' 4K 9.33. Cf. ῥαίνω, ἐπι~, περιρραντίζω, ῥαντισμός, πλύνω.

ῥαντισμός, οῦ. m. *
v.n. of ῥαντίζω (q.v.): ὕδωρ ~οῦ Nu 19.9. Cf. ῥαντίζω, ῥαίνω.

ῥαντός, ή, όν.
spotted, speckled: *s* goat (αἶξ) Ge 30.32; sheep, σποδοειδῆ ~ά 30.39, 31.12; he-goat (τράγος) and ram (κριός) 31.10.

ῥαπίζω
strike w. palm of hand, 'slap': ἐπὶ τὰς σιαγόνας αὐτοῦ 'his cheeks' Ho 11.4; + acc. pers., τὸν βασιλέα τῇ ἀριστερᾷ 'the king with her right hand' 1E 4.30. Cf. ῥάπισμα, πατάσσω: Schmidt 3.292.

ῥάπισμα, ατος. n.ʃ
blow w. palm of hand: δέδωκα .. τὰς σιαγόνας μου εἰς ~ατα 'turned .. my cheeks ..' Is 50.6 (|| μάστιξ). Cf. ῥαπίζω.

ῥαπτός, ή, όν.ʃ
stitched: *s* εἴδωλον Ez 16.16. Cf. ῥάπτω.

ῥάπτω: aor. ἔρραψα, inf. ῥάψαι.
to sew together: + acc. rei, φύλλα συκῆς 'leaves of a fig-tree' Ge 3.7 (as a piece of clothing); opp. ῥήγνυμι 'to tear' Ec 3.7. Cf. ῥαπτός, συ~, ὑπορράπτω.

ῥάσσω: fut. ῥάξω; aor.impv. ῥάξον, pass. ἐρράχθην.
1. *to break into pieces*: + acc., τέκνα (of defeated army) Is 13.16, ὑμᾶς καὶ τὴν πόλιν Je 23.39; 'to crush (militarily),' τοὺς ἐχθρούς Is 9.11, αὐτῶν τὴν ἰσχὺν ἐν δυνάμει σου Ju 9.8 (|| κατάγνυμι); mountains and pass., Da 8.11 LXX (TH θυσία).
2. *to hurl violently downwards*: *o* κέρας 'horn' and pass., ἐπὶ τὴν γῆν ἀπὸ τῶν ἄστρων '.. from the stars' Da 8.10 LXX (TH ἔπεσεν).
Cf. συντρίβω, καταβάλλω, κατάγνυμι. Del. Ju 16.10 v.l.

ῥαφιδευτής, οῦ. m.ʃ *
embroiderer: ποικιλία τοῦ ~οῦ 'marking with various colours by the embroiderer' Ex 27.16. Cf. ῥαφιδευτός and ποικιλτής.

ῥαφιδευτός, ή, όν.ʃ *
embroidered: ὑφαντὰ .. ~ὰ .. ποικιλτὰ .. 'woven .. embroidered .. multicoloured ..' Ex 37.21. Cf. ῥαφιδευτής.

ῥάχις, εως/ιος. f.
spine, backbone: Jb 40.18. Cf. Shipp 482f. Del. 1K 5.5 v.l.

ῥέγχω.ʃ
to snore: Jn 1.6; + καθεύδω 1.5.

ῥεμβασμός, οῦ. m. * ʃ
insecure wavering: Wi 4.12. Cf. ῥεμβεύω.

ῥεμβεύω: aor.impv. ῥέμβευσον.ʃ *
to roam about: *s* prostitute, Is 23.16. Cf. καταρρεμβεύω, ῥέμβομαι, ῥεμβασμός.

ῥέμβομαι.ʃ
syn. of ῥεμβεύω: *s* prostitute, Pr 7.12. Cf. ῥεμβεύω.

ῥεῦμα, ατος. n.ʃ
that which flows, 'stream': Si 39.13. Cf. ῥέω, ποταμός.

ῥέω: fut. ῥυήσομαι; aor. ἐρρύην, impv. ῥεύσον.
1. *to flow forth*: οἱ ὀφθαλμοὶ αὐτῶν ῥυήσονται ἐκ τῶν ὀπῶν αὐτῶν 'their eyes will melt out of their sockets' Zc 14.12; *s* ὕδωρ Is 48.21; aromatic substance, Ct 4.16.
2. *to become exhausted*: *s* wealth, Ps 61.11. Cf. ἐκλείπω **5**.
3. *to have* or *produce* liquid: + acc. rei, γῆν ῥέουσαν γάλα καὶ μέλι 'a land flowing with milk and honey' Ex 3.8, 13.5, 33.3, De 6.3, 11.9; οἱ βουνοὶ ῥυήσονται γάλα καὶ πᾶσαι αἱ ἀφέσεις Ιουδα ὕδατα 'the hills will flow with milk and all the watercourses of Judah with water' Jl 3.18; νέφη .. δρόσους 'clouds .. dew' Pr 3.20; ῥέων γόνον 'having a discharge of semen' Le 15.3, ῥύσιν αἵματος 'menstrual discharge' 15.25; τὰ βλέφαρα ἡμῶν ῥείτω ὕδωρ 'let our eyelids ..' Je 9.18; + dat. of fluid, γυνὴ .. ῥέουσα αἵματι Le 15.19 - on the dat., see LS s.v. **1a**.
Cf. ῥύσις, ῥεῦμα, ἀπο~, ἐπι~, παρα~, περιρρέω, ῥοῦς: Chadwick 247-53.

ῥῆγμα, ατος. n.
that which is torn: 3K 11.30. Cf. ῥήγνυμι. Del. Am 6.12 v.l.

ῥήγνυμι, ῥήσσω: fut. ῥήξω, pass. ῥαγήσομαι; aor. act. ἔρρηξα, impv. ῥῆξον, inf. ῥῆξαι, ptc. ῥήξας, pass. ἐρράγην, subj. ῥαγῶ; pf. ἔρρωγα, ptc. ἐρρηγώς
I. tr. *to split into two parts*: + acc., sea, Ex 14.16, ἄβυσσοι 'deep seas' Pr 3.20, whirlpools of rivers (by jumping into them?) Jb 28.10; ground 3K 1.40B; τὴν βασιλείαν 11.31; asps' eggs, Is 59.5; garment Jb 2.12 (gesture of grief); σε ῥήξει 'a secret report kept with you will try to burst out' Si 19.10; into more than two parts, and w. a second acc. (cogn.), ^ἱμάτιον^ δώδεκα ῥήγματα 3K 12.24°; pass., ἐρράγη ἀπὸ τοῦ οἴκου Δαυιδ 'split from the house of D.' 4K 17.21.
2. *to allow to burst out*: *o* εὐφροσύνην 'joy' Is 49.13, 52.9, θυμὸν .. ἔναντι κυρίου Jb 15.13; φωνήν 'break into speech' 6.5, cf. Renehan 1.175. **b**. intr., ῥῆξον καὶ βόησον 'Cry your heart out' Is 54.1.
II. pass. and pf.act. ἔρρωγα with intr. force: *to burst forth*, what holds sth together having snapped and its contents emerging: ἐρράγησαν πᾶσαι αἱ πηγαὶ τῆς ἀβύσσου 'all the springs of the abyss burst forth' Ge 7.11; ἐρράγη ἡ γῆ Nu 16.31; ποταμῶν ῥαγήσεται γῆ 'the land of rivers will be torn asunder' Hb 3.9; *s* wineskin, Jo 9.13, woven cloth, Ex 28.28; thongs of shoes, Is 5.27; cords,

33.23; water and valley, 35.6; light, 58.8; city conquered after a siege, Je 46.2 mountains Ez 38.20.

Cf. ῥάγμα, ῥῆγμα, ῥακώδης, δια~, κατα~, περιρρήγνυμι, σπαράσσω, σχίζω, ἄρρηκτος: Schmidt 3.303-7.

ῥῆμα, ατος. n.

1. *word spoken*: ἀπέκτεινα αὐτοὺς ἐν ~ασι στόματός μου 'I killed them with the words of my mouth' Ho 6.5; λαλῶν ~ατα προφάσεις ψευδεῖς 'uttering words (which amount to) false excuses' 10.4; πολὺς ἐν ~ασιν 'talkative' Jb 11.3; ‖ λόγος– λαλοῦντι ἐν ἐμοὶ ~ατα καλὰ καὶ λόγους παρακλητικούς Zc 1.13. **b**. subsequently written down: τὰ ~ατα τοῦ νόμου τούτου τὰ γεγραμμένα ἐν τῷ βιβλίῳ τούτῳ De 28.58.

2. *statement*: τὰ δέκα ~ατα 'the Decalogue' De 4.13.

3. *thought or intent uttered verbally*: σκληρὸν ἐφάνη τὸ ῥ. Ge 21.11; ἐγενήθη κατὰ τὸ ῥ. Ιωσηφ, καθὼς εἶπεν 44.2; φυλάξεσθε τὸ ῥ. τοῦτο νόμιμον σεαυτῷ 'you shall keep this pronouncement as binding to yourself' Ex 12.24; τὸ ῥ. τὸ πονηρὸν τοῦτο 'this harsh message' 33.4; ~ατα πονηρά 'unfavourable report' Nu 14.36; speech, 1E 3.5.

4. *matter, affair*: ~ατα κρίσεως 'juridical matters' De 17.8; τὸ γεγονὸς ῥ. 'that which has happened' 1K 4.16.

5. pl., *events verbally presented*: μετὰ τὰ ~ατα ταῦτα 'following the events recounted just now; thereafter' Ge 15.1, 22.1 +; ἀπήγγειλεν .. κατὰ τὰ ~ατα ταῦτα 24.28; Jo 23.15*bis*.

6. *course of action* already taken or yet to be taken: ἐποίησας ὡς τὸ ῥ. τοῦτο '(act) like this' Ge 22.16; διηγήσατο ὁ παῖς τῷ Ισαακ πάντα τὰ ~ατα, ἃ ἐποίησεν 24.66; πῶς ποιήσω τὸ ῥ. τὸ πονηρὸν τοῦτο ..; 39.9; Is 42.16, 1M 5.37; 2K 11.27B (*L* πρᾶγμα).

7. *dealings with men and matters*: ἕως τοῦ λαλῆσαί με τὰ ~ατά μου 'until I have told about my business' Ge 24.33.

*8. *palpable object*, 'thing,' Hebraism for דָּבָר: οὐκ ἐπεδεήθης ~ατος 'you did not lack a thing' De 2.7.

*9. *something unspecified*: sg., μῶμος, πᾶν ῥ. πονηρόν 'a defect, anything wrong' De 17.1; often w. a negator, μὴ ἀδυνατεῖ παρὰ τῷ θεῷ ῥ.; 'is anything impossible with God?' Ge 18.14; μὴ ἀφέλῃς ῥ. 'don't delete anything (out of οἱ λόγοι)' Je 33.2; ἐρωτήσω λόγον, καὶ μὴ κρύψῃς ἀπ' ἐμοῦ ῥῆμα 'I'm going to ask you about something. Don't hide from me anything' 45.15, sim. 49.4.

Cf. λόγος, μεγαλορρημονέω, ῥῆσις, ῥητός, εἶπον: Schmidt 1.97-100; Repo 1951-54, esp. I.108-93.

ῥῆσις, εως. f.

verbal message: sent as letter, 2E 5.7; σοφῶν 'sages' sayings' Pr 1.6. Cf. ῥῆμα, λόγος.

ῥητίνη, ης. f.

resin of the pine: valuable commodity, Ge 37.25 (+ θυμίαμα 'spice' and στακτή 'myrrh'); valuable gift, 43.11 (+ μέλι 'honey,' θυμίαμα, στακτή etc.); famous product of Gilead, 37.25, Je 8.22, 26.11; medicine, 28.8; μέλι καὶ ἔλαιον καὶ ῥ. Ez 27.17.

ῥητός, ή, όν.∫

stated, specified: οὐ τελευτήσει .. ~όν 'none of the stated things .. will die' Ex 9.4; πᾶν ~ὸν ἀδίκημα 'every stated unlawfulness' 22.9. Cf. λέγω, ῥῆμα: LSG s.v.

ῥῖγος, ους. n.∫

extremely low temperature: as a disease and divine punishment, 'hypothermia, chill, shivering', De 28.22; personified natural phenomenon, εὐλογεῖτε, ῥ. καὶ ψῦχος, τὸν κύριον '.. chill and coldness, ..' Da LXX 3.67 (:: πῦρ καὶ καῦμα vs. 66).

Cf. ψῦχος, θέρμη.

ῥίζα, ας. f.

1. *root* of plant: ἄνω φύουσα 'growing upwards' De 29.18; τὰς ~ας αὐτοῦ ἐξηράνθη 'it has dried up at its roots' Ho 9.16, cf. τὰς ~ας αὐτοῦ ὑποκάτωθεν Am 2.9 (‖ καρπός); βαλεῖ τὰς ~ας αὐτοῦ 'will cast forth its roots' Ho 14.6, sim. Je 17.8, Jb 5.3; ‖ κλῆμα 'branch' Ma 4.1. **b**. *that which is at the base*, 'foundation': ἐκ ~ῶν 'from the foundations (of mountains)' Jb 28.9; ὑπὸ τὴν ~αν τοῦ ὄρους 'at the foot of the mountain' Ju 6.13; metaph., τῆς φρονήσεως 'of prudence' Wi 3.15, ἀθανασίας 'of immortality' 15.3.

2. fig. *that from which a living organism multiplies*, 'stock, family': Is 5.24 (‖ ἄνθος), Si 40.15 (‖ κλάδος 'branch'), τῶν δικαίων Pr 12.3. **b**. *a leading clan* or *family*: ἐκ τῆς ~ης Ιεσσαι Is 11.1 (‖ ἄνθος), ἐκ ~ης μεγάλης (𝔊[II] ἀγάθης) εἶ σύ To 5.14 𝔊[I]. **c**. *origin*: ‖ γένεσις Ez 16.3; ῥ. σοφίας Si 1.6.

3. *the farthest end*: ῥ. τῶν ποδῶν Jb 13.27.

Cf. (ἐκ)ριζόω, ἄρριζος, ὁλόρριζος.

ῥιζόω: aor. ἐρρίζωσα, pass. ἐρριζώθην, subj. ῥιζωθῶ; pf. ἐρρίζωκα, ptc.pass. ἐρριζωμένος.∫

pass. *to strike root*: μὴ ῥιζωθῇ εἰς τὴν γῆν ἡ ῥίζα Is 40.24. ***b**. act. = pass. and metaph., *s* φυτὸν πονηρίας 'a plant of evilness' Si 3.28; 24.12, Ps 47.3 (see Ra ad loc.). **c**. *to execute with sound and deep roots*: pass., *o* φυτεία 'tree-planting' PSol 14.4.

Cf. ῥίζα, ἐκριζόω.

ῥίζωμα, ατος. n.∫

1. *group of people with shared ancestors*: Ps 51.7.

2. *bottom*: ~ατα τῆς θαλάσσης Jb 36.30¶.

Cf. βυθός, ἔδαφος, πυθμήν.

ῥιπίζω: aor. ἐρρίπισα.ʃ
to fan by blowing at: + acc., *s* wind, Da 2.35 LXX.

ῥιπιστός, ή, όν.ʃ*
well-ventilated: *s* ὑπερῷον 'attic; penthouse' Je 22.14.

ῥῖπος, ου. m.ʃ
wicker-work, 'mat': as a cover on top of a cistern, 2K 17.19*L* (B: ἐπικάλυμμα).

ῥιπτέω = ῥίπτω, q. v. Only in pres.

ῥίπτω: fut. ῥίψω, pass. ῥιφήσομαι; aor. ἔρριψα, subj. ῥίψω, ptc. ῥίψας, impv. ῥῖψον, 2pl ῥίψατε, pass. ἐρρίφην, ptc. ῥιφείς, subj. ῥιφῶ; pf.pass.3s ἔρριπται, ptc.pass. ἐρριμμένος, ῥεριμμένος.

1. *to cast, throw*: + acc., τὸ παιδίον ὑποκάτω μιᾶς ἐλάτης '.. under a silver fir' Ge 21.15 (out of despair); εἰς τὸν λάκκον 'into the pit' 37.24 (ǁ ἐμβάλλω vs. 22, sim. Da 6.17 LXX and vs. 16 TH); εἰς τὸν ποταμόν Ex 1.22, εἰς μέσον τοῦ Εὐφράτου Je 28.63, ἵππον καὶ ἀναβάτην .. εἰς θάλασσαν Ex 15.1 'horses and their riders ..,' εἰς τὸ πῦρ 32.24, ^τὴν ἀνομίαν^ ἐν μέσῳ τοῦ μέτρου .. τὸν λίθον .. εἰς τὸ στόμα αὐτῆς Zc 5.8; ἐπὶ τὴν γῆν Ex 4.3; ἀπὸ τῶν χειρῶν αὐτοῦ 32.19. **b**. *to throw to the ground* in a combat *and defeat*: pass., Je 27.30 (ǁ πίπτω), Jd 4.22 B (A: πίπτω), cf. Ez 19.12. **c**. as useless or despicable: *o* pers., Wi 11.14; money, ἐν ταῖς πλατείαις 'on to the streets' Ez 7.19, τὸν νόμον σου ὀπίσω σώματος αὐτῶν Ne 9.26; *o* the dead without a proper burial, ἐν τοῖς ὄρεσιν ὡς νεκρός Is 14.19, ἐπέκεινα τῆς πύλης Ιερουσαλημ 'opposite the gate of J.' Je 22.19, ἐν ταῖς διόδοις Ιερουσαλημ 14.16, ἐρριμμένον ὀπίσω τοῦ τείχους Νινευη, ἔθαπτον αὐτόν To 1.17, ἐν τῇ ἀγορᾷ 'in the marketplace' 2.3; into the commoners' mass-grave Je 33.23, sim. 48.9; ἐπὶ τῆς χελωνῖδος ἐρριμμένον νεκρόν 'on the threshhold lying dead' Ju 14.15; + ἐπί τινι Jb 16.11; *o* weapons, 1M 7.44; corpse, ἐν τῷ καύματι τῆς ἡμέρας Je 43.30, τὰ σώματα ἐρριμμένα 1M 11.4; virtually dead, πάσης ἐστερεωμένος ἐλπίδος καὶ σωτηρίας ἔρριπτο 'he lay there with every hope of recovery gone' 2M 3.29; wounded and killed troops, Is 34.2; τοῖς λέουσι 'to the lions' Da 6.24 LXX; *o* justice, 8.12. **d**. as burden: clothes and baggage of fleeing soldiers, 4K 7.15. **e**. *to set and place as a sacrificial offer*: + acc., τὴν ψυχὴν αὐτοῦ ἐξ ἐναντίας 'his own life in front of others' Jd 9.17 A (B: ἐκ~). **f**. + ἑαυτόν 'to prostrate oneself': 2M 3.15, but not 4M 12.19.

2. *to bring under notice*, 'present': Ῥίπτω ἐγὼ τὸ ἔλεός μου κατ' ὀφθαλμοὺς τοῦ βασιλέως 'I make my entreaty ..' Je 45.26, sim. Da 9.18, 20 TH (LXX: δέομαι), τὸν οἰκτιρμὸν ἡμῶν 18 TH, cf. an analogous use of καταβάλλω **4** (Ba 2.19) and πίπτω **4** (Je 43.7, 44.20, 49.2)

Cf. ἀπο~, ἐκ~, ἐπι~, ὑπορρίπτω, βάλλω: Schmidt 3.153; Spicq 3.221-4.

ῥίς, ινός. f.
nostril: of hum., Is 37.29; an organ for smelling, Ps 113.14; channel for inhalation of air, Wi 2.2, ǁ ὄμματα 'eyes' 15.15; of animals, Jb 40.24, Pr 11.22.

ῥόα, ας. f.

1. *pomegranate-tree*: Ex 28.29; ῥ. καὶ φοῖνιξ καὶ μῆλον καὶ τὰ πάντα τὰ ξύλα τοῦ ἀγροῦ 'apple-tree and palm-trees and all wild trees' Jl 1.12 (also ǁ ἄμπελος and συκῆ, so Nu 20.5, De 8.8); ἡ ἄμπελος καὶ ἡ συκῆ καὶ ἡ ῥ. καὶ τὰ ξύλα τῆς ἐλαίας 'the vine and the fig-tree .. and the olive-trees' Hg 2.19.

2. *fruit of pomegranate*: ǁ συκῆ 'fig' Nu 13.24; also ǁ ἄμπελος 'grape' 20.5, De 8.8. **b**. temple-ornament shaped like pomegranate: Je 52.22.

Cf. ῥοΐσκος, ῥοών: Schnebel 315; Caird 1969. 32f.

ῥόαξ, κος. m.ʃ
conduit for liquid: Ez 40.40.

ῥόδον, ου. n.
rose: Si 24.14, ἄνθος ~ων 'a flower of ..' 50.8, ~ων κάλυξ 'rosebud' Wi 2.8.

ῥοδοφόρος, ον.ʃ*
rose-bearing: nickname of Ptolemais (Acre), 3M 7.17.

ῥοιζέω.ʃ
to make a whistling sound: *s* mountain stream, Ct 4.15. Cf. βομβέω, ἠχέω, ῥοῖζος, φωνέω: Schmidt 3.342f. Del. 4K 13.17 v.l.

ῥοῖζος, ου. m.ʃ

1. *rushing sound*: χειμάρρου 'of a wadi' Ez 47.5, πνεύματος 'of wind' Bel 36 TH. Cf. ῥοιζέω.

2. *very fast movement*: Wi 5.11, 2M 9.7.

ῥοΐσκος, ου. *
ornamental *knob* or *tassel shaped like a pomegranate*: Ex 28.29; on priestly garment, Si 45.9. Cf. ῥόα.

ῥομφαία, ας. f.
sword: **a**. weapon, Nu 22.23 (ǁ μάχαιρα vs. 31), Ho 1.7 (ǁ τόξον and πόλεμος); ὡς ~αν μαχητοῦ Zc 9.13; Mi 4.3[1] (ǁ δόρα and ǁ μάχαιρα Is 2.4); Jl 3.10 (ǁ σειρομάστης); "a nation will no longer raise a sword against another nation, and they will no longer learn the art of war" Mi 4.3[2]; στιλβούσης ~ας 'flashing sword' Na 3.3 (ǁ ὅπλα). **b**. destructive, ἀποκτεῖναι ἡμᾶς Ex 5.21; πεσοῦνται ἐν ~ᾳ Am 4.10, cf. 9.4; ἐν ~ᾳ τελευτήσει 7.11; ἐξολεθρεύσει σε ῥ. Na 3.15; εἰς ~αν παραδοθήσονται Mi 6.14; τοὺς λέοντάς σου καταφάγεται Na 2.14; τραυματίαι ~ας 'the slain by sword' Zp 2.12; meton. for armed conflict, Si 40.9.

Cf. μάχαιρα, ξίφος, δόρα, ὅπλον, and σειρομάστης.

ῥόπαλον, ου.ʃ
cudgel: instrument for discipline and punishment, Pr 25.18. Cf. ῥάβδος.

ῥοπή, ῆς. f.ʃ
1. *fall* of the scale-pan: ζυγοῦ Pr 16.11; metaph., 'outcome, end-result,' τοῦ θυμοῦ 'of anger' Si 1.22.
2. *small additional weight*: ῥ. ζυγοῦ '.. of a balance' Is 40.15; Wi 11.22.
3. *decisive, critical moment*: πρὸς μίαν ~ήν 'in one moment' Wi 18.12, ὑστάτην βίου ~ὴν αὐτοῖς 'their last moment of life' 3M 5.49; Jo 13.22.

ῥο/ωποπώλης, ου. m.ʃ *
dealer in petty wares: 3K 10.15, Ne 3.31, 32.

ῥοῦς, οῦ. m.ʃ
flow of water, current: ποταμοῦ Si 4.26. Cf. ῥέω, ποταμός.

ῥοών, ῶνος. m. ʃ *
pomegranate orchard: Zc 12.11. Cf. ῥόα.

ῥύδην. adv.ʃ
with unhampered, swift movement: of an attacking horse, φερόμενος 2M 3.25.

ῥυθμίζω: aor. ἐρρύθμισα.ʃ
to put together and shape in orderly fashion: + acc. (timber), ἐν κόλλῃ 'with glue' Is 44.13.

ῥυθμός, οῦ. m.
1. *fixed measurement*, 'blueprint' or *shape, form*: κατὰ τὸν ~ὸν τῆς ἐπωμίδος Ex 28.15; ‖ μέτρον 4K 16.10.
2. *rhythm*: of rushing water, Wi 17.18.
3. *shape*: μηρῶν 'of thighs' Ct 7.2.
Cf. ῥυθμίζω, μορφή: Renehan 1.177.

ῥύμη, ης. f.
street: Is 15.3 (‖ πλατεῖα), πόλεως Si 9.7; by metonymy, inhabitants of a street, To 13.18 𝔊[I] (‖ πλατεῖα 13.17). Cf. ὁδός, πλατεῖα: Shipp 486.

ῥύομαι: fut. ῥύσομαι, pass. ῥυσθήσομαι; aor. ἐρρυσάμην, impv. ῥῦσαι, inf. ῥύσασθαι, ptc. ῥυσάμενος, opt. ῥύσαιμι, subj. ῥύσωμαι, pass. ἐρρύσθην, subj. ῥυσθῶ, opt. ῥυσθείην.
to rescue from danger, a state of distress, discomfort etc.: + acc. pers., τὸν ἀδικούμενον Is 1.17; ἐκ πάντων τῶν κακῶν Ge 48.16 (*s* ἄγγελος), Ex 2.17; ἐκ δουλείας 6.6 (‖ λυτρόομαι), ἐκ πάσης θλίψεως 'out of every distressful situation' Ps 53.9; ἀπὸ τῶν ποιμένων 'from the shepherds' Ex 2.19, ἀπὸ ⌜*L* ἐκ χειρὸς⌝ πάντων τῶν ἐχθρῶν 2K 19.10, ἀπὸ ῥομφαίας .. ἐκ χειρὸς κυνός '.. from a dog's paw' Ps 21.21; ἐκ χειρὸς Αἰγυπτίων Ex 14.30, ἐκ χειρὸς ᾅδου Ho 13.14 (‖ λυτρόομαι), ἐκ χειρὸς ἁμαρτωλοῦ Ps 81.4 (‖ ἐξαιρέω); ἐκεῖθεν Mi 4.10 (‖ λυτρόομαι); ἐξ ἁμαρτίας Wi 10.13, ἀπὸ πασῶν τῶν ἀνομιῶν Ez 37.23, ἀπὸ ἀκαθαρσίας ἐχθρῶν βεβήλων 'from the impurity of abominable enemies' PSol 17.45; from predatory animals, Is 5.29, ἐκ στόματος λεόντων 1M 2.60, ἐκ παγίδος θηρευτῶν 'from a hunters' trap' Ps 90.3; from death, Ep Je 35 (‖ ἐξαιρέω); from defilement, *o* bones of a buried hum., 4K 23.18 (*L* διασῴζω); ‖ σῴζω Ps 6.5, ‖ φυλάσσω 24.20, σκεπάζω 'protect' 90.14; *s* God Ex 5.23, pagan gods 4K 18.33; God's arm, Is 63.5; hum., Ex 2.17, Jo 22.31, 2K 14.16 (‖ ἐξαιρέω), Is 1.17, 1M 5.17; hum. acts of charity, Si 40.24. Cf. ῥῦσις, ῥύστης, ἐξαιρέω, λυτρόομαι, σῴζω, φυλάσσω.

ῥυπαρός, ά, όν.ʃ
filthy, unclean: *s* ἱμάτια 'clothes' Zc 3.3, 4. Cf. ῥύπος, καθαρός: Spicq 3.225f.

ῥύπος, ου. m.ʃ
filth, dirt: metaph., ἐκπλυνεῖ κύριος τὸν ~ον τῶν υἱῶν .. Σιων 'the Lord will wash off the filth ..' Is 4.4; ἐν ~ῳ με ἔβαψας 'you have plunged me in filth' Jb 9.31, ἐκδύσῃ ~ον 'divest thyself of ..' 11.15 (:: καθαρὸν ὕδωρ), καθαρὸς .. ἀπὸ ~ου 14.4. Cf. ῥυπαρός, κηλίς, μύσος: Schmidt 2.206-10.

ῥύσις, εως. f.
1. *discharge of fluid*: of nocturnal discharge of male semen, ἐκ τοῦ σώματος Le 15.2, οὐκ ἔσται καθαρὸς ἐκ ~εως αὐτοῦ νυκτός De 23.10; of menstruation, Le 15.19, αἵματος 20.18.
2. *channel for flowing* of fluid: of rain water, Jb 38.25.
Cf. ῥέω, πηγή: Schmidt 1.633-40.

ῥῦσις, εως. f.ʃ *
v.n. of ῥύομαι, *rescue*: θανάτου 'from death' Si 51.9.

ῥύστης, ου. m.*
he who rescues: *s* God, Ps 17.3, ‖ ἀντιλήμπτωρ 143.2; ἐξ ἐχθρῶν 17.49. Cf. σωτήρ, ῥύομαι.

Ῥωμαῖος, α, ον.
Roman: subst. m. pl., Da 11.30 LXX, 1M 8.1.

ῥωμαλέος, α, ον.ʃ
strong of body: *s* νεανίαι 'youths' 2M 12.27. Cf. ῥώμη.

ῥώμη, ης. f.ʃ
bodily strength: of hum., 2M 3.26; of giants, 3M 2.4; ~η ἀσθενής 'weak' Pr 6.8*c*. Cf. ῥωμαλέος, ῥώννυμι, δύναμις, κράτος, σθένος, ἄρρωστος: Schmidt 3.659f. Del. 3M 3.14 v.l.

Ῥώμη, ης. f.
Rome: 1M 1.10.

ῥώννυμι: pf.pass. ἔρρωμαι, inf. ἐρρῶσθαι.
pass. *to be in good condition*: *s* hum. (health), 2M 9.19; battle-front, τινι 3M 1.4; in an epistolary greeting formula, χαίρειν καὶ ἐρρῶσθαι 3M 3.12, 7.1. Cf. ἐπιρρώνυμι, ῥώμη, ὑγιαίνω: Schmidt 3.658f.

ῥώξ, γός. m./f.ʃ
berry: ῥ. ἐλαίας 'olive' Is 17.6. **b**. spec., *grape*: οὐδὲ τοὺς ῥῶγας τοῦ ἀμπελῶνός σου συλλέξεις 'nor shall you gather grapes of your vineyard' Le 19.10; ἐν βότρυϊ 'as a bunch' Is 65.8. Cf. Shipp 481.

Σ

σαβαωθ.

Transliteration of צְבָאוֹת used in combination with κύριος: Is 1.9 +; τῷ κυρίῳ θεῷ ὑψίστῳ θεῷ σαβαωθ παντοκράτορι 1E 9.46.

σαββατίζω: fut. σαββατιῶ; aor. ἐσαββάτισα, inf. σαββατίσαι.*

1. *to observe a sabbath*: Ex 16.30; + cogn. obj., ἀπὸ ἑσπέρας ἕως ἑσπέρας σαββατιεῖτε τὰ σάββατα ὑμῶν Le 23.32; 2M 6.6.

2. *to lie inactive*, 'lie fallow': ***s*** agricultural land, ἡ γῆ Le 26.34; the land of Israel during the Exile, 1E 1.55.

Cf. σάββατον.

σάββατον, ου. n.* < Heb. שַׁבָּת, Ar. שַׁבְּתָא.

1. *sabbath*: often pl., Μνήσθητι τὴν ἡμέραν τῶν ~ων Ex 20.8; the seventh day following six working days, 20.10; holiday to be celebrated, Ho 2.11 (‖ ἑορτή, νουμηνία, and πανήγυρις); when trading is forbidden, Am 8.5 (‖ μήν); σάββατα ~ων Le 16.31, 23.32; τῇ ἡμέρᾳ τῇ ἑβδόμῃ ~α κυρίῳ τῷ θεῷ σου De 5.14. **b**. sg. τὸ σ. σου τὸ ἅγιον Ne 9.14, σ. ἐκ ~ου Is 66.23, ἐν Σιων ἑορτῆς καὶ ~ου La 2.6; 1M 1.43, 6.49, and 5x in 2M exc. 15.3.

2. *week*: δευτέρᾳ ~ου 'to the second day of the week' Ps 47 tit.; pl. τῆς μιᾶς ~ων 'on the first day of the week' 23.1.

Used mostly in the pl., the sg. being a wrong back formation from the pl., a pseudo-plural reflecting the Ar. sg.st.det.: see Pelletier 1972, cf. Mateos.

Cf. ἑορτή, νουμηνία, πανήγυρις, προσάββατον, σαββατίζω: Schwyzer 1935; Shipp 491.

σαγή, ῆς. f.ʃ

pack-saddle: of a horse, 2M 3.25. Cf. σάγμα.

σαγήνη, ης. f.*

large drag-net for fishing: ***o*** of βάλλω and ‖ ἄγκιστρον 'fishing-hook' Is 19.8; to which an offering is made, Hb 1.16 (‖ ἀμφίβληστρον); fig. of trap, ~αι καρδία αὐτῆς [= woman's] Ec 6.26. Cf. ἀμφίβληστρον, δίκτυον: Trench 236f.

σάγμα, ατος. n.ʃ

saddle-bag: of camel Ge 31.34. Cf. σαγή.

σαθρός, ά, όν.ʃ

unsound, 'rotten': ***s*** ξύλον Jb 41.19, Wi 14.1. Cf. σαπρία.

σαθρόω: aor. ἐσάθρωσα.ʃ *

to sap the strength of: + acc. pers., Jd 10.8 A (B: θλίβω).

σάκκος, ου. m. < Heb. שַׂק.

1. *coarse fabric* worn by mourner: round the waist, ἐπέθετο ~ον ἐπὶ τὴν ὀσφὺν αὐτοῦ Ge 37.34; Am 8.10; νύμφην περιεζωσμένην ~ον Jl 1.8; needed in order to be dressed properly, Is 20.2.

2. *oblong garment made of coarse fabric*: worn as a mark of penitence, Le 11.32 (‖ ἱμάτιον, δέρμα); ἐν ~οις, clothed in such, Jl 1.13; ἐνεδύσαντο ~ους Jn 3.5; περιεβάλετο ~ον 3.6 (opp. στολή); ~ον καὶ σποδὸν ὑποστρώσῃ 'you strew .. and ashes' Is 58.6, περιζώσασθε ~ους καὶ κόψασθε 'gird yourselves with .. and beat your chests' Je 30.3; worn by a mourner, Ps 29.12.

3. *sack* as container: for grain, Ge 42.25.

Cf. στολή, μάρσιππος: Shipp 488f.

σαλεύω: fut. σαλεύσω, pass. σαλευθήσομαι; aor.inf. σαλεῦσαι, pass. ἐσαλεύθην, subj. σαλευθῶ, impv. σαλεύθητι, inf. σαλευθῆναι, opt.act. 3s σαλεύσαι; pf.pass. σεσάλευμαι.

to set in commotion, violent movement: of earth tremor, Am 9.5. Pass.: ***o*** sea waters, Am 8.12, Si 29.18; of earthquake, Hb 3.6; mountains, Mi 1.4; hills, Na 1.5 (‖ σείω); πρόθυρα σαλευόμενα 'shaking front-doors' Zc 12.2; τὰ θεμέλια τῆς γῆς 'the foundations ..' Ps 81.5; trees, Is 7.2. **b**. *to shake violently*: fruit tree in order to shake fruits off, Na 3.12; ***o*** head, Ps 108.25 (a gesture of contempt and dislike), cf. κινέω **A**; foot, 4K 21.8; feet and pass., so that a walker loses balance, Ps 72.2 (‖ ἐκχέω); out of intoxication, 106.27 (‖ ταράσσομαι), Je 28.7; out of fear and awe, Ps 32.8. **c**. mentally, *to cause to lose equilibrium or stability*: + acc. pers., Si 28.14; pass., ἐσαλεύθη ἡ ψυχὴ αὐτοῦ Ju 12.16, cf. ἐν ἐμοὶ ἐσαλεύθη πάντα τὰ ὀστᾶ μου ('my bones') Je 23.9, καρδίαι καὶ χεῖρες Si 48.19; οὐ μὴ σαλευθῶ 'my position is ever secure' Ps 9.27; 14.5; + ἔντρομος γίνομαι 17.8 (***s*** γῆ); ***s*** διάβημα 'step' 16.5.

Cf. διασαλεύω, σάλος, σείω, ἀσάλευτος: Schmidt 3.143.

σάλος, ου. m.

tossing motion: of the rolling swell of rough sea, Jn 1.15, θαλασσῶν PSol 6.3, κυμάτων 'of waves' Ps 88.10; ἐν ~ῳ ἀπειλῆς αὐτοῦ 'by shaking himself menacingly' or 'with his menacing tempest' Zc 9.14; μὴ δόντος εἰς ~ον τοὺς πόδας μου 'not allowing my feet to totter' Ps 65.9. **b**. metaph. of commotion and instability: political, La 1.8; personal, Ps 54.23, + ταραχή Si 40.5.

Cf. σαλεύω.

σάλπιγξ, ιγγος. f.

trumpet: silver, Nu 10.2; war-trumpet, Σαλπίσατε σάλπιγγι 'Blow a trumpet' Ho 5.8, Jl 2.1, 15; ἐν ~γι σαλπιεῖ Zc 9.14; φωνὴ ~γος Am 2.2; φωνήσει σ. 'a trumpet sounds' 3.6; *s* of σημαίνω Jb 39.24, 25; ἡμέρα ~γος καὶ κραυγῆς Zp 1.16. See *BA* 9.1, p. 85f. Cf. σαλπίζω, κερατίνος.

σαλπίζω: fut. σαλπιῶ; aor. ἐσάλπισα, impv. σάλπισον, subj. σαλπίσω.

to produce the sound of a trumpet: σάλπιγγι Nu 10.8, Ho 5.8; ἐν σάλπιγγι Zc 9.14, σάλπιγξι 1M 9.12; ἐν κερατίνῃ 'with a horn trumpet' Jd 6.34, κερατίνῃ 7.18 A (B: ἐν ..); *s* θεμέλια τῆς γῆς Is 44.23 (‖ βοάω). **b.** *to send* a message *by blowing a trumpet*: + acc., σημασίαν 'a signalling call' Nu 10.6 ‖ σημασίᾳ ib.

Cf. σάλπιγξ, ἠχέω, σημαίνω.

Σαμάρεια, ας.

Samaria: Ho 7.1.

σαμβύκη, ης. f. < Ar. שַׂבְּכָא, סַבְּכָא.

small arched harp (LSG s.v.): Da 3.5.

σανδάλιον, ου. n.ʃ

sandal: pl. Jo 9.5, Is 20.2, Ju 10.4; sg. 16.9. Cf. ὑπόδημα.

σανίδωμα, ατος. n.ʃ

plank: of a ship's deck, πυκνός 'thick' 3M 4.10. Cf. σανίς, σανιδωτός.

σανιδωτός, ή, όν.ʃ *

planked, boarded over: *s* altar, Ex 27.8. Cf. σανίς, σανίδωμα.

σανίς, ίδος. f.ʃ

board, plank: ταινίαι ~ίδων κυπαρίσσου 'boards of cypress timber' Ez 27.5 (of ships), κεδρίνη 'of cedar' Ct 8.9; lid of a wooden chest, 4K 12.10. Cf. σανίδωμα, σανιδωτός: Spicq 3.227f.

σαπρία, ας. f. *(σαπρός: Hipponax +)

rotten, decayed state immediately following death: ἐν ~ίᾳ σκωλήκων κάθησαι 'you sit amongst rotten worms' Jb 2.9ca; ‖ θάνατος 17.14; ‖ σκώληξ 25.6, cf. σ. σκωλήκων 2.9c; ‖ βρόμος 'stench' Jl 2.20. **b.** morally: PSol 14.7, 16.14.

Cf. σαπρίζω, σαθρός, σήπω: Schmidt 2.363; Lindhagen 27-69, esp. 42-5.

σαπρίζω: fut. σαπριῶ.ʃ

to make rotten, to make stink: *s* flies, + acc., Ec 10.1. Cf. σαπρία, σήπω.

σάπφιρος, ου. f. < Ar. סַפִּיר. On the spelling, see Walters 36.

lapis lazuli: Ex 24.10; ἄνθραξ καὶ σ. καὶ ἴασπις 'carbuncle, sapphire and jasper' 28.18, 36.18; ζώνη ~ου 'girdle of ..' Ez 9.2; + σμάραγδος To 13.16.

σαράβαρα, ων. n.pl.ʃ < Ar. סַרְבָּלִין.

loose trousers: Da 3.21 TH, 94. Cf. Shipp 491f.

σάρδιον, ου. n.

the Sardian stone: a precious stone, λίθος ~ου Ex 25.6, 35.8; ‖ τοπάζιον, σμάραγδος 28.17, 36.17; πολυτελές 'highly-valued' Pr 25.12.

σάρκινος, η, ον.

made of flesh (σάρξ): *s* καρδία Ez 11.19, 36.26, Si 17.16¶ (living, receptive; opp. λίθινος 'stony, i.e. hard and not pliable'); βασιλεύς Es C 21 (mere human); μάχαιρα γλῶσσα βασιλέως καὶ οὐ σαρκίνη Pr 24.22c, μετ' αὐτοῦ βραχίονες ~οι, μεθ' ἡμῶν δὲ κύριος ὁ θεὸς ἡμῶν .. 'he has mere arms of flesh, but ..' 2C 32.8. Cf. σάρξ, σωματικός, ψυχικός: Renehan 2.124f.

σαρκοφαγέω.ʃ

to eat unlawful *meat*: 4M 5.26. Cf. subs.

σαρκοφαγία, ας. f.ʃ

eating of meat: 4M 5.8, ἔκθεσμος 'unlawful' 4M 5.14. Cf. prec.

σάρξ, κός. f.

1. *soft substance between skin and bones*, 'flesh': τὰ δέρματα αὐτῶν .. καὶ τὰς ~ας αὐτῶν ἀπὸ τῶν ὀστέων αὐτῶν 'their skins .. and their flesh from their bones' Mi 3.2, sim. Jb 2.5; φάγεται τὰ ὄρνεα τοῦ οὐρανοῦ τὰς ~ας σου ἀπὸ σοῦ Ge 40.19; βόες .. ἐκλεκταὶ ταῖς ~ξίν 'cows of top-quality flesh' 41.2, λεπταὶ ταῖς ~ξίν 'skinny, lean' 41.3, ἰσχυροὶ ταῖς ~ξίν 'stout of body' Da 1.15 TH (LXX σῶμα), αἱ ~ες μού εἰσιν χάλκειαι 'my muscles are bronze' Jb 6.12; τηκήσονται αἱ ~ες αὐτῶν 'their flesh will decompose' Zc 14.12 (‖ ὀφθαλμός and γλῶσσα); for hum. consumption, Mi 3.3*a*; Ps 77.27 (‖ birds), Jb 31.31; cannibalism - Le 26.29, Zc 11.9, Dt 28.55 (‖ κρέας 53), Je 19.9; to be cooked, Mi 3.3*b*; σπλαγχνοφάγον ἀνθρωπίνων ~ῶν θοῖναν καὶ αἵματος 'a sacrificial meal of human flesh and blood' Wi 12.5; ‖ αἷμα Zp 1.17. **b.** A figure for blood-relationship: ἐκ τῶν ὀστῶν μου καὶ ἐκ τῆς ~ός μου εἶ σύ 'you are a very close relation of mine' Ge 29.14, sim. 2.23; ἀδελφὸς ἡμῶν καὶ σ. ἡμῶν ἐστιν 37.27; ἀπὸ τῶν οἰκείων τῶν ~ῶν αὐτοῦ 'sbd out of his kinsmen' Le 25.49, ὡς σ. ἀδελφῶν ἡμῶν σ. ἡμῶν Ne 5.5; πονηρὸς ἐν σώματι ~ὸς αὐτοῦ 'guilty of incest' Si 23.16. Cf. Lys 1986.168. **c.** In the literal sense, the pl. is the norm as in Homer, but sg. referring to a specific part of human body, ἀκροβυστίας 'of foreskin' Ge 17.11, Le 12.3, cf. ἀπεριτμήτους ~κί Ez 44.7 and ἐκσπάσω τὴν καρδίαν τὴν λιθίνην ἐκ τῆς ~ὸς αὐτῶν 'I shall pull out the stony heart from their body' 11.19, sim. 36.26, but ὡς ὄνων αἱ ~ες αὐτῶν 'their phallus is like that of asses' 23.20 (‖ αἰδοῖα), and cf. μεγαλόσαρκος 16.26; ~ες σώματός σου Pr 5.11.

2. *physical living being*: hum., "the two shall become one σάρξ" Ge 2.24 (cf. Dafni 2001b), ‖ ψυχή Ps 62.2, ‖ καρδία – ἡ κ. μου καὶ ἡ σ. μου ἠγαλλιάσαντο ἐπὶ θεὸν ζῶντα '.. have rejoiced in the living God' 83.3, cf. Ez 36.26; ἐν κοιλίᾳ μητρὸς ἐγλύφην σ. 'I was carved as flesh in my mother's womb' Wi 7.1; opp. divine spirit (πνεῦμα), Ge 6.3, Ez 37.6, 8 (last two, pl. and || νεῦρα 'sinews' and δέρμα 'skin'); animals included, καταφθεῖραι πᾶσαν ~κα, ἐν ᾗ ἐστιν πνεῦμα ζωῆς Ge 6.17, πατάξαι πᾶσαν ~κα ζῶσαν 8.21, ἀπὸ πάσης ~κός .. ἀπὸ ἀνθρώπου ἕως κτήνους Nu 18.15, sim. Si 40.8; animals only, Ge 7.15; specified by the pl. genitive, πᾶσα σ. .. τῶν πετεινῶν καὶ τῶν κτηνῶν καὶ τῶν θηρίων, and distinct from πᾶν ἑρπετὸν .. καὶ πᾶς ἄνθρωπος 7.21.

***3**. *human being*: πᾶσα σ. 'everybody' Jl 2.28, Zc 2.13, Is 49.26, οὐκ ἔστιν εἰρήνη πάσῃ ~κί 'nobody has peace' Je 12.12; || πᾶσα ἡ γῆ Is 66.16; || ἄνθρωπος Ge 6.12 (resumed by a masc. pron., αὐτοῦ), Si 28.5; οὐ διαφωνήσει τῶν ἀνδρῶν αὐτοῦ σ. μία 'he would lose not even one of his men' Ju 10.13. **b**. as against the divine: De 5.26; οὐ φοβηθήσομαι, τί ποιήσει μοι σ. 'I shall have no fear. What can a mere human do to me?' Ps 55.5; "gods whose dwelling is not with any flesh (μετὰ πάσης ~κός)" Da TH 2.11. **c**. ephemeral existence, || πνεῦμα πορευόμενον 'passing wind' Ps 77.39, πᾶσα σ. χόρτος 'all people are grass' Is 40.6, τελευτήσει πᾶσα σ. ὁμοθυμαδόν 'death is a lot common to all' Jb 34.15; σ. καὶ αἷμα Si 14.18, sim. 17.31 (|| γῆ καὶ σποδός 'dust and ashes' vs. 32), cf. Ps 72.26. **b**. concords with the pl.: ἐπιγνώσονται πᾶσα σ. Ez 20.48 (|| sg. 21.5).

Cf. κρέας, σῶμα, πνεῦμα, ψυχή, σάρκινος: Spicq 3.231-41, esp. 233f.; Scharbert 1972.121-4; Lys 1986.

σατανᾶς, ᾶ. m.ʃ* < Heb. שָׂטָן.

enemy, adversary: not military, Si 21.27. Cf. διάβολος, ἐχθρός: MM and *ND* 3.83.

σάτον, ου. n. * < Ar. סָאתָא.

a Hebrew dry measure: ἐγένετο κριθῆς δέκα σάτα Hg 2.16.

σατραπ(ε)ία, ας. f.

satrapy: designation of a non Hamito-Semitic geopolitical entity, 1E 3.2 (Persian), 2M 9.25 (formerly Persian); πέντε ~αις Φυλιστιιμ Jo 13.3, τῶν ἀλλοφύλων Jd 3.3 (Philistine). Cf. σατράπης.

σατράπης, ου. m.

satrap: of the Persian Empire, + τοπάρχης 1E 3.2; applied to Philistine warlords, Jd 16.5A (B: ἄρχων); to rulers in general, 5.3 (|| βασιλεύς). Cf. σατραπεία.

σαύρα, ας. f.ʃ

lizard: ceremonially unclean, Le 11.30.

σαυτοῦ, ῆς, οῦ.

Marked form of σου, *of yourself*: σὺ τὴν ψυχὴν σαυτοῦ ἐξῄρησαι 'you have saved your own soul' Ez 33.9; σαυτοῦ γενοῦ 'Pull your socks up!' 3K 20.7, cf. ἐν σαυτοῦ γενοῦ 'Be yourself' Soph., *Phil.* 950.

σαφής, ές.

clear and distinctly identifiable as such: τὸ σαφὲς ἐπιγνόντες 'recognising the plain truth' Su 48; *s* πνεῦμα Wi 7.22; state of affairs, 2M 12.40. Cf. σαφῶς, τρανός, φανερός.

σαφῶς. adv.ʃ

1. *in lucid manner*: γράψεις .. σ. De 27.8; Γράψον ὅρασιν καὶ σ. εἰς πυξίον 'Write a vision clearly on a tablet' Hb 2.2; σ. ἐπεγνωκὼς .. 'having obtained a clear picture of ..' 2M 4.33; σ. .. πεισθῆναι 'clearly convinced' 3M 4.19. Cf. σαφής, φανερῶς.

2. *it is manifest that*, 'clearly, undoubtedly': ἀληθὴς σ. 'undoubtedly true' De 13.14.

σβέννυμι: fut. σβέσω, ptc. σβέσων, pass. σβεσθήσομαι; aor. ἔσβεσα, inf. σβέσαι, ptc. σβέσας, impv. σβέσον, subj. σβέσω, pass. ἐσβέσθην, inf. σβεσθῆναι, ptc. σβεσθείς, subj. σβεσθῶ; pf.ptc. pass. ἐσβεσμένος.

1. *to cause to cease burning or being aflame*: Le 6.9, Am 5.6, ἐν τῷ πάντα σβεννύντι ὕδατι 'with water which quenches all' Wi 16.17; ***o*** φλόξ 'flame' Ez 20.47, Si 28.23 (latter: pass.); burning object, Is 1.31, Jb 34.26 (ἀσεβεῖς 'the ungodly') + Ez 32.7 (humans as divine punishment), λύχνος 'lamp' Jb 18.6, λαμπτήρ 'torch' Pr 20.9a, σπινθήρ 'spark' Wi 2.3 + Si 28.12, φῶς Pr 13.9, burning coals 4M 9.20; ἡ γῆ καιομένη 'the burning land' Is 34.10 (pass.), λίνον καπνιζόμενον 'smoking flax' 42.3. **b**. fig.: ψυχὴ θερμὴ ὡς πῦρ καιόμενον οὐ μὴ σβεσθῇ .. 'hot passion like a burning fire cannot be put out ..' Si 23.16, ὕδωρ πολὺ οὐ δυνήσεται σβέσαι τὴν ἀγάπην Ct 8.7, anger Je 4.4; 4M 3.17; with double acc., τὴν πυριπνοῦν τόλμαν ἐσβεσμένοι 'having their fire-breathing daring quenched' 3M 6.34.

2. fig., *to do away with*: + acc., κλέος ἐσβεσμένον ἀπὸ γῆς 'their fame is ..' Jb 30.8, ὄνομα Pr 10.7, δόξαν οἴκου σου καὶ θυσιαστήριόν σου Es C 20, γαυρίαμα δρακόντων 'boasting of snakes' Jb 4.10, τὸ σθένος μου 'my strength' 16.15, ὑπερήφανον 'the haughty' 40.12, ἀσεβεῖς 'the ungodly' 34.26.

Cf. ἀπο~, κατασβέννυμι, σβεστικός, ἀφανίζω, ἄκαυστος: Lang, *TDNT* 7.166f.; Spicq 3.242f.

σβεστικός, ή, όν.ʃ

having to do with extinguishing: Wi 19.20. Cf. σβέννυμι.

σεαυτοῦ, ~ῆς; ~ῷ, ~ῇ; ~όν, ~ήν.

Pronoun of reflexive reference, referring to the person spoken to; used only in oblique cases.

Ποίησον σεαυτῷ κιβωτόν 'Make yourself an ark' Ge 6.14; θεοὺς χωνευτοὺς οὐ ποιήσεις σεαυτῷ Ex 34.17 ‖ .. οὐ ποιήσετε ὑμῖν Le 19.4; λάβε ~ῷ Ho 1.2; πρὸς ~όν Ex 28.1.

σέβασμα, ατος. n.ʃ

that which is worshipped with reverence: Bel 27 TH, Wi 14.20, 15.17. Cf. σέβομαι.

σέβομαι (act. only once [4M 5.24] in the LXX).

to worship with reverence: ***o*** God, + acc., Is 29.13 (‖ τιμάω), Jo 4.24, Jn 1.9, Jb 1.9, 3M 3.4; opp. ἀπειθέω 'disobey' Is 66.14; pagan god, Jo 24.33[b], Bel 3 LXX. Cf. σέβασμα, εὐλαβέομαι, εὐσεβής, ἀσεβής, σεμνός, προσκυνέω, φοβέομαι: Schmidt 4.344f.; Foerster, *TDNT* 7.171.

σειρά, ᾶς. f.

long, fairly thin object used for catching or tying, 'cord': metaph., ἑκάστου ἁμαρτιῶν 'of one's own sins' Pr 5.22; lock of hair, κεφαλῆς Jd 16.13; 16.14B (A: βόστρυχος). Cf. βόστρυχος.

σειρήν, ῆνος. f.ʃ

some kind of wild bird noted for its singing sound: ‖ θηρία Is 13.21; ‖ στρουθός 'ostrich'(?) 34.13, Jb 30.29; inhabits wilderness, Is 43.20 (‖ στρουθός); ‖ ἴνδαλμα 'phantom' Je 27.39; ὡς θυγατέρων σειρήνων Mi 1.8 (in a description of a wailing mourner and ‖ δράκων 'sea-snake'). Cf. σειρήνιος: Kaupel 1935-6.

σειρήνιος, ον.ʃ

of σειρήν (q.v.): ***s*** μελῳδία 'melody,' + κύκνειος 'of a swan' 4M 15.21. Cf. σειρήν.

σειρομάστης. ⇒ σιρομάστης.

σεῖσμα, ατος. n.ʃ

shaking to and fro: of a sieve, Si 27.4. Cf. σείω.

σεισμός, οῦ. m.

vibration: τροχῶν 'of wheels' Na 3.2; of earthquake, Am 1.1, Zc 14.5, πυρφόρου 'of firebrand' Jb 41.21; βασάνων 'of torturings' 4M 17.3; + βροντή 'thunder' Is 29.6. Cf. σείω, σεῖσμα, σάλος, and τρόμος.

σείω: fut. σείσω, pass. σεισθήσομαι; aor.pass. ἐσείσθην, impv. σείσθητι, subj.pass. σεισθῶ.

to shake: + acc., βασιλεῖς Is 14.16 (out of awe?); ***o*** city or its walls, Am 1.14, πόλεις Is 10.14 (military operation), σκηναί 33.20 (‖ κινέω); earth, ἐκ τῶν θεμελίων αὐτῆς 'to its foundations' 13.13, τὰ θεμέλια τῆς γῆς 24.18; gateway, Am 9.1; heaven Jl 2.10, cf. 3.16, Hg 2.6, 21; mountains, Na 1.5 (‖ σαλεύω); men, διασαλεύθητι καὶ σείσθητι 'Shake and tremble(, and wake up to the stark prospect)' Hb 2.16 (cf. Cyr. II 111); out of consternation, 3.14, ***s*** animals and humans, ἀπὸ προσώπου κυρίου Ez 38.20. **b**. pass. intr. *to move with shaky steps*, 'totter': ***s*** ὁ μεθύων καὶ κραιπαλῶν 'a drunken, inebriate man' Is 24.20, cf. ἀπὸ τῆς μέθης τοῦ σικερα 28.7. **c**. pass. intr., *to quake, tremble*: ***s*** the earth, Jd 5.4 (A: ‖ ἐξίστημι), + ταράσσομαι 2K 22.8.

Cf. ἀπο~, ἐκ~, συσσείω, σεῖσμα, σεισμός, σαλεύω, ταράσσω, τρέμω, κινέω: Schmidt 3.133, 139.

σελήνη, ης. f.

the moon as heavenly luminary: ὁ ἥλιος καὶ ἡ σ. καὶ ἕνδεκα ἀστέρες Ge 37.9; ὁ ἥλιος καὶ ἡ σ. συσκοτάσουσι 'the sun and the moon will grow dark' Jl 2.10, 3.15; ‖ ἥλιος Hb 3.11, Is 13.10, + ἀστήρ Je 38.36, Ps 8.4, and w. implicit ref. to its paleness, μεταστραφήσεται .. ἡ σ. εἰς αἷμα Jl 2.31; object of worship, τὸν ἥλιον καὶ τὴν ~ην καὶ τοὺς ἀστέρας καὶ πάντα τὸν κόσμον τοῦ οὐρανοῦ De 4.19, sim. 17.3; changeable, Si 27.11 (w. ref. to its phases). Cf. ἥλιος, ἀστήρ, ἄστρον, κόσμος: Shipp 494-6.

σελίς, ίδος. f.ʃ

column of writing in a papyrus-roll: Je 43.23.

σεμίδαλις, εως. f.

the finest wheaten flour: material for cakes, τρία μέτρα ~εως 'three measures of fine flour' Ge 18.6; σ. ἐκ πυρῶν Ex 29.2; ingredient of choice cuisine and + ἔλαιον, μέλι Ez 16.13; cultic offering, Le 2.1, Is 1.12; θυσία ~εως Nu 15.4; for unleavened bread, Nu 6.15. Cf. σταῖς: Battaglia 66f.

σεμνολογέω: aor.ptc. ~λογήσας.ʃ

to speak solemnly: abs., 4M 7.9. Cf. σεμνός.

σεμνός, ή, όν.ʃ

1. *worthy of reverence*: σεμνοτάτη ἡμέρα 'a most sacred day' 2M 6.11 (ref. to sabbath), σ. καὶ ἅγιος νόμος 6.28; God's name, 8.15 (+ μεγαλοπρεπής); ***s*** hum., 4M 17.5; subst. n., ‖ ὀρθά Pr 8.6.

2. *worthy of dedication*: ***s*** ἐργασία 'work' Pr 6.8*a*, cf. Aes. *Supp*. 1037 ἔργῳ ~ῷ.

3. *worthy of respect and high estimation*: ***s*** ῥήσεις 'pronouncements' Pr 15.26 (:: βδέλυγμα κυρίῳ 'abomination ..'); a martyr's mouth 4M 5.36, a martyr's high age 7.15 (‖ μακάριος), martyrs' mother 17.5.

Cf. ἅγιος, σεμνῶς: Schmidt 4.216-8, 344f.; Trench 346-8; Foerster, *TDNT* 7.193f.; Shipp 496; Spicq 3.244-8.

σεμνότης, ητος. f.ʃ

augustness, dignity: of the Jerusalem temple, ‖ ἁγιωσύνη and + ἀσυλία 'inviolability' 2M 3.12. Cf. σεμνός.

σεμνῶς. adv.ʃ

with attitude of reverence: μανθάνω 'to learn' 4M 1.17. Cf. σεμνός.

σευτλίον, ου. n.ʃ

beet: Is 51.20. Cf. Shipp 496f.

σηκός, οῦ. m.ʃ

sacred enclosure: 2M 14.33 (‖ θυσιαστήριον; vs. 35 ναός). Cf. ἱερόν, ναός.

σημαία. ⇒ σημέα.

σημαίνω: fut. σημανῶ; aor. ἐσήμανα, impv. σήμανον, subj. σημάνω, pass. ἐσημάνθην; pf.pass.3s σεσήμανται.

1. *to give signal, indicate*: + dat. instr., σάλπιγξιν 'with trumpets' Nu 10.9, cf. Jb 39.24 (*s* σάλπιγξ), φωνῇ μεγάλῃ 2E 3.11, ποδί Pr 6.13 (|| διδάσκω); || κράζω Je 4.5; + dat. pers., Zc 10.8.

2. *to point to by way of instruction*: + dat. pers. and acc. rei, αὐτοῖς τὰς ὁδούς, ἐν αἷς πορεύσονται .. καὶ τὰ ἔργα, ἃ ποιήσουσιν 'them the paths in which they shall walk .. and the works which they shall perform' Ex 18.20; Da 2.23, 45 LXX (TH γνωρίζω); + inf., 1E 2.4 (|| ἐντέλλομαι 2C 36.23).

3. *to name, mention*: *o* facts, 2M 2.1; + acc. and dat. pers., Es B 6; pass., *o* action noun, 1E 8.48.

Cf. σημεῖον, σημειόω, δια~, ἐννεύω, γνωρίζω, δείκνυμι, προσημειόομαι.

σημασία, ας. f.

1. *visible, concrete symptom*: of a disease, οὐλὴ ~ας τηλαυγής 'shining scar as symptom' Le 13.2; οὐλὴ καὶ σ. 14.56. **b**. *sth clearly marked*: of a jubilee year of remission, ἐν τῷ ἔτει ἀφέσεως σημασίᾳ αὐτῆς 'in the year of remission, (a year) marked for it' Le 25.13, cf. 25.10; elliptically, ἀφέσεως σ. 25.11, 12 (at the latter with a n.sg. predicate, ἅγιον).

2. *signal*: sounded by a trumpet on a battlefield, σαλπίζω ~αν Nu 10.5, 6, ~ᾳ 10.6[4], 7; σάλπιγξ ~ας 31.6; at a religious festival, ἡμέρα ~ας 'a day ushered in by some audible signal' 29.1; εὐφροσύνης 2E 3.13.

σημέα, ας. f. Also spelled σημεία, σημαία.ʃ

military standard, banner: Nu 2.2; ~αίαν φέρων ἐπὶ βουνοῦ 'carrying a banner on a hill' Is 30.17. Cf. σημεῖον **1b**.

σημεῖον, ου. n.

1. *that which signals*: of the sun and the moon signalling the distinction between day and night and the change of seasons, Ge 1.14, τὰ ~α τοῦ οὐρανοῦ Je 10.2; an extraordinary event caused (ultimately) by God and carrying some message, Ex 4.8, 17, σημεῖα καὶ τέρατα 7.3, De 7.19, sim. 4.34, 26.8, Is 8.18, σ. ἢ τέρας Ex 7.9; || μνημόσυνον 'reminder' 13.9; οὐ πιστεύουσίν μοι ἐν τοῖς σημείοις, οἷς ἐποίησα ἐν αὐτοῖς Nu 14.11; "this is the sign from the Lord (to convince you) that God is going to do it" Is 38.7; || θαυμάσια Si 33.6; wrought by a human, σ. ἢ τέρας De 13.1. **b**. *flag, standard*: Nu 21.8, ἐπ' ὄρους πεδινοῦ ἄρατε ~ον 'On hilltops in a plain hoist a flag' Is 13.2, cf. σημέα.

2. *that which serves for identification*, 'mark': ἔθετο κύριος .. σ. τῷ Καιν Ge 4.15; τῆς διαθήκης 9.12; 17.11 (of circumcised foreskin); δὸς τὸ σ. ἐπὶ τὰ μέτωπα τῶν ἀνδρῶν 'Put the mark on the foreheads of the men' Ez 9.4; a sign to mark the temporary burial spot, 39.15, cf. ἐστὶν σ. τῆς ταφῆς *P.Paris* 18bis, 10. Cf. χαρακτήρ: LSG s.v. **II 1b**; Merkelbach 1970.

Cf. σημαίνω, σημειόω, τέρας, παρά~, σύσσημον, σύμβολον, τεκμήριον, ἄσημος: Trench 339-43; Spicq 3.249-54; Youtie 1970; Dorival 1996.537.

σημειόω: aor.pass. ἐσημειώθην.ʃ

to send as signal: pass., *o* light, Ps 4.7. Cf. σημείωσις, σημαίνω.

σημείωσις, εως. f.ʃ

signal: for inducing an action, Ps 59.6; περισσὸς ἐν ~ει 'excessive in gestures' PSol 4.2. Cf. σημειόω, σημεῖον.

σήμερον. indecl.

today: ἐκβαλεῖς με σ. 'you cast me out today' Gn 4.14; σήμερον ὡς ἐχθὲς καὶ τρίτην ἡμέραν 'today like yesterday and the day before' 1M 9.44; ἕως τῆς σ. ἡμέρας Ge 19.37, Nu 22.30. **b**. adv. 'today': apart from the bare σήμερον one encounters various forms: τὸ τῆς σ. Ex 5.14, ἐν τῇ σ. 13.4, ἐν τῇ σ. ἡμέρᾳ Jo 5.9, ἐν τῇ ἡμέρᾳ τῇ σ. Ju 7.28, cf. ἀπὸ τῆς ἡμέρας τῆς σ. Ez 24.2 (|| ἀπὸ τῆς ἡ. ταύτης), ἀπὸ τῆς σ. 1M 10.30. **c**. as subject: ἡμέρα θλίψεως .. ἡ σ. ἡμέρα Is 37.3, cf. τῷ τῆς σ. ὕπνῳ 'by today's sleep' 3M 5.20.

Cf. αὔριον, ἐπαύριον, ἐχθές, πρώην.

σήπη, ης. f.ʃ *

putrid humour, 'puss': + σκώληξ 'maggot' Si 19.3. Cf. σήπω.

σήπω; fut.pass. σαπήσομαι; aor.impv. σῆψον, pass. ἐσάπην, subj.pass. σαπῶ; pf.ptc. σεσηπώς.ʃ

to make rot: + acc. pers., Jb 40.12. **b**. pass. *to rot*: *s* purple and marble, Ep Je 71, roots and fruits of a plant, Ez 17.9, bruises, Ps 37.6 (+ προσόζω); hum. Jb 16.7, hum. flesh 19.20, 33.21; ἔργον 'artefact' Si 14.19.

Cf. σήπη, σῆψις, σαπρίζω, ἄσηπτος: Schmidt 2.360-3.

σής, σητός. m.

moth: σ. ἐκτρώγων 'devouring moth' Mi 7.4, σ. καταφάγεται ὑμᾶς Is 50.9; σ. ἐπὶ ἱματίου 33.1; ὀστέων 'of bones' Pr 14.30; fig. of sth ephemeral, 27.18 (|| ἀράχνη 'spider's web'). Cf. σητόβρωτος: Shipp 497.

σητόβρωτος, ον.ʃ*

moth-eaten: *s* garment, Jb 13.28, cf. Is 51.8, Jas 5.2. Cf. βιβρώσκω.

σῆψις, εως. f.ʃ

that which has putrefied: Is 14.11 (|| σκώληξ). Cf. σήπω.

σθένος, ους. n.

bodily *strength*: λέοντος 'of a lion' Jb 4.10, cf. Ziegler 1985.112, Orlinsky 1962.128f.; βροντῆς 'of thunder' 26.14; + θράσος 3M 2.2; πόλις ~ους 'a city conquered through military might' (?) PSol 17.14. Cf. σθένω, δύναμις, ἰσχύς, κράτος, ῥώμη, ἀσθένεια, μεγαλοσθενής: Schmidt 3.689-91; Shipp 497.

σθένω.ʃ

to be strong: *s* hum., βοηθεῖν '(strong enough) to help' 3M 3.8. Cf. σθένος, ἰσχύω, ἀσθενέω.

σιαγόνιον, ου. n.ʃ

part under or near the jaw: part of a sacrificial animal, De 18.3. Cf. σιαγών.

σιαγών, όνος. f.

1. *fleshy part on either side of face*, 'cheek': of hum., ἐν ῥάβδῳ πατάξουσιν ἐπὶ ~όνα τὰς φυλὰς τοῦ Ισραηλ 'they shall strike the tribes of Is. on the cheek with a rod' Mi 5.1, cf. δώσει τῷ παίοντι αὐτὸν ~όνα 'turns the cheek to the one who hits him' La 3.30, δέδωκα .. τὰς ~ας μου εἰς ῥαπίσματα '.. for blows' Is 50.6, cf. Mt 5.39; pl. Ho 11.4; τὰ δάκρυα αὐτῆς ἐπὶ τῶν ~ων αὐτῆς La 1.2.

2. *jaw* (or: **1**): Jb 21.5.

Cf. σιαγόνιον: BDAG, s.v.

σίαλον, ου. n.ʃ

spittle: 1K 21.14; sth worthless, Si 26.22¶. Cf. προσσιελίζω, πτύω, πτύελος.

σιγάω: pres.impv. σίγα; fut. σιγήσω; aor. ἐσίγησα, subj. σιγήσω.

1. *to keep silence, refrain from speech*: Ex 14.14, Am 6.10; refrain from speaking in public, Ps 31.3; Σίγα ἀπ' ἐμοῦ 'Shut up, and leave me alone' To 10.7 𝔊II; opp. λαλέω Ec 3.7, Si 13.23, ἐσίγησεν οὕτως εἴπας 'having said this, he stopped speaking' 1E 3.24.

2. *to stop* engaging in activity: + ptc. pres., ἐσίγησεν κλαίουσα 'stopped crying' To 6.1 𝔊II (𝔊I ἐπαύσατο); + ἔκ τινος - ἐξ ἀγαθῶν Ps 38.3; *s* roaring billows, 106.29.

Cf. σιγή, σιγηρός, σιωπάω, ἡσυχάζω, παύω, λαλέω: Schmidt 1.215-22; Krischer 1981.

σιγή, ῆς. f.ʃ

refraining from speaking: opp. λόγος 3M 3.23; Wi 18.14. Cf. σιγάω.

σιγηρός, ά, όν.ʃ

quiet: *s* γυνή Si 26.14. Cf. σιγάω. Del. Pr 18.18 v.l.

σιδήριον, ου. n.ʃ

iron tool: blade of an axe, De 19.5, 4K 6.5, 6, Ec 10.10. Cf. σίδηρος, σκέπαρνον.

σιδηρόδεσμος, ον.ʃ *

constraining as bonds of iron: ~οις ἀνάγκαις 'tied with iron bonds against their will' 3M 4.9. Cf. σίδηρος.

σίδηρος, ου. m.

1. *iron* as metal: χαλκεὺς χαλκοῦ καὶ ~σιδήρου Ge 4.22; τοῦ χρυσίου καὶ τοῦ ἀργυρίου καὶ χαλκοῦ καὶ ~ου καὶ μολίβου καὶ κασσιτέρου Nu 31.22; less valuable than silver, Is 60.17; χαλκὸς καὶ σ. in a fig. of hardened, obstinate character, Je 6.28, cf. Is 48.4. **b**. as material, χαλκὸς καὶ σ. τὸ ὑπόδημα .. 'the sandal is made of ..' De 33.25.

2. *iron tool*: axe, De 20.19; 27.5; razor, Jd 16.17B (A: ξυρόν), 13.5; sword, Bel 26 LXX (TH μάχαιρα), Ju 6.6, Jb 5.20; fetters (?), Ps 104.18.

Cf. σιδήριον, σιδηρόδεσμος, σιδηροῦς, στόμωμα, χαλκός.

σιδηροῦς, ᾶ, οῦν.

made of iron: *s* bed, De 3.11; collar, 28.48; saw, Am 1.3; horn, Mi 4.13 (ǁ χαλκοῦς); bolts, Is 45.2 (ditt.); walls, 2M 11.9; fig. of hardness, Is 48.4 (ǁ χαλκοῦς), ζυγός 'yoke' (ditt.) Si 28.20; of dryness in drought, θήσω τὸν οὐρανὸν ὑμῖν ~οῦν Le 26.19 (ǁ χαλκοῦς), ἔσται .. ἡ γῆ .. ~ᾶ De 28.23 (dit.; of parched, hard soil?); ἐκ τῆς καμίνου τῆς ~ᾶς 'out of the iron furnace' 4.20. Cf. χαλκοῦς.

Σιδών, ῶνος.

Sidon: Ez 28.22.

Σιδώνιος, α, ον.

Sidonian: subst.m., 1E 5.53.

σίελον ⇒ σίαλον.

σίκερα. n., indecl. Heb. loanword (שֵׁכָר).*

strong alcoholic drink: οἶνος καὶ σ. Le 10.9, Nu 6.3; De 14.25, 29.6, Is 5.11. Cf. οἶνος, μέθυσμα.

σίκλος, ου. m. < Heb. שֶׁקֶל.

1. a Hebrew weight, *shekel*: Ex 30.23; κατὰ τὸν ~ον τὸν ἅγιον 39.1; ἐν τῷ ~ῳ τῶν ἁγίων Nu 7.85; equivalent of two drachms, Ex 39.2.

2. a Hebrew monetary value: ζημιώσουσιν αὐτὸν ἑκατὸν ~ους 'they shall fine him 100 shekels' De 22.19.

σικυήρατον, ου. n.ʃ

cucumber-bed: Is 1.8, Ep Je 69. Cf. σίκυος.

σίκυος, ου. m. Also σίκυς.ʃ

cucumber: as food, Nu 11.5. Cf. σικυήρατον.

σινδών, όνος. f. < Heb. סָדִין.

linen garment: Pr 31.24; + στολή Jd 14.12; 14.13A (B: ὀθόνιον). Cf. ὀθόνιον. Del. 1M 10.64 v.l.

σιρομάστης, ου. m. Also spelled σειρομάστης.

barbed lance: Nu 25.7, Jd 5.8A (B: λόγχη); converted from sickle, Jl 3.10 (ǁ ῥομφαία). Cf. λόγχη.

σισόη, ης. f.ʃ *

roll of hair (?): σ. ἐκ τῆς κόμης τῆς κεφαλῆς Le 19.27, cf. Frankel, *Einfl.* 152.

σιτέομαι.ʃ

to live on sth (acc.) *as food*: χορτώδη τροφήν 'grass as food' 2M 5.27, σῖτα Pr 4.17. Cf. ἐσθίω.

σιτευτός, ή, όν.

fatted: *s* calf (μόσχος) Je 26.21, sheep 3K 5.3B.

σιτίον, ου. n.ʃ

food: Pr 30.22. Cf. σῖτος, βρῶμα, ἔδεσμα.

σιτοβολών, ῶνος. m.∫
facility for storing grain, 'granary': ἀνέῳξεν .. πάντας τοὺς ~ῶνας Ge 41.56. Cf. σῖτος.

σιτοδεία, ας. f.∫
want of food, 'famine': ἐν τῷ θλῖψαι ὑμᾶς ~ᾳ ἄρτων 'by harrowing you with shortage of food' Le 26.26; ‖ δίψα 'thirst' Ne 9.15. Cf. λιμός, δίψα

σιτοδοσία, ας. f.∫
allowance of grain: ἀγορασμὸν ~ας 'purchased ..' Ge 42.19, 33. Cf. σῖτος.

σιτομετρέω.∫
to measure out grain: + dat. pers., Ge 47.14; and + acc. rei, 47.12 (σῖτον). Cf. σῖτος and μετρέω.

σιτοποιός, οῦ. m.∫
baker: Ge 40.17. Cf. σῖτος; Battaglia 201-3.

σῖτος, ου. m. Pl. also σῖτα.
1. *grain* as agricultural produce: πλῆθος σίτου καὶ οἴνου 'abundance of grain and wine' Ge 27.28; ‖ βρώματα 41.35, Is 62.58 and ‖ γενήματα Ge 41.34; ἅλων ~ου 'threshing floor ..' Ho 9.1, cf. Jl 2.24 and σ. ἀπὸ ἅλωνος Nu 18.27; basic food for humans, along w. οἶνος and ἔλαιον, De 7.13, Ho 2.8; 7.14, Zc 9.17 (‖ οἶνος); σ., οἶνον, ἔλαιον, τὰ βουκόλια τῶν βοῶν .. καὶ τὰ ποίμνια τῶν προβάτων De 28.51; produce of the earth, ἐπὶ τὸν ~ον καὶ ἐπὶ τὸν οἶνον καὶ ἐπὶ τὸ ἔλαιον καὶ ὅσα ἐκφέρει ἡ γῆ Hg 1.11; Ge 27.37, De 11.14; cultic offerings, οἴσεις τὰ ἐπιδέκατα τοῦ ~ου σου καὶ τοῦ οἴνου σου καὶ τοῦ ἐλαίου σου 14.22.
2. *food served*: ~οι Jb 3.24.
Cf. σιτοβολών, σιτοδεία, σιτοδοσία, σιτομετρέω, ἀσιτί, σιτοποιός, ἐπισιτισμός, ἐνσιτέομαι, οἶνος, ἔλαιον: Shipp 499; Moussy 91-7; Battaglia 41f.

σιωπάω: fut. σιωπήσομαι; aor. ἐσιώπησα, impv. σιώπησον, subj. σιωπήσω, opt.mid.3s σιωπήσαιτο; pf. σεσιώπηκα.
1. *to keep quiet, not speaking*: Σιώπα καὶ ἄκουε De 27.9; ὁ συνίων .. σιωπήσεται 'the prudent will keep silence' Am 5.13; + dat. pers., Nu 30.15*b*; ‖ παρασιωπάω 30.15*a*; ‖ ἀνέχομαι Is 42.14; ἐξ ἀγαθῶν 'malicious (utterances)' Ps 38.3 (euphemism: Cyr. PG 69.972).
2. *to cease* or *fail* to engage in activity: oral and + ptc., οὐ σιωπήσονται μιμνησκόμενοι κυρίου 'will not cease mentioning ..' Is 62.6; + inf., τοῦ λαλεῖν 1E 4.41; Σιώπα 'Say no more' Jd 3.19B (L Σίγα), Σιωπᾶτε 'Stop (weeping)' Ne 8.11; not oral, + a negated inf., τοῦ ⸢μὴ⸣ (B: om.) λαβεῖν 3K 22.3. **b**. general: *s* hum., Jd 18.9 A (B: ἡσυχάζω), 2K 19.11*L*; eyes, La 2.18.
Cf. σιωπή, ἀπο~, κατα~, παρασιωπάω, σιωπή, σιγάω, κωφεύω: Schmidt 1.215-22; Krischer 1981.

σιωπή, ῆς. f.∫
abstinence from speech, 'silence': ἐπιρρίψω ~ήν 'I shall impose silence' Am 8.3; Si 41.19. Cf. σιωπάω.

σιώπησις, εως. f.∫*
**veil*: used by a woman, Ct 4.1, 3, 6.7. Cf. θέριστρον, (κατα)κάλυμμα: Ceulemans and de Crom 2007.

σκάλλω.∫
to search, probe: *s* τὸ πνεῦμά μου Ps 76.7. Cf. ζητέω, ἐρευνάω.

σκαμβός, ή, όν.∫
crooked: metaph., *s* καρδία Ps 100.4. Cf. σκολιός, στρεβλός.

σκανδαλίζω: fut.pass. ~λισθήσομαι; aor.subj.pass. ~λισθῶ.∫
to bring to a fall: fig., + acc. pers., ἄφρονα 'the silly' PSol 16.7; pass., ἐν τοῖς ἐπιτιμίοις αὐτῆς 'through the damages to be paid on account of her' Si 9.5; ἐν τοῖς χείλεσιν 23.8; 35.15. Cf. σκάνδαλον, σκελίζω: Stählin, esp. 105-35.

σκάνδαλον, ου. n.*
1. *an object deliberately placed to make sbd trip*, 'stumbling-block': ἀπέναντι τυφλοῦ οὐ προθήσεις ~ον 'in front of a blind person you shall not place ..' Le 19.14; ἔθηκεν ἑαυτῷ ~α Ho 4.17; ‖ παγίς 'trap, snare', ἐχόμενα τρίβου σ. ἔθεντό μοι 'near the path they set ..' Ps 139.6, sim. Ju 5.1; φύλαξόν με .. ἀπὸ ~ων τῶν ἐργαζομένων τὴν ἀνομίαν 'guard me .. from the trap set by those who practise lawlessness' Ps 140.9; fig., *an occasion for calamity or sin*, heathen nations left surviving, ἔσονται ὑμῖν εἰς παγίδας καὶ εἰς ~α Jo 23.13; pagan idols, εἰς ~α ψυχαῖς ἀνθρώπων καὶ εἰς παγίδα ποσὶν ἀφρόνων Wi 14.11; pagan way of life, Ps 48.14.
2. *that over which one's reputation or public image might suffer*: θήσεις σ. ἐν εὐθύτητί σου 'you would mar your integrity' Si 7.6, ἐν τοῖς λόγοις σου δώσει σ. 'he will cast your words in a bad light' 27.23; also verbally, Ps 49.20 (‖ καταλαλέω); Ju 5.20 (‖ ἀνομία 21).
Cf. σκανδαλίζω, παγίς, ἀντίπτωμα, πρόσκομμα, σκῶλον: Lindblom; Stählin, esp. 23-74.

σκάπτω: aor.pass.subj. σκαφῶ.∫
to dig about in sth for cultivation: pass., *o* ἀμπελών 'vineyard' Is 5.6. Cf. ὀρύσσω: Ziegler 1934. 181.

σκάφη, ης. f.∫
deep-shaped basin, 'bowl': for holding liquid, Bel 33. Cf. κρατήρ.

σκάφος, ους. n.∫
boat: for passengers, 2M 12.3, 6. Cf. ναῦς, πλοῖον.

σκελίζω.ʃ*

to cause the downfall of: + acc. pers., ἐν θλίψει Je 10.18. Cf. ὑποσκελίζω, πίπτω, πτερνίζω, σκανδαλίζω, ὑποσχάζω.

σκέλος, ους. n.

leg: of animal, Am 3.12; ἀνώτερον τῶν ποδῶν 'above the feet' Le 11.21; ‖ πούς Ez 1.7; of hum., 1K 17.6, Pr 26.7. Cf. πούς, περισκελής.

σκεπάζω: fut. σκεπάσω, pass. ~πασθήσομαι; aor. ἐσκέπασα, subj. ~πάσω, inf. ~πάσαι, pass. ἐσκεπάσθην, subj. ~πασθῶ, inf. ~πασθῆναι, ptc. ~πασθείς, opt.act.3s ~πάσαι.

to provide protective covering or *shield for*: + acc. pers., Ex 2.2, 12.13, 27 (‖ ῥύομαι), De 13.8; ὡς ἀετὸς σκεπάσαι νοσσιὰν αὐτοῦ 'as an eagle would shield its brood' De 32.11; παρεμβολήν 'military camp' 1M 3.3; ‖ ὑπερασπίζω Wi 5.16; + ἐπί τινα – σκεπάσω τῇ χειρί μου ἐπί σε Ex 33.22; καταπετάσματι 'with a curtain' 40.3; *s* God's right hand, PSol 13.1 (‖ φείδομαι 'to spare'); pass., ὅπως σκεπασθῆτε ἐν ἡμέρᾳ ὀργῆς κυρίου Zp 2.3; ὑπό τινος Is 30.2 (‖ βοηθέω), ἀπὸ καύματος 'against the heat' Si 14.27; ὑπό τι– ὑπὸ τὴν σκιὰν τῆς χειρός μου 'under the shade of my hand' Is 51.16; μετά τινος (pers.) 1K 26.1 (*L* κρύπτομαι); τῷ ψεύδει Is 28.15; ἐν σκέπῃ Ps 16.8, 60.5; ἀπὸ ^γλώσσης^ 'from a (slanderous) tongue' Si 28.19; πανοπλίαις 'with armour' 2M 10.30. Cf. σκέπασις, σκέπη, σκεπαστής, σκεπεινός, ἐπισκεπάζω, σκιάζω, ὑπερασπίζω, βοηθέω: Lee 76f.

σκέπαρνον/ς, ου. n./m.ʃ

carpenter's axe, 'adze,' used for hewing and smoothing: Is 44.12; used as an instrument of torture (cf. βασανιστήριον), ἐν ~οις σιδήροις 'with iron ..' 1C 20.3 (‖ πρίων 'saw'), ‖ 2K 12.31*L*. Cf. πέλεκυς, σιδήριον.

σκέπασις, εως. f.ʃ *

protection provided: θεοῦ ἀρχῆς 'by ancient God' De 33.27. Cf. σκέπη.

σκεπαστής, οῦ. m.ʃ *

one who provides protection: alw. of the divine, βοηθὸς καὶ σ. ἐγένετό μοι εἰς σωτηρίαν Ex 15.2; βοηθησάτωσαν ὑμῖν, καὶ γενηθήτωσαν ὑμῖν ~αί 'let them aid you and become your protectors' De 32.38; ἀπεγνωσμένων σ. 'protector of the forsaken' Ju 9.11 (‖ βοηθός, ἀντιλήμπτωρ, σωτήρ); Ps 70.6, Si 51.2; τῶν ὅλων 3M 6.9. Cf. σκέπη, σκεπάζω.

σκεπεινός, ή, όν.ʃ

sheltered: subst.n.pl., 'sheltered places' Ne 4.13. Cf. σκεπάζω.

σκέπη, ης. f.

that which provides protection: a leather curtain spread over the tabernacle, Ex 26.7 (‖ κατακάλυμμα vs. 14); a tree providing shade, Ho 4.13; thickly grown forest, Ez 31.12; πένθου 'for the time of sorrow' Is 16.3; ἀπὸ προσώπου διώκοντος 'from a pursuer' 16.4; καθιοῦνται ὑπὸ τὴν ~ην αὐτοῦ 'will sit in its shade' Ho 14.8; + ἀπόκρυφον and ‖ σκιά Is 4.6, ‖ βοηθός 25.4, + βοήθεια Es 4.14 o'; διψώντων 'of the thirsting' Is 25.4; ἐν ~ῃ τῶν πτερύγων σου '.. of your wings' Ps 16.8, τοῦ ὄρους 1M 9.38; ἀπὸ καύσωνος 'from a sirocco' Si 31.19 (‖ σκιά); provided by wisdom, 14.26; a piece of defensive weapon, 2K 1.21*L* (B: θυρεός 'shield'). Cf. σκεπάζω, σκέπασις.

σκέπτομαι: fut. σκέψομαι; aor.impv. σκέψαι.ʃ

1. *to examine, consider*: εἰ δόκιμόν ἐστιν 'whether it is genuine or not' Zc 11.13; σκέψαι μή τι σοι ἀσύμφωνον γεγένηται '.. whether something not to your liking has happened or not' Bel 15-17 LXX.

2. *to look for carefully*: + acc., ἄνθρωπον φρόνιμον καὶ συνετόν 'a prudent and intelligent man' Ge 41.33; σὺ σεαυτῷ σκέψαι ἀπὸ παντὸς τοῦ λαοῦ ἄνδρας δυνατοὺς θεοσεβεῖς .. Ex 18.21.

Cf. σκοπεύω, ἐπισκέπτω, ζητέω.

σκέπω. ⇒ σκεπάζω.

σκευάζω: aor. ἐσκεύασα; pf.ptc.pass. ἐσκευασμένος.ʃ

to manufacture by regular process: ***o*** incense, Si 49.1; meal, 3M 5.31. Cf. ἑτοιμάζω, ποιέω.

σκευασία, ας. f.ʃ

food prepared for a meal: ἐλαίου ἡδύσματος 'with fragrant oil' Ec 10.1. Cf. βρῶμα.

σκεύασμα, ατος. n.ʃ

pl. **furniture*: Ju 15.11. Cf. σκεῦος.

σκεῦος, ους. n.

1. *implement, tool*: hunter's gear, τὸ σ. σου, τήν τε φαρέτραν καὶ τὸ τόξον 'your gear, the quiver and bow' Ge 27.3, κεραμέως 'potter's' Ps 2.9; ~η πολεμικά 'weapons' De 1.41, πολέμου Je 28.20, just σκεύη 1K 17.54, 30.24, Is 10.29; τῶν βοῶν '(the gear) of the oxen' 2K 24.22; ψαλμοῦ 'of praise' Ps 70.22 (‖ κιθάρα); ἄχρηστον 'useless' Ho 8.8; ~η ποιμενικά 'shepherd's gear' Zc 11.15; δερμάτινον .. ξύλινον 'leather .. wooden' Nu 31.20; χρυσοῦν 'golden' 31.50; εἰς ἔργον Is 54.16, ~η ἐξολεθρεύσεως '.. of destruction' Ez 9.1; fig., σ. ὀργῆς Je 27.25. **b**. in pl. *household belongings, furniture*: σκεύη ἀργυρᾶ καὶ χρυσᾶ καὶ ἱματισμόν Ge 24.53, Ex 3.22, 11.2, 12.35; ἀπὸ πάντων τῶν σκευῶν τοῦ οἴκου σου Ge 31.37; τὰ ~η τὰ ἐπιθυμητὰ αὐτοῦ 'his desirable belongings' Ho 13.15 (‖ γῆ), Na 2.10 (‖ "silver and gold"). **c**. for cultic use: τραπέζης Ex 38.12; 25.8, 39; chair or stool, Le 15.4; τὴν σκηνὴν (sc. τοῦ μαρτυρίου) καὶ πάντα τὰ ~η αὐτῆς Nu 1.50; ~η ἅγια 4.15, 31.6, λειτουργικά 4.26, cf. κατασκευή **2**, χορηγία **3**.

2. *goods, cargo* of ship: Jn 1.5 (rather than 'tackle' or 'gear'; cf. Th 179 τὰ ἐνόντα τῷ πλοίῳ).
*3. Hebraism, *pieces of outfit* worn on body: ~η ἀνδρός De 22.5 (‖ στολὴ γυναικεία); Ez 16.17.
Cf. ἐργαλεῖον, κατασκευή, (κατα)σκεύασμα, ἱμάτιον, σκευοφύλαξ.

σκευοφύλαξ, ακος. m.ʃ
he who guards temporarily deposited σκεύη: weapons, 1K 17.22*L* (A: φύλαξ). Cf. φύλαξ.

σκηνή, ῆς. f.
1. *tent, booth* as temporary dwelling: opp. οἰκία Je 42.7; κτηνοτρόφων 'of cattlemen' Ge 4.20; ‖ ἔπαυλις 25.16; ‖ οἶκος Nu 24.5; for livestock, τοῖς κτήνεσιν αὐτοῦ ἐποίησεν ~άς Ge 33.17; Jn 4.5; Hb 3.7 (‖ σκήνωμα); τὴν ~ὴν Δαυιδ τὴν πεπτωκυῖαν Am 9.11; erected on festivals, κατοικιῶ σε ἐν ~αῖς καθὼς ἡμέρα ἑορτῆς Ho 12.9, cf. ἑορτὴ τῶν ~ῶν De 16.13; used for religious services, τοῦ μαρτυρίου 'of the testimony' Ex 27.21 +; σ. τοῦ Μολοχ Am 5.26; part of nomad's possessions, πρόβατα καὶ βόες καὶ ~αί Ge 13.5 (= τὰ ὑπάρχοντα vs. 6); divine residence, Le 26.11.
2. *space for dwelling*: in a hewn-out rock, Is 22.16.
Cf. σκῆνος, σκήνωμα, σκηνοπηγία, σκήνωσις, (κατα)σκηνόω.

σκηνοπηγία, ας. f.
setting up of booth or *tent* (σκηνή, q.v.): ἑορτὴ (τῆς) ~ας 'the feast of tabernacles' De 16.16, Zc 14.16, 1M 10.21, ~ας ἑορτή 1E 5.50; ἵνα ἄγητε τὰς ἡμέρας τῆς ~ας 2M 1.9. Cf. σκηνή, πήγνυμι: Deissmann 1923.92f.

σκῆνος, ους. n.ʃ
= σκηνή: hum. body as a dwelling on the earth, Wi 9.15.

σκηνόω: fut. σκηνώσω; aor. ἐσκήνωσα.ʃ
to pitch a tent as settler: Jd 5.17B (A: κατα~), ἐν Σοδόμοις Ge 13.12. **b.** *to live in a tent*: ἐν σκηναῖς Jd 8.11B (A: κατοικέω). Cf. σκηνή, ἀπο~, κατασκηνόω, σκήνωσις.

σκήνωμα, ατος. n.
dwelling-place, abode, often pl.: De 33.18 (:: ἐξοδία); Ma 2.12; τοῦ κατακληρονομῆσαι ~ατα οὐκ αὐτοῦ Hb 1.6; ἄκανθαι ἐν τοῖς ~ασιν αὐτῶν Ho 9.6; σ. Αἰθιόπων Hb 3.7 (‖ σκηνή); humbler than οἶκος, Zc 12.7; = the Jerusalem temple, Ps 14.1 (‖ τὸ ὄρος τὸ ἅγιον); military, Ju 10.18. **b.** σκηνωμάτων 'the feast of tabernacles' (ἑορτή understood) 2M 10.6 (‖ σκηνῶν ἑορτή). **c.** people dwelling in σκήνωμα: ἔθνη καὶ ~ατα 2K 7.23.
Cf. σκηνή.

σκήνωσις, εως. f.ʃ
act of dwelling: 2M 14.35. Cf. σκηνόω.

σκῆπτρον, ου. n.
sceptre as a symbol of rulership: σ. Αἰγύπτου Zc 10.11; held by judge, Ep Je 13; + θρόνος Wi 6.21, 7.8, βασιλείας 'of dominion' 10.14. ***b.** by Hebraising metonymy, *group of people under the authority of a sceptre-bearing person*: Jd 18.19 *L* (A: συγγενεία), 1K 2.28B (*L* φυλή), cf. *BA* 9.1, pp. 47-9.
Cf. ῥάβδος, σκυτάλη, συγγενεία, φυλή.

σκιά, ᾶς. f.
1. *greater or smaller area darkened by an object blocking the light*, 'shade,' often associated with its protective function: created by a tent, Jn 4.5; by a plant and providing protection, 4.6; πτερύγων 'of wings' Ps 56.2; ἀπὸ καύματος 'against burning heat' Is 4.6, ἀπὸ μεσημβρίας 'from midday (heat)' Si 31.19 (‖ σκέπη); τῆς ἑσπέρας Je 6.4; metaph., ζησόμεθα .. ὑπὸ τὴν ~ὰν .. βασιλέως Ba 1.12, ἐν τῇ ~ᾷ ^χριστοῦ κυρίου^ La 4.20.
2. *dark figure on a surface reflecting some object*, 'shadow': βάλλω ~άν 'to cast a shadow' Jb 15.29. **b.** fig. of evanescent existence: Ps 143.4, Jb 8.9, 1C 29.15, Wi 2.5.
3. *darkness*: σ. θανάτου 'utter darkness (of night)' (?) Am 5.8 (opp. τὸ πρωΐ), Je 13.16 (‖ σκότος and :: φῶς), Is 9.2, Ps 22.4, cf. Cyr. I 459 ad Am 5.8; + σκότος, ‖ γνόφος Jb 3.5; ἐπὶ βλεφάροις 'on eyelids' 16.16 (due to fatigue).
Cf. γνόφος, ἐπι~, συ~, σκιάζω, κατάσκιος, σκέπη, and σκότος.

σκιαγράφος, ου. m.ʃ *
scene-painter: Wi 15.4.

σκιάδ(ε)ιον, ου. n.ʃ
sunshade of a carriage: of λαμπήνη ἡμιόνων 'carriage drawn by a mule' Is 66.20.

σκιάζω: fut. σκιάσω; aor. ἐσκίασα.
1. *to cast a shadow*, 'to overshadow': + acc., "the cloud overshadowing the encampment" Wi 19.7, τοὺς ὀφθαλμοὺς ἡμῶν 2K 20.6B (in order to blind us; *L* σκεπασθῇ ἀφ' ἡμῶν); σκιάζει ἡ νεφέλη ἐπὶ τῆς σκηνῆς Nu 9.18 (‖ καλύπτω 9.15 and ἐπισκιάζω Ex 40.29); νάπαι σκιάζουσαι 'shady glens' Nu 24.6; + ἐπί τινος, *s* νέφη 'clouds' Jb 36.28; cherubim, ἐπὶ τῆς κιβωτοῦ διαθήκης κυρίου 1C 28.18. **b.** *mid. = act.: δένδρα μεγάλα Jb 40.22.
b. *to provide protective shade*: + dat. com. pers. and *s* δρυμοὶ καὶ ξύλον Ba 5.8. **c.** fig., + ἐπί and acc. and *s* cherubs, σκιάζοντας ταῖς πτέρυξιν αὐτῶν ἐπὶ τὸ ἱλαστήριον '.. with their wings' Ex 38.8; + dat. com. pers. σκιάζειν αὐτῷ ἀπὸ τῶν κακῶν αὐτοῦ 'to provide him with a cover against his calamities' Jn 4.6; *s* God, ἐπ' αὐτῷ De 33.12.
*2. *to seek shade* as shelter: "under it [= a tree] all the animals .. would seek shade" Da 4.9 LXX (TH: κατασκηνόω).
Cf. σκιά, ἐπισκιάζω, κατάσκιος, σκεπάζω, καλύπτω.

σκιρτάω: fut. σκιρτήσω; aor. ἐσκίρτησα.ʃ
to leap about: *s* foetuses in a womb, Ge 25.22; ζῷα 'animals' Wi 17.19; βοΐδια 'calves' Je 27.11; δαμάλεις 'heifers' Jl 1.17; τὰ ὄρη ἐσκίρτησαν ὡσεὶ κριοί 'the mountains leapt like rams' Ps 113.4; out of joy, ὡς μοσχάρια ἐκ δεσμῶν ἀνειμένα 'like calves let loose from tethers' Ma 4.2; sbd kicking and struggling in his agony of death, Jd 5.27 *L*. Cf. διασκιρτάω, ἅλλομαι, πηδάω: Schmidt 1.536-46.

σκληρία, ας. f.ʃ
obstinacy: Ec 7.25. Cf. σκληρός.

σκληροκαρδία, ας. f.ʃ *
stubbornness of attitude: in refusing to do God's will, περιτεμεῖσθε τὴν ~αν ὑμῶν 'circumcise ..' De 10.16; Si 16.10. Cf. σκληρός, σκληροκάρδιος.

σκληροκάρδιος, ον.ʃ *
stubborn of attitude: *s* hum., φιλόνεικοι καὶ ~οι Ez 3.7, ἔθνη Si 16.9¶; Pr 17.20. Cf. σκληροκαρδία.

σκληρός, ά, όν.
1. *hard to the touch*: *s* stone, Wi 11.4.
2. *hard* (of a person's character): σ. αὐθάδης 'hard, arrogant' Ge 49.3; φωνὴ ἡμέρας κυρίου πικρὰ καὶ ~ά Zp 1.14; κύριος 'master' Is 19.4, βασιλεὺς ἰσχυρὸς καὶ σ. 1E 2.23.
3. *hard to bear and mentally painful*: *s* thought verbally expressed, ~ὸν ἐφάνη τὸ ῥῆμα Ge 21.11; work, ἐν τοῖς ἔργοις τοῖς ~οῖς Ex 1.14; δουλεία 'servitude' Is 14.3, ὅραμα 'vision' 21.2 (ǁ φοβερός); πνεῦμα 'spirit' 27.8 (ǁ π. θυμοῦ), γυνή, ἧ ~ὰ ἡμέρα 'a woman having a hard time' 1K 1.15; σκότος 'darkness' Is 5.30, θυμὸς κυρίου 28.2; λόγος To 13.12 𝔊[II]; ἄνεμος 'wind' Pr 27.16; subst. n. ἐβουλεύσαντο ~ά 'planned cruel things' Ju 9.13; a fact, μηδὲ ~ὸν φανήτω ὅτι ἀπέδοσθέ με ὧδε 'Don't think it was too cruel of you to sell me down here' Ge 45.5. **b**. n.pl. adv. *in a harsh manner*: ἐλάλησεν αὐτοῖς ~ρά 'gruffly' Ge 42.7, ἥξει ἐφ' ὑμᾶς ~ὰ λιμός Is 8.21; ἀποκρίθη 1K 20.7*L* (B: σκληρῶς).
4. *stubborn*: *s* hum., Nu 16.26, Is 48.4; τράχηλος 'neck' De 31.27, νῶτος 'back' Ba 2.33, καρδία Si 3.26f.; horse, ἵππος ἀδάμαστος 'untamed ..' 30.8 (ǁ προαλής 'impetuous'); ζῆλος 'jealousy (or: affection)' Ct 8.6 (ǁ κραταιός). **b**. Positively viewed: σ. γενόμενος ἐναντίου αὐτοῦ ὑπέμεινεν 'having put his foot down, he held up against him' Jb 9.4, sim. 22.21.
5. *hard of execution*: *s* hum., + epexegetic inf., σ. φέρεσθαι 'hard to put up with' Ge 49.3; ἔργα ~ά 'hard tasks' De 26.6; ῥῆμα 'a court-case hard (to deal with)' 1.17; πόλεμος 2K 2.17, ὁδός Ps 16.4.
Cf. σκληρία, σκληρῶς, σκληρότης, σκληρύνω, σκληρυσμός, σκληροκαρδία, σκληροτράχηλος, δύσκολος, πωρόω, κοῦφος, ἀπηνής, χαλεπός, μαλακός: Trench 46-9; Spicq 3.258-62.

σκληρότης, τος.ʃ f.
1. *harshness*: of climatic conditions, ἀπὸ ~τος καὶ ὑετοῦ '.. and from rain' Is 4.6; treatment, 28.27.
2. *stubbornness* in refusing to do God's will: σ. τοῦ λαοῦ τούτου .. ἀσεβήματα .. ἁμαρτήματα De 9.27.
3. *condition and situation hard to bear*: pl., θανάτου 'deadly' 2K 22.6B.
Cf. σκληρός, σκληρυσμός.

σκληροτράχηλος, ον. *
stiff-necked: *s* λαός Ex 33.3, De 9.6 +; individual, Si 16.11, Pr 29.1. Cf. σκληρός, σκληρύνω.

σκληρύνω: fut. ~ρυνῶ; aor. ἐσκλήρυνα, subj. ~ρύνω, pass. ἐσκληρύνθην, ptc. ~ρυνθείς, opt.3s ~ρυνθείη.
to harden: lit. and pass. of intr. force, Ps 89.6 (*s* vegetation under a scorching sun; + ξηραίνομαι). **b**. fig.: *o* anger (μῆνις) Ge 49.7; *s* God, ἐγὼ σκληρυνῶ τὴν καρδίαν τινός Ex 4.21, 7.3, 14.4 (leading to his refusal to act in a certain way); ἐσκλήρυνεν .. τὸ πνεῦμα αὐτοῦ καὶ κατίσχυσεν τὴν καρδίαν αὐτοῦ De 2.30; elliptically with the verb alone, ἐσκλήρυνεν Φαραω ἐξαποστεῖλαι ἡμᾶς Ex 13.15; fig. and *s* hum. and *o* τράχηλον 'neck' De 10.16 (ǁ σκληροκαρδία 'stubbornness of attitude'), καρδίαν Ps 94.8, τράχηλον καὶ καρδίαν 1E 1.46, cf. τοῦ μὴ ἀκοῦσαί μου Je 17.23, τοῦ μὴ εἰσακούειν τῶν ἐντολῶν μου 19.15, and σκληρυνθεὶς ἀπειθήσῃ σοι 'having hardened, he might disobey you' Si 30.12; *s* God, ἐσκλήρυνας ἡμῶν τὰς καρδίας τοῦ μὴ φοβεῖσθαί σε Is 63.17, *o* hum., Φαραω Si 16.15¶; deed, ἐσκλήρυνας τοῦ αἰτήσασθαι 'you have made a difficult request' 4K 2.10. **b**. *to add to the harshness of*: τὸν ζυγὸν ἡμῶν 'our yoke' 2C 10.4. **c**. pass. intr. *to intensify in severity*: ἐσκληρύνθη ἐπ' αὐτοὺς τὰ κακά 1M 2.30; *s* hand w. ref. to military strength, Jd 4.24, cf. κραταιόομαι ib. *L*; argument, 2K 19.44.
Cf. σκληρός, σκληροτράχηλος, ἀποσκληρύνω, βαρύνω, κατισχύω, προκατασκιρόομαι.

σκληρυσμός, οῦ. m.ʃ
obduracy: + ὑπερηφανία Si 10.21¶. Cf. σκληρότης.

σκληρῶς. adv.ʃ
1. *with difficulty*: ἐν τῷ αὐτὴν σ. τίκτειν 'while she was having difficulties in delivery' Ge 35.17.
2. *harshly*: treatment, δεδεμένος 'incarcerated' Is 22.3; mode of speech, 1K 20.7, 10 (*L* σκληρά); ἀπειλήσαντος αὐτοῖς ~ρότερον 'having threatend them rather severely' 3M 4.19, sim. 7.6.
Cf. σκληρός.

σκνίψ, σκνιφός, πός. m.
a kind of insect, "found under the bark of trees, eaten by the woodpecker" (LSJ acc. to Aristoteles), traditionally "gnat": Ex 8.16, Ps 104.31, Wi 19.10.

σκολιάζω. *

to walk in crooked ways: metaph., Pr 10.8; opp. πορεύομαι ὀρθῶς 14.2. Cf. σκολιός, ὀρθῶς.

σκολιός, ά, όν.

not straight, 'crooked': *s* παγίς 'a (twisted) trap' Ho 9.8, δράκων 'snake' Is 27.1, τρίβος 'path' Pr 2.15 (‖ καμπύλος 'bent'), ὁδός 21.8, ξύλον 'timber' Wi 13.13; opp. εὐθής 'even (terrain)' Is 40.4, 42.16; metaph., *s* hum. Jb 9.20 (:: ἄμεμπτος 'faultless'), γενεὰ ~ὰ καὶ διεστραμμένη 'an obstinate and perverse generation' De 32.5, γενεὰ ~ὰ καὶ παραπικραίνουσα '.. infuriating' Ps 77.8; στόμα '(devious) speech' Pr 4.24, λογισμός 'thought' Wi 1.3; subst. n., *irregularity, defect*, Jb 4.18. Cf. σκολιῶς, σκολιότης, διαστρέφω, εὐθύς, καμπύλος, ὀρθός, πλάγιος, σκαμβός: Spicq 1.387-9.

σκολιότης, τος. f.ʃ

perversity: τῆς ψυχῆς σου Ez 16.5, καρδίας Ps 80.13 Aq. Cf. σκολιός.

σκολιῶς. adv.ʃ

adv. of σκολιός (q.v.): ἀνήκοοι, πορευόμενοι σ. 'disobedient ..' Je 6.28. Cf. σκολιός.

σκόλοψ, οπος. m.ʃ

thorn: irritating and painful, ἐν τοῖς ὀφθαλμοῖς καὶ βολίδες ἐν ταῖς πλευραῖς '.. and darts in your sides' Nu 33.55; obstacle for pedestrians, Ho 2.6; ~όπων ἄκρα 'points of thorns' Si 43.19; σ. πικρίας καὶ ἄκανθα ὀδύνης 'a thorn of bitterness and painful briars' Ez 28.24.

σκόπελος, ου. m. Also ~ον, ου. n.ʃ

mound: serving as a grave, 4K 23.17. Cf. σωρός, χελώνη.

σκοπεύω: aor.impv. σκόπευσον.

to watch, look out: Ex 33.8; + acc., ὁδόν Na 2.2; εἰς τὰς τροχιάς 'the paths' Pr 5.21; + acc. pers. and *s* God's eyes, 15.3; *s* vulture's eyes, Jb 39.29¶. Cf. φυλάσσω, σκοπέω, σκοπός, σκοπιά, ἀποσκοπεύω, and σκέπτομαι.

σκοπέω. Used in the pres.ʃ

1. *to observe and notice*: + acc. rei, Es E 7.

2. *to look out for*: + acc. rei, τὸ σύμφορον 'the benefit' 2M 4.5.

Cf. ἀποσκοπέω, σκοπέω.

σκοπή, ῆς. f.ʃ

watch-tower: Si 37.14. Cf. σκοπιά: Shipp 503f.

σκοπιά, ᾶς. f.

1. *watch-out*: ἐν ἡμέρᾳ ~ᾶς σου Mi 7.4.

2. *group of watchmen*: παγὶς ἐγενήθητε τῇ ~ᾷ 'you have become a trap for the watchmen' Ho 5.1.

3. *look-out place* on an elevated ground: ἀγροῦ Nu 23.14; 3K 15.22.

4. *elevated ground*, 'peak': Is 41.9 (‖ ἄκρον); site of cult, Nu 33.52.

Cf. σκοπός, σκοπή, σκοπεύω, φυλακή.

σκοπός, οῦ. m.

1. *watchman, guard*: λίθος σ. '(pagan) protective stone' Le 26.1; σ. Εφραιμ μετὰ θεοῦ Ho 9.8; Is 21.6, Je 6.17, Ez 3.17, 33.2.

2. *target*: εἰς βέλος 'for an arrow' La 3.12; Wi 5.12.

Cf. σκοπιά, τερατοσκόπος, σκοπεύω: Harl, *Langue* 226-9.

σκορακισμός, οῦ. m.ʃ*

act of treating with contempt: λήμψεως καὶ δόσεως 'of receiving and giving gifts' Si 41.19. Cf. μυκτηρισμός.

σκόρδον, ου. n.ʃ

garlic: as food, Nu 11.5.

σκορπίδιον, ου. n.ʃ

engine of war for discharging arrows: 1M 6.51.

σκορπίζω: fut. σκορπιῶ, aor. ἐσκόρπισα, inf. σκορπίσαι, pass. ἐσκορπίσθην, subj. σκορπισθῶ, opt. 3pl σκορπισθείησαν; pf.pass.ptc. ἐσκορπισμένος.

to scatter abroad, scatter around: *o* water, Hb 3.10; ἔνυστρον ἐπὶ τὰ πρόσωπα ὑμῶν 'cud (of ruminating animal) on your faces' Ma 2.3; arrows (to be made ineffective), Ps 17.15; possessions for charity, 111.9; troops without a leader, 2M 14.13; pass., *o* corpses, PSol 4.19, bones of the deceased, 12.4. Cf. διασκορπίζω, διασκεδάζω, σκορπισμός, διασπορά: Shipp 504.

σκορπίος, ου. m.

scorpion: ὄφις δάκνων καὶ σκορπίος De 8.15; dangerous, Si 39.30; instrument of torture (cf. βασανιστήριον), ‖ μάστιξ 'whip' 3K 12.11.

σκορπισμός, οῦ. m.ʃ

v.n. of σκορπίζω: PSol 17.18.

σκοτάζω: fut. σκοτάσω; aor. ἐσκότασα.

to grow dark: σκοτάσει ἐν σοί 'you will experience moments of gloom'(?) Mi 6.14; *s* eyes, La 5.17 (from grief); wooded mountain mourning, and + ἐπί τινα Ez 31.15. Cf. σκότος and συσκοτάζω.

σκοτεινός, ή, όν.

1. *shrouded in darkness*: *s* θησαυροί 'treasures (laid up in darkness)' Is 45.3 (‖ ἀπόκρυφος), ὄρη Je 13.16; subst. n. ~ά 'dark places, i.e. Sheol' La 3.6, Ps 142.3, cf. πορευθῆναι .. εἰς γῆν ~ὴν καὶ γνοφεράν 'into a dark and gloomy land' Jb 10.21.

2. *inscrutable, indescribable*: φόβος ~ὸς μέγας 'great, dark fear' Ge 15.12, λόγος '(obscure) matter' Pr 1.6; subst. n.pl., ἀνακαλύπτων τὰ βαθεῖα καὶ ~ά 'revealing the profound and ..' Da 2.22 LXX (TH ἀπόκρυφα).

Cf. σκότος, ἀφεγγής, γνοφερός.

σκοτία, ας. f.

= σκότος (q.v.): ‖ νύξ Mi 3.6; μεσημβρινή 'midday' Is 16.3. Cf. σκότος.

σκοτίζω: fut.pass. σκοτισθήσομαι; aor.pass.impv. σκοτίσθητι, subj. σκοτισθῶ; pf.ptc.pass. ἐσκοτισμένος.

1. *to make dark*: + acc. pers. and pass., ἐσκοτισμένοι τοὺς ὀφθαλμούς 'having their eyes deprived of light' 3M 4.10.

2. pass. intr. *to grow dark*: impers., Is 13.10; *s* eyes, σκοτισθήτωσαν οἱ ὀφθαλμοὶ αὐτῶν τοῦ μὴ βλέπειν Ps 68.24; σκότος οὐ σκοτισθήσεται 138.12 (:: φωτίζομαι); ὁ ἥλιος καὶ τὸ φῶς Ec 12.2; metaph., spiritually, Ps 73.20.

Cf. σκότος. Del. Wi 17.3 v.l.

σκοτομήνη, ης. f.*

moonless night: Ps 10.2.

σκότος, ους. n.

absence of light, 'darkness': σ. καὶ οὐ φῶς Am 5.18; σ. καὶ γνόφος Ex 14.20, Is 60.2; ἡμέρα ~ους καὶ γνόφου Jl 2.2, Zp 1.15, γῆ ~ους αἰωνίου οὗ οὐκ ἔστιν φέγγος '.. where there is no light' Jb 10.22 (ref. to Hades, cf. ᾅδης καὶ σ. PSol 14.9); juxtaposition of three nouns, σ. γνόφος θύελλα 'pitch-dark stormy cloud(?)' Ex 10.22, De 4.11, 5.22; absence of sunlight, ὁ ἥλιος μεταστραφήσεται εἰς σ. 'the sun will turn into darkness' Jl 2.31; adversary or hostile force, τοὺς ἐχθροὺς αὐτοῦ διώξεται σ. 'darkness will pursue his enemies' Na 1.8; fig. of helpless, hopeless situation, θλῖψις καὶ στενοχωρία καὶ σ., ἀπορία στενὴ καὶ σ. ὥστε μὴ βλέπειν Is 8.22; ὁ λαὸς ὁ πορευόμενος ἐν ~ει, ἴδετε φῶς μέγα 9.2; fig. of secretiveness, ἔσται ἐν ~ει τὰ ἔργα αὐτῶν 29.15. Cf. σκοτία, σκοτάζω, σκοτόω, συσκοτάζω, γνόφος, φέγγος, φῶς: Schmidt 1.599-608; Shipp 504f.

σκοτόω: aor.pass. ἐσκοτώθην, opt.3s σκοτωθείη; pf.pass.3s ἐσκότωται.ʃ

1. *to make dark*: πονηρία γυναικὸς .. σκοτοῖ τὸ πρόσωπον αὐτῆς ὡς ἄρκος 'a woman's wickedness .. darkens her face like a bear' Si 25.17; pass., 'to become dark, lose light *or* brightness, lustre', σκοτωθείη τὰ ἄστρα 'may the stars lose light' Jb 3.9, τὸ δέρμα μου 'my skin' 30.30; fig. "over the blow suffered by the daughter(s) of my people I became despondent (ἐσκοτώθην)" Je 8.21; 14.2.

2. *to make dizzy*: resulting from a fatal blow and pass., ἐξεστὼς ἐσκοτώθη καὶ ἀπέθανεν 'having lost consciousness, ..' Jd 4.21B. Cf. περιφέρω **3**.

Cf. σκότος : Shipp 504f.

σκυβαλίζω: aor.subj.pass. σκυβαλισθῶ.ʃ

to look on as dung, disregard contemptuously: ***o*** hum., Si 26.28. Cf. σκύβαλον, καταφρονέω.

σκύβαλον, ου. n.ʃ

refuse: metaph., 'sheer nonsense, crap' Si 27.4 (ǁ κοπρία). Cf. κοπρία, περικάθαρμα, περίψημα: Lang, *TDNT* 7.445-7; Spicq 3.263-5.

σκυθρωπάζω: fut. ~πάσω.

to look gloomy and sad: πενθῶν καὶ σκυθρωπάζων 'mourning and ..' Ps 34.14; *s* the face of one who is in sorrow, Pr 15.13; σκυθρωπάζων ἐπορευόμην Ps 37.7; + συρίζω 'to hiss' Je 19.8, 27.13. Cf. σκυθρωπός, σκυθρωπόω, στυγνάζω, and εὐφραίνομαι.

σκυθρωπός, ον.ʃ

gloomy-looking: τί ὅτι τὰ πρόσωπα ὑμῶν ~ὰ σήμερον; 'why are you looking gloomy today?' Ge 40.7; καρδία ταπεινὴ καὶ πρόσωπον ~ὸν 'low spirit and gloomy face' Si 25.23; *s* face, Da 1.10 TH (LXX διατετραμμένον). Cf. σκυθρωπάζω, σκυθρωπῶς, μελανία.

σκυθρωπόω: pf.ptc.pass. ἐσκυθρωπωμένος.ʃ*

= σκυθρωπάζω: *s* hum., Es 6.20 *L*.

σκυθρωπῶς. adv.ʃ

sullenly: 3M 5.34. Cf. σκυθρωπός.

σκυλεία, ας. f.ʃ *

act of plundering: possesions of defeated troops, 1M 4.23. Cf. σκυλεύω.

σκυλεύω: fut. σκυλεύσω; aor. ἐσκύλευσα, impv. σκύλευσον, inf. σκυλεῦσαι, ptc. σκυλεύσας.

1. *to despoil*: abs. Is 8.3 (ǁ προνομεύω); + acc. pers. Ex 3.22, 12.36; ἔθνη πολλά Hb 2.8 (slain enemy); 2K 23.10*L* (B: ἐκδιδύσκω), 1C 10.8 (ǁ ἐκδιδύσκω 1K 30.8).

2. *to take possession of by force*: + acc. rei, τὰ ὑπάρχοντά σου 'your possessions' Ez 26.12 (ǁ προνομεύω), τὰ σκεῦλα αὐτῆς 29.19, sim. 1M 5.68; ἅγιον νεῴ 'holy temple' 2M 9.16.

Cf. (δι)αρπάζω, σκῦλον, σκυλεία, ἐκδιδύσκω, προνομεύω: *ND* 4.26-8.

σκυλμός, οῦ. m.

annoying treatment accompanied by physical violence: pl., + ὕβρις 3M 3.25; meted out to slaves, 7.5. Cf. Passoni dell'Acqua 1974.

σκῦλον, ου. n. Alw. pl.

spoils to be had of slain enemy or victims: μεριῶ ~α 'I shall divide spoils' Ex 15.9, διαμερισθήσεται τὰ ~α σου 'your spoils will be divided up' Zc 14.1; ǁ προνομή Nu 31.11, ǁ αἰχμαλωσία, προνομή 31.12; τῆς αἰχμαλωσίας 31.26; προνομὴ ~ων Is 8.1; τὰ ~α τῶν πόλεων ἐλάβομεν De 2.35; τῷ ἐμῷ λαῷ .. ποιῆσαι ~α 'to take spoils .. of my own people' (dat. incom., not to be construed with συντάξω) Is 10.6. **b.** gen., *gain, profit*: Pr 31.11.

Cf. σκυλεύω, προνομή.

σκύμνος, ου. m.

young of predatory animal: of lion, σ. λέοντος Ge 49.9, De 33.22, Na 2.12; λέων ἥρπασε τὰ ἱκανὰ τοῖς ~οις αὐτοῦ 'a lion carried off enough prey for its cubs' 2.13; Nu 23.24, Am 3.4 (ǁ λέων); ὡς σ. ἐν ποιμνίοις προβάτων 'like a cub amongst flocks of sheep' Mi 5.8 (|| λέων); αἱ μύλαι αὐτοῦ ~ου 'its back teeth are those of a (lion's) whelp' Jl 1.6 (|| λέων); of snake (δράκων) La 4.3; fig. of hum. enemy, Ps 56.6. Cf. λέων.

σκυτάλη, ης. f.ʃ
long, slender rounded piece: pole used for bearing an object and keeping it in place: ὥστε αἴρειν αὐτὸ ἐν αὐταῖς Ex 30.4; made of incorruptible wood, 30.5. **b**. staff to lean on for support: 2K 3.29. **c**. symbol of authority: ἄρχων ~ης 'the chief officer in charge' 3K 12.24[b], cf. σκῆπτρον.

σκώληξ, κος. m.
worm: ἐξέζεσεν ~κας καὶ ἐπώζεσεν 'it [= left-over food] boiled out worms and stank' Ex 16.20; devours grapes, De 28.39; ~κι ἑωθινῇ 'early-morning worm' Jn 4.7; maggots devouring a human corpse, Si 10.11 (+ ἑρπετά, θηρία), 19.3 (+ σήπη 'puss'), Is 66.24; lives inside timber, Pr 12.4; a form of divine punishment, πῦρ καὶ σ. Si 7.17, Ju 16.17; fig. of worthlessness, Jb 25.6¶.
Cf. σῆψις: *ND* 3.83); Amigues 2005.

σκῶλον, ου. n.
1. *thorn in the flesh, painful annoyance*: of a situation, Ex 10.7; foreign religion, De 7.16.
2. *stumbling-block, hindrance*: Is 57.14; Jd 8.27B (A: σκάνδαλον).
Cf. σκάνδαλον: Shipp 507; Caird 1969.33; *BA* 2.38f.

σκώπτω.ʃ
to make mockery of: + acc., Si 10.10.

σμαραγδίτης, ου. m.ʃ
of the kind of or *of the colour of* σμάραγδος: σ. λίθος Es 1.6 o' (*L* σμάραγδος). Cf. σμάραγδος.

σμάραγδος, ου. f.
emerald: λίθος ~ου Ex 28.9; precious stone, Ju 10.21; || σάπφειρος To 13.16; σφραγὶς ~ου 'a seal of ..' Si 35.6; delightful stone, Ez 28.13. Cf. σμαραγδίτης.

σμῆγμα, ατος. n.
soap: part of women's toilet accessories, Su 17 TH, τῶν γυναικῶν Es 2.12 o'.

σμικρύνω: aor. ἐσμίκρυνα, impv. σμίκρυνον, subj. σμικρύνω, pass. ἐσμικρύνθην, subj. σμικρυνθῶ.
to reduce the quantity of: + acc., τὰς ἡμέρας τοῦ χρόνου αὐτοῦ 'his life-span' Ps 88.46; cattle, 106.38 (:: πληθύνω), πρόσκομμα 'offence' Si 17.25, ἀπαρχὴν χειρῶν 'offerings' 32.10. **b**. pass. *to suffer decrease*: *s* population, Je 36.6, Ba 2.34 (:: πληθύνομαι), sim. Da 3.37; 1C 16.19 (|| ὀλιγοστοὶ γίνομαι); *to pale in significance*, 17.17.
Cf. ἐλαττόω, ὀλιγόω, and πληθύνω.

σμῖλαξ, ακος. f.ʃ
bindweed (LSJ): σ. περιπλεκομένη 'twisted b.' Na 1.10; Jer 26.14.

σμιρίτης, ου. m.ʃ
emery powder: σ. λίθος Jb 41.7.

σμύρνα, ης. f.
myrrh: for cultic use, Ex 30.23; aromatic used to scent garments, σ. καὶ στακτὴ καὶ κασία ἀπὸ τῶν ἱματίων σου Ps 44.9; fragrant substance, ὡς σ. ἐκλεκτὴ διέδωκα εὐωδίαν 'as choice myrrh I gave out fragrance' Si 24.15. Cf. σμύρνινος.

σμύρνινος, η, ον.ʃ *
of myrrh: *s* ἔλαιον Es 2.12 o'. Cf. σμύρνα.

σορός, οῦ. f.ʃ
coffin: ἔθηκαν αὐτὸν ἐν τῇ ~ῷ Ge 50.26; ἐπὶ ~ῷ ἠγρύπνησεν 'he kept vigil by a coffin' Jb 21.32¶.

σός, σή, σόν.
belonging or *pertaining to you*, with stressed notion of ownership and claim, and sg. of ὑμέτερος, q.v.: ἀπὸ πάντων τῶν σῶν 'out of all that belongs to you' Ge 14.23; σὺ καὶ πάντα τὰ σά 'you and all that belongs to you' 20.7; more emphatic than σου and when used attributively, often precedes the noun head, τῇ σῇ εἰσόδῳ 'through your arrival' 30.27; τοῖς σοῖς οἰκέταις Ex 5.15; δώσω διαστολὴν ἀνὰ μέσον τοῦ ἐμοῦ λαοῦ καὶ ἀνὰ μέσον τοῦ σοῦ λαοῦ 'I shall discriminate between ..' 8.23; τῶν σῶν οἰκετῶν 'your servants' 32.13; τῆς σῆς ἐπιστήμης Jb 39.26; anarthrous, σὴ ἀσχημοσύνη 'your own pudenda' Le 18.10; postposition, τὸ ὄνομα τὸ σόν Is 4.1. **b**. pred.: σή ἐστιν ἡ γῆ Ps 88.12 (|| σοί εἰσιν οἱ οὐρανοί). **c**. esp. frequent in Pr, and often anarthrous: 1.9, 2.10*a*+; postpositive, 27.10; articular, 1.14, 2.10*b*+.

σοφία, ας. f.
wisdom: of practical and technical nature, σοφίαν καὶ σύνεσιν καὶ ἐπιστήμην Ex 31.3 (of an architect); spinning skill, 35.26, Jb 38.36 (|| ἐπιστήμη); stonemason, Ex 35.33; σ. καὶ ἐπιστήμη 36.1; divine and applied at the creation of the world, Je 10.12 (|| φρόνησις); statesman, σ. συνέσεως Is 10.13; || σύνεσις 29.4, Je 28.15. **b**. *branch of science*, 'discipline': ἐπιστήμων ἐν πάσῃ ~ᾳ Da 1.4 LXX. **c**. of moral character and in relation to God: ἡ σ. ὑμῶν καὶ ἡ σύνεσις ἐναντίον πάντων τῶν ἐθνῶν De 4.6; divine gift, Is 11.2; σ. καὶ ἐπιστήμη καὶ εὐσέβεια 33.6; created by God, Si 1.9; σ. δικαιοσύνης PSol 17.23. **d**. personified: Si 4.17.
Cf. σοφός, σύνεσις, ἐπιστήμη, φρόνησις: *BA* 2:36f.

σοφίζω: fut.pass. σοφισθήσομαι; aor.inf. σοφίσαι, mid. ἐσοφισάμην.
1. fact. of σοφός, = σοφόω: + acc. pers., νήπια 'infants' Ps 18.8 (*s* μαρτυρία κυρίου); || παιδεύω 104.22.
2. *to teach*: *+ acc. pers. et rei, με τὴν ἐντολήν σου Ps 118.98. Cf. διδάσκω.

3. mid. *to show off one's knowledge, play the wise man*: παρὰ βασιλεῖ Si 7.5; 10.26 (|| δοξάζομαι). **b**. with no derogatory nuance, *to prove to be wise, act wisely*: 3K 5.11, Ec 7.16, Si 18.29; ἐν λόγοις 'in speech' 37.20; *to grow in wisdom*, 38.24, Pr 16.17.

4. mid. *to come to realise and conclude*: + ὅτι 1K 3.8, cf. ὁράω **I 3**.

σοφιστής, οῦ. m.

wise person, 'sage' of non-Israelite background: τοὺς ~ὰς Αἰγύπτου καὶ τοὺς φαρμάκους Ex 7.11; + φιλόσοφος Da 1.20 LXX, τῆς Βαβυλωνίας 2.14 as against Daniel and his colleagues called σοφοί (*BA* 2:37).

Cf. σοφός, ἐπιστήμων.

σοφός, ή, όν.

1. *skilled in any handicraft, expert*: *s* hum. engaged in construction and maintenance of cultic installations, τῇ διανοίᾳ 'intelligent' Ex 28.3, 35.9; οἱ ~οὶ οἱ ποιοῦντες τὰ ἔργα τοῦ ἁγίου 36.4; women, ταῖς χερσὶν νήθειν 'to spin with hands' 35.25; enchanter, Ps 57.6 (|| ἐπᾴδων 'snake-charmer'); ἀρχιτέκτων Is 3.3 (|| συνετός). **b**. metaph. σ. τοῦ κακοποιῆσαι Je 4.22.

2. *wise*: *s* man, ἄνδρας ~οὺς καὶ ἐπιστήμονας καὶ συνετοὺς .. De 1.13, 15; λαὸς σ. καὶ ἐπιστήμων 4.6; ἀπολῶ ~οὺς ἐκ τῆς Ἰδουμαίας Ob 8 (|| σύνεσις); τίς σ. καὶ συνήσει ταῦτα; Ho 14.10 (|| συνετός); λαὸς μωρὸς καὶ οὐχὶ σ. 'a foolish and not wise nation' De 32.6; God, Si 1.8; ῥῆμα 'speech' 1E 3.5; subsr. m.pl. οἱ ~οί σου 'your sages' Is 19.12.

Cf. συνετός, σοφία, σοφιστής, σοφόω, πάνσοφος, ἐπιστήμων, φρόνιμος, σώφρων, ἀνόητος, μωρός, νοήμων, φαῦλος.

σοφόω.ʃ*

to make wise: κύριος σοφοῖ τυφλούς Ps 145.9. Cf. σοφός, σοφίζω.

σοφῶς. adv. ʃ

in a wise and skilful manner: of a carpenter, Is 40.20; manner of speech, Pr 31.28 (|| νομοθέσμως). Cf. σοφός, σωφρόνως.

σπάδων, οντος. m.ʃ

eunuch: in a royal court, τῷ ~οντι Φαραω, ἀρχιμαγείρῳ Ge 37.36 (|| εὐνοῦχος 39.1); σ. ἐν τῷ οἴκῳ τοῦ βασιλέως τῶν Βαβυλωνίων Is 39.7, 4K 20.18*L* (B: εὐνοῦχος). Cf. εὐνοῦχος: Schmidt 4.35-7.

σπαίρω.ʃ

to twitch: *s* hands and toes of a dying person, 4M 15.15. Cf. Renehan 2.127.

σπανίζω: aor. inf. σπανίσαι, pass. ἐσπανίσθην; pf. ptc.pass. ἐσπανισμένος.ʃ

1. *to be in want of, lack*: pass., gram. *s* πᾶν ὕδωρ Ju 11.12; *o* hum. in want, 4K 14.26; "with the passage of time the sea waters become scarce" Jb 14.11. Cf. ὑστερέω,

2. *to be dealt with and removed*: : *s* unlawful deeds, Da 9.24 LXX (TH: σφραγίζω).

Cf. σπάνις, II ἐνδέω, περισσεύω.

σπάνιος, α, ον.ʃ

rare: subst.n.sg., adv. *infrequently*, Pr 25.17. Cf. πυκνός.

σπάνις, εως. f.ʃ

unsatisfied need: + gen., τῶν ὑδάτων Ju 8.9. Cf. σπανίζω.

σπαράσσω: aor. ἐσπάραξα, pass. ἐσπαράχθην; pf. ptc.pass. ἐσπαραγμένος.ʃ

to tear: + acc. Da 8.7 LXX; metaph., σπαράσσεται ἡ καρδία μου Je 4.19; pass. and *o* τὰ θεμέλια τοῦ οὐρανοῦ 'the foundations of heaven' 2K 22.8 (|| συνταράσσω; *L* ἐφώνησεν); metaph. of martyrs of faith ἐσπαραγμέναι σκυλμοῖς ἀλλοεθνέσιν '.. by cruelties at the hands of aliens' 3M 4.6. Cf. ῥήγνυμι.

σπάργανον, ου. n.ʃ

swaddling-bands: Ez 16.4; ἀνετράφην ἐν ~οις 'I was nursed ..' Wi 7.4. Cf. σπαργανόω: Shipp 509.

σπαργανόω: aor. ἐσπαργάνωσα, pass. ἐσπαργανώσθην.ʃ

to swaddle: *o* baby, σπαργάνοις Ez 16.4; ὁμίχλῃ αὐτὴν [= θάλασσαν] ἐσπαργάνωσα 'I enveloped it with mist' Jb 38.9. Cf. σπάργανον.

σπαρτίον, ου. n.

small cord: || σφαιρωτὴρ ὑποδήματος 'shoe thong' Ge 14.23; κόκκινον 'scarlet' Jo 2.18, Ct 4.3; γεωμετρίας 'used to measure land' Is 34.11; measuring cord, Je 52.21, οἰκοδόμου 'builder's' Ez 40.3, || μέτρον Jb 38.5; ἀποτινάγματος 'of a piece of flax' Jd 16.9*L*. Cf. σχοινίον.

σπασμός, οῦ. m.ʃ

v.n. of σπάω: μαχαιρῶν 'of swords' 2M 5.3.

σπαταλάω.ʃ*

to live in excessive comfort: ἐν πλησμονῇ ἄρτων καὶ ἐν εὐθηνίᾳ ἐσπατάλων 'they indulged in abundant supply of bread and plenty' Ez 16.49; Si 21.15. Cf. κατασπαταλάω, σπατάλη, τρυφάω: Trench 201f.; MM and BDAG, s.v.

σπατάλη, ης. f.ʃ*

luxury, indulgent life-style: ὁ γέλως αὐτῶν ἐν ~ῃ ἁμαρτίας 'their joke is about sinful luxury (or: unbridled sin)' Si 27.13. Cf. σπαταλάω, τρυφή.

σπάω: aor. ἔσπασα, inf. σπάσαι, subj. σπάσω, mid. ἐσπασάμην, impv. σπάσαι, ptc. σπασάμενος; pf. ptc.mid. ἐσπασμένος.

1. *to pull out*, 'draw': + acc., sword, ῥομφαίαν Nu 22.23 (|| μάχαιραν vs. 31), Jd 20.2 A (B: ἕλκω), μάχαιραν 8.20 A (B: ῥομφαίαν), ἐπὶ φίλον Si 22.21. **b**. mid. *to pull out* one's own sword: ἀνδρῶν ἐσπασμένων ῥομφαίαν Jd 8.10A; but also act. in the same sense, 8.20B (*L* mid.).

2. *to draw in*, 'inhale': + acc., ἀέρα 'air' Wi 7.3. Cf. ἐκ~, ἐπισπάω, σπασμός, ἕλκω, σύρω: Schmidt 3.253-8.

σπεῖρα, ας. f.

tactical unit: of soldiers, Ju 14.11, 2M 8.23.

σπειρηδόν. adv.ʃ

in groups of 60 or 120 troops: 2M 5.2, 12.20.

σπείρω: fut.act. σπερῶ, pass. σπαρήσομαι; aor. ἔσπειρα, impv. σπεῖρον, subj. σπείρω, ptc. σπείρας, opt. σπείραιμι; pf. ἔσπαρκα, ptc.pass. ἐσπαρμένος.

1. *to sow* seeds: abs. Ge 26.12; ἐν τῷ ἀγρῷ Ex 23.16, σπείρατε .. τρυγήσατε .. 'Sow .. harvest' Ho 10.12, σπείρατε .. θερίσατε Je 12.13, σὺ σπερεῖς καὶ οὐ μὴ ἀμήσῃς '.. but not reap' Mi 6.15; + acc., σπέρματα 'seeds' Le 26.16; ἐσπείρατε πολλὰ καὶ εἰσηνέγκατε ὀλίγα 'you sowed much but reaped a little' Hg 1.6; fig. of descendants, and pass. οὐ σπαρήσεται ἐκ τοῦ ὀνόματός σου ἔτι 'there will arise no more bearing your name' Na 1.14; impers. pass., τόπος, οὗ οὐ σπείρεται Nu 20.5. **b**. *to sow seeds of*: + acc., πυρὸν καὶ κριθὴν .. 'wheat, barley ..' Is 28.26, πᾶν τὸ σπειρόμενον διὰ τοῦ ποταμοῦ '.. through the river (Nile)' Is 19.7 (|| ἄχι 'reed-grass'); acc. pers., ***s*** hum. father, 4M 10.2 (|| γεννάω ***s*** mother). **c**. w. double acc. (acc. of field and acc. of seed): σπερῶ τὸν Ισραηλ .. σπέρμα ἀνθρώπου καὶ σπέρμα κτήνους Je 38.27.

2. *to plant* field by sowing: + acc., τὴν γῆν Ge 47.23; Ex 23.10; ἀγρόν 'the field' Ps 106.37 (|| φυτεύω), Le 25.3; φάραγγα 'wadi' De 21.4.

3. *to scatter abroad, disperse*: + acc. pers., σπερῶ αὐτοὺς ἐν λαοῖς Zc 10.9, cf. Ho 10.12; + acc. rei, σπεῖρον σπέρμα Ge 1.11, 29 || σπέρμα σπόριμον ib.; ἐπὶ τὸ ὕδωρ Ex 32.20; ***o*** one's possessions as alms, Pr 11.24. **b**. + double acc.: ^τὴν πόλιν^ ἅλας (B: εἰς ἅλας) '.. salt' Jd 9.45 A.

Cf. δια~, κατασπείρω, σπέρμα, σπορά, σπόρος, διασκεδάζω, (δια)σκορπίζω, ἐκριπτέω.

σπένδω: fut. σπείσω; aor. ἔσπεισα, inf. σπεῖσαι.

to pour a drink-offering: abs. Ex 25.29; + acc. rei, ἔσπεισεν ἐπὶ ^τὴν στήλην^ σπονδήν Ge 35.14 (|| ἐπιχέω); σπονδὴν σίκερα κυρίῳ Nu 28.7; τῷ κυρίῳ οἶνον Ho 9.4, σπονδὰς θεοῖς ἀλλοτρίοις Je 7.19; ὕδωρ 2K 23.16; τὸ πόμα τῷ θεῷ 'the drink ..' 4M 3.16. Cf. σπονδή, σπονδεῖον, θύω, and θυσιάζω.

σπέρμα, ατος. n.

1. *seed*: καρπὸν, οὗ τὸ σ. αὐτοῦ ἐν αὐτῷ 'fruit the seed of which is in it' Ge 1.12; τὸ γένημα καὶ τὸ σ. 'the produce and the seed(s)' De 22.9.

2. sg. used collectively, *offspring*: of humans and animals, σοὶ δώσω αὐτὴν καὶ τῷ ~ατί σου ἕως τοῦ αἰῶνος Ge 13.15; τῷ σπέρματί σου μετὰ σέ 48.4; Ιακωβ καὶ πᾶν τὸ σ. αὐτοῦ 46.6 (specified as υἱοὶ καὶ οἱ υἱοὶ αὐτοῦ .., θυγατέρες καὶ θυγατέρες τῶν υἱῶν αὐτοῦ), sim. Nu 18.19; ἀνὰ μέσον τοῦ ~ατός σου [= Αδαμ] καὶ ἀνὰ μέσον τοῦ σπέρματος αὐτῆς [= ἡ ὄφις] Ge 3.15: on a possible individuation here, see *BA* 1.109, Wevers *Notes* 44, and Rösel 1994.94; ὄφεων 'of snakes' Is 14.29; αὐτῶν ὄνομα καὶ κατάλειμμα καὶ σπέρμα 14.22, || κατάλοιπος 15.9, || τέκνα 44.3; σ. μεταβόλων 'descendants of tradesmen' 23.3. Cf. ἀπό~, ἔκγονος, φυτόν **2**. **b**. rarely pl.: τῶν Αβραμιαίων σπερμάτων ἀπόγονοι 'the descendants of the seed of Abraham' 4M 18.1. **c**. the notion of descendants weakened and alm. = ἔθνος, λαός: σ. πονηρόν Is 1.4, 14.20. **d**. agricultural *crops* generally: 1K 8.15, Ps 125.6, Is 61.11. **e**. κοίτη σπέρματος 'ejaculated semen': Le 15.16, originally intended to mean 'sleeping to produce offspring'?; 'sexual intercourse,' γυνή, ἐὰν κοιμηθῇ ἀνὴρ μετ' αὐτῆς ~ην σπέρματος 15.18

3. *act of sowing*: σ. καὶ θερισμός 'sowing and harvesting' Ge 8.22.

Cf. σπείρω, σπορά, ἐπιγονή, σπερματισμός, τέκνον: LSG s.v. **I 1**.

σπερματίζω: aor.pass.subj. σπερματισθῶ.ʃ

I. *to implant seeds*: ***o*** woman, 'to have semen implanted' leading to pregnancy, σπερματισθῇ καὶ τέκῃ ἄρσεν 'to become pregnant and bear a male' Le 12.2.

II. intr. *to form seeds*: ***s*** flax (λίνον), Ex 9.31.

Cf. σπέρμα, σπερματισμός.

σπερματισμός, οῦ.ʃ

production of offspring (σπέρμα): Le 18.23. Cf. σπέρμα.

σπεύδω: fut.act. σπεύσω; aor. ἔσπευσα, impv. σπεῦσον, ptc. σπεύσας; pf. ἔσπευκα.

1. *to move with speed*: ἐπὶ τὴν σκηνὴν πρὸς Σαρραν Ge 18.6; Mi 4.1; ἐπὶ τὰ τείχη 'on to the walls' Na 2.6.

2. *to act with speed*: abs., Ex 15.15; the action indicated by the following verb joined by καί - Σπεῦσον καὶ φύρασον 'Knead quickly' Ge 18.6; ἔσπευσεν καὶ καθεῖλεν τὴν ὑδρίαν 'quickly let the pitcher down' 24.18; 24.20, 44.11; 2M 11.37; by a τοῦ inf., σπεῦσον τοῦ σωθῆναι Ge 19.22, with no τοῦ - Ju 10.15, 2M 4.14, Pr 28.22; σπεύδω as a conjunctive ptc., σπεύσασα καθεῖλεν τὴν ὑδρίαν Ge 24.46, σπεύσαντες ἀνάβητε .. 45.9, σπεύσας Μωυσῆς κύψας ἐπὶ τὴν γῆν προσεκύνησεν 'Moses, quickly bending to the ground, prostrated himself' Ex 34.8, sim. Ju 12.14; poss. opp. ὑστερέω 'to run late' Si 11.11. On the syntax, cf. ταχύνω **1a**.

*3. *to become mentally unsettled*: ***s*** pers., Ex 15.15 (|| τρόμος ἔλαβεν αὐτούς 'trepidation gripped them' and cf. Syh *estarhav*); ἐπ' αὐτῷ 'over him' Je 38.20, cf. ἐπ' αὐτῷ ἐσπούδακα Jb 23.15; 1K 28.20, 21. Cf. Ge 43.30 ἐταράχθη = יִמָּהֵר; Taylor 2004.

4. tr. *to strive after, seek eagerly* or *to promote vigorously*: + acc., δικαιοσύνην Is 16.5 (|| ἐκζητέω κρίμα).

5. tr. *to accelerate*: + acc., καιρόν Si 33.10.

Cf. σπουδή, σπουδάζω, ἐπι~, κατασπεύδω, (κατα) ταχύνω, τρέχω. Cf. Walters 144-8.

σπήλαιον, ου. n.

cavern: ᾤκησεν ἐν τῷ ~ῳ Ge 19.30; burial-place, σ. διπλοῦν 'double ..' 23.9; purchased as part of a field, 25.10; family cemetery, 49.29; hiding-place, Ps 56.1; place for concealing treasures (cf. Th 271) or fig. of privy parts of a male (?), ὅπως ἐπιβλέπῃ ἐπὶ τὰ ~α αὐτῶν Hb 2.15 (cf. *DJD* 8.55 ἀσχημοσύνην[?], Ach and Thph PG 126.867); σ. λῃστῶν 'robbers' den' Je 7.11; || τρώγλη, ῥαγάς Is 7.19; site of divination, 65.4 (+ μνῆμα 'grave'). Cf. LSG s.v. **2**.

σπιθαμή, ῆς. f.

linear distance between the thumb and little finger, 'span': of horizontal dimension, Ex 28.16; a unit of measurment, Is 40.12, Ez 43.13; χειρός Si 18.3¶.

σπιλόω: aor.ptc.pass. σπιλωθείς.ʃ

to stain: pass., *o* idol, χρώμασιν διηλλαγμένοις 'with various colours' Wi 15.4. Cf. μολύνω.

σπινθήρ, ῆρος. m.

spark: ~ῆρες πυρός as a figure of sth evanescent, Is 1.31, sim. Si 11.32, Wi 2.2, but also as a figure of sth splendidly shining, Si 42.22, ~ῆρες ὡς ἐξαστράπτων χαλκός '.. like flashing brass' Ez 1.7, ὡς ~ῆρες ἐν καλάμῃ Wi 3.7, ~ῆρας ἀστράπτοντας 11.18; a son to keep the family flag flying, 2K 14.7*L*.

σπλάγχνα. n.pl.

1. *the inner organs* of a body: hum., τῶν ~ων ἀλγηδών 'pain ..' 2M 9.5 (|| τὰ ἔνδον); and animated by πνεῦμα, Ba 2.17.

2. *the seat of feelings and affections*: Je 28.13; ταραχθήσεται τὰ ~α αὐτοῦ Si 30.7; + κοιλία PSol 2.14. **b**. *compassion*: τέκνου 'for one's child' Wi 10.5; Pr 12.10, cf. *ND* 3.84.

Cf. σπλαγχνίζω, εὔσπλαγχνος, κοιλία, ἔλεος, οἶκτος: Spicq 3.273-5.

σπλαγχνίζω.ʃ *

to eat inner organs: of sacrificial animals, 2M 6.8. Cf. σπλάγχνα, σπλαγχνισμός, σπλαγχνοφάγος. Del. Pr 17.5 v.l.

σπλαγχνισμός, οῦ. m.

v.n. of σπλαγχνίζω: of sacrificial animals, 2M 6.7; unlawful, 6.21. Cf. σπλαγχνίζω.

σπλαγχνοφάγος, ον.ʃ

consisting of eating the internal organs: *s* θοῖνα 'meal' Wi 12.5.

σποδιά, ᾶς. f.ʃ

ashes: remains of burnt sacrificial animals, Le 4.12, Nu 19.10, 17. Cf. σποδός.

σποδοειδής, ές.ʃ

ash-coloured: *s* πρόβατον - σ. ῥαντά 'having ash-coloured spots' Ge 30.39; τράγος 'he-goat' and κριός 'ram' 31.10, 12. Cf. σποδός.

σποδόομαι: aor. ἐσποδωσάμην, ptc. σποδωθείς.ʃ

to strew oneself or part of one's body *with ashes*: as a gesture of grief, abs. Es 4.2 *L*; + acc., κεφαλάς Ju 4.11. Cf. σποδός.

σποδός, οῦ. f.

Alw. used in the sg.

1. *ashes*: resulting from the burnt suet of a sacrificial animal, δαμάλεως 'of a heifer' Nu 19.9; Le 1.16; περιεβάλετο σάκκον καὶ ἐκάθισεν ἐπὶ ~οῦ 'he put on a sack-cloth and sat on ashes' (as a mark of penitence) Jn 3.6, opp. δόξα Is 61.3 (as a mark of grief), σάκκον καὶ ~ὸν ὑποστρώσῃ 'you strew sack-cloth and ashes' 58.6, sim. Da 9.3 LXX (also + νηστεία 'fast'), Je 6.26; fig. of sth worthless, Is 44.19, Wi 15.10.

2. *dust*: sth of negligible account, ἔσονται ~ὸς ὑποκάτω τῶν ποδῶν ὑμῶν Ma 4.3; in self-depreciation, ἐγώ εἰμι γῆ καὶ ~ός 'I am soil and dust' Ge 18.27; Si 10.9, 40.3.

Cf. αἰθάλη, σποδιά, σποδοειδής, σποδόομαι, κονία, κονιορτός, τέφρα.

σπονδεῖον, ου. n.

cup from which the σπονδή *was poured* (LSJ): Ex 25.28; ~εῖα, ἐν οἷς σπείσει 38.12; Nu 4.7; golden, 1E 2.12; silver, ib.

σπονδή, ῆς. f.

libation, drink offering to God: as cogn. obj. of σπένδω, Ge 35.14, Ex 30.9, Je 19.13; οἴνου Ex 29.40, οἶνος εἰς ~ήν Nu 15.5, οἶνος σπονδῶν De 32.38; εἰς θυσίαν καὶ ~ήν Nu 28.9; ἐξῆρται θυσία καὶ σ. ἐξ οἴκου κυρίου 'sacrifices and libations have been removed from the house of the Lord' Jl 1.9; ἐξέχεας ~άς 'you poured out ..' Is 57.6. Cf. σπένδω and θυσία.

σπόνδυλος, ου. m.ʃ

vertebra: 4M 10.8. Cf. ἐκσπονδυλίζω, σφόνδυλος.

σπορά, ᾶς. f.ʃ

1. *seed*: 1M 10.30.

2. *act of sowing*: + ἄμητος 'harvesting' 4Ki 19.29.

Cf. σπείρω, σπέρμα.

σπόριμος, ον.ʃ

1*. *seed-producing*: *s* χόρτος 'grass' Ge 1.29; *s* σπέρμα Le 11.37; subst. n.pl. Da 1.12 LXX (Zgl-Munnich: ὄσπρια, cf. Hamm 103-5).

2. subst. *sown field*: χλόη ~ου 'herbage of ..' Si 40.22, v.l. for σπόρου.

Cf. σπέρμα and ἀγρός.

σπόρος, ου. m.

1. *act of sowing seed*: τῷ ~ῳ καὶ τῷ ἀμήτῳ κατάπαυσις 'you shall not engage in seeding and harvesting' Ex 34.21.

2. *season for sowing*: ὁ τρύγητος καταλήμψεται τὸν ~ον 'the harvesting will continue up to the sowing' Le 26.5; περκάσει ἡ σταφυλὴ ἐν τῷ ~ῳ 'the grapes will ripen at seedtime' Am 9.13 (|| τρύγητος).

3. *harvest, crop*: οὐ δώσει ἡ γῆ τὸν ~ον αὐτῆς Le 26.20; ἀποδώσει τὸν ~ον Jb 39.12; Is 32.10 (|| τρυγητός).

4. *seed*: coll., σπείρωσιν τὸν ~ον De 11.10; χλόη ~ου 'the first green shoot of ..' Si 40.22; Is 28.24.

5. *offspring*: coll., Jb 21.8 (|| τέκνα).

Cf. σπείρω, σπέρμα, ἄμητος, τρύγητος.

σπουδάζω: aor. ἐσπούδασα, subj. σπουδάσω; pf. ἐσπούδακα.

1. *to act with speed*: ἐσπούδασεν ὁ πούς μου εἰς δόλον 'my foot sped towards deception' Jb 31.5; the action indicated by a τό-inf., ἐσπούδασα τὸ μὴ βλέπειν 'I lost no time in closing my eyes' Is 21.3; a τοῦ-inf., καταβῆναι Ju 13.12; a bare inf., ἀναλύειν 'to retire for the night' Ju 13.1, οὐκ ἐσπούδασεν εὐθέως γενέσθαι περὶ τὴν ἄφοδον 'they did not immediately make haste to depart' 3M 7.10.

*2. *to become mentally unsettled*: ***s*** pers., ἐπ' αὐτῷ 'over him' Jb 23.15; 4.3, 21.6; μὴ σπεύσῃς ἐν καιρῷ ἐπαγωγῆς 'do not panic in time of calamity' Si 2.2 (or: 'do not act rashly ..'). **b**. tr. *to unsettle mentally*: + acc. pers., ἐσπούδασέν σε πόλεμος ἐξαίσιος 'a fierce battle made you panic' Jb 22.10.

Cf. σπεύδω, ἐπισπουδάζω, σπουδή: Spicq 3.276-85.

σπουδαῖος, α, ον.ʃ

of good, fine quality: ***s*** ξύλα 'wood' Ez 41.25. Cf. σπουδαιότης, σπουδαίως: Spicq 3.283.

σπουδαιότης, τος. f.ʃ

good, fine quality: τῇ ~τι καὶ εὐπρεπείᾳ καταπλαγείς 'struck by its excellence and beauty' 3M 1.9. Cf. σπουδαῖος.

σπουδαίως. adv.ʃ

in good manner and making one's best efforts: χρησώμεθα τῇ κτίσει .. σ. 'let's make good use of the creation ..' Wi 2.6 (or: 'with ardour' Spicq 3.281 or 'let us lose no time in ..', cf. Vulg. *celeriter*). Cf. σπουδαῖος.

σπουδή, ῆς. f.

1. *great speed*: μετὰ ~ῆς 'in haste' Ex 12.11, Ps 77.33, 3M 5.24; σπουδῇ 'as soon as possible' 12.33, ~ῇ ἔσπευσαν Jd 5.22 B; ἐν ~δῇ De 16.3; κατὰ ~ὴν ἥξει Si 20.18, κατὰ ~ὴν ἐν τάχει 27.3; in a hendiadys, συντέλειαν καὶ ~ὴν ποιήσει 'will bring about swift destruction' Zp 1.18.

*2. *loss of composure*, 'panic, fright': ἐπέρριψα ἐπ' αὐτὴν ἐξαίφνης τρόμον καὶ ~ήν 'cast upon her suddenly trepidation and ..' Je 15.8, "we gathered for a time of healing, but ἰδοὺ σ." 8.15; ἀπέδρασαν ἐν ~ῇ 'ran away ..' Da 10.7 LXX (or: 'in haste'?, but TH ἐν φόβῳ); ἀκοαὶ καὶ ~αί, hendiadys for "disconcerting reports" (?) 11.44 TH.

3. *earnest commitment in discharge of a task*, 'eagerness, zeal': ἐπὶ ~ῆς 1E 6.9 (|| ἐπιδέξιον 2E 5.8); Wi 14.17. Cf. προθυμία.

Cf. σπεύδω, σπουδάζω, ὀξύς, τάχος, ταχύς, ἔξστασις: Spicq 2.276-85.

σταγών, όνος. f.

1. *drop* of liquid: ὡσεὶ ~όνες στάζουσιν Ps 71.6 (|| ὑετός), ὑετοῦ Jb 36.27 (ὑετοῦ implied, Pr 27.15), ὕδατος ἀπὸ θαλάσσης Si 18.10 (fig. of small quantity), αἵματος 'of blood' 4M 10.8.

*2. *small number*: τοῦ λαοῦ τούτου Mi 2.11.

Cf. στάζω, ῥανίς, σταλαγμός, ψεκάς.

στάδιον, ου. n.

1. measure of length, 'stadium': 2M 12.9.

2. *area*: κυκλοῦντες τὸ σ. 'walking round ..' Su 37 LXX, or 'taking our walk around (in the garden).'

στάζω: pres.opt.3s στάζοι; fut. στάξω; aor. ἔσταξα, inf. στάξαι, subj. στάξω.

1. *to fall in small drops, drip*: ὁ ὑετὸς οὐκ ἔσταξεν ἔτι ἐπὶ τὴν γῆν 'the rain fell no more on the earth' Ex 9.33; ***s*** dew, Jd 6.38 B. **b**. fig., στάξει ὁ θυμός μου ἐφ' ὑμᾶς Je 49.18; 51.6, ἐν Ιερουσαλημ 2C 12.7.

2. tr. *to cause to flow down in small quantities*: ***o*** understood, tears of a suppliant, στάζοι μου ὁ ὀφθαλμός Jb 16.20; rain (?) and ***s*** οἱ οὐρανοί Ps 67.9 (|| Jd 5.4B + δρόσους), PSol 17.18; σμύρναν 'myrrh' Ct 5.5; οἰκία '(leaking) house' Ec 10.18.

Cf. πίπτω, σταγών, σταλάσσω: Schmidt 2.264-6.

σταθμάω: pf.ptc.pass. ἐσταθμωμένος.ʃ

to calculate and determine the weight of: pass., 3K 6.23. Cf. σταθμός.

στάθμιον, ου. n.

weight of balance: μεγαλῦναι ~α 'to enlarge weights' Am 8.5 (|| μέτρον and ζυγός); Le 19.35; ζυγὰ δίκαια καὶ ~α δίκαια 19.36; ζυγὸν ~ίων Ez 5.1; ἅγιον Le 27.25; σ. καὶ σ. 'double standard' De 25.13; σ. ἀληθινὸν καὶ δίκαιον 25.15 (|| μέτρον ἀ. καὶ δ.). Cf. ζυγός, σταθμός, and μέτρον.

σταθμός, οῦ. m.

1. *weight* numerically expressed: of silver, ἐν ~ῷ 'having been correctly weighed' Ge 43.21, .. καὶ ἐν ἀριθμῷ '.. and having been counted' 2E 8.34 (|| ὁλκή 1E 8.64); || ἐν μέτρῳ Ez 4.16, μέτρῳ καὶ ἀριθμῷ καὶ ~ῷ Wi 11.20; ἐν ἀκριβείᾳ 'with precision' Si 16.25; ~ῷ ἁγίῳ 'by sacred weight' Le 27.3; of baked bread, 26.26; of winds, Jb 28.25 (|| μέτρον); οὐκ ἔστιν σ. τινος '.. is of immeasurable value' Si 6.15; σ. ἀργυρίου 'a quantity of silver weighed out' 2E 8.30; ‖ ὁλκή 1C 28.16.

2. *doorpost*: Ex 12.7 (there are two of them), τῆς θύρας Is 57.8; ‖ θύρα Pr 8.34.

3. *doorway*: οἱ ἱερεῖς οἱ φυλάσσοντες τὸν ~όν 4K 12.10.

4. *place where a marching army had its quarters*: τῶν υἱῶν Ισραηλ Nu 33.1; τὰς ἀπάρσεις αὐτῶν καὶ τοὺς ~οὺς αὐτῶν 'their departures and their stages' 33.2. See Dorival 1996.537f. **b**. gen., *a lodging-station on a journey*: Je 9.2.

5. *instrument for determining weight*, 'balance': Is 40.12, 46.6, Si 28.25 (‖ ζυγός).

6. fig. *yardstick, standard* of practice: pl., Is 28.17.

Cf. σταθμά/όω, στάθμιον, μέτρον, ὁλκή; Chadwick 253-61.

σταθμόω. ⇒ σταθμάω.

σταῖς, τός. n.

flour of spelt mixed and made into dough (LSJ): πρὸ τοῦ ζυμωθῆναι 'prior to fermentation' Ex 12.34; ἔπεψαν τὸ σ. 'baked ..' 12.39; τρίβουσι σ. τοῦ ποιῆσαι χαυῶνας 'knead .. to make cakes' Je 7.18. Cf. σεμίδαλις.

στακτή, ῆς. f.

oil of myrrh: valuable commodity, αἱ κάμηλοι αὐτῶν ἔγεμον θυμιαμάτων καὶ ῥητίνης καὶ ~ῆς 'their camels were fully laden with spices, resins and ..' Ge 37.25, σ. καὶ ποικίλματα ἐκ Θαρσις '.. and multicoloured garments ..' Ez 27.16; valuable gift, Ge 43.11; part of royal treasures, Is 39.2; aromatic ingredient of incense, Ex 30.34, Si 24.15; part of royal treasures, Is 39.2; used on royal garments, Ps 44.9.

σταλαγμός, οῦ. m.ʃ

that which drops constantly in small quantities: of gore, 4M 9.20. Cf. σταλάσσω, ῥανίς, σταγών.

σταλάσσω: aor. ἐστάλαξα. On the form, cf. Thack. 222f.ʃ

intr. *to drop in small quantities* (of liquid), 'drip': εἰς οἶνον 'to become wine' Mi 2.11. Cf. ἀποσταλάσσω, στάζω, σταλαγμός: Schmidt 2.264-6.

στάμνος, ου. m.

jar: χρυσοῦς 'golden' Ex 16.33 (for keeping the manna); μέλιτος 'of honey' 3K 12.24[h]; οἴνου Da LXX Bel 33.

στασιάζω: aor. ἐστασίασα.ʃ

to rebel: abs. and in military situation, Ju 7.15, 2M 4.30, 14.6. Cf. στάσις **7**, ἀνθίστημι, ἀπονοέω, συναφίστημι.

στάσιμος, η, ον.ʃ

solid, stable: ***s*** ἡλικία 'physique, figure' (of a woman) Si 26.17.

στάσις, εως. f.

1. *pause in movement*: οὐδὲ μὴ γένηται σ. τῷ ἴχνει τοῦ ποδός σου '.. the sole of your foot' De 28.65; Jo 10.13. Cf. κατάπαυσις **1**.

2. *military station* for defensive purpose: ἐξ ἐχθρῶν '(to escape an attack) of enemies' Na 3.11.

3. *office held*: Is 22.19 (or: room occupied by an office-holder).

4. *standing posture*: ἐν ~ει Ne 8.7; ‖ καθέδρα 'sitting posture' 3K 10.5. **b**. *act of remaining standing*: οὐκ ἔστιν ὑμῖν σ. ποδὸς κατὰ πρόσωπον ἡμῶν 'you cannot withstand us' 1M 10.72 (‖ ὑφίστημι). **c**. *sth that is standing erect*, 'pillar': Jd 9.6 (*L* οὔσης 'to be found'), or poss. **2** above, cf. Caird 1969.34.

5. *place where sbd or sth is situated*: Da 8.17 TH, 10.11 TH (LXX τόπος); ποδῶν 'for feet' 1C 28.2.

6. *agreed position to be followed*, 'statute, decree': ‖ ὁρισμός Da 6.7; ‖ ὅρκος 1M 7.18. **b**. *agreed venue* or *location* for some activity: 2C 23.13, 30.16, 3M 1.23.

7. *sedition*: + μάχη Pr 17.14, cf. στασιάζω.

Cf. ἵστημι, καθέδρα: Spicq 3.286-8.

σταυρόω: aor.impv.pass.3s σταυρωθήτω; pf.inf.pass. ἐσταυρῶσθαι.

to crucify: ***o*** hum., Es 7.9 o'. Cf. ἀνασκολοπίζω.

σταφίς, ίδος. f.

dried grapes, raisins: πέμματα μετὰ ~ίδων 'cakes stuffed with raisins' Ho 3.1; opp. fresh grapes, Nu 6.3. Cf. σταφυλή.

σταφυλή, ῆς. f.

grapes: βότρυς ~ῆς 'a cluster of grapes' Ge 40.10, Nu 13.24; food, De 23.25; σ. ἐν ἐρήμῳ Ho 9.10; περκάσει ἡ σ. ἐν τῷ σπόρῳ 'the grapes will ripen at seedtime' Am 9.13; + καρπός Ez 36.8; αἷμα ~ῆς ‖ οἶνος Ge 49.11, De 32.14; χολῆς 'of bile' 32.32. Cf. βότρυς, στέμφυλον: Shipp 163-5.

στάχυς, υος. m.

ear of corn: ἑπτὰ ~υες ἀνέβαινον ἐν πυθμένι ἑνὶ ἐκλεκτοὶ καὶ καλοί 'seven ears of corn began to come up on one stem, excellent and good' Ge 41.5; λεπτοὶ καὶ ἀνεμόφθοροι 'lean and blasted by wind' 41.6; συλλέξεις ἐν ταῖς χερσίν σου σ. 'collect with your hands ..' De 23.24. Cf. Shipp 515; Caird 1969.34f.

στέαρ, ατος. n.

1. *fat attached to animal meat*, 'suet': ἀρνῶν καὶ κριῶν, υἱῶν ταύρων καὶ τράγων 'of lambs and rams, of calves and kids' De 32.14; + πιότης Ps 62.6; as cultic offering, Ge 4.4, Ex 23.18; θυσιῶν De 32.38; τὸ σ. τὸ ἐπὶ τῆς κοιλίας 'the fat on the surface of the intestines' Ex 29.13; κατακαλύπτον τὴν κοιλίαν Le 3.3. **b**. *the fat underneath the skin of a hum. body*, Jd 3.22, 2K 1.22; metaph., τὸ σ. αὐτῶν 'the best of their humanity' Ps 16.10, cf. Thdt ad loc. at PG 80.969.

2. *dough made from flour of spelt*: ἀπὸ φυράσεως ~ατος 'from the kneading of dough' Ho 7.4, πυροῦ 'of wheat' Ps 80.17.

Cf. στεατόω: Shipp 515.

στεατόω: pf.ptc.pass. ἐστεατωμένος.ʃ *

to fatten: ***o*** μόσχος 'calf' Ez 39.18. Cf. στέαρ.

στεγάζω: aor. ἐστέγασα, inf. στεγάσαι.

to provide with roof: + acc., Ps 103.3, οἴκους 2C 34.11, πύλας Ne 2.8. Cf. στέγη, φατνόω.

στέγη, ης. f.

flat, protective structure over above: 'roof,' κιβωτοῦ 'of ark' Ge 8.13; εἰσῆλθον ὑπὸ τὴν ~ην τῶν δοκῶν μου 'entered under the roof of my rafters (for protection)' 19.8, cf. ὑπὸ σκέπην δοκῶν 'under the cover of ..' Si 29.22; of a temple, 1E 6.4; ἐπὶ στύλους 'over columns' 4M 17.3; over a slaughtering-table against rain and heat, Ez 40.43. Cf. ἄστεγος, στεγάζω, δῶμα **1**, ὄροφος, τέγος, φάτνωμα: Shipp 515.

στεγνός, ή, όν.ʃʃ

impeccable, difficult to pick holes in (?): ***s*** διατριβαὶ οἴκων αὐτῆς 'the ways her household is managed' or poss. lit. 'the buildings on her estate are waterproof (against leakage)' Pr 31.27.

στέγω: aor.inf. στέξαι.ʃ

to keep secret: + acc., λόγον '(no) matter' Si 8.17. Cf. κρύπτω: Spicq 3.289f.

στεῖρα, ας.

woman who has not given birth to a child, 'barren': σ. ἡ οὐκ τίκτουσα '.. who does not give birth' Is 54.1, ἦν Σαρα σ. καὶ οὐκ ἐτεκνοποίει 'S. was barren and was not producing children' Ge 11.30; ‖ ἄγονος Ex 23.26; opp. γεννῶσα Is 65.9; including animals, οὐκ ἔσται ἐν ὑμῖν ἄγονος οὐδὲ στεῖρα καὶ ἐν τοῖς κτήνεσίν σου De 7.14. Cf. ἄγονος, ἀτεκνία, στειρόω.

στειρόω: aor.subj.pass. στειρωθῶ.ʃ*

pass. *to fail to produce young*: ***s*** woman, Si 42.10. Cf. στεῖρα.

στελεός, οῦ. m.ʃ

oblong part of an instrument to hold it with: of an axe, 4K 6.5*L*. Cf. στέλεχος.

στέλεχος, ους. n.

oblong, erect object: trunk of a tree, ἀνειμένον 'set free' Ge 49.21 (thus growing luxuriantly); φοινίκων 'of date-palms' Ex 15.27, Nu 33.9. **b**. *column*: καπνοῦ 'of smoke' Ct 3.6.

Cf. στελεός, στῦλος: Schmidt 2.459f.

στέλλομαι: aor. ἐστειλάμην; pf.ptc. ἐσταλμένος.ʃ

A. act. **1**. *to keep away* (out of fear or awe): ἀπὸ προσώπου τοῦ ὀνόματός μου Ma 2.5 (‖ φοβέομαι).

2. *to set out*: on a military expedition, + acc., ἔφοδον 2M 5.1, cf. Soph. *Ph*. 1416 ὁδὸν ἣν στέλλῃ; εἰς τὴν χώραν 'into the countryside' 3M 4.11.

B. mid. *to make oneself ready*: + inf., Wi 14.1; ***s*** woman, for wedding 3M 1.19. **b**. *to create* a condition to one's advantage and *conducive to*: + acc. rei, πρὸς θεὸν φιλίαν 'friendship with God' Wi 7.14, τάξιν .. τῇ γλώσσῃ αὐτῆς 'orderliness .. to her own tongue' Pr 31.25.

Cf. φοβέομαι: BDAG, s.v. στέλλω.

στέμφυλον, ου. n.ʃ

pl. *mass of pressed grapes*: οἶνος ἀπὸ ~ων Nu 6.4. Cf. σταφυλή: Shipp 517.

στεναγμός, οῦ. m.

sighing, groaning: uttered by woman in labour, Ge 3.16 (‖ λύπη), Je 4.31; by oppressed people, Ex 6.5; Ma 2.13 (‖ δάκρυα and κλαυθμός); ὀδύνη καὶ λύπη καὶ σ. Is 51.11; ‖ ἀρά 'accursed condition' PSol 4.13. Cf. στενάζω.

στενάζω: fut. στενάξω; aor. ἐστέναξα, subj. στενάξω, inf. στενάξαι, impv. στέναξον, ptc. στενάξας.

to bemoan, express sorrow: abs., Is 30.15, ‖ πενθέω 19.8, στενάξας ἔκλαυσα To 3.1 𝔊[II]; ἐν ὀδύναις 'in pain' Ez 21.6; *for* (+ τινα), τίς στενάξει αὐτήν; 'who is going to bemoan her?' Na 3.7; + ἐπί acc., ἐπὶ ἡμέρας αἰσχύνης 'over the days of shame' Je 38.19; + ἐπί τινι - ἐπ' ἐμοί Jb 31.38 (***s*** exploited land, ‖ κλαίω), ἐπὶ τῇ ἀγγελίᾳ Ez 21.7; ***s*** the dying, Is 59.10; + dat., πένθει ἀώρῳ 'untimely sorrow (of death)' Si 16.3¶. Cf. στεναγμός, ἀνα~, καταστενάζω, στένω, θρηνεύω, κλαίω: Schmidt 3.391-5.

στενακτός, ή, όν.ʃ

mournful: ***s*** pers., Ez 5.15 (+ δηλαϊστός). Cf. δηλαϊστος.

στενός, ή, όν.

1. *lacking in space or scope for freedom of movement or manœuvring*, 'narrow, cramped': ***s*** τόπος Nu 22.26, Is 49.20, ἀπορία 8.22, θάλασσα Zc 10.11, χρόνος Je 37.7; options, 1C 21.13. **b**. subst.n.pl.: lit.(?), *narrow passes* 1K 23.14; metaph., ψυχὴ ἐν ~οῖς 'a soul in dire straits' Ba 3.1 (‖ ἀκηδιάω); ~ά μοι 'I'm stuck, I've been cornered' 2K 24.14, Su 22 TH.

2. *liable to constraint*: ***s*** hunger, famine Jb 18.11.

3. *scanty*: ὕδωρ ~όν Is 30.20 (‖ ἄρτος θλίψεως).

Cf. στενότης, στενοχωρία, στενῶς, εὐρύχωρος.

στενότης, ητος. f.ʃ

narrowness: of place, 2M 12.21. Cf. στενός.

στενοχωρέω: fut. ~ρήσω.ʃ

1. *to make feel lack of elbow-room*: + acc. pers., στενοχωρεῖ σε τὸ ὄρος τὸ Εφραιμ 'you find the Ephraim mountains too narrow' Jo 17.15.

2. *to drive into a corner*: + acc. pers., ἐστενοχώρησεν αὐτόν 'she drove him into a corner' Jd

16.16 B (A: παρηνώχλησεν); pass., στενοχωρούμενοι 'hard pressed' Is 28.20; τὸ πνεῦμα στενοχωρούμενος 'gasping for air' 4M 11.11.

3. intr. *to be hard pressed*: ἀπὸ τῶν κατοικούντων Is 49.19 (overpopulation).

Cf. στενοχωρία.

στενοχωρία, ας. f.ʃ

state of finding onself in exceedingly frustrating difficulty: Joseph in Egypt, ἐν καιρῷ ~ίας αὐτοῦ 1M 2.53; imposed by enemies, ἐν τῇ ~ίᾳ σου καὶ ἐν τῇ θλίψει σου De 28.53, 55, 57; θλῖψις καὶ σ. Es A 7 ο', Is 30.6; θλῖψις καὶ σ. καὶ σκότος 8.22*a*; ἱμάτια στενοχωρίας καὶ πένθους Es C 13 ο'; τοὺς πολέμους καὶ τὰς ~ίας 1M 13.3; διὰ ~ίαν πνεύματος στενάξουσιν 'they will sigh out of mental distress' Wi 5.3; ὁ ἐν ~ίᾳ ὤν Is 8.22*b*; ἐν καιρῷ ~ίας σου Si 10.26. Cf. στενός, ἀπορία, θλῖψις: Trench 202f.

στένω.

to groan in sorrow: στένων καὶ τρέμων Ge 4.12, 14; ‖ κάμνω 'be weary' Jb 10.1. Cf. στενάζω.

στενῶς. adv.ʃ

finding oneself in dire straits: 1K 13.6. Cf. στενός.

στέργω: aor.impv. στέρξον.ʃ

to show affection for: + acc., φίλον Si 27.17. Cf. στοργή, ἀγαπάω, φιλέω: Schmidt 3.480-8.

στερεός, ά, όν.

1. *firm, solid*: *s* lampstand, Ex 38.14; rock, De 32.13, Is 2.21, 5.28, 50.7; valley (φάραγξ) 17.5 (of hard soil not suited for cultivation, cf. Eus. 115).

2. *physically strong*: ἐκ χειρὸς στερεωτέρων αὐτοῦ 'from the hand of those who are stronger than he' Je 38.12; *s* god, on battlefield 1K 4.8; subst. m. Ps 34.10.

3. *not amenable to (medical) treatment*: *s* πληγή 'blow' Je 15.18, cf. παιδεία (‖ πληγή) στερεά 37.14.

Cf. στερεόω, στερέωμα, ἰσχυρός, ἀνίατος.

στερεόω: fut. στερεώσω, pass. στερεωθήσομαι; aor. ἐστερέωσα, ptc. στερεώσας, impv. στερέωσον, pass. ἐστερεώθην; pf.ptc.pass. ἐστερεωμένος.

1. *to make firm, solid*, + τι: of God's creative act, στερεῶν οὐρανὸν καὶ κτίζων γῆν Ho 13.4, ὁ θεὸς ὁ ποιήσας τὸν οὐρανὸν καὶ πήξας αὐτόν, ὁ στερεώσας τὴν γῆν .. Is 42.5, τῷ στερεώσαντι τὴν γῆν ἐπὶ τῶν ὑδάτων Ps 135.6, τοὺς στύλους αὐτῆς 'its columns' [= τῆς γῆς] 74.3, ναόν '(shaky) temple' Si 50.1, ἐγὼ στερεῶν βροντὴν καὶ κτίζων πνεῦμα Am 4.13; ἐστερέωσαν αὐτά, καὶ οὐ κινηθήσονται '.. they will not move' Je 10.4, cf. Ps 92.1; δεξιὰν αὐτοῦ 'his right hand' La 2.4, τὸν βραχίονά σου 'your arm' Ez 4.7, μάστιγας '(punishing) whips' Si 39.28; πόλεμον '(to wage) a determined, fierce battle' 1M 10.50; metaph., κρίσιν μητρός Si 3.2, φυλακήν 'watch' 26.10, στερέωσον λόγον 'keep (your) promise' 29.3. **b**. pass.: ἐστερεώθησαν ὑπὲρ ἐμέ 'they became more powerful than I' Ps 17.18; *o* one's heart gaining confidence, 1K 2.1; conspiratory design, 15.12*L*. **c**. *secure against loss and damage*: *o* possessions, Si 34.11; fortified city, 1K 6.18.

2. *to make unreceptive*, 'harden': + acc., τὰ πρόσωπα αὐτῶν ὑπὲρ πέτραν '.. harder than a rock' Je 5.3 (‖ οὐκ θέλω). Cf. βαρύνω **3**.

3. *intensify*: pass., *o* famine (λιμός), Je 52.6, cf. ἐνισχύω **II 3**.

Cf. στερέωμα, στερεός, and κτίζω.

στερέω: fut. στερήσω, pass. ~ρηθήσομαι; aor. ἐστέρησα, subj. στερήσω, inf. στερῆσαι, pass. ἐστερήθην, inf. στερηθῆναι, ptc. στερηθείς; pf.pass. 3pl ἐστέρηνται, ptc. ἐστερημένος.

1. *to withhold, refuse to give*: *s* God and + acc. pers. and acc. rei., ἐστέρησέν σε καρπὸν κοιλίας '.. fruit of womb, i.e. children' Ge 30.2; pass., τὸ ζῆν ἐστερήθης 'you would have been deprived of life' 3M 5.32; + gen. rei, ἐστέρησέν σε κύριος τῆς δόξης Nu 24.11; + gen. pers., πεινώντων .. ψωμόν 'the hungry .. food' Jb 22.7; pass. τοῦ προσώπου σου οὐκ ἐστερήθην 'I was not deprived of a chance to see you' Ge 48.11, πάσης σοφίας Si 37.21; + ἀπό τινος Ps 77.30. Cf. ὑποστέλλω.

2. *to deprive*: + acc. pers., gen., not on purpose, Si 28.15, 2M 3.29, pass. 4M 12.6; on purpose, 2M 13.11.

Cf. στεῖρα, στερίσκω.

στερέωμα, ατος. n.

***1**. *firmament*: called οὐρανός Ge 1.8; τοῦ οὐρανοῦ Ex 24.10; De 33.26, Ps 18.2 (‖ οὐρανός), Dan 12.3 TH (LXX ‖ οὐρανός).

2. *solid, steadfast support*: *s* God, Ps 17.3 (‖ καταφυγή 'refuge,' ῥύστης 'rescuer'), 79.3. **b**. *firm, secure position*: 1E 8.78.

3. *attitude of firm commitment, steadfastness*: οὐκ ἔστησαν ἐν ~ατι Ez 13.5.

4. *bodily tenacity and resilience*: Ps 72.4. **b**. *strong section* of an army: 1M 9.14.

5. *written confirmation of a decision taken*: τῆς ἐπιστολῆς Es 9.29.

Cf. στερεόω and οὐρανός: Rösel 36f.

στερέωσις, εως. f.ʃ *

intensity: μάχης 'of strife' Si 28.10.

στερίσκω.ʃ

to deprive: + acc. and ἀπό τινος, τὴν ψυχήν μου ἀπὸ ἀγαθωσύνης 'my soul of pleasure' Ec 4.8. Cf. στερέω.

στεφάνη, ης. f.

1. *continuous narrow space* round sth, 'border, rim': round an altar, Ex 27.3; στρεπτὴ σ. κύκλῳ 'twisted border all round' Ex 30.3; 'railing on rooftop,' δώματι De 22.8.

*2. *edge*: παλαιστοῦ 'of the size of a palm' Ex 25.23.

Cf. στέφανος.

στεφανηφορέω.ʃ

to bear a crown on one's head: ***s*** victor in an athletic game, Wi 4.2. Cf. στέφανος.

στέφανος, ου. m.

1. *that which surrounds*: σ. ἀδελφῶν 'colleagues standing in a circle (round him)' Si 50.12.

2. *crown*: reward for perseverance, Zc 6.14; part of a uniform, τὴν στολήν σου καὶ τὸν ~όν σου τὸν ἔνδοξον Is 22.17; royal and mark of honour, ἀπὸ κεφαλῆς .. σ. δόξης Je 13.18, ‖ δόξα Jb 19.9; ἐκ λίθου τιμίου 'made from a precious stone' Ps 20.4; women's accessory, Ez 16.12; fig. σ. ὕβρεως Is 28.1, κάλλους 62.3 (‖ διάδημα), Ez 28.12, ἀγαλλιάματος 'of joy' Si 1.11, σοφίας 1.18; fig. of choice agricultural produce, Ps 64.12.

Cf. στεφάνη, στέφος, στεφανόω, στεφανοφορέω, καταστέφω: Trench 78-81.

στεφανόω: fut.pass. στεφανωθήσομαι; aor. ἐστεφάνωσα, mid. ~νωσάμην.

to invest with crown: + acc. pers., ἀθλητάς 'athletes' 4M 17.15; Ps 5.13, δόξῃ καὶ τιμῇ 8.6, ἐν ἐλέει 102.3, σκεύεσιν ἰσχύος 'with vessels of authority' Si 45.8; τῆς ἐλευθερίας (gen. pretii) 3M 3.28; + acc. rei, τείχη ^Ιερουσαλημ^ PSol 8.17; τὴν ζωὴν αὐτοῦ Si 19.5¶; mid., *to crown oneself with*: + acc., τὴν ἐλαίαν 'olive wreath' Ju 15.13. Cf. στέφανος, στέφω.

στέφος, ους. n.ʃ

= στέφανος: worn by a bridegroom, 3M 4.8.

στέφω: aor.subj.mid. στέψωμαι.ʃ

mid. *to crown oneself*: ῥόδων κάλυξιν 'with rosebuds' Wi 2.8 Cf. στεφανόω, στέφανος.

στηθοδεσμίς, ίδος. f.ʃ*

brassière: Je 2.32 (‖ κόσμος).

στῆθος, ου. n.

part of the body enclosed by ribs, 'chest': of a snake crawling on it, Ge 3.14 (‖ κοιλία); of a human body, Ex 28.23. Cf. στηθύνιον.

στηθύνιον, ου. n.

Dim. of στῆθος: of sacrificial animals, ἀπὸ τοῦ κριοῦ 'of the ram' Ex 29.27. Cf. στῆθος.

στήκω.ʃ See Thackeray 224f.

to stand firm: ***s*** edifice, Jd 16.26B. Cf. ἵστημι **I 1**.

στήλη, ης. f.

perpendicular block: σ. ἁλός 'salt pillar' Ge 19.26; λιθίνη 'stone' 35.14; of stone set up for pagan worship, συντρίψεις τὰς ~ας αὐτῶν 'thou shalt demolish their pillars' Ex 23.24, sim. 34.13, De 7.5 (‖ καθαιρέω, κατακαίω and βωμός, ἄλσος, γλυπτά), 12.3; ἐρημώσω τὰς ~ας ὑμῶν Le 26.30 (‖ ξύλινα χειροποίητα 'wooden, handmade'); τοῦ Βααλ Nu 22.41; οὐ στήσεις σεαυτῷ ~ην De 16.22; ᾠκοδόμησαν ~ας Ho 10.1 (‖ θυσιαστήριον); ‖ γλυπτά 'engraved idols' Mi 5.13; σ. μνημείου 'grave-stone' Ge 35.20; with an inscribed message thereupon, 3M 2.27. **b**. τῷ κυρίῳ Is 19.19 (‖ θυσιαστήριον).

Cf. θυσιαστήριον: Daniel 1966. 33-53.

στηλογραφία, ας. f.

inscription on the surface of στήλη: a genre of psalm, Ps 15.1+.

στηλόω: aor. ἐστήλωσα, impv. στήλωσον, pass. ἐστηλώθην, impv. στηλώθητι; pf.ptc.pass. ἐστηλωμένος.

to erect: abs., στήλην or suchlike understood, ὑπὲρ τῶν τεθνηκότων 'for the dead' 2K 1.19, σωρὸν λίθων 'a mound of stones' 2K 18.17B (*L* ἐφίστημι); + acc., με ὡς σκοπὸν εἰς βέλος 'me as a target for arrows' La 3.12. **b**. *to position*: pass., ***o*** hum., 2K 18.30B; armed troops deployed Jd 18.16A (B: pf. ἵστημι), 2K 23.12B (*L* 2aor. καθίστημι; ‖ 2aor. ἵστημι 1C 11.14). ‖ φρουρά 'garrison' 2K 8.14*L*. Cf. ἵστημι **II 3** and ἀνίστημι **I 5**.

στήμων, ονος. m.

warp: ‖ κρόκη 'woof' Le 13.48. Cf. κρόκη.

στήριγμα, ατος. n.

support provided: βοηθὸς σ., wife for her husband, To 8.6; material, συντρίβω σ. ἄρτου 'I shall break off steady supply of bread' Ez 4.16, sim. Ps 104.16; psychological support, Si 31.18, σ. ἰσχύος 31.19 (‖ ὑπερασπισμός); military, 4K 25.11B, 1M 2.43. Cf. ἀντι~, ἐπιστήριγμα: Caird 1969.35.

στηρίζω: fut. στηριῶ, στηρίσω, pass. στηριχθήσομαι; aor. ἐστήρισ/ξα, mid. ἐστηρισάμην, impv. act. στήρισον, pass. ἐστηρίχθην, inf. ~ριχθῆναι, subj. ~ριχθῶ; pf. ἐστήρικα, pass. ἐστήριγμαι,2s ἐστήρισαι, inf. ἐστηρίχ/σθαι, ptc. ἐστηριγ/σμένος; plpf.pass.3s ἐστήρικτο.

1. *to place firmly and determinedly*: τοὺς ὀφθαλμούς μου ἐπ' αὐτοὺς εἰς κακά 'to aim my eyes determinedly at them to their disadvantage' Am 9.4, sim. Je 24.6 + Pr 16.30, τὸ πρόσωπον Je 3.12 + Ez 6.2, cf. Lk 9.51; ***o*** exhausted hands of a commander, Ex 17.12[1]; pass. κλῖμαξ ἐστηριγμένη ἐν τῇ γῇ 'a ladder firmly planted in the ground' Ge 28.12, metaph., καρδία ἐστηριγμένη ἐπὶ διανοήματος βουλῆς '.. intelligent thought' Si 22.16; ***o*** disease, Le 13.55, arrogance 1M 2.49; subject matter, τὸ ῥῆμα ἐν τῇ καρδίᾳ μου ἐστήριξα Da 7.28 LXX (TH διετήρησα); God's commandments Ps 110.8; fame, Si 4.19; σάρκα βραχίονος 'physical (or: military) strength' Je 17.5; office-holder, ὁ ἄνθρωπος ὁ ἐστηριγμένος ἐν τόπῳ πιστῷ 'the person established in a secure position' Is 22.25; ὄνομα Si 40.19. **b**. *to establish and mark firmly*: + acc. rei, ὅριον 'boundary'

Pr 15.25. **c**. mid. *to form a firm and enduring link with*: ἐν Σιων ἐστηρίχθην Si 24.10; ἴσθι ἐστηριγμένος ἐν συνέσει σου 'hold firmly on to your understanding' Si 5.10.

2. *to sustain* sbd (acc.) *by making abundant provisions of*: σίτῳ καὶ οἴνῳ ἐστήρισα αὐτόν Ge 27.37, στηρίσατέ με ἐν ἀμόραις 'sweet cakes' Ct 2.5 (ǁ στοιβάσατέ με ἐν μήλοις 'stuff me with apples').

3. *to support* morally: "a father's blessing supports (στηρίζει) his children's homes" Si 3.9 (:: ἐκριζόω 'to undermine'), ἄρτος καρδίαν ἀνθρώπων στηρίζει Ps 103.15 (ǁ εὐφραίνω), Jd 19.5; τὴν ψυχήν μου PSol 16.12; pass. and ***o*** a weakened person, Ex 17.12[2]; πλούσιος σαλευόμενος στηρίζεται ὑπὸ φίλων 'a faltering rich man is supported by friends' Si 13.21, υἱοῖς καὶ ἀδελφοῖς 1M 2.17; τὴν καρδίαν σου Si 6.37, ἐστήρικται ἡ καρδία αὐτοῦ, οὐ μὴ φοβηθῇ Ps 111.8; τοὺς ταπεινοὺς τοῦ λαοῦ 1M 14.14. **b**. pass. *to become convinced*: Si 39.32.

4. mid. *to seek support and rely* on: στηριχθήσεται ἐπ' αὐτήν [= σοφίαν] Si 15.4; 4K 18.21 (*L* ἐπι~).

5. intr. *to stand firm and hold on to one's course of action*: abs., ***s*** national leader, 1M 14.26.

Cf. ἐπι~, κατα~, ὑποστηρίζω, ἐρείδω, στήριγμα, τίθημι, τάσσω: Anz 20f.; Spicq 3.291-5.

στιβαρός, ά, όν.ʃ

forceful: ***s*** hum., τῇ γλώσσῃ Ez 3.6. Cf. στιβαρῶς, βία.

στιβαρῶς. adv.ʃ

by applying considerable physical force: βαρύνων τὸν κλοιὸν αὐτοῦ σ. 'making his collar very heavy' Hb 2.6. Cf. στιβαρός, βιαίως.

στίβι, εως/ιος. n., a variant spelling of στίμμι.ʃ

powdered antimony, used for eye-paint (LSJ): Je 4.30. Cf. στιμίζομαι.

στιβίζομαι: ⇒ στιμίζομαι.

στίγμα, ατος. n.ʃ

stud: of silver, Ct 1.11.

στιγμή, ῆς. f.ʃ

very short duration of time: ἔσται ὡς σ. παραχρῆμα Is 29.5; κατὰ ~ήν 'every moment' 2M 9.11. Cf. χρόνος, χρονίσκος.

στικτός, ή, όν.ʃ

tattooed: γράμματα ~ά 'tattoo marks' (on hum. body) Le 19.28, cf. Jones 142-5, 154f.

στιλβόω: fut. στιλβώσω.ʃ*

caus. of στίλβω, q.v.: + acc., ῥομφαίαν 'sword' Ps 7.13 (by polishing). Cf. στίλβω.

στίλβω: aor.subj. στίλψω.ʃ

to gleam, glitter: ***s*** sword, Na 3.3 (ǁ ἐξαστράπτω), Ez 21.33; gilded pagan idols, Ep Je 23; χαλκός 'brass' Da 10.6 TH (LXX: ἐξαστράπτω), 2E 8.27, Ez 40.3; brass utensils, 1E 8.56; the sun reflecting on shields, 1M 6.39, mountain reflecting shields, ib. Cf. αὐγέω, ἐξαστράπτω, στιλβόω, στίλβωσις, φαίνω, χρυσαυγέω: Schmidt 1.563-98.

στίλβωσις, εως. f.ʃ *

v.n. of στιλβόω, q.v.: Ez 21.10, 15. Cf. στίλβω.

στιμίζομαι: aor. ἐστιμισάμην.ʃ

to paint the eyes: ***s*** woman, ὀφθαλμούς 4K 9.30, + λούομαι, κοσμέομαι Ez 23.40. Cf. στίβι.

***στιππύϊνος**, η, ον.ʃ

made of fibre: ***s*** ἱμάτιον Le 13.47, 59. Cf. στιππύον.

στιππύον, ου. [= στυππεῖον].*

the coarse fibre of flax, 'tow': καλάμη ~ου as a figure of sth frail, Is 1.31; συνηγμένον 'gathered' Si 21.9; fuel, + νάφθα, πίσσα, κληματίς Da 3.46. Cf. στιππύϊνος.

στιχίζω: pf.ptc.pass. ἐστιχισμένος.ʃ*

to arrange in a row: ***o*** ἐξέδρα 'chamber' Ez 42.3.

στίχος, ου. m.

more or less straight line of objects, 'row, course': λίθων Ex 28.17; δεύτερος 28.18, κέδρου 'cedar' 3K 6.36. Cf. τετράστιχος.

στοά, ᾶς. f.

roofed colonnade: Ez 40.18.

στοιβάζω: fut. στοιβάσω; aor. ἐστοίβασα, impv. στοίβασον; pf.ptc.pass. ἐστοιβασμένος.* (but δια~ in Hdt. and στοιβή in Eupolis [5th c. BCE])

to place large quantities of sth on sth large one on top of the other, 'to pile up': + acc., ἐπὶ ^τοῦ θυσιαστηρίου^ τὴν ὁλοκαύτωσιν 'the (animal offered as) wholly burned offering' Le 6.12; flax, Jo 2.6; cleft wood, 3K 18.33. **b**. *to supply abundantly*: + acc., με ἐν μήλοις 'me with apples' Ct 2.5.

Cf. ἐπιστοιβάζω, σωρεύω.

στοιβή, ῆς. f.ʃ

1. *thorny burnet*, branches of which were used to make brooms: Is 55.13.

2. *a quantity of grain brought together*: Jd 15.5A, Ru 3.7.

στοιχεῖον, ου. n.ʃ

basic component: of the universe, Wi 7.17, 19.18; of hum. body, 4M 12.13. Cf. στοιχείωσις: Delling, *TDNT* 7.670-83; Shipp 518.

στοιχείωσις, εως. f.ʃ

teaching of fundamentals: 2M 7.22. Cf. στοιχεῖον.

στοιχέω: fut. στοιχήσω.ʃ

to meet the expectation or standard set*: ***s* agricultural product, Ec 11.5.

στολή, ῆς. f.

robe: of good quality, καλή Ge 27.15 (ǁ ἱμάτια vs. 27); ἐξαλλασσούσας ~άς 'extraordinary robes' 45.22; ǁ περιβολή 49.11; δοξῶν 'stately' Ex 33.5; sg. collectively used, ἁγία 'sacerdotal' worn by priests in office, 28.2 || τοῦ ἁγίου 29.29; λειτουργική 31.10; τὴν ~ὴν τὴν λινῆν, ~ὴν ἁγίαν Le 16.32; regal, Jn 3.6, Jb 2.12; of any quality, γυναικεία De 22.5; πένθους 'for mourners' Ba 5.1. Cf. ἔνδυμα, ἐπενδύτης, ἐπίβλημα, ἱμάτιον, ἱματισμός, περιβολή, περιστολή, στολισμός, στολίζω: Wilckens, *TDNT* 7.688-90; Trench 186f.

στολίζω: fut. στολιῶ; aor. ἐστόλισα, inf. ~λίσαι, impv.3s στολισάτω; pf.ptc.pass. ἐστολισμένος.

to dress: + acc. pers., 1E 1.2; also + acc. (fine or formal clothes), πορφύραν Da 5.16 LXX (TH, vs. 29 LXX ἐνδύω), βασιλικὴν στολήν Es 8.15 o'. **b**. mid., *to dress oneself*: ἔν τινι (garment) Ju 10.3. Cf. ἐνδύω.

στολισμός, οῦ. m.

dress: Si 19.30; priestly uniform, Ez 42.14. Cf. στολή.

στολιστής, οῦ. m.ʃ *

he who is in charge of robes: of cultic uniforms, 4K 10.22. Cf. στολή.

στόλος, ου. m.

armada: 1M 1.17, + πλῆθος 2M 14.1.

στόμα, ατος. n.

1. *mouth*: as organ of speech, τὸ σ. μου τὸ λαλοῦν πρὸς ὑμᾶς Ge 45.12; ἐλάλησας τῷ ~ατί σου De 23.23; σ. κατὰ σ. λαλήσω αὐτῷ 'I shall have a tête-à-tête with him' Nu 12.8; ἐν ῥήμασι ~ατός μου 'with the words of my mouth' Ho 6.5; κατὰ σ. τινός 'in accordance with sbd's instruction' Nu 4.27; ἐπὶ ~ατος δύο μαρτύρων 'on the basis of a testimony of two witnesses' De 19.15; ἐπὶ στόμα / στόματός τινος 'as directed by': 2C 36.4[a] || 4K 23.35; ἐν στόματί τινος 'in the opinion of ..' Si 13.24; ἐπιθήσουσι χεῖρας ἐπὶ σ. αὐτῶν 'they will put their hands on their mouths (speechless)' Mi 7.16, χεῖρα θήσω ἐπὶ στόματί μου Jb 40.4, cf. Si 5.12; || χεῖλος Ma 2.6; with a tongue inside it Zc 14.12; to kiss with, Jb 31.27; anthropomorphically of God, De 8.3, Is 1.20, Mi 4.4. **b**. inlet for food: ἐκ ~ατος τοῦ λέοντος 'from a lion's mouth' Am 3.12; εἰς σ. ἔσθοντος 'into the mouth of an eater' Na 3.12. Fig. of that of the earth, Ge 4.11, Nu 16.30. **c**. the top part of a well: ἀπεκύλιον τὸν λίθον ἀπὸ τοῦ ~ατος τοῦ φρέατος 'they would roll the stone away from the top of the well' Ge 29.3; πηγῆς Ne 2.13, λάκκου 'of a pit' Da 6.17. **d**. the top of a bag: money-bag, ἐπάνω τοῦ ~ατος τοῦ μαρσίππου Ge 42.27. **e**. the entrance of a cave: σπηλαίου Jo 10.18, βοθύνου Je 31.28.

2. *mouth-shaped receptacle*: of ephah Zc 5.8.

3. *lip-shaped oblong, narrow and thin object*: σ. μαχαίρας 'the blade of a sword' Ge 34.26, Je 21.7 (or: *the foremost part*, 'the edge of a sword'), Jd 1.8 B (A: μαχαίρας), ῥομφαίας 1M 5.28.

4. *the farthest end*: σ. εἰς σ. 'from one end to the other' 4K 10.21, 21.16, also σ. ἐπὶ σ. ib. *L*, ἀπὸ ~ατος ἐπὶ σ. 2E 9.11.

Cf. χεῖλος and ὀδούς.

στόμωμα, ατος. n.ʃ

steel: Si 34.26. Cf. σίδηρος.

στοργή, ῆς. f.

sense of intimate affection: among people brought up together, 3M 5.32; φιλοτεκνίας 4M 14.13. Cf. στέργω, ἀγάπη, φιλία, φιλοστοργία.

στοχάζομαι: aor.impv. στόχασαι, ptc. στοχασάμενος, inf. στοχάσασθαι.ʃ

1. *to investigate and determine the extent* or *size* or *nature of*: + acc., τὴν ὁδόν De 19.3, τὸν αἰῶνα 'the world' Wi 13.9; στόχασαι τοὺς πλησίον 'size up your colleagues' Si 9.14.

2. *to have regard to*: + gen. pers., 2M 14.8.

στοχαστής, οῦ. m.ʃ*

diviner: προφήτην καὶ ~ήν Is 3.2. Cf. μάντις.

στραγγαλάω: pf.pass. ἐστραγγάλημαι, ptc. ἐστραγγαλωμένος.ʃ

to strangle: ***o*** hum., To 2.3. Cf. ἀποπνίγω.

στραγγαλιά, ᾶς. f.ʃ

constraining entanglement: metaph., βιαίων συναλλαγμάτων 'of powerful associations' Is 58.6; pl. and of wicked nature, Ps 124.5.

στραγγαλίς, ίδος. f.ʃ

some kind of personal ornament consisting of knots: Jd 8.26 A. Cf. Russo 221-5.

στραγγαλώδης, ες.ʃ *

twisted, knotty: metaph., + σκολιός Pr 8.8.

στραγγεύω: aor.impv. στράγγευσον, pass. ~γεύθητι.ʃ

to delay action: Jd 19.8 v.l. (Ra: < στρατεύω). Cf. χρονίζω: Schleusner s.v. στρατεύομαι; *BA*.ad loc. and Sym. ad Ge 19.16, Hb 2.3 with התמהמה).

στραγγίζω: fut. στραγγιῶ.ʃ

to squeeze out fluid: ***o*** blood of sacrificial animal, πρὸς τὴν βάσιν τοῦ θυσιαστηρίου Le 1.15 (after having nipped its head).

στρατεία, ας. f.ʃ

warfare: as cogn. obj. of στρατεύω 4M 9.24. Cf. στρατεύω, στράτευμα, μάχη, πόλεμος: Bauernfeind, *TDNT* 7.701-6.

στράτευμα, ατος. n.

1. *conduct of warfare*: πολέμου Ju 10.8.

2. *group of soldiers*: 2M 5.24.

Cf. στρατεία.

στρατεύω: aor. ἐστράτευσα, impv. στράτευσον, mid. 2pl στρατεύσασθε, pass. ~τεύθητι.

1. *to wage war*: ἐπὶ Πέρσας 4M 18.5; mid., Is 29.7; || πολεμέω 1E 4.6; + cogn. obj., στρατείαν περὶ τῆς εὐσεβείας 'for the cause of piety' 4M 9.24.

*__2__. *to set out on an uphilll journey* (?): στρατεύθητι Jd 19.8A (B: στράτευσον).

Cf. ἐκ~, ἐπιστρατεύω, στρατεία, μάχομαι, πολεμέω, παρατάσσω.

στρατηγέω: pf.pass. ἐστρατήγημαι.ʃ

1. *to serve as army general*: 2M 10.32.

2. *to outwit or outmanoeuvre*: + acc. pers. (general), 2M 12.31.

Cf. στρατηγός.

στρατήγημα, ατος. n.ʃ

strategem: 2M 14.29.

στρατηγία, ας. f.ʃ

office of military commander: 2K 8.16*L* (B: στρατιά). Cf. στρατηγός. Del. Ju 5.3 v.l.

στρατηγός, οῦ. m.

1. *commander of an army*: ἡγεμὼν καὶ σ. Je 28.23, + ἡγούμενοι Ez 23.6. Cf. πρωταγωνιστής, φυλάρχης.

2. *governor of a region or province*: 2M 10.11.

Cf. στρατηγέω, ~γία.

στρατιά, ᾶς. f.

band of numerous individuals: army of soldiers, Ex 14.4; a group of people including armed ones, Nu 10.28; esp. τοῦ οὐρανοῦ 'constellation' consisting of the sun, the moon, and the stars, 4K 17.16*L* (B: δύναμις), Ho 13.4, Zp 1.5; Je 7.18 (objects of illicit worship), cf. δύναμις **3** and κόσμος **1**. Cf. ἐπιστρατεύω. Del. 4M 16.10 v.l.

στρατιώτης, ου. m.

warrior: 2M 5.12. Cf. στρατιῶτις, μαχητής, πολεμιστής.

στρατιῶτις, ιδος. f.ʃ

female warrior: 4M 16.13. Cf. στρατιώτης.

στρατοκῆρυξ, υκος. m.ʃ

herald of an army: 3K 22.36. Cf. κῆρυξ.

στρατοπεδεία, ας. f.ʃ

place where troops are encamped: Jo 4.3 (‖ παρεμβολή vs. 8), 2M 13.14.

στρατοπεδεύω: fut. ~δεύσω; aor. ἐ~δευσα, subj. ~δεύσω, impv. ~δευσον; pf.ptc. ἐ~δευκώς; plpf. ἐ~δεύκειν.

1. *to encamp*: ἐν τῇ ἐρήμῳ Ge 12.9; ἐπὶ τῆς θαλάσσης Ex 14.2.

***2**. *to set out on military expedition*: εἰς τὴν ἔρημον De 1.40; 2M 9.23. **b**. gen., *to set up a base* for some operation: Pr 4.15.

Cf. παρεμβάλλω, στρατοπεδεία. Del. 4M 18.6 v.l.

στρατόπεδον, ου. n.

a body of troops on a military expedition: Je 41.1; πολεμίων 'of enemies' 4M 3.13. Often with πᾶς or ἅπας: e.g., Je 41.1, 2M 9.9. Cf. δύναμις, στρατιά, στρατός, τάγμα.

στρατός, οῦ. m.

army of troops: 2M 8.35. οὐράνιος 'heavenly,' i.e. angels 4M 4.11. Del. 1M 4.35 v.l.

στρέβλη, ης. f.

instrument of torture: + βάσανος Si 30.35; + αἰκισμός 4M 7.4; μετὰ ~ῶν ἀποθανεῖν 8.11. Mostly pl. Cf. αἰκία, βάσανος, and βασανιστήριον.

στρεβλός, ή, όν.

crooked and not straight: ***s*** bow, Ps 77.57. **b**. metaph., *perverse* in character: ***s*** hum., Ps 17.27; hum. heart, Si 36.25.

Cf. στρεβλόω, σκαμβός, σκολιός, εὐθής, ὀρθός.

στρεβλόω: fut.pass. στρεβλωθήσομαι; aor.inf. ~λῶσαι, ptc.pass. ~λωθείς.

1. *to torture*: τινα 4M 12.11; αἰκίαις 'with tortures' 3M 4.14. Cf. βασανίζω.

2. mid. *to conduct oneself perversely*: 2K 22.27 (*L* διαστρέφω).

στρεβλωτήριον, ου. n.ʃ *

rack: instrument of torture, 4M 8.13. Cf. βασανιστήριον.

στρέμμα, ατος. n.ʃ

**thread*: Jd 16.9 B.

στρεπτός, ή, όν.

twisted: κυμάτια ~ὰ χρυσᾶ 'small twisted, golden mouldings' Ex 25.10 (engraved on the ark of testimony); ~ὴν στεφάνην χρυσῆν 'golden, twisted crown' 30.3, 4 (on an altar). **b**. subst. n.: 'tassel' on a garment, De 22.12; ***s*** hair, Es C 13 o'; wreathed decorative work on the capital of a column, 3K 7.27.

στρέφω: fut. στρέψω, pass. στραφήσομαι; aor. ἔστρεψα, ptc.act. στρέψας, impv. στρέψον, pass. ἐστράφην, subj. στραφῶ, ptc. στραφείς.

I. *to transform*: + τι εἴς τι– τὴν πέτραν εἰς λίμνας ὑδάτων 'the rock into pools of water' Ps 113.8, πένθος εἰς χαρμονήν Je 38.13; pass. *to undergo a change and become* sth, τὴν ῥάβδον .. τὴν στραφεῖσαν εἰς ὄφιν 'the staff which has turned into a snake' Ex 4.17, 7.15; ἐστράφη αὐτοῖς εἰς ἔχθραν 'became their enemy' Is 63.10; νύκτα Jb 34.25¶ (εἰς ἡμέραν understood?); impers., ἐστράφη αὐτοῖς ἀπὸ πένθους εἰς χαράν Es 9.22 o'.

2. *to cause to face*: + acc., ἐπ' ἐμὲ νῶτα καὶ οὐ πρόσωπα αὐτῶν 'their backs to me, not their faces' Je 2.27; defeated and in flight, 31.39.

3. *to cause to turn round and move* towards: τὴν βουλὴν αὐτῶν ἐπ' αὐτούς 'their design back to themselves' Es C 22, τὴν καρδίαν τοῦ λαοῦ τούτου ὀπίσω (*L* + σου) 3K 18.37.

4. *to twist and turn*: ***o*** the sick in bed so as to ease his discomfort, Ps 40.4, cf. Ibn Ezra ad loc.; pass., ἡ καρδία μου ἐστράφη ἐν ἐμοί 'my heart was turned upside down' La 1.20.

II. mid. *to revolve*: ***s*** sword, Ge 3.24; a piece of cake, Jd 7.13B; axle, Si 36.5, door on its hinge Pr 26.14; the sun, 1E 4.34; ὀργή Je 37.23.

2. *to change from one side to another*, 'turn': 3K 2.15; ἀπὸ τοῦ πλευροῦ σου ἐπὶ τὸ πλευρόν σου Ez 4.8.

3. *to turn round and move in a different direction*: backwards in flight, ἐν ἡμέρᾳ πολέμου Ps 77.9; εἰς τὰ ὀπίσω 113.3.

4. *to turn* towards *and focus one's attention and efforts* to: *s* ὠδῖνες 'pains of labour,' ἐπ' αὐτήν 1K 4.19*L* (B: ἐπι~); οὗ ἂν ἐστράφη 'in whichever direction he turned' 14.47 (*L* ἐπιβλέπω), sim Pr 12.7.

Cf. ἀνα~, ἐπιστρέφω.

στρῆνος, ους. n.ʃ

insolence: 4K 19.28. Cf. ὑπερηφανία.

στρίφνος, ου. m.ʃ *

tough or *gristly meat* (LSJ): Jb 20.18.

στροβέω: fut. στροβήσω.

to throw off mental balance, 'upset': + acc. pers., ὁ φόβος μού σε στροβήσει Jb 33.7; *s* ἡμέρα σκοτεινή 'dark day' 15.23. Cf. συγχέω.

στρογγύλος, η, ον.

round in shape: *s* "the sea" in Solomon's temple, 2C 4.2. Cf. Schmidt 4.457f.; Shipp 521.

στρουθίον, ου. n.

1. dim. of στρουθός, q.v.: Je 8.7, La 4.3, poss. Ps 83.4.

2. *small bird*: child's plaything, Jb 40.29 (ǁ ὄρνεον). Cf. Fehling, esp. 219; Bain 131.

Cf. ὄρνεον.

στρουθός, οῦ. m./f.

sparrow: forbidden as food, Le 11.15, De 14.14; inhabiting ruins, Is 34.13, Je 10.22; ǁ ὄρνεον Pr 26.2. Cf. στρουθίον.

στροφεύς, έως. m.ʃ

socket in which the pivot of a door moves (LSJ): 3K 6.34, 1C 22.3.

στροφή, ῆς. f.ʃ

meandering path: παραβολῶν 'of parables' Si 39.2; λόγων '(twists) of words' Wi 8.8, Pr 1.3, cf. PSol 12.2.

στρόφιγξ, ιγγος.ʃ

pivot: hinge of a door, Pr 26.14.

στρόφος, ου.m ʃ

colic: Si 34.20.

στροφωτός, ή, όν.ʃ*

capable of turning on pivots: *s* θύρωμα 'door' Ez 41.24.

στρῶμα, ατος. n.ʃ

that which is spread to sleep on: Pr 22.27, 4K 8.15*L*. Cf. κλίνη.

στρωμνή, ῆς. f.

1. *spread bed*: ἐμίανας τὴν ~ήν 'you defiled ..' Ge 49.4; κατασπαταλῶντες ἐπὶ ~αῖς 'leading too comfortable a life, sleeping in spread beds' Am 6.4 (ǁ κλίναι ἐλεφάντιναι); ἐπὶ κλίνης ~ῆς Ps 130.3; Ju 13.9.

2. *bed-cover* or *bed-sheet*: Ez 27.7, Es 1.6 o'.

Cf. κλίνη, στρῶμα, and στρώννυμι.

στρώννυμι: fut. στρώσω; aor. ἔστρωσα; pf. ἔστρωκα, pass. ἔστρωμαι, ptc. ἐστρωμένος.

to place sth *over a wide surface*, 'spread': + acc., σάκκον καὶ σποδόν 'sackcloth and ashes' Es 4.3; pass., ἐπὶ κλίνης ἐστρωμένης 'on a spread bed' Ez 23.41, ἔστρωταί μου ἡ στρωμνή Jb 17.13; ***o*** understood, ἔστρωσεν 'she made the bed' Ju 12.15, To 7.16 𝔊II; ἀμφιτάποις 'with double tapestry' Pr 7.16; metaph., Is 14.11, Ez 28.7. **b**. ***o*** = the surface: pass., ὁδοὶ .. ἐστρωμέναι ἀκάνθαις 'ways .. strewn with thorns' Pr 15.19.

Cf. στρωμνή, δια~, ὑποστρώννυμι, κατασήθω.

στυγέω.ʃ

to dislike intensely: + acc. rei, 3M 2.31; pass., ***o*** hum. 2M 5.8 (ǁ βδελύσσω). Cf. βδελύσσω, μισέω.

στυγνάζω: fut. στυγνάσω; aor. ἐστύγνασα.*

to turn a gloomy, lowering look (LSJ): + ἐπί τινα Ez 26.16, 27.35. Cf. στυγνός, σκυθρωπάζω.

στυγνός, ή, όν.ʃ

1. *gloomy, sullen*: *s* hum., ἐπορεύθη ~ός Is 57.17.

2. *hated, abhorrent*: *s* night, Wi 17.5.

Cf. μισητός.

στῦλος, ου. m.

oblong structure which is positioned erect: 'pillar' of a temple, Jd 16.25A (B: κίων), Je 52.17, ἐπὶ τοῦ ~ου 'next to the pillar' 4K 11.14; of a house, Pr 9.1; σ. νεφέλης .. πυρός 'of cloud .. of fire' Ex 13.21, Nu 14.14, πυριφλεγής 'burning in flames' Wi 18.3; Si 24.4; τῆς ^γῆς^ Ps 74.4, Jb 9.6, οὐρανοῦ 26.11¶; ἀναπαύσεως Si 36.29; πάρινος 'of marble stone' Es 1.6. **b**. supports sth above, 'post': of a tabernacle and wooden, τῇ σκηνῇ Ex 26.15.

Cf. στυλόω, κίων, στέλεχος: Wilckens, *TDNT* 7.732-4.

στυλόω: aor.pass. ἐστυλώθην.ʃ

pass. *to position oneself like a pillar*: *s* tall hum., 1K 17.16.

στυράκινος, η, ον.*ʃ

made of the wood of the tree στύραξ "Styrax officinalis" (LSJ): *s* ῥάβδος 'rod' Ge 30.37.

σύ; σοῦ, σου; σοί, σοι; σέ, σε.

Reference to a person being addressed. The usage is similar to that of ἐγώ, q.v.: the ἐ- forms such as ἐμοῦ correspond to the accented σοῦ, σοί, and σέ.

συγγελάω: fut.~γελάσω.ʃ

to laugh out of pleasure with: + dat. pers., Si 30.10 (father with child; opp. συνοδυνάομαι). Cf. γελάω.

συγγένεια, ας. f.

group of people bound by family ties, '(somewhat distant) kinsfolk': ἐκ τῆς ~ας σου καὶ ἐκ τοῦ οἴκου τοῦ πατρός σου Ge 12.1; Ex 6.14; brothers, for instance, excluded, and mentioned alongside livestock, Ge 50.8; ἡ σ. αὐτῶν 'their ilk' Ps 73.8. **b.** *affinity, kinship*: 2M 5.9; ἀθανασία ἐστιν ἐν ~ᾳ σοφίας 'immortality has close affinity with ..' Wi 8.17; ἀδελφότητος 'of brotherhood' 4M 10.3.

Cf. οἶκος, συγγενής: Michaelis, *TDNT* 7.736-8; Spicq 301-7.

συγγενής, ές.

of the same kin: subst. σ. σου Le 18.14; 20.20, 25.45. **b.** not related by blood, but applied to a king's close associate: subst. m. 1M 10.89, 11.31, 1E 3.7; + ἐπίτροπος τοῦ βασιλέως 'the king's trustee' 2M 11.1.

Cf. συγγένεια, ἀγχιστεύς, ἀλλογενής: Spicq 308-11.

συγγηράω.ʃ

to grow old together with: τινι Si 11.16¶.

Cf. γηράσκω.

συγγίνομαι: aor.inf. ~γενέσθαι, subj. ~γένωμαι.ʃ

to have sexual intercourse with: abs., *s* a man and a woman, Da TH Su 39; + dat. pers., καθεύδειν μετ' αὐτῆς τοῦ συγγενέσθαι αὐτῇ Ge 39.10; Da TH Su 11; μετά τινος Ju 12.16; men with men, Ge 19.5. Alw. ref. to illicit intercourse; cf. γίνομαι **4**.

συγγίνωσκω: fut.mid. ~γνώσομαι; aor.ptc. ~γνούς.ʃ

1. *to become aware of a fact*: ὅτι 2M 14.31.

2. *to judge leniently*: + dat. pers., 4M 8.22.

Cf. συγγνώμη, συγγνωμονέω, συγγνωστός: Metzler, esp. 224-34.

συγγνώμη, ης. f.ʃ

lenient judgement: ~ην ἔχω 'judge kindly (by making allowances)' Si prol. 16, 3.13; ὁμοιόψηφος 'universal' 2M 14.20 (v.l. γνώμη). Cf. συγγίνωσκω, συγγνωμονέω.

συγγνωμονέω: aor.opt.3s ~νήσειεν.ʃ *

to deal leniently with: + dat. pers., ἐπὶ πάσῃ παρανομίᾳ 'over every transgression of the law' 4M 5.13. Cf. συγγνώμη.

συγγνωστός, όν.ʃ

pardonable: *s* hum., Wi 13.8, ἐλέους 'for the sake of mercy' 6.6 (gen. causae).

συγγραφεύς, έως. m.ʃ

he who gathers and writes down historical facts: 2M 2.28. Cf. συγγράφω.

συγγραφή, ῆς. f.ʃ

written document: 1M 13.42; contract, 14.43, ἄδικος Is 58.6; charge, κατά τινος Jb 31.35. **b.** *draft document*: of marriage contract, To 7.13 𝔊II.

Cf. συγγράφω.

συγγράφω: aor.inf. ~γράψαι.ʃ

to put together in writing: + acc. rei, Si prol. 12. Cf. συγγραφεύς, ~φή.

συγγυμνασία, ας. f.ʃ *

act of gaining more experience of: ὁμιλίας ^τῆς σοφίας^ 'of the company of Wisdom' Wi 8.18.

συγκάθημαι.ʃ

to sit together: μετ' ἐμοῦ Ps 100.6. Cf. κάθημαι and συγκαθίζω.

συγκαθίζω: aor. συνεκάθισα, inf. συγκαθίσαι.ʃ

1. *to sit in company with*: + dat., beside pieces of sacrificed animals in order to guard them, Ge 15.11; *s* πᾶν τὸ πλῆθος 'the entire congregation' 1E 9.6 (at a meeting); ἐτάσαι τὸ πρᾶγμα 'to examine the matter' 9.16; for a banquet, μετ' αὐτῶν τοῦ φαγεῖν καὶ πιεῖν Je 16.8.

2. *to sit in a court of justice*: as judge, κρίνειν τὸν λαόν Ex 18.13.

3. *to crouch*: *s* ass, ὑποκάτω Βαλααμ 'beside Balaam' Nu 22.27.

Cf. καθίζω and συγκάθημαι.

συγκαθυφαίνω: pf.ptc.pass. ~υφασμένος.ʃ *

to interweave with sth else: σὺν χρυσίῳ καὶ ὑακίνθῳ 'with gold and purple' Is 3.23. Cf. ὑφαίνω.

συγκαίω: fut. ~καύσω, pass. ~καυθήσομαι; pf.pass. ~κέκαυμαι.ʃ

to burn, blaze: abs., πνεύματι καύσωνος συγκαίοντι 'a hot scorching wind' Jn 4.8; + acc., ἡμέρας ὁ ἥλιος οὐ συγκαύσει σε οὐδὲ ἡ σελήνη τὴν νύκτα Ps 120.6; of the effect of alcoholic drink, ὁ οἶνος αὐτοὺς συγκαύσει Is 5.11, cf. ἡ γαστήρ μου συγκέκαυται ἀπὸ κλαυθμοῦ 'my belly is burnt from weeping' Jb 16.16 and νυκτὶ δέ μου τὰ ὀστᾶ συγκέκαυται 'my bones ..' 30.17; συγκαιόμενος τῷ καύματι καὶ παγετῷ 'being burned by heat and frost' Ge 31.40, καλάμη .. συγκαυθήσεται ὑπὸ φλογός 'stubble .. will be burnt by a flame' Is 5.24 (‖ καίω), ὡς φλόξ Pr 24.22e; ***o*** γῆ Is 9.19 (‖ κατακαίω). Cf. καίω.

συγκαλέω: fut. ~καλέσω; aor. συνεκάλεσα, ptc. ~καλέσας.

1. *to summon, call in*: + acc. pers., συνεκάλεσεν Φαραω τοὺς σοφιστὰς Αἰγύπτου καὶ τοὺς φαρμάκους 'Ph. summoned the wise men of Egypt and the magicians' Ex 7.11.

2. *to invite* a guest: συγκαλέσετε ἕκαστος τὸν πλησίον αὐτοῦ ὑποκάτω ἀμπέλου 'you are going to invite each his own colleague (to sit) under a vine' Zc 3.10.

Cf. καλέω, σύγκλητος.

συγκάλυμμα, ατος. n.ʃ *

that which covers as a protection: a garment provided by a man for his wife, οὐκ ἀνακαλύψει σ. τοῦ πατρὸς αὐτοῦ 'shall not uncover ..' De 22.30 (an injunction against sexual intercourse with one's stepmother), sim. 27.20. Cf. συγκαλύπτω, κάλυμμα.

συγκαλύπτω. fut. ~καλύψω; aor. συνεκάλυψα, mid. ~καλυψάμην, subj.act. συγκαλύψω; pf.ptc.pass. ~κεκαλυμμένος.

to place a cover: abs., ἐπί τι 2C 5.8; συγκαλύπτον ἐπὶ τὰ πλάγια τῆς σκηνῆς ἔνθεν καὶ ἔνθεν 'covering the sides of the tabernacle on either side' Ex 26.13; + acc. rei, τὸν λουτῆρα καὶ τὴν βάσιν αὐτοῦ 'the basin and its pedestal' Nu 4.14; in order to make the object invisible, τὴν γύμνωσιν τοῦ πατρὸς αὐτῶν 'the naked body of their father' Ge 9.23, cf. Su 39 LXX ('dressed':: 'naked'); *o* τὸ πρόσωπόν σου Ez 12.6, cf. Jb 9.24¶; + acc. pers., ἐν δέρρει 'with a leather garment' Jd 4.18A. **b**. mid. *to wrap oneself up*: in order to disguise oneself, 1K 28.8, 3K 22.30 (‖ 2C 18.29 κατα~).

Cf. (κατα)καλύπτω, συγκάλυμμα.

συγκάμπτω: aor. συνέκαμψα, impv. ~καμψον.ʃ

to bend: + acc., τὸν νῶτον αὐτῶν 'their backs' Ps 68.24, ἐν νηστείᾳ τὴν ψυχήν μου 'with fasting ..' 68.11. **b**. intr. *to bend down*: συγκάμψας ἔπεσεν Jd 5.27A, ἐπὶ τὸ παιδάριον 4K 4.35B (*L*: ἠνδρίσατο), 4.34*L* (B: δια~). Cf. κάμπτω.

συγκαταβαίνω: fut. ~βήσομαι; aor. ~κατέβην.ʃ

to descend together with: + dat. pers., Ps 48.18 (into Hades), εἰς λάκκον Wi 10.14, + ἅμα τινι Da 3.49. Cf. καταβαίνω.

συγκαταγηράσκω: aor.inf. ~γηρᾶσαι.ʃ

to grow old together with: + dat. pers., To 8.7 𝔊[I], κοινῶς 𝔊[II]. Cf. γηράσκω.

συγκατακληρονομέομαι: fut. ~μηθήσομαι.ʃ *

to become co-heir: Nu 32.30. Cf. (συγ)κληρονομέω.

συγκαταμίγνυμι: aor.subj.pass. ~μιγῶ.ʃ

to form relationship through intermarriage: + dat. pers., Jo 23.12. Cf. γαμβρεύω.

συγκατατίθημι: fut.mid. ~θήσομαι; aor.mid.impv. ~θου.ʃ

to come to an agreement: on a joint course of action, μετά τινος and + inf., Ex 23.1; expressed as διαθήκη - οὐ συγκαταθήσῃ αὐτοῖς καὶ τοῖς θεοῖς αὐτῶν διαθήκην 23.32; ἡμῖν Su 20 TH. Cf. συντίθημι.

συγκαταφέρω.ʃ

to carry down together: χάλαζα συγκαταφερομένη βίᾳ 'hail carried down together violently' Is 30.30. Cf. καταφέρω **1**.

συγκατεσθίω: fut. ~καταφάγομαι.ʃ

to eat up: *s* fire and + acc., Is 9.18. Cf. κατεσθίω.

σύγκειμαι.ʃ

to exist together as a coherent unit: *s* τὰ πάντα 'the entire creation' Si 43.26. **b**. *to be banded together in conspiracy*: ἐπ' ἐμέ 'up against me' 1K 22.8; 2K 15.31*L* (B: συστρέφομαι), cf. συστρέφω **1**.

συγκεντέω.ʃ

to stab more than one person *together*: + acc. pers., 2M 12.23. Cf. κεντέω.

συγκεράννυμι: aor.pass.inf. ~κραθῆναι, ptc. ~κερασθείς.ʃ

to mix, blend: pass., + dat., οἶνος ὕδατι 2M 15.39; Da 2.43 LXX. Cf. κεράννυμι, σύγκρασις, μίγνυμι.

συγκερατίζομαι: fut. ~τισθήσομαι.ʃ*

to engage in a fight with: *s* hum., + τινι Da 11.40 LXX (TH μετά τινος). Cf. πολεμέω.

συγκεραυνόω: aor. συνεκραύνωσα.ʃ

to strike as with a thunderbolt: + acc. pers., 2M 1.16.

συγκλασμός, οῦ. m.ʃ *

breaking: *o* fruit-tree, Jl 1.7. Cf. συγκλάω.

συγκλάω: fut. ~κλάσω; aor. συνέκλασα, pass. συνεκλάσθην.ʃ

to break: destructive action and + acc., μοχλοὺς σιδηροῦς 'iron bolts' Is 45.2, Ps 106.16 (‖ συντρίβω), ἐν ὀργῇ θυμοῦ αὐτοῦ πᾶν κέρας Ισραηλ '.. every horn ..' La 2.3, τὰ κέρατα τῶν ἁμαρτωλῶν Ps 74.11, ὀσφῦν 'hip' Ez 29.7, ὅπλον 'weapon' Ps 45.10 (‖ συντρίβω); pass., σφῦρα 'hammer' Je 27.23 (‖ συντρίβω); metaph., πληγὴ γλώσσης συγκλάσει ὀστᾶ 'a blow of the tongue crushes bones' Si 28.17. Cf. συγκλασμός, συντρίβω, ἀφανίζω.

σύγκλεισμα, ατος. n. *

bordering area: 3K 7.16. Cf. συγκλειστός.

συγκλεισμός, οῦ. m. *

1. *that which encloses*, 'enclosure': διαρρήξω ~ὸν καρδίας αὐτῶν 'I will tear apart their pericardia (or: their closely formed heart)' Ho 13.8 (cf. Eth *šerw*).

2. *hole* in which a snake confines itself, Mi 7.17; hiding-place for humans, 2K 22.46 (*L* δεσμός). Cf. LSG s.v.

*__3__. *that which is securely closed and locked*, 'a chest of treasures'(?): Jb 28.15 (or 'concentrated gold, gold bullion'?, cf. χρυσίον συγκεκλεισμένον 3K 6.21 [זָהָב סָגוּר] ‖ χ. καθαρόν 2C 4.20.

*__4__. *state of being shut up*, 'siege': Ez 4.3,1M 6.21. Cf. συγκλείω.

συγκλειστής, οῦ. m.ʃ

lock-smith (?): 4K 24.16*L*.

συγκλειστός, ή, όν.ʃ

subst.n. *border*: 3K 7.15, 36. Cf. σύγκλεισμα.

συγκλείω: fut. ~κλείσω, pass. ~κλεισθήσομαι; aor. ~έκλεισα, subj. ~κλείσω, inf. ~κλεῖσαι, impv. ~κλεισον, ptc. ~κλείσας, pass. συνεκλείσθην, inf. ~κλεισθῆναι, ptc. ~κλεισθείς; pf. ~κέκλεικα, ptc. ~κεκληκώς, pass. ~κεκλεισμένος, inf. ~κεκλεῖσθαι.

1. *to close off*: + acc., συνέκλεισεν κύριος .. πᾶσαν μήτραν 'every womb' (resulting in sterility) Ge 20.18, τὰ περὶ τὴν μήτραν αὐτῆς 1K 1.6 (‖ vs. 5 ἀποκλείω), cp. Jb 3.10; *o* doors, Ma 1.10; roads, Ju 5.1, pass. συγκλεισθήσεταί σου τὰ διαβήματα 'you will come to a dead end' Pr 4.12; cities, Jo 6.1,

Is 45.1 (to resist conquest), Je 13.19 (poss. to surround and besiege and :: ἀνοίγω); tent, Ju 13.1; τὸ στέαρ αὐτῶν 'their fat' Ps 16.10 (meaning 'the best of their humanity'?, cf. Tht, PG 80. 969); + ἐξ ἐναντίας τινός 34.3, town 2M 12.7. **b.** ὁ συγκλείων 'lock-smith'(?): 4K 24.14 ‖ vs. 16 συγκλειστής. **c.** χρυσίον συγκεκλημένον or χρυσίῳ συγκεκλεισμένος mechanically translating /zāhāv sāgur/ 3K 6.20, 10.21 ‖ χ. καθαρόν 'pure gold' 2C 4.20.

2. *to confine to a narrow space, blocking a way out*: + acc., συγκέκλεικεν αὐτοὺς ἡ ἔρημος Ex 14.3; + εἰς, Am 1.6, 9, εἰς θάνατον Ps 77.50 (‖ παραδίδωμι vs. 48), εἰς ῥομφαίαν 77.62, εἰς χεῖρας ἐχθροῦ 30.9, sim. 1K 17.46*L* (B: ἀπο~); of blocking the way of the defeated trying to escape, Ob 14, 1M 15.25; people under siege, Je 21.9, mid. 1M 6.49; into a private chamber, To 8.4 𝔊[I]. Cf. συνέχω **4**.

3. *to block the way to achieving a goal*: + acc. pers. and negative inf., συνέκλεισέν με ὁ κύριος τοῦ μὴ τίκτειν 'the Lord has prevented me from bearing' Ge 16.2; + κατά τινος (pers.), Jb 3.23; pass., ὑπὸ τῆς ὥρας 'under the time constraint' 2M 8.25.

Cf. (ἀπο)κλείω, συγκλειστής: Michel, *TDNT* 7.744f.

συγκληρονομέω: aor.subj. ~μήσω.ʃ *

to become co-heir: ἐν τῇ κληρονομίᾳ αὐτοῦ 'to share his inheritance' Si 22.23. Cf. (συγκατα)κληρονομέω.

σύγκλητος, ον.ʃ

summoned: ~οι βουλῆς 'council members' Nu 16.2 (‖ ἀρχηγοὶ συναγωγῆς). Cf. συγκαλέω, ἐπίκλητος.

συγκλύζω: fut. ~κλύσω.*

to wash over, engulf: + acc., ποταμοὶ οὐ συγκλύσουσί σε Is 43.2. Cf. κατακλύζω: Renehan 2.128.

συγκοιμάομαι.ʃ

to sleep together: for sex, *s* male, μετὰ γυναικῶν 1K 2.22 *L*. Cf. κοιμάομαι.

σύγκοιτος, ου. m./f.ʃ

bedfellow: of female spouse, Mi 7.5 (‖ φίλος); fem. companion in bed, 3K 1.4*L* (v.l. θάλπουσα 'keeping warm'). Cf. κοίτη.

συγκολλάω.ʃ

to glue together: + acc., ὄστρακον 'potsherds' Si 22.9. Cf. LSG s.v.

συγκομίζω: aor.ptc.pass. ~κομισθείς.ʃ

to gather: *o* harvested crops, Jb 5.26 (‖ θερίζω). Cf. συνάγω.

συγκόπτω: fut. συγκόψω; aor. συνέκοψα, impv. σύγκοψον, inf. συγκόψαι.

1. *to cut up into small pieces*, 'crush, grind': *o* spices (ἡδύσματα) Ex 30.36, burned calf (μόσχος) De 9.21; αὐχένας ἁμαρτωλῶν 'the necks of sinners' Ps 128.4; κέρατα 'drinking-horns' Je 31.12; metal object, ἄροτρα ὑμῶν εἰς ῥομφαίας 'your ploughshares into swords' Jl 3.10, τὰς μαχαίρας αὐτῶν εἰς ἄροτρα Is 2.4 (‖ Mi 4.3 κατακόπτω).

2. *to deal a severe blow to*: + acc. pers., Ge 34.30, Ju 5.22; ἐχθρούς Ps 88.24.

Cf. κόπτω and συντρίβω.

σύγκρασις, εως. f.ʃ

mixed compound: Ez 22.19. Cf. συγκεράννυμι.

σύγκριμα, ατος. n.

1. *sth formed by combination*: σ. μουσικῶν 'musical concert' Si 35.5.

2. = σύγκρισις *interpretation*: Si 35.17, Da 5.26.

*__3.__ *binding decision*, 'decree': Da 4.14 TH, τοῦ βασιλέως 1M 1.57 (death sentence).

Cf. σύγκρισις, συγκρίνω.

συγκρίνω: aor. συνέκρινα, inf. ~κρῖναι, subj.pass. ~κριθῶ.

1. *to compare*: pass. and + dat., φωτὶ συγκρινομένη 'compared with light' Wi 7.29. Cf. συμβάλλω **3**.

2. *to interpret*: *o* dream, vision (ἐνύπνιον), Ge 40.8; ὀρθῶς 40.16; συγκρίνων ἐνύπνια καὶ ἀναγγέλλων κρατούμενα καὶ λύων συνδέσμους 'interpreting dreams and telling what is held together (?) and untying knots' Da 5.12 TH; + dat. pers., Ge 40.22; + cogn. obj., τὸ σύγκριμα τῆς γραφῆς .. συγκρῖναι τῷ βασιλεῖ 'to interpret the meaning of the writing to the king' Da 5.7 LXX. Cf. Polyb. 14.3.7.

3. *to consider and adjudge*: ἀνοίᾳ συγκρινόμενα 'when considered by (their) lack of intelligence' Wi 15.18.

4. *to decide*: οὐ συνέκριναν τί ποιήσωσιν αὐτόν 'they did not decide what to do with him' Nu 15.34.

5. mid.: συγκριθῶμεν ἑαυτοῖς ἐκεῖ 'Let us contend with each other there' 1M 10.71.

Cf. σύγκρισις, σύγκριμα, κρίνω, διασαφέω.

σύγκρισις, εως. f.

1. *interpretation*: + gen. (ἐνύπνιον 'dream') Ge 40.12.

2. *decision made*: κατὰ τὴν ~ιν αὐτοῦ 'in accordance with the decision pertaining to it [= the Passover celebration]' Nu 9.3; 29.6 +; τῶν Σιδονίων '(nonbelligerency?) agreement with the S.' Jd 18.7A (B: κρίσις).

3. *act of assessing and comparing* multiple entities: Wi 7.8.

Cf. συγκρίνω, σύγκριμα, ἐπίκρισις, διασάφησις, δήλωσις: Lieberman 1962.58-62.

συγκροτέω: aor. συνεκρότησα.ʃ

to strike together: ταῖς χερσίν '(to clap) the hands' Nu 24.10 (angry gesture); mid. *s* τὰ γόνατα 'the knees' Da TH 5.6 (angst). Cf. κροτέω.

συγκρουσμός, οῦ. m.ʃ *
colliding with one another: w. ref. to noise arising therefrom, ὅπλων 'of weapons' 1M 6.41.

συγκρύπτω.ʃ
to hide oneself and avoid contact with: τινα 2M 14.30. Cf. κρύπτω.

συγκτίζω: aor.pass. συνεκτίσθην; pf.pass. συνέκτισμαι.ʃ
to create together with: + dat., *o* wisdom, Si 1.14, error and darkness 11.16¶. Cf. κτίζω.

συγκύπτω: fut. ~κύψω; pf.ptc. ~κεκυφώς.ʃ
to stoop: προσώπῳ 'with face down' Jb 9.27; gesture of dejection, Si 12.11, μελανίᾳ 'in mourning' 19.26. Cf. κύπτω, συγκύφω.

συγκυρέω.
to be contiguous to: + dat., ἐν Εσεβων καὶ ἐν πάσαις ταῖς συγκυρούσαις αὐτῇ 'in Heshbon and all its satellite cities' Nu 21.25; τὰ συγκυροῦντα χειμάρρῳ Ιαβοκ 'the areas adjacent to Wadi Jabok' De 2.37; τὰ συγκυροῦντα τῶν πόλεων 'the areas adjacent to the cities' Nu 35.4 (τὰ ὅμορα τῶν πόλεων vs. 5; τὰ προάστια τῶν πόλεων vs. 2). Cf. ὅμορος, προάστιος, προσκυρέω: Lee 78-81.

συγκύφω.ʃ
= συγκύπτω: πρόσωπον Si 19.27.

συγχαίρω: fut. ~χαροῦμαι, ptc. ~χαρησόμενος.ʃ
to show that one shares joy with: + dat. pers., συγχαρεῖταί μοι Ge 21.6; ἐπὶ τοῖς συμβεβηκόσι συγχαρησομένους 'who were to congratulate him over what had happened' 3M 1.8. Cf. χαίρω, συνευφραίνομαι. On the morphology, see Walters 105.

συγχέω: fut.act. συγχεῶ, pass. ~χυθήσομαι; aor. συνέχεα, inf. ~χέαι, subj. συγχέω, pass. συνεχύθην, impv.3pl συγχυθήτωσαν, ptc. συγχυθείς; pf.pass. (or mid.?) συγκέχυμαι, ptc. ~κεχυμένος; plpf.pass. 3s συνεκέχυτο.ʃ
1. *to throw into confusion*: συνέχεεν κύριος τὰ χείλη πάσης τῆς γῆς 'the Lord confused the speeches of the whole earth' Ge 11.9; τὴν γλῶσσαν 'the language' 11.7; pass. τὰ ἅρματα Na 2.5 (‖ θορυβέω), ἔθνη Wi 10.5 (‖ Ge 11.7); ἀορασίᾳ 'through blindness' 2M 10.30; ἐν πολέμῳ 'through a verbal warfare' PSol 12.3.
2. *to disturb composure* or *temper of* (sbd τινα), 'to upset': pass. *o* person, Jn 4.1 (‖ ἐλυπήθη), Mi 7.17, Jl 2.1, 2M 13.23, 14.28; συνεχύθη καὶ ἠθύμει 'was upset and despondent' 1M 4.27, συγκεχυμένος καὶ ἐκλελυμένος 'upset and exhausted' 3K 21.43; συγχυθήσεται ἡ γῆ (‖ σείω) Jl 2.10.
3. *to demolish*: τὸν οἶκον τὸν περίπτερον ἐπὶ τὸν οἶκον τὸν θερινόν '(I will demolish) the house with a single row of columns (and make it collapse) on to the summer house' Am 3.15, cf. a doublet, πατάξω as a v.l.
Cf. ἀφανίζω, διατρέπω, θορυβέω, ἐκχέω, ἐξίστημι, κατασπεύδω, στροβέω, σύγχυσις, ἐπι~, συνταράσσω.

συγχρονίζω: aor.ptc. ~χρονίσας.ʃ
to spend some time in a place: Si prol. 23.

σύγχυσις, εως.
1. *confusion, mixing up*: ἐκλήθη τὸ ὄνομα αὐτῆς Σύγχυσις 'its name was called Confusion' Ge 11.9.
2. *commotion and disquiet*: due to a calamity, θανάτου 1K 5.6 (‖ τάραχος vs. 9), μεγάλη σφόδρα 'utter pandemonium' 14.20.
Cf. συγχέω, ταραχή.

συγχωρέω: aor. συνεχώρησα, inf.pass. ~χωρηθῆναι; pf. συγκεχώρηκα.
1. *to give permission* to do: + dat. pers., *s* king, Bel 26; + acc. pers. and inf., Es 5.23 *L*. Cf. ἀφίημι **3**, δίδωμι **16**.
2. *to concede as right*: + acc. rei, 2M 11.15, 18; also + dat. pers., 11.24, 35.
Cf. συγχωρητέον.

συγχωρητέον.ʃ
one ought to permit: 2M 2.31. Cf. συγχωρέω.

συζεύγνυμι: pf.ptc.pass. συνεζευγμένος.ʃ
to couple one another: pass., *o* bird's wings, πρὸς ἀλλήλας Ez 1.11. Cf. ζεύγνυμι.

συζυγής, οῦς. m./f.ʃ
consort, spouse: male, 3M 4.8.

συζώννυμι: aor. συνέζωσα, mid. συνεζωσάμην.ʃ
1. act. *to gird up*: + acc. pers., Le 8.7.
2. mid. *to gird on about oneself*: σκεύη πολεμικά 'battle outfit' 1M 3.3.
Cf. ζώννυμι.

συκάμινον, ου. n.ʃ
fruit of sycamore-fig: κνίζων ~α 'scratching ..' Am 7.14, see LSG s.v.

συκάμινος, ου. f.
sycamore: building material and + κέδρος 'cedar', Is 9.10; Ps 77.47.

συκῆ, ῆς. f. Cf. Shipp 521f.
fig-tree: ‖ ῥόα Nu 13.24; ‖ ῥόα, ἄμπελος 20.5, De 8.8; ‖ ἄμπελος Ho 2.12, Mi 4.4, Jl 1.7, 12 (also ‖ ῥόα, φοῖνιξ, μῆλον, and other fruit-trees, sim. Hg 2.19), Jl 2.22; Hb 3.17 (also ‖ ἐλαία), Zc 3.10; ἀναπαύσεται ἕκαστος .. ὑποκάτω ~ῆς αὐτοῦ 'each will have rest .. under his fig-tree' Mi 4.4; protected by watchman, ~αῖ σκοποὺς ἔχουσαι Na 3.12, cf. Ho 9.10. Cf. συκών, σῦκον: Shipp 521f.; Schnebel 300-2.

σῦκον, ου. n.
fruit of the συκῆ, 'fig': 4K 20.7, Is 28.4. Cf. συκῆ.

συκοφαντέω: fut. ~τήσω; aor.inf. ~τῆσαι, impv.3pl ~τησάτωσαν.
1. *to accuse falsely*: + acc. pers., Ge 43.18; Le 19.11 (‖ κλέπτω 'steal' and ψεύδομαι 'lie').

2. *to make financial gain by laying false charges against*: + acc. pers., such a target not necessarily being rich, μὴ συκοφαντησάτωσάν με ὑπερήφανοι 'the overbearing ..' Ps 118.122, πένητα 'a poor man' Pr 22.16; pass., ἀπὸ πλήθους συκοφαντούμενοι κεκράξονται Jb 35.9¶. Cf. συκοφάντης, συκοφαντία: Nestle 1903; MM, s.v.; Walters 184f.

συκοφάντης, ου. m.ʃ

one who engages in συκοφαντέω (**2**): ταπεινώσει ~ην Ps 71.4; Pr 28.16. Cf. συκοφαντέω.

συκοφαντία, ας. f.

extortion: οἶνος ἐκ ~ῶν 'wine obtained through extortion' Am 2.8; λύτρωσαί με ἀπὸ ~ίας ἀνθρώπων Ps 118.134, πένητος 'of the poor' Ec 5.7. Cf. συκοφαντέω.

συκών, ῶνος. m.ʃ *

fig-yard: || κῆπος, ἀμπελών, and ἐλαιών Am 4.9; Je 5.17. Cf. κῆπος.

συλάω: aor.subj.pass. συληθῶ.ʃ

to strip sth *off*: pass., ***o*** gilt images, Ep Je 17. Or: *to carry off unlawfully valuable contents of*, 'plunder, pillage': pass., ***o*** temples, ib. Cf. ἄσυλος: Spicq 3.312-6.

συλλαλέω: aor. συνελάλησα, ptc. ~λαλήσας.

to converse with sbd: + dat. pers., Ex 34.35, Is 7.6; + acc. rei, ῥήματα κατὰ τῆς ψυχῆς μου Je 18.20. Cf. λαλέω: Lee 95f.

συλλαμβάνω: fut. συλλήμψομαι, pass. ~λη(μ)φθήσομαι; aor. act. συνέλαβον, impv.2pl ~λάβετε, ptc. συλλαβών, inf. ~λαβεῖν, subj. ~λάβω, mid. συνελαβόμην, pass. συνελή(μ)φθην, impv.3pl συλλημφθήτωσαν, inf. ~λημφθῆναι, ptc. ~λημφθείς; pf.ptc.act.f. συνειληφυῖα, pass. συνειλημμένος.

1. *to become pregnant*: συλλαβοῦσα ἔτεκεν τὸν Καιν Ge 4.1; εἰσῆλθεν πρὸς Αγαρ καὶ συνέλαβεν '.. and she became pregnant' 16.4, sim. Ho 1.3, 6, 8; συνέλαβον αἱ δύο θυγατέρες Λωτ ἐκ τοῦ πατρὸς αὐτῶν Ge 19.36; τοῦ τεκεῖν 'about to give birth' 1K 4.19. **b**. tr. *to conceive*: ***o*** hum., υἱόν Jd 13.3 B; pass., Ps 50.7 (|| κισσάω). **c**. tr. *to conceive mentally*, 'plot, design': + acc., πόνον 'pain (to others)' Ps 7.15 (|| ὠδίνω, τίκτω), cf. Jas 1.15.

2. *to catch*: ***s*** trap, Am 3.5, Je 5.26 || ἐν παιγίδι 31.44, Ps 9.16 (***o*** foot); + cogn. dat., συλλήψει συλλημφθήσῃ Je 41.3; ***o*** lion, Ez 19.4; metaph., ἐν διαβουλίοις Ps 9.23.

3. *to catch red-handed*: + acc. pers. (adulteress), Nu 5.13; pass., ἐν τοῖς ἔργοις τῶν χειρῶν αὐτοῦ (sinner) Ps 9.17. Cf. ἁλίσκομαι **1**, φωράω.

4. *to apprehend*: so as to take a legal action against: + acc. pers., De 21.19 (parents and their recalcitrant child); so as to harm, 1M 12.48, ζῶντα 14.2.

5. *to capture, conquer*: militarily - ἰσχὺν βουνοῦ ὑψηλοῦ 'the fortress on a high hill' Je 29.17, πόλεις Da 11.15 TH (LXX λαμβάνω); + acc. pers., Jd 7.25.

6. *to take in addition*: + acc., συλλήψεται μεθ' ἑαυτοῦ τὸν γείτονα τὸν πλησίον αὐτοῦ 'he shall bring his nextdoor neighbour along (to meet the quorum)' Ex 12.4.

7. *to take* somewhere with oneself: + acc., Ju 6.10, 1M 5.26.

8. mid. *to come to the aid of*: + dat. pers., ***s*** God, Ge 30.8.

Cf. σύλλημψις, λαμβάνω, κισσάω, κύω, ἔγκυος, γαστήρ.

συλλέγω: fut. συλλέξω; aor. συνέλεξα, impv. σύλλεξον, inf. συλλέξαι, ptc.pass. ~λεγείς; pf.ptc.pass. συνειλεγμένος; plpf.pass.3s συνελέλεκτο.

to collect: abs., Nu 11.8; + acc., συνέλεξαν λίθους καὶ ἐποίησαν βουνόν 'they collected stones and made a cairn' Ge 31.46; ἄρτους Ex 16.4 (|| συνάγω vs. 5), ξύλα Nu 15.32, στάχυς 'corn' De 23.24, δράγματα 'sheaves' Ps 128.7; + dat. com., συλλέγετε ἑαυτοῖς ἄχυρα 'Gather straw for yourselves' Ex 5.11 (|| συνάγω vs. 12); gleanings, Le 19.9, 23.22. **b**. *to put together*, 'compose': + acc., βίβλον 'book' Si prol. II. **c**. mid. *to come together as a united group*: πρός τινα Jd 11.3 A (B: συστρέφομαι), Ju 4.3, 3M 1.21.

Cf. συνάγω, συλλογή.

σύλλημψις, εως. f.ʃ

1. *pregnancy*: || τόκος 'childbirth' and ὠδίνη 'birthpang' Ho 9.11; μήτρα ~εως αἰωνίας 'womb of eternal conception' Je 20.17.

2. *act of catching* (with a trap or by stealth?): Jb 18.10¶, Je 18.22, 41.3.

Cf. συλλαμβάνω, συναγωγή.

συλλογή, ῆς. f.ʃ

act of bringing and keeping together: 1K 17.40. Cf. συλλέγω, συναγωγή.

συλλογίζομαι: fut. ~λογιοῦμαι, pass. ~λογισθήσομαι.

1. *to calculate*: abs., Le 25.50; + acc., τὰ ἔτη 'the years' 25.27.

2. *to consider carefully*: + acc. rei, τὰ ἀρχαῖα 'the past' Is 43.18 (|| μνημονεύω).

3. *to consider as belonging together* with (ἐν): ἐν ἔθνεσιν οὐ συλλογισθήσεται 'he shall not be counted among nations' Nu 23.9.

Cf. συλλογισμός, λογίζομαι.

συλλογισμός, οῦ. m.ʃ

act of counting up: λάβῃς τὸν ~ὸν τῶν υἱῶν Ισραηλ Ex 30.12; ἁμαρτημάτων 'of misdeeds' Wi 4.20. Cf. συλλογίζομαι.

συλλοχάω: aor. συνελόχησα.ʃ *

to get together for a military operation: + acc. pers. (troops), 1M 4.28. Cf. συνάγω.

συλλοχισμός, οῦ. m.ʃ

**list of members associated as a group*, 'muster-roll': 1C 9.1.

συλλυπέομαι: fut. ~πηθήσομαι.ʃ

to share the grief of: + dat. pers., Is 51.19 (|| παρακαλέω); Ps 68.21. Cf. λυπέω.

συλλύω: fut.ptc. ~λύσων; aor.pass. συνελύθην.ʃ

1. *to come between and resolve conflict*: ἀνὰ μέσον αὐτῶν 2K 14.6*L* (B: ἐξαιρέομαι).

2. mid. *to come to a settlement*: abs. 2M 11.14, 13.23; + dat. pers., 1M 13.47.

συμβαίνω: fut. συμβήσομαι, ptc. ~βησόμενος; aor. συνέβην, ptc. συμβάς, subj. ~βῶ, inf. ~βῆναι; pf. συμβέβηκα, ptc. ~βεβηκώς.

1. *to happen, turn out*: + inf., συνέβη, ἐμέ τε ἀποκατασταθῆναι ἐπὶ τὴν ἀρχήν μου .. 'it resulted in my being restored to my office ..' Ge 41.13; συμβήσεται αὐτὸν μαλακισθῆναι 'he might just fall ill' 42.38

2. *to happen, befall*: abs., μὴ γένηται τὸ ῥῆμα καὶ μὴ συμβῇ 'what has been said does not materialise and happen' De 18.22; + dat. pers., πάντα τὰ συμβάντα αὐτοῖς 'all that had happened to them' Ge 42.29; Es 6.13 o' (*L* γίνομαι); *s* sth untoward or unpleasant and + dat. pers., Μήποτε συμβῇ αὐτῷ μαλακία 'I fear that he might fall ill' Ge 42.4, 44.29; συμβῇ ἡμῖν πόλεμος Ex 1.10; 3.16, 24.14; πονηρά 'calamity' Is 3.11, κακά Je 39.24, Si 22.26. Cf. συναντάω **4**, συντελέω **4**, τυγχάνω **3**, ὑπαντάω **3**, and φθάνω **4**.

Cf. γίνομαι, προσπίπτω **2**.

συμβάλλω: aor. συνέβαλον, pass. συνεβλήθην; pf. ptc. συμβεβληκώς, mid. συμβέβλημαι.ʃ

1. *to bring into conflict*, 'pit': τινα πρός τινα Je 50.3.

2. *to get involved in*: ἐν κακίᾳ 2C 25.19.

3. *to compare*: + dat., Si 22.1. Cf. συγκρίνω **1**.

4. intr. *to come to blows, fight*: abs., 1M 4.34; + dat. pers., 2M 8.23, 14.17. Cf. μάχομαι.

5. mid. *to contribute*: + acc., χρυσίον Is 46.6; + dat., Wi 5.8 (|| ὠφελέω).

Cf. συμβολή.

συμβαστάζω: fut.pass. ~ταχθήσομαι.ʃ*

to regard as of comparable value: + dat. and pass., ***o*** σοφία Jb 28.16, 19 (|| ἰσόω). Cf. ἰσόω.

συμβιβάζω: fut. ~βιβάσω, ~βιβῶ; aor. συνεβίβασα, inf. ~βιβάσαι, impv.3s ~βιβασάτω.ʃ

**to teach, instruct*: + acc. pers., De 4.9 (|| διδάσκω vs. 10), Is 40.13 (|| σύμβουλος γίνομαι 'to become adviser'), 14 (|| συμβουλεύω); and + acc. rei [=subject matter of instruction], συμβιβάσω σε ἃ μέλλεις λαλῆσαι 'I shall instruct you what you are going to speak' Ex 4.12; σε ἃ ποιήσετε 4.15; αὐτοὺς τὰ προστάγματα τοῦ θεοῦ καὶ τὸν νόμον αὐτοῦ 18.16; τοὺς υἱοὺς Ισραηλ πάντα τὰ νόμιμα Le 10.11; σὲ σύνεσιν Da 9.22 TH (|| LXX ὑποδείκνυμι); + indir. question, Jd 13.8 B (A: φωτίζω); + ἕν τινι– σε ἐν ὁδῷ ταύτῃ Ps 31.8 (|| συνετίζω). Cf. διδάσκω, προβιβάζω, συνετίζω: Renehan 1.183 s.v. συμβίβασις.

συμβιόω: fut. ~βιώσομαι.ʃ

to live with: + dat. pers., Si 13.5.

Cf. συμβίωσις, ~βιωτής, βιόω, ζάω.

συμβίωσις, εως. f.ʃ

close, intimate company or *association*: θεοῦ 'with God' Wi 8.3; with Wisdom, 8.9, 16. Cf. συμβιόω: Poland. Del. Si 31.22 v.l.

συμβιωτής, οῦ. m.

one who lives with sbd else: + gen., royal companion, Bel 2.

σύμβλημα, ατος. n.ʃ *

a joint of metal- or woodwork: Is 41.7. Cf. σύμβλησις.

σύμβλησις, εως. f.ʃ*

place at which two things are joined together, 'joint': architectural t.t., Ex 26.24. Cf. σύμβλημα, συμβολή.

συμβοηθός, ον.ʃ *

assisting: μετ' αὐτοῦ 3K 21.16. Cf. βοηθός.

συμβολή, ῆς. f.

1. *that which joins and couples* two adjacent things: Ex 26.4. Cf. σύμβλησις.

2. *joint meal*: μνημόσυνον ἔναντι κυρίου 'commemorative' Is 23.18 (μ. in app.); Pr 23.20.

3. *expenses incurred and their payment*: Si 18.32.

Cf. συμβάλλω.

συμβολοκοπέω: aor.subj. ~πήσω.ʃ *

to be given to feasting: De 21.20; μετ' αὐτῆς ἐν οἴνῳ Si 9.9; ἐκ δανεισμοῦ 'with borrowed money' 18.33.

σύμβολον, ου. n.

that which signifies or *indicates sth*, 'token': used in divination, ἐν ~οις ἐπηρώτων 'they inquired by means of tokens' Ho 4.12 (*pace* Zgl συμβούλοις), cf. Muraoka 1983.45; ~α τῆς εὐφροσύνης 'signs of happiness' Wi 2.9. Cf. σημεῖον.

συμβόσκω: fut.pass. ~βοσκηθήσομαι.ʃ*

pass. intr. *to feed together*: λύκος μετὰ ἀρνός 'a wolf with a lamb' Is 11.6. Cf. βόσκω.

συμβουλευτής, οῦ.ʃ

adviser: of a king, 1E 8.11.

Cf. συμβουλεύω, σύμβουλος, βουλευτής.

συμβουλεύω: fut. ~λεύσω; aor. συνεβούλευσα, opt. ~λεύσαιμι, mid. συνεβουλευσάμην; pf. ~βεβούλευκα, mid. ~βεβούλευμαι.

1. *to advise* a course of action: + dat. pers., συμβουλεύσω σοι, τί ποιήσει ὁ λαὸς οὗτος Nu 24.14; Ex 18.19; + cogn. acc., συμβουλίαν 3K 1.12; + a ὅπως-clause, 4M 1.1; + inf., 8.5. **b**. mid. *to seek advice*: πρός τινα Is 40.14 (‖ συμβιβάζω 'to instruct'); συβεβουλεύσαντο ἕκαστος πρὸς τὸν πλησίον αὐτοῦ 'they consulted one another' Je 43.16; μετά τινος Si 8.17; + dat. pers., Jb 26.3; = act., with the advice indicated by λέγων and dir. speech, Jo 15.18.

2. *to agree after consultation*: + inf., Da 6.7 TH.

Cf. βούλομαι, βουλή, συμβουλευτής, σύμβουλος, συμβουλία.

συμβουλία, ας. f.

advice: cogn. acc. of συμβουλεύω 3K 1.12; παρὰ φρονίμου To 4.18; ‖ γνώμη Si 6.23. Cf. συμβουλεύω, βουλή.

συμβούλιον, ου. n.ʃ

official body where deliberation takes place and decisions are taken: 4M 17.17. Cf. βουλή **1c**.

σύμβουλος, ου. m.

adviser, counsellor: ‖ κριτής Is 1.26; θαυμαστὸν ~ον καὶ σοφὸν ἀρχιτέκτονα .. 3.3; king's, σοφοὶ ~οι τοῦ βασιλέως 19.11; God's, σ. αὐτοῦ (= κυρίου), ὃς συμβιβᾷ αὐτόν '.., who instructs Him' 40.13; *s* Moses, 4M 9.2; commercial consultant, Ez 27.27; mother for her boy, 2M 7.25. Cf. (συμ)βουλευτής.

συμβραβεύω: aor. συνεβράβευσα.ʃ *

to act as co-judge or *-assessor with*: + dat. pers., 1E 9.14. Cf. βραβεύω.

συμμαχέω: fut. ~μαχήσω; aor.inf. ~μαχῆσαι.

to act as military ally: 1M 8.25; + dat. pers., Jo 1.14; 1M 11.43' + inf. indicating the nature of the fight, τὸ μὴ καμφθῆναι τῇ κακοηθείᾳ 'not to bow to malice' 4M 3.4.

συμμαχία, ας. f.

1. military *ally*: sg.coll., Is 16.4 (‖ ἄρχων), Ju 7.1, 1M 11.60.

2. *auxiliary troops*: sg.coll., Ju 3.6.

3. military *alliance*: στῆσαι αὐτοῖς φιλίαν καὶ ~αν 'to establish with them friendship ..' 1M 8.17 (‖ μετά τινος vs. 20, πρός τινα 14.24), μνημόσυνον εἰρήνης καὶ ~ας 'a memorial of peace ..' 8.22; cooperation in general, τῶν θεῶν 3M 3.14.

σύμμαχος, ον.

allied militarily: *s* φίλος 1M 8.31; + dat. pers., 2M 10.16; subst.m. φίλος καὶ σ. 1M 10.16. Cf. συμμαχία.

συμμείγνυμι. ⇒ συμμίγνυμι.

σύμμεικτος, ον. On the spelling, see Walters 31.

commingled, lacking uniformity: subst., ὁ ~ς σου 'your mixed crowd' Na 3.17, ἀπὸ πλήθους τοῦ ~ου σου 'from your large variety of trading partners' Ez 27.16; irregular troops, τοὺς μαχητὰς αὐτῶν καὶ .. τὸν ~ον τὸν ἐν μέσῳ αὐτῆς Je 27.37; :: ὁ λαός 'the regular army' 32.6. Cf. μίσγω, συμμίγνυμι, συναναμίγνυμι.

συμμετέχω: aor.ptc. ~μετασχών.ʃ

to have a share of experiencing together: + gen. rei, δυσπετημάτων 'misfortunes' 2M 5.20 (‖ κοινωνέω). Cf. κοινωνέω, μετέχω.

συμμετρία, ας. f.ʃ

right measure: PSol 5.16. Cf. μέτρον.

σύμμετρος, ον.ʃ

of generous proportions and size: *s* οἶκος Je 22.14. Cf. μέγας.

συμμιαίνω: aor.pass. συνεμιάνθην.ʃ

to defile together with: + dat., τοῖς νεκροῖς 'with the dead' Ba 2.11. Cf. μιαίνω.

συμμιγής, ές.ʃ

mixed together: συμμιγεῖς ἔσονται ἐν σπέρματι ἀνθρώπων 'will be mixed together into human seed' Da TH 2.43; .. εἰς γένεσιν ἀνθρώπων LXX ib. Cf. συμμίγνυμι.

συμμίγνυμι: fut. ~μιγήσομαι; aor. συνέμι/ειξα, subj. ~μείξω, ptc. ~μείξας; pf.ptc.pass. ~μεμιγμένος.

1. *to mix together with*: + dat., Da 2.41 LXX (TH ἀναμίγνυμι). **b**. through marriage: Da 11.6 TH.

2. *to come into contact*: + dat. pers., ἀλλήλοις Ex 14.20; to join battle, 2M 15.26. **b**. *to meet personally*: + dat. pers., 2M 3.7.

3. intr. *to attach oneself to* for joint action: + dat. pers., 2M 13.3. **b**. abs. *to form* fighting *units*: 2M 15.20. **c**. mid. *to become deeply involved in*: + dat., ^μέθη^ 'intoxication' Pr 20.1.

Cf. σύμμικτος, συμμιγής, συναναμίγνυμι, συμμίσγω.

σύμμικτος: ⇒ σύμμεικτος.

σύμμιξις, εως. f.ʃ

commingling: υἱὸς ~εως 'child of mixed marriage' 4K 14.14 ‖ 2C 25.24. Cf. συμμίσγω: Caird 1969.37.

συμμίσγω.ʃ

1. *to meet for conversation*: 1M 11.22.

2. *to enter close relationship with*: + dat. pers., 2M 14.14.

3. *to engage in battle with*: + dat. pers., 2M 14.16.

Cf. συμμίγνυμι.

συμμισοπονηρέω.ʃ*

to feel common hatred of what is bad: ὑπέρ τινος 2M 4.36.

συμμολύνω: aor.subj.pass. ~μολυνθῶ.ʃ

to defile together with sbd else: pass., *o* hum., Da LXX 1.8 (‖ ἀλισγέω). Cf. μολύνω.

συμπάθεια, ας. f.

compassion aroused by sbd else's distress and misery: 4M 6.13; mothers towards her children, πρὸς τὰ τέκνα 14.17, ‖ τέκνων 14.20, εἴς τινα 15.7; triggered by φιλοτεκνία 15.11. Cf. συμπαθής, συμπαθέω, ὁμοιοπαθής: Michaelis, *TDNT* 5.935.

συμπαθέω.ʃ
to display kind and thoughtful disposition towards: + dat. pers., *s* God, 4M 5.25. Cf. συμπαθής: Spicq 3.319f. Del. 4M 13.23 v.l.

συμπαθής, ές.ʃ
unanimously or *mutually felt*: *s* brotherhood, 4M 13.23a; + dat. pers., 15.4. Cf. συμπάθεια.

συμπαίζω: aor.impv. ~παιξον.ʃ
to engage in relaxed and lively activities with: + dat. pers. (father with child), Si 30.9. Cf. παίζω.

συμπαραγίνομαι: aor. ~εγενόμην.ʃ
to come together as ally: μετά τινος Ps 82.9.

συμπαραλαμβάνω: aor.act.ptc. ~λαβών, subj.pass. ~λημφθῶ.ʃ
to take along together: + acc. pers. 3M 1.1; συμπαραλαβόντες ἅμα καὶ τὰς τρεῖς ἀδελφὰς αὐτῶν 'having taken their three sisters along at the same time' Jb 1.4; μήποτε συμπαραλημφθῇς 'so that you will not be taken along together (to destruction)' Ge 19.17; PSol 13.5. Cf. (παρα)λαμβάνω.

συμπαραμένω: fut. ~μενῶ.ʃ
to endure or *last as long as*: + dat., τῷ ἡλίῳ Ps 71.5. Cf. παραμένω.

συμπάρειμι.ʃ
to be present together with sbd: + dat. pers., To 12.12 𝔊[I], Pr 8.27, Wi 9.10. Cf. I πάρειμι **1**.

συμπαρίστημι: fut.mid. ~παραστήσομαι.ʃ
to stand beside in support of: + dat. pers., μοι ἐπὶ ἐργαζομένους τὴν ἀνομίαν Ps 93.16. Cf. παρίστημι.

σύμπας, ~ασα, ~αν.
the whole of: articular but with no noun head, ἡ σύμπασα (sc. γῆ mentioned earlier) καὶ πάντες οἱ κατοικοῦντες ἐν αὐτῇ Na 1.5; f. and γῆ or οἰκουμένη understood (so Soph. *Frg*. 411) – Διαπορευθεὶς τὴν ὑπ' οὐρανὸν καὶ ἐμπεριπατήσας τὴν ~σαν πάρειμι 'I am here, after having gone through the world under the sky and journeyed through the entire world' Jb 2.2, ἡ Ἑλλὰς καὶ ἡ ~σα 'Greece and the whole world' Ez 27.13; Is 11.9; n.pl. 'everything'– τὰ ~τα ματαιότης 'everything is vanity' Ps 38.6; including animate entities, χρηστὸς κύριος τοῖς ~σιν 'the Lord is kind to all' 144.9. **b**. articular and foll. by a noun head, κατὰ τὸν σύμπαντα κόσμον 'throughout the world' 2M 3.12, τὸ σύμπαν ἡμῶν γένος 'our entire nation' 14.8. Cf. ἅπας, πᾶς, ὅλος: Schmidt 4.547f., 549f.

συμπατέω: fut. ~πατήσω, pass. ~πατηθήσομαι; aor. συνεπάτησα, pass.impv. συμπατήθητι.
to tread together: + acc., 4K 7.17 (*L* κατα~), 20; ποσίν 'with feet' Da 7.7, 19 TH; pass., συμπατήθητι ἐν ἀχύροις 'Be trampled in straw' Na 3.14. Cf. πατέω.

συμπείθω: aor. συνέπεισα.ʃ
to win by persuasion: abs., 2M 13.26; + τινα εἰς τὸ inf., 3M 7.3. Cf. πείθω.

συμπεραίνω: aor. συνεπέρανα.ʃ
to destroy completely: + acc. pers. λαοὺς πολλούς Hb 2.10. Cf. ἀφανίζω.

συμπεριλαμβάνω: aor.subj.mid. ~λήμψωμαι.ʃ
to place together in: ἀναβολῇ '(to embrace in) a mantle' Ez 5.3.

συμπεριφέρομαι: fut.inf. ~ενεχθήσεσθαι; aor.ptc. pass. ~ενεχθείς.ʃ
1. *to be understanding and accommodating in attitude*: *s* husband and wife, + dat. pers., ἑαυτοῖς Si 25.1; 2M 9.27, + dat. rei, τῇ τούτων ἀνοίᾳ 'their folly' 3M 3.20.
2. *to go about and busy oneself with*: + dat., τῷ ἑαουτοῦ οἴκῳ Pr 11.29; ἐν τῇ ταύτης φιλίᾳ 'her friendship' 5.19.

συμπίνω: aor.inf. ~πιεῖν.ʃ
to drink together with: at a party, + dat. pers., Es 7.1 o'. Cf. πίνω, συμπόσιον, συμπότης.

συμπίπτω: fut. ~πεσοῦμαι; aor. συνέπεσον, impv. σύμπεσον; pf. συμπέπτωκα.
1. *to become despondent*: *s* pers., συνέπεσεν τῷ προσώπῳ Ge 4.5 ‖ *s* πρόσωπον 4.6, Ju 6.9, 1K 1.18; καρδία .. ἐπ' αὐτόν '.. over him' 17.32; hum., τῇ καρδίᾳ ἀπὸ τῆς μερίμνης 'out of worry' 1M 6.10.
2. *to confront* with hostile intention: ἄνθρωπος πρὸς ἄνθρωπον Is 3.5.
3. *to collapse*: *s* ἡ Ιουδαία Is 3.8, πάντα τὰ ἔνδοξα 'all the glorious things' 64.11, θεμέλια 'foundations' Ez 30.4.
4. *to fall slaughtered together* with: *s* οἱ ἁδροί 'the fattened, stout (animals)' Is 34.7.
5. *to arrive at same place*, 'to converge': *s* troops, 2K 5.18.
Cf. πίπτω.

συμπλεκτός, ή, όν.ʃ *
plaited: *s* collar of garment, Ex 36.31. Cf. συμπλέκω.

συμπλέκω: fut.pass. ~πλακήσομαι; aor.pass. συνεπλάκην; pf.pass. συμπέπλεγμαι, ptc.pass. ~πεπλεγμένος.
1. *to embrace* (μετά τινος): μετὰ πόρνης 'a harlot' Ho 4.14. Cf. περιλαμβάνω **1**.
2. *to mix up*: pass. συμπλακήσονται '(the chariots) will get jammed into one another' Na 2.5.
3. *to join*: pass. συμπλακήσεται ἡ χεὶρ αὐτοῦ πρὸς χεῖρα τοῦ πλησίον αὐτοῦ 'his hand will be joined to the hand of his neighbour' Zc 14.13; τὰ νεῦρα αὐτοῦ συμπέπλεκται 'its [= an animal's] nerves are tightly packed' Jb 40.17; metaph., *o* transgressions, La 1.14; Pr 20.3.

4. *to plait*: ***o*** tassles, fringe (κροσσός), Ex 28.22, 36.22; τρίχωμα 'hair' Ez 24.17.
5. *to interweave*: pass. εἰς ἄλληλα συμπεπλεγμένον καθ' ἑαυτό 'alternately interwoven by itself' Ex 36.11.
6. fig. *to put components together, produce and effect*: ἀδικίαν αἱ χεῖρες ὑμῶν συμπλέκουσιν Ps 57.3.
Cf. συμπλεκτός, (περι)πλέκω and συμφύρω.

συμπλήρωσις, εως. f.ʃ
1. *complete elapse* of a period of time: ἐτῶν ἑβδομήκοντα 'of 70 years' 1E 1.55, 2C 36.21 (*L* simp.). Cf. ἀναπληρόω **5**.
2. *act of reaching the full extent of* and subsequent suspension of: ἐρημώσεως Ιηρουσαλημ 'the desolation of J.' Da 9.2 TH (LXX: ἀναπλήρωσις).
Cf. ἀναπλήρωσις.

συμπλοκή, ῆς. f.ʃ
close engagement: with idolatrous practices, 3K 16.28[d]. Cf. συμπλέκω.

συμποδίζω:fut. ~ποδιῶ, pass. ~ποδισθήσομαι; aor. συνεπόδισα, pass. ~εποδίσθην, ptc. ~ποδίσας.
to tie the feet of: ***o*** a human sacrifice, Ge 22.9; fig. of a parent accompanying a toddler, as it begins to learn to walk, Ho 11.3; in order to stop a child from walking off, Zc 13.3 (see Muraoka 1991.211f. and Harl 1992.62f, 65); in order to immobilise, Ps 17.40, 19.9, + ἐπιδέω To 8.3𝔊[II], Da 3.20 LXX (TH: πεδάω).

συμποιέω.ʃ
to work jointly with: + dat. pers.,1E 6.27. Cf. ποιέω.

συμπολεμέω: aor. συνεπολέμησα.ʃ
to fight together on the side of: ***s*** God, + dat. pers., Jo 10.14, 42. Cf. πολεμέω. Del. Wi 5.20 v.l.

συμπονέω.ʃ
to toil with: + dat., φίλῳ Si 37.5. Cf. πονέω.

συμπορεύομαι: fut. ~πορεύσομαι; aor. συνεπορεύθην, ptc. ~πορευθείς, impv. ~πορεύθητι, 3s ~πορευθήτω.
to journey together: abs. De 31.11; μετά τινος, Ge 13.5, Ex 33.16, Nu 16.25, De 31.8; on a military expedition, Da 11.6 LXX; + dat. pers., 1E 8.10; πρὸς ἀλλήλους Jb 1.4. Cf. πορεύομαι, συνέρχομαι.

συμπορπάω: pf.ptc.pass. ~πεπορπημένος.ʃ *
to fasten together: pass. and ***o*** stone, Ex 36.13.

συμποσία, ας. f.
banquet: royal, 3M 5.15. Cf. συμπόσιον, πότος.

συμπόσιον, ου. n.
drinking-party: οἴνου Si 34.31, 49.1. Cf. συμπίνω, συμποσία.

συμπότης, ου. m.ʃ
drinking-mate: + ἑταῖρος 3M 2.25. Cf. συμπίνω.

συμπραγματεύομαι.ʃ
to be jointly involved in business: 3M 3.10. Cf. πραγματεύομαι.

συμπροπέμπω: aor.inf. ~πέμψαι.ʃ
to go part of the way together, escorting a departing guest or traveller: + acc. pers., ἐνετείλατο Φαραω ἀνδράσιν περὶ Αβραμ συμπροπέμψαι αὐτὸν .. Ge 12.20; Αβρααμ δὲ συνεπορεύετο μετ' αὐτῶν συμπροπέμπων αὐτούς 18.16. It is not certain that *joining* others in escort is meant at Ge 18.16. Cf. ἐξαποστέλλω **6**, πέμπω, and συμπορεύομαι.

συμπρόσειμι: fut. ~έσομαι.ʃ *
to be present together with: + dat. pers., ***s*** θρόνος Ps 93.20; Ec 8.15.

συμπροσπλέκομαι: fut. ~πλακήσομαι.ʃ *
to get entangled in a battle: Da 11.10 TH.

σύμπτωμα, ατος. n.ʃ
1. *chance happening*: 1K 6.9, 20.26.
2. *mishap, accident*: Ps 90.6, Pr 27.9.

συμφερόντως. adv.ʃ
profitably: μανθάνω 'to learn' 4M 1.17. Cf. συμφέρω.

συμφέρω.
to be useful, beneficial: + dat., συμφέροντα αὐτοῖς 'things useful to them' De 23.6; Je 33.14 (‖ βελτίων); τὸ συμφέρον 'benefit, advantage' 2M 11.15. Cf. ἀγαθός, καλός, σύμφορος, συμφερόντως, ὠφελέω: Schmidt 4.162-7.

συμφεύγω: aor. συνέφυγον, ptc. ~φυγών.
to take refuge: from danger, 1M 10.84, 2M 10.18. Cf. φεύγω.

συμφλέγω.ʃ
to burn to cinders: + acc., Is 42.25.

συμφλογίζω: aor.pass. συνεφλογίσθην.ʃ *
to burn together: pass., ***o*** hum. 2M 6.11. Cf. κατακαίω, φλογίζω.

συμφορά, ᾶς. f.
calamitous mishap: Es E 5, 2M 6.12; torture, 9.6. Cf. ἀτυχία, δυσημερία.

συμφοράζω: fut. ~ράσω.ʃ*
to bewail: ἕτερος πρὸς τὸν ἕτερον 'one another' Is 13.8. Cf. θρηνέω.

σύμφορος, ον.ʃ
beneficial: + dat. pers., 2M 4.5. Cf. συμφέρω, ἀσύμφορος.

συμφράσσω: fut. ~φράξω.ʃ
to fence in all round: Is 27.12. Cf. φράσσω.

συμφρονέω.ʃ
to conspire: 3M 3.2. Cf. ἐπισυνίστημι **II**.

συμφρύγω: aor.pass. συνεφρύγην.ʃ
to burn or *parch up*: metaph., ***s*** yearning for water, + acc. pers., 4M 3.11; pass., ***o*** hum. bones, Ps 101.4. Cf. φρύγω, φρύγιον.

συμφύρω ʃ
mid. *to have frequent dealings*, 'associate, mix': + μετά – μετὰ τῶν πορνῶν συνεφύροντο 'they associated with harlots' Ho 4.14 (‖ συμπλέκω); προ-

σπορευόμενον ἀνδρὶ ἁμαρτωλῷ καὶ συμφυρόμενον ἐν ταῖς ἁμαρτίαις αὐτοῦ 'goes to a sinner and gets involved in his sins' Si 12.14; ref. to incest, PSol 8.9. Cf. συναναμίγνυμι, συναναστρέφω, συναναφύρω.

σύμφυτος, ον.ʃ

1. *thickly wooded*: *s* βουνοί Am 9.13; δρυμός 'thicket' Zc 11.2.

2. *innate, born with*: *s* κακοήθεια 'malice' 3M 3.22.

Cf. φυτεύω: Spicq 2.321-3.

συμφύω: pf.ptc. ~πεφυκώς.ʃ

to grow together with: + dat., Wi 13.13. Cf. φύω.

συμφωνέω: aor. συνεφώνησα.ʃ

1. *to indicate consent*: + inf., τοῦ μὴ λαβεῖν ἀργύριον 4K 12.9; πρός τινα, Is 7.2; πρός τι 4M 14.6. Cf. νεύω.

*2. *to converge* (Wevers ad Ge 14.3 and cf. אזדמנו לעמק .. 1QapGen 21.25): *s* military commanders, ἐπὶ τὴν φάραγγα 'on to the valley' Ge 14.3 (or: pregnantly, 'agreed [to come] to the valley,' cf. Mortari ad loc.). Cf. ἐξεκλησιάζω **2**.

Cf. συνέρχομαι: Spicq 3.324-8.

συμφωνία, ας.ʃ f.

1. *concord*: of attitude and outlook, περὶ τῆς εὐσεβείας 'for the sake of piety' 4M 14.3.

2. some kind of musical instrument: Da 3.5 LXX.

σύμφωνος, ον.ʃ

consonant, concordant: τινι Ec 7.14; + gen., *s* hum., νόμου 4M 7.7; brothers in harmony, 14.7. Cf. συμφωνία, συμφώνως.

συμφώνως. adv.ʃ

jointly in harmony: to move, 4M 14.6. Cf. σύμφωνος, ὁμοθυμαδόν.

συμψάω: aor.pass. συνεψήσθην, ptc. ~ψησθείς, subj. ~ψησθῶ.ʃ

to drag away for destruction: pass. and *o* corpse, Je 22.19, sheep 29.21; fig., joy 31.33.

σύν. Prep. with dat, far less common than μετά + gen. (Johannessohn, *Präp.*, 202).

1. *in concert with, jointly with*: πενθήσει ἡ γῆ σὺν τοῖς κατοικοῦσιν αὐτήν 'the earth will mourn together with its inhabitants' Ho 4.3, μεγαλύνατε τὸν κύριον σ. ἐμοί 'Glorify ..' Ps 33.4.

2. *along with, including*: πᾶσα ἡ ἐπίσκεψις τῶν παρεμβολῶν σ. ταῖς δυνάμεσιν αὐτῶν 'the total of the people in the encampments together with their troops' Nu 2.32; ἐξαρῶ πόλιν σ. τοῖς κατοικοῦσιν αὐτήν 'I shall eradicate a city along with its inhabitants' Am 6.8, sim. Mi 7.13; συναχθήσεται Ιακωβ σ. πᾶσιν 'Jacob will be gathered together with all others' 2.12; δίδωμί σε εἰς μετοικίαν σ. πᾶσι τοῖς φίλοις σου '.. into exile ..' Je 20.4; τὴν γῆν σ. τῷ πληρώματι αὐτῆς Ez 30.12 v.l. (for καὶ); νεανίσκος σ. παρθένῳ 'a laddie with a lassie' De 32.25 (|| μετά); ὀσφραίνεται πολέμου σ. ἅλματι καὶ κραυγῇ 'smells a war along with (a sound of horses?) hopping about and a clamour' Jb 39.25; ἐπέγνωσαν προπεπτωκότα Νικάνορα σ. πανοπλίᾳ 'they recognised N., fallen in full armour' 2M 15.28; τὸ πραχθὲν σ. τῷ δράσαντι κολασθήσεται 'the deed shall be punished along with the perpetrator' Wi 14.10. **b.** at the end of multiple terms: δῶρα .. καὶ πᾶν χρυσίον καὶ ἀργύριον .. σ. τῷ δεδωρημένῳ .. 'gifts .. along with that which had been donated ..' 1E 8.13, ἐν χρυσίῳ καὶ ἐν ἀργυρίῳ ἐν δόσεσιν <u>μεθ</u>' ἵππων καὶ κτηνῶν σ. τοῖς ἄλλοις '.. with gifts along with horses and cattle together with the other things' 2.6. **c.** with a reinforcing καί: σὺν καὶ τοῖς λοιποῖς συνδούλοις 2E 4.7; + τε - σύν τε τούτοις 'on top of that' 3M 1.22.

3. *by involving and making use of*: ἐξάξω σ. δυνάμει μου τὸν λαόν μου .. σ. ἐκδικήσει μεγάλῃ 'I shall lead my people out with my army .. meting out a great punishment at the same time' Ex 7.4.

4. *accompanied by*, indicating a trait, or an accompanying action which characterises an action: σ. ἐξηγορίᾳ 'with a confession' Jb 33.26; ἡγήσεται ὁ θεὸς Ισραηλ <u>μετ</u>' εὐφροσύνης <u>τῷ</u> φωτὶ τῆς δόξης αὐτοῦ <u>σὺν</u> ἐλεημοσύνῃ καὶ δικαιοσύνῃ '.. will guide Is. with joy, with the light .. with mercy and justice' Ba 5.9, cf. s.v. μετά **I 2**. ***b.** *carrying with oneself*: σ. ταῖς ἐπιστολαῖς 2C 30.6.

*5. *in spite of*, a Hebraism [= עִם]: σ. τούτοις 'despite these circumstances' Ne 5.18.

*6, marker of a direct (accusative) object, calqued on Heb. אֵת: εἶδον σὺν πάντα Ec 1.14. **b.** once + gen.: σὺν τοῦ ἀνδρός Ec 9.15.

Cf. ἅμα, μετά: Johannessohn, *Präp.* 202-16.

συναγελάζομαι.ʃ

to herd together: *s* hum., 4M 18.23. Cf. συνάγω.

σύναγμα, ατος. n.ʃ

what has been collected and brought together: Ec 12.11. Cf. συναγωγή.

συνάγω: fut. ~άξω, pass. ~αχθήσομαι; aor. ~ήγαγον, ~ῆξα, subj. ~αγάγω, impv. ~άγαγε, inf. ~αγαγεῖν, pass. ~ήχθην, subj. ~αχθῶ, ptc. ~αχθείς, inf. ~αχθῆναι, impv. ~άχθητι; pf. συναγείοχα, pass.3s ~ῆκται, ptc. ~ηγμένος.

1. *to bring together*: *o* people, ἐπὶ τὸ αὐτὸ 'together' Ho 1.11; for public meeting, γερουσίαν τῶν υἱῶν Ισραηλ Ex 4.29, συναγωγὴν υἱῶν Ισραηλ Nu 8.9; πρεσβυτέρους Jl 1.14, for feast Ge 29.22; Jl 2.16*bis*; πάντα τὰ ἔθνη 3.2; for a military campaign, πάντα τὸν λαὸν αὐτοῦ Nu 21.23; of exiles (αἰχμαλωσία), Hb 1.9, τὴν διασπορὰν Ισραηλ PSol 8.28, cf. Zc 2.6; cattle to a secure place, Ex 9.19, ἔνδον εἰς τὴν οἰκίαν σου De 22.2; timber, 19.5; w. hostile

intent, εἰς αὐτοὺς κακά 32.23, ὡς δράγματα ἅλωνος 'like sheaves of a threshing-floor' Mi 4.12; 5.7, cf. Th 221 ἐπιχειρῆσαι τῷ κατ' αὐτῶν πολέμῳ; ἐπί τινα, Ho 10.10; συνήχθη ἀτιμία ἐπὶ τὴν δόξαν σου 'dishonour has collected on your glory' Hb 2.16; flock (ποίμνια) Ge 29.3, cattle (κτήνη) 29.7; of harvesting, ***o***. γενήματα 'crops' Ex 23.10, Le 25.20; καρπόν Le 25.3, καλάμην ἐν ἀμήτῳ 'straw in harvest' Mi 7.1, καλάμην εἰς ἄχυρα 'stalk to get straw from' Ex 5.12; ἀμητὸν ἑστηκότα 'standing crop' Is 17.5; ἐν ταῖς σαγήναις αὐτοῦ 'with his drag-nets' Hb 1.15; an obj. understood, οἱ συνάγοντες 'the harvesters' Is 62.9; ***o*** food Ge 6.21 (πρὸς σεαυτόν), 41.35 (βρώματα .. σῖτος), Ex 16.16 (|| συλλέγω); silver (ἀργύριον) Ge 47.14; wealth (ἰσχύς), Zc 14.14, πλοῦτος Pr 28.8; || σφραγίζω De 32.34; λύπας 'griefs' Pr 10.10. **b.** ***o*** wages: μισθούς Hg 1.6*bis*; ἐκ μισθωμάτων πορνείας συνήγαγε 'she brought together earnings of whoredom' Mi 1.7; pass. and ***o*** merchandise and profts, 'to hoard' Is 23.18; effort, "unanimous outcry" 3M 1.28. **c.** pass. with intransitive force, *to come together, assemble*: ***s*** hum., Συνάχθητε ἐπὶ τὸ ὄρος Σαμαρείας Am 3.9; Mi 2.12; 5.7; || ἀθροίζομαι Ge 49.1; || συναθροίζομαι Jl 3.11; || συνδέομαι Zp 2.1 +; πρός τινα Je 28.44; with hostile intent, συναχθέντες ἐπ' ἐμὲ συγκόψουσίν με 'they will gang up against me and cut me down' Ge 34.30, ἐπὶ τὸ αὐτὸ κατὰ τοῦ κυρίου 'together against the Lord' Ps 2.2; an army, Is 29.7, || μάχομαι 28.20; commander with his troops, Da 11.40 TH; water, Συναχθήτω τὸ ὕδωρ .. εἰς συναγωγὴν μίαν Ge 1.9. **d.** pass. *to join one's ancestors on one's death*: pregnantly, εἰς τὸν τάφον σου '(to be buried) in your grave' 4K 22.20. **e.** *to hold a funeral for* by gathering the bones of the fallen scattered on the ground: + acc. hum., Ez 29.5 (pass.), Je 32.19 v.l. (|| κόπτομαι).

*__2__. *to invite, receive* (guest): ***o*** one in need of care, τὴν συντετριμμένην 'the bruised' (|| εἰσδέχομαι) Mi 4.6; Zp 3.18, traveller Jd 19.15, a semantic development most likely infl. by MH *hiḵnis* (= Late BH *kānas* 'to gather' = BH *'āsaf*, and cf. Ar. *knaš*), and cp. De 22.2 συνάξεις αὐτὸν ἔνδον εἰς τὴν οἰκίαν σου, and Jd 19.15, 18, 2K 11.27 (*L* λαμβάνω; cf. MH הַכְנָסַת כַּלָּה 'wedding ceremony'), Mt 25.35, 38, 43. Cf. MM, s.v., where the example quoted from *OGIS* 130.5 does not appear to be of the same usage.

Cf. subs., συγκομίζω, συστρέφω, συλλέγω, ~λοχάω, συναθροίζω, ἀθροίζω, συναγελάζομαι.

συναγωγή, ῆς. f.

1. *assemblage* or *collection of large size*: of people, Ex 38.22; Ob 13 (|| λαοί); δέσμιοι τῆς ~ῆς Zc 9.12; ~ὰς ἐθνῶν Ge 28.3, Zp 3.8, ἐθνῶν πολλῶν Ez 26.7; υἱῶν Ισραηλ Ex 12.3 +, πᾶν τὸ πλῆθος ~ῆς υἱῶν Ισρ. 12.6; σ. Ισραηλ 12.19; τῆς πόλεως Su 28 LXX; θεῶν Ps 81.1; of water Ge 1.9, Le 11.36, Is 19.6; of troops, Ez 32.22 (|| δύναμις vs. 23, ἰσχύς vs. 26); of stones, Jb 8.17; of bees, Jd 14.8 B (A: συστροφή).

2. *act of assembling, bringing together*: of harvesting, τῶν ἔργων σου ἐκ τοῦ ἀγροῦ σου Ex 23.16; ἑορτὴ ~ῆς 34.22; χρημάτων 'of possessions' Si 34.3.

Cf. ἀγέλη, ἐκκλησία, ἐπισυναγωγή, συνάγω, σύναγμα, σύνοδος, σύστημα, ἄθροισμα, ὄχλος, πλῆθος: Trench 1-6; Katz, *TDNT* 5.584f., Schrage ib. 7.802-5; Harl 2001.871f.

συνᾴδω.ʃ

to express mutual agreement: ὅπως συνᾴδωσιν ὡς συνᾴδοντες τῇ καρδίᾳ αὐτῶν Ho 7.2.

συναθροίζω: fut. ~αθροίσω, pass. ~αθροισθήσομαι; aor. ~ήθροισα, impv. ~άθροισον, ptc. ~αθροίσας, pass. ~ηθροίσθην, ptc. ~αθροισθείς, inf. ~αθροισθῆναι; pf.ptc.pass. ~ηθροισμένος; plpf.mid./pass.3s ~ήθροιστο.

1. intr. (pass.) *to come together, assemble*: συναθροισθήσονται δύο καὶ τρεῖς πόλεις εἰς πόλιν μίαν 'inhabitants of two or three cities shall come together to one city' Am 4.8; || συνάγω Jl 3.11; w. hostile intent, ἐπί τινα 'against sbd' 3K 11.14.

2. tr. *to bring together*: + acc., πᾶσαν συναγωγὴν υἱῶν Ισραηλ Ex 35.1; pass. πᾶσα ἡ συναγωγή σου ἡ συνηθροισμένη πρὸς τὸν θεόν Nu 16.11; || συνάγω 2M 10.24; ***o*** troops, Jd 12.4 A (B: συστρέφω).

Cf. συνάγω, ἀθροίζω.

συναινέω: aor.ptc.~νέσας.ʃ

to express agreement with that which has been said by sbd else: abs., 3M 7.12; || παραδέχομαι 5.21. **b.** *to consent to a request made by* sbd: τινι 3M 6.41.

Cf. ὁμοιόω **3**, ὁμολογέω **4**, προσδέχομαι **3**, συνᾴδω, συνευδοκέω, συνθέλω, συντίθημι.

συνακολουθέω.ʃ

to move together with: abs., 2M 2.6; + dat. pers., 2.4. Cf. ἀκολουθέω, συνέπομαι.

συναλγέω: fut. ~αλγήσω.ʃ

to share pain with: + dat. pers., Si 37.12. Cf. ἀλγέω.

συνάλλαγμα, τος. n.

1. pl., *dealings, transactions*: Is 58.6.

2. *agreement reached*: γράφειν ἐν συγγραφαῖς καὶ ~ασιν 'to write in documents and contracts' 1M 13.42; μεθ' ὅρκου 'by swearing' PSol 4.4. Cf. συναινέω.

συναλοάω: aor. συνηλόησα.ʃ

to crush into pieces: + acc. rei, Da 2.45 LXX (TH λεπτύνω). Cf. καταλοάω, λεπτύνω, συντρίβω.

συναναβαίνω: fut. ~βήσομαι; aor. συνανέβην, ptc. συναναβάς, subj. ~βῶ, inf. ~βῆναι.

1. intr. *to move upwards together with* sbd: μετά τινος Ge 50.7, Ex 33.3; + dat. pers. 12.38; εἰς Ιερουσαλημ 1E 8.5.

***2**. *to set out on a military campaign together with*: *s* an army, + dat. pers., Jd 6.3 B (A: simp.).

Cf. ἀναβαίνω, συμπορεύομαι, συνέρχομαι

συνανάκειμαι.ʃ *

to be seated at a dinner-table together: 3M 5.39. Cf. ἀνάκειμαι.

συνανάμειξις, εως. f.ʃ

relationship forged as allies: πρός τινα Da 11.23 TH. Cf. συναναμίγνυμι.

συναναμίγνυμι: impf.mid. 3s συνανεμείγνυτο.ʃ

to have dealings with, become active part of: + ἔν τινι - ἐν τοῖς λαοῖς συνανεμείγνυτο 'assimilated among the peoples' Ho 7.8.

Cf. συμμίγνυμι, μίσγω, συνανάμειξις, συμφύρω, συναναστρέφω.

συναναμίσγω. ʃ

mid. = prec.: ἐν τοῖς ἐπιτηδεύμασι αὐτῶν μὴ συναναμίσγεσθε 'Do not have anything to do with their practices' Ez 20.18. Cf. μίσγω.

συναναπαύω: fut.mid. ~παύσομαι.ʃ

mid. *to take rest together*: + dat., παρδάλις .. ἐρίφῳ 'a leopard with a kid' Is 11.6. Cf. ἀναπαύω.

συναναστρέφω: aor.pass. συνανεστράφην.ʃ

pass. *to live together and associate with*: + dat. pers. τῇ ἀδελφῇ μου Ge 30.8 (as a rival wife); παροικίαις ἀσεβῶν 'with communities of the godless' Si 41.5; ἐν τοῖς ἀνθρώποις Ba 3.38.

Cf. ἀναστρέφω **6**, συναναμίγνυμι, συμφύρω, συναναστροφή.

συναναστροφή, ῆς. f.

act of maintaining association with sbd: + dat. pers., 3M 2.31, κοινή 2.33; + gen. pers., ^τῆς σοφίας^ Wi 8.16. Cf. συναναστρέφω.

συναναφέρω: fut. συνανανοίσω.ʃ

to carry with oneself to a higher position: + acc., τὰ ὀστᾶ μου ἐντεῦθεν μεθ' ὑμῶν 'my bones ..' Ge 50.25 (to the land of Canaan), sim. Ex 13.19; cultic offerings, 2K 6.18 (*L* ἀνα~). Cf. ἀναφέρω.

συναναφύρω.ʃ

mid. *to get deeply involved*: Ez 22.6. Cf. συμφύρω: LSG s.v.

συναντάω: fut. ~τήσω, mid. ~τήσομαι; aor. συνήντησα, subj. ~τήσω, impv. ~τησον, inf. ~τῆσαι, ptc. ~τήσας.

1. *to present oneself to*: + dat. pers., συνήντησαν αὐτῷ οἱ ἄγγελοι τοῦ θεοῦ Ge 32.1; for a formal meeting, 46.28; for a hostile action, Ex 4.24, Pr 12.13a, εἰς πόλεμον πρός τινα (enemies) Jo 11.20; for personal encounter or interaction, Is 8.14 (with God); πρὸς αὐτόν Ju 1.6 (as allies in war). **b**. w. a pl. subj., *to meet each other*: ἔλεος καὶ ἀλήθεια συνήντησαν Ps 84.11, ἔλαφοι 'the deer' Is 34.15; ἀλλήλοις Pr 22.2.

2. *to meet* sbd *with signs of welcome* or *salutation*: + dat. pers. (in transit), παρὰ τὸ μὴ συναντῆσαι αὐτοὺς ὑμῖν μετὰ ἄρτου καὶ ὕδατος ἐν τῇ ὁδῷ ἐκπορευομένων ὑμῶν .. 'because they did not welcome you with bread and water when you were on the way out ..' De 23.4 ‖ ἐν ἄρτῳ καὶ ὕδατι Ne 13.2, ἄρτοις Is 21.14.

3. *to meet by chance, run into*: + dat., συνήντησαν Μωυσῇ καὶ Ααρων ἐρχομένοις εἰς συνάντησιν αὐτοῖς 'they ran into M. and A. as they were coming to meet them' Ex 5.20; τῷ βοῒ τοῦ ἐχθροῦ σου ἢ τῷ ὑποζυγίῳ αὐτοῦ πλανωμένοις 'chance upon your enemy's stray ox or his donkey' 23.4; νοσσιᾷ ὀρνέων 'a birds' nest' De 22.6; + sth incorporeal, ἀραῖς 'curses' Pr 12.23, ἀγαθοῖς 17.20.

4. *to befall*: + dat. pers. and *s* a misfortune, συναντήσῃ ἡμῖν θάνατος ἢ φόνος Ex 5.3, θάνατος Pr 24.8, φόβος Jb 3.25, σκότος 5.14, ὀδύναι 'sufferings' 27.30, ἡμέραι κακῶν 30.26; mid., τὰ κακά De 31.29, cf. Ec 2.14, 9.11. Cf. συμβαίνω **2**.

5. *to confront and deal with personally*: + dat. pers., Jd 8.21 B (A: ἀπ~); with harmful intent, ἐν ἐμοί 15.12 B (A: ἀπαντάω).

Cf. συνάντησις, συνάντημα, εὑρίσκω, συντυγχάνω, ἀπαντάω.

συνάντημα, τος. n.

that which befalls sbd: Ec 2.14. **b**. grievous in nature,, 'calamity, adversity': ἐξαποστέλλω πάντα τὰ ~ατά μου εἰς τὴν καρδίαν σου 'I am sending all my calamities into your heart (to terrorise you)' Ex 9.14. Cf. συναντάω **4**, ἀπάντημα.

συνάντησις, εως. f.

1. *coming face to face with*: εἰς ~ίν τινι often following a verb of physical movement and with hostile intent: 'to challenge in a battle' Ge 14.17, Nu 20.18 (ἐξέρχομαι), 2C 35.20 (‖ ἀπάντησις 1E 1.23), 1M 3.16 (‖ .. τινος vs. 17); in order to welcome a guest, Ge 19.1, To 11.16 𝔊^{I} (𝔊^{II} εἰς ἀπάντησίν τινος); εἰς ~ιν αὐτῆς 'in order to meet her' Ge 24.17 (ἐπιτρέχω), 4K 4.26*L* (εἰς ἀπάντησιν αὐτῆς and B: εἰς ἀπαντὴν αὐτῆς); εἰς ~ιν διψῶντι ὕδωρ φέρετε 'when meeting sbd thirsty, take water (to him)' Is 21.14, ἄρτοις συναντᾶτε τοῖς φεύγουσι 'welcome fugitives with bread' ib. Other verbs are: ἀναβαίνω Ge 46.29, ἀνίστημι 19.1, ἐκπορεύομαι Zc 2.3, ἔρχομαι Ge 32.6, πορεύομαι 24.65, προστρέχω 18.2, τρέχω 29.13. Exceptions: ἐξήγαγεν Μωυσῆς τὸν λαὸν εἰς ~ιν τοῦ θεοῦ Ex 19.17; σύ μοι ἀνθέστηκας .. εἰς ~ιν Nu 22.34; εἴ μοι φανεῖται ὁ θεὸς ἐν ~ει 23.3.

2. *group of people who come together for a purpose*: 2K 2.25B (*L* συναγωγή).

Cf. συναντάω, ἀπαντή, ἀπ~, ὑπάντησις.

συναντιλαμβάνομαι: fut. ~λήμψομαι.ʃ

to assist: + dat. pers., Ex 18.22; ἡ χείρ μου συναντιλήμψεται αὐτῷ Ps 88.22 (ǁ κατισχύω). **b**. by carrying together: + acc. (burden), συναντιλήμψονται μετὰ σοῦ τὴν ὁρμὴν τοῦ λαοῦ 'they will help you (by carrying) the overwhelming demand made by the people' Nu 11.17.

Cf. ἀντιλαμβάνομαι, βοηθέω: *ND* 3.84f.

συναπάγω: aor. συναπήγαγον.ʃ

to lead away together: + acc. pers. and μεθ' ἑαυτοῦ Ex 14.6. Cf. ἀπάγω.

συναποθνῄσκω: aor.impv.3s ~ποθανέτω.ʃ

to die with sbd: *s* report heard, συναποθανέτω σοι 'Enter the grave with it' Si 19.10. Cf. ἀποθνῄσκω.

συναποκρύπτω: aor.pass.subj. ~κρυβῶ.ʃ

pass. *to hide oneself together with* sbd: from danger, μετ' αὐτῶν Ep Je 48. Cf. ἀποκρύπτω.

συναπόλλυμι: fut.mid.2s ~απολῇ; 2aor.act.subj. ~απολέσω, mid.3s ~απώλετο, subj.2s ~απόλῃ, inf. ~απολέσθαι.

Often with a note of protest against unfair bundling together; tr. (2aor.) *to destroy along* with (μετά τινος), δίκαιον μετὰ ἀσεβοῦς 'the righteous with the impious' Ge 18.25, ἵνα μὴ συναπολέσῃ ὁ ἁμαρτωλὸς τὸν ἀναμάρτητον 'so that the sinner will not destroy the sinless' De 29.19, μετὰ ἀσεβῶν τὴν ψυχήν μου Ps 25.9; 27.3. **b**. intr. (mid.): abs. χάριν τοῦ συναπολέσθαι 'in order to get them destroyed (along with others)' Da LXX 2.13, ἐν πάσῃ τῇ ἁμαρτίᾳ αὐτῶν Nu 16.26; + dat., ἵνα μὴ καὶ σὺ συναπόλῃ ταῖς ἀνομίαις τῆς πόλεως '.. along with the lawless deeds of the city' Ge 19.15, cf. Wi 10.3, Si 8.15.

Cf. ἀπόλλυμι, ἀφανίζω.

συναποστέλλω: fut. ~στελῶ; aor. ~απέστειλα.ʃ

to send to go together with sbd: + acc. pers., τὸν ἄγγελόν μου πρότερόν σου 'my angel ahead of you' Ex 33.2; μετά τινος 33.12, 1E 5.2. Cf. ἀποστέλλω.

συνάπτω: fut. συνάψω; aor. ~ῆψα, subj. ~άψω; pf. ptc.pass. ~ημμένος.

1. *to join together*: + acc., τὰς αὐλαίας ἑτέραν τῇ ἑτέρᾳ 'the curtains with one another' Ex 26.6; πρός τι 29.5; οἰκίαν πρὸς οἰκίαν Is 5.8 (appropriating another man's property, and ǁ ἐγγίζω).

2. *to bring together as a group for an action*: conspiracy, + cogn. acc., σύναψιν 3K 16.20, 4K 10.34ʃ.

3. *to challenge* sbd to sth: + acc., πρὸς αὐτοὺς πόλεμον De 2.5, 9 (ǁ αὐτοῖς εἰς πόλεμον vs. 19), sim. 24, 1M 5.7; μάχην 10.53, παράταξιν Jd 20.22 B (A: παρατάσσομαι πόλεμον). **b**. abs. *to join battle*: 1M 4.14, εἰς πόλεμον 7.43, 10.78, 13.14; + dat. pers., Jd 20.20 B, 1K 31.2, cf. ἡ παράταξις Ισραηλ συνῆπτεν αὐτοῖς εἰς πόλεμον Jd 20.42*L*.

4. *to reach* a point on the way: συνῆψε ἡ βοὴ τὸ ὅριον .. 'the cry reached the region of ..' Is 15.8; οὐ μὴ συνάψητε 'you'll never make it' 16.8; ἕως νεφέλων 'as far as the clouds' Si 32.20.

5. *to border on*: + gen., Ne 3.19; + ἐπί (case unknown) Jo 17.10 (ǁ dat. loc.). **b**. *to come very close* mid. *to*: so as to assail, + dat. pers., 2K 1.6.

Cf. σύναψις.

συναριθμέω: fut. ~αριθμήσομαι.ʃ

to include in enumeration, 'to count up together': mid., Ex 12.4. Cf. ἀριθμέω.

συναρπάζω: aor.ptc. ~πάσας, pass. ~πασθείς, subj. pass. ~πασθῶ.ʃ

to grasp: physically, + acc., 2M 3.27, 4.41; 'apprehend, arrest' pl. obj., 4M 5.4 (ǁ vs. 2 ἐπισπάω). **b**. mentally, 'to captivate': ἀπὸ τῶν αὐτῆς βλεφάρων 'by her eyelids' Pr 6.2, cf. αἰχμαλωτίζω.

Cf. ἁρπάζω.

συναρχία, ας. f.ʃ

rule free from dissention and discord: Es B 4 o' (*L* εὐστάθεια). Cf. ἀρχή **2**.

συνασπίζω: fut.inf. ~πιεῖν.ʃ

to shield from danger: abs., 3M 3.10. Cf. προασπίζω.

συναυλίζομαι.ʃ

to keep company of: + dat. pers., Pr 22.24.

συναύξω.ʃ

to help increase: + acc., κακίαν 2M 4.4; 4M 13.27. Cf. αὐξάνω.

συναφίστημι: 2aor.ptc. ~αποστάς.ʃ

to rise up in rebellion together: To 1.5 𝔊[I]. Cf. ἀνθίστημι, ἀπονοέω, στασιάζω.

σύναψις, εως. f.ʃ

v.n. of συνάπτω **2**: as cogn. obj., 3K 16.20, 4K10.34. Cf. συνάπτω.

συνδάκνω: aor.pass. ~δήχθην.ʃ

pass. *to feel a sudden, sharp pain together*, 'smart': *s* eyes, To 11.12 𝔊[I].

συνδειπνέω: aor. συνεδείπνησα.ʃ

to dine together: + μετά τινος - τοῖς συνδειπνοῦσιν μετ' αὐτοῦ Ge 43.32; + dat. pers., Pr 23.6; + acc. rei, ἄρτον μετ' αὐτῶν 2K 12.17*L* (B: συνεσθίω). Cf. δειπνέω, σύνδειπνος, and συνεσθίω.

σύνδειπνος, ου. m.ʃ

companion at dinner-table: Si 9.16. Cf. συνδειπνέω.

σύνδεσμος, ου. m.

1. *that which binds together*: joint, ligaments, ὀσφύος 'of a hip' Da 5.6 TH; the back of an animal tightly packed with scales, Jb 41.7. **b**. *conspiracy*: Is 58.9, ἀδικίας 58.6, Je 11.9, 4K 11.14.

2. *knotty problem*: λύων ~ους 'unravelling ..' Da 5.12 TH.

συνδέω: fut. ~δήσω; aor. συνέδησα, impv. ~δησον, pass. ~εδέθην, impv. ~δέθητι; pf.ptc.pass. ~δεδεμένος.

1. *to bind together*: ***o*** wheels, making a vehicle immobile, τοὺς ἄξονας τῶν ἁρμάτων αὐτῶν Ex 14.25; thief, Jb 17.3; tongue to be made speechless, Ez 3.26; ornamental precious stones and ἐν χρυσίῳ 'with gold' Ex 28.20, χρυσίῳ 36.20; παιδείαν 'all that one has learned (so as to draw upon it as a resource)' Si 36.4; κέρκον πρὸς κέρκον 'a tail to a tail (of a fox)' Jd 15.4.

2. pass. *to form close union*: συνάχθητε καὶ συνδέθητε Zp 2.1; of close personal bond, + dat., συνεδέθη ἡ ψυχὴ αὐτοῦ τῇ ψυχῇ Δαυιδ 1K 18.1.

Cf. δέω.

συνδιώκω: aor.ptc. ~διώξας.ʃ

to chase together: + acc. pers., 2M 8.25. Cf. διώκω.

σύνδουλος, ου. m.

fellow-servant: fairly high-ranking in a king's service, 2E 4.7. Cf. δοῦλος.

συνδρομή, ῆς. f.ʃ

excited movement of people from place to place: Ju 10.18, 3M 3.8.

συνδυάζω: aor.subj. ~δυάσω.ʃ

to act in unison with (μετά): Ps 140.4.

συνεγγίζω: aor.subj. ~γγίσω, ptc. ~γγίσας.

to draw near: + dat., 2M 10.27; and reach destination, Si 32.21. Cf. ἐγγίζω.

σύνεγγυς. adv.ʃ

close to, near: ἀπὸ παντὸς ὕδατος τοῦ σ. 'from any water close by' Si 26.12; + gen., οἴκου Φογωρ De 3.29; τῆς πύλης Νινευη To 11.15 𝔊[II]; τοῦ οἴκου αὐτῆς Si 14.24; ᾅδου 51.6, πυλῶν ᾅδου 'the gates of ..' PSol 16.2; Ez 43.8 967 (Zgl συνεχόμενον; < ἐχόμενον?). Cf. ἐγγύς, ἔχω **II 2.**

συνεγείρω: fut. συνεγερῶ; aor.pass. ~ηγέρθην.ʃ *

1. *to cause to rise* from a seated position: pass., σοι 'to welcome you' or 'together with you' Is 14.9.

2. *to assist in causing to rise* from a fallen position: + acc., συνεγερεῖς αὐτὸ μετ' αὐτοῦ Ex 23.5, τὰ πεπτωκότα 4M 2.14.

Cf. ἐγείρω.

συνεδρεύω: aor. συνήδρευσα.ʃ

1. *to act as councillor*: ἀνὰ μέσον μεγιστάνων Si 23.14; 11.9, Su 28 LXX.

2. *to sit in sbd's company*: ἐν μέσῳ γυναικῶν Si 42.12.

Cf. καθίζω συνεδριάζω.

συνεδρία, ας.ʃ

conference held for discussion: Ju 6.1,17, 11.9.

συνεδριάζω.ʃ

to keep company and close relationship: ἐν δικαίοις 'among the righteous' Pr 3.32.

Cf. συνεδρεύω.

συνέδριον, ου. n.

group of people formally gathered to discuss matters and take decisions: ἐκάθισα μετὰ ~ου ματαιότητος Ps 25.4 (|| ἐκκλησία 25.5). **b.** *meeting* of such a body: ἐκάθισα ἐν ~ῳ αὐτῶν 'attended their meeting' Je 15.17, sim. Pr 31.23; προσκληθεὶς εἰς σ. 'invited to ..' 2M 14.5.

Cf. ἐκκλησία, συναγωγή.

σύνεδρος, ον.ʃ

sitting with others in council: subst.m., Jd 5.10B, 4M 5.1. Cf. καθίζω.

συνεθίζω: aor.subj.~θίσω, pass. ~θισθῶ.ʃ

to make accustomed to: + double acc., ἀπαιδεσίαν .. τὸ στόμα σου Si 23.13. **b.** pass. *to get into the habit of*: + dat., ὀνομασίᾳ τοῦ ἁγίου Si 23.9, λόγοις ὀνειδισμοῦ 23.15. Cf. ἐθίζω.

συνείδησις, εως. f.ʃ

inner consciousness: ἐν ~ει 'quietly in heart' Ec 10.20; capable of moral judgement, 'conscience' Wi 17.11. Cf: Mauer, *TDNT* 7.898-910; Spicq 3.332-6; *ND* 3.85.

συνεῖδον: ptc. ~ιδών.

to perceive visually and become aware of: + acc. pers., Da 3.14 LXX; + acc. rei, 1M 4.21a, 2M 4.41; + acc. and adj., 1M 14.21b; + acc. and ptc., 2M 14.30 (|| νοέω). Alw. as conjunctive ptc. nom. Cf. συνοράω, νοέω.

συνείκω: aor.ptc. ~είξας.ʃ

to give way to sbd who is superior to oneself: τινι 4M 8.5. Cf. (ὑπ)εικω.

σύνειμι: pres.impv.3s συνέστω.ʃ

1. *to live with*: + dat. pers. and *in wedlock*, ὁ συνὼν αὐτῇ 'her spouse' Je 3.20, ***s*** wife, Pr 5.19 (|| ὁμιλέω); τοῖς συνοῦσιν ἡμῖν τέκνοις καὶ κτήνεσιν 'the children and cattle that were with us' 1E 8.50. Cf. συνοικέω, συνουσιασμός.

2. *to accompany*: on a journey, ***s*** heavenly judgment, + dat. pers., 2M 9.4; in an undertaking, 1E 6.2 (|| βοηθέω).

συνεῖπον: aor.mid. συνειπάμην.ʃ

mid. *to agree among themselves*: ἀλλήλοις 'mutually' Su 38 LXX; + inf., Da 2.9 LXX. Cf. ὁμοιόω **3**.

συνεισέρχομαι: fut. ~ελεύσομαι; aor.subj. ~έλθω.ʃ

1. *to enter together* with sbd else: ***s*** slave entering service, μετ' αὐτοῦ Ex 21.3; + dat. pers., Es 2.13 o'; εἰς κρίσιν Jb 22.4.

2. *to penetrate* as an enquirer: ἐν στροφαῖς παραβολῶν 'into the subtleties of parables' Si 39.2.

Cf. εἰσέρχομαι. Del. 1M 12.48 v.l.

συνεκκεντέω: aor. συνεξεκντησα.ʃ*
to stab at once: acc. pers., 2M 5.26. Cf. ἐκκεντέω.

συνεκπολεμέω: fut. ~μήσω; aor.inf. ~μῆσαι.ʃ
to fight a joint battle against: + acc. pers. and *s* God, μεθ' ὑμῶν De 1.30; ὑμῖν τοὺς ἐχθροὺς ὑμῶν 20.4; + ἐπί τινα– συνεκπολεμήσει αὐτῷ ὁ κόσμος ἐπὶ τοὺς παράφρονας 'the creation will fight jointly with him against the deranged' Wi 5.20. Cf. πολεμέω, ἐκπολεμέω.

συνεκπορεύομαι.ʃ
to go out together with sbd: so as to assist, μετά τινος Jd 11.3 A (B: ἐξέρχομαι), τινι 13.25 B (A: συμπορεύομαι). Cf. ἐκορεύομαι, συνεξέρχομαι.

συνεκτρέφω: aor.ptc.pass. ~τραφείς.ʃ
to bring up together: *s* hum., 2C 10.8 (|| 3K 12.8 ἐκτρέφω, 24ʳ σύντροφος). Cf. συνέκτροφος, ἐκτρέφω.

συνεκτρίβω: aor.inf. ~τρῖψαι.ʃ*
to destroy utterly together: + acc., Wi 11.19. Cf. ἐκτρίβω, συντρίβω.

συνέκτροφος, ον.ʃ*
brought up together: *s* sons, ἀπὸ νεότητος 'since his youth' 1M 1.6. Cf. συνεκτρέφω, σύντροφος.

συνελαύνω: aor. συνήλασα, ptc.pass. ~ελασθείς; plpf.pass.3s συνήλαστο.ʃ
to force to move away into an undesirable situation: + acc. pers., εἰς φύγην '(force) to flee' 2M 4.42; 2K 11.21 *L*; pass., *o* hum., 2M 4.26, defeated troops 5.5.

συνέλευσις, εως. f.ʃ
an installation where troops come together: Jd 9.46, 49 B (A: ὀχύρωμα).

συνέλκω: aor.subj. ~ελκύσω.ʃ
to put into the same category as sbd else *and treat accordingly*: μετὰ ἁμαρτωλῶν τὴν ψυχήν μου Ps 27.3.

συνεξέρχομαι: fut. ~ελεύσομαι; aor. ~ῆλθον.ʃ
to exit together with: + dat., *s* locusts, Ju 2.20; νεῖκος 'quarrel' Pr 22.10. Cf. ἐξέρχομαι, συνεκπορεύομαι.

συνεξορμάω: aor.impv.3pl ~μάτωσαν.ʃ
to set out together: 1E 8.11.

συνεπακολουθέω: aor. συνεπηκολούθησα.ʃ
to follow closely: ὀπίσω τινός– in adhering to his instruction, Nu 32.11, 12. Cf. (ἐπ)ακολουθέω.

συνεπισκέπτω: fut.mid. ~σκέψομαι; aor.pass. ~επεσκέπην.
to count together with sbd else in census-taking: ἐν τοῖς υἱοῖς Ισραηλ 'among the children of Is.' Nu 1.47. Cf. ἐπισκέπτομαι **4**, ἀριθμέω.

συνεπίσταμαι.ʃ
to know perfectly well: abs., Jb 9.35; + acc. rei, ἃ ἐγὼ ἐμαυτῷ συνεπίσταμαι 19.27. Cf. ἐπίσταμαι.

συνεπισχύω: aor. συνεπίσχυσα.ʃ
to provide military reinforcements: + dat. pers., Es E 20 o' (*L* ἐπι~), 2C 32.3.

συνεπιτίθημι: 2aor.mid.3pl ~επέθεντο, subj.act.3s or mid.2s ~επιθῇ, 3pl ~επιθῶνται.ʃ

1. mid. *to join in attacking*: abs. De 32.27, Zc 1.15*bis*; + dat. pers., Ps 3.7; *+ ἐπί τι - ἐπὶ τὴν δύναμιν αὐτῶν 'against their forces' Ob 13. Cf. ἐπιτίθημι **6**.

2. act. *to impute*: μὴ συνεπιθῇ ἡμῖν ἁμαρτίαν 'may he [= Moses, i.e. you] impute no sin to us' Nu 12.11 (taking ἐπιθῇ as subj.act.3s, honorific 3rd person). If mid.2s, 'Do not allow sin to be imputed to us.'

συνέπομαι.
to move along together, following sbd: τινι, *s* hum., 2M 15.2. Cf. ἕπομαι, (συν)ακολουθέω, συνέρχομαι.

συνεργέω.ʃ
to work together with: + dat. pers., 1E 7.2; 1M 12.1 ('in his favour'). Cf. ἐργάζομαι.

συνεργός, όν.ʃ
suited and advantageous for accomplishing a task: *s* nighttime, 2M 8.7, καιρός '(propitious) moment' 14.5.

συνερείδω: aor.ptc. ~ρείσας.ʃ
to meet in close conflict, 'come to close quarters with': + dat. (enemy troops), 2M 8.30, cf. Plb. 5.84.2.

συνέρχομαι: fut. ~ελεύσομαι; aor. ~ῆλθον, inf. ~ελθεῖν, ptc. ~ελθών.
to come together: συνῆλθον πρὸς αὐτὸν πάντες οἱ υἱοὶ Λευι Ex 32.26; "the inhabitants of five cities will come together to one city" Zc 8.21; ἐπί τινα 'to converge with ..' Je 3.18; + dat. pers., Jb 6.29, ἀλλήλοις Pr 29.13, εἰς τὸν πόλεμον Ju 1.11; + dat. rei and *s* ἡδονή 'pleasure of sexual intercourse,' ὕπνῳ Wi 7.2. Cf. συμφωνέω **2**. **b**. *to travel together with*: + dat. pers., To 5.10 𝔊II.

Cf. ἔρχομαι, συμπορεύομαι, συνοδεύω, συνέπομαι.

συνεσθίω: aor. ~έφαγον, inf. συμφαγεῖν.
to eat together: + acc. rei, μετὰ τῶν Ἑβραίων ἄρτους Ge 43.32 (|| συνδειπνέω); Ex 18.12; + dat. pers., Ps 100.5; ἐπὶ τῆς τραπέζης μου 'at my table' 2K 9.7. Cf. ἐσθίω and συνδειπνέω.

σύνεσις, εως. f.

1. *intellectual quality* or *capability conducive to sensible conduct*: ἡ σοφία ὑμῶν καὶ ἡ σ. ἐναντίον πάντων τῶν ἐθνῶν De 4.6; πνεῦμα ~εως 34.9; οὐκ ἔστι σ. ἐν αὐτῷ Ob 7; of possessors of σ., ib. 8 (|| σοφοί); Jb 28.20 (|| ἐπιστήμη vs. 12). διανοῖξαι ~ιν αὐτῆς 'to open up her mind' Ho 2.15; σοφία ~εως Is 10.13; || σοφία Je 28.15. ***b**. *that which one could deduce from a word or event*: Da 9.22 TH (LXX διάνοια).

2. *capability to arrive at sensible solution in practical, technical matters*: of architect and a divine gift, πνεῦμα θεῖον σοφίας καὶ ~εως καὶ ἐπιστήμης Ex 31.3; ἐνέπλησεν (sc. ὁ θεὸς) αὐτοὺς σοφίας καὶ ~εως διανοίας πάντα συνιέναι ποιῆσαι τὰ ἔργα τοῦ ἁγίου 35.35; + γνῶσις Pr 2.6.

Cf. συνίημι, συνετός, σοφία, ἐπιστήμη.

συνεταιρίς, ίδος. f.ʃ

female companion: of a fem., Jd 11.37, 38.

Cf. συνέταιρος, ἑταῖρος.

συνέταιρος, ου. m.

comrade: in office, 1E 6.3, Da 2.17 LXX (TH φίλος).

Cf. συνεταιρίς, ἑταῖρος.

συνετίζω: fut. ~ετιῶ; aor. ~έτισα, ptc. ~ετίσας, impv. ~έτισον, inf. ~ετίσαι.*

to cause to understand: + acc. pers., *s* God, Ps 15.7 (‖ παιδεύω), νηπίους 'infants' 118.130; ‖ συμβιβάζω 31.8, ‖ ὑποδιδάσκω Ne 8.7; + double acc., ὁδὸν δικαιωμάτων σου .. με Ps 118.26, ἐκεῖνον τὴν ὅρασιν Da 8.16 (*s* Gabriel), 10.14 TH (LXX ὑποδείκνυμι). Cf. διδάσκω, παιδεύω, συμβιβάζω, ὑποδείκνυμι.

συνετός, ή, όν.

intelligent: *s* person, ἄνθρωπον φρόνιμον καὶ ~όν Ge 41.33; παντὶ ~ῷ καρδίᾳ δέδωκα σύνεσιν 'I have given understanding to everyone intelligent of mind' Ex 31.6, ~οὶ καρδίας Jb 34.10, 34; ἄνδρας σοφοὺς καὶ ἐπιστήμονας καὶ ~ούς De 1.13, 15; τίς .. σ. καὶ ἐπιγνώσει αὐτά; Ho 14.10; subst. m.pl. Is 19.11, ‖ σοφόι 29.14, opp. ἄφρων Je 4.22, ‖ ἱερεύς, προφήτης 18.18; n.pl. Is 32.8. Cf. συνίημι, συνετῶς, ἐπιστήμων, σοφός, and φρόνιμος.

συνετῶς. adv.ʃ

in an intelligent way: Οὐ σ. με ἐποίησας Is 29.16, ψάλατε σ. Ps 46.8. Cf. συνετός.

συνευδοκέω.

to consent to: + dat., τῷ νόμῳ 1M 1.57; 2M 11.24; + ὑπέρ τινος 11.35. Cf. συναινέω.

συνευφραίνομαι.ʃ *

to rejoice together: μετά τινος (pers.), Pr 5.18. Cf. εὐφραίνω, συγχαίρω.

συνεχής, ές.ʃ

conjoined, contiguous: ποταμοὺς ~εῖς '(I dried) river after river' 4K 19.24*L* (B: περιοχῆς). Cf. συνέχω **3b**.

συνέχω: fut. ~έξω, pass. συσχεθήσομαι; aor. συνέσχον, subj. συσχῶ, impv.3s συσχέτω, pass. ~εσχέθην, inf. συσχεθῆναι, subj. συσχεθῶ.

1. *to keep under control*: *o* anger (ὀργή) Mi 7.18; τὴν πόλιν 2M 9.2.

2. *to hold back from acting*: *o* rain, συνεσχέθη ὁ ὑετὸς ἀπὸ τοῦ οὐρανοῦ 'rain was withheld from the sky, i.e. the sky was not allowed to send down rain' Ge 8.2; *s* sky, συσχῇ τὸν οὐρανόν, καὶ οὐκ ἔσται ὑετός De 11.17, sim. 3K 8.35; τοὺς οἰκτιρμοὺς αὐτοῦ 'his mercies' Ps 76.10; fountains, PSol 17.19; ἀπὸ τῆς ψυχῆς αὐτοῦ 'from his own enjoyment' Si 14.4; *o* σῖτον 'grain' (without giving to the needy) Pr 11.26. **b**. *to cause to stop* that which is already happening: pass., *o* θραῦσις 'calamitous blow' 2K 24.21B (*L* ἐπέχω; ‖ 1C 21.22 παύομαι), 25 (*L* ἐπε~).

3. *to hold together* to prevent dislocation and falling away: abs. Ex 36.11; + acc., ἑτέρα τὴν ἑτέραν 28.7; *s* God's spirit, τὸ συνέχον τὰ πάντα Wi 1.7. **b**. pass. *to be continuous by being joined together one to the next*: ἐξ ἀλλήλων συνεχόμεναι ἑτέρα ἐκ τῆς ἑτέρας 'joined to one another' Ex 26.3, cf. ⸢ὡς συνεχόμενον ἐμοῦ⸣ (967 συνεγγύς μου) καὶ αὐτῶν Ez 43.8 (see also ὡς **15** and ἔχω **II 2b**), cf. συνεχής.

4. *to confine inside a limited space and deny freedom of movement*: *o* pers., 1M 13.15, φόβῳ Jb 3.24 (*s* φόβος κυρίου 31.23); water in a cistern, Je 2.13; pass., Ne 6.10, ἐν σχοινίοις 'with cords' Jb 36.8¶ (‖ πεδάομαι); ἀγκάλαις '(throw yourself into a tight grip of) the arms (of a woman who is not your own)' Pr 5.20; 4M 15.32. **b**. metaph.: 1K 16.14*L* (‖ πνίγω 'to vex'), pass., Jb 7.11 (‖ εἰμί ἐν ἀνάγκῃ).

5. *to bring components tightly together and deny freedom of action*: *o* τὸ στόμα 'to hold the tongue, remain speechless' Is 52.15 (cf. τὰ ὦτα i.e. refusing to listen, Acts 7.57), Ez 33.22 (:: ἀνοίγω); συσχέτω ἐπ' ἐμὲ φρέαρ τὸ στόμα αὐτοῦ Ps 68.16 (preventing my exit); crocodile's(?) scales, Jb 41.9¶; + acc. pers., 2.9d. **b**. pass. *to have one's hands tied*: οὐκ ἔστιν τῷ κυρίῳ συνεχόμενον σῴζειν 'it is not impossible for the Lord to rescue' 1K 14.6; 1C 12.1. Cf. συγκλείω **2**, συνοχή.**c**. mid. *to occupy oneself fully with*: + dat., ἔργοις Wi 17.20.

6. *to affect in injurious* or *painful manner*, 'to distress, afflict': τὰ συνέχοντα τῶν πολέμων κακά 'the distressful calamities of wars' 2M 10.10; pass., ἀπὸ οἴνου Je 23.9, συνειδήσει '(cornered and harassed) by conscience' Wi 17.11, cf. ὑπὸ κακοῦ συνειδότος κατεχόμενος 'troubled by bad conscience' *P.Oxy*. 532, 23.

Cf. συνοχή: Köster, *TDNT* 7.879-81; Spicq 3.337-41.

συνήθεια, ας. f.

close, intimate relationship: hum., φίλων 4M 2.13; of brothers, 13.22.

συνήθης, ες.ʃ

subst.m. *friend*: 2M 3.31. Cf. φίλος.

συνῆλιξ, ικος; n.pl. συνήλικα.ʃ

of equal or *like age*: *s* παιδάριον Da TH 1.10 (or subst. and appos., *playmates*). Cf. ἡλικία **1**.

συνηχέω: aor.ptc.~ηχήσας.ʃ
to echo: 3M 6.17. Cf. ἠχέω.

συνθέλω: fut. ~θελήσω.ʃ. A poetic form of συνεθέλω.
to consent: + dat. pers., De 13.8 (|| εἰσακούω τινός). Cf. θέλω, εἰσακούω, νεύω, συναινέω.

σύνθεσις, εως. f.
1. *act of making compound substance with diverse ingredients*: unguent, Ex 30.32; incense, 30.37. **b.** *compound substance*: Ex 35.28; θυμιάματος 'of incense' 35.28, Si 49.1; θυμίαμα ~εως Ex 31.11.
2. *assortment*: σ. τοῦ κόσμου τῆς δόξης 'a wardrobe of glorious dresses (for ladies)' or 'an assortment of glorious cosmetic accessories' Is 3.20.
Cf. σύνθετος, μίγνυμι.

σύνθετος, ον.ʃ
compounded, composite: θυμίαμα ~ον λεπτόν 'powdery, compound incense' Ex 30.7. Cf. σύνθεσις.

συνθήκη, ης. f. Mostly pl.
mutual agreement entered: ~ην ἔθεντο πρὸς αὐτόν 'entered an agreement with him [= death personified]' Wi 1.16, Ἐποιήσαμεν .. μετὰ τοῦ θανάτου ~ας Is 28.15 (|| διαθήκη), ὧν τοῖς πατράσιν ὅρκους καὶ ~ας ἔδωκας ἀγαθῶν ὑποσχέσεων 'to whose ancestors you gave oaths and covenants of good promises' Wi 12.21. **b.** a political, military treaty and || βουλή Is 30.1; ποιήσασθαι ~ας Da 11.6 LXX (|| TH ποιῆσαι ~ας μετ' αὐτοῦ); συνετηρήσατε τὰς πρὸς ἡμᾶς ~ας 'you kept to our agreements' 1M 10.26, ἐπένευσαν ταῖς ~αις 'indicated their consent to ..' 2M 14.20; a document of agreement, τὰς γενομένας ~ας λαβὼν ἧκε .. 'taking the document of agreement drawn up went ..' 14.26.
Cf. διαθήκη, ὅρκος: Penna.

σύνθημα, ατος. n.
word or brief phrase mutually agreed upon in advance: password, Jd 12.6A; watchword, 2M 8.23. Cf. συνθήκη **b**.

συνθλάω: fut. ~θλάσω; aor. συνέθλασα.
to crush together: ***o*** τὰ ὀστᾶ αὐτῶν 'their bones' Mi 3.3, lions' molars (μύλη) Ps 57.7 (|| συντρίβω); kings, 109.5; enemies' heads, 67.22, snakes' heads 73.14 (|| συντρίβω), κρανίον 'skull' Jd 9.53 A (B: simp.). Cf. θλάσμα, καταθλάω, συντρίβω. Del. 1M 15.14 v.l

συνθλίβω: fut.pass. ~θλιβήσομαι; aor.subj.pass. ~θλιβῶ.ʃ
to squeeze in: "a sin is bound to creep in between sale and purchase" Si 27.2 (Zgl: ~τριβήσεται); ***o*** flower, Ec 12.6.

συνίημι: pres.inf. ~ιέναι, συνίειν, ptc. συνιείς, συνίων; fut. συνήσω; aor. συνῆκα, subj. συνῶ, impv.2s σύνες, pl. σύνετε.
1. *to comprehend, understand*: συνίειν καὶ γινώσκειν ὅτι .. Je 9.24; + acc. rei, τίς σοφὸς καὶ συνήσει ταῦτα; Ho 14.10; οὐ συνῆκαν τὴν βουλὴν αὐτοῦ Mi 4.12 (|| γινώσκω), γνῶσιν Jb 29.7 (|| ἐπίσταμαι); act. ptc. = συνετός 'prudent, intelligent,' Am 5.13, cf. ὁ οὐ συνίων Ho 4.14; + acc. pers., ὁ λαός με οὐ συνῆκεν Is 1.3 (|| γινώσκω), τὸν κύριον 1K 2.10 (+ γίνωσκω); *+ ἐν - ἐν τῇ ἀναγνώσει 'the text being read' Ne 8.8 (or: 'during the recitation'), ἐν ὁδῷ ἀμώμῳ Ps 100.2, ἐν τῇ πονηρίᾳ Ne 13.7, ἐν τῷ λαῷ 2E 8.15, ἐν τοῖς λόγοις Da TH 10.11;*+ ἀνὰ μέσον - ἀνὰ μέσον ἀγαθοῦ καὶ κακοῦ '(distinguish) between good and bad' 3K 3.9; *+ εἰς Ps 27.5, 32.15, 72.17, Da 11.33; after having heard (ἀκούω), τῇ καρδίᾳ Is 6.10. **b.** + inf.: ποιῆσαι '(intelligent enough) to do' Ex 35.35, 36.1; + ptc., To 3.8 𝔊[I].
2. *to take notice of*: *+ ἐπί τινα - Da 11.37 TH (LXX προνοέομαι); favourably, ἐπὶ πτωχόν Ps 40.2, ἐπὶ παρθένον Jb 31.1¶; with hostile intent, Da 11.30 TH; + gen. rei, τῆς κραυγῆς μου Ps 5.2; + ὅτι 2K 12.19 (*L* εἶδον); + pred. ptc., Οὐ συνίεις ἀποπνίγουσα ..; 'Don't you realise that you're strangling ..?' To 3.8 𝔊[I].
3. *to ponder* so as to comprehend: abs., Da 8.5 TH (LXX διανοέω). **b.** *to examine* so as to comprehend the nature of: + acc., νεφροὺς καὶ καρδίας 'kidneys and hearts' Je 20.12 (|| δοκιμάζω), De 32.7 (? || μιμνήσκω).
Cf. συνετός, σύνεσις, σοφός, αἰσθάνομαι, γινώσκω, ἐπίσταμαι, καταλαμβάνω **8**, κατανοέω **2**: Schmidt 1.293f.; Conzelmann, *TDNT* 7.890f.

συνίστημι: 1aor. συνέστησα, ptc. συστήσας, mid. συνεστησάμην, inf. συστήσασθαι, ptc. ~τησάμενος; 2aor. συνέστην, inf. συστῆναι, ptc. συστάς, pass. συσταθείς; pf. συνέστηκα, ptc. συνεστηκώς.
I. tr.(1aor.) **to place in the charge of*: + acc. pers. and dat. pers., συνέστησεν ὁ ἀρχιδεσμώτης τῷ Ιωσηφ αὐτούς Ge 40.4; 2M 8.9.
2. *to appoint* to an office: + acc. pers., Nu 27.23, 32.28.
3. *to put together into a well-ordered whole*: εὖ ^τῆς σοφίας^ τὴν ὁδὸν Jb 28.23, τὸν ἑαυτοῦ λαόν 2M 14.15, δόλον 'deception' Pr 26.26; mid., + acc., πόλιν κατοικεσίας Ps 106.36, παγίδα 'snare' 140.9.
4. *to establish logically to be so and so*: + acc. pers. and ptc., αὐτοὺς .. ψευδομάρτυρας ὄντας Su 61 TH (LXX: καθίστημι).
5. *to commend*: + acc. and dat. pers., 1M 12.43; pass. 2M 4.24.
6. mid. *to organise and hold* an event or activity: + acc., ἑορτήν 'festival' Ps 117.27, πόλεμον Da 7.21 LXX (TH ποιέω), 1E 1.26, πολιορκίας 'blockades' 2.19, δρόμον 'running' 3M 1.19, εὐωχία 'festivity' 4.1, συμπόσια 'drinking-parties' 4.16, χορούς

'dances' 6.32, ἀπώλειαν 'destruction' 6.38. Cf. ποιέω **10**.

7. mid. *to put togther* a group for an action: + acc., δύναμιν 'an army' 1M 2.44, γυμνάσιον καὶ ἐφηβίαν 'a gymnasium and a youth club' 2M 4.9.

8. *to erect* an edifice: + acc., τρόπαιον 'war monument' 2M 15.6. Cf. ἀνίστημι **I 5**.

9. *to cause to come into being*: + acc. and dat. (incom.), ταραχὰς .. πόλει 'troubles ..' Pr 6.14; mid., δυσφημίας 'malicious reports' 3M 2.26.

II. intr. (2aor., pf. in the present sense) *to be concentrated, collected*: συνεστηκὸς ὕδωρ 'reservoir of water' Ex 7.19.

2. *to band together*: ἐπὶ Ααρων 'stormed A. together' Ex 32.1, sim. Nu 16.3; 3M 4.18.

3. *to meet in fight*: ἐναντίον μου Ps 38.2.

4. *to harden*: *s* penis (?), Le 15.3.

5. *to stand together*: Da 2.25 TH.

6. *to be in session, proceeding*: *s* συμπόσιον 'party' Es 1.11 *L*.

7. pf. *to come into existence*: τοσούτων συνεστηκότων 'against such a background' 2M 4.30.

Cf. (καθ)ίστημι: Lee 1990.

συνίστωρ, ορος. m.ʃ

one who knows along with sbd else: w. ref. to God, Jb 16.19 (|| μάρτυς). Cf. μάρτυς, σύνοιδα.

συννεφέω.ʃ

to gather clouds: *s* God and + acc. rei, ἐν τῷ συννεφεῖν με νεφέλας ἐπὶ τὴν γῆν 'when I gather clouds over the earth' Ge 9.14. Cf. νεφέλη and συννεφής.

συννεφής, ές.ʃ

clouded: ὁ οὐρανὸς αὐτῷ σ. δρόσῳ 'the sky shall be covered for him with dewy cloud' De 33.28. Cf. νεφέλη and συννεφέω.

συννοέω: aor.ptc. ~νοήσας.ʃ

to become aware and realise: + inf., 2M 5.6, 11.13, + ὅτι 14.3.

σύννους, ουν.ʃ

gloomy or *pensive*: *s* hum., σ. καὶ περίλυπος '.. deeply sorrowful' 1E 8.68, Da 2.12 LXX.

σύννυμφος, ου. f.ʃ *

husband's brother's wife: Ru 1.15. Cf. νυμφίος.

συνοδεύω: fut. ~δεύσω; aor.opt.3s ~δεύσαι.ʃ

to journey together with: + dat. pers., φθόνῳ τετηκότι 'rotten envy' Wi 6.23, ὁ ἄγγελος συνοδεύσαι ὑμῖν To 5.17 𝔊[II]. (𝔊[I] συμπορεύομαι). Cf. ὁδεύω, συνοδία, συνέρχομαι.

συνοδία, ας. f.ʃ

group of people journeying together: Ne 7.5, 64. Cf. συνοδεύω, παρεμβολή **3**: Caird 1969.36.

σύνοδος, ου. m./f.ʃ

1. *group, assemblage*: 3K 15.13; ἀθετούντων 'of rebels' Je 9.2.

2. *converging, conjunction*: μηνῶν 'of months' De 33.14.

Cf. ἐκκλησία, συναγωγή.

συνοδυνάομαι: aor.subj. ~οδυνηθῶ.ʃ

to suffer pain with: + dat. pers., Si 30.10 (:: συγγελάω). Cf. ὀδυνάω.

σύνοιδα. Pf. with present sense.ʃ

to know sth about a person, esp. as a potential witness: μάρτυς ἢ ἑώρακεν ἢ σύνοιδεν 'a witness whether he has seen or is acquainted (with the matter)' Le 5.1. **b**. + dat. and ptc., οὐ σύνοιδα ἐμαυτῷ ἄτοπα πράξας 'I am not aware of having done anything improper' Jb 27.6.

Cf. οἶδα, συνίστωρ: Maurer, *TDNT* 7.898-910.

συνοικέω: fut. ~οικήσω, ptc. ~οικήσων; aor.subj. ~οικήσω, inf. ~οικῆσαι; pf.ptc.f. συνῳκηκυῖα.

1. *to enter marital relationship*, 'marry' (+ τινι): συνῳκηκυῖα ἀνδρί 'married to a man' Ge 20.3. See *ND* 3.85f.

2. *to live in wedlock* (+ τινι): ἐὰν δέ τις λάβῃ γυναῖκα καὶ συνοικήσῃ αὐτῇ De 22.13, 24.1; 25.5, Si 25.8; μετὰ γυναικός 25.16. **b**. *to live in companionship*: λέοντι καὶ δράκοντι 'with a lion and a serpent' Si 25.16, σοφίᾳ Wi 7.28, cf. *ND* 3.85f ..

Cf. οἰκέω, συνοίκησις, συνοικίζω, γαμέω.

συνοίκησις, εως. f.ʃ

marriage: βιβλίον ~εως 'marriage certificate' To 7.13 𝔊[II]. Cf. συνοικέω: Casevitz 1985.197.

συνοικίζω: fut.pass. ~οικισθήσομαι; aor. ~ῴκισα, subj. ~οικίσω; pf.ptc.pass. ~ῳκισμένος.

to unite: in marriage, + acc. pers. (male) and to consummate marriage, pass., αὐτῇ De 21.13; acc. (fem.), 22.22, 1E 8.89; τὰς θυγατέρας αὐτῶν .. τοῖς υἱοῖς ὑμῶν 8.81; as a city, ἀπὸ ἑνὸς συνετοῦ συνοικισθήσεται πόλις Si 16.4. **b**. *to enter marital relationship*: μετὰ τῶν θυγατέρων αὐτῶν 1E 8.67.

Cf. συνοικέω, γαμέω.

συνοικοδομέω: fut. ~μήσω.ʃ

to build together with: + dat. pers., 1E 5.65. Cf. οἰκοδομέω.

συνολκή, ῆς. f.ʃ

act of drawing in, 'inhaling': ἀερός 'of air' Wi 15.15.

σύνολος, ον.

altogether, alw. τὸ σύνολον: πᾶσα πόλις ἢ χώρα τὸ ~ον 'every city or country, without exception' Es E 24; τίς νομὸς .. τὸ ~ον 'what district .. at all?' 3M 4.3. **b**. + neg., μὴ κάθου τὸ ~ον 'Don't sit under any circumstances' Si 9.9; 3M 4.11, 7.8, 21.

Cf. ὅλος, πᾶς: Schmidt 4.549f.

συνομολογέω.ʃ

to express agreement to a certain view: pass. impers., + πανταχόθεν ὅτι, 'it is generally agreed that ..' 4M 13.1. Cf. ὁμολογέω.

συνοράω.

1. *to be become aware of*: + acc., τὸ χύμα τῶν ἀριθμῶν 'mass of figures' 2M 2.24; 4.4.

2. *to look on*: abs., 2M 7.4.

Cf. βλέπω, ὁράω.

συνούλωσις, εως. f.ʃ *

complete healing: + ἴαμα Je 40.6, cf. 37.17. Cf. ἴαμα.

συνουσιασμός, οῦ. m.ʃ *

sexual intercourse: 4M 2.3. **b**. *libido, sexual drive*: + gluttony, Si 23.6. Cf. σύνειμι **1**.

συνοχή, ῆς. f.ʃ

act of confining inhabitants and/or an army within a place, 'siege': ~ὴν ἔταξεν ἐφ' ἡμᾶς 'they laid siege against us' Mi 5.1; ἦλθεν ἡ πόλις εἰς ~ήν Je 52.5; + ἄνυδρον, ταλαιπωρία Jb 30.3¶. **b**. *a group of individuals bent on denying others freedom of movement*: Jd 2.3, cf. Caird 1969.36.

Cf. συνέχω, περιοχή.

συνταγή, ῆς. f.ʃ

directive specifying a course of action: + dat. pers., Jd 20.38A (B: σημεῖον); ἀπὸ ~ῶν 2E 10.14; κακίας 'concerning a wrongdoing' PSol 4.5. Cf. σύνταξις **3**.

σύνταγμα, ατος. n.ʃ

1. *body of doctrine*: κυρίου Jb 15.8.

2. *literary composition*, 'book; treatise': 2M 2.23 (|| βιβλίον), Si prol. II. Cf. σύνταξις **4**.

σύνταξις, εως. f.

1. *assigned amount of work, quota*: τὴν ~ιν τῆς πλινθείας ἀποδώσετε 'you shall deliver the assigned quota of bricks' 5.18; 5.8, 14. **b**. of meal, 'ration': Je 52.34.

2. *mutually agreed amount of money to be paid*: as subvention, allowance, ~ιν δίδοσθαι τούτοις τοῖς ἀνθρώποις 1E 6.28; χορηγήσειν 'will defray' 2M 9.16 (|| δαπανήματα 'expenses incurred' 3.3).

3. *an instruction* or *order given* as to how to do a certain thing: αὕτη ἡ σ. τῆς σκηνῆς τοῦ μαρτυρίου 'this is the instruction pertaining to the tent of testimony' Ex 37.19; ποιήσει τὸ πάσχα .. κατὰ τὴν ~ιν αὐτοῦ Nu 9.14. Cf. συνταγή, ἐντολή.

4. *that which has been put together*, '(literary) composition' 2M 15.38, 39. Cf. σύνταγμα **2**.

Cf. συντάσσω.

συνταράσσω: fut. ~ταράξω; aor. συνετάραξα, pass. ~εταράχθην.

1. *to throw into confusion* or *disorder*: + acc. pers., τὴν παρεμβολὴν τῶν Αἰγυπτίων 'the camp of the Egyptians' Ex 14.24; *o* the earth, Ps 59.4; the depth of the sea, 64.8, the foundations of the sky, 2K 22.8; mentally, Da 4.2 TH. Cf. συγχέω.

2. *to excite and arouse*: συνεταράχθη ἡ μεταμέλειά μου 'I have been moved to regret' Ho 11.8.

3. *to cause to move in agitation*: *o* lightnings, Ps 17.15; arrows, 143.6.

Cf. ταράσσω.

συντάσσω: fut. ~τάξω; aor. συνέταξα, impv. σύνταξον, ptc. ~τάξας, mid. ~εταξάμην, pass. συνετάγην, ptc.1aor. ~ταχθείς, 2aor. ~ταγείς; pf. ~τέταχα, pass. ~τέταγμαι.

1. *to give orders*, 'command' (+ dat. pers.): Ex 1.17; Nu 27.23 (|| ἐντέλλομαι vs. 22), 36.2 (|| ἐντέλλομαι); + πρός τινα, 15.23; αὐτοῖς πρὸς τοὺς κυρίους αὐτῶν '(commanded) them (to take the message) for their masters' Je 34.3; the content of the order expressed by καί + a finite verb, καὶ φυλάξουσιν τὰς ὁδούς Ge 18.19, καὶ δώσουσιν .. Nu 35.2; + λέγων and direct speech – Ge 26.11, Ex 5.6, 35.4; + inf., τὰ ἔργα, ὅσα συνέταξεν κύριος ποιῆσαι αὐτά 35.29; pass. καθὰ συνετάγη Μωυσῇ 37.19; 1E 6.4 (|| προστάσσω vs. 10). **b**. + acc. rei, 'concerning': πάντων, ὧν συνέταξέν σοι κύριος 'all concerning which the Lord gave you orders' De 4.23.

2. *to communicate as order*: + dat. pers. and acc. rei, πάντας τοὺς λόγους τούτους, οὓς συνέταξεν αὐτῷ ὁ θεός Ex 19.7. **b**. *as binding*: ἡ ἀρά, ἣν συνέταξε κύριος Μωυσῇ Ba 1.20.

3. *to draw up for battle*: pass., *o* troops, Ju 2.16. Cf. παρατάσσω **1**.

4. *to place* sth (acc.) *at the disposal of* sbd (dat.): μοι τὰ δέοντα 'what I need' Pr 30.8.

5. mid. *to order oneself together with* or *on the side of*: + dat., οἱ τούτοις συντασσομένοις 'their colleagues' 1E 2.15 (|| σύνδουλος 2E 4.7); δῆμος συνταγεὶς μετ' αὐτοῦ 'people allied with him' Da 11.23 LXX.

6. mid. *to arrange together and agree on*: + acc., καιρόν Su 14 TH.

Cf. ἐντέλλομαι, ἐνυπο~, ἐπι~, προστάσσω, σύνταξις: Lee 2003.517-23; Muraoka 2006.

συντέλεια, ας. f.

1. passively, *cessation of existence*: brought about violently, *s* territory, city, etc., ἐν ἡμέρᾳ ~ας αὐτῆς Am 1.14; people, σ. εἰς ἀσεβεῖς ἥξει Hb 1.9. **b**. not necessarily violently: ἡμέρα ~ας ἡμερῶν ζωῆς σου Si 30.32; ἀνθρώπου 11.27; μέχρι ~ας φωτὸς μετὰ σκότους 'until light fades away with the onset of darkness' Jb 26.10¶.

2. actively, *wiping out of existence, annihilation*: ἐν ~ᾳ καὶ ἐν συσσεισμῷ ἡ ὁδὸς αὐτοῦ 'His way is in annihilation and earthquake' Na 1.3; ἐν κατακλυσμῷ πορείας ~αν ποιήσεται τοὺς ἐπεγειρομένους 'by flooding the path he will wipe out those who rise up (against him)' 1.8; ἀναβήσεται ὡς ποταμὸς σ. 'an end will come up like a (flooding) river' Am 8.8; ~αν καὶ σπουδὴν ποιήσει ἐπὶ πάντας .. Zp 1.18; ~αν ἐν ἀγκίστρῳ ἀνέπαυσε, i.e. he pulled up a fish with a hook, thereby causing its destruction, Hb 1.15; ὀργὴ ~ας Ps 58.14; + ἀπώλεια 1M 3.42. **b**. ποιέω τινα εἰς ~αν 'to annihilate sbd': Je 5.18, Ez 20.17 (ǁ without εἰς 11.13). **c**. by metonymy, fire and smoke indicative of destruction: τῆς πόλεως Jd 20.40.

3. *bringing to a conclusion*: of yearly agricultural cycle, ἑορτὴν ~ας ἐπ' ἐξόδου τοῦ ἐνιαυτοῦ 'an end-of-year concluding feast' Ex 23.16; of work, Si 37.11, 38.28, ~αν λειτουργῶν 'by way of the conclusion of the rites' 50.14, τῆς διαβάσεως 'of the crossing' Jo 4.8; λόγων 'all that one can say at the end' 43.27; of a building work - οὐκ ἔλαβεν ~αν 'is still unfinished' 1E 6.19, σ. μία 'identical finish' 3K 6.25. **b**. εἰς ~αν 'to the end' = 'for ever'(?, cf. Eth *lazalāfu*) Hb 3.19; ἀπ' ἀρχῆς τοῦ ἐνιαυτοῦ καὶ ἕως ~ας τοῦ ἐνιαυτοῦ 'from the beginning of the year to the end ..' De 11.12; ἐπὶ ~ᾳ 'at the conclusion (of a discourse)' Si 22.10; κατὰ τὴν ~αν καιροῦ ἐνιαυτοῦ 'after a year's time' Da 11.13 LXX (TH εἰς τὸ τέλος ..); εἰς ~αν ἐνιαυτῶν [= ἐν ~ᾳ ..] 'after some years' 11.6 LXX (TH μετὰ τὰ ἔτη αὐτοῦ). **c**. *end-product*: Si 21.11.

4. v.n. of συντελέω: Ez 22.12.

5. *ideal perfection, the highest reach*: καυχήματος 'that which deserves the highest pride' Si 45.8, 50.11; μέχρι ~ας 47.10, cf. Ps 118.96; ἔκλαυσεν .. ἕως ~ας μεγάλης 'cried their hearts out' (?) 1K 20.41; εἰς ~αν 'utterly' Si 40.14, but Heb. לנצח and Vulg. *in consummatione*.

6. *coming true* of what has been promised or foretold: ῥήματος κυρίου 1E 2.1 (ǁ πληρωθῆναι 2C 36.22).

7. *contribution made for a public purpose, either pecuniary or in kind*: 1K 8.3, cf.Caird 1969.36f. and *BA* ad loc.

Cf. συντελέω, τέλος, ἀναπλήρωσις: Delling, *TDNT* 8.64-6.

συντελέω: fut. ~τελέσω, pass. ~τελεσθήσομαι; aor. act. συνετέλεσα, inf. ~τελέσαι, ptc. ~τελέσας, subj. ~τελέσω, impv. ~τέλεσον, mid. ~ετελεσάμην, inf., ~τελέσασθαι, pass. συνετελέσθην, subj. ~τελεσθῶ, impv.3s ~τελεσθήτω, inf. ~τελεσθῆναι, ptc. ~τελεσθείς; pf.mid./pass.3s συντετέλεσται, inf. ~τετελέσθαι, ptc. συντετελεσμένος.

1. *to complete, finish*: abs. 1C 27.24 (:: ἄρχομαι), οὐ μὴ συντελέσουσι 'they will never finish it off' Jl 2.8; pass., ὁ οὐρανὸς καὶ ἡ γῆ καὶ πᾶς ὁ κόσμος αὐτῶν Ge 2.1; ***o*** craftsman's product, ἔργα τεκτόνων συντετελεσμένα αὐτοῖς 'carpenters' works produced for them' Ho 13.2; process or action, + inf., καταφαγεῖν Ge 43.2, Am 7.2; + ὥστε and inf., Nu 7.1; + ptc. pres., λαλῶν Ge 17.22, 24.45; Le 16.20, Nu 4.15, De 31.1, 24, 32.45, Jo 3.17, 4.1 (ǁ inf., vs. 11), Jd 3.18, 15.17 A (B: παύομαι), 1K 10.13, 2K 6.18, 11.19*L* (B: inf.), 3K 8.54, Is 10.12, To 8.1 𝔊[I] (𝔊[II] τὸ φαγεῖν καὶ πιεῖν), but aor. Jo 21.42[a] (v.l. inf.); ***o*** τὰ ἔργα αὐτοῦ Ge 2.2; τὰ ἔργα τὰ καθήκοντα 'the prescribed jobs, assignments' Ex 5.13; συντάξεις 'quotas' 5.14; νόμος Si 31.8; τὸ ταχθὲν 'the assignment' Ep Je 61; συντέλεσον τὰ ἕβδομα ταύτης 'Sit through the seven-day marriage feast of this (girl)' Ge 29.27, ἡμέρας τοῦ βίου αὐτοῦ Jb 14.14, ἐν ἀγαθοῖς τὸν βίον αὐτῶν 21.13; λόγον 'what has been pledged' Is 10.22, ῥήματα La 2.17; συντετελεσμένα καὶ συντετμημένα πράγματα 'finished and concluded matters' Is 28.22. **b**. pass. *to reach fulness*: ***s*** flower, 'to come into full bloom' Is 18.5, κάλλος '(female) beauty' Ez 16.14. **c**. *to reach a firm decision*: ἐπὶ ^τὸν Δαυιδ^ 1K 20.34 (*L* βουλεύομαι .. συντελέσαι ..), cf. συντετέλεσται ἡ κακία αὕτη παρὰ τοῦ πατρὸς αὐτοῦ θανατῶσαι τὸν Δαυιδ 'this evil deliberation on the part of his father to put David to death had now come to an end' 20.33, sim. 25.17.

*__2__. *to make an end of, destroy*: ***o*** building, Zc 5.4, wickedness, Ps 7.10; pers., 2K 22.38 (ǁ ἀφανίζω; ἐκλείπω Ps 17.38), Je 15.16, 1K 15.18, PSol 7.5; pass., Συντετέλεσται, ἐξῆρται 'he is finished, he has been removed' Na 2.1; τὸ ἔθνος συνετελέσθη Ma 3.9; ǁ συντρίβω Is 1.28; ἐν λιμῷ 'in famine' and ǁ ἀποθνήσκω Je 14.15, ǁ ἀναλίσκω Ez 5.12, cf. Lampe, s.v. **5**, **6**; LSG s.v. **I 4**. **b**. *to slaughter*: animals for food, To 8.19 𝔊[II] (prob. mistranslation of Heb. עָשָׂה or Ar. עֲבַד 'to cook').

3. *to perpetrate*: + acc. ἀδικίαν Ge 49.5, ἄνομα Is 32.6, Je 6.13, ἀποστάσεις καὶ πολέμους 1E 2.23; κακά 'damages' Es B 5, τὰ ἄνομα Pr 1.19, ὕβριν 'outrage' 2M 8.17, φόνους 'murders' 4.3, πρός τινα 1M 10.5; mid. πονηρά Ge 44.5, ἁμαρτήματα 'sins' 2M 13.8, συνετελέσω συντέλειαν κακίας σου τὴν ἐν καταδυναστείᾳ 'you have thoroughly indulged in your wickedness through oppression' Ez 22.12, ǁ ποιέω 22.13; εἴς τινα 'against them' 1M 8.31.

4. pass., *to happen, occur*: Ge 18.21 (or **3**), Jb 19.26, Da 4.30 TH; To 12.20 𝔊[I] (𝔊[II] συμβαίνω), Ju 15.4.

5. *to make a thorough job of*: + acc., θερισμόν Le 19.9 (leaving no gleaning behind), cf. πληγὴν ἔργων αὐτοῦ συντελέσει 'he will be roundly punished for his deeds' Pr 22.8 (ǁ θερίσει κακά 'he will harvest misfortunes'), ματαιότητα ἔργων αὐτοῦ 22.8a; συνετέλεσεν ἀποικίαν τελείαν 'went through the whole process of deportation' Je 13.19; + inf., γνῶναι Si 24.28, 1E 1.53. Cf. τελεσιουργέω.

6. *to cause to produce the full effect*: ἐν τῷ συντελέσαι με τὴν ὀργήν μου ἐπ' αὐτούς Ez 5.13, sim. 6.12, ἐν σοί 7.5; θυμόν La 4.11; pass., 6.12, Da 11.36 LXX; συντέλεσον τὴν ζωὴν αὐτῶν ἐν ὑγιείᾳ 'Grant them to make the best of their life in health' To 8.17 $\mathfrak{G}^{I}$.

7. *to use up*: τὰ βέλη μου συντελέσω εἰς αὐτούς 'I shall empty my arrows on them' De 32.23.

8. *to rob of strength*, 'exhaust': + acc. pers., Je 5.3.

***9**. *to come to an agreement with*: + acc., μετὰ τὸ συντέλεσαι τὸν βασιλέα .. διαθήκην πρὸς τὸν λαόν 'after the king concluded an agreement with the people' Je 41.8.

10. *to hold* or *celebrate* a religous rite: θυσίας 3M 5.43, τὰ τῆς θυσίας 1E 1.16, ἑορτήν 2C 30.22. Cf. ποιέω **I 11**.

11. *to spend* a period of time and reach *its end*: + acc., "the three-week period' Da 10.3 LXX. **b**. pass. *to come to the end of* a period of time:; συνετελέσθησαν αἱ ἡμέραι πένθους '.. of mourning' De 34.8; αἱ ἡμέραι τοῦ συγκλεισμοῦ '.. of the confinement' Ez 4.8; Jb 1.5; To 8.20 $\mathfrak{G}^{I}$ (|| πληρόομαι). Cf. πληρόω **7**.

Cf. συντέλεια, τελέω, διαπράσσω, κατανύω, παύω, ἀφανίζω: Delling, *TDNT* 8.63; Muraoka 2008b.232.

συντέμνω: aor.pass. ~ετμήθην; pf.pass. ~τέτμημαι, ptc. ~τετμημένος.ʃ

1. *to shorten the duration of*: ***o*** βασιλεία 'reign,' συντέτμηται καὶ συντετέλεσται Da 5.27 LXX (|| ἀπολήγω 'to cease' vs. 26), πόλεμος 9.26 TH (or **3**).

2. *to summarise*: + acc., 2M 10.10.

***3**. *to determine as appropriate*: pass., λόγον συντετμημένον ποιήσει Is 10.23, cf. λόγον συντελῶν καὶ συντέμνων ἐν δικαιοσύνῃ 10.22 and συντετελεσμένα καὶ συντετμημένα πράγματα .. ἃ ποιήσει 'matters definitively determined upon, which he is going to execute' 28.22; ἑβδομήκοντα ἑβδομάδες συνετμήθησαν ἐπὶ τὸν λαόν 'seventy weeks ..' Da 9.24 TH. Cf. MH גָּזַר.

Cf. συντελέω: LSG, s.v.

συντήκω: pf. ~τέτηκα.ʃ

to become extremely weak: mentally, 2K 13.4*L* (B: ἀσθενής).

συντηρέω: fut. ~τηρήσω, pass. ~τηρηθήσομαι; aor. συνετήρησα, impv. ~τήρησον, inf. ~τηρῆσαι, pass. ~ετηρήθην.

1. *to adhere to* a command *and practise* it: + acc., πάντα τὰ νόμιμά μου Ez 18.19, νόμον Si 32.1; τὰς ὁδοὺς ^κυρίου^ 2.15; a relationship once established, φιλίαν 1M 8.12, 10.20, τὰς πρὸς ἡμᾶς συνθήκας 10.26, πρὸς ἡμᾶς πίστιν 10.27, τῷ ἔθνει αὐτοῦ 14.35.

2. *to cleave to and not let go of*: ἀνθρώπῳ .. ὀργήν Si 28.3, || διατηρέω μῆνιν 28.5, εὔνοιαν 'goodwill' 2M 9.26, 11.18.

3. *to watch out for*: abs. and + προσέχω, Si 13.13; + acc., καιρόν 'opportune moment' Si 4.20.

4. *to maintain carefully* in a certain condition: + double acc., ὑγιῆ 'healthy' Si 26.19¶; ἐμαυτὴν αὐτῷ γυναῖκα 'myself as his (potential) wife' To 3.15; + inf., ἁυτοὺς ἀναμαρτήτους εἶναι 'themselves free from sin' 2M 12.42.

5. *to watch over and keep from danger*: pass., ***o*** hum., Da 3.23 LXX; τὴν ψυχήν μου To 1.11; one's tongue (speech), Pr 15.4.

6. *to store in memory*: + acc., τοὺς λόγους ἐν τῇ καρδίᾳ Da 4.25 LXX, cf. διατηρέω 7.28 TH and Lk 2.19.

Cf. τηρέω, προσέχω, φυλάσσω.

συντίθημι: aor. ~έθηκα, mid. συνεθέμην, ptc. ~θέμενος, inf. ~θέσθαι, subj. ~θῶμαι.

1. *to place together*: + acc., To 9.5 $\mathfrak{G}^{II}$; so as to store, 2M 8.31.

2. mid. *to agree* to do: abs., 3K 16.28[c], Su 19 LXX; + inf., Da 2.9 TH (LXX: συνείπομαι), 1K 22.13, 4M 4.17 (+ inf. fut.). **b**. *to accept and agree to the terms of*: + acc. rei, πρὸς αὐτὸν εἰρήνην 1M 9.70, πρὸς ἑαυτοὺς διαθήκην 11.9; + dat. pers. 15.27; αὐτοῖς συνθήκας PSol 8.10. Cf. συναινέω.

Cf. δια~, συγκατα~, τίθημι, συνθήκη.

συντίμησις, εως. f.

total value: Le 27.4, 18, Nu 18.16. Cf. τιμή.

σύντομος, ον.

1. *concise*: subst.n., λέξεως 'brevity of expression' 2M 2.31.

2. *soon to arrive*: ***s*** τέλος 'end' Wi 14.14; δύναμις 'of immediate efficacy' 4M 14.10.

Cf. συντόμως.

συντόμως. adv.

forthwith, without delay: Pr 13.23, 3M 5.25. Cf. σύντομος, εὐθέως.

συντρέφω: aor.pass. συνετράφην, ptc. ~τραφείς.

to nourish together w. sbd else: Da 1.10 LXX; ***s*** lamb, μετά τινος 2K 12.3. Cf. τρέφω, συντροφία, σύντροφος.

συντρέχω: fut. ~δραμοῦμαι; aor. συνέδραμον, ptc. ~δραμών.

to run together with: + dat. pers., Ps 49.18. Cf. τρέχω.

συντριβή, ῆς. f. *

crushing, destruction: + gen. obj. τέκνων Ho 13.13, cf. Am 6.6; παρὰ τοῦ θεοῦ Is 13.6; || κακά Je 4.6. **b**. *injury*: "there is no cure for your bruise" Na 3.19 (cf. Zc 11.16 and see under συντρίβω), ὀσφύος 'of hip' Ez 21.6. **c**. mental, psychological: πνεύματος Is 65.14.

Cf. συντρίβω and σύντριμμα.

συντρίβω: fut. ~τρίψω, mid. ~τρίψομαι, pass. ~τριβήσομαι; aor. συνέτριψα, subj. συντρίψω, inf.

~τρῖψαι, ptc. ~τρίψας, impv. ~τριψον, pass. συνετρίβην, subj. ~τριβῶ, inf. ~τριβῆναι, ptc. ~τριβείς, impv.3s ~τριβήτω, opt.3s ~τριβείη, 3pl ~τριβείησαν; pf.pass.ptc. συντετριμμένος.

1. *to shatter, break to pieces, crush*: ***o*** person, τοὺς ὑπεναντίους 'the enemies' Ex 15.7, cf. ὀδόντας '(enemies') teeth' Ps 3.8, κεφαλὰς ἀρχόντων ἐχθρῶν Si 33.12, κέρας'horn' 47.7; pass. and not necessarily total slaughter, but serious military failure, 1M 4.14, ἐνώπιον τῶν ἐχθρῶν ὑμῶν 'before your enemies' De 1.42, ***o*** οἱ ἄνομοι καὶ οἱ ἁμαρτωλοί Is 1.28 (|| συντελέω), ἔθνη Ez 26.2 (|| ἀπόλλυμι); things, ξύλα ἐν τοῖς πεδίοις 'trees in the fields' Ex 9.25 (*s* hail); θύραν 'door' Ge 19.9; ὀστοῦν 'bone' Ex 12.10, 46, Nu 9.12 (of sacrificial sheep), the bones of a human victim mauled by a lion, Is 38.13; στήλας 'stone pillars (of pagan worship)' 23.24; 34.13 (|| βωμοί, ἄλσος, γλυπτά and καθαιρέω, ἐκκόπτω, κατακαίω), sim. De 12.3; σκεῦος ὀστράκινον 'earthen vessel' Le 6.28; πλάκας 'stone tablets' Ex 32.19; δεσμὸν ζυγοῦ 'band of yoke' Le 26.13; ζυγόν Je 5.5 (|| διαρρήγνυμι), Is 14.5, 29; βραχίονα καὶ ἄρχοντα 'arm and leader' De 33.20; τόξον 'bow' Ho 1.5; τόξον καὶ ῥομφαίαν καὶ πόλεμον 'bow and sword and war' 2.18; πολέμους 'wars' Ex 15.3, Ju 9.7, 16.2, sim. Is 42.13; μοχλούς 'bars (of a gate)' Am 1.5; πλοῖον 'ship' Jn 1.4; ῥάβδον 'rod' Na 1.13, σκῆπτρα Si 32.23; ᾠά 'eggs' Is 59.5 (|| ῥήγνυμι); λάκκον 'cistern' Je 2.13; ὀστέα μου 'my bones' La 3.4; κύματα 'waves' Jb 38.11; τὸ συντετριμμένον οὐ μὴ ἰάσηται 'will not heal what is crushed' (|| ἐκλιμπάνον 'abandoned' and διεσκορπισμένον 'scattered') Zc 11.16; + cogn. dat., συντρίμματι Je 14.17, + cogn. acc. and acc. pers. 17.18, Jo 10.10 (on battlefield). **b**. incorporeal things: τὴν ὕβριν τῆς ὑπερηφανίας ὑμῶν 'the haughtiness of your pride' Le 26.19. **c**. metaph. συνάξω τὴν συντετριμμένην 'I will gather that which is shattered' (|| τὴν ἐξωσμένην 'that which is rejected') Mi 4.6, sim. 4.7, Zp 3.18; ἰάσασθαι τοὺς συντετριμμένους τῇ καρδίᾳ 'to heal ..' Is 61.1, τὴν καρδίαν 57.15, so Ps 33.19 (|| ταπεινὸς τῷ πνεύματι), 146.3, τὰς ψυχάς 3M 2.20; καρδίαν συντετριμμένην καὶ τεταπεινωμένην '.. humbled' Ps 50.19, ἀνὴρ συντετριμμένος Je 23.9 (τῇ καρδίᾳ or τὴν καρδίαν understood?), τὰς ψυχάς 3M 2.20; πνεῦμα συντετριμμένον Ps 50.19; καρδίαν or ψυχήν understood, Ne 2.13, 15.

2. *to break a limb* or *limbs of* by accident: pass. and ***o*** animal, Ex 22.10; sacrificial animal, Le 22.22; grazing sheep, Ez 34.4.

Cf. συντριβή, σύντριμμα, συντριμμός, σύντριψις, κατα~, (συν)θλάω, διαθρύπτω, θραύω, καταλεαίνω, (κατ)αλέω, κατάγνυμι, (συγ)κλάω, λεπτύνω, κατακόπτω, (κατ)αράσσω, συνεκτρίβω, κατα~, συναλοάω, ἀφανίζω.

σύντριμμα, ατος. n. *

1. *fracture*: σ. χειρὸς ἢ σ. ποδός, a physical defect disqualifying a person so handicapped for priesthood, Le 21.19; caused by an act of violence, 24.20. **b**. *one who has been crushed*: Je 37.12. **c**. in gen., *wound, injury*: Je 3.22, 6.14.

2. *crushed grain*: "no crushed grain will fall on to the ground" Am 9.9.

3. *act of being crushed*: of earthen vessel, Is 30.14; in military, political sense, 22.4, θυγατρὸς λαοῦ μου La 2.11, τοῦ λαοῦ μου .. καὶ τῆς πόλεως τῆς ἁγίας 1M 2.7; + πτῶμα Is 57.19, + ταλαιπωρία 59.7, 60.18, + ὄλεθρος Je 31.3; as cogn. dat. of συντρίβω 14.17 (|| πληγή), cogn. acc., 17.18; in general, moral sense, 'loss of one's cause' Wi 3.3 (|| κάκωσις 'misery').

Cf. συντρίβω, συντριμμός, πληγή.

συντριμμός, οῦ. m.ʃ *

1. *ruin*: διαιρῶν ~ὸν ἐπ' ἰσχύν 'dispensing ruin to strength' (|| ταλαιπωρία 'hardship') Am 5.9, cf. Je 4.20; σ. πολέμου 'brought about by warfare' Mi 2.8.

2. *act of crushing*: σ. μέγας ἀπὸ τῶν βουνῶν 'a mighty din of crushing from the hills' (|| φωνὴ κραυγῆς and ὀλολυγμός) Zp 1.10. **b**. *that which results from crushing and fragmenting*: ~οὶ ὑδάτων 'billows' 2K 22.5*L* (B: θανάτου 'deadly').

Cf. συντρίβω, συντριβή, σύντριμμα.

σύντριψις, εως. f.ʃ

act of crushing on battlefield: + acc. pers. and acc. cogn., αὐτοὺς ~ιν μεγάλην Jo 10.10. Cf. συντρίβω.

συντροφία, ας. f.ʃ

act of being raised and brought up together: 4M 13.22; w. king, 3M 5.32. Cf. συντρέφω, σύντροφος.

σύντροφος, ον.ʃ

brought up together with: subst.m., τινος 3K 12.24[r] (|| vs. 8 ἐκτρεφείς), 2M 9.29. Cf. συνέκτροφος, συντρέφω: *ND* 3.37-9. Del. 1M 1.6.

συντροχάζω: aor.subj. ~τροχάσω.ʃ

to move continuously forward: *s* wheel with a well-rope, Ec 12.6.

συντυγχάνω: aor.inf. ~τυχεῖν.ʃ

to meet with sbd: abs., 2M 8.14. Cf. συναντάω.

συνυφαίνω: aor.inf. ~υφᾶναι, pass. ~υφάνθην; pf. ptc.pass. ~υφασμένος.ʃ

to weave into one piece: τὴν συμβολὴν συνυφασμένην 'the binding interwoven' Ex 28.28; σὺν τῇ ὑακίνθῳ 'together with the blue fabric' 36.10; ἐν αὐτῷ 'into it' 36.17. Cf. ὑφαίνω and συνυφή.

συνυφή, ῆς. f.ʃ

that which holds separate parts together: ἐπωμίδος 'of ephod' Ex 36.28.

συνωμότης, ου. m.∫
confederate: τινος, Ge 14.13.

συνωρίς, ίδος. f.∫
pair of horses: ἀναβάτης ~ίδος Is 21.9. Cf. ἵππος.

Συρία, ας. GN
1. *Aram*: Ge 28.5 +.
2. *Syria*: Κοίλη Σ. 1E 216+.

Συριακός, ή, όν.
Aramaic: *s* βίβλος 'Bible' Jb 42.17bα.

σύριγμα, ατος. n.∫
v.n. of συρίζω (q.v.): derisive act, Je 18.16. Cf. συρισμός, συριγμός.

συριγμός, οῦ. m.
= συρισμός, q.v.: ἑρπετῶν 'of reptiles' Wi 17.9. **b**. derisive hissing, Je 19.8 (+ ἀφανισμός); 25.9 (also + ὀνειδισμός), 32.4 (+ ἄβατον, ἐρήμωσις). Cf. συρισμός, συρίζω.

σύριγξ, ιγγος. f.
whistle: Da 3.5. Cf. συρίζω.

συρίζω: fut. συριῶ; aor. ἐσύρισα
to hiss: in derision, Zp 3.1, La 2.16, + acc. pers., Ez 27.36, Jb 27.23¶; ὑπέρ τινος 'over sth' Je 19.8, ἐπί τινα 'at sbd' 29.18; + ἐξίστημι 'to be astonished' 3K 9.8; to signal, Is 5.26 (‖ αἴρω σύσσημον), μυίαις .. καὶ τῇ μελίσσῃ 'to flies .. and bees (directing to launch an attack)' 7.18; *s* snake, Je 26.22. Cf. συρισμός, συριγμός, σύριγμα, σύριγξ, δια~, ἐκσυρίζω, ἠχέω, ψιθυρίζω.

συρισμός, οῦ. m.*
hissing: Jd 5.16; indicative of derision: παραδῶ σε .. εἰς ~όν Mi 6.16 (‖ ἀφανισμός 'obliteration' and ὄνειδος 'disgrace'). Cf. συρίζω, σύριγμα, συριγμός.

Συριστί. adv.∫
in Aramaic: 4K 18.26 ‖ Is 36.11, Da 2.4, 2E 4.7.

Σύρος, α.
Aramaean: subst.m. Ge 25.20; Σύροι *Syria*, Is 17.3.

συρράπτω: aor.subj.pass. συρραφῶ.∫
to stitch together: + acc., προσκεφάλαια ἐπὶ πάντα ἀγκῶνα χειρός 'pillows on to every elbow' Ez 13.18; pass., *o* οὐρανός Jb 14.12. Cf. ῥάπτω.

σύρω: fut. συρῶ; aor. ἔσυρα.∫
1. tr. *to pull along, drag*: + acc., τοὺς χιτῶνας 'the garments' Is 3.16 (ostentatiously); *o* hum., roughly, ἐπὶ τὰ βασανιστήρια 'to the torturing instruments' 4M 6.1; enemy troops, 2K 17.13B (*L* ἐπισπάομαι).
2. intr. *to move along slowly but firmly over a surface*: *s* serpent and + acc. of space, σύροντες γῆν Mi 7.17; predatory animals, μετὰ θυμοῦ συρόντων ἐπὶ γῆς De 32.24; torrent, ὕδατος πολὺ πλῆθος σῦρον χώραν 'a large mass of water sweeping over a tract of land' Is 28.2, ὕδωρ ἐν φάραγγι σῦρον 'water sweeping along in a valley' 30.28, cf. χειμάρρου δίκην 'in the manner of a wadi' Plut. 2.5f.
Cf. ἐκσύρω, ἕλκω, σπάω: Schmidt 3.259; Trench 72-4.

σῦς, υός. m./f.∫
= ὗς 'wild boar' ἐκ δρυμοῦ Ps 79.14.

συσκήνιος, ον.∫
living in the same tent: subst. 'tentmate' Ex 16.16. Cf. σύσκηνος, subs.

σύσκηνος, ου. m.∫
one who lives in the same house: ‖ γείτων 'neighbour' Ex 3.22. Cf. γείτων, πλησίον, σκηνή, prec.

συσκιάζω.∫
to provide thick shade: *s* cherubs, ταῖς πτέρυξιν αὐτῶν ἐπὶ τοῦ ἱλαστηρίου 'with their wings over the propitiatory' Ex 25.19; veil, Nu 4.5; tree, κατὰ .. δένδρου συσκιάζοντος Ho 4.13. Cf. σκιά, σύσκιος.

σύσκιος, ον.∫
providing abundant shade: *s* δένδρον 'leafy tree' Ez 6.13, ξύλον 3K 14.23; hum., Ct 1.16. Cf. συσκιάζω.

συσκοτάζω: fut. συσκοτάσω; aor. συνεσκότασα, inf. ~τάσαι, impv.3s ~τασάτω.
*__1__. tr. *to make dark*: + acc., ἡμέραν εἰς νύκτα Am 5.8; *o* ἄστρα 'stars' Ez 32.7.
2. intr. *to become dark*: impers., Je 13.16; συσκοτάσει ἐπὶ τῆς γῆς ἐν ἡμέρᾳ τὸ φῶς 'the daylight will darken upon the earth' Am 8.9; συσκοτάσει ἐπ' αὐτοὺς ἡ ἡμέρα Mi 3.6, sim. Ez 32.8. **b**. *to lose light*: *s* heavenly luminaries, ὁ ἥλιος καὶ ἡ σελήνη Jl 2.10, 3.15 (‖ δύειν τὸ φέγγος), ὁ οὐρανός Je 4.28.
Cf. σκοτάζω and σκότος.

συσσεισμός, οῦ. m. *
commotion: of air, 'tempest,' ἐν συντελείᾳ καὶ ~ῷ ἡ ὁδὸς αὐτοῦ Na 1.3; ‖ σεισμός Je 23.19. **b**. of the ground, 'earthquake': Si 22.16.
Cf. σεισμός.

συσσείω: fut. συσσείσω; aor. συνέσεισα.∫
tr. *to shake*: + acc. pers., *s* God, πάντα τὰ ἔθνη Hg 2.7; *o* ἔρημον Ps 28.8, τὴν γῆν 59.4 (‖ συνταράσσω) τρόμῳ 'with a trembling' Si 16.19; μου τὰ ὀστᾶ 'my bones' Jb 4.14. Cf. σείω and συσσεισμός.

σύσσημον, ου. n.∫
signal: ἀρεῖ σ. ἐν τοῖς ἔθνεσιν 'he will raise a signal among the nations' Is 5.26 (‖ συρίζω 'to hiss'), εἰς τὰς νήσους ἀρῶ σ. μου 49.22, ἐξάρατε σ. εἰς τὰ ἔθνη 62.10. Cf. σημεῖον, πυρσός.

συσσύρω.∫
to make off with all of: + acc. rei, temple vessels, 2M 5.16 (‖ λαμβάνω).

σύστασις, εως. f.∫
1. *plan of action drawn up jointly*: ἐπὶ τῇ ~ει αὐτῶν μὴ ἐρείσαι 'may not hold fast to their plot' Ge 49.6 (‖ βουλή), cf. LSG s.v.
2. *coming into existence, formation*: τοῦ κόσμου

Wi 7.17; ~ιν ποιησάμενος αὐτοῦ 'having established it' 3M 2.9.

Cf. συνίστημι.

συστέλλω: aor. συνέστειλα, pass. συνεστάλην; pf. ptc.pass. συνεσταλμένος.

1. *to draw back*: *o* hands pulled back, refusing to help, Si 4.31 (:: ἐκτείνω).

2. *to bring low*: in terms of military prestige, *o* hum., 1M 5.3, ἐνώπιόν τινος Jd 8.28B (A: ἐντρέπομαι), ἀπὸ προσώπου τινός 11.33B. **b**. *to depress* psychologically: 2M 6.12; as manifest in facial expressions, 3M 5.33.

3. pass. *to shrink back*: ἀπὸ τοῦ φόβου αὐτοῦ 'for fear of him' 1M 3.6.

Del. 1M 2.32 v.l.

σύστημα, ατος. n. Also spelled σύστεμα.

a whole that has accumulated: ~ατα τῶν ὑδάτων Ge 1.10 (which was called by God θαλάσσαι); pool of water, Ez 31.4; cistern or reservoir of water, Je 28.32; army of soldiers, 1C 11.16 (*L* σύστρεμμα, ‖ 2K 23.14 ὑπόστημα), 2M 8.5, nation 15.12, community 3M 3.9. Cf. συναγωγή: LSG s.v.

σύστρεμμα, ατος. n.

group of men banded together for a purpose: ἀνθρώπων ἁμαρτωλῶν Nu 32.14; 2E 8.3; troops, 1K 30.8*L* (B: γεδδουρ for ~δ); conspirators, 4K 14.19. Cf. συστρέφω, συστροφή.

συστρέφω: aor. συνέστρεψα, ptc. ~στρέψας, pass. ~εστράφην, ptc. ~στραφείς; pf.ptc.pass. συνεστραμμένος.

1. *to collect, bring together*: ἐκ μισθωμάτων πορνείας συνέστρεψεν '.. earnings of whoredom' (‖ συνάγω) Mi 1.7, cf. Thph στερεός .. σταθηρὸς γέγονεν, PG 126.1061, and Eth *tagabrat*; *o* hums., 2M 14.30, troops Jd 12.4 B (A: συναθροίζω), σύστρεμμα ἐπί τινα 4K 15.30; pass., Is 33.18; mid., *to come together and form a group*, πρός τινα Jd 11.3 B (A: συλλέγομαι); as conspirators, 2K 15.31B (*L* σύγκειμαι), ἐπί τινα 4K 14.19; act. in the same sense, ἐπί τινα 'against sbd' 3K 16.9.

2. *to cause to rotate*: + acc., ἐν ποσὶν αὐτοῦ τροχόν '(potter's) wheel with his feet' Si 38.29.

3. pass. *to become tight* as a result of components coming close together: συνεστρέφετο τὰ ἔντερα αὐτοῦ ἐπὶ τῷ ἀδελφῷ αὐτοῦ 'his intestines were contracting over his brother' Ge 43.30; ὀργὴ .. συστρεφομένη (‖ στρεφομένη 37.23) ἐπὶ τοὺς ἀσεβεῖς ἥξει 'fury will come over the impious with full force' Je 23.19; Ez 1.13; *s* troops in close formation, 1M 12.50.

4. pass. *to form a coalition*: ἐπὶ τὸν βασιλέα 'against the king' Bel 28 TH; 4K 9.14*L* (B: πρός τινα).

Cf. συνάγω, συστροφή, σύστρεμμα: LSG s.v.

συστροφή, ῆς. f.

gathering: of people, σ. ἀδικίας 'a wicked gathering' Ho 13.12; ~ὰς ποιεῖται 'he is engaged in plots' Am 7.10; πονηρευομένων Ps 63.3 (‖ πλῆθος); conspiracy, cogn. acc. of συστρέφω, 4K 15.15B; μελισσῶν 'of bees' Jd 14.8 A (B: συναγωγή). **b**. σ. πνεύματος 'a whirlwind' Ho 4.19, Si 43.17.

Cf. συστρέφω, σύστρεμμα, συναγωγή, πλῆθος.

συσφίγγω: aor. συνέσφιγξα, subj. συσφίγξω.ʃ

to bind close together: + acc., λόγιον Ex 36.29; τὴν χεῖρά σου ἀπὸ τοῦ ἀδελφοῦ σου De 15.7 (to deny him a helping hand and :: ἀνοίγω), τὴν ὀσφῦν αὐτοῦ 'his loin' (so as to run steadily) 3K 18.46; + acc. pers., ἐν αὐτῇ [= ἐν τῇ ἐπωμίδι 'with the ephod'] Le 8.7. Cf. LSG s.v.

συχνός, ή, όν.ʃ

many: subst.m., 2M 5.9. Cf. πολύς.

σφαγή, ῆς. f.

slaughter, butchering, murder: of humans, Ob 10 (‖ ἀσέβεια), ‖ ἀναίρεσις, ἀφανισμός 2M 5.12, ‖ ὄλεθρος PSol 8.1 (on battlefield), ‖ ἀπόλλυμι Is 34.2, ‖ θυσία 34.6, ‖ μάχαιρα 65.12, ‖ διασπασμός 'tearing apart,' βρῶσις 'devouring,' διαφθορά 'destruction' Je 15.3; of animals, but not for cultic purpose, πρόβατα ~ῆς Zc 11.4, 7, Ps 43.23. Cf. σφάγιον, σφάζω, σφαγιάζω, ἀποκτείνω, θυσία, ὄλεθρος: Michel, *TDNT* 7.935f.

σφαγιάζω: aor.inf. σφαγιάσαι, pass. σφαγιασθῆναι.ʃ

to slaughter: *o* hum. sacrifice, 4M 13.12. Cf. σφαγή, σφάζω.

σφάγιον, ου. n.

1. *slaughtered animal* or *human* in general: animal, ~α ποιήσεις αὐτὰ σεαυτῷ Le 22.23; hum., σ. ῥομφαίας Ez 21.15 (‖ σφαγή); 21.28; cogn. obj. of σφάζω, 21.10.

2. *animal victim slaughtered for offering*: ~α καὶ θυσίας προσηνέγκατέ μοι Am 5.25.

Cf. σφαγή, σφάζω, and θυσία.

σφάζω: fut. σφάξω, pass. σφαγήσομαι; aor. ἔσφαξα, impv. σφάξον, subj. σφάξω, inf. σφάξαι, pass. ἐσφάγην, ptc. σφαγείς, inf. σφαγῆναι; pf.ptc.pass. ἐσφαγμένος.

1. *to slaughter*: + acc., a human sacrifice, Ge 22.10 (with a knife [μάχαιρα]), *o* τέκνα Is 57.5, Ez 23.39; sacrificial animal, ἔριφον αἰγῶν 'kid' Ge 37.31; an animal for meat, θύματα 43.16; μόσχον ἢ πρόβατον Ex 22.1; αἷμα θυσιασμάτων 'animals with their blood undrained' 34.25; πρόβατα καὶ βόες Nu 11.22; ὁλοκαύτωμα Le 14.19, σφάγια Ez 21.10; τὸ πάσχα 1E 7.12; ἔναντι κυρίου Le 1.5; ἐνώπιον αὐτοῦ [= priest] Nu 19.3. **b**. with the notion of sacrifice absent: *o* μόσχους Is 22.13 (‖ θύω), hum., 14.21; prophets, 3K 18.40, the righteous, Ps 36.14; in battle, Jd 12.6 A (B: θύω), 1M 1.2.

2. *to bring to naught*: + acc., βουλήν 'plan, design' Je 19.7.

Cf. σφαγή, σφάγιον, ἀπο~, κατασφάζω, σφαγιάζω, ἀποκτείνω, θύω, ἀφανίζω: Shipp 525; Michel, *TDNT* 7.929-32.

σφαιρωτήρ, ῆρος. m.*

1. *thong* for tying shoes: σ. ὑποδήματος Ge 14.23 (|| σπάρτιον and as an object of negligible value).

2. *knop* as ornamental component of lampstand in a tabernacle: Ex 25.30, cf. Boyd-Taylor 2001.77.

Cf. Masson 1986; LSG s.v.

σφακελίζω.ʃ

to suffer from gangrene: ***s*** the eyes, and divine punishment, Le 26.16, De 28.32 (|| ἐκλείπω vs. 65). Cf. Shipp 524f.

σφαλερός, ά, όν.ʃ

likely to cause one to stumble, 'slippery': ***s*** path, Pr 5.6. Cf. σφάλλω.

σφάλλω: fut. σφαλῶ; aor. ἔσφαλα for Attic ἔσφηλα, pass. ἐσφάλην, subj.pass. σφαλῶ, ptc.pass. σφαλείς, opt.act.3s σφάλαι. See Thack. 286.

1. *to lose balance and move downwards involuntarily*, 'fall': ***s*** foot, De 32.35; nation, Am 5.2 (|| πίπτω). **b**. *to fail to achieve its end*: ***s*** plan, counsel Jb 18.7; w. ref. to miscarriage, 21.10 (|| ὠμοτοκέω). **c**. metaph., *to fall from high positions in society*: ***s*** the rich, Si 13.22.

2. pass. *to commit a* moral *error*: Wi 10.8.

Cf. σφάλμα, ἐπισφαλής, πίπτω, σκανδαλίζω, σκελίζω, ὑποσκελίζω.

σφάλμα, ατος. n.ʃ

that which is effected by σφάλλω **1**: Pr 29.25. Cf. σφάλλω.

σφενδονάω: aor. ἐσφενδόνησα.ʃ

to assail with a sling: abs., 1K 17.49; metaph., + acc., ψυχὴν ἐξθρῶν 'the souls of enemies' 25.29. Cf. σφενδόνη, ἀποσφενδονάω.

σφενδόνη, ης. f.

sling as weapon: 1K 17.40, λίθοι ~ης Zc 9.15, sim. Si 47.4; + ἀσπίς, γαῖσος, τόξον Ju 9.7. Cf. σφενδονήτης, σφενδονάω.

σφενδονήτης, ου. m.

soldier using a sling as weapon, 'slinger': Ju 6.12; || τοξότης 'archer' 1M 9.11; ἐν λίθοις καὶ τόξοις 'with stones and bows' 1C 12.2. Cf. σφενδόνη.

σφηκιά, ᾶς. f.ʃ

swarm of wasps (LSG): as instrument of warfare, Ex 23.28, Jo 24.12; De 7.20. Cf. σφήξ.

σφήν, ηνός. m.

wedge: used as an instrument of torture, 4M 8.13. Cf. βασανιστήριον.

σφηνόω: aor. ἐσφήνωσα; pf.ptc.pass. ἐσφηνωμένος.ʃ

to bolt: ***o*** doors, + κλείω Ne 7.3, + ἀποκλείω Jd 3.23.

σφήξ, κός. m.ʃ

wasp: agent of divine punishment, Wi 12.8. Cf. σφηκιά: Shipp 526.

σφιγγία, ας. f.ʃ*

careful management of finances, frugality: Si 11.18.

σφίγγω: aor. ἔσφιγξα.ʃ

to bind tight: abs., 4K 12.11 (κιβωτόν 'chest' understood?); metaph., Pr 5.22.

σφόδρα. adv.

very, very much, indicating intensity of degree: + vb which indicates some measurable or gradable quality or property, πληθύνεσθαι 'to increase' Ge 7.18; ἐνίσχυσεν ὁ λιμὸς σ. 'the famine got severe' 47.13; ἠτιμωμένος Ob 2; λελύπησαι, ~μαι Jn 4.4, 9*bis*; ἄνδρισαι τῇ ἰσχύι Na 2.2; εὐφρόνησαν Zc 9.2; ὀδυνηθήσεται 9.5; χαῖρε 9.9; ἐξερευνήσεις σ. 'you shall investigate thoroughly' De 13.14. **b**. + adj.: Ge 12.14, Jl 2.11*bis*; Je 24.2 (|| λίαν vs. 3). **c**. with a comparative, δυνατώτερος ἡμῶν ἐγένου σ. 'you have become much stronger than we' Ge 26.16. **d**. + prep. phrase: εἰς πλῆθος σ. Zc 14.14, 2C 4.18. **e**. σ. may be removed from its head, which precedes: ἠτιμωμένος σὺ εἶ σ. Ob 2; Jl 2.11*a*. It may immediately follow its head (Jl 2.11*b*, Na 2.2, Zp 1.14, Zc 9.2, 5, 9, 14.14) or precede it (Jn 4.9*bis*). **f**. qualifying a noun: πλῆθος σ. 'a large number indeed' Nu 32.1, Is 31.1. **g**. reinforced by σφοδρῶς– ἐπεκράτει σ. σφοδρῶς Ge 7.19. **h**. reinforced by repetition, αὐξανῶ σε σ. σ. 'I shall increase you very much' Ge 17.6; ἐπλούτησεν .. σ. σ. 30.43; Nu 14.7. **i**. at a remove from the nucleus, πονηροὶ καὶ ἁμαρτωλοὶ ἐναντίον τοῦ θεοῦ σ. Ge 13.13; ὁ μισθός σου πολὺς ἔσται σφόδρα 15.1; σκληρὸν δὲ ἐφάνη τὸ ῥῆμα σ. 21.11; μέγας ἐγενήθη σ. Ex 11.3. ***j**. ἕως σ. 'exceedingly': ὠργίσθη 'became angry' La 5.22; ἐπένθησαν 'grieved' 1M 2.39, μεθύων '(utterly) drunk' 1K 25.36, καλή 3K 1.4 (*L* at both latter: om. ἕως); μὴ .. ἕ. σ. 'by no means' Ps 118.43.

Cf. σφοδρῶς, ἐξόχως, λίαν, πάνυ, περισσῶς, ὑπεράγαν, ὑπερβαλλόντως.

σφοδρός, ά, όν.ʃ

vehement, very strong: ***s*** ἄνεμος 'wind' Ex 10.19; sea water, 15.10, Ne 9.11, Wi 18.5, all referring to the same incident; fire of cauldron, 4M 5.32. Cf. ἰσχυρός.

σφοδρῶς. adv.ʃ

very much, exceedingly, indicating intensity of degree: reinforcing σφόδρα– ἐπεκράτει σφόδρα σφοδρῶς 'gained strength exceedingly' Ge 7.19; μακρὰν σφόδρα σ. 'very, very far' Jo 3.16; πρόσχε σ. 'pay careful attention' Si 13.13; 4M 6.11. Cf. σφόδρα.

σφόνδυλος, ου. m.ʃ
vertebra including the neck: of bird, Le 5.8. Cf. σπόνδυλος.

σφραγίζω: fut.mid.2s σφραγιῇ; aor.act. ἐσφράγισα, impv. σφράγισον, inf. σφραγίσαι, mid. ἐσφραγισάμην, ptc. σφραγισάμενος, pass. ἐσφραγίσθην, subj. σφραγισθῶ; pf.pass.3s ἐσφράγισται, ptc. ἐσφραγισμένος.
1. *to affix a seal on*: abs. Es 3.10 o'; *o* a document - βιβλίον ἐσφραγισμένον Is 29.11; only to be forgotten about and + acc. rei, τὸν νόμον τοῦ μὴ μαθεῖν 8.16; δακτυλίῳ 'with a signet-ring' Es 8.8 o', σφραγῖδι 'with a seal' 3K 20.8. **b**. so as to withhold access to contents: Da 6.17, + ἐμφράσσω 12.9 TH. **c**. so as to certify the quantity or quality: + acc., silver, 4K 22.4B.
2. *to store securely*: pass. and ‖ συνάγω – ἐν τοῖς θησαυροῖς μου De 32.34.
3. *to close off* an area or building: + acc., τὸν ναόν Bel 14 LXX; τὴν ἄβυσσον Od 12.3 (‖ πεδάω; + κλείω).
Cf. σφραγίς, κατασφραγίζω: cf. *ND* 2.191.

σφραγίς, ῖδος. f.
seal or *signet-ring* with a marking and closely guarded by its owner: γλύμμα ~ῖδος 'engraved seal' Ex 28.11; ‖ ἐπίσημος PSol 2.6; θήσομαί σε ὡς ~ῖδα, διότι σὲ ᾑρέτισα 'I will make you like a signet-ring because I have chosen you' Hg 2.23; woman's accessory, ~ῖδας καὶ ἐνώτια καὶ δακτυλίους καὶ ἐμπλόκια καὶ περιδέξια Ex 35.22; valuable, ‖ κόρη 'pupil of the eye' Si 17.22; prevents contents inside from coming out, 22.27. Cf. σφραγίζω, ἀποσφράγισμα, δακτύλιος: Russo 190-5.

σφῦρα, ας. f.
hammer: χαλκεὺς τύπτων ~ᾳ 'a coppersmith striking with ..' Is 41.7; ἐν ~αις καὶ ἥλοις 'with .. and nails' Je 10.4; symbol of hardness, ὡς καλάμην ἐλογίσθησαν ~αι 'hammers were counted as stubble' Jb 41.21¶, cf. Je 27.23. Cf. σφυροκόπος and σφυροκοπέω.

σφυροκοπέω: aor. ἐσφυροκόπησα.ʃ *
to beat with a hammer: + acc. pers., Jd 5.26 B. Cf. σφῦρα.

σφυροκόπος, ου.ʃ.
one who beats with a hammer: glossed as χαλκεὺς χαλκοῦ καὶ σιδήρου Ge 4.22. Cf. σφυροκοπέω.

σχάζω: fut. σχασθήσομαι.ʃ
pass. *to move suddenly when there is no more constraint*: *s* trap, εἰ σχασθήσεται παγὶς ἐπὶ τῆς γῆς .. 'Would a trap on the ground spring ..?' Am 3.5.

σχεδία, ας. f.
raft: means of transport across the sea, 3K 5.23, 1E 5.53; for transport of men, Wi 14.5.

σχεδιάζω.ʃ
to act carelessly: Ba 1.19.

σχεδόν. adv.
almost: μετὰ προφήτας σ. ἅπαντας 'after alm. all the prophets' Si prol. II; σ. ἐφ' ἡμέρας τεσσεράκοντα 'for alm. 40 days' 2M 5.2; after a nucleus phrase, 3M 5.14.

σχετλιάζω.ʃ
to complain bitterly: ἐπί τινι 'over sth' 4M 3.12; πρός τι 4.7. Cf. γογγύζω.

σχέτλιος, α, ον.ʃ
abominable: *s* βούλημα 'design' 2M 15.5. Cf. βδελυκτός, βδελυρός.

σχῆμα, ατος. n.ʃ
outward shape: of a female body, ἀποκαλύψω τὸ σ. αὐτῶν Is 3.17. Cf. μορφή: Schmidt 4.351-4; Trench 262-6.

σχίδαξ, ακος. f.
wood cleft into small pieces: firewood, 3K 18.33.

σχίζα, ης. f.
dart: 1K 20.20, 1M 10.80. Cf. βέλος.

σχίζω: fut. σχίσω, pass. σχισθήσομαι; aor. ἔσχισα, ptc. σχίσας, pass. ἐσχίσθην; pf.ptc.mid. ἐσχισμένος.
to split, cleave apart: + acc., ξύλα εἰς ὁλοκάρπωσιν 'firewood ..' Ge 22.3; τὰ ἱμάτια Is 37.1; σε μέσον 'you right down the middle' Su 55 TH; mid. τοὺς χιτῶνας Ge 36.22; ἔνθα καὶ ἔνθα 'on both sides' 1M 6.45; pass. ἐσχίσθη τὸ ὕδωρ Ex 14.21, σχισθήσεται τὸ ὄρος Zc 14.4, πέτρα Is 48.21, Ισραηλ εἰς δύο 1K 15.29*L* (B: διαιρέω); air by flying birds, Wi 5.11. Cf. ἀνα~, ἀπο~, δια~, κατα~, περισχίζω, σχιστός, σχισμή, ῥήγνυμι, τέμνω, διαιρέω.

σχῖνος, ου. f.ʃ
mastic tree: Su 54.

σχισμή, ῆς. f.ʃ
cleft, crevice: σ. ὀρέων Jn 2.6; πετρῶν 'of rocks' Is 2.19 (‖ σπήλαια 'caves'), 21 (‖ τρῶγλαι 'holes'). Cf. σχίζω.

σχιστός, ή, όν.ʃ
torn: *s* fishing-net Is 19.9. Cf. σχίζω.

σχοινίον, ου. n.
1. *cord*: with which firmly to bind a clothing round the body, Am 2.8; ἀντὶ ζώνης σχοινίῳ ζώσῃ 'you shall gird with a cord instead of a belt' Is 3.24; plain hairband, PSol 2.20; with which to pull sth towards onself, 5.18 (‖ ἱμάς); of a trap, Ps 139.6; symbol of constraint, πενίας 'of poverty' Jb 36.8¶ (‖ χειροπέδη 'handcuff').
2. *land-measure*: σ. γεωμετρικόν Zc 2.1; ἡ γῆ σου ἐν ~ῳ καταμετρηθήσεται Am 7.17; βάλλω ~ον Mi 2.5.
Cf. σχοίνισμα, σχοινισμός, σπαρτίον, σχοῖνος and μέτρον.

σχοίνισμα, ατος. n. *

1. *long narrow area*: τὸ σ. τῆς θαλάσσης 'the coastal strip' Zp 2.5, 7.

2. *piece of land measured out*, see σχοῖνος **4**: σ. κληρονομίας (ǁ μερίς) De 32.9; Ez 47.13, Ps 104.11.

3. *long narrow object*, symbolic name of a shepherd's staff, Zc 11.7, 14.

4. *line of people* picked for a certain treatment: for execution or survival, 2K 8.2.

On the semantic development of this lexeme, see σχοῖνος used in Egypt in the sense of 'land-measure' (LSJ, s.v., III). Cf. σχοινίον and σχοῖνος.

σχοινισμός, οῦ. m.ʃ

piece of land measured out by the σχοῖνος: Jo 17.5. Cf. σχοῖνος: Rupprecht 1994.82f.; *BA* 6.60.

σχοῖνος, ου. f.ʃ

1. *rush, reed*: τὸν χειμάρρουν τῶν ~ων Jl 3.18; a place-name or a mechanical rendering, Mi 6.5.

2. *reed-pen, stylus*: σ. ψευδὴς τοῖς γραμματεῦσιν 'a false pen of the scribes' Je 8.8.

***3**. *path*: ǁ ὁδός, τρίβος Je 18.15; ǁ τρίβος Ps 138.3.

4. a land-measure of unknown length: ἀπέχοντι ὡσεὶ ~ους πέντε 'about five ?'s away' 2M 11.5.

Cf. σχοίνισμα, σχοινισμός, and σχοινίον: Renehan 1.187; Aitken 2000; LSG s.v.

σχολάζω: aor.impv.2pl σχολάσατε.ʃ

1. *to take it easy*: Ex 5.8; σχολάζετε, σχολασταί ἐστε 5.17.

2. *to take time, to devote time to study*: σχολάσατε καὶ γνῶτε ὅτι .. Ps 45.11.

Cf. σχολαστής, σχολή, μανθάνω.

σχολαστής, οῦ. m.ʃ

lazy person, 'lazy-bones': Σχολάζετε, ~αί ἐστε Ex 5.17. Cf. σχηολάζω.

σχολή, ῆς. f.ʃ

freedom from strenuous work and activity, 'leisure': κατὰ ~ὴν τῆς πορεύσεως 'with a leisurely pace of the march' Ge 33.14; σοφία γραμματέως ἐν εὐκαιρίᾳ ~ῆς 'the wisdom of a scribe lies in the opportunity of leisure, i.e. freedom from the mundane routine' Si 38.24; w. negative connotation, Pr 28.19. Cf. ἀγρία.

σῴζω: fut.act. σώσω, pass. σωθήσομαι; aor. ἔσωσα, inf. σῶσαι, impv. σῶσον, subj. σώσω, pass. ἐσώθην, subj. σωθῶ, inf. σωθῆναι, ptc. σωθείς; pf. σέσωκα, ptc.pass. σεσῳσμένος. On the orthography, cf. Renehan, 1.187.

I. act. and pass. *to save, rescue* out of some difficult situation: + acc. pers., Ho 14.4, Mi 6.9, Jl 2.32, Ob 21, Hb 1.2, 3.13, Ma 3.15; ἐκ χειρὸς μισούντων Ps 105.10, ἐκ τῶν ἐχθρῶν μου 17.4, ἑαυτοὺς ἐκ πολέμου .. ἐκ κακῶν Ep Je 49, με ἐξ ἀπωλείας Si 51.12 (ǁ ἐξαιρέομαι); ἀπὸ βασιλέως 'Ασσυρίων Is 20.6; motivated by a sense of pity and mercy, Ho 1.7*a*, Is 63.8; by military means, Ho 1.7*b*; τὴν ψυχὴν αὐτοῦ Am 2.14, 15, τὴν σεαυτοῦ ψυχήν Ge 19.17, ψυχὰς πενήτων Ps 71.13 (ǁ φείδομαι); τὴν ἐκπεπιεσμένην καὶ τὴν ἀπωσμένην 'one who was oppressed and rejected' Zp 3.19; τὰ σκηνώματα Ιουδα Zc 12.7; οἱ σωθέντες τοῦ Ιακωβ Is 10.20 (ǁ τὸ καταλειφθὲν τοῦ Ιακωβ vs. 21); + cogn. acc., σωτηρίαν αἰώνιον Is 45.17. **b**. God of Israel as (ὁ) σῴζων: Ho 13.4, cf. Zp 3.17 (resulting in harmonious and happy relationship with Him) and λαὸς σῳζόμενος ὑπὸ κυρίου De 33.29; ǁ δίκαιος, Zc 9.9; 9.16, 10.6, 12.7; moral rescue, ἐκ ἀκαθαρσιῶν Ez 36.29. **c**. leads to "life": Ge 19.20, 22. **d**. opp. destruction (ἐκκόπτω): Ge 32.8.

II. mid. *to flee for life*: εἰς ὄρος σῴζου Ge 19.17 (ǁ σῷζε τὴν σεαυτοῦ ψυχήν); 1K 27.1, 4K 19.37 (*L* διασῴζομαι).

2. *to save one's own skin and come out victorious*: 1K 14.47.

Cf. ἀνα~, διασῴζω, σωτήρ, σωτηρία, σωτήριον, ἐξαιρέω, ἰάομαι, ῥύω, σῷος: Fohrer, *TDNT* 7.970-3; ib. 1969.275-93; Spicq 3.344-57.

σῶμα, ατος. n.

1. *physical body*: ~ατα νεκρά 4K 19.35 ǁ Is 37.36 (slain soldiers); ἀσθενήσουσιν ἐν τοῖς ~ασιν αὐτῶν 'they will grow physically weak' Na 3.3; Da 3.95; πρόσεχε τῷ ~ατι αὐτῶν 'keep an eye on their [= young daughters'] chastity' Si 7.24; 51.2, Jb 33.17; Pr 11.17, Wi 1.4, 2M 6.30 (:: ψυχή); of animals, Jb 40.32, σάρκες ~ατος 41.15; οἱ σωματοφύλακες οἱ φυλάσσοντες τὸ σ. τοῦ βασιλέως 'the royal bodyguards' 1E 3.4, cf. 1C 28.1. **b**. specifically w. ref. to the hum. sexual organ: Le 6.10, so poss. 15.2f., 19.

2. *dead body*, 'carcass, corpse': of a hum., De 21.23, 1K 31.10, of sacrificed animals, τὰ ~ατα, τὰ διχοτομήματα Ge 15.11; of a slain animal, Da 7.11; food for lions, Bel 32 TH (LXX τῶν ἐπιθανατίων ~ατα 'of those condemned to death').

3. *torso* of a graven image: Ep Je 21 (:: κεφαλή).

4. *slave*: τὰ ~ατα αὐτῶν .. ᾐχμαλώτευσαν Ge 34.29 (ǁ ἀποσκευὴν .. καὶ γυναῖκας); τὰς γυναῖκας αὐτοῦ καὶ τοὺς υἱοὺς καὶ τὰς θυγατέρας καὶ πάντα τὰ ~ατα τοῦ οἴκου αὐτοῦ καὶ πάντα τὰ ὑπάρχοντα καὶ πάντα τὰ κτήνη .. 36.6; To 10.10 𝔊[I] (παῖδας καὶ παιδίσκας 𝔊[II]), 2M 8.11. See Scholl 1983.13f.

5. *person* as living, physical entity: κατὰ σ. 'according to the number of persons' Ge 47.12; to be owned and exploited by others, 47.18, Ne 9.37.

Cf. σωματικός, σάρξ, ψυχή, θνησιμαῖος, κῶλον, πτῶμα: Grobel; Baumgärtel and Schweizer, *TDNT* 7.1044-8; Scharbert 121-4; Gundry 9-23; Spicq 1978.224f.; Ziesler; Lys 1986.

σωματικός, ή, όν.ʃ
pertaining to σῶμα, 'bodily, physical': opp. ψυχικός 'psychic,' *s* ἐπιθυμία 'desire' 4M 1.32, πάθος 'passion' 3.1. Cf. σῶμα, σάρκινος, ψυχικός: Spicq 3.358.

σωματοποιέω: aor. ἐσωματοποίησα.ʃ
to provide with bodily strength: *o* sickly sheep, Ez 34.4. Cf. ἐνισχύω, ἰάομαι.

σωματοφύλαξ, ακος. m.
bodyguard: 1E 3.4. Cf. φύλαξ.

σῷος, η, ον.ʃ
undamaged, unharmed, intact: *s* seal, Bel 17 TH; deposits, ~α διαφυλάξαι 'to keep safe' 2M 3.15; hum., 12.24, 3M 2.7. Cf. ἀπήμαντος, ἀσινής, σῴζω.

σωρεύω: fut. σωρεύσω; aor. ἐσώρευσα.ʃ
to heap sth on sth else: αὐτὰ [= furniture] ἐπ' αὐτῶν [= carts] Ju 15.11; ἄνθρακας ἐπὶ τὴν κεφαλήν αὐτοῦ 'coals on his head' Pr 25.22. Cf. σωρός, σωρηδόν, στοιβάζω, ἐπιτίθημι.

σωρηδόν. adv.ʃ
in heaps: + πίπτω Wi 18.23. Cf. σωρεύω.

σωρός, οῦ. m.
heap: mound of stones, Jo 7.26; of coal, 4M 9.20; ~οὺς ~ούς 'heap upon heap' 2C 31.6. Cf. σωρεύω, σκόπελος, χελώνη.

σωτήρ, ῆρος. m.
saviour: of God of Israel, ἀπὸ θεοῦ ~ῆρος αὐτοῦ De 32.15; ǁ ὁ θεός μου Mi 7.7, Hb 3.18; ἀπηλπισμένων 'of the hopeless' Ju 9.11. **b**. of hum. saviour, Jd 3.9; pl. Ne 9.27, cf. van der Kooij 1987.141. On σ. w. ref. to physicians, see Merkelbach 1971; on its application to secular rulers, see *BA* 7.22f.
Cf. σῴζω: Forher, *TDNT* 7.1012f.

σωτηρία, ας. f.
1. *rescue, deliverance* out of some difficulty: κυρίου 'by the Lord' Ge 49.18; παρὰ τοῦ θεοῦ Ex 14.13; ἐν τῷ ὄρει Σιων ἔσται ἡ σ. Ob 17; ἡ ἱππασία σου σ. 'your cavalry is your salvation' Hb 3.8; ἐξῆλθες εἰς ~αν λαοῦ σου 'you went out to save your people' 3.13; σ. ἐκ πάσης θλίψεως Is 63.8, cf. Jn 2.10; ǁ φυγή Je 32.21; *s* God Is 12.2, cf. κύριε τῆς ~ας μου 38.20; opp. ἀπώλεια Wi 18.7. Cf. *ND* 3.28f.
2. *security, safety*: ἀποστρέψῃ με μετὰ ~ας εἰς τὸν οἶκον τοῦ πατρός μου 'bring me back safely to my father's house' Ge 28.21; 26.31.
Cf. σῴζω, σωτήριον.

σωτήριον, ου. n.
1. *deliverance, security*: Ge 41.16; ἄγω ~α 'to celebrate deliverance' Es 1 5 *L*, 3M 6.31.
2. *thank-offering for deliverance*: ὁλοκαυτώματα .. καὶ σωτήρια Ex 20.24; ὁλοκαυτώματα .. θυσίαν ~ου 24.5; σ. κυρίῳ δεκτὸν εἰς ὀσμὴν εὐωδίας Le 17.4; ~ου ἐπιφανείας 'displays of ..' Am 5.22. **b**. σωτηρίου - ὁλοκαυτώματα understood, Ez 45.15, τὰ τοῦ σωτηρίου 45.17, 46.2.
Cf. σῴζω, σωτηρία: Foerster and Fohrer, *TDNT* 7.1021-4; Daniel 281-7; Spicq 3.642f.

σωτήριος, ον.
pertaining to deliverance from danger: *s* κώθων 'drinking bout' 3M 6.31, πότος 'party' 7.18; εὐπείθεια 'submission (conducive to deliverance)' 4M 12.6; γενέσεις 'creatures' capable of, or meant for, perpetual existence, Wi 1.14.

σωφρόνως. adv.ʃ
wisely: Wi 9.11. Cf. σώφρων, σοφῶς.

σωφροσύνη, ης. f.
1. *soundness in judgement*, 'prudence': Es B 3.
2. *moderation in sensual desires*, 'temperance, self-control': 4M 1.3; in a list of Stoic moral ideals, + ἀνδρεία, δικαιοσύνη 1.6, also + φρόνησις 1.18, cf. Wi 8.7; defined as ἐπικράτεια ἐπιθυμιῶν 'control of desires' 4M 1.31.
Cf. σώφρων, σοφία: North; Spicq 3.359-65.

σώφρων, ονος; n. σῶφρον.
capable of controlling excesses and deviations from the right path: *s* hum., Joseph vis-à-vis Potyphar's wife, 4M 2.2, ǁ δίκαιος, ἀνδρεῖος 'courageous' 15.10; νοῦς 'mind' 1.35, 2.16, 3.17; λογισμός 'reason' 3.19; βασιλεία 'rule, control' 2.23 (ǁ δίκαιος, ἀγαθός, ἀνδρεῖος).
Cf. σωφρόνως, σωφροσύνη, σοφός, φρόνιμος, ἄφρων: Luck, *TDNT* 7.1100-2; Spicq 3.359-65. Del. 4M 7.23.

T

τάγμα, ατος. n.
body of soldiers, 'division, brigade': Nu 2.2, 10.14. Cf. δύναμις, στρατόπεδον, τάξις **4**: Taylor 2003.80-2.

ταινία, ας. f.
fascia: σανίδων κυπαρίσσου 'of cypress planks' Ez 27.5.

τακτικός, ή, όν.
suited and authorised to issue orders: ***s*** hum., Da 6.2 TH (ranked higher than satrap).

τακτός, ή, όν.ʃ
prescribed: εἰς χρόνον ~όν 'for an appointed period' Jb 12.5. Cf. τάσσω.

ταλαιπωρέω: fut. ~ρήσω; aor. ἐταλαιπώρησα, ptc. ~ρήσας; pf. τεταλαιπώρηκα.

1. *to suffer misery*: μεγάλως μεγιστᾶνες ἐταλαιπώρησαν 'mighty men have greatly suffered' Zc 11.2, ἐταλαιπώρησα καὶ κατεκάμφθην ἕως τέλους 'I was wretched and was brought utterly low' Ps 37.7, οὐαὶ ἡμῖν, ὅτι ταλαιπωροῦμεν Je 4.13; ‖ καταισχύνομαι 9.19; + cog. dat. ταλαιπωρίᾳ Mi 2.4; ***s*** nature, τὰ πεδία .. σῖτος Jl 1.10 (‖ πενθέω), πᾶσα ἡ γῆ Je 4.20, cf. αἱ στῆλαι 'the columns (of altars)' Ho 10.2.

2. *to make suffer misery*: ptc. and/or + acc. pers., ἀπὸ προσώπου ἀσεβῶν ταλαιπωρησάντων με Ps 16.9, οὐαὶ τοῖς ταλαιπωροῦσιν ὑμᾶς 'Woe unto those who ..' Is 33.1 (‖ ποιέω ταλαιπώρους); Je 12.12.

Cf. ταλαιπωρία, ταλαίπωρος, πενθέω: Spicq 3.366-8.

ταλαιπωρία, ας. f.
wretched, miserable condition: ~αν καὶ ἀσέβειαν Hb 1.3 (‖ κόπος and πόνος); ἀδικίαν καὶ ~αν Am 3.10, Ez 45.9 (:: κρίμα καὶ δικαιοσύνη at latter); τ. θηρίων πτοήσει σε 'distress caused by wild beasts will scare you' Hb 2.17; τ. Αἰγύπτου Ho 9.6; brought on by outside enemies, Je 6.26; + σύντριμμα Is 59.7; ‖ ὀνειδισμός Ps 68.21. Cf. ταλαιπωρέω.

ταλαίπωρος, ον.

1. *suffering misery and misfortune*, 'wretched': due to some calamity, national or personal and ***s*** pers., Is 33.1; Ps 136.8 (:: μακάριος); as a result of ungodliness, Wi 3.11, 13.10; subst.m. To 13.10, 2M 4.47.

2. *causing misery*: ὦ ~ων κακῶν 'what miserable calamities!' To 7.7 𝔊II; ἐπίπονον καὶ ~ον .. καταστροφήν 'painful and pitiful destruction' 3M 5.47.

Cf. ταλαιπωρέω, τάλας, δηλαϊστός, δυσάθλιος, μακάριος: Schmidt 4.443-5. Del. 3M 5.5 v.l.

τάλαντον, ου. n.
definite measure of weight: of gold, Ex 25.39; μολίβου 'of lead' Zc 5.7.

τάλας, ~αινα, ~αν; gen. ~ανος, ~αίνης, ~ανος.ʃ
wretched, miserable: ***s*** hum., 4M 8.17, 12.3; Ὦ τάλας ἐγώ 'o, what a wretch I am!' Is 6.5; subst.m., ἀφρονέστατοι καὶ ~ανες ὑπὲρ ψυχὴν νηπίου 'the most foolish and more miserable than the soul of an infant' Wi 15.14. Cf. ταλαίπωρος, τρισάθλιος, μέλεος: Schmidt 4.446-50.

ταμίας, ου. m.ʃ
treasurer, paymaster: Is 22.15.

ταμιεῖον, ου. n. On the accentuation, see Walters 94f.

1. *storehouse*: De 28.8; for grains, Pr 3.10.

2. *private, small room*, 'closet, chamber': εἰσελθὼν εἰς τὸ τ. ἔκλαυσεν ἐκεῖ 'having entered the closet, he wept there' Ge 43.30; τ. κοιτώνων 'recesses of bed-chambers' Ex 8.3, Ec 10.20; τ. κλινῶν 'bedchamber' 4K 11.2; royal, 3K 1.15B (*L* κοιτών); bridal chamber, To 7.15; ‖ κοιτών 2K 13.10B; νότου 'of the south' Jb 9.9 (astronomical t.t.); τοῦ θανάτου Pr 7.27. **b**. not readily accessible and visible: metaph., κοιλίας 'one's inner being' Pr 20.27, σπλάγχνων 26.22; καρδίας 'the innermost (secrets) of the heart' PSol 14.8.

Cf. κοιτών.

ταμιεύω: fut. ταμιεύσομαι.ʃ
mid. *to deal out*: abs. (***o*** one's emotions implied), κατὰ μέρος 'bit by bit' Pr 29.11. **b**. τινά (for sbd) τινί (sth as retribution): 4M 12.12. Cf. μερίζω.

τανύω: aor. ἐτάνυσα, ptc. τανύσας.ʃ
to stretch out, extend: + acc., τὸν οὐρανόν Jb 9.8; rainbow, Si 43.12. Cf. (ἐκ)τείνω: Shipp 528.

τάξις, εως. f.

1. *assigned position* or *post*: ἀνὴρ ἐν τῇ ἑαυτοῦ ~ει Nu 1.52; ἡ σελήνη ἔστη ἐν τῇ ~ει αὐτῆς 'the moon stood in her course' Hb 3.11; ~ιν ἔθετο σκότει 'he assigned a position to darkness' Jb 28.3; κατὰ τὴν ~ιν Μελχισεδεκ Ps 109.4; of temple staff, 1E 1.14 (‖ στάσις 2C 35.15).

2. *regularity*: ἐν ~ει 'in orderly fashion' 1E 1.6; in speech, Pr 31.25.

3. *general character, nature*: τ. ἄνυδρον 'dry in character' 2M 1.19, 9.18, cf. Wilhelm 15-7.

4. *division of an army*: 2M 8.22, 10.36, cf. τάγμα.

Cf. ἡγεμονία, τάσσω and τόπος.

ταπεινός, ή, όν.

1. *situated low*: physically, ἡ ὄψις τῆς ἁφῆς ~ὴ ἀπὸ τοῦ δέρματος τοῦ χρωτός 'the visible symptom of the infection is beneath the surface of the skin' Le 13.3; opp. ὑψηλός 1M 6.40. **b.** subst.n.pl., 'low-lying region, i.e. to the west of the Judaean hills' Jo 11.16; (water resources in) the low-lying region (of the Negev) Jd 1.15 (:: μετέωρα); affairs down on the earth, Ps 112.6, sim. 137.6 (:: ὑψηλός). **c.** in social status, 'lowly,' λαὸν πραῢν καὶ ~όν 'a meek and lowly people' Zp 3.12 (opp. φαυλίσματα τῆς ὕβρεως, vs. 11), sim. and subst., Is 26.6, Am 2.7, 8.6, Si 13.21 (|| πτωχός); ~οὶ γῆς Zp 2.3; + πένης Ps 81.3; + ὀρφανός 9.39; oppressed by foreign powers, Ju 16.11; opp. ἔνδοξος 1K 18.23, ὕψος Ec 10.6. **d.** in value: τιμῇ 'in value' Le 27.8. **e.** *vertically short*, 'low': *s* ξύλον Ez 17.24 (:: ὑψηλός).

2. *humble* in attitude: opp. ὑπερήφανος 'haughty' Pr 3.34; 11.2; ὅσιοι καὶ ~οὶ καρδίᾳ 'pious ..' Da 3.87.

3. *despondent, depressed*: *s* hum. and + ἀκατάστατος 'unsettled' Is 54.11; καρδία Si 25.23; subst. and τῷ πνεύματι Ps 33.19 (|| συντετριμμένος τὴν καρδίαν).

Cf. ταπεινόω, ταπεινότης, ταπεινοφρονέω, πτωχός, πραΰς, ὑπερήφανος, ὕβρις, δυσγένεια: Grundmann, *TDNT* 8.9-10; Rehrl 1961.147-73; Leivestad 1966; Spicq 3.369-71.

ταπεινότης, ητος. f.ʃ

humility: βδέλυγμα ὑπερηφάνῳ τ. 'humility is an abomination to the proud' Si 13.20. Cf. ταπεινός, ὑπερηφανία.

ταπεινοφρονέω.ʃ

to be humble-minded: *s* hum., Ps 130.2 (:: ὑψοῦμαι). Cf. ταπεινός, ταπεινόφρων, ὑψόω.

ταπεινόφρων, ον, gen. ονος.ʃ

humble-minded: *s* hum., Pr 29.23 (:: ὕβρις). Cf. ταπεινοφρονέω, ὕβρις.

ταπεινόω: fut.act. ~νώσω, pass. ~νωθήσομαι; aor. ἐταπείνωσα, subj. ~νώσω, inf. ~νῶσαι, impv. ~νωσον, ptc. ~νώσας, pass. ἐταπεινώθην, impv. ~νώθητι, subj. ~νωθῶ, inf. ~νωθῆναι, ptc. ~νωθείς, opt.3s ~νωθείη; pf.ptc.pass. τεταπεινωμένος

1. *to bring low*: + acc., high city-wall to be demolished, Is 25.12, voice Si 29.5 (:: ὑψόω); pass. ***o*** πᾶν ὄρος καὶ βουνός 'every mount and hill' Is 40.4, τὸ ἔδαφος τῆς γῆς κάτω 'the base of the earth downwards' Je 38.35. **b.** metaph.: τὴν κεφαλήν σου Si 4.7 (mark of diffidence); pass., ***o*** hum. worshippers, Is 2.12 (|| κύπτω 'bend forward'), ὀφθαλμοὶ μετέωροι 'proudly raised eyes' 5.15[b], ἐπὶ μετεώρων 2K 22.28 (|| ὑψηλῶν; ὑπερηφάνων Ps 17.28); ὕβριν 'pride' Ho 5.5, Is 25.11; τὸ ὕψος τῶν ἀνθρώπων 2.11 (:: ὑψόω and vs. 17 || πίπτω); δόξα 3.8; *to devalue*, τὸ ὑψηλόν Ez 21.26 (:: ὑψόω). **c.** *to cause to feel to be low in estimation*: + acc., τινα 1K 2.7 (*s* God; opp. ἀνυψόω, cf. Si 7.11), Pr 25.7, ὑβριστήν Jb 40.11; ψυχήν Si 2.17 (|| φοβέομαι); and w. ref. to a fast, ψυχήν Le 16.29, 31, Is 58.3; Le 23.27 (|| Nu 29.7 with κακόω), ἐν νηστείᾳ Ps 34.13, cf. Si 7.17, 31.31; ὑπερηφάνους ταπεινώσω Is 1.25; former elite, 5.15[a] (|| ἀτιμάζομαι), cf. "grovel in dust and ashes" Si 40.3; as a result of poverty, Le 25.39, cf. 27.8, Pr 13.7 (:: πλουτίζω), 10.4; πνεῦμα – ἐν ψυχῇ συντετριμμένῃ καὶ πνεύματι τεταπεινωμένῳ Da 3.29 LXX (TH: ταπεινώσεως), καρδία Ps 50.19. **d.** *to bring under control and to submission*: τινα Jd 16.5; Ho 14.9 (|| κατισχύω); through a military defeat, 1C 20.4. **e.** mid. *to submit oneself* to sbd's authority: ὑπὸ τὰς χεῖρας αὐτῆς Ge 16.9, cf. 1 Pet 5.6; "I lay low" Ps 38.3. **f.** mid. *to take a humble, low view of one's own value out of a sense of awe or respect for sbd else*: ἀπὸ προσώπου θεοῦ 2C 33.12, ^ἐναντίον κυρίου^ (*L* om.) 33.23, ἐνώπιόν τινος Es 6.13 o'; ταπεινώθητε said to rulers, Je 13.18.

2. *to subject to humiliation*: + acc. pers. Ge 15.13 (|| δουλόω, κακόω); Ho 14.9 (:: κατισχύω), Ps 74.8, Is 3.17 (:: ὑψόω); ὑπὸ τοὺς πόδας αὐτοῦ 'under his feet' La 3.34; εἰς γῆν 'utterly' Ps 142.3; pass. ***o*** woman Ho 2.15, sexually violated La 2.5, Ez 22.10, 11; by having premarital sexual relationships and without her family's consent, Ge 34.2, De 22.24, cf. 21.14; defeated soldiers, Jd 11.33 *L* (A: ἐντρέπομαι), Is 3.25; of ill-treatment, ὑπὸ τὰς χεῖρας αὐτῆς Ge 16.9, cf. ὀστᾶ τεταπεινωμένα Ps 50.10; Ex 1.12; De 26.6 (|| κακόω) ἕως καὶ ταπεινωθῇ ἐκ σκηνωμάτων Ιακωβ 'until he is even humiliated (and cast) out of the tents of Jacob' Ma 2.12; ἐν πόδαις τοὺς πόδας αὐτῶν 'their feet with fetters' Ps 104.18; opp. δοξάζω La 1.8.

Cf. ταπεινός, ταπείνωσις, ἀτιμάζω, ἀν~, ὑψόω: Grundmann, *TDNT* 8.6-9.

ταπείνωσις, εως. f.

1. *humiliating situation*: ἐπήκουσεν ὁ κύριος τῇ ~ει σου 'the Lord took note of ..' Ge 16.11; εἶδέν μου κύριος τὴν ~ιν 29.32, sim. 1K 1.11 (also of a barren wife); τὴν ~ίν μου καὶ τὸν κόπον τῶν χειρῶν μου εἶδεν ὁ θεός 'God saw .. and the toil of my hands' Ge 31.42; γῆ ~εώς μου 41.52; εἶδεν τὴν ~ιν ἡμῶν καὶ τὸν μόχθον ἡμῶν καὶ τὸν θλιμμὸν ἡμῶν 'he saw .. and our hardship and our affliction' De 26.7; || δουλεία La 1.3; + πένθος 'sorrow' 1M 3.51, + κόπος Ps 24.18, ἀνάγκαι 'dire straits' 30.8. **b.** v.n. of ταπεινόω **2**: PSol 2.35.

2. *humility* of attitude: ἐν ψυχῇ συντετριμμένῳ καὶ πνεύματι ~εως Da 3.39 TH (LXX: τεταπεινωμένῳ).

*__3.__ *fasting*: 2E 9.5; ψυχῆς || νηστεία PSol 3.8.

Cf. ταπεινός, ταπεινόω, ἀτιμία, θλιμμός, κόπος, μόχθος: Grundmann, *TDNT* 8.10f.

ταράσσω: fut. ταράξω, pass. ταραχθήσομαι; aor. ἐτάραξα, subj. ταράξω, inf. ταράξαι, ptc. ταράξας, pass. ἐταράχθην, inf. ταραχθῆναι, ptc. ταραχθείς, subj. ταραχθῶ, impv.3pl ταραχθήτωσαν, opt.3pl ταραχθείησαν; pf.pass. τετάραγμαι, ptc. τεταραγμένος.

1. *to stir, set in motion*: ***o*** ὕδωρ, Ho 6.8, Hb 3.15; τὸ ὕδωρ τοῖς ποσί σου '.. with your feet' Ez 32.2, τὴν θάλασσαν Is 51.15 (causing howling billows), cf. Je 5.22; pass. of earthquake - οὐ ταραχθήσεται ἡ γῆ Am 8.8, sim. Is 24.19, Ps 45.3; τὰ ὄρη 45.4, τὰ θεμέλια τῶν ὀρέων 'the foundations of the mountains' 17.8, ἄβυσσοι 'the depth of the sea' 76.17; βουνοί Je 4.24 (|| τρέμω). **b**. of mental agitation, ***o*** hum., Ps 2.5, 38.7, 82.16, αἰσχυνθείησαν καὶ ταραχθείησαν οἱ ἐχθροί μου 'may my enemies be ashamed and dismayed' 6.11; and pass., 'became alarmed' Ge 19.16, 'became deeply moved' 43.30, 45.3; πρὸς ἀλλήλους 42.28; ἦσαν τεταραγμένοι 40.6; Is 8.12 (|| φοβέομαι), Ps 47.6 (|| θαυμάζω, σαλεύομαι), ἐν τῷ ὕπνῳ Da 2.1 LXX (TH ἐξέστη τὸ πνεῦμα αὐτοῦ), cf. αἱ ὁράσεις .. ἐτάρασσόν με Da 7.15 TH and ἐπὶ τοῖς γεγενημένοις 'over what had happened' Es 4.1*L*, ἐπὶ πάσῃ βοῇ Si 30.7; ἀπὸ προσώπου σου Is 64.2, ἀπὸ τοῦ βασιλέως Es 7.6 o'; ἐταράχθη ἡ ψυχὴ αὐτοῦ Ge 41.8, τὸ πνεῦμα τῶν Αἰγύπτων Is 19.3, sim. Hb 3.2, ἡ καρδία μου 37.11, 108.22, ταύτης 'over this matter' Jb 37.1¶, τὸ θράσος αὐτῆς 'by her daring' Ju 16.10; psychosomatic effect - ἡ κοιλία μου Si 51.21, La 1.20, τὰ ὀστᾶ μου 'my bones' Ps 6.3, ἀπὸ θυμοῦ ὁ ὀφθαλμός μου 6.8, ὁ ὀφθαλμός .. ἡ ψυχή .. ἡ γαστήρ μου 30.10, σπλάγχνά αὐτοῦ 'his entrails' Si 30.7, ἡ μήτρα αὐτῆς 3K 3.26; associated with fear and angst, Ps 54.5; φόβῳ δεινῷ 'with tremendous fear' Wi 5.2; ἡ ἕξις μου 'my body' Hb 3.16; ***o*** πρόσωπον '(he has lost) his orientation (?)' Ec 10.10.

2. *to confuse*: ***o*** τὴν τρίβον τῶν ποδῶν ὑμῶν 'the path of your feet' Is 3.12 (|| πλανάω), also La 3.9?, cf. Albrektson 133.

3. *to destabilise*: acc., τρίβους 'paths' La 3.9; metaph., τὸ δίκαιον 'justice' Jb 8.3, 34.10, κρίσιν 34.12, φίλους '(relatioship between) friends' Si 28.9.

Cf. ἐπιταράσσω, ταραχή, τάραχος, ταραχώδης, ἀταραξία, σείω, τρέμω, θαυμάζω, συγχέω: Spicq 3.372-6. Del. Wi 17.4 v.l.

ταραχή, ῆς. f.

upheaval: political and military, Je 14.19 (:: εἰρήνη, ἴασις), ἡμέρα ~ῆς καὶ ἀπωλείας καὶ καταπατήματος Is 22.5; earthquake, 24.19; mental, La 3.59, + δειλία 'fear' 3M 6.19; δὸς ἐν αὐταῖς ~ήν 'Give them a bit of shock' Ez 23.46; μάχης 'of a strife' Pr 26.21. **b**. *cause of upheaval*: ἐγὼ ὡς τ. τῷ Εφραιμ Ho 5.12 (|| κέντρον). Cf. ταράσσω, τάραχος, σεισμός, σύγχυσις.

τάραχος, ου. m.

commotion: physical, σεισμός, τ. ἐπὶ τῆς γῆς Es A 4; mental, Jd 11.35 B; caused by a calamity, 1K 5.9 (|| σύγχυσις vs. 6). Cf. ταραχή and ταράσσω.

ταραχώδης, ες.ʃ

liable to disturb: ***s*** λόγος Ps 90.3; subst.n., Wi 17.9 (|| ταραχή vs. 8). Cf. ταράσσω.

ταριχεύω.ʃ

to preserve food *by salting*: abs., Ep Je 27. Cf. ἁλίζω.

ταρσός, οῦ. m.ʃ

flat surface: of the outstreched wings of a bird, Wi 5.11.

τάρταρος, ου. m.ʃ

the netherworld: τῆς ἀβύσσου Jb 41.24; 40.20; τ. καὶ γῆ Pr 30.16. Cf. ἄβυσσος.

τάσσω, τάττω: fut. τάξω, mid. τάξομαι; aor. ἔταξα, inf. τάξαι, impv. τάξον, ptc. τάξας, subj. τάξω, mid. ἐταξάμην, impv. τάξαι, ptc. ταξάμενος, subj. τάξωμαι, ptc.pass. ταχθείς; pf.act. τέταχα, pass. τέταγμαι, ptc. τεταγμένος.

1. *to position, station in a fixed place*: abs. ἐξ αὐτοῦ ἔταξε, of uncertain meaning, Zc 10.4; + acc. τάξαι εἰς ὕψος νοσσιὰν αὐτοῦ 'to set his nest high up' Hb 2.9; συνοχὴν ἔταξεν ἐφ' ἡμᾶς 'he has laid siege against us' Mi 5.1; βδελύγματα 'objects of abominable worship' Je 7.30, βωμούς 11.13. **b**. *to put in place* sbd charged with a certain task: ***s*** God, + acc., κριτὰς ἐπὶ τὸν λαόν μου 2K 7.11. **c**. metaph.: τάξατε δὴ τὰς καρδίας ὑμῶν εἰς τὰς ὁδοὺς ὑμῶν 'Set your hearts on your paths' Hg 1.5 (|| τίθημι vs. 7), cf. 2.18, Ez 44.5; τὸ πρόσωπόν τινος + inf., 4K 12.18B (*L* τίθημι); εἰς τὴν καρδίαν σου '(lay) to your heart' Ez 40.4, 44.5; 'to set out in orderly fashion' - ἡγεμονία .. τεταγμένη 'orderly government' Si 10.1. **d**. *to put in order ready for a battle* (?): + ^τὰς πόλεις^ ἐν σκεύεσιν ὀχυρώσεως 'with means for fortification' 1M 14.10.

2. *to consign, condemn* (*to* εἰς): εἰς κρίμα Hb 1.12, εἰς ἀφανισμόν 'annihilation' Zc 7.14, Ma 1.3.

***3**. *to cause to become*: + double acc., τὸν τάξαντα ἄμμον ὅριον τῇ θαλάσσῃ 'one who made the sand (on the beach) the boundary for the sea' Je 5.22; ὑμᾶς .. ἑκατοντάρχους 'you .. centurions' 1K 22.7; + acc. and adj. τὴν καρδίαν αὐτῶν ἔταξαν ἀπειθῆ 'they made their heart disobedient' Zc 7.12; + acc. and ὡς– τάξω αὐτὴν ὡς γῆν ἄνυδρον 'waterless land' Ho 2.3 (|| τίθημι); τάξει αὐτοὺς ὡς ἵππον εὐπρεπῆ 'comely horse' Zc 10.3; + acc. and εἰς– τὴν γῆν αὐτοῦ εἰς ἔρημον Je 2.15, εἰς ἀφανισμόν 18.16; mid. 2M 10.28; pass. τέτακται δυνατή Zp 1.14.

4. *to assign as task*: τὸ ταχθέν 'the assignment' Ep Je 61 (‖ συνταχθέν vs. 62).

5. *to give charge* (over): + acc. pers., "over (ἐπὶ πᾶσαν) all the accounts of his kingdom" To 1.21; ἐπὶ τῶν πραγμάτων 'over the running of the state' Es B 6; πρός τινι (task) 2M 6.21.

6. *to institute*: + acc., ὁρισμόν 'decision' Da 6.12 TH.

7. mid. *to indicate by way of instruction*: τάξαι πρός με, πότε εὔξωμαι περὶ σοῦ 'Tell me when I should pray about you' Ex 8.9; *s* God, τάξομαι .. τοῖς υἱοῖς Ισραηλ 29.43.

8. mid. *to indicate as binding* or *standard*: abs., καθὼς ἐτάξατο 'as he had instructed' 1K 20.35; ὁδὸς ἡμερῶν δύο τεταγμένων 'a journey of two customary days' To 5.6 𝔊II; ταξάμενος ἡμέραν 'having set a day' 2M 3.14, sim. 14.21.

Cf. τάξις, τίθημι, ἐντάσσω, ἐντέλλομαι, βάλλω, ἐμβάλλω, ποιέω, and ὑποτάσσω.

τάττω: ⇒ τάσσω.

ταυρηδόν. adv.ʃ

like a bull: to look at, 4M 15.19. Cf. ταῦρος.

ταῦρος, ου. m.

bull: Ge 32.15 (+ βοῦς); πρωτότοκος ~ου De 33.17; sacrificial animal, αἷμα ταύρων καὶ τράγων 'blood of bulls and goats' Is 1.11. Cf. βοῦς, ταυρηδόν.

ταφή, ῆς. f.

1. *burial* of a dead person: αἱ ἡμέραι τῆς ~ῆς Ge 50.3; De 21.23 (dat. cogn.), ~ὴν ὄνου 'ass's' Je 22.19 (contemptible and acc. cogn.).

2. *burial-place*: De 34.6; θήσομαι ~ήν σου Na 1.14.

Cf. θάπτω, τάφος, and μνημεῖον.

τάφος, ου. m.

burial-place, 'grave, tomb': privately owned, κτῆσιν ~ου Ge 23.4 (‖ μνημεῖον vs. 9), Ez 37.13 (‖ μνῆμα vs. 12). Cf. ταφή, ἐνταφιάζω, ἐπιτάφιος, θάπτω, μνῆμα, μνημεῖον, πολυανδρεῖον.

τάφρος, ου. f.ʃ

irrigation ditch: of ἡ γῆ τοῦ Νεβρωδ 'Nimrod,' i.e. Mesopotamia, Mi 5.6. Cf. διῶρυξ, ὑδραγωγός.

τάχα. adv.ʃ

perhaps: not clause-initial, Wi 13.6, 14.19. Cf. ἴσως: Schmidt 1.329-32.

ταχέως. adv.

swiftly: Jl 3.4; Is 8.3 (‖ ὀξέως). Cf. ταχύς, ταχινός, ὀξέως, βραδέως.

ταχινός, ή, όν.

fast-moving: τὸ ἔθνος τὸ πικρὸν καὶ τὸ ~όν 'the bitter and swift people' Hb 1.6; ἐν ὥρᾳ ~ῇ 'promptly' Si 11.22; *s* feet, Is 59.7 and Pr 1.16 (‖ ὀξύς Ps 13.3), ἀήρ 'air' Wi 13.2. Cf. ταχύς.

τάχος, ους. n.

swiftness, speed: τάχει 3M 5.43; ἐν τάχει De 9.3; κατὰ σπουδὴν ἐν ~ει Si 27.3; διὰ ~ους Ps 6.11, διὰ ~ους ἐξάπινα 'instantly and all of a sudden' Si 11.21; ἕως ~ους Ps 147.4; adv. τὸ τ. 'with speed,' κατάβηθι τὸ τ. Ex 32.7; Nu 16.46, De 7.4; 7.22 (:: κατὰ μικρὸν μικρόν 'little by little'); sim. τ. foll. by an acc., "Fetch sbd quickly" 3K 22.9 (‖ 2C 18.8). **b**. *speedy movement*: Wi 18.14. Cf. σπουδή, ταχύς.

ταχύνω: fut. ταχυνῶ; aor. ἐτάχυνα, ptc. ταχύνας, impv. τάχυνον, subj. ταχύνω, opt.3s ταχύναι.

1. *to be quick* in action: + τοῦ inf., τοῦ ποιῆσαι αὐτό Ge 18.7, 41.32, τοῦ παραγενέσθαι Ex 2.18; 1M 13.10; *+ a finite verb, ἐτάχυναν ἐπελάθοντο 'they quickly forgot' Ps 105.13; + καί, Jd 13.10; + τ. as conjunctive ptc., ταχύναντες καταγάγετε .. 'Quickly bring down ..' Ge 45.13; ταχύνας πορεύου καὶ μὴ στῇς 'Go quick, and don't stop' 1K 20.38. On the syntax cf. σπεύδω **2**. **b**. *to execute fast*: + acc., πόλεμον 1M 2.35; τὸ ἔλεος 'the mercy' PSol 17.45.

2. *to cause to move fast*: + acc., ἀστραπάς 'lightnings' Si 43.13 (‖ κατασπεύδω).

Cf. ταχύς, σπεύδω, βραδύνω, ἐποξύνω, μακροθυμέω, χρονίζω.

ταχύς, εῖα, ύ; adv. comp. n. θᾶττον, τάχιον.

swift in movement or action: *s* an approaching day, Zp 1.14; a witness, Ma 3.5, πονηρία 'disaster' Je 31.16; hum., ἐν λόγοις 'quick-tongued' Pr 29.20 (not complimentary), ἐν ἀκροάσει 'in listening to others' Si 5.11, cf. τ. εἰς τὸ ἀκοῦσαι Jas 1.19; εἰς οἰκίαν Si 21.22; γραμματεὺς τ. ἐν νόμῳ 2E 7.6; εἰσόδῳ '(quick) to enter' PSol 4.5; n. sg. ταχύ used adv., ταχὺ εὗρες Ge 27.20; Ex 32.8, Is 9.1, 3M 2.20. **b**. comp. w. elative force: 1M 2.40, 2M 4.31. **c**. superl. w. elative force: adv., τὴν ταχίστην 'as soon as possible' 1M 11.22; ὡς τάχιστα w. same meaning, 3M 1.8.

Cf. ταχέως, ταχινός, ὀξύς, νωθρός: Schmidt 2.151f.

τε. Enclitic particle of juxtaposition and coordination.

1. Used alone in conjunction with the following (but separated from) καί: **a**. connects phrases, ὅ τε Αδαμ καὶ ἡ γυνὴ αὐτοῦ 'both Adam and his wife' Ge 3.1; τόν τε οὐρανὸν καὶ τὴν γῆν De 4.26; τὸ σκεῦός σου, τήν τε φαρέτραν καὶ τὸ τόξον 'your gear, (i.e.) the quiver and bow' Ge 27.3, τὴν βασιλείαν τῆς τε γῆς καὶ τῆς θαλάσσης Es 10.1; before the first term - εἴς τε τὴν τοῦ νόμου καὶ τῶν προφητῶν .. ἀνάγνωσιν 'to the reading of both ..' Si prol. 8-10; with more than two members, ᾠκοδόμησαν πόλεις ὀχυρὰς τῷ Φαραω, τήν τε Πιθωμ και Ραμεσση και Ων Ex 1.11; θυμοῦ τε καὶ φόβου καὶ πόνου 4M 1.4. **b**. connects clauses: ἐμέ τε ἀποκτενοῦσιν 'and so they might kill me' Ge 20.11;

τά τε πρωτοτόκιά μου εἴληφεν, καὶ νῦν εἴληφεν τὴν εὐλογίαν μου 'he has taken my primogeniture, and now he has taken my blessing' Ge 27.36. **c.** with καί immediately following: ἐγώ τε καὶ ὁ λαός σου Ex 33.16; Ge 41.10, Ex 35.34, Nu 20.19, 1E 1.12, 4.53, 8.11, 13, 50, 51, 9.41, Es 7.4, Jb 5.9, 9.4, 10, 34.24, Si 45.21, Ep Je 17, 19, Da TH 3.5, 1M 8.7, 2M 3.1, 10, 5.13, 11.20, 3M 1.1, 4, 18, 28, 3.10, 23, 6.30: see Blomqvist 1974. **d.** = καί: αἰσχύνονταί τε καὶ οἱ θεραπεύοντες αὐτὰ .. 'those who minister to him also get embarrassed' Ep Je 25 (the τε goes with the verb). **e.** A B τε = 'A and B': σχετλιάζοντος ἀντιλέγοντός τε 'complaining and protesting' 4M 4.7.

2. in conjunction with δέ: ἐμέ τε ἀποκατασταθῆναι .., ἐκεῖνον δὲ κρεμασθῆναι 'for me to be restored .. but for him to be hanged' Ge 41.13; τοὺς δύο υἱοὺς αὐτοῦ, τόν τε Εφραιμ .. τὸν δὲ Μανασση 48.13.

3. ἐάν τε .. ἐάν τε .. in a disjunctive statement, *whether .. or ..*: ἐάν τε κτῆνος ἐάν τε ἄνθρωπος, οὐ ζήσεται 'whether it be an animal or a human, it shall not live' Ex 19.13; ἐάν τε ἄρσεν ἐάν τε θῆλυ 'whether male or female' Le 3.1; 24.16; De 18.3, 1E 8.24 (repeated 4 times || 2E 7.26), Si 13.25.

4. indicates a range of possibilities: ἀπό τε .. ἕως .. - τὸ κλέμμα ἀπό τε ὄνου ἕως προβάτου 'the stolen object ranging from donkey to sheep' Ex 22.4; ἀδίκημα περί τε μόσχου καὶ ὑποζυγίου καὶ προβάτου .., ὅ τι οὖν ἂν ᾖ 'a wrongdoing relating to a bull or ass or sheep .. or whatsoever it might be' Ex 22.9.

Cf. καί: Blomqvist 1974.

τέγος, ους. n.ʃ

roof: of a building, Ep Je 10. Cf. στέγη, φάτνωμα.

τείνω: pf. τέτακα, ptc.pass. τεταμένος.

to pull tight: ***o*** bow, τείνων τόξον 'archer' Je 27.14 (|| ἐντείνων τ. vs. 29). **b.** *to stretch out and extend*: + acc., τοὺς βραχίονας αὐτοῦ τοὺς ἰσχυροὺς καὶ τοὺς τεταμένους 'his strong and stretched out arms' Ez 30.22, τὰς χεῖρας εἰς τὸν οὐρανόν 3M 5.25 (in prayer); κλίνην 'bed' Pr 7.16.

Cf. ἀνα~, ἐκ~, προ~, προσεπικατατείνω, χειροτονία.

τειχήρης, ες.

protected by walls: ***s*** city, Nu 13.20 (:: ἀτείχιστος), Je 4.5; πόλεις μεγάλας καὶ ~εις ἕως τοῦ οὐρανοῦ 'large cities with sky-high walls' De 9.1 (|| τετειχισμένη 1.28). Cf. τεῖχος and τειχίζω.

τειχίζω: aor. ἐτείχισα; pf.pass.ptc. τετειχισμένος.

to build defensive walls round: ***o*** πόλις τετειχισμένη Le 25.29, Ho 8.14, Ez 17.4; πόλις understood, 33.27; πόλεις μεγάλαι καὶ τετειχισμέναι ἕως τοῦ οὐρανοῦ De 1.28 (|| τειχήρης 9.1); πόλεις ὀχυραὶ τετειχισμέναι 'strong, walled ..' Nu 13.29; κώμας Ju 4.5. Cf. τεῖχος and περιτειχίζω.

τειχιστής, οῦ. m.*

builder of wall: 4K 12.13. Cf. τεῖχος.

τεῖχος, ους. n.

protective wall: τὸ ὕδωρ αὐτοῖς τ. ἐκ δεξιῶν .. 'the water served them as a wall on the right..' Ex 14.22, cf. Na 3.8; round a city, τείχη ὑψηλά De 3.5; round a land, Is 15.1, cf. van der Kooij 1998.68; τ. πυρός 'a wall of fire (which would repel enemy attack)' Zc 2.5; pl. target of military attack, τείχη .. ὑψηλὰ .. ὀχυρά 'high.. and solid' De 28.52, πύργος ὑψηλὸς .. τ. ὑψηλόν Is 2.15; ἐξαποστελῶ πῦρ ἐπὶ τὰ ~η Γάζης Am 1.7; ἀναβήσονται ἐπὶ τὰ ~η; where defence installations are located, Na 2.6. Cf. τειχίζω, τειχήρης, τειχιστής, προτείχισμα, and τοῖχος.

τεκμήριον, ου. n.ʃ

symptom or signal indicative of a certain state of affairs or activity: 3M 3.24; of activity Wi 5.11 (|| σημεῖον), 19.13. Cf. σημεῖον.

τέκνον, ου. n.

1. *immediate offspring*: δώσω σοι ἐξ αὐτῆς ~ον Ge 17.16; in relation to parents, esp. mother, ἡ τεκοῦσα αὐτά Ho 2.5; ~α ἀλλότρια 'strange, i.e. illegitimate' 5.7; ἐκθρέψωσι τὰ ~α αὐτῶν 'raise their children' 9.12; || μήτηρ 10.14. **b.** voc. without a posses. pron.: Τί ἐστιν, τέκνον; 'What is the matter, child?' Ge 22.7; 22.8; said to a daughter about to marry, To 7.17 𝔊ᴵ (|| θύγατερ). **c.** of animal, οὐ λήμψῃ τὴν μητέρα μετὰ τῶν ~ων 'thou shall not take the mother (bird) with its young' De 22.6 (|| νοσσοί); τέκνα αἰγῶν 'kids' 2C 35.7; Jl 1.3.

2. *descendant*: τέκνα καὶ .. τέκνα τέκνων Ex 34.7 (:: πατέρες).

3. *one who adheres to the principle of, and given up to*: ~ ἀδικίας Ho 10.9.

4. *member of* community (τινος): ~α ^Ισραηλ^ Ho 11.1 (|| νήπιος); τὰ ~α Σιων 'the inhabitants of Zion' Jl 2.23; ~α ὑδάτων 'fishes'(?; cf. Cyr. I 239, Tht PG 81.1613, and Thph PG 126.768) Ho 11.10, see υἱός **4**.

5. an endearing address to a youth: Ὁ θεὸς ἐλεήσαι σε, τέκνον 'May God show mercy to you, child' Ge 43.29 (Joseph to Benjamin); defined as παιδάριον 1K 4.17, cf. vs. 16. **b.** teacher to his pupil: as voc., τέκνον Si 2.1+ (|| υἱέ Pr 1.8+), rarely pl. τέκνα Si 3.1, 23.7, 41.14; priest to his apprentice, 1K 3.9. Cf. Schmidt 2.423; BDAG s.v. **3**.

Cf. υἱός, θυγάτηρ, μήτηρ, νήπιος, παιδάριον, πατήρ, τίκτω, τεκνοποιέω, ἐπιγονή, εὐτεκνία, ἀτεκνόω: Shipp 434f., 530; Stanton 463-80.

τεκνοποιέω: fut. ~ποιήσω, mid. ~ποιήσομαι; aor. ἐτεκνοποίησα, subj. ~ήσω, impv.2pl ~ποιήσατε, mid. ~ήσωμαι.ʃ *to produce a child*: Is 65.23; indicative of wellbeing, Jer 12.2 (‖ ποιέω καρπόν); + acc. pers., ὄχλον πολύν 38.8; *s* a hum. female, ἦν Σαρα στεῖρα καὶ οὐκ ἐτεκνοποίει 'S. was barren ..' Ge 11.30; through a surrogate mother, τεκνοποιήσομαι κἀγὼ ἐξ αὐτῆς 30.3 (mid.); a hum. male, ἵνα τεκνοποιήσῃς ἐξ αὐτῆς 16.2; + acc. pers., λάβετε γυναῖκας καὶ τεκνοποιήσατε υἱοὺς καὶ θυγατέρας Je 36.6. Cf. τέκνον.

τεκνοφόνος, ον.ʃ*

involving infanticide: *s* τελετή 'mystic rite' Wi 14.23. Cf. φόνος.

τεκταίνω: aor.subj.mid. τεκτήνωμαι.

1. *to work as a smith on*: + acc. (metal), Ba 3.18, cf. ἐργάζομαι **2a**. **b**. *to work in general*: fig. of cruel maltreatment, ἐπὶ τοῦ νώτου μου Ps 128.3.

2. *to effect, bring about*: + acc., διαφθοράν Ez 21.31, πονηρά Si 11.33, κακά 27.22, ἐπὶ σὸν φίλον κακά Pr 3.29. **b**. mid. = act., ἀγαθά Pr 11.27, ἔλεον καὶ ἀλήθειαν 14.22; mentally, λογισμοὺς κακούς 'evil designs' Pr 6.18, ἐν τῇ καρδίᾳ δόλους '.. deceptions' 26.24. Cf. ποιέω.

τεκτονικός, ή, όν.ʃ

pertaining to carpenter or *joiner*: ἔργα ~ά Ex 31.5 (‖ λιθουργικός). **b**. subst.f. *carpentry, joiner's work*: τοῖχος ~ῆς 'wall made by carpenter' 4K 3.25 *L*.

Cf. τέκτων and λιθουργικός.

τέκτων, ονος. m.

craftsman: σιδήρου 'ironsmith' 1K 13.19, ξύλων .. λίθων (*L* τοίχου) 'carpenter .. and mason' 2K 5.11; he who fashions idols, χώνευμα ἐκ τοῦ ἀργυρίου αὐτῶν κατ' εἰκόνα εἰδώλων, ἔργα ~όνων 'a molten image from silver fashioned after idols, works of craftsmen' Ho 13.2; 8.6, Zc 1.20; + λατόμος 'stone-cutter' 2E 3.7; of intangible entities, κακῶν Pr 14.22. Cf. τεκτονικός, ἀρχιτέκτων, λιθουργικός.

τελαμών, ῶνος. m.ʃ

broad bandage: 3K 21.38, 41.

τέλειος, α, ον.

1. *perfect, impeccable*: in moral character and religious beliefs and practices and *s* pers., Ge 6.9, Si 44.17 (Noah; ‖ δίκαιος); measured against divine standards, τ. ἔσῃ ἔναντι κυρίου τοῦ θεοῦ σου De 18.13; could be wanting in divine wisdom, Wi 9.6; καρδία .. πρὸς κύριον 3K 8.61; sacrificial animal, πρόβατον τ. Ex 12.5; subst.f., θυσία understood, Jd 20.26 B; m., *accomplished in skill*, 1C 25.8 (:: μανθάνων 'apprentice').

2. *approximating to the ultimate*: ~ον μῖσος 'utter hatred' Ps 138.22, ἀποικία 'exile' Je 13.19; ἐν καρδίᾳ ~ᾳ 'whole-heartedly' 1C 28.9, cf. ἐν καρδίᾳ πλήρει 2C 25.2; ~εία μου 'my ideal girl' Ct 5.2; subst.n.pl., 'infallible truths' (?) 2E 2.63.

Cf. τελειότης, τελείως, ἄμεμπτος, δίκαιος: Trench 74-7; Du Plessis, esp. 94-103; Delling, *TDNT* 8.72; Chadwick 266-71.

τελειότης, ητος. f.ʃ

state of being complete and not deficient: φρονήσεως τ. 'perfect wisdom' Wi 6.15; 12.17; ἐν ἀληθείᾳ καὶ ~ητι 'in complete sincerity' Jd 9.16, 19 (hendiadys?). Cf. τέλειος.

τελειόω: fut. τελειώσω, pass. ~ωθήσομαι; aor. ἐτελείωσα, inf. τελειῶσαι, subj. ~ώσω, opt.3s τελειώσαι, pass. ἐτελειώθην, inf. ~ωθῆναι, ptc. ~ωθείς, subj. ~ωθῶ; pf.ptc.pass. τετελειωμένος.

1. *to help bring to successful conclusion*: *s* God and + acc., τὰ ἐπιτηδεύματά σου 'your mission' Ju 10.8.

2. *to bring to conclusion, complete*: + acc., οἶκον 2C 8.16, λειτουργίαν Si 50.19; pass., *o* work, task, τελειωθῆναι τὸ ἔργον τοῦτο Ne 6.16. **b**. *to bring to full realisation*: pass., *o* ἡ εὐλογία σου 'the blessing promised to you' Si 7.32.

3. *to bring to perfection*: + acc., σου τὸ κάλλος 'your beauty' Ez 27.11; pass., *o* hum., w. ref. to moral character, 2K 22.26B, Si 34.10, 4M 7.15, cf. Da 3.40 LXX.

4. pass. *to die*: ἐν ὀλίγῳ 'young' Wi 4.13 (‖ τελέομαι vs. 16).

5. *+ τὰς χεῖράς τινος 'to consecrate sbd as priest': Ex 29.9, Le 8.33; ‖ χρίω Ex 29.29, cf. ὁ ἱερεὺς ὁ χριστὸς ὁ τετελειωμένος τὰς χεῖρας Le 4.5; ‖ ἁγιάζω Ex 29.33; ἱερατεύειν Nu 3.3. **b**. without τὰς χεῖράς τινος: Le 21.10. The switching to τελειόω in preference to the more literal ἐμπίμπλημι (e.g. Ex 28.37) is due to one of the senses of the former, 'to come to maturity.'

Cf. τελείωσις, τελέω, τελεσιουργέω, τελεσφορέω, συντελέω, περαίνω, πληρόω: Schmidt 4.504; Delling, *TDNT* 8.80f.

τελείως. adv.

1. *thoroughly*: Ju 11.6, 2M 12.42.

2. *perfectly*: 3M 7.22.

Cf. τέλειος.

τελείωσις, εως. f.

1. *act of executing and completing*: τῶν λόγων Ju 10.9; Si 31.8 (‖ συντελέω), τοῦ σωτηρίου 2C 29.35, τοῦ ἱεροῦ 2M 2.9.

2. *mature age*: opp. νεότης 'youth' Je 2.2.

*3. *installation, consecration as priest*, an elliptical Hebraism based on τελειόω τὰς χεῖράς τινος (q.v. sub τελειόω): Ex 29.22; κριὸς ~εως a ram offered on such an occasion, 29.26 +; ὁλοκαυτώματα ~εως Le 8.28; κανοῦν ~εως, a basket containing ritual offerings for such an occasion, Le 8.26.

Cf. τελειόω, ἀνήνυτος.

τέλεος, α, ον.ʃ

subst.n.sg. ~ον, adv., *to full measure*: + neg., 'absolutely not' 3M 1.22. Cf. τέλειος.

τελεσιουργέω.ʃ

to accomplish fully: + acc. rei, κακίαν Pr 19.7. Cf. τελειόω, συντελέω **5**, **6**.

τελεσφορέω: aor.ptc.pass. τελεσφορηθείς.ʃ

to bring to a goal and accomplishment: pass., ***o*** baby about to be born, 4M 13.20. Cf. τελειόω.

τελεσφόρος, ον.ʃ

pertaining to mystery rites: subst.f., a gloss on πόρνη 'temple prostitute' and ‖ τελισκόμενος De 23.17. Cf. τελίσκω: Waanders § 190.

τελετή, ῆς. f.

pagan *mystic rite*: ~αὶ τοῦ Ισραηλ ἐξερημωθήσονται 'the mystic rites of I. shall fall into decay' Am 7.9 (‖ βωμοὶ γέλωτος); ἔχθιστα πράσσειν, ἔργα φαρμακειῶν καὶ ~ὰς ἀνοσίους 'to practise detestable things, practices of sorcery and profane ..' Wi 12.4, μυστήρια καὶ ~άς 14.15, τεκνοφόνους ~ὰς ἢ κρύφια μυστήρια '.. involving infanticides and secret mysteries' 14.23. Cf. Zijderveld 39-96, esp. 81-3.

τελευταῖος, α, ον.ʃ

last in order: ***s*** milk, 3M 5.49. **b**. subst.n.pl., *endpoint* reached: Pr 14.12, 16.25; ἐν τοῖς ~οις 'in the end' 20.9b (:: ἐν πρώτοις); adv., *~α (Cl. Gk ~ον, τὸ ~ον, τὰ ~α.), *in the end* 14.13. Cf. τελευτή, τέλος, ἔσχατος, πρῶτος: Schmidt 4.524-6.

τελευτάω: pres.impv. τελεύτα; fut. τελευτήσω; aor. ἐτελεύτησα, inf. τελευτῆσαι, ptc. ~τήσας, impv.3s ~τησάτω, subj. ~τήσω; pf. τετελεύτηκα, ptc. τετελευτηκώς.

to come to the end of one's life: Ex 2.23; natural death, Jo 1.2; not as a result of natural death, Ge 6.17; out of extreme hunger, 25.32; τελευτήσω 30.1 (threat of suicide?); θανάτῳ τελευτήσει Ex 19.12 (punishment); 35.2 (‖ θανατόω pass. 31.15); ἐν ῥομφαίᾳ Am 7.11, 9.10; ‖ ἐν ῥομφαίᾳ πίπτω 7.17; De 25.6 (‖ θνήσκω vs. 5), 32.50 (‖ ἀποθνήσκω); ***s*** river fish Ex 7.18; frogs, ἐκ τῶν οἰκιῶν 8.13; beasts fallen into a pit, 21.34; a bull gored by another, 21.35; ψυχή '(human) soul' Le 21.11, Nu 6.6; σοφία Jb 12.2. Cf. τέλος, τελευτή, (ἀπο)θνήσκω, and ἐκλείπω: Schmidt 4.58-60, 500f.

τελευτή, ῆς. f.

1. *end, limit*: Ba 3.25.

2. *death*: natural, οὐ γινώσκω τὴν ἡμέραν τῆς ~ῆς μου Ge 27.2 (‖ ἀποθανεῖν vs. 4); De 31.29 (‖ θάνατος vs. 27); πρὸ τῆς ~ῆς αὐτοῦ 33.1, μετὰ τὴν ~ὴν Ἰούδου 1M 9.23.

Cf. τελευτάω, τελευταῖος, θάνατος: Schmidt 4.497-501.

τελέω: fut.ptc. τελέσων; aor. subj. τελέσω, inf. τελέσαι, pass. ἐτελέσθην, impv.3s τελεσθήτω, inf. τελεσθῆναι, ptc. τελεσθείς; pf.pass. τετέλεσμαι, ptc. τετελεσμένος.

1. *to accomplish, effect*: + acc., ἔργον μέγα Si 7.25.

2. *to bring to an end and settlement*: ***o*** temple, 2E 5.16; pass., ***o*** λόγος τετέλεσται 'a matter has been settled' 7.12, τὸ πρᾶγμα 'the business' To 7.9 𝔊I; 2M 4.23. **b**. *to give effect*: + acc. rei, τὸ ῥῆμα Ru 3.18; pass., ***o*** λόγος κυρίου 2E 1.1. **c**. metaph. of death: pass., ***o*** youth, Wi 4.16 (‖ τελειόομαι vs. 13).

3. *to consecrate* to deity: ***o*** hum. and pass., τῷ Βεελφεγωρ Nu 25.3, 5, Ps 105.28, μετὰ τῶν τετελεσμένων ἔθυον 'they offered sacrifices along with the devotees' Ho 4.14.

Cf. ἐκτελέω, τελειόω, τελίσκω, συντελέω: Schmidt 4.499; Grundmann, *TDNT* 8.58f.; Dorival 1996.539f.

τελίσκω.ʃ

to dedicate or *offer*: as temple prostitute, τελισκόμενος De 23.17 (a gloss on πορνεύων and ‖ τελεσφόρος). Cf. τελεσφόρος, τελέω.

τέλος, ους. n.

1. *the full amount*: τῆς τιμῆς 'of the assessment' Le 27.23.

2. *levy*: κυρίῳ Nu 31.28, 37, 38, 39, 40; τὸ τ. κυρίῳ τὸ ἀφαίρεμα τοῦ θεοῦ 31.41; Es 10.1 *L*. Cf. τελωνέω.

3. *the close of a period* or *process*, 'end': ποιήσει κεφαλὴν καὶ οὐράν, ἀρχὴν καὶ τ. 'he will make head and tail, beginning and end' Is 19.15, ἀρχὴν καὶ τ. καὶ μεσότητα χρόνων 'the beginning, the end, and the middle of times' Wi 7.18; γενεᾶς ἀδίκου χαλεπὰ τὰ ~η 'the end of an unrighteous generation is painful' 3.18; οὐκ ἔστιν τ. τῆς κτήσεως αὐτῶν 'there is no end to their acquisition' Ba 3.17; ἀπονοίας '(result) of thoughtlessness' 4M 12.3; military victory, εἰς τὸ τέλος 'on the occasion of *or* to mark the victory' Ps 4.1+, cf. Cyr. ad loc. (PG 69.733), but **b iv** below; 3M 1.26; ἄγω ἐπὶ τέλος '(to execute and) bring to a (successful) conclusion' 1C 29.19, 3M 3.14, 5.19; ἔλθοιμι εἰς τέλος 'I might reach the goal (or: come to the end of the matter, τέλος λόγου Ec 12.13)' Jb 23.3. **b**. with various prepositions: **i**. μετὰ τὸ τ. τῶν ἑπτὰ ἐτῶν 'at the end of the seven years' 4K 8.3, μετὰ τ. δύο μηνῶν 'at the end of two months' Jd 11.39 A (B: ἐν ~ει ..); **ii**. ἐπὶ τέλει τῶν ἐκβάσεων 'at the end of the events' Wi 11.14; **iii**. εἰς τέλος, 'in the end', ἀναβιβάσω σε εἰς τ. 'I shall bring you up in the end' Ge 46.4; 'never (in future),' οὐ ἐγκαταλείψει ἡμᾶς εἰς τ. 'he will never abandon us' Ju 7.30; ἕως εἰς τ. 'till the end' De 31.24, 30, 'thoroughly' 2C 31.1; *until a process begun reaches its logical conclusion*, 'utterly, completely; to its bitter end,' ἕως εἰς τ. ἀποθάνωμεν 'die to a man' Nu 17.13, cf. ἵνα ἐξολεθρευθῶσιν εἰς τ. Ju 14.13 and ἀπολέσαι εἰς τ. Da 7.26; ἕως οὗ εἰς τ. ἐκκαῇ 'until it burns out' 3.19 TH; Am 9.8, Hb 1.4; καταλλαγῆναι 'to be reconciled' 2M 8.29; **iv**. εἰς τὸ τ. as (part of) the title of many psalms: '(looking forward) to the finish' (?) Ps 4+, cf. Rösel 2001; **v**. διὰ τέλους 'completely' Es B 7 o' (*L*: 'never [in future]'), δ. ~ους οὐ σιωπήσονται 'will never cease' Is 62.6; **vi**. ἕως τέλους 'utterly' Ps 37.7, see above, **iii**.; **vii**. μέχρι ~ους 'till the end' Wi 16.5, 19.1; **viii**. πρὸς τέλος ἀφικομένων ἡμῶν τῶν ἁμαρτιῶν 'with our sins having reached their height' 2M 6.15; **ix**. ἀπὸ τέλους 'at the end of,' calqued on -מִקְצֵה: 4K 18.10B (*L* εἰς τ.). **c**. adv. acc., 'in the end': τ. 2M 5.5, 13.16, τὸ τ. 5.7, or 'result won at the end.'

Cf. ἀρχή, μεσότης, ὅριον, πέρας, συντέλεια, τελευταῖος, τέρμα, ἀτελής, ἀτέλεια: Schmidt 4.497-501, 517-20; Waanders § 108; Du Plessis 56-67; Delling, *TDNT* 8.51f.

τελωνέω.ʃ

to collect as tax: pass., 1M 13.39. Cf. τέλος **2**.

τέμενος, ους. n.

piece of land marked off from common uses and dedicated to god, 'precinct' (LSJ): of pagan religion, ᾠκοδόμησαν ~η Ho 8.14; Ez 6.4 (‖ θυσιαστήριον); τῶν ἐθνῶν 2M 11.3; βωμοὺς καὶ ~η καὶ εἰδώλια 1M 1.47; serving as refuge, 5.43. Cf. ἅγιος, ἄλσος, αὐλή, θυσιαστήριον, ἱερός, ναός.

τέμνω: fut. τεμῶ; aor.pass. ἐτμήθην, subj. τμηθῶ, ptc. τμηθείς.

to split: + acc., ἄμπελον '(prune) grape-vine' Le 25.3, 4; ξύλα 'trees' 4K 6.4; μου τὰ μέλη 'my limbs' 4M 9.17; pass. and ***o*** πέταλα χρυσίου 'leaves of gold' Ex 36.10, ἀμπελών [prob. an impersonal passive meant: "no pruning will take place"] Is 5.6; ἐτμήθη λίθος ἐξ ὄρους 'a stone was hewn out of a mountain' Da 2.34 LXX (TH ἀπεσχίσθη), 'the air' (ἀήρ) Wi 5.12 (by a flying arrow). Cf. ἀπο~, κατα~, περιτέμνω, τομή, τόμος, σχίζω: Chadwick 271-9; Borthwick.

τένων, οντος. m.ʃ

sinew, tendon: 4M 9.28, 15.15. Cf. τόνος, νεῦρον.

τέρας, ατος. n.

portentous, extraordinary event with some symbolic meaning performed by God, or by man (though ultimately by God): Ex 4.21; σημεῖα καὶ ~ατα 7.3; σημεῖον ἢ τέρας Ex 7.9, sim. De 4.34, 13.1; σημεῖα καὶ τέρατα μεγάλα 7.19; ποιῶν ~ατα Ex 15.11; δώσω ~ατα ἐν τῷ οὐρανῷ καὶ ἐπὶ τῆς γῆς, αἷμα καὶ πῦρ .. Jl 2.30; ‖ ἔργα Si 48.14. Cf. τερατοσκόπος, τερατοποιός, θαυμαστός, σημεῖον: Schmidt 4.179-81; Trench 339-43; Rengstorff, *TDNT* 8.119f.; Fernández Marcos.

τερατεύομαι.ʃ

to play the pretentious humbug: 3M 1.14.

τερατοποιός, ον.ʃ *

performing τέρας (q.v.): ***s*** God, 2M 15.21, 3M 6.32. Cf. τέρας.

τερατοσκόπος, ου. m.ʃ

diviner, one who inspects signs (τέρατα): ἐπᾴδων ἐπαοιδήν, ἐγγαστρίμυθος καὶ τ. De 18.11; ἄνδρες ~οι Zc 3.8. Cf. σκοπός, τέρας, ἐγγαστρίμυθος, and ἐπαοιδός.

τερέβινθος. ⇒ τερέμινθος.

τερέμινθος, ου. f. On the spelling variation, see LSJ s.v., p. 1777a. and Shipp 531f.

terebinth: tree, Ge 14.6; fruits thereof, 43.11 ('pistachio nuts'?); ‖ βάλανος 'oak' Is 6.13; full of vitality, Si 24.16, cf. Is 1.30.

τέρετρον, ου. n.ʃ

borer, gimlet: carpenter's tool, Is 44.12. Cf. τετραίνω.

τέρμα, ατος. n.ʃ

end or *limit beyond which there is no further progress*: οὐκ ἦν τ. τῷ σταθμῷ 'there was no end to the weight' 3K 7.32; τὸ τ. τῆς καταδίκης 'the severest possible sentence' Wi 12.27. Cf. τέλος, πέρας: Schmidt 4.514-20; Shipp 229-31.

τερπνός, ή, όν.ʃ

pleasant: ***s*** ψαλτήριον Ps 80.3; brotherly companionship, ‖ καλός 132.1. Cf. τέρπω, ἡδύς, λυπηρός: Schmidt 2.560.

τερπνότης, ητος. f.ʃ*

pleasantness: pl., Ps 15.11; τοῦ κυρίου 26.4. Cf. τέρπω, τερπνός.

τέρπω: fut. τέρψω, mid. τερφθήσομαι; aor.mid. ἐτέρφθην, impv.3pl ~φθήτωσαν.

to give pleasure, delight: + acc., Ps 64.9, καρδίαν Si 1.12. **b**. mid. *to enjoy, have pleasure*: τέρπου καὶ εὐφραίνου Zc 2.10; + ἐπί τινι Ps 34.9 (‖ ἀγαλλιάομαι); ἐν εὐφροσύνῃ 67.4; + ἔν τινι, 118.14 (‖ ἐπὶ πλούτῳ); τινι, ***s*** καρδία Pr 27.9.

Cf. ἀγαλλιάομαι, κατατέρπω, τέρψις, τερπνότης, εὐφραίνω, χαίρω: Schmidt 2.570f.

τέρψις, εως. f.

enjoyment: εὐφρανθήσεται ἐπὶ σὲ ἐν ~ει ὡς ἐν ἡμέρᾳ ἑορτῆς 'he will rejoice over you with delight as in a day of festival' Zp 3.17; opp. γόος 'bewailing' 3M 4.6; Wi 8.18 (‖ εὐφροσύνη καὶ χαρά vs. 16). Cf. τέρπω, εὐφροσύνη, γέλως, and χαρά.

τεσσαράκοντα: indecl. num.

forty: Ge 5.13.

τεσσαρακοστός, ή, όν.
fortieth: Jo 14.10, 1M 1.20.

τέσσαρες. num. m./f.nom.; gen. ~άρων, dat. τέσσαρσι(ν), acc. ~ας; n.nom./acc. τέσσαρα.
four: πορεύεται ἐπὶ ~άρων 'walks on fours' Le 11.20. Cf. τέταρτος and τετράς.

τεσσαρεσκαιδέκατος, η, ον.
fourteenth in order: ἐν τῷ ~ῳ ἔτει 'in the fourteenth year' Ge 14.5; ~ῃ ἡμέρᾳ τοῦ μηνός 'on the fourteenth day of the month' Nu 28.16.

τεταγμένως. adv.ʃ
in orderly, well-coordinated manner: w. ref. to troops' movement, 1M 6.40. Cf. ἀκόσμως, ἐναρμόνιος.

τέταρτος, η, ον.
1. *fourth* in order: ἐν τῷ ἅρματι τῷ ~ῳ 'in the fourth carriage' Zc 6.3; ~ῃ γενεᾷ 'in the fourth generation' Ge 15.16; γενεά understood, ἕως τρίτης καὶ ~ης Nu 14.18.
2. subst. *one quarter*: τοῦ ἵν 'of a hin' Ex 29.40, Nu 28.5; τὸ ~ον τοῦ ἶν οἴνου Le 23.13.
Cf. τέσσαρες and τετράς.

τετράγωνος, ον.
having four angles, 'square': κιβωτὸν ἐξ ξύλων ~ων 'an ark made from square, i.e. trimmed timber' Ge 6.14; *s* altar (θυσιαστήριον), Ex 27.1; oracular breastplate (λόγιον) 28.16; ἀναπτυσσόμενος ~α 'with an entry at four corners (?)' Ez 41.21. **b.** subst. n., *a square plot of land*: Ez 45.2, 48.20, cf. χῶραι ~οι 3K 7.42.
Cf. τέσσαρες and γωνία.

τετράδραχμον, ου. n.ʃ
silver coin of 4 drachma: Jb 42.11.

τετραίνω: fut. τρήσω; aor. ἔτρησα; pf.ptc.pass. τετρημένος.ʃ
to bore through: + acc., ἐν τερέτρῳ 'with a gimlet' Is 44.12; *o* ῥῖνα 'a nose' Jb 40.24¶; πίθος 'wine-jar' Pr 23.27; ῥάβδος 'staff' 4K 18.21. **b.** *to effect by boring through*: + acc., τρώγλην 'hole' 4K 12.10.
Cf. τέρετρον and τρυπάω.

τετρακισμύριοι, αι, α. num.ʃ
forty thousand: Jo 4.13.

τετρακισχίλιοι, αι, α. num.
four thousand: Ez 48.16.

τετρακόσιοι, αι, α. num.
four hundred: ἔτη τετρακόσια τριάκοντα '430 years' Ge 11.13.

τετρακοσιοστός, ή, όν.ʃ
fourhundredth: 3K 6.1.

τετραμερής, ές.ʃ
consisting of four parts: *s* army, 2M 8.21.

τετράμηνος, ον.ʃ
lasting four months: subst.n., *four-month period* Jd 19.2 A, 20.47 A (B: τέσσαρες μῆνες).

τετράπεδος, ον.ʃ
having four sides, 'squared': *s* λίθοι 2C 34.11.

τετραπλασίων, ον; gen., ~ονος.ʃ *
fourfold: n.pl. ~α used adv., 2K 12.6*L*.

τετραπλῶς. adv.ʃ
in fourfold fashion: 3K 6.33.

τετράποδος, ον.ʃ
= τετράπεδος, q.v.: *s* λίθοι '(squared) stones' 1M 10.11 (cf. 2C 34.11 τετράπους); subst., a kind of scaffolding for military attack, Je 52.4.

τετράπους, ουν, gen. οδος.
four-footed, used mostly as subst.: *s* λίθοι '(squared) stones' 2C 34.11 (cf. 1M 10.11 τετραπόδος); of animals, Ge 1.24 (‖ ἑρπετὰ καὶ θηρία); 34.23 (+ κτήνη καὶ ὑπάρχοντα); ‖ ἄνθρωπος Ex 8.16, 17, 18. Cf. θηρίον, ἑρπετόν.

τετράς, άδος. f.
1. *fourth*: adjectivally, νηστεία ἡ τ. 'the fourth fast' Zc 8.19.
2. *the fourth day* of month: τῇ ~άδι καὶ εἰκάδι τοῦ μηνὸς τοῦ ἕκτου 'on the twenty-fourth of the sixth month' Hg 2.1, see LSG s.v.; σαββάτων 'of the week' Ps 93.1.
Cf. τέταρτος and τέσσαρες.

τετράστιχος, ον.ʃ *
in four rows or *courses*: ὕφασμα κατάλιθον ~ον 'a woven piece set with four rows of precious stone' Ex 28.17, 36.17; ἐπὶ ~ου λίθων γλυφῆς 'on stones engraved in four rows' Wi 18.24. Cf. στίχος.

τέφρα, ας. f.
ashes: to be besprinkled on an area, Bel 14 TH (LXX σποδός), θυμιαμάτων 'of incense' To 6.17; resulting after the death of a hum., Wi 2.3. Cf. σποδός.

τεχνάζω: aor.mid.impv.2pl τεχνάσασθε.ʃ
to employ art and cunning: Is 46.5. Cf. τέχνη.

τεχνάομαι: aor.ptc.mid. τεχνησάμενος.ʃ
to apply τέχνη (q.v.): *s* woodcutter (ὑλοτόμος) Wi 13.11. Cf. τέχνη.

τέχνη, ης. f.
body of knowledge and skills needed to execute work: λιθουργική 'stonemason's' Ex 28.11; μυρεψοῦ 'of one who prepares unguents, perfumer' 30.25; 3K 7.2; possessed by seamen, Wi 14.4, sculptor 14.19, magicians 17.7; literary, Da 1.17 LXX. Cf. τεχνάζω, τεχνάομαι, τεχνίτης, τεχνῖτις.

τεχνίτης, ου. m.
artisan: one who makes stone, wooden or metal idols, De 27.15, Je 10.9; Creator, Wi 13.1; part of builders' gang, 4K 22.6, 1C 22.15. Cf. τέχνη, τεχνῖτις.

τεχνῖτις, ιδος. f.
fem. of τεχνίτης: title given to wisdom as creator, ἡ πάντων τ. ἐδίδαξέν με σοφία Wi 7.22; τῶν ὄντων 'of things which exist' 8.6; τ. σοφία κατεσκεύασεν 14.2. Cf. τεχνίτης.

τηγανίζω.ʃ
to fry: *o* hum., 2M 7.5 (torturing). Cf. τήγανον.

τήγανον, ου. n. See Shipp 527.
frying-pan: cultic instrument, Le 2.5; ἐν ἐλαίῳ 6.21. **b.** of fairly large size and instrument of torture: + λέβης 'cauldron' 2M 7.3, cf. βασανιστήριον.
Cf. τηγανίζω.

τήκω: fut. τήξω, pass. τακήσομαι; aor.impv. τῆξον, opt.2s τήξειας, pass. ἐτάκην, ptc. τακείς, subj. τακῶ; pf.ptc. τετηκώς.
1. intr. *to melt* or *crumble and disappear*: Jb 7.5. **b.** pass. *s* snow and ice, Wi 16.22; αἱ κοιλάδες τακήσονται ὡς κηρός 'the valleys will melt away like wax' Mi 1.4; βουνοί 'hills' Hb 3.6, ὄρη Is 64.1, ἡ γῆ Ps 74.4, πλίνθος 'bricks (of a city-wall) Is 24.23; of putrefying flesh, τακήσονται αἱ σάρκες αὐτῶν ἑστηκότων αὐτῶν ἐπὶ τοὺς πόδας αὐτῶν 'their flesh will fall away, as they stand on their feet' Zc 14.12; eyes from sorrow and distress, ἐφ' υἱοῖς 'over my sons' Jb 17.5; food heated by the sun, Ex 16.21 ("manna"); *s* hum., ἐν ταῖς ἀδικίαις αὐτῶν Ez 4.17 (ǁ ἀφανίζομαι here and ἐντήκομαι 24.23); ψυχή Ps 106.26, καρδία Es 5.11 *L* (ο' ταράσσομαι), ὀφθαλμοί Jb 11.20. **c.** of military or physical annihilation, ἐτάκησαν πάντες οἱ κατοικοῦντες Χανααν Ex 15.15; ǁ καταφθείρομαι 'perish' Le 26.39; λιμῷ καὶ βρώσει ὀρνέων 'by hunger and eating by birds' De 32.24; opp. ζάω Ez 33.10.
2. mid. *to fade away*: τηκομένη ψυχή 'languishing spirit' De 28.65 (ǁ καρδία ἀθυμοῦσα); *s* διάνοια 'mind' Jo 5.1; Jonah in the belly of a fish, 3M 6.8; πονηρία Je 6.29.
3. mid. *to lose firm grip*: "the cords slipped off from his hands" Jd 15.14 B (A: διαλύομαι).
4. act.tr. *to cause to melt and disappear*: + acc. rei, Ps 147.7; ὁ θυμὸς αὐτοῦ τήκει ἀρχάς 'His anger brings dominions to naught' Na 1.6; σάρκας 'flesh (of hum. body)' Si 38.28 (*s* fire), cf. 4M 5.30; + acc. rei, θράσος 'courage' 1M 4.32.
Only rarely literally, 'melt and decompose through exposure to heat': Wi 16.22, poss. Ps 147.7, and cf. Mi 1.4.
Cf. δια~, ἐν~, ὑπερτήκω, εὔτηκτος, ἀφανίζω.

τηλαύγημα, ατος. n.ʃ *
state of being τηλαυγής: Le 13.23. Cf. τηλαυγής.

τηλαυγής, ές.ʃ
shining and conspicuous: *s* scar on a leper's skin, Le 13.2; τ. λευκή 'shining white' 13.4, 24; λευκὴ ἢ τ. 13.19; φῶς Jb 37.21¶; fig. ἡ ἐντολὴ κυρίου τ., φωτίζουσα ὀφθαλμούς Ps 18.9. Cf. τηλαύγημα, τηλαύγησις.

τηλαύγησις, εως. f.ʃ
shining brightness: divine attribute, Ps 17.13. Cf. τηλαυγής.

τηλικοῦτος, αύτη, οῦτον.ʃ
of such a considerable degree or extent: δυσσέβημα 'ungodliness' 2M 12.3, σύστεμα 'community' 3M 3.9, τὰ τοσαῦτα καὶ ~αῦτα πάθη 'so many and such intense emotions' 4M 16.4.

τηρέω: fut. τηρήσω; aor. ἐτήρησα, impv. τήρησον, subj. τηρήσω.
1. *to watch* (so as to attack at an opportune moment): abs. ἀγρυπνεῖτε καὶ τηρεῖτε 'be alert and watch out' 2E 8.29, cf. Pr 8.34; + acc. αὐτός σου τηρήσει κεφαλήν, καὶ σὺ τηρήσεις αὐτοῦ πτέρναν 'he will watch your head, and you will watch his heel' Ge 3.15; τὸν Δανιηλ Da 6.11 LXX (TH παρα~). **b.** *to remain alert and wait for*: ἐτήρει καιρὸν τοῦ ἀπατῆσαι αὐτήν 'he kept watching for a chance to seduce her' Ju 12.16, εὔκαιρον ἐτήρει .. τοῦτ' ἐπιτελέσαι '.. a chance to execute this plan' 2M 14.29. **c.** *to watch out for dangers to*: abs., *s* guard, Ct 3.3 (ǁ 5.7 φύλαξ); + acc., θύραν Es A 16 *L*, καρδίαν Pr 4.23, ψυχήν 13.3; + acc. pers., 2.11 (ǁ φυλάσσω), αὐτὸν ἄμεμπτον θεῷ 'blameless ..' Wi 10.5 (dit.); σε ἀπὸ γυναικὸς ἀλλοτρίας '.. against a strange woman' Pr 7.5; κύκλῳ περὶ ^τὸν βασιλέα^ 'round the king' 1E 4.11. **d.** *to watch out for loss of*: + acc., τὰ ῥήματά μου Pr 3.1 (:: ἐπιλανθάνομαι 'forget'). **e.** *to observe closely*: + acc., *s* farmer, ἄνεμον Ec 11.4; Je 20.10; hum. eyes, ἐμὰς ὁδούς 'my ways of life' Pr 23.26.
2. *to act and conduct oneself in conformity with*: + acc., ἐντολάς Si 29.1, τὸν νόμον καὶ τὰ προστάγματα 'the law and the commandments' To 14.9 𝔊[I], τοὺς λόγους μου 1K 15.11; *s* God, τὴν διαθήκην Da 9.4 LXX (TH φυλάσσω).
3. *to retain without letting go of*: + acc. rei, Ct 7.14; τὰ κακά μοι Od 12.13.
Cf. τήρησις, παρα~, συντηρέω, φρουρέω, φυλάσσω: Schmidt 4.686-8.

τήρησις, εως. f.ʃ
v.n. of τηρέω: ἐντολῶν Si 35.23, νόμων Wi 6.18; military guard, 1M 5.18, 3M 5.44, γαζοφυλακίου 'of treasury' 2M 3.40. Cf. τηρέω.

τιάρα, ας. f.ʃ
head-dress: worn by Chaldaean noblemen, Ez 23.15, Da 3.21.

τίθημι: fut.act. θήσω, inf. θήσειν, mid. θήσομαι, inf. θήσεσθαι, pass. τεθήσομαι; 1aor.act. ἔθηκα, ἔθηκαν (on the pl. forms, see Thack. 255), pass. ἐτέθην, inf. τεθῆναι, subj. τεθῶ, impv.3s τεθήτω; 2aor.act. inf. θεῖναι, ptc. θείς, impv. θές, subj. θῶ, opt.3s θείη; 2aor.mid. ἐθέμην, impv. θοῦ, 3s θέσθω, 2pl θέσθε, subj. θῶμαι, θῆσθε, inf. θέσθαι, ptc. θέμενος; pf.act. τέθεικα, mid./pass. τέθειμαι.
I. act. **1.** *to place, lay* (+ acc.): τόξον '(rain)bow' Ge 9.13; βρώματα 'foods' 41.48; ἔχθραν 'enmity'

3.15; τὴν χεῖρά σου ὑπὸ τὸν μηρόν μου 'your hand under my thigh' 24.2; χεῖρα .. ἐπὶ σιαγόνι Jb 21.5, see s.v. ἐπιτίθημι **1**; σκάνδαλα 'stumbling-blocks' Ho 4.17, παγίδα 'snare' Ps 118.110, ἔνεδρα 'ambush' Ob 7, νοσσιάν 'nest' 4; ὅρια 'borders' Ex 23.31; τράπεζαν 'table' 26.35, θρόνον 'throne' Je 25.18; ἐν βιβλίῳ '(to record) in a book' Jb 19.23 (ll γράφω). **b.** *to lay aside*: ***o*** capital, τὸν θησαυρόν σου Si 29.11, cf. θέμα ἀγαθὸν θησαυρίζεις σεαυτῷ εἰς ἡμέραν ἀνάγκης 'you are laying up a good treasure .. for a day of emergency' To 4.9. **c.** metaph., ἐπὶ τὴν καρδίαν 'turn one's thoughts on sth (acc.)' Ez 14.4 (ll τάσσω; see below **II 1 b**), Si 50.28, ἐπὶ διανοίᾳ Wi 4.14, εἰς (B: ἐφ') ἡμᾶς 2K 18.3*L*; ***o*** obligation, τὸν φόβον ^κυρίου^ ἐπὶ πάσης σαρκὸς καὶ inf., Si 17.4, ἐπὶ τὰς καρδίας αὐτῶν 17.8; μετὰ μοιχῶν τὴν μερίδα σου '(share) a portion with adulterers' Ps 49.18. **c.** idiom., + ***o*** πρόσωπον 'to fix one's stance':, τὸ πρόσωπον αὐτῶν εἰς γῆν Αἰγύπτου Je 49.17 (to look to Egypt as allies and ll δίδωμι vs. 15); ***s*** priests, θεῖναι (v.l. εἶναι) εὐλογίας ὑμῶν ἐπὶ τοὺς οἴκους ὑμῶν Ez 44.30.

2. *to institute*: ἐγὼ τίθημί σοι διαθήκην Ex 34.10, μήποτε θῇς διαθήκην τοῖς ἐγκαθημένοις .. 34.12; πρός τινα Si 44.18; συνθήκην .. πρὸς αὐτόν Wi 1.16; δικαιοσύνην εἰς γῆν ἔθηκε Am 5.7. ἐπὶ τῆς γῆς κρίσιν Is 42.4; εἰρήνην μετά τινος 1M 10.4; γνώμην 'official decision, directive' 1E 5.3, 2E 4.21, 6.1.

*__3.__ *to cause to be, render*: **a.** + double acc., πατέρα πολλῶν ἐθνῶν τέθεικά σε Ge 17.5, σωτηρίαν ἡμῶν θήσει τεῖχος Is 26.1; adj. as 2nd acc., θήσω τὸν οὐρανὸν ὑμῖν σιδηροῦν '.. steely' Le 26.19, θεῖναι τὴν οἰκουμένην .. ἔρημον Is 13.9. **b.** + εἰς– θήσω σε εἰς ἔθνη Ge 17.6, θεῖναι ^τὰς πόλεις^ εἰς κονιορτόν '.. dust' Is 10.6, εἰς οὐδέν '(think) nothing of' Jb 24.25¶; pass. Je 12.11. **c.** + ὡς/ ὡσεί– θήσω τὸ σπέρμα σου ὡς τὴν ἄμμον τῆς θαλάσσης Ge 32.12; θήσω τὸν οὐρανὸν ὑμῖν σιδηροῦν καὶ τὴν γῆν ὡσεὶ χαλκήν '.. steely .. copperlike' Le 26.19.

4. *to designate as, categorise as*: + double acc., οἱ τιθέντες τὸ σκότος φῶς καὶ τὸ φῶς σκότος Is 5.20 (ll λέγω); τὸ ὄνομα αὐτοῦ Αβιμελεχ Jd 8.31 B (A: ἐπι~).

5. *to direct* sbd to do sth: + acc. and inf., τίς με θήσει φυλάσσειν .. Is 27.4, see LSJ s.v. **B I 4**.

6. *to allow* sth to happen: + acc. and inf., κάμψαι με καὶ ἀπωσθῆναι ἡμᾶς 'for me to bend and for us to be rejected' La 3.45.

II. mid., hardly different in function from act. **1.** *to place*: **a.** + acc. lit., ἐκεῖ τὸν ἄνθρωπον Ge 2.8; εἰς τὸ δεσμωτήριον 40.3; ἐν φυλακῇ 41.10; φυλακήν .. θύραν Ps 140.3; λίθον ἐπὶ λίθον Hg 2.15*b*; Zc 5.11; αὐτοῖς ⌜κακά⌝ (Ra om.) Ps 72.18; με ἐπὶ τὸν θρόνον 3K 2.24. **b.** metaph. and idiom. w. *καρδία: abs. θέσθε εἰς τὰς καρδίας ὑμῶν 'Consider, Lay to your hearts' Hg 2.15*a* (ll ὑποτάσσω vs. 18), ἐν καρδίᾳ Je 12.11; Θέσθε τὰς καρδίας ὑμῶν εἰς τὰς ὁδοὺς ὑμῶν 'Put your minds to your ways, Consider your behaviour carefully' Hg 1.7 (ll τάσσω vs. 5), Ps 47.14; τὴν καρδίαν αὐτοῦ ἐπὶ τὸν ἄνθρωπον 1K 25.25; w. obj. clause, εἰ .. 'whether ..' Hg 2.19; + inf., ἐὰν μὴ θῆσθε εἰς τὴν καρδίαν ὑμῶν τοῦ δοῦναι δόξαν τῷ ὀνόματί μου 'unless you consider showing respect to my name' Ma 2.2*a*; θέσθε ἐπὶ τὰς καρδίας ὑμῶν Ma 1.1, Ez 14.7 (last ll act. vs. 4), cf. ἔθεντο ἐπὶ ψυχὴν Is 42.25; εἰς τὰ εἴδωλα ἔθετο τοὺς ὀφθαλμοὺς αὐτοῦ Ez 18.12, cf. Ps 16.11; τὸ πρόσωπον αὐτοῦ + inf., 4K 12.18*L* (B: τάσσω), ἐπ' ἐμὲ ἔθετο πᾶς Ισραηλ τὸ πρόσωπον αὐτοῦ (*L*: αὐτῶν) εἰς βασιλέα 'the entire Israel looked towards me as their (future) king' 3K 2.15; θῶνται ἐπὶ τὸν θεὸν τὴν ἐλπίδα αὐτῶν 'to pin their hope on ..' Ps 77.7, ὄνειδος (*L* pr. εἰς) ἐπὶ Ισραηλ 'a reproach ..' 1K 11.2, τιμὴν θέσθαι ἁδροῖς 'to show respect to the great' Jb 34.19, ζωὴν καὶ ἔλεος ἔθου παρ' ἐμοί 10.12. **c.** θέσθαι ἐπὶ τὰ σκῦλα 'to go for (or: aim at) the spoils' 1K 15.19, ellipsis of τὴν καρδίαν σου or τοὺς ὀφθαλμούς σου (?). **d.** *to entrust*: ἐν αὐτοῖς τοὺς λόγους Ps 104.27.

2. *to institute* (law etc.): θήσομαι τὴν διαθήκην μου ἀνὰ μέσον ἐμοῦ καὶ ἀνὰ μέσον σοῦ Ge 17.2; τέθειμαί σοι διαθήκην Ex 34.27; ἔθετο αὐτῷ δικαιώματα καὶ κρίσεις 15.25; ἔθετο ^δικαιώματα^ τῇ Βααλ Ho 13.1, νόμον Ps 77.5, δόγμα 'decree' 4M 4.23; ὥραν 'fixed season' Jb 36.26. **b.** + inf., ἔθετο αὐτοῖς .. εἰς πρόσταγμα .. ἀποπεμπτοῦν τῷ Φαραω 'he set them a rule .. (for them) to set off a fifth part for Ph.' Ge 47.26.

*__3.__ *to cause to be, render*, a causative transform of εἰμί: **a.** + double acc., θήσομαι τὴν Ιερουσαλημ λίθον καταπατούμενον 'I shall make a trampled stone of Jerusalem' Zc 12.3, ἐθήκαμεν ψεῦδος τὴν ἐλπίδα ἡμῶν Is 28.15; 29.21. **b.** + acc. and ὡς– θήσομαι αὐτὴν ὡς ἔρημον Ho 2.3 (ll τάσσω); 11.8, Am 8.10, Hg 2.23, Zc 12.2, 6. Cf. γίνομαι **3b**, ποιέω **I 9** and παρέχω **3**.

*__4.__ *to cause to become*, a causative transform of γίνομαι: **a.** + acc. and εἰς: εἰς μαρτύριον Ho 2.12; τὴν δόξαν αὐτῶν εἰς ἀτιμίαν 4.7; "I shall turn Samaria into an orchard-guard's shed" Mi 1.6. **b.** + acc. and adj. τὰ κέρατά σου θήσομαι σιδηρᾶ 'I will make your horns iron' Mi 4.13*a*, sim. 4.13*b*. Cf. γίνομαι **3**, ποιέω **I 9**. **c.** + double acc.: τὰ θνησιμαῖα τῶν δούλων σου βρώματα τοῖς πετεινοῖς 'your servants' corpses food for birds' Ps 78.2.

*5. *to destine* or *consign* to a certain fate or unfavourable treatment: + acc. and εἰς– πάντα τὰ εἴδωλα αὐτῆς θήσομαι εἰς ἀφανισμόν 'I shall condemn all her idols to destruction' Mi 1.7, sim. Jl 1.7, Zp 2.13; θήσομαί σε εἰς παράδειγμα 'I shall make an example of you' Na 3.6, εἰς παραβολήν Ps 43.15 (|| + acc. vs. 14).

6. *to make appointment of* (officer): + dat. com. θήσονται ἑαυτοῖς ἀρχὴν μίαν 'they will appoint a ruler for themselves' Ho 1.11; ἄρχοντας τοῦ πολέμου ἐπὶ τὸν λαόν 'military leaders ..' 1C 32.6. Cf. καθίστημι **I 4**.

7. *to put it* to sbd (τινι) to do, 'propose, suggest': + inf., θέσθαι Σίμωνι ποιῆσαι κατὰ τοὺς λόγους τούτους '.. to act in these terms' 1M 14.46.

8. *to cause to happen, bring about*: + acc., ἔθετο ἐν Αἰγύπτῳ τὰ σημεῖα Ps 77.43, τὰ ἔργα κυρίου, ἃ ἔθετο τέρατα ἐπὶ τῆς γῆς 45.9; cf. ἐπὶ τὸ αὐτὸ θήσομαι τὴν ἀποστροφὴν αὐτῶν 'I shall effect their return together' Mi 2.12; ἑαυτῷ ὄνομα μέγα 1C 17.21.

9. *to consider as*: + double acc., 3M 1.17; + acc. and inf., αὐτὸν εἶναι ἀσεβῆ 'him to be an infidel' Jb 32.3; Si prol. 30, 3M 6.34. **b**. *to consider as belonging to, categorise as*: + ἐν - ἐν οὐδενί '(to think) nothing of' 2M 4.15, 7.12.

10. *to allot*: τόπον τῷ λαῷ μου 2K 7.10.

11. periphrastically with a v.n.: ἀπειλὰς πικρὰς θέμενος 'having uttered bitter threats' 3M 2.24, μετάνοιαν Od 12.8. Cf. ποιέω **II 1**.

Cf. ἀνα~, ἀντι~, ἀπο~, ἐν~, ἐπι~, μετα~, περι~, συντίθημι, ἀπερείδομαι, ποιέω, τάσσω, θέμα, θέσις.

τιθηνέω: aor.impv. τιθήνησον, mid.inf. ~νήσασθαι.ʃ

1. *to bring up* an infant: + acc. pers., τέκνον Si 30.9, παιδείᾳ 'through education' 17.18¶; pass. La 4.5.

2. *to cultivate relationship with*: mid. and + acc. pers., ἔθνη 3M 3.15.

Cf. τιθηνός, τιθηνία.

τιθηνία, ας. f.ʃ *

act of rearing infants: 4M 16.7. Cf. τιθηνέω.

τιθηνός, όν.ʃ

subst., *one who nurses*: m., father, ὡσεὶ ἄραι τ. τὸν θηλάζοντα 'just as a father might pick up his babe' Nu 11.12; king Is 49.23 (|| τροφός), 'guardian' for king's children - 4K 10.1, 5; prob. nanny, 3M 1.20 (|| μήτηρ), cf. ἐγενήθη αὐτῷ εἰς ~όν Ru 4.16 (of Naomi taking Ruth's baby in her charge) and (f.) ἡ ~ὸς αὐτοῦ 2K 4.4 (for a handicapped 5-year-old child of Jonathan). Cf. τιθηνέω, ὑποτίθιος, τροφός: *BA* 4.78f.

τίκτω: fut. τέξομαι, ptc.pass. τεχθησόμενος; aor. ἔτεκον, inf. τεκεῖν, ptc.f. τεκοῦσα, subj. τέκω, pass. ἐτέχθην, subj. τεχθῶ, ptc. τεχθείς; pf. τέτοκα, ptc. τετοκώς, pass. τετεγμένος.

to give birth to: ***s*** woman, abs. Ge 17.17; ἐν λύπαις 'in pains' 3.16; τέξεται ἐπὶ τῶν γονάτων μου 'as a surrogate mother for me' 30.3; mother, Ho 2.5, Je 16.3 (latter || γεννάω ***s*** father); hum. male, Nu 11.12 (|| ἐν γαστρὶ λαμβάνω); ἐπὶ μηρῶν Ιωσηφ 'on J.'s thighs' Ge 50.23; ὠδῖνες ὡς τικτούσης 'pangs like those of a woman in labour' Ho 13.13, || ὠδίνω Is 54.1; + acc. pers., συνέλαβε ἔτι καὶ ἔτεκεν θυγατέρα 'she conceived again and bore a daughter' Ho 1.6; παιδίον De 25.6; τέκνον Ge 3.16; υἱόν 19.37; animal, Le 22.27, De 15.19; acc. rei, βώλους δρόσου 'drops of dew' Jb 38.28, ἀνομίαν Is 59.4 (|| κύω), Ps 7.15; + dat. (the husband) Ge 16.1, 22.20, 29.32; τέξεταί σοι υἱόν 17.19; metaph. τί τέξεται 'what is going to result' Si 8.18, sim. τί τέξεται ἡ ἐπιοῦσα 'what tomorrow has in store' Pr 3.28, 27.1; ἡ σοφία ἀνδρὶ τίκτει πρόνησιν 'wisdom brings forth prudence ..' 10.23. Cf. τέκνον, τόκος, τεκνοποιέω, πρωτοτοκέω, πρωτότοκος, γεννάω, ἀνα~, ἀποτίκτω, κύω, λοχεύομαι, μήτηρ: Schmidt 4.62-5.

τίλλω: aor.pass. ἐτίλην; pf.ptc.pass. τετιλμένος.ʃ

to pull and remove: ***o*** hair, ἀπὸ τῶν τριχῶν τῆς κεφαλῆς μου 2E 9.3 (as a gesture of sorrow), σάρκας 'pieces of flesh (of a victim)' PSol 13.3; pass., ***o*** πτερά 'feathers' Da 7.4 LXX; pass., ἐκ λαοῦ .. τετιλμένου 'a people .. with their hairs plucked (a form of punishment, torture?)' or mid. '.. who plucked their own hair out (as a gesture of mourning and sorrow)' Is 18.7. Cf. ἐκ~, κατατίλλω: Spicq 3.379f.

τιμάω: pres.impv.2s τίμα; fut. τιμήσω, mid. τιμήσομαι, pass. τιμηθήσομαι; aor. ἐτίμησα, inf. τιμῆσαι, ptc. τιμήσας, impv. τίμησον, mid.subj. τιμήσωμαι, pass. ἐτιμήθην, ptc. τιμηθείς; pf.pass.3pl τετίμηνται, ptc. τετιμημένος

1. act. *to treat respectfully*: + acc. pers., τίμα τὸν πατέρα σου καὶ τὴν μητέρα Ex 20.12, sim. De 5.16, ἄνδρα ἴδιον 'own husband' Si 26.26¶ (:: ἀτιμάζω); θεόν Da 11.38 LXX (TH δοξάζω), ὡς θεόν Wi 14.15, through offerings, Pr 3.9 (|| ἀπάρχομαι), 2M 13.23, 3M 3.17, with kindness, Es E 2 (pass.); + acc. rei, πρόσωπον πρεσβυτέρου Le 19.32; ***o*** temple, 2M 3.12, 3M 3.16, + δοξάζω 2M 3.2. **b**. *to attach great value to*: + acc., σοφίαν Pr 6.8c, πεδίον 'field' 27.26; pass., ***o*** friends, Ps 138.17. **c**. *to help win respect*: + acc. pers., ἔναντι τοῦ βασιλέως 1E 8.26.

2. *to consider as equal to*: + acc., pred. and pass., τὸν .. τιμηθέντα ἄνθρωπον 'one who was regarded to be human' Wi 14.20 (|| λογίζομαι).

3. mid. *to assess the value of*: abs. and + gen., ἀργυρίου 'in terms of silver' Is 55.2; + acc. pers., Le

27.8; + acc. rei ἀνὰ μέσον καλοῦ καὶ ἀνὰ μέσον πονηροῦ 'whether it is good or bad' 27.12 (cultic offering).

Cf. τιμή, προ~, ὑπερτιμάω, δοξάζω, ἀτιμάζω, ἀσκέω.

τιμή, ῆς. f.

1. *compensation paid*: τ. τοῦ προσώπου 'compensation for the (loss of) face suffered' Ge 20.16.

2. *that which is given as payment for commodity* or *service rendered*, 'price': τοῦ σίτου 'of the grain' Ge 44.2; ~ὴν δώσεις Ex 34.20; ἄνευ ἀργυρίου καὶ ~ῆς 'without paying silver ..' Is 55.1; λυτρώσεως '(paid) for manumission' Ps 48.9; honoraria (?) Ez 22.25. **b**. *tax imposed on*: ἁλός 'salt-(tax)' 1M 10.29. **c**. *value*: τῆς ψυχῆς αὐτοῦ 'of his own life' Le 27.2.

3. *high esteem*: arising from outward splendour, εἰς ~ὴν καὶ δόξαν Ex 28.2, 36 (of priest's garments); ἄνθρωπος ἐν ~ῇ ὤν Ps 48.13; opp. ἀτιμία Is 10.16 (|| δόξα); in general, + εὔνοια 'goodwill' 2M 9.21; δόξαν καὶ ~ήν 'glorious and worthy offerings' (metonymy) Ps 95.7, cf. 1Tim 1.17; conferred on humans as God's creation, Ps 8.6; social standing, Wi 8.10. Cf. φιλοτιμία.

4. *respect shown*: to one's own parents, Si 3.11; by wives to husbands, Es 1.20.

Cf. τιμάω, τίμημα, συντίμησις, τιμογραφέω, δόξα, ἀξία.

τίμημα, ατος. n.ʃ

value: Le 27.27 (|| τιμή). Cf. τιμή.

τίμιος, α, ον.

precious, valuable: *s* hum., La 4.2; God's infrequent verbal revelation, 1K 3.1; in an official title, 2E 4.10; λίθος Da 11.38 TH (LXX πολυτελής), Ps 18.11, σοφία Pr 3.15, ψυχή 6.26, ἱερωσύνη 'priesthood' 4M 5.35; subst. τὰ ~α αὐτοῦ Ho 11.7, τὸ πρῶτον ~ον 'the first-rate treasure' PSol 17.43; opp. ἀνάξιος 'worthless' Je 15.19. **b**. *profitable*: *s* soul of a harlot's client, Pr 6.26. Cf. ἔντιμος, πολυτελής.

τιμογραφέω: aor. ἐτιμογράφησα.ʃ

to assess the value of: + acc., τὴν γῆν 4K 23.35. Cf. τιμή.

τιμωρέω: fut.mid. τιμωρήσομαι; aor. act.opt. 3s τιμωρήσειεν, mid. ἐτιμωρησάμην, pass.inf. τιμωρηθῆναι; pf.pass. τετιμώρημαι.

to punish: *s* divine providence, 4M 9.24; pass. and *o* hum., Pr 22.3, 4M 18.5 (|| κολάζω), 17.21; τὸ σῶμα 2M 7.7. **b**. mid. + acc. hum., *s* hum. Jd 5.14 AL, *s* God, Wi 12.20, 4M 12.18; Ez 5.17, *o* ^τὴν γῆν^ 14.15.

Cf. εὐθύνω, κολάζω, τιμωρητής, τιμωρία, ἀτιμώρητος: Schmidt 4.172-5.

τιμωρητής, οῦ. m.ʃ *

he who punishes: + πολέμιος 'enemy' 2M 4.16. Cf. τιμωρέω.

τιμωρία, ας. f.

1. *punishment*: corporeal, 3M 4.4, also 1E 8.24?, || μάστιγες 'whips' Pr 19.29; plagues visited upon Egypt, 3M 2.6.

2. *aid*: from God, Da 2.18 LXX.

Cf. βοήθεια, κόλασις, εὔθυνα, ὄφλησις, πρόστιμον: Schmidt 4.159f.; Trench 24-6.

τίναγμα, ατος. n.ʃ*

shake, quake: caused by a thunder (?), Jb 28.26¶. Cf. ἐκτιναγμός.

τίνω: fut. τείσω, mid. τείσομαι. On the spelling, see LSJ s.v. τίω ad finem.ʃ

to pay a penalty: + acc., ζημίαν Pr 27.12. **b**. mid. *to punish*: *s* God and kings, + acc. pers., τὸν ἐχθρόν Pr 20.9c, τοὺς ἀσεβεῖς 'the impious' 24.22.

Cf. ἀποτίνω, κολάζω, τιμωρέω: Schmidt 4.172-5.

τίς, τίνος m.f.; τί, τίνος n.

Reference to unknown entity in a question.

I. τίς, referring to an unknown person, *Who?*: τίς ἐξ ὑμῶν .. 'Who amongst you ..?' Hg 2.3; τίνες καὶ τίνες 'who exactly ..?' Ex 10.8; τίνος ἕνεκεν 'On whose account?' Jn 1.7, 8 (or poss. 'why?', i.e. τίνος neuter, cf. Thph PG 126.925 and Syh at Jn 1.8 *meṭṭul mānā'*); rhetorically = someone– Τίς οἶδεν εἰ .. Jn 3.9; 'what kind of person?'– τίνες ἦτε; Hg 2.16. **b**. = τί, where the noun referred to is of masc. or fem. gender: τίς σου ἡ ἐργασία ἐστί; 'what is your occupation?' Jn 1.8; τίς ἡ ἀσέβεια τοῦ Ιακωβ; Mi 1.5; ὄψεσθε τὴν γῆν τίς ἐστιν 'Look at the land what it is like' Nu 13.19; Jb 13.23.

II. τί, referring to an unknown object, *What?*: τί ἐστιν; 'What is the matter?' Ge 21.17; τί σοι ποιήσω, Εφραιμ; Ho 6.4; in indirect question, μνήσθητι δὴ τί ἐβουλεύσατο .. Βαλακ 'Do remember what B. decided' Mi 6.5; τί αὐτῷ ἔτι καὶ εἰδώλοις; 'What has he still to do with idols?' Ho 14.9, τί σοι καὶ τῇ ὁδῷ Αἰγύπτου τοῦ πιεῖν ὕδωρ Γηων; 'What have you got to do with the way of Egypt that you should drink the water of G.?' Je 2.18; asking about the character or office of a person, Τί οἱ ἄνθρωποι οὗτοι ..; Nu 22.9. **b**. *Why?*, *for what purpose?* (= διὰ τί), Jn 1.6, Is 1.5, 3.14, Ne 2.16, cf. Shipp 533f. ***c**. *in what manner?* (= πῶς)– τί δικαιωθῶμεν 'how could we justify ourselves?' Ge 44.16; τί ἀράσομαι ..; 'how shall I curse ..?' Nu 23.8; τί σε διαθῶ 'how shall I deal with you?' Ho 11.8 (so Eth Bo); Si 30.19, 38.25. **d**. ἕως τίνος *Until when?, How much longer?*: ἕως τίνος οὐ βούλεσθε εἰσακούειν .. 'How much longer do you refuse to listen ..?' Ex 16.28; Hb 1.2; 2.6. **e**. ἵνα τί *Why? For what purpose?*: ἵνα τί εἶπας .. Ge 12.19; ἵνα τί ἔγνωκας κακά; Mi 4.9; Hb 1.3, 13; see under ἵνα. ***f**. τί ὅτι *Why?, Why is it that ..?*: τί ὅτι τὰ πρόσωπα ὑμῶν σκυθρωπὰ σήμερον; 'why are you looking gloomy today?' Ge 40.7; τί ὅτι ἐγκατελίπετε ἕκαστος τὸν ἀδελφὸν αὐτοῦ ..; 'Why is it that you abandoned one another ..?' Ma 2.10; cf. BDAG, s.v., **1 β**, ה end. Cf. Vulg *cur* at Ge 3.1. In Cl. Gk one finds ὅτι τί: LSJ s.v. ὅτι **B 1 b**. **g**. διὰ τί *why?*: Le 10.17. **h**. The neuter interrogative τί is only rarely used in the pl.: τίνα ἐστιν τὰ ὀνόματα ..; 2E 5.4, cf. τί οὗτοι (referring to horses) ..; .. Ἐγὼ δείξω σοι τί ἐστι ταῦτα Zc 1.9. **i**. On τίς/τί combined with the demonstrative οὗτος/τοῦτο, see under the latter, **1e**.

III. The interrogative may occupy a non-initial position: Ὑμεῖς δὲ τί ἐνεπυρίσατε .. 'You, why did you burn ..?' Is 3.14 (with an accusing finger pointed at the defendants), καὶ σὺ τί ποιήσεις .. Je 4.30.

IV. = relative pron.: Ἐκ τοῦ ἀνθρώπου, τίνος (v.l. οὗτινος) ταῦτά ἐστιν, ἐγὼ ἐν γαστρὶ ἔχω 'By the person, to whom these belong, I am pregnant' Ge 38.25; τίνος ἐστίν, αὐτῷ ἀποδώσει 'To one to whom it belongs, he shall give back' Le 6.5; ἥξει τίνος αὐτοῦ ἡ οἰκία 'the owner of the house shall come along' 14.35; τίνι ἐὰν ᾖ ἐν αὐτῷ μῶμος, οὐ προσελεύσεται .. 'whosoever has a blemish shall not proceed ..' 21.17 (|| πᾶς ἄνθρωπος or only πᾶς + subj., vs. 18 and 21); ἀποδώσει τίνι ἐπλημμέλησεν αὐτῷ Nu 5.7; ἀνὴρ ἢ γυνὴ .., τίνος ἡ διάνοια ἐξέκλινεν .. De 29.18; 1E 4.54. **b**. antecedentless: οὐκ ἔστιν τίς ὁμοιωθήσεταί σοι 'there is none comparable with you' Ps 39.6. See Mayser II1.80.

V. = attrib. adj. interr., *what sort of?*: τίνι ὁμοιώματι 'to what sort of likeness ..?' Is 40.18, τίς εἰρήνη 'what kind of peace ..?' Si 13.18, τίς ὠφέλεια 'what sort of benefit' Ps 29.10, Si 20.30; Ec 1.3, 5.10, 15, 6.8.

τις, τι.

A pronoun of indefinite reference: indefiniteness reinforced by the addition of πᾶς: πᾶς τις διανοεῖται .. ἐπὶ τὰ πονηρά 'every single one that you may care to name is thinking of evil things' Ge 6.5, sim. Ps 28.9; πᾶν οἰκέτην τινὸς .. 'anybody's slave' Ex 12.44; ἕν τι τῶν ῥημάτων τοῦ κυρίου σου 'any one of ..' Ju 2.13. **b**. pl. indicating an unspecified number, but not many, 'several': ἡμέρας τινάς 'for some time' Ge 27.44. **c**. combined with a pl. noun in the gen. indicates an unspecified member belonging to the group - τινα τῶν υἱῶν Ισραηλ Ex 21.17, cf. Ἐὰν δὲ λοιδορῶνται δύο ἄνδρες, καὶ πατάξῃ τις τὸν πλησίον 'If two men were quarrelling and one (of them) struck the other' 21.18. **d**. tones down an utterance: Πόσον τινὰ εὗρες μισθὸν ..; 'How much wage have you found .., I wonder?' Ez 27.33, πόση τίς ἐστιν 'about how much is it?' Jb 38.18; with an adj. or adv., βραχύ τι 'just a little' Ps 8.6; indecl. - εἴ τι πεπλάνημαι 'if I have gone astray somewhat' Jb 6.24. **e**. + a subst.: prepositive, τι αἴτημα 'some request' 3K 3.5, τινα θεοῦ δύναμιν 'some kind of divine force' 2M 3.38, ἔν τινι τόπῳ 'in a certain place' 12.18; postpositive, μέρος τι 'a certain part' 1M 6.40. **f**. + an adj.: τι ἄλλο 'sth else' 1M 13.39, τι παράδοξον 'sth unusual' 2M 9.24. **g**. following a proper noun, introduces a person or place the audience or readership may be assumed not to be familiar with: πρὸς ἄνθρωπόν τινα Ὀδολλαμίτην 'to a certain Odollamite person' Ge 38.1, Σίμων δέ τις 2M 3.4, sim. 4M 4.1; 2M 10.11; τινος Αὐρανοῦ 'of a certain Auranus' 4.40.

τιτάν, ᾶνος. m.∫

Titan: || γίγας Ju 16.6; 2K 5.18, 22.

τιτρώσκω: fut. τρώσω, pass. τρωθήσομαι; aor. ἔτρωσα, subj. τρώσω, ptc. τρώσας, impv.3s τρωσάτω, op.3s τρώσαι; pf.pass. τέτρωμαι, ptc. τετρωμένος.

to wound: bodily, De 1.44, 7.21; on battlefield, 2M 11.9; and pass., Nu 31.19; mental and *s* μάχαιρα 'sword' (fig. of malicious speech) Pr 12.18, βολίς 'missile' Je 9.8 (fig. of harmful tongue), τόξον 'arrow' Jb 20.24; *o* τὸ κάλλος σου Ez 28.7, pass. ζωή Jb 36.14; ἀγάπης 'love-(sick)' Ct 2.5; τὴν διάνοιαν 'mentally' 2M 3.16. Cf. τραῦμα, τραυματίζω, κατατιτρώσκω, ἄτρωτος: Schmidt 3.300-2.

τμητός, ή, όν.∫

shaped by cutting: s stone to build an altar with, Ex 20.25. Cf. τέμνω.

τοι.

Rhetorical particle added so as to reinforce the veracity of a statement: only in 4M (7x) and always as γε τοί, e.g. 4M 2.17. Del. 4M 4.21 v.l.

τοιγαροῦν.

Inferential particle, 'therefore, for that very reason': clause-initial, Is 5.26(-), Si 41.16(-), Jb 22.10 (*a*), 2M 7.23; not clause-initial, Jb 24.22(-).

Cf. οὖν. *a*) עַל־כֵּן.

τοίνυν.

Inferential particle, *if that is the case, then*: Is 3.10(-), 5.13(*a*), 1C 28.10(*b*); reinforced by διὰ τοῦτο 27.4(-); by δή 4M 1.13 +.

Position: alw. clause-initial in Is (4x); non-initial in 1/2C, Jb, Wi, 4M. Cf. ἄρα, διότι.

a) לָכֵן; *b*) עַתָּה. Del. Je 7.14, 2M 3.1 v.l

τοιόσδε, άδε, όνδε. pron.

such as the following: 2M 11.27; n.pl., τοιάδε εἶπαν 'they said as follows' 2E 5.3.

τοιοῦτος, τοιαύτη, τοιοῦτο.

similar to what/who has been already mentioned or present, 'such as this,' mostly with connotation of sth striking or extraordinary: attr. and anarthrous – τοιαύτη τις ἡμέρα 'one such day' Ge 39.11; ἄνθρωπον τοιοῦτον 'a person such as this' 41.38, Μὴ εὑρήσομεν ἄνδρα τοιοῦτον ἕνα; 1M 10.16; τοιαύτη ἀκρίς 'so many locusts' Ex 10.14; with the article intervening – ἐν ἔθνει τῷ τοιούτῳ Je 5.9, 29, μισητὸς ἄνθρωπος ὁ τοιοῦτος 'such a person is hateful' Si 20.15; the pron. at the end – τὸ πάσχα τοιοῦτο 1E 1.18; with the pron. in the middle, διὰ τῶν τοιούτων ἔργων 'through such works' Wi 12.19. **b**. subst.– οἵας οὐκ εἶδον τοιαύτας ἐν ὅλῃ γῇ Αἰγύπτῳ αἰσχροτέρας 'the uglier than which as these I had not seen in the whole of Egypt' Ge 41.19; ἤκουσται τοιοῦτο De 4.32 (|| τὸ ῥῆμα τὸ μέγα τοῦτο); γέγονε τοιαῦτα Jl 1.2; articular, τὸ τοιοῦτο 'such a (serious) matter' 1E 2.18, πάντα τὰ τοιαῦτα 4.37; ἐκ τῶν τοιούτων 'because of such deeds' Si 7.35; τοιαῦτα πολλά 'many such things' Jb 16.2; || οὕτως Is 66.8; Pr 6.14 (|| ὁ αὐτός vs. 13), 31.10. **c**. coordinated with ὅστις– χάλαζαν πολλὴν σφόδρα, ἥτις τοιαύτη οὐ γέγονεν ἐν Αἰγύπτῳ 'an exceeding amount of hail, the like of which has never been in Egypt' Ex 9.18; 9.24; κραυγὴ μεγάλη .. ἥτις τοιαύτη οὐ γέγονεν καὶ τοιαύτη οὐ προστεθήσεται 'a great cry .. the like of which had never occurred and will not be repeated' 11.6. **d**. correlated with οἷος– πάσχα τοιοῦτο, οἷον ἤγαγεν Ἰωσίας 'a passover like that which Josiah celebrated' 1E 1.19; οὐδεὶς ἐκτίσθη ἐπὶ τῆς γῆς τοιοῦτος οἷος Ενωχ 'nobody such as Enoch was ever created on the earth' Si 49.14; οὐχ οἷα ἤθελεν, τοιαῦτα ἐγεγόνει τῷ Ισραηλ 'not what he wished for had happened to Israel' 1M 4.27. **e**. correlated w. ὥσπερ: "as (ὥσπερ) a man's broken vessel becomes useless, so are their gods (τοιοῦτοι ὑπάρχουσιν οἱ θεοὶ αὐτῶν)" Ep Je 15f.

Del. 2M 11.27, 3M 2.1 v.l.

τοῖχος, ου. m.

wall: of house, οἰκίας Le 14.37; λίθος ἐκ ~ου βοήσεται 'a stone shall cry out of the wall' Hb 2.11; Am 5.19; of altar, Ex 30.3, Le 5.9; round a vineyard, Is 5.5 (|| φραγμός 'fence, hedge'); round a country, 23.13, cf. van der Kooij 1998.68f. Cf. τεῖχος.

τοκάς, άδος. f.ʃ

for breeding: τ. ἵππος 'brood-mare' 3K 2.46[i].

τοκετός, οῦ. m.ʃ

childbirth: Ge 35.16; καιρὸς ~οῦ τραγελάφων πέτρας 'the time of delivery of rock goat-deer' Jb 39.1¶; μῆνας .. ~οῦ 'months of ..' 39.2; ἡμέραν τοῦ ~οῦ Si 23.14. Cf. τόκος, τίκτω.

τόκος, ου. m.

1. *childbirth*: || ὠδίνη 'birthpang' and σύλλημψις 'pregnancy' Ho 9.11.

2. *interest on lent money* or *goods*: οὐκ ἐπιθήσεις αὐτῷ ~ον 'thou shalt not impose interest on him' Ex 22.25; οὐ λήμψῃ παρ' αὐτοῦ ~ον Le 25.36; τὸ ἀργύριόν σου οὐ δώσεις αὐτῷ ἐπὶ ~ῳ '.. with interest' 25.37, sim. Ez 18.8; μετὰ ~ου ἔδωκε καὶ πλεονασμὸν ἔλαβε '.. made profit' 18.13; δανείζων χωρὶς ~ων 4M 2.8; ἐκτοκιεῖς .. ~ον ἀργυρίου καὶ ~ον βρωμάτων καὶ παντὸς πράγματος De 23.20. **b**. perceived as a form of social injustice, 'usury': ἐκ ~ου καὶ ἐξ ἀδικίας λυτρώσεται .. Ps 71.14, cf. Ez 18.8, 12f., 17; τ. καὶ δόλος '.. and deception' Ps 54.12, cf. Je 9.6. See Caird 1969.37 *pace* LSG s.v.

Cf. τίκτω, ἐκτοκίζω, πλεονασμός.

τόλμα, ης. f.

challenging and daring attitude: Jb 21.27¶; on battlefield, Ju 16.10 (|| θάρσος), 2M 8.18. Cf. τολμάω, τολμηρός: Schmidt 3.543-7.

τολμάω: fut. τολμήσω; aor. ἐτόλμησα, ptc. τολμήσας.ʃ

to challenge and dare to aim at: + acc. rei, Jb 15.12 (*s* καρδία), ἀπείθειαν 'disobedience' 4M 8.18; + inf., Ju 14.13, Es 1.18, 7.5, 2M 4.2; with no connotation of improper audacity, 3M 3.21. Cf. τόλμα, τολμηρός, κατατολμάω, εὐτολμία.

τολμηρός, ά, όν.

reckless: subst.m., Si 8.15; *s* ψυχή 19.3. Cf. τολμάω, ἴταμος.

τολύπη, ης. f.ʃ

a kind of gourd: 4K 4.39. Cf. κολόκυνθα.

τομή, ῆς. f.ʃ

1. *act of cutting, pruning*: Ct 2.12.

2. *part cut off* from a vine: Jb 15.32.

Cf. τέμνω.

τομίς, ίδος. f.ʃ *

knife: as weapon, || μάχαιρα Pr 30.14.

τόμος, ου.ʃ

1. *piece cut off* from sth else: μεγάλου καινοῦ (v.l. + χάρτου 'of a papyrus roll') Is 8.1. Cf. τέμνω.

2. *roll* of papyrus: 1E 6.22.

τόνος, ου. m.ʃ

sinew, tendon: of hum. body, 4M 7.13 (|| νεῦρον). Cf. τένων, νεῦρον: Renehan 1.192.

τόξευμα, ατος. n.

arrow: κύριοι τοξευμάτων 'archers' Ge 49.23, μετὰ βέλους καὶ ~ατος Is 7.24; + τόξον 'bow' Ez 39.3, 9. Cf. τόξον, βέλος.

τοξεύω: fut. τοξεύσω; aor. ἐτόξευσα, impv. τόξευσον.

to shoot with the bow: ἐπί τινα 'at sbd' Je 27.14, πρός τινα 2K 11.24B; + acc. βέλος 'arrow' 4K 19.32. Cf. τόξον, κατατοξεύω.

τοξικόν, οῦ. n.ʃ

narrow vertical slit in wall for looking through: Jd 5.28 B.

τόξον, ου. n.

bow: as instrument of warfare, ὡσεὶ ~ου βολήν 'about a bow-shot' Ge 21.16; ἐν μαχαίρᾳ μου και ~ῳ 'with my sword and bow' 48.22; συνετρίβη .. τὰ

~α αὐτῶν 'their bows were broken' 49.24; ~ον καὶ ῥομφαίαν καὶ πόλεμον συντρίψω ἀπὸ τῆς γῆς Ho 2.18, τ. καὶ ἐγχειρίδιον '.. hand-weapon' Je 27.42; τ. πολεμικόν Zc 9.10; ἐντεταμένον 'bent' Ho 7.16, sim. Is 5.28 (|| βέλος 'arrow'), Je 4.29 (|| ἱππεύς 'horseman'); + τοξεύματα 'arrows' Ez 39.3, 9; w. ref. to rainbow (?) – τὸ τ. μου τίθημι ἐν τῇ νεφέλῃ Ge 9.13; Si 43.11. **b.** hunter's gear: τὸ σκεῦός σου, τήν τε φαρέτραν καὶ τὸ ~ον 'your gear, the quiver and bow' Ge 27.3.

Cf. τοξότης, τόξευμα, τοξεύω, βέλος, φαρέτρα.

τοξότης, ου. m.

archer: Ge 21.20; || ἱππεύς Am 2.15, cf. ἱππεῖς ~τας 'mounted archers' Ju 2.15; || σφενδονήτης 1M 9.11. Cf. τόξον, σφενδονήτης.

τοπάζιον, ου. n.ʃ

topaz: Ex 28.17, 36.17; of Ethiopian origin, Jb 28.19¶; precious stone, ἠγάπησα .. ὑπὲρ χρυσίον καὶ τ. 'I loved .. more than gold and topaz' Ps 118.127; Ez 28.13.

τοπάρχης, ου. m.

governor of a district: appointed by Pharaoh, Ge 41.34; Is 36.9; + σατράπης 1E 3.2, + ὕπατος Da 3.2, + ἄρχων Es B 1 o' (*L* σατράπης).

τοπαρχία, ας. f.ʃ

district: 1M 11.28.

τόπος, ου. m.

1. *particular part of space occupied by sbd or sth whether permanently or temporarily*, 'place, locality': || πόλις, Am 4.6, cf. Zp 1.4; ἐν παντὶ ~ῳ 'everywhere' Am 8.3, Ma 1.11. With a place-name appositionally following: ἕως τοῦ ~ου Συχεμ Ge 12.6; τοῦ θυσιαστηρίου 13.4.

2. *place where sbd or sth is habitually found*, 'abode, quarters': οἱ ἄνδρες τοῦ ~ου 'the local folks' Ge 26.7, τοὺς ἄνδρας ἐκ τοῦ τόπου 38.21; ἀπεκαθίστων τὸν λίθον ἐπὶ τὸ στόμα τοῦ φρέατος εἰς τὸν ~ον αὐτοῦ 'they would put the stone back on to the top of the well in its place' 29.3; Ραμα ἐπὶ ~ου μενεῖ 'Rama will remain in its place'(?) Zc 14.10; Na 3.17, Zp 2.11; ἵνα ἀπέλθω εἰς τὸν ~ον μου καὶ εἰς τὴν γῆν μου Ge 30.25; κύριος ἐκπορεύεται ἐκ τοῦ ~ου αὐτοῦ Mi 1.3; τὸν ἑαυτοῦ ~ον 2M 10.7, 1E 4.34, sim. 1C 16.27 (|| Ps 95.6 ἁγίασμα 'sanctuary'); || οἶκος Jb 7.10.

3. *space, room* for an activity, accommodation: τ. ἡμῖν καταλῦσαι 'room for us to stay' Ge 24.23; ~ον, οὗ φεύξεται ἐκεῖ ὁ φονεύσας 'a refuge for the murderer' Ex 21.13, εἰσάξουσιν εἰς τὸν ~ον αὐτῶν Is 14.2, στενός μοι ὁ τ., ποίησόν μοι ~ον ἵνα κατοικήσω 'my place is crowded. Make me room for me to dwell' 49.20. **b.** provincial area under direct royal administration: 1M 10.40, Bengston 10.

4. *proper place*: ἦν ὁ τ. τ. κτήνεσι 'the spot was meant for cattle' Nu 32.1, ἔστι ἀργυρίῳ τ., ὅθεν γίνεται 'gold has its proper origin' Jb 28.1, ποῖος τ. τῆς καταπαύσεώς μου; 'where is the place where I can have decent rest?' Is 66.1 (|| οἶκος). Cf. χώρα **2**.

5. *opportunity for action, chance*: μὴ δῷς ~ον αὐτῷ καταράσασθαί σε 'don't give him a chance to curse you' Si 4.5; δὸς ~ον νόμῳ 'leave the final decision to the law' 19.17.

Cf. Schmidt 2.13-6; Köster, *TDNT* 8.193-200; Chadwick 280-6.

τορευτός, ή, όν.

worked in relief, chased: χερουβιμ χρυσᾶ ~ά 'golden, embossed cherubs' Ex 25.17; *s* lampstand (λυχνία) 25.30, 36; piece of silver, Je 10.5.

τορνευτός, ή, όν.ʃ On the spelling, see Walters 132.

worked with a chisel, turned on a lathe: *s* building stone, 3K 10.22; smooth hum. hand, Ct 5.14; κρατήρ 'bowl' 7.3.

τόσος, η, ον.ʃ

so much in degree: ~ῳ μᾶλλον 'so much more' Si 11.11, 13.9.

τοσοῦτος, αύτη, οῦτο(ν).

I. subst. **1.** *to the same degree, as much*: another, mostly preceding, clause sets a standard– καθότι αὐτοὺς ἐταπείνουν, τοσούτῳ πλείους ἐγίνοντο 'the more they humiliated them, the more numerous they would grow' Ex 1.12; ὅσῳ ἐνεχρίοσάν με τὰ φάρμακα, τοσούτῳ μᾶλλον ἐξετυφλοῦντο οἱ ὀφθαλμοί μου .. 'the more they smeared the medicines on to me, the more my vision became obscured' To 2.10 𝔊[II], ὅσῳ μέγας εἶ, τοσούτῳ ταπείνου σεαυτόν 'the greater you are, humble yourself the more' Si 3.18; ποιήσεις τοσοῦτο 'you shall do the same' Nu 15.5; τοσαῦτα εἰπὼν .. 'having said that much' 2M 6.28, 14.34.

2. *to the extent that, so much as*: ἐπὶ τοσοῦτον δεδηλώσθω 'Let this suffice by way of an exposition' 2M 7.42; ἔτυχεν .. φιλανθρωπίας ἐπὶ ~ον ὥστε ἀναγορεύεσθαι ἡμῶν πατέρα .. 'he enjoyed so much of goodwill that he was called our father ..' Es E 11 o', sim. ἐπὶ τοσοῦτον ὥστε + inf., 2M 4.3, 3M 2.26, 3.1; τοσοῦτον ἴσχυσαν εἰδέναι ἵνα δύνωνται .. 'were so capable of understanding as to be able to ..' Wi 13.9.

3. absolutely and without explicit reference to anything mentioned earlier, 'so much, very much': τοσοῦτον ἐπιζεύξαντες 'having added so much' 2M 2.32.

II. attrib., *of such a degree* or *quantity* as indicated or implied, mostly of considerable degree or quality: μετὰ τοσαύτης .. προσοχῆς 'with so much attention ..' Wi 12.20; τὰ τοσαῦτα κακά 'such gross evils' 14.22; πλῆθος τοσοῦτο ἰσχυρόν 'a multitude as strong as this' 1M 3.17.

Cf. οὗτος, οὕτως.

τότε. adv.

1. *at that time*, 'then': of the past, τ. ἢ νῦν 'then than now' Ho 2.7; of the future, + fut. Hb 1.11, Zp 3.9, 11, Is 65.25.

2. *after that* (w. ref. to future): καὶ τ. φάγεται ἀπ' αὐτοῦ 'only then he may eat of it' Ex 12.44. **b**. indicates that something will occur on completion of some other action: coordinating with ὅταν, Is 28.25.

Cf. νῦν.

τραγέλαφος, ου. m.ʃ

goat-stag: ritually clean food, De 14.5; Jb 39.1¶.

τράγος, ου. m.

he-goat: Ge 30.35; ‖ κριός 'ram' 31.10, Ez 34.17; cultic offering, Nu 7.17; ‖ ταῦρος 'bull' De 32.14, Is 1.11; food, + κριός, μόσχος Ez 39.18. Cf. πρόβατον, αἴξ.

τρανός, ή, όν.

clear, distinct: *s* γλῶσσα μογιλάλων 'tongue of stammerers' Is 35.6; Wi 10.21. Cf. σαφής.

τράπεζα, ης. f.

table on which an object or objects is or are placed: cultic, Ex 25.22, τῆς προθέσεως 39.18, θυμάτων Ez 40.41, ~αι ὁλοκαυμάτων λίθιναι 'stone tables for burnt-offerings' 40.42; dining-table, κάθημαι ἐπὶ ~ης 3K 13.20, δειπνεῖν ἐπὶ ~ης 'to dine ..' Pr 23.1, τ. κυρίου Ma 1.7, 12, κεκοσμημένη 'decorated' Ez 23.41. **b**. *meal served at a table*: ἐσθίω τὴν ~άν τινος 2K 19.29B, 3K 2.7, Da 1.13 TH (LXX δεῖπνιον), Es C 28 o' (LXX ἐπὶ ~ης), cf. *ND* 2.37. **c**. *company of guests at dinner-table*: 2K 19.29*L*.

Cf. δεῖπνον: Goppelt, *TDNT* 8.209-11.

τραῦμα, ατος. n.

physical *wound, hurt*: τ. ἐμοί 'inflicted upon me' Ge 4.23, Ju 9.13 (‖ μώλωψ); Ex 21.25 (‖ κατάκαυμα, μώλωψ), Is 1.6 (‖ μώλωψ, πληγή); μαχαίρας Ez 32.29. Cf. τραυματίας, τιτρώσκω, μώλωψ, ἕλκος.

τραυματίας, ου. m.

wounded person or *animal*: mortally wounded, Ge 34.27; ‖ νεκρός Nu 19.16, Is 34.3; ‖ αἰχμαλωσία De 32.42; ‖ πτῶσις Na 3.3; ῥομφαία Zp 2.12; αἷμα ~ῶν Nu 23.24; μαχαίρας Is 22.2 (‖ νεκρός), Ez 31.18 (‖ ἀπὸ μαχαίρας vs. 17), Je 14.18, ῥομφαίας La 4.9; ~αι πεπτωκότες μαχαίρᾳ Ez 32.22; not mortally, διεσώθησαν 'survived' 2M 11.12. **b**. casualty in general: λιμοῦ 'of famine' La 4.9 (‖ ~αι ῥομφαίας).

Cf. τραῦμα.

τραυματίζω: aor. ἐτραύματισα, pass. ἐτραυματίσθην; pf.pass. τετραυμάτισμαι, ptc. τετραυματισμένος.

to wound, injure: + acc. pers., Ct 5.7; ‖ μαλακίζομαι Is 53.5; ἐν μαχαίραις Ez 28.23. Cf. τιτρώσκω.

τραχηλιάω: aor. ἐτραχηλίασα.ʃ*

to arch the neck proudly: Jb 15.25. Cf. τράχηλος.

τράχηλος, ου. m.

neck: of a hum., προσέπεσεν ἐπὶ τὸν ~ον αὐτοῦ 'flung himself on his neck' Ge 33.4; with ἐπιπίπτω, 45.14, 46.29; of an animal, Ho 10.11; on which a yoke is laid, Ge 27.40, Mi 2.3, Hb 3.13; on which a rod is laid, Is 9.4; fig. τ. σκληρός 'obstinacy' De 31.27, ἐσκλήρυναν τὸν ~ον αὐτῶν Je 7.27, 17.23, cf. "your neck is an iron sinew" Is 48.4 (‖ μέτωπον 'forehead'); ὑψηλός 'haughty' Is 3.16. Cf. σκληροτράχηλος, τραχηλιάω.

τραχύς, χεῖα, ύ.

1. *not even or smooth*, 'rugged': *s* ὁδός Je 2.25, PSol 8.17; subst. f., γῆ or ὁδός understood, Is 40.4 (:: λεῖος).

2. *wildly flowing*: *s* φάραγξ 'valley' De 21.4.

3. *hard to take and handle*: ~εῖα .. σοφία τοῖς ἀπαιδεύτοις Si 6.20.

4. *harsh and savage in disposition*: *s* ὗς 'boar' 2K 18.8B.

Cf. λεῖος.

τραχύτης, ητος. f.ʃ

sharp exchange of views: 3M1.23.

τρεῖς, gen. τριῶν, dat.τρισίν, neut. τρία.

three: τρεῖς ἡμέρας καὶ τ. νύκτας Jn 2.1; τρία μέτρα σεμιδάλεως 'three measures of flour' Ge 18.6. Cf. τρίτος, τρίς, τρισσός.

τρέμω.

to tremble, shake with fear and angst: στένων καὶ τρέμων Ge 4.12, 14; ἔστην τρέμων 'I stood, shaking' Da 10.11 LXX; διὰ τὸν ἐνεστῶτα χειμῶνα 'because of the prevailing storm' 1E 9.6; σείεται καὶ τρέμει 'shakes and trembles' 4.36; + φρίττω Od 12.4; *s* the earth, Ps 103.32, mountains Je 4.24. **b**. *to stand in awe of*: + φοβέομαι Da 5.19 TH; + acc., τοὺς λόγους μου Is 66.2.

Cf. τρόμος, ἔντρομος, ταράσσω, τρομέω, σαλεύω, σείω: Schmidt 3.513-5.

τρέπω: fut.mid. τρέψομαι, pass. τραπήσομαι; aor. mid. ἐτρεψάμην, pass. ἐτράπην, inf. τραπῆναι, ptc. τραπείς.

1. *to turn* in a certain direction: in giving way to pressure, metaph., + acc. (rudders), 4M 7.3.

2. *to defeat*: + acc. pers., ἐν φόνῳ μαχαίρας 'with the slaughter of a sword' Ex 17.13; Nu 14.45; ἐτράπησαν εἰς φυγήν 'were put to flight' Ju 15.3.

3. mid. *to direct oneself* into a certain disposition or action: εἰς ἔχθραν 'into hostility' Si 37.2, εἰς κακά 39.27, εἰς ἱκετείαν 'to supplication' 2M 12.42, εἰς τὸν πότον 'to drinking' 3M 5.16; + εἰς τό + inf.,

1.27; πρὸς τὴν εὐωχίαν 'to the festivity' 5.3; εἰς τὸν λόγον 'to the topic' 4M 1.12.

4. mid. *to fall involuntarily* into a certain state: εἰς ἔκλυσιν καὶ δειλίαν 'into stupor and terror' 2M 3.24; τῆς ὀργῆς εἰς ἔλεον τραπείσης 'the wrath having changed to mercy' 8.5, ἐπὶ ἔλεος '(moved) to pity' 4.37.

Cf. τροπή, τροπόω.

τρέφω: fut. θρέψω; aor. ἔθρεψα, ptc. θρέψας, inf. θρέψαι, pass. ἐτράφην, subj. τραφῶ, ptc. τραφείς.

1. *to provide food and water for sustenance*: ***s*** God, ***o*** hum., Ge 48.15 (with no age restriction); De 32.18 (|| γεννάω 'to give birth to'); pass., ***o*** lions, Bel 31f. LXX; ἐξ αὐτοῦ ἐτρέφετο πᾶσα σάρξ 'every living being was being nourished by it (= tree)' Da 4.9 TH.

2. *to sustain physical life of, keep alive*: ***s*** hum., ***o*** animals, Ge 6.19; ***s*** food, Wi 16.26 (|| διατηρέω).

3. *to allow to grow*: + acc., κόμην τρίχα κεφαλῆς 'a shock of hair of head' Nu 6.5. **b**. *to raise*: ***o*** livestock, θρέψει ἄνθρωπος δάμαλιν βοῶν καὶ δύο πρόβατα '.. a heifer and two lambs' Is 7.21. **c**. *to bring up, educate*: abs., Pr 23.24; + acc. (sbd else's child), τὸν υἱὸν αὐτοῦ 1M 3.33, sim. 11.39. Cf. Da 1.5 TH (|| LXX ἐκπαιδεύω); pass., ἐτράφης ἐν χειρί μου Es 4.8 o'.

Cf. τροφή, τροφεῖα, δια~, συντρέφω, παντοτρόφος, χορτάζω, ψωμίζω: Schmidt 4.98-100, 102-5; Moussy 37-89; Demont; Spicq 3.381-3.

τρέχω: fut. δραμῶ (rather than R's δράμω), δραμοῦμαι; aor.act. ἔδραμον, ptc. δραμών, impv. δράμε, inf. δραμεῖν.

to move on foot at pace faster than walk, 'run': εἰς τὰς βόας 'into the cows' Ge 18.7, ἐπὶ τὸ φρέαρ 'to the well' 24.20, πρὸς τὸν ἄνθρωπον ἔξω ἐπὶ τὴν πηγήν 24.29, εἰς συνάντησιν αὐτῷ 'to meet him' 29.13, εἰς τὴν συναγωγήν Nu 16.47, ὀπίσω αὐτοῦ 4K 5,21; + acc., ὁδόν Ps 18.6, 118.32; out of excitement, Ge 29.12, 13; || βαδίζω 'to walk' Is 40.31; ***s*** letter-carrier, 2C 30.6, on horseback, Es 3.13 *L*; locusts compared to soldiers Jl 2.7, 9, hum. compared to horses Je 8.6; ἀπώλεια Jb 41.14; hum. feet, Pr 1.16, Is 59.7, Je 12.5; divine word, Ps 147.4. **b**. *to transport oneself with speed by riding a beast*: ***s*** hum., 4K 4.22. **c**. ἀγῶνα 'race' as acc. or κίνδυνον 'risk' understood: περὶ ψυχῆς 'for his life' Pr 7.23 (|| σπεύδω 'hurry'), see LSJ s.v. **II 2**.

Cf. ἀνα~, δια~, εἰσ~, ἐπι~, κατα~, παρα~, περι~, προ~, προσ~, συντρέχω, τροχός, δρομεύς, δρόμος, διώκω, σπεύδω: Schmidt 1.524-34; Bauernfeind, *TDNT* 8.229f.

τριακάς, άδος. f.ʃ

the thirtieth day of a month: 2M 11.30.

τριάκοντα. num.

thirty: ἔτη διακόσια τ. '230 years' Ge 5.3; τ. χιλιάδες 30,000' 1E 1.7.

τριακονταετής, ές.ʃ

thirty years old: 1C 23.3.

τριακόσιοι, αι, α. num.

three hundred: τ. δέκα καὶ ὀκτώ 'three hundred and eighteen' Ge 14.14. Cf. τρεῖς.

τριακοστός, ή, όν.

thirtieth: Ez 1.1.

τρίβολος, ου.ʃ

1. *caltrop, tribulus terrestris* (LSJ): growing on an altar in ruins - ἄκανθαι καὶ ~οι Ho 10.8; Ge 3.18; metaph., entangling, ἀνομίας 'of lawlessness' Wi 5.7, + παγίς 'snare' Pr 22.5.

2. *threshing-machine*: used as an instrument of torture, Jd 8.7*L*, 16*L*, 2K 12.31, cf. βασανιστήριον.

τρίβος, ου. f.

familiar path: ἐγκαθήμενος ἐπὶ ~ου 'sitting on ..' Ge 49.17; τὴν ~ον αὐτῆς οὐ μὴ εὕρῃ 'she will not find her path' Ho 2.6 (|| ὁδός), εὐθείας ποιεῖτε τὰς ~ους τοῦ θεοῦ ἡμῶν Is 40.3 (|| ὁδός); πορευσόμεθα ἐν ταῖς ~οις αὐτοῦ Mi 4.2 (|| ὁδός); οὐ μὴ ἐκκλίνωσι τὰς ~ους αὐτῶν 'will not turn off their course' Jl 2.7 (|| ὁδός); τῶν ποδῶν ὑμῶν Is 3.12; θαλασσῶν Ps 8.9; of birds, Jb 28.7; τῆς ἐρήμου Je 9.10; ἐπιστήμης Ba 3.21 (|| ὁδός). **b**. metaph. course of action: + βουλή To 4.19 𝔊[I]; || τροχιά 'path' Pr 2.15, δικαιοσύνης 2.20; || βίος 'life-style' Wi 2.15.

Cf. ὁδός: Schmidt 4.635f.

τρίβω: aor.impv. τρῖψον; pf.ptc.pass. τετριμμένος.ʃ

1. *to pound*: hard stuff: for food, ἐν τῇ θυείᾳ 'with the mortar' Nu 11.8; ***o*** fruit-cakes, Is 38.21; pass., ^ὁδοὶ^ τετριμμέναι 'well-beaten (smooth) paths' Pr 15.19. Cf. κοπανίζω.

2. *to knead*: + acc., σταῖς 'dough' Je 7.18.

τριετής, ές.ʃ

of three years: ***s*** three-year-old heifer (still full of vitality) Is 15.5 (|| τριετίζουσα Ge 15.9), ἀπὸ ~οῦς καὶ ἐπάνω 'from three years and older' 2C 31.16; μετὰ ~ῆ χρόνον 'after a period of three years' 2M 4.23. Cf. τριετίζω.

τριετίζω.ʃ

to be three years old: ***s*** animal, δάμαλιν τριετίζουσαν καὶ αἶγα τριετίζουσαν .. 'a three-year-old heifer and a three-year-old goat ..' Ge 15.9 (|| τριετής Is 15.5); sacrificial calf (μόσχος), 1K 1.24.

τριημερία, ας. f.ʃ *

period of three days: Am 4.4.

τριήρης, εος. f.ʃ

trireme: 2M 4.20.

τρικυμία, ας.ʃ

soaring wave: threatening, pl., 4M 7.2. Cf. κῦμα.

τριμερίζω: fut. τριμεριῶ.ʃ
to divide into three parts: + acc., τὰ ὅρια τῆς γῆς De 19.3. Cf. μερίζω.

τρίμηνος, ον.
subst.n.sg., *period of three months*: Ge 38.24; 2C 36.2 (‖ μῆνας τρεῖς 1E 1.33).

τριόδους, gen. όδοντος. m./f.ʃ *
three-pronged: *s* κρεάγρα 'flesh-hook' 1K 2.13.

τριπλασίως. adv.ʃ
three times as much: Si 43.4.

τριπλοῦς, ῆ, οῦν.ʃ
threefold, triple: *s* στοά Ez 42.6. Cf. τρισσός, διπλοῦς.

τρίς. adv.
three times: δὶς ἢ τ. 'twice or thrice' Si 13.7; 1K 20.41 (*L* τρίτον). Cf. τρεῖς.

τρισάθλιος, α, ον.ʃ
thrice-unhappy: *s* hum., ‖ μέλεος 4M 16.6.

τρισαλιτήριος, ον.ʃ *
thrice-sinful: *s* hum., Es E 15, 2M 8.34, 15.3.

τρισκαίδεκα. num.
thirteen: 3K 7.38.

τρισκαιδέκατος, η, ον.
thirteenth: τῷ ~ῳ ἔτει 'in the thirteenth year' Ge 14.4.

τρισμύριοι, αι, α.ʃ
thirty thousand: Es 1.7 o'.

τρισσεύω: fut. τρισσεύσω; aor. ἐτρίσσευσα.ʃ
1. *to act three times* or *for the third time*: 1K 20.19, 20.
*2. *to divide into three*: + acc., army 2K 18.2*L*.
Cf. τρεῖς.

τρισσός, ή, όν.
1. *threefold*: στοαὶ ~αί 'triple porticos' Ez 42.3.
2. *pertaining to* τριστάτης (?): ὄψις ~ή Ez 23.15; subst.m., 23.23, τοῦ βασιλέως 4K 11.10 (*L* δόρατα).
Cf. τρεῖς, τριστάτης, τριπλοῦς: LSG s.v.

τρισσόω: aor.impv. τρίσσωσον.ʃ *
= τρισσεύω (q.v.): 3K 18.34.

τρισσῶς. adv.
in threefold fashion: Ez 16.30; repeating three times, Pr 22.20.

τριστάτης, ου. m. *
military *officer* of high rank (LSG): ἐπὶ πάντων 'charged with all' Ex 14.7; ἐκλέκτους ἀναβάτας ~άτας 'first-class, mounted officers' 15.4; 4K 7.2. Cf. *BA* 2.55f.

τρισχίλιοι, αι, α. num.
three thousand: Ex 32.28.

τριταῖος, α, ον.ʃ
on the third day: ἀπολωλώς 'missing now three days' 1K 9.20, ἠνωχλήθην ~ος 'have been unwell the past three days' 30.13. Cf. τρίτος.

τρίτος, η, ον.
1. *third* in order: τῇ ἡμέρᾳ τῇ ~ῃ 'on the third day' Ge 22.3; ἕως ~ης καὶ τετάρτης Nu 14.18. **b.*** Hebraistically τρίτη ἡμέρα 'the day before yesterday' in an idiom ὡς ἐχθὲς καὶ ~ην ἡμέραν 'as previously, as before' Ge 31.2, 5 = καθάπερ ἐ… Ex 5.7, 14, cf. the same phrase meaning 'yesterday and the day before' Xen., *Cyr*. 6.3.11 and so perh. at 1M 9.44; οὐχ .. πρὸ τῆς ἐ. οὐδὲ πρὸ τῆς ~ης ἡμέρας 'not in the recent nor remote past' 4.10; πρὸ τῆς ἐ. καὶ πρὸ τῆς ~ης 'in the past, previously' Ex 21.29, De 19.4, 6; πρὸ τῆς ἐ. καὶ ~ης 4.42, see also under ἐχθές.
2. n. adv. τρίτον 'thrice': τοῦτο τρίτον 'now three times' Nu 22.28, 32, Jd 16.15; τρίτον τοῦτο Nu 22.33, 24.10; also without τοῦτο, 1K 20.41*L*, 3K 17.21*L* (B+ τρίς), 4K 13.18*L* (and also ‖ πεντάκις, ἑξάκις); ἤδη τρίτον 3M 5.40.
3. *one third in quantity*: 4K 11.5, 1M 10.30.
Cf. τρεῖς, τριταῖος.

τρίχαπτος, η, ον.ʃ
plaited or *woven of hair*: subst.n., *fine veil of hair* (LSJ) for women, Ez 16.10, 13.

τρίχινος, η, ον.ʃ
made of hair: δέρρις τ. 'hairy leather garment' Ex 26.7, Zc 13.4. Cf. θρίξ.

τρίχωμα, ατος. n.ʃ
hair: Ez 24.17, κεφαλῆς 1E 8.68; Da 7.9 LXX (TH: θρίξ). Cf. θρίξ.

τριώροφος, ον.ʃ
situated at third level: subst. pl.n., of cabins of ship, Ge 6.16 (‖ κατάγαια and διώροφα); chambers, Ez 41.7 (‖ ὑπερῷος), 3K 6.8. Cf. κατάγαιος, ὑπερῷος, διώροφος.

τρομέω: aor. ἐτρόμησα.ʃ
to tremble: *s* νεφροί 'kidneys' 1M 2.24 (out of indignation). Cf. τρέμω. Del. Es 5.9 v.l.

τρόμος, ου. m.
trembling caused by alarm: ἔλαβεν αὐτοὺς τ. 'a shiver caught them' Ex 15.15; εἰσῆλθε τ. εἰς τὰ ὀστᾶ μου 'trembling penetrated my bones' Hb 3.16; ‖ φόβος with gen. obj. pers., Ge 9.2, De 2.25, 11.25; φόβος καὶ τ. Ex 15.16, Ju 2.28, ἀπὸ προσώπου τινός Is 19.16; τ. καὶ φόβος De 2.25, δέος καὶ τ. 2M 15.23; caused by stormy rain-water, Jb 38.34. Cf. τρέμω, σεισμός, φόβος, ἔντρομος.

τρόπαιον, ου. n.ʃ
public monument marking the enemy's defeat: 2M 5.6, 15.6. Cf. τροπή, μνημεῖον.

τροπή, ῆς. f.
1. *rotation*: ~αὶ ἡλίου 'solar cycle' De 33.14; οὐρανοῦ Jb 38.33; ~ῶν ἀλλαγὰς καὶ μεταβολὰς καιρῶν 'the alternations of solstices and the changes of the seasons' Wi 7.18.

2. *act of putting to flight, routing*: Ex 32.18; οἴσω τὴν ~ὴν αὐτῶν Je 30.10; τ. καὶ ἀπώλεια 'rout and destruction' 2M 12.27. **b**. *act of taking to flight*: λαοῦ Si 45.23; 1M 4.35; μεγάλη 5.61.

Cf. τρέπω, τρόπαιον, τροπόω. An error for τρυπῆς 'of piercing' or κοπῆς 'of a blow' at 3K 22.35?

τρόπις, ιος. f.ʃ

ship's keel: Wi 5.10.

τρόπος, ου. m.

1. *custom*: κατὰ τρόπον τοῦ θυσιαστηρίου 'in accordance with what is customarily done with the altar' Nu 18.7. Cf. ἐθισμός.

2. *manner of acting* in a certain way: 1K 25.33; πραῢς τὸν ~ον 'gentle of manners' 2M 15.12; διὰ τούτων τῶν τρόπων 'in these ways' Es E 14; 2M 1.24. **b**. in the phrase ὃν τρόπον and introducing a clause, *just as*, *exactly as* emphasising comparability and analogy: ὃν τρόπον ἐχρησάμεθά σοι καλῶς 'just as we treated you well' Ge 26.29; ὃν τ. εἴπατε 'as you said' Am 5.14, "just as you drank upon my holy mount, all the nations will drink wine" Ob 16; with the correlating οὕτως: Ex 39.23, Am 3.12, Is 33.4; the logical relationship between the two members can be that of antithetical contrast, "as (ὃν τ.) you were a curse among the nations .. so (οὕτως) I will save you and you shall be a blessing" Zc 8.13, sim. 8.14f. **c**. a verb understood: ὃν τ. οἱ διαιρούμενοι σκῦλα 'as those who divide spoils among themselves (rejoice)' Is 9.3; ὃν ~ον κἀγώ Is 38.19. **d**. followed by another conj., ὃν τ. ὅταν ἐξεγερθῇ ἄνθρωπος 'as when a man is awakened' Zc 4.1, sim. Am 3.12, Is 7.2; ὃν τ. ἐὰν φύγῃ ἄνθρωπος 'as if a man should flee' Am 5.19. **e**. κατὰ πάντα ~ον 'in every way' 3M 3.24; κατ' οὐδένα ~ον 'in no way whatsoever' Ep Je 68, 2M 11.31; τὸν αὐτὸν ~ον 'in the same way' 11.70. **f**. τοῦτον τὸν ~ον *in this manner*: 2M 6.31, τὸν ~ον τοῦτον 7.7; πάντα ~ον 'thoroughly' 4M 1.29. **g**. τρόπον + prec. gen., *in the manner of, as*: σητὸς τρόπον 'like a moth' Jb 4.19, θηρίων ~ον 'like wild animals' 2M 5.27, δραπέτου ~ον 'like a fugitive' 8.35; 4M 11.10.

Cf. καθά, ὡς.

τροπόω: fut. τροπώσω, mid. τροπώσομαι; aor.act. ἐτρόπωσα, mid. ἐτροπωσάμην, inf. τροπώσασθαι, pass. ἐτροπώθην, ptc. τροπωθείς; pf.pass. τετρόπωμαι, ptc. τετροπωμένος.

1. *to put to flight*: + acc. pers., Ps 88.24; Da 7.21 LXX (TH ἰσχύω), enemy troops Jo 11.6; ‖ ἐλαττονόω 'to defeat' 2M 13.19; Jd 20.36 A (B: πλήσσω), 39 A (B: πίπτω); pass., ***o*** enemy troops, ἔφυγεν καὶ ἐτροπώθη 'he fled ..' 1M 11.55; Jd 20.32*L* (A: προσκόπτω, B: πίπτω); mid. = act., 2K 8.1, 1C 18.1, 2C 25.8, Ps 88.24, 2M 8.6, ἐτροπώσατο αὐτοὺς καὶ ἔφυγον 1M 11.72.

*__2__. mid. *to reach a turning-point* (LSG s.v.): ***s*** battle, 3K 22.35 ‖ 2C 18.34.

Cf. τρέπω, τροπή, τρόπωσις, φεύγω, φυγαδεύω.

τρόπωσις, εως. f.ʃ

act of being put to flight: 3K 22.35*L*. Cf. τροπόω.

τροφεία, ας. f.ʃ

woman who nurtures a baby: 4M 15.13. Cf. τρέφω and τροφός.

τροφεύω: aor.ptc. τροφεύσας.ʃ*

to serve as a wet-nurse: γυναῖκα τροφεύουσαν .. καὶ θηλάσει Ex 2.7; ***s*** God and + acc. pers., ἐπελάθεσθε τὸν τροφεύσαντα ὑμᾶς θεὸν αἰώνιον 'you have forgotten the eternal God who suckled you' Ba 4.8. Cf. τροφός, θηλάζω: LSG s.v.; Moussy 73f.

τροφή, ῆς. f.

1. *food*: διαδώσει ~ήν 'will distribute food' Ge 49.27; ἀγγέλων ~ὴν .. ἄρτον ἀπ' οὐρανοῦ Wi 16.20.

2. *upbringing*: Si 22.7¶.

Cf. ἔδεσμα, τρέφω: Moussy 85-8.

τροφός, οῦ. f.

wet-nurse: Ῥεβέκκας Ge 35.8 (in her service); Is 49.23 (‖ τιθηνός). Cf. τροφεύω, τροφοφορέω, τροφεία, and τιθηνός.

τροφοφορέω: aor. ἐτροφοφόρησα, ptc. ~ρήσας, opt. 3s ~ρήσαι.ʃ*

to sustain by providing food: s God and + acc. pers., De 1.31*a*; hum. father, ὡς εἴ τις τροφοφορήσαι ἄνθρωπος τὸν υἱὸν αὐτοῦ 'as a man might sustain his son' 1.31*b*; ***s*** hum. mother, 2M 7.27 (‖ θηλάω, ἐκτρέφω). Cf. ἐκτρέφω, τρέφω, τροφός.

τροχαντήρ, ῆρος. m.ʃ

instrument of torture: 4M 8.13. Cf. βασανιστήριον.

τροχηλάτης, ου. m.ʃ

carriage-driver: Si 20.32¶.

τροχιά, ᾶς. f.

path to be followed: ὀρθή 'right' Pr 4.11 (‖ ὁδός). Cf. ὁδός.

τροχιαῖος, α, ον.ʃ*

worked by a wheel: ***s*** wedge, 4M 11.10. Cf. τροχός.

τροχίας, ου. m.ʃ

cast iron or *shaft* (*GI*): Ez 27.19.

τροχίζω: aor.ptc.pass. τροχισθείς.ʃ

to torture on the wheel: pass, ***o*** hum., 4M 5.3. Cf. αἰκίζω and βασανίζω.

τροχίσκος, ου. m.ʃ

small wheel: of ear-ring, Ez 16.12.

τροχός, οῦ. m.

wheel: of chariot, οἱ ~οὶ τῶν ἁρμάτων Is 5.28, ἁμάξης 'of a wagon' 41.15, fig. of fickleness Si 36.5; φωνὴ σεισμοῦ ~ῶν 'the sound of rattling wheels' Na 3.2; instrument of torture, Pr 20.26, 4M 5.32, cf. βασανιστήριον and τροχιαῖος.

τρύβλιον, ου. n.

bowl: fixture of a cultic table, Ex 25.28; τὰ σκεύη τῆς τραπέζης, τά τε ~α καὶ τὰς θυίσκας 38.12; ἀργυροῦν 'silver' Nu 7.13; a piece of dinner-set, Si 34.14. Cf. κρατήρ.

τρυγάω: fut. τρυγήσω; aor. ἐτρύγησα, subj. τρυγήσω, impv. τρύγησον, opt.pass.3s τρυγηθείη.

to harvest: lit., + acc. rei (τὰ ἡγιασμένα αὐτῆς) and || ἀμάω Le 25.11; ἀμπελῶνα 'vineyard' De 24.21, ἄμπελον Ps 79.13; pass. ὡς ὄμφαξ πρὸ ὥρας 'like unripe grape before the season' Jb 15.33. **b**. fig. σεαυτῷ Ho 6.11; εἰς καρπὸν ζωῆς, following seeding and in order to gather in fruits of life, 10.12; τὰς ἀδικίας αὐτῆς 10.13.

Cf. τρύγητος, τρυγητής, ἐκ~, ἐπανατρυγάω, ἀμάω, εἰσφέρω, συνάγω.

τρυγητής, οῦ. m.*

harvester: without specifying what fruit to gather in, Ob 5; Si 30.25. Cf. τρυγάω and τρύγητος.

τρύγητος, ου. m.ʃ

act of harvesting (of grapes): Am 4.7, Is 24.13; followed immediately by threshing season, Am 9.13; by sowing season, Le 26.5; ὡς ἐπιφυλλίδα ἐν ~ῳ 'like small grapes left during a vintage' Mi 7.1 (|| ἄμητος); ἐν ἡμέραις ~ου 'in a harvest season' Si 24.27 (|| θερισμός vs. 26). Cf. τρυγητός, τρυγάω, and ἄμητος. On the distinction between τρύγητος and τρυγητός, see Walters 95, 226.

τρυγητός, οῦ. m.

crop which has been (or: *is to be*) *harvested*: ἀπόλωλε τ. ἐξ ἀγροῦ 'crop has vanished from a field' Jl 1.11; παρέστηκε τ. 'the crop is ripe (for harvesting)' 3.13; || θερισμός Is 16.9; || σπόρος 32.10; ἕτοιμος τοῦ θερίζειν 'ready to be harvested' 1K 13.21. Cf. τρύγητος.

τρυγίας, ου. m.ʃ

lees of wine, dregs: ὁ. τ... οὐκ ἐξεκενώθη '.. were not emptied out' Ps 74.8.

τρυγών, όνος. f.(m. Ca 2.12, LSG s.v.).

turtle dove: φωνὴ ~όνος Ca 2.12; ~όνα καὶ περιστεράν Ge 15.9; cultic offerings, Le 1.14, 5.7. Cf. περιστερά.

τρυμαλιά, ᾶς. f. *

hole: of a rock as a hiding-place, Je 13.4, Jd 6.2B (A: μάνδρα); 15.8B (A: σπήλαιον), 11B (A: ὀπή).

τρυπάω: fut. τρυπήσω; pf.ptc.pass. τετρυπημένος.ʃ

to make hole(s) through: ***o*** ear, Ex 21.6; τρυπήσεις τὸ ὠτίον αὐτοῦ πρὸς τὴν θύραν 'you shall bore his ear through to the door' De 15.17; lip, ψελίῳ τρυπήσεις τὸ χεῖλος αὐτοῦ 'will you bore his lip with a ring?' Jb 40.26; δεσμὸν τετρυπημένον 'holey purse' Hg 1.6. Cf. τετραίνω.

τρυφαλίς, ίδος. f.ʃ

fresh cheese: γάλακτος 'of milk' 1K 17.18*L*. Cf. τυρός.

τρυφάω: fut. τρυφήσω; aor. ἐτρύφησα, subj. τρυφήσω.ʃ

to indulge in material comfort: ἐν ἀγαθωσύνῃ σου τῇ μεγάλῃ Ne 9.25 (|| λιπαίνομαι 'to anoint oneself'), ἐν τοῖς ἀγαθοῖς αὐτοῦ Si 14.4; ἀπὸ εἰσόδου δόξης αὐτῆς 'her glorious influx' Is 66.11 (|| ἐμπίμπλημι). Cf. τρυφή, (κατα)σπαταλάω, ἐν~ κατατρυφάω: Trench 201f.

τρυφερεύομαι.ʃ *

to be delicate of constitution and physique: Es D 3.

τρυφερός, ά, όν.

1. *having been used to comfortable life and not prepared for harsh or rough life-style*: ***s*** pers. οἱ ~οί μου ἐπορεύθησαν ὁδοὺς τραχείας 'my delicate children have gone rough ways' Ba 4.26; τὰ τέκνα τὰ ~ά σου Mi 1.16; || ἁπαλός De 28.54 (*s* man), 56 (*s* woman), Is 47.1; ἡ Σουσάννα ἦν ~ὰ σφόδρα καὶ καλὴ τῷ εἴδει 'S. was very delicate and good-looking' Da TH Su 31.

2. *affording much pleasure*: of sabbaths when one may refrain from physical work, Is 58.13.

Cf. τρυφερότης, τρυφή, and ἐντρυφάω.

τρυφερότης, τος. f.ʃ

quality of τρυφερός, **1**.: De 28.56 (|| ἁπλότης).

τρυφή, ῆς. f.

abundance of material comfort, luxury: οἰκία ~ῆς 'luxurious home (of the ruling class)' Mi 2.9; παράδεισος τῆς ~ῆς 'luxuriant garden' Ge 3.23, 24, Jl 2.3 (cf. Ge 2.15); delicacies of food, La 4.5. Cf. τρυφερός, τρύφημα, τρυφάω, ἐν~, κατατρυφάω, σπατάλη: Husson 1988.64-73.

τρύφημα, ατος. n.ʃ

that which provides material comfort and pleasure: ἐν τῇ ἀναπαύσει ἐμπίπλαται ~άτων αὐτοῦ 'when he [= a rich man] rests he thoroughly enjoys his dainties' Si 34.3. Cf prec.

τρύχω.ʃ

to wear out: pass., ***o*** hum., Wi 11.11, ἀώρῳ πένθει 'with grief at an untimely bereavement' 14.15.

τρώγλη, ης. f.

deep hole: in the ground, 'pit': τῆς γῆς Is 2.19, τῆς στερεᾶς πέτρας 'of the solid rock' 2.21 (hiding depot); τῶν πετρῶν 7.19 (|| σπήλαιον 'cave' as temporary resting place from the heat of the sun?), Jb 30.6 (thieves' den); ἀσπίδων 'of vipers' Is 11.8; in a chest, 4K 12.10 (*L* ὀπή). Cf. βόθρος.

τυγχάνω: fut.ptc.mid. τευξόμενος; 1aor.mid.inf. τεύξασθαι; 2aor. ἔτυχον, inf. τυχεῖν, subj. τύχω; pf. ptc. τετευχώς.

1. *to move and reach* an object, 'chance upon': ***s*** iron head of an axe, + gen. pers., De 19.5. **b**. *to attain* *what one desires*: abs., Jb 3.21, 17.1; + gen., ἀνδρὸς ἀγαθοῦ 'good husband' Pr 30.23, εὐκαιρίας 'a propitious moment' 1M 11.42, εὐιλάτου 'favourable treatment' 1E 8.53, φιλανθρωπίας 'friendly treatment' 2M 6.21, εἰρήνης 14.10; ταφῆς 'burial' Bel 31-32 LXX, σκέπης 'protection' 2M 5.9, ἀντιλήμψεως 'assistance' 15.7, βοηθείας 'help' 3M 5.35. **c.** *to have* sth (gen.) undesirable *meted out*: κακῆς ἀναστροφῆς 'a miserable end' 2M 5.8, κολάσεως 'punishment' 3M 7.10, σκιᾶς 'shadow' Jb 7.2.

2. *to turn out* to be on examination: + ptc., τυγχάνεις ἀδελφὸς ὤν 'you happen to be a kinsman' To 5.14 𝔊^{II} (𝔊^{I} > ὤν); ἐτύγχανε πεπρακώς 'it was emerging that he had sold' 2M 4.32, ἀναλελυκώς 'that he had left' 9.1; 3.9. **b.** the ptc. ὤν omitted: Wi 15.19.

3. *to befall, happen to*: + dat. pers., ἔτυχεν αὐτοῖς νὺξ μία 'the first night of their journey came round' To 6.2 𝔊^{II}, cf. συμβαίνω.

4. οὐ τυχών *not commonly met with*: *s* ψόγος 'reproach' 3M 3.7.

Cf. ἐπι~, κατατυγχάνω: Bauernfeind, *TDNT* 8.240f. Del. 2M 6.2 (> ἐντυγχάνω).

τυλόω: aor.pass. ἐτυλώθην.ʃ

to make callous: *o* foot with long walk, De 8.4.

τυμπανίζω.ʃ *

to play the drum: 1K 21.14. Cf. τύμπανον.

τυμπανίστρια, ας. f.ʃ

feminine drum player: Ps 67.26. Cf. τύμπανον.

τύμπανον, ου. n.

1. *drum*: used on festive occasions, ∥ κιθάρα Ge 31.27, ∥ κύμβαλον Ju 16.1, μετὰ κιθάρας καὶ ψαλτηρίου καὶ ~ων καὶ αὐλῶν Is 5.12, μετὰ μουσικῶν, ~ων καὶ αὐλῶν 'with music, drums and flutes' (or: 'musical instruments, [such as] ..') 1E 5.2; εὐφροσύνη ~ων Is 24.8 (∥ κιθάρα); ∥ χορός Ex 15.20*b*; held in a hand, Ex 15.20*a*; + χορός Jd 11.34. Cf. *BA* 9.1, p. 83.

2. *block* or *stake* to which those who were beaten for punishment were fastened: 2M 6.19, 28, see Owen 1929.260f.

Cf. κιθάρα, τυμπανίζω, and τυμπανίστρια.

τύπος, ου. m.ʃ

1. *pattern* or *model to be followed*: ποιήσεις κατὰ τὸν ~ον τὸν δεδειγμένον σοι 'you shall construct in accordance with the pattern shown to you' Ex 25.40 (∥ παράδειγμα vs. 8); ἀσεβείας 'of ungodliness' 4M 6.19 (∥ παράδειγμα). Cf. παράδειγμα **1** and ὑπόδειγμα **2**: Roux 1961a, 1961b.114f.

2. *carved figure resembling its original*: τοὺς ~ους αὐτῶν οὓς ἐποιήσατε ἑαυτοῖς Am 5.26.

3. *text of a document*: ὁ τῆς ἐπιστολῆς τ. 3M 3.30.

Cf. εἴδωλον, τυπόω: Goppelt, *TDNT* 8.246-8, 256-9; Spicq 3.384-7.

τυπόω: fut. τυπώσω; aor. ἐτύπωσα.ʃ

to mould: + acc., πηλόν 'clay' Si 38.30; Wi 13.13. Cf. διατυπόω, τύπος.

τύπτω. Only in the pres. or impf.: note esp. τύπτων (*L* πατάξας) ἐπάταξας 4K 14.10 and Stählin, *TDNT* 8.260, n. 7.

to hit, strike: τῇ ῥάβδῳ .. ἐπὶ τὸ ὕδωρ τὸ ἐν τῷ ποταμῷ 'with the staff ..' Ex 7.17 (∥ πατάσσω vs. 20), σφύρῃ 'with a hammer' Is 41.7; *o* metal so as to mint a coin, Pr 25.4; in order physically to harm and + acc. pers., Ex 2.11, 21.15; Nu 22.27 (∥ παίω here and πατάσσω at vs. 24), *o* enemy troops 1K 11.11, abs. ἐν τῷ πολέμῳ 2K 5.24 (B: κόπτω); ∥ ἀναιρέω Da 5.19 TH; δόλῳ 'in some devious manner' De 27.24; effected obj., τραυματίας 'wounded troops' Jd 20.39 A (B: πατάσσω); *s* God as punisher, Ez 7.6. **b.** metaph.: τύπτει σε ἡ καρδία σου 1K 1.8, cf. τυπτόμενον καρδίᾳ Is 66.2 Th and τὸν δ' ἄχος ὀξὺ κατὰ φρένα τύψε βαθεῖαν 'an acute pain smote him deep at heart' Hom. *Il.* 19.125.

Cf. ἀφανίζω, κόπτω, παίω, πατάσσω, πλήσσω: Schmidt 3.278-82; Stählin, *TDNT* 8.260-2.

τυραννέω: fut. ~ήσω.

to be ruler of: + gen. pers., Wi 10.14, Pr 28.15, ∥ δεσπόζω 4M 5.38. Cf. ἄρχω, δεσπόζω, κρατέω.

τυραννικός, ή, όν.ʃ

tyrannical or despotic of character: *s* διάθεσις 'state' 3M 3.8; deed, 4M 5.26. Cf. τύραννος.

τυραννίς, ίδος. f.

1. *wife of* τύραννος, 'first lady': Es 1.18.

2. *domain of rule*: Si 47.21.

3. *powerful, despotic rule*: κατὰ τοῦ ἔθνους 4M 1.11.

Cf. ἀρχή.

τύραννος, ου. m.

powerful ruler: ~οι παίγνια αὐτοῦ 'princes are his playthings' Hb 1.10; ∥ βασιλεύς Jb 2.11, 42.17eγ; τ. μέγας Da 3.3 TH. **b.** savage and cruel: 3M 6.24, 4M 1.11.

Cf. ἄρχων, βασιλεύς, τυραννίς, τυραννικός.

Τύριος, α, ον.

Tyrian: ἀνὴρ Τ. 3K 7.2; subst.m., 1E 5.53.

τυρός, οῦ. m.ʃ

cheese: Jb 10.10. Cf. τυρόω and τρυφαλίς.

τυρόω: aor. ἐτύρωσα, pass. ἐτυρώθην; pf.ptc.pass. τετυρωμένος.ʃ

to curdle: *o* hum. at his creation, Jb 10.10; mountain, Ps 67.16; hardened and insensible hum. heart, ὡς γάλα 118.70. Cf. τυρός, ἀμέλγω.

τυφλός, ή, όν.

blind: subst. of person, βλέποντα καὶ τυφλόν 'seeing and blind' Ex 4.11; ψηλαφῆσαι .. ἐν τῷ σκότει 'grope .. in the dark' De 28.29; disqualifying for priesthood, Le 21.18 (∥ χωλός, κολοβόρις, ὠτότμητος); Zp 1.17; of ceremonially unsuitable sacrifical animal, Ma 1.8 (|| χωλός and ἄρρωστος), sim. De 15.21. Cf. ἀποτύφλωσις, ἀποτυφλόω, ἐκτυφλόω, ἀορασία: Schrage, *TDNT* 8.279-82; Chadwick 290-2.

τυφλόω: aor.pass. ἐτυφλώθην.ʃ
to cause the loss of sight: ***o*** pers. and pass., To 7.7 𝔊II (𝔊I: ἀπόλλυμι τοὺς ὀφθαλμούς); Is 42.19. Cf. τυφλός, ἀπο~, ἐκτυφλόω, ἀπαμαυρόω. Del. Wi 2.21 v.l.

τῦφος, ου. m.ʃ
arrogance: 3M 3.18. Cf. ὕβρις: Spicq 3.388f.

τύχη, ης. f.ʃ
good fortune: ἐν ~η Ge 30.11; deified, πληροῦντες τῇ ~η κέρασμα 'filling (a cup of) mingled drink to Fortune' Is 65.11 (|| δαίμων), cf. Seeligmann 1948. 99f. Cf. δαίμων, μόρος: Schmidt 4.375f.; Bauernfeind, *TDNT* 8.240f. Del. 2M 7.37 v.l.

Y

ὕαινα, ης. f.ʃ

"striped *hyena*" (LSJ): σπήλαιον ~ης Je 12.9; at loggerheads with dogs, Si 13.18.

ὑακίνθινος, η, ον.

blue-coloured: *s* skin, hide (δέρμα) Ex 25.5, Nu 4.6; undergarment (ὑποδύτης) Ex 28.27; subst. ~α (sc. ἱμάτια) Is 3.23 (+ βύσσινα, κόκκινα), Ez 23.6. Cf. ὑάκινθος: Schmidt 3.22f.

ὑάκινθος, ου. f.

1. "precious stone of blue colour, perh. *sapphire*" (LSG): Ex 25.4.

2. *expensive blue fabric*: Ex 26.1, 28.5 (|| βύσσος, πορφύρα, κόκκινος); material for a veil of the tabernacle, 26.31; Is 3.23 (+ χρυσίον); of footwear, Ez 18.10.

Cf. ὑακίνθιος.

ὕαλος, ου. m.ʃ

a kind of crystalline stone or glass: Jb 28.17¶. Cf. Shipp 581.

ὑβρίζω: aor. ὕβρισα, inf.pass. ὑβρισθῆναι.

1. *to conduct oneself arrogantly*: ὑβρίζειν καὶ ἀδικεῖν Is 23.12; + cogn. acc., λίαν ὕβριν αὐτοῦ Je 31.29 (|| ὑπερηφανία).

2. tr. *to cause sbd loss of honour*: + acc. pers., 2K 19.44 (*L* ἀτιμάω); pass. τῆς ἰδίας εὐγενείας ἀναξίως ὑβρισθῆναι 'to be subjected to insults unworthy of his noble birth' 2M 14.42; 3M 6.9.

Cf. ὕβρις, ἐξ~, καθυβρίζω, and ὑπερηφανέω.

ὕβρις, εως. f.

1. *arrogance, insolence*: ~ιν ὑπερηφάνων ταπεινώσω Is 13.11; ταπεινωθήσεται ἡ ὕ. τοῦ Ισραηλ 'the arrogance of Is. will be brought low' Ho 5.5; manifested in violation of justice, μέτρον ~εως 'a (false) measure (used out of moral) arrogance (?)' Mi 6.10; obj. of ἀποστρέφω Na 2.3; of ἀφαιρέω Zc 10.11; of συντρίβω - ὕ. τῆς ὑπερηφανίας Le 26.19; φαυλίσματα τῆς ~εώς σου 'disdainful expressions of your pride' Zp 3.11; + ὑπερηφανία Pr 8.13. **b**. not necessarily with negative connotation: ὑμῶν ἡ ὕ. 'your pride' Is 23.7; God's, φωνὴ ~εως αὐτοῦ Jb 37.4¶.

2. *violent and outrageous treatment*: against deportees, + σκυλμός 3M 3.25; target of such treatment, Wi 4.19; + βάσανος 'torture' 2.19. **b**. with no moral overtone: violence done by overtowering billows, PSol 2.27.

Cf. ὑβριστής, ὑβρίζω, ὑβριστικός, ὑβρίστρια, ὑπερηφανία, ὑψόω, μίσυβρις, ἀγερωχία, τῦφος, and ταπεινός: Schmidt 4.273-5; Bertram 1964-66; id., *TDNT* 8.299-302; Fisher; Chadwick 292-7.

ὑβριστής, οῦ. m.

arrogant, insolent person: ~ὴν καὶ ὑπερήφανον καὶ .. ὑψηλὸν καὶ μετέωρον Is 2.12; ~ὴν ταπείνωσον Jb 40.11 (|| ὑπερήφανος vs. 12). Cf. ὕβρις, ὑβρίστρια, ἀλαζών, ὑπερήφανος:Trench 98-105.

ὑβριστικός, ή, όν.ʃ

conducive to violence or *outrage*: *s* intoxication, Pr 20.1 (|| ἀκόλαστος 'incorrigible'). Cf. ὕβρις.

ὑβρίστρια, ας.ʃ *

f. of ὑβριστής, q.v.: Je 27.31.

ὑγιάζω: fut. ὑγιάσω; aor. ὑγίασα, subj. ὑγιάσω, pass. ὑγιάσθην, subj. ὑγιασθῶ, ptc. ὑγιασθείς, inf. ὑγιασθῆναι; pf. ὑγίακα.

to make healthy, 'cure' (sbd τινα): Ho 6.2 (|| ἰάομαι vs. 1); and *o* ἕλκος 'festering wound' Le 13.18; too salty water, Ez 47.8; pass. 'to become healthy again' Jb 24.23 (opp. μαλακίζομαι); after circumcision, Jo 5.8. Cf. ὑγιαίνω, ἰάομαι and ἀσθενέω.

ὑγιαίνω.

1. *to be in sound health*: as a greeting asking after sbd, Ὑγιαίνει; 'Is he well?' Ge 29.6; 43.27, 2K 20.9. **b**. in a greeting formula at meeting: Ὑγιαίνων ἔλθοις 'Welcome!' To 5.14 𝔊[I] (𝔊[II] + σῳζόμενος, and also || χαίρων ἔλθοις); on parting, Βάδιζε ὑγιαίνων 'Bon voyage!' Ex 4.18, cf. To 8.21 𝔊[II]. **c**. in an opening formula of a letter: χαίρειν καὶ ὑγιαίνειν 2M 1.10.

2. *to be in a condition causing no worry*: ὑγιαίνουσιν οἱ ἀδελφοί σου καὶ τὰ πρόβατα Ge 37.14, ὑγιαίνει ὁ λαὸς .. ὁ πόλεμος 2K 11.7*L*; *s* ὁ οἶκός σου καὶ πάντα τὰ σά 1K 25.6.

Cf. ὑγιάζω, ὑγιής, ὑγίεια, ῥώννυμι, ἀσθενέω: Luck, *TDNT* 8.310f.

ὑγίεια, ας. f.

sound health: + εἰρήνη Is 9.6, Si 1.18; σώματος 30.16; in a forceful affirmation, νὴ τὴν ~αν Φαραω 'by the health of Ph.' Ge 42.15, 16. Cf. ὑγιάζω, ὑγιής, ἀρρώστημα, ἀσθένεια, μαλακία.

ὑγιής, ές.

1. *being in sound health*: *s* hum., Is 38.21; opp. plagued with physical infirmities, Si 30.14 (+ ἰσχύων).

2. *having live organisms*: *s* σάρξ Le 13.10; χρώς '(leper's) skin (with open wounds)' 13.15 (|| ζῶν vs. 14).

Cf. ὑγιαίνω, ὑγίεια.

ὑγιῶς. adv.ʃ

by exercising sound mind: κρίνω Pr 31.8 (|| δικαίως vs. 9).

ὑγραίνω.ʃ

mid. *to become wet*: Jb 24.8¶. Cf. ὑγρός.

ὑγρασία, ας. f.ʃ

urine*: κάθισον ἐν ~ᾳ 'Sit in ..' Je 31.18; μολυνθήσονται ~ᾳ 'will be polluted with .. (becoming incontinent from shock)' Ez 7.17, 21.7. Cf. ὕδωρ **3: LSG s.v.

ὑγρός, ά, όν.

moist: *s* ῥεῦμα 'stream' Si 39.13, νευρά 'cord' Jd 16.7. Cf. ξηρός.

ὑδραγωγός, όν.

subst.m., *channel through which water flows*: aqueduct, Is 36.2; irrigation channel, 41.18; || διῶρυξ Si 24.30. Cf. διῶρυξ, τάφρος: Schnebel 32f.

ὑδρεύομαι: fut. ὑδρεύσομαι; aor. ὑδρευσάμην, inf. ὑδρεύσασθαι.

to fetch water from a well: *s* woman, abs., Ge 24.11; lad, Ru 2.9; + dat. com. Ge 24.19 (for animals); + acc. ὕδωρ 24.43; *s* soldiers, 2K 23.16. Cf. ὕδωρ, ἀντλέω.

ὑδρία, ας. f.

portable container of water, 'pitcher, jug': Ἐπίκλινόν μοι τὴν ~αν σου, ἵνα πίω 'Incline your pitcher for me, so that I may drink' Ge 24.14; Πότισόν με ὕδωρ ἐκ τῆς ~ας σου 24.17; carried on the shoulders, 24.15; filled, 24.16; lowered on an arm, 24.18; emptied, 24.20; containing wheat-meal, 3K 17.12. Cf. ὕδωρ, ὑδρίσκη, κάλπη.

ὑδρίσκη, ης. f.ʃ

Dim. of ὑδρία 'pitcher': 4K 2.20. Cf. ὑδρία.

ὑδροποτέω.ʃ

to drink water instead of alcoholic drink: Da 1.12 LXX (TH πίνω ὕδωρ).

ὑδροφόρος, ον.ʃ

subst. *water-carrier*: || ξυλοκόπος De 29.11, Jo 9.21, 27.

ὕδωρ, ὕδατος. n.

1. *water*: drinking water, for humans Ge 21.19, for animals 24.44; ποσίν 'for (washing) feet' 24.32; for purification Ex 29.4, ῥαντισμοῦ 'for sprinkling (and cleansing)' Nu 19.9, ἁγνισμοῦ 'of purification' 8.7; θαλάσσης Am 5.8, 9.6, cf. σαλευθήσονται ~τα ὡς θαλάσσης 8.12, ποταμοῦ Ex 4.9; λάκκου οὐκ ἔχοντος ὕ. 'cistern with no water in it' Zc 9.11; πηγὴ τοῦ ~τος 'spring of .. ' Ge 24.13, φρέαρ ~ος 'well of ..' 21.19, κολυμβήθρα ~τος 'pool of water' Na 2.9, χείμαρροι ~ων 'torrents of ..' De 8.7; πρόσωπον ~τος 'the surface of water' Ho 10.7; of flooding, κατακλυσμὸς ~ος Ge 7.6, ἡμέρα ~τος καὶ θορύβου Mi 7.12; ἀφέσεις ~των 'water holes'(?) Jl 1.20, cf. ib. 3.18; fish in water Ge 1.20; τέκνα ~των, w. ref. to fishes Ho 11.10 (so Tht PG 81.1613 and Thph PG 126.768); essential for physical subsistence, ἄρτους καὶ ἀσκὸν ~τος 'bread and a bag of water' Ge 21.14; ἄρτοι καὶ ὕ. De 23.4; Ho 2.5 (+ ἄρτοι, ἱμάτια, ὀθόνια, ἔλαιον), cf. Am 8.11; δίψα ~τος 'thirst for water' Am 8.11; περιοχῆς 'stored for fear of siege' Na 3.14; ζῶν 'living, i.e. fresh, flowing' Le 14.5, cf. ὕ. ζωῆς Je 2.13; πολλὰ 'abundant' Na 1.12; rain as divine gift, ~τα θεοῦ 2K 21.10*L*; as ***o*** of ἀντλέω 'to draw' Ge 24.13, ἐκχέω 'to pour out' Ho 5.10, περιχέω 'to pour around' Jn 2.6, πίνω Am 4.8, Jn 3.7, ταράσσω 'to disturb, muddy' Ho 6.8, Hb 3.15, ὑδρεύομαι 'to draw and fetch' Ge 24.43; *s* of κατακαλύπτω 'to cover' Hb 2.14, κυλίζω 'to roll' Am 5.24, and cf. ὡς ὕ. καταφερόμενον ἐν καταβάσει 'like water running down a slope' Mi 1.4. **b**. *water-reservoir*: Is 22.11. **c**. *area or expanse full of water*: pool, Je 48.12; sea or lake for shipping, Wi 5.10. **d**. Pl., of masses of water: τὰ ὕδατα ἐν θαλάσσαις Ge 1.22; ἐπὶ τὰ ~ατα Αἰγύπτου καὶ ἐπὶ τοὺς ποταμοὺς αὐτῶν Ex 7.19; ἐν τοῖς ~ασιν specified as ἐν ταῖς θαλάσσαις καὶ ἐν τοῖς χειμάρροις Le 11.9, 10; summing up ποταμοί, διώρυγες, ἕλη 'rivers, canals, marshes' Ex 8.6. **e**. *well-watered soil*: σπείροντες ἐπὶ πᾶν ὕ. Is 32.20; Ez 19.10. **f**. metaph., ὕ. σοφίας Si 15.3 (|| ἄρτος συνέσεως).

2. *river*: ἐκπορεύεται ἐπὶ τὸ ὕ. 'he goes out to the river' Ex 7.15; 8.20.

3. *urine*: ὕ. ἀποκαθημένης '.. of a menstruating woman' Is 30.22 (|| κόπρος 'excrement'; poss. w. ref. to blood, see Jer. PL 24.359); pl., Ez Sym 7.17, 21.7 (LSG, s.v.). Cf. ὑγρασία.

4. *tears*: Je 9.18.

Cf. ὑδρεύομαι, οὖρον: Goppelt, *TDNT* 8.317-22

ὕειος, α, ον.

pertaining to ὗς 'pig, swine': κρέα ~α 'pork' as (forbidden) meat Is 65.4, ἀπὸ τῶν ἀθεμίτων ~ων κρεῶν ἐφάπτεσθαι 'partake of unlawful pork' 2M 7.1, αἷμα ~ον Is 66.3 (unclean offering); subst. n.pl. 'pigs' – θύειν ~α καὶ κτήνη κοινά 'to slaughter pigs and unclean animals' 1M 1.47. Cf. ὗς.

ὑετίζω: aor.inf. ὑετίσαι.ʃ *

1. *to descend as rain*: *s* rain, ἐπὶ γῆν Jb 38.26.

2. *to cause to rain*: *s* god, Je 14.22.

Cf. ὕω, ὑετός, βρέχω.

ὑετός, οῦ. m.

rain: punitive and destructive, ἐπάγω ~ὸν ἐπὶ τὴν γῆν Ge 7.4; ἐγένετο ὁ ὑ. 7.12; χάλαζα καὶ ὑ. 'hail and ..' Ex 9.29, ὑ. κατακλύζων καὶ λίθοι χαλάζης 'flooding rain and hailstones' Ez 38.22; to moisten the soil, ὑ. πρόϊμος καὶ ὄψιμος Ho 6.3, Jl 2.23, Zc 10.1*a*; ὑ. χειμερινόν 'winter rain' Zc 10.1*b*; its provision controlled by God, Le 26.4, De 28.12, Am 4.7, Zc 10.1*a*; obj. of βρέχω 'to send rain' Jl 2.23; source of drinking water, τοῦ οὐρανοῦ De 11.11; long awaited, 32.2 (|| δρόσος, ὄμβρος, νιφετός), ὑ. εὐλογίας Ez 34.26; ὑ. ^χιόνος^ 'sleet' Si 43.18. Cf.

δρόσος, ὄμβρος, ὄμβρημα, βροχή, ὑετίζω, ὕω: Schmidt 1.623-7.

υἱός, οῦ. m.

1. *male descendant*: hum., Λαβαν τὸν ~ὸν Ναχωρ Ge 29.5 (L. being a grandson of N.'s); 31.43 (children, girls included); 'son,' ἔτεκεν αὐτῷ ~όν 'she bore him a son' Ho 1.3; vs. πατήρ Ma 1.6; opp. θυγάτηρ and preceding it, ἐγέννησεν ~οὺς καὶ θυγατέρας Ge 5.4, σὺν τοῖς ~οῖς καὶ θυγατράσιν καὶ προβάτοις καὶ βουσίν Ex 10.9; adopted, 2.10. On οἱ ~οὶ τοῦ θεοῦ Ge 6.2, see *BA* 1:125. **b**. of animals: υἱ. ταύρων 'calves' De 32.14, Si 38.25, κριῶν 'of rams' Ps 28.1; 28.6.

*__2__. *member of community* defined in ethnic, racial, religious or political terms, mostly used in the pl.: ~οὶ Χετ 'Hittites' Ge 27.46; ~οὶ Ισραηλ 'Israelites' Ex 1.7, Ob 20; cf. female members, αἱ θυγατέρες Ισραηλ De 23.17, τῶν ~ῶν καὶ τῶν θυγατέρων Σιων Is 4.4; τοὺς ~οὺς Λευι 'the Levites' Ma 3.3; υἱοὶ Ιακωβ 3.7; τοῦ λαοῦ σου Le 19.18. Cf. Renehan 1.156f., s.v. παῖς. **b**. υἱ. ἀνθρώπου 'a (mere) human being' Je 28.43 (|| οὐδείς), 29.19 and Ps 8.5 (|| ἄνθρωπος); with focus on his limitations, frailty or worthlessness: Is 51.12 (|| ἄνθρωπος θνητός 'mortal man'), οὐκ ἀθάνατος Si 17.30, υἱ. γηγενοῦς Je 30.11, υἱ. ἀνδρός La 3.33, υἱ. ἀνθρώπου σκώληξ '.. worm' Jb 25.6¶, cf. Colpe, *TDNT* 8.400-77; BDAG, s.v. **2 d γ**; pl. ~οὶ ἀνθρώπων Ge 11.5, Jl 1.12, Ps 11.2.

*__3__. *person characterised by a certain property*: ~οὶ θεοῦ De 32.43 (|| ἄγγελοι θεοῦ; || ἅγιοι Wi 5.5), ~ὸς τοῦ θεοῦ Je 42.4, 3K 12.22 (*L*: ἄνθρωπος τ. θ., MT אִישׁ הָאֱלֹהִים, and w. ref. to a prophet); ~οὶ τῆς πιότητος 'embodiments of abundance, those blessed with abundance (?)' Zc 4.14, cf. *BA* ad loc.; ~οὶ ἀνομίας Ps 88.23, ~οὶ ἄνομοι Is 1.4 (|| σπέρμα πονηρόν), ~οὶ ψευδεῖς 30.9; υἱ. θανάτου '.. deserving death' 2K 12.5 (*L*: ἄξιος θανάτου), 1K 20.31, θανατώσεως 26.16 (*L*: θανάτου); δυνάμεων 1K 10.26; σοφίας Si 4.11. Cf. Souter, s.v. **b**. age: υἱ. ἑκατὸν ἐτῶν '100 years old' Ge 11.10. Cf. θυγάτηρ **4**.

*__4__. *one who* or *that which constitutes an integral part of* sth: ~οὶ φαρέτρας lit. 'sons of a quiver,' i.e. arrows La 3.13 (|| βέλος vs. 12), cf. τέκνα θαλάσσης 'fishes' Ho 11.10; ~οὶ τῆς ἄκρας 'men stationed at the citadel' 1M 4.2.

Cf. τέκνον, θυγάτηρ, πατήρ: Schweizer, *TDNT* 8.340-57.

ὑλακτέω.ʃ

to bark: *s* dog, Is 56.10. Cf. ἠχέω: Schmidt 3.349f.

ὕλη, ης. f.

1. *forest, woodland*: ravaged by bush-fire, Is 10.17, cf. κατὰ τὴν ~ην τοῦ πυρός Si 28.10; lairs of wild beasts, Jb 38.40 (pl.); metaph., ἠθῶν καὶ παθῶν 'of (wild) habits and passions' 4M 1.29. Cf. δρυμός.

2. *material to be processed*: documentary, 2M 2.24; raw material, κτίσασα τὸν κόσμον ἐξ ἀμόρφου ~ης 'creating the world from amorphous ..' Wi 11.17, cf. Jb 19.29; w. ref. to potter's clay, Wi 15.13.

Cf. Shipp 547-9.

ὑλοτόμος, ον.ʃ

cutting wood: *s* τέκτων 'carpenter' Wi 13.11.

ὑλώδης, ες.ʃ

prosperous, thriving: *s* hum., Jb 29.5.

ὑμεῖς; ὑμῶν; ὑμῖν; ὑμᾶς.

Reference to the persons being addressed or spoken to. On the contrastive, emphatic nominative, see under ἐγώ, **I**. There exists no morphological distinction between the free-standing and enclitic forms as in, e.g. ἐμέ vs. με.

ὑμέναιος, ου. m.ʃ

song sung at wedding: opp. θρῆνος 'mourning' 3M 4.6.

ὑμέτερος, α, ον.ʃ

belonging or *appertaining to you* (pl.), with stressed notion of ownership and claim, and pl. of σός, q.v.: τὸ ~ον αἷμα 'your blood' Ge 9.5; πλείονα .. τῶν ~ων ὁρίων 'greater than your territory' Am 6.2; Pr 1.26, To 8.21 𝔊[II]. Used as synonym of ὑμῶν for contrast's sake, cf. Ba 4.24 (|| ὑμῶν). Cf. ὑμῶν.

ὑμνέω: fut. ὑμνήσω, inf. ὑμνήσειν; aor. ὕμνησα, impv. ὕμνησον, subj. ὑμνήσω.

to express adoration for in hymns, alw. to do with God: abs., ἐν πάσῃ καρδίᾳ καὶ στόματι Si 39.35 (|| εὐλογέω), ἐν ἐξμολογήσει 51.11 (|| αἰνέω); + acc. pers., κύριον Is 12.4 (|| βοάω); + acc. rei, τὸ ὄνομα κυρίου 12.5, τὸ ὄ. σου 25.1 (|| δοξάζω), τὸ ὄ. τὸ ἅγιόν σου Wi 10.20 (|| αἰνέω), τὴν δόξαν σου Ps 70.8; pass. *o* σοφία Pr 1.20, 8.3; + acc. pers., Ps 21.23 (in public); + dat. pers., ^τῷ κυρίῳ^ 1C 16.9 (|| ᾄδω); + acc. cogn., τῷ κυρίῳ ὕμνον καινόν Ps 42.10 (|| δοξάζω); + εὐλογέω and foll. by a text of a hymn, 1M 4.24, 13.47. **b**. not necessarily accompanied by singing: πᾶσί τε ἀνθρώποις ὑμνήσειν .. τὴν τοῦ ἱεροῦ τόπου μακαριότητα 'the blessedness of the sacred site .. in front of all the people' 4M 4.12; + ὅτι recitativum, Jd 16.24 B (A: αἰνέω).

Cf. ᾄδω, αἰνέω, δοξάζω, ἐπιψάλλω, ἐξ~, καθυμνέω, ὑμνός, ὑμνῳδέω, ψάλλω: Delling, *TDNT* 8.493-5.

ὕμνησις, εως. f.ʃ

v.n. of ὑμνέω, q.v.: Ps 70.6. **b**. object of such an act: *s* God, Ps 117.14. Cf. ὑμνέω, αἴνεσις.

ὑμνητός, ή, όν.

sung of in praise: *s* God, + δεδοξασμένος Da 3.56. Cf. ὑπερυμνητός.

ὑμνογράφος, ου. m.ʃ
composer and/or writer of hymns: 4M 18.15. Cf. ὕμνος.

ὕμνος, ου. m.
hymn sung in praise of sbd: of God, Ὑμνήσατε κυρίῳ ~ον καινόν Is 42.10 (‖ δοξάζω), ‖ ᾆσμα Ps 39.3; πατέρων Si 44; sung on battlefield after victory, 2M 10.38 (+ ἐξομολόγησις). Cf. ὑμνογράφος, ᾠδή.

ὑμνῳδέω.ʃ
to sing a song of praise: in temple service, 1C 25.6. Cf. ὑμνέω.

ὑπαγορεύω: aor.subj. ~ρεύσω.ʃ
to indicate verbally: 1E 6.29. Cf. λέγω.

ὑπάγω: aor. ὑπήγαγον, ptc.pass. ὑπαχθείς.
1. tr. *to drive back, push back*, military t.t.: τὴν θάλασσαν ἐν ἀνέμῳ νότῳ βιαίῳ 'the sea with a strong southerly wind' Ex 14.21.
2. *to influence sbd's disposition into a certain direction*: pass., ***o*** hum., τούτοις τοῖς λόγοις '(moved) by these words' 4M 4.13.
3. intr. *to leave and go*: ὕπαγε ὑγιαίνων πρὸς τὸν πατέρα σου 'Go safely to your father' To 8.21 𝔊II. Cf. Lee 127, n. 17.
Cf. ἀπέρχομαι, οἴχομαι, and πορεύομαι.

ὕπαιθρος, ον.ʃ
in the open air: ***s*** γωνία Pr 21.9 ('unroofed'); subst.n., open space as battlefield as against fortified position, 2M 15.19.

ὑπακοή, ῆς. f.ʃ
v.n. of ὑπακούω: ***s*** God, 2K 22.36.

ὑπακούω: fut. ὑπακούσομαι; aor. ὑπήκουσα, impv. ὑπάκουσον, inf., ὑπακοῦσαι, subj. ὑπακούσω, mid. ~ακούσωμαι.
to take heed of, pay heed to: + gen. rei, the message (τῆς φωνῆς τινος), Ge 16.2 (suggestion, proposal); ὑπήκουσα τῆς φωνῆς κυρίου τοῦ θεοῦ μου, ἐποίησα καθότι ἐνετείλω μοι '.. just as you commanded me' De 26.14, τῆς φωνῆς μου Jd 2.20A (B: εἰσακούω), τοῦ προστάγματος τοῦ βασιλέως 'the king's order' 2M 7.30 (‖ ἀκούω); τῶν λόγων μου Je 13.10; wisdom, Si 4.15 (‖ προσέχω 'to heed'). **b**. + gen. pers. and with a sense of awe and respect to sbd who carries authority: towards God, ἐὰν .. πορεύησθε πλάγιοι καὶ μὴ βούλησθε ὑπακούειν μου 'should you walk perversely and refuse to obey me' Le 26.21; priest and judge, De 17.12. **c**. + φωνήν τινος, syn. with **b**.: υἱὸς ἀπειθὴς καὶ ἐρεθιστὴς οὐχ ὑπακούων φωνὴν πατρὸς καὶ φωνὴν μητρὸς .. 'a disobedient and quarrelsome son not obeying his father and mother' De 21.18 (‖ τῆς φωνῆς ἡμῶν vs. 20). **d**. + dat. pers., 'to take notice (of an order issued by sbd): οὐχ ὑπήκουεν αὐτῇ καθεύδειν μετ' αὐτῆς 'he would not give in to her to sleep with her' Ge 39.10; De 20.12; τρόμῳ 'trembling' Ba 3.33; syn. and Hebraism (Helbing, *Kasus*. 156)– ἐπὶ τῷ στόματί σου [= עַל־פִּיךָ] ὑπακούσεται 'will obey your orders' Ge 41.40, or 'to act obediently, comply with deference to your directive' (ἐπί **II 7**). **e**. + dat. rei: τῷ δόγματί σου Da 3.12 TH. **f**. Often accompanied, whether implicitly or explicitly, by acting or refusing to act in conformity with what one is told to do: μὴ ὑπακούσητέ μου, μηδὲ ποιήσετε τὰ προστάγματά μου ταῦτα, ἀλλὰ ἀπειθήσητε αὐτοῖς καὶ τοῖς κρίμασίν μου προσοχθίσῃ ἡ ψυχὴ ὑμῶν Le 26.14f.; ὑπακούω mentioned last - πορεύεσθαι ἐν ταῖς ὁδοῖς αὐτοῦ καὶ φυλάσσεσθαι τὰ δικαιώματα καὶ τὰ κρίματα αὐτοῦ καὶ ὑπακούειν τῆς φωνῆς αὐτοῦ De 26.17. **g**. *to respond when called or addressed*: ἐκάλεσα καὶ οὐκ ἦν ὁ ὑπακούων Is 50.2, sim. 65.12, 66.4, Jb 9.16, 19.16; σοι 5.1, μου Ct 5.6.
Cf. ἀκούω, προσέχω, εἰσακούω, ὑπήκοος, πειθαρχέω, πείθω, ἀπειθέω, παρακούω: Schmidt 4.132-5.

ὕπανδρος, ον.
subject to husband's authority: ***s*** woman, μετὰ ~ου γυναικὸς μὴ κάθου 'Don't dine with a married woman' Si 9.9; 41.21. See Shipp 547.

ὑπαντάω: fut. ὑπαντήσω; aor. ὑπήντησα.ʃ
1. *to go to meet*: + dat. pers., Si 9.3, Wi 6.16; arriving guest, To 7.1𝔊I.
2. *to treat and look after*: + dat. pers., ὡς μήτηρ Si 15.2 (‖ προσδέχομαι).
3. *to befall*: + dat. pers., ***s*** κακά 'misfortune' Si 12.17, ὅ τι 'that which' Da 10.14 LXX (TH ἀπ~), cf. συμβαίνω.
Cf. ἀπ~, συναντάω, ὑπάντησις.

ὑπάντησις, εως. f.ʃ
v.n. of prec., **1**: εἰς ~ιν (A: ἀπ~) Jd 11.34B. Cf. ἀπ~, συνάντησις.

ὕπαρξις, εως. f. Alw. in the sg.
1. *creatures*, hums. prob. excluded: φωνὴ ~εως Je 9.10.
2. *possessions, property*: 2E 10.9; ‖ ἀγαθά Pr 8.21; Ps 77.48 and 1M 12.23 (‖ κτήνη 'livestock'). **b**. *estate*: κατέμεινεν ἐπὶ τῆς ~εως αὐτῆς Ju 16.21. **c**. *financial resources*: ἐν δυνάμει μεγάλῃ καὶ ~ει πολλῇ 'with a huge army ..' Da 11.13 TH (‖ LXX .. ἐν χρήμασιν πολλοῖς), προνομὴν καὶ σκῦλα καὶ ~ιν 'booty and spoils ..' 11.24 (‖ LXX .. χρήματα).
Cf. ὑπάρχω, κτῆμα, κτῆσις, ὑπόστημα, χρῆμα.

ὑπάρχω: fut. ὑπάρξω; aor. ὑπῆρξα, subj. ὑπάρξω, impv.3s ὑπαρξάτω, inf. ὑπάρξαι, ptc. ὑπάρξας.
1. *to exist*: παρὰ τὸ μὴ ὑπάρχειν μνήματα ἐν γῇ Αἰγύπτῳ 'on account of there being no graves in the land of Egypt' Ex 14.11; πάντα, ὅσα ἂν ὑπάρχῃ ἐν τῇ πόλει De 20.14; εἶναι ὡς οὐχ ὑπάρχων 'to be

virtually non-existent' Am 5.5; Ob 16, Hg 2.3 (w. καθώς for ὡς), ὡς οὐχ ὑπάρξαντες 'as if they had never existed' Si 44.9 (|| ὡς οὐ γεγονότες 'as if they had never been born'); ἔτι ὑπάρχει παρὰ σοί 'there is still another left with you' Am 6.10; Mi 7.1, 2, Hb 3.17; Zp 3.6 (|| κατοικέω), Ma 1.14; ὑπάρχων φίλος 'current, i.e. not new, friend' Pr 19.4. Mostly w. a negator and an indeterminate subject noun, but ὁ ἕτερος οὐχ ὑπάρχει 'the other is not to be found' Ge 42.13 (of absolute non-existence || ὁ νεώτερος μετὰ τοῦ πατρὸς ἡμῶν σήμερον with a location specified), sim. 42.32; ὁ μισθὸς τῶν κτηνῶν οὐχ ὑ. Zc 8.10 (|| εἶναι); || εὑρίσκομαι Je 27.20, cf. Ps 36.10; πρὸ τοῦ με ἀπελθεῖν καὶ οὐκέτι μὴ ὑπάρξω 'before I depart and be no more around (in life)' 38.14, ἕως ὑπάρχω 'as long as I am alive' 103.33 and 145.2 (|| ἐν τῇ ζωῇ μου). **b.** τὰ ὑπάρχοντα [ptc., n.pl.] 'material possessions, property': πάντα τὰ ὑπάρχοντα αὐτῶν, ὅσα ἐκτήσαντο 'all their possessions that they had acquired' Ge 12.5; ἦν τὰ ὑπάρχοντα αὐτῶν πολλά 13.6; owned by a woman, Ρεβεκκαν .. καὶ τὰ ὑ. αὐτῆς 24.59; κατακληρονομῇ τοῖς υἱοῖς τὰ ὑπάρχοντα αὐτοῦ 'bequeathes to the sons his possessions' De 21.16, cf. Ge 25.5; + ἀποσκευή 31.18; separate from humans and beasts, τὰς γυναῖκας αὐτοῦ καὶ τοὺς υἱοὺς καὶ τὰς θυγατέρας καὶ πάντα τὰ σώματα τοῦ οἴκου αὐτοῦ καὶ πάντα τὰ ὑ. καὶ πάντα τὰ κτήνη καὶ πάντα, ὅσα ἐκτήσατο 36.6; household furniture, agricultural land, cattle etc., πᾶσιν τοῖς ὑπάρχουσιν αὐτῷ ἐν τῷ οἴκῳ καὶ ἐν τῷ ἀγρῷ 39.5; + κτῆσις 46.6; separate from silver (ἀργύριον), 47.18.

2. *to be*, mere copula in an equational sentence: ἐν τῇ δόξῃ τοῦ ὀνόματος κυρίου .. ὑπάρξουσιν 'they will be in the glory of the name of the Lord ..' Mi 5.4; by nature, Ep Je 16; To 3.5 𝔊^II (𝔊^I εἰμί), 5.20 𝔊^I (𝔊^II >); in a periphrasis with a ptc., Jo 4.6. Cf. προϋπάρχω.

3. w. dat. to indicate possession or availability: ἐὰν δὲ μὴ ὑπάρχῃ αὐτῷ 'but if he have no (means of making amends)' Ex 22.3; Εἴ τινι ὑπάρχει χρυσία 'should anybody have gold' 32.24; τοῖς παισίν σου κτήνη ὑπάρχει 'your servants have livestock' Nu 32.4, οὐχ ὑπῆρχε νομὴ αὐτοῖς 'they had no pasture' Jl 1.18; 2K 15.3*L* (|| B: εἰμί).

Cf. εἰμί, ἔχω, ἀποσκευή, κτῆσις, ὕπαρξις: Schmidt 2.538f.

ὑπασπιστής, οῦ. m.ʃ

shield-bearing guard: pl., 4M 3.12, 9.11. Cf. ἀσπίς.

ὕπατος, ου.ʃ

very high-ranking official: prefect (?), listed after τόπαρχος 1E 3.14, Da 3.2 LXX (TH ἡγούμενος), before τ. 6.7 TH; Roman consul, 1M 15.16.

ὑπείκω: aor. ὑπεῖξα,ʃ

to concede a point to sbd: + dat. pers. and a ὅτι-clause, Je 38.19; + acc. rei, 4M 6.35. Cf. εἴκω.

ὑπεκρέω.ʃ

to move away gradually and quietly: *s* hum. 3M 5.34.

ὑπεναντίος, α, ον.

opposed: + dat. pers., Jb 13.24; mostly subst. τὰς πόλεις τῶν ὑπεναντίων 'the cities of the enemies' Ge 22.17, 24.60; τοὺς ~ους τοὺς ἀνθεστηκότας ὑμῖν '.. who are opposed to you' Nu 10.9; || ἐχθρός De 32.27, Is 1.24, Ps 73.10; ἐκδικῶν κύριος τοὺς ~ους αὐτοῦ 'the Lord is a revenger ..' Na 1.2 (|| ἐχθροί). Cf. ἐχθρός, ἐναντίος, and μισέω.

ὑπεξαιρέω: pf.pass. ὑπεξῄρωμαι.ʃ

to deny access to, 'withhold': ὑπεξῄρηται ἀπ' ἐμοῦ οὐδὲν 'nothing is denied to me' Ge 39.9.

ὑπέρ. prep.

I. + gen., *at a level higher than*, but not touching: ὁ οὐρανὸς ὑ. τῆς κεφαλῆς σου De 28.23(*c*); ἐπληθύνθησαν ὑ. κεφαλῆς ἡμῶν 'multiplied and piled up higher than ..' 2E 9.6; Jn 4.6(*c*).

2. *concerning*, indicating a subject-matter: + διηγέομαι 'to narrate' Jl 1.3(*c*); θρηνέω 'to lament' 1.11(*c*); διακρίνομαι 'to adjudge' 3.2(*c*); ἐντέλλομαι 'to command' Na 1.14(*c*); Am 1.1(*c*); Mi 1.1 (|| περί τινος)(-); δέομαι 'to entreat' Si 51.9, ἐντυγχάνω 'to appeal' + inf., 2M 4.36. **b.** indicates a matter in respect of which some emotion is displayed: φείδομαι 'to pity' Jn 4.10(*c*), 11(*c*); εἰς οἶκτρον καὶ δάκρυα ὑ. τῶν ἔμπροσθεν αὐτῷ μεμηχανευμένων 'into pity and tears over what had been earlier devised by him' 3M 6.22. **c.** ὑπὲρ οὗ *with regard to the fact that*: ἠθύμησεν 'was disheartened' 2K 6.8(*c*), εὐλογῆσαι 'to congratulate' 8.10(*c*).

3. *in relation to*: "as I was put to the test in relation to them" Zc 11.13(*b*).

4. *in the interest of, for the cause of*: Οὐκ ἀποθανοῦνται πατέρες ὑ. τέκνων De 24.16(*c*), πολεμήσατε .. ὑ. τῶν ἀδελφῶν ἡμῶν 1M 5.32, ὑ. σοῦ Si 4.28(*f*); ἀποθανόντας ἡμᾶς ὑ. τῶν αὐτοῦ νόμων 2M 7.9; δότε τὰς ψυχὰς ὑμῶν ὑ. διαθήκης πατέρων ἡμῶν 1M 2.50; τὰ ὑ. ἁμαρτίας 'sin-offerings' Ez 40.39(-), sim. 43.22(*f*) (|| περὶ ἁμαρτίας vs. 19, 21), cf. BDAG, s.v. **A 1 a ε**.

5. marks a cause or motive: ὑ. τοῦ οὐθενός 'on no account' Ps 55.8(*c*).

6. marks a reason: "because of the people (supporting his opponent)" 4M 4.1, see Deissmann 1921 ad loc.

II. + acc. *more than*: ἰσχύει ὑ. ἡμᾶς 'is stronger than we' Ex 1.9(*d*); "Lament to me more (bitterly) than a virgin girt with sackcloth" Jl 1.8(?); "they became heavier than all its desirable vessels (= σκεῦα πολεμικά 'weapons'(?)" Na 2.10(*d*); θαυμάσια ὑ. ἐμέ 'things wonderful beyond me' Ps 130.1(*d*); "Make it stronger than brick" 3.14(*d*); μετὰ δυνάμεως πολλῆς ὑ. τὸ πρότερον 'with a force larger than before' 1M 12.24; ὑ. ἅπαν 'more than anything else' 2M 8.35; "they multiplied beyond reckoning (ὑ. ἀριθμόν)" Ps 39.6(*d*), "more than the hairs of my head" 39.13(*d*); ὑ. ἄνθρωπον ἀλαζονεία 'superhuman boastfulness' 2M 9.8. **b**. w. comparative, ὑ. ταύτας τὰς πληγὰς πλείους 'more than those beatings' De 25.3(*c*); ὀξύτεροι ὑ. τοὺς λύκους τῆς Ἀραβίας 'swifter than Arabian wolves' Hb 1.8*b*(*d*), cf. 1.8*a*(*d*); "the latter splendour of the house will be greater than the former" Hg 2.9(*d*); ‖ ἤ Si 30.17(*d*).

2. *extending farther than*, 'beyond': ὑ. τὰ ὅριά σου 'beyond your borders' Is 57.9(fr).

Cf. ἀντί περί, ὑπεράνω: Trench 310-3; Johannessohn, *Präp*. 216-9; Riesenfeld, *TDNT* 8.507-16.

a) בְּעַד; *b*) מֵעַל; *c*) עַל; *f*) לְ; + acc. *d*) מִן; *e*) עַל.x∫

ὑπεράγαν. adv.∫

above measure, 'very much': + verb, 2M 10.34, 13.25. Cf. λίαν, σφόδρα. Del. 2M 8.35 v.l.

ὑπεραγόντως. adv.∫

in particular: 2M 7.20.

ὑπεράγω.∫

1. *to be superior to*: + acc., 1M 6.43; ὑπέρ + acc., Si 36.27.

2. *to be pre-eminent, excel*: ἐν πᾶσιν τοῖς ἔργοις σου Si 30.31.

Cf. προέχω, ὑπέρκειμαι, and ὑπερφερής.

ὑπεραινετός, όν.∫*

highly praiseworthy: *s* God's name, Da 3.52 (‖ αἰνετός, + ὑπερυψόω).

ὑπεραίρω: fut.pass. ~αρθήσομαι; aor. ὑπερῆρα, pass. ~ήρθην.

1. *to exceed*: + acc., "my deeds of lawlessness piled up higher than my head" Ps 37.5; Pr 31.29 (+ ὑπέρκειμαι), "nothing was too hard for him" Si 48.13; pass., in estimation, ὑπὲρ τὸν Λίβανον 'above ..' Ps 71.16.

2. mid. *to treat in a high-handed manner*: + dat. pers., 2M 5.23.

ὑπεράλλομαι: fut. ~αλοῦμαι.∫

to win a prominent position: Si 38.33.

ὑπεράνω.

I. prep. w. gen. **1**. *higher above*: εἶναί σε ὑ. πάντων τῶν ἐθνῶν De 26.19; μετεωρισθήσεται ὑ. τῶν βουνῶν 'shall tower over the hills' Mi 4.1, sim. Is 2.2; fig. ἐμεγαλύνθη κύριος ὑ. τῶν ὁρίων τοῦ Ισραηλ Ma 1.5 (but Cyr. II 554: ἐν ..).

2. *over* a surface: τοῦ εἶναι σκιὰν ὑ. τῆς κεφαλῆς αὐτοῦ Jn 4.6.

***3**. *situated to the north of*: To 1.2, cf. ἐπάνω **II 4**.

II. adv. *beyond* a specified point in time and further into the future: ἀπὸ τῆς ἡμέρας ταύτης καὶ ὑ. 'from this day and beyond' Hg 2.15 (‖ ἐπέκεινα vs. 18).

Cf. ὑπέρ, ὑπεράνωθεν, ὑποκάτω, ἄνω, ἐπάνω, ἐπάνωθεν, and ἐπέκεινα.

ὑπεράνωθεν.∫

I. adv. *higher above*: νεφέλαις ὑ. 'to clouds high above' Ps 77.23.

II. prep. w. gen., *higher above*: Ez 1.25.

Cf. ὑπεράνω.

ὑπέραρσις, εως. f.∫

high-water mark: Ez 47.11. See Caird 1969.37f.

ὑπερασπίζω: fut. ~ιῶ; aor.subj. ~πίσω, inf. ~πίσαι, opt.3s ~πίσαι; pf.ptc. ~ησπικώς.

to provide protection, defend: *s* God, abs., ὁ βοηθός σου De 33.29; + gen. pers., κύριος παντοκράτωρ ὑπερασπιεῖ αὐτῶν Zc 9.15, sim. Ju 6.2 (‖ ὑπὲρ αὐτῶν 5.21); ἐγὼ ὑπερασπίζω σου Ge 15.1 (God to Abram), Ho 11.8; + gen. rei, τοῦ ἱεροῦ 'the temple' 4M 4.9; ‖ σκεπάζω Wi 5.16; + ὑπέρ τινος 3M 7.6 (‖ + gen.), Zc 12.8, Is 37.35; + acc., τὴν πορείαν αὐτῶν 'their journey' Pr 2.7; *s* God's name, Ps 19.2; rational will, 4M 74. On the combination with ὑπέρ, see Helbing, *Kasus*., 189. **b**. in general, *to cover*: ἵνα .. στεφάνῳ τρυφῆς ὑπερασπίσῃ σου 'so that .. he may cover you with a garland of delight' Pr 4.9. Cf. ὑπερασπισμός, ὑπερασπιστής, ὑπερασπίστρια, and σκεπάζω.

ὑπερασπισμός, οῦ. m.∫ *

protection provided: σωτηρίας 'of salvation' Ps 17.36 (‖ 2K 22.36B, *L*: ὅπλον); *s* God, ὑ. δυναστείας καὶ στήριγμα ἰσχύος Si 31.19; sarcastically (?), ὑ. καρδίας, ‖ μόχθος La 3.65. Cf. ὑπερασπίζω.

ὑπερασπιστής, οῦ. m., voc. ~ά. *

protector: *s* God, Ps 17.3 (‖ ἀντιλήμπτωρ), τῆς ζωῆς μου 26.1, ‖ βοηθός 27.7, σωτηρίων 27.8, ἐν καιρῷ θλίψεως 36.39. **b**. attr. adj.: θεὸς ὑ. Ps 30.3, 70.3.

Cf. ὑπερασπίζω and ὑπερασπίστρια. Del. 4M 3.12 v.l.

ὑπερασπίστρια, ας. f.∫ *

female who champions for a cause: τῆς εὐσεβείας 'of religion' 4M 15.29. Cf. ὑπερασπιστής.

ὑπερβαίνω: fut. ~βήσομαι; aor. ~έβην, subj. ~βῶ; pf. ~βέβηκα.

1 *to move beyond* a border or limit: abs., Jb 14.5, 38.11; + acc., ὅριον Je 5.22, οἶκον 4M 18.7, καιρόν 'jump the gun' Si 20.7. **b**. *to cross over*: + acc., river Pr 9.18b (‖ διαβαίνω). **c**. *to overtake*: τινα 2K 18.23 (*L* παρέρχομαι). **d**. *to outstrip*: + acc. pers., τυράννους .. ὠμότητι 'tyrants .. in cruelty' 3M 6.24, cf. ὑπερισχύω and ὑπέρκειμαι.

2. *to mount and move* to the other side, 'scale': + acc., τεῖχος 'wall' Ps 17.30, χάρακας 'ramparts' 4M 3.12.

*3. *to pass over, overlook intentionally*: *s* God and + acc. ἀσεβείας 'iniquities' Mi 7.18.

Cf. ὑπεροράω: *ND*, 2.148f.

ὑπερβαλλόντως. adv.∫

exceedingly: Jb 15.11. Cf. ὑπερβάλλω, σφόδρα.

ὑπερβάλλω: aor.ptc. ~βαλών.∫

1. *to surpass*: ὑπέρ τι Si 25.11; + double acc., τὸν Ἰάσωνα τάλαντα .. τριακόσια 'outbidding J. by 300 talents ..' 2M 4.24. **b**. pres. ptc. *exceeding*: "exceeding impurity" 2M 4.13; 7.42; *s* φόβος 'fear' 3M 2.23. Cf. ὑπερφέρω.

2. mid. *to postpone*: ἡμέραν ἐξ ἡμέρας 'from one day to another' Si 5.7 (‖ ἀναμένω 'delay'). Cf. ὑστερέω **1b** and χρονίζω.

Cf. prec., ὑπερβολή, ἀνυπέρβλητος, περιγίνομαι, I περίειμι **2**.

ὑπερβολή, ῆς. f.∫

excess: καθ' ~ήν 'to extreme measure' 4M 3.18.

ὑπερδυναμόω: aor. ὑπερεδυνάμωσα.∫ *

to overpower: + acc. pers. and *s* λόγοι ἀνομιῶν Ps 64.4.

ὑπερεῖδον: aor.ptc. ~ιδών, inf. ~ιδεῖν, subj. ~ίδω.

1. *to neglect, choose to take no notice of* sbd or sth that calls for attention: + acc. pers., ^τὸν θεόν^ Le 26.40, αὐτούς 26.44, De 21.16, *o* elderly, widowed mother To 4.3 𝔊^I (𝔊^II ἐγκαταλείπω); + acc. rei, τὴν θλῖψιν τῆς ψυχῆς αὐτοῦ 'the agony of his soul' Ge 42.21; τὴν δέησίν μου 'my supplication' Ps 54.2; τὰ κρίματά μου 'my decisions' Le 26.43; τὰς πόλεις Ιουδα Zc 1.12; ἀποστῆσαι καὶ ὑπεριδεῖν τὸ ῥῆμα κυρίου 'to revolt and disregard the word of the Lord' Nu 31.16; stray cattle, De 22.1; πόνους 'pains' 4M 1.9 (out of bravery); + *ἀπό τινος– τοῖς ὀφθαλμοῖς αὐτῶν ἀπὸ τοῦ ἀνθρώπου ἐκείνου Le 20.4. **b**. *to handle without due attention and in perfunctory fashion*: + acc., τὴν τάφην αὐτοῦ 'his burial' Si 38.16.

2. *to look down, disdain*: + acc. pers., Nu 5.12 (*s* adulterous wife).

Cf. ὑπεροράω: Spicq 2.899f.; Walters 262-4.

ὑπερείδω: aor. ὑπήρεισα, subj. ~είσω.∫

1. *to under-prop, support*: + acc., οἰκίαν Jb 8.15, cf. Caird 1969.38.

2. *to place vertically* as part of an edifice: + acc., στύλους 'columns' Pr 9.1.

ὑπερεκχέω: fut. ~χυθήσομαι.∫ *(but attested in Diodorus Siculus+ [1 c. BCE])

pass.intr. *to overflow*: ὑπερεκχεῖται τὰ ὑπολήνια 'the vats are overflowing' Jl 3.13; + *gen. ὑπερεκχυθήσονται οἱ ληνοὶ οἴνου καὶ ἐλαίου 'the tubs will overflow with wine and oil' ib. 2.24; *s* ὕδατα Pr 5.16.

ὑπερένδοξος, ον.∫ *

exceedingly glorious: *s* God, Da 5.54 LXX (+ ὑπερυμνητός). Cf. ἔνδοξος.

ὑπερέχω: fut. ὑπερέξω.

1. *to be more powerful than*: + gen., λαὸς λαοῦ ὑπερέξει Ge 25.23; οὐχ ὑπερέχει ἐν τῇ οἰκίᾳ ταύτῃ οὐθὲν ἐμοῦ 'there is nothing in this house which is beyond me' 39.9; πλὴν τὸν θρόνον ὑπερέξω σου ἐγώ 'only with respect to the throne I shall have an edge over you' 41.40; ptc., ὁ ὑπερέχων 'the holder of a high office' Wi 6.5; Jd 5.25 B (A: ἰσχυρός). **b**. *to outstrip, exceed*: + acc. pers., Da 5.11 LXX, πάσας τὰς βασιλείας 7.23 TH (LXX διαφέρω). **c**. *to stick out*: *s* staves, ‖ βλέπομαι 'to be visible' 2C 5.9, cf. 3K 8.8.

2. *to constitute excess*: ὃ ὑπερέχει 'the difference' Le 25.27; Ex 26.13.

Cf. ὑπεροχή, κατακρατέω, ὑπερισχύω, ὑπέρκειμαι.

ὑπερηφανέω: aor. ὑπερηφάνησα.

1. *to act arrogantly*: ἐπί τινα Ne 9.10.

2. *to treat disdainfully*: pass., *o* νόμος 4M 5.21.

Cf. ὑπερηφανεύομαι and ὑβρίζω.

ὑπερηφανεύομαι: aor. ὑπερηφανευσάμην, inf. ~νεύσασθαι, ptc. ~νευσάμενος.*

to act arrogantly: *s* the impious, Ps 9.23, hum. as dust and ashes Si 10.9. **b**. + inf., *to treat with contempt the idea of*: To 4.13 𝔊^I, cf. Joseph., *JA* 4.8.23.

Cf. ὑπερηφανέω, ὑπερηφανία, and ἐπαίρω.

ὑπερηφανία, ας. f.

arrogance, pride: μισοῦντας ~αν Ex 18.21; ὕβρις τῆς ~ας Le 26.19, + ὕβρις Je 31.29; ὀμνύει κύριος καθ' ~ας Ἰακωβ 'the Lord swears against [rather than by] the pride of Jacob' (so Tht Th Syh and Eth) Am 8.7; ἐν χειρὶ ~ας Nu 15.30; τῆς καρδίας Ob 3 (‖ ἰταμία Je 29.17); ἐν ~ᾳ τοῦ μὴ ὑπακοῦσαι .. De 17.12; manifested in speech, τὸ στόμα αὐτοῦ ἐλάλησεν ~αν Ps 16.10, ἐν ~ᾳ καὶ ἐξουδενώσει '.. with disdain' 30.19, γλώσσης 3M 2.17. **b**. not in derogatory sense: τὸ σημεῖον τῆς ~ας Es C 27 (ref. to the royal crown).

Cf. ὑπερήφανος, ὕβρις, φρύαγμα, αὐθάδεια, καύχημα, στρῆνος, ταπεινότης, πραΰς: Bertram, *TDNT* 8.525-7; Spicq 3.390-5.

ὑπερήφανος, η, ον.

1. *arrogant*: *s* hum., ἐν διαφθορᾷ κατέσπασα ~ους 'with destruction I cut down the arrogant' Zp 3.6, ~ους ταπεινώσω Is 1.25; ὑβριστὴν καὶ ~ον καὶ .. ὑψηλὸν καὶ μετέωρον 2.12; ‖ ἄνομος Is 29.20; an attitude liable to end up in a murder, Si 27.15; *s* ὀφθαλμός Ps 100.5, ὀφθαλμοὺς ~ων 17.28 (:: ταπεινός); μὴ ἁμάρτῃς λόγῳ ~ῳ 'do not sin with arrogant speech' Si 35.12; ‖ ὑβριστής Jb 40.12; subst. n.pl., 2M 9.12.

2. *outstanding* of quality: *s* ἡδύσματα 'fragrant unguents' Es C 13.

Cf. ὑπερηφανία, ~άνως, ἀγέρωχος, ἀλαζών, αὐθάδης, μεγαλόφρων, ταπεινός, ὑψηλός: Schmidt 4.272f.; Trench 98-105; Schoonheim.

ὑπερηφάνως. adv.
arrogantly: λαλέω 1M 7.34. Del. 2M 9.12 v.l. Cf. ὑπερήφανος.

ὑπέρθυρον, ου. n.ʃ
lintel of a door: Is 6.4.

ὑπερισχύω: fut. ~ισχύσω; aor. ὑπερίσχυσα.
1. *to be very strong*: *s* hum., Ge 49.26; λόγος 'idea, theory' 1E 3.5, 'opinion' πρός τινα, εἴς τινα 'over against (the opinion) of ..' 2K 24.4 (*L* κατακρατέω ὑπέρ τινα). **b.** + gen. pers. *to outstrip*: Jo 15.18, Da 11.23 TH, cf. ὑπερβάλλω, ὑπέρκειμαι, and ὑπερκρατέω.
2. *to be taken and acted upon in real earnest*: Da 3.22 TH (LXX ἐπείγω).
Cf. ἰσχύω.

ὑπέρκειμαι.ʃ
to excel, outstrip: *s* hum. and + acc. pers., Pr 31.29 (ǁ ὑπεραίρω), ἐν πάσαις ταῖς ὁδοῖς σου Ez 16.47. Cf. προέχω, ὑπερβάλλω, ὑπερισχύω, ὑπέρκειμαι.

ὑπερκεράω: aor. ὑπερεκέρασα.ʃ
to outflank: + acc. (enemies), Ju 15.5, 1M 7.46.

ὑπερκρατέω: aor. ὑπερεκράτησα.ʃ *
to become more powerful than: τινα 3K 16.21. Cf. ὑπερισχύω.

ὑπερμάχεω.ʃ
to fight in defence of: ὑπὲρ τοῦ ἔθνους ἡμῶν 1M 16.3. Cf. ὑπέρμαχος. Del. 3M 7.6 v.l.

ὑπέρμαχος, ον.ʃ
fighting in defence of sbd else: *s* χείρ Wi 10.20 (God's hand), the universe defending the righteous, 16.17; subst. m., on battlefield, 2M 8.36 (= God), τοῦ ἔθνους ἡμῶν 'of our nation' 14.34. Cf. (ὑπερ)μαχέω.

ὑπερμεγέθης, ες.ʃ
immensely great: in size, *s* hum., 1C 20.6; in value or importance, *s* πράγματα Da 4.34a LXX. Cf. μέγας and μέγεθος.

ὑπερμήκης, ες.ʃ
exceedingly tall: *s* hum., Nu 13.33. Cf. ὑψηλός, πανυπέρτατος.

ὑπέρογκος, ον.
1. *extremely large*: metaph., subst.n., λαλήσει ~α 'he will talk big' Da 11.36 TH (LXX ἔξαλλα 'strange things').
2. *rather difficult*: *s* ῥῆμα 'matter' Ex 18.22 (:: βραχύς), 26 (:: ἐλαφρός); ἐντολή De 30.11; σύγκριμα 'interpretation' Da 5.12 LXX (TH κραταιούμενον); inf. clause, 2K 13.2B.
Cf. σκληρός, χαλεπός, βραχύς,. and ἐλαφρός.

ὕπερον, ου. n.ʃ
pestle: Pr 23.31.

ὑπερόρασις, εως.ʃ
v.n. of ὑπεροράω: as cogn. dat., Nu 22.30. Cf. ὑπεροράω and ὑπέροψις.

ὑπεροράω: fut. ὑπερόψομαι, pass. ~οφθήσομαι; pf. pass.ptc. ὑπερεωραμένος.
to pass over, take no notice of: + acc. pers., Le 26.37; person in trouble or need, Ps 9.22, ǁ ἀποστρέφω πρόσωπον Si 14.8 (*s* miser); Jo 1.5 (ǁ ἐγκαταλείπω); pass. ἔσῃ ὑπερεωραμένη Na 3.11; + *ἀπό τινος, Is 58.7, but not Ju 8.20 (partitive ἀπό). **b.** out of disdain: pass., *o* τὸ χρυσίον αὐτῶν Ez 7.19. **c.** *to be willing to part with*: + acc. rei, 2M 7.11.
Cf. ὑπερόρασις, ὑπέροψις, ὑπερβαίνω, λανθάνω, παρεῖδον, παροράω: Spicq 3.396f.

ὑπεροχή, ῆς. f.ʃ
prominence: μῆκος ὑ. 'height' Je 52.22; w. ref. to social standing and estimation, 2M 3.11, 15.13; arising from old age, 6.23; *extremely high degree*, τινων ἄλλων κακῶν ~ὴν πεποιημένον 'having distinguished themselves in any other kind of wrongdoing' 13.6. Cf. ὑπερέχω.

ὑπέροψις, εως. f.ʃ*
v.n. of ὑπεροράω: as cogn. dat., Le 20.4. Cf. prec., ὑπερόρασις.

ὑπερπλεονάζω: aor.subj. ~πλεονάσω.ʃ *
to have too much: *s* hum., PSol 5.16.

ὑπερτήκω.ʃ
to melt exceedingly: pass., *o* hum., διὰ τοῦ πυρός 4M 7.12. Cf. τήκω.

ὑπερτίθημι.ʃ
mid. *to delay*: + acc., συνέδρια 'council meetings' Pr 15.22. Cf. ὑστερέω **1**, χρονίζω.

ὑπερτιμάω.ʃ
to think very highly of: + acc. rei, 4M 8.5. Cf. τιμάω.

ὑπερυμνητός, όν.ʃ *
highly worthy of adoration in hymns: *s* God, Da 3.54 LXX, 53 TH (+ ὑπερένδοξος). Cf. ὑμνητός.

ὑπερυψόω: aor.pass. ὑπερυψώθην; pf.ptc.pass. ~υψωμένος.*
to exalt exceedingly: *o* divinity, and + δοξάζω τὸν βασιλέα τοῦ οὐρανοῦ Da 4.34 TH, + ὑμνέω 3.57; pass. 3.52 (+ αἰνετός, ὑπεραινετός), σφόδρα .. ὑπὲρ πάντας τοὺς θεούς Ps 96.9. **b.** poss. mid.: Ps 36.35 (ǁ ἐπαίρομαι).
Cf. ὑψόω.

ὑπερφερής, ές.ʃ*
pre-eminent: *s* πρόσοψις 'appearance' Da 2.31. Cf. ὑπεράγω **2**.

ὑπερφέρω: fut. ὑπεροίσω; aor. ὑπερήνεγκα.
to surpass others: abs., "our errors have exceeded those of anybody else, reaching as high as the sky" 1E 8.72; + acc., κακοῖς πάντας τοὺς ἔμπροσθεν 'all his predecessors in terms of wicked deeds' Da 7.24 TH (LXX: διαφέρω); + gen., τῶν σοφιστῶν 1.20 LXX. Cf. ὑπερβάλλω, ὑπέρκειμαι.

ὑπέρφοβος, ον.ʃ
very frightening: *s* animal, Da 7.19 LXX (TH φοβερὸς περισσῶς 'exceedingly fearful'). Cf. φοβερός, δεινός.

ὑπερφρονέω: aor. ~εφρόνησα.
to think litttle of: + gen., πόνων 'pains' 4M 13.1. Cf. ἐξουδενέω. καταφρονέω.

ὑπερφωνέω.ʃ *
**to sing loudly*: + acc., αἴνεσιν 'praise' Ju 15.14. Cf. ᾄδω.

ὑπερχαρής, ές.ʃ
overjoyed: Es 5.9 o', 3M 7.20. Cf. χαρά.

ὑπερχέω: aor.pass. ὑπερεχύθην.ʃ
to pour upon: ὑπερεχύθη ὕδωρ ἐπὶ κεφαλήν μου La 3.54.
Cf. (ἐπι)χέω.

ὑπέρχομαι: pf.ptc. ~εληλυθώς.ʃ
to get under: + acc., γαμικὸν παστόν 'bridal canopy' 3M 4.6.

ὑπερωμία, ας. f.ʃ (ed. R: ὑπὲρ ὠμίαν)
shoulder: 1K 9.2, 10.23. Cf. ὦμος.

ὑπερῷος, ον.
located higher up: *s* house, Je 20.2, περίπατος 'walk' Ez 42.5. **b**. subst.n., *upper part of a dwelling*: penthouse (of the well-to-do) Jd 3.20, Je 22.13, ῥιπιστόν 'well-ventilated' 22.14; upper chamber, Ez 41.7, Da 6.10, Ps 103.3, To 3.10 𝔊II.

ὑπεύθυνος, ον.ʃ
liable to: + dat. rei, ἐλέγχοις 'reproaches' Pr 1.23.

ὑπευλαβέομαι.ʃ*
to be somewhat scared: + inf., 2M 14.18. Cf. εὐλαβέομαι.

ὑπέχω: fut. ὑφέξομαι; aor.act. ὑπέσχον, mid. ὑπεσχόμην.ʃ
1. act. *to be subjected to*, 'suffer': + acc., ἄδικον ζημίαν 'unjust penalty' 2M 4.48; humiliation (ὀνειδισμός) Ps 88.51; penalty for lawlessness, La 5.7. **b**. mid. in the same sense: παιδείαν ἐν πενίᾳ 'discipline through poverty' PSol 16.13.
2. mid. *to pledge*: + inf. and μετ' ὅρκου Es 7.7.
Cf. ὑπόσχεσις. Del. Wi 12.21 v.l.

ὑπήκοος, ον.
owing obedience: subject to tributes, Jo 17.13; + gen. pers., σοι φορολόγητοι καὶ ~οί σου 'your tributaries and subjects' De 20.1. **b**. *obedient*: + dat. and *s* hum., υἱὸς .. ὑ. πατρί Pr 13.1 (:: ἀνήκοος).
Cf. ὑπακούω and ἀνήκοος.

ὑπηρεσία, ας. f.ʃ
1. *body of servants* or *attendants*, 'retinue': Jb 1.3.
2. *service rendered*: ζωῆς 'for daily life' Wi 13.11; 15.7.
Cf. ὑπηρέτης and δοῦλος. Del. Wi 13.12 v.l.

ὑπηρετέω: fut. ὑπηρετήσω.
to render services: ἀνὰ μέσον μεγιστάνων 'among important people' Si 39.4. **b**. *to further the cause of*: + dat., Wi 16.21, 25.
Cf. θεραπεύω and λειτουργέω.

ὑπηρέτης, ου. m.ʃ
one who is in service to another or *in subservient position*, 'servant, attendant': Is 32.5; τοῦ βασιλέως Da 3.46 TH, βασιλεῖ Pr 14.35; τῆς ^κυρίου^ βασιλείας Wi 6.4.
Cf. διάκονος, δοῦλος, θεράπων, λειτουργός, παῖς, ὑπηρεσία, ὑπουργός: Schmidt 4.135-7, 141-7; Trench 33f.; Rengstorf, *TDNT* 8.530-5; Spicq 3.398-402.

ὑπισχνέομαι.
to promise: + inf. 2M 4.9, Wi 17.8. Cf. ἐπαγγέλλω and ὑπόσχεσις.

ὕπνος, ου. m.
1. *sleep*: ἐν ~ῳ τὴν νύκτα 'in sleep at night' Ge 20.3 (time of theophany) ‖ καθ' ~ον 20.6; εἶδον τοῖς ὀφθαλμοῖς μου ἐν τῷ ~ῳ 31.10; ἐξεγερθῇ ἄνθρωπος ἐξ ~ου αὐτοῦ 'a man is aroused from his sleep' Zc 4.1; ὅλην τὴν νύκτα ~ου Εφραιμ ἐνεπλήσθη 'E. slept soundly all night' Ho 7.6. **b**. *state of death*: Jb 14.12¶; αἰώνιος Je 28.39 (as cogn. obj.).
2. *sexual intercourse*: ἡδονῆς 'delectable' Wi 7.2; ἄνομος 'illicit' 4.6.
Cf. ὑπνόω, ὑπνώδης, ἐνύπνιον, νύσταγμα, καταφορά: Balz, *TDNT* 8.550f.

ὑπνόω: fut. ὑπνώσω; aor. ὕπνωσα, subj. ὑπνώσω, inf. ὑπνῶσαι, impv. 2pl ὑπνώσατε, ptc. ὑπνώσας.
to sleep: *s* hum., Ge 2.21 (caused by God), Jl 1.13, εἰς θάνατον Ps 12.4; God, οὐ νυστάξει οὐδὲ ὑπνώσει 120.4; out of intoxication and + cogn. acc., ὕπνον αἰώνιον Je 28.39 (+ καρόομαι); of death, Si 46.20; metaph. of inactivity, PSol 3.1 (:: γρηγορέω 'to stay awake' vs. 2). Cf. ὕπνος, καθεύδω, νυστάζω, ἐξ~, καθυπνόω, καρόω: Schmidt 1.442-70; Shipp 547f.

ὑπνώδης, ες.ʃ
fond of sleep: fig. of laziness, *s* hum., Pr 23.21. Cf. ὕπνος.

ὑπό. prep.
I. + gen., *because of*: "because of the multitude of your iniquities" Ho 9.7.
2. *through the agency of*, 'by': with a passive verb, κατασταθέντες ὑ. τῶν ἐπιστατῶν 'appointed by the supervisors' Ex 5.14, πληγέντες ὑ. κυρίου 'smitten by ..' 16.3, λαὸς σῳζόμενος ὑ. κυρίου De 33.29. **b**. with a non-passive verb, but with a passive signification: ἀναστήσεσθαι ὑπ' αὐτοῦ 'to rise again ..' 2M 7.14, ἔσονται τραυματίαι ὑ. κυρίου Je 32.19, ἐὰν κακὸν πάθωσιν ὑπό τινος .. ἀγαθόν 'if they suffer evil .. or good at sbd's hands' Ep Je 33, ὑπέπεσεν 'fell defeated' Ju 16.6, θανεῖται 'will die'

Pr 13.14, ἀπολεῖται 'will perish' 19.9; τῶν ὑπὸ σοῦ γενομένων κτισμάτων 'the creatures brought into being by you' Wi 9.2, cf. ὑφ' ὑμῶν αὐτῶν καὶ μὴ ὑ. τῶν πολεμίων τοῦτο παθεῖν 'to endure this at your hands of all people and not at the enemies'' Thuc. 4.64 and BDAG, s.v. πάσχω **3aβ**, **b** and s.v. ὑπό **Ab**. **c**. with an adjective of passive signification and || διά τινος– πάντα τὰ ἀρτὰ ὑπ' αὐτῶν 'all that which is carried by them' Nu 4.27. **d**. a passive verb understood: τὰς ὑ. τοῦ θεοῦ .. ἐλπίδας 'the hopes granted .. by God' 2M 7.14.

3. *subject to, under the authority of*: of wife, ὑπ' ἀνδρὸς οὖσα Nu 5.20, 29 (|| + acc., vs. 19).

II. + acc. **1**. of static position, *under*: τὰ ὑ. τοὺς πόδας αὐτοῦ 'that which was at his feet' Ex 24.10; συνέτριψεν αὐτὰς ὑ. τὸ ὄρος 'smashed them at the foot of the mountain' 32.19; ὑ. τὸν ἄνδρα τὸν σεαυτῆς 'under your own husband' Nu 5.19 (|| ὑπ' ἀνδρὸς οὖσα vs. 20); "they will sit under his shade" Ho 14.8; "under a single yoke" Zp 3.9; 'at the foot of'– ἔστητε ὑ. τὸ ὄρος De 4.11; ἐκ τῆς ὑ. τὸν οὐρανόν 25.19, τὴν γῆν .. ὁ ποιῶν τὴν ὑπ' οὐρανόν Jb 34.13; ὑ. τὸν ἥλιον Ec 1.3. **b**. dynamic – placing under: moving under, Ex 23.5; ἐὰν μὴ ἐμβάλωσι τὸν τράχηλον αὐτῶν ὑ. τὸν ζυγὸν βασιλέως Βαβυλῶνος Je 34.6; Ez 32.27. **c**. fig., ὑ. χεῖρας ὑμῖν δέδωκα 'I have handed (them) over to your control' Ge 9.2, ταπεινώθητι ὑ. τὰς χεῖρας αὐτῆς 'submit yourself to her' 16.9; ὑ. τὰς χεῖράς σου .. ὑ. σέ εἰσιν De 33.3; ὑ. τὴν χεῖρά σου 'at your disposal' 1K 21.4; Ge 41.35; πεσοῦνται ὑ. τοὺς πόδας μου 'fall at my feet' Ps 17.39, ταπεινῶσαι ὑ. τοὺς πόδας αὐτοῦ πάντας δεσμίους γῆς 'to subjugate all the prisoners of the land ..' La 3.34; τοὺς ὑπὸ τὴν βασιλείαν Ἰουδαίους 'the Jewish subjects in the kingdom' 3M 7.3.

2. *on to the other side of*: ἤγαγεν τὰ πρόβατα ὑ. τὴν ἔρημον Ex 3.1.

3. of time, *in the course of, during*: ὑ. νύκτα 'by night' Jn 4.10*bis*, ὑ. τὴν νύκτα To 7.11 𝔊^I (𝔊^II om. ὑ.), μιᾶς ὑ. καιρὸν ἡμέρας 'in the course of a single day' 2M 7.20, 3M 4.14; ὑ. τὴν ἐπερχομένην ἡμέραν 'on the following day' 5.2, ὑ. τοῦτον τὸν καιρόν 'about this time' Jo 5.2.

4. *under the protection of*: ὑ. τὴν μητέρα Ex 22.30, Le 22.27 (of newborn young animals); ὑ. τὰς πτέρυγας αὐτοῦ ἐλπιεῖς 'under his wings you will find hope' Ps 90.4.

5. *under the authority of, being subject to*: ὑ. τὰς χεῖράς σου .. ὑ. σέ εἰσιν De 33.3; ὑποτάσσων τὸν λαόν μου ὑπ' ἐμέ Ps 143.2, γενέσθαι ὑφ' ἕνα 'to come under one ruler' 1M 10.38, πάντας τοὺς ὑ. τὴν Ἀρταξέρξου βασιλείαν Ἰουδαίους Es 3.6.

6. Idiomatic: ὑφ' ἓν ἐκτρῖψαι 'to destroy at a single stroke' Wi 12.9; ὑπ' ὄψιν τεθεαμένος 'having seen with his own eyes' 2M 3.36, cf. τὰ ὑ. τὴν ὄψιν ἐρχόμενα 'what comes to one's notice' Es E 9.

Cf. Johannessohn, *Präp*. 174-84.

ὑποβάλλω.ʃ

to lay the foundation for: + acc., ναόν 1E 2.17.

ὑποβλέπομαι.ʃ

to eye suspiciously: + acc. pers., 1K 18.9, Si 37.10. Cf. βλέπω.

ὑπόγαιος, ον.ʃ

subterranean: ***s*** οἰκία Je 45.11.

ὑπογραμμός, οῦ. m.ʃ *

guideline to be followed: 2M 2.18.

ὑπογράφω: pf.ptc.pass. ~γεγραμμένος.

1. *to write below*: ὑπογεγραμμένη ἐπιστολή 'letter below' 1E 2.15; τὰ ὑπογεγραμμένα 2.21.

2. *to indicate as appropriate* or *right*: ὡς ἂν ὁ καιρὸς ὑπογράφῃ αὐτοῖς 'as the occasion might dictate to them' 1M 8.25. **b**. *to endorse in writing*: pass., ***o*** decision, 2M 11.17.

Cf. γράφω: Schrenk, *TDNT* 1.772f.

ὑπόγυος, ον.ʃ

near at hand, imminent: ***s*** festival, 2M 12.30. Cf. ἐγγύς.

ὑπόδειγμα, ατος. n.ʃ

1. *that which is laid out and structured in orderly fashion*: τοῦ οἴκου Ez 42.15 (a model for the future temple), cf. 1C 28.11.

2. *model to be followed*: μετανοίας ταῖς γενεαῖς Si 44.16, ὑ. γενναιότητος καὶ μνημόσυνον ἀρετῆς καταλιπών 'leaving an example of nobility and a memory of virtue' 2M 6.31, τοῖς νέοις ὑ. γενναῖον καταλελοιπώς 'having left a noble example for the young people' 6.28; 4M 17.23. Cf. παράδειγμα **1** and τύπος **1**.

Cf. Schlier, *TDNT* 2.32f.; Spicq 3.403-5.

ὑποδείκνυμι: fut. ~δείξω; aor. ὑπέδειξα, inf. ~δεῖξαι, impv. ~δειξον, ptc. ~δείξας, subj. ~δείξω, pass. ὑπεδείχθην.

1. *to make known*, 'inform': + acc. rei, Da 5.6 LXX; surreptitiously or in private, + τινί τι Si 17.7, and pass., 3.23; + τινι ὅτι Da 9.23 LXX (TH ἀναγγέλλω); τινι περί τινος Es A 13 o' (*L* ἀπαγγέλλω), To 4.2 𝔊^II; also + ὅτι .. 1.19; 4.19 𝔊^II (𝔊^I + acc. rei); τινι λέγων and dir. speech, 2C 20.2; τινί τινα and ptc. acc., Es 3.4 o'; + inf., B 3.17 *L*, 2M 13.4. **b**. *to inculcate*: ***s*** priest, 2C 15.3.

2. *to draw attention to, point out*: τινι διότι 1E 2.20 (|| γνωρίζω 2E 4.16); + acc. rei and ptc., 3M 5.15.

3. *to cause to see visually*: + acc. and dat. pers., ὅρασιν .. αὐτῷ 'a vision ..' Si 49.8; 1C 28.18.

Cf. δείκνυμι, γνωρίζω, συμβιβάζω, ἀν~, ἀπαγγέλλω.

ὑποδέχομαι: fut. ~δέξομαι; aor. ὑπεδεξάμην.ʃ

to receive a visitor: + acc. pers., μετὰ δόλου 'treacherously' 1M 16.15; in friendly manner, προθύμως 'eagerly' To 7.8 𝔊^I (= 7.9 𝔊^II), Ju 13.13, 4M 13.17. Cf. δέχομαι.

ὑποδέω: aor. ὑπέδησα.ʃ

to equip sbd w. footwear: + acc. pers., 2C 28.15; + double acc., σε ὑάκινθον 'dark blue sandal' Ez 16.10. Cf. ὑπόδημα.

ὑπόδημα, ατος. n. Often pl.

sandal: relatively inexpensive commodity, λῦσαι τὸ ὑ. ἐκ τῶν ποδῶν σου 'Take the sandal off your feet' Ex 3.5 (sg. used collectively, but not at De 25.9); τὰ ~ατα ἐν τοῖς ποσὶν ὑμῶν 12.11; ἀπέδοντο .. πένητα ἕνεκεν ~άτων 'sold .. the poor for sandals' Am 2.6; 8.6; ‖ ἱμάτια De 29.5; made of iron and bronze, De 33.25. Cf. πέδιλον, σανδάλιον.

ὑποδιδάσκω.ʃ*

to teach: + acc. pers., Ne 8.7, see Hanhart 2003. 402-4. Cf. διδάσκω.

ὑποδύτης, ου. m.

undergarment: part of the high priest's outfit, ποδήρης 'falling over the feet' Ex 28.27; worn under ἐπωμίς 'ephod' 36.30; worn by princesses, 2K 13.18*L* (B: ἐπενδύτης). Cf. χιτών.

ὑποδύω: aor.impv. ~δυσον, ptc. ~δύσας.ʃ

to position oneself under sth for a cover: ὑποκάτω τοῦ ὄρους Ju 6.13; ὑπὸ τὴν σκέπην 'under the cover' Jd 9.15 (A: πεποίθατε 'Trust').

ὑποζύγιον, ου. n.

ass: ‖ κτῆνος, ἵππος, κάμηλος, βοῦς, πρόβατον Ex 9.3; 34.20 (‖ ὄνος 13.13); ‖ πῶλος Zc 9.9; humble possession, ὀρφανῶν 'of orphans' Jb 24.3 (‖ βοῦς χήρας 'a widow's ox'); means of private transport, Jd 1.14.

Cf. ὄνος, πῶλος: Lee 140-3.

ὑποζώννυμι: aor.impv. ~ζῶσον; pf.ptc.mid .. ὑπεζωσμένος.ʃ

to fasten a piece of fabric under some part of body: + acc. rei, ὑπὸ τοὺς μαστοὺς σάκκους 'sackcloth under the breasts' 2M 3.19; metaph., τινά τι - αὐτὸν ἰσχύν '.. strength' PSol 17.22. Cf. ζώννυμι.

ὑπόθεμα, ατος. n.ʃ

lowest part of a structure on which the latter is set, 'base': of a lampstand, Ex 25.38. Cf. θεμέλιον and ὑποτίθημι.

ὑπόθεσις, εως. f.ʃ

1. *plan of action*: Es 6.3 *L*.

2. *rule of action, principle*: 4M 1.12.

ὑποκαίω/κάω.ʃ

1. *to heat from underneath*: ***o*** and pass., λέβης 'cauldron' Am 4.2, Je 1.13; κάμινος 'furnace' Da 3.25 LXX.

2. *to burn underneath* sth: + acc., τὰ ὀστὰ ὑποκάτω αὐτῶν Ez 24.5, νάφθαν Da 3.46 LXX (TH: καίω); ***o*** hum., 4M 11.18. **b**. *to burn*: pass., ***o*** hair, Da 3.94 LXX (TH φλογίζω).

Cf. καίω.

ὑποκαλύπτω: fut. ~καλύψω.ʃ *

to let hang down to cover sth: + acc. Ex 26.12 (‖ καλύπτω vs. 13). Cf. καλύπτω.

ὑποκάτω

I. prep. w. gen., *under, underneath* some object under which **a**. an activity takes place: ἔθυον ὑ. δρυός 'they would offer sacrifices under an oak tree' Ho 4.13; ἀναπαύσεται ἕκαστος ὑ. ἀμπέλου αὐτοῦ καὶ ἕκαστος ὑ. συκῆς αὐτοῦ 'each will rest under his vine and each under his fig-tree' Mi 4.4; ἐκάθητο ὑ. αὐτῆς 'sat under it' Jn 4.5. **b**. where some object is placed or located: τοῦ ὕδατος, ὃ ἦν ὑ. τοῦ στερεώματος Ge 1.7 (:: ἐπάνω), τὰ ὄρη τὰ ὑψηλά, ἃ ἦν ὑ. τοῦ οὐρανοῦ 'all the high mountains that were under the sky' 7.19; ἐν τῷ οὐρανῷ ἄνω καὶ .. ἐν τῇ γῇ κάτω καὶ .. ἐν τοῖς ὕδασιν ὑ. τῆς γῆς Ex 20.4; ἔθηκαν ἔνεδρα ὑ. σου 'they laid snares underneath you' Ob 7; ἔσονται σποδὸς ὑ. τῶν ποδῶν ὑμῶν 'they will be ashes underneath your feet' Ma 4.3. **c**. where some object is moved or moves to: κυλίω ὑ. ὑμῶν 'I roll under you' Am 2.13; συγκαλέσετε ἕκαστος τὸν πλησίον αὐτοῦ ὑ. ἀμπέλου καὶ ὑ. συκῆς Zc 3.10.

2. marks a place where sbd or sth is located, with the notion of *under* being absent: ἀποθνήσκει ὑ. αὐτοῦ 'he died where he was' 2K 2.23.

II. adv. *underneath*: fig. of inferiority, ἔσῃ τότε ἐπάνω καὶ οὐκ ἔσῃ ὑ. De 28.13; Ba 2.5.

Cf. ὑπό, ὑποκάτωθεν, ἐπάνω: Johannessohn, *Präp.* 183.

ὑποκάτωθεν.

I. prep. + gen., *from under*: ὑ. τοῦ οὐρανοῦ De 9.14, Je 10.11; ὑ. χειρὸς Φαραω 4K 17.7. **b**. *under, underneath*: σαλευθήσεται τὰ ὄρη ὑ. αὐτοῦ 'the mountains will be shaken under him' Mi 1.4, sim. Hb 3.16; ὑ. αὐτοῦ ἀνατελεῖ 'he will shoot up under it (or: from under it)' Zc 6.12.

II. adv. *below*: ἐξῆρα .. τὰς ῥίζας αὐτοῦ ὑ. 'I dried up .. his roots below' Am 2.9 (:: ἐπάνωθεν).

Cf. ὑπό, ἐπάνωθεν: Johannessohn, *Präp.* 183.

ὑποκάω: ⇒ ὑποκαίω.

ὑπόκειμαι.ʃ

1. *to be given below* in the text: τὸ ὑποκείμενον 'the following' 1E 8.8; 1M 12.7.

2. *to exist*: ***s*** soul, Jb 16.4.

3. *to be subject to, submit oneself to*: ἀπὸ (read: ὑπὸ) ἁμαρτίας PSol 16.8.

ὑποκρίνομαι: aor.subj. ~κριθῶ, ptc. ~κριθείς, inf. mid. ~κρίνασθαι, pass. ~κριθῆναι.ʃ

to act as hypocrite*: Si 1.29, 35.15, 36.2, PSol 4.20. **b. *to perform* an act *merely out of false profession*: abs. 2M 6.24; + acc., ἀπρεπὲς ἡμῖν δρᾶμα 'a role not befitting us' 4M 6.17; ψυχὰς ἀκάκων παραλογισμῷ 'innocent souls by means of twisted argument' PSol 4.22. **c.** *to pretend to be*: τὸν εἰρηνικόν 'peaceful man' 2M 5.25. **d.** *to pretend to do*: + ὡς and ptc., 2M 6.21; + ptc., 4M 6.15.

Cf. ὑπόκρισις, ὑποκρίτης, ἀνυπόκριτος: Wilckens, *TDNT* 8.559-64; Spicq 3.406-13.

ὑπόκρισις, εως. f.ʃ

act of pretending to be what one actually is not: 2M 6.25, PSol 4.6. Cf. ὑποκρίνομαι, εἰρωνεία.

ὑποκριτής, οῦ. m.ʃ

**hypocrite*: Jb 34.30, 36.13. Cf. ὑποκρίνομαι.

ὑπολαμβάνω: aor. ὑπέλαβον, ptc. ~λαβών, subj. ~λάβω, opt.3s~λάβοι; pf.ptc. ὑπειληφώς.

1. *to come upon suddenly*: *s* sth threatening and + acc. pers., ὑπέλαβόν με ὡσεὶ λέων ἕτοιμος εἰς θήραν 'they came upon me like a lion ready for game' Ps 16.12.

2. *to render support* to sbd in trouble, 'uphold': + acc. pers. and *s* God, Ps 29.2.

3. *to react orally to what has been said*, 'to respond': ὑπολαβὼν δὲ ὁ διάβολος εἶπεν τῷ κυρίῳ Jb 2.4, Ὑπολαβὼν δὲ Ελιφας ὁ Θαιμανίτης λέγει 4.1, sim. 6.1 +, Da 3.95 LXX (|| TH ἀποκρίνομαι); οὐχ οὕτως ὑπελάμβανον ἀντερεῖν σε ταῦτα Jb 20.2; 40.6 || ἀποκρίνομαι 40.1. Cf. ἀναλαμβάνω **7**.

4. *to assume mentally*: abs., ταῖς ψυχαῖς ὑμῶν 'mentally' Je 44.9; ὡς αὐτοὶ ὑπελάμβανον 'in their view' 2M 6.29; + acc., ἃ ὑπέλαβες τῇ καρδίᾳ σου Da LXX 2.30; + ὅτι-clause, To 6.18; + inf., καλῶς ἔχειν ὑπολαμβάνομεν .. 'we consider it appropriate that ..' 1E 2.18; wrong assumption, ἐκφεύξεσθαι δίκην 'to escape justice' Es E 4 o', also 2M 6.24; an inf. (εἶναι) understood, θεοὺς ὑπολαμβάνοντες τὰ .. ἄτιμα 'assuming that the undeserving things .. are gods' Wi 12.24, sim. 13.3 (|| νομίζω vs. 2) and 2M 12.12. Cf. ὑπονοέω **1**.

5. *to form an assumption* or *view about*: + acc., ὑπελάβομεν τὸ ἔλεός σου 'we came to know what your mercy means' Ps 47.10; the content of the assumption or view formed further specified – ὑπέλαβες ἀνομίαν ὅτι ἔσομαί σοι ὅμοιος 'you assumed wickedness (of me) that I might become like you' 49.21; ὑπολαμβάνετε .. τὸ ὄρος ὃ εὐδόκησεν ὁ θεὸς κατοικεῖν ἐν αὐτῷ 'you assume (that you are) that mountain, in which God was pleased to live' 67.17.

6. *to undertake* some task: + inf., ὑπέλαβον τοῦ γνῶναι τοῦτο 'I set about getting to know this' Ps 72.16; βασιλεῦσαι 1M 1.16; 2C 25.8, Wi 17.2.

Cf. ἀποκρίνομαι, βοηθέω, ἀντιλαμβάνω, νομίζω, οἴομαι, ὑπόληψις.

ὑπόλειμμα, ατος. n.

residue, remainder: of food, 1K 9.24, Jb 20.21¶; ὑ. πνεύματος αὐτοῦ Ma 2.15; collectively of survivors, 4K 21.14, || ἔθνος ἰσχυρόν Mi 4.7; ὑ. τοῦ Ιακωβ 5.7, 8. Cf. λεῖμμα, κατά~, ὑπόλοιπος, ὑπολείπω: Schrenk, *TDNT* 4.194f.

ὑπολείπω: fut. ~λείψομαι, pass. ~λειφθήσομαι; aor. act. ὑπέλιπον, mid. ὑπελιπόμην, impv.2pl ~λίπεσθε, opt. 3s ~λίποιτο, pass. ὑπελείφθην, ptc.pass. ~λειφθείς, subj. ~λειφθῶ; pf.pass./mid. ~λέλειμμαι, ptc. ~λελειμμένος.

1. tr. *to leave remaining*: + acc. ὑπολείψομαι ἐν σοὶ λαὸν πραῢν καὶ ταπεινόν 'I shall leave amongst you a modest and humble people' Zp 3.12; μοι εὐλογίαν Ge 27.36; ὑπολείψεται ὀπίσω αὐτοῦ εὐλογίαν Jl 2.14; alone, ὑπελείφθη Ιακωβ μόνος Ge 32.24, sim. Da TH 10.8 (LXX κατα~); *o* fruit left behind by harvesters, Ob 5 (mid.); undamaged by hail, τὸν καρπόν, ὃν ὑπελίπετο ἡ χάλαζα Ex 10.12 (|| ὃ κατέλιπεν ὑμῖν ἡ χ. vs. 5), ὃς ὑπελείφθη ἀπὸ τῆς χαλάζης 10.15, cf. ὑπολείπεσθαι ὑμῶν κατάλειμμα ἐπὶ τῆς γῆς Ge 45.7; legacy left to a widow, Ju 8.7; an amount remaining after removing a part, ὑπολειφθήσονται ἑκατόν Am 5.3, sim. 6.9*bis*; πᾶσαι αἱ φυλαὶ αἱ ὑπολελειμμέναι 'all the remaining families' Zc 12.14; οὐ μὴ ὑπολειφθῇ ἐξ αὐτῶν ῥίζα οὐδὲ κλῆμα 'neither root nor twig will remain of them' Ma 4.1; οἱ ὑπολελειμμένοι λαοί 'the surviving nations' Hb 2.8; τὸ τρίτον ὑπολειφθήσεται 'the third portion will survive' Zc 13.8; τὸ ὑπολειφθὲν ἐν Σιων καὶ τὸ καταλειφθὲν ἐν Ιερουσαλημ Is 4.3. **b.** in a certain state without changing: ὑπολειφθήσεται καὶ οὗτος τῷ θεῷ ἡμῶν 'this also will remain for our God' Zc 9.7. **c.** abandoned and forgotten: οὐ μὴ ὑπολειφθῇ ἐξ αὐτῶν οὐδὲ εἷς Zc 10.10. **d.** object of lesser value: Ge 50.8. **e.** πλὴν τῶν προβάτων καὶ τῶν βοῶν ὑπολείπεσθε 'but leave some of the sheep and cattle behind(?)' Ex 10.24. **f.** mid.: for one's own use, + acc. rei, 2K 8.4.

2. intr.mid. *to remain, stay put*: οὐχ ὑπελίποντο εἰς τὸ πρωΐ 'they did not stay on till the morning' Zp 3.3.

Cf. ὑπόλειμμα, (κατα)λείπω, and κατάλειπος.

ὑπόλημψις, εως. f.ʃ

(false) *supposition, speculation*: Si 3.24 (|| ὑπόνοια 'conjecture'). Cf. ὑπολαμβάνω **4**, ὑπονόημα, ὑπόνοια: Caird 1969.38f.

ὑπολήνιον, ου. n. *

container placed under a wine-press to collect wine: ὑπερεκχεῖται τὰ ~α 'the wine-vats are overflowing' Jl 3.13 (|| ληνός); οὐ μὴ πατήσουσιν οἶνον εἰς τὰ ~α 'they will not tread wine into the vats' Is 16.10. Cf. ληνός: Mayerson 2000.162f.

ὑπόλοιπος, ον.ʃ

subst.n., *that which is left over*: τὸ καταλειφθὲν ~ον τοῦ λαοῦ 'that which has survived and is left over of the people' Is 11.11. Cf. κατάλοιπος, ὑπολείπω, ὑπόλειμμα: Schmidt 4.569.

ὑπόλυσις, εως. f.ʃ *

loosening, putting out of joint: fig. of mentally debilitating experience, ὑ. γονάτων '.. of knees' Na 2.11. Cf. ὑπολύω.

ὑπολύω: fut. ~λύσω; aor.mid. ~ελυσάμην, impv.mid. ὑπόλυσαι, ptc.pass. ~λυθείς.ʃ

to loosen beneath: + acc., τὸ ὑπόδημα αὐτοῦ .. ἀπὸ τοῦ ποδὸς αὐτοῦ 'sandal ..' De 25.9; 25.10; mid. + acc. rei (one's own footwear), τὰ σανδάλιά σου ὑπόλυσαι ἀπὸ τῶν ποδῶν σου Is 20.2; ὑπόδημα Ru 4.7, 8. Cf. λύω and ὑπόλυσις.

ὑπομαστίδιος, ον.ʃ

hanging at the breast: subst.m., *suckling*, + νήπιος 'infant' 3M 3.27. Cf. μαστός and ὑποτίτθιος.

ὑπομένω: fut. ~μενῶ; aor. ὑπέμεινα, impv. ὑπόμεινον, subj. ~μείνω, inf. ~μεῖναι, ptc. ~μείνας, opt.3s ~μείναι.

1. *to wait for*: abs., La 3.21; + acc. of something beneficial, ἡμέραν εἰσόδου αὐτοῦ 'the day of his entrance' Ma 3.2, τὴν βουλὴν αὐτοῦ Ps 105.13, τὴν ψυχήν μου 'my life' 55.7 (with hostile design), ἐμὲ .. τοῦ ἀπολέσαι με 118.95; ἔλεον Is 64.4; + acc. dei (God as helper), χρηστὸς κύριος τοῖς ~νουσιν αὐτὸν ἐν ἡμέρᾳ θλίψεως 'the Lord is kind to those who count on him in the day of trouble' Na 1.7, sim. La 3.25 with ἀγαθός (|| ζητέω); Hb 2.3, Zp 3.8; Is 51.5 (|| ἐλπίζω); + εἰς– εἰς εἰρήνην .. εἰς καιρὸν ἰάσεως Je 14.19. **b**. *to wait in ambush*: + dat. incom., Jb 20.26. **c**. + inf., for a chance to act: Jb 32.5.

2. *to continue to count on for support*: abs., Jb 6.11 (|| ἀνέχομαι); + ἐπί τινι - ἐπὶ τῷ θεῷ τῷ σωτῆρί μου 'God my saviour' Mi 7.7; + dat., τῷ κυρίῳ Ps 32.20, 4K 6.33 (*L* δέομαι); + εἰς– εἰς τὸν λόγον σου Ps 129.5 (|| ἐλπίζω vs. 6): + acc., τὸν κύριον Pr 20.9c, σε, κύριε Ps 129.5, τὸ ὄνομά σου 51.11.

3. *to remain temporarily without setting off on a journey*: ὑπομείνατε αὐτοῦ τὴν νύκτα 'Stay here tonight' Nu 22.19 (|| καταλύω, καταμένω vs. 8).

4. *to submit* to a difficult or undesirable task: + inf., 1E 2.18, 2M 6.20, Wi 17.5, 4M 13.12; + acc., πόνον ἑκουσίως 'suffering willingly' 4M 5.23; 6.9; παιδείαν 'discipline' PSol 10.2.

5. *to hold one's own* without collapsing or being defeated: Jb 8.15 (|| ἵστημι intr.), 41.3, Jo 19.48a. **b**. *to withstand*: + acc., πῦρ 'fire' Wi 16.22, βασανισμούς 'tortures' 4M 9.6, κλύδωνας 'waves' 15.31, χειμῶνας 'storms' 15.32.

6. *to acquiesce in*: + acc., ἀνομίαν Su 57 TH.

Cf. ἐλπίζω, καταλύω,ἐγκαρτερέω, ἐπι~, καταμένω, μένω, ὑπομονή: Spicq 3.414-20.

ὑπομιμνήσκω: aor.ptc. ~μνήσας.ʃ

to cause to call back into memory, 'remind': + acc. rei, Wi 12.2, 18.22; ὑπομιμνήσκων 'secretary' 2K 20.25*L* (B: ἀναμιμνήσκων), 3K 4.3; τινά τι 4M 18.14.

Cf. μιμήσκομαι, ὑπόμνησις, γραμματεύς: Schmidt 1.317f.

ὑπόμνημα, ατος. n.ʃ

= ὑπομνηματισμός, q.v.: pl., 2K 8.16, 1E 2.19, 2E 6.2.

ὑπομνηματίζω: plpf.pass.3s ὑπεμνημάτιστο.ʃ

to record in writing: pass. 1E 6.22. Cf. ὑπομνηματισμός.

ὑπομνηματισμός, οῦ. m.

written record kept for future: βιβλίον ~οῦ 2E 4.15 (|| ὑπόμνημα 1E 2.19). Cf. ὑπομνηματίζω.

ὑπομνηματογράφος, ου. m.

recorder, name of a great official in the Egyptian king's household, and the corresponding official in the office of the minister of finance, and prob. in those of other high officials (LSJ): || οἰκονόμος, γραμματεύς Is 36.3, 22; 1C 18.15.

ὑπόμνησις, εως. f.

act of recalling into memory: 2M 6.17, Wi 16.11. Cf. ὑπομιμνήσκω: Behm, *TDNT* 1.348f.

ὑπομονή, ῆς. f.

1. *act of calmly enduring* sufferings: εὐσεβοῦς 'of the pious' Si 16.13; ἐκλείποντας ~ήν 'those who are about to give up' 17.24. **b**. *strength to endure calmly*: ἀπολωλεκὼς ~ήν 'having lost ..' Si 41.2 (of the elderly), sim. 2.14, ὑ. ἀνθρώπου Jb 14.19¶; + ἀνδρεία 'courage' 4M 1.11.

*__2__. *that which helps one endure, source of strength to endure*: = God of Israel, σὺ εἶ ἡ ὑ. μου, κύριε Ps 70.5 (|| ἐλπίς), τῶν πενήτων 'of the poor' 9.19; 38.8, 61.6, Je 14.8.

3. *remaining behind without vanishing*: οὐκ ἔστιν ὑ. 1C 29.15 (of ephemeral human existence), cf. 2E 10.2.

Cf. ὑπομένω, ἀνεξικακία, ἀνυπομόνητος, μακροθυμία, ἐλπίς: Trench 195-9; Chadwick 307-11; LSG s.v.

ὑπονοέω: aor. ὑπενόησα.ʃ

1. *to believe without adequate evidence*, 'suspect': abs., To 8.16, Si 23.21; + inf., Ju 14.14. Cf. ὑπονόημα and ὑπολαμβάνω **4**.

2. *to have a secret design* of doing sth: + inf., Da 7.25 TH (LXX: προσδέχομαι).

ὑπονόημα, ατος. n.ʃ

that which one regards plausible: Si 25.7. Cf. ὑπονοέω, ὑπόνοια, and ὑπόληψις.

ὑπονοθεύω: aor. ὑπενόθευσα, ptc. ~νοθεύσας, pass. ~νοθευθείς.ʃ

1. *to obtain by corruption*: + acc., ἀρχιερωσύνην 'high-priesthood' 2M 4.7.

2. *to remove from office and take over by underhand means*: + acc. pers., 2M 4.26.

ὑπόνοια, ας. f.

speculation, supposition: πονηρά Si 3.24 (ǁ ὑπόλημψις). **b**. *suspicion*: Da 4.16 LXX, 5.6 LXX.

Cf. ὑπονόημα and ὑπόλημψις.

ὑπονύσσω.ʃ

to cause acute pain wilfully: + acc. pers., Is 58.3.

ὑποπίπτω: aor. ὑπέπεσον.ʃ

1. *to fall defeated*: ὑπὸ νεανίσκων 'by youths' Ju 16.6. Cf. πίπτω **2**.

2. *to cringe*: ἀπόκρισις ὑποπίπτουσα 'submissive reply' Pr 15.1.

3. *to come to the notice of*: + dat. pers., 1E 8.17; τὰ ὑποπίπτοντά μοι 'my impressions' Su 51[a] LXX.

ὑποπόδιον, ου. n.ʃ

footstool: God's, τῶν ποδῶν Is 66.1 (w. ref. to the earth), La 2.1 (w. ref. to Zion); Ps 98.5; to be trodden upon, τοὺς ἐχθρούς σου ὑ. τῶν ποδῶν σου 109.1.

ὑποπτεύω: aor. ὑπώπτευσα, subj. ~τεύσω.ʃ

to stand in fear of sth undesirable that might materialise: + acc. rei, τὸν ὀνειδισμόν μου Ps 118.39, φόβον θανάτου 'frightening death' Si 9.13. Cf. ὑφοράω and φοβέομαι.

ὕποπτος, η, ον.ʃ

fearful that sth undesirable might happen: + μήποτε + subj. 2M 3.32. **b**. *liable to arouse suspicion that sth might go wrong*: μηδὲν ~ον ἐχόντων 'they suspecting nothing' 2M 12.4.

Cf. ὑποπτεύω and ὑποψία.

ὑποπυρρίζω.ʃ

to be reddish: ***s*** leprous skin, ὑποπυρρίζον ἢ ἔκλευκον '.. or rather white' Le 13.24. Cf. πυρρίζω.

ὑπορράπτω: aor. ὑπέρραψα.ʃ

to patch by way of repair: + acc., οἶκον Si 50.1. Cf. ῥάπτω.

ὑπορρίπτω: aor. ὑπερρίπτοσα.ʃ

to hurl downwards: τινα 4M 6.25. Cf. ῥίπτω.

ὑποσκελίζω: fut.pass. ~σκελισθήσομαι; aor.inf. ~λίσαι, impv. ~λισον, pass. ὑπεσκελίσθην.

to trip up, causing to stumble and fall: ***o*** διάβημα 'step' Ps 139.5, pass. 36.31; hum. and + πίπτω Je 23.12. **b**. *to upset an evil design of*: + acc. pers., ***s*** God, Ps 16.13.

Cf. σκελίζω, ὑποσκέλισμα, πίπτω, σφάλλω, ὑποσχάζω.

ὑποσκέλισμα, ατος. n.ʃ *

act of stumbling: Pr 24.17 (ǁ πίπτω). Cf. ὑποσκελίζω and πτῶμα.

ὑπόστασις, εως. f.ʃ

1. *rebellion, resistance*: De 1.12.

2. *foundation* (of building): ἡ ὑ. ἀπεκαλύφθη 'the f. has been exposed' Na 2.8; Ez 43.11(?), 26.11, cf. θεμέλιον.

*3. *possessions, property*: τὴν ~ιν τὴν μετ' αὐτῶν De 11.6; Jb 22.20¶ (ǁ κατάλειμμα); ὑ. ζωῆς 'means of subsistence' Jd 6.4; Je 10.17.

4. *existence*: ἡ ὑ. μου ὡσεὶ οὐθὲν ἐνώπιόν σου 'my existence counts for almost nothing in your eyes' Ps 38.6; 88.48, 138.15; ἡ ὑ. μου παρὰ σοῦ ἐστιν 'my existence is derived from you' 38.8; "I am trapped in the slime of the depth, and οὐκ ἔστιν ὑ. 'I have no foothold'" 68.3; PSol 15.5, 17.24.

5. *support* rendered: divine, Wi 16.21, ἔστησαν ἐν ~ει μου 'they stood by me as their support' Je 23.22 (ǁ ὑπόστημα vs. 18).

6. *good chance* of sth happening: ἔστιν μοι ὑ. τοῦ γενηθῆναί με ἀνδρί '.. of me finding a husband' Ru 1.12, ἀπώλετο ἡ ὑ. αὐτῆς Ez 19.5.

*7. *mutually agreed tariff*: 1K 13.21, cf. LSG, s.v.

*8. *troops stationed at a military base*: 1K 13.23, cf. ὑπόστημα.

Cf. ὑφίστημι, ὑπόστημα, ὕπαρξις: Witt; Dörrie; Köster, *TDNT* 8.572-83; Perlitt, esp. 310f.; Spicq 3.421-23.

ὑποστέλλω: fut.mid. ὑποστελοῦμαι; aor.subj.mid. ~στείλωμαι.

1. *to hold back and refuse to grant* (sth τι): ἡ γῆ ὑποστελεῖται τὰ ἐκφόρια αὐτῆς 'the earth will withhold its produce' Hg 1.10 (ǁ ἀνέχω). Cf. στερέω, συνέχω **1**.

2. *to shrink before, flinch before, hold in undue awe*: + acc. pers., Ex 23.21; πρόσωπον ἀνθρώπου De 1.17, sim. Wi 6.7 (ǁ ἐντρέπομαι).

3. intr. *to draw back, stand back* in hesitation: Hb 2.4, Jb 13.8; + inf., 'to refrain from doing, dare not do' 2K 19.4*L* (B: διακλέπτομαι).

Cf. ἀνέχω.

ὑπόστεμα. ⇒ ὑπόστημα.

ὑπόστημα, ατος. n.ʃ Also spelled ὑπόστεμα.

1. = ὑπόστησις **1**: Je 23.18 (ǁ ὑπόστησις vs. 22).

2. *military camp*: 2K 23.14 (ǁ σύστημα vs. 15), cf. παρεμβολή.

Cf. ὑπόστασις, ὑπόστησις.

ὑποστήριγμα, ατος. n.*

underprop of city wall: defence installation, Je 5.10, Da 11.7 TH; of part of a building, 3K 7.11.

ὑποστηρίζω.ʃ *

to provide support for: + acc. pers., τοὺς δικαίους Ps 36.17, τοὺς καταπίπτοντας 144.14. Cf. στηρίζω.

ὑποστρέφω: fut. ~στρέψω; aor.act. ὑπέστρεψα.

intr. *to return to the point of origin*: πρὸς αὐτὸν εἰς τὴν κιβωτόν Ge 8.9; 43.10; Jd 3.19B (A: ἀνα~).

Cf. ἀνα~, ἐπιστρέφω.

ὑποστρώννυμι: fut. ~στρώσω, mid. ~στρώσομαι; aor. ὑπέστρωσα, subj. ~στρώσω, mid. ~στρώσωμαι.

to spread under on the ground or floor: + acc. and dat., ταῦτα λέγοντι πῦρ ὑπέστρωσαν 'they spread fire under him while he was saying these things' 4M 9.19; fig., μὴ ὑποστρώσῃς ἀνθρώπῳ μωρῷ σεαυτόν 'do not fall flat on your face before a fool' Si 4.27 (obsequious gesture); mid. and + acc. rei, σάκκον καὶ σποδόν 'sackcloth and ashes' Is 58.5. Cf. στρώννυμι.

ὑποσχαζω: fut. ~σχάσω.ʃ *

to trip up: + acc., πτέρναν σου 'your heel' Si 12.17. Cf. (ὑπο)σκελίζω.

ὑπόσχεσις, εως. f.ʃ

that which has been promised: Wi 12.21, 4M 15.2. Cf. ὑπέχομαι, ὑπισχνέομαι.

ὑποτάσσω: fut. ~τάξω, pass. ~ταγήσομαι; aor. ὑπέταξα, impv.2pl ~τάξατε, ptc. ~τάξας, pass. ὑπετάγην, impv. ~τάγηθι; pf.ptc.pass. ~τεταγμένος.

1. act. *to place*: + acc. ὑποτάξατε τὰς καρδίας ὑμῶν 'Set your minds (to the matter)' Hg 2.18, cf. 1.5, 7. **b**. *to place below* in a document: ***o*** ἐπιστολή Es 3.14 *L*. **c**. *to place* under the authority and rule of, 'subordinate, subjugate': + acc. pers., πάντα ὑπέταξας ὑποκάτω τῶν ποδῶν αὐτοῦ 'under his feet' Ps 8.7, λαοὺς ὑπ' ἐμέ 17.48; τὰς καρδίας ὑμῶν Hg 2.18; ὑπὸ πέτασον '(making .. wear) a petasus hat' 2M 4.12; + dat. pers., ὑπέταξεν λαοὺς ἡμῖν Ps 46.4; οἱ ὑποτεταγμένοι 'the (ruled) subjects' 3K 10.15, Es B 2 o'.

2. mid. *to submit oneself to*: + dat., τῷ θεῷ ὑποταγήσεται ἡ ψυχή μου Ps 61.2; 2M 9.12; πᾶσαι ἐξουσίαι ὑποταγήσονται αὐτῷ Da 7.27 LXX (TH δουλεύω); ἐναντίον κυρίου καὶ ἐναντίον λαοῦ αὐτοῦ 1C 22.18. Cf. χράω **II 4**. **b**. *to give in to the other party's terms*: abs., 2M 13.23.

Cf. (προυπο)τάσσω, (ὑπο)τίθημι, δαμάζω: Spicq 3.424-6.

ὑποτίθημι: fut. ὑποθήσω; 1aor.act. ὑπέθηκα, 2aor. impv., ὑπόθες, mid. ὑπεθέμην, ptc. ὑποθέμενος.

1. *to lower and place* in a certain position, 'put down': + acc., τὸν λίθον, ὃν ὑπέθηκεν ἐκεῖ πρὸς κεφαλῆς Ge 28.18 (|| τίθημι vs. 11); ὑπόθες τὴν χεῖρά σου ὑπὸ τὸν μηρόν μου 'Put your hand under my thigh' 47.29; τὸν ὦμον αὐτοῦ εἰς τὸ πονεῖν 'his shoulder to labour' 49.15; Si 6.25; τὸν τράχηλον ὑμῶν ὑπόθετε ὑπὸ ζυγόν '.. your neck under the yoke' 51.26.

2. *to place* under: + acc., ὑπ' αὐτόν 'under him' Ex 17.12 (λίθον 'a stone' understood); ὑπέθηκεν ἑαυτῷ τὸ ξίφος 'fell upon his own sword' 2M 14.41.

3. *to risk one's life against*: τὴν ψυχήν understood and + dat., αὐτῷ [= elephant] 1M 6.46.

4. mid. *to advise* or *suggest* a course of action: + dat. pers., ὑπέθεντο τῷ βασιλεῖ πρὸς τὸ μὴ κατακαῦσαι .. 'advised the king not to burn ..' Je 43.25, Πτολεμαίου ὑποθεμένου 'at P.'s suggestion' 2M 6.8.

Cf. τίθημι, ὑποτάσσω.

ὑποτίτθιος, ον.ʃ

subst. *child at the breast*: Ho 14.1. Cf. τέκνον, τιθηνός, βρέφος, and ὑπομαστίδιος.

ὑπουργός, όν.ʃ

rendering service: subst.m., Joshua in relation to Moses, Jo 1.1, cf. *BA* 6.25f. Cf. δοῦλος, διάκονος, θεράπων, λειτουργός, παῖς, ὑπηρέτης: Schmidt 4.147f.

ὑποφαίνω.ʃ

to begin to appear: ***s*** new day, 2M 10.35, 13.17. Cf. διαφώσκω.

ὑπόφαυσις, εως. f.ʃ

that which allows a glimpse: slit in a wall, Ez 41.16.

ὑποφέρω: fut.act. ὑποίσω; aor.act. ὑπήνεγκα, inf. ὑπενεγκεῖν, ptc. ὑπενέγκας.

1. *to endure, put up with*: abs., Ps 54.13; + acc. rei, οὐ μὴ δύνηται ἡ γῆ ὑπενεγκεῖν πάντας τοὺς λόγους αὐτοῦ 'the land cannot bear all of what he says' Am 7.10; ὀργὴν κυρίου ὑποίσω 'I shall endure God's anger' Mi 7.9, ὀνειδισμόν 'humiliation' Ps 68.8 (|| ἐντροπή); κακοπάθειαν 'hard work' 2M 2.27, ἀλγηδόνας 'pains' 6.30 (|| πάσχω), πόνον 7.36, ὀδύνας καὶ ἀτιμίας 'pains and humiliations' Pr 6.33, πολλά 14.17, τὰ κακά 'hardships' Jb 2.10; ἰσχὺν ῥημάτων 4.2; + acc. pers., Si 22.15, Pr 18.14; + ἀπό τινος (rei), either partitive ἀπό **3b** or a Heb. calque, Jb 31.23.

2. *to experience and suffer*: + acc., δόλον Jb 15.35, ἀπείλην 'threat' 3M 5.33.

Cf. ἀναντλέω, ἀνέχω, φέρω: Schmidt 1.424-41.

ὑπόφρικος, ον.ʃ*

shuddering a little: ***s*** hum. body, 3M 6.20. Cf. φρίττω.

ὑποχείριος, ον.

under the control of, subordinate to (+ dat.): παρέδωκεν τοὺς ἐχθρούς σου ~ους σοι Ge 14.20; Ἐάν μοι παραδῷς τὸν λαὸν τοῦτον ~ον Nu 21.2; gen. for dat., παρέδωκεν τὸν Χανανὶν ~ον αὐτοῦ ib. 3, sim. Jo 6.2; ἔλαβον τὴν πόλιν ~ον 'got the city under control' 2M 12.28.

ὑποχόνδριος, ον.ʃ

pertaining to abdomen: subst.n., 'abdomen' 1K 31.3. Cf. γαστήρ, κοιλία.

ὑπόχρεως, ων.ʃ

being in debt: Is 50.1; 1K 22.2 (|| ἐν ἀνάγκῃ). Cf. χρέος.

ὑποχυτήρ, ῆρος. m.ʃ*

vessel from which to pour oil into a lamp: Je 52.19.

ὑποχωρέω: aor.inf.~χωρῆσαι.ʃ
 1. *to retreat*: military operation, Jd 20.37B.
 2. *to be reserved in disposition* or *action*: Si 13.9. Del. 2M 12.12 v.l.

ὑποψία, ας. f.ʃ
 fear and apprehension that sth untoward might happen: 2M 4.34. Cf. ὑποπτεύω.

ὑπτιάζω.ʃ
 to bend back: + acc., χεῖρας πρὸς αὐτόν Jb 11.13.

ὕπτιος, α, ον. n.ʃ
 lying on the back of: subst.n.pl., ~α τοῦ χώματος 'the top-soil of the dike' Jb 14.19¶.

ὑπώπιον, ου. n.ʃ
 a blow in the face, 'black eye': + συντρίμματα 'fractures', ‖ πληγή 'blows'Pr 20.30.

ὗς, ὁς, acc. ὗν. m./f.
 pig: forbidden food, Le 11.7, De 14.8. Cf. ὕειος, σῦς.

ὕσσωπος, ου. m. < Heb. אֵזוֹב. On the gender, see Wevers 1986.119.
 hyssop, Origanum hirtum (LSJ): δεσμὴ ~ου 'bundle of ..' Ex 12.22; cultic offering, Le 14.4 +; detergent, ῥαντιεῖς με ~ῳ 'thou shalt wash me with ..' Ps 50.9.

ὑστερέω: fut. ὑστερήσω; aor. ὑστέρησα, subj. ὑστερήσω, impv.3s ὑστερησάτω.
 1. *to be behind schedule*: in arriving, Hb 2.3 (of the end-time, and ‖ χρονίζω); + gen. rei (task to be executed), διατάξεως 2K 20.5*L* (B: χρονίζω). **b**. *to postpone, defer*: *+ inf., ποιῆσαι τὸ πάσχα 'to celebrate the Passover' Nu 9.13; 9.7. Cf. βραδύνω, ὑπερβάλλω **2**, ὑπερτίθημι, and χρονίζω.
 2. *not to be had, to be unavailable, wanting*: + dat. pers., οὐχ ὑστέρησεν αὐτοῖς οὐδέν 'they lacked nothing' Ne 9.21; + acc. pers., οὐδέν με ὑστερήσει Ps 22.1, cf. ἕν σε ὑστερεῖ Mk 10.21. **b**. *to be absent*: + ἀπό – μὴ ὑστέρει ἀπὸ κλαιόντων 'do not absent yourself from a mourners' gathering' Si 7.34, οὐχ ὑστερήσει ἀπὸ δικαίων κρίμα 'the righteous shall not be deprived of justice' Jb 36.17.
 3. *to lack, not have*: abs., ἐὰν ὑστερήσῃς 'should you be in need' Si 13.4, πολεμιστὴς ὑστερῶν δι' ἔνδειαν 'warrior in need due to poverty' 26.28, εὑρέθη ὑστεροῦσα 'it was found deficient' Da TH 5.27; τί ὑστερῶ ἐγώ Ps 38.5, + ἐν – τί ἔτι ὑστερεῖτε ἐν τούτοις; 'why do you still lack these?' (?) Si 51.24, cf. ὥστε μὴ ὑμᾶς ὑστερεῖσθαι ἐν μηδενὶ χαρίσματι 1Cor 1.7; + ἀπό - ὑστερῶν τῇ ψυχῇ αὐτοῦ ἀπὸ πάντων, ὧν ἐπιθυμήσει Ec 6.2; + dat., ἰσχύι Si 11.12 (:: περισσεύω). **b**. mid.: Si 11.11.
 Cf. καθυστερέω, ὑστέρημα, λείπω, περισσεύω, ἀπορέω, ἐνδέω II, σπανίζω: Spicq 3.427-31; Wilckens, *TDNT* 8.594f.; Helbing, *Kasus*. 173-6.

ὑστέρημα, ατος. n.*
 that which is wanting: Ps 33.10, οὐκ ἔστιν ἐκεῖ ὑ. παντὸς ῥήματος 'nothing is lacking there' Jd 18.10, πᾶν (τὸ) ὑ. σου 'all that you lack' 19.19. Cf. ὑστερέω.

ὑστεροβουλία, ας. f. * ʃ
 deliberation after the fact: Pr 31.3.

ὕστερον.
 I. prep. + gen., *after* in time, *in the wake of, following*: ὕ. αἰχμαλωσίας μου '.. my captivity' Je 38.19; + τοῦ inf., ὕ. τοῦ γνῶναί με 'following my realisation' ib.; *+ ptc. phrase, ὕ. ἐξελθόντος Ιεχονίου .. ἐξ Ιερουσαλημ 'after J. had left .. J.' 36.2.
 II. adv., *thereafter, afterwards*: Si 1.23, 27.23, 2M 5.20, 6.15, 3M 1.3; ἐν χρόνῳ ὕστερον 'at a later stage' 2.24; μετὰ μικρὸν ὕστερον 'a little later' 4M 12.7.
 Cf. ὕστερος, μετά.

ὕστερος, α, ον, superl. ὕστατος, η, ον.ʃ
 relatively *late* in sequence, *latter*: ὁ πρῶτος .. οὗτος ὁ ὕστερος .. Je 27.17; ἐξ ~ου *'eventually, in the end' Ep Je 71; *ἐφ' ὑστέρῳ 'later, afterwards' Wi 19.11. **b**. subst. n., *that which eventuates at the end*: PSol 2.28. **c**. superl. 'the last': ὑστάτην βίου ῥοπὴν αὐτοῖς 'the last moment of their life' 3M 5.49.
 Cf. ἔσχατος, ὕστερον, and πρότερος.

ὑφαίνω: aor. ὕφανα, subj. ὑφάνω, inf. ὑφᾶναι; pf.ptc. pass. ὑφασμένος.
 to form into fabric or sth similar by interlacing: + acc. rei, locks of hair, Jd 16.13. **b**. *to produce* sth *by weaving*: + acc., τῷ κοκκίνῳ καὶ τῇ βύσσῳ 'with scarlet and fine linen' Ex 35.35, 37.21; ἱμάτιον ἐκ δύο ὑφασμένον 'a garment woven from two (sorts) of stuff' Le 19.19; ἱστὸν ἀράχνης ὑφαίνουσιν 'they weave a spider's web' Is 59.5.
 Cf. ὑφάντης, ὑφαντός, ὕφασμα, δι~, καθ~, συγκαθ~, συνυφαίνω.

ὑφαιρέω: aor. ὑφεῖλον, mid. ὑφειλάμην.
 to take away: + acc. and ἀπό τινος Ec 2.10; κονιορτός, ὃν ὑφείλατο λαῖλαψ Jb 21.18. **b**. *to pilfer, steal*: + acc. rei, Ep Je 9. Cf. αἴρω and ὑφαιρέω.

ὑφάντης, ου. m.
 weaver: ἐργασία ~ου 'weaver's workmanship' Ex 26.1 (‖ ἔργον ὑφαντόν vs. 31, 37.3, 5); ἔργον ~ου 28.28. Cf. ὑφαίνω.

ὑφαντός, ή, όν.
 woven: ἔργον ~όν 'woven work' Ex 26.31; τὰ ~ὰ καὶ τὰ ποικιλτά 'the woven and embroidered (things)' 35.35; ‖ ῥαφιδευτός 'stitched' (needle-works) and ποικιλτός 'embroidered' 37.21. Cf. ὑφαίνω.

ὑφάπτω: aor. ὑφῆψα.ʃ
 to set on fire: + acc. pers., 2M 8.33; + acc. rei, harbour 12.9, gates, 14.41. Cf. ἀνάπτω, καίω.

ὕφασμα, ατος. n.

woven work: ἐπωμίδων 'of shoulder-pieces' Ex 28.8; κατάλιθον 'set with precious stones' 28.17, 36.17; ἔδωκεν γυναιξὶν ~ατος σοφίαν 'gave women the skill of ..' Jb 38.36. Cf. ὑφαίνω.

ὑφίστημι: fut.mid. ὑποστήσομαι; 2aor. ὑπέστην, subj. ὑποστῶ, inf. ~στῆναι, impv. ~στηθι.

1. *to withstand, stand the ground, resist*, often in military context: + acc. pers. (enemy), 1M 5.40, 7.25; *o* τὸ κράτος τῶν ἵππων ἡμῶν 'the strength of our horses' Ju 6.3, τὴν ἵππον καὶ δύναμιν τοιαύτην 'such a powerful cavalry and troops' 1M 10.73; τὸ βάρος αὐτῶν 'their weight' Ju 7.4; ἀπειλήν 'threat' Pr 13.8. **b**. with various prepositions: ἀπὸ προσώπου ὀργῆς αὐτοῦ τίς ὑποστήσεται; 'who could withstand his anger?' Na 1.6, κατὰ πρόσωπόν τινος [= enemy] Jo 7.12 (ǁ ἀνθίστημι vs. 13), 1M 3.53, κατὰ πρόσωπον ψύχους αὐτοῦ 'against his chill' Ps 147.6, ἐναντίον καύματος αὐτοῦ 'against his heat' Si 43.3. **c**. abs.: τίς ὑποστήσεται; Ps 129.3, εἰ ὑποστήσεται ἡ καρδία σου; 'could your heart stand it?' Ez 22.14; μηδὲ ὑποστῇ ἐν υἱοῖς ἀνθρώπων 'nor will anybody resist' Mi 5.7; Am 2.15; ἐν συντριβῇ τέκνων Ho 13.13 (or: *to bear up, endure* [suffering]); ἐν ταλαιπωρίαις 'in distressful situations' Ps 139.11; ἐν τῇ ὀπτασίᾳ αὐτοῦ 'on his appearance' Ma 3.2; προσώπῳ '(defies every criticism so as to save) his face (?)' Pr 21.29; ὑφίστατο "would not move away, bearing acute pain" 2K 2.23 (*L* ἐφ~). **d**. mid.: τινα Pr 27.4.

2. *to take up a position*, facing the enemy: Nu 22.26; ἐν τῇ σκιᾷ μου Jd 9.15B (A: πεποίθατε). **b**. so as to assume and execute duties: ἐν τόποις δυναστῶν 'in offices of men of authority' Pr 25.6.

3. tr. *to erect under*: ὑποστήσομαι τῷ οἴκῳ μου ἀνάστημα Zc 9.8 (s.v. ἀνάστημα).

Cf. ἵστημι, ὑπόστασις, ἀνυπόστατος.

ὑφοράω.ʃ

mid. *to secretly suspect*: + acc. rei, 2M 7.24 (v.l. ὑπεροράομαι 'take no notice of,' cf. Kamphausen ad loc.); + inf., 3M 3.23. Cf. ὑποπτεύω.

ὑψαυχενέω.ʃ

to carry the neck high arrogantly: 2M 15.6; + dat. pers. (kings), 3M 3.19.

ὑψηλοκάρδιος, ον.ʃ *

arrogant: Pr 16.5. Cf. ὑψηλός, ὑπερήφανος, ὑβρίστης.

ὑψηλός, ή, όν.

1. *high, elevated* physically: *s* ὄρη 'mountains' Ge 7.19, βουνός 'hill' Je 29.17; as suited for public pronouncement, Ho 5.8 (ǁ βουνός); ǁ μετεωρός Is 30.25; γῆ 'region' Ge 22.2; τείχη 'walls' De 3.5, 28.52; πύργος 'tower' Is 2.15; τὰς γωνίας τὰς ~άς Zp 1.16, ξύλον Ez 17.24 (:: ταπεινός); of divine strength, ἐν χειρὶ κραταιᾷ .. καὶ ἐν βραχίονι ~ῷ 'with a mighty hand .. and an uplifted arm' Ex 6.1; ἐν χειρὶ ~ῇ 'enjoying military superiority, having the upper hand' Nu 33.3, ἔτι ἡ χεὶρ ~ή Is 9.12, cf. Ex 17.11; οἱ ὀφθαλμοὶ κυρίου ~οί Is 2.11 (fig. of self-confidence and preeminence; opp. ταπεινός); subst. τὰ ~ά 'high grounds' Hb 3.19 (cf. πόλεις ~άς Ju 2.24), 'elevated cultic sites' τῆς Βααλ Je 19.5; ὁ θεὸς ὁ κατοικῶν ἐν ~οῖς Is 33.5, cf. ὁ ~ός as divine title, Ps 17.14; sg., τῷ Χαμως 3K 11.5; with no cultic significance, ἐφ' ~οῦ 'on a high place' PSol 11.2, ἀφ' ~οῦ 'from high on' Is 32.15. **b**. *tall*: *s* hum., 1K 9.2. ***c**. *loud*: *s* κήρυγμα 'announcement' Pr 9.3, cf. s.v. ὑψόω **1f**.

2. *puffed-up, arrogant*: *s* pers., ὑβριστὴν καὶ ὑπερήφανον καὶ .. ~ὸν καὶ μετέωρον Is 2.12; ἐπορεύθησαν ~ῷ τραχήλῳ 'walked with their necks bent back' 3.16, ὀφθαλμοί Pr 30.13; ἐφ' ὕβρει καὶ ὑψηλῇ καρδίᾳ 'in haughtiness ..' Is 9.9, ὑ. τῇ ὕβρει 10.33; subst., οἱ ~οὶ ταπεινωθήσονται 10.33; μὴ λαλεῖτε ~ά 1K 2.3 (ǁ καυχάομαι). Cf. ὑπερήφανος.

3. metaph. *worthy of high esteem*: subst. m., ὑ. ἐν οὐρανῷ (= God?) La 3.41; 'the foremost leaders,' οἱ ~οὶ τῆς γῆς Is 24.4; n.pl., ~ὰ ἐποίησεν 12.5.

Cf. ὕψος, ὑψόω, ὕψιστος, μετεωρός, ὑψηλοκάρδιος.

ὕψιστος, η, ον.

highest in rank, superlative of ὑψηλός: *s* God, ἱερεὺς τοῦ θεοῦ τοῦ ~ου Ge 14.18; κύριος ὕ. Is 57.15; subst., *s* God, Nu 24.16 (ǁ θεός), De 32.8, υἱοὶ ~ου Ps 81.6, see BDAG, s.v., **2**, and *ND* 1.25-9; voc., ~ε Ps 9.3; subst. n.pl., *higher region* Jb 16.19, Si 43.9 (ǁ οὐρανός), Wi 9.17, cf. Lk 2.14 (:: γῆ). Cf. ὑψηλός: Kraabel 87-93: Bertram, *TDNT* 8.617f.

ὕψος, ους. n.

1. *vertical measure*, 'height': of boat, Ge 6.15 (ǁ μῆκος 'length' and πλάτος 'width'); καθὼς ὕ. κέδρου ('cedar') τὸ ὕ. αὐτοῦ Am 2.9. **b**. *relatively great height*: Ez 31.7.

2. *elevated part*: τὸ ὕ. τῆς γῆς Si 46.9, τὰ ὕψη .. Am 4.13, Mi 1.3 (of heavenly sphere); ὕ. ὀρέων 'mountain-top' Ps 94.4, Is 37.24; ὕ. τῆς κέδρου 'of a cedar' ib.; ὕ. μέρους τοῦ δρυμοῦ 'the highest region of the forest' ib., τὸ ὕ. τοῦ οὐρανοῦ 38.14; ὕ. ἰσχύος 'mighty (fortress situated) high up' Je 28.53; εἰς ὕ. (= ἐν ὕψει) Am 5.7 (:: εἰς γῆν); τάξαι εἰς ὕ. νοσσιάν 'to build a nest high up' Hb 2.9; εἰς βάθος ἢ εἰς ὕ. Is 7.11; = οὐρανός an abode of God, εἰς ὕψος .. εἰς τὸν ἅγιον τοῦ Ισραηλ 4K 19.22, cf. Ps 72.8, 1C 15.16, Si 43.1. **b**. fig., ἐν τῷ ~ει τῶν ἡμερῶν μου 'in the prime of my life' Is 38.10; ἐν ~οις μεγάλοις 'in important, high offices' Ec 10.6.

3. *haughtiness*: τῶν ἀνθρώπων Is 2.11; τὸ ὕ. τῆς δόξης τῶν ὀφθαλμῶν αὐτοῦ 'the arrogant look arising from his glory' 10.12; τῆς καρδίας αὐτοῦ 2C 32.26.

4. *exalted status*: of God, Is 35.2 (ǁ δόξα); ηὐξήθη εἰς ὕ. 'grew in standing' 1C 14.2, ἐμεγάλυνεν αὐτὸν εἰς ὕ. 2C 1.1; Ju 13.20, Ez 31.2; ὕ. φαντασίας 'prominent appearance' Hb 3.10.

Cf. ὑψηλός, ὕψιστος, ὑψόω, ὕψωμα, ὕψωσις, πανυπέρτατος, εὖρος, κορυφή, μῆκος, πλάτος: Bertram, *TDNT* 8.603.

ὑψόω: fut. ὑψώσω, pass. ὑψωθήσομαι; aor. ὕψωσα, inf. ὑψῶσαι, subj. ὑψώσω, impv. ὕψωσον, pass. ὑψώθην, ptc. ὑψωθείς, impv. ὑψώθητι, subj. ὑψωθῶ, inf. ὑψωθῆναι.

1. tr. *to move to a higher position*: + acc. and *s* rock-dwellers, κατοικίαν 'to live in an elevated location' Ob 3, cf. Nu 32.35, and νοσσιάν 'nest' Je 29.17 (ǁ μετεωρίζω Ob 4); pass. and of the raising of a hand to attack, ὑψωθήσεται ἡ χείρ σου ἐπί τινα Mi 5.9, τὴν δεξιὰν τῶν ἐχθρῶν Ps 88.43, τὸ πρόσωπόν μου πρὸς σέ 2E 9.6; *o* πρίων 'saw' Is 10.15; heaven, εἰς τὸ μετέωρον Je 38.35 (:: ταπεινόω), κέρας 'horn' La 2.17, κέρας χριστοῦ αὐτοῦ '.. of his anointed one' 1K 2.10. **b**. *to build and erect* some high structure: + acc., ὕψος μέγα 'massive wall' 1M 12.36. **c**. pass., physically *to raise oneself, get up*: ὁ λέγων .. τῷ λίθῳ ὑψώθητι Hb 2.19 (ǁ ἐξεγέρθητι), Ps 7.7 (also ǁ ἀνάστηθι); *s* ship (κιβωτός) being pushed up by rising flood-water and getting off the ground, ὑψώθη ἀπὸ τῆς γῆς Ge 7.17; flood-water, 7.20, 24; waves of the sea, Ps 106.25; rivers, Es A 8 *L*; ὑψώθη ἡ κραυγὴ αὐτῶν ἐναντίον κυρίου 'the uproar against them ..' Ge 19.13; ὑπεράνω τῶν βουνῶν 'above the hills' Is 2.2; pass. = mid. *to grow tall*: *s* a plant, cypress ἐν νεφέλαις 'up into the clouds' Si 50.10; Jb 8.11, eagle soaring into the sky, 39.27; 'to rouse oneself into action' (?) Is 30.18. **d**. metaph.: + acc. pers. (in estimation): τοῦ ὑψῶσαι καὶ δοξάσαι Is 4.2; κατενώπιόν τινος Jo 3.7 (ǁ αὐξάνω 4.14); ὑψώθη Ge 24.35, 26.13 (as a result of divine blessing and consisting in increased possessions or abundant harvest); ἢ Γωγ 'than G.' Nu 24.7 (ǁ αὐξάνω); Ho 11.7; opp. ταπεινόω Ps 74.8; *o* God, Ex 15.2 (ǁ δοξάζω), Is 2.11 (:: ταπεινόω), 5.16 (ǁ δοξάζω), + εὐλογέω To 12.6 𝔊[I]; vain comfort, Is 28.29 (sarcasm?); ὑψωθήτω ἡ ἰσχύς σου Nu 14.17; κέρας 'horn' Ps 74.5 (ǁ ἐπαίρω εἰς ὕψος vs. 6), 11, τὴν κεφαλήν τινος 3.4 (ǁ δόξα); sbd else's head = 'to restore sbd to a favourable situation' 4K 25.27; τὸ ὄνομα αὐτοῦ Is 12.4; γάμους '(grandiose) wedding celebrations' Es 2.18 o'; ἀτιμίαν '(reach) the height of ignominy' Pr 3.35. **e**. of arrogance: ἡ γλῶσσα αὐτῶν ὑψώθη Mi 6.12 (cf. Th 226: ὑπερηφάνῳ κεχρημένοι διανοίᾳ); cf. also ὑψωθῇ ἡ καρδία αὐτοῦ De 17.20, ἐν ὑπερηφανίᾳ Da 4.19 LXX, + ἐπαίρω 1M 1.3, but at 2C 17.6 (ἐν ὁδῷ κυρίου) in a favourable sense; *s* pers., ὑψωθῇς τῇ καρδίᾳ De 8.14; Is 3.16 (:: ταπεινόω vs. 17), οὐ μὴ ὑψωθῇ ἐπὶ τὰ ἔθνη 'over against ..' Ez 29.15, ἐπὶ τὸν κύριον Da 5.23 TH; ἐφ' ἵππῳ 'about horses' Ju 9.7 (ǁ γαυριάω). **f**. + φωνήν Ge 39.15, Ju 16.11 (of raised tone and + βοάω), ὕψωσον τῇ ἰσχύι τὴν φωνήν σου Is 40.9, cf. ἀνυψοῖ φωνὴν αὐτοῦ Si 21.20; πρός τινα Is 37.23; φωνήν understood, 2E 10.1; ᾠδήν 3.12. ***g**. a calque on Heb. /hērim/ 'to offer (to God)': 2E 8.25.

***2**. *to help grow physically and socially*, 'bring up (a child), raise': υἱοὺς ἐγέννησα καὶ ὕψωσα Is 1.2, παρθένους 23.4 (ǁ ἐκτρέφω); ἡμέρας ἡμῶν ἐκ μήτρας '(accompany) our growth from the time when we were in our mother's womb' Si 50.22.

***3**. *to lift = to remove* (?), cf. ἀναβαίνω **4**: + acc., ματαίαν παράκλησιν 'baseless enouragement' Is 28.29, but cf. above, **1c**.

Cf. ὕψος, ὕψιστος, ὑψηλός, ἀν~, ἐξ~, προσ~, ὑπερυψόω, μετεωρίζω, δοξάζω, ταπεινόω, and ὕβρις: Bertram, *TDNT* 8.606f.

ὕψωμα, ατος. n.ʃ

exalted status: brings about elation, ὕ. Ιερουσαλημ Ju 10.8, 15.9 (ǁ γαυρίαμα, καύχημα), 13.4; hurts others, Jb 24.24. Cf. ὕψος: Bertram, *TDNT* 8.613.

ὕψωσις, εως. f.ʃ *

that which characterises exalted status: pl., αἱ ~εις τοῦ θεοῦ Ps 149.6. Cf. ὕψος.

ὕω.ʃ

to cause to descend in small shapes and large numbers: *s* God and + acc., χάλαζαν 'hail' Ex 9.18 (ǁ βρέχω vs. 23); ὕω ὑμῖν ἄρτους ἐκ τοῦ οὐρανοῦ 16.4. Cf. ὑετίζω, βρέχω and ὑετός.

Φ

φαιδρός, ά, όν.ʃ

beaming with joy: *s* hum., + θαρραλέος 'undaunted' 4M 13.13. Cf. εὐφραίνω.

φαίνω: fut. act. φανῶ, mid. φανοῦμαι, pass. φανήσομαι; 1aor.act. ἔφανα, subj. φάνω, 2aor.pass. ἐφάνην, subj. φανῶ, impv.3s φανήτω, inf. φανῆναι, ptc. φανείς, opt. 3pl φανεῖεν.

I. act. *to shine*: *s* heavenly bodies, ἐπὶ τῆς γῆς Ge 1.15; lamp, Ex 25.37; Da 13.3 LXX (TH ἐκλάμπω).

***2**. *to cause to shine*: σελήνη οὐ μὴ φάνῃ τὸ φῶς αὐτῆς· [8]πάντα τὰ φαίνοντα φῶς ἐν τῷ οὐρανῷ συσκοτάσουσιν 'the moon shall not give her light. [8]all that emits light in the sky shall darken' Ez 32.7f. Or poss.: *to cause to appear*, as in ἔφην' ἄφαντον φῶς 'I made the hidden flash appear' Soph. *Ph*. 297. Cf. ἐπιφαύσκω. **b**. obj. understood: ἔφαναν αἱ ἀστραπαὶ αὐτοῦ τῇ οἰκουμένῃ 'his lightnings gave light to the world' Ps 96.4.

II. mid./pass. *to come into view*, 'appear': Ge 30.37, To 6.18 𝔊[II]; ἐν τούτῳ φανεῖσθε 'this way your colours will show' Ge 42.15; theophany, Nu 23.3, 4; *s* ἔχθρα 'enmity' 1M 11.12; + dat. pers. ἐφάνη ὁ θεὸς τῷ Βαλααμ Nu 23.4; ἐπὶ σὲ φανήσεται κύριος Is 60.2.

2. *to be adjudged as*: σκληρὸν ἐφάνη τὸ ῥῆμα σφόδρα ἐναντίον Αβρααμ 'what was said sounded to A. rather harsh' Ge 21.11; πονηρὸν ἐφάνη ἐναντίον τοῦ θεοῦ 'it appeared to God wrong' 38.10, ἐνώπιον κυρίου 2K 11.27*L* (B: ἐν ὀφθαλμοῖς κυρίου); + dat. pers., πᾶσι Si 26.26¶; ἑαυτῷ δίκαιος Pr 21.2; + ptc., φαινέσθω ὑπακούουσα 'let it be seen paying heed' Es 1.18 *L*; 3M 2.30; visually perceived, 2M 3.25, 4M 4.23; impers., πονηρὸν ἐφάνη ἐναντίον τοῦ θεοῦ περὶ τοῦ πράγματος 1C 21.7. **b**. *to appear sound and right*: ὃ ἂν φανῇ σοι δοῦναι 'which you think ought to be given' 2E 7.20; impers., ἐὰν φαίνηταί σοι 'with your approval' 1E 2.18, see MM s.v. **c**. *to be seen to be, to prove oneself to be*: σύμμαχον 'ally' 2M 12.36.

Cf. φῶς, ἀνα~, δια~, ἐπι~, κατα~, προφαίνω, φάσμα, φαῦσις, ὁράω, ὀπτασία, ἀφανής, αὐγάω, λάμπω, στίλβω, δοκέω, ἔοικα: Schmidt 1.321-4; Trench 304-8; Renehan 1.196.

φαιός, ή, όν.

grey in colour: *s* πρόβατον Ge 30.32. Cf. πολιός: Schmidt 3.28f.

φακός, οῦ. m.

1. *lentil*: ἕψεμα ~οῦ 'boiled lentil' Ge 25.34; food, Ez 4.9.

2. *container looking like lentil*: for oil, 1K 10.1, for water 26.11.

φάλαγξ, γγος. f.

phalanx: 1M 6.35 +.

φαλακρός, ά, όν.

lacking hair, 'bald': *s* hum., Le 13.40; head, Ez 29.18 (result of physical exhaustion and ‖ μαδάω). Cf. μαδάω, φαλάκρωμα.

φαλάκρωμα, ατος. n.*(φαλακρόομαι: Anacreon [6th c.] +)

loss of bodily hair: of the head and ‖ ἀναφαλάντωμα 'forehead-baldness,' Le 13.42; ἐπὶ κεφαλὴν φ. Am 8.10; symbol of humiliation, Is 3.24, 15.2, Ez 7.18; a sign of mourning, ἀνὰ μέσον τῶν ὀφθαλμῶν ὑμῶν ἐπὶ νεκρῷ De 14.1. Cf. θρίξ, φαλακρός, ἀναφαλάντωμα.

φανερός, ά, όν.

1. *clarified and comprehensible*: ἕως τοῦ ~ὰ γενέσθαι τὰ ῥήματα ὑμῶν, εἰ ἀληθεύετε ἢ οὔ 'until your statement has been clarified as to whether you are telling the truth or not' Ge 42.16; + dat. pers., τὰ ~ὰ ἡμῖν De 29.29 (:: κρυπτός), τοῖς ἔθνεσι πᾶσι ~ὸν ἔσται ὅτι .. Ep Je 50, opp. κεκρυμμένος 2M 12.41.

2. *clearly recognisable and identifiable as such*: *s* hum., Is 8.16; wisdom, Si 6.22; πρᾶγμα 'affair' 2M 1.33; hum. hearts, παρὰ τῷ κυρίῳ Pr 15.11.

Cf. φανερόω, φανερῶς, ἐπίδηλος, σαφής, ἀμαυρός, κρυπτός.

φανερόω: fut. φανερώσω; aor.inf. φανερῶσαι, pass. ἐφανερώθην.ʃ

to reveal: + dat. pers., Je 40.6, pass. Si 1.7¶ (‖ ἀποκαλύπτομαι vs. 6). **b**. *to make public*: + acc., μετάνοιαν 'repentance' Si 20.8¶. Cf. φανερός, ἀποκαλύπτω, ὁράω.

φανερῶς. adv.ʃ

in a clearly comprehensible fashion: φ. τὴν τοῦ θεοῦ δυναστείαν ἐπεγνωκότες 'having clearly recognised God's sovereignty' 2M 3.28. Cf. φανερός, σαφῶς.

φαντάζομαι.ʃ

1. *to picture in one's mind*, 'fantasise': *s* hum. heart, Si 31.5.

2. *to become visible, make appearance*: + dat. pers., Wi 6.16.

Cf. ὁράω, φαίνω.

φαντασία, ας. f.ʃ

1. *what one pictures in one's mind*, 'imagination': of idols as objects of worship, φ. ψευδής 'deceptive imagination' Hb 2.18.

2. *product of imagination*: *s* idols, Hb 2.19 (‖ ἔλασμα χρυσίου καὶ ἀργυρίου).

3. *what visibly manifests itself*, 'image': of some unusual natural phenomenon, Hb 3.10; κύριος ἐποίησε ~ας Zc 10.1; ~αι ὀνείρων 'in dreams' Wi 18.17.

Cf. φάντασμα, φάσμα: Shipp 552.

φαντασιοσκοπέω.ʃ*

to look at suspiciously: ἐν τοῖς οἰκέταις σου 'your domestic servants' Si 4.30.

φάντασμα, ατος. n.ʃ

what manifests itself in imagination: τέρασιν ἠλαύνοντο ~άτων 'were driven by monstrous apparitions' Wi 17.15. Cf. φαντασία.

φάραγξ, αγγος. f.

chasm, cleft: in the ground, called θεμέλια τῆς γῆς 'the foundations of the earth' Mi 6.2; valley at the base of adjoining mountains– ἐπὶ τὴν φάραγγα τὴν ἁλυκήν 'on to the salt valley' Ge 14.3, φ. ἀνὰ μέσον τῶν πετρῶν Is 57.5; Zc 14.5 (see under ἐμφράσσω); ‖ τρώγλη, σπήλαιον, ῥαγάς Is 7.19 (for insects); + ὄρη, βουνοί, νάπαι Ez 6.3; + χειμάρρους Ju 2.8. Cf. κοιλάς, νάπη, χάος, and χειμάρρους.

φαρέτρα, ας.

quiver: τήν τε ~αν καὶ τὸ τόξον 'the quiver and the bow' Ge 27.3; ἡτοίμασαν βέλη εἰς ~αν 'prepared arrows for ..' Ps 10.3; πληροῦτε τὰς ~ας 'fill the quivers' Je 28.11; ἐπιστήσατε ~ας 'set up ..' 28.12; ~ας ἐκρέμασαν ἐπὶ τῶν ὅρμων 'hung .. on the battlements' Ez 27.11; for securing arrows, Is 49.2; ἀνοίξας ~αν Jb 30.11; υἱοὺς ~ας 'sons of q.', i.e. arrows La 3.13. **b**. euphemism for female private parts: ἔναντι βέλους ἀνοίξει ~αν 'open (her) quiver for an arrow' Si 26.12.

Cf. βέλος, τόξευμα, τόξον.

φαρμακεία, ας. f.

magical potion: used by Egyptian ἐπαοιδός 'enchanter, charmer' Ex 7.11, cf. Is 47.9, 12; pagan practices, ἔργα φαρμακειῶν 'practices of sorcery' Wi 12.4. Cf. φάρμακον, φάρμακος, ἐπαοιδός.

φαρμακεύω: aor.ptc. φαρμακεύσας.ʃ

1. *to administer a poisonous drug to*: + acc. pers., ἑαυτόν 2M 10.13.

2*. *to prepare* a magical potion: pass. and + acc., φαρμάκου τε φαρμακευομένου παρὰ σοφοῦ 'a potion prepared by a wise man' Ps 57.6. **b. m. *to practise magic with potions*: 2C 33.6.

Cf. φάρμακον.

φάρμακον, ου. n.

1. *medicine*: ζωῆς 'with which to sustain life' Si 6.16; herbal, 38.4.

2. *enchanted potion*: administered by prostitute, πόρνη καλὴ .. ἡγουμένη ~ων 'a pretty harlot .. making masterly use of enchanted potions' Na 3.4.

3. *poison*: ὀλέθρου 'resulting in perdition' Wi 1.14.

Cf. φάρμακος: Schmidt 4.106-9.

φάρμακος, ου. c. On the position of the accent, see Walters 95f. *

sorcerer: + σοφιστής Ex 7.11; in a catalogue of practitioners of various pagan arts and skills, De 18.10; female, Ma 3.5 (‖ μοιχαλίς); illicit and + ψευδοπροφήτης, ἐνυπνιαζόμενος, μαντευόμενος, οἰώνισμα Je 34.7; + ἐπαοιδός, μάγος Da 2.2. Cf. φάρμακον.

φάρυγξ, γγος. m.

throat: held fast to cause suffocation, 1K 17.35; where a sense of taste resides, φ. γεύεται βρώματα θήρας 'the palate tastes foods of game' Si 36.24, metaph. Pr 8.7; where thirst is keenly felt,.Je 2.25, La 4.4. Cf. λάρυγξ.

φάσις, εως. f.ʃ

that which has been announced: orally by God, Su 55 TH; in writing, 2E 4.17 (see Hanhart 2003. 292, n. 2). Cf. φημί, ῥῆμα.

φάσκω. Used only as ptc.ʃ

to assert with conviction and defiantly: + inf., φάσκοντες αὐτῶν εἶναι τὸ φρέαρ 'claiming that the well is theirs' Ge 26.20; Δανιηλ ὁ φάσκων μὴ ἐσθίεσθαι αὐτὰ .. Da LXX Bel 9; 2M 14.27, 32, 3M 3.7. Cf. εἶπον, λέγω, φημί: Schmidt 1.88.

φάσμα, ατος. n.

unusual vision: ἐν ~ατι δείξει κύριος Nu 16.30; νυκτερινόν 'nocturnal' Jb 20.8 (‖ ἐνύπνιον). Cf. ὅραμα, φαντασία.

φάτνη, ης. f.

1. *manger*: for oxen, βόες ἐπὶ ~αις Hb 3.17; heifer, Jl 1.17; ass, Is 1.3; humans (!), Jb 39.9.

2. *stall*: for livestock, 2C 32.28 (‖ μάνδρα 'pen, fold').

Cf. ἔπαυλις, μάνδρα: Hengel, *TDNT* 9.51.

φατνόω: aor. ἐφάτνωσα; pf.ptc.pass. πεφατνωμένος.ʃ

to furnish with roof or *ceiling*: + acc., τὸν οἶκον 3K 7.40; pass., Ez 41.15. Cf. φάτνωμα, στεγάζω.

φάτνωμα, ατος. n.

1. *ceiling*: opp. ἔδαφος 'floor' Ez 41.20; 2M 1.16. Cf. στέγη, τέγος.

2. *coffer* in ceiling: τοῦ ναοῦ Am 8.3; habitation of chameleons and hedgehogs, Zp 2.14.

φαυλίζω: aor.act. ἐφαύλισα, ptc. φαυλίσας; pf.ptc. pass. πεφαυλισμένος.

to hold in contempt, treat with disdain: + acc., πρωτοτόκια 'birthrights as first-born' Ge 25.34; τὸ ῥῆμα κυρίου Nu 15.31 (‖ διασκεδάζω); τὸ ὄνομά μου [= τοῦ θεοῦ] Ma 1.6*a*; 1.6*b*; λαόν Is 33.19, τὴν ψυχὴν αὐτοῦ 49.7; ‖ μυκτηρίζω 37.22; ‖ ἄτιμος Jb 30.4; κρίμα 'court-case' 31.13. Cf. ἐκφαυλίζω, φαυλισμός, φαύλισμα, καταφρονέω, μυκτηρίζω, and ὑπερηφανία.

φαύλισμα, ατος. n.ʃ *

manifestation of contemptuous attitude: τὰ ~ατα τῆς ὕβρεώς σου 'disdainful expressions of your pride' Zp 3.11. Cf. φαυλίζω and φαυλισμός.

φαυλισμός, οῦ. m.ʃ*

v.n. of φαυλίζω, *contemptuous treatment*: Ho 7.16; verbally expressed, χειλέων 'of lips' Is 28.11; ‖ ὀνειδισμός 'humiliation' 51.7. Cf. φαυλίζω.

φαυλίστρια, ας. f.ʃ*

showing contempt: used as adj., ἡ πόλις ἡ φ. Zp 3.1. Cf. φαυλίζω.

φαῦλος, η, ον.

low in estimation: *s* ῥήματά μου Jb 6.3; hum., 9.23; w. ref. to social rank, γυνή Pr 5.3; morally, 13.6; *s* καρδία Es 3.7 *L*; ref. to educational background, Pr 16.21 (:: σοφὸς καὶ συνετός); γλῶσση Si 20.16; poor-quality seeds, Pr 22.8; subst.n., morally, opp. τὸ καλόν 3M 3.22. Cf. κακός, πονηρός, σοφός, συνετός, τίμιος, φαυλότης: Trench 317f.

φαυλότης, ητος.ʃ

morally low character: Wi 4.12. Cf. φαῦλος.

φαῦσις, εως. f.ʃ*

1. *act of lighting, illuminating*: performed by heavenly bodies, φ. τῆς γῆς (obj. gen.) Ge 1.14; glossed as ὥστε φαίνειν ἐπὶ τῆς γῆς 1.15; πῦρ εἰς ~ιν 'a fire for a light' Ju 13.13.

2. *source of light, luminary body*: σὺ κατηρτίσω ~ιν καὶ ἥλιον 'you made light and the sun' Ps 73.16.

Cf. φῶς, φαίνω.

φέγγος, ους. n.

brightness of light-emitting object: γνόφος οὐκ ἔχων φ. 'darkness which has no brightness' Am 5.20; φ. αὐτοῦ ὡς φῶς ἔσται Hb 3.4; of the sun, 2K 23.4, of stars, Jl 2.10; of lightning, Hb 3.11; of divine glory, Ez 10.4. **b**. *bright object*: Ez 43.2; πυρός φ. Ho 7.6.

Cf. φῶς, γνόφος and σκότος: Schmidt 1.563-98.

φείδομαι: fut. φείσομαι; aor. ἐφεισάμην, subj. φείσωμαι, inf. φείσασθαι, impv. φεῖσαι, ptc. φεισάμενος.

1. *to spare* sbd misfortune, destruction etc.: + gen., οὐκ ἐφείσω τοῦ υἱοῦ σου τοῦ ἀγαπητοῦ Ge 22.12; τοῦ λαοῦ σου Jl 2.17, sim. 2.18; *ἀπό τινος (victim), 1K 15.3 (*L* gen.); + inf. ἐφεισάμην ἐγώ σου τοῦ μὴ ἁμαρτεῖν σε εἰς ἐμέ 'I have spared you from sinning against me' Ge 20.6; ἀπὸ θανάτου Jb 33.18; abs., *s* πληγή 'a blow' Is 14.6.

2. *to show sympathies for, take pity on*: + gen. pers., Ge 19.16, Ex 2.6, χήρας 'widow' Wi 2.10 (‖ ἐντρέπομαι), ‖ ἀγαπάω Is 63.9; *s* ὁ ὀφθαλμός + *ἐπί τινι– De 7.16; 13.8 (‖ ἐπιποθέω), 19.13, 25.12, ἐπὶ τοῖς τέκνοις Is 13.18 (‖ ἐλεέω); + ἐπί τινα Ju 2.11; *ὑπέρ τινος– ὑπὲρ τῆς κολοκύνθης Jn 4.10, ὑπὲρ Νινευη 4.11; *ἐπί τινα, Zc 11.6, Je 28.3; *περί τινος, "he couldn't care less, hurting you or throwing you into a prison" Si 13.12; 16.8; + ἐπιποθέω, οἰκτιρέω Je 13.14. **b**. *to take a charitable view of*: ἐπὶ τοῖς ἀγνοήμασίν μου 'my errors of ignorance' Si 23.2.

3. *to feel too attached to part with*: + gen. rei, μὴ φείσησθε τοῖς ὀφθαλμοῖς τῶν σκευῶν ὑμῶν Ge 45.20, τῆς ψυχῆς σου Ju 13.20, cf. **1** above. **b**. *to make sparing use of*: *ἐπί τινι– ἐπὶ τοῖς τοξεύμασιν 'the arrows' Je 27.14. **c**. + neg., *to make liberal use of*: "they spat left and right in my face" Jb 30.10.

4. *to spare efforts*: ἀναβόησον ἐν ἰσχύι καὶ μὴ φείσῃ 'shout with all your might' Is 58.1; οὐδὲ φείσομαι τῷ στόματί μου 'Nor shall I restrain my mouth, I shall speak up' Jb 7.11; οὐκ ἐφείσαντο 'spared (no efforts)' Je 14.10. **b**. *to make sparing, restrained use of*: + gen., χειλέων 'lips' Pr 10.19 (:: πολυλογία), βακτηρίας 'rod (for disciplining)' 13.24, δώρων 'gifts' 21.14. **c**. + τοῦ inf., *to refrain*: from doing sth, τοῦ λαβεῖν ἐκ τοῦ ποιμνίου αὐτοῦ 2K 12.4 *L* (B: om. τοῦ); Pr 17.27, with no τοῦ Hb 1.17; ἐφείσατο ὁ ὀφθαλμός μου ἐπ' αὐτοὺς τοῦ ἐξαλείψαι αὐτούς Ez 20.17, cf. **2**; ἀπὸ θανάτου '(he did not shrink) from making an end (of their lives)' Ps 77.50, ἀπὸ καταλαλιᾶς Wi 1.11.

Cf. ἐλεέω, φειδώ, ἀφειδῶς, φειδωλός, προδίδωμι **1**.

φειδώ, οῦς. f.ʃ

1. *sparing from harsh treatment*: ἄνευ παντὸς οἴκτου καὶ φειδοῦς 'without any pity or sparing' Es B 6 o'; μετὰ πολλῆς ~οῦς Wi 12.18.

2. *disinclination to part with* sth valuable: ἐν ~οῖ 'grudgingly' PSol 5.13 (‖ γογγυσμός).

Cf. φείδομαι, οἶκτος, ἔλεος.

φειδωλός, ή, όν.ʃ

miserly: *s* hum., 4M 2.9. Cf. φείδω.

φερνή, ῆς. f.ʃ

bride-price, 'dowry': Ge 34.12, Ex 22.16, Jo 16.10, 2M 1.14; τῶν παρθένων Ex 22.17. Cf. φερνίζω: Shipp 552f., and *ND* 6.1-18.

φερνίζω: fut. φερνιῶ.ʃ

to take a woman as wife by *paying her price*: + dat. cogn., φερνῇ φερνιεῖ αὐτὴν αὐτῷ γυναῖκα Ex 22.16. Cf. φερνή.

φέρω: fut. οἴσω; aor. ἤνεγκα, subj. ἐνέγκω, impv. ἔνεγκε, ἔνεγκον, ἐνέγκατε, inf. ἐνέγκαι, ptc. ἐνέγκας, ἐνεγκών, opt.3pl ἐνέγκαισαν, pass. ἠνέχθην, ptc. ἐνεχθείς; pf. ἐνήνοχα. Cf. Shipp 553f.

1. *to cause to move* to a certain place: + acc. rei, ***o*** water (for washing feet), Ge 43.24; cultic offerings, ἠνέγκατε .. θυσίας ὑμῶν Am 4.4; αἴνεσιν 'praise' Je 17.26; + dat. pers. θυσίαν τῷ κυρίῳ Ge 4.3; τῆς πλημμελείας Le 5.15 (|| προσάγω 19.22); τῷ κυρίῳ δόξαν καὶ τιμήν Ps 28.1; τὰς εὐλογίας μου, ἃς ἤνεγκά σοι Ge 33.11; φόβον ἐπὶ σέ Je 30.5; σῖτος 'corn', Ge 43.2 (ἐξ Αἰγύπτου); + πρός τινα, Ex 32.2. **b**. *to transport*: ἔλαβεν ὧν ἔφερεν δῶρα 'he picked up gifts out of what he was transporting' Ge 32.13; ὡς φερόμενος χνοῦς ὑπὸ ἀνέμου 'like dust carried by wind' Wi 5.14, πνεύματι Jb 17.1; leaf of a plant, φωνὴ φύλλου φερομένου 'sound of a leaf borne along (by the wind)' Le 26.36. **c**. pass. with intr. force: καταιγὶς φερομένη 'a moving whirlwind' Is 28.15, 18 || κ. φέρουσα 17.13; ὕδωρ 32.2, ποταμός ib.; *s* hum., τάχει 'fast' Da 9.21 LXX (TH πέτομαι 'to fly'), attacking horse 2M 3.25, streaming blood 14.45. **d**. intr. *to transport oneself enthusiastically*: 2K 18.27 *L* (B: ἔρχομαι).

2. *to have about oneself for ready use*, 'carry': οἴσει Ααρων τὰς κρίσεις τῶν υἱῶν Ισραηλ ἐπὶ τοῦ στήθους Ex 28.26, cf. δορατοφόρος, θυρεοφόρος, ὁπλοφόρος, but with αἴρω in verbal phrases as in δύναμις ὁπλοφόρων αἰρόντων θυρεοὺς καὶ δόρατα 2C 14.7. **b**. as permanent quality: || ἔχω 2M 4.25.

3. *to produce, bear* (fruit, τι): τὰ ξύλα τῆς ἐλαίας τὰ οὐ φέροντα καρπόν 'the olive-trees which do not bear fruit' Hg 2.19; Ho 9.16, Jl 2.22, Ma 1.13; φέρετε (*L* Δότε) ἑαυτοῖς βουλήν 'Make your minds up' 2K 16.20. Cf. ποιέω **I 5**.

4. *to sustain materially*: *s* land, οὐκ ἐδύνατο ἡ γῆ .. φέρειν αὐτούς Ge 36.7. **b**. *to provide sufficient space to accommodate*: + acc., 2C 2.5.

5. *to endure, bear*: physically, ἀλγηδόνας 'pains' 4M 6.7; mentally, σκληρὸς φέρεσθαι Ge 49.3; μαλακίαν 'infirmity' Is 53.3, ὀνειδισμὸν ἐθνῶν 'insult by nations' Ez 34.29, ὀνειδισμοὺς λαῶν 36.15, ὑπερηφανίαν '(not having been able to contain) arrogance (within himself any longer) Es E 12; abs., Je 20.9 (?), 51.21, 2M 7.20.

6. *to maintain a certain attitude in reaction to*: Μὴ βαρέως φέρε, κύριε 'No offence, sir' Ge 31.35; πικρῶς ἐπὶ τῷ μυκτηρισμῷ 'bitterly at the scorn' 2M 7.39; + acc., πικρῶς .. τὴν παρρησίαν 'bitter at the boldness' 4M 10.5.

7. *to bear the responsibility for*: as leader and + τινα, De 1.9, Nu 11.14, 17; to take care of difficulties and + τι– τὸν κόπον ὑμῶν καὶ τὴν ὑπόστασιν ὑμῶν καὶ τὰς ἀντιλογίας ὑμῶν 'your hardship, rebelliousness, and quarrels' De 1.12; τὰς ἁμαρτίας ἡμῶν Is 53.4.

8. *to cause to apply*: + acc. rei, τοὺς λόγους μου ἐπὶ τὴν πόλιν ταύτην εἰς κακὰ Je 46.16.

9. *to acquire and bring*: + acc., Ba 3.30.

10. intr. *to be favourably disposed* towards a certain course of action: ἔφερεν αὐτῶν ἡ καρδία Ex 35.21 (|| ἔδοξεν τῇ ψυχῇ [vs. 26 διανοίᾳ] αὐτῶν); ἔφερεν ἡ διάνοια αὐτῶν .. ποιεῖν πάντα τὰ ἔργα .. 35.29. Cf. LSJ s.v. **A III 2**.

11. *to be en route* in a certain direction: ἐπὶ λίβα 'to the south' Jo 15.2, πρὸς νότον 'leading to the south' Ez 40.44.

12. mid. *to conduct oneself* in a certain manner: ὕβρει 'arrogantly' Jb 22.12; σκληρὸς φέρεσθαι 'hard to get on with' Ge 49.3.

Cf. ἄγω, αἴρω, ἀνα~, ἀπο~, δια~, εἰσ~, ἐκ~, ἐπι~, κατα~, μετα~, παρα~, περι~, προ~, προσ~, ὑποφέρω, φορέω, φορεύς, ἀφορία, ἀφόρητος, καρποφορέω, πνευματοφόρος, πυρφόρος, βαστάζω, (παρα)κομίζω: Trench 212f.; Schmidt 1.424-41, 3.167-73, 175-80; Shipp 32-8, 553f.

φεύγω: fut. φεύξομαι; aor. ἔφυγον, subj. φύγω, inf. φυγεῖν, ptc. φυγών, impv.3pl φυγέτωσαν; pf. πέφευγα, ptc. πεφευγώς.

to flee some danger, *run away* from undesirable situation: abs., Ge 14.10, 39.13, Am 9.1, Ob 14 (|| ἀνασῴζω in both); Na 2.6, 9; ἀπὸ ^ὄφεως^ 'snake' Ex 4.3, ἀπὸ πολέμου Le 26.36, ἀπὸ τῆς φωνῆς αὐτῶν Nu 16.34, ἀπὸ γῆς βορρᾶ 'from the land of the north' Zc 2.6, ἀπὸ ἁμαρτίας To 4.21 𝔊II (𝔊I ἀφίστημι), Si 21.2; ἀπὸ προσώπου τινός Ex 14.25, De 28.7, ἀπὸ τοῦ προσώπου σου ποῦ φύγω; Ps 138.7; ἐκ προσώπου τινός, a lion, Am 5.19; God Jn 1.10; ἔμπροσθέν τινος 2K 24.13B; *to* (εἰς) a place, Jn 1.3, 4.2, εἰς τὸν τόπον σου Is 24.11; πόρρω 'afar' 22.3; + acc., τὸν φόβον 24.18; + dat. cogn., Je 26.5. **b**. Fig., 'fleeting' (as against 'permanent') Am 6.5. **c**. *to avoid*: + acc., ἁμάρτημα Si 20.8¶, κενοδοξίαν 'vainglory' 4M 8.19; δόλον 'deceit' Wi 1.5.

Cf. ἀναχωρέω, φυγή, φυγάς, ἀπο~, δια~, ἐκ~, κατα~, συμφεύγω, φυγαδεύω, φυγαδεῖον, φυγαδευτήριον, φυγαδεία, φευκτός, ἀπο~, διαδιδράσκω, αὐτομολέω, τροπόω.

φευκτός, ή, όν.ʃ

avoidable: *s* ἀήρ 'air' Wi 17.10. Cf. φεύγω **c**.

φήμη, ης. f.

that which is talked about openly, 'report, rumour': ἀγαθή Pr 15.30; δυσμενής 'malicious' 3M 3.2; 2M 4.39. Cf. ἀκοή.

φημί: highly literary pres.mid.ptc. φάμενος (Jb 24.25), pres.3s φησίν; impf./aor.3s ἔφη, ἔφησεν, pl. ἔφασαν.

With a few exceptions, confined to the 3s φησί(ν) and ἔφη, rare, literary or poetic synonyms of εἶπεν or λέγει, and mostly to mark direct speech.

to say: ἡ δὲ ἔφη Ge 24.47 (|| καὶ εἶπεν αὐτῷ vs. 24); Φησὶν Βαλααμ υἱὸς Βεωρ Nu 24.3. **b**. contents of utterance in the form of an inf. clause:

ἐξελεύσεσθαι γὰρ ἔφη .. 'she said she was going out ..' Ju 13.4; ὁ φάμενος ψευδῆ με λέγειν 'one who says that I talk lies' Jb 24.25. **c.** ἔφη οὕτως 1E 3.16. **d.** φησὶ κύριος inserted in the middle of divine message: Je 31.12, 35, 38, 36.23, 37.3, 17, 38.27, 28 +, cf. Κἀγώ, φησι, δυνάστης .. ὁ προστάσσων αἴρειν .. 'I, he said, am a sovereign, being the one who commands you to take up ..' 2M 15.5; at the conclusion of such, Je 37.21, 38.20 +. ***e.** φ. ἐν ἑαυτῷ *to resolve* to do sth: + inf., φησὶν .. ἁμαρτάνειν ἐν ἑαυτῷ Ps 35.2; Wi 15.12, cf. εἶπον **1 d.**

Cf. λέγω, εἶπον, φάσκω.

φθάνω: aor. ἔφθασα, subj. φθάσω, ptc. φθάσας, impv. mid. φθάσαι; pf. ἔφθακα.

1. *to outstrip*: + acc. pers., ἔφθασας Ez 16.52 (*pace* Zgl ἔφθειρας), so also Cornill ad loc. and cf. Sym. ὑπερέβαλες. **b.** *to be the first to arrive*: Si 30.25. **c.** *to surprise* by sth happening *with speed*: + acc. pers., Wi 6.13; no acc., 3K 12.18.

2. *to act ahead of time and too early*: + inf., Wi 4.7.

***3.** *to arrive*: *s* a month of the year, 2E 3.1; καιρὸς τῆς τομῆς 'the pruning season' Ct 2.12; + dat., 'to arrive eagerly and obtain (?)' To 5.19; ἔτη Ec 12.1 (|| ἔρχομαι). **b.** *to reach*: ἕως τοῦ οὐρανοῦ 'as high as the sky' Da 4.8 TH (LXX ἐγγίζω), εἰς τὸν οὐρανόν 4.17 TH, εἰς τὸ ἔδαφος τοῦ λάκκου 'the bottom of the pit' 6.24 TH; ἐκ τῆς τρίβου '(he was cleared) from the way' 2K 20.13, prob. a mechanical translation of הגיע < MT הֹוגָה.

4. *to befall*: πρός τινα Ec 8.14, ἐπί τινα Da 4.21, 25 TH, *s* κακία 'calamity' Jd 20.34 B (A: ἀφάπτομαι). Cf. συμβαίνω **2**.

Cf. κατα~, προφθάνω, ἔρχομαι, ἀφικνέομαι: Fitzer, *TDNT* 9.88f.; Shipp 555.

φθάρμα, ατος. n.ʃ *

corrupt feature: bodily defects of animals unfit for offering, Le 22.25 (|| μῶμος). Cf. φθείρω.

φθαρτός, ή, όν.ʃ

1. *damaged*: *s* σκεῦος 'work-tool' Is 54.17.

2. *perishable*: *s* human being, 2M 7.16; human body, Wi 9.15; subst. n., idol for worship, 14.8.

Cf. εὔφθαρτος.

φθέγγομαι: fut. φθέγξομαι; aor. ἐφθεγξάμην, opt.3s φθέγξαιτο, impv.2pl φθέγξασθε, 3pl φθεγξάσθωσαν.

1. *to utter sounds*: abs. and *s* κύριος ἐξ Σιων ἐφθέγξατο Am 1.2 (|| φωνὴν δίδωμι); + λαλέω Ps 93.4, opp. σιγάω 'to remain silent' Wi 8.12; doves, Na 2.8. **b.** *to make an oracular pronouncement*: Je 9.17.

2. *to give vocal expression to*: + acc., κάνθαρος ἐκ ξύλου φθέγξεται αὐτά 'a dung beetle (?) will tell them out of timber' Hb 2.11 (|| βοάω), δόλον 'deceit' Jb 13.7 (|| λαλέω), ἄδικα Wi 1.8, σύνεσιν Si 13.22, ἀπόκρισιν 5.11, φωνήν Jd 5.11A (B: διηγέομαι); *s* tongue, ἡ γλῶσσά μου τὸ λόγιόν σου Ps 118.172 (|| ἐξερεύγομαι).

Cf. ἀποφθέγγομαι, βοάω, λαλέω, κράζω, λέγω, φωνέω, φθέγμα. φθόγγος: Schmidt 1.54, 92-5.

φθέγμα, ατος. n.ʃ

that which is uttered: ῥήματος 'of word(s)' Jb 6.26; Wi 1.11. Cf. φθέγγομαι, λόγος, ῥῆμα.

φθειρίζω: fut. φθειριῶ.ʃ

to pick the lice off: + acc., ποιμὴν τὸ ἱμάτιον αὐτοῦ 'a shepherd .. his garment' Je 50.12.

φθείρω: fut. φθερῶ, pass. φθαρήσομαι; aor. ἔφθειρα, inf.act. φθεῖραι, pass. ἐφθάρην, subj. φθαρῶ.

1. *to damage physically, disfigure* (+ acc.): ***o*** τὴν ὄψιν τοῦ πώγωνος 'the look of the beard' Le 19.27 (regarded as pagan practice), hum., Da 8.24 LXX (TH δια~); through a military operation, τὴν χώραν 'the country' 1C 20.1. **b.** pass. *to be physically ruined and devastated*: *s* the earth (γῆ) Ex 10.15 (by a swarm of locusts), + cogn. dat., Is 24.3; ἡ οἰκουμένη 24.4, βασιλεία Da 2.44 LXX. **c.** *to fail to function*: *s* eye, De 34.7 (in old age and || ἀμαυρόω).

2. *to disable*: + acc., ὕβριν 'pride, arrogance' Je 13.10.

3. *to morally corrupt*: + acc., τὰς ἀδελφάς σου Ez 16.52; through sexual seduction, ***o*** woman, 4M 18.8. **b.** pass. *to become morally corrupt*: *s* hum., ἐναντίον τοῦ θεοῦ and manifested by ἀδικία Ge 6.11 (|| καταφθείρω vs. 12); Ho 9.9.

Cf. φθορά, φθάρμα, δια~, καταφθείρω, ἀφθαρσία, ἄφθορος, ἀφανίζω: Schmidt 4.83f., 86-91; Harder, *TDNT* 9.98-100.

φθίνω.ʃ

to wane: *s* σελήνη 'moon' Jb 31.26 (|| ἐκλείπω).

φθόγγος, ου. m.ʃ

1. *clear, distinct sound* with a message: || ῥήματα Ps 18.5.

2. pl., *notes* on a musical instrument: Wi 19.18.

Cf. φθέγγομαι, φωνή.

φθονερός, ά, όν.ʃ

unduly possessive of and unwilling to part with: ἐπ' ἄρτῳ Si 14.10 (|| ἐλλιπής). Cf. φθόνος, φθονέω.

φθονέω: aor.impv.3s φθονεσάτω.ʃ

to be unwilling to act generously: *s* the eye of a benefactor, To 4.7, 16 𝔊[I]. Cf. φθόνος.

φθόνος, ου. m.ʃ

malevolent envy: 3M 6.7, Wi 6.23; + ζῆλος 1M 8.16; διαβόλου 'of the devil' Wi 2.24. Cf. (δια)-φθονέω, ἄφθονος, ζῆλος: Trench 86-90; Spicq 3.435f.

φθορά, ᾶς. f.
1. *ruin*: ζωῆς μου Jn 2.7.
2. *physical and mental exhaustion*: cogn. dat. of καταφθείρω, Ex 18.18.
3. *moral decay*:; cogn. dat. διεφθάρητε ~ᾷ 'you have been utterly ruined' Mi 2.10.
Cf. καταφθορά, (δια)φθείρω.

φθορεύς, έως. m.ʃ
corrupter, seducer: ***o*** women, 4M 18.8 (‖ λυμεών). Cf. φθείρω, λυμεών.

φιάλη, ης. f.
bowl: for pouring libations, Ex 27.3; πλήσουσιν ὡς ~ας θυσιαστήριον 'they will fill the altar as bowls' Zc 9.15; ἀργυρᾶ 'silver' Nu 7.13; for wine, + ποτήριον Pr 23.31. Cf. κρατήρ.

φιλάγαθος, ον.ʃ
loving the good: ***s*** spirit of Wisdom, Wi 7.22. Cf. μισοπόνηρος and ἀγαθός: Spicq 3.437-9.

φιλαδελφία, ας. f.
love of one's brother(s): 4M 13.23. Cf. φιλάδελφός.

φιλάδελφος, ον.
loving one's brothers: ***s*** hum., 2M 15.14, + φιλομήτωρ 15.10; ψυχή 4M 13.21. Cf. *ND* 1.118, 3.87. Cf. φιλαδελφία, ἀδελφός.

φιλαμαρτήμων, ον, gen. ονος.ʃ *
fond of sins: ***s*** hum., Pr 17.19. Cf. ἁμαρτία.

φιλανθρωπέω: aor. ἐφιλανθρώπησα.ʃ
to treat generously: by way of donations, + acc. (the temple), 2M 13.23. Cf. φιλανθρωπία.

φιλανθρωπία, ας. f.
kindliness: displayed by a ruler to his subject(s), Es E 11, 2M 6.22, 3M 3.15. Cf. εὐεργεσία: Bell; Le Déaut; Spicq 3.440-5.

φιλάνθρωπος, ον.
1. *humane*: τὰ ~α κρίνας 'having made the humane decision' 1E 8.10.
2. *friendly towards humans*: ***s*** God's spirit of wisdom, Wi 1.6, ***s*** spirit of Wisdom, 7.23.
3. subst.n.pl. *privileges, concessions*: βασιλικά 'royal' 2M 4.11.
Cf. φιλανθρώπως.

φιλανθρώπως. adv.ʃ
in humane manner: + ἐπιεικῶς 'in fairness' 2M 9.27; ἀπαντάω 'to treat' 3M 3.20. Cf. φιλάνθρωπος.

φιλαργυρέω: aor.ptc. ~ρήσας.ʃ
to show oneself to be fond of money: 2M 10.20. Cf. φιλαργυρία, φιλάργυρος: Spicq 1.245f.

φιλαργυρία, ας.ʃ
fondness of money: 4M 1.26. Cf. φιλαργυρέω: Spicq 3.446f. Del. 4M 2.15 v.l.

φιλάργυρος, ον.ʃ
fond of money: ***s*** hum., Si 10.8¶, 4M 2.8. Cf. φιλαργυρέω.

φιλαρχία, ας. f.ʃ
lust for power: 4M 2.15. Cf. ἀρχή.

φιλελεήμων, ον.ʃ *
compassionate: ***s*** hum., To 14.9 𝔊[I]. Cf. ἐλεήμων.

φιλεχθρέω: aor.subj. ~ρήσω.ʃ *
to exercise enmity: πρός τινα Pr 3.30. Cf. ἔχθρα.

φιλέω: aor. ἐφίλησα, impv. φίλησον, inf. φιλῆσαι.
1. *to find agreeable, feel attracted to*: + acc. rei, πέμματα 'cakes' Ho 3.1 (‖ ***o*** pers., ἀγαπάω), ἀγαπᾷ εὐφροσύνην .. φιλῶν οἶνον καὶ ἔλαιον Pr 21.17; ***o*** wisdom personified, ^τὴν σοφίαν^ ἐφίλησα .. ἐραστὴς ἐγενόμην τοῦ κάλλους αὐτῆς .. καὶ ὁ πάντων δεσπότης ἠγάπησεν αὐτήν 'I loved her .. became a lover of her beauty .. the lord of all loved her' Wi 8.2f., cf. ὑπὸ τῶν ἀγαπώντων ^σοφίαν^ 6.12, ἀγάπησις σοφίας Si 40.20, ἐγὼ [= ἡ σοφία] τοὺς ἐμὲ φιλοῦντας ἀγαπῶ Pr 8.17 (‖ ζητέω; and ἀγαπάω vs. 21); ποίησόν μοι ἐδέσματα ὡς φιλῶ ἐγώ 'make me food to my taste' Ge 27.4; + inf., κύνες .. φιλοῦντες νυστάξαι 'dogs .. fond of slumber' Is 56.10, see s.v. ἀγαπάω **3**. **b**. + acc. pers., αὐτὸν ὁ πατὴρ φιλεῖ ἐκ πάντων τῶν υἱῶν αὐτοῦ Ge 37.4 (‖ ἠγάπα vs. 3); To 6.19 𝔊[I] (‖ 𝔊[II] ἀγαπάω); subst. ptc., 'lover' Je 22.22 (‖ ἐραστής vs. 20); verbal ptc., La 1.2 (‖ ἀγαπῶν); pass. Es 10.3; ***s*** δαιμόνιον, ***o*** woman, To 6.15 𝔊[I]. **c**. opp. μισέω: καιρὸς τοῦ φιλῆσαι καιρὸς τοῦ μισῆσαι Ec 3.8. Not attested in the impv. in this sense.
2. *to kiss*: ***s*** son and ***o*** father, φίλησόν με, τέκνον Ge 27.26; 50.1; ***s*** son and ***o*** parents, To 5.17 𝔊[II] (goodbye kiss); a man to an unmarried woman on first encounter, Ge 29.11; an uncle to a nephew of his, 29.13; reconciled brothers, 33.4; ἐφίλησεν αὐτοὺς καὶ περιέλαβεν αὐτούς 'he kissed them and embraced them' 48.10 (an aged father and grandchildren); following an embrace – περιλαβὼν αὐτὸν ἐφίλησεν 29.13, 33.4; a gesture of courtesy, ἐφίλησεν αὐτόν, καὶ ἠσπάσαντο ἀλλήλους 'he kissed him [= father-in-law], and they greeted each other' Ex 18.7; + obj. rei, πέλματα ποδῶν αὐτοῦ 'the soles of his feet' Es C 6.
Cf. καταφιλέω, φίλος, φιλία, φιλιάζω, φίλημα, ἔραμαι, ἀγαπάω, στέργω, μισέω, προσφιλής: Schmidt 3.476-80; Trench 41-4; Shipp 126f.; Steinmueller 406-13; Paeslack; Joly 1968; Stählin, *TDNT* 9.113-28; Swinn 1990; Muraoka 2001a:16f.

φιληκοΐα, ας. f.ʃ
fondness for listening: 4M 15.21.

φίλημα, ατος. n.ʃ
kiss: στόματος αὐτοῦ Ct 1.2; Pr 27.6. Cf. φιλέω.

φιλία, ας. f.
intense attachment to and predilection towards sbd or sth: ***o*** pretty woman, φ. ὡς πῦρ ἀνακαίεται 'love flares up like fire' Si 9.8; with an adulteress, Pr 7.18 (‖ ἔρως); πρὸς γαμετήν 'for (one's) wife' 4M

2.11 (ǁ + gen., vs. 13), ἔλαφος ~ας 'deer ..' Pr 5.19. **b.** *friendship*: Si 6.17, διαλύσει ~αν 'will break up ..' 22.20, τῶν πλησίον 'among neighbours' 25.1; πρὸς θεὸν ἐστείλαντο ~αν 'won friendship ..' Wi 7.14; αὐτῆς 'with her [= wisdom]' 8.18 (ǁ ὁμιλία 'companionship' and κοινωνία 'association'); Pr 15.17 (:: ἔχθρα 'enmity'); + συμμαχία 'military alliance' 2M 4.11, 1M 8.17, + ἀδελφότης 'brotherhood' 12.10; opp. μῖσος Pr 10.12.

Cf. φιλέω, φίλτρον, μῖσος: Paeslack 74-82; Stählin, *TDNT* 9.155-9; Mitchell.

φιλιάζω: aor. ἐφιλίασα.ʃ*

to be a friend: abs. Si 37.1; + dat. pers. Jd 5.30A (B: οἰκτιρέω), φίλοις καὶ ἀδελφοῖς 1E 3.21; μισουμένῳ 2C 19.2; 20.37. Cf. φιλέω.

φιλογέωργος, ον.ʃ

fond of agriculture: *s* hum., 2C 26.10.

φιλογύναιος, ον.ʃ

fond of women: 3K 11.1.

φιλοδοξία, ας. f.ʃ

fondness of good reputation: + ὕβρις, ὑπερηφανία Es C 5 o'; + ἀλαζονεία, φιλαργυρία, φιλονεικία, βασκανία 4M 1.26. Cf. δόξα.

φιλόκοσμος, ον.ʃ

fond of cosmetic ornaments: *s* παρθένος Ep Je 8. Cf. κόσμος **3**.

φιλόλογος, ον.ʃ

fond of learning: subst.m., + σοφιστής Da LXX 1.20 (v.l. φιλόσοφος). Cf. Spicq 3.452f.

φιλομαθέω.ʃ

to be fond of learning: *s* Bible scholars, Si prol. 5, 34. Cf. φιλομαθής, μανθάνω: Wagner 130-3.

φιλομαθής, ές.ʃ

fond of learning: subst.m., Si prol. 13. Cf. φιλομαθέω.

φιλομήτωρ. ορος. m./f.ʃ

loving one's mother: + φιλάδελφος 4M 15.10.

φιλονεικέω.ʃ

to be fond of strife: Pr 10.12. Cf. φιλονεικία.

φιλονεικία, ας.

fondness of strife: rivalry, contentiousness in a catalogue of vices, 4M 1.26. Cf. φιλονεικέω, φιλόνεικος, νεῖκος.

φιλόνεικος, ον.ʃ

fond of strife: *s* hum., Ez 3.7. Cf. φιλονεικέω.

φιλοπολίτης, ου. m.ʃ *

one who is fond of one's compatriots: 2M 14.37. Cf. πολίτης.

φιλοπονέω: pf.ptc.pass. πεφιλοπονημένος.ʃ

to toil eagerly: κατά τι 'over' Si prol. 20. Cf. φιλοπονία, φιλόπονος, πονέω **3**.

φιλοπονία, ας. f.ʃ

eagerness to toil: + σπουδή 'zeal' Si prol. 31. Cf. φιλοπονέω: Wagner 133f.

φιλόπονος, ον.ʃ

diligent: *s* hum., Si prol. II.

φίλος, ου. m.ʃ

friend: fig. of a relationship between God and Moses, Ex 33.11; ~ους θεοῦ καὶ προφήτας Wi 7.27, see Paeslack 94-96, Larcher ad loc. and Winston ad loc.; ὁ φ. ὁ ἴσος τῆς ψυχῆς σου 'as valuable as your own life' De 13.6 (ǁ one's brother, children and wife); μὴ καταπιστεύετε ἐν ~οις 'Do not trust friends' Mi 7.5, οἱ φίλοι σου ἐπελάθοντό σου '.. have forgotten about you' Je 37.14; ǁ ὁ πλησίον, ἀδελφός 9.4, ὁ πλησίον Ps 37.12, also γνωστοί 87.19, + οἰκεῖος Pr 17.9, + γείτων 'kinsman' 3M 3.10; Δανιηλ καὶ τοὺς ~ους αὐτοῦ Da 2.13 TH (LXX οἱ μετ' αὐτοῦ), 2.17 (LXX συνεταῖροι); ~ον ἡγησάμενοι αὐτόν 'having considered him [= death] to be a friend' Wi 1.16; + πλησίον Ps 87.19; opp. ἐχθρός Si 6.1. **b.** in political network: φίλος βασιλέως 'king's close counsellor': Es 1.13 o' +, 1M 2.18 +, 2M 1.14, 3M 2.23 +, 4M 12.5; Da 3.91 LXX (TH μεγιστάν), 94 (TH δυνάστης); ἑπτὰ φίλοις συμβουλευταῖς 1E 8.11, σύμβουλος τοῦ βασιλέως .. πρῶτος φ. τοῦ βασιλέως 1C 27.33 (*L* ἀρχιέταιρος and ǁ ἑταῖρος Δαυιδ 2Sm 15.37 [*L* ἀρχιέ.]), ἑταῖρος καὶ φ. Si 37.2; ~οι καὶ σύμμαχοι καὶ ἀδελφοί, an honorary Roman title for the Jewish nation, 1M 14.40.

Cf. φιλέω, ἑταῖρος, συνήθης: Schmidt 3.464-8; Paeslack 82-96; Stählin, *TDNT* 9.146-55; Spicq 3.448-51.

φιλοσοφέω: fut. ~φήσω.

1. *to live and conduct oneself as philosopher*: 4M 5.7.

2. *to contemplate* over: + acc. rei, ἀλήθειαν 4M 5.11.

Cf. ἀντιφιλοσοφέω.

φιλοσοφία, ας. f.

philosophical exposition: 4M 1.1. **b.** *philosopher's way of life*: 4M 5.4 v.l., 7.21.

Cf. φιλόσοφος: Malingrey.

φιλόσοφος, ον.

concerned with philosophy: *s* λόγος 'subject-matter' 4M 1.1, 'reason' 5.25. Cf. φιλογοφία.

φιλοστοργία, ας. f.ʃ

1. *tender love and affection*: shown by mother for her children, πρὸς αὐτούς 4M 15.6, ἐν αὐτοῖς 15.9.

2. *intense desire*: πρὸς τὸ ζῆν 'to stay alive' 2M 6.20.

Cf. φιλόστοργος, στοργή: *ND* 2.101-3.

φιλόστοργος, ον.ʃ

characterised by tender love and affection: γένεσι 'towards offspring' 4M 15.13. Cf. φιλοστοργία, ~όργως: Spicq 3.462-5; *ND* 2.101-3, 3.41f.

φιλοστόργως. adv.ʃ

Adv. of prec.: 2M 9.21.

φιλοτεκνία, ας. f.*
affection for children: shown by mother, 4M 14.13. Cf. φιλότεκνος.

φιλότεκνος, ον.
having to do with φιλοτεκνία: *s* πάθη 'emotions' 4M 15.4. Cf. φιλοτεκνία: *ND* 3.42f.

φιλοτιμία, ας. f.ʃ
eagerness driven by pursuit of honour: Wi 14.18. Cf. φιλότιμος, φιλοτίμως. Del. Wi 18.3 v.l.

φιλότιμος, ον.ʃ
1. *indicative of* φιλοτιμία (q.v.): *s* προσεδρεία 'assiduity' 3M 4.15.
2. *conducive to great honour and estimation*: *s* living abroad, Wi 18.3.
Cf. φιλοτιμία, τιμή **3**.

φιλοτίμως. adv.ʃ
with intense desire, 'eagerly': Su 12 TH, 2M 2.21. Cf. φιλοτιμία.

φιλοφρονέω.ʃ
to be favourably and well disposed: εἰς τὸ .. ἀναλαβεῖν 'to take up' 2M 2.25.

φιλοφρόνως. adv.ʃ *
in friendly manner: reception of guests, 2M 3.9; 4M 8.5.

φιλόψυχος, ον.ʃ
soul-loving: *s* God, Wi 11.26.

φίλτρον, ου. n.
affection: ἀδελφότητος 'of brotherhood' 4M 13.19. Alw. pl. Cf. φιλία.

φιμός, οῦ. m.
1. *muzzle*: φ. ἐν στόματι Si 20.29.
2. *nose-band*: ἐμβαλῶ ~ὸν εἰς τὴν ῥῖνά σου καὶ χαλινὸν εἰς τὰ χείλη σου 'I shall place a nose-band on your nose and a bit in your lips' Is 37.29.
Cf. φιμόω.

φιμόω: fut. φιμώσω; aor. ἐφίμωσα.ʃ
to muzzle: + acc., βοῦν ἀλοῶντα 'a threshing ox' De 25.4; + acc. pers., so as disallow to speak, Da LXX Su 61. **b**. metaph., *to deny complete freedom of action*: pass., *o* movements of body, 4M 1.35.
Cf. φιμός, ἀνέχω **I b**, συνέχω, κωλύω.

φλεγμαίνω: aor.act. ἐφλέγμανα.ʃ
to become purulent: *s* πληγή 'wound' Is 1.6, Na 3.19.

φλεγμονή, ῆς. f.ʃ
heat: metaph., οἴστρων 'of frenzied desires' 4M 3.17.

φλέγω: fut. φλέξω.
I. tr. *to burn*: + acc. and *s* ἡμέρα κυρίου, Ma 4.1; *s* πῦρ – θεμέλια ὀρέων 'the foundations of mountains' De 32.22 (ǁ κατεσθίω).
II. intr. *to burn*: πῦρ φλέγον 'a burning fire' Ex 24.17, πῦρ καιόμενον φλέγον Je 20.9; Da 7.9 (ǁ φλὸξ πυρός), Ps 103.4; ὑπὲρ τὴν πυρὸς δύναμιν 'more powerfully than fire' Wi 16.19.
Cf. καίω, δια~, ἐκ~, καταφλέγω, φλογίζω, and φλόξ.

φλέψ, βός. f.ʃ
spring or stream of water: ἀναξηρανεῖ τὰς ~ας 'will dry up the springs' Ho 13.15 (ǁ πηγή). Cf. κρήνη, πηγή and φρέαρ.

φλιά, ᾶς. f. Cf. Shipp 556.
1. *lintel* (?): + σταθμός 'doorpost' Ex 12.7; τῶν οἰκιῶν and + πύλη De.6.9 (to inscribe on it).
2. *doorpost*: part of the temple along with πρόθυρον 'porch' Ez 43.8; where the blood of sacrificial animals is placed, τοῦ οἴκου .. τῆς πύλης τῆς αὐλῆς 45.19; 1K 1.9. Alw. pl. in this sense even where the MT has a sg. form.

φλογίζω: fut. φλογιῶ; aor. ἐφλόγισα, pass. ἐφλογίσθην.ʃ
I. tr., *to set on fire*: + acc. land and rivers, πόλεμος κυρίου ἐφλόγισεν τὴν Ζωοβ καὶ τοὺς χειμάρρους Αρνων Nu 21.14; *o* hum., πῦρ φλογιεῖ κύκλῳ τοὺς ἐχθροὺς αὐτοῦ Ps 96.3; 1M 3.5.
2. metaph. *to awaken intense desires of* sbd *to act*: τινα - παρανόμους PSol 12.3, cf. Kittel ad loc.
***II**. intr., *to burn*: τὸ πῦρ φλογίζον ἐν τῇ χαλάζῃ 'the fire was burning in the hail' Ex 9.24, cf. φλέγον Wi 16.22; mid. πῦρ φλογιζόμενον Si 3.30; *s* hair, Da TH 3.94 (LXX ὑποκαίω).
Cf. φλόξ, φλέγω, καίω, κατα~, συμφλογίζω, πῦρ.

φλόγινος, η, ον.ʃ
in flames, fiery: φ. ῥομφαία protecting the access to the tree of life, Ge 3.24. Cf. φλόξ.

φλοιός, οῦ. m.ʃ
bark of trees: Wi 13.11.

φλόξ, γός. f.
flame: Ge 15.17; of oven, Ho 7.4; ἄστρων 'of stars' Wi 10.17, 17.5. **b**. of conflagration as destructive force, ǁ πῦρ, Nu 21.28, Jl 1.19, Ob 18, ἀναπτομένη 'kindled' Jl 2.3; ὡς φωνὴ ~γὸς πυρὸς κατεσθιούσης καλάμην 'like the sound of a fire consuming stubble' 2.5; ἐν πυρὶ ~γός 'in the fire in the form of a flame' Ex 3.2. **b**. *gleaming object*: w. ref. to the blade of a sword, Jd 3.22 (v.l. παραξιφίς, q.v.), cf. Caird 1969.39.
Cf. φλέγω, φλόγινος, φλογίζω, πῦρ, πυριφλεγής: Renehan 2.137.

φλύαρος, ον.ʃ
foolish: *s* φιλοσοφία 4M 5.11 (ǁ λῆρος). Cf. ἄφρων, μωρός: Spicq 3.466.

φλυκτίς, ίδος. f.ʃ
boil on the skin: + ἕλκη 'festering wounds'– ἀναζέουσαι 'breaking out' Ex 9.9, 10 (affecting both humans and animals).

φοβέομαι: fut. φοβηθήσομαι; aor. ἐφοβήθην, ptc. φοβηθείς, subj. φοβηθῶ, inf.act. φοβῆσαι, pass. φοβηθῆναι; pf. πεφόβημαι.

1. *to dread, become terrified*: abs. Ge 18.15, 42.35; De 1.21 (ll δειλιάω); Am 3.8 (at a roaring lion), Jn 1.5, Zc 9.5 (ll ὀδυνάω); μὴ φοβοῦ 'Fear not!' Ge 15.1, 26.24; + acc. pers., 32.11, Nu 14.9, Is 33.7 (last ll ἀπό τινος); + acc. rei, κακά Ps 22.4, ἀπώλειαν 'perdition' Ez 26.16, ὀνειδισμόν 'humiliation' Is 51.7, τὸ πρόσωπον τοῦ θυμοῦ 'the face of anger' 51.13; ἀπό τινος (pers.) De 1.29, 20.1, ἀπὸ μυριάδων λαοῦ 'tens of thousands of people' Ps 3.7, on ἀπό, cf. ὁ ἀπὸ τῶν πολεμίων φόβος Xen. *Cyr*. 3.3.53; Mi 7.17 (ll ἐξίσταμαι); + ἀπό τινος (rei) - ἀπὸ τῶν λόγων, ὧν ἤκουσας Is 37.6 ll 4K 19.6, ἀπὸ φωνῆς πτώσεως Je 29.22; ἀπὸ προσώπου + gen. pers., De 7.19, Ez 3.9 (latter ll πτοέω pass.), but ἀπὸ προσώπου τοῦ πυρός De 5.5; ἔν τινι (pers.) Jo 10.2 (v.l. ἀπό τινος); + cogn. obj., φόβον Ps 52.6, φόβον μέγαν Jn 1.10, τὸν φόβον αὐτοῦ 'that which he fears' Is 8.12 (ll ταράσσομαι); + cogn. dat. φόβῳ μεγάλῳ Jn 1.16; + inf., Ge 19.30, 20.2, 26.7, 46.3, Ex 34.30, Nu 12.8, Jd 7.10, To 2.8 𝔊[I]; + an interrog. clause, οὐ φοβηθήσομαι, τί ποιήσει μοι σάρξ (vs. 12 ἄνθρωπος) Ps 55.5; *s* καρδία 26.3, cf. τῇ καρδίᾳ σου Ju 11.1; τοῖς προσώποις αὐτῶν 'showing their fear on their faces' or 'prostrating on the ground' Je 10.3; + a ptc., πτόησιν ἐπελθοῦσαν 'a terror coming upon you' Pr 3.25; + a μή-clause, To 6.15.

2. *to become filled with a sense of awe* in relation to God: Hb 3.2 (ll ἐξίσταμαι); ἀπὸ προσώπου κυρίου 'in the presence of the Lord' Hg 1.12; + acc., τὸν κύριον, καὶ ἐπίστευσεν τῷ θεῷ Ex 14.31.

3. *to act respectfully and out of a sense of* (*religious*) *awe towards*: abs., ἡσύχασα φοβηθείς 'I held my tongue out of diffidence (for your seniority)' Jb 32.6; + acc., τὸν θεόν Ge 22.12, 42.18, Ex 1.17, To 4.21 𝔊; τὸν κύριον Ho 10.3, Jn 1.16 (+ cogn. dat.), cf. Ma 2.5 (+ ἐν φόβῳ); Zp 3.7; ll εὐλαβέομαι Je 5.22; ll εὐλαβέομαι τὸ ὄνομα ^τοῦ κυρίου^ Ma 3.16; τὸ ὄνομα αὐτοῦ (= God's) Mi 6.9, sim. Ma 4.2; τὸ ῥῆμα κυρίου Ex 9.20 (opp. οὐ προσέχω vs. 21); τὸ ὄνομα τὸ ἔντιμον καὶ τὸ θαυμαστὸν τοῦτο, κύριον τὸν θεόν σου De 28.58; φοβεῖσθαί με καὶ φυλάσσεσθαι τὰς ἐντολάς μου 5.29; + acc. hum., πατέρα αὐτοῦ καὶ μητέρα αὐτοῦ Le 19.3 (ll τιμάω Ex 20.12, De 5.16), 2.4 (ll εὐλαβέομαι). **b**. + ἀπό τινος– ἀπὸ τῶν ἁγίων μου Le 19.30, 26.2.

4. act. *to frighten*': τινα 2C 32.18, Wi 17.9.

Cf. φόβος, φοβερός, φοβερίζω, ἐκφοβέω, δείδω, δειλιάω, δειλιόομαι, πτήσσω, πτοέω, στέλλομαι, ἐκσοβέω, εὐλαβέομαι, θαρσέω: Schmidt 3.512f.; Trench 35-7.

φοβερίζω: aor. ἐφοβέρισα, impv. φοβέρισον, inf. φοβερίσαι.*

to instil a sense of awe or *angst into* sbd: + acc. pers., ἐν ἐντολαῖς θεοῦ ἡμῶν 2E 10.3; Ne 6.9. Cf. φοβέομαι.

φοβερισμός, οῦ. m.ʃ*

act of terrifying: God's, Ps 87.17. Cf. prec., φόβος.

φοβεροειδής, ές.ʃ *

possessed of awe-inspiring appearance: *s* angels, 3M 6.18. Cf. φοβερός.

φοβερός, ά, όν.

awe-inspiring, formidable, frightful: *s* a place with divine presence, ὡς ~ὸς ὁ τόπος οὗτος 'How awesome this place is!' Ge 28.17; τὴν ἔρημον τὴν μεγάλην καὶ τὴν ~άν De 1.19; a foreign army, + ἐπιφανής (q.v.) Hb 1.7; κύριος Ps 46.3; God's name, 110.9, Od 12.3 (+ ἔνδοξος). **b**. *capable of instilling a sense of dread and fear*: *s* λόγος Pr 12.25.

Cf. φοβεροειδής, φοβέομαι, φοβερῶς, φόβητρον, ὑπέρφοβος.

φοβερῶς. adv.ʃ

in awesome manner: Ps 138.14, 3M 5.45. Cf. φοβερός.

φόβητρον, ου. n.ʃ

sth or *sbd that instills dread*: *s* hum., Is 19.17. Cf. φοβερός: Shipp 557.

φόβος, ου. m.

1. *fear, dread*: φ. σκοτεινὸς μέγας 'great, dark fear' Ge 15.12; φ. καὶ τρόμος Ex 15.16, ~ον καὶ δειλίαν Si 4.17; τῆς καρδίας De 28.67; of a thing, stormy sea, Jn 1.10 (as cogn. acc.), 16 (as cogn. dat.); of a human, Ge 9.2 (ll τρόμος); opp. εἰρήνη Je 37.5; of punitive God, κυρίου Is 2.19.

2. *religious fear, awe, reverence*: + gen. obj. φ. θεοῦ Ge 35.5, πνεῦμα ~ου θεοῦ Is 11.3; ποῦ ἐστιν ὁ φ. μου; Ma 1.6; ἐν ~ῳ φοβεῖσθαί με 'to fear me reverently' 2.5; ἐν ~ῳ .. ἐν τρόμῳ '.. trembling' Ps 2.11.

3. *one who* or *that which is feared*: ὁ φ. Ισαακ Ge 31.42; τὸν ~ον αὐτοῦ οὐ μὴ φοβηθῆτε 'what they fear ..' Is 8.12; αὐτός [= κύριος] ἔσται σου φ. 8.13; τὸ ἅγιον τοῦ ~ου Da 11.31 LXX; pl. Jb 20.25¶, Wi 18.17.

Cf. φοβέομαι, ἀφοβία, ἄφοβος, εὐλάβεια, εὐσέβεια, δειλία, δεῖμα, δέος, πτόη, τρόμος, φρίκη.

φοιβάω: fut. φοιβήσω.ʃ

to cleanse (?): De 14.1, cf. *BA* ad loc.

Φοινίκη, ης. f. GN

Phoenicia: Is 23.2.

φοινικοῦς, ῆ, οῦν.ʃ

purple-red, crimson: subst.n. 'purple-red dye'(?), *s* sins, Is 1.18 (ll κόκκινος:: λευκός). Cf. ἐρυθρός: Schmidt 3.48-50.

φοινικών, ῶνος. m.

palm-grove: τὴν .. ~ῶνος Ez 47.18 (ref. to Jericho).

φοῖνιξ, κος. m.

1. *date-palm*: στελέχη φοινίκων 'palm trees' Ex 15.27, Nu 33.9; πόλις φοινίκων i.e. Jericho, De 34.3; ῥόα καὶ φ. καὶ μῆλον καὶ πάντα τὰ ξύλα τοῦ ἀγροῦ Jl 1.12. **b**. *fruit of date-palm*: 2K 16.2B. Cf. Schnebel 294-300.

2. *Phoenician*: De 3.9.

φονεύς, έως. m.ʃ

= φονευτής: 4K 9.31*L* (B: φονευτής); τέκνων Wi 12.5. Cf. φονευτής, ἀνδροφόνος, αὐθέντης, μιαιφόνος.

φονευτής, οῦ. m.*

one who has killed a human: Nu 35.11 (‖ ὁ φονεύων vs. 12; ὁ φονεύσας vs. 6); De 4.42; of homicide, Nu 35.16, 17, 18. Cf. φονεύω, φονεύς, φόνος.

φονεύω: fut. φονεύσω, pass. ~νευθήσομαι; aor. ἐφόνευσα, subj. φονεύσω, inf. φονεῦσαι, pass. φονευθῆναι, ptc. φονεύσας, pass. φονευθείς; pf. πεφόνευκα, pass. πεφόνευμαι, ptc.pass. πεφονευμένος.

to kill: abs. Ex 20.15, + acc. pers., Ho 6.9; manslaughter, Ex 21.13, οὐκ εἰδώς De 4.42; ψυχήν 22.26; ‖ ἀποκτείνω Ps 93.6, Jd 20.5; metaph., 'to ruin,' τινα Pr 7.26 (‖ καταβάλλω). Cf. ἀποκτείνω, φονευτής, φόνος, and φονώδης.

φονοκτονέω: aor.subj. ~νήσω, pass. ἐφονοκτονήθην.ʃ *

to pollute with murder: + acc., τὴν γῆν Nu 35.33 (‖ μιαίνω vs. 34 and cf. Syh *ṭṭanfunāh b-qaṭlē*); pass. ἐφονοκτονήθη ἡ γῆ ἐν τοῖς αἵμασιν Ps 105.38. Cf. φονεύω, φονοκτονία.

φονοκτονία ας. f.ʃ*

deed of murder: 1M 1.24. Cf. φονοκτονέω, φόνος.

φόνος, ου. m.

wilful termination of human life: active, Ex 22.2; οὐ ποιήσεις ~ον 'shall not occasion manslaughter' De 22.8; ἀρὰ καὶ ψεῦδος καὶ φ. καὶ κλοπὴ καὶ μοιχεία 'cursing, deception, murder, theft, and adultery' Ho 4.2; + πορνεία Ez 43.7. **b**. passive: 'being killed', μήποτε συναντήσῃ ἡμῖν θάνατος ἢ φ. Ex 5.3; on battlefield, πεσοῦνται .. ~ῳ Le 26.7; ~ῳ μαχαίρας 'by sword' Nu 21.24, ἐν ~ῳ μαχαίρας De 13.15, 20.13; divine punishment, 28.22.

Cf. φονεύω, φονώδης, φονοκτονία, and τεκνοφόνος.

φονώδης, ες.ʃ

murderous: *s* hum., + αἱμοβόρος 'bloodthirsty' 4M 10.17. Cf. φόνος.

φορβεά, ᾶς.f.ʃ

halter: put round a crocodile's(?) nose, Jb 40.25.

φορεῖον, ου. n.*

litter, sedan-chair: 2M 3.27; ἐν ~ῳ παρεκομίζετο 'was transported in a litter' 9.8; royal, Ct 3.9.

φορεύς, έως. m.ʃ

that which bears (αἴρω Ex 27.7) *a structure*, 'pole': of altar, Ex 27.6, 7 (2x). Cf. φέρω.

φορέω: fut. φορέσω; aor. ἐφόρεσα.ʃ

to carry habitually: + acc., νόμον καὶ ἔλεον ἐπὶ γλώσσης φορεῖ Pr 3.16a, ἐπὶ χείλεσιν 'on his lips' 16.23, ἐπὶ .. στόματι 16.26; 'to wear,' διάδημα Si 11.5, ὑακίνθινον καὶ στέφανον 40.4, *o* royal crown Es C 27. Cf. φέρω: Trench 212f.

φορολογέω: aor. ἐφορολόγησα.

to levy tribute from: + acc. pers., Κοίλην Συρίαν 1E 2.23; 2C 36.4[a]. Cf. φόρος, φορολόγητος, φορολογία, φορολόγος.

φορολόγητος, ον.ʃ *

obliged to pay a tribute, 'tributary': subst. σοι De 20.11 (‖ ὑπήκοος). Cf. φορολογέω.

φορολογία, ας. f.

tribute payable: ~αν .. δοῦναι 1E 2.18; 6.28; ‖ ἐπιβολή 'impost' 8.22; ἄρχων ~ας 'chief collector of tributes' 1M 1.29. Cf. φορολογέω, φόρος.

φορολόγος, ου. m.

collector of tributes: 2E 4.7. Cf. φορολογέω: Wooden 254-6.

φόρος, ου. m.

1. *tribute* to be paid by a vassal or a subject: ἤγαγον αὐτοὺς ὑπὸ ~ον 'reduced them to the status of vassals' 1M 8.2; δίδωμί τινι ~ον 'pay ..' 8.4; ἐπέβαλεν ~ον .. ἐπὶ τὴν γῆν 'imposed ..' 2C 36.3; 2E 4.13, 1M 3.29; τῶν τεταγμένων 'paid by the subjects' 3K 10.15; ‖ τιμή 'tax' and στέφανοι 'crown levies' 1M 10.29. ***b**. coll. sg., *those obliged to pay tributes*: Jo 19.48a, Jd 1.28, 29, 1M 1.4.

2. *imposed labour*, 'corvée': 2C 8.8; φ. δουλείας 3K 9.21 v.l. **b**. coll. sg. *those obliged to provide labour free*: Jd 1.28, 3K 5.27, La 1.1.

Cf. φορολογέω, τιμή, στέφανος: Weiss, *TDNT* 9.80.

φορτίζω.ʃ

to load: + acc. pers., of a harlot loading her clients with gifts as inducement for further patronage (?) Ez 16.33. Cf. φορτίον.

φορτίον, ου. n.

load, burden: αἴρετε .. ὡς φ. 'carry .. like ..' Is 46.1; *s* one's iniquities, βαρύ 'heavy' Ps 37.5, ἐν ὁδῷ 'on a journey' Si 21.16, ὄνῳ 'for a donkey' 30.33; fig. εἰμὶ ἐπὶ σοὶ φ. 'I am a burden to you' Jb 7.20, ἐπὶ τὸν κύριόν μου 2K 19.36. **b**. *a quantity to be carried and transported*: ξύλων 'of timber' Jd 9.48 A.

Cf. βάσταγμα, φορτίζω, διγομία.

φραγμός, οῦ. m.

barrier preventing free movement between the two sides of it: of part of a womb holding a foetus within, Ge 38.29; 'hedge,' ἔστη ὁ ἄγγελος τοῦ θεοῦ ἐν ταῖς αὔλαξιν τῶν ἀμπελώνων, φ. ἐντεῦθεν καὶ φ. ἐντεῦθεν 'the angel of God stood in the furrow of the vineyard, with a hedge on either side' Nu 22.24; ἀκρὶς ἐπιβεβηκυῖα ἐπὶ ~όν 'locust which has landed on a hedge' Na 3.17; ~ὸν περιέθηκα 'I set a hedge round it [= vineyard]' Is 5.2, protective, 5.5, Si 36.30, Ps 79.13, 88.41 (ǁ ὀχυρώματα), κατάπτωμα ~ου 'collapse of ..' 143.14; τοίχῳ κεκλιμένῳ καὶ φραγμῷ ὠσμένῳ 'with a leaning wall and a tottering fence' 61.4 (sth life-threatening); λίθων 'of stone' Pr 24.31; φ. Ὠρίωνος 'the orbit of Orion' Jb 38.31. **b**. *an area marked off*: δοῦναι ἡμῖν ~ὸν ἐν Ιουδα καὶ ἐν Ιερουσαλημ 2E 9.9.

Cf. φράσσω and ἐμφραγμός: Ziegler 1934.179.

φράζω: fut. φράσω; aor.impv. φράσον, subj. φράσω.ʃ.

to communicate orally: + dat. pers., Jb 6.24, 12.8; + acc. rei, Da 2.4 LXX (TH ἀναγγέλλω).

Cf. λέγω: Schmidt 1.60f., 90f.; *BA* ad Jd 5.8.

φράξις, εως. f.ʃ

barricade: obstructing free passage, La 3.9 (see Albrektson 132f.). Cf. φράσσω, φραγμός.

φράσσω: aor. ἔφραξα; pf.ptc.pass. πεφραγμένος.

1. *to build a hedge along* (a way in order to make it impossible for it to be crossed): τὴν ὁδὸν αὐτῆς ἐν σκόλοψι 'a hedge of thorns on either side of its way' Ho 2.6; θάλασσαν πύλαις 'the sea with gates' Jb 38.8; πηγήν 'fountain' Pr 25.26; pass., ***o*** hum., πεφραγμένος 'hedged round for protection, i.e. well prepared for defence' 2K 22.30*L* (B: μονόζωνος).

2. metaph. *to deny access to*: ***o*** ὅραμα 'vision' Da 8.26 LXX (TH σφραγίζω 'to seal'); τὰ ὦτα '(to stop) the ears (so as not to hear)' Pr 21.13.

Cf. φραγμός, φράξις, ἀνα~, ἐμ~, περιφράσσω.

φρέαρ, ~ατος. n.

cavity made by excavating in the ground: 'well' from which water is drawn – τὸ φ. τοῦ ὅρκου 'the well of oath' Ge 21.14 (= φ. ὁρκισμοῦ vs. 31), Am 5.5; ὕδατος Ge 21.25; ὕδατος ζῶντος 'of running water' 21.19, 26.19; 'pit(s)' dotting a valley, ἡ κοιλὰς ἡ ἁλυκὴ ~ατα ~ατα ἀσφαλτῶν 'the salt valley is (dotted with) pits of tar' Ge 14.10; πηγῆς Pr 5.15; metaph., φ. διαφθορᾶς Ps 54.24. Cf. πηγή, κρήνη, and φλέψ: Schmidt 1.628-32; Shipp 449f.

φρενόω: pf.ptc.pass. πεφρενωμένος.ʃ

to make elated: pass., + dat., 2M 11.4.

φρήν, ένος. f.

mental faculty: 3M 4.16, 5.47; pl., Pr 6.32, Da 4.31 TH, ἐνδεεῖς ~ῶν 'have no brains' Pr 9.4 (ἄφρων), 12.11. Cf. φρόνιμος, ἄφρων, καρδία, λόγος, νοῦς: Schmidt 3.628-33.

φρικασμός, οῦ. m.ʃ *

act of shuddering out of fear: σώματος 2M 3.17 (+ δέος). Cf. φρίττω.

φρίκη, ης. f.ʃ

shivering fear: ǁ τρόμος 'trembling' Jb 4.14; Am 1.11. Cf. φρίττω, τρόμος and φόβος.

φρικτός, ή, όν.ʃ

to be shuddered at: subst.n., Je 18.13 (*s* deeds); and + ἔκστασις 'consternation' 5.30; *s* τύραννοι Wi 8.15. Cf. φρίττω, φρικτῶς.

φρικτῶς. adv.ʃ *

in a manner likely to cause shuddering: + ταχέως 'swiftly' Wi 6.5. Cf. φρικτός.

φρικώδης, ες.ʃ

causing shuddering, horrifying: subst., Ho 6.10. Cf. φρίκη, φρίττω.

φρίττω: aor. ἔφριξα.

to shudder: out of horror, ἐξέστη ὁ οὐρανὸς ἐπὶ τούτῳ καὶ ἔφριξεν 'heaven was amazed at this ..' Je 2.12; + τρέμω Od 12.4; + acc., τὴν τόλμαν αὐτῆς 'at her boldness' Ju 16.10 (ǁ ταράσσομαι); *s* μου τρίχες καὶ σάρκες 'my hair and flesh' Jb 4.15, τὸ πνεῦμά μου Da TH 7.15. Cf. φρίκη, φρικώδης, φρικασμός, ὑπόφρικος, and ἐξίστημι.

φρονέω: aor. ἐφρόνησα, inf. φρονῆσαι, ptc. φρονήσας, impv.2pl φρονήσατε.

1. *to be wise*: οὐκ ἐφρόνησαν συνιέναι ταῦτα 'were not wise enough to comprehend these matters' De 32.29; σφόδρα Zc 9.2.

2. *to conduct oneself wisely*: Is 44.18.

3. *to give thought* to: abs., εὖ φρονήσας Es A 13 *L*; + acc. rei, τὰ ἡμέτερα '(have) our interests close to their hearts' E 1, sim. 2M 14.7; ὑπερήφανα 'arrogant schemes' 2M 9.12 (v.l. ἰσόθεα); περί τινος Wi 1.1.

Cf. (ἐν)νοέω, λογίζομαι, φρόνησις, φρόνιμος, πολύφροντις, φροντίζω, and σοφός.

φρόνημα, ατος. n.

way of thinking: Es 1.18 *L*, 7.25 *L*; γενναῖον 'noble' 2M 7.21. **b**. *that which one forms in one's mind*, 'thought, idea': 2M 13.9.

Cf. φρήν.

φρόνησις, εως. f.

state of being wise: divine attribute, Is 40.28, at the creation of the universe, Pr 3.19 and Je 10.12; hum. quality and ǁ ἐπιστήμη Ez 28.4, Si 19.22; σύνεσις ~εως 1.4; + σοφία 3K 2.35[a]; + σοφία, γνῶσις Da 1.4 TH. **b**. *practical wisdom*: Pr 1.2; "they were at their wits' end" Jo 5.1 (ǁ διάνοια).

Cf. γνῶσις, σοφία, σύνεσις, φρόνιμος.

φρόνιμος, η, ον.

shrewd in judgement: *s* snake (ὄφις) Ge 3.1; hum., ἄνθρωπον ~ον καὶ συνετόν Ge 41.33; υἱός Ho 13.13; καρδία and + σοφός 3K 3.12.

Cf. φρονέω, σοφός, συνετός, ἀνόητος, ἄφρων: Bertram, *TDNT* 9.224-6.

φροντίζω: fut. φροντιῶ; aor. ἐφρόντισα, inf. φροντίσαι, ptc. φροντίσας, impv. φρόντισον.

to exercise the mind, 'think': abs., ταῦτα λογισάμενος ἐν ἐμαυτῷ καὶ φροντίσας ἐν καρδίᾳ μου Wi 8.17, ὡς ἀποτείσων φρόντιζε 'start thinking how to repay' Si 8.13; περὶ ἡμῶν 'about us' 1K 9.5. **b**. *to give thought to*: + gen., Jb 23.15, τῆς καθ' αὐτὸν ἀσφαλείας 'the security around himself' 2M 4.21, τοῦ συμφέροντος 'the benefits' 11.15. **c**. *to think and give caring attention to*: + gen. pers., κύριος φροντιεῖ μου Ps 39.18, τοῦ λαοῦ αὐτοῦ ἀπὸ πτώσεως 'how to save his people from ruin' Si 50.4; 35.1; worried, περὶ ἡμῶν 1K 9.5. **c**. *to consider, ponder*: + acc., φόβος Jb 3.25, τὰ τῆς ἐπιμελείας αὐτῶν 'the affairs pertaining to their interests' 1M 16.14. **d**. *to think and devise*: + acc., τοῖς βουλομένοις ἀναγινώσκειν ψυχαγωγίαν 'amusement for those wishing to read' 2M 2.25.

Cf. φρήν, φροντιστέον, ἐπιμελέομαι, λογίζομαι, μελετάω, μεριμνάω, φροντίζω.

φροντίς, ίδος.

act of giving thought: + gen. obj., Wi 5.15; μέριμνα καὶ φ. Jb 11.18, so Aristeas 271; dat., ~ίσιν 'carefully' Wi 7.4. **b**. *matter to which thought is given*, 'concern, worry': pl., + λύπη 'sorrow' Wi 8.9; ἔστιν αὐτῷ φ. οὐχ ὅτι .. 'he is not concerned about the fact that ..' 15.9.

Cf. φροντίζω, φροντιστέον.

φροντιστέον.ʃ

one must give thought to: + gen., 2M 2.29. Cf. φροντίζω.

φρουρά, ᾶς. f.

garrison: 2K 8.6, 1M 6.50.

φρουρέω: aor. ἐφρούρησα.

to keep watch over: + acc., πόλιν 1E 4.56. Cf. φρουρά, φυλάσσω: Schmidt 4.683-6. Del. 1M 11.3 v.l.

φρούριον, ου. n.

citadel: 2M 10.32; ὀχυρόν 'solid' 13.19. Cf. ἄκρα.

φρύαγμα, ατος. n.ʃ

1. *insolence*: ἠγάπησαν ἀτιμίαν ἐκ ~ατος αὐτῆς 'she preferred ignominy out of her insolence' Ho 4.18.

2. *that which one takes pride in*: τὸ φ. τοῦ Ιορδάνου 'the glory of the Jordan river' Zc 11.3 (w. ref. to the dense thickets of the Jordan Valley), Je 12.5 (haunted by lions and leopards); τῆς ἰσχύος αὐτῶν 'of their strength' Ez 7.24, 24.21 (w. ref. to the sanctuary); τῆς δυνάμεως 'of the military might' or 'the pride of the army' 3M 6.16.

Cf. φρυάσσω, καύχημα and ὑπερηφανία.

φρυάσσω, φρυάττω: aor. ἐφρύαξα; pf.ptc.mid. πεφρυαγμένος.ʃ

to be haughty or *act haughtily*, verbally manifested: *s* hum., Ps 2.1; mid. 2M 7.34 (|| μετεωρίζομαι), θράσει καὶ σθένει πεφρυαγμένος 'puffed up with audacity and power' 3M 2.2. Cf. φρύαγμα, καυχάομαι.

φρύγανον, ου. n.ʃ

1. *dry stick*: fig. of an object easy to manipulate, ἀπέρριψε Σαμαρεια βασιλέα αὐτῆς ὡς ~ον ἐπὶ προσώπου ὕδατος 'S. cast her king as a dry stick (floating) on the surface of the water' Ho 10.7, cf. LSG s.v.; ὡς ~να φερόμενα ὑπὸ ἀνέμου '.. borne by a wind' Je 13.24; Is 40.24; sth of little value, ὡς ~α ἐξωσμένα τὰ τόξα αὐτῶν 'their bows as castaway sticks' 41.2; firewood, ὡς ~α ἐπὶ πυρὶ κατακαήσονται '.. will burn on a fire' 47.14.

2. *undershrub*: pl., ἄγρια 'wild' Jb 30.7 (a dwelling for thieves)

φρύγιον, ου. n.ʃ *

firewood: ὡσεὶ φ. συνεφρύγησαν 'parched like firewood' Ps 101.4. Cf. φρύγω.

φρύγω: pf.ptc.pass. πεφρυγμένος.ʃ

to roast or *parch*: νέα πεφρυγμένα χίδρα 'new, roasted, unripe wheaten-groats' Le 2.14, sim. 23.14. Cf. φρύγιον, συμφρύγω.

φυγαδεία, ας.ʃ

banishment, exile: ἀποστάσεις καὶ ~εῖαι 'riots and ..' 2E 4.19. **b**. *group of banished fugitives*: δούλων 2E 4.15.

Cf. φεύγω.

φυγαδεῖον, ου. n.ʃ *

place of refuge: Nu 35.15. Cf. φυγαδευτήριον.

φυγαδευτήριον, ου. n.*

place of refuge: πόλεις τῶν ~ίων Nu 35.6; for cases of unmeditated murder, φ. φυγεῖν ἐκεῖ τὸν φονευτὴν 35.11; ἀπὸ ἀγχιστεύοντος τὸ αἷμα 'from the blood-relation' 35.12. Cf. φυγαδεῖον, φεύγω, καταφυγή: Moatti-Fine 321-3; *BA* 6.44f.

φυγαδεύω: aor. ἐφυγάδευσα, ptc. ~δεύσας; pf.ptc. πεφυγαδευκώς.

to flee from danger or misery: abs., Ps 54.8; + acc. pers., 2M 14.14; ἀπὸ τῶν κακῶν 1M 2.43; εἰς τὴν ἀκρόπολιν 'into the citadel' 2M 5.5. **b**. tr. *to put to flight*: + acc. pers., 2M 9.4.

Cf. φεύγω, τροπόω.

φυγάς, άδος. m./f.

one in flight running away out of fear: δώσω πάντας τοὺς ὑπεναντίους σου ~άδας 'I shall put all your opponents to flight' Ex 23.27; ~άδα ὀργῆς ἀδελφοῦ δίκαιον 'a righteous man fleeing from his brother's wrath' Wi 10.10, τῆς αἰωνίου προνοίας 'from eternal providence' 17.2, ὡς ~ας ἐδιώκον 19.3; οὐκ ἐν ἀσφαλείᾳ 'not safe' Pr 28.17. Cf. φεύγω.

φυγή, ῆς. f.

act of fleeing: ἀπολεῖται φ. ἐκ δρομέως 'a runner will lose strength to flee' Am 2.14; οὐκ ἔστι πέρας τῆς ~ῆς 'there is no end (Thph τέλος, PG 126.1032) to the flight, i.e. she will still be fleeing' Na 3.9; cogn. dat., Je 26.5; || σωτηρία 32.21. **b.** *means of escape*: Ps 141.5.

Cf. φεύγω: Schmidt 3.249.

φυή, ῆς. f.

1. *stately shape*: ἀνέβη ἡ φ. τοῖς τείχεσιν 'the walls rose in respectable shape' Ne 4.7.

2. *that which has grown* out of sth: τῶν ῥιζῶν 'from the roots' Da TH 4.12.

φῦκος, εος. n.ʃ

orchil: || μίλτος Wi 13.14.

φύλαγμα, ατος. n.

what is to be observed and followed* (see under φυλάσσω, **4): καταφρονοῦντας ἐπὶ τὰ ~ατα αὐτῶν 'despising ordinances incumbent upon them' Zp 1.12 (cf. Th 287: προστάγματα and Cyr. II 185: νόμοι), hardly 'that which has been entrusted for good-keeping'; φυλάξεσθε τὰ ~ατα κυρίου Le 8.35; || δικαίωμα, ἐντολή De 11.1, also || κρίσις 11.1; Ma 3.14; obligation imposed by a military treaty, 1M 8.26, 28. Cf. φυλάσσω.

φυλακή, ῆς. f.

1. *act of keeping guard* or *state of being kept under guard*: ἔθετο αὐτοὺς ἐν ~ῇ παρὰ τῷ ἀρχιμαγείρῳ εἰς τὸ δεσμωτήριον 'he put them into the prison cell under house arrest at the chief cook's' Ge 40.3; ἐξ οἴκου φυλακῆς Is 42.7, εἰς οἰκίαν ~ῆς Je 44.15; τοῦ οἴκου 'of the temple' Ez 40.45, τοῦ θυσιαστηρίου 40.46; as sentinel, ἐπὶ τῆς ~ῆς μου στήσομαι 'I will stand on my watch' Hb 2.1; cogn. acc. of φυλάσσω, Nu 1.53, 3.7, 31.30, 4K 11.5; βαλεῖ ~ήν ἐπὶ σὲ κύκλῳ 'will place you under close watch (by laying siege)' Ez 23.24, ἐθέμην τῷ στόματί μου ~ήν Ps 38.2, δώσει ἐπὶ στόμα μου ~ήν Si 22.27.

2. *division of night-time*, 'watch': ἑωθινή 'early-morning' Ex 14.24, sim. πρωινή 1K 11.11; "the stars shone in their watches" Ba 3.35; φ. ἐν νυκτί Ps 89.4.

3. *place and area which one is charged with guarding*, 'post, station': Nu 3.25; ἡ φ. αὐτῶν ἡ κιβωτός 'their beat is the ark' 3.31.

4. *place where one is confined and guarded*: Ne 3.25, 2C 16.10; cage for animals, Ez 19.9. Cf. δεσμωτήριον.

5. *watchman, guard, sentinel*: Je 28.12; coll. sg., 1C 26.16. **b.** *that which provides security and protection*: ἀπὸ προσκόμματος 'from stumbling' Si 31.19 (|| βοήθεια); ***s*** ἐλεημοσύνη καὶ ἀλήθεια Pr 20.28.

6. *act of adhering to and acting in conformity with* divine instruction, law etc.: φυλάσσω τὴν ~ὴν Κυρίου 3K 2.3; περὶ τὸν νόμον 4M 13.13.

Cf. φυλάσσω, φυλακίζω, φύλαξ, σκοπιά: Bertram, *TDNT* 9.242f.

φυλακίζω: aor.inf.pass. φυλακισθῆναι.ʃ *

to keep confined and guarded: pass., ***o*** hum., σκότει 'in darkness' Wi 18.4. Cf. φυλακή, φυλάσσω.

φυλάκισσα, ας. f.ʃ *

fem. of φύλαξ: ἐν ἀμπελῶσιν 'in vineyards' Ct 1.6. Cf. φύλαξ.

φύλαξ, λακος. m. and f.

one who keeps watch to protect: φ. τοῦ ἀδελφοῦ μου Ge 4.9; οἰκίας 'of a house' Ec 12.3, γυναικῶν 'warden of harem' Es 2.3 o'; ἐν πύργοις 'in towers' Ez 27.11; ***s*** God, ***o*** hum., 2K 22.3. Cf. φυλάσσω, ἀκρο~, ἀρχιδεσμο~, ἀρχισωματο~, γαζο~, θησαυρο~, ἱματιο~, νομο~, προ~, σωματοφύλαξ, φυλάκισσα.

φυλάρχης, ου. m.ʃ

commander: of a military unit, 2M 8.32. Cf. στρατηγός.

φύλαρχος, ου. m.

1. *chief of tribe*: || πρεσβύτερος, κριτής, γραμματοεισαγωγής De 31.28; 1E 7.8.

2. *chief*: τῶν ἱερέων 1E 8.54, 58.

Cf. ἀρχίφυλος.

φυλάσσω: fut. φυλάξω, mid. φυλάξομαι, pass. φυλαχθήσομαι; aor. ἐφύλαξα, inf. φυλάξαι, ptc. φυλάξας, impv. φύλαξον, mid. ἐφυλαξάμην, impv. φύλαξαι, pass.3s φυλαχθήτω, subj. φυλάξω, mid. φυλάξωμαι, pass. φυλαχθῶ, opt.act. φυλάξαι; pf. πεφύλακα, pass. πεφύλαγμαι, ptc. πεφυλαγμένος.

1. *to guard, watch*: in order to protect and ***o*** a way to sth of value, Ge 3.24 (***s*** sword); τὰ σκεύη τῆς σκηνῆς τοῦ μαρτυρίου 'the vessels and implements of the tent of testimony' Nu 3.8; hum., Ex 23.20 (***s*** guardian angel); πρόβατα Ge 30.31, ***s*** (shepherding) God, Je 38.10, cf. Ps 11.8 (|| διατηρέω), 16.8 (|| σκεπάζω), 24.20 (|| ῥύομαι), σε ἀπὸ παντὸς κακοῦ 120.7, || εὐλογέω Nu 6.24, :: ἐξολεθρεύω Ps 144.20, ***s*** God's "angel," ἐν τῇ ὁδῷ Ex 23.20, wisdom Wi 10.5 (|| τηρέω), good counsel Pr 2.11 (dit.), δικαιοσύνη 13.6; "cattle" as ***o*** understood, Ho 12.12; pass., ***o*** τὰ πρόβατα τὰ φυλασσόμενα Zc 11.11; παράδεισος 'garden' Ge 2.15; πεφύλαξαι σὺ παρ' ἐμοί 'you are safe with me' 1K 22.23; + acc. (sth vulnerable or potential hazard) φύλαξον τὴν ψυχήν σου .., μὴ ἐπιλάθῃς .. '.. in case you forget ..' De 4.9 (|| πρόσεχε σεαυτῷ), τὸ ἑαυτοῦ στόμα 'one's own mouth' Pr 13.3, πόδα σου '(Mind) your step' Ec 4.17, τὰς ὁδούς μου τοῦ μὴ ἁμαρτάνειν Ps 38.2; pass., ***o*** ἔργα χειρῶν αὐτοῦ PSol 6.2. **b.** with hostile intent: τὴν ψυχήν μου Ps 70.10; Je 39.2 (pass.); protective, τὰς ψυχὰς ὑμῶν 17.21; τὴν πτέρναν μου 'to trip me' Ps 55.7; ἐπὶ τὴν πόλιν 2K 11.16. **c.** + ἀπό τινος 'against ..': σε ἀπὸ παντὸς κακοῦ Ps 120.7, cf. ἐκ χειρὸς ἁμαρτωλοῦ

139.5. **d**. with anticipation: πρός τινα (as a source of help) Ps 58.10. **e**. mid.: φυλασσόμενος λαλέω 'speak cautiously' Pr 21.28. ***f**. poss. w. double obj.: ἡμερῶν, ὧν με ὁ θεὸς ἐφύλαξεν 'the days which G. protected for me' Jb 29.2.

2. mid. (in one's own best interests), *to be on guard* against, *beware* a potential hazard, error etc.: abs. Hb 3.16; + ἀπό τινος– φυλάξῃ ἀπὸ παντὸς ῥήματος πονηροῦ De 23.9, ἀπὸ τῆς ἀνομίας μου Ps 17.24; ἀπὸ τῆς συγκοίτου σου φύλαξαι τοῦ ἀναθέσθαι τι αὐτῇ 'be on guard against your bedfellow so as not to communicate to her anything' Mi 7.5, ἕκαστος ἀπὸ τοῦ πλησίον αὐτοῦ φυλάξασθε καὶ .. μὴ πεποίθατε '.. and do not trust ' Je 9.4, cf. Φύλαξαι τοῦ ἡσυχάσαι καὶ μὴ φόβου Is 7.4; ἀπὸ γυναικός 1K 21.5 (abstinence; ‖ ἀπέχομαι vs. 6), ἀπὸ τῆς μαχαίρας 2K 20.10*L* (B: acc.); φυλάξασθε ἐν τῷ πνεύματι ὑμῶν Ma 2.15, 16; + acc., ὁδοὺς σκληράς 'hard ways' Ps 16.4 (act.); τὴν ὁδὸν αὐτῶν πορεύεσθαι .. 'their own way ..' 3K 2.4; + inf. and neg., Φύλαξαι μὴ παρελθεῖν .. 4K 6.9 (*L* προσέχω); without a negator, Ec 12.12; + μή and subj., μὴ πράξῃς ἄτοπα Jb 36.21¶; Si 26.11, Jd 13.4; Φύλαξαι σεαυτόν, μήποτε + subj. 'Beware not to ..' Ge 31.24, 29.

3. *to preserve as valuable, cherish*: + acc. βρώματα 'foods' Ge 41.35 (stored for future emergency), 36 (+ dat. com.); μάταια καὶ ψευδῆ Jn 2.9; ἔλεον καὶ κρίμα φυλάσσου Ho 12.6; πορνείαν 4.10 (see Muraoka 1983.43); δικαιοσύνην .. ἀλήθειαν Is 26.2, εἰρήνην 26.3 (‖ ἀντιλαμβάνομαι); τὸ ὅρμημα Am 1.11; με ὡς κόραν ὀφθαλμοῦ '.. as the apple of the eye' Ps 16.8.

4. *to adhere to and act in conformity with* divine instruction, law etc.: + acc. ἐντολήν Ex 12.17, De 7.9; διαθήκην Ex 19.5; τὰ προστάγματα Am 2.4 (+ neg. ‖ ἀπωθέω τὸν νόμον κυρίου), Zc 3.7; τὰ προστάγματά μου καὶ τὰς ἐντολάς μου καὶ τὰ δικαιώματά μου καὶ τὰ νόμινά μου Ge 26.5 (‖ ὑπακούω φωνῆς τινος); τὰς ὁδοὺς κυρίου 18.19; Ma 3.7 (νόμιμα understood), τὴν ὁδὸν κυρίου πορεύεσθαι Jd 2.22; τὰ φυλάγματα κυρίου Le 8.35; Ma 3.14; obligations imposed by a military treaty, 1M 8.26, 28; ***o*** laws of nature, καιροὺς εἰσόδων 'seasons for arrival' Je 8.7; ***s*** God, τὴν διαθήκην καὶ τὸ ἔλεος τοῖς ἀγαπῶσιν αὐτόν De 7.9, φύλαξον .. τῷ Δαυιδ .. ἃ ἐλάλησας αὐτῷ 3K 8.25. **b**. A foll. inf. indicates what such an attitude entails: φυλάξουσιν τὰς ὁδοὺς κυρίου ποιεῖν δικαιοσύνην καὶ κρίσιν Ge 18.19; τὰ προστάγματά μου φυλάξεσθε πορεύεσθαι ἐν αὐτοῖς Le 18.4; τοῦτο φυλάξῃ λαλῆσαι Nu 23.12. **c**. the collocation with ποιέω can take various forms: (A) paratactic and (i) abs., φυλάξεσθε καὶ ποιήσετε De 4.6; (ii) + acc. rei, φυλάξεσθε καὶ ποιήσετε αὐτά 26.16; (iii) + acc. with φύλασσω and the pron. repeated with ποιέω– φυλάσσεσθαι πάσας τὰς ἐντολὰς .. ποιεῖν αὐτά 17.19; φυλάξεσθε πάντα τὰ προστάγματά μου .. καὶ ποιήσετε αὐτά Le 18.5; (B) hypotactic with the inf. ποιεῖν and (i) abs., ὃν τρόπον ἐνετειλάμην ὑμῖν, φυλάξεσθε ποιεῖν De 24.8b; φυλάξῃ σφόδρα ποιεῖν κατὰ πάντα τὸν νόμον 24.8a; (ii) + acc. rei, φυλάξεσθε ποιεῖν αὐτά 5.1; Πάσας τὰς ἐντολάς, .. φυλάξεσθε ποιεῖν 8.1; φυλάσσεσθαι πάσας τὰς ἐντολὰς ταύτας καὶ τὰ δικαιώματα ταῦτα ποιεῖν αὐτά 17.19, see Muraoka - Malessa 2002.

5. *to keep stored, reserve* for future: χείλη ἱερέως φυλάξεται γνῶσιν 'the lips of a priest shall preserve knowledge' Ma 2.7; τινα Si 12.6¶ (for future punishment), εἰς ἡμέραν κακήν Pr 16.9; ἐν ᾅδῃ με Jb 14.13.

6. *to guard against oblivion* or *neglect*: mostly mid. and ***o*** days of religious significance, τὴν ἑορτὴν τῶν ἀζύμων φυλάξασθε ποιεῖν Ex 23.15; without ποιεῖν 'to celebrate' 34.18; φύλαξαι τὴν ἡμέραν τῶν σαββάτων ἁγιάζειν De 5.12 (‖ μνήσθητι Ex 20.8); τὸν μῆνα τῶν νέων De 16.1; λόγον 'words (of instruction?)' Pr 24.22a. **b**. act.: φυλάξουσιν οἱ υἱοὶ Ισραηλ τὰ σάββατα ποιεῖν αὐτά Ex 31.16 (‖ mid. 31.13, 14); φυλάσσων τὰ σάββατα μὴ βεβηλοῦν '.. against desecration' Is 56.2 (‖ mid. τοὺς φυλασσομένους τὰ σάββατά μου μὴ βεβηλοῦν vs. 6); εἰς τὸν αἰῶνα φυλάξω αὐτῷ τὸ ἔλεός μου Ps 88.29.

7. *to attend to*: + acc. rei, ἱερατείαν 'priesthood' Nu 3.10; + cogn. acc., φυλακὴν τῆς σκηνῆς 1.53, ἐν τῇ σκηνῇ κυρίου 31.30; τὰς φυλακὰς ^Ααρων^ καὶ τῶν υἱῶν Ισραηλ 3.7; 3.8.

8. *to keep eyes fixed on*: out of interest, + acc. pers. Jb 10.14; + acc. rei, τὸ στόμα αὐτῆς 1K 1.12; the calving of the deer, Jb 39.1; 13.27, 33.11.

NB. It seems that the active and the middle are interchangeable, and this not just in respect of the sense **7**. Cp. De 28.1 and 28.13, Zc 3.7 and Ma 3.7, Ho 4.10 and Jn 2.9, Jd 2.22 A and B.

Cf. δια~, προφυλάσσω, ὀπωροφυλάκιον, παρα~, προφυλακή, φύλαγμα, φυλακή, φυλακίζω, δια~, συν~, τηρέω, εὐλαβέομαι, σκοπεύω: Schmidt 4.683-6; Bertram, *TDNT* 9.237f.

φυλή, ῆς. f.

community of people: **a**. generally and in pl., πᾶσαι ~αὶ τῆς γῆς Ge 12.3 (‖ τὰ ἔθνη 18.18, 22.18, 26.4, Ez 20.32), Am 3.2, Zc 14.17; Na 3.4 (‖ ἔθνη v.l. λαούς). **b**. of common ancestry: εἰς τὴν ~ήν μου Ge 24.4; τις ἐκ τῆς ~ῆς Λευι Ex 2.1; φ. οἴκου Δαυιδ Zc 12.12; of the twelve tribes of Israel, and in pl., εἰς τὰς δώδεκα ~ὰς τοῦ Ισραηλ Ex 24.4; αἱ ~αὶ τοῦ Ισραηλ Ho 5.9, Mi 5.1; πάσας ~ὰς τοῦ Ισραηλ

Zc 9.1; in sg. and w. ref. to the whole nation of Israel, λογίζομαι ἐπὶ τὴν ~ὴν ταύτην κακά Mi 2.3; 6.9 (ǁ πόλις); of an individual tribe, φ. Ιουδα Hg 1.12, 14; φ. οἴκου Λευι Zc 12.13. **c.** united by local habitation: φ. ἐξ ἀνδρῶν Χαρραν Am 1.5; ἐξ Ἀσκάλωνος 1.8; οἱ κατοικοῦντες ἐν Σαμαρείᾳ κατέναντι ~ῆς 'those who dwell in Samaria next to a local group(?)' Am 3.12; φ. Αἰγύπτου Zc 14.18. **d.** w. emphasis on a large number: Si 16.4 (:: εἷς).

Cf. δῆμος, ἔθνος, λαός, φῦλον, πάμφυλος, οἶκος: Maurer, *TDNT* 9.246-8.

φύλλον, ου. n.

leaf (of a plant): ~α συκῆς 'leaves of a fig-tree' Ge 3.7; ἐλαίας ib. 8.11; φωνὴ ~ου φερομένου 'sound of a leaf borne (by the wind)' Le 26.36. Cf. πέταλον: Schmidt 2.480-2.

φῦλον, ου. n.ʃ

race of individuals: Jewish, 3M 4.14, 5.5. Cf. ἔθνος, φυλή.

φύραμα, ατος. n.

dough: Ex 8.3; as a cultic offering, Nu 15.20. Cf. φυράω.

φύρασις, εως. f.ʃ *

kneading: στέατος 'of dough' Ho 7.4. Cf. φυράω.

φυράω: aor. ἐφύρασα, impv. φύρασον; pf.pass. πέφυρμαι, ptc. πεφυραμένος.

to knead: + acc., τρία μέτρα σεμιδάλεως 'three measures of flour' Ge 18.6; ἄλευρα 'wheat-meal' 1K 28.24; ἄρτους ἀζύμους πεφυραμένους ἐν ἐλαίῳ 'unleavened breads kneaded in oil' Ex 29.2, Le 2.4. Cf. φύραμα, φύρασις.

φύρδην. adv.ʃ

in utter confusion: 2M 4.41.

φυρμός, οῦ. m.ʃ *

disorderly mixture: Ez 7.23, ἀναμείξεως PSol 2.13. Cf. φύρω.

φύρω: pf.pass. πέφυρμαι, ptc. πεφυρμένος.

to mix sth *dry with* sth *wet*, mostly with a sense of *mixing so as to spoil* or *defile* (LSJ): mid., + acc. rei and ἔν τινι– ἱμάτιον ἐν αἵματι πεφυρμένον Is 14.19, + acc. pers., εἶδόν σε πεφυρμένην ἐν τῷ αἵματι Ez 16.6; pass., φύρεται μου τὸ σῶμα ἐν σαπρίᾳ σκωλήκων 'my body is covered with rotten worms' Jb 7.5, πεφυρμένος ἐν τῷ αἵματι αὐτοῦ 'wallowing in his own blood' 2K 20.12; two dry objects (dat. and acc.), κόνει τὴν μυροβρεχῆ πεφυρμέναι κόμην 'having their myrrh-perfumed hair sullied with ashes' 3M 4.6; metaph. ἐν ὀδύναις πέφυρμαι 'I am all sorrows' Jb 30.14. Cf. μίγνυμι.

φυσάω: aor.subt. φυσήσω.ʃ

1. *to blow at*: + acc., χαλκεὺς φυσῶν ἄνθρακας 'a coppersmith blowing at coals' Is 54.15, κάμινον 'furnace' Si 43.4; + εἰς– εἰς σπινθῆρα 'on a spark' 28.12.

2. *to breathe out*: + acc., πύρπνοον ἄσθμα 'fiery breath' Wi 11.18.

Cf. ἐκφυσάω, φυσητήρ.

φυσητήρ, ῆρος. m.ʃ

bellows: Je 6.29; χαλκέως 'of a coppersmith' Jb 32.19. Cf. φυσάω.

φύσις, εως.

1. *natural, living organism*: θνητή 'mortal' 3M 3.29.

2. *inherent nature* or *property*: Wi 19.20, 4M 13.27; κατὰ ~ιν 'by nature' 5.25, cf. μάταιοι .. ~ει 'senseless ..' Wi 13.1; ἱερά 4M 15.13, τῆς φιλοτεκνίας 'of love for children' 16.3.

3. *that which grows* out of sth: παθῶν 'of passions' 4M 1.20, cf. vs. 28.

4. *the physical world as it exists*: 4M 5.8, 9.

Cf. Köster, *TDNT* 9.266f.

φυτεία, ας. f.ʃ

1. v.n. of φυτεύω (q.v.): ἀμπελῶνος 'of a vineyard' Mi 1.6, 4K 19.29B; ^ξύλων^ PSol 14.4.

2. *plot of land for growing fruits*: σὺν τῷ βώλῳ τῆς ~ας αὐτῆς 'with the soil where it [= vine] is planted' Ez 17.7.

Cf. φυτεύω, κῆπος, παράδεισος.

φύτευμα, ατος. n.ʃ

that which is planted for crops: φ. ἄπιστον 'unpromising ..' Is 17.10 (ǁ σπέρμα ἄπιστον), φ., ἔργα χειρῶν 60.21; fig. of Israel, φ. κυρίου εἰς δόξαν 61.3. Cf. φυτεύω.

φυτεύω: fut. φυτεύσω; aor. ἐφύτευσα, impv. φύτευσον, inf. φυτεῦσαι, ptc. φυτεύσας, subj. φυτεύσω; pf. πεφεύτευκα, ptc.pass. πεφυτευμένος.

1. *to plant, establish*: + acc. and plot of ground for growing fruits, παράδεισον Ge 2.8; ἀμπελῶνα 9.20, De 28.30, 39, Am 5.11, ǁ καταφυτεύω Is 65.22; ἄρουραν 'tilled land' Ge 21.33; κήπους Am 9.14. **b.** ἄλσον 'sacred grove' De 16.21; νήσους 'islands' Si 43.23. **c.** fruit-growing plant: φύτευμα ἄπιστον καὶ σπέρμα ἄπιστον 'unpromising ..' Is 17.10, ἄμπελον 'grape-vine' 5.2, ξύλον Ps 1.3. **d.** trees: Is 44.14.

2. + acc. pers., *to help settle securely*: ἐν τῇ γῇ ταύτῃ Je 39.41; opp. ἐκτίλλω 51.34; as ruler, Si 10.15 (:: ἐκτίλλω).

3. *to place firmly for a purpose*: **o** τὸ οὖς 'the ear' Ps 93.9 (*s* God, ǁ πλάσσω τὸν ὀφθαλμόν), ἧλος 'nail' Ec 12.11.

Cf. φυτεία, φύτευμα, φυτόν, ἐπι~, κατα~, περιφυτεύω, σύμφυτος, ἐκτίλλω.

φυτόν, οῦ. n.

1. *plant*: Ge 22.13, Ez 31.4; ~ὰ ῥόδου 'rose bushes' Si 24.14.

2. *offspring*: hum., ἐκ τῆς ῥίζης αὐτοῦ Da 11.7 LXX. Cf. ἀπό~, ἔκγονος, σπέρμα. **b**. *branch* of a tree or plant: δένδρου 'of a tree' 2K 18.9*L*.

Cf. βοτάνη, φύω, νεόφυτος, παραφυάς: Shipp 561f.

φύω: fut. φυήσω; pf. πέφυκα, ptc. πεφυκώς

I. intr. *to grow*: ῥίζα ἄνω φύουσα ἐν χολῇ καὶ πικρίᾳ 'a root growing upwards with gall and bitterness' De 29.18; *s* sth intangible, 4M 1.20; mid. ξύλον φυόμενον ὑμῖν ἐπὶ τῆς γῆς 'tree growing (producing food) for you on the ground' Ex 10.5, sim. Da 3.76.

II. tr. *to cause to grow*: ῥίζαν 'a root' Is 37.31, δένδρον 'tree' Pr 11.30.

Cf. ἀνατέλλω, ἀνα~, προσ~, συμφύω.

φωνέω: fut. φωνήσω; aor.inf. φωνῆσαι, ptc. φωνήσας, impv. φώνησον.

1. *to utter* or *give out sound*: ἐν λάρυγγι 'with a throat' Ps 113.15; *s* hum., 1E 4.41, δι' ὕμνων 'through hymns' 5.58; σάλπιγξ 'trumpet' Am 3.6, σάλπιγξι 'with trumpets' 1M 9.12 (|| σαλπίζω); θηρία 'animals' Zp 2.14, χελιδών 'swallow' Is 38.14; of heathen divination, ἀπὸ τῆς γῆς (|| ἐκ τῆς γῆς 19.3) .. ἐκ τῆς κοιλίας '.. out of the stomach' 8.19.

2. *to invite in*: + acc. pers., πρός με To 5.9 𝔊I (𝔊II καλέω).

3. *to urge orally* to act: + inf., 3M 1.23.

4. *to speak to* sbd: τινα 4M 15.21.

Cf. φωνή, ἀναφωνέω, φθέγγομαι, ἠχέω, λαλέω, καλέω, προσαγορεύω: Betz, *TDNT* 9.302.

φωνή, ῆς. f.

1. *sound*: verbal and of a hum., φ. μία πᾶσιν "everybody had one speech sound, i.e. a system of sounds perceived as homogeneous" Ge 11.1 (|| χεῖλος); μεγάλη 'loud' 39.14; ~ῇ μιᾷ 'unanimously' Ex 24.3; πολέμου 32.17; αἰνέσεως καὶ ἐξομολογήσεως Jn 2.10; θρηνούντων ποιμένων 'of mourning shepherds' Zc 11.3*a*; προσευχῆς χειλέων μου Hb 3.16; κραυγῆς Zp 1.10, Is 30.19; of animals, δώσει σκύμνος ('a whelp') ~ὴν αὐτοῦ Am 3.4, ποιμνίου 1K 15.14, στρουθίου 'of a bird' Ec 12.4, ὠρυομένων λεόντων 'of howling lions' Zc 11.3*b*; of God, θεοῦ Ge 15.4; ἔδωκε ~ὴν αὐτοῦ Am 1.2 (|| φθέγγομαι), sim. Jl 2.11, 3.16, Je 12.8; κυρίου Mi 6.9; πικρὰ καὶ σκληρά 'bitter and harsh' Zp 1.10; 'message' Hg 1.12; ἤκουσας τῆς ~ῆς τῆς γυναικός Ge 3.17; αἵματος τοῦ ἀδελφοῦ σου 4.10. **b**. non-verbal, 'noise': of musical instrument, σάλπιγγος 'of a trumpet' Ex 19.19, τῶν ὀργάνων 'of musical instruments' Am 6.5, κιθάρας 'of a lyre' Is 24.8; of wagons - ἁρμάτων Jl 2.5*a*; cracking sound of fire, φλογὸς πυρός 2.5*b*; φ. μαστίγων καὶ φ. σεισμοῦ τροχῶν 'the sound of whips and the sound of rattling wheels' Na 3.2; the rustling of flying leaves, Le 26.36; pl., thunder, + ὑετός 'rain' 1K 12.17; ἔδωκεν ἡ ἄβυσσος τὴν ~ὴν αὐτῆς Hb 3.10; of river, Ps 92.3 (pl.); of pedestrian's steps, Ge 3.8.

2. *that which is said*: ὑπακούω τῆς ~ῆς τινος 'to accept sbd's advice or follow his instruction' Ge 16.2, 22.18; εἰσακούσωσιν τῆς ~ῆς τοῦ σημείου τοῦ πρώτου 'heed the message of the first sign' Ex 4.8; διὰ ~ῆς κυρίου ἐν χειρὶ Μωυσῆ 'by divine order given to Moses' Nu 4.37; 9.20 (|| διὰ προστάγματος κυρίου).

3. *news*: διεβοήθη ἡ φ. εἰς τὸν οἶκον Φαραω Ge 45.16.

4. *language as a system of verbal communication*: πατρία 'ancestral' 2M 7.8, 12.37, Συριακή 'Aramaic' 15.36; Ex 19.19.

Cf. ἀλαλαγμός, ἦχος, ἠχώ, λόγος, φθόγγος, χεῖλος, γλῶσσα, διάλεκτος, ψόφος: Betz, *TDNT* 9.280-5, 290.

φωράω: aor.subj.pass. φωραθῶ.ʃ

to catch red-handed: + ptc., 3M 3.29; Pr 26.19. Cf. ἁλίσκομαι **1**, εὑρίσκω, καταλαμβάνω **1a**, συλλαμβάνω **3**.

φῶς, φωτός. n.

1. *light*, which makes objects visible: created by God, γενηθήτω φ. 'Let there be light' Ge 1.3, ἐγὼ ὁ κατασκευάσας φ. καὶ ποιήσας σκότος Is 45.7, φ. ποιήσας ἐκ σκότους Jb 37.15, cf. τὸ φ. τοῦ θεοῦ To 3.17 𝔊II, τὸ φ. σου Is 58.8 and ἀνατολὴ ~ός Wi 16.28 (the last two of the break of day, cf. τὸ πρωὶ ἐν τῷ ~ί Da 6.19 TH and φ. τοῦ πρωΐ 4K 7.9); of daytime (as against night) Ps 138.12, Is 60.19; τῶν ὀφθαλμῶν Ps 37.11, Ba 3.14, To 10.5; seen for the first time on birth, νήπιοι, οἳ οὐκ εἶδον φ. 'babes ..' Jb 3.16; emitted by an oil-lamp, τὸ ἔλαιον τοῦ ~ός Ex 39.17, Nu 4.16; Le 24.2; || λαμπάς Is 62.1; φ. λύχνου 'of a lamp' Je 25.10, λυχνία ~ός 'candelabrum ..' 1M 1.21; by a burning fire, φ. πυρὸς καιομένου Is 4.5; by heavenly bodies, τῆς σελήνης .. τοῦ ἡλίου 30.26, οἱ ἀστέρες τοῦ οὐρανοῦ .. τὸ φ. οὐ δώσουσι 13.10, cf. metaph. ἔσται σοι κύριος φ. αἰώνιον Is 60.19; stored away in the sky, Je 10.13, 28.16; opp. darkness, διεχώρισεν .. ἀνὰ μέσον τοῦ ~ὸς καὶ ἀνὰ μέσον τοῦ σκότους '.. divided between the light and the darkness' Ge 1.4, σκότος καὶ οὐκ φ. Am 5.18; called ἡμέρα 'daytime' Ge 1.5, ἀπὸ ἡλίου Si 36.7. **b**. fig. ἐξάξει με εἰς τὸ φ., ὄψομαι τὴν δικαιοσύνην αὐτοῦ 'he will lead me out into the light, I shall see his righteousness' Mi 7.9 (cf. τὸ δικαιοσύνης φ. Wi 5.6), ὁ λαὸς ὁ πορευόμενος ἐν σκότει, ἴδετε φ. μέγα Is 9.2; || φέγγος 'brightness' Hb 3.11; opp. blindness, φ. ἐθνῶν ἀνοῖξαι ὀφθαλμοὺς τυφλῶν Is 42.6f.; a guide along a path, Λύχνος τοῖς ποσίν μου ὁ λόγος σου καὶ φ. ταῖς τρίβοις μου Ps 118.105, πορευθῶμεν τῷ ~ὶ κυρίου Is 2.5, πορεύεσθε τῷ ~ὶ τοῦ πυρὸς ὑμῶν καὶ τῇ φλογί 50.11, τῷ ~ὶ αὐτοῦ ἐπορευόμην ἐν σκότει Jb 29.3; ἡγήσεται ὁ θεὸς Ισραηλ .. τῷ ~ὶ τῆς δόξης .. Ba 5.9, φ. ἀγαπήσεως Si 17.18¶; of illuminating divine law, τὸ κρίμα μου ὡς φ. ἐξελεύσεται Ho 6.5, cf. φ. γνώσεως 10.12, τὸ φ. σου καὶ τὴν ἀλήθειάν σου Ps 42.3, γινώσκων τὰ ἐν τῷ σκότει, καὶ τὸ φ. μετ' αὐτοῦ ἐστι Da TH 2.22, ἀπαύγασμα .. ~ος ἀιδίου 'a reflection of eternal light' Wi 7.26, διόδευσον πρὸς τὴν λάμψιν κατέναντι τοῦ ~ὸς αὐτῆς [= ἡ βιβλίος τῶν προσταγμάτων τοῦ θεοῦ] Ba 4.2; οὐκ ἔσται φ. Zc 14.6 (of the end-time); glimmer of hope, Jb 3.20 (|| ζωή), ἡ ζωή μου φ. ὄψεται 33.28¶, ἡ ζωή μου ἐν ~ὶ αἰνῇ αὐτόν 33.30, ἐν ~ὶ ζώντων Ps 55.14. **c.** idiom τὸ φ. τοῦ προσώπου as an expression of satisfaction and pleasure, ἐν τῷ ~ὶ τοῦ προσώπου σου πορεύσονται Ps 88.16, cf. 4.7 and Nu 6.25, ὁ φωτισμὸς τοῦ προσώπου σου, ὅτι εὐδόκησας ἐν αὐτοῖς Ps 43.4, and Jb 29.24¶; φ. καὶ εὐφροσύνη Es 8.16 o', || εὐφροσύνη Ps 96.11.

2. *source of light, object which emits light*: of heavenly body - συσκοτάσει ἐπὶ τῆς γῆς ἐν ἡμέρᾳ τὸ φ. Am 8.9 (|| ἥλιος); τὰ φῶτα ^τοῦ οὐρανοῦ^ Je 4.23. Cf. φωστήρ.

3. *aperture, opening*: Ez 41.11.

Cf. φωτίζω, φωτεινός, φωστήρ, φωτισμός, φέγγος, ἀπαύγασμα, σκότος: Schmidt 1.563-98; Spicq 3.470-91.

φωστήρ, ῆρος. m. *

that which gives out light, 'luminary': heavenly body, ἐποίησεν ὁ θεὸς τοὺς δύο ~ῆρας Ge 1.16, ~ῆρας οὐρανοῦ Wi 13.2; of the moon, Si 43.7; fig. of a source of hope, τοῦ ἀνακαλύψαι ~ῆρα ἡμῶν 1E 8.76; of wise men compared to φωστῆρες τοῦ οὐρανοῦ Da LXX 12.3. Cf. φῶς **2.**

φωταγωγέω: aor.ptc. φωταγωγήσας.ʃ *

to guide with a light: τινα 4M 17.5. Cf. ἄγω.

φωτεινός, ή, όν.ʃ

1. *emitting light, shining*, 'bright': *s* ἥλιος 'sun', τί φωτεινότερον ἡλίου 'what is brigher than the sun?' Si 17.31; 23.19.

2. *reflecting light*: *s* eyes, ὀφθαλμοὶ κυρίου μυριοπλασίως ἡλίου φωτεινότεροι '.. ten thousand times brighter ..' Si 23.19.

Cf. φῶς.

φωτίζω: fut. φωτιῶ, φωτίσω, pass. φωτισθήσομαι, ptc. φωτίσων; aor. ἐφώτισα, inf. φωτίσαι, impv. φώτισον, pass.2pl φωτίσθητε.

1. *to illumine, provide light*: *s* λύχνος 'lamp' Nu 8.2, σελήνη Ep Je 66 (|| λάμπω); + dat., κύριος φωτιεῖ μοι Mi 7.8; + obj. cogn. φωτίσατε ἑαυτοῖς φῶς γνώσεως Ho 10.12; + acc., ἐν στύλῳ πυρὸς τὴν νύκτα φωτίσαι αὐτοῖς τὴν ὁδόν 'with a column of fire ..' Ne 9.12, cf. πῦρ τοῦ φωτίσαι αὐτοῖς τὴν νύκτα Ps 104.39; metaph., ὀφθαλμοὺς ἡμῶν 2E 9.8, Ba 1.12, sim. Ps 12.4; ἡ ἐντολὴ κυρίου τηλαυγής, φωτίζουσα ὀφθαλμούς 18.9; πρόσωπον Ec 8.1; ἡ δήλωσις τῶν λόγων σου φωτιεῖ Ps 118.130 (|| συνετιεῖ); + acc. pers., ἐν νόμῳ αὐτοῦ Si 45.17. **b.** impers. 'it becomes light with sunrise': φωτισάτω ὑμῖν 1K 29.10. **c.** *to cause to emit light and shine*: + acc., σὺ φωτιεῖς λύχνον μου .. φωτιεῖς τὸ σκότος μου Ps 17.29; 2K 22.29*L* (|| ἀναλάμπω).

2. pass. *to become bright and shine*: νὺξ ὡς ἡμέρα φωτισθήσεται Ps 138.12 (:: σκοτίζομαι), *s* Jerusalem Is 60.1.

3. metaph. *to instruct and explain*: + acc. rei, μυστήρια Da 2.28 LXX; τινα 4K 12.3; + double acc., φωτισάτω ἡμᾶς τί ποιήσωμεν '.. what we should do' Jd 13.8A (B: συμβιβασάτω), αὐτοὺς πῶς φοβηθῶσιν τὸν κύριον 4K 17.28; ἐφώτισεν ἡμᾶς πάντα ταῦτα Jd 13.23A (B: ἔδειξεν), φωτιοῦσιν αὐτοὺς (*L* αὐτοῖς) τὸ κρίμα τοῦ θεοῦ 4K 17.27; pass. φωτίσθητε 'receive instruction' Ps 33.6.

Cf. φῶς.

φωτισμός, οῦ. m.*

syn. of φῶς **1**, 'light': εἰς ~ὸν μὴ ἔλθοι 'may it not be made bright' Jb 3.9, φ. πυρός 'fiery light' Ps 77.14; metaph., κύριος φ. μου καὶ σωτήρ μου 26.1; φ. τοῦ προσώπου, indicative of pleasure and favourable estimation, 43.4 (continued by ὅτι εὐδόκησας ἐν αὐτοῖς and cf. Nu 6.26 || Ps 66.2), same idiom with a different connotation, ὁ αἰὼν ἡμῶν εἰς ~ὸν τοῦ προσώπου σου 'our past is facing your observing light' 89.8; opp. νύξ, 138.11, φ. ὑγιείας 'of health' Si 17.26¶ (:: σκότος). Cf. φῶς: Spicq 3.490f.

X

χαβραθα.

A transliteration of כִּבְרַת of unknown meaning: Ge 35.16, 48.7.

χαίνω: aor. ἔχανον, impv. χάνε. Cf. χάσκω, which supplies the present tense.ʃ

to open widely: *o* mouth in order to eat or drink, χάνε τὸ στόμα σου Ez 2.8; ἀπὸ τῆς γῆς, ἣ ἔχανεν τὸ στόμα αὐτῆς δέξασθαι τὸ αἷμα τοῦ ἀδελφοῦ σου Ge 4.11. Cf. ἀναχαίνω, ἀνοίγω, (ἐγ)χάσκω, ἀχανής.

χαιρετίζω: aor. ἐχαιρέτισα.ʃ

to greet by saying χαῖρε: + acc. pers. (visitor), To 5.10 𝔊II, 7.1. Cf. χαίρω.

χαίρω: fut. χαρήσομαι (with composita ~χαροῦμαι, and occasionally also as simplex as v.l., e.g. Zc 10.7 where χαρήσομαι also occurs); aor. ἐχάρην, impv. χάρηθι, 2pl χάρητε, opt. χαρείην.

to rejoice, be cheerful: abs. Ge 45.16, Ho 9.1; ἐν ἑαυτῷ Ex 4.14; + ἐπί τινι Jl 2.23, Jn 4.6 (also w. cogn. obj. χαρὰν μεγάλην), Hb 3.18, Zc 10.7*b*; + dat., Pr 6.16, 17.19; + cogn. dat., χαρᾷ Is 66.10; often ‖ εὐφραίνω, Ho 9.1, Jl 2.21, 23, Hb 1.16, Je 7.34; malicious joy at others' misfortune, La 1.21, Ba 4.33; *s* καρδία – χαρήσεται ἡ καρδία αὐτῶν ὡς ἐν οἴνῳ Zc 10.7*a*; τὰ πεδία 'the fields' Ps 95.12; opp. θρηνέω Ez 7.12. **b.** χαίρειν as an opening formula of a letter: Βασιλεὺς Δημήτριος Σίμωνι ἀρχιερεῖ .. χαίρειν 1M 13.36, Τοῖς ἀδελφοῖς τοῖς κατ' Αἴγυπτον .. χαίρειν οἱ ἀδελφοὶ οἱ ἐν Ἱεροσολύμοις .. εἰρήνην ἀγαθήν 2M 1.1; 1E 6.7; χαίρειν καὶ ὑγιαίνειν 2M 1.10, χαίρειν καὶ ὑγιαίνειν καὶ εὖ πράττειν 9.19. **c.** in a welcoming salutation: χαίρων ἔλθοις 'Welcome' To 5.14 𝔊II (‖ ὑγιαίνων ἔλθοις καὶ σῳζόμενος), χαίρετε πολλά 7.1 𝔊II, cf. Mt 26.49.

Cf. χαρά, ἐπι~, προσ~, συγχαίρω, χαιρετίζω, ἀγαλλιάομαι, ἀσμενίζω, εὐφραίνω, κατατέρπομαι, τέρπομαι: Schmidt 2.566f.; Croughs 2002.63; BDAG, s.v., **2b**.

χάλαζα, ης. f.

hail: destructive, ἐγὼ ὕω .. ~αν πολλὴν Ex 9.18; πέσῃ ἐπὶ ^τὰ κτήνη^ ἡ χ. 9.19; χ. καὶ ὑετός '.. and rain' 9.29; ἐπάταξα ὑμᾶς .. καὶ ἐν ~ῃ πάντα τὰ ἔργα τῶν χειρῶν ὑμῶν 'I smote you .. and all the works of your hands with hail' Hg 2.17; λίθοι ~ης Jo 10.11, Si 43.15; harmful to crops, Ps 77.47 (‖ πάχνη 'frost').

χαλαστόν, οῦ. n.ʃ

festoon: 2C 3.5, 16. Cf. Russo 101-6.

χαλάω: fut. χαλάσω; aor. ἐχάλασα.ʃ

1. *to loosen from a fixed position*: + acc., οὐ χαλάσει τὰ ἱστία 'it [= a mast] will not loosen the sails' Is 33.23. **b.** *to come loose and get detached*: mid. and + ἀπό τινος, Ex 36.29.

2. *to allow to have free play*: + acc., ἐπὶ τίνα ἐχαλάσατε τὴν γλῶσσαν ὑμῶν; 'upon whom have you dropped your tongue out?' Is 57.4 (in mockery or a French kiss?).

3. *to cause to move downwards*: + acc. pers., εἰς τὸν λάκκον 'into the cistern' Je 45.6 (‖ ῥίπτω).

Cf. κατα~, προχαλάω, καταβιβάω, ἀνίημι: Schmidt 3.261-3; Shipp 564f.

χαλβάνη, ης. f.ʃ < Heb. חֶלְבְּנָה.

"*the* resinous *juice of all-heal, Ferula galbaniflua*" (LSJ): χ. ἡδυσμοῦ Ex 30.34; Si 24.15.

Χαλδαῖος, α, ον.

Chaldaean: *s* διάλεκτος 'language' Da 1.4 LXX; subst. ~οι 'Chaldaea' Ge 11.28, Is 13.19 +; known for skills in divination, + μάγος, ἐπαοιδός, σοφός Da 2.10.

Χαλδαϊστί. adv.

in the Chaldaean [i.e. Babylonian] *language*: Da 2.26 LXX.

χαλεπαίνω.ʃ

to be violently agitated: *s* hum., κατά τινος (hum.) 4M 9.10 (anger); 16.22 (‖ ὀργίζομαι). Cf. χαλεπός, ὀργίζομαι.

χαλεπός, ή, όν.ʃ

1. *difficult or awkward to deal with*: *s* hum., πρὸς .. ξένον λαὸν καὶ ~όν Is 18.2; instrument of torture, 4M 8.1; φροντίς 'thought given' 16.8; business, ~πώτερά σου 'what is beyond you' Si 3.21 (‖ ἰσχυρός 'tough'); subst. n., τὰ ~ά 'the difficulties' Wi 17.11.

2. *grievous in effect*: *s* one's final destiny, Wi 3.19; mistreatment of guests, 19.13; situation, 2M 4.16, 6.3.

3. *dangerous*: *s* rivalry, 2M 4.4; death and transgression of the law, 4M 9.4.

Cf. κοῦφος, σκληρός, ὑπέρογκος, εὔκοπος, εὐχερής, ῥᾴδιος: Schmidt 3.562f.; Spicq 3.494f.

χαλινός, οῦ. m.

bridle: Hb 3.14; ἵππου Zc 14.20, + κημός 'muzzle' Ps 31.9; metaph. *restraining influence*: τοῦ προσώπου μου 'of my presence' Jb 30.11¶. Cf. ἡνία, κημός, χρυσοχάλινος.

χάλιξ, ικος. m./f.ʃ

small stone, pebble: Jb 8.17 (‖ λίθος), χειμάρρου 21.33¶; Si 22.18. Cf. κόλαξ, λίθος, ψῆφος.

χαλκεῖον. ⇒ χαλκίον.

χάλκειος, η, ον.

of copper: *s* hum. flesh, Jb 6.12, fetters Si 28.20 (|| σιδηροῦς 'iron'), Jd 16.21B. Cf. χαλκός.

χαλκεύς, έως. m.

coppersmith: χ. χαλκοῦ καὶ σιδήρου Ge 4.22; τέκτων καὶ χ. Is 41.7. Cf. χαλκοῦς: Spicq 3.496f.

χαλκεύω.ʃ

to fabricate a metal tool: + acc. rei, 1K 13.20.

χαλκίον, ου. n.

bronze cauldron: cooking utensil, + λέβης 'cauldron' 1K 2.14, 1E 1.11; Jb 41.23. Cf. LSG s.v.

χαλκοπλάστης, ου. m.ʃ *

worker in bronze: || χρυσουργός .. ἀργυροχόος 'goldsmith .. silversmith' Wi 15.9.

χαλκός, οῦ. m.

1. *copper*: χαλκεὺς ~οῦ καὶ σιδήρου Ge 4.22; χρυσίον, ἀργύριον, ~όν as offerings to God, Ex 25.3; building material, 31.4; sandal made of .., χ. καὶ σίδηρος τὸ ὑπόδημα .. De 33.25; less valuable than gold, but more valuable than stones, Is 60.17; χ. καὶ σίδηρος in a fig. of hardened, obstinate character, Je 6.28, cf. Is 48.4.

2. *anything made of copper*: fetter, La 3.7.

3. *money*: Ez 16.36; || πλοῦτος Ep Je 34.

Cf. χαλκεύς, χαλκοῦς, κατα~, περιχαλκόω, σίδηρος, ἀργύριον, χρυσίον.

χαλκοῦς, ῆ, οῦν.

made of copper: *s* curtain-ring, Ex 26.11; weapon, Mi 4.13 (|| σιδηροῦς), helmet 1K 17.38, door Is 45.2; of mountain, Zc 6.1; earth at a time of drought, Le 26.19 (|| σιδηροῦς), sky, De 28.23 (dit.); forehead in a fig. of hardness, Is 48.4, cf. Je 6.28. Cf. σιδηροῦς, χαλκεύς, χαλκός: Meyer 1984.

χαμαί. adv.

downwards *in the direction of the ground*: πίπτω Jb 1.20; ἕως χ. Da LXX 8.11, ἐκοιμήθην ἐπὶ πρόσωπον χ. 8.18 LXX (TH: ἐπὶ τὴν γῆν); metaph., ἐρρίφη χ. ἡ δικαιοσύνη 8.12. **b**. static: ἰδοὺ Ὀλοφέρνης χ. Ju 14.18.

χαμαιλέων, οντος. m.ʃ

chameleon: ceremonially unclean, Le 11.30; Zp 2.14.

χαμαιπετής, ές.ʃ

kneeling on the ground: 1E 8.88.

Χαναναῖος, α, ον.

1. *belonging to Canaan*: θυγατέρα ἀνθρώπου Χαναναίου Ge 38.2; subst. 'a Canaanite', αἱ φυλαὶ τῶν Χαναναίων 10.18; ἀπὸ τῶν θυγατέρων τῶν Χαναναίων 'from the daughters of the Canaanites' 36.2 (Wevers ad loc.).

2. *pedlar, travelling merchant*: Pr 31.24.

Χανανίς. m.; acc. ίν.ʃ

a Canaanite: ὁ Χ. βασιλεὺς Nu 21.1, 33.40; 21.3.

Χανανῖτις, ιδος. f.ʃ

Canaanite: λαλοῦσαι τῇ γλώσσῃ τῇ Χανανίτιδι 'speaking in the Canaanite language' Is 19.18; subst., 'Canaanite woman' Ge 46.10; 'the land (γῆ) of Canaan' Zc 11.7. Cf. Χανααν, Χαναναῖος.

χάος, ους. n.

chasm: in the ground, χ. μέγα σφόδρα Zc 14.4; Mi 1.6. Cf. κοιλάς, φάραγξ, χάσμα.

χαρά, ᾶς. f.

joy: εὐφροσύνη καὶ χ. Jl 1.16; as cogn. obj. ἐχάρη ~ὰν μεγάλην Jn 4.6; associated w. drinking and festivity, and verbally manifested, ἐξῆρται ἐκ στόματος ὑμῶν εὐφροσύνη καὶ χ. Jl 1.5; εἰς ~ὰν καὶ εἰς εὐφροσύνην καὶ εἰς ἑορτὰς ἀγαθάς Zc 8.19; ᾔσχυναν ~άν '(because of a general famine) they denigrated (i.e. detracted from?) joyous festivities' (?) Jl 1.12. Cf. χαίρω, χαρμοσύνη, χαροποιός, ὑπερχαρής, ἀγαλλίαμα, γέλως, εὐφροσύνη, τέρψις, λύπη: Schmidt 2.564f.; Spicq 3.498f.

χαραδριός, οῦ. m.ʃ

thick-knee, Charadrius oedicnemus (LSJ): Le 11.19, De 14.17.

χαρακοβολία, ας. f.ʃ*

building of palisade: Ez 17.17. Cf. βάλλω χάρακα, subs.

χαρακόω: aor. ἐχαράκωσα.ʃ

to build a palisade: abs. Is 5.2 (|| περιτιθέναι φραγμόν 'to set a fence around'); ἐπὶ Ιερουσαλημ Je 39.2 (siege). Cf. χάραξ, χαράκωσις, χαρακοβολία, περιχαρακόω, φράσσω: Ziegler 1934.179.

χαρακτήρ, ῆρος. m.ʃ

distinctive mark: + gen., Le 13.28 (|| οὐλή 'scar'). **b**. *distinctive style*: life-style, Ἑλληνικός 'Hellenic' 2M 4.10; personal character, 4M 15.4. Cf. σημεῖον.

χαράκωσις, εως. f.ʃ

palisade: De 20.20. Cf. χάραξ, χαρακόω, φραγμός.

χάραξ, κος. m.

palisade: De 20.19; βαλῶ περὶ σὲ ~ακα Is 29.3, κυκλώσῃ ἐπὶ ^τὴν πόλιν^ ~ακα 37.33; 2K 20.15 *L* (B: πρόσχωμα); + προμαχών 'battlement' Je 40.4. Cf. χαράκωσις.

χαράσσω: aor. ἐχάραξα.ʃ

to write by scratching: abs., 4K 17.11; εἰς τὸ σῶμα 'on the body' 3M 2.29. **b**. *to write*: + acc. rei, παιδείαν 'a teaching' Si 50.27. Cf. γλύφω, γράφω.

χαρίεις, εσσα, εν.ʃ

accomplished of character: morally or intellectually (?), *s* hum., 4M 8.3.

χαρίζομαι: aor. ἐχαρισάμην, inf. χαρίσασθαι, ptc. χαρισάμενος; pf. κεχάρισμαι, ptc. κεχαρισμένος.

1. *to act kindly by giving*: + acc., ἐλεημοσύνην 'alms' Si 12.3; property, Es 8.7 (+ δίδωμι); and +

dat. pers., 2M 3.31; + cogn. acc., χάριτας ἡμῖν 4M 11.12.

2. *to regard and treat favourably*: + dat. pers., 2M 1.35.

Cf. χάρις, χαριστήριον.

χάρις, τος. f.

1. *outward beauty*: of stone, Zc 4.7; + κάλλος Si 40.22.

2. *charming or attractive quality*: τὸ πρόσωπόν σου ~ων μεστόν '.. full of charms' Es D 14; of a woman, χ. γυναικὸς τέρψει ἄνδρα αὐτῆς 'the wife's charm is her husband's delight' Si 26.13; 7.19, 26.15; marking speech by an intelligent person, 21.16, cf. ἐξεχύθη χ. ἐν χείλεσίν σου Ps 44.3, λόγοις πρὸς ~ιν Pr 7.5, and τοῖς λόγοις τῆς ~τος Lk 4.22; μισθὸς ~ων '.. reward' Pr 17.8.

3. *kindness*: shown by a hum., Zc 6.14; by God, πνεῦμα ~τος καὶ οἰκτιρμοῦ '.. of mercy' 12.10; + ἔλεος Wi 3.9. **b**. *kind deed*: hum., ǁ ἐλεημοσύνη Si 17.22, 40.17. **c**. *favour offered*: χ. δόματος Si 7.33, pl., 3.31, 20.13, φύσεως 'of nature' 4M 5.9. Cf. χρηστός.

4. *favourable estimation*: in the idiom εὑρίσκω χάριν, see under εὑρίσκω, **7 i**; ~ιν ἔχεις παρ' ἐμοί 'you are a favourite of mine' Ex 33.12; ἔσχοσαν ~ιν 'were treated favourably' 1E 6.5; τὰ πρὸς ~ιν 'pleasing things' Ez 12.24. **b**. δίδωμί τινι[1] χάριν ἐναντίον τινός[2] 'to dispose sbd[2] favourably towards sbd[1]' Ge 39.21, 43.14, Ex 3.21, 11.3, 12.36, κατὰ πρόσωπόν τινος Ba 2.14; ἐποίησαν ἡμᾶς ἐν ~ιτι ἐνώπιον τῶν βασιλέων 'brought us into favour with the kings' 1E 8.77.

5. *sense of gratitude*: Πολλὰς Ονίᾳ .. ~τας ἔχε 'Be ever grateful to Onias ..' 2M 3.33, εὔχομαι τῷ θεῷ τὴν μεγίστην ~ιν 'I express my most profound gratitude to God' 9.20; τοῖς ἀγαθοῖς 'for kindnesses' Si 20.16; 3M 5.20. **b**. *token of gratitude*: 1M 14.25; thank-offering to God, 3M 1.9.

6. χάριν as causal postposition c. gen.: ὧν χάριν .. 'on account of which ..' Ju 8.19, 3M 5.41, τούτου χάριν 'for this reason' 1M 12.45, 13.4, τούτων χ. Si 31.13; ἔχθρας χ. 'out of hatred' 1M 13.6; οὐ πότου χ. καὶ λιχνείας 'not for the sake of drinking and gluttony' 3M 6.36. **b**. as prep. with same meaning: χάριν τούτου 'for this reason' To 2.14 𝔊II, 1M 6.24, χάριν τῆς διχοστασίας 'because of the dissention' 3.29, χ. τῶν νομίμων 'on account of the laws' 6.59, ἀποθάνωμεν .. χ. τῶν ἀδελφῶν ἡμῶν 9.10; χάριν τίνος 'for what reason?' 2C 7.21. **c**. + inf., χάριν τοῦ ἐπιθυμῆσαι αὐτὸν τῆς βασιλείας αὐτοῦ 'because he coveted his kingdom' 1M 11.11; Wi 18.2 where χάριν can hardly mean 'pardon, favour' as an obj. of ἐδέοντο, which would require a gen., cf. Scarpat 3.279f.; with final force, χάριν τοῦ λαβεῖν τὰ χρήματα 'in order to secure its treasures' 2M 1.14; Da 2.13 LXX.

Cf. εὐχαριστέω, εὐχάριστος, εὔχαρις, χαρίζομαι, χαριστήριον, χαριτόω, ἔλεος: Trench 166-71; Spicq 3.500-6.

χαριστήριον, ου. n.∫

that which is awarded as a token of favour: = resurrection, 2M 12.45. Cf. χαρίζομαι.

χαριτόω: aor.impv. χαρίτωσον; pf.ptc.pass. κεχαριτωμένος.∫ *

1. *to treat favourably*: ἀνὴρ κεχαριτωμένος 'exceedingly favoured (by God)' Si 18.17.

***2**. *to cause to be accepted favourably*: + acc., τὰ ῥήματά μου ἐνώπιον τοῦ βασιλέως Es 4.25 *L*.

Cf. χάρις.

χαρμονή, ῆς. f.

joy: πλήρεις ~ῆς 3M 6.31; opp. πένθος 'sadness' Je 38.13; opp. ὀδύνη, ǁ εὐφροσύνη Jb 3.7; experienced by animals, 40.20. Cf. χαρά, χαρμοσύνη.

χαρμοσύνη, ης. f.∫ * [but χαρμόσυνος Hdt +].

joy: εὐχὴ ~ης 'joyous vow' Le 22.29; + εὐφροσύνη Ba 4.23, Je 31.33; φωνὴ εὐφροσύνης καὶ φ. ~ης 40.11, Ba 2.23; accompanied by music, 1K 18.6B (*L*: χαρμονή). **b**. *joyous occasion*: + ἑορτή Ju 8.6.

Cf. χαρά.

χαροποιός, ή, όν.∫

gladdening: *s* human eyes, Ge 49.12. Cf. χαρά.

χαρτηρία, ας. f.∫*

papyrus as writing material: + κάλαμος 'pen' 3M 4.20. Cf. χαρτίον.

χάρτης, ου. m.∫

papyrus-roll: writing material, Je 43.23. Cf. χαρτίον.

χαρτίον, ου. n. Dim. of χάρτης.

papyrus roll: as writing material, χ. βιβλίου Je 43.2. Cf. χάρτης, χαρτηρία.

χάσκω. Only in the pres.∫

to open widely: ***o*** mouth of admiring onlooker, χάσκοντες τὸ στόμα θεωροῦσιν αὐτήν 1E 4.19; ib. 31. Cf. ἐγχάσκω and χαίνω, which latter is a later and less sophisticated synonym (Anz 22f.) and, in the LXX, is attested only in the aor

χάσμα, ατος. n.

yawning chasm: in the ground, 2K 18.17. Cf. χάος.

χαῦνος, η, ον.∫

having little substance: 'insignificant,' *s* ἀήρ '(thin) air' Wi 2.3. Cf. κοῦφος, παχύς: Schmidt 4.670f.

χαυών, ῶνος.∫ * (< Heb. כַּוָּן)

a kind of cake for a cultic purpose: Je 7.18, 51.19. Cf. πέμμα.

χεῖλος, ους. n.

1. *lip*: pl., organ of speech, τὰ ἐκπορευόμενα διὰ τῶν ~έων σου 'that which comes out through your lips' De 23.23; τὰ ~η ὑμῶν ἐλάλησεν ἀνομίαν Is 59.3; καρπὸν ~έων 'fruit of lips' Ho 14.3; ἀπὸ φωνῆς προσευχῆς ~έων 'from the sound of a prayer said with lips' Hb 3.16; Ma 2.6 (‖ στόμα); ~η ἱερέως φυλάξεται γνῶσιν 'the lips of a priest will preserve knowledge' 2.7.

2. *speech community*: sg., ἦν πᾶσα ἡ γῆ χ. ἕν Ge 11.1 (‖ φωνή).

3. *a flat, oblong surface along* sth else: τὸ χ. τῆς θαλάσσης'the seashore, beach' Ge 22.17, Ex 14.30; παρὰ τὸ χ. τοῦ ποταμοῦ 'by the river-bank' Ge 41.3; rim of an altar, Ez 43.13, of a cup 2C 4.5[2].

4. *the far end of a flat surface*: of a curtain, Ex 26.4; of a lake, 3K 7.10.

Cf. στόμα, φωνή, αἰγιαλός.

χειμάζω.ʃ

to cause distress to, 'batter': pass., *o* hum. body, Pr 26.10. Cf. λυπέω, πονέω.

χειμάρρους, ον. Also χείμαρρος, ον.

Used alw. as subst.m., but n. at Ez 47.5 (967).

1. *winter-flowing*: *s* stream, διέβη τὸν ~ουν 'crossed the wadi' Ge 32.23; εἰς τὸν ~ουν τὸν καταβαίνοντα ἐκ τοῦ ὄρους De 9.21; χ. ἄβατος 'impassable wadi' Am 5.24; the river-bed of a wadi, even when dry, Nu 34.5; + φάραγξ Ju 2.8; metaph. of an entity of limited width and with considerable length, ἐν μυριάσι ~ων πιόνων 'ten thousand rows (?) of fat animals' Mi 6.7.

2. possibly syn. of ποταμός 'river, stream' in any season: ἐν ταῖς θαλάσσαις καὶ ἐν τοῖς ~οις Le 11.9; χείμαρροι ὑδάτων De 8.7, γῆ ~ου ὑδάτων 10.7, καταγάγετε ὡς ~ους δάκρυα 'Let tears flow down like rivers' La 2.18. **b**. threateningly large quantity: ἀνομίας Ps 17.5.

Cf. χειμερινός, πηγή, ποταμός, φάραγξ: Schmidt 1.633-40; Caird 1969.39.

χειμερινός, ή, όν.ʃ

wintry: *s* ὑετός 'rain' Zc 10.1; καιρός 'season' 2E 10.13, ὥρα 1E 9.11, ἡμέρα Pr 27.15; οἶκος Je 43.22. Cf. χειμών, χειμάρρους.

χειμέριος, α, ον.ʃ

= χειμερινός, q.v.: *s* πάχνη 'frost' Wi 16.29. Cf. χειμών.

χειμών, ῶνος. m.

1. *winter*: characterised by much rainfall, ὁ χ. παρῆλθεν 'the winter is past' Ct 2.11 (‖ ὑετός).

2. *storm*: χ. ὑετῶν 'rain-storm' Jb 37.6¶; τρέμοντες διὰ τὸν ἐνεστῶτα ~να 'shivering from the prevailing storm' 1E 9.6; metaph., ὑπὲρ τῆς εὐσεβείας ~νας 'trying, stormy times for religion' 4M 15.32.

Cf. θέρος: Spicq 2.97f.

χείρ, ός. f.

1. *hand* as a limb of body: κροτέω χεῖρας ἐπί τινα 'to clap hands against sbd' Na 3.19; flat object placed over a surface to cover it, ἐπιθήσουσι ~ας ἐπὶ στόμα αὐτῶν Mi 7.16; holds an object, κράτησον τῇ ~ρί σου αὐτό 'Grip it with your hand' Ge 21.18; ἐν τῇ ~ρὶ αὐτοῦ σχοινίον 'a string' Zc 2.1; moves sth, ἡ χ. μου ἀνασπάσει αὐτούς 'my hand will drag them up' Am 9.2; is stretched out to offer sth (in pl.), δέξαι τὰ δῶρα διὰ τῶν ἐμῶν χειρῶν Ge 33.10, θυσίαν οὐ προσδέξομαι ἐκ τῶν ~ῶν ὑμῶν Ma 1.10; λαβεῖν δεκτὸν ἐκ τῶν ~ῶν ὑμῶν 2.13; carriage and transport, τὸ ἀργύριον ἡμῶν .. ἀπεστρέψαμεν .. ἐν ταῖς χερσὶν ἡμῶν Ge 43.21; δίδωμί τινι ~α 'to submit oneself to sbd' 4K 8.22*L*, cf. 10.15 and δεξιός **II a**; κυνός 'a dog's (paw)' Ps 21.21; 'paw' Le 11.27. **b**. author of a deed (often in pl.): ἐν καθαρᾷ καρδίᾳ καὶ ἐν δικαιοσύνῃ ~ῶν ἐποίησα τοῦτο Ge 20.5; τῆς ἀδικίας τῆς ἐν χερσὶν αὐτῶν Jn 3.8; τὰ ἔργα τῶν ~ῶν σου De 24.19; τοὺς πόνους τῶν ~ῶν αὐτῶν Hg 1.11; αἱ ~ρες Ζοροβαβελ ἐθεμελίωσαν τὸν οἶκον τοῦτον Zc 4.9; of hostile action, ἡ χ. σου ἐπὶ τοὺς θλίβοντάς σε 'your hand will be raised against those who harass you' Mi 5.9, cf. Ge 16.12; ἐκτενεῖ τὴν ~α αὐτοῦ ἐπὶ βορρᾶν καὶ ἀπολεῖ .. 'he will stretch out his hand against the north and will destroy ..' Zp 2.13; ἐπέβαλε τὴν ~ρα αὐτοῦ ἐπ' αὐτούς Is 5.25, ἡ χ. ὑψηλή 'the hand is raised' ib.; ἐπιφέρω τὴν ~α μου ἐπ' αὐτούς Zc 2.9; εἶδεν Ισραηλ τὴν ~α τὴν μεγάλην, ἃ ἐποίησεν κύριος τοῖς Αἰγυπτίοις Ex 14.31, cf. ταῖς χερσὶν καὶ τοῖς λόγοις 'by their words and deeds' Wi 1.16; perform manual labour, αἱ λύπαι τῶν ~ῶν Ge 5.29; deed itself, κατήρξατο ~ῶν ἀδίκων 'initiated unjust (military) actions' 2M 4.40, cf. Xen. *Cyr* 1.5.13 ἄρχοντες ἀδίκων χειρῶν. **c**. Idiomatically: ἐὰν δὲ μὴ εὕρῃ ἡ χεὶρ αὐτοῦ τὸ ἱκανὸν ὥστε ἀποδοῦναι αὐτῷ 'should he not manage to put together enough to repay him' Le 25.28, see under εὑρίσκω **7 iv**; ἰσχύει ἡ χ. τινος 'be capable': see under ἰσχύω **2,** δύναμαι **1c**, and ἐκποιέω **1c**. **d**. ἐν χειρί τινος denotes agency, 'through': ἐγένετο λόγος κυρίου ἐν ~ὶ Ἀγγαίου 'a pronouncement of the Lord was made through Haggai' Hg 1.1; + ἀποστέλλω Ge 38.20, 1K 11.7; + λαλέω Hg 2.1, Je 44.2; + συντάσσω 'issue a command' Nu 15.23; λῆμμα λόγου κυρίου .. ἐν ~ὶ ἀγγέλου αὐτοῦ Ma 1.1; ἐν νόμῳ τοῦ θεοῦ, ὃς ἐδόθη ἐν ~ὶ Μωυσῆ .. Ne 10.29; ἐν χερσίν in the case of multiple agents, ἐν ~σὶν ὑμῶν γέγονε ταῦτα Ma 1.9, ἐλάλησε ἐν ~σὶν τῶν προφητῶν Zc 7.7, but ἐν ~ὶ τῶν παίδων σου Ba 2.20 (:: ἐν ~σὶ τῶν παίδων σου 2.24) and ἐν χερσὶν βασιλέως Je 39.3 (‖ εἰς χεῖρας vs. 4); leadership, Nu 33.1: cf. Sollamo, *Semiprep.*, 162-5, 335-7. **e**. possession: εὑρεθῇ ἐν τῇ ~ὶ αὐτοῦ 'found in his possession' Ex 22.4; τοὺς θεοὺς τοὺς ἀλλοτρίους, οἳ ἦσαν ἐν ταῖς ~σὶν αὐτῶν 'the alien gods which were in their possession' Ge 35.4; ἔτι ἐν ~ὶν ἔχοντες τὰ πένθη 'while still keenly feeling the sorrow' Wi 19.3. **f.** διὰ χειρός denotes intermediacy– ἔδωκεν διὰ ~ὸς τῶν υἱῶν αὐτοῦ Ge 30.35; διὰ ~ὸς τοῖς παισὶν αὐτοῦ 32.16; 39.4 ‖ εἰς τὰς χεῖράς τινος vs. 8; ἐλάλησεν .. διὰ χειρὸς Μωυσῆ Le 10.11; distinct from δέξαι τὰ δῶρα διὰ τῶν ἐμῶν χειρῶν Ge 33.10. **g.** denotes sphere of control and authority: κυριεύσει ἡ χ. μου 'my hand shall dominate' Ex 15.9; λελύτρωταί σε ἐκ ~ὸς ἐχθρῶν σου 'he has liberated you from the grip of your enemies' Zp 3.15; ἐν ~ὶ αὐτοῦ ψυχὴ πάντων τῶν ἀνθρώπων Jb 12.10, ἄνθρωποι ἐν ~ὶ τοῦ ποιήσαντος αὐτούς Si 36.13; "I am in your hands (ἐν ~ὶν ὑμῶν). Do to me as is expedient and as it is best for you" Je 33.13; ὑπὸ ~ας ὑμῖν δέδωκα 'I have handed (them) over to your control' Ge 9.2; ἡ παιδίσκη σου ἐν ταῖς χερσίν σου 16.6; ταπεινώθητι ὑπὸ τὰς χεῖρας αὐτῆς 'submit yourself to her authority' (Wevers) 16.9; ἀποθάνῃ ὑπὸ τὰς ~ας αὐτοῦ 'die whilst in his charge' Ex 21.20; παραδίδωμι τοὺς ἀνθρώπους ἕκαστον εἰς ~ας τοῦ πλησίον αὐτοῦ καὶ εἰς ~ας (pl.) τοῦ βασιλέως αὐτοῦ .. οὐ μὴ ἐξέλωμαι ἐκ ~ὸς (sg.) αὐτῶν 'I turn the people each over to his king .. and will not rescue (them) from them' Zc 11.6 (‖ παραδίδωμί τινα ἐν ~ί τινος Is 36.15, 2E 9.7, 1M 5.50); ἐπέτρεψεν ('entrusted') πάντα .. εἰς ~ας Ιωσηφ Ge 39.6; πάντα .. ἔδωκεν εἰς τὰς ~άς μου 39.8; δὸς αὐτὸν εἰς τὴν ~ά μου 42.37; παραδοθήσονται εἰς ~ας ῥομφαίας Ps 62.11, εἰς ~ας μαχαίρας Je 18.20, sim. εἰς ~ας πτώσεως αὐτοῦ 'to his fall' Si 4.19; ἐκζητήσω ἐκ ~ός τινος 'I shall demand from ..' Ge 9.5; ἐκ ~ός μου ζήτησον αὐτόν 43.9; ἐκσπασθῆναι ἐκ ~ὸς κακῶν Hb 2.9; μὴ παρείσθωσαν αἱ ~ές σου 'Do not allow your hands to lose their grip' Zp 3.16; ἐρρύσατο .. ἐκ ~ὸς Αἰγυπτίων 'rescued ..' Ex 14.30; πορεύεται κατὰ χεῖράς σου 'follows your lead' Si 25.26; Δέκα μοι ~ες ἐν τῷ βασιλεῖ 'I have ten votes in his kingdom' 2K 19.44*L*. Cf. Sollamo, *Semiprep.*, 167-9, 191-8, 333-5, 340-42. **h.** denotes power and strength: ἐὰν μὴ μετὰ ~ὸς κραταιᾶς 'unless with brute force' Ex 3.19; ἐν ~ὶ κραταιᾷ .. καὶ ἐν βραχίονι ὑψηλῷ 'with a mighty hand .. and an uplifted arm' 6.1, sim. De 3.24, 7.19; ἐν ~ὶ ὑψηλῇ 'enjoying military superiority, having the upper hand' Ex 14.8, Nu 33.3; esp. the right hand, ἡ δεξιά σου .. δεδόξασται ἐν ἰσχύι· ἡ δεξιά σου χείρ .. ἔθραυσεν ἐχθρούς '.. has been glorified with might .. crushed enemies' Ex 15.6. ***i.** ἐπὶ χεῖρα(ς), calqued on Heb. /ʿal yad-/ 'beside, alongside': + gen., 1C 6.16, 23.28 (as assistant), Ne 3.2, 4; syn., ἀνὰ χεῖρα (= /l-yad/) + gen., 2K 15.2B; /ʿal ydē/ 'following the rules of' 2E 3.10. ***j.** *unit or group of people organised for action*: 4K 11.7.

2. *hand-shaped object*: τῶν δύο μυξωτήρων 'of the two (oil-)pipes' Zc 4.12; handle of a bar, Ct 5.5; spokes of a wheel, 3K 7.18; claw as instrument of torture, 4M 8.13, cf. βασανιστήριον.

***3**. *signpost*: ἐν ἀρχῇ ὁδοῦ πόλεως 'at the top of a city-street' Ez 21.20.

***4**. *monument*: ἀνέστακεν αὐτῷ χεῖρα 'set up a monument for himself' 1K 15.12, ἐκάλεσεν τὴν στήλην Χεὶρ Αβεσσαλωμ 2K 18.18, cf. *BA* ad loc.

Cf. βραχίων, δράξ, πυγμή, χειροποίητος: Schmidt 1.389-96; LSG s.v.

χειραγωγέω.ʃ *

to lead by the hand: + acc. (sbd blind), Jd 16.26A (B: κρατέω τὴν χεῖρά τινος), To 11.16 𝔊[II]. Cf. ἄγω: Spicq 3.507.

χειρίζω.ʃ

to administer public affairs: + acc. rei, πράγματα 'state affairs' Es E 5.

χείριστος, η, ον. Super. of χείρων, q.v.

χειρίστως. adv.ʃ

in worse manner: of cruelty and harshness of treatment, 2M 7.39. Cf. χείρων.

χειρόγραφον, ου. n.ʃ

handwritten note: pertaining to monetary transaction, To 5.3, 9.2𝔊[II], 9.5. Cf. Spicq 3.508-10.

χειρονομία, ας. f.ʃ

hand-to-hand military encounter: 3M 1.5, cf. χειρῶν νομή 2M 5.14.

χειρόομαι: aor. ἐχειρωσάμην, inf. ~ρώσασθαι, ptc. ~ρωσάμενος.

to overpower, subdue: + acc. pers., Jb 13.15; giant fish, 3.8; w. collateral notion of killing, 2M 4.34, 42, 3M 7.15.

χειροπέδη, ης. f.

handcuff: δεθήσονται ~αις 'will be handcuffed' Na 3.10, δῆσαι .. ἐν ~αις σιδηραῖς 'to bind .. with iron handcuffs' Ps 149.8, ἐν πέδαις καὶ ~αις χαλκαῖς 'with fetters and bronze ..' Da LXX 4.14[a]; δεδεμένοι ~αις 'bound ..' Is 45.14, πεπεδημένοι ἐν ~αις 'bound ..' Jb 36.8¶; ἐπὶ χειρὸς δεξιᾶς 'on the right hand' Si 21.19; ἔλυσά σε ἀπὸ τῶν ~ων τῶν ἐπὶ τὰς χεῖράς σου 'released you ..' Je 47.4. Cf. πέδη.

χειροποίητος, ον.

made by hand, alw. with negative connotation of not being live, genuine or natural, and w. ref. to idols: προσκυνοῦσιν θεοῖς ~τοις Ju 8.18; εὐλογοῦσαν τὰ εἴδωλα τὰ ~τα αὐτῶν, καὶ τὸν θεὸν τοῦ αἰῶνος οὐκ εὐλόγησαν Da LXX 5.4; τὰ εἴδωλα τὰ ~τα τῶν ἀνθρώπων 5.23; subst. n.pl. (εἴδωλα understood), οὐ ποιήσετε ὑμῖν αὐτοῖς ~τα οὐδὲ γλυπτά Le 26.1; ξύλινα ~τα 'handmade, wooden idols' 26.30 (‖ στήλη), τὰ ~τα αὐτῶν τὰ ἀργυρᾶ καὶ τὰ χρυσᾶ, ἃ ἐποίησαν αἱ χεῖρες αὐτῶν Is 31.7; ἀγάλματα καὶ ~τα 21.9. No such pejorative connotation is indicated by ἐκ χειρός meaning the same: ἐν σκεύει ξυλίνῳ ἐκ χειρός 'with a wooden, handmade vessel' Nu 35.18.

χειροτονία, ας. f.ʃ

act of putting a hand out to grab by force or harm: Is 58.9, cf. Tht. PG 81.457. Cf. τείνω.

χείρων, ον; superl. χείριστος, η, ον.

worse: τὰ χείριστα κακά 'the worst damages' Es B 5; *s* μόρος 'death (by torture)' 3M 3.1. Cf. χειρίστως, κακός, ἥσσων, ἄριστος: Schmidt 4.316-20.

χελιδών, όνος. f.ʃ

swallow: twittering in a sorrowful tone, Is 38.14; knows its seasons, Je 8.7, perched on heads of idols, Ep.Je 21.

χελώνη, ης. f.ʃ

arched protrusion over the ground, 'mound, hillock': τὰ θυσιαστήρια αὐτῶν ὡς ~αι ἐπὶ χέρσον ἀγροῦ 'their altars are like mounds on a parched field' Ho 12.11, cf. 'tortoises' *BA* 23.1 ad loc. Cf. σκόπελος, σωρός.

χελωνίς, ίδος. f.ʃ

**threshold*: Ju 14.15.

χερουβ. m./n.;pl., βιμ, ~ν.

Transliteration of Heb. כְּרוּב, 'cherub': Ge 3.24 (n.)+; Ex 25.18 (m.‖ n. vs. 17), 3K 6.31*L* (n.).

χερσαῖος, α, ον.ʃ

inhabiting dry land: κροκόδιλος χ. 'lizard ..' Le 11.29 (ceremonially unclean); subst. n.pl. ~α 'land animals' Wi 19.19 (:: ἔνυδρα 'water animals'). Cf. χέρσος.

χέρσος, ον.

dry and barren: subst. χ. ἀγροῦ '.. of a field' Ho 10.4, 12.11; ~ος used as f. subst., land unproductive for agriculture Wi 10.7; where thorns (ἄκανθα) grow and thrive, Is 5.6; ἀπὸ τῆς ~ου καὶ ἀκάνθης 5.25, sim. 7.23, 24. Cf. χερσαῖος, χερσόω, ἔρημος, ξηρός: Shipp 569; Schnebel 9-24; Ziegler 1934.181.

χερσόω: fut.pass. χερσωθήσομαι; pf.pass.ptc. κεχερσωμένος.*

to cause to become barren and desolate: ***o*** land, ἕως θεμελίου αὐτῶν χερσωθήσεται 'it will be made barren down to their foundation' Na 1.10; ἔρημος .. γῆ κεχερσωμένη Je 2.31; Pr 24.31. Cf. χέρσος, ἐρημόω.

Χετταῖος, α, ον.

Hittite: Ez16.3+.

χέω: fut.act. χεῶ, pass. χυθήσομαι; pf.pass. κέχυμαι, ptc. κεχυμένος.

to pour, shed: ***o*** metal into a smelter, χεεῖ αὐτοὺς ὡς τὸ χρυσίον καὶ ὡς τὸ ἀργύριον Ma 3.3; frost as salt, Si 43.19. **b**. pass. and metaph. *to spread* (intr.): μοιχεία κέχυται ἐπὶ τῆς γῆς 'adultery has spread widely over the earth' Ho 4.2; χυθήσεται ἐπὶ τὰ ὄρη λαὸς πολύς 'a numerous nation will spread out over the mountains' Jl 2.2; ***o*** anger, ὀργή καὶ θυμός μου χεῖται ἐπὶ τὸν τόπον τοῦτον Je 7.20; ἐν θυμῷ κεχυμένῳ Ez 20.33, 34, cf. ἐκχεῶ ἐπὶ σὲ ὀργήν μου 21.31.

Cf. δια~, ἐκ~, ἐν~, ἐπι~, μετα~, προσ~, ὑπερεκ~, ὑπερχέω, χύτρα, and χωνεύω.

χηλή, ῆς. f.ʃ

hoof: κτῆνος .. ὀνυχιστῆρας ὀνυχίζον δύο ~ῶν 'animal with a hoof cloven into two claws' Le 11.3, De 14.6. Cf. ὁπλή, ὀνυχιστήρ.

χήρα, ας. f.

widow: vulnerable member of society, πᾶσαν ~αν καὶ ὀρφανὸν οὐ κακώσετε 'thou shalt not maltreat any widow or orphan' Ex 22.22; Zc 7.10 (+ πένης 'the poor'); in a similar listing, De 10.18, 14.28, Ma 3.5; εὐχὴ ~ας καὶ ἐκβεβλημένης 'a vow of a widow and a divorcee' Nu 30.10; w. pleonastic γυνή (q. v. **1 c**) 2K 14.5, 4M 16.10; ~αι ζῶσαι 'living widows (deliberately separated from their husband)' 2K 20.3. Cf. χηρεία, χήρευσις, χηρεύω.

χηρεία, ας. f.ʃ

state of being a widow, 'widowhood': ἐμπλάτυνον τὴν ~αν σου 'Widen your widowhood' (?) Mi 1.16; χ. καὶ ἀτεκνία Is 47.9; ὄνειδος τῆς ~ας 'humiliation of ..' 54.4. Cf. χήρα.

χήρευσις, εως. f.ʃ *

= χηρεία, q.v.: ἱμάτια ~εως 'clothes of ..' Ge 38.14, 19, Ju 8.5; 10.3 (:: ἱμάτια εὐφροσύνης); στολὴν ~εως 16.7; πάσας τὰς ἡμέρας τῆς ~εως αὐτῆς 8.6. Cf. χήρα.

χηρεύω: aor. ἐχήρευσα.ʃ

to become widow and live as such: Ju 8.4; χηρεύουσα καὶ ἐκψυχοῦσα '.. utterly depressed' 2K 13.20*L*. **b**. *to suffer severance of intimate relationship with* (ἀπό): ἀπὸ θεοῦ Je 28.5.

χθές. ⇒ ἐχθές.

χθιζός, ή, όν.ʃ

of χθές 'yesterday': ***s*** hum. Jb 8.9 (in a fig. of brevity of hum. existence). Cf. (ἐ)χθές.

χῖδρον, ου. n.ʃ On the accent, see Walters 48.

"*wheaten-groats*" (LSJ, LSG): νέα πεφρυγμένα ~α 'new, roasted, wheaten-groats' Le 2.14, sim. 23.14; 2.16.

χιλιαρχία, ας. f.ʃ

1. *office* or *post of* χιλίαρχος (q.v.): Nu 31.48.

2. *a unit consisting of a thousand soldiers*: 1M 5.13.

Cf. χιλίαρχος.

χιλίαρχος, ου. m.

leader over thousand men: military, Ex 18.21, Zc 9.7; ‖ ἄρχων Nu 1.16, ‖ ἑκατόνταρχος 31.14; ἑκατόνταρχος, πεντηκόνταρχος, δεκάδαρχος De 1.15. **b**. civic: 1E 1.9.

Cf. χιλιάς, χίλιοι, χιλιαρχία, ἑκατόνταρχος, πεντηκόνταρχος, δεκάδαρχος.

χιλιάς, άδος, pl.dat. χιλιάσιν. f.

1. *one thousand*: pl. as hyperbole, χιλιάσι κριῶν 'with thousands of rams' Mi 6.7 (ǁ μυριάδες); γίνου εἰς ~άδας μυριάδων 'Grow to thousands of myriads' Ge 24.60; εἰς ~άδας 'up to a thousand generations' De 5.10, Ex 20.6, 34.7.

2. *population consisting of one thousand households*: ἐν ~άσιν Ιουδα Mi 5.2; Jd 6.15. **b**. *contingent consisting of one thousand soldiers*: ἑπτὰ χιλιάδας ἱππεῶν '7,000 horsemen' 2K 8.4 (:: χίλια ἅρματα 'a thousand chariots'); + ἑκατοντάς 1K 29.2, cf. *BA* 7.65-9 on a difference between χιλιάς and χίλιοι. The latter, χίλιοι, is used when not specified further, but in the sense of 'thousands': εἴκοσι ~άδας πεζῶν .. χιλίους ἄνδρας .. δώδεκα χιλιάδας ἀνδρῶν '20,000 horsemen .. thousands of men .. 12,000 men' 2K 10.6, cf. τρεῖς ~άδες ἀνδρῶν Jd 15.11A (B: τρισχίλιοι ἄνδρες); 1K 13.2. The accompanying noun for the entity counted is usually in the gen. pl.

Cf. χίλιοι, χιλίαρχος, and μυριάς.

χίλιοι, αι, α: num.

thousand: χίλια δίδραχμα 'a thousand half-shekels' Ge 20.14, ~α τάλαντα ἀργυρίου '1,000 talents of silver' 4K 15.19; Am 5.3. In counting soldiers χιλίας is preferred except when an exact thousand-figure is given: see s.v. χιλιάς. Cf. χιλιάς, χιλίαρχος, χιλιοπλασίως.

χιλιοπλασίως. adv.ʃ

thousandfold, thousand times as many or *much*: De 1.11.

χίμαιρα, ας. f.

young she-goat: cultic offering, χίμαιραν ἐξ αἰγῶν· θήλειαν ἄμωμον Le 4.28; τῆς ἁμαρτίας 4.29. Cf. χίμαρος, αἴξ.

χίμαρος, ου. m.

young he-goat: χ. ἐξ αἰγῶν, ἄρσεν ἄμωμον Le 4.23; De 14.4 (ǁ μόσχος, ἀμνός). Cf. αἴξ, χίμαιρα, τράγος: Shipp 569f.

χιονόομαι: fut. ~νωθήσομαι.ʃ *

to cover with snow: Ps 67.15. Cf. χιών: Caird 1969.39f.

χιτών, ῶνος. m. Cf. Heb. כְּתֹנֶת, Akkadian *kitintu* 'linen garment.'

garment worn next to the skin, 'tunic': δερμάτινος 'leather' Ge 3.21; ποικίλος 'multicoloured' 37.3 (costly); priestly garment, κοσυμβωτός 'tasseled' Ex 28.4; ποδήρης 'so long as to reach down to the feet' 29.5; τῆς ἱερατείας 35.19; λινοῦν ἡγιασμένος Le 16.4; ǁ ἱμάτιον Is 61.10. Cf. ἱμάτιον, ὑποδύτης, χλαῖνα: Trench 184f.

χιών, όνος. f.

snow: ὡσεὶ χ. Ex 4.6; Nu 12.10 (of a leper and in both w. ref. to white colour); ὡς ~όνα λευκανῶ 'I shall make (them) as white as snow' Is 1.18 (:: φοινικοῦς 'crimson'); ǁ ὑετός 'rain' descending from the sky and watering the soil, 55.10. Cf. χιονόομαι.

χλαῖνα, ης. f.ʃ

upper-garment: Pr 31.22. Cf. χιτών.

χλαμύς, ύδος. f.ʃ

short mantle: worn by soldiers, 2M 12.35.

χλευάζω: aor.ptc. χλευάσας.

to scoff at: + acc., 2M 7.27, 4M 5.22. Cf. χλεύασμα, χλευασμός, μυκτηρίζω: Schmidt 3.460-2; *ND* 2.104.

χλεύασμα, ατος. n.ʃ *

target of scoffing: Jb 12.4. Cf. χλευάζω.

χλευασμός, οῦ. m.

that which causes one to be scoffed at: + ὀνειδισμός Je 20.8. **b**. target of scoffing: + μυκτηρισμός Ps 78.4.

Cf. χλευάζω, μυκτηρισμός.

χλιδών, ῶνος.

kind of ornament, armlet or anklet: ǁ ψέλιον, δακτύλιος Nu 31.50; female accessories, χ. .. ἐνώτια καὶ πάντα τὸν κόσμον Ju 10.4, sim. Is 3.20; ἐπὶ βραχίονι δεξιῷ 'on the right arm' Si 21.21; golden, 2K 8.7 (ǁ κλιοιός 1C18.7). Cf. κόσμος **3**.

χλόη, ης. f.

young grass: Ps 22.2, λάχανα ~ης 36.2, δωμάτων 'on roof-tops' 4K 19.26; fig. of evanescence, Ps 89.5. Cf. χλοηφόρος, βοτάνη, χόρτος.

χλοηφόρος, ον.ʃ

bearing green grass or *leaves*: *s* πεδίον 'a tract of plain' Wi 19.7. Cf. χλόη.

χλωρίζω ʃ *

to be greenish: *s* part affected by leprosy and ǁ πυρρίζω, Le 13.49, 14.37. Cf. χλωρός.

χλωρός, ά, όν.

green in colour: *s* vegetation, χόρτος Ge 1.30, Is 15.6, ἄχι 19.7; ῥάβδος 'rod' Ge 30.37, ξύλον Ez 17.24; subst. πᾶν ~ὸν ἀγροῦ 'all greenery of the field' Ge 2.5; οὐχ ὑπελείφθη ~ὸν οὐδὲν ἐν τοῖς ξύλοις 'no green thing was left on the trees' Ex 10.15; περισύρων τὸ ~όν 'tearing the green part around' Ge 30.37; in pasture, Is 27.11; ἐκλείξαι ὁ μόσχος τὰ ~ὰ ἐκ τοῦ πεδίου 'the calf licks up the greenery off the field' Nu 22.4; De 29.23, cf. LSG. Cf. χόρτος, χλωρίζω, χλωρότης, πράσινος: Schmidt 3.51-3; Shipp 572f.; LSG s.v.

χλωρότης, ητος. f.ʃ *

green colour: χρυσίου 'of gold' Ps 67.14. Cf. χλωρός.

χνοῦς, οῦς. m.
chaff: χ. ἀποφυσώμενος ἀφ' ἅλωνος 'chaff blown away from a threshing-floor' Ho 13.3; χ. ἀχύρου 'of straw' Is 17.13; χ. φερόμενος 'blown about' 29.5, ὑπὸ ἀνέμου 'by a wind' Wi 5.14.

χοεύς. ⇒ II χοῦς.

χοῖνιξ, ικος. f.
a choenix (a dry measure): + ζυγός, μέτρον Ez 45.10; = one tenth of homer, 45.11. Cf. Shipp 573.

χοιρογρύλλιος, ου. m.ʃ *
"Hyrax syriacus, coney" (LSJ): forbidden food, Le 11.6, De 14.7; Ps 103.18, Pr 30.26.

χολάω: aor. ἐχόλησα.ʃ
to be very angry: ***s*** hum., 3M 3.1. Cf. χόλος, θυμόω, ὀργίζομαι: *ND* 4.175f.

χολέρα, ας. f.ʃ
nausea caused by overeating: Nu 11.20; πόνος ἀγρυπνίας καὶ ~ας 'distress of insomnia and nausea' Si 34.20; ἡ ἀπληστία ἐγγιεῖ ἕως ~ας 'gluttony leads to ..' 37.30. Cf. Dorival 1996.540f.

χολή, ῆς. f.
gall: of fish, To 6.5; fig. of sth highly repugnant and unbearable, χ. καὶ πικρία '.. and bitterness' De 29.18, sim. La 3.20; σταφυλὴ ~ῆς 'grapes of ..' De 32.32 (ǁ πικρία), πικρότερον ~ῆς 'more bitter than ..' Pr 5.4; ὕδωρ ~ῆς Je 8.14, 9.14 (ǁ ὕ. πικρόν 23.15); ǁ ὄξος Ps 68.22. Cf. πικρία.

χόλος, ου. m.
bitter anger: hum., + ὀργή 3M 5.1; Ec 5.16; ǁ θυμός Wi 18.22. Cf. χολάω, θυμός, ὀργή: Schmidt 3.558f. Del. 2M 3.28 v.l.

χονδρίτης, ου. m.ʃ
bread made of groats or *coarse meal*: τρία κανᾶ ~τῶν 'three reed baskets of ..' Ge 40.16.

χορδή, ῆς.ʃ
string (of musical instrument and made of guts): ἅρμοσαι ~ήν 'Tune the chord' Na 3.8; αἰνεῖτε αὐτὸν ἐν ~αῖς καὶ ὀργάνῳ 'Praise him with ..' Ps 150.4.

χορεία, ας. f.ʃ
dance: Ju 15.13. Cf. χορεύω, χορός.

χορεύω: aor.inf. χορεῦσαι.
to dance: ***s*** women, 1K 18.6 (*L* + ᾄδω), ἐν χοραῖς Jd 21.21; πᾶς ὁ λαός and + εὐφραίνομαι 3K 1.40. Cf. χορεία, χορός.

χορηγέω: fut. ~γήσω, inf. ~γήσειν, pass. ~γηθήσομαι; aor. ἐχορήγησα, ptc. ~γήσας, subj. ~γήσω; pf.ptc.pass. κεχορηγημένος.
to give liberally: + dat. pers. and acc. rei, σοφίαν Si 1.10, 26; εὐδοκίαν ἐπιθυμίας 'satisfaction of desire' 18.31, χρείαν '(amply satisfy) the need' 39.33, ταῖς πόλεσιν .. βρώματα 1M 14.10; τὰ πρὸς τὴν κηδείαν 'the costs of funeral' 2M 4.49; pass., ***o*** pers., ἐν ἰσχύι Si 44.6. **b**. *to collect and raise public funds*: τῷ βασιλεῖ καὶ τῷ οἴκῳ αὐτοῦ 3K 4.7.
Cf. ἐπιχορηγέω, χορηγία.

χορηγία, ας. f.
1. *official expenses*: 1E 4.54.
2. *sth supplied and provided*: οἴνου 3M 5.10.
3. *facilities and provisions*: available at a gymnasium, 2M 4.14, at the Jerusalem temple, 2E 5.3. Cf. κατασκευή **2**, σκεῦος **1c**.
Cf. Robert 1937.290f.; GLS s.v.; Shaw 2004-5.

χορηγός, οῦ. m.ʃ
one who meets every need: = God, 2M 1.25.

χόριον, ου. n.ʃ
afterbirth: De 28.57.

χορός, οῦ. m.
band of dancers and singers: μετὰ τυμπάνων καὶ ~ῶν Ex 15.20; 32.19; prophets accompanied by musicians, 1K 10.5; fig. of joy and pleasure, La 5.15, Ps 29.12 (:: κοπετός), εὐφροσύνης σημεῖον 'indicative of joy' 3M 6.32. Cf. χορεία, χορεύω: Perpillou-Thomas.

χορτάζω: fut. χορτάσω, pass. ~τασθήσομαι; aor. ἐχόρτασα, inf. χορτάσαι, pass. ἐχορτάσθην.
to supply abundantly: + acc., Je 5.7, ψυχὴν κενήν Ps 106.9 (ǁ ἐμπίμπλημι); + acc. pers. and gen. rei, τοὺς πτωχοὺς .. ἄρτων 131.15, + double acc., 80.17 (ǁ ψωμίζω), pass. ἀπὸ καρποῦ and ***o*** ἡ γῆ 103.13; ǁ πίμπλημι 16.14; wilderness to be watered for vegetation to grow, Jb 38.27¶, cf. ***o*** ξύλα Ps 103.16; ζωῆς To 12.9 𝔊[II] (𝔊[I] πλήννυμι pass.); metaph., πικρίας 'bitterness' La 3.15 (gen. and ǁ μεθύσκω), pass. ὀνειδισμῶν 3.30. Cf. χορτασία, χόρτασμα, τρέφω, ψωμίζω.

χορτασία, ας. f.ʃ
v.n. of χορτάζω: κοιλίας 'of belly' Pr 24.15.

χόρτασμα, ατος. n. *(?). Alw. pl.
food: fodder for livestock, ἄχυρα καὶ ~ατα ταῖς καμήλοις 'straw and fodder for the camels' Ge 24.32; δοῦναι ~ατα τοῖς ὄνοις 42.27; δώσει ~ατα ἐν τοῖς ἀγροῖς σου τοῖς κτήνεσίν σου 'he will provide straw in your fields for your cattle' De 11.15; ὄνῳ 'for a donkey' Si 30.33, δαμάλεων 'of young cows' 38.26. Cf. ἄχυρον, χορτάζω, ἔδεσμα: LSG s.v.

χορτομανέω: fut. ~νήσω.ʃ *
to become overgrown with grass and weeds: ***s*** agricultural field, vineyard, Pr 24.31. Cf. χόρτος.

χόρτος, ου. m. (possibly n. at Ge 1.11, 29, on which see Thack. 174 and Shipp 289).
grass: βοτάνη ~ου 'grass' Ge 1.11; χ. σπόριμον 1.29, τοῦ ἀγροῦ 'of the field' Je 12.4, δωμάτων 'on roof-tops' Ps 128.6; as animal fodder, καταφαγεῖν τὸν ~ον τῆς γῆς Am 7.2; λάχανα ~ου 'vegetables as food' Ge 9.3; but also inferior human food, 3.18; ǁ

βοτάνη Je 14.6, ‖ λάχανον Ps 36.2. Cf. πόα, λάχανον, βοτάνη, χορτώδης, χορτομανέω: Schnebel 211-8; Paradise 191f.

χορτώδης, ες.ʃ *

pertaining to grass: *s* τροφή 'foods' 2M 5.27. Cf. χόρτος.

I. χοῦς, gen. χοός, dat. χοΐ. m.

1. *layer of tiny particles lying on the ground*, 'soil': χοῦν ἀπὸ τῆς γῆς Ge 2.7 (material from which the first man was fashioned); τὰ πατοῦντα ἐπὶ τὸν χοῦν τῆς γῆς 'tread upon ..' Am 2.7; λείξουσιν ~ν ὡς ὄφις 'they will lick the dust like a snake' Mi 7.17; in a simile of enormous quantity, ἐκχεεῖ τὸ αἷμα αὐτῶν ὡς ~ν 'he will pour out their blood as dust' Zp 1.17, ἐθησαύρισεν ἀργύριον ὡς χοῦν 'amassed silver like dust' Zc 9.3 (‖ πηλός), λαὸν πολὺν ὡς ὁ χ. τῆς γῆς 2C 1.9; Si 44.21; sprinkled on one's head as a sign of remorse, Jo 7.6. **b.** crumbled remains of the dead: Ps 29.10. **c.** descends from the sky as divine punishment: De 28.24 (‖ κονιορτός).

2. *a quantity of* usually valueless *particles*: plaster dust scraped off walls, Le 14.41; ashes, 4K 23.4.

Cf. χόω, γῆ, πηλός, κονιορτός: Alexandre 236f.

II. χοῦς, χοός. m.; pl.acc. χοεῖς.ʃ

liquid measure: χ. δίκαιος Le 19.36 (‖ ζυγὰ δίκαια καὶ στάθμια δίκαια), 3K 7.24.

χόω: aor.inf. χῶσαι.ʃ

to throw earth into and cover: + acc., grave dug up To 8.18. Cf. I χοῦς.

χράω: fut. χρήσομαι, pass. χρησθήσομαι; aor. ἔχρησα, mid. ἐχρησάμην, ptc. χρησάμενος, impv. χρῆσαι, 2pl χρήσασθε, subj. χρήσωμαι, pass. χρησθῶ, opt.1pl χρησαίμεθα; pf.mid. κέχρημαι, ptc. κεχρημένος.

I. act. *to supply, furnish on request*: + dat. pers., Ex 11.3, 12.36.

2. *to put at sbd else's disposal for long-term use or service*: + cogn. obj. (χρέος), τῷ κυρίῳ 1K 2.20; pass., 4K 6.5.

II. mid. *to act towards* in a certain manner, 'treat': + dat. pers., τῷ Αβραμ εὖ ἐχρήσαντο δι' αὐτήν 'they treated A. well on account of her' Ge 12.16; χρῶ αὐτῇ, ὡς ἄν σοι ἀρεστὸν ᾖ 'Treat her as you see fit' 16.6, sim. 19.8; καλῶς 26.29; of sexual intercourse (so Hdt. 2.181), ὡσεὶ πόρνῃ χρήσονται τῇ ἀδελφῇ ἡμῶν; 'are they going to treat our sister like a whore?' 34.31, also 19.8, Si 26.22¶; ὀργῇ .. μοι 'with anger ..' Jb 10.17, δεινῶς μοι ὀργῇ 'in horrifying manner ..' 19.11, δυεῖν μοι 'in two ways ..' 13.20, ἐν ἀπειλῇ 'with threats' 23.6; κέχρηταί σοι ὀργή 'you allowed yourself to be dictated by anger' 18.4; τὸν τρόπον τοῦτον 'in this manner' Da 1.14 LXX; κατὰ τὸ ἔλεός σου 1M 13.46. **b.** the manner of treatment unspecified: ἑαυτῇ χρήσηται 'she treats herself to it [= freedom]' Si 26.10 (or: of onany, Ryssel 1900 ad loc., and cf. MH תַּשְׁמִישׁ 'sexual intercourse'). **c.** in gen. and not particularly towards sbd: ἄλλως 'in some other way' Es 1.19, 9.27; ὀργῇ Jb 16.9, παρανόμως 'unlawfully' 34.20, διαφόρως 'differently' Da 7.7 LXX. Cf. ποιέω **I 2**.

2. *to use*: + dat., διακόνῳ 'servant' Pr 10.4a; μεταβολαῖς 'changes' E 9 o' (*L* διαβολαῖς 'prejudices'), κτίσει 'creation' Wi 2.6, παραλογισμῷ 'deception' 2M 1.13; + acc., 2M 4.19; + ἐπί τινι Ep Je 58; + ἔν τινι 3M 4.20; pass., εἰς οὐθέν Je 13.7.

3. *to perform* a certain action: + v.n. (dat.), βάσει 'to take a step' Wi 13.18; + acc. rei, ^παρανομίαν^ Pr 10.26. Cf. ποιέω **II 1**.

4. *to submit oneself to*: + dat., νόμοις Es 8.11, τοῖς ἑαυτῶν νομίμοις E 19, cf. νόμοις τοῖς ἰδίοις *Riv. Fil.* 58.472 (iii BC); θρησκείᾳ 'religion' 4M 5.7; Moses the counsellor, 9.2. Cf. ὑποτάσσω **2**.

5. *to have intimate dealings with*: + dat. pers. (harlot), Pr 5.5.

6. *to experience*: dat., συμφοραῖς 'calamities' 4M 3.21.

Cf. καταχράομαι, κιχράω, κίχρημι, χρῆσις, χρεία.

χρεία, ας. f.

1. *need*: + gen., οὐδὲ χρυσίου ~αν ἔχουσι 'nor do they have need of gold' Is 13.17, οὐκ ἔστι χ. αὐτοῦ Je 22.28; ἐν καιρῷ ~ας 'when necessary' Si 4.23, 8.9, 29.2; + inf., "we need not answer you" Da 3.16; + ἵνα - ~αν ἔχω ἵνα βαδίσῃς 'I need you to go' To 6.7 𝔊II. **b.** *that which is needed*: Si 29.3, εἰς ζωὴν ἀνθρώπου 39.26.

2. *assignment*: ἀποστελλόμενα ἐπὶ ~ας 'sent on business' Ep Je 59; ~αν ποιέω Si 35.2; ἐμπιστεύω ~ας 'to entrust ..' 2M 7.24. **b.** οἱ πρὸς ταῖς ~αις 'the military (or: naval) officers' Ju 12.10, sim. οἱ ἐπὶ τῶν ~ῶν 1M 12.45; 10.37; οἱ ἀπὸ τῶν ~ῶν 10.41. **c.** *military engagement*: ἐπὶ τὴν ~αν ἦλθον 'went into action' 2M 8.20.

3. *way in which sbd or sth can be put to use*: Si 38.1.

Cf. χράω: Pelletier 1962.303-5.

χρεμετίζω: aor.impv. χρεμέτισον.ʃ

to neigh, whinny (at sbd ἐπί τινα): *s* horse and fig., ἕκαστος ἐπὶ τὴν γυναῖκα τοῦ πλησίον αὐτοῦ ἐχρεμέτιζον 'everyone would neigh at his neighbour's wife' Je 5.8; Si 36.6; expression of joy, Εὐφράνθητε καὶ χρεμετίσατε ἐπὶ κεφαλὴν ἐθνῶν Je 38.7. Cf. χρεμετισμός.

χρεμετισμός, οῦ. m.ʃ

v.n. of prec.: ἵππων Am 6.7; ἵππος κάθιδρος ἐν ~ῷ αὐτοῦ 'a horse profusely sweating as he whinnies' Je 8.6; ἀπὸ φωνῆς ~οῦ ἱππασίας 8.16; fig. of lovers calling each other, μοιχεία σου καὶ χ. σου 13.27. Cf. χρεμετίζω.

χρεοκοπέομαι.ʃ
to cancel a debt: + acc., δάνειον 'debt' 4M 2.8. Cf. ἀφίημι **2**.

χρέος, ους. n.ʃ
1. *debt*: ἴδιον 'private' De 15.2 (*o* of ἀφίημι and ὀφείλω); ἄφεσις .. τοῦ χρέους 'the writing off of the debt' 15.3; τὸ τῆς ψυχῆς χ. 'the soul which was on loan' Wi 15.8.
2. *that which has been put at sbd else's disposal for long-term use or service*: for cultic service, *o* of χράω 1K 2.20 (ǁ χρῆσις 1.28).
Cf. ὀφείλημα, ὑπόχρεως, χρῆσις, χράω.

χρεοφειλέτης, ου. m.ʃ
debtor: Jb 31.37; opp. δανιστής Pr 29.13.

χρή. Impers.ʃ
it is necessary, required: + inf., Pr 25.27. Cf. ἀναγκαῖος, II δέω: Schmidt 3.702-5. Del. 4M 8.26 v.l.

χρῄζω.ʃ
to be in need of urgent help: *s* hum., Jd 11.7 B (A: θλίβομαι), 1K 17.18 v.l.

χρῆμα, ατος. n. Alw. pl.
1. *material possessions*: Jb 6.20, 27.17, Si 14.3, Pr 17.6a; πλοῦτος ~άτων 2C 1.11 (ǁ vs. 12 π. καὶ ~ατα).
2. *funds*: for public expenses, 4M 3.20.
Cf. κτῆμα, ὕπαρξις.

χρηματίζω: fut. ~ματιῶ; aor. ἐχρημάτισα, inf. χρηματίσαι; pf.inf. κεχρηματικέναι.ʃ
1. *to make a solemn pronouncement*: *s* God, ἀφ' ὑψηλοῦ 'from high above' Je 32.16[1]. **b**. *to utter* sth in a solemn manner: + acc. and *s* God, λόγον Je 32.16[2], τὰ κακὰ ταῦτα ἐπὶ τὸν τόπον τοῦτον 47.2; *s* king, 33.2, + dat. pers., ib., πρὸς σέ 37.2, ἐν τῷ ὀνόματί μου 36.23.
2. *to deal with*: + dat. pers., Jb 40.8.
3. *to be busily engaged*: 3K 18.27.
Cf. χρηματισμός, χρηματιστήριον, χρησμολογέω.

χρηματισμός, οῦ. m.ʃ
solemn annoucement communicated: divine utterance, 2M 2.4; in writing, 11.17; royal, Pr 31.1. Cf. χρηματίζω: *ND* 4.176.

χρηματιστήριον, ου. n.ʃ
council-chamber: 1E 3.14.

χρησιμεύω: fut. ~μεύσω; aor.subj. ~μεύσω.ʃ
to be useful: *s* hum., Si 13.4, Wi 4.3. Cf. χρήσιμος.

χρήσιμος, η, ον.
useful, beneficial: Τί χρήσιμον, ἐὰν .. 'What is the use of ..?' Ge 37.26; Zc 6.10, 14; εἰς ἐργασίαν 'for work' Ez 15.4; *s* σκεῦος Ep Je 58, Wi 13.11; hum., Si 10.4, Pr 17.17; advice, To 4.18 𝔊[I]; medicine, 6.5 𝔊[II]; + dat., Si prol. 5, 7.22; inf. cl. and dat. pers., To 3.10 𝔊[II]. Cf. ἀχρεῖος, ἄχρηστος, εὔχρηστος, συμφέρω, ὠφελέω: Schmidt 4.170f.

χρῆσις, εως. f.
1. *ability* or *permission to use*: ἔλαβον ~ιν τῶν πέντε 'received the use of the five (senses)' Si 17.5¶; Wi 15.15.
2. *purpose for which sth or sbd can be used*: τί ἡ χ. ^ἀνθρώπου^; Si 18.8; πάντα τὰ πρὸς τὴν ~ιν 'everything useful' To 1.13𝔊[II]; Wi 15.7.
3. *lending, loan*: τῷ κυρίῳ 1K 1.28.
Cf. χράω, χρέος, κιχράω.

χρησμολογέω.ʃ
to utter an oracle of: + acc., εἰρήνην 'to preach peace' Je 45.4. Cf. χρηματίζω.

χρηστεύομαι.ʃ *
to act kindly to sbd: *s* God, τινι PSol 9.6. Cf. χρηστός, χρηστοήθεια.

χρηστοήθεια, ας. f.ʃ*
kindheartedness: Si 37.11. Cf. χρηστός.

χρηστός, ή, όν.
1. *benevolent of character*: *s* God, χ. κύριος τοῖς ὑπομένουσιν αὐτὸν ἐν ἡμέρᾳ θλίψεως 'the Lord is benevolent to those who count on Him on the day of adversity' Na 1.7, χ. ὁ κύριος Ps 33.9; + εὐθής 24.8, + ἐπιεικὴς καὶ πολυέλεος 'fair ..' 85.5, + ἀληθής, μακρόθυμος Wi 15.1, + ἐλεήμων PSol 5.2; hum., χ. ἀνὴρ ὁ οἰκτίρων Ps 111.5; Je 51.17 (well-to-do enough to be able to be kind to the needy?). **b**. *expressive of benevolent character*: ~ὸν τὸ ἔλεός σου Ps 68.17, τὰ κρίματά σου ~ά 118.39, God's name 51.11; subst. n.pl., ἐλάλησε αὐτῷ ~ά 'he spoke to him kindly' Je 52.32 (*s* hum.). Cf. χάρις **3**.
2. *of good quality*: σκεύη χαλκᾶ ἀπὸ ~οῦ χαλκοῦ 'bronze vessels of fine bronze' 1E 8.56, μετὰ πρώτων ἡδυσμάτων καὶ λίθων ~ῶν 'with first-rate spices ..' Ez 27.22, χρυσίου ~ου Da 2.32; *s* fruits, Je 24.2 (:: πονηρός); hum., Τοῖς ~οῖς Ἰουδαίοις τοῖς πολίταις 'To the worthy Jewish citizens' 2M 9.19. **b**. *morally good*, 'decent': *s* hum., Pr 2.21 (ǁ εὐθής, ἄκακος).
Cf. ἀγαθός, ἐλεήμων, καλός, χρηστεύομαι, χρηστότης, χρηστῶς: Spicq 1947.321-4; Spicq 3.511-6; Weiss, *TDNT* 9.483-6; Mayerson 2002.102-5.

χρηστότης, ητος. f.
benevolence: εὐλογίαι ~ητος Ps 20.4, τῶν εὐεργετούντων 'of the benefactors' Es E 2; attribute of God, Ps 24.7 (ǁ ἔλεος), + ἔλεος PSol 8.28; of hum., 5.13. **b**. *deed* or *manifestation of benevolence*: hum., Ps 13.1, 36.3; divine, 103.28, 118.65, ǁ καρπὸς ^τῆς γῆς^ 84.13, ǁ πιότης 'fatness' 64.12.
Cf. χρηστός, ἀγαθωσύνη: Weiss, *TDNT* 9.489f.

χρηστῶς. adv.ʃ

in proper manner, 'well': Wi 8.1. Cf. χρηστός.

χρῖσις, εως. f.

v.n. of χρίω: ἔλαιον ~εως oil used for the consecration of priests and their vestments, Ex 29.21; used on priests and cultic utensils, ἔλαιον ἄλειμμα ~εως ἅγιον 30.31 (ǁ ἔλαιον χρῖσμα ἅγιον vs. 25); ǁ σύνθεσις θυμιάματος 'concoction of incense' 38.25, 39.16; Ααρων 'of A.' Le 7.25; David as king, Ps 151.4. Cf. χρίω.

χρῖσμα, ατος. n.

1. = χρῖσις, q.v.: + acc., ἔλαιον ~ατος 'oil for smearing' Ex 29.7; = ἔλαιον χρῖσμα 30.25; = ἔ. χρίσεως 38.25; ἱερατείας 'accompanying the ceremony of instalment as priest' 40.13; 'glazing' (done by a potter) Si 38.30.

2. *one on whom* χρίσις *was performed*: Da 9.26 (ǁ χριστός TH 9.25).

Cf. χρίω.

χριστός, ή, όν.

1. *applied by smearing*: ***s*** oil used to consecrate a priest, τὸ ἅγιον ἔλαιον τὸ ~ὸν τοῦ θεοῦ Le 21.12.

2. subst., *one on whom the act of* χρίσις *has been performed*: priest, ὁ ἱερεὺς ὁ χ. ὁ τετελειωμένος τὰς χεῖρας 'the priest who has been installed after anointment' Le 4.5 (ǁ κεχρισμένος vs. 3), 16, 6.22; τῷ ~ῷ μου Κύρῳ Is 45.1; τοῦ ἐλαίου τοῦ ~οῦ καὶ τετελειωμένου Le 21.10. **b**. God's: τὸν ~ὸν αὐτοῦ Am 4.13, κυρίου La 4.20; τοὺς ~ούς σου Hb 3.13.

Cf. χρίω, and Karrer 2006, § 4.2 on La 4.20 and PSol 17.32.

χρίω: fut.act. χρίσω, mid. χρίσομαι, pass. χρισθήσομαι; aor. ἔχρισα, subj. χρίσω, inf. χρῖσαι, mid. ἐχρισάμην, pass. ἐχρίσθην, inf. χρισθῆναι, subj. mid. χρίσωμαι; pf. κέχρικα, pass.3s κέχρισται, ptc.pass. κεχρισμένος.

to apply sticky fluid to,'to smear': + acc., λάγανα ἄζυμα κεχρισμένα ἐν ἐλαίῳ 'unleavened cakes smeared with oil' Ex 29.2, Nu 6.15, weapon 2K 1.21, τὴν πόλιν Ez 43.3; ἐν μίλτῳ 'with red ochre' Je 22.14; so as to appoint as king, σε εἰς βασιλέα 1K 15.1; + double acc., ἔχρισέν σε ὁ θεὸς .. ἔλαιον ἀγαλλιάσεως '.. oil of joy' Ps 44.8. **b**. mid.: abs., 2K 12.20 *L* (B: ἀλείφομαι); + acc. rei, ἔλαιον οὐ χρίσῃ 'you will have no occasion to apply oil to yourself' De 28.40; τὰ πρῶτα μῦρα χριόμενοι 'anoint themselves with the first-rate myrrh' Am 6.6. **c**. act./pass. 'to invest with office by performing the act of χρίω': + acc. pers. and for priesthood, Ex 28.37, 29.7, 29; Ααρων καὶ τοὺς υἱοὺς αὐτοῦ χρίσεις, καὶ ἁγιάσεις αὐτοὺς ἱερατεύειν μοι 30.30; ἐπὶ σάρκα ἀνθρώπου οὐ χρισθήσεται 'it shall not be applied to the body of an ordinary person' 30.32; ὁ ἀρχιερεὺς ὁ κεχρισμένος Le 4.3 (ǁ ὁ ἱερεὺς ὁ χριστός vs. 5); ἐπέχεεν Μωυσῆς ἀπὸ τοῦ ἐλαίου τῆς χρίσεως ἐπὶ τὴν κεφαλὴν Ααρων, καὶ ἔχρισεν αὐτὸν καὶ ἡγίασεν αὐτόν 'M. poured some of the oil of anointing on to A.'s head ..' 8.12; ὁ ἱερεύς, ὃν ἂν χρίσωσιν αὐτὸν καὶ ὃν ἂν τελειώσωσιν τὰς χεῖρας αὐτοῦ ἱερατεύειν 'the priest whom they might anoint and install to serve as priest' 16.32, cf. Nu 7.88 with the reverse order of the two verbs; τῷ ἐλαίῳ τῷ ἁγίῳ Nu 35.25; βασιλέα καὶ ἄρχοντας Ho 8.10; + double acc., κέχρισται Δαυιδ βασιλέα 2K 5.17. **d**. act., in order to consecrate for exclusively cultic use: ***o*** various parts of the place of cult and associated utensils, ἐξ αὐτοῦ [= ἔλαιον χρῖσμα ἅγιον vs. 25] τὴν σκηνὴν τοῦ μαρτυρίου καὶ τὴν κιβωτόν .. καὶ τὴν λυχνίαν καὶ πάντα τὰ σκεύη αὐτῆς [+ καὶ ἁγιάσεις αὐτήν ǁ 40.7] καὶ τὸ θυσιαστήριον Ex 30.26f.; χρίσεις αὐτὸ [= τὸ θυσιαστήριον] ὥστε ἁγιάσαι αὐτό 29.36.

Cf. χρίσμα, χρίσις, χριστός, δια~, ἐγ~, καταχρίω, ἀλείφω, λιπαίνω.

χρόα, ας. f.ʃ

colour: of the skin of a hum. body, Ex 4.7, 2M 3.16; Wi 13.14. Cf. χρῶμα.

χρονίζω: fut. χρονιῶ; aor. ἐχρόνισα, subj. χρονίσω; pf. κεχρόνικα.

1. *to tarry*: ἐχρόνισα ἕως τοῦ νῦν Ge 32.4; ἐπὶ τῆς γῆς De 4.25.

2. *to fail to arrive for a long time*: Hb 2.3 (of the end-time, and ǁ ὑστερέω); ταχὺ ἔρχεται καὶ οὐ χρονιεῖ Is 13.22; ***s*** divine wrath, Si 7.16; hum., ἀπὸ τοῦ καιροῦ '(fell behind) the schedule (set by the king)' 2K 20.5B (*L* ὑστερέω).

3. *to fail to act immediately* or *speedily*, often negated: + inf. aor., οὐκ ἐχρόνισεν ὁ νεανίσκος ποιῆσαι τὸ ῥῆμα τοῦτο 'the lad did not wait long to do this' Ge 34.19; κεχρόνικεν Μωυσῆς καταβῆναι 'M. had been delayed in descending' Ex 32.1; De 23.21; μὴ χρονίσῃς 'Don't take too long' To 5.8; οὐ στήσεται οὐδὲ χρονιεῖ 'he will not stand still nor be delayed' Is 51.14. **b**. *to be made wait long* before sth happens: οὐκ ἐχρόνισα ἕως .. PSol 2.26.

Cf. ὑστερέω, παρέλκυσις, βραδύνω, μακροθυμέω, στραγγεύω, ὑπερβάλλω **2**, and ὑπερτίθημι.

χρονίσκος, ου. m.ʃ*

Dim. of χρόνος, *a short while*: 2M 11.1. Cf. χρόνος, στιγμή.

χρόνος, ου. m.

1. *a period of time*: ἐν τῷ ~ῳ τοῦ πατρὸς αὐτοῦ 'at the time of his father' Ge 26.15; εἰς τὸν αἰῶνα ~ον 'for a long time to come' Ex 14.13, Ju 15.10, Is 9.7; πάντα τὸν ~ον, ὅσον ἂν ζῇς ἐπὶ τῆς γῆς 'so long as you live on the earth' De 12.19; τὸν ἅπαντα ~ον 22.19, 29; εἰς τὸν ἐπιόντα ~ον 'for the future time' 32.29; μέχρι ~ου 'for a while' To 14.4 𝔊[I]

(ǁ ἕως ~ου); χ. ἀνθρώπου 'man's (average) life-span' Is 23.15; νεώτερος τῷ χρόνῳ 'younger in age' Jb 32.6, Οὐχ ὁ χ. ἐστὶν ὁ λαλῶν 'it is not one's age that qualifies one to speak' 32.7 (ǁ ἔτη); ~ῳ 'in the course of time' 14.11, ἐν ~ῳ Wi 2.4, 14.16. **b**. with quantifiers: ~ου πολλοῦ Jb 2.9, ~ον ἔτι μικρόν 2.9aα; πολὺν ~ον 29.18, Is 27.10; διὰ ~ου πολλοῦ 49.1; πάντα τὸν ~ον De 12.19; εἰς τὸν ἅπαντα ~ον 1M 10.30; μετ' οὐ πολὺν ~ον 2M 6.1; πρὸ μικροῦ ~ου 10.6.

2. *a point in time*: ἐν τῷ ~ῳ ἐκείνῳ 'on that occasion' Is 54.9, ἐν αὐτῷ τῷ ~ῳ 'at that very time' 1E 6.3. **b**. ǁ καιρός **4e**, sg. Ec 3.1, + κ. Da 7.12; pl., ǁ κ. Wi 7.18, + κ. 8.8, Da 2.21.

Cf. χρονίσκος, καιρός, ἡμέρα, στιγμή, ὥρα: Trench 209-12; Shipp 290-2; Delling, *TDNT* 9.586f.; Eynikel and Hauspie 1997.

χρυσαυγέω.ʃ*

to shine like gold: *s* clouds, Jb 37.22. Cf. στίλβω.

χρύσεος. ⇒ χρυσοῦς.

χρυσίον, ου. n.

gold as metal, often ǁ ἀργύριον: καθαρόν 'pure' Ex 28.13; material for making images, Ho 8.4, Hb 2.19; "you will take silver and gold, and make crowns" Zc 6.11; "as gold is tested" 13.9, cf. Ma 3.3*bis*; valuable possessions, Jl 3.5, Na 2.10, Zp 1.18; χ. καὶ ἀργύριον καὶ ἱματισμόν Zc 14.14; κτήνεσιν καὶ ἀργυρίῳ καὶ ~ῳ Ge 13.2; more valuable than copper, Is 60.17. Cf. χρυσοῦς, χρυσός, χρυσοειδής, χαλκός, ἀργύριον.

χρυσοειδής, ές.ʃ

looking like gold: *s* temple vessels, 1E 8.56. Cf. χρυσίον.

χρυσόλιθος, ου. m. *

yellow topaz (?): Ex 28.13. Cf. BDAG s.v.

χρυσός, οῦ. m.

gold as metal: ἐν πυρὶ δοκιμάζεται χ. 'gold is tested in the fire' Si 2.5; διὰ ~οῦ καὶ λίθων πολυτελῶν 'through gold and precious stones' Es D 6. **b**. *golden bed*: 1E 3.6. Cf. χρυσίον.

χρυσουργός, οῦ. m.ʃ *

goldsmith: ǁ ἀργυροχόος .. χαλκοπλάστης 'silver-smith .. coppersmith' Wi 15.9.

χρυσοῦς, ῆ, οῦν. Also χρύσεος.

made of gold: *s* ἐνώτια 'ear-rings' Ge 24.22; σκεύη ἀργυρᾶ καὶ ~ᾶ 'silver and golden implements' Ex 3.22; κλοιός 'collar' Ge 41.42, κόσμος 'ornaments' Si 6.30; λυχνία ~ῆ ὅλη 'a candlestick made wholly of gold' Zc 4.2; subst. ἀργυρᾶ καὶ ~ᾶ ἐποίησα τῇ Βααλ 'she fashioned silver and golden (images) for Baal' Ho 2.8. **b**. subst. 'gold coin or piece': paid, Ge 37.28, 45.22. See Lee 63-5. Cf. χρυσίον, χρύσωμα, ἀργυροῦς.

χρυσοφορέω.ʃ

to wear golden ornaments or *apparel*: *s* high priest 1M 14.43.

χρυσοχάλινος, ον.ʃ

having a golden bridle: *s* chariot, 1E 3.6; horse, 2M 10.29.

χρυσοχόος, ου.

goldsmith: Is 40.19, 46.6; Je 10.9 (ǁ τεχνίτης), Ep Je 45 (ǁ τέκτων). Cf. ἀργυροχόος.

χρυσόω: fut. χρυσώσω; aor. ἐχρύσωσα; pf.ptc.pass. κεχρυσωμένος.

to cover with gold-leaf, 'gild': *o* (acc.) the ark of testimony, Ex 25.10 (ǁ καταχρυσόω); post, pole, χρυσίῳ 26.32. Cf. καταχρυσόω and χρυσίον.

χρύσωμα, ατος. n.

that which is made of gold: 1E 8.56; wine-glass, 3.6; plate, + ἀργύρωμα 1M 15.32; temple furnishings, 2M 5.32. Cf. χρυσοῦς, ἀργύρωμα.

χρῶμα, ατος. n.ʃ

colour of skin: μετέβαλεν τὸ χ. αὐτῆς 'she turned pale' Es D 7; σπιλωθὲν ~ασιν διηλλαγμένοις 'stained with various colours' Wi 15.4. Cf. χρόα.

χρώς, ωτός. m.

fleshy surface, 'skin': of human body, Ex 28.38; δέρμα χρωτός Le 13.2; of human face, 34.29. Cf. δέρμα.

χυδαῖος, ον.ʃ

abundant: *s* population, ~οι ἐγένοντο Ex 1.7. Cf. πολύς, πληθύνω.

χυλός, οῦ. m.ʃ

liquid in general: stinking, 4M 6.25. Cf. ὕδωρ.

χύμα, ατος. n.

1. *that which is poured over* an area: metaph., καρδίας 'extensive intellectual capacity (?),' + φρόνησις, σοφία 3K 5.9 (ǁ B 2.35[a] πλάτος κ.).

2. *unclassified, unprocessed mass*: ἀριθμῶν 'of figures' 2M 2.24.

χυτός, ή, όν.

melted, cast: *s* iron, Jb 40.18.

χύτρα, ας. f.ʃ Also spelled κύθρα.

earthen pot: cooking utensil, Nu 11.8, + λέβης, χαλκίον 1K 2.14; receptacle for meat, Mi 3.3, Si 13.2 (ǁ λέβης); ὡς πρόσκαυμα ~ας 'like burnt earthenware' Jl 2.6, Na 2.11; for soup, Jd 6.19.

χυτρόγ/καυλος, ου. m.

a kind of pot: 3K 7.24.

χυτρόπους, ποδος. ⇒ κυθρόπους.

χωλαίνω: fut. χωλανῶ; aor. ἐχώλανα, pass. ἐχωλάνθην.

to become lame: Ps 17.46; pass. = act., 2K 4.4B (*L* act.). **b**. *to go limping*: 1K 17.39*L* (B: κοπιάω 'to act awkwardly, clumsily'), 3K 18.21.

Cf. χωλός.

χωλός, ή, όν.
lame in the feet: *s* hum., ὀφθαλμὸς ἤμην τυφλῶν ποὺς δὲ ~ῶν Jb 29.15; disqualifying for priesthood, Le 21.18; ἀμφοτέροις τοῖς ποσὶν αὐτοῦ 'in both of his feet' 2K 9.13 (*L* acc.); subst., Is 33.23, ἁλεῖται ὡς ἔλαφος ὁ χ. 'the lame shall leap like a hart' 35.6; unsuitable sacrificial animal, De 15.21 (|| τυφλός); Ma 1.8 (|| ἄρρωστος and τυφλός); 1.13 (|| ἐνοχλούμενος). Cf. χωλαίνω.

χῶμα, ατος. n.
elevation consisting of soil: dike, τῆς γῆς Ex 8.16; thrown up to build an embankment, βαλεῖ χ. Hb 1.10; 'tel, mound,' ruins of a destroyed city - Is 25.2, ἀοίκητον Jo 8.28; grave, Jb 17.16¶. Cf. χωματίζω: Shipp 576f.; *BA* 2.37f.

χωματίζω: pf.ptc.pass. κεχωματισμένος.ʃ
to fortify with mounds: pass., *o* city, Jo 11.13. Cf. χῶμα.

χώνευμα, ατος. n.*
molten image: object of worship, ἐποίησαν ἑαυτοῖς χ. De 9.12 (|| χωνευτόν vs. 16); ἔπλασεν αὐτὸ χ. 'he fashioned it as a molten image' Hb 2.18; ἔργον τέκτονος καὶ χ. 'work of a carpenter ..' Je 10.3. Cf. χωνεύω, χωνευτός.

χώνευσις, εως. f.ʃ
manufacturing by melting and casting of metal: τῶν κεφαλίδων τῆς σκηνῆς 'of the capitals of the tent' Ex 39.4; 2C 4.3. Cf. χωνεύω.

χωνευτήριον, ου. n.ʃ *
smelting-furnace: 3K 8.51, Zc 11.13*bis*; πῦρ ~ου Ma 3.2; ὡς χρυσὸν ἐν ~ῳ ἐδοκίμασεν αὐτούς 'tested them like gold in ..' Wi 3.6. Cf. χωνεύω.

χωνευτής, οῦ. m.ʃ *
artisan who works metal: Jd 17.4 A (B: ἀργυροκόπος). Cf. χωνεύω.

χωνευτός, ή, όν.*
molten: *s* image for worship, μόσχος 'calf' Ex 32.4; θεοὺς ~οὺς οὐ ποιήσεις σεαυτῷ 34.17; εἴδωλον Nu 33.52; subst. n., ἐποιήσατε ὑμῖν ἑαυτοῖς ~όν De 9.16 (|| χώνευμα vs. 12); ποιήσει γλυπτὸν καὶ ~όν '.. engraved and ..' 27.15; ἐξολεθρεύσω τὰ γλυπτὰ καὶ ~ά Na 1.14. Cf. χωνεύω, χώνευμα.

χωνεύω: fut. χωνεύσω, pass. χωνευθήσομαι; aor. ἐχώνευσα, ptc. χωνεύσας, impv. χώνευσον, inf. pass. χωνευθῆναι.
1. *to smelt, cast*: *o* metal, Ma 3.3 (|| καθαρίζω), ἐν μέσῳ καμίνου 'inside a furnace' Ez 22.21; metaph. and + acc. pers., 22.20.
2. *to fit* sth (dat.) with cast metal (acc.): αὐτοῖς πέντε βάσεις χαλκᾶς 'them [= pillars] with five copper bases' Ex 26.37; 38.3.
3. *to produce by processing and working metal*: + acc., ψευδῆ 'false objects (of worship)' Je 10.14.
Cf. χώνευμα, χώνευσις, χωνευτήριον, χωνευτής, χωνευτός.

χώρα, ας. f.
1. *country, territory of a nation*: χ. τῶν Χαλδαίων Ge 11.28; ἐκ ποίας ~ας Jn 1.8; εἰς γῆν Σηιρ εἰς ~αν Εδωμ Ge 32.3; Mi 5.5, Is 2.7 (|| γῆ); Αἰγύπτου 19.20 (|| Αἰγυπτίων vs. 19), τῶν Ἰουδαίων 19.17, τῆς Ἰουδαίας 1E 6.8 (|| ἡ Ἰουδαία χ. 2E 5.8). **b**. *smaller district within a country, region*: ~αις ἐν Ἀσσυρίοις .. ~ας τῆς Αἰγύπτου Am 3.9; 3.10, 11 (|| γῆ), 6.8.
2. *place proper* to a person or thing: ἀπεκατέστη τὸ ὕδωρ .. ἐπὶ ~ας 'the water reverted .. to (its) place' Ex 14.27. Cf. τόπος **4**.
3. *space, area*: κατὰ ~αν μείνῃ 'be confined locally' Le 13.23; Is 28.2.
4. *countryside* as opp. to urban areas: ἐν ~ᾳ Ἀσσυρίων Is 7.18 (habitat of bees), ἐν ταῖς φάραγξι τῆς ~ας 'in the valleys of ..' 7.19; opp. Alexandria, 3M 3.1.
Cf. γῆ, τόπος, χωρίον: Shipp 577f.

χωρέω: aor. ἐχώρησα, ptc. χωρήσας.
1. *to provide sufficient space* ('Lebensraum') *for*: + acc. pers., *s* land, οὐκ ἐχώρει αὐτοὺς ἡ γῆ κατοικεῖν ἅμα 'the land did not offer space enough for them to live together' Ge 13.6; γαστήρ '(hum.) belly' 4M 7.6. **b**. *to hold, contain* a certain amount: 3K 7.24.
2. *to turn out* in a certain way at the end: οὕτως 2M 3.40, 15.37. Cf. ἐκβαίνω **2**.
3. *to move far and abroad*: *s* spirit of Wisdom, 7.23, || διήκω 24.
Cf. δύναμαι.

χωρίζω: aor. ἐχώρισα, ptc. χωρίσας, pass. ἐχωρίσθην, subj. χωρισθῶ, ptc. χωρισθείς, impv. χωρίσθητι; pf.ptc.pass. κεχωρισμένος.
1. *to set apart*: + acc. pers. and gen. pers. (a group from which to choose), 1E 8.54; babies from their mothers' breasts, 3M 5.50; *o* leper, κεχωρισμένος καθήσεται ἔξω τῆς παρεμβολῆς 'he shall remain outside of the camp in isolation' Le 13.46; ἀπὸ τῶν βδελυγμάτων 'from the abominations' 1E 7.13. **b**. mid.: + gen., τῆς ἀκαθαρσίας 2E 6.21, "said farewell to everything just" 3M 2.25; ἀπὸ φίλων Pr 18.1.
2. *to exclude*: *o* hum. and pass., τοῦ ἱερατεύειν 'to serve as priest' 1E 5.39. **b**. *to deny approach* to: ἀπὸ θεοῦ Wi 1.3.
3. pass. *to depart*: εἰς τὴν Ἀντιόχειαν 2M 5.21. **b**. *to part with sbd and join sbd else*: ἀπό τινος .. πρός τινα 1C 12.9.
Cf. χωρισμός, δια~, ἐκχωρίζω, ἀφορίζω, διαστέλλω.

χωρίον, ου. n.
fairly large area: *s* town of Joppa, 2M 12.7; οἴνου 'wine-producing' 1C 27.27, cf. Bagnall. Cf. χώρα.

χωρίς prep. c. gen.

1. *besides, in addition to*: ἐγένετο δὲ λιμὸς .. χ. τοῦ λιμοῦ τοῦ πρότερον 'there occurred now a famine .. other than the previous one' Ge 26.1; Le 9.17; Nu 6.21, 16.49; 2E 2.65 (‖ πάρεξ Ne 7.67).

2. *excepting, not including*: χ. τῶν γυναικῶν υἱῶν Ιακωβ 'the wives of Jacob's sons excluded' Ge 46.26; χ. τῆς γῆς τῶν ἱερέων μόνον 'with the sole exception of the priests' land' 47.22, 26; οὐ δύνανται οἱ ἄνθρωποι εἶναι χ. τῶν γυναῖκων 'the menfolk can't do without the womenfolk' 1E 4.17.

Cf. ἀλλά, ἄνευ, ἐκτός, πάρεξ, πλήν.

a) מִלְּבַד; *b*) רַק; *c*) לְבַד מִן.

χωρισμός, οῦ. m.ʃ

1. *seclusion*: of menstruating woman, κατὰ τὰς ἡμέρας τοῦ ~οῦ τῆς ἀφέδρου Le 12.2; γυναῖκα ἐν ~ῷ ἀκαθαρσίας 18.19.

2. *keeping away and not mingling*: ~ὸν ἐποίουν ἐπὶ τῷ κατὰ τὰς τροφάς 'kept themselves apart in matters pertaining to foods' 3M 3.4.

Cf. χωρίζω: LSG s.v.

χωροβατέω: aor. ἐχωροβάτησα, inf. ~βατῆσαι, impv. ~βάτησον.ʃ

to survey on foot: + acc., τὴν γῆν Jo 18.8, 9. Cf. van der Meer 2006.72f.

Ψ

ψαλίς, δος. f.

"*U-shaped band* for affixing hangings to columns or the like" (LSG): Ex 27.10. Cf. Shipp 579.

ψάλλω: fut. ψαλῶ; aor.impv.2pl ψάλατε, subj. ψάλω.

1. *to perform music*: with a musical instrument, ἐν κινύρᾳ 1K 16.16; τῷ ὀνόματι κυρίου Ps 7.18 (|| ἐξομολογέομαι), τῷ κυρίῳ 9.12, + ᾄδω 26.6, 56.8; mocking, εἰς ἐμέ 68.13 (|| ἀδολεσχέω 'chatter'). **b**. professionally: ἡ ψάλλουσα 'songstress, geisha' Si 9.4.

2. *to praise with music*: + dat., τῷ κυρίῳ Ps 9.12; τῷ ὀνόματι κυρίου 7.18; ἐν κιθάρᾳ 'with a lyre' 70.22, ἐν ψαλτηρίῳ 'with a harp' 32.2, ἐν κιθάρᾳ καὶ φωνῇ ψαλμοῦ 97.5; + acc., τὰς δυναστείας σου 20.14; || αἰνέω 149.3; *s* ἡ δόξα μου 29.13.

Cf. ψαλμός, ψάλτης, ἐπιψάλλω, ψαλτῳδέω, μελῳδέω, ὑμνέω, ᾠδός.

ψαλμός, οῦ. m.

music made with an instrument: ψ. ὀργάνων Am 5.23 (|| ἦχος ᾠδῶν). **b**. cultic, ψ. ἐν οἴκῳ κυρίου Zc 6.14; Is 66.20; + αἶνος Ju 16.1. **c**. mocking song: La 3.14 (|| γέλως), 3.63.

Cf. ψάλλω, θρῆνος, δίψαλμα, ᾠδή.

ψαλτήριον, ου. n.

harp: ψ. καὶ κιθάραν Ge 4.21; used on festive occasions, αὐλὸς καὶ ψ. ἡδύνουσιν μέλη 'flutes and harps accompany sweet melodies' Si 40.21, μετὰ κιθάρας καὶ ~ίου καὶ τυμπάνων καὶ αὐλῶν Is 5.12, in praising God, 38.20. Cf. ψαλτός: LSG s.v.

ψάλτης, ου. m.ʃ

singer: + ψαλτῳδός 1E 5.41. Cf. ψάλλω, ψαλτῳδός, ᾠδός.

ψαλτός, ή, όν.ʃ*

sung to the harp: *s* τὰ δικαιώματά σου Ps 118.54. Cf. ψαλτήριον.

ψαλτῳδέω. ʃ *

to sing to the harp: in cultic service, 2C 5.13. Cf. ψάλλω.

ψαλτῳδός, όν. *

serving as singer or psalmist: subst.m., (temple-) *singer* Si 47.9; + ψάλτης 1E 5.41. Cf. ψάλλω.

ψάμμος, ου. f.ʃ

sand: fig. of small value, Wi 7.9; of large quantity, θαλάσσης Od 12.9. Cf. ἄμμος.

ψαρός, ά, όν.

dapple-grey: *s* horse, Zc 1.8. Cf. Shipp 579.

ψαύω: aor.opt.3s ψαύσειεν.ʃ

to touch: + gen., 4M 17.1. Cf. ἅπτομαι.

ψεκάς, άδος. f.ʃ

particle of liquid: ὀρέων '(raindrops) in mountains' Jb 24.8¶; of dew, Ct 5.2 (|| δρόσος 'dew'). Cf. ῥανίς, σταγών.

ψέλιον, ου. n.

U-shaped armlet, i.e. in the form of an interrupted circle (LSG): an ornament worn by women, δύο ~ια ἐπὶ τὰς χεῖρας Ge 24.22, sim. Ez 23.42, περὶ τὰς χεῖρας Ge 24.47, Ez 16.11; with other ornamental items, Nu 31.50, Ju 10.4, Is 3.20; ~ῳ τρυπήσεις τὸ χεῖλος αὐτοῦ; 'will you bore his lip with a ring?' Jb 40.26. Cf. κόσμος **3**: Taillardat 1978; Russo 135-52.

ψελλίζω.ʃ

to falter in speech: *s* γλῶσσα Is 32.4. Cf. λαλέω, ἰσχνόφωνος: Schmidt 3.370-2.

ψευδής, ές.

1. *different from what a person or an object professes or purports to be*, **'**false, lying': *s* persons, Ps 61.10 (|| μάταιος), Ho 12.11, μάρτυς 'witness' Pr 19.5; pagan gods, Ep Je 7, 58; λαλῶν ῥήματα προφάσεις ~εῖς Ho 10.4; καταλαλέω ~ῆ 7.13; μαρτυρία 'testimony' Ex 20.16, De 5.20; ὅρκος 'oath' Zc 8.17; ἐνύπνια 'dreams' 10.2; ὅρασις 'vision' ib. (|| κόπος); things, καρπός 'deceptive fruit' Ho 10.13, ὕδωρ Je 15.18; σάββατα Am 6.3; of idols and images, φαντασία ψ. Hb 2.18; military horses, Ps 32.17; *subst. n.pl., *deceptive deeds* - ἐργάζομαι ~ῆ Ho 7.1 (a manifestation of ἀδικία and κακία), and possibly μάταια καὶ ~ῆ Jn 2.9; untruths, Je 34.8, λαλέω ~ῆ Mi 6.12, Zc 13.3.

2. *given to deception and lying*: *s* πόλις Je 6.6, πόλις ψ. ἀδικίας πλήρης Na 3.1, χείλη 'lips' Pr 8.7, 17.4.

Cf. ψεῦδος, ψεύδομαι, ψευδοπροφήτης, ψευδολογέω, ψεύστης, δόλιος, μάταιος, ἀληθής.

ψευδοθύριον, ου. n.ʃ *

= ψευδοθυρίς: Bel 21 LXX (TH κρυπτὴ θύρα). Cf. ψευδοθυρίς.

ψευδοθυρίς, ίδος. f.ʃ *

secret door: Bel 15-17 LXX. Cf. θυρίς, ψευδοθύριον.

ψευδολογέω: fut. ~λογήσω.ʃ

to speak falsely: *s* hum., Da 11.27 LXX (TH ψευδῆ λαλέω). Cf. ψεύδομαι: Spicq 3.517.

ψεύδομαι: fut. ψεύσομαι; aor. ἐψευσάμην, subj. ψεύσωμαι, ptc.pass. ψευσθείς.

1. *to lie, speak falsely*: abs. Le 19.11; περί τινος, 6.3; 'to deceive, beguile' and + acc. pers., De 33.29,

Is 57.11; + cogn. acc., ψεῦδος Si 7.13, cf. Renehan 2.141; + dat. pers., Je 5.12, τῷ θεῷ σου Jo 24.27, + κατά τινος Bel 12 TH; *s* prophets, Zc 13.4.

2. *to make a false statement about*: + acc. rei, τὰ πρὸς τὸν πλησίον 'things which are at the neighbour's' Le 6.2; Jb 27.11; + acc. pers., Ps 65.3, Jb 8.18. **b**. *to utter as falsehood*: + acc. rei, ^τοὺς λόγους τούτους^ Ne 6.8.

3. *to disappoint, balk*: *s* ὁ οἶνος ἐψεύσατο αὐτούς Ho 9.2; ἔργον ἐλαίας 'work on olive' (or poss. 'olive-grove') Hb 3.17; 4M 5.34.

4. *to go back on, renege on*: + acc. rei, πάντα, ὅσα εἶπε 1M 11.53.

Cf. ψευδής, ψεῦδος, ψεύστης, δια~, καταψεύδομαι, ψευδολογέω, ψευδομαρτυρέω, δολιόω, παραλαλέω, ἀληθεύω.

ψευδομαρτυρέω: fut. ~ρήσω; aor.ptc. ~ρήσας.ʃ

to bear false witness: + cogn. obj., κατὰ τοῦ πλησίον σου μαρτυρίαν ψευδῆ Ex 20.16, De 5.20. Cf. ψευδομάρτυς, ψευδής, μαρτυρέω: Corssen.

ψευδομάρτυς, υρος. m.ʃ

lying witness: Su 61. Cf. ψευδομαρτυρέω, μάρτυς.

ψευδοπροφήτης, ου. m. *

false prophet: Zc 13.2 (|| τὸ πνεῦμα τὸ ἀκάθαρτον); classed with various categories of pagan diviners, Je 34.7, 36.8. Cf. ψευδής, μάντις, προφήτης: Reiling; Corssen.

ψεῦδος, ους. n.

act of lying, deception: Mi 2.11; ἀρὰ καὶ ψ. καὶ φόνος καὶ κλοπὴ .. 'cursing, .. murder and theft ..' Ho 4.2; 7.3 (|| κακία), 11.12 (|| ἀσέβεια); ἐπὶ ~δει '(to swear) falsely' Zc 5.4, Ma 3.5. **b**. Ψεῦδος or Ψεύδη as an interjection of disbelief, 'That's a lie!' Je 44.14, 50.2. **c**. *deceptive attitude or behaviour which sows mistrust*: ψ. καὶ οὐκ πίστις Je 9.3. **d**. *false statement*: + πλάνος Je 23.32. **e**. *false object of worship*: 2C 30.14.

Cf. ψευδής, δόλος, ἀλήθεια.

ψεύστης, ου. m.

liar: Ps 115.2; used attr., πλούσιος ψ. Si 25.2, Pr 19.22. Cf. ψεύδομαι.

ψηλαφάω: fut.act. ~φήσω, pass. ~φηθήσομαι; aor. ἐψηλάφησα, inf. ~φῆσαι, subj. ~φήσω, opt.3s ~φήσαι.

to feel after: abs., with hands, Ps 113.15; *s* a blind person, μεσημβρίας .. ἐν τῷ σκότει 'at midday .. in the dark' De 28.29, sim. Is 59.10, Jb 5.14; *o* θήρα 'game' Na 3.1; πᾶσαν τὴν ἀδικίαν τῆς γῆς Zc 3.9; in order to investigate, + acc. pers. ψηλαφήσω σε, εἰ σὺ εἶ ὁ υἱός μου Ησαυ ἢ οὔ 'let me feel you (to see) if you are ..' Ge 27.21; 27.12; σε ὡς ῥομφαίαν μαχητοῦ Zc 9.13; + acc. rei, σκότος Jb 12.25; ἐπὶ τοὺς στύλους 'the pillars' Jd 16.26 A (B: acc.). Cf. Schmidt 1.240f.; Trench 58-60.

ψηλάφησις, εως. f.ʃ

v.n. of ψηλαφάω, 'groping': with fingers, Wi 15.15. Cf. ψηλαφάω.

ψηλαφητός, ή, όν.ʃ

palpable: *s* σκότος Ex 10.21. Cf. ψηλαφάω.

ψήφισμα, ατος. n.

decision made: by casting lots, Es 3.7 o'; + κλῆρος, *o* of τίθημι 9.24 o'; casting of lots not implied, 2M 10.8 (+ πρόσταγμα), κοινόν 'public' 15.36. Cf. πρόσταγμα.

ψηφολογέω: fut. ~λογηθήσομαι.ʃ *

to pave with cobble-stones: pass., *s* street of Jerusalem, To 13.17. Cf. ψῆφος.

ψῆφος, ου. f.

1. *pebble*: used to perform circumcision, Ex 4.25; ἄμμου 'of sand' (fig. of tiny object) Si 18.10. **b**. used in taking a decision: 4M 15.26.

2. *outcome of enquiry or investigation*: Ec 7.25.

Cf. ψηφολογέω, κόχλαξ, λίθος, χάλιξ.

ψιθυρίζω.ʃ

to whisper slanders: abs., 2K 12.19, Si 21.28, κατά τινος Ps 40.8. Cf. διαψιθυρίζω, ψίθυρος, ψιθυρισμός, συρίζω: Schmidt 3.367f.

ψιθυρισμός, οῦ.ʃ

act of whispering by a snake-charmer: Ec 10.11. Cf. ψιθυρίζω.

ψίθυρος, ον.ʃ

subst. *slanderer*: *s* hum., Si 5.14, + παράνομος PSol 12.1; + δίγλωσσος 'double-tongued' Si 28.13; hum. lips, PSol 12.3. Cf. ψιθυρίζω.

ψιλή, ῆς. f.ʃ *

carpet of superb quality: Jo 7.21. Cf. ἀμφίταπος.

ψιλόω: fut. ψιλώσω.ʃ

pluck off, pull out: + acc., κόμας 'hair' Ez 44.20.

ψόα, ας. f. See also ψύα.

muscle of the loins: of sacrificial animal, Le 3.9, of a hum., Ps 37.8.

ψογίζω: aor. ἐψόγισα, inf. ψογίσαι.ʃ *

to censure, say censorious things against: + acc. pers., 1M 11.5, 11. Cf. ψόγος, ἐλέγχω.

ψόγος, ου. m.

censure: κατήνεγκεν .. ~ον πονηρόν Ge 37.2; ἤκουσα ~ον πολλῶν παροικούντων κυκλόθεν Ps 30.14, sim. Je 20.10; δημοσίᾳ κατὰ τοῦ ἔθνους διαδοῦναι ~ον 'openly to spread a censorious opinion against the nation' 3M 2.27 (|| δυσφημία vs. 26). Cf. ψογίζω, δυσφημία, ἔλεγχος, ὄνειδος, ἔπαινος.

ψοφέω: aor.impv. ψόφησον.ʃ

to make noise: ψόφησον τῷ ποδί 'Make noise with your foot' Ez 6.11 (|| κροτέω 'to clap'). Cf. ψόφος and κροτέω.

ψόφος, ου. m.ʃ

sound, noise: ἁρμάτων καὶ ἱππευόντων 'of

chariots and horsemen' Mi 1.13. Cf. ψοφέω, ἦχος, φωνή: Schmidt 3.313-5.

ψύα. Spelled also ψόα, q.v.

ψυγμός, οῦ. m.ʃ

drying-ground: σαγηνῶν 'of drag-nets' Ez 26.5, 14, 47.10. **b**. a mechanical rendering of the Hebrew: Nu 11.32, cf. Caird 1969.40.

Cf. ψύχω.

ψυκτήρ, ῆρος. m.ʃ

wine-cooler: golden and silver, 2E 1.8.

ψύλλος, ου. m.ʃ *

flea: fig. of insignificant entity, + κύων 'dog' 1K 24.15; 26.20*L*.

ψυχαγωγία, ας. f.ʃ

sth amusing and attractive: w. ref. to studying of history, 2M 2.25.

ψυχή, ῆς. f.

1. *physical life, life-force*: of a human, Jn 1.14; as *o* of φονεύω 'to murder' De 22.26, λαμβάνω 'to take sbd's life, kill him' Ho 4.8 (on which see Muraoka 1983.36-8), Jn 4.3, πατάσσω 'to strike' Nu 35.11, ἀναιρέω 'to kill' Le 31.19, ἐξαίρω 'to do away with' Ps 39.15, ἐξολεθρεύω Ge 17.14; σῴζω Ge 19.17, Am 2.14, Jb 33.28¶ (at latter ‖ ζωή), ἐξαιρέω 'to rescue' Ps 63.2, ῥύομαι (ῥύσασθαι ἐκ θανάτου τὰς ~ὰς αὐτῶν 'to rescue ..') 32.19, Jb 33.30 (at latter ‖ ζωή), φείδομαι 'to spare' 33.18, φυλάσσομαι 'to guard' Ps 24.20, Je 17.21; ζητέω Ex 4.19, 1K 24.10 (to kill), παγιδεύω 'to ensnare' 28.9, τὰ χείλη αὐτοῦ [= ἄφρονος] παγὶς τῇ ~ῇ αὐτοῦ Pr 18.7, θηρεύω 'to ambush' Ps 58.4, φυλάσσω 'to watch for' 70.10, ὑπομένω 'to watch for' 55.7, καταδιώκω 'to hunt for' 7.6 (‖ ζωή); ἐνεχυράζω 'to take as pawn' De 24.6; ἀπελέγετο τὴν ~ὴν αὐτοῦ 'he felt like giving up on his own life' Jn 4.8; ἐν τῷ ἀφιέναι αὐτὴν τὴν ~ήν 'as she was about to breathe her last' Ge 35.18; ἀποθάνοι ἡ ψ. μου 'may my life die' Nu 23.10, ἔφυγον πρὸς τὴν ~ὴν ἑαυτῶν [*L*: κατὰ τὰς ~ας αὐτῶν; on κατά, see 3K 19.3] 4K 7.7, ἔθετο τὴν ~ὴν αὐτοῦ ἐν τῇ χειρὶ αὐτοῦ 'he put his life on the line' 1K 19.5, 28.21, Jb 13.14, cf. Ps 118.109; ἥψατο ἡ μάχαιρα ἕως τῆς ~ῆς αὐτῶν 'the sword befell them fatally' Je 4.10; οὐ πατάξομεν αὐτὸν εἰς ~ήν 'we shan't harm his life' 37.21, ὃς ἂν πατάξῃ ~ὴν ἀνθρώπου, καὶ ἀποθάνῃ Le 24.17; δώσει ~ὴν ἀντὶ ~ῆς 'he shall pay a life for a life' Ex 21.23, sim. Le 24.18 and cf. ἡ Φιλουμένη ψυχὴν ἀντὶ ψυχῆς καὶ σῶμα ἀντὶ σώματος ἀντέδωκε, τὰ αὑτῆς ἀντὶ τῶν ἐμῶν Aristides, 27.352[9]; πλὴν ὅσα ποιηθήσεται ~ῇ 'except that which is done for (minimum) sustenance' De 16.8, sim. Ex 12.16. **b**. of non-human animates: πᾶσαν ~ὴν ζῴων ἑρπετῶν 'every life of creeping animals' Ge 1.21, ψ. κτήνους Le 24.18; ~ὴν ζῶσαν 'living being(s)' Ge 1.24 (animals) ‖ 2.7 (human); ψ. ζωῆς 'energy for life' 1.30; αἷμα ~ῆς 'blood of life' 9.4.

2. *living being*: non-human, πάσῃ ~ῇ τῇ ζώσῃ μεθ' ὑμῶν 'every living being living with you' Ge 9.10 (specified as birds and livestock); πάσης ~ῆς τῆς κινουμένης ἐν τῷ ὕδατι καὶ πάσης ~ῆς ἑρπούσης ἐπὶ τῆς γῆς Le 11.46. See above **1 b**.

3. man's *incorporeal, inner existence and strength*: περιεχύθη μοι ὕδωρ ἕως ~ῆς 'water was poured round me, reaching my soul' Jn 2.6; "as my inner strength was about to fail me" 2.8; ἀπὸ ~ῆς ἕως σαρκῶν 'totally' Is 10.18. Cf. .. σῶμα νέρθεν, πνεῦμα καὶ ψυχὴ μένει 'the body of PN is below, but (his) spirit and soul remain' on an epitaph (*ND* 4.38). **a**. involved in moral, ethical or religious aspects, ἁμαρτία ~ῆς μου Mi 6.7, cf. ἐξήμαρτεν ἡ ψ. σου Hb 2.10; yearning for God, Ps 62.2 (:: σάρξ); :: σῶμα Wi 1.4, 2M 6.30, Pr 11.17; 25.20 (‖ καρδία); ἀγαπήσεις κύριον .. ἐξ ὅλης τῆς καρδίας σου καὶ ἐξ ὅλης τῆς ~ῆς σου καὶ ἐξ ὅλης τῆς δυνάμεώς σου De 6.5, sim. 13.4, 30.2, cf. ἀπὸ τῆς ~ῆς φιλεῖν Thphr. *Char.* 17.3 (Renehan 2.142), ἀπὸ ~ῆς 'on purpose' Si 19.16, ἐκ ~ῆς 'willingly' 1M 8.27 and ἐκ ~ῆς σου Is 58.10, λατρεύειν κυρίῳ .. ἐξ ὅλης τῆς ~ῆς σου De 10.12, ζητῆσαι κύριον .. ἐξ ὅλης τῆς καρδίας καὶ ἐξ ὅλης τῆς ~ῆς 2C 15.12 (‖ ἐν πάσῃ θελήσει vs. 15); ἄφαψαι αὐτοὺς ἐπὶ σῇ ~ῇ 'Fasten them [= instructions] to your ..' Pr 6.21; ἐκολλήθη ἡ ψ. μου ὀπίσω σου Ps 62.9; ἔλπισον ἐπὶ τὸν θεόν 41.6; ἡ ψ. ἡμῶν ὑπομένει τῷ κυρίῳ 32.20; ἡ ψ. μου αἰνέσει σε 118.175, ~ὴν ἐξομολογουμένην σοι 73.19, ἀγαλλιάσεται ἐπὶ τῷ κυρίῳ 34.9, sim. Is 61.10; τῷ θεῷ ὑποτάγηθι 'Submit yourself to ..' Ps 61.6, εἰς ὕβριν μὴ ἐπαίρου τῇ ~ῇ σου 'don't get worked up into an arrogant attitude' Pr 19.18; πρὸς σὲ ἦρα τὴν ~ήν μου Ps 24.1, ἐξέχεα ἐπ' ἐμὲ τὴν ~ήν μου 'I poured out ..' 41.5, ἐφύλαξεν ἡ ψ. μου τὰ μαρτύριά σου 118.167, ἐμβαλεῖτε τὰ ῥήματα ταῦτα εἰς τὴν καρδίαν ὑμῶν καὶ εἰς τὴν ~ὴν ὑμῶν De 11.18; *s* of πέποιθα (< πείθω) 'to trust' Ps 56.2, πλημμελέω 'to err' Nu 5.6, ἁμαρτάνω Le 4.2, ἁμαρτία ~ῆς μου Mi 6.7, δολία 'deceitful' Pr 13.9, αἵματα ~ῶν ἀθῴων 'murders of innocent ..' Je 2.34, μόσχον ἕνα περὶ ἁμαρτίας περὶ τῶν ~ῶν αὐτῶν 'one bull ..' Jb 1.5; *o* of μιαίνω 'to defile' Le 11.44, δικαιόω Je 3.11, ἰάομαι 'to heal' Ps 40.5, λυτρόομαι 'to redeem' 68.19, σῴζω 71.13 (‖ φείδομαι). **b**. desire: ἔχετε τῇ ~ῇ ὑμῶν ὥστε .. 'you are so minded to ..' Ge 23.8, cf. 4K 9.15 ms. 93 and οὐκ ἔστιν ἡ ψ. μου πρὸς αὐτούς 'my heart is not with them' Je 15.1; πάντα, ὅσα ἠθέλησεν ἐν τῇ ~ῇ 'all that he willed ..' 2C 7.11; ὁ σπόρος αὐτῶν κατὰ ~ήν 'their offspring are to their satisfaction' Jb 21.8; ἐμοὶ ἐγένετο ἐπὶ ~ῇ τοῦ οἰκοδομῆσαι οἶκον 'I thought of building ..' 1C 22.7; ὁ υἱός μου προείλατο τῇ ~ῇ τὴν θυγατέρα ὑμῶν 'my son has deliberately chosen your daughter' Ge 34.8; καταθύμιον ~ῆς αὐτοῦ 'his inner desire' Mi 7.3; ἐπιθυμία ~ῆς De 12.20 + Ps 9.24, ἐπιθυμεῖ ἡ ψ. μου Is 26.9, ἐπιποθεῖ ἡ ψ. μου πρὸς σέ '.. yearns after you' Ps 41.2; ἐπλάτυνε καθὼς ὁ ᾅδης τὴν ~ὴν αὐτοῦ Hb 2.5, sim. Is 5.14; ὅσον ~ήν σου ἐμπλησθῆναι 'as much as your appetite is satisfied' De 23.25, "a righteous diner fills his ψ., but the ψ. of the impious are in need" Pr 13.25, cf. ψ. ἀεργοῦ πεινάσει 'the soul of the idle will be hungry' Pr 19.15, ἐχόρτασεν ~ὴν κενὴν καὶ ~ὴν πεινῶσαν ἐνέπλησεν ἀγαθῶν 'he fed an empty soul and sated a hungry soul with good things' Ps 106.9, sim. Je 38.14, 25, Pr 38.39, ‖ κοιλία 'belly' Ez 7.19; οἱ ἄρτοι αὐτῶν ταῖς ~αῖς αὐτῶν '.. for their own enjoyment' Ho 9.4, cf. τὴν γῆν .. εὔχονται ταῖς ~αις αὐτῶν Je 22.27; of disgust, προσοχθίσῃ ἡ ψ. ὑμῶν 'your soul loathes' Ge 26.15, προσώχθισαν τῇ ~ῇ αὐτῶν Le 26.43; Nu 21.5, οὐ βδελύξεται ἡ ψ. μου ὑμᾶς 'my soul will not loathe you' Le 26.11, πᾶν βρῶμα ἐβδελύξατο ἡ ψ. αὐτῶν Ps 106.18; βαρύνομαι 'to be unfriendly' Zc 11.8. **c.** intellectual, mental or emotional reaction: ὅπως εὐλογήσῃ σε ἡ ψ. μου Ge 27.4 (‖ εὐλογήσω vs. 7); ἐταράχθη ἡ ~ὴ αὐτοῦ 41.8, ταραχθῆναι τὴν ~ήν μου ἐν ὀργῇ Hb 3.2; ἐξεκινήθη ἡ ψ. βασιλέως 'the king was rather upset' 4K 6.11 (*L* ἐξέστη ἡ καρδία ..), ἐξέστη ἡ καρδία .. ἐσαλεύθη ἡ ψ. αὐτοῦ Ju 12.16; οὐκ εὐδοκεῖ ἡ ψ. μου ἐν αὐτῷ 'I am not pleased with him' Hb 2.4; ἐπέχαρας ἐκ ~ῆς σου 'you rejoiced heartily' Ez 25.6; εἰρήνη ~ῆς 'inner peace' Hg 2.9, ἐν ~ῇ εἰρηνικῇ 'firmly determined' 1C 12.39, θλῖψις ~ῆς 'inner agony' Ge 42.21; πόνος ~ῆς Is 53.10, πικρία ~ῆς Jb 7.11; βαρυνθήσεται ἡ ψ. μου ἐπ' αὐτούς, καὶ γὰρ αἱ ~αὶ αὐτῶν ἐπωρύοντο ἐπ' ἐμέ 'I shall be gravely distressed over them, for their souls howled at me' Zc 11.8; ‖ καρδία Ex 35.21, De 6.6, 13.3, Je 4.19, cf. Πᾶν τὸ ἐν τῇ ~ῇ σου ποίει 'Do all that is on your mind' 1C 17.2 (‖ 2K 7.3 καρδία), ἐλάλησεν πάντα, ὅσα ἐν τῇ ~ῇ αὐτῆς 'she discussed with him all that was on her mind' 2C 9.1 (‖ 3K 10.2 καρδία); πονηρίαι ἐν τῇ ~ῇ αὐτοῦ 'evil designs ..' Pr 26.25, ἀφέλετε τὰς πονηρίας ἀπὸ τῶν ~ῶν ὑμῶν 'remove ..' Is 1.16; ‖ διάνοια Ex 35.22; ἐξουδένωσεν αὐτὸν ἐν τῇ ~ῇ αὐτῆς 'she despised him ..' 1C 15.29 (‖ 2K 6.16 καρδία); ***s*** of προαιρέομαι 'to favour' Ge 34.8, προσδοκέω 'to expect' Ps 68.21, προσδέχομαι 'to look forward to' Is 42.1, ἐλπίζω 29.8, θέλω 66.3, ἐπιθυμέω 'to desire' De 14.26, κολλάομαι 'to attach oneself' Ps 62.9, συνδέομαι 'to be bound' 1K 18.1*L*, ἐκκρέμαμαι 'to be dependent' Ge 44.30, μισέω Is 1.14, βδελύσσομαι 'to loathe' Je 14.19, ἀφίστημι 'to distance oneself' 6.8, ἀπαναίνομαι 'to refuse' Ps 76.3, ἐκδικέω 'to revenge' Je 5.9, ἀνέχομαι 'to endure' Jb 6.11, ἐντρυφάω 'to enjoy' Is 55.2, εὐφραίνομαι 'to rejoice' Pr 23.24, εὐφραινόμενοι τὴν ~ήν Is 24.7, ζάω Ps 68.33, ἔγκοπος 'wearied' Jb 19.2, πενθέω 'to pine' 14.22, κατώδυνος ~ῇ 'in agony' 1K 1.10, λυπηρός 'distressful' Pr 14.10 (‖ καρδία), περίλυπος 'very sad' Ps 41.6, ἐκλείπω 'to languish' 81.5, 83.3, Je 4.31, ἐξίστημι 'to be stunned' Is 7.2, δειλιάω 'to fear' 13.7, ἡ ψυχή μου ἐφέστηκεν εἰς φόβον 'my soul is staring fear in the face' 21.4, ἀσθενέω 'to become feeble' 7.4, ἔδοξεν τῇ ~ῇ αὐτῶν 'was thought by them good and right' Ex 35.21 (τῇ καρδίᾳ 25.2, τῇ διανοίᾳ 35.22, 26), τῇ ~ῇ οὐχ οὕτως λελόγισται 'he did not think that way' Is 10.7 (‖ νοῦς), sim. 44.19 (‖ τῇ καρδίᾳ and γινώσκω τῇ φρονήσει), οὐδὲ ἔθεντο ἐπὶ ~ήν 'nor did they take note of it' 42.25 (cf. οὐκ οἶδα τῇ ~ῇ 'I have no idea' Jb 9.21), μελετάω 'to ponder' Is 33.18, Jb 27.4, καταδολεσχέω 'to chatter' La 3.20, ἐπιλανθάνομαι 'to forget' Ps 102.2, πρόσχες τῇ ~ῇ μου καὶ λύτρωσαι αὐτήν 'Be mindful of .. and redeem it' 68.19, ἐξερευνάω 'to investigate' 118.129; ***o*** of πικραίνω 'to embitter' Jb 27.2 (cf. πικρία ~ῆς μου 10.1), παροργίζω 'to anger' 3K 16.33, ἀπωθέω 'to reject' La 3.17, παρακαλέω 'to comfort' Ps 76.3, εὐφραίνω 'to gladden' 85.4, ταράσσω 'to disturb' 6.4, θλίβω 142.12, ἐνδιαβάλλω 'to calumniate' 70.13, ἐπιφυλλίζω ἐπὶ τὴν ~ήν 'to ravage ..' La 3.51, πονέω 'to distress' Is 19.10, ἐκτήκω 'to exhaust' Ps 38.12, ἐκθλίβω 'to afflict' Pr 12.13, ἐπιστρέφω 'to bring back' Ps 18.8; μίσθιος διδοὺς ~ὴν αὐτοῦ 'a devoted employee' Si 7.21, μὴ δῷς γυναικὶ τὴν ~ήν σου 'don't abandon yourself to a woman' 9.2. **d.** of sense perception: ἤκουσεν ἡ ψ. μου Je 4.19, but preceded by σπαράσσεται ἡ καρδία μου 'my heart is torn'; ἡ ψ. ὑμῶν ὄψεται Is 53.10, cf. the foll. ἀπὸ τοῦ πόνου τῆς ~ῆς αὐτοῦ. **e.** almost *alter ego*: ἵνα τί περίλυπος εἶ, ψυχή, καὶ ἵνα τί συνταράσσεις με; 'O soul, why are you so sad, and why do you disquieten me so?' Ps 41.6, 42.5. **f.** ἡ ψ. τινος in these places is no substitute for "I," "he" etc. In some cases, however, including many of those cited under **3**, ψ. with a gen. with a personal referent may be *translated* accordingly, though with emphasis on his or her non-physical existence: thus οἱ ἐχθροί μου τὴν ~ήν μου περιέσχον 'my foes encircled me [but not "myself"] Ps 16.9, cf. κύριος φυλάξει σε ἀπὸ παντὸς κακοῦ, φυλάξει τὴν ~ήν σου 120.7 and ὃς ἀπωθεῖται παιδείαν, μισεῖ ἑαυτόν· ὁ δὲ τηρῶν ἐλέγχους ἀγαπᾷ ~ὴν αὐτοῦ Pr 15.32; τὴν ~ήν σου ‖ σεαυτόν Si 30.21; To 12.10 𝔊[II] (𝔊[I] ζωή). **g.** extended to God: προσοχθιεῖ ἡ ψ. μου ὑμῖν 'my soul will become weary of you' Le 26.30, sim. 26.11; μισεῖ ἡ ψ. μου Is 1.14; Je 5.9, Ez 23.18, 3K 16.33; τὴν ἠγαπημένην ~ήν μου Je 12.7 (God speaking). **h**. extended to animals: ἐπιγνώσῃ ~ὰς ποιμνίου σου Pr 27.23, cf. **1 b** above; δίκαιος οἰκτίρει ~ὰς τῶν κτηνῶν αὐτοῦ 'the righteous have compassion ..' 12.10; οἱ κυνὲς ἀναιδεῖς τῇ ~ῇ 'the dogs unashamed ..' Is 56.11.

*__4__. *corpse* as sth ritually harmful: ἁπτόμενος πάσης ἀκαθαρσίας ~ῆς 'touches any unclean corpse' Le 22.4, ἀκάθαρτοι ἐπὶ ~ῇ ἀνθρώπου Nu 9.6, sim. 9.10, ἥμαρτεν περὶ τῆς ~ῆς 6.11; τοῦ τεθνηκότος πάσης ψυχῆς ἀνθρώπου 'a dead person, any human corpse' 19.11; Hg 2.13 (so Cyr. II 272, and cf. Ez 44.25 ψ. = MT *mēt*).

*__5__. *dead person*: Le 19.28, 21.1, cf. 21.5, 11. That not a mere corpse is meant is manifest in ἐπὶ πάσῃ ~ῇ τετελευτηκυίᾳ Le 21.11, but cp. ἐντομίδας οὐ ποιήσετε ἐν τῷ σώματι ὑμῶν 19.28 and ἐπὶ τὰς σάρκας αὐτῶν οὐ κατατεμοῦσιν ἐντομίδας 21.5.

*__6__. *individual person*: πᾶσαι ~αί, υἱοὶ καὶ θυγατέρες, τριάκοντα τρεῖς 'all the persons ..' Ge 46.15; Ex 1.5; κατὰ ἀριθμὸν ~ῶν 'according to the number of persons' 12.4; ἐξολεθρευθήσεται ἡ ψ. ἐκείνη 12.19 (|| πᾶς, ὅς ..), Nu 19.20, Le 17.4 (|| ἄνθρωπος 17.9). **b**. referring to domestic staff, personnel, and used collectively: πᾶσαν ~ήν, ἣν ἐκτήσαντο Ge 12.5; ~ὴν ἔγκτητον ἀργυρίου '.. purchased by money' Le 22.11; ἐνεπορεύοντο .. ἐν ~αῖς ἀνθρώπων 'traded in slaves' Ez 27.13. **c**. = τις: Ἐὰν δὲ ψ. προσφέρῃ .. Le 2.1 (|| ἄνθρωπος 1.2); resumed by a masc. pron., Ψ. ἐὰν λάθῃ αὐτὸν λήθῃ 'should somebody inadvertently act, having not been aware of the matter' 5.15; resumed by ἄνθρωπος, 6.2f.; κλέπτων ~ὴν τῶν ἀδελφῶν αὐτοῦ 'kidnapping one of his fellowmen' De 24.7.

Cf. ζωή, καρδία, πνεῦμα, ψυχικός, ψυχικῶς, ἄψυχος, φιλόψυχος, σῶμα: Bratsiotis; Lys 1966; Lee 1969.234f.; Scharbert 125-35; Dihle, *TDNT* 9.632-4; Chadwick 311-20; Alexandre 242-4; Harl 2001.864-6; Muraoka 2005.60-5.

ψυχικός, ή, όν.ʃ

pertaining to ψυχή, 'psychic, mental': opp. σωματικός, *s* ἐπιθυμία 'desire' 4M 1.32. Cf. ψυχή, σάρκινος, σωματικός.

ψυχικῶς. adv.ʃ

at heart: ἐπιλυπηθείς 'grieved' 2M 4.37, προσεκέκλιτο 'attached' 14.24. Cf. ψυχή.

ψῦχος, ους: pl. ~χη. n.

condition of being cold: ψ. καὶ καῦμα 'cold and heat' Ge 8.22; of ice (κρύσταλλον) [rather than of God] and unbearable, κατὰ πρόσωπον ~ους αὐτοῦ τίς ὑποστήσεται; Ps 147.6; originates in high mountain tops (ἀκρωτήρια), Jb 37.9; personified, εὐλογεῖτε, ψ. καὶ καύσων Da 3.67 TH, cf. πάγος καὶ ψ. 69 LXX, ῥῖγος καὶ ψ. 67 LXX. **b**. *cold weather*: || πάγος 'frost' Zc 14.6.

Cf. ψύχω, ψυχρός, πάγος, ῥῖγος, καῦμα, καύσων.

ψυχουλκέομαι.ʃ *

to be at the last gasp: *s* hum., 3M 5.25.

ψυχρός, ά, όν.

having low temperature: *s* ἄνεμος 'wind' Si 43.20; water, Pr 25.25. Cf. ψῦχος, θερμός.

ψύχω: fut. ψύξω; aor. ἔψυξα.ʃ

1. *to cool*: + acc., ὡς ψύχει λάκκος ὕδωρ, οὕτως ψύχει κακίαν αὐτῆς 'As a cistern cools water, so does she cool her evil' Je 6.7. **b**. intr. *to seek the cool air*: 4K 19.24B.

2. *to dry*: in the cool open air and *o* meat, Nu 11.32; baked cakes, 2K 17.19*L*; human bones, πρὸς τὸν ἥλιον καὶ πρὸς τὴν σελήνην 'under the sun and under the moon' Je 8.2.

Cf. ψυχρός, ψῦχος, θερμαίνω.

ψωμίζω: fut. ψωμιῶ; aor. ἐψώμισα, ptc. ψωμίσας, impv. ψώμισον.

1. *to feed* by providing food: + double acc., Τίς ἡμᾶς ψωμιεῖ κρέα; 'Who is going to give us meat as food?' Nu 11.4; 11.18 || δώσει κύριος ὑμῖν κρέα φαγεῖν; ἐψώμισέν σε τὸ μάννα De 8.3; αὐτοὺς γεννήματα ἀγρῶν '.. the produce of fields' 32.13 (|| θηλάζω), cf. σε τὴν κληρονομίαν Ιακωβ Is 58.14; ἀγγέλων τροφήν 'angels' food' Wi 16.20; + ἐκ– αὐτοὺς ἐκ στέατος πυροῦ 'with the dough of wheat' Ps 80.17 (|| χορτάζω); metaph. and *o* ἀνάγκας 'hardships' Je 9.15 (|| ποτίζω), ὀδύνην 'suffering' 23.15 (|| ποτίζω), ἄρτον δακρύων 'bread of tears' Ps 79.6.

2. *to serve food for* sbd (acc.): 2K 13.5, Si 29.26.

Cf. ἐσθίω, τρέφω, ψωμός: Harl, *Langue*, 138f.

ψωμός, οῦ. m.

small piece of food: ~όν μου ἔφαγον μόνος Jb 31.17, πεινώντων ἐστέρησας ~όν 'you withheld .. from the hungry' 22.7, ~ὸν ἀφείλαντο 'deprived ..' 24.10; modest meal, Pr 17.1, ἄρτου 28.21, Jd 19.5 B (A: κλάσμα 'broken piece'). Cf. ψωμίζω, ἔδεσμα: Shipp 582-4.

ψώρα, ας. f.ʃ

itch: bodily defect the sufferer of which is disqualified for priesthood, ψ. ἀγρία 'malignant itch' Le 21.20; divine punishment, De 28.27; Le 26.16 (|| ἴκτερος 'jaundice'). Cf. ψωραγριάω.

ψωραγριάω.ʃ * [ψώρα: Hdt +]

to suffer from malignant itch: rendering such an animal as offering inappropriate, Le 22.22. Cf. ψώρα.

Ω

ὦ, ὤ interj.

I. ὦ marks a person or an entity named immediately after as orally addressed: **a.** + voc., σὺ δέ, ὦ ἀνόσιε καὶ πάντων ἀνθρώπων μιαρώτατε 'O, you, impious fellow and the most defiled of all mortals!' 2M 7.34, ὦ ὀκνηρέ 'O sluggard!' Pr 6.6, ὦ μήτερ δι' εὐσέβειαν στρατιῶτι 'O mohter, divine warrior for piety's sake!' 4M 16.14. **b.** + nom. (?), ὦ ἄνθρωποι Pr 8.4, Τί τοῦτο, ὃ ταχὺ εὗρες, ὦ τέκνον; 'What is this that you've found so quickly, O child?' Ge 27.20, ὦ φίλοι Jb 19.21, ὦ τύραννοι Wi 6.9; Ὦ Δανιηλ Da 6.20 LXX.

II. ὤ expresses the speaker's emotion such as joy, surprise or pain: + gen. ὢ ταλαιπώρων κακῶν 'what miserable calamities!' To 7.7 $\mathfrak{G}^{II}$; ὢ μακαρίου γήρως .. 'What an amazingly blessed old age ..!' 4M 7.15. **b.** ὤ repeated with no proper or common noun referring to an animate entity immediately following: Ὢ ὤ, τίς ζήσεται; Nu 24.23, ὢ ὢ φεύγετε 'Now there, flee!' Zc 2.6, Ὢ ὤ, ἡ ἡμέρα Ez 30.2. **c.** with no proper or common noun referring to an animate entity immediately following: ὢ τίνα τρόπον ἠθολογήσαιμι 'How can I characterise?' 4M 15.4, ὢ τάλας ἐγώ 'I am wretched' Is 6.5. **d.** even foll. by a voc.:Ὦ, κύριε, ῥῦσαι τὴν ψυχήν μου Ps 114.4, Ὢ λογισμὲ τέκνων παθῶν τύραννε 4M 15.1. **e.** a mechanical rendition of Heb.: ὢ ὅτι κέκληκεν .. for .. אֲהָה כִּי קָרָא 4K 3.10.

Cf. Kraft in Kraft 1972b.173-5; BDF, § 146–"omitted .. in invoking God"; for the spelling distinction from the vocative ὦ, see Walters 228-36.

ᾦα, ας. f.

border or *fringe of a garment*: Ex 28.28; ἐνδύματος 'of a garment' Ps 132.2. Cf. Shipp 584.

ὧδε. adv.

1. *to this place*: ἐξελεύσονται ὧδε Ge 15.14; ἔλθῃ ὧδε 42.15; Μὴ ἐγγίσῃς ὧδε Ex 3.5; εἰσελήλυθεν ὧδε Zc 7.3.

2. *in this place*: Ἔστιν τίς σοι ὧδε ..; 'Have you anyone here ..?' Ge 19.12; 38.22 (|| vs. 21 ἐνταῦθα); μετ' ἐμοῦ ὧδε Nu 14.23.

3. ἕως ὧδε 'up to here' Ge 22.5.

4. ὧδε καὶ ὧδε 'once this way and then that way': περιβλεψάμενος ὧδε καὶ ὧδε 'looking around this way and that' Ex 2.12.

Cf. ἐνταῦθα, ἐκεῖ, ἐνθάδε, αὐτός **4**.

ᾠδή, ῆς. f.

song: didactic, De 31.19, 30; joyous, μεταστρέψω .. τὰς ~ὰς ὑμῶν εἰς θρῆνον 'I shall turn .. your songs into a dirge' Am 8.10 (|| ἑορτή), quoted at To 2.6 $\mathfrak{G}^{II}$ ($\mathfrak{G}^{I}$ εὐφροσύνη); ἀγαλλιάματος 13.18 $\mathfrak{G}^{II}$; ἦχος ~ῶν Am 5.23 (|| ψαλμός); Ps 4.1; χειλέων 'with lips' Si 39.15; triumphant, Jd 5.1 A. Cf. ᾆσμα, θρῆνος, μέλος, ψαλμός.

ὠδίν, ~ῖνος. f. Mostly (in the LXX) in pl.

pains of childbirth: ὠδῖνες ὡς τικτούσης ἥξουσιν αὐτῷ 'he will experience something like the pains of a woman in labour' Ho 13.13; ἐκ τόκων καὶ ~νων καὶ συλλήμψεων 'from childbirth and pains of labour and pregnancy' 9.11; πόνος ~ων Is 66.7; felt around the loins, ὑπόλυσις γονάτων καὶ ~νες ἐπὶ πᾶσαν ὀσφῦν Na 2.11; sg., Is 37.3; of animals, Jb 39.1. **b.** acute pain in general: mental, ὠδῖνες ἔλαβον κατοικοῦντας Φυλιστιιμ 'pains seized the inhabitants of Philistia' Ex 15.14, sim. Is 21.3; ~νες αὐτοὺς ἕξουσιν ὡς γυναικὸς τικτούσης '.. will grip them' 13.8; ~νας ἕξουσιν ἀπὸ προσώπου σου 'they will have angst at your sight' De 2.25; || θόρυβος Ez 7.4; θανάτου 'life-threatening' Ps 17.5 (|| ~νες ᾅδου 17.6), 114.3 (|| κίνδυνοι ᾅδου).

Cf. ὠδίνω, λύπη: Bertram, *TDNT* 9.668-70.

ὠδίνω: fut. ὠδινήσω; aor. ὠδίνησα.

1. *to suffer pains of childbirth*: ὤδινε καὶ ἀνδρίζου Mi 4.10; πρὶν ἢ τὴν ὠδίνουσαν τεκεῖν, πρὶν ἐλθεῖν τὸν πόνον τῶν ὠδίνων 'before the woman in labour gives birth, before the pain of labour comes' Is 66.7; || τίκτω 26.18, 54.1; 23.4 (also || ἐκτρέφω).

2. *to have extreme pains*: ὄψονταί σε καὶ ὠδινήσουσι λαοί 'people will watch you and agonise' Hb 3.10; ὡς .. ἡ τίκτουσα Si 19.11.

3. *to give birth to after painful labour*: + acc., Ct 8.5; εἰς Σαρραν τὴν ὠδίνουσαν ὑμᾶς Is 51.2; τί .. 45.10 (|| γεννάω), γῆν Si 43.17, ἀδικίαν Ps 7.15 (|| τίκτω).

Cf. ἀλγέω, ὠδίν, γεννάω, τίκτω.

ᾠδός, οῦ. m.

singer: 3K 10.12; + ὑμνοῦντες αἶνον 2C 23.13. Cf. ᾄδω, ψάλλω, ψάλτης.

ὠθέω: fut. ὤσω; aor. Ion. ὦσα, Att. ἔωσα, subj. ὤσω, ptc.pass. ὠσθείς; pf.ptc.pass. ὠσμένος.ʃ

1. *to push with considerable physical force*: + acc. pers., δι' ἔχθραν 'with hostile intent' Nu 35.20; ἐξάπινα οὐ δι' ἔχθραν 'not on purpose ..' 35.22; εἰς τέλος 'to an end' Jb 14.20; τοίχῳ κεκλιμένῳ καὶ φραγμῷ ὠσμένῳ 'with a leaning wall and a fence pushed on the ground' Ps 61.4; ὠσθεὶς ἀνετράπην τοῦ πεσεῖν 'having been pushed, I was overthrown nearly to fall' 117.13. **b**. metaph.: ἔωσαν αὐτοὺς εἰς παῖδας καὶ παιδίσκας 'forced them into slavery' Je 41.10.

2. *to thrust out* as useless: + acc. rei, ὡς κόπρον ὤσεις αὐτά 'you shall thrust them [= idols] out as dung' Is 30.22.

Cf. ἀπ~, δι~, ἐξ~, ἐπ~, προσ~, προσαπωθέω.

ὠμία, ας. f.*

shoulder: of a hum. body, 1K 9.2B. **b**. part of a building projecting like hum. shoulder, 3K 6.8.

Cf. ὦμος: Renehan: 1.208.

ὠμόλινον, ου. n.ʃ

piece of coarse linen: as plain dress, Si 40.4 (opp. ὑακίνθινος).

ὦμος, ου. m.

1. *shoulder*: Ma 2.3; on which to carry a burden, water and a child, Ge 21.14, a pitcher, 24.15 (pl.); ὑπέθηκεν τὸν ~ον αὐτοῦ εἰς τὸ πονεῖν 'put his shoulder to labour' 49.15; a yoke, ἀπὸ τοῦ ~ου σου .. ἀπὸ τῶν ~ων ὑμῶν Is 10.27; to be whipped, Pr 19.29.

2. *shoulderstrap* of an ephod: τῆς ἐπωμίδος Ex 28.12.

3. *slope* of a mountain as against its summit: ὦ. Μωαβ Ez 25.9.

Cf. παρωμίς, ὑπερωμία.

ὠμός, ή, όν.

1. *uncooked, raw*: *s* meat, Ex 12.9.

2. *unrefined, uncultured, rough*: *s* hum., τύραννος 2M 4.25, 7.27.

3. *cruel*: *s* λέβης 'cauldron (for burning martyrs in)' 4M 18.20.

Cf. ὠμότης, ὠμόφρων, ἄγριος.

ὠμότης, ητος. f.ʃ

cruelness: of treatment, Es 7.24 *L*, 2M 12.5, 3M 7.5; hum. character, 5.20. Cf. ὠμός.

ὠμοτοκέω: aor. ὠμοτόκησα.ʃ *

to suffer miscarriage: *s* cow, Jb 21.10.

ὠμόφρων, ον.ʃ

cruel of mind: *s* hum., 4M 9.15. Cf. ὠμός.

ᾠόν, οῦ. n.

egg: of bird, νοσσοῖς ἢ ᾠοῖς 'young birds or eggs' De 22.6; Jb 39.14 ¶, Is 10.14; of viper, 59.5.

ὥρα, ας. f.

1. *time when something regularly happens*, 'season': πᾶσαν ~αν 'on every opportunity' Ex 18.22; τὸν σῖτόν μου καθ' ~αν αὐτοῦ 'my corn in its season' Ho 2.9 (ǁ ἐν καιρῷ αὐτοῦ); ὑετὸν καθ' ~αν 'seasonal rainfall' Zc 10.1, cf. ὑετὸν καθ' ~αν πρόϊμον καὶ ὄψιμον '.. early and late (rain)' De 11.14; καθ' ὥραν γενημάτων ἡλίου τροπῶν 33.14, καθ' ~αν γῆς 33.16; ǁ καιρός Jb 5.26.

2. *time when something is due to happen*: "the previously appointed time (of destruction)" 3M 5.13; εἰς ~ας 'on time, in good time (for the birth of a child)' Ge 18.10, 14 (cf. Hdt. 1.31 ἐν ὥρῃ), '(we seem to have come) at the right moment' 1K 25.6, μενεῖ εἰς ~ας 'will bide his time (?)' Da 11.6; ἐν ~ᾳ Si 35.11; sim., ὡς ἡ ὥρα 4K 4.16, 17; πρὸ ~ας 'prematurely' 4M 12.4.

3. *a point in time*: αὐτῇ τῇ ~ᾳ 'then and there' Da 3.6 TH, 15 (LXX αὐθωρί), 4.33 TH, ἐν αὐτῇ τῇ ~ᾳ (LXX ἐκείνῃ) 5.5 TH; ᾗ ἂν ~αν ⌜LXX ὅταν⌝ ἀκούσητε 'the moment you hear' 3.5 TH; ἐν τῇ ~ᾳ ταύτῃ 'here and now' Ju 13.4, κατὰ τὴν ~αν ταύτην 3M 2.19.

4. "= τὰ ὡραῖα, the *products of the season, fruits of the year*" (LSJ): οὐρανοῦ De 33.13 (ǁ δρόσος 'dew').

5. *prime of the year, springtime*: Is 52.7.

6. *a period of short duration*: κάκωσις ~ας 'brief hardship' Si 11.27, ~αν μετὰ σοῦ διαμενεῖ 'he will stand by you just a while' 12.15, ~αν μίαν Da 4.16 LXX.

7. *one of the twelve divisions of daytime*: δεκάτη 'tenth' 3M 5.14.

Cf. καιρός, χρόνος, ὥριμος: Delling, *TDNT* 9.676f.

ὡραιόομαι: aor. ὡραιώθην.ʃ *

to be beautiful in outward appearance: *s* hum., male 2K 1.26; maiden, Ct 7.7 (ǁ ἡδύνομαι), part of hum. body, 1.10; marching step, 7.2. Cf. ὡραῖος.

ὡραῖος, α, ον.

1. *beautiful* (of outward appearance): *s* tree, ξύλον ~ον εἰς ὅρασιν 'tree beautiful to gaze at' Ge 2.9, καρπὸν ξύλου ~ον Le 23.40 (poss. 'ripe'), olive-tree, Je 11.16; temple furniture, 2C 36.19 (ǁ ἔνδοξος 1E 1.53); woman, ὡ. τῇ ὄψει 'good-looking' Ge 26.7; man, καλὸς τῷ εἴδει καὶ ~ος τῇ ὄψει 39.6, ǁ καλός Ct 1.16, ~ος κάλλει Ps 44.3; ǁ εὐπρεπής 2K 1.23B; subst. and of flora, τὰ ~α τῆς ἐρήμου Jl 1.19, 20, Ps 64.13; more generic La 2.2.

2. *timely*: *s* ἔλεγχος 'rebuke' Si 20.1.

3. *fitting, in its place*: "a praise is not in its place, when said by a sinner" Si 15.9; *s* God's mercy, 32.26.

4. *pleasing* to listen to: *s* λαλιά 'talk' Ct 4.3.

Cf. καλός, ὡραιόομαι, ὡραιότης, ὡραϊσμός, εὐπρεπής: Shipp 585.

ὡραιότης, τος. f. *

beauty: ~τα ἀνθρώπου 'a beautifully sculptured man' Is 44.13 (ǁ μορφὴ ἀνδρός); of woman, Ez 16.14 (ǁ εὐπρέπεια), ἀγροῦ 'of fields' Ps 49.11; + κάλλος 44.4. Cf. ὡραῖος.

ὡραϊσμός, οῦ. m.ʃ *

adornment with cosmetics and attractive apparel: Je 4.30. Cf. ὡραῖος.

ὥριμος, ον.ʃ

having reached the right moment for action, 'ripe, ready': *s* ἅλων 'threshing-floor' Je 28.33; σῖτος ὥ.

κατὰ καιρὸν θεριζόμενος 'ripe corn harvested in season' Jb 5.26. Cf. ὥρα, καιρός.

Ὠρίων, ωνος. m.∫

Orion: Is 13.10, Jb 38.31.

ὤρυμα, ατος. n.∫*

roaring: of lion, φωνὴ ~ατος Ez 19.7. Cf. ὠρύομαι.

ὠρύομαι: fut. ὠρύσομαι.

to roar: *s* lion, οἱ ἄρχοντες αὐτῆς .. ὡς λέοντες ὠρυόμενοι Zp 3.3, sim. Ez 22.25; ἐπί + acc. (prey), Je 2.15 (‖ δίδωμι φωνήν); ‖ ἐρεύγομαι Ho 11.10; *s* hum. mourner, Ep Je 31. Cf. ἐπωρύομαι, ὤρυμα, ἐρεύγομαι, ὀλολύζω: Schmidt 3.351f.; Shipp 586.

ὡς.

I. *as, like* (of similarity or identity).

1. Often foll. by a fragment of a clause, except: ὡς ἄν σοι ἀρεστὸν ᾖ 'as you please' Ge 16.6; ὡς Ρουβην καὶ Συμεων ἔσονταί μοι 48.5; ὡς καθήκει πάσῃ τῇ γῇ 'as it ought to happen throughout the land' 19.31; ὡς καθήκει 'as it is/was proper' Le 5.10, 9.16; πυρώσω αὐτοὺς ὡς πυροῦται τὸ ἀργύριον, καὶ δοκιμῶ αὐτούς, ὡς δοκιμάζεται τὸ χρυσίον Zc 13.9. This latter usage is more commonly represented by καθά, καθότι, and partly καθώς (q.v.). **b**. + opt.: ὡς ἄν τις ἴδοι πρόσωπον θεοῦ 'as if one might be looking at God's face' Ge 33.10; ὡς ἐκλείξαι ὁ μόσχος .. 'just as the calf might lick up ..' Nu 22.4; De 1.31, 32.11, Is 21.1, 66.20, cf. Joosten 1996.229-33; Evans 1999; id. 2001.190-7. **c**. + gen. abs., Is 23.3, 17.13², 59.10². **d**. ὡς εἰ = ὡσεί Is 66.13, Ps 82.15.

2. Introduces an adverbial phrase: εὐφρανθήσεται .. ὡς ἐν ἡμέρᾳ ἑορτῆς Zp 3.17; χαρήσεται ἡ καρδία αὐτῶν ὡς (> MT) ἐν οἴνῳ Zc 10.7; sim. 12.10, Ho 4.16.

3. Often a missing word or phrase can be supplied from the context: ὠδῖνες ὡς τικτούσης (i.e. ὡς ὠδῖνες τικτούσης) Ho 13.13, Mi 4.9; ἡ ὀσφρασία ὡς Λιβάνου Ho 14.7, sim. Mi 1.8*bis*. Cp. αὗται εἶχον πτέρυγας ὡς πτέρυγας ἔποπος Zc 5.9; ὁ οἶκος Δαυιδ ὡς οἶκος (> MT) θεοῦ 12.8; ὡς ὅρασις ἵππων ἡ ὅρασις αὐτῶν Jl 2.4 as against ἡ ὅρασις αὐτῶν ὡς λαμπάδες Na 2.5. **b**. the head noun is to be supplied: οὐκ ἔστιν ὡς ἐγὼ ἄλλος Ex 9.14; ὡς ῥῶγες ἐλαίας δύο ἢ τρεῖς 'something like two or three olive berries' Is 17.6; ὡς υἱὸς ἀνθρώπου Da 7.13, ὡς ὁμοίωσις χειρὸς ἀνθρώπου 10.16 LXX; ὡς σὺ .. ὅμοιός σοι 'sbd like you .. one comparable to you' 3K 3.12 (‖ vs. 13 ἀνὴρ ὅμοιός σοι).

4. The ὡς phrase follows the main phrase or clause except in ὡς δάμαλις παροιστρῶσα παροίστρησεν Ho 4.16, ἀνεκαύθησαν ὡς κλίβανος αἱ καρδίαι αὐτῶν 7.6 and ὡς ὅρασις ἵππων ἡ ὅρασις αὐτῶν Jl 2.4.

5. Only rarely is the *tertium comparationis* expressed: ἦν Εφραιμ ὡς περιστερὰ ἄνους οὐκ ἔχουσα καρδίαν Ho 7.11; ἰσχυρὸς ἦν ὡς δρῦς 'was mighty as an oak-tree' Am 2.9.

6. In similes the noun following ὡς is usually anarthrous, though the Heb. often has *ka-*: ὡς πῦρ Am 5.6 (MT: *kā'ēš*), ὡς ὕδωρ 5.24 (MT: *kammayim*) etc.; ‖ ὡσεί De 32.2. Exceptions: καθαρίζων ὡς τὸ ἀργύριον καὶ ὡς τὸ χρυσίον .. χεεῖ αὐτοὺς ὡς τὸ χρ. καὶ τὸ ἀρ. Ma 3.3, also Ho 1.10.

7. Introduces the predicate in an equational sentence: **a**. with εἰμί or γίνομαι – ἦν ὁ ἀριθμὸς τῶν υἱῶν Ισραηλ ὡς ἡ ἄμμος τῆς θαλάσσης Ho 1.10; ἔσται ὡς οὐχ ὑπάρχουσα 'will be virtually non-existent' Am 5.5; ἐγένοντο .. ὡς μετατιθέντες ὅρια Ho 5.10*a*; παγὶς ἐγενήθητε .. καὶ ὡς δίκτυον ἐκτεταμένον ἐπὶ τὸ Ιταβυριον 'you became a snare .. and like a net spread over Itaburion' Ho 5.1; ‖ ὥσπερ Je 23.14. **b**. Without εἰμί or γίνομαι: ὁ λαός μου ὡς ἀντιλεγόμενος ἱερεύς Ho 4.4. **c**. Related to this is the use of the particle with verbs of *finding, perceiving* an object to be in a certain state: ὡς σταφυλὴν ἐν ἐρήμῳ εὗρον τὸν Ισραηλ καὶ ὡς σκοπὸν ἐν συκῇ .. 'I found Israel (to be) like grapes in a desert and saw their fathers (to be) like an early signal on the fig-tree' (?; s.v. σκοπός) Ho 9.10.

8. With a correlative οὕτως: ὡς ἱππεῖς οὕτως καταδιώξονται Jl 2.4. See under οὕτως, **A b**.

9. One can detect a subtle drift from the notion of similarity to that of identity. **a**. εἰμί τινι ὡς 'play for sbd the role of ..' as in ἔσομαι αὐτοῖς ὡς ῥαπίζων ἄνθρωπος Ho 11.4; see also 13.7*bis*, 14.6, Am 9.7. **b**. with ὁμοιόομαι: ὡμοιώθη ὁ λαός μου ὡς οὐκ ἔχων γνῶσιν Ho 4.6. **c**. with τίθημι or τάσσω: θήσομαι αὐτὴν ὡς (> B) ἔρημον καὶ τάξω αὐτὴν ὡς γῆν ἄνυδρον Ho 2.3; likewise 11.8*bis*, Am 8.10*bis*, Mi 1.16 v.l. (for εἰς), 3.12*b* (v.l. εἰς), 12 v.l. (for εἰς), τίθημι τὴν Ιερουσαλημ ὡς (> MT) πρόθυρα σαλευόμενα Zc 12.2; with both εἰς and ὡς– in θήσει τὴν Νινευη εἰς ἀφανισμὸν ἄνυδρον ὡς ἔρημον Zp 2.13. **d**. with ποιέω: ποιήσεις τοὺς ἀνθρώπους ὡς τοὺς ἰχθύας τῆς θαλάσσης Hb 1.14. **e**. with λογίζομαι: ὡς ἑστῶτα ἐλογίσαντο καὶ οὐχ ὡς φεύγοντα 'they thought them to be permanent and not ephemeral' Am 6.5.

10. *in such a way as*: ποίησόν μοι ἐδέσματα ὡς φιλῶ ἐγώ 'cook my meals to my taste' Ge 27.4.

11. *in conformity to, in agreement with*: ποιήσεις ὡς τὸ ῥῆμα τοῦτο Ge 18.24, cf. κατὰ τὸ ῥῆμα τοῦτο λαλήσατε 32.19. **b**. with a collateral οὕτως: ὡς λέγετε, οὕτως ἔσται Ge 44.10., see above **8**. **c**. *in proportion to*: ὡς ἡ δύναμις αὐτῶν = κατὰ τὴν ~ιν .. 2E 2.69, sim. Ec 9.10.

12. with a ptc. gives the reason or motive of the action expressed by the lead verb, 'on the ground that ..': ἔθετο ἡμᾶς ἐν φυλακῇ ὡς κατασκοπεύοντας τὴν γῆν 'he put us in custody on the assumption that we were spying on the land' Ge 42.30; false motive, 1M 10.77; + gen. abs., Su 41 LXX, ὡς ἄν 2M 12.4 (the gen. of the ptc. may be due to gen. ptc. of the lead verb), 3M 4.1; ἐνυπνιάζεται ὁ διψῶν ὡς πίνων 'a thirsty man dreams of himself drinking sth' Is 29.8 belongs under **1** above. **b**. *to make look as if*: ὡς δυνατοῦ ὄντος αὐτοῦ .. 'as if he were capable ..' Ep Je 40; 2M 5.5, 12.3. **c**. with fut. ptc. to mark a purpose: Is 59.18.

13. ὡς τί 'why?; for what purpose?': 2K 16.10B (*L* τί ὅτι).

14. following a negator, not *so much as, but rather*: οὐ βούλομαι τὸν θάνατον τοῦ ἀσεβοῦς ὡς τὸ .. ζῆν αὐτόν 'I do not so much wish for the death of the ungodly as for him to live' Ez 33.11.

15. redundantly with a prep. marking a direction: ὡς πρὸς θάλασσαν Ez 41.12, ὡς πρὸς ἀνατολάς 2C 4.10, ἀνάγειν .. ὡς εἰς τὸν οὐρανόν 4K 2.1, ὡς εἰς ἔρημον Ho 2.14 (Zgl. εἰς), ὡς ἐπὶ τὴν αὐλήν Es 4.2 *L*, see Muraoka 1964.70f.

16. with a superlative, marks the highest possible degree: "your cup is sated as well as it can be (ὡς κράτιστον)" Ps 22.5; ὡς τάχιστα 'as soon as possible' 3M 1.8, cf. Kilpatrick 1990.73-5; ὡς μάλιστα διψῶν 'as thirsty as he could be' 4M 3.10; ἐν .. εὐχαῖς ὡς πλείσταις 'with as many votive offerings as possible' 1E 2.8. **b**. ὡς ἔνι μάλιστα χαίροιεν 'they were ecstatic' 4M 4.22.

17. with a temporal adjunct, 'precisely, just': ὡς σήμερον 'already today' (Germ. *schon heute*) Ne 5.11, ὡς νῦν 1K 13.13 (but cf. below **IV**), ὡς ἡ ὥρα αὕτη αὔριον 4K 7.1.

18. with an inf. marks a purpose: 2M 3.8, 3M 1.2. **b**. ὡς εἰπεῖν 'so to speak' 3M 5.45.

19. redundantly with an adv.: ὡς ἀληθῶς 'truly' 2M 12.12, 4M 6.5, ὡς ὁμοίως 'equally' 5.21, cf. ὡς μικρόν 'for a while' 2C 12.7 (prob. calqued on Heb. /kimʻaṭ/.

20. with a numeral, *approximately*: Ru 1.4, 2M 14.4.

II. a temporal conj.: ὡς ἄν + impf., 'every time that'– ὡς ἂν εἰσεπορεύοντο οἱ υἱοὶ τοῦ θεοῦ .. Ge 6.4; + aor. ind., ὡς ἂν εἰσῆλθεν Ex 33.9; + sub. aor., ἔσται ὡς ἂν ἴδωσίν σε .. 'when they see you ..' Ge 12.12; 30.38, Ex 9.29, De 30.1, Is 8.21; ὡς + ind. aor., ὡς ἐπαύσατο 'when he finished' Ge 18.33; ὡς ἐξῆλθεν 27.30; ἐγένετο ὡς ἔτεκεν 30.25; 38.29, Ex 16.32; ὡς + impf., ὡς ἐξεπορευόμην 'as I was departing' Ex 13.8; 34.29; De 32.8 (‖ ὅτε and precedes the main clause); + ind. pres., Si 30.12.

III. introduces an object clause: mostly marking a past event— οἴδατε ὡς κατῳκήσαμεν .. De 29.16; Μνήσθητι .. ὡς .. 'Remember .. that ..' Is 38.3; Ps 77.43; ‖ ὅτι To 11.15𝔊II; but πεποιθέτω .. ὡς .. ἔσται Jb 12.6, θεώρει .. ὡς .. βασανιεῖ 2M 7.17; ἐκακολόγει .. ὡς αὐτός τε εἴη .. 2M 4.1.

IV. introduces a causal clause: + pres. indic., Si prol. 4, poss. 1K 13.13 (but cf. above **17**).

V. marks an intention: + subj., "he made his mind up not to get defiled (ὡς οὐ μὴ ἀλισγηθῇ)" Da 1.8 TH (LXX ὅπως).

VI. exclamatory, 'how ..!, what a ..!': + adj., ὡς φοβερὸς ὁ τόπος οὗτος 'How awesome this place is!' Ge 28.17; ὡς καλοί Nu 24.5; ὡς θαυμαστὸν .. Ps 8.2, Ὡς ἀγαθός 72.1; with an adj. at a remove, ὡς .. ἐπιθυμητά Si 42.22; + adjectival verb, ὡς ἐπλήθυνας Ps 35.8, ὡς ἐμεγαλύνθη 103.24.

VII. prep. marking a destination: + acc. pers., 2M 4.5. See LSJ **C III**.

Cf. ὥς, καθώς, καθάπερ, καθό, καθότι, ὡσεί, ὥσπερ, οἷος, ὅμοιος, ὅτι, τρόπος: Muraoka 1964. Del. Ho 2.14 v.l.

ὥς adv.ʃ

Adv. *so*, mostly in the refrain οὐδ᾽ ὧς 'even so .. not': οὐδ᾽ ὧς ὄντων αὐτῶν ἐν τῇ γῇ τῶν ἐχθρῶν αὐτῶν, οὐχ ὑπερεῖδεν αὐτούς 'even while they were thus in the land of their enemies, He did not overlook them' Le 26.44; οὐδ᾽ ὧς ἐπεστρέψατε πρός με 'even so you did not return to me' Am 4.8, 9, 10, 11; Jb 9.11, Ec 9.2*bis*, Ez 16.47, 3M 1.12. The spelling ὧς may also be found. Cf. οὐδ᾽ οὕτως s.v. οὐδέ **f**. **b**. Ὡς σύ, ὡς αὐτοὶ .. Jd 8.18 B; Ec 9.2a; ὡς .. καθὼς .. 9.2b.

Cf. ὡς, ὡσεί, οὕτως.

ὡσανεί. adv.ʃ

as if: + a prep. phrase, Es A 9.

ὡσαύτως. adv.

in similar fashion, 'likewise': ἐποίησαν .. ὡ. Ex 7.11; ὡς ἐποίησεν αὐτῷ, ὡ. ἀντιποιηθήσεται αὐτῷ Le 24.19 (‖ καθότι .. οὕτως vs. 20); De 12.22 (‖ ἐπὶ τὸ αὐτό vs. 15); ὡ. καί Ep Je 21.

ὡσεί

1. *similar(ly) to*: ὡ. ἀτμὶς καμίνου 'like steam of a furnace' Ge 19.28; ὅλος ὡσεὶ δορὰ δασύς 'entirely like a shaggy hide' 25.25; reinforced by καί – ὡσεὶ καὶ μία φυλή 49.16; ὡ. τὰ ἄστρα τοῦ οὐρανοῦ τῷ πλήθει 'like the stars of heaven in abundance' Ex 32.13, De 1.10; ‖ ὡς 32.2. The case of the noun is that of the *primum comparationis* – ὡ. πόρνῃ χρήσονται τῇ ἀδελφῇ ἡμῶν; 'should they treat our sister like a whore?' Ge 34.31. **b**. the case of the noun following ὡσεί is determined by the main verb: ὡσεὶ στέατος (gen.) .. ἐμπλησθείη ἡ ψυχή μου 'may my soul be sated as if with the fat ..' Ps 62.6; Je 28.14.

2. With a quantifier or temporal expression, *about, approximately*: ὡ. τόξου βολήν 'about a bow-shot' Ge 21.16; ἡμέρας ὡσεὶ δέκα 24.55; ὡ. (v.l. ὡς) πορείας ὁδοῦ ἡμερῶν τριῶν Jn 3.3; ὡ. πορείαν ἡμέρας μιᾶς 3.4 (both passages lack a Heb. equivalent); ὡ. ὥραν θυσίας ἑσπερινῆς 'about the time of the evening sacrifice' Da 9.21 TH.

3. conj. *just as*: + opt., ὡ. ἄραι τιθηνὸς τὸν θηλάζοντα 'just as a foster-father might pick up his babe' Nu 11.12; ὡ. ψηλαφήσαι ὁ τυφλὸς ἐν τῷ σκότει 'just as the blind might grope in the dark' De 28.29. Cf. ὡς **I 1 b**; ὥσπερ **IIb**. **b**. + subj., ὡ. σημεῖον ἀπ' ὄρους ἀρθῇ 'just as a signal is taken from a mountain' Is 18.3.

Cf. ὡς.

ὥσπερ.

I. prep. **1**. *like, as* of similarity: Μήποτε ἀποθάνῃ καὶ οὗτος ὥ. οἱ ἀδελφοὶ αὐτοῦ Ge 38.11; κακωθήσεται Ισραηλ ὥ. ὁ προφήτης '.. in the manner of ..' Ho 9.7; τίς θεὸς ὥ. σύ; 'what god is like you?' or 'who is a god like you?' Mi 7.18; || ὡς Je 23.14; Ma 3.3*c*, *d* v.l. for ὡς; + a prepositional phrase, ὥ. ἐκ τοῦ ποταμοῦ 'as if out of the river' Ge 41.2. **b**. a noun head understood: ὥ. ἁφὴ ἑώραται 'something like an infection has appeared' Le 14.35. **c**. elliptical: ὥ. μισθίου = ὥ. ἡ ζωὴ μισθίου Jb 7.1. **d**. the notion of similarity reinforced by καί: τοὺς ἀδελφοὺς ὑμῶν ὥ. καὶ ὑμᾶς De 3.20; Is 14.10. **e**. foll. by a coordinating οὕτως: Pr 19.12 (|| ὅμοιος). **f**. + ptc.: ὥ. οὐχὶ .. μαθών 'as if you have not learned ..' 4M 9.5.

2. *comparable, equal* in estimation: with an otiose καί– ἔσται ὥ. καὶ ὁ αὐτόχθων τῆς γῆς 'he shall be equal to an indigenous person of the land' Ex 12.48; ὥ. καὶ σύ De 5.14.

3. *approximately*, 'about': + a numeral, ὥ. ἑπτὰ στάχυες 'about seven ears of corn' Ge 41.22.

II. conj., *in similar manner as*: ὥσπερ ἀποτρέχουσιν αἱ δοῦλαι Ex 21.7; Je 31.13; foll. by a correlative οὕτως, Si 23.10, Pr 17.3. **b**. + εἰ and opt., Pr 25.26.

2. pleonastically preceding an adverbial: ὥ. σπουδῇ 'with great speed, all of a sudden' La 4.6.

3. *as if*: leading a gen. abs., 4M 5.22.

Cf. ὡς.

ὥστε.

1. *with the aim of, for the purpose of*: + inf. pres., ὥ. φαίνειν ἐπὶ τῆς γῆς 'in order to shine upon the earth' Ge 1.15; Ex 36.2; + inf. aor., ὥ. δοῦναι Ge 15.7; 45.27; .. ὥ. πιεῖν ὕδωρ, καὶ οὐκ ἠδύναντο πιεῖν ὕδωρ '.. in order to drink water, but they were not able to ..' Ex 7.24; οὐχ εὕρισκον ὕδωρ ὥ. πιεῖν 15.22. **b**. || ἵνα + subj.: ὥ. νίπτεσθαι Ex 30.18 || ἵνα νίπτωνται 38.27. **c**. εἶναι ὥ. and inf., 'to be charged with the task of ..': Nu 5.8, 8.11. **d**. + inf. as a complement of a verb of command: Ne 23.19.

2. *resulting in*: + inf. aor., οὐκ ἔσται ἔτι τὸ ὕδωρ εἰς κατακλυσμὸν ὥ. ἐξαλεῖψαι πᾶσαν σάρκα 'there shall be no repetition of that water leading to a flooding resulting in the obliteration of every living being' Ge 9.15; ἐξέλθῃ ἐξ αὐτοῦ κοίτη σπέρματος ὥ. μιανθῆναι ἐν αὐτῇ 'has an ejaculation of semen so that he gets defiled thereby' Le 15.32; + subj. aor., Jb 6.21. **b**. Logical consequence: ἐὰν δὲ ὀλιγοστοὶ ὦσιν οἱ ἐν τῇ οἰκίᾳ ὥ. μὴ ἱκανοὺς εἶναι εἰς πρόβατον 'should those present in the household be so few that they do not suffice for one sheep' Ex 12.4; + a fin. verb, Jb 21.27; preceded by a cataphoric correlative οὕτως, "I am not that old .. so as not to .." 4M 5.31, sim. 5.33.

3. *so that* (epexegetic): + inf. aor., ἔχετε τῇ ψυχῇ ὑμῶν ὥ. θάψαι .. 'you are so minded as to bury ..' Ge 23.8; εἰσακούσομαι τῆς φωνῆς αὐτοῦ ὥ. ἐξαποστεῖλαι τοὺς υἱοὺς Ισραηλ 'to heed what he says so as to let the Israelites go' Ex 5.2; 12.42; τὴν διαθήκην μου πρὸς αὐτούς, ὥ. δοῦναι αὐτοῖς τὴν γῆν τῶν Χαναναίων 6.4; τίς δώσει εἶναι οὕτως τὴν καρδίαν αὐτῶν .. ὥ. φοβεῖσθαί με ..; De 5.29.

4. with an adj. or adv., *to the extent that, so much .. that*: εὑρεῖς τοῖς διωστῆρσιν ὥ. αἴρειν αὐτὴν ἐν αὐτοῖς 'wide enough for the poles for them to carry it' Ex 38.4; ἐὰν δὲ μὴ εὕρῃ ἡ χεὶρ αὐτοῦ τὸ ἱκανὸν ὥ. ἀποδοῦναι αὐτῷ 'should he not manage to put together enough to repay him' Le 25.28. Cf. εὔξηται εὐχὴν ὥ. τιμὴν τῆς ψυχῆς αὐτοῦ 'makes a vow equivalent to the value of his own life' Le 27.2; ὥ. λίαν 2K 2.17. **b**. with a correlative, cataphoric οὕτως and an inf., 'so much .. as to ..': 4M 5.31, 9.17, 10.14. **c**. an adj. or adv. understood: ἔσται ἡ παρεμβολὴ αὐτοῦ πληρῶσαι τὸ πλάτος τῆς χώρας σου 'his encampment will be so huge as to fill up your country from one end to the other' Is 8.8.

5. redundant: συνετέλεσεν .. ὥ. ἀναστῆσαι .. 'finished erecting' Nu 7.1; ἐπιθυμήσῃ ἡ ψυχή σου ὥ. φαγεῖν κρέα De 12.20; νομιστέον ὥ. θεοὺς αὐτοὺς ὑπάρχειν Ep Je 44.

6. adv. *to an extent as this*: Ὥστε καὶ τὴν γυναῖκα βιάζῃ 'So here you are, even violating my wife' Es 7.8 o'.

Cf. ἵνα, ὅπως: Muraoka 1973b.

ὠτίον, ου. n.

ear: λοβὸν ~ου 'ear-lobe' Am 3.12; organ for aural perception, Is 50.4, 55.3, εἰς ἀκοὴν ~ου Ps 17.45. Cf. οὖς.

ὠτότμητος, ον.ʃ *

having slit ears: *s* person (disqualified for priesthood), Le 21.18; sheep, edible but not suited for cultic offering, 22.23.

ὠφέλεια, ας. f.

1. *being beneficial, useful*: ‖ βοήθεια Is 30.5; as cogn. obj., Je 23.32. Cf. ὄφελος.

2. *spoils of war*: 2M 8.20.

ὠφελέω; fut.act. ὠφελήσω, pass. ὠφεληθήσομαι, inf. ὠφελήσειν; aor. ὠφέλησα, inf. ὠφελῆσαι, pass. ὠφεληθῆναι

1. *to benefit, be of use* to sbd (acc.), often in a negative sentence or a rhetorical question: abs., τί ὠφελεῖ γλυπτόν; 'what use is a sculpture?' Hb 2.18; οὐκ ὠφέλησάν με 'they [= physicians] were of no help to me' To 2.10 𝔊[I], οὐκ ὠφελήσει αὐτοὺς οὔτε εἰς βοήθειαν οὔτε εἰς ὠφέλειαν Is 30.5, cf. ὠφέλειαν οὐκ ὠφελήσουσιν τὸν λαόν Je 23.32; + double acc., μάταια καὶ κενὰ ὠφελήσουσιν ὑμᾶς 'they will be only of dubious use to you' Is 30.7; pass., ὠφεληθήσεσθε 'you will be benefited' Wi 6.25, + ἔκ τινος Je 2.11, + ὅθεν 7.8.

2. *act. *to derive as benefit*: + acc., τί ὠφέλησαν πλεῖον ἢ πόνους; 'what did they gain more than toil?' Si 31.28; 31.30, 31.

Cf. ὠφέλεια, ὠφέλημα, συμφέρω, χρήσιμος, ἀνωφελής: Schmidt 4.169f.

ὠφέλημα, ατος. n.ʃ

that which is beneficial or *useful*: οὐκ ἔστιν ἐν αὐτοῖς ὠ. Je 16.19. Cf. ὠφελέω.

ὤχρα, ας. f.ʃ

**mildew*: divine punishment and ‖ ἀνεμοφθορία 'blight' De 28.22.

LIST OF LEXEMES NOT INCLUDED IN THIS LEXICON

This is a list of Greek entry words entered in Hatch and Redpath's concordance but not covered in this lexicon. Almost all of them are found as variant readings in one or more manuscripts. With a few exceptions all transliterations of Semitic words have not been covered, either.

The symbol > signifies that the lexeme or form mentioned after it is to be preserved. This information, however, is given sparingly.

"simp." is an abbreviation for "simplex" as against a compound form.

ἄβλαστος
Ἀβρααμίθιος
ἀγάγω
ἀγανάκτησις
ἀγγέλλω
ἀγκαινισμός
ἀγκύλος > σκῦλον
ἁγνιασμός > ἁγνισμός
ἄγνους > ἄπνοος
ἀγύναιος > γύναιος
ἀδελφιδοῦς
ἀδιάφορος
ἀδρανία
ἄδυτον
ἀθεΐα > ἀθεσία
ἀθετίζω
ἀθέω > ἀθετέω
αἰθρίζω > διορίζω
αἵρεμα > εὕρεμα
αἴσθομαι
αἰχμάλωσις > αἰχμαλωσία
αἰχμαλώτισσα
ἀκάθεκτος > ἀκατάσχετος
ἀκαίριος > ἀκαριαῖος
ἀκαταπάτητος > ἀκαπάποτος
ἀκινάκις
ἀκλινῶς > ἀκλινής
ἄλκιμος > Ἄλκιμος
ἀλόη > αλωθ
ἀμείνων > μεῖζον
ἄμειψις > ἀντάμειψις
ἀμνημοσυνέω > ἀμνημονέω
ἄμνησις > ἀνάμνησις
ἀμπλάκημα
ἀναγεννάω > παραγίνομαι
ἀναδύω > ἀναλύω
ἀναθαυμάζω > ἀπο~
ἀνάλλαγμα > simp.
ἀναμαρυκάομαι > simp.
ἀναφαιρέω > ἀφ.
ἀναφυράω > ἀναποιέω
ἀνδραγάθησις
ἀνδραλογία
ἀνδρογύναιος
ἀνδρολογεῖον
ἀνεπιτρέπτως
ἀνέργεια
ἀνθράκιον
ἀνθρωπότης > ἀδελφότης
ἄνοιγμα
ἀνοίκητος > ἀοίκητος
ἀνταποδισμός > ἀναπ.
ἀντιδοκέω
ἀντιπεριβάλλω > ~παρα~
ἀντιστάτης
ἀντισχύω > κατισυχύω
ἀντίτυπος > ~θετος
ἀξιοδυναστεύω
ἀπαραιτήτως > ~τοις
ἀπαρτίζω
ἀπαρχία > ἀπαρχή
ἀπαστία > ἁγιαστία
ἀπατηλός > ἀπάτη
ἀπείθω > ἀπειθέω
ἀπέλκω > ἐφελκύω
ἀπεριτέτμητος > ἀπερίτμ~
ἀποδημέω > ~πηδάω
ἀποδιαιρέω
ἀποδιαστέλλω
ἀποικέω > ~κίζω
ἀπόκλειστος
ἀποκρύνω
ἀποκρύφιος
ἀπολανθάνω
ἀπολήνιον
ἀποξέω > ξύω
ἀποπέμπω > ~μέμφομαι
ἀπορρωγάς
ἀποσκορπίζω > ~σκορακίζω
ἀπόστολος
ἀποσυρίζω
ἀποτεκνόομαι > ἀτεκνόω
ἀποτρέμω > ~τρέπω
ἀποφορίζω > ἀφορίζω
Αραβα
Αραβω
ἀρεταλόγιον
ἄρης
ἀροτριόω
ἀρχιεταῖρος
ἀρχός > ἄρχων
ἄσβεστος > ἄκαυστος
ἄσοφος
ἀστυγής > ~γείτων
ἀσυνετέω
ἀτενής
ἀτενόω
ἀτμός
ἀτονέω.
ἀτράπελος
αὔξων > ἄξων
ἀφέστιος

βάθρον
βαθύγλωσσος
βαρέομαι
βελοστασία
βόλος

γεφυρόω
γονορρυέω

δαίμων
δειλιάζω
δέκαρχος > δεκάδαρχος
δεκάς
δεσμοφύλαξ
δημαγωγέω
διαβουλή > ~βολή
διαβουλία > ~βούλιον
διαζωννυμι > simp.
διαίρω > simp.
διακαλέω > ἐπι~
διακρίβεια
διακριβέω
διακρύπτω > simp.
διάλογος > simp.
διάλυτος > ἀδια.
διαναφέρω
διαξαίνω > ~τάσσω
διαπέτομαι > διΐπταμαι
διάπηγος
διάραντος
διασαφηνίζω > ~σαφέω
διασαφίζω > ~σαφέω
διαστηρίζω > ~τηρέω
διασφραγίζομαι > simp.
διαφαιρέω
διαφρύγω > συν~
διεκκύπτω > δια~
διηχέω > διαχέω

διεῖδον
διορθρίζω > simp.
διορύγη > διώρυξ
δισχιλίας > ~χίλιος
δίφορος > διάφορος
διχηλεύω
δούλιος > δοῦλος
δράσος
δυνατόω
δυσάτακτος > δυσαίακτος
δυσημερέω > εὐη~

ἐγγελάω > ἐκ~, ἐπεγ~
ἐγγεννάω > simp.
ἐγγίγνομαι
ἔγγονος > ἔκγονος
ἐγκαίνωσις
ἐγκαλύπτω > ἐκ~
ἐγκατακρύπτω ἐγκαταλοχίζω
ἐγκατασκηνόω
ἐγκόλαμμα > ἐκ~
ἔγκτημα
ἐγχειρίζω
ἐγχειρόω > ἐγχειρέω
ἔδρασμα
εἴλη > ἴλη
εἰλικρίνεια > εἰλικρινής
εἱλικτός > ἑλ.
εἰσαγωγή > συν~
εἰσβεβηλόω
εἰσηγέομαι
εἰσηγορέομαι > ἰσ.
εἰσκολάπτω > ἐκ~
εἰσόδιον
ἐκβεβηλόω
ἐκβραγμός
ἐκβύζω
ἐκδικησία
ἔκθλιψις
ἐκκλείω
ἐκκολαπτός
ἐκκοσμέω
ἐκμαίνομαι
ἐκμελῶς > ἐπι~
ἔκρημα > ἔκρηγμα
ἐκστραγγίζω
ἐκφορέω
ἐκφόρτιον
ἐκφύσημα
ἐκχαίνω
ἐκχολάω > simp.
ἔλλειμμα
ἐλλήν < θελητής?
ἐμβαθύνω
ἐμπαίρω
ἐμπαρρησιάζομαι
ἐμπεποδεστάτη
ἐμπλάσσω
ἐμπολιορκέω
ἐμπροθέσειος
ἐμφιλόνεικος

ἐμφύρομαι
ἐνάγω
ἔναρα
ἐναρίθμητος
ἐνάρμοστος
ἐνδελεχιστός
ἐνδιαλλάσσω
ἐνδιασπείρω
ἐνδοσθιαῖος
ἐνδυάζω
ἐνεμπορεύομαι
ἔνηχος
ἐνικός
ἐνιουδαΐζω
ἐνορκίζω
ἐνσκηνόω
ἐντίναγμα
ἐντότερος
ἐντυπόω
ἐνυποκρίνομαι
ἐνυψόω > ἀν~
ἐξαίρεσις
ἐξακριβόομαι
ἐξαμαρτωλός
ἔξαρξις
ἐξατιμάζω
ἐξαφίστημι
ἐξερεύομαι
ἐξευφραίνομαι
ἐξισάζω
ἐξισχύω
ἐξορίζω
ἐξουσιαστής
ἐπαίτιος
ἐπαναγωγή
ἐπανακαλέω
ἐπανάστασις
ἐπανγέλτερος
ἐπαρκῶς
ἔπαρξις
ἐπαρχία
ἐπείσχυσις
ἐπέκτασις
ἐπενδέω > ἐπι~
ἐπηχέω
ἐπίβατος
ἐπιδέησις > ἐπιδέω
ἐπιδιηγέομαι
ἐπιθαυμάζω
ἐπικατάγω
ἐπίκουφος
ἐπικρύπτω
ἐπιλαλέω
ἐπιλείπω
ἐπιμέλομαι
ἐπιμερίζω
ἐπιμεσόω
ἐπιμιξία
ἐπίμιξις
ἐπιμύλιος
ἐπινύσσομαι

ἐπιπαρέρχομαι
ἐπιπληθύνω
ἐπίποκος
ἐπισκευή
ἐπισκορπίζω
ἐπιστέλλω
ἐπιστερέω
ἐπισύνειμι
ἐπιταφή
ἐπιτιτρώσκω
ἐπιτρίβω
ἐπίτριψις
ἐπιφαυλίζω
ἐπιφώσκω
ἐπίχαρις
ἐποικτειρέω
ἐπταπλοῦς
ἔρδω
ἐρεμάζω
ἐριστής
ἐριστός
ἔστε
ἐσχαρίς
ἑτεροκωφέω > ἐθελο~
εὐγεννασία > εὐγενίζω
εὐδοξία
εὐηχοῖος
εὐθαρσέως
εὔκληρος
εὐλογίζω
εὐλόγως
εὐμελῶς
εὐπειθής
εὐπορία
εὐπόρφυρος
εὔριζος
εὐσεβῶς
εὐτρεπῶς
εὐτυχία
εὐφρονεύομαι
εὐχαρής
εὐχαριστήριον
ἐφέστιος
ἐφικνέομαι
ἐφορμάζω
ἔχθος
ἐχθράζω

ζήτημα
ζώω

ἡγεμονίδης
ἡγεμόνος
ἦδος
ἥρεμος
ἥτησις

θεωρητός
θράζω
θρασύγνωστος
θραῦμα

θραυμός
θυάζω
θύπη

ἱερουργέω
ἱκεσία
ἵκτηρ
ἱλαστήριος > ~ον
ἱλαστής
ἱλατής
ἱμείρομαι
ἱμερόομαι
ἰσαστήρ > ἰσάστερος
ἰσόθεος
ἰσοπαλίς
ἰσοπολίτης > ~πολῖτις
ἰχθυϊκός

καθάρισις > κάθαρσις
καθαρότης > ~ρειότης
κάθαρτος
καθήλωμα
κάθησις > κάθισις
καθίγω
κακότης
κάματος
καπνοδόχη
κάπτω
καταβέννω > ~βαίνω
κατακοπή > κατάκοπος
κατακράζω
κατάκριμα > κατὰ κρίμα
καταληγέω > καταλήγω
καταλειμμάνω
καταλείφω > ~λαμβάνω
κατάλημμα
κατανοίγνυμι
καταπείθω > simp.
καταπείρομαι > ~σπείρω
καταρεμβεύω > καταρρεμ~
καταρομβεύω
καταρχή > ταραχή
κατασιγάω
κατασκήνεσις > ~σκήνωσις
κατατενίζω
κατατρέπω
κατατρόπος
καταφθονέω
καταχρύσεα
κατειλέω > ~λαμβάνω
κατελαύνω
κατενισχύω
κατερευνάω
κατηγόρημα
κατοίομαι > κατοινόομαι
κατοικτίζω > κατοικίζω
κατόπτης
κατόρθωμα
κενίζω
κενότης
κηδιάω

κηρία
κληρουχία
κλιτύς
κλώδαλον
κοθωνός
κολαιός
κολαστήριον
κολλύρα
κραυάζω
κρεμνάω
κρόκινος
κρύβδην
κρύβω
κυδίων
κυκλωπάζω
κυλίκινος
κυνέω
κυριακός

λαγωός
λεόντινος
λῆξις
λιγμίζω > λικμίζω
λυρίζω

μαθητής
μάκρυνσις
μαρσυπεῖον
μάσσω
μαστιστής
μεγαλοημέρευσις
μεγαλοποιέω
μεθλά
μελετητικός
μελύνω
μεσοπο/ωρέω
μεσόπωρος
μεταγινώσκω
μετακρίνομαι
μεταστενάζω
μεταστέφω
μεταφρονέω
μετοχετεύω
μῆνιμα
μηρυκάομαι > μαρυκάομαι
μητριά
μιαροφονία
μίξις > ἐπιμίξ
μνήσκομαι
μόλυβος > μόλιβος
μονήμερος
μυστάθεια
μώκημα > δώρημα
μώμημα > δώρημα

νεκριμαῖος
νίκημα
νομόθεσμος
νομοφαγία > μονο.
νουά

ξενητία
ξενία
ξέω
ξυνωρίς
ξυρός

οἰκεσία
οἰκιάζω
οἰκίον
οἴκτιστος > οἰκτρός
οἰνόβρωτος
οἰνοδόχος
οἰνόομαι
ὀλέθρευσις
ὁλοκληρία
ὁμόψηφος, ὁμοιόψηφος
ὅλως
ὀνομαστί
ὀξυσθενής
ὁπλιστής
ὀργιάω
ὀρθρόω
ὁρκόω
ὀροφόω
οὐκοῦν
οὔπου
ὀφείλησις
ὀχεῖον
ὀχληρία
ὀχυράζω

πάθμη, πάθνη
παιδευσία
παιδιόθεν
παιδοχαρακτήρ
πανεπόπτης
πανέχινος
πανηγύριος
πανοικί
πανούργημα, ~γευμα
παντεπίσκοπος
παντοκρατέω
παραβαπτός
παραβιωτής
παραγινώσκω
παραδειπνίζω
παράδωσις > ~δοσις
παρακαθίστημι
παρακλίνω
παράνους
παραφορά > περι~
παρεγκλίνω
παρελέγχω
παρέξω
παρθένιος
πάτραρχος
πεδία
πελιδνός
περάω
περιβώμιον
περίγλυφον

περιδίδωμι
περιεῖδον
περιεργασία
περικρατής
περιπέτομαι
περιπιλέω
περισκέλιον
περισώζω
περιτήκω
πεταλόω
πετηνός
πήσσω
πικρόω
πίναξ
πλανῆτις
πλώστης
ποῖ
ποιμνημίον
πολεμία > πολέμιος
πολλύς
πολυοχία
πολύπειρα
πολυτρόπως
πονεύω
πονήριος
πρᾶος
πρεσβυτέριον
πρῆν
προαγορεύω
προαναπληρόω
προβλητός
πρόδομος
προέχω
προθύρα
προκαθήκω
πρόκαιρος
προκαλέομαι
προκαταχωρίζω
πρόκλησις
προπύλαιον
προσαπειλέω
προσαπέρχομαι
προσγεννάω > ~γίνομαι
προσγράφω
προσδοκέω
προσεγκρούω
πρόσειμι
προσενέχομαι
προσεπιαπατάω
προσηγέομαι
προσκαταβαίνω
προσκαταλαμβάνω
προσκατατείνω
προσμηνύω
προσοικέω
προσπλάσσω
προσπροάγω
προσσημειόω
προσστατέω
πρόστομα
προστρέπω
προσυμνέω
προσυμπλέκομαι
πρόσχεσις
προσώτιον
προτάσσω
προφιλής
πρόχωμα
πρω ϊόθεν
πτέρνον > πτέρνη
πύδαργος
πυρισμός
πυρογενής
πυρόπνους
πυροφορός
πυρπνέω
πω

ῥαβδίον
ῥοδοφόνος
ῥύαξ

σαπριόω > σαπρίζω
σέβημα
σειρομάστρα
σημανίζω
σήψ
σίγα > σιγάω
σίδηρον > σιδήριον
σίκυς
σιτοδοτεία
σιτόω > σιτέομαι
σκεύασις
σκευαστός
σκεύη
σκληροπρόσωπος
σκολαβρίζω
σκοτωμένη
σπάλαξ
σπινόω
σπόριον
σταθμόν > στάθμιον
σταλάζω > σταλάσσω
στέγος > τέγος
στερεοκάρδιος
στέρνον
στεφανηφόρος
στήκω
στήλωσις
στίμη
στοιχίζω
στομίς
στραγγαλιώδης
στραγγαλόομαι
στρατοπεδίον
στρογγυλόω
στρογγύλωσις
στρυφαλίς
στρύχνος
συγγενεύς
σύγκλιμα
συγκύφω
συζητέω
συκήρατος
συλλοιδορέω
συμβασιλεύω
σύμβολος
συμβράσσω
συμμένω
συμμερίζομαι
συμμίσσω
συμπαράγω
συμπληρόω
συμπροπορεύομαι
συμφρυγίζω
συμφυτέω
συμψηφίζω
συναίρω
συναιτέω
συναποκλείω
συνδέομαι
συνδοιάζω
συνεκφαίνω
συνερίζω > ~ερείδω
συνηθίζω
σύνηθος > συνήθης
συνήλικος > συνῆλιξ
σύνθεμα
συντελμάω
συρράσσω
συρρέμβρομαι
σύρρηγμα
συσκευάζω
συσπάω
συσστράτευμα
συστροφία
σφυρόν
σωτηρίαγμα
σωτήρισμα

ταλαιπωρίζω
ταπεινοφορέω
ταφνόω
ταών
τέ
τεθνήκω
τελέως > τελείως
τερατώδης > ταραχώδης
τεταρταῖος
τηκτός
τηνικαῦτα
τινάσσω
τίω > τίνω
τοῖος > τοιόσδε
τριηραρχία
τρομάζω
τροποφορέω
τροχαῖος
τροχαντήριον
τρυπητής
τυραννία

ὑβρίστια
ὕλις

ὑπαίρω
ὑπανθέω
ὕπαρ
ὕπαρχος
ὑπεξερέομαι
ὑπερασπίστεια
ὑπερειδέναι
ὑπερκύκλῳ
ὑπερυμνέω
ὑπευθύνω
ὑποθραύομαι
ὑπολυπέομαι
ὑπομάσθιος, ~μαστιαῖος
ὑπονομεύω
ὑποσκελισμός
ὑποσημαίνω > ἀπο~
ὑποταγή
ὑποτομεύς
ὑποφυλλίς
ὑποφωνέω
ὕποψ
ὑσσωπίον

φαλακρόω
φαλάντωμα
φαρμακόω
φάτνωσις
φθέγγος > φέγγος
φιαλίζω
φιλοτιμέομαι
φλέξ
φλυαρία
φοβερόω
φοράζω
φρουρόω
φρύττω > φρυάσσω
φυγάδιον
φυσητής

χάζομαι
χαλαβώτης
χάρα > καρρον
χαρβάνη
χάρισμα
χειμάρρουν > ~μάρρους
χελύνιον
χθών
χορεῖον
χορίδιον
χρηματιστηρί
χρησιμολογέω > χρησμο~
χρονέω
χρυσοτορευτός
χύσις
χώρημα
χῶρος

ψαλμῳδός
ψαμμωτός
ψέγω
ψηφίζω

ὤμιον
ὠμίς
ὡραΐζομαι
ὡρηδόν

PRINTED ON PERMANENT PAPER • IMPRIME SUR PAPIER PERMANENT • GEDRUKT OP DUURZAAM PAPIER - ISO 9706
N.V. PEETERS S.A., WAROTSTRAAT 50, B-3020 HERENT